The Good Pub Guide
2007

The Good Pub Guide 2007

Edited by

Alisdair Aird and Fiona Stapley

Managing Editor: Karen Fick
Senior Associate Editor: Robert Unsworth
Associate Editor: Tim Locke
Editorial Assistance: Fiona Wright

EBURY PRESS
LONDON

Please send reports on pubs to

The Good Pub Guide
FREEPOST TN1569
WADHURST
East Sussex
TN5 7BR

or contact our website:
www.goodguides.co.uk

Good Guide publications are available at special discounts for bulk purchases or for sales promotions or premiums. Special editions, including personalised covers, excerpts of existing Guides and corporate imprints, can be created in large quantities for special needs. Enquiries should be sent to the Sales Development Department, Random House, 20 Vauxhall Bridge Road, London SW1V 2SA (020 7840 8400).

This edition first published in 2006 by Ebury Press,
Random House, 20 Vauxhall Bridge Road,
London SW1V 2SA

The Random House Group Limited Reg. No. 954009

www.randomhouse.co.uk

1 3 5 7 9 10 8 6 4 2

A CIP catalogue record for this book is available from the British Library.

ISBN 0091909244
ISBN 9780091909246 (after Jan 2007)

Typeset from author's disks by Clive Dorman
Edited by Pat Taylor Chalmers
Printed and bound in Great Britain by Cox and Wyman Ltd, Reading, Berkshire

Contents

Introduction

This edition is a celebration. It's our 25th. So we have been looking back on this last quarter-century, to put today's pub scene in perspective.

HOW IT ALL STARTED

Back in the early 1970s one of the present editors, Alisdair Aird, started the magazine *Holiday Which?*. When he sent his researchers to explore holiday areas of the UK, Alisdair used to ask them to find a few good pubs that people would enjoy, perhaps to have a bite to eat in. Naturally, they asked how they were to find such pubs. Though Alisdair initially suggested looking in guide books, it emerged that at that time there was no reliable guide to the sort of pubs he had in mind – pubs that were appealing in their own right, as well as providing decent drinks, and food if they had it.

Alisdair knew that there were plenty of such places. So he put at the back of his mind the idea that one day he'd set about finding them, and writing a book about them. Some years later, wanting a complete break after heading a series of heavyweight public policy research projects for the Government, he decided to take a year off and write the pub book. Which?, his old employers, agreed to publish it, and put a note in the magazine asking for readers' suggestions. That 'year off' then turned into quite a lot longer, as Alisdair delved in libraries and quizzed pub-loving friends and friends of friends, amassing lists of promising-sounding places, and then driving off to investigate. Much of that first edition was written in a small car, on a portable typewriter, sometimes by the light of a lamp plugged into the car's lighter socket. And Alisdair quickly learned the first hard rule: that for every Good Pub, there are an awful lot that aren't.

The book, originally intended as a one-off, turned into an annual which Alisdair has been writing ever since. Its crucial ingredient has been the combination of suggestions or reports from readers with anonymous inspections, initially always by Alisdair himself. This has meant that pubs are always judged against a single standard, and that the text has always been written from a single viewpoint – even though the reported experience and opinions of thousands of readers underlies it.

At the end of 1984 Fiona Stapley joined Alisdair, and has worked with him ever since – now as joint Editor. She has inspected hundreds of pubs together with him, and now occasionally inspects pubs on her own. So do Karen Fick (Managing Editor), who joined us in 1993, and Robert Unsworth (Senior Associate Editor), who joined us in 1992 – Rob now works primarily as a TV series producer, but still has a big hand in the book's preparation.

Other landmarks have been our first computer, a then state-of-the-art Superbrain, bought in 1985, weighing about 45lb, which had a 64kB memory; and our 1991 move from Which? to Random House/Ebury Press, when Which? wanted to take control of our copyright (we wanted to keep our independence).

The correspondence with readers is in many ways the part of the work which we enjoy most. Over 4,000 people have helped with this present edition, many of them writing frequently (often now by email), and many of them have been writing for years. As we always write back, we feel quite a close relationship with our readers. We'd reckon that about 2,000 people are 'regulars', in their way equivalent to other guides' inspectors; and, after years of two-way correspondence, we'd reckon to know about 600 of them pretty well, from the point of view of their tastes, their likes and dislikes.

The correspondence has its dramatic moments. We well remember the report card which arrived with an apology for the brown stains on it: 'My tie was pressed into service as a tourniquet when someone knifed the barman'. There was the reader/reporter who told us that although she had escaped, all her luggage was lost, including her cherished *Guide*, when the inn she was asleep in and had planned to report to us on was destroyed by an explosion and fire. Another described a meal in a sleepy Kent village pub interrupted by a hooded man bursting in and firing a shotgun at the landlord from close range.

Reporting for the *Guide* has its lighter moments, too. There was the letter we had describing 'a lovely evening playing dominoes with the dalmatians under the table'. Often, people squeezing information into telegraphese say things that Frankie Howerd would certainly take the wrong way: 'recently refurbished new landlady...' 'the omelette was tasty but I didn't like the cat...' 'good steak well hung landlord v good fun...'

HOW BEER PRICES VARY

Twenty-five years ago, we first drew attention to the sharp difference in beer prices from one part of the country to another. As we said then, 'In a month in which we were paying 46p a pint in the West Midlands, we paid up to 78p a pint in London'. Alas, even in the West Midlands the days of the 46p pint are now just a dim memory. But the price differences have survived. The following Table, based on our annual survey of prices in 1,134 pubs, shows current average prices in each area:

COUNTY	£
Lancashire, Staffordshire	2.10
Nottinghamshire, West Midlands	2.11
Cheshire	2.13
Cumbria	2.14
Yorkshire	2.15
Derbyshire	2.19
Worcestershire	2.21
Northumbria	2.23
Herefordshire	2.25
Shropshire	2.26
Lincolnshire, Wales	2.27
Leicestershire and Rutland	2.30
Devon, Gloucestershire	2.31
Cornwall, Warwickshire	2.32
Wiltshire	2.33
Dorset, Northamptonshire, Somerset	2.34
Essex	2.35
Norfolk	2.37
Cambridgeshire, Isle of Wight, Scotland	2.39
Oxfordshire	2.40
Sussex	2.41
Bedfordshire, Kent	2.42
Hertfordshire	2.43
Suffolk	2.45
Hampshire	2.46
Berkshire	2.49
Buckinghamshire	2.50
London	2.55
Surrey	2.57

If price changes in the next 25 years come to echo those of our first quarter-century, what prices can you expect in our 50th edition? Be prepared for a national average beer price of £8.40 a pint, with Londoners paying up to £10.60 – and, with Surrey now steaming ahead of London as the most expensive area for drinks, goodness only knows what people there will be paying for their pints then.

WHERE TO FIND THE BEST BEER

In our first edition, 25 years ago, even the best pubs had a much more restricted range of beers than we've now become used to. We ran a check in a typical county (Berkshire), and found that, for the same number of pubs, you will now find beers from over twice as many different breweries as back then. And a major change is that beers from big national brewers, which used to be the dominant feature, have given way to beers from smaller – often much smaller – ones, either local or from more distant parts of the country.

Another big change is that, whereas in that first edition just a handful of pubs brewed their own beers, now several dozen do. We find these consistently cheaper than their local competitors. Against a national average beer price of £2.32, beers brewed at the pub typically cost just £2.

Among the best are the Brewery Tap in Peterborough (Cambridgeshire), the John Thompson near Melbourne (Derbyshire – still brewing happily as it was in our very first edition), the Church Inn at Uppermill (Lancashire – remarkably cheap), the Grainstore in Oakham (Leicestershire and Rutland), the Keelman in Newburn (Northumbria), the Burton Bridge Inn in Burton (Staffordshire), the Old Cannon in Bury St Edmunds and St Peters Brewery in South Elmham (Suffolk), the Beacon in Sedgley (Warwickshire chapter), the Talbot at Knightwick (Worcestershire – using hops from their brothers' farm), the New Inn at Cropton and the Fat Cat in Sheffield (Yorkshire), and the Fox & Hounds in Houston (Scotland). The Brewery Tap in Peterborough, supplying its splendid beers to quite a lot of other good pubs too, takes the award of **Own Brew Pub of the Year 2007**.

Almost all the pubs in this *Guide* serve a fine pint of real ale, and for many people this is a good pub's life-blood. Some make a real speciality of their beers, keeping a considerable range, tracking down obscure brews with strange names, running multi-beer festivals with morris dancers, music and barbecues, and taking a pride in changing their beers so frequently that they can paper their walls with pump-clips. Ones which seem to have just the right atmosphere and surroundings for enjoying good beer are the Bhurtpore at Aston (Cheshire), the Old Ale House in Truro (Cornwall), the Watermill at Ings (Cumbria), the Brunswick in Derby (Derbyshire), the Bridge on the edge of Topsham (Devon), the Old Spot in Dursley (Gloucestershire), the Station Buffet in Stalybridge (Lancashire chapter), the Fat Cat in Norwich (Norfolk), the Victoria in Beeston (Nottinghamshire), the Nags Head in Malvern (Worcestershire), the Market Porter in South London, and the Bon Accord in Glasgow (Scotland). The Market Porter in London (Stoney Street, SE1), with its splendid range of quickly changing beers and thriving atmosphere, is **Beer Pub of the Year 2007**.

BREWERIES AND PUB GROUPS

This year has seen further brewery amalgamations, with Greene King adding the family-owned Nottinghamshire brewers Hardys & Hansons to their portfolio, which we've seen expand year by year to include Morlands, Ruddles, Belhaven and Ridleys. Thus it ever was: not long after our first edition, the family-owned Theakstons brewery in Masham, Yorkshire, was taken over by Matthew Browns, in turn shortly afterwards swallowed up by the Scottish & Newcastle (S&N) brewing giant. Then in the 1990s one of the Theakstons started his own rebel brewery in Masham, ironically calling it Black Sheep. Much more recently, other Theakston family members have bought Theakstons back from S&N, and it now operates independently again, like Black Sheep. Black Sheep supplies about one in ten of our main entries with its good beer (rather more than get beer from Theakstons, incidentally). Black Sheep, with a good dining bar attached to the brewery, and a shining example of independence in times when the trend has been for breweries to be taken over by their bigger brethren, is **Brewery of the Year 2007**.

In our 25 years, there have been just a few different examples of successful pub groups which in their development have turned out to be very good news for their customers. Back in the 1980s readers tipped us off about a pub called the White Lion of Mortimer, in rather an unpromising part of North London, which when we tried it out surprised us by having solid clean furnishings (rare enough in London pubs back then) in an attractively converted building, no piped music (ditto), and decent food (all day) and beer at much lower prices than the London norm. This turned out to be a very early example of a chain which went on to prove extremely popular with customers: Wetherspoons. A much smaller and much more upmarket group of pubs is the Huntsbridge group, focused on and around Cambridgeshire. These sophisticated dining pubs, with good modern food and a fine range of wines, have been a model for many others. Then there's the rather newer Brunning & Price group, quite widely spread away from their Cheshire base. Their pubs, laid out to look interesting, and usually to give plenty of well furnished and attractively lit separate areas for people to relax in, have an enterprising range of food all day, super wines by the glass, and a good choice of real ales and other drinks. As we have said, this is the sort of approach that looks to be the future way forward for many of the better pubs. Brunning & Price is **Pub Group of the Year 2007**.

WINE NOW REALLY COUNTS IN PUBS

The first edition of *The Good Pub Guide* scarcely mentioned wine – with good reason. Twenty-five years ago, pub wine was on the whole best not talked about, nor drunk. Right through the 1980s pubs were rather slow to catch on to the possibilities – even with wine bars proving a big draw, with women beginning to come for a pub meal but not really fancying a beer with it, and with shop wine sales booming as millions back from holidays abroad developed a taste for it. In the 1990s things started looking up. In the 1993 edition we introduced our Wine Award. But we were very tentative about it. As we said, the Award 'should mean that a glass of wine should be at least palatable' – hardly high praise for these, the best wine pubs of those days. We said then that we hope the Wine Award would encourage other pubs to join 'this sadly small minority'.

Over the following decade, wine really did take off in pubs. And now, it's a passionate interest for some licensees, many others now choose wisely and can give good advice, and some specialist suppliers have been enormously encouraging and helpful. Today the Wine Award means that their wines should be reliably enjoyable, usually with a good carefully chosen range by the glass. The fact that nearly 400 pubs now qualify for the Award shows how much things have changed.

Both the Huntsbridge and the Brunning & Price pubs mentioned above have a super choice of wines by the glass. Other pubs that are outstanding for wine are the Royal Oak at Bovington Green and the Stag at Mentmore (Buckinghamshire), the Nobody Inn at Doddiscombsleigh (quite a wine pioneer, and one of the very few pubs where we mentioned the wine as a plus point in our first edition), the Culm Valley at Culmstock and the Harris Arms at Portgate (all Devon), the Museum at Farnham and the Cow in Poole (Dorset), the Wykeham Arms at Winchester (Hampshire), the Stagg at Titley (Herefordshire), the Olive Branch at Clipsham (Leicestershire and Rutland), the Wig & Mitre in Lincoln and the George of Stamford (Lincolnshire), the Crown in Southwold (Suffolk – it was among the very first pubs to have a really good range of well kept wines by the glass), Woods in Dulverton (Somersetshire), and the Angel at Hetton (Yorkshire). With a really remarkable choice by the glass, Woods in Dulverton is **Wine Pub of the Year 2007**.

WHISKY, SCOTLAND'S NATIONAL DRINK

A prime drink on a cold day is whisky with hot water – something many pubs in upland walking areas are quick to offer. There are hundreds of different malts, each with its own character, but very few pubs sell more than the well known brands – well known, it has to be said, because they are enjoyable. However, the subtleties of the more obscure brands can be a revelation. Even in England and Wales, some pubs have made something of a speciality of their whisky collection: the Nobody Inn at Doddiscombsleigh (Devon), the Britons Protection in Manchester (Lancashire chapter), the Marton Arms at Thornton in Lonsdale (Yorkshire), the Dinorben Arms at Bodfari (Wales small print section). Of course it's in Scotland that you are most likely to find pubs with an interesting choice of what is after all the national drink – and many would say that it's here that whisky slips down best of all. Three excellent places here for whisky are the Bon Accord (Glasgow), Bow Bar (Edinburgh) and Fox & Hounds (Houston). The congenial Bow Bar in Edinburgh is **Whisky Pub of the Year 2007**.

THE UNSPOILT PUB IS HERE TO STAY – WE HOPE

When we set about researching the first *Guide* we, along with many others, worried that unspoilt thoroughly old-fashioned pubs were a dying breed. Back then – and indeed every year since then – we have found a reassuringly large number. So we can confidently say that at the moment the unspoilt pub is very much alive, even if you do need to know exactly where to look. There are many dozens in the main entries, and hundreds more among the Lucky Dips. Our one worry is that many of these special places are run by people who are not exactly spring chickens. These venerable landlords and landladies are happy to serve a few pints of beer in an evening, and maybe the odd snack, just as they have done for decades. But for anyone who buys one of these pubs in the future, paying off a big loan will need much more substantial takings. The temptation to switch to a more contemporary dining pub operation is obvious. Making ends meet while keeping such a pub's unspoilt charm intact needs lots of imagination and hard work.

Our hope is that there will always be people keen to take up this challenge. There are certainly people today who through their wholehearted commitment are keeping classic unspoilt pubs not just alive but on top form. Fine examples are the Bell at Aldworth (Berkshire), the Queens Head at Newton (Cambridgeshire), the Barley Mow at Kirk Ireton and the Bear at Alderwasley (Derbyshire), the London at Molland, the Bridge on the outskirts of Topsham and the Rugglestone near Widecombe (Devon), the Square & Compass at Worth Matravers (Dorset), the Red Lion at Ampney St Peter and the Boat at Ashleworth Quay (Gloucestershire), the Harrow at Steep (Hampshire), the Carpenters Arms at Walterstone (Herefordshire), the Gate at Boyden Gate (Kent), the Three Horseshoes at Warham (Norfolk), the Crown at Churchill and the Tuckers Grave at Faulkland (Somerset), the Turf in Bloxwich and the Case is Altered at Five Ways (Warwickshire), the Birch Hall at Beck Hole, the White Horse in Beverley and the Olde White Harte in Hull (Yorkshire), the Colton Arms in West London, and the Plough & Harrow at Monknash (Wales). Several of these pubs figured in the first book, and in all the years since have hardly changed. Our three favourites are the Bell at Aldworth, the Queens Head at Newton and the Bridge at Topsham; after 25 years with us – and over 200 years in the same family – it's the 14th-c Bell at Aldworth which is **Unspoilt Pub of the Year 2007.**

HOW TOWN PUBS HAVE CHANGED

Twenty-five years ago, pubs in towns and cities were often fairly grotty: smoky, somewhat shabby, very blokey, and with a characteristic sticky finish to table and bar tops – not appealing to strangers or casual visitors. There were good pubs to be found in towns, and we included quite a few even in that first book. But you now stand a much better chance of finding somewhere pleasant and welcoming. Some favourites are the Brewery Tap and Charters in Peterborough (Cambridgeshire), the Albion in Chester (Cheshire), the Black Boy and the Wykeham Arms in Winchester (Hampshire), the Britons Protection in Manchester (Lancashire chapter), the Victoria in Beeston (Nottinghamshire), the Anchor in Henley and the Turf Tavern in Oxford (Oxfordshire), the Old Green Tree in Bath (Somerset), the Nutshell in Bury St Edmunds (Suffolk), the Old Joint Stock in Birmingham (Warwickshire etc), the Nags Head in Malvern (Worcestershire), the Maltings in York, the Cittie of Yorke, Jerusalem Tavern and Seven Stars (London), the Café Royal in Edinburgh (Scotland), and Kilverts in Hay-on-Wye (Wales). The Nags Head in Malvern, warm-hearted and interesting, with good food, drink and service, is the sort of place one hopes to find in every town but rarely does; the Nags Head is **Town Pub of the Year 2007.**

THE PUB FOOD REVOLUTION

The last quarter-century has seen a dramatic change in pub food. Today, the quality in the better pubs is top-notch, outclassing many restaurants. Twenty-five years ago, things were much bleaker. Back then in our first edition, the star items on a foody pub's menu were typically things like spaghetti bolognese or egg and prawn mayonnaise (£1.65), and trout or goujons of plaice (£2.20) – this is a real example, from a smart and relatively expensive Gloucestershire pub. The general run of pub food then was even simpler, maybe sandwiches (65p) and home-made shepherd's pie (85p).

A few landmark developments have been vital to this massive change in pub food quality.

Through the late 1980s and the 1990s, a huge growth in foreign travel opened many more people's eyes to the possibility of there being more to a meal than meat and two veg. Also, TV cookery programmes, mass-sale cookery books and magazines raised people's awareness of what was possible in the kitchen. So there was a huge new potential market.

At the same time, partly because of drink/driving laws, partly because of changes to the structure of their industry, many pub licensees were finding it less easy to make a good living from drink sales.

It was also this period that saw a significant increase in the number of retired people who had time on their hands, money in their pockets, and an active interest in getting out and about – all potential lunchers. And women no longer saw pubs automatically as male territory (as they had done in previous decades); they were more likely to think of eating than boozing.

Initially, it was the microwave, and the supplies for it from the catering companies (most notably Brake Bros), which brought these three strands together. Without needing any particular skill, pubs could offer much more interesting menus. They found plenty of willing customers.

The novelty of these huge menus gradually wore off, as adventurous home cooks found catering-pack pub meals less satisfactory than their own cooking, and as the less adventurous found that what the pubs had to offer was little different from supermarket ready-made meals. This opened the way for a new wave of keen young (and not so young) chefs to woo customers with real hands-on and imaginative cooking. As part of this process, the *nouvelle cuisine* fashion briefly touched the pub scene in the early to mid 1990s – but while people enjoyed eating pretty food the small helpings struck so many customers as poor value that the fashion passed quite quickly.

The 1990s made food scares frequent front-page news – BSE, salmonella in eggs, foot and mouth, the whole GM issue. Suddenly many more people started questioning what they were eating and where it came from. This is the most recent development. Ten years ago it was hardly even on people's radar. So very few pubs bothered much about this. Indeed, so few pubs used organic produce that, in our 1996 edition's Introduction, we drew particular attention to the one or two that did.

Now, most pubs which serve good food do take great care to secure the best possible fresh produce. And many of the best now list their individual suppliers and farms, often organic.

This brings us to the present – masses of talent in pub kitchens, excellent fresh produce, customers who know and care about food. For a short while, it all nearly went terribly wrong. Thinking to please these gourmet customers, in the early 2000s many pub chefs, even in some top pubs, went through a phase in which taste was overshadowed by absurdly elaborate presentation and description. All too often, what you got on your plate didn't live up to the ambitious descriptions – and what you put in your mouth didn't taste as special as its fancy appearance promised. We are now past that. Today, taste is paramount, however imaginative the recipe.

The best food pubs can often be very restaurant – both in their style and atmosphere, and in their price. But many have instead kept the relaxed informality and style of their pub roots, with a genuine welcome for people just popping in for a chat and a drink. Certainly, these are the ones which our readers enjoy most. To us, this looks like the way forward. It is this style of pub which will be flourishing in ten years' time – and, we hope, in 25: friendly easy-going informality, comfortable places for a chat and a drink (not necessarily an alcoholic drink), and good freshly made food.

Of the 247 pubs in this edition with such good food that they have earned our Food Award, those which stand out as particularly memorable are the Gate Inn at Yanwath (Cumbria), the White Horse at Frampton Mansell (Gloucestershire), the Plough at Sparsholt (Hampshire), the Stagg at Titley (Herefordshire), the New Inn at Shalfleet (Isle of Wight), the Victoria at Holkham (Norfolk), the Burlton Inn (Shropshire), the Boat near Lichfield (Staffordshire), the Angel at Stoke-by-Nayland (Suffolk), the Kings Head at Aston Cantlow (Warwickshire), the Pear Tree at Whitley (Wiltshire), the Three Acres near Shelley (Yorkshire), the Masonic Arms in Gatehouse of Fleet (Scotland), and the Olde Bulls Head in Beaumaris (Wales). It's nice to see, in this top list, one pub – but there is only one – which featured also in our very first edition 25 years ago: the New Inn at Shalfleet. It is a rather newer entry that wins the title of **Dining Pub of the Year 2007**, the Pear Tree at Whitley.

A hundred or so pubs in this edition have our Bargain Award, showing that they do decent food at remarkably low prices. Twenty of these also figured in our first edition. Their prices are now typically about five times as high as they were back then, for the same sort of bargain pub food. Some of these old stagers have held their prices remarkably steady over all those years – the Olde Mitre in London with its very cheap sandwiches, for instance, and the John Thompson near Melbourne (Derbyshire), still doing very much the same sort of food at little more than twice the price, such as its £5 buffet lunch. Throughout the 25 years that their price has inched up from 35p to £2, those delicious hot crusty rolls in the Bell at Aldworth (Berkshire) have been a particular favourite. Some of the bargain food specialists (usually pubs which have not been in the *Guide* for quite so long) manage to produce cheap meals that are not merely good, and good value, but also show real imagination. Prime examples are the Brewery Tap and Charters in Peterborough, both doing good thai food (Cambridgeshire), the Old Ale House in Truro (Cornwall), the White Horse in Hertford, the Head of Steam in Newcastle (Northumbria), the Lincolnshire Poacher in Nottingham, the Basketmakers Arms in Brighton and the Six Bells at Chiddingly (Sussex), and the Fat Cat in Sheffield (Yorkshire). With its immaculate open kitchen doing rewarding and interesting food at very low prices, the bustling Old Ale House in Truro is **Bargain Pub of the Year 2007.**

TODAY'S TOP PUBS AND TOP PUBLICANS

Good pubs don't always stay good. Managements change; even without a change of management, standards can slip. Only 66 pubs have managed to keep their places in every edition of the *Guide* since it started – a great achievement by each of those pubs, but underlining how difficult it is to keep standards up over a long period. Nearly 600 pubs which have featured in at least one edition as main entries have fallen by the wayside, and no longer appear in even its Lucky Dip sections. Over a thousand more, once solid main entries, have been eclipsed by others, and are now in the Lucky Dip sections; even if they are no longer quite in the top flight, they are still perfectly decent pubs, and well worth knowing.

It's obvious that this fairly rapid rate of attrition would by now have left us with a very slender *Guide* indeed – if we had not been able to add to it each year with a healthy crop of new entries, initially tracked down for us by reports from eagle-eyed readers (over the years well over 27,000 people have written to us, and some have sent us hundreds, a few even thousands, of reports). This year we have added just under 1,900 new entries to the Lucky Dip sections, and well over another hundred to the main entries.

Some of these new main entries are absolute crackers. We have particularly enjoyed the Plough at Bolnhurst (Bedfordshire), the Royal Oak at Knowl Hill (Berkshire), the Pineapple in Dorney (Buckinghamshire), the Globe in Lostwithiel (Cornwall), the New Inn at Brampton, the Punch Bowl at Crosthwaite and the Strickland Arms at Levens (Cumbria), the Old Poets Corner in Ashover (Derbyshire), the Turtley Corn Mill at Avonwick and the Rose & Crown at Yealmpton (Devon), the Greyhound at Sydling St Nicholas (Dorset), the Henny Swan at Great Henny (Essex), the Royal Oak in Prestbury (Gloucestershire), the New Harp at Hoarwithy (Herefordshire), the Sun at Hulverstone (Isle of Wight), the Three Fishes at Great Mitton and the Sun in Lancaster (Lancashire), the Victoria at Holkham (Norfolk), the Battlesteads at Wark (Northumbria), the Chequers at Aston Tirrold, the Bell at Langford and the Baskerville Arms at Shiplake (Oxfordshire), the Fox at Chetwynd Aston (Shropshire), the King William in Bath and Woods in Dulverton (Somerset), the Anchor at Walberswick (Suffolk), the Mill at Elstead (Surrey), the Fox Hounds near East Knoyle (Wiltshire), the Swan at Hanley Swan (Worcestershire), the Bay Horse at Kirk Deighton and the Pipe & Glass at South Dalton (Yorkshire), and the Masonic Arms in Gatehouse of Fleet (Scotland). The Masonic Arms in Gatehouse of Fleet, with its attractive and cheerfully civilised bar, good drinks, and comfortable informal and more formal areas for eating its good food, is **New Pub of the Year 2007.**

In our 25 years, bedrooms in pubs and inns have improved tremendously, particularly in the last decade or so. The main change is that you now almost always get your own bathroom, instead of having to share one down the corridor – often with the licensees' family. Back when we started the *Guide*, it was quite normal for even smartish inns and market town hotels to have bedrooms without their own bathrooms. And in those days the bedrooms themselves were at best simple and functional, with no extra comforts. A kettle to make yourself tea was high luxury. Now, the smarter places give you all sorts of mod cons, and even in the humbler ones a good deal of thought has gone into the décor, so that an overnight stay becomes something of a treat rather than just a necessity.

A second change is that rather more pubs do now have bedrooms, and particularly in recent years many which don't are either converting existing outbuildings or building new bedroom wings or blocks from scratch.

The consequence of these changes is that there is now a splendid choice of places to stay in, throughout Great Britain (even in London a couple of our main entries have bedrooms). Well over two hundred of the main entries now have our Stay Award. Places that are especially enjoyable include the Port Gaverne Inn near Port Isaac (Cornwall), the Pheasant at Bassenthwaite Lake and the Punch Bowl at Crosthwaite (Cumbria), the Inn at Whitewell (Lancashire), the George of Stamford (Lincolnshire), the Victoria at Holkham (Norfolk), the Cock & Hoop/Lace Market Hotel (Nottingham), the Burlton Inn and the Inn at Grinshill (Shropshire), the Royal Oak at Luxborough (Somerset), the Star at Harome, the Charles Bathurst at Langthwaite, White Swan in Pickering and the Sportsmans Arms at Wath in Nidderdale (Yorkshire), the Applecross Inn and the Plockton Hotel (Scotland), the Harbourmaster in Aberaeron and the Groes at Ty'n-y-groes (Wales), and the Fleur du Jardin on Guernsey (Channel Islands). The Port Gaverne Inn, the Inn at Whitewell and the George of Stamford all featured as good places to stay in our first edition – praise to them for keeping the flag flying so strongly. It's a newer entry, the beautifully placed and utterly distinctive Victoria at Holkham, which earns the title of **Inn of the Year 2007**.

Pubs whose all-round appeal have made them top favourites this year are the Punch Bowl at Crosthwaite (Cumbria), the Lathkil at Over Haddon (Derbyshire), the Duke of York at Iddesleigh (Devon), the Five Mile House at Duntisbourne Abbots and the Bell at Sapperton (Gloucestershire), the Inn at Whitewell (Lancashire), the Feathers in Hedley on the Hill and the Olde Ship in Seahouses (Northumbria), the Cat Head at Chiselborough (Somerset), the Angel at Stoke-by-Nayland (Suffolk), the Three Horseshoes at Elstead and the Queens Head at Icklesham (Sussex), the Compasses at Chickgrove and the Pear Tree at Whitley (Wiltshire), the Fleece at Bretforton and the Nags Head in Malvern (Worcestershire), the Sandpiper in Leyburn (Yorkshire), and the Masonic Arms in Gatehouse of Fleet (Scotland). The Five Mile House at Duntisbourne Abbots, run well by father and son, and with a thoroughly pubby little bar and rewarding food and drink, is **Pub of the Year 2007**.

In our 25 years, one thing has become clear above all: however charming the building, however comfortable, however good the food and drink, it all falls flat without a good landlord or landlady. This year, these special people have injected real warmth and enjoyment into their pubs: Robert Grigor-Taylor in the Lathkil at Over Haddon (Derbyshire), Peter and Angela Gatling in the Merry Harriers at Clayhidon, Jamie Stuart and Pippa Hutchinson in the Duke of York at Iddesleigh and Andy and Rowena Whiteman in the Harris Arms at Portgate (Devon), John Ford and Karen Trimby in the Greyhound at Sydling St Nicholas (Dorset), André and Liz Large in the Cross House at Doynton and Jo and Jon Carrier in the Five Mile House at Duntisbourne Abbots (Gloucestershire), Mary Holmes in the Sun at Bentworth and Hassan Matini in the Trooper near Petersfield (Hampshire), Christopher Smith in the Gate Inn at Boyden Gate (Kent), Lucille and Barry Carter in the Woolpack at Terrington St John (Norfolk), Maggie Chandler in the George at Kilsby (Northamptonshire), Josh and Kay Reid in the Chequers in Chipping Norton and Graham and Mary Cromack in the Baskerville Arms at Shiplake (Oxfordshire), Paul and Jo Stretton-Downes in the Bottle & Glass at Picklescott (Shropshire), Roxy Beaujolais in the Seven Stars in London, and Michael, Margaret and Simon Key of the Nags Head in Usk (Wales). The touch of whimsical individuality which Paul and Jo Stretton-Downes bring to the Bottle & Glass at Picklescott, which they run with such unforced professionalism, earns them the accolade of **Licensees of the Year 2007**.

LONG SERVICE AWARD

As we have said, keeping standards high over a long period is extremely difficult. All the more remarkable that a few individual licensees and their families have run their pubs so consistently well that they have achieved main entries in every single edition since we started. These remarkable landlords and landladies are: H E Macaulay of the Bell at Aldworth, Berkshire; David and Juliet Short of the Queens Head at Newton, Cambridgeshire; Steph Barton of the Drunken Duck near Hawkshead, Cumbria; John Thompson of the John Thompson Inn at Ingleby, near Melbourne, Derbyshire;

Nick Borst-Smith of the Nobody Inn at Doddiscombsleigh, Devon; Penny Doe and her family in the Bell in Castle Hedingham, Essex; Claire and Denise McCutcheon in the Harrow at Steep, Hampshire; Charles Bowman of the Inn at Whitewell, Lancashire; the Hope family at the Wig & Mitre in Lincoln, and Ivo Vannocci at the George of Stamford, Lincolnshire; Alan and Jean Glen at the Olde Ship in Seahouses, Northumbria; Alan East of the Yew Tree at Cauldon, Staffordshire; Anthony Leroy at the Haunch of Venison in Salisbury, Wiltshire; and Graham and Anne Henderson at Burts Hotel in Melrose, Scotland.

Back in the 1983 edition, we were immensely impressed by the Olde Ship in Seahouses, with its fascinating ship's gear, lovely harbour-view position, and buoyant atmosphere. It has been delighting readers ever since, producing another fat file of several dozen enthusiastic reports from happy readers for this special anniversary edition. The Olde Ship in Seahouses is the pub which wins our **25 Year Award**.

We've included a special 25 year symbol in this edition to pick out not just these pubs, but also other pubs that have been in every edition since we started, even though their management has changed.

LANDLORDS AND LANDLADIES HAVE THEIR SAY

Year after year we have said what we think about pubs. Sometimes we've had hard words – particularly about service. So for this celebration edition we invited licensees to get their own back, and let off steam about us, the customers. We expected a very fat postbag, full of diatribes. But there was hardly a word of complaint. Lots said – and meant – 'We only have lovely customers'. The people who run good pubs must be an extremely relaxed and tolerant bunch. Or perhaps they are just philosophical about it – as one veteran landlord put it: Everyone brings joy to this pub, some when they enter, and others when they leave.

There certainly are at least some Customers From Hell around. Mostly, it seems, they bring wry laughter rather than grief to the long-suffering publicans who have so politely put up with them. Here are a few trying incidents that we did hear about:

The lady who insisted on her whitebait having their heads and tails removed

'My wife is being sick! I hope you didn't put any dairy products in her cauliflower cheese!'

The couple sharing the same plate of vegetables – one complained to the landlord that they were overcooked, the other complained to the landlady that they were undercooked

The man seen by another customer hiding a spent match in the last of his food, then 'spotting' it and refusing to pay, even hoping for compensation – luckily the other customer spoilt his game

'I've just burnt myself on this pipe – three times!'

One pub charges £10.95 for an adult helping of roast beef, £5 for a child's helping – so one customer asked for five child's helpings, for himself, his wife and one child

An elderly customer's foot slipped on her accelerator pedal as she reversed. She slammed into the forecourt's ornamental pillar, and a half-ton stone ball toppled off, through her sun roof, and on to the passenger seat. Presumably in shock, she drove 55 miles home, ball and all.

Customers do complain about broccoli soup tasting of broccoli, and more than one landlord told us of customers complaining about fish being 'too fishy' – not off, not bad, nothing wrong with it, just too fishy. When one of these landlords was fielding this complaint, the next table beckoned him over, with a customer complaining that his duck was 'too ducky' – 'I just knew it was going to be one of those nights!' In another pub, famous for its game, the most common question is 'What's in the rabbit pie'?

One pub had a Saturday night 21st birthday party of ten in – this pub does parties proud, with a rollicking do, photographs and all. The meal ended with some specially bought-in sassily coloured fruit sundaes, and Birthday Girl (Kate, let's call her) chose a gorgeous red and white raspberry one. Suddenly the landlady spotted all ten people crashing out of the restaurant, through the crowded pub, and piling into three cars; she rushed after, shouting 'What's the matter?' 'Kate forgot she's allergic to red food colouring, she's got 20 minutes to get to hospital!' 'Go... but ring me!' They did ring, at 1am: Kate was safe, but kept in hospital overnight. As the landlady said: 'AAAAAaaaaaargh!!'

In one pub, a customer asked if the (very thin) smoked salmon in their avocado and smoked salmon fan could be served unsmoked. When the impossibility of this was explained, the customer asked if it could at least be fried. The chef felt a real sense of achievement in serving up something remotely acceptable even if it did look more like crispy bacon. Then the customer, for pudding, asked for the speciality home-made key lime pie to be served hot (the point of this dish being that it needs hours of chilling to hold its shape). The customer being always right, the chef rose to the challenge with a very clever and artistic decoration to hold together the rather runny and gooey result.

A Sunday story, with a happy ending (Sunday lunches being a busy time, with both food and drink ordered from the one barmaid):

Customer: What can I have to eat?
Barmaid: As it's Sunday, only what's on this board – three roasts and a vegetarian option.
Customer: *(after some time looking at board)* Do you do cheese sandwiches?
Barmaid: No madam, only the roasts and vegetarian option, only what's on the board.
Customer: Right, in that case I'd like a jacket potato.
Barmaid: I'm sorry madam, on Sundays we only do the roasts; the kitchen's too small to prepare for more.
Customer: Then could you get the chef to make me a sandwich?
Barmaid: Unfortunately we don't have any fresh bread and the chef is quite busy doing the roasts.
Customer: Surely he can make one sandwich!
Barmaid: I'm sorry madam, but we don't do sandwiches.
Customer: What do you serve then?
Barmaid: As I mentioned, only the roasts written on the board.
Customer: What do you have to drink then?
Barmaid: Well, we're a pub, so pretty much anything; what do you like?
Customer: I don't normally come to a pub. What do most people drink?
Barmaid: It's difficult to say – a nice glass of red wine?
Customer: I couldn't possibly have that, it's got alcohol in it!
Barmaid: How about an orange juice?
Customer: I can't drink fizzy drinks, or fruit juices.
            (quite a queue was by now building up behind...)
Barmaid: How about a mineral water then?
Customer: That would be fine, and could I also order the roast chicken...
Barmaid: Fine, I'll bring it over as soon as it's ready...
Customer: Just a moment, the chicken but without the meat!
Barmaid: !!!!?

The customer had her meal and her water. When she left she came over to the barmaid and said: Thank you so much! You know I think that was one of the best meals I've ever had. I'm so pleased you persuaded me not to have that sandwich!

The one ominous point that did come up was the concern of some licensees that the compensation culture is beginning to affect pubs. One couple said they feared that a small proportion of people now seemed to go out with almost the express purpose of finding fault and expecting compensation. Another told us about the five-year-old who clambered up the slide the wrong way, and fell off the steps, and his mother who then threatened to sue – as a result of which they have now taken out all their play equipment.

REGULATIONS

We also asked pubs if they had any views on the current balance of regulation and red tape, as it affects their customers. This did produce some explosions. We heard from just under 100 – only a small sample of pubs, and what they told us has no statistical significance. But it does strongly suggest that there are some serious problems with the current degree and system of regulation. As one landlord wryly put it to us: 'What's the best way of making a small fortune from running a good pub? Start with a large fortune.' We asked pubs which of three statements came closest to describing the present set-up:

One in nine pubs agreed that *The way pubs are regulated and licensed is fair, and gives our customers a good deal.*

Rather more than half the pubs said that *The way pubs are regulated and licensed does give some problems, but we can cope.*

About one in three pubs said that *The way pubs are regulated and licensed now causes needless expense which ends up by giving customers a bad deal.*

The general theme was that, every year, the number of forms publicans have to fill in and file grows. A major change has been that instead of the old licence granted by local licensing magistrates, now pub premises need a different much more complex and expensive licence from the local authority, and on top of that pub managers now need their own personal licence. Besides the growing number of regulations affecting most other small businesses, covering asbestos, disability, maternity, health and safety, gas safety, money laundering, financial services, and so forth, they have had to cope with a raft of new food safety requirements, new and stricter fire regulations around the time this edition is published, and during 2007 will have to deal with the effects of the smoking ban. As one publican put it, pubs are very small businesses but are being treated as if they were big companies, so have to meet regulations designed for big business without having a big-business income, hiring solicitors, accountants, surveyors, risk consultants, fire safety officers and trainers.

Moreover, in pubs bank holidays have traditionally been treated as working days. The new legislation which will effectively add eight days a year to paid holiday entitlement will have a fairly dramatic effect on their staff costs, and we expect to see this pushing up pub food and drink prices more than usual in the coming year.

Besides the extra financial costs (which as in all businesses get passed on to us, the customers), all this costs them time, more and more time. So, as one told us, the increased load of paperwork, and ensuring compliance with the 'rules', means that the people best at looking after customers, the management teams, 'can't spend as much time at the "sharp end". It is inevitable that, as a result, problems may slip through the net.' Many others said much the same – they can no longer be with their customers as much as they'd like to be, with the result that standards are compromised, or chef/landlords have to leave more of the cooking to other people.

One landlord told us that he thought the cost of all this was such a serious threat to the village pub that it might not survive. Others said it took a lot of the fun out of running a pub – an often-repeated theme. Another said that 'the regulations are stifling all the creativity, imagination and eccentricity that the british pub is world-famous for. We are replacing common sense with rules, regulations and form-filing.'

To put a figure on what it's costing pubs, one landlord said that while under the old system it used to cost £37.50 for a seven-year licence, under this year's new system it cost him £3,900 – and he still hasn't seen anyone or got any sort of certificate. Another group of three small pubs told us that because of the increased work load they have had to recruit a new staff member dedicated to training and legislation, just to make sure that they keep on top of everything. Even though they're sticking to their old closing times, the new licensing regime took an inordinate amount of management time, and for the three pubs cost well in excess of £10,000.

Finally, the new system clearly has scope for unfortunate local variation. While some licensees were full of praise for their local licensing authority, others were not: 'The system now is a flagrant licence to print money by the local authority. We are now at the mercy of political parties, petty bureaucracy and ill-informed clerks who have difficulty in understanding the needs of the licensed trade.'

To summarise all this, it seems that the main risks of the increased burden of red tape affecting pubs are: less management time available for looking after customers properly; and increased costs leading to higher prices. These do seem to us to be real potential threats, so we will obviously be keeping a close eye on both of them. There is a third risk, mentioned by some publicans – that the extra cost and paperwork burden, and its impact on the 'fun' element of pub-keeping, will simply drive some small country pubs out of business.

So finally, warm thanks to all the publicans who manage to put so much effort into keeping us all so happy, while coping with all these new problems.

What is a Good Pub?

The main entries in this *Guide* have been through a two-stage sifting process. First of all, some 2,000 regular correspondents keep in touch with us about the pubs they visit, and double that number report occasionally. We also get quite a flow of reports through our www.goodguides.co.uk website. This keeps us up-to-date about pubs included in previous editions – it's their alarm signals that warn us when a pub's standards have dropped (after a change of management, say), and it's their continuing approval that reassures us about keeping a pub as a main entry for another year. Very important, though, are the reports they send us on pubs we don't know at all. It's from these new discoveries that we make up a shortlist, to be considered for possible inclusion as new main entries. The more people that report favourably on a new pub, the more likely it is to win a place on this shortlist – especially if some of the reporters belong to our hard core of about 600 trusted correspondents whose judgement we have learned to rely on. These are people who have each given us detailed comments on dozens of pubs, and shown that (when we ourselves know some of those pubs too) their judgement is closely in line with our own.

This brings us to the acid test. Each pub, before inclusion as a main entry, is inspected anonymously by one of the editorial team. They have to find some special quality that would make strangers enjoy visiting it. What often marks the pub out for special attention is good value food (and that might mean anything from a well made sandwich, with good fresh ingredients at a low price, to imaginative cooking outclassing most restaurants in the area). The drinks may be out of the ordinary (pubs with several hundred whiskies, with remarkable wine lists, with home-made country wines or good beer or cider made on the premises, with a wide range of well kept real ales or bottled beers from all over the world). Perhaps there's a special appeal about it as a place to stay, with good bedrooms and obliging service. Maybe it's the building itself (from centuries-old parts of monasteries to extravagant Victorian gin-palaces), or its surroundings (lovely countryside, attractive waterside, extensive well kept garden), or what's in it (charming furnishings, extraordinary collections of bric-a-brac).

Above all, though, what makes the good pub is its atmosphere – you should be able to feel at home there, and feel not just that *you're* glad you've come but that *they're* glad you've come. A good landlord or landlady makes a huge difference here – they can make or break a pub.

It follows from this that a great many ordinary locals, perfectly good in their own right, don't earn a place in the *Guide*. What makes them attractive to their regular customers (an almost clubby chumminess) may even make strangers feel rather out-of-place.

Another important point is that there's not necessarily any link between charm and luxury – though we like our creature comforts as much as anyone. A basic unspoilt village tavern, with hard seats and a flagstone floor, may be worth travelling miles to find, while a deluxe pub-restaurant may not be worth crossing the street for. Landlords can't buy the Good Pub accolade by spending thousands on thickly padded banquettes, soft music and menus boasting about signature dishes nesting on beds of trendy vegetables drizzled by a jus of this and that – they can only win it, by having a genuinely personal concern for both their customers and their pub.

Using the *Guide*

THE COUNTIES

England has been split alphabetically into counties, mainly to make it easier for people scanning through the book to find pubs near them. Each chapter starts by picking out the pubs that are currently doing best in the area, or are specially attractive for one reason or another.

The county boundaries we use are those for the administrative counties (not the old traditional counties, which were changed back in 1976). We have left the new unitary authorities within the counties that they formed part of until their creation in the most recent local government reorganisation. Metropolitan areas have been included in the counties around them – for example, Merseyside in Lancashire. And occasionally we have grouped counties together – for example, Rutland with Leicestershire, and Durham with Northumberland to make Northumbria. If in doubt, check the Contents.

Scotland and Wales have each been covered in single chapters, and London appears immediately before them at the end of England. Except in London (which is split into Central, East, North, South and West), pubs are listed alphabetically under the name of the town or village where they are. If the village is so small that you probably wouldn't find it on a road map, we've listed it under the name of the nearest sizeable village or town instead. The maps use the same town and village names, and additionally include a few big cities that don't have any listed pubs – for orientation.

We always list pubs in their true locations – so if a village is actually in Buckinghamshire that's where we list it, even if its postal address is via some town in Oxfordshire. Just once or twice, when the village itself is in one county but the pub is just over the border in the next-door county, we have used the village county, not the pub one.

A small number of pubs have featured as main entries in every single edition of the *Guide*. This year, we've included a special symbol to let you know which they are.

STARS ★

Really outstanding pubs are picked out with a star after their name. In a few cases, pubs have two stars: these are the aristocrats among pubs, really worth going out of your way to find. The stars do NOT signify extra luxury or specially good food – in fact some of the pubs which appeal most distinctively and strongly of all are decidedly basic in terms of food and surroundings. The detailed description of each pub shows what its particular appeal is, and this is what the stars refer to.

FOOD AND STAY AWARDS ⑪ 🛏

The knife-and-fork rosette shows those pubs where food is quite outstanding. The bed symbol shows pubs which we know to be good as places to stay in – bearing in mind the price of the rooms (obviously you can't expect the same level of luxury at £60 a head as you'd get for £100 a head). Pubs with bedrooms are marked on the maps as a square.

🍷

This wine glass symbol marks out those pubs with particularly enjoyable wines by the glass, and usually a good choice.

The beer tankard symbol shows pubs where the quality of the beer is quite exceptional, or pubs which keep a particularly interesting range of beers in good condition.

This symbol picks out pubs where we have found decent snacks at £3 or less, or worthwhile main dishes at £6.45 or less.

RECOMMENDERS

At the end of each main entry we include the names of readers who have recently recommended that pub (unless they've asked us not to).

Important note: the description of the pub and the comments on it are our own and not the recommenders'; they are based on our own personal inspections and on later verification of facts with each pub. As some recommenders' names appear quite often, you can get an extra idea of what a pub is like by seeing which other pubs those recommenders have approved. In the rare instances where we have discovered a good pub which has no reader recommenders, or judge that a pub deserves to stay in the main entries despite a very recent management change we include the acronym BOB (buyer's own brand) as a recommender.

LUCKY DIPS

The Lucky Dip section at the end of each county chapter includes brief descriptions of pubs that have been recommended by readers, with the readers' names in brackets. As the flood of reports from readers has given so much solid information about so many pubs, we have been able to include only those which seem really worth trying. Where only one single reader's name is shown, in most cases that pub has been given a favourable review by other readers in previous years, so its inclusion does not depend on a single individual's judgement. In all cases, we have now not included a pub in the list unless readers' descriptions make the nature of the pub quite clear, and give us good grounds for trusting that other readers would be glad to know of the pub. So the descriptions normally reflect the balanced judgement of a number of different readers, increasingly backed up by similar reports on the same pubs from other readers in previous years. Many have been inspected by us. In these cases, LYM means the pub was a main entry in a previous edition of the *Guide*. The usual reason that it's no longer one is that, although we've heard nothing really condemnatory about it, we've not had enough favourable reports to be sure that it's still ahead of the local competition. BB means that, although the pub has never been a main entry, we have inspected it, and found nothing against it. In both these cases, the description is our own; in others, it's based on the readers' reports. This year, we have deleted many previously highly rated pubs from the *Guide* simply because we have no very recent reports on them. This may well mean that we have left out some favourites – please tell us if we have!

Lucky Dip pubs marked with a ☆ are ones where the information we have (either from our own inspections or from trusted reader/reporters) suggests a firm recommendation. Roughly speaking, we'd say that these pubs are as much worth considering, at least for the virtues described for them, as many of the main entries themselves. Note that in the Dips we always commend food if we have information supporting a positive recommendation. So a bare mention that food is served shouldn't be taken to imply a recommendation of the food. The same is true of accommodation and so forth.

The Lucky Dips (particularly, of course, the starred ones) are under consideration for inspection for a future edition – so please let us have any comments you can make on them. You can use the report forms at the end of the book, the report card which should be included in it, or just write direct (no stamp needed if posted in the UK). Our address is The Good Pub Guide, FREEPOST TN1569, WADHURST, East Sussex TN5 7BR. Alternatively, you can get reports to us immediately, through our website www.goodguides.co.uk.

MAP REFERENCES

All pubs outside the big cities are given four-figure map references. On the main entries, it looks like this: SX5678 Map 1. Map 1 means that it's on the first map in the book (see first colour section). SX means it's in the square labelled SX on that map. The first figure, 5, tells you to look along the grid at the top or bottom of the SX square for the figure 5. The third figure, 7, tells you to look down the grid at the side of the square to find the figure 7. Imaginary lines drawn down and across the square from these figures should intersect near the pub itself.

The second and fourth figures, the 6 and the 8, are for more precise pin-pointing, and are really for use with larger-scale maps such as road atlases or the Ordnance Survey 1:50,000 maps, which use exactly the same map reference system. On the relevant Ordnance Survey map, instead of finding the 5 marker on the top grid you'd find the 56 one; instead of the 7 on the side grid you'd look for the 78 marker. This makes it very easy to locate even the smallest village.

Where a pub is exceptionally difficult to find, we include a six-figure reference in the directions, such as OS Sheet 102, map reference 654783. This refers to Sheet 102 of the Ordnance Survey 1:50,000 maps, which explain how to use the six-figure references to pin-point a pub to the nearest 100 metres.

MOTORWAY PUBS

If a pub is within four or five miles of a motorway junction, and reaching it doesn't involve much slow traffic, we give special directions for finding it from the motorway. And the Special Interest Lists at the end of the book include a list of these pubs, motorway by motorway.

PRICES AND OTHER FACTUAL DETAILS

The *Guide* went to press during the summer of 2006, after each pub was sent a checking sheet to get up-to-date food, drink and bedroom prices and other factual information. By the summer of 2007 prices are bound to have increased a little – to be prudent, you should probably allow at least 5% extra by then. But if you find a significantly different price please let us know.

Breweries or independent chains to which pubs are 'tied' are named at the beginning of the italic-print rubric after each main entry. That generally means the pub has to get most if not all of its drinks from that brewery or chain. If the brewery is not an independent one but just part of a combine, we name the combine in brackets. When the pub is tied, we have spelled out whether the landlord is a tenant, has the pub on a lease, or is a manager. Tenants and leaseholders of breweries generally have considerably greater freedom to do things their own way, and in particular are allowed to buy drinks including a beer from sources other than their tied brewery.

Free houses are pubs not tied to a brewery, so in theory they can shop around to get the drinks their customers want, at the best prices they can find. But in practice many free houses have loans from the big brewers, on terms that bind them to sell those breweries' beers. So don't be too surprised to find that so-called free houses may be stocking a range of beers restricted to those from a single brewery.

Real ale is used by us to mean beer that has been maturing naturally in its cask. We do not count as real ale beer which has been pasteurised or filtered to remove its natural yeasts. If it is kept under a blanket of carbon dioxide to preserve it, we still generally mention it – as long as the pressure is too light for you to notice any extra fizz, it's hard to tell the difference. (For brevity, we use the expression 'under light blanket pressure' to cover such pubs; we do not include among them pubs where the blanket pressure is high enough to force the beer up from the cellar, as this does make it unnaturally fizzy.)

Other drinks: we've also looked out particularly for pubs doing enterprising non-alcoholic drinks (including good tea or coffee), interesting spirits (especially malt whiskies), country wines (elderflower and the like), freshly squeezed juices, and good farm ciders.

Bar food refers to what is sold in the bar, not in any separate restaurant. It means a place serves anything from sandwiches and ploughman's to full meals, rather than pork scratchings or packets of crisps. We always mention sandwiches in the text if we know that a pub does them – if you don't see them mentioned, assume you can't get them.

The **food listed** in the description of each pub is an example of the sort of thing you'd find served in the bar on a normal day, and generally includes the dishes which are currently finding most favour with readers. We try to indicate any difference we know of between lunchtime and evening, and between summer and winter (on the whole stressing summer food more). In winter, many pubs tend to have a more restricted range, particularly of salads, and tend then to do more in the way of filled baked potatoes, casseroles and hot pies. We always mention barbecues if we know a pub does them. Food quality and variety may be affected by holidays – particularly in a small pub, where the licensees do the cooking themselves (May and early June seems to be a popular time for licensees to take their holidays, and lots seek winter sun in February).

What we call OAP meals are usually available for all 'seniors', not only people of pensionable age.

Any separate **restaurant** is mentioned. But in general all comments on the type of food served, and in particular all the other details about bar food at the end of each entry, relate to the pub food and not to the restaurant food.

Children's Certificates exist, but in practice **children** are allowed into at least some part of almost all the pubs included in this *Guide* (there is no legal restriction on the movement of children over 14 in any pub, though only people over 18 may get alcohol). As we went to press, we asked the main-entry pubs a series of detailed questions about their rules. **Children welcome** means the pub has told us that it simply lets them come in, with no special restrictions. In other cases we report exactly what arrangements pubs say they make for children. However, we have to note that in readers' experience some pubs make restrictions that they haven't told us about (children only if eating, for example). Also, very occasionally pubs which have previously allowed children change their policy altogether, virtually excluding them. If you come across this, please let us know, so that we can clarify the information for the pub concerned in the next edition. Beware that if children are confined to the restaurant, they may occasionally be expected to have a full restaurant meal. Also, please note that a welcome for children does not necessarily mean a welcome for breast-feeding in public. If we don't mention children at all, assume that they are not welcome. All but one or two pubs (we mention these in the text) allow children in their garden or on their terrace, if they have one. In the Lucky Dip entries we mention children only if readers have found either that they are allowed or that they are not allowed – the absence of any reference to children in a Dip entry means we don't know either way.

We asked all main entries what their policy was about **dogs**, and if they allow them we say so. Generally, if you take a dog into a pub you should have it on a lead. We also mention in the text any pub dogs or cats (or indeed other animals) that we've come across ourselves, or heard about from readers.

Parking is not mentioned if you should normally be able to park outside the pub, or in a private car park, without difficulty. But if we know that parking space is limited or metered, we say so.

We say if a pub does **not** accept **credit cards**; some which do may put a surcharge on credit card bills, as the card companies take quite a big cut. We also say if we know that a pub tries to retain customers' credit cards while they are eating. This is a reprehensible practice, and if a pub tries it on you, please tell them that all banks and card companies frown on it – and please let us know the pub's name, so that we can warn readers in future editions.

Telephone numbers are given for all pubs that are not ex-directory.

Opening hours are for summer; we say if we know of differences in winter, or on particular days of the week. In the country, many pubs may open rather later and close earlier than their details show unless there are plenty of customers around (if you come across this, please let us know – with details). Pubs are allowed to stay open all day Mondays to Saturdays if licensed to do so. However, outside cities many English and

Welsh pubs close during the afternoon. We'd be grateful to hear of any differences from the hours we quote.

Bedroom prices normally include full English breakfasts (if these are available, which they usually are), VAT and any automatic service charge that we know about. If we give just one price, it is the total price for two people sharing a double or twin-bedded room for one night. Otherwise, prices before the / are for single occupancy, prices after it for double. A capital B against the price means that it includes a private bathroom, a capital S a private shower. As all this coding packs in quite a lot of information, some examples may help to explain it:

£70	on its own means that's the total bill for two people sharing a twin or double room without private bath; the pub has no rooms with private bath, and a single person might have to pay that full price.
£70B	means exactly the same – but all the rooms have private bath
£65(£70B)	means rooms with private baths cost £5 extra
£40/£65(£70B)	means the same as the last example, but also shows that there are single rooms for £40, none of which has a private bathroom

If there's a choice of rooms at different prices, we normally give the cheapest. If there are seasonal price variations, we give the summer price (the highest). During the winter, many inns, particularly in the country, will have special cheaper rates. And at other times, especially in holiday areas, you will often find prices cheaper if you stay for several nights. On weekends, inns that aren't in obvious weekending areas often have bargain rates for two- or three-night stays.

MEAL TIMES

Bar food is commonly served from 12-2 and 7-9, at least from Monday to Saturday (food service often stops a bit earlier on Sundays). If we don't give a time against the *Bar food* note at the bottom of a main entry, that means that you should be able to get bar food at those times. However, we do spell out the times if we know that bar food service starts after 12.15 or after 7.15; if it stops before 2 or before 8.45; or if food is served for significantly longer than usual (say, till 2.30 or 9.45).

   Though we note days when pubs have told us they don't do food, experience suggests that you should play safe on Sundays, and check first with any pub before planning an expedition that depends on getting a meal there. Also, out-of-the-way pubs often cut down on cooking during the week, especially the early part of the week, if they're quiet – as they tend to be, except at holiday times. Please let us know if you find anything different from what we say!

NO SMOKING

All Scottish pubs are now no smoking throughout. The same will become true in England and Wales during the summer of 2007. So what we say about smoking in England and Wales refers to the time before the smoking ban becomes law. However, we have found that about one in eight English pubs have already gone completely no smoking, ahead of the ban, so you may find many more going completely no smoking in advance of the law.

DISABLED ACCESS

Deliberately, we do not ask pubs questions about this, as their answers would not give a reliable picture of how easy access is. Instead, we depend on readers' direct experience. If you are able to give us help about this, we would be particularly grateful for your reports.

PLANNING ROUTES WITH THE GOOD PUB GUIDE

Computer users may like to know of a route-finding programme, Microsoft® MapPoint™ European Edition, which shows the location of *Good Pub Guide* pubs on detailed maps, works out the quickest routes for journeys, adds diversions to nearby pubs – and shows our text entries for those pubs on screen. Some in-car navigation systems use post codes so we include these for all entries.

OUR WEB SITE (www.goodguides.co.uk)

Our Internet website uses material from *The Good Pub Guide* in a way that gives people who do not yet know it at least a taste of it. It includes a map to find each pub and you can use it to send us reports – this way they get virtually immediate attention. We are hoping for major developments to the site in the forthcoming year.

CHANGES DURING THE YEAR – PLEASE TELL US

Changes are inevitable during the course of the year. Landlords change, and so do their policies. We very much hope that you will find everything just as we say. But if you find anything different, please let us know, using the tear-out card in the middle of the book (which doesn't need an envelope), the report forms at the back of the book, or just a letter. You don't need a stamp: the address is The Good Pub Guide, FREEPOST TN1569, WADHURST, East Sussex TN5 7BR. As we have said, you can also send us reports by using our website **www.goodguides.co.uk**

The Good Pub Guide
25th Anniversary Quiz

This quiz is all about pubs. Some of the questions can be quite easily answered if you skim through the *Guide*, some – we hope – are harder. The person who sends the first complete set of correct answers to be opened by us at COMPETITION, Good Pub Guide, The Forge, Stonegate, Wadhurst, TN5 7EA will win the prize of 12 bottles of Pol Roger champagne. No other entries will be acknowledged. So don't forget to include your own address!

The competition is open to anyone except the staff of *The Good Pub Guide* itself, their relations and connections, or other people employed in its production. The editors' decision will be final. The correct answers and winner's name will be published as soon as possible on our website. No other entries will be acknowledged.

In the unlikely event that we do not receive a correct set of answers by the publication date of the following (2008) edition, we shall devote the prize to a future quiz or quizzes, possibly on our website.

The internet takes a lot of the fun out of quizzes, and almost all the skill. For instance, with a question that we would have liked to use, such as 'Where might misfortune's lightened steps wander wild?', a couple of clicks on Google and you're in the Kenmore Inn. Or what improbable pub-related boat sailed from Darwin to Singapore in 1977? The internet quickly throws up the answer: Can-Tiki, built entirely from beer cans. So for this quiz we have tried as far as possible to avoid questions that the internet can quickly answer. The result – we hope – is that some of the questions will really stretch your imagination.

1. Which pub, a main entry in this edition, has a big tilework portrait of Robert Peel?

2. There is a Royal Oak in Barrington, Cambridgeshire, and a Royal Oak in Barrington, Somerset. Name four other pairs like this – same pub name and same locality name, in quite different localities. We don't count nearly-the-same names, such as the Ships in Porlock/Porlock Weir, the Skinners Armses in Hindley/Hindley Green, the Fairmiles at Fairmile/Fairmile Common, the Ploughs in Normanton on the Wolds/Normanton on Soar, or the Victoria at Roch/Roche.

3. Which brewery brews a beer called Hobgoblin?

4. Which current main entry has murals by an artist better known for his connection with a particular drink?

5. Which current Lucky Dip entry brews a beer with quite a buzz in its head?

6. Where were two hikers famously silly?

7. Which current main entry shows receipts from the former John Brown Clyde shipyard?

8. What begins inside the Garter Inn?

9. Which three main entries, according to this edition, sell pickled eggs?

10. What tenuous pubby connection has there been between Storrington in Sussex and Southwater in Sussex?

11. Which main entry is in a village where *The Vicar of Dibley* and *Chitty Chitty Bang Bang* were filmed?

12. Which three pubs have some sort of claim to be the oldest in Edinburgh?

13. Which inn includes an enormous neolithic monolith which the original monastic builders are said to have built around?

14. What do these beers have in common: Blackawton, Carlsberg Burton, Dartmoor Best, K&B Sussex and Oakham?

15. Which pub was a great anti-war play written in?

16. Which Essex pub is run by the parents of probably the most famous TV chef?

17. Which ancient Lucky Dip pub, once a hospice for Abingdon Abbey, had a landlord who, condemned to be hanged, boasted that he had murdered dozens of customers while they slept?

18. Which main entry started life as a folly built to commemorate a Civil War battle?

19. Name a pub with an indoor shooting range.

20. Which pub stands on the site of a hospice for the nearby nunnery where Henry II's mistress is said to have been forced to drink poison by his wife Queen Eleanor?

21. What recent pubby connection is there between bad behaviour and Dylan Thomas?

22. What connection is there between the Cow & Plough in Oadby and the Victory in Hereford?

23. Which pub gave unplanned refuge to the Queen in a snow storm, and when?

24. Which main entry features visibly in a famous children's book?

25. Who wrote 'And the Dublin stout is genuine', and where did he find it was genuine?

26. Which hotel, included in this *Guide* for its splendid pubby bar, stands beside a castle that's been in the licensee's family for well over six centuries?

27. Which landlord of a good Oxfordshire pub was once a Director of the brewing firm Courage?

28. Which station buffet on the main Manchester—Huddersfield railway line stocks up to 20 or so changing guest beers a week?

29. What linked Churchill, a pub landlady, and Upper Oddington?

30. Which good pub is actually a converted grain barge?

31. Which pub was formerly home of the priests of St Lawrence church?

32. In which edition of *The Good Pub Guide* did we first include Lucky Dip entries?

33. Which is Britain's highest pub?

34. Name two Norfolk pubs which are owned by direct descendants of a man who revolutionised farming.

35. What London pub, a main entry in this edition, was included in an earlier edition under an entirely different name?

36. Which new main entries in this edition of the *Guide* are tied to Fullers?

37. In what year was the first edition of *The Good Pub Guide* published?

38. What different name has the Lough Pool at Sellack appeared under, in an earlier edition of the *Guide*?

Authors'
Acknowledgements

The *Guide* has gained immensely over the years from the hugely generous help we have from the many thousands of readers who report to us on the pubs they visit, often in great detail. For the special help they have given us this year, we are deeply grateful to Ian Phillips, N R White, Tracey and Stephen Groves, the Didler, Dr and Mrs M E Wilson, Guy Vowles, Paul Humphreys, Susan and John Douglas, George Atkinson, Michael Doswell, Liz and Brian Barnard, Martin and Karen Wake, Phil and Jane Hodson, Gerry and Rosemary Dobson, Steve Whalley, G Coates, Paul A Moore, Andy and Claire Barker, Bruce Bird, Pete Baker, Michael and Jenny Back, Rona Murdoch, Derek and Sylvia Stephenson, Howard Dell, Bruce and Penny Wilkie, Nick Holding, Michael Dandy, Donna and Roger, Dave Irving, Ewan McCall, Tom McLean, Joan and Michel Hooper-Immins, Dennis Jenkin, Peter Meister, JJW, CMW, Ann and Colin Hunt, Joe Green, Colin Moore, John Wooll, Tony and Wendy Hobden, Comus and Sarah Elliott, Brian and Janet Ainscough, B and K Hypher, Kevin Thorpe, W W Burke, Paul and Ursula Randall, LM, MLR, Val and Alan Green, Bob and Margaret Holder, John Beeken, Tom and Jill Jones, Rob Winstanley, Phyl and Jack Street, J R Ringrose, Mike Gorton, Keith and Chris O'Neill, John Foord, Phil and Sally Gorton, C and R Bromage, Neil and Anita Christopher, Tina and David Woods-Taylor, MDN, Andy and Jill Kassube, Eric Larkham, John Saville, Michael Butler, Rob and Catherine Dunster, Michael and Alison Sandy, Fr Robert Marsh, KC, Duncan Cloud, Simon and Mandy King, Mike and Mary Carter, Pat and Tony Martin, Edward Mirzoeff, John Evans, Barry and Anne, Les and Sandra Brown, Charles and Pauline Stride, R T and J C Moggridge, Dr and Mrs A K Clarke, Ted George, Martin and Pauline Jennings, Keith and Sue Ward, Mike Ridgway, Sarah Miles, Richard Fendick, J F M and M West, Dr and Mrs C W Thomas, Theocsbrian, Tony and Jill Radnor, Joel Dobris, Ray and Winifred Halliday, David and Pauline Brenner, Mayur Shah, Bill Strang, Stuart Pearson, Richard Atherton, Chris Flynn, Wendy Jones, Margaret Dickinson, Dave Braisted, E A and D C T Frewer, Russell Grimshaw, Kerry Purcell, David Barnes, M G Hart, Meg and Colin Hamilton, Jenny and Brian Seller, Ben and Helen Ingram, Simon Collett-Jones, Roger Thornington, R M Corlett, Roger Brown, Clive and Fran Dutson, Terry Buckland, David Glynne-Jones and Peter and Audrey Dowsett.

Warm thanks too to John Holliday of Trade Wind Technology, who built and looks after our database.

As this 25th Anniversary edition is something of a special event, we'd also like to record our heartfelt thanks to David Perrott who has made our maps throughout that period; to Pat Taylor Chalmers who has with an eagle eye edited our work for nearly as long; to Clive Dorman who has typeset it for 15 years now; to Claire Bowles, long our brilliant ambassador; and to Hannah MacDonald, Ken Barlow, Nicky Thompson, Fiona MacIntyre, Gail Rebuck and all at Random House who have given the *Guide* so much support over the years.

Alisdair Aird and Fiona Stapley

ENGLAND

Bedfordshire

This year's batch of new main entries brings Bedfordshire up a good couple of notches on the food front – an area where it's always lagged a little. The ancient Plough at Bolnhurst, reopened after careful refurbishment and back in the *Guide* after quite a break, now combines good food with charmingly distinctive surroundings. The French Horn at Steppingley, also old but with an enjoyable contemporary feel, has some interesting bar snacks alongside the restaurant which is its main food focus. The stylish Birch just outside Woburn aims high and scores well with its imaginative cooking. These three newcomers are all good choices for an enjoyable meal out. But despite the competition from these, and from the cheery Red Lion at Milton Bryan, the beautifully run Hare & Hounds at Old Warden, with its splendid cooking, this year keeps its crown as Bedfordshire Dining Pub of the Year. Yet another new main entry, the Falcon at Bletsoe, is well worth noting as a rewarding all-rounder. In the Lucky Dip section at the end of the chapter, pubs to note particularly are the Black Horse at Ireland, Swan at Radwell, Sow & Pigs in Toddington and reopened Three Fyshes at Turvey. Overall drinks prices in the county are rather higher than the national average – expect to pay about 10p a pint extra.

BIDDENHAM TL0249 Map 5
Three Tuns ㉕
Village signposted from A428 just W of Bedford; MK40 4BD

'Wonderfully ordinary' is the gentle commendation from one reader about this pleasantly straightforward thatched village pub. The low-beamed lounge has wheelback chairs round dark wood tables, window seats and pews on a red turkey carpet, and country paintings. The green-carpeted oak panelled public bar (readers have found it a bit smoky in here) has photographs of local sports teams, also darts, skittles, board games and dominoes. The dining area and lounge bar are no smoking; piped music. Standard but enjoyable food is served in generous helpings and includes dishes such as soup (£4), sandwiches (from £4; soup and sandwich £6), ploughman's (£5.50), home-made dishes such as quiche of the day (£8), steak and kidney pie, steak braised in tarragon and red wine, poached salmon, and meat or vegetable lasagne (£8.50), daily specials such as lamb shank in red wine and mint with horseradish mash (£9.50), and puddings (£4). On handpump, Greene King Abbot is kept under light blanket pressure alongside a guest such as Everards. There are seats in the attractively sheltered spacious garden, and a big decked terrace has lots of picnic-sets. The very good children's play area has swings and a climbing frame; more reports please. *(Recommended by John Saville, Mr and Mrs John Taylor, Richard Greaves)*

Greene King ~ Tenant Kevin Bolwell ~ Real ale ~ Bar food (not Sun evening) ~ Restaurant ~ (01234) 354847 ~ Children in dining room ~ Dogs allowed in bar ~ Open 11.30-2.30, 6-11; 12-3, 7-10.30 Sun

---

Post Office address codings confusingly give the impression that some pubs are in Bedfordshire, when they're really in Buckinghamshire or Cambridgeshire (which is where we list them).

BLETSOE   TL0157   Map 5
Falcon
Rushden Road (A6 N of Bedford); MK44 1QN

We were rather taken aback, arriving for our anonymous inspection in early summer 2006, to see a big board outside claiming 'Good Pub Guide 2006 Accredited' – jumping the gun a bit, as in that edition the pub was just an unstarred Lucky Dip entry and certainly had not been 'accredited' by us. However, all is forgiven, as it turns out to be well worth knowing, with kind service, good value food, a decent range of drinks, pleasant ambiance and a nice riverside garden. The welcoming carpeted bar, with a cheerfully relaxed atmosphere, has low beams and joists, a pleasant mix of sturdy dark tables and of seating from cushioned wall/window seats to high-backed settles, and in winter a couple of open fires – in summer the brick inglenook on the left is instead decorated with copperware and fat church candles. A little side snug on the right has a couple of leather wing armchairs and a sofa, and through on the left is a quiet and comfortable beamed and timbered dining room. Besides good lunchtime sandwiches (from £4.75) and ploughman's (£6.95), the day's menu, on a lectern in the bar, might include soup (£3.95), chicken liver and wild mushroom pâté (£4.95), seared scallops with bacon (£6.95), sausage and mash or steak burger (£8.95), salmon and haddock fishcakes (£9.50), steak and kidney pie (£10.25), braised lamb shank (£10.95), beef stroganoff (£13.95) and puddings such as sticky toffee pudding or pecan pie (£3.95). On Fridays they have an additional fresh fish menu with dishes such as tiger prawn kebab (£6.95) or baked cod fillet with herb oil (£11.95). They have Charles Wells Eagle and Bombardier on handpump, with a guest such as Highgate Davenport, a decent choice of wines by the glass, and good coffee, with daily papers; unobtrusive piped music. The big garden, with plenty of trees and shrubs and perhaps strolling peafowl, has picnic-sets in its main area, with one stone table and seats, and a couple of teak seats on a lower stretch of grass running down to the slow River Ouse. On our visit they were just about to open a smart new terrace overlooking the water. *(Recommended by Sarah Flynn, Michael Dandy)*

Charles Wells ~ Lease Jonathan Seaton-Reid, Lisa Sutcliffe and Lianne Poole ~ Real ale ~ Bar food (12-2, 6.30-9; 12-5, 7-9 Sun) ~ Restaurant ~ (01234) 781222 ~ Children welcome in dining areas ~ Open 12-3, 6-11; 12-11 Sat; 12-10.30 Sun

BOLNHURST   TL0858   Map 5
Plough ♀
Kimbolton Road; MK44 2EX

Those of you who know the Huntsbridge group of pubs will quickly recognise the high standards and style that the experienced and charming new licensees have introduced at this fine old pub. Helpful staff cope happily with the buzzing crowd that's already been attracted by the stylishly relaxed atmosphere, contemporary light and airy interior design (you can see into the kitchen) and carefully considered food and drinks. Beautifully presented food is prepared using thoughtfully sourced ingredients, and as well as tasty drinks, snacks such as devils on horseback (£2) and complimentary home-made bread, the well balanced changing menu includes sensibly imaginative dishes such as double-baked goats cheese soufflé with apple and walnut salad (£4.95), tuna in tempura with wasabi and sesame and soy dipping sauce (£6.95), sausage and mash (£9.95), shallot and girolle mushroom tart with thyme crème fraîche and spinach (£9.50), braised free-range pork and vegetables (£12.50), grilled bass with creamed leeks (£15.50), fillet steak (£18.95), puddings such as rhubarb crumble with stem ginger ice-cream or chocolate tart with double cream (from £4.50) and good cheese platters (£5.50); set lunch menu (two courses £11, three courses £15). An interesting range of carefully chosen drinks includes well kept Batemans XB, Potton Village Bike and a guest such as Adnams Regatta on handpump, a very good wine list including well over a dozen by the glass, home-made lemonade (in summer) and tomato juice, and local apple juice. The lovely tree-shaded garden looks on to the pond where you can still see the remains of the moat that used to surround the pub. *(Recommended by K Carr-Brion, Eithne Dandy, Ryta Lyndley, John and Gillian Browne, Michael Sargent, Ken Carr-Brion)*

Free house ~ Licensees Martin and Jayne Lee and Michael Moscrop ~ Real ale ~ Bar food (12-2(2.30 Sun), 6.30-9.30) ~ Restaurant ~ (01234) 376274 ~ Children welcome ~ Dogs allowed in bar ~ Open 12-3(3.30 Sun), 6.30-11; closed Sun evening, Mon

BROOM   TL1743   Map 5

Cock ★ £

High Street; from A1 opposite northernmost Biggleswade turn-off follow Old Warden 3, Aerodrome 2 signpost, and take first left signposted Broom; SG18 9NA

Readers love the sense they get that little has changed over three centuries at this simple village green pub. There's no bar counter, so the very well kept Greene King IPA, Abbot and Ruddles County are tapped straight from casks by the cellar steps off a central corridor. Original latch doors lead from one cosy little room to the next (four in all), inside which you'll find warming winter open fires, low ochre ceilings, stripped panelling, and farmhouse tables and chairs on antique tiles. Straightforward but well liked bar food includes sandwiches (from £3.25), soup (£3.75), ploughman's (from £5.95), scampi or vegetarian curry (£5.95), breaded plaice (£7.95) and chicken balti or filled yorkshire pudding (£8.45). The restaurant is no smoking; piped (perhaps classical) music, darts and board games. There are picnic-sets and flower tubs on the terrace by the back lawn, and caravanning and camping facilities are available. *(Recommended by Michael Dandy, Mrs Jane Kingsbury, Derek and Sylvia Stephenson, the Didler, Peter and Jean Hoare, John Robertson, Pete Baker, Geoff and Carol Thorp)*

Greene King ~ Tenants Gerry and Jean Lant ~ Real ale ~ Bar food (12-2.30, 7-9; not Sun evening) ~ Restaurant ~ (01767) 314411 ~ Children welcome ~ Dogs allowed in bar ~ Open 12-3(4 Sat), 6-11; 12-4, 7-10.30 Sun

HENLOW   TL1738   Map 5

Engineers Arms ◖ £

A6001 S of Biggleswade; High Street; SG16 6AA

Besides their house beer (Everards Tiger), the fabulous range of up to nine beautifully kept guest ales at this charmingly spick and span pub will probably be from smaller far-flung brewers such as Black Sheep, Breconshire, Bridge of Allan, Northern, Thornbridge, Triple fff or York. Their good drinks range is rounded off with four ciders and a perry, many belgian bottled beers, decent wines by the glass, a good value wine of the month by the bottle, good coffee, and those splendid Tyrrells crisps. If you're stuck for choice the helpful staff are very knowledgeable. The comfortable green-carpeted no smoking front room has lots of old local photographs on its green fleur-de-lys wallpaper, tidily kept and interesting bric-a-brac collections, traditional green-cushioned wall seats, settles and other dark seats, armchair-style bar stools, daily papers and a good log fire. A small tiled inner area has wide-screen sports TV, and beyond is a step up to another comfortable carpeted area, with a second TV, juke box, silenced fruit machine, board games and other games such as table football. Sausage rolls (£1), pork pies (£1.50), hot pies (£1.60) and panini (£2.40) are served most of the time, and service is hospitable and helpful; the good-natured spaniel is called Chico. They run quarterly bank holiday beer festivals, and a bigger one in mid-October. The back terrace has picnic-sets and heaters; more reports please. *(Recommended by Michael Dandy, Bruce Bird)*

Free house ~ Licensees Kevin Machin and Claire Sturgeon ~ Real ale ~ Bar food (snacks when open) ~ No credit cards ~ (01462) 812284 ~ Children welcome in back room ~ Dogs allowed in bar ~ Live blues every third Fri ~ Open 12-12(1 Fri, Sat)

If we know a pub does summer barbecues, we say so.

HOUGHTON CONQUEST TL0441 Map 5
Knife & Cleaver ♀
Between B530 (old A418) and A6, S of Bedford; MK45 3LA

After a bit of a blip last year we're delighted to report that all seems to be back on track at this nice-looking 17th-c dining pub. You may well have to book, and do be aware that they may not serve bar meals if the restaurant is full on Saturday evenings and Sunday lunchtimes. With emphasis on good quality ingredients, the food here is very well prepared. The nicely balanced seasonally changing bar menu might include smoked haddock soup (£4.95), chicken and rabbit terrine (£5.25), antipasti (£6), minute steak baguette (£6.95), mushroom, cheese and hazelnut parcels with sweet red pepper sauce, beef daube or thai-style seafood noodles (£7.25), grilled bass with sweetcorn and chive fritters and yoghurt and ginger sauce (£17.95), and puddings such as milk chocolate refrigerator cake, sticky toffee pudding or home-made ice-creams (£4.25). Batemans XB and a beer from Potton are well kept on handpump alongside Stowford Press farm cider, around 30 good wines by the glass, and over 20 well aged malt whiskies. The rather lovely dark panelling in the comfortably civilised bar is reputed to have come from nearby ruined Houghton House. Maps, drawings and old documents on the walls, as well as lamps, comfy seating and a blazing winter fire add a cosy feel. The airy white-walled no smoking conservatory restaurant has rugs on the tiled floor and lots of hanging plants. There's also a family room, and tables on a terrace alongside a neatly kept attractive garden; unobtrusive piped music. *(Recommended by Dr Michael Smith, David and Ruth Shillitoe, Mr and Mrs John Taylor, Andrew Kell, Iain R Hewitt, Michael Dandy, Ryta Lyndley, Karen Eliot, Mr and Mrs D S Price)*

Free house ~ Licensees David and Pauline Loom ~ Real ale ~ Bar food (12-2.30(2 Sat), 7-9.30; not Sun evening; see note in text about weekends) ~ Restaurant ~ (01234) 740387 ~ Children welcome ~ Dogs allowed in bedrooms ~ Open 12-2.30(2 Sat, 3 Sun), 7-11; closed Sun evening, 27-30 Dec ~ Bedrooms: £59B/£74B

KEYSOE TL0762 Map 5
Chequers
Pertenhall Road, Brook End (B660); MK44 2HR

This simple village local, sunnily painted in yellow and cherry brown, is friendly, and the food is tasty. Now completely no smoking, its two simple beamed rooms (usually fairly quiet at lunchtime unless a group is in) are divided by a stone-pillared fireplace. Well worn carpets and furnishings in one room and piped local radio or music lend a homely 1960s air; darts and board games. Batemans XB and Fullers London Pride are served from handpumps on the stone bar counter, they have a few malt whiskies, and their short wine list is very reasonably priced. Good value bar food includes sandwiches (plain or toasted £3), home-made soup (£3.50), garlic mushrooms on toast or ploughman's (£4), chilli or home-made steak and ale pie (£6.50), chicken breast stuffed with stilton in chive sauce (£8.50), steaks (from £11), and blackboard specials. Tables and chairs on the back terrace look over the garden (which one reader felt could do with a bit of attention), which has a play tree and swings. *(Recommended by Michael and Jenny Back, Mr and Mrs John Taylor, Margaret and Roy Randle)*

Free house ~ Licensee Jeffrey Kearns ~ Real ale ~ Bar food (12-2, 6.30-9.30(7-9 Sun)) ~ No credit cards ~ (01234) 708678 ~ Children welcome away from bar ~ Open 11.30-2.30, 6.30-11; 12-2.30, 7-10.30 Sun; closed Tues

MILTON BRYAN SP9730 Map 4
Red Lion ⑪ ♀
Toddington Road, off B528 S of Woburn; MK17 9HS

Run with true loving pride, this much-enjoyed attractive old pub is well positioned in a pretty little country village near Woburn Abbey and Safari Park. In summer, a plethora of carefully tended floral hanging baskets makes a spectacular show, and there are plenty of tables, chairs and picnic-sets out on the terrace and lawn, which looks across to a delightful row of thatched black and white timbered cottages. The immaculately kept beamed bar area has a relaxed and happily welcoming atmosphere, cream-coloured walls, some exposed brickwork, polished wood and part flagstoned floors, and cheery fresh flowers on the round wooden tables. Using carefully sourced ingredients, bar food (nearly all home made and served by very pleasant staff) includes soup (£3.95), sandwiches (from £3.95), thai fishcakes (£4.95), ploughman's or caramelised onion and cherry tomato tartlet with taleggio cheese (£5.50), toulouse sausage and crème fraîche mash (£8.50), steak and kidney pudding (£9.50), grilled rib-eye steak or smoked haddock fillet on cabbage with poached egg and butter sauce (£12.50), and puddings such as summer fruit pudding or warm chocolate fudge brownie with preserved cherries and mascarpone cream (from £4.95). Greene King IPA, Abbot and Old Speckled Hen are kept under a light blanket pressure, and ten wines and a local apple juice are sold by the glass. *(Recommended by Michael Dandy, F D Smith, N R White, Dr S Lightfoot, Brian Staton, B R and M F Arnold)*

Greene King ~ Tenant Paul Ockleford ~ Real ale ~ Bar food (12-2.30(3 Sun), 7-9.30) ~ Restaurant ~ (01525) 210044 ~ Children welcome ~ Open 11.30-3, 6(6.30 winter)-11; 12-4 Sun; closed Sun evening, Mon evening in winter

NORTHILL TL1446 Map 5
Crown
Ickwell Road; village signposted from B658 W of Biggleswade; SG18 9AA

This jolly nice black and white pub stands just across from the church in a green and peaceful village, with picnic-sets under cocktail parasols out in front looking over the village pond. The smallish bar has a big open fire, flagstones and low heavy beams, comfortable bow window seats, and well kept Greene King IPA and Abbot and Old Speckled Hen and a guest such as Brains Reverend James on handpump from the copper-topped counter. On the left is a small dining area while on the right, the airy main no smoking dining room has elegantly laid tables on bare boards, with steps up to a smaller more intimate side room. The atmosphere throughout is warm and relaxed with fairly unobtrusive piped music. Bar food includes lunchtime sandwiches and baguettes (from £3.99), sausage and mash (£7.95), daily roast (£8.95), tomato, basil, mushroom and cheese in filo pastry with pesto cream sauce (£9.95), and daily specials such as grilled cod with white wine and parsley sauce (£11.95) or duck breast with red wine gravy (£13.95). A sheltered side terrace has more picnic-sets and opens into a very large garden with a few widely spaced canopied tables, plenty of trees and shrubs, a good play area, and masses of room for children to run around. *(Recommended by Michael Dandy, Pete Baker, Jeff Rix, John Cadge)*

Greene King ~ Tenant Kevin Blois ~ Real ale ~ Bar food (12-2.30(3 Sun), 6.30-9.30; not Sun evening) ~ Restaurant ~ (01767) 627337 ~ Children welcome away from main bar ~ Dogs allowed in bar ~ Open 11.30-3, 6-11; 11.30-12 Sat; 11.30-11 Sun; 11-4 Sun, cl Sun evening; 11.30-3.30, 6-11 Sat in winter

OLD WARDEN TL1343 Map 5
Hare & Hounds 🍴 ♟
Village signposted off A600 S of Bedford and B658 W of Biggleswade; SG18 9HQ

Bedfordshire Dining Pub of the Year

Readers are full of praise for the splendid food served at this beautifully kept and rather elegant pub. Breads and ice-cream are home made, and where possible they use local ingredients such as pork from the Shuttleworth estate. The changing bar menu might include saffron risotto (£5.95), whitebait (£6.95), roasted garlic polenta with grilled mediterranean vegetables (£8.95), pie of the day, sausages or salmon tagliatelle (£9.95),fried pigeon with wild mushroom risotto and truffle oil (£13.95), sirloin steak with pepper butter (£15.95), side orders (£2), puddings such as apple crumble or vanilla crème brûlée (£5.95) and british and irish cheeses

(£6.95). Service from well turned out staff remains attentive and friendly throughout the session. Rambling around a central servery, in cosy reds and creams, the four beamed rooms (now completely no smoking) have dark standing timbers, comfortable upholstered armchairs and sofas on stripped flooring, light wood tables and coffee tables, a woodburning stove in an inglenook fireplace and fresh flowers on the bar. Prints and photographs depict the historic aircraft in the Shuttleworth Collection just up the road. Although the accent is firmly on dining, you can pop in for just a drink. Charles Wells Eagle and Bombardier and a guest such as Greene King Old Speckled Hen are well kept on handpump, with eight or so wines by the glass including some from a local vineyard; piped music. The village itself is part of the Shuttleworth estate and was built about 200 years ago in a swiss style. The glorious sloping garden (with tables on a terrace) which stretches up to pine woods behind the pub, dates back to the same period and style, and there are some substantial walks nearby. Though there's an ample car park you may need to use the village hall parking as an overflow. (Recommended by Michael Dandy, John and Patricia White, David and Ruth Shillitoe, Alex and Irene Harvey, Bob and Maggie Atherton, B and M Kendall)

Charles Wells ~ Lease Jane Hasler ~ Real ale ~ Bar food (12-2(3 Sun), 6.30-9.30; not Sun evening, not Mon) ~ (01767) 627225 ~ Children welcome away from bar ~ Dogs allowed in bar ~ Open 12-3, 6-11; 12-10.30 Sun; closed Mon except bank hols; 26 Dec-1 Jan

RISELEY   TL0362   Map 5
Fox & Hounds
High Street; village signposted off A6 and B660 N of Bedford; MK44 1DT

The speciality at this cheery bustling pub is their steaks: you choose your own piece and pay by weight – say, £11.60 for 8oz rump, £12.60 for 8oz of sirloin and £14.20 for 8oz of fillet – and watch it cooked on an open grill. Other good food is listed on blackboards and might include parsnip and ginger soup (£3.75), whitebait (£4.95), ploughman's (£6.95), beef curry (£8.95), steak and stilton pie (£9.50), salmon in champagne sauce or chicken with pesto (£9.75), beef stroganoff (£11.25), and puddings such as jam roly-poly or spotted dick and custard (£3.75). Even if you don't see anything you fancy, it's worth asking: they're very obliging here, and will try to cope with particular food requests. Service is normally very attentive and friendly, but it does get busy, and as they don't take bookings on Saturday night you may have to wait for your table and food. A relaxing lounge area, with comfortable leather chesterfields, lower tables and wing chairs, contrasts with the more traditional pub furniture spread among timber uprights under the heavy low beams; unobtrusive piped classical or big band piped music. Charles Wells Eagle and Bombardier are kept well on handpump alongside a decent collection of other drinks including bin-end wines and a range of malts and cognacs. An attractively decked terrace with wooden tables and chairs has outside heating, and the pleasant garden has shrubs and a pergola. (Recommended by Michael Dandy, Philip Denton, Michael Sargent, Margaret and Roy Randle, A J Bowen)

Charles Wells ~ Managers Jan and Lynne Zielinski ~ Real ale ~ Bar food (11.30-1.45, 6.30-9.30 (12-2, 7-9 Sun)) ~ Restaurant ~ (01234) 708240 ~ Children welcome ~ Dogs allowed in bar ~ Open 11.30-2.30, 6.30-11; 12-3, 7-10.30 Sun

STANBRIDGE   SP9623   Map 4
Five Bells
Station Road, at junction with A505 – and pub signposted off A5 N of Dunstable; LU7 9JF

Although this cream-fronted pub with its striking grey woodwork appears to be a perfectly traditional pub from the outside, inside has been comprehensively updated with a stylish, contemporary look. Very low exposed beams are complemented by careful spotlighting, rugs on wooden floors, armchairs and sofas, and neatly polished tables. The airy, elegant no smoking restaurant leads into a large garden with plenty of good wooden tables and chairs, and big perfectly mown lawns with fruit trees. Smoking in the bar only and an enjoyable atmosphere throughout. Very good bar food might include soup (£3.75), mushroom, bacon and stilton rarebit (£4.65), sandwiches (£5.25), tagliatelle puttanesca or vegetable lasagne (£6.95), beef and ale pie (£7.75), grilled bass with herb butter (£11.95) and puddings such as chocolate brownie (£4.95). Well kept Greene King IPA, Timothy Taylors Landlord and guest such as Fullers London Pride on handpump, and ten wines by the glass; one reader found the piped music obtrusive. *(Recommended by Gerry and Rosemary Dobson, Dave Braisted, Annabel Viney, Michael Dandy, David and Ruth Shillitoe)*

Tetleys ~ Manager Luke Davy ~ Real ale ~ Bar food (12-9.30(9 Sun)) ~ Restaurant ~ (01525) 210224 ~ Children welcome ~ Dogs allowed in bar ~ Open 12-12(10.30 Sun)

STEPPINGLEY   TL0135   Map 5

French Horn ♀

Village signposted off A507 just N of Flitwick; Church End; MK45 5AU

Going into this old pub, snuggled down below the quiet village's church, brings a real surprise. Yes, there are the low heavy beams you'd expect, the flagstones and the inglenook fireplace (with a solid fuel stove), and staff are friendly and interested in the proper old-fashioned way. But the style of the place is thoroughly up to date, with big brown leather bucket armchairs, comfortable bar stools to match, squishy leather sofas in a jungly back corner of lilies and house plants, and a bright bare-boards dining area with a couple of big abstracts on plain cream walls. They serve only light snacks such as goats cheese tart (£6.50), caesar salad (£6.95) and some interesting open ciabattas (£6.95) in the bar, with a more extensive restaurant menu. They have Greene King IPA and Old Speckled Hen on handpump, ten or so wines by the glass, and showpiece modern lavatories; piped music and TV for major sporting events only. The little public bar on the left is a nice exercise in modernity, too, with its minimalist décor and admirably blocky dark seats and tables. There are tables outside front and back, with a good children's play area at the back, and this is fairly handy for Woburn. *(Recommended by Michael Dandy, Ian Phillips, Geoff and Carol Thorp)*

Greene King ~ Lease Stephan Marriott ~ Real ale ~ Bar food (12-3, 6.30-9.30; 12-4 Sun) ~ (01525) 712051 ~ Children welcome ~ Dogs allowed in bar ~ Open 12-3, 5.30-11; 12-12 Sat; 12-10.30 Sun

WOBURN   SP9433   Map 4

Birch ♀

3.5 miles from M1 junction 13; follow Woburn signs via A507 and A4012, then in village turn right and head out on A5130 (Newport Road); MK17 9HX

This well run and stylishly upscale dining pub, now no smoking throughout, describes itself accurately as a Bar and Restaurant. The bar part, looping around the front servery, has deep armchairs, sofas and bar stools, all in soft brown leather, with good dark hardwood flooring, handsome flower arrangements, and modern prints on its cream walls. It has a good range of interesting wines by the glass, Adnams and Fullers London Pride on handpump, good coffees, and daily papers; there may be unobtrusive piped music, and the service by neatly dressed staff is helpful and efficient. The main emphasis here is unquestionably on the food side. The carefully lit back part consists of an extensive and comfortable dining area, the central part given an airy conservatory feel by its ceramic tile floor, lightly ragged plank panelling and glazed pitched roof, with a step up either side to carpeted or bare-boards sections with attractive artwork on their soft canary walls. The good food includes soup (£4.95), filled ciabattas (£5.95), prawn and monkfish fishcake with lemon cream (£6.95), wild mushroom risotto with thyme and truffle oil (£7.95), smoked haddock with poached egg, spinach and hollandaise or battered fish of the day (£8.95), fried chicken with red pepper mash and béarnaise sauce (£9.95), veal escalope with blue cheese potato rösti (£13.50), venison steak or bass (£17.95). There are tables out on a sheltered terrace. *(Recommended by Michael Dandy, Michael Sargent)*

Free house ~ Licensee Mark Campbell ~ Real ale ~ Bar food (12-2.30, 6-10; 12-5 Sun) ~
Restaurant ~ (01525) 290295 ~ Children welcome ~ Open 11.30-3, 6-11; 12-6 Sun;
closed Sun evening

LUCKY DIP

Besides the fully inspected pubs, you might like to try these Lucky Dips recommended to
us and described by readers (if you do, please send us reports: www.goodguides.co.uk).

AMPTHILL [TL0338]
Prince of Wales MK45 2NB [Bedford St (B540
N from central crossroads)]: Welcoming new
landlord and cheerful staff happy to discuss
make-up of their good imaginative food, small
bar with easy chairs and settees, larger no
smoking flagstoned dining room,
contemporary décor, Charles Wells Eagle and
Bombardier, good choice of wines by the glass
(Michael Dandy, Stephen Cavender)
BEDFORD [TL0550]
Park MK40 2PF [Park Ave/Kimbolton Rd]:
Large modernised pub with mix of furnishings
inc leather sofas in partly flagstoned linked
areas, Charles Wells Eagle and Bombardier,
daily papers, conservatory eating area; sizeable
garden with tables on decking *(Eithne Dandy)*
Wellington Arms MK40 2JX [Wellington St]:
Traditional corner local with Adnams, B&T
and up to eight guest beers, also continental
beers on tap and in bottle, darts, dominoes,
hood skittles; tables outside, open all day
(Brian and Jean Hepworth)
CLOPHILL [TL0838]
Stone Jug MK45 4BY [N on A6 from A507
roundabout, after 200 yds 2nd turn on right
into Back St]: Secluded stone-built local, cosy
and welcoming, with good value lunchtime
food from sandwiches and baked potatoes up,
B&T Shefford, Courage Directors or John
Smiths and changing ales such as Everards
Beacon, Marlow Rebellion Wrecked and
Wadworths 6X, pleasantly unpretentious
comfortable bar with family area and darts in
small games extension; piped music; small
pretty back terrace, roadside picnic-sets too
(Michael Dandy, Geoff and Carol Thorp)
DUNSTABLE [TL0122]
Globe LU6 1LS [Winfield St]: Back-to-basics
real ale pub, a dozen handpumps with B&T
and changing guest ales, good landlord and
conversation, darts, dominoes, cards; dogs
welcome *(John Flowers)*
GREAT BARFORD [TL1252]
Golden Cross MK44 3JD [Bedford Rd]:
Thriving atmosphere in main-road pub with
pretty back restaurant/bar serving good chinese
food (worth booking), cheerful attentive
service, pristine tables, white linen cloths and
napkins, special deals Mon-Thurs
(Sarah Flynn)
HENLOW [TL1738]
Crown SG16 6BS [High St]: Small Chef &
Brewer with their usual décor and food,
Adnams Broadside, Courage Directors and
Fullers ESB, good coffee and choice of wines
by the glass, nice log fire, daily papers; piped

music; terrace and small garden
(Michael Dandy)
HUSBORNE CRAWLEY [SP9635]
White Horse MK43 0XE [Mill Rd, just off
A507]: Open-plan pub with Flowers IPA,
reasonable wine choice, usual bar food from
baguettes and baked potatoes up, pool in
games area; piped music, TV; tables outside,
lovely hanging baskets, open all day wknds
(Michael Dandy)
IRELAND [TL1341]
☆ *Black Horse* SG17 5QL [off A600 Shefford—
Bedford]: Busy and attractive dining pub
consistently reliable for wide choice of plentiful
food from sandwiches, ciabattas and
interesting light dishes up, good fresh
ingredients, up-to-date presentation, wider
evening menu, comfortable seats and plenty of
space including stylish garden-view extension,
Fullers London Pride, Greene King IPA and a
guest such as Potton Village Bike, good range
of wines and good coffee, pleasant attentive
staff; smoking allowed in bar; plenty of tables
in neat front garden with play area, cottage
bedrooms – nice peaceful rural setting
*(Michael Dandy, BB, Michael Sargent,
Peter and Margaret Glenister, John Saul,
Bob and Maggie Atherton)*
KEMPSTON [TL0347]
Slaters Arms MK43 8RS [Box End Rd (A5134,
off A4218 W of Bedford)]: Extensive modern
refurbishment giving comfortable carpeted bar
and family restaurant area, wide choice of pub
food from baguettes and baked potatoes up
using some local and organic ingredients, cut-
price Sun lunch for children, Greene King IPA
and Abbot and St Austell Tribute, speciality
coffees; picnic-sets in big back tree-shaded
garden with plenty for children inc well
equipped fenced-off play area, pets corner and
summer ice-cream bar, has been open all day
at least in summer *(Michael Dandy,
Mike Ridgway, Sarah Miles)*
LANGFORD [TL1840]
Plough SG18 9QA [Church St]: Small simply
and comfortably refurbished two-bar pub with
Greene King IPA and Old Speckled Hen and
good choice of wines by the glass from central
servery, attractively priced pubby food from
sandwiches and wraps up; piped music, TV;
good-sized garden, bedrooms *(Michael Dandy,
Emma Chippendale)*
LINSLADE [SP9125]
Hunt LU7 2LR [Church Rd]: Hotel with
refurbished traditional pubby bar enjoyed by
locals, well kept ales, enjoyable home-made
food in restaurant; bedrooms *(Brian Root)*

LUTON [TL0921]
Bricklayers Arms LU2 0DD [Hightown Rd]:
Convivial local with long-serving landlady, five
real ales, lunchtime bar food, décor evoking
living room/library; sports TV, very busy for
Luton home matches *(John Flowers)*

MAULDEN [TL0538]
Dog & Badger MK45 2AD [Clophill Rd]:
Attractive thatched village pub, refurbished
bare-boards bar, steps down to two carpeted
areas and no smoking restaurant, Fullers
London Pride and Greene King IPA, good
choice of wines by the glass, wide range of
good value food (all day Sun – best to book
wknds), friendly quick service; piped music;
tables in front garden *(Michael Dandy)*
White Hart MK45 2DH [Ampthill Rd]:
Thatch and low beams, large well divided
partly no smoking dining area, big fireplace
dividing bar, wide food choice from good
value hot ciabattas, baguettes and baked
potatoes up, friendly helpful service, Fullers
London Pride, Greene King IPA and a guest
such as Ringwood Fortyniner, good choice of
wines by the glass; tables outside front and
back, open all day wknds *(Michael Dandy)*

MILLBROOK [TL0138]
Chequers MK45 2JB: Two-room village pub
opp golf club, log fire and plate collection in
small low-beamed carpeted bar, Flowers IPA
and Stonehenge Pigswill, good coffee,
reasonably priced food inc lunch deals, quick
cheerful service, back restaurant
(Michael Dandy)

ODELL [SP9657]
Bell MK43 7AS [off A6 S of Rushden, via
Sharnbrook; High St]: Several low-beamed
rooms around central servery, mix of old
settles and neat modern furniture, log or coal
fires, good service under friendly new licensees,
Greene King IPA and Abbot and perhaps a
guest beer, good choice of usual food from
sandwiches and baked potatoes up (not Sun
evening); children welcome away from counter,
delightful big garden backing on to River
Ouse, handy for Harrold-Odell country park
(Steve Nye, LYM, Michael Dandy)

PEGSDON [TL1130]
☆ *Live & Let Live* SG5 3JX [B655 W of
Hitchin]: Extended dining pub with wide
choice if not cheap, real ales such as Adnams,
Brakspears, Fullers London Pride and
Theakstons, good wine choice, friendly staff,
snug traditional tiled and panelled core; piped
music; attractive hanging baskets and garden
below Deacon Hill, open all day *(David and
Ruth Shillitoe, Michael Dandy, LYM, Mr and
Mrs John Taylor)*

PULLOXHILL [TL0634]
Cross Keys MK45 5HB [High St; off A6 N of
Barton le Clay]: Friendly local, lots of
timbering and flower baskets, rambling front
bars, very welcoming long-serving landlord
and family, wide choice of good value usual
food inc tasty pies and OAP bargain lunches,
children in big back no smoking dining room,
Adnams Broadside and Charles Wells
Bombardier and Eagle, daily papers; garden

with play area (and field for caravans), pretty
part of village in nice countryside
*(Michael Dandy, Geoff and Carol Thorp,
Gerry and Rosemary Dobson)*

RADWELL [TL0057]
☆ *Swan* MK43 7HS [signed off A6 Bedford—
Rushden; Felmersham Rd]: Friendly new
young licensees in small thatched dining pub,
appealingly simple décor in comfortable
flagstoned bar and bare-boards eating rooms
either side, good food from short choice of
simple and rewarding bar lunches to interesting
evening menu (Sat evening usually fully booked
now), Sun carvery, helpful service, Charles
Wells Eagle, good wines by the glass and
coffee, some nice prints; informal garden with
tables and play area, attractive quiet village,
cl Mon *(Michael Dandy, Mr and Mrs G Swire,
BB, John Saville)*

RIDGMONT [SP9736]
☆ *Rose & Crown* MK43 0TY [2 miles from M1
junction 13: A507, follow Ampthill signs –
High St]: Useful off-motorway standby with
comfortable furniture and open fire in neat
lounge, traditional public bar, well kept
Adnams, Charles Wells Eagle and Bombardier
and a couple of guests such as St Austells
Tinners, usual food from sandwiches up (not
Sun evening), no smoking areas; piped music
and machines, darts; children and dogs
allowed, good wheelchair access, long and
attractive sheltered back garden, camping and
caravanning, open all day wknds
*(Michael Dandy, Dave Braisted,
Philip Denton, LYM, Andy Lickfold,
Michael and Alison Sandy, Geoff and
Carol Thorp)*

SHARPENHOE [TL0630]
☆ *Lynmore* MK45 4SH [Sharpenhoe Rd]: This
low-beamed rambling pub, long popular with
readers (and walkers) for its enjoyable food,
good service and drinks range, fine views of
The Clappers from its big back no smoking
dining area, and good garden for children, was
under complete refurbishment by new owners
as we went to press in 2006 *(BB)*

SHILLINGTON [TL1234]
Crown SG5 3LP [High Rd, S end]: Small
flagstoned bar and attractive lounge area,
Greene King IPA and Old Speckled Hen and
Timothy Taylors Landlord, good choice of
wines by the glass, good value generous
straightforward food from baguettes and
baked potatoes up, quick friendly helpful
service, no smoking restaurant; pleasant garden
with heaters *(Michael Dandy)*
Musgrave Arms SG5 3LX [Apsley End Rd,
towards Pegsdon and Hexton]: Low-beamed
village local with settles, tables, prints and
horsebrasses in friendly and civilised lounge,
woodburner in comfortable public bar, small
no smoking dining room, Greene King IPA
and Abbot, generous home-made pubby food
from sandwiches and baked potatoes up,
cheerful service, daily papers; piped music;
big back garden with picnic-sets, cl Mon
lunchtime *(Michael Dandy, Geoff and
Carol Thorp)*

SILSOE [TL0835]
Star & Garter MK45 4DR [High St]: Smart
pub by village church, large bar and raised no
smoking dining area, good value usual bar
food from sandwiches and baguettes up,
separate evening menu, quick service, Adnams,
B&T Shefford and a seasonal ale and Greene
King IPA, darts; piped music; nice good-sized
terrace *(Michael Dandy)*

SOUTHILL [TL1441]
White Horse SG18 9LD [off B658 SW of
Biggleswade]: Cosy and comfortable country
pub with extensive eating area, wide range of
enjoyable generous food inc lunchtime
favourites, welcoming staff, well kept Greene
King IPA and Old Speckled Hen and perhaps
guests such as Black Sheep, good wine choice;
piped music; lots of tables in large pleasant
neatly kept garden with good play area
*(Michael Dandy, LYM, Peter and
Margaret Glenister)*

STANFORD [TL1541]
Green Man SG18 9JD [Southill rd]: L-shaped
bar with big fireplace, adjoining games area
with pool, bar food from generous sandwiches,
hot baguettes and baked potatoes up, smart
restaurant with beams and stripped brick, OAP
lunchtime bargains, Courage Best and
Theakstons, friendly service; terrace with
barbecue, big garden with lots of play
equipment, 11 bedrooms in chalet block
(Michael Dandy)

STREATLEY [TL0728]
Chequers LU3 3PS [just off A6 N of Luton;
Sharpenhoe Rd]: Popular partly panelled open-
plan L-shaped local, mix of chairs and table
sizes, old-fashioned prints, books and old local
photographs, good value food from bargain
sandwiches up, four Greene King ales, cheerful
staff, daily papers, open fire in public bar;
piped music, games, TV, Tues quiz night; nice
front terrace, small back garden
(Michael Dandy)

STUDHAM [TL0215]
Bell LU6 2QG [Dunstable Rd]: Well worn in
village pub dating from 16th c, big public bar
with pool, darts, TV and games machine,
plenty of brasses and bric-a-brac in partly no
smoking beamed and timbered dining lounge
on right, wide choice of enjoyable fresh food
from sandwiches to good value Sun lunch,
Adnams and Greene King IPA and Abbot,
helpful staff, daily papers; piped music; views
from picnic-sets in big back garden, good
walks, handy for Whipsnade and the Tree
Cathedral *(Michael and Alison Sandy)*
Red Lion LU6 2QA [Church Rd]: Open-plan
pub in attractive setting below grassy common,
bright and cheerful décor in bare-boards front
bar and back carpeted dining area, Adnams,
Fullers London Pride, Greene King IPA and
Tring Colleys Dog, pubby food from
sandwiches to steaks, pleasant service, darts in
small side area; quiet piped music; garden
tables, handy for Whipsnade *(LYM,
Michael Dandy)*

TEMPSFORD [TL1652]
Wheatsheaf SG19 2AN [Church St]: 18th-c

village pub with open fire in cosy lounge,
Special Operations Executive memorabilia
(nearby World War II base), friendly service,
good value straightforward pub food from
sandwiches and baked potatoes up, small
helpings available, Courage and Greene King
IPA, pleasant restaurant; piped music; tables
on decking and in big garden (some traffic
noise) *(Michael Dandy)*

THURLEIGH [TL0558]
Jackal MK44 2DB [High St]: Friendly village
pub with easy chairs and good fire in tiled-
floor bar (where dogs allowed), another in
comfortable carpeted dining lounge, enjoyable
pubby food from lunchtime rolls and wraps
up, good service, well kept Charles Wells Eagle
and Bombardier; piped music; roadside seats
out in front, more in nice rambling back
garden *(Michael Dandy, Mark Kiteley)*

TILSWORTH [SP9824]
Anchor LU7 9PU [just off A5 NW of
Dunstable]: Bright and airy, good value quickly
served usual food from sandwiches, baguettes
and baked potatoes up, real ales such as
Greene King IPA, St Austell Tribute and Tom
Woods Bomber County, friendly staff, daily
papers, dining conservatory; pool and TV in
games end; picnic-sets on terrace and side
lawn, more paddocky part with play area
(Michael Dandy)

TODDINGTON [TL0128]
Angel LU5 6DE [Luton Rd]: Contemporary
furnishings inc a good-sized no smoking eating
area and a log-fire area with sofas and
comfortable seats, Greene King IPA and
Morlands Original with a guest such as Tom
Woods Bomber County, good coffee and
choice of wines by the glass, wide range of
food, daily papers, pub games; tables in garden
with terrace and heaters, overlooking village
pond and green *(Michael Dandy)*
☆ *Sow & Pigs* LU5 6AA [Church Sq]: Quaint
19th-c pub named after carving on church opp,
lots of pig decorations, also old books and
knick-knacks, mixed bag of furnishings inc
pews, two armchairs and a retired chesterfield,
friendly chatty landlady and pub dog,
particularly well kept Greene King ales, good
coffee, home-made lunchtime food from good
cheap rolls up (not Sun; back Victorian-style
dining room can be booked for parties), two
log fires, games; smoking allowed throughout;
children allowed, games in small garden,
bedrooms, open all day *(JJW, CMW,
Conor McGaughey)*

TOTTERNHOE [SP9721]
☆ *Cross Keys* LU6 2DA [off A505 W of A5;
Castle Hill Rd]: Thatched and timbered two-
bar pub below remains of a motte and bailey
fort, reopened after beautiful restoration
following 2004 fire damage; low beams, cosy
furnishings, good straightforward food, several
real ales, friendly service, no smoking dining
room; big-screen TV; good views from big
attractive garden *(LYM)*

TURVEY [SP9452]
Three Cranes MK43 8EP [off A428 W of
Bedford]: Comfortably worn in two-level pub

with quickly served pub food all day from good value sandwiches up, Greene King IPA and Abbot, guest beers such as Ridleys Old Bob and St Austell Tribute, good choice of other drinks, log fire, darts and games; piped music, TV; children in no smoking restaurant area, tables in secluded tree-shaded garden with climber, bedrooms *(Michael Dandy, LYM, George Atkinson, B C Robertson)*

☆ *Three Fyshes* MK43 8ER [A428 NW of Bedford; Bridge Street, W end of village]: Early 17th-c beamed pub reopened after careful refurbishment by small pub group, big inglenook in small bar, no smoking lounge, plenty of character with mix of easy chairs and upright chairs around tables on carpet or ancient flagstones, Adnams, Caledonian Deuchars IPA, Fullers London Pride and Greene King IPA, very wide choice of pub food from baguettes and baked potatoes up, daily papers; piped music; decking and canopy in charming garden overlooking bridge and mill on Great Ouse *(Mr and Mrs D Price, Michael Dandy, LYM, George Atkinson, Sarah Flynn)*

WESTONING [SP0332]
Chequers MK45 5LA [Park Rd (A5120 N of M1 junction 12)]: Neatly refurbished multi-gabled thatched pub with black bargeboards, Greene King IPA and Fullers London Pride, good choice of wines by the glass, enjoyable pub food from ciabattas up, cask tables in small low-beamed front bar, good-sized back bar inc some settees, big stables restaurant; piped music; courtyard tables, open all day *(Michael Dandy)*

WHIPSNADE [TL0018]
Old Hunters Lodge LU6 2LN [B4540 E]: Extended thatched pub with sofas in small carpeted bar, big old-world no smoking dining room in beamed original core dating from 15th c, pubby bar food from sandwiches and baguettes up, more extensive restaurant menu, Greene King IPA and Abbot and a guest such as Black Sheep or Nethergate Old Chap, cheerful service; handy for zoo, with tables in sheltered front garden, bedrooms, open all day Sun *(Michael Dandy)*

WOBURN [SP9433]
Bell MK17 9QJ [Bedford St]: Good value generous food from sandwiches and pubby bar lunches to restaurant dishes, Greene King IPA

and Abbot, good choice of wines by the glass, good coffee, efficient friendly service, small bar area, longer bare-boards dining lounge up steps, pleasant décor and furnishings; piped music, games; children welcome at lunchtime, tables on back terrace, hotel part across road, handy for Woburn Park *(Michael Dandy, Ian Phillips)*

☆ *Black Horse* MK17 9QB [Bedford St]: Friendly and smartly kept 19th-c food pub, sandwiches (all day) and wide choice of enjoyable mealtime dishes inc enterprising deli board, Greene King IPA, Abbot and Old Speckled Hen, good choice of wines by the glass, coal fire, several areas with steps down to pleasant back restaurant; children in eating areas, summer barbecues in attractive sheltered back courtyard, open all day *(Michael Dandy, Mr and Mrs John Taylor, LYM)*

Flying Fox MK17 9HD [Sheep Lane (actually A5 Bletchley—Hockliffe, well away from village)]: Well run Vintage Inn dining pub with hop-hung beams, pictures and artefacts in well arranged linked areas, pleasant atmosphere and attentive service, decent food from open sandwiches up (good fish and chips), fine choice of wines by the glass, Bass; piped music, pub games; tables out on grass *(B H and J I Andrews, Michael Dandy)*

Inn at Woburn MK17 9PX [George St]: Attractive Georgian hotel with sofas and high-backed leather seats in beamed bar, former fireplace now a seating alcove, good choice of wines by the glass, CharlesWells Eagle, good service, baguettes, ploughman's and up-to-date snacks, brasserie-style restaurant; nice bedrooms *(Michael Dandy)*

Magpie MK17 9QB: Small low-ceilinged traditional bar, sofas in small lounge with popular restaurant beyond, Greene King Ruddles County and Marstons Pedigree, nice choice of food from sandwiches and wraps to local river trout; TV, radio; tables in neatly kept back courtyard, bedrooms, open all day *(Michael Dandy)*

WRESTLINGWORTH [TL2547]
Chequers SG19 2EP [High St]: Carpeted bar with Greene King IPA and Ridleys Rumpus from central servery, food from bargain baguettes and toasties up, open fire, side dining area, pool and darts in games end; garden tables, cl Sun evening *(Michael Dandy)*

Real ale to us means beer which has matured naturally in its cask – not pressurised or filtered. We name all real ales stocked. We usually name ales preserved under a light blanket of carbon dioxide too, though purists – pointing out that this stops the natural yeasts developing – would disagree (most people, including us, can't tell the difference!)

Berkshire

This county has something ideal for almost every taste. There are delightfully unspoilt taverns, bustling places liked by families, and dining pubs offering imaginative modern cooking. Three new entries are the Crown & Horns at East Ilsley (a lively country pub, relaxed and unpretentious, back in the *Guide* after a break), the bistroish Royal Oak at Knowl Hill (quite a discovery, with good inventive cooking and kind service), and the Olde Red Lion at Oakley Green (a well run and inviting country inn, good all round). At the Royal Oak at Knowl Hill, we enjoyed our anonymous inspection meal so much that it takes the title of Berkshire Dining Pub of the Year. Other pubs doing well here this year include the unspoilt and unchanging Bell at Aldworth (a great favourite and with very low prices), the Sun in the Wood, Ashmore Green (hard-working licensees and enjoyed by all ages of customers), the Green Man at Hurst (popular food and fair prices), the Crown & Garter at Inkpen (particularly friendly, helpful staff), the Little Angel at Remenham (smart, modern and comfortable), the tiny Magpie & Parrot at Shinfield (the plant nursery has now closed, sadly), the Beehive at White Waltham (a nice little country local), and the well run Winterbourne Arms, Winterbourne (new landscaped garden). Quite a few pubs in the Lucky Dip section at the end of the chapter are also attracting particular attention at the moment – most of these already inspected and approved by us: the Bell at Boxford, Horns at Crazies Hill, Swan at Great Shefford, White Hart at Hamstead Marshall, Belgian Arms in Holyport, Red Lyon at Hurley, Swan at Inkpen, restauranty Hare near Lambourn, Sweeney & Todd in Reading, Bull in Sonning (quite a favourite), Carpenters Arms in Windsor and Wheelwrights Arms in Winnersh. Though beer here does tend to cost quite a bit more than the national average, the excess isn't now as pricey as it used to be. This may partly be because of the growing success of the small West Berkshire brewery. You can find its beers in more and more of the county's better pubs, and they are usually attractively priced.

ALDWORTH   SU5579   Map 2
Bell ⑳ ★ ♀ ◧ £
A329 Reading—Wallingford; left on to B4009 at Streatley; RG8 9SE

A favourite with many of our readers, this warmly friendly 14th-c country pub is a very special place. It's quite unspoilt and unchanging and has been run by the same family for over 200 years, who make sure that mobile phones, piped music and games machines are banned. With a good mix of customers, it's at its quietest on weekday lunchtimes, and the rooms have benches around the panelled walls, an ancient one-handed clock, beams in the shiny ochre ceiling, and a woodburning stove – and rather than a bar counter for service, there's a glass-panelled hatch. Well priced Arkells BBB and Kingsdown are superbly kept alongside Old Tyler, Dark Mild and a monthly guest on handpump from the local West Berkshire Brewery; Upton farm cider; no draught lager. They also serve good house wines and winter mulled wine (£2.25). Excellent value bar food is limited to filled hot crusty rolls such as honey-roast ham, wild mushroom and port pâté, cheddar, stilton or brie (£2), smoked salmon, crab, tongue or salt beef (£2.30), and a variety

of ploughman's (from £4.50); in winter they also do home-made soup (£3). Darts,
shove-ha'penny, and dominoes. The quiet, old-fashioned cottagey garden is by the
village cricket ground, and behind the pub there's a paddock with farm animals. In
summer there may be occasional morris dancers, while at Christmas local
mummers perform in the road by the ancient well-head (the shaft is sunk 365 feet
through the chalk). It tends to get very busy at weekends; dogs must be kept on
leads. *(Recommended by Stan Edwards, Ray J Carter, Rob Winstanley, Dick and
Madeleine Brown, Guy Vowles, Dr and Mrs A K Clarke, the Didler, Pete Baker, Kevin Thorpe,
Paul Humphreys, Richard Endacott, Keith Wright, Angela Copeland, Anthony Longden,
Susan and John Douglas, AP Seymour, Andrew Hollingshead, Ian Phillips)*

Free house ~ Licensee H E Macaulay ~ Real ale ~ Bar food (11-2.30, 6-10.30; 12-2.30,
7-10 Sun; not Mon) ~ No credit cards ~ (01635) 578272 ~ Children in Tap Room ~
Dogs welcome ~ Open 11-3, 6-11; 12-3, 7-10.30 Sun; closed Mon

ASHMORE GREEN   SU5069   Map 2
Sun in the Wood ♀

NE of Newbury, or off A4 at Thatcham; off A34/A4 roundabout NW of Newbury, via
B4009 Shaw Hill, then right into Kiln Road, then left into Stoney Lane after nearly 0.5
miles; or get to Stoney Lane sharp left off Ashmore Green Road, N of A4 at W end of
Thatcham via Northfield Road and Bowling Green Road; RG18 9HF

You can be sure of a genuinely warm welcome from the hard-working licensees and
their 'team' at this particularly well run and very popular country pub – now totally
no smoking. It's the sort of place where customers of any age feel at home and
where you can drop in for a drink and chat on a sofa after work, entertain family
and friends or even enjoy a game of crazy golf at their nine-hole woodland course.
The high-beamed front bar has bare boards on the left, carpet on the right, and a
mix of nice old chairs, padded dining chairs and stripped pews around sturdy
tables. It opens into a big back dining area which has the same informal feel,
candles on tables, and some interesting touches like the big stripped bank of
apothecary's drawers. There's a small conservatory sitting area by the side entrance.
Served by friendly, helpful staff, the enjoyable bar food might include daily specials
and good freshly baked filled baguettes (Tuesday-Saturday lunchtimes, £5.25), as
well as home-made soup (£3.95), baked brie in filo pastry with a port and
redcurrant dressing (£5.25), home-made chicken liver and foie gras pâté with
caramelised orange and green peppercorn reduction (£5.35), salmon and red pepper
fishcake on a dill and lemon potato cake with lime and crab dressing (£5.50; main
course £10.50), roasted butternut squash with roasted mediterranean vegetables
(£10.50), chicken breast stuffed with brie and smoked bacon with a tarragon cream
sauce (£11.50), fillet of pork baked in puff pastry with herb and mushroom pâté
and apple and onion gravy (£13.95), and 10oz sirloin steak with a choice of sauces
(£14.95); puddings such as warm dark chocolate fudge cake with clotted cream,
baked alaska with mango sorbet and strawberry coulis or apple and blackberry
crumble (£4.95), Sunday lunch (two courses £13.50, three courses £16.50),
children's menu (£4.50), and Thursday steak nights (from £10.50). Well kept
Wadworths IPA, 6X, and a changing seasonal guest on handpump, and a fine
choice of wines by the glass. The decked terrace with its outdoor heaters and old-
fashioned street lights has proved very successful, and there's a big woodside garden
with plenty of picnic-sets. It's hard to believe the pub is only a few minutes away
from the centre of Newbury. *(Recommended by Mike and Heather Watson, Ray J Carter,
P Price, Mr and Mrs A Silver, Tim Hawkins, Sue and Roger Bourne, Peter and Jean Hoare,
Angus and Rosemary Campbell)*

Wadworths ~ Manager Philip Davison ~ Real ale ~ Bar food (12-2(2.30 Sat), 6(5.30 Sat)-
9.30(9.45 Sat); 12-8.30 Sun; not Mon) ~ Restaurant ~ (01635) 42377 ~ Children welcome
~ Open 12-2.30, 5.30-11; 12-4, 5.30-11 Sat; 12-10.30 Sun; closed Mon

BRAY SU9079 Map 2

Crown

1¾ miles from M4 junction 9; A308 towards Windsor, then left at Bray signpost on to B3028; High Street; SL6 2AH

Well run and friendly, this bustling 14th-c pub is a popular place for an enjoyable meal. There are lots of beams (some so low you have to mind your head), plenty of old timbers handily left at elbow height where walls have been knocked through, and three roaring winter log fires. The partly panelled main bar has oak tables and leather backed armchairs, and one dining area has photographs of WWII aeroplanes; the area around the bar counter is no smoking. Promptly served by helpful staff, the good food might include home-made soup (£4.50), pâté of the day (£6.85), a platter of cheese (£8.95), tagliatelle with various sauces (from £8.95), wild boar sausages or wild mushrooms on bruschetta with fresh parmesan (£9.95), home-made beef and Guinness pie (£11.85), oriental warm chicken salad (£11.95), moules marinière and frites or fresh crab salad (£12.95), sirloin steak with a green peppercorn sauce (£16.95), and daily specials such as natural smoked haddock with wholegrain mustard sauce (£15.95). Best to arrive early as it does get busy, and they recommend you book if you want to eat in the no smoking restaurant. Well kept Brakspears Special, and Courage Best and Directors on handpump along with a decent choice of wines. There are tables and benches out in a sheltered flagstoned front courtyard (which has a flourishing grape vine), and in the large back garden. *(Recommended by Michael Dandy, Jarrod and Wendy Hopkinson, R T and J C Moggridge, Chris and Susie Cammack, Susan and John Douglas)*

Scottish Courage ~ Lease John and Carole Noble ~ Real ale ~ Bar food (not Sun or Mon evenings) ~ Restaurant ~ (01628) 621936 ~ Children at weekends only in restaurant and eating area of bar ~ Open 11-3, 6-11; 12-3, 7-10.30 Sun; closed 25 and 26 Dec, 1 Jan

Hinds Head ⊕ ♀

High Street; car park opposite (exit rather tricky); SL6 2AB

With a relaxed and decorous atmosphere, this handsome old pub (now no smoking throughout) has a thoroughly traditional L-shaped bar – dark beams and panelling, polished oak parquet, blazing log fires, red-cushioned built-in wall seats and studded leather carving chairs around small round tables, and latticed windows. As well as lunchtime snacks like scotch quail eggs or devils on horseback (£1.50) and lunchtime sandwiches (from £4.50, not Sunday), the interesting food here includes pea and ham soup (£5.50), soused herrings with beetroot and horseradish (£7.50), rabbit and bacon terrine or steamed mussels (£7.75), potted shrimps (£8.25), salt beef stovey with fried egg and mustard sauce (£12), roast cod with champ and parsley sauce (£13.50), oxtail and kidney pudding (£14), pot-roast chicken with bacon, mushrooms and tarragon (£14.50), puddings such as eton mess (£5.95), and a cheese board (£7.50); their triple-cooked chips are popular (£4.50). They have a dozen interesting wines by the glass including two champagnes, well kept Greene King IPA and Abbot and a couple of guests such as Adnams Broadside and Rebellion Mutiny on handpump, 24 malt whiskies, an excellent bloody mary, and Sheppy's farm cider; service is quick and efficient, and the lavatories are smart and stylish. A spacious restaurant area spreads off to the left. This is under the same ownership as the highly praised Fat Duck restaurant nearby. *(Recommended by Michael Dandy, Michael and Alison Sandy, Paul Humphreys, Bob and Maggie Atherton, Jarrod and Wendy Hopkinson, Simon Collett-Jones, Ian Phillips, Susan and John Douglas)*

Free house ~ Licensees Mr and Mrs A Proctor ~ Real ale ~ Bar food (12-2.30, 6.30-9.30; Sun 12-4; not Sun evening) ~ Restaurant ~ (01628) 626151 ~ Children welcome ~ Dogs allowed in bar ~ Open 11-11; 12-10.30 Sun

---

Pubs with particularly interesting histories, or in unusually interesting buildings, are listed at the back of the book.

EAST ILSLEY SU4981 Map 2
Crown & Horns 🍺 🛏

Just off A34, about 5 miles N of M4 junction 13; Compton Road; RG20 7LH

Right in the heart of horse-training country, this bustling pub has lots of interesting racing prints and photographs on the walls, and the side bar may have locals (including stable lads) poring over the day's races. The rambling set of snug beamed rooms is relaxed and unpretentious, with soft lighting, a blazing log fire, and tables tucked into intimate corners. There's also a separate no smoking snug (ideal for a small party), and an oak panelled dining room, as well as two more formal dining rooms. Bar food includes soup (£4.50), filled baguettes (from £4.50), filled baked potatoes (£5.50), vegetable lasagne, ham and eggs, and sausage and mash (£7.50), as well as more elaborate choices such as chicken liver and pistachio pâté with red onion marmalade (£5), sautéed mushrooms with chorizo (£5.50), tiger prawns with garlic, chilli and sambucca (£6), sun-dried tomato, olive, spinach and pine nut risotto (£8), steaks (from £11.50), slow-roasted lamb shank in red wine and rosemary gravy or chicken breast stuffed with black pudding and whisky with a tarragon and cream sauce (£12.50), specials like steak, mushroom and Guinness casserole (£10), and puddings such as sticky toffee pudding or apple crumble (£4). They have Adnams Regatta, Brakspears and Timothy Taylors Landlord on handpump, and over 150 whiskies from all over the world (some of the bottles have clearly been here for ages). Piped music, TV and games machine. Under two chestnut trees, there is a paved courtyard with comfortable new furniture; the surrounding countryside is laced with tracks and walks. *(Recommended by P Price, Chris Kay, Angus Johnson, Carol Bolden, Mrs S A Brooks, Robert and Jill Kennedy, David Cannings, Gerry and Rosemary Dobson, Howard and Margaret Buchanan, Jack Clark, Andrea and Guy Bradley, A P Seymour, Gill and Keith Croxton, John Cook)*

Free house ~ Licensee Sally Allsop ~ Real ale ~ Bar food (12-2.30, 6-9.30) ~ Restaurant ~ (01635) 281545 ~ Children welcome ~ Dogs allowed in bar and bedrooms ~ Open 11-11; 12-10.30 Sun ~ Bedrooms: £60S/£70B

FRILSHAM SU5573 Map 2
Pot Kiln 🍴 🍺

From Yattendon take turning S, opposite church, follow first Frilsham signpost, but just after crossing motorway go straight on towards Bucklebury ignoring Frilsham signposted right; pub on right after about half a mile; RG18 0XX

Although the emphasis in this no smoking country dining pub is now so much on the imaginative modern cooking that it's almost best thought of as a restaurant, there is still a little bar where the friendly locals gather to enjoy one of the five well kept real ales on handpump. From the West Berkshire brewery (which started life behind the pub but has now moved to larger premises), they serve well kept Brick Kiln Bitter, Maggs Mild, and Mr Chubbs Lunchtime Bitter, plus guests like Crouch Vale Oregan Best and Greene King Morlands Original. Darts. The comfortable bar area has wooden floorboards, bare benches and pews, and a good winter log fire, and the extended lounge is open plan at the back and leads into a large, pretty dining room with russet painted walls, a nice jumble of old tables and chairs, and an old-looking stone fireplace. Using seasonal local produce, a small choice of bar food includes filled rolls (from £2.95), home-made soup (£4.50), cornish pasty (£6), ploughman's (£7.50), smoked salmon platter (£8), and sausage and mash (£8.95); from the more exotic restaurant menu there might be grilled goats cheese and fig salad (£6), warm salad of pigeon, crispy bacon and black pudding (£6.50), risotto of morels, peas and broad beans (£13), ham hock with pease pudding, parsley and caper sauce (£13.50), slow-braised wild rabbit with rosemary and garlic or roast hake with pickled potatoes and braised savoy cabbage (£15.50), pavé of fallow venison with a smoked garlic sauce (£16), and puddings such as sticky toffee pudding or tonka bean rice pudding with stewed prunes (£6). Sunday roast (two courses £13.50, three courses £19.50) and a weekday lunchtime special menu (two courses £13.50, three courses £16.50). This is a charming rural spot, and seats in the big suntrap garden have good views of the nearby forests and meadows; plenty of nearby walks. *(Recommended by Mr and Mrs G S Ayrton, the Didler, Susan and John Douglas, Franklyn Roberts)*

Free house ~ Licensees Mr and Mrs Michael Robinson ~ Real ale ~ Bar food (not Sun evening) ~ Restaurant ~ (01635) 201366 ~ Children in restaurant ~ Dogs allowed in bar ~ Open 12-3, 6-11; 12-11 Sat; 12-10.30 Sun

HURST SU8074 Map 2
Green Man
Hinton Road, off A321 just outside village; RG10 0BP

In summer, even on cooler, damper evenings you can now enjoy meals outside this bustling pub under their giant new umbrellas; the sheltered terrace also has outdoor heaters. There are plenty of picnic-sets, too, under big oak trees in the large garden, and a good sturdy children's play area. Inside, the old-fashioned bar has black standing timbers and dark oak beams around cosy alcoves, cushioned wall seats and built-in settles around copper-topped and other pub tables, attractive prints, Edwardian enamels and decorative plates on cream or terracotta walls, and a hot little fire in one fireplace and a nice old iron stove in another. Beyond is a light and airy no smoking dining room, and the appealing no smoking cellar room, with just four tables and lots of pictures on its cream-painted brickwork. Well kept Brakspears PA, Special, and a seasonal ale on handpump, and half a dozen wines by the glass. Popular bar food includes lunchtime sandwiches (from £2.95; the hot sausage baguette is good) and filled baked potatoes (from £3.40), as well as soup (£2.95), warmed goats cheese with walnut salad (£4.50), crispy prawns with a sweet and sour dip (£4.75), ploughman's (£6.45), chicken, gammon and leek pie (£7.25), butternut bake (£7.95), lamb tagine (£9.25), steaks (from £9.75), and well liked daily specials like steak, mushroom and Guinness pudding (£7.95), roast pork fillet stuffed with onion and mushroom on a creamy wholegrain mustard sauce with leek mash (£8.95), and roast monkfish with a crème fraîche, saffron and vermouth sauce (£9.75). Best to book to be sure of a table. On Sunday lunchtimes the pub is totally no smoking. *(Recommended by Paul Humphreys, Kevin Thomas, Nina Randall, June and Robin Savage, Kim Mead, D J and P M Taylor, Mark and Diane Grist, R Lake, Mrs L M Beard)*

Brakspears ~ Tenants Simon and Gordon Guile ~ Real ale ~ Bar food (12-2.30, 6.30-9.30; 12-9 Sun) ~ Restaurant ~ (0118) 934 2599 ~ Children in eating area of bar and in restaurant until 8.30pm ~ Open 11-3, 5.30-11; 12-10.30 Sun

INKPEN SU3864 Map 2
Crown & Garter 🍲 🛏
Inkpen signposted with Kintbury off A4; in Kintbury turn left into Inkpen Road, then keep on into Inkpen Common; RG17 9QR

Run by friendly people, this 16th-c brick pub has a lovely long side garden with picnic-sets and a play area, and there are plenty of good downland walks nearby. It is surprisingly substantial for somewhere so remote-feeling, and has an appealing low-ceilinged bar with a few black beams and a relaxed central bar serving well kept West Berkshire Mr Chubbs Lunchtime Bitter and Good Old Boy plus a guest such as Fullers London Pride or Timothy Taylors Landlord on handpump; decent wines by the glass and several malt whiskies. Three areas radiate from here; our pick is the parquet-floored part by the raised log fire, which has a couple of substantial old tables, a huge old-fashioned slightly curved settle, and a neat little porter's chair decorated in commemoration of the Battle of Corunna (the cats' favourite seat – they've two). Other parts are slate and wood, with a good mix of well spaced tables and chairs, and nice lighting. Well liked bar food includes soup (£4.75), home-made onion and goats cheese tart (£5.75), natural smoked haddock topped with welsh rarebit (very popular, £5.95), a vegetarian dish of the day (£9.45), quite a few thai curries (£9.75), liver and bacon with onion gravy (£9.95), chicken breast filled with parma ham and mozzarella (£11.95), lamb shank with redcurrant jus (£12.95), puddings such as peach soup with raspberry sorbet or tipsy bread and butter pudding (£4.95), and daily specials like home-made pie of the day (£9.95) and half a roast duck with brandy and fresh orange sauce or fried bass with roasted sweet pepper and sunblush tomato pesto (£13.95); children's menu (£5.45). In a separate single-storey building, the well equipped bedrooms form an L around a pretty garden. James II is reputed to have used the pub on his way to visit his mistress locally. *(Recommended by Douglas and Ann Hare, Mary Rayner, Paul Bruford, Bruce and Sharon Eden, A P Seymour, Pam and John Smith, Pat and Tony Martin, Jane and Emma Macdonald, J Stickland)*

Free house ~ Licensee Gill Hern ~ Real ale ~ Bar food (not Mon-Tues lunchtime) ~ Restaurant ~ (01488) 668325 ~ Children welcome ~ Dogs allowed in bar ~ Open 12-3, 5.30-11; 12-5, 7-10.30 Sun; closed Mon and Tues lunchtime ~ Bedrooms: £55B/£80B

KINTBURY   SU3866   Map 2

Dundas Arms 🍴 ♈ 🛏

Station Road; RG17 9UT

In fine weather the setting here by the canal is well liked by our readers and there are seats on the jetty or waterside terrace. Inside, the partly panelled and carpeted bar is popular with locals, and one of the walls has a splendid collection of blue and white plates. Good bar food includes soup (£4.50), country pâté (£4.95), grilled goats cheese on italian bread (£5.75), home-potted shrimps (£6.60), spinach and red pepper lasagne (£7.50), dressed dorset crab salad (£7.95), steak and kidney pie (£10.50), slow-roast shoulder of lamb with rosemary and garlic sauce (£10.75), grilled free-range pork chop with bubble and squeak and grain mustard sauce (£11), salmon fishcakes with parsley sauce (£11.50), calves liver with bacon and onion gravy (£11.80), and puddings such as raspberry crème brûlée or fruit crumble (£5). Well kept Adnams Best, West Berkshire Mr Chubbs Lunchtime Bitter, and a couple of changing guests like Ramsbury Gold and Sharps Eden Ale on handpump, and a decent range of wines. The former barge-horse stables have been converted into comfortable, quiet bedrooms, which look out through french windows on to their own secluded terrace. The pub takes its name from Admiral Lord Dundas who, along with his brother, was responsible for the creation of the Kennet & Avon Canal. *(Recommended by Bruce and Sharon Eden, Rob Winstanley, Phyl and Jack Street, Lynn Sharpless, Paul Humphreys, Mrs J H S Lang, John Robertson, Paul Bruford, V Brogden, Angus and Rosemary Campbell, Susan and John Douglas, Chris Smith, Franklyn Roberts)*

Free house ~ Licensee David Dalzell-Piper ~ Bar food (not Sun) ~ Restaurant ~ (01488) 658263 ~ Children allowed but must be very well behaved ~ Open 11-2.30, 6-11; 12-2.30 Sun; closed Sun evening, 25 and 31 Dec ~ Bedrooms: £80B/£90B

KNOWL HILL   SU8279   Map 2

Royal Oak 🍴 ♈

Pub signed off A4 in village; coming from E, first unmarked turning on left by St Peter's Church just after limit sign, after Shottesbrooke turn-off; RG10 9YE

Berkshire Dining Pub of the Year

The French chef/landlord's good cooking is unquestionably the main thing at this restauranty little no smoking dining pub, but there is a proper corner bar, complete with bar stools, and Loddon Hoppit on handpump as well as a good interesting range of fairly priced wines by the glass (two glass sizes). Bar lunches might include baguettes with aberdeen angus cold beef, steak, parma ham or cajun chicken (£4.75), a home-made burger (£5.95) or fresh wild mushroom and bacon tagliatelle (£7.25). Besides some more adventurous starters which could also do as a light lunch, the landlord's skills come into their own with deftly flavoured main dishes such as chicken supreme with cherry tomato and basil sauce or wild mushroom stroganoff (£8.95), calves liver and bacon (£11.95), bass with a vanilla beurre blanc (£14.25) and fillet steak bordelaise (from 5oz £14.95). The breads baked here are delicious and interesting, and vegetables are fresh, tender and sometimes slightly unusual. A

two-course Sunday lunch, perhaps with mulled wine, is £11.95. The restaurant is
no smoking. Down by the bar is a brown leather fireside sofa, but otherwise the
softly lit carpeted room is all pale wood modern dining tables with comfortable
rather elegant matching chairs. Unless you count the candles, and an intriguingly
techno clock, décor is limited to just a couple of monochrome prints (a tulip, a
sunflower) on the buttery walls. Service by the friendly landlady is punctilious; well
reproduced piped music is carefully chosen. Outside a good-sized informal garden
has picnic-sets, and a sturdy play installation in quite a meadow. They are hoping
to add eight bedrooms. (Recommended by Paul Humphreys)

Free house ~ Licensees Franck Chauvin and Diane Raynsford ~ Real ale ~ Bar food (12-2,
6-9) ~ Restaurant ~ (01628) 822010 ~ Children welcome ~ Open 12-2.30, 6-11; 12-3
Sun; closed Sun evening and all day Mon

OAKLEY GREEN   SU9276   Map 2
Olde Red Lion 🛏
**4 miles from M4 junction 8 (and also junction 6); B3024, off A308 just W of Windsor;
SL4 4PZ**

Tiled and black-shuttered, this is set well back from the road, leaving space for a
biggish front car park – but even so, the pub's popularity fills that quickly at
weekends. The low-ceilinged bar is quite compact, with just two or three sturdy
tables, and seating including comfortable wall seats, and bar stools by the counter
which serves Adnams and Bass from handpump. They have a decent range of wines
by the glass, and do good coffees; service is attentive and friendly, and the piped
music not too obtrusive. On the right a snugly narrow sloping-ceiling side area has
white tablecloths on its tables, but is designated for drinking as well as eating. On
the left, past a cosy corner with a brown leather sofa and coal-effect fire, is an
extensive carpeted dining area. The enjoyable food includes a commendable range
of sandwiches (from £3.60; fillet steak £7.50), home-made soup (£4.50), chicken
liver pâté with red onion marmalade or smoked chicken and avocado salad (£7.25),
thai crab cake with mango chilli salsa (£7.50), home-made tomato and basil
tortellini (£10), home-made steak and Guinness pudding (£10.95), baked salmon in
a white wine and dill sauce (£12.25), slow-baked half shoulder of lamb in garlic,
rosemary and red wine (£16.95), and puddings such as raspberry crème brûlée or
sticky toffee pudding with butterscotch sauce (£4.75). Booking is advised for the
popular Sunday lunch; the restaurant is no smoking. A good-sized sheltered back
garden has plenty of picnic-sets under cocktail parasols on the grass, and green
plastic tables on a terrace under a fairy-lit arbour. If you stay, you get a good
breakfast. (Recommended by Andy Blackburn, Simon Collett-Jones)

Punch ~ Tenant Andrew Deeley ~ Real ale ~ Bar food (12-2.30, 6.30-10) ~ Restaurant ~
(01753) 863892 ~ Well behaved children welcome ~ Open 11-11; 11.30-9 Sun; closed
25 and 26 Dec, 1 Jan ~ Bedrooms: /£50B

READING   SU7272   Map 2
Hobgoblin 🍺
2 Broad Street; RG1 2BH

It's the fine choice of eight regularly changing real ales that draws customers into
this basic and cheerful back street pub. Served by friendly staff, there are three beers
from West Berkshire alongside five interesting guests such as Downton Mad Hare,
Fugelestou Two Hats, Fuzzy Duck Stout, Sharps Doom Bar, and Tryst IPA. If that
isn't enough, they've also lots of different bottled beers, czech lager on tap,
Weston's farm cider and perry, and country wines. Pump clips cover practically
every inch of the walls and ceiling of the simple bare-boards bar – a testament to
the enormous number of brews that have passed through the pumps over the past
few years (now over 5,100). Up a step is a small seating area, but the best places to
sit are the three or four tiny panelled rooms reached by a narrow corridor leading
from the bar; cosy and intimate, each has barely enough space for one table and a
few chairs or wall seats, but they're very appealing if you're able to bag one; the

biggest also manages to squeeze in a fireplace. It does get very busy, especially at weekends. They don't do any food at all, and they don't allow children or mobile phones. Piped music (very much in keeping with the rough and ready feel of the place), and TV. More reports please. *(Recommended by Pete Walker, the Didler, Mark and Diane Grist, Catherine Pitt)*

Community Taverns ~ Manager Rob Wain ~ Real ale ~ No credit cards ~ (0118) 950 8119 ~ Open 11-11; 12-10.30 Sun

REMENHAM   SU7682   Map 2
Little Angel ♀
A4130, just over bridge E of Henley; RG9 2LS

This attractive pub is all very roomy and relaxed. Several areas link openly together so you feel part of what's going on, yet each has its own distinct individual feel. There are well spaced seats and tables on the bare boards or ochre tiles, and furnishings are mainly in pale fabrics or soft suede, running from comfortable bar seats through tub chairs to deep sofas, with just a few prints on walls painted mainly in gentle seaside pastels. In one corner a case of art books and the like helps to set the tone. The no smoking conservatory has unusual patterned tablecloths and grey Lloyd Loom wicker seating. Good modern food at lunchtime includes soup (£4.50), toasted muffins with smoked salmon, poached egg, prawns and hollandaise (£4.40; large £7.25), mushroom, pea, tomato and parmesan risotto with a sweet potato crisp (£6.95; main course £9.95), chicken and foie gras terrine with pear and sauterne chutney (£7.25), ploughman's (£8.50), smoked chicken caesar salad (£8.95), haddock and crab fishcake with creamy watercress sauce or beefburger with applewood cheese glaze, bacon and fries (£9.95), cumberland sausages with sage, apple and roast tomato gravy (£10.25), steamed selection of fish with pak choi and sweet chilli, ginger and coriander noodles (£12.95), and puddings like dark chocolate pot with Tia Maria cream and shortbread or rhubarb and ginger crumble with vanilla custard (£5.50). The attractive curved bar counter has a good choice of a dozen wines by the glass (plus champagne), and Brakspears Bitter and Special on handpump; board games, unobtrusive piped music, and TV; live music Wednesday evenings. Service is friendly, helpful and unhurried – mildly continental in style. A sheltered floodlit back terrace has tables under cocktail parasols, looking over to the local cricket ground. *(Recommended by Ian Phillips, Michael Dandy, Chris Glasson, Tracey and Stephen Groves, Dave Braisted, Tom and Ruth Rees)*

Brakspears ~ Lease Douglas Green ~ Real ale ~ Bar food (12-3, 7-9.30; 12-4, 7-9 Sun) ~ Restaurant ~ (01491) 411008 ~ Children allowed but must be well behaved and must be over 10 in evening ~ Dogs allowed in bar ~ Live music Weds ~ Open 11-11; 12-10.30 Sun

RUSCOMBE   SU7976   Map 2
Royal Oak
Ruscombe Lane (B3024 just E of Twyford); RG10 9JN

The majority of customers come to this smartened-up village pub to enjoy the wide choice of popular food. Throughout, it's open plan and carpeted (not the cheerful side garden room), and well laid out so that each bit is fairly snug, yet keeps the overall feel of a lot of people enjoying themselves. A good variety of furniture runs from dark oak tables to big chunky pine ones, with mixed seating to match – the two sofas facing one another are popular. Contrasting with the exposed ceiling joists, mostly unframed modern paintings and prints decorate the walls, mainly dark terracotta over a panelled dado; one back area has a big bright fruity cocktail mural. As well as lunchtime snacks such as pâté (£5.95), sandwiches (£4.50; panini £5.95), grilled goats cheese salad (£5.95), burgers (from £6.95), ham and egg or chicken curry (£7.95), and bangers and mash with caramelised onion gravy (£8.95), there's home-made soup (£3.95), home-made fishcakes with a sweet chilli dressing (£6.50), lamb shank with red wine and rosemary (£11.95), salmon with a chive and cream sauce (£13.95), tomato risotto (£14.50), half a roast duck with orange and Grand Marnier sauce (£16), and daily specials like cured meats, olives and bread

(£6.95), king prawns in garlic citrus butter (£9.95) or halibut in a prawn and asparagus cream sauce (£14.50). Two-course set menu (£13.50) and three courses (£16.95); friendly staff. Well kept Brakspears Bitter, Fullers London Pride, and a guest beer on handpump, and half a dozen nicely chosen wines in two glass sizes; the restaurant and conservatory are no smoking. Picnic-sets are ranged around a venerable central hawthorn in the garden behind (where there are ducks and chickens); summer barbecues, spit roasts and morris dancing. Please note, they no longer offer bedrooms. *(Recommended by F and K Portnall, Mrs L M Beard, Paul Humphreys, Simon Collett-Jones, Susan and John Douglas)*

Enterprise ~ Lease Jenny and Stefano Buratta ~ Real ale ~ Bar food (12-2.30, 7-9.30; 12-4 Sun; not Sun or Mon evenings) ~ Restaurant ~ (0118) 934 5190 ~ Children welcome ~ Dogs allowed in bar ~ Open 12-3, 6-11; 12-4 Sun; closed Sun and Mon evenings

SHINFIELD   SU7367   Map 2
Magpie & Parrot ◥

2.6 miles from M4 junction 11, via B3270; A327 just SE of Shinfield – heading out on Arborfield Road, keep eyes skinned for small hand-painted green Nursery sign on left, and Fullers 'bar open' blackboard; RG2 9EA

Unless you already knew, you'd never guess that this little brick roadside cottage contained a genuine pub (as indeed it has done since the 17th c). Go in through the lobby (with its antiquated telephone equipment), and you find a cosy and inviting high-raftered room with a handful of small polished tables – each with a bowl of peanuts (they don't do any food) – and a comfortable mix of individualistic seats from Georgian oak thrones to a red velveteen sofa, not to mention the armchair with the paw-printed cushion reserved for Spencer the dog. It's a charming and relaxed place to while away an hour or so in the afternoon beside the warm open fire. Everything is spick and span, from the brightly patterned carpet to the plethora of interesting bric-a-brac covering the walls: miniature and historic bottles, dozens of model cars, veteran AA badges and automotive instruments, and mementoes of a pranged Spitfire (ask about its story – they love to chat here). Well kept Fullers London Pride and a changing guest on handpump from the small corner counter, a good range of malt whiskies and of soft drinks; very hospitable landlady. There are teak tables on the back terrace, and an immaculate lawn beyond. There are hog roasts and morris men at various summer events, and an annual beer festival in May with 22 real ales; aunt sally. Note the unusual opening hours; no children inside. *(Recommended by Mayur Shah, Mark and Diane Grist, Martin and Pauline Jennings)*

Free house ~ Licensee Mrs Carole Headland ~ Real ale ~ No credit cards ~ (0118) 988 4130 ~ Dogs allowed in bar ~ Open 12-7; 12-3 Sun; closed Sun evening

STANFORD DINGLEY   SU5771   Map 2
Bull ⇐

Off A340 via Bradfield, coming from A4 just W of M4 junction 12; RG7 6LS

The half-panelled lounge bar of this attractive 15th-c brick pub reflects the motorsport and classic car interests of the licensees, and on Saturdays between April and October, owners of classic cars and motorcycles gather in the grounds. The main part of the building has an old brick fireplace, cushioned seats carved out of barrels, a window settle, wheelback chairs on the red quarry tiles, and an old station clock; a carpeted section has an exposed wattle and daub wall. The beamed tap room is firmly divided into two by standing timbers hung with horsebrasses. Well kept Bass, Brakspears-Bitter, Greene King Morlands Original, and West Berkshire Good Old Boy and Skiff (exclusive to the pub) on handpump, and up to eight wines by the glass. As well as lunchtime sandwiches and filled baguettes (from £3.50; steak and onion baguette £6.50), ploughman's (£6), and ham and egg (£7), the menu might include home-made dishes such as soups (£4.25), warm bacon, mushroom and stilton salad or chicken caesar salad (£5.50; main course £8.50), chilli con carne (£7), fishcakes (£9), broccoli and stilton pasta bake or a pie of the day (£9.50), steaks (from £14), and puddings like treacle tart or crème brûlée (£5);

Sunday roast (£9). The dining room (which has waitress service at weekends only) and saloon bar are both no smoking; dominoes, ring the bull and piped music. In front of the building are some big rustic tables and benches, and to the side the big garden has plenty of seats. Morris men visit in August, and on St George's Day and New Year's Day. *(Recommended by John and Joan Nash, David and Sue Smith, Martin and Pauline Jennings, Philip and June Caunt, M Sage, Julia and Richard Tredgett, P Price, B and M Kendall, Paul Humphreys, Dr D Scott, Nigel Clifton, Simon Collett-Jones)*

Free house ~ Licensees Robert and Kate Archard ~ Real ale ~ Bar food (12-2.30, 6.30-9.30; not winter Sun evenings) ~ (0118) 974 4409 ~ Children in saloon bar and dining room ~ Dogs allowed in bar ~ Folk/blues second Weds of month ~ Open 12-3, 6-11; 12-3, 7-10.30 Sun ~ Bedrooms: £68S/£85S

Old Boot

Off A340 via Bradfield, coming from A4 just W of M4 junction 12; RG7 6LT

In warm weather you can sit in the quiet sloping back garden or on the terrace here and enjoy the pleasant rural views; there are more tables out in front. It's a stylish, 18th-c pub and very neatly kept inside, and the beamed bar has two welcoming fires (one in an inglenook), fine old pews, settles, old country chairs, and well polished tables. The fabrics for the old-fashioned wooden-ring curtains are attractive, and there are some striking pictures and hunting prints, boot ornaments in various sizes, and fresh flowers. The well liked bar food might include filled baguettes (£5.50), omelettes (£7.50), lasagne (£8.50), steak and kidney pie or curries (£8.95), fillet of cod in parsley sauce (£9.50), bass fillet (£10.95), and skate wing (£11.95). The dining conservatory is no smoking. Well kept West Berkshire Good Old Boy, Youngs Bitter, and a guest on handpump, and ten wines by the glass. *(Recommended by John and Joan Nash, John Baish, P Price, Paul Humphreys)*

Free house ~ Licensees John and Jeannie Haley ~ Real ale ~ Bar food ~ Restaurant ~ (0118) 974 4292 ~ Children welcome ~ Dogs allowed in bar ~ Open 11-3, 6-11

WHITE WALTHAM   SU8477   Map 2

Beehive 🍺

Waltham Road (B3024 W of Maidenhead); SL6 3SH

The relaxed and neatly kept bar on the left in this country local is brightened up by cheerful scatter cushions on its comfortable seating – built-in wall seats, captain's chairs and a leather wing armchair. It has well kept Brakspears, Fullers London Pride, Greene King Abbot and a changing guest from maybe Hogs Back, Loddon or Rebellion on handpump, welcoming service, and a good choice of soft drinks, nuts and so forth; piped music, fruit machine, and board games. On the right there's a lot more space, with country kitchen chairs around sturdy tables in several comfortably carpeted areas including a conservatory. The eating areas are no smoking. Honest bar food includes sandwiches (from £3.95), soup or pâté (£4.95), ploughman's, home-cooked ham and eggs or home-made lasagne (£7.95), local sausages (£8.95), cod in light lemon batter (£9.95), and seared venison steak with parmesan mash and smoked bacon (£16.95). In summer the garden is an extra draw. Besides the few picnic-sets and teak seats out by the topiary on the front grass, there are more on a good-sized sheltered back lawn. It's just by the village cricket field. Good disabled access and facilities. *(Recommended by Dr and Mrs A K Clarke)*

Enterprise ~ Lease Guy Martin ~ Real ale ~ Bar food (11.30-2.30, 5.30-9.30; all day weekends) ~ Restaurant ~ (01628) 822877 ~ Children allowed but not in restaurant area after 9pm ~ Dogs allowed in bar ~ Open 11-3, 5-11; 11-11 Sat; 12-10.30 Sun

---

Post Office address codings confusingly give the impression that some pubs are in Berkshire, when they're really in Buckinghamshire, Oxfordshire or Hampshire (which is where we list them).

WINTERBOURNE   SU4572   Map 2
Winterbourne Arms ♀

3.7 miles from M4 junction 13; A34 S, then cutting across to B4494 Newbury—
Wantage from first major slip-road (bearing left in Chieveley towards North Heath
when the main road bends round to the right), and follow Winterbourne signs;
RG20 8BB

Charming both inside and out, this bustling country pub is run by friendly people.
The bars have a collection of old irons around the fireplace, early prints and old
photographs of the village, and a log fire; piped music. The peaceful view over the
rolling fields from the big bar windows cleverly avoids the quiet road, which is
sunken between the pub's two lawns. There's a good wine list with 16 by the glass
(served in elegant glasses and including sparkling and sweet wines), and well kept
Fullers London Pride, Ramsbury Gold, Wadworths 6X, and West Berkshire Good
Old Boy on handpump. Enjoyable bar food at lunchtime includes soup (£3.95),
filled baguettes (from £4.50), sautéed garlic mushrooms in white wine cream sauce
on toasted brioche (£5.75), ploughman's (£7.25), chargrilled chicken, bacon and
avocado salad or home-made burger (£7.95), lamb, leek and dumpling hotpot with
minted mash (£10.95), and mediterranean vegetable lasagne (£11.45); evening
choices such as wild mushroom risotto (£9.80), grilled lemon sole with parsley
butter sauce (£13.95), and entrecote steak with pepper sauce (£15.50), daily
specials like poached eggs benedict (£5.45), confit of duck legs on spicy egg noodles
(£5.95), roast pheasant with bacon, pâté on toast and red wine jus (£13.95), and
grilled bass fillets with anchovy butter (£14.95), and puddings such as violet crème
brûlée or blackberry and apple crumble (from £4.95); Sunday brunch breakfast
(£7.95). A large landscaped garden has been created this year to the side of the
building and the furniture has been refurhished; pretty flowering tubs and hanging
baskets. The surrounding countryside here is lovely and there are nearby walks to
Snelsmore Common and Donnington. *(Recommended by Mr and Mrs J S Roberts,
Ray J Carter, Jenny Major, V B Side, Dave Braisted, John Robertson, Mark and Joanna,
Michael and Judy Buckley, Basil and Jarvis, J R Parker, P Price, W J Taylor, Martin and
Karen Wake)*

Free house ~ Licensee Frank Adams ~ Real ale ~ Bar food (12-2.30, 6-10; all day Sun and
bank hols) ~ Restaurant ~ (01635) 248200 ~ Children in restaurant ~ Dogs allowed in bar
~ Open 12-3, 6-11; 12-10.30 Sun

YATTENDON   SU5574   Map 2
Royal Oak ㉕ ♀ 🛏

The Square; B4009 NE from Newbury; turn right at Hampstead Norreys, village
signposted on left; RG18 0UG

Certainly more of a place to come for a meal rather than drop into for a quick pint,
this handsome inn has a panelled and prettily decorated brasserie/bar with a nice
log fire and striking flower arrangements. Staff are attentive and welcoming, they
keep West Berkshire Good Old Boy and Mr Chubbs Lunchtime Bitter on
handpump, and seven wines by the glass. As well as a two (£12) and three-course
(£15) set lunchtime menu, there's an à la carte choice (not available on Monday
lunchtimes) which might include soup (£6), chicken liver parfait, baked polenta
with mushroom sauce and brie or black cuttlefish risotto with olives and rocket
salad (£6.50), pasta with goats cheese, baked cherry tomatoes and fresh herbs
(£12.75), roast supreme of duck with black pudding, caramelised apple and parsley
and cider sauce (£15.50), poached cod fillet wrapped in lettuce with dual
champagne sauce, bubble and squeak and asparagus (£16), and puddings such as
chocolate crème brûlée with mint sorbet or vanilla cheesecake with spiced berry
sauce (from £6). It's best to book for the no smoking restaurant. In summer, you
can eat at tables in the pleasant walled garden, and there are more in front by the
peaceful village square. The bedrooms are attractive and well appointed, and some
overlook the garden. The poet Robert Bridges once lived in the village. More
reports please. *(Recommended by John Braine-Hartnell, Dr and Mrs A K Clarke, the Didler,*

Richard Atherton, Len and Di Bright, Heather Couper, Mrs E A Macdonald, V Brogden, Dr D Scott, Denise White, Karen and Graham Oddey)

Free house ~ Licensee William Boyle ~ Real ale ~ Bar food (not Sun evening) ~ Restaurant ~ (01635) 201325 ~ Well behaved children welcome ~ Open 11-11; 12-10.30 Sun; closed 1 Jan ~ Bedrooms: £85B/£110B

LUCKY DIP

Besides the fully inspected pubs, you might like to try these Lucky Dips recommended to us and described by readers (if you do, please send us reports: www.goodguides.co.uk).

ALDWORTH [SU5579]
☆ *Four Points* RG8 9RL [B4009 towards Hampstead Norreys]: Attractive thatched pub with low beams and standing timbers, good value home-made food from baguettes up, Adnams Best and Wadworths 6X, quick service, fresh flowers on tidy array of polished tables in good-sized eating area (bar area not so big), no piped music, games room; children very welcome, neat garden over road *(LYM, Mrs Ann Gray, Stan Edwards)*

ARBORFIELD [SU7666]
Swan RG2 9PQ [Eversley Rd (A327), Arborfield Cross]: Friendly and attractive, reminiscent of 1960s with small rooms and lots of glinting brassware, above-average enterprising food in two peaceful dining bars (one a mezzanine), Adnams Broadside, Caledonian Deuchars IPA, Courage Best and Fullers London Pride *(Ian Phillips, Martin and Pauline Jennings)*

ASTON [SU7884]
☆ *Flower Pot* RG9 3DG [small signpost off A4130 Henley—Maidenhead at top of Remenham Hill]: Roomy old-fashioned two-bar pub with fine array of stuffed fish and other river-inspired decorations in bright bare-boards public bar and (children allowed here) bigger blue-carpeted saloon, lots of close-set tables in tiled-floor adult dining area, Brakspears ales inc a seasonal beer, reasonably priced food from sandwiches to lots of fish and game in season; may be unobtrusive piped music, very busy with walkers and families wknds; lots of picnic-sets giving quiet country views from nice big dog-friendly orchard garden, side field with chickens, ducks and guinea fowl *(BB, Bob and Laura Brock, Richard Greaves, Susan and John Douglas, Jeremy Woods)*

BAGNOR [SU4569]
☆ *Blackbird* RG20 8AQ [quickest approach is from Speen on edge of Newbury]: Chatty no smoking country pub in peaceful setting nr Watermill Theatre (with pre-show menu), friendly service, changing ales inc West Berkshire, home-made food, simple unfussy traditional bar with log fire and old farm tools and firearms, more formal eating area off; tables in pleasant side garden and on green in front *(Emma Newsome, BB)*

BEENHAM [SU5868]
Six Bells RG7 5NX: Cosy and attractive village pub with Brakspears ales, reasonably priced food, no smoking lounge bar *(Mark and Ruth Brock)*

BINFIELD [SU8271]
Warren RG40 5SB [Forest Rd (B3034 W)]: Well laid out and spacious family dining pub, comfortably refurbished and popular under new management, with good friendly service, decent food from enterprising ciabattas up, good house wines and good range of soft and hot drinks; plenty of garden tables *(Paul Humphreys, R Lake, Jack Clark, Alistair Forsyth)*

BISHAM [SU8585]
Bull SL7 1RR: Good-sized L-shaped bar with some booth seating and wide choice of pubby food, Brakspears and good choice of wines by the glass, good service, separate small bar for sizeable french restaurant; piped music; pleasant garden *(Michael Dandy)*

BOXFORD [SU4271]
☆ *Bell* RG20 8DD [back road Newbury—Lambourn]: Relaxed and civilised country local with great choice of wines and champagnes by the glass as well as four real ales and plenty of other drinks, wide choice of bar food from sandwiches and snacks to steak, some interesting bric-a-brac and racing pictures, rather smart no smoking restaurant area, pool, cribbage, shove-ha'penny, dominoes; TV, piped music; children and dogs welcome, attractive covered and heated prettily lit terrace, bedrooms, open all day (Sun afternoon break) *(Mr and Mrs J S Roberts, Dr and Mrs A K Clarke, Dr and Mrs M Savidge, Dr D and Mrs B Woods, LYM, Bill and Jessica Ritson)*

BRACKNELL [SU8566]
Golden Retriever RG12 7PB [Nine Mile Ride (junction A3095/B3430)]: Attractively antiquated largely thatched Vintage Inn with comfortable farmhouse-style décor, decent food all day, Bass and Fullers London Pride, plenty of wines by the glass, lots of young well trained staff, log fires, daily papers; open all day *(Ian Phillips, R Lake, Martin Wilson)*

BRIMPTON [SU5662]
☆ *Pineapple* RG7 4RN [Kingsclere Rd, Brimpton Common – B3051, W of Heath End]: Busy thatched and low-beamed pub with stripped brick and timbering, tiled floor, heavy elm furnishings, log fire, reasonably priced traditional food, welcoming attentive service, real ales such as Flowers, Gales HSB, Greene King IPA and Ringwood, decent wines; piped music; children allowed in no smoking dining extension, tables on sheltered lawn, play area, open all day *(J V Dadswell, LYM, Mr and Mrs Bentley-Davies)*

CHADDLEWORTH [SU4177]
Ibex RG20 7ER [Main St]: Quiet village pub with enjoyable food, good choice of beers and soft drinks, welcoming landlady, traditional games in public bar; wheelchair access, dogs and walkers welcome, tables out on sheltered lawn and floodlit terrace *(LYM, Andrew Jones)*

CHEAPSIDE [SU9469]
☆ *Thatched Tavern* SL5 7QG [off A332/A329, then off B383 at Village Hall sign]: Civilised dining pub with good interesting up-to-date food, friendly service, good choice of wines by the glass, Brakspears and Fullers London Pride, big inglenook log fire, low beams and polished flagstones in cottagey core, three smart carpeted dining rooms off, daily papers, no games or piped music; children in restaurant, rustic tables on attractive sheltered back lawn, open all day wknds, handy for Virginia Water *(N R White, LYM, Robert Hay)*

CHIEVELEY [SU4773]
☆ *Olde Red Lion* RG20 8XB [handy for M4 junction 13 via A34 N-bound; Green Lane]: Thriving local with good value straightforward food, welcoming staff, Arkells ales, comfortably worn in low-beamed L-shaped bar with lots of brassware, couple of old sewing machines, roaring log fire, back restaurant with paintings for sale, pool; piped music, games machine, TV *(BB, J V Dadswell)*

COOKHAM [SU8985]
Ferry SL6 9SN [Sutton Rd]: Splendidly placed riverside pub with smart modern décor, Adnams Broadside and Bass, enjoyable if not cheap food (very popular Sun lunchtime), contemporary artwork, blue sofas and armchairs, solid teak furnishings in light and airy Thames-view dining areas upstairs and down, dark décor and small servery in beamed core; piped music may be rather loud; children welcome, attractive waterside garden and decking *(BB, Simon Collett-Jones, Susan and John Douglas)*

COOKHAM DEAN [SU8785]
Chequers SL6 9BQ [Dean Lane]: Small pleasantly refurbished dining bar with beams, flagstones, old fireplace, traditional furniture and decorations, imaginative and enjoyable food, real ale, good friendly service, good value wines; small garden, and seats out among hanging baskets *(Mr Waterman)*

☆ *Jolly Farmer* SL6 9PD [Church Rd, off Hills Lane]: Traditional pub owned by village consortium, old-fashioned unspoilt bars with open fires, friendly helpful staff, real ales such as Brakspears and Courage Best, decent wines and coffee, stylishly simple back dining room (sandwiches and baguettes too, even on Sun), pub games, no music or machines; well behaved children welcome away from bar, good quiet garden with play area *(Paul Humphreys, LYM, David Tindal, Susan and John Douglas)*

CRAZIES HILL [SU7980]
☆ *Horns* RG10 8LY [Warren Row Rd off A4 towards Cockpole Green, then follow Crazies Hill signs]: Comfortable and civilised beamed bars with enterprising fresh food (not Sun evening) from lunchtime baguettes to Billingsgate fish, Brakspears Bitter, Special and seasonal ales, decent wines by the glass, plenty of character and warm décor in dark colours, stripped furniture and open fires, raftered no smoking barn room where children allowed; dogs allowed lunchtime, pleasant seats in large garden with play area, cl Sun evening in winter *(LYM, Ray J Carter, Richard Marjoram, T R and B C Jenkins, P Price, Roy and Gay Hoing, Martin and Karen Wake)*

DONNINGTON [SU4668]
☆ *Castle Inn* RG14 3AA [Oxford Rd (B4494 N of Newbury); handy for M4 junction 13)]: Smart open-plan pub with good pubby bar lunches from baguettes up, wider evening menu, Flowers Original, Fullers London Pride, Timothy Taylors Landlord and Wadworths 6X, decent wines by the glass, attentive and welcoming young staff, plenty of pleasant nooks and corners, no smoking area; tables under cocktail parasols on attractive suntrap walled terrace *(Mark and Ruth Brock, John and Rosemary Haynes)*

EAST ILSLEY [SU4981]
Swan RG20 7LF [just off A34 Newbury—Abingdon; High St]: Traditional, attractive pub that has been a popular food stop, with Greene King ales, but now under new management; tables in courtyard and walled garden with play area, good bedrooms, some in house down road *(LYM, Dennis Jenkin)*

EASTBURY [SU3477]
Plough RG17 7JN: Large lively locals' bar, quieter lounge and no smoking restaurant, changing ales such as Archers and Morlands, friendly staff, good value food from snacks up; children welcome *(Mark and Ruth Brock)*

ETON [SU9677]
George SL4 6AF [High St]: Friendly well staffed family dining pub with neat dining tables on stripped wood, bar area with Brakspears, Fullers London Pride and Wadworths 6X, good wine choice, sensible food from ciabattas and baked potatoes up; piped music; children welcome, big back terrace with heaters *(Simon Collett-Jones, Mike and Sue Richardson, Esther and John Sprinkle)*

☆ *Gilbeys* SL4 6AF [High St]: Not a pub, but well worth knowing for imaginative home-made bar meals (their good vegetarian dishes often tempt even meat-eaters), nice sensibly priced house wines (bottled beers), friendly unstuffy family service; can be very busy if there's an event at the school, best to book for light and airy back restaurant down long corridor *(Mrs Ann Gray, Mike and Sue Richardson, BB)*

New College SL4 6BL [High St]: Pleasantly refurbished local with bare boards, lots of panelling and glazed partitions, college blue décor, enjoyable straightforward sensibly priced food from baguettes up, Brakspears and Fullers London Pride, friendly staff, back no smoking area; piped music; nice terrace *(Michael and Alison Sandy)*

☆ *Watermans Arms* SL4 6BW [Brocas St]: Large friendly panelled pub facing Eton College boat house, horseshoe servery with Brakspears, Fullers London Pride, Hogs Back TEA and a guest, prompt friendly service, good reasonably priced usual food (all day Fri/Sat, not Sun eve), bright roomy no smoking back dining area, overhead Thames map and lots of old river photographs; children welcome *(Michael and Alison Sandy, LYM, Bruce Bird)*

FIFIELD [SU9076]
Fifield Inn SL6 2NX [just off B3024 W of Windsor]: Neat and attractive old stone-built village local with welcoming staff, Greene King IPA and Abbot, lots of wines by the glass, good value fresh restaurant and bar food inc interesting dishes (no snacks on Sun), daily papers, flame-effect fire; live jazz Sun evening; children welcome, picnic-sets in lovely garden *(June and Robin Savage, D J and P M Taylor, Simon Collett-Jones)*

GREAT SHEFFORD [SU3875]
☆ *Swan* RG17 7DS [2 miles from M4 junction 14 – A338 towards Wantage (Newbury Rd)]: Low-ceilinged bow-windowed pub with good range of lunchtime snacks and evening meals (can have just a starter), real ales inc local Butts, good wine choice, prompt friendly service, good log fire, daily papers, well laid out no smoking river-view restaurant; good wheelchair access, children in eating areas, tables on attractive waterside lawn and terrace *(Mark and Ruth Brock, Mr and Mrs J S Roberts, Simon Jones, LYM, A and B D Craig, Ann and Colin Hunt, John and Jill Perkins)*

HALFWAY [SU4068]
Halfway Inn RG20 8NR [A4 Hungerford—Newbury]: Nicely refurbished Badger dining pub with well divided back dining area, chef/landlord doing wide choice of enjoyable food inc some imaginative dishes, good range of wines and beers, smiling helpful landlady, daily papers and log fire in attractive rambling bar; may be faint piped music; picnic-sets on side terrace and neat back lawn *(BB)*

HAMSTEAD MARSHALL [SU4165]
☆ *White Hart* RG20 0HW [off A4 W of Newbury]: Comfortable dining pub with good fresh food, french influences on english menu and adaptable chef happy to modify recipes, friendly and obliging staff, Hook Norton Best and Wadworths 6X, L-shaped bar with good central log fire, attractively cottagey no smoking dining room; children welcome, pretty tree-sheltered walled garden, quiet and comfortable beamed bedrooms in converted barn *(A J Murray, Pauline and Philip Darley, James Morrell, LYM, N R White)*

HERMITAGE [SU5072]
White Horse RG18 9TB [Newbury Rd]: Completely reworked and now comfortable, attractive and interesting, with enjoyable traditional food (freshly made so may be a wait), real ales and decent wines, friendly caring licensees; well behaved dogs welcome *(Philip and Susan Chauncy)*

HOLYPORT [SU8977]
☆ *Belgian Arms* SL6 2JR [handy for M4 junction 8/9, via A308(M) and A330]: Traditional chatty low-ceilinged pub with friendly attentive tenants, enjoyable efficiently served pubby food from good sandwiches up (small helpings for children available), well kept Brakspears Bitter and Special, good local atmosphere, interesting belgian military uniform prints, cricketing memorabilia and a good log fire, occasional events such as hog roasts with steel band and bouncy castle; children in eating areas, pleasant outlook over pond and charming green from garden *(Stan Edwards, LYM, Simon Collett-Jones, Kevin Blake, M G Hart, Gordon Prince, KC)*
George SL6 2JL [1½ miles from M4 junction 8/9, via A308(M)/A330; The Green]: Extended open-plan low-beamed pub, pleasantly old-fashioned without being self-conscious about it, nice old fireplace, enjoyable usual food from baguettes up, some more restauranty evening dishes, Adnams, Courage Best and Fullers London Pride, good service, no smoking area; piped music; picnic-sets on attractive terrace, lovely village green, open all day *(Michael and Alison Sandy, Michael Dandy, T J and L Baddeley)*

HUNGERFORD [SU3368]
Bear RG17 0EL [3 miles from M4 junction 14; town signed at junction]: After changing hands this hotel now has a minimalist more contemporary neo-scandinavian décor, a useful stop for all-day bar food inc good range of sandwiches, restaurant; bedrooms comfortable and attractive *(Colin and Janet Roe, LYM)*
Plume of Feathers RG17 0NB [High St]: Big well run open-plan family pub, lots of tables around central bar, bare boards and lack of fabrics giving a slight brasserie feel, good food from soup, well made sandwiches and pubby favourites to more adventurous dishes, Greene King ales, friendly staff, cosy fire towards the back; garden tables, bedrooms *(Nick and Lynne Carter, Charles and Pauline Stride, A P Seymour, Stan Edwards)*

HURLEY [SU8183]
Black Boys SL6 5NQ [A4130 E of Henley]: Restaurant not pub now (you can't just drop in for a drink), clean, bright and smart in the modern bare-boards style, manageable choice of good if not cheap food esp fresh west country fish, Brakspears Bitter, great range of wines by the glass, friendly service, woodburner separating main eating area from small bar; piped music; garden tables, walks to Thames, nine bedrooms *(Mr and Mrs Gordon Turner, Mr Waterman, Michael Dandy)*
☆ *Red Lyon* SL6 5LH [A4130 SE, just off A404]: Comfortable pub reopened 2005 after transformation giving some seven cosy and traditional partly double areas, largely no smoking, with low beams, two log fires, attractive medley of seating, friendly helpful service, decent homely food from sandwiches and generous starters up, Brakspears and a changing guest beer, good wine choice, nice coffee, daily papers, country magazines; piped music (can be turned down for your table); children welcome, picnic-sets in good-sized

garden behind, open all day *(Michael Dandy, Susan and John Douglas, Richard Greaves, Ian Phillips)*

Rising Sun SL6 5LT [High St]: Open-plan refurbishment, low beams and flagstones in bar with Adnams Broadside, Black Sheep and Fullers London Pride, economical simple food from sandwiches and baguettes up, pleasant service, small eating area, sofas in bare-boards back area, pub games; piped music; seats in small tree-shaded garden, attractive spot nr Thames, open all day *(BB, Michael Dandy)*

INKPEN [SU3564]

☆ *Swan* RG17 9DX [Lower Inkpen; coming from A338 in Hungerford, take Park St (first left after railway bridge, coming from A4)]: Rambling beamed country pub, largely no smoking, with strong organic leanings in its wines as well as the food from sandwiches and pubby things to more upscale dishes (the farming owners also have an interesting organic shop next door), cosy corners, three log fires, helpful service, good Butts and West Berkshire ales, local farm cider, pleasant restaurant, flagstoned games area; piped music; well behaved children welcome in eating areas, picnic-sets out in front, small quiet garden, well equipped bedrooms, open all day in summer *(LYM, Betsy and Peter Little, Pete Baker, Guy Vowles)*

KNOWL HILL [SU8178]

☆ *Bird in Hand* RG10 9UP [A4, quite handy for M4 junction 8/9]: Relaxed, civilised and roomy, with cosy alcoves, heavy beams, panelling and splendid log fire in tartan-carpeted main area, enjoyable home-made straightforward food even Sun evening from sandwiches and baguettes up, several real ales, good wines by the glass, good choice of other drinks, polite prompt staff in colourful waistcoats, much older side bar, no smoking buffet (children allowed), smart restaurant; tables out on front terrace, tidy modern bedrooms *(Simon Collett-Jones, LYM, Mrs E A Macdonald, Tracey and Stephen Groves, M G Hart)*

LAMBOURN [SU3175]

☆ *Hare* RG17 7SD [aka Hare & Hounds; Lambourn Woodlands, well S of Lambourn itself (B4000/Hilldrop Lane)]: Emphasis on good enterprising food, not cheap but worth it, from short choice of sophisticated light lunches to more elaborate evening menu, several nicely individual rooms inc a proper bar, elegant décor, furnishings, glass and china, welcoming landlord and friendly efficient service, Bass and Wadworths IPA or 6X, nice wines, exemplary lavatories; piped music; children welcome, garden behind with decent play area, cl Sun evening *(Mark and Ruth Brock, Dr D and Mrs B Woods, LYM, Dr and Mrs Geoff Ayrey)*

LITTLEWICK GREEN [SU8379]

☆ *Cricketers* SL6 3RA [not far from M4 junction 9; A404(M) then left on to A4, from which village signed on left; Coronation Rd]: Proper old-fashioned pub with wholesome good value pubby food (not Sun evening) from good range

of sandwiches, ciabattas and baked potatoes up, well kept Badger ales, good choice of wines by the glass, daily papers, darts, lots of cricketing prints, friendly local atmosphere, docile pub alsatian; piped music; charming spot opp cricket green, bedrooms, open all day wknds *(Paul Humphreys, LYM, Susan and John Douglas, Michael Dandy)*

Shire Horse SL6 3QA [Bath Rd; 3 miles from M4 junction 9; A404(M) then left on to A4]: Chef & Brewer taking its name from Courage's former adjoining shire horse centre, comfortable and attractive linked areas with old beams and tiled floors, good choice of sensibly priced wines by the glass, cafetière coffee, decent food all day inc interesting baguettes; tables out on side lawn *(Paul Humphreys, LYM)*

MAIDENHEAD [SU8683]

Lemon Tree SL6 6NW [Golden Ball Lane, Pinkneys Green – off A308 N]: Low-beamed linked rooms and good-sized smart airy dining area, Marlow Rebellion and Smuggler, good coffee and choice of wines by the glass, helpful service, food from light lunchtime dishes such as sandwiches and wraps to steaks; picnic-sets out on grass behind, open all day *(Michael and Alison Sandy, Michael Dandy)*

MARSH BENHAM [SU4267]

☆ *Red House* RG20 8LY [off A4 W of Newbury]: Attractive place, nowadays restaurant rather than pub (and they no longer serve real ale); comfortable bar, appealing library-style front no smoking restaurant lined with bookcases and paintings, modern food, lots of wines by the glass; piped music; terrace with teak tables and chairs over long lawns sloping to water meadows and the River Kennet *(LYM)*

PALEY STREET [SU8675]

Bridge House SL6 3JS: Small cottagey black and white pub with warm beamed bar, friendly landlady and helpful service even when busy, Brakspears and Fullers London Pride, good value home-made food from lunchtime baguettes and baked potatoes up, pleasant no smoking back dining room; children welcome, big garden *(June and Robin Savage)*

PANGBOURNE [SU6376]

Swan RG8 7DU [Shooters Hill]: Attractive Thames-side pub dating from 17th c, good choice of wines by the glass, Greene King ales, friendly staff, lounge with open fire, river-view dining balcony and conservatory (food all day); piped music, sports TV; picnic-sets on terrace overlooking weir and moorings, open all day *(Roy and Lindsey Fentiman)*

PEASEMORE [SU4577]

☆ *Fox & Hounds* RG20 7JN [off B4494 Newbury—Wantage]: Civilised yet properly pubby country local tucked away in racehorse country, good honestly priced varied food, particularly good house wines, real ales, good service *(LYM, Stan Edwards)*

READING [SU7173]

Brewery Tap RG1 7SB [Castle St]: Big simply furnished beamed pub spreading back to games area with darts and four pool tables, Fullers London Pride and Greene King IPA, sensibly priced pubby food from double-decker sandwiches up, daily papers, log fire; open all day *(Ian Phillips)*

☆ *Fishermans Cottage* RG1 3DW [Kennet Side – easiest to walk from Orts Rd, off Kings Rd]: Friendly local well worth knowing for its nice spot by canal lock and towpath; modern furnishings, pleasant stone snug behind woodburning range, good value lunches inc lots of hot or cold sandwiches (very busy then but service quick), full Fullers beer range, small choice of wines, light and airy conservatory, small darts room, SkyTV; dogs allowed (not in garden), waterside tables, lovely big back garden *(the Didler, Susan and John Douglas)*

Griffin RG4 7AD [Church Rd, Caversham]: Roomy good value chain dining pub with Courage Best and Directors and Wadworths 6X, cafetière coffee, good friendly service, separate areas with several log fires; tables in attractive courtyard garden, beautiful spot on Thames overlooking swan sanctuary *(D J and P M Taylor, Tony Hobden)*

☆ *Hop Leaf* RG1 2QZ [Southampton St]: Friendly bustling local next to Hop Back of Wiltshire with their full beer range, may be occasional Reading Lion beers brewed on the premises, farm cider, nice family atmosphere, simple bar snacks, no smoking area, family room, darts, bar billiards; one-way system making parking close by difficult *(Pete Walker)*

Retreat RG1 4EH [St Johns St]: Friendly 1960ish backstreet local with several particularly well kept changing ales such as Caledonian Deuchars IPA and Ringwood, farm ciders, back bar with darts; open all day Fri-Sun *(Mark and Diane Grist, the Didler)*

☆ *Sweeney & Todd* RG1 7RD [Castle St]: Successful cross between café and pub with exceptional value home-made pies all day, also ploughman's, casseroles and roasts, in warren of little period-feel alcoves and other areas on various levels, cheery staff, small well stocked bar with Adnams Best, Badger Tanglefoot, Wadworths 6X and a changing guest beer, children welcome in restaurant area, open all day (cl Sun and bank hols) *(D J and P M Taylor, Ray J Carter, P Price, the Didler, Susan and John Douglas, LYM)*

SANDHURST [SU8461]

Wellington Arms GU47 9BN [Yorktown Rd (A321)]: Congenial suburban local with good bar food from good value sandwiches to steaks, Brakspears, friendly staff; good-sized garden and park view, comfortable bedrooms *(Maggie Ainsley)*

SONNING [SU7575]

☆ *Bull* RG4 6UP [off B478, by church; village signed off A4 E of Reading]: Classic old-fashioned inn in pretty setting nr Thames, low heavy beams, cosy alcoves, cushioned antique settles and low-slung chairs, inglenook log fires, several changing ales such as Fullers and Gales, enjoyable food from baguettes and baked potatoes to steaks, quick friendly service, no smoking back dining area (children allowed); charming courtyard, five attractive recently refurbished bedrooms, open all day

summer wknds *(LYM, Susan and John Douglas, Simon Collett-Jones, P and J Shapley, A P Seymour, G Robinson)*

SUNNINGHILL [SU9367]

Dog & Partridge SL5 7AQ [Upper Village Rd]: Real ales such as Fullers London Pride, good range of wines, good friendly staff, enjoyable reasonably priced food inc popular Sun lunch and good value take-aways *(R Bowles)*

SWALLOWFIELD [SU7364]

☆ *George & Dragon* RG7 1TJ [Church Rd, towards Farley Hill]: Relaxed and cottagey pub with enjoyable fresh food inc some good interesting recipes, Brakspears, Fullers London Pride and Youngs, good wines, big log fire, charming and well meaning young staff, stripped beams, red walls, rugs on flagstones and plenty of character and atmosphere; very popular with business diners, piped music; well behaved children welcome, open all day *(KC, LYM, PL, Stephen Allford, Richard Endacott, David and Sue Smith)*

THEALE [SU6168]

Winning Hand RG7 5JB [A4 W, opp Sulhamstead turn; handy for M4 junction 12]: Friendly pub with enjoyable food from sandwiches, baguettes and light meals to interesting main dishes, good service, Arkells and Hook Norton, varied wine list, restaurant; quiet piped music; bright gardens, four bedrooms *(John Baish, Mike and Sue Richardson)*

TIDMARSH [SU6374]

Greyhound RG8 8ER [A340 S of Pangbourne]: Pretty thatched pub, warm and inviting, with good service, good choice of enjoyable food, Fullers ales inc seasonal ones, back dining extension; good walks nearby *(Robert Turnham)*

WALTHAM ST LAWRENCE [SU8376]

☆ *Bell* RG10 0JJ [B3024 E of Twyford; The Street]: Heavy-beamed and timbered village pub with cheerful chatty locals, good log fires, good value pubby bar food (not Sun evening) from good sandwich range up inc interesting pizzas, fine choice of changing ales inc West Berkshire, perhaps its own wheat beer, plenty of malt whiskies, good wine, daily papers, compact panelled lounge, no smoking front snug, quiz night; they may try to keep your credit card while you eat; children and dogs welcome, tables in back garden with extended terrace, open all day wknds *(Simon Collett-Jones, LYM, Paul Humphreys, Mark and Diane Grist, A P Seymour)*

Star RG10 0HY [Broadmoor Rd]: Tidy old pub with enjoyable food from substantial starters to restaurant dishes, friendly licensees, beams, brasses, daily papers, open fire, Wadworths ales *(Mr and Mrs A Silver)*

WEST ILSLEY [SU4782]

Harrow RG20 7AR [signed off A34 at E Ilsley slip road]: Friendly village pub in peaceful spot overlooking cricket pitch and pond, Victorian prints in appealing deep-coloured knocked-through bar, some antique furnishings, log fire, Greene King ales, good choice of wines by the glass; children in eating areas, dogs allowed in bar, picnic-sets in big garden, more seats on pleasant terrace, cl Sun evening (F D Smith, Bridget Nichols, LYM, Ian Phillips, Susan and John Douglas, A G Marx)

WICKHAM [SU3971]

Five Bells RG20 8HH [3 miles from M4 junction 14, via A338, B4000; Baydon Rd]: Welcoming thatched pub in racehorse-training country, real ales such as Adnams, Fullers London Pride and ESB and Ringwood Best, good choice of reasonably priced wines, keen chatty landlord and good service, pubby food from sandwiches up, big log fire, stylish décor with some tables tucked into low eaves, no smoking at bar; children in eating area, informal garden with decking and good play area, good value bedrooms, interesting church nearby with overhead elephants (Mark, Amanda, Luke and Jake Sheard, LYM, J Iorwerth Davies, R T and J C Moggridge)

WINDSOR [SU9676]

☆ *Carpenters Arms* SL4 1PB [Market St]: Town pub ambling around central servery with particularly well kept changing ales such as Adnams, Bath Gem, Caledonian Deuchars IPA and Mauldons May Bee, good value pubby food all day from sandwiches and baked potatoes up (can take a while when busy), good choice of wines by the glass, sturdy pub furnishings and Victorian-style décor inc two pretty fireplaces, no smoking family areas up a few steps, also downstairs beside former tunnel entrance with suits of armour; piped music, no nearby parking; tables out on cobbled pedestrian alley opp castle, handy for Legoland bus stop, open all day (Michael and Alison Sandy, Michael Dandy, Keith and Janet Morris, Bruce Bird, BB, Esther and John Sprinkle)

Three Tuns SL4 1PB [Market St]: Courage Best from central servery, kind helpful service, sensibly priced pubby food from good sandwiches up, lots of games; piped music; relaxing tables out on pedestrianised street (Michael Dandy, Esther and John Sprinkle)

☆ *Two Brewers* SL4 1LB [Park St]: Bustling old-fashioned pub with lots to look at in three quaint and cosily civilised bare-board rooms, Courage Best, Fullers London Pride and a guest, quite a few wines by the glass, daily papers, straightforward food (not wknd evenings); no children inside; tables out by pretty Georgian street next to Windsor Park's Long Walk, has been open all day (Jeremy Woods, Fr Robert Marsh, Ray J Carter, Michael Dandy, LYM, Michael and Alison Sandy, Ian Phillips, Simon Collett-Jones, John Saville)

Windsor Castle SL4 2AP [Kings Rd]: Pleasant informal atmosphere, areas for drinkers and diners, decent food from good home-made pâté up, real ales such as Adnams, Caledonian Deuchars IPA and Hogs Back TEA, kind helpful staff, log fire; sports TV; dogs very welcome (handy for the Park with view over Royal Paddocks to Frogmore House), good parking (a real bonus here), small outside deck (John Millwood, Dr R W Pickles, Jeremy Woods)

WINNERSH [SU7871]

☆ *Wheelwrights Arms* RG10 0TR [off A329 Reading—Wokingham at Winnersh crossroads by Sainsbury's, signed Hurst, Twyford; then right into Davis Way]: Cheerfully bustling beamed local with big woodburner, bare black boards and flagstones, Wadworths IPA, 6X and guest beers, great value lunchtime food from huge doorstep sandwiches up, quick friendly service, cottagey no smoking dining area; may keep your credit card, can be a bit smoky by bar; children welcome, picnic-sets in smallish garden with terrace, disabled parking and facilities, open all day wknds (R T and J C Moggridge, John Baish, BB, Paul Humphreys)

WOKINGHAM [SU8266]

☆ *Crooked Billet* RG40 3BJ [Honey Hill]: Busy country pub with pews, tiles, brick serving counter, crooked black joists, generous enjoyable honest lunchtime food inc good family Sun lunch, Brakspears ales, efficient friendly service; nice outside in summer, very busy wknds (LYM, Betty Cantle)

Dukes Head RG40 2BQ [Denmark St]: Well refurbished keeping cosy feel and adding no smoking eating extension to back bar, Brakspears, enjoyable food using local ingredients, popular Sun lunch; improved sunny garden, five comfortable and well equipped new bedrooms in old coach house (J Lister)

WOODSIDE [SU9271]

Duke of Edinburgh SL4 2DP [Woodside Rd (narrow turn off A332 Windsor—Ascot S of B3034)]: Welcoming local with Arkells 2B, 3B and Kingsdown, good choice of wines by the glass, friendly service, solidly furnished main bar, sofas in middle lounge, no smoking area, usual bar food from good range of proper sandwiches up, small no smoking area and separate no smoking bistro restaurant; big-screen TV, quiz night; children welcome, tables out in front and in pleasant garden with summer marquee (John and Joyce Snell, Tracey and Stephen Groves, Gerry and Rosemary Dobson)

☆ *Rose & Crown* SL4 2DP [Woodside Rd, Winkfield, off A332 Ascot—Windsor]: Thriving pub with low-beamed bar and extended no smoking dining area, enjoyable food (not Sun or Mon evening) from lunchtime sandwiches and baguettes to more elaborate evening restaurant dishes and popular Sun lunch, Greene King IPA and Morlands Original and a guest beer, interesting affordable wines; piped music, games machine; children in eating areas, tables and swing in side garden backed by woodland, bedrooms, open all day, cl Sun evening (Gerry and Rosemary Dobson, Bob and Margaret Holder, LYM, Les and Barbara Owen)

WRAYSBURY [TQ0074]

Perseverance TW19 5DB [High St]: Comfortable bar areas, enjoyable attractively priced food from sandwiches up, good choice of beers and wines, prompt service, small restaurant; tables in back garden (Angela Winton)

Buckinghamshire

There's a fine choice of proper friendly country pubs in pretty walking country here – as well as some very smart dining pubs. Pubs on top form this year include the Three Horseshoes at Bennett End (the new licensee/chef is working hard, smartening up rooms and the garden), the welcoming Royal Oak at Bovingdon Green (among many other virtues a fantastic choice of pudding wines), the Red Lion at Chenies (run by long-standing and friendly people), the Swan in Denham (super imaginative food), the Palmers Arms in Dorney (delicious, impeccably presented meals), the Royal Standard of England in Forty Green (lots of fascinating history evident here), the White Horse in Hedgerley (fine choice of real ales in a real country local), the cheerfully run and simple Crown at Little Missenden, the bustling Polecat in Prestwood (a good local following), the very popular Frog at Skirmett (a super pub run by cheerful people), and the civilised Boot at Soulbury. Many of the county's pubs, as you can see, specialise in good food; the title of Buckinghamshire Dining Pub of the Year 2007 goes to the Palmers Arms in Dorney. The very same village of Dorney holds a nice new entry that is quite a contrast: the Pineapple's speciality is excellent sandwiches – and this appealingly traditional pub's good beers are far cheaper than the norm for this otherwise expensive county. The other two new entries in the county also mark a striking contrast with each other. Hidden away in the centre of Aylesbury, the Kings Head is an ancient inn owned by the National Trust and now well run as a good value pub by the local small Chiltern Brewery. The Grove Lock by the canal at Grove is at the opposite end of the time spectrum, a fine new all-day Fullers pub. In the Lucky Dip section at the end of the chapter, pubs to note particularly are the Old Thatched Inn at Adstock, Chester Arms at Chicheley, Hampden Arms at Great Hampden, Stag & Huntsman at Hambleden, Rising Sun at Little Hampden, restaurantry Hand & Flowers in Marlow, Swan in Olney, Hit or Miss at Penn Street, Old Swan at The Lee, Chequers at Wheeler End and Royal Standard at Wooburn Common. We have inspected (and enjoyed) almost all of these.

AYLESBURY   SP8113   Map 4
Kings Head ◀

Kings Head Passage (narrow passage off Bourbon Street), also entrance off Temple Street; no nearby parking except for disabled; HP20 2RW

Hidden away behind the shops and offices of this modern town centre is this real surprise – a handsome 15th-c inn owned by the National Trust. Only a part of the building is used as a pub (other parts include a coffee shop, arts and crafts shop, and conference rooms, and besides striking early Tudor window lighting the former Great Hall has even more ancient stained glass showing the Royal Arms of Henry VI and Margaret of Anjou). Since 2005 the three-room pub part, entirely no smoking, has been run by the small local Chiltern Brewery. It has been restored with careful and unpretentious simplicity – stripped boards, cream walls with little decoration, gentle lighting, a variety of seating which includes softly upholstered sofas and armchairs, cushioned high-backed settles and little dove-grey café chairs. Most of the bar tables are of round glass, supported on low cask tops; the left-hand room has simple modern pale dining tables and chairs. It's all nicely low-key – not smart, but thoroughly civilised. The neat corner bar has Chiltern Ale, Beechwood Bitter, 300s Old Ale, and perhaps John Hampdens on handpump, and some interesting bottled beers; service is friendly, and there's no piped music or machines; disabled access and facilities. Interestingly, they include their own beer in much of the food (which is locally sourced): home-made soup (£3.95), sandwiches (from £4.60), ploughman's with beer cheese and beer bread (£5.95), three different sausages made with three different beers and spiced ale gravy (£6.80), a proper steak in ale pie (£6.95), chicken in lemon and paprika (£7.95), and puddings such as barley wine fruit cake (£1.95), and peach and cherry crumble (£3.95). The original cobbled courtyard has teak seats and tables, some under cover of a pillared roof. No children inside. *(Recommended by Tim and Ann Newell, Mike Pugh, Caren Harris)*

Chiltern ~ Manager Claire Bignell ~ Real ale ~ Bar food (12-2(3 Sat), 6-9; not Sun or Mon evenings) ~ (01296) 718812 ~ Occasional live music ~ Open 11-11; 12-10.30 Sun; closed 25 and 26 Dec and Easter Sunday

BENNETT END   SU7897   Map 4

Three Horseshoes

Horseshoe Road; from Radnage follow unclassified road towards Princes Risborough and turn left into Bennett End Road, then right into Horseshoe Road; HP14 4EB

A new chef/patron has taken over this quietly set old country inn and the food promises to be very good. The no smoking restaurant is to be redecorated and the garden has been replanted and smartened up – though the rather endearing red telephone box that is gradually sinking into one of the duck ponds has remained. There are several separate seating areas: to the left of the entrance (mind your head) is the flagstoned snug bar, liked by walkers (muddy boots to be left outside), with a log fire in the raised stone fireplace, and original brickwork and bread oven. To the right of the entrance are two further sitting areas, one with a long wooden winged settle and the other enclosed by standing timbers with wooden flooring and a woodburning stove. The two-part dining room overlooks the garden and valley beyond. Well kept Adnams Broadside, Rebellion Zebedee and Charles Wells Bombardier on handpump, and a seasonally changing wine list. As well as sandwiches (from £3.75; the sirloin of beef with wild rocket is well liked, £4.50), the imaginative food, using fresh local produce, might include home-made soup (£3.75), arborio rice risotto with broad beans and peas (£4.50), chicken liver parfait with home-made piccalilli and pickles (£4.95), asparagus and scallop in a puff pastry case with chive butter sauce (£6.50), grilled fillets of bass with roasted salsify and truffle jus (£12.50), roast rack of lamb cutlets with potato rösti, spiced aubergine and baby vegetables (£14.95), thin strips of aberdeen angus fillet with wild mushrooms and madeira jus (£16.50), and puddings such as chocolate mousse, raspberry crème brûlée and passion fruit ice-cream or bread and butter pudding with marmalade ice-cream (£5.50). More reports on the new regime, please. *(Recommended by Brian Young, Brian Root, Janet Cameron, Tim and Ann Newell, Ken and Pat Headley, Susan and John Douglas, Tracey and Stephen Groves, Peter Abbott, J Simmonds, Heather Couper, Mr and Mrs R J Timberlake, Bruce and Sharon Eden, Roy and Gay Hoing, Paul Humphreys)*

Free house ~ Licensee Simon Crawshaw ~ Real ale ~ Bar food (not winter Sun evening or winter Mon) ~ Restaurant ~ (01494) 483273 ~ Children welcome ~ Open 12-3, 6-11; 12-11 Sat; 12-10.30 Sun; may not be open all day weekends in winter; closed Sun evening and all day Mon Oct-April ~ Bedrooms: £65S/£78B

BOVINGDON GREEN   SU8286   Map 2

Royal Oak 🍴 ♈

¾ mile N of Marlow, on back road to Frieth signposted off West Street (A4155) in centre; SL7 2JF

For those who enjoy their pudding wines, this friendly and rather civilised whitewashed pub is just the place to come to – they have a fantastic range of ten by two sizes of glass. There are 17 other wines by the glass, too, plus Brakspears, Fullers London Pride and the local Rebellion IPA on handpump. Several attractively decorated areas open off the central bar, the half-panelled walls variously painted in pale blue, green or cream: the cosiest part is the low-beamed room closest to the car park, with three small tables, a woodburner in an exposed brick fireplace, and a big pile of logs. Throughout there's a mix of church chairs, stripped wooden tables and chunky wall seats, with rugs on the partly wooden, partly flagstoned floors, co-ordinated cushions and curtains, and a very bright, airy feel; thoughtful extra touches set the tone, with a big, square bowl of olives on the bar, smart soaps and toiletries in the lavatories, and carefully laid out newspapers – most tables have fresh flowers or candles. The raised dining area is no smoking. Using as much local produce as possible, the popular food might include soup (£4.25), wild mushroom filo parcels with tarragon cream (£5.75), a plate of tapas (£6), sautéed tiger prawns and baby squid on spring onion, chilli and coriander noodles (£6.75), free-range pork and herb sausage with red wine gravy (£10.50), tempura spring vegetables on baked herb pancake with saffron and basil yoghurt (£11), cajun-spiced chicken supreme with roast red pepper sauce (£11.50), crispy skinned salmon fillet on warm new potato and spinach salad with truffle oil (£12), grilled lamb cutlets on pea and chickpea purée with mint jus (£14.25), grilled rib-eye steak with fat chips (£14), and puddings such as warm banana pudding with toffee sauce, tangy rhubarb compote or chilli-poached pineapple with mango sauce and ginger biscuits (from £5); side orders of vegetables or salad (from £2.50). A good few tables may have reserved signs (it's worth booking ahead, especially on Sundays); quick, helpful service, and piped music. A terrace with good solid tables leads to an appealing garden with plenty more, and there's a smaller garden at the side as well. The pub is part of a little group which comprises the Alford Arms in Frithsden (see Hertfordshire main entries), the Old Queens Head in Penn (Buckinghamshire), and the Swan at Denham (see Buckinghamshire main entries). *(Recommended by Mike and Nicky Pleass, Mrs Ann Gray, A J Murray, Tracey and Stephen Groves, Michael Dandy, Stephen Moss, Simon Collett-Jones, Jeff and Wendy Williams, Mrs E A Macdonald, Heather Couper, Bob and Maggie Atherton)*

Salisbury Pubs ~ Lease Trasna Rice Giff ~ Real ale ~ Bar food (12-2.30(4 Sun), 7-10) ~ Restaurant ~ (01628) 488611 ~ Children welcome ~ Dogs allowed in bar ~ Open 11-11; 12-10.30 Sun; closed 25-26 Dec

CADMORE END   SU7892   Map 4
Old Ship 🍺
B482 Stokenchurch—Marlow; HP14 3PN

The two little low-beamed rooms of the bar in this tiny and carefully restored 17th-c no smoking cottage are separated by standing timbers, and have plenty of unpretentious charm. They are simply furnished with scrubbed country tables and bench and church chair seating (one still has a hole for a game called five-farthings), and have well kept ales from Archers, Sharps and Youngs tapped straight from the cask down in the cellar and carried upstairs; shove-ha'penny. Simple bar food includes home-made soup or pâté (£4.95), filled baguettes, local ham and eggs (£7.95), local sausages (£8.95), hand-made pies (£9.50), sirloin steak (£11.95), and puddings such as treacle sponge or spotted dick (£4.95). Outside, there are seats in the sheltered garden with a large pergola, and a terrace at the end of the bar with cushioned seats and clothed tables. Parking is on the other side of the road. More reports please. *(Recommended by Michael Dandy, the Didler, Pete Baker, Angus Johnson, Carol Bolden, Alan and Anne Driver)*

Free house ~ Licensee Philip Butt ~ Real ale ~ Bar food (not Mon lunchtime except bank hols) ~ Restaurant ~ (01494) 883496 ~ Open 12(11.30 Sat)-2.30(3 Sat), 5.30-11; 11.30-3, 7-10.30 Sun; closed Mon lunchtime

Pubs staying open all afternoon at least one day a week are listed at the back of the book.

CHALFONT ST GILES   SU9893   Map 4
White Hart
Three Households (main street, W); HP8 4LP

The civilised bar here has been refurbished this year with chocolate leather seats and sofas and modern artwork on the mushroom coloured walls. There's quite an emphasis on the food, and the extended, spreading no smoking dining room (similarly furnished to the bar) is mainly bare boards – the bright acoustics make for a lively medley of chatter – sometimes rather on the noisy side when it's busy. As well as sandwiches (from £5), the good modern food at lunchtime might include smoked salmon and asparagus quiche (£6.95), chicken caesar salad (£7.25), moules marinière (£7.95), and stir-fried thai chicken (£9.25); daily specials like home-made broccoli and stilton soup (£4.50), goats cheese, artichoke and baby spinach salad (£7.25), smoked haddock florentine (£16.50), and fried duck breast with pak choi, portabella mushrooms and thyme and rosemary jus (£17.95), with puddings such as warm chocolate fondant with pistachio crème fraîche or sticky toffee pudding with butterscotch sauce (from £4.95). Greene King IPA, Abbot and Morlands Original on handpump, and several wines by the glass; broadsheet daily papers, piped music, and neatly dressed young staff. A sheltered back terrace has squarish picnic-sets under cocktails parasols, with more beyond in the garden, which has a neat play area. Please note, no under 21s (but see below for children). More reports please. *(Recommended by Mr and Mrs A Curry, Mrs Ann Gray, Tracey and Stephen Groves, Roy and Gay Hoing)*

Greene King ~ Lease Scott MacRae ~ Real ale ~ Bar food ~ Restaurant ~ (01494) 872441 ~ Children allowed if with an adult ~ Dogs allowed in bar ~ Open 11.30-2.30, 6-11; 12-10.30 Sun; closed evening 25 Dec, 26 Dec ~ Bedrooms: £77.50S/£97.50S

CHENIES   TQ0198   Map 3
Red Lion ★ 🍺
2 miles from M25 junction 18; A404 towards Amersham, then village signposted on right; Chesham Road; WD3 6ED

The long-standing and friendly licensees here are determined to keep this well run place as a traditional pub serving good home-made food rather than a restaurant serving beer. The bustling, unpretentious L-shaped bar has comfortable built-in wall benches by the front windows, other traditional seats and tables, and original photographs of the village and traction engines; there's also a small back snug and a no smoking dining room (where, for the first time in 20 years, they now take bookings). Very well kept Rebellion Lion Pride (brewed for the pub), Vale Best Bitter, Wadworths 6X, and a guest beer on handpump, and at least ten wines by the glass. Popular food from quite a wide menu includes lunchtime filled baguettes and baps (bacon and beetroot £5.50, steak and onions £6.95), field mushrooms topped with stilton and prawns (£5.95), quorn lasagne (£8.95), lamb pie or bangers and mash (£9.50), game pie or thickly sliced gammon topped with a poached egg and served with parsley sauce (£10.95), grilled bass with wholegrain mustard sauce (£12.95), Orkney Isle steaks, and home-made puddings like chocolate roulade, crumbles or apple pie (from £3.95). The hanging baskets and window boxes are pretty in summer, and there are picnic-sets on a small side terrace. No children, games machines or piped music. *(Recommended by Val and Alan Green, Colin and Alma Gent, Ian Phillips, Tracey and Stephen Groves, Michael B Griffith, M G Hart, Lynn Elliott, Peter Abbott, Susan and John Douglas, Roy and Gay Hoing, Charles Gysin, Brian P White)*

Free house ~ Licensee Mike Norris ~ Real ale ~ Bar food (12-2, 7-10(9.30 Sun)) ~ (01923) 282722 ~ Dogs allowed in bar ~ Open 11-2.30, 5.30-11; 12-3, 6.30-10.30 Sun; closed 25 Dec

DENHAM TQ0486 Map 3

Swan ⚐ ♀

¾ mile from M40 junction 1 or M25 junction 16; follow Denham Village signs; UB9 5BH

With particularly good food and friendly, helpful staff, this civilised dining pub is, not surprisingly, very popular and it's best to book a table in advance. The rooms are stylishly furnished with a nice mix of antique and old-fashioned chairs and solid tables, individually chosen pictures on the cream and warm green walls, rich heavily draped curtains, inviting open fires (usually lit), newspapers to read, and fresh flowers. Promptly served, the interesting food includes soup (£4.25), potted ham hock with toasted rye bread (£5.75), crab gnocchi with truffle cream sauce (£6.25; main course £12), seared king scallops with cauliflower purée and beetroot syrup (£7.50), free-range pork and herb sausages with red onion gravy (£10.50), halloumi, sweet pepper, tomato and broad bean pastry stack with jalapeno and pumpkin seed pesto (£10.75), fish pie topped with applewood cheese and buttered leeks (£11.75), pot-roast lamb rump on caramelised roots with puy lentil and balsamic jus (£13.75), chargrilled rib-eye steak with straw chips and herb butter (£14), and puddings such as warm chocolate brownie with white chocolate milkshake or vanilla panna cotta with mixed berries (from £4.75); side orders of salad or vegetables (from £2.50); the dining room is no smoking. A smashing choice of 17 wines plus ten pudding wines by two sizes of glass, and Courage Best, Rebellion IPA and Wadworths 6X on handpump; piped music. The extensive garden is floodlit at night, and leads from a sheltered terrace with tables to a more spacious lawn. It can get busy at weekends, and parking may be difficult. The wisteria is very pretty in May. The pub is part of a little group which comprises the Royal Oak, Bovingdon Green and the Old Queens Head in Penn (also in Buckinghamshire) and the Alford Arms in Frithsden (see Hertfordshire main entries). *(Recommended by Jill Bickerton, John Saville, Martin and Karen Wake, Peter Saville, Geoffrey Kemp, Susan and John Douglas, Nigel Howard, Ian Phillips, Grahame Brooks)*

Salisbury Pubs ~ Lease Mark Littlewood ~ Real ale ~ Bar food (12-2.30(4 Sun), 7-10) ~ Restaurant ~ (01895) 832085 ~ Children welcome ~ Dogs allowed in bar ~ Open 11-11; 12-10.30 Sun; closed 25 and 26 Dec

DORNEY SU9279 Map 2

Palmer Arms ⚐ ♀

2.7 miles from M4 junction 7; turn left on to A4, then left on B3026; Village Road; SL4 6QW

Buckinghamshire Dining Pub of the Year

Handy for the motorway, this extended and smartly modernised dining pub (totally no smoking now) places much emphasis on its excellent and impeccably presented food. But they do have Greene King IPA, Abbot and a guest beer on handpump kept under light blanket pressure, 14 wines by the glass, and country wines. The bar is civilised and relaxed with several separate-seeming areas around a central counter: a nicely polished wooden floor, newspapers, a couple of fireplaces and the occasional sofa, fresh flowers, mirrors, and art for sale on the walls. At the back is a more elegant dining room, with exposed brick walls, long red curtains, solid wooden tables and brown leather armchairs. Lunchtime meals might include cheese, smoked meat and fish or vegetarian platters (from £7.50 small, from £14.50 large), as well as spicy tomato, chorizo and chickpea broth (£4.50), smooth chicken liver parfait with home-made chutney (£5), crayfish and blood orange salad with pea shoots and citrus dressing (£6; main course £11.50), home-cooked honey roasted ham and eggs (£9), trio of local sausages with roast garlic mash and onion gravy (£10.50), asparagus and mascarpone risotto with shredded sorrel and parmesan crisp (£11), and fish pie with a herb brioche crust (£13.50); evening extras such as a warm chicken and pomegranate salad (£5.50; main course £10.50), a trio of smoked duck, venison and ham with home-made relishes (£6), baked cod with soft herb crust on cabbage, bacon and pea broth (£14), and 21-day aged rib-eye steak with foie gras butter or seared yellowfin tuna with niçoise vegetables and dijon mustard dressing (£15); puddings like white chocolate crème brûlée with lavender shortbread or honey and rhubarb eton mess (from £4.50). Side orders of vegetables or salad (from £2.25) and set menus: two courses £12, three courses £15, and the monthly 'Bubbles with Jazz' Sunday lunch (when lunch includes unlimited bubbles). Service may incur a 10% surcharge. The terrace overlooks a very attractively landscaped palm-filled garden, with plenty of stylish tables and chairs. The drive from here to Eton throws up splendid views of Windsor Castle. *(Recommended by Kevin Thomas, Nina Randall, A J Murray, Simon Collett-Jones, Susan and John Douglas, Michael Dandy, E B Ireland, I D Barnett)*

Greene King ~ Lease Elizabeth Dax ~ Real ale ~ Bar food (12-9.30(7 Sun)) ~ Restaurant ~ (01628) 666612 ~ Children welcome ~ Jazz first Sun of month ~ Open 11-11; 12-9 Sun

Pineapple 🍺

2.4 miles from M4 junction 7; turn left on to A4, then left on B3026 (or take first left off A4 at traffic lights, into Huntercombe Lane S, then left at T junction on main road – shorter but slower); Lake End Road; SL4 6QS

It's the sandwiches which come in for highest praise at this nicely old-fashioned and unpretentious pub – a choice of five different fresh breads, good generous fillings, and at £5.95 quite a bargain as they come with your choice of hearty vegetable soup, salad or chips. Up to 1,000 varieties run from cream cheese with beetroot to chicken, avocado, crispy bacon and lettuce with a honey and mustard dressing. They do good Sunday roasts, and puddings such as spiced apple, or banana sliced with dates and maple syrup, or pineapple (of course) perhaps with chocolate and hazelnuts (£3.75). China pineapples join the decorations on a set of shelves in one of three cottagey carpeted linked rooms, all no smoking, on the left. It's bare boards on the right, where the bar counter has Greene King IPA, Fullers London Pride and Hook Norton Old Hooky on handpump, good wines by the glass, and good coffee. Throughout there are low shiny Anaglypta ceilings, black-panelled dadoes and sturdy country tables – one very long, another in a big bow window. There is a woodburning stove at one end, a pretty little fireplace in another room; half the pub is no smoking. Plenty of young staff, a quietly friendly black labrador; the piped pop music is fairly unobtrusive; disabled access and facilities. A roadside verandah has some rustic tables, and there are plenty of round picnic-sets out in the garden, some on fairy-lit decking under an oak tree; the nearby motorway makes itself heard out here. *(Recommended by Mike and Sue Richardson, Karen Keen, Michael Dandy)*

Punch ~ Lease Stuart Jones ~ Real ale ~ Bar food (12-9) ~ (01628) 662353 ~ Children welcome ~ Dogs welcome ~ Open 11-11; 11-10.30 Sun

EASINGTON SP6810 Map 4
Mole & Chicken 🍴 🍷 🛏️

From B4011 in Long Crendon follow Chearsley, Waddesdon signpost into Carters Lane opposite the Chandos Arms, then turn left into Chilton Road; HP18 9EY

The no smoking restaurant in this bustling dining pub has been extended and refurbished this year, and new french doors now open on to a wooden deck which leads to the garden (where they sometimes hold summer barbecues and pork and lamb roasts); the views and sunsets from here are lovely. The open-plan layout is cleverly done, so that all the different parts seem quite snug and self-contained without being cut off from what's going on, and the atmosphere is relaxed and sociable. The beamed bar curves around the serving counter in a sort of S-shape, and there are oak and pine tables on flagstones, rag-washed terracotta walls with lots of big antique prints, lit candles, and good winter log fires. Generous helpings of consistently excellent food might include sandwiches, home-made soup (£3.50), field mushrooms with spinach and cheese or squid rings with spicy dressing (£5.95), good creamed chilli mussels or skewers of chicken and prawn with peanut dip, chilli, and garlic mayonnaise (£6.95), sun-dried tomato and asparagus tart with grilled goats cheese (£8.95), rack of pork ribs in barbecue sauce or home-made smoked chicken and mushroom pie (£9.95), bass fillet stuffed with roasted vegetables (£10.95), crispy gressingham duck with orange sauce or 10oz rib-eye steak (£12.95), popular shoulder of lamb with a special sauce (£13.95), daily specials, and puddings (£4.95). A good choice of wines (with decent french house wines), over 40 malt whiskies, and well kept Greene King Old Speckled Hen, Hook Norton Best, and Vale Best Bitter on handpump; piped music. Readers enjoy staying here. *(Recommended by Neil and Angela Huxter, R E Dixon, Paul Humphreys, Donna and Roger, Cathryn and Richard Hicks, John Reilly, Angus Johnson, Carol Bolden, David and Pam Lewis, Jeff and Wendy Williams, Karen and Graham Oddey)*

Free house ~ Licensees A Heather and S Ellis ~ Real ale ~ Bar food (all day Sun) ~ Restaurant ~ (01844) 208387 ~ Children welcome ~ Open 12-3, 6-11; 12-10.30 Sun; closed 25 Dec ~ Bedrooms: £50B/£65B

FORD   SP7709   Map 4
Dinton Hermit 🛏️
SW of Aylesbury; HP17 8XH

Tucked away in pretty countryside this carefully extended 16th-c stone building is now perhaps more of a restaurant with bedrooms than pub – though they do keep Adnams, Brakspears Bitter and Youngs on handpump. The bar has scrubbed tables and comfortable cushioned and wicker-backed mahogany-look chairs on a nice old black and red tiled floor, a huge inglenook fireplace, and white-painted plaster on very thick uneven stone walls. There's an old print of John Bigg, the supposed executioner of Charles I and the man later known as the Dinton Hermit. The no smoking back dining area with smart linen tablecloths and napkins has similar furniture on quarry tiles. A nice touch is the church candles lit throughout the bar and restaurant, and there are hundreds of wine bottles decorating the walls and thick oak bar counter. At lunchtime the attractively presented food might include soup (£3.95), chicken liver parfait with plum compote or slow-roasted duck leg with chilli mash and hoisin sauce (£5.95), sandwiches (from £6.25), bruschetta of goats cheese with sun-dried tomato and rocket (£6.95), chicken, bacon and avocado salad with green pesto dressing (£7.95), tagliatelle carbonara (£9.90), and braised lamb shank on saffron risotto with tarragon jus (£12.95); also, grilled fillet of mackerel topped with chilli, garlic and thyme wrapped in pancetta and served with sweet and sour reduced cherry tomatoes (£5.95), home-made asparagus and ricotta open ravioli of basil pasta with roasted red pepper and mascarpone sauce (£6.95), calves liver with caramelised onion and bacon tart, confit of apple, thyme mash and port jus (£13.50), roasted duck breast with glazed peaches, pommes anna, roasted baby leeks and port jus (£13.95), and baked halibut fillet topped with black olive and herb crust with black linguini, steamed mussels and fish velouté (£14.50); a decent choice of wines. Plenty of picnic sets in the garden, and the bright, well decorated bedrooms are in a sympathetically converted barn. More reports please. *(Recommended by Peter and Gill Helps, Helen Hodson, Barry Collett, Julia and Richard Tredgett, Howard Dell)*

Free house ~ Licensees John and Debbie Colinswood ~ Real ale ~ Bar food (not Sun evening) ~ Restaurant ~ (01296) 747473 ~ Well behaved children in eating areas but must be over 12 in evening ~ Jazz every other Weds evening ~ Open 12-11; 12-10.30 Sun; closed 25-26 Dec, 1 Jan ~ Bedrooms: /£100S

FORTY GREEN   SU9292   Map 2
Royal Standard of England ㉕ 🍷
3½ miles from M40 junction 2, via A40 to Beaconsfield, then follow sign to Forty Green, off B474 ¾ mile N of New Beaconsfield; keep going through village; HP9 1XT

Once known as The Ship, this ancient place was given its current name by Charles II as a reward for the support the pub had given to his executed father and his cavaliers, and it's the oldest free house in England. There's certainly lots to look at – both in the layout of the building itself and in the fascinating collection of antiques which fills it. The rambling rooms have huge black ship's timbers, finely carved old oak panelling, roaring winter fires with handsomely decorated iron firebacks, and there's a massive settle apparently built to fit the curved transom of an Elizabethan ship; you can also see rifles, powder-flasks and bugles, ancient pewter and pottery tankards, lots of brass and copper, needlework samplers and stained glass. A fine choice of up to eight real ales on handpump might include Brakspears Bitter, Marstons Pedigree, Rebellion IPA and Mild, and guests such as Crouch Vale Brewers Gold or Springhead Puritans Porter; a good range of bottled beers, too, 11 wines by two sizes of glass, Thatcher's cider, and Weston's perry; shove-ha'penny. Bar food such as country terrine or devilled lambs kidneys (£4.95), sandwiches (from £4.95), pint of prawns (£5.95), ploughman's (£6.75), ham and free-range eggs, sausage and mash or chicken caesar salad (£7.95), home-made cottage pie or mushroom risotto (£8.95), braised lamb shank (£11.95), and puddings like spotted dick or jam roly-poly (£3.95). The pub is totally no smoking on Sunday lunchtimes and at other times there is just one small room where smokers are allowed. Seats outside in a neatly hedged front rose garden or in the shade of a tree. *(Recommended by Heather Couper, Tracey and Stephen Groves, Simon Collett-Jones, Paul Humphreys, John and Glenys Wheeler, Mrs Ann Gray, Piotr Chodzko-Zajko, the Didler, Susan and John Douglas, Keith Barker, E V Lee, Jarrod and Wendy Hopkinson, John Reilly, Michael Dandy, T R and B C Jenkins)*

Free house ~ Licensee Matthew O'Keeffe ~ Real ale ~ Bar food (all day (including Sat breakfasts from 9am)) ~ Restaurant ~ (01494) 673382 ~ Children welcome ~ Dogs allowed in bar ~ Live music once a month ~ Open 11-11; 12-11 Sun

GROVE SP9122 Map 4
Grove Lock ♀ ◖

Pub signed off B488, on left just S of A505 roundabout (S of Leighton Buzzard); LU7 0QU

Alone by the Grand Union Canal, this modern open-plan pub is a good all-day refuge. The extensive main area, largely no smoking and with diagonal oak floor boarding and a lofty high-raftered pitched roof, gives you a choice between pleasant modern dining tables (all with flowers) and more laid-back seating such as squishy brown leather sofas, bucket chairs and drum stools around low tables. Steps take you up to a further three-room no smoking restaurant area, partly flagstoned, looking down on the narrow canal lock. They have Fullers London Pride, ESB, Discovery and HSB on handpump and were adding another four pumps as we went to press; a good changing range of wines by the glass. Dependable food such as home-made soup (£3.95), sandwiches (from £4.95), roasted mushrooms, red onion, sweet potato and brie in a filo parcel with a rocket and balsamic glaze (£4.95), chicken liver pâté with chutney or cod and pancetta fishcakes (£5.95), beanburger (£7.95), beef curry (£8.95), beer battered fish (£9.25), pork chop (£9.50) and fillet steak (£13.95); efficient young staff; piped music (not too obtrusive); disabled access and facilities. A couple of games machines are tucked away at one end, as is the TV for sports. In winter there's a big open-standing log fire under an impressive steel chimney canopy. In summer a partly terraced waterside garden has plenty of circular picnic-sets, some on canopied decking. *(Recommended by Michael Dandy, Lynda Payton, Sam Samuells)*

Fullers ~ Managers Daniel and Anne Toner ~ Real ale ~ Bar food (all day – best to check in winter) ~ Restaurant ~ (01525) 380940 ~ Children welcome ~ Open 11-11; 12-10.30 Sun

HADDENHAM SP7408 Map 4
Green Dragon ⑪ ♀

Village signposted off A418 and A4129, E/NE of Thame; then follow Church End signs; HP17 8AA

There is still some provision for drinkers in this well run, totally no smoking place, but most customers do come to enjoy the particularly good, imaginative cooking. The neatly kept opened-up bar, in colours of pale olive and antique rose, has an open fireplace towards the back of the building and attractive furnishings throughout; the dining area has a fine mix of informal tables and chairs. Using seasonal ingredients, the high quality food might include home-made soup (£4.25), sandwiches (from £4.95), home-smoked pigeon breast with celeriac remoulade (£5.50), gravadlax with crayfish and avocado with a caper and mustard dressing (£6.50), warm roasted mediterranean vegetable tart with gruyere (£9.95), steak and kidney pudding (£10.50), fish and chips (£11), gressingham duck breast with apple confit and blackcurrant jus (£14.50), bass with fennel, sweet potato fondant and watercress sauce (£14.95), and puddings such as pina colada panna cotta or ginger and rhubarb crème brûlée with home-made shortbread biscuits (£5.50). Well kept Caledonian Deuchars IPA, Vale Wychert Ale (brewed in the village) and Wadworths 6X on handpump, and around eight wines by the glass. A big sheltered gravel terrace behind the pub has white tables and picnic-sets under cocktail parasols, with more on the grass, and a good variety of plants. This part of the village is very pretty, with a duck pond unusually close to the church. *(Recommended by Mike and Sue Richardson, B H and J I Andrews, Mr and Mrs J E C Tasker, B Brewer, Peter and Jan Humphreys, Keith Rutter, Inga Davis, Jonathan and Virginia West, John Reilly, Ian Arthur)*

Enterprise ~ Lease Peter Moffat ~ Real ale ~ Bar food ~ Restaurant ~ (01844) 291403 ~ Children over 7 in restaurant lunchtime only ~ Open 12-2.30, 6.30-11; 12-2.30 Sun; closed Sun evening, 1 Jan

HAWRIDGE COMMON   SP9406   Map 4
Full Moon 🍺

Hawridge Common; left fork off A416 N of Chesham, then follow for 3.5 miles towards Cholesbury; HP5 2UH

This is a pretty setting, best enjoyed in summer when you can sit out on the terrace (which has an awning and outside heaters for cooler evenings), and gaze over the windmill nestling behind; plenty of walks over the common, too. The six real ales on handpump are also quite a draw: Adnams, Bass, Brakspears Special, Fullers London Pride and Original and Greene King Ruddles County. The low-beamed rambling bar is the heart of the building, with oak built-in floor-to-ceiling settles, ancient flagstones and flooring tiles, hunting prints and an inglenook fireplace. At lunchtime the enjoyable food might include sandwiches (£4.25), filled baked potatoes or spare ribs in hoisin sauce (£5.50), battered cod or wild mushroom pasta (£9.25), and beef stew with herb dumplings or chicken curry (£9.95), with evening choices like salmon fishcakes with lime crème fraîche dip or duck and plum parcels (£5.50), sausage and mash (£9.95), and szechuan sirloin stir fry or gilt-head bream with white wine and saffron sauce (£12.95), and daily specials such as goats cheese and sunblush tomato salad with a fig, pear and white balsamic dressing or grilled sardines (£5.50), and steak and kidney pudding or grilled salmon fillet with pesto (£9.25); puddings like apple dumplings with crème anglaise, mixed berry soufflé or caramel bavarois (£4.95), and Sunday roast (£8.95). They hold supper evenings with films or sports events shown on a 50-inch plasma screen, and there are eight wines by the glass; good service, cribbage, and piped music. Both the restaurants and one bar area are no smoking. *(Recommended by Mike Pugh, Peter and Giff Bennett, Mel Smith, D J and P M Taylor, Roy and Gay Hoing, Tracey and Stephen Groves)*

Enterprise ~ Lease Peter and Annie Alberto ~ Real ale ~ Bar food ~ Restaurant ~ (01494) 758959 ~ Children welcome ~ Dogs allowed in bar ~ Open 12-11; 12-10.30 Sun; closed 25 Dec

HEDGERLEY   SU9686   Map 2
White Horse ★ 🍺

2.4 miles from M40 junction 2; at exit roundabout take Slough turn-off then take Hedgerley Lane (immediate left) following alongside M40; after 1.5 miles turn right at T junction into Village Lane; SL2 3UY

It's a very pleasant surprise to come across an old-fashioned drinkers' pub such as this in the Gerrards Cross commuter belt. There's a good mix of customers and a fine range of seven real ales all tapped from the cask in a room behind the tiny hatch counter: Greene King IPA and Rebellion IPA are well kept alongside five daily changing guests from anywhere in the country, with good farm cider and perry, and belgian beers too; their regular ale festivals are very popular. The cottage main bar has plenty of character, with lots of beams, brasses and exposed brickwork, low wooden tables, some standing timbers, jugs, ballcocks and other bric-a-brac, a log fire, and a good few leaflets and notices about future village events. There is a little flagstoned public bar on the left; darts. On the way out to the garden, which has tables and occasional barbecues, they have a canopy extension to help during busy periods. The atmosphere is jolly with warmly friendly service from the cheerful staff. At lunchtimes they do bar food such as sandwiches (from £3.95), ploughman's (from £5), cold meats and quiches, and changing straightforward hot dishes. In front are lots of hanging baskets and a couple more tables overlooking the quiet road. There are good walks nearby, and the pub is handy for the Church Wood RSPB reserve. It can get crowded at weekends. *(Recommended by Chris Glasson, Anthony Longden, Brian Young, Dennis Jenkin, Mr and Mrs John Taylor, Paul Humphreys, N R White, Tracey and Stephen Groves, the Didler, Susan and John Douglas, Keith Barker, Simon Collett-Jones, Michael B Griffith, Nina Randall, Roy and Gay Hoing)*

Free house ~ Licensees Doris Hobbs and Kevin Brooker ~ Real ale ~ Bar food (lunchtime only) ~ (01753) 643225 ~ Children in canopy extension area ~ Dogs allowed in bar ~ Open 11-2.30, 5-11; 11-11 Sat; 12-10.30 Sun

LEY HILL   SP9802   Map 4

Swan 🍺

Village signposted off A416 in Chesham; HP5 1UT

Spotlessly kept with gleaming furniture, this charming little timbered 16th-c pub has a nice old-fashioned and chatty atmosphere. The main bar has black beams (mind your head) and standing timbers, an old range, a log fire and a collection of old local photographs; there's a cosy snug. Well liked bar food includes warm asparagus wrapped in a spring onion pancake (£5.95), baked brie wrapped in filo pastry with cranberry sauce (£6.95), grilled scottish king scallops (£7.50), chicken club sandwich or sirloin steak baguette (£7.95), chicken pasta (£8.50), wild mushroom risotto (£9.50), a plate of mixed fish (£9.95), grilled bass fillet on crab risotto (£13.25), fillet steak with a blue cheese crust (£15.95), and puddings (from £4.25); there's also a two-course set menu (£12.50; not Friday or Saturday evenings or Sunday lunch). The restaurant is no smoking; occasional live jazz. Well kept Adnams, Brakspears, Fullers London Pride and Timothy Taylors Landlord on handpump, and several wines by the glass. In front of the pub amongst the flower tubs and hanging baskets there are picnic-sets, with more in the large back garden. There's a cricket pitch, a nine-hole golf course, and a common opposite. More reports please. *(Recommended by Joe and Agnes Walker, Anthony Barnes, B Brewer, Tracey and Stephen Groves, Roy and Gay Hoing)*

Punch ~ Lease Nigel Byatt ~ Real ale ~ Bar food (not Sun evening) ~ Restaurant ~ (01494) 783075 ~ Children welcome ~ Open 12-11; 12-10.30 Sun; 12-3.30, 5.30-11 in winter

LITTLE MISSENDEN   SU9298   Map 4

Crown ★ 🍺 £

Crown Lane, SE end of village, which is signposted off A413 W of Amersham; HP7 0RD

There's a proper traditional and often cheery pubby feel in this small brick cottage which has been run by the same family for more than 90 years. The bustling bars are kept spotless by the friendly licensee, and the well kept real ales on handpump or tapped from the cask might come from Adnams, Hook Norton, St Austell, Vale and Youngs breweries; several malt whiskies. There are old red flooring tiles on the left, oak parquet on the right, built-in wall seats, studded red leatherette chairs, and a few small tables. You'll find darts, shove-ha'penny, cribbage and dominoes, but no piped music or machines. Straightforward bar food includes good fresh sandwiches (from £3), buck's bite (a special home-made pizza-like dish, £4.75), filled baked potatoes (from £4.95), ploughman's (from £5), steak and kidney pie (£5.25), and winter soup (£3.75). The large attractive sheltered, garden behind has picnic-sets and other tables, and the interesting church in the pretty village is well worth a visit. No children. (*Recommended by Tracey and Stephen Groves, Brian Root, Anthony Longden, Paul Humphreys*)

Free house ~ Licensees Trevor and Carolyn How ~ Real ale ~ Bar food (lunchtime only, not Sun) ~ No credit cards ~ (01494) 862571 ~ Open 11-2.30(3 Sat), 6-11; 12-3, 7-11 Sun

MENTMORE SP9119 Map 4

Stag ♀

Village signposted off B488 S of Leighton Buzzard; The Green; LU7 0QF

All the 50 wines on the list in this pretty village pub are available by the glass; they offer champagne cocktails, too. If it's just a drink you are after, you must go to the bustling public bar where they serve Charles Wells Bombardier, Eagle IPA and maybe St Austell Tribute on handpump; board games. There's a small, civilised no smoking lounge bar with a relaxed atmosphere, low oak tables, attractive fresh flower arrangements and an open fire, though this tends to be used by customers heading for the restaurant. Bar food at lunchtime includes sandwiches (£5.50), cheeseburgers, fishcakes, chicken curry and big omelettes (£8.75), with evening choices such as vegetable chilli, barbecue pork and spiced mexican chicken (£8.75). The restaurant is no smoking. There are seats out on the pleasant flower-filled front terrace looking across towards Mentmore House, and a charming, well tended, sloping garden. More reports please. (*Recommended by Mrs Ann Gray, Doreen and Haydn Maddock, Ian Phillips*)

Charles Wells ~ Lease Jenny and Mike Tuckwood ~ Real ale ~ Bar food ~ Restaurant ~ (01296) 668423 ~ Children in eating areas but not in restaurant on weekend evenings ~ Dogs allowed in bar ~ Open 12-11(10.30 Sun); may be shorter opening hours in winter

OVING SP7821 Map 4

Black Boy

Village signposted off A413 out of Whitchurch, N of Aylesbury; HP22 4HN

This appealing and no smoking 16th-c pub stretches further back than you might expect from the outside, with the old parts at the front the most atmospheric, especially the cosy red and black-tiled area around the enormous inglenook. The low heavy beams have mottoes chalked on them, and, up a couple of steps, another snug corner has a single table, some exposed stonework, and a mirror over a small brick fireplace. The long, light wooden bar counter is covered with posters advertising sales of agricultural land; opposite, two big, comfortable leather armchairs lead into the lighter, more modern dining room, with good-sized country kitchen pine tables set for eating, and picture windows offering the same view of the gardens. Throughout are plenty of candles and fresh flowers. There's some emphasis on food which might include soup (£4.50), sandwiches (from £5.50), chicken liver pâté with onion marmalade (£6.25), meats and seafood with assorted breads and olives (£7.50), cumberland sausages or home-cured ham and eggs (£7.75), pasta in cream, garlic and cheese (£11.50), baked cod topped with welsh rarebit, steak and kidney pie or mixed grill (£12.25), sizzling beef, chicken or tiger prawns (£12.75), steaks (from £12.75), and daily specials like spicy meatballs in tomato sauce, whole mackerel or venison sausages (£9.95); side orders £2.50. Gales Swing Low or Wadworths IPA on handpump, and half a dozen wines by the glass; piped music. The impressive garden has tables on its spacious sloping lawns and terrace with remarkable views down over the Vale of Aylesbury. The licensees breed and train chocolate labradors. More reports please. (*Recommended by R E Dixon, B H and J I Andrews, Brian Root, Gerry and Rosemary Dobson*)

Free house ~ Licensees Sally and David Hayle ~ Real ale ~ Bar food (till 4 Sun; not Sun evening or Mon) ~ Restaurant ~ (01296) 641258 ~ Well behaved children welcome ~ Dogs allowed in bar ~ Open 12-3, 6-11; 12-11 Sat; 12-5.30 Sun; closed Sun evening and all day Mon (exc bank hols)

PENN SU9193 Map 4

Crown

B474 Beaconsfield—High Wycombe; HP10 8NY

Under a new licensee, this creeper-covered dining pub has nicely decorated bars unusually laid out in an old-fashioned style; one comfortable low-ceilinged room used to be a coffin-maker's workshop. Bar food now includes home-made soup (£3.25), sandwiches or hot baguettes (from £3.25), mushroom rarebit (£4.25), chicken liver pâté with scottish heather honey or smoked salmon fishcake with celeriac remoulade (£4.45), fish and chips (£7.45), aberdeen angus steakburger (£7.95), tomato and mascarpone gnocchi (£8.25), chicken with goats cheese and tagliatelle (£8.95), salmon delice with lime and coriander salsa (£9.25), outdoor reared double pork chop (£10.25), rack of lamb (£14.95), and puddings such as hot chocolate pudding (£4.45). Well kept Fullers London Pride, Greene King Old Speckled Hen, Ringwood Old Thumper, and Timothy Taylors Best on handpump, and 16 wines by the glass; piped classical music, and two roaring log fires. The staff are friendly and helpful, and there's a pleasant atmosphere. Tables in front of the building, amongst pretty roses, face a 14th-c church which has a fine old painting of the Last Judgement; pleasant country views. More reports please. *(Recommended by Geoff and Sylvia Donald, Mrs Ann Gray, Susan and John Douglas, B Brewer, Roy and Gay Hoing, Brian P White)*

Spirit Group ~ Manager Richard Harold ~ Real ale ~ Bar food (all day) ~ Restaurant ~ (01494) 812640 ~ Children away from bar ~ Open 11-11; 12-10.30 Sun

PRESTWOOD SP8700 Map 4

Polecat 🍴

170 Wycombe Road (A4128 N of High Wycombe); HP16 0HJ

There's a good mix of chatty customers in this friendly and rather civilised pub – and an especially loyal local following. Opening off the low-ceilinged bar are several smallish rooms with an assortment of tables and chairs, various stuffed birds as well as the stuffed white polecats in one big cabinet, small country pictures, rugs on bare boards or red tiles, and a couple of antique housekeeper's chairs by a good open fire; the Gallery room and Drover Bar are no smoking. Popular and enjoyable, the food includes sandwiches (from £3.50), soup (£3.90), filled baked potatoes (from £4.90), kipper pâté with toasted lemon brioche (£4.95), ploughman's (£5.50), home-made steak and kidney pie or parsnip and stilton croquettes (£8.90), pork spare ribs in barbecue sauce (£9.90), smoked haddock and prawn filo parcels with creamed leek sauce (£10.20), roast barbary duck breast with orange and cognac sauce (£12.40), daily specials such as stilton soufflé with red onion marmalade (£4.95), greek spinach and feta pie with tomato and basil sauce (£8.90), beef casserole with steamed onion pudding (£9.90), and seafood tagliatelle (£10.90), and puddings like passion fruit syllabub with stem ginger biscuit or roulade of date and pecan with butterscotch sauce (£4.50). Well kept Brakspears Bitter, Flowers IPA, Greene King Old Speckled Hen, and Marstons Pedigree on handpump, quite a few wines by the glass, and 20 malt whiskies; piped music. The attractive garden has lots of bulbs in spring, and colourful hanging baskets, tubs and herbaceous plants; quite a few picnic-sets under parasols on neat grass out in front beneath a big fairy-lit pear tree, with more on a big well kept back lawn. *(Recommended by Tracey and Stephen Groves, Michael Dandy, Alan and Anne Driver, Howard Dell, B Brewer, Paul Humphreys, Mel Smith, John Branston, Heather Couper, Roy and Lindsey Fentiman, Roy and Gay Hoing, Brian P White, Peter Saville)*

Free house ~ Licensee John Gamble ~ Real ale ~ Bar food (not Sun evening) ~ No credit cards ~ (01494) 862253 ~ Children in Gallery Room and Drovers Bar ~ Dogs welcome ~

Open 11.30-2.30, 6-11; 12-3 Sun; closed Sun evening, evenings 25 and 31 Dec, all day 26 Dec and 1 Jan

SKIRMETT SU7790 Map 2

Frog 🍽 ♀ 🛏

From A4155 NE of Henley take Hambleden turn and keep on; or from B482 Stokenchurch—Marlow take Turville turn and keep on; RG9 6TG

Our readers enjoy this bustling and friendly country pub – as somewhere to drop into for a pint after a walk along one of the many hiking routes, to enjoy a leisurely meal or stay overnight. The neatly kept beamed bar area has a mix of comfortable furnishings, a striking hooded fireplace with a bench around the edge (and a pile of logs sitting beside it), big rugs on the wooden floors, and sporting and local prints around the salmon-painted walls. The function room leading off is sometimes used as a dining overflow. Although brightly modernised, there is still something of a local feel with leaflets and posters near the door advertising raffles and so forth. The imaginative food might include lunchtime baguettes, soup (£3.95), bruschetta of avocado, parma ham and soft poached egg with rocket salad (£5.95; main course £7.95), watercress pancake with smoked haddock filling glazed with saffron chive sauce (£6.50; main course £9.75), grilled goats cheese with roasted beetroot (£6.75), linguini with wild mushrooms, shallots, artichoke hearts and parmesan (£9.50), seared salmon with curried lentils and coriander cream sauce (£10.95), supreme of chicken on rösti potato with ratatouille and thyme sauce (£11.50), daily specials such as grilled mackerel fillet with marinated cucumber and dill crème fraîche (£5.95), ham hock and lentil terrine with piccalilli and baby gerkhins (£6.85), slow-roasted belly pork with apple mash and cider sauce (£14.50), and steamed halibut on spinach in a mussel and marjoram broth (£14.95), and puddings like mascarpone and fruit crème brûlée or knickerbocker glory (from £4.95). They also offer a good value weekday two- and three-course set menu (£12.50 and £14.95); you must book to be sure of a table. All the food areas are no smoking; piped music. Well kept Adnams, Rebellion IPA, and Sharps Doom Bar on handpump, 15 wines by the glass (including champagne), and 20 malt whiskies. A side gate leads to a lovely garden with a large tree in the middle, and the unusual five-sided tables are well placed for attractive valley views. Henley is close by, and just down the road is the delightful Ibstone windmill. (*Recommended by Dr and Mrs P Reid, Michael Dandy, Paul Humphreys, Martin and Karen Wake, Peter Abbott, Mike and Sue Richardson, Jeremy Woods, Ned Kelly, Anthony Longden, Mike and Mary Carter, T R and B C Jenkins*)

Free house ~ Licensees Jim Crowe and Noelle Greene ~ Real ale ~ Bar food (12-2.30, 6.30-9.30; not winter Sun evening) ~ Restaurant ~ (01491) 638996 ~ Children welcome ~ Dogs allowed in bar ~ Open 11-3, 6-11; 11-11 Sun; 11-4 Sun in winter; closed Sun evening Oct-May ~ Bedrooms: £55B/£70B

SOULBURY SP8827 Map 4

Boot ♀

B4032 W of Leighton Buzzard; LU7 0BT

Well run with smartly dressed and friendly staff, this is a civilised village pub with attractive and contemporary furnishings. The partly red-tiled bar has a light, sunny feel, thanks mainly to its cream ceilings and pale green walls, and there's a nice mix of smart and individual furnishings, as well as sporting prints and houseplants, and neat blinds on the windows. Well kept Greene King IPA and Abbot, and Shepherd Neame Spitfire on handpump from the modern, light wood bar counter, and a fantastic choice of around 40 wines and a couple of champagnes by the glass; Old Rosie cider. One end of the room, with a fireplace and wooden floors, is mostly set for diners, and then at the opposite end, by some exposed brickwork, steps lead down to a couple of especially cosy rooms for eating – a yellow one with beams and another fireplace, and a tiny red one. All the eating areas are no smoking; piped music. Popular bar food includes pubby choices such as filled ciabatta, onion baps or multigrain baguettes (from £5.75), home-roasted ham with two free-range eggs (£7.50), goats cheese salad (£7.95), beer battered fish and chips (£8.50), and home-made british beefburger (£8.75), as well as home-made soup (£4.25), sautéed mushrooms, herbs and cream and a roast red pepper cup (£5.95), venison and apricot terrine with home-made piccalilli (£6.25), salmon and spring onion fishcakes with parsley sauce (£10.50), a filo basket with roast mediterranean vegetables, goats cheese and tomato sauce (£10.95), chicken, leek and tarragon pie (£11.25), thai green lamb and chickpea curry (£11.50), duck breast with kumquat and peach sauce (£12.50), and puddings such as orange and Cointreau brûlée with a mini chocolate muffin or blueberry and elderflower cheesecake (from £4.25). Overlooking peaceful fields, there are tables behind in a small garden and on a terrace (with heaters for cooler weather), and a couple more in front. *(Recommended by Mrs Julie Thomas, John Baish, Bob and Maggie Atherton, Susan and John Douglas, John Branston)*

Pubmaster ~ Lease Greg Nichol, Tina and Paul Stevens ~ Real ale ~ Bar food (12-2.30, 6.30-9.30; all day Sun) ~ Restaurant ~ (01525) 270433 ~ Children welcome ~ Open 11-11; 12-10.30 Sun; closed 25-26 Dec

STOKE MANDEVILLE SP8310 Map 4
Woolpack
Risborough Road (A4010 S of Aylesbury); HP22 5UP

The contemporary furnishings inside this partly thatched old pub are a triumphant blend of the traditional with the trendy. It's all very stylish, and original stripped beams, timbers and a massive inglenook log fireplace comfortably jostle for attention with gleaming round copper-topped tables, low leather armchairs, and rich purple walls. In the comfortable, knocked-through front areas by the bar it's the wood and low beams that make the deepest impression, but there are also substantial candles artfully arranged around the fireplace, and illuminated Mouton Rothschild wine labels (designed by top artists) on the walls. Beyond here is a big, busily chatty dining room with chunky wooden tables, a dividing wall made up of logs of wood, thick columns with ornate woodcarvings, and a real mix of customers; it's no smoking in here. The good modern food includes sharing plates of baked camembert and rustic bread (£8.50) or italian antipasti (£9), as well as soup (£4), squid with pineapple, pomegranate and chilli salsa (£5.50), chicken liver and foie gras parfait with fig chutney (£7), salads of crispy duck, watercress, spring onion and plum sauce or salmon and crayfish with lemon mayonnaise (£7; main course £10.50), wood-fired pizzas (from £7), scallops of the day (£8), chicken, chorizo and tomato gnocchi (£9), wild mushroom, spinach and ricotta lasagne (£9.50), fillet steak burger or spit chicken with garlic confit and belgian frites (£10), five spice slow-roast pork belly with noodles, honey and soy (£11), and rib-eye steak with gorgonzola butter (£14.50); prompt obliging service from uniformed young staff. Fullers London Pride and a changing guest on handpump, decent wines and various coffees; piped music. Tables in the neatly landscaped back garden and on the new front terrace where there are outside heaters; large car park. More reports please. *(Recommended by B H and J I Andrews, Susan and John Douglas)*

Mitchells & Butlers ~ Manager Abby Selby ~ Real ale ~ Bar food (12-2.30, 6-9.30; Sun 12-7.30) ~ Restaurant ~ (01296) 615970 ~ Children allowed but must be quiet and well behaved ~ Dogs allowed in bar ~ Open 12-11; 12-10 Sun

TURVILLE SU7691 Map 2
Bull & Butcher ♀
Off A4155 Henley—Marlow via Hambleden and Skirmett; RG9 6QU

There are plenty of walks in the lovely Chilterns valley around this black and white timbered pub – which is handily open all day; no muddy boots inside. There are two low-ceilinged, oak-beamed rooms both with inglenook fireplaces (the Windmill lounge is no smoking), and the bar has a 50ft well incorporated into a glass-topped table, with tiled floor and cushioned wall settles. Brakspears Bitter, Special and a

seasonal guest, and Hook Norton Hooky Dark on handpump, and a good choice of wines by the glass; piped music. Popular bar food includes duck liver pâté with apple brandy chutney (£5.95), beer battered asparagus (£6.95), a good ploughman's, crayfish cocktail (£7.95), cod and chips, bangers and mash or burger on a granary bap (£9.95), chicory and fennel with beans and rosemary (£11.95), shank of lamb or fresh tuna with lime and coriander dressing (£12.95), and puddings (£4.95). They may serve cream teas and light bar snacks through the day during the summer months. There are seats on the lawn by fruit trees in the attractive garden and a children's play area. The village is popular with television and film companies; *The Vicar of Dibley*, *Midsomer Murders* and *Chitty Chitty Bang Bang* were all filmed here. The pub does get crowded at weekends.
(Recommended by R T and J C Moggridge, Dominic Lucas, Michael Dandy, Tom and Jill Jones, Darren and Jane Staniforth, Jeremy Woods, Angus Johnson, Carol Bolden, Mrs Carolyn Dixon, Susan and John Douglas, Tracey and Stephen Groves, Tim Maddison)

Brakspears ~ Tenant Lydia Botha ~ Real ale ~ Bar food (12-2.30, 6.30-9.30; 12-4, 7-9.30 Sun and bank hol Mon) ~ Restaurant ~ (01491) 638283 ~ Children in eating area of bar and restaurant ~ Dogs allowed in bar ~ Open 12-11; 12-10.30 Sun

WOOBURN COMMON   SU9187   Map 2
Chequers 🛏

From A4094 N of Maidenhead at junction with A4155 Marlow road keep on A4094 for another ¾ mile, then at roundabout turn off right towards Wooburn Common, and into Kiln Lane; if you find yourself in Honey Hill, Hedsor, turn left into Kiln Lane at the top of the hill; OS Sheet 175 map reference 910870; HP10 0JQ

The thriving hotel and restaurant side here brings quite a good mix of customers into the busy, friendly bar. Standing timbers and alcoves break up the low-beamed room that is furnished with comfortably lived-in sofas (just right for settling into) on its bare boards, a bright log-effect gas fire, and various pictures, plates, a two-man saw, and tankards. The restaurant and part of the lounge bar are no smoking. They offer a sizeable wine list (with champagne and good wines by the glass), a fair range of malt whiskies and brandies, and well kept Greene King Abbot, IPA, Ruddles County and a guest on handpump; piped music. Bar food includes sandwiches (from £4.95; steak and stilton baguette £8.50), ploughman's (from £5.95), chicken caesar salad (£8.95), salmon and crayfish risotto or home-made burger (£9.95), slow-roasted lamb shank (£10.95), tuna steak with tomato salsa (£12), and confit of duck (£12.95), and puddings such as rhubarb and ginger panna cotta or chocolate brownie with chocolate sauce (£4.50). The spacious garden, set away from the road, has cast-iron tables. *(Recommended by A J Murray, Michael Dandy, Simon Collett-Jones, Peter and Giff Bennett, Chris Glasson, Steve Derbyshire, Fr Robert Marsh, Mrs Jane Kingsbury)*

Free house ~ Licensee Peter Roehrig ~ Real ale ~ Bar food (12-2.30, 6-9.30; all day Sat, Sun and bank hols) ~ Restaurant ~ (01628) 529575 ~ Children welcome ~ Open 11-11 ~ Bedrooms: £72.50B/£77.50B

LUCKY DIP

Besides the fully inspected pubs, you might like to try these Lucky Dips recommended to us and described by readers (if you do, please send us reports: www.goodguides.co.uk).

ADSTOCK [SP7229]
Folly MK18 2HS [A413 SE of Buckingham]: Dining tables in roomy L-shaped beamed bar, nice light furniture in bright and airy further dining area, wide choice of enjoyable food from baguettes and baked potatoes to tempting puddings, Greene King ales, quick friendly service; good play area in good-sized garden with fruit and other trees, bedrooms in separate back block *(Michael Dandy, Gill and Keith Croxton)*

☆ *Old Thatched Inn* MK18 2JN [Main St, off A413]: Good generous food from sandwiches up at reasonable prices, Adnams, Greene King IPA and Hook Norton Old Hooky, good choice of wines by the glass, enthusiastic landlord and friendly helpful service, beams and flagstones, cosy corners and open fires, part comfortably pubby, and part with easy chairs and settees leading to modern back conservatory restaurant; children in eating areas, tables in garden with sheltered terrace

(Michael Dandy, LYM, Ian Phillips, George Atkinson, Jess and George Cowley, Ken and Jenny Simmonds)

AMERSHAM [SU9698]

Boot & Slipper HP6 5JN [Rickmansworth Rd]: Chef & Brewer with their usual food and décor inc plenty of cosy corners, wide choice of wines by the glass, Greene King Ruddles Best, Smiles IPA and Theakstons Old Peculier, good coffee, good-sized no smoking areas; piped music, games; tables outside *(Michael Dandy)*

Eagle HP7 0DY [High St]: Cosy rambling low-beamed pub, landlady doing decent food, log fire, simple décor with a few old prints, friendly helpful staff and quick service even when busy, Adnams, Fullers London Pride and Greene King Old Speckled Hen, good choice of wines by the glass, pub games; pleasant streamside walled back garden *(Michael Dandy)*

☆ *Saracens Head* HP7 0HU [Whielden St (A404)]: Neat and friendly 17th-c beamed local, massive inglenook with roaring fire in ancient decorative fire-basket, interesting décor, good fresh food from sandwiches and baked potatoes up, Greene King real ales, good choice of wines by the glass, pleasant staff, cheery chatty landlord; soft piped music; little back courtyard, bedrooms *(LYM, Steve and Liz Tilley, Michael Dandy)*

ASTON CLINTON [SP8712]

☆ *Oak* HP22 5EU [Green End St]: Cosy and attractive beamed pub, Fullers ales and good choice of wines by the glass, friendly efficient staff, enjoyable home-made food (not Sun pm) cooked to order inc good value lighter lunches, real fire, no music or machines, no smoking dining room *(Brian Root, Mrs Roxanne Chamberlain)*

ASTWOOD [SP9547]

☆ *Old Swan* MK16 9JS [Main Rd]: Appealing and stylish low-beamed pub with Everards Tiger and Beacon and two interesting guest beers, interesting choice of enjoyable fairly priced food, friendly quick service, flagstones, inglenook woodburner and nice collection of blue china, two attractive dining areas, warm cosy atmosphere; large garden *(LYM, Michael Dandy, John Saul)*

BEACHAMPTON [SP7736]

Bell MK19 6DX [Main St]: Good choice of ales inc local ones such as Oxfordshire Marshmallow in big pub with pleasant view down attractive streamside village street, log fire dividing bar from lounge and attractive dining area, nice range of home-made pubby food, friendly service, pool in small separate games room; piped music; open all day, terrace and play area in big garden *(Gill and Keith Croxton)*

BEACONSFIELD [SU9489]

Greyhound HP9 2JN [a mile from M40 junction 2, via A40; Windsor End, Old Town]: Well run rambling former coaching inn, real ales inc Marlow Rebellion, daily papers, small no smoking middle bar room, some emphasis on modern cooking in partly no smoking back bistro area, pool room upstairs *(Chris Glasson, LYM, Tracey and Stephen Groves)*

BLEDLOW [SP7702]

Lions of Bledlow HP27 9PE [off B4009 Chinnor—Princes Risboro; Church End]: Great views from bay windows of well worn Chilterns pub, unsmart and relaxed, with low 16th-c beams, ancient floor tiles, inglenook log fires and a woodburner, real ales such as Marlow Rebellion and Wadworths 6X, good value bar food from sandwiches up, games room, no smoking dining room; well behaved children allowed, picnic-sets out in attractive sloping garden with sheltered terrace, nice setting, good walks *(Peter J and Avril Hanson, LYM, the Didler)*

BUTLERS CROSS [SP8407]

Russell Arms HP17 0TS [off A4010 S of Aylesbury, at Nash Lee roundabout; or off A413 in Wendover, passing stn; Chalkshire Rd]: Pleasantly renovated, with beams and flagstones, wide food choice in bar and separate modern light and roomy restaurant, real ales, two open fires; small sheltered garden, well placed for Chilterns walks *(LYM)*

CALVERTON [SP7939]

Shoulder of Mutton MK19 6ED [just S of Stony Stratford]: Friendly open-plan L-shaped pub with beams and stripped brickwork, wide food range from sandwiches up inc wkdy bargain lunches and lots of curries, half a dozen or more good real ales, good choice of other drinks, quick attentive service, small aquarium in nicely laid out dining area, darts; piped music, TV, games machines, live music Fri/Sun; big attractive back garden with pleasant view and play area, well equipped bedrooms, open all day wknds *(JJW, CMW, George Atkinson)*

CHALFONT ST GILES [SU9895]

☆ *Ivy House* HP8 4RS [A413 S]: Smart 18th-c dining pub, wide range of good if not cheap freshly cooked food (can take a long time), friendly service, good wines by the glass, changing ales such as Bass and Fullers London Pride, espresso coffee, attractive open-plan layout with comfortable fireside armchairs in elegantly cosy L-shaped tiled bar, lighter flagstoned no smoking dining extension; pleasant terrace and sloping garden (can be traffic noise), five bedrooms *(Howard Dell, BB, J and S French)*

CHALFONT ST PETER [SU9990]

White Hart SL9 9QA [High St]: Old low-beamed pub, said to be haunted, pleasantly updated, with civilised atmosphere, some sofas, primrose walls above panelled dado, nice inglenook fireplace, Greene King ales, daily papers, efficient service, daily papers, large back dining area *(Sarah Booker, Simon Collett-Jones)*

CHEARSLEY [SP7110]

Bell HP18 0DJ [The Green]: Traditional cosy beamed pub on attractive village green, Fullers Chiswick, London Pride and seasonal brews, good wines by the glass, bar food from sandwiches up, enormous fireplace, cribbage, dominoes; children in eating area, dogs welcome, plenty of tables in spacious back garden, terrace and attractive play area

(Roy Butler, LYM, Barry Collett)

CHICHELEY [SP9045]

☆ *Chester Arms* MK16 9JE [quite handy for M1 junction 14]: Cosy and pretty low-beamed pub, largely no smoking, with rooms off semi-circular bar, log fire, comfortable settles and chairs, good friendly service, wide choice of good popular home-made meals inc daily fresh fish and aberdeen angus beef (order any fish or cut of meat if you book ahead), separate snack menu, children's helpings, Greene King ales, decent wines, good coffee, daily papers, interesting back dining room down steps; darts, games machine, quiet piped music; picnic-sets in small back garden and out in front *(Michael Dandy, Gerry and Rosemary Dobson, B A Lord, Michael Sargent, BB, Andrea and Guy Bradley, Colin and Janet Roe, Mr and Mrs D S Price)*

CLIFTON REYNES [SP9051]

☆ *Robin Hood* MK46 5DR [off back rd Emberton—Newton Blossomville; no through road]: Unpretentious stone-built village pub, dark beams, woodburner in small lounge's inglenook, welcoming licensees, he cooks well with some interesting recipes, Greene King IPA and Abbot, lots of *Robin Hood* film stills, nice grapevine conservatory, table skittles in simple public bar; very big garden with plenty of tables and play area, riverside walks to Olney, cl Mon *(BB, William Naylor)*

COLESHILL [SU9594]

Mulberry Bush HP7 0LU [A355]: Modern family-friendly roadside dining pub with wide range of generous food all day from sandwiches and melts up inc good children's choice, staff cheerful and helpful even when busy, Courage Best and Directors, no smoking restaurant; piped music; children welcome, disabled facilities, large fenced garden with terrace and good play area (wknd bouncy castle), good walking country, open all day *(Michael Dandy, James Orme)*

☆ *Red Lion* HP7 0LH [Village Rd]: Small traditional two-room local, relaxed, unspoilt and warmly welcoming, with wide choice of good value food (not Sun eve) from sandwiches and baked potatoes up, changing ales such as Greene King IPA and Vale Wychert, interesting helpful licensees, blazing fire, thriving darts and dominoes teams, Tues quiz nights; TV for racing, fruit machine; picnic-sets out in front and in back garden with sturdy climbing frames outside, good walks, open all day wknds *(Mrs Ann Gray, Michael B Griffith, BB, Roy and Gay Hoing)*

COLNBROOK [TQ0277]

Ostrich SL3 0JZ [1¼ miles from M4 junction 5 via A4/B3378, then 'village only' rd; High St]: Striking and popular Elizabethan pub, modernised but still interesting, with intriguing history, good log fire in massive fireplace, Archers Trafalgar 200, Fullers London Pride and Greene King Old Speckled Hen, friendly atmosphere, some pubby dishes with emphasis on upstairs restaurant; quiet piped music *(LYM, Ian Phillips)*

CUBLINGTON [SP8322]

Unicorn LU7 0LQ [High St]: Friendly and attractive low-beamed 16th-c village pub owned by consortium of local people and supposedly haunted, with prompt friendly service, good value food inc tapas and mezze, five real ales, long rustic bare-boards room with wooden seating and handsome fireplace at one end; picnic-sets in peaceful attractive enclosed garden behind, open all day wknds *(MP)*

CUDDINGTON [SP7311]

☆ *Crown* HP18 0BB [village signed off A418 Thame—Aylesbury; Spurt St]: Small convivial thatched village pub, attractively olde-worlde with candles, low beams, good tables, nicely cushioned settles, pleasant décor and inglenook log fires, prompt friendly service, unusual choice of good if not cheap food inc interesting hot sandwiches and specials, Fullers Chiswick, London Pride and ESB; appealing small terrace, open all day Sun *(Giles and Annie Francis, R E Dixon, Mike and Jennifer Marsh, B Brewer, Susan and John Douglas)*

DOWNLEY [SU8495]

☆ *Le De Spencers Arms* HP13 5YQ [The Common]: Unpretentious and softly lit 18th-c Fullers local hidden away from High Wycombe on Chilterns common, their good beers, prompt cheerful service, good bar food, big pine tables, pictures and bric-a-brac, some stripped masonry, low ceilings; fairy-lit loggia overlooking lawn with picnic-sets, woodland walks to nearby Hughenden Manor *(Tracey and Stephen Groves, LYM)*

FARNHAM COMMON [SU9584]

Stag SL2 3TA [Hawthorn Lane]: Food upgraded by new chef, good inexpensive Sun lunch, no smoking conservatory; children welcome *(Peter and Eleanor Kenyon)*

FINGEST [SU7791]

☆ *Chequers* RG9 6QD [signed off B482 Marlow—Stokenchurch]: Traditional Chilterns pub with several rooms around old-fashioned Tudor core, roaring log fire in vast fireplace, sunny lounge by good-sized charming and immaculate country garden with lots of picnic-sets, small no smoking room, interesting furniture, Brakspears and guest ales, dominoes and cribbage, lunchtime food (not Mon, and can take a while when busy) from sandwiches and lots of cheeses up, reasonable prices, cheerful service, daily papers, attractive restaurant; children in eating area; interesting church opp, picture-book village, good walks – can get crowded wknds *(Michael Dandy, Derek Harvey-Piper, the Didler, LYM, Roy and Gay Hoing, Peter Saville)*

FRIETH [SU7990]

Prince Albert RG9 6PY [off B482 SW of High Wycombe]: Old-fashioned cottagey Chilterns local with low black beams and joists, high-backed settles, big black stove in inglenook, big log fire in larger area on the right, pubby food from baguettes up, Brakspears; children and dogs welcome, nicely planted informal side garden with views of woods and fields, open all day *(the Didler, LYM, Pete Baker, Paul Humphreys, Anthony Longden)*

FULMER [SU9985]

Black Horse SL3 6HD [Windmill Rd]: Small traditional stepped bar areas with plenty of nooks and crannies, beams, woodburner, chequered tables, some sofas, Greene King IPA and Abbot and a seasonal beer, helpful service, modest sensibly priced food from sandwiches and baguettes up, decent wines, good décor; small garden, attractive village, open all day wknds *(Howard Dell)*

GREAT BRICKHILL [SP9029]

☆ *Red Lion* MK17 9AH [Ivy Lane]: Experienced new landlord aiming at reasonably priced proper pub food in friendly pub with simple décor, Greene King and guest beers, good service, daily papers, log fire in small bar, woodburner in restaurant; fabulous view over Buckinghamshire and beyond from neat walled back lawn *(Nick and Lynne Carter, LYM, Roy and Lindsey Fentiman, Michael Dandy)*

GREAT HAMPDEN [SP8401]

☆ *Hampden Arms* HP16 9RQ [off A4010 N and S of Princes Risborough]: Civilised dining pub opp village cricket pitch, wide choice of enjoyable food made by landlord from lunchtime sandwiches to substantial main dishes, cheerful speedy service, Adnams, a seasonal Vale ale and Addlestone's cider from small corner bar, good choice of wines by the glass, big woodburner in more spacious back room, may be free olives; children and dogs welcome, tree-sheltered garden, good walks nearby *(LYM, William Goodhart, Anthony Longden, Paul Humphreys, Jarrod and Wendy Hopkinson, John Franklin, Peter Saville)*

GREAT HORWOOD [SP7731]

Crown MK17 0RH [off B4033 N of Winslow; The Green]: Comfortable Georgian pub with striking inglenook fireplace, Adnams, Courage Directors and Greene King IPA, good choice of wines by the glass, friendly service, good value usual food from sandwiches and baked potatoes up, daily papers, dining room with big wooden tables; piped music; tables on neat front lawn, pretty village, very handy for Winslow Hall *(Michael Dandy, BB)*

Swan MK17 0QN [B4033 N of Winslow]: Updated former coaching inn, low beams and two feature fireplaces (one a big inglenook) in open-plan lounge/dining area, Everards Tiger and Charles Wells Eagle, usual food from sandwiches up, friendly landlord, back bar with darts and pool; TV; nice side garden, open all day wknds *(Michael Dandy)*

GREAT KIMBLE [SP8206]

☆ *Bernard Arms* HP17 0XS [Risborough Rd (A4010)]: Friendly and unpretentious, with popular freshly-made food in bar and restaurant, up to four changing real ales, decent wines, good range of malt whiskies and bottled beers, good log fire, daily papers, photographs of fairly recent prime ministers dropping in for a drink, games room, pianist doing old favourites Sat eve and Sun lunch; children welcome, no dogs, particularly

attractive fairy-lit gardens, good walks, well equipped bedrooms *(George Atkinson, BB, Mel Smith, Howard Dell)*

GREAT MISSENDEN [SP8901]

☆ *Cross Keys* HP16 0AU [High St]: Relaxed and unspoilt beamed bar divided by standing timbers, bric-a-brac, traditional furnishings inc high-backed settle and open fire in huge fireplace, Fullers Chiswick, London Pride and ESB, good wines, good interesting modern food from tasty baguettes up, attractive and spacious no smoking beamed restaurant (children allowed here), cheerful helpful staff; back terrace *(John Baish, LYM, Howard Dell, J B C Williams, Roy and Gay Hoing)*

White Lion HP16 0AL [High St]: Pleasantly refurbished, with comfortable atmosphere and furniture, good choice of enjoyable food using local produce, good value small plates, quick efficient service, good coffee; can get smoky; children welcome, cl Sun evening *(Martin and Pauline Jennings)*

HAMBLEDEN [SU7886]

☆ *Stag & Huntsman* RG9 6RP [off A4155 Henley—Marlow]: Handsome brick and flint pub in pretty Chilterns village, congenial old-fashioned front public bar with masses of beer mats, big fireplace in low-ceilinged partly panelled lounge bar, Rebellion IPA, Wadworths 6X and a guest beer, farm cider, good wines, friendly efficient staff, decent food (not Sun evening), darts, dominoes, cribbage, shove-ha'penny; piped music; provision for children and dogs, spacious and attractive garden with some raised areas and decking, good walks, bedrooms with own bathrooms *(Tracey and Stephen Groves, Michael Dandy, LYM, Anthony Longden, Robert Turnham, Roy and Gay Hoing, Tim Maddison)*

HAWRIDGE [SP9505]

Rose & Crown HP5 2UG [signed from A416 N of Chesham; The Vale]: Roomy open-plan pub dating from 18th c, enthusiastic youngish licensees, wide choice of enjoyable home-made food, Fullers London Pride, two guest beers, good range of wines, attentive service, big log fire, peaceful country views from restaurant area; children allowed, broad terrace with lawn dropping down beyond, play area *(Geoff and Elaine Colson, LYM)*

HIGH WYCOMBE [SU8693]

Bell HP13 5DQ [Frogmoor (off A4128)]: Town-centre pub carefully extended from 16th-c core, low beams and lighting, bare boards, comfortable sofas and stylish high-backed chairs, full Fullers beer range, thai restaurant, good landlord; five bedrooms, open all day *(Tracey and Stephen Groves)*

HUGHENDEN VALLEY [SU8697]

Harrow HP14 4LX [Warrendene Rd, off A4128 N of High Wycombe]: Bare-boards low-ceilinged L-shaped public bar, larger carpeted dining lounge, Brakspears, Courage Best and a guest beer, good atmosphere; tables out in front, more in garden with play area, water feature and sculptures, good valley views and walks *(Tracey and Stephen Groves)*

KINGSWOOD [SP6819]
Plough & Anchor HP18 0RD [Bicester Rd (A41 NW of Aylesbury)]: Enjoyable food from sandwiches up, simple smart décor, variety of well spaced heavy wooden tables, beams and flagstones, friendly staff, real ales such as Fullers London Pride and Greene King, good wine list; children welcome *(Mrs Jean Mitchell)*

LACEY GREEN [SP8201]
☆ *Pink & Lily* HP27 0RJ [from A4010 High Wycombe—Princes Risboro follow Loosley sign, then Gt Hampden, Gt Missenden one]: Charming little old-fashioned taproom (a Rupert Brooke favourite – see his tipsy poem framed here) in much-extended Chilterns pub with airy and plush main dining bar, well presented good food, Brakspears and guest beers, good well priced wines, friendly efficient service, log fires, dominoes, cribbage, ring the bull; piped music; children and dogs now welcome, conservatory, big garden *(Heather Couper, LYM, the Didler, B Brewer, Mike and Jennifer Marsh, Mel Smith, Roy and Gay Hoing)*

LAVENDON [SP9153]
Green Man MK46 4HA [A428 Bedford—Northampton]: Attractive thatched 17th-c pub in pretty village, roomy and relaxed open-plan wood-floored bar with no smoking area, beams, lots of stripped stone and open woodburner, Greene King IPA, Abbot and Old Speckled Hen, good choice of wines by the glass, good coffee, generous food, quick friendly service even when busy, big carpeted evening/wknd restaurant with no smoking area; children welcome, tables and heaters outside, open all day *(Michael Dandy, George Atkinson)*
Horseshoe MK46 4HA [A428 Bedford—Northampton; High St]: Sizeable low-beamed village pub with log fire in no smoking lounge, airy dining extension, decent food from baguettes and baked potatoes to lots of fish, Charles Wells Eagle and Bombardier, small but interesting wine list, quick cheerful service, skittles in public bar; piped music; appealing good-sized garden behind with terrace, new decking and play area, cl Sun evening *(BB, Michael Dandy, George Atkinson)*

LITTLE BRICKHILL [SP9029]
George MK17 9NB [Watling St, off A5 SE of Milton Keynes]: Settees, pine tables and woodburner in roomy front bar, L-shaped restaurant opening into big back conservatory with striking ceiling canopy, friendly service, Adnams Broadside and Greene King IPA, good choice of wines by the glass, enjoyable food (not Sun evening or Mon lunchtime) from wkdy sandwiches up, daily papers; quiet piped music, TV; heated terrace, play equipment in large mature garden *(Eithne Dandy, Andrea and Guy Bradley)*
Old Green Man MK17 9LU [just off A5 SE of Milton Keynes]: Large pub recently tastefully refurbished for emphasis on good value food (inc unusual sandwiches) in pleasant surroundings, Greene King ales, decent wines by the glass, friendly neatly turned out staff, log fire *(John Saul, Andy Chapman)*

LITTLE CHALFONT [SU9997]
Sugar Loaves HP7 9PN [Chalfont Station Rd]: Recently reopened after refurbishment as no smoking dining pub, bright and spacious, with wide choice from light dishes up, helpful service *(anon)*

LITTLE HAMPDEN [SP8503]
☆ *Rising Sun* HP16 9PS [off A4128 or A413 NW of Gt Missenden; OS Sheet 165 map ref 856040]: Comfortable no smoking dining pub in delightful setting, opened-up bar with woodburner and log fire, good food inc interesting dishes and popular Sun lunch (can be very busy wknds), Adnams, Brakspears and a seasonal beer, good short wine list, home-made mulled wine and spiced cider in winter, friendly service; piped music; tables out on terrace, lovely walks, bedrooms with own bathrooms, cl Sun evening and all Mon exc bank hols *(Kevin Thomas, Nina Randall, Mrs Ann Gray, LYM, John and Glenys Wheeler, B Brewer, John and Joyce Snell)*

LITTLE MARLOW [SU8788]
☆ *Kings Head* SL7 3RZ [A4155 about 2 miles E of Marlow; Church Rd]: Long flower-covered pub with bustling open-plan low-beamed bar, wide blackboard choice of good value food from plenty of sandwiches, panini and baked potatoes to popular Sun roasts, smart no smoking red dining room, Adnams Broadside, Fullers London Pride and Timothy Taylors Landlord, quick cheerful service, log or coal fires, Sun bar nibbles, cricket memorabilia; children welcome; big attractive garden behind popular with families, nice walk down to church *(BB, Ian Phillips, Paul Humphreys, Michael Dandy, Edward Mirzoeff, Howard Dell, Tracey and Stephen Groves)*
☆ *Queens Head* SL7 3RZ [Church Rd/Pound Lane; cul de sac off A4155 nr Kings Head]: Current licensees doing wide food choice from chunky rustic rolls to some interesting main dishes in charming small quietly placed pub with real ales such as Adnams Broadside and Jennings Cumberland, quick friendly service, cosy lighter dining room on right with biggish new no smoking back extension, lots of books in saloon; darts and TV in public bar on left, no dogs; picnic-sets in appealing cottagey front garden, a couple more tables on secluded terrace across lane – short walk from River Thames *(Paul Humphreys, Mark Percy, Lesley Mayoh, Michael Dandy, BB, Ian Phillips)*

LITTLE MISSENDEN [SU9298]
☆ *Red Lion* HP7 0QZ: Small traditional 15th-c local, two coal fires, real ales, decent wines, generous good value standard food inc nice fairly proper pepper sandwiches, preserves for sale; piped music; tables and busy aviary in sunny side garden by river with ducks, swans and fat trout *(Brian Root, Mike Turner, B Shelley, Roy and Gay Hoing)*

LITTLE TINGEWICK [SP6432]
Red Lion MK18 4AG [off A421 SW of Buckingham; pub towards Finmere, over the Oxon border]: 16th-c thatched and stone-built

Fullers pub with their full beer range, decent wines by the glass, helpful service, good choice of food from sandwiches to popular Sun lunch, recently refurbished bar and adjacent no smoking eating area, big log fire, low beams, mix of new furniture on wood floor; piped music; small garden, open all day wknds *(Michael Dandy, Colin and Jo Howkins)*

LITTLEWORTH COMMON [SP9386]

☆ *Blackwood Arms* SL1 8PP [3 miles S of M40 junction 2; Common Lane, OS Sheet 165 map ref 937864]: Nicely kept dining pub in lovely spot on edge of beech woods – good walks, stylish décor in cream and mulberry, dark woodwork and blinds, almost all tables now smartly set for the good home cooking from open sandwiches (enough for two) and simple lunchtime dishes to pricier evening meals and great puddings, two-sitting Sun lunch usually fully booked, helpful staff, Brakspears and Hook Norton Mild from handsome oak counter, roaring log fire; quiet piped music; children and dogs welcome, views from chunky tables in pleasant back garden *(Michael Dandy, Peter and Eleanor Kenyon, LYM, Simon Collett-Jones, Steve Derbyshire)*

Jolly Woodman SL1 8PF [2 miles from M40 junction 2; off A355]: Good site by Burnham Beeches; Brakspears, Fullers London Pride and interesting changing ales, wide food choice from sandwiches and baked potatoes up, efficient service, reasonable wine choice, rambling beamed and timbered linked areas with log fire, central woodburner and rustic woody décor, pub games; unobtrusive piped music, jazz Mon; picnic-sets out in front and secluded garden behind, open all day *(Michael Dandy, LYM)*

MARLOW [SU8486]

Chequers SL7 1BA [High St]: Attractive pub with large air-conditioned front bar, bare boards and heavy beams, leather settees, Brakspears ales, good choice of wines by the glass, friendly service, good food range from basics to more exotic things in bright and pleasant bar restaurant area, daily papers; piped music, TV, games – popular with young people (stays open late wknds); children welcome, pavement tables, bedrooms *(Michael Dandy)*

☆ *Hand & Flowers* SL7 2BP [West St (A4155)]: Restaurant rather than pub now (Greene King IPA and Abbot from bar counter, but not a place to sit with a drink), well worth knowing for very good but expensive meals inc short choice of lunchtime bar food, pleasant rustic no-frills furnishings and careful decorations, informal service, log fire; piped music; tables in small garden *(Cindy Cottman, Kevin Deacon, Michael Dandy)*

☆ *Hare & Hounds* SL7 2DF [Henley Road (A4155 W)]: Big inglenook in homely little quarry-tiled beamed bar, small carpeted eating room on left, much bigger no smoking dining area on right, sandwiches (not Sun) and more ambitious dishes, Brakspears, lots of wines by the glass; piped music, games machine; front terrace with picnic-sets under cocktail parasols

(the road isn't too busy), a few more in side garden *(Michael Dandy, LYM, Catherine and Richard Preston, Ian Phillips, Fr Robert Marsh)*

☆ *Two Brewers* SL7 1NQ [St Peter St, first right off Station Rd from double roundabout]: Busy low-beamed pub with shiny black woodwork, nautical pictures, gleaming brassware and interesting layout, most tables set for good food inc particularly good choice of sandwiches and light snacks, Brakspears, Fullers London Pride, Hook Norton Old Hooky and Marlow Rebellion, good wines, welcoming service, relaxed atmosphere; children in eating area, unobtrusive piped music; tables in sheltered back courtyard with more in converted garage, front seats with glimpse of the Thames – pub right on Thames Path *(Michael Dandy, LYM)*

MEDMENHAM [SU8084]

Dog & Badger SL7 2HE [Bockmer (A4155)]: Comfortably refurbished low-beamed pub under new licensees, carpeted eating area one side of central open fire, up-to-date pubby food at fair prices, Caledonian Deuchars IPA, Fullers London Pride and Marlow Rebellion, daily papers; piped music; children welcome, some tables outside, cl Mon *(Michael Dandy, LYM, David Twitchett)*

MILTON KEYNES [SP8739]

Barge MK15 0AE [Newport Rd, Woolstone]: Large beamed Vintage Inn, rustic furnishings in various rooms and alcoves, no smoking areas inc modern conservatory, Hook Norton Old Hooky and Wadworths 6X, lots of wines by the glass, wide food choice, daily papers, friendly staff, good food service (not in garden); piped music; picnic-sets on spacious tree-dotted lawns, village setting, open all day *(Michael Dandy)*

Olde Swan MK6 3BS [Newport rd, Woughton on the Green]: Spacious and picturesque timber-framed thatched Chef & Brewer, largely no smoking, with attractive furnishings, good log fires and nice nooks and corners, their usual wide menu, pleasant service, good wine choice and real ales such as Adnams Flagship, Caledonian Deuchars IPA, Courage Directors and Greene King Old Speckled Hen; TV; picnic-sets in back garden, footpaths to nearby lakes *(Michael Dandy, Heather Couper)*

Ship Ashore MK15 9JL [Granville Sq, Willen]: Well designed modern Ember Inn, half a dozen distinct areas, mix of sofas and dining tables, big log-effect gas fires, Adnams Flagship, Caledonian Golden Promise, Fullers London Pride, Greene King IPA and Moorhouses Pendle Witches Brew, good range of wines by the glass and good value coffee, their usual well priced food, daily papers; piped music, pub games; picnic-sets under parasols on small lawn, open all day *(Michael Dandy, Ian Phillips)*

MOULSOE [SP9141]

☆ *Carrington Arms* MK16 0HB [1¼ miles from M1 junction 14: A509 N, first right signed Moulsoe; Cranfield Rd]: Good interesting if not cheap pub majoring on all sorts of meats, also fresh fish, sold by weight from refrigerated display then cooked on indoor barbecue, good puddings, helpful service, Greene King IPA and Old Speckled Hen and a guest such as Woodfordes Nelsons Revenge, champagnes by the glass, friendly helpful staff, open-plan layout with comfortable mix of wooden chairs and cushioned banquettes; children allowed, long pretty garden behind, open all day Sun, decent bedrooms in adjacent block *(Michael Dandy, LYM, Mr and Mrs D S Price)*

NEWTON LONGVILLE [SP8431]

☆ *Crooked Billet* MK17 0DF [off A421 S of Milton Keynes; Westbrook End]: Thatched pub doing lunchtime sandwiches and wraps as well as the good enterprising restauranty dishes it focuses on without being pretentiously foody, Greene King ales with a guest such as Ridleys Old Bob, brightly modernised extended pubby bar with games, log-fire dining area; piped music, TV; dogs in bar (no children), tables out on lawn, cl Mon lunchtime, open all day Sat *(Michael Dandy, Ian Phillips, LYM, Karen and Graham Oddey, Hunter and Christine Wright)*

OLNEY [SP8851]

☆ *Swan* MK46 4AA [High St S]: Friendly beamed and timbered pub with good choice of excellent value generous food from sandwiches, baguettes and baked potatoes up, real ales such as Adnams, Batemans XB, Fullers London Pride and Shepherd Neame Bitter and Spitfire, good value wines by the glass, quick helpful service, daily papers, attractive flowers; several rooms off bar, candles on rather close-set pine tables, log fires, small no smoking back bistro dining room (booking advised for this); very busy at lunchtime, no under-10s; back courtyard tables, one under cover *(Michael Dandy, Michael Sargent, BB, Sue and Keith Campbell)*

Two Brewers MK46 4BB [High St (A509)]: Double-fronted proper pub, large public bar and lounge, big dining area with plenty of different-sized tables, good value home-made traditional food from sandwiches up, keen and welcoming landlord, Bass, Brains, Courage Directors and Greene King IPA, decent wines by the glass, pub games; piped music; attractive courtyard interestingly decorated to show its brewery past, tables in small garden too *(Michael Dandy, Earl and Chris Pick)*

PENN [SU9093]

Old Queens Head HP10 8EY [Hammersley Lane]: Attractive old building recently taken on by the small local group that includes three good foody main entries, so well worth a try though we've not yet had reports on it – see Bovingdon Green, Denham and (in Herts) Frithsden *(anon)*

PENN STREET [SU9295]

☆ *Hit or Miss* HP7 0PX [off A404 SW of Amersham, then keep on towards Winchmore Hill]: Well laid out low-beamed pub with own cricket ground, enjoyable freshly made food (can take a while when busy) inc interesting dishes, good fish and popular all-day Sun lunch, Badger ales, decent wines, friendly helpful young staff, cheerful atmosphere in three clean linked rooms, log fire, charming décor inc interesting cricket and chair-making memorabilia, good-sized no smoking area; piped music can be tiresome; picnic-sets out in front, pleasant setting, open all day *(Mrs Ann Gray, LYM, Howard Dell, Kevin Thomas, Nina Randall, Di and Mike Gillam, Tracey and Stephen Groves)*

Squirrel HP7 0PX: Now run by the same people as the Hit or Miss (above), friendly open-plan bar with flagstones, log fire, comfortable sofas as well as tables and chairs, good value home-made traditional food from baguettes up (not Sun evening), good children's meals, real ales, free coffee refills, bric-a-brac and cricketing memorabilia, darts; big garden with good play area, handy for lovely walks (and watching cricket), open all day wknds *(Paul Humphreys, Mary Priest)*

SHABBINGTON [SP6606]

Old Fisherman HP18 9HJ [off A418 Oxford—Thame; Mill Rd]: Busy modern dining pub in pretty riverside setting, roomy and attractive, with generous home-made food inc popular all-day Sun lunch and (no puddings) separate garden menu, Greene King ales, good choice of wines by the glass, good coffee, no smoking areas; lots of picnic-sets in large waterside garden with play area, open all day wknds and summer *(Grahame Brooks)*

SHERINGTON [SP8846]

Swan MK16 9NB [High St]: Tidily redone with emphasis now on the food side, traditional bar food as well as more french-style cooking for the separate back restaurant, Wadworths 6X and Charles Wells Bombardier in smallish front bar, good choice of wines by the glass *(Michael Dandy)*

White Hart MK16 9PE [off A509; Gun Lane]: Small and friendly, with good changing ales such as Batemans Combined Harvest, Fullers London Pride, Marstons Bitter, Oldershaws Mowbray Mash and Youngs, attentive landlord and good service, good pub food (not Sun evening) from sandwiches up, bright fire, two-room bar, contemporary dining area; children and dogs welcome, picnic-sets in garden with terrace, pretty hanging baskets, bedrooms in adjacent building *(Michael Dandy, Michael B Griffith)*

STOKE GOLDINGTON [SP8348]

☆ *Lamb* MK16 8NR [High St (B526 Newport Pagnell—Northampton)]: Proper down-to-earth village pub with good changing ales such as Frog Island Shoemaker, Nethergate IPA and Timothy Taylors Landlord, Weston's farm cider, good generous home-made food (not Sun/Tues evenings) at appealing prices from baguettes to bargain Sun lunch, welcoming landlady, good public bar with table skittles and small pleasant no smoking dining room, quiet lounge with log fire and sheep decorations; piped radio, TV; terrace and sheltered garden behind, open all day wknds *(JJW, CMW, BB, Gerry and Rosemary Dobson, George Atkinson, Steve Willis)*

White Hart MK16 8NR [High St (B526 NW of Newport Pagnell)]: Friendly 18th-c thatched and beamed pub with cheerful attentive service, good value food from baguettes and baked potatoes up (freshly made so may be a wait), Charles Wells Eagle and seasonal beers, good choice of wines by the glass, comfortable banquettes, open fire, tiled bar with stripped stone, pictures and brasses, games room with table football and skittles, no smoking restaurant; piped music; picnic-sets on sheltered back lawn with play area, footpath network starts just across road *(LYM, JJW, CMW)*

STOKE POGES [SU9885]
Fox & Pheasant SL2 4EZ [Gerrards Cross Rd (B416, Stoke Common)]: Good value carvery restaurant, other decent food too, good service, small quiet bar with Charles Wells Bombardier *(Geoff and Sylvia Donald, Marjorie and David Lamb)*

STONE [SP7912]
Bugle Horn HP17 8QP [Oxford Rd, Hartwell (A418 SW of Aylesbury)]: Long low 17th-c stone-built family dining pub, warm and friendly series of comfortable rooms, pleasant furnishings, good choice of modestly priced home-made food from good daytime sandwiches (not Sun) up, Brakspears and Hook Norton Old Hooky, lots of wines by the glass, quick efficient service, several log fires, prettily planted well furnished conservatory; lovely trees in large pretty garden, horses grazing in pastures beyond *(E A and D C T Frewer, Tim and Ann Newell, Mel Smith, Michael Dandy)*

THE LEE [SP8904]
Cock & Rabbit HP16 9LZ [back roads 2½ miles N of Great Missenden, E of A413]: Warmly welcoming italian-run dining pub, stylish and comfortable, with reasonably priced home-made food (not Sun or Mon evenings) inc good fresh fish, pasta, real ales such as Fullers and Greene King, decent wines, good lively staff, panelled bar, two separate back dining areas welcoming children; big garden with tables on verandah, terraces and lawn *(LYM, Paul Humphreys)*

☆ *Old Swan* HP16 9NU [Swan Bottom, back rd ¼ mile N of The Lee]: Charming civilised 16th-c dining pub well off the beaten track, with very good interesting food esp seafood cooked by long-serving landlord, good value, and sandwiches (not Sun) too; four simply but attractively furnished linked rooms, low beams and flagstones, cooking-range log fire in inglenook, particularly well kept Adnams and Brakspears, decent wines, cheerful landlady, friendly relaxed service, TV etc tucked nicely away; spacious prettily planted back lawns with play area, good walks *(JJW, CMW, LYM, Marjorie and David Lamb, Tracey and Stephen Groves, Victoria Taylor, Anthony Longden, Mike Turner, Paul Humphreys)*

WADDESDON [SP7416]
☆ *Five Arrows* HP18 0JE [High St (A41)]: More restaurant-with-rooms or small hotel than pub, elegant and civilised series of light and airy well furnished high-ceilinged rooms with Rothschild family portrait engravings and lots of old estate-worker photographs, excellent wines (Fullers London Pride and Discovery too), good coffee, helpful polite staff, ciabattas and baguettes as well as light dishes and full meals; no smoking area, children allowed; appealing back garden, comfortable bedrooms, handy for Waddesdon Manor; has been cl last wknd Aug *(Neil and Angela Huxter, David and Jean Hall, Michael Dandy, John Robertson, LYM, Karen and Graham Oddey)*

WEEDON [SP8118]
Five Elms HP22 4NL [Stockaway]: Cottagey low-beamed two-room pub with Adnams, enjoyable home-made food, old photographs and prints, separate dining room; pretty village *(Pat Sweeney)*

WEST WYCOMBE [SU8394]
☆ *George & Dragon* HP14 3AB [High St; A40 W of High Wycombe]: Centrepiece of beautifully preserved Tudor village, thriving atmosphere in rambling bar with massive beams and sloping walls, big log fire, Adnams, Courage Best and Charles Wells Bombardier, prompt friendly service even when busy, good fairly priced food choice from fresh lunchtime sandwiches and wraps to some exotic specials, small no smoking family dining room (wknd children's menu); spacious peaceful garden with fenced play area, character bedrooms (magnificent oak staircase) and good breakfast, handy for West Wycombe Park *(LYM, Ian Phillips, Alan and Anne Driver)*

WESTON TURVILLE [SP8510]
Chequers HP22 5SJ [Church Lane]: Cosy two-level traditional bar with good welcoming service, Adnams, Boddingtons, Fullers London Pride, Gales HSB and Wadworths 6X, enjoyable bar food, large log fire, flagstones, low beams and stylish solid wooden furniture, adjoining restaurant (not cheap) with good food esp fish, tables in nice garden; tucked away in attractive part of village *(Peter and Jan Humphreys, Lin Carroll, Tricia North)*

WESTON UNDERWOOD [SP8650]
☆ *Cowpers Oak* MK46 5JS [signed off A509 in Olney; High St]: Attractive wisteria-covered beamed pub in pretty thatched village, popular and friendly, with generous good value food (all day wknds) from tasty choice of imaginative soups up, changing ales such as Fullers London Pride, Greene King IPA, Oldershaws Isaacs Gold and Theakstons Old Peculier, nice medley of old-fashioned furnishings, woodburners, dark red walls, dark panelling and some stripped stone, no smoking back restaurant, good games room with darts, bar billiards, hood skittles and table football, daily papers; piped light classics, TV; children very welcome, dogs in main bar, small suntrap front terrace, more tables on back decking and in big orchard garden (no dogs) with play area and farm animals, bedrooms, open all day wknds, pretty thatched village *(LYM, George Atkinson, Colin and Janet Roe,*

Michael Sargent)

WHADDON [SP8034]

Lowndes Arms MK17 0NA: Small bar with inglenook fireplace, beams, brasses and bric-a-brac, Bass, Everards Tiger, Fullers London Pride and Greene King IPA and Abbot, good choice of wines by the glass, enterprising range of food, attractive restaurant; piped music; tables on small heated terrace, small garden with great views, refurbished bedroom block *(Michael Dandy)*

WHEELER END [SU8093]

☆ *Chequers* HP14 3NH [off B482 NW of Marlow]: Neatly kept 17th-c pub with inglenook log fire in convivial low-ceilinged little bar, bigger back no smoking dining room, candlelit tables and hunting prints, enjoyable bar food (not Sun evening) using their garden herbs, good fish choice and local game, sandwiches and snacks as well as Sun roast, Fullers London Pride, ESB and a seasonal beer, decent wines, brisk friendly service even when busy, dominoes and cribbage; can get crowded Sat in rugby season; children welcome in eating areas, dogs in bar, two charmingly kept gardens (M40 noise), open all day *(Martin and Karen Wake, Tracey and Stephen Groves, LYM)*

WOBURN SANDS [SP9236]

Weatheroak MK17 8SH: Friendly and comfortable, with good value food, Greene King IPA and Abbot, good service, two no smoking areas on one side of central bar, attractive dining room the other; children welcome *(John Dorrell)*

WOOBURN COMMON [SU9387]

☆ *Royal Standard* HP10 0JS [about 3½ miles from M40 junction 2]: Particularly well kept Adnams Broadside, Black Sheep, Caledonian

Deuchars IPA, Everards Tiger and Charles Wells Bombardier, with several guest beers tapped from the cask, in busy low-ceilinged local with good value pubby food from baguettes and baked potatoes up, welcoming helpful staff, well chosen wines, lots of daily papers, open fire, daily papers and crosswork reference books, neat dining area; picnic-sets on pretty front terrace and in back garden, open all day *(Michael Dandy, LYM, Mr Waterman, Jarrod and Wendy Hopkinson, Steve Derbyshire, Roy and Gay Hoing, Nina Randall)*

WOOBURN GREEN [SU9188]

Glory Mill HP10 0HH [Wycombe Lane (A4094)]: Neat bare-boards front bar with leather settees by log fire, Adnams and Fullers London Pride, reasonably priced wines, darts and pub games, enjoyable food, no smoking carpeted back dining area; small garden *(Michael Dandy, D and M T Ayres-Regan)*

☆ *Old Bell* HP10 0PL [Town Ln]: Light, airy and friendly, with cheerful Thai landlord, enjoyable generous thai and english food inc single-price lunchtime menus, pleasant bar, separate restaurant *(John and Glenys Wheeler)*

WORMINGHALL [SP6308]

☆ *Clifden Arms* HP18 9JR [Clifden Rd]: 16th-c beamed, timbered and thatched pub in pretty gardens, charmingly unpretentious inside with old-fashioned seats, rustic memorabilia and roaring log fires, attractive lounge bar leading to further no smoking dining area, decent food inc bargain wkdy lunches, good changing real ales, traditional games in public bar, children allowed; good play area, aunt sally, attractive village *(Brian Root, LYM, Marjorie and David Lamb, Susan and John Douglas)*

Post Office address codings confusingly give the impression that some pubs are in Buckinghamshire, when they're really in Bedfordshire or Berkshire (which is where we list them).

Cambridgeshire

An astonishing one-third of the main entries in this county have leapt ahead of legislation and are already completely no smoking – indeed pubs in this county have always been rather progressive about that. One of this year's new main entries here, the charming Chequers in St Neots, is among this smoke-free advance guard. The other, the very restauranty Three Horseshoes at Madingley back in the *Guide* after a break, is not cheap, but thoroughly enjoyed for its italian-oriented menu and tremendous wine list. Other pubs with great food are the Old Bridge in Huntingdon, the Pheasant at Keyston and the Anchor up at Sutton Gault, but it's the imaginative food at the Cock at Hemingford Grey that has recently been winning the highest praise, and so takes the award for Cambridgeshire Dining Pub of the Year. At the other end of the spectrum, the welcoming Queens Head at Newton, in the same family for three generations and a pillar of the *Guide* since its very first edition, is as well loved and unspoilt as ever. The Lucky Dip section at the end of the chapter includes some pubs currently on great form, particularly the Duke of Wellington at Bourn, Crown at Broughton, Castle in Cambridge, John Barleycorn at Duxford, White Horse in Eaton Socon, Mermaid at Ellington, George & Dragon at Elsworh, Crown at Elton, Three Tuns at Fen Drayton, Pheasant at Great Chishill, Tavern on the Green at Great Staughton, Hole in the Wall at Little Wilbraham and (on a grander scale) Haycock at Wansford. In general drinks prices tend to be a little higher than the national average here. Do keep an eye open for the tasty Oakham beers that you can see being brewed at the very laid-back Brewery Tap in Peterborough; their flavour (and reasonable price) is winning friends farther and farther from their heartland.

CAMBRIDGE   TL4658   Map 5

Cambridge Blue 🍺 £

85 Gwydir Street; CB1 2LG

The two peaceful rooms and attractive little conservatory at this friendly back street pub (which is completely no smoking) are simply decorated with old-fashioned bare-boards style furnishings, candles on the tables, and a big collection of oars; there's also the bow section of the Cambridge boat that famously rammed a barge and sank before the start of the 1984 boat race, and such a nice selection of rowing photographs you feel you're browsing through someone's family snaps; cribbage and dominoes. The interesting range of seven well kept real ales on handpump includes Adnams Bitter, Elgoods Black Dog, Woodfordes Wherry and changing guests from brewers such as Cottage, Hadrian & Border, Oakham and Old Cannon; they also have Aspall's farm cider, malt whiskies and fresh orange juice. Straightforward bar food includes home-made soup (from £3.25), filled baked potatoes (from £3.80), filled ciabatta rolls (from £4), vegetable chilli (£5), sausage and mash (£5.50) and specials such as parsnip, sweet potato and chestnut bake (£6.75) and steak and ale or seafood pie (£7); Sunday roast (£6.75). Children like the surprisingly rural feeling and large back garden. *(Recommended by Dr David Cockburn, Andy and Jill Kassube, Mark Farrington, the Didler, Eric Robinson, Jacqueline Pratt, Helen McLagan)*

Free house ~ Licensees Chris and Debbie Lloyd ~ Real ale ~ Bar food (12-2.30, 6-9.30) ~ (01223) 505110 ~ Children welcome in conservatory ~ Dogs welcome ~ Open 12-2.30 (3 Sat), 5.30-11; 12-3, 6-10.30 Sun

Eagle ♀ £
Bene't Street; CB2 3QN

The rambling rooms of this old coaching inn can get very busy (and smoky) in the evening and during lunchtimes, so as they serve food all day, it's worth aiming for an off peak hours visit. As well as saving you from a long queue at the servery for your meal, this will also give you a better chance to appreciate the many charming original architectural features, from the lovely worn wooden floors to plenty of pine panelling, two fireplaces dating back to around 1600, two medieval mullioned windows, and the remains of two possibly medieval wall paintings. Don't miss the high dark red ceiling which has been left unpainted since World War II to preserve the signatures of British and American airmen worked in with Zippo lighters, candle smoke and lipstick. Creaky old furniture is nicely in keeping with it all, and there are several no smoking areas. Straightforward but good value bar food comes in generous helpings and includes filled baked potatoes (from £4.70), filled baguettes (from £5.45), and vegetarian quiche, steak in ale pie, ham and eggs or lasagne (all £6.45), with evening dishes such as giant battered cod (£8.25) and steaks (from £9.85); Sunday carvery. Drinks include well kept Greene King IPA, Abbot, Old Speckled Hen and a guest such as Brains Reverend James on handpump, and around a dozen wines by the glass. An attractive cobbled and galleried courtyard, screened from the street by sturdy wooden gates and with heavy wooden seats and tables, heaters and pretty hanging baskets, takes you back through the centuries – especially at Christmas, when they serve mulled wine and you can listen to the choristers from King's College singing here; children may be welcome in no smoking areas if eating though reader's have experienced mixed rules so do check beforehand. *(Recommended by John Wooll, Dr David Cockburn, Andy and Jill Kassube, Michael Dandy, John Saville, Rosanna Luke, Matt Curzon, the Didler, Christine and Neil Townend, Eric Robinson, Jacqueline Pratt, Hazel Morgan, Bernard Patrick)*

Greene King ~ Managers Steve Ottley and Sian Crowther ~ Real ale ~ Bar food (12-10 (8 Fri and Sat); 9-11 weekday breakfast)) ~ (01223) 505020 ~ Open 9-11; 12-10.30 Sun

Free Press £
Prospect Row; CB1 1DU

This unspoilt little pub has a homely tucked-away atmosphere, and is completely no smoking. In winter you can sit peacefully reading a newspaper by the log fire (no piped music, mobile phones or games machines), and in summer the sheltered paved garden at the back is quite a suntrap. In a nod to the building's history as home to a local newspaper, the walls of its characterful bare-board rooms are hung with old newspaper pages and printing memorabilia, as well as old printing trays that local customers are encouraged to top up with little items. Well kept Greene King IPA, Abbot and Mild and a guest or two such as Caledonian 80/- and Titanic White Star on handpump, around 20 malt whiskies, and winter mulled wine; TV and quite a few assorted board games. Good value tasty bar food is served in generous helpings: soup or filled ciabattas (£3.25), ploughman's (from £6.50), spinach and ricotta tortellini or stuffed peppers (£6.50), gammon with bubble and squeak (£6.25) and baked trout or lamb shank (£7.95). *(Recommended by John Wooll, Dr David Cockburn, Michael Dandy, the Didler, Mark Harrington, A J Bowen)*

Greene King ~ Tenant Donna Thornton ~ Real ale ~ Bar food (12-2, 6-8.30; not Sun evening) ~ (01223) 368337 ~ Children welcome till 8pm ~ Dogs allowed in bar ~ Open 12-2.30(3 Sat, Sun), 6-11(7-10.30 Sun)

Information about no smoking areas is for the period before summer 2007, when smoking inside pubs will become illegal throughout England.

Live & Let Live ◖ £

40 Mawson Road; off Mill Road SE of centre; CB1 2EA

The landlord at this down-to-earth but popular old local is a real ale enthusiast so there's usually an interesting selection of seven very well kept beers from thoughtfully sourced brewers such as Cropton, Dark Star, Fenland or Tring, plus around 20 belgian beers, and a dozen malt whiskies. The atmosphere is relaxed and friendly, and the heavily timbered brickwork rooms have sturdy varnished pine tables with pale wood chairs on bare boards, and real gas lighting. An assortment of collectables takes in lots of interesting old country bric-a-brac and some steam railway and brewery memorabilia, and posters advertise local forthcoming events; cribbage and dominoes. The eating area of the bar is no smoking until 9pm, and simple but good value home-made food includes sandwiches and filled baked potatoes (from £2.50), home-made soup (£3.50), ploughman's (£5), sausage or ham and egg (£6), lambs liver and bacon with bubble and squeak or vegetable lasagne (£6.50), chicken and mushroom pie (£7.50), and puddings (£3.75); all day breakfast on Saturday and roast lunch on Sunday. *(Recommended by John Wooll, Dr David Cockburn, Giles and Annie Francis, Keith and Janet Morris, Helen McLagan, Revd R P Tickle)*

Burlison Inns ~ Lease Peter Wiffin ~ Real ale ~ Bar food (12-2, 6(7 Sun)-9) ~ (01223) 460261 ~ Children in eating area of bar ~ Dogs welcome ~ Open 11.30-2.30, 5.30(6 Sat)-11; 12-2.30, 7-11 Sun

ELTON   TL0893   Map 5

Black Horse ♀

B671 off A605 W of Peterborough and A1(M); Overend; PE8 6RU

This well run dining pub has all you'd expect of a country inn from its welcoming atmosphere and roaring fires to hop-strung beams, a homely and comfortable mix of furniture (no two tables and chairs seem the same), antique prints, and lots of ornaments and bric-a-brac including an intriguing ancient radio set. Dining areas at each end of the partly no smoking bar have parquet flooring and tiles, and the stripped stone back lounge towards the restaurant has an interesting fireplace. Consider booking, especially on Sunday, as the emphasis is very much on the good (though not cheap) food, which ranges from bar snacks such as filled baked potatoes (from £3.50), sandwiches (from £4.95), ploughman's or caesar salad (£8.25), and a home-made pie of the day (£8.95), to bangers and mash (£11.95), pork medallions stuffed with garlic and herbs wrapped in bacon with stilton sauce (£14.95) or tuna loin with red pesto and balsamic (£15.95). They may ask you to leave your credit card behind the bar, or pay on ordering. As well as a good choice of 15 wines by the glass, the four real ales on handpump such as Barnwell (brewed locally), Bass, Everards Tiger or Nethergate Suffolk County do attract the odd local for a pint at the bar. The big garden has super views across to Elton Hall park and the village church, there are seats on the terrace, some tables shaded by horse chestnut trees, and a couple of acres of grass for children to play. *(Recommended by J C M Troughton, Gene and Kitty Rankin, Fiona McElhone, Phil and Jane Hodson, Gerry and Rosemary Dobson, Oliver and Sue Rowell)*

Free house ~ Licensee John Clennell ~ Real ale ~ Bar food (12-2(3 Sun), 6-9; not Sun evening) ~ Restaurant ~ (01832) 280240 ~ Children welcome ~ Dogs allowed in bar ~ Open 12-11(12 Sat, 8 Sun); closed Sun evening

ELY   TL5380   Map 5

Fountain ◖

Corner of Barton Square and Silver Street; CB7 4JF

This simple yet genteel 19th-c corner pub, despite being very close to the cathedral, manages to escape the tourists and maintain a local following. Old cartoons, local photographs, regional maps and mementoes of the neighbouring King's School punctuate the elegant dark pink walls, and neatly tied-back curtains hang from gold colour rails above the big windows. Above one fireplace is a stuffed pike in a case, and there are a few antlers dotted about – not to mention a duck at one end of the bar. A recent extension at the back provides much needed additional seating. Everything is very clean and tidy, and there's no music, fruit machines or even food. Well kept Adnams Bitter and Broadside, Fullers London Pride and a changing guest such as Timothy Taylors Landlord on handpump. Note the limited opening times below. More reports please. *(Recommended by the Didler)*

Free house ~ Licensees John and Judith Borland ~ Real ale ~ No credit cards ~ (01353) 663122 ~ Children welcome away from bar until 8pm ~ Dogs welcome ~ Open 5-11(closed weekday lunchtimes); 12-2, 6-11.30 Sat; 12-2, 7-10.30 Sun

FEN DITTON   TL4860   Map 5
Ancient Shepherds
Off B1047 at Green End, The River signpost, just NE of Cambridge; CB5 8ST

The nicest room at this solidly beamed old pub (now completely no smoking) is the softly lit central lounge, where you can't fail to be comfortable on one of the big fat dark red button-back leather settees or armchairs which are grouped round low dark wood tables. The warm coal fire, and heavy drapes around the window seat with its big scatter cushions add to the cosiness. Above a black dado the walls (and ceiling) are dark pink, and decorated with comic fox and policeman prints and little steeplechasing and equestrian ones. On the right the smallish more pubby bar, with its coal fire, serves Adnams and Greene King IPA, while on the left is a pleasant restaurant (piped music in here). Generously served bar food is fairly priced and includes home-made soup (£3.95), lunchtime filled baguettes (from £4.40), ploughman's (from £5.95) and ham, egg and chips (£7.50), with daily specials such as smoked haddock and spring onion fishcakes, sausage and mash or brie, almond and courgette bake (£8.95). The licensee's west highland terrier, Billie, might be around outside food service times. *(Recommended by Roger and Anne Newbury, Dr Phil Putwain, Helen and Ian Jobson)*

Punch ~ Tenant J M Harrington ~ Real ale ~ Bar food (12-2(2.30 Sun), 6.30-9) ~ Restaurant ~ (01223) 293280 ~ Children welcome with restrictions ~ Dogs allowed in bar ~ Open 12-2.30, 6-11; 12-5 Sun; closed Sun evening

FORDHAM   TL6270   Map 5
White Pheasant ♀
A142 (may be bypassed by the time this edition is published) at junction with B1102 to Burwell, north of Newmarket; Market Street; CB7 5LQ

The exterior is somewhat unassuming, but inside, this smallish open-plan dining pub is light, airy and gently stylish in its simplicity, with an attractive mix of well spaced big farmhouse tables and chairs on bare boards, some stripped brickwork, and a cheery log fire at one end. One or two steps lead down to a small similarly furnished but carpeted room; piped music. Though the emphasis is fairly restauranty, very pleasant young staff impart the relaxed friendliness of a pub, with Fenland St Audreys and a guest beer, four ciders and a dozen carefully chosen wines (including champagne) by the glass served from the horseshoe bar that faces the entrance. Very enjoyable food might include whitebait (£4.75), locally smoked salmon with coriander corn fritter (£5.50), pork tenderloin topped with mozzarella and pesto (£13.95), organic risotto with saffron and wild mushrooms (£14.50), fillet steak with leeks, mushrooms and peppercorn sauce (£19.50), a few lighter lunch dishes such as interestingly filled breads (from £5.50), sausage and mash (£7.50), tagliatelle carbonara or celery, blue cheese and bacon salad (£7.95), and full breakfast (£9.95). We mention in passing that one reader found the pub closed for a private function. *(Recommended by Richard Storey, John Saville, Mr and Mrs S Wilson, David and Judith Stewart, Michael Dandy, Ben and Helen Ingram, Stephen Woad)*

Free house ~ Licensee Elizabeth Trangmar ~ Real ale ~ Bar food (12-2.30, 6-9.30(7-9 Sun)) ~ Restaurant ~ (01638) 720414 ~ Well behaved children welcome ~ Open 12-3(3.30 Sat), 6-11(11.30 Sat); 12-4, 7-10 Sun

FOWLMERE   TL4245   Map 5
Chequers ㉕ 🍴 🍷
B1368; SG8 7SR

Though not the cheapest in the county, the imaginative food at this lovely 16th-c coaching inn is first-rate, and starters can double as light snacks if you're not so hungry: soup (£4.50), niçoise salad with quails eggs (£7.95), fried foie gras on potato cake and wilted spinach with veal jus (£8.50), celery, apple, walnut, gorgonzola and ricotta strudel (£10.95), fried pollock on crushed new potatoes and chorizo with white wine sauce and rocket or fresh crab linguini with rocket and chilli (£12.95), fillet steak with creamed peppercorn and armagnac sauce (£18.95), and puddings such as apple strudel (£4.50) or hot date sponge with toffee sauce (£6); the restaurant cover charge (£2.50 a head) includes bread, olives and a bottle of mineral water. Two comfortably furnished downstairs rooms are warmed by an open log fire, and upstairs there are beams, wall timbering and some interesting moulded plasterwork above the fireplace. One area is no smoking. The airy conservatory overlooks tables with cocktail parasols on a terrace and among flowers and shrub roses in a neatly kept floodlit garden. Historic aeroplanes flying from Duxford pass over here during the summer months. Drinks include Adnams, three or four guests from brewers such as Green Jack (tapped from the cask by friendly staff), 18 wines by the glass and 30 malt whiskies. *(Recommended by Adele Summers, Alan Black, Mrs P J Pearce, Michael Butler, Jennie Challacombe, Mrs Joyce Ferguson, Marion and Bill Cross, Eric Robinson, Jacqueline Pratt, Gerry and Rosemary Dobson, Pat Flynn, Jeremy Whitehorn, Andy Millward)*

Free house ~ Licensee Paul Beaumont ~ Real ale ~ Bar food (12-2, 7-9.30(9 Sun)) ~ Restaurant ~ (01763) 208369 ~ Children over 10 welcome ~ Open 12-3, 6-11(7-10.30 Sun)

GODMANCHESTER   TL2470   Map 5
Exhibition
London Road; PE29 2HZ

Don't be deterred by the unassuming exterior, as once inside you'll find an unexpectedly attractive, even amusing, choice of rooms. The main bar has its walls humorously decorated with re-created shop-fronts – a post office, gallery, and wine and spirit merchant – complete with doors and stock in the windows. It's cosy with big flagstones on the floor, cushioned wall benches, fresh flowers and candles on each of the tables and white fairy lights on some of the plants; piped music. At lunchtime, the enjoyable food might include sandwiches (from £3.95; steak baguette with teriyaki sauce £5.25), soup (£3.95), chargrilled burger in a seeded bun (£5.50), duck and chicken liver terrine with home-made chutney (£5.75), pasta of the day (£8.95), thai salmon fishcakes with soured cream and sweet chilli jam (£10.95), vegetarian bake (£10.95), and cornfed chicken supreme wrapped in pancetta with a wild mushroom and mixed herb sauce (£11.25), with evening choices such as emmenthal cheese and vegetable terrine (£4.95), prawn and crab tian with fresh gazpacho sauce (£5.45), globe artichoke with butter bean cassoulet (£9.75), duck breast glazed with orange and soya sauce (£13.35), chargrilled sirloin steak (£13.75), and halibut fillet with spinach, potato purée, muscat grapes and fish cream sauce (£14.85). The dining room, with smart candelabra and framed prints, is no smoking. Well kept Fullers London Pride, Greene King IPA on handpump. There are picnic-sets on the back lawn, some shaded by pergolas, and a couple in front as well, and they hold barbecues in summer. *(Recommended by Karen Eliot, Michael Dandy, M and GR, R T and J C Moggridge, Keith and Chris O'Neill, Christopher Turner, Richard Siebert, Mrs Jane Kingsbury, Derek and Sylvia Stephenson, Peter and Jean Hoare)*

Enterprise ~ Lease Paul Dyer ~ Real ale ~ Bar food (12-3, 6.30-9.30) ~ Restaurant ~ (01480) 459134 ~ Children welcome ~ Dogs allowed in bar ~ Open 11.30-11(12 Thurs-Sat); 12-11 Sun

HELPSTON   TF1205   Map 5
Blue Bell 🍴
Woodgate; off B1443; PE6 7ED

Cheery service and reasonably priced food, including a senior citizens' two-course lunch (£5.95), draw a happy crowd at this friendly bustling pub: soup (£2.50), salmon and dill fishcakes (£4.25), ploughman's (£6.95), steak and ale pie or fried king prawns (£7.95), lasagne (£8.25), chicken breast in creamy tarragon sauce (£8.45) and sirloin steak (£9.95). Comfortable cushioned chairs and settles, plenty of pictures, ornaments, mementoes and cart-wheel displays, and piped music give a homely atmosphere to the lounge, smoking parlour and snug. The dining extension is light and airy with a sloping glass roof; no smoking except in the bar. Adnams Southwold, Everards Tiger and Old Original and a couple of guests from brewers such as Batemans and Greene King Abbot are served from handpumps, and there may be jam and marmalade for sale; darts, pool and board games; wheelchair access. A sheltered terrace has plastic garden tables and outdoor heaters. *(Recommended by Michael and Jenny Back, Ben and Helen Ingram, Ian Stafford)*

Free house ~ Licensee Aubrey Sinclair Ball ~ Real ale ~ Bar food (not Sun evenings) ~ Restaurant ~ (01733) 252394 ~ Children welcome in dining areas ~ Dogs allowed in bar ~ Open 11.30-2.30, 5-11; 11.30-3, 6-12 Sat; 11-3.30, 6.30-11 Sun

HEMINGFORD GREY   TL2970   Map 5
Cock 🍴 ☂ 🍴
Village signposted off A14 eastbound, and (via A1096 St Ives road) westbound; High Street; PE28 9BJ

Cambridgeshire Dining Pub of the Year
Although there's quite an emphasis on the very good imaginative food at this pretty little pub, the public bar on the left is still a traditional drinking room, with an open woodburning stove on the raised hearth, bar stools, wall seats, a carver, some cock photographs, and steps down to more seating below black beams. Earl Soham Victoria, Woodfordes Wherry and a couple of guests from brewers such as Potbelly and Wolf are well kept on handpump, alongside a good choice of 15 good wines by the glass from an extensive list. In marked contrast, the stylishly simple spotless restaurant on the right has clattery pale bare boards, canary walls above a powder-blue dado, and another woodburning stove. There's a friendly, bustling atmosphere, a good mix of locals and visitors, and the pub is no smoking throughout. As well as a very useful two- or three-course lunch menu (£9.95/£12.95), changing dishes might include soup (£3.95), warm venison salad (£4.95), three or four different home-made sausages and mash with a choice of gravy (£9.95), gnocchi with buffalo mozzarella, sun-dried tomatoes and mint (£10.95), and loin of lamb with marinated grilled aubergines, pea and mint blini and port sauce (£15.95); you may need side orders (£1.95), with puddings such as fig and muscat crème brûlée or chocolate tart with amaretto crème anglaise (from £4.95). There are tables out behind in a neat garden. *(Recommended by MJB, Michael Dandy, J Stickland, Dr David Cockburn, Margaret and Roy Randle, John Saul, P Clements)*

Free house ~ Licensees Oliver Thain and Richard Bradley ~ Real ale ~ Bar food (12-2.30, 6.30-9.30) ~ Restaurant ~ (01480) 463609 ~ Children in restaurant ~ Dogs allowed in bar ~ Open 11.30-3, 6-11; 12-10.30 Sun; 12-4, 6-10.30 Sun in winter

HEYDON   TL4340   Map 5
King William IV
Off A505 W of M11 junction 10; SG8 7RY

A charming assortment of rustic jumble fills the rambling rooms at this neatly kept dining pub. Its beamed nooks and crannies (warmed in winter by a log fire) are filled with ploughshares, yokes and iron tools, cowbells, beer steins, samovars, brass or black wrought-iron lamps, copper-bound casks and milk ewers, harness, horsebrasses, and smith's bellows – as well as decorative plates, cut-glass and china ornaments; piped music. Adnams Best, Fullers London Pride, Greene King IPA and Timothy Taylors Landlord are well kept on handpump. The menu (with more vegetarian dishes than at most pubs) might include soup (£4.25), filled ciabattas or panini (from £5.65), thai-style mussels (£5.95), crispy duck pancakes (£6.25), fish pie (£9.95), tempura vegetables on sweet chilli noodles with an oriental dipping sauce (£10.65), grilled pork chops with apple and cider sauce with lyonnaise potatoes (£10.95), confit of duck leg with apple and black pudding mash with beetroot and honey duck liver jus or 8oz fillet (£13.95), baked bass with thai spices and stir-fried vegetables (£14.95), with puddings such as apple and rhubarb crumble or tiramisu with fruit coulis (£4.50). The restaurant and snug areas are no smoking; you will need to book at weekends. A wooden deck has teak furniture and outdoor heaters, and there are more seats in the pretty garden. *(Recommended by Mike and Shelley Woodroffe, Richard Siebert, Gillian Grist, Mrs Margo Finlay, Jörg Kasprowski, Margaret and Roy Randle, M R D Foot, B N F and M Parkin)*

Free house ~ Licensee Elizabeth Nicholls ~ Real ale ~ Bar food (12-2, 6.30-9.30) ~ Restaurant ~ (01763) 838773 ~ Children welcome with restrictions ~ Dogs allowed in bar ~ Open 12-2.30(3 Sat), 6-11; 12-3, 7-10.30 Sun

HINXTON   TL4945   Map 5
Red Lion

2 miles off M11 junction 9 northbound; take first exit off A11, A1301 N, then left turn into village – High Street; a little further from junction 10, via A505 E and A1301 S; CB10 1QY

The calmly quiet atmosphere at this carefully extended pink-washed 16th-c inn makes a restful break from the nearby M11, and it's not far from the Imperial War Museum at Duxford. Its dusky, mainly open-plan beamed bar has leather chesterfields on wooden floors, Adnams Best, Greene King IPA, Woodfordes Wherry and a guest such as City of Cambridge Hobson's Choice on handpump, ten wines by the glass, and Aspall's cider. Off here there are high-backed upholstered settles in an informal dining area (no smoking on Sundays), and the smart no smoking restaurant is filled with mirrors, pictures and assorted clocks. Bar food, served by friendly helpful staff, might include home-made soup (£3.95), sandwiches (from £4.50), vegetable terrine (£4.25), filled baked potatoes (from £5.50), sausage and mash (£7.95), chicken curry (£9.95), 8oz sirloin (£13.95), and puddings such as baked blueberry cheesecake or sticky toffee pudding (from £4.25). It's peaceful too in the neatly kept big garden which has a pleasant terrace with picnic-sets, a dovecote and views of the village church. *(Recommended by Roy Bromell, Peter and Jean Dowson, Anthony Barnes, Eric Robinson, Jacqueline Pratt, Stephen and Jean Curtis, Mrs Margo Finlay, Jörg Kasprowski, LM, B C Robertson, Mrs M Hatwell, Louise Medcalf)*

Free house ~ Licensee Alex Clarke ~ Real ale ~ Bar food (12-2, 6.45-9(9.30 Fri, Sat); 12-2.30, 7-9 Sun) ~ Restaurant ~ (01799) 530601 ~ Well behaved children welcome ~ Dogs allowed in bar ~ Open 11-3, 6-11; 12-4, 7-10.30 Sun

HUNTINGDON   TL2371   Map 5
Old Bridge Hotel ★ ⑪ ♀ 🛏

1 High Street; ring road just off B1044 entering from easternmost A14 slip road; PE29 3TQ

This very civilised ivy-covered Georgian hotel is top notch all round. Although not strictly a pub, the bar is still somewhere that customers are happy to drop into for a pint. It has fine polished floorboards, a good log fire and a quietly chatty atmosphere. The splendid range of drinks includes well kept Adnams Bitter, Hobsons City of Cambridge and a guest from a brewer such as Nethergate on handpump, 18 wines by the glass, ten sweet ones, and two champagnes. But it's the excellent imaginative (though not cheap) food, beautifully served by friendly efficient staff, that most people come to enjoy. You can eat in the big airy Terrace (an indoor room, but with beautifully painted verdant murals suggesting the open air) or in the slightly more formal panelled restaurant (both are no smoking). As well as a two- and three-course lunch menu (£13.50/£16.75), there might be olives or home-made crisps (£1.95), inventive sandwiches (from £5), soup (£5.95), thai squid and pork salad (£7.95), sausage and mash (£9.95), cod and chips (£11.95), sautéed leg of rabbit with creamed endive (£13.95), aberdeenshire sirloin steak with watercress and béarnaise sauce and hand-cut chips or roast rump of cornish lamb with sweetbreads, peas and mint (£16.95) or halibut with herb crust, boulangère potatoes and beurre blanc (£18.95). The building is tucked away in a good spot by the River Great Ouse with its own landing stage, and tables on waterside terraces (unfortunately there may be traffic noise). *(Recommended by MJB, Michael Dandy, J F M and M West, Michael Sargent, Alan Clark, Martin and Pauline Jennings, Les and Barbara Owen, Fred and Lorraine Gill, Christopher Turner, Anthony Longden, Richard Siebert, Mr and Mrs Ladley)*

Huntsbridge ~ Licensee John Hoskins ~ Real ale ~ Bar food (12-2.15, 6.30-10) ~ Restaurant ~ (01480) 424300 ~ Children welcome ~ Dogs allowed in bar ~ Open 11.30-11; 12-10 Sun ~ Bedrooms: £95B/£125B

KEYSTON   TL0475   Map 5
Pheasant 🍽 ♀
Just off A14 SE of Thrapston; village loop road, off B663; PE28 0RE

The highly thought-of robustly flavoured modern cooking is the focus at this long low thatched inn. Although they do keep real ales, and its look is quite pubby, this is essentially a restaurant (now completely no smoking). Using carefully sourced ingredients, food (not cheap) might include drinks snacks such as warm olives or salted almonds (from £2.50), white bean, cep and truffle oil soup (£4.95), warm salad of confit of duck with chicory, green beans and soft boiled egg (£5.75), snails with garlic and parsley butter (£5.95), moroccan spiced ricotta cannelloni with marinated pumpkin, courgettes and red peppers (£11.75), crisp haddock with skordalia, shaved fennel, crab and chilli salad (£14.50), pot roast rabbit with onion, tomato, gremolata and rosemary potato (£14.95), and peppered steak with hand-cut chips (£19.75). Service is cheerful and efficient. The immaculately kept spacious oak-beamed bar has a comfortably civilised atmosphere, open fires, simple wooden tables and chairs on deep coloured carpets, guns on pale pink walls, and country paintings. An excellent range of drinks includes a fine wine list with an interesting choice of reasonably priced bottles and 16 wines by the glass (plus eight sweet wines and two champagnes), fine port and sherry, freshly squeezed or locally pressed juices and Adnams Bitter and a couple of changing guests such as Oakham JHB and Potton Village Bike on handpump. There are seats out in front of the building (which has been owned by the Hoskins family for over 40 years). *(Recommended by Martin and Pauline Jennings, J F M and M West, M and GR, Ryta Lyndley, Michael Sargent, Dave Braisted, Dr and Mrs M E Wilson, John and Enid Morris, Mr and Mrs D S Price, Martin and Sue Day, Oliver and Sue Rowell, Bill and Marian de Bass, Paul and Margaret Baker, Mrs Roxanne Chamberlain)*

Huntsbridge ~ Licensees Johnny Dargue and John Hoskins ~ Real ale ~ Bar food (12-2(2.30 Sun), 6-9.30) ~ Restaurant ~ (01832) 710241 ~ Children welcome ~ Dogs allowed in bar ~ Open 12-3, 6-11(10.30 Sun)

KIMBOLTON   TL0967   Map 5
New Sun ♀
High Street; PE28 0HA

Gently smartened up since the last edition, this nice old pub fits in well with Kimbolton's delightfully harmonious High Street. The low-beamed front lounge is perhaps the cosiest, with a couple of comfortable armchairs and a sofa beside the fireplace, standing timbers and exposed brickwork, books, pottery and brasses, and maybe mid-afternoon sun lighting up the wonkiest corners. This leads into a narrower locals' bar, with well kept Charles Wells Bombardier and Eagle, and a guest such as Greene King Old Speckled Hen on handpump, and about a dozen wines by the glass; piped music. Opening off here are a dining room and a bright, busy tiled no smoking conservatory, with wicker furniture, an unusual roof like a red and yellow striped umbrella, and plenty of tables for eating. A short tapas menu includes a handful of dishes such as tortilla or marinated anchovies (from £2.50), otherwise there are lunchtime sandwiches (from £2.75) and filled baked potatoes (from £2.95), and possibly fried squid with rocket and harissa (£5.50), pasta with goats cheese, tomatoes, basil and toasted pine nuts (£9.25), seared tuna steak with roast artichokes, basil pesto, parmentier potatoes and dijon sauce (£11.75), roast rack of lamb with dauphinoise potatoes (£16.95), beef stroganoff (£17.25), daily specials such as lamb and mint sausages (£8.95) or thai-style baked bass (£12.95), and puddings such as sherry trifle, spotted dick and custard or Malteser cheesecake (from £4.50). There's a very pleasant garden behind, with plastic tables and chairs. Some of the nearby parking spaces have a 30-minute limit. *(Recommended by Michael Dandy, John Picken, Sarah Flynn)*

Charles Wells ~ Tenant Stephen Rogers ~ Real ale ~ Bar food (12-2.15(2.30 Sun), 7-9.30; not Sun or Mon evenings) ~ Restaurant ~ (01480) 860052 ~ Dogs allowed in bar ~ Open 11.30-2.30, 6-11; 12-10.30 Sun

LONGSTOWE TL3154 Map 5
Red House 🍺

Old North Road; A1198 Royston—Huntingdon, S of village; CB3 7UT

A local artist painted the rather charming sporting murals that you can see in the bar and restaurant area at this very easy-going creeper-covered pub. Bits and pieces dotted around the informal interior follow the same theme – there's a fox mask and horse tack, stuffed hare, quite a few good hunting prints, and rosettes mounted proudly behind the bar. From the bar (no smoking) with its red-tiled floor and cottagey window you go round to the right, past the big log fire with its fat back kettle and a couple of tables beside it, and step down into another dark-tiled area with chintzy easy chairs and settees. This looks onto a sheltered little garden with picnic-sets; piped music and daily papers. Well kept Greene King IPA and three or four interesting guests on handpump, and ten wines by the glass. As well as lunchtime sandwiches (from £3.95), a short menu includes sausage and mash, beef in ale pie or chicken curry (£9.50) and sirloin steak (£13.95). The largest doll's house museum in the world and Wimpole Hall are nearby. *(Recommended by Michael Dandy, Phil and Jane Hodson)*

Free house ~ Licensee Martin Willis ~ Real ale ~ Bar food (12-2, 6-9.30; 12-9.30 Sat; 12-8 Sun) ~ Restaurant ~ (01954) 718480 ~ Children welcome away from bar and if seated ~ Dogs allowed in bar ~ Open 12-2.30(3 Fri), 5.30-11(12 Fri); 12-12(10.30 Sun) Sat

MADINGLEY TL3960 Map 5
Three Horseshoes 🍴 ♓

Off A1303 W of Cambridge; High Street; CB3 8AB

Emphasis at this civilised white thatched place is on the sophisticated italian cooking, with prices right up at restaurant levels. It's a very popular place so it's worth booking. The daily changing menu might include starters such as tomato salad with mascarpone and olive crostini (£6.50), hand-filled pea and ricotta ravioli (£7.50), roast quail (£8.50), main courses such as roast gressingham duck with parmesan and garlic potato cake and duck liver crostini (£16.50), grilled leg of lamb with mint and chilli sauce (£16.95), monkfish and scallop skewer with lentils, braised spinach and anchovy and rosemary sauce (£21.95), side orders (from £2.75), puddings such as caramelised lemon tart with raspberries in prosecco (£7.50) and pressed chocolate cake with burnt caramel ice-cream (£7.95), and a cheese platter (£7.95). They may have a handful of cheaper dishes. Not just the food but the wine list too is outstanding, with over 18 by the glass, plus sweet wines and ports. The pleasantly relaxed little airy bar (which can be a bit of a crush at busy times) has an open fire, simple wooden tables and chairs on bare floorboards, stools at the bar and pictures on green walls. Friendly efficient service;

well kept Adnams Southwold plus a guest on handpump. *(Recommended by Michael Dandy, John and Elisabeth Cox, Adele Summers, Alan Black, Ryta Lyndley, Richard Siebert, Bob Sadler, Eamonn and Natasha Skyrme, Michael Butler)*

Huntsbridge ~ Licensee Richard Stokes ~ Real ale ~ Bar food (12-2, 7-9(6.30-9.30 Fri, Sat; 6.30-8.30 Sun)) ~ Restaurant ~ (01954) 210221 ~ Children welcome ~ Open 11.30(12 Sun)-3, 6-11

NEWTON   TL4349   Map 5
Queens Head ㉕ ★ ◨ £
2½ miles from M11 junction 11; A10 towards Royston, then left on to B1368; CB2 5PG

This lovely old pub has been kept traditionally unspoilt by the same welcoming family for three generations now. Comfortably worn and low key, but always spotlessly clean, the peaceful main bar has a low ceiling and crooked beams, bare wooden benches and seats built into the walls, paintings on the cream walls, and bow windows. A curved high-backed settle stands on yellow tiles, a loudly ticking clock marks the unchanging time, and a lovely big log fire crackles warmly. The little carpeted saloon is similar but even cosier. Drinks include Adnams Bitter and Broadside, with any one of the Adnams range on as a guest, tapped straight from the barrel, ten wines by the glass, interesting fruit juices and a couple of ciders. Darts are in a no smoking side room, with shove-ha'penny, table skittles, dominoes, cribbage and nine men's morris. There's a limited range of basic but well liked food, which comes in hearty and very fairly priced helpings: toast and beef dripping (£2), lunchtime sandwiches (from £2.40, including things like banana with sugar and lemon or herb and garlic), a mug of their famous home-made brown soup (£3), and filled Aga-baked potatoes (£3). In the evening and on Sunday lunchtime you can get plates of excellent cold meat, smoked salmon, cheeses and pâté (from £4). There are seats in front of the pub, with its vine trellis. This is a popular place so you will need to get here early for a seat during peak times, and there may be a queue of people waiting for the doors to open on a Sunday. *(Recommended by Mr and Mrs T B Staples, Michael Butler, Keith and Janet Morris, Mark Harrington, Eric Robinson, Jacqueline Pratt, Annabel Viney, Michael and Marion Buchanan, Helen McLagan)*

Free house ~ Licensees David and Robert Short ~ Real ale ~ Bar food ~ No credit cards ~ (01223) 870436 ~ Very well behaved children welcome in games room ~ Dogs welcome ~ Open 11.30-2.30, 6-11; 12-2.30, 7-10.30 Sun

PETERBOROUGH   TL1999   Map 5
Brewery Tap ◨ £
Opposite Queensgate car park; PE1 2AA

An impressive range of 12 real ales is served at this enormous brewpub. Nine guests come from a plethora of thoughtfully sourced countrywide brewers, and the three Oakham beers (Bishops Farewell, JHB and White Dwarf) are produced here. They also keep a good number of bottled belgian beers, and a fun wine list with quite a few by the glass. The first thing that will probably grab your attention at this striking modern conversion of an old labour exchange is the vast two-storey high glass wall that divides the bar and brewery, giving fascinating views of the massive copper-banded stainless brewing vessels. There's an easy going relaxed feel to the open-plan contemporary interior, with an expanse of light wood and stone floors for drinkers, blue-painted iron pillars holding up a steel-corded no smoking mezzanine level, and hugely enlarged newspaper cuttings on light orange or burnt red walls. It's stylishly lit by a giant suspended steel ring with bulbs running around the rim, and steel-meshed wall lights. A band of chequered floor tiles traces the path of the long sculpted light wood bar counter, which is boldly backed by an impressive display of bottles in a ceiling-high wall of wooden cubes. A sofa seating area downstairs provides a comfortable corner for a surprisingly mixed bunch of customers from young to old; there's a big screen TV for sporting events, piped music and games machines and DJs or live bands at the weekends. It gets very busy in the evening. The comprehensive range of very tasty thai food runs from snacks such as chicken satay or tempura vegetables (from £2.99) to soups (tom yum £3.99) to main courses such as pad thai noodles to panang curry (mostly £5.99) and rice dishes (from £1.59). The pub is owned by the same people as Charters (below). More reports please. *(Recommended by Andy and Jill Kassube, the Didler, P Dawn, Rona Murdoch, Mike and Sue Loseby, Ben and Helen Ingram, Andy Lickfold)*

Own brew ~ Licensees Stuart Wright, Jessica Loock, Paul Hook ~ Real ale ~ Bar food (12-2.30, 6-9.30; 12-10.30 Fri, Sat) ~ Restaurant ~ (01733) 358500 ~ Children welcome during food service times ~ Dogs allowed in bar ~ DJs or live bands weekends ~ Open 12-11; 12-10.30 Sun

Charters 🍺 £
Town Bridge, S side; PE1 1FP

This sizeable timbered bar is housed in the hold of a remarkable conversion of a sturdy 1901 dutch grain barge, which is moored on the River Nene. Old wooden tables and pews provide plenty of seating; piped music, games machines and darts. Above deck a rather nice glazed oriental restaurant has been built where tarpaulins would have covered the hold. A third of the bar and the restaurant are no smoking. An impressive range of real ales includes three Oakham beers and around nine quickly changing guests from an interesting variety of brewers. They also keep around 30 foreign bottled beers, and hold regular beer festivals. Good value oriental-style food (you order upstairs from the restaurant menu in the evening or if you prefer at lunchtime) includes snacks such as crispy seaweed, spring rolls, tempura prawns or salt and pepper crispy squid (£1.95-£4.65), pitta bread with fillings such as oriental duck or beef in black bean sauce (£3.95), and singapore chicken curry or lamb rendang curry (£5.95). Adjacent to the mooring is what is thought to be the biggest pub garden in the city, making this a great place for a summer visit. *(Recommended by Andy and Jill Kassube, the Didler, P Dawn, Rona Murdoch, Ben and Helen Ingram, Barry Collett, Alastair Gibson)*

Free house ~ Licensees Stuart Wright, Paul Hook and Gerry Cairns ~ Real ale ~ Bar food (12-2.30, 6-10) ~ Restaurant ~ (01733) 315700 ~ Children welcome ~ Dogs allowed in bar ~ Live bands Fri, Sat ~ Open 12-11(1 Fri, Sat)

REACH   TL5666   Map 5
Dyke's End 🍺
From B1102 E of A14/A1103 junction, follow signpost to Swaffham Prior and Upware – keep on through Swaffham Prior (Reach signposted from there); Fair Green; CB5 0JD

Peaceful and cosy, this 17th-c farmhouse is in a charming village-green setting next to the church, with picnic-sets under big green canvas parasols out in front on the grass. Inside, a high-backed winged settle screens off the door, and the simply decorated ochre-walled bar has stripped heavy pine tables and pale kitchen chairs on dark boards with one or two rugs, a few rather smarter dining tables on parquet flooring in a panelled section on the left, and on the right a step down to a red-carpeted bit with the small red-walled servery, and sensibly placed darts at the back. All the tables have lit candles in earthenware bottles, and there may be a big bowl of lilies to brighten up the serving counter. Adnams Bitter and a couple of guests from breweries such as Archers or Youngs are well kept on handpump alongside a good wine list, and Old Rosie cider. Enjoyable bar food includes sandwiches, soup or spare ribs (£4.50), potted ham and toast (£4.95), local bangers and mash with onion gravy or baked ham and egg (£6.95), cod in beer batter with mushy peas (£8.50), roast tomato and vegetable tart with caramelised red onion (£8.95), venison casserole with parsley dumplings or roast chicken with grappa and sweet potato mash (£9.95), and steaks (from £9.95). The entire pub is no smoking except for a small area by the bar. *(Recommended by M and GR, Mrs P J Pearce, John and Bettye Reynolds, Paul Humphreys, Pam and David Bailey)*

Free house ~ Licensee Simon Owers ~ Real ale ~ Bar food (not Sun evening or Mon lunchtime) ~ Restaurant ~ (01638) 743816 ~ Children welcome with restrictions ~ Dogs allowed in bar ~ Open 12-3, 6-11(7-10.30 Sun); closed Mon lunchtime

ST NEOTS TL1859 Map 5

Chequers 🍺

St Marys Street, Eynesbury (B1043 S of centre); PE19 2TA

The small carpeted bar at this charming 16th-c pub has lots of traditional character, with its dark heavy beams, an appealing mix of seats including an unusually shaped rocking chair and a dark carved oak settle, and a log fire in a big inglenook fireplace. The pub is completely no smoking. Particularly kind and welcoming licensees give good service, and a continually changing roster of carefully chosen ales on handpump such as Nethergate Greedy Pike and Youngs are kept well; also a dozen wines by the glass. Bar food might include sandwiches or soup (£4.95), ploughman's (£7.50), green lentil patty (£9.25), pork and apple patty (£9.95), scampi (£11.50), honey and lemon salmon on noodles (£12.25) and puddings (from £4.25). A lot of energy goes into the communicating back restaurant area, which has attractively set tables, fresh flowers throughout, and rugs on its brick floor; piped music. There are tables out in the sheltered garden behind, some on a terrace. *(Recommended by Martin and Alison Stainsby, Michael Dandy)*

Free house ~ Licensees David and Ann Taylor ~ Real ale ~ Bar food (12-2, 7-9.30) ~ Restaurant ~ (01480) 472116 ~ Children welcome ~ Open 10.30(12 Sun)-2.30, 7-11; closed Sun evening

STILTON TL1689 Map 5

Bell ♀ 🛏️

High Street; village signposted from A1 S of Peterborough; PE7 3RA

Well run and gently civilised, this elegant 16th-c stone coaching inn has two neatly kept bars (smoking in these areas only) with bow windows, sturdy upright wooden seats on flagstone floors as well as plush button-back built-in banquettes, and a good big log fire in one handsome stone fireplace. The partly stripped walls have big prints of sailing and winter coaching scenes, and a giant pair of blacksmith's bellows hangs in the middle of the front bar; shove-ha'penny, dominoes, cribbage, and piped music. There's also a residents' bar and a bistro. Bar food might include stilton and leek soup with garlic croûtons (£3.95), welsh rarebit with poached quail eggs (£4.75), chicken liver parfait with red onion marmalade (£4.95), fish and chips with mushy peas (£9.95), roast chicken breast on green vegetable mashed potato with oyster mushroom, garlic and stilton cream sauce or aubergine lasagne with rocket and olive salad (£10.95), marinated tuna loin in black rice wine and on pak choi with spring onions and noodles (£12.50) and 10oz sirloin steak (£15.50). Well kept Adnams, Fullers London Pride, Greene King Abbot, Oakham JHB and a guest such as Youngs Kew Brew on handpump, and around eight wines by the glass. Through the fine coach arch is a very pretty sheltered courtyard with tables, and a well which supposedly dates back to Roman times. *(Recommended by Michael Dandy, Phil and Jane Hodson, Ian Phillips, David Glynne-Jones, Ray and Winifred Halliday)*

Free house ~ Licensee Liam McGivern ~ Real ale ~ Bar food ~ Restaurant ~ (01733) 241066 ~ Children in eating area of bar only ~ Open 12-2.30, 6-11(5-12 Sat); 12-3, 7-11 Sun ~ Bedrooms: £72.50B/£99.50B

SUTTON GAULT TL4279 Map 5

Anchor ★ 🍽️ ♀ 🛏️

Village signed off B1381 in Sutton; CB6 2BD

This appealing inn (completely no smoking) is quietly tucked away down what looks almost like a farm track. The emphasis here is on the thoughtfully prepared changing food. It's not cheap but ingredients are carefully sourced and the modern style cooking is very good. The weekday lunch menu includes a handful of more reasonably priced dishes such as venison and orange casserole with chestnut mash or salmon or prawn red thai curry (£8.50) with puddings at £4.95, while the main menu might include soup (£4.95), rillettes of local smoked eel with melba toast, yoghurt and piccalilli (£6.95), mozzarella and roast pepper lasagne (£12.50), fried bass with wok-fried vegetables and noodles, plum and ginger sauce (£15.95), local venison loin with celeriac and chestnut gateau, braised red cabbage and crème de cassis jus (£18.50) and puddings such as cinnamon panna cotta with spiced pannetone and apple sorbet (£5.95) or sticky figgy pudding with rum and raison ice-cream (£6.25). Four heavily timbered rooms are stylishly simple with two log fires, antique settles and well spaced candlelit pine tables on gently undulating old floors and good lithographs and big prints on the walls. A great range of drinks includes well kept City of Cambridge Boathouse Bitter or Hobson's Choice tapped straight from the cask, a thoughtful wine list with quite a few (including champagne) by the glass, winter mulled wine and freshly squeezed fruit juice. This is a delightful place to stay, with comfortable bedrooms, nice walks along the high embankment by the river, and the bird-watching is said to be good. There are seats outside. *(Recommended by Mrs Carolyn Dixon, M and GR, B N F and M Parkin, A J Bowen, Earl and Chris Pick, Glenys and John Roberts, Richard Siebert, Jill Hurley, Stephen Woad, Anthony Longden, Paul and Annette Hallett, Jeff and Wendy Williams, Derek Thomas)*

Free house ~ Licensees Robin Moore and Carlene Bunten ~ Real ale ~ Bar food (12-2, 7-9; 6.30-9.30 Sat) ~ Restaurant ~ (01353) 778537 ~ Children welcome ~ Open 12-3.30, 7-11; 12-4, 6.30-11 Sat; 12-4, 7-10.30 Sun ~ Bedrooms: £55(£55S)(£65B)/£75(£85S) (£110B)

THRIPLOW TL4346 Map 5

Green Man

3 miles from M11 junction 10; A505 towards Royston, then first right; Lower Street; SG8 7RJ

The exterior of this cheery no smoking Victorian pub is painted a striking dark blue, with window boxes and potted plants looking particularly nice against this strong background. The interior is comfortably laid out with a mix of tables and attractive high-backed dining chairs and pews on a flowery red carpet, and shelves full of artefacts on deeply coloured walls. To the right of the bar a cosy little room has comfortable sofas and armchairs, while two arches lead through to a restaurant on the left. Using local produce and served in hearty helpings, the homely bar food includes lunchtime baguettes (from £5), home-made burger (£5.50) and sausage and mash (£6), and daily specials such as sautéed potato, chorizo sausage and spinach salad (£6), pork loin with mustard mash and cider gravy (£9.50) and roast lamb shoulder with minted gravy (£13). In the evening you can mix and match sauces, such as creamy mushroom or port sauce, with your choice of dish, which might be chicken, stuffed pepper or steak and so on (from £8.50). Four regularly changing real ales are likely to be from brewers such as Archers, Dark Star and Nethergate; darts. There are tables and an outdoor heater outside. More reports please. *(Recommended by Mark Farrington, Eric Robinson, Jacqueline Pratt, Gerry and Rosemary Dobson)*

Free house ~ Licensee Ian Parr ~ Real ale ~ Bar food (not Mon or Sun eve) ~ Restaurant ~ (01763) 208855 ~ Children welcome away from the bar ~ Open 12-3, 6-11; closed all day Mon, Sun evening

---

LUCKY DIP

Besides the fully inspected pubs, you might like to try these Lucky Dips recommended to us and described by readers (if you do, please send us reports: www.goodguides.co.uk).

ARRINGTON [TL3250]
Hardwicke Arms SG8 0AH [Ermine Way (A1198)]: Handsome coaching inn built incrementally since 13th c (more recently shrinking to make room for a cul de sac), dark-panelled no smoking dining room, huge central fireplace, decent food from bar snacks to pheasant and marlin, Greene King IPA and

guests such as Batemans and Woodfordes, good friendly service, daily papers; piped music; bedrooms with own bathrooms, handy for Wimpole Hall, open all day *(Michael Dandy, LYM)*

BABRAHAM [TL5150]
George CB2 4AG [High St; just off A1307]: Nicely restored beamed and timbered dining

pub, new landlord emphasising local produce, comfortably refurbished lounge and new no smoking restaurant; heated terrace tables, attractive setting on quiet road *(Adele Summers, Alan Black)*

BARRINGTON [TL3849]

Royal Oak CB2 5RZ [turn off A10 about 3¾ miles SW of M11 junction 11, in Foxton; West Green]: Rambling thatched Tudor pub with tables out overlooking classic village green, heavy low beams and timbers, some new furniture inc leather sofa in one updated area, friendly helpful landlord, prompt service, enjoyable if not cheap food from sandwiches to steak, children's helpings, Adnams, Greene King IPA and Old Speckled Hen and Potton Gold, good coffee, light and airy no smoking dining conservatory; may be piped music; children welcome, open all day Sun *(Michael Dandy, David Barnes, LYM, Jill McLaren)*

BARTON [TL4055]

White Horse CB3 7BG [High St]: Former coaching inn with old-fashioned bare-boards bar and carpeted lounge leading into restaurant, Greene King ales, wide food choice from some interesting sandwiches up, daily papers, pub games and TV; tables on small back terrace and in larger front garden, bedrooms, cl Tues *(Michael Dandy)*

BOURN [TL3256]

☆ *Duke of Wellington* CB3 7SH [signed off B1046 and A1198 W of Cambridge; at N end of village]: Consistently good food cooked with real care and imagination at appealing prices in neat and civilised relaxing dining pub divided by arches and so forth, Adnams and Greene King ales, welcoming young licensees eager to please, some special evenings; piped music; small back terrace *(David Collison, Mr and Mrs D Scott, Richard Atherton, BB, Dr and Mrs T C Dann)*

BOXWORTH [TL3464]

Golden Ball CB3 8LY [High St]: Attractive thatched pub/restaurant recently refurbished and extended, contemporary bar with pine tables on tiles, sizeable restaurant in original core, well presented food inc baguettes, baked potatoes and interesting light dishes, Adnams and Greene King IPA, helpful service; big well kept garden and heated terrace, nice setting, ten bedrooms in new block *(Michael Dandy)*

BRANDON CREEK [TL6091]

☆ *Ship* PE38 0PP [A10 Ely—Downham Market]: Prime summer pub, in lovely spot on Norfolk border at confluence of Great and Little Ouse, plenty of tables out by the moorings; spacious tastefully modernised bar with massive stone masonry in sunken former forge area, big log fire one end, woodburner the other, good choice of enjoyable food, friendly attentive staff, real ales such as Adnams, Buckleys Best and Shepherd Neame Spitfire, interesting old photographs and prints, evening restaurant; bedrooms *(LYM, George Atkinson)*

BROUGHTON [TL2877]

☆ *Crown* PE28 3AY [off A141 opp RAF Wyton; Bridge Rd]: Attractively tucked away opp church (pub owned by village consortium), fresh and airy décor, sturdy furnishings inc nicely set dining end, real ales such as Elgoods Black Dog and good enterprising food, good service; disabled access and facilities; tables out on big stretch of grass behind, cl Mon/ Tues, open all day wknds *(Nick and Ginny Law, BB)*

BUCKDEN [TL1967]

George PE19 5XA [Old Gt North Rd]: Stylish and elegant modern revamp of handsome former coaching inn, wide range of good wines (and choice of champagnes) by the glass, Adnams and a guest ale, log fire, brasserie food all day; large integral boutique, tables out on sheltered pretty terrace, nice bedrooms *(Michael Dandy, Mike and Mary Carter, Michael Sargent, BB, Gerry and Rosemary Dobson)*

☆ *Lion* PE19 5XA [High St]: Partly 15th-c coaching inn, black beams and big inglenook log fire in airy and civilised bow-windowed entrance bar with plush bucket seats, wing armchairs and settees, decent bar food inc good value lunchtime sandwiches, good choice of wines, Greene King IPA and a guest such as Skinners, friendly staff, no music or machines, panelled no smoking back dining room beyond latticed window partition; children welcome, bedrooms *(Michael Dandy, BB, Michael Sargent, David and Ruth Shillitoe, Sarah Flynn, Anthony Double, Gerry and Rosemary Dobson)*

CAMBRIDGE [TL4458]

Baron of Beef CB2 1UF [Bridge St]: Friendly traditional front bar, old wooden furnishings, scrubbed floor, panelling, lots of old photographs, Greene King ales with a guest such as Caledonian 80/- from uncommonly long counter, good choice of wines by the glass, daily papers, all-day bar food, pub games; piped music, TV; tables in small back courtyard, open all day *(Michael Dandy)*

Carlton Arms CB4 2BY [Carlton Way]: Well run local with three or four real ales such as Timothy Taylors Landlord, decent food (not Sun evening), smart easy chairs in no smoking lounge, pool and pub games in bar, dining room; outside tables, open all day wknds and summer *(Keith and Janet Morris)*

☆ *Castle* CB3 0AJ [Castle St]: Large and airy bare-boards pub, several simple and pleasantly decorated rooms, full Adnams ale range and lots of guest beers, wide choice of good value quick pubby food from sandwiches up inc a popular bargain burger, friendly staff, peaceful no smoking area upstairs (downstairs can be noisy, with piped pop music – live jazz Sun night); picnic-sets in good walled back courtyard *(Dr David Cockburn, P and D Carpenter, Michael Dandy, the Didler)*

Clarendon Arms CB1 1JX [Clarendon St]: Quaint partly flagstoned pub with friendly landlord and staff, nice mix of customers, Greene King and guest beers, wide choice of good value food, carpeted dining area, darts, cribbage; simple good value bedrooms, open all day *(Dr David Cockburn)*

Flying Pig CB2 1LQ [Hills Rd]: Individual small local with pig emblems everywhere, Adnams, Fullers London Pride and Greene King Old Speckled Hen, young friendly staff, daily papers, back games room with pool; eclectic piped music; seats outside front and back *(Dr David Cockburn)*

☆ *Kingston Arms* CB1 2NU [Kingston St]: U-shaped pub with some emphasis on the food side (many tables booked for this) inc popular light lunches, thriving atmosphere, fine choice of real ales inc four or five changing guest beers, good choice of wines by the glass, friendly service, no music or children inside; wkdy lunchtime free internet access (two terminals and wireless access); small torch-lit and heated back terrace, open all day Fri-Sun *(Dr David Cockburn, John Wooll, Steve Nye)*

Maypole CB5 8AF [Portugal Pl/Park St]: Welcoming two-bar pub with tasty filling italian food, Adnams, Courage Directors and Charles Wells Bombardier, good value cocktails, prompt friendly service even when crowded with students, big 18th-c print of maypole dancing; fruit machines, darts and TV in public bar; ice-cream hatch for tables outside *(Fiona Davenport-White)*

☆ *Old Spring* CB4 1HB [Ferry Path; car park on Chesterton Rd]: Old-fashioned scrubbed-wood décor, bare boards, gas lighting, lots of old pictures, enjoyable food inc good vegetarian options and Sun roasts, Greene King IPA and Abbot, good coffee and choice of wines by the glass, two log fires, no smoking area inc long back conservatory, summer barbecues; no children *(LYM, Mrs Jane Kingsbury)*

Pickerel CB3 0AF [Magdelene St]: Low-beamed two-room local with cosy corners, friendly staff, good choice of wines by the glass, real ales, limited lunchtime food inc good baguettes; heated courtyard *(Rosanna Luke, Matt Curzon)*

Vine CB1 1DB [East Rd]: Fairly recently refurbished in City wine bar style, enjoyable food, good beer and wines *(Bob Sadler)*

Volunteer CB2 2EX [Trumpington Rd]: Recently refurbished, with good choice of enjoyable food, good quick service by helpful cheerful staff; tables outside *(Sarah Flynn)*

CASTOR [TL1298]
Royal Oak PE5 7AX [Peterborough Rd, off A47]: Pretty beamed and part-thatched local, partly 16th-c, with Bass, Tetleys and guest beers such as Adnams Broadside and Timothy Taylors Landlord, bar food from simple sandwiches up, chatty licensees, open fires and several small traditional bar areas; picnic-sets out in front, quiet attractive village *(LYM, Ben and Helen Ingram)*

CHATTERIS [TL3986]
Cross Keys PE16 6BA [Market Hill]: Welcoming and attractive 16th-c coaching inn opp church in fenland market town, friendly service and atmosphere, good value food in bar and candlelit restaurant inc good Sun lunches, long bar with fireside armchairs, Greene King beers, inexpensive wine, tea and coffee; pleasant back courtyard, comfortable

bedrooms *(Robert Turnham, Christine and Neil Townend)*

CLAYHITHE [TL5064]
Bridge Hotel CB5 9HZ [Clayhithe Rd]: Well run no smoking Chef & Brewer dining pub with small bar area, beams and timbers, attentive service; picturesque spot by River Cam with pretty waterside garden, comfortable bedroom extension *(LYM, Trevor Swindells, Peter and Liz Holmes)*

CONINGTON [TL3266]
☆ *White Swan* CB3 8LN [signed off A14 (was A604) Cambridge—Huntingdon; Elsworth Rd]: Attractive and quietly placed country local with quick friendly service, Greene King IPA and Old Speckled Hen and guest beers tapped from the cask, good value straightforward food from baps, generous baguettes and baked potatoes up, cheerful traditional bar, neat eating areas inc no smoking ones on right, games inc bar billiards and darts on left; good big front garden with terrace, play area and play house, open all day *(Michael Dandy)*

CROYDON [TL3149]
☆ *Queen Adelaide* SG8 0DN [off A1198; High St]: Big beamed dining area very popular for its wide food range inc upmarket dishes, mainstream real ales, impressive array of spirits, prompt service, standing timbers dividing off part with settees, banquettes and stools; garden, play area *(P and D Carpenter)*

DRY DRAYTON [TL3862]
Black Horse CB3 8DA [signed off A428 (was A45) W of Cambridge; Park St, opp church]: Low-beamed village pub with central woodburner in compact carpeted bar, tiled floor in good-sized no smoking restaurant, Adnams Bitter and Broadside and Greene King IPA, reasonably priced usual food from good baguettes up, prompt cheerful service, pool in games area; piped music; tables on pretty back terrace and neat sheltered lawn *(Michael Dandy, BB, Keith and Janet Morris, Ian and Nita Cooper, P and D Carpenter)*

DUXFORD [TL4746]
☆ *John Barleycorn* CB2 4PP [handy for M11 junction 10; signed off A505 E at Volvo junction]: Thatch, shutters, low beams, charming old-world furnishings, prints and china, gentle lighting, good reasonably priced food from open sandwiches up all day (cooked to order, so may be a wait), nice staff, Greene King IPA and Abbot and a guest beer, decent wines; may be piped music; tables out among flowers, open all day, pleasantly simple beamed bedrooms *(David Twitchett, Mike and Margaret Banks, B N F and M Parkin, Erica Castle, LYM, Paul and Marion Watts)*

EATON SOCON [TL1658]
☆ *White Horse* PE19 8EL [B4128]: Rambling, comfortable and interestingly furnished low-beamed rooms dating from 13th c, nice high-backed traditional settles around big inglenook log fire in end room, relaxing atmosphere, enjoyable reasonably priced fresh food from sandwiches and baked potatoes up, Flowers IPA and Original and Wadworths 6X, decent

wines, quick friendly service, daily papers, pub games; play area in back garden, children in eating areas *(Michael Dandy, LYM, Marion and Bill Cross, Conor McGaughey)*

ELLINGTON [TL1671]

☆ *Mermaid* PE28 0AB [High St]: Properly pubby atmosphere, friendly and chatty, in comfortable old bow-windowed local's bar and puce-walled dining areas, good traditional food, real ales (perhaps one at bargain price) such as Caledonian Deuchars IPA, Cotleigh Tawny and Fullers London Pride, helpful service; faint piped music; picnic-sets in pleasant garden with terrace between the quaint building and the church – lovely spot *(BB, Margaret and Roy Randle)*

ELSWORTH [TL3163]

☆ *George & Dragon* CB3 8JQ [off A14 NW of Cambridge, via Boxworth, or off A428]: Sympathetically refurbished old no smoking dining pub, wide choice of enjoyable generous food from sandwiches and baguettes up (popular OAP wkdy lunchtime discount card), attentive helpful service, Greene King IPA, Ruddles County and Old Speckled Hen, decent wines, neatly refurbished carpeted rooms with some stripped masonry, plenty of ornaments and open fire, light and airy garden room; piped music; disabled access (step down to lavatories), nice terraces, play area in garden, attractive village *(Michael Dandy, Michael and Jenny Back, LYM, M and GR, Dr Phil Putwain)*

Poacher CB3 8JS [Brockley Rd]: Unpretentious 17th-c thatched and beamed pub with polished pine and neat pews and settles on bare boards, lots of carving inc nicely done birds on bar front, nice pictures, Adnams Broadside, Greene King IPA and Old Speckled Hen and Shepherd Neame Spitfire, cheerful staff, popular traditional food from baguettes and baked potatoes up, no smoking area; piped music; plenty of tables in pretty garden with play area and barbecues, good walks *(BB, Michael Alcott, Michael Sargent)*

ELTON [TL0894]

☆ *Crown* PE8 6RQ [Duck St]: New chef/landlord doing good food (not Sun evening or Mon) from baguettes up inc some interesting dishes in carefully rebuilt thatched stone pub, pleasant layout with big log fire, more formal no smoking conservatory restaurant, welcoming landlady and staff, good changing ales such as Goffs Jouster, Greene King IPA and Woodfordes Great Eastern, well chosen wines; tables out on terrace opp green of beautiful small village *(Michael and Jenny Back)*

ELY [TL5479]

Cutter CB7 4BN [Annesdale, off Station Rd just towards centre from A142 roundabout; or walk S along Riverside Walk from Maltings car park]: Refurbished under new management, enjoyable generous food in no smoking carpeted dining bar, Greene King real ales, fairly lively bare-boards main bar; plenty of tables outside, lovely riverside setting *(Rev John Hibberd, LYM)*

FEN DRAYTON [TL3468]

☆ *Three Tuns* CB4 5SJ [off A14 NW of Cambridge at Fenstanton; High St]: Well preserved thatched pub in charming village, heavy Tudor beams and timbers, inglenook fireplaces, tiled-floor bar, comfortable settles and other seats, well laid out no smoking dining end (children welcome here), Greene King IPA and Abbot or Old Speckled Hen, sensibly placed darts, good value usual bar food (not Sun evening) from lunchtime sandwiches to steaks; piped music; tables on covered terrace and neat back lawn, good play area, open all day *(Mike and Heather Watson, Martin and Pauline Jennings, Michael Dandy, Christopher Turner, Gill and Keith Croxton, LYM, Comus and Sarah Elliott, Mrs Hazel Rainer)*

GIRTON [TL4262]

☆ *Old Crown* CB3 0QD [High St]: Attractive thatched 1930s restaurant/pub, roomy and popular, with good value generous food (best to book wknds), well chosen menu with fish emphasis, Greene King IPA, good wine choice, prompt smiling service, real fires, antique pine on polished boards; children welcome, disabled facilities, pleasant terrace overlooking countryside *(Eric George, Keith and Janet Morris)*

GODMANCHESTER [TL2470]

White Hart PE29 2BW [Cambridge Rd]: Roomy pub with enjoyable traditional food, good-sized helpings, friendly attentive staff, good beer range inc Timothy Taylors Landlord, pleasant atmosphere and décor *(W K Wood)*

GRANTCHESTER [TL4355]

Blue Ball CB3 9NQ [Broadway]: Small bare-boards village local, said to be the oldest in the area, log fire, Adnams and a guest beer, friendly landlord, traditional games; tables on small terrace with lovely views to Grantchester meadows a short stroll away, nice village *(Ian Frowe)*

Green Man CB3 9NF [High St]: Heavily beamed pub dating from 16th c, log fire and individual furnishings, good choice of ales such as Adnams and Greene King, good value food, friendly staff, no smoking dining room; disabled facilities, tables out behind *(Andrei, LYM)*

Red Lion CB3 9NF [High St]: Comfortable and spacious family food pub with quick friendly service, wide menu inc lots of nice puddings, real ales such as Greene King Old Speckled Hen, good wine choice; sheltered terrace, good-sized lawn *(LYM, John Saville, J A West)*

Rupert Brooke CB3 9NQ [Broadway; junction Coton rd with Cambridge—Trumpington rd]: Welcoming open-plan pub with enjoyable food from good lunchtime sandwiches and light dishes up, helpful staff, Greene King Old Speckled Hen and Charles Wells Bombardier, good choice of wines by the glass, central log fire in comfortable beamed bar, family eating area and smarter sympathetic dining extension; piped music *(Sarah Flynn, Tony and Margaret Cross)*

GRAVELEY [TL2463]
Three Horseshoes PE19 6PL [High St]:
Pleasantly furnished long narrow bar with two
fish tanks, good choice of usual food from
baguettes to steaks, Adnams and Theakstons,
good coffee, helpful licensees, low-beamed
restaurant; piped music; a few tables outside
(Michael Dandy)

GREAT CHISHILL [TL4239]
☆ *Pheasant* SG8 8SR [follow Heydon signpost
from B1039 in village]: Good freshly made
food using local produce in popular split-level
flagstoned pub with beams, timbering and
some elaborately carved though modern seats
and settles, welcoming landlady and friendly
service, real ales such as Adnams, Courage Best
and Directors and Theakstons, good choice of
wines by the glass, small no smoking dining
room, darts, cribbage, dominoes; children
welcome, charming back garden with small
play area *(LYM, Mrs Margo Finlay,
Jörg Kasprowski, Ross and Christine Lovedary)*

GREAT STAUGHTON [TL]
☆ *Tavern on the Green* PE19 5DG [The Green;
B645/B661]: Now under same ownership as
Snooty Fox at Lowick (see Northants main
entries), with comfortably up-to-date and
uncluttered open-plan layout, good simply
cooked fresh food inc fish from display and
aberdeen angus steaks cut to order,
sandwiches, ploughman's and appealing light
dishes too, good range of wines by the glass,
Greene King ales, polite service, a few
children's toys; unobtrusive piped music;
children welcome, some picnic-sets outside
(Michael Dandy, BB)

GUYHIRN [TF3903]
☆ *Oliver Twist* PE13 4EA [follow signs from
A47/A141 junction S of Wisbech]:
Comfortable open-plan lounge with good
generous home-made food from crusty
baguettes to steaks, cheerful attentive service,
interesting changing real ales, big open fires,
neat sturdy furnishings, no smoking restaurant;
may be piped music; six bedrooms
(Barry Collett, BB, Phil and Jane Hodson)

HADDENHAM [TL4675]
Three Kings CB6 3XD [Station Rd]: Popular
village pub, well run and friendly, with nice
staff, particularly well kept Greene King IPA
and Old Speckled Hen, enjoyable varied home-
made food with fresh veg *(K Christensen)*

HEMINGFORD ABBOTS [TL2870]
Axe & Compass PE28 9AH [High St]: 15th-c
two-bar thatched pub with flagstones and
inglenook seats, contemporary fittings in
extension dining areas (one no smoking),
friendly service, Fullers London Pride, Greene
King IPA and Wychwood Hobgoblin Mild,
good choice of wines by the glass, good value
pubby lunchtime food from baguettes up,
wider evening menu, pool and bar billiards;
piped music, TV, quiz or live music nights;
garden tables, pretty village *(Michael Dandy)*

HILDERSHAM [TL5448]
☆ *Pear Tree* CB1 6BU [off A1307 N of Linton]:
Friendly landlady in spotless and airy Victorian
pub with odd crazy-paved floor and plenty of

curios, good value changing home cooking
from ploughman's up, Greene King ales, daily
papers, board games; children welcome, tables
and aviary in garden behind, picturesque
thatched village, cl Mon lunchtime *(BB,
Stephen Woad)*

HOLME [TL1907]
Admiral Wells PE7 3PH [Station Rd]:
Picturesque and well refurbished, with three
seating areas, cheerful friendly atmosphere,
over half a dozen changing real ales, obliging
service, enjoyable reasonably priced bar food,
conservatory; lively summer beer festival,
tables out on gravel and in pleasant side garden
(Inter-City trains hurtling by); open all day
wknds *(Sarah Knight)*

HOLYWELL [TL3370]
Old Ferry Boat PE27 4TG [signed off A1123]:
Much refurbished partly thatched chain pub in
lovely setting, low beams, open fires and side
areas, dozens of carpenter's tools, window
seats overlooking Great Ouse, Greene King
IPA, Ruddles County and Abbot, decent wines
by the glass, good coffee, good no smoking
eating areas (reasonably priced food all day in
summer); quiet piped music, games; children
welcome, plenty of tables and cocktail parasols
on front terrace and riverside lawn, moorings,
bedrooms, open all day wknds
*(Michael Dandy, Robert Turnham, LYM,
J Stickland, Peter and Jean Dowson)*

HORNINGSEA [TL4962]
☆ *Plough & Fleece* CB5 9JG [just NE of
Cambridge: first slip-road off A14 heading E
after A10, then left; or B1047 Fen Ditton road
off A1303; High St]: Rambling low-beamed
country pub with good pubby food under
newish tenants, some high-backed settles and
other sturdily old-fashioned wooden
furnishings, dark cool recesses in summer, log
fires in winter, more modern no smoking back
dining room and comfortable conservatory,
Greene King ales; garden tables
(Robert Turnham, LYM)

HOUGHTON [TL2872]
Three Horseshoes PE28 2BE [The Green]:
Cosy village pub with low black beams and
inglenook, good-sized L-shaped eating area
with no smoking conservatory, Greene King
ales with a guest such as Timothy Taylors
Landlord, fine choice of wines by the glass,
pubby lunchtime food from baguettes and
baked potatoes to lots of fish, different evening
menu, friendly service, pool in small second
bar, darts; quiet piped music; tables outside,
next to Houghton watermill (NT) and Ouse
walks, bedrooms, open all day
(Michael Dandy, LYM)
Three Jolly Butchers PE28 2AD [A1123,
Wyton]: Log fire in L-shaped beamed pub with
leather sofas as well as tables and chairs,
Adnams, Fullers London Pride and Greene
King IPA and Old Speckled Hen, friendly
attentive service, usual food from baguettes
and baked potatoes up (not Sun/Mon
evenings), daily papers; piped music may be
loud, TV; children and dogs allowed in one
area, pool table on covered back terrace, huge

back garden with play area and occasional barbecues, pretty village *(Michael Dandy)*

HUNTINGDON [TL2371]

☆ *George* PE29 3AB [George St]: Relaxed, friendly and comfortable hotel lounge bar, generous reasonably priced sandwiches and simple bar meals, wider choice in brasserie, Greene King IPA and Abbot, good choice of wines by the glass, good coffee (or tea and pastries), helpful staff; magnificent galleried central courtyard, comfortable bedrooms *(Michael Dandy, LYM)*

LINTON [TL5546]

Dog & Duck CB1 6HS: Picturesque traditional thatched 16th-c pub, low beams and log fire, Greene King ales, welcoming staff, popular food from baguettes up *(Neil and Sally Onley)*

LITTLE WILBRAHAM [TL5458]

☆ *Hole in the Wall* CB1 5JY [off A14 at Stow cum Quy turn, turning right off A1303 Newmarket rd; High St]: New licensees bringing new life and very good if not cheap food to appealing 15th-c pub, heavy beams, timbering and stripped brickwork, log fire in big fireplace, charming service, good choice of wines by the glass, real ales such as Courage Best and Elgoods Golden Newt, restaurant; sturdy seats and tables in pretty garden, interesting fenland walks nearby, cl Mon *(P and D Carpenter)*

MARHOLM [TF1402]

Fitzwilliam Arms PE6 7HX [Stamford Rd]: Handsome and spotlessly kept thatched stone-built Vintage Inn, its rambling three-room bar comfortably opened up and modernised, wide choice of good value food, fine range of wines by the glass, efficient service; good big garden *(P Tailyour)*

NEEDINGWORTH [TL3571]

☆ *Pike & Eel* PE27 4TW [pub signed from A1123; Overcote Rd]: Marvellous peaceful riverside location with spacious lawns and small marina; plush bar opening into room with easy chairs, settees and big open fire, civilised eating area (also separate smart restaurant) in light and airy glass-walled block overlooking water, boats and swans, immaculate service, Adnams Broadside, Greene King IPA and Woodfordes Wherry, good coffee and wines; children welcome, clean simple bedrooms, good breakfast *(Michael Dandy, LYM, Mike and Mary Carter)*

OAKINGTON [TL4064]

White Horse CB4 5AB [Longstanton Rd]: Friendly pub with something of a mexican feel, good wine choice; appealing outside area *(Sarah Knight)*

PETERBOROUGH [TL1897]

Coalheavers Arms PE2 9BH [Park St, Woodston]: Small friendly traditional flagstoned alehouse, Milton and guest beers, farm cider, good range of continental imports and malt whiskies; pleasant garden, cl Mon-Weds lunchtimes, open all day wknds *(the Didler)*

Goodbarns Yard PE1 5DD [St Johns St, behind Passport Office]: Friendly two-room local popular for its Adnams, Black Sheep and changing guest beers tapped from the cask, annual beer festival, enjoyable wkdy bar lunches, big-screen sports TV, big no smoking conservatory; open all day *(the Didler)*

Palmerston Arms PE2 9PA [Oundle Rd]: Partly 17th-c stone-built pub with Batemans and lots of guest ales tapped from the cask, good choice of malt whiskies, good pork pies, welcoming service, old-fashioned furnishings and décor in carpeted lounge, tiled-floor public bar, no music or machines; steps down into pub, steps to lavatory; picnic-sets in small garden, open all day *(the Didler)*

ST IVES [TL3171]

White Hart PE27 5AH [Sheep Market]: Small local with enjoyable sensibly priced home cooking, warm friendly service *(Robert Turnham)*

STAPLEFORD [TL4651]

Rose CB2 5DG [London Rd]: Wide range of good plain well presented food in family-friendly dining pub, prompt smiling service, tap room on left of small bar with good ales such as Adnams and Fullers London Pride, reasonably priced wines, nicely decorated lounge with low beams, big inglenook log fire and roomy adjacent dining area; picnic-sets out on grass *(Stephen Woad)*

STILTON [TL1689]

Stilton Cheese PE7 3RP [signed off A1; North St]: Enjoyable food from sandwiches up inc lots of fish; Tetleys and guest beers such as Newby Wyke Bear Island and Timothy Taylors Landlord, decent wines, welcoming staff, interesting old interior with log fire in unpretentious central bar, good tables in two rooms off (one no smoking), and separate two-room restaurant; tables out in back garden with sheltered decking, bedrooms *(Michael Dandy)*

STRETHAM [TL5072]

Lazy Otter CB6 3LU [Elford Closes, off A10 S of Stretham roundabout]: Big rambling nicely furnished family pub in fine spot on the Great Ouse, with good views from waterside conservatory and tables in big garden with neat terrace; good value generous food, friendly attentive staff, real ales such as Greene King and Nethergate, warm fire; piped music; bedroom annexe, open all day *(Frank W Gadbois, LYM)*

Red Lion CB6 3LD [High St (off A10)]: Neat village pub popular for wide daily-changing choice of good generous traditional food inc children's and Sun lunch, friendly attentive service, five good real ales, solid pine furniture and old village photographs in lively locals' bar, marble-topped tables in pleasant no smoking dining conservatory; children welcome, picnic-sets and barbecues in garden, attractive and comfortable bedrooms, open all day bank hols *(Brian Root, M and GR, Keith and Janet Morris, Andy Chapman)*

SWAVESEY [TL3668]

White Horse CB4 5QG [signed off A14 (ex A604) NW of Cambridge; Market St]: Welcoming village pub with Caledonian Deuchars IPA, guest beers such as Rudgate

Battleaxe and Wychwood Hobgoblin, and good soft drinks choice, good value generous pub food, quick friendly service, spacious nicely decorated lounge, central woodburner, no smoking dining area beyond, games, TV and log fire in attractively traditional public bar; children allowed, garden with play area, open all day wknds *(Michael Dandy, Keith and Janet Morris)*

UFFORD [TF0904]

Olde White Hart PE9 3BH [back rd Peterborough—Stamford, just S of B1443]: Recently refurbished 17th-c village pub brewing its own Ufford ales such as Idle Hour and Setting Sun, others such as Adnams and Oakham JHB, enjoyable pubby food all day, good short wine list, log fire and railway memorabilia in busy flagstoned bar, back dining area, attractive new conservatory link to new barn bedroom block; informal service; children welcome, big garden with terrace and play area, open all day *(Ray and Winifred Halliday, LYM)*

WANSFORD [TL0799]

☆ *Haycock* PE8 6JA [just off A1 W of Peterborough]: Handsome old coaching inn greatly extended and kept up to date as smart hotel and conference centre, useful break for enjoyable bar food all day from good sandwiches and ciabattas up, helpful staff, Adnams, Bass and a guest beer, good wine choice, variety of relaxing seating areas with plenty of character, big log fire, no smoking restaurant with airy conservatory; children in eating areas, attractive courtyard and garden near river, dogs allowed in bar and comfortable bedrooms, open all day *(Michael Dandy, Dr and Mrs R G J Telfer, LYM, Eithne Dandy, Eric Robinson, Jacqueline Pratt, David Glynne-Jones)*

Paper Mills PE8 6JB [London Rd]: Front bar with two woodburners, no smoking eating area, Bass, Hancocks Hadrian & Border and a guest such as Fullers Discovery, usual bar food inc good baguettes and baked potatoes, good friendly service, separate menu for larger back restaurant; piped music; tables out in front and on back terrace *(Michael Dandy)*

WARESLEY [TL2454]

☆ *Duncombe Arms* SG19 3BS [Eltisley Rd (B1040, 5 miles S of A428)]: Comfortable and welcoming old pub, long main bar, fire one end, good range of good value generous wholesome food from lunchtime sandwiches up, consistently well kept Greene King ales, good choice of wines by the glass, good service, no smoking back room and restaurant; occasional live music; picnic-sets in small shrub-sheltered garden *(BB, John Westwood, Michael Dandy, Margaret and Roy Randle, Gerald and Valerie Pepper, JWAC)*

WICKEN [TL5670]

Maids Head CB7 5XR [High St]: Neatly kept dining pub with friendly local atmosphere, real ales such as Adnams, fair-priced wines, no smoking restaurant; quiet piped music; tables outside, lovely village-green setting, handy for Wicken Fen nature reserve (NT) *(Brian Root)*

Post Office address codings confusingly give the impression that some pubs are in Cambridgeshire, when they're really in the Leicestershire or Midlands groups of counties (which is where we list them).

Cheshire

Cheshire hosts an enjoyable range of pubs, with a good diversity of strengths, and each place expressing its own robustly distinct character – though a warm welcome is a Cheshire pub trademark. This is home territory for the Brunning & Price group, who are so strong in the field of effortlessly chatty dining pubs. So it's fitting that it's one of their flagships, the Grosvenor Arms in Aldford, with its sensibly imaginative and sensibly priced menu, that is Cheshire Dining Pub of the Year. Indeed, another of their pubs, the Dysart Arms at Bunbury, was close in the running. Back in the *Guide* after quite a few years, the Roebuck at Mobberley is now well worth knowing for its well liked thoughtfully prepared food in a relaxed traditional setting. The enthusiastically run Bhurtpore at Aston is a beacon with its fantastic range of drinks and real ales, and the Dog at Peover Heath, though largely a dining pub, gets a new beer award this year in acknowledgement of its small but interesting range of ales, with Hydes at a remarkable £1.60 a pint. Drinks prices here are well below the national average, with the flourishing regional brewers Hydes, Robinsons and Thwaites all competing on price. Pubs currently showing strongly in the Lucky Dip section at the end of the chapter include the Blue Bell at Bell o' th' Hill, Combermere Arms at Burleydam, Bear & Billet and Mill in Chester, Alvanley Arms at Cotebrook, Duke of Portland at Lach Dennis, Harp near Neston, Highwayman at Rainow, Swettenham Arms at Swettenham and Boot at Willington.

ALDFORD   SJ4259   Map 7

Grosvenor Arms ★ ⑪ ♀ ◨

B5130 Chester—Wrexham; CH3 6HJ

Cheshire Dining Pub of the Year

As this bustling place is so popular it's worth visiting just outside peak times as they do serve food all day, otherwise it's best to book. A buoyantly chatty atmosphere fills its spacious open-plan interior, with good solid pieces of traditional furniture, plenty of interesting pictures, and attractive lighting adding a personal feel. The huge no smoking panelled library area has tall bookshelves lining one wall, and lots of substantial tables well spaced on the handsomely boarded floor. Lovely on summer evenings, the airy terracotta-floored no smoking conservatory has lots of gigantic low hanging flowering baskets and chunky pale wood garden furniture. This opens on to a large elegant suntrap terrace (delightful for a summer evening drink), and a neat lawn with picnic-sets, young trees and a tractor. A particularly comprehensive range of drinks includes around 16 wines (largely new world and all served by the glass) a tempting range of whiskies (including 100 malts, 30 bourbons, and 30 irish whiskeys) as well as Flowers IPA, Caledonian Deuchars IPA, Weetwood and a couple of guests from brewers such as Beartown and St Austell. The menu is not ridiculously elaborate; it's sensibly imaginative, well balanced and fairly priced with something for everyone: sandwiches (from £4.50), celeriac and potato soup (£4.50), duck rillette with orange marmalade (£5.95), tempura-battered cod with tartare sauce (£6.25), wild mushroom risotto (£8.75), chilli or steak burger topped with mozzarella and bacon (£8.95), sweet potato and vegetable curry (£9.95), grilled salmon with saffron mussels and fennel mash (£13.45), 10oz rump steak (£14.45), side orders (from £2.50), and puddings such as chocolate chip pudding with chocolate sauce or baked lemon and raspberry cheesecake (£4.95). Service is friendly, attentive and reliable. They keep a good selection of board games. *(Recommended by R G Stollery, Revd D Glover, J S Burn, Clive Watkin, Paul Boot, Mrs Maricar Jagger, Therese Flanagan, Bruce and Sharon Eden, Derek and Sylvia Stephenson, Steve Whalley)*

Brunning & Price ~ Managers Gary Kidd and Jeremy Brunning ~ Real ale ~ Bar food (12-10(9 Sun and bank hols)) ~ (01244) 620228 ~ Children welcome till 7pm, no prams or pushchairs ~ Dogs allowed in bar ~ Open 11.30-11; 12-10.30 Sun

ASTBURY SJ8461 Map 7
Egerton Arms 🛏
Village signposted off A34 S of Congleton; CW12 4RQ

Handy if you're looking for a break from the M6, this friendly village inn (about 15 minutes from the motorway) is in a pretty spot overlooking an attractive old church. Rambling round the bar, the cream-painted rooms have a cheery family-run atmosphere. Walls sport the odd piece of armour, shelves of books, and mementoes of the Sandow Brothers, who performed as 'the World's Strongest Youths' (one of them was the landlady's father). In summer dried flowers fill the big fireplace; most of the pub is no smoking. Robinsons Double Hop, Hartleys XB and Unicorn are well kept on handpump; piped music, fruit machine, TV. Straightforward reasonably priced bar meals could include soup (£2.75), sandwiches (from £3.25), sausage and chips (£4), steak and kidney pudding, battered haddock or vegetable stroganoff (£6.50). They also do OAP lunches Mon-Fri (two courses £5, three £6), as well as children's meals (£3.25). Out in front, you'll find a few well placed tables, and a play area with a wooden fort. Despite the large car park you might struggle to get a place Sunday lunchtime. More reports please. *(Recommended by Dr D J and Mrs S C Walker, Liz Blackadder, K M Crook)*

Robinsons ~ Tenants Alan and Grace Smith ~ Real ale ~ Bar food (11.30-2, 6.30-9) ~ Restaurant ~ (01260) 273946 ~ Children welcome away from bar ~ Open 11.30-11; 12-3, 6.45-11 Sun ~ Bedrooms: £40S/£60S

ASTON SJ6147 Map 7
Bhurtpore ★ ♀ 🍺
Off A530 SW of Nantwich; in village follow Wrenbury signpost; CW5 8DQ

You're bound to feel completely spoilt for choice when it comes to ordering a drink at this enthusiastically run red brick freehouse. Each year, over 1,000 different superbly kept real ales – anything from Moorhouses to Wentworth – pass through the 11 handpumps. They also stock dozens of unusual bottled beers and fruit beers, a great many bottled ciders and perries, over 100 different whiskies and carefully selected soft drinks, and have a good wine list. If you're a very keen real ale enthusiast it's worth going during their summer beer festival. The pub takes its unusual name from the town in India, where a local landowner, Lord Combermere, won a battle, and in the carpeted lounge bar a collection of exotic artefacts has an indian influence, with one turbaned statue behind the counter proudly sporting any sunglasses left behind by customers; also good local period photographs, and some attractive furniture. Tables in the comfortable public bar are reserved for people not eating; several no smoking areas; darts, dominoes, cribbage, pool, TV and fruit machine. At lunchtime and early weekday evenings the atmosphere is cosy and civilised, and on weekends, when it gets packed, the cheery staff cope superbly. The enjoyable menu has snacks (not Friday or Saturday night) such as sandwiches (from £2.65, hot filled baguettes £3.95) and sausage, egg and chips (£4.95), as well as cheese and leek cakes with creamy dijon sauce (£8.25), a choice of five different tasty curries (from £8.25), steak and kidney pie (£8.50) and steaks (from £10.95), with daily changing specials such as black pudding on sweet potato mash with madeira sauce (£4.75) and monkfish in red wine sauce with mushrooms and bacon (£10.95), as well as puddings such as banoffi pie with toffee sauce (£3.95). *(Recommended by Andy Chetwood, Rick Capper, Dr B and Mrs P B Baker, Sue Holland, Dave Webster, Jeremy King, the Didler, John and Helen Rushton, Martin Grosberg)*

Free house ~ Licensee Simon George ~ Real ale ~ Bar food (12-9) ~ Restaurant ~
(01270) 780917 ~ Children welcome in dining room till 8pm ~ Dogs allowed in bar ~
Folk session third Thurs ~ Open 12-2.30(3 Sat), 6.30-11.30(12 Fri, Sat); 12-11 Sun

BARTHOMLEY   SJ7752   Map 7

White Lion ㉕ ★ £

**A mile from M6 junction 16; from exit roundabout take B5078 N towards Alsager, then
Barthomley signposted on left; CW2 5PG**

We're hoping that a tidy up at this lovely old 17th-c black and white thatched place
won't detract from its unpretentious charm. Up till now the main bar has kept a
lovely timeless feel, with its blazing open fire, heavy low oak beams dating back to
Stuart times, attractively moulded black panelling, Cheshire watercolours and prints
on the walls, latticed windows and thick wobbly old tables. Up some steps, a second
room has another welcoming open fire, more oak panelling, a high-backed winged
settle, a paraffin lamp hinged to the wall, and shove-ha'penny, cribbage and
dominoes; local societies make good use of a third room. Outside, seats and picnic-
sets on the cobbles have a charming view of the attractive village, and the early
15th-c red sandstone church of St Bertiline across the road is well worth a visit. Very
good value lunchtime food includes sandwiches (from £4.25), sausage and mash,
fresh salmon, beef and yorkshire pudding (£5.95) and ploughman's (£6.50). It's best
to arrive early on weekends to be sure of a table. Well kept real ales on handpump
include Marstons Bitter and Pedigree, Mansfield and a couple of guests such as
Everards Tiger and Jennings Snecklifter. *(Recommended by Leslie G Smith, Edward
Mirzoeff, Dave Braisted, Sue Holland, Dave Webster, G K Smale, Dr and Mrs A K Clarke,
the Didler, MLR, Jo Lilley, Simon Calvert, Dr and Mrs M E Wilson, John Saul, Philip and
Cheryl Hill, Roger Thornington, John and Yvonne Davies, Jack Clark, Simon Jones, Peter and
Gill Helps, Rob Stevenson, Paul Humphreys, Simon and Sally Small, Richard Smith, Clare Rosier)*

Union Pub Company ~ Tenant Laura Cowdliffe ~ Real ale ~ Bar food (lunchtime only) ~
(01270) 882242 ~ Children welcome with restrictions ~ Dogs welcome ~ Open 11.30-11;
12-10.30 Sun

BICKLEY MOSS   SJ5650   Map 7

Cholmondeley Arms ♀

**Cholmondeley; A49 5½ miles N of Whitchurch; the owners would like us to list them
under Cholmondeley Village, but as this is rarely located on maps we have mentioned
the nearest village which appears more often; SY14 8HN**

The cross-shaped high-ceilinged bar, high gothic windows, huge old radiators and
old school desks on a gantry above the bar refer back to this imaginatively
converted building's past as a schoolhouse. An eclectic mix of seats runs from cane
and bentwood to pews and carved oak settles, and the patterned paper on the
shutters matches the curtains. There's a stag's head over one of the side arches, an
open fire and masses of Victorian portraits and military pictures; piped music and
no smoking area. Generously served bar food includes lunchtime sandwiches
(£4.95) and steak baguettes (£7.50), stuffed pancakes (£7.25) and lasagne (£8.95),
with daily specials such as watercress soup (£3.95), baked prawns in sour cream
and garlic (£5.50), steak and kidney pie (£8.75), wild mushroom stroganoff
(£8.95), fishcakes with hollandaise (£9.50), leg of lamb with red wine gravy and
garlic mash (£10.95) and cod from Whitby (£11.95). Adnams, Marstons Pedigree,
Weetwood and a guest from the local Woodlands are well kept on handpump
alongside around eight interesting and reasonably priced wines by the glass, which
are listed on a blackboard. There are seats outside on the sizeable lawn, and more
in front overlooking the quiet road. The pub is handy for Cholmondeley Castle
Gardens. For a pub that has done so very well in previous editions we were
surprised to receive a handful of disappointed reports, but we're hoping this was
just a blip. *(Recommended by Ray and Winifred Halliday, Alistair and Kay Butler,
Rob and Catherine Dunster, Mrs P J Carroll, Richard Cole, Mike and Mary Carter, A G Roby,
Peter Neate, Susan Brookes, Richard Smith)*

Free house ~ Licensee Carolyn Ross-Lowe ~ Real ale ~ Bar food (12-2.30, 6.30-10) ~
(01829) 720300 ~ Children welcome ~ Dogs welcome ~ Open 10-3, 6-11; 12-3, 6-10.30
Sun ~ Bedrooms: £50S(£50B)/£70S(£70B)

BUNBURY   SJ5758   Map 7
Dysart Arms 🍴 ♀ 🏮
Bowes Gate Road; village signposted off A51 NW of Nantwich; and from A49 S of
Tarporley – coming this way, coming in on northernmost village access road, bear left in
village centre; CW6 9PH

This civilised dining pub is just the place for a relaxed chatty meal. An
immaculately kept series of well laid out knocked-through cream-walled rooms
rambles around the pleasantly lit central bar, furnished with an attractive variety of
well spaced sturdy wooden tables and chairs, a couple of tall filled bookcases, a
small amount of carefully chosen bric-a-brac, properly lit pictures and good winter
fires. Under deep venetian red ceilings, some areas have red and black tiles, some
stripped boards and some carpet. They've lowered the ceiling in the more
restaurant end room (with its book-lined back wall), and there are lots of plants
on the window sills. Service is efficient and friendly, and most of the pub is no
smoking. From a changing menu, food is tasty, just imaginative enough, attractively
presented, and fairly priced: soup (£3.95), sandwiches (from £4.50), ploughman's
(£6.95), leek and smoked haddock tartlet with welsh rarebit (£5.95), spinach and
ricotta lasagne (£8.95), steak, kidney and ale pie or battered haddock, chips and
mushy peas (£9.95), grilled rib-eye steak (£13.95), puddings such as sticky toffee
pudding with butterscotch sauce or chocolate and orange crème brûlée with
shortbread (£4.75) and cheeseboards from four British dairies (£6.50). Thwaites
and Weetwood and a couple of guests such as Humpty Dumpty and Phoenix
Arizona are very well kept on handpump, alongside a good selection of ten wines
by the glass, around 20 malts and fresh apple juice. Sturdy wooden tables on the
terrace and picnic sets on the lawn in the neatly kept slightly elevated garden are
lovely in summer, with views of the splendid church at the end of the pretty village,
and the distant Peckforton Hills beyond. *(Recommended by Revd D Glover, Bruce and
Sharon Eden, John Kane, Mrs P J Carroll, Sue Holland, Dave Webster, J S Burn, Clive Watkin,
Gwyn and Anne Wake, Ann and Tony Bennett-Hughes, Dennis Jones, JWAC, Dave Irving,
Dr D Scott, H and P Cate, Steve Whalley, Joyce and Maurice Cottrell, Selwyn Roberts,
Gerry and Rosemary Dobson, A Darroch Harkness, Rob Stevenson, Mr Tarpey, Richard Smith,
Mr and Mrs Gerry Price, Dr Phil Putwain)*

Brunning & Price ~ Managers Darren and Elizabeth Snell ~ Real ale ~ Bar food (12-9.30
(9 Sun)) ~ (01829) 260183 ~ No children under 10 after 6pm ~ Dogs allowed in bar ~
Open 11.30-11; 12-10.30 Sun

CHESTER   SJ4166   Map 7
Albion ★ 🏮
Park Street; CH1 1RQ

With a layout that's little changed since Victorian times, this strongly traditional
pub is tucked away on a quiet street corner just below the Roman Wall, and has
been leased by the same landlord for some 35 years. Most unusually, it's the
officially listed site of four war memorials and attracts a handful of veterans during
commemorative events. Throughout the peacefully quiet rooms (no games
machines or children here) you'll find an absorbing collection of World War I
memorabilia, from big engravings of men leaving for war, and similarly moving
prints of wounded veterans, to flags, advertisements and so on. Even the ancient
pub cat is called Kitchener. The post-Edwardian décor is appealingly muted, with
dark floral William Morris wallpaper (designed on the first day of WWI, a cast-iron
fireplace, appropriate lamps, leatherette and hoop-backed chairs, a period piano
and cast-iron-framed tables; there's an attractive side dining room too. Service is
friendly, though this is a firmly run place: groups of race-goers are discouraged
(opening times may be limited during meets), and they don't like people rushing in

just before closing time. Three or four well kept real ales on handpump might be
from brewers such as Batemans, Black Sheep and St Peters, with over 25 malt
whiskies, new world wines, and fresh orange juice. Served in generous helpings, the
wholesome good value bar food includes doorstep sandwiches (from £3.90), filled
staffordshire oatcakes (£4.20), cottage pie, creamy coconut chicken and rice or
lambs liver, bacon and onions in cider gravy with creamed potatoes (all £6.95), and
daily specials such as hot thai chicken curry (£6.95), with puddings such as
chocolate torte or bread and butter pudding with marmalade (£3.50). The eating
area is no smoking in the evening. It can get very busy at lunchtime. If you stay
here please tell us about the bedrooms. *(Recommended by J S Burn, Sue Holland,
Dave Webster, Rob and Catherine Dunster, the Didler, Nigel Epsley, A Darroch Harkness,
Joe Green, Mr and Mrs Gerry Price)*

Punch ~ Lease Michael Edward Mercer ~ Real ale ~ Bar food (12-2, 5(6 Sat)-8; 12-4 Sun,
not Sun evening) ~ No credit cards ~ (01244) 340345 ~ Dogs allowed in bar ~ Open
12-3, 5(6 Sat)-11; 12-11 Fri; 12-3, 7-10.30 Sun ~ Bedrooms: £60B/£70B

Old Harkers Arms ♀ 🍺

**Russell Street, down steps off City Road where it crosses canal – under Mike Melody
antiques; CH3 5AL**

You can watch canal and cruise boats glide past from this big converted early
Victorian canalside warehouse which takes its name from a Mr Harker, who once
ran a canal-boat chandler's in the building. Lofty ceilings and tall windows give an
appealing light and spacious feel, though tables are carefully arranged to create a
sense of privacy. Walls are covered with frame to frame old prints, and the usual
Brunning & Price wall of books features at one end. Attractive lamps add cosiness,
and the bar counter is apparently constructed from salvaged doors. As well as a
good range of sandwiches (from £4.45), nicely presented bar food from a changing
menu could include cauliflower and stilton soup (£3.95), whitebait with lemon
soured cream (£5.25), rollmops with pear and roasted walnut salad (£6.95),
polenta with roasted vegetables and parmesan (£7.95), salmon and smoked
haddock fishcakes (£8.45), ploughman's (£8.65), faggots with leek mash (£8.95),
10oz rump steak with hand-cut chips (£14.50), side orders (from £2.50), and
puddings such as chocolate terrine with cherry compote or ginger parkin with
rhubarb and custard (£4.95), and a cheeseboard (£7.25). A great choice of nine real
ales on handpump includes Flowers, Thwaites Original, Wapping and Weetwood,
with up to six regularly changing guests from brewers such as Brains, Kelham
Island, Roosters and Salopian. They also do around 100 malt whiskies, decent well
described wines (with around 20 by the glass), farmhouse ciders and local apple
juice. *(Recommended by Bruce and Sharon Eden, Darren and Jane Staniforth, Sue Holland,
Dave Webster, Lawrence Pearse, Mrs Maricar Jagger, Tony Hobden, Nigel Epsley,
David Collison, Roger and Anne Newbury, Mrs Hazel Rainer, A Darroch Harkness, Joe Green,
Mr and Mrs Gerry Price)*

Brunning & Price ~ Manager Paul Jeffery ~ Real ale ~ Bar food (12-9.30(9 Sun)) ~
(01244) 344525 ~ Children in eating area of bar till 5pm, no pushchairs ~ Dogs allowed in
bar ~ Open 11.30-11; 12-10.30 Sun

COTEBROOK   SJ5865   Map 7
Fox & Barrel

A49 NE of Tarporley; CW6 9DZ

The original part of this pretty white cottage comprises a snug little bar, which is
dominated by a big log fireplace, and interestingly furnished with a good mix of
tables and chairs including two seats like Victorian thrones, a comfortable
banquette corner, and rather nice ornaments and china jugs; silenced fruit machine,
unobtrusive piped music. The much bigger uncluttered candlelit no smoking dining
area is a later addition to the building, and has attractive rugs on bare boards,
rustic tables, comfortable dining chairs, rustic pictures above the panelled dado,
and an extensively panelled section. Neatly uniformed staff serve well kept Jennings

Cumberland, John Smiths and Marstons Pedigree and a guest such as Cains through a sparkler (though you can ask for it to be taken off), and there's a decent choice of wines, with 15 by the glass. As well as lunchtime sandwiches (from £4.25), ploughman's (£6.35), and burgers (£7.50), well presented dishes from a changing menu might include soup (£3.50), smoked salmon and asparagus risotto or tempura king prawns (£5.75), tandoori chicken salad (£8.25), steak, ale and mushroom pie (£9.50), chicken breast stuffed with cream cheese and chives, wrapped in bacon, with tarragon and grape cream sauce (£12.50), barbary duck breast with apple, honey grain mustard and cream (£14.25) and 8oz fillet (£15.95); side orders (from £1.50). It's a popular place so you may need to book, particularly for Sunday lunch. *(Recommended by Ray and Winifred Halliday, Brian and Anna Marsden, Peter Fitton)*

Punch ~ Lease Chris Crossley ~ Real ale ~ Bar food (12-2.30, 6-9.30; 12-8 Sun) ~ Restaurant ~ (01829) 760529 ~ Children in restaurant ~ Live jazz first and third Mon, 50s and 60s music second Mon ~ Open 12-3, 6-11; 12-11 Sat; 12-10.30 Sun

EATON   SJ8765   Map 7
Plough 🛏
A536 Congleton—Macclesfield; CW12 2NH

The neatly converted bar at this attractive 17th-c village pub has plenty of beams and exposed brickwork, a couple of snug little alcoves, comfortable armchairs and cushioned wooden wall seats on red patterned carpets, long red curtains, mullioned windows, and a big stone fireplace. Moved here piece by piece from its original home in Wales, the heavily raftered barn at the back is a striking restaurant. The entire pub is no smoking. The big tree-filled garden is attractive, with good views of nearby hills, and there are picnic-sets on the lawn and a smaller terrace. Very good home-made bar food, where possible using local ingredients, includes lunchtime sandwiches (from £2.95), soup (£2.95), prawns in garlic butter (£5.15), steak and kidney pudding or chilli (£7.95), thai green curry (£8.50), 10oz rib-eye steak (£11.95), some interesting daily specials, and a three-course Sunday lunch (£11.95). Changing beers might include Copper Dragon, Hydes Bitter (very reasonably priced) and Moorhouses on handpump, and a decent wine list (ten by the glass). Service is friendly and attentive, and spare a few words for Thunder, the resident black labrador; piped music, TV. The appealingly designed bedrooms are in a converted stable block. *(Recommended by Mark and Ruth Brock, Mrs P J Carroll, Dr David Clegg)*

Free house ~ Licensee Mujdat Karatas ~ Real ale ~ Bar food (12-2.30, 6-8.30; 12-8 Sun) ~ Restaurant ~ (01260) 280207 ~ Children welcome ~ Dogs allowed in bedrooms ~ Open 11.30-11.30; 12-1 Sat; 12-11 Sun ~ Bedrooms: £55B/£70B

HAUGHTON MOSS   SJ5855   Map 7
Nags Head 🍴 ♀ £
Turn off A49 S of Tarporley into Long Lane, at 'Beeston, Haughton' signpost; CW6 9RN

Dating back in parts to the 16th c, this immaculately kept black and white pub is nicely tucked away down winding country lanes. It has gleaming black and white tiles by the serving counter (this is the only area where you can smoke), pews and a heavy settle by the fire in a small quarry-tiled room on the left, and button-back wall banquettes in the carpeted room on the right, which also has logs burning in a copper-hooded fireplace. Below heavy black beams are shelves of pewter mugs, attractive Victorian prints and a few brass ornaments, and the front window of the pub is full of charmingly arranged collector's dolls. On the right is a sizeable carpeted dining area, and an oak beamed conservatory extension serves as the dining room; maybe very quiet piped music. Alongside a well chosen wine list (with ten by the glass) and a dozen malts, Boddingtons, Flowers and Greene King Abbot and possibly a guest are well kept on handpump. The generously served tasty bar food is popular (attentive service and atmosphere remain calm even when it's busy) particularly between 12 and 2 on weekdays when they run the bargain-priced self-service buffet (£6.25). Snacks, which are served till 4.30, include sandwiches (£4.25), filled baked potatoes (£4.25), omelettes (£3.60) and ploughman's (£6.20). Main menu items include soup (£3.45), fishcakes (£4.35), roasted peppers filled with vegetable risotto (£7.90), gammon and egg (£8.70), pork medallions on roasted peppers with sweet soy sesame sauce (£9.90), fried monkfish on stir-fried vegetables with thai cream sauce (£10.25), and steak (£11.85); there's a puddings trolley (£3.85) and various ice-cream sundaes (£3.40). A big immaculately kept garden has well spaced picnic-sets and a bowling green. *(Recommended by Leo and Barbara Lionet, Gill and Keith Croxton, Mr and Mrs M Stratton, Herbert and Susan Verity)*

Free house ~ Licensees Rory and Deborah Keigan ~ Real ale ~ Bar food (12-10) ~ Restaurant ~ (01829) 260265 ~ Children welcome ~ Open 12-11(12 Sat)

HIGHER BURWARDSLEY   SJ5256   Map 7

Pheasant ♀

Burwardsley signposted from Tattenhall (which itself is signposted off A41 S of Chester) and from Harthill (reached by turning off A534 Nantwich—Holt at the Copper Mine); follow pub's signpost on up hill from Post Office; OS Sheet 117 map reference 523566; CH3 9PF

Readers love the fantastic views from this half-timbered and sandstone 17th-c pub. On a clear day the telescope on the terrace (with nice hard wood furniture) lets you make out the pier head and cathedrals in Liverpool, while from inside you can see right across the Cheshire plain. The nicely timbered interior has an airy modern feel, with wooden floors and well spaced furniture including comfy leather armchairs and nice old chairs. They say the see-through fireplace houses the largest log fire in the county, and there's a pleasant no smoking restaurant. Four local Weetwood beers are well kept on handpump alongside a guest from a brewer such as Mallard, a selection of bottled beers, nine wines by the glass and around 20 malts; piped music, daily newspapers. A big side lawn has picnic-sets, and on summer weekends they sometimes have barbecues. Besides sandwiches (from £4.25, steak £5.95), the menu might include soup (£3.75), chicken satay (£5.25), chilli (£8.25), steakburger (£8.50), battered cod (£8.95) and 10oz rib-eye steak (£13.45). Popular with walkers, the pub is well placed for the Sandstone Trail along the Peckforton Hills. *(Recommended by Margaret and Roy Randle, Richard Cole, Brian and Anna Marsden, Dave Irving, John and Hazel Williams, Edward Leetham)*

Free house ~ Licensee Andrew Nelson ~ Real ale ~ Bar food (12-3, 6-9.30 Mon; 12-9.30 (10 Fri/Sat, 8.30 Sun)) ~ (01829) 770434 ~ Children welcome till 6pm ~ Dogs allowed in bar and bedrooms ~ Open 12-11(12 Sat) ~ Bedrooms: £65B/£80B

LANGLEY   SJ9569   Map 7

Hanging Gate ♀

Meg Lane, Higher Sutton; follow Langley signpost from A54 beside Fourways Motel, and that road passes the pub; from Macclesfield, heading S from centre on A523 turn left into Byrons Lane at Langley, Wincle signpost; in Sutton (½ mile after going under canal bridge, ie before Langley) fork right at Church House Inn, following Wildboarclough signpost, then 2 miles later turning sharp right at steep hairpin bend; OS Sheet 118 map reference 952696; SK11 0NG

Given its remote location high on a Peak District ridge, it's not surprising that this welcoming old drover's inn is popular with hikers. It was first licensed around 300 years ago, though it's thought to have been built long before that. Still in their original layout, its three cosy little low-beamed rooms are simply furnished, and have attractive old prints of Cheshire towns, and big coal fires. The first traditional room houses the bar (with well kept Hydes Bitter and Classic on handpump, quite a few malt whiskies and ten wines by the glass) and is so small there's barely space for seating, the second room has a section of bar in the corner and three or four tables, and the third, the appealingly snug blue room, with its little chaise longue, is no smoking. Down some stone steps, an airy garden room extension (also no smoking) has panoramic views over a patchwork of valley pastures to distant moors and the tall Sutton Common transmitter above; piped music. Good straightforward bar food, served by very friendly attentive staff, could include soup (£3.25), fried camembert (£4.75), fried cod (£8.65), gammon and eggs (£8.95), 10oz rib-eye steak (£11.95), with puddings (£3.45). It does get busy so it's best to book on weekends. Seats out on the crazy-paved terrace also have terrific views. *(Recommended by Mr and Mrs Colin Roberts, the Didler, DJH)*

Hydes ~ Tenants Peter and Paul McGrath ~ Real ale ~ Bar food (not Sun evening) ~ Restaurant ~ (01260) 252238 ~ Children welcome away from snug bar ~ Open 12-3, 7-11(12-11 Sat, Sun)

MACCLESFIELD   SJ9271   Map 7
Sutton Hall Hotel   ★

Leaving Macclesfield southwards on A523, turn left into Byrons Lane signposted Langley, Wincle, then just before canal viaduct fork right into Bullocks Lane; OS Sheet 118 map reference 925715; SK11 0HE

The 16th-c baronial hall which forms the heart of this attractive building is beautifully impressive – particularly in the entrance space. The bar is divided into separate areas by tall oak timbers, and has some antique squared oak panelling, lightly patterned art nouveau stained-glass windows, broad flagstones around the bar counter (carpet elsewhere), and a raised open fire. It's mostly furnished in a straightforward way with ladderback chairs around sturdy thick-topped cast-iron-framed tables, but there are a few unusual touches such as a suit of armour by a big stone fireplace, a longcase clock, a huge bronze bell, and a brass cigar-lighting gas taper on the bar counter itself. Beers include Hydes and Marstons and a guest such as Bass on handpump, and they also stock over 50 malt whiskies, decent wines and freshly squeezed fruit juice, and serve a well prepared Pimms. There's a good relaxed atmosphere, and the staff are friendly and efficient; piped music. Generously served bar food might include soup (£3.50), sandwiches (from £4.25), fried sardines with a herb crust and anchovy butter (£5.45), fried chicken livers on a croûton with mustard sauce (£5.95), lasagne (£7.25), beef and ale pie (£7.95), courgette and herb risotto with balsamic vine tomatoes and forest mushrooms (£8.25), battered cod and chips (£8.95) and sirloin steak (£12.95). The dining room, overlooking lovely grounds with tables on a tree-sheltered lawn and ducks and moorhens swimming in the pond, is no smoking. *(Recommended by Michael Butler, Dave Irving, the Didler, Dennis Jones, Ian Dutton, Rob Stevenson)*

Free house ~ Licensee Robert Bradshaw ~ Real ale ~ Bar food (12-2.30, 7-10) ~ Restaurant ~ (01260) 253211 ~ Children in bar Sat, Sun and bank hol lunchtimes only ~ Dogs allowed in bedrooms ~ Open 11-11 ~ Bedrooms: £79.95B/£94.95B

MOBBERLEY   SJ7879   Map 7
Roebuck

Mill Lane; down hill from sharp bend on B5085 at E edge of 30mph limit; WA16 7HX

A comfortable mix of farmhouse furnishings, from cushioned long wood pews that were rescued from a redundant welsh chapel to scrubbed pine tables and a mix of old chairs, and old tiled and boarded floors, give a relaxed country feel to this nice white-painted pub, which is in a quiet spot down a bypassed lane. It's here though that the simplicity ends. Readers have sent us enthusiastic praise for the thoughtfully sourced and prepared food, which, as well as lunchtime sandwiches (from £5.25, not Sunday), might include soup (£4.25), asparagus with poached egg and hollandaise sauce (£5.95), scallops (£8.55), steak and ale pie (£8.75), avocado and crème fraîche soufflé omelette (£9.95), lamb shank (£13.65), fillet steak with foie gras (£18.95), and puddings such as warm chocolate brownie with mascarpone ice-cream (£5.30). Staff are polite, friendly and helpful, two areas are no smoking, and you will probably need to book; piped music. Greene King Old Speckled Hen, Tetleys, Timothy Taylors Landlord and a guest such as Charles Wells Bombardier are well kept alongside a dozen wines by the glass. There is a cobbled courtyard with benches and tables and, at the back of the pub, an enclosed beer garden with picnic-sets – and more by the car park; also a play area for small children with a sandpit and play equipment. *(Recommended by Mrs P J Carroll, H and P Cate, Dr D Scott)*

Free house ~ Licensee Jane Marsden ~ Real ale ~ Bar food (12-2.30, 6-9.30; 12-9.30 Sat; 12-4, 6-9 Sun) ~ Restaurant ~ (01565) 873322 ~ Well behaved children welcome ~ Open 12-3, 5-11; 12-11 Sat; 12-10.30 Sun

PEOVER HEATH   SJ7973   Map 7

Dog 🍺

Off A50 N of Holmes Chapel at the Whipping Stocks, keep on past Parkgate into Wellbank Lane; OS Sheet 118 map reference 794735; note that this village is called Peover Heath on the OS map and shown under that name on many road maps, but the pub is often listed under Over Peover instead; WA16 8UP

A cheery welcome and tasty food are the principal attractions at this dining pub. It's pleasing however that their remarkably well priced and rather interesting range of very well kept real ales (Copper Dragon Scotts 1816, Hydes, Moorhouses Black Cat and Weetwood Best) has earned them a new beer award this year. They also have Addlestone's cider, 35 different malt whiskies and eight wines by the glass. It can be busy, so it's worth arriving early to try for a seat in the slightly more spacious feeling main bar. This is comfortably furnished with easy chairs and wall seats (including one built into a snug alcove around an oak table), and two wood-backed seats built in either side of a coal fire, opposite which logs burn in an old-fashioned black grate. You may have a short wait for the generous helpings of bar food, which might include soup (£2.95), sandwiches (from £3.05, hot baguettes from £4.15), ploughman's (from £4.55), chilli (£6.55), sausage of the day and mash (£8.25), steak and kidney pie (£10.25), braised lamb shank (£10.45), roast of the day (£10.75), king cod with chips and mushy peas (£10.95), and puddings such as strawberry pavlova (£3.95). The dining room is no smoking; games machine, darts, pool, dominoes, TV and piped music. There are picnic-sets beneath colourful hanging baskets on the peaceful lane, and more out in a pretty back garden. It's a pleasant walk from here to the Jodrell Bank Centre and Arboretum. *(Recommended by John Wooll, Martin Hann, Gerry and Rosemary Dobson, Mike and Linda Hudson, Tom and Jill Jones, Peter F Marshall, Dr Phil Putwain, Dave Braisted, H and P Cate, Steve Whalley)*

Free house ~ Licensee Steven Wrigley ~ Real ale ~ Bar food (12-2.30, 6-9; 12-8.30 Sun) ~ Restaurant ~ (01625) 861421 ~ Children welcome ~ Dogs allowed in bar ~ Live music monthly Fri ~ Open 11.30-3, 4.30-11; 11.30-11 Sat; 12-11 Sun ~ Bedrooms: £55B/£75B

PRESTBURY   SJ8976   Map 7

Legh Arms 🛏

A538, village centre; SK10 4DG

This beautifully kept inn has been elegently worked in a comfortably smart traditional style. The relaxing bar, though opened up, is well divided into several distinctive areas, with muted tartan fabric over a panelled dado on the right, ladderback dining chairs, good solid dark tables, elegant french steam train prints, italian costume engravings and a glass case of china and books; brocaded bucket seats around similar tables, antique steeplechase prints, staffordshire dogs on the stone mantelpiece and a good coal fire on the left; a snug panelled back part has cosy wing armchairs and a grand piano, and a narrow side offshoot has pairs of art deco leather armchairs around small granite tables, and antique costume prints of french tradesmen. The bar, towards the back on the left, has well kept Robinsons Unicorn and Hatters Mild on handpump and nice house wines (eight by the glass), a good range of malts and whiskies, good coffee, and maybe genial regulars perched on the comfortable leather bar stools; this part looks up to an unusual balustraded internal landing. There are daily papers on a coffee table, and magazines on an antique oak dresser; piped music. The lounge is no smoking. Very tasty bar food might include soup (£3.25), spicy fishcakes with sweet chilli sauce (£4.95), fish broth (£5.50), dips for two (£7.95), thai chicken curry (£7.25), fish and chips or tomato and vegetable tagliatelle (£7.50), wild mushroom risotto with asparagus (£7.95), salmon and dill linguini (£8.25), duck confit (£10.95) or lamb on rosemary and olive mash with red wine jus (£12.50). A garden behind has a terrace with outdoor heating, tables and chairs. *(Recommended by Mrs P J Carroll, DJH, Mr and Mrs Robert Jamieson, Rob Stevenson, Joan York)*

Robinsons ~ Tenant Peter Myers ~ Real ale ~ Bar food (12-2, 7-10; 12-9.30 Sun) ~ Restaurant ~ (01625) 829130 ~ Children welcome with restrictions ~ Open 11-11 ~ Bedrooms: /£95B

TARPORLEY   SJ5563   Map 7
Rising Sun
High Street; village signposted off A51 Nantwich—Chester; CW6 0DX

The nice old interior of this friendly bustling pub is cosily furnished with well chosen tables surrounded by eye-catching old seats including creaky 19th-c mahogany and oak settles, an attractively blacked iron kitchen range, sporting and other old-fashioned prints on the walls, and a big oriental rug in the back room. The wide-ranging menu includes soup (£2.30), sandwiches (from £2.65), toasties and filled baked potatoes (from £3.10), half a dozen tasty pies or fish and chips (from £6.65), poached salmon with prawn and tomato sauce (£8.25), a dozen spicy dishes such as fruit beef curry (£8.25), over a dozen vegetarian dishes such as vegetable stroganoff (£8.50) and 12oz sirloin (£11.75); no smoking dining room, helpful service, piped music and TV. Two or three Robinsons beers are well kept on handpump. *(Recommended by the Didler)*

Robinsons ~ Tenant Alec Robertson ~ Real ale ~ Bar food ~ Restaurant (evening) ~ (01829) 732423 ~ Children welcome with restrictions ~ Open 11.30-3, 5.30-11; 11.30-11 Sat; 12-10.30 Sun

WETTENHALL   SJ6261   Map 7
Boot & Slipper
From B5074 on S edge of Winsford, turn into Darnhall School Lane, then right at Wettenhall signpost: keep on for 2 or 3 miles; OS Sheet 118 map reference 625613; CW7 4DN

There's a friendly interested welcome from the chatty licensee couple and staff at this traditionally pleasant old pub. The knocked-through beamed main bar has three shiny old dark settles, straightforward chairs, and a fishing rod above the deep low fireplace with its big warming log fire. The modern bar counter also serves the left-hand communicating beamed room with its shiny pale brown tiled floor, cast-iron-framed long table, panelled settle and bar stools; darts and piped music. An unusual trio of back-lit arched pseudo-fireplaces forms one stripped-brick wall, and there are two further areas on the right, as well as an attractive back restaurant with big country pictures. Drinks include Bass and Tetleys on handpump, a good choice of malt whiskies and a decent wine list. Straightfoward but tasty bar food could include home-made soup (£3.35), chicken liver pâté (£5.95), pie of the day (£8.95), vegetable lasagne (£9.25), curry of the day (£9.50), 8oz fillet (£15.75), and puddings such as sherry trifle or sticky toffee pavlova (£3.95). You may need to book at the weekend. There are picnic-sets out on the cobbled front terrace by the big car park; children's play area. *(Recommended by Dr Phil Putwain)*

Free house ~ Licensee Joan Jones ~ Real ale ~ Bar food (12-2, 6-9.30; 12-2.30, 6-9 Sun) ~ Restaurant ~ (01270) 528238 ~ Children welcome with restrictions ~ Open 12-3, 5.30-11; 12-12 Sat; 12-10.30 Sun ~ Bedrooms: £40S/£60S

Post Office address codings give the impression that some pubs are in Cheshire, when they're really in Derbyshire (and therefore included in this book under that chapter) or in Greater Manchester (see the Lancashire chapter).

WINCLE SJ9666 Map 7
Ship 🍺
Village signposted off A54 Congleton—Buxton; SK11 0QE

The two simple little tap rooms at this attractive 16th-c pub have an enjoyably welcoming atmosphere, thick stone walls and a coal fire. It's in an area of lovely countryside so can get very busy at weekends with walkers (they sell their own book of local walks, £3) and tourists so you may need to book. Served by efficient young staff, tasty bar food could include home-made soup (£3.50), grilled goats cheese topped with honey and toasted pine nuts (£4.95), grilled duck breast marinated in five spice with thai noodles (£6.25), battered haddock with hand-cut chips, home-made gnocchi with basil and parmesan sauce with roasted courgettes and peppers (£10.95), lamb shank braised in red wine with orange and cumin on parsnip mash with roasted mediterranean vegetables (£11.95) or pork fillet topped with stilton and red onions (£12.95). A couple of thoughtfully sourced guest beers from brewers such as Titanic and Thornbridge are well kept alongside Fullers London Pride and Lancaster Duchy, belgian beers, Weston's farm cider and fruit wines; no smoking area. A small garden has wooden tables. *(Recommended by Mrs P J Carroll, Richard, the Didler, Ian Dutton, Rob Stevenson, Jeremy Whitehorn, DJH)*

Free house ~ Licensee Giles Henry Meadows ~ Real ale ~ Bar food (12-2.30, 6.30-9.30; 12-3, 6.30-9.30(5.30-8 Sun) Sat; not Mon) ~ Restaurant ~ (01260) 227217 ~ Children in family room ~ Dogs allowed in bar ~ Open 12-3, 6.30-11; 12-11 Sat; 12-10.30 Sun; closed Mon

WRENBURY SJ5948 Map 7
Dusty Miller
Village signposted from A530 Nantwich—Whitchurch; CW5 8HG

This substantial brick building, right next to the Shropshire Union Canal, is a neatly converted 19th-c corn mill – you can still see the old lift hoist up under the rafters. The River Weaver runs in an aqueduct under the canal at this point, and it was the river that once powered the millrace. These days a constant stream of boats slipping through the striking counter-weighted canal drawbridge, just outside here, provides entertainment if you're sitting at picnic-sets among rose bushes on the gravel terrace or at one of the tables inside by the series of tall glazed arches. The atmosphere is low-key restauranty, with some emphasis on the generously served food, though drinkers are welcome, and in summer the balance may even tip. The monthly changing menu might include soup (£3.75), chicken liver parfait with beetroot and port compote (£4.95), filled rolls (£4.95), cheese platter (£7.25), aberdeen angus beefburger with melted cheese, pear and apple chutney (£8.95), gammon steak with black pudding and fried egg (£9.25), baked cod fillet with mash and white wine and parsley sauce (£10.25), rib-eye steak with garlic butter (£13.50), a few daily specials such as local mutton cooked in ale (£9.95) and puddings such as orange and bread and butter pudding or sloe gin and damson ice-cream with warm berries (from £3.75). The spacious modern main bar area is comfortably welcoming, including long low-hung hunting prints on green walls, and a mixture of seats flanking the rustic tables that includes tapestried banquettes, oak settles and wheelback chairs. Further in, a quarry-tiled part by the bar counter has an oak settle and refectory table. All the dining areas are no smoking. Friendly staff serve three well kept Robinsons beers on handpump; eclectic piped music and dominoes. *(Recommended by JCW, Gwyn and Anne Wake, Philip and Cheryl Hill, Roger and Pauline Pearce, Frank and Chris Sharp, Gerry Price)*

Robinsons ~ Tenant Mark Sumner ~ Real ale ~ Bar food (12-2, 6.30-9.30; not Mon in winter) ~ Restaurant ~ (01270) 780537 ~ Children in dining area ~ Dogs allowed in bar ~ Open 11.30-3, 6.30-11; 11.30-11 Sat; 12-11 Sun; 11.30-3, 6.30-11 Sat and 12-3, 7-11 Sun winter; closed Mon lunchtime in winter

---

Tipping is not normal for bar meals, and not usually expected.

LUCKY DIP

Besides the fully inspected pubs, you might like to try these Lucky Dips recommended to us and described by readers (if you do, please send us reports: www.goodguides.co.uk).

ACTON BRIDGE [SJ5974]
Hazel Pear CW8 3RA [Hill Top Rd]:
Welcoming country pub with good value home cooking, Marstons Pedigree and Timothy Taylors Landlord, good wine choice, pleasant attentive service, no smoking restaurant; children welcome, open all day *(A Harding)*

ALDERLEY EDGE [SJ8176]
☆ *Stags Head* SK9 7TY [Mill Lane, off A535 SW]: Friendly and relaxing traditional pub in rich countryside, nice mix of regulars and visitors, enjoyable generous food inc proper steak pie, fresh fish and local specialities, efficient obliging service, good beer *(A J W Smith, John Trevor and Susan Rispin)*

ALPRAHAM [SJ5759]
Travellers Rest CW6 9JA [A51 Nantwich—Chester]: Unspoilt four-room country local with friendly staff and veteran landlady (same family for three generations), particularly well kept Tetleys Bitter and Mild and a guest beer, low prices, leatherette, wicker and Formica, some flock wallpaper, fine old brewery mirrors, darts and dominoes, back bowling green; no machines, piped music or food (apart from crisps and nuts), cl wkdy lunchtimes *(the Didler, Pete Baker)*

ALVANLEY [SJ4973]
☆ *White Lion* WA6 9DD [Manley Rd; handy for M56 junction 14]: Neatly kept and comfortable 16th-c Chef & Brewer dining pub with low beams, cosy corners and candlelight, friendly service and atmosphere, real ales, good choice of wines by the glass; tables on terrace, play area, duck pond *(LYM, D Watson)*

AUDLEM [SJ6543]
Shroppie Fly CW3 0DX [Shropshire St]:
Beautifully placed by locks 12/13 of Shrops Union Canal, friendly relaxed atmosphere and keen staff, good choice of real ales, tasty pub food, one bar shaped like a barge, canal photographs, brightly painted bargees' china and bric-a-brac, mainly modern furnishings, three rooms and pool room; piped music; provision for children, tables on waterside terrace, cl winter lunchtimes, open almost all day summer *(LYM, David and Sue Smith)*

BELL O' TH' HILL [SJ5245]
☆ *Blue Bell* SY13 4QS [just off A41 N of Whitchurch]: Heavily beamed partly 14th-c country local, cheerful and relaxed, with changing ales such as Black Sheep, Hanby Drawell, Old Swan Mrs Pardoes Original and Woods, reliable well priced food from sandwiches and baguettes up, friendly licensees, two cosy and attractive rooms, well behaved alsatian; dogs and children welcome, pleasant garden and surroundings, cl Mon *(MLR, LYM, Dr Phil Putwain)*

BOLLINGTON [SJ9477]
☆ *Poachers* SK10 5BU [Mill Lane]: Charming stone-built village local prettily set in good walking area, good imaginative food (not

Mon) from bargain lunches to exotics such as ostrich, Copper Dragon, Timothy Taylors Landlord and three guest beers, decent wines, friendly atmosphere and helpful attentive young licensees, no smoking dining room (best to book wknds); attractive secluded garden and terrace behind, cl Mon lunchtime *(Roy and Lindsey Fentiman)*
Vale SK11 0AW [heading N off B5091 by railway viaduct]: Pleasantly modernised local with well kept Storm and Timothy Taylors Landlord, home-made food (all day Sat), friendly young licensees, log fire; can be smoky; children welcome till 7pm, neat woodside lawn, canal walks nearby *(Brian and Anna Marsden, LYM)*

BURLEYDAM [SJ6042]
☆ *Combermere Arms* SY13 4AT [A525 Whitchurch—Audlem]: Well redesigned and roomy 18th-c beamed dining pub, largely no smoking, with good imaginative home-made food all day, half a dozen good ales, good choice of wines by the glass, distinctive and comfortable linked areas – in same good small group as Grosvenor Arms, Aldford; open all day *(Sue Holland, Dave Webster, D Weston, LYM)*

CHESTER [SJ4065]
☆ *Bear & Billet* CH1 1RU [Lower Bridge St]:
Handsome timbered building reopened under new management, Okells and other interesting changing ales such as Copper Dragon Best Bill, belgian and US imports, nice range of wines by the glass, wide range of reasonably priced pubby food, interesting features and some attractive furnishings in friendly and comfortable open-plan bar, log fire in front room; pleasant courtyard tables behind, open all day *(Paul Davies, Richard and Margaret McPhee, Nigel Epsley, BB)*
Carlton CH4 7BN [Hartington St]: Friendly and lively traditional pub with three real ales, open fires, darts, pool, table football, pinball and board games; live music, quiz nights *(anon)*
☆ *Mill* CH1 3NF [Milton St]: Early 19th-c mill converted to hotel, neat and comfortable sizeable bar on right, five regular beers inc ones brewed for them by Coach House and Phoenix, up to nine changing guest ales, reasonable prices, good value ciabattas and enjoyable hot dishes till late evening, charming service, relaxed mix of customers, canalside restaurant and dining barge; quiet piped music, unobtrusively placed big-screen sports TV, jazz Mon; children looked after well, benches out by water, good bedrooms, open all day *(Sue Holland, Dave Webster, BB, Colin Moore, the Didler, Nigel Epsley, Joe Green)*
Olde Boot CH1 1LQ [Eastgate Row N]:
Down-to-earth and relaxed pub in lovely 17th-c Rows building, heavy beams, lots of dark woodwork, oak flooring, flagstones,

some exposed Tudor wattle and daub, black-leaded kitchen range in lounge beyond decent lunchtime food servery (not Tues), old-fashioned settles and oak panelling in no smoking upper area popular with families, good service, Sam Smiths; piped music; children allowed (*Michael Dandy, the Didler, Nigel Epsley, LYM, Joe Green*)

Pied Bull CH1 2HQ [Upper Northgate St]: Roomy open-plan carpeted bar, attractive mix of individual furnishings, divided inner area with china cabinet and lots of pictures, nice snug by pillared entrance, imposing intriguingly decorated fireplace; wide choice of generous reasonably priced food all day inc afternoon teas, real ales, attentive welcoming staff, no smoking area; fruit machines, may be piped music; open all day, handsome Jacobean stairs up to bedrooms (*BB, David Glynne-Jones*)

Telfords Warehouse CH1 4EZ [Tower Wharf, behind Northgate St nr rly]: Well kept ales such as Harviestoun Bitter & Twisted, Timothy Taylors Landlord, Thwaites Original and Weetwood Eastgate in large converted canal building, freshly made generous up-to-date food, efficient friendly staff, bare brick and boards, high pitched ceiling, big wall of windows overlooking water, massive iron winding gear in bar, some old enamelled advertisements, good photographs for sale, steps to heavy-beamed area with sofas, more artwork and restaurant; late-night live music; tables out by water, open all day (*BB, Colin Moore*)

Union Vaults CH1 3ND [Francis St/Egerton St]: Basic local notable for its reasonably priced changing ales inc Caledonian and Phoenix, friendly knowledgeable staff, bagatelle, dominoes, cards and two TV sports channels, back games room with pool, two quieter upper rooms with old local photographs; piped music; open all day (*the Didler, Nigel Epsley, Joe Green*)

CHILDER THORNTON [SJ3678]

☆ *White Lion* CH66 5PU [off A41 S of M53 junction 5; New Rd]: Low two-room whitewashed country pub, an old-fashioned and unpretentious surprise for the area, with welcoming atmosphere and staff, Thwaites Bitter, Mild and Lancaster Bomber, good value sensible wkdy lunches from good ciabattas and hot filled rolls up, open fire, framed matchboxes, no music or machines (small TV for big matches); children welcome, tables out in secluded back garden, play area, open all day (*MLR*)

CONGLETON [SJ8663]

Beartown Tap CW12 1RL [Willow St (A54)]: Tap for nearby Beartown small brewery, their interesting beers well priced, and perhaps a guest microbrew, changing farm cider, bottled belgians, bare boards in friendly bar and two light and airy rooms off, no games or music; upstairs lavatories; open all day Fri-Sun (*the Didler, Rob Stevenson*)

Railway Inn CW12 3JS [Biddulph Rd (A527)]: Well kept frequently changing real ales and

good basic home-made food in friendly pub nr station and Macclesfield Canal (*Rob Pointon, G V Price*)

COTEBROOK [SJ5765]

☆ *Alvanley Arms* CW6 9DS [A49/B5152 N of Tarporley]: Fine old sandstone inn, 16th-c behind its Georgian façade, with good Robinsons ales, friendly helpful young staff, good value generous straightforward food from baguettes and light lunches up, three attractive beamed rooms (two no smoking areas), big open fire, chintzy little hall, shire horse décor (plenty of tack and pictures – adjacent stud open in season); garden with pond and trout, pleasant walks, seven comfortable bedrooms (*Michael and Jenny Back, Mrs P J Carroll, LYM, Dennis Jones, Richard Endacott, Denis Golden*)

CREWE [SJ7055]

Borough Arms CW1 2BG [Earle St]: Well kept interesting changing ales inc ones from its own microbrewery, five or six foreign beers on tap and dozens in bottle, friendly enthusiastic landlord, two small plain rooms off central bar, railway theme, green décor; games machine, sports TV; tables outside, cl wkdy lunchtimes (*the Didler, Rob Stevenson*)

Rising Sun CW2 8SB [Middlewich Rd (A530), Wistaston]: Olde-worlde Chef & Brewer with plenty of individuality, beamery, panelling, prints, two log fires and lots of separate areas, nine particularly well kept real ales inc one brewed for the pub by Titanic, occasional beer festivals, good choice of wines by the glass, wide range of enjoyable food, raised eating area; children's facilities, good disabled access (inc lift), tables and play area outside, quiet countryside, open all day (*Edward Leetham*)

CROFT [SJ6393]

Horseshoe WA3 7HQ [Smithy Lane; left just after the Noggin, right at next T junction]: Wide choice of enjoyable food at good prices in comfortable and interesting village pub, friendly and well run, with several separate rooms, good choice of wines and ales; children welcome (*Alvin Morris*)

DARESBURY [SJ5782]

Ring o' Bells WA4 4AJ [B5356, handy for M56 junction 11]: Chef & Brewer with wide choice of food all day from sandwiches, baguettes and baked potatoes up, friendly staff, several real ales, lots of wines by the glass, generous coffee, comfortable library-style areas (largely no smoking) and part more suited to walkers (canal is not far); children in eating areas, good disabled access, plenty of tables in long partly terraced garden, pretty village, church with *Alice in Wonderland* window, open all day (*June and Ken Brooks, Dr and Mrs A K Clarke, Roger Thornington, Mrs Phoebe A Kemp, LYM, Mrs Hazel Rainer, Frank and Chris Sharp, Mart Lawton*)

DAVENHAM [SJ6670]

Bulls Head CW9 8NA [London Rd]: Picturesque old coaching inn, clean and bright, with cheerful helpful staff, Theakstons and a guest beer such as Caledonian Deuchars IPA, decent wines, several low-beamed rooms, nicely placed tables, sympathetic décor, interesting prints, small library under stairs, upstairs no smoking dining room; tables out on back terrace *(Mr and Mrs John Taylor)*

FADDILEY [SJ5852]

✩ *Thatch* CW5 8JE [A534 Wrexham—Nantwich]: Attractive thatched, low-beamed and timbered dining pub carefully extended from medieval core, open fires, candlelit barn-style dining room with no smoking area (children allowed), friendly helpful service, relaxing atmosphere, real ales inc local Weetwood, enjoyable food (all day Sun) inc children's helpings; charming country garden, open all day Sun *(LYM, Dr Phil Putwain)*

FRODSHAM [SJ5177]

Netherton Hall WA6 6UL [A56 towards Helsby]: Large converted town-edge farmhouse popular for flexible chef's good imaginative well presented food all day, with changing real ales such as Jennings and Timothy Taylors Landlord, good choice of wine by the glass, friendly attentive young staff, calm relaxed atmosphere no smoking rooms; well behaved children welcome, nice setting *(Pat and Tony Hinkins)*

GAWSWORTH [SJ8869]

✩ *Harrington Arms* SK11 9RJ [Church Lane]: Rustic 17th-c farm pub with two small basic rooms (children allowed in one), bare boards and panelling, fine carved oak bar counter, Robinsons Best and Hatters Mild, friendly service, pickled onions, pork pies, chunky lunchtime sandwiches; Fri folk night; sunny benches on small front cobbled terrace *(LYM, the Didler)*

GLAZEBURY [SJ6796]

Raven WA3 5LA [Warrington Rd (A574)]: Small and welcoming, all food freshly made from lunchtime sandwiches with home-made crisps to good specials, real ales and decent wines, no smoking area *(Rachel Rigby)*

GOOSTREY [SJ7869]

✩ *Olde Red Lion* CW4 8PJ [Station Rd]: Comfortable open-plan bar and restaurant with relaxed atmosphere and well presented nourishing food inc Thurs OAP lunches, friendly efficient service, real ales, winter mulled wine; children welcome, nice garden with play area *(LYM, Joan York)*

Red Lion CW4 8PJ [Station Rd, towards A535]: Open-plan family-friendly pub taking real care of children (even their fish fingers are home-made), with enjoyable adult food too, real ales, friendly efficient service, spotless restaurant; nice garden with play area *(Mr and Mrs Wroe, LYM)*

GURNETT [SJ9271]

✩ *Old Kings Head* SK11 0HQ [just S of Macclesfield]: Beamed former coaching house and smithy, now a welcoming split-level local by Macclesfield Canal aqueduct (moorings), friendly attentive landlord, pleasant staff, Banks's and Marstons Pedigree, very generous reasonably priced good food, old-fashioned kitchen range, restaurant; quiet piped music; tables outside *(John Bell)*

HANDLEY [SJ4657]

✩ *Calveley Arms* CH3 9DT [just off A41 S of Chester]: Good changing food from sandwiches and baguettes to interesting specials and fresh fish in black and white beamed country pub licensed since 17th c, friendly efficient staff, Boddingtons and Theakstons Black Bull with occasional guest beers, good wines by the glass and nice soft drinks, reasonable prices, open fire, cosy alcove seating, traditional games; piped music; very well behaved children allowed, secluded garden with boules *(LYM, Jill Sparrow)*

HANKELOW [SJ6645]

White Lion CW3 0JA [A529 Audlem—Nantwich]: Pleasantly refurbished pub opp village green and pond, enjoyable food in comfortable dining areas, good service, open fires *(Margaret and Allen Marsden)*

HASSALL GREEN [SJ7858]

Romping Donkey CW11 4YA: Picturesque black-and-white pub by locks on Trent & Mersey Canal, with timbers, bevelled beams and ledged doors in bustling bar neatly furnished to match appearance, Bass, Greene King Old Speckled Hen and Tetleys Bitter and Mild, freshly squeezed orange juice, good wines by the glass, usual food; garden with terrace and play area *(G V Price, LYM)*

HELSBY [SJ4874]

✩ *New Helsby Arms* WA6 0JE [Chester Rd (A56, handy for M56 junction 14)]: Well kept Black Sheep and three changing ales, good wine choice, good fresh food, not a hugely wide choice but changing daily, young friendly staff, good log fire, no smoking area *(Pete Wright, Myke and Nicky Crombleholme, Sue and Alex)*

HIGH LEGH [SJ7084]

Bears Paw WA16 0RT [Warrington Rd (A50 E of M6 junction 20)]: Comfortable and welcoming old roadside pub, two carpeted dining rooms off bar, popular for enjoyable food cooked to order (so may take a while), Marstons Pedigree; tables out behind *(Mr and Mrs Colin Roberts)*

KELSALL [SJ5268]

Olive Tree CW6 0RS [Chester Rd (A54)]: Rambling old low-beamed pub with comfortable country furnishings, clean spare modern décor and relaxed civilised atmosphere, two bars, wine bar area and restaurant, good local and other beers, friendly staff, lovely log fires *(Dennis Jones)*

Royal Oak CW6 0RR [Chester Rd]: Impressive building with some emphasis on enjoyable all-day food, Sun carvery, Worthington and two or three guest beers; children welcome, courtyard tables, six bedrooms, camping, open all day *(Dennis Jones)*

KETTLESHULME [SJ9879]

✩ *Swan* SK23 7QU [Macclesfield Rd (B5470)]: Delightful little traditional beamed 16th-c pub run by consortium of locals, Marstons and two guest beers, lunchtime soup and good sandwiches, log fires, old settles and pews, Dickens prints; children welcome, garden tables, good walks, cl Mon lunchtime, open all day wknds *(Dennis Jones, Ian and Liz Rispin)*

KINGSLEY [SJ5474]

Horse Shoe WA6 8EF [Hollow Lane]: Friendly village pub handy for Delamere Forest, warm and welcoming, with generous attractively priced food running up to beef wellington, Burtonwood ales, fresh flowers; piped music; garden tables *(Michael Daley)*

LACH DENNIS [SJ7072]

☆ *Duke of Portland* CW9 7SY [Holmes Chapel Rd (B5082, off A556 SE of Northwich)]: Great atmosphere in stylish and relaxing country dining pub with beautifully presented fresh traditional and more unusual food using local supplies, from interesting sandwiches and light lunches up, super chips made with local potatoes, young attentive helpful staff, four or more changing ales inc Marstons Pedigree and Weetwood, good choice of wines by the glass, daily papers, attractive L-shaped bar with leather seats and sofas and balustraded eating areas (one no smoking), little dance floor for special nights *(A Jones, Mrs P J Carroll, Simon J Barber)*

Three Greyhounds WA16 9JY [B5082 Northwich rd off A50]: Enjoyable food and good service, getting to be more of a dining pub but still has a busy proper bar area *(Tom and Jill Jones)*

LANGLEY [SJ9471]

☆ *Leathers Smithy* SK11 0NE [off A523 S of Macclesfield, OS Sheet 118 map ref 952715]: Isolated pub up in fine walking country, spotless flagstoned bar and carpeted dining room, interesting local prints and photographs, pleasant relaxing atmosphere, log fire, winter glühwein and lots of whiskies, Courage Directors, Marstons Pedigree, Theakstons Best and a guest beer, farm cider, cheerful service, decent food (all day Sun) from sandwiches up; unobtrusive piped music; family room, no dogs, picnic-sets out on grass opposite *(David Crook, LYM)*

LITTLE BOLLINGTON [SJ7387]

Swan With Two Nicks WA14 4TJ [2 miles from M56 junction 7 – A56 towards Lymm, then first right at Stamford Arms into Park Lane; use A556 to get back on to M56 westbound]: Extended village pub full of beams, brass, copper and bric-a-brac, some antique settles, log fire, welcoming helpful service, good choice of generous food from filling baguettes up, several good ales inc one brewed for the pub, decent wines, good coffee; tables outside, open all day, attractive hamlet by Dunham Hall deer park, walks by Bridgewater Canal *(LYM, John and Sylvia Harrop)*

LOWER PEOVER [SJ7474]

Bells of Peover WA16 9PZ [just off B5081; The Cobbles]: Chef & Brewer well worth a look for its appearance and position, a lovely wisteria-covered building with plenty of old-fashioned character inside, panelling, antiques and two small coal fires, real ale; piped music; children and dogs welcome, terrace tables and big side lawn with trees, rose pergolas and a

little stream, on quiet cobbled lane opposite fine black and white 14th-c church, open all day *(Nikki Wild, Spider Newth, Michael Dugdale, Revd D Glover, LYM, the Didler, Rob Stevenson, Stan and Hazel Allen, Rev Michael Vockins)*

Crown WA16 9QB [B5081, off A50]: Enjoyable food (all day Sun), fresh-cooked so can take a while, good choice of real ales inc Boddingtons, Greene King Old Speckled Hen and Timothy Taylors Landlord, friendly and attractive L-shaped bar with two rooms off, low beams and flagstones, lots of bric-a-brac inc interesting gooseberry championship memorabilia, darts and dominoes; tables outside, open all day Sun *(Tom and Jill Jones)*

LYMM [SJ7087]

Barn Owl WA13 0SW [Agden Wharf, Warrington Lane (just off B5159 E)]: Comfortably extended former canal building in picturesque setting by Bridgewater Canal, good value fresh food all day inc OAP bargains, Marstons Bitter and Pedigree and a guest beer, decent wines by the glass, friendly atmosphere, pleasant service even though busy; disabled facilities, little ferry for customers (and may be canal trips), open all day *(Ben Williams)*

☆ *Spread Eagle* WA13 0AG [not far from M6 junction 20; Eagle Brow (A6144, in centre)]: Big cheerful rambling beamed pub, charming black and white façade, good value home-made food all day from sandwiches and baguettes through two-course bargains to steaks, particularly well kept Lees Bitter and Red Dragon, good choice of wines, good service, comfortable two-level lounge, proper drinking area by central bar, coal fire, lots of brasses, separate games room with pool; piped music; attractive village, open all day *(BB, Pete Baker, Caroline and Gavin Callow)*

MACCLESFIELD [SJ9272]

Railway View SK11 7JW [Byrons Lane (off A523)]: Half a dozen or more unusual changing ales in pair of 1700 cottages knocked into roomy pub with attractive snug corners, farm cider, good value simple home-made food, friendly service; back terrace overlooking railway, remarkably shaped gents'; cl lunchtime Mon-Thurs and Sat, open all day Fri and Sun *(the Didler)*

Waters Green Tavern SK11 6LH [Waters Green, opp stn]: Quickly changing real ales such as Copper Dragon, Phoenix, Rooster and Whim in large L-shaped open-plan local, home-made lunchtime food (not Sun), friendly staff and locals, back pool room; open all day *(the Didler)*

MADELEY HEATH [SJ7845]

Old Swan CW3 9LD [Crewe Rd]: Good authentic italian food (not Tues) in bistro pub conversion, friendly efficient service, good wines *(John and Paula Miller, Susan Brookes)*

MARBURY [SJ5645]

Swan SY13 4LS [NNE of Whitchurch]: Old-fashioned farmhouse pub with welcoming new landlords, enjoyable fresh food in roomy partly panelled lounge and pretty candlelit restaurant, local Woodlands ales, good range of well priced wines, log fire in copper-canopied fireplace; venerable oak on green opposite, delightful village a half-mile's country walk from the Llangollen Canal, Bridges 23 and 24 *(LYM, John Goodison, Liz Webster, Edward Leetham)*

MARTON [SJ8568]

Davenport Arms SK11 9HF [A34 N of Congleton]: Comfortable, roomy and tasteful pub with good choice of home-made food in bar and restaurant inc their speciality venison and black pudding salad and good value Sun lunch, friendly obliging service, real ales, no smoking area; no dogs; nr ancient half-timbered church (and Europe's widest oak tree) *(Mrs P J Carroll, Dr D J and Mrs S C Walker)*

MOBBERLEY [SJ8079]

Bird in Hand WA16 7BW [Knolls Green; B5085 towards Alderley]: Cosy well managed low-beamed pub with good plain honest fairly priced food, Sam Smiths, lots of malt whiskies, decent house wines, linked rooms with comfortably cushioned heavy wooden seats, warm coal fires, small pictures on Victorian wallpaper, little panelled snug, good no smoking top dining area, pub games; children allowed, open all day *(LYM, Mrs P J Carroll)*

Church Inn WA16 7RD [Church Lane]: Cheerful and welcoming, with enjoyable fresh food from good baguettes up, real ales, big log fire; children welcome, disabled facilities, tables outside, play area, own bowling green *(Mr and Mrs A Silver)*

Plough & Flail WA16 7DB [Paddock Hill; small sign off B5085 towards Wilmslow]: Refurbished and extended in 2005, light and airy, all no smoking, with enjoyable home-made food (they even bake the biscuits for your coffee), good wines by the glass, Bass and Boddingtons; children welcome, good garden with play area *(Helen Cobb, Mark and Lynette Davies)*

MOULDSWORTH [SJ5170]

Goshawk CH3 8AJ [Station Rd (B5393)]: Plushly comfortable family dining pub with up-to-date character décor in extensive series of rooms, attentive young manager and uniformed staff, enjoyable generous food from sandwiches to restaurany dishes using local supplies (free rail travel from Chester if you eat), enterprising range of wines by the glass, Greene King IPA and Old Speckled Hen; piped music may obtrude; good spot nr Delamere Forest with big outdoor area inc good play area and bowling green *(Mr and Mrs A H Young, J S Burn)*

NANTWICH [SJ6452]

☆ *Black Lion* CW5 5ED [Welsh Row]: Three little rooms alongside main bar, old-fashioned nooks and crannies, beams, bare floors and timbered brickwork, big grandfather clock, coal fire; three local Weetwood ales and Titanic White Star, farm cider, may be cheap sandwiches, chess; dogs welcome, open all day from 4 (1 Fri-Sun) *(the Didler, BB, Pete Baker, Rob Stevenson)*

Cronkinsons Farm CW5 7GZ [corner Pear Tree Field and new link road]: Attractive and friendly modern neo-traditional pub reopened after restoration of fire damage and now all no smoking, large central bar serving several different lounge areas, wide range of food all day, Banks's, Marstons Pedigree and a guest beer; handy for Stapeley Water Gardens, open all day *(Edward Leetham)*

☆ *Red Cow* CW5 5NF [Beam St]: Well renovated and welcoming proper pub in low-ceilinged former Tudor farmhouse, three Robinsons ales, good value coffee, good log or coal fire, enjoyable home-made food inc less usual dishes in no smoking dining area away from the bar, smallish lounge; terrace with pergola and play area, bedrooms *(Gwyn and Anne Wake, Edward Leetham, Keith and Maureen Trainer)*

NESTON [SJ2976]

☆ *Harp* CH64 0TB [Quayside, SW of Little Neston; keep on along track at end of Marshlands Rd]: Tucked-away country local with particularly well kept ales such as Fullers London Pride, Holts and Timothy Taylors Landlord, good malt whiskies, good value home-made wknd lunchtime food, charming landlady, woodburner in pretty fireplace, pale quarry tiles and simple furnishings (children allowed in room on right); picnic-sets up on grassy front sea wall look out over the Dee marshes to Wales, glorious sunsets with wild calls of wading birds; open all day *(Ann and Tony Bennett-Hughes, BB, Paul Humphreys, Derek and Sylvia Stephenson, Dr Phil Putwain)*

Hinderton Arms CH64 7TA [Chester High Rd (A540)]: Large Chef & Brewer, well divided and tastefully decorated, with good generous all-day food (freshly made so can take quite a while) from sandwiches and baguettes to some interesting hot dishes, cheerful attentive service, Courage Directors, splendid choice of wines by the glass, sensibly priced soft drinks *(Tom and Jill Jones, Paul Humphreys)*

OLLERTON [SJ7776]

☆ *Dun Cow* WA16 8RH [Chelford Rd; outskirts of Knutsford towards Macclesfield]: Attractive country pub with reliable up-to-date food, pleasant helpful service, real ales inc a guest beer, decent wines, modern décor, leather sofas and easy chairs, two fine log fires, no smoking area; good disabled access, open all day in summer *(Mrs P J Carroll, LYM, H and P Cate, Simon J Barber)*

PARKGATE [SJ2778]

☆ *Red Lion* CH64 6SB [The Parade (B5135)]: Comfortable and neatly kept Victorian local on attractive waterfront, big windows look across road to silted grassy estuary with Wales beyond, typical pub furnishings, shiny brown beams hung with lots of china, copper and brass, standard food inc sandwiches, OAP lunches and other bargain offers, Adnams, Tetleys and Charles Wells Bombardier, decent wines by the glass, flame-effect fire in pretty fireplace, good games room off public bar; picnic-sets out on small front terrace, open all day *(Keith and Sue Campbell, BB)*

Ship CH64 6SA [The Parade]: Bow-window estuary views from long bar of large hotel, good changing beer range, good value bar food inc local fish (and afternoon teas), quick pleasant service, open fire, restaurant, quizzes, perhaps karaoke; 24 bedrooms, open all day *(Paul Humphreys)*

PLUMLEY [SJ7275]

☆ *Golden Pheasant* WA16 9RX [Plumley Moor Lane (off A556 by the Smoker)]: Friendly and efficient, with Lees Bitter and Mild and decent food in comfortable lounge areas, wider menu in roomy restaurant and conservatory, dark timbering of extensions blending well with older part; children welcome, spacious gardens inc play area and bowling green, good well equipped bedrooms *(LYM, Mike Jones, Paul and Margaret Baker)*

☆ *Smoker* WA16 0TY [A556 S of M6 junction 19]: Attractive 16th-c pub with dark panelling, open fires in impressive period fireplaces, deep sofas as well as other comfortable seats in three partly no smoking linked rooms, good choice of wines and whiskies, Robinsons and a guest ale, food (all day Sun) from sandwiches up in bar and restaurant; piped music; children welcome, good-sized garden with good play area, open all day Sun *(LYM, Alistair and Kay Butler, Dennis Jones, Hugh and Susan Ellison, Mart Lawton)*

RAINOW [SJ9678]

☆ *Highwayman* SK10 5UU [A5002 Whaley Bridge—Macclesfield, NE of village]: Warmly welcoming 17th-c moorside pub with good value generous food from good sandwiches up, Thwaites Original and Lancaster Bomber, cosy low-beamed rooms with lovely log fires, plenty of atmosphere, grand views; open all day Thurs-Sun *(LYM, the Didler, Brian and Anna Marsden, Peter F Marshall)*

RUNCORN [SJ5081]

Prospect WA7 4LD [Weston Rd, Weston, just off A557 expressway]: Cains and four other good ales inc a Mild, good value standard food lunchtime and early evening and two open fires in village local with partly no smoking lounge bar and good public bar with darts, dominoes, cribbage and pool; tables outside, open all day *(Colin Boardman, Pete Baker)*

SMALLWOOD [SJ7861]

☆ *Legs of Man* CW11 2UG [A50 S of Sandbach]: Good home-made bar food inc some imaginative dishes in comfortable roadside pub with carefully matched chairs, banquettes, carpet, curtains and wallpaper, fin de siècle tall white nymphs on columns, lush potted plants, Robinsons ales, good friendly service even when busy, separate restaurant menu; children truly welcome, well spaced tables on side lawn with barbecue and play area *(BB, Leo and Barbara Lionet)*

STOAK [SJ4273]

Bunbury Arms CH2 4HW [Little Stanney Lane; a mile from M53 junction 10, A5117 W then first left]: Small snug and big but cosy beamed lounge with interesting antique furniture, lots of pictures and books, enjoyable reasonably priced food (all day Sun) from enterprising sandwiches and unusual starters to pheasant and paella, good changing real ales,

jovial landlord, open fires, board games; garden tables (some motorway noise), short walk for canal users from bridge 136 or 138, handy for Cheshire Oaks shopping outlet, open all day *(D Watson)*

STRETTON [SJ6282]

☆ *Stretton Fox* WA4 4NU [Spark Hall Cl, Tarporley Rd, just off M56 junction 10 exit roundabout]: Particularly good Vintage Inn in spaciously converted farmhouse, surprisingly rural setting, interesting variety of rooms pleasantly done in their usual faux-old style, generous well priced food, quick friendly service, real ales and good choice of wines *(Roger and Anne Newbury, Pat and Stewart Gordon)*

SWETTENHAM [SJ7967]

☆ *Swettenham Arms* CW12 2LF [off A54 Congleton—Holmes Chapel or A535 Chelford—Holmes Chapel]: Attractive old country pub in pretty setting by scenic Quinta wildlife arboretum, wide choice of good food from sandwiches up in charming line of individually furnished rooms from sofas and easy chairs to no smoking dining area (must book Sun), well spaced tables, changing real ales such as Beartown, Hydes Light, Moorhouses, Storm and Timothy Taylors Landlord, good wine choice, efficient friendly service, log fires; may have two evening sittings, 7.15 and 9.15; children welcome, picnic-sets on quiet side lawn, open all day Sun *(LYM, Brian and Anna Marsden, K M Crook, Edward Leetham)*

TARPORLEY [SJ5562]

Crown CW6 0AT [High St]: More hotel than pub, relaxed atmosphere, extensive good value food, real ales, good service, lots of pictures, conservatory; bedrooms *(Mrs Jane Kingsbury)*

WARRINGTON [SJ6185]

London Bridge WA4 5BG [Appleton; London Rd (A49)]: Canalside pub with half a dozen real ales inc Caledonian Deuchars IPA and Timothy Taylors Landlord, wide choice of food inc huge all-day brunch *(Ben Williams)*

WESTON [SJ7352]

White Lion CW2 5NA [not far from M6 junction 16, via A500]: Busy black and white timbered inn, low-beamed main room divided by gnarled black oak standing timbers, fine 18th-c style settles as well as more modern seating (some tables rather low), two no smoking side rooms, efficient friendly service, generous bar food from sandwiches up, Bass and Jennings Cumberland, dominoes; piped music may obtrude, TV; children in eating areas, lovely garden with bowling green *(Dave Braisted, LYM)*

WHITELEY GREEN [SJ9278]

☆ *Windmill* SK10 5SJ [off A523 NW of Bollington; Hole House Lane]: Extended open-plan pub, airy contemporary décor with light wood tables, wood and stone floors, heavy-beamed core, real ales such as Black Sheep and Timothy Taylors Landlord, good wine choice, enjoyable food using local produce (not cheap but worth it), efficient friendly staff, good-sized no smoking area; TV, piped music; children welcome, big attractive garden with plenty of picnic-sets and summer bar, usually open all day wknds *(G V Price, LYM, Dr K P Tucker, Gary Lee)*

WILLASTON [SJ3277]

Pollards CH64 2TU [Village Sq, off B5151 just S of B5133 junction]: Striking partly 14th-c building with cheerily comfortable beamed and flagstone bar, unusual cushioned wall seats with some stone armrests, welcoming service, wide choice of enjoyable food, Theakstons, good value wines by the glass, restaurant with dining conservatory overlooking sizeable pleasant garden; bedrooms *(Paul Humphreys)*

WILLINGTON [SJ5367]

Boot CW6 0NH [Boothsdale, off A54 at Kelsall]: Popular dining pub in terrific hillside setting, views over Cheshire plain to Wales, good if not cheap food (all day wknds and bank hols) from panini up, good service, real ales such as Greene King and Weetwood, decent wine list, plenty of malt whiskies, small unpretentiously furnished areas around central bar, woodburner, no smoking area, log fire in charming restaurant; no under-8s; garden with picnic-sets on suntrap raised stone terrace (they do make you pay as you order course by course out here), two donkeys, golden retriever H and cat called Sooty *(Mrs P J Carroll, LYM, Ann and Tony Bennett-Hughes, Mike Tucker, Derek and Sylvia Stephenson)*

WILMSLOW [SJ8480]

Coach & Four SK9 1PA [Alderley Rd]: Large open-plan pub with quiet corners around the edge, good value pub food from baguettes and baked potatoes up, Hydes ales; children welcome, bedrooms in separate new block behind *(Dave Irving)*

WINTERLEY [SJ7557]

Forresters Arms CW11 4RF [A534]: Welcoming low-beamed village local with cheerful attentive landlord, inventive good value bar lunches from open-view kitchen, Tetleys ales inc Dark Mild; darts and quiz night, Weds raffle; pleasant garden with dovecote and retired tractor *(Sue Holland, Dave Webster)*

WYBUNBURY [SJ6949]

Swan CW5 7NA [B5071]: Family-friendly bow-windowed pub with nooks and crannies in comfortable rambling lounge, pleasant public bar, plenty of bric-a-brac, log fires (not always lit), Robinsons Cumbria Way, Old Stockport and Unicorn and a guest such as Wards, bar food (not Sun evening) inc interesting specials, no smoking area, darts; young serving staff, piped music, TV, games machine; tables in garden by beautiful churchyard, bedrooms, open all day (cl Mon lunchtime) *(Sue Holland, Dave Webster, Alistair and Kay Butler, LYM, M and GR, Roy and Lindsey Fentiman, Martin Grosberg, John and Sylvia Harrop, Rob Stevenson)*

Cornwall

A good crop of new entries here (some of them back in the *Guide* on top form after a break) includes the warm-hearted old Globe in Lostwithiel, the charming Roseland at Philleigh (doing well under its new landlords, with good food), the Blue Peter in Polperro (a classic fishing-village pub), the Rising Sun at Portmellon Cove (an interesting bar and good food, overlooking the sea), and the Tinners Arms near a magnificent stretch of coast at Zennor. Like these last three, many other pubs here are in lovely positions by or close to fine beaches or creeks: the Cadgwith Cove close to the working fishing boats at the bottom of the village, the Heron at Malpas (try to bag a seat to watch the sunset over the water), the idyllically set Pandora near Mylor Bridge, the popular and well run Rashleigh in Polkerris just a few steps from a lovely beach, the bustling Ship built into the cliffs by Porthleven harbour, the light and airy Blue (more a contemporary bar than traditional pub) right on the sand at Porthtowan, the Turks Head on St Agnes in the Isles of Scilly (steps down to the slipway so you can take your drink to the shore), the straightforward Old Success by Sennen Cove's magnificent beach, and the lively bar at Port Gaverne hotel near Port Isaac (just back from the sea with fine cliff walks). Other pubs doing well this year include the Blisland Inn at Blisland (cheerfully run with a fine choice of real ales and well liked food), the Olde Plough at Duloe (quite an emphasis on the popular food), the Crown at Lanlivery (genuinely friendly and now totally no smoking), the bustling Royal Oak in Lostwithiel (fine choice of beers), the Miners Arms in Mithian (good food and a nice atmosphere), the civilised Royal Oak in Perranwell, and the particularly well run Old Ale House in Truro (great food at very low prices, and ten real ales). Tops for pub food here is now the Roseland at Philleigh: it is Cornwall Dining Pub of the Year. There are dozens more really fine pubs in the Lucky Dip section at the end of the chapter, many of them well up to main entry standard – if only we didn't have to keep the *Guide* to a manageable size. One of them, the Boot at Calstock, was all set to be our choice as Cornwall's Dining Pub of the Year – until the landlord told us he was planning to leave. Other favourites, almost all inspected by us, are the Cross Keys in Cawsand, Coombe Barton at Crackington Haven, Old Albion at Crantock, Smugglers Den at Cubert, Old Quay at Devoran, Seven Stars in Falmouth, Lamorna Wink at Lamorna, Top House at Lizard, White Hart at Ludgvan, Red Lion at Mawnan Smith, Bush at Morwenstow (much changed recently), Old Coastguard in Mousehole (hotel rather than pub) and cheerful Ship there, Racehorse at North Hill, Kings Arms at Paul, Cornish Arms at Pendoggett, Admiral Benbow in Penzance, Polgooth Inn, Five Pilchards at Porthallow, Rising Sun in St Mawes and London at St Neot. Drinks prices in the county are close to the national average, with locally brewed ales from Sharps, Skinners or St Austell usually the cheapest on offer. Another local brewery, Organic, is exactly that, and uses its own spring water as well as entirely organic ingredients.

ALTARNUN   SX2182   Map 1
Rising Sun ◨ £

Village signposted off A39 just W of A395 junction; pub itself NW of village, so if coming instead from A30 keep on towards Camelford; PL15 7SN

Very popular with cheery locals (and their dogs), this is a pretty straightforward inn on the edge of Bodmin Moor. The low-beamed L-shaped main bar has plain traditional furnishings, bare boards and polished delabole slate flagstones, some stripped stone, guns on the wall, and a couple of coal fires. The central bar has well kept Bass, Cotleigh Golden Eagle and Tawny, Flowers Original, Greene King IPA, and Sharps Doom Bar on handpump, and decent house wines. Hearty home-made bar food includes burgers (from £2.20), soup or locally made pasties (£3), decent sandwiches (£3; baguettes £4.50), three-egg omelette (£4), home-cooked ham and eggs or chicken and chips (£6), meat pie or vegetable chilli (£6.50), and steaks (from £8). A small back area has darts, games machine, juke box and a pool table, with a second pool table in the carpeted room beyond (no dogs allowed in that one); cribbage and dominoes. The main bar can get a bit smoky sometimes. There are tables outside; the field opposite has space for caravans, though screened off by high evergreens. The village itself (with its altarless church – hence the name) is well worth a look. *(Recommended by Dennis Jenkin, the Didler)*

Free house ~ Licensee Jim Manson ~ Real ale ~ Bar food ~ No credit cards ~ (01566) 86636 ~ Children in family room only ~ Dogs allowed in bar ~ Open 11-3, 5.30-11; 11-11 Sat; 12-10.30 Sun ~ Bedrooms: £22/£40

BLISLAND   SX0973   Map 1
Blisland Inn ◨

Village signposted off A30 and B3266 NE of Bodmin; PL30 4JF

The present licensees of this welcoming local have offered over 2,000 guest beers during their time here. They keep up to eight at any one time tapped from the cask or on handpump and from all over the country, too: two are named for the pub (brewed by Sharps), as well as Cottage Normans Conquest, Itchen Valley Fagins, Larkins Best, Thwaites Mild, St Austell Black Prince, and one from Uncle Stuarts. Every inch of the beams and ceiling is covered with beer badges (or their particularly wide-ranging collection of mugs), and the walls are similarly filled with beer-related posters and memorabilia. They also have a changing farm cider, fruit wines and real apple juice. Above the fireplace another blackboard has the choice of enjoyable, hearty home-made food, which might include hot meat baps (from £4.45; the breakfast bap of bacon, egg, sausage, mushroom and tomato is liked), lasagne, moussaka or leek and mushroom bake (£6.95), and various pies like rabbit or steak in ale (from £6.95); service is cheerful and friendly. The carpeted no smoking lounge has a number of barometers on the walls, a rack of daily newspapers for sale, a few standing timbers, and a good chatty atmosphere. The family room has pool, table skittles, euchre, cribbage and dominoes; piped music. Plenty of picnic-sets outside. The popular Camel Trail cycle path is close by – though the hill up to Blisland is pretty steep. As with many pubs in this area, it's hard to approach without negotiating several single-track roads. *(Recommended by Peter Meister, the Didler, DAV, Canon Michael Bourdeaux, A P Seymour, R V T Pryor, W F C Phillips, David Crook)*

Free house ~ Licensees Gary and Margaret Marshall ~ Real ale ~ Bar food (12-2.30(2 Sun), 6.30-9.30; may not do Sun evening food Jan/Feb) ~ (01208) 850739 ~ Children in family room only ~ Dogs welcome ~ Live music Sat evening ~ Open 11.30-11; 12-10.30 Sun

---

'Children welcome' means the pub says it lets children inside without any special restriction. If it allows them in, but to restricted areas such as an eating area or family room, we specify this. Some pubs may impose an evening time limit. We do not mention limits after 9pm as we assume children are home by then.

BODINNICK   SX1352   Map 1
Old Ferry

Across the water from Fowey; coming by road, to avoid the ferry queue turn left as you go down the hill – car park on left before pub; PL23 1LX

To make the most of the views over the pretty Fowey river from either the front terrace or the restaurant here, you must arrive promptly and bag a seat. The binoculars in the guest lounge make the most of any water activity or birdlife. Three simply furnished little rooms have quite a few bits of nautical memorabilia, a couple of half model ships mounted on the wall, and several old photographs, as well as wheelback chairs, built-in plush pink wall seats, and an old high-backed settle; there may be several friendly cats and a dog. The family room at the back is actually hewn into the rock, and the restaurant is no smoking; piped music and TV. Bar food includes pasties (£3.10), home-made soup (£3.80), sandwiches (from £3.50; toasties 45p extra), quite a few dishes with chips (from £4.95; home-cooked ham and egg £7.25), home-made cream cheese and broccoli pasta bake or curry of the day (£7.50), home-made steak and kidney in ale pie (£7.95), fresh smoked haddock with scrambled egg (£8.95), puddings (£3.95), and daily specials such as smoked salmon, crab and prawn cocktail (£5.50), cashew nut paella (£9.25), home-made pork loin wellington (£11.75), and fresh medley of local fish (£15.25). Sharps Own on handpump, kept under light blanket pressure. The lane beside the pub, in front of the ferry slipway, is extremely steep and parking is limited, and some readers suggest parking in the public car park in Fowey and taking the little ferry to the pub. *(Recommended by Jim Abbott, Roger Thornington, Mayur Shah, Mr and Mrs A H Young, Gill and Keith Croxton, Charles and Pauline Stride, A P Seymour)*

Free house ~ Licensees Royce and Patricia Smith ~ Real ale ~ Bar food (12-3, 6-9; sandwiches all day) ~ Restaurant ~ (01726) 870237 ~ Children welcome ~ Dogs allowed in bar ~ Open 11-11; 12-10.30 Sun; 12-10.30 weekdays in winter; closed 25 Dec ~ Bedrooms: £70S/£60(£75B)

CADGWITH   SW7214   Map 1
Cadgwith Cove Inn

Down very narrow lane off A3083 S of Helston; no nearby parking; TR12 7JX

Before – or after – a visit to this old-fashioned, bustling local you could enjoy one of the superb coastal walks in either direction. The two snugly dark front rooms have plain pub furnishings on their mainly parquet flooring, a log fire in one stripped stone end wall, lots of local photographs including gig races, cases of naval hat ribands and of fancy knot-work, and a couple of compass binnacles. Some of the dark beams have ship's shields and others have spliced blue rope hand-holds. Well kept Flowers IPA, Greene King Abbot, Sharps Doom Bar, and maybe a guest on handpump. A plusher pink back room has a huge and colourful fish mural. One room and the area by the bar counter are no smoking. Home-made bar food includes soup (£3.85; crab soup £6.95), sandwiches (from £3.95; white crab £6.45), lasagne (£7.55), home-made stilton and broccoli quiche (£8.50), sirloin steak (£11.45), daily specials such as lamb shank (£9) or fish casserole (£10.50), and puddings (£4); best to check food times in winter. The left-hand room has darts, euchre, and maybe piped music. A good-sized front terrace has green-painted picnic-sets, some under a fairy-lit awning, looking down to the fish sheds by the bay. The pub is set at the bottom of a steep working fishing cove; you can park at the top and walk down but it's quite a hike back up again. More reports please. *(Recommended by Charles Gysin, Derek and Heather Manning, Sue Holland, Dave Webster, Victoria Hatfield)*

Punch ~ Lease David and Lynda Trivett ~ Real ale ~ Bar food ~ (01326) 290513 ~ Children welcome away from main bar ~ Dogs welcome ~ Live music frequently in summer ~ Open 12-11(midnight Sat); 12-10.30 Sun; 12-3, 7-11 weekdays in winter (but open all day Fri then) ~ Bedrooms: £27.50/£55(£75S)

DULOE SX2358 Map I
Olde Plough House
B3254 N of Looe; PL14 4PN

There's quite an emphasis on the popular food in this neatly kept, well run pub.
Served by friendly, efficient staff, the lunchtime choice might include home-made
soup (£3.10), local pasty (£3.65), white or granary baguettes (from £4.05; breakfast
sausage, bacon and egg £5.35), ploughman's (from £5.80), a roast of the day
(£5.95), a trio of local sausages and fried egg (£6.95), vegetable lasagne (£7.45),
vietnamese sweet chilli chicken (£7.75), beef and stilton pie (£7.95), and scallops
in garlic butter (£8.25); there's also devilled whitebait (£4.95), mushrooms in
creamy garlic sauce (£4.85), home-made chicken pancakes (£5.25), a duo of stuffed
peppers (£8.25), steaks on hot stones (from £9.95), wild boar with grain mustard
sauce (£11.95), and beef wellington (£13.25). The small more modern restaurant is
no smoking; piped music. Butcombe Bitter and Sharps Doom Bar on handpump
and eight wines by the glass; local cider. The three communicating rooms have
lovely dark polished delabole slate floors, some turkey rugs, a mix of pews, modern
high-backed settles and smaller chairs, foreign banknotes on the beams, and three
woodburning stoves. The décor is restrained – prints of waterfowl and country
scenes, and copper jugs and a fat wooden pig perched on window sill. There are a
few picnic-sets out by the road. The friendly jack russell is called Jack, and the two
cats, Amy and Tia. (Recommended by Ray and Winifred Halliday, Jim Abbott, John and Joan
Calvert, Jacquie and Jim Jones, Julia and Richard Tredgett, David Lewis, Nick Lawless, Paul and
Shirley White, Geoff Calcott, Glenwys and Alan Lawrence)

Free house ~ Licensees Gary and Alison Toms ~ Real ale ~ Bar food ~ Restaurant ~
(01503) 262050 ~ Children welcome away from main bar ~ Dogs allowed in bar ~
Open 12-2.30, 6.30-11; 12-2.30, 7-10.30 Sun; closed 25 Dec, evening 26 Dec

EGLOSHAYLE SX0172 Map I
Earl of St Vincent
Off A389, just outside Wadebridge; PL27 6HT

To find this tucked away, pretty pub, just head for the church. There's plenty
of interest inside – golfing memorabilia, art deco ornaments, all sorts of rich
furnishings, and around 200 antique clocks, all in working order. Well kept
St Austell HSD, Tinners and Tribute on handpump; piped music. Bar food includes
soup (£3.50), sandwiches (from £4), ploughman's (from £5), mushroom and
broccoli au gratin or ham and egg (£6.50), fish dishes (from £7.50), and grills (from
£11.50). The snug is no smoking. In summer, there are picnic-sets in the lovely
garden and marvellous flowering baskets and tubs. (Recommended by R J Herd,
Brian and Bett Cox, the Didier, M A Borthwick, Mayur Shah, George Tucker, Mike Tucker,
R M Corlett, Kevin Blake, Liz and Tony Colman, R V T Pryor)

St Austell ~ Tenants Edward and Anne Connolly ~ Real ale ~ Bar food (not Sun evening)
~ (01208) 814807 ~ Well behaved children allowed at lunchtime ~ Open 11-3, 6.30-11;
12-3, 7-10.30 Sun

FALMOUTH SW8132 Map I
5 Degrees West ♀
Grove Place, by the main harbourside car park; TR11 4AU

This is an up-to-date light and airy bar with young and friendly staff, all neatly clad
in black. It's open plan with an expanse of stripped wood flooring but there are
several different areas: squashy sofas around low tables, some modern leatherette
cushioned dining chairs around chunky pine tables, a few leather-topped high steel
benches and stools dotted about (one table has a nice metal fish leg), and a log fire
in a driftwood-effect fireplace. The contemporary artwork and photographs are
local, there's a relaxed informal atmosphere, lots of steel and etched glass, and good
lighting. From the long bar counter they serve St Austell HSD and Tribute on
handpump, 14 good wines by two sizes of glass, plenty of locally produced drinks,

lots of coffees and teas, and hot chocolate with marshmallows and a flake. Using local seasonal produce, the enjoyable food might include home-made soup (£3.95), chargrilled chicken wings in home-made barbecue sauce or tapas (£5.95), toasted ciabattas with various fillings (£5.95; served between 12 and 6), home-made carrot, cashew nut and goats cheese terrine or stuffed vine leaves with olive tapenade, roasted spicy almonds and local bread (£6.95), trio of sausages with caramelised onion and ale gravy or double burger with bacon, mozzarella and an organic egg (£8.95), steamed cod with chilli, lemon grass and ginger (£10.95), marinated lamb steak with home-grown rosemary and mint gravy (£11.95), and puddings (£4.50); a little people's menu (£4.95). A back dining area is similar in style, with long built-in side pews and a couple of little semi-open booths; doors lead to a sheltered back terraced area with seating. A side ramp gives good wheelchair access; disabled facilities. There's a useful short-term car park across the road by the marina. *(Recommended by N Taylor, David Crook)*

St Austell ~ Manager Justine Stockton ~ Real ale ~ Bar food (all day) ~ Restaurant ~ (01326) 311288 ~ Children welcome ~ Dogs welcome ~ Open 11-11.30pm(midnight Fri and Sat); 12-11 Sun; closed 25 Dec

HELSTON SW6522 Map 1
Halzephron ♀ ⇔

Gunwalloe, village about 4 miles S but not marked on many road maps; look for brown sign on A3083 alongside perimeter fence of RNAS Culdrose; TR12 7QB

To be sure of a table in this popular former smugglers' haunt you must book beforehand or get there early. It does get packed at the height of the season. Seating is comfortable, the rooms are spotlessly clean with copper on the walls and mantelpiece, and there's a warm winter fire in the big hearth. Bar food includes lunchtime sandwiches (from £3.20; crab when available £8.40), as well as home-made soup (£3.95), pâté of the day with home-made toasted brioche (£5.70), ploughman's (from £5.85), tagliatelle bolognese (£8.85), evening sirloin steak (£12.95), and evening specials such as crab, corn and coriander cakes with sweet chilli sauce or duck leg confit on an olive and sun-dried tomato salad (£6.50), goats cheese and red onion tart (£8.50), grilled whole rainbow trout on mascarpone polenta with chargrilled vegetables (£11.95), and peppered venison haunch steak with celeriac purée and redcurrant sauce (£13.95); half helpings are available on some of the specials. All the eating areas are no smoking. Well kept Organic Halzephron Gold (this local brewer only supplies organic beers), Sharps Special, Doom Bar and Wills Resolve, and St Austell Tribute on handpump, seven wines by the glass, and 40 malt whiskies; darts and board games. Some readers have been disappointed in the family room recently. There are lots of lovely surrounding unspoilt walks with fine views of Mount's Bay, Gunwalloe fishing cove is just 300 yards away, and there's a sandy beach one mile away at Church Cove. The church of St Winwaloe (built into the dunes on the seashore) is also only a mile away, and well worth a visit. *(Recommended by Derek and Heather Manning, Walter and Susan Rinaldi-Butcher, Colin and Alma Gent, Martin and Pauline Jennings, Brian and Bett Cox, Jacquie and Jim Jones, Andrew Shore, Maria Williams, W M Paton, Sue Demont, Tim Barrow, J K and S M Miln, Stuart Turner, Mel Smith, J and S French, Jan and Alan Summers, John and Joan Nash, R V T Pryor, Matthew Hegarty, Roger Brown)*

Free house ~ Licensee Angela Thomas ~ Real ale ~ Bar food ~ Restaurant ~ (01326) 240406 ~ Children in family room ~ Open 11-2.30, 6(6.30 winter)-11; 12-2.30, 6(6.30 in winter)-10.30 Sun ~ Bedrooms: £50B/£90B

LANLIVERY SX0759 Map 1
Crown ◖

Signposted off A390 Lostwithiel—St Austell (tricky to find from other directions); PL30 5BT

This is a proper old-fashioned pub (now no smoking) with a lovely chatty-buzzy atmosphere and a genuinely warm welcome from the licensees and their staff. The small, dimly lit public bar has heavy beams, a slate floor and built-in wall settles, and an attractive alcove of seats in the dark former chimney. A much lighter room leads off, with beams in the white boarded ceiling, cushioned black settles, and a little fireplace with an old-fashioned fire; there's also another similar small room. Well liked bar food includes lunchtime pasties (£3.95) and sandwiches (from £3.95; fresh local crab £6.95), as well as pork, apple and calvados pâté (£4.95), seared local scallops or specially made burger with garlic and thyme (£6.95), steak in ale pie or chicken caesar salad (£7.95), wild mushroom stroganoff (£8.95), fish pie (£9.95), steaks (from £9.95), slow-cooked shoulder of lamb (£10.95), fowey crab salad (£11.95), and puddings (from £3.95). Well kept Sharps Doom Bar and Eden Ale, and Skinners Betty Stogs and Cornish Knocker on handpump, seven wines by the glass, and local cider; board games. The slate-floored porch room has lots of succulents and a few cacti, and wood-and-stone seats, and at the far end of the restaurant is a sun room, full of more plants, with tables and benches. There's a sheltered garden with granite faced seats, white cast-iron furniture, and several solid wooden tables. The Eden Project is only ten minutes away. *(Recommended by John Evans, Dennis Jenkin, Andy and Claire Barker, Dr Graham Thorpe, Mike and Mary Carter, Jacquie and Jim Jones, Nick and Meriel Cox, R and S Bentley, Keith and Maureen Trainer, Charles and Pauline Stride, Brian Dawes, David Crook, Paul Rampton, R V T Pryor, Ian Wilson, Mrs Frances Pennell, B and M A Langrish, Ron and Sheila Corbett, Ian Phillips)*

Wagtail Inns ~ Licensee Andrew Brotheridge ~ Real ale ~ Bar food (12-2.30, 6-9.30) ~ Restaurant ~ (01208) 872707 ~ Children welcome but must be away from bar ~ Dogs allowed in bar ~ Live music Sun lunchtime ~ Open 12-11; 12-10.30 Sun; 12-3, 6.30-11 in winter ~ Bedrooms: £39.95S/£69.95S

LOSTWITHIEL SX1059 Map 1
Globe ♀ 🍺
North Street (close to medieval bridge); PL22 0EG

This traditional local has a cheerfully relaxed and unassuming bar, and a comfortable and attractive no smoking back restaurant – surprisingly roomy, but so popular that it's well worth booking. The food is interesting, using fresh fish from Fowey and other local produce. As well as lunchtime snacks, there might be home-made soup (£4), sautéed mushrooms and mature stilton baked in ruby port (£5.75), moules marinière (£6.95), home-made chicken curry or vegetarian tortellini in a creamy tomato and basil sauce (£8.95), smoked haddock, spinach and parmesan fishcakes (£9.95), honey roast duck (£11.95) and specials such as venison, hazelnut and burgundy sausages (£8.95), rabbit pie, beef in beer, brie and redcurrant tart or roasted vegetable lasagne (£9.95), and lamb shank or pork chop with stuffing (£11.95). The long somewhat narrow bar has a good mix of pubby tables and seats, with customers' photographs on pale green plank panelling at one end, nice more-or-less local prints (for sale) on canary walls above a coal-effect stove at the snug inner end, and a small red-walled front alcove. The ornately carved bar counter, with comfortable chrome and leatherette stools, dispenses well kept Sharps Doom Bar and Atlantic IPA, Skinners Betty Stogs and Charles Wells Bombardier from handpump, with 12 reasonably priced wines by the glass; friendly licensees and attentive staff. Piped music, darts, board games, TV, and Sunday evening quiz. The sheltered back courtyard, with a dogs' water bowl, is not large, but has some attractive and unusual pot plants, and is a real suntrap (with an extendable overhead awning, the first of its kind in the UK, and outside heaters). The lovely ancient river bridge just a stone's throw away is well worth a look. *(Recommended by Reg Fowle, Helen Rickwood, PL, Bob Monger)*

Free house ~ Licensee William Erwine ~ Real ale ~ Bar food ~ Restaurant ~ (01208) 872501 ~ Children welcome ~ Dogs allowed in bar ~ Cornish music Weds ~ Open 12-2.30, 6(7 Sun)-midnight ~ Bedrooms: /£70B

Royal Oak ♨

Duke Street; pub just visible from A390 in centre – best to look out for Royal Talbot Hotel; PL22 0AG

As well as a fine choice of bottled beers from around the world, they keep up to six real ales on handpump in this bustling and friendly town local: Bass, Fullers London Pride and Marstons Pedigree, and changing guests such as Adnams Broadside and Sharps Doom Bar. Under the new licensees, tasty bar food includes sandwiches (from £2.20; crab £4.45), soup (£3.95), ploughman's (from £5.10), field mushrooms, bacon and goats cheese on toast (£5.25), baked aubergine with wild cornish yarg and basil dressing (£7.95), deep-fried haddock (£8.25), roasted organic chicken with butternut squash and herb dressing (£10.95), steaks (from £12.25), and daily specials such as slow-cooked duck leg with hazelnut dressing (£5.25), seared scallops with spiced lentils (£5.95), sardines with red onion salad and parsley and lime butter (£8.25), chargrilled pork chop with black pudding and apple sauce (£8.95). The neat no smoking lounge is spacious and comfortable, with captain's chairs and high-backed wall benches on its patterned carpet, and a couple of wooden armchairs by the log-effect gas fire; there's also a delft shelf, with a small dresser in one inner alcove. The flagstoned and beamed back public bar (also no smoking) has darts, fruit machines, TV and piped music. On a raised terrace by the car park are some picnic-sets. *(Recommended by Ray and Winifred Halliday, Andy and Claire Barker, Dennis and Gill Keen, Mick and Moira Brummell, David M Cundy, Jodie Phillips, B J Harding, David Crook, Ron and Sheila Corbett, Edward Mirzoeff, Ian Phillips)*

Free house ~ Licensees Joe Lade and Steve Pitt ~ Real ale ~ Bar food ~ Restaurant ~ (01208) 872552 ~ Children welcome ~ Dogs allowed in bar ~ Open 11-midnight(1am Fri and Sat); 12-11.30 Sun ~ Bedrooms: £45B/£79.50B

MALPAS SW8442 Map 1

Heron

Trenhaile Terrace, off A39 S of Truro; TR1 1SL

The creekside position here is lovely – best enjoyed from one of the seats on the terrace or from the window tables inside. The bar is long and narrow with several areas leading off and a raised part at one end, and it's all very light and airy with blue and white décor and furnishings throughout. Two gas fires, mainly wooden floors with flagstones by the bar, modern yacht paintings on the wood-planked walls, some brass nautical items, heron pictures and a stuffed heron in a cabinet, and a chatty brasserie-type atmosphere; half the pub is no smoking. At lunchtime, bar food includes filled rolls or wraps (from £5.50; hoisin duck wrap with plum sauce £6.95), cheese omelette (£6.10), sausages on honey and mustard mash (£6.75), roast ham and eggs (£7.70), and lasagne (£8.75); also, fresh tuna niçoise (£5.25), antipasti (£5.90), thai fishcakes with sweet chilli sauce (£5.95), and evening dishes like steak, mushroom and ale pudding (£6.95), tandoori vegetable masala (£7.95), and fillet steak (£13.25). St Austell IPA, HSD and Tribute on handpump, and ten good wines by the glass; piped music. Parking is extremely difficult at peak times. More reports please. *(Recommended by Malcolm Taylor, Mayur Shah, Jenny and Brian Seller, David Crook, A P Seymour, R V T Pryor, Ian Phillips)*

St Austell ~ Tenant F C Kneebone ~ Real ale ~ Bar food ~ (01872) 272773 ~ Children welcome ~ Open 11-3, 6-11; 12-3, 7-11 Sun

MITCHELL SW8654 Map 1

Plume of Feathers 🛏

Just off A30 Bodmin—Redruth, by A3076 junction; take the southwards road then turn first right; TR8 5AX

As we went to press, we heard that a new licensee had taken over this dining pub, but no major changes were planned. The attractive bars are contemporary and appealing with Farrow & Ball pastel-coloured walls, paintings by local artists, stripped old beams, painted wooden dado and two fireplaces. The restaurant is no smoking. From quite a choice of daily specials there might be ciabatta with goats cheese and sun-dried tomato (£6.75), local scallops with five spice (£6.95), home-cooked ham with local free-range eggs (£7.50), home-made chicken, leek and ham pie (£7.95), locally shot rabbit braised in cider (£11), poached corn-fed chicken breast in a wild garlic and baby vegetable broth (£13.25), and roasted whole bass with crispy fennel salad and herb crushed potatoes (£16.50). The menu includes sandwiches, home-made soup (£3.95), greek mezze plate (£5.25), chargrilled burger with red onion jam (£8.75), fresh pasta with wild mushrooms, truffle oil and parmesan (£8.95), and chargrilled angus rib-eye steak (£14.95). Bass, Courage Directors and Sharps Doom Bar on handpump, and ten wines by the glass; piped music, games machine and TV. The well planted garden areas have plenty of seats, and the bedrooms are very comfortable. *(Recommended by Bernard Stradling, Michael and Maggie Betton, Andy and Claire Barker, David Rule, Dr and Mrs A K Clarke, M G Hart, Will and Kay Adie, Mrs Sheela Curtis, R J Herd, Andy Sinden, Louise Harrington, Dr C C S Wilson, R M Corlett, Mayur Shah, Paul and Shirley White, Betsy and Peter Little, Roger and Anne Newbury, H W Roberts, A P Seymour, David Swift, R V T Pryor, Ian Wilson)*

Free house ~ Licensee Joe Musgrove ~ Real ale ~ Bar food (12-5, 6-10; not evening 25 Dec) ~ Restaurant ~ (01872) 510387/511125 ~ Children welcome but must be away from bar ~ Dogs allowed in bar and bedrooms ~ Open 10.30-11(midnight Sat); closed evening 25 Dec ~ Bedrooms: £48.75S(£56.25B)/£65S(£75B)

MITHIAN SW7450 Map 1

Miners Arms ㉕

Just off B3285 E of St Agnes; TR5 0QF

A new garden area has been opened here and there are also seats on the back terrace, with more on the sheltered front cobbled forecourt. Inside, several cosy little rooms and passages are warmed by winter open fires, and the small back bar has an irregular beam and plank ceiling, a wood block floor, and bulging squint walls (one with a fine old wall painting of Elizabeth I); another small room has a decorative low ceiling, lots of books and quite a few interesting ornaments. The restaurant areas are no smoking. Served by helpful, friendly staff the good bar food (using only fresh local produce) includes lunchtime sandwiches (from £4.95; crab and prawn £6.50), ploughman's (£6.95), ham and egg (£7.95), salads (from £7.95; fresh crab £9.50), and home-made steak in ale or spinach and feta pies (£8.95), with evening choices such as soup (£3.95), tiger prawns with chilli butter (£5.50), smoked fish platter or wild mushroom and courgette risotto (£9.95), chicken with pineapple, banana and peppers in a coconut and fresh herb sauce (£10.50), calves liver with crispy pancetta (£10.75), steaks (from £10.95), and daily specials like monkfish wrapped in parma ham with a garlic and mushroom sauce (£11.50), and dover sole with flaked almonds and nut brown butter (£12.95). Well kept Adnams Broadside, Bass, and Sharps Doom Bar on handpump, and several wines by the glass. *(Recommended by Steve Harvey, Dennis Jenkin, N Taylor, Mike Tucker, Stephen and Jean Curtis, Paul and Shirley White, Ted George, Roger Brown)*

Punch ~ Lease Dyanne Hull and Chris Mitchell ~ Real ale ~ Bar food ~ (01872) 552375 ~ Children allowed until 9pm ~ Dogs allowed in bar ~ Open 12-midnight; 12-11.30 Sun

MYLOR BRIDGE SW8137 Map 1

Pandora ㉕ ★★ 🍷

Restronguet Passage: from A39 in Penryn, take turning signposted Mylor Church, Mylor Bridge, Flushing and go straight through Mylor Bridge following Restronguet Passage signs; or from A39 further N, at or near Perranarworthal, take turning signposted Mylor, Restronguet, then follow Restronguet Weir signs, but turn left down hill at Restronguet Passage sign; TR11 5ST

As well as driving to this idyllically placed pub, you can reach it by walking along the estuary amongst avenues of wild flowers or arrive (as do quite a few customers) by boat; in fine weather you can sit with your drink on the long floating pontoon and watch children crabbing. Inside, the several rambling, interconnecting rooms have low wooden ceilings (mind your head on some of the beams), beautifully polished big flagstones, cosy alcoves with leatherette benches built into the walls, old race posters, and three large log fires in high hearths (to protect them against tidal floods); part of the bar area is no smoking – as is the restaurant. Lunchtime bar food includes sandwiches (from £4.50; crab £7.95), home-made soup (£4.75), local mussels (£5.95), ploughman's (£7.95), vegetable stir fry (£9.50), lamb and mint sausages (£10.75), and crab cakes with rocket, orange and asparagus salad (£12.50), with evening dishes such as chargrilled lambs liver on creamed horseradish potato with red wine jus (£5.75), seared scallops with belly pork and a white onion sauce (£6.95), spinach and wild mushroom risotto (£9.95), roast cod with pea and mint purée (£11.50), veal escalopines with fried egg and anchovies and parsley beurre noisette (£11.75), and sirloin steak on thyme potato purée with hogs pudding (£14.95); puddings like coconut, treacle and lemon tart or marmalade bread and butter pudding (£4.75). Afternoon teas, too. Well kept St Austell HSD, Tinners and Tribute, and a guest beer on handpump, and a dozen wines by the glass. It does get very crowded and parking is difficult at peak times. *(Recommended by Steve Harvey, John Whiting, Dennis Jenkin, Martin Hann, Colin and Alma Gent, David Rule, Gene and Kitty Rankin, M Bryan Osborne, the Didler, Dr and Mrs M E Wilson, Andy Sinden, Louise Harrington, Mr and Mrs A H Young, Chris and Susie Cammack, Michael and Jeanne Shillington, Malcolm Taylor, Mayur Shah, Paul and Shirley White, J M Tansey, Bernard Stradling, A P Seymour, Simon Cleasby, Neil and Anita Christopher, R V T Pryor, Gary Rollings, Peter Johnson)*

St Austell ~ Tenant John Milan ~ Real ale ~ Bar food (all day) ~ Restaurant ~ (01326) 372678 ~ Children welcome away from bar area ~ Dogs allowed in bar ~ Jazz Fri evenings in winter ~ Open 10am-midnight; 10.30am-11pm in winter

PENZANCE SW4730 Map 1
Turks Head ㉕
At top of main street, by big domed building (Lloyds TSB), turn left down Chapel Street; TR18 4AF

This is the oldest pub in town and there has been a Turks Head here for over 700 years – though most of the original building was destroyed by a Spanish raiding party in the 16th c. Run by a friendly, cheerful licensee, the bustling bar has old flat irons, jugs and so forth hanging from the beams, pottery above the wood-effect panelling, wall seats and tables, and a couple of elbow rests around central pillars; piped music. Bar food includes soup (£3.75), lunchtime sandwiches and baguettes (from £4.50), and filled baked potatoes (from £4.95), omelettes (£5.95), various ciabattas (from £6.95), a pie of the day with a pint (£7.95), steaks (from £11.50), popular sizzler dishes (£10.95 chicken, £11.95 tandoori monkfish), and white crabmeat salad (£12.50). The restaurant area is no smoking. Well kept Adnams Bitter, Sharps Doom Bar, Wadworths 6X, and a guest on handpump; helpful service. The suntrap back garden has big urns of flowers. *(Recommended by Bruce and Penny Wilkie, Gene and Kitty Rankin, Michael and Alison Sandy, Pam and Alan Neale, Alan Johnson, Catherine Pitt, Paul and Shirley White)*

Punch ~ Lease Jonathan Gibbard ~ Real ale ~ Bar food ~ (01736) 363093 ~ Children in eating areas ~ Dogs allowed in bar ~ Open 11-midnight(1am Sat); 12-11 Sun; 11-3, 5.30-11 in winter

PERRANWELL SW7739 Map 1
Royal Oak ♀
Village signposted off A393 Redruth—Falmouth and A39 Falmouth—Truro; TR3 7PX

Although drinkers do get a look-in, most emphasis in this pretty and quietly set stone-built village pub is on the very good food. The roomy, carpeted bar is welcoming and relaxed, with a buoyant, gently upmarket atmosphere, horsebrasses and pewter and china mugs on its black beams and joists, plates and country pictures on its cream-painted stone walls, and cosy wall and other seats around its candlelit tables. It rambles around beyond a big stone fireplace (with a good log fire in winter) into a snug little nook of a room behind, with just a couple more tables. Well kept Bass, Flowers IPA and Sharps Special on handpump from the small serving counter and good wines by the glass (the wine list is well balanced and not over-long); prompt, friendly service and a particularly helpful landlord. Well presented, the interesting bar food includes super tapas like smoked anchovies, chorizo and olives, artichoke hearts in garlic butter, stuffed vine leaves, and guacamole (from £3.25), home-made soup (£4.25), smoked duck salad (£6.25), crab bake (£6.75), moules marinière or smoked salmon and crab gateau (£6.75), teriyaki chicken (£9.75), a trio of local fish (£10.25), steaks (from £12.95), and specials such as crab and sweetcorn bisque (£4.50), fresh steamed cockles (£6.95), paella (£9.95), a super bouillabaisse (£11.50), and lobster in garlic butter (£22). The restaurant area is no smoking; piped music, table football, and shove-ha'penny. There are tables out in front and in a secluded canopied garden. More reports please. *(Recommended by David Gunn, Andy Sinden, Louise Harrington, Mayur Shah, Dennis Jenkin, J M Tansey, R V T Pryor)*

Free house ~ Licensee Richard Rudland ~ Real ale ~ Bar food (12-2.30, 7-9.30) ~ Restaurant ~ (01872) 863175 ~ Children in dining areas only ~ Dogs allowed in bar ~ Open 11-3, 6-midnight; 12-3.30, 6-11 Sun

PHILLEIGH SW8739 Map 1

Roseland 🍴 ♀

Between A3078 and B3289, NE of St Mawes just E of King Harry Ferry; TR2 5NB

Cornwall Dining Pub of the Year

Happily back on track with a father and son now at the helm, this busy little pub has a good mix of customers enjoying the friendly atmosphere. The two bar rooms (one with flagstones and the other carpeted) have wheelback chairs and built-in red-cushioned seats, open fires, old photographs, and some giant beetles and butterflies in glass cases. The small lower back bar is liked by locals. Good food at lunchtime includes sandwiches, soup (£4), salmon and smoked haddock fishcakes with lemon zest tartare sauce, beefburger topped with local brie and bacon or pork and leek sausages with red wine gravy (£7), sticky ribs (£8), a whole baked camembert with dipping breads and sweet apricot chutney (enough for two to share, £9), and local scallops and crab (£10); evening choices such as aubergines stuffed with creamy mushrooms and topped with local cheese (£6), chinese-style crispy duck salad (£7), beef bourguignon (£10), creamy garlic chicken wrapped in local bacon or slow-roasted lamb shoulder with a redcurrant and port gravy (£12), crispy duck breast on braised red cabbage (£13), fillet steak with a rich red wine sauce (£15), daily specials, and puddings. Adnams Best, Sharps Doom Bar and Skinners Betty Stogs on handpump, and a dozen wines (plus champagne) by the glass. The pretty paved front courtyard is a very pleasant place on a sunny day, and the pub is handy for Trelissick Gardens and the King Harry ferry. *(Recommended by Steve Harvey, Walter and Susan Rinaldi-Butcher, Michael Cooper, Pete Walker, John and Jackie Chalcraft, Adrian Johnson, Mr and Mrs Bentley-Davies)*

Free house ~ Licensees Douglas and William Richards ~ Real ale ~ Bar food (12-2.30, 5.30-9.30; 12-3, 6-9 Sun) ~ Restaurant ~ No credit cards ~ (01872) 580254 ~ Children in restaurant ~ Dogs allowed in bar ~ Open 11.30-3, 5.30-11; 12-3, 6-10.30 Sun

POLKERRIS SX0952 Map 1

Rashleigh ㉕

Signposted off A3082 Fowey—St Austell; PL24 2TL

The position of this popular pub is lovely. There's a splendid beach with its restored jetty only a few steps away and safe moorings for small yachts in the cove. From the sun terrace, with its big awning and outside heaters, there are fine views towards the far side of St Austell and Mevagissey bays. Inside, the bar is snug and cosy, and the front part has comfortably cushioned seats and up to half a dozen well kept real ales on handpump: Sharps Doom Bar and a beer named for the pub, Timothy Taylors Landlord, and guests such as Ring o' Bells Dreckly and Skinners

Cornish Knocker; farm ciders, several whiskies, and eight wines by the glass. The more simply furnished back area has local photographs on the brown panelling, and a winter log fire; games machine. Well liked and reasonably priced bar food includes sandwiches (from £3.50; open salad sandwiches from £6.95), home-made soup (£3.60), local mushrooms stuffed with pâté and fried in a light batter (£4.95), ploughman's (from £5.95), hazelnut and vegetable crumble (£8.25), home-made daily specials like local crab and prawn cocktail (£5.75), beef curry (£8.50), fish or steak pies (from £8.75), plenty of fresh fish caught in the bay, and home-made puddings such as cherry trifle or treacle tart (£4.25). The restaurant is no smoking. Plenty of parking either at the pub's own car park or the large village one. This whole section of the Cornish Coast Path is renowned for its striking scenery. *(Recommended by Bob and Margaret Holder, Andy and Claire Barker, the Didler, Mayur Shah, David Lewis, Charles and Pauline Stride, Alan Sutton, A P Seymour, Rob Stevenson, Gary Rollings, Meg and Colin Hamilton, Edward Mirzoeff)*

Free house ~ Licensees Jon and Samantha Spode ~ Real ale ~ Bar food (12-2, 6-9; cream teas and snacks 3-5) ~ Restaurant ~ (01726) 813991 ~ Children welcome ~ Open 11-11; 12-10.30 Sun

POLPERRO SX2050 Map 1

Blue Peter

Quay Road; PL13 2QZ

Overlooking the sea and picturesque harbour, this is a bustling and friendly little pub with hard-working licensees. The cosy low-beamed bar has fishing regalia and photographs and pictures by local artists for sale on the walls, traditional furnishings including a small winged settle and a polished pew on the wooden floor, candles everywhere, a solid wood bar counter, and a simple old-fashioned local feel despite being in such a touristy village. One window seat looks down on the harbour, another looks out past rocks to the sea. Freshly prepared, well liked lunchtime bar food includes home-made soup (£3.95), doorstep sandwiches (from £3.95; lots of hot and cold filled baguettes; wraps (£5.95), cottage pie (£5.75), ploughman's (from £5.95), caribbean crab cakes or pitta bread filled with roast lamb, greek-style mint sauce, salad and feta cheese (£6.95), and vegetable fajitas or fish stew (£7.95), with evening choices such as home-made steak and Guinness pie (£8.25), pork chop in a peppered Boursin sauce (£10.95), and baked haddock and cod topped with melted brie and garlic mushrooms (£11.95). St Austell HSD, Sharps Cornish Coaster, Doom Bar and Wills Resolve, and Shepherd Neame Spitfire on handpump (they may keep only two ales during the winter), and local cider. Seats outside on the terrace. The pub is quite small, so it does get crowded at peak times. *(Recommended by John and Joan Calvert, the Didler, Jonathan Brown, Rob Stevenson)*

Free house ~ Licensees Steve and Caroline Steadman ~ Real ale ~ Bar food (12-3, 6.30-9) ~ (01503) 272743 ~ Children in upstairs family room ~ Dogs allowed in bar ~ Live music Fri and Sat evenings and Sun afternoon ~ Open 10.30-midnight

PORT ISAAC SX0080 Map 1

Port Gaverne Inn ♀ 🛏

Port Gaverne signposted from Port Isaac, and from B3314 E of Pendoggett; PL29 3SQ

Although the hotel side of this 17th-c inn, set just back from the sea, is very popular, what our readers enjoy a lot is the lively and chatty pub part which is full of locals – even on a winter Monday night. The bustling bar has big log fires and low beams, flagstones as well as carpeting, some exposed stone, and genuinely helpful, friendly staff. In spring the lounge is usually filled with pictures from the local art society's annual exhibition, and at other times there are interesting antique local photographs. Bar food includes sandwiches, chicken liver pâté (£5.75), ploughman's with home-made rolls (£6.50), roasted mediterranean vegetable lasagne or fishcakes with salsa (£8), home-cooked ham and eggs (£8.50), local crab salad (£10.95), and daily specials such as vegetable risotto (£7.95), lamb curry (£8), and chicken and mushroom pie or venison stew (£8.50). You can eat in the bar, the 'Captain's Cabin' – a little room where everything is shrunk to scale (old oak chest, model sailing ship, even the prints on the white stone walls) or on a balcony overlooking the sea. The restaurant is no smoking. Well kept St Austell Tribute, and Sharps Doom Bar, Cornish Coaster and Will's Resolve on handpump, a good wine list and several whiskies; cribbage and dominoes. There are outside heaters in the terraced garden. Splendid clifftop walks all around. *(Recommended by Betsy Brown, Nigel Flook, Bob and Margaret Holder, Peter Salmon, Theo, Anne and Jane Gaskin, M A Borthwick, Chris Glasson, Liz and Tony Colman, A P Seymour)*

Free house ~ Licensee Graham Sylvester ~ Real ale ~ Bar food ~ Restaurant ~ (01208) 880244 ~ Children in eating area of bar and restaurant ~ Dogs allowed in bar and bedrooms ~ Open 11-11; 12-10.30 Sun ~ Bedrooms: £60B/£100B

PORTHLEVEN   SW6225   Map 1
Ship   ㉕
Village on B3304 SW of Helston; pub perched on edge of harbour; TR13 9JS

This friendly old fisherman's pub is actually built into the base of the steep cliffs. So from seats inside you can watch the sea surging against the harbour wall only yards from the window. There are tables out in the terraced garden that make the most of the view too, and at night the harbour is interestingly floodlit. The knocked-through bar has log fires in big stone fireplaces and some genuine individuality. The no smoking family room is a conversion of an old smithy with logs burning in a huge open fireplace; piped music, games machine, cribbage and dominoes. Well liked bar food includes sandwiches or toasties (from £4.95; crusties from £5.95), smoked haddock fishcake with lime chilli salsa (£5.25), moules marinière (£5.95), ploughman's (from £7.50), home-made chilli (£9.25), fish pie or nut roast (£9.95), steaks (from £10.95), crab and prawn mornay (£12.95), daily specials such as home-made soups (from £4.50), lasagne (£9.50), and fresh fish (from £11.95), and puddings (£4.50); the candlelit dining room also looks over the sea. Well kept Courage Best, and Sharps Atlantic, Doom Bar and Eden Ale on handpump. *(Recommended by Derek and Heather Manning, Clifford Blakemore, Mike and Heather Watson, Theo, Anne and Jane Gaskin, the Didler, Catherine Pitt, Ann and Bob Westbrook, Paul and Shirley White, David and Nina Pugsley, Andy and Ali, Gary Rollings)*

Free house ~ Licensee Colin Oakden ~ Real ale ~ Bar food ~ (01326) 564204 ~ Children in family room only ~ Dogs allowed in bar ~ Open 11.30-11; 12-10.30 Sun

PORTHTOWAN   SW6948   Map 1
Blue
Beach Road, East Cliff; use the car park (fee in season), not the slippy sand; TR4 8AW

All sorts of customers of any age enjoy this bustling bar – by no means a traditional pub. It's right by a fantastic beach and huge picture windows look across the terrace to the huge expanse of sand and sea. It's very light and airy, with built-in pine seats in the front bays, chrome and wicker chairs around plain wooden tables on the stripped wood floor, quite a few high-legged chrome and wooden bar stools, and plenty of standing space around the bar counter; powder blue painted walls, ceiling fans, some big ferny plants, two large TVs showing silent surfing videos, and fairly quiet piped music; pool table. Perky, busy young staff and a chatty informal atmosphere. Good modern bar food includes puff pastry tartlet with goats cheese and red onion marmalade (£4.50), home-made fishcakes (£4.75), pizzas (from £4.75), lamb koftas on chunky tabouleh with tzatziki sauce (£5), grilled and topped ciabatta bread (lunchtime only, from £5), antipasti or mezze to share (£8.50), meaty or vegetarian burgers (£7), thai green chicken curry (£8.50), warm roasted squash, feta and chickpea salad on rocket and baby spinach with orange, cinnamon and honey vinaigrette (£9), chargrilled sirloin steak with herb or chilli butter (£10), daily specials such as home-made soup (£3.75), local cheese board (£3.95), moules marinière (£5.50; main course £9), and lemon sole with herb butter (£9), puddings like chocolate mousse with chilli shortbread (£4), children's choices (from £3.75), and all-day breakfasts at weekends with the newspapers. Quite a few wines by the glass, cocktails and shots, and giant cups of coffee. *(Recommended by Dr R A Smye, Andy Sinden, Louise Harrington, Tim and Ann Newell)*

Free house ~ Licensees Tara Roberts, Luke Morris and Alexandra George ~ Bar food (12(10 weekends)-3, 6-9; some food served all afternoon weekdays) ~ Restaurant ~ (01209) 890329 ~ Children welcome away from bar ~ Dogs welcome ~ DJs Fri evening, live bands Sat evening ~ Open 11-11; 10-midnight Sat; 11-10.30 Sun; closed first 3 weeks Jan

PORTMELLON COVE SX0143 Map 1
Rising Sun ♀ ⇦
Just S of Mevagissey; PL26 6PL

This spotless and appealing black-shuttered seaside pub combines plenty of atmosphere in its properly pubby main bar with real quality on the food side. Beside home-made cakes and raised pork pies, the food at lunchtime might include a large pasty (£4.25), soup (£4.95), filled foccacia or panini (from £5.25), home-made crab fishcakes with dipping sauces (£5.95), roasted red pepper and stilton lasagne, salmon and noodle salad or home-made shepherd's pie (£6.95), and local fresh fish in beer batter (£7.25); evening choices such as cracked local crab claws (£4.95), home-made mackerel and horseradish pâté (£5.50), teriyaki scallops (£6.25), local duck breast with a brandy and plum sauce or game casserole (£14.95), steaks (from £14.95), and poached cod with fresh mango (£15.95), and puddings like home-made lemon and basil cheesecake, rhubarb and date crumble or chocolate sponge with rich dark chocolate sauce (£5.25). They have well kept Adnams Bitter and Broadside, and a changing guest beer such as Sharps Doom Bar on handpump, and a dozen wines from a good choice and strong in new world ones. The helpful landlord is backed by friendly efficient staff. The bar has black beams (some with small bits of ropework), an unusual log fire at the far end, lots of small old local photographs along with a former local boatbuilder's sign and a variety of nautical hardware on the ochre walls above its dark panelled dado, and nice pub tables on the sealed crazy paving; piped music. Windows looking over the quiet shore road to the sea have a few house plants and musical instruments such as a saxophone and melodion. The attractive no smoking side restaurant, with a rewarding evening menu, has proper tablecloths and so on, and there's also a big upper family/games room (bar billiards and board games) and charming well shaded plant-filled conservatory. There are a few good solid tables and seats (and a water bowl for dogs) out by the side entrance steps, which are flanked by good tubs of flowers, and some more modern tables on the small front terrace. This sandy rock cove is much quieter than nearby Mevagissey even in summer, and very peaceful indeed out of season; some of the bedrooms overlook the water. The sea is safe for swimming and boating, with an August regatta; the pub has tide-time dials outside. *(Recommended by Alan and Paula McCully, Steve Pocock, Jane and Mark Hooper, Andy Sinden, Louise Harrington, Roger Brown, Gary Rollings)*

Free house ~ Licensees Clive and Christopher Walker and Daniel Tregonning ~ Real ale ~ Bar food (12-3(4 Sun), 6.30-9) ~ Restaurant ~ (01726) 843235 ~ Children welcome till 6pm (teens then allowed in snug bar and restaurant) ~ Dogs allowed in bar and bedrooms ~ Live music every second Fri evening ~ Open 12-11.30(midnight Fri and Sat); closed Nov-end Feb ~ Bedrooms: £42.50B/£55B

SENNEN COVE SW3526 Map 1
Old Success
Off A30 Land's End road; TR19 7DG

The view over Whitesands Bay, either from seats inside this old-fashioned seaside hotel or from the terraced garden, are super; Land's End is a pleasant walk away. The unpretentious beamed and timbered bar has plenty of lifeboat memorabilia, including an RNLI flag hanging on the ceiling; elsewhere are ship's lanterns, black and white photographs, dark wood tables and chairs, and a big ship's wheel that doubles as a coat stand. Straightforward bar food includes sandwiches (from

£2.75), soup (£3.95), filled baked potatoes (from £4.50), beer battered fresh cod (£7.75), vegetable lasagne (£7.95), seafood pie (£8.75), steaks (from £9.50), and puddings like jam roly-poly (£3.90). Well kept Sharps Doom Bar, Skinners Heligan Honey and a guest beer on handpump. The upper bar and restaurant are no smoking; piped music, TV, and darts. Bedrooms are basic but comfortable, enjoying the sound of the sea, and they have four self-catering suites. It does get crowded at peak times. *(Recommended by A and B D Craig, Andy and Claire Barker, Michael and Alison Sandy, Paul Goldman, Simon J Barber, J and D Waters, Matthew Hegarty, Roger Brown)*

Free house ~ Licensee Martin Brooks ~ Real ale ~ Bar food (12-2.30, 6-9.30; all day August) ~ Restaurant ~ (01736) 871232 ~ Children welcome ~ Dogs allowed in bar ~ Live music Sat and Thurs ~ Open 11-11(midnight Sat); 12-11(10.30 in winter) Sun ~ Bedrooms: £35(£44B)/£88B

ST AGNES   SV8807   Map 1

Turks Head   🍺   🛏

This is the St Agnes in the Isles of Scilly; The Quay; TR22 0PL

Particularly on a sunny day, this small converted boathouse – Britain's most south-westerly pub – is very special and a favourite with many readers. You can sit on the extended area across the sleepy lane or on terraces down towards the sea, and there are steps down to the slipway so you can take your drinks and food and sit right on the shore; the hanging baskets are very pretty. The simply furnished but cosy and very friendly pine-panelled bar has quite a collection of flags, helmets and headwear, as well as maritime photographs and model ships. The real ale arrives in St Agnes via a beer supplier in St Austell and a couple of boat trips, and the two well kept on handpump might include a beer named for the pub, Ales of Scilly Scuppered (from a local microbrewery), and Skinners Betty Stogs; decent house wines, a good range of malt whiskies, and hot chocolate with brandy. At lunchtime, the well liked bar food includes open rolls (from £3.25; local crab £6.25), ploughman's (£4.95), salads (from £6.50; local crab £9.95), cold ham with chips (£6.75), vegetable pasta bake (£7.50), and puddings (£3.25), with evening dishes like wild rice, spinach and honey roast (£7.95), crab cakes with sweet chilli dip (£8.25), and blackened swordfish steak or sirloin steak (£10.95). Ice-cream and cakes are sold through the afternoon, and in good weather they may do evening barbecues. The inn is totally no smoking, the cats are called Taggart and Lacey, and the collie, Tess. Darts, cribbage, dominoes and piped music. If you wish to stay here, you must book months ahead. Please note, they are now shut between November and March. *(Recommended by Pete and Rosie Flower, R J Herd, Margaret and Roy Randle, Roger and Pauline Pearce, Paul Humphreys, Catherine Pitt, Andy Sinden, Louise Harrington, David Hoult, David Swift)*

Free house ~ Licensees John and Pauline Dart ~ Real ale ~ Bar food (12-2.30, 6-9) ~ (01720) 422434 ~ Children welcome ~ Dogs allowed in bar ~ Open 10.30-11(11.30 Sat); 10.30-11 Sun; closed Nov-Mar ~ Bedrooms: /£64S(£70B)

ST ANNS CHAPEL   SX4170   Map 1

Rifle Volunteer

A390; PL18 9HL

The two front bars here have a pleasantly pubby feel. The main one on the left has a log fire in its big stone fireplace, cushioned pews and country kitchen chairs, a turkey rug on its parquet floor, and a relaxed ochre and green décor; on the right, the Chapel Bar has similar furnishings on its dark boards, another open fire, and motorcycle prints on its cream walls. Well kept Sharps Cornish Coaster and Doom Bar and Wadworths 6X are tapped from the cask, there are over 70 whiskies, local farm cider, and decent wines by the glass; pool, TV and skittle alley. Well liked home-made bar food includes lunchtime sandwiches, soup or hummous (£4.25), moules marinière (£5.50), wild mushroom pasta (£9.95), lamb casserole (£10.95), pork loin steaks with mustard, honey, leek and cream sauce, various curries or sweet and sour chicken (£10.50), fish crumble (£10.95), steaks (from £12.95), and daily specials. The modern back dining room has picture windows to take advantage of a very wide view that stretches down to the Tamar estuary and Plymouth. An elevated Astroturf deck beside it has some tables, with more in the garden which slopes away below. *(Recommended by Ted George, Alistair Caie, Jacquie and Jim Jones, Brian P White, Dr and Mrs P Truelove)*

Free house ~ Licensees Frank and Lynda Hilldrup ~ Real ale ~ Bar food ~ Restaurant ~ (01822) 832508 ~ Children in restaurant ~ Dogs allowed in bar ~ Open 12-2.30, 6-11 ~ Bedrooms: £35S/£50B

ST KEW   SX0276   Map 1
St Kew Inn
Village signposted from A39 NE of Wadebridge; PL30 3HB

A new licensee has taken over this rather grand-looking old stone building but doesn't plan any major changes. The neatly kept bar has winged high-backed settles and varnished rustic tables on the lovely dark delabole flagstones, black wrought-iron rings for lamps or hams hanging from the high ceiling, and a handsome window seat; there's also an open kitchen range under a high mantelpiece decorated with earthenware flagons. Bar food now includes soup (£3.50), pasty (£3.75), ploughman's (£6.75), filled baked potatoes (from £6.95), chicken kiev (£7.25), and 10oz sirloin steak (£13.95); evening choices such as garlic mushrooms (£4.50), home-made chicken liver pâté (£4.75), king prawns in garlic and ginger butter (£6.25), vegetarian curry (£7.95), beef stroganoff or port and stilton chicken (£9.25), and honey-roast duck (£13.50). St Austell HSD, Tinners and Tribute tapped from wooden casks behind the counter (lots of tankards hang from the beams above it), a couple of farm ciders, a good wine list, and several malt whiskies. The big garden has seats on the grass and picnic-sets on the front cobbles. *(Recommended by M Bryan Osborne, the Didler, M A Borthwick, Ian Wilson)*

St Austell ~ Tenant Justin Mason ~ Real ale ~ Bar food ~ (01208) 841259 ~ Children in dining room ~ Open 11-2.30, 6-11(all day July and Aug); 12-3, 7-10.30(all day in July and Aug) Sun

ST MAWGAN   SW8766   Map 1
Falcon
NE of Newquay, off B3276 or A3059; TR8 4EP

In a pretty village, this wisteria-clad old stone inn has seats in the front cobbled courtyard and a peaceful garden with plenty of seats and a wishing well. The neatly kept big bar has a log fire, large antique coaching prints and falcon pictures on the walls, and St Austell HSD, Tinners and Tribute on handpump; piped music, darts, pool, table football and board games. Lunchtime bar food includes home-made soup (£3.75), sandwiches (from £3.95), filled baked potatoes (from £4.50), pesto-filled pasta in tomato sauce (£7.95), home-made chicken and mushroom pie (£8.25), and local fresh cod fillet in beer batter (£8.95), with evening dishes such as garlic mushrooms (£4.75), deep-fried camembert with blackcurrant and port sauce (£5.50), vegetable and five bean chilli (£7.25), home-made curry or a trio of local sausages (£7.95), sirloin steak (£11.95), and puddings like home-made treacle tart or double chocolate and cherry gateau (£3.95). The restaurant is no smoking. *(Recommended by Andrew Curry, Brian and Bett Cox, Tim and Rosemary Wells, Theo, Anne and Jane Gaskin, Bob and Margaret Holder, Louise Daler-Finch, David Hoult, Brian Dawes, David Crook, Ron and Sheila Corbett, Mrs J R Williams, R V T Pryor)*

St Austell ~ Manager Andy Marshall ~ Real ale ~ Bar food (12-2.30, 6.30-9.30) ~ Restaurant ~ (01637) 860225 ~ Children welcome ~ Dogs allowed in bar and bedrooms ~ Open 11-3, 6-11; 12-5, 7-11 Sun ~ Bedrooms: /£68S

TREGADILLETT   SX2984   Map 1

Eliot Arms

Village signposted off A30 at junction with A395, W end of Launceston bypass; PL15 7EU

As we went to press the licensees of this creeper-covered inn were about to change again. Readers, though, have very much enjoyed their visits over the last year here so we are keeping our fingers crossed that the new people won't make any drastic changes. The series of small softly lit rooms are full of interest: 72 antique clocks (including seven grandfathers), 400 snuffs, hundreds of horsebrasses, old prints, old postcards or cigarette cards grouped in frames on the walls, quite a few barometers, and shelves of books and china. Also, a fine old mix of furniture on the delabole slate floors, from high-backed built-in curved settles, through plush Victorian dining chairs, armed seats, chaise longues and mahogany housekeeper's chairs, to more modern seats, and open fires. Several areas are no smoking. Bar food includes home-made soup (£3.50), lunchtime baguettes and filled baked potatoes (from £4.95), ploughman's (from £5.95), a curry of the day (£6.95), and a pie of the day, local pork sausages with mustard mash and onion gravy or spinach and mushroom lasagne (all £7.95). Courage Best and Sharps Doom Bar on handpump; piped music, games machine and darts. There are seats in front of the pub and at the back of the car park. Reports on the new regime, please. *(Recommended by Chris Glasson, Nigel Long, Roger Thornington, Colin and Alma Gent, John Urquhart, Peter Salmon, Jude Wright, John Evans, Paul Goldman, the Didler, Sue Demont, Tim Barrow, Alan Sadler, David Crook, Steve Whalley, J and S French, George A Rimmer, Betsy and Peter Little)*

Coast & Country Inns ~ Manager Michael Redding ~ Real ale ~ Bar food ~ Restaurant ~ (01566) 772051 ~ Children in eating area of bar ~ Dogs allowed in bar ~ Open 11.30-3, 6-11; 11-11 Sat; 12-10.30 Sun ~ Bedrooms: /£65S(£60B)

TRESCO   SV8915   Map 1

New Inn ♀ 🍺 🛏

New Grimsby; Isles of Scilly; TR24 0QG

A short stroll from the quay, this attractive inn does get very busy in high season. Visitors tend to head for the main bar room or the light, airy dining extension but locals prefer the little bar with its chatty and more cosy atmosphere. There are some comfortable old sofas, banquettes, planked partition seating and farmhouse chairs and tables, a few standing timbers, boat pictures, a large model sailing boat, a collection of old telescopes, and plates on the delft shelf. The Pavilion extension has cheerful yellow walls and plenty of seats and tables on the blue wooden floors, and looks over the flower-filled terrace where there's lots of teak furniture and views of the sea. Good bar food at lunchtime includes soup or garlic ciabatta topped with melted cheese (£3.50), garlic crevettes (from £5), sandwiches (from £6; chargrilled bacon, blue local cheese and pear £7.50; fresh crab £10), sticky barbecue spare ribs or moules marinière (£7.50), wild mushroom pasta (£8), chargrilled gammon with a free-range egg (£8.50), local beer battered fish (£9.50), beef in ale pie (£10), seafood tagliatelle (£12.50) and daily specials such as gnocchi with artichoke hearts, feta, and basil cream (£8.50), salmon with saffron and sunblush tomato mash (£10.50), and bouillabaisse (£12.50). Well kept Ales of Scilly Natural Beauty, St Austells Tribute, and a beer named for the pub on handpump, interesting wines by the glass, and several coffees; piped music, darts, pool and board games. Note that the price below is for dinner, bed and breakfast. *(Recommended by Bernard Stradling, R J Herd, Paul Humphreys, Catherine Pitt)*

Free house ~ Licensee Alan Baptist ~ Real ale ~ Bar food (all day in summer) ~ Restaurant ~ (01720) 422844 ~ Children welcome ~ Dogs allowed in bar ~ Open 11-11; 12-10.30 Sun; 11-3, 6-11 in winter ~ Bedrooms: /£228B

There are report forms at the back of the book.

TRURO   SW8244   Map 1
Old Ale House ♦ £
Quay Street; TR1 2HD

Particularly at lunchtime, there's a really good mix of customers and a tremendous atmosphere in this bustling and well run pub. Of course the ten well kept real ales on handpump or tapped from the cask are quite a draw: Skinners Kiddlywink plus changing guests like Bass, Courage Directors, Everards Tiger, Fullers Chiswick Bitter and London Pride, Greene King Abbot, Sharps Doom Bar and Skinners Cornish Knocker. Eleven wines by the glass and quite a few country wines. Tasty wholesome bar food prepared in a spotless kitchen in full view of the bar includes specials such as potato skins topped with bacon and melted cheese or cauliflower and broccoli bake (£3.95), all day breakfast or sautéed potatoes with bacon and mushrooms in a creamy garlic sauce (£4.25), tuna stuffed tomatoes with garlic mushrooms or beef stew (£4.75), and lamb and mint hotpot (£4.95); from the menu there might be doorstep sandwiches (from £3.25; 'hands' or half bloomers with toppings such as bacon, onions and melted cheese or tuna, mayonnaise and melted cheese up to £3.75), vegetable stir fry (£4.95 small, £5.95 large), sizzling skillets (£5.75 small, £6.95 large), and a pie of the day (£5.75). The dimly lit bar has an engaging diversity of furnishings, some interesting 1920s bric-a-brac, beer mats pinned everywhere, matchbox collections, and newspapers and magazines to read. Giant Jenga, giant Connect Four, and piped music. English Heritage have smartened up the building this year. (Recommended by Ted George, Andrew Curry, Dr and Mrs A K Clarke, Brian and Bett Cox, Jacquie and Jim Jones, the Didler, Alan Johnson, Mark Flynn, Mike Gorton, David Crook, Klaus and Elizabeth Leist)

Enterprise ~ Tenants Mark Jones and Beverley Jones ~ Real ale ~ Bar food (12-3, 6.30-9; not Sat or Sun evenings) ~ (01872) 271122 ~ Children allowed but away from bar ~ Jazz every second Weds, live band every second Thurs ~ Open 11-11; 12-11 Sun; closed 26 Dec

ZENNOR   SW4538   Map 1
Tinners Arms
B3306 W of St Ives; TR26 3BY

Originally built in 1271 to house the masons building the church next door, this is a friendly pub with a good mix of customers. The new licensees have gently refurbished the place but don't plan any major changes to the bar. There are wooden-ceilings, newly cushioned settles, benches, and a mix of chairs around wooden tables, antique prints on the stripped plank panelling, and a log fire in cool weather. Tasty bar food at lunchtime includes sandwiches (£3.50), soup (£3.75), ploughman's (£5.95), cottage pie (£6.95), home-cooked ham with free-range eggs (£7.25), and fish pie (£7.25), with evening dishes such as grilled goats cheese (£4.95), confit of duck with orange and ginger (£12.50), and sirloin steak (£13.50); daily specials and puddings like treacle tart (£4.25). The dining room is no smoking. Sharps Doom Bar and a beer named for the pub, and St Austell Tinners on handpump. You can sit on benches in the sheltered front courtyard, or at tables on a bigger side terrace. (Recommended by Richard, Jacquie and Jim Jones, Pete Walker, David Gunn, the Didler, Alan Johnson, Brian and Genie Smart, George A Rimmer, Roger Brown)

Free house ~ Licensee Grahame Edwards ~ Real ale ~ Bar food (12-2.30, 6.30-9) ~ (01736) 796927 ~ Children not allowed in main bar ~ Dogs allowed in bar ~ Open 11-11; 12-10.30 Sun; 11-3, 6.30-11 Mon-Sat in winter

---

If a service charge is mentioned prominently on a menu or accommodation terms, you must pay it if service was satisfactory. If service is really bad you are legally entitled to refuse to pay some or all of the service charge as compensation for not getting the service you might reasonably have expected.

LUCKY DIP

Besides the fully inspected pubs, you might like to try these Lucky Dips recommended to us and described by readers (if you do, please send us reports: www.goodguides.co.uk).

ANGARRACK [SW5838]
Angarrack Inn TR27 5JB [Steamers Hill]: Welcoming pub tucked below railway viaduct, enjoyable country cooking with local produce inc Newlyn fish, good choice changing daily (worth booking Sun lunch and evenings in season), St Austell beers, friendly landlord, log fire, well divided bar with interesting bric-a-brac and a couple of cockatiels; children and dogs welcome, picnic-sets outside, quiet pretty village in little secluded valley (*Keith and Chris Tindell, Mick and Moira Brummell*)

ASHTON [SW6028]
Lion & Lamb TR13 9RW [A394 Helston—Penzance]: Straightforward food from good sandwiches and baguettes up, several real ales, new young licensees, no smoking areas; dogs welcome in bar, lovely hanging baskets and flower beds, open all day, handy for SW Coastal Path (*Dennis Jenkin, Mick and Moira Brummell, Ann and Bob Westbrook*)

BODMIN [SX0767]
Hole in the Wall PL31 2DS [Crockwell St]: Former debtors' prison, masses of bric-a-brac inc old rifles, pistols and swords, arched 18th-c stonework, Bass, Sharps Doom Bar and a guest beer, good value fresh local food (not Mon), upstairs dining bar; well planted yard with small stream running past, open all day (*the Didler*)

BOSCASTLE [SX0991]
Cobweb PL35 0HE [B3263, just E of harbour]: Dim-lit two-bar pub with plenty of character, hundreds of old bottles hanging from heavy beams, two or three high-backed settles, flagstones and dark stone walls, cosy log fire, St Austell real ales, generous popular food at good prices, good friendly service, decent wine choice, pub games, sizeable no smoking family room with a second fire; open all day (*Glenn and Gillian Miller, LYM, the Didler, David Eagles, Betsy and Peter Little, Ted George*)
☆ *Napoleon* PL35 0BD [High St, top of village]: Low-beamed 16th-c pub with good value blackboard food from pasties to bistro dishes, St Austell ales tapped from the cask in no smoking bar, decent wines, good coffee, friendly service, log fires, interesting Napoleon prints, slate floors and cosy rooms on different levels, traditional games; piped music; dogs allowed in bar, children in eating areas, tables on small covered terrace, large sheltered garden, steep climb up from harbour (splendid views on the way), open all day (*LYM, Dr and Mrs M W A Haward, Mrs E M Richards, the Didler, Peter and Margaret Glenister*)
Wellington PL35 0AQ [Harbour]: Long tastefully redone low-beamed bar with eating area and no smoking area upstairs, Skinners Spriggan, Betty Stogs, Cornish Blonde and Admiral and St Austell Tribute, enjoyable food (interesting without being too fancy), log fire;

children welcome, big secluded garden, comfortable bedrooms (*Peter Meister, BB*)

BOTALLACK [SW3632]
☆ *Queens Arms* TR19 7QG: Friendly pub with good food choice inc good local seafood and Sun lunch, Sharps Doom Bar, Skinners and guest beers, cheerful helpful staff, log fire in unusual granite inglenook, comfortable settles and other dark wood furniture, tin mining and other old local photographs on stripped stone walls, attractive family extension; tables out in front and pleasant back garden with owl refuge, wonderful clifftop walks nearby, open all day wknds (*Ian and Joan Blackwell, Mick and Moira Brummell*)

BOTUSFLEMING [SX4061]
Rising Sun PL12 6NJ [off A388 nr Saltash]: Convivial low-ceilinged rural local in same welcoming family for many years, lively public bar and smaller quieter stripped stone room with good coal fire, Bass and changing guest beers; has been cl Mon-Thurs lunchtimes, open all day wknds (*Phil and Sally Gorton*)

BREAGE [SW6128]
Queens Arms TR13 9PD [3 miles W of Helston]: L-shaped local with Caledonian Deuchars IPA, Sharps Doom Bar and up to four guest beers from far afield, farm cider, wide range of good value hearty food from sandwiches and tasty baguettes (not Sun) to enjoyable specials and puddings, quick polite service even when busy, daily papers, good coal fires, ceiling festooned with interesting decorative plates, Queen Victoria memorabilia one end, plush banquettes, back games area with pool, paperback sales for silver band, no smoking restaurant area; piped pop music, quiz night Weds, jazz Thurs; dogs welcome, some picnic-sets outside, bedrooms, medieval wall paintings in church opp, open all day Sun (*Dennis Jenkin, BB, Patrick Renouf, Revd R P Tickle, R V T Pryor*)

BUDE [SS2203]
Bay View EX23 0EW: Varied generous fresh food using local produce cooked to order, cheerful and helpful neat staff; comfortable recently modernised bedrooms (*J R Storey*)
Brendon Arms EX23 8SD: Canalside, with two big friendly pubby bars, back family room, real ales inc Sharps, enjoyable food inc good crab sandwiches and interesting specials; picnic-sets on front grass, bedrooms (*Anon*)

CALSTOCK [SX4368]
☆ *Boot* PL18 9RN [off A390 via Albaston; Fore St]: A smashing find for Cornwall, and would have been a main entry, but landlord planned to leave as we went to press: 17th-c pub stylishly brought up to date in both décor and good food, fairly priced and using only local ingredients, carefully chosen wines by the glass, Sharps Doom Bar and Eden; may be piped jazz, little nearby parking; cl Mon (*Kate and Kevin Gamm, BB, Dr and Mrs P Truelove*)

CAMBORNE [SW6437]
☆ *Old Shire* TR14 0RT [Pendarves; B3303 towards Helston]: Largely extended family dining pub with decent generous food inc popular carvery, Bass, pleasant wines, friendly hands-on landlady, attentive young staff, modern back part with lots of easy chairs and sofas, pictures for sale and roaring coal fire, conservatory; picnic-sets on terrace, summer barbecues *(Colin Gooch)*

CANONS TOWN [SW5335]
Lamb & Flag TR27 6LU [A30 Hayle—Penzance; half a mile Penzance side of St Erth station]: Bright and clean, with well presented lunchtime food from baguettes and baked potatoes to good range of specials, smart welcoming service, real ales inc Caledonian Deuchars IPA, evening restaurant; dogs very welcome, large picnic-sets in courtyard (under cover) and out on grass *(C A Hall)*

CAWSAND [SX4350]
☆ *Cross Keys* PL10 1PF [The Square]: Pretty pub in picturesque square opp boat club, friendly and simple-smart, with wide range of enjoyable generous food esp fish and shellfish (well worth booking in season) in bar and attractive stripped-pine dining room, reasonable prices, west country and mainstream real ales, good value wines, flexible service; pool, may be piped music; dogs welcome, some seats outside, pleasant bedrooms *(Neil Doak, S P Watkin, P A Taylor, Roger Brown)*

CHAPEL AMBLE [SW9975]
. ☆ *Maltsters Arms* PL27 6EU [off A39 NE of Wadebridge]: Busy and enjoyable no smoking country food pub, not cheap but very popular under its friendly and hard-working new owners, beams, panelling, stripped stone and partly carpeted flagstones, Sharps and chilled St Austell Tribute, good wines, upstairs family room, attractive restaurant; dogs welcome in bar, benches out in sheltered sunny corner *(Jacquie and Jim Jones, Mick and Moira Brummell, M A Borthwick, Rachel, LYM)*

CONSTANTINE [SW7229]
Trengilly Wartha TR11 5RP [Nancenoy; off A3083 S of Helston, via Gweek then forking right]: As we went to press friendly new licensees finding their feet still in this previously very popular tucked-away inn, long low-beamed main bar with woodburner and attractive built-in high-backed settles boxing in polished heavy wooden tables, Sharps Cornish Coaster, Skinners Betty Stogs and perhaps a guest beer, some good seafood, bright no smoking conservatory liked by families; table football; children and dogs welcome, pretty garden with boules and lots of surrounding walks, has been open all day wknds *(LYM, M A Borthwick)*

COVERACK [SW7818]
Paris TR12 6SX [The Cove]: Old-fashioned pub above harbour in beautiful fishing village, spectacular bay views from dining room, enjoyable generous food from lunchtime baguettes to local fish and seafood specialities and good Sun lunch, friendly staff, real ales, nautical items inc large model of namesake

ship, interesting wooden moulds from Falmouth churchyard, no mobile phones; garden, bedrooms *(Paul and Shirley White, Meg and Colin Hamilton)*

CRACKINGTON HAVEN [SX1496]
☆ *Coombe Barton* EX23 0JG [off A39 Bude—Camelford]: Much-extended old inn in beautiful setting overlooking splendid sandy bay, welcoming modernised bar with plenty of room for summer crowds, neat and pleasant young staff, wide range of simple bar food inc local fish, Sharps Safe Haven (brewed for the pub) and St Austell, good wine choice, lots of local pictures, surfboard hanging from plank ceiling, big plain family room, enjoyable no smoking restaurant; darts, glazed-off pool table, fruit machines, piped music, TV; dogs allowed in bar, side terrace with plenty of tables, good cliff walks, comfortable bedrooms, open all day Sun, also Sat in school hols *(Pete Walker, LYM, Betsy and Peter Little, DAV, Michael H Legge, Peter and Margaret Glenister, G K Smale, Roger Brown)*

CRAFTHOLE [SX3654]
☆ *Finnygook* PL11 3BQ: Clean and comfortable much-modernised lounge bar, light and airy, Skinners Betty Stogs, good wines by the glass, cheering expert service, wide food choice from good generous open sandwiches up, interesting evening restaurant menu; discreet piped music, one car park is steep; dogs on leads allowed, tables in yard, good sea views from residents' lounge, low-priced bedrooms *(John and Joan Calvert, BB, Dennis Jenkin)*

CRANTOCK [SW7960]
☆ *Old Albion* TR8 5RB [Langurroc Rd]: Picture-postcard thatched village pub, low beams, flagstones and open fires, old-fashioned small bar with brasses and low lighting, larger more open room with local pictures, informal local feel despite all the summer visitors (and the souvenirs sold here), friendly fairly brisk service even when it's busy, generous basic home-made bar lunches inc good sandwiches and giant ploughman's, Sharps and Skinners real ales, farm cider, decent house wines, pool and darts at back of lounge; dogs welcome, tables out on small terrace, open all day *(Colin Gooch, Gloria Bax, LYM, Adrian Johnson)*

CREMYLL [SX4553]
☆ *Edgcumbe Arms* PL10 1HX: Super setting by foot-ferry to Plymouth, with good Tamar views and picnic-sets out by water; attractive layout and décor, with slate floors, big settles, comfortable fireside sofas and other old-fashioned furnishings, old pictures and china, no smoking area, plentiful food from sandwiches up, St Austell ales, cheerful staff, good family room/games area; children in eating area, bedrooms, *(LYM, S P Watkin, P A Taylor, Andy and Ali, Shirley Mackenzie)*

CUBERT [SW7857]
☆ *Smugglers Den* TR8 5PY [village signed off A3075 S of Newquay, then brown sign to pub (and Trebellan holiday park) on left]: Big open-plan 16th-c thatched pub, neat ranks of tables

(worth booking), dim lighting, stripped stone and heavy beam and plank ceilings, west country pictures and seafaring memorabilia, small barrel seats, steps down to no smoking area with enormous inglenook woodburner, another step to big side family dining room; neat helpful friendly staff, fresh generous enjoyable food inc local seafood, Sharps, Skinners and St Austell ales, farm cider, well lit pool area, darts; piped music, fruit machine; picnic-sets in small courtyard and on lawn with climbing frame, has been cl winter Mon–Weds lunchtime (*Steve Harvey, Peter Salmon, BB, the Didler, R V T Pryor, Paul and Shirley White*)

DEVORAN [SW7938]

⋆ *Old Quay* TR3 6NE [Quay Rd – brown sign to pub off A39 Truro—Falmouth]: Two light and fresh no smoking rooms off bar, good reasonably priced food made by landlord from nice lunchtime sandwiches and baguettes to Sun roasts and enterprising specials, changing real ales such as Flowers IPA, Fullers London Pride and Sharps Doom Bar, interesting wines by the glass, good friendly young staff, big coal fire, daily papers, boating bric-a-brac, some attractive prints, evening restaurant; imaginatively terraced suntrap garden behind making the most of the idyllic spot – peaceful creekside village, lovely views, walks nearby, and this ends a coast-to-coast cycle way; dogs welcome, open all day in summer (*Dennis Jenkin, Ian and Joan Blackwell, BB, Dr and Mrs M E Wilson, R and M Willes, David Crook*)

EDMONTON [SW9672]

⋆ *Quarryman* PL27 7JA [off A39 just W of Wadebridge bypass]: Welcoming three-room beamed bar, partly no smoking, around courtyard of former quarrymen's quarters, and part of a small holiday complex; interesting decorations inc old sporting memorabilia, Sharps, Skinners and a couple of good guest beers, some good individual cooking besides generous pubby lunchtime food inc good baguettes, salads and fish and chips, attentive staff; pool, cribbage and dominoes, cosy no smoking bistro; well behaved dogs and children welcome, open all day (*Mrs Sylvia Elcoate, LYM, J Kirkland*)

FALMOUTH [SW8132]

Blue South TR11 3JG [Arwenack St]: Offshoot of Blue at Porthtowan (see main entries), and like that not strictly a pub, though it does have bar as well as table service, with a good choice of food and drink all day (*Andy Acosta*)

Boathouse TR11 2AG [Trevethan Hill/Webber Hill]: Interesting two-level local with buoyant young atmosphere, lots of woodwork, nautical theme, log fire, two or three real ales, friendly bar staff; children welcome, smart chrome tables outside, upper deck with awning, heaters and great estuary views (*Dr and Mrs M E Wilson*)

⋆ *Chain Locker* TR11 3HH [Custom House Quay]: Fine spot by inner harbour with window tables and lots outside, real ales such as Sharps Doom Bar and Skinners Cornish

Knocker, well priced generous food from sandwiches and baguettes to fresh local fish, bargains for two, quick service, nautical bric-a-brac, darts alley; games machine, piped music; well behaved children welcome, self-catering accommodation, open all day (*Colin Gooch, Dr and Mrs M E Wilson, LYM, Neil and Anita Christopher, the Didler*)

⋆ *Quayside Inn & Old Ale House* TR11 3LH [ArwenackSt/Fore St]: Bare-boards dark-panelled bar with Fullers London Pride, Sharps Doom Bar and Skinners, decent wines, efficient service, good value food (all day in summer) from doorstep sandwiches to Sun roasts, friendly helpful staff, upstairs harbour-view lounge with armchairs and sofas one end; lots of pub games, piped music, TV, busy with young people evenings – esp Fri/Sat for live music; children welcome, plenty of waterside picnic-sets, open all day (*Dr and Mrs M E Wilson, Mike Gorton, Gene and Kitty Rankin, Colin Gooch, LYM, the Didler, Barry Collett*)

⋆ *Seven Stars* TR11 3QA [The Moor (centre)]: Quirky 17th-c local, unchanging and unsmart, with long-serving and entertaining vicar-landlord, no gimmicks (nor machines or mobile phones), warm welcome, Bass, Sharps and Skinners tapped from the cask, home-made rolls, chatty regulars, big key-ring collection, quiet back snug; corridor hatch serving tables on prime-site roadside courtyard (*the Didler, BB, Dr and Mrs M E Wilson, Sue Holland, Dave Webster*)

Star & Garter TR11 2AF [High St]: Thriving two-room local extending from narrow frontage into good-sized L-shaped bar with fine high views over harbour and estuary, friendly service, reasonably priced bar food, real ales some tapped from the cask, huge collection of teapots, local murals; theme and music nights (*Dr and Mrs M E Wilson, Sue Holland, Dave Webster*)

FOWEY [SX1251]

⋆ *Galleon* PL23 1AQ [Fore St; from centre follow Car Ferry signs]: Superb spot overlooking harbour and estuary, spotless solid pine and modern nautical décor with lots of wood, dining areas off, good value changing real ales inc Sharps, generous nicely priced food from good sandwiches to plenty of fish, fast service; pool, jazz Sun lunchtime; children welcome, disabled facilities, tables out on attractive extended waterside terrace and in sheltered courtyard with covered heated area, good estuary-view bedrooms (*Margaret and Roy Randle, BB, Ann and Bob Westbrook*)

⋆ *King of Prussia* PL23 1AT [Town Quay]: Handsome quayside building with good welcoming service in neat and roomy upstairs bar with bay windows looking over harbour to Polruan, good food inc splendid local seafood and meats in side family food bar and restaurant concentrating on local produce, St Austell ales, sensibly priced wines; may be piped music; seats outside, open all day at least in summer, pleasant bedrooms (*Margaret and Roy Randle, LYM,*

Alan Johnson, Jodie Phillips, Rob Stevenson, Edward Mirzoeff)

Lugger PL23 1AH [Fore St]: Spotless and interesting family-friendly pub with good mix of locals and visitors in unpretentious bar, comfortable small candlelit back dining area, St Austell ales, friendly service, wide choice of generous food inc lots of seafood, big waterfront mural; piped music; pavement tables, bedrooms *(BB, Margaret and Roy Randle, the Didler, Nick Lawless, Alan Sutton, Peter Meister)*

☆ **Ship** PL23 1AZ [Trafalgar Sq]: Friendly staff, good choice of good value generous food from sandwiches up inc fine local seafood, St Austell ales, coal fire in clean and tidy bar with lots of sea pictures and nauticalia, steps up to family dining room with big stained-glass window, pool/darts room; piped music, small TV for sports, bar can get a bit smoky; dogs allowed, old-fashioned bedrooms, some oak-panelled *(LYM, Margaret and Roy Randle, Alan Sutton, Rob Stevenson, Peter Meister)*

GOLANT [SX1254]

☆ **Fishermans Arms** PL23 1LN [Fore St (B3269)]: Bustling partly flagstoned waterside local with lovely views across River Fowey from front bar and terrace, good value generous home-made standard food from good crab sandwiches to curry specials and fresh local fish, all day in summer (cl Sun afternoon), Sharps Doom Bar and Ushers Best, good wines by the glass, friendly service (can slow on busy days), log fire, interesting pictures, fancy goldfish, back family room; piano, TV, may be piped radio; pleasant garden *(BB, Tim and Rosemary Wells, the Didler, Dr and Mrs M E Wilson, Charles and Pauline Stride, Rob Stevenson, Edward Mirzoeff)*

GORRAN HAVEN [SX0141]

☆ **Llawnroc** PL26 6NU [Chute Lane]: Comfortable and relaxed family-friendly granite hotel (try reading its name backwards), good choice of home-made food inc local fish and big Sun lunch in good-sized dining area, St Austell ales and a bargain light ale brewed for them by Sharps, good wine choice; sunny tables in good-sized garden overlooking the cove and quiet fishing village, barbecues, good value bedroom block, open all day *(Christopher Wright)*

GURNARDS HEAD [SW4337]

Gurnards Head Hotel TR26 3DE [B3306 Zennor—St Just]: Isolated hotel in bleak NT scenery, pubby bar, log and coal fires at each end, local pictures on plank panelling, real ales such as Skinners and St Austell, fine wines by the glass, good value bar and restaurant food inc good fresh fish, welcoming licensees and staff, no smoking family room; tables in garden behind, comfortable bedrooms with rugged moorland or sea views, glorious walks inland or along the cliffy coast *(Geoff and Teresa Salt, LYM, Sue Demont, Tim Barrow, Betsy and Peter Little, Stuart Turner)*

HELFORD [SW7526]

☆ **Shipwrights Arms** TR12 6JX [off B3293 SE of Helston, via Mawgan]: Thatched pub

overlooking beautiful wooded creek, at its best at high tide, terraces making the most of the view, plenty of surrounding walks – and there's a summer foot ferry from Helford Passage; nautical décor and winter open fire, real ale, a decent wine list, bar food inc summer barbecues and lunchtime buffet platters, separate dining area; quite a walk from nearest car park; dogs welcome on a lead, cl winter Sun and Mon evenings *(Derek and Heather Manning, LYM, the Didler, Paul and Shirley White)*

HELFORD PASSAGE [SW7626]

☆ **Ferry Boat** TR11 5LB [signed from B3291]: Big family bar in super position, about a mile's walk from gate at bottom of Glendurgan Garden (NT), by sandy beach with swimming, small boat hire, fishing trips and summer ferry to Helford, suntrap waterside terrace with covered area and barbecues; full St Austell range kept well, very good range of wines by the glass, popular food, friendly cheerful service, no smoking restaurant; may be piped music, games area with pool and SkyTV, steep walk down from the overflow car park; usually open all day summer (with cream teas and frequent live entertainment), bedrooms *(LYM, Dr and Mrs M E Wilson, George A Rimmer)*

HELSTON [SW6527]

☆ **Blue Anchor** TR13 8EL [Coinagehall St]: 15th-c no-nonsense thatched local, very popular for the distinctive and well priced Spingo IPA, Middle and specials they still brew in their ancient brewhouse; quaint rooms off corridor, flagstones, stripped stone, low beams and simple old-fashioned furniture, traditional games, family room, cheap lunchtime food (if not, they let you bring your own); seats out behind, bedrooms, open all day *(LYM, Pete Walker, the Didler, Tom McLean, David Crook)*

HESSENFORD [SX3057]

Copley Arms PL11 3HJ [A387 Looe—Torpoint]: Emphasis on good food from sandwiches, baguettes and baked potatoes to popular Sun lunch and restaurant dishes using local produce in modernised linked areas, St Austell ales, nice wine choice, variety of teas and coffee, log fires, one part with sofas and easy chairs; piped music, dogs allowed in one small area, big plain family room; sizeable and attractive streamside garden and terrace (but by road), play area, bedrooms *(S P Watkin, P A Taylor, Brian P White)*

KINGSAND [SX4350]

Devonport PL10 1NF [The Cleave]: Proper pub with lovely bay views from front bar, changing real ales such as Ring o' Bells Dreckly, good bar food, friendly service, scrubbed floorboards and Victorian décor, lots of ship photographs and bric-a-brac, mix of cast-iron-framed pub furniture with window seats and pine settles, log fire, back snug; tables out by sea wall, good value bedrooms *(Phil Hanson)*

☆ **Halfway House** PL10 1NA [Fore St, towards Cawsand]: Attractive well sited inn with simple mildly Victorian bar rambling around huge central fireplace, low ceilings and soft lighting, Sharps Doom Bar and guests such as Shepherd Neame Spitfire, decent wines, bar food from crab sandwiches and baguettes up, pleasant service, morning coffee, perhaps summer afternoon teas, no smoking restaurant; children and dogs welcome, picturesque village, marvellous walks, bedrooms, open all day in summer *(Mrs Sylvia Elcoate, Ian and Joan Blackwell, Charles and Pauline Stride, Geoff Calcott, LYM, Neil Hammacott)*

LAMORNA [SW4424]

☆ *Lamorna Wink* TR19 6XH [off B3315 SW of Penzance]: Great collection of warship mementoes, sea photographs, nautical brassware, hats and helmets in proper no-frills country local with Sharps Doom Bar and Eden, nice house wine, swift friendly service, enormous lunchtime sandwich platters and the like from homely kitchen area (may not be available out of season), coal fire, pool table, books and perhaps lots of local produce for sale; children in eating area, picnic-sets outside, short stroll above pretty cove with good coast walks *(LYM, David Crook, Paul Rampton, Paul and Shirley White)*

LELANT [SW5437]

Badger TR26 3JT [village signed off A30 W of Hayle; Fore St]: Spaciously extended dining pub with wide range of enjoyable food from sandwiches to fresh fish and OAP lunches, St Austell ales, cheerful efficient service, attractive softly lit modern L-shaped interior, partly no smoking, with panelled recesses, some high-backed settles, airy back conservatory; may be piped music; children welcome, good value pretty bedrooms, wonderful breakfast *(Alan Johnson, A P Seymour, John and Jackie Chalcraft)*

☆ *Old Quay House* TR27 6JG [Griggs Quay, Lelant Saltings; A3047/B3301 S of village]: Large neatly kept modern pub in marvellous spot overlooking bird sanctuary estuary, good value wholesome usual food, real ales, good service, dining area off open-plan bar, children allowed upstairs; garden tables, decent motel-type bedrooms, open all day in summer *(Mel Smith, John and Jackie Chalcraft)*

LERRYN [SX1356]

☆ *Ship* PL22 0PT [signed off A390 in Lostwithiel; Fore St]: Lovely spot esp when tide's in (boats from Fowey then, can radio your order ahead), newish chef doing good food choice using local produce from pasties and good sandwiches up, real ales such as Bass, Skinners and Sharps Eden, local farm cider, good wines, fruit wines and malt whiskies, no smoking area, huge woodburner, attractive adults-only dining conservatory (booked quickly evenings and wknds), games room with pool; dogs on leads and children welcome, picnic-sets and pretty play area outside, nr famous stepping-stones and three well signed waterside walks, decent bedrooms in adjoining building *(Mike Abbott, Andrew Shore, Maria Williams, LYM, Ann and Bob Westbrook, Clive and Vivienne Locks, Richard and Jean Phillips, A P Seymour)*

LIZARD [SW7012]

☆ *Top House* TR12 7NQ [A3083]: Neat and spotless, real ales such as Flowers IPA, Sharps Doom Bar and Wadworths 6X, reasonably priced wines, roaring log fire, generous food (particularly popular with older people) inc good crab sandwiches and regular theme nights, friendly helpful service (same family for over 40 years), lots of interesting local sea pictures, fine shipwreck relics and serpentine craftwork (note the handpumps), big no smoking area, no piped music (occasional live); tucked-away fruit machine, darts, pool; dogs welcome, tables on sheltered terrace, interesting nearby serpentine shop *(A and B D Craig, BB, Dave Braisted, J K and S M Miln, Paul and Shirley White, Sue Holland, Dave Webster)*

LUDGVAN [SW5033]

☆ *White Hart* TR20 8EY [off A30 Penzance—Hayle at Crowlas]: Unchanging 19th-c pub, friendly and well worn in, with great atmosphere in small unspoilt beamed rooms, paraffin lamps, masses of mugs, jugs and pictures, rugs on bare boards, two big blazing woodburners, Bass, Flowers IPA and Marstons Pedigree tapped from the cask, sensibly priced home cooking (not Mon evenings exc high season) from sandwiches to prized treacle tart, no piped music *(the Didler, Alan and Pat Newcombe, LYM, Paul and Shirley White)*

MANACCAN [SW7624]

New Inn TR12 6HA [down hill signed to Gillan and St Keverne]: Small thatched pub in attractive setting above sea and popular with sailing folk, bar with beam and plank ceiling, comfortably cushioned built-in wall seats and other chairs, Flowers IPA and Sharps Doom Bar, bar food, cribbage, dominoes; children and dogs welcome, picnic-sets in rose-filled garden, bedrooms *(Geoff Calcott, LYM, Gloria Bax, the Didler, Ned Kelly)*

MAWNAN SMITH [SW7728]

☆ *Red Lion* TR11 5EP [W of Falmouth, off former B3291 Penryn—Gweek; The Square]: Attractive old thatched pub with cosy series of softly lit linked beamed rooms, open-view kitchen doing wide choice of good food inc seafood, generous carvery roasts and inventive recipes (should book summer evening), quick friendly service, lots of wines by the glass, real ales such as Greene King Old Speckled Hen and Sharps Doom Bar, good coffee, daily papers, fresh flowers, woodburner, dark woodwork, country pictures, plates and bric-a-brac, back no smoking area; piped music, live Sat, TV; children welcome, picnic-sets outside, handy for Glendurgan and Trebah Gardens *(Roger Fox, LYM, Lee Turner, Mick and Moira Brummell, Neil and Anita Christopher)*

MEVAGISSEY [SX0144]

Fountain PL26 6QH [Cliff St, down alley by Post Office]: Unpretentious and interesting fishermen's pub, low beams, slate floor and some stripped stone, St Austell ales, good coal fire, lots of old local pictures, small fish tank, simple lunchtime bar food inc crab sandwiches, upstairs evening restaurant strong on fish, back locals' bar with glass-topped cellar (and pool, games machine and sports TV); occasional live music; dogs welcome, bedrooms, pretty frontage, open all day in summer *(Alan and Paula McCully, Ted George, the Didler, BB, Christopher Wright, J M Tansey, Adrian Johnson)*

☆ *Ship* PL26 6UQ [Fore St, nr harbour]: Lively 16th-c pub with interesting alcove areas in big open-plan bar, low beams and flagstones, nice nautical décor, open fire, friendly efficient uniformed staff, good range of generous quickly served food esp seafood, full St Austell range kept well; games machines, piped music, occasional live; children welcome in two front rooms, comfortable bedrooms, open all day in summer *(Alan and Paula McCully, Christopher Wright, Andy Sinden, Louise Harrington)*

MORWENSTOW [SS2015]
☆ *Bush* EX23 9SR [signed off A39 N of Kilkhampton; Crosstown]: Beautifully placed beamed pub near interesting village church and great cliff walks; now under new management and refurbished in pastel colours with light and tidy contemporary-feel dining room, but keeping the bar's massive flagstones and fireplace (in fact it's partly Saxon and one of Britain's most ancient pubs, with a serpentine Celtic basin in one wall); real ales, enjoyable food using local seasonal produce; garden with good views and solid wooden play things, two new bedrooms *(Jeremy Whitehorn, Nevill Pike, LYM)*

MOUSEHOLE [SW4726]
☆ *Old Coastguard* TR19 6PR [The Parade (edge of village, Newlyn coast rd)]: This light and airy place now thinks of itself as much more hotel than pub, though they do keep real ales and a fair choice of wines by the glass; lovely position with neat and attractive sizeable mediterranean garden by rocky shore with marble-look tables out on decking, good up-to-date food, polite service, modern furniture and potted plants on wood strip flooring, light artwork, lower dining part with glass wall giving great view out over garden to Mounts Bay; children in eating areas, comfortable bedrooms, good breakfast, open all day *(David Glynne-Jones, Dr R A Smye, Mike and Heather Watson, LYM, I A Herdman, David Gunn, Stuart Turner, David and Nina Pugsley, Andy and Ali, J and D Waters, David Booth, Matthew Hegarty)*

☆ *Ship* TR19 6QX [Harbourside]: Bustling harbourside local, the heart of the village, with welcoming landlord and staff, beams, panelling, flagstones and open fire, St Austell ales, one bar no smoking now, restaurant area busy early evening with families eating – the fish pie is good value, and they do a good crab soup; prominent TV and machines in one part; children and dogs welcome, plastic glasses for beach drinks, nice bedrooms, open all day *(Bruce and Penny Wilkie, Geoff Marston, LYM, Colin Gooch, Pete Walker, David Gunn, Mike and Heather Watson, Alan Johnson, Stuart Turner, Paul and Shirley White)*

MULLION [SW6719]
☆ *Old Inn* TR12 7HN [Churchtown – not down in the cove]: Extensive thatched and beamed family food pub with central servery doing generous good value food (all day July/Aug) from good doorstep sandwiches to pies and evening steaks, linked eating areas with lots of brasses, plates, clocks, nautical items and old wreck pictures, big inglenook fireplace, no smoking rooms, Sharps Doom Bar, Skinners Cornish Knocker and John Smiths, lots of wines by the glass, friendly attentive staff; children welcome, open all day Sat/Sun and Aug; picnic-sets on terrace and in pretty orchard garden, good bedrooms, open all day *(LYM, Gloria Bax)*

MULLION COVE [SW6618]
Mullion Cove Hotel TR12 7EP: Doing well under current management, good range of beer and wines, wide food choice inc seafood specialties and all-day tapas, comfortable sea-view dining room *(Clifford Blakemore)*

MYLOR BRIDGE [SW8036]
Lemon Arms TR11 5NA [Lemon Hill]: Traditional village pub with friendly helpful staff, enjoyable unfussy food, three St Austell ales, decent wine choice; handy for start or finish of very pretty walk *(Frank Plater, Lesley Piekielniak, J M Tansey)*

NEWQUAY [SW8061]
Lewinnick Lodge TR7 1NX [Pentire headland, off Pentire Rd]: Modern bar/restaurant built into the bluff above the sea, big picture windows for the terrific views, open uncluttered layout and furnishings, popular if not cheap food (lunch served till 4), decent drinks choice, good service and pleasant relaxed atmosphere even when busy; good outside seating *(Stephen Allford, Mick and Moira Brummell, Andy Sinden, Louise Harrington)*

Mermaid TR7 3NB [Alexandra Rd, Porth]: Lots of tables on beachside terrace, comfortable bar and lounge with separate no smoking area, real ales inc Sharps Doom Bar, wide range of modestly priced food; own amusement arcade; children welcome *(Colin Gooch)*

NORTH HILL [SX2776]
☆ *Racehorse* PL15 7PG [North Hill, off B3254 Launceston—Liskeard]: Pleasantly reworked beamed pub (once the gabled village school), well run and neatly kept, with cheerful attentive owners and Ollie the golden retriever, comfortable banquettes and cushioned settles, careful balance between eating and drinking, enjoyable sensibly priced food inc OAP deals, Sharps Doom Bar and St Austell Tribute, two coal fires, some nice local photographs by landlord, darts; quiz night, TV; picnic-sets under cocktail parasols out by quiet road, country views from more out on decking by separate restaurant *(Peter Stanning, BB)*

PADSTOW [SW9175]
Golden Lion PL28 8AN [Lanadwell St]: Cheerful black-beamed locals' bar, high-raftered back lounge with plush banquettes against ancient white stone walls, reasonably

priced simple bar lunches inc good crab and other sandwiches, evening steaks and fresh seafood, Bass, Sharps Doom Bar and Skinners, prompt friendly service, coal fire; pool in family area, piped music, games machines; terrace tables, bedrooms, open all day *(the Didler, BB, Michael B Griffith, Chris and Susie Cammack)*

☆ *London* PL28 8AN [Llanadwell St]: Down-to-earth fishermen's local with flower-filled façade, lots of pictures and nautical memorabilia, friendly atmosphere, St Austell ales, decent choice of malt whiskies, wknd lunchtime bar food inc good if pricey crab sandwiches, fresh local fish, more elaborate evening choice (small back dining area – get there early for a table), great log fire; games machines but no piped music – home-grown live music Sun night; dogs welcome in bar, open all day, bedrooms good value *(LYM, Andrew Curry, Alan Sadler, Chris and Susie Cammack, Kevin Blake)*

Old Custom House PL28 8BL [South Quay]: Large airy open-plan seaside bar, well divided, with rustic décor and cosy corners, bare boards, raised section, big family area and conservatory, good food choice from sandwiches and baguettes to bargain deals for two, St Austell ales, good service, adjoining fish restaurant, pool; big-screen TV, some live music; good spot by harbour, open all day, attractive sea-view bedrooms *(BB, Stephen Allford, Chris and Susie Cammack, Ted George, Chris Glasson)*

Old Ship PL28 8AE [Mill Sq, just off North Quay/Broad St]: Cheery mix of locals and visitors in hotel's bustling open-plan bar with St Austell ales, good range of reasonably priced food from sandwiches to plenty of good seafood, upstairs restaurant; back games room with SkyTV, may be piped radio, good live music Fri/Sat; tables in heated front courtyard tucked away just off harbour, open all day from breakfast on at least in summer, 15 bedrooms *(BB, Pete Walker, D W Stokes, Robert Wivell)*

PAR [SX0553]
Britannia PL24 2SL [Tregrehan (A390 St Austell—Lostwithiel, just E of A3092 roundabout)]: Modern refurbishment of 16th-c pub with several big-screen sports TVs in bright main bar, log-effect fire in comfortable partly stripped stone nautical-theme second bar (only over-21s here), wide choice of enjoyable bar food (snacks all day in summer), changing ales such as Fullers London Pride, Greene King Old Speckled Hen, Sharps and Skinners, good choice of wines by the glass, attentive friendly staff, family room and neat modern restaurant; plenty of picnic-sets in good-sized neatly kept enclosed garden with terrace and play area *(Andy Sinden, Louise Harrington)*

☆ *Royal* PL24 2AJ [Eastcliffe Rd (close to station, off A3082)]: Newly reopened after open-plan refurbishment, light and airy, with solid pale country furniture on flagstones and bare boards, some stripped stone, log-effect fire, restaurant opening into slate-floored

conservatory, good food, Cotleigh Golden Eagle, Sharps Doom Bar and Skinners Cornish Knocker, darts and pool; piped pop music may be on the loud side, big-screen TV, games machine; disabled access, picnic-sets on small heated terrace, well updated bedrooms *(Clare, BB)*

PAUL [SW4627]
☆ *Kings Arms* TR19 6TZ: Appealing beamed local opp church, cosy bustling atmosphere and friendly licensees, St Austell ales, enjoyable sensibly priced food; dogs welcome, tasteful bedrooms *(Paul and Karen Cornock, Dr R A Smye, Stuart Turner, Giles and Annie Francis, J and D Waters)*

PENDOGGETT [SX0279]
☆ *Cornish Arms* PL30 3HH [B3314]: Picturesque and friendly old coaching inn with traditional oak settles on civilised front bar's handsome polished slate floor, fine prints, above-average food from good soup and sandwiches to fresh fish, splendid steaks and great Sunday lunches, particularly welcoming helpful service, Bass and Sharps Doom Bar, good wines by the glass, comfortably spaced tables in small dining room, congenial back locals' bar with woodburner and games; provision for children, terrace with distant sea view, open all day, bedrooms *(Gloria Bax, Bart Thibadeau, Gail Giles, M R Dearman, LYM, M A Borthwick, Mick and Moira Brummell)*

PENELEWEY [SW8140]
☆ *Punch Bowl & Ladle* TR3 6QY [B3289]: Well run thatched dining pub in picturesque setting handy for Trelissick Gardens, wide choice of good value generous food from good sandwiches up (Thurs very popular with elderly lunchers), children's helpings, efficient helpful service, St Austell ales, good wine choice, comfortable olde-worlde bar with big settees, rustic bric-a-brac, several room areas; unobtrusive piped music; children and dogs on leads welcome, small back sun terrace, open all day summer *(LYM, Mick and Moira Brummell, Gill and Keith Croxton, Paul and Shirley White, Ian and Celia Abbott)*

PENTEWAN [SX0147]
Ship PL26 6BX [just off B3273 St Austell—Mevagissey; West End]: 17th-c pub opp tiny village's harbour, comfortable and clean, with three separate areas and dining room, four St Austell ales, lots of dark tables for the food (good choice with plenty of fish), open fire; pool room, piped music; views from tables outside (seagulls make it unwise to eat out there), nr good sandy beach and big caravan park *(Andy Sinden, Louise Harrington)*

PENZANCE [SW4730]
Admiral Benbow TR18 4AF [Chapel St]: Well run pub, full of life, with interesting nautical décor and appealingly rambling layout, cosy corners, friendly attentive staff, good value above-average food inc local fish, real ales such as Sharps, Skinners and St Austell, decent wines, downstairs restaurant, upper floor with pool, juke box and pleasant view from back room; children allowed, open all day summer *(LYM, Margaret and*

Roy Randle, Catherine Pitt, Matthew Hegarty)

☆ *Dolphin* TR18 4EF [The Barbican; Newlyn road, opp harbour after swing-bridge]: Roomy and welcoming, part old-fashioned pub and part bistro, with attractive nautical décor, good harbour views, good value food from good lunchtime sandwiches and baguettes to steaks and fresh local fish (landlady's husband is a fisherman), St Austell ales, generous wine glasses, helpful service, great fireplace, dining area a few steps down, cosy family room; big pool room with juke box etc, no obvious nearby parking; pavement picnic-sets, open all day *(Dr R A Smye, LYM, Michael and Alison Sandy, the Didler, Anne Morris, Valerie Baker)*

☆ *Globe & Ale House* TR18 4BJ [Queen St]: Small low-ceilinged tavern with changing real ales inc Bass, Sharps and Skinners, some tapped from the cask, lots of old pictures and artefacts, bare boards and dim lighting, enthusiastic helpful landlord, enjoyable simple prompt food; TV sports *(Pete Walker, the Didler, Catherine Pitt)*

Navy TR18 4DE [Queen St]: Interesting historic house with atmosphere, chef/landlord doing good local seafood and other restauranty food (sandwiches, ploughman's and light dishes too, and brunch from 10am), Batemans and Sharps Doom Bar, decent choice of wines, reasonable prices, pleasant service and setting *(Pete Walker, Brian and Genie Smart, Anne Morris)*

PERRANUTHNOE [SW5329]

☆ *Victoria* TR20 9NP [signed off A394 Penzance—Helston]: Comfortable and relaxed L-shaped pub, cosy low-beamed bar, some stripped stonework and no smoking part, coastal and wreck photographs, good food from freshly baked lunchtime baguettes and doorstep sandwiches up, interesting evening specials, friendly efficient service, real ales such as Bass and Sharps Doom Bar, nice wine choice, neat coal fire, good-sized no smoking room; quiet piped music; picnic-sets in sheltered pretty sunken garden, good bedrooms, handy for Mounts Bay *(LYM, Pete Walker, Eileen Goddard, John and Jackie Chalcraft)*

PILLATON [SX3664]

☆ *Weary Friar* PL12 6QS [off Callington—Landrake back road]: Pretty tucked-away 12th-c pub under welcoming newish management, enjoyable food in bar and big back restaurant, quick service, real ales such as Bass and Sharps Eden, farm cider, four spotless and civilised knocked-together rooms (one no smoking), appealing décor, comfortable seats around sturdy tables, easy chairs one end, log fire; children in eating area (no dogs inside), tables outside, Tues bell-ringing in church next door, comfortable bedrooms with own bathrooms *(Gerry Price, LYM, Ted George)*

POLGOOTH [SW9950]

☆ *Polgooth Inn* PL26 7DA [well signed off A390 W of St Austell; Ricketts Lane]: Popular and attractive country pub with St Austell ales, good

wine choice, efficient friendly service, enjoyable generous food from sandwiches to some interesting modern dishes (only roasts on Sun), children's helpings and appealing prices, eating area around biggish bar with woodburner, good big family room; fills quickly in summer (handy for nearby caravan parks), steps up to play area, tables out on grass, pretty countryside *(Michael and Jean Hockings, Mick and Moira Brummell, LYM, Mark Flynn, Jane and Mark Hooper, Christopher Wright)*

POLPERRO [SX2050]

☆ *Three Pilchards* PL13 2QZ [Quay Rd]: Welcoming low-beamed fishermen's local behind the fish quay, good value food from baguettes to nicely cooked local fish and seafood, real ales, quick service, lots of black woodwork, dim lighting, simple furnishings, open fire in big stone fireplace, regulars' photographs; piped music, can get very busy; tables on upper terrace (no sea view) up steep steps, open all day *(Jim Abbott, BB, Ivan Ericsson)*

POLRUAN [SX1250]

Russell PL23 1PJ [West St]: Fishermen's local, lively yet relaxing, with sensibly priced straightforward food using local produce from good sandwiches up, St Austell beers, friendly staff, log fire, large tidy bar with interesting photographs, no smoking section; dogs welcome (pub airedale), lovely hanging baskets *(Tim and Rosemary Wells, Nick Lawless, A Truelove, Edward Mirzoeff)*

PORT ISAAC [SX9980]

Edge PL29 3SB [New Rd]: Clifftop pub with picture-window coast views (may see basking sharks), light oak modern interior, enjoyable up-to-date food, Sharps Doom Bar tapped from the cask, good wine selection; children looked after well *(Simon Rhodes)*

☆ *Golden Lion* PL29 3RB [Fore Street]: Window seats and three balcony tables looking down on rocky harbour and lifeboat slip far below, good local atmosphere in simply furnished old rooms, open fire in back one, straightforward food inc fresh fish range, St Austell Tinners, HSD and Tribute, darts, dominoes, cribbage; piped music, games machine; children in eating areas, dramatic cliff walks from the door, open all day *(LYM, Mrs Julie Thomas, Betsy Brown, Nigel Flook, the Didler, Michael H Legge, Rob Stevenson)*

Slipway PL29 3RH [Middle St]: Small family-run hotel just across from delightful village's slipway and beach, small unpretentious cellar-like bar with low dark beams, flagstones and some stripped stonework, Sharps Doom Bar and Cornish Coaster, nice bar food, appealing watercolours for sale, no smoking restaurant; children welcome, crazy-paved heated terrace with awning, refurbished bedrooms, open all day in summer *(LYM, M A Borthwick, Geoff Calcott)*

PORTHALLOW [SW7923]

☆ *Five Pilchards* TR12 6PP [SE of Helston; B3293 to St Keverne, then village signed]: Sturdy old-fashioned stone-built local in secluded cove right by shingle beach, lots of salvaged nautical gear, interesting shipwreck memorabilia, enjoyable reasonably priced food (not winter), Sharps Doom Bar and Skinners Betty Stogs, good value wines, quick friendly service, conservatory with waterfall; children in eating area, seats out in sheltered yard, cl Sun evening/Mon in winter *(Derek and Heather Manning, LYM, Geoff Calcott, Roger Brown)*

PORTHLEVEN [SW6325]

☆ *Atlantic* TR13 9DZ [Peverell Terr]: Friendly pub in great setting up above harbour and now doing enjoyable restaurrary food, with pleasant helpful staff, real ales such as Bass, Skinners and St Austell, big open-plan lounge with well spaced seating and cosier alcoves, good log fire in granite fireplace, no smoking dining room with amazing trompe l'oeil mural; good bay views from front terrace, open all day *(Tony Byworth)*

Harbour Inn TR13 9JB [Commercial Rd]: Large neatly kept pub/hotel in outstanding harbourside setting, impressive dining area off expansive lounge and bar, quick service, St Austell ales, comprehensive wine list, restaurant; picnic-sets on big quayside terrace, decent bedrooms, some with harbour view, good breakfast *(Sue Demont, Tim Barrow, David and Nina Pugsley, Mick and Moira Brummell)*

PORTLOE [SW9339]

Ship TR2 5RA: Comfortably bright L-shaped local with sensibly priced generous food emphasising good local seafood, lunchtime sandwiches, three St Austell ales, decent wines, pleasant young staff, interesting nautical and local memorabilia and photographs; piped music may be intrusive; sheltered and attractive streamside picnic-sets over road, pretty fishing village with lovely cove and coast path above, open all day Fri-Sun in summer *(Christopher Wright, Neil Whitehead, BB, Mark Flynn, Paul and Shirley White)*

PORTSCATHO [SW8735]

Plume of Feathers TR2 5HW [The Square]: Comfortable and cheerful largely stripped stone pub in pretty fishing village, friendly service, St Austell and other ales, pubby food from sandwiches up, sea-related bric-a-brac in linked room areas, side locals' bar (can be very lively evenings), restaurant; very popular with summer visitors but perhaps at its best with warm local atmosphere out of season; dogs welcome, open all day in summer (and other times if busy), lovely coast walks *(Dr and Mrs M E Wilson, LYM, Mark Flynn, Paul and Shirley White)*

PRAZE AN BEEBLE [SW6335]

St Aubyn Arms TR14 0JR [The Square]: Has been traditional country local with Sharps and Skinners, wide choice of good value food inc lunchtime bargains, purple décor with interesting china, models and busts; recently changed hands, so things may change; two restaurants, one upstairs, public bar with games; piped music; children warmly welcomed, picnic-sets in large attractive garden *(Colin Gooch, David M Cundy, Mark Flynn)*

RILLA MILL [SX2973]

Manor House PL17 7NT: Welcoming newish licensees and staff, enjoyable changing fresh food with some nice recipes, two real ales, good wine choice, pleasant renovations *(Michelle Stearman)*

ROCK [SW9375]

Mariners PL27 6LD: Waterside hotel, very popular in summer, with beautiful views across Camel estuary to Padstow, enjoyable pub food in bar and restaurant, sensible prices, friendly staff; children and dogs welcome, bedrooms *(Mrs R Tordoff)*

RUAN LANIHORNE [SW8942]

☆ *Kings Head* TR2 5NX [off A3078]: Attractive beamed pub opp fine old church, comfortable and interesting, good log fire in front bar with teacups hanging on beams and sofa favoured by friendly cats Millie and George, welcoming efficient service, some unusual dishes as well as old favourites using local ingredients, Skinners ales (Steve Skinner brews one for the pub), decent wines, pleasant no smoking eating area with plenty to look at; piped music, traditional games – for children too; suntrap sunken garden, views over the Fal estuary, cl Mon lunchtime (and Mon evening in winter) *(Jennifer Sheridan, LYM, M Bryan Osborne, Jane and Mark Hooper, Basil and Sylvia Walden, Gordon Stevenson)*

ST BREWARD [SX0977]

☆ *Old Inn* PL30 4PP [off B3266 S of Camelford; Churchtown]: Broad slate flagstones, low oak beams, stripped stonework, two massive granite fireplaces dating from 11th c, straightforward bar food, Bass and Sharps Doom Bar and Eden, lots of wines by the glass, sensibly placed darts, roomy no smoking extended restaurant with tables out on deck; piped music, games machine; provision for dogs and children, moorland behind (cattle and sheep wander freely into the village), open all day Fri-Sun and summer *(Gloria Bax, Jacquie and Jim Jones, the Didler, LYM, Liz and Tony Colman, David Crook)*

ST BURYAN [SW4025]

St Buryan Inn TR19 6BA: Two-bar local with Courage and Sharps Rock, friendly cricket-loving landlord (pictures everywhere), solid-fuel stove, tractor seats by bar, kitchen chairs and a few plain tables, horse tack on modern stone wall, darts; TV *(Giles and Annie Francis)*

ST EWE [SW9746]

Crown PL26 6EY [off B3287]: Low-beamed pub with 16th-c flagstones, traditional furnishings, lovely log fire, voluble parrot and some nice decorative touches, St Austell full beer range, good house wines, generous if pricey food (can take a while) from crab sandwiches up, large no smoking back dining room up steps (heavily booked in season); bar can get smoky, outside gents', no dogs even in garden; children in eating areas, stone tables in good garden, geese and ducks outside, handy for the Lost Gardens of Heligan, one bedroom, open all day in summer *(Alan and Paula McCully, LYM, Mike Gorton, Andy Sinden, Louise Harrington, Gary Rollings)*

ST ISSEY [SW9272]

Pickwick PL27 7QQ [Burgois, signed off A389 at St Issey]: Rambling old hillside pub with views over Padstow and Camel estuary, generous all-day food inc good local lamb, beef and venison, three St Austell ales, decent wines, friendly helpful staff, log fire, Dickensian kitsch and dark oak beams, two bars (one allowing children) and pretty candlelit restaurant; quiet piped music, pool, machines; picnic-sets in sizeable garden with good play area, bowling green and tennis, bedrooms *(Alan M'Quillan, Ian and Sharon Shorthouse)*

ST IVES [SW5140]

Lifeboat TR26 1LF [Wharf Rd]: Refurbished harbourside pub, good atmosphere, wide choice of all-day food, three St Austell ales, friendly staff, cosy corners, nautical theme, good views; open all day *(Alan Johnson, Geoff Calcott)*

☆ *Pedn Olva* TR26 2EA [The Warren]: Hotel not pub, but has St Austell Bitter and Tribute in its roomy all-day bar, picture-window views of sea and Porthminster beach, esp from tables on rooftop terrace, tasteful modern mediterranean décor, good service, some emphasis on handsome restaurant's good modern cooking, particularly in the evenings; comfortable bedrooms *(Mick and Moira Brummell, Alan Johnson)*

☆ *Sloop* TR26 1LP [The Wharf]: Busy low-beamed and flagstoned harbourside pub with bright St Ives School pictures and attractive portrait drawings in front bar, booth seating in panelled back bar, good friendly service, well cooked down-to-earth food from sandwiches and baguettes to lots of fresh local fish, Bass, John Smiths, Greene King Old Speckled Hen and Sharps Doom Bar, good wine list and coffee; juke box or piped music, TV; children in eating area, a few beach-view seats out on cobbles, open all day (breakfast from 9am), clean cosy bedrooms, handy for Tate Gallery *(Steve Harvey, LYM, Gene and Kitty Rankin, Alan Johnson, David Crook, the Didler)*

Union TR26 1AB [Fore St]: Friendly low-beamed pub, roomy but cosy, with good value food worth waiting for from good soup and filled baguettes to local seafood specials, real ales inc Bass and Sharps, decent wines, coffee, daily papers, small hot fire, dark woodwork and masses of old local photographs; piped music *(Alan Johnson, Barry Collett, Tim and Ann Newell)*

ST JUST IN PENWITH [SW3731]

Kings Arms TR19 7HF [Market Sq]: Traditional local with friendly relaxed service, comfortable elderly furniture, plenty of character, good local photographs, good value bar meals from baguettes up, St Austell ales, some tapped from the cask; popular live music nights; dogs welcome, good value bedrooms with prodigious breakfast *(the Didler, Ann and Bob Westbrook, David Crook)*

☆ *Star* TR19 7LL [Fore St]: Relaxed and informal dimly lit low-beamed local with good value home-made food from sandwiches and pasties up (if no food, they let you bring your own), St Austell ales, farm cider in summer, mulled wine in winter, coal fire; traditional games inc bar billiards, nostalgic juke box, singalong Mon; tables in attractive back yard, simple bedrooms, good breakfast *(LYM, the Didler, Paul and Shirley White)*

ST MAWES [SW8433]

Idle Rocks TR2 5AN [Tredenham Rd (harbour edge)]: Comfortable waterfront hotel with superb sea views, Skinners Betty Stogs and good wines by the glass (at a price), enjoyable lunchtime food from sandwiches up, friendly helpful young staff, informal brasserie and smart leisurely evening restaurant; well behaved dogs allowed on sun terrace over harbour, good bedrooms *(Dennis Jenkin, BB, Mark Flynn, Mr and Mrs Bentley-Davies)*

☆ *Rising Sun* TR2 5DJ [The Square]: Long nicely fitted bare-boards bar with prized bow-window seat, good coal fire, St Austell ales, decent wines, good coffee, prompt service, interesting choice of reasonably priced good food here and in classy restaurant with pleasant conservatory, good crab sandwiches and unusual seafood snacks, great puddings; bar can be smoky; dogs and children welcome, teak seats and slate-topped tables on handsome sunny terrace just across lane from harbour wall, charming bedrooms, good breakfast, open all day summer *(Helen Sharpe, Mrs M Ainley, LYM, Mr and Mrs A H Young, Mark Flynn, Matthew Shackle)*

☆ *Victory* TR2 5DQ [Victory Hill]: Local bare-boards bar on left (can be smoky), no smoking dining area on right, enjoyable if pricey food from good crab sandwiches to carefully cooked fresh local fish, real ales such as Sharps Doom Bar, good service, warm log fires, plain wooden seating, upstairs dining room in season; piped music; pleasant picnic-sets outside, good value bedrooms, open all day *(LYM, J D O Carter, Brian and Genie Smart, Mr and Mrs A H Young, C J Jones, Stephen and Jean Curtis, Paul and Shirley White, Barry Collett, Jenny and Brian Seller, Alan Johnson)*

ST NEOT [SX1867]

☆ *London* PL14 6NG [N of A38 Liskeard—Bodmin]: Spotless 16th-c beamed country pub on Bodmin Moor, open-plan but well divided, with soft lighting, two log fires and some stripped stone, cheerful efficient staff, good home-made food from sandwiches (normal or doorstep) up, Courage Best, John Smiths, Sharps Doom Bar and Theakstons XB, decent house wines (choice of glass sizes), dining area behind timber divider; unobtrusive piped music; picnic-sets on small front terrace below 15th-c church with outstanding medieval stained glass, attractive village in wooded valley, bedrooms *(BB, DAV, Charles Gysin)*

ST TEATH [SX0680]

White Hart PL30 3JT [B3267]: Welcoming flagstoned village local with good value generous food from sandwiches to good steaks and Sun roasts, friendly helpful service, good range of real ales, decent wines, coal fire, neat dining room off; games bar, live music wknds;

children very welcome, open all day wknds, comfortably refurbished bedrooms, good breakfast *(Dr D Smith, LYM)*

ST TUDY [SX0676]

Cornish Arms PL30 3NN [off A391 nr Wadebridge]: Attractive low-beamed 16th-c local with Bass, Sharps and St Austell, decent food in flagstoned front bar and restaurant, pool room; children welcome *(the Didler)*

STITHIANS [SW7640]

Cornish Arms TR4 8RP [Frogpool, which is not shown on many roadmaps but is NE of A393 – ie opp side to Stithians itself]: Welcoming and comfortable village pub with good value generous food and local real ales; good bedrooms *(BB, John Marsh)*

Golden Lion TR16 6NW [Stithians Lake, Menherion]: Welcoming pub with good sensibly priced food from sandwiches and other bar food up, St Austell ales, friendly helpful licensees, neatly laid restaurant (busy Fri and wknds), no smoking area; large well maintained garden and lakeside terrace *(David Crook, PL)*

STRATTON [SS2306]

☆ *Tree* EX23 9DA [just E of Bude; Fore St]: Rambling and softly lit 16th-c beamed local with interesting old furniture and colourful décor, cheerful staff, friendly locals and relaxed atmosphere, great log fires, real ales inc Sharps Doom Bar and St Austell Tinners, good value generous home-made food using supplies from local farms, character Elizabethan-style evening restaurant with old paintings; big-screen sports TV; children welcome in back bar, seats alongside unusual old dovecote in attractive ancient coachyard, bedrooms *(Jeremy Whitehorn, BB, Pauline and Philip Darley, Ryta Lyndley)*

TREBARWITH [SX0586]

☆ *Mill House* PL34 0HD [signed off B3263 and B3314 SE of Tintagel]: Marvellously placed in own steep streamside woods above sea, convivial black-beamed bar with fine delabole flagstones, well worn mix of furnishings and interesting old pictures, restaurant area alongside, good rather upmarket food, Sharps and other real ales; piped music; provision for dogs and children, tables out on terrace and by stream, 12 bedrooms, open all day *(Peter Meister, BB, Canon Michael Bourdeaux, Robert Wivell, A P Seymour)*

TREBURLEY [SX3477]

☆ *Springer Spaniel* PL15 9NS [A388 Callington—Launceston]: Has been popular for its interesting food, friendly atmosphere and Sharps and Skinners real ales, but has recently changed ownership, and we have not yet had any reports on the new management (news please); nice décor, with a very high-backed settle by the woodburner, high-backed farmhouse chairs and other seats, olde-worlde stage-coach pictures, further cosy room with big solid teak tables, attractive furnished restaurant up some steps *(LYM)*

TREEN [SW3923]

☆ *Logan Rock* TR19 6LG [just off B3315 Penzance—Lands End]: Relaxed local well

worth knowing for its atmosphere, and position nr fine coast walks; low-beamed traditional bar with inglenook seat by hot coal fire, gorgeous pub dog usually lying across flagstoned passageway (others allowed on leads), pricey St Austell HSD and other ales, courteous service, wide food choice (all day in summer) from sandwiches up, lots of games in family room, no smoking in small back snug with cricket memorabilia; may be juke box or piped music, no children inside; tables in small and pretty sheltered garden *(Richard, LYM, the Didler, David Crook, Stuart Turner)*

TREGONY [SW9244]

Kings Arms TR2 5RW [Fore St (B3287)]: Newish licensees in 16th-c pub with long comfortable main bar, St Austell ales, mildly upscale pubby food using local produce, woodburners in two smart beamed and panelled front rooms, one a no smoking dining room, the other for families, back games room; tables in pleasant garden, charming village, open all day *(Christopher Wright)*

TREMATON [SX3960]

☆ *Crooked Inn* PL12 4RZ [off A38 just W of Saltash]: Down a long drive, this laid-back and decidedly not smart place has free-roaming horses, a pig and sheep, and swings, slides and a trampoline for children; more or less open-plan bar with lower lounge leading to conservatory and doors on to decked area overlooking garden and valley; beams, straightforward furnishings, open fire, and up to five real ales from St Austell and Sharps, wide food choice; bedrooms overlook courtyard, open all day *(Ted George, LYM, Ian Phillips)*

TREVAUNANCE COVE [SW7251]

Driftwood Spars TR5 0RT [off B3285 in St Agnes; Quay Rd]: 17th-c inn just up from beach and dramatic cove, great coastal walks; slate, granite and massive timbers, lots of nautical and wreck memorabilia, brews its own Cuckoo Ale, up to half a dozen or so other mainly cornish ales, over 100 malt whiskies, Addlestone's cider, 15 wines by the glass, log fires, bar food (all day in summer) from sandwiches and baguettes up inc good cornish cheeses, separate residents' areas and new fish restaurant; piped music, pool, fruit machine and TV in back bar, can get crowded, some live bands; children welcome, dogs allowed in bar, garden tables opposite, nautical-theme bedrooms, open all day *(Steve Harvey, the Didler, LYM, Kev and Gaye Griffiths, Steve Felstead, Jan and Alan Summers)*

TYWARDREATH [SX0854]

New Inn PL24 2QP [off A3082; Fore St]: Friendly and informal local atmosphere in what was once a private house, Bass tapped from the cask and St Austell ales on handpump, caring landlord, games and children's room; large secluded garden behind, nice village setting, bedrooms *(Ian and Joan Blackwell, BB, the Didler)*

UPTON CROSS [SX2772]

Caradon PL14 5AZ [B3254 N of Liskeard]:

Welcoming country pub with built-in banquettes and dark chairs, carpet over 17th-c flagstones, woodburner, pewter hanging from joists, decorative plates, good cheerful service, wide choice of enjoyable food inc some unusual dishes, Sharps real ale; children welcome, some picnic-sets outside *(BB, Nick and Meriel Cox)*

VERYAN [SW9139]

☆ *New Inn* TR2 5QA [village signed off A3078]: Neat and comfortably homely one-bar beamed local very popular for good generous nourishing food using local produce inc Sun lunch (must book), St Austell Tinners and Tribute, good value house wines and good coffee, leisurely atmosphere, inglenook woodburner, lots of polished brass and old pictures, no smoking dining area, friendly efficient service even when very busy; piped music, nearby parking unlikely in summer; quiet garden behind the pretty house, charming comfortable bedrooms, interesting partly thatched village *(Christopher Wright, the Didler, J D O Carter, BB, Nick Lawless, Mark Flynn, Gordon Stevenson, Barry Collett, Glenn and Julia Smithers, Roger Brown)*

WATERGATE BAY [SW8464]

Phoenix TR8 4AB: Spectacular coast and sunset views from open balcony, enjoyable restaurant food inc interesting fish dishes, pizzas from downstairs too, local real ales, decent wines, sensible prices, friendly efficient staff; live music Fri *(Simon Cole)*

WIDEMOUTH [SS1902]

☆ *Bay View* EX23 0AW [Marine Drive]: Open-plan pub overlooking magnificent stretch of sand, gorgeous sunset views, wide choice of tasty good value food in roomy dining area, light and summery, pleasant efficient service even when busy, Sharps Doom Bar and Own, Skinners Betty Stogs and a beer brewed for the pub; tables on front decking, open all day in summer, bedrooms *(Gloria Bax, Ryta Lyndley, the Didler, G K Smale)*

ISLES OF SCILLY

ST MARY'S [SV9010]

☆ *Atlantic Inn* TR21 0HY [The Strand; next to but independent from Atlantic Hotel]: Spreading cosily dark bar with good atmosphere, St Austell ales, enjoyable sea-view restaurant, friendly efficient service, low beams, hanging boat and lots of nautical bits and pieces, flowery-patterned seats, mix of locals and tourists – busy evenings, quieter on sunny lunchtimes; darts, pool, fruit machines; nice raised verandah with green cast-iron furniture and wide views over harbour, good bedrooms *(C A Hall, R J Herd, BB, Tom McLean, Mayur Shah, David Swift)*

Bishop & Wolf TR21 0LL [Hugh St/Silver St (A3110)]: Interesting sea/boating décor with secluded corners and gallery above road, nets, lots of woodwork and maritime bric-a-brac, lifeboat photographs, friendly helpful staff, St Austell Tinners and HSD, very wide food choice (attractive relaxed upstairs restaurant – no bar food after 7.30), games area with pool; piped music, popular summer live music, handy for day-trippers (nr coach tour start) *(Pete Walker, Tom McLean, Stuart Turner, J and S French, David Swift)*

Mermaid TR21 0HY [The Bank]: Picture-window views across town beach and harbour from all-day back restaurant extension (not Tues), thorough-going nautical theme in unpretentious bar with ceiling flags, lots of seafaring relics, rough timber, stone floor, dim lighting, big stove, real ales such as Ales of Scilly and Skinners Betty Stogs, simple bar food; packed on Weds and Fri when the gigs race; cellar bar with boat counter, pool table, TV and music for young people (live wknds) *(C A Hall, Pete Walker, Catherine Pitt)*

Porthcressa TR21 0JG [Little Porth, Hugh Town]: Watch the boats from terrace of former restaurant in superb position right on beach, beers inc St Austell Tribute, simple décor, takeaway food Sun; karaoke and disco some nights *(David Crook)*

A very few pubs try to make you leave a credit card at the bar, as a sort of deposit if you order food. They are not entitled to do this. The credit card firms and banks which issue them warn you not to let them out of your sight. If someone behind the counter used your card fraudulently, the card company or bank could in theory hold you liable, because of your negligence in letting a stranger hang on to your card. Suggest instead that if they feel the need for security, they 'swipe' your card and give it back to you. And do name and shame the pub to us.

Cumbria

Many of the pubs here are surrounded by glorious scenery and are warmly welcoming to walkers. There's a terrific choice from pretty basic taverns to civilised hotels, several brewing their own beer, and some excellent food using top-notch local produce – fell-bred lamb, beef from true beef breeds (not your usual dairy industry by-products), plenty of fresh fish, and super cheeses. In general this area is good value all round, with food usually cheaper than you'd pay for equivalent quality down south, and drinks prices well below the national average. You can still find a pint of beer for under £2 here and there – pubs brewing their own are as always a good bet, and beers from local brewers such as Jennings (now part of the Wolverhampton & Dudley group), Hawkshead and Yates often figure as a pub's cheapest beer. Pubs doing particularly well this year include the quietly placed little Barbon Inn at Barbon (readers enjoy staying here), the smart Pheasant at Bassenthwaite Lake (mainly a comfortable hotel but with a thriving pubby bar), the cheerful White Hart at Bouth (very popular and well run), the extended Highland Drove at Great Salkeld (manages to be a good local and super dining pub), the busy Watermill at Ings (a fantastic choice of 16 real ales on handpump), the very simple Old Dungeon Ghyll at Langdale (walkers love it), the Kirkstile Inn at Loweswater (own-brewed beer and a good mix of customers), the friendly Bridge at Santon Bridge (more a hotel than pub but none the worse for that), the bustling Newfield Inn at Seathwaite (consistently well run with reasonable prices, too), the much enjoyed Queens Head at Troutbeck (a nice place to stay), and the popular Gate Inn at Yanwath (a relaxed pubby atmosphere plus delicious food). We can add to these five very varied new main entries (some of them back in the *Guide* after a break): the charming little New Inn at Brampton (the small one up by Appleby), newly taken over by welcoming and enthusiastic licensees, the Punch Bowl at Crosthwaite, reworked most tastefully by new owners (good food, and nice bar), the bustling good value Dog & Gun in Keswick, the newly reopened Strickland Arms at Levens, already looking all set to become one of Lakeland's top pubs, and the beautifully set White Horse at Scales (a rewarding all-rounder). Our current top recommendations for a really enjoyable meal out, with first-rate imaginative food, are the Pheasant by Bassenthwaite Lake, the Highland Drove in Great Salkeld, the Drunken Duck near Hawkshead, its new sister pub the Strickland Arms, the Queens Head at Troutbeck, both the Bay Horse and the Farmers Arms in or just outside Ulverston, and the Gate Inn at Yanwath. The award of Cumbria Dining Pub of the Year goes to the Gate Inn at Yanwath. In the Lucky Dip section at the end of the chapter, pubs currently showing well (most of them already inspected and vouched for by us) include the New Inn up at Blencogo, Wheatsheaf at Brigsteer, Weary Sportsman at Castle Carrock, Black Bull and Sun in Coniston, Sportsmans at Cowgill, Sun at Crook, Sawrey Hotel at Far Sawrey, Prince of Wales at Foxfield, Royal Oak at Lindale, Herdwick at Penruddock, Eagles Head at Satterthwaite and Dalesman in Sedbergh.

AMBLESIDE NY3804 Map 9
Golden Rule
Smithy Brow; follow Kirkstone Pass signpost from A591 on N side of town; LA22 9AS

The main bar with its warm log fire and cosy atmosphere is the place to head for in this no-frills town local. There are lots of local country pictures decorating the butter-coloured walls, horsebrasses on the black beams, built-in wall seats, and cast-iron-framed tables. Also, a no smoking back room with TV (not much used), a left-hand room with darts and a fruit machine, and a further room down a few steps on the right with lots of seats. Robinsons Hatters Dark, Hartleys XB, Cumbrian Way, Old Stockport, Unicorn and Double Hop on handpump; pork pies (55p or 85p), jumbo scotch eggs (£1.20), and filled rolls (£2.50). The back yard has some benches and especially colourful window boxes. The golden rule referred to in its name is a brass measuring yard mounted over the bar counter. *(Recommended by Pierre Richterich, Andy and Jill Kassube, David and Sue Smith, Helen Clarke, Mike and Sue Loseby, Mark Harrington, MLR)*

Robinsons ~ Tenant John Lockley ~ Real ale ~ Bar food ~ No credit cards ~ (015394) 32257 ~ Children welcome until 9pm ~ Dogs welcome ~ Open 11-midnight

APPLEBY NY6921 Map 10
Royal Oak ㉕
B6542/Bongate is E of the main bridge over the River Eden; CA16 6UN

With new licensees, this old-fashioned coaching inn is still a friendly place with a good mix of customers. As we went to press, some refurbishments were taking place but the oak-panelled public bar still has a relaxed and chatty atmosphere with a good open fire, and the beamed lounge has old pictures on the timbered walls, some armchairs and a carved settle, and a panelling-and-glass snug enclosing part of the bar counter. Well liked bar food includes lunchtime filled ciabattas or baguettes (from £3.95), home-made salmon and crab fishcakes with a sweet chilli dip (£4.95); main course £8.95), cumberland sausage ring (£7.95), home-made lamb burger (£8.50), chicken breast stuffed with sausage, spinach and ricotta cannelloni or steak in ale pie (£8.95), and baked cod (£9.50); prices are slightly higher in the evening. The restaurant is no smoking. Black Sheep Bitter, Jennings Cumberland and John Smiths on handpump; piped music, board games, dominoes (very popular) and TV. There are seats on the front terrace, and attractive flowering tubs, troughs and hanging baskets. You can get here on the scenic Leeds/Settle/Carlisle railway (best to check times and any possible delays to avoid missing lunch). *(Recommended by Andy and Jill Kassube, Tony and Betty Parker, Roger Braithwaite, Maggie Chandler, Carl Van Baars, Karen Eliot, B and M Kendall, Pat and Tony Martin, David Swift, Guy Vowles, Ann and Tony Bennett-Hughes)*

Enterprise ~ Tenants Kyle Macrae and Janice Hunter ~ Real ale ~ Bar food (11.45-2.30, 5.30-9.30; all day Sun) ~ Restaurant ~ (01768) 351463 ~ Children welcome ~ Dogs allowed in bar ~ Open 11-midnight ~ Bedrooms: £35S/£69B

ARMATHWAITE NY5046 Map 10
Dukes Head
Off A6 S of Carlisle; CA4 9PB

Every couple of months, they hold tasting nights here with samples of local food and interesting drinks – Hot & Spicy, Fish Feast or Food from France (four courses plus coffee from £16.50). The civilised, no smoking lounge bar has oak settles and little armchairs among more upright seats, oak and mahogany tables, antique hunting and other prints, and some brass and copper powder-flasks above the open fire. Good, popular food includes soup (£3.55), sandwiches (from £3.65), butter bean and black olive pâté (£4.25), hot potted solway shrimps (£4.50), cold meat platter with gooseberry preserve (£5.80), ploughman's (£7.95), filo parcels filled with roasted red pepper, red onion and a mild goats cheese (£8.25), fresh cod in a light basil and olive crumb with home-made tartare sauce (£8.95), local steaks (from £8.95), salmon on leeks with dry vermouth and prawns (£9.95), duckling with apple sauce and stuffing (£12.95), and interesting daily specials. The restaurant is no smoking. Black Sheep and Jennings Cumberland on handpump, home-made lemonade and ginger cordial and blackcurrant liqueur; dominoes, and a separate public bar with darts and table skittles. This year there's a new heated and lit up outside seating area with more seats on the lawn behind; boules. Day tickets for fishing are available. *(Recommended by Dr and Mrs T E Hothersall, Helen Clarke, A Harding, Ann and Tony Bennett-Hughes, Hugh and Susan Ellison, John and Margaret Priestley, JWAC, Christine and Phil Young)*

Punch ~ Tenant Henry Lynch ~ Real ale ~ Bar food ~ Restaurant ~ (016974) 72226 ~ Children welcome ~ Dogs allowed in bar and bedrooms ~ Open 11.30-11.30(midnight Sat) ~ Bedrooms: £38.50B/£58.50B

BARBON   SD6282   Map 10
Barbon Inn 🛏

Village signposted off A683 Kirkby Lonsdale—Sedbergh; OS Sheet 97 map reference 628826; LA6 2LJ

In a charming village setting below the fells, and with plenty of surrounding tracks and paths, this 17th-c coaching inn is a smashing little place. Our readers enjoy staying here and some of the quiet and comfortable little bedrooms overlook the lovely sheltered and prettily planted garden. The simple bar has several small rooms that lead off, each individually and comfortably furnished: carved 18th-c oak settles, comfortable sofas and armchairs, a Victorian fireplace. Fairly priced bar food might include hot and cold filled baguettes, morecambe bay potted shrimps (£4.95), hot chicken and bacon salad (£6.95), lamb or steak in ale pies (£7.50), and gammon platter (£8.75); the restaurant is no smoking. Well kept Theakstons Black Bull and a changing beer from Dent on handpump; dominoes and piped music. *(Recommended by Michael Doswell, Ann and Tony Bennett-Hughes, David and Lin Short, Michael Dugdale, Dr and Mrs T E Hothersall, Maurice and Gill McMahon)*

Free house ~ Licensee Lindsey MacDiarmid ~ Real ale ~ Bar food ~ (015242) 76233 ~ Children welcome ~ Dogs allowed in bar and bedrooms ~ Open 12-3, 6.30-11(midnight Sat, 10.30 Sun); closed 25 Dec ~ Bedrooms: £45B/£70B

BASSENTHWAITE LAKE   NY1930   Map 9
Pheasant ★ 🍽 ♇ 🛏

Follow Pheasant Inn sign at N end of dual carriageway stretch of A66 by Bassenthwaite Lake; CA13 9YE

This civilised hotel is a lovely peaceful place and the restaurant food is excellent but thankfully, the little bar remains as pleasantly old-fashioned and pubby as ever, with plenty of customers enjoying a quiet pint or informal lunch. There are mellow polished walls, cushioned oak settles, rush-seat chairs and library seats, hunting prints and photographs, and Bass, Jennings Cumberland and Theakstons Best on handpump; 12 good wines by the glass and over 60 malt whiskies. Several comfortable no smoking lounges have log fires, fine parquet flooring, antiques, and plants. Enjoyable lunchtime bar food includes freshly made soup with home-made bread (£4.35), stilton, walnut and apricot pâté (£5.35), open sandwiches with home-made crisps (from £6.25; prawn with avocado and lemon mayonnaise and a mango and chilli salsa £6.95), ploughman's (£6.95), their own potted silloth shrimps (£7.55), deep-fried breaded goats cheese with red onion marmalade (£7.95), braised venison and cumberland sausage and mash (£9.95), shepherd's pie (£10.35), poached naturally smoked haddock on buttered spinach with a light cheese sauce and poached egg (£11.75), and puddings (£5.25). The restaurant is no smoking. Dogs are allowed in the residents' lounge at lunchtime and they do let them into the bar during the day too, unless people are eating. There are seats in the garden, attractive woodland surroundings, and plenty of walks in all directions. *(Recommended by W K Wood, Revd D Glover, Tina and David Woods-Taylor, Pat and Stewart Gordon, Helen Clarke, Andy and Jill Kassube, Mike and Sue Loseby,*

Mr and Mrs Woodhead, Peter F Marshall, Jack Clark, Patrick and Phillipa Vickery,
Mrs Phoebe A Kemp, Martin and Sue Day, Geoff and Brigid Smithers, Sylvia and Tony Birbeck,
Christine and Phil Young, Sheila Stothard)

Free house ~ Licensee Matthew Wylie ~ Real ale ~ Bar food (not in evening – restaurant
only then) ~ Restaurant ~ (017687) 76234 ~ Children in eating area of bar if over 8 ~
Dogs allowed in bar and bedrooms ~ Open 11-2.30, 5.30-10.30(11 Sat); 12-2.30, 6-10.30
Sun; closed 25 Dec ~ Bedrooms: £82B/£144B

BEETHAM   SD5079   Map 7
Wheatsheaf ♀ ⇌
Village (and inn) signposted just off A6 S of Milnthorpe; LA7 7AL

The timbered cornerpiece of this neatly kept 17th-c coaching inn is very striking –
a two-storey set of gabled oriel windows jettied out from the corner into the quiet
village street. Now totally no smoking, there's an opened-up front lounge bar with
fresh flowers and candles on the tables, and lots of exposed beams and joists; the
main, recently refurbished bar with an open fire is behind on the right. Jennings
Cumberland, Tirril Brougham Ale and a weekly changing guest beer on handpump,
ten wines by the glass and quite a few malt whiskies. Upstairs are two dining rooms
(open at weekends); piped classical or jazz music. Enjoyable bar food includes
lunchtime fresh baked rustic rolls (£4.95; open sandwich of freshly grilled fish and
lemon mayonnaise or soup and a sandwich £7.95), plus home-made soup (£3.70),
tomato, rocket and parmesan tart or black pudding rarebit (£4.95), local potted
shrimps (£5.95), sautéed large garlic prawns (£6.95), cumberland sausage and mash
or mushroom, pepper, courgette and aubergine tian (£7.95), steak and mushroom
in ale pie (£8.95), minted lamb henry (£11.50), pork fillet with prunes wrapped in
bacon with a cream sauce and bubble and squeak (£13.95), gressingham duck with
plum compote tarte tatin (£14.50), tournedos rossini (£16.50), daily specials, and
puddings such as crème brûlée with boozy berries or rich chocolate pot (£4.95).
Early bird and Saturday at Six menus: two courses £10.35 and three courses
£12.95. *(Recommended by Mr and Mrs C R Little, Malcolm Taylor, W K Wood, Dr and
Mrs T E Hothersall, Karen Eliot, Michael Doswell, G Dobson, Jo Lilley, Simon Calvert,
R M Corlett, T Walker, Graham and Doreen Holden, J F M and M West, Maurice and
Gill McMahon, Chris Smith, Anthony Waters)*

Free house ~ Licensees Mark and Kath Chambers ~ Real ale ~ Bar food (12-2, 6-9(8.30
Sun)) ~ Restaurant ~ (015395) 62123 ~ Children welcome but must be over 10 after 7pm
~ Open 11.30-2.30, 5.30-11; 12-2.30, 6-10.30 Sun; closed 25 Dec, 1-18 Jan ~ Bedrooms:
£55S(£65B)/£69.50S(£95B)

BOUTH   SD3386   Map 9
White Hart ◀
Village signposted off A590 near Haverthwaite; LA12 8JB

Much enjoyed by our readers, this is a well run and cheerful place with a thoroughly
authentic Lakeland feel. No smoking throughout. The sloping ceilings and floors
show the building's age, and there are lots of old local photographs and bric-a-brac –
farm tools, stuffed animals, a collection of long-stemmed clay pipes – and two
woodburning stoves. Good bar food includes home-made soup (£3.95), sandwiches
(from £4.75; ciabattas £5.75), five bean chilli (£8.75), home-made steak and Guinness
pie (£8.95), halibut steak in garlic and parsley butter (£10.25), cumberland sausage
with rich onion and cranberry gravy (£8.95), rare breed sirloin steak (£13.95), and
daily specials such as lamb in fresh thyme and red wine (£13.95), a good children's
menu. Well kept Black Sheep, Jennings Cumberland, Tetleys, and guests like Copper
Dragon Black Gold Hawkshead Gold, and York Stonewall on handpump; 30 malt
whiskies, and Weston's cider. The games room (where dogs are allowed) has darts,
pool, dominoes, fruit machine, TV and juke box; piped music. There are some seats
outside and fine surrounding walks. *(Recommended by Pat and Stewart Gordon, Andy and
Jill Kassube, Ron Gentry, Dr and Mrs A K Clarke, JDM, KM, Malcolm Taylor, Dennis Jones,
Mike Pugh, Lee and Liz Potter, Ann and Tony Bennett-Hughes, Pip King, Bob Ellis)*

Free house ~ Licensees Nigel and Peter Barton ~ Real ale ~ Bar food (12-2, 6-8.45; not Mon or Tues lunchtime except bank hols) ~ (01229) 861229 ~ Children in eating area of bar and restaurant ~ Dogs allowed in bedrooms ~ Open 12-2, 6-11; 12-11 Sat; 12-10.30 Sun; closed Mon and Tues lunchtimes (except bank hols) ~ Bedrooms: £47.50S(£37.50B)/ £80S(£60B)

BRAMPTON NY6723 Map 10

New Inn 🍺

Note: this is the small Brampton near Appleby, not the bigger one up by Carlisle. Off A66 N of Appleby – follow Long Marton 1 signpost then turn right at church; village also signposted off B6542 at N end of Appleby; CA16 6JS

As the cheerful, hard-working licensees were so popular running another of our main entries, this attractive place looks like doing particularly well under them. There's an open-plan bar with a mix of wooden dining chairs around traditional pub tables on the wood-boarded floor, some upholstered cushions, photographs of the pub and country pictures on the wall, and Tirril Bewshers and Brougham Ale on handpump; they will have three guest beers, too. Weston's cider; piped music, darts and dominoes. The interesting low-beamed and flagstoned dining room has an ancient cooking range by a massive old oak settle. Tasty bar food at lunchtime includes home-made soup (£3.75), sandwiches (from £4), cumberland sausage on spring onion mash or leek and potato bake (£8.50), steak in ale pie (£8.95), and gammon and egg (£9.95); evening choices such as garlic mushrooms topped with stilton (£3.95), pork and chicken liver pâté with cumberland sauce (£4.50), chicken on braised leeks with a blue cheese sauce (£10.50), tuna steak with lime and ginger butter (£10.95), locally reared fillet steak (£14.95), and puddings like sticky toffee pudding (from £4). Picnic-sets in the garden and views over the Pennines. By the time this book is published, they hope to have opened up bedrooms. (Recommended by Tony and Betty Parker)

Free house ~ Licensees Dan Ingham and Tom Mitchell ~ Real ale ~ Bar food (12-2, 6-9) ~ Restaurant ~ (017683) 51231 ~ Children welcome if well behaved ~ Dogs allowed in bar ~ Open 12-3, 6-11; 12-11 Sat and Sun

BROUGHTON MILLS SD2190 Map 9

Blacksmiths Arms

Off A593 N of Broughton-in-Furness; LA20 6AX

After you've enjoyed one of the fine nearby walks, this charming little pub is a smashing place to relax. Three of the four simply but attractively decorated small rooms have open fires, ancient slate floors, and Dent Aviator, Hawkshead Bitter and Jennings Cumberland on handpump, and summer farm cider. Using local produce, the good bar food includes lunchtime sandwiches or ciabattas (from £3.50; hot bacon and brie melt £3.95), ploughman's (from £5.75), and cajun chicken salad (£6.25), as well as soup (£2.95), oriental spare ribs (£3.95), home-made cod cake with apricot chutney (£4.25), cumberland sausage with red onion gravy (£7.25), steak in ale pie (£7.75), tomato, basil and mixed bean casserole (£8.25), minted lamb henry (£9.75), daily specials such as hock terrine with spicy tomato chutney (£3.95), gammon and egg or green pea and parmesan risotto (£8.25), roast duck with a Cointreau and orange sauce (£10.95), rump steak with creamy wild mushrooms and a red wine sauce (£13.45), and puddings like home-made sticky toffee pudding or fresh fruit créme brûlée (£3.95). There are three smallish dining rooms (the back one is no smoking). Darts, dominoes, and cards. Pretty summer hanging baskets and tubs of flowers in front of the building. More reports please. (Recommended by Tina and David Woods-Taylor, Derek Harvey-Piper, Karen Eliot, Christine and Phil Young)

Free house ~ Licensees Mike and Sophie Lane ~ Real ale ~ Bar food (12-2, 6-9; not Mon lunchtime) ~ Restaurant ~ (01229) 716824 ~ Children welcome ~ Dogs allowed in bar ~ Open 12-11; 12-10.30 Sun; 5-11 Mon (closed winter Mon), 12-2.30, 5-11 Tues-Fri in winter

BUTTERMERE NY1817 Map 9
Bridge Hotel
Just off B5289 SW of Keswick; CA13 9UZ

First licensed as a coaching inn in 1735, this bustling place – totally no smoking this year – has unrestricted walking for all levels as soon as you step outside; Crummock Water and Buttermere are just a stroll away. The beamed bar has built-in wooden settles and farmhouse chairs around traditional tables, a panelled bar counter, and a few horsebrasses – as well as a dining bar with blue plush armchairs around copper-topped tables and brass ornaments hanging from the beams, and a guest lounge. Lunchtime bar food includes home-made burgers, filled baked potatoes or hot panini (from £5.20), open sandwiches (from £5.45), platters (from £6.55), vegetable lasagne (£7.40), cumberland sausage and egg (£7.55), and cumbrian hotpot (£7.95), with evening dishes such as soup with home-made bread (£2.95), home-made chicken liver pâté (£4.15), mushroom stroganoff (£6.95), chicken and mushroom pie (£7.55), home-made steak and kidney pudding (£8.25), steaks (from £12.50), and daily specials like chilli con carne or cottage pie (£7.50), and fresh fish (£7.95). Black Sheep, Theakstons Old Peculier and a guest beer on handpump, several malt whiskies and a decent wine list. Outside, a flagstoned terrace has new furniture by a rose-covered sheltering stone wall. Please note, the bedroom prices are for dinner, bed and breakfast; several of the bedrooms and the self-catering apartments have been newly decorated this year. *(Recommended by Helen Clarke, Geoff and Angela Jaques, A S and M E Marriott, Patrick and Phillipa Vickery, John Foord, Geoff and Carol Thorp, Sylvia and Tony Birbeck)*

Free house ~ Licensees Adrian and John McGuire ~ Real ale ~ Bar food (12-9.30) ~ Restaurant ~ (017687) 70252 ~ Children in eating area of bar and, if over 7, in restaurant ~ Open 10.30-11(10.30 Sun) ~ Bedrooms: £75B/£150B

CARTMEL SD3879 Map 7
Kings Arms
The Square; LA11 6QB

In fine weather, the seats outside this rather grand little black and white pub make the most of the lovely square. Inside, the rambling bar has small antique prints on the walls, a mixture of seats including old country chairs, settles and wall banquettes, and tankards hanging over the bar counter. Bar food includes sandwiches (£4), baguettes (from £5.50), steak pie (£9.50), chicken with mascarpone and sun-dried tomatoes (£9.95), barramundi with a sweet thai chilli sauce (£11.25), and smoked haddock with cheese sauce or duck with cumberland sauce (£11.95). The snug and restaurant are no smoking. Black Sheep, Coniston Bluebird, Hawkshead Bitter, and maybe a couple of guest beers on handpump, and several wines by the glass; piped music. This ancient village has a grand priory church, and close to the pub is a fine medieval stone gatehouse; the race track is 200 yards away. More reports please. *(Recommended by John Foord, Alan and Paula McCully, Michael Doswell, Dennis Jones, Steve and Liz Tilley)*

Enterprise ~ Lease Richard Grimmer ~ Real ale ~ Bar food (12-2.30, 5.30-8.45; 12-8.45 weekends) ~ Restaurant ~ (01539) 536220 ~ Children welcome ~ Dogs allowed in bar ~ Open 11-11; 11-10.30 Sun; 11-3, 5-11 in winter; closed 25 Dec

CARTMEL FELL SD4189 Map 9
Masons Arms
Strawberry Bank, a few miles S of Windermere between A592 and A5074; perhaps the simplest way of finding the pub is to go uphill W from Bowland Bridge (which is signposted off A5074) towards Newby Bridge and keep right then left at the staggered crossroads – it's then on your right, below Gummer's How; OS Sheet 97 map reference 413895; LA11 6NW

The view down over the Winster Valley to the woods below Whitbarrow Scar is really quite special and can be enjoyed from the rustic benches and tables on the

terrace here. Inside, the main bar has plenty of character, with low black beams in
the bowed ceiling, and country chairs and plain wooden tables on polished
flagstones. A small lounge has oak tables and settles to match its fine Jacobean
panelling, there's a plain little room beyond the serving counter with pictures and a
fire in an open range, a family room with an old-parlourish atmosphere, and an
upstairs dining room; piped music. Black Sheep, Hawkshead Bitter and Gold, and
guests like Thwaites Lancaster Bomber or Timothy Taylors Landlord on
handpump; quite a range of foreign bottled beers, and locally produced damson gin
and strawberry vodka. Bar food includes home-made soup (£3.85), sandwiches
(£4.95; peking duck wrap £6.25), ploughman's (from £4.95), chicken liver pâté
with red onion marmalade (£5.95), home-made burger (£7.95), gratin of macaroni
in a creamy wild mushroom sauce (£9.95), beef and beer cobbler (£11.95), slow-
cooked lamb in mint (£13.95), steaks (from £13.95), daily specials such as warm
cajun chicken and bacon salad (£6.25) and roast pork with apple sauce (£9.95),
and puddings (£4.25). Self-catering cottages and apartments behind. More reports
please. *(Recommended by Rob & Sue Hastie, Andy and Jill Kassube, Helen Clarke,
Chris Evans, Jenny and Peter Lowater, Jo Lilley, Simon Calvert, Tessa Allanson,
Mark Harrington, Nigel Stevenson, Dennis Jones, Tom Halsall, Ewan McCall, Simon Cleasby,
Ewan and Moira McCall, Helen and Brian Edgeley, David and Sue Atkinson, M J Winterton)*

Free house ~ Licensees John and Diane Taylor ~ Real ale ~ Bar food (12-2, 6-9; all day
weekends) ~ Restaurant ~ (015395) 68486 ~ Children welcome ~ Open 11.30-11;
12-10.30 Sun; 11.30-3, 6-11 Mon-Thurs in winter

CASTERTON   SD6279   Map 7

Pheasant ♀ 🍽

**A683 about 1 mile N of junction with A65, by Kirkby Lonsdale; OS Sheet 97 map
reference 633796; LA6 2RX**

Courteous and helpful people run this pleasant place that is no smoking except for
one small bar. The beamed rooms of the main bar are neatly kept and attractively
modernised, with wheelback chairs, cushioned wall settles, a nicely arched oak
framed fireplace (gas effect fires now), and Dent Aviator, Theakstons Bitter,
Timothy Taylors Landlord and a guest beer on handpump; over 20 malt whiskies
and an extensive wine list. There's quite an emphasis on the restaurant food which
at lunchtime might include home-made soup (£3.25), sandwiches (from £3.25),
home-made pâté (£4.55), ploughman's (£6.25), cannelloni stuffed with chopped
mushrooms and asparagus spears in parsley cream sauce (£6.45), steak in ale pie
(£6.75), roast chicken with apple sauce and stuffing (£6.95), and crispy battered
haddock (£7.75); evening dishes such as poached fresh pears with stilton dressing
(£4.15), hors d'oeuvres (£5.35), spinach, feta and mushroom strudel (£8.25), roast
pork fillet in pepper cream sauce (£11.25), crispy duckling with sage and onion
stuffing (£11.95), seafood mixed grill (£12.95), and home-made puddings (£4).
Piped music and board games. There are some tables with cocktail parasols outside
by the road, with more in the pleasant garden. The nearby church (built for the
girls' school of Brontë fame here) has some attractive pre-Raphaelite stained glass
and paintings. *(Recommended by John and Yvonne Davies, G Dobson, Margaret and
Roy Randle, Roger Thornington, Jo Lilley, Simon Calvert, Tom and Jill Jones)*

Free house ~ Licensee The Dixon Family ~ Real ale ~ Bar food (12-2, 6-9(9.30 Fri and
Sat)) ~ Restaurant ~ (015242) 71230 ~ Children welcome ~ Open 12-3.30, 6-11(10.30
Sun); closed two weeks Jan for redecorating ~ Bedrooms: £38B/£74B

CHAPEL STILE   NY3205   Map 9

Wainwrights 🍺

B5343; LA22 9JH

The position here is lovely with fells rising directly behind this white-rendered
lakeland house, and you can enjoy the views from the picnic-sets out on the terrace;
good surrounding walks. Inside, the characterful slate-floored bar has plenty of
room, and it is here that walkers and their dogs are welcomed. There's a relaxed

and friendly atmosphere, an old kitchen range, cushioned settles, and well kept Jennings Cumberland Ale and Sneck Lifter, and up to four changing guests on handpump or tapped from the cask; eight wines by the glass and summer fruit smoothies. Bar food includes soup (£2.50), lunchtime sandwiches (from £3.50), filled baked potatoes (from £4.60), ploughman's, curry of the day, steak and mushroom pie or mushroom and spinach lasagne (all £7.95), cumberland sausage (£8.75), slow-braised lamb in honey and mint (£9.25), and daily specials like home-made hotpot, chicken caesar salad or liver and onion casserole (£7.95). The family dining area is no smoking; piped music, darts, dominoes and TV. More reports please. (Recommended by Ewan and Moira McCall, David and Katharine Cooke, Tony and Penny Burton, Jack Clark, W W Burke)

Free house ~ Licensees Mrs C Darbyshire and B Clarke ~ Real ale ~ Bar food (12-2(2.30 Sun), 6-9) ~ 015394 38088 ~ Children in family dining area ~ Dogs allowed in bar ~ Open 11.30-11; 11.30-11 Sat; 12-10.30 Sun; 11.30-3, 6-11 in winter

COCKERMOUTH NY1231 Map 9
Bitter End ◀
Kirkgate, by cinema; CA13 9PJ

The Victorian-style window at the back of this bustling and friendly pub gives a view into their own little brewery: Cuddy Luggs, IPA and Cockermouth Pride. The licensee also keeps guests such as Coniston Bluebird, Derwent Pale Ale, Hawkshead Gold and Jennings Cumberland on handpump in good condition; quite a few bottled beers from around the world, and eight wines by the glass. The three main rooms have a different atmosphere in each – from quietly chatty to sporty, with the décor reflecting this, such as unusual pictures of a Cockermouth that even Wordsworth might have recognised, to more up-to-date sporting memorabilia, various bottles, jugs and books, and framed beer mats. The snug is no smoking. Good value traditional bar food includes toasted panini bread with fillings (from £2.95), filled baked potatoes (£3.75), chilli lamb (£5.50), pasta in a spicy tomato sauce (£6.50), cumberland sausage or battered haddock (£6.95), steak, mushroom and ale pie (£7.50), and puddings such as sticky toffee pudding (£2.50); piped music and free Tuesday evening quiz. The public car park round the back is free after 7pm. More reports please. (Recommended by Helen Clarke, Andy and Jill Kassube, Paul Davies, Steve Kirby, P S Hoyle, John Foord, Barry Collett, Edward Mirzoeff)

Own brew ~ Licensee Susan Askey ~ Real ale ~ Bar food (12-2, 6-8.30) ~ (01900) 828993 ~ Children welcome but must be well behaved ~ Open 12-2.30, 6-11.30; 11.30-midnight Sat; 12-3, 6-11 Sun; 11.30-3, 6-11 Sat in winter

CROSTHWAITE SD4491 Map 9
Punch Bowl ⊕ ♀ ⇦
Village signposted off A5074 SE of Windermere; LA8 8HR

Given a stylish and sympathetic up-to-date makeover, this is an appealing no smoking dining pub with good food, yet with no pressure to eat if you just drop in for a drink. Reopened late in 2005 by the owners of the Drunken Duck near Hawkshead, it has an enlarged raftered and hop-hung bar with a couple of eye-catching rugs on its flagstones, and bar stools by the slate-topped counter, which has Barngates Cat Nap and Tag Lag (brewed at their sister pub) and a guest beer on handpump, and a good range of wines by the glass. This opens on the right into two linked carpeted and beamed rooms with well spaced country pine furnishings of varying sizes, including a big refectory table. The walls, painted in restrained neutral tones, have an attractive assortment of prints, with some copper objects, and there's a dresser with china and glass. There's a winter log fire, they have daily papers, and service by young staff is prompt, friendly and attentive. On the left is the wooden-floored restaurant area, also attractive, with comfortable leather seating. Throughout, the pub feels relaxing and nicely uncluttered. For most people, it will be the wide choice of food which is the main attraction. This might include soup with home-made bread (£4.25), caesar salad (£4.95; main course £8.95), sandwiches (from £4.95), ham hock and pear terrine, gingerbread and pineapple chutney (£5.25), chicken livers in creamy leek, prune and brandy sauce (£5.95), ploughman's (£6.95), pea and roasted tomato risotto (£9.75), fish pie (£9.95), brisket braised in their own beer with a horseradish cream (£11.25), roast chump of lamb with hotpot vegetables (£11.95), roast chicken breast, boulangère potatoes and a chicken cream (£12.50), and puddings such as warm chocolate brownie with dark chocolate ice-cream and white chocolate sauce or poached pear rice pudding with rum and raisin ice-cream (£5.95). There are some tables on a terrace stepped into the hillside, overlooking the lovely Lythe Valley. *(Recommended by Leslie G Smith, Rob Bowran, Dr K P Tucker, Hugh Roberts, Dr and Mrs A K Clarke, Michael Doswell, Helen Clarke, Tessa Allanson)*

Free house ~ Licensee Stephen Carruthers ~ Real ale ~ Bar food (12-3, 6-9) ~ Restaurant ~ (015395) 68237 ~ Children welcome ~ Dogs allowed in bar ~ Open 12-11 ~ Bedrooms: £75B/£100B

ELTERWATER   NY3305   Map 9
Britannia ㉕ ◗
Off B5343; LA22 9HP

This is a fine spot in the heart of the Lake District, close to Langdale and the central lakes, and with tracks over the fells to Grasmere and Easedale. As well as a small and traditionally furnished back bar, there's a front one with a couple of window seats looking across to Elterwater itself through the trees: coal fires (which may not always be lit), oak benches, settles, windsor chairs, a big old rocking chair, and Coniston Bluebird, Isle of Skye Coruisk, Jennings Bitter, Shepherd Neame Spitfire and Timothy Taylors Landlord on handpump; quite a few malt whiskies. The lounge is comfortable. Bar food includes lunchtime filled rolls, home-made soup (£3.30), home-made cumberland pâté (£4.95), home-made mushroom stroganoff (£8.90), cumberland sausage with onion gravy (£9.50), home-made steak in ale pie (£9.90), lamb in mint and spices (£11.50), daily specials, and puddings like home-made apple crumble (£4.60). The main bar, hall, dining room and residents' lounge are no smoking. Plenty of seats outside and summer morris and step and garland dancers. The pub does get very crowded with long queues for service at busy times, and as the location virtually guarantees a constant stream of customers, people occasionally feel that the staff are rather less concerned about any customer disappointments than they might otherwise be. *(Recommended by Tina and David Woods-Taylor, Chris Willers, C J Pratt, David and Sue Smith, Tom and Jill Jones, Ewan and Moira McCall, Jo Lilley, Simon Calvert, Alan Sadler, Peter and Eleanor Kenyon, Mr and Mrs Richard Osborne, Jack Clark, TOH, W W Burke, Steve and Liz Tilley, David and Jean Hall, Malcolm and Jane Levitt, Dr David Clegg)*

Free house ~ Licensee Clare Woodhead ~ Real ale ~ Bar food (all day) ~ Restaurant ~ (015394) 37210 ~ Children welcome ~ Dogs allowed in bar and bedrooms ~ Open 10-11 ~ Bedrooms: £78S/£96S(£88B)

GREAT SALKELD   NY5536   Map 10
Highland Drove ⑪
B6412, off A686 NE of Penrith; CA11 9NA

This is a smashing place and deservedly popular with both the cheerful locals enjoying a chat and a pint and visitors keen to sample the particularly good food. A new downstairs eating area has been opened up with cushioned dining chairs around wooden tables on the pale wooden floorboards, brick walls and ceiling joists, and a two-way fire in a raised brick fireplace that separates this room from the new no smoking coffee lounge with its comfortable leather chairs and sofas. The convivial main bar has sandstone flooring, brick walls, cushioned wheelback chairs around a mix of tables, an open fire in a raised stone fireplace, and John Smiths, Theakstons Black Bull and Timothy Taylors Landlord on handpump; a good choice of wines and 25 malt whiskies. Piped music, TV, juke box, darts, pool, games machine and dominoes. Using the best local produce, the downstairs bar food might include home-made soup (£2.95; large £3.95), chicken liver parfait (£4.25), black pudding with garlic crushed potatoes and a Black Bull sauce (£4.95), cream cheese and spinach cannelloni (£4.50), charcuterie plate (£6.25), ploughman's (£6.95), cumberland sausage with spring onion mash (£6.95), roast ham and egg or home-made beefburger (£7.95), and lamb shank on vegetable mash (£10.95); more elaborate dishes upstairs such as spring roll of duck with summer cabbage and pickled fresh cherries with a rocket dressing (£5.25), wild mushroom and pesto pasta with a tempura of courgette and a chilli tomato dressing (£9.95), and duck breast with vanilla and lime mash and white onion ice-cream with red wine juniper berry jus (£14.95). Puddings like brownie with warm chocolate sauce with white chocolate and cardamom ice-cream or fresh strawberry panna cotta with lemon ice-cream (£4.25). The eating areas are no smoking. There are lovely views over the Eden Valley and the Pennines – best enjoyed from seats on the upstairs verandah. *(Recommended by Robert and Susan Phillips, Richard J Holloway, Kevin Tea, Michael Doswell, Dr K P Tucker, Helen Clarke, Les and Sandra Brown, Tony and Maggie Harwood)*

Free house ~ Licensees Donald and Paul Newton ~ Real ale ~ Bar food (12-2, 6.30-8.45; not Mon lunchtime, 25 Dec, 1 Jan) ~ Restaurant ~ (01768) 898349 ~ Children welcome ~ Dogs allowed in bar ~ Open 12-2.30(3 Sun), 6-midnight; 12-midnight Sat; closed Mon lunchtime ~ Bedrooms: £32.50B/£60B

HAWKSHEAD NY3501 Map 9

Drunken Duck ㉕ 🍽 🍷 🍴 🛏

Barngates; the hamlet is signposted from B5286 Hawkshead—Ambleside, opposite the Outgate Inn; or it may be quicker to take the first right from B5286, after the wooded caravan site; OS Sheet 90 map reference 350013; LA22 0NG

With so much emphasis in this civilised totally no smoking inn being placed on the beautifully appointed bedrooms and three restaurant areas, it cannot be thought of as a pub. But it does have a small, stylish bar where they serve their own-brewed Barngates Cat Nap, Cracker, Red Bull Terrier, Tag Lag and Westmorland Gold plus local microbrewery ales on handpump; belgian and german draught beers, 20 wines by the glass, and several malt whiskies. There are beams and oak floorboards, leather-topped bar stools by the slate-topped bar counter, leather club chairs, photographs, coaching prints and hunting pictures, and some kentish hop bines. The only nod to bar food comes in the form of pre-made sandwiches wrapped in greaseproof paper (home-cooked meats, local cheeses, free-range eggs, from £4.25) and soup (£3.75). From the imaginative à la carte menu there might be pigeon marinated with liquorice on prune and parmesan risotto (£6.25), potted flookburgh shrimps with toasted malt bread (£6.95), crab and chive cake with sweet sherry vinegar dressing and a warm green bean and sunblush tomato salad (£7.95), goats cheese and slow-roast tomato tartlet on roast onion and asparagus with red pepper sauce (£14.45), venison fillet with chestnut polenta, caramelised figs and espresso pistachio nuts (£14.95), and diver-caught seared king scallops with local air-dried ham and burnt orange sauce (£17.95), with puddings such as banana fritters with banoffi tart and iced banana parfait, a trio of lemon puddings, and Bailey's bread and butter pudding with chocolate malt ice-cream and hot chocolate sauce (from £5.95). Rustic seating on the grass bank opposite the building offers spectacular views across the fells, and there are thousands of spring and summer bulbs. *(Recommended by Leslie G Smith, Noel Grundy, Mrs Suzy Miller, Mr and Mrs P Eastwood, Mike and Sue Loseby, Mark Harrington, Nigel Stevenson, Mr and Mrs Woodhead, Alan Sadler, Maggie Chandler, Carl Van Baars, Jo Lilley, Simon Calvert, T Walker, Tina and David Woods-Taylor, Derek and Heather Manning, W W Burke, Janet Walters, Karen and Graham Oddey, W M Lien, David and Sue Atkinson, Dr K P Tucker)*

Own brew ~ Licensee Steph Barton ~ Real ale ~ Restaurant ~ (015394) 36347 ~ Children welcome ~ Dogs allowed in bar ~ Open 11.30-11; 12-10.30 Sun; closed 25 Dec except between 12 and 2 ~ Bedrooms: £71.25B/£95B

Kings Arms
The Square; LA22 0NZ

You can sit on the terrace outside this 16th-c inn and look over the central square of the lovely Elizabethan village. There are some fine original features, traditional pubby furnishings, and an open log fire: Black Sheep, Coniston Bluebird and Hawkshead Bitter and Red on handpump, 33 malt whiskies, a decent wine list and organic soft drinks. Piped music, games machine, TV and board games. Decent bar food at lunchtime includes soup (£2.95), filled focaccia, baps or ciabatta (from £4.75), and hot meals such as home-made fish pie (£7.50), lamb chops (£8.25), and roast beef (£8.25); evening choices like pâté with home-made chutney (£4.25), chilli ginger chicken goujons with roast garlic, cream cheese and chive dip (£4.50), mushroom ravioli in tomato, basil and oregano sauce (£6.75), steak in ale pie (£8.25), and duck breast in plum sauce (£9.25). The restaurant is no smoking. As well as bedrooms, they offer self-catering cottages. There are free fishing permits for residents. *(Recommended by Nick Lawless, Alan and Paula McCully, Ron Gentry, Andy and Ali)*

Free house ~ Licensees Rosalie and Edward Johnson ~ Real ale ~ Bar food (12-2.30, 6-9.30) ~ Restaurant ~ (015394) 36372 ~ Children in eating area of bar and restaurant ~ Dogs allowed in bar and bedrooms ~ Live music last Thurs in month ~ Open 11-11(midnight Sat); closed evening 25 Dec ~ Bedrooms: £45S/£80S

Queens Head
Main Street; LA22 0NS

Particularly at lunchtime, this lovely black and white timbered pub has a good bustling atmosphere and plenty of customers. There's quite a local following as well as a mix of visitors, and the low-ceilinged bar has heavy bowed black beams, red plush wall seats and plush stools around heavy traditional tables, lots of decorative plates on the panelled walls, and an open fire; a no smoking snug little room leads off. Lunchtime food served in either the bar or more formal no smoking restaurant includes sandwiches, home-made soup (£3.25), chicken liver pâté with orange and tequila (£5.25), ciabatta topped with bacon and melted stilton (£5.75), croque monsieur or cumberland sausage with white onion sauce (£7.25), vegetarian pasta (£7.50), deep-fried haddock with home-made chips (£7.75), and slow-roasted lamb with rosemary scented sauce (£11.50); ambitious evening dishes such as game terrine wrapped in local air-dried ham with tomato chutney (£5.45), locally smoked salmon and halibut on a chive and buttermilk pancake with dill dressing (£6.45), chicken and king prawns in thai spices and cream with saffron rice (£13.50), and local venison on root vegetable mash with a juniper and red wine glaze (£16.50). Robinsons Cumbria Way, Double Hop, Unicorn and Young Tom on handpump; piped music. As well as bedrooms in the inn, they have three holiday cottages to rent in the village. The summer window boxes are very pretty. Residents can get a parking pass from the inn for the public car park about 100 yards away. *(Recommended by Helen Clarke, Alan and Paula McCully, Tom and Jill Jones, Ian and Jane Irving, Mr and Mrs P Eastwood, David Carr, W W Burke, Andy and Ali, Bruce and Sharon Eden)*

Robinsons ~ Tenants Mr and Mrs Tony Merrick ~ Real ale ~ Bar food (12-2.30, 6.15-9.30) ~ Restaurant ~ (015394) 36271 ~ Children welcome ~ Open 11-midnight ~ Bedrooms: £60B/£90B

Bedroom prices normally include full English breakfast, VAT and any inclusive service charge that we know of. Prices before the '/' are for single rooms, after for two people in double or twin (B includes a private bath, S a private shower). If there is no '/', the prices are only for twin or double rooms (as far as we know there are no singles). If there is no B or S, as far as we know no rooms have private facilities.

HESKET NEWMARKET NY3438 Map 10
Old Crown ♥
Village signposted off B5299 in Caldbeck; CA7 8JG

One of the main draws to this bustling, unfussy local are their own-brewed beers. Well kept on handpump, these include Hesket Newmarket Blencathra Bitter, Doris's 90th Birthday Ale, Great Cockup Porter, Helvellyn Gold, Skiddaw Special Bitter, Old Carrock Strong Ale, Catbells Pale Ale and Sea Fell Blonde. Reasonably priced bar food such as sandwiches, mediterranean pasta bake, ham and egg or cumberland sausage (£5.25), steak in ale pie (£6.50), somerset chicken or salmon fillet with lemon and dill, and specials like vegetable stir fry (£5.25) or slow-cooked lamb in mint and rosemary (£7.50). The dining room is no smoking, and a new garden dining room should be open by the time this book is published. The little bar has a few tables, a coal fire and shelves of well thumbed books, and a friendly atmosphere; darts, pool and dominoes. The pub is in a pretty setting in a remote, attractive village. You can book up tours to look around the brewery; £10 and a minimum of six people. More reports please. *(Recommended by Helen Clarke, Tina and David Woods-Taylor, Mike and Sue Loseby, Mrs C E Godfrey, Peter F Marshall, Martin and Sue Day, Simon Cleasby)*

Own brew ~ Licensees Lou and Linda Hogg ~ Real ale ~ Bar food (12-2, 6.30-8.30; not Sun evening or all day Mon) ~ Restaurant ~ (016974) 78288 ~ Children welcome ~ Dogs allowed in bar ~ Folk first Sun of month ~ Open 12-3, 5.30-11; 12-3, 7-10.30 Sun; closed Mon evening all year and Tues evening in winter

INGS SD4599 Map 9
Watermill ♥
Just off A591 E of Windermere; LA8 9PY

'This is the one pub I will come to every time I visit the Lake District,' said one happy reader who regularly walks in this area. It's a particularly well run and very popular pub run by an enthusiastic and hard-working landlord. They keep a fantastic range of 16 real ales on handpump with regulars such as Black Sheep Bitter and Special, Coniston Bluebird, Hawkshead Bitter, Moorhouses Black Cat, and Theakstons Best and Old Peculier, guests like Batemans XB, Brakspears Bee Sting, Cotleigh Tawny Owl, Fyne Highlander, Harviestoun Navigator, Jennings Cumberland, Loddon Flight of Fancy, Wadworths 6X and Yates Fever Pitch, and their own-brewed A Bit of Ruff, Collie Wobbles and Ruff Nite. Sixty foreign bottled beers and over 50 whiskies. The building is cleverly converted from a wood mill and joiner's shop, and the partly no smoking bars have a friendly, bustling atmosphere, a happy mix of chairs, padded benches and solid oak tables, bar counters made from old church wood, open fires and interesting photographs and amusing cartoons by a local artist. The spacious no smoking lounge bar, in much the same traditional style as the other rooms, has rocking chairs and a big open fire; two areas are no smoking. Using locally sourced produce, the generous helpings of well liked bar food include home-made soup (£3.40), lunchtime filled rolls or ciabatta (from £3.75), filled baked potatoes (from £4.50), and ploughman's (£5.95), as well as home-made pâté (£4.75), broccoli and onion pasta (£7.50), cumberland sausage with beer and onion gravy (£8.25), fresh beer-battered haddock (£8.50), home-made beef in ale pie (£8.75), daily specials such as toasted brioche topped with a creamy smoked bacon and mushroom sauce or filo prawns with a sweet chilli dip (£4.75), game casserole (£8.50), steamed escolar with a seafood medley (£9.50), lamb chops with a roasted shallot, red wine and rosemary jus (£11.25), and puddings like warm pancakes filled with fruits and a raspberry compote (£3.75). Darts and board games. Seats in the gardens, and lots to do nearby. *(Recommended by Helen Clarke, Andy and Jill Kassube, J S Burn, Bob Broadhurst, JDM, KM, Tom and Jill Jones, G Dobson, Paul Boot, P Dawn, Mr and Mrs J N Graham, MLR, Jo Lilley, Simon Calvert, Phil and Jane Hodson, Adrian Johnson, Andrew and Christine Gagg, Mark Harrington, Dennis Jones, Mike Pugh, Douglas Keith, A S and M E Marriott, Mr and Mrs Maurice Thompson, Paul and Gloria Howell, Pam and John Smith, Len Beattie, Dr David Clegg)*

Free house ~ Licensee Brian Coulthwaite ~ Real ale ~ Bar food (12-4.30, 5-9) ~
(01539) 821309 ~ Children in lounge area ~ Dogs allowed in bar and bedrooms ~
Storytelling first Tues of month ~ Open 12-11(10.30 Sun); closed 25 Dec ~ Bedrooms:
£35S/£68B

KESWICK   NY2623   Map 9
Dog & Gun
Lake Road; CA12 5BT

There's a good bustling atmosphere in this unpretentious town pub. The bar has
low beams, a partly slate floor (the rest are carpeted or bare boards), some high
settles, a fine collection of striking mountain photographs by the local firm
G P Abrahams, brass and brewery artefacts, and coins in beams and timbers by the
fireplace (which go to the Mountain Rescue Service). Well kept Theakstons Best
and Old Peculier and Yates Bitter, with a couple of guests like Fullers London Pride
and Greene King Old Speckled Hen on handpump, and a dozen wines by the glass.
Tasty bar food includes soup (£2.95), nachos with toppings (from £3.95),
sandwiches and filled baked potatoes (until 6pm, from £3.95), sausage and mash
with red onion gravy (£6.45), aberdeen angus burgers (until 6pm, from £6.45),
vegetarian pasta or a pie of the day (£6.95), their not-to-be-missed goulash (£7.95),
daily specials, and puddings (from £3.45). *(Recommended by Fred and Lorraine Gill,
P Dawn, Phil Merrin, Steve Kirby, Andy and Jill Kassube, Patrick Renouf)*

Scottish Courage ~ Manager Peter Ede ~ Real ale ~ Bar food (12-9) ~ (017687) 73463 ~
Children allowed if dining ~ Dogs welcome ~ Open 12-11(11.30 Thurs); 12-midnight Fri
and Sat; 12-11 Sun; closed 25 Dec

LANGDALE   NY2906   Map 9
Old Dungeon Ghyll ㉕ ◧
B5343; LA22 9JY

The position of this straightforward local is smashing. It is at the heart of the Great
Langdale Valley and surrounded by fells including the Langdale Pikes flanking the
Dungeon Ghyll Force waterfall. The whole feel of the place is basic but cosy – and
once all the fell walkers and climbers crowd in, full of boisterous atmosphere.
There's no need to remove boots or muddy trousers, and you can sit on the seats in
old cattle stalls by the big warming fire, and enjoy well kept Jennings Cumberland,
Theakstons Old Peculier and XB, Yates Bitter and a couple of changing guests on
handpump; up to 30 malt whiskies, and farm cider. Straightforward food includes
home-made soup (£3.75), lunchtime sandwiches (£4), and various hot dishes like
curries, stews, lasagne or a pie of the day (from £6.50); darts. It may get lively on a
Saturday night (there's a popular National Trust campsite opposite). *(Recommended
by Helen Clarke, David and Sue Smith, David and Katharine Cooke, Hugh Roberts, B Shelley,
Ewan and Moira McCall, Dr D J and Mrs S C Walker, Len Beattie, Dr David Clegg)*

Free house ~ Licensee Neil Walmsley ~ Real ale ~ Bar food (12-2, 6-9) ~ Restaurant ~
(015394) 37272 ~ Children in eating area of bar and restaurant ~ Dogs allowed in bar ~
Folk first Weds of month ~ Open 11-11(10.30 Sun); closed Christmas ~ Bedrooms:
£45/£90(£96S)

LEVENS   SD5087   Map 9
Strickland Arms ♀ ◧
4 miles from M6 junction 36, via A590; just off A590, by Sizergh Castle gates;
LA8 8DZ

Closed since the late 1990s, this has now been reopened after sympathetic
refurbishment by the owner of the Eagle & Child down at Bispham Green (see
Lancashire main entries), who has leased it from its owners, the National Trust. It's
now a no smoking dining pub, and word has quickly got around locally about its
friendly service and atmosphere, good food and drink. Largely open plan, it has

oriental rugs on the flagstones of the bar on the right, which has a log fire and serves Thwaites Original and Lancaster Bomber from handpump, with two local guest beers such as Coniston Bluebird or Hawkshead Gold, 25 malt whiskies, and good wines by the glass. On the left are polished boards, and another log fire (they have central heating, too), and throughout there's a nice mix of sturdy country furniture, with candles on tables, hunting scenes and other old prints on the walls, heavy fabric for the curtains, and some staffordshire china ornaments. There is a further dining room upstairs. The good food relies strongly on fresh produce from local farms and estates, and besides good value lunchtime soup (£3.95), doorstep sandwiches and baguettes, might include smoked salmon pâté or fish goujons with garlic mayonnaise (£4.50), baked mushrooms with tomato concasse and goats cheese (£5.95), potted shrimps to their own recipe, scallops with black pudding (£7), avocado, pine nut and smoked cheese salad (£7.95), chicken breast stuffed with goats cheese and wrapped in smoked bacon or steak in ale pie (£9.95), fell-bred lamb chump chop with redcurrant sauce (£11), daily specials such as asparagus fishcakes with lobster vinaigrette (£5.25), vegetable stir fry (£8), and wild boar and plum sausage on roast onion mash with red wine and rosemary gravy (£11.95), and puddings (from £5) such as chocolate tart or passion fruit crème brûlée. Service is friendly and personal, they have disabled access and facilities, and there are tables out in front on a new flagstone terrace. The Castle, in fact a lovely partly medieval house with beautiful gardens, is open in the afternoon (not Friday/Saturday) from April to October. *(Recommended by Ray and Winifred Halliday, Michael Doswell, John and Sylvia Harrop)*

Free house ~ Licensees Emma Bigland and Martin Ainscough ~ Real ale ~ Bar food (12-2, 6-9; all day weekends) ~ (015395) 61010 ~ Children welcome ~ Dogs welcome ~ Open 12-3, 5.30-11; 12-midnight(11pm Sun) Sat

LITTLE LANGDALE   NY3204   Map 9

Three Shires ⑳ ⇌

From A593 3 miles W of Ambleside take small road signposted The Langdales, Wrynose Pass; then bear left at first fork; LA22 9NZ

Readers enjoy their visits to this pleasantly placed stone-built inn – totally no smoking now. There are lovely views over the valley to the partly wooded hills below Tilberthwaite Fells from seats on the terrace, with more seats on a well kept lawn behind the car park, backed by a small oak wood. Inside, the comfortably extended back bar has stripped timbers and a beam-and-joist stripped ceiling, antique oak carved settles, country kitchen chairs and stools on its big dark slate flagstones, and lakeland photographs; there's a warm winter fire in the modern stone fireplace. An arch leads through to a small, additional area. Good lunchtime bar food includes sandwiches or baguettes (from £3.95; a filled baguette plus soup £6.25), home-made fishcake with lime and cucumber crème fraîche (£5.95), ploughman's (£6.75), and cumberland sausage or beef in ale pie (£7.95); evening choices such as rich tomato tart topped with melting goats cheese, toasted pine nuts and basil pesto (£8.95), chargrilled guinea fowl with a wild mushroom porridge and whiskied raisins (£10.95), baked salmon fillet with lemon grass, spinach and ginger (£11.95), and roast half duckling with an orange, honey and thyme glaze (£14.50); puddings like sticky toffee pudding crème brûlée or creamy rice pudding topped with apple strudel syrup (from £4.95). Well kept Jennings Bitter and Cumberland, and maybe Hawkshead Red or Theakstons Black Bull on handpump, over 30 malt whiskies, and a decent wine list; darts and board games. The three shires are the historical counties Cumberland, Westmorland and Lancashire, which meet at the top of the nearby Wrynose Pass. The summer hanging baskets are very pretty. *(Recommended by Louise English, R M Corlett, Tina and David Woods-Taylor, J S Burn, Ron Gentry, Ewan and Moira McCall, Michael Doswell, Tony and Penny Burton, Jo Lilley, Simon Calvert, Jack Clark, TOH, Christine and Phil Young, Barry Collett, Dr David Clegg)*

Free house ~ Licensee Ian Stephenson ~ Real ale ~ Bar food (12-2, 6-8.45; no evening meals Dec and Jan) ~ Restaurant ~ (015394) 37215 ~ Children welcome ~ Dogs allowed

in bar ~ Open 11-10.30(11 Sat); 12-10.30 Sun; 11-3, 8-10.30 Dec and Jan winter ~
Bedrooms: /£80S(£78B)

LOWESWATER   NY1421   Map 9
Kirkstile Inn   ㉕   🍺   🛏️

From B5289 follow signs to Loweswater Lake; OS Sheet 89 map reference 140210;
CA13 0RU

In a glorious spot between Loweswater and Crummock Water, this popular little
no smoking country inn is surrounded by arresting peaks and fells. The bustling bar
is low-beamed and carpeted, with a good mix of customers, a roaring log fire,
comfortably cushioned small settles and pews, and partly stripped stone walls; slate
shove-ha'penny board. Enjoyable food at lunchtime includes home-made soup (£3),
filled baked potatoes and baguettes (£4.50), mackerel parfait with red onion
chutney (£4.25), lamb stew with pickles (£6.25), vegetable moussaka (£7), steak in
ale pie (£7.50), and liver and bacon with bubble and squeak (£8.25), with evening
dishes such as smooth duckling pâté (£4.25), pork fillet with brandy sauce or local
salmon fillet on a purée of yams with a sweet pepper tapenade (£8.75), and baked
lamb in honey and mint (£9.75); daily specials like vegetable bake (£7.75), fish
crumble (£8.50), and steak laced with whisky cream (£11.95) and puddings such as
panna cotta with a strawberry and kirsch compote, home-made fruit crumble or
home-made bread and butter pudding (£3.95). Their own-brewed and well kept
Loweswater Grasmoor Dark and Melbreak Bitter plus Coniston Bluebird, and
Yates Bitter on handpump. You can enjoy the view from picnic-sets on the lawn,
from the very attractive covered verandah in front of the building, and from the
bow windows in one of the rooms off the bar. *(Recommended by Mr and Mrs*
John Taylor, G J and M M Hill, Edward Mirzoeff, Richard Tosswill, Mike and Sue Loseby,
Dennis Jones, Mrs Judith Smith, T Walker, Geoff and Carol Thorp, Maurice and Gill McMahon,
Bob and Sue, Sylvia and Tony Birbeck, Patrick Renouf)

Own brew ~ Licensee Roger Humphreys ~ Real ale ~ Bar food (12-2, 6-9) ~ Restaurant ~
(01900) 85219 ~ Children welcome ~ Dogs allowed in bar ~ Open 11-11; 12-10.30 Sun;
closed 25 Dec ~ Bedrooms: £55B/£78B

MUNGRISDALE   NY3630   Map 10
Mill Inn

Off A66 Penrith—Keswick, a bit over 1 mile W of A5091 Ullswater turn-off; CA11 0XR

There's a fantastic choice of 13 varieties of home-made shortcrust pastry pies on
offer in this bustling and popular inn. These might include wild venison, pheasant
and rabbit, steak and haggis in a whisky gravy, herdwick lamb and redcurrants,
and gloucester old spot pork with pineapple and ginger, and they all come with a
jug of gravy (from £5.45). At lunchtime you can also have home-made soup
(£3.10), filled rolls, open sandwiches or toasted muffins (from £3.35; toasted
muffin with bacon and fried eggs £4.10), home-made fishcakes (£4.95), three-egg
omelette (£4.90), local cumberland sausage (£5.60), and ploughman's (£5.75), with
evening choices such as chicken liver pâté (£4.20), black pudding scotch egg
(£4.95), chicken breast with a mushroom, garlic, stilton, white wine and cream
sauce (£9.45), shoulder of lamb in mint and rosemary (£11.35), and steaks
(from £13.75), and daily specials like smoked haddock rarebit with black pudding
(£5.25), chicken balti (£10.95) and baked bass with citrus butter or supreme of
pheasant with calvados sauce (£12.95). Two-course Sunday lunch (£11), and
friendly, efficient service. The traditionally furnished and neatly kept bar has a
wooden bar counter with an old millstone built into it, an open fire in the stone
fireplace, and well kept Jennings Bitter and Cumberland, and a guest beer on
handpump; over 30 malt whiskies and seven wines by the glass. Piped music and
darts. The restaurant and part of the bar are no smoking. There are tables on the
gravel forecourt and neat lawn sloping to a little river; good walks nearby and some
strenuous hillwalking further on. They also own the Pie Mill in Threlkeld. Please
note that there's a quite separate Mill Hotel here. *(Recommended by G J and M M Hill,*

Helen Clarke, J S Burn, Eileen McCall, Mike and Sue Loseby, Geoff and Angela Jaques, Peter Abbott, Jim Abbott, Sally and Mark Bramall, Mike and Penny Sutton, Tracey and Stephen Groves, Mr and Mrs W D Borthwick, Mrs Phoebe A Kemp, Maurice and Gill McMahon, Tina and David Woods-Taylor, Jed Scott, Pip King, Patrick Renouf, David J Cooke)

Free house ~ Licensees Jim and Margaret Hodge ~ Real ale ~ Bar food (12-2, 6-8.30) ~ (017687) 79632 ~ Children welcome ~ Dogs allowed in bar and bedrooms ~ Open 12-11; 12-10.30 Sun; closed 25 and 26 Dec ~ Bedrooms: £42.50B/£70B

NEAR SAWREY SD3796 Map 9

Tower Bank Arms ㉕ ◖

B5285 towards the Windermere ferry; LA22 0LF

A new licensee has taken over this no smoking little country inn and has freshened up the décor to give a much brighter feel. The low-beamed main bar has plenty of rustic charm, settles and other seats on the rough slate floor, game and fowl pictures and postcards of Beatrix Potter, a grandfather clock, an open fire, and fresh flowers. Many illustrations in the Beatrix Potter books can be traced back to their origins in this village, including this pub which features in *The Tale of Jemima Puddleduck*. Well kept Barngates Cat Nap, Dent Bitter, Hawkshead Bitter and Theakstons Old Peculier on handpump. Lunchtime bar food now includes soup (£3.75), sandwiches (from £4.25), freshly battered haddock (£6.50), a trio of sausages with onion gravy (£6.95), and beef in ale stew (£7.50), with evening dishes such as chicken and asparagus tagliatelle (£9.95), spinach and ricotta cannelloni (£10.75), calves liver with root vegetable mash (£11.50), roast loin of cod on wilted spinach with a tomato sauce (£13.50), and puddings like sticky toffee pudding (£3.75). Cards and dominoes. Seats outside have pleasant views of the wooded Claife Heights. More reports on the new regime, please. *(Recommended by Ron Gentry, Dr A J and Mrs Tompsett, Tina and David Woods-Taylor, Jason Caulkin, Alice Carruthers)*

Free house ~ Licensee Anthony Hutton ~ Real ale ~ Bar food (12-2, 6-9; snacks served all day) ~ Restaurant ~ (015394) 36334 ~ Children welcome until 9pm ~ Dogs welcome ~ Open 10-11(all day); 12-10.30 Sun; 10-3, 6-11 Nov-Jan ~ Bedrooms: £45B/£70B

SANDFORD NY7316 Map 10

Sandford Arms ⇔

Village and pub signposted just off A66 W of Brough; CA16 6NR

A former farmhouse, this is a neat little inn tucked away in a very small village by the River Eden. The compact and comfortable no smoking dining area is on a slightly raised balustraded platform at one end of the L-shaped carpeted main bar, which has stripped beams and stonework, Black Sheep and a guest from Hesket Newmarket on handpump, and a good range of malt whiskies. The two sons do the cooking, and the food might include sandwiches, home-made soup (£3.25), grilled black pudding with mustard sauce (£3.95), hot spicy prawns (£5.65), local cumberland sausage with onion gravy (£7.75), home-made steak in ale pie (£8.25), mushroom and pepper stroganoff (£8.50), chicken with mushrooms, smoked bacon and cream (£8.95), steaks (from £13.75), and puddings such as fruit crumble or sticky toffee pudding (from £3.50); popular three-course Sunday lunch (£10.50). There's also a more formal separate dining room (open if pre-booked), and a second bar area with broad flagstones, charming heavy-horse prints, an end log fire, and darts, dominoes, board games and piped music. The eating areas are no smoking. Some picnic-sets outside. Please note the restricted opening times; they may open longer at weekend lunchtimes if there are enough customers. More reports please. *(Recommended by Richard Gibbs)*

Free house ~ Licensee Susan Stokes ~ Real ale ~ Bar food (12-1.45, 6.30-8.30; not weekday lunchtimes) ~ Restaurant ~ (017683) 51121 ~ Children welcome ~ Dogs allowed in bar ~ Open 6.30-11; 12-1.45, 6.30-11 Sat; 12-2, 7-10.30 Sun; closed Tues and weekday lunchtimes; 3-12 June ~ Bedrooms: £50B/£60B

SANTON BRIDGE NY1101 Map 9
Bridge Inn
Off A595 at Holmrook or Gosforth; CA19 1UX

With cheerful, helpful staff and a friendly atmosphere, this busy little black and white hotel is popular with our readers. The turkey-carpeted bar has stripped beams, joists and standing timbers, a coal and log fire, and three rather unusual timbered booths around big stripped tables along its outer wall, with small painted school chairs and tables elsewhere. Bar stools line the long concave bar counter, which has well kept Jennings Bitter, Cocker Hoop, Cumberland and Sneck Lifter, and a guest such as Golden Host on handpump; good big pots of tea, speciality coffees, and eight wines by the glass. Piped music, pool, games machine, TV and board games. Well liked bar food includes filled baguettes, home-made soup (£2.50), greek salad (£4.20), crab and prawn medley (£4.50), cumberland sausage, curry of the day or steak and kidney pie (£7.95), and specials such as vegetarian sausages (£9.95), and organic rare breed pork steaks in a rich mushroom sauce, organic lamb chops with mint gravy or halibut on thai red curry sauce (all £13.95). The italian-style bistro is no smoking (children must be over 10 in here), the small reception hall has a rack of daily papers, and there's a comfortable more hotelish lounge on the left. There are fell views and seats out in front by the quiet road, and plenty of surrounding walks. *(Recommended by J S Burn, W K Wood, Helen Clarke, David Heath, Phil and Jane Hodson, Stuart Orton, Mary Kirman and Tim Jefferson, Mr and Mrs Maurice Thompson)*

Jennings (W & D) ~ Lease John Morrow and Lesley Rhodes ~ Real ale ~ Bar food (12-2.30, 6-9.30) ~ Restaurant ~ (01946) 726221 ~ Children allowed in bar and Esk Room but must be over 10 in bistro ~ Dogs allowed in bar and bedrooms ~ Open 10-midnight ~ Bedrooms: £50(£58S)/£60(£70B)

SCALES NY3426 Map 9
White Horse
A66 W of Penrith; CA12 4SY

A bonus for walkers coming down from Blencathra is that this traditional lakeland pub (now totally no smoking) is open all day in summer; the flowering window boxes and tubs are pretty then. The little snug and old kitchen have all sorts of farming implements such as a marmalade slicer, butter churns, kettles and a black range, and the comfortable beamed bar has warm winter fires, hunting pictures and photographs of the pub on the walls. Camerons Castle Eden Ale and Strongarm and a guest like Charles Wells Bombardier on handpump. Well liked bar food might include sandwiches (from £2.95), home-made soup (£3.95), spinach pancake with cheese sauce (£3.95; main course £7.50), ploughman's (£5.95), steak in ale pie (£6.95), chicken in tarragon and cream or pork fillets in brandy sauce (£9.95), and puddings such as sticky toffee pudding (£3.95). From the cluster of pub and farm buildings, tracks lead up into the splendidly daunting and rocky fells with names like Foule Crag and Sharp Edge; muddy boots should be left outside. *(Recommended by Mike and Penny Sutton, JWAC, Patrick Renouf)*

Camerons ~ Lease Kevin Martindale ~ Real ale ~ Bar food (12-2.30, 6-9; all day July-Sept) ~ Restaurant ~ 017687 79241 ~ Children welcome ~ Open 12-11; 12-3, 6-10 in winter

SEATHWAITE SD2396 Map 9
Newfield Inn 🍺
Duddon Valley, near Ulpha (ie not Seathwaite in Borrowdale); LA20 6ED

As food is served all day in this cottagey and friendly 16th-c inn, there's nearly always a good bustling atmosphere; it is particularly popular with walkers and climbers at weekends. The slate-floored bar has a genuinely local and informal atmosphere, wooden tables and chairs, some interesting pictures, well kept Caledonian Deuchars IPA, Jennings Cumberland and Theakstons Old Peculier on handpump, and half a dozen wines by the glass. There's a comfortable side room and a games room with shove-ha'penny and board games; piped music. Good value bar food using only local meat from named butchers includes soup (£2.55), filled rolls (from £3.10), beans on toast (£3.55), double egg and chips (£3.95), home-made spicy bean casserole (£5.95), cumberland sausage (£6.45), home-made steak pie (£7.55), and daily specials such as liver and bacon (£6.95), and four-cheese lasagne or home-made casseroles (£8.95). The dining room and one bar are no smoking. Tables outside in the nice garden have good hill views. The pub owns and lets the next-door self-catering flats, and there are fine walks from the doorstep. *(Recommended by Tina and David Woods-Taylor, David Field, Christine and Phil Young, Nigel Howard, Rona Murdoch)*

Free house ~ Licensee Paul Batten ~ Real ale ~ Bar food (12-9) ~ (01229) 716208 ~ Children welcome ~ Dogs allowed in bar ~ Open 11-11; 11-10.30 Sun; closed lunchtimes 25 and 26 Dec

STAVELEY   SD4798   Map 9
Eagle & Child   🍺 🛏
Kendal Road; just off A591 Windermere—Kendal; LA8 9LP

Even on a dreary day there's usually a bustling atmosphere and a welcoming fire under an impressive mantelbeam in this little inn. The roughly L-shaped flagstoned main area has plenty of separate parts to sit in, and pews, banquettes, bow window seats and some high-backed dining chairs around polished dark tables; also, some nice photographs and interesting prints, just a few farm tools and a delft shelf of bric-a-brac, and another log fire. Quite a few areas are no smoking. Good bar food includes sandwiches, home-made soup (£2.95), chicken liver, thyme and port pâté with seville orange chutney or terrine of roasted garlic vegetables with flaked parmesan and sunblush tomato dressing (£4.50), a home-made pie of the day or home-made beefburger (£6.95), cumberland sausage with caramelised red onion sauce (£7.95), parcel of thai vegetables on coconut and coriander noodles with garlic cream (£8.50), moroccan beef (£8.95), chicken, rabbit and pheasant casserole (£9.95), cod fillet wrapped in beech-smoked salmon and grilled with lemon butter (£10.50), fillet steak with shallots and basil oil, finished with cream and brandy (£14.95), and puddings like jamaican chocolate cheesecake or home-made mulled apple crumble (£3.95). They also offer Lunch for a Fiver (Monday-Saturday lunchtimes) and a two-course meal (£10.95, Monday-Wednesday). Well kept Barngates Cat Nap, Hawkshead Bitter, Yates Bitter and a changing guest on handpump or tapped from the cask; quite a few wines by the glass, a dozen bottled foreign beers, and four farm ciders. An upstairs barn-theme dining room (with its own bar for functions and so forth) doubles as a breakfast room. There are picnic-sets under cocktail parasols in a sheltered garden by the River Kent, with more on a good-sized back terrace, and second garden behind. *(Recommended by Dave Braisted, RJH, Bob Broadhurst, P Dawn, Jo Lilley, Simon Calvert, Alan and Carolin Tidbury, Mike Pugh, Paul and Gloria Howell)*

Free house ~ Licensees Richard and Denise Coleman ~ Real ale ~ Bar food ~ Restaurant ~ (01539) 821320 ~ Children welcome ~ Dogs allowed in bar ~ Open 11-11 (midnight Sat); 12-midnight Sun ~ Bedrooms: £40B/£60B

STONETHWAITE   NY2613   Map 9
Langstrath   🍺 🛏
Off B5289 S of Derwent Water; CA12 5XG

New licensees have taken over this civilised little no smoking inn. It's in a lovely spot in the heart of Borrowdale and en route for the Cumbrian Way and the Coast to Coast Walk; plenty of fine surrounding walks. At it's pubbiest at lunchtime, the neat and simple bar has a welcoming coal and log fire in a big stone fireplace, just a handful of cast-iron-framed tables, plain chairs and cushioned wall seats, and on its textured white walls maybe quite a few walking cartoons and attractive lakeland mountain photographs. Well kept Black Sheep and Jennings Bitter on handpump, with a couple of guest beers such as Coniston Bluebird or Hawkshead Bitter,

25 malt whiskies, and half a dozen wines by the glass; piped music. A little oak-boarded room on the left reminded us almost of a doll's house living room in style – this is actually the original cottage built around 1590. Bar food might include home-made soup (£3.50), sandwiches (from £4.50), asparagus with parmesan cheese or goats cheese salad (£4.50), morecambe bay potted shrimps (£5.50), roast fennel, red onion and mozzarella tart (£8.50), cumberland sausage (£8.95), lamb in mint and honey (£11.95), and beef fillet with mushrooms in a red wine gravy (£12.50). It is essential to book a table in advance. There is also a separate back restaurant, by the residents' lounge. Outside, a big sycamore shelters a few picnicsets. They may not always be open, so you must phone before setting out. More reports please. *(Recommended by Tina and David Woods-Taylor, Dr and Mrs D Ash, John Knighton, John and Enid Morris, Christine and Phil Young, Glenys and John Roberts, Guy Vowles, Malcolm and Jane Levitt)*

Free house ~ Licensees Sarah and Mike Hodgson ~ Real ale ~ Bar food ~ Restaurant ~ (017687) 77239 ~ Children in bar during the day but only in restaurant at night ~ Open 12.30-10.30 ~ Bedrooms: £30/£60(£80B)

TALKIN   NY5557   Map 10
Blacksmiths Arms ♀ 🛏
Village signposted from B6413 S of Brampton; CA8 1LE

This former blacksmiths is by the green in an attractive village. It's a welcoming, well run place and readers enjoy staying here. The neatly kept, warm lounge is on the right with a log fire, upholstered banquettes, tables and chairs, and country prints and other pictures on the walls; the restaurant to the left is pretty, there's a long lounge opposite the bar with smaller round tables, and a well lit garden room. All areas are no smoking except the bar. Well kept Jennings Cumberland, Yates Bitter, and a guest beer on handpump, over 20 wines by the glass, and 40 malt whiskies; piped music. As well as lunchtime sandwiches, toasties and filled baked potatoes, the enjoyable food might include home-made soup (£2.70), chicken and pistachio paté (£3.95), fresh haddock in home-made beer batter (£6.55), steak and kidney pie or vegetable curry (£6.85), sweet and sour chicken (£7.95), beef stroganoff (£11.95), steaks (from £13.45), daily specials, and Sunday roast (£6.25). There are a couple of picnic-sets outside the front door with more in the back garden. Good surrounding walks. *(Recommended by Tony and Maggie Harwood, Ken Richards, JWAC, Steve Whalley, Pat and Stewart Gordon, Mark and Lynette Davies)*

Free house ~ Licensees Donald and Anne Jackson ~ Real ale ~ Bar food (12-2, 6-9) ~ Restaurant ~ (016977) 3452 ~ Children welcome ~ Open 12-3, 6-midnight ~ Bedrooms: £35B/£50B

TROUTBECK   NY4103   Map 9
Queens Head ★ ⑪ ♀ 🍺 🛏
A592 N of Windermere; LA23 1PW

Very well run and extremely popular, this rather civilised old inn remains a smashing place for either a drink, a good meal or somewhere to spend a few days. The big rambling original U-shaped bar (partly no smoking) has beams and flagstones, a very nice mix of old cushioned settles and mate's chairs around some sizeable tables (especially the one to the left of the door), and a log fire in the raised stone fireplace with horse harness and so forth on either side of it; there's another log fire, some trumpets, cornets and saxophones on one wall with country pictures on others, stuffed pheasants in a big glass case, and a stag's head with a tie around his neck. A massive Elizabethan four-poster bed is the basis of the finely carved counter where they serve around five or six real ales well kept on handpump such as Black Sheep Bitter, Boddingtons Bitter, Coniston Bluebird, Hawkshead Red, Jennings Bitter and Tirril Academy Ale. Interesting and enjoyable food at lunchtime includes home-made soup (£3.95), rustic rolls (£4.75), cheeses with their own cheese biscuits and malt loaf, grapes and home-made chutney (£5.95), fresh sardines with garlic and thyme and mixed bean salad (£7.25), risotto of mushrooms, peas and parmesan with a free-range egg (£8.25), corn-fed chicken breast with a leek and prune broth (£8.75), and home-made cumberland sausage with their own black pudding, roast apples and wholegrain mustard sauce (£8.95); evening dishes such as terrine of lamb shank with toasted brioche and apricot chutney or confit of duck leg with chilli jam (£6.25), cider battered goats cheese on a roast squash and pumpkin seed salad (£6.95), sautéed herbed gnocchi, red onion, fennel and smoked garlic cream (£12.95), local beef on horseradish mash with crispy bacon, onion rings and a mustard and local ale cream (£13.95), and fillet of bass with rösti potato and a sautée of fine beans and air-dried ham with gremolata dressing (£15.95), with puddings like soft centred hot chocolate pudding with boozy mandarins and a crème chantilly or passion fruit brûlée with pistachio biscotti (£4.95). The newer dining rooms (where you can also drop in for just a drink) are similarly decorated to the main bar, with oak beams and stone walls, settles along big tables, and an open fire. Piped music. Seats outside have a fine view over the Trout valley to Applethwaite moors. *(Recommended by Liz and Tony Colman, Revd D Glover, Helen Clarke, Pierre Richterich, Chris Willers, Noel Grundy, Paul Boot, Dr and Mrs R G J Telfer, Michael Doswell, Adrian Johnson, Margaret and Jeff Graham, Ann and Tony Bennett-Hughes, Dennis Jones, David Field, Mike Pugh, John and Enid Morris, Barry and Patricia Wooding, Mrs S E Griffiths, Mr and Mrs Hyde-Moxon, Patrick and Phillipa Vickery, Douglas Keith, Fred and Lorraine Gill, Bruce and Sharon Eden, Linda and Rob Hilsenroth)*

Free house ~ Licensees Mark Stewardson and Joanne Sherratt ~ Real ale ~ Bar food ~ Restaurant ~ (015394) 32174 ~ Children welcome ~ Dogs allowed in bar ~ Open 11-11; 12-10.30 Sun; closed 25 Dec ~ Bedrooms: /£105B

ULVERSTON SD2978 Map 7

Bay Horse 🍲 ♀ 🛏

Canal Foot signposted off A590 and then you wend your way past the huge Glaxo factory; LA12 9EL

Once a staging post for coaches crossing the sands of Morecambe Bay to Lancaster, this is a smart and civilised hotel on the water's edge of the Leven Estuary; the views of both the lancashire and cumbrian fells are lovely. It's at its most informal at lunchtime, and the bar, notable for its huge stone horse's head, has a relaxed atmosphere despite its smart furnishings: attractive wooden armchairs, some pale green plush built-in wall banquettes, glossy hardwood traditional tables, blue plates on a delft shelf, and black beams and props with lots of horsebrasses. Magazines are dotted about, there's an open fire in the handsomely marbled green granite fireplace, and decently reproduced piped music; board games. Imaginative lunchtime bar food might include home-made soup (£3.75), sandwiches (from £3.95), chicken liver pâté with cranberry and ginger purée (£6.50), hot filled ciabattas, baguettes or filled baked potatoes (£6.75), deep-fried chilli prawns on a sweet and sour sauce (£7.95), red and green peppers stuffed with a mushroom and onion pâté, served on a tomato provençale with a garlic and chive cream, breadcrumb and pine nut topping (£10.50), fresh crab and salmon fishcakes in a white wine and fresh herb cream sauce or medallions of pork, leek and lancashire cheese on a rich madeira sauce (£10.95), and aberdeen angus steak and kidney puff pastry pie (£12.75). The breakfasts are good. Well kept Coach House Rabbits Punch, Marstons Double Drop and Moorhouses Pendle Witches Brew on handpump, and a dozen wines by the glass (champagne, too) from a carefully chosen and interesting wine list. The no smoking conservatory restaurant has fine views over Morecambe Bay (as do the bedrooms) and there are some seats out on the terrace. *(Recommended by Andrew Beardsley, Alison Lawrence, Tina and David Woods-Taylor, W K Wood, Carol and Dono Leaman, Mr and Mrs P Eastwood, Mary Kirman and Tim Jefferson, Jo Lilley, Simon Calvert, Michael Doswell, Neil Ingoe, M J Winterton)*

Free house ~ Licensee Robert Lyons ~ Real ale ~ Bar food (12-2(4 weekends); only restaurant food at night) ~ Restaurant ~ (01229) 583972 ~ Children in eating area of bar but must be over 10 in restaurant at night ~ Dogs allowed in bar and bedrooms ~ Open 11-11; 12-10.30 Sun ~ Bedrooms: £80B/£95B

Farmers Arms ⑪ ♀ ◖
Market Place; LA12 7BA

Once you step inside this straightforward looking town pub, it's quite a surprise as it has been appealingly modernised and extended. The original fireplace and timbers blend in well with the more contemporary furnishings in the front bar – mostly wicker chairs on one side, comfortable sofas on the other; the overall effect is rather unusual, but somehow it still feels like a proper village pub. A table by the fire has newspapers, glossy magazines and local information, and a second smaller bar counter leads into a big raftered eating area, part of which is no smoking; piped music. Up to six swiftly changing well kept real ales on handpump from breweries such as Coniston, Hawkshead, Moorhouses, Theakstons and Yates, and around a dozen wines by the glass. Good food includes lunchtime hot and cold sandwiches (from £4.75), plus soup (£3.75), chicken caesar salad with parmesan and croûtons (£4.25), greek mezze or home-made burger with bacon, pineapple and salsa (£7.95), grilled salmon topped with whole green beans stir-fried in chilli marmalade (£8.95), stir-fried chicken strips with cajun spices, red onions and mushrooms or pasta with leeks, mushrooms, wine and cream (£8.95), and steaks (from £14.95). In front are a very attractive terrace with plenty of good wooden tables looking on to the market cross, big heaters, and lots of colourful plants in tubs and hanging baskets. If something's happening in town, the pub is usually a part of it, and they can be busy on Thursday market day. More reports please. *(Recommended by David Carr, Jo Lilley, Simon Calvert, Michael Doswell)*

Free house ~ Licensee Roger Chattaway ~ Real ale ~ Bar food (10-3, 6-8.30) ~ Restaurant ~ (01229) 584469 ~ Children allowed but with restrictions ~ Open 10-midnight

YANWATH NY5128 Map 9
Gate Inn ⑪ ♀
2¼ miles from M6 junction 40; A66 towards Brough, then right on A6, right on B5320, then follow village signpost; CA10 2LF

Cumbria Dining Pub of the Year

The atmosphere in this bustling and neatly kept old place is relaxed and pubby, and you can be sure of a warm welcome from the helpful and cheerful staff. It's totally no smoking with the emphasis very much on the good, imaginative food – but they do keep Dent Aviator, Hesket Newmarket Doris's 90th Birthday Ale and Tirril Bewshers on handpump, a dozen wines by the glass, scrumpy cider and organic soft drinks. Using local suppliers and producers, the menu at lunchtime might include soup (£4.25), smoked haddock and fresh mussel skink (£7.95), italian aubergine and sweet potato quesadilla (£7.95 or £14.95), cumbrian sausage, black pudding and mash (£8.50), a platter of bread and chutney with local cheeses and smoked meats (£8.95 or £15.96), pure bred cumbrian galloway beefburger with bacon, local brie and a poached egg (£9.95), and fish of the day in beer batter (£13.95); evening choices such as chicken liver parfait with cumberland sauce (£5.95), king scallops with chilli, lime and baby fennel (£8.95), vegetable and lentil suet pudding or wild rabbit in cider and cream with pear chutney (£13.95), fillet of bass with wilted greens, salsify chips, oyster fritter and saffron cream (£14.95), and roast goosnargh corn-fed duck with parsnip fritters, sweet potato purée and blood orange jus (£15.95). Plenty of fresh fish and seafood on the specials board, and puddings like a brûlée of the day or chocolate pot with tuiles and fresh berries (from £5.95). The two carefully refurbished restaurant areas have oak floors, panelled oak walls and heavy beams, and the cosy bar has country pine and dark wood furniture, lots of brasses on the beams, church candles on all the tables, and a good log fire in the attractive stone inglenook; piped music. There are seats on the terrace and in the garden. *(Recommended by Helen Clarke, Peter Mueller, Richard J Holloway, David and Katharine Cooke, Kerry Law, Simon Smith, J S Burn, Christine and Neil Townend, Hugh and Susan Ellison, Sally and Mark Bramall, Maurice and Gill McMahon, Jed Scott)*

Free house ~ Licensee Matt Edwards ~ Real ale ~ Bar food (12-2.30, 6-9) ~ Restaurant ~ (01768) 862386 ~ Children welcome ~ Dogs allowed in bar ~ Open 12-11

LUCKY DIP

Besides the fully inspected pubs, you might like to try these Lucky Dips recommended to us and described by readers (if you do, please send us reports: www.goodguides.co.uk).

AMBLESIDE [NY4008]

☆ *Kirkstone Pass Inn* LA22 9LQ [A592 N of Troutbeck]: Lakeland's highest pub, in grand scenery, hiker-friendly décor of flagstones, stripped stone and simple furnishings with lots of old photographs and bric-a-brac, two log fires, friendly service, cheap hearty food all day from 9.30, well kept Jennings and occasional guest beers, good coffee, hot chocolate, mulled wine, daily papers, games and books; piped music, pool room; dogs welcome, tables outside, three bedrooms, open all day *(David and Sue Smith, John and Hiro Charles, LYM, Rob and Catherine Dunster)*

☆ *Wateredge* LA22 0EP [Borrans Rd]: Lovely spot with sizeable garden running down to the edge of Windermere, lots of tables and some bench swings out here, same splendid view through big windows in much-modernised bar with Coniston Bluebird, Greene King Old Speckled Hen and Marstons Pedigree, several wines by the glass, quickly served food, cosy beamed area down steps with fireside sofa; piped music; children welcome in eating areas, open all day, comfortable bedrooms *(Chris and Amy Johnson, Dr and Mrs R G J Telfer, LYM)*

ARNSIDE [SD4578]

Albion LA5 0HA [Promenade]: Neatly kept extended pub with Thwaites Bitter and Lancaster Bomber, wide choice of enjoyable food from hot and cold sandwiches up, quick friendly service, great views over estuary to Lakeland mountains from bar and terrace tables *(John Tavernor)*

BAMPTON [NY5118]

☆ *Mardale* CA10 2RQ: Smart and neatly kept small village inn, entirely no smoking, with local real ales such as Hawkshead and Yates, lots of whiskies, good wines and coffee, small choice of enjoyable evening food inc splendid hearty puddings, informal friendly atmosphere, helpful young licensees, log fire and oak beams, dominoes, other games, wooden puzzles and things to read left out, shelves of interesting knick-knacks; unobjectionable piped music; children welcome, three comfortable well equipped bedrooms, hearty breakfast, lovely countryside, cl wkdy lunchtimes *(BB, Nigel Scott, Jed Scott)*

BARROW-IN-FURNESS [SD2270]

Crofters LA13 0RE [Holbeck Park Ave]: Ex-farmhouse pub, reopened after refurbishment with soft leather seating in up-to-date bar, games area with pool and darts, popular dining area with emphasis on generous traditional food inc good Sun lunch, good wines by the glass, helpful staff, hands-on landlady; no dogs; disabled access, children welcome *(anon)*

BASSENTHWAITE [NY2332]

Sun CA12 4QP [off A591 N of Keswick]: Opened-up rambling bar with charming new Scottish landlord, lively atmosphere, wide range of quickly served up-to-date food from sandwiches up, Jennings ales, good wines by the glass, two big log fires, low 17th-c beams, interesting local photographs; provision for children, tables in pretty front yard with lovely fell views *(Helen Clarke, LYM, Paul Jeffery)*

BECKERMET [NY0206]

Royal Oak CA21 2XB: Well presented fresh food, good service, pleasant ambiance *(Dodie and Cliff Rutherford)*

BLENCOGO [NY1948]

☆ *New Inn* CA7 0BZ [signed off B5302 Wigton—Silloth]: Very good food, with interesting choice, good helpings and reasonable prices, in bright and simply modernised country pub, log fire, real ale, decent wines and whiskies, a few big Cumbrian landscapes, pleasant service; well worth booking; cl Mon *(Helen Clarke, BB, Matthew and Pippa Oakeshott)*

BOOT [NY1701]

Boot Inn CA19 1TG [aka Burnmoor; signed just off the Wrynose/Hardknott Pass rd]: New licensees for comfortably modernised beamed pub with ever-burning fire, Black Sheep, Jennings Bitter and Cumberland and a guest beer, decent wines and malt whiskies, good mulled wine, reasonably priced home-made lunchtime bar food from sandwiches and baked potatoes up, no smoking restaurant and dining conservatory; games room with pool and TV; children and dogs welcome, seats out on sheltered front lawn with play area, good walks, lovely surroundings, open all day *(LYM, Jo Lilley, Simon Calvert, Mark and Debra Davies, Christine and Phil Young)*

☆ *Brook House* CA19 1TG: Converted small Victorian hotel with friendly family service, wide choice of good generous home-made food inc some interesting dishes (breakfast for nearby campers too), log fires, four real ales such as Black Sheep, Coniston, Theakstons and Yates, decent wines, small no smoking plushly modernised bar, comfortable hunting-theme lounge, peaceful separate restaurant, good views; handy for Ravenglass rly and great walks, eight good bedrooms with own bathrooms – and good drying room *(Jenny and Brian Seller, J S Burn, Jo Lilley, Simon Calvert, Robert Ager, Mark and Debra Davies)*

BOTHEL [NY1839]

Greyhound CA7 2HS: Jennings Cumberland, good choice of wines, enjoyable food inc real chips and proper shortcrust pies *(Helen Clarke)*

BOWLAND BRIDGE [SD4189]

☆ *Hare & Hounds* LA11 6NN [signed from A5074]: Good enterprising food in neatly attractive country dining pub with good friendly service, real ales inc Black Sheep, Boddingtons and a beer brewed for the pub, roaring log fire in small bar, eating areas off with polished flagstones or red carpet, some stripped stone; owners thinking of retiring, though; children welcome, picnic-sets in spacious side garden, bedrooms, quiet hamlet in lovely scenery *(John and Verna Aspinall, Michael Doswell, LYM, Mrs P Gostling)*

BOWNESS-ON-WINDERMERE [SD4096]

☆ *Hole in t' Wall* LA23 3DH [Lowside]: Enjoyable good value pub food from sandwiches to steak in ancient beamed pub, stripped stone and flagstones, lots of country bric-a-brac and old pictures, lively bustle, splendid log fire under vast slate mantelpiece, upper room with attractive plasterwork (and dominoes and juke box), well kept Robinsons ales, may be home-made lemonade or good winter mulled wine; very busy in tourist season; no dogs or prams, sheltered picnic-sets in tiny flagstoned front courtyard *(LYM, Robert Wivell, Ron Gentry)*

BRAITHWAITE [NY2323]

☆ *Coledale Hotel* CA12 5TN [signed off A66 W of Keswick, pub then signed left off B5292]: Bustling inn below Whinlatter Pass, welcoming to walkers, with coal fire, little 19th-c Lakeland engravings, plush banquettes and studded tables, real ales such as Jennings and Yates, friendly staff, hearty promptly served food, no smoking dining room; darts, dominoes, piped music; fine Skiddaw views, garden with slate terrace and sheltered lawn, pretty bedrooms, open all day *(A J Bowen, LYM, Geoff and Angela Jaques, John and Angie Millar, David J Cooke)*

Royal Oak CA12 5SY: Friendly and pubby flagstoned bar with good choice of good value food (best to book evenings), prompt helpful service, Jennings; dogs welcome exc at mealtimes *(A J Bowen, Tony and Maggie Harwood, W M Lien)*

BRAMPTON [NY5261]

Howard Arms CA8 1NG [Front St]: Well kept Thwaites and enjoyable generous food from baguettes and ploughman's up, rustic décor; bedrooms *(Tony and Maggie Harwood)*

BRIGSTEER [SD4889]

☆ *Wheatsheaf* LA8 8AN: Quiet no smoking dining pub with good food inc interesting sandwiches, fresh fish, game and good value Sun lunch inc splendid fish hors-d'oeuvre, nice breads baked here, takeaways some nights, cheerful attentive staff, a local ale perhaps with a guest such as Greene King IPA, good choice of wines by the glass, attractive dining room; pretty village *(Michael Doswell, Malcolm Taylor, Clive Gibson, Jenny and Peter Lowater, Peter Abbott, Jim Abbott, Robert Ager, Maurice and Gill McMahon, Pat and Graham Williamson)*

BROUGHTON-IN-FURNESS [SD2087]

High Cross LA20 6ES [A595 towards Millom]: Low-beamed inn with hard-working new owners, up to five good ales from small and local breweries, lots of whiskies, good choice of imported vodkas, wholesome reasonably priced food, open fire, Lakeland pictures and soft lighting, separate estuary-view restaurant, some live music; disabled access (one small step), picnic-sets on front terrace and in garden, bedrooms overlooking Duddon fells

(G Coates, Dr B and Mrs P B Baker)

☆ *Manor Arms* LA20 6HY [The Square]: Outstanding choice of good changing well priced ales from local microbreweries and further afield in neat and comfortable open-plan pub on quiet sloping square, flagstones and nice bow window seats in no smoking front bar, coal fire in big stone fireplace, chiming clocks, good sandwiches, pizzas and bockwurst sausages, winter soup, pool table; children allowed, stairs down to lavatories (ladies' has baby-changing); well appointed good value bedrooms, big breakfast, open all day *(BB, Mr and Mrs Maurice Thompson, Ben and Helen Ingram)*

CALDBECK [NY3239]

☆ *Oddfellows Arms* CA7 8EA [B5299 SE of Wigton]: No-nonsense modernised split-level pub with fine old photographs and woodburner in comfortable front bar full of locals and visitors, big no smoking back dining room, generous competitively priced home cooking from lunchtime sandwiches up inc good proper chips, Jennings Bitter and Cumberland and Youngers, good choice of wines by the glass, affable landlord, quick pleasant service; piped music, games area with darts, pool and TV; children welcome, open all day Fri-Sun and summer, low-priced bedrooms, nice village *(Mrs C E Godfrey, Helen Clarke)*

CARTMEL [SD3778]

☆ *Cavendish Arms* LA11 6QA [Cavendish St, off main sq]: Friendly local atmosphere in civilised well organised bar with roaring fire, promptly served enjoyable food from sandwiches up, real ales, good coffee, no smoking restaurant; children truly welcome, tables out in front and behind by stream, ten comfortable bedrooms, good walks, open all day *(R Davies, Michael Doswell, Mr and Mrs P Eastwood, LYM, Margaret Dickinson, Ann and Tony Bennett-Hughes)*

Royal Oak LA11 6QB [The Square]: Low beams and flagstones, cosy nooks, pleasant décor, generous good value food from baguettes up, good choice of real ales, decent wines, welcoming helpful staff, log fire; modern public bar with games, TV and piped music; nice big riverside garden, bedrooms *(BB, M J Winterton)*

CASTLE CARROCK [NY5455]

☆ *Weary Sportsman* CA8 9LU: Smart modern pub/brasserie with comfortable sofas and bucket chairs on bare boards of refreshingly light and airy bar, ambitious choice of good upmarket food, good lunchtime sandwiches too, a real ale such as Black Sheep or Greene King, interesting wines, welcoming service, good modern prints and wall of glassware and objets, smart conservatory dining room; good tables in back japanese garden, comfortable well equipped bedrooms *(A J Bowen, Michael Doswell, Dr K P Tucker, Nigel and Jean Eames)*

CONISTON [SD3097]

☆ *Black Bull* LA21 8DU [Yewdale Rd (A593)]: Good Coniston Bluebird, XB and Old Man brewed here, lots of Donald Campbell water-speed memorabilia, bustling flagstoned back area (dogs allowed), banquettes and open fire in partly no smoking carpeted lounge bar (no smoking restaurant area), quick cheerful service, simple good value food inc children's, good sandwiches and more enterprising specials, farm ciders, quite a few bottled beers and malt whiskies; children and dogs welcome, tables out in suntrap former coachyard, bedrooms, open all day *(John Foord, Nikki Wild, Maggie Chandler, Carl Van Baars, Dave Braisted, Len Beattie, LYM, Mike and Lynn Robinson, Mr and Mrs Maurice Thompson)*

☆ *Sun* LA21 8HQ: Friendly mix of locals and walkers in16th-c pub in terrific setting below dramatic fells, interesting Donald Campbell and other Lakeland photographs in old-fashioned back bar with beams, flagstones, good log fire in 19th-c range, cask seats and old settles, big no smoking conservatory restaurant off carpeted lounge (children allowed here), Coniston Bluebird, Hawkshead and three good guest beers, decent wines, darts, cribbage, dominoes; dogs in bar, tables on pleasant front terrace, big tree-sheltered garden, comfortable bedrooms, good hearty breakfast, open all day *(Jarrod and Wendy Hopkinson, Tina and David Woods-Taylor, Steve Kirby, Chris Evans, LYM, Len Beattie, Jo Lilley, Simon Calvert, Christine and Phil Young, Mrs Phoebe A Kemp, Mr and Mrs Maurice Thompson, Malcolm and Jane Levitt)*

COWGILL [SD7686]

☆ *Sportsmans* LA10 5RG [nr Dent Station, on Dent—Garsdale Head rd]: Cosy and beautifully placed Dentdale local with good nearby walks, friendly straight-talking landlord, substantial bargain home-made food using local organic supplies from sandwiches up, good vegetarian dishes, Black Sheep and Copper Dragon, decent wine, log fires, simple bar/lounge with darts in snug at one end and pool room at the other, no piped music; tidy bedrooms overlooking lovely river, camp site, cl wkdy lunchtimes out of season *(Robert Wivell, Mr and Mrs Maurice Thompson, T J Smith, Rona Murdoch, Ann and Tony Bennett-Hughes)*

CROOK [SD4695]

☆ *Sun* LA8 8LA [B5284 Kendal—Bowness]: Good atmosphere and good varied food (all day wknds – nice to have full menu choice on Sun) from unusual sandwiches to enterprising hot dishes, winter game and lovely puddings, prompt cheerful helpful service, Coniston Bluebird and Courage Directors, good value wines, roaring log fire, two bustling no smoking dining areas off low-beamed bar, fresh flowers *(Hugh Roberts, Michael Doswell, Margaret and Roy Randle, LYM, Tony and Penny Burton, Les and Barbara Owen, David and Jean Hall, Lee and Liz Potter, Sheila Stothard)*

DACRE [NY4526]

Horse & Farrier CA11 0HL [between A66 and A592 SW of Penrith]: 18th-c black-beamed village local with Jennings ales, straightforward home-made pub food from nice sandwiches up, cheery front room with lovely fire in big old-fashioned range, more modern dining extension down steps on the left; darts, dominoes, bridge and quiz nights; children welcome, integral post office, pretty village *(David and Katharine Cooke, BB, Geoff and Angela Jaques)*

DALTON-IN-FURNESS [SD2376]

☆ *Black Dog* LA15 8JP [Broughton Rd, well N of town]: Unpretentious local with fine range of interesting changing real ales, simple tiled and flagstoned bar with beer mats on beams, no smoking eating area and breakfast room, hearty good value food, traditional games; children and dogs welcome, side terrace tables, handy for South Lakes Wild Animal Park; bedrooms, open all day Sun and summer, may be cl winter wkdy lunchtimes *(Andrew Beardsley, Alison Lawrence, LYM, Geoffrey Tyack, Hugh Roberts)*

Brown Cow LA15 8LQ [Goose Green]: Picturesque old-world village local nr church, warmly welcoming long-serving licensees, five real ales such as Coniston Bluebird, Greene King Old Speckled Hen and Theakstons Best (samples may be offered), lots of whiskies, big helpings of good value home-made food all day inc some bargains, log fire, upstairs restaurant; pleasant good-sized terrace, bedrooms, open all day *(G Coates, Carol and Dono Leaman, M J Winterton)*

Red Lion LA15 8AE [Market St]: Low beams, huge fireplace, several distinct areas served by single bar with Coniston Bluebird, Jennings Snecklifter and a guest beer, tasty evening home-cooked food; good disabled access, picnic-sets out in front, bedrooms with own bathrooms *(G Coates)*

DENT [SD7086]

Sun LA10 5QL [Main St]: Popular old-fashioned local with four good Dent ales brewed nearby, good value usual food from sandwiches up, well worn in beamed traditional bar with coal fire and darts; children welcome, open all day in summer *(Dudley and Moira Cockroft, LYM, Margaret Dickinson, Mr and Mrs Maurice Thompson)*

DOCKRAY [NY3921]

Royal CA11 0JY [A5091, off A66 or A592 W of Penrith]: Bright open-plan bar, straightforward food served quite quickly, Black Sheep, Coniston and Jennings Fish King, two dining areas (one no smoking), walkers' part with stripped settles on flagstones, attractive restaurant, darts, cribbage and dominoes; piped music; picnic-sets in large peaceful garden, great setting, open all day, comfortable bedrooms *(J Hudson, LYM, Derek and Sylvia Stephenson, Maurice and Gill McMahon)*

ENNERDALE BRIDGE [NY0615]

☆ *Shepherds Arms* CA23 3AR [off A5086 E of Egremont]: Walkers' inn well placed by car-free dale, with footpath plans, weather-forecast blackboard and appropriate books, lots of pictures, log fire and woodburner, Coniston Bluebird, Jennings, Timothy Taylors Landlord and guest beers, good wine choice, panelled dining room and conservatory; may be piped music, main bar can be smoky; children and dogs welcome, bedrooms, open all day (may be winter afternoon break Mon-Thurs) *(Pat and Stewart Gordon, LYM, Evan and Marjorie Lisovskis, TOH, John and Enid Morris, Mark and Debra Davies, Paul and Gloria Howell, Tina and David Woods-Taylor, Sylvia and Tony Birbeck)*

ESKDALE GREEN [NY1200]
☆ *Bower House* CA19 1TD [½ mile W]: Civilised old-fashioned stone-built inn with friendly mix of holiday-makers, locals and businessmen, good log fire in main lounge bar extended around beamed and alcoved core, real ales such as Theakstons, good value pubby food, biggish no smoking restaurant; bar can be smoky, may be piped music; nicely tended sheltered garden by cricket field, charming spot with great walks, bedrooms, open all day *(Tina and David Woods-Taylor, LYM, TOH, Mark and Debra Davies)*

FAR SAWREY [SD3795]
☆ *Sawrey Hotel* LA22 0LQ: Comfortable, warm and welcoming stable bar with tables in wooden stalls, harness on rough white walls, even water troughs and mangers, big helpings of good value simple lunchtime bar food, Black Sheep, Jennings and Theakstons, good coffee, pleasant attentive staff, appealingly relaxed and old-fashioned second bar in main hotel, log fires in both, restaurant; seats on nice lawn, beautiful setting, walkers, children and dogs welcome, bedrooms comfortable and well equipped *(G Coates, LYM)*

FOXFIELD [SD2085]
☆ *Prince of Wales* LA20 6BX [opp stn]: Convivial bare-boards pub with half a dozen good ales inc bargain beers brewed in the former stables here and at their associated Tigertops brewery, bottled imports, farm cider and regular beer festivals, enthusiastic licensees, enjoyable home-made food inc lots of unusual pasties, hot coal fire, maps, customer snaps and beer awards, pub games inc bar billiards, daily papers and beer-related reading matter, back room with one huge table; children very welcome, games for them; steps up to door; cl Mon/Tues, opens 5 Weds/Thurs, open all day Fri-Sun, reasonably priced bedrooms with own bathrooms *(MLR, BB, Christopher Goddard, Mr and Mrs Maurice Thompson)*

GARRIGILL [NY7441]
☆ *George & Dragon* CA9 3DS [off B6277 S of Alston]: Distinctive little 17th-c inn in attractive quiet village, popular with walkers and mountain-bikers; Black Sheep and guests such as Hop Back Summer Lightning, Jennings Fishking and Tetleys, good wines, great log fire in flagstoned bar and attractive stone-and-panelling dining room; pleasant bedrooms, open all day Sat, has been cl winter wkdy

lunchtimes *(LYM, Mike and Lynn Robinson, Mr and Mrs Maurice Thompson)*

GOSFORTH [NY0703]
Lion & Lamb CA20 1AL [The Square]: Thriving local with half a dozen good changing ales at attractive price inc one brewed for them by Moorland, good value pubby food inc home-made proper pies, darts; tables outside, open all day *(Ben and Helen Ingram)*

GRASMERE [NY3406]
☆ *Travellers Rest* LA22 9RR [A591 just N]: Cheerful and popular, with settles, banquettes, upholstered armchairs and log fire, local watercolours, old photographs, suggested walks, bar food (all day in summer), Greene King and Jennings ales, children welcome in big dining area and games area; dogs in bar, open all day, comfortable quiet bedrooms, good breakfast *(Mr and Mrs John Taylor, Nikki Wild, LYM, Jack Clark, W W Burke, Mr and Mrs Maurice Thompson, Walter and Susan Rinaldi-Butcher)*

GREAT URSWICK [SD2674]
☆ *General Burgoyne* LA12 0SZ [Church Rd]: Flagstoned early 18th-c village pub overlooking small tarn, four small cosy rambling rooms with log fires, bustling cheerful country atmosphere, mugs, glasses and hop bines hanging from beams, friendly efficient service, good value generous standard food, Robinsons Hartleys XB and guest beers, board games; piped music *(Andrew Beardsley, Alison Lawrence, BB)*

GRIZEBECK [SD2385]
Greyhound LA17 7XJ: Warmly welcoming 17th-c local, beams and flagstones, good value imaginative food, four real ales, good service, woodburners, no smoking dining room; well behaved dogs welcome, tables in pleasant garden behind, good value smart bedrooms with big breakfast *(Dr B and Mrs P B Baker)*

HALE [SD5078]
Kings Arms LA7 7BH [A6 S of Beetham]: Traditional pub with new management making an impression, good generous pubby food at attractive prices, real ales, plenty of brass, china and hunting prints, two open fires, restaurant section *(Rev John Hibberd)*

HAVERTHWAITE [SD3284]
Anglers Arms LA12 8AJ [just off A590]: Busy and friendly split-level pub with good choice of fairly priced generous fresh food from sandwiches to steak, fine choice of real ales, helpful staff, overflow upstairs dining room, lower area with pool *(Ron Gentry, Dennis Jones)*

HEVERSHAM [SD4983]
☆ *Blue Bell* LA7 7FH [A6]: Beamed and partly panelled lounge bar, warm log fire, big bay-windowed no smoking area, enjoyable bar food (all day during hols), friendly service, low-priced Sam Smiths OB, no smoking restaurant, long public bar (games, TV, piped music); children and dogs welcome, comfortable roomy bedrooms, open all day *(Dr and Mrs T E Hothersall, Mr and Mrs C R Little, LYM, Roger and Maureen Kenning, JWAC, Sylvia and Tony Birbeck, Neil Ingoe)*

HIGH NEWTON [SD4082]
Crown LA11 6JH [just off A590 Lindale—Newby Bridge, towards Cartmel Fell]: Well run and attractive 18th-c former coaching inn, said to be haunted, with friendly young staff, changing ales inc Jennings and Yates, enjoyable food inc quickly served Sun lunch, spacious bars and dining area; children welcome, comfortable bedrooms with own bathrooms *(Mr and Mrs P Eastwood, Ron Gentry)*

KENDAL [SD5192]
Burgundys Wine Bar LA9 4DH [Lowther St]: Small attractive multi-level bar with (despite the name) interesting changing local ales such as Dent, Derwent, Hawkshead and Yates, enthusiastic landlord happy to talk about them, bottled imports, ciders and unusual wines too, lunchtime food from sandwiches to light hot dishes, welcoming service; cl Mon evening and Sun-Weds lunchtimes *(Mr and Mrs Maurice Thompson, Andy and Jill Kassube, Hugh Roberts, Christopher Goddard)*
Castle LA9 7AD [Castle St]: Well run bustling local by River Kent and nr castle, Jennings, Tetleys and guests such as Black Sheep and Dent, good value popular bar lunches from sandwiches up, TV and games in bar, dining tables in adjoining lounge area; roadside tables *(Mr and Mrs Maurice Thompson, MLR, Chris Evans)*
Duke of Cumberland LA9 6ES [Appleby Rd]: Traditional pub with good service, enjoyable food; tables outside, parking *(Paul Little)*
Miles Thompson LA9 4JH [Allhallows Lane]: Well appointed Wetherspoons, entirely no smoking now, in interesting conversion of substantial Victorian public baths with towering chimney, plain wood and chrome furniture, high-raftered stripped-stone upper room, ten reasonably priced real ales and speciality bottled beers, their usual food, family room; busy with young people Fri/Sat night *(Hugh Roberts, Michael Doswell)*
Riflemans Arms LA9 4LD [Greenside]: New landlord keen to promote real ales – Caledonian, Tetleys and two guest beers; welcoming staff *(Hugh Roberts)*
Vats Bar LA9 4HE [Brewery Arts Centre, Highgate]: Unusual light and airy bar in good arts centre, seating in huge vats around tables, good changing real ale range, enjoyable food inc good pizzas made to order here and in adjoining restaurant, relaxed atmosphere, friendly staff; terrace tables overlooking garden *(Chris Evans)*

KESWICK [NY2623]
Bank Tavern CA12 5DS [Main St]: Low-beamed L-shaped carpeted bar, spotless and well run, with Jennings ales, simple pub food (very popular for this at lunchtime), lots of nooks and crannies, log-effect gas fire, no smoking area and children's room; bedrooms, open all day *(Fred and Lorraine Gill, Tony and Maggie Harwood, Steve and Liz Tilley)*
☆ *George* CA12 5AZ [St Johns St]: Handsome old place with attractive traditional black-panelled side room, open-plan main bar, old-

fashioned settles and modern banquettes under Elizabethan beams, daily papers, Jennings Bitter, Cocker Hoop, Cumberland, and Sneck Lifter, big log fire, no smoking restaurant; piped music, fruit machine; children welcome in eating areas, dogs in bar, bedrooms with own bathrooms, open all day *(LYM, P Dawn, Mike and Lynn Robinson, David Carr, B Shelley, Robert Ager, Mr and Mrs John Taylor, Paul and Gloria Howell)*
Keswick Lodge CA12 5HZ [Main St]: Hotel lounge bar with Thwaites real ales, wide choice of reasonably priced bar food all day, pleasant service; 20 bedrooms with own bathrooms *(Mr and Mrs Maurice Thompson)*
Oddfellows CA12 5BL [Main St]: Long busy open-plan bar with masses of horse-racing memorabilia, friendly staff, four Jennings ales, plentiful food all day, upstairs dining room; piped music, live nightly; huge beer garden, open all day *(P Dawn, Tony and Maggie Harwood, Mr and Mrs John Taylor)*
☆ *Swinside Inn* CA12 5UE [Newlands Valley, just SW]: Brilliant peaceful valley setting; new licensees still settling in as we went to press, long bright public bar, traditionally furnished, with Jennings Cumberland, Theakstons Best and a guest beer, games area beyond central log fire (two more elsewhere), two no smoking dining rooms; piped music; children and dogs welcome, open all day, bedrooms, tables in garden and on upper and lower terraces giving fine views across to the high crags and fells around Grisedale Pike *(LYM, David and Katharine Cooke, Mark Lubienski)*

KIRKBY LONSDALE [SD6178]
Sun LA6 2AU [Market St (B6254)]: Low-beamed partly stripped-stone bar, cosy pews, two good log fires, real ales such as Black Sheep and Timothy Taylors Landlord, lots of malt whiskies, cheerful helpful staff, attractive no smoking back dining room; quiet piped music; bedrooms *(LYM, John and Yvonne Davies, Jo Lilley, Simon Calvert)*

KIRKOSWALD [NY5541]
Crown CA10 1DQ: Friendly 16th-c beamed village local with new tenants doing wider choice of fresh generous food using local suppliers (same menu in bar and small no smoking restaurant), Caledonian Deuchars IPA and Theakstons Best, games area *(Kevin Tea, Michael Doswell)*

LANGWATHBY [NY5633]
Shepherds CA10 1LW [A686 Penrith—Alston]: Cheerful village pub with good quickly served reasonably priced food, friendly efficient service, real ales, decent wine choice, comfortable banquettes, bar down steps from lounge, games room; tables and chairs outside, attractive spot on huge green of Pennines village, play area *(Sarah and Peter Gooderham)*

LEECE [SD2469]
Copper Dog LA12 0QP: Three changing real ales, fresh food (worth the wait if it's busy) in bar and pleasant restaurant with country views towards Coniston Fells; children welcome *(Andrew Beardsley, Alison Lawrence)*

LINDALE [SD4180]

☆ *Royal Oak* LA11 6LX: New licensee doing surprisingly good unusual food – serious cooking at its best; pleasant atmosphere *(John Lane, Peter Burton)*

LORTON [NY1526]

☆ *Wheat Sheaf* CA13 9UW [B5289 Buttermere—Cockermouth]: Smartly furnished no smoking bar, good atmosphere with locals and visitors, four Jennings ales, good generous food (not Mon–Weds lunchtimes) from sandwiches up inc fresh local produce, good value wines, separate restaurant, pool, no piped music; tables outside *(BB, Sylvia and Tony Birbeck)*

LOWTHER [NY5423]

Lowther Castle Inn CA10 2HX: Attractively refurbished, with good value generous food, stately upstairs evening Courthouse dining room *(Helen Boyes)*

LUPTON [SO5581]

Plough LA6 1PJ [A65, nr M6 junction 36]: Impressive oak beams and stonework, Black Sheep, good home-made food, attractive conservatory; disabled access, garden tables, beautiful spot *(Margaret Dickinson)*

MELMERBY [NY6137]

Shepherds CA10 1HF [A686 Penrith—Alston]: Country pub with comfortable heavy-beamed no smoking room off flagstoned bar, spacious end room with woodburner, generous food, Black Sheep, Jennings Cumberland and a guest beer, quite a few malt whiskies, games area; children welcome *(LYM, John Foord, Mr and Mrs Maurice Thompson)*

MIDDLETON [SD6286]

☆ *Swan* LA6 2NB [A683 Kirkby Lonsdale—Sedbergh]: Quaint two-roomed beamed pub built as a 16th-c farm, clean and friendly, with lots of individuality, good real ales such as Harviestoun Bitter & Twisted, Timothy Taylors Landlord and Theakstons Best, fine log fire in lovely fireplace, decent sandwiches, panini and hot dishes, great fell views *(LYM, Michael Doswell, Margaret Dickinson)*

NETHER WASDALE [NY1204]

☆ *Screes* CA20 1ET: Interesting and welcoming locals' bar and steps up to long plush lounge, stunning views of mountains and along Wasdale, particularly well kept Black Sheep, Coniston, Derwent and Yates Best, friendly licensees and staff, good enterprising home-made food inc lunchtime sandwiches, decent piped music; picnic-sets out on large front green, five bedrooms, open all day *(David J Cooke, David Field, Dr and Mrs S G Barber, Mr and Mrs Maurice Thompson, David and Katharine Cooke)*

OULTON [NY2451]

Bird in Hand CA7 0NR [N of Wigton]: Unpretentious and homely local, with enjoyable simple home cooking (especially the chips), Jennings ales, friendly service *(Helen Clarke)*

OUTGATE [SD3599]

☆ *Outgate Inn* LA22 0NQ [B5286 Hawkshead—Ambleside]: Attractively placed, neatly kept and very hospitable country pub with three pleasantly modernised rooms, Robinsons Best,

Frederics and Hartleys XB, friendly licensees and helpful staff, popular food inc sandwiches; trad jazz Fri (very busy then), open all day wknds, comfortable bedrooms, good breakfast, nice walks *(Maggie Chandler, Carl Van Baars, BB)*

OXENHOLME [SD5390]

☆ *Station Inn* LA9 7RF [½ mile up hill, B6254 towards Old Hutton]: Reliable generous home-made food inc hearty sandwiches and winter game as well as the standards in spruce and roomy dining pub, thoughtful children's dishes, good friendly service, well kept ales such as Black Sheep, Flowers Original and Tirril, nice wine list, log fire; children welcome, large garden with extensive play area, bedrooms, good walks *(Michael Doswell, Clive Gibson, Jim Abbott)*

PENRITH [NY5130]

Lowther Arms CA11 7XD [Queen St]: Handsome 17th-c local, friendly and comfortable, with reliable reasonably priced home cooking, real ales such as Courage Directors, Fullers London Pride and Theakstons, good value house wine, prompt friendly service, three or four linked rooms with log fire *(John and Hiro Charles, Guy Vowles)*

Stoneybeck CA11 8RP: Big comfortable and friendly pub with generous food and Youngers Scotch *(Mr and Mrs Colin Roberts)*

PENRUDDOCK [NY4227]

☆ *Herdwick* CA11 0QU [off A66 Penrith—Keswick]: Attractively cottagey and sympathetically renovated 18th-c inn, Jennings and summer guest beers from unusual curved bar, decent wines, bar food from lunchtime sandwiches, baguettes and baked potatoes to more elaborate evening dishes and popular all-day Sun carvery, friendly efficient service, good open fire, stripped stone and white paintwork, nice no smoking dining room with upper gallery, games room with pool and darts; children in eating areas, five good value bedrooms *(Mrs C E Godfrey, Ken Marshall, David Gunn, Geoff and Angela Jaques, LYM, Andy and Jill Kassube, Mike and Sue Loseby, D Morriss, Anthony Waters, Dodie and Cliff Rutherford)*

RAVENSTONEDALE [SD7401]

☆ *Fat Lamb* CA17 4LL [Crossbank; A683 Sedbergh—Kirkby Stephen]: Attractively isolated, with pews in cheerful relaxing bar, coal fire in traditional black inglenook range, good local photographs and bird plates, friendly helpful staff, wide choice of good proper food from filled baguettes to enjoyable restaurant meals, Tetleys, decent wines; facilities for disabled, children welcome, tables out by nature-reserve pastures, good walks, bedrooms *(John and Yvonne Davies, M and GR, BB, Jack Clark, Margaret Dickinson, Helen and Brian Edgeley)*

RYDAL [NY3606]

Glen Rothay Hotel LA22 9LR: Attractive small 17th-c hotel with enjoyable pubby lunchtime food from baguettes up in popular and well furnished back bar, fireside armchairs in beamed lounge bar, real ales, no smoking restaurant; tables in pretty garden, boats for residents on nearby Rydal Water, comfortable bedrooms *(LYM, Alan and Paula McCully)*

SANDSIDE [SD4781]

☆ *Ship* LA7 7HW [B5282]: Roomy modernised beamed pub with glorious view over estuary to mountains beyond, relaxed atmosphere, good value generous standard food from baguettes up, Marstons Pedigree and Theakstons, decent reasonably priced wines; subdued piped music; children allowed, barbecues and picnic-sets out on grass by good play area, bedrooms *(LYM, Ray and Winifred Halliday)*

SATTERTHWAITE [SD3392]

☆ *Eagles Head* LA12 8LN: Unpretentious small beamed pub in pretty village on edge of Grizedale Forest (beautiful scenery), particularly welcoming and obliging landlord, good sensibly priced pubby food (not Mon), wider evening choice, local real ales inc Barngates Tag Lag or Hawkshead and a beer brewed for the pub, big log fire, lots of local photographs and maps; children welcome, picnic-sets outside, comfortable bedrooms *(Mr and Mrs Hughes, Maggie Chandler, Carl Van Baars, Alan and Paula McCully, Tom Maddocks)*

SEDBERGH [SD6592]

☆ *Dalesman* LA10 5BN [Main St]: Linked rooms well used by visitors, stripped stone and beams, log fire, sporting prints, no smoking buttery area with good value generous traditional food (all day Sun) from sandwiches to aberdeen angus steaks, Tetleys and their own Dalesman, dominoes; piped music, jazz nights; children in eating areas, picnic-sets out in front, bedrooms, open all day *(Andy and Jill Kassube, Rob Bowran, John and Yvonne Davies, Michael Doswell, Jim Abbott, LYM, Derek Stafford)*

☆ *Red Lion* LA10 5BZ [Finkle St (A683)]: Cheerful family-run beamed local, down to earth and comfortable, with good value generous home-made food from baguettes to bargain Sun lunch using local meats, full Jennings range kept well, helpful and friendly staff, splendid coal fire, sports TV *(BB, Dr D J and Mrs S C Walker, John and Yvonne Davies)*

SHAP [NY5614]

☆ *Greyhound* CA10 3PW [A6, S end]: Unpretentious former coaching inn, good local food from sandwiches to slow-cooked local lamb and nice puddings in open-plan bar or restaurant (chef happy to share his recipes), hearty helpings, Jennings and up to half a dozen guest beers, good reasonably priced house wines, cheerful bustle and quick helpful service; unobtrusive piped classical music, resident collie, dogs welcome; comfortable bedrooms, bunkhouse, popular with coast-to-coast walkers *(Mr and Mrs Maurice Thompson, J S Burn, MLR, Alison Hoy, Evan and Marjorie Lisovskis, Andy and Jill Kassube)*

SILLOTH [NY1053]

Golf CA7 4AB [Criffel St]: Substantial well run hotel with portraits of young Queen Elizabeth II and Churchill and comfortable deco chairs in amazing time-warp bar, local Derwent Carlisle State ale, good choice of wines by the glass, decent food, restaurant, games and snooker rooms; 22 bedrooms, open all day *(Helen Clarke)*

TEBAY [NY6104]

Cross Keys CA10 3UY: Comfortable beamed former coaching inn, handy for M6 junction 38, with promptly served usual food, friendly chatty staff, Black Sheep and Tetleys, decent wine, coal fire, separate eating area, games room with darts and pool; picnic-sets in back garden, good value bedrooms *(Danny Savage)*

THRELKELD [NY3225]

Horse & Farrier CA12 4SQ: Comfortably extended and neatly kept 17th-c pub with Jennings and guest ales, good house wines, enjoyable restauranty food, cosy snug, fairly close-set tables in eating area, polite service; open all day, dogs allowed when restaurant is closed, tables out on green, good value bedrooms and breakfast *(Steve Godfrey, J A Hooker, Rob and Catherine Dunster, Tony and Maggie Harwood, Ann and Tony Bennett-Hughes)*

Salutation CA12 4SQ [old main rd, bypassed by A66 W of Penrith]: Low-beamed pub below Blencathra, friendly mix of locals and visitors (busy wknds), Jennings Cumberland, quite a few malt whiskies, pubby food from sandwiches and baguettes up, good coal or log fire, padded wall seats in three areas divided by standing timbers, back games room; piped music, TV; dogs welcome, spacious upper children's room, tables out on decking in pleasant outside area *(LYM, Tina and David Woods-Taylor, Ann and Tony Bennett-Hughes)*

TIRRIL [NY5026]

Queens Head CA10 2JF [B5320, not far from M6 junction 40]: Quite a few recent changes here, and we look forward to things settling down under the new licensees; low beams, black panelling, flagstones, bare boards, high-backed settles and four open fireplaces inc a roomy inglenook, good Tirril ales (formerly brewed here, now from Appleby), popular bar food and no smoking restaurant; piped music and pool in back bar; children welcome in eating areas, bedrooms, has been open all day Fri-Sun and summer *(Kerry Law, Simon Smith, Helen Clarke, LYM, Christine and Neil Townend)*

TODHILLS [NY3662]

Highland Laddie CA6 4HB [off A74 4 or 5 miles N of M6]: Small cheerful bar with amiable chatty landlord, attractively priced food inc some unusual combinations in bar and well laid out restaurant *(Phil and Jane Hodson)*

TROUTBECK [NY4103]

Mortal Man LA23 1PL [A592 N of Windermere; Upper Rd]: Pleasant partly panelled beamed hotel bar with friendly efficient staff, real ales such as Jennings, John Smiths and Theakstons Best, decent food, big log fire, comfortable mix of seats inc a cushioned settle, copper-topped tables, no smoking picture-window restaurant, darts, dominoes; piped music, TV room, Sun folk/blues night; children welcome, great views from sunny garden, lovely village, comfortable bedrooms, open all day *(Ewan and Moira McCall, Dr and Mrs R G J Telfer, LYM, Jack Clark)*

ULDALE [NY2436]
Snooty Fox CA7 1HA: Comfortable two-bar village inn, friendly helpful landlord, changing real ales inc one brewed for them in Hesket Newmarket, good value wines, wide choice of good generous food using local ingredients; good value bedrooms with own bathrooms *(Martin and Sue Day)*

WABERTHWAITE [SD1093]
Brown Cow LA19 5YJ [A595]: Recently refurbished, warm friendly atmosphere, enjoyable pubby food using local ingredients *(J and E Dakin)*

WALTON [NY5264]
Centurian CA8 2DH: Recently totally refurbished, with welcoming atmosphere, enjoyable lunchtime snacks and evening meals using good local produce, real ales, good service; large terrace with attractive country views *(Dr and Mrs R G J Telfer)*

WARWICK BRIDGE [NY4756]
George CA4 8RL: Well kept village local with attentive licensee, enjoyable straightforward home cooking; dogs welcome *(Mike and Lynn Robinson)*

WARWICK-ON-EDEN [NY4656]
Queens Arms CA4 8PA [junction 43; A69 towards Hexham, then village signposted]: Pleasantly unpretentious two-room bar with friendly landlord, enjoyable food from lunchtime baguettes, interesting open sandwiches and light dishes up, Thwaites Original and Lancaster Bomber, good log fires; children welcome, picnic-sets and swings in side garden *(Michael Doswell)*

WASDALE HEAD [NY1807]
Wasdale Head Inn CA20 1EX [NE of Wast Water]: Mountain hotel worth knowing for its stunning fellside setting and the interesting Great Gable beers it brews; roomy walkers' bar with side hot food counter (all day in summer, may be restricted winter), decent choice of wines and malt whiskies, striking mountain photographs, traditional games, old-fashioned residents' bar, lounge and restaurant; children welcome, dogs allowed in bar, open all day *(Helen Clarke, LYM, Ben and Helen Ingram, Mr and Mrs Maurice Thompson)*

WATERMILLOCK [NY4523]
Brackenrigg CA11 0LP [A592, Ullswater]: Opened-up 19th-c inn in lovely spot with spectacular Ullswater and mountain views, good service with friendly young summer staff, food from generous lunchtime filled rolls and sandwiches up, Jennings Cumberland and Tirril Old Faithful, good range of wines by the glass, pleasant partly panelled bar with log fire and darts, carpeted lounge and good-sized dining room; no dogs inside; comfortable bedrooms, self-catering *(Dr D J and Mrs S C Walker, Jane and Neil Kendrick, Geoff and Angela Jaques, Michael Doswell, BB, Tina and David Woods-Taylor)*

WELTON [NY3544]
Royal Oak CA5 7ES [B5299 S of Dalston]: Carefully extended and updated, with log fire in beamed and panelled bar, reasonably priced usual food, real ales, appealing and comfortable dining area, friendly family service; picnic-sets outside, four comfortable bedrooms, attractive village surroundings *(anon)*

WESTNEWTON [NY1344]
Swan CA7 3PQ [B5301 N of Aspatria]: Attractive 18th-c inn in small village, good restaurant food using local ingredients, small bar with Yates *(Mark Gradwell)*

WINDERMERE [NY3902]
Holbeck Ghyll Hotel LA23 1LU [Holbeck Ghyll, off A591 N]: Nicely placed hotel, well worth knowing for its particularly good fresh food, impeccable service, breathtaking views; bedrooms *(Helen Clarke, Anthony Rickards Collinson)*

'Children welcome' means the pub says it lets children inside without any special restriction. If it allows them in, but to restricted areas such as an eating area or family room, we specify this. Places with separate restaurants often let children use them, hotels usually let them into public areas such as lounges. Some pubs impose an evening time limit – let us know if you find this.

Derbyshire

This is a fine area for those who like good beer, with plenty of pubs notable for the quality of their real ales – particularly the three main entries in Derby, the Alexandra, the Brunswick (brewing its own bargain ales), and the Olde Dolphin. Others we'd recommend highly for their beer quality are the well run Old Poets Corner in Ashover (a new find for us this year), the Dead Poets at Holbrook, the unspoilt Barley Mow in Kirk Ireton, the John Thompson by the River Trent near Melbourne (another place brewing its own), the popular Monsal Head Hotel, the bustling Lathkil at Over Haddon (the friendly licensees have been there 25 years now), and the basic and simple Three Stags Heads at Wardlow. Derbyshire drinks prices tend to be comfortably below the national average, with some good small local brewers such as Whim and Leatherbritches. There is of course some stunning walking country in the county, and quite a few of the pubs doing well here are also perfectly set for walkers: the Quiet Woman at Earl Sterndale, the Scotsmans Pack in Hathersage, the Lantern Pike at Hayfield, the Cheshire Cheese at Hope (an appealing new entry, which hasn't featured in the main entries for quite a few years), the Barley Mow at Kirk Ireton, the Red Lion at Litton, the Monsal Head Hotel, and the Lathkil at Over Haddon. Food is hearty and warming, and much better value than many other counties in this book: another new entry, the Old Pump at Barlow, typifies this approach – food value that's hard to resist, in welcoming surroundings. Pubs doing particularly well for food include the very popular and distinctive Bear at Alderwasley, the no smoking Chequers at Froggatt Edge, and the well run Plough at Hathersage. For its imaginative dishes in charming surroundings, the unspoilt Bear at Alderwasley takes the title of Derbyshire Dining Pub of the Year. Current favourites in the Lucky Dip section at the end of the chapter include Smiths Tavern in Ashbourne, the Duke of York at Elton, Shady Oak at Fernilee, Crispin at Great Longstone, Miners Arms at Milltown (we have had to leave this nice pub out of the main entries this year purely because of a lack of recent readers' reports), Royal Oak at Ockbrook and Old Crown at Shardlow.

ALDERWASLEY   SK3153   Map 7
Bear ★ 🍴 ♀
Village signposted with Breanfield off B5035 E of Wirksworth at Malt Shovel; inn ½ mile SW of village, on Ambergate—Wirksworth high back road; DE56 2RD

Derbyshire Dining Pub of the Year

Charmingly unspoilt and extremely popular, this busy village pub has a good mix of both locals and visitors. The dark, low-beamed rooms have a cheerful miscellany of antique furniture including high-backed settles and locally made antique oak chairs with derbyshire motifs, and there are staffordshire china ornaments, old paintings and engravings, and a trio of grandfather clocks; the warm open fires in stone fireplaces are welcoming on a cold, dull day. One little room is filled right to its built-in wall seats by a single vast table. It's all very easy-going with dominoes players clattering about beside canaries trilling in a huge Edwardian-style white cage (elsewhere look out for the budgerigars and talkative cockatoos). There's a large choice of particularly good often imaginative food: sandwiches (from £3.75;

panini £5.95 and the super big hot roast beef crusty with onion rings and gravy
£5.95), soup (£3.95), smoked salmon fishcakes (£5.50), melted stilton and crispy
bacon en croûte with orange and strawberry chutney or crab claws in garlic butter
(£5.95), pork and black pudding sausages or vegetable stew with cheddar mash
(£8.95), slow-cooked lamb in red wine, rosemary and tomato sauce (£10.95),
chicken breast wrapped with bacon and stuffed with smoked cheese in a chasseur
sauce (£12.95), monkfish tails in a creamy thai curry sauce (£14.95), and puddings
such as chocolate torte, crème brûlée or bakewell pudding (£4.50); service is
friendly and helpful, and the restaurant is no smoking. You must book to be sure of
a table. Well kept Bass, Black Sheep, Greene King Old Speckled Hen, Marstons
Pedigree and Whim Hartington Bitter on handpump, and quite a few wines by the
glass; darts and board games. Well spaced picnic-sets out on the side grass with
peaceful country views. There's no obvious front door – you get in through the
plain back entrance by the car park. *(Recommended by Bernard Stradling,
Peter F Marshall, Deb and John Arthur, Jeff and Wendy Williams, Fred and Lorraine Gill,
Rob and Catherine Dunster, the Didler, Derek and Sylvia Stephenson, John and Karen
Wilkinson, Janet and Peter Race, Alan Bowker, Theocsbrian, Cathryn and Richard Hicks,
Brian and Jean Hepworth, Wendy Dye, Kevin Blake, Martha Hoyer Millar, Richard)*

Free house ~ Licensee Nicky Fletcher-Musgrave ~ Real ale ~ Bar food (12-9.30) ~
Restaurant ~ (01629) 822585 ~ Children welcome away from bar areas ~ Dogs welcome
~ Open 12-midnight ~ Bedrooms: £45S/£70S

ASHOVER   SK3462   Map 7

Old Poets Corner 🍺 🛏

Butts Road (B6036, off A632 Matlock—Chesterfield); S45 0EW

The dramatic rise in fortunes of this splendidly enjoyable village pub is entirely
down to the licensees who bought it two years ago. They've very quickly stamped
their personalities on the place, and their enthusiasm and enjoyment of their work
are both obvious and infectious; even fleeting visitors are made to feel like the most
valued of regulars. The most obvious draw is the range of perfectly kept real ales,
never fewer than six and often running to eight, typically including beers brewed
for the pub by Leatherbritches and Tower, Greene King Abbot, Sarah Hughes Dark
Ruby and Timothy Taylors Landlord, and rapidly changing brews like Abbeydale
Belfry, Archers Crystal Clear and Funfair Gallopers. Other carefully chosen drinks
include at least four farm ciders, a dozen bottled belgian beers and a good choice of
malt whiskies and fruit wines. They have regular beer festivals – and plans for their
own microbrewery. The landlord's other chief interest is very much in evidence
with the twice-weekly music nights (mostly acoustic, folk and blues), and posters
around the walls list the range of what's coming up, the busy calendar also taking
in weekly quiz nights and occasional poetry evenings and morris dancers. We
visited on a quieter winter Saturday night, when there was a steady murmur of laid-
back chat, and candles in bottles flickering on the tables. With a cosy, lived-in feel,
the bar has a mix of chairs and pews with well-worn cushions, a pile of board
games by a piano, a big mirror above the fireplace, plenty of blackboards, and lots
of hops around the counter; there's also a simple no smoking dining room. A small
room opening off the bar has another fireplace, a stack of newspapers and vintage
comics (our bedroom had a 1970 edition of the *Beano* in the wardrobe), and a
french door leading to a tiny balcony with a couple of tables. Good honest home-
made bar food includes soup (£2.95), hot baguettes (£4.25), a good choice of
vegetarian meals like five bean chilli (£5.45) or goats cheese and red pepper
cannelloni (£6.35), meat and potato pie (£5.65), pork and black pudding sausage,
braised liver and onions or devilled kidneys (£5.85), and a Sunday carvery. The
bedrooms are attractive, and at breakfast they do big helpings of pretty much
whatever you fancy. The village is pretty, with good walks nearby. *(Recommended by
the Didler, JJW, CMW)*

Free house ~ Licensees Kim and Jackie Beresford ~ Real ale ~ Bar food (12-2(3 Sat),
6.30-9; not Sun evening) ~ (01246) 590888 ~ Dogs allowed in bar ~ Live music Sun and
Tues evenings ~ Open 12-2.30, 5-11; 12-11 Sat; 12-10.30 Sun ~ Bedrooms: /£65S

BARLOW SK3474 Map 7
Old Pump
B6051 (Hackney Lane) towards Chesterfield; S18 7TD

Unexpected mid-March snowstorms had made the roads quite treacherous when we visited this villagey dining pub, but it hadn't put anyone off – the bar and dining room were packed with people eating, and there was a particularly vibrant, chatty atmosphere. There's a reddish hue to the long, narrow beamed bar, which has a clock sticking out from above the counter, fresh flowers, quite a few dark tables and stools, and a tiny alcove with a single table tucked beside the neatly curtained windows. It's book-ended by the dining room and two comfortably traditional little rooms, the first with big cushioned wall-benches, the other with salmon-painted walls and more substantial wooden tables for larger groups; tables are candlelit at night, and the entire pub is no smoking. Enjoying quite a reputation locally, the bar food at lunchtime might include home-made soup (£3.50), chicken liver pâté (£4.50), hot pannini or baguettes (from £4.50), steak and onion or homity pies (£6.95), and beer battered haddock (£7.50), with evening choices such as field mushrooms with stilton and sour cream or thai-spiced crab cake (£4.50), pork in sage and sherry in a filo basket or chicken wrapped in bacon with a chive and white wine sauce (£10.95), and breast of duck with black pudding and a port and cumberland sauce (£11.95); they recommend booking at weekends. Everards Tiger and Jennings Golden Host on handpump, served by friendly young staff. The pub has a few tables in front. Barlow is well known for its August well-dressing festivities, and there are good walks nearby. *(Recommended by David Carr, Keith and Chris O'Neill)*

Union Pub Company ~ Lease Mike Norie ~ Real ale ~ Bar food (12-2, 6-9) ~ Restaurant ~ (0114) 289 0296 ~ Children welcome if well behaved ~ Open 12-3, 6-11; 12-3, 7-10.30 Sun; closed 25 Dec, evening 26 Dec and 31 Dec

BEELEY SK2667 Map 7
Devonshire Arms
B6012, off A6 Matlock—Bakewell; DE4 2NR

Although a new licensee has taken over this no smoking place, little seems to have changed. It's a handsome old stone building in a pretty village and within strolling distance of Chatsworth and its huge park. Dickens is said to have been a regular visitor and Edward VII is rumoured to have often met his mistress Alice Keppel here. Big log fires cheerfully warm the cosy black-beamed rooms and antique settles and simpler wooden chairs stand on old flagstoned floors. The enjoyable food includes home-made soup (£3.80), sandwiches (£4.95), roasted field mushroom crumble (£5.35), red onion, tomato and rarebit tartlet (£5.85), chicken liver pâté or smoked haddock and spring onion fishcake (£6), ploughman's (from £6), chicken caesar or pear, stilton and walnut salads (£7; main course £11), daily changing sausage and mash (£7.95), steak in ale pie or slow-roasted vegetable risotto (£9), ham and eggs (£9.55), steaks (from £12.75), and puddings (from £4). Friday night is fish night from 7pm. Well kept Black Sheep Best and Special, Theakstons Old Peculier and a guest like Peak Ales Bakewell Best Bitter on handpump; house wines and about 30 malt whiskies. The excellent Chatsworth estate produce shop is to be found in nearby Pilsley. They plan to have bedrooms by the time this edition is published. *(Recommended by Andrew Beardsley, Alison Lawrence, Roger Yates, the Didler, Ian and Jane Irving, Keith and Chris O'Neill, Mike and Sue Loseby, B M Eldridge, Wendy Dye, Dr P C Rea, A and B D Craig, Mike and Mary Carter, Adrian White, Fred and Lorraine Gill)*

Free house ~ Licensee Richard Palmer ~ Real ale ~ Bar food (all day) ~ Restaurant ~ (01629) 733259 ~ Children welcome ~ Open 11-11; 12-9.30 Sun

---

People named as recommenders after the main entries have told us that the pub should be included. But they have not written the report – we have, after anonymous on-the-spot inspection.

BRASSINGTON SK2354 Map 7

Olde Gate ★

Village signposted off B5056 and B5035 NE of Ashbourne; DE4 4HJ

Just a five-minute drive from Carsington Water, this cosy ivy-clad inn is popular with walkers. The traditionally furnished public bar is prettily candlelit at night and has a fine ancient wall clock, rush-seated old chairs, antique settles, including one ancient black solid oak one, and roaring log fires. Gleaming copper pots sit on a 17th-c kitchen range, pewter mugs hang from a beam, and a side shelf boasts a collection of embossed Doulton stoneware flagons. To the left of a small hatch-served lobby, another cosy beamed room has stripped panelled settles, scrubbed-top tables, and a blazing fire under a huge mantelbeam. Bar food, from a regularly changing menu, is mostly home made (some with a new england influence: the landlady, Evie, is from Connecticut) and could include well presented lunchtime sandwiches, baguettes or soup (from £3.50), new england clam chowder (£5.95), ploughman's (£7.95), fidget pie, made of baked sliced potato, honey roast ham and cheese (£8.45), vegetarian chilli (£8.95), barbecued cajun spiced butterflied chicken (£10.95), rump steaks (from £12.95), and puddings such as boston brownie or treacle sponge (£4.50). The panelled room and bar area are no smoking. Well kept Marstons Pedigree and a guest such as Wychwood Wychcraft on handpump, and a good selection of malt whiskies; board games. Stone-mullioned windows look out across lots of tables in the pleasant garden to small silvery-walled pastures, and there are some benches in the small front yard. Maybe Sunday evening boules in summer and Friday evening bell-ringers. Although the date etched on the building reads 1874, it was originally built in 1616, from magnesian limestone and timbers salvaged from Armada wrecks, bought in exchange for locally mined lead. *(Recommended by Peter F Marshall, the Didler, Richard, Brian and Julie Shurmer, John Dwane, Tich Critchlow, John and Fiona McIlwain)*

Marstons (W & D) ~ Lease Paul Burlinson ~ Real ale ~ Bar food (12-1.45, 7-8.45; not Mon) ~ (01629) 540448 ~ Children over 10 only ~ Dogs welcome ~ Open 12-2.30(3 Sat and Sun), 7-11; closed Mon except bank hols

DERBY SK3435 Map 7

Alexandra ◨ £

Siddals Road, just up from station; DE1 2QE

A new licensee has taken over this lively Victorian town pub and has given the place a thorough spring clean. Two simple rooms have a buoyantly chatty atmosphere, good heavy traditional furnishings on dark-stained floorboards, shelves of bottles, breweriana, and lots of railway prints and memorabilia about Derby's railway history. The lounge is no smoking. Six well kept and constantly changing real ales from all sorts of small countrywide breweries, plus continental bottled beers and belgian and german beers on tap; quite a few malt whiskies, too. Darts, piped music and fruit machine. Bar food includes filled rolls (from £2.95; the warm baguette with sausage, egg, beans and chips is popular, £3.75), sausage and mash with onion gravy (£3.75), and home-made shepherd's pie or lasagne (£4.25). Derby station is just a few minutes away. *(Recommended by David Carr, the Didler, Mark and Diane Grist, C J Fletcher)*

Tynemill ~ Licensee Jonathan Hales ~ Real ale ~ Bar food (lunchtimes only (not Sun or Mon)) ~ No credit cards ~ (01332) 293993 ~ Children in lounge ~ Dogs allowed in bar ~ Open 11.45-11; 12-3, 7-10.30 Sun ~ Bedrooms: /£40S

Brunswick ◨ £

Railway Terrace; close to Derby Midland station; DE1 2RU

Up to 16 real ales on handpump or tapped from the cask are well kept in this former railwaymen's hostelry. Seven are brewed here (Father Mikes Dark Rich Ruby, Old Accidental, Second Brew Usual, Mild, Pilsner, Triple Hop and Triple Gold), with regularly changing guests like Batemans, Everards Tiger, Holdens

Golden Glow, Marstons Pedigree and Timothy Taylors Landlord. You can tour the brewery – £7.50 including a meal and a pint. Weston's Old Rosie farm cider is tapped from the cask. The welcoming high-ceilinged bar has heavy well padded leather seats, whisky-water jugs above the dado, and a dark blue ceiling and upper wall, with squared dark panelling below. The no smoking room is decorated with little old-fashioned prints and swan's neck lamps, and has a high-backed wall settle and a coal fire; behind a curved glazed partition wall is a chatty family parlour (also no smoking) narrowing to the apex of the triangular building. Informative wall displays tell you about the history and restoration of the building, and there are interesting old train photographs. Lunchtime bar food includes toasties (from £1.45), filled baguettes (from £2), burgers (from £2.25), home-made soup (£2.55), filled baked potatoes (from £2.70), cumberland sausage (£3.95), all-day breakfast (£4.25), home-made quiche (£4.45), and home-made beef stew (£4.95). There are two outdoor seating areas, including a terrace behind. They'll gladly give dogs a bowl of water. *(Recommended by David Carr, Kevin Blake, the Didler, Mark and Diane Grist, Brian and Jean Hepworth, C J Fletcher, Keith and Chris O'Neill, Bob)*

Everards ~ Licensee Graham Yates ~ Real ale ~ Bar food (11.30-2.30 Mon-Thurs; 11.30-5 Fri and Sat) ~ No credit cards ~ (01332) 290677 ~ Children in family room ~ Dogs welcome ~ Blues Mon evenings, jazz Thurs evenings ~ Open 11-11; 12-10.30 Sun

Olde Dolphin ◧ £
Queen Street; nearest car park King Street/St Michaels Lane; DE1 3DL

As the cathedral and main pedestrianised area are very close, this quaint old timber-framed pub is a useful place to enjoy a drink or good value meal. The rambling layout encompasses four snug old-fashioned rooms (two with their own separate street doors), with big bowed black beams, shiny panelling, cast-iron-framed tables, opaque leaded windows, lantern lights and coal fires; there are varnished wall benches in the tiled-floor public bar, and a brocaded seat in the little carpeted snug. The lounge bar and restaurant are no smoking. Seven well kept real ales on handpump such as Adnams, Bass, Black Sheep, Caledonian Deuchars IPA, Greene King Abbot, Jennings Cumberland and Marstons Pedigree, and there's a beer festival in the last week of July with some 80 brews. Good value tasty bar food includes triple-decker sandwiches (from £2.65), home-made soup (£2.85), filled baguettes (from £3.65), giant yorkshire puddings (from £3.90), all-day breakfast (£4.30), battered cod (£4.80), and 10oz rump steak (£10.95). There are seats on the terrace. No children and no noisy games machines or piped music. *(Recommended by David Carr, Kevin Blake, the Didler, Mark and Diane Grist)*

Mitchells & Butlers ~ Lease James and Josephine Harris ~ Real ale ~ Bar food (11-10; 9.30am-10pm Sat, 10-6 Sun) ~ Restaurant ~ (01332) 267711 ~ Open 10.30(9.30 Sat)-midnight; 10am-11pm Sun

EARL STERNDALE SK0967 Map 7
Quiet Woman
Village signposted off B5053 S of Buxton; SK17 0BU

For those who enjoy proper unspoilt pubs with genuine village character and plenty of friendly locals, this is the place to be. It's very simple inside, with hard seats, plain tables (including a sunken one for dominoes or cards), low beams, quarry tiles, lots of china ornaments and a coal fire. There's a pool table in the family room (where you may be joined by two friendly jack russells eager for a place by the fire), darts and board games. Archers, Jennings Dark Mild and Marstons Best and Pedigree are well kept on handpump, and bar food is limited to locally made pork pies. There are picnic-sets out in front, and the budgies, hens, turkeys, ducks and donkeys help keep children entertained. You can buy free-range eggs, local poetry books and even silage here, and sometimes local dry-cured bacon and raw sausages; they have a caravan for hire in the garden, and you can also arrange to stay at the small campsite next door. Needless to say, it's a popular place with walkers, with some very rewarding hikes across the Dove valley towards Longnor and Hollinsclough. *(Recommended by DC, the Didler, Rona Murdoch, P Dawn, Barry Collett)*

Free house ~ Licensee Kenneth Mellor ~ Real ale ~ Bar food ~ No credit cards ~ (01298) 83211 ~ Children allowed but with restrictions ~ Jamming sessions most Sun lunchtimes ~ Open 12-3(4 Sat), 7-1am; 12-5, 7-1am Sun

FENNY BENTLEY SK1750 Map 7
Coach & Horses
A515 N of Ashbourne; DE6 1LB

A new conservatory dining room with pine chairs and tables had been opened up in this 17th-c rendered stone house. It's a cosy pub with blazing log fires, exposed brick hearths, flagstone floors and hand-made pine furniture that includes flowery-cushioned wall settles; wagon wheels hang from the black beams amid horsebrasses, pewter mugs and prints. Quiet piped music and dominoes. Well kept Caledonian Deuchars IPA and Marstons Pedigree with a couple of guests like Abbeydale Moonshine and Thornbridge Blackthorn on handpump, and 24 malt whiskies. Served by efficient uniformed staff, the well liked bar food might include home-made soup (£3.25), warmed goats cheese salad (£4.25), pork and leek sausages with red onion gravy, chicken korma or three cheese vegetable tart (£7.95), fried tuna with vegetable salsa (£9.50), barbary duck breast with fruits of the forest and port sauce (£10.50), Friday fish specials such as steamed mussels in white wine, garlic and cream (£8.50) or natural smoked haddock on cheesy mash with lemon butter (£8.75), and puddings like spotted dick, home-made summer pudding or panna cotta with pears (£3.75). The eating areas are no smoking. Outside, there are views across fields from picnic-sets in the side garden by an elder tree, and wooden tables and chairs under cocktail parasols on the front terrace. The ever-popular Tissington Trail is a short stroll away. *(Recommended by Martin and Alison Stainsby, Andrew Beardsley, Alison Lawrence, I J and S A Bufton, P M Newsome, the Didler, P Dawn, Cathryn and Richard Hicks, Mr and Mrs John Taylor, Jan and Alan Summers, Geoff and Linda Payne, Bob)*

Free house ~ Licensees John and Matthew Dawson ~ Real ale ~ Bar food (12-9; not 25 Dec) ~ (01335) 350246 ~ Children welcome ~ Open 11-11; 12-10.30 Sun

FOOLOW SK1976 Map 7
Bulls Head ♛
Village signposted off A623 Baslow—Tideswell; S32 5QR

This village pub, close to a small green with a duck pond, has a simply furnished flagstoned bar plus a couple of quieter areas for eating. A step or two takes you down into what may once have been a stables with its high ceiling joists, stripped stone and woodburning stove. On the other side, a smart no smoking dining room has more polished tables set in cosy stalls. Interesting photographs include a good collection of Edwardian naughties. They tell us prices have not changed for food, which includes lunchtime snacks such as sandwiches (from £3.95), hot filled baps (£5.25), and ploughman's (£5.50), as well as soup (£3.25), thai fishcakes with sweet chilli sauce (£4.50), chicken with lemon cream sauce or minted lamb casserole (£7.25), and rump steak (£10.75). Adnams, Black Sheep, Shepherd Neame Spitfire and a guest beer on handpump; piped music and darts. The jack russells are called Honey and Jack. Picnic-sets at the side have nice views, and from here you can follow paths out over rolling pasture enclosed by dry-stone walls. More reports please. *(Recommended by John Wooll, Mrs J Clarke-Williams, Russell Grimshaw, Kerry Purcell, Barbara Ronan, Richard, Derek and Sylvia Stephenson, C E Reid, JWAC)*

Free house ~ Licensee William Leslie Bond ~ Real ale ~ Bar food (12-2, 6.30-9; 12-2, 5-8 Sun) ~ Restaurant ~ (01433) 630873 ~ Children welcome ~ Dogs allowed in bar ~ Live folk Fri evening and Sun ~ Open 12-3, 6.30-11; 12-10.30 Sun; closed Mon ~ Bedrooms: £50S/£70S

FROGGATT EDGE SK2476 Map 7

Chequers 🍴 🛏

A625 (busy even at night with quarry traffic), off A623 N of Bakewell; OS Sheet 119
map reference 247761; S32 3ZJ

The public areas and bathrooms in this bustling and smart no smoking dining pub
have been refurbished this year. There are solid pale wooden farmhouse chairs
around circular tables on the partly carpeted and partly wooden boarded floors,
antique prints on the walls, an attractive richly varnished beam-and-board ceiling
and a grandfather clock. One corner has a nicely carved oak cupboard. Enjoyable
food includes imaginative sandwiches (from £5.50), daily specials such as chicken
and mushroom roulade with sage and bacon sauce (£5.95), crayfish terrine with dill
and fennel seed yoghurt dressing or good seared scallops with basil pesto (£6.50),
trout and sole paupiettes with prawn and Pernod sauce or fillet of pork wrapped in
basil and parma ham with apple jus (£14.95), and calves liver with celeriac purée
and red pepper sauce (£15.95); from the menu there might be pasta with sun-dried
tomato and spinach sauce (£7.75), warm tandoori chicken salad with mango and
mint salsa (£8.95), local sausage with red wine gravy and red onion jam (£9.25),
grilled bacon steak with pineapple and chilli marmalade and homecut chips
(£9.95), and puddings such as cappuccino mousse in a two chocolate cup or baked
alaska (£5.95). Caledonian Deuchars IPA and Charles Wells Bombardier on
handpump, and nine wines by the glass; piped music. The wooded slopes of
Froggatt Edge provide a wonderful backdrop and there are picnic sets in the
garden. *(Recommended by David Carr, Noel Dinneen, W M Lien, Roger Yates, Bob, Mr and
Mrs M Wall, Richard, Annette and John Derbyshire, Geoff and Kaye Newton, Mike and
Linda Hudson, M G Hart, C E Reid, Dave Braisted, Adrian White)*

Pubmaster ~ Lease Jonathan and Joanne Tindall ~ Real ale ~ Bar food (12-2, 6-9.30;
12-9.30(9 Sun) Sat) ~ Restaurant ~ (01433) 630231 ~ Children welcome ~ Open 12-2,
6-10; 12-10 Sat and Sun ~ Bedrooms: /£70B

HARDWICK HALL SK4663 Map 7

Hardwick Inn

3 miles from M1 junction 29: at roundabout A6175 towards Clay Cross; after ½ mile
turn left signed Stainsby and Hardwick Hall (ignore any further sign for Hardwick Hall);
at sign to Stainsby follow road to left; after 2½ miles turn left at staggered road junction;
S44 5QJ

Handy for the M1, this 17th-c golden stone house was originally built as a lodge
for the nearby Elizabethan Hall (owned by the National Trust). There are plenty of
customers in the cosy but fairly old-fashioned rooms (all no smoking) – the most
comfortable being the carpeted lounge with its upholstered wall settles, tub chairs
and stools around varnished wooden tables; one room has an attractive 18th-c
carved settle. Bar food includes soup (£2.95), sandwiches (from £3.35), home-made
chicken liver pâté (£3.60), filled baked potatoes (from £3.75), ploughman's (from
£5.70), lambs liver and kidney with button onions and rich gravy or home-made
lasagne (£7.25), vegetable curry (£7.50), beer battered cod (£7.75), steaks (from
£11.95), and daily specials such as venison steak with a wild mushroom and
burgundy sauce (£12.75), and duck breast with orange, plum and brandy sauce
(£12.95); afternoon tea (£3.50). A huge range of some 220 malt whiskies, 24 wines
by the glass, and Greene King Old Speckled Hen and Ruddles County, Marstons
Pedigree and Theakstons XB and Old Peculier on handpump; piped music. There's
a very pleasant back garden and plenty of seats at the front. *(Recommended by
D P and M A Miles, Andrew Beardsley, Alison Lawrence, Andy and Ali, Fred and Lorraine Gill,
John Saville, the Didler, Mark and Diane Grist, DFL, Mr and Mrs J E C Tasker, J Stickland,
Keith and Chris O'Neill, Peter F Marshall, Alison and Pete, Brian and Jacky Wilson, Susan and
Nigel Wilson, A J Ward)*

Free house ~ Licensees Peter and Pauline Batty ~ Real ale ~ Bar food (11.30-9.30; 12-9
Sun) ~ Restaurant ~ (01246) 850245 ~ Children allowed but with restrictions ~ Open
11.30-11; 12-10.30 Sun

HASSOP   SK2272   Map 7

Eyre Arms

B6001 N of Bakewell; DE45 1NS

This creeper-clad 17th-c stone inn – totally no smoking now – is in the centre of the
Peak District National Park. The Eyre coat of arms (painted above the stone
fireplace) dominates the beamed dining bar, and there's also a longcase clock,
cushioned settles around the walls, comfortable plush chairs and lots of brass and
copper. A smaller public bar has an unusual collection of teapots and another fire.
Black Sheep Special, Marstons Pedigree and John on handpump; piped classical
music. Bar food includes sandwiches, soup (£3.65), thai-style crab cakes with sweet
pepper sauce (£3.65), deep-fried garlic mushrooms (£4.65), breaded plaice (£7.45),
steak and kidney pie (£8.20), mushroom stroganoff (£8.45), steaks (from £9.75),
and specials such as lamb stuffed with apricots and honey (£9.75) or rabbit pie
(£13.45). There's a fountain in the small garden and tables looking out over
beautiful peak district countryside; colourful summer hanging baskets.
*(Recommended by Peter F Marshall, Martin and Alison Stainsby, DC, Kevin Blake, the Didler,
Annette and John Derbyshire, M G Hart, W W Burke, Derek and Sylvia Stephenson, Richard)*

Free house ~ Licensee Lynne Smith ~ Real ale ~ Bar food (12-2, 6.30-9) ~ Restaurant ~
(01629) 640390 ~ Children allowed but with restrictions ~ Open 11-3, 6.30-11; closed
Mon evenings in winter

HATHERSAGE   SK2380   Map 7

Plough 🍽 ♀ 🛏

Leadmill; B6001 towards Bakewell, OS Sheet 110 map reference 235805; S32 1BA

There's no doubt that the emphasis in this neatly kept dining pub is placed firmly
on the interesting, very popular food – though they do keep Adnams, Batemans,
Theakstons and Youngs on handpump. As well as lunchtime sandwiches, there are
bar meals such as a trio of sausages with onion gravy or spinach and ricotta
cannelloni (£7.95), a roast of the day (£8.50), and steak and kidney pudding
(£8.95), plus more elaborate choices such as crab cakes with mango and sweet corn
salsa (£6.95), ham hock and foie gras terrine with home-made piccalilli (£7.50),
mixed hors d'oeuvres for sharing (£8.95), butternut squash risotto cake, goats
cheese with a shallot glaze and warm sage dressing (£11.95), rabbit with cider,
rosemary and cream (£12.95), lamb shank with pea and mint risotto and mint jus
(£14.95), and steamed halibut with ginger and spring onion (£16.50). Sixteen wines
(plus champagne) by the glass and 40 malt whiskies. One attractive room, on two
levels, has dark wood tables and chairs on a turkey carpet, with a big log fire at one
end and a woodburning stove at the other; friendly staff, piped music and TV.
There are picnic-sets in the pretty secluded garden going right down to the River
Derwent. The bedrooms are comfortable and the breakfasts good. *(Recommended by
Mrs L Aquilina, M G Hart, DC, Tom and Ruth Rees, Paul Wilson, Bob, John and Sarah Webb,
B and M Kendall, Christine Shepherd, DFL, Jo Lilley, Simon Calvert, Cathryn and
Richard Hicks, Annette and John Derbyshire, Peter F Marshall, Gerry and Rosemary Dobson,
Keith and Chris O'Neill, John and Elisabeth Cox, Mike and Mary Carter, Avril Burton,
Brian and Jacky Wilson, Fred and Lorraine Gill)*

Free house ~ Licensees Bob, Cynthia and Elliott Emery ~ Real ale ~ Bar food (11.30-2.30,
6.30-9.30; 12-9 Sun) ~ Restaurant ~ (01433) 650319 ~ Children welcome ~ Open
11.30-11; 12-10.30 Sun; closed 25 Dec ~ Bedrooms: £59.50B/£89.50B

Scotsmans Pack 🛏

School Lane, off A6187; S32 1BZ

This is a perfect centre for walkers with plenty of surrounding footpaths, and the
bedrooms in this friendly and civilised inn are very comfortable. Perhaps the nicest
area is on the left as you enter, with a fireplace, and patterned wallpaper somewhat
obscured by a splendid mass of brasses, stuffed animal heads and the like.
Elsewhere there's plenty of dark panelling, lots of mugs and plates arranged around

the bar, and a good few tables, many with reserved signs (it's worth booking ahead, particularly at weekends). Good, enjoyable food includes sandwiches, home-made soup (£2.95), button mushrooms in a peppercorn, cream and brandy sauce (£3.95), feta cheese, parma ham and plum salad (£4.25), home-made lasagne (£7.50), a sausage of the day (£7.80), peppers filled with aromatic couscous on a tomato sauce or niçoise salad (£7.95), home-made steak in ale pie (£8.50), gammon with pineapple and egg (£9.25), grilled salmon steak with tomato and herb hollandaise (£9.95), and 10oz sirloin steak or chicken in leek and stilton sauce (£10.95). Well kept Jennings Cumberland and Lakeland, Marstons Pedigree, and a couple of changing guests on handpump; service remains prompt and cheery even when busy. Some tables are no smoking; piped music, games machine and darts. Outside is a small but very pleasant terrace, next to a trout-filled stream. This is close to the church where Little John is said to be buried. *(Recommended by David Carr, Mrs U Pentelow, M G Hart, Peter F Marshall, Mrs J Clarke-Williams)*

W&D ~ Lease Nick Beagrie, Steve Bramley and Susan Concannon ~ Real ale ~ Bar food (12-2, 6-9; 12-5, 6-9 Sat and Sun) ~ (01433) 650253 ~ Children welcome ~ Jazz first Mon evening of month ~ Open 11.30-3, 5.30-11; 11.30-11 Sat ~ Bedrooms: £35S/£63B

HAYFIELD   SK0388   Map 7

Lantern Pike 🍺

Glossop Road (A624 N) at Little Hayfield, just N of Hayfield; SK22 2NG

Tables on a stonewalled terrace behind this welcoming pub look over a big-windowed weaver's house to the Lantern Pike itself, and there are plenty of walks on to the moors of Kinder Scout. The bar is unpretentious but cosy with a warm fire, plush seats, flowers on the tables, and lots of brass platters, china and toby jugs. Black Sheep, Caledonian Deuchars IPA, Tetleys and Timothy Taylors Landlord on handpump, and several malt whiskies; TV and piped music. Reasonably priced bar food includes home-made soup (£2.95), sandwiches (from £3.95), mixed vegetable balti (£6.50), home-made steak and kidney pie (£7.95) and 8oz rump steak (£10.95), while specials might feature thai green curry or salmon in white wine and cream (£7.95), and lamb on the bone (£8.95). The restaurant is no smoking. More reports please. *(Recommended by Michael Lamm, Christine Mills, Derek and Sylvia Stephenson, Donald and Margaret Wood, Kevin Blake)*

Enterprise ~ Lease Chris and Katherine Middleton ~ Real ale ~ Bar food (12-9(8.30 Sun)) ~ Restaurant ~ (01663) 747590 ~ Children welcome ~ Live entertainment monthly Sat ~ Open 12-midnight(1am Sat) ~ Bedrooms: £40B/£55B

Royal

Market Street, just off A624 Chapel-en-le-Frith—Buxton; SK22 2EP

Run by friendly new licensees, this large, bustling inn has a genuinely pubby feel and is very much the centre of local life. As a former vicarage there are many original features, so there's lots of dark panelling in the separate-seeming areas around the central island bar counter, as well as several fireplaces, bookshelves, brasses and house plants, and newspapers to read; the family room is no smoking. Boddingtons Bitter and Hydes Bitter on handpump, and maybe a beer festival in early October; piped music. Bar food includes home-made soup (£3.25), home-made chicken liver pâté (£3.50), creamy stilton mushrooms (£3.95), sandwiches (from £4.50), roast beef and yorkshire pudding or field mushrooms with a tomato sauce (£6.95), home-made steak and kidney pie (£7.95), chicken in white wine and cream (£8.95), steaks (from £9.95), specials such as stir-fried monkfish with oyster sauce (£9.95) and whole plaice with a tomato and prawn sauce (£10.95), and puddings like bread and butter pudding with vanilla custard or strawberry and toffee meringue nest (£3.95). They also offer a set two-course (£10.95) and three-course (£12.95) meal; tea and coffee are served all day. On fine days, drinkers spill out on to the terrace in front which has lots of picnic-sets. The River Sett runs alongside the car park. Bedrooms are comfortable, and it's a useful base for exploring the local scenery. More reports please. *(Recommended by Derek and Sylvia Stephenson)*

Free house ~ Licensees Bernadette Meredith and Paul Ash ~ Real ale ~ Bar food (12-9
(6 winter Sun, 8 summer Sun)) ~ Restaurant ~ (01663) 742721 ~ Children welcome with
restrictions ~ Open 12-11; 12-10.30 Sun ~ Bedrooms: £45B/£60B

HOLBROOK   SK3644   Map 7
Dead Poets 🍺 £

Village signposted off A6 S of Belper; Chapel Street; DE56 0TQ

There's a thoroughly good mix of customers of all ages in this old-fashioned place –
most are keen to enjoy one of the eight well kept real ales on handpump or served in
a jug from the cellar: Bass, Greene King Abbot and Marstons Pedigree with guests
from breweries such as Church End, Everards, Exmoor and Ossetts. Farm cider and
country wines. It's quite a dark interior with low black beams in the ochre ceiling,
stripped stone walls and broad flagstones. There are candles on scrubbed tables, a
big log fire in the end stone fireplace, high-backed winged settles forming snug
cubicles along one wall, and pews and a variety of chairs in other intimate corners
and hideaways. The décor makes a few nods to the pub's present name (it used to be
the Cross Keys) including a photo of W B Yeats and a poem dedicated to the pub by
Les Baynton, and there are old prints of Derby. Alongside cobs (from £2, nothing
else on Sundays), bar food is limited to a few good value hearty dishes such as home-
made soup (£2) and chilli con carne, casserole or chicken jalfrezi (£4.25); piped
music. Behind is a sort of verandah room with lanterns, fairy lights and a few plants,
and more seats out in the yard with outdoor heaters. More reports please.
(Recommended by the Didler, JJW, CMW, Derek and Sylvia Stephenson)

Everards ~ Tenant William Holmes ~ Real ale ~ Bar food (lunchtime only) ~ No credit
cards ~ (01332) 780301 ~ Children in family room ~ Dogs welcome ~ Open 12-3, 5-11;
12-11 Fri-Sat; 12-10.30 Sun

HOPE   SK1783   Map 7
Cheshire Cheese 🛏

Off A6187, towards Edale; S33 6ZF

In an attractive village, this 16th-c pub is close to the Pennine Way and well placed
for a walk in the lovely Edale Valley. The friendly chatty landlord will make you
feel welcome, and each of the three very snug oak-beamed rooms has its own coal
fire. As well as lunchtime snacks such as sandwiches (from £4.50; toasties from
£4.75), filled baked potatoes (from £4.50), and ploughman's (£6.25), the enjoyable
food might include home-made soup (£3.50), cream cheese and broccoli bake
(£7.95), steak and kidney pudding or pork steak in porcini mushroom sauce
(£8.95), mixed grill (£10.25), roasted lamb shank in minted gravy (£10.95), daily
specials, and puddings such as spotted dick or chocolate pudding in chocolate sauce
(£3.95). The restaurant is no smoking. Well kept Black Sheep Bitter and Whim
Hartington plus guests like Coach House Coachmans Best Bitter, Greene King IPA
and Salamander Cloud Nine on handpump, and a good range of spirits; piped
music. When it's busy, parking can be a problem. *(Recommended by Dr Ann Henderson,
Peter F Marshall, the Didler, Pete Baker, Mrs Julie Thomas)*

Free house ~ Licensee David Helliwell ~ Real ale ~ Bar food (12-2(2.30 Sat), 6.30-9; all day
Sun) ~ Restaurant ~ (01433) 620381 ~ Children in eating area till 9pm ~ Dogs allowed in
bar ~ Open 12-3, 6.30-midnight; 12-midnight Sat; 12-10.30 Sun ~ Bedrooms:
£50S/£65S(£75B)

KIRK IRETON   SK2650   Map 7
Barley Mow 🍺 🛏

Village signed off B5023 S of Wirksworth; DE6 3JP

In a pretty hilltop village and surrounded by good walks, this is an unspoilt and
unchanging rural inn that has been welcoming travellers since 1750. The dimly lit
passageways and narrow stairwells have a timeless atmosphere, helped along by

traditional furnishings and civilised old-fashioned service. It's a place to sit and chat and there's a good mix of customers of all ages. The small main bar has a relaxed pubby feel, with antique settles on the tiled floor or built into the panelling, a roaring coal fire, four slate-topped tables and shuttered mullioned windows. Another room has built-in cushioned pews on oak parquet and a small woodburning stove, and a third room has more pews, a tiled floor, beams and joists, and big landscape prints. One room is no smoking. In casks behind a modest wooden counter are six or seven well kept (and reasonably priced) real ales: Archers, Burton Bridge, Cottage, Eccleshall Slaters, Hook Norton Old Hooky, Storm and Whim Hartington IPA; Thatcher's farm cider too. Lunchtime filled rolls (85p) are the only food; the decent evening meals are reserved for residents staying in the comfortable rooms. There's a good-sized garden, and a couple of benches out in front, and a post office in what used to be the pub stables. Handy for Carsington Water. *(Recommended by the Didler, John Dwane, Brian and Jacky Wilson, Pete Baker, Tich Critchlow, Mark and Mary Fairman, Simon Fox, T Stone, David and Sue Smith)*

Free house ~ Licensee Mary Short ~ Real ale ~ No credit cards ~ (01335) 370306 ~ Children in side rooms lunchtime only ~ Dogs allowed in bar and bedrooms ~ Open 12-2, 7-11(10.30 Sun); closed 25 Dec and 1 Jan ~ Bedrooms: £35S/£55B

LADYBOWER RESERVOIR   SK1986   Map 7
Yorkshire Bridge 🛏
A6013 N of Bamford; S33 0AZ

Just a short stroll away from the Ladybower Dam and close to the Derwent and Howden reservoirs, this is a friendly and pleasantly old-fashioned hotel. One area has a country cottage feel with floral wallpaper, sturdy cushioned wall settles, staffordshire dogs and toby jugs above a big stone fireplace, china on delft shelves, and a panelled dado. Another extensive area, also with a fire, is lighter and more airy with pale wooden furniture, good big black and white photographs and lots of polished brass and decorative plates on the walls. The Bridge Room (with yet another coal-effect fire) has oak tables and chairs, and the Garden Room gives views across a valley to steep larch woods. Two areas are no smoking. Well liked bar food includes home-made soup (£3.50), large yorkshire pudding filled with creamy onion sauce and gravy (£3.95), lunchtime sandwiches or filled baked potatoes (from £4; soup and a sandwich £6.95), ploughman's (£7.25), lasagne or cheese and broccoli pasta bake (£7.95), home-made steak and kidney pie (£8.25), pot-roasted lamb with minted gravy (£10.95), steaks (from £11.25), daily specials such as quiche (£7.75), grimsby haddock or local sausages (£8.75), and baked halibut with lemon butter (£9.25), and puddings like crumbles, trifles and sticky toffee pudding (£3.75). Black Sheep, Copper Dragon Best Bitter, Fullers London Pride, Theakstons Old Peculier on handpump; darts, games machine, board games and piped music; disabled lavatories. *(Recommended by Derek and Sylvia Stephenson, Andrew Beardsley, Alison Lawrence, B M Eldridge, Alan and Paula McCully, Brian Brooks, Jan and Alan Summers, Irene and Ray Atkin, Bob)*

Free house ~ Licensees Trevelyan and John Illingworth ~ Real ale ~ Bar food (12-2, 6-9(9.30 Fri, Sat); 12-8.30 Sun) ~ Restaurant ~ (01433) 651361 ~ Children in dining areas only ~ Dogs allowed in bedrooms ~ Open 10am-11pm ~ Bedrooms: £50B/£68B

LITTON   SK1675   Map 7
Red Lion
Village signposted off A623, between B6465 and B6049 junctions; also signposted off B6049; SK17 8QU

You can be sure of a warm welcome at this 17th-c stone-built village pub, popular with locals and walkers. The two inviting homely linked front rooms have low beams and some panelling, and blazing log fires. There's a bigger back room (no smoking during food service) with an amusing collection of pigs, good-sized tables, and large antique prints on its stripped stone walls. The small bar counter has well kept Barnsley real ale on handpump, plus three guests that usually include Black

Sheep, Timothy Taylors and another often from a small brewery such as Kelham Island, with decent wines and several malt whiskies; darts and board games. Tasty bar food includes steak and ale pie or well liked steak and kidney pudding (£6.95), rabbit casserole or braised steak in Black Sheep ale (£7.20), pork and apricot casserole (£7.40) and garlic and rosemary lamb (£8.95). A particularly rewarding time to visit is during the annual village well-dressing carnival (usually the last weekend in June), when villagers create a picture from flower petals, moss and other natural materials, and at Christmas a brass band plays carols. It's such a small pub that it's not ideal for children. *(Recommended by Richard, the Didler, B and M Kendall, J R Ringrose, Keith and Chris O'Neill, Derek and Sylvia Stephenson, Barry Collett, Brian and Jacky Wilson)*

Free house ~ Licensees Terry and Michele Vernon ~ Real ale ~ Bar food (12-2, 6-8 (not Sun evening)) ~ (01298) 871458 ~ No children under 6 ~ Dogs welcome ~ Open 11.30-midnight ~ Bedrooms: /£65S(£60B)

MELBOURNE   SK3427   Map 7
John Thompson   ㉕   🍴   £
Ingleby, which is NW of Melbourne; turn off A514 at Swarkestone Bridge or in Stanton by Bridge; can also be reached from Ticknall (or from Repton on B5008); DE73 1HW

Both the own-brewed beers and popular food continue to draw customers to this welcoming pub. It's simple but comfortable, and the big modernised lounge has ceiling joists, some old oak settles, button-back leather seats, sturdy oak tables, antique prints and paintings, and a log-effect gas fire; piped music. A couple of smaller cosier rooms open off; piano, fruit machine, TV, and pool in the conservatory. Two areas are no smoking. From the JT brewery behind, they produce JTS XXX, Rich Porter and Summer Gold, and keep guests from other breweries such as Leatherbritches and Shardlow. The menu is very short but the food is home made and decidedly tasty: sandwiches (from £2), soup (£2.50), beef, ham or cheese salads (£5), roast beef with yorkshire pudding (£6), and puddings like home-made crumble or dark chocolate and raspberry tart (from £2.20). Outside are lots of tables by flowerbeds on the neat lawns or you can sit on the partly covered terrace. *(Recommended by Margaret and Allen Marsden, Brian and Jacky Wilson, the Didler, P Dawn, C D Bowring, Lynn Sharpless, Rona Murdoch, Michael Lamm, Brian and Ruth Archer, Paul and Gloria Howell, Rob Berridge)*

Own brew ~ Licensee John Thompson ~ Real ale ~ Bar food (lunchtime only – not Sun or Mon) ~ (01332) 862469 ~ Children welcome but with restrictions ~ Open 11-2.30, 6-11; 11-11 Sat; 12-10.30 Sun; closed Mon lunchtime

MONSAL HEAD   SK1871   Map 7
Monsal Head Hotel   🍴   🛏
B6465; DE45 1NL

The views from here are terrific as this busy extended hotel is perched high above the steep valley of the River Wye. It's the cosy stable bar (once housing the horses that used to pull guests and their luggage up from the station at the other end of the steep valley) that readers head for – and walkers and their dogs are welcome here too: stripped timber horse-stalls, harness and brassware, and lamps from the disused station itself, all hint at those days. There's a big warming woodburning stove in the inglenook, and cushioned oak pews around the tables on the flagstones. They keep between six and eight real ales on handpump such as Lloyds Bitter, Theakstons Best and Old Peculier, Timothy Taylors Landlord, Thornbridge Blackthorn Ale, Jaipur, and Lord Marples, and Whim Hartington Bitter; a good choice of german bottled beers, and a dozen wines by the glass. Well liked bar food includes lunchtime sandwiches (from £4.50; steak melt £7.10; peking duck hoisin wrap £7.90), plus home-made soup (£3.70), chicken caesar or butternut squash and roquefort salad (£4.80 small, £8.50 large), chicken liver pâté (£4.30), smoked haddock fishcake (£4.50), pasta with ricotta, walnuts, lemon and parsley (£7.80), spicy thai vegetable curry (£8.50), beef in ale pie (£9.60), chicken with stilton wrapped in smoked bacon with a white wine, cream and chive sauce (£11.20), slow-roasted shoulder of lamb (£11.90), and specials such as chorizo, feta and fried artichoke salad (£4.90), wild boar sausage (£8.50), wild mushroom, sweet potato, celeriac and spinach pie (£9.40), and seared duck breast (£12.80). The boundary of the parishes of Little Longstone and Ashford runs through the hotel, and the spacious no smoking restaurant and smaller lounge are named according to which side of the line they sit; beer garden. The best places to admire the terrific view are from the big windows in the lounge, the garden, and from four of the seven bedrooms. *(Recommended by Peter F Marshall, the Didler, Brian and Jacky Wilson, Russell Grimshaw, Kerry Purcell, Keith and Chris O'Neill, Mike and Sue Loseby, DFL, Leigh and Gillian Mellor, M G Hart, Mr and Mrs R B Berry, Richard, Janet and Peter Race, David Martin, Andrew Wallace, Fred and Lorraine Gill, Dr David Clegg)*

Free house ~ Licensee Victor Chandler ~ Real ale ~ Bar food (12-9.30(9 Sun)) ~ Restaurant ~ (01629) 640250 ~ Children welcome ~ Dogs allowed in bar and bedrooms ~ Open 11.30-11.30; 12-11 Sun; closed 25 Dec ~ Bedrooms: /£70B

OVER HADDON   SK2066   Map 7

Lathkil 🍺

Village and inn signposted from B5055 just SW of Bakewell; DE45 1JE

Particularly at lunchtime, there's a chatty, cheerful atmosphere as the many socked customers discuss their walk through Lathkill Dale, a gorgeously secretive limestone valley; dogs are welcome, too, though muddy boots are not and must be left in the lobby. The walled garden is a good place to sit and soak in the views. The licensees have been running this much loved inn for 25 years now and readers continue to sing its praises. The airy room on the right as you go in has a nice fire in the attractively carved fireplace, old-fashioned settles with upholstered cushions and chairs, black beams, a delft shelf of blue and white plates, original prints and photographs, and big windows. On the left, the spacious and sunny no smoking dining area doubles as an evening restaurant. Well kept Charles Wells Bombardier and Whim Hartington Bitter plus guests like Adnams Explorer, Everards Tiger and Thornbridge Lord Marples on handpump, a few unusual malt whiskies, and decent range of wines. The popular buffet-style lunch menu includes filled rolls (from £2.65), soup (£3.20), brie, broccoli and cauliflower crumble or quiche and salad (£6.35), home-cooked ham with chips (£6.50), steak and kidney pie or lasagne (£6.60), minty lamb casserole (£6.70), daily specials, and puddings (from £3). More elaborate restaurant food in the evening. Piped music, darts, bar billiards, shove-ha'penny, and card and board games. *(Recommended by Richard and Margaret McPhee, Peter F Marshall, the Didler, John and Karen Wilkinson, Russell Grimshaw, Kerry Purcell, Dr D J and Mrs S C Walker, Jo Lilley, Simon Calvert, Richard, A and B D Craig, Alan and Paula McCully, Mrs P J Carroll, Mark and Mary Fairman)*

Free house ~ Licensee Robert Grigor-Taylor ~ Real ale ~ Bar food (lunchtime) ~ Restaurant ~ (01629) 812501 ~ Children allowed away from bar ~ Dogs allowed in bar ~ Open 11.30-11; 12-10.30 Sun; 11.30-3, 6.30-11 in winter ~ Bedrooms: £40B/£65S(£80B)

SHELDON   SK1768   Map 7

Cock & Pullet £

Village signposted off A6 just W of Ashford; DE45 1QS

It's quite a surprise to discover that this family-run place was only converted into a pub around ten years ago – the bar with its flagstones and cheerful assembly of deliberately mismatched furnishings makes it feel much older. As well as low beams, exposed stonework, scrubbed oak tables and pews, and an open fire, the small, cosy rooms have 24 fully working clocks (one for every hour of the day). Black Sheep, Timothy Taylors Landlord and a guest such as Thornbridge Lord Marples on handpump. Bar food includes soup (£2.25), sandwiches (from £2.25), fish pie (£5.50), a curry of the day, a vegetarian dish, steak in ale pie, and chicken in stilton sauce (all £5.75), minted lamb casserole (£5.95), and specials such as brisket with yorkshire pudding (£5) and chilli con carne (£5.75); Sunday roast

(£5.95). A fireplace is filled with flowers in summer, and around it are various representations of poultry, including some stuffed. A plainer room has pool and a TV; there's also a no smoking snug, and darts and dominoes. At the back is a pleasant little terrace with tables and a water feature. The pub is a year-round favourite with walkers (it can be busy at weekends); the pretty village is just off the Limestone Way. *(Recommended by Peter F Marshall, DC, Martin Sherwood, Richard, John Yates, Brian and Jacky Wilson)*

Free house ~ Licensees David and Kath Melland ~ Real ale ~ Bar food (12-2.30, 6-9) ~ No credit cards ~ (01629) 814292 ~ Children allowed until 8.30pm ~ Dogs allowed in bar ~ Open 11-11; 12-10.30 Sun ~ Bedrooms: /£60B

WARDLOW   SK1875   Map 7

Three Stags Heads ㉕ ▇

Wardlow Mires; A623 by junction with B6465; SK17 8RW

Genuinely traditional, this is a real find if you like your pubs basic and full of character, and enjoy a chat with the locals at the bar. It's situated in a natural sink, so don't be surprised to find the floors muddied by boots in wet weather (and the dogs even muddier). Warmed right through by a cast-iron kitchen range, the tiny flagstoned parlour bar has old leathercloth seats, a couple of antique settles with flowery cushions, two high-backed windsor armchairs and simple oak tables (look out for the petrified cat in a glass case). Abbeydale Absolution, Black Lurcher (brewed for the pub at a hefty 8% ABV), Brimstone and Matins on handpump, and lots of bottled continental and english beers. Home-made hearty food includes various soups or mutton stew (£3.50), toad-in-the-hole (£6.50), pigeon breasts (£7.50), and rabbit in chocolate and tomato sauce (£8.50); the hardy plates are home-made (the barn is a pottery workshop). The front terrace looks across the main road to the distant hills. Please note the opening times. More reports please. *(Recommended by the Didler, Pete Baker, Chris Reading, Derek and Sylvia Stephenson, Richard, John Dwane)*

Free house ~ Licensees Geoff and Pat Fuller ~ Real ale ~ Bar food (12.30-3.30, 7-9 when open) ~ No credit cards ~ (01298) 872268 ~ No toddlers; children allowed away from bar room ~ Dogs welcome ~ Folk music most Sat evenings and alternate Fri ~ Open 7-11 Fri; 12-11 Sat, Sun and bank hols; closed Mon-Thurs (all day)

WOOLLEY MOOR   SK3661   Map 7

White Horse

Badger Lane, off B6014 Matlock—Clay Cross; DE55 6FG

New licensees have done some refurbishment in this attractive old pub but the tap room is still very much in its original state and has a chatty, pleasant atmosphere. Black Sheep, St Austell Tribute and Timothy Taylors Landlord on handpump, and piped music in the lounge and conservatory (great views of the Ogston reservoir from here). Bar food now includes soup (£3.20), creamy garlic mushrooms or fishcakes (£3.95), sandwiches (£4.95), steak in Guinness pie (£6.95), red onion and goats cheese tart with roast tomato sauce (£7.70), fish and chips or chicken wrapped in parma ham with a creamy carbonara sauce (£7.95), fillet of red mullet with ratatouille sauce (£11.95), and puddings like chocolate trifle (£3.95). The pub looks over the Amber valley, there are picnic-sets in the garden, and a good children's play area. More reports on the new regime, please. *(Recommended by Michael and Maggie Betton, the Didler, Keith and Chris O'Neill, Peter F Marshall, Robert F Smith)*

Musketeers ~ Manager John Parsons ~ Real ale ~ Bar food (12-2, 5-9; not Sun evening) ~ Restaurant ~ (01246) 590319 ~ Children welcome away from tap room ~ Dogs allowed in bar ~ Open 12-3, 5-11; 12-10.30 Sun

Post Office address codings confusingly give the impression that a few pubs are in Derbyshire, when they're really in Cheshire (which is where we list them).

LUCKY DIP

Besides the fully inspected pubs, you might like to try these Lucky Dips recommended to us and described by readers (if you do, please send us reports: www.goodguides.co.uk).

ASHBOURNE [SK1846]

Olde Vaults DE6 1EU [Market Pl]: Imposing and attractive building, welcoming landlord and staff, good generous reasonably priced bar food, particularly well kept Bass, farm cider, good local atmosphere in open-plan bar; open all day wknds and summer, bedrooms, huge breakfast *(Steve Jennings)*

☆ *Smiths Tavern* DE6 1GH [bottom of market place]: Neatly kept traditional pub, chatty and relaxed, stretching back from heavily black-beamed bar (which can get quite smoky) through lounge to attractive light and airy end no smoking dining room, friendly efficient staff, above-average sensibly priced food using local produce from fresh sandwiches up, Banks's, Marstons Pedigree and a guest beer, lots of whiskies and vodkas, daily papers, traditional games; children welcome, open all day summer Sun *(I J and S A Bufton, Michael Lamm, John and Yvonne Davies, DJH, LYM)*

ASHFORD IN THE WATER [SK1969]

☆ *Bulls Head* DE45 1QB [Church St]: Busy 16th-c dining pub kept spotless, with enjoyable blackboard meals and lunchtime sandwiches, friendly helpful service, Robinsons Best, Old Stockport and Hartleys XB, cosy beamed lounge and thriving bar, daily papers; may be piped music; tables out behind and by front car park, attractive village *(DJH, Mrs Sylvia Elcoate, Martin and Alison Stainsby, Peter F Marshall, the Didler, Annette and John Derbyshire, Mrs Jennifer Hurst, Derek and Sylvia Stephenson)*

ASHOVER [SK3463]

Crispin S45 0AB [Church St]: Tastefully extended old building with very welcoming landlord, reasonably priced enjoyable food, Mansfield real ale, real fires, several areas from beamed original core to back conservatory *(Robert F Smith, Barry Steele-Perkins)*

BAKEWELL [SK2168]

Castle Inn DE45 1DU [Bridge St]: Bay-windowed Georgian-fronted 17th-c pub with three candlelit rooms, flagstones, stripped stone and lots of pictures, Black Sheep and Greene King IPA and Abbot, enjoyable food inc interesting vegetarian dishes, friendly staff, two real fires, daily papers; dogs welcome, tables outside *(Russell Grimshaw, Kerry Purcell, B M Eldridge)*

Peacock DE45 1DS [Bridge St]: Clean, bright and cheerful, Theakstons and guest beers such as Adnams Bitter and Broadside, good value food (not Mon-Weds evenings), quick service even when it's busy *(Mike Dean , Lis Wingate Gray, Bob, A and B D Craig, Janet and Peter Race)*

Rutland Arms DE45 1BT [The Square]: Handsome stone-built Georgian hotel with impressive service from welcoming young staff, enjoyable bar food and restaurant meals; recently refurbished bedrooms *(Adrian White)*

BARLBOROUGH [SX4779]

Pebley S43 4TH [A618 towards Killamarsh, nr Woodhall service area access rds]: Good value blackboard food (not Mon/Tues lunchtime) inc some unusual dishes, three real ales such as Fullers Discovery and Timothy Taylors Landlord, L-shaped lounge with woodburner and no smoking dining area up two steps; piped music, games machine; children and dogs welcome, garden with picnic-sets and play area, open all day *(JJW, CMW)*

BARLOW [SK3375]

Tickled Trout S18 7SL [Valley Rd, Common Side; B6051 NW of Chesterfield]: Beamed dining pub under promising new landlord, enjoyable food, choice of real ales, decent wines, comfortable banquettes and good-sized tables, old-world prints, no smoking dining area; unobtrusive piped music; terrace tables *(Keith and Chris O'Neill, LYM)*

BELPER [SK3349]

Bulls Head DE56 2DL [Belper Lane End]: Good choice of enjoyable food in smallish two-bar pub extended into large and attractive conservatory restaurant high above town, well kept beers, pianist some nights *(John and Karen Wilkinson)*

Cross Keys DE56 1FZ [Market Pl]: Two-room pub with Bass, Batemans and a guest beer, bar food, coal fire in lounge, bar billiards; summer beer festival, open all day *(the Didler)*

Queens Head DE56 1FF [Chesterfield Rd]: Warm and cosy three-room pub with five real ales such as Caledonian Deuchars IPA, Carlsberg Burton, Jennings Cumberland and Sharps Doom Bar, nourishing rolls (may even be goose at Christmas), constant coal fire, local photographs; good upstairs wknd band nights, beer festivals; good views from terrace tables, open all day *(the Didler, C J Fletcher)*

Thorntree DE56 1FF [Chesterfield Rd (B6013)]: Comfortable two-bar local with congenial licensees, five changing ales inc Bass and Greene King *(the Didler)*

BIRCHOVER [SK2362]

Druid DE4 2BL [off B5056; Main St]: No smoking two-storey dining pub with four spacious areas, very wide choice of food worth its price, friendly helpful staff, real ale such as Marstons Pedigree, good choice of malt whiskies and wines; piped music, no dogs; children welcome, picnic-sets out in front, good area for walks, has been cl Mon *(M L Rantzen, LYM, Derek and Sylvia Stephenson, James A Waller, B and M A Langrish)*

Red Lion DE4 2BN [Main St]: Friendly local with affable landlord, Black Sheep and a beer brewed for them by Shardlow, good choice of straightforward food from sandwiches up, dogs welcome in cosy tile-floor tap room *(Russell Grimshaw, Kerry Purcell)*

BONSALL [SK2758]

Barley Mow DE4 2AY [off A6012 Cromford—Hartington; The Dale]: Friendly tucked-away pub with well kept Whim Hartington and guest beers, fresh sandwiches and other good value plain food, character furnishings, coal fire, tiny pool room; live music wknds inc landlord playing accordion or keyboards, organises local walks inc UFO spotting; small front terrace, cl wkdy lunchtimes and Mon, open all day wknds *(Kevin Blake, the Didler, Richard, Derek and Sylvia Stephenson, Mark and Mary Fairman)*

BRASSINGTON [SK2354]

Miners Arms DE4 4HA [off B5035/B5056 NE of Ashbourne; Miners Hill]: Thriving opened-up local with welcoming helpful staff, enjoyable home-made food from hot meat rolls to huge plates of daily roasts, Banks's Original, Marstons Pedigree and two guest beers, central log fire; children welcome, tables out among flower tubs, bedrooms, open all day *(John Dwane, Gwyn and Anne Wake, Duncan Chappell)*

BUXTON [SK1266]

☆ *Bull i' th' Thorn* SK17 9QQ [Ashbourne Rd (A515) 6 miles S of Buxton, nr Flagg and Hurdlow]: Medieval hall doubling as straightforward roadside dining pub, all sorts of antique features to look at, handsome panelling, old flagstones and big open fire, also games room and simple no smoking family room; friendly licensees, wide range of food all day from baguettes to restaurant dishes, Robinsons Best; children and dogs welcome, terrace and big lawn, bedrooms with own bathrooms, big breakfast, open all day from 9.30am *(Dave Simmonds, the Didler, Jenny Berki, B M Eldridge, Alan and Paula McCully, Paul and Margaret Baker)*

☆ *Old Sun* SK17 6HA [33 High St]: Interesting old building with several small dimly lit traditional areas off central bar inc no smoking dining area, enjoyable food from sandwiches and baked potatoes up usefully served till 10, friendly helpful staff, five good ales inc Banks's and Marstons Best and Pedigree, good choice of reasonably priced wines by the glass, farm cider, low beams, open fires, bare boards or tiles, stripped wood screens, old local photographs; piped music, TV; children in back bar, open all day *(Paul Goldman, the Didler, Andy and Cath Pearson, LYM, Barry Collett, Peter and Pat Frogley)*

BUXWORTH [SK0282]

☆ *Navigation* SK23 7NE [S of village towards Silkhill, off B6062]: Popular and cheery pub by restored canal basin, linked low-ceilinged flagstoned rooms with canalia and brassware, lacy curtains, coal and log fires, flagstone floors, good attractively priced changing ales, summer farm ciders, winter mulled wine, enjoyable generous bar food all day from nice sandwiches up, no smoking restaurant, games room; quiet piped music; tables on sunken flagstoned terrace, play area and pets corner, open all day *(Michael Lamm, LYM, Derek and Sylvia Stephenson, Gerry and Rosemary Dobson, Keith and Chris O'Neill, Peter F Marshall, Barry Collett, Bob and Laura Brock)*

CASTLETON [SK1582]

Bulls Head S33 8WH [Cross St (A6187)]: Recently well refurbished roomy bar with enjoyable reasonably priced food, Robinsons, helpful service, log fire; four bedrooms *(Ian Thurman, Tony Goff)*

Castle Hotel S33 8WG [High St/Castle St]: Neat and spacious Vintage Inn, largely no smoking, with log fires, stripped-stone walls, beams and some ancient flagstones. Bass, Black Sheep and Charles Wells Bombardier, lots of wines by the glass, useful all-day food from sandwiches up, fast efficient service; piped music; children welcome, heated terrace, comfortable bedrooms, open all day *(LYM, M G Hart, Mrs Julie Thomas, Guy Vowles, Brian Brooks, Richard, Ian and Nita Cooper, Peter and Pat Frogley)*

☆ *George* S33 8WG [Castle St]: Friendly and relaxed, good value food from hearty sandwiches to imaginative main dishes, Wadworths 6X, two good-sized rooms, one mainly for eating, ancient beams and stripped stone, no music; tables on wide forecourt, lots of flower tubs; dogs, children and muddy boots welcome, may be cl Mon lunchtime *(Keith and Chris O'Neill, B M Eldridge, A and B D Craig)*

Olde Cheshire Cheese S33 8WJ [How Lane]: Two simple linked beamed areas, cosy and spotless, with real ales, good value food all day, good house wine, log fire, lots of photographs, toby jugs and local paintings, sensibly placed darts, back dining room; piped music, and they may try to keep your credit card while you eat; children welcome (and dogs in bar), bedrooms *(Bob, BB, Lynda Payton, Sam Samuells, N R White)*

☆ *Olde Nags Head* S33 8WH [Cross St (A6187)]: Small solidly built hotel dating from 17th c, interesting antique oak furniture and coal fire in small civilised bar with nice pictures on dark red walls, real ales such as Black Sheep, Edale and Timothy Taylors, good coffee, impressive sensibly priced bar food from sandwiches up, cosy Victorian restaurant; open all day till late, comfortable bedrooms *(Ian Thurman, LYM, Lynda Payton, Sam Samuells)*

CHELMORTON [SK1170]

Church Inn SK17 9SL [between A6 and A515 SW of Buxton]: Comfortable split bar with good range of enjoyable generous food, Adnams, Marstons Pedigree and a guest beer, companionable atmosphere, friendly landlord and golden labrador; piped music, outside lavatories; tables out in pleasant sloping garden with terrace, well tended flower boxes, superb walking country, open all day summer wknds *(J R Ringrose, Barry Collett)*

CHESTERFIELD [SK3871]

Barley Mow S40 1JR [Saltergate]: Largely no smoking, with original Wards stained glass, wide choice of enjoyable food from sandwiches, cobs, baguettes and baked potatoes up, low prices, Greene King IPA, Marstons Pedigree and John Smiths, good hot drinks; sunny picnic-sets outside *(Keith and Chris O'Neill)*

Portland S40 1AY [New Sq]: Landmark hotel reopened as well laid out Wetherspoons with their usual food and ale ranges; nicely planted terrace, bedrooms, open all day *(Keith and Chris O'Neill)*

Rutland S40 1XL [Stephenson Pl]: Well run ancient L-shaped pub next to crooked-spire church, Badger Best, Timothy Taylors Landlord and three or more interesting guest beers, farm cider, low-priced pub food all day from sandwiches and baguettes up, friendly polite service even when busy, rugs and assorted wooden furniture on bare boards, old photographs, no smoking eating area, darts; piped music; children welcome, open all day *(Keith and Chris O'Neill, Alan Johnson)*

Woodside S40 4DB [Ashgate Rd]: Enjoyable reasonably priced food (not Sun evening) from traditional pubby things to the current exotics, Marstons Pedigree and Charles Wells Bombardier, good choice of wines by the glass, civilised contemporary layout inc sofas and wing armchairs; great terrace, open all day *(Keith and Chris O'Neill)*

CRICH [SK3454]

Cliff DE4 5DP [Cromford Rd, Town End]: Cosy and unpretentious two-room pub with real fire, Hardys & Hansons Bitter and Mild, good value generous straightforward food inc children's; great views, handy for National Tramway Museum *(the Didler)*

CROMFORD [SK2956]

☆ *Boat* DE4 3QF [Scarthin, off Mkt Pl]: Traditional 18th-c waterside pub (though no view of water) under new licensees, changing ales such as Derby Falstaff, Springhead and Whim Hartington, relaxed atmosphere, coal fire, good value food (not Sun evening), long narrow low-beamed bar with stripped stone, bric-a-brac and books, darts and pool room, cool cellar bar (used for easter, summer and Nov beer festivals); TV; children and dogs welcome, back garden, open all day wknds *(the Didler, BB, JJW, CMW, Jeremy Beckett)*

DENBY [SK3847]

Old Stables DE5 8PX [Park Hall Rd, just off B6179 (former A61) S of Ripley]: Friendly tap for Leadmill microbrewery in raftered former stable barn in Park Hall grounds, their full impressive range, some from the cask, at low prices, two or three guest beers, fresh filled cobs, bench seating and sawdust on floor, plenty of brewery memorabilia, visits of the 1800s former mill brewery opposite; tables outside, open only Fri evening and all day wknds *(the Didler)*

DERBY [SK3538]

☆ *Abbey Inn* DE22 1DX [Darley St, Darley Abbey]: Interesting former abbey gatehouse, massive 15th-c or older stonework remnants, brick floor, studded oak doors, big stone inglenook, stone spiral stair to upper bar with handsome oak rafters and tapestries (and the lavatories with their beams, stonework and

tiles are worth a look too); cheap Sam Smiths, decent low-priced lunchtime bar food, coal fire; piped music; children welcome, opp Derwent-side park, pleasant riverside walk out from centre, open all day wknds *(the Didler, LYM)*

Babington Arms DE1 1TA [Babington Lane]: Large well run open-plan Wetherspoons, usual style and comfortable seating, good welcoming service, particularly good choice of real ales, well priced food; open all day *(the Didler)*

Falstaff DE23 6UJ [Silver Hill Rd, off Normanton Rd]: Basic full-blooded local aka the Folly, brewing its own good value ales such as 3 Faze and Phoenix, guest beers too; left-hand bar with games and occasional discos, right-hand lounge with coal fire usually quieter; open all day *(the Didler)*

☆ *Flower Pot* DE1 3DZ [King St]: Extended real ale pub with up to a dozen or so good reasonably priced changing beers mainly from small breweries – glazed panels show cellarage, regular beer festivals; friendly staff, three linked rooms inc comfortable back bar with lots of books, side area with old Derby photographs and brewery memorabilia, good value food cooked to order till early evening, daily papers, pub games; piped music/juke box, separate concert room – good live bands Fri/Sat and busy then; disabled access and facilities, tables on cherry-tree terrace, open all day *(Bob, David Carr, G Coates)*

Rowditch DE22 3LL [Uttoxeter New Rd (A516)]: Good value friendly local with well kept Hardys & Hansons, Marstons Pedigree and guest beers, country wines, attractive small snug on right, coal fire, piano, downstairs cellar bar; pleasant garden *(the Didler)*

☆ *Smithfield* DE1 2BH [Meadow Rd]: Friendly and comfortable bow-fronted local with big bar, snug, back lounge full of old prints, curios and breweriana, fine choice of well kept changing ales, filled rolls and hearty lunchtime meals, real fires, daily papers; piped music, pub games inc table skittles, board games, TV and games machines, quiz nights, summer blues nights; children welcome, riverside terrace, open all day *(C J Fletcher)*

☆ *Standing Order* DE1 3GL [Irongate]: Spacious no smoking Wetherspoons in grand and lofty former bank, central bar, booths down each side, elaborately painted plasterwork, pseudo-classical torsos, high portraits of mainly local notables; usual popular food all day, good range of real ales, reasonable prices, daily papers, neat efficient young staff; very busy wknds; good disabled facilities, open all day *(David Carr, Kevin Blake, the Didler, Bob, BB)*

Station Inn DE1 2SN [Midland Rd, below station]: Friendly and basic local with good food lunchtime and early evening in large back lounge, particularly well kept Bass (in jugs from cellar) and other ales such as Black Sheep and Caledonian Deuchars IPA, long tiled floor bar, side room with darts, pool and TV, ornate façade; piped music; open all day Fri *(the Didler)*

EDLASTON [SK1842]

☆ *Shire Horse* DE6 2DQ [off A515 S of Ashbourne, just beside Wyaston]: Properly pubby but gently sophisticated rambling timbered pub run by hospitable sisters, blazing fires and gleaming brass in well furnished long beamed bar with unusual slate-roofed counter and cottagey areas off, good very popular bar food and some interesting recipes for evening conservatory restaurant, reasonable prices, efficient attentive service, Bass, Marstons Pedigree and a guest such as St Austell Tribute; piped music; children welcome, tables out in front and in back garden with terrace, peaceful spot (D P and M A Miles, BB, Dr David Clegg)

ELMTON [SK5073]

Elm Tree S80 4LS [off B6417 S of Clowne]: Softly lit and popular country pub with good value bar food all day, Black Sheep and Youngs, quietly welcoming service, stripped stone and panelling, no smoking area, back barn restaurant (Fri/Sat evening and for good Sun lunch); children welcome if eating, garden tables, open all day Weds-Sun (Keith and Chris O'Neill, Ian and Nita Cooper)

ELTON [SK2260]

☆ *Duke of York* DE4 2BW [village signed off B5056 W of Matlock; Main St]: Classic old-fashioned spotless local in charming Peak District village, very long-serving friendly landlady, lovely little quarry-tiled back tap room with coal fire in massive fireplace, glazed bar and hatch to corridor, nice prints and more fires in the two front ones – one like private parlour with piano and big dining table (no food, just crisps); Adnams Broadside and Mansfield, welcoming regulars, darts, dominoes; lavatories out by the pig sty; open 8.30pm-11pm, and Sun lunchtime (the Didler, John Dwane, Pete Baker, Tich Critchlow)

FENNY BENTLEY [SK1850]

Bentley Brook DE6 1LF [A515 N of Ashbourne]: Sizeable place changing hands so may well change character, but has had Banks's, Marstons Pedigree and perhaps its own Leatherbritches beers in big open-plan bare-boards bar/dining room, central log fire, communicating restaurant, popular food inc herbs and produce from the garden (sold kitchen/meat products too); piped music; dogs have been welcome, terrace picnic-sets, barbecue, good play area, 11 bedrooms, open all day (LYM)

FERNILEE [SK0179]

☆ *Shady Oak* SK23 7HD [A5004 Whalley Bridge—Buxton]: Attractive and welcoming roadside pub in glorious countryside, doing well under new management – generous quality food from uncomplicated menu, not expensive, big side helping of steaming vegetables, good service, several Jennings ales and Marstons Pedigree, range of coffees and teas, log fires, daily papers, traditional décor, restful atmosphere, no music or machines; tables out in front overlooking Goyt valley, plans for new courtyard garden, three smartly comfortable new bedrooms (W K Wood,

Steve Redfern, BB, Andi Strain)

FOOLOW [SK2078]

☆ *Barrel* S32 5QD [Bretton, N of village]: Friendly new unassuming landlord in magnificently placed stone-roofed turnpike inn, old-fashioned low-beamed and flagstoned bar with lots of pictures and cosy log-fire end, Hardys & Hansons ales and Marstons Pedigree, good range of malt whiskies, decent bar food; piped music; children welcome, front terrace and courtyard garden, five-county views and good walking, good value bedrooms, open all day wknds (LYM, Mrs J Clarke-Williams, Phil and Anne Nash, Jo Lilley, Simon Calvert)

FROGGATT EDGE [SK2577]

Grouse S11 7TZ [Longshaw, off B6054 NE of Froggatt]: Plush front bar, log fire and wooden benches in back bar, big dining room, good home cooking from sandwiches to imaginative dishes, good value smaller helpings, Banks's and guest beers, friendly service, handsome views; verandah and terrace, neatly kept bedrooms, good moorland walking country (C J Fletcher, J S Bethell)

GLOSSOP [SK0294]

Globe SK13 8HJ [High St W]: Good interesting choice of changing ales and farm ciders, comfortable relaxed atmosphere, friendly licensees, frequent live music; open till late Fri/Sat (the Didler)

Star SK13 7DD [Howard St]: Interesting changing real ales such as local Howard Town, Pictish, Shaws and Whim and farm ciders in bare-boards alehouse opp station, friendly knowledgeable staff; piped music; open all day (the Didler, Dennis Jones)

GREAT HUCKLOW [SK1777]

Queen Anne SK17 8RF: Comfortable and friendly 17th-c stone-built pub, beams, big log fire and gleaming copper, Adnams and two good changing guest beers, good soft drinks choice, good simple food (may be just soup and sandwiches, winter lunchtimes), walkers' bar, pub games; piped music; dogs welcome, french windows to small back terrace and charming garden with picnic-sets and lovely views, two quiet bedrooms, good walks, cl Tues lunchtime (the Didler, Derek and Sylvia Stephenson, JJW, CMW, Mrs S Fairbrother, B M Eldridge, Richard, John Dwane)

GREAT LONGSTONE [SK1971]

☆ *Crispin* DE45 1TZ [Main St]: Spotless pub doing very well under welcoming and popular new landlord, good generous food inc OAP lunches, Robinsons ales, punctilious service, log fire; picnic-sets out in front, nice spot at top of *Peak Practice* village (Peter F Marshall, Iain Greenhalgh)

HARTINGTON [SK1260]

Devonshire Arms SK17 0AL [Market Pl]: Attractive old pub with good choice of real ales such as Greene King and Charles Wells, enjoyable home-made food, friendly staff, log fires, flagstoned public bar welcoming walkers and dogs; comfortable bedrooms, tables out in front facing village duck pond, more in small garden behind, good walks *(Keith and Chris O'Neill, Alan Johnson, Dr D J and Mrs S C Walker, Richard)*

HATHERSAGE [SK2381]
Millstone S32 1DA [Sheffield Rd (A6187 E)]: Good generous food in bar and side brasserie with interesting menu, courteous service, adventurous choice of real ales, wines and whiskies, lots of knick-knacks and antiques (many for sale); tables outside with excellent Hope Valley views, bedrooms *(DC)*

HAYFIELD [SK0387]
☆ *Pack Horse* SK22 2EP [off A624 Glossop—Chapel-en-le-Frith; Market St]: Smartly modernised dining pub with good fresh food all day at reasonable prices, from baguettes to some interesting main dishes and Sun lunch, Black Sheep, Greene King IPA and Fullers London Pride, good choice of spirits and wines, friendly efficient service, nice chatty atmosphere, cosier areas near door; piped music; open all day *(BB, Dr M A Turner, Ivan Sangster)*
Sportsman SK22 2LE [Kinder Rd]: Roomy traditional pub, tidy and well run, with wide choice of enjoyable food, friendly staff, Thwaites beers, decent wines, lots of malt whiskies, two coal fires; handy for Kinder Scout walks *(A J Girling)*

HEANOR [SK4345]
Mundy Arms DE75 7LX [Ilkeston Rd (A6007 S)]: Smart dining pub with enjoyable food in pleasant atmosphere, sensible prices, three Hardys & Hansons ales, beams and alcoves, country dressers with china and ornaments *(Derek and Sylvia Stephenson)*

HIGHAM [SK3959]
Greyhound DE55 6EF [A61 N of Alfreton]: Large dining pub with wide food choice (free tortilla chips and dip while you wait), Marstons Pedigree, no smoking areas; piped pop music; disabled access and facilities, heated covered terrace, small garden with play area *(JJW, CMW)*

HOGNASTON [SK2350]
☆ *Red Lion* DE6 1PR [Village signposted off B5035 Ashbourne—Wirksworth]: Open-plan beamed bar with three open fires, attractive mix of old tables, old-fashioned settles and other seats on ancient flagstones, Marstons Pedigree and changing ales such as two from Derby, no smoking conservatory restaurant (the food can be a plus point); piped music; handy for Carsington Water; bedrooms *(Fred and Lorraine Gill, Mrs P J Carroll, Brian and Jacky Wilson, LYM, Brian and Jean Hepworth, M G Hart, Jeff and Wendy Williams, Richard, Peter Cole, Derek and Sylvia Stephenson, Philip and Susan Philcox, Dr David Clegg)*

HOLYMOORSIDE [SK3369]
Lamb S42 7EU [Loads Rd, just off Holymoor Rd]: Small, cosy and spotless two-room village pub in leafy spot, up to half a dozen or so particularly well kept ales such as Adnams, Fullers London Pride and John Smiths, friendly landlady, coal fire, pub games; tables outside, cl wkdy lunchtimes *(the Didler)*

HORSLEY WOODHOUSE [SK3944]
Old Oak DE7 6AW [Main St (A609 Belper—Ilkeston)]: Attractively basic two-bar beamed pub reopened by Leadmill, their interesting ales and two guest beers, farm cider, may be cobs and pork pies, coal fires, friendly locals, back rooms with toys, games and pool, no piped music (occasional live); children and dogs welcome, hatch to covered courtyard tables, cl wkdy lunchtimes, open all day wknds *(the Didler, Rona Murdoch)*

HULLAND WARD [SK2647]
Black Horse DE6 3EE [Hulland Ward; A517 Ashbourne—Belper]: 17th-c pub with good fresh food at sensible prices inc local game in low-beamed quarry-tiled bar or back country-view dining room, popular Sun carvery, Bass, Harviestoun Bitter & Twisted and other changing ales, friendly licensees; children welcome, garden tables, comfortable bedrooms, nr Carsington Water, open all day Fri-Sun *(Martin and Alison Stainsby, the Didler)*

ILKESTON [SK4643]
Bridge Inn DE7 8RD [Bridge St, Cotmanhay; off A609/A6007]: Welcoming two-room local by Erewash Canal, popular with fishermen and boaters for early breakfast and sandwich lunches; low-priced Hardys & Hansons Bitter and Mild, interesting photographs in lounge, darts and dominoes; well behaved children allowed, nice back garden with play area, open all day *(the Didler)*

KIRK LANGLEY [SK2937]
Bluebell DE6 4LW [Adams Rd/B5020]: Two-bar country pub with enjoyable reasonably priced blackboard food inc children's dishes and Sun lunch, Bass, Greene King Old Speckled Hen and Marstons Pedigree, friendly staff; garden picnic-sets, small play area *(Deb and John Arthur)*

KNOCKERDOWN [SK2351]
Knockerdown Inn DE6 1NQ [1½ miles S of Brassington on B5035]: Well organised and busy family pub with teacups on beams, pictures and bric-a-brac inc Harley-Davidson memorabilia, wide choice of reasonably priced generous home-made food in bar and restaurant using own free-range eggs, Marstons, no piped music; garden with good views and playground, farm animals, even ostriches, nr Carsington reservoir *(Michael and Maggie Betton, Martin and Alison Stainsby, Steve Jennings)*

LADYBOWER RESERVOIR [SK1986]
Ladybower S33 0AX [A57 Sheffield—Glossop, junction with A6013]: Fine views of attractive reservoir from open-plan stone-built pub, clean and spacious, with good value food, real ales, red plush seats; children welcome, stone seats outside, good walks *(Richard)*

MAPLETON [SK1647]
☆ *Okeover Arms* DE6 2AB [back rd just NW of Ashbourne]: Attractively refurbished two-room pub with nice woodburner and candles on pale wood tables, comfortable dining room, tasty food using named local suppliers from ciabattas to restaurant dishes and Sun roasts,

real ales from local Thorndale brewery plus
Adnams Broadside and Timothy Taylors
Landlord, dozens of malt whiskies (some very
rare), good wines, friendly efficient service,
daily papers, magazines and books; piped
music; pleasant garden with good timber play
area and views up sheep-dotted hill, pleasant
village with interesting domed church, good
riverside walks (pub has bootwash outside)
(D P and M A Miles, BB, A C Johnstone)

MATLOCK [SK2960]
Crown DE4 3AT [Crown Sq]: Welcoming
child-friendly Wetherspoons, useful for real
ales and their usual value food; open all day
(Fred and Lorraine Gill, DFL)

MAYFIELD [SK1444]
Rose & Crown DE6 2JT [Main Rd (B5032 off
A52 W of Ashbourne)]: Comfortable pub with
welcoming newish chef/landlord and wife,
good food with plenty of choice, Marstons
Pedigree and good range of reasonably priced
wines by the glass, good service, log fire and
thriving atmosphere in carpeted bar, no
smoking restaurant; children welcome, garden
tables, local walks leaflets, four good
bedrooms (John and Karen Wilkinson)

MELBOURNE [SK3826]
Olde Packhorse DE73 8BZ [Main Street,
King's Newton]: Unpretentious pub with wide
choice of bargain food inc popular carvery
(best to book wknds), Robinsons ales, friendly
staff, two main rooms; bar can get a bit smoky
(David Barnes)

MILLERS DALE [SK1473]
Anglers Rest SK17 8SN [just down Litton
Lane; pub is PH on OS Sheet 119, map ref
142734]: New licensees putting more emphasis
on the food side in creeper-clad two-bar pub
enjoyed for its lovely quiet riverside setting on
Monsal Trail, wonderful gorge views and
riverside walks; real ales such as Storm
Damage, efficient service, open fire, no
smoking dining room; children welcome,
attractive village (David Crook, John Wooll,
Peter F Marshall, the Didler)

MILLTOWN [SK3561]
☆ *Miners Arms* S45 0HA [off B6036 SE of
Ashover; Oakstedge Lane]: Only a lack of
recent reader reports keeps this nice no
smoking pub out of the main entries, L-shaped
layout with a local feel up nearer the door,
enjoyable proper home cooking (best to book),
friendly service, Archers and Greene King
Abbot; may be quiet piped classical music;
children welcome, attractive country walks
right from the door, cl Sun evening, Mon/Tues,
winter Weds, and ten days Aug (Tony Fisher,
the Didler, LYM)

MONYASH [SK1566]
Bulls Head DE45 1JH [B5055 W of Bakewell]:
Well worn in high-ceilinged local with
unpretentious furnishings, horse pictures, shelf
of china, mullioned windows, sensibly priced
food inc sandwiches and help-yourself Sun
buffet, real ales such as Carlsberg Burton,
Tetleys Mild and Whim Hartington, good log
fire; two-room dining room, darts, dominoes,
pool in small back bar; may be quiet piped

music; children and muddy dogs welcome,
long pews out facing small green, simple
bedrooms, attractive village in fine walking
country, open all day (BB, Mrs S Fairbrother,
Alan and Paula McCully, Pam and John Smith,
Mark and Mary Fairman)

MORLEY [SK3941]
Three Horseshoes DE7 6DF: Friendly open-
plan stone-built pub with wide choice of
generous enjoyable food (not Sun evening),
three Marstons beers from central no smoking
bar, dining one end, darts, TV and games
machine the other; quiet piped music, Mon
quiz night; children welcome, picnic-sets in
small garden with play area (JJW, CMW)

NEW MILLS [SJ9886]
Fox SK22 3AY [Brookbottom; OS Sheet 109
map ref 985864]: Tucked-away traditional
country local with good value simple food (not
Tues evening) from toasties up, a few extra hot
dishes recently, good long-serving landlord,
particularly well kept Robinsons, log fire, darts
and pool; children welcome, good walking
area (so can get crowded wknds)
(John Fiander, Bob Broadhurst, David Hoult,
the Didler)

NEWTON SOLNEY [SK2825]
Brickmakers Arms DE15 0SJ [Main St (B5008
NE of Burton)]: Friendly new licensees doing
good choice of enjoyable food from upgraded
kitchen inc small helpings for children, Bass
and Hardys & Hansons Bitter and 1832, good
service, three comfortable rooms inc
restaurant, beams and brasses; tables on small
terrace, open all day (Sun afternoon break)
(the Didler, Deb and John Arthur)

OAKERTHORPE [SK3856]
Amber DE55 7LL: Charming old-fashioned
pub with friendly landlady, Abbeydale
Absolution and Timothy Taylors Landlord,
limited bar snacks, blazing winter fires, lots of
antiques inc a piano, well-worn seating; good
views from the back terrace (Kevin Blake)
Anchor DE55 7LP: Comfortable partly 18th-c
dining pub with linked rooms and bookable
back restaurant extension, good choice (not
Sun/Mon evenings) inc game and good Sun
carvery, Cropton ales (unique for this part of
the world), relaxed pleasant service; open all
day wknds (can be busy then) (Derek and
Sylvia Stephenson)

OCKBROOK [SK4236]
☆ *Royal Oak* DE72 3SE [village signed off B6096
just outside Spondon; Green Lane]: Quiet
18th-c village local run by same welcoming
family for half a century, small unspoilt rooms
(one no smoking), bargain honest food (not
wknd evenings) from super lunchtime rolls to
steaks, Sun lunch and OAP meals, Bass and
four interesting guest beers, good soft drinks
choice, tiled-floor tap room, turkey-carpeted
snug, inner bar with Victorian prints, larger and
lighter no smoking side room, nice old settle in
entrance corridor, open fires, darts and
dominoes, no music or machines; tables in
sheltered cottage garden, more on cobbled front
courtyard, separate play area (Robert F Smith,
the Didler, BB, Pete Baker)

OWLER BAR [SK2978]

☆ *Peacock* S17 3BQ [A621 2 miles S of Totley]: Warm, welcoming and attractive Chef & Brewer in moorland setting with panoramic views of Sheffield and Peak District, traditional character and layout with big log fires, usual wide food choice all day from huge sandwiches up, helpful attentive staff, good beer choice, large no smoking area away from central bar; open all day *(R T and J C Moggridge, Keith and Chris O'Neill, Irene and Ray Atkin)*

PARWICH [SK1854]

Sycamore DE6 1QL: Chatty old country pub with cheerful landlady, good log fire in simple but comfortable main bar, generous wholesome food lunchtimes and most Weds-Sat evenings, Robinsons and Theakstons, lots of old local photographs, hatch-served tap room with games; tables out in front and on grass by car park, quiet village not far from Tissington *(the Didler, Pete Baker)*

PENTRICH [SK3852]

☆ *Dog* DE5 3RE [Main Rd (B6016 N of Ripley)]: Extended traditional pub, cosy and smartly fitted out, very popular for its fresh up-to-date food (best to book), reasonable prices, Bass, Marstons Pedigree and a guest beer (you can choose to have it with or without a head), nice wines by the glass, friendly and attentive well turned out staff, beams and panelling; tables in attractive garden behind, quiet village, good walks *(the Didler, Robert F Smith, Derek and Sylvia Stephenson, John E Robson)*

PILSLEY [SK2371]

Devonshire Arms DE45 1UL [off A619 Bakewell—Baslow; High St]: Good value generous home cooking worth waiting for inc interesting fish and Thurs-Sat evening carvery (may need to book), appealing lounge bar with warm atmosphere and bric-a-brac, public bar area for walkers and children, open fires, Boddingtons, Mansfield and a guest beer, San Miguel on tap; quiz and music nights; bedrooms, handy for Chatsworth farm and craft shops, lovely village *(Peter F Marshall)*

RIPLEY [SK3950]

Pear Tree DE5 3HR [Derby Rd (B6179)]: Full Hardys & Hansons range inc seasonal beers in friendly unspoilt two-room local, two good coal fires, darts and dominoes; open all day *(the Didler)*

ROWARTH [SK0189]

Little Mill SK22 1EB [pub now signed well locally; off A626 in Marple Bridge at Mellor sign, sharp left at Rowarth sign]: New landlord in beautifully tucked-away family pub with unusual features inc working waterwheel, big open-plan bar with plenty of seating, good choice of real ales, popular food inc upstairs restaurant, big log fire, pub games; frequent live music; children welcome, pretty garden dell across stream great for them, with good play area, vintage Pullman-carriage bedrooms, open all day *(LYM, David Hoult, Dennis Jones)*

ROWSLEY [SK2565]

Grouse & Claret DE4 2EB [A6 Bakewell—Matlock]: Attractive and spotless no smoking family dining pub in old stone building,

spacious and comfortable, with friendly helpful staff, enterprising food (all day wknd) from sandwiches and light dishes up as well as the usual pubby dishes, decent wines, open fires, taproom popular with walkers; tables outside, good value bedrooms *(David Carr)*

SAWLEY [SK4833]

Harrington Arms NG10 4QB [Derby Rd (B6540)]: Open-plan pub with beams and panelling, wide choice of food all day, Hardys & Hansons ales, no smoking areas, Sun quiz night; quiet piped music, no dogs; disabled access and facilities, garden and heated terrace, open all day *(JJW, CMW)*

SHARDLOW [SK4430]

☆ *Malt Shovel* DE72 2HG [3½ miles from M1 junction 24, via A6 towards Derby; The Wharf]: Busy old-world beamed pub in 18th-c former maltings, interesting odd-angled layout, Banks's and Marstons Pedigree, quick friendly service, good value food (not Sat evening) from baguettes and baked potatoes up, good central open fire, farm tools and bric-a-brac; no small children; lots of tables out on terrace by Trent & Mersey Canal, pretty hanging baskets and boxes *(the Didler, John Beeken, LYM)*

Navigation DE72 2HA [London Rd]: Comfortable high-beamed pub with decent food inc wider evening choice, real ales, pictures and bric-a-brac in big split-level lounge, dining room, games room; picnic-sets and play area in garden by marina *(Brian and Jean Hepworth)*

☆ *Old Crown* DE72 2HL [off A50 just W of M1 junction 24; Cavendish Bridge, E of village]: Masses of jugs and mugs on the beams, lots of other interesting bric-a-brac, half a dozen or more real ales such as Bass, Burtonwood, Marstons Pedigree, Thwaites and Wychwood Hobgoblin, nice choice of malt whiskies, very friendly service, good value sandwiches, baguettes and standard pub dishes (not wknd evenings); children and dogs welcome, simple good value bedrooms (with videos inc children's ones), good breakfast, open all day *(Blaise Vyner, the Gray family, Kevin Blake, the Didler, Ian Phillips, Alan and Sue Folwell, Brian and Ruth Archer, Mr and Mrs John Taylor, Bren and Val Speed, R T and J C Moggridge, Michael and Marion Buchanan, LYM, Michael J Caley)*

Shakespeare DE72 2GP [old A6]: Friendly service, good pubby lunchtime food inc children's, evening restaurant (not Sun/Mon), good real ale range *(Brian and Jean Hepworth)*

SMISBY [SK3419]

Smisby Arms LE65 2UA [Nelsons Sq]: Ancient low-beamed no smoking pub with good friendly village atmosphere and no frills, Marstons Pedigree and guest beers, sensible choice of enjoyable food from lunchtime sandwiches up inc delicious puddings and Mon steak night, pleasantly bright little dining extension *(Brian and Jean Hepworth, John and Hazel Williams)*

SOUTH NORMANTON [SK4456]

Clock DE55 2AA [off M1 junction 28 via B6019; Market St]: Friendly two-bar pub with two real ales, no smoking lounge; back garden, open all day (no food Mon/Tues) *(JJW, CMW)*

SPONDON [SK3935]

☆ *Malt Shovel* DE21 7LH [off A6096 on edge of Derby, via Church Hill into Potter St]: Unspoilt traditional pub with decent cheap food, Bass, Burtonwood Top Hat and guest beers from hatch in tiled corridor with cosy panelled and quarry-tiled or turkey-carpeted rooms off (one no smoking), old-fashioned décor, huge inglenook, steps down to big games bar with full-size pool table; lots of picnic-sets, some under cover, in big well used back garden with good play area *(the Didler, BB)*

STANTON IN PEAK [SK2364]

Flying Childers DE4 2LW [off B5056 Bakewell—Ashbourne; Main Rd]: Cosy and unspoilt beamed right-hand bar with fireside settles, comfortable lounge, changing ales such as Adnams, Black Sheep and Charles Wells Bombardier, friendly service, good value lunchtime soup and rolls, dominoes and cribbage; in delightful steep stone village overlooking rich green valley, good walks, may be cl Mon and Thurs lunchtimes *(the Didler)*

STARKHOLMES [SK3058]

White Lion DE4 5JA [Starkholmes Rd]: Well run open-plan village pub in exceptional location, views over Matlock Bath and Derwent valley, enjoyable wholesome food at reasonable prices, Burtonwood, Marstons Pedigree, Whim Hartington and a guest beer, attentive staff, low ceilings and stripped stone, coal fire in restaurant; pleasant tables outside, boules, bedrooms (with fridge for good self-serve continental breakfast), open all day wknds *(B M Eldridge, the Didler, Mark and Mary Fairman, David and Sue Smith)*

STONEY MIDDLETON [SK2375]

Moon S32 4TW [Townend (A623)]: Good sensibly priced food inc OAP lunchtime bargains, real ales such as Black Sheep and Charles Wells Bombardier, reasonably priced wines, friendly staff, nice décor with old photographs; handy for dales walks *(Richard, A and B D Craig)*

SUTTON CUM DUCKMANTON [SK4371]

Arkwright Arms S44 5JG [A632 Bolsover—Chesterfield]: Friendly mock-Tudor pub with bar, pool room and no smoking dining room (children welcome here), all with real fires, good value food (not Sat/Sun evenings), four or five changing real ales; quiet piped music; garden and play area, open all day *(JJW, CMW, Derek and Sylvia Stephenson)*

SWANWICK [SK4053]

Steam Packet DE55 1AB [Derby Rd (B6179/B6016)]: Chatty 19th-c local popular for its good real ale range inc Adnams, Black Sheep and Jennings (beer festivals Apr and Oct), comfortable traditional bar with coal fire, cosy lounge, food (not Sun evening to Weds lunchtime); open all day (not till 2pm Mon-Weds) *(the Didler)*

SWARKESTONE [SK3628]

Crewe & Harpur Arms DE73 7JA [Woodshop Lane]: Tidy bow-windowed family dining pub with wide choice of enjoyable food, friendly

atmosphere, Marstons ales; big parasols in walled garden over road with play area, good value bedrooms, handy for Calke Abbey *(Dave Braisted)*

TANSLEY [SK3259]

Tavern DE4 5FR [A615 Matlock—Mansfield]: Well run dining pub with good value well prepared traditional food from lunchtime baguettes and baked potatoes to duck, bass, steaks and good Sun lunch, relaxed atmosphere, friendly staff, Marstons Pedigree, Tetleys and another real ale, Weston's farm cider, good value wines, no smoking restaurant *(Steve Nye, Kobi Thompson, Brian Coleman)*

TICKNALL [SK3523]

Staff of Life DE73 1JH [High St (Ashby Rd)]: Recently completely refurbished, with small areas off main bar, some emphasis on enjoyable food (Sun lunch particularly popular – worth booking), real ales such as Batemans and Timothy Taylors Landlord, good friendly service, open fire; bedrooms, handy for Calke Abbey *(David Barnes)*

TIDESWELL [SK1575]

George SK17 8NU [Commercial Rd (B6049, between A623 and A6 E of Buxton)]: Unpretentious L-shaped bar/lounge inc dining area and linked no smoking room, three Hardys & Hansons ales, modestly priced wines, open fires, paintings by local artists, separate bar with darts and pool; piped music; children and dogs welcome, by remarkable church, tables in front overlooking pretty village, sheltered back garden, pleasant walks *(BB, Michael Butler, the Didler, Alan Johnson, Mrs S Fairbrother)*

Horse & Jockey SK17 8JZ [Queen St]: Recently refurbished with beams, bare boards and coal fires, real ales inc Theakstons, modestly priced food; four bedrooms, good walks *(Michael Butler)*

Star SK17 8LD [High St]: Several unspoilt rooms with local paintings (most for sale) and old photographs, three real ales, short good value wine list, brisk cheerful service; unobtrusive piped music, public bar with TV and games machine; reasonably priced bedrooms *(Alan Johnson, Dennis Jones)*

WENSLEY [SK2661]

Red Lion DE4 2LH [B5057 NW of Matlock]: Friendly and utterly unspoilt no smoking farm pub with chatty brother and sister owners, assorted 1950s-ish furniture, piano in main bar (landlord likes sing-songs), unusual tapestry in second room (usually locked, so ask landlady), no games or piped music, just bottled beer, tea, coffee, soft drinks and filled sandwiches or home-baked rolls perhaps using fillings from the garden – may be their fruit for sale, too; outside gents'; open all day *(the Didler, Pete Baker, Richard and Margaret McPhee)*

WHITTINGTON [SK3875]

Cock & Magpie S41 9QW [Church Street N, behind museum]: Old stone-built dining pub with good choice from sandwiches and OAP bargains up, friendly well organised service, particularly well kept Banks's and Marstons Pedigree, good soft drinks choice, conservatory, separate public bar with games room; piped music, no dogs; children welcome in dining areas, next to Revolution House museum *(Keith and Chris O'Neill, JJW, CMW)*

WHITTINGTON MOOR [SK3873]

☆ *Derby Tup* S41 8LS [Sheffield Rd; B6057 just S of A61 roundabout]: Spotless no-frills Tynemill pub with up to ten good changing ales, good choice of other drinks, pleasant service, simple furniture and lots of standing room, two small no smoking rooms (children allowed here), daily papers, good value basic bar lunches; can get very busy wknd evenings; dogs welcome, open all day Fri-Sun *(the Didler, LYM, Peter F Marshall)*

Red Lion S41 8LX [Sheffield Rd (B6057)]: Friendly two-room 19th-c stone-built local tied to Old Mill with their real ales, hard-working landlady, thriving atmosphere, old local photographs; sports TV; open all day *(the Didler, Keith and Chris O'Neill)*

WINSTER [SK2460]

Bowling Green DE4 2DS [East Bank, by NT Market House]: Pleasantly traditional refurbished local with character landlord and cheerful staff, real ales such as Whim Hartington, enjoyable generous food, efficient service even when busy, log fire, dining area and family conservatory; open all day wknds, cl Mon/Tues *(Theocsbrian, Andrew Beardsley, Alison Lawrence)*

Miners Standard DE4 2DR [Bank Top (B5056 above village)]: Comfortable 17th-c local with

friendly family service, Marstons Pedigree, Storm and a guest beer, good value generous food inc huge pies, big open fires, lead-mining photographs and minerals, ancient well, restaurant; children allowed away from bar, attractive view from garden, interesting stone-built village below, open all day wknds *(the Didler)*

WIRKSWORTH [SK2854]

Blacks Head DE4 4ET [Market Pl]: Civilised local with coal fires, pleasant staff, Hardys & Hansons ales, sensible prices *(S Holder)*

Royal Oak DE4 4FG [North End]: Traditional small backstreet local with key fobs, old copper kettles and other bric-a-brac, friendly licensees and locals, changing ales inc Bass, Marstons Pedigree, Timothy Taylors Landlord and Whim Hartington, dominoes, may be filled cobs; opens 8pm, cl lunchtime exc Sun *(the Didler)*

YOULGREAVE [SK2164]

☆ *George* DE45 1WN [Alport Lane/Church St]: Handsome stone-built 17th-c inn opp Norman church, friendly landlord and locals, wide range of good straightforward low-priced home-made food all day inc game, real ales inc John Smiths and Theakstons Mild, comfortable banquettes, flagstoned tap room (walkers and dogs welcome), games room; juke box, live music Sat; attractive village handy for Lathkill Dale and Haddon Hall, roadside tables, simple bedrooms, open all day *(the Didler, Russell Grimshaw, Kerry Purcell)*

Devon

This huge county is one of Britain's best-loved areas for pubs. It offers a great choice, whatever you want: unspoilt and simple, ancient and picturesque, or stylish and civilised. What shines through all these is a genuine friendliness, whether it's from the licensees, the staff or the local regulars. The food here is extremely good, there are a lot of interesting small independent brewers, and it's nice to come across proper farm ciders, too. All this amid some lovely scenery ranging from quiet sheltered creeks to windswept moorland, with plenty of walks all round. Pubs on top form this year include the attractively placed Masons Arms at Branscombe, the fishy Drewe Arms in Broadhembury, the thriving Coach & Horses in Buckland Brewer, the friendly Old Thatch Inn at Cheriton Bishop, the very popular Anchor at Cockwood, the chatty New Inn in Coleford, the not-so-easily reached Turf Hotel at Exminster, the laid-back Duke of York at Iddesleigh, the quirky London at Molland, the waterside Ship in Noss Mayo, the interesting Harris Arms at Portgate, the well run Tower at Slapton, the busy Sea Trout at Staverton, the rather special Bridge Inn at Topsham, the packed-out Start Bay in Torcross, and the local Rugglestone near Widecombe. For an enjoyable meal out with super food, there's the Masons Arms at Branscombe, the Drewe Arms at Broadhembury, the Merrie Harriers at Clayhidon, the New Inn at Coleford, the Culm Valley at Culmstock, the Dartmoor Union at Holbeton, the Harris Arms at Portgate, the Jack in the Green at Rockbeare, the Tower at Slapton, the Kings Arms at Strete, and the Diggers Rest at Woodbury Salterton. A clutch of new entries for this year, which also offer good or in some cases very good food, include the Turtley Corn Mill at Avonwick (a stylish and extensive conversion of a tall mill house), the unusual Old Chapel at St Anns Chapel (part of the building is a 13th-c wayfarers' chapel), the riverside Steam Packet in Totnes, the prettily placed Maltsters Arms at Tuckenhay, and the thoroughly up-to-date Rose & Crown at Yealmpton (owned by the same people as the Dartmoor Union at Holbeton). Indeed, it is one of these new entries, the Rose & Crown at Yealmpton, which takes the top title of Devon Dining Pub of the Year, giving you a dining choice between the pub itself and its separate accompanying fish restaurant. There are so many good pubs in the Lucky Dip section at the end of the chapter that it's worth marking your card with ones on particularly good current form: the Court Farm at Abbotskerswell, Beaver in Appledore, Cricket at Beesands, Chichester Arms at Bishop's Tawton, Poltimore Arms at Brayford, Rockford Inn at Brendon, Pilchard on Burgh Island, Ring o' Bells in Chagford, Linny at Coffinswell, Ferry Boat at Dittisham, Fortescue Arms at East Allington, Double Locks just outside Exeter, Poachers at Ide, Grove at King's Nympton, Royal Oak at Meavy, Ring of Bells at North Bovey, Stag at Rackenford, Blue Ball at Sandy Gate, Highwayman at Sourton, Oxenham Arms at South Zeal, Tradesmans Arms at Stokenham, Golden Lion at Tipton St John, Passage House in Topsham and Lymington Arms at Wembworthy. The Old Ship in Sidmouth is another good place, and perhaps a replacement for the same owner's Blue Ball at Sidford, whose proud run of 25 years in the *Guide* without a break has sadly been ended by a disastrous fire. Drinks prices in Devon are more or less in line with the national average – very much less in the case of Wetherspoons' Imperial in Exeter, which has beers at bargain prices. In most pubs, we found that the cheapest beer on offer was usually a local one, such as Otter (now the top Devon brew), Branscombe Vale, Teignworthy, Summerskills, Princetown or Blackdown; or from Cornwall or Somerset brewers such as Sharps, Cotleigh, St Austell (who brew Dartmoor Best), Butcombe, Blackawton (from Cornwall despite its name), Skinners or Exmoor.

ASHPRINGTON SX8156 Map 1
Durant Arms 🏠
Village signposted off A381 S of Totnes; OS Sheet 202 map reference 819571; TQ9 7UP

It would be stretching the imagination a bit to describe this attractive Victorian gabled place as a pub, but readers continue to enjoy their visits here. It's more of a small country hotel with a busy dining side and attached bar but they still stock St Austell Dartmoor Best and Tribute on handpump. The charming and helpful licensees keep the three linked areas spotlessly clean, and there are turkey carpets throughout, comfortably upholstered red dining chairs around clothed tables, and a small corner bar counter in one area with a couple of bar stools in front; piped music. Popular food includes sandwiches, home-made soup (£4.25), chicken liver pâté (£4.95), fresh crab cocktail (£5.95), smoked duck and chicken salad with roasted vegetables (£6.25), moussaka, roast rib of local beef with yorkshire pudding or smoked haddock and broccoli bake (£7.95), steak and kidney pie (£8.95), fresh poached salmon in prawn sauce (£11.25), venison fillet with shallots and port (£16.95), and puddings such as rhubarb crumble, raspberry brûlée or bread and butter pudding (£4.20); best to book if you want to be sure of a table. Good, attentive service. The no smoking dining room has lots of oil and watercolours by local artists on the walls. The flagged back courtyard has teak furniture, and the bedrooms are carefully decorated and comfortable. *(Recommended by Gerry and Rosemary Dobson, Howard and Lorna Lambert, Ann and Bob Westbrook, MP, Brian Green, Bob and Margaret Holder)*

Free house ~ Licensees Graham and Eileen Ellis ~ Real ale ~ Bar food ~ Restaurant ~ (01803) 732240 ~ Children welcome with restrictions ~ Dogs allowed in bar ~ Open 11.30-2.30, 6.30-11; 12-2.30, 7-10.30 Sun ~ Bedrooms: £45B/£75B

AVONWICK SX6958 Map 1
Turtley Corn Mill ♀
½ mile off A38 roundabout at SW end of S Brent bypass; TQ10 9ES

This huge newly reworked pub, no smoking throughout, is a very promising venture by the people who have the Ship at Noss Mayo. The careful conversion of the tall mill house (with its waterwheel now standing idle) gives a spreading series of linked areas, each with some individuality – bookcases, fat church candles and oriental rugs in one area, dark flagstones by the bar, a strategic woodburning stove dividing one part, a side enclave with a modern pew built in around a really big table, and so on. Throughout, lighting is good, with plenty of big windows looking out over the grounds, a pleasant array of prints and some other decorations (framed 78rpm discs, elderly wireless sets, house plants) on pastel walls, and a mix of comfortable dining chairs around heavy baluster-leg tables in a variety of sizes. They have a commendable range of wines and sherries including good french house wines, Butcombe Blonde, Princetown Jail and IPA, St Austell Tribute and Summerskills Tamar on handpump, 50 malt whiskies and decent coffee. The food, using local produce, largely follows the pattern which has proved a hit with readers at the Ship, and besides sandwiches (from £4.25) and warm panini (from £5.25) might include chicken liver pâté with toasted brioche and red onion marmalade (£5.75), potted shrimps on a toasted crumpet (£6.50), ploughman's (£8.25), vegetarian homity pie (£8.50), sausages with herb mash, black pudding and gravy (£8.95), ham hock with parsley sauce (£9.50), thai pork rissoles with lime leaves, chillies and mint (£9.75), local haddock in real ale batter with minted mushy peas (£11.25), 10oz rib-eye steak with bèarnaise sauce (£16.95), and puddings such as apricot, walnut and ginger pudding with butterscotch sauce or deep chocolate and orange cheesecake (£5.25); as we went to press, they were celebrating greek food with specials like mezze for two (£8.75), moussaka (£10.95), and baklava (£5.25). On our visit in late spring 2006, everything was still pristine – all neat and new; the service then, although efficient and faultless, perhaps needed time to develop a more personal and friendly touch. The extensive gardens, spreading down to a lake, have well spaced picnic-sets and a giant chess set, and some landscaping work continues: they will be a big plus in summer, as will the good parking area. The only serious minus is that they try to keep your credit card if you eat outside. With its sister pub the Dartmoor Union at Holbeton this comes from the Wykeham Inns stable, a new small local group. *(Recommended by John Evans)*

Free house ~ Licensees Lesley and Bruce Brunning ~ Real ale ~ Bar food (12-9.30(9 Sun) or a little earlier if busy) ~ Restaurant ~ (01364) 646100 ~ Children welcome until 7pm ~ Dogs welcome ~ Open 11.30-11; 12-10.30 Sun

BRANSCOMBE   SY1888   Map 1

Fountain Head ◧

Upper village, above the robust old church; village signposted off A3052 Sidmouth—Seaton, then from Branscombe Square follow road up hill towards Sidmouth, and after about a mile turn left after the church; OS Sheet 192 map reference SY188889; EX12 3BG

Popular with both locals and visitors, this 500-year-old stone pub remains old-fashioned and unspoilt. The Branscombe Brewery still supply their own-brewed beers such as Branoc, Jolly Geff, and summer Summa That, and there are guests such as Fullers London Pride or Loddon Flight of Fancy on handpump; the annual beer festival takes place in June. The room on the left – formerly a smithy – has forge tools and horseshoes on the high oak beams, a log fire in the original raised firebed with its tall central chimney, and cushioned pews and mate's chairs. On the right, an irregularly shaped, more orthodox snug room has another log fire, white-painted plank ceiling with an unusual carved ceiling-rose, brown-varnished panelled walls, and rugs on its flagstone-and-lime-ash floor. Lunchtime bar food includes sandwiches (from £3.95), chicken liver pâté (£4.25), ploughman's (£5.95), home-cooked ham and eggs (£7.50), and beef in ale pie (£7.75), with evening dishes such as filo prawns with a sweet chilli dip or warm salad with bacon and stilton (£4.50), wild boar and apple sausages with mustard mash and onion gravy (£7.25), home-made curry of the day or duck and bacon pie (£7.75), and lamb steak with an orange and rosemary sauce (£10.50). There are seats out on the front loggia and terrace, and a little stream rustling under the flagstoned path; pleasant nearby walks. *(Recommended by Mrs Sylvia Elcoate, Wendy Straker, Phil and Sally Gorton, Di and Mike Gillam, the Didler, Richard Pitcher, Pete Walker, Bruce Horne, Mary Kirman and Tim Jefferson, Mike and Mary Carter, John and Jane Hayter, Jeremy Whitehorn, Revd R P Tickle, Gary Rollings, Sue and Keith Campbell)*

Own brew ~ Licensee Andy Hearn ~ Real ale ~ Bar food ~ (01297) 680359 ~ Children allowed but with restrictions ~ Dogs allowed in bar ~ Open 11-3, 6-11; 12-3, 6-10.30 Sun

Masons Arms ⊛ ⊻ ◧ ⊨

Main Street; signed off A3052 Sidmouth—Seaton, then bear left into village; EX12 3DJ

This pretty 14th-c longhouse is in a village surrounded by little wooded hills and close to the sea. At the heart of the building is the rambling low-beamed main bar with a massive central hearth in front of the roaring log fire (winter spit roasts), windsor chairs and settles, slate floors, ancient ship's beams, and a good bustling atmosphere. The no smoking Old Worthies bar also has a slate floor, a fireplace with a two-sided woodburning stove, and woodwork that has been stripped back to the original pine. There's also the original no smoking restaurant (warmed by one side of the woodburning stove), and a new beamed restaurant that has been opened above the main bar. Good bar food includes sandwiches (from £3.25; panini £5.95), braised field mushrooms with garlic, thyme and red wine or crispy fried black pudding and smoked bacon with a lightly poached egg (£4.95), steamed mussels with green curry and coconut sauce (£5.95), ploughman's (from £5.95), chickpea and sweet pepper biryani (£7.95), crispy cod in beer batter (£9.25), a trio of sausages (£9.50), thai sour orange chicken curry (£9.75), braised lamb shank with creamy root vegetable dauphinoise (£11.95), daily specials such as smoked chicken and pistachio nut terrine (£5.95), seared brixham scallops (£6.95), steamed venison and wild mushroom pudding (£11.95), and fried brill fillet (£13.95), and puddings like tempura fried banana or white chocolate and toffee tart (£3.95). Well kept Branscombe Vale Branoc, Otter Bitter, St Austell Tribute, Wolf Coyote Bitter, and a beer named for the pub on handpump, 14 wines by the glass, and 33 malt whiskies; darts, shove-ha'penny, cribbage and dominoes. Outside, the quiet flower-filled front terrace has tables with little thatched roofs, extending into a side garden. They may insist that you leave your credit card behind the bar. *(Recommended by Neil and Lorna Mclaughlan, Chris and Ann Coy, Brenda and Stuart Naylor, Wendy Straker, the Didler, John and Enid Morris, Richard Pitcher, Mike Gorton, Pete Walker, Peter Craske, Di and Mike Gillam, W W Burke, Barry Steele-Perkins, Alan and Paula McCully, Mike and Chris Higgins, Melanie Ginger, Mrs Sylvia Elcoate, Anthony Moody, Simon J A Powis, Canon Michael Bourdeaux, Peter Titcomb, Gary Rollings, Jo Rees, Tracey and Stephen Groves, Lawrence Pearse)*

Free house ~ Licensees Colin and Carol Slaney ~ Real ale ~ Bar food ~ Restaurant ~ (01297) 680300 ~ Children in bar with parents but not in restaurant ~ Dogs allowed in bar ~ Open 11-11; 12-10.30 Sun; 11-3, 6-11 weekdays in winter ~ Bedrooms: £40(£55S) (£70B)/£60(£75S)(£90B)

BRIXHAM SX9256 Map 1

Maritime

King Street (up steps from harbour – nearby parking virtually non-existent); TQ5 9TH

There's just one bar in this enjoyable little pub – and it's crammed full of interest: hundreds of key fobs and chamber-pots hang from the beams, there's a binnacle by the door, cigarette cards and pre-war ensigns from different countries, toby jugs and horsebrasses, mannequins, pictures of astronomical charts and plenty of mugs and china jugs. Both the african grey parrot (mind your fingers) and the lively terrier may be around, and there are two warming coal fires, cushioned wheelback chairs and pink-plush cushioned wall benches, flowery swagged curtains. The small TV might be on if there's something the landlady wants to watch; darts, piped music and board games. It's all very informal and relaxed. Well kept Badger Best and Fursty Ferret, and and St Austell Dartmoor on handpump, 78 malt whiskies, and home-made smoothies; no food. Fine views down over the harbour and almost non-existent nearby parking. More reports please. *(Recommended by Kevin Blake)*

Free house ~ Licensee Mrs Pat Seddon ~ Real ale ~ No credit cards ~ (01803) 853535 ~ Well behaved children allowed ~ Dogs allowed in bar ~ Open 11-3, 6.30-midnight ~ Bedrooms: £20/£40

BROADHEMBURY ST1004 Map 1

Drewe Arms ★ ⑪ ♀

Signposted off A373 Cullompton—Honiton; EX14 3NF

Even if you drop into this civilised place for just a drink or a sandwich, you will be made just as welcome as those here to enjoy one of the delicious fish dishes. It's a consistently well run place and the small bar has neatly carved beams in its high ceiling and handsome stone-mullioned windows (one with a small carved roundabout horse). On the left, a high-backed stripped settle separates off a little room with flowers on the three sturdy country tables, plank-panelled walls painted brown below and yellow above with attractive engravings and prints, and a big

black-painted fireplace with bric-a-brac on a high mantelpiece; some wood
carvings, walking sticks, and framed watercolours for sale. The flagstoned entry has
a narrow corridor of a room by the servery with a couple of tables, and the cellar
bar has simple pews on the stone floor. By the time this edition is published, all
rooms will be no smoking. Unfailingly good (if not cheap), the food might include
open sandwiches (from £5.25; crab £7.25), daily specials such as spicy crab soup
(£5), cornish sardines, warm salmon salad or smoked haddock with stilton rarebit
(£7; main course £13.50), wing of skate with black butter (£13.50), whole
langoustines (£7; main course £16.50), lyme bay crab or seared tuna salad (£15),
and sea bream with orange and chilli (£16); there are a few meaty choices, and
puddings such as bread pudding with whisky butter sauce or hazelnut parfait
(£5.50). Best to book to be sure of a table. Well kept Otter Bitter, Ale, and Bright
plus O'Hanlon's Yellowhammer tapped from the cask, and a very good wine list
laid out extremely helpfully – including around half a dozen by the glass. There are
picnic-sets in the lovely garden which has a lawn stretching back under the shadow
of chestnut trees towards a church with its singularly melodious hour-bell.
Thatched and very pretty, the 15th-c pub is in a charming village of similar cream-
coloured cottages. (*Recommended by M G Hart, S J and B S Highmore, Mr and Mrs
C Barwell, Rev D E and Mrs J A Shapland, Bob and Margaret Holder, John Urquhart, Gene and
Kitty Rankin, the Didler, Jacquie and Jim Jones, John and Enid Morris, Richard Pitcher,
Pete Walker, Robin and Ann Taylor, Jo Lilley, Simon Calvert, Dr Ian S Morley, Dr and Mrs
M E Wilson, Barry Steele-Perkins, John and Diana Head, R I C Skinner, John and Vivienne Rice,
Alan Cowell, John and Fiona Merritt, Anthony Barnes, Gary Rollings, Mike Turner*)

Free house ~ Licensees Kerstin and Nigel Burge ~ Real ale ~ Bar food (not Sun evening) ~
Restaurant ~ (01404) 841267 ~ Children in eating area of bar, restaurant and family room
~ Dogs allowed in bar ~ Open 11-3, 6-11; 12-5 Sun; closed Sun evening

BUCKFAST SX7467 Map 1

Abbey Inn ♀

Just off A38 at A384 junction; take B3380 towards Buckfastleigh, but turn right into
Buckfast Road immediately after bridge; TQ11 0EA

On a fine day, try to bag one of the tables on the terrace overlooking the River Dart
here. The pub is a sizeable, pleasant place and the bar has partly panelled walls
with some ships' crests there and over the gantry (Mr Davison was in the Royal
Navy for many years), two chequered green and beige wooden-armed settees, a mix
of high-backed chairs and captain's chairs around a few circular tables, and a
woodburning stove in an ornate fireplace. The big no smoking dining room also
has a woodburning stove, as well as more panelling and river views. There's quite
an emphasis on the well liked bar food: home-made soup (£3.25), filled rolls (from
£3.95), mussels in salsa (£4.95), home-cooked ham and egg (£6.95), fish of the day
in home-made batter (£7.50), spinach and feta cheese in a filo pastry pie (£8.50),
lasagne or home-made steak in ale pie (£8.95), chicken on tagliatelle with a wild
mushroom sauce (£11.95), steaks (from £11.95), pork steak with cider (£12.95),
and puddings such as warm chocolate brownies or cheesecake flavoured with
Baileys and served with chocolate sauce (£3.50). Well kept St Austell Dartmoor
Best, HSD and Tribute on handpump, 13 wines by the glass and local cider; piped
music and board games. The pub is reached down a steep little drive from the car
park. (*Recommended by Mike Gorton, Mayur Shah, E B Ireland, Glenn and Gillian Miller*)

St Austell ~ Tenants Terence and Elizabeth Davison ~ Real ale ~ Bar food ~
Restaurant ~ (01364) 642343 ~ Children welcome ~ Dogs allowed in bar and bedrooms
~ Open 11-midnight(11pm Sun); 11-2.30, 6-11 Mon-Thurs in winter; closed 26 Dec ~
Bedrooms: £50S/£80S

Stars after the name of a pub show exceptional quality. One star means most people
(after reading the report to see just why the star has been won) would think a special
trip worth while. Two stars mean that the pub is really outstanding – for its particular
qualities it could hardly be bettered.

BUCKLAND BREWER   SS4220   Map I

Coach & Horses

Village signposted off A388 S of Monkleigh; OS Sheet 190 map reference 423206;
EX39 5LU

This is an enjoyable and friendly village old pub with a good mix of regulars and
visitors. The heavily beamed bar has comfortable seats (including a handsome antique
settle) and a woodburning stove in the inglenook – there's also a good log fire in the
big stone inglenook of the cosy lounge. A small back room has darts and pool. Well
liked bar food includes home-made soup (£2.95), sandwiches (from £2.95), large
home-made pasty (£3.95), chicken liver pâté (£4.50), ploughman's (£5.50), ham and
egg (£6.95), home-made curries (£8.25), steaks (from £12.50), and home-made daily
specials such as bolognese and cheddar pasta bake (£7.95), beef, ale and stilton pie
with herb crust (£8.50), pork in honey and ginger sauce or salmon, cod and prawn
pancakes in a creamy cheese sauce (£8.95), and bass fillets in lime and sage butter
(£13.95). The restaurant and lounge bar are no smoking. Well kept Cotleigh Golden
Eagle, Fullers London Pride and Shepherd Neame Spitfire on handpump, and around
six wines by the glass; games machine, skittle alley (that doubles as a function room),
piped music, and occasional TV for sports. Tables on a terrace in front and in the side
garden, and a self-contained flat above the pub to rent out. Nearby moorland walks
and the beaches of Westward Ho! are close by. *(Recommended by Jean Barnett,
David Lewis, Rev D E and Mrs J A Shapland, Tony and Jill Radnor, the Didler, Brian and
Karen Thomas, Gene and Kitty Rankin, Peter Robinson, Peter and Margaret Glenister, W W Burke)*

Free house ~ Licensees Oliver Wolfe and Nicola Barrass ~ Real ale ~ Bar food
(not 25 Dec) ~ Restaurant ~ (01237) 451395 ~ Children welcome ~ Dogs allowed in bar
~ Open 12-3, 6(7 Sun)-11.30

BUCKLAND MONACHORUM   SX4868   Map I

Drake Manor 🍺

Off A386 via Crapstone, just S of Yelverton roundabout; PL20 7NA

The friendly landlady has now been running this charming little pub for 17 years.
The heavily beamed public bar on the left has plenty of local customers as well as
those from Tavistock and Plymouth, brocade-cushioned wall seats, prints of the
village from 1905 onwards, some horse tack and a few ship badges on the wall, and
a really big stone fireplace with a woodburning stove; a small door leads to a low-
beamed cubbyhole. The snug Drakes Bar has beams hung with tiny cups and big
brass keys, a woodburning stove in an old stone fireplace, horsebrasses and
stirrups, a fine stripped pine high-backed settle with a partly covered hood, and a
mix of other seats around just four tables (the oval one is rather nice). On the right
is a small, beamed no smoking dining room with settles and tables on the
flagstoned floor. Shove-ha'penny, darts and fruit machine. Well liked bar food
includes lunchtime baguettes (from £4.25), ploughman's (from £4.95), and snacks
like sausage and chips (£3.50), as well as crab cakes with a lemon and dill cream
dressing or home-made goats cheese and red onion filo parcels with gooseberry
chutney (£4.25), grilled whole lemon sole with black pepper and lemon butter or
scallops on spinach with light mustard and chive sauce (£9.25), venison steak with
cranberries and port (£9.50), medallions of beef fillet with mushrooms, chilli and
Guinness sauce (£9.75), rib-eye steak with red onion sauce and dolcelatte glaze
(£10.25), and puddings such as vanilla cheesecake with fruit coulis and ginger
pudding with caramelised pineapple and butterscotch sauce (£3.50). Well kept
Courage Best, Greene King Abbot and Sharps Doom Bar on handpump, around
40 malt whiskies, and eight wines by the glass. The sheltered back garden – where
there are picnic-sets – is prettily planted, and the floral displays in front are very
attractive all year round. *(Recommended by A Mathews, Jacquie and Jim Jones, D M Heath,
Brian and Bett Cox, Tracey and Stephen Groves, Dr and Mrs P Truelove)*

Punch ~ Lease Mandy Robinson ~ Real ale ~ Bar food (12-2, 7-10(9.30 Sun)) ~
(01822) 853892 ~ Children in restaurant and cellar bar ~ Dogs allowed in bar ~
Open 11.30-2.30(3 Sat), 6.30-11; 12-10.30 Sun

CHERITON BISHOP   SX7793   Map 1
Old Thatch Inn
Village signposted from A30; EX6 6JH

Just as we were going to press we heard that this pub had been very badly damaged by fire. They were hoping to open again at the end of 2006. Several of our readers now time their journeys to Cornwall to fit in with a lunchtime stop at this friendly and old-fashioned 16th-c pub. You can be sure of a warm welcome from the landlord, and the lounge and the rambling beamed bar are separated by a large open stone fireplace (lit in the cooler months): Otter Ale, Sharps Doom Bar, and a guest like O'Hanlons Yellowhammer or Princetown Jail Ale on handpump, and ten wines by two sizes of glass. As well as sandwiches and other bar snacks, they offer good, interesting daily specials such as home-made soup (£3.95), warm mozzarella and tomato stack with pesto dressing (£4.95), chicken liver pâté with red onion marmalade (£5.25), home-made fresh crab open ravioli with lemon grass butter cream (£6.95), goats cheese and asparagus filo tartlet with tomato coulis (£10.25), chicken supreme with a fresh mussel and chardonnay sauce (£10.95), braised lamb shank with rosemary and garlic jus or pheasant breast wrapped in bacon with an apple and thyme sauce (£11.50), fried duck breast with sweet chilli and pineapple cream (£12.50), and bass fillet on pak choi with a balsamic dressing (£14.95). The sheltered garden has lots of pretty flowering baskets and tubs. *(Recommended by Dr and Mrs M E Wilson, David Crook, Dr and Mrs M W A Haward, David and Ruth Shillitoe, Andrew Curry, Martin and Pauline Jennings, W M Paton, M G Hart, Dave Braisted, DAV, Neil and Anita Christopher, Dr C C S Wilson, DP and RA Pascoe, OPUS, Sue Demont, Tim Barrow, Ross and Christine Loveday)*

Free house ~ Licensees David and Serena London ~ Real ale ~ Bar food ~ Restaurant ~ (01647) 24204 ~ Children welcome away from bar area ~ Dogs allowed in bar ~ Open 11.30-3, 6-11; 12-3, 6.30-10.30 Sun; closed winter Sun evenings ~ Bedrooms: £45B/£60B

CLAYHIDON   ST1817   Map 1
Merry Harriers
3 miles from M5 junction 26: head towards Wellington; turn left at first roundabout signposted Ford Street and Hemyock, then after a mile turn left signposted Ford Street; at hilltop T junction, turn left towards Chard – pub is 1½ miles on right; EX15 3TR

New licensees are now running this charmingly laid out dining pub, and readers have been quick to voice their enthusiasm. There's a bustling, convivial atmosphere in the several small linked green-carpeted areas, comfortably cushioned pews and farmhouse chairs, lit candles in bottles, a woodburning stove with a sofa beside it, and plenty of horsey and hunting prints and local wildlife pictures. Two dining areas have a brighter feel with quarry tiles and lightly timbered white walls; the restaurant is no smoking. Using local produce, the food is very good and might include lunchtime sandwiches or filled baguettes (from £4), ploughman's or ham and free-range eggs (£6.50), and beer-battered fish (£8.50), as well as local potted duck and cognac pâté with cranberry jelly (£4 or £7), grilled goats cheese and pomegranate salad with black rice dressing (£4.50 or £8.50), home-made ravioli with asparagus and pecorino with goats cheese and mushroom sauce (£11.50), steaks (from £11.50), and brixham scallops on ginger, chilli and coriander linguini or free-range chicken breast wrapped in parma ham and filled with a roasted pepper stuffing and white wine, leek and cream sauce (£12). Puddings like Cointreau and vanilla crème brûlée, rhubarb crumble or triple nut chocolate brownie with white chocolate sauce (£4.50), and they also have a firm favourites menu: organic pork and apple sausages on mustard mash with onion gravy (£7.50), chicken korma with home-made chutney or chilli beef with sour cream and cheese (£8.50), and steak and kidney pie (£9.50). Well kept Blackdown Devons Pride, Exmoor Hound Dog and Otter Head on handpump, 14 wines by the glass, local cider and juice, and 25 malt whiskies. Picnic-sets on a small terrace, with more in a sizeable garden sheltered by shrubs and the old skittle alley; this is a good walking area. *(Recommended by Stuart Turner, Martin and Pauline Jennings, Rev D E and Mrs J A Shapland, Mike Gorton, John and Enid Morris, Mr and Mrs W Mills, Christine and Neil Townend, Mr and Mrs Colin Roberts, Richard and Jean Phillips, M Incledon, M G Hart, G K Smale)*

Free house ~ Licensees Peter and Angela Gatling ~ Real ale ~ Bar food (not Sun evening or Mon (except bank hol lunchtime)) ~ Restaurant ~ (01823) 421270 ~ Children allowed away from bar but no under-6s Fri or Sat evening ~ Dogs allowed in bar ~ Open 12-3, 6-11; 12-3 Sun; closed Sun evening, Mon (but open lunchtime bank hols)

CLYST HYDON ST0301 Map 1

Five Bells

West of the village and just off B3176 not far from M5 junction 28; EX15 2NT

The immaculate cottagey garden in front of this attractive thatched pub is a fine sight with its thousands of spring and summer flowers, big window boxes and pretty hanging baskets; up some steps is a sizeable flat lawn with picnic-sets, a play frame, and pleasant country views. Inside, the partly no smoking bar is divided at one end into different seating areas by brick and timber pillars; china jugs hang from big horsebrass-studded beams, there are many plates lining the shelves, lots of copper and brass, and a nice mix of dining chairs around small tables, with some comfortable pink plush banquettes on a little raised area. Past the inglenook fireplace is another big (but narrower) room they call the Long Barn with a series of prints on the walls, a pine dresser at one end, and similar furnishings. Well liked bar food includes soup (£3.95), filled cottage rolls or panini (from £4.50), black pudding and bacon in apple and cider sauce on a potato cake (£4.95), filled baguettes (from £5.95), roasted mediterranean vegetable tart (£7.95), steak and kidney pudding or beer battered cod (£8.95), fillet of salmon with asparagus and white wine sauce (£9.50), and coq au vin or lamb shank with sherry, orange and rosemary (£10.50); there's also a good value two-course meal (£7.95). Well kept Cotleigh Tawny, O'Hanlon's Royal Oak and Otter Bitter on handpump, several wines by the glass; piped music and board games. *(Recommended by Ian Phillips, Dr and Mrs A K Clarke, Mike Gorton, Ian and Deborah Carrington, John and Fiona McIlwain, D M Heath, Brian Dawes, Simon J A Powis, M Joyner)*

Free house ~ Licensees Mr and Mrs R Shenton ~ Real ale ~ Bar food ~ (01884) 277288 ~ Children allowed away from bar ~ Live jazz second Weds of the month ~ Open 11.30-3, 6.30-11; 12-3, 7-10.30 Sun; evening opening 7 in winter

COCKWOOD SX9780 Map 1

Anchor 25

Off, but visible from, A379 Exeter—Torbay; EX6 8RA

Even in mid-winter, this former ex-seaman's mission – totally no smoking now – remains immensely popular, and you must arrive early to be sure of a table (and even a parking space). There's often a queue to get in but they do two sittings in the restaurant on winter weekends and every evening in summer to cope with the crowds. They are still hoping to build a large extension. There are 30 different ways of serving mussels (£7.75 normal size helping, £12.50 for a large one), 13 ways of serving scallops (from £5.75 for a starter, from £13.45 for a main course), and five ways of serving oysters (from £7.25 for a starter, from £14.25 for a main course), as well as crab and brandy soup (£4.50), and smoked haddock steam pudding (£7.25), and potted seafood pie (£7.50). Non-fishy dishes feature as well, such as sandwiches (from £3.25), home-made chicken liver pâté (£4.25), cheese and potato pie (£5.50), home-made steak and kidney pudding (£7.25), rump steak (£9.95), and children's dishes (£4.50). But despite the emphasis on food, there's still a pubby atmosphere, and they keep six real ales on handpump or tapped from the cask: Bass, Fullers London Pride, Greene King Abbot and Old Speckled Hen, Otter Ale and Timothy Taylors Landlord. Also, a fine wine list of 300 (bin ends and reserves and 12 by the glass), 20 brandies and 20 ports, and 130 malt whiskies. The small, low-ceilinged, rambling rooms have black panelling, good-sized tables in various alcoves, and a cheerful winter coal fire in the snug. Darts, dominoes, cards, fruit machine and piped music. From the tables on the sheltered verandah you can look across the road to the bobbing yachts and crabbing boats in the harbour. *(Recommended by R J Walden, Hugh Roberts, Di and Mike Gillam, Graham and*

Glenis Watkins, Peter and Margaret Lodge, Norman and Sarah Keeping, Dr Ian S Morley,
Ann and Bob Westbrook, Mr and Mrs A H Young, John and Fiona McIlwain, Dr and Mrs
M E Wilson, Dr A J and Mrs Tompsett, the Didler, Gary Rollings, Meg and Colin Hamilton)

Heavitree ~ Tenants Mr Morgan and Miss Sanders ~ Real ale ~ Bar food (all day) ~
Restaurant ~ (01626) 890203 ~ Children in snug ~ Dogs allowed in bar ~ Open 11-11;
12-10.30 Sun; closed evening 25 Dec

COLEFORD   SS7701   Map 1
New Inn 🍽 ⏲ 🛏
Just off A377 Crediton—Barnstaple; EX17 5BZ

In an attractive hamlet of thatched cottages, this 13th-c inn strikes a good balance
between a proper pub and restaurant. It's an L-shaped building with the servery in
the 'angle', and interestingly furnished areas leading off it: ancient and modern
settles, spindleback chairs, plush-cushioned stone wall seats, some character tables –
a pheasant worked into the grain of one – and carved dressers and chests; also,
paraffin lamps, antique prints and old guns on the white walls, and landscape plates
on one of the beams, with pewter tankards on another. The chatty resident parrot
Captain is most chatty when it's quieter. As well as snacks such as filled baguettes
and ciabattas (from £4), omelettes (from £5.25), and ploughman's (from £6), the
good food includes soup (£4), chicken liver and bacon pâté (£5), smoked haddock
chowder or chilli prawns (£5.25), creamy fish pie (£8.50), 6oz sirloin steak and
fries (£8.75), pork and leek sausages with bubble and squeak (£9), parmesan
crusted pork medallions, thai green chicken curry (£10), and puddings such as
profiteroles in chocolate sauce (£5). The end-of-the-month pig roasts are popular;
good, cheerful service. The restaurant is no smoking. Well kept Badger Best, Otter
Ale and Sharps Doom Bar on handpump; piped music and darts. There are chairs,
tables and umbrellas on decking under the willow tree along the stream, and more
on the terrace. *(Recommended by Mark Flynn, Mrs L M Lefeaux, Betsy Brown, Nigel Flook,*
Mike and Mary Carter, Bob and Margaret Holder, Peter Craske, Peter and Margaret Lodge,
John Robertson, J F Stackhouse, Derek Harvey-Piper, Dennis Jenkin)

Free house ~ Licensees Simon and Melissa Renshaw ~ Real ale ~ Bar food ~ Restaurant ~
(01363) 84242 ~ Children welcome ~ Dogs allowed in bar ~ Open 12-3, 6-11; 12-3,
7-10.30 Sun; closed 25 and 26 Dec ~ Bedrooms: £55B/£70B

COMBEINTEIGNHEAD   SX9071   Map 1
Wild Goose ⏲ 🍺
Just off unclassified coast road Newton Abbot—Shaldon, up hill in village; TQ12 4RA

To find this well run and welcoming pub, just head for the 14th-c church next
door. The back beamed spacious lounge has a mix of wheelbacks, red plush dining
chairs, a decent mix of tables, and french windows to the garden, with nice country
views beyond; the front bar has seats in the window embrasures of the thick walls,
flagstones in a small area by the door, some beams and standing timbers, and a step
down on the right at the end, with dining chairs around the tables and a big old
fireplace with an open log fire. There's a small carved oak dresser with a big white
goose, chess, backgammon and shove-ha'penny, and also a cosy section on the left
with an old settee and comfortably well used chairs. Well liked bar food, using local
produce where possible, includes home-made soup (£3.75), sandwiches (from
£3.75), three-egg omelette (from £5.25), garlic mushrooms (£5.50), ham and egg or
ploughman's (£5.95), steak and kidney pie (£8.25), leek and mushroom crumble
(£8.50), fresh haddock in herb batter (£8.75), smoked chicken in a rich creamy
stilton sauce (£10.75), steaks (from £12.95), and specials such as whole rack of
barbecue ribs or local mussels (£9.95), whole lemon sole or brixham plaice £12.95,
and bass fillet with thermidor sauce (£14.95); they also have a bargain £5 meal
each day such as corned beef hash. The dining room is no smoking. A fine choice of
regularly changing real ales on handpump such as Archers Mild, Cottage Golden
Arrow, Otter Bright, RCH PG Steam, Skinners Betty Stogs, Teignworthy Martha's
Mild and Youngs Bitter, plus 15 wines by the glass, 40 malt whiskies and two

village ciders. The garden behind has plenty of seats and there are outdoor heaters for chillier evenings. *(Recommended by Prof H G Allen, John and Helen Rushton, Ken Flawn, D M Heath, the Didler)*

Free house ~ Licensees Jerry and Kate English ~ Real ale ~ Bar food ~ (01626) 872241 ~ Well behaved children in restaurant ~ Dogs allowed in bar ~ Live jazz/folk Fri evenings ~ Open 11-3, 5.30-11(midnight Sat); 12-3, 7-11 Sun

CORNWORTHY SX8255 Map 1
Hunters Lodge
Off A381 Totnes—Kingsbridge ½ mile S of Harbertonford, turning left at Washbourne; can also be reached direct from Totnes, on the Ashprington—Dittisham road; TQ9 7ES

This is a particularly friendly place that our readers enjoy very much. The small low-ceilinged bar has two rooms with an engagingly pubby feel and a combination of wall seats, settles and captain's chairs around heavy elm tables; there's also a small and pretty cottagey dining room with a good log fire in its big 17th-c stone fireplace. Half the pub is no smoking. Cooked by the landlord and using local produce, the good food might include lunchtime sandwiches (from £4; brixham crab with lemon mayonnaise £6) and ploughman's (£7.50), as well as home-made soup (£3.75), chicken and duck pâté with apricot chutney (£4.50), local mussels in a thai broth (£5.50; main course £9.50), gammon, egg and beans (£7.95), home-made sausages with mustard mash and onion gravy (£8.50), stuffed red pimento with ricotta and rocket and a sun-dried tomato and pine nut dressing (£7.95), and fresh squid ink tagliolini of salmon, mussels and local crab with a light chive cream sauce (£8.50), with daily specials like lightly grilled oysters topped with spinach, nutmeg and parmesan (£5.80), half a pot-roasted guinea fowl with smoked bacon and root vegetables (£9.50), rib-eye steak with café de paris butter and madeira sauce (£14.50), and puddings such as walnut, stem ginger and rum dark chocolate terrine with rasberry coulis and cinnamon mascarpone or rosemary crème brûlée (£4.50); seafood barbecue monthly Fridays. We expect the food to be worth an award but would like more feedback from readers, please. Well kept Teignworthy Reel Ale and a couple of guests on handpump, 50 malt whiskies, a dozen wines by the glass, and local Hogwash cider; piped music. In summer, there is plenty of room to sit outside, either at the picnic-sets on a big lawn or on the flower-filled terrace closer to the pub. *(Recommended by J P Greaves, Richard and Sheila Brooks, M Sage, B J Harding, Simon Hollis)*

Free house ~ Licensees J Reen and G Rees ~ Real ale ~ Bar food ~ Restaurant ~ (01803) 732204 ~ Children welcome ~ Dogs allowed in bar ~ Monthly live music ~ Open 11.30-3, 6.30-11; 12-3, 7-10.30 Sun

CULMSTOCK ST1013 Map 1
Culm Valley 🍴 🍷 📷
B3391, off A38 E of M5 junction 27; EX15 3JJ

Idiosyncratic and far from smart, this isn't an obvious dining out place. So that makes the good food all the more appreciated by those who like a really unfussy country atmosphere. The salmon-coloured bar has a hotch-potch of modern and unrenovated furnishings, a big fireplace with some china above it, newspapers, and a long stripped wooden bar counter; further along is a dining room with a chalkboard menu, a small front conservatory, and leading off here, a little oak-floored room with views into the kitchen. You may smoke in the bar but nowhere else. Board games and maybe TV for major sporting events. The landlord and his brother import wines from smaller french vineyards, so you can count on a few of those (they offer 50 wines by the glass), as well as some unusual french fruit liqueurs, somerset cider brandies, vintage rum, good sherries and madeira, local ciders and around six well kept real ales tapped from the cask: Branscombe Vale Branoc, Dark Star American Pale Ale, Dorset Weymouth Harbour Master, O'Hanlons Firefly and Royal Oak, Otter Bitter and Woodfordes Great Eastern. They may hold a May bank holiday weekend beer festival. Enjoyable, imaginative food includes sandwiches, home-made soup (£4), risotto with sage, onion and butter (£6; large helping £9), grilled goats cheese salad (£6; large helping £10), tea-smoked wild venison, moules marinière or thai duck (£7; large helping £11), scallops with crème fraîche and sweet chilli sauce (£8; large helping £16), beef rendang (£9), pollack fillet with puy lentils and salsa verde (£10), whole grilled lemon sole or local lamb with anchovies, garlic and rosemary (£12), shellfish platters (from £16), and puddings such as crème brûlée, honey and ginger pudding or chocolate nut brownie (£4.50). Outside, tables are very attractively positioned overlooking the bridge and the River Culm. The gents' are in an outside yard. *(Recommended by David Collison, Simon Watkins, Tony and Tracy Constance, Jacquie and Jim Jones, Sue Demont, Tim Barrow, B Phenin, M Fairbairn, John and Fiona Merritt, John and Fiona McIlwain, R M Corlett, Ian and Meg Ainsworth, M G Hart)*

Free house ~ Licensee Richard Hartley ~ Real ale ~ Bar food (not Sun evening) ~ Restaurant ~ No credit cards ~ (01884) 840354 ~ Children allowed away from main bar ~ Dogs welcome ~ Occasional impromptu piano and Irish music ~ Open 12-3, 7-11(may open all day in good weather); 12-11(10.30 Sun) Sat ~ Bedrooms: £30B/£55B

DALWOOD ST2400 Map 1
Tuckers Arms
Village signposted off A35 Axminster—Honiton; keep on past village; EX13 7EG

Customers tend to come back to this pretty, cream-washed and thatched old inn time and time again, and the courteous licensees have now been here 20 years. The fine flagstoned bar has a lot of atmosphere, plenty of beams, a random mixture of dining chairs, window seats and wall settles (including a high-backed winged black one), and a log fire in the inglenook fireplace. The back bar has an enormous collection of miniature bottles. Well liked bar food includes home-made soup (£3.55), freshly baked baguettes or granary torpedoes (from £4.25), home-made pâté (£4.95; large £5.95), kidneys in garlic or smoked haddock rarebit (£4.95; large £7.95), ploughman's (£5.25), pork sausages with black pudding and eggs (£7.95), beef and mushroom in ale (£9.95), braised lamb shank (£11.95), steaks (from £14.95), and puddings such as date and banana sponge pudding or treacle and walnut tart (£4.95). From a more elaborate menu they offer two courses (£17.95) and three courses (£20.95). The restaurant is no smoking. Well kept Courage Best, Greene King Old Speckled Hen and Otter Bitter on handpump, eight wines by the glass, and farm cider; piped music and skittle alley. In summer, the hanging baskets, flowering tubs and window boxes in front of the building are lovely, and there's a covered pergola with outdoor heating. *(Recommended by Mr and Mrs W Mills, Anthony Longden, Frogeye, Bob and Margaret Holder, Pete Walker, John Waters, Stephen and Jean Curtis, Glenwys and Alan Lawrence)*

Free house ~ Licensees David and Kate Beck ~ Real ale ~ Bar food (all day Sun) ~ Restaurant ~ (01404) 881342 ~ Children in restaurant and family room ~ Open 12-2.30, 6.30-11; 12-10.30 Sun; 12-3, 7-10.30 Sun in winter ~ Bedrooms: £42.50S/£69.50S

DARTMOUTH SX8751 Map 1
Cherub
Higher Street; TQ6 9RB

Already 300 years old when Francis Drake used it, this striking inn is Dartmouth's oldest building. It's a fine sight in summer, particularly, with each of the two heavily timbered upper floors jutting further out than the one below, and very pretty hanging baskets. The bustling bar has tapestried seats under creaky heavy beams, leaded-light windows, a big stone fireplace, and Sharps Doom Bar, a beer named for the pub and a changing guest on handpump; quite a few malt whiskies and 14 wines by the glass. Upstairs is the fine, low-ceilinged and no smoking restaurant; piped music. Good bar food includes home-made soup (£4.25), well liked sandwiches (from £4.50; crab £5.95), smoked haddock in a saffron and herb sauce topped with cheese (£5.95), local scallops roasted with shredded leeks, butter and muscat on a brioche croûte (£6.95), beer-battered cod, lambs liver and bacon on bubble and squeak or home-made bangers and mash with apple and honey sauce (£9.95), peppered steak pudding (£10.95), and pasta with langoustines, pancetta, basil and sunblush tomatoes (£12.95). It does get very crowded at peak times. *(Recommended by John Evans, Geoff Calcott, John and Helen Rushton, Paul and Shirley White, David Carr, Di and Mike Gillam, Sue Heath, M Sage, Mr and Mrs Colin Roberts, Glenn and Gillian Miller, Jim and Janet Brown, Emma Kingdon)*

Free house ~ Licensee Laurie Scott ~ Real ale ~ Bar food ~ Restaurant ~ (01803) 832571 ~ Children over 5 in restaurant by appointment ~ Dogs allowed in bar ~ Open 11(12 Sun)-midnight(1am Sat); 11-2.30, 5-11 in winter

DODDISCOMBSLEIGH   SX8586   Map 1
Nobody Inn ㉕ ★ ♀ ◀
Village signposted off B3193, opposite northernmost Christow turn-off; EX6 7PS

There's still an extraordinary choice of whiskies and wines on offer here: around 800 wines by the bottle and 20 by the glass, and 260 whiskies. Also, local ciders, and well kept Topsham & Exminster Ferryman, an ale from Cottage and a beer named for the pub on handpump or tapped from the cask. The two rooms of the lounge bar have handsomely carved antique settles, windsor and wheelback chairs, benches, carriage lanterns hanging from the beams, and guns and hunting prints in a snug area by one or the big inglenook fireplaces. Bar food includes soup (£4.20), smoked bacon, rosemary and butterbean risotto (£4.90; main course £8.50), toasted ham, cheese and tomato sandwich (£5), a choice of six local cheeses (£6.50), ploughman's (£6.90), fish pie (£7.90), fillet of salmon with ham and braised peppers (£8.50), lamb shank or beef casserole (£9.50), and puddings such as treacle tart or apple and blackcurrant crumble (£4.50). The restaurant is no smoking. Several readers have felt the staff could be more welcoming and helpful. There are picnic-sets on the terrace with views of the surrounding wooded hill pastures. The medieval stained glass in the local church is some of the best in the West Country. This has been a star pub for many years, but over the last few months one or two readers have wondered whether its legendary friendliness might be fading a little. We do hope this has been just a temporary blip. No children. *(Recommended by Lynn Sharpless, Mrs Bridget Cushion, Gareth Lewis, Dr and Mrs T E Hothersall, Peter Salmon, John Whiting, Peter Burton, J D O Carter, John Brooks, Betsy Brown, Nigel Flook, the Didler, Andrew Shore, Maria Williams, Sue Demont, Tim Barrow, Dr and Mrs M E Wilson, DAV, Ann Holdsworth, Ann and Bob Westhrook, Steve Whalley, Ian and Jane Irving, Simon Cleasby, Adrian Johnson, Tracey and Stephen Groves)*

Free house ~ Licensee Nick Borst-Smith ~ Real ale ~ Bar food ~ Restaurant ~ (01647) 252394 ~ Open 12-2.30, 6-11; 12-3, 7-10.30 Sun; closed 25, 26, evening 31 Dec, 1 Jan ~ Bedrooms: £25(£45B)/£40(£80B)

EAST BUDLEIGH   SY0684   Map 1
Sir Walter Raleigh
High Street; EX9 7ED

This is a nice bustling little local in a pretty thatch-and-cob village. There's a lively local atmosphere, pleasant staff, and a low-beamed bar with lots of books on shelves, and well kept Adnams Broadside and Explorer and Otter Bitter on handpump. The attractive restaurant down a step from the bar is no smoking. Bar food is very good and changes every couple of months: sandwiches (from £2.40), soup (£3.50), filled baked potatoes (from £3.50), duck pâté with cherries (£4.95), cumberland sausage with horseradish mash and port gravy or roasted pepper and butternut squash risotto with tomato salsa (£7.95), fresh grilled plaice with sautéed banana (£8.95), monkfish and mushroom brochette with pesto dressing (£9.95), grilled partridge on a honey and mustard sauce (£10.95), and puddings such as light chocolate and orange mousse or apple and blackberry flapjack pudding (£3.75). They are hoping to re-do the garden. There's a fine church with a unique collection of carved oak bench ends, and the pub is handy for Bicton Park gardens. Raleigh himself was born at nearby Hayes Barton, and educated in a farmhouse

300 yards away. Parking is about 100 yards away. No children. *(Recommended by Dr and Mrs M E Wilson, Paul and Shirley White, Mike Gorton, John and Enid Morris, Barry Steele-Perkins, John Waters, Ian and Joan Blackwell, John and Jane Hayter)*

Enterprise ~ Lease Lindsay Mason ~ Real ale ~ Bar food ~ Restaurant ~ (01395) 442510 ~ Dogs allowed in bar ~ Open 11.45-2.30, 6-11; 12-2.30, 7-10.30 Sun

EXETER   SX9292   Map 1

Imperial   🍽 £

New North Road (St David's Hill on Crediton/Tiverton road, above St David's station); EX4 4AH

Standing in its own six-acre hillside park, this early 19th-c mansion is reached along a sweeping drive; there are plenty of picnic-sets in the grounds and elegant garden furniture in the attractive cobbled courtyard. Inside, there's a light and airy former orangery with an unusual lightly mirrored end wall, and various different areas including a couple of little clubby side bars, a left-hand bar that looks into the orangery, and a fine ex-ballroom filled with elaborate plasterwork and gilding brought here in the 1920s from Haldon House (a Robert Adam stately home that was falling on hard times). Half the pub is no smoking. The furnishings give Wetherspoons' usual solid well spaced comfort, and there are plenty of interesting pictures and other things to look at. They always have Greene King Abbot and Marstons Burton and Pedigree on handpump, plus a beer from Cotleigh, Exmoor and O'Hanlon's, and three national guests; friendly, efficient staff – even when the place is hopping with students. Standard bar food includes filled panini (from £3.19), meaty or vegetarian burgers (£3.99 which includes a pint), battered cod or ham and eggs (£4.79), chicken caesar salad (£5.09), and mediterranean pasta bake or sausages and mash (£5.39). *(Recommended by Pete Walker, Donna and Roger, Mike Gorton, Ian Phillips, Dr and Mrs A K Clarke, the Didler, Mrs Sylvia Elcoate, E B Ireland, R T and J C Moggridge)*

Wetherspoons ~ Manager Paul Dixey ~ Real ale ~ Bar food (all day) ~ (01392) 434050 ~ Children in family area ~ Open 9am-midnight; 9am-1am Fri and Sat

EXMINSTER   SX9686   Map 1

Turf Hotel   ★

Follow the signs to the Swan's Nest, signposted from A379 S of village, then continue to end of track, by gates; park, and walk right along canal towpath – nearly a mile; there's a fine seaview out to the mudflats at low tide; EX6 8EE

The friendly licensees of this very popular pub have now been here for 17 years and have opened a new outside bar with six beers tapped from the cask: Otter Bitter and Ale, O'Hanlons Yellowhammer, Princetown Dartmoor IPA, Skinners Betty Stogs and Topsham & Exminster Ferryman. Also, local Green Valley cider, local juices, local rosé wine, and jugs of Pimms. The main outdoor barbecue area is much used in good weather (there are smaller barbecues, too) and there are plenty of picnic-sets spread around the big garden and a children's play area built using a lifeboat from a liner that sank off the Scilly Isles around 100 years ago. Inside, the end room has a slate floor, pine walls, built-in seats, lots of photographs of the pub, and a woodburning stove; along a corridor (with an eating room to one side) is a simply furnished room with wood-plank seats around tables on the stripped wooden floor. The tables in the bay windows are much prized so get there early if you want to bag one. Two rooms are no smoking. Bar food is very good indeed (there may be quite a wait at peak times) and might at lunchtime include sandwiches (from £3.65; ham, cheese and pineapple toastie £5.25), home-made soup (£3.95), hummous and cracked olives or guacamole and spicy salsa (£4.25), vegetarian cottage pie (£6.25), chargrilled lamb harissa in pitta bread (£7.50), and chilli nachos (£7.95), evening choices such as wild mushroom and tarragon risotto (£5.45; main course £7.95), fresh local mussels (£7.95), thai green chicken curry (£9.50), and rack of lamb with ratatouille, bubble and squeak and thyme jus (£13.95), and daily specials like thai fishcakes with lime mayonnaise (£5.95), cannelloni with spinach and ricotta (£7.95), beer battered hake (£9.50), and bass on chorizo with potato cream (£12.95). To get to the pub you must either walk (which takes about 20 minutes along the ship canal) or cycle, and there's a 60-seater boat which brings people down the Exe estuary from Topsham quay (15-minute trip, adult £3, child £2); there's also a canal boat from Countess Wear Swing Bridge every lunchtime. Best to phone the pub for all sailing times. For those arriving in their own boat there is a large pontoon as well as several moorings. Although the pub and garden do get packed in good weather and there are inevitable queues, the staff remain friendly and efficient. *(Recommended by Dr and Mrs M E Wilson, Neil and Lorna Mclaughlan, Phil and Sally Gorton, Brenda and Stuart Naylor, Mike Gorton, the Didler, David Field)*

Free house ~ Licensees Clive and Ginny Redfern ~ Real ale ~ Bar food (12-2.30 (3 weekends), 7-9(9.30 Fri and Sat); not Sun evening) ~ (01392) 833128 ~ Children welcome ~ Dogs welcome ~ Open 11.30-11; 11.30-10.30 Sun; closed Nov-Feb but open weekends in March

HAYTOR VALE SX7677 Map 1

Rock ★ ⇌

Haytor signposted off B3387 just W of Bovey Tracey, on good moorland road to Widecombe; TQ13 9XP

Being on the edge of Dartmoor National Park, this civilised and rather smart inn (totally no smoking now) is less formal at lunchtime when customers are more likely to drop in for a drink or a meal after a walk. In the evening, most people are here to stay overnight in the comfortable bedrooms or to enjoy the good restaurant food. The two communicating, partly panelled bar rooms have lots of dark wood and red plush, polished antique tables with candles and fresh flowers, old-fashioned prints and decorative plates on the walls, and warming winter log fires (the main fireplace has a fine Stuart fireback). Good lunchtime bar food includes home-made soup (£3.50), chicken liver parfait (£4.95), smoked salmon and cream cheese sandwich (£5.95), ciabatta filled with sirloin of beef and mustard or smoked chicken and pine nut salad (£6.95), ploughman's (£7.50), venison sausages or chicken curry (£8.50), beef in ale pie or whole grilled plaice with lemon butter (£8.95), and puddings such as apple crumble or vanilla crème brûlée (£4.50). Greene King Old Speckled Hen and St Austell Dartmoor Best on handpump, and several malt whiskies. There are seats in the large, pretty garden opposite the inn, with tables and chairs on a small terrace next to the pub itself. Parking is not always easy. *(Recommended by Frank Plater, Lesley Piekielniak, M G Hart, Brian and Bett Cox, Doug Kennedy, Peter and Margaret Lodge, Mrs Viv Haigh, Dr Ian S Morley, Hugh Roberts, M Sage, Dr C C S Wilson, Gene and Tony Freemantle, Bill Smith, Pat and Robert Watt, B J Harding)*

Free house ~ Licensee Christopher Graves ~ Real ale ~ Bar food ~ Restaurant ~ (01364) 661305 ~ Children welcome ~ Open 11(12 Sun)-11; closed 25 and 26 Dec ~ Bedrooms: £66.95B/£95.95B

HOLBETON SX6150 Map 1

Dartmoor Union ⑪ ♀ ◀

Village signposted off A379 W of A3121 junction; Fore Street; PL8 1NE

This is a civilised place with a smart and rather chic spreading bar and plenty of young neat staff all dressed in black. There's a nice mix of dining chairs around several wooden tables on the stripped wood floor, squashy leather sofas and armchairs in front of the log fire in the brick fireplace, witticisms and old photographs of the village on the elegant, pale yellow walls, and a dark wood, brass and black slate bar counter; table skittles and board games. The no smoking restaurant leads off here with big yachting photographs by Beken on the dark red walls and white-clothed tables and high-backed leather dining chairs; stylish flower arrangements. The atmosphere is chatty and relaxed, and there's a good mix of customers. Under the new licensee, the imaginative modern food might include home-made soup (£4.25), twice-baked goats cheese soufflé with chive oil (£5.25), pressed chicken and smoked bacon terrine with pickled wild mushrooms (£5.50), tempura of mixed vegetables (£9.95), roasted cod, braised lentils, caramelised shallots and wine jus (£10.95), rack of lamb with dauphinoise potatoes, ratatouille and madeira jus (£12.95), chargrilled fillet of beef with a wild mushroom and red wine risotto (£16.95), daily specials such as thai chicken salad with fresh coriander dressing (£5.95), seared scallops with salt cod brandade and tomato gazpacho (£7.95; main course £12.95), line-caught mackerel with mixed herb butter (£10.95), and puddings like iced rhubarb parfait, sticky toffee pudding or vanilla crème brûlée with raspberry sorbet (£5.25). Two-course lunch (£9.95) and three courses (£12.95). Nine wines by two sizes of glass from a carefully chosen list, and Otter Bitter and St Austell Dartmoor IPA on handpump; as we went to press, they still had not opened their microbrewery. There's smart teak furniture on a sheltered back terrace. Note that the back car park may not be signed from the street and there's no inn sign – just a brass plaque. *(Recommended by David M Cundy, John Evans, J F Stackhouse, Brian and Bett Cox)*

Wykeham Inns ~ Licensee Allyson Wray ~ Real ale ~ Bar food (12-3.30, 6.30-9) ~ Restaurant ~ (01752) 830288 ~ Children in restaurant and bar until 9pm ~ Dogs allowed in bar ~ Open 12-3, 5.30-11; 12-11 Sun

HOLNE   SX7069   Map 1

Church House

Signed off B3357 W of Ashburton; TQ13 7SJ

After a walk on Dartmoor, this medieval inn is a welcome place to drop in to and you'll find a friendly welcome from the licensees; there are fine moorland views from the pillared porch (where regulars tend to gather). The lower bar has stripped pine panelling and an 18th-c curved elm settle, and is separated from the lounge bar by a 16th-c heavy oak partition; open log fires in both rooms. Bar food includes lunchtime sandwiches and baguettes (from £4.50) and ploughman's (from £5.95), as well as soup (£4.25), home-made pâté (£4.95), favourites like steak in ale pie or rabbit casserole (£8.95), and daily specials such as local venison, redcurrant and rosemary sausages (£8.95), deep-fried brixham cod in beer batter (£9.50), and roasted rump of local lamb on sweet potato purée (£13.50); more elaborate choices in the evening, and Sunday lunch (£8.95). Only one bar is for smoking. Well kept Butcombe Bitter and Teignworthy Reel Ale on handpump, several wines by the glass, and organic cider, apple juice and ginger beer; darts. You may see morris men and clog dancers in the summer. Charles Kingsley (of *Water Babies* fame) was born in the village. *(Recommended by R J Walden, Phil and Sally Gorton, Glenn and Gillian Miller)*

Free house ~ Licensee J Silk ~ Real ale ~ Bar food (not Sun evening or Mon in winter) ~ Restaurant ~ (01364) 631208 ~ Children in eating area of bar and restaurant ~ Dogs allowed in bar and bedrooms ~ Open 12-2.30(3 Sat and Sun), 7-11; closed Sun evening and Mon in winter ~ Bedrooms: £33S/£55(£66B)

HORNDON   SX5280   Map 1

Elephants Nest ⑳ ◖

If coming from Okehampton on A386 turn left at Mary Tavy Inn, then left after about ½ mile; pub signposted beside Mary Tavy Inn, then Horndon signposted; on the Ordnance Survey Outdoor Leisure Map it's named as the New Inn; PL19 9NQ

From benches on the spacious lawn in front of this isolated 16th-c inn, you can look over dry-stone walls to the pastures and the rougher moorland above; plenty of surrounding walks. Inside, the bar has original stone walls, flagstones, three woodburning stoves and a beam-and-board ceiling; there's a no smoking dining room and garden room. Well kept Otter Bright, Palmers IPA and Copper Ale, and a guest such as Princetown Jail Ale on handpump, farm cider and a few wines by the glass; piped music. Bar food includes soup (£4.25), lunchtime baguettes or tortilla wraps (not Sunday, from £4.50), chicken liver pâté (£4.95), home-made burger with red onion marmalade (£8.95), home-made fish pie (£9.95), 10oz local sirloin steak (£13.95), daily specials such as aubergine and coconut or lamb curries (£8.95), fillets of fresh bass (£15.95), and fillet of local beef with green peppercorn sauce (£16.95); Sunday roast (£9.95). New bedrooms have been added this year. *(Recommended by Dr and Mrs M W A Haward, John and Bernadette Elliott, Peter and Margaret Lodge, DAV, Rev D E and Mrs J A Shapland)*

Free house ~ Licensee Hugh Cook ~ Real ale ~ Bar food (12-2.15, 6.30-9) ~ (01822) 810273 ~ Children allowed but with restrictions ~ Dogs welcome ~ Jazz second Weds of month ~ Open 12-3, 6.30-11(10.30 Sun) ~ Bedrooms: /£65B

IDDESLEIGH SS5708 Map 1
Duke of York ★ ♀
B3217 Exbourne—Dolton; EX19 8BG

Bustling and unspoilt, full of chatty, friendly regulars (and their dogs), this pub is a throwback to old-fashioned hospitality. The enjoyably unfussy bar has a lot of homely character: rocking chairs by the roaring log fire, cushioned wall benches built into the wall's black-painted wooden dado, stripped tables and other simple country furnishings. Well kept Adnams Broadside, Cotleigh Tawny and Sharps Doom Bar tapped from the cask, and quite a few wines by the glass. Good, honest bar food includes home-made soup (£3 small, £4 large), sandwiches (from £4.50), chicken liver pâté (£5.50), ham and eggs (£6), grilled or battered fish and chips (£6 small, £8 large), scallops wrapped in smoked bacon or crab mayonnaise (£6 small, £10 large), cottage pie or ploughman's (£7), vegetable korma, smoked haddock or beef in Guinness (£8), steak and kidney pudding (£9), and double lamb chop with rosemary and garlic gravy (£9.50); it does get pretty cramped at peak times. Darts. Through a small coach arch is a little back garden with some picnic-sets. Fishing nearby. The bedrooms are quirky and in some cases very far from smart, so their appeal is very much to people who enjoy taking the rough with the smooth. *(Recommended by R J Walden, Louise English, Jamie Turner, Ruth Hooper, Anthony Longden, John and Mary Ling, the Didler, Rona Murdoch, David and Pauline Brenner, Mark Flynn, Ann Holdsworth, DAV, Peter and Jean Dowson, Stuart Turner, Peter and Margaret Glenister, Rev D E and Mrs J A Shapland, Sue Demont, Tim Barrow, W W Burke, PL)*

Free house ~ Licensees Jamie Stuart and Pippa Hutchinson ~ Real ale ~ Bar food (all day) ~ Restaurant ~ (01837) 810253 ~ Children welcome ~ Dogs welcome ~ Open 11-11(11.30 Sat); 12-11 Sun; closed evening 25 Dec ~ Bedrooms: £30B/£60B

KINGSTON SX6347 Map 1
Dolphin ⇌
Off B3392 S of Modbury (can also be reached from A379 W of Modbury); TQ7 4QE

Half a dozen tracks lead from this peaceful shuttered 16th-c inn down to the sea and unspoilt Wonwell Beach about a mile and a half away. Inside, several knocked-through beamed rooms have a good mix of customers, and the cheerful landlady offers a warm welcome to all. There are amusing drawings and photographs on the bared stone walls, and rustic tables and cushioned seats and settles; half the pub is no smoking. Decent bar food includes sandwiches, home-made soup (£4.25), tasty crab bake (£5.95), ploughman's (£6.75), mushroom gratin (£7.95), steak in ale or fish pie or caribbean chicken (£8.95), and braised lamb chump chop with red wine and rosemary jus (£10.95). Butcombe Bitter, Courage Best and Sharps Doom Bar on handpump. Tables outside. *(Recommended by Roger Wain-Heapy, Gene and Kitty Rankin, Jacquie and Jim Jones, David Uren, Sue Demont, Tim Barrow, George Atkinson, Alan and Anne Driver, Tracey and Stephen Groves)*

InnSpired ~ Lease Janice Male ~ Real ale ~ Bar food (12-2.30, 6-9; not Sun or Mon evenings in winter) ~ (01548) 810314 ~ Children welcome ~ Open 12-3, 6-11(10.30 Sun); Sunday opening 7 in winter ~ Bedrooms: £42.50B/£60B

Pubs brewing their own beers are listed at the back of the book.

LOWER ASHTON   SX8484   Map 1
Manor Inn   ◀

Ashton signposted off B3193 N of Chudleigh; EX6 7QL

This is a friendly creeper-covered pub with a good, bustling atmosphere and welcoming licensees. Locals tend to head for the left-hand room with beer mats and brewery advertisements on the walls, whereas on the right, two rather more discreet rooms have a wider appeal. Well kept Princetown Jail Ale, RCH Pitchfork and Teignworthy Reel Ale with a couple of guests such as O'Hanlons Yellowhammer and Teignworthy Martha's Mild; Gray's farm cider, several wines by the glass and local organic fruit juice and ginger beer. Well liked home-made food (they tell us prices have not changed) might include sandwiches (from £3), home-made soup (£3.50), lots of filled baked potatoes (from £3.95), home-made burger (£4.75), ploughman's (from £6.75), vegetable bake (£6.95), home-cooked ham and egg (£7.75), beef, mushroom and Guinness pie (£7.95), chicken in a creamy stilton sauce (£8.75), steaks (from £9.95), duck breast in port and cranberry sauce (£10.95), home-made puddings (£3.50), and a good cheese platter with five different local cheeses to share (£5.95). The garden has lots of picnic-sets under cocktail parasols (and a fine tall scots pine), and pretty hanging baskets. No children inside. *(Recommended by David and Jean Hall, Mike Gorton, the Didler, Richard and Sheila Brooks, David M Cundy, Ann Holdsworth, DAV)*

Free house ~ Licensee Mark Quilter ~ Real ale ~ Bar food (12-1.30, 7-9; not Mon except bank hols) ~ (01647) 252304 ~ Dogs welcome ~ Open 12-2(2.30 Sat), 6.30-11; 12-2.30, 7-10.30 Sun; closed Mon

LUSTLEIGH   SX7881   Map 1
Cleave

Village signposted off A382 Bovey Tracey—Moretonhampstead; TQ13 9TJ

As this charming thatched no smoking pub is popular with walkers, it's best to get here early. The low-ceilinged lounge bar has attractive antique high-backed settles, cushioned wall seats, and wheelback chairs around the tables on its patterned carpet, granite walls and a roaring log fire. A second bar has similar furnishings, a large dresser, harmonium, an HMV gramophone, and prints, and there's a family room with toys for children. Bar food includes sandwiches, home-made soup (£4.50), home-made chicken liver pâté (£5.50), local butcher's sausages (£7.95), spinach and feta cheese pie (£9.50), game pie (£10.50), poached salmon fillet with lemon and tarragon sauce (£10.95), half a honey-roasted duckling (£14.95), and puddings such as orange tart with marmalade ice-cream (£4.50). Otter Ale, Timothy Taylors Landlord and Wadworths 6X on handpump kept under light blanket pressure, quite a few malt whiskies, several wines by the glass, and local organic soft drinks. In summer, you can sit in the sheltered garden – the hanging baskets and flower beds are lovely. Until the car parking field in the village is opened during the summer, parking can be very difficult. More reports please. *(Recommended by David and Paula Russell, DAV, Dr and Mrs M E Wilson, Geoff and Marianne Millin)*

Heavitree ~ Tenant A Perring ~ Real ale ~ Bar food (not Mon) ~ (01647) 277223 ~ Children in family room ~ Dogs welcome ~ Open 11.30-3, 6-11; 11-11 Sat; 12-10.30 Sun; closed Mon

LYDFORD   SX5184   Map 1
Castle Inn

Off A386 Okehampton—Tavistock; EX20 4BH

There's plenty of character and charm in this bustling pink-washed Tudor inn – probably helped by its position next to the daunting, ruined 12th-c castle. The twin-roomed bar has country kitchen chairs, high-backed winged settles and old captain's chairs around mahogany tripod tables on big slate flagstones. One room has low lamp-lit beams, a sizeable open fire, masses of brightly decorated plates, some Hogarth prints and, near the serving counter, seven Lydford pennies hammered out in the old Saxon mint in the reign of Ethelred the Unready, in the 11th c. The bar area has a bowed ceiling with low beams, a polished slate flagstone floor and a stained-glass door with the famous Three Hares; there's also a snug with high-backed settles. Bar food includes toasted open sandwiches (£3.95), filled baked potatoes (£4.95), crab and avocado salad with lime, coriander and chilli dressing (£5.95; large £8.95), home-cooked ham and eggs (£6.95), sausages with herby mash and creamed leek and onion sauce (£7.95), a pie of the day (£8.25), and wild boar and apple burger topped with bacon and cheese (£8.75). The snug, restaurant and lounge are no smoking. Fullers London Pride, Greene King IPA and Otter Ale on handpump, and ten wines by the glass; darts, board games, and Wednesday quiz night. You can walk in the beautiful nearby river gorge (owned by the National Trust; closed November-Easter). *(Recommended by David and Paula Russell, Tony and Tracy Constance, Mrs J H S Lang, Mrs M Ainley, Ian Clare, Mary Ellen Cummings, DAV, Dr and Mrs M E Wilson, David Eberlin)*

Heavitree ~ Tenant Richard Davies ~ Real ale ~ Bar food ~ Restaurant ~ (01822) 820241 ~ Children allowed in snug, restaurant and lounge ~ Dogs allowed in bar and bedrooms ~ Open 11.30-11; 12-10.30 Sun ~ Bedrooms: £45B/£65B

MARLDON   SX8663   Map 1

Church House 🍽 ♀

Just off A380 NW of Paignton; TQ3 1SL

The spreading bar in this attractive no smoking inn has several different areas that radiate off the big semi-circular bar counter. The main part has interesting windows, some beams, dark pine chairs around solid tables on the turkey carpet, and yellow leather bar chairs; leading off here is a cosy little candlelit room with just four tables on the bare-board floor, a dark wood dado and stone fireplace; next to this is the restaurant with a large stone fireplace. At the other end of the building, a similarly interesting room is split into two parts with a stone floor in one bit and a wooden floor in another (which has a big woodburning stove). Well liked bar food includes sandwiches, home-made soup (£5.50), home-made chicken liver pâté with apple and date chutney or cornish blue cheesecake with pickled gooseberry compote (£6.50), roasted vegetable lasagne (£8.50), supreme of chicken in lemon and rosemary with a roasted garlic sauce (£12.50), slow-cooked lamb shoulder with fresh mint sauce (£14), and fillet steak topped with cornish yarg and a red wine and thyme sauce (£17.50). Bass, Fullers London Pride, Otter Ale and St Austell Dartmoor Best on handpump, and 12 wines by the glass; piped music. There are three grassy terraces with picnic-sets behind. More reports please. *(Recommended by JMC, M Sage, Mike and Mary Carter, Mr and Mrs Colin Roberts, Alan and Paula McCully, Emma Kingdon)*

Enterprise ~ Lease Julian Cook ~ Real ale ~ Bar food (12-2, 6.30-9.30) ~ Restaurant ~ (01803) 558279 ~ Children welcome ~ Dogs allowed in bar ~ Open 11.30-2.30, 5-11(11.30 Sat); 12-3, 5.30-10.30 Sun

MOLLAND   SS8028   Map 1

London 🍺

Village signposted off B3227 E of South Molton, down narrow lanes; EX36 3NG

Tucked away down narrow lanes, this is a proper Exmoor inn and much enjoyed by those who don't like uniformity. It's a bit quirky and very much huntin', shootin' and fishin', with a water bowl by the good log fire for the working dogs that come in with their keepers, a Crufts working-dog rosette won by one of the regulars sitting proudly on a shelf, and a really good mix of customers (Princess Anne dropped in for lunch just before we went to press). You can be sure of a genuinely warm welcome from the licensees, and they keep proper farm cider as well as Cotleigh Tawny and Exmoor Ale tapped from casks. The two small linked rooms by the old-fashioned central servery have lots of local stag-hunting pictures, tough carpeting or rugs on flagstones, cushioned benches and plain chairs around rough stripped trestle tables, a table of shooting and other country magazines, ancient stag and otter trophies, and darts, table skittles and dominoes. On the left an attractive beamed room has accounts of the rescued stag which lived a long life at the pub some 50 years ago, and on the right, a panelled dining room with a great curved settle by its fireplace has particularly good hunting and gamebird prints, including ones by McPhail and Hester Lloyd. Honest bar food includes home-made soup (£3.25), sandwiches (from £3.70), ham and egg (£5), ploughman's (£5.30), filled baked potatoes (£5.50), savoury pancakes (£6.20), and a dish of the day such as cottage or steak and kidney pie or curry (£6.50); evening choices such as steak, pigeon and mushroom pie, tuna steak chargrilled with salsa verde or lamb chop with port and redcurrant sauce (£10.80). The dining room and lower bar are no smoking. A small hall with stuffed birds and animals and lots of overhead baskets has a box of toys, and there are good country views from a few picnic-sets out in front. The low-ceilinged lavatories are worth a look, with their Victorian mahogany and tiling (and in the gents' a testament to the prodigious thirst of the village cricket team). And don't miss the next-door church, with its untouched early 18th-c box pews – and a spring carpet of tenby daffodils in the graveyard. Readers in tune with the down-to-earth style of the pub have enjoyed staying here. *(Recommended by the Didler, Heather and Dick Martin, Dave Braisted, Geoff and Teresa, Barry Steele-Perkins, Bob and Margaret Holder, David and Sheila Pearcey, Jeremy Whitehorn, George Atkinson)*

Free house ~ Licensees Mike and Linda Short ~ Real ale ~ Bar food (not Sun evening) ~ Restaurant ~ No credit cards ~ (01769) 550269 ~ Children welcome ~ Dogs allowed in bar and bedrooms ~ Open 11.30-2.30, 6-11.30; 12-2.30, 7-10.30 Sun ~ Bedrooms: /£50B

NEWTON ABBOT SX8468 Map 1
Two Mile Oak ♦
A381 2 miles S, at Denbury/Kingskerswell crossroads; TQ12 6DF

There's a relaxed atmosphere in this pleasant old coaching inn – as well as a beamed lounge and an alcove just for two, a mix of wooden tables and chairs, and a fine winter log fire. The beamed and black-panelled bar is traditionally furnished, again with a mix of seating, lots of horsebrasses and another good log fire. The no smoking restaurant has been smartened up with padded chairs, new tables, and sofas in front of the fire. Adnams, Bass, Flowers IPA and Otter Ale tapped from the cask, and decent wines. Well liked bar food includes home-made soup (£3.50), filled baguettes (from £4.95), ploughman's (from £5.95), ham and eggs (£7.25), lasagne (£7.95), lamb curry or steak and kidney pudding (£8.95), and daily specials such as trout fillets topped with mussels, prawns and squid with a light curry butter (£9.95), chicken breast in a honey, mushroom and cream sauce (£10.95), and grilled bass with prawns and lemon (£11.95). Piped music, TV, games machine, and darts. Picnic-sets on the terrace and a lawn with shrubs and tubs of flowers. More reports please. *(Recommended by Mrs Sylvia Elcoate, Mr and Mrs Colin Roberts, the Didler, Pamela and Merlyn Horswell)*

Heavitree ~ Manager Karen Brown ~ Real ale ~ Bar food (12-2.30, 6-9.30; all day Sat and Sun) ~ Restaurant ~ (01803) 812411 ~ Children welcome ~ Dogs allowed in bar ~ Open 11-11; 11-11 Sat; 12-10.30 Sun

NEWTON FERRERS SX5447 Map 1
Dolphin
Riverside Road East – follow Harbour dead end signs; PL8 1AE

By day, the two terraces across the lane from this friendly 18th-c pub have a grandstand view of the boating action on the busy tidal River Yealm below the cottages on these steep hillsides, and at night the floodlit church over in Noss Mayo makes a lovely focal point. Inside, the L-shaped bar has a few low black beams, slate floors, some white-painted plank panelling, and simple pub furnishings including cushioned wall benches and small winged settles; chatty and relaxed out of season, it can get packed in summer. Well liked food includes sandwiches (from £4; filled baguettes from £5.20), filled baked potatoes (from £5), sausage and chips

(£5.50), ploughman's (from £5.95), home-made vegetable lasagne (£7.45), fresh cod (£7.50), daily specials such as madras curry (£8.45), home-smoked salmon fillet (£9.45), and scallops in garlic butter (£10.95), and puddings like treacle sponge (£4). Sharps Doom Bar, a beer from Skinners named after the pub, and a guest beer on handpump, Heron Valley cider, and eight wines by the glass; darts, a popular quiz night on winter Wednesdays, local card games on Monday evenings, and lots of coastal watercolours. The carpeted no smoking dining room is up a few steps at the back. Parking by the pub is very limited, with more chance of a space either below or above. More reports please. *(Recommended by B J Harding, David M Cundy, MP)*

Free house ~ Licensee Sandra Dunbar Rees ~ Bar food ~ (01752) 872007 ~ Children in dining room until 9pm; no children in bar ~ Dogs allowed in bar ~ Open 12-3(2.30 in winter), 6-11; 12-3, 7-10.30 Sun; opens 12.30 in winter

NOMANSLAND   SS8313   Map 1
Mount Pleasant
B3137 Tiverton—South Molton; EX16 8NN

As we went to press, we heard that the long-standing licensees were thinking of selling this friendly pub, so we'd be grateful for any news on the forthcoming new people. The long bar here is divided into three with huge fireplaces each end, one with a woodburning stove under a low dark ochre black-beamed ceiling, the other with a big log fire, and there are tables in a sizeable bay window extension. A nice mix of furniture on the patterned carpet includes an old sofa with a colourful throw, old-fashioned leather dining chairs, pale country kitchen chairs and wall pews, and tables all with candles in attractive metal holders; country prints and local photographs including shooting parties. The bar, with plenty of bar stools, has Cotleigh Tawny, Greene King IPA and Sharps Doom Bar on handpump, and nine wines by the glass. Well liked bar food includes sandwiches, chicken liver pâté or oriental prawns in filo pastry (£4.95), sausages and onion gravy (£6.95), steak and kidney pie or pasta with smoked salmon in tomato and basil sauce (£7.95), mushroom stroganoff (£8.95), chicken breast with a choice of sauces such as garlic, mushrooms, spring onions, brie, Benedictine and cream (£9.95), lamb shank with redcurrant and orange sauce (£12.50), daily specials such as soups (£2.95), all-day breakfast or quiche (£5.95), ham and egg (£6.50), lamb chops with minted mash (£7.95), and puddings such as treacle tart or chocolate brownie (£4.50). On the left, a high-beamed stripped stone no smoking dining room was once a smithy and still has the raised forge fireplace. Piped music, darts and board games; picnic-sets under smart parasols in the neat back garden. *(Recommended by R J Walden, Bob and Margaret Holder, Jan Multon, Mr and Mrs M G Lipton, Jeremy Whitehorn)*

Free house ~ Licensees Anne, Karen and Sarah Butler ~ Real ale ~ Bar food (all day) ~ Restaurant ~ (01884) 860271 ~ Children welcome ~ Dogs allowed in bar ~ Open 11.30-11.30; 12-10.30 Sun; closed evening 25 Dec, 1 Jan

NOSS MAYO   SX5447   Map 1
Ship ♀ ◧
Off A379 via B3186, E of Plymouth; PL8 1EW

Almost as soon as this bustling pub opens, all the seats are taken. The front terrace is extremely popular in fine weather – you can sit at the octagonal wooden tables under parasols and look over the inlet, and visiting boats can tie up alongside (with prior permission); there are outdoor heaters for cooler evenings. Inside it's all no smoking, and the two thick-walled bars have a happy mix of dining chairs and tables on the wooden floors, log fires, bookcases, dozens of local pictures, newspapers and magazines to read, and a friendly, chatty atmosphere; board games. Changing daily, the popular food might include sandwiches (from £4.75; minute steak and crispy onion baguette £6.75), blue cheese and apple pâté (£5.25), chicken satay with peanut sauce (£6.75), three bean and vegetable casserole with suet dumplings or cumberland sausages with mustard mash and onion gravy (£8.95), fish pie (£10.25), crispy belly of pork with bubble and squeak and cider and apple gravy (£10.50, steak burger topped with gruyère cheese and bacon (£10.95), local haddock in ale batter and minted mushy peas (£11.25), 10oz sirloin steak with béarnaise sauce (£16.50), and puddings such as white chocolate cheesecake with raspberry compote, vanilla panna cotta with wild berries, and rhubarb fool (£5.25). Well kept Butcombe Blonde, Princetown Jail Ale, St Austell Tribute and Summerskills Tamar on handpump, lots of malt whiskies, and ten wines by the glass. Parking is restricted at high tide. They also own the Turtley Corn Mill at Avonwick, a new main entry this year. *(Recommended by Mrs Bridget Cushion, John Evans, B J Harding, Gene and Kitty Rankin, David Rule, Alan and Anne Driver, Dr and Mrs M E Wilson, Lynda and Trevor Smith, Mike Gorton, Mr and Mrs J E C Tasker, Charles and Pauline Stride, Geoff and Marianne Millin, Steve Whalley, Karen and Graham Oddey, Bruce Bird, Jennifer Sheridan, Tracey and Stephen Groves)*

Free house ~ Licensees Lesley and Bruce Brunning ~ Real ale ~ Bar food (all day) ~ (01752) 872387 ~ Children allowed before 7pm unless eating ~ Dogs allowed in bar ~ Open 11.30-11; 12-10.30 Sun

PARRACOMBE SS6644 Map 1
Fox & Goose ♀
Village signposted off A39 Blackmoor Gate—Lynton (actually a short cut, but winding and rather narrow); EX31 4PE

This quietly placed inn is run by friendly young licensees. The log fire, wooden ceiling, assorted mounted antlers, horns and ex-wildlife in some variety give a proper Exmoor feel to the relaxed and informal bar, and seating is mainly wheelback carver chairs around solid tables, with more tables at a comfortable height for people eating over on the left, and rambling around behind; there are some interesting black and white photographs. Tasty bar food might include home-made soup (£3.95), greek salad or home-made chicken liver pâté (£4.75), dressed crab salad (£5.95), mushroom stroganoff (£8.95), venison casserole (£10.75), fish stew or wild mushroom and game pie (£11.95), steaks (from £11.95), cod fillet with tiger prawns on a fresh basil and tomato sauce (£12.95), and puddings such as truffly peppermint and chocolate pots, rich toffee sauce sponge pudding or creamy rice pudding with fresh orange (£4.25); good breakfasts. Well kept Cotleigh Barn Owl and Exmoor Gold tapped from the cask, local farm cider and ten wines by the glass. The no smoking dining room on the right looks down on a little stream, and the front verandah has a couple of picnic-sets, with hanging baskets and flower tubs. *(Recommended by Ian Phillips, Mehefin, Geoff and Teresa, Rev D E and Mrs J A Shapland, Bob and Margaret Holder, Trevor and Diane Waite, David and Kay Griffiths, B M Eldridge, W W Burke, Janice and Phil Waller, Margit Severa, Felicity Stephens, David Fox)*

Free house ~ Licensees N Baxter and P Houle ~ Real ale ~ Bar food (12-2, 6-9) ~ (01598) 763239 ~ Well behaved children allowed but must be with parents at all times ~ Dogs allowed in bar ~ Open 12-3, 6(7 Sun)-11; closed 25 Dec ~ Bedrooms: £30S/£45S

PETER TAVY SX5177 Map 1
Peter Tavy Inn ♀
Off A386 near Mary Tavy, N of Tavistock; PL19 9NN

New licensees have taken over this attractive old stone pub but have kept on the chef and quite a few of the senior staff. The low-beamed bar has high-backed settles on the black flagstones by the big stone fireplace (a fine log fire on cold days), smaller settles in stone-mullioned windows, and a good bustling atmosphere; there's also a snug, no smoking dining area and restaurant. Good food at lunchtime might include leek and sweet potato soup (£4.25), filled baguettes or baked potatoes (from £4.95), ham and egg or game terrine with pear and ginger chutney (£5.75), roast beef with yorkshire pudding (£7.95), and minted lamb and orange casserole or peppers tuffed with roasted vegetables and mozzarella (£8.95); evening choices such as camembert wrapped in pancetta with chilli jam or moules marinière (£5.95), caramelised red onion tart tatin or pork tenderloin with apples and stilton sauce (£13.95), mexican fajitas (£12.95), duck breast with an orange and red fruit sauce (£13.45), and lamb shank with gooseberry and mint gravy (£13.95); home-made puddings (£4.25). Blackawton Original Bitter, Princetown Jail Ale, Sharps Doom Bar and a guest like St Austell HSD on handpump, kept under light blanket pressure; local farm cider, 20 malt whiskies and ten wines by the glass; piped music. From the picnic-sets in the pretty garden, there are peaceful views of the moor rising above nearby pastures. *(Recommended by Gillian Rodgers, Gene and Kitty Rankin, Mick and Moira Brummell, Alistair Caie, Jacquie and Jim Jones, Peter and Margaret Lodge, Pam and Alan Neale, Alan and Paula McCully, Leo and Barbara Lionet)*

Free house ~ Licensees Chris and Joan Wordingham ~ Real ale ~ Bar food ~ Restaurant ~ (01822) 810348 ~ Children welcome ~ Dogs welcome ~ Open 12-3(4 Sat and Sun), 6-11(10.30 Sun)

PORTGATE SX4185 Map 1

Harris Arms 🍴 🍷

Turn off A30 E of Launceston at Broadwoodwidger turn-off (with brown Dingle Steam Village sign), and head S; Launceston Road (old A30 between Lewdown and Lifton); EX20 4PZ

A large new decking area has been opened up behind this white-painted roadside pub. There are olive trees, pots of lavender, huge umbrellas and outdoor heaters, and on the sloping back garden, plenty of picnic-sets looking out over the rolling wooded pasture hills. Twenty-four young vines have been planted, too. Inside, you can expect a warm welcome from the chatty and helpful licensees. One of their great loves is wine, and as qualifield wine-makers they are happy to help you through their eclectic wine list. There are a dozen of their favourite house wines (all available by the glass) plus plenty of gems from all over the world. With burgundy end walls and cream ones in between, the partly no smoking bar has some rather fine photographs, a log fire in a big stone hearth with a woodburning stove in another, a huge table at one end (brought back from New Zealand) and a long red-plush built-in wall banquette; afghan saddle-bag cushions are scattered around a mixture of other tables and dining chairs. On the left, steps lead down to the recently refurbished no smoking dining room with elegant beech dining chairs (and more afghan cushions) around stripped wooden tables, and some unusual paints on the walls collected by the Whitemans on their travels. Using local seasonal produce, the good food at lunchtime might include home-made soup (£3.75), game terrine with home-made red onion and apricot chutney (£5.75), ham and egg or wild boar sausages and mash (£7.50), ploughman's (£7.75), fish and chips (£8.25), and steak frites (£8.95), with evening choices such as grilled goats cheese with garlic croûtons and olives (£5.75), home-made fishcakes on creamed leeks (£6.50), roast breast of guinea fowl with braised fennel and herbed lemon shallot butter (£12.50), and griddled local rib-eye steak or lamb shank with orange and thyme jus (£13.50), and daily specials like grilled marinated cornish sardines (£6.50), seared scallops with sage, lemon and capers (£6.95), roasted leg of venison with chestnuts and spiced red cabbage (£14.50), and italian fish stew (£14.50). Puddings are home made: very berry brûlée, stem ginger pudding and double chocolate brownies (from £4.50). Well kept Sharps Doom Bar and a beer from Ring o' Bells on handpump, Luscombe organic soft drinks, summer cider, and a pile of country magazines. *(Recommended by M and R Thomas, Charles and Isabel Cooper, R J Walden, John Whiting, Andy and Claire Barker, Mr and Mrs Ron Patterson, Alistair Caie)*

Free house ~ Licensees Andy and Rowena Whiteman ~ Bar food (12-2, 6(7 Sun)-9; not Mon) ~ Restaurant ~ (01566) 783331 ~ Children welcome ~ Dogs allowed in bar ~ Open 12-3, 6-11; 12-3, 7-10.30 Sun; closed Mon all day, winter Sun evenings

---

We checked prices with the pubs as we went to press in summer 2006. They should hold until around spring 2007 – when our experience suggests that you can expect an increase of around 10p in the £.

POSTBRIDGE   SX6780   Map 1
Warren House
B3212 ¾ mile NE of Postbridge; PL20 6TA

This no-frills place is handy for a drink after a damp hike on Dartmoor. The cosy bar has a fireplace at either end (one is said to have been kept almost continuously alight since 1845), and is simply furnished with easy chairs and settles under a beamed ochre ceiling, wild animal pictures on the partly panelled stone walls, and dim lighting (fuelled by the pub's own generator); there's a no smoking family room. Standard bar food and Badger Tanglefoot, Otter Ale and Ringwood Old Thumper on handpump, local farm cider and malt whiskies. Darts, board games, and piped music. There are picnic-sets on both sides of the road that give pleasant moorland views. *(Recommended by Andrea Rampley, John Robertson, Ian and Ruth Laurence, Anthony Longden, Ken Flawn)*

Free house ~ Licensee Peter Parsons ~ Real ale ~ Bar food (all day summer and all day Thurs-Sun in winter; 12-4 Mon-Weds in winter) ~ (01822) 880208 ~ Children in family room ~ Dogs allowed in bar ~ Open 11-11; 12-10.30 Sun; 11-5 Mon-Weds in winter

POUNDSGATE   SX7072   Map 1
Tavistock Inn
B3357 continuation; TQ13 7NY

After enjoying one of the many moorland hikes, walkers (and their boots and dogs on leads) are made welcome in this picturesque old pub. Some original features include a narrow-stepped granite spiral staircase, original flagstones, ancient log fireplaces, and beams, and there's a friendly atmosphere and a good mix of locals and visitors; one small room is no smoking. Brakspears, Courage Best, Greene King Old Speckled Hen and Wychwood Hobgoblin Best on handpump, decent wines, and a few malt whiskies. Traditional bar food includes filled baguettes (from £3.90; sausage and onion £4.10), filled baked potatoes (from £4.90), home-made lasagne or vegetarian pasta bake (£6.90), locally made burger (£7.10), beef in ale pie (£7.90), and steaks (from £11); summer afternoon teas. Tables on the front terrace and pretty flowers in stone troughs, hanging baskets and window boxes, and more seats (and ducks) in the quiet back garden; lovely scenery. Sir Arthur Conan Doyle wrote *The Hound of the Baskervilles* while staying here. *(Recommended by Paul and Shirley White, Dr R C C Ward, JHW, Geoff and Marianne Millin)*

InnSpired ~ Lease Peter and Jean Hamill ~ Real ale ~ Bar food (all day in summer) ~ Restaurant ~ (01364) 631251 ~ Children in eating area of bar ~ Dogs allowed in bar ~ Open 11-3, 6-11; 11-11 Sat; 12-10.30 Sun

RATTERY   SX7461   Map 1
Church House
Village signposted from A385 W of Totnes, and A38 S of Buckfastleigh; TQ10 9LD

Dating back to 1028, this is one of Britain's oldest pubs, and the spiral stone steps behind a little stone doorway on your left as you come in date back to that time. The original building here probably housed the craftsmen who built the Norman church, and may then have served as a hostel for passing monks. There are massive oak beams and standing timbers in the homely open-plan bar, large fireplaces (one with a little cosy nook partitioned off around it), windsor armchairs, comfortable seats and window seats, and prints on the plain white walls; the dining room is separated from this room by heavy curtains, and there's also a no smoking lounge area. Bar food (with prices unchanged since last year) includes soup (£3.75), sandwiches (from £4.25; toasties £4.50; filled baguettes from £4.75), devilled whitebait (£4.95), ploughman's (from £5.75), sausages with onion gravy (£7.25), creamy coconut chicken curry or steak and kidney pie (£7.75), vegetable lasagne (£8.25), steaks (from £10.75), citrus and olive lamb shank (£11.75), daily specials, and puddings (£3.50). Well kept Greene King Abbot, Otter Ale, Princetown Jail Ale and St Austell Dartmoor Best on handpump, several malt whiskies, and eight wines by the glass; obliging service. The garden has picnic benches on the large hedged-in lawn, and peaceful views of the partly wooded surrounding hills. *(Recommended by B J Harding, Mr and Mrs J Curtis, Hugh Roberts, MP, Mrs J H S Lang, M Sage, Mick and Moira Brummell, George Atkinson, Richard May, Tracey and Stephen Groves, Clare Rosier)*

Free house ~ Licensee Ray Hardy ~ Real ale ~ Bar food ~ Restaurant ~ (01364) 642220 ~ Children welcome ~ Dogs allowed in bar ~ Open 11-2.30, 6-11; 12-2.30, 6-10.30 Sun

ROCKBEARE   SY0295   Map 1
Jack in the Green 🍴 ♀
Signposted from new A30 bypass E of Exeter; EX5 2EE

Although many customers come to this big, neatly kept roadside dining pub for a meal, those dropping in for a quick pint are made just as welcome by the friendly landlord. The neat and comfortable good-sized bar has wheelback chairs, sturdy cushioned wall pews and varying-sized tables on its dark blue carpet, a dark carved oak dresser, and sporting prints and nice decorative china; piped music. The larger dining side is similarly traditional in style: some of its many old hunting and shooting photographs are well worth a close look and there are button-back leather chesterfields by the big woodburning stove. You may smoke in only one bar. Popular, if not cheap, bar food includes soup (£4.25), peppered duck liver and orange parfait (£5.25), bangers and mash with onion gravy (£9.50), grilled goats cheese salad with grape chutney and spicy walnuts (£9.75), crisp fried confit of duck leg with stir-fried noodles and mangetout with a sweet and sour sauce (£9.95), steak and kidney pie, wild bass fishcake with soy and ginger dressing or thai chicken curry (all £12.50), peppered rib-eye steak with beetroot fondant (£16.50), and daily specials such as fillet of brill with lightly curried or whole grilled lemon sole with pesto (£16.50). Greene King Ruddles Best and Otter Ale on handpump, and ten wines by the glass. There are some tables out behind, by a back skittle alley. *(Recommended by Mick and Moira Brummell, Mrs Sylvia Elcoate, Dr Donald Ainscow, Ian Phillips, Dr and Mrs A K Clarke, Dr and Mrs M E Wilson, Barry Steele-Perkins, Alan Sadler, John and Fiona McIlwain, Piotr Chodzko-Zajko, Gill and Keith Croxton, OPUS, Oliver and Sue Rowell, Lucien Perring)*

Free house ~ Licensee Paul Parnell ~ Real ale ~ Bar food (12-2, 6-9.30(10 Fri and Sat) but all day Sun) ~ Restaurant ~ (01404) 822240 ~ Well behaved children in no smoking bar and in restaurant for Sun lunch ~ Open 11-2.30(3 Sat), 6-11; 12-9.30 Sun; closed 25 Dec-4 Jan

SANDY PARK   SX7087   Map 1
Sandy Park Inn 🛏
A382 Whiddon Down—Moretonhampstead; TQ13 8JW

There's a super mix of customers and a terrific bustling atmosphere in this little thatched inn – all helped along by the friendly and enthusiastic young landlord. The small bar on the right has rugs on the black-painted composition floor, black beams in the cream ceiling, varnished built-in wall settles forming separate areas around nice tables, and bar stools by the chatty bar with Otter Bitter and St Austell Tribute, and perhaps a couple of guests like Exe Valley Dobs Best or O'Hanlons Yellowhammer on handpump, local cider, and a decent choice of wines by the glass; big blow-ups of old golfing pictures and some smaller interestingly annotated Dartmoor photographs. The back snug has one big table that a dozen people could just squeeze around, stripped stone walls, and a cream-painted bright-cushioned built-in wall bench. On the left is a small dining room with golfing and other prints on the red walls and just a few tables, and an inner private no smoking dining room with lots of prints, and one big table. Enjoyable food includes home-made soup or roast beef and horseradish sandwich (£4.95), fresh calamari rings with sweet chilli (£6.50), local sausages and mash (£7.50), roasted red pepper and asparagus risotto or lambs liver and bacon (£7.95), beer battered cod (£8.50), braised lamb shank (£9.50), sirloin steak with blue cheese (£11.50), and rack of lamb with redcurrant jus (£14). Board games. There's a large garden with fine views. This is a nice place to stay and the decent breakfasts are cooked by the landlord. They may have preferential fishing rates on the River Teign. More reports please. *(Recommended by Will and Kay Adie, Barry Steele-Perkins, Gordon and Glynis Casey, Sally Jenkin, Derek Allpass)*

Free house ~ Licensee Simon Saunders ~ Real ale ~ Bar food (12-2.30, 6-9) ~ Restaurant ~ (01647) 433267 ~ Children in snug or dining room ~ Dogs allowed in bar and bedrooms ~ Open 12-11.30; 12-11 Sun ~ Bedrooms: /£80B

SIDBURY   SY1595   Map 1
Hare & Hounds 🏮
3 miles N of Sidbury, at Putts Corner; A375 towards Honiton, crossroads with B3174; EX10 0QQ

Extremely popular, this very well run roadside pub is so much bigger inside than you could have guessed from outside. There are two good log fires (and rather unusual wood-framed leather sofas complete with pouffes), heavy beams and fresh flowers throughout, some oak panelling, plenty of tables with red leatherette or red plush-cushioned dining chairs, window seats and well used bar stools too; it's mostly carpeted, with bare boards and stripped stone walls at one softly lit end. At the opposite end, on the left, another big dining area has huge windows looking out over the garden. The two dining areas are no smoking. They tell us prices for food have not changed at all this year: the much enjoyed daily carvery counter has a choice of joints and enough turnover to keep up a continuous supply of fresh vegetables (lunchtime £7.85, evening £8.35, Sunday lunch £8.50). Other food includes sandwiches or baguettes (from £3.75), home-made soup (£3.95), home-made chicken liver pâté (£4.45), filled baked potatoes (from £4.45), home-made pie of the day (£7.25), home-made curry (£7.45), nut roast or ploughman's (£7.50), home-made lasagne (£7.75), local steaks (from £10.75), and daily specials. Well kept Branscombe, O'Hanlons Yellowhammer, and Otter Ale and Bitter tapped from the cask; a side room has a big-screen sports TV. The big garden, giving good valley views, has picnic-sets, a new children's play area, and a new marquee; maybe a small strolling flock of peafowl. *(Recommended by Edna Jones, Louis Hertzberg, Michael and Marion Buchanan)*

Free house ~ Licensee Peter Cairns ~ Real ale ~ Bar food (all day) ~ Restaurant ~ (01404) 41760 ~ Children welcome with restrictions ~ Dogs allowed in bar ~ Live music Sun lunchtimes in marquee ~ Open 10-11.30; 11.30-11.30 Sun

SLAPTON   SX8244   Map 1
Tower ★ 🍽
Signposted off A379 Dartmouth—Kingsbridge; TQ7 2PN

Although many customers come to this atmospheric old place to enjoy the interesting food, they do keep Badger Tanglefoot, Butcombe Bitter and St Austell Tribute on handpump and plenty of our readers drop in with their dogs after a walk. The low-ceilinged beamed bar has armchairs, low-backed settles and scrubbed oak tables on the flagstones or bare boards, open log fires, and farm ciders and several wines by the glass. At lunchtime, the popular food includes home-made soup (£3.95), sandwiches (from £4.50; hot sausage and caramelised onions £5.25), a platter of locally smoked fish (£5.50; main course £9.25), duck liver and smoked duck pâté with spicy fruit and nut chutney (£5.95), pork and leek sausages with cheddar mash (£8.95), chicken and mushroom pie (£9.75), warm leek and gruyère tart (£9.95), and slow-cooked lamb shank with redcurrant rosemary jus (£12.95); evening choices such as caramelised onion tartlet topped with goats cheese (£5.25), thai-flavoured prawns with a sweet lime and coconut dip (£5.50), spicy borlotti bean, lentil and butternut stew (£9.95), baked salmon fillet with parmesan and hazelnut crust and a lemon and white wine cream sauce (£10.95), venison bourguignon with blue cheese dumplings (£11.95), and fillet steak with marsala sauce (£17.95); piped music and board games. The picnic-sets on the neatly kept lawn in the pretty back garden are overlooked by the ivy-covered ruin of a 14th-c chantry – lovely in summer. The lane up to the pub is very narrow and parking is difficult. *(Recommended by Peter and Giff Bennett, Mr and Mrs J Curtis, Roger Wain-Heapy, Gerry and Rosemary Dobson, Mrs Carolyn Dixon, Dr R C C Ward, Bob and Margaret Holder, Mayur Shah, Mike Gorton, the Didler, Terry and Linda Moseley, Marguerite Pointer, Nick Lawless, Ann Holdsworth, Lynda and Trevor Smith, Lizzie Parker-Clarke, Mark Bramley, Mike Ambrose, Chris and Helena Cooke, Alan and Anne Driver, Mike and Shelley Woodroffe, David Eberlin, Wendy and Carl Dye)*

Free house ~ Licensees Annette and Andrew Hammett ~ Real ale ~ Bar food ~ Restaurant ~ (01548) 580216 ~ Children not allowed in bar ~ Dogs allowed in bar ~ Open 12-2.30(3 Sat), 6-11; 12-3, 7-10.30 Sun; closed Sun evening and Mon in winter ~ Bedrooms: £50S/£70S

ST ANNS CHAPEL   SX4170   Map 1

Old Chapel ♀ 🛏

B3392 Modbury—Bigbury-on-Sea; TQ7 4HQ

This takes its name from the 13th-c wayfarers' chapel which now serves as a central entrance area – bar on one side, dining room on the other. Small and simple, the chapel is now white-painted, with just a couple of pillars, what looks like a little sleeping alcove up above your head on one side, and opposite that a patch of the high ceiling where the ancient hand-cut laths have been roughly exposed (by a 2005 lightning strike). The sisal-carpeted beamed bar, mainly 18th-c but in part dating back to the time of the chapel itself, has been attractively restored: sconces with lighted candles and some fleurs-de-lis and other stencils on walls of red-ragged plaster or stripped dark stone, a log fire in a neat raised stone fireplace, red cushions on black built-in high-backed settles (one topped with a lighted candelabrum that makes an alluring sight from the road – candles really do set the mood here), chunky farm chairs, long black-painted tables, nicely carved high stools on dark slate flagstones by the bar counter – which has Sharps Doom Bar and South Hams Devon Pride on handpump, good wines by the glass, and on its gantry some stylish monochrome chapel and church photographs (that look french rather than english). The family room is no smoking. Good up-to-date bar food using local supplies includes sandwiches, roasted red pepper, tomato and chorizo soup (£3.95), chicken liver and mushroom terrine (£5.50), mussels steamed in cider with home-smoked bacon and garlic (£5.75), ploughman's (£6.95), roast local beef with yorkshire pudding or local sausages with onion gravy (£7.95), fish and chips (£8.25), chicken breast with black pudding hash and a leek and bacon sauce (£12.95), fillet of salmon on crayfish and crab risotto with a red pepper and vermouth sauce (£13.95), daily specials like hearty fish stew (£8.95), lambs liver on butter-braised savoy cabbage with a bacon, mushroom and tarragon fricassee (£9.50), and whole ham hock with wholegrain mustard mash (£10.50), and puddings such as rhubarb and apple crumble or ginger sponge with butterscotch sauce (£4.50); they do nice simple proper food for children. Service is friendly and relaxed. The light and airy modern no smoking dining room, with comfortable seating and a grand piano, leads into a conservatory. There are picnic-sets in a neat back terraced garden. The five bedrooms are furnished in character. *(Recommended by Mr and Mrs Davies)*

Free house ~ Licensees Paul and Britt Clement ~ Real ale ~ Bar food (12-2.30, 6-9.30) ~ Restaurant ~ (01548) 810241 ~ Children welcome ~ Dogs allowed in bar ~ Open 11 (12 Sun)-3, 6-11; Closed Sun evenings and all day Mon in winter; closed first two weeks Jan ~ Bedrooms: £55S/£85B

STAVERTON   SX7964   Map 1

Sea Trout ♀

Village signposted from A384 NW of Totnes; TQ9 6PA

Even when this old village pub is busy – which it usually is – staff remain efficient and friendly. The neatly kept rambling beamed lounge bar has sea trout and salmon flies and stuffed fish on the walls, cushioned settles and stools, a stag's head above the fireplace, and a cheerful mix of locals and visitors. The main bar has low banquettes, soft lighting and an open fire, and there's also a public bar with darts, pool, fruit machine, TV, shove-ha'penny, bar billiards, board games and a juke box. Enjoyable food includes lunchtime sandwiches, soup (£3.75), roast tomato, red onion and herb bruschetta (£4.95), chicken caesar salad (£5.25), home-made steak and Guinness pie, beer battered haddock with home-made chips, chicken breast stuffed with spicy chorizo or baked red pepper and aubergine stuffed with vegetable risotto (all £9.95), steaks (from £13.95), daily specials such as creamy saffron fish pie (£9.95) and free-range pork chops with apple and cider sauce (£10.95), and puddings like strawberry crème brûlée, dark chocolate mousse or sticky toffee pudding with caramel sauce (£4.50). The conservatory, restaurant and all food bars are no smoking. Palmers IPA, Copper and Gold on handpump, a dozen wines by the glass, quite a few whiskies, and farm cider. There are seats under parasols on the attractive paved back garden. A station for the South Devon Steam Railway is not too far away. *(Recommended by Dennis Jenkin, Mike and Mary Carter, Norman and Sarah Keeping, E B Ireland, the Didler, Mrs A P Lee, Tony Baldwin, Henry and Fiona Dryden, Mrs S Gudgeon)*

Palmers ~ Tenants Nick and Nicky Brookland ~ Real ale ~ Bar food (12-2, 7-9; 12-2.30, 6.30-9.30 Fri and Sat) ~ Restaurant ~ (01803) 762274 ~ Children allowed away from bar ~ Dogs allowed in bar and bedrooms ~ Open 11-3.30, 6-11.30; 10-4, 5.30-12.30 Sat; 11-4, 7-11 Sun; closed evenings 25 and 26 Dec ~ Bedrooms: £49.50B/£64B

STOCKLAND   ST2404   Map 1

Kings Arms ♀

Village signposted from A30 Honiton—Chard; and also, at every turning, from N end of Honiton High Street; EX14 9BS

As we went to press, we heard that this 16th-c inn was up for sale. It's been much enjoyed by our readers over the years so we are keeping our fingers tightly crossed that the new people will not change too much. The dark beamed, elegant Cotley Bar has had solid refectory tables and settles, attractive landscapes, a medieval oak screen (which divides the room into two), and a great stone fireplace across almost the whole width of one end; the cosy no smoking restaurant has a huge inglenook fireplace and bread oven. Enjoyable bar food has been served lunchtime only (not Sunday) and has included soup (£3), open sandwiches with ciabatta bread (£4.50), omelettes (from £4.50), ploughman's (£6.50), lasagne or sausage and mash with onion gravy (£7.50), mascarpone and spinach linguini (£8.50), daily specials, and puddings (£5); in the evening, only the restaurant menu has been available. Exmoor Ale, O'Hanlons Fire Fly and Yellowhammer, and Otter Ale on handpump, lots of malt whiskies, a comprehensive wine list, and farm ciders. At the back, a flagstoned bar has cushioned benches and stools around heavy wooden tables, and leads on to a carpeted darts area, another room with dark beige plush armchairs and settees (and a fruit machine), and a neat ten-pin skittle alley; TV and piped music. There are tables under cocktail parasols on the terrace in front of the white-faced thatched pub and a lawn enclosed by trees and shrubs. Reports please. *(Recommended by Dr and Mrs T E Hothersall, Derek and Heather Manning, Bob and Margaret Holder, David and Elizabeth Briggs, Alan Sadler, Michael B Griffith, Mike and Mary Carter, Dr and Mrs R Booth, Pat and Robert Watt, Chris Bell, John and Fiona Merritt, John and Wendy Hamilton)*

Free house ~ Licensees Heinz Kiefer and Paul Diviani ~ Real ale ~ Bar food ~ Restaurant ~ (01404) 881361 ~ Children welcome ~ Dogs allowed in bar ~ Open 12-3, 6.30-11 (midnight Sat); closed 25 Dec ~ Bedrooms: £45B/£70B

STOKE GABRIEL   SX8457   Map 1

Church House

Village signposted from A385 just W of junction with A3022, in Collaton St Mary; can also be reached from nearer Totnes; TQ9 6SD

Bustling and cheerful, this friendly old local always has a good mix of customers. The lounge bar has an exceptionally fine medieval beam-and-plank ceiling, as well as a black oak partition wall, window seats cut into the thick butter-coloured walls, decorative plates and vases of flowers on a dresser, and a huge fireplace still used in winter to cook the stew; darts. The mummified cat in a case, probably about 200 years old, was found during restoration of the roof space in the verger's cottage three doors up the lane – one of a handful found in the West Country and believed to have been a talisman against evil spirits. Straightforward, good value bar food includes home-made soup (£2.95), a big choice of sandwiches and toasties (from £2.95; ham, cheese, pineapple and onion toastie £3.95), filled baked potatoes (from £4.25), ploughman's (from £4.95), daily specials such as steak and kidney or fish pies, wild mushroom ravioli or chilli con carne (all £6.95), and puddings (£3.75). Bass, Skinners Figgys Brew and Worthington Best on handpump, and 20 malt whiskies. Euchre in the little public locals' bar. There are picnic-sets on the small terrace in front of the building. The church is very pretty, and relations with the Church of England and this pub go back a long way – witness the priest hole, dating from the Reformation, visible from outside. Parking is very limited. No children. *(Recommended by Dr and Mrs M E Wilson, David and Karen Cuckney, H Frank Smith, Di and Mike Gillam, M Sage, Sheila Newbury, Alan and Paula McCully, Peter Titcomb)*

Free house ~ Licensee T G Patch ~ Real ale ~ Bar food (11(12 Sun)-2.30, 6(7 Sun)-10) ~ No credit cards ~ (01803) 782384 ~ Dogs allowed in bar ~ Open 11-3, 6-11.30; 11-11.30 Sat; 12-4, 7-11 Sun

STRETE SX8446 Map 1
Kings Arms 🍴 ♀
A379 SW of Dartmouth – car park is S of pub; TQ6 0RW

With its wrought-iron work and canopied upper balcony, this family run pub is very pretty, and there's a back terrace and garden with views over Start Bay. Inside, the L-shaped bar has country kitchen chairs and tables, some comfortable brocaded dining chairs, very nice fish prints on the dark salmon pink walls, and bar stools by the attractively carved oak bar counter where the chatty locals gather. Well kept Adnams Best, Fullers London Pride and Otter Ale on handpump, 15 wines by the glass (including sweet ones) from a carefully chosen list, a dozen malt whiskies, and local Heron Valley cider; board games. You go up some stairs to the little no smoking restaurant decorated in cool blue/green colours with dark green padded plush and pale wood chairs around wooden tables. They use local and regional produce and bake their own breads, brioche, oatcakes and biscuits, and the main menu is the same throughout. From the bar and terrace menu, there might be local oysters and sausages (£4.95), crab bisque (£6.50), moules marinière (£7.50), scallops with crispy bacon (£7.95), fish in beer batter with home-made tartare sauce (£8.95), caesar salad (£9.25), fillet of sea trout on noodles with yellow beans, lemon grass, ginger and spring onions or slow-roasted belly of pork in masala, honey and root vegetables (£11.95), and rib-eye steak with café de paris butter (£16.95). The pub is on the South West Coastal Path. *(Recommended by Alastair Beck, Charles Moore, Roger Wain-Heapy)*

Heavitree ~ Tenant Rob Dawson ~ Real ale ~ Bar food (12-2 (3 Sun), 6.30-9.30) ~ Restaurant ~ (01803) 770377 ~ Children welcome ~ Dogs allowed in bar ~ Open 11.30-2.30(3 Sat), 6.30(6 Sat)-11; 12-4, 7-10.30 Sun closed; Sun evening and all day Mon in winter

TOPSHAM SX9688 Map 1
Bridge Inn ★ 🍺
2¼ miles from M5 junction 30: Topsham signposted from exit roundabout; in Topsham follow signpost (A376) Exmouth on the Elmgrove Road, into Bridge Hill; EX3 0QQ

The very friendly landlady here – she is the fifth generation of her family to run this wonderful old place – has introduced third-pint glasses (all custom made and stamped by the government) so that customers can taste her strong beers 'without going over the top and getting drunk'; the glasses are popular with drivers, too. This remains an absolute favourite with many readers for its utterly old-fashioned layout and character – and of course for the perfectly kept eight or nine real ales.

Tapped from the cask, these might include Adnams Broadside, Blackawton Merryweather, Branscombe Vale Branoc, Old Man of the Sea and Summa That, Jollyboat Privateer, O'Hanlons Broad Oak and Yellowhammer, and Weltons Dragons Gold; country wines, non-alcoholic pressés, and decent wines by the glass. It's totally no smoking now, and there are fine old traditional furnishings (true country workmanship) in the little lounge partitioned off from the inner corridor by a high-backed settle; log fire, and a bigger lower room (the old malthouse) is open at busy times. Simple, tasty bar food such as pasties (£2.50), sandwiches (3.50; the ham with gooseberry and elderflower chutney is particularly good), a hearty winter soup (£3.95), and various ploughman's (from £5.50); the local hand-fried crisps are excellent. No noisy music, games machines or mobile phones – just a chatty, relaxed atmosphere. Outside, riverside picnic-sets overlook the weir. *(Recommended by Phil and Sally Gorton, David Crook, Barry Steele-Perkins, Tony and Jill Radnor, Dr and Mrs A K Clarke, the Didler, Richard Pitcher, Will and Kay Adie, Pete Baker, Dr and Mrs M E Wilson, Michael Rowse, Mike Gorton, John and Fiona McIlwain, John and Jane Hayter, David Swift, Peter Titcomb, OPUS, R T and J C Moggridge)*

Free house ~ Licensee Mrs C Cheffers-Heard ~ Real ale ~ Bar food (lunchtime only) ~ No credit cards ~ (01392) 873862 ~ Children welcome ~ Dogs allowed in bar ~ Occasional live music ~ Open 12-2, 6(7 Sun)-10.30(11 Fri/Sat)

TORBRYAN SX8266 Map 1
Old Church House
Most easily reached from A381 Newton Abbot—Totnes via Ipplepen; TQ12 5UR

Quietly set next to the part-Saxon church with its battlemented Norman tower, this Grade II* listed 13th-c inn is doing very well at the moment. The particularly attractive bar on the right of the door is neatly kept and bustling, and has benches built into the fine old panelling as well as a cushioned high-backed settle and leather-backed small seats around its big log fire. On the left there is a series of comfortable and discreetly lit lounges, one with a splendid deep Tudor inglenook fireplace with a side bread oven. The restaurant is no smoking; piped music. Enjoyable bar food includes home-made soup (£3.95), sandwiches (from £4.50; filled baguettes £5.95), ploughman's, mushroom risotto or lasagne (£7.95), beef in ale pie (£8.50), haddock mornay (£9.90), and rack of lamb or 10oz sirloin steak with beer-battered onion rings (£14.95); curry night is Tuesday (£8.95). Well kept Skinners Betty Stogs and Cornish Knocker and maybe a guest beer on handpump, 25 malt whiskies, and quite a few wines; friendly service. Plenty of nearby walks. *(Recommended by E B Ireland, Graham and Glenis Watkins, Andrew Shore, Maria Williams, Peter and Margaret Lodge, J D O Carter, Mr and Mrs T A Watson, Emma Kingdon)*

Free house ~ Licensees Kane and Carolynne Clarke ~ Real ale ~ Bar food ~ Restaurant ~ (01803) 812372 ~ Children welcome but with restrictions ~ Dogs allowed in bar ~ Accoustic guitar Thurs evening, open music night Sun ~ Open 11-11; 12-10.30 Sun ~ Bedrooms: £54B/£69B

TORCROSS SX8241 Map 1
Start Bay
A379 S of Dartmouth; TQ7 2TQ

Although Paul Stubbs (who was here for 28 years) has now retired, his son-in-law and daughters continue to run this extremely popular dining pub. The main emphasis remains on the fresh fish which is delivered to the door by local fishermen (who work off the beach in front of the pub) and from a local crabber; Mr Jacob is aiming to carry on the diving for scallops. Queues usually form even before the doors open and the straightforward main bar is always packed. It is very much set out for eating with wheelback chairs around plenty of dark tables or (round a corner) back-to-back settles forming booths; some photographs of storms buffeting the pub and country pictures on the cream walls and a winter coal fire. A small chatty drinking area by the counter has a brass ship's clock and barometer, there's a winter games room with pool and darts, and more booth seating in a no smoking family room with sailing boat pictures. Their speciality is fish in light batter: cod or haddock (medium £5.50; large £7.50; jumbo £9.70), plaice (from £5.50), and lemon sole (£8.90), with other fish dishes as available. Also, sandwiches (from £3.50), filled baked potatoes (from £3.80), ploughman's (from £5.50), vegetable lasagne (£6.50), steaks (from £9.70), and mixed seafood platter (£10.90); they do warn of delays at peak times. Bass, Flowers Original and Otter Ale on handpump, Heron Valley cider, and local wine from the Sharpham Estate. There are seats (highly prized) out on the terrace overlooking the three-mile pebble beach, and the freshwater wildlife lagoon of Slapton Ley is just behind the pub. *(Recommended by Mayur Shah, Mike Gorton, Mike and Mary Carter, Geoff Calcott, Sheila Newbury, Jack Clark, Fred and Lorraine Gill, Sue Demont, Tim Barrow)*

Whitbreads ~ Tenant Stuart Jacob ~ Real ale ~ Bar food (11.30-2, 6-10 (9.30 in winter)) ~ (01548) 580553 ~ Children in family room ~ Open 11.30-11; 12-10.30 Sun; 11.30-2.30, 6-11 weekdays and Sat in winter

TOTNES SX8059 Map 1
Steam Packet
St Peters Quay, on W bank (ie not on Steam Packet Quay); TQ9 5EW

In summer, the terrace in front of this bustling pub overlooking the quay is quite a bonus – plenty of modern tables and chairs, flowering tubs and outdoor heaters. Inside has stripped wood floors throughout, and is interestingly laid out. The end part has an open coal fire, fancy knotwork in a case above the fireplace, a squashy leatherette sofa with lots of cushions against a wall of books, and a similar seat built into a small curved brick wall (which breaks up the room). The main bar has built-in wall benches and plenty of stools and chairs around traditional pubby tables, and a further section with another small fire and plain dark wooden chairs and tables leads into the no smoking conservatory restaurant. Butcombe Bitter, Courage Best, Otter Bright and a guest like Youngs Waggle Dance on handpump, and ten wines by the glass. Served by friendly, helpful staff, the well liked food might include home-made soup (£4.50), poached button mushrooms with garlic, herbs and cream (£5.50), sandwiches (from £5.50), moules marinière (£5.75), venison burger with carrot and sweetcorn relish (£7.95), asparagus, roast fennel and sun-dried tomato tagliatelle (£9.95), tuna loin with red pepper salsa (£12.50), grilled bass fillet with crab and lime butter (£12.95), and daily specials; piped music. *(Recommended by Frogeye, David Crook, Lesley and Peter Barrett, George Atkinson, Ken Flawn, Jo Rees)*

Buccaneer Holdings ~ Manager James Pound ~ Real ale ~ Bar food (12-2.30, 6-9.30) ~ Restaurant ~ (01803) 863880 ~ Children welcome ~ Dogs allowed in bar ~ Live jazz every second Sun lunchtime ~ Open 11-11; 12-10.30 Sun ~ Bedrooms: £59.50B/£79.50B

TUCKENHAY SX8156 Map 1
Maltsters Arms ♀
Take Ashprington road out of Totnes (signed left off A381 on outskirts), keeping on past Watermans Arms; TQ9 7EQ

This is a lovely spot by a peaceful wooded creek with tables by the water, and in summer there are barbecues and regular live music concerts on the quayside. Inside, the long, narrow bar links two other rooms – a little snug one with an open fire and plenty of bric-a-brac, and another with red-painted vertical seats and kitchen chairs on the wooden floor; there are nautical charts and attractive local photographs on the walls. Well kept Princetown Dartmoor IPA, Sharps Atlantic, South Hams Devon Pride and Teignworthy Springtide on handpump, 19 wines by the glass, a dozen malt whiskies, local farm cider, and summer Pimms and cocktails. As well as nice bar nibbles, the good, enjoyable bar food includes lunchtime double-decker sandwiches (from £4.95) and ploughman's (from £6.25), as well as home-made soups (from £4.25), local mussels and cockles marinière (£5.75), duck and chicken pâté with kirsch cherries (£5.95), smoked fish platter (£6.95), sweet potato, aubergine and spinach korma (£9.25), local rabbit in ale pie or cajun-style pork steak (£10.25), whole local dab grilled with lemon and herb butter (£13.50), T-bone steak with blue cheese sauce (£18.25), half a dozen healthy meals for children, and puddings such as raspberry, redcurrant and apple crumble, brandy and orange crème brûlée or treacle tart (from £4.25). The restaurant is no smoking. Darts, board games, and TV for sports. *(Recommended by Gareth Lewis, Hannah Selinger, Sue Heath, Alan and Anne Driver, MP, Andrew Barker, Claire Jenkins, Mike Gorton, the Didler, OPUS)*

Free house ~ Licensees Denise and Quentin Thwaites ~ Real ale ~ Bar food (12-3, 7-9.30; all day summer weekends) ~ Restaurant ~ (01803) 732350 ~ Children welcome away from bar and must be over 12 in main restaurant ~ Dogs welcome ~ Live music first and third Fri of month; outside events in summer ~ Open 11-11; closed evening 25 Dec ~ Bedrooms: /£85S

WIDECOMBE SX7276 Map 1
Rugglestone
Village at end of B3387; pub just S – turn left at church and NT church house, OS Sheet 191 map reference 720765; TQ13 7TF

In rural surroundings, though just up the road from the bustling tourist village, this is a genuinely unspoilt local with a chatty landlord and plenty of cheerful customers. The small bar has a strong country atmosphere, just four little tables, a few window and wall seats, a one-person pew built into the corner by the nice old stone fireplace, and a rudimentary bar counter dispensing well kept Butcombe Bitter, St Austell Dartmoor Best and Sharps Doom Bar tapped from the cask; local farm cider and a decent little wine list. The room on the right is a bit bigger and lighter-feeling with another stone fireplace, beamed ceiling, stripped pine tables and a built-in wall bench. There's also a small no smoking room which is used for dining. Well liked home-made bar food includes soup (£3.50), filled baked potatoes (from £4.95), and daily specials such as liver and bacon (£6.95), steak and kidney or chicken and leek pies or beef stew (all £7.95), and fish pie (£8.95). Outside across the little moorland stream is a field with lots of picnic-sets. Tables and chairs in the garden. *(Recommended by R J Walden, Theocsbrian, Donna and Roger, David and Paula Russell, Mike Gorton, the Didler, Michael and Judy Buckley, Ann and Bob Westbrook, JHW, Dr and Mrs M E Wilson, Ken Flawn)*

Free house ~ Licensees Rod and Diane Williams ~ Real ale ~ Bar food ~ No credit cards ~ (01364) 621327 ~ Children welcome ~ Dogs welcome ~ Open 11.30-3.30, 6.30-12.30; 12-3.30, 6.30-11.30 Sun

WINKLEIGH SS6308 Map 1
Kings Arms
Village signposted off B3220 Crediton—Torrington; Fore Street; EX19 8HQ

There's a welcome for all from the friendly licensees here – children and dogs included. The attractive beamed main bar has some old-fashioned built-in wall settles, scrubbed pine tables and benches on the flagstones, and a woodburning stove in a cavernous fireplace; another woodburning stove separates the bar from the no smoking dining rooms (one has military memorabilia and a mine shaft). Popular bar food includes burgers (from £2.95), home-made soup (£3.75), chicken liver pâté (£3.95), sandwiches and baguettes (from £3.95; steak and onion £5.95), ploughman's (£5.95), filled baked potatoes or omelettes (from £5.95), a trio of sausages with eggs (£6.75), vegetable shepherd's pie (£7.95), fish and chips or curry of the day (£8.25), steak and kidney parcel or chicken breast filled with brie and spinach (£9.95), steaks (from £9.95), and puddings such as marmalade bread and butter pudding or rich chocolate mousse with chocolate sauce (£3.95). Well kept Butcombe Bitter, and Sharps Cornish Coaster and Doom Bar on handpump, local cider and decent wines; darts, board games, shut-the-box, and Jenga. There are seats out in the garden. *(Recommended by R J Walden, Alan and Ruth Hooper, Mark Flynn, W M Paton, Mr and Mrs Syson)*

Enterprise ~ Lease Chris Guy and Julia Franklin ~ Real ale ~ Bar food (all day) ~ Restaurant ~ (01837) 83384 ~ Children welcome ~ Dogs allowed in bar ~ Open 11-11; 12-10.30 Sun

WONSON SX6790 Map 1
Northmore Arms ♀ ◀

A30 at Merrymeet roundabout, take first left on old A30, through Whiddon Down; new roundabout and take left on to A382; then right down lane signposted Throwleigh/Gidleigh. Continue down lane over hump-back bridge; turn left to Wonson; OS Sheet 191 map reference 674903; EX20 2JA

Tucked away down narrow lanes, this secluded cottage is perhaps nicest on a sunny day when you can sit out in the sloping rustic and peaceful garden. The two small connected beamed rooms – modest and informal – have wall settles, up to three tables in each room, and an open fire and woodburning stove; the granite stone walls are hung with some attractive photographs. Well kept Adnams Broadside, Cotleigh Tawny and Exe Valley Dobs tapped from the cask, and good house wines; darts and board games. With prices unchanged since last year, the simple food includes sandwiches (from £1.75; toasties from £2.25), garlic mushrooms or pâté (£2.65), ploughman's (£4.25), filled baked potatoes (from £4.25), ham and egg (£4.75), liver and onions (£5.50), and roast lamb with garlic potatoes or Tuesday curries (£6.95). The ladies' lavatory is up steep steps. Excellent walking from the pub (or to it, perhaps from Chagford or Gidleigh Park). Castle Drogo is close by. Although the pub is open all day, readers have occasionally found it shut, so it might be best to phone before setting out. More reports please. *(Recommended by R J Walden, the Didler, Paul Goldman, Ann Holdsworth, Anthony Longden)*

Free house ~ Licensee Mrs Mo Miles ~ Real ale ~ Bar food (all day Mon-Sat; 12-2.30, 7-9 Sun) ~ (01647) 231428 ~ Children allowed away from bar ~ Dogs allowed in bar ~ Open 11-11; 12-10.30 Sun ~ Bedrooms: /£40

WOODBURY SALTERTON SY0189 Map 1
Diggers Rest ⑪

3½ miles from M5 junction 30: A3052 towards Sidmouth, village signposted on right about ½ mile after Clyst St Mary; also signposted from B3179 SE of Exeter; EX5 1PQ

There's no doubt that most customers do come to this thatched village pub to enjoy the very good food, but locals happily gather around the bar for a chat and a pint. Readers like the main bar with its antique furniture, local art on the walls, and cosy seating area by the open fire with its extra large sofa and armchair. Well kept Butcombe Bitter, Otter Bitter and Scatter Rock Scatty Bitter on handpump, and up to 14 wines by the glass; fine service from young antipodean staff. Using local produce where possible, the popular food at lunchtime includes sandwiches (from £4.50), home-made hummous and tzatziki with olives, crudités and chargrilled pitta bread (£6.50), ploughman's or home-cooked ham and free-range egg (£7.25), pasta in a mushroom, garlic, parmesan and cream sauce with fresh spinach (£8.35), super burgers, fresh haddock and herb fishcakes with crème fraîche and dill tartare sauce, steak and kidney pie or local sausages and onion gravy (£8.95), and thai chicken curry (£9.25); daily specials such as green pea soup with a mint pesto croûton (£4.50), spinach koftas in a mildly spicy yoghurt sauce and home-made flat breads (£9.75), free-range chicken and ham pie with rosemary new potatoes (£11.25), toad in the hole with red onion gravy (£11.75), leg of lamb stuffed with figs and feta cheese and slow cooked with red wine (£13.75), and 10oz rib-eye steak with shallot and red wine butter (£15.50). You may smoke only in the public bar; piped music. Contemporary garden furniture under canvas parasols in the terraced garden, and lovely countryside views. *(Recommended by Glenn and Gillian Miller, Brenda and Stuart Naylor, John and Jackie Chalcraft, Paul and Shirley White, David and Pauline Brenner, Mike Gorton, Hugh Roberts, M G Hart, John and Sarah Perry, M and GR, David Hall, Sue and Alex, Geoffrey Medcalf, Phil and Jane Hodson, Dr and Mrs M E Wilson, Mr and Mrs W Mills, J Kirkland, Tracey and Stephen Groves)*

Free house ~ Licensee Stephen Rushton ~ Real ale ~ Bar food (12-2.15, 6.30-9.30; all day weekends) ~ (01395) 232375 ~ Children welcome ~ Dogs allowed in bar ~ Open 11-3, 6-11; 11-11 Sat; 12-10.30 Sun

WOODLAND   SX7968   Map 1

Rising Sun ♀ 🍴

Village signposted off A38 just NE of Ashburton – then keep eyes peeled for Rising Sun signposts (which may be hidden in the hedges); pub N of village itself, near Combe Cross; TQ13 7JT

Friendly new licensees have taken over this bustling pub but happily not much seems to have changed. There's an expanse of softly lit red plush button-back banquettes and matching studded chairs, partly divided by wooden banister rails, masonry pillars and the odd high-backed settle. A forest of beams is hung with thousands of old doorkeys, and a nice part by the log fire has shelves of plates and books, and old pictures above the fireplace. Princetown Jail Ale and a local guest beer on handpump, ten wines by the glass, and Luscombe cider. The family area has various toys. Bar food now includes home-made soup (£3.75), pork and liver terrine with apple chutney (£4.95), sandwiches (from £4.95), ploughman's or home-cooked ham and free-range egg (£6.95), honey-roast sausages with leek and garlic mash (£7.50), risotto of wild mushrooms (£8.95), spaghetti, cockles, prawns, and squid with a chilli and tomato concasse (£9.95), wild bass with prawn and chive butter (£11.95), and belly of pork slow-roasted with bramley apples (£12.95). You may smoke only in the bar area. There are some picnic-sets in the spacious garden which has a play area including a redundant tractor. (Recommended by Gareth Lewis, E B Ireland, Frogeye, Donna and Roger, Mike and Mary Carter, Alain and Rose Foote, Melanie Ginger, S P Watkin, P A Taylor)

Free house ~ Licensees Simon and Hazel Towle ~ Real ale ~ Bar food (12-2.15(3 Sun), 6(7 Sun)-9.15; not Mon) ~ Restaurant ~ (01364) 652544 ~ Children welcome ~ Dogs allowed in bar ~ Open 12-3, 6-11; 12-3, 7-10.30 Sun; closed Mon ~ Bedrooms: £38B/£65B

YEALMPTON   SX5851   Map 1

Rose & Crown 🍴 ♀

A379 Kingsbridge—Plymouth; PL8 2EB

Devon Dining Pub of the Year

An offshoot of the Dartmoor Union over at Holbeton, this newly reopened pub is now a stylish place for a drink or a meal, satisfyingly civilised without being at all formal or overbearing. The big central bar counter, all dark wood and heavy brass with good solid leather-seated bar stools, has a splendid range of wines by the glass, Courage Best and Sharps Doom Bar on handpump, a fine choice of other drinks, and Burts crisps. Service by neatly aproned black-dressed staff is quick and friendly. There's an attractive mix of tables and old dining chairs, with good lighting, and some leather sofas down on the left. With its stripped wood floor and absence of curtains and other soft furnishings, the open-plan bar's acoustics are lively; beige carpeting keeps the two dining areas on the right rather quieter, and here smart leather high-backed dining chairs, flowers on the tablecloths and framed 1930s high-life posters take you a notch or two upscale. The food might include open baguettes (from £4.25), thai vegetable broth (£4.50), flaked salmon and caper fishcake with cucumber salsa (£5.25; main course £10.50), wok-fried green pepper and bean sprouts with noodles and soy (£6.95), pork and leek sausages with caper jus (£8), roasted chicken with basil pesto and pasta (£8.75), vine ripened tomato tart with parmesan and rocket (£10.25), seared fillet of salmon with truffled potatoes (£12.95), roast duck breast with vanilla purée and armagnac jus (£14.50), and puddings such as chocolate and raspberry mousse, white chocolate sabayon and blackcurrant sorbet or hot apricot soufflé with vanilla ice-cream (from £4.50); two-course set lunch (£9.95) and three courses (£12.95). They also have an attractive adjacent seafood restaurant with super big fishing photographs, lobster pots and nets on decking, and high-backed powder blue cushioned dining chairs around white clothed tables. *(Recommended by John Evans)*

Free house ~ Licensee Jason Poore ~ Real ale ~ Bar food (12-2, 6.30-9.30; 12-3.30, 6.30-9 Sun) ~ Restaurant ~ (01752) 880223 ~ Children welcome ~ Dogs allowed in bar ~ Open 12-11(10.30 Sun)

LUCKY DIP

Besides the fully inspected pubs, you might like to try these Lucky Dips recommended to us and described by readers (if you do, please send us reports: www.goodguides.co.uk).

ABBOTSHAM [SS4226]
Thatched Inn EX39 5BA: Popular extensively refurbished family pub with friendly staff, choice of real ales, enjoyable reasonably priced food inc fresh fish and good value Sun lunch, mix of modern seating and older features (dates from 15th c); garden tables, handy for the Big Sheep *(June and Robin Savage)*

ABBOTSKERSWELL [SX8568]
☆ *Court Farm* TQ12 5NY [Wilton Way; look for the church tower]: Attractive neatly extended 17th-c former farmhouse tucked away in picturesque hamlet, various rooms off long crazy-paved main beamed bar, partly no smoking, good mix of furnishings, good helpings of well presented food from sandwiches to steaks and bargain Sun lunch, half helpings for children, friendly helpful staff, several real ales, farm cider, decent wines and wide choice of other drinks, woodburners; piped music; children in eating area, picnic-sets in pretty garden, open all day *(LYM, Ken Flawn)*

APPLEDORE [SS4630]
☆ *Beaver* EX39 1RY [Irsha St]: Relaxed good-humoured harbourside pub, good value generous honest cooking esp fresh local fish and good puddings, friendly helpful staff, St Austell or other local ales and Bass in summer, farm cider, decent house wines, great range of whiskies, cuddly beaver toys on bar shelves, lovely estuary view from popular raised dining area; pool in smaller games room; children and dogs welcome, disabled access, tables on small sheltered water-view terrace *(R J Walden, Paul and Ursula Randall, Bob and Margaret Holder, Rona Murdoch, Peter and Margaret Glenister, Mark Flynn, John and Fiona McIlwain, Roger Brown)*
☆ *Royal George* EX39 1RY [Irsha St]: Simple but good fresh food inc local fish in no smoking dining room with superb estuary views, real ales, decent wines, quick helpful service, thriving narrow bar (dogs allowed) with attractive pictures and well worn in front room; disabled access, picnic-sets outside, picturesque street sloping to sea *(Rona Murdoch, Michael and Ann Cole, Roger Brown)*

ASHBURTON [SX7569]
Exeter Inn TQ13 7DU [West St]: Friendly pleasantly old-fashioned beamed pub with bargain straightforward food from sandwiches up, Badger Best, good local chilled ciders; attractive little suntrap back courtyard *(Rona Murdoch)*

AVONWICK [SX7158]
Avon TQ10 9NB [off A38 at W end of South Brent bypass]: Comfortable light and airy dining pub with good food in sensible helpings in restaurant and bar, French chef/landlord doing some interesting specials, friendly smart staff, real ales such as Badger Best and Teignworthy, decent wine choice, log fire; picnic-sets in meadow by River Avon, adventure playground *(John Evans, LYM, John Riddell)*

AXMINSTER [SY2998]
Axminster Inn EX13 5AH [Silver St]: Friendly old local just behind the minster church, Palmers ales, simple bar food, skittle alley, busy on Thurs market day; children welcome, open all day *(Anthony Double)*

BAMPTON [SS9520]
☆ *Exeter Inn* EX16 9DY [A396 some way S, at B3227 roundabout]: Long low stone-built roadside pub under steep hill overlooking River Exe, fairly handy for Knightshayes Court, several friendly and comfortable linked rooms, mainly flagstoned, sensible choice of good reasonably priced bar food inc plenty of fresh fish, large pleasant restaurant, Cotleigh Tawny and Exmoor Ale and a monthly guest beer, decent coffee, quick bar service, log fire, daily papers, no piped music; tables out in front, good value bedrooms, good breakfast, open all day *(BB, Jodie Phillips, Di and Mike Gillam, Paul Rampton)*

BANTHAM [SX6643]
Sloop TQ7 3AJ [off A379/B3197 NW of Kingsbridge]: Popular updated beamed and flagstoned pub in great spot across dunes from lovely beach, character bar and new pine furniture in side area, real ales, good wines, woodburner, no smoking dining room (two evening sittings, 6.30 and 8.30), lots of (well behaved) children; dogs warmly welcomed, seats outside, bedrooms, plenty of surrounding walks *(Mr and Mrs J Curtis, Roger Wain-Heapy, Theocsbrian, Stephen Woad, H G H Stafford, Bob and Margaret Holder, Lawrence Pearse, LYM, Alan and Anne Driver, Ann and Bob Westbrook, Lynda and Trevor Smith, W Taylor, Ian and Ruth Laurence, Geoff and Marianne Millin, Ian and Jane Irving, Martin and Sue Day)*

BARNSTAPLE [SS5633]
Ebberley Arms EX32 7BZ [Bear St]: Busy and unpretentiously pubby, with popular bargain bar lunches *(Mark Flynn)*

BEER [ST2289]
Anchor EX12 3ET [Fore St]: Neatly refurbished sea-view dining pub with wide choice of standard food from sandwiches and baked potatoes up inc good local and Brixham

fish, Greene King IPA and Abbot and Otter, decent wines, genial management, prompt and friendly young staff, rambling open-plan layout with old local photographs, large no smoking eating area; sports TV, piped music; reasonably priced bedrooms, lots of tables in nice area out across road, delightful seaside village - parking may not be easy *(Neil and Lorna Mclaughlan, LYM, John Branston, Mary Kirman and Tim Jefferson, Pat and Tony Martin, Lawrence Pearse)*

☆ *Barrel o' Beer* EX12 3EQ [Fore St]: Lively family-run pub with good interestingly cooked local fish and seafood (they cure and smoke their own) as well as simpler more ▪ straightforward dishes, helpful attentive staff, Exe Valley Bitter and Devon Glory and Timothy Taylors Landlord, choice of ciders, log fire, very small no smoking back dining area; piped music; dogs welcome, open all day *(Alain and Rose Foote, Michael Doswell, Mike Gorton, BB, Howard and Margaret Buchanan, Mike and Chris Higgins, Cynthia and Stephen Fisher)*

Dolphin EX12 3EQ [Fore St]: Open-plan local quite near sea, no smoking in front bar, old-fashioned décor, oak panelling, nautical bric-a-brac and interesting nooks inc marvellous old distorting mirrors and antique boxing prints in corridors leading to back antique stalls, good value food from lunchtime sandwiches up, Cotleigh real ales, decent wine; piped music; children and dogs welcome, one or two tables out by pavement, bedrooms *(Mike Gorton, LYM, Ian and Joan Blackwell)*

BEESANDS [SX8140]
☆ *Cricket* TQ7 2EN: Friendly open-plan pub, really well run, in old-fashioned fishing village above a sandy beach (the parking's free); light and airy décor, interesting photographs, good fresh food from sandwiches up inc local meat and veg and nice choice of fresh fish and shellfish, summer cream teas, real ales such as Bass and Skinners Admiral, local farm cider, decent wines, log fire, family room; unobtrusive piped music; dogs welcome, picnic-sets out by sea wall, bedrooms, at start of coast path to Hallsands and Start Point *(Mr and Mrs J Curtis, Mayur Shah, Roger Wain-Heapy, David and Karen Cuckney, Stephen Gutteridge, BB, Fred and Lorraine Gill)*

BERRYNARBOR [SS5546]
☆ *Olde Globe* EX34 9SG [off A399 E of Ilfracombe]: Rambling dim-lit rooms, low ceilings and ancient walls and flagstones, high-backed oak settles, cushioned cask seats around antique tables, lots of old pictures, cutlasses, swords, shields and rustic bric-a-brac, Golden Hill Exmoor, Shepherd Neame Spitfire and Wadworths 6X, straightforward bar food, no smoking dining room, darts and pool; piped music; children welcome in family area, crazy-paved front terrace with some old-fashioned garden seats, play area, pretty village *(LYM, Ann Holdsworth, Chris and Ann Coy, Brian and Ruth Archer, Sue Demont, Tim Barrow, Andy and Ali)*

BICKINGTON [SX8072]
Dartmoor Half Way TQ12 6JW [A383 Ashburton—Newton Abbot]: Big helpings of well cooked reasonably priced food, warm welcome, Batemans, Fullers London Pride and Otter, log fires, pleasant environment; space for touring caravans, bedrooms *(Ann and Bob Westbrook)*

BISHOP'S TAWTON [SS5629]
☆ *Chichester Arms* EX32 0DQ [signed off A377 outside Barnstaple; East St]: Friendly 15th-c cob and thatch pub carefully restored after 2005 fire, well priced good generous food from home-made soup and sandwiches to fresh local fish and seasonal game (all meat from named local farms), plenty of choice in the popular price bracket, quick obliging service even when crowded, Greene King Abbot and other ales, decent wines, heavy low beams, large stone fireplace with log fire, partly no smoking restaurant; children welcome, picnic-sets on front terrace and in back garden, open all day *(LYM, Mark Flynn)*

BISHOPSTEIGNTON [SX9073]
Cockhaven Manor TQ14 9RF [off A380 Teignmouth—Newton Abbot; Cockhaven Rd]: Friendly family and staff in 16th-c former manor, warm atmosphere, real ales such as Butcombe and Wadworths 6X, good range of other drinks, enjoyable food from bar snacks to bargain four-course Sun lunch; bedrooms *(John and Helen Rushton, B M Eldridge)*

BOLBERRY [SX6939]
☆ *Port Light* TQ7 3DY: Alone on dramatic NT clifftop, nr fine beaches, right on the coast path, bright, clean, spacious and busy, with superb picture-window views and conservatory, real ales such as Teignworthy Reel, friendly efficient eager-to-please service, interesting memorabilia of its time as a radar station, decent lunchtime bar food in oversized helpings, evening functions more as a restaurant; children and dogs welcome (they host dog wknds), picnic-sets on quiet terrace and in garden with splendid fenced play area, five bedrooms *(George Atkinson, Helen and Brian Edgeley)*

BOVEY TRACEY [SX8178]
Old Thatched TQ13 9AW: Attractive 15th-c pub with welcoming new landlady, good beer and enjoyable food *(Ken Flawn)*

Riverside TQ13 9AD [Fore St]: Cottagey hotel by River Bovey, mill stream visible under large attractive L-shaped bar with food from sandwiches up, real ales, good wines by the glass, plenty of spirits, friendly helpful staff, nice restaurant; may be piped music; waterside garden, comfortable bedrooms *(Ken Flawn)*

BRAYFORD [SS7235]
☆ *Poltimore Arms* EX36 3HA [Yarde Down; 3 miles towards Simonsbath]: Old-fashioned 17th-c two-bar beamed local, so remote it generates its own electricity, friendly landlord and cheerful obliging staff, enticing good value blackboard food inc good Sun roast, real ales such as Adnams, Cotleigh Tawny and Exmoor and Greene King Abbot tapped from the cask, good wines by the glass, basic traditional

furnishings, fine woodburner in inglenook, interesting ornaments, two attractive restaurant areas; children welcome, also dogs on leads (pub has own dogs), picnic-sets in side garden, has been cl winter lunchtimes *(LYM, Stan and Hazel Allen, Mark Flynn, Andrew Scott, George Atkinson)*

BRENDON [SS7547]

☆ *Rockford Inn* EX35 6PT [Rockford; Lynton—Simonsbath rd, off B3223]: Welcoming and interesting series of small linked rooms in unspoilt 17th-c beamed inn by East Lyn river, limited low-priced homely food from good proper sandwiches and baked potatoes up, cream teas (all day in summer), friendly staff, Cotleigh Barn Owl and a beer brewed for the pub tapped from the cask, Addlestone's cider, good house wines and choice of malt whiskies, farm cider, woodburners, lots of local pictures, darts, pool, shove-ha'penny, cribbage, dominoes, restaurant; children in eating areas, quiet dogs on leads welcome (sweet resident springer), good walks, bedrooms, cl Sun evening and Mon out of season *(Sheila Topham, LYM, B M Eldridge, Dennis Jenkin, George Atkinson)*
Staghunters EX35 6PS: Hotel in idyllic setting with gardens by East Lyn river, neat traditional bar with woodburner, generous popular food, Exmoor Ale and Gold, family room with pool table, restaurant; can get very busy; walkers and dogs welcome, good value bedrooms *(Gaynor Gregory, Lynda and Trevor Smith, George Atkinson)*

BRIXHAM [SX9256]

Long Bar TQ5 8DY [Union Ln]: Wide choice of ales as well as usual lagers and spirits, open fire, chatty locals, usual pub games, frequent live music *(Leon Shaw)*

BRIXTON [SX5552]

Foxhound Clipper PL8 2AH: Popular and welcoming village local with good value food, good range of real ales; live music and other events *(Lisa Sherwin)*

BROADCLYST [SX9897]

Red Lion EX5 3EL [B3121, by church]: Extended and pleasantly refurbished while keeping its heavy beams, flagstones and woodburner, friendly efficient service, several real ales, enjoyable food from lunchtime bar snacks to good evening choice, attractive mix of furnishings; picnic-sets on front cobbles below fine wisteria, more in small enclosed garden across quiet lane, nice village and church, not far from Killerton (NT – they own the pub too) *(LYM, David Hall)*

BROADHEMPSTON [SX8066]

☆ *Coppa Dolla* TQ9 6BD: Good ambitious food inc two-in-one pies and fine steaks, very reasonable prices, children's helpings, comfortable and welcoming beamed bar divided by sturdy timber props, real ale such as Fullers London Pride tapped from the cask, good choice of wines by the glass, cheery service, log fires, small no smoking area, pleasant upstairs restaurant; well spaced picnic-sets in attractive garden with country views *(BB, Mrs Bridget Cushion, Mr and Mrs S Smith, Gerry and Rosemary Dobson)*

BURGH ISLAND [SX6444]

☆ *Pilchard* TQ7 4BG [300 yds across tidal sands from Bigbury-on-Sea; walk, or summer Tractor if tide's in – unique bus on stilts]: No smoking pub in unbeatable setting high above sea on tidal island, with lanterns, roaring log fire in back bar, ancient beams and flagstones and a parrot called Oscar all giving nice smuggly feel despite the neat refurbishment; Sharps, Thwaites Lancaster Bomber and an ale brewed for the pub, local farm cider, friendly chatty staff, decent food inc lunchtime baguettes and some interesting evening dishes, family room – useful for trippers by day, warm local atmosphere at night; Sat evening barbecues, some tables down by beach, unspoilt cliff walks, bedrooms in associated flamboyantly art deco hotel, open all day *(David Eberlin, Guy Vowles, the Didler, Ian and Ruth Laurence, Sue Demont, Tim Barrow, George Atkinson)*

BUTTERLEIGH [SS9708]

Butterleigh Inn EX15 1PN [off A396 in Bickleigh]: Small-roomed country pub with nice pictures, big fireplace, pine dining chairs around country kitchen tables in one room, attractive elm trestle table and darts in another, two no smoking areas (one a lunchtime family room), Cotleigh and Greene King Abbot and Ruddles County, usual food; they may try to keep your credit card if you eat outside; attractive gardens, up-to-date bedrooms *(David and Jean Hall, LYM, Revd R P Tickle)*

CALIFORNIA CROSS [SX7053]

☆ *California* PL21 0SG: Well restored 18th-c or older no smoking pub with beams, stripped stone and log fire, wide choice of enjoyable food in bar and restaurant, local ales as well as Fullers London Pride and Greene King Old Speckled Hen, decent wines, friendly efficient staff; garden and back terrace, open all day *(Jonathan Bell, Neil and Anita Christopher)*

CHAGFORD [SX6987]

☆ *Bullers Arms* TQ13 8AW [Mill St]: Cheery panelled local with good value food servery, Bass, Butcombe and Courage Directors, decent coffee, very friendly efficient staff, militaria, copper and brass, darts; summer barbecues *(LYM, Ian and Joan Blackwell)*

☆ *Ring o' Bells* TQ13 8AH [off A382 Moretonhampstead—Whiddon Down]: Well run black-and-white medieval pub with appealing oak-panelled bar much as one reader remembers from 45 years ago, welcoming landlord and staff, Butcombe, St Austell Dartmoor Best and Teignworthy Reel, Addlestone's cider, enjoyable bar food, nice photographs, copper and brass, log-effect fire, traditional games, small no smoking candlelit dining room; dogs in bar, sunny walled garden behind with seats on lawn, good value bedrooms, good breakfast *(JMC, John Stirrup, LYM, J Poirrette, Sheila Newbury, David Uren, Prof Keith and Mrs Jane Barber, Ken Flawn)*

CHALLACOMBE [SS6941]

☆ *Black Venus* EX31 4TT [B3358 Blackmoor Gate—Simonsbath]: Low-beamed 16th-c pub with good varied food from sandwiches and baguettes to blackboard specials (may take a while), friendly staff, two changing ales, Thatcher's farm cider, pews and comfortable chairs, woodburner and big open fire, roomy and attractive dining area; garden tables, grand countryside *(Stan and Hazel Allen, BB, P K Clark, Merle Abbott)*

CHAWLEIGH [SS7112]

Earl of Portsmouth EX18 7HJ [B3042]: Small unpretentious local with changing real ales such as Barum Firing Squad, Beer Engine Rail and Thwaites Lancaster Bomber, farm cider, warm woodburner, bar food from baked potatoes up – they cook with fresh local ingredients (worth the wait) and bake their own bread, dining room on left, darts, skittle alley; TV, games machine; children welcome, a couple of picnic-sets outside, open all day *(Mark Flynn, Nick, BB)*

CHIP SHOP [SX4375]

Chip Shop Inn PL19 8NT [1½ miles N of Gulworthy, towards Lamerton]: Cheery little no-nonsense country local (once the mine shop where tin miners had to use their pay chips – hence the name) with real ales inc Sharps Doom Bar, welcoming service, lots of mirrors, well placed darts; can get smoky; children welcome, garden tables *(Phil and Sally Gorton)*

CHITTLEHAMHOLT [SS6420]

Exeter Inn EX37 9NS [off A377 Barnstaple—Crediton, and B3226 SW of South Molton]: Spotless old inn with friendly staff and long-serving licensees, enjoyable food from sandwiches, baguettes and baked potatoes to good local steaks and Sun roast, no smoking restaurant, Dartmoor Best, Greene King Abbot and a guest beer, farm ciders, good wine choice, open stove in huge fireplace, side area with booth seating; traditional games, piped music; children and dogs welcome, benches out on terrace, decent bedrooms with showers *(Mark Flynn, LYM)*

CHITTLEHAMPTON [SS6325]

Bell EX37 9QL [signed off B3227 S Molton—Umberleigh]: Cheerful family-run village local, good value food from huge filled rolls to bargain steaks, Bass and guest beers, outstanding range of malt whiskies, competent staff; children and dogs welcome, nice quiet garden *(Mark Flynn)*

CHRISTOW [SX8385]

☆ *Teign House* EX6 7PL [Teign Valley Rd (B3193)]: Attractive former farmhouse in country setting, open fire in beamed bar, consistently good fresh food (all day Sat) using local fish and other produce here and in partly no smoking family dining room, friendly helpful staff, real ales such as Cotleigh 25, Princetown Jail and Sharps Doom Bar, decent wines; pretty garden, cl Tues lunchtime *(Mr and Mrs Roy Davies)*

CHUDLEIGH [SX8679]

Bishop Lacey TQ13 0HY [Fore St, just off A38]: Quaint partly 14th-c low-beamed church house with cheerful staff, changing ales such as Branscombe Vale, Princetown, Skinners and Fullers London Pride, some tapped from casks

in back bar, enjoyable food using local produce cooked by landlord, good strong coffee, two log fires, dark décor, no smoking dining room; live bands in next-door offshoot; children welcome, garden tables, winter beer festival, bedrooms, open all day *(JDM, KM, John Urquhart, the Didler)*

CHUDLEIGH KNIGHTON [SX8477]

Claycutters Arms TQ13 0EY [just off A38 by B3344]: Attractive 17th-c thatched two-bar village pub with real ales such as Fullers London Pride and Otter, home-made food from sandwiches and baguettes up (can take a while), polite service, decent wines by the glass, stripped stone, interesting nooks and crannies, pleasant restaurant; needs a no smoking area, piped pop music may be loud; dogs and children welcome, tables on side terrace and in orchard *(Alain and Rose Foote, LYM, David M Cundy, E B Ireland)*

CHURCHSTOW [SX7145]

Church House TQ7 3QW [A379 NW of Kingsbridge]: Long pub dating from 13th c (and remembered by one reader from when its cider was 4d a pint), warmly helpful staff, quickly served generous food from sandwiches to plenty of fish and (Weds-Sat nights, Sun lunch) popular carvery, local ales, decent wines, much refurbished though keeping heavy black beams and stripped stone, back conservatory with floodlit well feature; well behaved children and dogs welcome, tables outside *(Bob and Margaret Holder, LYM, Nick Lawless)*

CHURSTON FERRERS [SX9056]

☆ *Churston Court* TQ5 0JE [off A3022 S of Torquay; Church Rd]: Interesting converted manor house, largely early 17th-c, in pretty spot next to ancient church; warren of largely no smoking candlelit rooms, plenty of beams, flagstones and open fires inc a massive inglenook, suits of armour, historic portraits, faded tapestries, long wooden tables, sofas, gilt-framed mirrors, Greene King Abbot, Princetown Dartmoor and Jail, huge carvery choice plus local fish, good sandwiches, friendly service; piped classical music; children allowed, lots of tables in attractive walled lawn, quirky individual bedrooms, good walks nearby, open all day *(Dr and Mrs M E Wilson, LYM, David M Cundy, Alan and Paula McCully, Kevin Blake, Emma Kingdon)*

CLAYHIDON [ST1615]

Half Moon EX15 3TJ: Pretty village pub recently renovated by new licensees, warm friendly atmosphere, good choice of enjoyable home-made food, real ales, tasteful furniture and inglenook fireplace in comfortable bar; children and dogs welcome, delightful calming views from picnic-sets in tiered garden over road *(David Griffiths, Dr Peter Crawshaw)*

CLEARBROOK [SX5265]

Skylark PL20 6JD [village signed down dead end off A386 Tavistock—Plymouth]: Simple two-room pub in pretty cottage row tucked right into Dartmoor, real ales, log fire, usual food running up to big steaks; piped music; pleasant family room in big back garden with plenty of picnic-sets and other seats, small adventure play area, wandering ponies *(BB, Ted George)*

CLYST ST GEORGE [SX9888]

St George & Dragon EX3 0QJ: Spaciously extended open-plan low-beamed bar divided by timbers into smaller olde-worlde areas, welcoming landlord and helpful young staff, Bass and Wadworths 6X, good wine list, open fires *(Dr and Mrs M E Wilson)*

CLYST ST MARY [SX9791]

☆ *Half Moon* EX5 1BR [under a mile from M5 junction 30 via A376]: Attractive and genuine old pub beside disused multi-arched bridge (Devon's oldest) over Clyst, Bass, Fullers London Pride and Otter, generous home-made food, cheerful attentive service, friendly unpretentious local atmosphere, red plush seating, log fire; wheelchair access, bedrooms *(Dr and Mrs M E Wilson)*

COCKWOOD [SX9780]

Ship EX6 8RA [off A379 N of Dawlish]: Comfortable 17th-c pub overlooking estuary and harbour, partitioned beamed bar with big log fire and ancient oven, decorative plates and seafaring prints and memorabilia, small no smoking restaurant, generous reasonably priced food from open crab sandwiches up inc good evening fish dishes and good puddings (freshly made so takes time), Greene King Abbot and Old Speckled Hen and Sharps Doom Bar, friendly helpful staff; piped music; good steep-sided garden *(Mrs Bridget Cushion, Charles and Pauline Stride)*

COFFINSWELL [SX8968]

☆ *Linny* TQ12 4SR [just off A380 at Kingskerswell S of Newton Abbot]: Very pretty newly rethatched partly 14th-c country pub under friendly and attentive newish landlord, wide choice of good generous food inc lots of fresh fish, good steaks and fine local cheeseboard, Bass and Fullers London Pride, big beamed bar with traditional settles and other comfortable and individual seats, smaller areas off, cosy log fires, lots of twinkling brass, no smoking area, children's room, upstairs restaurant extension (not always open); some tables outside, picturesque village *(Mr and Mrs Colin Roberts, BB, Darren and Jane Staniforth)*

COLATON RALEIGH [SY0787]

Otter EX10 0LE [A376 Newton Poppleford—Budleigh Salterton]: Much-modernised family pub with well priced food inc popular carvery in long airy bar and restaurant, good service, several real ales, fireside leather sofa, tall window bar tables, modern artwork; lovely big garden, handy for Bicton Park *(Basil Minson, Louis Hertzberg, Christine and Neil Townend, Grace and Michael Upton, Dave Rutlidge)*

COLYTON [SY2494]

Gerrard Arms EX24 6JN [St Andrews Sq]: Well worn in open-plan local with Bass, Branscombe Vale Branoc and a guest beer tapped from the cask, skittle alley, lunchtime food inc Sun roasts; public bar can get smoky; tables in courtyard and informal garden *(the Didler, Pete Walker)*

☆ *Kingfisher* EX24 6NA [off A35 and A3052 E of Sidmouth; Dolphin St]: Well run low-beamed village pub with enjoyable food from generous baguettes and baked potatoes to fresh local crab (nice to have snacks as well as full meals in the evening too), Badger and Otter ales, farm cider, good wines by the glass, polite service, big open fire, stripped stone, plush seats and elm settles, pub games, upstairs family room, skittle alley; parking can be a problem, outside gents'; tables out on terrace, garden with water feature *(Alun Evans, the Didler, LYM, Pete Walker, Michael Doswell, Meg and Colin Hamilton)*

COMBE MARTIN [SS5846]

Pack o' Cards EX34 0ET [High St]: Straightforward pub with usual food, Barnstaple Barum and Fullers London Pride, three bars and restaurant; originally built late 17th c to celebrate card winnings, with four floors, 13 doors and 52 windows; pretty garden with play area *(Ian Phillips)*

COMBEINTEIGNHEAD [SX9072]

Coombe Cellars TQ12 4RT [Shaldon rd, off A380 opp main Newton Abbot roundabout]: Big bustling Brewers Fayre, roomy, comfortable and particularly good value for families, with lots for children inc indoor play area, their own menu, fun days and parties with entertainment, outside play galleon and fenced-in playground; friendly efficient staff, very wide choice of good usual food all day, real ales, lots of wines by the glass, plenty of sporting and nautical bric-a-brac, lovely estuary views, various events; good disabled facilities, tables out on pontoons, jetties and big terraces, water sports, open all day *(LYM, Mr and Mrs Colin Roberts)*

COUNTISBURY [SS7449]

Exmoor Sandpiper EX35 6NE [A39, E of Lynton]: Beautifully set rambling heavy-beamed pub, friendly staff, several handsome log fires, good range of enjoyable food in bar and restaurant, decent wines, real ales such as Exmoor, reasonable prices; children in eating area, views from terrace tables, good nearby cliff walks, comfortable bedrooms, open all day *(LYM, Cathy Robinson, Ed Coombe, George Atkinson)*

DARTINGTON [SX7861]

Cott TQ9 6HE [Cott signed off A385 W of Totnes, opp A384 turn-off]: Picturesque long 14th-c thatched pub, nice heavy-beamed core with flagstones and big log fires, Greene King IPA and Abbot, dining area with plenty of close-set tables for the popular daily carvery, wide choice of other food from sandwiches and baked potatoes up; children and dogs on leads welcome, picnic-sets in garden and on pretty terrace, open all day at least in summer *(Clifford Blakemore, David M Cundy, LYM, Ian and Ruth Laurence)*

DARTMOUTH [SX8751]

Dartmouth Arms TQ6 9AN [Lower St, Bayards Cove]: Thriving friendly local (popular with naval students evening) with efficient service, log fire, panelling and boating memorabilia; best thing is that you can have their good beer and good value basic bar food inc lots of pizzas out at tables in prime harbour-wall spot overlooking the estuary – the Pilgrim Fathers set sail from here *(Kevin Flack)*

Floating Bridge TQ6 9PQ [Coombe Rd]: Friendly well worn in pub by upper ferry, good Dart views, real ales, good value wines, wide range of decent reasonably priced food inc fish and shellfish; dogs welcome *(Ken Flawn)*

Royal Castle Hotel TQ6 9PS [the Quay]: Rambling 17th-c or older hotel behind Regency façade overlooking inner harbour, Galleon dining bar on right with all-day food from plain sandwiches to good steaks, perhaps winter lunchtime spit-roasts from their 300-year-old Lidstone range, bustling Harbour Bar on left (TV, piped music may be a bit loud, can get smoky, dogs very welcome – no children), Bass and Exe Valley Dobs Best; comfortable bedrooms with secure parking, open all day *(Russell Grimshaw, Kerry Purcell, David and Karen Cuckney, David Carr, Hugh Roberts, LYM)*

DAWLISH WARREN [SX9778]

Mount Pleasant EX7 0NA [Mount Pleasant Rd]: Marvellous view from lounge and garden over the Warren, Exe estuary and sea, welcoming staff, good choice of enjoyable food and of real ales, two pool tables, darts *(Alain and Rose Foote)*

DITTISHAM [SX8654]

☆ *Ferry Boat* TQ6 0EX [Manor St; best to park in village – steep but attractive walk down]: Well refurbished family-friendly pub in idyllic waterside setting, big windows making the most of it, beams and bare boards, lots of interesting bric-a-brac, warmly welcoming landlord and family, good value simple home-made food using local produce from baguettes to fresh fish, home-made cakes, real ales such as Bass, Wychwood Hobgoblin and Youngs, organic drinks, impromptu jam sessions; no parking, quite a walk down; nr little foot-ferry you call by bell, good walks, open all day *(Peter and Giff Bennett, Di and Mike Gillam, Sue Heath, LYM)*

Red Lion TQ6 0ES: Lovely location looking down over attractive village and River Dart, friendly licensees, decent food and drinks, open fires, restaurant; reasonably priced bedrooms *(Brian and Bett Cox)*

DREWSTEIGNTON [SX7390]

Drewe Arms EX6 6QN [off A30 NW of Moretonhampstead]: New licensees again in old thatched pub smartened up while keeping its log fire and nicely old-fashioned layout, real ales such as Bass, Gales and Otter from casks in back tap room, sizeable back restaurant (children welcome); open all day, handy for Castle Drogo *(Ian and Joan Blackwell, Peter and Margaret Lodge, LYM)*

☆ *Fingle Bridge Inn* EX6 6PW [E of village; OS Sheet 191 map ref 743899]: Idyllic wooded Teign valley spot by 16th-c pack-horse bridge, lovely walks and a magnet for summer visitors; much extended former tea pavilion (aka Anglers Rest), with tourist souvenirs and airy café feel, but has Exe Valley ales and reliable

substantial food (may be a wait when busy) from baguettes and good local cheese ploughman's up, Sun carvery, friendly helpful service, log fire; children and dogs welcome, waterside picnic-sets, has been cl winter evenings *(Dr and Mrs M E Wilson, Robert Gomme, LYM, Ian and Ruth Laurence)*

DUNSFORD [SX8189]

☆ *Royal Oak* EX6 7DA [signed from Moretonhampstead]: Relaxed village inn with good generous food cooked to order, good choice of changing ales inc Princetown and Sharps, local farm cider, friendly landlord, light and airy lounge bar with woodburner and view from small sunny dining bay, simple dining room, steps down to games room with pool; quiz nights, piped music; children welcome, sheltered tiered garden, good value bedrooms in converted barn *(the Didler, LYM, Barry Steele-Perkins, Dr and Mrs M E Wilson)*

EAST ALLINGTON [SX7648]

☆ *Fortescue Arms* TQ9 7RA [off A381 Totnes–Kingsbridge]: Pretty village pub well upgraded by chatty new landlords, good informal atmosphere in charming beamed and flagstoned bar, real ales inc Butcombe, good value sandwiches and flavourful country cooking and log fire, another in comfortable contemporary restaurant; piped classical music; dogs very welcome, disabled facilities, picnic-sets in attractive sheltered garden with decking, three bedrooms being refurbished, cl Mon lunchtime, open all day in summer *(David and Sandra Rockell, John Vereker, MP, Mike and Shelley Woodroffe)*

EAST PRAWLE [SX7836]

Pigs Nose TQ7 2BY [Prawle Green]: Homely and relaxed, with low beams and flagstones, real ales tapped from the cask, enjoyable if limited food from good ploughman's and sandwiches up, friendly laid-back service, open fire, easy chairs and sofa, interesting bric-a-brac and local pictures, jars of wild flowers and candles on tables, bird log, darts, small family area with small box of unusual toys, nice dogs; unobtrusive piped music, hall for live bands; tables outside, nice spot on village green *(Roger Wain-Heapy, Mike Turner)*

ERMINGTON [SX6353]

Crooked Spire PL21 9LP [The Square]: Cheerful Scots landlord, Sharps Doom Bar and Cornish Coaster, good reasonably priced straightforward food from sandwiches to Sun roasts, small no smoking restaurant, open-plan layout with up-to-date colour scheme; pleasant heated back courtyard, comfortable bedrooms with shared bathroom *(David Oakley)*

EXETER [SX9292]

Chaucers EX4 3LR [basement of Tesco Metro, High St]: Large dim-lit modern olde-worlde pub/bistro/wine bar down lots of steps, comfortable furnishings, candles in bottles, several levels inc no smoking areas, Otter, good range of reasonably priced generous food inc adventurous dishes, quick friendly service, pleasant atmosphere; piped music *(Dr and Mrs A K Clarke, R T and J C Moggridge)*

Countess Wear EX2 6HE [on B3181 ring rd roundabout]: Well run pub/restaurant with real ale, reliable food, good quick service; good value comfortable bedrooms in attached Travel Inn *(Dr and Mrs A K Clarke)*

☆ *Double Locks* EX2 6LT [Canal Banks, Alphington, via Marsh Barton Industrial Estate; OS Sheet 192 map ref 933901]: Remote and unpretentious refuge by ship canal, attentive friendly staff, Youngs and guest ales often tapped straight from the cask, farm cider in summer, good value plain home-made bar food from sandwiches and hot filled rolls up all day; piped music, live wknds; children welcome in eating areas, dogs very welcome too, seats out on decking with distant view to city and cathedral (nice towpath walk out), good big play area, camping, open all day *(Phil and Sally Gorton, Steve Felstead, Peter Titcomb, Dr and Mrs A K Clarke, the Didler, LYM, Pete Walker, Mrs Sylvia Elcoate)*

Georges Meeting House EX1 1ED [South St]: Comfortable no smoking Wetherspoons in grand former 18th-c chapel dominated by tall pulpit one end; stained glass, original pews in three-side gallery, some leather settees, their usual food and good west country cheese, fish and meat, half a dozen real ales, good wine choice; children welcome when eating, quality furniture in attractive side garden, open all day *(Dr and Mrs A K Clarke, John Fiander, Mike Gorton, Dr and Mrs M E Wilson)*

☆ *Great Western* EX4 4NU [St Davids Hill]: Up to a dozen or so changing real ales usually inc Adnams, Bass, Exmoor, Fullers London Pride and Teignworthy in large hotel's small split-level convivial bar, wholesome good value fresh food all day from sandwiches and generous baked potatoes up (kitchen also supplies the hotel's restaurant), daily papers, no music; bedrooms fresh and warm, open all day *(Phil and Sally Gorton, Dr and Mrs A K Clarke, the Didler, Colin Gooch)*

☆ *Hour Glass* EX2 4AU [Melbourne St, off B3015 Topsham Rd]: Thriving bistro-feel 19th-c pub doing well under newish owners, beams, bare boards, panelling, candles and open fire, interesting blackboard food inc delicatessen meats and good fish, also good tapas and nibbles, Adnams Broadside, Otter and Sharps Doom Bar, good choice of wines by the glass, cheerful helpful young staff; can be smoky *(Mike Gorton, Dr and Mrs A K Clarke, the Didler, Dr and Mrs M E Wilson)*

Mill on the Exe EX4 3AB [Bonhay Rd (A377)]: Good spot by pedestrian bridge over weir, heated waterside terrace, bar comfortably done out in current style with bare boards, old bricks, beams and timbers, large airy river-view conservatory restaurant, good sensibly priced food inc good value lunchtime light dishes, St Austell ales, good house wines, friendly young staff; children welcome *(BB, Dr and Mrs A K Clarke, Pete Walker)*

Prospect EX2 4AN [The Quay (left bank, nr rowing club)]: Good quayside spot, plenty of comfortable tables, modern colour-scheme and prints contrasting with the old building's

beams, good value up-to-date bar food from baguettes with chips and baked potatoes up, Adnams and Otter, friendly helpful young staff, raised river-front dining area; gentle piped music; tables out by historic ship-canal basin *(Roger Thornington, Peter Titcomb, Dr and Mrs A K Clarke, Michael and Alison Sandy)*

Welcome EX2 8DU [Haven Banks, off Haven Rd (which is first left off A377 heading S after Exe crossing)]: Venerable two-room pub near the gasometers and little changed since the 1960s (ditto the juke box), gas lighting and flagstones, very friendly old-school landlady, changing real ales; a few tables out overlooking basin on Exeter Ship Canal, and can be reached on foot via footbridges from The Quay *(Phil and Sally Gorton, Dr and Mrs A K Clarke, the Didler)*

Well House EX1 1HB [Cathedral Yard, attached to Royal Clarence Hotel]: Big windows looking across to cathedral in open-plan bar divided by inner walls and partitions, lots of interesting Victorian prints, good choice of local real ales such as Otter, quick service, wide range of reasonably priced upscale lunchtime food inc good sandwiches and salads, daily papers, sofa; may be piped music, popular with young smokers; Roman well below (can be viewed when pub not busy) *(Dr and Mrs A K Clarke, BB, Dr and Mrs M E Wilson, Pete Walker, R Michael Richards, Michael and Alison Sandy)*

EXMINSTER [SX9587]

Swans Nest EX6 8DZ [Station Rd, just off A379 on outskirts]: Huge well arranged food pub very popular for wide choice of reasonably priced food from sandwiches, baked potatoes and children's dishes to extensive carvery, friendly staff, Otter Best and Youngs Special, no smoking areas; especially good for family groups, handy for M5 *(LYM, David Carr, Alain and Rose Foote, Mrs Sylvia Elcoate)*

EXMOUTH [SX9980]

Beach EX8 1DR [Victoria Rd]: Old quayside local with Bass, Greene King Old Speckled Hen and Otter, food, friendly landlord and staff, shipping and lifeboat memorabilia and photographs, beams, posts and panelling, cast-iron framed tables *(Dr and Mrs M E Wilson, Mrs Hazel Rainer)*

Powder Monkey EX8 1RJ [The Parade]: Well managed Wetherspoons with long bar, armchairs in two smaller front rooms (children allowed in one), five real ales, low prices; very popular with young people wknds; a few tables on roadside terrace, open all day *(John Fiander, Tony and Wendy Hobden)*

EXTON [SX9886]

Puffing Billy EX3 0PR: Brightly decorated dining pub with good helpings of good inventive modern food using named local organic suppliers, imaginative puddings, compact bar; close-set picnic-sets on terrace, small back garden *(D P and M A Miles, Dr and Mrs M E Wilson)*

FILLEIGH [SS6727]

☆ *Stags Head* EX32 0RN [off A361, via B3226 N of S Molton; large-scale maps name the hamlet

Stags Head]: Pretty 16th-c thatched and flagstoned pub, helpful staff, good value home-made food from sandwiches up, Cotleigh, reasonably priced wines, friendly local bar with very high-backed settle, separate lounge bar, lots of tables in cottagey dining room up a couple of steps, pool and darts; rustic tables out in fairy-lit honeysuckle arbour by big tree-sheltered pond with ducks and fish; children welcome, bedrooms comfortable and good value, good breakfast (Tracey and Stephen Groves, BB, Mark Flynn, D G Brown, June and Robin Savage)

FROGMORE [SX7742]
Globe TQ7 2NR [A379 E of Kingsbridge]: Nautical décor, some built-in settles creating corner booths, mix of simple tables, quick friendly service, generous good value food from sandwiches to steak, Exmoor Ale and Greene King Abbot, local farm cider in summer, good wines, fine log fire in cosy restaurant; piped music, TV, games machine; terrace tables with play area, plenty of walks, comfortable bedrooms (LYM, Mr and Mrs R J Kynaston)

GEORGEHAM [SX4639]
Lower House EX33 1JJ [B3231 Croyde—Woolacombe]: Former Kings Arms reopened under new ownership after major refurbishment, St Austell and local guest ales such as Barum and Exmoor, no food yet as we went to press but plans for full range (Paul and Ursula Randall)
☆ *Rock* EX33 1JW [Rock Hill, above village]: Well restored oak-beamed pub with real ales such as Bass, Cotleigh, Fullers London Pride, Greene King IPA and Abbot and Timothy Taylors Landlord, local farm cider, wide range of good value generous food from baguettes to plenty of fish, friendly quick-witted landlady and cheerful staff, open fire, old red quarry tiles, pleasant mix of rustic furniture, lots of bric-a-brac, separate vine-adorned back family conservatory (children allowed in pool room too); piped music, darts, fruit machine, juke box; dogs welcome, tables under cocktail parasols on flower-decked front terrace (Mark Flynn, BB, Bob and Margaret Holder, Chris and Ann Coy, Peter and Margaret Glenister, Roona Murdoch)

HARBERTON [SX7758]
☆ *Church House* TQ9 7SF [off A381 S of Totnes]: Ancient partly Norman village pub under new licensees, real ales such as Butcombe, Courage Best, Marstons Pedigree and St Austell Tribute, good choice of wines by the glass, farm cider, decent bar food, woodburner in big inglenook, medieval latticed glass and oak panelling, attractive 17th- and 18th-c pews and settles, no smoking family room; bedrooms (LYM, Peter and Margaret Lodge)

HATHERLEIGH [SS5404]
George EX20 3JN [A386 N of Okehampton; Market St]: Timbered pub with huge oak beams, enormous fireplace, easy chairs, sofas and antique cushioned settles in original core, more modern main bar, more settles and woodburner in L-shaped beamed back bar,

good value simple generous food inc bargain wkdy OAP lunches, cheery staff, Bass, St Austell Dartmoor Best and a beer named for the pub, lots of malt whiskies, farm cider, restaurant; piped music may obtrude; children in eating area, dogs in bar, rustic tables in pretty courtyard and walled cobbled garden, bedrooms, open all day (Ryta Lyndley, LYM, the Didler, Liz Tull)
☆ *Tally Ho* EX20 3JN [Market St (A386)]: Attractive heavy-beamed and timbered linked rooms, sturdy furnishings, big log fire and woodburner, ample enjoyable food from lunchtime sandwiches up, local Clearwater ales, welcoming staff, no smoking restaurant, traditional games; piped music; tables in nice sheltered garden, three pretty bedrooms (LYM, David Ashton, the Didler, Brian Coleman, DAV)

HAWKCHURCH [ST3400]
Old Inn EX13 5XD [off B3165 E of Axminster, nr Dorset border]: Cosy and welcoming 16th-c local opp church, log fires in long low-beamed main bar, Cotleigh ales, decent house wines, good choice of food, good-sized dining room; picnic-sets in flower-filled back courtyard, cl winter Sun/Mon evenings (Nigel Long)

HIGH BICKINGTON [SS6020]
Old George EX37 9AY: Pretty beamed local with friendly helpful staff, Fullers London Pride and Sharps Doom Bar, good value blackboard food (can take a while), chatty bar, quiet dining room (Mark Flynn)

HOLBETON [SX6150]
Mildmay Colours PL8 1NA [off A379 W of A3121]: Local beers inc one brewed for the pub by Skinners, local farm cider, generous food from sandwiches and baguettes up (and chinese restaurant behind), stripped stone and timbers, woodburner, small no smoking family room, games area; piped music, TV, fruit machine, no credit cards; dogs and children welcome, colourful front terrace, well kept back garden, bedrooms with own bathrooms (B J Harding, LYM, Geoff and Marianne Millin, Bruce Bird, Tracey and Stephen Groves, Jeremy Whitehorn)

HOLSWORTHY [SS3403]
Kings Arms EX22 6EB [Fore St/The Square]: 17th-c village pub with Victorian fittings, etched windows and coal fires in three interesting traditional bars, friendly regulars, particularly well kept Bass and Sharps Doom Bar, food inc proper fresh sandwiches, old pictures and photographs, 40s and 50s beer advertisements, lots of optics behind ornate counter with snob screens; dogs welcome, open all day, Sun afternoon closure (the Didler, Dennis Jenkin)

HONITON [SY1198]
Greyhound EX14 3BJ [Fenny Bridges, B3177 4 miles W]: Big busy thatched family dining pub under new management, wide food choice all day from good open sandwiches and baked potatoes up, good range of beers inc Otter, heavy beams and stylish décor, attractive restaurant with no smoking area; bedrooms

(Miss A G Drake, Meg and Colin Hamilton, LYM, Gill and Keith Croxton)
Honiton Motel EX14 1BL [Turks Head Corner, Exeter Rd]: More pubby than many pubs, with Otter in two bars, freshly made food *(Bob and Margaret Holder)*

HOPE COVE [SX6740]

Hope & Anchor TQ7 3HQ: Simple inn, friendly and comfortable, in lovely seaside spot, good open fire, kind quick service, good value straightforward food inc good crab sandwiches, Sharps Doom Bar, reasonably priced wines, flagstones and bare boards, great bay views to Burgh Island from no smoking dining room, no piped music; children and dogs welcome in family room, sea-view tables out on decking, great coast walks, bedrooms, open all day *(LYM, David and Karen Cuckney, Lawrence Pearse)*

HORNS CROSS [SS3823]

Hoops EX39 5DL [A39 Clovelly—Bideford, W of village]: Picturesque thatched inn with oak settles, beams and inglenook log fires in pleasant bar, Sharps and other ales tapped from the cask, good wine choice, welcoming staff, daily papers, darts; what we call piped music (actually separate CD players in both bar and no smoking restaurant), TV; well behaved children in eating area till 8, dogs allowed in bar, tables in small courtyard, bedrooms, open all day *(R J Walden, John and Jackie Chalcraft, Peter and Margaret Lodge, LYM, John and Joan Calvert, JMC, Peter and Margaret Glenister)*

HORSEBRIDGE [SX4074]

☆ **Royal** PL19 8PJ [off A384 Tavistock—Launceston]: Peaceful rustic spot these days (this was once the main Tamar bridge between Devon and Cornwall), with cheerful slate-floored rooms, interesting bric-a-brac and pictures, simple good value food from baguettes and baked potatoes to fresh scallops, friendly landlord and staff, real ales inc Sharps Doom Bar and Special, farm cider, log fire, bar billiards, cribbage, dominoes, no smoking café-style side room, no music or machines; no children in evening, picnic-sets on back terrace and in big garden *(R M Yard, LYM, Alistair Caie, Mrs J H S Lang, DAV, G Coates)*

IDE [SX8990]

☆ **Poachers** EX2 9RW [3 miles from M5 junction 31, via A30; High St]: Friendly and individual, with nice informal mix of old chairs and sofas, good generous food, both traditional and inventive, from sandwiches to good fish choice (worth booking evenings), Bass, Branscombe Vale Branoc, Otter and one brewed locally for the pub, good value house wines, big log fire; picnic-sets in pleasant garden, attractive and comfortable bedrooms, small quaint village, cl Mon lunchtime *(Phil and Sally Gorton, Cheryl Haddy, the Didler)*

Twisted Oak EX2 9RG [off Balls Farm Rd/Little Johns Cross Hill, N of A30]: Well modernised old country pub, light wood furniture and pale stripped flooring, L-shaped main bar with log fire in lower section, big family dining extension, friendly staff, real ales,

good value food inc OAP bargains; garden picnic-sets *(Dr and Mrs M E Wilson, Bob and Margaret Holder)*

IDEFORD [SX8977]

☆ **Royal Oak** TQ13 0AY [2 miles off A380]: Unpretentious thatched and flagstoned village local with friendly helpful landlord and staff, Bass, Timothy Taylors Landlord and two guest beers, good generous simple food inc bargain steaks, interesting Nelson and Churchill memorabilia, log fire; children and dogs welcome, tables out by car park over road *(Phil and Sally Gorton, the Didler, Ian and Ruth Laurence, Darren and Jane Staniforth)*

INSTOW [SS4730]

☆ **Boat House** EX39 4JJ [Marine Parade]: Airy modern high-ceilinged café/bar with huge tidal beach just across lane and views to Appledore, Bass, Flowers IPA and a local guest beer, good choice of popular food from sandwiches to steaks inc plentiful fish, open fire, friendly prompt service even when crowded, big old-fashioned nautical paintings on stripped stone wall, lively family bustle – children very welcome; piped music, roof terrace *(LYM, Rev D E and Mrs J A Shapland, Mike and Mary Clark)*

KENN [SX9285]

☆ **Ley Arms** EX6 7UW [signed off A380 just S of Exeter]: Extensively rambling thatched pub in quiet spot nr church, attractive inside and out, beams and polished granite flagstones, ploughs on the walls, plush black-panelled lounge with striking log fireplace, relaxed atmosphere, good wines, real ales, friendly efficient staff, enjoyable bar lunches, interesting if not cheap evening menu, sizeable smartish restaurant side; piped music, no smoking family room, games area *(David and Karen Cuckney, LYM)*

KENNFORD [SX9185]

Gissons Arms EX6 7UD [well signed off A38 at end of M5]: Busy well run dining pub, good choice of food all day, breakfast from 8am, helpful neatly dressed staff, good range of real ales and of malt whiskies and other spirits, low beams and lots of old oak, thick carpets and plush furnishings, various levels; tables outside, bedrooms, open all day *(Phil and Jane Hodson)*

KENTON [SX9583]

Devon Arms EX6 8LD [Fore St; A379 Exeter—Dawlish]: Comfortable 16th-c beamed bar with old farm tools, animal photographs and hunting trophies, sound good value food from sandwiches and baguettes up, good mainstream and interesting local beers, short choice of decent wine, friendly helpful service, dining area; small back garden with play area and aviary, bedrooms, handy for Powderham Castle *(Alain and Rose Foote)*

KILMINGTON [SY2698]

New Inn EX13 7SF: Traditional thatched pub, originally three 14th-c cottages but carefully rebuilt after 2004 fire, with Palmers ales, pub food, friendly service; large garden with aviaries *(Pete Walker)*

Old Inn EX13 7RB [A35]: Thatched pub with enjoyable food using local supplies, St Austell and other changing ales, small character polished-floor front bar with traditional games, back lounge with leather armchairs by inglenook log fire, small no smoking restaurant; children welcome, two gardens *(LYM, Pete Walker)*

KING'S NYMPTON [SS6819]

☆ *Grove* EX37 9ST [off B3226 SW of S Molton]: Attractive thatched village pub with flagstones, low beams and two log fires, sensibly priced food from sandwiches and various ploughman's to good proper cooking, Exmoor ale, decent wine by the glass, bookmark collection and interesting photographs of old-time villagers on red walls, welcoming service and atmosphere, skittle alley; small pretty enclosed terrace (defibrillator in porch), picturesque village *(LYM, Mrs J Ekins-Daukes, Mark Flynn, Jeremy Whitehorn)*

KINGSBRIDGE [SX7343]

Crabshell TQ7 1JZ [Embankment Rd, edge of town]: Lovely waterside position, charming when tide in, big windows and tables outside; simple bar with plainly furnished eating area, wide choice of food from good fresh lunchtime shrimp or crab sandwiches to local fish and shellfish, helpful staff, real ales, feature open fire, upstairs restaurant with good views *(Ken Flawn, BB)*

KINGSKERSWELL [SX8666]

☆ *Bickley Mill* TQ12 5LN [Stoneycombe, Abbotskerswell— Compton/Marldon]: Tucked-away pub with wide choice of good reasonably priced food from sandwiches or baguettes to fine main dishes, sensible prices, good real ales, friendly efficient staff, buoyant atmosphere in spotless rambling beamed rooms with lots of copper and brass, log fire; children welcome, disabled access and facilities, courtyard tables, subtropical-style hillside garden, comfortable bedrooms *(LYM, Phil and Anne Nash, Mrs Sylvia Elcoate)*

KINGSTEIGNTON [SX8674]

Ten Tors TQ12 3NP [Exeter Rd]: Large extended 1930s pub, wide choice of good value typical food (may take a while) from doorstep sandwiches to OAP specials, end restaurant, Courage and local beers, cheerful efficient bar staff *(Meg and Colin Hamilton)*

KINGSWEAR [SX8851]

Royal Dart TQ6 0AA [The Square]: Fine setting by ferry and Dart Valley Railway terminal, great view of Dartmouth from balcony outside upstairs restaurant, enjoyable food inc seafood here and in modern bar, South Hams ale *(Dave Braisted)*

Ship TQ6 0AG [Higher St]: Tall and attractive old two-bar pub with interesting décor, quiet little lounge, real ales inc Otter, farm cider, nice wines, friendly service, usual food (best views from upstairs bar); a couple of tables outside *(Pete Walker)*

KNOWLE [SY0582]

☆ *Britannia* EX9 6AL [B3178 NW of Budleigh Salterton]: Victorian pub thriving under new ex-RM landlord/chef and his vivaceous wife, enjoyable food inc speciality sausages, some interesting starters and puddings, new sofa in small public bar with log fire and pool, small

lounge bar leading to attractively done no smoking dining room (former skittle alley); picnic-sets out on lawn *(Dr and Mrs M E Wilson)*

KNOWSTONE [SS8223]

Masons Arms EX36 4RY: No longer a pub, but now a pricey restaurant – and under its excellent new chef/landlord particularly enjoyed as that by many readers; so (unless there is a change) it will not be mentioned in future editions of the *Guide* *(LYM)*

LAKE [SX5288]

☆ *Bearslake* EX20 4HQ [A386 just S of Sourton]: Welcoming family in thatched stone-built Dartmoor inn dating from 13th c, beams, flagstones, inglenook fireplace, pews and plenty of locals in friendly character bar, wide choice of home-made food from generous baguettes to good restaurant dishes, mainstream and local real ales, good service; picnic-sets in sizeable streamside garden with terrace, six olde-worlde bedrooms, filling breakfast *(Peter and Margaret Lodge, DAV)*

LIFTON [SX3885]

☆ *Arundell Arms* PL16 0AA [Fore St]: Good interesting lunchtime bar food in substantial and warmly welcoming country-house fishing hotel with real personality, rich décor, nice staff and sophisticated service, good choice of wines by the glass, evening restaurant; can arrange fishing tuition – also shooting, deer-stalking and riding; pleasant bedrooms *(Mrs J H S Lang, Oliver and Sue Rowell)*

LITTLEHEMPSTON [SX8162]

Pig & Whistle TQ9 6LT [Newton Rd (A381)]: Large former coaching inn with beams and stripped brick, extensive dining area with reasonably priced home-made food from generous sandwiches to good value set meals, friendly efficient staff, Sharps Special and Charles Wells Bombardier from long bar with comfortable pews boxing in large old table; pleasant little front terrace *(E B Ireland, Steve Whalley)*

LUPPITT [ST1606]

☆ *Luppitt Inn* EX14 4RT [back roads N of Honiton]: Unspoilt little basic farmhouse pub, amazing survivor of past times, friendly chatty landlady who keeps it open because she (and her cats) like the company; tiny room with corner bar and a table, another not much bigger with fireplace, cheap Otter tapped from the cask, intriguing metal puzzles made by neighbour, no food or music, lavatories across the yard; cl lunchtime and Sun evening *(the Didler, Richard Pitcher)*

LUTON [SX9076]

☆ *Elizabethan* TQ13 0BL [Haldon Moor]: Charming low-beamed old-world pub with welcoming owners and friendly efficient staff, good well presented food, real ales inc a local guest beer, reasonably priced house wines, thriving atmosphere; garden tables *(Mrs Bridget Cushion)*

LYDFORD [SX5285]

☆ *Dartmoor Inn* EX20 4AY [Downton, A386]: Attractive restaurant-with-rooms, not a pub now (though there is a small front log-fire bar), no smoking throughout, with several small civilised and relaxed stylishly decorated contemporary areas, good wines by the glass; the food, priced at restaurant levels, went through an inconsistent patch, though our most recent reports have been warmly favourable; children welcome, dogs allowed in bar, terrace tables, cl Sun evening, Mon *(Jacquie and Jim Jones, LYM, Victoria Hatfield)*

LYMPSTONE [SX9984]

☆ *Redwing* EX8 5JT [Church Rd]: Bustling village local with good value well prepared food inc lots of local fish and good puddings, may be Sun bar nibbles, Greene King Abbot, Otter, Palmers and a guest beer, local farm cider, good house wines, caring licensees and helpful efficient staff, brightly painted lounge, thriving bar and neat little no smoking dining area; may be discreet piped music, live music most wknds, some bank hols, good jazz Tues; pretty enclosed garden behind, unspoilt village with shore walks, open all day wknds *(Peter Burton, BB, Kevin Flack, Dr and Mrs M E Wilson, Donna and Roger, the Didler)*
Swan EX8 5ET [The Strand]: Pleasan olde-worlde décor, welcoming staff, sensibly priced enjoyable food in bar and restaurant inc good fresh fish and italian specials (esp Fri evening – Italian chef), real ales; piped music, live Weds; pretty flower troughs and hanging baskets *(Grace and Michael Upton)*

LYNMOUTH [SS7249]

Rising Sun EX35 6EG [Harbourside]: Wonderful position overlooking harbour, concentration on the upmarket hotel side and the attractive cosy no smoking restaurant; Exmoor Bitter, Fox and Gold, wide lunchtime choice of blackboard food inc plenty of fish, good fire; may be quiet piped music, bar can get smoky, parking can be a problem – expensive by day, sparse at night; children allowed away from bar, bedrooms in cottagey old thatched terrace stepped up hills, gardens up behind *(LYM, Comus and Sarah Elliott, Keith and Margaret Kettell, June and Robin Savage, Edward Leetham)*
Village EX35 6EH [Lynmouth St]: Welcoming and neatly kept, with good fires, good value food, friendly landlord; bedrooms *(John and Jackie Chalcraft)*

LYNTON [SS7249]

Crown EX35 6AG [Market St/Sinai Hill]: Relaxed chatty atmosphere in hotel lounge bar, open fire, decent reasonably priced bar food all day from baguettes up, small comfortable restaurant, five changing real ales such as Cotleigh, Greene King Ruddles and Marstons Pedigree, farm cider, horse tack; no pushchairs allowed, even for disabled children; good bedrooms, open all day *(A and B D Craig, Stan and Hazel Allen, Comus and Sarah Elliott)*

☆ *Hunters* EX31 4PY [pub well signed off A39 W of Lynton]: Superb Heddon Valley position by NT information centre down very steep hill, great walks inc one, not too taxing, down to the sea; big spreading bar with some plush banquettes and so forth, enjoyable fresh generous food from soup and baguettes to local seafood (may be a wait when crowded), cheerful young staff, Exmoor ales, woodburner, no smoking area; piped music; bedrooms, picnic-sets on balconied terrace overlooking attractively landscaped pondside garden with peacocks, open all day summer, hours may be restricted when season tails off *(Gillian Rodgers, BB, Andy and Ali)*

MAIDENCOMBE [SX9268]

☆ *Thatched Tavern* TQ1 4TS [Steep Hill]: Much extended well run three-level thatched pub, Bass, Flowers IPA and Original and Fullers London Pride in pubby bar, good value generous food inc local fish (can be a wait) and tempting puddings in two cosy eating areas, one no smoking, quick friendly service even when busy, big family room, pleasant restaurant; children allowed, no dogs inside, nice garden with small thatched huts, small attractive village above small beach *(Mike and Mary Carter, Dr and Mrs M E Wilson, Brian and Ruth Archer)*

MANATON [SX7580]

Kestor TQ13 9UF: Modern Dartmoor-edge inn in splendid spot nr Becky Falls, warm-hearted family giving it a welcoming homely feel, attractive dining room with good range of enjoyable food, real ales, farm cider, good wine choice, open fire, good mix of locals and visitors; piped music; nice bedrooms *(Alan Swann, Dennis and Jean Bishop)*

MARSH [ST2510]

☆ *Flintlock* EX14 9AJ [pub signed just off A303 Ilminster—Honiton]: Long open-plan dining pub popular for wide choice of good varied reasonably priced food inc well cooked Sun lunches, welcoming landlord and staff, Fullers London Pride and Otter, neat furnishings, woodburner in stone inglenook, beamery and mainly stripped stone walls, plenty of copper and brass; piped music, cl Mon *(BB, Brian and Bett Cox)*

MEAVY [SX5467]

☆ *Royal Oak* PL20 6PJ [off B3212 E of Yelverton]: Heavy-beamed partly 15th-c pub owned by the Parish Council (with pews from the next-door church), engaging new landlord, small flagstone bar with log fire in big fireplace, good reasonably priced traditonal food using local ingredients in roomy and well appointed dining area (best to book), particularly well kept ales inc St Austell, attractive cottage décor with some bric-a-brac hoping for buyers; tables out by pretty green *(LYM, J F Stackhouse, Tracey and Stephen Groves)*

MERRIVALE [SX5475]

☆ *Dartmoor Inn* PL20 6ST [B3357, 4 miles E of Tavistock]: Well run and carefully refurbished pub in tranquil spot with high Dartmoor views; generous lunchtime food from sandwiches and good ploughman's up, quick polite service, Greene King IPA, decent wines, water from their 36-metre (120-ft) deep well, open fire; dogs on leads allowed, good views from tables out in front (very popular summer evenings) good walks – near Bronze-Age hut circles, stone rows and pretty river *(Dennis Jenkin, Dr and Mrs M E Wilson)*

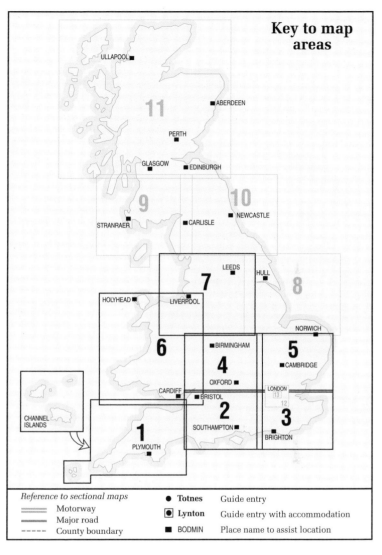

Key to map areas

ULLAPOOL

11

ABERDEEN

PERTH

GLASGOW — EDINBURGH

9 **10**

STRANRAER — CARLISLE — NEWCASTLE

LEEDS — HULL

7 **8**

HOLYHEAD — LIVERPOOL

NORWICH

BIRMINGHAM

6 **4** **5**

CAMBRIDGE

OXFORD

CARDIFF — BRISTOL — LONDON **13** **12**

2 **3**

SOUTHAMPTON

BRIGHTON

CHANNEL ISLANDS

1 PLYMOUTH

Reference to sectional maps	● **Totnes**	Guide entry
Motorway	◉ **Lynton**	Guide entry with accommodation
Major road		
County boundary	■ **BODMIN**	Place name to assist location

MAPS IN THIS SECTION

For Maps 8 – 13 see later colour section

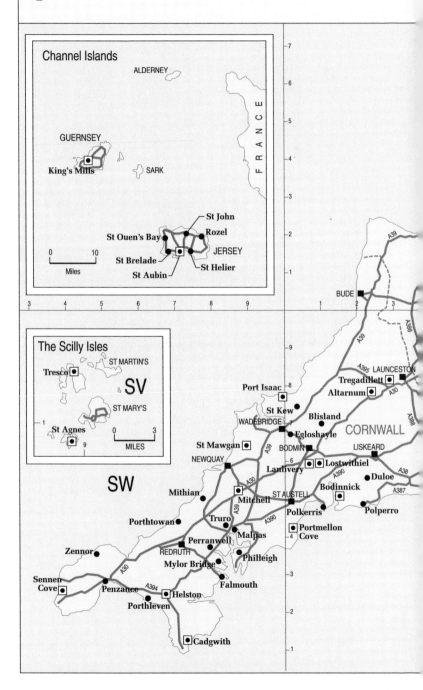

1

Channel Islands

ALDERNEY

F
R
A
N
C
E

GUERNSEY

King's Mills

SARK

St John
Rozel

St Ouen's Bay

St Brelade   JERSEY

St Aubin   St Helier

0   10
Miles

The Scilly Isles

ST MARTIN'S

Tresco

SV

ST MARY'S

St Agnes

0   3
MILES

SW

BUDE

A39

A38

A388

A395   LAUNCESTON

Tregadillett

Altarnum   A30   A388

Port Isaac

St Kew   Blisland

WADEBRIDGE   CORNWALL

Egloshayle

St Mawgan   BODMIN   LISKEARD

NEWQUAY   Lanlivery   Lostwithiel   A38

Mithian   A390   Duloe

Mitchell   ST AUSTELL   Bodinnick   A387

Porthtowan   Truro   Polkerris   Polperro

Perranwell   Malpas   Portmellon
Cove

Zennor   REDRUTH   Mylor Bridge   Philleigh

Sennen
Cove   Penzance   A394   Falmouth

Porthleven   Helston

Cadgwith

SW

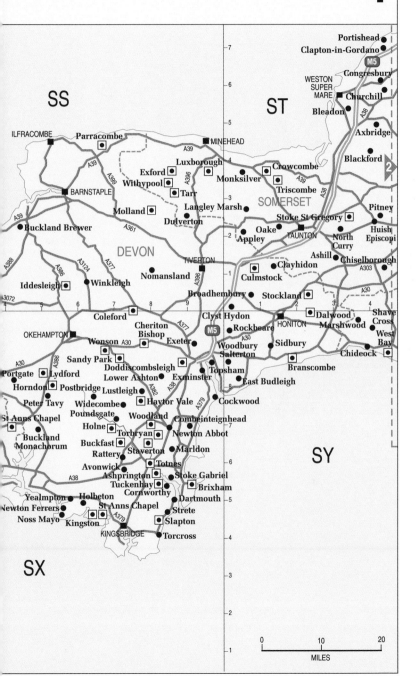

2

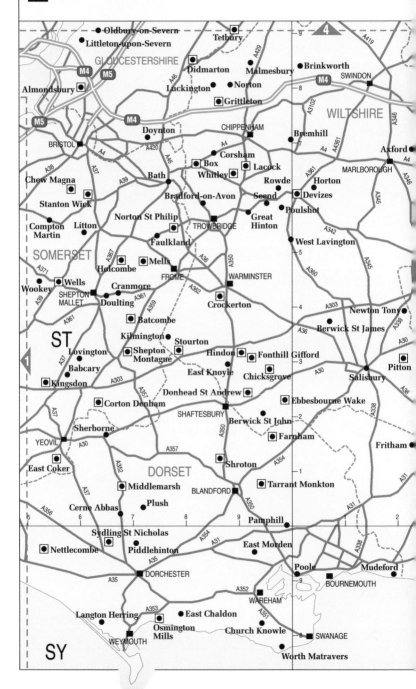

Oldbury-on-Severn
Littleton-upon-Severn
Tetbury
GLOUCESTERSHIRE
Didmarton
Malmesbury
Brinkworth
Almondsbury
Luckington
Norton
SWINDON
Grittleton
WILTSHIRE
Doynton
CHIPPENHAM
Bremhill
BRISTOL
Axford
Corsham
MARLBOROUGH
Box
Lacock
Chew Magna
Bath
Whitley
Rowde
Horton
Bradford-on-Avon
Seend
Devizes
Stanton Wick
Poulshot
Compton
Martin
Litton
Norton St Philip
TROWBRIDGE
Great
Hinton
West Lavington
SOMERSET
Faulkland
Mells
Holcombe
FROME
WARMINSTER
Wells
Cranmore
Wookey
SHEPTON
MALLET
Doulting
Crockerton
Batcombe
Kilmington
Newton Tony
Stourton
Berwick St James
ST
Lovington
Shepton
Montague
Hindon
Fonthill Gifford
Babcary
East Knoyle
Chicksgrove
Pitton
Kingsdon
Donhead St Andrew
Salisbury
Corton Denham
SHAFTESBURY
Ebbesbourne Wake
Sherborne
Berwick St John
YEOVIL
Farnham
Fritham
East Coker
Shroton
DORSET
Middlemarsh
BLANDFORD
Tarrant Monkton
Cerne Abbas
Plush
Pamphill
Sydling St Nicholas
East Morden
Nettlecombe
Piddlehinton
Poole
Mudeford
BOURNEMOUTH
DORCHESTER
WAREHAM
Langton Herring
East Chaldon
Osmington
Mills
Church Knowle
SWANAGE
SY
WEYMOUTH
Worth Matravers

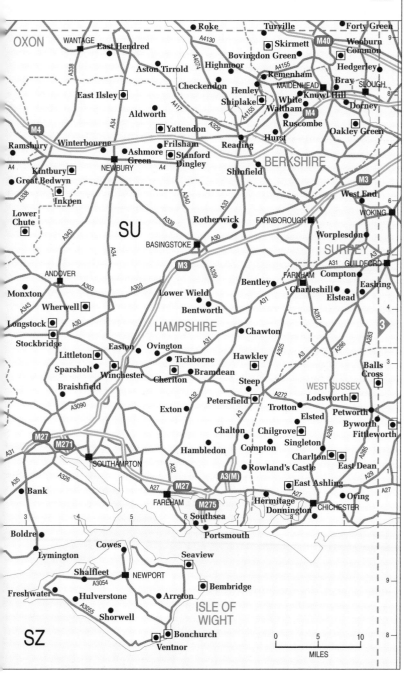

2

3

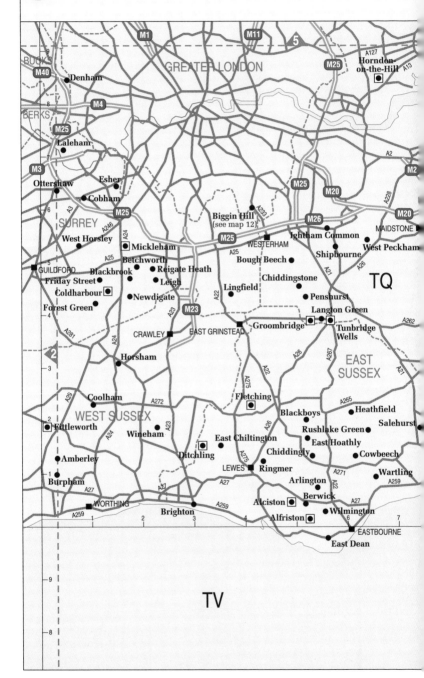

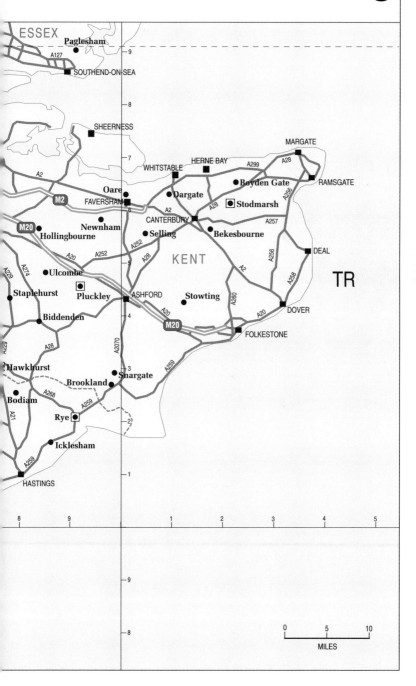

3

ESSEX

Paglesham

A127

SOUTHEND-ON-SEA

SHEERNESS

MARGATE

WHITSTABLE   HERNE BAY   A299   A28

M2   Oare   Dargate   Boyden Gate   RAMSGATE
      FAVERSHAM   A256
                          A2   A28   Stodmarsh
M20   Newnham   CANTERBURY   A257
Hollingbourne   Selling   Bekesbourne
      A20   A252   A252   A28   A256   DEAL

A274   Ulcombe   KENT   A2   A258

Staplehurst   TR
      Pluckley   ASHFORD   Stowting   A260
Biddenden   A20
      A28   A2070   M20   FOLKESTONE   DOVER

Hawkhurst   Snargate   A259

Brookland
Bodiam   A268   A259

A21   Rye

Icklesham

A259

HASTINGS

0   5   10
MILES

4

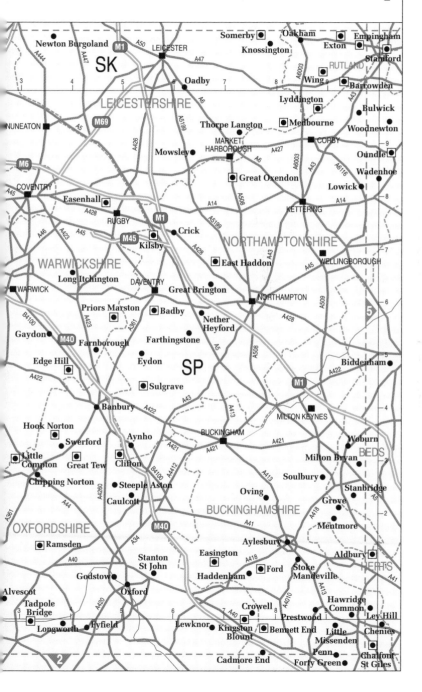

Newton Burgoland · **M1** A50 LEICESTER · Somerby · Oakham · Empingham
A444 A47 · Knossington · Exton · Stamford
SK A47 · RUTLAND
A447 · A6003 · Wing · Barrowden
LEICESTERSHIRE · Oadby · A6 · Lyddington · A43 · Bulwick
NUNEATON · **M69** A5 · Thorpe Langton · Medbourne · Woodnewton
A426 · MARKET HARBOROUGH · A427 · CORBY · Oundle
M6 A5199 · Mowsley · A6 · A6003 · A6116 · Wadenhoe
COVENTRY · Great Oxendon · A43 · Lowick
A45 · Easenhall · A508 · A14 · KETTERING · A14
A428 · RUGBY · A5199
M1 · Crick · **NORTHAMPTONSHIRE**
M45 · Kilsby · A428 · WELLINGBOROUGH
WARWICKSHIRE · East Haddon · A43 · A45
Long Itchington · DAVENTRY · Great Brington · A5 · NORTHAMPTON · A509
WARWICK · Priors Marston · Badby · Nether Heyford · A428
A46 · A423 · A45 · A361 · Farthingstone · A5 · A508
Gaydon · **M40** · Farnborough · Eydon · **SP**
B4100 · Edge Hill · Sulgrave · Biddenham
A422 · A4422 · **M1**
Hook Norton · Banbury · A422 · A43 · A413 · MILTON KEYNES
Little Compton · Swerford · Aynho · BUCKINGHAM · Woburn
Great Tew · Clifton · A421 · A421 · Milton Bryan · BEDS
Chipping Norton · A4412 · B4100 · A413 · Soulbury · Stanbridge
A4260 · Steeple Aston · Oving · Grove · A5
A361 · Caulcott · **BUCKINGHAMSHIRE** · A418 · Mentmore
OXFORDSHIRE · **M40** · A41
Ramsden · A34 · Aylesbury · Aldbury · **HERTS**
A40 · Stanton St John · Easington · A418 · Ford · Stoke Mandeville
Alvescot · Godstow · Haddenham · A4010 · Hawridge Common · A413
Tadpole Bridge · Oxford · A40 · Crowell · Prestwood · Ley Hill
A420 · Lewknor · Kingston Blount · Bennett End · Little Missenden · Chenies
Longworth · Fyfield · Penn · Chalfont St Giles
Cadmore End · Forty Green

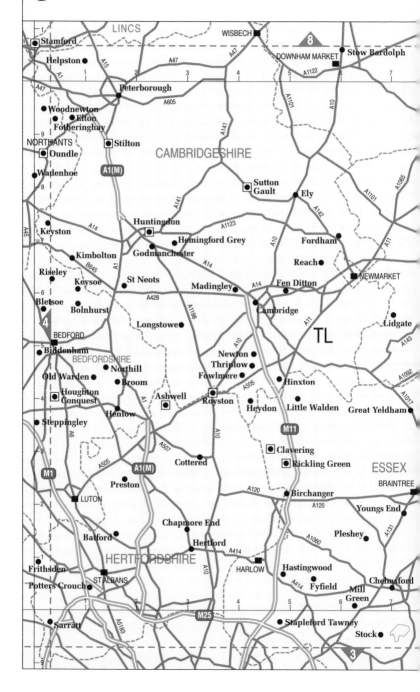

LINCS

Stamford

Helpston

WISBECH

DOWNHAM MARKET

Stow Bardolph

Peterborough

Woodnewton
Elton
Fotheringhay

Stilton

CAMBRIDGESHIRE

NORTHANTS
Oundle

Wadenhoe

Sutton Gault

Ely

Keyston

Huntingdon

Hemingford Grey

Fordham

Kimbolton
Godmanchester

Reach

Riseley
Keysoe

St Neots

Madingley

Fen Ditton

NEWMARKET

Bletsoe
Bolnhurst

Longstowe

Cambridge

TL

Lidgate

BEDFORD

Biddenham

BEDFORDSHIRE

Newton
Thriplow
Fowlmere

Hinxton

Old Warden
Northill
Broom

Ashwell

Royston

Heydon

Little Walden

Great Yeldham

Houghton
Conquest

Henlow

Steppingley

Cottered

Clavering

Rickling Green

ESSEX

BRAINTREE

Preston

LUTON

Birchanger

Youngs End

Chapmore End

Pleshey

Batford

Hertford

HERTFORDSHIRE

HARLOW

Hastingwood

Chelmsford

Frithsden

Potters Crouch

ST ALBANS

Fyfield

Mill Green

M25

Sarratt

Stapleford Tawney

Stock

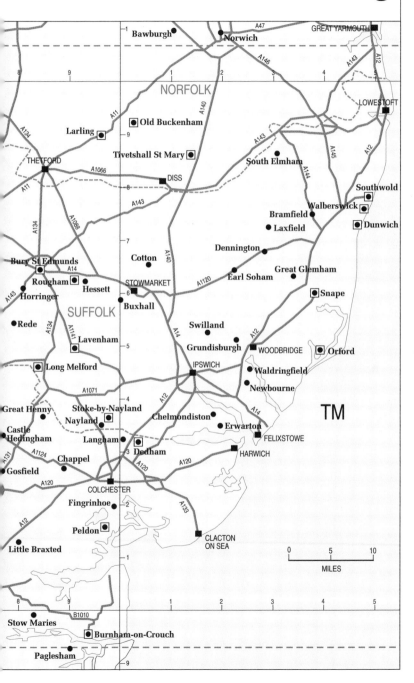

5

Bawburgh

Norwich

GREAT YARMOUTH

A47

A146

A143

A12

LOWESTOFT

NORFOLK

A11

A140

A143

A145

A12

Larling

Old Buckenham

THETFORD

A134

A11

A1066

Tivetshall St Mary

South Elmham

A143

DISS

A144

Southwold

Walberswick

Bramfield

Dunwich

A134

A1068

A143

A140

Laxfield

Dennington

Bury St Edmunds

A14

Cotton

STOWMARKET

Great Glemham

Rougham

Hessett

Earl Soham

A143

Horringer

SUFFOLK

Buxhall

A1120

Snape

Rede

A1141

Lavenham

Swilland

A14

Grundisburgh

WOODBRIDGE

Orford

Long Melford

A1071

IPSWICH

Waldringfield

Newbourne

Great Henny

Stoke-by-Nayland

A12

Nayland

Chelmondiston

Erwarton

TM

Castle Hedingham

Langham

Dedham

FELIXSTOWE

A131

A1124

Chappel

A120

A120

HARWICH

Gosfield

A120

COLCHESTER

Fingrinhoe

A12

A133

Peldon

CLACTON ON SEA

Little Braxted

0   5   10

MILES

A12

B1010

Stow Maries

Burnham-on-Crouch

Paglesham

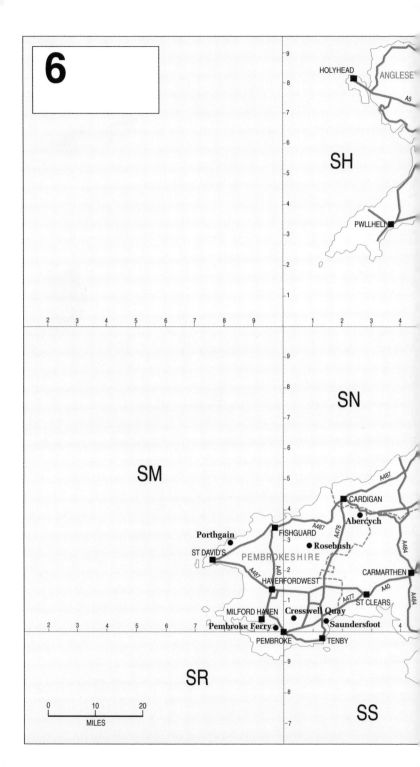

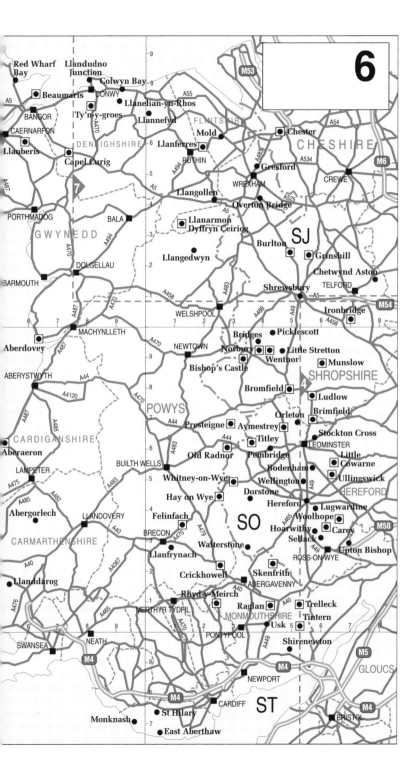

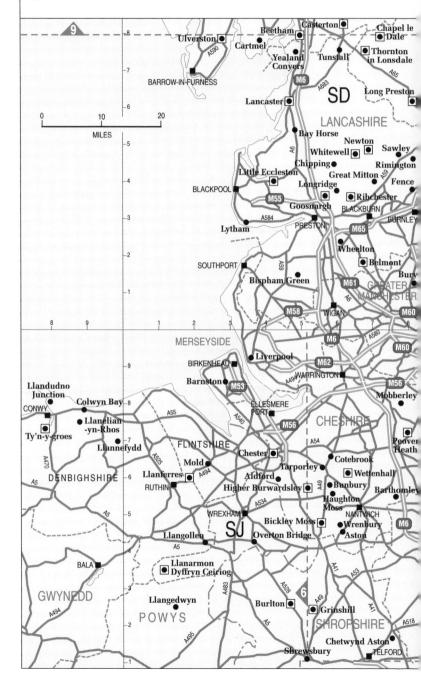

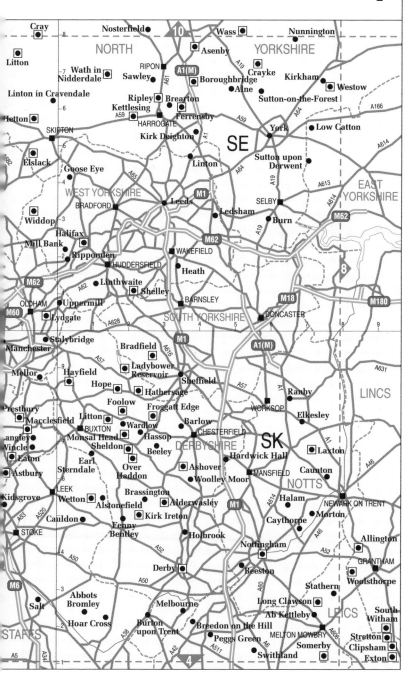

Cray
Litton
Nosterfield
NORTH
10
Wass
Asenby
Nunnington
YORKSHIRE
Wath in Nidderdale
RIPON
A1(M)
Sawley
Crayke
Kirkham
Linton in Cravendale
Boroughbridge
Alne
Westow
Hetton
Ripley
Brearton
Sutton-on-the-Forest
A166
SKIPTON
Kettlesing
HARROGATE
Ferrensby
A59
York
Low Catton
Kirk Deighton
A1
SE
A614
Elslack
Goose Eye
Linton
Sutton upon Derwent
EAST YORKSHIRE
WEST YORKSHIRE
M1
A64
A19
A613
A614
BRADFORD
Leeds
Ledsham
SELBY
Burn
M62
Widdop
Halifax
Mill Bank
Ripponden
WAKEFIELD
HUDDERSFIELD
Heath
M62
Linthwaite
Shelley
M62
Uppermill
BARNSLEY
M18
M180
OLDHAM
Lydgate
SOUTH YORKSHIRE
DONCASTER
M60
Stalybridge
M1
A1(M)
Manchester
Bradfield
A631
Mellor
Hayfield
Ladybower Reservoir
Sheffield
Ranby
LINCS
Hope
Hathersage
WORKSOP
Elkesley
Presthury
Foolow
Froggatt Edge
Barlow
Macclesfield
Litton
Wardlow
CHESTERFIELD
Langley
BUXTON
Hassop
DERBYSHIRE
SK
Laxton
Wincle
Monsal Head
Sheldon
Beeley
Eaton
Hardwick Hall
Astbury
Earl Sterndale
Over Haddon
Ashover
MANSFIELD
Caunton
Woolley Moor
NOTTS
LEEK
Brassington
Alderwasley
M1
Halam
NEWARK ON TRENT
Kidsgrove
Wetton
Alstonefield
Kirk Ireton
Caythorpe
Morton
Cauldon
Fenny Bentley
Holbrook
Allington
STOKE
A52
Nottingham
GRANTHAM
M6
A50
Derby
Beeston
Woolsthorpe
A50
Stathern
Abbots Bromley
Melbourne
Long Clawson
Salt
Ab Kettleby
South Witham
Hoar Cross
Burton upon Trent
Breedon on the Hill
LEICS
STAFFS
Peggs Green
MELTON MOWBRAY
Stretton
A5
A34
Somerby
Clipsham
Swithland
Exton
4

IF YOU HAVE A MOBILE PHONE, THERE'S A QUICK AND EASY WAY TO FIND A PUB NEAR YOU

Text **goodpub** to **60300** to find your nearest good pub.

Text **goodpub food** to **60300** to only include pubs where meals are served – serving times vary – ring pub to check.

(Texts cost 50p plus standard network charges. Involves a location look-up on your mobile – further details can be found at **www.goodguides.co.uk**)

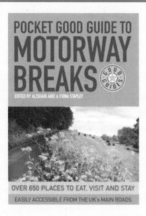

If you would like to order a copy of
Pocket Good Guide to Motorway Breaks (£5.99)
or the
Good Guide to Dog Friendly Pubs, Hotels and B&Bs 2005/2006 (£9.99)
direct from Ebury Press (p&p free), please call our credit-card hotline on

01206 255 800

or send a cheque/postal order made payable to
Ebury Press to
Cash Sales Department, TBS Direct,
Frating Distribution Centre,
Colchester Road, Frating Green,
Essex CO7 7DW

For more information about these titles,
please refer to the back of the next colour section.

MILTONCOMBE [SX4865]

☆ *Who'd A Thought It* PL20 6HP [village signed off A386 S of Yelverton]: Attractive 16th-c thatched pub, black-panelled bar with interesting bric-a-brac, woodburner, barrel seats and high-backed winged settles, separate no smoking lounge and dining conservatory, wide choice of food, friendly efficient staff, five real ales, good choice of reasonably priced wines by the glass; quiet piped music; children welcome, well planted garden with water feature (flaming torches may light your way from the car park on summer nights), more tables out in front; folk club Sun *(Peter Salmon, LYM)*

MODBURY [SX6551]

Modbury Inn PL21 0RQ [Brownston St]: Friendly helpful licensees, enjoyable food, small traditional bar with Bass, Courage and Otter, reasonable prices; attractive garden, comfortable bedrooms *(John and Joan Calvert)*

MORCHARD BISHOP [SS7607]

London EX17 6NW [signed off A377 Crediton—Barnstaple]: Open-plan low-beamed 16th-c coaching inn in picturesque village position, helpful friendly service, good generous traditional home-made food, real ales such as Fullers London Pride and Sharps Doom Bar, big carpeted red plush bar with rather dark décor, plenty of locals and pool, darts and skittles, woodburner in large fireplace, small dining room *(Miss A G Drake)*

MORELEIGH [SX7652]

New Inn TQ9 7JH [B3207, off A381 Kingsbridge—Totnes in Stanborough]: Busy and old-fashioned country local with attentive landlady (same family for several decades), limited choice of wholesome generous home cooking, reasonable prices, Palmers tapped from the cask, good inglenook log fire, character old furniture, nice pictures, candles in bottles; may be cl Sat lunchtime/race days *(Roger Wain-Heapy, LYM, Mike and Shelley Woodroffe)*

MORETONHAMPSTEAD [SX7586]

White Hart TQ13 8NF [A382 N of Bovey Tracey; The Square]: Smartly reworked old coaching inn, stripped floor bar, elegant relaxing lounge (pianist some evenings), helpful friendly service, real ales, enjoyable bar food (not Mon) from toasties and hot meat sandwiches up, attractive brasserie; courtyard tables, 13 well equipped country-style bedrooms with own bathrooms, well placed for Dartmoor, good walks *(LYM, Alec and Barbara Jones, Sally Jenkin)*

MORTEHOE [SS4545]

Chichester Arms EX34 7DU [off A361 Ilfracombe—Braunton]: Interesting old local photographs in plush and leatherette panelled lounge and comfortable no smoking dining room, quick friendly service, wide choice of pubby food, real ales such as local Barum Original, reasonably priced wine, pubby locals' bar with darts and pool, no piped music; skittle alley and games machines in summer children's room, tables out in front and in shaded pretty garden, good coast walks *(Stan and Hazel Allen, Bob and Margaret Holder, Felicity Stephens, David Fox)*

☆ *Ship Aground* EX34 7DT [signed off A361 Ilfracombe—Braunton]: Comfortably worn in open-plan beamed village pub, real ales such as Cotleigh Tawny, Burton Bridge and Greene King Abbot, decent wine, wide choice of food from good crab sandwiches up, upstairs carvery some days, big log fires, massive rustic furnishings, interesting nautical brassware, children allowed in big back family room with pool in games area; tables on sheltered sunny terrace with good views, by interesting church, wonderful walking on nearby coast footpath *(Rona Murdoch, LYM, Comus and Sarah Elliott, Chris and Ann Coy, Felicity Stephens, David Fox)*

NEWTON ABBOT [SX8571]

Dartmouth TQ12 2JP [East St]: Thriving three-room pub with changing local real ales, farm cider, decent wines, log fires, enjoyable food; children welcome till 7pm, tables and barbecues in nice outside area, open all day *(the Didler)*

☆ *Olde Cider Bar* TQ12 2LD [East St]: Basic old-fashioned cider house with casks of interesting low-priced farm ciders (helpful landlord may give you samples), a couple of perries, more in bottles, good country wines, baguettes and pasties etc, dark stools, barrel seats and wall benches, flagstones and bare boards; small games room with machines *(the Didler, Meg and Colin Hamilton)*

NORTH BOVEY [SX7483]

☆ *Ring of Bells* TQ13 8RB [off A382/B3212 SW of Moretonhampstead]: Attractive bulgy-walled 13th-c thatched inn, low beams, flagstones, sturdy rustic tables and winding staircases, good interesting fresh food strong on local produce, friendly relaxed service, real ales inc Otter, Gray's farm cider and warm log fire, stylish no smoking dining room, longer more functional room with pool and TV; by lovely tree-covered village green below Dartmoor, garden picnic-sets, good walks from the door, five big comfortably refurbished bedrooms *(LYM, Stephen R Holman, Sybil Williams, Mr and Mrs Colin Roberts, Prof Keith and Mrs Jane Barber)*

NORTH TAWTON [SS6600]

Railway Inn EX20 2BE [Whiddon Down Rd]: Happy local with particularly welcoming licensees, enjoyable food using local supplies from bar lunches to evening meals (not Thurs), real ales such as Teignworthy and Wye Valley, farm cider; cl lunchtime Mon-Thurs *(R J Walden, DAV)*

NOSS MAYO [SX5447]

☆ *Swan* PL8 1EE [off B3186 at Junket Corner]: Very family-friendly small two-room beamed pub right on the creek, lovely harbour views and good terraces facing the sunset, with wide choice of enjoyable food inc good low-priced fresh fish, Sharps Doom Bar, good-humoured landlord, open fire, unpretentiously traditional décor with plenty of individuality; can get crowded, with difficult parking; children and dogs on leads welcome, terrace tables facing the sunset *(Nicola Hull, Alistair Milne, MP, Martin and Pauline Jennings, Hugh Roberts)*

OKEHAMPTON [SX5895]

Plymouth EX20 1HH [West St]: Cheery beer-oriented local with attractive façade, enterprising low-cost food, Palmers IPA and St Austell Tribute tapped from the cask (May and Nov beer festivals), daily papers, no smoking area, provision for children; open all day wknds *(David Carr, BB, B C Head)*

OTTERTON [SY0885]

Kings Arms EX9 7HB [Fore St]: Big open-plan pub handy for families from extensive nearby caravan site, quick food service from sandwiches up, Otter, friendly staff; TV and darts in lounge, good skittle alley doubling as family room; dogs welcome, beautiful evening view from picnic-sets in good-sized attractive back garden with play area, bedrooms, charming village *(Meg and Colin Hamilton)*

PAIGNTON [SX8860]

Isaac Merritt TQ3 3AA [Torquay Rd]: Spacious efficiently run open-plan Wetherspoons conversion of former shopping arcade, food all day, good range of real ales, low prices, no piped music, no smoking area *(Rev John Hibberd)*

PLYMOUTH [SX4854]

☆ *China House* PL4 0DW [Sutton Harbour, via Sutton Rd off Exeter St (A374)]: Attractive conversion of Plymouth's oldest warehouse, super boaty views day and night over harbour and Barbican, great beams and flagstones, bare slate and stone walls, good log fire, generous pubby food all day from ciabattas and filled baguettes up, real ales, good choice of wines by the glass; piped music; good parking and disabled access and facilities, tables out on waterside balconies, open all day *(Gareth Lewis, LYM, Ken Flawn, Hugh Roberts, Andy and Ali)*

Dolphin PL1 2LS [Barbican]: Basic local with good range of beers inc Bass tapped from the cask, coal fire (not always lit), Beryl Cook paintings inc one of the friendly landlord; open all day *(the Didler)*

Duchy of Cornwall PL1 5JT [Anstis St]: Friendly little local with good beer, farm cider, good atmosphere *(David Ellerington)*

Lounge PL1 4QT [Stopford Pl, Stoke]: Unspoilt open-plan backstreet local, Bass and a guest beer from oak-panelled counter, popular lunchtime food, friendly landlord, local artwork *(the Didler)*

Minerva PL4 0EA [Looe St (nr Barbican)]: Lively low-ceilinged backstreet pub dating from 16th c, good choice of mainstream and less common ales, coal fire, good nostalgic juke box; quite small so can get packed; open all day *(the Didler)*

Navy PL1 2LE [Southside St, Barbican]: Waterside local worth knowing for its bargain cheap and cheerful fry-up; friendly service, Charles Wells Bombardier, cosy corner seats, tables out on balcony, handy for aquarium *(David Crook)*

Thistle Park PL4 0LE [Commercial Rd]: Welcoming bare-boards pub nr National Maritime Aquarium, South Hams ales (used to be brewed next door), tasty food all day, friendly South African landlady, interesting décor, live music wknds; children welcome, open all day till very late *(the Didler)*

POSTBRIDGE [SX6578]

East Dart PL20 6TJ [B3212]: Central Dartmoor hotel by pretty river, in same family since 1861; big comfortable open-plan bar, good value generous food using local ingredients from sandwiches with chips up, prompt pleasant service, St Austell ales inc Dartmoor, good wines by the glass, good fire, hunting murals and horse tack, pool room; can take coaches; dogs welcome, tables out in front and behind, decent bedrooms, some 30 miles of fishing *(Dennis Jenkin, BB, Mike Turner)*

PRINCETOWN [SX5973]

☆ *Plume of Feathers* PL20 6QQ [Plymouth Hill]: Bustling extended four-room local with wide choice of good value generous food inc Sun carvery, cheerful attentive service even when busy, real ales inc Princetown Jail, good choice of wines by the glass, two log fires, solid slate tables, big family room; children welcome, play area, good value bedrooms, also bunkhouse and good camp site, open all day *(David and Karen Cuckney, Ken Flawn)*

RACKENFORD [SS8518]

☆ *Stag* EX16 8DT [pub signed off A361 NW of Tiverton]: Intriguing 13th-c low-beamed newly rethatched pub with original flagstoned and cobbled entry passage between massive walls, huge fireplace flanked by ancient settles, relaxed atmosphere, cheerful Yorkshire landlord, nicely served hearty food in big helpings, Cotleigh Tawny and a guest beer such as Otter (may be more in summer), good soft drinks choice, cottagey dining room (children allowed); quiet views from a few tables out behind, simple bedrooms *(JJW, CMW, Rev D E and Mrs J A Shapland, LYM, Rona Murdoch, Michael Rowse, J C Brittain-Long)*

RINGMORE [SX6545]

☆ *Journeys End* TQ7 4HL [signed off B3392 at Pickwick Inn, St Anns Chapel, nr Bigbury; best to park up opp church]: Ancient village inn with character panelled lounge, enjoyable food, good friendly service, half a dozen changing local ales from casks behind bar, local farm cider, decent wines, log fires, bar billiards (for over-16s), sunny back family dining conservatory with board games; pleasant big terraced garden with boules, attractive setting nr thatched cottages not far from the sea, bedrooms antique but comfortable and well equipped *(LYM, the Didler, Edward Leetham)*

SALCOMBE [SX7438]

Ferry Inn TQ8 8JE [off Fore St nr Portlemouth Ferry]: Good visitors' pub in splendid estuary position, lovely view from tiers of stripped-stone bars rising from sheltered and attractive flagstoned waterside terrace, inc top one opening off street, and middle dining bar, classic seaside pub menu, Palmers and farm cider, good house wine, helpful friendly staff; piped music, can get busy, may be cl part of winter *(Peter and Giff Bennett, B J Harding, JMC, LYM)*

☆ *Fortescue* TQ8 8BZ [Union St, end of Fore St]:
Good proper pub with five linked nautical-
theme rooms, friendly service, popular
promptly served food from hot-filled rolls up,
real ales such as Bass, Courage Directors and
Otter, decent wines, good woodburner, lots of
old local black and white shipping pictures, big
public bar with games, small no smoking
dining room; children welcome, picnic-sets in
courtyard *(Roger Wain-Heapy, Gerry and
Rosemary Dobson, Bruce Bird)*
Victoria TQ8 8BU [Fore St]: Neat and
attractive 19th-c pub opp harbour car park,
colourful window boxes, comfortable
furnishings, usual food from sandwiches up,
St Austell ales, decent wines, good coffee, no
smoking area, nautical décor; piped music;
large sheltered tiered garden behind with good
play area, bedrooms *(Roger Wain-Heapy,
Dudley and Moira Cockroft, J M Tansey,
George Atkinson, Bruce Bird)*

SAMPFORD COURTENAY [SS6300]
New Inn EX20 2TB [B3072 Crediton—
Holsworthy]: Attractive 16th-c thatched pub
with friendly atmosphere and hospitable
landlord, Otter, good food, pleasant décor in
low-beamed open-plan bar, open fires; dogs
welcome, nice garden with play area,
picturesque village *(David Ashton, Peter and
Margaret Lodge)*

SAMPFORD PEVERELL [ST0314]
☆ *Globe* EX16 7BJ [a mile from M5 junction 27,
village signed from Tiverton turn-off; Lower
Town]: Spacious and comfortable village pub
with thriving atmosphere, enjoyable good
value home-made food from sandwiches to
massive mixed grill and popular Sun lunch,
Otter, good wine choice, friendly staff, lounge
largely for eating, big-screen sports TV in
bar, restaurant; piped music, can get smoky;
children and dogs welcome, picnic-sets out in
front, open all day *(Pete and Sue Robbins,
Paul Goldman, LYM, Mike and Jenny Beacon,
Mike and Mary Clark)*

SANDFORD [SS8202]
Lamb EX17 4LW: Relaxed informal local with
small choice of enterprising home cooking, real
ales, village farm cider, friendly service, log
fire, fresh flowers, books and magazines;
upstairs skittle alley *(Dr and Mrs J Mitchell,
Miss N Myers)*

SANDY GATE [SX9690]
☆ *Blue Ball* EX2 7JL [from M5 junction 30, take
A376 and double back from A376/A3052
roundabout, turning off left towards Topsham
just before getting back to M5 junction]:
Extended thatched dining pub, handy and
relaxing escape from the M5, warm and
friendly, with good rather upmarket food,
good helpings, old wood and tile floors, beams,
candles and lovely settles, big inglenook log
fire, O'Hanlons Yellowhammer and Otter,
well priced wine, friendly attentive young staff,
no smoking section; good gardens inc good
play area *(Dr and Mrs M E Wilson, BB)*

SHALDON [SX9472]
London TQ14 8AW [Bank St/The Green]:
Lively and cheerfully bustling pub with good

value generous food from good sandwiches to
fresh fish, good friendly service even when
busy, Greene King Abbot IPA and Abbot and
Otter, decent wines; pool, juke box; children
welcome, good value bedrooms, opp bowling
green in pretty waterside village *(John and
Helen Rushton, Roy and Lindsey Fentiman,
David Field)*
Ness House TQ14 0HP: Hotel on Ness
headland, with two Badger ales in comfortable
bar areas, good range of food inc good fish in
restaurant or brasserie overlooking
Teignmouth harbour; splendid setting, superb
on a summer evening, bedrooms *(John and
Helen Rushton)*
Shipwrights Arms TQ14 0AQ [B3195 to
Newton Abbot]: Friendly village pub unusual
for its locally popular thai restaurant, obliging
service, local real ales, character bar; pleasant
River Teign views from back garden
(John and Helen Rushton, LYM)

SHEEPWASH [SS4806]
Half Moon EX21 5NE [off A3072
Holsworthy—Hatherleigh]: Ancient
fisherman's hotel with 10 miles of River
Torridge fishing (salmon, sea trout and brown
trout), rod and drying rooms and fishing
supplies; big log fire in beamed bar, good
sandwiches and other simple lunchtime snacks,
Courage Best, Greene King Ruddles County
and a local ale, farm cider, fine choice of malt
whiskies, black oak woodwork polished to
perfection in stylish evening restaurant with
extensive wine list, games room; children in
eating areas, good value annexe bedrooms,
good breakfast *(Richard Pierce, LYM, DAV,
S G N Bennett)*

SHOBROOKE [SS8601]
Red Lion EX17 1AT: Pleasant village local
with good value food, Skinners real ale,
friendly service *(Andrew Kings)*

SIDBURY [SY1391]
Red Lion EX10 0SD [Fore St]: Small quiet
village local with some surprisingly good food
inc interesting dishes, palatable house wine
(Robin and Ann Taylor)

SIDFORD [SY1389]
☆ *Blue Ball* EX10 9QL [A3052 just N of
Sidmouth]: Very sad news is that this fine old
pub, a *Guide* favourite since its first edition
25 years ago, burned down in early 2006.
Good luck to them as they press ahead with
rebuilding; they hope that it may possibly
reopen by Easter 2007 *(LYM)*

SIDMOUTH [SY1090]
Bowd EX10 0ND [junction B3176/A3052]:
Big thatched family dining pub with wide
choice of food in bar and restaurant, efficient
friendly service, real ales; children welcome,
tables in sizeable garden with play area, open
all day *(LYM)*
Dukes EX10 8AR [Market Pl]: Good central
spot nr esplanade, one side no smoking with
comfortable leather sofas and armchairs, the
other side a modern coffee/wine bar with
flagstones and big-screen TV; Branscombe
Vale Branoc and Princetown Jail, pubby food
all day from lunchtime sandwiches and baked

potatoes to steak, small conservatory; prom-view terrace tables, bedrooms, open all day *(Dr and Mrs M E Wilson, Joan and Michel Hooper-Immins)*

☆ *Old Ship* EX10 8LP [Old Fore St]: Partly 14th-c, with low beams, mellow black woodwork and early 17th-c carved panelling, sailing ship prints, good inexpensive food (not Sun evening) from simple snacks and huge crab sandwiches to local fish, real ales such as Otter, St Austell Dartmoor and Wadworths 6X, decent wine choice, prompt courteous service even when busy, quietly friendly atmosphere, no piped music; close-set tables and can get smoky downstairs, but raftered upstairs family area is more roomy and airy; dogs allowed, in pedestrian zone just moments from the sea (note that around here parking is limited to 30 mins) *(Dr and Mrs M E Wilson, BB, W W Burke, Mike Turner, Gary Rollings, Tracey and Stephen Groves, Meg and Colin Hamilton)*

☆ *Swan* EX10 8BY [York St]: Cheerful backstreet local, pleasant staff, decent food from doorstep sandwiches up, Youngs, lounge bar with interesting pictures and memorabilia, darts in bigger light and airy public bar with boarded walls and ceilings, warm fire, separate dining area; nice small flower-filled garden *(Phil and Sally Gorton, Di and Mike Gillam, Dr and Mrs M E Wilson)*

SILVERTON [SS9503]

Lamb EX5 4HZ [Fore St]: Friendly flagstoned local with two or three changing real ales such as Bass and Exe Valley Dobs Best tapped from the cask, food from sandwiches to good steaks, helpful family service, separate eating area; handy for Killerton (NT), open all day wknds *(the Didler)*

Three Tuns EX5 4HX [Exeter Rd]: 17th-c or older, with comfortable settees, period furniture and log fire in attractively old-fashioned beamed lounge, food here or in cosy restaurant welcoming children, Exe Valley and guest beers, fair-sized public bar; lovely flower displays, tables in pretty inner courtyard, handy for Killerton *(the Didler, Dr and Mrs M E Wilson, Mick and Moira Brummell)*

SLAPTON [SX8245]

Queens Arms TQ7 2PN: Neat and friendly modernised village local with snug comfortable corners, inexpensive straightforward food using local suppliers inc good Sun roast, Princetown, Teignworthy and perhaps a local guest ale, interesting World War II pictures and brassware; parking needs skill; plenty of tables in lovely suntrap stepped back garden *(Bob and Margaret Holder, MP, Nick Lawless, Fred and Lorraine Gill, Bruce Bird)*

SOURTON [SX5390]

☆ *Highwayman* EX20 4HN [A386, S of junction with A30]: Believe-it-or-not décor in warren of dimly lit stonework and flagstone-floored burrows and alcoves, all sorts of things to look at, even a make-believe sailing galleon; local farm cider (perhaps a real ale in summer), organic wines, good proper sandwiches or pasties, friendly chatty service, old-fashioned penny fruit machine, 40s piped music, no smoking at bar counters; outside has fairy-tale pumpkin house and an old-lady-who-lived-in-the-shoe house – children allowed to look around pub but can't stay inside; period bedrooms with four-posters and half-testers, bunk rooms for walkers and cyclists *(the Didler, Richard Atherton, Clive Godwin, LYM, Richard Baldwin, DAV)*

SOUTH BRENT [SX6960]

Royal Oak TQ10 9BE [Station Rd]: Largely no smoking, with popular food inc Sun carvery, four changing ales such as Bass and Teignworthy Reel, good choice of wines by the glass, helpful service, restaurant; children and dogs welcome, small courtyard *(anon)*

Woodpecker TQ10 9ES [A38]: Pleasant décor, booth tables, no smoking area, friendly new management, wide choice of enjoyable good value food using local ingredients, real ales, reasonably priced wines *(M G Hart, Dudley and Moira Cockroft)*

SOUTH MOLTON [SS7125]

George EX36 3AB: Well kept ales in former coaching inn's friendly compact bar, enjoyable bar food, thriving atmosphere, live music nights; comfortable bedrooms *(anon)*

SOUTH POOL [SX7740]

☆ *Millbrook* TQ7 2RW [off A379 E of Kingsbridge]: Charming little creekside pub with dining area off cheerful compact bar, good food using much local produce from generous lunchtime crab sandwiches, ploughman's and so forth to wider range of interesting simple modern evening cooking, with Bass, Fullers London Pride, Wadworths 6X and a changing guest beer tapped from the cask, local farm cider, no piped music; children and dogs welcome, covered seating and heaters for front courtyard and waterside terrace, bedrooms *(B J Harding, David Eberlin, Mr and Mrs J Curtis, Roger Wain-Heapy, LYM)*

SOUTH ZEAL [SX6593]

☆ *Oxenham Arms* EX20 2JT [off A30/A382]: Stately and interesting building with elegant mullioned windows and Stuart fireplaces in friendly beamed and partly panelled front bar, small beamed family room with another open fire, Sharps and guest ales tapped from the cask, quite a few wines by the glass, good bar food from good baguettes up, restaurant; dogs allowed in bar, imposing garden with lovely views, bedrooms with own bathrooms *(Phil and Sally Gorton, David Rule, Paul Williams, David Carr, the Didler, Pete Baker, Ann Holdsworth, Elizabeth and Roy Russell, Ian and Jane Irving, LYM, Karen and Graham Oddey, Dr and Mrs P Truelove)*

STICKLEPATH [SX6494]

Devonshire EX20 2NW [off A30 at Whiddon Down or Okehampton]: Old-fashioned 16th-c thatched village local next to foundry museum, low-beamed slate-floored bar with big log fire, longcase clock and easy-going old furnishings, sofa in small snug, Bass and St Austell ales tapped from the cask, farm cider, magazines to read, good value sandwiches, bookable Sun lunches and evening meals, games room with piano and bar billiards, lively folk night 1st Sun in month; dogs welcome, open all day Fri/Sat, bedrooms, good walks *(the Didler, LYM, Phil and Sally Gorton)*

STOKE FLEMING [SX8648]

☆ *Green Dragon* TQ6 0PX [Church St]: Relaxed village pub at its best when yachtsman landlord is not away on epic voyages, beams and flagstones, boat pictures and burmese cats, snug with sofas and armchairs, adult board games, grandfather clock, open fire, Flowers IPA, Otter and Wadworths 6X, good choice of wines by the glass, no smoking restaurant; children welcome, tables out on partly covered heated terrace, climbing frame *(Roger Wain-Heapy, Marguerite Pointer, LYM, E B Ireland, George Atkinson, John and Fiona Merritt)*

STOKEINTEIGNHEAD [SX9170]

☆ *Church House* TQ12 4QA [signed from Combeinteignhead, or off A379 N of Torquay]: 13th-c thatched pub with heavy beams, inglenook fireplace, antique furnishings, ancient spiral stairs and relaxed informal atmosphere, friendly obliging staff, Adnams, Bass and Greene King Abbot, farm cider, good coffee, food from sandwiches and baked potatoes up, smart extended no smoking dining room, simple public bar with traditional games and TV; quiet piped music; children in eating area, neat interestingly planted back garden, unspoilt village *(Prof H G Allen, John and Helen Rushton, LYM, David Field)*

STOKENHAM [SX8042]

☆ *Church House* TQ7 2SZ [opp church, N of A379 towards Torcross]: Large welcoming restaurant pub next to interesting church, open-plan but well divided with cosy part by bar and good no smoking area, good range of food from generous sandwiches and filled baked potatoes to fresh local seafood and good steaks, good value children's dishes, friendly efficient service, real ales such as Brakspears and Otter, good wine choice, farm cider; unobtrusive piped music, Weds jazz night; attractive garden with fishpond and appealing play area *(B J Harding, David and Karen Cuckney, Roger Wain-Heapy, LYM, MP, Fred and Lorraine Gill)*

☆ *Tradesmans Arms* TQ7 2SZ [just off A379 Dartmouth—Kingsbridge]: Picturesque 15th-c thatched and low-beamed pub overlooking village green, good pubby atmosphere, enjoyable reasonably priced food from traditional favourites to lots of local fish, good Sun roasts and puddings, four good ales such as Brakspears and South Hams Devon Pride, local farm cider, well chosen wines, woodburner, nice antique tables and interesting old pictures, lovely cat called Mr Black, no smoking dining room; attractive garden *(Mrs Carolyn Dixon, David and Karen Cuckney, Roger Wain-Heapy, Mrs J Ekins-Daukes, Marguerite Pointer, LYM, Torrens Lyster, Nick Lawless, Fred and Lorraine Gill, Wendy and Carl Dye)*

TALATON [SY0699]

Talaton Inn EX5 2RQ [former B3176 N of Ottery St Mary]: Enjoyable food (not

Sun/Mon) inc interesting dishes and good service in simply modernised country pub dating from 16th c, large carpeted public bar with pool in skittle alley beyond, roomy and comfortable no smoking timbered lounge bar/restaurant area on right with fresh flowers and candles, real ales such as Greene King Old Speckled Hen and Otter; picnic-sets out in front *(Dr and Mrs M E Wilson)*

TAVISTOCK [SX4975]

Trout & Tipple PL19 0JS [Parkwood Rd, towards Okehampton]: Good food with great emphasis on trout (nearby trout farm), four real ales such as Princetown Jail, decent wines (friendly licensees may offer samples), attractive bar décor with fly-fishing theme, ex-stables dining room *(Ken Flawn)*

TEDBURN ST MARY [SX8194]

Red Lion EX6 6EQ: Friendly village pub with local real ales, good value food, light polished woodwork and fresh décor, end dining area; tables outside *(Dr and Mrs M E Wilson)*

TEIGNMOUTH [SX9372]

☆ *Ship* TQ14 8BY [Queen St]: Upper and lower decks like a ship, good friendly atmosphere, nice mix of locals, families and tourists, good reasonably priced food (all day in summer) esp simply cooked local fish and good Sun lunch, good service from obliging staff, real ales inc Bass and Greene King Abbot, interesting wine list, fresh coffee, gallery restaurant; open all day, fine floral displays, lovely riverside setting, beautiful views *(David Field)*

TIPTON ST JOHN [SY0991]

☆ *Golden Lion* EX10 0AA [signed off B3176 Sidmouth—Ottery St Mary]: Individually run beamed village pub with French chef/landlord doing good sensibly priced food using local fish, game and organic veg, light lunches and small helpings for children, Bass, Greene King IPA and Otter or St Austell Tribute, well chosen wine list, early coffee, quick friendly helpful service, blazing log fire, attractive décor and mix of furnishings joining olde-worlde with art deco and nouveau in spacious and relaxing two-part bar with subtle lighting and quiet back room, no smoking restaurant; piped music, winter jazz nights Sun; well behaved children welcome, river walks nearby, garden and terrace tables with heaters *(Dr and Mrs M E Wilson, LYM, John and Doris Couper, Mrs A P Lee, Tracey and Stephen Groves)*

TOPSHAM [SX9687]

☆ *Globe* EX3 0HR [Fore St; 2 miles from M5 junction 30]: Substantial traditional inn dating from 16th c, thriving local atmosphere and solid comfort in heavy-beamed bow-windowed bar, good interesting home-cooked food from tasty sandwiches and toasties up, reasonable prices, Bass, Sharps Doom Bar and guest beers, good value house wines, prompt service, log-effect gas fire, snug little dining lounge, good value separate restaurant, back extension; children in eating area, open all day, well priced attractive bedrooms *(Barry Steele-Perkins, Dr and Mrs M E Wilson, LYM, the Didler, David Field)*

☆ *Lighter* EX3 0HZ [Fore St]: Big comfortable

pub with tall windows looking out over tidal flats and lots of tables out in lovely spot on old quay, quickly served food from good sandwiches and light dishes to fresh fish, some small helpings available, Badger ales, nautical décor, panelling and central log fire, raised enclosed no smoking area, good children's area; games machines, piped music; handy for antiques centre *(Mrs Sylvia Elcoate, Barry Steele-Perkins, the Didler, Edward Leetham, Pete Walker, Michael and Alison Sandy, Dr and Mrs M E Wilson, BB, B J Harding)*

☆ *Passage House* EX3 0JN [Ferry Rd, off main street]: Attractive 18th-c pub much enjoyed by locals and visitors for its good fresh fish choice, nice simple cooking, other pubby food from sandwiches up, thriving atmosphere, Otter and other ales, good wines, traditional black-beamed bar and no smoking slate-floored lower bistro area (children welcome here), pleasant service; may be piped music; peaceful terrace looking over moorings and river (lovely at sunset) to nature reserve beyond, open all day wknds and summer *(Dr and Mrs M E Wilson, Barry Steele-Perkins, LYM, Tony and Jill Radnor, the Didler, Peter Burton, OPUS)*

Steam Packet EX3 0JQ [Monmouth Hill]: Well priced bar food, several real ales, dark flagstones, scrubbed boards, panelling, stripped masonry, a lighter dining room; on boat-builders' quay *(David Carr, LYM)*

TORQUAY [SX9166]

Crown & Sceptre TQ1 4QA [Petitor Rd, St Marychurch]: Friendly two-bar local in 18th-c beamed and stone-built coaching inn, eight mainstream and other changing ales, interesting naval memorabilia and chamber-pot collection, good-humoured long-serving landlord, basic good value lunchtime food (not Sun), snacks any time, frequent wknd jazz; dogs very welcome, children too *(the Didler, Kevin Blake, Margaret Mason, David Thompson)*

London TQ1 2AA [Strand]: Vast Wetherspoons bank conversion overlooking harbour and marina, big local ship paintings and a couple of reproduction ship's figureheads, good value food all day, bargain coffee as well as usual real ales, no piped music; small back no smoking area, family area up two flights of stairs; open all day *(Hugh Roberts)*

TORRINGTON [SS4919]

☆ *Black Horse* EX38 8HN [High St]: Unpretentious twin-gabled pub dating from 15th c, overhanging upper storeys, beams hung with stirrups, solid furniture, no smoking lounge with striking ancient black oak partition wall and a couple of attractive oak seats, oak-panelled back restaurant with aquarium, good value generous food inc OAP wkdy lunchtime bargains and good evening dishes, good friendly service, Courage Best and Directors, John Smiths and changing guest beers, darts, shove-ha'penny, cribbage, dominoes; well reproduced piped music, friendly cat and dogs; children really welcome,

disabled access, open all day Sat *(LYM, Michael and Judy Buckley, June and Robin Savage)*

Torridge EX38 8AW [Mill St]: Hard-working and welcoming newish licensees now doing good choice of enterprising food using local ingredients in small village pub, real ales inc Sharps, good service, friendly cat, occasional pianist *(R J Walden, Dr and Mrs A K Clarke, Jason Muxworthy)*

TOTNES [SX8060]

King William IV TQ9 5HN [Fore St]: Warm, spacious and comfortably carpeted, popular (esp with older people) for enjoyable bargain main dishes, quick cheerful service, real ales such as Fullers London Pride and St Austell Cousin Jack, new world wines, colourful décor, stained glass windows; big-screen sports TV; bedrooms with own bathrooms *(Mr and Mrs Colin Roberts, Joan and Michel Hooper-Immins, Ken Flawn)*

TRUSHAM [SX8582]

Cridford Inn TQ13 0NR [off B3193 NW of Chudleigh, just N of big ARC works]: Interesting 14th-c longhouse, Norman in parts, with Britain's oldest domestic window, lots of stripped stone, flagstones and stout timbers, pews and chapel chairs around kitchen and pub tables, big woodburner, cheerful landlady, Otter, enjoyable food, cribbage, dominoes; children in no smoking eating area, tables out on raised front terrace *(Mike Gorton, LYM)*

UFFCULME [ST0513]

Waterloo Cross EX15 3ES [A38, just off M5 junction 27]: Large roadside pub with linked areas, one with World War II memorabilia, others with old advertisements, pleasant efficient service, real ales, extensive menu from tapas to slow roasts; covered terrace outside, bedrooms *(Neil and Anita Christopher)*

UGBOROUGH [SX6755]

Ship PL21 0NS [off A3121 SE of Ivybridge]: Reliable open-plan dining pub extended from cosy 16th-c flagstoned core, bright smartish bar, wide choice of enjoyable home-made food, willing pleasant service, Bass and Butcombe; tables outside *(Brian P White)*

UMBERLEIGH [SS6023]

Portsmouth Arms EX37 9ND [A377 by Portsmouth Arms Stn]: Attractive pub reopened after another change of management, friendly competent service, reasonably priced food, real ale, log fire; bedrooms *(Mark Flynn)*

☆ *Rising Sun* EX37 9DU [A377 S of Barnstaple]: Civilised fishing inn with five River Taw salmon and sea trout beats, lots of stuffed fish and fishing memorabilia in relaxed partly no smoking divided bar with woodburner, flagstones and magazines to read, friendly staff, good food inc lunchtime sandwiches and light dishes, real ales inc Cotleigh Barn Owl, good wines by the glass and farm cider; children in eating areas, tables outside, good bedrooms, open all day summer *(Mark Flynn, LYM, B M Eldridge, JMC)*

WELCOMBE [SS2317]

☆ *Old Smithy* EX39 6HG [signed off A39 S of Hartland]: Thatched pub with good enterprising fresh food using local fish and other local produce, real ales, good coffee, buoyant atmosphere combining local regulars with the surfing contingent in simple open-plan family bar with old dark wood tables and open fires; plenty of seats in pretty terraced garden, self-catering, lovely setting by lane leading eventually to attractive rocky cove *(LYM, Ryta Lyndley, Tansy Spinks, Nick Rampley)*

WEMBURY [SX5349]

Odd Wheel PL9 0ED [Knighton Hill]: Very friendly village pub with several real ales such as Courage Best, Princetown and Skinners tapped from the cask, popular food from sandwiches to fresh fish in big plush lounge, traditional front locals' bar with pool; disabled access, children's eating area, tables on back terrace with chickens running around, may be more animals in paddock, open all day Sat *(David Oakley, Hugh Roberts)*

WEMBWORTHY [SS6609]

☆ *Lymington Arms* EX18 7SA [Lama Cross]: Large beamed dining pub, clean and bright, with wide choice of good reasonably priced food (not Sun evening or Mon), friendly helpful service, Princetown Dartmoor IPA and Sharps Doom Bar, Winkleigh farm cider, decent wines, comfortably plush seating and red tablecloths in partly stripped stone bar, big back evening restaurant (not Sun/Mon); children welcome, picnic-sets outside, pleasant country setting, bedrooms *(Mark Flynn, BB)*

WEST ALVINGTON [SX7243]

☆ *Ring o' Bells* TQ7 3PG: Extraordinarily wide choice of good attractively priced food inc half helpings in extended modernised pub with wide views, helpful friendly staff, relaxing atmosphere, good housekeeping, Sharps Doom Bar; children and dogs welcome, terrace tables, comfortable bedrooms in motel-style upper bedroom wing with great breakfast – also B&B in licensees' own converted barn *(B J Harding, BB, George Atkinson, Gary Fairbairn)*

WEST DOWN [SS5142]

☆ *Crown* EX34 8NF [the one up nr Ilfracombe]: 17th-c village pub with current chef/landlord doing enjoyable home-made food, local real ales, alcovey lounge, log fires, small red plush dining area, family room, back games room; large pleasant garden behind with play area and good shelter *(E Clark)*

WESTCOTT [ST0204]

Merry Harriers EX15 1SA [B3181 S of Cullompton]: Small country pub with very wide range of good food cooked by landlord, welcoming service by wife and daughter, big log fire, real ales, good house wines and whiskies, attractive restaurant *(David and Helen Sawyer)*

WESTON [ST1400]

☆ *Otter* EX14 3NZ [off A373, or A30 at W end of Honiton bypass]: Great family pub with heavy low beams, reasonably priced enjoyable food from light dishes to substantial meals, OAP specials, quick cheerful helpful service, Fullers London Pride and Otter, good value wines, good log fire, roomy no smoking extension; piped music can obtrude; children

welcome, disabled access, picnic-sets on big lawn leading to River Otter and its ducks and skipping-rocks, play area *(Nicholas and Dorothy Stephens, B Pike, LYM, Bob and Margaret Holder, Dr and Mrs M E Wilson)*

WHIMPLE [SY0497]

Thirsty Farmer EX5 2QQ: Welcoming and helpful young licensees doing enjoyable food, inventive without being too clever, in tall brick-built pub with log fires and dark oak in large L-shaped bar, Otter ale, side dining area; piped music (turned down on request), some band nights; garden tables *(Dr and Mrs M E Wilson)*

WIDECOMBE [SX7176]

Old Inn TQ13 7TA [B3387 W of Bovey Tracey]: Busy and comfortable, with 14th-c stonework, big log fires, olde-worlde pubby front bar, some concentration on large adjoining eating area with wide choice of good value hearty food, real ales inc Wadworths 6X, local farm cider, decent wines, large attractive no smoking side conservatory; in pretty moorland village – get there before about 12.30 in summer to miss the tourist coaches; room to dance on music nights, nice garden with water features and pleasant terrace; great walks *(LYM, Andy Ferguson, Dr and Mrs M E Wilson)*

WILMINGTON [ST2199]

White Hart EX14 9JQ [A35 Honiton—Axminster]: Handsomely restored after 2004 fire, good choice of reasonably priced food inc OAP wkdy lunches, friendly staff, Cotleigh or Courage Directors and Otter tapped from the cask, spacious bar with rooms off, beams and log fires; disabled access, three bedrooms *(Mr and Mrs R B Berry, Anthony Double)*

WOODBURY [SY0087]

White Hart EX5 1HN [3½ miles from M5 junction 30; A376, then B3179; Church St]: Popular unpretentious local with good choice of good value straightforward food (not Sun), Bass and Everards Tiger, decent wines, plain public bar, comfortable quieter dining lounge, log fire; attractive small walled garden with aviary, skittle alley, nice spot by church in peaceful village *(Dr and Mrs M E Wilson)*

LUNDY

LUNDY [SS1344]

☆ *Marisco* EX39 2LY: One of England's most isolated pubs (yet full every night), great setting (steep trudge up from landing stage where the boat with you and perhaps 250 others docks), galleried interior with lifebelts and other paraphernalia from local shipwrecks; two St Austell ales labelled for the island, also Lundy spring water on tap, good value house wines, welcoming staff, good food using island produce and lots of seafood fresh from immaculate kitchen, fine views; children welcome, tables outside, self catering and camping available; souvenir shop, and doubles as general store for the island's few residents *(Dave Braisted, D Cheesbrough, Phil and Sally Gorton)*

Dorset

Two new entries to watch here: the beautifully placed Marquis of Lorne at Nettlecombe, back in the *Guide* after a break, is in top form, with its locally sourced food and good beer both much appreciated; and the Greyhound at Sydling St Nicholas looks all set for a starring role under its new owners, with particularly good food and drink and a very warm-hearted atmosphere. Both are nice places to stay. Other pubs doing well here these days, particularly on the food side, include the busy and friendly George at Chideock, the interesting and ancient New Inn at Church Knowle, the rustic Cock & Bottle at East Morden, the stylish Museum at Farnham, the good value rambling Hunters Moon at Middlemarsh, the Thimble at Piddlehinton (a nice all-rounder), the contemporary Cow in Poole (splendid wine choice), and the ancient Shave Cross Inn (surprising to find such Caribbean influences here). All these, including the two newcomers, are rewarding for a meal out; though it's by no means cheap, for a special occasion the Museum at Farnham takes the title of Dorset Dining Pub of the Year. Some other Dorset favourites, prized above all for their character, include the Bottle at Marshwood (nice food here too), the simple family-run Vine at Pamphill, the Digby Tap in Sherborne (great changing beer choice, and now open all day), and the classic Square & Compass at Worth Matravers. Some pubs from the Lucky Dip section at the end of the chapter also deserve a special note: the Worlds End at Almer (typical of the well run Badger dining pubs which can be found throughout Dorset), White Lion at Bourton, Three Horseshoes at Burton Bradstock, Fox & Hounds at Cattistock, Fleur-de-Lys at Cranborne, Blue Raddle in Dorchester, Countryman at East Knighton, Harbour Inn, Royal Standard and Victoria in Lyme Regis, Three Horseshoes at Powerstock, Mitre at Sandford Orcas, Bankes Arms at Studland, Ilchester Arms at Symondsbury and Riverhouse at Upwey. Dorset drinks prices are close to the national average; the county's main brewers are Palmers and Badger, with Ringwood from Hampshire also often turning up as a pub's cheapest beer here.

CERNE ABBAS ST6601 Map 2
Royal Oak
Long Street; DT2 7JG

Under new licensees since early in 2006, this cheery Tudor inn focuses on dining, with a range of changing food that is sourced locally and changes within the seasons. The son of the licensees does the cooking, and sometimes catches the fish himself (all the fish is wild). As well as lunchtime panini (£4.95-£8.95) and ploughman's (£7.95, including one with a selection of west country cheeses), food might include starters like soup (£3.95), goats cheese and tomato tart (£5.95) and hand-dived scallops (£6.95), with main courses such as mackerel, slow-cooked lamb shank or venison bourguignon (£12.95), sirloin steak (£15.50) and bass (£16.95); some home-made puddings (£4.25). The three flagstoned communicating rooms have sturdy oak beams, lots of shiny black panelling, an inglenook with an oven, and warm winter log fires. Stone walls and the ceilings are packed with all sorts of small ornaments from local photographs to antique china, brasses and farm tools; candles on tables, fresh flowers; occasional piped music. Four Badger beers are served from handpumps on the uncommonly long bar counter. From an extensive wine list, they do 16 wines by the glass. The enclosed back garden is very pleasant, with comfortable chairs and tables under cocktail parasols, and outdoor heaters on purbeck stone terracing and cedarwood decking. On sunny summer afternoons they sometimes serve drinks and snacks out here. Parking can be a problem at busy times. *(Recommended by John Coatsworth, P Dawn, the Didler, John and Sheila Packman, Mrs J H S Lang, Andy and Yvonne Cunningham, Andrew Turnbull)*

Badger ~ Tenants Maurice and Sandra Ridley ~ Real ale ~ Bar food (12-3, 7-9) ~ (01300) 341797 ~ Children welcome ~ Dogs welcome ~ Open 11-11; 11-3, 6.30-11 in winter

CHIDEOCK SY4292 Map 1
George
A35 Bridport—Lyme Regis; DT6 6JD

You might find locals playing a game of table skittles in the snug of this pleasantly chatty, thatched 17th-c inn, and in summer you can eat out on the terrace. The dark-beamed lounge bar has comfortable blue plush stools and wall and window seats, pewter tankards hanging from the mantelpiece above the big fireplace (with good winter log fires), boat drawings and attractively framed old local photographs on its cream walls, high shelves of bottles, plates, mugs and so forth. Palmers ales – Copper Ale, IPA, Palmers 200 and Tally Ho – are served on handpump from the horseshoe-shaped counter. Much enjoyed by readers, bar food includes lunchtime soup (£4.45), sandwiches (from £4.95), ploughman's (from £6.95), scampi (£8.95; small portion £6.95), battered haddock (£9.75), thai-style chicken (£10.95) and seafood pasta (£11.95); children's menu (£4.95). The evening blackboard menu might include additional dishes such as starter courses of whitebait or moules marinière (£6.95), and main courses like chargrilled pork chops with apple and cinnamon sauce (£12.95), locally dived scallops (£14.95), barbary duck (£15.95), 10oz sirloin steak stuffed with stilton (£18.95); puddings (£4.25). The pub is now predominantly no smoking, including all dining areas except the snug bar; unobtrusive piped music. *(Recommended by Jacqueline Waller, Terry and Linda Moseley, Louise English, W W Burke, Nick Lawless, Julie and Bill Ryan, Bruce Bird, Dave Mower)*

Palmers ~ Tenant Paul Crisp ~ Real ale ~ Bar food (12-2, 6-9) ~ Restaurant ~ (01297) 489419 ~ Children in no-smoking areas only ~ Dogs allowed in bar ~ Live folk country, jazz and blues Sat ~ Open 11-2.30, 6-11.30(11 in winter); 12-3, 6-11 Sun; closed 25, 26 Dec evenings

CHURCH KNOWLE SY9481 Map 2
New Inn ♀
Village signposted off A351 just N of Corfe Castle; BH20 5NQ

Walkers often stop off at this usefully placed partly thatched 16th-c inn in a quiet village beneath a fold of the Purbeck Hills and not far from the Dorset Coast Path. The good food includes a great choice of fresh fish: whitebait (£4.65), whole gurnard (£10.50), half a pint of prawns (£7.50), trout (£9.25), fruits de mer (£9.50, as a starter for two, or a light main course), large haddock in batter (£13.50), locally caught sea bream (£13.95), and bass (£14.95). Other meals might include sandwiches (from £4), dorset blue vinny soup (£4.25), home-made faggots or sausages and mash (£7.95), spinach and ricotta cannelloni (£8.45), venison, rabbit, pheasant and pigeon pie (£9.25), lamb casserole (£9.95), szechuan chicken or curry of the day (£10.95) and steaks (from £12.95); children's menu (from £4.25); puddings (from £4.50). The two main areas, linked by an arch, are attractively furnished with farmhouse chairs and tables, lots of bric-a-brac (including stuffed pheasants and a glass case with some interesting memorabilia, including ration books) and a log fire at each end; the dining area, itself a former farmhouse, is no smoking. You can choose wines from a tempting display in the wine cellar, which often includes interesting bin ends from their wine shack (they also do off sales from here), and they serve several wines by the glass. Flowers Original, Greene King Old Speckled Hen and Wadworths 6X on handpump. There are disabled facilities, though there's a step down to the gents'. The good-sized garden has plenty of tables and fine views of the Purbecks, and you can camp in two fields behind (you must book). *(Recommended by Clive Watkin, John and Joan Calvert, Joan and Michel Hooper-Immins, Pat and Robert Watt, JDM, KM, Mike and Sue Loseby, Peter and Margaret Glenister, Janet Whittaker, Gerry and Rosemary Dobson, Ned Kelly, John Balfour, Derek and Maggie Washington, Pam and Alan Neale)*

Badger ~ Managers Maurice and Rosemary Estop ~ Real ale ~ Bar food (12-2, 6(7 Sun)-9) ~ (01929) 480357 ~ Children allowed in main bar ~ Dogs allowed in bar ~ Open 11-3, 5.30-11; 12-3, 7-10.30 Sun; closed Mon evening in winter

EAST CHALDON   SY7983   Map 2
Sailors Return
Village signposted from A352 Wareham—Dorchester; from village green, follow Dorchester, Weymouth signpost; note that the village is also known as Chaldon Herring; OS sheet 194 map reference 790834; DT2 8DN

This extended rural thatched pub is a pleasant place to stop for a drink, perhaps as part of a walk over the downs to join the coast path above the cliffs between Ringstead Bay and Durdle Door. The flagstoned bar still keeps much of its original country-tavern character, while the newer part has unfussy furnishings, old notices for decoration, and open beams showing the roof. Half a dozen well kept real ales include Hampshire Strongs Best and Ringwood Best, alongside guests such as Dorset Durdle Door and Palmers Dorset Gold, and they also have country wines and several malt whiskies. Straightforward bar food includes ploughman's or filled baked potatoes (£5.75), ham and egg or breaded plaice (£7.25) and a handful of daily specials such as half a lamb shoulder (£10.95). The no smoking restaurant has solid old tables in nooks and corners; darts, TV and piped music. Picnic-sets, benches and log seats on the grass in front of the pub look down over fields to the village. Although fairly isolated, it gets very busy at weekends, especially in fine weather. *(Recommended by Edna Jones, Mark Flynn, Sue Heath, Alan Cowell, Mike and Sue Loseby, Alec and Joan Laurence, Alex and Irene Harvey, Matthew Beard, Pat and Robert Watt, Alan M Pring, Pam and Alan Neale)*

Free house ~ Licensees Mike Pollard and Claire Kelly ~ Real ale ~ Bar food (12-2, 6-9(9.30 weekends); 12-9.30 weekends in summer) ~ Restaurant ~ (01305) 853847 ~ Children in restaurant ~ Dogs allowed in bar ~ Open 11-11; 12-10.30 Sun

EAST MORDEN   SY9195   Map 2
Cock & Bottle 🍴 ♀ 🍺
B3075 between A35 and A31 W of Poole; BH20 7DL

Originally a longhouse, this popular dining pub has plenty to suggest its rustic origins. There's a pubby wood-floored bar (fruit machine, and sensibly placed darts alcove), while the rest of the interior comprises two dining areas, with heavy rough beams, some stripped ceiling boards, squared panelling, a mix of old furnishings in various sizes and degrees of antiquity, small Victorian prints and some engaging bric-a-brac, some reflecting the landlord's passion for vintage cars and motorcycles (the pub hosts meetings for such vehicles in summer). There's a roaring log fire, and comfortably intimate corners, each with just a couple of tables. From an imaginative changing bar menu and using local produce where possible (booking advisable), dishes might include starters like home-made sweet potato soup (£4.50), crispy duck and green onion spring roll (£5.95) or spicy thai crab cake (£6.95), and main courses such as deep-fried smoked goats cheese fritter with roasted mediterranean vegetables and pesto (£9.95), steak and kidney suet pudding (£11.95), roast duck supreme with blood orange and Cointreau sauce (£14.25), venison wellington (£15.95) and grilled fillet steak with red wine and ratatouille sauce (£16.25), with puddings such as Baileys cheesecake or seasonal fruit pie (£4.75). The restaurant areas are no smoking. Badger Best, King and Barnes and

Tanglefoot are on handpump, and they have several wines by the glass; helpful service from the pleasant staff. There are a few picnic-sets outside, a garden area, and an adjoining field with a nice pastoral outlook. *(Recommended by M Joyner, Peter Meister, Betsy and Peter Little, Mr and Mrs Peter Llewellyn, Mrs H E Cunliffe, Dr Stephen Jolles, T and P, Peter Titcomb, Pat and Robert Watt)*

Badger ~ Tenant Peter Meadley ~ Real ale ~ Bar food (12-2, 6(7 Sun)-9) ~ Restaurant ~ (01929) 459238 ~ Children in restaurant ~ Dogs welcome ~ Open 11-2.30, 6-11; 12-3, 7-10.30 Sun

FARNHAM ST9515 Map 2
Museum 🍽 🍷 🍴 🛏
Village signposted off A354 Blandford Forum—Salisbury; DT11 8DE
Dorset Dining Pub of the Year
Once owned by General Pitt Rivers – the father of modern archaeology – to offer accommodation and refreshment for his nearby museum, this dining pub is a stylish place for a treat, priding itself as it does on innovative dishes that source local and organic ingredients. Apart from lunchtime focaccias and baguettes from (£6.50), the changing menu is by no means cheap, especially if you add a vegetable side dish (£2.50). It might include starters such as french onion soup (£6), chicken liver parfait with toasted focaccia bread (£6.50) and dorset crab and prawn ravioli (£9), with main courses like roasted sweet potato and butternut squash strudel or chicken, ham, leek and grain mustard pie (£14), whole grilled plaice with caper and parsley butter (£16) and 10oz rib-eye steak (£16.50); puddings include warm plum and almond tart and banana bavarois of caramelised banana and toffee sauce (£5.50). It's a good idea to book if you want to eat in the no smoking restaurant. The attractively extended building has been opened up into a series of appealing interconnecting rooms and bars (rooms off the bar are also no smoking, as are all bedrooms). Cheery yellow walls and plentiful windows give the place a bright, fresh feel. The flagstoned bar has a big inglenook fireplace, light beams, good comfortably cushioned furnishings and fresh flowers on all the tables. To the right is a dining room with a fine antique dresser, while off to the left is a cosier room, with a very jolly hunting model and a seemingly sleeping stuffed fox curled in a corner. Another room feels rather like a contemporary baronial hall, soaring up to a high glass ceiling, with dozens of antlers and a stag's head looking down on a long refectory table and church-style pews. This leads to an outside terrace with more wooden tables. As well as an excellent choice of some 150 wines, with a dozen by the glass, three real ales will probably be Hop Back Summer Lightning, Ringwood Best Bitter and Timothy Taylors Landlord; prompt service from antipodean staff. *(Recommended by John and Vivienne Rice, Noel Grundy, Tony Orman, Terry and Linda Moseley, P Dawn, Mrs J H S Lang, Dr A J and Mrs Tompsett, Keith and Jean Symons, Gaynor Gregory, M N Sugarhood, Pat and Robert Watt, J Stickland, Karen Eliot)*

Free house ~ Licensees Vicky Elliot and Mark Stephenson ~ Real ale ~ Bar food (12-2.30(not weekdays), 7-9.30) ~ Restaurant (Fri and Sat evening and Sun lunch) ~ (01725) 516261 ~ Children over 8 ~ Dogs allowed in bar and bedrooms ~ Open 12-3, 6-11; 12-3, 7-10.30 Sun; closed 25 Dec, 1 Jan evening ~ Bedrooms: £85B/£95B

LANGTON HERRING SY6182 Map 2
Elm Tree
Signed off B3157; DT3 4HU
Outside this spotless, character-laden beamed dining pub are flower tubs, hanging baskets and a very pretty flower-filled sunken garden. The Portland spy ring is said to have met in the main beamed and carpeted rooms, which have walls festooned with copper, brass and bellows, cushioned window seats, red leatherette stools, windsor chairs, and lots of big old kitchen tables; one has some old-fashioned settles and an inglenook. The traditionally furnished extension gives more room for diners; the dining areas are no smoking. Daily specials might include soup (£3.50), pork tenderloin stuffed with mushroom duxelle and wrapped in bacon (£10.95)

and bass fillets with sautéed spinach, pine nuts and balsamic vinegar (£11.95). The more pubby menu includes sandwiches (from £3.50), filled panini (from £5.75), ploughman's (£5.95), lasagne or steak and ale pie (£7.45), cod mornay, vegetable bake or thai green chicken curry (£7.95) and 10oz rump or sirloin steak (£10.95 or £12.95). Puddings might be treacle tart and clotted cream, apple pie or chocolate rum pot (£4.95). Adnams Best Bitter and Courage Directors on handpump and a dozen wines by the glass; piped music, darts. A track leads down to the Dorset Coast Path, which here skirts the eight-mile lagoon enclosed by Chesil Beach. *(Recommended by Peter J and Avril Hanson, Janet Whittaker, W W Burke, Fred and Lorraine Gill)*

Punch ~ Lease Paul and Jo-Ann Riddiough ~ Real ale ~ Bar food (12-2(3 Sun), 7-9) ~ Restaurant ~ (01305) 871257 ~ Children welcome except at bar ~ Folk music night first Tues in month ~ Open 11-3, 6-11; 12-4, 7-10.30 Sun

MARSHWOOD SY3799 Map 1
Bottle
B3165 Lyme Regis—Crewkerne; DT6 5QJ

Not much has changed over the years at this enjoyably straightforward local, in attractive rolling country, beneath Lambert's Castle, one of several imposing iron-age hill forts in the area. The simple cream-walled interior has down-to-earth furnishings including cushioned benches and one high-backed settle, and there's an inglenook fireplace with a big log fire in winter; also pool, fruit machine, TV, a skittle alley and piped music. Otter Bitter and up to three guests such as O'Hanlons Firefly and Royal Oak are on handpump. A wide range of tasty bar food includes soup (£3.95), recommended baguettes (from £5.20), filled baked potatoes (from £4.95), and ploughman's (from £6.25), a vegetarian pie or roast of the day (£6.95), salmon fillet with hollandaise sauce (£8.45), medallions of pork fillet with stilton sauce (£10.50), chicken breast stuffed with smoked salmon in whisky cream and mustard sauce (£11.95), steak (from £11.45) and puddings (from £2.75); the dining area and front bar are no smoking. A good big back garden has a play area, and beyond it a field for camping. The annual world stinging-nettle eating championships are held at the same time as their beer festival, on the weekend before the summer solstice. *(Recommended by Terry and Linda Moseley, Pat and Tony Martin, OPUS, Meg and Colin Hamilton, Roland and Wendy Chalu, David Eberlin)*

Free house ~ Licensees Shane and Ellen Pym ~ Real ale ~ Bar food (12-2, 6.30-9) ~ (01297) 678254 ~ Children welcome ~ Live music monthly ~ Open 12-3, 6.30-11(12 Sat); Sun 12-3, 7-10.30 winter; closed Mon except bank hols

MIDDLEMARSH ST6607 Map 2
Hunters Moon 🍴 £ 🛏
A352 Sherborne—Dorchester; DT9 5QN

West Country ales feature large at this peaceful and delightfully attired village pub, with typically Sharps Doom Bar, St Austell Tribute and Tinners, and Otter on handpump. The comfortably welcoming interior rambles around in several linked areas, with a great variety of tables and chairs, plenty of bric-a-brac from decorative teacups, china ornaments and glasses through horse tack and brassware, to quite a collection of spirits miniatures. Beams, some panelling, soft lighting from converted oil lamps, three log fires (one in a capacious inglenook), and the way that some attractively cushioned settles form booths all combine to give a cosy relaxed feel. The food is good and reasonably priced, and includes soup (£2.95), sandwiches and baguettes (from £3.95), salmon and cod fishcakes (£6.50), spinach and mascarpone lasagne (£7.95), home-made meat pie (£8.25), fresh lamb shank (£10.50) and steaks (from £11.95) and they often have local game specials like rabbit pie (£7.25) or game pie (£8.25); they also serve children's meals (£4.25) and a bargain range of 'smaller appetite meals' such as sausage and mash (£4.95), and curry or home-made beef lasagne (£5.95); puddings (£3.50). Also decent wines by the glass, proper coffee, and a good range of spirits and soft drinks; faint piped music. A neat lawn has circular picnic-sets as well as the more usual ones, and the bedrooms are in what was formerly a skittle alley and stable block. *(Recommended by M G Hart, Joan and Michel Hooper-Immins, David Fulford-Brown, John A Barker)*

Free house ~ Licensee Brendan Malone ~ Real ale ~ Bar food (6-9.30) ~ Restaurant ~ (01963) 210966 ~ Children welcome ~ Dogs allowed in bar ~ Open 11-3, 6-11.30; 12-10.30 Sun ~ Bedrooms: £48S/£60S

MUDEFORD   SZ1892   Map 2
Ship in Distress ♀
Stanpit; off B3059 at roundabout; BH23 3NA

Unassuming from outside, this cheerful cottagey place is full of entertaining bits and pieces, with nautical bric-a-brac from rope fancywork and brassware through lanterns, oars and ceiling nets and ensigns, to an aquarium, boat models (we particularly liked the Mississippi steamboat), and the odd piratical figure. Besides a good few boat pictures, the room on the right has masses of snapshots of locals caught up in various waterside japes, under its glass tabletops. The wide choice of carefully cooked fresh local fish and seafood is good and imaginative: sandwiches (£4.50), breton-style fish soup or a pint of prawns (£6.50), fish and chips (£8.95), seafood pancake (£9.50), tagliatelle with wild mushroom, garlic, parsley, lemon and truffle oil or fried smoked haddock fishcake on rocket and tomato salad with poached egg and chive butter sauce (£9.50), smoked trout and asparagus risotto or lemon sole filled with crab (£13.50), 8oz fillet steak with wild mushroom, shallot and red wine jus (£15.50) and puddings such as Cointreau orange mascarpone cheesecake or banana tart tatin (£5.50). Service is friendly, and they have Adnams, Bass, Ringwood and a guest such as Shepherd Neame Spitfire on handpump, and good wines by the glass; darts, fruit machine, a couple of TV sets – the dated piped pop music seems to fit in rather well; they also have live jazz on Sundays. A spreading two-room no smoking restaurant area, as cheerful in its way as the bar, has a light-hearted mural sketching out the impression of a window open on a sunny boating scene, and another covering its dividing wall with vines. There are tables out on the back terrace; look out for the two springer spaniels. More reports please. *(Recommended by Janet Whittaker, Brian and Ruth Archer, Mrs C Sleight)*

Punch ~ Tenants Sally Canning, Colin Pond, Ed Blanchard ~ Real ale ~ Bar food (12-2.30, 7-9.30) ~ Restaurant ~ (01202) 485123 ~ Children welcome until 9pm ~ Dogs allowed in bar ~ Live jazz on Sun ~ Open 11-11

NETTLECOMBE   SY5195   Map 2
Marquis of Lorne 🍽 🍺 🛏
Off A3066 Bridport—Beaminster, via W Milton; DT6 3SY

In deep and unspoilt country within strolling distance of Eggardon Hill, one of Dorset's most evocative Iron-Age hillfort sites, this pub has recently been giving a lot of pleasure with its locally sourced food and very well kept beer, and also has good bedrooms. The comfortable bustling main bar has a log fire, mahogany panelling, and old prints and photographs around its neatly matching chairs and tables; two dining areas lead off, the smaller of which has another log fire. The wooden-floored snug has cribbage, dominoes, board games and table skittles; gentle piped music. In addition to sandwiches (from £3.95), baguettes (£5.95) and ploughman's (£6.50), tasty home-made food includes starters like soup (£4.50), grilled local goats cheese (£5.25) and scallops with bacon risotto (£6.95), and main courses such as filo pastry parcel with spinach, brie, courgette and tomato (£9.95), pork medallions with apple and red onions in cider sauce (£11.95), baked haddock with herb crust on tomato ragout (£12.45) and local organic rack of lamb (£13.95); puddings such as sticky toffee pudding (£3.95); they may also have locally made chutneys and marmalade for sale. Four real ales from Palmers are on handpump, with Copper, IPA and 200 alongside Gold in summer or Tally Ho in winter, and Thatcher's Gold cider or perhaps a cloudy farm cider; a good wine list with about a dozen by the glass, and several malt whiskies. The maturing big garden is full of pretty herbaceous borders, and has a rustic-style play area among the picnic-sets under its apple trees. It is all no smoking apart from one bar (to which dogs are also allowed). *(Recommended by Dorothy Clarkson, Terry and Linda Moseley, Pete Walker, Alan and Pat Newcombe, R M Corlett, Mr and Mrs S Jones, Brian Lord, Michael Bayne)*

Palmers ~ Tenants David and Julie Woodroffe ~ Real ale ~ Bar food (12-2.30, 7-9.30 (9 winter)) ~ Restaurant ~ (01308) 485236 ~ Children in eating area of bar and restaurant ~ Dogs allowed in bar ~ Open 11.30(12 in winter)-2.30, 6.30(7 Sun in winter)-11 ~ Bedrooms: £45S/£80S

OSMINGTON MILLS   SY7381   Map 2

Smugglers
Off A353 NE of Weymouth; DT3 6HF

Open all day and no smoking throughout, this family-friendly inn is a very popular place for a meal in high season (if you prefer a quieter atmosphere it may be better to visit off-peak), but the staff cope with the crowds very well. Woodwork divides the spacious bar into cosy, welcoming areas, with logs burning in two open stoves and old local pictures scattered about, and various quotes and words of wisdom painted on the wall ('a day without wine is a day without sunshine'). Some seats are tucked into alcoves and window embrasures. The games machines are kept sensibly out of the way; piped music. Handily served all day, bar food (they will do smaller helpings for children) includes soup (£2.99), a starter portion of crab and salmon fishcake (£4.25), fish and chips or sausage and mash (£6.99), wilted spinach, mushroom and brie tart (£7.45), tomato mozzarella chicken (£8.25) and steak (from £8.25), with weekly changing specials ranging in price from chilli con carne (£7.50) to grilled haddock (£13.70). Badger Dorset Best, Tanglefoot and a third Badger ale like Stinger or Fursty Ferret are on handpump. There are picnic sets out on crazy paving by a little stream, with a thatched summer bar (which offers quick-service bottled drinks and where they sometimes have summer barbecues and hog roasts) and a good play area (including a little assault course) over on a steep lawn. The licensee moved here in winter 2006; more reports on the new regime please. *(Recommended by John and Joan Nash, Mark Percy, Lesley Mayoh, Ian Phillips, the Didler, OPUS, John Fiander, Pam and Alan Neale)*

Badger ~ Manager Sonia Henderson ~ Real ale ~ Bar food (12-9) ~ (01305) 833125 ~ Children welcome ~ Open 11-11; 12-10.30 Sun ~ Bedrooms: /£75B

PAMPHILL   ST9900   Map 2

Vine 🍺
Off B3082 on NW edge of Wimborne: turn on to Cowgrove Hill at Cowgrove signpost, then turn right up Vine Hill; BH21 4EE

The atmosphere is really special in this enchantingly unchanged and simple pub, run by the same family for three generations (although it's now owned by the National Trust as part of the Kingston Lacy estate). Its two tiny bars have that well cared-for feel and friendly service that make little places like this feel so special. One, with a warm coal-effect gas fire, has only three tables, the other just half a dozen or so seats on its lino floor, some of them huddling under the stairs that lead up via narrow wooden steps to an upstairs games room; darts; no smoking throughout. Local photographs (look out for the one of the regular with his giant pumpkin) and notices decorate the painted panelling. On our weekday inspection visit, piped Classic FM mingled quietly with a blackbird's song drifting in through the french window, though at weekends and in summer it can get very busy. One beer from Fullers London Pride, Hidden or Archers Best on handpump together with a guest such as Archers Golden from the cask, real cider, and good fresh sandwiches (from £2) and ploughman's (from £3.50) are on offer. There are picnic-sets and benches out on a sheltered gravel terrace, and more share a fairy-lit, heated verandah with a grapevine. Round the back a patch of grass has a climbing frame; outside lavatories. The National Trust estate includes Kingston Lacy house and the huge Badbury Rings Iron-Age hill fort (itself good for wild flowers), and there are many paths. They don't accept credit cards or cheques. *(Recommended by the Didler, John and Jane Hayter, Peter Titcomb)*

Free house ~ Licensee Mrs Sweatland ~ Real ale ~ Bar food (11(12 Sun)-2) ~ No credit cards ~ (01202) 882259 ~ Well behaved children welcome, except in bar ~ Dogs welcome ~ Open 11-3, 7-10.30(11 Fri, Sat)

PIDDLEHINTON   SY7197   Map 2

Thimble   £

B3143; DT2 7TD

This friendly, partly thatched pub stands on the banks of the memorably named River Piddle amid winding country lanes, and inside the attractive low-beamed bar is roomy enough to accommodate crowds at busier times. There are two handsome brick fireplaces, and a deep glassed-over well; darts and cribbage. Badger Gold and Tanglefoot, Palmers Copper and IPA, and Ringwood Old Thumper are kept under a light blanket pressure (look out for the original Eldridge Pope keg founts), along with quite a few fruit wines and 15 malt whiskies. Straightforward bar food includes sandwiches (from £2.80), soup (from £3), filled baked potatoes (from £3.70), ploughman's (from £4.60), home-made beefburger (£5.75), battered or breaded plaice (£6.15), steak pie or game pie (£7.95), grilled bass (£9.95), fillet steak (£13.10) and puddings (£4.10); they also do children's meals (from £4.10) and a Sunday roast (£7.25). The garden is floodlit at night. *(Recommended by M Joyner, David Thornton, Joan and Michel Hooper-Immins, Gene and Kitty Rankin, Peter Neate, Bill Smith, John A Barker)*

Free house ~ Licensees N R White and V J Lanfear ~ Real ale ~ Bar food ~ (01300) 348270 ~ Children welcome ~ Dogs welcome ~ Open 12-2.30, 7-11(10.30 Sun); closed 25 Dec, 26 Dec and 1 Jan evenings

PLUSH   ST7102   Map 2

Brace of Pheasants

Off B3143 N of Dorchester; DT2 7RQ

New owners took over this charmingly placed 16th-c thatched country pub in spring 2006, and they were converting the skittle alley into ensuite accommodation as we went to press (we understand the bedrooms will be ready by the end of 2006). There's a fairly upmarket but relaxed atmosphere (with no piped music or games machines) in the airy beamed bar, which has good solid tables, windsor chairs, fresh flowers, a huge heavy-beamed inglenook at one end with cosy seating inside, and a good warming log fire at the other. A usefully pubby bar menu includes snacks such as soup (£3.95), sandwiches (from £5.50) and ploughman's (£6.50), starters like fried lamb kidneys in cream mustard sauce (£5.95) and main courses like warm cheddar, basil and tomato tart (£8), sausages and mash with apple and tomato compote (£8.25), beer-battered haddock (£8.60), and 8oz rump steak (£8.25), with specials like battered scallops with sweet chilli dipping sauce (£7.95) or fricasee of lambs sweetbreads with chervil cream and pilaf rice (£9.75), and puddings (£4.95). The restaurant and family room are no smoking. Three changing real ales such as Dorset Weymouth, Ringwoods Best and Sharps Doom Bar are tapped from the cask. A decent-sized garden and terrace include a lawn sloping up towards a rockery. The pub lies alongside Plush Brook, and an attractive bridleway behind goes to the left of the woods and over to Church Hill. More reports on the new regime, please. *(Recommended by John and Joan Nash, Rob Winstanley, the Didler, Maggie Chandler, Carl Van Baars, Mike and Sue Loseby, OPUS, Peter Neate, Stuart and Alison Ballantyne, Sue and Keith Campbell)*

Free house ~ Licensees Phil and Carol Bennett ~ Real ale ~ Bar food (12-2.30, 7-9.30) ~ Restaurant ~ (01300) 348357 ~ Children welcome ~ Dogs allowed in bar ~ Open 12-3, 7-11(10.30 Sun); closed Mon exc bank hols

---

We say if we know a pub allows dogs.

POOLE SZ0391 Map 2

Cow ♀

Station Road, Ashley Cross, Parkstone; beside Parkstone Station; BH14 8UD

From a sensibly short menu, the good modern lunchtime bar food at this imaginatively revamped and nicely relaxed one-bar pub includes soup (£4.25), hog-roast sandwich with stuffing (£5.50), glazed goats cheese crostini, club sandwich or filled baguettes (£5.95), sausages and mash with onion gravy (£6.95), bacon, bubble-and-squeak and free-range eggs, fishcakes or sweet chilli beef stir fry (£7.50), fried fillet of bass (£12.95), rib-eye of beef (£13.50) and puddings such as dark chocolate mousse or warmed lemon and almond sponge pudding (£3). Don't be put off by the unpromising exterior and location next to the railway station: the décor inside comes as a pleasant surprise. Ochre ragged walls are hung with a vintage songsheet of *Three Acres and a Cow*, Twickenham Rugby Museum replicas of 1930s and 1940s rugby prints, and big modern cow prints in bright pinks, yellows and blues. There are a mix of wooden tables and dining chairs, a couple of low tables by some comfortable squashy sofas with huge colourful cushions, and high leatherette bar chairs. A gas-effect coal fire in a brick fireplace, with another in the entrance hall, and quite a discreet flat-screen TV in one corner; piped music, board games and a good array of newspapers. Fullers London Pride, Ringwood Best and a guest such as Loddons Hoppit on handpump, and an extensive wine list with about ten wines by the glass and many remarkable bottles (the most expensive being a Château Pétrus at £650). In the evening you can eat in the sizeable no smoking bistro, where there are more heavy stripped tables on bare boards, and plenty of wine bottles lining the window sills. *(Recommended by W W Burke, Terry and Linda Moseley, Janet Whittaker)*

Free house ~ Licensee David Sax ~ Real ale ~ Bar food (12.30-2.30) ~ Restaurant ~ (01202) 749569 ~ Children allowed in bistro, and in bar until 7.30pm ~ Dogs allowed in bar ~ Live bands bank hols ~ Open 11(12 Sun)-11(12 Sat)

SHAVE CROSS SY4198 Map 1

Shave Cross Inn

On back lane Bridport—Marshwood, signposted locally; OS Sheet 193 map reference 415980; DT6 6HW

There's a distinctively caribbean slant to several aspects of this historic flint and thatch inn, which dates back to the 14th c. The building is traditionally english: the original timbered bar is a lovely flagstoned room, surprisingly roomy and full of character, with country antiques, two armchairs either side of a warming fire in an enormous inglenook fireplace and hops round the bar – a scene little altered from the last century. The origins of the chef show in some of the caribbean seasonings, spices and recipes of the tasty home-made food. Bar food includes soup (£4.50), filled baguettes (£6.95) and main courses like caribbean chicken, lamb curry with calypso rice, guyanese stew with pork or chicken, or caribbean jerk chicken salad (all £10.95); the home-made puddings such as dorset apple cake or lemon meringue pie (£4.95) are nicely english. They also have a more elaborate evening restaurant menu (£22.50 for two courses, £26 for three). They serve Branscombe Vale Branoc and their own-label 4Ms and Dorset Marshwood Vale on handpump, alongside half a dozen wines by the glass, Thatcher's and Old Rosie farm cider, several vintage rums and a caribbean beer; piped music (jazz or caribbean). The refurbished skittle alley has pool, darts and a juke box, and the dining area and restaurant have tablecloths, and caribbean pictures (for sale). Lovingly tended, the sheltered flower-filled garden with its thatched wishing-well, carp pool and children's play area is very pretty. Bedrooms are planned for 2007. More reports please. *(Recommended by Terry and Linda Moseley, H Frank Smith, Marjorie and David Lamb, Mr and Mrs M Shirley, W W Burke, Mrs A P Lee, Revd L J and Mrs Melliss, Roland and Wendy Chalu)*

Free house ~ Licensee Mel Warburton ~ Real ale ~ Bar food (11-3, 6-7; not Sun evenings) ~ Restaurant (7-9.30) ~ (01308) 868358 ~ Children in restaurant and skittle alley ~ Dogs

allowed in bar ~ Jazz and discos some nights ~ Open 11-3, 6-11.30; 12-3, 7-11.30 Sun;
closed Mon except bank hols

SHERBORNE ST6316 Map 2
Digby Tap ◗ £
Cooks Lane; park in Digby Road and walk round corner; DT9 3NS

A couple of minutes' walk from the famous abbey and now open all day, this is a
delightfully unpretentious alehouse that serves an interesting range of beer. Its
simple flagstoned bar is full of character, with a good mix of chatty customers. The
beers are quite cheap and change regularly, with four pumps serving around 20 to
25 different ones a week, and might include Cottage, Hop Back, Slaters or Youngs.
A little games room has pool and a quiz machine, and there's a TV room. Large
helpings of reasonably priced, straightforward bar food might include tasty soup
(£1.95), sandwiches or baguettes (from £1.75, toasted from £1.80), filled baked
potatoes (from £2.80), potato wedges (£2.95), with daily specials such as chicken
tikka (£3.95), lasagne, tuna mozzarella fishcakes or steak and chips (£4.50); they
don't do puddings apart from ice-cream. There are some seats outside.
*(Recommended by Guy Vowles, Donna and Roger, Theo, Anne and Jane Gaskin,
Michael B Griffith, John A Barker, Mr and Mrs A Silver, Brian and Bett Cox, Phil and
Sally Gorton)*

Free house ~ Licensees Oliver Wilson and Nick Whigham ~ Real ale ~ Bar food (12-1.45,
not Sun) ~ No credit cards ~ (01935) 813148 ~ Children welcome lunchtimes only ~
Dogs welcome ~ Open 11-11; 12-3, 7-11 Sun

SHROTON ST8512 Map 2
Cricketers ♀ ◗ ⇌
Off A350 N of Blandford (village also called Iwerne Courtney); follow signs; DT11 8QD

Facing the village green, this welcoming red-brick pub nestles beneath the slopes of
Hambleton Hill, and from here a walk up to the Iron-Age ramparts on the summit
reveals terrific views (walkers will need to leave their boots outside). The bright
divided bar has a big stone fireplace, alcoves and cricketing memorabilia. Greene
King IPA and Youngs Best are alongside a couple of guests such as Brains Rev
James and Charles Wells Bombardier, served from pumps made into little cricket
bats. They've also a dozen wines by the glass, and quite a few malt whiskies; good
friendly service from the attentive landlord and his neatly uniformed staff. Besides
filled baguettes (£5.50), good, reasonably priced changing dishes could include soup
(£3.95), garlic mushrooms or cullen skink soup (£3.95), avocado and prawn bake
(£5.25), moroccan lamb tagine and couscous (£8.95), salmon pancake, fish pie or
thai crab cakes (£9.25), mushroom-stuffed chicken breast with tomato and basil
sauce or roast pheasant with cider sauce (£8.95), sirloin steak with stilton and
shallot glaze (£14.95) and puddings such as fresh tropical fruit pavlova with mango
sauce or rhubarb crumble (£4.25). The comfortable no smoking back restaurant
overlooks the garden and has a fresh neutral décor, and a sizeable games area has
pool, darts, board games, fruit machine and piped music; the bar area is also no
smoking. Secluded and pretty, the garden has big sturdy tables under cocktail
parasols, with well tended shrubs, and a well stocked (and well used) herb garden
by the kitchen door. *(Recommended by Stan Edwards, KN-R, Terry and Linda Moseley,
Mike and Shelley Woodroffe, W W Burke, J Stickland, Mrs H E Cunliffe, Pat and Robert Watt,
Richard and Nicola Tranter)*

Free house ~ Licensees George and Carol Cowie ~ Real ale ~ Bar food ~ Restaurant ~
(01258) 860421 ~ Children welcome ~ Open 11.30-3, 6.30-11; 12-3, 6.30(7 in winter)-
10.30 Sun ~ Bedrooms: £40S/£70S

Post Office address codings confusingly give the impression that some pubs are in
Dorset, when they're really in Somerset (which is where we list them).

SYDLING ST NICHOLAS SY6399 Map 2

Greyhound 🍴 ♟ 🛏

Off A37 N of Dorchester; High Street; DT2 9PD

The new owners of this attractively kept village inn won a great many friends among our readers at their last place, the West Bay. Here, you get an instant sense of welcome, with everyone from the adept barmen to the cheerful kitchen and serving staff obviously keen to give you a good time. That can be practically guaranteed if you're eating, with good attractively presented, seasonally changing and locally sourced food such as lunchtime sandwiches and baguettes, soup (£5.95), wild mushroom risotto (starter £5.95, main course £10.95), seared scallops (£6.95), beef stew (£8.95), green thai chicken curry (£10.50), deep-fried cod stuffed with basil pesto (£10.50), steak (from £13.50), roasted duck breast (£13.95) and rack of lamb on potato rösti (£15.95); specials might include guinea fowl in shallot marmalade (£14.95) or turbot fillets on fresh scallops (£15.95); puddings (from £3.50). They have Palmers Copper, Wadworths 6X and a monthly guest such as Youngs St George on handpump at the long brick bar counter, and a good range of fairly priced wines by the glass; this beamed and flagstoned serving area is airy and alluring, with its big bowl of lemons and limes, backdrop of gleaming bottles and copper pans, and plenty of bar stools, with more opposite ranging against a drinking shelf. On one side a turkey-carpeted area with a warm coal fire in a handsome portland stone fireplace has a comfortable mix of straightforward tables and chairs and country decorations such as a stuffed fox eyeing a collection of china chickens and a few farm tools. There may be fairly unobtrusive piped music; board games. At the other end, a cosy separate dining room with smart white table linen has some books and a glass-covered well set into its floor. Apart from the small bar area the pub is no smoking. A garden room with succulents and other plants on its sills has simple modern café furniture, and the small front garden has a wooden climber and slide alongside its picnic-sets. The new bedrooms are in a separate block; this is a quiet and very pretty streamside village. *(Recommended by Mr and Mrs Peter Larkman, Kerry Murray)*

Free house ~ Licensees John Ford and Karen Trimby ~ Real ale ~ Bar food (12-2(2.30 Sun), 6.30-9(9.30 Sat)) ~ Restaurant ~ (01300) 341303 ~ Children welcome ~ Dogs allowed in bar ~ Open 11-2.30, 6-11; 12-3 Sun; closed Sun evening ~ Bedrooms: /£65S(£75B)

TARRANT MONKTON ST9408 Map 2

Langton Arms 🍺 🛏

Village signposted from A354, then head for church; DT11 8RX

This 17th-c thatched dining pub has been refreshed with cream walls and has more of an airy, contemporary look than you might expect from outside. It's now all no smoking apart from one bar, and the light oak beamed bar has flagstone floors, a light oak counter with recessed lighting, and fresh flowers on light wood furniture; paintings for sale (by a local artist) are displayed on the walls. There is one guest beer such as Hampshire Lionheart on handpump alongside brews from Hop Back, Hidden and Ringwood. The public bar has a juke box, darts, pool and TV. The bistro restaurant is in an attractively reworked barn, and the skittle alley doubles as a family room during the day; piped music. Bar food includes soup (£3.95), baguettes (from £4.50), a starter of smoked haddock and spring onion fishcake (£4.95), filo prawns (£5.95), ploughman's or baked potatoes (from £6.95), roast beef (£8.50), local faggots in onion gravy (£8.75), chicken curry, steak and ale pie or home-made broccoli, brie and mushroom lasagne (£8.95), wild rabbit braised on the bone or crispy lemon sole goujons with avocado and tomato dip (£9.25), game pie (£9.75), poached fillet of salmon (£10.20) and home-made puddings such as mango mousse or warm chocolate cake (£4.65). Tarrant Monkton is a charming village (with a ford that can flow quite fast in wet weather), and is well located for local walks and exploring the area. There's a very good wood-chip children's play area in the garden, and the comfortable ensuite bedrooms are in a modern block at the back; good breakfasts. They are licensed for weddings; service can be erratic at times. *(Recommended by Graham Holden, Julie Lee, Colin and Janet Roe, M G Hart, Mrs L M Beard, Mrs Pat Crabb, Peter Titcomb, John A Barker, Pat and Robert Watt, W W Burke)*

Free house ~ Licensees Barbara and James Cossins ~ Real ale ~ Bar food (11.30-2.30, 6-9.30; all day Sat, Sun) ~ Restaurant ~ (01258) 830225 ~ Children welcome ~ Dogs allowed in bedrooms ~ Open 11.30(12 Sun)-12 ~ Bedrooms: £60B/£80B

WEST BAY   SY4690   Map 1
West Bay 🍴 🛏
Station Road; DT6 4EW

New tenants have taken over this popular seaside dining pub, with their son Mike running the kitchen – which is still on good form. It continues to specialise in fish, with a typical selection (not cheap) perhaps including starters like smoked haddock and herb fishcakes with warm tomato and basil sauce (£4.95), and main courses like fish pie (£12.45), whole grilled bream stuffed with herbs (£12.50), fried wing of skate with shrimps and caper beurre noisette (£13.50) and pan-roasted monkfish with pickled dill cucumber and red pepper sauce (£15.50); non-fish main courses could be steak and ale pie (£11.75), steak (from £12.95), pork loin with black pudding, apple and vanilla compote (£14.95), with puddings (£3.75). The short lunchtime and snack menu includes sandwiches (£4.25), baguettes (£4.95), soup (£4.45), and lasagne or ploughman's (£7.50). The pub is largely set out for eating. An island servery separates the fairly simple bare-boards front part, with its coal-effect gas fire and mix of sea and nostalgic prints, from a cosier carpeted no smoking dining area with more of a country kitchen feel; piped music. Though its spaciousness means it never feels crowded, booking is virtually essential in season. Palmers IPA, Copper and 200 are served on handpump alongside good house wines (with seven by the glass) and Thatcher's farm cider. A local team meets to play in the skittles alley. There are tables outside on a dining terrace, with more in a large garden; plenty of parking. The bedrooms, quiet and comfortable, have recently been refurbished. *(Recommended by PRT, John and Liz Wheeler, David and Julie Glover, Terry and Linda Moseley, W W Burke, Marje Sladden, Tony Baldwin, Charles Gysin)*

Palmers ~ Tenants Richard and Lorraine Barnard ~ Real ale ~ Bar food (12-2(3 Sun); 6.30-9.30) ~ Restaurant ~ (01308) 422157 ~ Children allowed in restaurant if well behaved ~ Dogs allowed in bar ~ Open 11.30-3, 6-11; 12-3, 6-10 Sun ~ Bedrooms: £65B/£70B

WORTH MATRAVERS   SY9777   Map 2
Square & Compass ★ 🍺
At fork of both roads signposted to village from B3069; BH19 3LF

For those who like country pubs unchanged and simple, the bewitchingly unsophisticated charms and fine range of drinks of this village local are worth quite a journey. It's been in the hands of the Newman family some 90 years and to this day there's no bar counter, so the Ringwood Best and two or three guests from brewers such as Palmers and RCH Steam, and up to ten ciders they keep, are tapped from a row of casks and passed to you in a drinking corridor through two serving hatches; several malt whiskies. A couple of basic unspoilt no smoking rooms opposite have simple furniture on the flagstones, a woodburning stove and a loyal crowd of friendly locals; darts, cribbage, shove-ha'penny and table skittles. Bar food is limited to tasty home-made pasties and pies (£2.50, served till they run out). A little museum (free) exhibits local fossils and artefacts, mostly collected by the current friendly landlord and his father; mind your head on the way out. The pub is on a peaceful hilltop, with a fantastic view from benches out in front (you may find free-roaming hens, chickens and other birds clucking around your feet), looking down over the village rooftops to the sea between the East Man and the West Man (the hills that guard the coastal approach) and out beyond Portland Bill. There are wonderful walks from here to some exciting switchback sections of the coast path above St Aldhelm's Head and Chapman's Pool; you will need to park in the public car park 100 yards along the Corfe Castle road. *(Recommended by John and Joan Nash, Richard Siebert, Bernard Stradling, P Dawn, the Didler, JDM, KM, Mike and Sue Loseby, Pete Baker, W W Burke, Mr and Mrs M Clark, Alex and Irene Harvey, Tich Critchlow, Paul Goldman, Derek and Maggie Washington, Jeremy Whitehorn)*

Free house ~ Licensee Charlie Newman ~ Real ale ~ Bar food (all day) ~ No credit cards ~ (01929) 439229 ~ Children welcome ~ Dogs welcome ~ Live music most Sats ~ Open 12-11(10.30 Sun); 12-3, 6-11 winter

LUCKY DIP

Besides the fully inspected pubs, you might like to try these Lucky Dips recommended to us and described by readers (if you do, please send us reports: www.goodguides.co.uk).

ABBOTSBURY [SY5785]

Ilchester Arms DT3 4JR [B3157]: Rambling stone-built pub with old pine tables and settles, lots of rustic bric-a-brac, prints of the famous swans; real ales inc Gales HSB tapped from the cask, wide choice of food from doorstep sandwiches, ciabattas and huge ploughman's up, good house wines in three glass sizes, large games room, no smoking conservatory restaurant; quiet piped music, TV, games machine; children in eating areas, nice views from suntrap terrace picnic-sets, ten bedrooms, open all day *(Colin Gooch, LYM, Stephen R Holman, Sarah and Peter Gooderham, Roland and Wendy Chalu)*

ALMER [SY9098]

☆ *Worlds End* DT11 9EW [B3075, just off A31 towards Wareham]: Handsome thatched Badger family dining pub, beams and flagstones in long busy smoke-free bar with panelled alcoves and candles, very wide choice of enjoyable reasonably priced food all day (you can choose generous or smaller helpings), Badger ales, pleasant helpful hard-working staff (lots of tables, even so you may have to wait); open all day, picnic-sets and heaters out in front and behind, outstanding play area *(Stuart Turner, BB, Michael and Robin Inskip, Mrs Ruth Lewis, Jennifer Banks)*

ANSTY [ST7603]

Fox DT2 7PN [NW of Milton Abbas]: Hotel rather than pub but with flourishing bar side, recently reopened after complete refurbishment, high-ceilinged partly no smoking main bar, lots of toby jugs, Badger Best, Tanglefoot and a seasonal beer, good wines by the glass, very wide choice of inexpensive food; piped music, separate bar with pool and TV, skittle alley; children welcome in no smoking restaurant, garden tables, bedrooms, attractive countryside, open all day *(LYM, Stuart and Alison Ballantyne, Richard and Liz Dilnot, Pat and Robert Watt)*

ASKERSWELL [SY5393]

Spyway DT2 9EP [off A35 Bridport—Dorchester]: Beamed country pub in pretty setting with old-fashioned high-backed settles, cushioned wall and window seats, old-world décor, real ales such as Dorset Weymouth Best and Otter, sensibly priced pubby food from sandwiches and baguettes up, good service, no smoking dining area with steps down to overflow area; may be soft piped music; disabled access, children in eating areas, spectacular views from back terrace and large informal garden, good walks *(Peter Neate, LYM, Barry and Anne, N R White, Roland and Wendy Chalu)*

BEAMINSTER [ST4801]

Greyhound DT8 3AW [A3066 N of Bridport; The Square]: Well run compact local on market square, friendly landlord, full Palmers ale range, wide blackboard choice of reasonably priced standard food from good crab sandwiches and baked potatoes up, flagstones and simple furnishings on right, plusher on left, coal-effect gas fires, small back family room, darts; piped music; dogs welcome *(BB, Christine and Neil Townend, Roland and Wendy Chalu, John A Barker)*

BERE REGIS [SY8494]

Royal Oak BH20 7HQ [West St]: Open-plan pub freshened up under friendly new family, real ales inc Fullers London Pride, good atmosphere, enjoyable reasonably priced food, comfortably refurbished dining room *(BB, John and Joan Nash)*

BLANDFORD FORUM [ST8806]

Crown DT11 7AJ [West St]: Best Western hotel's well furnished spacious bar areas used by locals as pub, large no smoking area, Badger beers from nearby brewery, good range of reasonably priced straightforward bar food inc good sandwiches and light meals, separate restaurant; bedrooms *(Colin and Janet Roe, W W Burke, Gerry and Rosemary Dobson)*

Greyhound DT11 7EB: Popular pub between Thurs/Sat market and main car park, Badger Best and Tanglefoot, good choice of generous sensibly priced food, friendly staff, long central bar, stripped brick, carved wood, comfortable seats, end restaurant *(Stan Edwards)*

BLANDFORD ST MARY [ST8805]

Hall & Woodhouse DT11 9LS: Visitor centre for Badger brewery, their full beer range in top condition inc interesting bottled beers, varied food from well filled baguettes up, friendly staff; spectacular chandelier made of Badger beer bottles, lots of memorabilia in centre and upper gallery; popular brewery tours *(Joan and Michel Hooper-Immins)*

BOURNEMOUTH [SZ0891]

Goat & Tricycle BH2 5PF [West Hill Rd]: Comfortable and roomy two-level rambling

Edwardian local (actually two separate pubs knocked together) with cheerful atmosphere, full Wadworths range and interesting guest beers kept well from handsome pillared bar's impressive rank of ten or more handpumps, farm cider, low-priced generous pubby food from sandwiches and baked potatoes up inc Sun lunch and OAP deals, good coffee, coal fire, lots of bric-a-brac inc hundreds of hats and helmets; can get rather noisily studenty and smoky; good disabled access, heated yard with flower tubs, water feature and covered bower *(G Coates, Joan and Michel Hooper-Immins, Steve Jackson, Michael and Alison Sandy)*

BOURTON [ST7731]

☆ *White Lion* SP8 5AT [High St, off old A303 E of Wincanton]: 18th-c stripped stone dining pub under newish landlord, good interesting fairly priced blackboard food using good fresh ingredients, Fullers London Pride, Greene King IPA, a guest beer, two farm ciders and good wines, quick friendly service, several nicely lit pubby beamed rooms around bar with fine inglenook log fire, no smoking beamed restaurant; dogs welcome, well spaced tables in pleasant garden, two neat bedrooms with own bathrooms *(Colin and Janet Roe, Edward Mirzoeff, LYM, John and Joan Calvert)*

BRIDPORT [SY4692]

Greyhound DT6 3LF [East St]: Bustling old pub smartly converted by Wetherspoons (smaller than most of theirs), with three changing real ales, good coffee, enjoyable food from panini up, polite friendly young staff *(Edna Jones)*

Hope & Anchor DT6 3RA [St Michaels Lane]: Thriving and friendly refurbished local with four real ales and two farm ciders, popular lunchtime food inc good ploughman's and bargain family Sun lunch *(David Ellerington, Jacqueline Hampton, Timothy Jan, D M Paterson)*

BROADWINDSOR [ST4302]

☆ *White Lion* DT8 3QD [The Square (B3163/B3164)]: New licensees doing enjoyable food in 17th-c stone-built pub with Palmers beers, decent wines by the glass, pews and flagstones on left, pine booth seating and big inglenook with log fire in no smoking carpeted dining area on right, pleasant décor, no machines or music; disabled facilities, picnic-sets in small courtyard *(BB, Roland and Wendy Chalu, Frank and Pat Shepherd)*

BUCKLAND NEWTON [ST6804]

☆ *Gaggle of Geese* DT2 7BS: Comfortable country local with good atmosphere and attractive décor, friendly helpful staff, Badger Best, Butcombe and Ringwood Best and Fortyniner, decent wines and spirits, good reasonably priced usual bar food, smartish restaurant, no music; goose auction May and Sept, spacious pool and skittle rooms, small garden but sizeable grounds (room for caravans) *(BB, Nick and Lynne Carter, Edward Mirzoeff)*

BURTON BRADSTOCK [SY4889]

☆ *Anchor* DT6 4QF [B3157 SE of Bridport]: Part gastropub specialising in upmarket seafood, not cheap but usually very good, part lively village pub with games and sports TV; friendly licensees, wide choice of other generous food (may be all day in summer, Sun choice limited) from baguettes up, several real ales such as Ushers Best and Wychwood Hobgoblin, Thatcher's farm cider, lots of malt whiskies, decent wines by the glass, friendly licensees, no smoking restaurant; children and dogs welcome, comfortable bedrooms, open all day *(Alec and Barbara Jones, Peter Meister, Glenn and Julia Smithers, Alun Evans, Paul and Shirley White, Pamela and Merlyn Horswell, D Crook, LYM, Roger and Maureen Kenning, M A Lightfoot, Roland and Wendy Chalu)*

☆ *Three Horseshoes* DT6 4QZ [Mill St]: Attractive and comfortable thatched inn in charming village, unusual in stocking Palmers' complete ale range, all particularly well kept (coincidence that head brewer lives nearby?), welcoming helpful staff, plentiful food from crab and other sandwiches to freshly caught fish and favourite local organic pork chops, good wines by the glass, log fire, homely and roomy layout with low beams and doorways, nice no smoking dining room; may be piped music, crowded on Fri live music nights; picnic-sets out on lawn, pleasant shingle beach a few minutes' drive away (with NT car park), bedrooms *(Glenn and Julia Smithers, LYM, Joan and Michel Hooper-Immins, Ron and Val Broom, Roger and Maureen Kenning, N R White, Roland and Wendy Chalu, Guy Vowles)*

CATTISTOCK [SY5999]

☆ *Fox & Hounds* DT2 0JH [off A37 N of Dorchester]: Friendly helpful service in attractive 17th-c or older pub, enjoyable food from baguettes to enterprising specials and generous OAP meals, Palmers ales from attractively carved counter, Taunton cider, good value wine choice, flagstones and nicely moulded Jacobean beams, stripped stone, log fire in huge inglenook, minimal décor, table skittles, pleasant no smoking side dining room, back public bar with well lit darts and TV, immaculate skittle alley; piped pop music, live some Sats; dogs allowed on back terrace, comfortable bedrooms, cl Mon lunchtime, open all day wknds *(BB, Mark and Sarah Desmond, J S Burn, R T and J C Moggridge)*

CERNE ABBAS [ST6601]

☆ *New Inn* DT2 7JF [14 Long Street]: Handsome Tudor inn with mullioned window seats in friendly beamed bar, Palmers ales, small choice of good wines, enjoyable sensible food strong on local ingredients from traditional standbys to some interesting dishes, big helpings, helpful staff, comfortable no smoking restaurant; children welcome, lots of tables on raised coachyard platform and sheltered lawn behind, play area, eight bedrooms with own bathrooms, open all day wknds and summer

*(Richard and Jean Green, LYM,
Rosanna Luke, Matt Curzon, Alan Johnson,
John Coatsworth)*

CHARMOUTH [SY3693]

George DT6 6QE [off A35 W of Bridport; The
Street]: Friendly and comfortable open-plan
village local, prompt cheerful service, good
value usual food, real ales, pool, table skittles;
dogs welcome, garden with play area
*(Terry and Linda Moseley, BB, Sarah and
Peter Gooderham)*

Royal Oak DT6 6PE [off A3052/A35 E of
Lyme Regis; The Street]: Chatty three-room
village local with quite some character,
welcoming staff and regulars, Palmers,
traditional games, usual food (lunchtimes
only), no TV or piped music
*(Terry and Linda Moseley, W W Burke,
John Joseph Smith)*

CHEDINGTON [ST4805]

☆ *Winyards Gap* DT8 3HY [A356 Dorchester—
Crewkerne]: Cheerful new licensees in well
refurbished dining pub, generous enjoyable
food particularly popular with older wkdy
lunchers, Cotleigh, Exmoor and perhaps guest
ales, no smoking dining area welcoming
children, skittle alley; spectacular view over
Parrett Valley and into Somerset from tables
out in front, good walks nearby *(Mr and Mrs
Peter Larkman, LYM)*

CHIDEOCK [SY4191]

Anchor DT6 6JU [Seatown signed off A35
from Chideock]: Outstanding spot, with
dramatic sea and cliff views and big front
terrace; pub itself unpretentious and
straightforward, with Palmers ales, local farm
cider, reasonably priced bar food (all day in
summer) from lunchtime sandwiches up,
interesting local photographs; unobtrusive
piped music; children and dogs welcome, open
all day in summer *(Miss A G Drake,
David Thornton, Edna Jones, LYM, Di and
Mike Gillam, PRT, Sue Heath, Marjorie and
David Lamb, R M Corlett, Susan Loppert,
Jane Caplan, Pamela and Merlyn Horswell,
Mrs L M Beard, Andy Trafford, Louise Bayly,
Dr Stephen Jolles, Steve Derbyshire, Barry and
Anne, N R White, Roland and Wendy Chalu)*

COLEHILL [SU0302]

☆ *Barley Mow* BH21 7AH [Colehill signed from
A31/B3073 roundabout; Long Lane]: Part-
thatched and part-tiled former drovers' cottage
with low-beamed main bar, open fire in brick
inglenook, attractively moulded oak panelling,
some Hogarth prints, Badger real ales, bar
food (can take a while), family area; piped
music; pleasant enclosed lawn behind with
terrace and boules pitch *(Stan Edwards, LYM,
Andy and Yvonne Cunningham)*

CORFE CASTLE [SY9681]

☆ *Fox* BH20 5HD [West St]: Old-fashioned take-
us-as-you-find-us stone-built local with tiny
front bar dominated by bar-stool regulars, real
ales such as Timothy Taylors Landlord and
Wadworths 6X tapped from the cask, good log
fire in early medieval stone fireplace, generous
simple food from sandwiches and baguettes
up, glassed-over well in lounge (many tables

reserved for eaters); dogs but not children
allowed inside, informal castle-view garden
*(M Joyner, J S and S Chadwick, Joan and
Michel Hooper-Immins, the Didler, LYM)*

☆ *Greyhound* BH20 5EZ [A351]: Bustling and
picturesque old pub in centre of tourist village,
three small low-ceilinged panelled rooms, steps
and corridors, changing real ales such as
Ringwood and Timothy Taylors Landlord,
reasonably priced generous food from
baguettes to steaks, friendly well managed
staff, traditional games inc purbeck long board
shove-ha'penny, no smoking family room;
piped music, live Fri; garden with fine castle
and countryside views, pretty courtyard
opening on to castle bridge, open all day
wknds and summer *(LYM, the Didler,
W W Burke, Peter and Margaret Glenister,
J M Tansey)*

CORFE MULLEN [SY9798]

Coventry Arms BH21 3RH [A31 W of
Wimborne; Mill St]: Reasonably priced bistro-
style food from named suppliers with some
unusual dishes and enterprising children's
dishes, things like olives too, in beamed dining
pub, candlelit at night, with friendly efficient
service, changing real ales such as Gales BB,
Greene King Abbot and Timothy Taylors
Landlord tapped from the cask, decent wines,
four low-ceilinged rooms with large central
open fire, flagstones and bare boards, fishing
décor, board games and books to browse;
tables out by small river *(John Haslam, Linda
Drew, Pat and Robert Watt, W W Burke)*

Holme Bush BH21 3RZ [Old Wareham Rd]:
Neatly kept country pub with real ales such as
Flowers, Gales and Ringwood, decent wines,
good value straightforward food from bar
menu to restaurant dishes inc OAP lunches and
fresh fish, well organised service, two bar areas
each with a log-effect gas fire, beamed
restaurant extension; piped music; picnic-sets
in garden with animals and aviaries, open all
day *(B and K Hypher)*

CORSCOMBE [ST5205]

☆ *Fox* DT2 0NS [towards Halstock]: Picturesque
old thatched country pub just out of the
village, beams and flagstones, big inglenooks,
antlers and stuffed owls, Butcombe and
Exmoor, farm cider, good wine list, charming
dining room with Aga, conservatory; pricy
food (can take a while); children over 5
welcome in dining areas, tables out by a little
stream, good bedrooms *(Dr A McCormick,
LYM, Andy Booth, Mrs J H S Lang)*

CRANBORNE [SU0513]

☆ *Fleur-de-Lys* BH21 5PP [Wimborne St (B3078
N of Wimborne)]: Attractive 17th-c inn with
long panelled lounge, flagstones and log fire,
welcoming licensees, thriving atmosphere,
good home-made pubby food from baguettes
and sandwiches up inc children's, Badger
Tanglefoot and First Gold, farm cider, decent
wines, evening restaurant; games and TV in
simple cheerful beamed public bar, piped
music; nice setting on edge of Cranborne
Chase, comfortable pretty bedrooms
(M and R Thomas, Joan and Michel Hooper-

Immins, LYM, Mr and Mrs A H Young, Phyl and Jack Street, Martin and Alison Stainsby)

DEWLISH [SY7798]

Oak DT2 7ND [off A354 Dorchester—Blandford Forum]: Light and airy village pub with helpful licensees, real ales such as Ringwood Best, farm cider, good basic bar food at pine tables, small no smoking dining room; dogs welcome, good-sized garden *(Mrs Diane M Hall)*

DORCHESTER [SY6990]

☆ *Blue Raddle* DT1 1JN [Church St, nr central short stay car park]: Cheerful unpretentious local with good attractively priced food from generous sandwiches to game and good Sun roast, Otter, Sharps Doom Bar and guest beers such as Smiles or Timothy Taylors Landlord, good wines, obliging landlord, coal-effect gas fire; no credit cards, piped music may be a bit loud; disabled access, but one step *(Mr and Mrs D Renwick, Joan and Michel Hooper-Immins, the Didler, BB)*

Kings Arms DT1 1HF [High East St]: Hotel bar with thriving atmosphere, appealing old-world décor, Courage Directors and guest beers, decent wines, enjoyable food from sandwiches up, two-for-one deals and Sun carvery, attentive service, open fire; close associations with Nelson and Hardy's *Mayor of Casterbridge*; bedrooms (the Lawrence of Arabia suite and the Tutenkhamen are pretty striking) *(LYM, the Didler, John and Joan Nash)*

☆ *Poet Laureate* DT1 3GW [Pummery Sq, Poundbury]: New tenants for substantial building in the Prince of Wales's Poundbury development, new chef doing enjoyable food inc some interesting dishes, Fullers London Pride, Palmers Copper and Ringwood Fortyniner, decent wines by the glass, proper coffee, pleasant attentive service, largely no smoking light and airy L-shaped bar with good décor, lots of chandeliers, good solid tables and chairs, daily papers, flame-effect stove, agreeable restaurant area; unobtrusive piped music; wheelchair access, a few picnic-sets on side terrace *(Mr and Mrs R B Berry, Joan and Michel Hooper-Immins)*

EAST KNIGHTON [SY8185]

☆ *Countryman* DT2 8LL [signed off A352 Dorchester—Wareham]: Big bustling family food pub with popular carvery (not Mon, or lunchtime Tues, must book wknds), some comfortable sofas in pleasant bar area, log fires, Courage Best, Greene King Old Speckled Hen and Ringwood Best and Old Thumper, farm cider, good well priced wines, young friendly well trained staff, no smoking restaurant; piped music; good provision for disabled, comfortable bedrooms, good breakfast *(John and Joan Nash, John and Joan Calvert, Andy and Yvonne Cunningham, Mrs Pat Crabb, LYM, Cathy Robinson, Ed Coombe, Jason Caulkin, W W Burke, Ed and Alan Neale)*

EAST STOUR [ST8123]

Kings Arms SP8 5NB [B3095, 3 miles W towards Shaftesbury; The Common]: Recently reopened after refurbishment, enjoyable

sensibly priced food inc all-day Sun roasts, Fullers London Pride and Palmers ales, decent wines, friendly informal service, large bar with good eating area and new carvery; children welcome; lots of flowers in front, tables in big garden, bedrooms *(Colin and Janet Roe, Paul and Annette Hallett)*

EVERSHOT [ST5704]

Acorn DT2 0JW [off A37 S of Yeovil]: Charmingly placed pub with Branscombe Vale ales, interesting wines and other drinks, front part all set for restaurant meals, with up-to-date décor despite the log fires and oak panelling, bar snacks from open sandwiches to salads and pubby hot dishes in back bar with games and juke box, skittle alley; they may try to keep your credit card while you eat; children allowed in eating areas, dogs in bar, terrace with dark oak furniture, bedrooms, pretty village, good surrounding walks, open all day *(Edna Jones, LYM, Rob Winstanley, Alan Johnson, Joan and Michel Hooper-Immins, Roland and Wendy Chalu, OPUS)*

FONTMELL MAGNA [ST8616]

Crown SP7 0PA: Attractively modernised, with emphasis on enjoyable reasonably priced food using fresh local supplies from bar snacks to full meals, friendly service, interesting wines, good beer; reasonably priced bedrooms *(Mrs G C Kohn, Paul and Caroline Marland)*

GILLINGHAM [ST7926]

Buffalo SP8 4NJ [off B3081 at Wyke 1 mile NW of Gillingham, pub 100yds on left]: Smartly refurbished Badger pub with popular sensibly priced food (not Sun evening) from sandwiches and baked potatoes up, their ales kept well; pleasant garden with picnic-sets and play area, open all day Sun *(Ian Phillips)*

GUSSAGE ALL SAINTS [SU0010]

☆ *Drovers* BH21 5ET [8 miles N of Wimborne]: Attractively placed thatched pub with good value generous food, Ringwood beers, friendly staff, pleasant country furnishings and good log fire in extended two-room bar; pretty village, tables on pretty front lawn with views across the Dorset hills *(LYM, Pat and Robert Watt)*

HAZELBURY BRYAN [ST7408]

Antelope DT10 2EB: Appealing village local with inglenook log fire and traditional wooden furnishings in main bar, enterprising newish licensees, well done straightforward food using local farms, Badger real ales, decent wine choice, no smoking area, pool in separate skittle alley; large garden with pleasant views and pet rabbits *(Rob Winstanley)*

HINTON ST MARY [ST7816]

White Horse DT10 1NA [just off B3092 a mile N of Sturminster]: Old-fashioned village pub with enjoyable reasonably priced blackboard food, changing real ales, several wines by the glass, unusual inglenook fireplace in cheerful tiled bar, extended dining lounge, darts; tables in flower garden, attractive setting *(Richard May, Colin and Janet Roe, Pat and Robert Watt)*

HOLT [SU0304]

Old Inn BH21 7DJ: Well run beamed Badger dining pub, their real ales, helpful friendly service even when busy, good choice of enjoyable well priced food inc good oriental dishes and fresh fish, plenty of comfortable tables, winter fires, good atmosphere; children welcome *(Stan Edwards, M and R Thomas)*

IBBERTON [ST7807]

Crown DT11 0EN: Good range of local beers, friendly helpful staff, enjoyable reasonably priced food inc interesting dishes; lovely garden, beautiful spot under Bulbarrow Hill *(Howard Johnson)*

LITTON CHENEY [SY5490]

☆ *White Horse* DT2 9AT: Relaxed and unpretentious, with good value traditional food from sandwiches up, good fresh local ingredients, particularly well kept Palmers ales, decent reasonably priced wines by the glass, cheerful landlord, big woodburner, lots of pictures, some pine panelling, stripped stone and flagstones, country kitchen chairs in dining area, table skittles; may be piped jazz; good spot on quiet lane into quaint village, picnic-sets on pleasant streamside front lawn *(C and R Bromage, Edna Jones, BB, Gavin Robinson, Roland and Wendy Chalu)*

LONGBURTON [ST6412]

☆ *Rose & Crown* DT9 5PD [A352 Sherborne—Dorchester]: Pleasantly modernised thatched village pub with friendly helpful staff, enjoyable food (limited Mon), freshly made and generous, from sandwiches to imaginative restaurant dishes inc unusual puddings, Badger beers, attractive back dining room with booth seating, interesting well feature and inglenook fireplace, long open-plan bar with pool and skittle alley; disabled access *(Richard and Jean Green, Jason Muxworthy, Jean and David Darby)*

LYME REGIS [SY3391]

☆ *Harbour Inn* DT7 3JF [Marine Parade]: Good food inc fresh local fish (great fish soup), friendly efficient service, good house wines, Otter and St Austell real ale, farm cider, clean-cut modern décor keeping original flagstones and stone walls (so can be a bit noisy when busy), thriving atmosphere, sea and coast views from front windows *(Bruce Horne, Joan and Michel Hooper-Immins)*

Pilot Boat DT7 3QA [Bridge St]: Popular and reliable modern all-day family food place nr waterfront, plenty of tables in cheery nautically themed bars with no smoking dining areas, Palmers real ales, good choice of wines by the glass, low prices, skittle alley; piped music; children and dogs welcome, tables out on terrace, open all day *(Alain and Rose Foote, Meg and Colin Hamilton, Sue and Mike Todd, Dave Irving, LYM, Pat and Tony Martin, Sarah and Peter Gooderham, Tim and Ann Newell)*

Royal Lion DT7 3QF [Broad St]: Coaching inn dating from 17th c, comfortably old-fashioned many-roomed bar with log fire and dark panelling, Bass, good value pub meals, efficient service, games room, upstairs restaurant; good bedrooms *(LYM, Tim and Ann Newell)*

☆ *Royal Standard* DT7 3JF [Marine Parade, The Cobb]: Right on broadest part of beach,

properly pubby bar with fine built-in stripped high settles and even old-fashioned ring-up tills, quieter no smoking area with stripped brick and pine, quick friendly service, three Palmers ales, good choice of wines by the glass, reasonably priced popular food from sandwiches to good local crab and fish, good cream teas, open fire, darts, prominent pool table; may be piped pop; children welcome, good-sized sheltered suntrap courtyard with own servery and wendy house – and you can keep an eye on your children on the beach just feet away *(Sue and Mike Todd, BB, Dave Irving, Marjorie and David Lamb, Colin and Janet Roe, Peter Salmon, Tim and Ann Newell, Dave Mower)*

☆ *Victoria* DT7 3LP [Uplyme Rd (B3165)]: Well remodelled yet pleasantly unpretentious Victorian pub/hotel, good reasonably priced food from lunchtime panini (not Mon) and other bar meals to well prepared and imaginative restaurant dishes (can be eaten in bar too) strong on fresh local seafood and carefully chosen local produce from named farms, reasonable prices, Fullers London Pride, Greene King Abbot and Otter, good wines by the glass, friendly licensees and staff, attractive neatly kept open-plan bar, big-windowed restaurant looking down on town; may be faint piped music; nicely planted sheltered terrace, bedrooms *(BB, Terry and Linda Moseley, Mr and Mrs P Stephens)*

Volunteer DT7 3QE [top of Broad St (A3052 towards Exeter)]: Easy-going local atmosphere in long cosy low-ceilinged bar, nice broad mix of customers, enjoyable food inc lots of modestly priced fresh local fish in no smoking dining lounge (children allowed here), changing real ales such as Sharps Doom Bar and farm ciders, roaring fires; dogs welcome, open all day *(Phil and Sally Gorton, LYM)*

LYTCHETT MINSTER [SY9693]

St Peters Finger BH16 6JE [Dorchester Rd]: Well run beamed two-part Badger roadhouse with good service, sensibly priced standard food from sandwiches and baguettes up, real ale inc Tanglefoot, cottagey mix of furnishings in different sections and end log fire giving a cosy feel despite its size; good skittle alley, tables on big terrace, part covered and heated *(Douglas and Ann Hare)*

MANSTON [ST8116]

☆ *Plough* DT10 1HB [B3091 Shaftesbury—Sturminster Newton, just N]: Good-sized traditional country pub with friendly considerate licensees and prompt service, plentiful appetising food from sandwiches up, Palmers ales, richly decorated plasterwork, ceilings and bar front; garden tables *(Paul Goldman, Glen and Nola Armstrong, Colin and Janet Roe)*

MARNHULL [ST7719]

☆ *Blackmore Vale* DT10 1JJ [Burton St, via Church Hill off B3092]: Comfortably modernised pub with pleasantly opened-up beamed and flagstoned no smoking dining bar with woodburner, cosy smaller bar with settles, sofas and pub games, friendly helpful service, enjoyable generous home-made food inc OAP lunches Tues and Thurs, Badger beers, good choice of reasonably priced wines; piped music, Weds quiz night; children welcome, tables in attractively reworked garden, open all day wknds *(LYM, Pat and Robert Watt)*

☆ *Crown* DT10 1LN [about 3 miles N of Sturminster Newton; Crown Rd]: Part-thatched 17th-c dining pub, new chef/landlord doing good value generous food, friendly attentive service, Badger Best and Tanglefoot, good wine choice, linked rooms with oak beams, huge flagstones or bare boards, old settles, stuffed animals and old prints and plates, log fire in big stone hearth in oldest part, more modern furnishings and carpet elsewhere; skittle alley, may be piped music; tables in peaceful enclosed garden, children welcome *(LYM, John and Gloria Isaacs)*

MORETON [SY7789]

Frampton Arms DT2 8BB [B3390 nr stn]: Relaxed and neatly kept, with generous food from sandwiches and baguettes to fish and seafood, Palmers, log fire, good service even on a busy Sun, steam railway pictures in lounge bar, Warmwell Aerodrome theme in public bar, bright and airy conservatory restaurant; tables on front terrace, comfortable bedrooms, nearby campsite *(Oliver Richardson)*

MOTCOMBE [ST8426]

Coppleridge SP7 9HW: Enjoyable food from sandwiches to speciality steaks, Boddingtons and Butcombe, decent wines and welcoming service in former 18th-c farmhouse's bar/lounge and two smallish dining rooms; big airy bedrooms, good-sized grounds *(Colin and Janet Roe, Pat and Robert Watt)*

NORDEN HEATH [SY94834]

☆ *Halfway* BH20 5DU [A351 Wareham—Corfe Castle]: Cosily laid out thatched pub with friendly staff, Badger beers, good wines by the glass, decent food all day, pitched-ceiling back serving bar where the locals congregate, front rooms with flagstones, log fires, stripped stonework, snug little side area; picnic-tables outside with play area, good nearby walks, open all day *(Richard Wyld, BB)*

OKEFORD FITZPAINE [ST8011]

Royal Oak DT11 0RN [Lower St]: Well kept Ringwood Best, Wadworths 6X and weekly changing guest beer, farm cider, bar food from baguettes and baked potatoes up, huge fireplace with copper-hooded stove in small traditional beamed and flagstoned front bar, no smoking green-painted L-shaped eating area with three very small cottagey interconnected rooms off, steps up to refurbished skittle alley, pool; quiz night, beer festival first wknd in July, tables on back lawn with play area, charming village *(BB, Peter Titcomb)*

OSMINGTON [SY7282]

Sunray DT3 6EU [A353 Weymouth—Wareham]: Good-sized Badger pub with good friendly service under hardworking newish landlord, generous good value food inc fish specialities and imaginative dishes for children, relaxing atmosphere and pleasant contemporary décor, card games; children

welcome, large garden and terrace, play area *(Cathy Robinson, Ed Coombe)*

PIDDLETRENTHIDE [SY7198]

European DT2 7QT: Unpretentious traditional beamed pub with cheerful service, enjoyable food from baguettes up, Ringwood Best, decent wines, log fire in attractive copper-hooded fireplace, willow-pattern china; dogs very welcome, tables in neatly kept front garden, three bedrooms with own baths and good views *(BB, Dennis Jenkin)*

☆ *Piddle* DT2 7QF [B3143 N of Dorchester]: Good food with emphasis on fish, Greene King ales tapped from the cask, most tables set for eating but comfortable leatherette sofas in refurbished bar, children's room, end pool room with SkyTV; informal streamside garden with picnic-sets and play area, good bedrooms *(BB, John Fiander, Marianne and Peter Stevens, M G Hart)*

☆ *Poachers* DT2 7QX [B3143 N of Dorchester]: Smart bright modern décor, luxurious seating in new lounge end, Butcombe, Palmers Tally Ho and Ringwood Fortyniner, welcoming service and good atmosphere, roomy and popular beamed no smoking restaurant with local artwork for sale; piped music; dogs welcome, garden with tables on decking and stream at bottom, 20 comfortable good value motel-style bedrooms around residents' heated swimming pool, good breakfast, open all day *(Rob Winstanley, Joan and Michel Hooper-Immins, Nick and Lynne Carter)*

PIMPERNE [ST9009]

☆ *Anvil* DT11 8UQ [well back from A354]: Attractive 16th-c thatched family pub with wide choice of appetising food from enterprising and generous lunchtime baguettes and ciabattas to piping hot substantial main dishes, real ales such as Butcombe, Palmers Copper and Timothy Taylors Landlord, cheerful efficient young staff, bays of plush seating in bright and welcoming bar, neat black-beamed restaurant; fruit machine, piped music; good garden with fish pond and big weeping willow, 12 bedrooms with own bathrooms, nice surroundings *(John and Joan Nash, BB, Stan Edwards)*

POOLE [SZ0190]

Angel BH15 1NF [Market St, opp Guildhall which is signed off A348]: Well run, spacious and relaxed, with fresh modern décor, good lighting, four Ringwood ales from visible cellar, fairly priced up-to-date food 12-7 (just lunchtime Sun), decent wines, quick efficient service; disabled facilities, heated back courtyard, modern bedrooms *(LYM, G Coates)*

Antelope BH15 1BP [High St]: Former coaching inn just off quay, Greene King IPA and Abbot, Ringwood Best and John Smiths, enjoyable reasonably priced food in neatly kept character bar and refurbished back restaurant with more elaborate dishes, lots of RNLI photographs; bedrooms *(W W Burke)*

Bermuda Triangle BH14 0JY [Parr St, Lower Parkstone (just off A35 at Ashley Cross)]: Old-fashioned bare-boards local with four interesting and particularly well kept changing real ales, two or three good continental lagers on tap and many other beers from around the world, good lunchtime food, friendly landlady, various snug old corners and lots of nautical and other bric-a-brac, cloudscape ceiling, back room with sports TV; a bit too steppy for disabled access; pavement picnic-sets, open all day wknds *(G Coates, Michael and Alison Sandy)*

☆ *Inn in the Park* BH13 6JS [Pinewood Rd, off A338 towards Branksome Chine, via The Avenue]: Popular open-plan bar in substantial Edwardian villa (now a small hotel), Wadworths and other ales, good value generous standard food (not Sun evening) from good sandwiches to fresh seafood, cheerful young staff, log fire, oak panelling and big mirrors, airy and attractive restaurant (children allowed) and Sun carvery; tables on small sunny terrace, comfortable bedrooms, quiet pine-filled residential area just above sea, open all day *(LYM, W W Burke)*

Nightjar BH13 7HX [Ravine Rd, Canford Cliffs]: Ember Inn attractively refurbished with leather armchairs, sofas and so forth, several separate areas, good wines by the glass, Bass and other good ales such as Fullers London Pride and Charles Wells Bombardier from long bar, usual food from sandwiches up; piped music, machines, two quiz nights; picnic-sets on pleasant shaded lawn, nice quiet spot in upmarket district *(Betsy Brown, Nigel Flook, W W Burke, Michael and Alison Sandy)*

Shah of Persia BH15 2HS [Longfleet Rd/Fernside Rd (A35)]: Spacious roadhouse under go-ahead new management, substantial and enjoyable food from sandwiches, baguettes and baked potatoes up, carvery counter and Mon-Thurs bargain lunches, Ringwood Best and Fortyniner, quick pleasant service, several mainly carpeted and largely no smoking areas on varying levels, pleasant décor with lots of prints, plates and other ornaments, art deco lighting; modern bedroom block *(B and K Hypher)*

PORTLAND [SY6872]

☆ *George* DT5 2AP [Reforne]: Cheerful 17th-c stone-built local mentioned by Thomas Hardy and reputed to have smugglers' tunnels running to the cliffs, very low doorways and beams, flagstones, small rooms, old scrubbed tables carved with names of generations of sailors and quarrymen, interesting prints and mementoes, Greene King Abbot and Old Speckled Hen with a guest such as Adnams Broadside, Addlestone's cider, big coffee mugs, chatty local landlord, good value food (not Weds lunchtime) from big filled baps to cheap home-made hot dishes, children's room; picnic-sets in pleasant back garden, open all day *(Ian Phillips, Joan and Michel Hooper-Immins, Roland and Wendy Chalu)*

Mermaid DT5 1HS [Wakeham]: Unpretentious friendly local nr cove with intriguing ruined churchyard, Adnams Best, Bass and Greene King Old Speckled Hen, good value food inc local scallops and choice of Sun

carvery roasts, two for one deals Mon night, pleasant back restaurant with extended evening menu, real fire in stone fireplace, two chesterfields, old photographs and interesting bric-a-brac inc ship models; suntrap back terrace, lovely flower displays, three bedrooms *(Cathy Robinson, Ed Coombe)*

PORTLAND BILL [SY6768]

Pulpit DT5 2JT: Welcoming extended traditional pub at end of Weymouth bus route in great spot nr Pulpit Rock, picture-window views, dark beams and stripped stone, Bass, Fullers London Pride, Greene King Old Speckled Hen or Ringwood Best, generous quickly served food from separate counter (they shout your name when it's ready), from good local crab sandwiches to fine steak and kidney pie, wide evening choice, friendly long-serving licensees; may be piped music; tiered sea-view terrace, short stroll to lighthouse and cliffs *(Colin Gooch, A and B D Craig, Joan and Michel Hooper-Immins, Meg and Colin Hamilton)*

POWERSTOCK [SY5196]

☆ *Three Horseshoes* DT6 3TF [off A3066 Beaminster—Bridport via W Milton]: Landlord/chef cooking good enterprising meals using fresh fish and other local ingredients, generous interesting lunchtime baguettes too, Palmers ales, good range of wines by the glass, friendly helpful landlady and staff, good log fires and stripped panelling, children welcome in no smoking pine-plank dining room, no music; level access, dogs welcome (two resident springers), fabulous view from back terrace (steps down to this) and big sloping garden, three pleasant bedrooms with own bathrooms, good walks, open all day *(Rob Winstanley, Pam and Alan Neale, LYM, R M Corlett, Barry and Anne, Roland and Wendy Chalu)*

PRESTON [SY7082]

Spyglass DT3 6PN [Bowleaze Coveway]: Big busy family dining pub on Furzy Cliff, bright and airy, with picture-window views over Weymouth Bay, wide choice of enjoyable generous food with plenty for children, real ales inc Ringwood Fortyniner; piped music; tables outside, big adventure play area *(Colin Gooch)*

PUNCKNOWLE [SY5388]

☆ *Crown* DT2 9BN [off B3157 Bridport—Abbotsbury]: Recently refurbished 16th-c thatched inn, inglenook log fires each end of low-beamed stripped stone lounge with local paintings for sale, steps up to public bar with books and magazines, no smoking family room with children's books, decent pubby food from sandwiches and baked potatoes up, full Palmers ale range, ten wines by the glass; views from peaceful pretty back garden, good walks, bedrooms *(LYM, Terry and Linda Moseley, Alan Johnson, Roland and Wendy Chalu, Peter Titcomb)*

PYMORE [SY4794]

Pymore Inn DT6 5PN [off A3066 N of Bridport]: Attractive Georgian beamed and stone-built pub justly popular with older local people for good value hearty traditional food (most tables laid for eating), lunchtime toasties and baguettes, friendly prompt service, changing real ales such as Badger Best and Youngs, good choice of wines by the glass, prints on panelled walls, woodburner, small pretty dining room; soft piped music; wheelchair access, big garden *(Bob and Margaret Holder, Roland and Wendy Chalu)*

SANDFORD ORCAS [ST6220]

☆ *Mitre* DT9 4RU [off B3148 and B3145 N of Sherborne]: Tucked-away country local with flagstones and fresh flowers throughout, thriving atmosphere, quick friendly service, good choice of reasonably priced wholesome home-made food inc local mackerel and good puddings, real ales, country wines, log fires, small bar and larger pleasantly homely dining area; tables out on pretty terrace, has been cl Mon lunchtime *(LYM, Janet Topp, Marjorie and David Lamb, Mrs S Gudgeon)*

SHAFTESBURY [ST8622]

Two Brewers SP7 8HE [St James St]: Nicely tucked away below steep famously photogenic Gold Hill, friendly well divided open-plan plush-seated bar, lots of decorative plates, pleasant staff, Fullers London Pride, Greene King Old Speckled Hen, Ringwood, Sharps and a guest beer, decent food from baguettes up (children's helpings of any dish), good value wines, no smoking back dining room, skittle alley; children in eating areas, dogs in bar, picnic-sets in attractive good-sized garden with pretty views *(LYM, Alan and Paula McCully, John A Barker)*

SHAPWICK [ST9301]

☆ *Anchor* DT11 9LB [off A350 Blandford—Poole; West St]: Appealing pub in heart of pretty thatched village, varnished pine tables on quarry tiles, courteous helpful service, good interesting generous food (not Mon, and can take a while as freshly made), good wine choice, Greene King Abbot and Ringwood Best, several small rooms with pleasant end dining room; piped music, occasional live; children welcome, brightly painted tables in front, more in attractive good-sized garden with terrace and play area behind, handy for Kingston Lacy *(BB, B and K Hypher, John and Joan Nash, A and H Piper)*

SHERBORNE [ST6316]

Half Moon DT9 3LN [Half Moon St]: Handy food pub with good choice of decent reasonably priced food from sandwiches, baguettes and baked potatoes up, real ales such as Otter, efficient friendly staff, bright and airy no smoking restaurants; 16 bedrooms with own bathrooms *(Mark Flynn, Dr and Mrs M E Wilson, Guy Vowles)*

☆ *Skippers* DT9 3HE [A352 link rd, W of centre; Terrace View, Horsecastles]: Comfortable extended pub with long stripped-stone bar partly laid for eating, good value food inc fresh fish and (not Sun) bargain OAP lunch, Butcombe and Wadworths IPA and 6X, daily papers, coal-effect gas fire, lively décor inc interesting helicopter and other mainly RNAS photographs; can get smoky, may be unobtrusive piped radio; children welcome in

eating areas, tables outside *(LYM, John A Barker)*

STOBOROUGH [SY9286]

Kings Arms BH20 5AB [B3075 S of Wareham; Corfe Rd]: Good Ringwood and other ales, late May beer festival, enjoyable food with good choice of specials inc local fish in bar and no smoking restaurant, good service and atmosphere; disabled access, garden with terrace by River Frome, open all day wknds *(Gerry and Rosemary Dobson, Liz and Tony Colman, Pam and Alan Neale)*

STOURPAINE [ST8609]

White Horse DT11 8TA [Shaston Rd; A350 NW of Blandford]: Friendly recently extended country pub with landlord/chef doing enjoyable food from lunchtime sandwiches to ambitious dishes (particularly evenings), Badger ales, nice layout and décor, scrubbed tables; bedrooms *(Stan Edwards)*

STRATTON [SY6593]

Saxon Arms DT2 9WG [off A37 NW of Dorchester; The Square]: Traditional (but recently built) thatched local, open-plan, bright and spacious, with open fire, part flagstones, part carpet, light oak tables and comfortable settles, large comfortable no smoking dining section on right, pleasant efficient service, Timothy Taylors Landlord and Charles Wells Bombardier, good value wines, traditional games; piped music; children and dogs welcome, tables out overlooking village green *(C and R Bromage, LYM, Alec and Joan Laurence, James A Waller, Mrs A P Lee)*

STUDLAND [SZ0382]

☆ *Bankes Arms* BH19 3AU [off B3351, Isle of Purbeck; Manor Rd]: Very popular spot above fine beach; outstanding country, sea and cliff views from huge pleasant garden over road with masses of seating; comfortably basic and easy-going big bar with raised drinking area, very wide choice of decent food (at a price) all day from good baguettes to local fish and good crab salad, half a dozen or more changing ales inc its own Isle of Purbeck ones brewed here, local farm cider, good wines by the glass, helpful young staff, great log fire, darts and pool in side games area; they may try to keep your credit card while you eat, can get very busily trippery wknds and in summer, parking in season can be complicated or expensive if you're not a NT member, piped music, machines, big-screen sports TV; children welcome, just off Coast Path, big comfortable bedrooms *(M Joyner, Betsy Brown, Nigel Flook, Bernard Stradling, John and Joan Calvert, Andy and Yvonne Cunningham, Liz and Tony Colman, Gerry and Rosemary Dobson, Mr and Mrs John Taylor, Dr D E Granger)*

STURMINSTER MARSHALL [SY9499]

Black Horse BH21 4AQ [A350]: Good value food from good sandwiches up, Badger real ales, welcoming attentive staff, comfortable long bar, interesting pictures and local artefacts in dining area *(Bill Smith, G Jones)*

STURMINSTER NEWTON [ST7813]

☆ *Bull* DT10 2BS [A357, S of centre]: Busy low-

beamed thatched 16th-c country inn by River
Stour, good bar food, Badger Best and Harveys,
soft lighting; children welcome in eating area,
roadside picnic-sets out in front, more in
pleasant fenced garden *(Stan Edwards, LYM)*

SWANAGE [SZ0278]

Red Lion BH19 2LY [High St]: Low-beamed
two-bar pub doing well under current
management, enjoyable sensibly priced food,
reasonably priced real ale; piped music;
children's games in large barn, picnic-sets in
extended garden with partly covered back
terrace *(the Didler, J M Tansey, JMM)*

SYMONDSBURY [SY4493]

☆ *Ilchester Arms* DT6 6HD [signed off A35 just
W of Bridport]: Attractive partly thatched old
inn with carefully prepared good food strong
on local fish and other local ingredients,
moderate prices, friendly obliging service,
Palmers ales, reasonably priced wines, snugly
rustic open-plan low-beamed bar with high-
backed settle built in by big inglenook, pretty
no smoking restaurant with another fire (worth
booking wknds – food not served in bar Sat
night), pub games, skittle alley doubling as
family room (no children in bar); fairly quiet
piped music; level entrance (steps from car
park), tables in nice informal brookside back
garden with play area, peaceful village, good
walks nearby *(Neil and Anita Christopher,
J Radford, LYM, Roland and Wendy Chalu,
Malcolm and Kate Dowty)*

TARRANT KEYNSTON [ST9204]

True Lovers Knot DT11 9JG [B3082
Blandford—Wimborne]: Recently refurbished
and extended Badger pub, light and spacious,
with their ales from long L-shaped counter in
largely carpeted bar with some beams and
flagstones, helpful friendly service, good
generous straightforward food using local
supplies, some small helpings available, new
uncluttered open-plan no smoking dining area;
children welcome, picnic-sets in good-sized
garden with enclosed play area and camp site,
four well equipped new bedrooms
(B and K Hypher)

TOLPUDDLE [SY7994]

Martyrs DT2 7ES [former A35 W of Bere
Regis]: Modest creeper-covered pub with
Badger beers, good choice of wines by the
glass, wide range of food (readers generally
praise the fish and seafood) in bar and busy
restaurant, pleasant attentive service; shame
about the piped music, no credit cards;
children welcome, picnic-sets on heated front
terrace, nice garden, quiet bypassed village,
open all day *(Bernard Stradling, Derek and
Maggie Washington, Dave Mower,
Peter Neate)*

UPLODERS [SY5093]

☆ *Crown* DT6 4NU [signed off A35 E of
Bridport]: Newish tenants and chef doing good
food with a french accent inc fresh local
seafood, in appealing low-beamed flagstoned
pub with steps down to pretty no smoking
restaurant, cheerful décor, friendly prompt
service, Palmers IPA and Copper, ten wines by
the glass, log fires, daily papers, table skittles;

picnic-sets in small attractive two-tier garden
*(G F Couch, Terry and Linda Moseley, LYM,
Peter Neate, David and Julie Glover,
Roland and Wendy Chalu)*

UPWEY [SY6785]

Old Ship DT3 5QQ [off A354; Ridgeway]:
Quiet beamed pub with lots of alcoves, log
fires each end, Greene King Old Speckled Hen
and a guest beer, food from lunchtime
baguettes up, quick friendly service; picnic-sets
in garden with terrace, interesting walks
nearby *(Terry and Linda Moseley,
Alan Johnson, LYM, Mrs Joyce Robson)*

☆ *Riverhouse* DT3 5QB [B3159, nr junction
A354]: Coal-effect gas fireplace dividing
flagstoned bar side from neat carpeted no
smoking dining side, charming licensees and
friendly staff, main emphasis on wide range of
good quickly served food from lunchtime
baguettes through familiar dishes to italian
specialities and gorgeous puddings, good
relaxed gently upmarket atmosphere, Courage
Best and Wadworths 6X, adventurous wine
choice, good coffees; well reproduced piped
pop music; disabled access, sizeable garden
with play area and water for dogs, cl Sun
evening *(Elizabeth and Gordon Foote,
Jean Barnett, David Lewis, BB, Joan and
Michel Hooper-Immins)*

WAREHAM [SY9287]

Duke of Wellington BH20 4NN [East St]:
Small traditional 18th-c pub with good friendly
service, real ales such as Castle Eden,
Ringwood Best and Sharps Atlantic and
Special, wide choice of reasonably priced food
esp fish, some original features; piped music,
and they may try to keep your card while you
eat; open all day *(John and Joan Nash,
Barry and Anne)*

WEST BEXINGTON [SY5386]

☆ *Manor Hotel* DT2 9DF [off B3157 SE of
Bridport; Beach Rd]: Relaxing quietly set hotel
with long history and fine sea views, good no
smoking restaurant with smart Victorian-style
conservatory, comfortable log-fire lounge and
bustling black-beamed cellar bar with another
log fire, helpful staff kind to children, bar food
from sandwiches and good ploughman's up,
Butcombe Gold and Quay Harbour Master,
quite a few malt whiskies and several wines by
the glass; piped music; dogs allowed in bar,
plenty of picnic-sets on lawns with play area,
comfortable bedrooms, open all day
*(Gordon Prince, LYM, Andy and
Yvonne Cunningham, John and Joan Nash,
Alex and Irene Harvey, Roland and
Wendy Chalu)*

WEST STAFFORD [SY7289]

Wise Man DT2 8AG [signed off A352
Dorchester—Wareham]: This 16th-c beamed
pub nr Hardy's cottage, with lovely walks
nearby, suffered a bad thatch fire in spring
2006, but should reopen after rebuilding some
time in 2007 *(BB)*

WEST STOUR [ST7822]

☆ *Ship* SP8 5RP [A30]: Friendly newish landlord
in attractively placed pub/hotel, good
imaginative reasonably priced food (may take a

while as cooked fresh) from panini up, real ales such as Ringwood and Timothy Taylors Landlord, spotless attractive furnishings, big log fire, lovely views from chatty bright and airy bar, intimate split-level dining room; comfortable bedrooms *(Neil Crux, Alan M Pring, Dennis Jenkin, Pat and Robert Watt, Colin and Janet Roe, Steve Jackson)*

WEYMOUTH [SY6778]

Boot DT4 8JH [High West St]: Friendly bare-boards local nr harbour dating from early 1600s, beams and hooded stone-mullioned windows, Ringwood ales with a guest beer from fine brass handpumps, Cheddar Valley farm cider; pavement tables, open all day *(Joan and Michel Hooper-Immins, the Didler)*

☆ *Nothe Tavern* DT4 8TZ [Barrack Rd]: Roomy and comfortable local with good atmosphere, wide range of enjoyable food inc local fresh fish and good value roast lunch deals, friendly service, Courage Best, Ringwood Best, Otter and Wadworths 6X, decent wines, good choice of malt whiskies, lots of whisky-water jugs on ceiling, interesting prints and photographs, no smoking restaurant (children welcome here) with distant harbour glimpses; may be quiet piped music; garden tables *(M G Hart, Joan and Michel Hooper-Immins, BB, Phil and Jane Hodson)*

☆ *Red Lion* DT4 8TR [Hope Sq]: Bare-boards pub with Courage Best and Dorset beers from smart touristy complex in former brewery opp, quickly served bargain lunches, good crab sandwiches too, interesting RNLI and fishing stuff all over the walls and ceiling (even two boats), coal fire, daily papers, friendly laid-back atmosphere, good staff, darts; can get a bit smoky, may be piped pop music; dogs welcome, plenty of picnic-sets on sunny front terrace (more than inside), open all day wkdys, food all day then too *(PRT, Pete Walker, BB, the Didler, Mr and Mrs M Clark, Roland and Wendy Chalu)*

Wellington Arms DT4 8PY [St Alban St]: Unpretentious mid 19th-c panelled town pub, good value lunchtime food (all day summer wkdys) from toasted sandwiches and baked potatoes to bargain pubby hot dishes inc daily roasts, Ringwood Best, Wadworths 6X and Youngs Special, lots of old local photographs; children welcome in no smoking back dining room, open all day *(Joan and Michel Hooper-Immins)*

WIMBORNE MINSTER [SZ0099]

Albion BH21 1HR [High St]: Small friendly local based on coaching inn dating from 17th c, pleasant décor, polite helpful staff, real ales, good value lunches, separate dining area *(G Jones)*

Green Man BH21 1EN [Victoria Rd, W of

town]: Splendid flower-draped façade, three linked areas with nooks and alcoves, usual pub furnishings, prints and lots of brasses, John Smiths, Wadworths and ciders, friendly staff, good value limited lunchtime food inc fine ploughman's, wider evening choice, small dining area, relaxed atmosphere; no dogs, lavatories up steps; benches out under ivy trellis *(W W Burke)*

WIMBORNE ST GILES [SU0212]

Bull BH21 5NF [off B3078 N of Wimborne]: Comfortable and attractive former private house, friendly staff, enjoyable food using local fresh ingredients, Badger ales, farm cider; small pleasant garden *(Dr Michael Smith)*

WINFRITH NEWBURGH [SY8085]

Red Lion DT2 8LE [A352 Wareham—Dorchester]: Comfortable and warmly welcoming Badger family dining pub with beamy décor and wide choice of generous enjoyable food inc fresh fish, good atmosphere and service, real ales, reasonably priced wines; TV room, piped music; tables in big sheltered garden (site for caravans), bedrooms *(M Joyner, Paul and Helen Spry, Brian and Bett Cox, Jack Kitching, Marjorie and David Lamb, Pam and Alan Neale)*

WINKTON [SZ1696]

☆ *Fishermans Haunt* BH23 7AS [B3347 N of Christchurch]: Thriving well run big-windowed bar, neat and well divided, with hands-on landlord, relaxed friendly atmosphere, good value standard food from sandwiches and filled baked potatoes up, good real ales, lots of country wines, wknd restaurant; disabled facilities, children and dogs welcome, well kept gardens, comfortable bedrooms, open all day *(LYM, Sara Fulton, Roger Baker, Mr and Mrs A P Reeves, Francis Johnston, T and P, Joan and Michel Hooper-Immins)*

WOOL [SY8486]

Ship BH20 6EQ [A352 Wareham—Dorchester]: Roomy open-plan thatched and timbered family pub, good reasonably priced choice of generous locally sourced food all day from baguettes and baked potatoes to seafood in low-ceilinged linked areas of long dining lounge and plush back restaurant, friendly quick service, Badger ales, decent wines, good coffee; quiet piped music; picnic-sets overlooking railway in attractive fenced garden with terrace and play area, handy for Monkey World and Tank Museum, pleasant village *(Gloria Bax)*

YETMINSTER [ST5910]

White Hart DT9 6LF [High St]: Lots of nooks and crannies in comfortable low-beamed stone and thatched village pub with real ales, proper pub food, friendly staff and locals; well behaved children allowed, tables on back terrace, garden with play area *(Paul and Annette Hallett, OPUS)*

If you report on a pub that's not a main entry, please tell us any lunchtimes or evenings when it doesn't serve bar food.

Essex

Essex includes quite a mix of pubs, many of them still rather traditional in a plush, rather than unspoilt sort of way. The Queens Head at Fyfield, run by enthusiastic young licensees, is a cheerful bustling all-rounder that represents the best of this sort of place. That's not to say there aren't charmingly unspoilt places: the friendly Viper at Mill Green is a lovely old country pub, and the Crown at Little Walden, with its two or three beers tapped straight from the cask, represents simplicity at its best – both serve good value tasty food. Three new entries show rather different approaches. Back in the *Guide* after a longish break, the Rose at Peldon combines a real sense of antiquity in its rambling bar with fresh modernity in its attractive conservatory; creative food using local supplies, good wines, nice bedrooms. The Henny Swan tucked away by the river at Great Henny is a stylish dining pub, also with good imaginative food. And the Cricketers Arms at Rickling Green, reopened a couple of years ago under new management, injects up-to-date comfort and style into its handsome Elizabethan framework, with rewarding food and good bedrooms. All three newcomers gain Food Awards. Another Cricketers, the one at Clavering, is also a front-runner in the Essex pub food stakes, as is the Sun at Dedham. However, it's one of the new entries, the Henny Swan at Great Henny, which takes the top prize of Essex Dining Pub of the Year. Pubs in the Lucky Dip section at the end of the chapter to note particularly are the Black Bull at Fyfield, Swan at Little Totham, restauranty Thorn at Mistley, Plough at Radwinter and Fleur de Lys at Widdington. Drinks prices in the county are perhaps a fraction higher than the national norm. Greene King is the dominant brewer in Essex pubs (and has now bought and closed the smaller-scale local rival Ridleys); beers from small local brewers such as Nethergate, Crouch Vale and Mighty Oak can be found fairly frequently, and Adnams from nearby Suffolk is quite common here.

BIRCHANGER TL5022 Map 5

Three Willows

Under a mile from M11 junction 8: A120 towards Bishops Stortford, then almost immediately right to Birchanger Village; don't be waylaid earlier by the Birchanger Services signpost! CM23 5QR

The name of this pub refers to the wood used to make cricket bats, and the spacious, carpeted main bar is full of cricketing prints, photographs, cartoons and other memorabilia. A small public bar has pool and sensibly placed darts, and there's a fruit machine. Friendly attentive staff serve well kept Greene King IPA and a guest on handpump, and there are decent house wines. The generously served food draws a quite crowd, so it's best to arrive early if you want to eat. Besides a wide selection of more standard bar food such as lunchtime sandwiches (from £2.50), filled baked potatoes (from £3.50), ploughman's (£4.95), chilli (£5.95) and other dishes such as steak and ale pie or vegetable curry (£8.95), and steaks (from £10.95), you can choose from a list of about 12 deliciously fresh simply cooked fish specials (served with chunky chips and plain salads) such as crab salad (£7.95), haddock (£8.95), and monkfish cutlets (£10.95); desserts (£3.90). Booking is a good idea if you want to eat in the no smoking restaurant. There are picnic-sets out on a terrace (with heaters) and on the lawn behind, which also has a sturdy climbing frame, swings and a basketball hoop (you can hear the motorway out here). *(Recommended by Edward and Deanna Pearce, Mrs Margo Finlay, Jörg Kasprowski, KC, Stephen and Jean Curtis, Dave Lowe, George Atkinson, Eric Robinson, Jacqueline Pratt, Mrs Hazel Rainer, Charles Gysin, Neil Marshall, Peter and Jean Dowson, B N F and M Parkin)*

Greene King ~ Tenants Paul and David Tucker ~ Real ale ~ Bar food (12-2, 6-9.30, not Sun evening) ~ Restaurant ~ (01279) 815913 ~ Open 11.30-3, 6-11; 12-3, 7-10.30 Sun

BURNHAM-ON-CROUCH   TQ9596   Map 5
White Harte
The Quay; CM0 8AS

It's worth popping into this cosy old-fashioned hotel, which sits right by the water's edge, to take in the views from the garden of the yacht-filled River Crouch. A summer's evening can bring few better sounds than that of the water lapping against their private jetty. Inside, the relaxed partly carpeted bars (cushioned seats around oak tables) carry assorted nautical bric-a-brac and hardware, from models of Royal Navy ships, to a ship's wheel and a barometer, to a compass set in the hearth. The other traditionally furnished high-ceilinged rooms have sea pictures on panelled or stripped brick walls, and one room is no smoking. An enormous log fire makes it cosy in winter. Adnams and Crouch Vale Best are well kept on handpump. Bar food includes steak and kidney pie, lasagne or baked lamb chops (£6.80) or fried skate or cod (£9.80). *(Recommended by John Wooll, OPUS, Keith and Chris O'Neill, Ian Phillips)*

Free house ~ Licensee G John Lewis ~ Real ale ~ Bar food ~ Restaurant ~ (01621) 782106 ~ Children welcome ~ Dogs welcome ~ Open 11-11; 12-8.30 Sun ~ Bedrooms: £19.80(£56B)/£45(£74B)

CASTLE HEDINGHAM   TL7835   Map 5
Bell ㉕
B1058 E of Sible Hedingham, towards Sudbury; CO9 3EJ

This interesting old coaching inn has changed little in the 36 years that it's been run by the same welcoming family. The beamed and timbered saloon bar is furnished with Jacobean-style seats and windsor chairs around sturdy oak tables, and beyond standing timbers left from a knocked-through wall, steps lead up to an unusual little gallery. Behind the traditionally equipped public bar, a games room has dominoes, cribbage, shove-ha'penny and other board games; piped music. Each of the rooms has a warming log fire, and one bar is no smoking; look out for Portia, the sociable german pointer. During their mid-July beer festival they bring in around 15 real ales, but the rest of the year you'll find well kept Adnams, Greene King IPA and Mighty Oak Oscar Wilde Mild, along with a guest or two such as Downton Chimera Gold and Unicorn Old Stockport, tapped from the cask, and they stock a good selection of malts. Tasty, good value bar food includes home-made soup (£3.50), black olive, red bean and chilli pâté (£4.50), ploughman's (£6), sausage and mash (£6.95), coq au vin or steak and ale or fish pie (£8.95), daily specials such as chicken, green pepper and tomato casserole or turkish lamb casserole, and puddings such as vanilla and poppyseed cheesecake (£4.25). Dogs are welcome but you must phone first. A delightful big walled garden is a special highlight with an acre or so of grass, trees and shrubs, as well as toys for children, and there are more seats on a vine-covered terrace. More reports please. *(Recommended by Ian Phillips, David Randall)*

Grays ~ Tenants Penny Doe and Kylie Turkoz-Ferguson ~ Real ale ~ Bar food (12-2(2.30 Sat, Sun), 7-9.30(9 Sun, Mon)) ~ (01787) 460350 ~ Children welcome ~ Dogs welcome ~ Live music Fri evening and last Sun in month ~ Open 11.45-3, 6-11; 11.45-12 Fri; 12-11.30(11 Sun) Sat

---

Pubs with attractive or unusually big gardens are listed at the back of the book.

CHAPPEL   TL8927   Map 5

Swan

Wakes Colne; pub visible just off A1124 Colchester—Halstead; CO6 2DD

The low-beamed rambling bar at this spacious old pub has standing oak timbers dividing off side areas, plenty of dark wood chairs around lots of dark tables for diners, a couple of swan pictures and plates on the white and partly panelled walls, and a few attractive tiles above the very big fireplace. The central bar area keeps a pubbier atmosphere, with regulars dropping in for a drink; fruit machine, cribbage, dominoes and piped music. The restaurant and one of the lounge bars are no smoking. As well as just under two dozen malt whiskies they keep Greene King IPA and Abbot and a guest on handpump. The menu features a good range of fresh fish, served in generous helpings, including fried squid (£3.95), grilled sardines (£4.50), scallops grilled with bacon (£6.95; large £13.95), fried rock eel (£9.45, large £13.95), haddock (£9.45, large £13.45), skate (£9.95, large £13.95) and specials such as fried tuna with garlic mushrooms or grilled lemon sole (from £13.95). Other bar food includes parma ham and melon (£6.45), sweet and sour chicken (£7.45), calves liver and bacon (£10.45) and sirloin steak (£12.45), with home-made puddings such as sticky toffee pudding (£3.95). The River Colne runs through the garden from where you can see a splendid Victorian viaduct. Flower tubs and french street signs lend the suntrap cobbled courtyard a continental feel, and gas heaters mean that even on cooler evenings, you can sit outside. The Railway Centre (a must for train buffs) is only a few minutes' walk away. More reports please. (Recommended by Michael Butler, Marion and Bill Cross, Colin and Dot Savill, Matthew Eglise, Richard Siebert, Charles Gysin, Mrs P J Pearce)

Free house ~ Licensee Terence Martin ~ Real ale ~ Bar food (12-2.30, 6.30-10; 12-3, 6.30-9.30 Sun) ~ Restaurant ~ (01787) 222353 ~ Children welcome away from bar ~ Dogs allowed in bar ~ Open 11-3, 6-11; 11-11 Sat; 12-10.30 Sun

CHELMSFORD   TL7006   Map 5

Alma ♀

Arbour Lane, off B1137 (Springfield Road); CM1 7RG

Since the last edition, this town centre dining pub has been completely refurbished in a more contemporary style. Cream walls give a bright airy feel, with warm orange blinds, two open fires, a trompe l'oeil fireplace, flagstoned flooring, candle-topped dark wood tables, leather sofas and comfortable dining chairs keep it inviting. The more formal no smoking restaurant now has a very sophisticated feel. They serve decent wines (with 11 by the glass), as well as Greene King IPA, Shepherd Neame Spitfire and a guest such as Marstons Pedigree on handpump; piped music. Bar food includes soup (£4.50), lunchtime ciabattas (£5.95), sausage and mash (£7.95), beef and Guinness pie (£8.95), fish pie (£9.95), and there's a less pubby restaurant menu; Sunday roast. You can sit on the newly smartened up terrace at the front, or in a small secluded enclosed garden at the back. (Recommended by Sheila Robinson-Baker, Mr Taylor, Ian Phillips, Sam and Christine Kilburn)

Free house ~ Licensees David and Sheila Hunt ~ Real ale ~ Bar food (12-2.30, 6-9.30; 12-8 Sun) ~ Restaurant ~ (01245) 256783 ~ Children in restaurant ~ Open 11am-11.30pm(12 Sat); 12-10.30 Sun

CLAVERING   TL4731   Map 5

Cricketers 🍴 🛏

B1038 Newport—Buntingford, Newport end of village; CB11 4QT

The main draw at this comfortably modernised and immaculately kept 16th-c dining pub is the delicious food. From a seasonally changing menu, there might be soup (£4), lamb samosas with mango chutney and cucumber and caraway yoghurt (£5.75), mussel and eel fillet salad (£6.50), salmon and dill filo pastry tart with roasted red peppers (£6.25), braised oxtail (£12.75), fresh herb risotto with roast spring vegetables (£13.50), medallions of pork with paprika, tomato, olive and caper sauce (£14), grilled halibut on kedgeree rice with creamy curry sauce (£16.50), half roast duck with orange marmalade sauce (£17.50), and puddings such as caramelised orange and lemon tart with marinated orange salad or pannetone bread and butter pudding (£5). The roomy L-shaped beamed bar is very traditional, in appearance at least, with standing timbers resting on new brickwork, and pale green plush button-backed banquettes, stools and windsor chairs around shiny wooden tables on a pale green carpet, gleaming copper pans and horsebrasses, dried flowers in the big fireplace (open fire in colder weather), and fresh flowers on the tables; the restaurant and most of the bar are no smoking; piped music. Greene King IPA and a couple of guests, maybe from Adnams, are well kept on handpump, and they've decent wines (13 by the glass) and freshly squeezed juices. It can get very busy, which perhaps explains why one or two readers found the service to be a little cold and businesslike. The attractive front terrace has picnic-sets and umbrellas among colourful flowering shrubs. The no smoking bedrooms are in the adjacent cottage. The pub is run by the parents of Jamie Oliver, and signed copies of his cookbook are on sale. *(Recommended by Paul Humphreys, Dr and Mrs A K Clarke, Les and Sandra Brown, Mrs Margo Finlay, Jörg Kasprowski, Roy and Lindsey Fentiman, John Saville, Martin and Karen Wake, John and Enid Morris, Alex and Irene Harvey)*

Free house ~ Licensee Trevor Oliver ~ Real ale ~ Bar food (12-2, 7-10) ~ Restaurant ~ (01799) 550442 ~ Children welcome ~ Open 10.30-11 ~ Bedrooms: £70B/£100B

DEDHAM   TM0533   Map 5

Sun

High Street (B2109); CO7 6DF

Stylishly simple décor allows the structure of this handsome Tudor inn to speak for itself – indeed carefully observed quality rather than elaboration seems to be the thing here, throughout. The main draw is probably the robustly flavoured cooking, which focuses on top notch locally sourced incredients rather than complicated cooking. The daily changing menu might include chickpea, tomato and sage soup (£4.50), cheese platter (£7.50), squid and mussel linguini (£9), roast pork chop with sage, white wine, garlic and milk and grilled polenta or lamb stew (£12.50), poached skate wing with peas, fennel and salsa verde (£15), and puddings such as rhubarb and custard trifle or a very tasty molten chocolate pudding (£4.50); children's helpings are available, and young staff offer friendly relaxed but efficient service. Adnams Broadside and Crouch Vale Brewers Gold are well kept on handpump alongside a couple of guests from brewers such as Oakham and Phoenix, and they've a very good selection of more than 60 wines (30 by the glass) and some interesting soft drinks. A window seat in the bar looks across to the church which is at least glimpsed in several of Constable's paintings. Elsewhere you'll find high carved beams, squared panelling, wall timbers and big log fires in splendid fireplaces. A variety of seats takes in high settles and easy chairs. The entire pub is no smoking apart from the Oak Room; maybe piped music, cribbage, dominoes and board games. On the way out to picnic-sets on the quiet and attractive back lawn, notice the unusual covered back staircase, with what used to be a dovecote on top. If you have time, beautiful walks into the heart of Constable country lead out of the village, over water meadows towards Flatford Mill. The panelled bedrooms are nicely done and have abundant character; we would welcome reports from any readers who have stayed here. *(Recommended by Tim Wellock, Robert and Susan Phillips, Trevor and Sheila Sharman, Peter Guy, Jill Franklin, Peter and Margaret Glenister, N R White, Marion and Bill Cross, John Saville, Pam and David Bailey, J and D Boutwood, Simon Cleasby, Adrian White)*

Free house ~ Licensee Piers Baker ~ Real ale ~ Bar food (12-2.30(3 Sat and Sun), 6.30-9.30) ~ Restaurant ~ (01206) 323351 ~ Children welcome ~ Dogs allowed in bar ~ Open 12-11(6 Sun) ~ Bedrooms: £60B/£120B

If we know a pub has an outdoor play area for children, we mention it.

FINGRINGHOE TM0220 Map 5

Whalebone

Follow Rowhedge, Fingringhoe signpost off A134, the part that's just S of Colchester centre; or Fingringhoe signposted off B1025 S of Colchester; CO5 7BG

Attractively redecorated since the last edition, the three airily opened-together rooms here have cream walls above aubergine dado, some timber studding, and leather dining chairs and oak and cream-painted tables on oak floors. Served by friendly staff, the tasty bar food might include roast red pepper soup or devilled lambs kidneys (£4.95), battered plaice and chips (£9.95), pork chop with stilton and walnut crust (£10.25), wild boar sausages (£10.45) or red snapper with artichoke and rocket salad (£10.95). Caledonian Deuchars and Greene King IPA are well kept alongside a couple of guests from brewers such as Archers or Mersea Island, and there are decent house wines; piped music. The rather lovely back garden, with gravel paths winding through the grass around a sizeable old larch tree, has picnic-sets with a peaceful valley view, and the newly finished front terrace has bistro-style tables and chairs with gingham parasols. The pub is no smoking throughout. *(Recommended by Bob Richardson, Tina and David Woods-Taylor, Charles Gysin, MDN, R T and J C Moggridge)*

Free house ~ Licensees Sam and Victoria Burroughes ~ Real ale ~ Bar food (10-2.30, 7-9.30(9 Sun, Mon)) ~ Restaurant ~ (01206) 729307 ~ Children welcome with restrictions ~ Dogs allowed in bar ~ Open 11-3, 5.30-11; 12-11 Sat; 12-10.30 Sun

FYFIELD TL5706 Map 5

Queens Head ♀ ◀

Corner of B184 and Queen Street; CM5 0RY

The enthusiastic young licensees at this characterful 15th-c pub generate a happy enjoyable atmosphere. Though the emphasis is mostly on the very good food, a pubby balance is maintained by their good range of real ale. Adnams Bitter and Broadside are well kept alongside four guests from brewers such as Cottage, Dark Star, Hop Back and Nethergate. They've also Weston's Old Rosie farm cider, and good wines by the glass including champagne – most of the pictures have a humorous wine theme, including a series of Ronald Searle cartoons. But it's mainly the generously served well prepared food that draws the bustling crowd. Besides good lunchtime sandwiches (from £3.25, toasted baguettes £4.50), and baked potatoes or ploughman's (£6.25), dishes from the daily changing menu might include soup (£4.25), asparagus with smoked salmon (£6), fennel cooked in cream with mozzarella and herb crust (£8.95), steak and kidney pie (£9.95), smoked haddock on chive mash (£11.50), roast garlic rack of lamb (£13.95) or fillet steak (£15.95). The low-beamed, compact L-shaped bar has some exposed timbers in the terracotta-coloured walls, fresh flowers and pretty lamps on its nice sturdy elm tables, and comfortable seating, from button-back wall banquettes to attractive and unusual high-backed chairs, some in a snug little side booth. Two facing log fireplaces have lighted church candles instead in summer; the licensees have a cat and two dogs; piped music. At the back, a neat little prettily planted garden by a weeping willow has a teak bench and half a dozen picnic-sets under canvas parasols, and beyond a picket fence, the sleepy River Roding flowing past. *(Recommended by Mr and Mrs C F Turner, Lucy Moulder, Richard Siebert, David Twitchett, Dave Lowe, Reg Fowle, Helen Rickwood, H O Dickinson)*

Free house ~ Licensees Daniel Lemprecht and Penny Miers ~ Real ale ~ Bar food (12-2.30, 7-9.30; not Sun evenings) ~ Restaurant ~ (01277) 899231 ~ Open 11-3.30, 6-11; 12-3.30, 7-10.30 Sun

GOSFIELD TL7829 Map 5

Green Man ♀

3 miles N of Braintree; CO9 1TP

The help-yourself cold buffet table (lunchtimes March-December) makes a change at this traditional dining pub: you can choose from home-cooked ham and pork, turkey, tongue, beef and poached or smoked salmon, as well as game pie, salads and home-made pickles (from £7.95). If you want something hot, big helpings from a mostly traditional english menu include breaded tiger prawns with sweet chilli dip (£4.95), duck and brandy pâté (£5.25), toad in the hole or cottage pie (£7.95) and casserole of the day, fried halibut or seafood bake (£8.95). A happy relaxed atmosphere is generated by friendly staff and licensees, and the two little oak beamed bars, one with an inglenook fireplace, feel warmly welcoming. Many of the decent nicely priced wines are available by the glass, and they've very well kept Greene King IPA and Abbot on handpump. The main bar and restaurant are no smoking; piped music; garden. *(Recommended by David Twitchett, Mrs J M Joyce, David J Bunter, Ian Phillips, Richard Siebert)*

Greene King ~ Tenants Debbie With and Tony Bowen ~ Real ale ~ Bar food ~ Restaurant ~ (01787) 472746 ~ Children welcome with restrictions ~ Dogs allowed in bar ~ Open 11-3, 6-11; 12-4.40 Sun; closed Sun evening; closed Mon evening in winter

GREAT HENNY   TL8738   Map 5
Henny Swan 🍴 ♀

Henny Street, signposted off A131 at traffic lights just SW of Sudbury, at the bottom of Ballingdon Hill; OS Sheet 155 map reference 879384; CO10 7LS

Essex Dining Pub of the Year

Now a stylish dining pub, this peaceful riverside former barge-house has come a long way from the simple country tavern we used to know it as, some 25 years ago. The smallish L-shaped contemporary bar has soft leather settees, armchairs and drum stools, with carefully lit big bright modern prints contrasting with its stripped beams and dark walls, a woodburning stove in a big brick fireplace, Adnams and Greene King IPA on handpump, good coffee, and a fine choice of wines by the glass including a champagne and a pudding wine. They do a good jug of Pimms. The restaurant is bigger, bright and airy – thanks to french windows along two walls. It has comfortable rather elegant modern dining chairs and tables well spaced on polished oak boards, more modern artwork, and another woodburning stove. Good food includes lunchtime baguettes (from £2.75) and changing bar specials such as deep-fried king prawns with an oriental dip (£5.50), haddock (£9.95) and lamb kleftiko (£13.50), or from the restaurant menu soup (£3.95), grilled haloumi cheese in parma ham (£4.95), duck liver pâté or salmon and smoked salmon fishcakes with sweet chilli dip (£5.25), spinach and feta filo parcels with roasted tomato sauce (£9.25), seared salmon (£11.50), 8oz rump steak (£12.95), and roast lamb rump (£13.95), with puddings including ice-creams (£4.25) and pecan pie, crème brûlée or chocolate fudge brownie (£4.35). Vegetables are carefully chosen and done just right; chips are good chunky ones. The staff are warmly welcoming and attentive; disabled access and facilities. There are stylish metal tables and chairs, some under canvas parasols, out on the good-sized side terrace, with picnic-sets across the quiet lane on a large informal lawn, beside which the River Stour flows gently past the willow trees and over a low weir. In summer they have Sunday barbecues, with late afternoon jazz . *(Recommended by Rosemary McRobert, Dave and Chris Watts)*

Punch ~ Lease Harry and Sofia Charalambous ~ Real ale ~ Bar food (12-2.30, 6.30-9.30; 12-4 Sun) ~ Restaurant ~ (01787) 269238 ~ Children welcome ~ Jazz outside summer Suns late afternoon ~ Open 11-3, 6-11; 11-11 Sat; 12-10.30(12-4 in winter) Sun; cl Mon in winter

GREAT YELDHAM   TL7638   Map 5
White Hart ♀

Poole Street; A1017 Halstead—Haverhill; CO9 4HJ

Watch your head as you enter this striking old black and white timbered dining pub, the door into the bar is very low. The main areas have stone and wood floors with some dark oak panelling or cream walls and a lovely old brick fireplace. In fine weather, the attractive landscaped garden is a pleasant place to sit, with well tended lawns and pretty seating. Emphasis is very much on the food (most tables are laid for dining) which includes club sandwich, ploughman's, fish pie, pasta with creamy pesto sauce or breaded plaice (all £8.50); the restaurant is no smoking. Drinks include Adnams and one or two guests from brewers such as Black Sheep and Highgate, nine wines by the glass, a good choice of bottled beers and organic fruit juices. *(Recommended by Adele Summers, Alan Black, Michael Dandy, Marion and Bill Cross, B N F and M Parkin)*

Free house ~ Licensee Mathew Mason ~ Real ale ~ Bar food (12-3, 6-9.30) ~ Restaurant ~ (01787) 237250 ~ Children welcome ~ Jazz last Fri monthly ~ Open 11-12.30

HASTINGWOOD   TL4807   Map 5

Rainbow & Dove £

¼ mile from M11 junction 7; Hastingwood signposted after Ongar signs at exit roundabout; CM17 9JX

Three little low-beamed rooms at this 16th-c cottage-style pub open off the main bar area. The one on the left is particularly beamy, with the lower part of its wall stripped back to bare brick and decorated with brass pistols and plates. Courage Directors, Greene King IPA and a guest such as Elgoods Greyhound are well kept on handpump. Unfortunately the piped music has been a bit loud for a couple of readers; darts. As well as lunchtime sandwiches (from £2.75), bar food includes soup (£3.50), lasagne (£6.35), steak, kidney and ale pie (£6.65), mushroom and cheese ravioli with cheese and mushroom sauce (£6.75), cajun-style chicken (£8.95), daily specials such as rabbit and cider casserole (£8.95), skate wing (£9.50), and puddings such as apple pie or spotted dick (£3.50); no smoking restaurant. Hedged off from the car park, a stretch of grass has picnic-sets and you can also eat outside in front of the pub. *(Recommended by John Robertson, Adele Summers, Alan Black, Jeremy King, Ian Phillips, Bob and Margaret Holder, Anthony Longden, B N F and M Parkin, Mrs Hazel Rainer, W W Burke, H O Dickinson)*

Punch ~ Lease Andrew Keep and Kathryn Chirvall ~ Real ale ~ Bar food (12-2(3 Sun), 7-9) ~ (01279) 415419 ~ Children in restaurant till 9pm ~ Dogs allowed in bar ~ Open 11.30-3, 6-11; 12-3.30, 6-11 Sat; 12-4 Sun; closed Sun evening

HORNDON-ON-THE-HILL   TQ6683   Map 3

Bell ♀ ◼ 🛏

M25 junction 30 into A13, then left into B1007 after 7 miles, village signposted from here; SS17 8LD

The heavily beamed bar at this ancient pub maintains a strongly pubby appearance with some antique high-backed settles and benches, rugs on the flagstones or highly polished oak floorboards, and a curious collection of ossified hot cross buns hanging from a beam. They also keep a very good range of drinks, including Greene King IPA and Bass and five guests from brewers such as Archers, Crouch Vale, Shepherd Neame and Youngs (the pub holds occasional beer festivals) and over a hundred well chosen wines from all over the world, including 16 by the glass. However it's here that the pubbiness ends as the frequently changing menu (the same in the bar and restaurant) is fairly elaborate, not especially cheap, and you will need to book. There might be leek and potato soup (£4.95), beef carpaccio (£7.25), globe artichoke stuffed with wild mushrooms and poached egg (£10.50), bass with herb crust (£13.50), roast suckling pig (£13.95), venison fillet with thyme jus (£14.10) and puddings such as pecan pie with chocolate sauce or lemon tart (£5.95). Note the accommodation is a couple of hundred yards away from the pub itself. *(Recommended by R E Dixon, Andy and Jill Kassube, David and Ruth Shillitoe, Geoff and Teresa Salt, Ian Phillips, W Andrew, Tina and David Woods-Taylor, Adrian White)*

Free house ~ Licensee John Vereker ~ Real ale ~ Bar food (12-2, 6.30(7 Sun)-9.45; not bank hol Mon) ~ Restaurant ~ (01375) 642463 ~ Children in eating area of bar and restaurant ~ Dogs allowed in bar and bedrooms ~ Open 11-2.30(3 Sat), 5.30(6 Sat)-11; 12-4, 7-10.30 Sun ~ Bedrooms: /£64B

LANGHAM   TM0233   Map 5

Shepherd & Dog

Moor Road/High Street; village signposted off A12 N of Colchester; CO4 5NR

The spick and span L-shaped bar at this bustling village pub (now under a new licensee) embraces an appealing hotchpotch of styles, including engaging collections of continental bottled beers and brass and copper fire extinguishers. Bar food includes sandwiches (from £2.50), ploughman's or salads (£4.75), scampi or cod and chips (£7.95) and steak and chips (£8.95). Greene King IPA, Abbot and three seasonal beers from Greene King and Nethergate on handpump; piped music. In summer, there are very pretty window boxes, and a shaded bar in the enclosed side garden. *(Recommended by Marion and Bill Cross, Roy and Lindsey Fentiman, R E Dixon, N R White, Liz and Brian Barnard, Comus and Sarah Elliott)*

Free house ~ Licensee Sav Virdi ~ Real ale ~ Bar food (12-2.15, 6-9.30; 12-9 Sun) ~ Restaurant ~ (01206) 272711 ~ Children welcome ~ Dogs allowed in bar ~ Open 11-3, 5.30-11; 12-10.30 Sun

LITTLE BRAXTED   TL8413   Map 5

Green Man   £

Kelvedon Road; village signposted off B1389 by NE end of A12 Witham bypass – keep on patiently; OS Sheet 168 map reference 848133; CM8 3LB

The traditional little lounge at this pretty brick house has an interesting collection of bric-a-brac, including 200 horsebrasses, some harness, mugs hanging from a beam, and a lovely copper urn; it's especially cosy in winter when you'll really feel the benefit of the open fire. The tiled public bar has books, darts, cribbage and dominoes; the saloon bar is no smoking till 9.30. Welcoming staff serve two Greene King beers and a guest such as Titanic White Star. Reasonably priced bar food includes sandwiches (from £2.75), filled baguettes or baked potatoes (from £3.55), ploughman's (£5.75), cottage pie (£4.25), sausages and creamed potatoes (£4.95), lasagne (£6.95), and a couple of daily specials such as steak and ale pie (£7.95) and minted lamb shank (£8.95), while puddings might be treacle tart (£3.25); picnic sets in pleasant sheltered garden. *(Recommended by John and Bettye Reynolds, David Twitchett, Alan and Carolin Tidbury)*

Greene King ~ Tenant Neil Pharaoh ~ Real ale ~ Bar food ~ (01621) 891659 ~ Dogs allowed in bar ~ Open 11.30-3, 6-11; 12-4, 7-10.30 Sun

LITTLE WALDEN   TL5441   Map 5

Crown

B1052 N of Saffron Walden; CB10 1XA

In winter months the cosy low-beamed bar at this friendly white 18th-c country cottage is cosily welcoming with two blazing log fires in brick fireplaces. Bookroom-red walls, flowery curtains and a mix of bare boards and navy carpeting add to the homely snugness. Seats ranging from high-backed pews to little cushioned armchairs are spaced around a good variety of closely arranged tables, mostly big, some stripped. The small red-tiled room on the right has two little tables; piped local radio. City of Cambridge Boathouse, Greene King IPA and possibly a guest are tapped straight from casks racked up behind the bar. Hearty bar food is popular, so you may need to book at weekends: sandwiches (from £3.50), soup (£3.95), ploughman's (from £6.25) and steak and ale pie (£7.95), with blackboard specials such as vegetable curry (£7.95), smoked haddock mornay (£8.25), home-made lasagne or chicken cacciatore (£8.95), cold seafood platter (£9.75) and beef stroganoff (£10.25); puddings might be tasty apple crumble or bread and butter pudding (from £4.25). There is a no smoking restaurant, and in summer you can eat outside at tables on the terrace, whilst taking in the tranquil countryside. *(Recommended by Mrs Margo Finlay, Jörg Kasprowski, the Didler, Ken Millar, Dave Lowe, Eric Robinson, Jacqueline Pratt, Colin and Penny Smith)*

Free house ~ Licensee Colin Hayling ~ Real ale ~ Bar food (not Sun or Mon evening) ~
Restaurant ~ (01799) 522475 ~ Children welcome with restrictions ~ Dogs allowed in bar
~ Trad jazz Weds evening ~ Open 11.30-3, 6-11; 12-10.30 Sun

MILL GREEN   TL6401   Map 5

Viper 🍺 £

**The Common; from Fryerning (which is signposted off north-east bound A12
Ingatestone bypass) follow Writtle signposts; CM4 0PT**

They have an interesting range of five well kept beers on handpump at this lovely
old local, which is quietly tucked away in the woods. As well as Viper (produced
for the pub by Nethergate), and local microbrewery Mighty Oak Hissed Off and
Jake the Snake, a couple of quickly changing guests might be from thoughtfully
sourced brewers such as Nethergate and RCH. And they have Wilkins' farm cider
too, straight from the barrel. The two timeless cosy lounge rooms have spindleback
seats, armed country kitchen chairs, and tapestried wall seats around neat little old
tables, and there's a log fire. Booted walkers are directed towards the fairly basic
parquet-floored tap room, which is more simply furnished with shiny wooden
traditional wall seats, and beyond that another room has country kitchen chairs
and sensibly placed darts; shove-ha'penny, dominoes, cribbage. There's an easy-
going welcoming atmosphere, and it's the kind of place where you're quite likely to
fall into casual conversation with the sociable locals or welcoming licensee; the
friendly pub cats are Molly and Millie. Simple but tasty bar snacks might include
sandwiches (from £3.25), home-made soup (£3.50), ploughman's (from £4.95),
chicken and leek pie or steak and ale pie (£5.95), puddings (£3) and the tasty bread
comes from a local baker a mile or so down the road; Sunday roast (£7.95), and
they do a popular barbecue at summer weekends. Tables on the lawn overlook a
beautifully tended cottage garden which is a dazzling mass of colour in summer,
further enhanced at the front by overflowing hanging baskets and window boxes.
*(Recommended by Andy and Jill Kassube, Bob Richardson, Sally and Mark Bramall, the Didler,
David Twitchett, Pete Baker, Dave Lowe, Richard Pitcher, Daniel Myers, Ian Phillips)*

Free house ~ Licensee Donna Torris ~ Real ale ~ Bar food (12-2(3 Sat, Sun); not
evenings) ~ No credit cards ~ (01277) 352010 ~ Dogs allowed in bar ~ Open 12-3, 6-11;
12-11 Sat; 12-10.30 Sun

PAGLESHAM   TQ9293   Map 5

Punchbowl

**Church End; from the Paglesham road out of Rochford, Church End is signposted on
the left; SS4 2DP**

The cosy beamed bar at this secluded white weatherboarded pub is traditional, with
exposed brick walls, low beams, pews, barrel chairs and other seats, and lots of
pictures and memorabilia. In winter, a woodburner warms its darker corners. A
lower room is laid out for dining. Besides Adnams, a couple of guests might be
from brewers such as Cottage or Nethergate; cribbage, shove-ha'penny, darts, and
piped music playing mostly 1960s and 70s classic hits. Straightforward but fairly
priced bar food includes rolls, sandwiches and filled baguettes (from £2.95), soup
(£3.25), filled baked potatoes (£4.50) and ploughman's (£4.95), with daily specials
such as skate (£7.50), mild lamb curry (£7.95) and rump steak (from £10.50);
puddings (from £3.50); the restaurant is no smoking. Be warned that they
sometimes close a few minutes early at lunchtime during the week. More reports
please, particularly on the food. Tables in the little front garden take in a lovely
rural view. *(Recommended by George Atkinson)*

Free house ~ Licensees Bernie and Pat Cardy ~ Real ale ~ Bar food ~ Restaurant ~
(01702) 258376 ~ Children welcome with restrictions ~ Open 11.30(12 Sun)-3,
6.30-11(10.30 Sun, Mon)

If we know a pub does summer barbecues, we say so.

PELDON TM0015 Map 5

Rose ⊕ ♈ ⇌

B1025 Colchester—Mersea; CO5 7QJ

This lovely old pastel-washed inn is held by the family-owned Essex wine merchant Lay & Wheeler, so not surprisingly they have a very good wine list, with about 25 by the glass, listed with helpful descriptions on a blackboard. Helpful staff also serve Adnams Best and Broadside, Greene King IPA and a weekly guest, often interesting, such as Springhead Charlies Angel. The rambling bar areas feel nice and traditional with standing timbers supporting the heavy low ceilings with their dark bowed 17th-c oak beams, alcoves that conjure up smugglers discussing bygone contraband, little leaded-light windows, and brass and copper on the mantelpiece of a gothick-arched brick fireplace. There are creaky close-set tables, and some antique mahogany and padded wall banquetes. The very spacious airy conservatory dining area, with views over the garden, has a much more modern feel, and is no smoking. Changing bar food, home-made and where possible using locally sourced ingredients, is popular, and might include parma ham, asparagus and parmesan salad (£5.25), cornish dressed crab (£6.75), half a dozen rock oysters (£8.25), pea, broad bean and asparagus risotto (£8.25), chicken cordon bleu with tomato coulis (£9.95), lamb chop with rosemary jus or confit of duck on chinese vegetables with hoi sin (£10.95), black bream with chilli, ginger and coriander baked in a banana leaf (£12.75), and puddings such as treacle tart with ice-cream or coconut and raspberry fool with shortbread biscuit (£4.25). Staff are friendly and efficient, though as it does get very busy you may need to book. The spacious garden is very relaxing, with good teak seats and a nice pond with white ducks. *(Recommended by Richard C Morgan, John Wooll, Ken Millar, Janice and Phil Waller)*

Lay & Wheeler ~ Licensee Craig Formoy ~ Real ale ~ Bar food (12-2.15(6 Sun), 6.30-9.30) ~ (01206) 735248 ~ Children welcome away from bar ~ Open 11-11; 12-7; cl evening Sun ~ Bedrooms: £40B/£60B

PLESHEY TL6614 Map 5

White Horse ♈

The Street; CM3 1HA

Nooks and crannies at this friendly feeling 15th-c pub are hugely cluttered with jugs, tankards, antlers, miscellaneous brass, prints, books, bottles and an old ship's bell. It even has its own little art gallery, with works by local artists, and sells crafts. Furnishings take in wheelback and other chairs and tables with cloths, and a fireplace has an unusual curtain-like fireguard. A snug room by the tiny bar counter has brick and beamed walls, a comfortable sofa, some bar stools and a table with magazines to read. Youngs Best and maybe a Youngs guest are swiftly served by helpful staff, and they've a dozen wines by the glass; piped music. At lunchtime you can choose from enjoyable home-made bar snacks such as toasted sandwiches (from £3.50), tasty herring roes fried in butter or prawn cocktail (£5.25), ploughman's (£6), smoked ham and eggs (£6.75), cottage pie or home-made lasagne (£6.95) and steak and kidney pie or fried plaice (£8.50), or you can eat from the more elaborate lunchtime and evening à la carte menu, which includes dishes such as smoked salmon salad (£5.50), pork escalope or duckling casserole (£9.75), roast rack of lamb (£14.75). Puddings might include home-made fruit crumble or apple and spice pie (£3.75); two-course set Sunday lunchtime menu (£11). Glass cabinets in the big sturdily furnished no smoking dining room are filled with lots of miniatures and silverware, and there are flowers on tables. Doors from here open on to a terrace and a grass area with trees, shrubs and tables. The pub hosts various events, including jazz buffets and barbecues. More reports please. *(Recommended by Richard Siebert, Tina and David Woods-Taylor, Sharon and Alan Corper, Paul and Ursula Randall)*

Free house ~ Licensees Mike and Jan Smail ~ Real ale ~ Bar food (12-5 Sun) ~ Restaurant ~ (01245) 237281 ~ Children welcome with restrictions ~ Dogs allowed in bar ~ Open 11.30-3, 6.30-11; 12-5 Sun; closed Mon-Weds evening and Sun evening

RICKLING GREEN   TL5129   Map 5
Cricketers Arms 🍴 🛏️
Just off B1383 N of Stansted Mountfichet; CB11 3YG

Refurbished with fresh clean lines a couple of years ago, this Elizabethan timbered
pub is agreeably relaxed with leather sofas and stripped pine trunks as coffee tables
on stone floors, an open fire, a handful of carefully selected prints on cream walls,
thoughtful lighting and modern stools at the counter. Greene King IPA, Jennings
Cumberland and a guest are racked behind the bar and tapped straight from the
cask, and they keep around eight wines by the glass. You can eat in the bar but they
encourage you to eat in one of the two smallish restaurants, which are gently
contemporary with softly coloured walls and solid uniform wood tables and chairs
on well finished (if slightly clattery) new wooden floors. Imaginative well presented
food from a changing menu might include lunchtime steak baguette (£6.95), baked
onion stuffed with mozzarella and beetroot with grated horseradish on rocket (£5),
crispy fried pigeon breast on polenta crackers with creamy chestnut and spring
onion reduction (£6), niçoise salad (£8.75), a boerewors (south african sausage),
toulouse and wild boar sausage with dijon mustard mash and red wine sauce
(£9.50), butternut purée risotto with tempura courgette flowers (£12), rosemary
and garlic lamb shank with spiced apple and red cabbage and potato croquette
(£13.95), fried bass with pak choi, sesame and ginger (£15.25), and prettily
arranged puddings such as apple and mixed berry crumble with crème anglaise or
baked rice pudding with honey cherry ragoût (from £5.25), and cheese platter with
quince jelly (£7.95). Staff are cheerfully welcoming and efficient; piped music.
Outside on a newly decked area, trellis screening and clusters of plants in pots
partition off private little areas which are set out with wood and metal tables and
chairs. Readers flying from Stansted have found this a useful place to stay.
*(Recommended by Mrs Roxanne Chamberlain, Grahame Brooks, Les and Sandra Brown,
Michael and Maggie Betton, Dr and Mrs D A Blackadder, Charles Gysin)*

Punch ~ Lease Barry Hilton ~ Real ale ~ Bar food (12-2.30, 7-9.30) ~ Restaurant ~
(01799) 543210 ~ Children welcome ~ Dogs allowed in bar ~ Open 11-12 ~ Bedrooms:
£95B/£65B

STAPLEFORD TAWNEY   TL5001   Map 5
Mole Trap 🍺
Tawney Common, which is a couple of miles away from Stapleford Tawney and is
signposted off A113 just N of M25 overpass – keep on; OS Sheet 167 map reference
500013; CM16 7PU

It's worth getting here early for a table as this isolated country pub fills up with an
older set weekday lunchtimes, and at the weekend their Sunday roast (£8.95) draws
quite a crowd too. Besides sandwiches (from £3.25, baguettes from £4), bar food
includes ploughman's (£5.25), lasagne, lamb curry and chilli (all £7.95), steak or
fresh daily fish such as plaice, cod or salmon (all £9.95), and puddings such as
crumbles or bakewell tart (£3.50). The smallish carpeted bar (mind your head as
you go in) has black dado, beams and joists, brocaded wall seats, library chairs and
bentwood elbow chairs around plain pub tables, and steps down through a partly
knocked-out timber stud wall to a similar area. There are a few small pictures, 3-D
decorative plates, some dried-flower arrangements and (on the sloping ceiling
formed by a staircase beyond) some regulars' snapshots, with a few dozen beermats
stuck up around the serving bar. It's especially cosy in winter, when you can fully
appreciate the three blazing coal fires. As well as Fullers London Pride on
handpump, they have three constantly changing guests from brewers such as Moles,
Moorhouses and Timothy Taylor; organic soft drinks; piped radio; one area is no
smoking. Outside are some plastic tables and chairs and a picnic-set, and a happy
tribe of resident animals, many rescued, including friendly cats, rabbits, a couple of
dogs, hens, geese, a sheep, goats and horses. The pub is run with considerable
individuality by forthright licensees and we have heard from a couple of readers
that food service on Sunday has ended earlier than times stated. Do make sure

children behave well here if you bring them, and note that they don't accept cheques or credit cards. *(Recommended by Evelyn and Derek Walter, the Didler, David Twitchett, Mrs Ann Gray, N R White, H O Dickinson)*

Free house ~ Licensees Mr and Mrs Kirtley ~ Real ale ~ Bar food (till 3 Sun, not Sun and Mon evening) ~ No credit cards ~ (01992) 522394 ~ Seated children welcome away from bar area ~ Open 11.30-2.30, 6-11; 12-4, 6.30-10.30 Sun

STOCK   TQ6998   Map 5

Hoop ☜

B1007; from A12 Chelmsford bypass take Galleywood, Billericay turn-off; CM4 9BD

They keep an interesting range of up to seven guest ales at this white weatherboarded inn. These might be from brewers such as Hampshire, St Peters, Tring and Youngs, and are well kept alongside Adnams, ten wines by the glass, farmhouse ciders and mulled wine in winter. Standing timbers and beams in the open plan bustling bar indicate the building's age and original layout as a row of three weavers' cottages. Stripped floors, a big brick fireplace, brocaded settles and stools and dark wood tables keep it feeling pubby. The airy restaurant (upstairs in the timbered eaves) and back bar are no smoking. Tasty bar food includes bread and olives (£2.95), tomato and pancetta bruschetta (£4.50), ploughman's or honey roast ham (£7.50), scampi (£7.50), spinach and garlic linguini with stilton (£9.95), tuna steak with braised octopus and chick pea sauté (£12.50), and puddings such as mango rice pudding or dark chocolate fondant (from £4.50). Prettily bordered with flowers, the large sheltered back garden has picnic-sets and a covered seating area. *(Recommended by Ian Phillips, John and Enid Morris, R T and J C Moggridge, Clare Rosier)*

Free house ~ Licensee Amanda Fenwick ~ Real ale ~ Bar food (12-2.30, 6-9(9.30 Fri, Sat); 12-7 Sun) ~ Restaurant ~ (01277) 841137 ~ Children welcome in back bar and restaurant ~ Dogs allowed in bar ~ Open 11-11(1 Fri, 12 Sat); 12-10.30 Sun

STOW MARIES   TQ8399   Map 5

Prince of Wales ☜

B1012 between S Woodham Ferrers and Cold Norton Posters; CM3 6SA

The chatty low-ceilinged rooms at this appealingly laid-back pub appear unchanged since the turn of the last century. Few have space for more than one or two tables or wall benches on their tiled or bare-boards floors, though the room in the middle squeezes in quite a jumble of chairs and stools. As well as five interesting, frequently changing real ales on handpump from brewers such as Dark Star, Deuchars and Hopback, you'll also find bottled and draught belgian beers, several bottled fruit beers and farm cider too. Besides sandwiches or ciabattas (from £3.95), enjoyable, generously served dishes (with good fish specials) could include ham, egg and chips (£5.95), sausage and mash (£7.95), beer-battered cod with mushy peas (£8.95), lamb shank with raspberry beer and mash (£9.75), sirloin steak (£11.25), and puddings such as sticky toffee pudding (£3.50); the restaurant and part of the bar area are no smoking. On Thursday evenings in winter they fire up the old bread oven to make pizzas in the room that used to be the village bakery (from £5.95), and on some summer Sundays, they barbecue steaks and unusual fish such as saupe, mahi-mahi and black barracuda. There are seats and tables in the back garden, and between the picket fence and the pub's white weatherboarded frontage is a terrace, with herbs in Victorian chimneypots, sheltered by a huge umbrella. There are live bands on most bank holidays and some Sundays. *(Recommended by Nick Lawless, David Twitchett, Reg Fowle, Helen Rickwood, Ian Phillips, Derek Thomas, Adrian White)*

Free house ~ Licensee Rob Walster ~ Real ale ~ Bar food (12-2.30, 6.30-9.30, 12-9.30 Sat, Sun) ~ Restaurant ~ No credit cards ~ (01621) 828971 ~ Children in family room ~ Dogs allowed in bar ~ Occasional live music ~ Open 11-11; 12-10.30 Sun

---

If you know a pub's ever open all day, please tell us.

YOUNGS END   TL7319   Map 5
Green Dragon

Former A131 Braintree—Chelmsford (off new bypass), just N of Essex Showground;
CM77 8QN

The two bars at this pleasant dining pub have cheery yellow walls and ordinary pub
furnishings, and there's an extra low-ceilinged snug just beside the serving counter.
Greene King Abbot, IPA and Old Speckled Hen and a guest such as Titanic White
Star are well kept on handpump; unobtrusive piped jazz; several no smoking areas.
Lunchtime dishes might include sandwiches (from £2.25, baguettes from £3.50),
home-made soup (£3.75), cottage pie (£5.65), ploughman's (£5.95), ham and eggs
(£7.95) and curry (£8.95), with other dishes such as faggots and gravy (£8.75),
battered cod and mushy peas (£9.50), venison casserole with dumplings (£11.50),
roast monkfish and pancetta (£14.25), and puddings (£4). A lawn at the back has
lots of picnic-sets under cocktail parasols, a terrace with outdoor heaters, and a
budgerigar aviary. (Recommended by Ian Phillips, Evelyn and Derek Walter, Paul and Ursula
Randall, Mrs Margo Finlay, Jörg Kasprowski, Roy and Lindsey Fentiman, Adrian White)

Greene King ~ Lease Bob and Mandy Greybrook ~ Real ale ~ Bar food (12-2.30, 6-9.30) ~
Restaurant ~ (01245) 361030 ~ Children welcome till 8pm ~ Open 12-3, 5.30-11; 12-11
Sun

LUCKY DIP

Besides the fully inspected pubs, you might like to try these Lucky Dips recommended to
us and described by readers (if you do, please send us reports: www.goodguides.co.uk).

ALTHORNE [TQ9000]
☆ *Huntsman & Hounds* CM3 6BJ [B1010 E of S
Woodham Ferrers]: Traditional thatched rustic
pub extended around low-beamed local-feel
core, Greene King ales, farm cider, good food
and coffee, good friendly service; piped music;
occasional barbecues in lovely big garden (BB,
James McGrane)
ARDLEIGH [TM0429]
☆ *Wooden Fender* CO7 7PA [A137 towards
Colchester]: Pleasantly refurbished and
extended old pub with emphasis on good
choice of good value food, friendly attentive
service, beams and log fires, three real ales such
as Adnams, decent wines; children welcome in
large no smoking dining area, good-sized
garden with water feature and play area (LYM,
N R White, David Eberlin)
ARKESDEN [TL4834]
☆ *Axe & Compasses* CB11 4EX [off B1038]:
Thatched village pub with easy chairs,
upholstered oak and elm seats, open fire and
china trinkets in cosy lounge bar, built-in
settles in smaller public bar with darts and
board games, good choice of wines by the
glass, Greene King IPA and Old Speckled Hen
and a guest beer, usual bar food, puddings
trolley and more elaborate menu in no
smoking restaurant allowing children; pretty
hanging baskets, seats on side terrace
(Nick Lawless, LYM, Grahame Brooks,
Eric Robinson, Jacqueline Pratt, Charles
Gysin, Ross and Christine Loveday)
BATTLESBRIDGE [TQ7896]
Lodge SS11 7QT [Hayes Chase, just off A132]:
Good food choice inc filling baguettes,
lunchtime bargains and several fish dishes,

Crouch Vale ales, separate restaurant; tables
and chairs on terrace and big protected lawn
with bouncy castles and other play things,
bedrooms (Adrian White)
BIRCHANGER [TL5122]
Stanstead Manor CM23 5ST [Birchanger
Lane]: Hotel worth knowing for its good well
priced bar meals, Boddingtons; children
welcome, bedrooms (KC)
BRAINTREE [TL7523]
White Hart CM7 9AB [A131/A120]: Well
restored old coaching inn, comfortable bar and
lounge, Greene King IPA and Abbot,
reasonably priced pubby bar food from
sandwiches and baguettes up, good service;
decent bedrooms, good breakfast (Ian Phillips)
BRENTWOOD [TQ5993]
Nags Head CM14 5ND [A1023, just off M25
junction 28]: Vintage Inn dining pub with
pleasant olde-worlde décor, good food and
wine choice, prompt friendly helpful service,
real ale; open all day (Andy and Jill Kassube)
CASTLE HEDINGHAM [TL7735]
Rising Sun CO9 3DP [Nunnery St]: Friendly
16th-c Greene King pub with new
chef/landlord doing enjoyable food; garden
with play area and awninged terrace (Anon)
CHELMSFORD [TL7006]
Queens Head CM2 0AS [Lower Anchor St]:
Lively well run Victorian backstreet local with
half a dozen or more changing ales inc three
from Crouch Vale, summer farm cider, friendly
service, winter log fires, cheap cheerful
lunchtime food (not Sun) from separate
counter; children welcome, open all day from
noon (11 Sat), terrace tables (the Gray family,
the Didler, Dave Lowe, Tony Hobden)

CHIGWELL [TQ4493]
Olde Kings Head IG7 6QA [High Rd (A113)]:
Large and handsome weatherboarded 17th-c
pub with some antique furnishings and
interesting Dickens memorabilia (features in
Barnaby Rudge), quick friendly service,
mainstream real ales, popular upstairs carvery
restaurant, conservatory; piped music; picnic-
sets in attractive back garden *(Robert Lester)*

COGGESHALL [TL8224]
☆ *Compasses* CM77 8BG [Pattiswick, signed off
A120 W]: Dining pub under friendly new
licensees who are doing good food, neatly
comfortable spacious beamed bars, partly no
smoking barn restaurant; children warmly
welcome, plenty of lawn and orchard tables,
rolling farmland beyond *(R T and
J C Moggridge, LYM, Francis Nicholls)*

COLCHESTER [TM9924]
Kings Arms CO3 3EY [Crouch St]: Simple
bare-boards town pub with good changing
ales, low-cost food; live music Thurs
(Peter Roberts)
Stockwell Arms CO1 1HN [W Stockwell St]:
Friendly timber-framed local, far from smart
but well worth knowing for its good interesting
changing real ales and cheap bar lunches from
snacks and baguettes to basic hot dishes and
popular Sun roast, heavy 14th-c beams and
lots of pictures and bric-a-brac; landlord
organises local walks; terrace tables, open all
day wkdys *(Pete Baker, Fr Robert Marsh,
Dr and Mrs M E Wilson)*

COOPERSALE COMMON [TL4702]
Garnon Bushes CM16 7QS: Reliable
reasonably priced food and Greene King ales in
welcoming beamed country local's bar and
small restaurant, log fires, brasses, fresh
flowers, World War II memorabilia from
nearby North Weald airfield; quiet piped
music; tables on front terrace *(B J Harding)*

DUTON HILL [TL6026]
☆ *Three Horseshoes* CM6 2DX [off B184
Dunmow—Thaxted, 3 miles N of Dunmow]:
Traditional village local with friendly licensee,
Everards and two guest beers, masses of
bottled beers, late spring bank hol beer festival,
central fire, aged armchairs by fireplace in
homely left-hand parlour, interesting theatrical
and 1940s memorabilia, breweriana and
enamel signs; darts and pool in small public
bar, pleasant views and pond in garden,
cl lunchtimes Mon-Weds *(BB, the Didler,
Pete Baker, Dave Lowe)*

EARLS COLNE [TL8628]
Carved Angel CO6 2PG [Upper Holt St]:
Welcoming dining pub popular for its fresh
blackboard food, good choice of wines by the
glass, real ales, big fireside sofas, pine tables in
eating area; pleasant tables outside
(Adrian White)

FEERING [TL8720]
☆ *Sun* CO5 9NH [Feering Hill, B1024]:
Interesting old pub with 16th-c beams (watch
out for the very low one as you enter), plenty
of bric-a-brac, woodburners in huge
inglenook fireplaces, nice carved bar counter
with Wolf and other good real ales, pleasant

helpful staff, wide food choice from
sandwiches up, daily papers, board games;
well behaved children allowed, tables out on
partly covered paved terrace and in attractive
garden behind, some wknd barbecues *(LYM,
the Didler, Comus and Sarah Elliott,
Mrs P J Pearce, Eric Robinson,
Jacqueline Pratt, John Allen)*

FRINTON [TM2319]
Lock & Barrel CO13 9PR [Connaught Ave]:
First and only pub in town (none here till
2000), café-bar feel, with Shepherd Neame
Bitter and Spitfire, good choice of wines by the
glass, reasonably priced pubby food from
sandwiches and baked potatoes up inc Sun
roasts *(Michael Dandy)*

FYFIELD [TL5707]
☆ *Black Bull* CM5 0NN [Dunmow Rd (B184,
N end)]: 15th-c pub doing well under new
management, wide range of consistently
enjoyable food, real ales such as Fullers
London Pride and Greene King, heavy low
beams and standing timbers in comfortably
opened-up pubby bar and no smoking country-
style dining area, open fire, traditional games;
may be quiet piped music; tables out among
flower tubs *(R E Dixon, LYM, DFL,
Anthony Longden, Adrian White)*

GOLDHANGER [TL9008]
Chequers CM9 8AS [off B1026 E of
Heybridge; Church St]: Old beamed village
pub looking across churchyard, enjoyable
fairly priced food (not Sun evening) inc fresh
fish Fri and delicious puddings, real ales such
as Brains Bread of Heaven, Caledonian
Deuchars IPA, Coach House Flintlock and
Titanic Lifeboat (Mar beer festival), cheerful
staff, central bar with simple rooms off, all
with real fires (darts in one, pool in another),
restaurant area; tables outside, good walks and
bird-watching nearby, open all day *(Paul and
Ursula Randall, Kevin Flack)*

GOSFIELD [TL7829]
Kings Head CO9 1TP [A1017 Braintree—
Halstead (The Street)]: Well extended and
refurbished, with enjoyable fairly priced food
(all day Sun and summer Sats) inc good
children's dishes, Greene King and guest ales,
cheerful staff, log fire, bookshelves and sofas in
part-panelled lounge with conservatory
restaurant beyond, pool in bare-boards public
bar, pub great dane; tables on pretty terrace,
open all day Sun and summer Sats *(Anon)*

GREAT BROMLEY [TM0923]
Snooty Fox CO7 7JW [Frating Rd (B1029)]:
Pleasant country pub popular for home-made
food esp Sun lunch, real ales, good wine
selection, friendly service, separate dining area;
good-sized garden *(J and E Dakin)*

GREAT CHESTERFORD [TL5142]
Crown & Thistle CB10 1PL [just off M11
junction 9 (A11 exit roundabout); High St]:
Busy village pub/restaurant, good value food,
friendly staff, range of wines by the glass,
nicely served tea and coffee, real ale, log fire,
simple furnishings on bare boards
*(Mrs Margo Finlay, Jörg Kasprowski,
Roy Bromell)*

GREAT EASTON [TL6025]

Swan CM6 2HG [off B184 N of Dunmow]: Small unpretentious beamed Tudor local in attractive village street, cosy and very friendly, with two clean and tidy traditional front rooms (smaller one with darts and pool only place smoking allowed), country bygones, log fire and sofas, good ordinary food (not Sun evening), Adnams and a guest beer, good tea and coffee perhaps with home-made chocolates, back restaurant *(Dave Lowe, Mrs Margo Finlay, Jörg Kasprowski)*

GREAT HORKESLEY [TL9732]

Yew Tree CO6 4EG [The Causeway (A134)]: Large and attractive thatched pub (rebuilt in the 1970s after a fire), friendly staff, real ales such as Adnams; tables in pleasant courtyard with fountain *(Tina and David Woods-Taylor)*

GREAT TEY [TL8925]

Chequers CO6 1JS [off A120 Coggeshall—Marks Tey]: Comfortable old pub with cheerful licensees and attentive staff, good value pub food from fresh sandwiches up, Greene King IPA and Abbot and a guest beer, darts and pool in public bar, restaurant; children and dogs welcome, fine walled garden, quiet village with plenty of country walks *(Marianne and Peter Stevens, Colin and Penny Smith)*

GREAT WAKERING [TQ9187]

Rose SS3 0PY [Wakering Rd]: Good for families, with good range of food and wines by the glass; climbing frames in pleasant garden *(Adrian White)*

HARWICH [TM2632]

Alma CO12 3EE [Kings Head St]: Ancient seafarers' local, pewter, hurricane lamps, nauticalia and old local photographs, Greene King ales, friendly service, good basic food; piped music; attractive well kept back courtyard *(Anon)*

New Bell CO12 3EN [Outpart Eastward]: Small, bright and shiny, with bar and back dining lounge, Greene King, Nethergate and guest beers such as Archers and Vale, short menu inc choice of huffers and of enterprising soups, bargain crab salad; tables on small terrace, open all day Sun in summer *(Trevor and Sheila Sharman)*

HATFIELD HEATH [TL5115]

Thatchers CM22 7DU [A1005 towards Bishop's Stortford]: Neat olde-worlde beamed and thatched pub with woodburner, copper kettles, jugs, brasses, plates and pictures in L-shaped bar, Greene King IPA and Charles Wells Bombardier from long counter, decent house wines, wide food choice from good sandwiches up, back dining area; no children in bar, may be piped music; at end of large green, tables out in front under cocktail parasols *(Eddie Edwards, Tina and David Woods-Taylor)*

HELIONS BUMPSTEAD [TL6541]

Three Horseshoes CB9 7AL [Water Lane]: Two-bar country pub dating from 17th c, nice choice of good value home-made food, Adnams and Greene King ales, friendly helpful licensees, small no smoking dining room up a step; tables in large attractive garden behind, charming unspoilt village, gypsy caravan among the flowers out in front, cl Mon lunchtime *(Adele Summers, Alan Black, Susan and Nigel Wilson)*

HERONGATE [TQ6391]

Boars Head CM13 3PS [Billericay Rd, just off A128]: Picturesque low-beamed dining pub with pleasant nooks and crannies, wide blackboard choice of popular traditional food all day from good choice of lunchtime baguettes to choice of Sun roasts, up to five changing real ales, reasonably priced wines, friendly staff; garden tables overlooking big attractive reed-fringed pond with ducks, swans and moorhens *(DFL, Roy and Lindsey Fentiman)*

☆ *Old Dog* CM13 3SD [Billericay Rd, off A128 Brentwood—Grays at big sign for Boars Head]: Dating from 16th c, carefully refurbished and moved gently upscale under new management, with enjoyable food, real ales, quick friendly service, comfortable back lounge area, long attractive dark-beamed bar, and appealing new raftered restaurant upstairs; pleasant front terrace and neat sheltered side garden *(R E Dixon, Nick Lawless, LYM, DFL)*

HEYBRIDGE BASIN [TL8706]

Old Ship CM9 4RX [Lockhill]: Decent food inc breakfast all morning, friendly service, pale wood chairs and tables, upstairs restaurant with estuary views; dogs and children welcome, seats outside, some overlooking water by canal lock with lovely views of the saltings and across to Northey Island, open all day 8am-midnight *(John Wooll)*

HOWE STREET [TL6914]

Green Man CM3 1BG [just off A130 N of Chelmsford]: Spacious beamed and timbered two-bar Greene King pub dating from 14th c, generous good value traditional food, comfortably plush lounge, nice brass and prints, log fire; garden with play area *(Paul and Ursula Randall)*

KNOWL GREEN [TL7841]

Cherry Tree CO10 7BY: Small thatched local on edge of pretty village, enjoyable food, good service, real ales such as Adnams and Greene King, step down to rustic split-level bar, 15th-c beams; garden with good play area, open all day *(Adele Summers, Alan Black)*

LAMBOURNE END [TQ4794]

Camelot RM4 1NH [off A1112; Manor Rd]: Roomy chain dining pub on edge of Hainault Forest, wide range of usual food from reasonably priced sandwiches and baked potatoes to steaks, efficient attentive young staff, good fire, several no smoking seating areas on varying levels; piped music; children welcome, garden with lots of picnic-sets and play area, open all day *(Adele Summers, Alan Black)*

LAYER DE LA HAYE [TL9720]

Donkey & Buskins CO2 0HU [off B1026 towards Colchester]: Friendly old-fashioned country pub with good range of reasonably priced hearty traditional food in two bars and dining room esp fresh fish and good Sun roasts, decent helpings, Adnams, Bass and Greene King IPA, pleasant service, general mix of furnishings and ornaments; pleasant garden, handy for Abberton Reservoir's fishermen and birders (E A and D C T Frewer)

LEIGH-ON-SEA [TQ8385]

☆ *Crooked Billet* SS9 2EP [High St]: Homely old pub with waterfront views from big bay windows, Adnams, Bass and a guest beer, good spring and autumn beer festivals, friendly attentive staff, log fires, beams and bare boards, local fishing pictures and bric-a-brac; piped music, live music nights, no under-21s; open all day, side garden and terrace, seawall seating over road shared with Osbornes good shellfish stall; pay-and-display parking (free Sat/Sun) by fly-over (N R White, LYM, Ian Phillips)

LITTLE TOTHAM [TL8811]

☆ *Swan* CM9 8LB [School Rd]: Good changing range of real ales tapped from the cask such as Adnams, Crouch Vale, Mauldons and Mighty Oak, farm ciders and country wines; welcoming service, enjoyable food (not Sun evening), low 17th-c beams, coal fire, tiled games bar with darts and bar billiards, dining extension, Jun beer festival; children and dogs welcome, small terrace and picnic-sets under cocktail parasols on sizeable front lawn, open all day (the Didler, MLR, Adrian White)

LITTLEY GREEN [TL6917]

Compasses CM3 1BU [off A130 and B1417 SE of Felsted]: Unpretentiously quaint and old-fashioned country pub with Greene King ales tapped from cellar casks, lots of malt whiskies, big huffers, ploughman's and baked potatoes, no machines; tables in big back garden, benches out in front (the Didler)

LOUGHTON [TQ4296]

Victoria IG10 4BP [Smarts Lane]: Popular traditional local with friendly service, good range of ales such as Everards Tiger and Timothy Taylors Landlord, wide blackboard choice of good value generous home-made food, chatty panelled bar with small raised end dining area; plenty of picnic-sets in pleasant neatly kept garden with views towards Epping Forest, good walks (N R White)

MALDON [TL8407]

☆ *Blue Boar* CM9 4QE [Silver St; car park round behind]: Quirky cross between coaching inn and antiques or auction showroom, luxurious main lounge with gilt and chenille love-seats, seductive paintings, Canova-look marble figures, dining room with chandeliers, pewter, more paintings and antique refectory table, beams and panelling; separate smallish dark-timbered bar with spectacular raftered upper room (both with interesting antique furnishings and pictures), Adnams tapped from the cask and Farmers Blue Boar and Pucks Folly brewed at the back, friendly helpful staff, fresh tasty food; jazz Sun lunchtime; open all day, parking £3 (Ian Phillips, Mrs Roxanne Chamberlain, LYM, Dave Braisted)

Jolly Sailor CM9 5HP [Church St/The Hythe]:

Charming timber-framed quayside pub, three Greene King ales and great choice of wines by the glass, friendly helpful landlady and up-beat staff, plenty of fish among other food from rolls, sandwiches and baked potatoes up; piped music; tables out overlooking Thames barges, play area and parakeet aviary (Ian Phillips, John Wooll)

MANNINGTREE [TM1031]

☆ *Crown* CO11 1AH [High St]: Bare-boards no smoking mealtime bar on left with plenty of old local photographs and advertisements, low-ceilinged lino-floored and ochre-walled front public bar, estuary views from brightly carpeted or tiled two-level back area with more dining tables and nautical stuff under high pitched ceiling, full range of Greene King ales, usual food inc interesting sandwiches, friendly efficient service, chatty local atmosphere; children welcome, picnic-sets on back terrace, attractively priced bedrooms, open all day (BB, N R White)

MARGARETTING TYE [TL6801]

White Hart CM4 9JX: Good value unpretentious food from sandwiches up, fine range of changing real ales and cheerful friendly service in pleasant L-shaped bar, bright and comfortable conservatory-roofed dining room; attractive garden with robust play area, well fenced duck pond and birds and animals to look at (Quentin and Carol Williamson, Mrs P J Pearce, Paul and Ursula Randall)

MISTLEY [TM1131]

☆ *Thorn* CO11 1HE [High St (B1352 E of Manningtree)]: Bistro-style no smoking restaurant and bar with short daily-changing choice of enterprising food inc local seasonal produce and seafood (American chef/landlady does cookery classes here), interesting sandwiches too, friendly service, good choice of wines by the glass, contemporary pictures for sale; evening booking recommended; children welcome, pavement tables, five well equipped bedrooms, open all day wknds (N R White, Judi Bell, Adrian White)

MORETON [TL5307]

Nags Head CM5 0LF [signed off B184, at S end of Fyfield or opp Chipping Ongar school]: Cosy and friendly country pub with good blackboard choice of good value food, friendly service, Greene King ales, three big log fires, extensive no smoking area with comfortable mix of tables and medley of salvaged rustic beams and timbers, restaurant; children welcome, picnic-sets on side grass (Gordon Neighbour, B N F and M Parkin, H O Dickinson)

NEWNEY GREEN [TL6506]

☆ *Duck* CM1 3SF [W of Chelmsford]: Quiet dining pub with attractive rambling bar full of hop-hung beams, timbering, panelling and interesting bric-a-brac, comfortable furnishings, enjoyable food inc good value set lunches, Shepherd Neame ales, decent wines by the glass, attentive service; tables out on attractive terrace (LYM, Roy and Lindsey Fentiman)

OLD HARLOW [TL4711]
Marquis of Granby CM17 0AH [Market St]:
Attractive and comfortable old tiled building
under new landlord, friendly staff, good choice
of sensibly priced real ales in no smoking bar
area, good value sensible pub food from
sandwiches up inc bargain offers, interesting
prints and memorabilia, back pool table; may
be piped music, TV; open all day
(Martin Grosberg, Craig Turnbull)

RADLEY GREEN [TL6205]
Cuckoo CM4 0LT [off A414]: Secluded two-
room local with simple wood tables and
brickwork, friendly landlord, decent
reasonably priced food, Greene King ales; dogs
welcome, tables outside, own football pitch,
good nearby walks *(Eddie Edwards)*

RADWINTER [TL6137]
☆ *Plough* CB10 2TL [Sampford Rd (B1053/54
crossroads E of Saffron Walden)]: Quietly
placed country pub with enjoyable food inc
game, fish and steaks in neat no smoking
dining room extension, good friendly service,
Greene King IPA and a changing guest beer,
red plush seating and warm log fire in open-
plan black-timbered beamed bar (can get
smoky); children and dogs welcome, very
attractive terrace and garden, comfortable
bedrooms *(Adele Summers, Alan Black, BB)*

RIDGEWELL [TL7340]
White Horse CO9 4SG [Mill Rd (A1017
Haverhill—Halstead)]: Friendly and
comfortable no smoking village pub, open plan
with low beams, good range of attractively
priced real ales tapped from the cask on cooled
stillage, good value generous food with
changing separate bar and restaurant menus,
friendly service, fireside sofa, no music; no
dogs; terrace tables, new bedroom block, open
all day *(Pam and David Bailey, MLR, Adele
Summers, Alan Black)*

SANDON [TL7404]
Crown CM2 7SH: Well run beamed village
pub recently reopened after fire restoration,
fresh plain décor, decent food all day, neat and
cheerful polite staff, Greene King IPA and Old
Speckled Hen and Shepherd Neame Spitfire,
quiet piped music; open all day *(Paul and
Ursula Randall)*

STISTED [TL7923]
☆ *Dolphin* CM77 8EU [A120 E of Braintree, by
village turn]: Friendly heavily beamed and
timbered bar, popular well priced
straightforward food (not Tues or Sun
evenings), log fire, bright eating area on left
(children allowed here), Greene King ales;
tables in pretty garden, nice hanging baskets
(LYM, the Didler, Pete Baker)

THAXTED [TL6031]
☆ *Swan* CM6 2PL [Bull Ring]: Attractively
renovated dark-beamed Tudor pub with
Adnams and Greene King, good choice of
whiskies and of enjoyable food, good-sized
helpings, light dishes all afternoon, welcoming
staff, plenty of well spaced tables in long open
bar, restaurant; may be piped music; open all
day, good bedrooms (ones at the back are
quieter), lovely church and windmill nearby

*(David Twitchett, M J Winterton, Dr and Mrs
M E Wilson)*

THEYDON BOIS [TQ4599]
Queen Victoria CM16 7ES [Coppice Row
(B172)]: Cosy beamed and carpeted traditional
lounge with roaring log fire, local pictures,
mug collection, popular good value food
servery, friendly efficient staff, McMullens ales,
decent house wines, bright end dining area
with interesting knick-knacks; piped music;
picnic-sets on well laid out front terrace
(N R White)

THORPE-LE-SOKEN [TM1722]
Rose & Crown CO16 0EF [High St]:
Welcoming mansard-roof pub with enjoyable
interesting food, several wines by the glass,
Greene King and Mauldons real ales
(Adrian White)

THRESHERS BUSH [TL5009]
John Barleycorn CM17 0NS [spelled
Thrushesbush on some maps]: Well
refurbished and extended old pub, pleasant
light and uncluttered décor, Greene King ales
inc Old Speckled Hen, good choice of good
value food; garden with terrace and water
feature, cl Mon *(Keith and Janet Morris)*

THUNDERSLEY [TQ7988]
Woodmans Arms SS7 3TA [Rayleigh Rd
(A129)]: Refurbished under new owners in
2005 and now no smoking, enjoyable
contemporary food using fresh local supplies,
four real ales, decent wines, friendly
atmosphere and polite service; may be soft
piped music; tables in garden *(David Ripo)*

UPSHIRE [TL4100]
Horseshoes EN9 3SN [Horseshoe Hill, E of
Waltham Abbey]: Friendly Victorian local,
simple and clean, with popular food (not
Mon), McMullens ales; can be smoky; tidy
garden overlooking Lea Valley, more tables out
in front, good walks *(N R White)*

WENDENS AMBO [TL5136]
☆ *Bell* CB11 4JY [B1039 just W of village]:
Small cottagey low-ceilinged pub with
ancient timbers, snug alcoves, quite a few
pictures and open fire, Adnams and
Woodfordes Wherry and a couple of
changing guest beers, bar food (not Sun/Mon
evenings), no smoking dining room, cribbage
and dominoes; piped music; children
welcome in restaurant and family room, dogs
in bar, big tree-sheltered garden with terrace
and plenty to keep children occupied, handy
for Audley End, open all day Fri-Sun *(LYM,
Dave Lowe, Eric Robinson, Jacqueline Pratt,
J L Wedel)*

WEST BERGHOLT [TL9528]
White Hart CO6 3DD [2 miles from
Colchester on Sudbury rd]: Pleasant mainly no
smoking village pub, former old coaching inn,
with good blackboard food choice inc plenty
of fish, Adnams ale, comfortable dining area;
children welcome, big garden *(Tony and
Shirley Albert)*

WEST MERSEA [TM0012]
Coast CO5 8NA [Coast Rd]: Two-bar pub in
attractive spot opp creek and mudflats, Greene
King IPA and Thwaites, half a dozen wines by

the glass, generous enjoyable food with quite a few fish dishes, friendly service, back dining extension; a few tables out in front *(John Wooll)*

WIDDINGTON [TL5331]

☆ *Fleur de Lys* CB11 3SG [signed off B1383 N of Stansted]: Welcoming new landlord in unpretentious low-beamed and timbered village pub, good short choice of well cooked food in bar and restaurant inc good Sun roasts and children's helpings, Adnams, Greene King

and guest beers, decent wines inc a local one, inglenook log fire, games in back bar; picnic-sets on pleasant side lawn, handy for Mole Hall wildlife park *(LYM, Grahame Brooks, Andrew Gardner)*

WRITTLE [TL6706]

Wheatsheaf CM1 3DU [The Green]: Thriving traditional two-room 19th-c local, Greene King, Mighty Oak and Mauldon ales, friendly knowledgeable landlord; terrace tables, open all day wknds *(the Didler)*

Gloucestershire

It's not just the beautiful buildings in pretty villages that pub-loving visitors enjoy so much here, but the friendly and relaxed atmosphere that seems to run through so many of the main entries, whether they are simple taverns or smart dining pubs. Doing particularly well this year are the Bowl at Almondsbury (very well run and popular under its new licensee), the Red Lion at Ampney St Peter (unchanging and unspoilt, with a charming landlord), the Queens Arms at Ashleworth (neatly kept and with good interesting food), the Boat at Ashleworth Quay (a delightfully unspoilt old place), the Red Hart at Blaisdon (a thoroughly nice atmosphere), the Halfway Inn at Box (back in the *Guide* after a break, well redeveloped by its new owners), the Seven Tuns at Chedworth (good value and handy for the Roman villa), the Five Mile House at Duntisbourne Abbots (a super all-rounder), the Old Spot in Dursley (a fine range of real ales), the White Horse at Frampton Mansell (delicious food using proudly traced produce), the handsome and handsomely placed Bell at Frampton on Severn (new to the *Guide*, with an extensive family dining area, and quite a menagerie in the garden), the Hollow Bottom at Guiting Power, the White Hart at Littleton-upon-Severn (a good mix of customers and very well run), the Weighbridge at Nailsworth (the two-in-one pies continue to draw warm praise), the Ostrich at Newland (the bouncy landlady keeps a good choice of beers), the Royal Oak in Prestbury (another new entry, nice all round), and the Bell at Sapperton (walkers and diners all mingle happily). Food is a prominent part of the Gloucestershire pub scene, and for a rewarding meal out you are really spoilt for choice. Narrowing things down as much as we can, we still have a splendid shortlist of over a dozen pubs that stand out for imaginative cooking. These are the Queens Arms at Ashleworth, the Village Pub at Barnsley, the Kings Head at Bledington, the Five Mile House at Duntisbourne Abbots, the White Horse at Frampton Mansell, the Inn for all Seasons at Little Barrington, the Fox at Lower Oddington, the Bathurst Arms at North Cerney, the Falcon at Poulton, the Bell at Sapperton, the Gumstool and Trouble House both just outside Tetbury, and the Horse & Groom at Upper Oddington. From this distinguished list, we name the White Horse at Frampton Mansell as Gloucestershire Dining Pub for 2007. The Lucky Dip section at the end of the chapter isn't short of pubs which have recently been gaining really warm plaudits: the Horse & Groom at Bourton-on-the-Hill, Bakers Arms in Broad Campden, Twelve Bells in Cirencester, Tunnel House at Coates, Puesdown Inn at Compton Abdale, Black Horse at Cranham, Fountain in Gloucester, Fox at Great Barrington, Bull at Hinton Dyrham, Dog at Old Sodbury, Royal Oak in Painswick, Plough at Prestbury, Cat & Custard Pot at Shipton Moyne, Swan at Southrop, Queens Head in Stow-on-the-Wold, Crown at Tolldown, Fleet at Twyning, Bell at Willersey, Old Corner Cupboard in Winchcombe and Ram at Woodchester. Almost all of these have now been inspected and approved by us. Drinks prices in the area are closely in line with the national average. Hook Norton, from just over the border in Oxfordshire, was the beer which we most often found as the cheapest on offer in pubs here. We also found the locally brewed Donnington and Goffs at bargain prices, and other local beers to look out for include Uley, Wickwar, Freeminer, Whittingtons and Nailsworth.

ALMONDSBURY ST6084 Map 2

Bowl

1¼ miles from M5 junction 16 (and therefore quite handy for M4 junction 20); from A38 towards Thornbury, turn left signposted Lower Almondsbury, then first right down Sundays Hill, then at bottom right again into Church Road; BS32 4DT

Even though a new licensee has taken over this very popular pub, little seems to have changed. It remains well run and cheerful with plenty of chatty customers and is much favoured by travellers on the M5. The long beamed no smoking bar is neatly kept, with terracotta plush-patterned modern settles, dark green cushioned stools and mate's chairs around elm tables, horsebrasses on stripped bare stone walls, and big winter log fire at one end, with a woodburning stove at the other. Up to seven real ales are well kept on handpump: Bass, Butcombe Bitter, Courage Best, Moles Best and Rucking Mole, and a couple of changing guests; piped music. Reasonably priced bar food includes filled baguettes (from £4.75; club sandwich from £6.95), ploughman's (from £4.95), mussels with cream, wine and garlic (£5.75; main course £8.95), chicken caesar salad (£7.50), pasta with mushrooms, spinach and parmesan cream sauce (£7.75), home-cooked ham and free-range eggs (£7.95), lasagne (£8.50), chicken curry or steak and Guinness pie (£8.95), 10oz rump steak (£13.95), and puddings such as lemon tart with raspberry coulis or triple chocolate mousse (£3.95); efficient service even when stretched, but it's a shame they still ask to keep your credit card behind the bar. This is a pretty setting with the church next door and lovely flowering tubs, hanging baskets and window boxes. *(Recommended by Gwen Griffiths, John and Helen Rushton, Gerry and Rosemary Dobson, Bob and Margaret Holder, Dave Braisted, Comus and Sarah Elliott, Len Clark, Roy and Lindsey Fentiman, Mrs Jane Kingsbury, Barry Steele-Perkins, Brian and Ruth Archer, Dr and Mrs A K Clarke, B and M Kendall, Matthew Hegarty, Ian Phillips)*

Free house ~ Licensee Mrs J Stephenson ~ Real ale ~ Bar food (all day Sun) ~ Restaurant ~ (01454) 612757 ~ Children welcome ~ Dogs allowed in bar and bedrooms ~ Open 11.30-3, 5-11; 12-10.30 Sun; closed 25 Dec ~ Bedrooms: £48.50S/£76S

AMPNEY ST PETER SP0801 Map 4

Red Lion 🍺

A417, E of village; GL7 5SL

Much loved by its loyal regulars, this is a totally unspoilt little roadside pub run by a very friendly long-serving landlord. It's the sort of place where it would be hard not to get drawn into easy conversation with either him or other customers. A central corridor, served by a hatch, gives on to the little right-hand tile-floor public bar. This has just one table, a wall seat, and one long bench facing a small open fire. Behind this bench is an open servery (no counter, just shelves of bottles and – by the corridor hatch – handpumps for the well kept Hook Norton Best and Timothy Taylors Landlord, and maybe Golden Best; reasonably priced wine. There are old prints on the wall, and on the other side of the corridor is a small saloon, with panelled wall seats around its single table, old local photographs, another open fire, and a print of Queen Victoria one could believe hasn't moved for a century – rather like the pub itself. There are seats in the side garden. Please note the limited opening hours. *(Recommended by R Huggins, D Irving, E McCall, T McLean, the Didler, Giles and Annie Francis, Richard Endacott)*

Free house ~ Licensee John Barnard ~ Real ale ~ No credit cards ~ (01285) 851596 ~ Children and dogs in the tiny games room ~ Open 6-10; 12-2, 6(7 Sun)-10 Sat; closed weekday lunchtimes

---

Bedroom prices normally include full English breakfast, VAT and any inclusive service charge that we know of. Prices before the '/' are for single rooms, after for two people in double or twin (B includes a private bath, S a private shower). If there is no '/', the prices are only for twin or double rooms (as far as we know there are no singles).

ASHLEWORTH   SO8125   Map 4

Queens Arms 🍴 ♀ 🍺

Village signposted off A417 at Hartpury; GL19 4HT

Consistently well run and spotlessly kept, this low-beamed country dining pub remains extremely popular. The comfortably laid out and civilised main bar has faintly patterned wallpaper and washed red ochre walls, big oak and mahogany tables and a nice mix of farmhouse and big brocaded dining chairs on a red carpet; at night it is softly lit by fringed wall lamps and candles. Using local produce, the good interesting bar food might include roast mediterranean vegetables in a garlic bread basket with basil and black olives or crispy whitebait in garlic butter (£5.50), seared chicken livers with bacon and mushrooms on a toasted brioche (£5.95), oxtail stew (£12.95), chicken breast stuffed with mushrooms, stilton and bacon topped with a rich port and cream sauce (£13.25), pork fillet escalopes with toasted sesame seeds and a ginger and honey marinade (£13.85), gressingham duck breast on a potato, spring onion and garlic rösti topped with a spicy plum and port sauce (£14.25), monkfish fillets wrapped in parma ham and mozzarella with a fresh herb beurre blanc (£14.50), and puddings such as pecan nut and maple syrup pie or orange and Cointreau cheesecake (from £4.95). Well kept Brains Reverend James, Donnington BB and Timothy Taylors Landlord on handpump, a dozen wines by the glass from a thoughtful wine list (including south african choices), and 22 malt whiskies; maybe summer home-made lemonade or winter mulled wine. Piped music, board games, and winter skittle alley; Bonnie, the little black pub cat, may entertain customers with her ping-pong football antics. Two perfectly clipped mushroom shaped yews dominate the front of the building. There are cast-iron tables and chairs in the sunny courtyard. *(Recommended by Bernard Stradling, RJH, John and Christine Lewis, Dr A J and Mrs Tompsett, Mrs Jill Wyatt, Conrad Meehan, Rod Stoneman, Jane and Martin Bailey, Pam and Alan Neale, J V Dadswell)*

Free house ~ Licensees Tony and Gill Burreddu ~ Real ale ~ Bar food (till 10 Fri and Sat; not Sun evening) ~ Restaurant ~ (01452) 700395 ~ Well behaved children allowed ~ Open 12-3, 7-11(10.30 Sun); closed Sun evening except bank hol weekends; 25 and 26 Dec

ASHLEWORTH QUAY   SO8125   Map 4

Boat ★ 🍺

Ashleworth signposted off A417 N of Gloucester; quay signed from village; GL19 4HZ

This is the kind of delightful, friendly place where strangers soon start talking to each other. It's unspoilt and unchanging and has been in the same family since it was originally granted a licence by Charles II. The front suntrap crazy-paved courtyard is bright with plant tubs in summer, with a couple of picnic-sets under cocktail parasols; there are more seats and tables under cover at the sides. Inside, the little front parlour has a built-in settle by a long scrubbed deal table that faces an old-fashioned open kitchen range with a side bread oven and a couple of elderly fireside chairs; there are rush mats on the scrubbed flagstones, houseplants in the window, fresh garden flowers, and old magazines to read. The pub is no smoking throughout; cribbage and dominoes in the front room. Two flower-cushioned antique settles face each other in the back room where four or five swiftly changing beers from breweries such as Archers, Arkells, Bath, Church End, Malvern Hills, RCH and Wye Valley are tapped from the cask, along with a full range of Weston's farm ciders. During the week, they usually do good lunchtime rolls (from £1.55) and cake (80p). *(Recommended by R Huggins, D Irving, E McCall, T McLean, Mike and Mary Carter, the Didler, Pete Baker, Pat and Tony Martin, Conrad Meehan, John Reilly, Annabel Viney, Ken and Jenny Simmonds, Dr A J and Mrs Tompsett, Mrs Joyce Robson, R T and J C Moggridge)*

Free house ~ Licensees Ron, Elisabeth and Louise Nicholls ~ Real ale ~ Bar food (lunchtime only; not Mon and Weds) ~ No credit cards ~ (01452) 700272 ~ Children allowed away from bar ~ Open 11.30-2.30(3 Sat), 6.30(7 winter)-11; 12-3, 7-10.30 Sun; evening opening 7 in winter; closed all day Mon, Weds lunchtime throughout year

AWRE SO7108 Map 4
Red Hart 🍴 ♟

Village signposted off A48 S of Newnham; GL14 1EW

Tucked away in a remote Severnside farming village, this red-brick building is surprisingly tall – with a chimney to match. The neat L-shaped bar has heavy old beams, flagstones, quarry tiles, a deep glass-covered illuminated well, stone fireplaces, and some exposed wattle and daub. Good interesting food using local produce might include home-made soup (£3.95), mussels in white wine, cream and garlic (£4.95), pressed duck terrine (£5.50), filled baguettes or panini or baked potatoes (£5.95), home-cooked ham and free-range eggs (£7.25), cod in beer batter or steak in ale pudding (£8.95), mushroom, rocket and goats cheese strudel with a tomato butter sauce (£9.95), fillet of bream with roasted vegetables (£10.95), loin of pork with honey-glazed apples and cider sauce (£11.95), and steaks (from £11.95); the dining areas are no smoking. Freeminer Bitter, Whittingtons Nine Lives and Wye Valley Butty Bach on handpump, 11 wines by the glass, and local cider; piped music and board games. Out in front are some picnic-sets. *(Recommended by Liz and Tony Colman, Bob and Margaret Holder, David Ashton, Bob Richardson, Graham Chamberlain)*

Free house ~ Licensees Marcia Griffiths and Martin Coupe ~ Real ale ~ Bar food (12-2.30(2 in winter), 6-9.30) ~ Restaurant ~ (01594) 510220 ~ Children welcome ~ Dogs allowed in bar ~ Open 12-3, 6-midnight; 12-midnight Sat; 12-4, 6-11 Sun; opens 6.30 winter evenings Mon-Sat and 12-4 Sun in winter; closed Sun evening and Mon and Tues lunchtimes in winter ~ Bedrooms: £50B/£80B

BARNSLEY SP0705 Map 4
Village Pub ㉕ 🍴 ♟

B4425 Cirencester—Burford; GL7 5EF

There's a good mix of customers in this smart and rather civilised pub – those popping in for a pint and a chat (with their dogs) and others looking forward to a special meal out. The low-ceilinged communicating rooms have oil paintings, plush chairs, stools and window settles around polished candlelit tables, and country magazines and newspapers to read. Using mainly local and organic produce, the enjoyable food might include lunchtime sandwiches, home-made soup (£4), farmhouse terrine with home-made chutney or aubergine and pepper roulade with mozzarella (£6.50), roasted quail with fried polenta, garlic and rosemary (£6.95), gnocchi with porcini cream sauce (£10.50), cumberland sausage ring with bacon, mushrooms, onions and sage (£14), calves liver, wild mushrooms and bacon sauce with peas and tarragon (£14.50), brill with asparagus, anchovy and rosemary (£14.95), roast rack of lamb with olive oil mash, spring cabbage, chilli, mint and garlic (£15), and puddings such as pear jelly with chocolate ice-cream or bramley apple crumble (£6); interesting cheeses. Adnams, Hook Norton Bitter and Wadworths 6X on handpump, and an extensive wine list with over a dozen by the glass. The sheltered back courtyard has plenty of good solid wooden furniture under umbrellas, outdoor heaters and its own outside servery. *(Recommended by Bernard Stradling, John Holroyd, John Kane, R Huggins, D Irving, E McCall, T McLean, Mr and Mrs G S Ayrton, Noel Grundy, Lynn Nisbet, Sebastian Snow, Derek Thomas, Iain R Hewitt, A G Marx, Mrs Joyce Robson, J Crosby, Karen and Graham Oddey, Mr and Mrs Martin Joyce)*

Free house ~ Licensees Tim Haigh and Rupert Pendered ~ Real ale ~ Bar food (12-2.30 (3 Fri-Sun), 7-9.30(10 Fri and Sat)) ~ Restaurant ~ (01285) 740421 ~ Children welcome ~ Dogs allowed in bar ~ Open 11-3, 6-11; 11-11 Sat; 11-11 Sun ~ Bedrooms: £75S/£105S(£115B)

Post Office address codings confusingly give the impression that some pubs are in Gloucestershire, when they're really in Warwickshire (which is where we list them).

BISLEY   SO9006   Map 4

Bear ◀

Village signposted off A419 just E of Stroud; GL6 7BD

The easiest way to find this elegantly gothic 16th-c inn is to head for the church. The meandering L-shaped bar has a friendly, bustling atmosphere, a long shiny black built-in settle and a smaller but even sturdier oak settle by the front entrance, and an enormously wide low stone fireplace (not very high – the ochre ceiling's too low for that); the separate no smoking stripped-stone area is used for families. Flowers IPA, Tetleys, Charles Wells Bombardier and Youngs Special on handpump; darts. Enjoyable bar food such as caesar salad (£5), cheeses and chutney with bread (£5.50), filled baguettes (from £5.75; black pudding, tomato and fried egg £6.50), bean or meat burgers (from £7), vegetable pasty (£10.50), rabbit or steak, kidney and Guinness pies (£10.95), and daily specials such as cottage pie with cheese and leek topping (£9.95), venison casserole with pickled walnuts (£10.95), and lamb rump or organic fishcakes (£11.95). A small front colonnade supports the upper floor of the pub, and the sheltered little flagstoned courtyard made by this has a traditional bench. The garden is across the quiet road, and there's quite a collection of stone mounting-blocks. The steep stone-built village is attractive. *(Recommended by Tom and Ruth Rees, Paul and Shirley White, R Huggins, D Irving, E McCall, T McLean, Brian McBurnie, Neil and Anita Christopher, M Joyner, Brian and Jacky Wilson, Guy Vowles)*

Punch ~ Lease Simon and Sue Evans ~ Real ale ~ Bar food ~ (01452) 770265 ~ Children in family room ~ Dogs welcome ~ Open 11.30-3, 6-11(midnight Sat); 12-3, 7-10.30 Sun; midday opening in winter ~ Bedrooms: £25/£50

BLAISDON   SO7017   Map 4

Red Hart ◀

Village signposted off A4136 just SW of junction with A40 W of Gloucester; OS Sheet 162 map reference 703169; GL17 0AH

Readers very much enjoy their visits to this bustling and friendly pub. The flagstoned main bar has cushioned wall and window seats, traditional pub tables, a big sailing-ship painting above the log fire, and a thoroughly relaxing atmosphere – helped along by well reproduced piped bluesy music and maybe Spotty the perky jack russell (who is now ten). On the right there's an attractive beamed two-room no smoking dining area with some interesting prints and bric-a-brac, and on the left you'll find additional dining space for families. Well kept Bath Ales SPA, Butcombe Bitter, Hook Norton Best, RCH Pitchfork and Tetleys on handpump (three of these change regularly), and a decent wine list; board games and table skittles. Good bar food includes sandwiches or filled baguettes (from £3.95; the steak one is popular £5.25), ploughman's (£4.75), sausages and egg (£5.25), pasta with tomato and basil sauce, chicken curry or grilled fresh cod (all £7.50), and daily specials such as salmon and coriander fishcakes (£5.25; main course £7.95), fried sardines on spinach (£5.75; main course £9.50), lemon chicken with stir-fried vegetables and noodles (£9.95), and pork loin with bacon and apple and a mustard and cider sauce (£11.95). There are some picnic-sets in the garden and a children's play area, and at the back of the building is a terrace for barbecues. The little church above the village is worth a visit. *(Recommended by A and B D Craig, Graham and Glenis Watkins, Guy Vowles, Dr A J and Mrs Tompsett, M J Winterton, Mike and Mary Carter, Di and Mike Gillam, Michael Doswell)*

Free house ~ Licensee Guy Wilkins ~ Real ale ~ Bar food ~ Restaurant ~ (01452) 830477 ~ Children allowed but must be well behaved ~ Dogs allowed in bar ~ Open 12-2.30, 6-11(11.30 Sat); 12-3.30, 7-10.30 Sun

---

Ideas for a country day out? We list pubs in really attractive scenery at the back of the book – and there are separate lists for waterside pubs, ones with really good gardens, and ones with lovely views.

BLEDINGTON   SP2422   Map 4
Kings Head (🍴) 🍷 🍺 🛏
B4450; OX7 6XQ

Originally a cider house, this rather smart 500-year-old inn is set back from the village green where there are usually ducks pottering about. The main bar is full of ancient beams and other atmospheric furnishings (high-backed wooden settles, gateleg or pedestal tables), and there's a warming log fire in the stone inglenook where a big black kettle hangs. To the left of the bar a drinking space for locals (popular with a younger crowd in the evening) has benches on the wooden floor, a woodburning stove, and darts. Well kept Hook Norton Best and guests like Goffs Jouster, Slaters Original and Vale Best Bitter on handpump, an excellent wine list with ten by the glass, 20 malt whiskies, interesting bottled ciders. Using as much free-range, organic and local produce as possible, the interesting bar food might include lunchtime sandwiches (from £5.50), toasted panini (from £5.95), and salads such as chargrilled pheasant breast with crispy bacon and pine nuts (£7.95), as well as soup (£4.50), smoked mackerel and caper pâté (£5.75), devilled lambs kidneys (£5.95; main course £10.50), cheese and herb fritters with sweet pepper marmalade (£9.95), home-made smoked haddock and prawn pie with fresh herb mash (£11.50), thai baked gilt-head bream fillets with ginger and leek salad or chargrilled venison steak with bubble and squeak and sage and mustard butter (£12.95), and steaks with beetroot crisps and shallot and port jus (from £13.50). The restaurant is no smoking; piped music. There are seats in the back garden. *(Recommended by Derek and Sylvia Stephenson, John and Jackie Chalcraft, Sean A Smith, Richard Wyld, Di and Mike Gillam, Keith and Sue Ward, Jacques and Huguette Laurent, Mr and Mrs John Taylor, Jane McKenzie, Noel Grundy, Lynn Nisbet, Richard Greaves, Tracey and Stephen Groves, Basil and Jarvis, Pam and David Bailey, Mr and Mrs Martin Joyce, Iain R Hewitt, A G Marx, Theocsbrian, M A and C R Starling, Gill Glover)*

Free house ~ Licensees Nicola and Archie Orr-Ewing ~ Real ale ~ Bar food ~ Restaurant ~ (01608) 658365 ~ Children allowed in restaurant and back bar only ~ Dogs allowed in bar ~ Open 11.30-3, 6-11; 11.30-11 Sat; 12-11 Sun; 12-3, 6.30-11 Sun in winter; closed 25 and 26 Dec ~ Bedrooms: £55B/£70S(£125B)

BOX   SO8500   Map 4
Halfway House
Edge of Minchinhampton Common; from A46 S of Stroud follow Amberley signpost, then after Amberley Inn turn right towards Box, then left along common edge as you reach Box; OS Sheet 162 map reference 856003; can also be reached from Brimscombe on A419 SE of Stroud; GL6 9AE

The new licensees in this tall 300-year-old house have created a downstairs no smoking restaurant which will have booths where customers can adjust the lighting or volume of music to suit themselves; there will be a disabled lavatory, a lift and new terrace, too. Upstairs, the light and airy open-plan bars wrap themselves around the central serving bar, and there are simple rush seated sturdy blond wooden chairs around good wooden tables, a built-in wall seat and long pew, a woodburning stove, and stripped wood floors. The bar has yellow cream walls and ceiling, the dining area is mainly a warm terracota, there are windows with views to the common, and an unusual pitched-roof area. Using only local produce (apart from fish from Cornwall), the totally home-made food now includes lunchtime sandwiches (from £4.50), filled panini (£5.50), and ploughman's (from £7), as well as cauliflower cheese (£6), home-made burger (£8), bangers and mash (£8.50), home-made cottage pie or lasagne (£9.50), and sirloin steak (£13). In the bar you can also eat from the more elaborate restaurant menu: home-made soup (£4.50), wild boar pâté with dark rum and ginger and rosemary and cranberry bread (£5), fresh oriental tiger prawns (£6.50), baked mediterranean crèpes (£9.90), fishcakes with sweet chilli sauce (£11.50), lamb stincotto with a strawberry and balsamic sauce (£11.90), bass with a wild fennel and pine nut condiment (£14.50), gressingham duck breast with a port and lampone sauce (£14.70), and puddings such as lavender sorbet with home-made shortbread, dark chocolate mousse with caramelised oranges and a bitter chocolate sauce or crème brûlée (£5.25). Well kept Nailsworth Artists Ale, Otter Bitter, Timothy Taylors Landlord, Wickwar BOB and Wychwood Englands Ale on handpump, and decent wines; piped music. There are seats in the landscaped garden. *(Recommended by Neil and Jenny Dury, Tom and Ruth Rees, R Huggins, D Irving, E McCall, T McLean)*

Free house ~ Licensee Dawn Winchester ~ Real ale ~ Bar food (no restaurant food Mon) ~ Restaurant ~ (01453) 832631 ~ Children welcome ~ Dogs allowed in bar ~ Open 11-11; 12-11 Sun

BRIMPSFIELD SO9413 Map 4

Golden Heart ♀

Nettleton Bottom (not shown on road maps, so we list the pub instead under the name of the nearby village); on A417 N of the Brimpsfield turning northbound; GL4 8LA

This is an enjoyable roadside pub of some genuine character and run by a friendly hands-on landlord. The main low-ceilinged bar is divided into five cosily distinct areas; there's a roaring log fire in the huge stone inglenook fireplace in one, traditional built-in settles and other old-fashioned furnishings throughout, and quite a few brass items, typewriters, exposed stone and wood panelling; newspapers to read. A comfortable parlour on the right has another decorative fireplace, and leads into a further room that opens on to the terrace; three areas are no smoking. A fair choice of bar food includes home-made soup (£3.95), doorstep sandwiches (from £4.25), baked potatoes (from £5.95), ploughman's (from £6.25), omelettes with free-range eggs (£6.95), steaks (from £11.95), and specials such as garlic mushrooms or crayfish tails in chilli sauce (£5.25), battered fish and chips (£8.50), mushroom stroganoff (£9.25), steak in ale pie (£10.95), chicken breast stuffed with blue cheese and wrapped in bacon (£11.25), and calves liver and bacon (£11.95). Well kept Archers Best Bitter, Marstons Pedigree, Timothy Taylors Golden Best and Wickwar BOB on handpump, and quite a few wines by the glass. From the rustic cask-supported tables on the suntrap terrace, there are pleasant views down over a valley; nearby walks. If you are thinking of staying here, bear in mind that the nearby road is a busy all-night link between the M4 and M5. *(Recommended by Martin and Karen Wake, R Huggins, D Irving, E McCall, T McLean, Theocsbrian, Ian Phillips, N R White, Colin Moore, Neil and Anita Christopher, Mr and Mrs I and E Bell, Guy Vowles)*

Free house ~ Licensee Catherine Stevens ~ Real ale ~ Bar food (12-3, 6-10; all day Sun) ~ (01242) 870261 ~ Children welcome ~ Dogs welcome ~ Open 11-3, 5.30-11; 11-11 Sat; 12-10.30 Sun; closed 25 Dec ~ Bedrooms: £35S/£55S

CHEDWORTH SP0511 Map 4

Seven Tuns

Village signposted off A429 NE of Cirencester; then take second signposted right turn and bear left towards church; GL54 4AE

Run by genuinely friendly people, this little 17th-c pub is handy for the famous nearby Roman villa, and there are nice walks through the valley. The snug little no smoking lounge on the right has comfortable seats and decent tables, sizeable antique prints, tankards hanging from the beam over the serving bar, a partly boarded ceiling, and a good winter log fire in a big stone fireplace. Down a couple of steps, the public bar on the left has an open fire, and this opens into a no smoking dining room with another open fire. Well kept Youngs Special and two seasonal guests on handpump, 12 wines by the glass, and 18 malt whiskies; darts, TV, skittle alley and piped music. Well liked bar food includes lunchtime sandwiches or filled baked potatoes (£4.95), and ploughman's (£6.95), as well as satay chicken kebab (£5.50), tian of fresh crab, coriander and spring onion (£5.95), home-made sage and rosemary beefburger with bacon and cheese, roasted mediterranean vegetable risotto and steak and kidney pie, ham and egg (all £7.95), battered fish and chips (£8.95), calves liver with bubble and squeak and onion and bacon gravy or teriyaki salmon with stir-fried vegetables (£10.95), and roasted lamb rump with garlic new potatoes and mint and rosemary sauce (£12.95); Sunday roast (£10.95). One sunny terrace has a boules pitch and across the road there's another little walled raised terrace with a waterwheel and a stream; plenty of tables and seats. *(Recommended by D P and M A Miles, Mrs Roxanne Chamberlain, R Huggins, D Irving, E McCall, T McLean, Guy Vowles, Keith and Sue Ward, DWT, John Reilly, Giles and Annie Francis)*

Youngs ~ Tenant Mr Davenport-Jones ~ Real ale ~ Bar food (12-2.30(3 Sun), 6.30-9.30 (10 Sat, 9 Sun)) ~ (01285) 720242 ~ Children welcome ~ Dogs allowed in bar ~ Open 11.30-midnight; 12-2am Fri and Sat; 12-10.30 Sun; 11.30-3, 6-midnight Mon-Fri in winter; closed 25 Dec

CHIPPING CAMPDEN SP1539 Map 4

Eight Bells 🍺 🛏

Church Street (which is one way – entrance off B4035); GL55 6JG

Neatly kept and handsome, this old inn is a pleasant place with heavy oak beams, massive timber supports, and stripped stone walls. It's totally no smoking now, and there are cushioned pews and solid dark wood furniture on the broad flagstones, daily papers, and log fires in up to three restored stone fireplaces. Part of the floor in the dining room has a glass inlet showing part of the passage from the church by which Roman Catholic priests could escape from the Roundheads. There's quite an emphasis on the food with menus on most tables: lunchtime sandwiches, home-made soup (£4.85), chicken liver parfait with apple and grape chutney (£6.25), warm salad of black pudding, peppers, bacon and chorizo (£6.50), fresh tagliatelle with roasted peppers, rocket pesto and melting goats cheese (£9.75), pork and chive sausages with mustard mash and rich onion gravy (£10), beer-battered fillet of plaice (£11.25), roast chicken breast with spicy bean cassoulet (£11.75), slow-braised lamb shank with rosemary mash and red wine jus (£14.95), and puddings such as apple and plum crumble with crème anglaise or dark chocolate cheesecake with Cointreau cream (£5.25). Well kept Goffs Jouster, Hook Norton Best and Old Hooky and Wickwar Cotswold Way on handpump from the fine oak bar counter, quite a few wines, Old Rosie cider and country wines. Piped music, darts and board games. There's a large terraced garden with plenty of seats, and striking views of the almshouses and church. The pub is handy for the Cotswold Way walk to Bath. *(Recommended by Gerry and Rosemary Dobson, Simon Collett-Jones, David and Jean Hall, Dr David Cockburn, David Howe, W W Burke, Michael Dandy, Tracey and Stephen Groves, Susan and John Douglas, Russell Grimshaw, Kerry Purcell, Roger Huggins, D M Heath, Bob Ellis, George Atkinson)*

Free house ~ Licensee Neil Hargreaves ~ Real ale ~ Bar food (12-2(2.30 Fri and Sat), 6.30-9(9.30 Fri and Sat); 12-2.30, 7-9 Sun) ~ Restaurant ~ (01386) 840371 ~ Children welcome until 9pm ~ Dogs allowed in bar ~ Open 12-11(10.30 Sun); closed 25 Dec ~ Bedrooms: £50S/£95S(£85B)

Volunteer 🍺

Lower High Street; GL55 6DY

New licensees have taken over this village pub and quite a bit of the old memorabilia has gone. The front bar now has oak flooring and has been repainted to give a more modern feel. There are cushioned seats in bay windows, a good log fire piled with big logs in the golden stone fireplace, proper old dining chairs with sage green plush seats and some similarly covered stools around a mix of tables, old army (Waterloo and WWI) paintings and bugles on the walls, some old local photographs, and quite a few brass spigots dotted about. The no smoking back room has been reworked into an eating area. Bar food now includes soup (£3.95), sandwiches or panini (from £4.25), garlic mushrooms (£4.75), ploughman's (£5.95), vegetarian lasagne (£6.95), fishcakes (£7.50), fish in beer batter, home-made steak and kidney pie or ham and egg (£7.95), and fillet steak (£13.95); there's also a take-away menu. Archers, Hook Norton Old Hooky, Goffs Jouster and Shepherd Neame Spitfire on handpump. Picnic-sets in a small brick-paved ivy courtyard with an arch through to the back garden where there are more seats. More reports please. *(Recommended by Derek and Sylvia Stephenson, Andy and Claire Barker, Michael Dandy, Simon Collett-Jones, Tracey and Stephen Groves, S Baranowski, E Slavid)*

Free house ~ Licensee Mark Gibson ~ Real ale ~ Bar food (12-2(2.30 Sat and Sun), 7-9) ~ Restaurant ~ (01386) 840688 ~ Children welcome ~ Dogs allowed in bar ~ Open 11-11(midnight Sat); 11-10.30 Sun; 12-3, 5-11 in winter ~ Bedrooms: £40B/£70B

COWLEY SO9714 Map 4
Green Dragon
Off A435 S of Cheltenham at Elkstone, Cockleford signpost; OS Sheet 163 map reference 970142; GL53 9NW

The two bars in this attractive stone-fronted dining pub have a cosy and genuinely old-fashioned feel: big flagstones and wooden boards, beams, two stone fireplaces (welcoming fires in winter), candlelit tables and a woodburning stove. The furniture and the bar itself in the upper Mouse Bar were made by Robert Thompson, and little mice run over the hand-carved chairs, tables and mantelpiece; the larger Lower Bar (and upstairs restaurant) are no smoking. Under the new licensees, lunchtime bar food now includes sandwiches (from £4.95; not Sunday), smoked haddock and spring onion fishcakes (£5.75), smoked salmon, crayfish and cream cheese parcel with a light lemon and parsley dressing (£5.75), and cheese and tomato omelette, steak burger in ciabatta with stilton and caramelised onions or turkey and mushroom pie (all £6.95); more elaborate dishes such as baked goats cheese, tomato and aubergine gateau with tomato coulis (£9.95), steak and kidney suet pudding (£10.75), garlic and mustard pork fillet with sweet apple jus (£12.25), and barbary duck breast with stir-fried vegetables, egg noodles and chilli plum sauce (£12.75); piped music. Terraces outside overlook Cowley Lake and the River Churn, and the pub is a good centre for the local walks. *(Recommended by Stuart Turner, KC, R Huggins, D Irving, E McCall, T McLean, Guy Vowles, Ian Phillips, Russell Grimshaw, Kerry Purcell, Bruce and Sharon Eden, Keith and Sue Ward, Peter and Audrey Dowsett, Jo Rees, John Reilly, Mr and Mrs J Brown, Theocsbrian, Michael Doswell)*

Buccaneer Holdings ~ Managers Simon and Nicky Haly ~ Real ale ~ Bar food (12-2.30 (3 Sat, 3.30 Sun), 6-10(9.30 Sun)) ~ Restaurant ~ (01242) 870271 ~ Children welcome ~ Dogs allowed in bar and bedrooms ~ Open 11-11; 12-10.30 Sun ~ Bedrooms: £57B/£75B

DIDMARTON ST8187 Map 2
Kings Arms ♀ 🛏
A433 Tetbury road; GL9 1DT

New licensees again for this busy pub, close to Westonbirt Arboretum. Several knocked-through rooms work their way around a big central counter with deep terracotta walls above a dark green dado, a pleasant mix of chairs on bare boards, quarry tiles and carpet, hops on beams, and a big stone fireplace. Bar food now includes soup (£3.95), tomato and mozzarella tian with pickled shallots and red pesto (£4.95), terrine of the day (£5.25), scallops on spring onion risotto with red pepper dressing (£6.25), calves liver on cabbage and onion mash, lasagne or chicken supreme in a rich bacon and cream sauce (all £9.95), steaks (from £9.95), wild mushroom and red pepper cannelloni (£10.25), half roast barbary duck with sweet cherry jus (£13.95), daily specials, and puddings such as brûlée of the day with cinnamon shortbread, marbled chocolate parfait with crushed honeycombe and brandied berries or rhubarb and apple crumble (from £4.95). Bath Ales Barnstormer, Sharps Wills Resolve and Uley Bitter on handpump, and ten wines by the glass; darts, TV and piped music. There are seats out in the pleasant back garden, and they have self-catering cottages in a converted barn and stable block. *(Recommended by Michael Doswell, Tom and Ruth Rees, Dr A McCormick, Donna and Roger, Alec and Barbara Jones, Jonathan Martin, Dr and Mrs C W Thomas, Barry and Anne, Bernard Stradling, Pamela and Alan Neale, Stephen Woad, Simon Jones, Sebastian Snow, Tom Evans, Andrew Scarr, Dr and Mrs A K Clarke, Malcolm Ward, Richard Wyld, J Crosby, Rod Stoneman)*

Free house ~ Licensee Nigel Pushman ~ Real ale ~ Bar food ~ Restaurant ~
(01454) 238245 ~ Children allowed but must be fully supervised at all times ~ Dogs
allowed in bar ~ Open 11-3, 6-11; 11-11 Sat; 12-10.30 Sun ~ Bedrooms: £55S/£80S

DOYNTON ST7174 Map 2
Cross House 🍺

**Village signposted with Dyrham off A420 Bristol—Chippenham just E of Wick; High
Street; BS30 5TF**

With a good welcome from the friendly and helpful landlord and his staff, this
18th-c village pub has a fine mix of customers. The softly lit carpeted bar, with
some beams and stripped stone, has a chatty atmosphere, simple pub furniture
brightened up with cheerful scatter cushions and a good woodburning stove in its
big stone fireplace. Two or three steps take you down to a cottagey candlelit dining
room with a small no smoking area. Besides good value traditional sandwiches
(from £2.40), good plain home cooking includes chicken liver pâté (£3.50), steak
and kidney pie or faggots (£7.25), rabbit pie (£8.25), chicken breast in white wine
and stilton sauce (£8.75), and mini leg of lamb with mint and barbecue sauce
(£8.95). Well kept Abbey Ales Bellringer, Bath Ales Gem Bitter, Courage Best,
Fullers London Pride and Greene King Old Speckled Hen on handpump, and 14
decent wines by the glass; darts, games machine, TV and piped music. There are
picnic-sets out by the road. This is good walking country, and Dyrham Park is quite
close. *(Recommended by Dr and Mrs C W Thomas, Andrew Shore, Maria Williams)*

Unique (Enterprise) ~ Lease Andre and Liz Large ~ Real ale ~ Bar food (11.30-2, 6(7 Sun)-
9.30(10 Fri and Sat)) ~ (0117) 937 2261 ~ Children in eating area of bar ~ Dogs allowed
in bar ~ Open 11.30-3, 6-11; 12-4, 7-10.30 Sun

DUNTISBOURNE ABBOTS SO9709 Map 4
Five Mile House 🍽 🍺

**Off A417 at Duntisbourne Abbots exit sign; then, coming from Gloucester, pass filling
station and keep on parallel to main road; coming from Cirencester, take Duntisbourne
Abbots services sign, then immediate right and take the underpass below the main road,
then turn right at T junction; GL7 7JR**

A favourite with many of our readers and somewhere they meet up with friends to
enjoy 'the larky atmosphere', good beer and food, and friendly welcome. It's an
imposing stone building with plenty of original character and a super mix of
customers, and the front room has a companionable bare-boards drinking bar on
the right (plenty of convivial banter from the locals), with wall seats around the big
table in its bow window and just one other table. On the left is a flagstoned hallway
tap room snug formed from two ancient high-backed settles by a woodburning
stove in a tall carefully exposed old fireplace; newspapers to read. There's a small
cellar bar, a back restaurant down steps, and a family room on the far side; darts.
The eating areas are no smoking. Cooked by the landlord, the enjoyable food at
lunchtime includes filled baked potatoes (from £5.25), open sandwiches (£5.50),
ploughman's (£6.50), free-range egg omelette (£7.50), and deep-fried cod and chips
or home-cooked smoked ham and eggs (£8.50); favourites such as home-made soup
(£3.75), home-made pâté or hot brie with cranberry sauce (£4.95), hot chicken
livers with bacon (£5.45), home-made pies, home-made fishcakes or local sausages
with bubble and squeak (£9.50), shoulder of lamb with redcurrant and mint or
chicken breast stuffed with stilton, wrapped in bacon and served on a mushroom
and brandy cream sauce (£10.95), lemon sole fillets stuffed with crab claw meat
and coriander in a light mustard sauce or bass fillets with garlic butter and fresh
asparagus (£13.50), and at least ten home-made puddings like lovely bakewell tart
(£4.95). Well kept Donningtons BB, Timothy Taylors Landlord and Youngs Bitter
with maybe a local guest from Cottage on handpump (the cellar is temperature-
controlled), and an interesting wine list (strong on new world ones). The gardens
have nice country views; the country lane was once Ermine Street, the main Roman
road from Wales to London. *(Recommended by Carol Broadbent, John Kane, Bren and*

Val Speed, Mr and Mrs I and E Bell, R Huggins, D Irving, E McCall, T McLean, Julie and
Bill Ryan, Guy Vowles, Neil and Anita Christopher, Dr A J and Mrs Tompsett, Nick and
Meriel Cox, Giles and Annie Francis, Keith and Sue Ward, the Didler, Mr and Mrs J Brown,
Tom and Ruth Rees, Gordon and Jay Smith, Mark and Joanna, Rod Stoneman, Gordon Prince,
J Crosby, W W Burke)

Free house ~ Licensees Jo and Jon Carrier ~ Real ale ~ Bar food (12-2.30, 6-9.30; 12-2.30,
7-9 Sun) ~ Restaurant ~ (01285) 821432 ~ Children welcome if well behaved ~ Dogs
allowed in bar ~ Open 12-3, 6-11; 12-3, 7-11 Sun

DURSLEY ST7598 Map 4
Old Spot ▣ £
By bus station; GL11 4JQ

Easy to miss, tucked away as it is behind a car park, this unassuming town pub has
a marvellous bouncy atmosphere and a good mix of customers. Most have come to
enjoy the fine choice of up to ten real ales well kept on handpump (and four annual
beer festivals). Alongside Uley Old Ric, a typical choice of beers might include
Butcombe Bitter and Blonde, Caledonian Six Nations, Fullers ESB, Goffs Jouster,
White Horse Village Idiot and Wickwar BOB; quite a few malt whiskies too. The
front door opens into a deep pink little room with stools on shiny quarry tiles along
its pine boarded bar counter, and old enamel beer advertisements on the walls and
ceiling; there's a profusion of porcine paraphernalia. A small room on the left
leading off from here has shove-ha'penny, cribbage and dominoes, and the little
dark wood floored room to the right has a stone fireplace. From here a step takes
you down to a cosy Victorian tiled snug and (to the right) the no smoking meeting
room. Bar food includes filled panini (£3.75), cauliflower cheese (£4.95), ratatouille
bake (£5.45), ploughman's (£5.75), sausage and mash with onion gravy, home-
cooked ham with parsley sauce or haddock and chive fishcakes (all £6.45), chicken
fajitas (£6.75), home-made pies (from £6.75), and home-made puddings like white
chocolate cheesecake or apple crumble (£3.75). *(Recommended by PL, Clive and*
Valerie Alpe, R Huggins, D Irving, E McCall, T McLean, Clare Rosier)

Free house ~ Licensee Steve Herbert ~ Real ale ~ Bar food (12-8 Mon-Thurs; 12-2
Fri-Sun) ~ No credit cards ~ (01453) 542870 ~ Children welcome with restrictions ~
Dogs welcome ~ Various live artists Weds evenings ~ Open 11-11; 12-11 Sun

EASTLEACH TURVILLE SP1905 Map 4
Victoria ♀
Village signposted off A361 S of Burford; GL7 3NQ

Picnic-sets in front of this old pub look down over a steep bank of spring daffodils
at the other stone-built houses and a couple of churches; there are also seats at the
back behind the car park. Low ceilinged and open plan, the rooms are nicely
divided and ramble cosily around a central bar, with sturdy pub tables of varying
sizes, and some attractive seats – particularly those built in beside the log fire in the
stripped stone chimneybreast. There are some unusual engravings and lithographs
of Queen Victoria around the back. Well kept Arkells 2B and a guest such as 3B on
handpump, and nine wines by the glass; may be unobtrusive piped music. The
right-hand area has been recently refurbished and has a stone floor and darts. Bar
food includes filled baguettes, home-made soup (£3.25), deep-fried camembert with
cranberry dip (£4.50), gammon and mozzarella (£7.75), steak and mushroom pie
(£8.25), mushroom stroganoff (£8.50), calves liver and bacon with red wine sauce
(£9.45), organic pork chop with apple and calvados (£9.50), and puddings (£4); the
restaurant is no smoking. *(Recommended by Michael Cooper, Gaynor Gregory,*
Julie and Bill Ryan, Paul and Shirley White, Maurice Holt, Lawrence Pearse)

Arkells ~ Tenants Stephen and Susan Richardson ~ Real ale ~ Bar food (not winter Sun
evenings) ~ Restaurant ~ (01367) 850277 ~ Children welcome ~ Dogs allowed in bar ~
Open 12-3, 7-11; 12-4, 7-10.30 Sun

EWEN   SU0097   Map 4
Wild Duck ♀
Village signposted from A429 S of Cirencester; GL7 6BY

Attractively civilised and usually very busy, this 16th-c inn is on the edge of a
peaceful village – though handy for Cirencester. The high-beamed main bar has a
nice mix of comfortable armchairs and other seats, paintings on the red walls,
crimson drapes, a winter open fire, and maybe candles on tables. The residents'
lounge, which overlooks the garden, has a handsome Elizabethan fireplace and
antique furnishings. Besides Duckpond Bitter (brewed especially for the pub), you'll
find well kept Archers Golden, Theakstons Old Peculier and a guest on handpump,
28 wines by the glass, and several malt whiskies; piped music and shove-ha'penny.
Bar food includes soup (£3.95), ardennes and porcini pâté with pickles or
ploughman's (£6.95), home-baked gloucester old spot ham salad or filled panini
(£8.50), thai vegetable curry (£9.50), home-made burger (£9.95), poached salmon
and asparagus salad with parma ham, parmesan and white crab dressing (£12.95),
aberdeen angus steaks (from £15.95), and daily specials such as wild boar sausages
with celeriac mash and grain mustard sauce (£10.95) and shark steak with citrus
curry sauce (£12.95). Pleasant in summer, the neatly kept and sheltered garden has
wooden tables and seats. You will be asked to leave your credit card behind the
bar. *(Recommended by R Seifas, Julie and Bill Ryan, Mrs Carolyn Dixon, Tom and Ruth Rees,
Richard and Sheila Fitton, Guy Vowles, Pat and Tony Martin, R Huggins, D Irving, E McCall,
T McLean, KC, Paul and Annette Hallett, Ian Phillips, Karen and Graham Oddey,
Mr and Mrs J Brown)*

Free house ~ Licensees Tina and Dino Mussell ~ Real ale ~ Bar food (12-2, 7-10; all day
weekends) ~ Restaurant ~ (01285) 770310 ~ Children welcome ~ Dogs allowed in bar
and bedrooms ~ Open 11-11(midnight Sat); 12-11 Sun ~ Bedrooms: £70B/£95B

FAIRFORD   SP1501   Map 4
Bull 🛏
Market Place; GL7 4AA

The sizeable main bar in this rather smart and civilised old hotel – redecorated this
year – is popular locally and has a thriving, chatty atmosphere. It's nicely laid out,
with beams and timbers, comfortably old-fashioned pubby furnishings including
dark pews and settles (try to sit at the big table in the bow window overlooking the
little market square), and on its ochre walls, aircraft pictures and photographs of
actors and actresses who have stayed here. The coal-effect gas fire is rather realistic.
The long bar has well kept Arkells 2B, 3B and Kingsdown on handpump, and
service is friendly. Up a few stone steps a nice little residents' lounge has some
attractive soft leather sofas and armchairs around its big stone fireplace, and fishing
prints and plates. The no smoking restaurant, in former stables, is charming. Quite
a choice of reasonably priced bar food includes lunchtime filled baked potatoes
(from £3.25) and baguettes (from £3.75), as well as soup (£2.95), home-made
chicken liver pâté (£3.75), bacon and stilton mushrooms (£3.95), a pie of the day
(£7.95), haddock wrapped in bacon on courgette and pepper ragoût or strips of
chicken with ham in a creamy garlic and tomato sauce (£8.95), steamed lamb and
mint suet pudding or courgette and mushroom pasta with cream (£9.95), fillet
steak (£14.95), and puddings (£3.75). Disabled lavatories have been installed. The
village is charming, and the church just along the street has Britain's only intact set
of medieval stained-glass windows. *(Recommended by Ian Phillips, Peter and
Audrey Dowsett)*

Arkells ~ Tenants Judy and Mark Dudley ~ Real ale ~ Bar food (12-2, 6-9) ~ Restaurant ~
(01285) 712535 ~ Children welcome ~ Dogs allowed in bar and bedrooms ~ Open
10am-11pm; 12-10.30 Sun; closed evening 25 Dec ~ Bedrooms: £39.50(£49.50B)/£79.50B

Soup prices usually include a roll and butter.

FORD SP0829 Map 4

Plough

B4077 Stow—Alderton; GL54 5RU

As this honey-coloured stone pub is opposite a well known racehorse trainer's yard, many of the customers are stable hands and jockeys – but there are plenty of visitors too, and the atmosphere is chatty and friendly. It does get packed on race meeting evenings. The beamed and stripped-stone bar has racing prints and photos on the walls, old settles and benches around the big tables on its uneven flagstones, oak tables in a snug alcove, four welcoming log fires (two are log-effect gas), and dominoes, cribbage, shove-ha'penny, pool, games machine, TV (for the races), and piped music. Very good, well presented bar food includes lunchtime filled baguettes (from £4.95), baked ham and free-range eggs (£8.50), and liver and smoky bacon with onion gravy or steak and mushroom in ale pie (£9.95), with evening dishes such as venison casserole, half a crispy duck with orange and Cointreau sauce (£13.95), and half a shoulder of lamb with mint and rosemary jus or scotch fillet with roquefort butter and a mushroom and red wine sauce (£14.95); the restaurant is no smoking. They offer breakfasts for travellers on the way to the Gold Cup meeting at Cheltenham, and have traditional asparagus feasts every April to June. Well kept Donnington BB and SBA on handpump, and Addlestone's cider; good efficient service, even when busy. There are benches in the garden, pretty hanging baskets, and a play area at the back. The Cotswold Farm Park is nearby. *(Recommended by Nigel and Sue Foster, Michael Cooper, Paul and Shirley White, Andy and Claire Barker, Roger Braithwaite, the Didler, Di and Mike Gillam, Peter and Margaret Glenister, Iain R Hewitt, Stephen Woad, A G Marx, Lawrence Pearse, Peter and Audrey Dowsett, John and Hazel Williams, R J Herd)*

Donnington ~ Manager Craig Brown ~ Real ale ~ Bar food (all day in summer and all day winter weekends) ~ Restaurant ~ (01386) 584215 ~ Children welcome ~ Dogs allowed in bar ~ Open 11-midnight(1am Sat); 12-10.30 Sun; closed 25 Dec ~ Bedrooms: £35S/£70S

FRAMPTON MANSELL SO9201 Map 4

White Horse 🍴 🍷

A491 Cirencester—Stroud; GL6 8HZ

Gloucestershire Dining Pub of the Year

Completely refurbished, this smart dining pub now has seagrass flooring, paintwork throughout in mulberry, cream and chocolate, new artwork, and fresh new tablecloths. Although there's quite an emphasis on the popular food, the atmosphere is cheerful and informal and a cosy bar area has a large sofa and comfortable chairs for those who just want a relaxing drink: Uley Bitter and a guest such as Arkells Summer Ale or Hook Norton Best on handpump, ten wines by the glass (plus house champagne) from a well chosen wine list (now with helpful notes against each wine), and quite a few malt whiskies. The seafood tank was just waiting to be replenished as we went to press and they will continue to serve fresh cornish lobsters, crabs, native oysters, clams and mussels. All of their meat originates from traceable sources. As well as lunchtime snacks such as croque monsieur, filled baguettes or panini (£4.95), home-glazed ham with two eggs and home-made chips (£8.95), battered cod (£9.95), and chicken caesar salad (£10.95), the excellent food might include pea and pear soup (£3.95), milano, jerusalem and goose salami with shallot, gherkin and tomato salsa (£5.95), fried chicken livers, potato pancake, sherry jus and crisp pancetta (£6.95), leek risotto with grilled goats cheese and basil pesto (£11.25), toulouse sausages, sweet potato mash and red wine cream sauce (£12.95), chicken breast with curried butternut squash and greek yoghurt with lime (£14.25), pork fillet stuffed with dates, celeriac purée and a soy, ginger and balsamic jus (£14.75), halibut fillet, roasted artichokes, red peppers and a crayfish tail and chive butter (£15.25), and puddings like white chocolate and cardamom mousse in a dark chocolate cup, elderflower and strawberry jelly with vanilla ice-cream, and sticky toffee pudding with butterscotch sauce (£4.95). Well liked rare breed meat Sunday roasts (from £10.50). The restaurant is no smoking.

The landscaped garden is a pleasant place for a meal or a drink. *(Recommended by Tom and Ruth Rees, Richard and Sheila Fitton, Rod Stoneman, Andy and Claire Barker, Martin and Sue Day)*

Free house ~ Licensees Shaun and Emma Davis ~ Real ale ~ Bar food (12-2.30(3 Sun), 7-9.45; not Sun evening) ~ Restaurant ~ (01285) 760960 ~ Children welcome ~ Dogs welcome ~ Open 11-3, 6-11; 12-4 Sun; closed Sun evening; first four days Jan

FRAMPTON ON SEVERN   SO7408   Map 4
Bell 🍺

3 miles from M5 junction 13; from A419 left on to A38 then following village signpost right on to B4071; The Green; GL2 7EP

This handsome creeper-covered three-storey Georgian inn stands at the top of a huge village cricket green – said to be England's longest village green. The building really makes the most of its position, now that they've moved the car park round to the back, so that picnic-sets under cocktail parasols have the sweep of forecourt to themselves. There are more in the garden, with a good play area behind, and what amounts to a kids' farm complete with dartmoor ponies, pigs, goats, sheep and ducks. Inside has recently been opened up and attractively refurbished, with some tub armchairs by the modern corner servery, which has real ales such as Greene King IPA, Hook Norton Old Hooky and a guest from Wickwar on handpump, and a good choice of other drinks including decent wines by the glass. Spreading out from here is an extensive carpeted dining area, with a mix of comfortable chairs around a variety of tables, some rather elegant. Enjoyable food using only local supplies includes home-made soup (£3.95), filled baguettes (from £4.95), deep-fried brie with cranberry coulis (£5.50), grilled sardines with sea salt (£5.95), steak in ale pie, ham and eggs or rice and vegetable nut loaf with provençale sauce (all £8.95), roast chicken in honey, pine nuts and thyme with roasted vegetable couscous (£10.50), fresh bass fillet with lemon and herb butter and pesto mash (£12.95), and puddings such as pistachio crème brûlée or chocolate and Cointreau mousse (£4.95); at lunchtime, they also offer a one-course (£5.95), two-course (£6.95) and three-course (£7.95) menu, Monday-Friday midday-6pm. The landlord and staff are friendly; there's a log fire, and table skittles. We have not yet heard from readers who have tried the three bedrooms here. The pub is a short walk away from the Sharpness Canal. *(Recommended by Mr and Mrs J Brown, A and B D Craig, Ken Marshall, Lynn Elliott, Jo Rees, Peter Neate, Michael Longman)*

Enterprise ~ Lease Easton Hoben ~ Real ale ~ Bar food (12-9) ~ Restaurant ~ (01452) 740346 ~ Well behaved children allowed ~ Open 11am-11.30pm; 11-1am Fri and Sat; 12-11 Sun ~ Bedrooms: /£90B

GUITING POWER   SP0924   Map 4
Hollow Bottom

Village signposted off B4068 SW of Stow-on-the-Wold (still called A436 on many maps); GL54 5UX

On the edge of an unspoilt village, this friendly 17th-c inn is extremely popular. The comfortable beamed bar has lots of racing memorabilia including racing silks, tunics and photographs (it's owned by a small syndicate that includes Peter Scudamore and Nigel Twiston-Davies), and a winter log fire in an unusual pillar-supported stone fireplace. The public bar has flagstones and stripped stone masonry and racing on TV; newspapers to read, darts, board games and piped music. Well kept Fullers London Pride, Wye Valley O'er the Sticks and a beer named for the pub (from Badger) on handpump, 15 malt whiskies, and seven wines (including champagne) by the glass; the staff are friendly and obliging. As well as specials like fresh fish (from £11.50), wild mushroom and spinach lasagne (£11.95), naturally smoked haddock in a light cheese sauce (£12.95), pork fillet in cider and cream (£13.95), slow-cooked shoulder of lamb in red wine, impala fillet in a cherry tomato and mushroom sauce or beef in brandy and green peppercorn sauce (£14.95), and ten home-made puddings (£4.95), the good food might include home-made soup (£4.75), filled baguettes (from £5.95), filled baked potatoes (from £6.95), ploughman's or home-made burger (£8.45), and ham and eggs or cottage pie (£8.95); on Sundays they only do a carvery (£11.95; you must pre-book). The restaurant is no smoking. From the pleasant garden behind are views towards the peaceful sloping fields, and there are decent walks nearby. *(Recommended by Mr and Mrs J Brown, C A Hall, Marian Higton, Roger Maskew, Michael and Jenny Back, Michael Sargent, Keith and Sue Ward, Tim Barrett, Lynn Nisbet)*

Free house ~ Licensees Hugh Kelly and Charles Pettigrew ~ Real ale ~ Bar food (all day) ~ Restaurant ~ (01451) 850392 ~ Children welcome ~ Dogs allowed in bar and bedrooms ~ Open 10am-12.30pm ~ Bedrooms: £45B/£70B

LITTLE BARRINGTON SP2012 Map 4
Inn For All Seasons 🍽 ♀
On the A40 3 miles W of Burford; OX18 4TN

This is a handsome and well run old inn with quite an emphasis on the popular food. The attractively decorated, mellow lounge bar has low beams, stripped stone, and flagstones, old prints, leather-upholstered wing armchairs and other comfortable seats, country magazines to read, and a big log fire. From a particularly good wine list, there are 20 wines by the glass (from a 120 bin list), 60 malt whiskies, and Sharps Own and Wadworths 6X on handpump with maybe a guest like Fullers London Pride on handpump; friendly, kind service. Fish is the speciality here and from quite a choice there might be grilled fresh sardines with garlic, port and parsley butter sauce (£6.25; main course £9.95), flash-fried squid with lime and baby spinach salad (£6.50; main course £9.95), irish rock oysters (£7.50 for 6), red thai fish curry (£9.95), fillet of river dart salmon with vermouth, smoked bacon and spinach sauce (£11.95), fillet of cod deep-fried with home-made chunky chips or grilled fillet of yellowfin tuna on niçoise salad (£12.95), and whole cock crabs (served only in the garden, £16.50); also, soup (£4.95), chicken liver parfait with grape chutney (£5.50), filled panini (£6.75), grilled mediterranean vegetables, rocket and balsamic syrup (£7.50), filo parcel of tofu and courgettes with tomato sauce (£9.95), braised shin of beef with mash (£12.95), free-range pork cutlet with a green peppercorn sauce (£13.75), rump of lamb with herb crust and minted jus (£15.75), roast chicken breast with chasseur sauce (£15.95), and puddings such as sticky toffee pudding with fudge sauce or apple and berry crumble (£4.75). The restaurant and conservatory are no smoking. Cribbage, board games and piped music. The pleasant garden has tables, a play area, and aunt sally, and there are walks straight from the inn. It gets very busy during Cheltenham Gold Cup Week. *(Recommended by KN-R, Peter and Audrey Dowsett, Dave Braisted, DWT, Keith and Sue Ward, Lewis Osborn, Derek Thomas, K Clarkson, B M Eldridge, Les and Barbara Owen, Karen and Graham Oddey, David Glynne-Jones, Dennis Jenkin)*

Free house ~ Licensees Matthew and Heather Sharp ~ Real ale ~ Bar food (12-2.30, 6-9.30; 12-2 Sun; not Sun evening) ~ Restaurant ~ (01451) 844324 ~ Children welcome ~ Dogs allowed in bar and bedrooms ~ Open 10.30-2.30, 6-10.30(11 Sat); 12-2.30, 7-10.30 Sun ~ Bedrooms: £59B/£102B

LITTLETON-UPON-SEVERN ST5990 Map 2
White Hart 🍺
3½ miles from M48 junction 1; B4461 towards Thornbury, then village signposted; BS35 1NR

There's always a really good mix of customers in this cosy 17th-c farmhouse – 'a delightful blend of village life' is how one reader put it. The three main rooms have log fires and some fine furnishings such as long cushioned wooden settles, high-backed settles, oak and elm tables, and a loveseat in the big low inglenook fireplace. There are flagstones in the front, huge tiles at the back, and smaller tiles on the left, plus some old pots and pans, and a lovely old White Hart Inn Simonds Ale sign. By the black wooden staircase are some nice little alcove seats, there's a black-panelled big fireplace in the front room, and hops on beams. Similarly furnished, a no smoking family room has some sentimental engravings, plates on a delft shelf, and a couple of high chairs; a back snug has pokerwork seats. Well kept Youngs Bitter, Special, and a seasonal beer plus maybe Hop Back Summer Lightning and St Austell Tribute on handpump, and several wines by the glass; bar billiards and board games. Good bar food includes lunchtime filled baguettes (from £3.50; melted goats cheese with honey and walnuts £4.95) and ploughman's (from £5.50), as well as potato and spinach curry with tomato, garlic and onions (£7.95), beer-battered haddock or local pork sausages with beer and onion gravy (£8.50), honey-roasted ham and eggs or beef in ale stew with dumplings (£8.95), braised lamb shank with red wine and mint jus (£10.95), and puddings such as home-made creamed rice pudding with jam or chocolate latte mousse (£3.95). Outside, there are picnic-sets on the neat front lawn with interesting cottagey flowerbeds, and by the good big back car park are some attractive shrubs and teak furniture on a small brick terrace; boules. Several enjoyable walks from the pub. *(Recommended by Andy and Jill Kassube, A and B D Craig, Donna and Roger, Mike and Mary Carter, R Huggins, D Irving, E McCall, T McLean, W F C Phillips, Pete Devonish, Ian McIntyre)*

Youngs ~ Managers Greg Bailey and Claire Wells ~ Real ale ~ Bar food (12-2(2.30 Sat/Sun), 6.30-9.30(9 Sun)) ~ (01454) 412275 ~ Children in family room only ~ Dogs allowed in bar ~ Open 12-2.30, 6-11; 12-11 Sat; 12-10.30 Sun

LOWER ODDINGTON   SP2326   Map 4

Fox 🍴 ♀

Signposted off A436 between Stow and Chipping Norton; GL56 0UR

There's no doubt that most people come to this smart, busy inn to enjoy the food but they do serve Greene King Abbot, Hook Norton and a beer from Wickwar on handpump, and there are some bar stools. The simply furnished rooms have fresh flowers and flagstones, hunting scene figures above the mantelpiece, a display cabinet with pewter mugs and stone bottles, daily newspapers and an inglenook fireplace. Well presented food served by neat, uniformed staff might include courgette and roquefort risotto (£5.75; main course £9.75), rough and smooth pâté with port, star anise and fig chutney (£5.95), chicken caesar salad with pancetta (£5.95; main course £10.95), home-made potted shrimps (£6.75), lasagne (£9.50), steak and kidney pie (£11.50), braised lamb shank with garlic, rosemary and red wine (£11.95), rabbit fricassee with dijon mustard cream sauce (£12.95), whole baked lemon sole with fresh herb butter (£13.95), and puddings such as crème brûlée, pear and apple crumble or bitter chocolate pudding with chocolate fudge sauce (£4.75). There's a good wine list with quite a few by the glass. The terrace has a custom-built awning and outdoor heaters, and the cottagey garden is pretty. A good eight-mile walk starts from here (though a stroll around the pretty village might be less taxing). *(Recommended by Mr and Mrs J Brown, Keith and Sue Ward, A Warren, Noel Grundy, Gaynor Gregory, Paul Boot, Brian and Pat Wardrobe, Rod Stoneman, John and Gloria Isaacs, Tom McLean, Karen and Graham Oddey, Tracey and Stephen Groves)*

Free house ~ Licensees James Cathcart and Ian MacKenzie ~ Real ale ~ Bar food (12-2 (3 Sun), 6.30-10(7-9.30 Sun)) ~ Restaurant ~ (01451) 870555 ~ Children welcome ~ Dogs allowed in bar ~ Open 12-11(midnight Fri and Sat); 12-10.30 Sun; closed 25 Dec ~ Bedrooms: /£68S(£95B)

MISERDEN   SO9308   Map 4

Carpenters Arms

Village signposted off B4070 NE of Stroud; also a pleasant drive off A417 via the Duntisbournes, or off A419 via Sapperton and Edgeworth; OS Sheet 163 map reference 936089; GL6 7JA

With new owners and a new licensee, this attractively placed pub remains the only building in this idyllic Cotswold estate village that is not owned by the Misarden Estate. The two open-plan bar areas have low beams, nice old wooden tables and some cushioned settles and spindlebacks on the bare boards; stripped stone walls, some interesting bric-a-brac, and two big log fires. The small dining room is no smoking. Bar food now includes lunchtime sandwiches or filled baguettes (from £4.75), filled baked potatoes (£5.75), and ploughman's (from £6.50), as well as baked field mushrooms with garlic and tarragon (£4.25), home-made vegetable terrine (£4.50), home-made fishcakes, honey-roast ham and eggs and lamb burgers with fresh mint (all £7.95), home-made pie of the day (£8.25), oriental chicken stir fry (£8.50), venison casserole (£8.95), rump steak (£10.95), and puddings such as crème brûlée or bread and butter pudding (£3.75). Three-course weekend set lunch (£14.95). Greene King IPA, Wadworths 6X and a guest on handpump. There are seats out in the garden; the nearby gardens of Misarden Park are well worth visiting. More reports on the new regime, please. *(Recommended by Neil and Angela Huxter, Michael Cooper, R Huggins, D Irving, E McCall, T McLean, Gaynor Gregory, Neil and Anita Christopher, Michael Dallas, John Reilly)*

Esteemed Pubs Ltd ~ Lease Miss M Barrett ~ Real ale ~ Bar food ~ Restaurant ~ (01285) 821283 ~ Children welcome ~ Dogs allowed in bar ~ Open 11.30-3, 6.30(6 Sat)-midnight(1am Sat); 12-midnight Sun

NAILSWORTH ST8599 Map 4

Egypt Mill 🛏

Just off A46; heading N towards Stroud, first right after roundabout, then left; GL6 0AE

An interesting place to stay overnight, this unusual building (totally no smoking now) is a stylish conversion of a three-floor stone-built mill still with working waterwheels and the millstream flowing through. The brick-and-stone-floored split-level bar gives good views of the wheels, and there are big pictures and lots of stripped beams in the comfortable carpeted lounge, along with some hefty yet elegant ironwork from the old mill machinery; piped music. Ideal for summer evenings, the floodlit terrace garden by the millpond is pretty, and there's a little bridge over from the car park. Bar food includes sandwiches, home-made soup (£3.95), slow-roasted tomato, basil and blue cheese risotto (£4.95), cured meats or chicken, pork and tarragon terrine (£5.95), a roast of the day (£8.95), tian of aubergine (£9.95), calves liver with smoked bacon, red onion marmalade and horseradish cream or chicken breast on creamy leek sauce (£10.95), deep-fried haddock in beer batter (£11.50), moroccan-style lamb (£12.95), peppered breast of duck with sweet cherry jus (£14.25), and puddings such as vanilla crème brûlée or sticky toffee pudding (£4.95). It can get quite crowded on fine weekends, but it's spacious enough to feel at its best when busy. Archers Best on handpump, and ten wines by the glass. *(Recommended by Mike and Heather Watson, Andy and Claire Barker, Ian Phillips, J Roy Smylie, B R and M F Arnold, Basil and Jarvis, Tim and Suzy Bower, Mr and Mrs W D Borthwick, Alison and Pete)*

Free house ~ Licensees Stephen Webb and Rob Aldridge ~ Real ale ~ Bar food (12-2, 6.30-9.30(9.45 Fri and Sat); all day Sun) ~ Restaurant ~ (01453) 833449 ~ Children welcome ~ Dogs allowed in bedrooms ~ Open 11-11; 12-10.30 Sun ~ Bedrooms: £65B/£80B

Weighbridge 🍴 ♀

B4014 towards Tetbury; GL6 9AL

The two-in-one pies at this busy pub remain a great favourite with customers. They come in a large bowl, and half the bowl contains the filling of your choice while the other is full of home-made cauliflower cheese (or broccoli mornay or root vegetables), and topped with pastry: turkey and trimmings, salmon in a creamy sauce, steak and mushroom, roast root vegetables, pork, bacon and celery in stilton sauce or chicken, ham and leek in a cream and tarragon sauce (from £9.40; you can also have mini versions from £7.40 or straightforward pies from £8) Other dishes include home-made soup (£3.95), filled baguettes or filled baked potatoes (from £3.90; not evenings), cauliflower cheese (£5.95), spinach and mushroom lasagne (£6.95), omelettes, cottage pie or ploughman's (from £6.95), moussaka (£8.95), salmon fishcakes (£11.95), and puddings such as banana crumble or bakewell tart (£4.45). Most of the pub is now no smoking, and the relaxed bar has three cosily old-fashioned rooms with stripped stone walls, antique settles and country chairs, and window seats. The black beamed ceiling of the lounge bar is thickly festooned with black ironware – sheepshears, gin traps, lamps, and a large collection of keys, many from the old Longfords Mill opposite the pub. Upstairs is a raftered hayloft with an engaging mix of rustic tables. No noisy games machines or piped music. Well kept Uley Old Spot and Laurie Lee and Wadworths 6X on handpump, 16 wines (and champagne) by the glass, Weston's cider, and ten malt whiskies; fast, friendly service. Behind the building is a sheltered landscaped garden with picnic-sets under umbrellas. Good disabled access and facilities. *(Recommended by Tom and Ruth Rees, PRT, James Read, Ginette Medland, Andrew Shore, Maria Williams, Andy and Claire Barker, Dr and Mrs C W Thomas, S P Watkin, P A Taylor, John Reilly, R Huggins, D Irving, E McCall, T McLean, John and Jane Hayter)*

Free house ~ Licensee Howard Parker ~ Real ale ~ Bar food (12-9.30) ~ (01453) 832520 ~ Children allowed away from the bars until 9pm ~ Dogs welcome ~ Open 12-11; 12-10.30 Sun; closed 25 and 31 Dec; 10 days Jan

NEWLAND   SO5509   Map 4
Ostrich ♀ ◀

Off B4228 in Coleford; or can be reached from the A466 in Redbrook, by the turning off at the England—Wales border – keep bearing right; GL16 8NP

In the middle of the village, opposite the church, this unspoilt country pub is very popular with walkers – and their dogs; Alfie the pub dog will probably be there to greet them. It's a friendly, relaxed place and the low-ceilinged bar is spacious but cosily traditional, with creaky floors, uneven walls with miners' lamps, window shutters, candles in bottles on the tables, and comfortable furnishings such as cushioned window seats, wall settles and rod-backed country-kitchen chairs. There's a fine big fireplace, newspapers to read, and perhaps quiet piped blues. Changing constantly, the eight well kept real ales might include Archers Swindon Strong Bitter and a seasonal beer, Fullers London Pride, Greene King Old Speckled Hen and Triumph, Hook Norton Old Hooky, RCH Pitchfork and Wye Valley Butty Bach on handpump. Popular home-made bar food includes soup (£5.50), pasta with fresh tomato and basil sauce (£6.50), ploughman's with home-made chutney or sausages with dauphinoise potato and onion gravy (£6.75), three-cheese tart with sun-dried tomatoes and basil (£7.95), sizzling pork ribs (£8), steak in ale pie (£8.50), and salmon and spinach fishcakes with parsley sauce (£8.50); you can also eat the restaurant menu in the bar. There are seats in a walled garden behind, and out in front; the church, known as the Cathedral of the Forest, is well worth a visit. *(Recommended by Marcus Bristow, David and Pauline Brenner, Jo Rees, Kevin Blake, GSB, V Brogden, Ken and Jenny Simmonds, LM, Rev Michael Vockins)*

Free house ~ Licensee Kathryn Horton ~ Real ale ~ Bar food (12-2.30, 6.30(6 Sat)-9.30) ~ Restaurant ~ (01594) 833260 ~ Children welcome ~ Dogs welcome ~ Open 12-3, 6.30(6 Sat)-11; 12-4, 6.30-10.30 Sun

NORTH CERNEY   SP0208   Map 4
Bathurst Arms ⑪ ♀

A435 Cirencester—Cheltenham; GL7 7BZ

The convivial landlord is sure to make you welcome in this handsome 17th-c inn. It's much enjoyed by a large number of our readers who feel the balance between the pubby side and the food is just right. The original beamed and panelled bar has a fireplace at each end (one quite huge and housing an open woodburner), a good mix of old tables and nicely faded chairs, and old-fashioned window seats. There are country tables in an oak-floored room off the bar, as well as winged high-backed settles forming a few booths around other tables; the restaurant is no smoking. Dominoes and piped music. A whole wall in the restaurant displays the fine wine list (with around ten wines and champagnes by the glass), and Hook Norton Best and Wickwar Cotswold Way are well kept alongside a guest such as Wickwar Premium Spring Ale on handpump. Good, enjoyable bar food includes soup (£3.95), mixed bread with italian olive oil, salsa fresca, olives and salted nuts (£4.35), duck liver parfait with red onion chutney and orange salad (£5.95), chicken caesar salad (£5.95; main course £8.95), ploughman's (£6.95), roasted vegetable hotpot, a trio of local old spot sausages with wholegrain mustard mash and red onion gravy, beef in ale pie or pure beefburger with avocado and barbecue sauce (all £8.95), chicken supreme stuffed with black pudding and wrapped in bacon with a haricot bean casserole and stilton sauce (£10.95), 10oz sirloin steak with a rich green peppercorn and brandy sauce (£14.95), and puddings such as lime crème brûlée with white chocolate cookie and fresh fruit or prune and armagnac black cap pudding (£4.95). The pleasant riverside garden has picnic-sets sheltered by trees and shrubs, and there are plenty of surrounding walks. The bedrooms have been refurbished this year. *(Recommended by J Graveling, R Huggins, D Irving, E McCall, T McLean, Guy Vowles, Howard and Lorna Lambert, Peter and Audrey Dowsett, Monica Cockburn, Mike Jefferies)*

Free house ~ Licensee James Walker ~ Real ale ~ Bar food (12-2(2.30 Fri and Sat, 3 Sun), 6(7 Sun)-9(9.30 Fri and Sat)) ~ Restaurant ~ (01285) 831281 ~ Children welcome ~ Dogs allowed in bar and bedrooms ~ Open 12-3, 6-11; 12-10.30 Sun; 12-3, 7-10.30 Sun in winter ~ Bedrooms: £50B/£70B

OLDBURY-ON-SEVERN   ST6292   Map 2

Anchor ♀ ⬛

Village signposted from B4061; BS35 1QA

Well priced for the area and kept on handpump in very good condition, the real ales here might include Bass, Butcombe Bitter, Otter Bitter, Theakstons Old Peculier and a guest such as Bath Ales Gem Bitter; also, 27 malt whiskies and a dozen wines by the glass. The neatly kept lounge has modern beams and stone, a mix of tables including an attractive oval oak gateleg, cushioned window seats, winged seats against the wall, oil paintings by a local artist, and a big winter log fire. Diners can eat in the lounge or bar area or in the no smoking dining room at the back of the building (good for larger groups) and the menu is the same in all rooms. Using local produce where possible, bar food might include soup (£3.25), ploughman's (£4.75), devilled kidneys and mushrooms on brioche toast (£4.95), ciabatta sandwiches (from £4.95), home-cooked honey-roast ham with two eggs and bubble and squeak (£6.95), sausages with red onion marmalade (£7.25), vegetable or meaty lasagne (£7.50), home-made steak and kidney pudding (£8.25), chargrilled rib-eye steak (£11.50), and puddings such as chocolate puddle pudding or white chocolate and raspberry trifle (£3.50). They also offer a midweek two-course lunch (£7.95). In summer you can eat in the pretty garden, and the hanging baskets and window boxes are lovely then; boules. They have wheelchair access and a disabled lavatory. Plenty of walks to the River Severn and along the many footpaths and bridleways, and St Arilda's church nearby is interesting, on its odd little knoll with wild flowers among the gravestones (the primroses and daffodils in spring are lovely). *(Recommended by Barry and Anne, Tom Evans, C A Hall, Bob and Margaret Holder, Dr and Mrs C W Thomas, James Morrell, Andrew Shore, Maria Williams, John and Gloria Isaacs, Mr and Mrs J Brown, Gloria Bax, Donald Godden)*

Free house ~ Licensees Michael Dowdeswell and Mark Sorrell ~ Real ale ~ Bar food (12-2(2.30 Sat and bank hols), 6.30(6 Sat and bank hols)-9.30; 12-3, 6-9 Sun) ~ Restaurant ~ (01454) 413331 ~ Children in dining room only ~ Dogs allowed in bar ~ Open 11.30-2.45, 6.30-11; 11.30-11 Sat; 12-10.30 Sun

POULTON   SP1001   Map 4

Falcon ⑪ ♀

London Road (A417 Fairford—Cirencester); GL7 5HN

This is a stylishly decorated no smoking pub with quite an emphasis on the interesting, popular food cooked by the landlord. At lunchtime this might include sandwiches on home-made white bread (from £3.50), smoked haddock chowder (£5.95), duck leg confit with watercress and orange salad, red onion and goats cheese tart or home-made burger with home-made chips (£6.95), beer-battered cod or wild mushroom risotto (£9.95), and home-made steak and kidney pie (£10.95); evening choices such as breast of pigeon, celeriac stuffed mushroom and crispy bacon (£5.95), seared scallops with cauliflower cream and beetroot vinaigrette (£8.50), slow-roasted belly of pork with parsnip purée, apple compote and sage and cider gravy (£12.95), braised shank of lamb with mashed vegetables and roasted shallots (£14.95), and fillet of cornish brill with courgette ribbons and wild mushroom sauce (£15.95). Also, daily specials, puddings like warm chocolate brownie, home-made honeycombe ice-cream and chocolate sauce or rhubarb trifle with home-made gingernut biscuits (from £5.95), a two-course set lunch (£12), and three-course Sunday lunch (£20). They have kept a proper beige-carpeted bar area on the left (liked by locals), with mixed bar stools, nicely waxed tables, chapel chairs and other more interesting seats, a restrained selection of photographs on watery grey-green walls, country magazines sharing a table with an aspidistra, and perhaps a big bunch of lilies on the unobtrusively modern bar counter: Hook Norton Best and maybe Ramsbury Bitter on handpump, good if not cheap wines by the glass, some interesting grown-up soft drinks, and Burts excellent crisps. It opens through into a similarly furnished dining area with flowers on the tables and a log fire in the imposing stone fireplace, with steps up to a further back dining room (and a view into the kitchen). Service is neat and friendly, piped music is sophisticated and unobjectionable, and the lavatories are good – what they call the 'Boys' is very blue. *(Recommended by Richard and Sheila Fitton, Bernard Stradling, Richard Atherton, Michael Dallas, Guy Vowles, Keith Rutter, Inga Davis, Rod Stoneman, Barry and Anne Cooper, Karen and Graham Oddey, Adrian White)*

Free house ~ Licensee Jeremy Lockley ~ Real ale ~ Bar food (not Sun evening) ~ Restaurant ~ (01285) 850844 ~ Children welcome ~ Dogs allowed in bar ~ Open 11-3, 7-11; 12-3, 7-10.30 Sun

PRESTBURY   SO9624   Map 4

Royal Oak ♀ ◧

Off B4348 just N of Cheltenham; The Burgage; GL52 3DL

In an upmarket village enclave just outside Cheltenham, this is the closest pub to the racecourse. It's an attractive cotswold stone building, already entirely no smoking, with a good atmosphere in its congenial low-beamed carpeted bar. Brightened by fresh flowers and polished brasses, this has a comfortable mix of seating, from country chairs and a cushioned pew to dark green wall banquettes built in on either side of its stone fireplace; there are some interesting pictures on the ochre walls. They keep Archers Best, Timothy Taylors Landlord and a guest beer such as Wye Valley Hereford Pale Ale on handpump, Thatcher's farm cider, and a good choice of good value wines by the glass and bottle. Service is friendly and efficient, with the good-natured landlord keeping a constant eye on things. Enjoyable and generous food might include home-made soup (£4.50), home-cured gravadlax (£5), filled baguettes or ciabattas or chicken satay (£5.25), home-cooked honey-roast ham, egg, tomato and chips, liver and bacon or three bean enchillada (all £7.50), fish and fennel pie (£11), lamb rump on celeriac purée with garlic and roast tomato sauce (£14.50), daily fresh fish dishes, and puddings such as lemon and ginger cheesecake (£4.50). In the winter they do good game dishes, and have a choice of roasts (with fish and vegetarian options) for Sunday lunch, which is served all afternoon. Dining room tables are nicely spaced so that you don't feel crowded; the restaurant has piped music. The skittle alley is used as a function room. There are picnic-sets under big parasols in a good-sized neat and sheltered garden behind. *(Recommended by Theocsbrian, Michael Sargent, Jo Rees, Andrew Barker, Claire Jenkins)*

Enterprise ~ Lease Simon and Kate Daws ~ Real ale ~ Bar food (all day Sun) ~ Restaurant ~ (01242) 522344 ~ Children in restaurant; can be in bar till 7pm ~ Open 11.30-3, 5.30(6 Sat)-11; 12-10.30 Sun; closed 25 and 26 Dec

---

We say if we know a pub has piped music.

SAPPERTON   SO9403   Map 4

Bell 🍽 ♀ 🍺

Village signposted from A419 Stroud—Cirencester; OS Sheet 163 map reference 948033; GL7 6LE

Being at the heart of lots of attractions and outdoor pursuits means this well run place has quite a mix of customers – summed up for us by a party of our readers sitting quite happily in their walking gear next to a table of smartly dressed lunchers out for a celebration meal. There are three separate, cosy rooms (all no smoking now) with stripped beams, a nice mix of wooden tables and chairs, country prints and modern art on stripped stone walls, one or two attractive rugs on the flagstones, and roaring log fires and woodburning stoves; fresh flowers and newspapers. They use traceable meat and fish, local seasonal vegetables, and make their own bread and puddings: lunchtime snacks such as soup (£4.50), bacon and cheese muffin with black pudding, free-range egg and home-made tomato ketchup (£6.95), ploughman's with home-made chutney and their own spiced onions (£7.25), and a basket of plaice goujons with fries and tartare sauce (£10.50), as well as home-made soup (£4.50), hand-pressed terrine of local game with shallot dressing (£6.50), crab beignets with lemon marmalade and yoghurt and chives (£7.75), twice-baked goats cheese soufflé with thyme and roasted butternut squash (£10.50), pure beefburger with home-spiced dill cucumber and tomato relish (£11.95), slow-braised belly of old spot pork with soy and balsamic and a sweet potato purée or marinated chicken breast with wild mushroom and garlic confit and pappardelle (£14.95), calves liver on a potato cake with smoked bacon and onions poached in red wine (£15.95), pure bred hereford rib-eye steak (£16.95), and puddings such as apple and rhubarb crumble tart, vanilla brûlée with passion fruit sorbet and vanilla shortbread or warm chocolate and banana bread pudding (£5.95). A plate of four west country cheeses (£7) and they sell their own home-made chutneys and jellies (£6.50). Four well kept ales from small local brewers like Bath, Butcombe, Uley and Wickwar, 16 wines by two sizes of glass from a large and diverse wine list with very helpful notes, Long Ashton cider, some interesting aperitifs, 20 malt whiskies and several armagnacs and cognacs. Harry the springer spaniel is very sociable but must not be fed for health reasons. There are tables out on a small front lawn and in a partly covered and very pretty courtyard, for eating outside. Horses have their own tethering rail (and bucket of water). *(Recommended by Mrs L Aquilina, Bernard Stradling, R Huggins, D Irving, E McCall, T McLean, Julie and Bill Ryan, Mr and Mrs J Brown, Richard and Jean Phillips, Gaynor Gregory, A G Marx, B R and M F Arnold, Ken Marshall, Stephen Woad, John Reilly, John Balfour, Andrew Barker, Claire Jenkins, Di and Mike Gillam, Drs M J and P M Cox, Michael Dallas, Adrian White)*

Free house ~ Licensees Paul Davidson and Pat Le Jeune ~ Real ale ~ Bar food ~ Restaurant ~ (01285) 760298 ~ Children allowed but not under 10 in evenings ~ Dogs welcome ~ Open 11-2.30, 6.30-11; 12-3, 7-10.30 Sun; closed 3-10 Jan

TETBURY   ST8494   Map 4

Gumstool 🍽 ♀ 🛏

At Calcot Manor Hotel; A4135 W; GL8 8YJ

Although attached to the very smart Calcot Manor Hotel, this civilised bar has an informally relaxed atmosphere and well kept Butcombe Blonde, Greene King IPA, Uley Best and Wickwar BOB on handpump; a dozen interesting wines by the glass, and lots of malt whiskies. It's been carefully and stylishly refurbished and the layout is well divided to give a feeling of intimacy without losing the overall sense of contented bustle: flagstones, elegant wooden dining chairs and tables, well chosen pictures and drawings on mushroom-coloured walls, and leather armchairs in front of the big log fire. Imaginative food includes several dishes that come in two sizes: chicken livers on toast with a garlic, shallot, tarragon and mustard cream (£6.75; generous £8.25), chicken caesar salad (£6.75; generous £8.95), plum tomato and caramelised red onion tart with taleggio and rocket (£6.75; generous £9). Also, sandwiches, home-made soup (£4), twice-baked ham and cheddar soufflé (£6.75), warm cornish crab and leek tart (£7.25), free-range pork and hop sausages with spring onion mash and beer gravy (£9.95), crispy duck confit with puy lentils and smoked bacon (£10.25), rabbit and root vegetable pie (£10.50), slow-braised beef with parsnip mash (£11.25), organic lamb tagine with pickled lemon (£11.95), and roast monkfish with creamy curried mussels and leeks (£12.25). The restaurant is no smoking; piped music. Westonbirt Arboretum is not far away. *(Recommended by Mrs L Aquilina, Bernard Stradling, Andy and Claire Barker, Tom and Ruth Rees, Dr and Mrs C W Thomas, M G Hart, Dr and Mrs A K Clarke)*

Free house ~ Licensees Paul Sadler and Richard Ball ~ Real ale ~ Bar food ~ Restaurant ~ (01666) 890391 ~ Children welcome ~ Open 12-3, 5.30-11; 12-11(10.30 Sun) Sat ~ Bedrooms: £170B/£195B

Snooty Fox ♀ ⇐

Market Place; small residents' car park, nearby pay & display; free car park some way down hill; GL8 8DD

Although this is more a hotel than pub, the high-ceilinged main bar on the left does score rather well with its bustling unstuffy atmosphere and three real ales on handpump: Bath Ales Barnstormer, Butcombe Bitter and Moles Best. Also, 20 wines by the glass (including rosé champagne as well as 'ordinary'), a fine collection of armagnac, cognac, calvados and port, and an espresso machine; good service from neat young staff and unobtrusive piped jazz. This front room – stripped stone, like much of the rest of the ground floor – has comfortable sturdy leather-armed chairs round the cast-iron tripod tables on its carpet, a big log fireplace flanked by an imposing pair of brass flambeaux, brass ceiling fans, and Ronald Searle pony-club cartoons. Behind is a similar room, with a colourful rug on bare boards, and a leather sofa among other seats; the no smoking restaurant is beyond. On the right a smaller quieter room has leather wing armchairs and sofas, and a couple of imposing portraits. Well liked bar food includes sandwiches and baguettes (from £4.50), soup (£4.25), portk satay with sweet chilli dip and soy sauce (£5.95; main course £9.95), parsnip, cheese, onion and sage tart with hazelnut and apple dressing (£6.50; main course £10.50), tapas plate (£6.95; main course £11.25), a proper ploughman's (£6.95), home-cooked ham and eggs (£7.50), tagliatelle with smoked chicken, chorizo, cream and parmesan (£10.25), steak, kidney and mushroom suet pudding (£10.75), mutton stew with horseradish dumplings (£11.50), 10oz hereford sirloin steak (£18.75), and puddings such as baked rhubarb brûlée with shortbread, walnut treacle tart with butterscotch ice-cream or winter berry pudding (£4.95). Outside, a sheltered entryway has teak tables and chairs facing the ancient central covered market. *(Recommended by John Dwane, Mrs Anne Callender, Peter and Audrey Dowsett, Mike and Heather Watson, R Huggins, D Irving, E McCall, T McLean)*

Free house ~ Licensee Marc Gibbons ~ Real ale ~ Bar food (12-2, 6-9; 12-8 Sun) ~ Restaurant ~ (01666) 502436 ~ Children welcome ~ Dogs allowed in bar and bedrooms ~ Open 11-11; 12-10.30 Sun ~ Bedrooms: £73B/£95B

Trouble House ⑪ ♀

A433 towards Cirencester, near Cherington turn; GL8 8SG

Popular with the country set, this smart and friendly pub places firm emphasis on its good, interesting food. Furnishings are mainly close-set stripped pine or oak tables with chapel chairs, some wheelback chairs and the odd library chair, and there are attractive mainly modern country prints on the cream or butter-coloured walls. The rush-matting room on the right is no smoking, and on the left there's a parquet-floored room with a chesterfield by the big stone fireplace, a hop-girt mantelpiece, and more hops hung from one of its two big black beams. In the small saggy-beamed middle room, you can commandeer one of the bar stools, where they have well kept Wadworths IPA and 6X on handpump, and a good wine list with helpful notes and 14 wines by the glass; piped music. From an ambitious menu, there might be shellfish minestrone (£4.95 small, £6.95 large), pork and chicken liver terrine with pickled cornichons (£6.25), scallops with crayfish and a crayfish cappuccino (£12), cornish lobster and pea risotto (£14), hake and spring greens with beef tortellini (£15), braised lamb with spiced couscous or guinea fowl sausages and breast (£16), and puddings such as hot chocolate tart or strawberry meringue with strawberry sorbet (£6); attentive service. You can also sit out at picnic-sets on the gravel courtyard behind. *(Recommended by Michael Cooper, Julie and Bill Ryan, Tom and Ruth Rees, Richard and Sheila Fitton, Paul Williams, Richard Stancomb, Derek Thomas, John and Hazel Williams, Frank Willy, Mary Rayner, Joyce and Maurice Cottrell, Tim and Suzy Bower, Richard Wyld, Michael Dallas, Karen and Graham Oddey, Adrian White)*

Wadworths ~ Tenants Michael and Sarah Bedford ~ Real ale ~ Bar food (not Sun evening or Mon) ~ Restaurant ~ (01666) 502206 ~ Children in restaurant only ~ Dogs welcome ~ Open 11-3, 6.30(7 winter)-11; 12-3 Sun; closed Sun evening, all day Mon; Christmas and New Year period

TODENHAM SP2436 Map 4
Farriers Arms ♀
Between A3400 and A429 N of Moreton-in-Marsh; GL56 9PF

New licensees have taken over this tucked away country pub. They've landscaped the garden, will redecorate the restaurant, and hope to open letting bedrooms. The bar has nice wonky white plastered walls, hops on the beams, fine old polished flagstones by the stone bar counter and a woodburner in a huge inglenook fireplace. A tiny room off to the side is full of old books and interesting old photographs. Bar food now includes home-made soup (£4), home-made chicken liver parfait with cumberland sauce, warm chicken caesar salad or crostini topped with grilled stilton and an apricot confit (£5), steak in ale pie, chicken breast on buttered spinach with a garlic and wild mushroom sauce or roast vegetable and goats cheese pasta bake (£10), whole grilled lemon sole topped with lemon, caper and herb butter (£11), braised lamb shank on parsnip purée (£13), barbecue-style rib-eye steak (£14), and home-made puddings such as white chocolate tart with milk chocolate top, sticky toffee pudding with caramel sauce or glazed lemon tart (£4); the restaurant is no smoking. Black Sheep, Hook Norton Best and Wye Valley Butty Bach on handpump, and ten wines by the glass; piped music, darts and board games. The pub has fine views over the surrounding countryside from the back garden (where you can play aunt sally), and there are a couple of tables with views of the church on a small terrace by the quiet little road. More reports please. *(Recommended by C and R Bromage, Andy and Claire Barker, Mike and Mary Carter, Martin and Pauline Jennings, John Holroyd, Susan and John Douglas, Paul Goldman, Ian and Nita Cooper, Lawrence Pearse, R Huggins, D Irving, E McCall, T McLean, R K Phillips, John Kane, Mr and Mrs P R Thomas)*

Free house ~ Licensees Nigel and Louise Kirkwood ~ Real ale ~ Bar food (12-2.30(4 Fri), 7-9.30; summer cream teas 2.30-4) ~ Restaurant ~ (01608) 650901 ~ Children welcome ~ Dogs allowed in bar ~ Open 12-4(3 Sat and winter weekdays), 6.30-11; 12-3, 7-10.30 Sun

UPPER ODDINGTON SP2225 Map 4
Horse & Groom ⊕ ♀
Village signposted from A436 E of Stow-on-the-Wold; GL56 0XH

This is an attractive 16th-c cotswold stone inn with quite an emphasis on the very good food, though they do keep Arkells 3B, Wickwar Cotswold Way and Wye Valley Butty Bach on handpump, and 30 wines by the glass. The bar has pale polished flagstones, a handsome antique oak box settle among other more modern seats, oak beams in the ochre ceiling, stripped stone walls and an inglenook fireplace. From a seasonally changing menu the lunchtime choices might include sandwiches (from £5.95), home-cured gravadlax with lime, avocado and cherry tomato salsa (£6.50; main course £12.50), smoked duck breast with a citrus and rocket salad and star anise dressing (£6.75; main course £13), ploughman's (£8.95), home-cooked ham with free-range eggs (£10.25), a trio of gloucester old spot pork sausages with wholegrain mustard mash and caramelised red onion gravy (£10.75), fish pie (£11.75), and chicken breast with garlic and basil mousse (£13.75); evening dishes such as home-made soup (£4.95), roast chicken and mushroom terrine with home-made piccalilli (£5.95), baked goats cheese and red onion tart (£6.75), wild mushroom and parmesan risotto (£11.50), and seared bass fillets with fish cream sauce and fresh egg tagliatelle or braised shoulder of lamb (£14), with daily specials like ham hock, sage and onion terrine (£5.95), deep-fried crab beignets with avocado, ginger and cherry tomato salsa (£7.25), hungarian goulash (£12.50), and slow-cooked belly of pork with apple and black pudding (£13.75); puddings such as iced dark and white chocolate parfait, vanilla crème brûlée or spiced fruit crumble (from £5.50). The restaurant is no smoking. There are seats on the terrace and in the pretty garden where there are grape vines bounded by dry-stone walls and cottages. *(Recommended by Bernard Stradling, Mr and Mrs J Brown, Dr and Mrs F Murgatroyd, Keith and Sue Ward, Gaynor Gregory, Mr and Mrs Martin Joyce, Rod Stoneman, Martin and Pauline Jennings, KC, Drs M J and P M Cox, Karen and Graham Oddey, P Michelson)*

Free house ~ Licensees Simon and Sally Jackson ~ Real ale ~ Bar food (12-2, 6.30-9.30) ~ Restaurant ~ (01451) 830584 ~ Children welcome ~ Open 12-3.30, 5-11; 12-11 Sat; 12-10.30 Sun ~ Bedrooms: £68S/£76S(£86B)

LUCKY DIP

Besides the fully inspected pubs, you might like to try these Lucky Dips recommended to us and described by readers (if you do, please send us reports: www.goodguides.co.uk).

ALDSWORTH [SP1510]
☆ *Sherborne Arms* GL54 3RB [B4425 Burford—Cirencester]: Cheerfully unpretentious, with quickly served good pubby food, generous and well priced, four mainstream real ales, farm cider, beams, stripped stone, central log fire between smallish bar and big dining area, attractive no smoking conservatory, walking sticks for sale; games area with darts, lots of board games, fruit machine, piped music; dogs welcomed kindly, pleasant front garden, lavatory for disabled *(R Huggins, D Irving, E McCall, T McLean, Jonathan Martin, David Gunn, BB, P and J Shapley)*

AMBERLEY [SO8401]
☆ *Amberley Inn* GL5 5AF [steeply off A46 Stroud—Nailsworth – gentler approach from N Nailsworth]: Doing well under new management (now linked to Tunnel House at Coates), good range of real ales, enjoyable generous food, not overpriced, from good baguettes to some interesting dishes, friendly efficient staff, comfortable panelled and carpeted lounge bar, beautiful views; comfortable bedrooms *(Steve and Marion Saviker, Richard Stancomb)*
☆ *Black Horse* GL5 5AL [off A46 Stroud—Nailsworth; Littleworth]: Unpretentious easy-going local under friendly new management, spectacular views from conservatory (foreground may be more workaday), Greene King IPA and Charles Wells Bombardier, decent lunchtime food, open fire, flagstones and high-backed settles, lots of cheerful sporting pictures (and TV for big matches), large no smoking family area on left, games room; plenty of tables on pleasant back terrace

with barbecue, more on lawn *(LYM, Gloria Bax, R Huggins, D Irving, E McCall, T McLean, Dr A Y Drummond, Colin McKerrow, John Beeken)*

AMPNEY CRUCIS [SP0701]
☆ *Crown of Crucis* GL7 5RS [A417 E of Cirencester]: Bustling food pub very popular particularly with older people, Sun lunchtime carvery, real ales in small neat bar, good house wines, efficient service, pleasant décor, split-level no smoking restaurant; children welcome, disabled facilities, lots of tables out on grass by car park, quiet comfortable modern bedrooms around courtyard, good breakfast, open all day *(Ted George, J S and S Chadwick, Roger Braithwaite, Richard and Sheila Fitton, LYM, Mr and Mrs J Brown)*

ANDOVERSFORD [SP0219]
☆ *Royal Oak* GL54 4HR [signed just off A40; Gloucester Rd]: Good value generous pub food using much local produce in cosy and attractive beamed village pub, real ales inc Hook Norton Best, prompt friendly service, lots of stripped stone, nice galleried raised dining room beyond big central open fire; popular quiz night, tables in garden *(Mr and Mrs J Brown, Mr and Mrs I and E Bell, BB)*

APPERLEY [SO8528]
☆ *Coal House* GL19 4DN [village signed off B4213 S of Tewkesbury; Gabb Lane]: Light and airy pub in splendid riverside position, welcoming staff, Hook Norton Best, Vale and Whittingtons Cats Whiskers, decent wines by the glass, plenty of blackboards for enjoyable inexpensive food from baguettes and light dishes up, walkers welcome, separate dining room; plenty of tables on front terrace and

lawn with Severn views, play area, moorings *(BB, Lawrence Pearse, Neil and Anita Christopher)*

ARLINGHAM [SO7011]

☆ *Old Passage* GL2 7JR [Passage Rd]: Good interesting food esp fish and seafood in upmarket restaurant rather than pub (they do keep a real ale, but you can't really go just for a drink – the serving counter is in the restaurant area), friendly helpful staff, nice clean décor; beautiful setting, french windows to pleasant terrace and big garden down to River Severn *(BB, Dr A J and Mrs Tompsett, Rod Stoneman, Dr A Y Drummond, Colin Morgan, Bernard Stradling)*

AUST [ST5788]

Boars Head BS35 4AX [½ mile from M48 junction 1, off Avonmouth rd]: Ivy-covered motorway break with wide food choice from baguettes to steak, quick friendly service, Courage Best and Otter, good house wines, dark furniture in series of linked rooms and alcoves, beams and some stripped stone, huge log fire; piped music; children in partly no smoking eating area away from bar, dogs on lead in bar, pretty sheltered garden *(LYM, Colin Moore, Meg and Colin Hamilton, Ian Phillips, Donald Godden)*

BERKELEY [ST6899]

Berkeley Arms GL13 9BP [Market Pl]: Nicely old-fashioned country-town hotel with chintzy lounge, high-backed settles and games in unpretentious public bar, local real ales; tables outside, bedrooms *(Giles and Annie Francis)*

BIBURY [SP1106]

☆ *Swan* GL7 5NW [B4425]: Hotel in lovely spot facing River Coln, comfortable and attractive side bar used by locals with Hook Norton Best, exemplary bar stools, coal fire, nice modern adjoining brasserie with enjoyable up-to-date food, good service, smart formal dining room; teak tables out on heated flagstoned terrace, pleasant waterside garden, luxurious bedrooms *(R Huggins, D Irving, E McCall, T McLean, BB)*

BIRDLIP [SO9316]

Air Balloon GL4 8JY [A417/A436 roundabout]: Busy no smoking chain dining pub, standard value food from sandwiches, baguettes and wraps up all day, changing ales such as Hook Norton Old Hooky, helpful service, many levels and alcoves inc separate restaurant and brasserie, pubbier front corner with open fire, beams and stripped stone; unobtrusive piped music; tables, some covered, on heated terrace and in garden with play area, open all day *(Mr and Mrs I and E Bell, R Huggins, D Irving, E McCall, T McLean, Tim and Ann Newell, Tony and Caroline Elwood, Ian and Joan Blackwell)*

BISLEY [SO9006]

Stirrup Cup GL6 7BL [Cheltenham Rd]: Long rambling well furnished local with real ales such as Wickwar Cotswold Way, friendly helpful staff, good modestly priced food from sandwiches and good baguettes to generous Sunday roasts, decent wines, no piped music; dogs welcome *(Guy Vowles)*

BOURTON-ON-THE-HILL [SP1732]

☆ *Horse & Groom* GL56 9AQ [A44 W of Moreton-in-Marsh]: Stone-built hilltop pub reopened after refurbishment by sons of the successful team at Howard Arms, Ilmington, airily high-ceilinged no smoking bistro yet with welcoming pub atmosphere, good changing restauranty food using local suppliers, changing ales such as Everards Tiger and Hook Norton Old Hooky, interesting choice of wines by the glass, friendly and eager young staff, scrubbed pine tables on bare boards, good log fire and separate woodburner; good-sized garden behind, comfortable bedrooms *(Michael and Anne Brown, LYM, Revd L and S Giller, Martin and Pauline Jennings, George Atkinson)*

BOURTON-ON-THE-WATER [SP1620]

Duke of Wellington GL54 2BY [Sherbourne St]: Large stone-built pub worth knowing for good choice of food and drinks inc Hook Norton real ale, friendly staff, open-plan carpeted bar with rustic furniture, back dining room, log fire; garden tables, bedrooms *(Ted George, Roger and Pauline Pearce)*

BROAD CAMPDEN [SP1537]

☆ *Bakers Arms* GL55 6UR [off B4081]: Chatty and relaxed traditional pub with enthusiastic licensees, real ales such as Donnington BB, Hook Norton Best, Stanway Stanney, Timothy Taylors Landlord and Charles Wells Bombardier, straightforward bar food (all day in summer) from lunchtime sandwiches and baguettes up, inglenook in snug beamed and stripped stone bar, no smoking beamed and stripped stone dining room, traditional games; no credit cards; children in eating areas, tables out on terrace and garden behind with play area, open all day Fri-Sun and summer *(DC, Theocsbrian, Lawrence Pearse, LYM, Di and Mike Gillam, H O Dickinson)*

BROADWELL [SP2027]

☆ *Fox* GL56 0UF [off A429 2 miles N of Stow-on-the-Wold]: Relaxing pub overlooking broad green in pleasant village, welcoming attentive service, good range of homely food (not Sun evening) from baguettes to popular Sun lunch, good fresh veg, low-priced Donnington BB and SBA, decent wines, good summer lemonade, nice coffee, cosy local feel, stripped stone and flagstones, beams hung with jugs, log fire, darts, dominoes and chess, plain public bar with pool room extension, pleasant separate restaurant; may be piped music; tables out on gravel, good big back family-friendly garden with aunt sally, meadow behind for Caravan Club members *(David A Hammond, Lawrence Pearse, BB, Bob Ellis)*

BROCKWEIR [SO5301]

Brockweir Inn NP16 7NG [signed just off A466 Chepstow—Monmouth]: Proper country local well placed for Wye Valley walkers (but no muddy boots), beams and stripped stonework, quarry tiles, sturdy settles, woodburner, snugger carpeted alcoves, Adnams, Bass, Hook Norton Best, Smiles and Worthington BB, Stowford Press cider, friendly landlord, upstairs restaurant, conservatory;

pool, machines and piped music in public bar; dogs allowed, children in eating area, small garden with interesting covered terrace; open all day Sat, bedrooms *(Bob and Margaret Holder, LYM)*

CAMBRIDGE [SO7403]
George GL2 7AL [3 miles from M5 junction 13 – A38 towards Bristol]: Big, busy and welcoming, with two spacious no smoking dining areas, good value generous food from filled rolls and baked potatoes up inc bargain lunches, Adnams, Greene King IPA and Old Speckled Hen and Hook Norton Old Hooky, helpful well organised service, log fire; garden with barbecues, fowl pen and play area, also camp site, handy for Slimbridge wildfowl centre, open all day Sun *(Neil and Anita Christopher, Michael and Jenny Back)*

CHALFORD [SO8903]
Old Neighbourhood GL6 8EN [Chalford Hill, Midway; OS Sheet 163 map ref 895032]: Light and airy linked rooms, generous food (can take a while) from good baguettes to dishes – can be eaten here – from integral indian take-away, welcoming easy-going atmosphere, three or four real ales, Stowford Press cider, solid pine tables on oak boards, log fire; high over village, views from lovely big terrace and garden, play area *(Guy Vowles)*

CHASTLETON [SP2629]
Cross Hands GL56 0SP [A44]: Friendly country pub with Hook Norton ales, coal fire, pool; soft piped music *(Giles and Annie Francis)*

CHEDWORTH [SP0608]
☆ *Hare & Hounds* GL54 4NN [Fosse Cross – A429 N of Cirencester, some way from village]: Good inventive food in rambling interestingly furnished stone-built dining pub, low beams, soft lighting, cosy corners and little side rooms, two big log fires, small conservatory; Arkells ales, good house wines, cheerful helpful service; children welcome away from bar, disabled facilities, open all day Fri-Sun *(LYM, Richard and Sheila Fitton, R Huggins, D Irving, E McCall, T McLean)*

CHELTENHAM [SO9422]
Overton Lodge GL50 3EA [St Georges Rd]: Former hotel, now pleasantly unassuming neighbourhood bar and dining room, useful pub alternative, with one or two real ales, good choice of wines by the glass, enjoyable sensibly priced food *(Guy Vowles)*
Restoration GL50 1DX [High St]: Long rambling 16th-c pub, much restored and useful for the two main shopping arcades, with lots of beams and dim-lit bric-a-brac, some leather sofas as well as simpler wooden furniture, good bustling atmosphere, St Austell Tribute and Wychwood Hobgoblin, good coffee and range of wines by the glass, daily papers, raised dining area with decent food inc two-for-one bargains, friendly young staff; piped music, TV *(Klaus and Elizabeth Leist, Michael Dandy)*
Sudeley Arms GL52 2PN [Prestbury Rd]: Chatty traditional pub with homely arch-divided lounge, proper public bar, real ales such as local Goffs Jouster, Timothy Taylors

Landlord and two or three changing guests, darts, cards; open all day *(Pete Baker)*

CHIPPING CAMPDEN [SP1539]
☆ *Kings Arms* GL55 6AW [High St]: Small hotel now calling itself just Kings, with inventive modern changing food from lunchtime snacks to wider evening menus (separate for lively bar/brasserie and larger no smoking restaurant), helpful and friendly young staff, Hook Norton beers, good log fire, charming décor; secluded back garden, bedrooms, open all day Sat *(LYM, Michael Dandy)*
☆ *Lygon Arms* GL55 6HB [High St]: Comfortable bar with very wide choice of enjoyable food till late evening from sandwiches and baked potatoes to interesting more pricey dishes, real ales such as Hook Norton Old Hooky and Wye Valley HBA, welcoming landlord and helpful staff, open fires, low beams and stripped stone, lots of horse pictures, small separate back restaurant; children welcome, tables in shady courtyard, open all day exc winter wkdys, comfortable well equipped beamed bedrooms, good breakfast *(Alain and Rose Foote, Gene and Kitty Rankin, Michael Dandy, LYM, Roger Huggins)*
Red Lion GL55 6AS [Lower High St]: Nicely refurbished and doing well under its current father-and-son owners, with good value fresh food from baguettes up in roomy flagstoned front eating area, Greene King IPA and Old Speckled Hen, decent wine choice, new stable bar, upstairs dining room; comfortable bedrooms in cottage annexe, plans for more *(Michael Dandy)*

CHIPPING SODBURY [ST7282]
Beaufort Hunt BS37 6AG [Broad St]: Partly divided by standing timbers, small back snug, local Codrington Codgers ale; piped music *(Donna and Roger)*

CIRENCESTER [SP0202]
☆ *Corinium* GL7 2DG [Dollar St/Gloucester St]: Civilised and comfortable, with big log fire, attractive antique coaching prints, good mix of tables, sofas and small armchairs, real ales inc strongish ones, decent wines, bar food from sandwiches, baguettes and baked potatoes up, nicely decorated restaurant; no piped music; entrance through charming courtyard with tables, attractive back garden, good bedrooms *(R Huggins, D Irving, E McCall, T McLean, BB)*
Drillmans Arms GL7 2JY [Gloucester Rd, Stratton]: Genuine and popular old two-room local, warm and relaxing, with low beams, good log fires, four real ales inc a guest beer, reasonable food, skittle alley doubling as eating area; tables out by small car park *(R Huggins, D Irving, E McCall, T McLean)*
Fleece GL7 2NZ [Market Pl]: Substantial old hotel, good choice of food in bar from baguettes to scampi and baked potatoes, bay window looking up market place to parish church, Hook Norton ales, substantial restaurant; terrace tables, bedrooms *(Craig Turnbull, BB, R Huggins, D Irving, E McCall, T McLean)*

Plough GL7 2LB [Stratton]: Opened-up Arkells pub with good service, their real ales, good value food inc generous ham ploughman's and OAP bargain lunches, rustic pine tables, separate dining room *(Guy Vowles)*

☆ *Twelve Bells* GL7 1EA [Lewis Lane]: Cheery backstreet pub made distinctive by Bob the no-nonsense pipe-smoking landlord, his son's cooking – bargain generous fresh food inc local produce and some unusual dishes lunchtime and early evening (may be goose around Christmas) – and Abbey Bellringer and five quickly changing interesting guest beers all in fine condition; good coal fires in all three small old-fashioned low-ceilinged rooms, sturdy pine tables and rugs on quarry tiles in back dining area, pictures for sale, clay pipe collection; can get smoky, piped music may be loud; small sheltered unsmart back terrace *(Giles and Annie Francis, R Huggins, D Irving, E McCall, T McLean, Roger Fox, Mike Pugh, BB, Pete Baker, Guy Vowles, Joyce and Maurice Cottrell, Canon Michael Bourdeaux)*

Waggon & Horses GL7 2PU [London Rd]: Comfortably cottagey stone-built pub with four good ales usually inc Caledonian Deuchars IPA and Fullers London Pride, back dining room with enjoyable food lunchtime and evening, lots of bric-a-brac in L-shaped bar *(R Huggins, D Irving, E McCall, T McLean)*

Wheatsheaf GL7 1JF [Cricklade St]: Busy local with five or so real ales, wide choice of inexpensive pub food from baguettes up until 4pm, quick service, no piped music, well used skittle alley; no children in bar, big-screen TV football in back room; tables, play area and car park out behind, open all day *(Peter and Audrey Dowsett)*

Woodbine GL7 1TR [Chesterton Lane]: Pleasant stone-built local with compact panelled snug, Shepherd Neame Spitfire and Wychwood Hobgoblin, decent low-priced food, big bar with corner pool and machines *(R Huggins, D Irving, E McCall, T McLean)*

CLEARWELL [SO5708]

Lamb GL16 8JU [off B4228; The Cross]: Old settles in cosy snug, larger high-ceilinged divided bar, three real ales from small breweries such as Freeminer tapped from the cask; cl Mon/Tues and lunchtimes Weds/Thurs, friendly service *(Pete Baker)*

CLEEVE HILL [SO9826]

Rising Sun GL52 3PX [B4632]: No smoking hotel with splendid view over Cheltenham to the Malvern Hills from conservatory, covered terrace and lawn; large carpeted bar with friendly efficient service, Greene King ales, decent wine choice, lower eating area, restaurant beyond, sports TV other end; bedrooms, good breakfast *(Jeff and Sue Evans, Neil and Anita Christopher)*

CLIFFORD'S MESNE [SO6922]

☆ *Yew Tree* GL18 1JS [out of Newent, past Falconry Centre]: Large open-plan divided pub on slopes of May Hill (NT), new licensees making it less restauranty but keeping quite an interesting choice of food (not Sun evening to

Tues lunchtime) from good ciabattas up, two real ales, good house wines; children welcome, tables out on sunny terrace, play area *(Mike and Mary Carter)*

COATES [SO9600]

☆ *Tunnel House* GL7 6PW [follow Tarleton signs (right then left) from village, pub up rough track on right after rly bridge; OS Sheet 163 map ref 965005]: Rambling country pub, quite a favourite, with beams and flagstones in idiosyncratic original bar, homely mix of chairs and settees, all sorts of unlikely bric-a-brac and memorabilia, log fire, more conventional pastel-décor eating extension and back conservatory (fills quickly), real ales such as Archers, Wickwar Cotswold Way and Wye Valley, Stowford Press cider, enjoyable food from sandwiches to interesting blackboard dishes, quick friendly service, amiable ambling black labrador; juke box, will improve with the new no smoking law, overrun with agriculture college students term-time wknd evenings; children and dogs welcome (play area and nice walled-in kids' lawn outside, too), impressive views from tables on pleasant terrace, big garden sloping down to former canal (under slow restoration), Sunday barbecues, good walks *(Julie and Bill Ryan, R Huggins, D Irving, E McCall, T McLean, Tom and Ruth Rees, Brian and Anita Randall, Andrew Shore, Maria Williams, John and Fiona McIlwain, Michael Dallas, LYM, Julia and Richard Tredgett, Theocsbrian, Meg and Colin Hamilton)*

COLEFORD [SO5813]

☆ *Dog & Muffler* GL16 7AS [Joyford, best approached from Christchurch 5-ways junction B4432/B4428, by church – B4432 towards Broadwell, then follow signpost; also signposted from the Berry Hill post office cross-roads; beyond the hamlet itself, bear right and keep your eyes skinned]: Very prettily set 17th-c country pub, cosy original beamed bar with log-effect gas fire in big fireplace, beamed and flagstoned back part with bright conservatory restaurant and verandah, cheerful helpful staff, good food from sandwiches and baguettes up, Sam Smiths and local Freeminers Speculation; children welcome, well spaced picnic-sets in large attractive sheltered garden with lovely views and good segregated play area, good value bedrooms, nice walks *(LYM, Mrs Sheela Curtis, Mr and Mrs M E Hawkins)*

COLESBOURNE [SO9913]

Colesbourne Inn GL53 9NP [A435 Cirencester—Cheltenham]: Civilised 18th-c grey stone gabled coaching inn with wide choice of enjoyable fresh food inc good Sun lunch and some enterprising cooking (can take a while), Wadworths IPA and 6X, good wine list, linked rooms with partly panelled dark red walls, log fires, soft lighting, comfortable mix of settles and softly padded seats, separate no smoking candlelit dining room; dogs welcome, views from attractive back garden and terrace, nice bedrooms in converted stable block *(LYM, Keith and Sue Ward, R Huggins, D Irving, E McCall, T McLean)*

COMPTON ABDALE [SP0717]

☆ *Puesdown Inn* GL54 4DN [A40 outside village]: Appealing and spacious series of stylish upmarket bar areas, wide choice of good imaginative food using local supplies from paninis up, neat staff, Hook Norton Best and Old Hooky, decent wines by the glass, good coffees, log fire and woodburner, leather or brightly upholstered sofas and armchairs, big art posters, bare boards, bright rugs and rafter-effect ceilings, cream and dark red walls, mainly stripped stone in extensive no smoking eating areas, well reproduced piped music, friendly chocolate labrador; nice garden behind, bedrooms *(DWT, BB, Ned Kelly)*

CRANHAM [SO8912]

☆ *Black Horse* GL4 8HP [off A46 and B4070 N of Stroud]: Unpretentious traditional 17th-c pub with hearty home cooking (not Sun evening, and other evenings they don't go on cooking indefinitely) from good sandwiches and omelettes using their own free-range eggs to fish and duck, cheaper small helpings, very fair prices, Archers Village, Hancocks, Sharps Doom Bar, Whittingtons Cats Whiskers and Wickwar BOB, convivial atmosphere, good log fire and high-backed wall settles in quarry-tiled public bar, cosy little lounge, shove-ha'penny, a couple of pub dogs, no smoking upstairs dining rooms; piped music; children welcome, may be cl Mon *(Mrs L Ferstendik, Andrew Shore, Maria Williams, Pete Baker, LYM, Di and Mike Gillam, Dennis and Gill Keen)*

EASTCOMBE [SO8904]

Lamb GL6 7DN: Two-bar pub with peaceful valley views from lovely terrace and garden, three or four real ales, enjoyable food, welcoming staff, flagstoned stripped-stone dining room and sunken conservatory-style area *(Dave Irving)*

EBRINGTON [SP1839]

Ebrington Arms GL55 6NH [off B4035 E of Chipping Campden or A429 N of Moreton-in-Marsh]: New management in well refurbished village pub handy for Hidcote and Kiftsgate, lively low-beamed bar with good wkdy lunchtime soup and baguettes, real ales such as Purity Pure UBU, Timothy Taylors Landlord and Charles Wells Bombardier, Thatcher's farm cider, stripped stone, flagstones and inglenooks, attractive dining room, sensible wine range; no dogs at meal times; children welcome, picnic-sets on pleasant sheltered terrace, good play area, bedrooms *(LYM, Clive and Fran Dutson, P J F Cooper, Michael Clatworthy, Therese Flanagan)*

EDGE [SO8409]

☆ *Edgemoor* GL6 6ND [Gloucester Rd (A4173)]: Tidy modernised dining place with panoramic valley view across to Painswick from picture windows and from tables on pretty terrace, wide choice of good value food inc fine home-made puddings, cheerful efficient service, orderly rows of tables, local real ales, good coffee, no smoking restaurant; children welcome, good walks nearby, has been cl Sun evening *(Neil and Anita Christopher, LYM)*

ELKSTONE [SO9610]

☆ *Highwayman* GL53 9PL [Beechpike; off northbound A417 6 miles N of Cirencester]: Interesting 16th-c building, a rambling and relaxing warren of low beams, stripped stone, cosy alcoves, antique settles, armchairs and sofa among more usual furnishings, full Arkells ale range, good house wines, friendly staff, good log fires, big back eating area; may be quiet piped music; disabled access, good family room, outside play area *(R Huggins, D Irving, E McCall, T McLean, Paul and Shirley White, the Didler, LYM, Brian McBurnie)*

FORTHAMPTON [SO8731]

Lower Lode Inn GL19 4RE: Brick-built Tudor pub with River Severn moorings and plenty of waterside tables (prone to winter flooding – hence the stilts for nearby caravan park), flagstones, enormous log fire and traditional seating, enjoyable usual pubby food, friendly helpful landlady, good ale choice such as Donnington, Goffs and Wickwar, back pool room and juke box; children and dogs welcome (lots of summer holiday families), good value bedrooms with good breakfast, cl Sun lunchtime and winter Mon to Tues lunchtime *(Nick and Lynne Carter, Gillian and Kenneth Green)*

FRAMPTON COTTERELL [ST6781]

Rising Sun BS36 2HN: Tucked-away popular village pub with good range of local ales in comfortable partly divided flagstoned bar, no smoking upper dining area and conservatory, skittle alley *(Donna and Roger)*

FRAMPTON ON SEVERN [SO7407]

Three Horseshoes GL2 7DY [The Green]: Cheerful little unpretentious 18th-c pub overlooking splendid green, welcoming landlord, lunchtime sandwiches and great ploughman's, Adnams, Hook Norton Old Hooky and Uley, good farm cider, lounge/dining room opened for evening meals *(Mrs R J Gray, Tom Evans, Blaise Vyner, Mr and Mrs A H Young)*

FROCESTER [SO7831]

George GL10 3TQ [Peter St]: Unassuming traditional coaching inn owned by a village consortium, welcoming atmosphere and service and plenty of character, good choice of changing real ales, tasty food, big but cosy main room with two log fires, daily papers, smaller no smoking room, large dining room on left; courtyard with boules, nice setting, huge shuttered bedrooms *(Mr and Mrs I and E Bell, R Huggins, D Irving, E McCall, T McLean)*

GLASSHOUSE [SO7121]

☆ *Glasshouse Inn* GL17 0NN [off A40 just W of A4136]: Homely beamed country pub with appealing and interesting old-fashioned and antique furnishings and décor, cavernous black hearth, flagstoned conservatory, Bass, Butcombe and Sharps Doom Bar tapped from the cask, decent food inc thai dishes; no children inside, no bookings, and landlord may move you on quickly when you've eaten; good disabled access, neat garden with interesting topiary and lovely hanging baskets, nearby paths up wooded May Hill, cl Sun evening *(Theocsbrian, LYM, the Didler, M J Winterton, Colin Moore, Martin and Pauline Jennings, Dr A J and Mrs Tompsett, Lucien Perring)*

GLOUCESTER [SO8218]

Dick Whittingtons House GL1 2PE: Unusual in being listed Grade I, early Tudor behind its 18th-c façade, probably former guild hall and mansion house; comfortably updated inside, wide range of customers from shoppers to rugby supporters, changing real ales, good basic food choice; open all day *(Theocsbrian)*

☆ *Fountain* GL1 2NW [Westgate St/Berkeley St]: Nice passageway entrance to friendly and civilised L-shaped bar, charming helpful service, real ales such as Caledonian Deuchars IPA, Fullers London Pride, Greene King Abbot, Timothy Taylors Landlord and Wickwar BOB, good range of whiskies, attractive prints, handsome stone fireplace (pub dates from 17th c), plush seats and built-in wall benches, log-effect gas fire; cheap usual food; tables in pleasant courtyard, good disabled access, handy for cathedral, open all day *(BB, Theocsbrian, B M Eldridge, Mrs Hazel Rainer)*

Royal Oak GL3 3TW [Hucclecote Rd, Hucclecote; quite handy for M5 junction 11A]: Bright modern décor in spacious open-plan pub, quite an emphasis on food now inc bargain Sun roasts, pleasant landlord, real ales; plenty of picnic-sets on attractive terrace and lawns *(B M Eldridge)*

Tall Ship GL1 2EX [Southgate St, docks entrance]: Extended Victorian pub near historic docks, raised dining area with emphasis on wide choice of good fresh fish (can take a while at busy times), plenty of other food from sandwiches up, morning coffee and afternoon tea, Wadworths and a guest beer; pool table and juke box on left; terrace, open all day *(Pat and Tony Martin, Pat Nelmes, Mrs Hazel Rainer)*

GREAT BARRINGTON [SP2013]

☆ *Fox* OX18 4TB [off A40 Burford—Northleach; pub towards Little Barrington]: 17th-c pub with stripped stone and simple country furnishings in low-ceilinged small bar, Donnington BB and SBA, farm cider, friendly staff, wide blackboard choice of promptly served food (all day Sun and summer Sat, not Mon night in winter) from sandwiches to good local game and puddings, river-view dining room in former skittle alley, traditional games; can get very busy, games machine, TV; children welcome, heated terrace by River Windrush (swans and private fishing), informal orchard with pond, open all day *(LYM, David Glynne-Jones, David Handforth, the Didler, Pete Baker, A G Marx, Mr and Mrs John Taylor, Mrs June Wilmers, Stuart Turner)*

GREAT RISSINGTON [SP1917]

☆ *Lamb* GL54 2LN [off A40 W of Burford, via Gt Barrington]: Partly 17th-c, with civilised low-beamed two-room bar, real ales such as Hook Norton Best and Charles Wells Bombardier, good wines by the glass, friendly staff, open fire, enjoyable imaginative food,

darts, dominoes, and cribbage, no smoking olde-worlde candlelit restaurant; children welcome, pretty and sheltered hillside garden, bedrooms *(LYM, Michael and Jenny Back, Mrs Frances Pennell)*

GUITING POWER [SP0924]

☆ *Farmers Arms* GL54 5TZ [Fosseway (A429)]: Stripped stone, polished tables on flagstones (carpeted back area), particularly well kept cheap Donnington BB and SBA, wide blackboard range of unpretentious good food from sandwiches and good ham ploughman's up inc children's dishes, prompt friendly service, good coal or log fire; skittle alley, games area with darts, pool, cribbage, dominoes, fruit machine; piped music; seats (and quoits) in garden, good walks; children welcome, bedrooms, lovely village *(LYM, Di and Mike Gillam, Guy Vowles, the Didler)*

HAWKESBURY UPTON [ST7786]

☆ *Beaufort Arms* GL9 1AU [High St]: Hook Norton, Wickwar BOB and good guest beers, local farm cider, good soft drinks choice, friendly landlord and staff, good value popular standard food, thriving local atmosphere, extended uncluttered no smoking dining lounge on right, darts in more spartan stripped-brick bare-boards bar, interesting local and brewery memorabilia, lots of pictures (some for sale), skittle alley; no cards; well behaved children welcome, disabled access and facilities, picnic-sets in pleasant smallish garden, on Cotswold Way, open all day *(JJW, CMW, Meg and Colin Hamilton, Matthew Shackle)*

HINTON DYRHAM [ST7376]

☆ *Bull* SN14 8HG [handy for M4 junction 18; A46 towards Bath, then first right]: Pretty 16th-c stone-built pub, two huge fireplaces, nice west country atmosphere, low beams and ancient flagstones, oak settles and pews, stripped stone back area with unusual cushioned cast-iron chairs, family room on the left, good value food from good sandwiches to interesting cooked dishes, Wadworths IPA, 6X and a guest, good wine choice, no smoking restaurant; piped music; dogs (and children till 7.30) welcome, plenty of picnic-sets and play equipment in sizeable sheltered upper garden, more on sunny front balcony; cl Mon lunchtime *(John and Joan Nash, Michael Cooper, Michael Doswell, Peter Dewhurst, LYM, Comus and Sarah Elliott, Nigel Long, Ian Moody, B and M Kendall, Martin and Karen Wake, Mrs Joyce Robson)*

HORSLEY [ST8497]

☆ *Tipputs* GL6 0QE [Tiltups End; A46 2 miles S of Nailsworth]: Doing well under current ownership, with Greene King ales, good wines by the glass, enjoyable food all day from wide range of sandwiches and light dishes to interesting evening meals, efficient young staff, beams and stripped stone in L-shaped bar with big log fire and abstract art, comfortable leather seats in anteroom to galleried restaurant; nice chairs and tables in pretty garden with raised deck, open all day

*(Miss M W Hayter, R Huggins, D Irving,
E McCall, T McLean, David and Gill Hatton,
Michael Doswell)*

HYDE [SO8801]

Ragged Cot GL6 8PE [Burnt Ash; off A419 E
of Stroud, OS Sheet 162 map ref 886012]:
Nicely placed 17th-c pub with comfortably
padded seat right round beamed and stripped
stone bar, log fire, Uley Old Spot and Wickwar
Cotswold Way, decent choice of wines,
friendly hospitable service even when busy,
sympathetic back no smoking modern dining
extension; picnic-sets (and interesting pavilion)
in garden, comfortable bedrooms in adjacent
converted barn *(Andy and Claire Barker,
LYM, R Huggins, D Irving, E McCall,
T McLean)*

KEMBLE [ST9899]

Thames Head GL7 6NZ [A433 Cirencester—
Tetbury]: Stripped stone, timberwork, log fire,
intriguing little front alcove (perhaps an ostler's
lookout), softly lit cottagey no smoking back
area with pews and log-effect gas fire in big
fireplace, country-look dining room with
another big gas fire, good value wines, Arkells
2B and 3B, decent bar food, pleasant staff,
skittle alley; TV; children welcome, tables
outside, good value four-poster bedrooms, nice
walk to nearby low-key source of River
Thames *(LYM, Stephen Woad, R Huggins,
D Irving, E McCall, T McLean)*

KILCOT [SO6925]

Kilcot Inn GL18 1NG [B4221, not far from
M50 junction 3]: Attractively renovated and
extended, with stripped beams, rustic bare
brick and terracotta paintwork, woodburner,
interesting modern yew chairs among other
wood furniture on bare boards or flagstones,
good service, Bass and Greene King Old
Speckled Hen, good value blackboard food
from good baguettes up in bar and no smoking
eating area; dogs welcome, garden picnic-sets
*(Theocsbrian, Neil and Anita Christopher,
Nigel Clifton, Alec and Joan Laurence)*

KILKENNY [SP0118]

☆ *Kilkeney Inn* GL54 4LN [A436 W of
Andoversford]: Spacious and reliable
modernised dining pub with some more
adventurous dishes and good puddings, Bass
and Hook Norton, good choice of wines by the
glass, efficient friendly service, pleasant relaxed
surroundings, log fire and comfortably light
and airy no smoking conservatory; well
behaved children allowed in eating areas,
tables outside, attractive Cotswold views, open
all day wknds *(LYM, Mr and Mrs J Brown,
Guy Vowles, Mike and Mary Carter,
Mrs T A Bizat)*

KINETON [SP0926]

☆ *Halfway House* GL54 5UG [signed from
B4068 and B4077 W of Stow-on-the-Wold]:
Unpretentious country pub with newish
tenants doing enjoyable traditional food using
local ingredients from baguettes up, cheap
Donnington BB and SBA from nearby brewery,
decent wines, farm cider, pub games,
restaurant; children welcome (lunchtime can
get very busy in school hols), attractive

sheltered back garden, tables on narrow front
terrace too, simple comfortable bedrooms,
good walks *(Theocsbrian, LYM, A G Marx)*

KINGSCOTE [ST8196]

☆ *Hunters Hall* GL8 8XZ [A4135 Dursley—
Tetbury]: Tudor beams, stripped stone, big log
fires and plenty of character in individually
furnished linked rooms, some sofas and easy
chairs, wide choice of food from lunchtime
sandwiches (not Sunday) to steak, Greene
King IPA and Abbot and Uley Hogs Head,
friendly and informal if not always speedy
service, no smoking areas inc restaurant,
flagstoned back bar with darts, pool, TV and
juke box; children and dogs welcome, garden
with good play area, bedrooms, open all day
*(Tom and Ruth Rees, R Huggins, D Irving,
E McCall, T McLean, John Dwane, LYM,
Neil and Anita Christopher, Mr and Mrs
M Stratton, Roger Wain-Heapy,
Simon Collett-Jones)*

LECHLADE [SU2199]

New Inn GL7 3AB [Market Sq (A361)]:
Imposing stone building with vast log fire in
big pleasantly plain front lounge, friendly
atmosphere and genial licensees, very wide
choice of good value generous food from good
filled baguettes up, changing real ales such as
Archers Best, Greene King and Youngs Special,
back restaurant; piped music, end games
machine, projector TV for sports; play area in
big garden extending to Thames, good walks,
29 comfortable bedrooms *(Peter and
Audrey Dowsett, Ian Phillips, Meg and
Colin Hamilton)*

Swan GL7 3AP [Burford St]: Oldest pub in
town, with friendly staff, good log fire, great
value proper bar food, bargain coffee,
restaurant; bedrooms, open all day
*(Mrs Angela Brown, Roger and
Pauline Pearce)*

☆ *Trout* GL7 3HA [A417, a mile E]: Three-room
pub dating from 15th c, olde-worlde décor
with low beams, flagstones, stuffed fish and
fishing prints, good log fire, pleasant landlord,
real ales such as Courage Best, Sharps Doom
Bar and Smiles, good value wines, enjoyable
generous food inc plenty of fish and vegetarian,
local paintings for sale, small charity book
stall, no smoking dining room; children in
eating areas, board games and magazines, jazz
Tues and Sun, fishing rights; nice big
Thamesside garden with boathouse bar,
boules, aunt sally, bouncy castle and swings,
camping, open all day summer Sat *(Paul and
Shirley White, Jennifer Banks, LYM, John and
Glenys Wheeler)*

LEIGHTERTON [ST8290]

Royal Oak GL8 8UN [off A46 S of
Nailsworth]: Sensitively refurbished and neatly
kept old stone-built pub, beams, log fires and
mullioned windows, good value pubby food
from soup and sandwiches to roasts,
Butcombe, Wickwar BOB and a weekly guest
beer, prompt pleasant service; piped music;
nice garden, quiet village, good walks, quite
handy for Westonbirt Arboretum *(J L Wedel,
Guy Vowles)*

MARSHFIELD [ST7773]

☆ *Catherine Wheel* SN14 8LR [High St; signed off A420 Bristol—Chippenham]: Traditional stripped stone pub with homely atmosphere, friendly staff, decent food inc imaginative dishes and good choice of Sun roasts, good range of real ales, farm cider, good choice of wines by the glass, plates and prints, medley of settles, chairs and stripped tables, open fire in impressive fireplace, cottagey back family bar, charming no smoking Georgian dining room, darts, dominoes, no music or machines; flower-decked back yard, unspoilt village, bedrooms, open all day Sat *(Guy Vowles, LYM, Dr and Mrs A K Clarke, Pamela and Merlyn Horswell, Nigel Long)*

Lord Nelson SN14 8LP [A420 Bristol—Chippenham; High St]: Spacious range of sympathetically lightened up beamed rooms (inc former stables still with runnel down middle of flagstones), wide choice of quickly served inexpensive and very generous food, good choice of real ales inc Bath Gem, friendly obliging service, open fires, bistro restaurant, games bar with pool and machines; live music Sun afternoon; charming small courtyard, bedrooms in cottage annexe *(Dr and Mrs A K Clarke, Guy Vowles)*

MAYSHILL [ST6882]

☆ *New Inn* BS36 2NT [Badminton Rd (A432 Coalpit Heath—Yate)]: Good food (all day Sun) and fine choice of interesting changing ales in popular 17th-c coaching inn with two comfortably carpeted bar rooms leading to restaurant, log fire; children welcome, garden with play area *(Donna and Roger, Charles Morrison)*

MEYSEY HAMPTON [SU1199]

☆ *Masons Arms* GL7 5JT [just off A417 Cirencester—Lechlade; High St]: 17th-c village pub with longish open-plan bar, painted stone walls, hops on beams, lots of farm tools, caps, beer mats and so forth, big inglenook log fire one end, good changing ales such as Archers Golden, Blindman Mine and Hop Back Odyssey, low-priced usual food, daily papers, no smoking restaurant; piped music, can be smoky; children welcome, compact bedrooms, cl winter Sun evening *(R Huggins, D Irving, E McCall, T McLean, LYM, Dr and Mrs M E Wilson, Colin McKerrow, Mary Rayner)*

MICKLETON [SP1543]

☆ *Kings Arms* GL55 6RT [B4632 (ex A46)]: Relaxed and civilised open-plan family lounge, wide choice of good locally sourced food from well filled sandwiches up (best to book at wknds), good value OAP lunches, friendly well organised service, Bass and Flowers, lots of good value wines by the glass, farm cider, nice mix of comfortable chairs, soft lighting, interesting homely décor, small log fire, no smoking area, small welcoming locals' bar with darts, dominoes and cribbage; piped music; tables outside, handy for Kiftsgate and Hidcote *(BB, Keith and Sue Ward, Andrew Barker, Claire Jenkins)*

Three Ways GL55 6SB [aka Randalls Hotel; B4632, junction with Pebworth rd]: Good bar food inc scrumptious puddings in cosy upmarket surroundings, nice log fire, Hook Norton; comfortable bedrooms *(George Atkinson)*

MORETON-IN-MARSH [SP2032]

Inn on the Marsh GL56 0DW [Stow Rd]: Reasonably priced food from baguettes, fishcakes, burgers and so forth to more restaurant things, may be some dutch dishes, Banks's, Marstons Bitter and Pedigree and a guest such as Shepherd Neame Spitfire, attentive helpful service, distinctive unpretentious beamed bar with inglenook woodburner, comfortable armchairs and sofa, lots of pictures particularly ducks, smartly attractive modern no smoking dining conservatory; small back garden, bedrooms *(Lynn Nisbet, Monica Cockburn, Mike Jefferies, Tony and Wendy Hobden, George Atkinson)*

☆ *Redesdale Arms* GL56 0AW [High St]: Handsome old coaching inn with good friendly service and atmosphere, interesting choice of good value generous food, prettily lit alcoves and big stone fireplace in solidly furnished comfortable panelled bar on right, log fires, real ales, small but good wine list, cafetière coffee, spacious back child-friendly restaurant and dining conservatory, darts in flagstoned public bar; piped music, fruit machine, TV; tables out on heated floodlit courtyard decking, comfortable well equipped bedrooms beyond *(BB, Keith and Sue Ward, Pat and Clive Sherriff, B M Eldridge)*

NAILSWORTH [ST8499]

☆ *Britannia* GL6 0DG [Cossack Sq]: Large popular open-plan food pub with wide range of good familiar bistro food, Fullers London Pride and Greene King IPA, good wines by the glass, friendly efficient service even when busy, thriving atmosphere, big log fire *(Tom and Ruth Rees, Ian Phillips, Keith and Sue Ward, Colin Moore)*

NAUNTON [SP1123]

☆ *Black Horse* GL54 3AD [off B4068 W of Stow]: Well run unspoilt stripped-stone pub with friendly staff, well priced Donnington BB and SBA, good simple fresh food from huge baguettes and baked potatoes to Sun roasts (veg may come from local allotments), plain tables on flagstones, black beams and log fire, darts, cribbage, dominoes, no smoking dining room; piped music; children and dogs welcome, some nice seating outside, bedrooms with own bathrooms, charming village, fine Cotswold walks *(Theocsbrian, Nick Lawless, LYM, Pete Baker, Monica Cockburn, Mike Jefferies, Patmos)*

NETHER WESTCOTE [SP2220]

New Inn OX7 6SD: A popular new main entry in our last edition, this pretty beamed cottage closed in 2005 for thorough-going refurbishment and extension, and looked as if it might not reopen before this edition is published; news please *(LYM)*

NEWENT [SO7225]

George GL18 1PU [Church St]: Old coaching inn with friendly local feel in partly no smoking open-plan L-shaped bar, quieter front part for the good value inexpensive lunchtime food from sandwiches up, changing real ales, big log fire, darts and TV at the back, separate restaurant; children welcome, bedrooms, nice location opp Shambles museum, open all day *(Theocsbrian)*

NORTH NIBLEY [ST7596]
New Inn GL11 6EF [E of village itself; Waterley Bottom – OS Sheet 162 map ref 758963]: Peacefully tucked away, with Bath Gem Bitter and SPA, Cotleigh Tawny and a guest beer from antique beer engines, friendly service, bar food inc good baguettes, pleasantly pubby furnishings in partly stripped stone lounge bar, simple public bar with traditional games (and TV); children and dogs welcome, lots of tables on lawn with neat new covered terrace (pool table here), open all day wknds, has been cl Mon lunchtime *(LYM, Neil and Lorna Mclaughlan, Theocsbrian, Paul Humphreys)*

NORTHLEACH [SP1114]
☆ *Sherborne Arms* GL54 3EE [Market Pl]: Neatly ranked tables stretching back from bare-boards bar on left, cosy lounge on right with wing armchairs and sofas around big stone fireplace, stripped stone restaurant area up a few steps beyond, interesting food using local meats and game, attentive staff, real ales such as Greene King Old Speckled Hen, Sharps Doom Bar and Shepherd Neame Spitfire, good wines and coffee; piped pop music, projector sports TV in back room which can get smoky; one or two picnic-sets out in front, bedrooms *(R Huggins, D Irving, E McCall, T McLean, Gene and Kitty Rankin, BB, Alec and Joan Laurence)*
☆ *Wheatsheaf* GL54 3EZ [West End]: Three big-windowed airy linked rooms, high ceilings, flagstones and bare boards, Black Sheep, Hook Norton and Wadworths 6X, good choice of wines by the glass, straightforward bar food from sandwiches up, no smoking restaurant; children welcome, picnic-sets in pretty garden, bedrooms, open all day (till very late Fri/Sat, winter afternoon closure Mon-Thurs) *(C and R Bromage, Jonathan Martin, LYM, Dennis Jenkin)*

NYMPSFIELD [SO7900]
Rose & Crown GL10 3TU [The Cross; signed off B4066 Stroud—Dursley]: Stone-built pub doing plentiful food (through Sun afternoon) from sandwiches, baguettes and baked potatoes up, Bath Gem, Otter and Uley, decent wines, local farm cider, wide choice of coffees and teas, pleasant service, daily papers, log fire, pine tables and bare boards in beamed front bar, pews and other seats in large no smoking back dining area; piped music can be obtrusive; children and dogs welcome, picnic-sets in side yard and on sheltered lawn with good play area, bedrooms adjacent, handy for Cotswold walks and Woodchester mansion and park (NT) *(BB, John and Gloria Isaacs, Paul Humphreys, Tom and Ruth Rees, J and F Gowers, Anne Morris, Jason Caulkin, Neil and Anita Christopher)*

OLD DOWN [ST6187]
Fox BS32 4PR [off A38 Bristol—Thornbury; Inner Down]: Low-ceilinged pub with good range of real ales, enjoyable very varied and well priced food, friendly staff *(Andy and Jill Kassube, James Morrell)*

OLD SODBURY [ST7581]
☆ *Dog* BS37 6LZ [3 miles from M4 junction 18, via A46 and A432; The Hill (a busy road)]: Two-level bar with low beams and stripped stone, no smoking room, real ales such as Fullers London Pride, Sharps Doom Bar, Wadworths 6X and Wickwar BOB, quick friendly young staff, extremely wide almost confusing choice of good value food from sandwiches up inc plenty of fish and vegetarian, log fires (not always lit), quiz nights Sun/Mon; games machine, juke box; children in eating area, big garden with barbecues and good play area, bedrooms, open all day *(Richard Fendick, Roger Smith, Gary Marchant, Donna and Roger, Dr and Mrs C W Thomas, Dr and Mrs A K Clarke, Cathy Robinson, Ed Coombe, Paul Humphreys, Dave Braisted, Sue and Mike Todd, John and Gloria Isaacs, LYM, Donald Godden, Stuart Paulley, Tom Evans, Stephen Woad)*

PAINSWICK [SO8609]
Falcon GL6 6UN [New St]: Sizeable old open-plan stone-built inn, friendly and largely no smoking, with panelling, high ceilings, cheerful bare-boards bar with stuffed birds and fish, mainly carpeted dining area with lots of prints, high bookshelves and shelves of ornaments by coal-effect fire, wide range of reasonably priced generous food from baguettes up, lots of wines by the glass, Badger and Otter ales, good coffee, daily papers; no dogs during meal times; bedrooms, opp churchyard famous for its 99 yews *(Martin and Pauline Jennings, DWT, BB)*
☆ *Royal Oak* GL6 6QG [St Mary's St]: Old-fashioned partly 16th-c three-room town local with appealing nooks and crannies, some attractive old or antique seats, plenty of prints, enjoyable good value food (not Sun) from filled rolls to interesting main dishes, friendly staff, Black Sheep, Moles Best and Shepherd Neame Spitfire, decent wines, open fire, no smoking lounge and small sun lounge; children in eating area, dogs welcome in public bar, suntrap pretty courtyard *(Giles and Annie Francis, Brian McBurnie, Neil and Anita Christopher, LYM, Eddie Edwards, Margaret and Roy Randle)*

PARKEND [SO6308]
Rising Sun GL15 4HN [off B4431]: Unpretentious friendly foresters' local with surprisingly good low-priced simple food; picnic-sets out in woodside garden, good walks *(Mike and Mary Carter)*

PAXFORD [SP1837]
Churchill Arms GL55 6XH [B4479, SE of Chipping Campden]: Simply furnished flagstoned bar and bare-boards back extension, assorted old tables and chairs, snug warmed by good log fire, Hook Norton Best and a couple

of guest beers, good choice of wines by the glass; imaginative food that can be most enjoyable, service usually friendly and helpful; children welcome, some seats outside (and aunt sally), charming good value bedrooms, good breakfast *(D C Leggatt, LYM, Derek Thomas, Steve Whalley, Mr and Mrs Martin Joyce, Canon Michael Bourdeaux, Michael and Anne Brown)*

PRESTBURY [SO9624]

☆ *Plough* GL52 3BG [Mill St]: Well preserved thatched village local opp church, cosy and comfortable front lounge, service from corner corridor hatch in locals' charming and basic flagstoned back tap room, grandfather clock and big log fire, consistently friendly service, Adnams Best and Broadside and Charles Wells Bombardier tapped from the cask, good choice of farm ciders, perhaps good sandwiches or simple hot dish; outstanding good-sized flower-filled back garden *(Donna and Roger, Jason Chess, R J Herd, B M Eldridge, Guy Vowles)*

RODBOROUGH [SO8502]

Bear GL5 5DE [Rodborough Common]: Comfortably cosy and pubby beamed and flagstoned bar in smart hotel, warm welcome, pleasant window seats, good log fire, hops hung around top of golden stone walls, interesting reproductions, Uley real ale, bar food that's reasonably priced considering the surroundings, afternoon teas, restaurant; children welcome, bedrooms *(Dave Irving, BB, Martin and Karen Wake)*

SAPPERTON [SO9303]

Daneway Inn GL7 6LN [Daneway; off A419 Stroud—Cirencester]: Flagstone-floored local in charming quiet wooded countryside, terrace tables and lovely sloping lawn; amazing floor-to-ceiling carved oak dutch fireplace, newly stripped and stained boards, sporting prints, Wadworths ales, Weston's farm cider, reasonably priced generous simple food from filled baps up, friendly landlord and staff, small no smoking family room, traditional games in inglenook public bar, Weds quiz night; no dogs; camping possible, good walks by canal under restoration with tunnel to Coates *(R Huggins, D Irving, E McCall, T McLean, Len Clark, LYM, Tim and Suzy Bower)*

SHEEPSCOMBE [SO8910]

☆ *Butchers Arms* GL6 7RH [off B4070 NE of Stroud]: Busy 17th-c pub with popular fresh food at fair prices from lunchtime filled rolls, bagels and wraps up, wider evening choice, Hook Norton Best and a couple of well chosen guest beers, roaring woodburner, seats in big bay windows, flowery-cushioned chairs and rustic benches, and lots of interesting oddments, refurbished no smoking restaurant, traditional games; can get crowded wknds; children in eating areas, tables outside, terrific views *(Bernard Stradling, LYM, Paul and Shirley White, Dr A J and Mrs Tompsett, R Huggins, D Irving, E McCall, T McLean, Neil and Anita Christopher, Andrew Shore, Maria Williams, John Reilly, Jason Caulkin, Rod and Chris Pring)*

SHIPTON MOYNE [ST8989]

☆ *Cat & Custard Pot* GL8 8PN [off B4040 Malmesbury—Bristol; The Street]: Well run pub with good choice of good value robust food from sandwiches and great ham and eggs to steaks and restaurant dishes (booking recommended even wkdy lunch), Fullers London Pride, Wadworths 6X and guest beers, Thatcher's cider, neat friendly staff, several dining areas, hunting prints, cosy back snug, no piped music; dogs welcome, picturesque village *(Richard Stancomb, Peter and Audrey Dowsett, BB, Gordon and Jay Smith, John and Gloria Isaacs)*

SIDDINGTON [SU0399]

☆ *Greyhound* GL7 6HR [Ashton Rd; village signed from A419 roundabout at Tesco]: Two linked rooms each with a big log fire, enjoyable food from sandwiches to bargain lunchtime carvery and unusual fish dishes, Badger Tanglefoot, Wadworths IPA and seasonal beers, welcoming service, public bar with slate floor, darts and cribbage; piped music; garden tables, open all day *(LYM, R Huggins, D Irving, E McCall, T McLean, Paul and Shirley White, Donna and Roger, Peter and Audrey Dowsett)*

SLIMBRIDGE [SO7204]

Tudor Arms GL2 7BP [Shepherds Patch; off A38 towards Wildfowl & Wetlands Trust]: Welcoming and obliging, with plentiful generous food (all day wknds), four or five changing ales such as Uley, Wadworths and Wickwar, good wines by the glass, typical modernised lounge, bar with billiards and TV, evening restaurant, skittle alley; children welcome, disabled facilities, handy for Wildfowl Trust and canal boat trips, bedrooms in small annexe, open all day *(Dr A J and Mrs Tompsett)*

SNOWSHILL [SP0933]

Snowshill Arms WR12 7JU: Spruce and airy carpeted bar in honeypot village, Donnington BB and SBA, reasonably priced straightforward food from sandwiches up (shame about the disposable plates), quick service even when busy, log fire, stripped stone, neat array of tables, local photographs; skittle alley, charming village views from bow windows and from big back garden with little stream and play area, friendly local feel midweek winter and evenings, can be very crowded other lunchtimes – nearby parking may be difficult; children welcome if eating, handy for Snowshill Manor and Cotswold Way walks *(LYM, Martin and Karen Wake, Guy Vowles, Martin and Pauline Jennings)*

SOUTH CERNEY [SU0496]

Royal Oak GL7 5UP [High St]: Thriving and sympathetically extended ancient local, welcoming landlord, decent range of changing real ales, woodburner, big back dining area; pleasant garden behind with big terrace and summer marquee *(R Huggins, D Irving, E McCall, T McLean, Ian Phillips)*

SOUTHROP [SP2003]

☆ *Swan* GL7 3NU: Charmingly refurbished low-ceilinged front dining rooms with log fire, flagstones, antiques and attractive pictures, particularly good interesting food (not Sun evening), pricey but generous, well spaced tables, good lively atmosphere, Greene King Abbot and Hook Norton from back bar, good wines, stripped stone skittle alley; children welcome, pretty village esp at daffodil time (R Huggins, D Irving, E McCall, T McLean, Julie and Bill Ryan, Paul and Shirley White, LYM, Richard and Sheila Fitton, Keith and Sue Ward, Gaynor Gregory, Noel Grundy, Mr and Mrs A H Young, Guy Vowles, A G Marx, Richard Greaves, Karen and Graham Oddey)

ST BRIAVELS [SO5504]
George GL15 6TA [High Street]: Rambling linked black-beamed rooms with old-fashioned seating, toby jugs and antique bottles, big stone open fireplace, very wide choice of wholesome food (can take a long while when busy), popular OAP lunches, Freeminer Bitter, Fullers London Pride, RCH Pitchfork and a couple of guest beers, Stowford Press cider, no smoking restaurant; piped music; children and dogs welcome, flagstoned terrace over former moat of neighbouring Norman fortress, bedrooms (LYM, Guy Vowles, Peter and Jean Dowson, Kevin Blake, Colin Morgan, Piotr Chodzko-Zajko, Denys Gueroult)

STANTON [SP0634]
☆ *Mount* WR12 7NE [off B4632 SW of Broadway; no through road up hill, bear left]: Stunning spot up steep lane from golden-stone village, heavy beams, flagstones and big log fire in original core, horseracing pictures and trappings and plenty of locals, roomy picture-window extensions, one no smoking with cricket memorabilia; welcoming landlord, Donnington BB and SBA, farm cider, decent bar food (not Sun evening) from super baguettes up; open all day Sat and summer Sun, well behaved children allowed, views to welsh mountains from large terrace (great on summer evenings), attractive garden with pets' corner (K H Frostick, LYM, Ian and Celia Abbott, Mrs Ann Gray, Martin and Pauline Jennings)

STOW-ON-THE-WOLD [SP1729]
☆ *Coach & Horses* GL56 0QZ [Ganborough (A424 about 2½ miles N)]: Beamed and flagstoned country pub alone on former coaching road, well priced Donnington BB and SBA, wide blackboard choice of popular generous well priced bar food from baguettes up, friendly staff, good fires, steps up to carpeted dining area with high-backed settles, no smoking area; children welcome, popular skittle alley, tables in garden (LYM, Keith and Sue Ward)
☆ *Eagle & Child* GL54 1BN [attached to Royalist Hotel, Digbeth Street]: Smart dining bar attached to handsome old hotel, woodburner, flagstones, low beams and dark pink walls, back conservatory, nice mix of tables (no bar as such), up-to-date food from baguettes up, Hook Norton Best, good if not cheap wine and malt whisky choice; may be piped music; children and dogs welcome, small

back courtyard, good bedrooms, open all day (David Hall, George Atkinson, Michael Dandy, Peter and Jean Hoare, Keith and Sue Ward, Mayur Shah, LYM, Mary Rayner, Lynn Elliott, John and Pat Morris)
Grapevine GL54 1AU [Sheep St]: Substantial hotel with relaxing small front bar, food from generous sandwiches, baguettes and wraps to steak and bass, helpful service, Hook Norton Old Hooky and a guest beer, good choice of wines by the glass, good coffee, separate brasserie and restaurant with live vine; pavement tables, bedrooms, open all day (David and Jean Hall, Michael Dandy, Colin and Janet Roe)
☆ *Kings Arms* GL54 1AF [The Square]: Reasonably priced good food from interesting baguettes to lots of fish, real food for children, good choice of wines by the glass, Greene King IPA and Old Speckled Hen, good coffee (opens early for this), cheerful friendly service, daily papers, some Mackintosh-style chairs on polished boards, bowed black beams, some panelling and stripped stone, log fire, charming upstairs dining room overlooking town; piped music; bedrooms, open all day (Michael Dandy, BB, Michael and Jeanne Shillington, Jane Taylor, David Dutton)
☆ *Queens Head* GL54 1AB [The Square]: Traditional unfussy local with good friendly service, heavily beamed and flagstoned back bar with high-backed settles, big log-effect fire, horse prints, lots of tables in bustling and chatty stripped stone front lounge, good value pub food (not Sun) from sandwiches up inc good home-made pies, low-priced Donnington BB and SBA, good if not so cheap wines by the glass, usual games; piped music; dogs and children positively welcome (pub dog lets herself in by opening back door), tables in attractive garden, occasional jazz Sun lunchtime (LYM, Paul and Shirley White, Tracey and Stephen Groves, Michael Dandy, the Didler, Gerry and Rosemary Dobson)
☆ *Talbot* GL54 1BQ [The Square]: Light, airy and spacious modern décor, relaxed brasserie/café bar feel, good reasonably priced continental-feel food, bright friendly service even when busy, Wadworths ales, lots of good value wines by the glass, good coffee, big log fire, plain tables and chairs on wood block floor, modern prints, daily papers; no children inside, may be piped radio, lavatories upstairs; bedrooms nearby, open all day (Michael Dandy, BB, Mel Smith)

STROUD [SO8404]
Clothiers Arms GL5 3JJ [Bath Rd]: Extended but still genuine 18th-c pub with Wychwood Hobgoblin and other ales in busy bar with old Stroud Brewery decorations, pleasant airy dining room; garden tables (Dave Braisted)

TEWKESBURY [SO8932]
Berkeley Arms GL20 5PA [Church St]: Pleasantly olde-worlde medieval timbered pub (most striking part down the side alley), with Wadworths and guest ales, friendly landlord and quick service, open fire, enjoyable

generous pubby food (not Mon), separate basic front public bar, raftered ancient back barn restaurant; open all day Fri/Sat, bedrooms *(Theocsbrian, Dave Braisted)*

☆ *Olde Black Bear* GL20 5BJ [High St]: The county's oldest pub, intricately rambling rooms with lots of atmosphere, ancient tiles, heavy timbering and low beams (one with leather-clad ceiling), armchairs in front of open fires, plenty of pictures and bric-a-brac, real ales (you may need to look around for the guest beers), reasonably priced wines; piped music; children welcome, terrace and play area in riverside garden, open all day *(Roger and Anne Newbury, the Didler, LYM, Gordon Prince)*

TODDINGTON [SP0432]
Pheasant GL54 5DT [A46 Broadway—Winchcombe, junction with A438 and B4077]: Attractive extended stone-built pub with emphasis on good choice of reasonably priced food, real ales, lots of railway prints – handy for nearby preserved Gloucestershire Warwickshire Railway station *(B M Eldridge)*

TOLLDOWN [ST7577]
☆ *Crown* SN14 8HZ [a mile from M4 junction 18 – A46 towards Bath]: No smoking heavy-beamed pub with simple furnishings and light fresh décor, welcoming efficient service, accent on generous interesting food from good ciabattas up, Wadworths ales, good house wines, good log fire, no smoking area; good disabled access, children in eating area and restaurant, good garden with play area, comfortable bedrooms *(LYM, Dr and Mrs A K Clarke, Pamela and Merlyn Horswell, Di and Mike Gillam, Mike and Mary Carter, Brian P White)*

TWYNING [SO8737]
☆ *Fleet* GL20 6FL [off westbound A38 slip rd from M50 junction 1]: Family holiday pub in superb setting at end of quiet lane though just off motorway, good river views from roomy high-ceilinged bars, interesting boating-theme décor, five real ales, wide choice of quickly served tasty bar food inc good value lunchtime baps and baguettes, woodburner, airy back restaurant area, tearoom and tuck shop; games room with darts and bar billiards, piped music, machines, entertainment Fri/Sat; children welcome, disabled access, picnic-sets in big waterside garden with two floodlit terraces, rockery cascade and safe enclosed children's area with chipmunk corner; stop on Tewkesbury—Bredon summer boat run, bedrooms, open all day *(Carol Broadbent, LYM, Neil and Anita Christopher, Carol and David Havard, Dr A J and Mrs Tompsett, Susan and Nigel Wilson)*

UPTON CHEYNEY [ST6969]
Upton Inn BS30 6LY [signed off A431 at Bitton]: Much-refurbished bar with good value interesting home-made food inc good fish choice, friendly helpful service, decent wines and real ale, smart unchanging restaurant with wall hangings, chandeliers and blackamoor statues; tables outside, picturesque spot *(Meg and Colin Hamilton, MRSM, Tom and Ruth Rees)*

WESTBURY-ON-SEVERN [SO7114]
☆ *Red Lion* GL14 1PA [A48, corner Bell Lane]: Substantial beamed and half-timbered traditional pub on busy road but by quiet church-side lane to river, welcoming atmosphere, genial landlord, generous interesting home cooking, real ales such as Bass and Fullers London Pride, decent wine, comfortable bar with button-back wall seats, velvet curtains, coal stove, big dining room with old pews; handy for Westbury Court gardens (NT) *(BB, M J Winterton, B M Eldridge)*

WESTONBIRT [ST8690]
Hare & Hounds GL8 8QL [A433 SW of Tetbury]: Substantial roadside hotel with separate entrance for end turkey-carpeted bar, with high-backed settles, snacks and good more substantial meals, Smiles Best and Wadworths 6X, central log-effect gas fire, sporting prints, games in public bar on left; small tweedy more central cocktail bar, pleasant gardens, good value bedrooms, handy for arboretum *(BB, Dr and Mrs C W Thomas, Meg and Colin Hamilton)*

WHITECROFT [SO6005]
Miners Arms GL15 4PE [B4234 N of Lydney]: Friendly unpretentious local with splendid changing range of real ales and farm ciders, piano in one of two rooms on either side of bar, lunchtime sandwiches and limited hot dishes; good gardens front and back, one with a pleasant little stream, handy for steam railway, open all day *(Pete Baker)*

WHITMINSTER [SO7607]
☆ *Frombridge Mill* GL2 7PD [Frombridge Lane (A38 nr M5 junction 13)]: No smoking mill-based dining pub with cosy and comfortable largely carpeted bar and dining areas, some tables overlooking river, decent reasonably priced pub food from sandwiches and baked potatoes up inc popular good value lunchtime carvery, charming helpful staff, Greene King real ales; picnic-sets in good-sized garden with play area, lovely setting overlooking weir *(Dr and Mrs C W Thomas, Peter Neate)*

WICK [ST7072]
☆ *Rose & Crown* BS30 5QH [High St (A420)]: Relaxed and well run Chef & Brewer, busy and roomy, with friendly attentive service, Courage Best, Greene King Old Speckled Hen, Charles Wells Bombardier and an unusual guest beer, good wines by the glass, plenty of character in largely untouched and mainly no smoking linked 17th-c rooms with low beams, mixed furnishings and candlelight, very wide food choice, coal fire in big stone fireplace, daily papers; good disabled access, picnic-sets out on terrace, open all day *(Pamela and Merlyn Horswell, BB, B N F and M Parkin)*

WILLERSEY [SP1039]
☆ *Bell* WR12 7PJ [B4632 Cheltenham—Stratford, nr Broadway]: Attractive stone-built pub, open-plan and neatly modernised, comfortable front part impressively set for the carefully prepared interesting and unpretentious home-made food (locally very popular – worth booking evenings), Aston

Villa memorabilia and huge collection of model cars in back area past the big L-shaped bar counter with its reasonably priced Hook Norton Best, Tetleys and Wadworths 6X, relaxed atmosphere, quick friendly helpful service; darts, Thurs evening chess ladder; overlooks delightful village's green and duck pond, lots of tables in big garden, bedrooms in outbuildings *(DC, Gerry and Rosemary Dobson, BB)*

WINCHCOMBE [SP0228]

☆ *Old Corner Cupboard* GL54 5LX [Gloucester St]: Attractive golden stone Tudor pub with generous reasonably priced food inc good specials and fresh fish in nice back partly no smoking eating area, friendly fast service, Fullers London Pride, Hook Norton Old Hooky and seasonal local Stanway ales, good choice of wines by the glass, comfortable stripped-stone lounge bar with heavy-beamed Tudor core, traditional hatch-service lobby, small side smoke room with woodburner in massive stone fireplace, traditional games; children welcome, tables in back garden, open all day *(Theocsbrian, LYM, Alan Bugler)*

Old White Lion GL54 5PS [North St]: Recently refurbished, light and pleasant, with small bar, interesting enjoyable food, real ale, separate restaurant; pleasant garden area (dogs allowed here), bedrooms *(Anon)*

☆ *White Hart* GL54 5LJ [High St (B4632)]: Unusual café-bar with big windows giving on to village street, small no smoking restaurant and downstairs bar with oak beams and stripped stone, friendly hard-working Swedish staff, Greene King IPA and Old Speckled Hen and Wadworths 6X, good wines by the glass, and useful all-day food inc scandinavian specialities; management seems to have been a bit erratic in recent months; children welcome, good bedrooms, open all day *(Guy Vowles, Stuart Turner, LYM)*

White Lion GL54 5PS [North St]: Enjoyable restaurant food inc good fish choice, friendly helpful staff, fair-priced wines *(Brian Jackson)*

WITHINGTON [SP0315]

Kings Head GL54 4BD [Kings Head Lane]: Thriving beamed local with Hook Norton Best and a changing Wickwar beer tapped from the cask, friendly service, neat divided partly stripped stone lounge with piano, long narrow basic bar with darts, shove-ha'penny, table skittles and pool; pleasant garden behind *(R Huggins, D Irving, E McCall, T McLean)*

WOODCHESTER [SO8403]

Old Fleece GL5 5NB [Rooksmoor; A46 a mile S of Stroud – not to be confused with Fleece at Lightpill a little closer in]: Emphasis on wide choice of interesting freshly made bar food from unusual lunchtime sandwiches up, informal bare-boards décor in open-plan line of several big-windowed room areas, largely no smoking, friendly welcome, three or four real ales from bar on right, good wines by the glass, local non-alcoholic drinks, big log fire, candles, daily papers, stripped stone or dark salmon pink walls; children welcome, two roadside terraces, one heated *(BB, Dave Irving, Neil and Anita Christopher)*

☆ *Ram* GL5 5EL [High St, South Woodchester]: Cheerful welcome from landlord and staff, half a dozen or more good ales such as Archers, Bath, Butcombe, Otter, Uley and Wadworths in relaxed L-shaped beamed bar with nice mix of traditional furnishings, stripped stonework, bare boards, three open fires, darts, friendly staff, good value food from generous baguettes to steaks and bargain Sun roast, well organised family dining extension, spectacular valley views from bar and terrace tables; some live music; children welcome, open all day Sat/Sun *(Andy and Claire Barker, Guy Vowles, LYM, Andrew Shore, Maria Williams, R Huggins, D Irving, E McCall, T McLean, Dave Irving)*

☆ *Royal Oak* GL5 5PQ [off A46; Church Road, N Woodchester]: Relaxing and comfortable low-beamed bar on right with oak tables, soft seats by big log fire in huge fireplace next to sprucely old-fashioned stripped stone dining area on left with enjoyable pub food, welcoming service, real ales such as Adnams Broadside, Greene King IPA and Sharps Doom Bar, fresh flowers, nice views; big-screen TV for special events, piped music; children and dogs welcome, open all day *(Andy and Claire Barker, Mrs Rosemary Reeves, LYM, R Huggins, D Irving, E McCall, T McLean, Tim and Suzy Bower)*

WOODCROFT [ST5496]

Rising Sun NP16 7HY: Wide choice of good food with emphasis on fish, welcoming landlord, good wines by the glass; large garden *(Drs Nigel and Gail Holgate)*

YATE [ST6983]

Codrington Arms BS37 7LG [North Rd]: Good value pubby food inc proper steak and kidney pudding, new dining room *(Alec and Barbara Jones)*

The letters and figures after the name of each town are its Ordnance Survey map reference. *Using the Guide* at the beginning of the book explains how it helps you find a pub, in road atlases or on large-scale maps as well as on our own maps.

Hampshire

There are quite a few changes here this year, with early reports looking promising on new management for the Red Lion at Boldre, the Red Lion at Chalton, the Vine in Hambledon, the smart Running Horse at Littleton and the Peat Spade at Longstock. We can't really count the landlord of the Black Swan at Monxton as new, as he was formerly assistant manager there – again, things are looking positive. Some pubs still in the same hands have been winning particularly warm praise in the last few months: the Oak at Bank (a nice individualistic all-rounder in a charming spot), the cosy Sun at Bentworth, the Wheatsheaf at Braishfield (again, refreshing individuality, with splendid staff), the Greyfriar opposite Jane Austen's house at Chawton (new to the *Guide*, enjoyable food in pleasant surroundings), the Flower Pots at Cheriton (unassuming charm – and good own-brew beers, even though their names are changing), the upmarket Chestnut Horse at Easton (a civilised place for a treat), the rustic Royal Oak at Fritham (fine choice of real ales), the welcoming Hawkley Inn, the quietly set Yew Tree at Lower Wield (very good food), the Bush at Ovington (good if pricey meals in appealing surroundings), the Trooper near Petersfield (a fine all-rounder, nice to stay in as well as to eat – and drink – at), the bustling and well run Plough at Sparsholt (good food), the lovely cottagey old Harrow at Steep, the beautifully placed riverside Mayfly near Wherwell (on splendid form, back in the *Guide* after a break), and the hugely popular Wykeham Arms in Winchester. For its interesting food at sensible prices in warm-hearted pubby surroundings, the Plough at Sparsholt keeps its title of Hampshire Dining Pub of the Year. Pubs to note particularly in the Lucky Dip section at the end of the chapter are the Green Dragon at Brook, Fox & Hounds in Bursledon, Mill Arms at Dunbridge, Hampshire Bowman at Dundridge, New Forest at Emery Down, Royal Oak at Langstone, Jolly Farmer in Locks Heath, Chequers near Lymington, Pilgrim at Marchwood, Trusty Servant at Minstead, Royal Oak at North Gorley, White Horse near Petersfield, restauranty Dukes Head in Romsey, Selborne Arms at Selborne, Duke of Wellington in Southampton and White Hart in Stockbridge. This tends to be one of the more expensive areas for drinks as well as for food. The main local brewer is Ringwood, with Flower Pots or Itchen Valley sometimes cropping up as the cheapest beer that a pub stocks. Gales was a major Hampshire brewer until this last year, when Fullers of London took over its beers (and pubs).

BANK SU2807 Map 2
Oak 🍺

Signposted just off A35 SW of Lyndhurst; SO43 7FD

Tapped from the cask, beers at this friendly, no smoking pub in a tranquil spot in the New Forest include a good representation of regional brews, with Hop Back Summer Lightning and Ringwood Best, three very frequently changing guests from small-scale brewers such as Cottage, Hop Back, Sharps and Welton; they also have beer festivals and stock country wines. It can get busy, despite its tucked-away location. On either side of the door in the bay windows of the L-shaped bar are built-in green-cushioned seats, and on the right, two or three little pine-panelled booths with small built-in tables and bench seats. The rest of the bar has more floor space, with candles in individual brass holders on a line of stripped old and blond newer tables set against the wall on bare floorboards, and more at the back; some low beams and joists, fishing rods, spears, a boomerang, and old ski poles on the ceiling, and on the walls are brass platters, heavy knives, stuffed fish and guns. There's also a big fireplace, cushioned milk churns along the bar counter, and little red lanterns among hop bines above the bar. Well liked bar food includes good lunchtime doorstep sandwiches (from £4.25) as well as baked brie with almonds and honey (£3.95), various cured meats with roasted red pepper and pickles (£6.75), pork and herb sausages with rich onion gravy (£7.50), a pie of the day (£8.95), greek salad topped with sliced grilled chicken breast (£8.95), fresh cod in beer batter (£10.95), roast cod on lentil curry with coriander rice (£11.95), grilled 12oz rib-eye steak (£12.95), and daily specials such as plaice (from £10), duck breast (£11) and crab and lobster in season (£15-£20). The side garden has picnic-sets and long tables and benches by the big yew trees. *(Recommended by Paul Goldman, Roger and Kate Sweetapple, Brian Root, Prof Keith and Mrs Jane Barber, Graham and Glenis Watkins, Dr Alan and Mrs Sue Holder, Louise English, D P and M A Miles, Mike and Sue Loseby, Sue Demont, Tim Barrow, Mayur Shah, Janet Whittaker, Roger and Pauline Pearce, C J Roebuck, Charles and Pauline Stride, Richard Waller, Pauline Smith, Pam and John Smith, Peter Titcomb, A G Marx)*

Free house ~ Licensee Karen Slowen ~ Real ale ~ Bar food (12-2.30, 6-9.30) ~ (023) 8028 2350 ~ Children welcome (with restrictions) ~ Dogs welcome ~ Open 11-11; 12-10.30 Sun; 11.30-3, 6-11 weekdays in winter

BENTLEY   SU8044   Map 2
Bull

A31 Alton—Farnham dual carriageway, east of village itself; accessible from both carriageways, but tricky if westbound; GU10 5JH

A welcoming haven from the busy A31 trunk road and now no smoking throughout, this cosy 16th-c country inn serves tasty food, with beef and lamb from local farms, together with a range of five real ales. The main room on the right, restful despite some traffic noise, has soft lighting, witty sayings chalked on low black beams in its maroon ceiling, lots of local photographs on partly stripped brick walls, and pub chairs around neat stripped pub tables. The back room on the left has a good log fire in a huge hearth, a cushioned pew by one long oak-planked table, and in a snug and narrow back alcove another pew built around a nice mahogany table; piped music. Good changing blackboard food includes sandwiches (from £4.45), soup (£4.50), ploughman's (£5.50), smoked haddock fishcakes or chicken liver and brandy pâté (£5.95), roasted vegetable and cheese wellington (£10.95), braised chunks of beef with seville oranges and horseradish mash (£11.95), confit of duck or pot-roasted poussin with apricot and bacon stuffing (£12.95), frequently changing daily specials such as chicken and leek pie (£9.25), beef stroganoff (£9.95), and a range of fish such as bass with tomato butter (£14.95), and puddings (£4.50). Courage Best, Fullers London Pride, Ringwood and Youngs Best are on handpump along with a guest such as Hogs Back TEA, and the friendly staff give free refills of the good filter coffee. There are plenty of pretty summer flowering tubs and hanging baskets outside, and picnic-sets and a teak table and chairs on the side terrace. More reports please *(Recommended by Ian Phillips, John and Rosemary Haynes, Janet Whittaker, Mike Park, William To, Susan Loppert, Jane Caplan, I D Barnett, Ann and Colin Hunt, Alan M Pring)*

Enterprise ~ Lease Grant Edmead ~ Real ale ~ Bar food (12-2.30, 6.30-9.30; 12-3, 6-8.30 Sun) ~ Restaurant ~ (01420) 22156 ~ Children in restaurant ~ Dogs allowed in bar ~ Open 10.30-11; 12-10.30 Sun

---

Pubs with outstanding views are listed at the back of the book.

BENTWORTH SU6740 Map 2
Sun 🍺

Sun Hill; from the A339 coming from Alton the first turning takes you there direct; or in village follow Shalden 2¼, Alton 4¼ signpost; GU34 5JT

Readers have been unanimous in praise for this charming 17th-c country pub – its welcoming landlady, the well kept beer she serves and the food too. There's a fine choice of eight changing real ales, some coming from local brewers; these might include Badger Fursty Ferret, Butcombe Best, Flower Pots, Fullers London Pride, Ringwood Best and Old Thumper, Stonehenge Pigswill and Timothy Taylors Landlord on handpump; several malt whiskies. Another strength at this delightful place is the promptly served good home-made bar food, which might include sandwiches, soup, creamy garlic mushrooms or pork liver pâté (all £3.95), yorkshire pudding with roast beef or pork and leek sausages (£7.50), fresh tagliatelle with smoked salmon, lemon and dill cream sauce or cumberland sausage with onion gravy (£8.95), home-made burger with relish (£9.95), steak and kidney pie, salmon wrapped in parma ham with pesto or avocado and stilton bake (all £10.95), steaks (from £11.95), and puddings (£3.95); specials might include medallions of scotch fillet in sherry and cranberry sauce with mustard mash or fillet of plaice filled with prawns in white wine and tarragon sauce (£12.95). Popular with both locals and visitors, the two little traditional communicating rooms have high-backed antique settles, pews and schoolroom chairs, olde-worlde prints and blacksmith's tools on the walls, and bare boards and scrubbed deal tables on the left; big fireplaces (one with a winter fire) and candles make it especially snug in winter; an arch leads to a brick-floored room with another open fire. There are seats out in front and in the back garden, and pleasant nearby walks. *(Recommended by Martin and Karen Wake, Ann and Colin Hunt, Tony and Jill Radnor, the Didler, Lynn Sharpless, Phyl and Jack Street, R Lake, Simon Fox, Mr and Mrs R W Allan)*

Free house ~ Licensee Mary Holmes ~ Real ale ~ Bar food (12-2, 7-9.30) ~ (01420) 562338 ~ Children welcome with restrictions ~ Dogs allowed in bar ~ Open 12-3, 6-11; 12-10.30 Sun

BOLDRE SZ3198 Map 2
Red Lion ♀

Village signposted from A337 N of Lymington; SO41 8NE

In warmer months, this pub on the edge of the New Forest is a lovely spot to sit outside, among the flowering tubs and hanging baskets: there are tables out in the back garden, and the new licensee has created a woodland garden and front and side terraces. The four black-beamed rooms reveal an entertaining collection of bygones, with heavy urns, platters, farm tools, heavy-horse harness, gin traps, ferocious-looking man traps and rural landscapes, as well as a dainty collection of old bottles and glasses in the window by the counter. Seating is on pews, wheelback chairs and tapestried stools. There's a fine old cooking range in the cosy little bar, and two good log fires. They have Bass, Ringwood Best and Fortyniner and perhaps a guest on handpump; several good wines by the glass. Straightforward food includes baguettes (from £4.75), ploughman's (£6.95), local sausages and mash (£7.25), roasted vegetable and butternut squash tartlet (£8.95), fresh dressed crab (£12.95) and home-made puddings (£3.95). There are allocated no smoking areas. More reports on the new regime please. *(Recommended by BOB)*

Eldridge Pope ~ Tenants Alan and Manda Pountney ~ Real ale ~ Bar food (12-2.30(4 Sun), 6.30-9.30(9 Sun)) ~ (01590) 673177 ~ Children in eating area of bar ~ Dogs allowed in bar ~ Open 11-11; 12-10.30 Sun

---

BRAISHFIELD   SU3724   Map 2
Wheatsheaf
Village signposted off A3090 on NW edge of Romsey, pub just S of village on Braishfield Road; SO51 0QE

In addition to using eggs from their own cotswold legbar chickens, the friendly owners of this nicely idiosyncratic pub have made this a charming place to eat, drink and chat: they source ingredients carefully and make good use of their own serious and sizeable herb garden, and you may be in luck and visit when their soft fruit cage is cropping. The décor is eclectic, with a miscellany of tables from elegant little oak ovals through handsome Regency-style drum tables to sturdy more rustic ones, with a similarly wide variety of chairs, and on the stripped brick or deep pink-painted walls a profusion of things to look at, from Spy caricatures and antique prints through staffordshire dogs and other decorative china to a leg in a fishnet stocking kicking out from the wall and a jokey 'Malteser grader' (a giant copper skimmer). It sounds a bit of a mish-mash, but in fact works well, making for an attractive and relaxed atmosphere – helped along by the way the efficient young staff clearly enjoy their work. Two of the dining areas are no smoking. In addition to snacks like sandwiches (from £3.95) and eggs benedict (£6.95), enjoyable and interesting food includes rustic breads with oils or soup (£3.95), field mushrooms baked with dolcelatte and basil rarebit (£5.95), millefeuille of salmon, chicken and langoustine pie or slow-roasted lamb shank with port, orange and red berry sauce (all £11.95), steak (from £12.95), daily specials such as hand-dived scallops (£7.95) and game dishes like local venison (£11.95); on Wednesdays they have burger evenings, where you customise your own burger (£5). They also do lots of snacks such as olives and nuts, and sell chocolates and sweets. Hook Norton Old Hooky, Ringwood Best, Timothy Taylors Landlord and a couple of guests such as Caledonian Deuchars IPA and Charles Wells Bombardier are on handpump, and they have 16 wines by the glass, speciality belgian beers and good coffee; daily papers and several reference books; piped music, TV; disabled access and facilities. Unusually, the chairs, tables and picnic-sets out on the terrace are painted in greek blue. There are woodland walks nearby, and the pub is handy for the Sir Harold Hillier Arboretum. *(Recommended by Glen and Nola Armstrong, Phyl and Jack Street, Lynn Sharpless, A and B D Craig, James Ponsford)*

Enterprise ~ Lease Peter and Jenny Jones ~ Real ale ~ Bar food (11-9.30; 12-9 Sun) ~ Restaurant ~ (01794) 368372 ~ Children welcome ~ Dogs allowed in bar ~ Open 11am-midnight

BRAMDEAN   SU6127   Map 2
Fox
A272 Winchester—Petersfield; SO24 0LP

This well heeled, weatherboarded dining pub continues to earn praise from readers for its friendly staff and as a civilised place for a meal. Booking is advisable if you want to eat here; the food (not cheap) includes lunchtime sandwiches (from £3.25), starters such as soup (£4.50), wild boar pâté (£4.95) or scallops fried with bacon or fresh figs baked with dolcellate and parma ham (£6.95), main courses like steak and kidney pie (£10.95, lunchtime only), roast confit of duck or grilled lamb cutlets (£13.95), fillet of monkfish with tarragon sauce (£14.95), and fillet steak (£17.95) and puddings such as panna cotta with fresh raspberries or apple and almond crumble (£4.95); on Sunday evenings they offer a shorter menu with two courses for £12.50 and three for £15. The carefully modernised black beamed open-plan bar is civilised and grown up (no children inside), with tall stools with proper backrests around the L-shaped counter, and comfortably cushioned wall pews and wheelback chairs – the fox motif shows in a big painting over the fireplace, and on much of the decorative china. Apart from a small section of the bar, the pub is no smoking. Greene King Ruddles County on handpump and piped music. At the back of the building is a walled-in terraced area, and a neatly kept spacious lawn spreading among the fruit trees; a play area has a climbing frame and slide. Good surrounding walks. *(Recommended by David Carr, Ann and Colin Hunt, Phyl and Jack Street, W W Burke, Janet Whittaker, J Stickland, Sue Demont, Tim Barrow, W A Evershed, Mr and Mrs R W Allan, Glenwys and Alan Lawrence)*

Greene King ~ Tenants Ian and Jane Inder ~ Real ale ~ Bar food ~ (01962) 771363 ~ Open 11-3, 6(6.30 winter)-11; 12-3.30, 7-10.30 Sun

CHALTON   SU7315   Map 2
Red Lion
Village signposted E of A3 Petersfield—Horndean; PO8 0BG

Hampshire's oldest pub (first licensed in 1503), this very pretty thatched dining pub has enchanting views of the South Downs, particularly from the dining room. Overflowing hanging baskets adorn a frontage of black beams and little windows, and on its wonky white frontage. Inside, the most distinctive part is the heavy-beamed and panelled front bar with high-backed traditional settles and elm tables, and an ancient inglenook fireplace with a frieze of burnished threepenny bits set into its mantelbeam. The old lounge and extended dining room have less character (the pink sofas in the lounge may not strike every visitor as the right choice), and are no smoking; piped music. Five Fullers and Gales beers are served from handpump, usually with Butser, HSB, London Pride and one or two seasonal brews, alongside 12 wines by the glass and 22 country wines by the glass. Served all day, food includes sandwiches (from £4.75), filled baked potatoes (from £4.95), ploughman's (from £5.35), steak baguettes (£6.95), and daily specials such as bean and vegetable chilli or two other vegetarian options (£6.95), organic pork and apple sausages on mustard mash (£8.95), grilled salmon fillet with prawn sauce (£9.95) and local fillet steak rossini (£15.95). The garden is pretty in summer and the farmland views are super. The pub is popular with walkers, mountain bikers and riders as it is fairly close to the extensive Queen Elizabeth Country Park. The car ferry is only about 20 minutes from here. The pub had friendly new licensees in March 2006; reports on this new regime please. *(Recommended by BOB)*

Gales (Fullers) ~ Managers Dave Browning and Clare Banner ~ Real ale ~ Bar food (12-9 (9.30 Fri, Sat; 8 Sun)) ~ (023) 9259 2246 ~ Children in dining areas only ~ Dogs allowed in bar ~ Open 11.30-11; closed 3-6 in winter

CHAWTON   SU7037   Map 2
Greyfriar
Signposted off A31/A32 roundabout just S of Alton; Winchester Road; GU34 1SB

In a quiet and attractive bypassed village straight opposite Jane Austen's house, this spotlessly kept open-plan pub is justly popular for its food. Besides well filled sandwiches, this might include baguettes (£4.95), ploughman's, beefburger with choice of topping or battered haddock (£7.95), prawn, crab and avocado salad (£8.50); children's meals (£3.95); more elaborate food might include starters like caramelised onion tart with melted goats cheese or chicken liver and brandy parfait (£5.50), scallops (£8.50), and main courses such as venison steak with rich chilli and chocolate sauce (£10.95), thai red curry with fillet of beef (£12.95), grilled red snapper fillets with lemon filling or crispy gressingham duck breast with cranberry and orange sauce (£13.95); Sunday roasts (£9.95). They bake their own bread, steaks are prime aberdeen angus, and in winter they have local game. The black-beamed bar part on the left has neat seating around sturdy varnished pub tables on its carpet, with a couple of pine farmhouse tables in recesses – one with a shelf of foodie books and guides. By the brick counter is a timber support studded with hundreds of coins – and a goodly row of comfortably backed bar chairs. Besides three Fullers beers there might be a guest such as Gales Festival Mild on handpump and decent wines by the glass; they do good coffees. There's a relaxed atmosphere, with quick helpful service by pleasant staff, and quite a few older midweek lunchers. The partly no smoking restaurant area on the right has more of the pine farmhouse furnishings, and a menu blackboard. There may be unobtrusive piped music. Behind is a small garden with terrace tables and a barbecue; there are good

nearby walks. *(Recommended by Tony and Jill Radnor, Phil and Jane Hodson, Roger and Pauline Pearce, Ann and Colin Hunt, B M Eldridge, Bruce Bird)*

Fullers ~ Lease Peter and Fran Whitehead ~ Real ale ~ Bar food (12-2, 7-9.30; 12-3, 6-8 Sun) ~ Restaurant ~ (01420) 83841 ~ Children welcome ~ Dogs allowed in bar ~ Open 12-11(10.30 Sun)

CHERITON SU5828 Map 2
Flower Pots ★ ▮ £
Pub just off B3046 (main village road) towards Beauworth and Winchester; OS Sheet 185 map reference 581282; SO24 0QQ

They serve very well kept own-brew beers from this bustling brick pub, tapped from casks behind the bar; you can tour the Flower Pots Brewery by arrangement. Homely and rustic, the two straightforward little rooms can attract a lively mix of customers, though the one on the left is a favourite, almost like someone's front room, with pictures of hounds and ploughmen on its striped wallpaper, bunches of flowers, and a horse and foal and other ornaments on the mantelpiece over a small log fire. Behind the servery is disused copper filtering equipment, and lots of hanging gin traps, drag-hooks, scaleyards and other ironwork. The neat extended plain public bar (where there's a covered well) has cribbage and dominoes. Very useful in fine weather (when the pub can fill up quickly), the pretty front and back lawns have some old-fashioned seats, and there's now a summer marquee; maybe summer morris dancers. Bar food from a fairly short straightforward menu includes sandwiches (from £3; toasties from £3.20), filled baked potatoes (from £4.60), ploughman's (from £5.10), hotpots such as lamb and apricot, chilli or spicy mixed bean (from £6.10), pork steak, onion and apple sauce bap (£6.60); popular curries on Wednesday evenings (£9.95); friendly service. The menu and serving times may be restricted at weekend lunchtimes, or when they're busy. The pub is near the site of one of the final battles of the Civil War, and it got its name through once belonging to the retired head gardener of nearby Avington Park. No children inside. *(Recommended by David Carr, Lynn Sharpless, R G Trevis, Mr and Mrs W D Borthwick, Tony and Jill Radnor, the Didler, Bruce Bird, MLR, Janet Whittaker, Michael B Griffith, Stephen Harvey, Jennifer Banks, Ann and Colin Hunt, Val and Alan Green, Paul and Shirley White, Francis Johnston, Patrick Hall, R T and J C Moggridge, Phil and Sally Gorton)*

Own brew ~ Licensees Jo and Patricia Bartlett ~ Real ale ~ Bar food (not Sun evening or bank hol evenings) ~ No credit cards ~ (01962) 771318 ~ Dogs welcome ~ Open 12-2.30, 6-11; 12-3, 7-10.30 Sun ~ Bedrooms: £40S/£60S

EASTON SU5132 Map 2
Chestnut Horse ❄ ♟
3.6 miles from M3 junction 9: A33 towards Kings Worthy, then B3047 towards Itchen Abbas; Easton then signposted on right – bear left in village; SO21 1EG

The open-plan interior manages to have a pleasantly rustic and intimate feel, with a series of cosily separate areas, making this upmarket country dining pub a cheering experience from the moment you walk in. Its really snug décor takes in candles and fresh flowers on the tables, log fires in cottagey fireplaces, comfortable furnishings, black beams and joists hung with all sorts of jugs, mugs and chamber-pots, and lots of attractive pictures of wildlife and the local area. Served by efficient and friendly staff, good (but by no means cheap) food from the lunchtime menu includes soup (£4.50), caesar salad (£4.95), dorset crab cocktail (£8.95), fish and chips (£11.95-£14.95), mussels (£14.95), fillet of salmon (£15.95), steak (from £14.95); Sunday roast (£11.95). The pricier evening menu might include tomato, roquefort and wild mushroom risotto (£14.95) and roast chicken supreme (£16.95). A much more reasonably priced two-course menu is good value, and a favourite with readers: £10, Mon-Sat lunchtime and Mon-Thurs evenings 6-7.30pm. Courage Best and Chestnut Horse (brewed for the pub by Itchen Valley) along with one or two guests from brewers like Itchen Valley or Ringwood on handpump, several wines by the glass, and around 60 malt whiskies; piped music. There are good tables out on a smallish sheltered decked area, with colourful flower tubs and baskets, and plenty of walks in the Itchen Valley from here. *(Recommended by Tom and Ruth Rees, Ann and Colin Hunt, James Price, Matthew Johnson, Phyl and Jack Street, Susan and John Douglas, Dr Alan and Mrs Sue Holder, Martin and Karen Wake, John Evans, David Sizer, Dr D and Mrs B Woods, Mayur Shah, Francis Johnston, W A Evershed, Patrick Hall, Lynn Sharpless, GHC, David and Sue Smith)*

Free house ~ Licensees John and Jocelyn Holland ~ Real ale ~ Bar food (12-2.30, 6-9.30; 12-8.30(4 winter) Sun) ~ Restaurant ~ (01962) 779257 ~ Children welcome ~ Dogs allowed in bar ~ Open 12-3.30, 5.30-12; 12-10.30 Sun; closed Sun evenings in winter

EXTON   SU6120   Map 2

Shoe

Village signposted from A32 NE of Bishop's Waltham – brown sign to pub into Beacon Hill Lane; SO32 3NT

You can sit out on picnic-sets and watch the ducks on the River Meon from beneath a floodlit sycamore across the road from this nicely located country pub. Well liked bar food, using local ingredients whenever possible, includes lunchtime sandwiches (from £3.95), ploughman's (from £5.25), ciabattas (from £5.50) and daily specials such as smoked ham and brie filo parcel (£5.95), broccoli, spinach and blue cheese tartlet with rocket, pine nut and caramelised pear salad (£8.95), breast of duck with cranberry and apple confit or baked cod with crab risotto (£12.95), with puddings such as chocolate brownie and bread and butter pudding. Bread comes with properly served butter, not messy little packets. Three linked rooms, no smoking except for the one on the left, have a friendly relaxed atmosphere, with comfortable pub furnishings, cricket and country prints, tea lights on tables, and in the right-hand room (which is panelled) a log fire. Well kept Wadworths 6X, Henrys IPA and a guest such as Wadworths Bishop's Tipple on handpump; helpful service. *(Recommended by Diana Brumfit, Peter Meister, Ann and Colin Hunt, Matt and Cathy Fawcett, Peter Salmon, W A Evershed)*

Wadworths ~ Tenants Mark and Carole Broadbent ~ Real ale ~ Bar food (12-2, 7-9(9.30 Fri, Sat);12-2, 6- 8.30 Sun, Mon) ~ (01489) 877526 ~ Children welcome ~ Dogs allowed in bar ~ Open 11-3, 6-11(10.30 Sun)

FRITHAM   SU2314   Map 2

Royal Oak 🍺

Village signed from exit roundabout, M27 junction 1; quickest via B3078, then left and straight through village; head for Eyeworth Pond; SO43 7HJ

It's surprising how many walkers and cyclists find their way to this remote thatched pub, in a delightfully rural location in the New Forest. It is part of a working farm so there are ponies and pigs out on the green, and plenty of livestock nearby. Locals (needless to say it still has a strong local following) and visitors alike are greeted with genuine warmth. Three neatly kept black beamed rooms (one is no smoking) are very simple but full of proper traditional character, with prints and pictures involving local characters on the white walls, restored panelling, antique wheelback, spindleback and other old chairs and stools with colourful seats around solid tables on new oak flooring, and two roaring log fires. The back bar has quite a few books. Seven well kept ales are tapped from the cask, with Flower Pots, Ringwood Best and Fortyniner, and Hop Back Summer Lightning along with guests from brewers such as Archers and RCH; also a dozen wines by the glass (mulled wine in winter), and they hold a beer festival in September. Simple lunchtime food is limited to home-made soup like home-baked bread (£4) and cumberland sausage ring, home-cooked pork pie or ploughman's (£6). Summer barbecues are put on in the neatly kept big garden, which has a marquee for poor weather; darts, board games and pétanque. *(Recommended by G Coates, Matthew Johnson, the Didler, W W Burke, Ann and Colin Hunt, Pete Baker, Dr A J and Mrs Tompsett, Mr and Mrs John Taylor, Mayur Shah, Mike Turner, Peter Titcomb)*

Free house ~ Licensees Neil and Pauline McCulloch ~ Real ale ~ Bar food (lunchtime only)

~ No credit cards ~ (023) 8081 2606 ~ Children welcome if well behaved ~ Dogs welcome ~ Open 11-11; 12-10.30 Sun; 11-3 weekdays in winter

HAMBLEDON SU6414 Map 2
Vine
West Street, just off B2150; PO7 4RW

New licensees took over this popular dining pub late in 2005, and are successfully preserving its nice village-local feel alongside producing interesting food that relies largely on local suppliers. They have a lunchtime menu with sandwiches (£4), fish pie or sausages and mash (£8) and rib-eye steak (£9.50), and the fortnightly changing lunchtime and evening menu features dishes like soup (£4), roast butternut squash with curry butter (£10.50) slow-cooked belly of hampshire pork (£12), roast rump of lamb with baked potato cake (£13.75) and puddings such as iced honey and Drambuie parfait with glazed fresh figs or sticky toffee pudding (£4). There's room for a few drinkers: Black Sheep Best, Fullers/Gales (called Vine Best here), Ringwood Best and a couple of guests like Ringwood Fortyniner and Wadworths Summersault are on handpump, alongside Addlestone's cider; there are 11 wines by the glass. Furnishings and décor include the usual pub tables and chairs plus a winged high-backed settle, a couple of log fires and a woodburning stove, quite a bit of bric-a-brac (signed cricket bats, decorative plates, banknotes, gin traps, a boar's head, snare drums and a sort of shell-based mandolin on the piano), with tankards and copper kettles (and even an accordion) hanging from old brown beams and joists, sporting and country prints, and some interesting watercolours of early 20th-c regimental badges on the cream or green walls. The whole pub is no smoking. There are tables in a small informal back garden. More reports on the new regime please. *(Recommended by Ann and Colin Hunt, Bruce Bird, Mrs Maricar Jagger)*

Union Pub Company ~ Tenants Tom and Vicki Faulkner ~ Real ale ~ Bar food (not Sun evening) ~ Restaurant ~ (023) 9263 2419 ~ Well behaved children welcome ~ Dogs allowed in bar ~ Open 11.30-3, 6-11; 12-4, 7-10.30 Sun

HAWKLEY SU7429 Map 2
Hawkley Inn 🍺
Take first right turn off B3006, heading towards Liss ¾ mile from its junction with A3; then after nearly 2 miles take first left turn into Hawkley village – Pococks Lane; OS Sheet 186 map reference 746292; GU33 6NE

'Welcoming enough so that you could feel comfortable going in on your own; wish it was our local,' enthuses one reader of this friendly pub, where the good real ale selection features usually seven constantly changing beers, and often from small local breweries such as Ballards, Flower Pots, Kings and Ringwood, as well as a couple of local ciders. The opened-up bar and back dining room have a simple and unassuming rather than smart décor – big pine tables, dried flowers, and prints on the mellowing walls. The snug can get a bit smoky when it's busy, but there is a no smoking area to the right of the bar – both sides now have a real fire; piped music, backgammon. Bar food includes soup or filled rolls (£4.95), ploughman's (£6.75), cider sausages with mash and onion gravy, spinach and ricotta tart or cottage pie (£8.50), sussex beef stew or minted lamb casserole (£9.50), rump steak (£10) and whole breast of duck with green peppercorn sauce (£12.50), with specials like fish pie (£8.50) and crab cakes (£9); friendly service; several malt whiskies and wines by the glass. The pub is on the Hangers Way Path, and at weekends there are plenty of walkers; tables in the pleasant garden. As we went to press a new kitchen was being built and new bedrooms were about to be completed; we would welcome reports from readers who stay here. *(Recommended by Derek and Sylvia Stephenson, Martin and Karen Wake, Mrs Margo Finlay, Jörg Kasprowski, Tony and Jill Radnor, the Didler, JMM, Lynn Sharpless, Ian Phillips, Tony and Wendy Hobden, W A Evershed)*

Free house ~ Licensee Nick Troth ~ Real ale ~ Bar food (12-2(4 Sat, Sun), 7-9.30) ~ (01730) 827205 ~ Children welcome until 8pm ~ Dogs allowed in bar ~ Live music Sat nights in winter ~ Open 12-3(5 Sat), 5.30-11; 12-5, 7-10.30 Sun ~ Bedrooms: /£69S

LITTLETON SU4532 Map 2

Running Horse 🍽 ♀

Village signposted off B3049 just NW of Winchester; Main Road; SO22 6QS

This crisply furnished dining pub, now in the hands of the expert publicans who run the Plough at Sparsholt so well, is now completely no smoking, offers bed and breakfast, and has widened its menu to include simple lunchtime bar food as well as gourmet options. The food is inventive and very rewarding, and they bake their own bread and use local produce where possible. In addition to lunchtime snacks like nachos or goats cheese with chilli pepper bruschetta (£5.50), mini chicken kebabs (£5.95) and moules marinière (£6.25), they have specials (available lunchtime and in the evening, in the bar or in the restaurant) such as sunblush tomato and garlic risotto (£10.95), fried bream (£14.95) and fillet of beef with roasted root vegetables and thyme jus (£18.50); Sunday roast (£12.50). The stylishly decorated bar has some deep leather chairs as well as ochre-cushioned metal and wicker ones around matching modern tables on its polished boards, up-to-date lighting, good colour photographs of hampshire landscapes and townscapes, a potted palm as well as a log fire, and venetian blinds in its bow windows. The neat modern marble and hardwood bar counter (with swish leather, wood and brass bar stools) has Itchen Valley Winchester Ale and Ringwood Best on handpump, ten wines by the glass, and an espresso machine. Linking openly from here, the back no smoking restaurant area has the same sort of elegant modern furniture, on flagstones. Good disabled access and facilities; there may be piped pop music. There are green metal tables and chairs out on terraces front and back, with picnic-sets on the back grass by a spreading sycamore. We would welcome reports from readers who have stayed here. *(Recommended by Phyl and Jack Street)*

Free house ~ Licensee Samantha Jowett ~ Real ale ~ Bar food (12-2, 6.30-9.30; 12-4.30 Sun) ~ Restaurant ~ (01962) 880218 ~ Children in eating area of bar and restaurant ~ Dogs allowed in bar ~ Open 11-3, 5.30-11; 11-11 Sat; 12-9.30 Sun ~ Bedrooms: /£65B

LONGSTOCK SU3537 Map 2

Peat Spade ♀

Village signposted off A30 on W edge of Stockbridge, and off A3057 Stockbridge—Andover; SO20 6DR

Right by the River Test, this is a popular haunt for anglers, and the fishing and shooting theme extends to the pictures on the walls, together with stuffed fish by the bar, and there's even a little fishing shop at the end of the garden for anyone who needs angling gear. The new owners here have made several changes, extending the terrace into the garden (to which they were about to add a gas pit – an open-air gas fire – just as we went to press), adding six letting rooms and creating a locals' bar. Residents and diners can also use the lounge upstairs, which has board games, cards, dominoes and chess. Local and seasonal produce features significantly on the imaginative menu (best to book a table in advance), which might typically include watercress soup (£4), whitebait (£4.90), double-baked cheese soufflé (£9.50), beer-battered cod or fish pie (£11.50) and rib-eye steak (£15.50), with puddings such as bread and butter pudding (£5.50) or an english cheese plate (£6.50); they usually have half a dozen specials; all the food apart from the bread and chips is home made. The roomy and attractive squarish main bar is airy and high-ceilinged, with pretty windows, well chosen furnishings and a nice show of toby jugs and beer mats around its fireplace. A rather elegant no smoking dining room leads off, and there are doors to the patio. Ringwood Best and Fortyniner together with a changing guest also from Ringwood on handpump, and eight wines by the glass from a carefully chosen list. There are plenty of surrounding walks, along the Test Way at the end of the road and in the water meadows around Stockbridge, and Longstock Water Gardens at the end of village. We would welcome reports from readers who stay here. *(Recommended by Simon and Mandy King)*

Free house ~ Licensees Andrew Clark and Lucy Townsend ~ Real ale ~ Bar food (12-2,
7-9.30) ~ Restaurant ~ (01264) 810612 ~ Children welcome if eating in restaurant; no
children under 10 in bedrooms ~ Dogs allowed in bar ~ Open 11-3, 6.30-11 ~ Bedrooms:
/£110B

LOWER WIELD   SU6339   Map 2
Yew Tree 🍽 ♀

**Turn off A339 NW of Alton at Medstead, Bentworth 1 signpost, then follow village
signposts; or off B3046 S of Basingstoke, signposted from Preston Candover; SO24 9RX**

In winter the crackling fire is a welcoming sight as you enter this beautifully placed
and relaxed tile-hung pub, while in summer you might see cricket in progress across
the road. The atmosphere is nicely informal: a small flagstoned bar area on the left
has a few military prints above its stripped brick dado, a steadily ticking clock and
a log fire. Around to the right of the serving counter – which has a couple of stylish
wrought-iron bar chairs – it's carpeted, with a few attractive flower pictures, and
throughout there is a mix of tables, including some quite small ones for two, and
miscellaneous chairs; piped music. Using fresh local ingredients, good bar food
includes lunchtime sandwiches, soup (£3.95), starters like mango and brie filo
parcels with salad and mango coulis (£5.25) or salmon and crab cake (£6.50), with
main courses such as local sausages and mash or spinach and ricotta cannelloni
(£8.95), red thai chicken curry (£9.95), baked whole bass (£13.95), pan-seared
gressingham duck with apricot and brandy compote (£14.50) and fillet steak with
blue cheese sauce (£17.95); puddings might include mocha, rum and chocolate
mousse or mixed berry and apple crumble (£4.50); children's menu. Vegetables are
good and seasonal, and nice breads come with good properly served butter; no
smoking dining area. The well chosen wine list, with a dozen or more by the glass,
is reasonably priced, and may include Louis Jadot burgundies from a shipper based
just along the lane; they generally have local beers, with Flower Pots and a guest
from one of 17 breweries such as Itchen Valley, Suthwyk or White Star on
handpump. Service is friendly and helpful, with a real personal touch – however
busy he is in the kitchen, the enthusiastic landlord always seems to find time to
come out and say hello. There are solid tables and chunky seats out on the front
terrace, with picnic-sets in a sizeable side garden and pleasant views. Nearby walks
include one around lovely Rushmoor Pond. *(Recommended by Martin and Karen Wake,
Richard Foskett, Stephanie Lang, Ann and Colin Hunt, Janet Whittaker, Phyl and Jack Street,
Roger Chacksfield)*

Free House ~ Tim Manktelow-Gray and Penny Appel-Billsberry ~ Real ale ~ Bar food
(12-2, 6.30-9(8.30 Sun)) ~ (01256) 389224 ~ Children welcome ~ Dogs allowed in bar ~
Open 12-3, 6-11; 12-10.30 Sun; 12-3, 6-10.30 Sun in winter; closed Mon

LYMINGTON   SZ3295   Map 2
Kings Head 🍺

**Quay Hill; pedestrian alley at bottom of High Street, can park down on quay and walk
up from Quay Street; SO41 3AR**

Tankards hang from great rough beams in this rambling, candlelit 17th-c pub, and
they serve Fullers London Pride, Gales HSB, Greene King Old Speckled Hen and
two guests from brewers such as Adnams and Ringwood on handpump, with
several wines by the glass. Up and down steps and through timber dividers, mainly
bare-boarded rooms with a rug or two contain a nice old-fashioned variety of
seating at a great mix of tables from an elegant gateleg to a huge chunk of elm, and
the local pictures include good classic yacht photographs. A cosy upper corner past
the serving counter has a good log fire in a big fireplace, its mantelpiece a shrine to
all sorts of drinking paraphernalia from beer tankards to port and champagne
cases. Enjoyable food includes home-made soup (£3.95), sandwiches (from £4.65),
duck salad (£7.95), home-made lasagne, lambs liver on mash or pasta with smoked
chicken and bacon in creamy parmesan sauce (£8.95), home-made steak and
mushroom in ale pie (£9.50), moules marinière (£9.95) and specials such as tiger

prawns in tempura batter with sweet chilli dip (£5.95), chicken breast with chilli, lime and coriander coconut cream or pork medallions in creamy honey and mustard sauce (£9.95), fried venison steak with shallots and bacon in redcurrant jus (£11.95) and monkfish in creamy white wine sauce (£12.50); puddings such as home-made apple crumble (£4.10). A wall rack holds daily papers; piped pop music; no smoking area. *(Recommended by David Carr, Diane Hibberd, Michael Sargent, Di and Mike Gillam, Mr and Mrs John Taylor, Pam and John Smith)*

Inn Partnership (Pubmaster) ~ Lease Paul Stratton ~ Real ale ~ Bar food (11-2.30(3 Fri-Sun), 6-10) ~ (01590) 672709 ~ Children welcome ~ Dogs welcome ~ Open 11-3, 6-12; 11-1am Sat; 12-11 Sun

MONXTON SU3144 Map 2
Black Swan ♀
Village signposted off A303 at Andover junction with A343; car park some 25 metres along High Street; SP11 8AW

In a row of whitewashed thatched cottages, this 17th-c inn has a lovely sheltered garden by the duck-populated Pillhill Brook. In addition to ten wines by the glass from a list of around 50 bottles, Fullers London Pride, Ringwood Best, Timothy Taylors Landlord and a guest such as Ringwood Fortyniner are on handpump. Besides lunchtime sandwiches (from £4.75), ploughman's (£6.50) and other lunchtime dishes such as home-made lasagne or fish platter (£7.95), the menu could include soup (£4.25), steak and ale pie, spinach and ricotta tortellini or sausages and mash (£10), fried calves liver with crispy bacon and mash, corn-fed chicken breast with chasseur sauce or grilled bass fillet (£12) and venison steak with redcurrant sauce (£14). Past a lobby with a settee and easy chairs, a couple of steps take you up to the small mansard-ceiling timbered bar, with the menu boards, a log fire, a table of daily papers and just a few pub tables. Angling off behind here is the main action: a triangular room with floor-to-ceiling windows looking out at picnic-sets in the garden, and a further good-sized restaurant, both carpeted and no smoking, with country-kitchen chairs and tables set for eating; piped music (can be intrusive). The former assistant manager took over the running of this pub shortly before we went to press; reports on the new regime please. *(Recommended by Stan Edwards, Phyl and Jack Street, Gerry and Rosemary Dobson, R T and J C Moggridge, S Topham, Gordon Prince, Mike Gorton, Michael and Jenny Back, Mr and Mrs R W Allan)*

Enterprise ~ Lease Tracey Attwood ~ Real ale ~ Bar food (12-2, 6-9.30, Mon-Thurs; 12-2.30, 6-10 Fri, Sat; 12-2.30, 7-9.30 Sun) ~ (01264) 710260 ~ Children welcome ~ Dogs allowed in bar ~ Open 12-11(10.30 Sun); closed 25 Dec evening and 1 Jan until 6pm

OVINGTON SU5631 Map 2
Bush
Village signposted from A31 on Winchester side of Alresford; SO24 0RE

The back garden runs down to the River Itchen, making this family-run pub a popular place to sit out on a sunny day. Inside it's delightfully cottagey, with a marked absence of piped music, fruit machines or similar intrusions. A low-ceilinged bar is furnished with cushioned high-backed settles, elm tables with pews and kitchen chairs, masses of old pictures in heavy gilt frames on the walls, and a roaring fire on one side with an antique solid fuel stove opposite. Three rooms are no smoking. Though not cheap the food is of high quality (note there's a minimum charge of £12 at Sunday lunchtime), where possible using local ingredients and typically includes soup (£4.95), sandwiches (from £5.25, with smoked salmon sandwiches at £9.25), crab and leek tart (£6.50, £13 as a main course), home-made chicken liver pâté (£6.95), ploughman's (from £7.45). king prawns in garlic, chilli and ginger butter (£10.75), and main courses such as french onion tart with goats cheese and olives (£11.50), beef, mushroom and red wine pie or bass fillet on saffron and smoked garlic purée with sautéed local mushrooms (£12.75), rib-eye steak (£13.50), fish pie or belly pork confit on braised cabbage and apple (£13.75), and home-made puddings such as fresh figs baked with balsamic vinegar and honey, or plum and port tart (£4.80); children's meals (£4.75). Three to five real ales on handpump such as Archers Bitter, JCB, Wadworths Henrys IPA, 6X or Summersault, with several country wines, 13 wines by the glass and malt whiskies; board games. Look out for the sociable scottish springer spaniel, Paddy. Please note that if you want to bring children it's best to book, as there are only a few tables set aside for families. *(Recommended by James Price, Lynn Sharpless, Tony and Jill Radnor, N R White, Ann and Colin Hunt, Patrick Hall, Dr D J and Mrs S C Walker, C J Roebuck, Francis Johnston, John Balfour, Martin and Karen Wake, W A Evershed, GHC, W W Burke)*

Wadworths ~ Managers Nick and Cathy Young ~ Real ale ~ Bar food (not Sun evening) ~ (01962) 732764 ~ No children in lower room, new room or bar ~ Dogs welcome ~ Open 11-3, 6-11; 12-3, 7-10.30 Sun

PETERSFIELD   SU7227   Map 2
Trooper 🍽 🍺 🛏

From B2070 in Petersfield follow Steep signposts past station, but keep on up past Steep, on old coach road; OS Sheet 186 map reference 726273; GU32 1BD

For its rural setting, welcoming landlord, comfortable accommodation (with good breakfasts) and satisfying food, this country dining inn receives very high praise. It's best to book to be sure of a table (particularly on Friday and Saturday evenings); food typically includes roasted red pepper and sweet potato soup (£5), poached mussels (£7 as a starter or £10 as a main course), chicken, bacon and mushroom pie or seared tuna steak with tomato and caper dressing (£10), fisherman's pie (£11), provençale vegetable stew (£12), free-range chicken poached in red wine with mushrooms and onions (£14), slow-roasted half shoulder of lamb (£14.50) or steak (from £16). Kept on handpump, the three or four beers change frequently but tend to be from local or fairly local brewers such as Flower Pots, Hogs Back, Hop Back and Itchen Valley, and they have decent house wines. There's an island bar, blond chairs and a mix of tripod tables on bare boards or red tiles, tall stools by a broad ledge facing big windows that look across to rolling downland fields, old film star photos and paintings by local artists for sale, little persian knick-knacks here and there, quite a few ogival mirrors, big baskets of dried flowers, lit candles all around, fresh flowers, a well tended log fire in the stone fireplace, and carefully chosen piped music; newspapers and magazines to read. The attractive raftered restaurant has french windows to a partly covered sunken terrace, and there are lots of picnic-sets on an upper lawn; the dining areas are no smoking. The horse rail in the car park ('horses and camels only before 8pm') does get used, though probably not often for camels. Note: as we went to press, one of the main access routes to the pub was closed because of a landslide. Until it is cleared, the pub will be closed on Sunday evenings and all day Monday. Best to contact the pub with regard to directions. *(Recommended by Bren and Val Speed, Ann and Colin Hunt, Karen Eliot, Mike and Mary Carter, Ray J Carter, Tony and Jill Radnor, Tracey and Stephen Groves, Keith and Chris O'Neill, Joan Thorpe, Bruce Bird, Phyl and Jack Street, Peter Fitton, Val and Alan Green, Brian and Janet Ainscough)*

Free house ~ Licensee Hassan Matini ~ Real ale ~ Bar food (12-2(2.30 Sun), 6-9(9.30 Fri, Sat)) ~ Restaurant ~ (01730) 827293 ~ Children welcome ~ Dogs allowed in bar ~ Open 12-3, 5-11; 12-3.30 Sun; closed Sun evening and all day Mon ~ Bedrooms: £69B/£89B

PORTSMOUTH   SZ6299   Map 2
Still & West

Bath Square, Old Portsmouth; PO1 2JL

Very handy if you are visiting the Historic Dockyard, this is a most atmospherically set pub with inspiring harbourside views across the water to the Isle of Wight, making it an excellent vantage point to enjoy the well kept real ales. The boats and ships fighting the strong tides in the very narrow mouth of Portsmouth harbour seem almost within touching distance. As well as seats on the terrace, the upper deck restaurant has fine views from all tables – best to book. The downstairs bar is decorated in nautical style, with paintings of galleons on the ceiling, ship models, old cable, and photographs of famous ships entering the harbour; most of the bar and all of the restaurant are no smoking. Butser, Fullers HSB and London Pride are on handpump together with a guest ale from the same brewery; several wines by the glass and country wines; piped music and fruit machine. Straightforward bar food includes soup (£3.95), baguettes (from £3.95), lasagne (£6.95), sausage and mash or steak and mushroom pie (£7.95) and cajun chicken (£8.95); puddings (£4.50). The pub can get busy on fine days and nearby metered parking can be difficult. (Recommended by David Carr, Colin Gooch, Ann and Colin Hunt, R M Corlett, A Wright, Susan and John Douglas, W A Evershed, Phyl and Jack Street)

Fullers ~ Manager Tina Blackhall ~ Real ale ~ Bar food (12-9 summer; 12-2.30, 6-9 winter) ~ Restaurant ~ (023) 9282 1567 ~ Children welcome until 9pm ~ Open 10-11; 11-10.30 Sun

ROTHERWICK SU7156 Map 2
Falcon
4 miles from M3 junction 5; follow Newnham signpost from exit roundabout, then Rotherwick signpost, then turn right at Mattingley, Heckfield signpost; village also signposted from B3349 N of Hook, then brown signs to pub; RG27 9BL

With sofas, a blazing fire and an open-plan layout, this country pub has a pleasantly relaxed atmosphere and you can sit out at tables and benches at the front and back – the sizeable informal back garden looks into grazing pastures. There's quite a mixture of dining chairs gathered around an informal variety of tables on varnished floorboards, big bay windows with sunny window seats, and minimal decoration on its mainly pale mustard-coloured walls; flowers on the tables, and perhaps a big vase of lilies on the terracotta-coloured central bar counter, are cheering. A rather more formal no smoking back dining area is round to the right, and on the left are an overstuffed sofa and a couple of ornate easy chairs by one log fire; piped music. Taking examples from the lunchtime snack menu, main menu and the specials board, bar food might include soup (£4), sandwiches (from £3.95), ploughman's (£5.50), beef chilli nachos (£5.25), moules marinière (£6.50 starter, £10.95 main course), chilli con carne or seafood lasagne (£8.50), roast vegetable lasagne (£9.50), sausage and mash (£9.95), king prawn stir fry (£11.50), braised shank of lamb marinated in garlic and rosemary (£11.75), fried bass fillet (£12.50) and 12oz rib-eye steak (£14.25); Sunday roast (£8.50). Two or three real ales on handpump might include Adnams Best, Brakspears, Ringwood and a guest such as Charles Wells Bombardier. Easy walks nearby. More reports please. (Recommended by Brian Dawes, Martin and Karen Wake, Mayur Shah)

Unique (Enterprise) ~ Lease Andy Francis ~ Real ale ~ Bar food (12-2, 6.45-9.30: Sun 12-2, 7-9 (not Sun evenings in winter)) ~ Restaurant ~ (01256) 762586 ~ Children welcome (small children and babies lunchtime only) ~ Dogs allowed in bar ~ Open 11-2.30, 6-11; 12-10.30 Sun

ROWLAND'S CASTLE SU7310 Map 2
Castle Inn
Village signposted off B2148/B2149 N of Havant; Finchdean Road, by junction with Redhill Road and Woodberry Lane; PO9 6DA

Now no smoking throughout, this friendly pub sets a cheerful mood from the moment you walk in, and the food is generously served and consistently good value. There are two appealing little eating rooms on the left. The front one has rather nice simple mahogany chairs around sturdy scrubbed pine tables, one quite long, rugs on flagstones, a big fireplace, and quite a lot of old local photographs on its ochre walls. The back one is similar, but with bare boards and local watercolour landscapes by Bob Payne for sale. There is a small separate public bar on the right with a good fire and Fullers London Pride, Gales Butser and HSB and a guest such as Fullers Discovery on handpump. Served by smartly dressed staff, the lunchtime menu includes filled baguettes (from £3.95), ploughman's (£5.50), beef and ale pie (£6.95) and lasagne or chicken balti (£6.50). Dishes are only a little pricier in the evening: starters like deep-fried mushrooms in garlic batter (£4.60), prawn and crabmeat cocktail (£5.25), pork stroganoff (£7.25) and lamb shoulder braised in honey and mint (£8.95); on Mondays they do a tex-mex buffet. The publicans' own ponies are in view from the largish garden, which is equipped with picnic-sets and a couple of swings; disabled access and facilities are good. *(Recommended by Colin Chapman, Claire Hardcastle, Bruce Bird, Ian Phillips, Ann and Colin Hunt, R M Corlett, Tony Hobden, Mrs Jane Kingsbury, Jess and George Cowley)*

Gales (Fullers) ~ Tenants Jan and Roger Burrell ~ Real ale ~ Bar food (12-9; not after 2pm on winter Sun) ~ Restaurant ~ (023) 9241 2494 ~ Children in eating area of bar ~ Dogs allowed in bar ~ Open 11-11(12 Fri, Sat)

SOUTHSEA   SZ6498   Map 2
Wine Vaults ♠
Albert Road, opposite Kings Theatre; PO5 2SF

Fullers brewery has now taken over this former free house, which still retains an impressive range of eight beers taken from a repertory of over thirty. There are four brews from Fullers, four from Gales and a couple of guests from Archers, Cottage and Dark Star. It's popular with a good mix of age groups. The straightforward bar has wood-panelled walls, a wood floor, and an easy-going, chatty feel, and the raised back area is no smoking. There are Sunday newspapers for you to read, plus pool, chess, draughts, backgammon and a football table; piped music. Handily served all day (but do bear in mind that beer is the forte here), good helpings of reasonably priced bar food include sandwiches (from £3.95), filled baked potatoes (from £3.95), fish dish of the day (£5.95-£10.95), mexican vegetable burrito (£6.25), steak and ale pie (£7.25), or vegetarian dish of the day (£6.95), with puddings (from £4.25). *(Recommended by Ian Phillips, David Carr, Ann and Colin Hunt, Michael B Griffith, the Didler)*

Fullers ~ Manager Sean Cochrane ~ Real ale ~ Bar food (12-9.30) ~ (023) 9286 4712 ~ Children welcome until 9pm ~ Dogs allowed in bar ~ Open 12-11(12, Fri Sat; 10.30 Sun)

SPARSHOLT   SU4331   Map 2
Plough ♚ ♀
Village signposted off B3049 (Winchester—Stockbridge), a little W of Winchester; SO21 2NW

Hampshire Dining Pub of the Year

'There were happy noises from all areas' and 'prices reasonable for the very high standard of food' are typical comments from readers in praise of this deservedly popular dining pub; it does get very busy, and booking is strongly recommended (you might have a wait for your food at peak times). Everything is neatly kept, and the main bar has an interesting mix of wooden tables and chairs, with farm tools, scythes and pitchforks attached to the ceiling; most of the pub is no smoking. As well as sandwiches, the interesting bar food (listed on daily changing blackboards) might include starters such as soup (£3.95), pigeon, bacon and mushroom salad or grilled goats cheese on a herb croûton (£5.95), and main courses like very tasty salmon and crab fishcake with saffron sauce, wild mushroom, potato and broccoli stroganoff, fried marinated salmon or green thai chicken curry (all £9.95), fillet of sea trout with horseradish cream or pork fillet with herb risotto and shallot and bacon sauce (£14.95) and prime scotch sirloin with wild mushroom sauce (£16.95), with tempting puddings such as chocolate, orange and brandy terrine or pecan pie with clotted cream (£4.95). Wadworths IPA, 6X and Summersault together with St Austell Tribute on handpump, and an extensive wine list with a good selection by the glass, including champagne and pudding wine. Disabled access and facilities; there's a children's play fort, and plenty of seats on the terrace and lawn. *(Recommended by John and Joan Calvert, James Price, M K Milner, Phyl and Jack Street, Ann and Colin Hunt, N Vernon, Susan and John Douglas, Keith Rutter, Inga Davis, Martin and Karen Wake, Lynn Sharpless, Keith and Jean Symons, Peter and Eleanor Kenyon, Peter and Jean Dowson, Patrick Hall, J Stickland, Francis Johnston, T D Soulsby, John Balfour, R Lake, GHC)*

Wadworths ~ Tenants Richard and Kathryn Crawford ~ Real ale ~ Bar food (12-2, 6-9(8.30 Mon, Sun; 9.30 Fri, Sat)) ~ (01962) 776353 ~ Children welcome except in main bar area ~ Dogs welcome ~ Open 11-3, 6-11

STEEP SU7425 Map 2

Harrow ㉕

Take Midhurst exit from Petersfield bypass, at exit roundabout first left towards Midhurst, then first turning on left opposite garage, and left again at Sheet church; follow over dual carriageway bridge to pub; GU32 2DA

This wonderfully unchanged pub has been run by the same family for some 70 years, and the two sisters who took it over from their mother not long ago have kept it going just as it was. The cosy public bar has hops and dried flowers hanging from the beams, built-in wall benches on the tiled floor, stripped pine wallboards, a good log fire in the big inglenook, and wild flowers on the scrubbed deal tables; dominoes. Flower Pots, Ringwood Best and maybe a guest such as Ballards Best are tapped straight from casks behind the counter, and they've local wine, and apple and pear juice. Good helpings of unfussy home-made bar food include sandwiches, home-made scotch eggs (£3.10), hearty ham, split pea and vegetable soup (£4.30), ploughman's, home-made cottage pie, lasagne or quiches (£7.75) and salads (£11), with puddings such as treacle tart or seasonal fruit pies (£3.70); staff are polite and friendly, even when under pressure. The big garden is left free-flowering so that goldfinches can collect thistle seeds from the grass. The Petersfield bypass doesn't intrude on this idyll, though you will need to follow the directions above to find it. No children inside, and dogs must be on leads. *(Recommended by Phil and Sally Gorton, Ann and Colin Hunt, Tony and Jill Radnor, the Didler, Charles and Pauline Stride, Irene and Derek Flewin, J L Wedel, Anthony Longden, W A Evershed, Simon Fox, David Gunn)*

Free house ~ Licensees Claire and Denise McCutcheon ~ Real ale ~ Bar food (not Sun evening) ~ No credit cards ~ (01730) 262685 ~ Dogs on leads welcome ~ Open 12-2.30, 6-11; 11-3, 6-11 Sat; 12-3, 7-10.30 Sun; closed winter Sun evenings

STOCKBRIDGE SU3535 Map 2

Grosvenor

High Street; SO20 6EU

Well divided into separate room areas (all no smoking apart from the bar), this comfortably old-fashioned Georgian coaching inn has a relaxing, high-ceilinged main bar with a good log fire. The restrained décor is entirely in keeping with the distinction of the building itself. Greene King IPA and Abbot are on handpump, alongside a dozen enjoyable wines by the glass, and decent coffee; piped music. As we went to press they were unable to give us specific information about the bar food as the menu was about to be completely changed, but it will continue to include soup (from £3.95) and sandwiches (from £4.95). The impressive oak-panelled restaurant has some hand-etched panels of horses done 200 years ago with a poker from the fire. A back conservatory has more tables. A couple of pavement tables stand out beside the imposing front portico, with more tables in the good-sized back garden, prettily laid out with attractive plantings. This is an appealing little town, with good antiques shops, the National Trust Common Marsh along the River Test, and downland walks all around. New licensees in 2006; reports on the new regime please, and tell us about the bedrooms if you stay here. *(Recommended by Edward Mirzoeff, Ian Phillips, N Vernon, Ann and Colin Hunt)*

Greene King ~ Managers David and Margo Fyfe ~ Real ale ~ Bar food (12-2.30, 6.30-9.30(8.30 Sun)) ~ Restaurant ~ (01264) 810606 ~ Children welcome ~ Dogs allowed in bar and bedrooms ~ Open 11-11; 12-10.30 Sun ~ Bedrooms: £85B/£99.50B

TICHBORNE SU5630 Map 2
Tichborne Arms
Village signed off B3047; SO24 0NA

You can expect to find quite a few walkers at this delightfully unspoilt country pub
during the day, as the Wayfarers Walk and Itchen Way pass close by, and the
countryside around is attractively rolling. The comfortable square-panelled room
on the right has wheelback chairs and settles (one very long), a stone fireplace and
latticed windows. On the left is a larger, livelier, partly panelled room used for
eating. Pictures and documents on the walls recall the bizarre Tichborne Case, in
which a mystery man from Australia claimed fraudulently to be the heir to this
estate. Home-made bar food includes sandwiches (from £3.50), prawn cocktail
(£5.50), ploughman's (£5.95), salmon escalope, chilli con carne or mushroom, leek
and red onion crumble (£8.25) and lamb shank (£12.50), with puddings such as
syrup sponge or fudge and walnut flan (from £3.50). Ringwood Best, Wadworths
6X and a couple of local guests are tapped from the cask, alongside a decent choice
of wines by the glass, country wines and farm cider; sensibly placed darts, bar
billiards, shove-ha'penny, cribbage and piped music; the long-haired german
shepherd is called Dylan. Picnic-sets outside in the big well kept garden. No
children inside. *(Recommended by David Carr, Lynn Sharpless, Ann and Colin Hunt,
the Didler, Susan and John Douglas, June and Geoffrey Cox, William Ruxton, Francis Johnston)*

Free house ~ Licensees Nigel and Sarah Burt ~ Real ale ~ Bar food ~ (01962) 733760 ~
Children welcome except in bars ~ Dogs allowed in bar ~ Open 11.30-2.30, 6-11; 12-3,
7-11 Sun; closed Mon evening in winter

WHERWELL SU3839 Map 2
Mayfly
Testcombe (over by Fullerton, and not in Wherwell itself); A3057 SE of Andover,
between B3420 turn-off and Leckford where road crosses River Test; OS Sheet 185
map reference 382390; SO20 6AX

The tables on the decking and the conservatory overlooking the duck-populated
and trout-filled River Test make this scenically placed pub a delightful place to
while away a summer afternoon. Inside, the spacious, beamed and carpeted bar has
fishing pictures on the cream walls, rustic pub furnishings, and a woodburning
stove, and most of the pub is no smoking; piped music. Efficient staff serve six real
ales on handpump, with Greene King Abbot, Ringwood Best, Wadworths 6X and
Wychwood Hobgoblin together with a couple of guests such as Gales HSB and
Ringwood Fortyniner; piped music. Handily available all day, tasty bar food comes
from a buffet-style servery: they do a choice of hot and cold meats, pies and
quiches, salads and they've a great selection of cheeses. The blackboard menu might
include mushroom and red pepper stroganoff (£7.95), lamb and mango curry
(£8.95), sausages and mash or fisherman's pie (£9.50), baked whole trout (£11.95),
fried duck breast with black cherry glaze (£12.50), lamb rump (£12.95), venison
steak (£13.95) and fillet steak with stilton sauce (£14.95), with puddings such as
bread and butter pudding or crumble (£4.50). *(Recommended by Lynn Sharpless,
Phyl and Jack Street, Barry and Molly Norton, B J Harding, Alec and Barbara Jones, R G Trevis,
Catherine FitzMaurice, Mrs Pam Mattinson, Mrs Ann Gray, Mrs Joyce Robson, Kate Evans,
Bill and Jessica Ritson, Ann and Colin Hunt, GHC)*

Enterprise ~ Manager Barry Lane ~ Real ale ~ Bar food (11.30-9) ~ (01264) 860283 ~
Children welcome ~ Dogs welcome ~ Open 10am-11pm

White Lion
B3420, in village itself; SP11 7JF

With good-natured and efficient staff and in an attractive village, this well run
17th-c pub is much appreciated by readers. The multi-level beamed bar has delft
plates, sparkling brass, fresh flowers, and Bass and Ringwood Best on handpump,
with 11 wines by the glass. The Village Bar has an open fire, and there are two no

smoking dining rooms; piped music. Tasty bar food includes soup (£4.25), ploughman's (£6.50), curry of the day (£8.75), pie of the day (£8.95), spinach and red pepper lasagne, grilled lamb rumps or fillet of salmon (£9.25), steak (from £13.25), alongside blackboard specials such as pork and apple casserole (£9.25) and hot crab with asparagus and cheese sauce salad (£10.50), and puddings (from £4.20); it's a good idea to book for their Sunday roast. Plenty of seats in the courtyard and on the terrace. The chocolate labrador is called Harley. There's a nice walk over the River Test and meadows to Chilbolton. *(Recommended by B J Harding, Phyl and Jack Street, Mike Gorton, Lynn Sharpless, OPUS, Mr and Mrs A Silver, Ann and Colin Hunt, Mike Turner)*

Punch ~ Lease Adrian Stent and Pat Fairman ~ Real ale ~ Bar food ~ Restaurant ~ (01264) 860317 ~ Children welcome in dining areas ~ Dogs welcome ~ Folk first and third Thurs of month ~ Open 11-2.30(3 Sat), 6-11; 12-3, 7-10.30 Sun; 6-10.30 Weds-Sun evenings in winter ~ Bedrooms: £42.50S/£54.50S

WINCHESTER   SU4828   Map 2

Black Boy ◀

1 mile from M3 junction 10 northbound; B3403 towards city then left into Wharf Hill; rather further and less easy from junction 9, and anyway beware no nearby daytime parking – 220 metres from car park on B3403 N, or nice longer walk from town via College Street and College Walk, or via towpath; SO23 9NQ

With its enchantingly quirky and eclectic collection of assorted bits and pieces and friendly staff, this interesting, old-fashioned pub is well worth seeking out. There are floor-to-ceiling books in some parts, lots of big clocks, mobiles made of wine bottles or strings of spectacles, some nice modern nature photographs in the lavatories and on the brightly stained walls on the way, and plenty of other things that you'll enjoy tracking down. Furnishings are similarly wide-ranging. Several different areas run from a bare-boards barn room with an open hayloft (now an evening dining room) down to an orange-painted room with big oriental rugs on red-painted floorboards. Lunchtime bar food includes sandwiches (£4.50), pasta (£6.50), and shepherd's pie or beer-battered cod and chips (£7.50); evening restaurant meals are more elaborate. The five well kept beers on handpump are more or less local: Flower Pots, Hop Back Summer Lightning and Ringwood Best alongside a couple of guests such as Hampshire Ironside and Triple fff Moondance; decent wines, two log fires. Well chosen and reproduced piped music; table football, ring and hook, shove-ha'penny, board games, cribbage and dominoes; a couple of slate tables out in front, more tables on an attractive secluded terrace with barbecues. No children. *(Recommended by David Carr, Peter Dandy, Ann and Colin Hunt, Sean A Smith, Len Beattie, family Buckle, Val and Alan Green)*

Free house ~ Licensee David Nicholson ~ Real ale ~ Bar food (not Sun evening, Mon, or Tues lunchtime) ~ Restaurant ~ (01962) 861754 ~ Dogs allowed in bar ~ Open 11-3, 5-11; 12-3, 7-10.30 Sun

Wykeham Arms ★ ⑪ ♀

Kingsgate Street (Kingsgate Arch and College Street are now closed to traffic; there is access via Canon Street); SO23 9PE

The imaginative food and good drinks make this stylish and civilised city-centre pub very popular, and booking is advisable even on the chilliest winter day. A series of bustling rooms radiating from the central bar has 19th-c oak desks retired from nearby Winchester College, a redundant pew from the same source, kitchen chairs and candlelit deal tables, and the big windows have swagged paisley curtains; all sorts of interesting collections are dotted around. A snug room at the back, known as the Jameson Room (after the late landlord Graeme Jameson), is decorated with a set of Ronald Searle 'Winespeak' prints, a second one is panelled, and all of them have log fires. Served by neatly uniformed staff, the lunchtime choice, prepared with carefully sourced ingredients, might include tempting sandwiches such as avocado and camembert with lemon and dill mayonnaise (from £4.25), starters like pan-seared pigeon breast with port wine dressing (£5.95) and haddock and toasted sesame risotto (£5.75), with main courses such as creamy wild mushroom, red onion, spinach and goats cheese linguini with rocket or grilled fillet of bass with stir-fried vegetables, egg noodles and sweet chilli sauce (£7.95), duo of cold poached and smoked salmon with lime and dill crème fraîche (£8.95), sirloin steak with garlic butter or peppercorn sauce (£12.95); vegetables are £1.95; they also have specials like cottage pie (£6.25) and beef, Guinness and root vegetable casserole (£6.50). The evening menu, served in the restaurant only, is more elaborate and pricier; the eating areas are no smoking. A fine choice of drinks includes four real ales on handpump, with, Gales Butser and HSB, Fullers London Pride and guests such as Timothy Taylors Landlord, and 19 wines by the glass (including champagne) from an extensive wine list. There are tables on a covered back terrace (they will serve food at lunchtime only here), with more on a small but sheltered lawn. No children inside. *(Recommended by Lynn Sharpless, James Price, David Carr, Peter Dandy, Martin and Karen Wake, Ann and Colin Hunt, M K Milner, Barry and Anne, Peter and Andrea Jacobs, Val and Alan Green, the Didler, Andy Booth, Richard Mason, John Oates, Denise Walton, Patrick Hall, Di and Mike Gillam, Chris Bell, Pam and John Smith, Bill and Jessica Ritson, W A Evershed, GHC, Simon Rodway)*

Gales (Fullers) ~ Managers Peter and Kate Miller ~ Real ale ~ Bar food (not Sun evening) ~ Restaurant ~ (01962) 853834 ~ Dogs allowed in bar and bedrooms ~ Open 11-11; 12-10.30 Sun ~ Bedrooms: £90B/£100B

LUCKY DIP

Besides the fully inspected pubs, you might like to try these Lucky Dips recommended to us and described by readers (if you do, please send us reports: www.goodguides.co.uk).

ALRESFORD [SU5832]
Bell SO24 9AT [West St]: Interesting good value food and good décor in relaxing Georgian coaching inn with polite attentive service, real ales inc Adnams, fairly priced wines, log fire, daily papers, smallish dining room; tables in attractively renovated back courtyard, comfortable bedrooms, open all day *(D and J Ashdown, Ron Shelton, Mr and Mrs R W Allan, Ann and Colin Hunt)*
Cricketers SO24 9LW [Jacklyns Lane]: Large friendly pub with good value appetising food (book ahead for Sun), real ales, good service, cottagey eating areas down steps; pleasant garden with covered terrace and good play area *(Phyl and Jack Street)*
☆ *Globe* SO24 9DB [bottom of Broad St (B3046)]: Comfortable dining pub doing well under current management, with smart lively staff, decent food (all day summer wknds), good range of ales inc Itchen Valley Godfathers and Wadworths 6X, good choice of wines by the glass, log fires each end, unusual pictures, no smoking restaurant allowing children; plenty of picnic-sets in garden with splendid outlook over historic Alresford Pond, open all day Sun and summer Sat *(David Carr, Ron Shelton, Ann and Colin Hunt, Jim and Janet Brown, LYM, Val and Alan Green, W A Evershed)*
ALTON [SU7139]
Eight Bells GU34 2DA [Church St]: Old-fashioned beamed local with real ales such as Ballards Best and Nyewood Gold, Ringwood Best and Shepherd Neame Spitfire, rolls served

most lunchtimes, helpful landlord; small back garden, open all day *(Derek and Sylvia Stephenson)*
Railway Arms GU34 2RB [Anstey Rd]: Hospitable tap for fff brewery, full range of their good ales and guest beers from small breweries all well kept, friendly staff willing to chat, panelling, simple seating; small garden, seats out in front with engine sculpture (handy for Watercress Line), open all day *(Bruce Bird)*
Swan GU34 1AT [High St]: Busy town pub with Greene King ales in modern bar, friendly helpful staff, pleasant restaurant; nice bedrooms, good breakfast *(Susan and Nigel Wilson)*
ARFORD [SU8236]
☆ *Crown* GU35 8BT [off B3002 W of Hindhead]: Welcoming and locally popular low-beamed pub with coal and log fires, steps up to homely eating area, enjoyable food from sandwiches to game and splendid puddings, Adnams, Fullers London Pride, Greene King Abbot and a guest beer, decent wines by the glass, friendly service, no smoking restaurant; piped music; children welcome in eating areas, picnic-sets out in peaceful dell by a tiny stream across the road *(LYM, Tony and Jill Radnor, J D Derry)*
AXFORD [SU6043]
Crown RG25 2DZ [B3046 S of Basingstoke]: Good service under new landlord, real ales, several wines by the glass, enjoyable food, three pleasantly refurbished linked rooms, small log fire; children welcome, suntrap terrace and sloping shrub-sheltered garden *(Mr and Mrs D Renwick, LYM)*

BASING [SU6653]

Bolton Arms RG24 7DA [The Street]: Pleasant village local with good atmosphere and decent basic food *(Tony and Jill Radnor)*

BATTRAMSLEY [SZ3098]

☆ *Hobler* SO41 8PT [Southampton Rd (A337 S of Brockenhurst)]: Attractively refurbished under new licensees, stylish furnishings and décor toning nicely with the ancient building's heavy beams, friendly relaxed service, good choice of wines and beers, good reasonably priced food from snacks to sophisticated main courses using fresh local ingredients; spacious lawn with play area, good Forest walks *(Mrs C Lintott, LYM, L Orchard)*

BEAUWORTH [SU5624]

☆ *Milbury's* SO24 0PB [off A272 Winchester/Petersfield]: Warmly welcoming licensees in attractive ancient pub, beams, panelling and stripped stone, massive 17th-c treadmill for much older incredibly deep well, log fires in huge fireplaces, changing real ales such as Archers, fff and Loddon, Addlestone's cider, good choice of wines and country wines, decent bar food, some south african dishes in smart restaurant; piped music; children in eating areas, garden with fine downland views, good walks, bedroom, open all day wknds and summer *(Ann and Colin Hunt, MLR, the Didler, LYM, Lynn Sharpless, Paul and Shirley White, Mrs Maricar Jagger, W A Evershed, Val and Alan Green)*

BIGHTON [SU6134]

Three Horseshoes SO24 9RE [off B3046 in Alresford just N of pond; or off A31 in Bishops Sutton]: Old-fashioned country local with very friendly licensees, Fullers and Gales, decent house wines, Sun bar nibbles, no smoking lounge with woodburner in huge fireplace, dining room, darts and pool in bare-boards stripped-stone back public bar; may be piped music; children welcome, good walks nearby, cl Mon lunchtime *(the Didler, W A Evershed)*

BISHOP'S SUTTON [SU6031]

Ship SO24 0AQ [B3047, former A31 on Alton side of Alresford – now bypassed]: Relaxed and simple, with welcoming obliging landlord, Ringwood Best and a guest beer, short sensible food choice inc lovely puddings, good fire, attractive small back dining room; well behaved dogs and children welcome, tables in garden with a couple of thatched parasols, handy for Watercress Line, good walks *(LYM, Ann and Colin Hunt)*

BISHOP'S WALTHAM [SU5517]

Barleycorn SO32 1AJ [Lower Basingwell St]: Comfortable and relaxed L-shaped main area with cheerful helpful landlady and staff, some ceiling panelling, Greene King IPA and Ruddles County, log fire, generous food (can take a while) from baguettes to popular Sun lunch, some two-for-one deals, log fire; TV and games in public bar; small beach garden and play area *(Ann and Colin Hunt, Stephen and Jean Curtis, Diana Brumfit)*

☆ *Bunch of Grapes* SO32 1AD [St Peters St – just along from entrance to central car park]:

Neatly kept small no smoking pub in attractive quiet medieval street, smartly updated furnishings and décor yet keeping individuality and unspoilt feel (run by same family for a century), Courage Best and Greene King IPA tapped from the cask, good chatty landlord and regulars; charming back terrace garden with own serving bar *(Phil and Sally Gorton, Stephen and Jean Curtis, the Didler, BB)*

White Horse SO32 1FD [Beeches Hill, off B3035 NE]: Friendly open-plan pub with central log fire, hop-hung beams and joists, fancy knotwork, candles in bottles, Adnams, Ringwood Best and Shepherd Neame Spitfire, country wines, good range of enjoyable food inc particularly wide vegetarian choice, all freshly made so may be a wait; unobtrusive piped music; picnic-sets on front terrace, small menagerie of rescued domestic animals, open all day *(Val and Alan Green, BB)*

BLACKNEST [SU7941]

Jolly Farmer GU34 4QD [Binsted Rd]: Bright and airy dining pub with interesting choice of good value food inc good two-course lunches, friendly staff, real ales, open fire one end, family room; tables on sheltered terrace and in garden *(Jennifer Banks, Betty Laker)*

BRAISHFIELD [SU3724]

Dog & Crook SO51 0QB [Crook Hill]: Imaginative and enjoyable if not cheap fresh food in spaciously refurbished pub with real ales, good wines by the glass and friendly service; garden with play area *(Dr Alan and Mrs Sue Holder)*

Newport Inn SO51 0PL [Newport Lane – from centre follow Michelmersh, Timsbury signpost]: Plain two-bar brick local, hard-used elderly furnishings, simple huge cheap sandwiches and bargain ploughman's, particularly well kept Gales, down-to-earth veteran licensees, cribbage; piped music, wknd piano singsongs; informal and relaxing tree-shaded garden with old furniture, busy bird feeder, may be geese, ducks or chickens *(Phil and Sally Gorton, Lynn Sharpless, the Didler, BB, Dr and Mrs A K Clarke)*

BRAMBRIDGE [SU4721]

☆ *Dog & Crook* SO50 6HZ [village signed off M3 junction 12 exit roundabout, via B3335]: Lots of neat tables under hop-hung beams around central bar, good food choice from pub standards to some more unusual and restaurant dishes inc lovely puddings (Sun lunch booked well ahead), relaxing atmosphere, quick friendly young staff, part kept as proper drinking area with Fullers London Pride, Gales HSB and Ringwood Best, country wines, cosy dining room; alloy tables and chairs out on deck and under fairy-lit arbour, grass beyond, Itchen Way walks nearby *(BB, Ann and Colin Hunt, Nicki Watson)*

BRANSGORE [SZ1997]

☆ *Three Tuns* BH23 8JH [opposite church, Ringwood Rd, off A35 N of Christchurch]: Pretty 17th-c thatched pub, wide range of above-average imaginative food from ciabattas up, cheerful efficient service, Caledonian

Deuchars IPA, Ringwood Fortyniner and Timothy Taylors Landlord, good range of wines and hot drinks, tastefully refurbished olde-worlde bar with stripped brickwork and beamery, comfortable partly no smoking dining area welcoming children, fresh flowers; dogs allowed, pleasant back lawn with play area and open country views, large flower-decked front terrace, bedrooms, open all day Sun *(Prof Keith and Mrs Jane Barber, Phyl and Jack Street, W A Evershed)*

BROCKENHURST [SU3002]

Snakecatcher SO42 7RL [Lyndhurst Rd]: Well run pub with enjoyable food from sandwiches to steaks cooked to order (so may be a wait), interesting split-level bar and restaurant areas inc cosy part with log fire and easy chairs, real ales, nice choice of wines by the glass, good service; garden tables, good walks nearby *(Kevin Flack)*

BROOK [SU2713]

☆ *Green Dragon* SO43 7HE [B3078 NW of Cadnam, just off M27 junction 1]: Big open-plan New Forest dining pub dating from 15th c and currently run by family with long record of turning Hampshire pubs into real successes, wide choice of enjoyable fresh food inc plenty of seasonal game and fish as well as sensibly priced pubby favourites, good service even when busy, Fullers London Pride, Gales HSB and Ringwood, pleasant décor in variety of areas with scrubbed pine tables or longer refectory tables, proper bar areas too; big attractive garden with good enclosed play area, picturesque village *(Dick and Madeleine Brown, JWAC)*

BURGATE [SU1515]

Tudor Rose SP6 1LX [A338 about a mile N of Fordingbridge]: Picturesque black and white thatched pub with very low well padded beams (and they say a ghost), wide choice of generous straightforward food all day, Ringwood beers, friendly attentive service, log-effect gas fire in big fireplace; children welcome, picnic-sets out in front, smallish back garden with play area, Avon Valley footpath passes the door, fine pedestrian suspension bridge, open all day *(Phyl and Jack Street)*

BURITON [SU7320]

☆ *Five Bells* GU31 5RX [off A3 S of Petersfield]: Low-beamed pub with welcoming staff, enjoyable food from baguettes to imaginative main dishes, Badger beers, good wines by the glass, big log fire, daily papers, fresh flowers and church candles on numbered tables, some ancient stripped masonry and woodburner on public side; fruit machine, piped music; children in eating areas, tables in nice garden behind with sheltered terraces, pretty village, good walks, self-catering in converted stables *(Wendy Arnold, LYM, MLR, Tony and Jill Radnor, Ian Phillips, Ann and Colin Hunt, Phyl and Jack Street, W A Evershed)*

BURLEY [SU2202]

☆ *White Buck* BH24 4AZ [Bisterne Close; ¾ mile E, OS Sheet 195 map ref 223028]: Long comfortable bar in 19th-c mock-Tudor hotel, very wide choice of reasonably priced good

generous food, Fullers/Gales ales and Ringwood Best, decent wines and country wines, cheap soft drinks, good coffee, log fire, courteous efficient staff, thriving atmosphere, pleasant end dining room with tables out on decking (should book – but no bookings Sun lunchtime); may be quiet piped music; dogs welcome, pleasant front terrace and spacious lawn, lovely New Forest setting, well equipped bedrooms, superb walks towards Burley itself and over Mill Lawn *(BB, Colin Chapman, Claire Hardcastle, D Marsh, Peter Titcomb)*

BURSLEDON [SU4809]

☆ *Fox & Hounds* SO31 8DE [Hungerford Bottom; 2 miles from M27 junction 8]: Rambling oak-beamed and partly flagstoned 16th-c Chef & Brewer, big log fires, Wadworths 6X, lots of wines, wide choice of enjoyable reasonably priced food from sandwiches up, cheerful obliging staff, daily papers; linked by pleasant family conservatory area to ancient back barn with cheerful rustic atmosphere, lantern-lit side stalls, lots of interesting and authentic farm equipment, wide choice from food bar; children allowed, tables outside *(Ann and Colin Hunt, Bruce and Penny Wilkie, LYM, Jess and George Cowley)*

☆ *Jolly Sailor* SO31 8DN [off A27 towards Bursledon Station, Lands End Rd; handy for M27 junction 8]: Busy well laid out Badger dining pub, bright and fresh, in superb spot overlooking yachting inlet, well presented food from sandwiches up (no bookings), four real ales, good wine choice, good friendly service; open all day *(Matthew Johnson, Lynn Sharpless, Ann and Colin Hunt, LYM, the Didler, Charles and Pauline Stride, Jess and George Cowley, A and B D Craig, Peter and Audrey Dowsett, Paul and Shirley White, Spider Newth, Ian Phillips, Peter Titcomb)*

CADNAM [SU2913]

Bartley Lodge SO40 2NR [A337 Lyndhurst Rd]: Hotel in 18th-c former hunting lodge, attractive compact bar open to non-residents, enjoyable lunches, coffee and biscuits all day, friendly staff, children and calm dogs welcome, bedrooms *(Dennis Jenkin)*

☆ *Sir John Barleycorn* SO40 2NP [Old Romsey Rd; by M27 junction 1]: Picturesque low-slung thatched pub extended from low-beamed and timbered medieval core on left, modern décor and stripped wood flooring, wide choice of enjoyable up-to-date food, real ales inc Ringwood, reasonably priced wines, two good log fires, no smoking restaurant end, prompt and friendly young staff; dogs and children welcome, can be very busy; suntrap benches in front and out in colourful garden, open all day *(LYM, Phyl and Jack Street)*

White Hart SO40 2NP [½ mile from M27 junction 1]: Big rambling food-oriented pub, all no smoking, with enjoyable food from good inventive sandwiches up, good choice of real ales and wines by the glass, pleasant efficient service, spotless simple furnishings on parquet floors, stripped brickwork; piped music turned down on request; children in eating area, garden tables, food all day *(Dr D and Mrs B Woods, LYM)*

CHARTER ALLEY [SU5957]

White Hart RG26 5QA [White Hart Lane, off A340 N of Basingstoke]: Quiet and friendly mainly no smoking beamed village pub with helpful staff, Otter, West Berkshire Maggs Mild and interesting guest beers, continental beers, summer farm cider, decent wines, impressive collection of whisky bottles, wide choice of enjoyable reasonably priced food (not Sun/Mon evenings) in dining area, comfortable lounge bar with woodburner in big fireplace, simple public bar with skittle alley; may be unobtrusive piped music; small garden with terrace tables *(J V Dadswell, Bruce Bird, Michael and Jeanne Shillington)*

CHILWORTH [SU4118]

Clump SO16 7JZ [Chilworth Rd (A27 S'ton—Romsey)]: Big reliable chain eating place, largely no smoking, with real ales such as Wadworths 6X, good choice of wines, two log fires, smart décor with sofas and easy chairs in one part, spacious conservatory; unobtrusive piped music; disabled facilities, large garden, open all day *(Phyl and Jack Street, A and B D Craig)*

COLDEN COMMON [SU4821]

Fishers Pond SO50 7HG [Main Rd (B3354)]: Big busy Brewers Fayre in style of a converted water mill, vast choice of sensibly priced generous food all day inc children's, real ales such as Greene King Old Speckled Hen and Wadworths 6X, decent coffee, efficient service; terrace tables, pretty wooded lakeside setting with ducks, handy for Marwell Zoo, open all day *(Phyl and Jack Street, Ann and Colin Hunt)*

COPYTHORNE [SU3115]

Empress of Blandings SO40 2PE [A337/Copythorne Crescent]: Large newish pub/restaurant getting popular locally for its moderately priced food; picnic-sets in garden front and back, open all day *(Phyl and Jack Street)*

CRAWLEY [SU4234]

Fox & Hounds SO21 2PR [off A272 or B3420 NW of Winchester]: Striking almost swiss-looking building in picturesque village with duck pond, mix of attractive wooden tables and chairs on polished floors in neat and attractive linked beamed rooms with three log fires, enjoyable reasonably priced food, affable young staff, good choice of real ales and wines by the glass, civilised atmosphere; garden tables, bedrooms in converted outbuildings *(J Stickland, LYM, Phyl and Jack Street)*

CRONDALL [SU7948]

Hampshire Arms GU10 5QU [village signed off A287 S of Fleet; Pankridge St]: Smartly refurbished as Greene King dining pub, with almost hotelish décor and furnishings for small bar, comfortable leather armchairs and sofa by splendid log fire, a dozen good wines by the glass, friendly staff; children welcome, heated tables in back garden *(BB)*

Plume of Feathers GU10 5NT [The Borough]: Attractive smallish 15th-c village pub,

courteous and helpful young staff, generous enjoyable food from interesting snacks up, beams and dark wood, prints on cream walls, log fire in big brick fireplace, Greene King ales, decent wines by the glass, smarter restaurant end; children welcome, two red telephone boxes in garden, picturesque village *(Betty Laker)*

CROOKHAM [SU7852]

Black Horse GU51 5SJ [The Street]: Friendly and spick and span beamed village local with good value straightforward lunchtime food (not Sun) from sandwiches up, Fullers London Pride, Hogs Back TEA and Youngs Special; tables out in nice back and side areas with some amusements for children, pleasant Basingstoke Canal towpath walks *(Ian Phillips)*

DAMERHAM [SU1016]

☆ *Compasses* SP6 3HQ [signed off B3078 in Fordingbridge, or off A354 via Martin; East End]: Appealing country inn with long pretty garden by quiet village's cricket ground, good food from sandwiches up esp soups, shellfish and cheeses, friendly obliging staff, five good ales from local brewers, good choice of wines by the glass, well over a hundred malt whiskies, neatly refurbished small lounge bar divided by log fire from pleasant dining room with booth seating (children allowed here), pale wood tables and kitchen chairs, separate locals' bar with pool; high downland walks, nice bedrooms *(Noel Grundy)*

DOWNTON [SZ2793]

Royal Oak SO41 0LA [A337 Lymington—New Milton]: Neat, bright and cheerful partly panelled family pub, half no smoking, with friendly staff, real ales, good wine choice, reasonably priced food, nice touches such as good-sized napkins, small restaurant; unobtrusive piped music; huge well kept garden with good play area *(Brian Root, D Marsh, Mr and Mrs R W Allan)*

DROXFORD [SU6018]

White Horse SO32 3PB [A32; South Hill]: Rambling pub with several small linked areas, low beams, bow windows, alcoves and log fires, two no smoking dining rooms, Greene King ales, wide food choice from good value ciabatta rolls up, pleasant staff, roomy separate public bar with plenty of games, also TV and CD juke box; children and dogs welcome, tables out in sheltered flower-filled courtyard, open all day, rolling walking country *(LYM, Steve Whalley, Jess and George Cowley, W A Evershed, Ann and Colin Hunt, Val and Alan Green)*

DUMMER [SU5846]

☆ *Queen* RG25 2AD [½ mile from M3 junction 7; take Dummer slip road]: Comfortable beamed pub well divided with lots of softly lit alcoves, Courage Best, Fullers London Pride and a guest such as Adnams Broadside or Wadworths 6X, good friendly service even on busy Sun lunchtime, log fire, queen and steeplechase prints, no smoking restaurant allowing children; fruit machine, well reproduced piped music, no mobile phones; picnic-sets under cocktail parasols on terrace and in extended back garden, attractive village with ancient church *(Martin and Karen Wake, Ian Phillips, Edward Mirzoeff, LYM, D O Parker, Stephen Allford, Ann and Colin Hunt, R Lake)*

DUNBRIDGE [SU3225]

☆ *Mill Arms* SO51 0LF [Barley Hill, just by stn on Portsmouth—Cardiff line]: High-ceilinged open-plan pub with good reasonably priced blackboard food inc some interesting dishes (fresh herbs from the garden), quietly friendly helpful service, Hampshire Mottisfont Meddler brewed for the pub, Ringwood Best and two or three changing ales, daily papers, dining area opening into conservatory, skittle alley and separate games room; full-scale refurbishment under way as we go to press in summer 2006, but has had nice mix of seating from stripped pews to soft sofas in cosy corner by log fire – reports on the changes, please; picnic-sets in pretty two-level garden with wendy house, bedrooms *(John Evans, J Metcalfe, John Pavey, Phyl and Jack Street, BB, Prof and Mrs Tony Palmer, Dr and Mrs A K Clarke, Ann and Colin Hunt)*

DUNDRIDGE [SU5718]

☆ *Hampshire Bowman* SO32 1GD [off B3035 towards Droxford, Swanmore, then right at Bishops W signpost]: Country local with great mix of customers, cosy unassuming bar with Ringwood Best and Fortyniner, a changing Flower Pots ale, two or three guest beers and farm cider tapped from the cask, decent house wines, country wines, some colourful paintings, new kitchen doing wider range of attractively priced home-made food (not Sun evening) inc some interesting dishes and good value Sun roast, new dining extension too; children and dogs welcome, picnic-sets on attractive lawn, peaceful downland walks, open all day Fri-Sun *(Phil and Sally Gorton, Wendy Straker, LYM, the Didler, Ron Shelton, Val and Alan Green, Ann and Colin Hunt, Charles and Pauline Stride, W A Evershed)*

DURLEY [SU5217]

Robin Hood SO32 2AA [Durley Street, just off B2177 Bishops Waltham—Winchester]: Attractive contemporary décor and atmosphere in smart lounge and bright and roomy dining area, good gently upmarket food (not Sun evening), cheerful attentive service, Greene King ales, reasonably priced wines, log fires, unusual modern lighting, darts in public bar; big pleasant garden with covered decking, country view and play area, good walks, open all day Fri-Sun *(Phyl and Jack Street)*

EAST BOLDRE [SU3700]

☆ *Turf Cutters Arms* SO42 7WL [Main Rd]: Small dim-lit New Forest country local, warmly welcoming and unpretentious, lots of beams and pictures, sturdy tables, rugs, bare boards and flagstones, log fire, huge helpings of simple local food from sandwiches and basic dishes to quite a lot of game, Gales HSB, Ringwood Best and Wadworths 6X, several dozen malt whiskies, no smoking room, fish tanks, friendly dogs; children welcome, garden

tables, some good heathland walks, three big old-fashioned bedrooms, simple but comfortable, good breakfast *(K H Frostick, BB, Sue Demont, Tim Barrow, Dick and Madeleine Brown)*

EAST MEON [SU6822]

☆ *George* GU32 1NH [Church St; signed off A272 W of Petersfield, and off A32 in West Meon]: Relaxing heavy-beamed rustic pub with particularly helpful and friendly staff and landlord, wide choice of generous good value food from sandwiches up, inglenook log fires, cosy areas around central bar counter, Badger ales, decent wines; soft piped music; children welcome, good outdoor seating arrangements, five small but comfortable bedrooms (book well ahead), good breakfast, pretty village with fine church, good walks *(MLR, William Ruxton, LYM, Michael and Robin Inskip, Peter Hacker, Neil and Debbie Cook, Paul and Shirley White, Mr and Mrs Hubling, W A Evershed, Ann and Colin Hunt)*

EAST TYTHERLEY [SU2927]

Star SO51 0LW [off B3084 N of Romsey]: Pretty if pricey no smoking country dining pub under new licensees, bar with attractive log fires, leather sofas and tub chairs, Ringwood Best and Fortyniner and a couple of guest beers; children welcome, smartly furnished terrace and play area, pleasant bedrooms overlooking cricket pitch, good nearby walks, cl Sun evening and Mon *(LYM)*

EASTON [SU5132]

☆ *Cricketers* SO21 1EJ [off B3047]: Thriving open-plan local with chatty and welcoming NZ landlord, Otter, Ringwood Best and interesting guest beers, reasonably priced wines, wide choice of good value generous food from sandwiches to piping hot dishes, prompt service, pleasant mix of pub furnishings, darts and shove-ha'penny one end, small bright no smoking restaurant, good wine range; well cared for bedrooms *(Lynn Sharpless, Ann and Colin Hunt, BB, Mr and Mrs R W Allan)*

ELLISFIELD [SU6345]

Fox RG25 2QW [Green Lane, Upper Common]: Village pub spruced up under considerate and friendly new management, pleasant lounge area on left, main dining area opposite, enjoyable food, nice range of wines by the glass, open fire; attractive garden, good walks (esp Bedlam Bottom to the W in spring, or Preston Oak Hills at bluebell time) *(Phyl and Jack Street)*

EMERY DOWN [SU2808]

☆ *New Forest* SO43 7DY [village signed off A35 just W of Lyndhurst]: Comfortable and spacious, in one of the best bits of the Forest for walking; sensible range of good generous food from filled baguettes to popular Sun lunch, welcoming staff, good choice of real ales inc Ringwood Best, wide choice of realistically priced house wines, proper coffee, attractive softly lit separate areas on varying levels, each with its own character, hunting prints, two log fires; children allowed, small pleasant three-level garden *(Ann and Colin Hunt, LYM, Rev Michael Vockins)*

EMSWORTH [SU7405]

Coal Exchange PO10 7EG [Ships Quay, South St]: Friendly bustle in comfortably compact L-shaped Victorian local, cheerful landlady proud of her well kept Fullers, Gales and guest ales, good fresh honest lunchtime food from generous baguettes to nice puddings, popular Sun lunch and Tues curry night, espresso coffee, coal fire each end, low ceilings, lots of locals and yachtsmen; tables outside, next to pay & display, handy for Wayfarers Walk and Solent Walk, open all day Fri-Sun *(Ann and Colin Hunt, Val and Alan Green, Minda and Stanley Alexander)*

EVERSLEY [SU7861]

Golden Pot RG27 0NB [B3272]: Enjoyable food from baguettes up in linked bar areas inc snug armchairs and sofa by log-effect gas fire, pretty no smoking restaurant, quick cheerful service, Greene King ales, nice wines by the glass; piped music; dogs allowed in bar, picnic-sets outside with masses of colourful flowers, cl winter Sun evening *(Mrs Angela Bromley-Martin, LYM, Mrs Pam Mattinson)*

EVERTON [SZ2994]

Crown SO41 0JJ [Old Christchurch Rd; pub signed just off A337 W of Lymington]: New management in quietly set New Forest-edge village pub, two attractive dining rooms with sturdy tables on polished boards off tiled-floor bar, log fires, real ales; picnic-sets on front terrace and back grass *(Brian Root, BB, C and R Bromage, Mr and Mrs A Silver)*

FACCOMBE [SU3958]

Jack Russell SP11 0DS [signed from A343 Newbury—Andover]: Light and airy creeper-covered pub in nice setting opp village pond by flint church, decorous bar with a few forestry saws and the like, well kept Greene King IPA and Shepherd Neame Spitfire, good coffee, decent bar food (not Sun evening), darts, sturdy oak tables in carpeted conservatory restaurant; disabled facilities, picnic-sets out on lawn by beech trees, bedrooms spotless and cheerful, good walks with rewarding views *(Phyl and Jack Street, BB)*

FAREHAM [SU5806]

Cob & Pen PO16 8SL [Wallington Shore Rd, not far from M27 junction 11]: Well kept Hook Norton Best and Ringwood ales, good value straightforward food, pleasant pine furnishings, flagstones and carpets, nice separate games room; large garden *(Stephen and Jean Curtis)*

Golden Lion PO16 7AE: Smartened up by Fullers, with their Butser, London Pride and HSB, decent food *(Val and Alan Green)*

Lord Arthur Lee PO16 0EP [West St]: Large open-plan Wetherspoons, attractively priced beers from small brewers, their usual good value food, no smoking family area; named for the local 1900s MP who presented Chequers to the nation *(Tony Hobden)*

FARNBOROUGH [SU8756]

☆ *Prince of Wales* GU14 8AL [Rectory Rd, nr Farnborough North station]: Impressive range

of changing real ales in friendly Edwardian local, small but lively, stripped brickwork, open fire and antiquey touches in its three small linked areas, popular lunchtime food (not Sun) from sandwiches to imaginative specials, good service, decent malt whiskies; open all day Sun *(Dr Martin Owton)*

FARRINGDON [SU7135]

Rose & Crown GU34 3ED [off A32 S of Alton; Crows Lane – follow Church, Selborne, Liss signpost]: Roomy L-shaped bar, bright and comfortable, with warmly welcoming efficient service even when busy, good choice of enjoyable food and real ales, reasonable prices, decent wines and coffee, log fire, fresh flowers, daily papers, neat back dining room; wide views from big well kept back garden *(BB, Peter Salmon, Ann and Colin Hunt)*

Royal Oak GU34 3DJ [Gosport Rd (A32 S of Alton), Lower Farringdon]: Warmly welcoming young landlady, wide choice of enjoyable food inc fresh fish and other local ingredients, sensible prices, quick cheerful service, real ales inc Ringwood Best, good coffee, log fire, pictures, brasses, fresh flowers and candles, nice good-sized separate restaurant; well behaved children and walking parties welcome *(Betty Laker, Ann and Colin Hunt)*

FINCHDEAN [SU7312]

George PO8 0AU: Cheerful smartly dressed staff, good value food in lounge and neat public bar, Bass and Youngs; good nearby walks, open all day Sun *(Ann and Colin Hunt, W A Evershed)*

FROGHAM [SU1712]

☆ *Foresters Arms* SP6 2JA [Abbotswell Rd]: Comfortably refurbished New Forest pub, flagstones and small woodburner, chef/landlord doing enjoyable blackboard food from sandwiches to very popular Sun lunch (get there early or book – the compact no smoking dining room fills quickly), reasonable prices, attentive young staff, Wadworths and guest ales, good wines by the glass; children welcome, pleasant garden and pretty front verandah; small camp site adjacent, nearby ponies and good walks *(LYM, John and Joan Calvert, Phyl and Jack Street)*

GOSPORT [SZ6098]

Anglesey PO12 2DH [Crescent Rd, Alverstoke]: Enjoyable reasonably priced pub food and real ale in friendly unpretentious bar, Jane Austen associations; attractive garden, bedrooms *(Peter and Audrey Dowsett)*

Queens PO12 1LG [Queens Rd]: Classic bare-boards local whose long-serving landlady keeps Ringwood, Roosters Yankee, Youngs and two more changing strong beers in top condition, quick service, Sun bar nibbles, perhaps huge filled rolls and other simple food, three areas off bar with good log fire in interesting carved fireplace, sensibly placed darts, docile pyrenean mountain dog; family TV room, quiz night Thurs; cl lunchtimes Mon-Thurs, open all day Sat *(Bruce Bird, Ann and Colin Hunt)*

HAMBLE [SU4806]

Olde Whyte Harte SO31 4JF [High St; 3 miles

from M27 junction 8]: Low-beamed 16th-c bar with big inglenook log fire and yachting memorabilia, well integrated no smoking flagstoned eating area allowing children, well priced fresh food all day inc plenty of fish, friendly relaxed staff, Fullers and Gales ales, good wines by the glass and country wines, decent coffee; piped music; some tables in small walled garden, handy for nature reserve, open all day (LYM, Ann and Colin Hunt, Bruce and Penny Wilkie, Val and Alan Green)

HAMBLEDON [SU6716]

☆ **Bat & Ball** PO8 0UB [Broadhalfpenny Down; about 2 miles E towards Clanfield]: Extended dining pub opp cricket's first-ever pitch (matches most summer Sundays), plenty of cricket memorabilia, log fires and comfortable modern furnishings in three linked rooms, genial landlord and good friendly service even when crowded, real ales, good wines by the glass, enjoyable meals inc fresh fish, panelled restaurant; children welcome, lovely downs views and walks (Ann and Colin Hunt, LYM, Richard Staveley, Jess and George Cowley, Mrs Maricar Jagger, Geoff and Sylvia Donald, W A Evershed, Paul and Shirley White)

HAVANT [SU6807]

Golden Lion PO9 3EY [Bedhampton Rd]: New landlord and chef with enjoyable home-made pubby food, pleasant lounge with central coal-effect fire, Shepherd Neame Spitfire and Youngs, public bar with pool etc (R M Corlett)

☆ **Old House At Home** PO9 1DA [South St]: Much modernised two-bar Tudor pub, low beams and nice rambling alcovey feel, low-priced lunchtime sandwiches, baked potatoes and bargain hot dishes, Fullers London Pride and Gales, good welcoming service, smallish no smoking area; piped music (may be live Sat – very popular with young people Fri/Sat night); pretty frontage with splendid hanging baskets, tables in back garden (Ann and Colin Hunt, LYM, Tony and Wendy Hobden)

Parchment Makers PO9 1HE [Park Road North]: Wetherspoons in former tax office, their usual food, up to ten low-priced real ales, good service, old books, long glazed frontage with double doors opening back in summer; open from breakfast on (R M Corlett, Tony Hobden)

Robin Hood PO9 1EE [Homewell]: Neat and relaxing rambling open-plan bar, Fullers/Gales ales tapped from the cask, reasonably priced simple lunchtime food, good service, open fire, sensibly placed darts; tables outside, open all day (Ann and Colin Hunt, R M Corlett, Tony Hobden)

HEDGE END [SU4912]

Barleycorn SO30 4FQ [Lower Northam Rd, nr M27 junction 8]: Greene King pub with their ales and a guest such as Courage Best, simple low-priced food from baguettes up; can get rather smoky (Val and Alan Green)

HERRIARD [SS6744]

Fur & Feathers RG25 2PN [pub signed just off A339 Basingstoke—Alton]: Open-plan Fullers pub, their ales kept well, friendly service, daily papers, bare boards, lots of pine furniture and panelling, log fire; picnic-sets out in front, big tree-sheltered garden behind (BB, Jill Hurley, Martin and Karen Wake, Bruce Bird)

HILL HEAD [SU5402]

Osborne View PO14 3JR [Hill Head Rd]: Modern extended clifftop Badger dining pub, three stepped-back levels and picture windows for stunning views to the Isle of Wight, Badger beers, friendly helpful staff, nautical prints and memorabilia, lots of stripped wood and red carpet, food inc children's and evening restaurant; may be piped music, busy wknds; garden and beach access, nr Titchfield Haven bird reserve, open all day (Dr Alan and Mrs Sue Holder, Val and Alan Green, Peter and Audrey Dowsett)

HORNDEAN [SU7013]

Ship & Bell PO8 0BZ [London Rd]: Comfortable and cheerful pub/hotel by former Gales brewery, Fullers and Gales ales, good range of wines, reasonably priced standard food, quick friendly service, relaxed pubby bar with deep well and log fire, broad low steps up to comfortable no smoking lounge and dining room, interesting photographs, separate public bar/games room; 14 bedrooms with own bathrooms, nice walk to Catherington church (R M Corlett, Bruce Bird, Ann and Colin Hunt)

HOUGHTON [SU3432]

☆ **Boot** SO20 6LH [S of Stockbridge]: Country local with good food from baguettes and croque monsieur to good salads with home-grown veg and more unusual dishes in log-fire bar with stuffed fish and other trophies or roomy and attractive restaurant on left, Ringwood and other real ales, friendly attentive staff; dogs welcome, long garden with half a dozen picnic-sets down by lovely (unfenced) stretch of River Test, where they have fishing – good walks, and opp Test Way cycle path (Julia and Richard Tredgett, Edward Mirzoeff, Phyl and Jack Street, Patrick Hall, Ann and Colin Hunt)

IBSLEY [SU1409]

Old Beams BH24 3PP [A338 Salisbury—Ringwood]: Big busy black-and-white thatched all-day family food pub, wide choice and reasonable prices, friendly helpful staff, no smoking dining areas with lots of modern pine furniture under aged oak beams, also pleasant bar with Greene King real ales and soft seating around log-effect fire, conservatory; plenty of garden tables, open all day (W W Burke, LYM, Pat and Robert Watt)

ITCHEN ABBAS [SU5332]

☆ **Trout** SO21 1BQ [4 miles from M3 junction 9; B3047]: Newish licensees giving good service in pleasant country pub with good river and downland walks nearby, enjoyable food using some local ingredients from baguettes and pubby favourites to contemporary dishes, Greene King ales, decent wines, simple but smartish décor in quiet no smoking lounge and dining room, chatty separate public bar; tables in sheltered pretty side garden, comfortable bedrooms (Phyl and Jack Street, LYM, Stephen Allford, Ann and Colin Hunt)

KEYHAVEN [SZ3091]

Gun SO41 0TP: Busy 17th-c pub looking over boatyard and sea to Isle of Wight, low-beamed bar with lots of nautical memorabilia and plenty of character (less in family rooms); good choice of generous food using local produce, real ales tapped from the cask such as Gales HSB, Greene King Old Speckled Hen, Ringwood and Wadworths 6X, well over a hundred malt whiskies, brisk service, bar billiards; back conservatory, garden with swings and fishpond *(A and B D Craig, Dr A J and Mrs Tompsett, JWAC)*

KINGSCLERE [SU5258]

Swan RG20 5PP [Swan St]: Old-fashioned 15th-c village inn, lots of beams, enthusiastic landlord and friendly helpful staff, Hampshire King Alfred, Theakstons XB and two guest beers, enjoyable reasonably priced home-made food (not Sun evening); dogs welcome, tables outside, nine bedrooms *(Bruce Bird)*

LANGSTONE [SU7104]

☆ *Royal Oak* PO9 1RY [off A3023 just before Hayling Island bridge; Langstone High St]: Charmingly placed no smoking waterside dining pub overlooking tidal inlet and ancient wadeway to Hayling Island, boats at high tide, wading birds when it goes out; real ales such as Flowers Original, Fullers London Pride, Gales HSB and Greene King IPA, good choice of wines by the glass, good pub food inc all-day sandwiches and snacks, plenty of cheerful young staff, spacious flagstoned bar and linked dining areas, log fire; children in eating areas, nice garden, good coastal paths nearby, open all day *(Ann and Colin Hunt, Colin M'Kerrow, LYM, OPUS, Ralph and Jean Whitehouse, Ian Phillips, Jenny Garrett, W A Evershed, David Sizer)*

☆ *Ship* PO9 1RD [A3023]: Busy waterside 18th-c former grain store, lovely views to Hayling Island from roomy softly lit nautical bar with upper deck dining room, good no smoking areas, quick friendly service, Fullers ales, good choice of wines by the glass, log fire, wide range of generous reasonably priced food; children welcome, plenty of tables on heated terrace by quiet quay, good coast walks, open all day *(Peter and Audrey Dowsett, Tony Hobden, Lynn Sharpless, Ian Phillips, Alain and Rose Foote, W A Evershed)*

LASHAM [SU6742]

Royal Oak GU34 5SJ: Friendly two-bar local with good changing ales such as fff, wide range of enjoyable home-made food (all day Sun), fair prices, log fire, much talk of aircraft and gliding (airfield nearby); may be quiet piped music; pleasant garden by church, attractive village, good walks, open all day *(Tony and Jill Radnor)*

LISS FOREST [SU7828]

Temple GU33 7BP [Forest Rd]: Welcoming refurbished local with lots of brass, reasonably priced bar food inc good fish and chips; children welcome, good garden with play area *(Mrs S M Prince)*

LOCKS HEATH [SU5006]

☆ *Jolly Farmer* SO31 9JH [2½ miles from M27

junction 9; A27 towards Bursledon, left into Locks Rd, at end T junction right into Warsash Rd then left at hire shop into Fleet End Rd]: Wide choice of enjoyable food from filled baps to fresh fish, local meats and good value very popular two-sitting Sun lunch in appealing series of linked softly lit rooms, nice old scrubbed tables (quite close-set) and masses of interesting bric-a-brac and prints, good quick friendly service, interesting long-serving landlord, Fullers London Pride, Gales HSB and a guest beer, decent wines and country wines, coal-effect gas fires, no smoking area; two sheltered terraces (one with a play area and children's lavatories), nice bedrooms *(Michael and Robin Inskip, LYM, Charles and Pauline Stride, Peter and Audrey Dowsett, Ann and Colin Hunt, Matt Long)*

LONG SUTTON [SU7447]

☆ *Four Horseshoes* RG29 1TA [signed off B3349 S of Hook]: Unpretentious well kept open-plan black-beamed country local with long-serving landlord cooking good choice of food inc a splendid cheese soup, very welcoming landlady, good range of changing real ales such as Gales, decent wines and country wine, two log fires, daily papers, no piped music, small glazed-in verandah; disabled access, picnic-sets on grass over road, boules pitch and play area *(Tony and Jill Radnor, BB)*

LONGPARISH [SU4344]

Cricketers SP11 6PZ: Two-bar village pub with wide choice of carefully cooked food from light snacks up, prompt service, real ales; good garden *(Mrs Belinda Mead)*

☆ *Plough* SP11 6PB [B3048, off A303 just E of Andover]: Comfortable open-plan food pub divided by arches, relaxed atmosphere, efficient friendly service, interesting food from good sandwiches up, Gales and Ringwood ales, decent house wines, log fire, partly no smoking restaurant, attractive watercolours; piped music; children in eating areas, tables on terrace and in nice garden, bedrooms *(Gareth Lewis, Neil and Angela Huxter, Dennis Jenkin, LYM, Mr and Mrs D S Price)*

LOWER FROYLE [SU7643]

☆ *Anchor* GU34 4NA [signed N of A31 W of Bentley]: 14th-c traditional pub with pleasant beamed and carpeted lounge on left, more room on right with big-windowed no smoking eating area, popular with older people lunchtime (esp Weds) for reasonably priced food with wide choice from sandwiches to fish, cheerful and efficient family service, Courage Best and Timothy Taylors Landlord, decent malt whiskies; white wrought-iron tables out on grass and by front car park, bedrooms *(David Cannings, BB, R B Gardiner)*

LYMINGTON [SZ3293]

☆ *Chequers* SO41 8AH [Ridgeway Lane, Lower Woodside – dead end just S of A337 roundabout W of Lymington, by White Hart]: Welcoming local atmosphere, friendly landlord and pleasant young staff, generous reasonably priced good food inc local fish, real ales such as Bass, Ringwood and Wadworths 6X, polished boards and quarry tiles, attractive pictures, plain chairs and wall pews, traditional games; may be piped music; well behaved children allowed, tables and summer marquee in neat walled back family garden, attractive front terrace, handy for bird-watching at Pennington Marshes *(Ian Blackwell, Jeff Hosier, LYM, Pam and John Smith, Peter Titcomb)*

☆ *Fishermans Rest* SO41 8FD [All Saints Rd, Woodside]: Wide choice of good traditional and more interesting food inc very popular Sun lunch (wknd booking recommended), friendly helpful staff, pleasant atmosphere, Ringwood ales, decent wines, plenty of locals at bar *(Graham and Glenis Watkins, D Marsh, Mr and Mrs A Silver)*

LYNDHURST [SU2908]

Crown SO43 7NF [top end of High St opposite church]: Best Western hotel, cheerful log fire in comfortable and attractive traditional panelled bar, pleasant and efficient young staff, Ringwood Best, good coffee, bar food as well as restaurant; bedrooms, fine Forest walks, open all day *(Ann and Colin Hunt)*

☆ *Crown Stirrup* SO43 7DE [Clay Hill; A337 ½ mile S]: 17th-c or older, thoughtfully taken in hand by newish licensees, good range of reasonably priced bar food with some unusual evening dishes, two friendly low-beamed rooms with pine furniture, real ales, good wine list and service, log fires, stripped brick in flagstoned dining room; children and dogs welcome, covered back terrace, picnic-sets in pleasant side garden with play area and gate to Forest *(Prof and Mrs Tony Palmer, Tony and Caroline Elwood)*

Fox & Hounds SO43 7BG [High St]: Big comfortable much modernised dining pub with promptly served reasonably priced food, Ringwood Best, decent wines, welcoming staff, lots of exposed brickwork, standing timbers as divisions, family room beyond former coach entry, no piped music, games room with pool, darts etc *(Ann and Colin Hunt)*

MAPLEDURWELL [SU6851]

Gamekeepers RG25 2LU [off A30, not far from M3 junction 6]: Dark-beamed dining pub with friendly new licensees doing enjoyable food, Badger Best and Tanglefoot, glass-topped well and various nooks and corners in flagstoned and panelled core, well spaced tables in large no smoking dining room; piped music; children welcome, picnic-sets on terrace and back grassy area, lovely thatched village with duckpond, good walks, open all day *(LYM, Guy Consterdine, N R White)*

MARCHWOOD [SU3809]

☆ *Pilgrim* SO40 4WU [Hythe Rd, off A326 at Twiggs Lane]: Picturesque immaculately kept thatched pub with wide choice of consistently good value changing blackboard food, good long-serving landlord, gleaming copper and brass and comfortable banquettes in long welcoming L-shaped bar, mainstream real ales, english wines, open fires, more expensive restaurant across road; can be crowded; neat garden *(Bruce and Penny Wilkie, Phyl and*

Jack Street, LYM, Meg and Colin Hamilton)

MEONSTOKE [SU6120]

☆ *Bucks Head* SO32 3NA [village signed just off A32 N of Droxford]: Partly panelled L-shaped dining lounge looking over road to water meadows, enjoyable sensibly priced food inc popular Sun roasts, Greene King IPA and Old Speckled Hen and a guest beer, log fire, decent wines, plush banquettes, rugs on bare boards and well spaced tables, unspoilt public bar with leather settee by another log fire, darts and juke box; tables and picnic-sets in small garden, lovely village setting with ducks on pretty little River Meon, good walks, comfortable bedrooms with own bathrooms, open all day wknds *(Ann and Colin Hunt, BB, Malcolm and Dorothy Hind, Phyl and Jack Street)*

MICHELDEVER [SU5138]

☆ *Half Moon & Spread Eagle* SO21 3DG [brown sign to pub off A33 N of Winchester]: Simply decorated village local with Greene King and guest beers, bar food, leather armchairs, solid seats and a woodburner in appealing beamed bar, games area; has been a popular main entry, but unaccountably no reader recommendations in recent months – news please; sheltered back terrace and garden, pleasant walks nearby *(LYM)*

MINSTEAD [SU2810]

☆ *Trusty Servant* SO43 7FY [just off A31, not far from M27 junction 1]: Relaxed and attractive 19th-c pub in pretty New Forest hamlet with interesting church and plenty of easy walks, pleasantly informal two-room bar and big airy separate dining room (children allowed here), friendly service, changing real ales such as Fullers London Pride, Ringwood Best and Wadworths 6X, decent house wines and country wines, generous food all day from sandwiches, baguettes and baked potatoes to good game dishes; dogs welcome in bar, good-sized side and back garden, open all day *(Don Manley, Kevin Flack, Brian Root, Evelyn and Derek Walter, Kath and Ted Warren, D P and M A Miles, LYM, Sue Demont, Tim Barrow, Claire Friend, David Adams, Ann and Colin Hunt)*

NEW MILTON [SZ2495]

House Martin BH25 6QF [Christchurch Rd (A337)]: Pleasantly refurbished dining pub with good value food all day, real ales inc Ringwood Best, good service, conservatory; open all day *(A Wright, David M Cundy)*

NORTH GORLEY [SU1611]

☆ *Royal Oak* SP6 2PB [Ringwood Rd; village signed off A338 S of Fordingbridge]: 17th-c thatched pub by New Forest, neatly refurbished no smoking lounge on left, busier main bar on right, attractive bare-boards L-shaped eating area, partly no smoking, with pine tables and old-fashioned chairs or booth seating, popular food (all day in school hols) from lunchtime sandwiches and baguettes up, Fullers London Pride, Ringwood Best and guests such as Hampshire Lionheart and Hop Back Summer Lightning, decent wines; piped music, TV, games machine; children and dogs welcome, neat sheltered back garden with play area for children, big duck pond over road, open all day *(Ian Phillips, Paul and Shirley White, W W Burke, Adrian and Christine Smithies, LYM, Tony and Wendy Hobden)*

NORTH WALTHAM [SU5645]

Fox RG25 2BE [signed off A30 SW of Basingstoke; handy for M3 junction 7]: Foxy décor in comfortable village pub with log fire in bright elongated dining area, real ales, welcoming landlord and well trained staff, enjoyable food from sandwiches and baguettes to venison and Sun roasts; children welcome, lovely garden with farmland views, pleasant village in nice spot (walk to Jane Austen's church at Steventon) *(Brian and Pamela Everett, Stephen Allford, Roger Huxtable, S Crowe)*

Sun RG25 2DJ [old A30]: Friendly, with good value pubby food all well done, real ale, nice wines by the glass, decent coffee, log fire in lounge *(Dr and Mrs Ewing)*

NORTH WARNBOROUGH [SU7351]

Swan RG29 1EX [Hook Rd, nr M3 junction 5]: Friendly village local by Basingstoke Canal, refurbished under current landlord, popular meals inc proper steak and kidney pie, pleasant service, beams and stripped brickwork, pubby front bar with Courage and Charles Wells Bombardier, restaurant area; picnic-sets in back courtyard, large well equipped play area beyond *(Tony and Jill Radnor)*

ODIHAM [SU7451]

Water Witch RG29 1AL [Colt Hill – quiet no through rd signed off main st]: Olde-worlde décor in nicely kept no smoking Chef & Brewer with good friendly staff, wide choice of reliable food, real ales; lovely hanging baskets, big garden with extensive children's facilities, very busy wknds, nr picturesque stretch of Basingstoke Canal *(Jennifer Banks, R T and J C Moggridge)*

OTTERBOURNE [SU4623]

Old Forge SO21 2EE [Main Rd]: Well run Vintage Inn, good layout, friendly staff, their usual good drinks range and food all day, great log fires *(Phyl and Jack Street, Lynn Sharpless)*

OWSLEBURY [SU5123]

Ship SO21 1LT [off B2177 Fishers Pond—Lower Upham; Whites Hill]: Popular family summer pub, plenty of space outside with play area, toddler zone, pets corner and garden kitchen doing burgers and so forth, 17th-c black oak beams and timbers inside, big central fireplace, particularly well kept Flower Pots and Greene King IPA, good choice of wines by the glass, good friendly service, cribbage, dominoes and alley skittles, comfortable dining area and restaurant (both no smoking) *(James Price, Ann and Colin Hunt, LYM, Paul and Shirley White, Phil and Sally Gorton, W A Evershed)*

PARK GATE [SU5108]

Talisman SO31 7GD [Bridge Rd, Park Gate (A27, a mile from M27 junction 9)]: Busy Badger dining pub, large and hospitable, with their real ales kept well, good choice of wines,

generous popular food, beams, oak panels, bare boards and carpets, flame-effect fire, no smoking area; quiet piped music; children welcome, large back garden with play area *(Jenny and Peter Lowater, Bruce and Penny Wilkie)*

PETERSFIELD [SU7423]

Good Intent GU31 4AF [College St]: Well kept Fullers London Pride and Gales HSB in 16th-c core with low oak beams and log fires, pleasant local atmosphere, decent food from sandwiches and ciabattas up, well spaced good-sized pine tables with flowers, camera collection, cosy family area; some live music *(Val and Alan Green, W A Evershed)*

☆ *White Horse* GU32 1DA [up on old downs rd about halfway between Steep and East Tisted, nr Priors Dean – OS Sheet 186 or 197 map ref 715290]: Charming country pub high and isolated on the downs, two relaxed and idiosyncratically old-fashioned rustic parlours (candlelit at night), attractive no smoking family dining room, open fires throughout, good range of real ales, enjoyable food (not Sun evening) from generous ciabattas to smartly served restaurant dishes, smart efficient staff; children welcome, rustic tables out by floodlit pond, open all day wknds. Note: as we went to press, a landslide had closed main access so best to phone for directions (01420) 588387 *(Tony and Jill Radnor, the Didler, LYM, Ann and Colin Hunt, W A Evershed, Val and Alan Green)*

PILLEY [SZ3298]

Fleur de Lys SO41 5QG [off A337 Brockenhurst—Lymington; Pilley St]: Upscale dining pub smartly updated revealing old boards and heavy beams, good food, Ringwood Best and Fortyniner, decent wines, friendly service, huge inglenook log fire in dining room, new furnishings and pretty contemporary décor; fine forest and heathland walks nearby *(LYM, Kevin Flack, Michael and Maggie Betton)*

PORTSMOUTH [SZ6399]

American Bar PO1 2JA [White Hart Rd]: Spacious colonial-theme bar and partly no smoking restaurant popular for reasonably priced food from all-day sandwiches, baguettes and bar meals to fresh local fish and seafood, Courage Directors and a guest beer, good friendly service; garden behind, handy for IOW ferry *(Colin Moore)*

Bridge Tavern PO1 2JJ [East St, Camber Dock]: Flagstones, bare boards and lots of dark wood, comfortable furnishings, good water views, Fullers and Gales ales, country wines, smiling service, straightforward food from baguettes and baked potatoes up, maritime theme; waterside terrace, nice position *(Mrs Maricar Jagger, Ann and Colin Hunt, Paul and Shirley White)*

Churchillian PO6 3LS [Portsdown Hill Rd, Widley]: Smallish open-plan dining pub with picture-window views over Portsmouth and its new Spinnaker Tower across to the Isle of Wight, Bass, Gales GB and HSB and

Wadworths 6X, generous pubby food, friendly bustle; may be piped music; handy for Fort Widley equestrian centre and nature trail (Bruce and Penny Wilkie, Val and Alan Green)

Fountain PO2 9AA [London Rd, North End]: Large bar with family room off, nicely polished brass, interesting pub pictures, mirrors each end, Badger Best and Gales HSB; seats outside (Ann and Colin Hunt)

George PO6 1BE [Portsdown Hill Rd, Widley]: Friendly Georgian local with half a dozen ales inc local Hidden and Ringwood, decent wines, cheap lunchtime food; handy for Portsdown Hill nature reserve, wonderful views of Hayling Island, Portsmouth and Isle of Wight from terrace (David Carr, Val and Alan Green)

Lady Hamilton PO1 3DT [The Hard, nr Gunwharf]: Nautical flavour, pictures of Lady H and Nelson, friendly staff and atmosphere (Peter and Audrey Dowsett)

Old Customs House PO1 3TY [Vernon Buildings, Gunwharf Quays]: Interesting conversion of handsome Georgian customs house, latterly an admin building for former RN mine clearance and diving school, in bright modern shopping centre by old quays and dockside, now a family dining pub with smoking and no smoking areas divided into small rooms, modern tables and chairs and some armchairs and sofas, quickly served reasonably priced usual food inc children's from central food counter or in upstairs restaurant, Fullers and Gales ales; piped music; nearby multi-storey car park (Peter and Audrey Dowsett, David Carr, Graham and Glenis Watkins, Ann and Colin Hunt, Tony Hobden, Val and Alan Green, Dr and Mrs M E Wilson)

Pembroke PO1 2NR [Pembroke Rd]: Buoyant atmosphere in well run traditional local, real ales such as Fullers London Pride, reasonably priced food; open all day (Ann and Colin Hunt)

Sallyport PO1 2LU [High St, Old Portsmouth]: Interesting old hotel's comfortable bar with leather chesterfields, soft lighting, lots of naval prints, chamber pots hanging from beams, attractively priced usual bar food from sandwiches and baked potatoes up, several real ales inc Fullers London Pride and Gales HSB, decent coffee, no smoking upstairs restaurant; bedrooms, open all day (Kevin Flack, Ann and Colin Hunt, Neil and Anita Christopher)

Spice Island PO1 2JL [Bath Sq]: Vast no smoking open-plan waterside pub, part dark and panelled in galleon style, part roomy modern bare-boards style, big windows overlooking passing ships, real ales, food all day, family room (one of the few in Portsmouth), bright upstairs restaurant; tables out in harbourside square (Mrs Maricar Jagger, Michael and Alison Sandy)

PRESTON CANDOVER [SU6041]

Purefoy Arms RG25 2EJ [B3046]: Cheerful pub in attractive village, good range of sensibly priced generous food inc bargain lunches, quick friendly service, real ale, attractively laid-out restaurant; big peaceful garden with play

area overlooking fields, nearby snowdrop walks, open all day Sun (Ken and Joyce Hollis)

RINGWOOD [SU1405]

Fish BH24 2AA [off A31 W of town]: Large well divided pub with welcoming staff, wide choice of reasonably priced food, several real ales, log fire, no smoking eating area allowing children; piped music; tables on riverside lawn (traffic noise) with play area, open all day (Mrs C Osgood, LYM)

Inn on the Furlong BH24 1EY [Meeting House Lane, next to supermarket]: Long flagstoned bar, stripped brick and oak timbering, simple décor, full range of Ringwood beers from nearby brewery kept well, log fire, daily papers, basic low-priced lunchtime food from soup and sandwiches up, daytime no smoking area, conservatory dining extension; quiet piped music; open all day (cl Sun afternoon), live music Tues, Easter beer festival (Bruce Bird, Sue and Mike Todd)

ROCKBOURNE [SU1118]

☆ Rose & Thistle SP6 3NL [signed off B3078 Fordingbridge—Cranborne]: Attractive 16th-c thatched pub with popular food, real ales such as Fullers London Pride and Hampshire Strongs Best, good range of wines, attentive staff, civilised flagstoned bar with antique settles, old engravings and cricket prints, good coal fire, traditional games, log fires in front restaurant with no smoking area; may be piped classical music; children and dogs welcome, tables by thatched dovecot in neat front garden, charming tranquil spot in lovely village, good walks (Colin Chapman, Claire Hardcastle, LYM, Andy Millward)

ROCKFORD [SU1608]

Alice Lisle BH24 3NA: Big well laid-out open-plan family dining pub attractively placed on green by New Forest (can get very busy, popular with older folk wkdy lunchtimes), emphasis on big conservatory-style eating area, generous helpings of usual food from sandwiches up, changing real ales, decent wines; baby-changing facilities, garden overlooking lake with peacock and other birds, ponies wander nearby, play area and summer children's entertainment, separate adults-only garden, handy for Moyles Court (BB, Mrs Susan Hunter, Peter Titcomb)

ROMSEY [SU3523]

☆ Dukes Head SO51 0HB [A3057 out towards Stockbridge]: Attractive 16th-c dining pub festooned with flowering baskets in summer, good enterprising food (not Mon) priced in round pounds and using local ingredients, friendly French landlady who tells you how it's cooked (all fresh so may take a while), picturesque series of small linked rooms each with its own distinct and interesting décor, good house wines, real ales inc Fullers London Pride and Ringwood, big log fire; may be quiet piped music; picnic-sets out in front, nicer tables on sheltered back terrace, attractive back garden (BB, Richard Atherton, J V Dadswell, David Sizer, Mr and Mrs P Stephens, Dr L Kaufman)

☆ Three Tuns SO51 8HL [Middlebridge St (but car park signed straight off A27 bypass)]:

Good interesting bistro food inc reasonably priced up-to-date bar lunches from baguettes and baked potatoes up in attractively furnished bow-windowed pub with panelling, flagstones and some low black beams, starched table linen, Ringwood ales, espresso machine, good amiable service; piped music; children allowed at lunchtime, good tables out on back terrace *(LYM, Mr and Mrs David Lewis, W W Burke, Patrick Hall)*

ROWLAND'S CASTLE [SU7310]

☆ *Robin Hood* PO9 6AB [The Green]: Modern-style bar, light and airy, with quarry tiles, bare boards and some carpet, candles on sturdy pine and other tables, nice contemporary retro artwork, enterprising up-to-date food inc plenty of fish on most days, changing real ales such as Adnams and Marstons Old Empire, good wine choice; piped music; disabled access and facilities, picnic-sets on heated front terrace, on green of pleasant village *(BB, Jess and George Cowley, Ann and Colin Hunt, Ian Phillips)*

SELBORNE [SU7433]

☆ *Selborne Arms* GU34 3JR [High St]: Character tables, pews and deep settles made from casks on antique boards in appealing bar, twinkly landlord and friendly staff, fine changing choice of largely local real ales, sensible range of enjoyable food from baguettes up, good choice of wines by the glass (three glass sizes), nice coffee, big log fire, daily papers, no smoking carpeted dining room with lots of local photographs; plenty of tables in garden with arbour, terrace, orchard and good play area, right by walks up Hanger, and handy for Gilbert White museum *(Chantal Croneen, Michael and Judy Buckley, Michael B Griffith, BB, Ann and Colin Hunt, W A Evershed, Brian and Janet Ainscough, Val and Alan Green)*

SETLEY [SU3000]

Filly SO42 7UF [Lymington Rd (A337 Brockenhurst—Lymington)]: Cheery pub, very popular wknds for wide choice of generous enjoyable home-made food inc Sun carvery, real ales, decent wines, quick service, nice no smoking eating area (interesting front bar can get smoky at busy times); some tables outside, New Forest walks, open all day *(LYM, John and Joan Calvert, Ann and Colin Hunt, Vince Eveleigh)*

SHALDEN [SU6941]

Golden Pot GU34 4DJ [on B3349 Odiham Rd N of Alton]: Fresh and airy décor with two log fires, beamery and plenty of pine, Greene King ales, enjoyable straightforward home-made food from good baguettes up, quick friendly service even when busy, skittle alley; terrace and garden, open all day *(Martin and Karen Wake, Tony and Jill Radnor)*

SHAWFORD [SU4724]

Bridge Hotel SO21 2BP: Large cheerful beamed Chef & Brewer, several interesting rooms, smart décor, cosy nooks and corners, enjoyable promptly served food all day, real ales such as Courage Best, Greene King IPA and Ringwood Fortyniner, decent wines;

pleasant terrace and large garden with play area, downland and Itchen Way walks *(Val and Alan Green, Phyl and Jack Street, Lynn Sharpless)*

SHERFIELD ON LODDON [SU6757]

Four Horseshoes RG27 0EX: Fairly small and simple, with tasty food in dining area *(Mayur Shah)*

SHIPTON BELLINGER [SU2345]

Boot SP9 7UF [High St]: Roomy traditional pub with home-made usual food from baked potatoes to steaks *(Jason Muxworthy)*

SILCHESTER [SU6262]

Calleva Arms RG7 2PH [The Common]: Spacious cheerful bar on left with interestingly carved bench seats, two smart no smoking dining areas on right, good value food, real ales inc Fullers/Gales, good choice of wines and country wines, games room with pool, no smoking family conservatory; handy for the Roman site, sizeable attractive garden with boules and big adventure play area *(J V Dadswell)*

SOBERTON [SU6116]

☆ *White Lion* SO32 3PF [School Hill; signed off A32 S of Droxford]: Cheerful Georgian-fronted 16th-c village pub in nice spot by green, enjoyable food from good panini to Sun roast and exotic meats, real ales such as Bass, Palmers 200 and one brewed for them by Hampshire, decent house wine, genial landlord, locals and border collies, unspoilt bare-boards low-ceilinged bar with built-in wooden wall seats and traditional games, more comfortable dining lounge and rambling no smoking restaurant; children in eating areas, small sheltered pretty garden with suntrap fairy-lit terrace and covered tables, good walks nearby, open all day *(Val and Alan Green, LYM, W A Evershed, Ann and Colin Hunt)*

SOPLEY [SZ1596]

☆ *Woolpack* BH23 7AX [B3347 N of Christchurch]: Pretty thatched pub with rambling open-plan low-beamed bar, rustic furniture, woodburner and little black kitchen range, friendly helpful staff, enjoyable food from sandwiches and ploughman's to steaks and Sun roasts, Flowers Original, Ringwood Best and Wadworths 6X, good house wine, no smoking conservatory; piped music, bustling Fri/Sat night; children in eating areas, charming garden, picnic-sets under weeping willows, stream with ducks and footbridges, open all day *(Brian Root, LYM, Mrs Pat Crabb, Glenwys and Alan Lawrence)*

SOUTHAMPTON [SU4111]

☆ *Duke of Wellington* SO14 2AH [Bugle St (or walk along city wall from Bar Gate)]: Ancient timber-framed building on 13th-c foundations, bare boards, log fire, friendly relaxed atmosphere, appealing enthusiastic landlord and really helpful service, full Wadworths ale range kept well and reasonably priced, good choice of wines by the glass, good varied bar food (not Sun evening), no smoking back area welcoming children (locals' front bar can get smoky); very handy for Tudor House Museum, open all day *(D J and P M Taylor, Val and*

Alan Green, Pam and John Smith)

Ship SO15 0NN [Old Redbridge Rd]: Fine unspoilt 15th-c building, a big surprise in the surrounding urban sprawl – heavy beams, panelling, some stripped brick, inglenook fireplaces, maritime memorabilia, enjoyable interesting food, friendly staff, changing real ales; picnic-sets out on cobbled terrace *(Prof and Mrs Tony Palmer)*

Standing Order SO14 2DF [High St]: Friendly efficient Wetherspoons with cosy corners (strange and intriguing collection of books in one), civilised atmosphere, their usual reasonably priced food, five good beers inc interesting guests, helpful efficient young staff, no smoking area *(Val and Alan Green)*

SOUTHSEA [SZ6498]

5th Hampshire Volunteer Arms PO5 2SL [Albert Rd]: Friendly two-bar backstreet local, Fullers/Gales ales and guests such as Greene King Abbot, old photographs of the regiment's members, good juke box; open all day *(R M Corlett, the Didler, Tony Hobden)*

Eldon Arms PO5 4BS [Eldon St/Norfolk St]: Well worn-in rambling tavern with half a dozen or more changing real ales and lots to look at – old pictures and advertisements, attractive mirrors, bric-a-brac and shelves of books, friendly service, lunchtime food (not Sat); sensibly placed darts, games machine; tables in back garden *(Ann and Colin Hunt)*

Hole in the Wall PO5 3BY [Gt Southsea St]: Small friendly and relaxed local in old part of town, with several changing real ales inc local Oakleaf and Southwyk, three farm ciders, speciality sausages and substantial home-made pies with mash (not Sun evening); can get smoky when crowded (there is a no smoking area), plans for live music; cl till 4 exc Fri, open all day wknds *(Mrs Maricar Jagger, R M Corlett, Jonathan Martin)*

Red White & Blue PO4 0DW [Fawcett Rd]: Busy open-plan corner local, Fullers/Gales ales, food till 5 (not Sun); games nights, often live bands wknd and monthly jazz night, can be smoky; open all day *(the Didler, Colin Moore)*

SOUTHWICK [SU6208]

Golden Lion PO17 6EB [High St; just off B2177 on Portsdown Hill]: Clean and welcoming local with large well worn bar and smarter lounge, good value simple food from good baguettes to Sun lunch, Fullers ESB and Hop Back Odyssey, friendly staff, antique pine, pleasant restaurant; where Eisenhower and Montgomery came before D-Day, picturesque estate village with scenic walks *(Val and Alan Green)*

Red Lion PO17 6EF [High St]: Hospitable low-beamed village pub, mainly no smoking, with wide choice of generous enjoyable food from good baguettes up inc substantial proper pies, Fullers/Gales ales, good choice of wines by the glass, prompt service from smart staff; good walks *(Bruce and Penny Wilkie, Lynn Sharpless, Ann and Colin Hunt)*

ST MARY BOURNE [SU4250]

George SP11 6BG: Comfortable and sociable brick-built village pub with Badger real ales

and good wines by the glass, attentive cordial service, pleasant bar eating area and attractively lit restaurant, enjoyable food inc good Sun carvery; tables outside, attractive village *(Mrs Viv Kington, Phil and Sally Gorton)*

STEEP [SU7325]

Cricketers GU32 2DW [Church Rd]: Reopened after light and airy refurbishment, some emphasis on good choice of generous hearty food inc fresh fish, real ales and decent wines, pine furniture and lots of cricket prints; picnic-sets on back lawn, comfortable good value bedrooms *(Andy Hedges)*

STOCKBRIDGE [SU3535]

☆ *Three Cups* SO20 6HB [High St]: Distinctive coaching inn dating from 1500, low-beamed bar, various country paraphernalia such as fishing gear, guns and taxidermy, Fagins, Gales, Ringwood and a guest beer, friendly atmosphere, bar food from baguettes up, no smoking evening restaurant; can be quite a wait for food when it's busy; cottage garden and streamside terrace, bedrooms, open all day *(James Price, Dennis Jenkin, John Coatsworth, LYM, Geoffrey Kemp, Ron Shelton, Mrs Angela Bromley-Martin, John and Julie Moon, Pam and David Bailey, Dr and Mrs A K Clarke, Alex and Irene Harvey, Patrick Hall, Edward Mirzoeff)*

☆ *White Hart* SO20 6HF [High St; A272/A3057 roundabout]: Roomy and welcoming divided bar, attractive décor with antique prints, oak pews and other seats, prompt friendly service, enjoyable freshly made food from sandwiches and delicious crispy baguettes up, Fullers and Gales ales, good coffee, decent wines and country wines, comfortable beamed restaurant with blazing log fire (children allowed); disabled access and facilities, dogs welcome (biscuits and water), tables in garden with terrace, bedrooms, open all day *(John and Joan Calvert, LYM, Fr Robert Marsh, John Balfour, Peter Neate, Stephen and Jean Curtis, GHC, Helen and Brian Edgeley)*

STRATFIELD SAYE [SU6861]

☆ *New Inn* RG7 2EH [signed off A33 Basingstoke—Reading; Bramley Rd]: Several semi-divided areas inc lounge with log fire in big fireplace, nice prints and plates, Badger and guest ales, welcoming service, interesting food choice, may be free bar nibbles; children welcome, attractive garden with play area, good barbecues, pleasant surroundings *(Pat and Robert Watt)*

SWANMORE [SU5815]

Rising Sun SO32 2PS [Hill Pound; off B2177 S of Bishops Waltham]: Affable new landlord, friendly efficient staff and thriving atmosphere in comfortably updated tile-hung pub with low beams, scrubbed pine, well separated partly stripped brick dining area, enjoyable generous food inc imaginative dishes, Bass, Greene King Old Speckled Hen, Marstons Pedigree and Ringwood Best, good range of wines by the glass, good log fires; pleasant side garden with play area, handy for Kings Way long distance path – best to head W (Val and Alan Green, Ann and Colin Hunt, Phyl and Jack Street)

SWANWICK [SU5109]

Elm Tree SO31 7DX [Swanwick Lane, off A3051 not far from M27 junction 9]: Comfortably unpretentious and friendly, with two bars and dining area, wide choice of enjoyable home-made food, helpful staff, Courage Best and Directors and Fullers London Pride; children welcome, tables in garden, handy for Hampshire Wildlife Reserve (Val and Alan Green, Charles and Pauline Stride)

SWAY [SZ2898]

Hare & Hounds SO41 6AL [Durns Town, just off B3055 SW of Brockenhurst]: Bright and airy comfortable New Forest family dining pub, lots of children, good value enjoyable fresh food, real ales inc Ringwood and Wessex, cheerful and enthusiastic young staff, log fires; dogs welcome, picnic-sets and play frame in good-sized neatly kept garden, open all day Sat (Brian Root, LYM, A D Lealan)

TANGLEY [SU3252]

☆ *Cricketers Arms* SP11 0SH [towards the Chutes]: Good local ales tapped from the cask and good value food from fresh baguettes to enterprising light and main dishes, hospitable landlord and good staff, relaxed atmosphere, character small front bar with tiled floor, massive inglenook log fire, bar billiards, friendly black labradors (Pots and Harvey), bistro-ish back flagstoned extension with a one-table alcove off, some good cricketing prints; dogs welcome, tables on neat terrace, good Nordic-style back bedroom block, unspoilt countryside (I A Herdman, LYM)

THRUXTON [SU2945]

White Horse SP11 8EE [Mullens Pond, just off A303 eastbound]: Attractive and relaxed 16th-c thatched pub rather dwarfed by A303 embankment, soft lighting, very low beams, horse-racing décor, log fire, nice staff, enjoyable food, good wines by the glass, real ales such as Fullers London Pride and Greene King IPA, separate dining area (Jim and Janet Brown)

TIMSBURY [SU3325]

☆ *Bear & Ragged Staff* SO51 0LB [A3057 towards Stockbridge; pub marked on OS Sheet 185 map ref 334254]: Well run chain roadside dining pub with wide blackboard choice of reliable food all day, friendly efficient service, real ales such as Ringwood Best and Wadworths 6X, lots of wines by the glass, log fire, good-sized beamed interior; children in eating area, tables in extended garden with good play area, handy for Mottisfont, good walks (Alec and Barbara Jones, Phyl and Jack Street, LYM, Lynn Sharpless, Mrs T A Bizat)

Malthouse SO51 0NG [A3057 N of village]: Spacious roadside family pub, very popular in good weather for its secluded lawn and terrace, pretty fishpond, barbecue house and big well equipped play area; fireside leather sofas in pleasant lounge area, real ales such as Gales, Ringwood and Wadworths from central bar, conservatory-style dining areas, wide choice of

decent blackboard food (best to book wknds); nr fine Norman church, pleasant paths to Michelmersh (Phyl and Jack Street, J Stickland)

TITCHFIELD [SU5305]

Bugle PO14 4RT [the Sq, off A27 nr Fareham]: Roomy and comfortable family pub, part flagstone, part carpet, popular good value bar food, friendly efficient service, several real ales, restaurant in old barn behind; dogs welcome, attractive village handy for Titchfield Haven nature reserve, fine walk by former canal to coast, bedrooms (Ann and Colin Hunt)

Fishermans Rest PO15 5RA [Mill Lane, off A27 at Titchfield Abbey]: Busy no smoking pub/restaurant with wide choice of good value fresh food (can take a while), Gales HSB, Greene King IPA and Old Speckled Hen, Ringwood Best and Wadworths 6X, cheerful staff, two log fires (not always lit), daily papers, fishing memorabilia, no music or machines; fine riverside position opp Titchfield Abbey, tables out behind overlooking water, open all day (Ann and Colin Hunt, LYM, Val and Alan Green)

Queens Head PO14 4AQ [High St; off A27 nr Fareham]: Ancient pub with good value straightforward food esp fish cooked by friendly landlord, good fresh veg, four changing real ales, reasonable prices, interesting smallish 1930s-feel bar with old local pictures, window seats and central brick fireplace, small attractive dining room; bar can get smoky; picnic-sets in prettily planted small back yard, bedrooms, pleasant conservation village nr nature reserve and walks to coast (Ann and Colin Hunt, A and B D Craig)

☆ *Titchfield Mill* PO15 5RF [A27, junction with Mill Lane]: Large popular Vintage Inn catering well for families in neatly kept converted watermill on River Meon, olde-worlde room off main bar, smarter dining room, upstairs gallery, stripped beams and interesting old machinery, friendly efficient service, Bass and Courage Best, good choice of wines by the glass, freshly squeezed orange juice; piped music; open all day, sunny terrace by mill stream with two waterwheels – food not served out here (Peter and Audrey Dowsett, Ann and Colin Hunt, Stephen Moss, Jess and George Cowley, Phyl and Jack Street)

TOTFORD [SU5737]

Woolpack SO24 9TJ [B3046 Basingstoke—Alresford]: Handy roadside pub, friendly and relaxing, with three real ales inc Palmers Best, open fire and flowers on tables in stripped-brick bar, large separate dining room, decent food inc good Sun roast; tables out by small pond, lovely setting in good walking country, bedrooms (Ann and Colin Hunt)

TURGIS GREEN [SU6959]

☆ *Jekyll & Hyde* RG27 0AX [A33 Reading—Basingstoke]: Bustling rambling pub with nice mix of furniture and village atmosphere in black-beamed and flagstoned bar, prompt cheerful service, Badger Best and IPA and Wadworths 6X, some interesting prints, blazing fire, daily papers, larger stepped-up three-room dining area with popular-priced food from sandwiches up all day inc breakfast, children's helpings (they are welcome); piped music; disabled facilities, lots of picnic-sets in good sheltered garden (some traffic noise) with terrace, play area and various games, bedrooms *(Michael Dandy, LYM, R C Livesey, Richard and Margaret, Martin and Karen Wake, John and Fiona Merritt)*

TWYFORD [SU4824]

Phoenix SO21 1RF [High St]: Cheerful open-plan local with lots of prints, bric-a-brac and big end inglenook log fire, friendly landlord and attentive staff, Greene King ales, decent wines, step up to no smoking dining area, side skittle alley; unobtrusive piped music; children allowed at one end lunchtime, garden *(Lynn Sharpless, Ann and Colin Hunt, David Coleman, Phyl and Jack Street)*

☆ **UPHAM** [SU5320]

Brushmakers Arms SO32 1JJ [off Winchester—Bishops Waltham downs rd; Shoe Lane]: Charming low-beamed L-shaped village pub under new landlord summer 2006 (too late for us to form any impression), has been very popular, with sensibly priced food, real ales such as Hampshire Brush and Uncle Bob, Ringwood Best and Charles Wells Bombardier, traditional games; children and dogs have been welcome, big well stocked tree-shaded garden with sheltered back terrace, good walks nearby; reports on new regime please *(LYM)*

UPPER CLATFORD [SU3543]

Crook & Shears SP11 7QL [off A343 S of Andover, via Foundry Rd]: Cosy two-bar 17th-c thatched pub, several homely olde-worlde seating areas, bare boards and panelling, good changing ale range, decent food from doorstep sandwiches up, woodburner, small dining room, back skittle alley with own bar; pleasant secluded garden behind *(Phyl and Jack Street, the Didler, N R White)*

UPTON [SU3555]

Crown SP11 0JS [N of Hurstbourne Tarrant]: Wide choice of consistently enjoyable fresh food in interesting evening dishes in friendly and attractive pub, linked rooms with pine tables and chairs, a pleasant modicum of sporting prints, horse tack and so forth, good log fires, good service, Fullers London Pride and Ringwood Best, good coffee, happy bustling atmosphere; may be piped music in public bar; conservatory, small garden and terrace, lovely walks *(J D G Isherwood, BB, Mrs Pat Crabb)*

WALHAMPTON [SZ3396]

Towles SO41 5RE [B3054 NE of Lymington; aka Walhampton Inn]: Large friendly roadhouse in rambling Georgian-style building with emphasis on enjoyable restaurant food inc reasonably priced carvery in raftered former stables and two adjoining areas, pleasant lounge on right, Fullers and Gales ales, good service; attractive courtyard, good walks nearby inc Solent Way, open all day *(Phyl and Jack Street)*

WALTHAM CHASE [SU5616]

Chase SO32 2LL [B2177]: Friendly young couple running two-bar pub with Greene King ales and a guest such as Hidden Quest, reasonably priced generous food, no smoking eating area *(Val and Alan Green)*

WARSASH [SU4906]

Ferryman SO31 9HX [Warsash Rd]: Real ales such as Gales, Loddon Ferrymans Gold, Ringwood and Charles Wells Bombardier in lively pub popular with young people, pleasant young staff, restaurant; games machines, some live music *(Simon Marley)*

Rising Sun SO31 9FT [Shore Rd; OS Sheet 196 map ref 489061]: Boating atmosphere in picture-window waterside pub, nautical charts and D-Day naval memorabilia, fine Hamble estuary views esp from summer restaurant up the spiral stairs, Greene King and Ringwood ales, enjoyable food, helpful friendly staff, long bar part tiled-floor and part boards, no smoking dining area; estuary walks, handy for Hook nature reserve *(Simon Marley)*

WELL [SU7646]

Chequers RG29 1TL [off A287 via Crondall, or A31 via Froyle and Lower Froyle]: Cosily low-beamed tavern with roaring log fire, panelled walls with 18th-c country-life prints and old sepia photographs, pews, brocaded stools and a few GWR carriage lamps, Badger beers and no smoking restaurant; recent management changes – we hope it's now settling down; picnic-sets on vine-covered terrace and in spacious back garden *(LYM, Janet Whittaker)*

WEST END [SU4714]

Southampton Arms SO30 2HG [Moorgreen Rd, off B3035]: Sizeable city-edge pub firmly run by friendly landlady, Ringwood ales, enjoyable reasonably priced food, comfortable and cosy bar, attractive conservatory restaurant; good garden *(Phyl and Jack Street)*

WEST MEON [SU6424]

Thomas Lord GU32 1LN [High St]: Pleasant layout with sofa by log fire on right, plenty of dining tables, cricket prints and memorabilia inc odd cricket match played by stuffed weasels and stoats, enjoyable fresh food from good sandwiches up, Bass, Greene King Abbot and Ringwood Best, good farm ciders, wines and coffee in great variety, cheerful service; unobtrusive piped jazz; picnic-sets in sheltered side garden, good walks W of village *(Ann and Colin Hunt, BB, Prof and Mrs Tony Palmer, W A Evershed)*

WHITCHURCH [SU4648]

Prince Regent RG28 7LT [London Rd]: Unpretentious L-shaped alehouse with Hop Back Summer Lightning, Otter and Stonehenge Pigswill, chatty locals, cards, piano, pool, valley view from back window; open all day *(Pete Baker)*

☆ *Red House* RG28 7LH [London St]: Very popular for landlord/chef's good daily-changing choice of food from home-baked baguettes and generous bar lunches to leaner more modern evening cuisine, in cheerful and chatty compact dining area up a step on right (big mirrored arches making it seem more extensive), sturdy tables on woodstrip flooring, a few big prints, friendly efficient service under on-the-ball landlady, Itchen Valley and guest beers, decent house wines, some very low beams, good log fire; separate traditional flagstoned public bar with juke box and TV; children welcome, tables on attractive back terraces with play area, own menu and hatch service *(Lynn Sharpless, Pete Baker, Jennifer Banks, BB, Guy Consterdine)*

WHITSBURY [SU1219]

Cartwheel SP6 3PZ [off A338 or A354 SW of Salisbury]: Welcoming and comfortable tucked-away pub with enjoyable food (not Mon evening), Ringwood ales, pitched high rafters in one part, lower beams elsewhere, snug little side areas, no smoking dining room; may be piped music, special events May-Dec; children welcome, garden with play area, open all day Sun *(LYM, Len and Di Bright, Peter Titcomb)*

WHITWAY [SU4559]

☆ *Carnarvon Arms* RG20 9LE [off A34 S of Newbury at Highclere Castle signs; Winchester Rd]: Roadside pub recently reworked in simple good taste, real ale, good choice of wines by the glass and leather sofas and armchairs on woodstrip floor in smart modern bar, enjoyable food from good choice of bar dishes to interesting if not cheap restaurant meals, raftered dining room with Victorian-style furnishings and big oriental rugs; neat comfortable modern bedrooms, handy for Sandham Memorial Chapel and Highclere Castle *(John and Rosemary Haynes)*

WINCHESTER [SU4728]

Bell SO23 9RE [St Cross Rd]: Unpretentious local giving more space over to its enjoyable freshly cooked food inc good value paninis, friendly helpful landlord, Greene King IPA and Old Speckled Hen and a guest such as Titanic White Star, decent wines by the glass, liner pictures in comfortable lounge, public bar and new sectioned-off dining area; big pleasant walled garden with swing and slide, handy for St Cross Hospital (ancient monument, not a hospital), lovely water meadows walk from centre *(David Carr, Lynn Sharpless, Val and Alan Green)*

☆ *Eclipse* SO23 9EX [The Square, between High St and cathedral]: Picturesque 14th-c local nicely cleaned up under good current landlord, massive 14th-c beams and timbers, oak settles, two small cheerful rooms, four real ales inc Fullers London Pride and Hampshire King Alfred, decent choice of wines by the glass, good choice of good value generous fresh lunchtime bar food; children in no smoking

back area, seats outside, very handy for cathedral *(A and B D Craig, Val and Alan Green, LYM, Ann and Colin Hunt)*

Old Gaol House SO23 8RZ [Jewry St]: Big very popular Wetherspoons with large no smoking area, food all day, good choice of local and other beers, low prices, no piped music; children welcome *(John Oates, Denise Walton, Tim and Ann Newell, Ann and Colin Hunt, Craig Turnbull)*

Old Vine SO23 9HA [Great Minster St]: Light and airy refurbishment opp cathedral, all no smoking, with local and other ales such as Timothy Taylors Landlord, full food choice from good soup and sandwiches up, good tables and chairs on oak boards *(Margaret McPhee)*

Royal Oak SO23 9AU [Royal Oak Passage, off upper end of pedestrian part of High St opp St Thomas St]: Otherwise standard pub with Greene King ales and usual food, notable for the no smoking cellar bar (not always open) whose massive 12th-c beams and Saxon wall give it some claim to be the country's oldest drinking spot; piped music, games machines, packed with young people Fri/Sat nights *(the Didler, Ian and Nita Cooper, LYM, Ann and Colin Hunt, Val and Alan Green, D J and P M Taylor)*

WOLVERTON [SU5658]

George & Dragon RG26 5ST [Towns End; just N of A339 Newbury—Basingstoke]: Comfortable rambling open-plan beamed and timbered pub with wide choice of enjoyable food, range of beers, decent wines, helpful service, log fires, pleasant dining area, no piped music, skittle alley; no children in bar; large garden with small terrace, bedrooms *(J V Dadswell, Jennifer Banks)*

WOODGREEN [SU1717]

☆ *Horse & Groom* SP6 2AS [off A338 N of Fordingbridge]: Nicely set New Forest pub with comfortably relaxed linked beamed rooms around servery, nature photographs, log fire in pretty Victorian fireplace, Badger ales, good choice of good value home-cooked food, friendly landlord; picnic-sets on front terrace and in spreading back garden *(Kevin Flack, LYM, A and B D Craig, Phyl and Jack Street)*

YATELEY [SU8160]

Dog & Partridge GU46 7LR [Reading Rd (B3272)]: Three or four changing real ales, a couple of farm ciders and Feb and Sept beer festivals in cheerful two-bar local with bar food, log fires, darts, pool and board games; sports TVs, juke box; children and dogs welcome, disabled access, bedrooms, open all day *(Anon)*

Real ale may be served from handpumps, electric pumps (not just the on-off switches used for keg beer) or – common in Scotland – tall taps called founts (pronounced 'fonts') where a separate pump pushes the beer up under air pressure.

Herefordshire

A couple of new entries here this year: the New Harp, beautifully set in the quiet village of Hoarwithy, reopened not long ago as a splendid country pub, appealing all round; and the Mill Race at Walford, another good reopening, successfully mixing old and very up-to-date both in its general style and in the food which is perhaps its main emphasis. The county does really well for pub food. Other more or less foody pubs which are currently on spanking form include the friendly Riverside Inn at Aymestrey (a lovely place to stay in), the peaceful Cottage of Content at Carey, the handsome Feathers in Ledbury (the dining bar has been well reworked, and a new chef is proving popular), the Three Horseshoes at Little Cowarne (the welcoming licensees base their home cooking on a strong network of fruitful local contacts), the unspoilt-feeling Crown & Anchor at Lugwardine, the Lough Pool at Sellack (the newish people have settled in really well, using local produce for their interesting food), the Stagg at Titley (a model country dining pub – gaining one of our Place to Stay Awards this year), the Three Crowns at Ullingswick (another top-notch dining pub, which now has a bedroom), and the Wellington (good value, whether you go for the bargain bar dishes, the lunchtime deals, or a more elaborate candlelit restaurant meal). For the second year running, the Stagg at Titley takes the top title of Herefordshire Dining Pub of the Year. However, it's certainly worth saying that in almost any other county several of the other pubs mentioned above would have an excellent claim to that Dining Pub title; at this top level, Herefordshire pub food really is rather special. Just as food, at whatever price level, seems generally to be fair value, drinks prices too are rather below the national average here. The cheapest beer we found was in the quirky Victory in Hereford, brewing its own. In other pubs, the beer we found cropping up most often as the cheapest on offer was another local brew, Wye Valley. A final note: in the Lucky Dip section at the end of the chapter, we'd like to draw attention particularly to the Hostelrie at Goodrich and the Olde Tavern in Kington, with a good few starred pubs to look out for too.

AYMESTREY   SO4265   Map 6
Riverside Inn   🍴   🍷   🛏

A4110, at N end of village, W of Leominster; HR6 9ST

In beautiful semi-wooded scenery, this is a lovely spot to stay, and the position by a double-arched bridge over the River Lugg is much enjoyed by readers – picnic-sets make the most of the view, and there are rustic tables and benches up above in a steep tree-sheltered garden. The rambling beamed bar has several cosy areas and the décor is drawn from a pleasant mix of periods and styles, with fine antique oak tables and chairs, stripped pine country kitchen tables, fresh flowers, hops strung from a ceiling wagon-wheel, horse tack and nice pictures; the eating areas are no smoking. Warm log fires in winter, while in summer big overflowing flower pots frame the entrances; fairly quiet piped pop music. Three beers from Woods and Wye Valley on handpump, two local farm ciders and more than 20 malt whiskies. The landlord likes to talk to his customers and service is good. Enjoyable food, with many ingredients locally sourced, includes freshly made baguettes (from £4.50) and ploughman's (from £5.50) as well as starters such as soup (£3.75), baked flat field mushrooms with Ragstone goats cheese, toasted pine nuts and balsamic dressing (£4.75) or cornish mussels in red wine and tomato sauce (£5.25), and main lunchtime courses like home-made beef lasagne (£7.25), cod in local ale batter with home-made chips (£8.95), confit of gressingham duck leg (£10.95) or rib-eye steak (£10.95); the evening menu is more elaborate with such items as supreme of chicken wrapped in local smoked bacon, stuffed with apricots and pistachios (£13.95), roasted rack of local lamb on parsnip chips with mint jus (£16.95) and fillet of local beef with smooth chicken liver pâté (£19.95). It does get busy at weekends, so booking would be wise. Residents can try fly-fishing on the river. *(Recommended by Tracey and Stephen Groves, Graham and Glenis Watkins, Rob Winstanley, Ian Stafford, B P Abrahams, Pam and David Bailey, Brian Wainwright, Guy Vowles, R M Corlett, J Jennings, Tony and Sally Hope)*

Free house ~ Licensees Richard and Liz Gresko ~ Real ale ~ Bar food (12-2.15, 7-9 Mon-Sat; 12-2.30, 6.30-8.30 Sun) ~ Restaurant ~ (01568) 708440 ~ Children welcome ~ Dogs welcome ~ Open 11-4, 6-11; 11-4, 6.30-10.30 Sun; closed Sun evening and Mon in winter ~ Bedrooms: £40B/£65B

BODENHAM SO5454 Map 4
Englands Gate
Just off A417 at Bodenham turn-off, about 6 miles S of Leominster; HR1 3HU

Thoroughly comfortable in feel, this half-timbered 16th-c coaching inn has a rambling, open-plan interior that looks every year of its age. It has a vast central stone chimneypiece, heavy brown beams and joists in low ochre ceilings, blazing fires, well worn flagstones, sturdy timber props, one or two steps, and lantern-style lighting. One nice corner has a comfortably worn leather settee and high-backed settle with scatter cushions; a cosy partly stripped-stone room has a long stripped table that would be just right for a party of eight; a lighter upper area with flowers on its tables has winged settles painted a cheery yellow or aquamarine. Decent bar food at lunchtime includes sandwiches (from £3.50; baguettes £4.75), chilli con carne or mushroom ravioli glazed in parmesan and herbs (£5.95), green thai king prawn curry or spicy cumberland sausage on mustard mash with onion gravy (£6.95) and deep-fried cod in beer batter (£8.50), with evening choices such as soup (£3.50), smoked salmon and herbed cream cheese roulade (£5.25), spinach and wild mushroom lasagne (£7.95), roasted marinated chicken breast (£10.75), baked salmon in filo pastry (£10.95) and individual fillet of beef wellington with tarragon and port sauce (£18.95); specials might include smoked fish platter or sausages and mash (£7.95), steak and Guinness pie (£8.95) and roast breast of guinea fowl (£9.95). Woods Shropshire Lad, Wye Valley Bitter and Butty Bach plus a guest such as Thwaites Thoroughbred on handpump, and they hold a beer and sausage festival in July; local wine, seven wines by the glass and malt whiskies; friendly staff; piped mellow pop music and TV; monthly quiz night for charity in winter; the bar area is no smoking. There are tables out in an attractive garden. More reports please. *(Recommended by Dr Michael Smith, Ken Millar, Pamela and Merlyn Horswell, Norman Lewis, Mr and Mrs J Tout)*

Free house ~ Licensee Evelyn McNeil ~ Real ale ~ Bar food (12-2.30, 6-9.30; 12-3 Sun; not Sun evening) ~ Restaurant ~ (01568) 797286 ~ Children welcome in dining area until 9pm ~ Dogs allowed in bar ~ Open 11-11(12 Thurs, Sat); 12-11 Sun

BRIMFIELD SO5368 Map 4
Roebuck Inn ⊕ ♀ ⇐
Village signposted just off A49 Shrewsbury—Leominster; SY8 4NE

You might find locals drinking and playing dominoes and cribbage by an impressive inglenook fireplace in the opened-out front bar of this smart dining pub (which has comfortable bedrooms). This bar merges into a light, contemporary-looking area, done in beige, green and cream colours, with a big bay window; TV, piped music. Pale oak panelling in the 15th-c no smoking lounge bar makes for a quietly relaxed atmosphere. There's also a brightly decorated cane-furnished dining room (also no smoking). At lunchtime, snacks might include sandwiches (£3.50) and platters with assorted cheeses, home-cooked ham or beef (£5.95). A more elaborate menu (available lunchtime or in the evening) includes items such as artichoke filled with field and wild mushrooms, shallots and cream (£5), smoked chicken and raspberry salad (£5.50), seared scallops (£6.50; £11 as a main course), chicken breast wrapped with parma ham on a bed of mediterranean vegetables (£9.95), and fillet steak with oyster mushroom and cognac sauce (£17.50), together with specials like bass on summer vegetable risotto (£12); puddings feature chocolate pudding, lemon tart or bread and butter pudding (all £5). Banks's and one or two guests such as Black Sheep or Marstons are on handpump. Seats are placed out on the enclosed terrace. As we went to press the pub's lease was about to be offered to a new landlord; reports on the new regime, please. *(Recommended by Mr and Mrs C W Widdowson, Chris Flynn, Wendy Jones, W H and E Thomas, Pam and Alan Neale, Rodney and Norma Stubington, Bernard Stradling, Elizabeth Carnie, Leo and Barbara Lionet)*

Union Pub Company ~ Lease Steve O'Donoghue ~ Real ale ~ Bar food (12-2.30(2 Sun), 6.9.30; not Sun evening) ~ Restaurant ~ (01584) 711230 ~ Children in eating area of bar and restaurant ~ Dogs allowed in bar and bedrooms ~ Open 11.30-3, 6.30-11; 12-3, 7-10.30 Sun ~ Bedrooms: £50B/£80B

CAREY   SO5631   Map 4
Cottage of Content
Village signposted from good back road betweeen Ross-on-Wye and Hereford E of A49, through Hoarwithy; HR2 6NG

Well tucked away in the countryside, this is an appealingly cottagey haven with a distinctly rustic character, and the recent addition of bedrooms prompted one local reader to comment, 'wish it was further away, then we might be able to stay there'. Country furnishings feature prominently, with stripped pine kitchen chairs, long pews by one big table, and various old-fashioned tables on flagstones, beams, prints and bare boards. Bar food includes lunchtime snacks such as soup (£3.95), filled baguettes and ciabattas (from £5.25), filled baked potatoes (from £6.50) and ploughman's (from £6.95), together with lasagne (£8.25), grilled supreme of salmon with chorizo sausage (£8.75), steak and kidney pie or chicken breast stuffed with brie and bacon (£9.25) and sirloin steak (£11.95); à la carte items, available in the restaurant or bar, change several times a week and might include chicken liver pâté with red onion jam (£5.25), fried bass with saffron and garden herb risotto (£12.25) and fillet of herefordshire beef on celeriac remoulade (£15.50). Hook Norton Best and Wye Valley Bitter on handpump and in summer they usually have a guest or two such as Whittingtons Nine Lives as well as farm cider; piped music. There are picnic-sets on the flower-filled front terrace, plus a couple more on a back terrace (they are hoping to build a conservatory on this). We would welcome reports from readers who have stayed here. *(Recommended by Mike and Mary Carter, Dr Michael Smith, Steve Bailey, the Didler, Alec and Joan Laurence)*

Free house ~ Licensee Svenia Wolf ~ Real ale ~ Bar food ~ Restaurant ~ (01432) 840242 ~ Children welcome ~ Dogs allowed in bar and bedrooms ~ Open 11.30-2.30, 6.30-11; 12-3 Sun; closed Sun evening and Mon ~ Bedrooms: £40B/£64B

DORSTONE   SO3141   Map 6
Pandy
Pub signed off B4348 E of Hay-on-Wye; HR3 6AN

Opposite the village green, this pretty half-timbered pub in the attractive Golden Valley can trace its roots to 1185, when it was reputedly built to house workers constructing Dorstone church in an act of atonement for one Richard de Brito for his part in plotting the murder of Thomas Becket. The neatly kept homely main room (on the right as you go in) has heavy beams in the ochre ceiling, stout timbers, upright chairs on its broad worn flagstones and in its various alcoves, and a vast open fireplace with logs; a side extension has been kept more or less in character. Home-made bar food includes lunchtime baguettes and focaccias with chips (£4.50) and ploughman's (£7.70), as well as soup (£3.95), smoked salmon with honey mustard and dill sauce (£5.50), thai butternut squash, pineapple and green bean curry (£8.95), fish pie (£9.95), lamb shank with redcurrant and rosemary gravy (£10.95), and puddings like blackberry and apple cobbler or chocolate truffle torte (£3.95); also pizzas and a children's menu, and half portions are available. Wye Valley Butty Bach and a guest such as St Austells Tribute are on handpump; quite a few malt whiskies, farm cider in summer, and decent wines; board games, quoits and piped music. The handsome red setter is Apache, and the neat side garden has picnic-sets and a play area. *(Recommended by Mrs Phoebe A Kemp, Sue Demont, Tim Barrow, Guy Vowles, MLR, Pam and David Bailey, the Didler, R Michael Richards, Ryta Lyndley, Dennis and Gill Keen, G W H Kerby, Ken Marshall)*

Free house ~ Licensees Bill and Magdalena Gannon ~ Real ale ~ Bar food ~ (01981) 550273 ~ Children welcome until 9pm ~ Dogs allowed in bar ~ Open 12-3, 6-11.30; 12-11.30 Sat; 12-4, 6-10.30 Sun; closed Mon lunchtime, all day Mon in winter

HEREFORD SO5139 Map 6

Victory 🍺 £

St Owen Street, opposite fire station; HR1 2QD

Be prepared for a surprise as you enter this home-brew city pub, as its exterior gives no hint of its extraordinary nautical décor. The counter re-creates a miniature galleon complete with cannon poking out of its top, and down a companionway the long back room is well decked out as the inside of a man o' war: dark wood, rigging and netting everywhere, benches along sides that curve towards a front fo'c'sle, stanchions and ropes forming an upper crow's nest, and appropriate lamps. The focus is very much on beer: the Spinning Dog brewery based here produces Herefordshire Light Ale, Herefordshire Old Bull, Herefordshire Organic Bitter, Mutleys Dark, Mutleys Revenge, Mutleys Springer and Mutts Nutts – they usually have six on handpump plus a couple of guest beers such as Corvedale Normans Pride, and three farmhouse ciders and a perry (also on handpump). Straightforward bar food (which may not always be available) includes sandwiches (from £2.50), chilli con carne or chicken curry (£5), ploughman's or fish of the day (£5.50) and 8oz steak (£6), with specials such as faggots, mash and peas (£5.50); they do a curry night on Friday. Service is friendly and informal (they'll show you around the brewery if they're not busy). Juke box (can be very loud), piped music, darts, fruit machine, TV, skittle alley, table skittles, board games and a back pool table; the bar area is no smoking. The garden has a pagoda, climbing plants and some seats. More reports please. *(Recommended by Gill and Tony Morriss)*

Own brew ~ Licensee James Kenyon ~ Real ale ~ Bar food (12-6 Weds-Sat, 12-5 Sun; not Mon, Tues) ~ Restaurant (Sun only) ~ No credit cards ~ (01432) 342125 ~ Children welcome ~ Dogs welcome ~ Live band Sat ~ Open 12(11 Sat)-12

HOARWITHY SO5429 Map 4

New Harp 🍷 🍺

Village signposted off A49 Hereford—Ross-on-Wye; HR2 6QH

Reopened after being closed for some years, this is now a delightful country pub, beautifully placed in a quiet village. Bow windows look up the hill to a remarkable italianate Victorian church with a tall tower, and the little stream which runs through the pretty tree-sheltered garden soon meets the nearby River Wye. There are plenty of picnic-sets, some on decking in a sort of arbour, and in summer they have barbecues. It's right on the new Herefordshire Trail (good walking, with a campsite close by). Inside, it's been completely reworked in a refreshing contemporary style, with brown leather tub armchairs in front of a woodburning stove, a mix of comfortable dining chairs around individual tables, stone floor tiling and stripped masonry in one wall, but mainly crisp off-white paintwork with nicely lit modern artwork, including cartoons and caricatures. The bar angles round to a cosy dining room, and the atmosphere is relaxed and welcoming throughout, with nicely informal service. The good blackboard food, carefully cooked and attractively presented, uses as much Herefordshire produce as possible, including organic vegetables from nearby Carey, with fresh fish from Brixham on Tuesday evenings. Besides good sandwiches (from £4.75, they cure their own ham and make their own chutneys), food might include soup (£3.95), smoked salmon and asparagus with hollandaise (£5.95), ploughman's with a pork pie (£6.50), filo basket filled with roast pepper and aubergine and topped with goats cheese (£8.95), herb-crusted sea trout (£11.50), chicken with wild mushroom and tarragon and white wine sauce (£11.75), rack of lamb on spring broth (£12.95), and puddings such as chocolate brownie with Jack Daniels milkshake and vanilla ice-cream (£4.95). They have three or four changing real ales on handpump such as Bath Gem, Hop Back Summer Lightning and St Austell Tribute, a growing collecting of unusual bottled beers, good Broome Farm ciders and perhaps perries, an interesting range of sensibly priced wines, and an enterprising choice of soft drinks, and you can get bowls of nuts and other nibbles. Muddy boots are no problem, and they stock bones for visiting dogs; Foxy the pub labrador is an indulgent host. There is a beer festival around the August bank holiday; unobtrusive piped music. *(Recommended by Andy and Claire Barker, Guy Vowles)*

Badger ~ Tenants Fleur and Andrew Cooper ~ Real ale ~ Bar food (12-2.30, 6-9.30 (9 Sun)) ~ (01432) 840900 ~ Children welcome ~ Dogs allowed in bar ~ Open 12-3, 6(5 Fri)-11; 12-11(10.30 Sun) Sat

LEDBURY   SO7138   Map 4

Feathers 🍽 ♀ 🛏

High Street, Ledbury, A417; HR8 1DS

In Ledbury's handsome main street, this black and white Tudor inn continues to do well for its food, and the lounge is a civilised place for afternoon teas, with high-sided armchairs and sofas in front of a big log fire, and newspapers to read. The bar, reception area and restaurant were thoroughly refurbished in 2006: they're hoping the changes haven't overly upset the two resident ghosts. At first sight it's predominantly comfortably hotel-like in character but the Top Bar has plenty of chatty and cheerful locals enjoying a pint quite uninhibited by those enjoying the food and wines at the brasserie tables behind them. There are beams and timbers, hop bines, some country antiques, 19th-c caricatures and fancy fowl prints on the stripped brick chimneybreast (lovely winter fire), copper jam pots hanging from the ceiling and fresh flowers on the tables – some very snug and cosy, in side bays. The recent refurbishment in the bar has given it an oak theme, with oak floor replacing the carpet, new oak tables and distressed internal shutters, and there are new furnishings in the lounge and no smoking restaurant too, together with Spy cartoons and ephemera such as 19th-c auction notices that they've unearthed; during the rebuilding work in the bar, they discovered a brick arch which has been preserved as a feature. In summer, abundant pots and hanging baskets adorn the sheltered back terrace. Fullers London Pride and a couple of guests such as Jennings or Thwaites on handpump; 14 wines by the glass and several malt whiskies. As well as a 'quickies' menu with home-made soup (£4.25), sandwiches (from £5.50) and deep-fried goats cheese, roasted beetroot and mixed leaf salad (£5.95, the enjoyable food includes starters like cornish mussels or chargrilled tuna loin (£6.95) and main courses such as penne pasta with cream and wild mushrooms or home-made salmon, cumin and coriander fishcakes (£8.50), grilled sea trout with roasted tomatoes and herb mash (£13.45), breast of chicken with wild mushroom risotto (£13.50), herefordshire sirloin steak (£14.50) and home-made puddings such as dark chocolate tart or sticky toffee pudding (£5.50). Nice breakfasts, and friendly, helpful staff. *(Recommended by Craig Turnbull, A S and M E Marriott, J E Shackleton, Bernard Stradling, Peter Cole, Derek Thomas, A D Lealan, J Crosby, Rod Stoneman)*

Free house ~ Licensee David Elliston ~ Real ale ~ Bar food (12-2(2.30 Sat, Sun), 7-9.30 (10 Fri, Sat)) ~ Restaurant ~ (01531) 635266 ~ Children welcome ~ Dogs allowed in bar and bedrooms ~ Open 11-11; 12-10.30 Sun ~ Bedrooms: £79.50B/£110B

LITTLE COWARNE   SO6051   Map 4
Three Horseshoes 🍷 🛏

Pub signposted off A465 SW of Bromyard; towards Ullingswick; HR7 4RQ

The licensees here have run this enchantingly placed pub for over 16 years, and it continues with its winning ways, with readers highlighting the garden, the food, the comfortable bedrooms and the welcoming staff for special praise. The quarry tiled L-shaped middle bar has leather-seated bar stools, upholstered settles and dark brown kitchen chairs around sturdy old tables, old local photographs above the corner log fire, and hop-draped black beams in the dark peach ceiling. Opening off one side is a skylit sun room with wicker armchairs around more old tables; the other end has a games room with darts, pool, juke box, fruit machine and games machine; also cribbage. For the well liked bar food the licensees get ingredients from local gamekeepers and fishermen, buy local eggs and vegetables (though they grow summer salads, tomatoes and herbs themselves), and make their own chutneys, pickles, jams and sloe gin. Enjoyable bar food includes sandwiches (from £2.25), salmon and lemon fishcake (£4.75), ploughman's (from £5.50), any starter from the blackboard menu, such as devilled kidneys, served with potatoes and vegetables or salad (£7.50), lasagne (£8.95), steak and ale pie (£9.50), salmon fillet (£9.95), pheasant breast in cider sauce with bacon or cod fillet with king prawns in dill and white wine sauce (£10.95), roast rack of lamb (£12.95) and fillet steak au poivre (£14.50); home-made ice-cream (£3.75) or home-made pudding such as damson soufflé (£3.95); children's menu (£3.95). Popular OAP pie lunch on Thursday. Besides Greene King Old Speckled Hen, Marstons Pedigree and Wye Valley Bitter on handpump, they have decent wines (including local ones, and ten by the glass), and Oliver's local farm ciders from named apple cultivars, and perry; obliging service, and disabled access. A roomy and attractive stripped-stone raftered restaurant extension has a Sunday lunchtime carvery. There are well sited tables on the terrace or the neat prettily planted lawn. *(Recommended by Michael Doswell, Theocsbrian, J E Shackleton, Carol Broadbent, Denys Gueroult, Ian Jones, Neil Kellett, Lucien Perring, Martin and Pauline Jennings)*

Free house ~ Licensees Norman and Janet Whittall ~ Real ale ~ Bar food ~ Restaurant ~ (01885) 400276 ~ No children in bar after 9pm ~ Dogs allowed in bar ~ Open 11-3, 6.30-12(1 Sat); 12-3, 7-10.30 Sun; closed Sun evening in winter ~ Bedrooms: £35S/£60S

LUGWARDINE   SO5541   Map 4
Crown & Anchor 🍴 🍷

Cotts Lane; just off A438 E of Hereford; HR1 4AB

No piped music or games machines disturb the atmosphere of this pleasantly cottagey half-timbered local, in what has become a dormitory village for Hereford. In addition to a pretty garden, it has several smallish and charming rooms, a big log fire, newspapers to read, and a bar furnished with an interesting mix of pieces. Butcombes, Timothy Taylors Landlord, Worthington and a couple of guests such as Adnams or Marstons Pedigree on handpump, a selection of malt whiskies and nine wines by the glass. As well as a huge choice of good lunchtime sandwiches (from £2.50), there might be ploughman's (£7), soup (£3.25), local smoked salmon, avocado and grapefruit salad (£4.75), salmon fishcakes (£5.50), cold hereford ham with free-range eggs (£8), poacher's pie with flaked salmon and potato and cheese topping (£8.50), cheese and spinach lasagne (£9), trout or steak and kidney pie (£9.50), chicken madras with fresh chillies (£10), roast breast of gressingham duck with redcurrants and lime (£11) and steak (from £11); most eating areas are no smoking. In ancient times the Lugg flats round here were farmed in strips by local farm tenants, and meetings with the lord of the manor were held in the pub. *(Recommended by Bernard Stradling, Denys Gueroult, Dr Michael Smith, Lucien Perring, Neil and Anita Christopher, Brian Brooks)*

Enterprise ~ Lease Nick and Julie Squire ~ Real ale ~ Bar food (12-2, 7-10) ~ (01432) 851303 ~ Children welcome ~ Open 12-11; 12-10.30 Sun; closed 25 Dec, 1 Jan

ORLETON   SO4967   Map 6
Boot
Just off B4362 W of Woofferton; SY8 4HN

'Warmth both from the open fire and the welcome,' commented one reader of this little 400-year-old village local. The traditional-feeling bar has a mix of dining and cushioned carver chairs around a few old tables on the red tiles, one very high-backed settle, hops over the counter, and a warming fire in the big fireplace, with horsebrasses along its bressumer beam. The lounge bar is up a couple of steps, and has green plush banquettes right the way around the walls, mullioned windows, an exposed section of wattle and daub, and standing timbers and heavy wall beams. There's a small and pretty no smoking restaurant on the left. Hobsons Best and Town Crier and a guest from a brewery like Wye Valley on handpump; cribbage, board games and dominoes. Lunchtime food includes home-made soup (£2.95), sandwiches (from £3.75); ploughman's (£5.50), baguettes (from £5.45), and steak and ale pie or scampi (£8.25), with evening choices such as home-made pâté (£3.95), smoked salmon salad (£5.25), home-made chicken and asparagus pie (£9.45), grilled duck breast with a black cherry and port sauce (£10.25), steaks (from £10.95) and mixed grill (£12.25); specials like deep-fried camembert with raspberry sauce (£4.75), giant yorkshire pudding filled with seasonal vegetables (£8.75), pork chop with red cabbage and onion sauce (£10.25) or poached fillet of smoked haddock with mornay sauce (£10.95). On Sunday they may be serving only hot food. There are seats in the garden under a huge ash tree, a barbecue area, and a fenced-in children's play area. (Recommended by Carol Broadbent, Rob Winstanley, R M Corlett)

Free house ~ Licensees Philip and Jane Dawson ~ Real ale ~ Bar food ~ Restaurant ~ (01568) 780228 ~ Children welcome ~ Dogs allowed in bar ~ Open 12-3, 6(7 Sun)-11

PEMBRIDGE   SO3958   Map 6
New Inn
Market Square (A44); HR6 9DZ

Despite its name this is anything but new, being one of an extraordinary number of half-timbered buildings in the village, and inside its wonderfully unchanged atmosphere simply oozes antiquity. Three simple but comfortable little beamed rooms have oak peg-latch doors and elderly traditional furnishings that include a fine antique curved-back settle on the worn flagstones; the log fire is the substantial sort that people needed long before central heating was reinvented. The homely no smoking lounge has sofas, pine furniture, family photos and books; darts, shove-ha'penny, board games and quoits in the bar; there's another no smoking dining room downstairs. Black Sheep, Fullers London Pride and John Roberts XXX, and perhaps a couple of guests from brewers such as Adnams or Dunn Plowman on handpump, 32 malt whiskies as well as local farm cider, wine and apple juice. Readers enjoy the food, which comes in generous helpings. Bar food at lunchtime includes sandwiches (from £3.75), ploughman's (from £4.95), creamed kidneys with toast (£6.95), battered fish and chips, or spinach and cream cheese lasagne (£7.50) and lamb and vegetable hotpot with herb dumplings (£7.75); evening choices include pork loin steak sautéed in apple, cider and cream (£9.50), whole prawns in garlic butter with crusty bread (£9), fillet of lamb (£10.50) and sirloin steak (£11.50); they also have specials such as pork, apple and cider casserole with sage dumplings (£7.75), trout (£8), braised lamb in redcurrant and port sauce (£8.95) and fish stew (£10). There's no pub garden as such, but a few tables are set out on the cobblestones by the tiny market place. (Recommended by Peter and Jean Hoare, David Eberlin, JWAC, Denys Gueroult, Anne Morris, Kevin Thomas, Nina Randall, M C and S Jeanes, Martin and Sue Day)

Free house ~ Licensee Jane Melvin ~ Real ale ~ Bar food ~ Restaurant ~ (01544) 388427 ~ Children in lounge and dining room ~ Open 11-3, 6-11; 12-2.30, 6-11 winter; closed first week in Feb

SELLACK SO5627 Map 4
Lough Pool ★ ⑪ ♀
Back road Hoarwithy—Ross-on-Wye; HR9 6LX

As well as producing good food using local and seasonal produce (including local meat, game, cream and fruit from Herefordshire and the welsh borders), this unspoilt timber-framed country pub is still somewhere you can feel at ease if you just want to enjoy a drink. The beamed central room has kitchen chairs and cushioned window seats around wooden tables on the mainly flagstoned floor, sporting prints, bunches of dried flowers and fresh hop bines, and a log fire at one end with a woodburner at the other. Other rooms lead off, gently brightened up with attractive individual furnishings and nice touches like the dresser of patterned plates; the bar area is no smoking; newspapers are left out for customers. The same interesting menu – which changes daily – is available in the chatty bar as well as the no smoking restaurant, and might include doorstep sandwiches and ciabattas, starters like cream of celery and apple soup (£4.25), herefordshire hop cheese and soufflé with cider and walnut cream (£6.25), ham hock and foie gras terrine with quince jelly (£6.95) and poached pigeon breast on mushroom risotto with beetroot and fresh truffle (£8.95), and main courses such as haddock in beer batter with hand-cut big chips (£10.95), confit shoulder and belly of pork (£13.45), roast free-range chicken breast on spinach and gruyère risotto (£13.50) or rib-eye steak (£15.25); puddings might include dark chocolate tart with crème anglaise, organic ice-creams, warm poached pears or sticky toffee pudding (all £5.25). They also have a lighter lunchtime menu (not Sunday), with items like poached free-range egg on toasted muffin with cotswold ham and hollandaise sauce (£7.95), confit of farm duck with stir-fried vegetables (£8.50), and lambs liver with streaky bacon and mash (£9.95). Adnams Explorer, and Wye Valley Bitter and Butty Bach plus a guest such as Greene King Old Speckled Hen or Theakstons XB on handpump, several malt whiskies, local farm ciders, perries and apple juices, and a well chosen reasonably priced wine list with ten by the glass. Service is good. There are plenty of picnic-sets on the neat front lawned area, and pretty hanging baskets; plenty of bridleways and surrounding walks. *(Recommended by Alec and Barbara Jones, Bren and Val Speed, Mike and Mary Carter, Bernard Stradling, Dr and Mrs A J Edwards, Lucien Perring, Mrs R Pearson, Pam and David Bailey, J Crosby, JMC, Bill and Jessica Ritson, Mrs Hazel Rainer)*

Free house ~ Licensees David and Janice Birch ~ Real ale ~ Bar food ~ Restaurant ~ (01989) 730236 ~ Children welcome ~ Dogs allowed in bar ~ Open 11.30-3, 6.30-11; 12-3, 6.30-10.30 Sun; closed Sun evening, all day Mon in winter

STOCKTON CROSS SO5161 Map 4
Stockton Cross Inn
Kimbolton; A4112, off A49 just N of Leominster; HR6 0HD

The long, heavily beamed bar of this attractive half-timbered pub features a handsome antique settle, and old leather chairs and brocaded stools by the huge log fire in the broad stone fireplace. Teme Valley This, Wye Valley Butty Bach and perhaps a guest such as Teme Valley T'Other are on handpump. At the far end is a woodburning stove with heavy cast-iron-framed tables and sturdy dining chairs, and up a step, a small area has more tables. Old-time prints, a couple of épées on one beam and lots of copper and brass complete the picture. The bar food includes soup (£4.25), locally made sausages (to the pub's own recipe) with mash (£7.25), home-made steak and kidney pie (£8.25) and cod and chips (£8.75); plus a more ambitious menu including starters like haddock and cheese smokie (£5.95), several vegetarian options such as pancake filled with ratatouille (£8.95), fisherman's pie (£11.25), tagine of lamb with apricots, honey and flaked almonds (£11.95), wild game casserole (£12.95), and steaks (from £16.75); puddings such as chocolate cake with hot chocolate fudge sauce (£4.95); half the eating area is no smoking; piped music. There are tables out in the pretty garden. *(Recommended by Mark and Lynette Davies, Dr Michael Smith, Bernard Stradling, Mike and Mary Carter)*

Free house ~ Licensees Stephen and Julia Walsh ~ Real ale ~ Bar food (12-2.15, 7-9.15) ~
(01568) 612509 ~ Well behaved children welcome ~ Dogs allowed in bar ~ Open 12-3,
7-11; closed Sun and Mon evenings

TITLEY   SO3360   Map 6

Stagg 🍽 ♀ 🛏
B4355 N of Kington; HR5 3RL

Herefordshire Dining Pub of the Year

With imaginative and skilful use of local and organic ingredients, the landlord/chef
here creates wonderful results and readers leave well satisfied with both the food
and the warm welcome. The pubbier blackboard menu (not available Saturday
evening or Sunday lunchtime) has eight to ten choices which, besides filled
baguettes (from £3.50), includes three-cheese ploughman's (£7.50), locally smoked
salmon salad or smoked chicken and crispy bacon salad (£7.90), and crispy duck
leg with cider sauce, smoked haddock risotto, scallops on parsnip purée or steak
sandwich with chips and garlic mushrooms (£8.50). On the more elaborate
restaurant menu (which can also be eaten in the bar) you might find starters like
soup (£3.70), cod on mustard lentils or pigeon breast with celeriac and apple
(£6.50) and foie gras two ways, pan-fried and port-marinated (£7.90); main courses
might feature herefordshire rump steak with béarnaise sauce (£13.90), pork
tenderloin stuffed with dried fruits with bacon and sherry vinaigrette (£14.50), fried
john dory with bouillabaisse sauce (£14.90) and saddle of venison with horseradish
gnocchi and braised fennel (£16.90). Puddings could include chocolate tart with
cardamom ice-cream, caramelised passion fruit tart with mango sorbet, or three
crème brûlées of vanilla, elderflower and lime (£5.20), and there's a choice of
around 21 british cheeses, mostly from Herefordshire and Wales. The extensive
dining rooms are no smoking. A carefully chosen wine list features ten wines and
champagne by the glass, as well as ports and pudding wines; Black Sheep and
Hobsons Town Crier are served on handpump, and they have local cider perry and
apple juice and a dozen malt whiskies. The bar, though comfortable and hospitable,
is not large, and the atmosphere is civilised rather than lively. They also have guest
accommodation in three double ensuite rooms above the pub and in a Georgian
vicarage four minutes away. The two-acre garden has a croquet lawn, chairs and
tables on the terrace, and a vegetable and herb garden for the kitchen. *(Recommended
by Chris Flynn, Wendy Jones, Blaise Vyner, Dr Michael Smith, Rob Winstanley, Tony Hall,
Melanie Jackson, Guy Vowles, Mike and Mary Carter, Mark Barker, Tom Halsall)*

Free house ~ Licensees Steve and Nicola Reynolds ~ Real ale ~ Bar food (12-2, 6.30-9.30)
~ Restaurant ~ (01544) 230221 ~ Children welcome ~ Dogs allowed in bar ~ Open 12-3,
6.30-11; closed Sun evening and Mon (exc bank hol weekends other than May Day bank
hol), Tues after bank hol weekends (exc May Day), first two weeks of Nov, 25 and 26 Dec,
1 Jan~ Bedrooms: £60B/£80B

ULLINGSWICK   SO5949   Map 4

Three Crowns 🍽 ♀
Village off A465 S of Bromyard (and just S of Stoke Lacy) and signposted off A417 N of
A465 roundabout – keep straight on through village and past turn-off to church; pub at
Bleak Acre, towards Little Cowarne; HR1 3JQ

Much appreciated by readers as somewhere for a special meal out, this dining pub
puts the accent on locally sourced organic ingredients in its very well presented
dishes. Lunchtime food (£12.95 for two courses, £14.95 for three) might include
starters like soup, mussels or terrine of pork and duck liver, with main courses like
lamb and barley stew with thyme and lemon dumplings, confit leg of duck or
smoked haddock fishcake, and puddings like rhubarb compote with strawberry
gratin. From a more elaborate daily changing menu (served at lunchtime and in the
evening), starters could include fish soup, smoked salmon with cornish crab or
cheddar and spinach soufflé (all £6) and sirloin steak, slow-roasted belly of pork
with black pudding and mustard mash, roast honey-glazed breast of duck with

rhubarb sauce or grilled fillet of bass on crisp risotto cake (all £14.25); it's best to book to be sure of a table. The landlord has extended part of the building, so that there's enough bar space for it to retain a cosily traditional pubby feel – with open fires, hops strung along the low beams of its smallish bar, traditional settles, a mix of big old wooden tables with small round ornamental cast-iron-framed ones, and more usual seats. It has one or two gently sophisticated touches such as candles on tables, and proper napkins; all of the pub is no smoking; cribbage. There are several wines by the glass, along with Hobsons Best and one or two monthly guests from Wye Valley and perhaps another brewer like Charles Wells on handpump, local farm ciders also on handpump and herefordshire apple juice. Nice summer views from tables out on the attractively planted lawn, and outside heaters for chillier evenings. We have not yet heard from anyone who has tried their new bedroom, above the restaurant – pretty, with sloping beams. *(Recommended by Andy and Claire Barker, J E Shackleton, Bernard Stradling, Peter and Jean Hoare, Denys Gueroult, Chris Flynn, Wendy Jones, Rodney and Norma Stubington, A J Ward)*

Free house ~ Licensee Brent Castle ~ Real ale ~ Bar food (12-3(2 Sun), 7-10(9 Sun)) ~ Restaurant ~ (01432) 820279 ~ Children welcome ~ Open 12-3, 7-11; 12-2, 7-9 Sun; closed Mon and 2 weeks from 24 Dec ~ Bedrooms: /£95S

UPTON BISHOP SO6527 Map 4
Moody Cow

2 miles from M50 junction 3 westbound (or junction 4 eastbound), via B4221; continue on B4221 to rejoin at next junction; HR9 7TT

Warmed by an open fire, the relaxing interior of this upmarket dining pub is laid out in snug areas that angle in an L around the bar counter, with rough sandstone walls, bare floorboards and a parade of cow-related ornaments and pictures. On the far right is a biggish rustic and candlelit restaurant, with rafters, and a fireside area with armchairs and sofas. The far left has a second smaller dining area, just five or six tables with antique pine tables and chairs; both rooms are no smoking. Home-made and cooked to order, the bar food typically includes sandwiches (from £4.95), soup (£4.75), thai crab fishcakes (£5.75), home-made ribbons of pasta with basil pesto sauce (£10.95), local sausages and wholegrain mustard mash (£11.50), steak, red wine and onion pie or fish and chips (£12.95), rib-eye steak and delicious puddings like bread and butter pudding (from £4.50); also more elaborate specials (not cheap) such as braised and glazed belly of local pork (£14.95) or breast of local duck with raspberry compote (£15.95). Hook Norton, Wye Valley Best and a guest such as Bass on handpump. *(Recommended by Theocsbrian, Mike and Mary Carter, Guy Vowles, Bernard Stradling, Julian Cox, Chris Flynn, Wendy Jones, LM)*

Free house ~ Licensee James Lloyd ~ Real ale ~ Bar food ~ Restaurant ~ (01989) 780470 ~ Well behaved children welcome ~ Dogs allowed in bar ~ Open 12-2.30, 6.30-11; 12-3 Sun; closed Sun evening and Mon

WALFORD SO5820 Map 4
Mill Race ♀

B4234 Ross—Lydney; HR9 5QS

Completely reworked since we'd last seen it a few years ago, this pink-washed building has now reopened as a contemporary no smoking pub, with some emphasis on the food side, but comfortable seating for those who want just a drink. As the blackboard by the entrance makes clear, they take pride in using named local suppliers for their careful mix of traditional dishes with up-to-date specialities, which might include soup (£3.95), pear, pine nut and stilton salad with lime dressing (£5.50), beef carpaccio (£6.50), shepherd's pie or mixed bean and tomato cassoulet (£8.95), ploughman's (£7.50), fricassee of rabbit loin on risotto or poached cod with braised lettuce, peas and potatoes in cream chowder sauce (£11.95), and puddings such as meringue nest with damson and sloe gin ice-cream or rhubarb crumble with custard (£4.50). Attentive smiling staff give good service. The layout and décor are now uncluttered and fresh, with a row of tall arched

windows giving an airy feel in the main part, which has some comfortable leather
armchairs and sofas on its flagstones, as well as stylish smaller chairs around broad
pedestal tables. The granite-topped modern bar counter stretching back from here
has Wye Valley Butty Bach on handpump, Weston's farm cider, and a good choice
of reasonably priced wines by the glass; opposite are a couple of tall nicely clean-cut
tables with matching chairs. The walls are mainly cream or dark pink, with just one
or two carefully placed prints, and good unobtrusive lighting. One wall stripped
back to the stonework has a woodburning stove, open also to the comfortable and
compact dining area on the other side. In keeping with the overall up-to-date style
of the pub, you can order weekday lunches on line (www.millrace.info), and they
have free wireless internet access. There are stylish tables out on the terrace; a
leaflet available at the pub details a pleasant round walk of an hour or so.
(Recommended by Martin and Pauline Jennings, Tony and Glenys Dyer)

Free house ~ Licensee C J Choremi ~ Real ale ~ Bar food (12-2(3 Sun), 6.30-9) ~
(01989) 562891 ~ Children welcome ~ Open 11-11; 11-10.30 Sun

WALTERSTONE   SO3425 Map 6
Carpenters Arms
**Village signposted off A465 E of Abergavenny, beside Old Pandy Inn; follow village signs,
and keep eyes skinned for sign to pub, off to right, by lane-side barn; HR2 0DX**

With a friendly landlady who always seems to have time for a chat, this stone
tavern on the edge of the Black Mountains has been in the same family for many
years and little has changed. The traditional rooms have ancient settles against
stripped stone walls, some pieces of carpet on broad polished flagstones, a roaring
log fire in a gleaming black range (complete with pot-iron, hot-water tap, bread
oven and salt cupboard), pewter mugs hanging from beams, and the slow tick of a
clock. The snug main no smoking dining room has mahogany tables and oak
corner cupboards, with a big vase of flowers on the dresser. Another little dining
area has old oak tables and church pews on flagstones; piped music. Breconshire
Golden Valley and Wadworths 6X are tapped from the cask. Reasonably priced
and tasty, the home-made food might include sandwiches and rolls (from £2), soup
(£4), steak roll (£4.50), ploughman's (£5), home-made dishes such as beef in
Guinness pie (£8), thick lamb cutlets with redcurrant and rosemary sauce (£10.95),
steaks (from £11), and home-made puddings (£4); also specials and a vegetarian
choice. The outside lavatories are cold but in character. *(Recommended by Chris Flynn,
Wendy Jones, Peter and Jean Hoare, MLR)*

Free house ~ Licensee Vera Watkins ~ Real ale ~ Bar food (12-2.30, 7-9.30) ~ Restaurant
~ No credit cards ~ (01873) 890353 ~ Children welcome ~ Open 12-11

WELLINGTON   SO4948 Map 6
Wellington 🍺
Village signposted off A49 N of Hereford; pub at far end; HR4 8AT

An unassuming red-brick pub from outside, this is a welcoming, child-friendly
place, with good food, and the beer is very well kept, with Hobsons Best, Wye
Valley Butty Bach and a couple of guests such as Bath Ales SPA and Timothy
Taylors Landlord on handpump. The carefully refurbished bar has big high-backed
dark wooden settles, an open brick fireplace with a log fire in winter and fresh
flowers in summer, and historical photographs of the village and antique farm and
garden tools around the walls. The charming candlelit restaurant is in the former
stables and is no smoking. From a short changing menu, inexpensive bar food
includes soup (£3.75), roast beef sandwich (£4.50), mustard-roasted ham with free-
range eggs and chips or locally made sausages (£5.95) and scrambled eggs with
oak-smoked salmon (£6.25); children's menu (£3.95; they also prepare smaller
helpings of most dishes); the more elaborate daily changing menu features
starters such as red onion marmalade and glazed goats cheese tart (£4.50) and
seared king scallops with pea and pancetta bubble and squeak (£6.50), with main
courses like roasted hand-made gnocchi with tomato, basil and mozzarella (£9.50),

honey-roasted belly of pork (£11.50) oak-smoked salmon with tarragon and peppercorn butter (£13.75) or fillet of local venison with balsamic roasted fig tart (£15.50); Sunday lunchtime carvery (no other food then); decent wines. Service is friendly; darts, board games and piped music in the bar. At the back is a pleasant garden with tables, where they have summer barbecues. *(Recommended by Peter and Jean Hoare, Ruth and Andrew Crowder, Nick and Meriel Cox, Ian Stafford)*

Free house ~ Licensees Ross and Philippa Williams ~ Real ale ~ Bar food (12-2, 7-9; 12.30-2.30 Sun; not Sun evening) ~ Restaurant ~ (01432) 830367 ~ Children welcome ~ Dogs allowed in bar ~ Open 12-3, 6(7 Sun)-11; closed Mon lunchtime

WHITNEY-ON-WYE SO2747 Map 6

Rhydspence ⇐

A438 Hereford—Brecon; HR3 6EU

This splendid 14th-c timber-framed building has always been a hostelry, and is thought to originate as a stopping place for pilgrims on their way between Abbey Cwmhir and Hereford Cathedral. Inside, the rambling, smartly kept rooms have heavy beams and timbers, attractive old-fashioned furnishings, and there's a log fire in the fine big stone fireplace in the central bar. There's a bistro-type eating area next to the bar, and this opens into the no smoking family room. The more formal restaurant is also no smoking; nice breakfasts. Bar food includes home-made soup (£3.85), home-made chicken liver pâté or lunchtime ploughman's (£5.95), leek and brie pancakes (£7.95), kedgeree or rabbit braised in cider and seed mustard sauce (£9.50), steak and kidney pie or a spicy curry (£9.95) and steaks (from £12.75); popular three-course Sunday lunch for £15.50 (booking strongly advised); also more elaborate restaurant food. Bass and Robinsons Best on handpump, local Dunkerton's cider on handpump, and a decent wine list; darts, cribbage, dominoes and shove-ha'penny. It's yards away from the border with Wales; in the garden, seats and tables make the most of the views over Wye valley. More reports please. *(Recommended by Duncan Cameron, Chris Flynn, Wendy Jones, G W H Kerby, Pam and David Bailey, Rodney and Norma Stubington)*

Free house ~ Licensee Peter Glover ~ Real ale ~ Bar food ~ Restaurant ~ (01497) 831262 ~ Children welcome ~ Open 11(12 Sun)-2.30, 7-11; closed 2 weeks in Oct ~ Bedrooms: £42.50S/£85B

WOOLHOPE SO6135 Map 4

Butchers Arms ◀

Signposted from B4224 in Fownhope; carry straight on past Woolhope village; HR1 4RF

They have five beers on handpump at this pleasantly 14th-c rural pub: Hook Norton Old Hooky, Shepherd Neame Spitfire, Wye Valley Butty Bach and a couple of guests such as Charles Wells Bombardier and a seasonal Wye Valley ale; also a good selection of malt whiskies. One of the spacious and welcoming bars has very low beams decorated with hops, old-fashioned well worn built-in seats with brocaded cushions, high-backed chairs and stools around wooden tables, and a brick fireplace filled with fresh flowers when it is not in use. Broadly similar though with fewer beams, the other bar has a large built-in settle and another log fire. Tables have fresh flowers; darts, board games and unobtrusive background music; the restaurant and part of the bar are no smoking. Lunchtime bar food includes sandwiches (from £3.95) and ploughman's (from £7.25); specials available at lunchtime and in the evening might include soup (£3.95), quiche of the day (£7.95), vegetable lasagne (£8.95), sausages with spring onion mash, or poached salmon fillet (£9.25), and steak (from £12.50); home-made puddings (£4.60); at quieter times of year they run occasional food nights. There's a relaxing beer garden with picnic-sets and cheerful flowering tubs and borders looking on to a tiny willow-lined brook. To enjoy some of the best of the surroundings, turn left as you come out and take the tiny left-hand road at the end of the car park; this turns into a track and then into a path, and the view from the top of the hill is quite something. *(Recommended by W H and E Thomas, Mr and Mrs J Tout, Denys Gueroult, R Davis)*

Free house ~ Licensees Cheryl and Martin Baker ~ Real ale ~ Bar food ~ Restaurant ~ (01432) 860281 ~ Children welcome until 8.30pm ~ Dogs allowed in bedrooms ~ Jazz and discos some evenings ~ Open 12-3, 6.30-11(12 Sat); 12-3, 7-11.30 Sun; closed Mon lunchtime in winter ~ Bedrooms: £35/£50

LUCKY DIP

Besides the fully inspected pubs, you might like to try these Lucky Dips recommended to us and described by readers (if you do, please send us reports: www.goodguides.co.uk).

ASTON CREWS [SO6723]

☆ *Penny Farthing* HR9 7LW: Partly 15th-c, roomy and relaxing, with lots of beams, horsebrasses, harness and farm tools, well in bar with skeleton at bottom; good generous competitively priced food from sandwiches to good fish choice, good friendly service, Greene King Abbot and Wadworths 6X, good value wines, easy chairs, log fires, two restaurant areas, one with pretty valley and Forest of Dean views; subdued piped music; tables in charming garden, bedrooms *(Lucien Perring, Mike and Mary Carter, BB, Kate Glozier, V Gapper)*

BOSBURY [SO6943]

☆ *Bell* HR8 1PX [B4220 N of Ledbury]: Chef/landlord doing good range of popular food, friendly attentive staff, attractively priced Hancocks HB and a guest beer, good choice of good value wines by the glass, tastefully decorated lounge with fresh flowers on tables, thriving public bar, restaurant; unobtrusive piped music *(Chris Flynn, Wendy Jones, Reg Fowle, Helen Rickwood, John Joyce-Townsend)*

BROMYARD [SO6554]

☆ *Falcon* HR7 4BT [Broad St]: Attractive timbered inn, several well laid out rooms with fascinating bulging walls and ancient windows, relaxed beamed and panelled bar enjoyed by local regulars, leather chairs and settees in small unrushed lounge, good food from good sandwiches (choice of home-baked breads) through honest hot dishes to popular Sun lunch, Wye Valley and an interesting small-brewery guest beer, helpful staff; comfortable bedrooms *(Dick and Madeleine Brown)*
Rose & Lion HR7 4AJ [New Rd]: Cheery local tied to Wye Valley brewery, their full range in top condition from central island servery, delightful landlady, simple comfortable lounge and games-minded public bar with darts, cards etc; tables out in pleasant courtyard, open all day wknds *(Nick and Lynne Carter, Pete Baker)*

CLODOCK [SO3227]

Cornewall Arms HR2 0PD [N of Walterstone]: Splendidly old-fashioned country local with landlady to match, by historic church and facing Black Mountains *(Anthony Double)*

COLWALL [SO7542]

Colwall Park WR13 6QG [Walwyn Rd (B4218 W of Malvern)]: Simple comfort in hotel's bar, enjoyable food inc good generous sandwiches in home-baked bread, good wines by the glass, Wye Valley ale, friendly staff; dogs allowed in bar and at terrace tables, bedrooms *(Dennis Jenkin, Theocsbrian)*
Wellington WR13 6HW [A449 Malvern—Ledbury]: Neat two-level bar and bright largely no smoking dining area, enjoyable italian and other dishes, Adnams and Greene King Ruddles, decent wines inc english ones *(Dave Braisted)*

CRASWALL [SO2736]

Bulls Head HR2 0PN [Hay-on-Wye—Llanfihangel Crucorney Golden Valley rd]: Remote stone-built country pub under new owners, low beams and flagstones in pleasantly simple rustic bar, log fire in old cast-iron stove, farm ciders and local real ales, traditional games, steps up to smarter dining area (not cheap); tables outside with play area, peaceful walking area, simple bedrooms, cl Mon *(Guy Vowles, MLR, LYM, David and Margaret Clark)*

EARDISLAND [SO4258]

Cross HR6 9BW [A44]: Friendly two-room local in lovely village, quick family service, good value honest food, a couple of real ales such as Fullers London Pride; open all day *(LYM, Dr Michael Smith)*
White Swan HR6 9BD [just off A44]: Interesting old traditional pub in lovely black-and-white village, good choice of real ales, enjoyable home-made food, armchairs and enormous fire in cosy inner core, two-room no smoking dining area, public bar with games; children welcome, good back garden *(BB, Liz Helm-Barnes)*

GOODRICH [SO5618]

Cross Keys HR9 6JB [just off A40 outside village]: Four real ales, good farm cider, good value generous home-made food, barn restaurant *(Lucien Perring)*

☆ *Hostelrie* HR9 6HX: Appealing and unusual Victorian building with turreted gothic extension, traditional softly lit panelled bar and lounge, roomy and individual with beams and stripped stone, good food cooked to order (so can take a while) inc local produce and imaginative dishes, sensible prices, good friendly service, two real ales and four ciders, good choice of wines, pretty dining room; children welcome, attractive garden, bedrooms, pleasant village nr Goodrich Castle and Wye Valley Walk *(Tom and Ruth Rees, Dr A J and Mrs Tompsett, Martin and Pauline Jennings, Mike and Mary Carter, Lawrence Bacon, Jean Scott, Mrs Veronica Mellor, Lucien Perring)*

HAMPTON BISHOP [SO5538]

Bunch of Carrots HR1 4JR: Spaciously refurbished beamed country pub by River

Wye, good helpful service, consistently good carvery and wide choice of other enjoyable food in bars and restaurant, real ales, local farm cider, lovely log fires; children and dogs welcome, garden with play area *(Lucien Perring, Mrs B Sugarman)*

HAREWOOD END [SO5227]

Harewood End Inn HR2 8JT [A49 Hereford—Ross]: Attractive and comfortable panelled dining lounge with wide food choice even Mon night, real ales and Wye Valley Butty Bach, good value wines; nice garden, good bedrooms with own bathrooms *(Tim and Sue Halstead, Dr Michael Smith)*

HEREFORD [SO5139]

Barrels HR1 2JQ [St Owen St]: Plain and cheery two-bar local with excellent low-priced Wye Valley Hereford and Dorothy Goodbodys ales (formerly brewed here), barrel-built counter also serving guest beers, several farm ciders, friendly efficient staff, may have sandwiches and pickled eggs, side pool room with games, juke box and big-screen sports TV, lots of modern stained glass; piped blues and rock, live music at beer festival end Aug; picnic-sets out on back cobbles, open all day *(Gill and Tony Morriss, the Didler, BB, Joe Green)*

Bay Horse HR4 0SD [Kings Acre Rd]: Cheerful and relaxed dining pub under new landlord, welcoming helpful service, enjoyable food from sandwiches up, real ales, local farm cider, large two-level main room, smaller side room, attractive upmarket décor; piped music *(Anon)*

Lichfield Vaults HR1 2LR [Church St]: Comfortable half-timbered traditional pub in picturesque pedestrianised street nr cathedral, sofas and armchairs at front, beams and inglenook tables behind, real ales such as Greene King Abbot, Marstons Pedigree and Wye Valley from long bar, generous enjoyable bar food, plenty of room, interesting memorabilia; pleasant back courtyard, open all day *(Anthony Double)*

Spread Eagle HR4 9BW [King St]: Busy beamed pub in side alley opp cathedral's west front, generous imaginative bar food, young friendly staff, Bass, Fullers London Pride and guest beers, comfortable upstairs restaurant; tables in back courtyard *(Gill and Tony Morriss, Dr Michael Smith, Anthony Double)*

Volunteer HR1 2QU [Harold St]: Warmly friendly local with generous bargain food inc Sun roasts, good choice of real ales and local ciders; tables outside *(Mary Randall)*

KENTCHURCH [SO4125]

Bridge Inn HR2 0BY [B4347 Pontrilas—Grosmont]: Ancient attractively refurbished rustic pub on new Herefordshire Trail, good bar food (not Sun evening) from enterprising open sandwiches up, Wye Valley and other ales, farm cider, welcoming service, big woodburner, games area, friendly local atmosphere, small pretty restaurant overlooking River Monnow (2 miles of trout fishing); waterside tables, bedrooms, cl Mon/Tues lunchtime *(Guy Vowles)*

KINGSTONE [SO4235]

Bull Ring HR2 9HE: Good value lunchtime bar food (not Sun/Mon) and good evening restaurant inc fresh fish and local lamb, Badger Tanglefoot, Bass and Wadworths 6X, attractive décor; children welcome, garden tables, pleasant village location *(M J Winterton)*

KINGTON [SO3056]

☆ *Olde Tavern* HR5 3BX [Victoria Rd, just off A44 opp B4355 – follow sign to Town Centre, Hospital, Cattle Mkt; pub on right opp Elizabeth Rd, no inn sign but Estd 1767 notice]: Splendidly old-fashioned, like stepping into an old sepia photograph of a pub (except for the strip lights – it's not at all twee), hatch-served side room opening off small plain parlour and public bar, plenty of dark brown woodwork, big windows, old settles and other antique furniture on bare floors, bargain real ales from Dunn Plowman and other small breweries, gas fire, china, pewter and curios, welcoming locals, no music or machines, plans for back food room; children welcome, though not a family pub; cl wkdy lunchtimes, outside gents' *(BB, MLR, the Didler, Pete Baker)*

Swan HR5 3AZ [Church St; note this is the Herefs Kington at SO3057]: Pleasantly refurbished airy bar overlooking square, good value food, several interesting ales, restaurant; children welcome, bedrooms *(Mark Percy, Lesley Mayoh)*

LEDBURY [SO7137]

☆ *Talbot* HR8 2DX [New St]: Relaxed local atmosphere in 16th-c inn's black-beamed bar rambling around island servery, antique hunting prints, plush wall banquettes or more traditional seats, log fire in big stone fireplace, good value food from baguettes to full meals, Wye Valley and other ales, good house wines, quick thoughtful service, smart no smoking black-panelled dining room, tales of a friendly poltergeist; piped music; decent bedrooms, open all day Sat *(Mary Randall, BB)*

LEOMINSTER [SO4959]

Bell HR6 8AE [Etnam St]: Beams and bare boards in recently opened-up pub with four mainly local real ales from central servery, good value simple lunchtime food from sandwiches up, log fire, friendly staff; tables out on good-sized back terrace, open all day *(MLR)*

Black Horse HR6 8JF [South St]: Well run bustling bar, comfortably well worn, with mainly local real ales, farm cider, good value food (not Sun evening) from good basic sandwiches up, traditional games, snug lounge and eating area; children welcome, open all day Sat *(MLR, BB, David and Sue Smith)*

LINTON [SO6525]

Alma HR9 7RY: Cheerful unspoilt local in small village, three real ales inc Butcombe, good fire, games room with pool, summer jazz festival; piped music; children very welcome, nice good-sized garden behind, cl wkdy lunchtimes *(Phil and Sally Gorton)*

MUCH MARCLE [SO6533]

☆ *Slip Tavern* HR8 2NG [off A449 SW of Ledbury]: Unpretentious country pub with splendidly colourful gardens overlooking cider orchards (Weston's Cider Centre is close by), charming newish licensees and very friendly informal service, good enterprising food, Wye Valley ale and local farm cider, attractive no smoking conservatory restaurant with fresh flowers and linen napkins; folk music first Thurs of month *(Denys Gueroult, Dr A J and Mrs Tompsett, LYM)*

PETERSTOW [SO5524]
Red Lion HR9 6LH [A49 W of Ross]: Doing well under present licensees, good choice of real ale and cider, enjoyable food, friendly staff, log fires, large open bar with dining area and conservatory; busy wknds; children welcome, back play area *(Anthony Double)*

ROSS-ON-WYE [SO5924]
Hope & Anchor HR9 7BU [Riverside; coming from A40 W side, 1st left after bridge (Rope Walk)]: Popular pub with big-windowed family extension looking out over gardens to River Wye, plenty of tables out here (and summer ice-cream bar and barbecues), boating-theme slate-floored main bar, steps up to servery with real ales, farm cider and good house wine, friendly prompt service, generous good value food inc good baguettes and good choice for children, Victorian-style upstairs parlour and dining room, cosy touches and good housekeeping; open all day *(LYM, M J Winterton, Guy Vowles)*
Kings Head HR9 5HL [High St]: Comfortably old-fashioned beamed and panelled hotel bar, blazing log fire, lots of old pictures and some cosy armchairs, generous good value pubby food from good sandwiches and baked potatoes up, two Wye Valley beers perhaps with a guest such as Freeminer or Whittingtons, swift friendly service, airy newer no smoking dining extension; bar can get smoky; dogs welcome, bedrooms, open all day *(Tony and Wendy Hobden, Derek and Sylvia Stephenson, Lucien Perring, Mr and Mrs A J Edwards, Kevin Blake)*
Mail Rooms HR9 5BS [Gloucester Rd]: Light and airy Wetherspoons, open and modern, with relaxing no smoking end, their usual food (using local ingredients) and attractively priced beers and wines, silenced TV; children in family area till 7, pleasant terrace with tables under big parasols, open all day *(Craig Turnbull, Reg Fowle, Helen Rickwood, Mike and Mary Carter)*
Royal HR9 5HZ [Royal Parade]: Enjoyable bistro bar as well as restaurant in substantial hotel, pleasant service, plans for complete refurbishment autumn 2006 (will probably then have Greene King real ales); fine views from outside decking (picnic-sets on steep lawn may not get this), some of the 41 bedrooms have river view *(Derek and Sylvia Stephenson, P and D Carpenter, Geoff Pidoux)*

STAUNTON ON WYE [SO3645]
New Inn HR4 7LR: Pleasantly relaxed old-fashioned 16th-c village inn, friendly helpful licensees, roomy bar with cosy alcoves, good value generous home-cooked food lunchtimes and Fri/Sat evenings in bar and restaurant inc

vegetarian and local ingredients and cheeses, changing beers inc Wye Valley, small no smoking eating area *(Reg Fowle, Helen Rickwood)*

STIFFORDS BRIDGE [SO7348]
Red Lion WR13 5NN [A4103 3 miles W of Gt Malvern]: Cosy beamed roadside pub with good value food inc good baguettes and OAP specials, prompt service, real ales, farm ciders inc a local organic one; children welcome, tables in well kept garden *(Guy Vowles)*

TARRINGTON [SO6140]
Tarrington Arms HR1 4HX [A438 E of Hereford]: Welcoming and cosy, with enjoyable and varied food in bar and well run restaurant; bellringers may be in at 9 after Fri practice *(Mike and Mary Carter, Neil Kellett)*

TILLINGTON [SO4645]
Bell HR4 8LE: Welcoming family-run and family-friendly local, good value food in bar and restaurant from nice baguettes to generous home-made hot dishes, Bass, Wye Valley Butty Bach and a guest beer, daily papers, comfortable banquettes in lounge extension; steps up to good big garden with play area *(Bruce Bird)*

TRUMPET [SO6639]
☆ *Trumpet Inn* HR8 2RA: Beautiful black and white timbered pub dating from 15th c, friendly and good value, with interesting horse-racing memorabilia, beams, log fires and stripped brickwork, sandwiches and good choice of enjoyable home-made food largely from local farms and own garden, changing real ales, nice house wines, good service; tables in big garden behind, camp site with hard standings *(Anthony Double)*
Verzons HR8 2PZ [A438 W of Ledbury]: Stylishly modernised country inn with low bucket seats in quiet comfortable lounge, attractive bar and subtly lit cocktail bar, two real ales, good wines by the glass, friendly staff, enjoyable food, upmarket restaurant; super views from verandah, spreading lawns behind, comfortable bedrooms *(A S and M E Marriott, LYM, Martin and Pauline Jennings)*

WEOBLEY [SO4051]
☆ *Salutation* HR4 8SJ [off A4112 SW of Leominster]: Beamed and timbered old inn in one of Herefordshire's most perfect-looking black and white villages, with Goffs Jouster, Spinning Dog Herefordshire PA and Wye Valley Butty Bach, good range of wines by the glass, bar food inc very local meat, big open fire, relaxed pubby lounge, no smoking restaurant conservatory, straightforward public bar with juke box, games machine and TV; children welcome, tables with parasols on sheltered back terrace, bedrooms, open all day *(Norman and Penny Davies, the Didler, Norman and Sarah Keeping, LYM, R T and J C Moggridge)*

WESTON-UNDER-PENYARD [SO6323]
☆ *Weston Cross Inn* HR9 7NU [A40 E of Ross]: Substantial creeper-covered stone-built pub overlooking picturesque village, good range of good value home-made food cooked by

friendly landlord's wife inc fresh fish (worth booking wknds), Stowford Press cider as well as a good range of real ales, pleasant and roomy beamed dining lounge opening to garden, big TV in separate bar; walkers welcome (they have a walks map), very pretty outside, plenty of picnic-sets on sweeping lawns, play area *(BB, Trevor, Guy Vowles, Mike and Mary Carter)*

WIGMORE [SO4169]

Compasses HR6 9UN [Ford St]: Walker-friendly inn, olde-worlde behind its modern façade, with welcoming landlord (knowledgeable about local walks), good Hobsons ale, enjoyable generous blackboard home cooking, daily papers, magazines and children's books, separate dining room, pool in plain public bar; good view from garden, four bedrooms, charming village with castle and lovely church *(Reg Fowle, Helen Rickwood, DFL)*

WOONTON [SO3552]

☆ *Lion* HR3 6QN [A480 SE of Kington]: Beautifully placed and well furnished country pub with friendly landlord and informal atmosphere, landlady cooks enjoyable home-made food using local produce from hot beef and other sandwiches up, also dishes (and wines and beers) suitable for vegans, and gluten-free dishes, local real ale, separate restaurant, good views; monthly vintage sports car meeting second Tues *(MLR, W H and E Thomas)*

Post Office address codings confusingly give the impression that some pubs are in Herefordshire when they're really in Gloucestershire or even in Wales (which is where we list them).

Hertfordshire

This county enjoys a rather endearing collection of soundly traditional pubs, many of them still nicely unspoilt. It's notable that, unless you count acquisitive Greene King, the big national combines don't own a single one of these individual little places. Indeed the Red Lion in Preston, which is now run by a devoted couple, was actually bought by the local community a couple of decades ago to avert a closure threat made by Whitbreads. With just under half the pubs in the county sporting a beer award, many would say this county has its priorities in exactly the right place. (Well, almost – the only slight snag is that beer prices tend to be rather above the national average.) The Valiant Trooper at Aldbury perhaps represents the pick of the bunch as a fine all-rounder, with its proper pubby welcome, generous tasty food and five real ales. The beautifully kept Holly Bush at Potters Crouch too is enjoyed by readers for its genuine homely feel. Food in this county, if good value, tends to be fairly straightforward, so the stylish Alford Arms at Frithsden (rescued from Enterprise by a small independent group), with its gently imaginative seasonally changing menu, stands out head and shoulders as Hertfordshire Dining Pub of the Year. In the Lucky Dip section at the end of the chapter, pubs gaining strong support recently are the Plough at Colney Heath, Horns near Datchworth, Beehive at Epping Green, Crown & Sceptre near Hemel Hempstead, Fox & Hounds at Hunsdon, Lytton Arms at Knebworth, Five Horseshoes at Little Berkhamsted, Bull at Much Hadham, Woodman at Nuthampstead, Six Bells in St Albans and Fox & Duck at Therfield. We have inspected and can vouch for almost all of these. And we'd add to them the Jolly Waggoner at Ardeley, all set to join the main entries until we found the landlord was changing just as we went to press in summer 2006.

ALDBURY   SP9612   Map 4

Greyhound

Stocks Road; village signposted from A4251 Tring—Berkhamsted, and from B4506; HP23 5RT

Back in the *Guide* after a short break, this spacious dining pub can draw quite a bustling crowd these days, though friendly staff stay on top of things well. The beamed interior shows some signs of considerable age (around the copper-hooded inglenook, for example), with plenty of tables in the two traditionally furnished rooms off either side of the drinks and food serving areas. Badger Best, Tanglefoot and a Badger seasonal beer are well kept on handpump; smoking in the public bar only, piped music and games machine. An airy oak floored restaurant at the back overlooks a suntrap gravel courtyard, and it's also well worth a winter visit, when the lovely warm fire and subtle lighting make it really cosy inside. As well as lunchtime panini (£5.50) and ploughman's (£6.95), the popular quickly served bar food might include fried halloumi with roast peppers and rocket (£5.75), seared smoked salmon with spiced guacamole (£6.50), spaghetti with king prawns, smoked bacon, sun-dried tomatoes and lemon oil (£11.25), smoked haddock on mushrooms and topped with a poached egg and butter sauce (£11.50) and beef fillet with pink peppercorn sauce on julienne vegetables (£16.50). Benches outside face a picturesque village green complete with stocks and lively duckpond.

(Recommended by Sheila Topham, John and Elisabeth Cox, Michael Dandy, John Baish, Ross Balaam, Ian Phillips, Tracey and Stephen Groves, David and Ruth Shillitoe, Gill and Keith Croxton)

Badger ~ Manager Tim O'Gorman ~ Real ale ~ Bar food (12-2.30(4 Sun), 6.30-9.30; not Sun evening) ~ Restaurant ~ (01442) 851228 ~ Children welcome ~ Dogs allowed in bar ~ Open 11-11; 12-10.30 Sun ~ Bedrooms: £65S/£75B

Valiant Trooper 🍺

Trooper Road (towards Aldbury Common); off B4506 N of Berkhamsted; HP23 5RW

This enjoyable place is a solid reminder of how a proper well run pub should be. A jolly decent range of very well kept beers is served alongside good tasty food, and there's a cheerful pubby welcome. The first room of its nicely unspoilt interior is beamed and tiled in red and black, and has built-in wall benches, a pew and small dining chairs around the attractive country tables, and an inglenook fireplace. The middle bar has spindleback chairs around tables on a wooden floor, some exposed brickwork, and signs warning you to 'mind the step'. The far room has nice country kitchen chairs around individually chosen tables, and a woodburning stove. Fullers London Pride, Oakham JHB, Tring Jack o' Legs and two guests from brewers such as Archers and Batemans are well kept on handpump, with around a dozen wines by the glass. The generously served food includes well filled baked potatoes, open sandwiches or ciabattas (from £4.50), ploughman's (£5.50), and home-made daily specials such as soup (£3.50), creamy mushroom carbonara (£8), roast chicken (£9.50) and steak and kidney pie (£9), with puddings such as chocolate and brandy torte (£3.95). One bar and the back barn conversion restaurant are no smoking; dominoes, cribbage and bridge on Monday nights. It's nicely positioned for walks through the glorious beech woods of the National Trust's Ashridge Estate, and the enclosed garden has a play house for children. (Recommended by Sheila Topham, David and Ruth Shillitoe, Brian Root, Michael Dandy, Colin McKerrow, Tracey and Stephen Groves, Julia and Richard Tredgett, John and Glenys Wheeler, Susan and John Douglas, Klaus and Elizabeth Leist, Paul Humphreys)

Free house ~ Licensee Tim O'Gorman ~ Real ale ~ Bar food (12-2(2.30 Sun), 6.30-9; not Sun or Mon evenings) ~ Restaurant ~ (01442) 851203 ~ Children in first bar and restaurant ~ Dogs allowed in bar ~ Open 11.30-11; 12-10.30 Sun

ASHWELL TL2639 Map 5
Three Tuns

Off A505 NE of Baldock; High Street; SG7 5NL

Relaxing chairs, big family tables, lots of pictures, stuffed pheasants and fish, and antiques lend an air of Victorian opulence to the cosy lounge at this flower-decked 18th-c inn; piped light classical music. The simpler more modern public bar has pool, darts, cribbage, dominoes, a fruit machine and Sky TV. Served by friendly efficient staff, generous helpings of tasty bar food might include soup (£4.25), filled baguettes (from £4.25), chicken liver pâté or devilled whitebait (£5.25), ploughman's (from £6.75), vegetarian pasta bake (£7.95), chicken curry (£9.45), grilled salmon fillet (£10.95), sirloin steak (£14.95), and puddings (from £4.75); no smoking dining room. There's a good choice of wines, as well as Greene King IPA, Abbot and a guest on handpump. A big terrace has metal tables and chairs, and the substantial shaded garden has boules, and picnic-sets under apple trees. The charming village is full of pleasant corners and is popular with walkers at summer weekends, as the landscape around rolls enough to be rewarding. (Recommended by Michael Dandy, Gordon Neighbour, Mike Dean , Lis Wingate Gray, Mrs Diane M Hall, Peter and Margaret Glenister, Jan and Alan Summers, Mary Rayner, N R White, Alison and Pete, Dave Braisted)

Greene King ~ Tenants Claire and Darrell Stanley ~ Real ale ~ Bar food (12-2.30, 6.30-9.30; all day Fri-Sun) ~ Restaurant ~ (01462) 742107 ~ Children welcome with restrictions ~ Dogs allowed in bar ~ Open 11-11; 12-10.30 Sun ~ Bedrooms: £39/£49(£59B)

BATFORD   TL1415   Map 5
Gibraltar Castle
Lower Luton Road; B653, S of B652 junction; AL5 5AH

Still pleasantly traditional, this neatly kept little roadside pub is stashed with an impressive collection of militaria including rifles, swords, medals, uniforms and bullets (with plenty of captions to read), and pictures depicting its namesake, and various moments in its history. The long carpeted bar has a pleasant old fireplace, comfortably cushioned wall benches, and a couple of snugly intimate window alcoves, one with a fine old clock; in one area the low beams give way to soaring rafters; several board games are piled on top of the piano, and they've piped music. Fullers Discovery, ESB, London Pride and an occasional guest beer are served on handpump, and they keep a good range of malt whiskies, and a thoughtful choice of wines by the glass. Reasonably priced tasty bar food might include lunchtime sandwiches (from £3.95, not Sunday) and ploughman's (£6.95), as well as sausage and mash (£7.95), chilli (£8), mushroom and mascarpone lasagne (£8.75), fish and chips or chicken and mushroom pie (£8.95), smoked fish salad (£9.95) and fillet steak (£14.95); booking is recommended for Sunday roast (£9.95). The pub is completely no smoking at lunchtime, with a few no smoking tables in the evening. There are tables and chairs on a decked back terrace, a few more in front by the road, and hanging baskets and tubs dotted around. *(Recommended by Michael Dandy, Angus Johnson, Carol Bolden, David and Ruth Shillitoe, Grahame Brooks, Derek Harvey-Piper, John and Joyce Snell, Terry Buckland, B and M Kendall, Mr and Mrs John Taylor)*

Fullers ~ Lease Hamish Miller ~ Real ale ~ Bar food (12-2.30(4 Sun) 7-9; not Sun evening) ~ Restaurant ~ (01582) 460005 ~ Children welcome at lunchtime only ~ Dogs welcome ~ Open 11.30-11; 12-10.30 Sun

CHAPMORE END   TL3216   Map 5
Woodman 🍷
Off B158 Wadesmill—Bengeo; 300 yards W of A602 roundabout keep eyes skinned for discreet green sign to pub pointing up otherwise unmarked narrow lane; OS Sheet 166 map reference 328164; SG12 0HF

Tucked away near the duck pond in a small hamlet, this peaceful early Victorian local takes you back through time. Two straightforward little linked rooms have plain seats around stripped pub tables, flooring tiles or broad bare boards, log fires in period fireplaces, cheerful pictures for sale, lots of local notices, and darts on one side, with a piano (and a couple of squeeze boxes) on the other. There's a refreshing lack of piped music and gimmicks, leaving you at peace to enjoy a game of boules, chess, backgammon, darts, shove ha'penny or cribbage. The lounge bar is no smoking. They have well kept Greene King IPA, Abbot and usually a guest such as Ridleys Prospect tapped from the cask, as well as several malt whiskies. Served by cheerful staff, the very short snacky lunchtime menu includes sandwiches (from £2.70), soup (£3.50), ploughman's (from £5.45) and caesar salad (£6), and on Thursday evening their very small kitchen might conjure up a themed evening, or a couple of main courses such as mixed grill or lamb tagine. In summer they have regular barbecues and tasty hog roasts. There are picnic-sets out in front under a couple of walnut trees, and a bigger garden behind has a good fenced play area (there are often toys left around by the publican's daughters, who generally don't mind other children playing with them). The car park has little room but there is usually plenty of on-street parking. *(Recommended by Jeremy Hemming, Robert Turnham, Ian Arthur, Mike Ridgway, Sarah Miles, Pat and Tony Martin)*

Greene King ~ Tenant Dr Danny Davis ~ Real ale ~ Bar food (lunchtime (not Mon) and Thurs evening) ~ No credit cards ~ (01920) 463143 ~ Children welcome in lounge bar till 8pm ~ Dogs welcome ~ Open acoustic night second Weds ~ Open 12-2.30, 5.30-11; cl Mon lunchtime; 12-11 Sat, Sun

---

Please let us know of any pubs where the wine is particularly good.

COTTERED TL3129 Map 5
Bull
A507 W of Buntingford; SG9 9QP

The airy low-beamed front lounge at this extended dining pub is well cared for, with polished antiques on a stripped wood floor, a good fire, Greene King IPA and Abbot and decent wines. A second bar has darts and a fruit machine; unobtrusive piped music. Thoughtfully presented bar food includes lunchtime sandwiches (from £3.25; open toasted sandwiches from £6.25), home-made burgers or ploughman's (£6.75) and sausage and mash (£8.50), as well as soup (£4.50), fresh crab (£6.75), wild mushroom risotto (£11), breaded pork fillet stuffed with bacon and cheddar (£13.50), fillet steak (£16.25) and bass on creamed leeks (£16.50); 5% service charge except if dining in the Hunt Bar; no smoking dining area. You can get tea here on summer Sunday afternoons (3-6). The pub is surrounded by trees and faces a row of pretty thatched cottages, and benches and tables in the attractive big garden make the best of the lovely setting. *(Recommended by Jack and Sandra Clarfelt, Mrs Margo Finlay, Jörg Kasprowski, Ian Phillips, John Saul, W Andrew, Alex and Irene Harvey, John Branston)*

Greene King ~ Lease Darren Perkins ~ Real ale ~ Bar food (12-2, 7-9.30; 12-9 Sun) ~ Restaurant ~ (01763) 281243 ~ No under-7s Mon-Sat ~ Open 12-3, 6.30-11; 12-10.30 Sun

FRITHSDEN TL0110 Map 5
Alford Arms 🍴 ♀
From Berkhamsted take unmarked road towards Potten End, pass Potten End turn on right, then take next left towards Ashridge College; HP1 3DD

Hertfordshire Dining Pub of the Year

It's worth booking to be sure of a table at this very popular dining pub, and as parking can be a problem we suggest getting there early. The fashionably elegant but understated interior has simple prints on pale cream walls, with blocks picked out in rich Victorian green or dark red, and an appealing mix of good antique furniture from Georgian chairs to old commode stands on bare boards and patterned quarry tiles. It's all pulled together by luxurious opulently patterned curtains, and piped jazz. The welcoming staff are thoughtful and conscientious, though a couple of readers found service slowed down at busy times. Where possible dishes are made from fresh local produce, and the seasonally changing temptingly imaginative menu might include soup (£4.25), roast red pepper gnocchi with gorgonzola, broad beans and cream (£5.75), scotch egg with pickle (£5.75), tapas plate (£6), sausage and mash (£10.25), mushroom and spinach lasagne with creamy mascarpone sauce (£10.75), roast pork belly on sweet potato dauphinoise with cider gravy (£12.75), grilled bass fillets on spiced aubergine with baby fennel and chorizo oil (£13.50), rib-eye steak with green peppercorn butter (£14); side orders (from £2.50). Puddings might include apple and blackberry crumble or treacle tart with lemon grass crème fraîche (£4.75) and dark chocolate fondant with clotted cream (£5.50); cheese platter (£6.25). The dining room is no smoking. A good wine list features ten good pudding wines and 15 other wines by the glass, and they've well kept Brakspears, Flowers Original, Marstons Pedigree and Rebellion on handpump. The pub stands by a village green, surrounded by lovely National Trust woodland, and there are plenty of tables out in front. *(Recommended by D J and P M Taylor, John and Joyce Snell, Michael Dandy, Professors Alan and Ann Clarke, John Baish, John Picken, Bob and Maggie Atherton, Andrew Scarr, Peter and Giff Bennett, Peter and Margaret Glenister, Annabel Viney, Alex and Irene Harvey, Susan and John Douglas, Tracey and Stephen Groves, Brian P White, Steven Page, Ian Phillips)*

Salisbury Pubs ~ Lease Richard Coletta ~ Real ale ~ Bar food (12-2.30(4 Sun), 7-10) ~ Restaurant ~ (01442) 864480 ~ Children welcome ~ Dogs allowed in bar ~ Open 11-11; 12-10.30 Sun

HERTFORD   TL3212   Map 5

White Horse 🍺 £

Castle Street; SG14 1HH

Despite this unpretentious town-centre pub's Fullers tie, they serve an impressive range of half a dozen thoughtfully sourced guests, with the choice often changing from one day to the next. As well as Chiswick, Discovery, ESB, London Pride, and their regular guest Adnams Southwold, you might find beers from brewers as far flung as Fyne, Orkney, Princetown and Sharps – no need to worry then if you can't make it here for their May or August bank holiday beer festivals. They also keep around 20 country wines. Parts of the building date from the 14th c, and you can still see Tudor brickwork in the three quietly cosy no smoking upstairs rooms. Downstairs, the two main rooms are small and homely. The one on the left is more basic, with some brewery memorabilia, bare boards, and a few rather well worn tables, stools and chairs, and an open fire separates it from the more comfortable right-hand bar, which has a cosily tatty armchair, some old local photographs, beams and timbers, and a red-tiled floor. Service can be quite chatty, and though it's quite a locals' pub, visitors are made to feel welcome; bar billiards, darts, shove-ha'penny, shut the box, cribbage and dominoes. The pub faces the castle, and there are two benches on the street outside. Another good reason to visit is the very inexpensive home-made bar food which includes sandwiches (from £2.40), soup (£2.50), baguettes (from £3.35), baked potatoes (from £3.75), ploughman's (£4.50) and daily specials such as beef and vegetable pie (£4), moroccan chicken, wild boar casserole, braised lamb shanks armenian style, and sausages and bubble and squeak with onion gravy (all £4.25). On Sunday they do a two-course lunch for £6.50, three courses for £7, and on Monday evenings they do a White Horse Gastronomic Tour, with one exotic dish such as curry for £5; they can do children's portions. *(Recommended by Andy and Jill Kassube, Pat and Tony Martin)*

Fullers ~ Lease Nigel Crofts ~ Real ale ~ Bar food (12-2(1-3 Sun); 6-8(Mon only)) ~ (01992) 501950 ~ Well supervised children in upstairs family room until 9pm ~ Dogs welcome ~ Open 12-2.30, 5.30-11; 12-11(10.30 Sun) Fri, Sat

POTTERS CROUCH   TL1105   Map 5

Holly Bush 🍺 £

2¼ miles from M25 junction 21A: A405 towards St Albans, then first left, then after a mile turn left (ie away from Chiswell Green), then at T junction turn right into Blunts Lane; can also be reached fairly quickly, with a good map, from M1 exits 6 and 8 (and even M10); AL2 3NN

Everything at this pretty wisteria-covered white cottagey building is spotless and well loved, giving the feeling of home away from home. Thoughtfully positioned fixtures create the illusion that there are lots of different rooms – some of which you might expect to find in a smart country house. In the evenings, neatly placed candles cast shadows over the mix of darkly gleaming varnished tables, all of which have fresh flowers, and china plates as ashtrays. There are quite a few antique dressers, several with plates on, a number of comfortably cushioned settles, the odd plant, a fox's mask, some antlers, a fine old clock, carefully lit prints and pictures, daily papers, and on the left as you go in, a big fireplace. The long, stepped bar counter (no smoking here) has particularly well kept Fullers Chiswick, ESB, London Pride and a Fullers seasonal beer on handpump, and the sort of reassuringly old-fashioned till you hardly ever see in this hi-tech age. Service is friendly, calm and efficient, even when they're busy. Straightforward, freshly prepared bar food, from a fairly short menu (see limited opening times below) includes sandwiches (from £2.60), burgers (from £4), filled baked potatoes (from £4.50), ploughman's (from £5.40), home-made chilli or very good generously sized fish or meat platters (from £6.20), apple pie (£2.90) and chocolate fudge cake (£2.90). Behind the pub, the fenced-off garden has a nice lawn, handsome trees, and sturdy picnic-sets – a very pleasant place to sit in summer. Though the pub seems to stand alone on a quiet little road, it's only a few minutes from the centre of St Albans. *More reports please.* *(Recommended by John and Joyce Snell, Gordon Prince, Professors Alan and Ann Clarke, Mr and Mrs Stevenson, Mr and Mrs Mike Pearson, John Picken, Mr and Mrs John Taylor)*

Fullers ~ Tenant R S Taylor ~ Real ale ~ Bar food (lunchtime only, not Sun) ~ (01727) 851792 ~ Open 11.30-2.30, 6-11; 12-2.30, 7-10.30 Sun

PRESTON TL1824 Map 5
Red Lion 🍺
Village signposted off B656 S of Hitchin; The Green; SG4 7UD

Bought by villagers when Whitbreads threatened closure in 1982, this delightful old village pub was the first in the country to be acquired by a local community. It's now managed by a conscientious committed couple, and has a good homely atmosphere. Readers very much enjoy it for the good value hearty food they serve, and the particularly well kept changing beers. Four interesting guests such as Castle Rock Harvest Pale, Crouch Vale Brewers Gold, Fullers London Pride and Mighty Oak English Oak are rotated alongside Youngs on handpump. They also tap farm cider from the cask, have eight wines by the glass including an english house wine, a perry, and mulled wine in winter. Food includes lunchtime sandwiches (£4) and ploughman's (£4.50), as well as soup (£3), grilled goats cheese or pâté (£4), stilton and asparagus quiche or chilli (£5.95), creamy haddock tart (£6.95), steak and kidney pie (£7.95), with specials such as lasagne (£5.95), salmon and dill fishcakes or steak and kidney pie (£6.95) and pheasant in red wine sauce or venison and cranberry casserole (£7.95). The main room on the left has sturdy well varnished pub furnishings including padded country-kitchen chairs and cast-iron-framed tables on its patterned carpet, a log fire in a brick fireplace, and foxhunting prints. The somewhat smaller room on the right has steeplechasing prints, and some varnished plank panelling, with brocaded bar stools on flagstones around the servery; dominoes. A few picnic-sets out on the front grass face across to lime trees on a peaceful village green, and there are many more, with some shade from a tall ash tree, in the good-sized sheltered garden behind, which is neatly kept, with a colourful herbaceous border. *(Recommended by Elizabeth Newbery, John and Joyce Snell, David and Ruth Shillitoe, John and Patricia White, Eithne Dandy, Steve Nye, Peter and Margaret Glenister)*

Free house ~ Licensee Tim Hunter ~ Real ale ~ Bar food (not Sun or Tues evenings) ~ No credit cards ~ (01462) 459585 ~ Children welcome away from bar ~ Dogs welcome ~ Open 12-2.30, 5.30-11; 12-3, 7-10.30 Sun

ROYSTON TL3540 Map 5
Old Bull £
High Street, off central A10 one-way system – has own car park, or use central car park; SG8 9AW

You'll find this fine bow-fronted early Georgian coaching inn tucked peacefully away from the traffic. The roomy high-beamed ceilinged bar, with handsome fireplaces, exposed timbers, big pictures and rather fine flooring, has easy chairs, a leather sofa and a table of papers and magazines (and ready-to-pour coffee) at the entrance end with the bar counter. Further in, tables are more set out for eating. They have well kept Greene King IPA and Old Speckled Hen plus a changing Greene King beer on handpump, and ten decent wines by the glass. The atmosphere is chatty and relaxed, the piped music is fairly unobtrusive, and half the pub is no smoking; cribbage and dominoes. Good-value bar food includes sandwiches (from £2.95), soup (£3.75), mixed pepper and mushroom pasta (£4.95), chicken curry and rice (£5.95), roast beef in yorkshire pudding (£7.95), and home-made puddings such as bread and butter pudding (£4.50). There is a separate more formal restaurant; Sunday lunches are £7.95 for one course, £9.95 for two and £11.95 for three, and the senior citizens' menu (Monday to Friday) is £6 for two courses. A sunny courtyard, originally a coachyard in the days when 100 horses were stabled here, is today equipped with outdoor heaters and modern tables and chairs.

(Recommended by John Branston, Margaret and Roy Randle, Pat and Tony Martin, Alistair and Kay Butler)

Greene King ~ Lease Clive Latter ~ Real ale ~ Bar food (12-2.30, 6.30-9.30; 12-9 Sat, Sun) ~ Restaurant ~ (01763) 242003 ~ Children welcome ~ Dogs allowed in bar ~ Open 11-11(12 Thurs-Sat, 10.30 Sun) ~ Bedrooms: £75S/£90S

SARRATT   TQ0499   Map 5
Cock
Church End: a very pretty approach is via North Hill, a lane N off A404, just under a mile W of A405; WD3 6HH

A new licensee has taken over this nicely positioned cream-painted 17th-c country local, so we're keeping our fingers crossed for the homely atmosphere that readers have enjoyed so much in the past. A latched front door opens into a carpeted snug with a vaulted ceiling, original bread oven, and a cluster of bar stools. Through an archway, the partly oak-panelled cream-walled lounge has a lovely log fire in an inglenook, pretty Liberty-style curtains, pink plush chairs at dark oak tables, and lots of interesting artefacts and several namesake pictures of cocks, and Badger Best, Sussex, Tanglefoot and a Badger guest on handpump; piped music, fruit machine and TV. Straightforward bar food includes soup (£3.95), sandwiches (from £4.25), cod fillet in batter (£8.25) and steak and ale pie (£8.95), plus specials such as chilli con carne (£7.95), vegetable lasagne (£8.95), bass (£9.95), and home-made puddings (£4.75). The no smoking restaurant is in a nicely converted barn. Picnic-sets in front look out across a quiet lane towards the churchyard, the terrace at the back gives open country views, and a pretty, sheltered lawn has tables under parasols. There's also a children's play area and (at summer weekends) a bouncy castle. *(Recommended by Howard Dell, N R White, Bob and Maggie Atherton, Peter and Margaret Glenister, Mr and Mrs John Taylor, Julie Ryan, Gill and Keith Croxton, John Saville, Ian Phillips)*

Badger ~ Tenant John Moir ~ Real ale ~ Bar food (12-2.30, 6-9; 12-3, 5-7 Sun; not Mon evening) ~ Restaurant ~ (01923) 282908 ~ No children under 5 in bar and restaurant ~ Dogs welcome ~ Live entertainment Mon evening ~ Open 12-11(9 Sun)

LUCKY DIP

Besides the fully inspected pubs, you might like to try these Lucky Dips recommended to us and described by readers (if you do, please send us reports: www.goodguides.co.uk).

ARDELEY [TL3027]
Jolly Waggoner SG2 7AH [off B1037 NE of Stevenage]: Relaxed traditional pub with beams, timbering, lots of nooks and corners; new licensees as we went to press but has had wide choice of enjoyable fresh home-made food in bar and restaurant, Greene King IPA and Abbot and decent wines; pleasant garden and terrace *(LYM, Alistair Forsyth, Margaret and Allen Marsden, Paul Melvin)*

ASHWELL [TL2639]
Rose & Crown SG7 5NP [High St]: Comfortable open-plan local with enjoyable bar food inc good baguettes, Greene King IPA and Abbot, 16th-c beams, lovely log fire, no smoking candlelit restaurant, games in plainer public end of L-shaped bar; tables in big pretty country garden *(Mike Turner)*

AYOT ST LAWRENCE [TL1916]
Brocket Arms AL6 9BT [off B651 N of St Albans]: Individualistic low-beamed 14th-c pub, simple and old-fashioned, with long-serving landlord, blazing log fires (one in big inglenook), a dozen or so wines by the glass, Greene King and guest ales, traditional games, lunchtime sandwiches and other bar food inc good winter game dishes, may be wider choice in no smoking evening restaurant, leisurely informal service; piped classical music; children and dogs welcome, nice suntrap walled garden with outside bar and play area, bedrooms, handy for Shaw's Corner, open all day *(David and Ruth Shillitoe, Margaret and Allen Marsden, LYM, Eric Robinson, Jacqueline Pratt)*

BALDOCK [TL2434]
Old White Horse SG7 5BS [Station Rd]: Bright and cheerful former coaching inn popular for pub lunches from sandwiches up, Adnams, B&T SOS, Flowers *(Ian Phillips)*

BARKWAY [TL3834]
Tally Ho SG8 8EX [London Rd (B1386)]: Smart cosy bar with three interesting changing ales from small breweries such as Buntingford, Hertford and Nethergate tapped from the cask, good choice of wines by the glass, good value

sandwiches and good home cooking, friendly staff, comfortable sofas, daily papers, log fire and a second in candlelit no smoking restaurant area, no music or machines; picnic-sets in good-sized garden *(Shirley Sandilands, Paul and Marion Watts)*

BENINGTON [TL3022]

Lordship Arms SG2 7BX [Whempstead Rd]: Comfortable and unpretentious, with eight good real ales inc several interesting guest beers, September beer festival, good value simple lunchtime food (can book Sun roast), Weds curry night, welcoming attentive landlord, lots of telephone memorabilia; no credit cards *(Mike Turner, Steve Nye, Peter and Betty Ford)*

BISHOP'S STORTFORD [TL4820]

Jolly Brewers CM23 3BQ [South St]: Friendly and well organised, with frequently changing real ales, enjoyable pubby food, pool in separate games area; terrace tables, open all day wknds *(Stephen and Jean Curtis)*

BRAUGHING [TL3925]

Axe & Compass SG11 2QR [just off B1368; The Street]: Drive through a ford to reach this simple unspoilt country local; two roomy and pleasant bars (one an unusual corner-shape) and restaurant, enjoyable straightforward food, real ales, charming landlord, friendly service; well behaved dogs and children welcome, pretty village *(Margaret and Allen Marsden)*

BROOKMANS PARK [TL2504]

Cock o' the North AL9 6NA [Great North Rd (A1000, Bell Bar)]: Well spaced stripped pine furnishings, comfy sofas, pleasant paintings and prints and log fire a contrast with its 1930s roadhouse exterior; McMullens ale; usual food, piped music *(David Hoult, Robert F Smith, Mrs E E Sanders)*

CHIPPERFIELD [TL0302]

Boot WD4 9LN [Tower Hill, towards Bovingdon]: Neatly kept traditional pub with good ales such as Adnams, enjoyable old-fashioned pub food in restaurant, open fires; big play area, bouncy castle *(Roger Clarke)*

CHISWELL GREEN [TL1304]

Three Hammers AL2 3EA [just S of St Albans; Watford Rd]: Ember Inn with choice of real ales, decent reasonably priced food, prompt helpful service, several areas on different levels around central bar, a few rather low beams, abstracts and photographs of old St Albans *(KC)*

CHORLEYWOOD [TQ0396]

☆ *Gate* WD3 5SQ [Rickmansorth Rd]: Newly refurbished, with thriving atmosphere, enjoyable proper food even late on Sun evening, good choice of wines by the glass, helpful staff; handy for walkers on well wooded common nearby *(LYM, Mr and Mrs M Lindsay-Bush)*

Land of Liberty Peace & Plenty WD3 5BS [Long Lane, Heronsgate; just off M25, junction 17]: Enthusiastic new licensees searching out four or five interesting real ales, belgian bottled beers, tapas menu and good crisps, seating inc cosy corner banquette, no music *(Tracey and Stephen Groves)*

Stag WD3 5BT [Long Lane/Heronsgate Rd]: Spacious open-plan Edwardian pub with large no smoking eating area extending into conservatory, quiet relaxed atmosphere, McMullens ales, decent wines and food, reasonable prices, cheery and helpful if not always speedy service; tables on back lawn, play area, open all day *(Howard Dell, Tracey and Stephen Groves, Keith Callard)*

White Horse WD3 5SD [A404 just off M25 junction 18]: Pleasantly decorated beamed and carpeted pub with Greene King IPA and Abbot, decent food, friendly landlady, daily papers, pub games, fish tank, no smoking area; piped music, TV, Tues quiz night; tables on neat back terrace *(Michael Dandy)*

COLNEY HEATH [TL2007]

☆ *Plough* AL4 0SE [handy for A1(M) junction 3; A414 towards St Albans, doubling back at first roundabout then turning off left]: Pleasantly refurbished 18th-c low-beamed thatched local, warm and cosy with big log fire, chatty atmosphere, good value generous standard food from sandwiches, baguettes and ciabattas up (lunchtime Mon-Sat, and Fri/Sat evening), well kept Greene King IPA and Abbot and Fullers London Pride, friendly efficient staff, small brighter back dining area; white iron tables on pretty front terrace, picnic-sets on sheltered back terrace and lawn *(BB, Peter and Margaret Glenister, John Picken, John Cadge, Monica Cockburn, Mike Jefferies, Ivan Ericsson)*

DATCHWORTH [TL2717]

☆ *Horns* SG3 6RZ [Bramfield Rd]: Pretty flower-decked Tudor pub facing small green, low beams and big inglenook one end, high rafters and rugs on patterned bricks the other, attractive décor, wide choice of good reasonably priced food from proper sandwiches up, quick friendly service, real ales such as Fullers London Pride; tables out on crazy-paved terrace among roses *(LYM, Frazer and Louise Smith, Mike Turner)*

ELSTREE [TQ1697]

Battleaxes WD6 3AD [Butterfly Lane]: Popular chain family dining pub with wide range of attractively priced food in bar and conservatory, Marstons Pedigree; garden tables *(Adele Summers, Alan Black, Brian P White, Mrs E E Sanders)*

EPPING GREEN [TL2906]

☆ *Beehive* SG13 8NB [back rd Cuffley—Little Berkhamsted]: Fresh fish the main attraction, with wide choice of other good value generous food inc impressive children's menu, friendly efficient staff, good range of wines by the glass and Adnams and Greene King IPA in cosy and popular pub with comfortable beamed dining area on left; tables overlooking fields *(Gordon Neighbour, Professors Alan and Ann Clarke, Geoff and Sylvia Donald, Mrs E E Sanders)*

FLAUNDEN [TL0101]

☆ *Bricklayers Arms* HP3 0PH [off A41; Hogpits Bottom]: Low-beamed and timbered country pub with good pub food inc sandwiches and good home-smoked fish lunchtime and

Mon/Tues evenings, restaurant meals other evenings, attractive décor and nice dining area adjoining bar/lounge, friendly attentive staff, Fullers London Pride and Greene King ales, good choice of wines by the glass, no piped music; children in eating areas, appealing old-fashioned garden, nearby walks (C J Woodhead, LYM, Alex and Irene Harvey)

GILSTON [TL4313]

Plume of Feathers CM20 2RD [Pye Corner]: Warm atmosphere, friendly staff, good choice of food, Adnams Broadside, good choice of wines by the glass; piped music (C Galloway)

GREAT OFFLEY [TL1427]

Gloucester Arms SG5 3DG [Luton Rd (A505)]: Interesting part clap-boarded building refurbished as smart dining pub, sofas in small bar, main no smoking eating area with good choice of modern often elaborate food from open kitchen, lunchtime carvery Sun, Greene King ales, good choice of wines by the glass; piped music, over-21s only in bar; small front garden, open all day. (Michael Dandy)

☆ *Green Man* SG5 3AR [signed off A505 Luton—Hitchin; High St]: Roomy and comfortable olde-worlde Chef & Brewer with peaceful country view from large flagstoned no smoking conservatory, picnic-sets on pleasant back terrace and garden; very wide choice of enjoyable food, well organised friendly staff, Courage Directors and Theakstons Best and Old Peculier, good choice of wines by the glass, good coffee, blazing log fires; may be unobtrusive piped classical music; children welcome, striking inn-sign, open all day (Michael Dandy, LYM, Wendy Cox)

Red Lion SG5 3DZ [Kings Walden Rd]: Friendly unpretentious local, low beams, big inglenook log fire, changing ales such as Thwaites and Youngs, good choice of wines by the glass, reasonably priced generous food from sandwiches up inc OAP wkdy lunches, small conservatory restaurant; piped music; picnic-sets in small sunny back garden, good walks from pub, simple bedrooms (Peter and Margaret Glenister, Steve Nye)

HARPENDEN [TL1413]

☆ *Carpenters Arms* AL5 1BD [Cravells Rd]: Compact and welcoming, with bargain food from good doorstep sandwiches to basic hot dishes, changing ales such as Adnams, Courage Best, Elgoods Black Dog Mild and Greene King Abbot from corner bar, special-issue bottled beers, chatty landlady and friendly efficient staff, two open fires, lovingly collected car memorabilia inc models and overseas number-plates; neat well planned side terrace (Michael Dandy, Monica Cockburn, Mike Jefferies, Terry Buckland)

Engineer AL5 1DJ [St Johns Rd]: Two-bar pub in residential area, Adnams, Black Sheep, Greene King IPA and Charles Wells Bombardier, good choice of wines by the glass, reasonably priced pubby bar food from sandwiches up, welcoming obliging staff, no smoking conservatory restaurant with different menu inc Sun roasts; piped music, games, TV; garden with terrace and small fishpond (Michael Dandy)

Fox AL5 3QE [Luton Rd, Kinsbourne Green; 2¼ miles from M1 junction 10; A1081 (ex A6) towards town]: Refurbished as contemporary dining pub, tiled floor, some leather armchairs and sofas, lots of modern dining tables, typical food inc platefuls of salads, pasta and pizzas, Bass and Greene King IPA, open fire; piped music; terrace tables (Michael Dandy)

Old Bell AL5 3BN [Luton Rd (A1081)]: Compact Chef & Brewer with decent food, good choice of wines by the glass, Courage Best, daily papers, pub games; large back tree-shaded garden (Eithne Dandy)

Old Cock AL5 2SP [High St]: Roomy low-beamed bare-boards town pub dating from early 17th c, real ales such as Buckleys Rev James, John Smiths and Wadworths Summersault, decent food, pub games; piped music, jazz Sun afternoon; pavement tables, more on back terrace (Michael Dandy)

Red Cow AL5 4ND [Westfield Rd]: Small spotless low-ceilinged pub with Fullers London Pride and Shepherd Neame Spitfire from long bar, generous low-priced pub food from baguettes and baked potatoes up, quick helpful service, lots of brasswork; TV; tables out in front among flower tubs and hanging baskets, more in small back garden with play area (Michael Dandy)

Rose & Crown AL5 1PS [Southdown Rd]: Enjoyable food from good baguettes up, Greene King IPA and Theakstons, good coffee, quick service, daily papers, contemporary décor and furnishings, small bar area with a couple of settees, airy back conservatory restaurant, games; piped music; side terrace and back garden (Michael Dandy, Terry Buckland)

Silver Cup AL5 2JF [St Albans Rd (A1081)]: Friendly and neatly refurbished pub with Adnams Regatta, Marstons Pedigree and Charles Wells Eagle and Bombardier, good choice of wines by the glass, wide choice of food from sandwiches, baguettes and pub lunches to restaurant dishes, ample breakfast even for non-residents, welcoming landlord and good staff, bare-boards bar and no smoking carpeted dining area, prints of old Harpenden, more expensive restaurant; piped music, TVs in bar; tables outside, four bedrooms, open all day from 7.30 (Michael Dandy, Ben Weedon, Brian and Janet Ainscough)

White Horse AL5 2JP [Hatching Green]: Timbered building refurbished as trendy dining pub, modern furniture and décor, front bar with Fullers London Pride and Tring Brock, good helpful service, daily papers, attractive main area with full restaurant menu, not cheap but with some unusual dishes; piped music; terrace tables (Mr and Mrs John Taylor, Michael Dandy, Mrs Anne Callender)

HEMEL HEMPSTEAD [TL0411]

☆ *Crown & Sceptre* HP2 6EY [Bridens Camp; leaving on A4146, right at Flamstead/Markyate sign opp Red Lion]: Cheerfully unpretentious rambling rooms, not at all smart but some oak panelling antique settles among more usual seating, Adnams Broadside, Greene King IPA and Abbot and a guest beer, reasonably priced pubby food from wide range of sandwiches and baguettes up, log fires, darts and dominoes, books and magazines; TV; children and dogs welcome, garden with play area, wandering chickens, rabbits and scarecrow, heated front picnic-sets, good walks, open all day summer wknds *(Michael Dandy, LYM, Dennis Jones)*

Olde Chequers HP2 6HH [Gaddesden Row; N, towards Markyate]: Recently refurbished attractive brick-built pub, Adnams Bitter and Broadside and Greene King IPA, good range of wines by the glass, wide choice of generous usual food from sandwiches up, small bar, large back dining areas with a mix of furnishings on carpet, flagstones or bare boards, log fires; picnic-sets and play area in garden *(Michael Dandy)*

HERTFORD [TL3213]

Hillside SG14 3EP [Port Hill, Bengeo (B158)]: No smoking dining pub with interesting modern cooking, good house wines, two northern real ales on electric pump, welcoming service, stripped beams and brickwork, leather sofas in pleasant log-fire lounge, pleasant quiet décor, bowls of olives and good nuts, side dining room with chunky scrubbed tables; piped music; children welcome, barn delicatessen, cl Mon, open all day wknds *(Grahame Brooks, Jack and Sandra Clarfelt)*

☆ *Old Cross Tavern* SG14 1JA [St Andrew St]: Eight particularly well kept real ales inc interesting guest beers, good home-made lunchtime food, friendly olde-worlde feel with log fire, brass, china etc (conversion from antiques shop); dogs welcome, small heated back terrace, open all day *(Ian Arthur)*

HEXTON [TL1030]

Raven SG5 3JB [signed off B655]: Big child-friendly dining pub matching this mock-Tudor estate village, four linked largely no smoking areas, plenty of dining tables, oil paintings (some for sale), wide range of good value food from baguettes and baked potatoes up, two children's menus, real ales such as Fullers London Pride, Greene King IPA and Old Speckled Hen and Charles Wells Bombardier, quick friendly service, daily papers, open fire, pool one end; piped music; big garden with heated terrace, barbecue, good play area *(Michael Dandy, Michael and Alison Sandy, Ian Phillips)*

HIGH WYCH [TL4614]

Rising Sun CM21 0HZ: Cosy old-fashioned local, serving hatch to carpeted lounge with coal or log fire, central area with Courage Best and good guest beers tapped from casks behind the counter, friendly landlord and locals, bare-boards games room (children allowed) with darts and woodburner; no food, no mobile phones or pagers, no music; tables in small garden *(the Didler, Pete Baker)*

HITCHIN [TL1828]

Half Moon SG4 9TZ [Queen St]: Welcoming open-plan pub with Adnams, Youngs Special

and guest ales, Weston's Old Rosie cider and perry, good choice of wines by the glass, bargain traditional food inc good sausage baguettes and pasta, open fires, congenial licensees; quiet piped jazz; open all day wknds *(Robert Killip)*

Sun SG5 1AF [Sun St]: Pleasantly refurbished beamed and timbered bar with mix of furniture inc sofas, Greene King IPA and Abbot, good choice of wines by the glass, adjacent brasserie; piped music, Sunday folk club; courtyard tables *(Michael Dandy)*

HUNSDON [TL4114]

☆ *Fox & Hounds* SG12 8NJ: Newly refurbished and reopened no smoking bistro pub with good enterprising fresh food, three real ales, good choice of wines by the glass, door to lavatories disguised as bookcases, no piped music *(LYM, Ian Arthur, Mrs Margo Finlay, Jörg Kasprowski, Kath Edwards)*

KIMPTON [TL1718]

White Horse SG4 8RJ [High St]: Welcoming refurbished pub with laminate floor and light décor, log fire, friendly helpful service, McMullens Best and AK with a guest such as Arkells 3B in small bar area, good choice of pub food from baguettes and pizzas up with some extra evening dishes in airy and spotless no smoking dining area, darts in games area up a few steps; some tables out by road or car park *(Michael Dandy, David and Ruth Shillitoe, Peter and Margaret Glenister)*

KNEBWORTH [TL2320]

☆ *Lytton Arms* SG3 6QB [Park Lane, Old Knebworth]: Several spotless big-windowed rooms around large central servery, changing real ales such as Adnams, Archers and Fullers London Pride, two farm ciders, good choice of wines, good value food from interesting choice of sandwiches, baguettes and baked potatoes up, friendly staff, good log fire, daily papers, no smoking conservatory; children and dogs welcome, picnic-sets on front terrace, back garden with play area, open all day wknds *(Dr P C Rea, Gerry and Rosemary Dobson, Deborah Shearly, LYM, Peter and Margaret Glenister)*

LITTLE BERKHAMSTED [TL2908]

☆ *Five Horseshoes* SG13 8LY [Church Rd]: Attractive and convivial largely no smoking Chef & Brewer nr church, 17th-c beams, dark wood and stripped brickwork, two log fires, Courage Best and Directors and two guest beers, decent wines, good value generous food from sandwiches and baguettes up, good service even on busy evenings, soft lighting; comfortable restaurant, cosy little upper dining room; garden with picnic-sets, busy in summer, attractive countryside *(Gordon Neighbour, Ross Balaam, Professors Alan and Ann Clarke, Robert Turnham, Jeremy King, Peter and Margaret Glenister, Mrs E E Sanders)*

LITTLE GADDESDEN [SP9913]

Bridgewater Arms HP4 1PD [Nettleden Rd, off B4506]: Recently decorated dining pub with enjoyable food from sandwiches and baked potatoes up, Greene King IPA and Abbot, good wine choice, good coffee, friendly service, daily papers, carpeted bar with log fire in smoking area, smart separate restaurant, darts and games in small bare-boards public area; piped music; garden tables, good walks straight from the pub *(Michael Dandy, LYM)*

LITTLE HADHAM [TL4322]
Nags Head SG11 2AX [Hadham Ford, towards Much Hadham]: 16th-c country dining pub with good value food inc fish in small linked heavily black-beamed rooms, small bar with three Greene King beers and decent wines, no smoking restaurant down a couple of steps; children in eating areas, tables in pleasant garden *(Gordon Neighbour, LYM)*

LONDON COLNEY [TL1803]
Green Dragon AL2 1RB [Waterside; just off main st by bridge at S end]: Good value generous straightforward food (not Sun), real ales such as Adnams, Fullers London Pride and Shepherd Neame Spitfire, decent wine, cheerful efficient service, lots of ancient timbers, beams and brasses, soft lighting, woodburner, separate dining room; prettily set riverside picnic-sets – would be even nicer without the parked cars *(Professors Alan and Ann Clarke, LYM, Stan Edwards)*

MUCH HADHAM [TL4219]
☆ *Bull* SG10 6BU [High St]: Nicely refurbished and neatly kept old dining pub with hard-working and cheerful young licensees, good food changing daily, good choice of wines by the glass inc champagne, Greene King IPA, inglenook log fire in unspoilt bar, roomy and civilised dining lounge and smaller back dining room; children welcome, good-sized garden *(LYM, Charles Gysin, Ross and Christine Loveday)*

NEWGATE STREET [TL3005]
Crown SG13 8RP: Attractive flower-decked building with colourful garden, cosy inside, with friendly staff and landlord, good varied home-made food, Greene King IPA and Abbot, good house wine; small well behaved dogs welcome, handy for Northaw Great Wood walks *(Lucien Perring)*

NUTHAMPSTEAD [TL4134]
☆ *Woodman* SG8 8NB [off B1368 S of Barkway]: Tucked-away thatched and weatherboarded village pub, welcoming and well run, sofa and other furnishings in comfortable unspoilt bar with worn tiled floor, nice inglenook log fire, another fire opposite and 17th-c low beams and timbers, old local photographs, enjoyable home-made food (not Sun evening), efficient friendly service, dining room, no music; interesting USAF memorabilia (nearby World War II airfield), inc a memorial outside; benches out overlooking tranquil lane, comfortable bedrooms, open all day Sat *(Margaret and Allen Marsden, BB, M R D Foot)*

PERRY GREEN [TL4317]
Hoops SG10 6EF [off B1004 Widford—Much Hadham]: Village pub opp Henry Moore Foundation (guided tours in summer by appt), stripped brick, terracotta walls, beams, standing timbers and inglenook, Fullers London Pride, Greene King IPA and a guest

beer, cosy no smoking dining area (children allowed); garden with large covered terrace, open all day Sun *(Gordon Neighbour, LYM, Dr P C Rea)*

POTTEN END [TL0108]
Martins Pond HP4 2QQ [The Green]: Small friendly traditional pub with enjoyable food inc nice twists on pubby favourites, Fullers London Pride and Tetleys; small garden with picnic-sets, opp pretty green and pond *(Ian Phillips)*

PUCKERIDGE [TL3823]
☆ *White Hart* SG11 1RR [Braughing Rd]: Rambling nicely updated 14th-c pub with enjoyable food inc steaks, duck and lots of fresh fish (fish and chips to take away, too), friendly welcome and relaxed informal atmosphere, McMullens ales and an occasional guest beer, good coffee, log fire, contemporary colour-scheme; children welcome, big garden, open all day *(Stephen and Jean Curtis, LYM, Mr and Mrs Hill)*

REDBOURN [TL1111]
Chequers AL3 7AD [St Albans Rd (A5183), nr M1 junction 9]: Small thatched Chef & Brewer family dining pub recently rebuilt after fire, flagstones and dark wood, Adnams, Camerons IPA and Charles Wells Bombardier, good choice of wines by the glass, quick helpful service; large back terrace and small pleasant garden *(Michael Dandy)*

REED [TL3636]
☆ *Cabinet* SG8 8AH [off A10; High St]: 16th-c weatherboarded pub housing attractive upmarket no smoking restaurant with current chef doing good food, very small bar with amiable french service, good choice of wines by the glass inc choice of two champagnes and prosecco, Adnams, Greene King IPA and a seasonal beer, inglenook log fire; piped music; charming big garden with pond *(Bob and Maggie Atherton, B N F and M Parkin, LYM, Adrian White)*

RICKMANSWORTH [TQ0594]
Druids WD3 1BB [High St]: Pub reworked on rugby theme, enjoyable food esp seafood *(Jerry Green)*
Pennsylvanian WD3 1AN [High St]: Roomy no smoking Wetherspoons with pleasant dark décor, nice leather seats near gas flame-effect fire in big baronial fireplace, attentive staff, real ales inc Hertford Red Squirrel, usual food deals; open all day *(Reg Fowle, Helen Rickwood, Tony Hobden)*
Rose & Crown WD3 1PP [Woodcock Hill/Harefield Rd, off A404 E of Rickmansworth at Batchworth]: Friendly low-beamed pub with warm coal fire and real ales such as Caledonian Deuchars IPA and Timothy Taylors Landlord in traditional country bar, quick service by helpful young staff, airy extension with good choice of restaurant food inc up-to-date dishes; large peaceful garden, wide views from big car park *(Tracey and Stephen Groves)*

RUSHDEN [TL3031]
☆ *Moon & Stars* SG9 0TA [Mill End; off A507 about a mile W of Cottered]: Cottagey beamed

country pub, all no smoking, with friendly and hard-working young licensees, good freshly made food (not Sun/Mon evenings) in neatly kept relaxed and welcoming lounge bar and small dining room (worth booking), inglenook log fire, Greene King ales with a guest such as Shepherd Neame Spitfire; well behaved children welcome, pleasant garden inc heated terrace, peaceful country setting *(LYM, Derek Walker)*

SARRATT [TQ0499]

☆ *Boot* WD3 6BL [The Green]: Attractive early 18th-c tiled pub, lively, cheery and unpretentious, with usual pub food inc some innovative sandwiches, friendly staff, Greene King ales, cosy rambling bar with unusual inglenook fireplace, more modern dining room; bar can be smoky; garden, pleasant spot facing green, handy for Chess Valley walks *(N R White, B Brewer, LYM, Ian Phillips, KC, Brian P White)*

SAWBRIDGEWORTH [TL4815]

Bull CM21 9BX [Cambridge Rd]: Attractive décor with lots of brass and beams, decent generous food; keg beer *(B N F and M Parkin)*
Gate CM21 9JJ [London Rd (A1184)]: 18th-c local with good range of real ales (hundreds of ceiling pump clips show how quickly they change), bank hol beer festivals with live music, farm cider, cheap fresh lunchtime food, roomy and relaxed front bar, back bar with pool and games, little snug tucked behind bar; open all day wknds *(Tony and Wendy Hobden)*

ST ALBANS [TL1307]

Blue Anchor AL3 4RY [Fishpool St]: Popular dining lounge with good value sandwiches and other bar food (not Sun evening), McMullens ales, attractive prices, welcoming landlord, daily papers, small locals' bar with sensibly placed darts, real fire; sizeable garden, handy for Roman remains *(the Didler, Mike and Jennifer Marsh)*
Farmers Boy AL1 1PQ [London Rd]: Bustling unpretentious bay-windowed pub brewing its own distinctive Verulam IPA, Farmers Joy and seasonal beers, also their own lager and continental bottled beers, lots of old prints on softly lit smoke-effect walls, imposing clock, log fire, back open kitchen serving straightforward food from sandwiches and baked potatoes up all day, helpful staff, no smoking area; SkyTV; open all day, suntrap back terrace with barbecues *(the Didler, John Dwane)*
Farriers Arms AL3 4PT [Lower Dagnall St]: Plain friendly two-bar local in no-frills old part, McMullens inc Mild and guest beers, bar food wkdys, lots of old pictures of the pub (Campaign for Real Ale started here in the early 1970s) *(the Didler)*
Garibaldi AL1 1RT [Albert St; left turn down Holywell Hill past White Hart – car park left at end]: Fullers local with their ales and guest beers, good house wines, some unusual cooking as well as traditional dishes, cheerful staff; may be piped music; children welcome, open all day *(the Didler, LYM)*

Goat AL1 1RN [Sopwell Lane, off Holywell Hill]: Neatly modernised rambling areas around central servery, traditional furnishings, open fire, cheery atmosphere, decent food, friendly staff, several real ales, good range of malt whiskies; games machines, piped music; children in eating area, tables in neat back garden, open all day *(Andy and Jill Kassube, LYM)*
Lower Red Lion AL3 4RX [Fishpool St]: Convivial chatty two-bar local dating from 17th c, lots of interesting changing ales, imported beers on tap and in bottle, May Day and Aug bank hol beer festivals, home-made food inc Sun lunches, red plush seats and carpet, Weds quiz night; tables in good-sized back garden, pleasant bedrooms, open all day wknds *(Andy and Jill Kassube, the Didler, John Dwane)*
☆ *Plough* AL4 0RW [Tyttenhanger Green, off A414 E]: Friendly village pub popular for its fine changing range of real ales, congenial prompt service even when it's busy, lovely longcase clock, good log fire, good value straightforward lunchtime food, interesting old beer bottles and mats, back conservatory; big garden with play area *(LYM, the Didler, Monica Cockburn, Mike Jefferies)*
☆ *Six Bells* AL3 4SH [St Michaels St]: Well kept rambling food pub with cheerful helpful service, real ales such as Adnams, Fullers London Pride and Greene King IPA and Abbot, big helpings of fresh food from lunchtime ciabattas and baked potatoes up inc good value pies, wider evening choice, low beams and timbers, log fire, quieter no smoking panelled dining room; children welcome, family room, occasional barbecues in small back garden, very handy for Roman Verulam Museum, open all day Fri-Sun *(Duncan Cloud, Professors Alan and Ann Clarke, LYM, Mike and Jennifer Marsh, Peter and Giff Bennett, Michael and Alison Sandy)*
White Hart Tap AL1 1QJ [Keyfield, round corner from Garibaldi]: Friendly neatly kept white-panelled Victorian pub with four changing ales, good value quickly served fresh lunchtime food; live band Sat, tables outside, open all day *(Andy and Jill Kassube, Derek Field, John Kearins)*

THERFIELD [TL3337]

☆ *Fox & Duck* SG8 9PN [signed off A10 S of Royston; The Green]: Open-plan bow-windowed pub with country chairs and big stripped-top dark tables on stone flooring, interesting food from enterprising sandwiches to seasonal game and some thai dishes, Greene King ales, decent wines and coffee, courteous helpful staff, good-sized carpeted back restaurant, darts in smaller boarded area on left (with TV and fruit machine); may be piped pop music; bedrooms with own bathrooms, a few picnic-sets in garden with good play equipment, more out on front green, quiet village, pleasant walks nearby *(BB, Mike Turner)*

TRING [SP9211]

Kings Arms HP23 6BE [King St]: Long-serving

landlord keeping half a dozen interesting changing ales in top condition, usually inc local Tring brews and Wadworths 6X direct from the brewers, sensibly priced wholesome home cooking (lunchtime emphasis on this, can phone order ahead) from hot baps up, ethnic and vegetarian leanings, simple décor with brewery memorabilia, pine and pews, no smoking area; busy with young people evenings; heated sheltered terrace *(Mike Pugh)*

☆ *Robin Hood* HP23 5ED [Brook St (B486)]: Modest local with short changing choice of surprisingly good food esp fish bought fresh each day, several small drinking areas, three Fullers beers, comfortable settles, lots of dark wood, slight nautical theme, dining conservatory with woodburner and diverse prints; piped music; no children or dogs inside, tables on small pleasant back terrace, free public car park nearby *(R E Dixon, BB, John Branston)*

WADESMILL [TL3517]
Sow & Pigs SG12 0ST [Cambridge Rd, Thundridge (A10 N of Ware)]: Neatly kept and cheerful dining pub, enjoyable food from sandwiches up, friendly efficient service, changing real ales, spacious pleasantly rustic beamed dining room off central bar with pig décor, log fire; no dogs, children in eating areas, tables outside, open all day *(Adele Summers, Alan Black, LYM, Mrs Margo Finlay, Jörg Kasprowski)*

WALKERN [TL2826]
White Lion SG2 7PA [B1037]: Comfortably cottagey open-plan 17th-c pub, low beams, bare boards, good inglenook log fire, Greene King IPA and Abbot and a guest beer, decent bar food from sandwiches and baguettes up, friendly staff, small no smoking restaurant; piped music; children in eating areas, open all day, lots of outdoor distractions for children inc good play areas *(LYM, Peter and Margaret Glenister)*

WATER END [TL2204]
Woodman AL9 7TT [B197 N of Potters Bar]:

Enjoyable reasonably priced food inc carvery and quick friendly service in comfortable two-bar pub, pretty village *(Professors Alan and Ann Clarke)*

WATTON-AT-STONE [TL3019]
☆ *George & Dragon* SG14 3TA [High St (B1001)]: Country dining pub popular for wide food choice from sandwiches up, Greene King IPA and Abbot and a guest beer, decent wines, good friendly service, interesting mix of antique and modern prints on partly timbered walls, big inglenook fireplace, daily papers; children welcome in eating areas, pretty shrub-screened garden with heaters and boules, open all day wknds *(LYM, Mike and Jennifer Marsh, Peter and Margaret Glenister, Peter Saville, Mrs E E Sanders)*

WHITWELL [TL1821]
Maidens Head SG4 8AH [High St (B651)]: Nice staff in old-fashioned local with McMullens and guest beers, usual food from simple sandwiches up, good coffee, interesting key-ring collection; tables in safe children's garden *(Ross Balaam, John Branston)*

WIGGINTON [SP9310]
Greyhound HP23 6EH [just S of Tring]: Friendly Rothschild estate pub in quiet village, wide choice of freshly made food using local supplies cooked to order, good range of wines, several real ales, good coffees; children welcome, garden with play area, Ridgeway walks *(BOB)*

WILDHILL [TL2606]
Woodman AL9 6EA [off B158 Brookmans Pk—Essendon]: Simple tucked-away country local with friendly licensees, attractively priced Greene King, McMullens and interesting changing guest ales, darts, lunchtime food (not Sun), open-plan bar and small back parlour; picnic-sets on long grassy bank above car park, walks from pub *(Tim Maddison)*

WILLIAN [TL2230]
Fox SG6 2AE: Enjoyable reasonably priced food, young lively staff, relaxed atmosphere *(Richard Pettengell)*

Isle of Wight

Over the years, with the help of our tireless reader-reporters, we have assessed well over a hundred pubs on the island. After numerous reports and careful editorial inspection, we have winnowed our selection down to just ten main entries. (But do look at the Lucky Dip entries too, more than half of them already inspected and approved by us.) This perky little set of pubs is run by enthusiastic licensees, and have the sort of cheery laid-back atmosphere you'd hope for during a relaxed holiday break. Several of them even boast terraces overlooking lovely waterside views. One new entry, the easy-going Folly at Cowes, back in the *Guide* under friendly new licensees and now offering tasty well liked food, is just such a place. The jovial Spyglass at Ventnor is another great all-rounder. It's in a splendid spot, with enjoyable food and a range of real ales that earns a new Beer Award this year. The strong grip that Enterprise seems to have on the island's better pubs may go some way towards explaining the fairly limited range of beers we found here, though our second new main entry, the unpretentious Sun at Hulverstone, puts up a valiant show – last year they got through over 280 different beers. Bar food seems to be up a notch on the island this year (last year we didn't make a Dining Pub award here). The Red Lion at Freshwater is as popular as ever with those looking for a good meal in a slightly more grown up atmosphere, but it's the rather cosmopolitan-feeling Seaview Hotel, and the buzzy New Inn at Shalfleet, which specialises in seafood, that lead the stakes. It's a close call, but the New Inn just pips its rival at the post for the award of Isle of Wight Dining Pub of the Year.

ARRETON SZ5486 Map 2
White Lion ㉕ £
A3056 Newport—Sandown; PO30 3AA

The pleasantly pubby beamed lounge bar at this welcoming white-painted village local has dark pink walls or stripped brick above stained pine dado, gleaming brass and horse tack, and lots of cushioned wheelback chairs on the patterned red carpet. There is very quiet piped music, and the public bar has a fruit machine and darts; Badger Best, Fullers London Pride and Wadworths 6X on handpump. Besides sandwiches and baguettes (from £3.50) and ploughman's (£5.75), straightforward food includes soup (£2.95), chilli (£5.95), lasagne, vegetable curry or haddock and chips (£6.45), pie of the day (£7.25), steaks (from £9.95), and a handful of specials. There's a no smoking restaurant and family room as well as a no smoking area in the stable room. The pleasant garden has a small play area. More reports please. *(Recommended by Tony and Penny Burton, Ian Phillips, Lew and Dot Hood)*

Enterprise ~ Lease Chris and Kate Cole ~ Real ale ~ Bar food (12-9) ~ (01983) 528479 ~ Children in family room ~ Dogs allowed in bar ~ Open 11-11; 12-10.30 Sun

BEMBRIDGE SZ6587 Map 2
Crab & Lobster 🛏
Foreland Fields Road, off Howgate Road (which is off B3395 via Hillgate Road);
PO35 5TR

Picnic sets on the terrace outside this well positioned inn, which is perched on low
cliffs within yards of the shore and prettily adorned with flower baskets in summer,
take in great views over the Solent. The dining area and some of the bedrooms
share the same views. Inside it's roomier than you might expect, and it's done out in
a civilised, almost parlourish style, with lots of yachting memorabilia and old local
photographs, and a blazing fire in winter months; darts, dominoes and cribbage.
They serve a very good choice of fresh local seafood specials every day, such as crab
cakes (£7.50), spicy baked local crab, lamb steak or grilled salmon fillet (£9.50),
seafood tagliatelle or veal escalope (£9.95), crab and lobster platter for two
(£22.95) and whole lobster (£23.50; half lobster £12.95). Other very well prepared
food includes sandwiches (from £4.25; very good crab ones for £5.50), filled
baguettes (from £4.95), soup (from £3.25), assorted pâté (£4.50), baked potatoes
(from £4.50), ploughman's (£6.95), home-made lasagne or vegetarian curry
(£7.50), mixed grill (£10.50), steak (from £12.95), and puddings such as treacle
sponge (£3.75); children's menu (£4.25); the restaurant is no smoking. Flowers
Original, Goddards Fuggle-Dee-Dum and Greene King IPA are on handpump, with
decent house wines, about 20 malt whiskies, farm cider and good coffee; piped
music (even in the lavatories). *(Recommended by Derek and Sylvia Stephenson, R G Trevis,
Julie and Bill Ryan, Glenwys and Alan Lawrence, B N F and M Parkin, Alan M Pring, Geoff and
Sylvia Donald)*

Enterprise ~ Lease Richard, Adrian and Pauline Allan ~ Real ale ~ Bar food (12-2.30, 6-10)
~ Restaurant ~ (01983) 872244 ~ Children welcome ~ Dogs allowed in bar ~ Open
11-11(12 Sat); 12-10.30 Sun ~ Bedrooms: £40B/£80B

BONCHURCH SZ5778 Map 2
Bonchurch Inn
Bonchurch Shute; from A3055 E of Ventnor turn down to Old Bonchurch opposite
Leconfield Hotel; PO38 1NU

The bar, no smoking restaurant, rooms and kitchens of this curious little place are
spread around a tucked away cobbled courtyard, and all snuggled below a steep,
rocky slope. Tables, a fountain and pergola out here are nicely enclosed, giving the
courtyard a slightly continental feel on warm summer days. The layout makes more
sense when you remember that before it gained its licence in the 1840s it was the
stables for the nearby manor house. The furniture-packed Victorian bar has a good
chatty local atmosphere, and conjures up images of salvaged shipwrecks, with its
floor of narrow-planked ship's decking, and seats like the ones that old-fashioned
steamers used to have. A separate entrance leads to the very simple no smoking
family room (a bit cut off from the congenial atmosphere of the public bar). As well
as Scottish Courage Directors and Best tapped from the cask, there are italian wines
by the glass, a few bottled french wines, darts, shove-ha'penny, dominoes and
cribbage. The welcoming landlord is Italian, and the menu reflects this with lasagne
(£7.50), tagliatelle carbonara (£7.95) or spaghetti with salmon or seafood risotto
(£8.95), as well as standard items such as sandwiches (from £3, toasted 30p extra),
soup (£4), grilled plaice (£8.95) and steak (from £10.50); there is a £1 charge for
credit cards. The pub owns a newly refurbished holiday flat for up to six people.
(Recommended by David Coleman, Dr D and Mrs B Woods, Geoff and Linda Payne)

Free house ~ Licensees Ulisse and Gillian Besozzi ~ Real ale ~ Bar food ~ Restaurant ~
(01983) 852611 ~ Children in family room ~ Dogs allowed in bar ~ Open 11-3, 6.30-11;
12-3, 7-10.30 Sun ~ Bedrooms: /£80B

COWES SZ5092 Map 2
Folly

Folly Lane – which is signposted off A3021 just S of Whippingham; PO32 6NB

The view from this splendidly positioned pub is worth a visit in itself. Seats on a waterside terrace look out to all sorts of nautical activity on the wide Medina estuary, and big windows in the bar share the same views. Rumour has it that the building originated from a french sea-going barge that beached here during a smuggling run in the early 1700s. The laid-back timbered interior certainly gives the sense of a ship's below decks. Straightforward but atmospheric furnishings include wooden tables (ready to be danced on come Saturday night) and chairs, and stools at the bar. All in all this is a cheery lighthearted place, with happy staff, and not surprisingly it gets very busy in summer. Breakfast is served first thing, followed by the lunchtime and evening menus, which, though varying slightly, seem to include a tasty dish to suit everyone: soup (£3.25), sandwiches (from £3.75), sausage and mash or lasagne (£6.95), cod and chips or beef and ale pie (£7.95), brie, mushroom and cranberry wellington (£8.45), 8oz sirloin steak (£10.95), daily specials such as cod loin with tomato parmesan crust (£8.45), red thai prawn curry (£8.75) and grilled halibut in creamy parsley sauce (£10.45), and good old favourite puddings such as sticky toffee pudding or chocolate mousse cake (£3.95). Greene King IPA and Old Speckled Hen and Goddards on handpump; no smoking area, pool and piped music. They set up a bouncy castle in the landscaped garden in summer. Watch out for the sleeping policemen along the lane if you're driving, and if you're coming along the river, they have moorings, a water taxi, long-term parking on the field, and showers, and they even keep an eye on weather forecasts and warnings. (Recommended by JDM, KM, Ian Pickard, Mrs Linda Campbell, OPUS)

Greene King ~ Managers Andy and Cheryl Greenwood ~ Real ale ~ Bar food (breakfast 9-11, 12-9.30(9 Sun)) ~ (01983) 297171 ~ Children welcome ~ Live entertainment Thurs and Sat evenings and Fri in summer ~ Open 11-11(11.30 Sat, 10.30 Sun)

FRESHWATER SZ3487 Map 2
Red Lion 🍴 ♟

Church Place; from A3055 at E end of village by Freshwater Garage mini-roundabout follow Yarmouth signpost, then take first real right turn signed to Parish Church; PO40 9BP

The grown-up atmosphere at this bustling pub tends to be appreciated by visitors without smaller children (unusually these days smoking is permitted throughout). Indeed it's so popular that if you want to eat it's a good idea to book ahead. Though the food is a big draw, chatting locals who fill the stools along the counter keep a pubby feel. The comfortably furnished open-plan bar has open fires, low grey sofas and sturdy country-kitchen style furnishings on mainly flagstoned floors, with bare boards at one end. The well executed paintings (between photographs and china platters) hung round the walls are by the licensee's brother and are well worth a look in themselves. The very enjoyable food is listed on blackboards behind the bar, and as well as lunchtime filled baguettes (from £4.95) and ploughman's (£5.95) might include soup (£4.50), whitebait (£6.25), crab-stuffed mushrooms (£6.50), sausage and mash, fish pie or steak and ale pie (£8.95), battered cod and mushy peas (£9.95), halibut steak with lemon butter (£12.95), and puddings such as apple crumble, black cherry trifle or bread and butter pudding (£4.50). Flowers Original, Fullers London Pride, Goddards and Wadworths 6X are kept under light blanket pressure, and the good choice of wines includes 16 by the glass. Fines on mobile phone users go to charity (they collect a lot for the RNLI); there's a games machine but no music. There are tables on a carefully tended grass and gravel area at the back (some under cover), beside which is the kitchen's herb garden, and a couple of picnic-sets in a quiet square at the front, overlooked by the church. The pub is virtually on the Freshwater Way footpath that connects Yarmouth with the southern coast at Freshwater Bay. (Recommended by Paul Boot, Di and Mike Gillam, JDM, KM,

Simon Collett-Jones, Gerry and Rosemary Dobson, Ian and Deborah Carrington, Peter Titcomb, Minda and Stanley Alexander)

Enterprise ~ Lease Michael Mence ~ Real ale ~ Bar food (12-2, 6.30-9) ~ (01983) 754925 ~ Children over 10 ~ Dogs allowed in bar ~ Open 11.30-3, 5.30-11; 11.30-4, 6-11 Sat; 12-3, 7-10.30 Sun

HULVERSTONE   SZ3984   Map 2
Sun
B3399; PO30 4EH

This thatched whitewashed country pub has a captivating position, with a view down from the charming secluded cottagey garden (which has a terrace and several picnic-sets) to a wild stretch of coast. It's very well positioned for some splendid walks along the cliffs, and up Mottistone Down to the prehistoric Long Stone. The bar (smoking in here only) is full of friendly chatter (with no piped music or games machines) and is unpretentiously traditional and low-ceilinged, with a fire blazing at one end and horsebrasses and ironwork hung around the fireplace, a nice mix of old furniture on flagstones and floorboards, and stone and brick walls; piped music, darts and board games. Leading off from one end is the more modern dining area, with large windows making the most of the view. Home-made bar food includes sandwiches (from £3.50), whitebait (£4.95), ploughman's (£6.25), sausage and mash or lasagne (£6.45), curry (£6.95), pie of day (£7.25) and mixed grill (£12.95); children's menu (£3.95). The specials board might include a range of starters such as duck and hoi-sin spring rolls, soup, or griddled black pudding with cranberry dip (all £3.95), vegetarian spring rolls and salad (£6.95), swordfish steak or whole trout (£8.95) and 8oz fillet steak (£13.95); Sunday roasts (£6.95). They also do an 'all you can eat' curry night on Thursdays (£6.95). The four quickly changing real ales are quite a feature here. Last year they got through 287 different ones from brewers such as Bass, Shepherd Neame, Timothy Taylors and Wadworths. Staff are helpful and friendly. *(Recommended by Sara Nicholls, Andy Moore, Phil Merrin)*

Enterprise ~ Lease Chris and Kate Cole ~ Real ale ~ Bar food (12-9) ~ (01983) 741124 ~ Children welcome ~ Dogs allowed in bar ~ Open 11-11; 12-10.30 Sun

SEAVIEW   SZ6291   Map 2
Seaview Hotel ⑪ ♀ ⇦
High Street; off B3330 Ryde—Bembridge; PO34 5EX

This smashing 200-year-old hotel is civilised yet enjoyably relaxed and very well run, with a bustling atmosphere, proper old-fashioned service, and reception rooms ranging from pubby to smart dining. The bay-windowed bar at the front has an impressive array of naval and merchant ship photographs, as well as Spy nautical cartoons for *Vanity Fair*, original receipts for Cunard's shipyard payments for the *Queen Mary* and *Queen Elizabeth*, and a line of close-set tables down each side on the turkey carpet. There's a more informal down-to-earth atmosphere in the simpler back bar, with traditional wooden furnishings on bare boards, lots of seafaring paraphernalia around its softly lit ochre walls, and a log fire. They keep Goddards, Youngs and a guest such as Gales HSB on handpump, a good selection of malt whiskies, a farm cider in summer and a good wine list (including a couple of local ones); TV, darts and board games. Using local ingredients wherever possible, and fish fresh from the sea, very good well presented and generously served bar food includes soup (£4.25), hot crab ramekin or sandwiches (£6.50), goats cheese and beetroot tart (£8.50), fish pie (£9.75), venison sausage and mash (£10.50), mussels and razor clams with garlic, herb and white wine sauce (£12.95) and rib-eye steak (£13.50), plus puddings such as sticky toffee pudding or cinnamon and jam rice pudding (from £4.50); Sunday roast (£9.95); the restaurant areas are no smoking. Tables on little terraces on either side of the path to the front door look down to the sea and along the coast, and some of the attractive bedrooms also have a sea view. *(Recommended by David H T Dimock, Dr Alan and Mrs Sue Holder, JDM, KM, Stephen R Holman, Michael Sargent, P Price, David Coleman, Michael B Griffith,*

Simon Collett-Jones, Gerry and Rosemary Dobson, B N F and M Parkin, Derek and Sylvia Stephenson, Peter Titcomb, David Glynne-Jones)

Free house ~ Licensee Andrew Morgan ~ Real ale ~ Bar food ~ Restaurant ~ (01983) 612711 ~ Children welcome ~ Dogs welcome ~ Open 10-11; 12-10.30 Sun ~ Bedrooms: £75B/£115B

SHALFLEET SZ4189 Map 2
New Inn ⊕ ♀ ◧
A3054 Newport—Yarmouth; PO30 4NS

Isle of Wight Dining Pub of the Year

A good set of enthusiastic reader reports makes this buzzing 18th-c fisherman's haunt, which is just a short stroll from the marshy inlets of the yacht-studded Newtown estuary, a pleasure to write about. Its strengths lie equally in its cheery welcome, great food and good beer. This year it's also completely no smoking. They're well known for their crab salad (£11.95), lobster salad (£19.95) and seafood platter (£19.95), and they also serve up to 12 different types of fresh fish a day, such as crab and prawn cocktail (£4.50), hake fillets with lemon and tarragon (£9.95), tuna steak with lime and chives (£10.95) and bass (£13.95). Other dishes on the changing menu might typically include soup (£3.25), sausage and mash (£5.95), steak and ale pie (£7.95), chicken breast with honey and cream (£8.95), lamb shank with garlic mash (£10.95) and 8oz fillet steak (£13.95). You will need to book, and there may be double sittings in summer. The partly panelled flagstoned public bar has yachting photographs and pictures, a boarded ceiling, scrubbed pine tables and a roaring log fire in the big stone hearth, and the carpeted beamed lounge bar has boating pictures and a coal fire. The snug and gallery have slate floors, bric-a-brac and more scrubbed pine tables. Bass, Goddards, Greene King IPA and Ventnor Golden are kept under a light blanket pressure, and they stock around 60 wines; piped music. *(Recommended by Steve Jones, Ron and Sheila Corbett, Julie and Bill Ryan, Paul Boot, David Coleman, Gerry and Rosemary Dobson, OPUS, B N F and M Parkin, Walter and Susan Rinaldi-Butcher, Mark and Mary Fairman, Martin and Karen Wake, Peter Titcomb, Minda and StanleyAlexander)*

Enterprise ~ Lease Mr Bullock and Mr McDonald ~ Real ale ~ Bar food (12-2.30, 6-9.30) ~ Restaurant ~ (01983) 531314 ~ Children welcome ~ Dogs welcome ~ Open 12-3, 6-11(10.30 Sun)

SHORWELL SZ4582 Map 2
Crown
B3323 SW of Newport; PO30 3JZ

In warmer months the tranquil tree-sheltered garden at this country pub draws quite a crowd of holidaymakers. Picnic-sets and white garden chairs and tables are closely spaced by a sweet little stream, that broadens out into a small trout-filled pool, and a decent children's play area blends in comfortably. Inside, four rooms spread pleasantly around a central bar, and the group of locals who gather here add character. The beamed two-room lounge has blue and white china in an attractive carved dresser, old country prints on the stripped stone walls, other individual furnishings, and a winter log fire with a fancy tile-work surround. Black pews form bays around tables in a stripped-stone room off to the left, with another log fire. Well kept Boddingtons, Flowers Original and Wadworths 6X, with a guest such as Badger Tanglefoot on handpump. Smoking is allowed only in the public bar. Enjoyable bar food includes sandwiches (from £3.50), soup (£3.50), pâté of the day (£4.95), crab cocktail (£5.25), ploughman's (from £5.50), lasagne or vegetable curry (£7.95), fisherman's pie (£8.50), and daily specials such as steak and kidney pie (£8.50), salmon with crab sauce (£9.50), lamb shank with mint gravy (£9.95), roast duck breast on pak choi with pineapple salad (£10.95), and puddings such as treacle tart or fruit crumble (£3.50); piped music. More reports please. *(Recommended by M and GR, Phil and Sally Gorton, Simon Collett-Jones)*

Enterprise ~ Lease Mike Grace ~ Real ale ~ Bar food (12-2.30, 6-9) ~ (01983) 740293 ~ Children welcome ~ Dogs welcome ~ Open 10-3.30, 5-11 (all day during school hols); 10.30-11 Sat, Sun; 10.30-3, 6-11 winter

VENTNOR SZ5677 Map 2

Spyglass 🍺

Esplanade, SW end; road down very steep and twisty, and parking nearby can be difficult – best to use the pay-and-display (free in winter) about 100 yards up the road; PO38 1JX

There seems to be something that appeals to nearly everyone at this cheerfully popular pub. It's in a super position, perched on the sea wall just above the beach – tables outside on a terrace have lovely views over the water. A fascinating jumble of seafaring memorabilia fills the snug quarry-tiled interior, with anything from wrecked rudders, ships' wheels, old local advertisements and rope-makers' tools to stuffed seagulls, an Admiral Benbow barometer and an old brass telescope; two no smoking areas, games machine and piped music. Generous helpings of very tasty bar food are promptly served and include sandwiches (from £4.25, baguettes from £5.25), soup (£4.25), filled baked potatoes (from £5.75), ploughman's (from £6.95), home-made chilli (£7.75), home-made fisherman's pie (£8.50) and sirloin steak (£11.95), with daily specials such as seafood chowder (£5.25), local sausages and mash (£7.50), steak and kidney pie (£7.95), crab tart or seafood stew (£8.95), and puddings (£4.25). Half a dozen well kept hand-pulled real ales include a couple from Badger and Ventnor, alongside three guests such as Badger Fursty Ferret, Goddards Fuggle-Dee-Dum and Ventnor Molly Downer. There are strolls westwards from here along the coast towards the Botanic Garden as well as heftier hikes up on to St Boniface Down and towards the eerie shell of Appuldurcombe House, and the pub owners don't mind muddy boots. *(Recommended by Colin Gooch, Tony and Penny Burton, Ian Phillips, B N F and M Parkin, Geoff and Linda Payne, Mark and Mary Fairman)*

Free house ~ Licensees Neil and Stephanie Gibbs ~ Real ale ~ Bar food (12-9.30) ~ (01983) 855338 ~ Children welcome away from main bar area ~ Dogs allowed in bar ~ Live entertainment every night except Mon ~ Open 10.30am-11pm ~ Bedrooms: /£60B

LUCKY DIP

Besides the fully inspected pubs, you might like to try these Lucky Dips recommended to us and described by readers (if you do, please send us reports: www.goodguides.co.uk).

ARRETON [SZ5484]
Fighting Cocks PO30 3AR [Hale Common, just S]: Newly refurbished and extended country pub with friendly licensees and staff, enjoyable food, real ales and good wines by the glass *(Helen Jukes)*
BRADING [SZ6086]
Yarbridge Inn PO36 0AA [Yarbridge, W]: Small pub full of local railway memorabilia, nice range of food esp home-made pizzas, good changing choice of wines by the glass and of real ales from small breweries such as Isle of Purbeck, Stonehenge and Ventnor; garden tables, open all day Sun and summer *(Derek and Sylvia Stephenson)*
CHALE [SZ4877]
☆ *Clarendon (Wight Mouse)* PO38 2HA [off A3055/B3399]: Popular and efficient family dining pub rambling around with flagstones here, carpet there, modern-look woody extension around attractive traditional core with log fire, four Badger and other ales from

long bar, good value food from good baked potatoes up, attentive cheerful service, entertaining quotes chalked up, plenty to keep children occupied, no smoking dining area; extensive outdoor seating with play area, great views out over cliffs, good bedrooms in adjoining hotel *(Quentin and Carol Williamson, Julie and Bill Ryan, LYM, Mark and Mary Fairman)*
COWES [SZ4996]
Fountain PO31 7AW [by hydrofoil terminal]: Hotel with open fire in large comfortably pubby bar overlooking high-speed ferry terminus, real ales, bar lunches, pleasant friendly staff, evening brasserie, live music Fri; tables out on covered deck, bedrooms *(Paul and Sue Dix)*
Union PO31 7QH [Watch House Lane, in pedestrian centre]: Small tucked-away local with good atmosphere, cheerful helpful staff, good value nicely prepared food (all day in summer) inc fine crab sandwiches, fresh local

fish and good OAP lunches, log fire, cosy areas around central bar, Fullers/Gales ales, farm cider and proper ginger beer shandies, dining room and conservatory; tables outside, bedrooms, may be open all day summer *(BB, Martin Ford)*

Vectis PO31 7AT [High St]: Smart little unspoilt flagstoned pub nr harbour, best at the front, with welcoming attentive service, lively local atmosphere, mainland and island real ales; tables outside *(David Ellerington)*

FISHBOURNE [SZ5592]

Fishbourne Inn PO33 4EU [from Portsmouth car ferry turn left into Fishbourne Lane no through road]: Spacious and neatly kept open-plan mock-Tudor pub with good fresh local fish and seafood, good value choice of other food (all day Sun) from sandwiches to grills, efficient friendly service even when packed, real ales such as Bass, Goddards and Wadworths 6X, comfortable modern repro furniture, open fire and large bright and airy dining area; tables in attractive front garden, useful setting nr ferry terminal and coast path, open all day wknds *(Bernard Phelvin, P Price, Liz and Brian Barnard, BB, John Coatsworth, Lew and Dot Hood)*

FRESHWATER [SZ3387]

Prince of Wales PO40 9ED [Princes Rd]: Small friendly old-fashioned local, real ales such as Boddingtons, Greene King Abbot and Wadworths 6X, summer farm cider, pickled eggs, pub games; garden tables, open all day *(Anon)*

HAVENSTREET [SZ5590]

☆ *White Hart* PO33 4DP [off A3054 Newport—Ryde; Main Rd]: Ancient village pub with good blackboard choice of reliably good food (not Sun evening or Mon; worth booking) all cooked by friendly landlady, lots of fresh veg, welcoming service, Badger real ales, cosy bar, tidy and comfortable, with locomotive prints and interesting beer-bottle collection, no piped music or machines; tables in secluded and attractive little garden behind *(Mrs Christa Sansom)*

NITON [SZ5075]

Buddle PO38 2NE [St Catherines Rd, Undercliff; off A3055 just S of village, towards St Catherines Point]: Plenty of character in pretty former smugglers' haunt, heavy black beams, big flagstones, broad stone fireplace, no smoking areas, friendly service, several real ales such as Adnams and Youngs, wide food choice (can be very busy at lunchtime), amiable dogs, games annexe; clifftop views from well cared for sloping garden and terraces, good walks; open all day *(Derek and Sylvia Stephenson, Steve Jones, LYM, Tony and Penny Burton, David Coleman, Mark Flynn, Alan M Pring, Geoff and Linda Payne)*

ROOKLEY [SZ5183]

Chequers PO38 3NZ [S of village, Chequers Inn Rd/Niton Rd]: Big family-oriented pub, largely no smoking, with mother-and-baby room and good children's games in plain and roomy family area as well as large safely fenced play area outside, downland views,

usual food all day from sandwiches and baked potatoes up, puddings in display cabinet, Courage Best and Directors, Gales HSB, Goddards, Ventnor and two guest beers, close-set tables in unpretentious dining lounge with log fire, flagstoned locals' bar with pool, darts and TV; children and dogs welcome, open all day *(LYM, Ian Phillips, Wendy Cox)*

SHANKLIN [SZ5881]

☆ *Chine* PO37 6BW [Chine Hill]: Great clifftop setting, with bright family conservatory and small terrace giving lovely views over sea, beach and chine (illuminated at dusk), nicely refurbished inside, low beams and flagstones, welcoming service, good interesting changing choice of real ales, woodburner, tiny sea-view snug one end; piped music, some live; cl winter lunchtimes, open all day summer wknds *(Paul Boot, BB)*

☆ *Fishermans Cottage* PO37 6BN [bottom of Shanklin Chine]: Thatched shoreside cottage in terrific setting surrounded by beached boats, tucked into the cliffs, steep walk down beautiful chine, lovely seaside walk to Luccombe; flagstones and some stripped stone, repro furniture, nets slung from low beams, old local pictures and bric-a-brac, simple bar lunches from sandwiches and baked potatoes up, more enterprising evening choice, Courage Directors and Goddards Fuggle-Dee-Dum, frequent entertainment; piped music; wheelchair access, children welcome, tables out on terrace, open all day in summer when fine *(BB)*

Village Pub PO37 6NS [High St, Old Village]: Pretty thatched building with real ales, pleasant staff, cheerful bustle, family dining area, overflow upstairs dining room; small pleasant back garden, open all day *(Paul Boot)*

TOTLAND [SZ3285]

High Down PO39 0HY [Highdown Lane]: Out-of-the-way pub in great spot at foot of NT Tennyson Down, real ales such as Wychwood Hobgoblin, cheerful service, food in bar and smart little dining room; piped music; dogs and walkers welcome, picnic-sets out in raised paddock area, good value bedrooms *(Liz and Brian Barnard, June and Malcolm Farmer, Peter Titcomb)*

VENTNOR [SZ5677]

Richmond PO38 1JX [Esplanade]: Newish pub with excellent sea views, real ales inc Yates Undercliff, fish inc local crab, daily papers, local memorabilia, friendly unpretentious bar, smart dining room *(Liz and Brian Barnard, Liz and John Soden)*

☆ *Volunteer* PO38 1ES [Victoria St]: Chatty and unpretentious little two-room local thriving under current cheerful and painstaking licensees, half a dozen or so changing ales such as Butcombe, Courage, Greene King Abbot and Ventnor Gold, reasonable prices, coal fire, comfortable red plush banquettes, darts, the local game of rings, perhaps sandwiches or finger buffet if you order specially; quiet piped music; no children, quiz nights, open all day *(David Ellerington, BB)*

WHITWELL [SZ5277]

White Horse PO38 2PY [High St]: Thatched pub popular for enjoyable generous food from pub staples to some more restaurant dishes and good Sun lunch, real ales such as Badger Best, Fullers London Pride, Greene King Abbot and Ventnor Golden, quick, helpful and friendly service, small beamed bar opening into large cheery high-ceilinged no smoking family dining area, and a second area (with darts) the other end; may be piped music; picnic-sets on pleasant lawn *(BB, Ian Phillips, Betty Laker)*

YARMOUTH [SZ3589]

☆ *Bugle* PO41 0NS [The Square]: Old inn with several different eating areas inc low-ceilinged panelled lounge and restaurant, enjoyable food from good soup and sandwiches to good fish and seafood choice, good service, decent house wines, Dunkerton's bottled organic cider, Greene King Abbot, Wadworths 6X and a beer brewed for them by Yates, lively public bar with nautical memorabilia and counter like galleon stern, games room with pool; piped music, little or no nearby parking, can be crowded Sat – get there early; children very welcome, sizeable garden, summer barbecues, bedrooms *(LYM, John Coatsworth, Joan and Michel Hooper-Immins, B N F and M Parkin)*

Kings Head PO41 0PB [Quay St]: Cosy low-ceilinged traditional pub opp car ferry, rather dark and quaint, with real ales, good food till quite late evening inc well prepared local fish, plush seats, friendly staff, children's eating area; unobtrusive piped music; bedrooms *(B N F and M Parkin)*

☆ *Wheatsheaf* PO41 0PH [Bridge Rd, nr ferry]: Victorian pub opened into one with light fresh décor, wide choice of generous reasonably priced family food all day inc plenty of fish, cheerful service, Goddards, Greene King Old Speckled Hen and Wadworths 6X, games area with pool in winter, no smoking glazed extension *(Alec and Barbara Jones, LYM, Liz and Brian Barnard)*

Kent

Kent is not a part of England where it's easy to find good value in pub food. You certainly can track down enjoyable meals, but you really have to know where to look (as the county is virtually on the *Guide*'s doorstep, we do have a bit of a local advantage). Pubs doing particularly well here this year include the foody old Three Chimneys just outside Biddenden, the ancient Wheatsheaf at Bough Beech, the simple and very friendly Gate Inn by the marshes at Boyden Gate, the largely unspoilt and old-fashioned Woolpack at Brookland (another marshland pub), the good value Mundy Bois near Pluckley (some readers will remember it as the Red Lion – the pub itself as well as the name has had a bit of a makeover recently), the civilised and up-to-date Chaser at Shipbourne, the pleasantly individualistic Red Lion at Stodmarsh, the charming Tiger at Stowting (this nicely set country pub is our new entry, this year), and the Pepper Box at Ulcombe (a very pleasant country inn). All of these, on their different levels, are pleasant for a pub lunch, even if with some the main charm is the overall style of the pub itself. For a special meal out, our top three choices in Kent would be the Three Chimneys near Biddenden, the Dove at Dargate, and Sankeys in Tunbridge Wells. It's the Dove at Dargate which consolidates its high reputation by again winning the title of Kent Dining Pub of the Year. Pubs we'd note particularly in the Lucky Dip section at the end of the chapter are the Fountain at Cowden, Kentish Rifleman at Dunks Green, Chafford Arms at Fordcombe, Green Cross near Goudhurst, Green Man at Hodsoll Street, Black Robin at Kingston, Cock at Luddesdown, Spotted Dog near Penshurst, Sportsman in Seasalter, Padwell Arms at Stone Street, White Lion in Tenterden and White Rock at Under River. Drinks prices, like pub food prices, tend to be rather higher in Kent than the national average. The main local brewer is Shepherd Neame, with good beer prices in its tenanted pubs (as well as decent wines). Larkins and – sometimes very attractively priced – Goachers are also becoming quite widely available.

BEKESBOURNE TR1856 Map 3

Unicorn

Coming from Patrixbourne on A2, turn left up Bekesbourne Hill after passing railway line (and station); coming from Littlebourne on A257, pass Howletts Zoo – Bekesbourne Hill is then first turning on right; turning into pub car park is at bottom end of the little terrace of houses on the left (the pub is the far end of this terrace); CT4 5ED

Run by friendly people with time to talk, this airy little pub remains happily unchanging. There are just a few scrubbed old pine tables and bentwood café chairs on worn floorboards, a canary ceiling and walls above a dark green dado, minimal décor, and a handful of bar stools against the neat counter. You can glimpse into the spick-and-span stainless kitchen where (using local produce where possible) the homely licensees produce their enjoyable food: home-made soup (£3.25), home-made chicken liver pâté (£3.50), soft herring roes on toast (£4.95), cauliflower cheese topped with grilled bacon or vegetable bake (£4.95), home-cooked ham and eggs (£5.95), lambs liver and bacon with rich onion gravy (£6.75), local cod fillet in beer batter (£8.95), daily specials such as grilled mushrooms with stilton (£3.25), butternut squash and black-eyed bean curry (£8.95), and smoked haddock pie with sweet potato topping or oxtail stew with herb dumplings (£9.25) and puddings like bramley apple crumble or steamed syrup and ginger sponge (from £3.50). Adnams Broadside and Harveys Best are well kept on handpump, with a short but carefully chosen wine list, local cider and apple and pear juice; perhaps piped radio, but no machines – unless you count the veteran penny-in-the-slot bagatelle machine – cribbage and dominoes. There's a piano in one corner, and a little Victorian fireplace. A side terrace, quite prettily planted, has teak tables and benches, and boules. Parking in front is tricky but there is a car park at the back. More reports please. *(Recommended by Fr Robert Marsh, Kevin Thorpe)*

Free house ~ Licensees Clive and Cheryl Barker ~ Real ale ~ Bar food (not Sun evening or Mon or Tues) ~ No credit cards ~ (01227) 830210 ~ Children welcome ~ Open 11.30-3, 7-11; 12-3 Sun; closed Sun evening, all day Mon and Tues

BIDDENDEN   TQ8538   Map 3

Three Chimneys ⑤ 🍴 ♈
A262, 1 mile W of village; TN27 8LW

After a visit to nearby Sissinghurst Gardens, this busy pub is just the place to head for. It's best to arrive early or book in advance to be sure of a table and the imaginative food is extremely good. As we went to press, prices had not changed since last year: soup (£3.95), baked field mushrooms with caramelised red onions and grilled goats cheese (£5.50), ploughman's (£6.50), thai-style crab cakes (£6.95), sautéed lambs liver and bacon with mash and port and red onion gravy (£11.95), duck leg confit with braised puy lentils, chorizo and bacon (£15.95), monkfish fillets with tomato and garlic, parma ham and mozzarella (£16.95), roast venison and parsnips with braised cabbage and port jus (£18.95), and puddings such as strawberry and vanilla crème brûlée (£5.25). Feeling quite pubby, with Adnams Best, Harveys Best and a guest like Fullers Discovery tapped straight from casks racked behind the counter, the series of low-beamed, very traditional little rooms has plain wooden furniture and old settles on flagstones and coir matting, some harness and sporting prints on the stripped brick walls, and good log fires. The simple public bar has darts, dominoes and cribbage. French windows in the civilised candlelit bare-boards restaurant open on to the garden (ploughman's only out here) with picnic-sets in dappled shade, and the smart terrace area has tables and outdoor heaters. They've a good wine list, with several by the glass, local Biddenden cider and several malt whiskies. *(Recommended by John Evans, Glenwys and Alan Lawrence, Kevin Thorpe, Alan Cowell, Michael and Anne Brown, Cathryn and Richard Hicks, the Didler, Brian Wainwright, M Sage, Alan Sadler, Anthony Longden, Alan and Anne Driver, B and M Kendall, J P Humphery)*

Free house ~ Licensee Craig Smith ~ Real ale ~ Bar food (12-2, 6.30-9.30; 12-2.30, 7-9 Sun) ~ Restaurant ~ (01580) 291472 ~ Children in eating area of bar and restaurant ~ Dogs welcome ~ Open 11.30-3, 6-11; 12-3.30, 7-10.30 Sun

BOUGH BEECH   TQ4846   Map 3

Wheatsheaf ⑤ ♈ 🍺
B2027, S of reservoir; TN8 7NU

The older part of this very popular pub is thought to have been a hunting lodge belonging to Henry V and the place is full of history with masses of interesting things to look at. The neat central bar and the long front bar (with an attractive old settle carved with wheatsheaves) have unusually high ceilings with lofty oak timbers, a screen of standing timbers and a revealed king post; dominoes and board games. Divided from the central bar by two more rows of standing timbers – one formerly an outside wall to the building – are the snug, and another bar. Other similarly aged features include a piece of 1607 graffiti, 'Foxy Holamby', thought to have been a whimsical local squire. There are quite a few horns and heads, as well as a sword from Fiji, crocodiles, stuffed birds, swordfish spears and a matapee on the walls and above the massive stone fireplaces. Thoughtful touches include piles of smart magazines, tasty nibbles and chestnuts to roast. It's appealing outside too, with plenty of seats, flowerbeds and fruit trees in the sheltered side and back gardens. Shrubs help divide the garden into various areas, so it doesn't feel too crowded even when it's full. Well kept Greene King Old Speckled Hen, Harveys Sussex Best, Shepherd Neame Master Brew, and from a village just three miles away, Westerham Brewery Grasshopper on handpump; three farm ciders (including a local one), a decent wine list, several malt whiskies, summer Pimms and winter mulled wine. As well as lunchtime dishes such as pie and mash (£5.95), thai dim sum (from £5.95), smoked haddock and spring onion fishcakes with lemon and parsley butter sauce (£6.95), and moules marinière and frites (£7.95), the large helpings of bar food might consist of soup (£4.95), grilled goats cheese on ciabatta with caramelised red onions and pesto (£5.95), vegetable curry (£8.95), local sausages (£9.95), beef bourguignon (£10.95), lambs liver, bacon and black pudding (£11.95), grilled gammon steak with cheesy potato bake (£12.95), and puddings like banana sponge with butterscotch sauce or chocolate truffle torte (£4.50). *(Recommended by B J Harding, Steve Godfrey, Bob and Margaret Holder, Mr and Mrs Mike Pearson, Tina and David Woods-Taylor, Michael and Anne Brown, Christopher Turner, Mike and Sue Loseby, Debbie and Neil Hayter, Richard Smye, M Sage, Alan Sadler, Mrs Jane Kingsbury, Mrs Susan Powell, Simon and Amanda Southwell, Ellen Weld, David London, John and Elisabeth Cox, Martin and Sue Day, Sue Demont, Tim Barrow, Oliver and Sue Rowell, Will Watson, Malcolm and Jane Levitt, GHC, Andrew Wallace, A J Ward)*

Enterprise ~ Lease Liz and David Currie ~ Real ale ~ Bar food (12-10) ~ (01732) 700254 ~ Children welcome with restrictions ~ Dogs welcome ~ Open 11am-11.30pm

BOYDEN GATE   TR2265   Map 3

Gate Inn ★ 🍺 £

Off A299 Herne Bay—Ramsgate – follow Chislet, Upstreet signpost opposite Roman Gallery; Chislet also signposted off A28 Canterbury—Margate at Upstreet – after turning right into Chislet main street keep right on to Boyden; the pub gives its address as Marshside, though Boyden Gate seems more usual on maps; CT3 4EB

The long-time tenant of this traditional and unchanging village pub (now no smoking) has a wonderful knack of making all his customers, locals or visitors, feel genuinely welcome and at home. The comfortably worn interior is properly pubby with an inglenook log fire serving both the well worn quarry-tiled rooms, flowery-cushioned pews around tables of considerable character, hop bines hanging from the beams and attractively etched windows. Well kept Shepherd Neame Bishops Finger, Master Brew, Spitfire and a seasonal ale are tapped from the cask and you can also get interesting bottled beers, half a dozen wines by the glass, and country wines; board games. Tasty bar food includes lots of different sandwiches (from £3; filled baguettes from £3.70; various melts from £4;), home-made soup (£3.50), a big choice of baked potatoes and burgers (from £3.30), ploughman's, salads, omelettes, home-made vegetable flan or grilled steak (all £5.95), and grills (from £5.95). The sheltered hollyhock flowered garden is bounded by two streams with tame ducks and geese (they sell bags of food, 10p), and on fine summer evenings you can hear the contented quacking of a multitude of ducks and geese, coots and moorhens out on the marshes. *(Recommended by Norman Fox, David and Ruth Shillitoe, Kevin Thorpe, Louise English, Bruce Eccles)*

Shepherd Neame ~ Tenant Christopher Smith ~ Real ale ~ Bar food ~ No credit cards ~ (01227) 860498 ~ Well behaved children in eating area of bar and family room ~ Dogs welcome ~ Open 11-3, 6-11; 10-3, 7-10.30 Sun

---

The 🍺 symbol shows pubs which keep their beer unusually well, have a particularly good range or brew their own.

BROOKLAND TQ9724 Map 3
Woolpack £

On A259 from Rye, about 1 mile before Brookland, take the first right turn signposted Midley where the main road bends sharp left, just after the expanse of Walland Marsh; OS Sheet 189 map reference 977244; TN29 9TJ

Bustling and friendly and very popular locally – though there's a warm welcome for visitors, too – this pretty 15th-c white cottage has plenty of marshland character. The ancient entrance lobby has an uneven brick floor and black-painted pine-panelled walls. To the right, the simple quarry-tiled main bar has basic cushioned plank seats in the massive inglenook fireplace (with a lovely log fire on chilly days), a painted wood-effect bar counter hung with lots of water jugs, some very early ships' timbers (maybe 12th c) in the low-beamed ceiling, a long elm table with shove-ha'penny carved into one end, other old and newer wall benches, chairs at mixed tables with flowers and candles, and photographs of locals on the walls. To the left of the lobby is a sparsely furnished little room, and an open-plan, no smoking family room; piped music. Well kept Shepherd Neame Master Brew, Spitfire and a seasonal brew on handpump; look out for the two pub cats Liquorice and Charlie Girl. Big helpings of good bar food include sandwiches or filled baguettes (from £3), home-made soup (£3.75), ploughman's (from £6.45), home-made steak pie, battered cod, chilli or stilton and vegetable bake (all £6.45), ham and egg (£6.95), lamb shank (£9.45), sirloin steak (£12.95), and puddings such as apple crumble or steamed treacle pudding (£3.75), or perhaps particularly good fresh local raspberries; there are also summer specials like various quiches (£6.45), cold pies (£7.45), dressed crab (£8.95), and 1kg moules marinière (£9.45). The big garden has plenty of picnic-sets, well developed shrubs, and pretty hanging baskets; it's all nicely lit up in the evenings. *(Recommended by Stephen Harvey, Peter Meister, Kevin Thorpe, MJVK, V Brogden, Jeremy Woods, Louise English)*

Shepherd Neame ~ Tenant Barry Morgan ~ Real ale ~ Bar food (12-2, 6-9; all day in summer and all day winter weekends) ~ (01797) 344321 ~ Children in family room ~ Dogs welcome ~ Open 11-11; 12-10.30 Sun

CHIDDINGSTONE TQ4944 Map 3
Castle Inn ♀

Village signposted from B2027 Tonbridge—Edenbridge; TN8 7AH

It's just around the corner from the castle in a pretty National Trust village, so this rambling old place can get busy at peak times. The handsome, carefully modernised beamed bar has well made settles forming booths around the tables, cushioned sturdy wall benches, an attractive mullioned window seat in one small alcove, and latticed windows (a couple of areas are no smoking); darts, shove-ha'penny, dominoes and cribbage. There are tables in front of the building facing the church, with more in the pretty secluded vine-hung garden. Larkins Traditional and winter Porter (both brewed in the village) and Harveys Best on handpump, an impressive wine list, and quite a few malt whiskies. Priced in euros and sterling, lunchtime bar food includes sandwiches, soup (£5.75), ham hock and black pudding terrine or timbale of dorset cock crab (£7.25), and mushroom risotto, slow-cooked lamb shank or corn-fed chicken on rösti potatoes (all £10.75); two-course set lunch (£9.95; not Sunday). Evening choices such as sautéed pigeon breasts or king prawns in garlic butter (£10.25), goats cheese, aubergine and basil roulade (£11.45), duck breast with kumquat compote (£13.25), and irish fillet steak wellington (£17.65); three courses are priced at £25. The licensees publish three circular walks from the village. *(Recommended by Dr Danny Nicol, N R White, Tony and Margaret Cross, Will Watson, GHC)*

Free house ~ Licensee Nigel Lucas ~ Real ale ~ Bar food (12-6, 7-9.30) ~ Restaurant ~ (01892) 870247 ~ Children welcome away from public bar ~ Dogs welcome ~ Open 11-11; 12-11 Sun

DARGATE TR0761 Map 3
Dove 🍴 ♇
Village signposted from A299; ME13 9HB
Kent Dining Pub of the Year
Even though this well run dining pub is tucked away down a network of narrow lanes in a quiet hamlet, it's pretty essential to book a table in advance. The very friendly landlady ensures a relaxed welcoming atmosphere in the charmingly unspoilt airy rambling rooms, which have flowers on stripped wood tables, photographs of the pub and its licensees throughout the past century on the walls, a good winter log fire, and plenty of seats on the bare boards; piped classical music. There are some lunchtime snacks such as croque monsieur (£5.25), minute steak baguette (£5.95), and warm salad of marinated chicken, caramelised pork with stir-fried vegetables or salt cod with a chorizo and flageolet bean sauce (all £7.95), but it's the exceptionally good restaurant-style food that most customers are here to enjoy. This might include leek and potato soup with crème fraîche, chives and lettuce (£4.75), glazed goats cheese on a tomato and red onion salad seasoned with pesto (£5.50), bayonne ham and oyster mushroom tart with a rocket, onion and herb salad (£6.99), risotto of spring onion and crab (£8.50), braised chicken breast on creamed leeks flavoured with shallots and pine nuts (£14.50), shank of lamb on potato purée with a tomato and basil jus flavoured with local beetroot (£15.50), grilled fillet of salmon with a tomato, caper and mussel butter sauce (£15.75), and local lemon sole flavoured with a caper, onion and herb butter (£18.99). Well kept Shepherd Neame Master Brew and Special on handpump. Lovely in fine weather, the sheltered garden has roses, lilacs, peonies and many other flowers, picnic-sets sets under pear trees, a dovecote with white doves, a rockery and pool, and a swing. A bridlepath leads up from the pub (along the quaintly named Plumpudding Lane) into Blean Wood. *(Recommended by Jonathan Lane, Richard Pitcher, Tina and David Woods-Taylor, Philip Denton, Uta and John Owlett, Richard Siebert, Kevin Thorpe, W Andrew, Clive Flynn)*

Shepherd Neame ~ Tenants Nigel and Bridget Morris ~ Real ale ~ Bar food (not Mon and maybe not Sun or Tues evenings) ~ Restaurant ~ (01227) 751360 ~ Children welcome ~ Dogs allowed in bar ~ Live music first Sun of month ~ Open 12-3.30, 6-11.30; 12-4, 7-11 Sun; closed Mon (but open bank hol Mon, when they then close Tues instead)

GROOMBRIDGE TQ5337 Map 3
Crown
B2110; TN3 9QH
This tile-hung pub is prettily positioned at the end of a horseshoe-shaped row of comely cottages, and there are picnic-sets out in front on a wonky but sunny brick terrace that look down over the steep village green. Inside, is a snug left-hand room with old tables on worn flagstones and a big brick inglenook with a cosy winter log fire – arrive early for a table in here. The low beamed rooms have roughly plastered walls, some squared panelling and timbering, and a quite a bit of bric-a-brac, from old teapots and pewter tankards to antique bottles. Walls are decorated with small topographical, game and sporting prints, and a circular large-scale map with the pub at its centre. The no smoking end room (normally for eaters) has fairly close-spaced tables with a variety of good solid chairs, and a log-effect gas fire in a big fireplace. Greene King Abbot and IPA, Harveys and Larkins on handpump, and ten wines by the glass. Bar food includes lunchtime toasted ciabattas and baked potatoes (from £5.50), as well as soup (£3.95), vegetarian pasta (£6.95), home-made pie of the day (£8.20), beer-battered cod (£8.80), and daily specials such as moules marinière (£5.50; main course £8.50), field mushrooms with peppers, tomatoes and mozzarella (£7.80), and cumberland sausage with onion gravy (£7.90). There's a back car park and pub garden. A public footpath across the road beside the small chapel leads through a field to Groombridge Place Gardens.
(Recommended by B J Harding, Peter Meister, B and M Kendall, Tina and David Woods-Taylor, Grahame Brooks)

Free house ~ Licensee Peter Kilshaw ~ Real ale ~ Bar food (12-3(4 Sun), 7-9; not Sun evening) ~ Restaurant ~ (01892) 864742 ~ Children welcome ~ Dogs allowed in bar ~ Open 11-3, 5-11; 11-11 Sat; 12-10.30 Sun; 11-3, 6-11 Sat and closed Sun evening in winter ~ Bedrooms: £40/£45(£60S)

HAWKHURST   TQ7630   Map 3

Queens
Rye Road (A268 E); TN18 4EY

Usefully open all day and with food available from 8.30am, this wisteria-covered old pub is a pleasant place. The spreading interior is opened up and appealingly decorated in keeping with its age (it was first recorded as an inn in the 16th c). There are comfortable fireside sofas at the front and further in, the mood is wine bar-ish: terracotta, sand or pea-green colourwashes give an airy feel despite the heavy low beams, and there's a nice mix of old oak tables (candlelit at night) on bare boards with plenty of scattered rugs. Around to the right, the no smoking piano bar is where they have the live music and serve breakfast and teas; newspapers to read and piped music. Fullers London Pride and Harveys Sussex Best on handpump. Bar food includes home-made soup, sandwiches or filled baguettes (£4.95), ploughman's (£5.95), antipasti (£7.95), home-made burger, sausage and mash or ham and egg (£8.95), lasagne (£9.95), roasted mediterranean vegetables (£10.95), lamb en croûte with redcurrant jus (£12.95), and steaks (£15.95); the restaurant is no smoking. There are tables on decking at the front, and in a side courtyard. More reports please. *(Recommended by Laurence Manning, Kevin Thorpe, Mr and Mrs Mike Pearson, Louise English, M Sage, Mayur Shah, Jason Caulkin)*

Enterprise ~ Lease Janelle Tresidder ~ Real ale ~ Bar food (8.30am-9.30pm(10 Sat and Sun)) ~ Restaurant ~ (01580) 753577 ~ Children welcome ~ Jazz Sun lunchtime ~ Open 11-midnight(1am Sat and Sun) ~ Bedrooms: £50S/£85S

HOLLINGBOURNE   TQ8354   Map 3

Windmill ♀
A mile from M20, junction 8: A20 towards Ashford (away from Maidstone), then left into B2163 – Eyhorne Street village; ME17 1TR

In a village with a good many handsome buildings, this pleasant no smoking place is very much a dining pub and mainly set out for food throughout. The pubby core can be found tucked up one or two steps towards the back with bar stools around the island serving bar: Flowers IPA, and Shepherd Neame Masterbrew and Sussex Best on handpump and eight wines by the glass. Under heavy low black beams, several small or smallish mainly carpeted areas link together around this core, sometimes partly separated by glazed or stained-glass panels; the solid pub tables have padded country or library chairs. Soft lighting, black timbers in ochre walls, shelves of books, and the good log fire in the huge inglenook fireplace add up to a pleasantly old-world feel. Bar food (they tell us prices have not changed) includes good weekday lunchtime sandwiches (from £3.95, sirloin steak £5.95), baguettes or filled baked potatoes (£5.95), liver and bacon (£8.95), steaks (from £8.95), cajun spiced chicken (£9.95), knuckle of ham with wholegrain mustard sauce (£12.75), cod fillet with cheese and parsley sauce (£12.95), and duck confit (£13.95), with puddings such as bread and butter pudding or treacle tart (£4.25); piped music. A neatly kept sunny little garden has picnic-sets under cocktail parasols, and a play area. More reports please. *(Recommended by Alan Cowell, Stephen Moss, John Branston)*

Enterprise ~ Lease Graham and Deana Godmon ~ Real ale ~ Bar food (12-2.30, 6-10; 12-10(9.30 Sun) Sat) ~ Restaurant ~ (01622) 880280 ~ Children welcome ~ Open 11-3, 5-11; 11-11 Sat; 12-10.30 Sun; closed 25 Dec

---

Planning a day in the country? We list pubs in really attractive scenery
at the back of the book.

IGHTHAM COMMON TQ5755 Map 3

Harrow ♀

Signposted off A25 just W of Ightham; pub sign may be hard to spot; TN15 9EB

There's quite an emphasis on food in this civilised country inn – which has had some redecoration this year. Two attractively decorated rooms have fresh flowers and candles, smart dining chairs on the new herringbone-patterned wood floor, and a winter fire (not always lit). The bigger room is painted a cheerful sunny yellow above the wood-panelled dado, the charming little antiquated conservatory no longer has the spreading vine, and the dining room is no smoking and laid with white cloths. Greene King IPA and Abbot on handpump and seven wines by the glass. Good, if not cheap, food might include soup (£5), crab and ginger spring rolls or pâté (£6.50), sausages and mash (£8.50), tagliatelle with spinach and wild mushrooms or beef and Guinness pie (£10.50), salmon and chive fishcake with lemon butter sauce (£11), roast lamb shank with red wine jus (£11.95), duck in a whisky and cherry sauce (£14.50), and beef sirloin with cracked peppercorn sauce (£15). There are tables and chairs out on a pretty little pergola-enclosed back terrace, and this is handy for Ightham Mote. More reports please. *(Recommended by Brian Root, John Evans, Heather and Dick Martin, Michael and Anne Brown, Andy and Claire Barker, M Sage, Derek Thomas, Catherine and Richard Preston, Comus and Sarah Elliott, N R White, GHC)*

Free house ~ Licensees John Elton and Claire Butler ~ Real ale ~ Bar food (12-2, 6-9; not Sun evening or Mon) ~ Restaurant ~ (01732) 885912 ~ Children in family room and dining room only ~ Open 12-3, 6-11; closed Sun evening and all day Mon

LANGTON GREEN TQ5538 Map 3

Hare ♀

A264 W of Tunbridge Wells; TN3 0JA

There's a good choice of drinks in this no smoking Edwardian roadside pub: Greene King IPA and Abbot with guests such as Belhaven Six Nations and Greene King Old Speckled Hen on handpump, over 50 malt whiskies, quite a few wines by the glass, and freshly squeezed juices. The front bar (piped music here) tends to be where drinkers gather, and the knocked-through interior has big windows and high ceilings giving a spacious feel. Décor, more or less in period with the building, runs from dark-painted dados below light walls, 1930s oak furniture, and turkey carpets on stained wooden floors to old romantic pastels, and a huge collection of chamber-pots hanging from one beam. Interesting old books, pictures and two huge mahogany mirror-backed display cabinets crowd the walls of the big room at the back, which has lots of large tables (one big enough for at least a dozen) on a light brown carpet; from here french windows open on to picnic-sets on a big terrace, and pretty views of the tree-ringed village green; shove-ha'penny, draughts and backgammon. Bar food such as soup (£4.50), sandwiches (from £4.95), mushroom risotto (£6), ploughman's (£7.50), steakburger (£8.95), smoked cod and bacon fishcakes (£9), salmon fillet with sweet and sour peppers (£11.95), and steaks (from £15.95). Parking is limited. More reports please. *(Recommended by Derek Thomas, Peter Meister)*

Brunning & Price ~ Tenant Christopher Little ~ Real ale ~ Bar food (12-9.30(9 Sun)) ~ (01892) 862419 ~ Children in eating area till 7pm ~ Dogs allowed in bar ~ Open 11-11; 12-10.30 Sun

NEWNHAM TQ9557 Map 3

George

The Street; village signposted from A2 just W of Ospringe, outside Faversham; ME9 0LL

A series of spreading open-plan rooms in this unchanging local have hop-strung beams, rugs on polished floorboards, stripped brickwork, gas-type chandeliers, open fires, candles and lamps on handsome tables and attractively upholstered mahogany settles. Shepherd Neame Master Brew, Spitfire, and a seasonal beer on handpump, and ten wines by the glass; piped music. Bar food includes lunchtime sandwiches or baguettes (from £4.75), filled baked potatoes (from £6.25), and ploughman's (from £6.75), as well as ham and eggs (£7.95), bangers and mash (£8.25), vegetable curry (£8.95), steak and kidney pudding (£9.50), specials such as calves liver with smoked bacon and wild mushroom and red wine sauce (£14.25), and half shoulder of lamb with mint and coriander gravy or bass fillets with fresh asparagus and hollandaise (£14.95), and home-made puddings such as cherry roly-poly and banoffi pie (£4.25); the restaurant is no smoking. The spacious sheltered garden has some picnic-sets and there are pleasant nearby walks. More reports please. *(Recommended by Jonathan Lane, Philip Denton, Fr Robert Marsh, David and Ruth Shillitoe, M Sage, Anthony Barnes, Colin Christie)*

Shepherd Neame ~ Tenants Chris and Marie Annand ~ Real ale ~ Bar food (12-2.30 (2 Mon), 7-9.30(9 Sun and Mon)) ~ Restaurant ~ (01795) 890237 ~ Children welcome ~ Occasional live music Mon evenings ~ Open 11-3.30, 6.30-11; 12-11 Sun; 12-3.30, 7-11 Sun in winter; closed evenings 25 and 26 Dec

OARE TR0163 Map 3

Shipwrights Arms ◨

S shore of Oare Creek, E of village; coming from Faversham on the Oare road, turn right into Ham Road opposite Davington School; or off A2 on B2045, go into Oare village, then turn right towards Faversham, and then left into Ham Road opposite Davington School; OS Sheet 178 map reference 016635; ME13 7TU

You can reach this unspoilt old place on foot from the village, by boat or by car. It's in the middle of marshland with lots of bird life and is actually 3ft below sea level. Three simple little bars are dark and cosy, and separated by standing timbers and wood partitions or narrow door arches. A medley of seats runs from tapestry cushioned stools and chairs to black wood-panelled built-in settles forming little booths, and there are pewter tankards over the bar counter, boating jumble and pictures, pottery boating figures, flags or boating pennants on the ceilings, several brick fireplaces, and a good woodburning stove. Look out for the electronic wind gauge above the main door, which takes its reading from the chimney. Well kept ales from Goachers, Hopdaemon and Whitstable Oyster Brewery Company, and maybe a couple of other kentish guests tapped from the cask, too; piped local radio. Standard bar food includes sandwiches (from £2.95), ploughman's or burger (£5.95), sausage and mash or battered cod (£6.95), vegetable tikka masala (£7.25), and puddings such as bread and butter pudding or cherry pancakes (from £3.75); the eating area is no smoking. Parking can be difficult at busy times. *(Recommended by N R White, the Didler, Colin Moore, Keith and Chris O'Neill, Louise English, B and M Kendall, Richard Siebert)*

Free house ~ Licensees Derek and Ruth Cole ~ Real ale ~ Bar food (not Sun or Mon evening) ~ Restaurant ~ (01795) 590088 ~ Children welcome if seated ~ Dogs allowed in bar ~ Open 11-3(4 summer Sat), 6-11; 12(11 in winter)-4, 6-11 Sun; closed Mon in winter

PENSHURST TQ5243 Map 3

Bottle House ⑪

Coldharbour Lane, Smarts Hill; leaving Penshurst SW on B2188 turn right at Smarts Hill signpost, then bear right towards Chiddingstone and Cowden; keep straight on; TN11 8ET

This is a tile-hung old house standing alone in quiet countryside. The low-beamed and neatly kept front bar has a well worn brick floor that extends behind the polished copper-topped bar counter and big windows that look on to a terrace with climbing plants, hanging baskets, and picnic-sets under cocktail parasols. The simply decorated red-carpeted main bar has massive hop-covered supporting beams, two large stone pillars with a small brick fireplace (with a stuffed turtle to one side), and old paintings and photographs on mainly plastered walls; quite a collection of china pot lids, with more in the no smoking low-ceilinged dining room. Several cosy little areas lead off the main bar – one is covered in sporting pictures right up to the ceiling and another has pictures of dogs. Good, popular food served by efficient staff might include filled baguettes, soup (£4.25), thai fishcake with chilli jam or prawn caesar salad (£5.25), camembert baked in its box (£6.50), three-cheese omelette, local sausages with caramelised onion gravy or home-baked honey and mustard ham with eggs (£7.95), moules marinière with chips (£8.95), barbecue chicken topped with bacon and cheese or beer-battered cod (£9.95), calves liver and bacon with garlic mash (£13.95), and fillet of beef wellington with wild mushroom sauce or herb-crusted rack of lamb with port and redcurrant sauce (£16.95). Well kept Courage Directors, Harveys and Larkins on handpump and several wines by the glass; piped music. Good surrounding walks. *(Recommended by Tina and David Woods-Taylor, Martin and Pauline Jennings, Sharon and Alan Corper, Louise English, Mrs G Bolton, Howard and Margaret Buchanan, Cathryn and Richard Hicks, Jason Caulkin, Alan Sadler, Derek and Maggie Washington, Tony Brace, B J Harding)*

Free house ~ Licensees Gordon and Val Meer ~ Real ale ~ Bar food (12(11.30 Sun)-9.30) ~ Restaurant ~ (01892) 870306 ~ Children welcome ~ Dogs allowed in bar ~ Open 11-11; 12-10.30 Sun; closed 25 Dec, evenings 26 and 31 Dec and 1 Jan

PLUCKLEY TQ9243 Map 3
Dering Arms ♀
Pluckley Station, which is signposted from B2077; The Grove; TN27 0RR

This striking old building was originally built as a hunting lodge on the Dering estate. The stylishly plain high-ceilinged main bar has a solid country feel, with a variety of good wooden furniture on stone floors, a roaring log fire in the great fireplace, country prints and some fishing rods. The smaller half-panelled back bar has similar dark wood furnishings, and an extension to this area has a woodburning stove, comfortable armchairs and sofas, and a grand piano; board games. Bar food, with quite an emphasis on fish, includes soup (£4.25), chicken livers in a brandy and cream sauce or sardines grilled with rosemary butter (£5.45), pie of the day (£9.45), confit of duck with wild mushroom sauce (£14.95), rib-eye steak (£15.95), daily specials such as chicken liver, bacon and mushroom pâté (£4.95), moules marinière (£5.95), salmon fishcakes with sorrel sauce or guinea fowl casserole (£12.95), and whole crab salad (£14.95), and puddings like rich chocolate truffle with brandy cream or tiramisu parfait with coffee sauce (£5.25). Goachers Gold Star, Old Ale and a beer named for the pub on handpump, a good wine list, home-made lemonade, local cider and over 25 malt whiskies. The big simple bedrooms have old ad hoc furnishings and breakfasts are good. Classic car meetings (the long-standing landlord has a couple) are held here on the second Sunday of the month. More reports please. *(Recommended by Derek Thomas, Mr and Mrs Mike Pearson, Kevin Thorpe, Grahame Brooks, Peter Meister, Philip and Cheryl Hill, M Sage, Brian and Ruth Archer, Martin and Sue Day, Louise English, Bruce Eccles, Ann and Colin Hunt)*

Free house ~ Licensee James Buss ~ Real ale ~ Bar food (not Sun evening, not Mon) ~ Restaurant ~ (01233) 840371 ~ Children welcome ~ Dogs allowed in bar ~ Open 11.30(11 Sat)-3, 6-11; 12-3 Sun; closed Sun evening, all day Mon, 25-27 Dec, 1 Jan ~ Bedrooms: £35/£45

Mundy Bois
Mundy Bois – spelled Monday Boys on some maps – off Smarden Road SW of village centre; TN27 0ST

Now renamed the Mundy Bois (it was the Rose & Crown), this quietly set pub has also had some refurbishment. The relaxed Village Bar is friendly and welcoming, with a massive inglenook fireplace (favourite spot of Ted the pub labrador) and chesterfield sofas. This leads on to a little pool room; TV and piped music. Using local produce and meats from traditional breeds, the enjoyable bar food is good value: home-made soup (£3.50), toasties, sandwiches or filled baguettes (from £3.95), home-made pâté (£4.95), four-egg omelette (£5.75), vegetable lasagne or ham and eggs (£6.25), sausages with onion gravy, aberdeen angus half-pound burger or home-made steak and kidney pie (£6.50), and mixed grill (£12.75); there's also a weekend brunch menu (from 10am) with vegetable fritatta (£5.95), buttermilk pancakes (£6.25), and corned beef hash and eggs or eggs benedict (£6.50) with drinks like bucks fizz, bloody mary special or an alcoholic iced 'tea' (£3.75 glass, £12.50 jug); Sunday roast (£7.95). You can also eat from the pricier and more elaborate restaurant menu in the bar. Shepherd Neame Master Brew, Wadworths 6X and a guest beer on handpump, and nine wines by the glass. There are seats in the rather nice garden, which has a good children's play area, and dining facilities on the terrace. More reports on the changes, please. (Recommended by Peter Farres, Lea Randolph, B and M Kendall)

Free house ~ Licensees Peter and Helen Teare ~ Real ale ~ Bar food (all day Sun) ~ Restaurant ~ (01233) 840048 ~ Children welcome ~ Dogs allowed in bar ~ Open 11.30-11; 10am-11pm Sat; closed 25 Dec

SELLING   TR0456   Map 3
Rose & Crown ★

Signposted from exit roundabout of M2 junction 7: keep right on through village and follow Perry Wood signposts; or from A252 just W of junction with A28 at Chilham follow Shottenden signpost, then right turn signposted Selling, then right signposted Perry Wood; ME13 9RY

New licensees have taken over this popular pub and, as we went to press, were hoping to open all day in summer and serve food all day then, too. Décor is in keeping with the age of the building – hop bines strung from the beams, interesting corn-dolly decorations amongst hand-made tapestries, winter log fires in two inglenook fireplaces, fresh flowers and comfortably cushioned seats. Steps lead down to the timbered no smoking restaurant. Adnams Southwold, Goachers Mild, Harveys Sussex Best, and Roosters Leghorn on handpump; piped music, cribbage, dominoes and board games. Bar food now includes home-made soup (£3.95), stilton, apple and walnut filo parcel (£4.50), filled rolls (from £4.50), filled baked potatoes (from £5), ploughman's (£5.25), spaghetti bolognese or chicken and leek pie (£6.50), steak and mushroom pudding or cod and smoked haddock mornay (£8.75), daily specials, and Sunday roast beef (£8). The cottagey garden behind is charmingly planted with climbers, ramblers and colourful plants, there's a fairy-lit pergola, plenty of picnic-sets, a neatly kept children's play area, bat and trap, and a small aviary. The flowering tubs and hanging baskets in front are pretty too, and the terrace has outdoor heaters. The pub is surrounded by natural woodland, with good walking; hitching rail for horses and drinking bowls for dogs. More reports on the new regime, please. (Recommended by the Didler, M and R Thomas, E D Bailey, N R White, Gerry and Rosemary Dobson, Michael and Judy Buckley, M Sage, Dr Danny Nicol, Peter Meister, Simon and Amanda Southwell)

Free house ~ Licensees Tim Robinson and Vanessa Grove ~ Real ale ~ Bar food (they hope to serve food all day in summer; 12-2, 7-9.30 winter; not Sun or Mon evenings) ~ Restaurant ~ (01227) 752214 ~ Children welcome ~ Dogs allowed in bar ~ Open 11-11(10.30 Sun); 11-3, 6.30-11 winter Mon-Sat; 12-3, 7-10.30 Sun in winter

SHIPBOURNE   TQ5952   Map 3
Chaser ♀

Stumble Hill (A227 N of Tonbridge); TN11 9PE

Bustling and rather smart, this attractively placed stone and tile-hung pub has several open-plan areas that meander into each other, all converging on a large central island bar counter. There are stripped wood floors and décor is comfortably relaxed with frame to frame pictures on deepest red and cream walls, stripped pine wainscoting, an eclectic mix of solid old wood tables (with candles) and chairs, shelves of books, and open fires. A striking school chapel-like restaurant, right at the back, has dark wood panelling and a high timber vaulted ceiling. French windows open on to a covered and heated central courtyard with teak furniture and big green parasols, and a side garden, with the pretty church rising behind, is nicely enclosed by hedges and shrubs. Good, popular bar food includes home-made soup (£3.95), sandwiches (from £4.95; chargrilled steak on toasted ciabatta £6.95), fig, parma ham, rocket and port salut salad or potted mackerel with pickled cucumber and chilli (£5.95), chicken liver and foie gras pâté with onion chutney (£6.95), green herb, mushroom and cheddar cheese omelette or ploughman's (£6.95), fishcakes with beef tomato and spring onion salad and lemon mayonnaise (£7.95), local bangers and mash with onion gravy (£8.95), whole honey-glazed ham hock with pease pudding or chicken breast wrapped in bacon with a field mushroom and asparagus with roasted garlic and rosemary sauce (£11.95), and home-made puddings such as butterscotch tart with toffee sauce and honeycombe ice-cream, vanilla crème brûlée or bread and butter pudding with orange sauce (£4.95). No smoking except in bar area. Well kept Greene King IPA and Abbot and perhaps Black Country Fireside or Ridleys Prospect on handpump, and 15 wines by the glass; piped music. There is a small car park at the back, or you can park in the lane opposite by a delightful green; farmer's market on Thursday morning. *(Recommended by Gerry and Rosemary Dobson, Bob and Margaret Holder, E D Bailey, Jerry Green, Derek Thomas, GHC)*

Whiting & Hammond ~ Tenant Darren Somerton ~ Real ale ~ Bar food (12-9.30(9 Sun)) ~ (01732) 810360 ~ Very well behaved children welcome ~ Dogs welcome ~ Open 12-11(midnight Sat); 12-10.30 Sun

SNARGATE   TQ9928   Map 3
Red Lion ★ ◨
B2080 Appledore—Brenzett; TN29 9UQ

The last time this completely unspoilt village local was modernised was in 1890 and it's been in the same family since 1911. Three simple little rooms still have their original cream tongue-and-groove wall panelling, a couple of heavy beams in a sagging ceiling, dark pine Victorian farmhouse chairs on bare boards, lots of old photographs and other memorabilia, and a coal fire; outdoor lavatories, of course. One small room, with a frosted glass wall through to the bar and a sash window looking out to a cottage garden, has only two dark pine pews beside two long tables, a couple more farmhouse chairs and an old piano stacked with books. Toad in the hole, darts, shove-ha'penny, cribbage, dominoes, nine men's morris and table skittles. Goachers Light and Mild, and a couple of guests from brewers such as Archers or Grand Union are tapped straight from casks on a low rack behind an unusual shop-like marble-topped counter (little marks it out as a bar other than a few glasses on two small shelves, some crisps and half a dozen spirits bottles); you can also get Double Vision cider from nearby Staplehurst, and country wines. No food. *(Recommended by Nick Lawless, Kevin Thorpe, Pete Taylor, the Didler, Pete Baker, Peter Meister, Richard Siebert, MP)*

Free house ~ Licensee Mrs Jemison ~ Real ale ~ No credit cards ~ (01797) 344648 ~ Children in family room ~ Dogs allowed in bar ~ Open 12-3, 7-11(10.30 Sun)

STAPLEHURST   TQ7847   Map 3
Lord Raglan
About 1½ miles from town centre towards Maidstone, turn right off A229 into Chart Hill Road opposite Chart Cars; OS Sheet 188 map reference 785472; TN12 0DE

Although unpretentious, this friendly country pub has a relaxed and rather civilised atmosphere. The interior is cosy but compact, with a narrow bar – you walk in almost on top of the counter and chatting locals – widening slightly at one end to a small area with a big log fire in winter. In the other direction it works its way round to an intimate area at the back, with lots of wine bottles lined up on a low shelf. Low beams are covered with masses of hops, and the mixed collection of comfortably worn dark wood furniture, on quite well used dark brown carpet tiles and nice old parquet flooring, is mostly 1930s. Goachers Light, Harveys Best and a guest like Westerham Brewery British Bulldog on handpump, a good wine list, and local farm cider. From the snack menu, bar food includes sandwiches (from £3.25;

filled baguettes from £5.50), macaroni cheese (£5.95), ploughman's or chilli
(£6.50), and ham and egg (£7.50). The main menu is pricier: garlic mushrooms
(£4.25), smoked venison and pickled walnut (£5.95), vegetarian pasta (£8.50),
poached salmon with lemon and herb sauce or duck breast with port and orange
sauce (£9.95), stir-fried beef (£10.95), king prawns with garlic and ginger (£11.95),
and puddings (£4.50). Small french windows lead out to an enticing little high-
hedged terraced area with green plastic tables and chairs, and there are wooden
picnic-sets in the side orchard; reasonable wheelchair access. More reports please.
(Recommended by Sue Williams, John and Joan Calvert, Martin and Sue Day, Louise English)

Free house ~ Licensees Andrew and Annie Hutchison ~ Real ale ~ Bar food (12-2.30,
7-10; not Sun) ~ (01622) 843747 ~ Children welcome ~ Dogs welcome ~ Open 12-3,
6.30(6 Sat)-11; closed Sun

STODMARSH   TR2160   Map 3
Red Lion 🛏
High Street; off A257 just E of Canterbury; CT3 4BA

This is a proper country pub with roaming ducks and chickens, a dog and cat,
chatty locals, and a warm welcome to all from the cheerful, slightly eccentric
landlord. Full of character, several idiosyncratic rooms wrap themselves around the
big island bar. You'll find hops all over the place, wine bottles (some empty and
some full) crammed along mantelpieces and along one side of the bar, all manner of
paintings and pictures, copper kettles and old cooking implements, well used
cookery books, big stone bottles and milk churns, trugs and baskets, and old tennis
racquets and straw hats; one part has a collection of brass instruments, sheet music
all over the walls, and some jazz records, and a couple of little stall areas have hop
sacks draped over the partitioning. There are green-painted, cushioned mate's
chairs around a mix of nice pine tables, lit candles in unusual metal candleholders,
a big log fire, and fresh flowers; piped jazz, and bat and trap. Well kept Greene
King IPA, Old Speckled Hen and a seasonal guest are tapped straight from the cask,
and they've a good wine list with several by the glass, excellent summer Pimms and
winter mulled wine, and cider. Using allotment vegetables and home-reared meat,
the good food might include filled baguettes (not Sunday lunch or Saturday
evening), baby spinach, streaky bacon and avocado salad (£6.25), scallops with
chopped chives and bacon (£7.25), fresh local asparagus with wild salmon and
lemon hollandaise (£7.95), bass with garlic and tarragon (£14.75), rabbit, pigeon,
pheasant and hare casserole (£14.95), and puddings such as bramley apple pie or
strawberry and raspberry mousse with mint (£3.95); they sell eggs and chutneys.
There are picnic-sets under umbrellas in the back garden, with pretty flowerbeds.
Please note that the bedrooms though much enjoyed by readers don't have their
own bathrooms. *(Recommended by John Saville, Kevin Thorpe, Mike and Linda Hudson,
Nick Lawless)*

Free house ~ Licensee Robert Whigham ~ Real ale ~ Bar food ~ Restaurant ~
(01227) 721339 ~ Children allowed but with restrictions ~ Dogs welcome ~
Open 10.30am-1am; 11-10.30 Sun; closed 18th March ~ Bedrooms: /£60

STOWTING   TR1241   Map 3
Tiger
3.7 miles from M20 junction 11; B2068 N, then left at Stowting signpost, straight across
crossroads, then fork left after ¼ mile and pub is on right; coming from N, follow
Brabourne, Wye, Ashford signpost to right at fork, then turn left towards Posting and
Lyminge at T junction; TN25 6BA

Deep in the heart of some lovely countryside, this is a peaceful old pub with
friendly, welcoming staff. It's traditionally furnished and decorated, with plain
chairs and dark pews built in against the walls, candles stuck into bottles, faded
rugs on the dark floorboards, and some floor-to-ceiling plank panelling; there's an
open fire at each end of the main bar, paintings for sale, and books meant to be
opened, rather than left as shelf decoration. Well kept Adnams, Fullers London

Pride, Harveys Sussex Best, and Shepherd Neame Early Bird, Master Brew and Spitfire on handpump, 50 malt whiskies and local cider. Well liked bar food at lunchtime includes home-made soup or chicken liver pâté (£4.95), doorstep sandwiches (from £5.95), tiger prawns with garlic butter (£6.95), filled baked potatoes (from £6.95), steak in ale pie or roasted peppers stuffed with spinach, goats cheese and tomatoes (£8.95), and whole grilled plaice with lemon butter (£10.95); evening choices such as crab and cod fishcakes with stir-fried vegetables or pork loin chops with a cheese and herb crust and dijon mustard sauce (£10.95), honey-roasted half shoulder of lamb with garlic and mint (£13.95), half a roast duck with beetroot and onion gravy (£13.95), and puddings such as banoffi pie, jam roly-poly or sticky toffee pudding (£4.50). Seats out on the front terrace. *(Recommended by Tony Brace, Mr and Mrs Mike Pearson, Tina and David Woods-Taylor, Clive W Greaves)*

Free house ~ Licensee Emma Oliver ~ Real ale ~ Bar food (12-2.30, 6-9; all day Fri-Sun) ~ Restaurant ~ (01303) 862130 ~ Children welcome ~ Dogs allowed in bar ~ Jazz Mon evenings ~ Open 12-11.30(10.30 Sun)

TUNBRIDGE WELLS   TQ5639   Map 3

Beacon ♀ ⇔

Tea Garden Lane; leaving Tunbridge Wells westwards on A264, this is the left turn-off on Rusthall Common after Nevill Park; TN3 9JH

In warm weather, the pergola-covered raised wooden deck behind this airy Victorian pub is a fine place to enjoy the hillside views. The dining area and spreading bar run freely into each other with stripped panelling, wooden floors and ornately built wall units giving a solidly comfortable feel; the sofas by the fireside are sought after in colder weather. Well kept Harveys Sussex Best, Larkins and Timothy Taylors Landlord on handpump, and decent wines. Good bar food includes lunchtime sandwiches (from £4.75), soup (£4.25), Guinness and chive-battered haddock and chips (£7.90), pasta with tomatoes, olives, mint and halloumi (£8.95), rib-eye steak or lambs liver and bacon with rich onion gravy (£10), pork, bacon and cider casserole with apple and sage mash (£11.25), and confit duck on bubble and squeak with a red wine sauce (£12). The grounds have footpaths between lakes and springs, as well as summer boules and (very rare for a pub these days) even rounders. *(Recommended by Peter Meister, B J Harding, V Brogden, Martin and Sue Day, B and M Kendall)*

Free house ~ Licensee John Cullen ~ Real ale ~ Bar food (all day in summer; 12-2.30, 6.30-9.30 in winter; 12-5, 6.30-9.30 Sun) ~ Restaurant ~ (01892) 524252 ~ Children allowed away from bar ~ Dogs allowed in bar ~ Open 11-11; 12-10.30 Sun ~ Bedrooms: £68.50B/£97B

Sankeys ⑪ ♀ ◧

Mount Ephraim (A26 just N of junction with A267); TN4 8AA

At lunchtime and early evening particularly, the downstairs flagstoned no smoking brasserie bar is full of lively, chatty customers – especially local business people. Big mirrors spread the light, and there are stripped brick walls, pews or chairs around sturdy tables, and french windows that open on to a nice suntrap deck (to be refurbished as we went to press). Light and airy with big windows and high ceilings, the street level Town Bar tends to attract a younger crowd and has comfortably laid-out leather sofas round low tables, pews round pubby tables on bare boards, a wine oriented décor, and a big flat screen TV for Sky sports (the landlord is a keen rugby fan, and runner). A fine collection of rare enamel signs, too. As well as lunchtime filled baked potatoes (£4) and ciabattas (from £4), the good (mainly fishy) food might include smoked haddock in mornay sauce (£4.95; main course £7.95), moules marinière, thai or indian style or with fries (from £6.50), steak and Guinness pie (£6.50), queenie scallops with garlic butter (£6.75), irish rock oysters (£7 for six), home-potted shrimps (£7.25), home-made fishcakes (£8.50), roasted vegetable risotto (£9.50), rib-eye steak (£11.50), cajun tuna steak

(£12.50), and delicious cornish cock crab (£16.50). Well kept Harveys Sussex Best and Larkins Traditional and Porter on handpump, a very good wine list with about eight by the glass, and lots of fruit beers and exotic brews; piped music. *(Recommended by Dr David Cockburn, Martin and Sue Day, John A Barker)*

Free house ~ Licensee Guy Sankey ~ Real ale ~ Bar food (12-3, 6-10.30; 12-3 Sun; not Sun evening) ~ Restaurant ~ (01892) 511422 ~ Children welcome ~ Dogs welcome ~ Live bands Sun evening ~ Open 12-11; 12-midnight Fri and Sat

ULCOMBE TQ8550 Map 3
Pepper Box 🍺
Fairbourne Heath; signposted from A20 in Harrietsham, or follow Ulcombe signpost from A20, then turn left at crossroads with sign to pub, then right at next minor crossroads; ME17 1LP

This cosy and traditional country pub is very nicely placed on high ground above the weald, looking out over a great plateau of rolling arable farmland. The homely bar has standing timbers and low beams hung with hops, copper kettles and pans on window sills, some very low-seated windsor chairs, and two leather sofas by the splendid inglenook fireplace with its lovely log fire. A side area, more functionally furnished for eating, extends into the opened-up dining room; all eating areas are no smoking. Well kept Shepherd Neame Master Brew, Spitfire and a seasonal beer on handpump, local apple juice, and several wines by the glass; piped music. The two cats are called Murphy and Jim. Well liked bar food includes sandwiches, home-made soup (£4), prawn and salmon cakes with sweet chilli sauce (£6.50), vegetables stir-fried with thai spices (£8.50), calves liver in sage butter (£11.50), chicken supreme in a smoked bacon and avocado sauce (£12), steaks (from £12.50), and specials such as fried sardines in garlic butter (£4.80), moules marinière (£8.50), steak and kidney pudding (£9.80), herb-crusted fillet of cod with parmesan mash (£10.50), and slow-cooked lamb shanks in port and rosemary (£10.80). There's a hop-covered terrace and a garden with shrubs, flowerbeds and a small pond. The name of the pub refers to the pepperbox pistol – an early type of revolver with numerous barrels, and the village church is worth a look. The Greensand Way footpath is nearby. No children inside. *(Recommended by P and D Carpenter, N R White, Philip and Cheryl Hill, Nigel and Olga Wikeley, Simon and Amanda Southwell, Jan and Alan Summers, Martin and Sue Day, Ian and Nita Cooper)*

Shepherd Neame ~ Tenants Geoff and Sarah Pemble ~ Real ale ~ Bar food (12-2.30, 7-9.30; not Sun evening) ~ Restaurant ~ (01622) 842558 ~ Dogs welcome ~ Open 11-3, 6.30-11; 12-4 Sun; closed Sun evening

WEST PECKHAM TQ6452 Map 3
Swan on the Green 🍺
From A26/A228 heading N, bear left at roundabout onto B2016 (Seven Mile Lane), then second left; ME18 5JW

There's a good mix of locals and visitors in this bustling pub and recently, a party of 16 bell ringers had a very cheery visit. The bar is light, airy, and open plan, with rush-seated dining chairs and cushioned church settles around an attractive mix of well spaced refectory and other pale oak tables on wood strip floors. Attractive decorations include lovely big bunches of flowers (one placed in the knocked-through brick fireplace), hops on beams, some modern paintings at one end and black and white photographs of regulars at the other end; piped classical music and daily papers. Their own brew beers include Bewick, Fuggles, Ginger Swan, Swan Mild, Trumpeter and Whooper Pale on handpump, alongside Biddenden's farm cider. Tasty bar food includes as lunchtime filled ciabattas or ploughman's (£6.95), fried chicken livers with caramelised red onions (£6.45), fresh cromer crab or tagliatelle with spinach, chicken and blue cheese (£7.50), warm chicken breast and chargrilled bacon salad (£8.50,) and steak (from £12.95); the eating areas are no smoking. Picnic-sets under parasols in front with more on the charming cricket green opposite; they take a £10 deposit for a rug if you want to eat outside. The nearby church is partly Saxon. *(Recommended by Simon and Sally Small, Mr and Mrs Mike Pearson, Martin and Pauline Jennings, Graham Burling, Bob and Margaret Holder, Christopher Turner, Kevin Thorpe, Ian Wilson, Martin and Sue Day, Jan and Alan Summers, Sue Demont, Tim Barrow, Malcolm and Jane Levitt, Ben and Helen Ingram)*

Own brew ~ Licensee Gordon Milligan ~ Real ale ~ Bar food (not Sun or Mon evenings) ~ Restaurant ~ (01622) 812271 ~ Children welcome ~ Dogs welcome ~ Open 11-3, 6-11; 11-4, 6-midnight Sat; 12-10.30 Sun; 12-4 Sun in winter; closed Sun evening in winter and 25 Dec

---

LUCKY DIP

Besides the fully inspected pubs, you might like to try these Lucky Dips recommended to us and described by readers (if you do, please send us reports: www.goodguides.co.uk).

APPLEDORE [TQ9529]

Black Lion TN26 2BU [The Street]: Compact 1930s village pub with bustling atmosphere, very welcoming helpful staff, wide range of food all day inc imaginative dishes, lamb from Romney Marsh and local fish, three or four changing ales such as Greene King, Biddenden farm cider, log fire, partitioned back eating area; tables out by attractive village street *(John Branston, Louise English, Mrs C Lintott)*
Railway Hotel TN26 2DF [Station Rd (B2080 E)]: Refurbished Victorian hotel with wicker seats, rail memorabilia and open fire in big front bar, Badger K&B and bar food, daily papers, pool, darts, big back children's room with toys and TV, separate restaurant; good disabled access and facilities, garden tables, 12 bedrooms with own bathrooms in small motel wing *(Kevin Thorpe, GHC)*

BIDBOROUGH [TQ5643]

Hare & Hounds TN3 0XB [Bidborough Ridge]: Extended local with rugs on boards, stripped brick and pine, prints and old photographs, Harveys Best and Shepherd Neame Spitfire, particularly good coffee, wide food range inc waitress-service restaurant, attentive landlord and neat staff, darts and pool in public bar; children welcome *(Pamela and Douglas Cooper)*

BODSHAM [TR1045]

☆ *Timber Batts* TN25 5JQ: 17th-c hilltop pub in lovely country, cosy and civilised beamed bar with big inglenook and good pub lunches, with a different menu for the french restaurant (also much enjoyed), good unrushed service with a french touch, real ales such as Fullers London Pride; children welcome, large garden with valley views *(Stephen Allford, John and Enid Morris)*

BOTOLPHS BRIDGE [TR1233]

Botolphs Bridge Inn CT21 4NL [W of Hythe]: Unpretentious Edwardian country pub notable for its wide choice of good generous home-made food at sensible prices inc Sun roasts, quick pleasant service, good value wines, real ales such as Greene King IPA and Old Speckled Hen, two log fires, airy chatty open-plan bar with games area, small dining room one end (children allowed here); small garden *(Grahame Brooks)*

BRASTED [TQ4755]

White Hart TN16 1JE [High St (A25)]: Carefully preserved Battle of Britain bar with signatures and mementoes of Biggin Hill fighter pilots in roomy largely no smoking Vintage Inn, several other snug areas, beams and log fires, helpful staff, good choice of wine by the glass, real ales, fresh orange juice; children welcome, big neatly kept garden with well spaced tables and play area; pretty village with several antiques shops, open all day *(LYM, Christine and Neil Townend, N R White)*

BRENCHLEY [TQ6841]

Halfway House TN12 7AX [Horsmonden Rd]: Attractive olde-worlde mix of rustic and traditional furnishings on bare boards, two log fires, particularly friendly landlord, enjoyable food inc very popular Sun carvery, real ales tapped from the cask such as Adnams Broadside, Elgoods Black Dog Mild, Harveys Best, Larkins and Westerham SPA, two eating areas; picnic-sets and play area in big garden, bedrooms *(Peter Meister, Richard Durrant)*

BRIDGE [TR1854]

Plough & Harrow CT4 5LA [High St]: Small popular local in 17th-c former maltings, friendly and unpretentious, with Shepherd Neame Bitter and good wine choice, coal fire and lots of sporting prints in open-plan brick-walled lounge, public bar with bar billiards and open fire, wi-fi internet access, back games room with darts, TV and woodburner – pub is HQ of over 30 clubs and groups; no food; children and dogs welcome away from bar, open all day Sat *(Kevin Thorpe, Mike and Lynn Robinson, Craig Turnbull)*

BROADSTAIRS [TR3866]

Brown Jug CT10 2EW [Ramsgate Rd]: Long-serving landlady in basic and unchanging old-style two-bar local, Greene King and guest beers, some tapped from the cask, board and quiz games; open all day wknds *(the Didler)*
Lord Nelson CT10 1HQ [Nelson Pl]: Early 19th-c, with lots of Nelson memorabilia in lower bar, smart stripped brick upper area with open fire, Greene King IPA and Abbot and a guest beer; TV, occasional live music; tables outside, open all day *(Kevin Thorpe)*
Neptunes Hall CT10 1ET [Harbour St]: Friendly early 19th-c two-bar Shepherd Neame

local with attractive bow windows and original shelving and panelling, carpeted back lounge with open fire, lunchtime snacks, real ales, friendly staff and regulars; occasional live folk (daily during Aug folk festival); children and dogs welcome, enclosed terrace, open all day *(N R White, Kevin Thorpe, the Didler)*

Tartar Frigate CT10 1EU [Harbour St, by quay]: Appealing stone-built harbourside pub with interesting local photographs and fishing memorabilia, hanging pots and brasses, soft lighting, bare boards, tiles and plush seating, local beers, generous local fish and seafood in busy upstairs restaurant with good view; locals' bar with pool (can get smoky), plastic glasses for outdoor drinkers *(N R White, Liz and John Soden)*

White Swan CT10 3AZ [Reading St, St Peters]: Much modernised 17th-c pub with armchairs in comfortable lounge, Adnams and five unusual changing beers, simple bargain food (not Sun) from sandwiches and rolls up, pool and darts (and cheaper beer) in plain public bar; dogs welcome, open all day Sat *(Kevin Thorpe)*

BROOKLAND [TQ9925]

☆ *Royal Oak* TN29 9QR [aka Yew & Ewe; High St]: Dating from 16th c, recently carefully refurbished as no smoking dining pub, good reasonably priced food from baguettes to set lunches and interesting contemporary dishes, real ales such as Adnams Best and Broadside or Fullers London Pride, good choice of wines, helpful staff, light and fresh bar with a couple of sofas and mixed tables and chairs, chatty atmosphere, rather more traditional beamed restaurant extension with open fire; worth booking Fri/Sat evenings; small garden with terrace, two bedrooms *(Peter Meister, M Coates)*

CANTERBURY [TR1458]

Dolphin CT1 2AA [St Radigunds St]: Smart dining pub, civilised and friendly, with newish owners and new furniture inc comfortable sofas, old and new pictures on warm red walls above stripped dado, books to read, bric-a-brac on delft shelf, popular blackboard food from baguettes to fish specials, Fullers London Pride and Greene King IPA, country wines, flagstoned conservatory with fine collection of advertising mirrors; disabled access, children welcome, good-sized garden behind *(Kevin Thorpe)*

Millers Arms CT1 2AA [St Radigunds St/Mill Lane]: Well run Shepherd Neame pub with their real ales, good wine choice, bar food, several pleasantly refurbished rooms inc restaurant, interesting pictures and sayings; unobtrusive piped music; decent bedrooms, quiet street nr river and handy for Marlow Theatre *(N R White)*

Old Gate CT1 3EL [New Dover Rd (A2050 S)]: Big reliable Vintage Inn, several distinct areas, stripped brick and beams, two large open fires, bookshelves, big prints, old wooden table and chairs, reasonably priced food all day, good choice of wines by the glass, real ales such as Adnams, Bass or Shepherd Neame, well trained staff, daily papers; some piped

music; easy disabled access, bedrooms, picnic-sets in small back garden *(Kevin Thorpe)*

Phoenix CT1 3DB [Old Dover Rd]: Unpretentious local with Greene King Abbot, Charles Wells Bombardier, Youngs and up to three recherché guest beers, low-priced food all day (not Thurs evening) inc bargain Sun roasts and OAP deals, friendly staff; sports TV; open all day *(Kevin Thorpe, Tony Hobden)*

Simple Simons CT1 2AG [Church Lane, St Radigunds]: Step down into basic pub in 14th-c building, no smoking front bar with heavy beams, broad floorboards, flagstones and some stripped masonry, two woodburners, dim-lit upstairs banqueting hall, good changing range of real ales, impressive pump clip collection, low-priced simple lunchtime food inc sandwiches and speciality home-made pies; may be piped classical music by day, more studenty evening, frequent live jazz or blues; dogs welcome, tables in brick-paved courtyard, open all day *(Kevin Thorpe)*

Three Tuns CT1 2UD [Watling St, opp St Margaret St]: Interesting 15th-c building with nice old-fashioned décor, Shepherd Neame Spitfire, friendly service, enjoyable well priced food; piped music *(Mrs Hazel Rainer)*

CAPEL-LE-FERNE [TR2538]

Lighthouse CT18 7HT [Old Dover Rd]: Family-run hotel in great clifftop spot overlooking Channel, large comfortable bar and restaurant serving wide food choice from good ciabattas and ploughman's up, good-sized area set aside for non-eaters, Greene King real ales, good wine choice, friendly staff, indoor play area; bedrooms, open all day *(Tony Brace)*

CHARTHAM [TR1054]

Artichoke CT4 7JQ [Rottington St]: Attractive and tastefully decorated pub with old timbers too in well matched extension, enjoyable reasonably priced food, good service and atmosphere, log fire, darts *(Ron and Sheila Corbett)*

CHARTHAM HATCH [TR1056]

☆ *Chapter Arms* CT4 7LT [New Town St]: Sizeable largely no smoking 18th-c pub overlooking orchards, enjoyable generous meals, Shepherd Neame and guest beers, decent wine, friendly service, flowers and candles on tables, heavily hop-hung ceiling with brass instruments and fairy lights, restaurant through doorway decorated in lilac, green and silver; quiet piped music, jazz Mon; neatly tended garden with good furniture and lots of flower tubs *(BB, Norman Fox, M Joyner)*

CHIDDINGSTONE CAUSEWAY [TQ5247]

Greyhound TN11 8LG [Charcott, off back rd to Weald]: Cheerful new licensees in quiet hamlet's smallish unpretentious traditional local, clean and comfortable, with enjoyable food (popular lunchtime with older people), Harveys and Youngs; tables out in front *(Gwyn Jones, Heather and Dick Martin)*

CHILLENDEN [TR2653]

☆ *Griffins Head* CT3 1PS: Good-sized helpings of consistently appealing food and Shepherd Neame real ales in attractive beamed, timbered and flagstoned 14th-c pub with three comfortable rooms, some good wines, big log fire, local regulars; small children not welcome; pleasant garden surrounded by wild roses, super Sun barbecues, attractive countryside *(Janey, Guy Vowles)*

CONYER QUAY [TQ9664]

Ship ME9 9HJ: Pleasant atmosphere in refurbished creekside pub on Saxon Shore Way, friendly service, selection of real ales, hot drinks, decent wines, good straightforward bar food (not wknds), upstairs restaurant; open all day, terrace tables facing waterfront – road can flood at spring tides *(LYM, N R White)*

COWDEN [TQ4640]

☆ *Fountain* TN8 7JG [off A264 and B2026; High St]: Attractive tile-hung country local in pretty village, steep steps to unpretentious dark-panelled corner bar with Harveys IPA, Best and a seasonal beer, decent wines, friendly young landlady, darts and good log fire, mix of tables in adjoining room, sensibly short blackboard choice of good freshly made food from ciabattas to Sun roast, woodburner in small beamed back dining room with one big table; piped music, may be TV sports; walkers and dogs welcome, annual flower show, cl Mon lunchtime *(BB, Gwyn Jones, Paul A Moore, Ian Phillips)*

☆ *Queens Arms* TN8 5NP [Cowden Pound; junction B2026 with Markbeech rd]: Friendly two-room country pub like something from the 1930s, with splendid landlady, Adnams, coal fire, darts; dogs welcome, occasional folk music or morris dancers; may be cl wkdy lunchtimes but normally opens 10am *(the Didler, Pete Baker, Martin and Sue Day)*

CROCKHAM HILL [TQ4450]

Royal Oak TN8 6RD [Main Rd]: Cosy village local popular lunchtime for good simple food from sandwiches and baked potatoes to steaks, particularly friendly and helpful landlord, Shepherd Neame ales, daily papers, comfortable high-backed seats, no smoking area, amazing cartoons by local artist, no music or fruit machines; dogs welcome, small garden, handy for walks and Chartwell *(Pamela and Douglas Cooper, N R White, William Ruxton, M Joyner)*

DEAL [TR3752]

☆ *Bohemian* CT14 6HY [Beach St]: Relaxed chatty bar opp pier popular for its four well chosen changing real ales, several continental beers on tap and wide range of wines, good service, leather sofas, open fire, wooden floors and abstract paintings on red walls, good seafront views from upstairs restaurant; easy wheelchair access, heated back terrace, open all day Fri-Sun and summer, cl Mon in winter *(N R White, Kevin Thorpe)*

Kings Head CT14 7AH [Beach St]: Handsome three-storey coaching inn just across from promenade and sea, interesting maritime décor and cricket memorabilia in comfortable areas around central servery with Fullers London Pride, Harveys Sussex and Shepherd Neame, friendly service, flame-effect gas fires,

reasonably priced straightforward food from sandwiches up; piped music, TV, popular with young locals wknd evenings; terrace with sea-view picnic-sets, bedrooms, open all day *(B J Harding, N R White, LYM, Craig Turnbull, Mike and Lynn Robinson, Christopher Turner, Geoff and Molly Betteridge)*

Ship CT14 6JZ [Middle St]: Neatly kept two-roomed alehouse, real ales such as Fullers ESB, Gadds, Hop Back Summer Lightning and Shepherd Neame Bitter, friendly landlord, lots of dark woodwork, stripped brick and local ship and wreck pictures, piano and woodburner, no piped music or machines; small pretty enclosed garden, open all day *(N R White, Kevin Thorpe)*

DENTON [TR2147]

Jackdaw CT4 6QZ [A260 Canterbury—Folkestone]: Imposing open-plan brick and flint pub useful for enjoyable family food all day, Shepherd Neame Spitfire, Tetleys Mild, Charles Wells Bombardier and a couple of guest beers, friendly young staff, cream and red décor with RAF memorabilia in front area, large back restaurant; quiet piped music; children welcome, tables in pleasant garden, open all day *(Kevin Thorpe, Eddie Edwards, Mrs Hazel Rainer)*

DOVER [TR3241]

Blakes CT16 1PJ [Castle St]: Four or five changing real ales such as Gadds, Hopdaemon and unusual microbrews in small flagstoned cellar bar, good value lunchtime bar food (not Sun), upstairs restaurant, good choice of wines by the glass and of malt whiskies, chatty new licensees and locals, daily papers, partly panelled brick and flint walls, friendly pub cat; quiet piped music; suntrap terrace tables, bedrooms, open all day (till 5 Sun) *(Kevin Thorpe)*

Fox CT16 3DU [Temple Ewell; High St]: Good varied choice of decent straightforward food and changing real ales, cosy welcoming atmosphere *(A Pickering)*

Three Cups CT17 0RX [Crabble Hill]: Friendly local with welcoming landlord emphasising good real ales; barbecue in garden behind *(David Ellerington, Timothy Jan)*

DUNGENESS [TR0916]

☆ *Pilot* TN29 9NJ [Battery Rd]: Bustling no-nonsense atmosphere – now entirely no smoking – and massive helpings of good value fresh fish and chips among wide choice of other simple food from sandwiches up in single-storey mid-20th-c pub looking on to shingle beach, two bars and barn family extension, dark plank panelling inc the slightly curved ceiling, Courage Best, Greene King IPA and Abbot, hard-working landlord and friendly service, lots of knick-knacks for sale; piped music, picnic-sets in side garden *(Stephen Harvey, Christopher Turner, Louise English)*

DUNKS GREEN [TQ6152]

☆ *Kentish Rifleman* TN11 9RU: Timbered Tudor pub, cosy and welcoming, with plenty of character, rifles on low beams, old high-backed seats in small public bar (dogs allowed here – amiable pub dog), log fire in well divided dining lounge, good friendly service, changing real ales such as Fullers London Pride, Greene King Abbot and Youngs Special, decent wine and coffee, enjoyable pubby food from soup and sandwiches to Sun roasts, no machines; children welcome, tables in well designed garden behind, good walks *(BB, Bob and Margaret Holder, Tina and David Woods-Taylor, Stephen Harvey, Louise English, N R White, GHC)*

DUNTON GREEN [TQ5156]

Bullfinch TN13 2DR [London Rd, Riverhead]: Useful family dining pub with carvery, friendly service; play area in garden *(GHC)*

EAST PECKHAM [TQ6648]

Man of Kent TN12 5LA [Tonbridge Rd]: Traditional country pub dating from 15th c, Harveys, Larkins and two guest beers, good choice of wines and other drinks, five shades of enjoyable fresh home-made food, log fire; large attractive garden, peaceful spot by River Bourne in orchard country, lots of walks *(Anon)*

EASTLING [TQ9656]

☆ *Carpenters Arms* ME13 0AZ [off A251 S of M2 junction 6, via Painters Forstal; The Street]: Pretty, cosy and cottagey 14th-c oak-beamed pub with good newish landlady and welcoming staff, decent food (not Sun evening) inc good generous Sun lunch, Shepherd Neame real ales, big log fireplaces front and back; children allowed in small candlelit restaurant, some tables outside, small but well equipped bedrooms in separate building *(LYM, Paul and Sue Merrick)*

ELHAM [TR1743]

Kings Arms CT4 6TJ [St Marys Rd]: Welcoming traditional pub with relaxing attractive lounge bar, good open fire, good value food, Flowers, Greene King and Harveys, unobtrusively attentive friendly service, steps down to big dining area, public bar with games; opp church in square of charming village, attractive sheltered garden *(Keith Wright, David Lowe)*

☆ *Rose & Crown* CT4 6TD [High Street]: Partly 16th-c inn in charming village in Kent's prettiest valley, low beams, uneven floors, inglenook log fire and woodburner, comfortable pleasantly random furnishings, four Shepherd Neame ales (it's tied to them now), several wines by the glass, decent bar food, cheery service, no smoking restaurant; children welcome, flagstoned back terrace with teak furniture, pleasant bedrooms in former stable block, open all day wknds *(Tina and David Woods-Taylor, Dave Braisted, LYM, Rob and Catherine Dunster, GHC)*

FARNINGHAM [TQ5467]

Chequers DA4 0DT [High St/Dartford Rd, just off A20]: Unpretentious one-bar local with good choice of real ales such as Fullers ESB, Greene King Abbot and Timothy Taylors Landlord, friendly staff; benches outside, picturesque village *(N R White)*

FAVERSHAM [TR0161]

Albion ME13 7DH [Front Brents]: Light and airy waterside pub with solid pine furnishings, local pictures on pale green walls, good plain bar food (not Sun evening) from sandwiches up, Shepherd Neame ales inc seasonal from the nearby brewery, genial staff, flowers and candles on tables; children welcome in restaurant area, disabled lavatories, picnic-sets out on riverside walkway (Saxon Shore long-distance path), open all day summer *(LYM, Mike and Lynn Robinson, Mike Gorton, Martin and Sue Day, N R White, B J Harding)*

Anchor ME13 7BP [Abbey St]: Friendly two-bar traditional local in attractive 17th-c street nr quay, several Shepherd Neame ales, good quiet relaxed atmosphere, bare boards, open fires, settles and part-panelling, enjoyable sensibly priced food (not Sun evening or Mon), no smoking candlelit tiled eating area, piano, pub games; may be piped music, some live; a couple of picnic-sets outside, pretty garden, open all day, cl Mon mid-afternoon *(N R White, the Didler, Kevin Flack)*

Bear ME13 7AG [Market Pl]: Friendly local dating from 16th c (front rebuilt last century), lounge, snug and public bar off side corridor, Shepherd Neame ales from the nearby brewery, basic good value lunchtime home cooking; tables outside, lively musical following, open all day Sat *(the Didler)*

Crown & Anchor ME13 8JN [The Mall]: Friendly open-plan local dating from 19th c, Shepherd Neame real ales, wkdy lunchtime food inc authentic goulash (long-serving Hungarian landlord), games area with darts and pool *(the Didler)*

Elephant ME13 8JN [The Mall]: Picturesque flower-decked terrace town pub under new landlady (she's planning to do food), five changing real ales, belgian beers on tap, local cider, central log fire, daily papers, modern prints on pastel walls, new tables and chairs, fresh flowers, darts; children welcome, suntrap enclosed terrace with fishpond, has been open from 3 wkdys, all day wknds *(BB, the Didler)*

Park Tavern ME13 8BE [Whitstable Rd, opp playing fields]: Recently opened as dining pub, with wide choice of enjoyable food inc local produce and some elaborate dishes in the current fashion, simple but stylish bar, smart restaurant *(Chandran Tanabalan)*

Sun ME13 7JE [West St]: Roomy and rambling old-world 15th-c weatherboarded town pub with good unpretentious atmosphere in small low-ceilinged partly panelled rooms, good value low-priced lunchtime food, Shepherd Neame beers inc seasonal one from nearby brewery, quick pleasant service, smart no smoking restaurant; unobtrusive piped music; wheelchair access possible (small step), tables in pleasant back courtyard, interesting street, nine bedrooms, open all day *(the Didler)*

FOLKESTONE [TR2336]

Mariners CT19 6AB [nr harbour]: Nicely placed by fishing-boat quay, good busy lunchtime atmosphere with fishermen among customers, varied food from good range of baguettes to super fresh fish in bar and restaurant with lovely view from upstairs part, Fullers London Pride, pleasant staff, two pianos (musical evenings), old photographs of Folkestone and sea *(Gwyn Jones)*

FORDCOMBE [TQ5240]

☆ *Chafford Arms* TN3 0SA [B2188, off A264 W of Langton Green]: After 40 years here the landlord was planning to leave this extremely picturesque tile-hung old favourite, and so we don't know at all what changes are afoot; certainly, it's hard to imagine it without the hanging baskets and carefully tended shrubs and perennials which have been so lovely, and the sheltered back garden is a summer boon; it's been simple and spacious inside, open all day wknds, with locals in the public bar of an evening, Larkins and Wadworths 6X, and straightforward food *(LYM)*

FOUR ELMS [TQ4748]

Four Elms TN8 6NE [B2027/B269 E of Edenbridge]: Large busy open-plan dining pub with wide choice of good value food (not Mon evening) from sandwiches and baguettes to grills, good home-baked breads, real ales such as Fullers London Pride, Greene King Abbot and Shepherd Neame Spitfire, decent wine and coffee, cheerful service, several rambling rooms, two big log fires, huge boar's head, family room, no music; tables outside, handy for Chartwell, open all day (Sun afternoon break) *(John Evans, GHC)*

GOUDHURST [TQ7037]

☆ *Green Cross* TN17 1HA [Station Rd (A262 W)]: Particularly good interesting restauranty food, especially fish and seafood, Harveys and Larkins, good wines, roomy and attractive back restaurant with good napkins, tablecloths etc, contrasting simple two-room bar with good fire and TV, pleasant informal service; bedrooms light and airy, good value; very handy for Finchcocks *(BB, Bill and Pauline Harvey)*

☆ *Star & Eagle* TN17 1AL [High St]: Striking medieval building, now a small hotel, with settles and Jacobean-style seats in attractive heavily beamed open-plan areas, wide choice of good generous freshly made food from crusty ciabattas to full meals, friendly efficient service, Adnams (the bar itself seems fairly modern), good coffee, interesting smuggling-days history, lovely views from roomy restaurant; children welcome, tables out behind with same views, character bedrooms, well furnished and comfortable, open all day *(R E Dixon, LYM, Roy and Lindsey Fentiman, Tina and David Woods-Taylor, Ann and Colin Hunt)*

GRAVESEND [TQ6473]

Crown & Thistle DA12 2BJ [The Terrace]: Friendly and chatty old-fashioned local with five interesting changing beers from small breweries, bar nibbles, brewery pictures, no juke box or machines, can order in meals from nearby indian/chinese restaurant; no children, occasional live music; handy for historic riverside, open all day *(Richard Pitcher, the Didler)*

HALSTEAD [TQ4861]

Cock TN14 7DD [Shoreham Lane]: Neatly kept open-plan linked rooms, enjoyable food from sandwiches to freshly prepared main dishes inc some interesting specials, real ales such as Fullers London Pride and Marstons Pedigree, welcoming staff, log fire, jugs and pewter hanging from ceiling, small restaurant area; children and dogs welcome, terrace and garden *(Stuart Fraser)*

HARBLEDOWN [TR1358]

Old Coach & Horses CT2 9AB [Church Hill]: Enjoyable food, good service, good beer; great views from garden, peaceful setting *(Mrs H Dean)*

HAWKHURST [TQ7531]

Great House TN18 5EJ [Gills Green, just off A229 N]: Pretty tucked-away country dining pub dating from 16th c, good often imaginative food using local produce inc good value two-course lunches or Mon-Weds suppers, helpful friendly French service (may be slower at lunchtime), well kept ales inc Harveys, two farm ciders, decent house wines, unusual foreign bottled beers, log fire in relaxed chatty bar, restaurant inc new orangery extension; some live music; picnic-sets under cocktail parasols in small sheltered garden *(BB)*

HEAVERHAM [TQ5758]

Chequers TN15 6NP [Watery Lane]: Cottagey old pub with pleasantly unpretentious and friendly locals' bar, decent food here or in beamed restaurant, Shepherd Neame ales; children welcome, picnic-sets in big garden *(Gwyn Jones, E D Bailey, Martin and Sue Day, N R White)*

HERNE [TR1865]

☆ *Butchers Arms* CT6 7HL [Herne St (A291)]: No smoking throughout in tiny new sawdust-floor pub with four or more particularly well kept changing real ales tapped from the cask, interesting bottled beers and Biddenden farm cider, just a couple of benches and butcher's-block tables, some wines too but no food (you can bring your own), no lagers, music or TV; dogs welcome, tables out under awning, cl Mon, Sun evening, and winter Sun lunchtime *(Kevin Thorpe)*

HERNHILL [TR0660]

☆ *Red Lion* ME13 9JR [off A299 via Dargate, or A2 via Boughton Street and Staplestreet]: Pretty Tudor inn by church and attractive village green, densely beamed and flagstoned, log fires, pine tables, enjoyable food, Fullers London Pride, Shepherd Neame and a guest beer, decent house wines, friendly attentive staff, no smoking upstairs restaurant; children welcome, big garden with boules and good play area, bedrooms *(LYM, Mrs Margo Finlay, Jörg Kasprowski, N R White)*

HEVER [TQ4743]

Greyhound TN8 7LJ [Uckfield Lane]: Well laid out bar with quiet corners, imaginative food at reasonable prices here or in more formal dining area, good beers; tables in garden behind, handy for Hever Castle *(D H Millett)*

☆ *Henry VIII* TN8 7NH [by gates of Hever

Castle]: Dating partly from 14th c, some fine
oak panelling and heavy beams, inglenook
fireplace, Henry VIII décor, enjoyable
reasonably priced food in bar and small dining
room, efficient welcoming service, Shepherd
Neame real ales; tables out on terrace and
pondside lawn (D H Millett, LYM, R and
S Bentley)

HIGHAM [TQ7171]
Gardeners ME3 7AS [off A226 Gravesend—
Rochester; Forge Lane]: Friendly pub with
enjoyable food inc good Sun lunch, real ales
inc Shepherd Neame Spitfire, good service
(Graham D Howard)

HODSOLL STREET [TQ6263]
☆ *Green Man* TN15 7LE [off A227 S of
Meopham]: Pretty no smoking pub by village
green with Flowers, Fullers London Pride,
Youngs and a guest beer, decent wines, good
food from lunchtime sandwiches, wraps and
baguettes to upmarket dishes and local game,
neat tables in big airy and relaxed rooms
around hop-draped central bar, interesting old
local photographs and antique plates, log fire;
piped music; children and dogs allowed, tables
out on lawn, play area, North Downs walks,
open all day Fri-Sun (Fiona McElhone,
Simon Pyle, Sherree Fagge, Gerry and
Rosemary Dobson, LYM, GHC)

HUCKING [TQ8458]
Hook & Hatchet ME17 1QT [village signed
off A249; Church Rd]: Isolated country pub in
enviable spot by Woodland Trust's Hucking
Estate, plenty of nearby interesting walks; now
under new management and tied to Shepherd
Neame, with their beers and standard food, an
open fire, well spaced seats on broad polished
boards, pleasant contemporary rustic décor, no
smoking dining room; piped music; children
welcome, tables out on heated verandah,
picnic-sets in neat garden, open all day
(Lesley and Peter Barrett, LYM)

HYTHE [TR1634]
Hope CT21 6DA [Stade St]: Proper pub with
enjoyable low-priced lunches in friendly
separately run simple restaurant (John and
Penelope Massey Stewart)

IDE HILL [TQ4851]
Cock TN14 6JN [off B2042 SW of Sevenoaks]:
Pretty village-green pub with warmly pubby
atmosphere, Greene King ales, wholesome
food (not Sun evening) from sandwiches and
ploughman's up, fine log fire, bar billiards;
piped music, no children; some seats out in
front, handy for Chartwell and nearby walks –
so gets busy (LYM, N R White, DJH,
David H T Dimock, GHC)
Woodman TN14 6BU [Whitley Row,
Goathurst Common; B2042 N]: Large mainly
no smoking Chef & Brewer, wide blackboard
choice of all-day food from hot baguettes to
some south african specialities (landlord's
from there), friendly young staff, decent wine,
real ales such as Greene King Old Speckled
Hen and Charles Wells Bombardier,
woodburner; manicured lawns, good walks
(Tina and David Woods-Taylor, N R White,
Tony Brace)

IGHTHAM [TQ5956]
☆ *George & Dragon* TN15 9HH [A227]:
Picturesque black and white timbered dining
pub, early 16th-c but much modernised, short
choice of good food from generous snacks (all
day till 6.30, not Sun) up, Shepherd Neame
Bitter, Spitfire and seasonal ales, decent wines,
good choice of fruit juices, sofas among other
furnishings in long sociable main bar, heavy-
beamed end room, woodburner and open fires,
partly no smoking restaurant; children in
family/restaurant areas, back terrace, open all
day, handy for Ightham Mote (NT), good
walks (LYM, Dave Braisted, Derek Thomas,
Martin and Sue Day, GHC)

IGHTHAM COMMON [TQ5955]
Old House TN15 9EE [Redwell, S of village;
OS Sheet 188 map ref 591559]: Basic two-
room country local tucked down narrow lane,
no inn sign, bare bricks and beams, huge log
fireplace filling one wall, four good changing
ales tapped from the cask, retired cash register
and small TV in side room; no food, music or
machines, cl wkdy lunchtimes, opens 7 (even
later Tues) (the Didler, BB)

IVY HATCH [TQ5854]
☆ *Plough* TN15 0NL [off A227 N of Tonbridge]:
Restauranty pub with good food and wines,
Harveys, pleasantly informal atmosphere and
décor, attractive conservatory; good garden
tables (Evelyn and Derek Walter, LYM,
Ian Wilson, Alan Sadler, Bob and
Margaret Holder, Darren Burrows, B and
M Kendall)

KINGSTON [TR2051]
☆ *Black Robin* CT4 6HS [Elham valley rd, off
A2 S of Canterbury at Barham signpost]: Great
atmosphere, good range of enjoyable food
from hot baguettes to smart main dishes, a
house beer (perhaps from Hopdaemon) and
interesting guest ales, decent wines by the glass,
local farm apple juice, cheerful helpful staff,
candles and flowers, stylish décor and nice mix
of seating inc leather armchair and chesterfield,
charming and cosy dim-lit inner room, no
smoking dining room; piped music; good
tables on terrace with standard roses and in
large garden, open all day (Mike and
Marion Higgins, BB)

KNOCKHOLT [TQ4658]
Crown TN14 7LS [Main Rd]: Cheerful old-
fashioned village pub, unchanged for decades,
with attractive dark ochre décor, friendly
relaxed service, good value home-made
comfort food lunchtimes and Sat evening inc
sandwiches and sensibly priced hot dishes,
Adnams Bitter and Broadside, walkers with
muddy boots welcome in public bar; picnic-sets
on lawn with fishpond, colourful flowers, path
to North Downs Way (Robert Gomme,
N R White)
Three Horseshoes TN14 7LD [Main Rd]:
Large friendly village pub with cosy bar, good
range of moderately priced food in no smoking
dining bar, real ale, welcoming service, live
music and quiz nights; pretty garden with
unusual fence mural, North Downs Way
footpath nearby (N R White)

LAMBERHURST [TQ6735]

Brown Trout TN3 8HA [B2169, off A21 nr entrance to Scotney Castle]: Pretty dining pub with biggish extension off small well worn-in beamed bar, good value food inc fish specialities and OAP deals, Adnams and Fullers London Pride, fair choice of decent wines, cheerful willing staff, good log fire, children in eating areas; picnic-sets in large safe garden with play area, open all day Sun and summer *(B J Harding, Ian Phillips, BB)*

Chequers TN3 8DB [A21]: Low limed beams and standing timbers in light open-plan main bar, parquet or flagstone floor, big leather sofa on turkey rug, variety of sturdy tables and dining chairs, big inglenook log fire, food from good sandwiches and panini to ambitious dishes, Shepherd Neame real ales, daily papers, similar public bar; piped jazz or pop; solid tables on back deck, pretty streamside garden beyond *(BB, Oliver and Sue Rowell, Jenny and Brian Seller)*

☆ *Elephants Head* TN3 8LJ [Hook Green; B2169 towards T Wells]: Ancient rambling timber-framed country pub, heavy beams, brick or oak flooring, big inglenook log fire, plush-cushioned pews etc, Harveys and other ales, pleasant staff, wide food choice inc generous and popular Sun dinner, darts and fruit machine in small side area, may be quiet piped music; children welcome, picnic-sets by front green and in big back garden with peaceful view, terrace and good play area, nr Bayham Abbey and Owl House *(Peter Meister, D Travis, Nigel and Jean Eames, LYM)*

Swan TN3 8EU [Lamberhurst Down]: Pleasantly refurbished family dining pub next to Lamberhurst vineyards, lots of english wines and good choice of others, wide range of food inc good starters and imaginative open sandwiches, friendly service, three real ales; children welcome, tables outside *(Nigel and Jean Eames)*

LEIGH [TQ5446]

Fleur de Lis TN11 8RL [High St]: Plain décor with scrubbed tables on flagstones, good range of food, Greene King real ales, efficient service *(Gwyn Jones)*

LEYSDOWN-ON-SEA [TR0266]

Ferry House ME12 4BQ [Harty Ferry Rd, Sheerness]: At seaside end of long bumpy single-track road through salt marshes full of birds, friendly staff, enjoyable if not cheap food, good beers and wine, restaurant recently extended into attractive new timbered barn-style structure; they may try to keep your credit card while you eat; tables outside looking across to Kent mainland, play area *(Dave Braisted, Colin Moore)*

LITTLE CHART [TQ9446]

Swan TN27 0QB [The Street]: Comfortable tucked-away 17th-c village inn with lots of beams, open fires in simple unspoilt front bar and interesting smarter bar, good-sized dining area, enjoyable food, Fullers London Pride, decent wines, friendly landlord and locals; dogs welcome, nice surroundings *(Ann and Colin Hunt)*

LUDDESDOWN [TQ6667]

☆ *Cock* DA13 0XB [Henley Street, N of village – OS Sheet 177 map reference 664672; off A227 in Meopham, or A228 in Cuxton]: Distinctive tucked-away early 18th-c country pub, homely bay-windowed lounge, quarry-tiled locals' bar with pews and other miscellaneous furnishings, lots of old posters, beer mats, bookshelves and bric-a-brac, several changing ales inc Adnams Bitter and Broadside and Goachers Mild, modestly priced generous food (not Sun evening) from sandwiches up, friendly service, traditional games inc bar billiards and three types of darts board, two woodburners, back dining conservatory; no children allowed in, picnic-sets on terrace and big secure garden with boules, open all day *(Dr Danny Nicol, LYM, N R White)*

MAIDSTONE [TQ7655]

Pilot ME15 6EU [Upper Stone St (A229)]: Busy old roadside pub, enjoyable low-priced simple home-made food (not Sun), Harveys ales, good friendly landlord, whisky-water jugs hanging from ceiling, darts and pool; tables on back terrace *(the Didler)*

Rifle Volunteers ME14 1EU [Wyatt St/Church St]: Old-fashioned backstreet pub tied to local Goachers, three of their ales inc Mild, good value simple home-made food, chatty long-serving landlord, two gas fires, darts, no machines; tables outside *(the Didler)*

MARDEN THORN [TQ7643]

Wild Duck TN12 9LH [Pagehurst Lane; off A229 in Staplehurst or B2079 in Marden]: Country pub with hard-working new young licensees doing enjoyable imaginative food inc cut-price smaller helpings, Shepherd Neame Spitfire, good-sized dining room; garden with climbing frame and slide, cl Tues *(Richard Durrant, Glenwys and Alan Lawrence, BB, Mark Conn, John and Joan Calvert)*

MARSHSIDE [TR2266]

Hog & Donkey CT3 4EH [North Stream]: Remote and idiosyncratic 18th-c pub with very long-serving landlord, Flowers tapped from the cask, no food, cottagey 1950s-feel front room with mix of tables, chairs, sofas and bright cushions strewn around, coal fire, may be 1960s radiogram playing; car park hedges gradually overtaking long-resident cars; handy for Stour Valley and Saxon Shore walks *(Eddie Edwards)*

MARTIN [TR3347]

Old Lantern CT15 5JL [off A258 Dover—Deal; The Street]: Pretty olde-worlde cottage, low beams and cosy corners in neatly kept bar with dining tables, popular home-made food, welcoming attentive staff, Shepherd Neame, decent wines; sizeable play area and wendy house in good-sized pretty gardens, beautiful setting, may cl Sun evening *(Janey, N R White)*

MAYPOLE [TR2064]

Prince of Wales CT3 4LN [S of Herne Bay]: Comfortable main bar with warm red décor and heavy curtains, two open fires, china and old photographs, Shepherd Neame Bitter and one or two guest beers, good staff, flowers on pine tables in small back dining area (best to book), pub games and working 78rpm gramophone; piped music; children and dogs welcome, garden tables, open all day *(Kevin Thorpe)*

NEWENDEN [TQ8327]
White Hart TN18 5PN [A268]: 16th-c pub with long beamed bar, real ales such as Harveys, Rother Valley, Skinners and St Austell, log fire in big stone fireplace, dining area with enjoyable food and quick service; popular with young people evenings, two sports TVs, pool in back games area, piped pop music; children welcome, large garden *(V Brogden, BB)*

NEWNHAM [TQ9557]
Tapster ME9 0NA [Parsonage Farm, Seed Rd]: Good interesting food in long recently redecorated bistro/bar, two changing beers from Archers, freshly squeezed orange juice and good wine choice, friendly staff and three entertaining dogs, huge log fireplace, candles, flowers and white linen, big pot plants and ferns, broad boards and reclaimed worn brickwork; piped jazz; dogs and children welcome, picnic-sets in big garden with cider press, bedrooms, open all day in summer, cl Mon in winter *(Kevin Thorpe)*

NORTHBOURNE [TR3352]
Hare & Hounds CT14 0LG [off A256 or A258 nr Dover; The Street]: Popular no smoking village local with good range of real ales such as Fullers London Pride, Gadds and Shepherd Neame Spitfire (Aug beer festival), log fires each end, sensibly priced and generous daily-changing blackboard food inc enterprising dishes (they try to cater for special needs), friendly attentive service; terrace tables, big play area *(N R White, Kevin Thorpe)*

OTFORD [TQ5259]
Bull TN14 5PG [High St]: Attractively laid out 15th-c no smoking Chef & Brewer, their usual huge food choice from sandwiches and baguettes up all day, good Sun lunch, friendly attentive staff, four real ales, decent wines, several quietly spacious rooms, log fires in two enormous fireplaces; nice garden behind *(B J Harding, N R White, Alan M Pring)*
Crown TN14 5PQ [High St, pond end]: 16th-c two-bar local opp village pond, relaxed lounge with sofas, real ales such as Black Sheep, cheerful friendly staff, reasonably priced lunchtime food inc good Sun roasts; walkers and dogs welcome, good walks nearby *(N R White)*

PENSHURST [TQ4943]
☆ *Rock* TN8 7BS [Hoath Corner, Chiddingstone Hoath; OS Sheet 188 map ref 497431]: Two charmingly old-fashioned and simple little beamed rooms with farmers and dogs, stripped brick and timbers, wonky brick floors, woodburner in inglenook, Larkins from the nearby brewery, good house wines, local farm cider, good blackboard food choice (not Sun), friendly staff, ring the bull (with a real bull's head), steps up to small dining room; children and dogs welcome, no mobile phones; front terrace, back garden, beautiful countryside

nearby (handy for Eden Valley walk), cl Mon *(N R White, GHC)*
☆ *Spotted Dog* TN11 8EP [Smarts Hill, off B2188 S]: Quaint old tiled pub, half no smoking, with welcoming helpful young mainly antipodean staff, good bar food changing daily, Harveys Best and Larkins Best and Traditional, cosy inglenook log fire, heavy low beams and timbers, antique settles and more straightforward furnishings, rugs and tiles, attractive moulded panelling, no smoking restaurant (very popular for Sun lunch); unobtrusive piped music; children welcome till 7, tables out in front and on attractive tiered back terrace, open all day summer Thurs-Sun *(Nigel and Jean Eames, Simon Pyle, LYM, N R White, Martin and Sue Day, J B Young)*

PLAXTOL [TQ6054]
☆ *Golding Hop* TN15 0PT [Sheet Hill (½ mile S of Ightham, between A25 and A227)]: Secluded country local, small and simple dim-lit two-level bar with hands-on landlord who can be very welcoming (but don't rely on this), Adnams, Youngs and a couple of guest beers, four local farm ciders (sometimes even their own), basic good value fresh bar snacks (not Mon/Tues evenings), woodburner, bar billiards; portable TV for big sports events, game machine; suntrap streamside lawn and well fenced play area over lane, open all day Sat *(B J Harding, Bob and Margaret Holder, LYM, N R White, Gwyn Jones, the Didler)*

PLUCKLEY [TQ9245]
Black Horse TN27 0QS [The Street]: Attractive and interesting old house said to be haunted, bare boards and flagstones, hops on beams, four log fires inc vast inglenook, plenty of old things to look at, cheery atmosphere, wide food choice from baguettes up (just roasts on Sun), real ales inc Adnams, roomy carpeted side and back dining areas; piped music, big-screen TV, fruit machine; children allowed if eating, picnic-sets in spacious informal garden by tall sycamores, good walks, open all day Fri-Sun *(BB, Louise English, Ann and Colin Hunt)*

RAMSGATE [TR3764]
Artillery Arms CT11 9JS [West Cliff Rd]: Chatty open-plan corner local under new licensees, Charles Wells Bombardier and four changing beers, farm cider, sandwiches all day, straightforward two-level bar with fire at top end, artillery prints and interesting stained-glass windows dating from Napoleonic wars; juke box can be loud; good wheelchair access, children and dogs welcome, open all day *(Kevin Thorpe)*
Churchill Tavern CT11 9JX [Paragon (seafront)]: Big clifftop pub rebuilt in the 1980s with old beams, bare bricks, pews and farm tools, long bar with Fullers London Pride, Ringwood Old Thumper, Charles Wells Bombardier and several changing guest beers, good value food in bar or popular back cottage restaurant, open fire, pool in games corner; occasional live music; children and dogs welcome, harbour, marina and Channel views, open all day *(Kevin Thorpe)*

Montefiore Arms CT11 7HJ [Trinity Pl]: Busy, friendly little backstreet pub, simply furnished single room, two changing ales usually from small breweries, keen landlord, chatty locals; darts, TV and piped radio; children welcome away from bar, cl Weds lunchtime *(Kevin Thorpe)*

SANDWICH [TR3358]

Fleur de Lis CT13 9BZ [Delf St]: Comfortable 18th-c former coaching inn with old stripped pine tables in smart split-level lounge end, open fire, wide food range (all day wknds) from sandwiches up, Fullers London Pride, Greene King IPA and a guest beer, pleasant uniformed staff, TV and games end, no smoking panelled back restaurant; piped music; 12 bedrooms with own bathrooms, open all day *(Mrs Hazel Rainer)*

SEASALTER [TR0864]

☆ *Sportsman* CT5 4BP [Faversham Rd, off B2040]: Good imaginative contemporary cooking (not Sun evening or Mon, and best to book other times) using local supplies in restauranty dining pub in caravan land, just inside the sea wall; relaxed atmosphere and friendly service in two simply furnished linked rooms and long conservatory, wooden floor, big film star photographs, pine tables, wheelback and basket-weave dining chairs, Shepherd Neame Bitter and Spitfire, well chosen wines; children welcome in no smoking areas, open all day Sun *(LYM, Derek Thomas, N R White, Louise English)*

SEVENOAKS [TQ5354]

Chequers TN13 1LD [High St]: Reasonably priced food worth waiting for in friendly beamed and flagstoned pub, nice change from the town's teen bars *(R Arnold)*

SHOREHAM [TQ5161]

Kings Arms TN14 7SJ [Church St]: Pretty and popular, with civilised bar, pleasant service, wide choice of decent usual food inc good value ploughman's, plates and brasses, bookable restaurant; picnic-sets outside, quaint unspoilt village on River Darent, good walks *(N R White)*

SISSINGHURST [TQ7937]

Bull TN17 2JG [The Street]: Good range of enjoyable food in bar and big pleasant dark-beamed restaurant area, quick pleasant service, Harveys and other ales, log fire, shelves of books and china; neat quiet garden with fenced duckpond, open all day *(M Joyner, Ann and Colin Hunt)*

SMARDEN [TQ8642]

☆ *Bell* TN27 8PW [from Smarden follow lane between church and Chequers, then left at T junction; or from A274 take unsignposted turn E a mile N of B2077 to Smarden]: Pretty rose-covered 17th-c inn with striking chimneys, rambling low-beamed little rooms, dim-lit and snug, nicely creaky old furnishings on ancient brick and flagstones or quarry tiles, warm inglenooks, nice atmosphere and friendly service, enjoyable bar food from ciabattas to steaks, Flowers IPA and several Shepherd Neame ales, local cider, country wines, winter mulled wine, no smoking room, end games

area; picnic-sets in attractive mature garden, simple bedrooms *(LYM, the Didler, Peter Meister, Ann and Colin Hunt)*

Chequers TN27 8QA: New management for refurbished low-beamed 14th-c inn in pretty village, Fullers London Pride, Greene King IPA and Harveys Sussex Best, straightforward food, flagstoned restaurant; piped music; attractive garden and seats on terrace, bedrooms, open all day *(LYM, Ann and Colin Hunt)*

ST MARGARET'S AT CLIFFE [TR3544]

Cliffe CT15 6AT [High St]: Attractive clapboard-and-brick inn opp church, good log fire in cosy bar leading to spacious dining room with claret-coloured fabrics and vineyard/grape pictures, enjoyable traditional food, friendly staff keen to please; secluded back walled garden, bedrooms, some in cottages across yard, good walks nearby *(LYM, Gloria Bax)*

ST MARGARET'S BAY [TR3744]

☆ *Coastguard* CT15 6DY [The Bay]: Cheery and lively modern nautical-theme seaside pub, enjoyable food inc plenty of fresh fish, children's helpings of most things, three changing real ales from small breweries, dozens of malt whiskies, good uniformed service even when busy, tremendous views to France – in the car park mobile phones have sometimes even picked up french not english transmitters, with calls billed as 'overseas'; children and dogs welcome, lots of tables on prettily planted balcony, more down by beach below NT cliff and nr Pines Garden, open all day *(LYM, Kevin Thorpe, A Pickering, David and Ruth Shillitoe)*

ST MARY IN THE MARSH [TR0627]

Star TN29 0BX [opp church]: Relaxed and remote down-to-earth pub, Tudor but very much modernised; friendly family service, good simple reasonably priced food from sandwiches to Sun lunch, Shepherd Neame beers, huge log fireplace, pool and darts, amiable pub labrador; tables in nice garden, good value attractive beamed bedrooms with Romney Marsh views, lovely setting opposite ancient church *(Kevin Flack, Michael and Jenny Back, David Lowe)*

ST NICHOLAS AT WADE [TR2666]

Bell CT7 0NT [just off A299; The Street]: Olde-worlde 16th-c beamed two-bar pub busy wknds for good value generous unfussy food from baguettes to fresh fish and good Sun roasts, stripped brickwork and lots of wood, big log fires, Adnams Broadside and Greene King IPA and Old Speckled Hen, friendly staff, restaurant, games and juke box in big back room; children and dogs welcome, open all day wknds *(Kevin Thorpe, Norman Fox, Paul and Ursula Randall)*

STALISFIELD GREEN [TQ9552]

Plough ME13 0HY [off A252 in Charing]: Well presented food from filled baguettes through bar dishes to more upmarket and restauranty italian dishes, pizza nights Tues-Thurs, pleasant service by friendly Italian family, peaceful atmosphere, four real ales, farm cider, big but tasteful side extension;

tables in big pleasant garden, attractive village green setting, good view and walks *(Paul and Sue Merrick)*

STANFORD [TR1238]

Drum TN25 6DN [B2068, ½ mile from M20 junction 11]: Recently reopened after refit, good atmosphere, enjoyable generous food inc local fish, Greene King ales, decent wines, friendly staff *(Stephen Allford)*

STONE STREET [TQ5755]

☆ *Padwell Arms* TN15 0LQ [off A25 E of Sevenoaks, on Seal—Plaxtol by-road; OS Sheet 188 map ref 569551]: Neatly kept orchard-view country pub with efficient friendly service by new family, wide choice of generous home-made food (served Sun evening too), good choice of changing real ales, nice wines and good coffee, comfortable banquettes and log fire, enlarged airy back dining area; tables on front terrace (lovely flowering baskets and window boxes), more in pleasant back garden, plenty of shade, good walks *(BB, Hugh Roberts, E D Bailey, DFL, B and M Kendall, Debbie and Neil Hayter, the Didler, Martin and Sue Day, Oliver and Sue Rowell, GHC)*

☆ *Snail* TN15 0LT: Well run pub/restaurant, wide choice of good food at big oak farmhouse tables, plenty of fish, good wines, Harveys and a guest beer, ad lib coffee, friendly staff and relaxed atmosphere, pleasant brasserie layout with beams, oak panelling and some stripped stone; attractive rambling garden, handy for Ightham Mote *(BB, E D Bailey, Melanie Ginger, John Marshall)*

STOWTING [TR1140]

Black Horse TN25 6AP [Fiddling Lane]: Friendly pub with enjoyable Sun carvery; smart comfortable furniture in attractive garden overlooking fields and llamas, timber play side, lovely surroundings *(Paul and Marie Spiller)*

SUTTON VALENCE [TQ8149]

Swan ME17 3AJ [Broad St]: Old two-bar pub under new landlord, enjoyable blackboard food using local supplies, several real ales, moderately priced wines, pub games; pretty village nr Leeds Castle *(Mr and Mrs Peter Radcliffe)*

TENTERDEN [TQ8833]

Eight Bells TN30 6BJ [High St]: Pleasant old inn popular with older people for lunch, enjoyable food with nice veg, real ales such as Adnams and Fullers, friendly and helpful young staff, long traditional bare-boards bar (can get smoky), central courtyard glazed in as further no smoking eating area; easy wheelchair access, good value old-world beamed bedrooms, tasty breakfast *(Peter Meister)*

☆ *White Lion* TN30 6BD [High St]: 16th-c inn, beams and timbers, masses of pictures, china and books, cheerful and helpful young staff, wide choice of generous popular food, Adnams Broadside, Bass and Greene King IPA, sensibly priced wines, big log fire, relaxed and friendly even when crowded with young people at night, smart no smoking softly lit back panelled restaurant; dogs welcome, bar can get a bit smoky; tables on heated terrace

overlooking street, 15 comfortably creaky beamed bedrooms, good breakfast, open all day *(W M Lien)*

William Caxton TN30 6JR [West Cross; top of High St]: Well worn in 15th-c local, heavy beams and bare boards, huge inglenook log fire, woodburner in smaller back bar, wide blackboard choice of enjoyable reasonably priced food, Shepherd Neame real ales, good service, pleasant small dining room; piped music; children welcome, tables in attractive front area, bedrooms, open all day *(V Brogden, the Didler, Peter Meister)*

TEYNHAM [TQ9562]

Plough ME9 0JJ [Lewson St]: Picturesque beamed pub in quiet village, friendly staff and atmosphere, full range of Shepherd Neame ales, good wines, wide choice of generous food from bar lunches to quality restaurant meals, log fires, comfortable and tasteful furnishings; music and quiz nights; children and dogs welcome, large well kept garden and terrace, attractive setting *(R J Snell)*

TONBRIDGE [TQ5945]

Cardinals Error TN9 2EP [Lodge Oak Ln]: Cottagey pub with steps and low beams, Greene King and Harveys ales, food from good sandwiches up; lovely garden *(Jenny and Brian Seller)*

TOYS HILL [TQ4752]

Fox & Hounds TN16 1QG [off A25 in Brasted, via Brasted Chart and The Chart]: Emphasis on generally good if not cheap food (not Sun evening), interesting blackboard choice, neat friendly and efficient staff, Greene King IPA and Abbot, tiled partly no smoking bar area with coal fire, smart comfortable modern dining extension; piped music, occasional live; disabled access and facilities, tree-sheltered garden, good walks nearby, open all day summer *(N R White, William Ruxton, LYM, Cathryn and Richard Hicks, Jenny and Brian Seller, A D McDowall, Mrs Susan Powell, Simon Rodway)*

TUNBRIDGE WELLS [TQ5739]

Mount Edgcumbe Hotel TN4 8BX [The Common]: Friendly tile-hung and weatherboarded hotel with enjoyable malaysian and thai food (and lunchtime sandwiches), extensive wine list, Harveys Best, friendly staff, small cosy bar, stripped brick and old town photographs, mini waterfall feature, tables (candlelit at night) in unusual grotto-like snug built into rock; children welcome, dogs in bar, tables out in pleasant setting with Common views, open all day *(LYM, Conor McGaughey)*

UNDER RIVER [TQ5552]

☆ *White Rock* TN15 0SB [SE of Sevenoaks, off B245]: Attractive and relaxed village pub, beams, bare boards and stripped brickwork in cosy original part with adjacent dining area, friendly service and interesting mix of customers, enjoyable well priced food from hot filled rolls to full meals lunchtime and evening inc Sun, coffee and cakes between times, Fullers London Pride, Harveys and Westerham SPA, public bar with pool in modern extension; quiet piped music; children welcome, pretty front garden, back terrace and big back lawn, handy for Knole Park and Greensand Way (walkers asked to use side door), open all day *(Tina and David Woods-Taylor, E D Bailey, John Tuck, DFL, Peter Meister, Debbie and Neil Hayter, Martin and Sue Day, N R White, GHC)*

UPSTREET [TR2363]
Grove Ferry CT3 4BP [off A28 towards Preston]: Big open-plan place under new management, variety of areas, up-to-date décor, comfortable well spaced tables (some very big), carpeted dining area behind central servery, reasonably priced food from club sandwiches up all day, uniformed staff, Shepherd Neame real ale, good wines by the glass, log fire in big fireplace; may be quiet piped music; french windows to heated deck with picnic-sets overlooking River Stour boats, more in big side garden with play area, barbecues Sun afternoon, handy for Stodmarsh national nature reserve *(BB, Kevin Thorpe, Keith and Chris O'Neill, Mrs Hazel Rainer)*

WEST MALLING [TQ6857]
Farmhouse ME19 6NA [High St]: Former Bear tastefully reworked as pub and brasserie (same management as Great House in Hawkhurst), pleasant atmosphere and good cross-section of customers, enjoyable food, nice wines by the glass, good beer choice on draught and in bottle *(Derek Thomas)*
Lobster Pot ME19 6JU [Swan St]: Open fire in carpeted traditional bar with old posters, nets and lobster pots, step up to pleasant small panelled dining room, friendly service, Adnams and five other changing ales usually inc Larkins, coffees in variety, enjoyable pub food (not Mon) from sandwiches up; darts and piped music down in small dark-panelled public bar (can get smoky when busy), upstairs skittle alley; open all day *(N R White, Kevin Thorpe)*

WHITSTABLE [TR1167]
Continental CT5 2BP [Beach Walk]: Interesting mix of 19th-c seafront hotel, pub/café and french-style brasserie restaurant on seafront, main outlet for Whitstable Bay brewery with their range of beers, meals, snacks and cakes, large windows looking over Thames estuary (on a clear day you can see Southend); children welcome, metal tables and chairs outside *(N R White)*

WICKHAMBREAUX [TR2258]
Rose CT3 1RQ [The Green]: Dating from 14th c and recently freshened up, good value home-made food from fine sandwich choice to stews and Sun roasts, quick service, Greene King IPA and two guest beers, three small rooms, stripped brick, beams and panelling, log fire in big fireplace, shove-ha'penny, piano (occasional live music); dogs on leads and children welcome, garden with barbecues, nice spot across green from church and watermill, open all day *(Kevin Thorpe)*

WINGHAM [TR2457]
☆ *Dog* CT3 1AB [Canterbury Rd]: Medieval building recently reopened as pub/restaurant, log fires in ancient fireplaces, uneven walls, heavy beams, old brickwork, leather sofas and armchairs, enjoyable food, Fullers London Pride and another real ale, good wines by the glass *(Rob and Catherine Dunster)*

WOODLANDS [TQ5159]
Rising Sun TN14 5JR [Twitton Lane, Twitton, W of Otford]: Traditional cottage local with cosy chatty atmosphere, real ale, bar food; seats out in front, back garden overlooking Darent Valley *(N R White)*

WORTH [TR3356]
☆ *St Crispin* CT14 0DF [signed off A258 S of Sandwich]: Comfortably refurbished bar with stripped brickwork, bare boards, low beams and central log fire, good value generous home-made food here and in restaurant from good baguettes to some imaginative dishes, welcoming and attentive staff, changing real ales, some tapped from the cask, such as Greene King Old Speckled Hen, Marstons Pedigree, Shepherd Neame and Charles Wells Bombardier, belgian beers, local farm cider, well chosen wines; good bedrooms (inc some chalet-style), charming big garden behind with terrace and barbecue, lovely village position *(N R White, Mrs Frances Pennell)*

WYE [TR0546]
☆ *Tickled Trout* [signed off A28 NE of Ashford]: Popular summer family pub with lots of picnic-sets (and hungry ducks) and occasional barbecues on pleasant lawn by River Stour, spacious modern conservatory/restaurant; modernised rustic-style bar with beams and stripped brickwork, friendly service, wide range of food, changing real ales, good open fire; children welcome *(LYM, N R White)*

Please tell us if the décor, atmosphere, food or drink at a pub is different from our description. We rely on readers' reports to keep us up to date. No stamp needed: The Good Pub Guide, FREEPOST TN1569, Wadhurst, E Sussex TN5 7BR.

Lancashire
(with Greater Manchester and Merseyside)

In last year's *Guide*, the introduction to the Lancashire chapter named eleven pubs from the Lucky Dip section as particularly bright prospects. Three of those are now new main entries: the Fence Gate at Fence, a good-natured pub with enjoyable food from bar snacks to more contemporary dishes; the Three Fishes at Great Mitton, a beautifully updated country pub, entirely no smoking, with particularly good food and drink – most impressive; and the Sun in Lancaster, another real winner, a splendidly renovated town pub, good all round, with new bedrooms too. Other pubs here on fine form these days are the civilised Bay Horse at Bay Horse (very good food using local ingredients, and gains a Wine Award this year), the Eagle & Child at Bispham Green (a most appealing all-rounder, with some interesting new developments), the Philharmonic Dining Rooms in Liverpool (this spectacular ornate Victorian showpiece now does evening as well as lunchtime bar food), the engaging and enterprising Britons Protection in Manchester (bargain food, and a great array of drinks), the restauranty Spread Eagle at Sawley (no smoking throughout here too now), the Station Buffet in Stalybridge (would that more stations had a match for this Victorian survivor, with its good beers and bargain snacks), the Lunesdale Arms up at Tunstall (winning friends with its thorough-going attention to detail on the food side), the Inn at Whitewell (recently attractively refurbished, top-notch all round), and the cottagey New Inn at Yealand Conyers (good food using local ingredients, all day – handy for M6 travellers). Of these, the Eagle & Child at Bispham Green, Spread Eagle at Sawley and Lunesdale Arms at Tunstall all stand out as particularly rewarding for a special meal out, and we'd add to them the smartly contemporary White Hart at Lydgate. But it's one of the new entries, the Three Fishes at Great Mitton, which gets top rating as Lancashire Dining Pub of the Year. This year's pick of the Lucky Dip entries at the end of the chapter are the Original Farmers Arms at Eccleston, Bay Horse at Fence, North Euston in Fleetwood, Red Lion in Hawkshaw, Ship at Lathom, Doctor Duncan in Liverpool, Mr Thomas Chop House in Manchester, Wheatsheaf at Raby, Arden Arms in Stockport, Old Sparrow Hawk at Wheatley Lane and restauranty Mulberry Tree at Wrightington Bar. The area scores very highly on value. Food tends to be better, for your money, than you'd get much further south. And drinks on average cost far less than the national norm. The cheerful Church Inn at Uppermill, which brews its own, has exceptionally low prices, and Holts and Hydes stand out for their bargain beers. Robinsons and Thwaites are the area's two main brewers – it's worth noting that Robinsons tend to have particularly good tenants in their pubs, often there for generations. There are plenty of thriving smaller local brewers. Moorhouses is probably the one you are most likely to come across. Others we found in our main entries this year included Bowland, Bank Top, Cains, Greenfield, Hart, Lees, Phoenix, Southport and Three Rivers.

BARNSTON SJ2783 Map 7
Fox & Hounds ♨ £

3 miles from M53 junction 3: A552 towards Woodchurch, then left on A551;
CH61 1BW

It's a good idea to arrive early if you want to sample the good-value lunchtime bar
food at this well kept pub; it includes open sandwiches (from £3.25), home-made
soup (£2.95), filled baked potatoes (from £3.95), quiche or various platters such as
greek salad (from £5.95), ploughman's (£6.50), with changing specials such as
curry or chilli (£5.95), lasagne (£6.25), hot pie of the day (£6.55), fish and chips or
salmon and broccoli fishcakes (£6.75), roasts (£6.95) and duck breast (£8.25); no
smoking during food times. There's an impressive array of drinks too, with
Marstons Pedigree, Theakstons Best and Old Peculier, and Websters Yorkshire,
along with a couple of guests such as Weetwood Cheshire Cat on handpump; 60
whiskies and 12 wines by the glass. Tucked away opposite the serving counter is a
charming old quarry-tiled corner with an antique kitchen range, copper kettles,
built-in pine kitchen cupboards, and lots of earthenware or enamelled food bins.
With its own entrance at the other end of the pub, a small locals' bar is worth a
peek for its highly traditional layout – as well as a collection of hundreds of metal
ashtrays on its delft shelf; beside it is a snug where children are allowed. The main
part of the roomy bay-windowed lounge bar has red plush button-back built-in
banquettes and plush-cushioned captain's chairs around the solid tables on its green
turkey carpet, and plenty of old local prints on cream walls below a delft shelf of
china, with a collection of police and other headgear; darts and board games. There
are some picnic-sets under cocktail parasols out in the yard behind, below a farm.
*(Recommended by Dr R A Smye, Clive Watkin, Paul Boot, Pat and Tony Martin, Steve Whalley,
Maurice and Gill McMahon)*

Free house ~ Licensee Ralph Leech ~ Real ale ~ Bar food (12-2) ~ (0151) 648 1323 ~
Children welcome with restrictions ~ Dogs welcome ~ Open 11-11; 12-10.30 Sun

BAY HORSE SD4952 Map 7
Bay Horse ⑪ ☲

1¼ miles from M6 junction 33: A6 southwards, then off on left; LA2 0HR

A good deal of thought goes into the food preparation at this justly popular dining
pub, with innovative use of locally sourced ingredients, and though the food is not
cheap the portions are generous and it represents good value for money. Beamed
and comfortable, its red-walled bar is attractively decorated, with a good log fire,
cushioned wall banquettes in bays, a friendly cat, and gentle lighting including table
lamps on window sills; the atmosphere is warm and cosy. As well as a decent, fairly
priced wine list (12 wines by the glass; fruit wines too), friendly staff serve Black
Sheep, Moorhouses Pendle Witches Brew and Thwaites Lancaster Bomber on
handpump, and 15 malt whiskies. There are usually fresh flowers on the counter,
and may be piped music. The main emphasis though is on the food, with a series of
small dining areas rambling around (including a no smoking dining room) – the feel
is of a civilised country restaurant, with a red décor, another log fire, candle-flame-
effect lights and nice tables, including one or two good-sized ones having an
intimate corner to themselves. As well as imaginative lunchtime sandwiches (from
£4.25) and soup (£3.95), they have lunch and evening menus with starters like
potted crab (£5.75), terrine of bowland lamb cannon and hotpot vegetables
(£6.25), smoked salmon and gravadlax with horseradish cream (£7.95) and main
courses like sausages and mash, fish pie with lancashire cheese mash or lamb
hotpot (£11.50), slow-cooked duck legs (£13.95), baked salmon fillet (£14.75) and
grilled bass (£17.95); puddings include chocolate pot, and bread and butter
pudding (£4.95). It's peacefully set, and there are tables out in the garden behind
(peaceful, though the railway is not far off). Note they don't accept lunchtime
bookings for parties of fewer than eight. *(Recommended by Revd D Glover, Mrs
P J Carroll, Dr D J and Mrs S C Walker, Jo Lilley, Simon Calvert, Rob and Catherine Dunster,
Christine and Neil Townend, D J Newth, Mike and Linda Hudson, Jane and Martin Bailey,
Sarah and Peter Gooderham, Peter and Jean Walker, Brian Wainwright, Michael Doswell)*

Mitchells ~ Tenant Craig Wilkinson ~ Real ale ~ Bar food (12-1.45(3 Sun), 7-9.30) ~
(01524) 791204 ~ Children welcome ~ Open 12-3, 6.30-11; 12-4.30, 9-11 Sun; closed
Mon, 25 Dec, 1 Jan

BELMONT   SD6716   Map 7

Black Dog 🛏

A675; BL7 8AB

Outside this unpretentiously cosy and atmospheric 18th-c inn, two long benches on
the sheltered sunny side of the building give delightful views of the moors above the
nearby trees and houses. In addition to Holts Bitter (at just £1.64 a pint) they also
have Mild and often a guest from the Holts range, all well kept on handpump. The
original cheery and traditional small rooms around the bar are packed with
antiques and bric-a-brac, from railwaymen's lamps, bedpans and chamber-pots to
landscape paintings. There are also service bells for the sturdy built-in curved seats,
rush-seated mahogany chairs, coal fires, and a plush turquoise banquette in the bay
opposite the bar. Three rooms (one very small) off the main bar are no smoking;
piped music, games machine. Enjoyably straightforward, generously served bar
food includes soup (£2.70), garlic mushroom in stilton (£3.95), cottage pie (£5.40),
lasagne (£6.70), steak and ale pie (£6.80), battered cod (£6.95), chicken and black
pudding stack (£7.35); puddings (£3.25); until 6pm you can also get sandwiches
(from £3.65) and baked potatoes (from £3.85). They also do a Sunday lunch
(£6.60). It tends to fill up quickly; they don't take bookings on Sunday, so get there
early for a table. The homely bedrooms are inexpensive too. A track leads from the
village up Winter Hill and (from the lane to Rivington) on to Anglezarke Moor,
and there are paths from the dam of the nearby Belmont Reservoir. *(Recommended by
Peter Abbott, Steve Whalley, Tom and Jill Jones, Pat and Tony Martin, Norma and Noel
Thomas, Pam and John Smith)*

Holts ~ Manager Victor Dewbrey ~ Real ale ~ Bar food (12-2, 6-8.30 Mon-Thurs (not
Tues evening); 12-8.30 Fri-Sat; 12-7 Sun) ~ (01204) 811218 ~ Children in no smoking
areas until 9.30pm ~ Open 12-11(10.30 Sun) ~ Bedrooms: /£50S

BISPHAM GREEN   SD4813   Map 7

Eagle & Child 🍴 ⛟ 🍺

Maltkiln Lane (Parbold—Croston road, off B5246); L40 3SG

Well liked for its food and drink, and free from piped music and similar intrusions,
this friendly pub has an interesting range of five changing beers typically including
ales such as Eccleshall Slaters Top Totty, Moorhouses Black Cat, Pheonix Arizona,
Southport Natterjack Premium Bitter, Thwaites Original and Timothy Taylors
Landlord, and they also have changing farm cider, decent wines, some country
wines and around 30 malt whiskies. The pub holds a popular beer festival over the
first May bank holiday weekend. Well divided by stubs of walls, the largely open-
plan bar is appealingly simple and civilised. Attractively understated old furnishings
include a mix of small oak chairs around tables in corners, an oak coffer, several
handsomely carved antique oak settles (the finest apparently made partly from a
16th-c wedding bed-head), and old hunting prints and engravings. There's coir
matting in the snug, and oriental rugs on flagstones in front of the fine old stone
fireplaces; two areas of the pub are no smoking. There's quite an emphasis on the
well cooked food, and besides snacks such as sandwiches with chips and salad
(from £4.25; not Friday or Saturday evenings), soup (£3.50), fish and chips,
cumberland sausage and mash or steak and ale pie (£8), the helpful staff serve more
elaborate specials such as mediterranean vegetable and saffron risotto (£8.50),
supreme of chicken stuffed with mozzarella and basil (£12.50), poached halibut
with king prawns in white wine, cream and black pasta or roast lamb rump
(£13.50). The handsome side barn was being converted into a deli, with an antiques
shop above, as we went to press. A nice wild garden has crested newts and nesting
moorhens; the pub's dogs are called Harry and Doris. You can try your hand at
bowls or croquet on the neat green outside this brick pub, but beware that the

crowns deceive even the most experienced players. *(Recommended by Revd D Glover, Mark Lowe, Mr and Mrs J N Graham, Johnny Cohen, Jo Lilley, Simon Calvert, Steve Whalley, Paul Humphreys, Mike Tucker, MLR, Jack Clark, Margaret and Jeff Graham, Brian Kneale)*

Free house ~ Licensees Monica Evans and David Anderson ~ Real ale ~ Bar food (12-2, 5.30-8.30(9 Fri, Sat); 12-8.30 Sun) ~ (01257) 462297 ~ Children welcome except in bar area ~ Dogs welcome ~ Open 12-3, 5.30-11; 12-10.30 Sun

BURY SD8115 Map 7
Lord Raglan 🍺

2 miles off M66 northbound junction 1; A56 S then left in Walmersley, up long cobbled lane to Mount Pleasant, Nangreaves; if coming from N, stay on A56 S instead of joining M66, and turn left in Walmersley as above; BL9 6SP

This neatly kept 18th-c pub, on the moors high above Bury, serves food all day at weekends and has a range of eight own-brew beers. On handpump alongside a seasonal guest are Leyden Balaclava, Black Pudding, Crowning Glory, Forever Bury, Light Brigade, Nanny Flyer, Raglan Sleeve and Sebastopol, and they hold a beer festival in June. They've also 20 malt whiskies and interesting foreign bottled beers; TV, board games and piped music. All sorts of bric-a-brac is dotted around the snug beamed front bar, with lots of pewter, brass and interesting antique clocks, and there's a mix of spindleback chairs and old wooden settles. The back room has a huge open fire, china on a high delft shelf and welsh dresser, and windows giving a splendid view down the valley. A plainer but more spacious dining room on the left is panelled in light wood. Available in the bar or the restaurant, bar food includes open sandwiches (£3.25), soup (£2.50), baked potatoes (£4.75), smoked fish platter (£5.40), ploughman's (£5.45), steak and ale pie (£6.35), prawn curry, red thai vegetable curry or chicken balti (£7.65), poached salmon fillet or fried plaice (£8.75), chicken chasseur (£8.95), and steaks (from £9.95); children's meals (£2.50). More reports please. *(Recommended by Graham Patterson, Mary Kirman and Tim Jefferson)*

Own brew ~ Licensee Brendan Leyden ~ Real ale ~ Bar food (12-2, 7(5 Fri)-9; Sat 12-9.30; Sun 12-8.30) ~ Restaurant ~ (0161) 764 6680 ~ Children welcome until 9pm ~ Dogs allowed in bar ~ Open 12-2.30, 7(5 Fri)-11; 12-11(10.30 Sun) Sat

CHIPPING SD6243 Map 7
Dog & Partridge ♀

Hesketh Lane; crossroads Chipping—Longridge with Inglewhite—Clitheroe; PR3 2TH

Within walking distance of the dramatic high moors of the Forest of Bowland, this comfortable and much-extended dining pub (the eating space spreads into a nearby stable) dates back to 1515. The comfortable main lounge has small armchairs around fairly close-set low tables on a blue patterned carpet, brown-painted beams, a good winter log fire, and multicoloured lanterns; the pub has piped music. Served by friendly and well trained staff, the enjoyable lunchtime bar food (not Sunday) includes home-made soup (£3.20), sandwiches (from £4.50), duck and orange pâté (£4.90), around four vegetarian dishes such as leek and mushroom crumble, and broccoli and stilton pancakes (£8.75), home-made steak and kidney pie with shortcrust pastry or roast chicken with stuffing (£9), roast duckling with apple sauce and stuffing (£12.50) and grilled sirloin steak with mushrooms (£13.75), with puddings such as home-made fruit pie or raspberry shortcake (£4), as well as daily lunchtime and evening specials like very good hot potted shrimps (£4.80), battered haddock (£9) or roast pheasant (£10.50). They have Tetleys Bitter and Mild with a weekly changing guest such as Black Sheep Bitter on handpump. Smart casual dress is preferred in the restaurant; dining areas are no smoking, and you may need to book. More reports please. *(Recommended by Dennis Jones, J F M and M West, Norma and Noel Thomas, Maurice and Della Andrew)*

Free house ~ Licensee Peter Barr ~ Real ale ~ Bar food (12-1.30; not Sun) ~ Restaurant (7(6.30 Sat)-9 Mon-Sat; 12-8.30 Sun) ~ (01995) 61201 ~ Children welcome ~ Open 11.45-3, 6.45-11; 11.45-10.30 Sun

FENCE   SD8237   Map 7

Fence Gate ♀

2.6 miles from M65 junction 13; Wheatley Lane Road, just off A6068 W; BB12 9EE

Smartly refurbished in recent years (with the addition of a highly thought of brasserie), this big, busy extended stone house is both bang up to date and determinedly pubby, cleverly blending its gently upmarket touches with more traditional features; on our visit there were as many cosmopolitan groups sipping Pimms as there were locals downing pints, but somehow both looked completely at home. The bar food is popular, and particularly the award-wining sausages made on the premises, blending organic meats with everything from local cheese or their own black pudding to blueberries and calvados or sun-dried tomato and chilli (all £8.25, served with a red wine gravy and bubble and squeak or mash). The rest of the menu also has an emphasis on local ingredients, and includes soup (£3.55), sandwiches (£3.85, more elaborate open sandwiches from £4.85), vegetable lasagne (£6.25), pies such as steak, ale and mushroom or local lamb and vegetable (£7.45), good home-made burgers (£8.45), cod and chips (£8.50), and daily specials; very good service. An almost bewildering array of blackboards above the bar counter shows off the good, comprehensive wine list (plenty by the glass), and they also have Caledonian Deuchars IPA, Courage Directors, Theakstons Best, two changing guests like Black Sheep or the local Bowland Bitter, and various teas and coffees. Plenty of polished panelling and timbers divide the carpeted bar into several distinct-feeling areas: there's an almost clubby corner with a small bookcase, a fish in a glass case, and a big fire, while just along from here is a part with sporting prints above the panelling, a number of stools, and a TV. Leading off the central section with its mix of wooden tables and chairs is a very comfortable area with red-patterned sofas and lots of cushions, and there's a more unusual bit with tables on a raised step beneath carved panelling; piped music. The imposing building dates from the 17th c and is said to be haunted by Horatio, the unfortunate victim of a shooting accident. The licensee celebrates his 25th year here in 2007. *(Recommended by Graham Patterson, D J Newth)*

Free house ~ Licensee Kevin Berkins ~ Real ale ~ Bar food (12-2.30 (3 Sun), 6.30-9.30 (10 Fri-Sun)) ~ Restaurant ~ 01282 618101 ~ Children welcome ~ Open 12-1am

GOOSNARGH   SD5839   Map 7

Horns ♀ 🍽

Pub signed from village, about 2 miles towards Chipping below Beacon Fell; PR3 2FJ

A few minutes' drive from the M6, this mock-Tudor former coaching inn now has real ale – Black Sheep, on handpump, and although food is the main attraction it's also a place you can just sit and enjoy a drink. Besides sandwiches (from £4.50) and ploughman's (£5.95), nicely presented dishes include soup (£4.25), home-made duck liver pâté (£4.75), creamy garlic shrimps (£4.95), prawns and salad (£8.25), home-made steak and kidney pie (£8.95), roast duckling with apple sauce and stuffing (£10.25) and scampi with home-made tartare sauce (£11.50), with specials such as black pudding with hot mustard sauce or smoked trout fillet (£5.50), home-made salmon fishcake (£5.75), battered cod with mushy peas (£8.95), halibut with prawn sauce (£9.25) and roast baby leg of lamb with cranberry (£9.50); home-made puddings (£4.95); they also have a more elaborate restaurant menu, from which you can choose a five-course dinner for £19.95. The neatly kept snug rooms have colourful flower displays and winter log fires, and a relaxing atmosphere; beyond the lobby, the pleasant front bar opens into attractively decorated middle rooms. The dining rooms and bedrooms are no smoking (the pub is hoped to be totally no smoking by the end of 2006); piped music. There's an extensive wine list with quite a few by the glass, and a fine choice of malt whiskies. *(Recommended by Nikki Wild, Revd D E and Mrs J A Shapland, Margaret Dickinson, Richard Endacott, Dr A McCormick, Ray and Winifred Halliday)*

Free house ~ Licensee Mark Woods ~ Real ale ~ Bar food ~ Restaurant ~ (01772) 865230 ~ Children in eating area of bar and restaurant ~ Open 11.45-3(4 Sun), 6.30-11(10.30 Sun); closed Mon lunchtime ~ Bedrooms: £59B/£79B

GREAT MITTON SD7139 Map 7

Three Fishes 🍴 ♀ 🛏

Mitton Road (B6246, off A59 NW of Whalley); BB7 9PQ

Lancashire Dining Pub of the Year

Smartly renovated by the people behind renowned restaurant-with-rooms Northcote Manor, since it reopened this 16th-c dining pub has quickly become one of the county's stand-out places to eat, thanks to its very good regional cooking. The emphasis is on traditional Lancastrian dishes with a modern twist, with all ingredients carefully sourced from small local suppliers – many of whom are listed on the back of the menu, or immortalised in black and white photographs on the walls. They've already won various awards and accolades (particularly for the way they look after children, who have their own good menu), and readers have very much enjoyed coming here over the last few months, praising not only the food, but also the décor, the range of drinks, and the efficient service and organisation. They don't take bookings, but write your name on a blackboard when you arrive, and find you when a table becomes free; it works rather well, even at the busiest times, and the polite staff are pretty good at remembering the names of people waiting. The menu includes soup (£3.50), lunchtime sandwiches (from £4), various salads (from £6.50), a platter of home-cured meats with home-made bread, pickle and piccalilli (small helping £7.50, large £9), forest mushroom, celeriac and spinach pancakes with lancashire cheese and spicy white cabbage (£7.50), free-range sausages and mash (£8.75), a very tasty hotpot with pickled red cabbage (£9.95), braised oxtail in red wine with horseradish mash and buttered root vegetables (£10.95), steaks (from £11.75), and seasonal specials like pan-fried sea bass or veal casserole with white wine, purple sprouting broccoli and carrots (£12.50); the beef is exclusive to here, coming from a unique herd of British Whites. You may need to order side dishes with some main courses. Completely no smoking, the pub stretches back much further than you'd initially expect; the areas closest to the bar are elegantly traditional with a couple of big stone fireplaces, rugs on polished floors, newly upholstered stools, and a good chatty feel, then there's a series of individually furnished and painted rooms with exposed stone walls and floors, careful spotlighting, and wooden slatted blinds, ending with another impressive fireplace. You order at various food points dotted around, and there's lots of space, but they do get busy (the big car park is sometimes overflowing). The long bar counter has elaborate floral displays and three real ales, usually including one or two from Thwaites, and guests like the local Three Bs Bobbins; also, various cocktails, a good choice of wines by the glass, and unusual soft drinks. The lavatories are smart, and they have facilities for the disabled and parents with young children. Overlooking the Ribble Valley, the garden has tables and perhaps its own menu in summer. *(Recommended by J F M and M West, Mrs P J Carroll, Rob Bowran, Brian Wainwright, Jo Lilley, Simon Calvert, Nigel Stevenson, Alyson and Andrew Jackson)*

Free house ~ Licensees Nigel Haworth, Andy Morris ~ Real ale ~ Bar food (12-2, 6-9; 12-8.30 Sun) ~ Restaurant ~ (01254) 826888 ~ Children welcome ~ Dogs allowed in bar ~ Open 12-11(10.30 Sun); closed 25 Dec

LANCASTER SD4761 Map 7

Sun ♀ 🛏

Church Street; LA1 1ET

Beautifully restored and extended over the last couple of years, this historic hotel in the heart of the city imaginatively blends its oldest features with some that are bang up to date. It's both warmly traditional and comfortably contemporary – and the food and drinks are impressive too. The beamed bar is atmospheric and characterful, with plenty of panelling, chunky modern tables on the part flagged and part wooden floors, several fireplaces (the biggest filled with a huge oak cask), and subtly effective spotlighting. The size of the bar counter belies the range of drinks available: you'll generally find four real ales from the Lancaster Brewery (set up in 2005 by the company behind the pub's transformation), as well as four changing guests like Jennings Dark Mild, Thwaites Lancaster Bomber and Titanic Iceberg, a good few belgian and bottled beers, 18 or so well chosen wines by the glass, lots of whiskies and spirits, and some unique teas and coffees from a local wholesaler. There's a discreet TV in a corner. A passageway leads to a long narrow room that's altogether cooler, still with exposed stone walls, but this time covered with changing art exhibitions; the furnishings in here are mostly soft and low, with lots of dark brown pouffes and stools. Some more substantial wooden tables and high-backed chairs lead into a no smoking conservatory; piped music, fruit machine. Bar food kicks off with an unusual breakfast menu where you pay for the number of items you have, encouraging you to try less common things like devilled kidneys (five items £8, eight items £11); at lunch a typical choice might be soup (£3.50), ciabattas (from £4.80), ploughman's (£7), cheese and onion pie with white wine and mustard gravy (£7.50), steak and ale pie or sausage and mash (£8.50), and changing specials like goats cheese, tomato and spinach quiche or black pudding on mash with dijon mustard and smoked bacon sauce (£7), pan-fried sardines with greek salad (£8), and seared tuna steaks with a red onion, tomato and basil sauce (£8.50). There isn't a full evening menu, but the excellent cheese and pâté menu is served pretty much all day (it stops earlier on Friday and Saturday), with lots of local flavours (two helpings £5.80, four £10). We've yet to hear from anyone who's stayed in the stylish bedrooms, but would be very surprised if they didn't deserve a stay award. *(Recommended by Jo Lilley, Simon Calvert, Mike Pugh)*

Free house ~ Licensee Dominic Kiziuk ~ Real ale ~ Bar food (12-3 (12.30-3.30 Sun), plus cheeseboards 12-9 Sun-Thurs, 12-7 Fri/Sat, and breakfast) ~ (01524) 66006 ~ Live punk jazz every third Weds of month ~ Open 10-midnight (12.30 Fri/Sat); 10am-11.30pm Sun ~ Bedrooms: £50S/£55S(£65B)

LITTLE ECCLESTON   SD4139   Map 7
Cartford 🍺 £ 🛏

Cartford Lane, off A586 Garstang—Blackpool, by toll bridge; PR3 0YP

Readers enjoy the range of real ales at this pub, and the tranquil setting by a toll bridge over the River Wyre is very attractive; there are tables out in a garden (not by the water), with a play area. Aside from a couple from Hart (from the pub's own good microbrewery behind the building, with brewery tours by arrangement), you'll find Fullers London Pride and up to six changing ales mostly from smaller brewers such as Bank Top, Bradfield, Greenfield, Moorhouses and Roosters; also decent house wines and several malt whiskies. The rambling interior has oak beams, dried flowers, a log fire and an unusual layout on four different levels, with uncoordinated seating areas; pool, darts, games machine, small TV and piped music. Two levels are largely set for dining. Straightforward low-priced bar food (you may have a wait at busy times) includes soup (£2.60), sandwiches (from £3.85; hot sandwiches from £5.85; hot baguettes £6.35), battered cod (£5.65), cumberland sausage and mash (£5.95), spinach and ricotta cannelloni (£6.85), red snapper with mediterranean sauce (£8.35) and 10oz rump steak (£9.95); specials board. The pub has fishing rights along 1½ miles of the river. *(Recommended by John Butterfield, Brian Wainwright, MLR, Keith and Chris O'Neill, Pam and John Smith, Maurice and Gill McMahon)*

Own brew ~ Licensee Andrew Mellodew ~ Real ale ~ Bar food (12-2, 6.30-9.30; 12-9 Sun) ~ (01995) 670166 ~ Children welcome ~ Dogs welcome ~ Open 12-3, 6.30-11; 11.30-3, 6.30-11.45 Sat; 12-10.30 Sun ~ Bedrooms: £36.95B/£48.95B

Bedroom prices normally include full English breakfast, VAT and any inclusive service charge that we know of. Prices before the '/' are for single rooms, after for two people in double or twin (B includes a private bath, S a private shower). If there is no '/', the prices are only for twin or double rooms (as far as we know there are no singles).

LIVERPOOL SJ4395 Map 7

Philharmonic Dining Rooms ㉕ ★ 🍺

36 Hope Street; corner of Hardman Street; L1 9BX

A wonderful period piece, this spectacular marble-fronted Victorian pub attracts a pleasant mix of customers, with theatre-goers, students, locals and tourists making up the contented bustle, and there's an impressive range of beer. The centrepiece is a mosaic-faced serving counter, from which heavily carved and polished mahogany partitions radiate under the intricate plasterwork high ceiling. The echoing main hall is decorated with stained glass including contemporary portraits of Boer War heroes Baden-Powell and Lord Roberts, rich panelling, a huge mosaic floor, and copper panels of musicians in an alcove above the fireplace. More stained glass in one of the little lounges declares 'Music is the universal language of mankind', and backs this up with illustrations of musical instruments; there are two plushly comfortable sitting rooms; two side rooms are called Brahms and Liszt (the latter and the bar counter are no smoking). Don't miss the original 1890s Adamant gents' lavatory (all pink marble and glinting mosaics; ladies are allowed a look if they ask first. They have up to ten changing guest ales on handpump, with usually a Cains beer and others such as Adnams, Batemans and Caledonian. Straightforward food (which can be eaten only in the table-service grand lounge dining room; best to phone first to check if they're serving in the evenings) could include soup (£2.95), baked potatoes (from £4.25), sandwiches (from £5.25, hot sandwiches from £5.95), ploughman's (£5.95), steak pie or fish and chips (£6.50) and puddings (from £2.75); they also have evening restaurant food; quiz machine and mellow piped jazz or blues. No children inside. *(Recommended by Clive Watkin, the Didler, P Dawn, Eric Robinson, Jacqueline Pratt, Joe Green, Dr Phil Putwain)*

Mitchells & Butlers ~ Manager Marie-Louise Wong ~ Real ale ~ Bar food (12-3, 5-8 (not every evening; best to phone first to check)) ~ Restaurant ~ (0151) 707 2837 ~ Open 12-12

LONGRIDGE SD6039 Map 7

Derby Arms ♀

Chipping Road, Thornley; 1½ miles N of Longridge on back road to Chipping; PR3 2NB

Overlooking the Forest of Bowland, this nicely unchanged and unfailingly welcoming country pub has a main bar with a hunting and fishing theme. Old photographs commemorate notable catches, and there's some nicely mounted bait above the comfortable red plush seats, together with a stuffed pheasant that seems to be flying in through the wall. To the right is a smaller room with sporting trophies and mementoes, and a regimental tie collection, while off to the left are a couple of no smoking dining areas. The gents' has dozens of riddles on the wall; you can buy a sheet of them in the bar (the money goes to charity). Enjoyable food might include sandwiches (from £3.95), soup (£3.75), ploughman's (£5.95), fresh dressed crab (from £7.95), ham, egg and chips, spicy chicken satay or vegetarian hotpot (£8.95), seafood pasta or steak and kidney pudding (£9.95), chargrilled lamb chops (£11.25), 10oz sirloin steak (£13.50), crisp roast goosnargh duckling (£14.95), aberdeen angus fillet steak rossini (£17.95); puddings such as home-baked fruit pies (£3.95); they also have pheasant, hare, rabbit, partridge, woodcock, rabbit and mallard in season. Along with a good range of wines including several half-bottles and a dozen or so by the glass (they're particularly strong on south african), you'll find Black Sheep and Marstons Pedigree on handpump. A few tables out in front, and another two behind the car park have fine views across to the Forest of Bowland. Note that they sometimes close earlier than midnight during the week. More reports please. *(Recommended by Peter and Jean Walker, Dennis Jones, Alyson and Andrew Jackson, Maurice and Gill McMahon, Margaret Dickinson)*

Punch ~ Lease Mrs G M Walne ~ Real ale ~ Bar food (12-2.15, 6.30-9.30(10 Sat); 12-9.30 Sun) ~ Restaurant ~ (01772) 782623 ~ Children allowed in dining area ~ Live jazz some nights ~ Open 12-3, 6(5 Sat)-12; 12-11 Sun

LYDGATE   SD9704   Map 7
White Hart   🍴 ♈ 🛏

Stockport Road; Lydgate not marked on some maps so not to be confused with the one near Todmorden; take A669 Oldham—Saddleworth, and after almost 2.5 miles turn right at brow of hill on to A6050, Stockport Road; OL4 4JJ

Keeping up its reputation for quality food, this striking upmarket stone-built inn overlooks Saddleworth Moor. Though it feels a little like a smart restaurant-with-rooms, it's very much a proper pub too, with a good few locals clustered round the bar, or in the two simpler rooms at the end. Many of the building's older features remain, but the overall style is more contemporary than traditional, so beams and exposed stonework are blended skilfully with deep red or purple walls, punctuated with a mix of modern paintings, black and white photos, and stylised local scenes; most rooms have a fireplace, and fresh flowers; all dining areas, bedrooms and half the bar are no smoking. The warmly elegant brasserie is the biggest of the main rooms. The thoughtfully prepared meals are pricier than in most pubs around here, but the quality is consistently high; a typical menu might include open sandwiches (from £6.25), starters like soup (£5.25), baked beetroot and goats cheese with red chard and horseradish salad (£6.25), terrine of home-smoked ham shank and mushroom or ravioli of spinach and ricotta with oregano and tomato compote (£6.50), crispy duck and hoi sin spring roll (£6.95) or a platter of six oysters (£7.50), followed perhaps by sausage and mash or celeriac fondant with griddled asparagus, glazed mozzarella and shallot beans (£13.75), fillet of haddock in beer batter with fried potatoes, minted peas and caper beurre blanc (£14.75) and best end of lamb and braised shoulder (£16.95). They do a two-course lunch for £14.25 (£3.50 for an extra course; also available Monday to Thursday evening until 6.45pm), and a fish menu on Tuesday evenings. Copper Dragon, Lees Bitter, Tetleys, Timothy Taylors Landlord and perhaps a changing guest on handpump; the wine list includes around 15 by the glass. Good service from smartly dressed staff. There are picnic sets on the lawn behind. Bedrooms are comfortable, with free internet access. The lavatories are extremely smart. The pub has plenty of special events based around themed menus, including wine and beer tastings, comedy acts and even a brass band contest. More reports please. *(Recommended by Revd D Glover)*

Free house ~ Licensee Charles Brierley ~ Real ale ~ Bar food (12-2.30, 6-9.30 Mon-Sat; 1-8 Sun) ~ Restaurant ~ (01457) 872566 ~ Children welcome ~ Open 12-11(10.30 Sun) ~ Bedrooms: £90B/£120B

LYTHAM   SD3627   Map 7
Taps   🍺 £

A584 S of Blackpool; Henry Street – in centre, one street in from West Beach; FY8 5LE

Open all day, this efficiently run and positively thriving seaside pub has on handpump its own Taps Best and Mild specially brewed by Titanic, along with six other ever-changing real ales from breweries such as Batemans, Hopback and Nethergate (a view-in cellar lets you see the beers); they also usually serve some country wines and a farm cider. It can get full to capacity, but even then it tends to cope with admirable efficiency. With a good mix of visitors, the Victorian-style bare-boarded bar has a sociable unassuming feel, plenty of stained-glass decoration in the windows, depictions of fish and gulls reflecting the pub's proximity to the beach (a couple of minutes' walk away), captain's chairs in bays around the sides, open fires, and a coal-effect gas fire between two built-in bookcases at one end. There's also an expanding collection of rugby memorabilia with old photographs and portraits of rugby stars on the walls; shove-ha'penny, dominoes, a quiz machine and a fruit machine. There are seat belts on the bar and headrests in the gents' to help keep you out of harm's way if you have one too many. Served only at lunchtime, a few cheap, straightforward bar snacks include sandwiches (from £2.25; soup and a hot roast sandwich from £3.95), filled baked potatoes or burgers (from £2.50), and chilli or curry (£3.95). There are a few seats and a heated canopied area outside. Parking is difficult near the pub so it's probably best to park at the West Beach car park on the seafront (free on Sunday), and walk. More reports please. *(Recommended by Steve Whalley, Pat and Tony Martin, Pam and John Smith)*

Greene King ~ Manager Ian Rigg ~ Real ale ~ Bar food (12-2, not Sun) ~ No credit cards ~ (01253) 736226 ~ Children welcome until 8pm ~ Open 11-11(12 Fri, Sat)

MANCHESTER   SJ7796   Map 7
Britons Protection ♀ £
Great Bridgewater Street, corner of Lower Mosley Street; M1 5LE

Handy for Bridgewater Hall and well known to many orchestral musicians, this busy city-centre pub is run with considerable gusto. The plush little front bar has a fine chequered tile floor, some glossy brown and russet wall tiles, solid woodwork and elaborate plastering. A tiled passage lined with battle murals depicting the Peterloo Massacre of 1819, which took place a few hundred yards away, leads to two cosy inner lounges, both served by hatch, with attractive brass and etched glass wall lamps, a mirror above the coal-effect gas fire in the simple art nouveau fireplace, and again good solidly comfortable furnishings. As something of a tribute to Manchester's notorious climate, the massive bar counter has a pair of heating pipes as its footrail. Although it's busy at lunchtime, it's usually quiet and relaxed in the evenings; the atmosphere is welcoming, and the staff are friendly (children may be allowed in the beer garden, but it's not really a family-oriented pub). As well as a terrific range of around 235 malt whiskies and bourbons, they have Jennings, Robinsons, Tetleys and two changing guests such as Coach House Dick Turpin and Robinsons Hatters on handpump, and good wines too. Straightforward, inexpensive bar food includes home-made soup (£1.85), sandwiches (from £2), ploughman's (£4), ham and egg or leek and mushroom crumble or various pies (£4.95) and home-made daily specials (from £4.95); piped music. There are tables out on the garden behind. On various evenings the pub hosts a range of events, including poetry readings, storytelling, silent film shows and acoustic gigs. They exclude football supporters on match days. *(Recommended by David Carr, Stephen and Jean Curtis, John Fiander, GLD, the Didler, Jo Lilley, Simon Calvert, Dennis Jones, Pam and John Smith)*

Punch ~ Lease Peter Barnett ~ Real ale ~ Bar food (11-2 weekdays, 12-3 Sat, 12-3.30 Sun) ~ (0161) 236 5895 ~ Monthly film shows, music hall, storytelling nights and poetry readings; acoustic gigs at various times ~ Open 11-11(12 Fri, Sat); 12-10.30 Sun

Dukes 92 £
Castle Street, below the bottom end of Deansgate; M3 4LZ

There's a tangibly upbeat feel nowadays to the revived area around the Rochdale Canal basin where this splendidly sited waterside pub stands, in a converted stable block by revamped warehouses. Tables outside make the best of the view over the bottom lock of the canal. Inside, black wrought-iron work contrasts boldly with whitewashed bare plaster walls, the handsome bar is granite-topped, and an elegant spiral staircase leads to an upper room and balcony. Down in the main room the fine mix of furnishings is mainly rather Edwardian in mood, with one particularly massive table, elegantly comfortable chaises-longues and deep armchairs. They do an excellent range of over three dozen cheeses and several pâtés with a generous helping of granary bread (£5.50, served till 9.30pm, and until 8pm on Fridays and Saturdays). Other good value bar food includes soup (£2.95), sandwiches (from £4.95), salads (from £6.50) and specials like fish and chips or chicken curry (from £6) as well as stone-baked pizzas (from £6.50, until 10pm); puddings include chocolate fudge cake (£3.50) and home-made sticky toffee pudding (£3.75). There might be a real ale on handpump such as Marstons Pedigree or Moorhouses (though some readers found no real ale available on the day of their visit), and they've decent wines, a wide choice of malt whiskies, and the belgian wheat beer Hoegaarden on tap; piped jazz. The gallery has temporary exhibitions of local artwork. *(Recommended by G V Price, Roger Yates, Mrs Hazel Rainer)*

Free house ~ Licensee James Ramsbottom ~ Real ale ~ Bar food (12-3(5 Fri-Sun); cold
food 12-9.30 Sun-Thurs,12-8 Fri and Sat; pizzas until 10pm) ~ (0161) 839 8646 ~ Children
welcome until 7pm ~ Dogs allowed in bar ~ Open 11.30-11(1 Sat); 12-10.30 Sun

Marble Arch ■ £

**Rochdale Road (A664), Ancoats; corner of Gould Street, just E of Victoria Station;
M4 4HY**

This alehouse takes its name from the porphyry entrance pillars that hint at the
admirably preserved Victorian splendours inside. Readers also enjoy it for its
outstanding range of well kept real ales (including the pub's own brew), sensibly
priced food and friendly atmosphere. The interior has a magnificently restored
lightly barrel-vaulted high ceiling, and extensive marble and tiling – the frieze
advertising various spirits and the chimneybreast above the carved wooden
mantelpiece particularly stand out. Furniture is a cheerful mix of rustic tables and
chairs, with a long, communal table conducive to conversation, and all the walls are
stripped back to the glazed brick; there's a collection of breweriana, and a cabinet
has a display of pump clips; a separate back room for eating is no smoking, as is
the bar area. The sloping mosaic floor in the bar can be a bit disconcerting after a
few pints; fruit machine, piped music and a juke box. From windows at the back,
you can look out over the brewery (tours by arrangement) where they produce the
distinctive Lagonda IPA, Manchester Bitter, Marble Bitter, Marble Ginger Ale as
well as a seasonal brew and they also have four guest ales such as Abbeydale
Absolution, Copper Dragon Black Gold, Oakham White Dwarf and Rebellion;
farm cider. Good-value food includes soup (£3.50), generously filled sandwiches
(£4.95), light bites like lamb kebab with flat bread or crayfish tails on mixed leaves
(£4.95), and main courses like steak and ale pie or spicy beefburger (£6.95), grilled
cod with sauté potatoes (£9.95) and grilled duck breast with hoi sin noodles
(£11.95). There's a little garden. The Laurel and Hardy Preservation Society meet
here on the third Wednesday of the month and show old films. *(Recommended by
Revd D Glover, the Didler, Pat and Tony Martin, Miss Schofield, Mr Robinson)*

Own brew ~ Licensee John Rogers ~ Real ale ~ Bar food (12-7.30(5.30 Sun)) ~
(0161) 832 5914 ~ Children welcome ~ Open 11.30-11(12 Fri); 11.30-12am Sat;
12-11 Sun

MELLOR   SJ9888   Map 7
Oddfellows Arms

**Heading out of Marple on the A626 towards Glossop, Mellor is the next road after the
B6102, signposted off on the right at Marple Bridge; keep on for nearly 2 miles up
Longhurst Lane and into Moor End Road; SK6 5PT**

Warmed by open fires, the pleasant low-ceilinged flagstoned bar at this pub makes
a civilised place for a meal and there's no piped music; there's also a small no
smoking restaurant upstairs. The main menu features a wide choice of dishes
including soup (£3.25), field mushrooms grilled with mozzarella, parmesan and
pesto (£4.95), black pudding salad (£4.95 or £7.50 as a main course), caesar salad
(£5.95 starter, £8.95 main course), club sandwich with chicken, bacon, egg,
avocado, peppers, served with chips (£6.25), sausage and champ (£7.95), fish and
chips (£9.25), proper cassoulet of duck, pork, ham and haricot beans (£10.95), and
specials such as roast of the day (£8.95), pan-seared salmon (£13.95), or moroccan
mullet (£14.95). Adnams Southwold, Marstons Best, Phoenix Arizona and a weekly
changing guest such as Cottage Best are on handpump. There are a few tables out
by the road. It can be tricky to secure a parking space when they're busy; get here
early to be sure of a table. More reports please. *(Recommended by Mrs P J Carroll,
Roger Yates, David Hoult, Jo Lilley, Simon Calvert)*

Free house ~ Licensee Olivier Berton ~ Real ale ~ Bar food (12-2, 6.30-9.30; not Sun
evening) ~ Restaurant ~ (0161) 449 7826 ~ Children welcome ~ Dogs allowed in bar ~
Open 12-3, 5.30-11; 12-7 Sun; closed Sun evening and Mon

NEWTON SD6950 Map 7
Parkers Arms
B6478 7 miles N of Clitheroe; BB7 3DY

A range of pets – pygmy goats, hens, pheasants, a parrot and ducks – is in residence at this beautifully placed pub (which is under a new licensee). The view from the garden and restaurant towards the Hodder valley and the distant fells (with scarcely another building in sight) is a reason in itself for coming here. Inside it's comfortably furnished, with red plush button-back banquettes, a mix of chairs and tables, stuffed animals, prints, and an open fire; piped music, pool. Beyond an arch is a similar area with sensibly placed darts, a log fire and TV; it can get smoky. Flowers IPA and a guest such as Copper Dragon are on handpump, and they have a good range of malt whiskies. Predominantly home-made bar food includes lunchtime sandwiches (from £3.95), basket meals such as scampi or chicken (£5.50), and steak and Guinness pie (£7.95), bass (£12.95) and lamb shank (£13.95), with puddings such as sticky toffee pudding (£3.75); the charming restaurant is no smoking. More reports please. (Recommended by Ann and Tony Bennett-Hughes, Norma and Noel Thomas, Melanie Lawrenson)

Enterprise ~ Lease Stuart Thacker ~ Real ale ~ Bar food (12-2.30, 6-9; 12-9 Sat-Sun) ~ Restaurant ~ (01200) 446236 ~ Children welcome ~ Open 11-3, 5-11; 11-11 Sat; 12-10.30 Sun ~ Bedrooms: £52S/£74S

RIBCHESTER SD6435 Map 7
White Bull 🛏
Church Street; turn off B6245 at sharp corner by Black Bull; PR3 3XP

In summer the garden of this efficiently run 18th-c pub makes a pleasant spot to sit and contemplate the ruins of the adjacent Roman bathhouse, and not far away are the museum and other remains of a 3rd-c fort. The spacious main bar has comfortable old settles, Victorian advertisements and various prints, and a stuffed fox in two halves that looks as if it's jumping through the wall. Most areas are set out for eating during the day, and food, from a reasonably priced menu, includes home-made soup (£2.95), sandwiches (£4.25), filo tiger prawns with plum sauce (£4.50), whole pizza with up to five toppings (£6.50; half pizza £3.25), spinach and ricotta cannelloni (£7.50), and steak and ale suet pudding or sausages and mash (£7.95); specials might include starters like beef chilli with cajun wedges and sour cream (£3.50) or mango and brie filo parcels (£4.50) and main courses like roast beef (£6.95), chicken curry (£8.95) or mixed grill (£13.95); puddings (£3); children's menu. The two dining areas are no smoking; TV, games machine and pool. Black Sheep, Marstons Pedigree and Timothy Taylors Landlord are on handpump. Look out for the tuscan pillars in the pub's porch: they are also thought to be of Roman origin and were originally from a nearby building. More reports please. (Recommended by Dennis Jones, Joan York, Roy and Lindsey Fentiman, Keith and Chris O'Neill, Martin and Sue Day)

Enterprise ~ Lease Jason Keen ~ Real ale ~ Bar food (12-9(8 Sun)) ~ Restaurant ~ (01254) 878303 ~ Children welcome with restrictions ~ Open 12-11(12 Fri, Sat) ~ Bedrooms: £35B/£50B

RIMINGTON SD8045 Map 7
Black Bull
Off A59 NW of Clitheroe, at Chatburn; or off A682 S of Gisburn; BB7 4DS

An astonishing collection of model trains, planes, cars, ships, and assorted railway memorabilia fills this pub, and the new owner who acquired it shortly before we went to press has kept most of the collection (though what had been set up as a separate little museum is no longer, most items having been moved into the pub itself). Exhibits are dotted around the airy, rather elegant rooms of the pub (they have a special night for rail buffs on the last Thursday of each month in winter, with pie and peas, film shows and soundtracks of vintage locos, for £3.50 all in).

The big, old-fashioned and civilised main bar has a model locomotive in a glass case beside an attractively tiled fireplace, a plane hanging from the ceiling, various platform signs on the walls, and comfortable banquettes and window seats; a central area with leatherette chairs leads through to a quietly refined dining room, with an exhibition of wildlife art on the walls; piped music; the restaurant is no smoking. It may all sound rather unpubby, but in the evenings it does feel very much like a village local, just as happy serving local lads a pint. Theakstons Best and up to three guests such as Caledonian Deuchars, Copper Dragon Challenger IPA and Timothy Taylors Landlord are served on handpump. From a printed menu are soup (£3.50), sandwiches (from £3.95), bouillabaisse fish soup (£5.95), roast of the day (£7.95) and game casserole (£8.95), and there's a changing à la carte board with items like fried lambs liver with baby onions (£6.95) and fried chicken breast in cranberry sauce (£8.95), with several fresh fish specials like grilled hake or lemon sole (prices vary; under £10); puddings change regularly too, and might include raspberry pavlova or apple and sultana strudel (£4.50); they also serve high tea on Sundays (4-7pm). Reports on the new regime please. *(Recommended by Steve Whalley, John and Sylvia Harrop)*

Free house ~ Licensee Neil Buckley ~ Real ale ~ Bar food (12-3(2.30 Sun), 7-10; not Sun evening) ~ Restaurant ~ (01200) 445220 ~ Children welcome ~ Open 12-3, 6-11; 12-11 Fri, Sat; 12-10.30 Sun

SAWLEY SD7746 Map 7

Spread Eagle (🍴) 🍷

Village signposted just off A59 NE of Clitheroe; BB7 4NH

'I've never had a disappointing visit; I've always found the service, drinks and (particularly) food to be superb,' remarks one reader who's been visiting this classy dining pub for many years. The location, by the River Ribble and ruins of a 12th-c cistercian abbey, is enjoyable too, and inside the pub is now entirely no smoking. The light and airy continental-feeling main bar has comfortable banquette seating, plenty of paintings and prints and lovely photographs of local views on the walls, a roaring winter coal fire, and Black Sheep, and Sawleys Drunken Duck (brewed for the pub by local microbrewery Bowland), on handpump; piped music. The impressive wine list has 150 bottles (12 wines by the glass), and the whiskies number over 50. The short lunchtime bar menu might include soup (£3.25), filled rolls (from £3.95), grilled black pudding medallion (£4.95), duck leg confit salad or grilled goats cheese niçoise (£5.50) and a fish plate with a selection including smoked trout, gravadlax, rollmop herring and crab (£6.95). In the restaurant, which overlooks the river, you can choose from more dishes such as roasted vegetable plate (£9.25), fried fillet of salmon with broad bean gnocchi (£9.95), grilled duck breast with chunks of poached pineapple, spring onions and aniseed sauce (£11.25) and fillet steak with peppercorn sauce (£16.50); two-course menu (£9.75 Tuesday to Friday lunch, £11.50 Tuesday to Thursday dinner, £12.50 Friday dinner and Saturday lunch, £13.50 Sunday lunch). They have various theme and gourmet evenings and you get swift service from the smartly dressed and attentive staff. The pub is very handy for the Forest of Bowland, an upland with terrific scope for exhilarating walks. *(Recommended by Paul Edwards, Ann and Tony Bennett-Hughes, Margaret Dickinson, Norma and Noel Thomas, Jo Lilley, Simon Calvert, John and Sylvia Harrop, Maurice and Gill McMahon, Steve Whalley)*

Free house ~ Licensees Nigel and Ysanne Williams ~ Real ale ~ Bar food (12-2 Tues-Sat only) ~ Restaurant ~ (01200) 441202 ~ Children welcome ~ Open 12-3, 6-11; 12-3 Sun; Closed first week in winter; closed Sun evening, all day Mon

'Children welcome' means the pub says it lets children inside without any special restriction. If it allows them in, but to restricted areas such as an eating area or family room, we specify this. Some pubs may impose an evening time limit. We do not mention limits after 9pm as we assume children are home by then.

STALYBRIDGE SJ9698 Map 7

Station Buffet 🍴 £

The Station, Rassbottom Street; SK15 1RF

On platform one of this Victorian station on the line from Manchester to Huddersfield, this enchantingly unpretentious railway-age institution is, as one reader puts it, 'well worth missing a few trains for'. The staff serve a marvellous range of up to 20 interesting guest ales a week (and are continually being approached by microbreweries to stock their latest brew) and usually have around seven or eight alongside Bass, Boddingtons and Flowers on handpump. You can also get farm cider, and belgian and other foreign bottled beers; beer festivals are held in early May and late November. The bar has a welcoming fire below an etched-glass mirror, newspapers and magazines to read, and old photographs of the station in its heyday and other railway memorabilia; there's a little conservatory. An extension along the platform leads into what was the ladies' waiting room and part of the station-master's quarters, with original ornate ceilings and a dining/function room with Victorian-style wallpaper; board games, cards; one room is no smoking. On a sunny day you can sit out on the platform. They do cheap old-fashioned snacks such as tasty black peas (50p) and sandwiches (from £1.95), and three or four daily specials such as home-made pie with peas (£2.50), bacon casserole (£3.20) and all day breakfast (£3.25); freshly made coffee and tea by the pot. Quiz nights on Mondays at 9pm. *(Recommended by John Fiander, the Didler, Dennis Jones)*

Free house ~ Licensees John Hesketh and Sylvia Wood ~ Real ale ~ Bar food (all day until 9pm) ~ No credit cards ~ (0161) 303 0007 ~ Children welcome ~ Dogs allowed in bar ~ Open 11-11; 12-10.30 Sun

TUNSTALL SD6173 Map 7

Lunesdale Arms ♀

A683 S of Kirkby Lonsdale; LA6 2QN

The food is prepared with admirable attention to detail at this civilised dining pub in the Lune valley, using locally sourced ingredients, and even the home-made bread and chips are singled out for praise by readers. The bright, homely atmosphere is helped along by bare boards and lively acoustics. There are big unframed oil paintings (some for sale) and pews and armchairs. On one side of the central bar part, a white-walled area (where the pictures are framed) has a good mix of stripped and sealed solid dining tables, and sofas around a lower table with daily papers, by a woodburning stove with a stone mantelpiece. At the other end, an airy games section has pool, table football, board games and TV, and a snugger little flagstoned back part has another woodburning stove; live piano most Thursday evenings. Enjoyable dishes from a constantly changing menu, where everything except the ice-cream is home-made, might include lunchtime soup (£3.75), open sandwiches (from £4), filled baked potatoes (£5.50), ham and cheese melt (£5.75), sausage and mash (small £5.95, large £8.50), home-made focaccia with smoked ham leek confit topped with free-range fried egg (£6) and steak and kidney pie (£9.50), with evening dishes such as chicken liver pâté (£4.25), clam and mussel marinière (£5.25), mediterranean bean stew (£8.50), slow-roasted shoulder of lamb on vermont baked beans with mash (£11.50), sirloin steak with béarnaise sauce (£11.90), and fillets of plaice stuffed with salmon and tomato on langoustine sauce (£14.50) as well as delicious puddings such as rhubarb fool or cappuccino crème brûlée (£4.25); Sunday lunch (around £9). They do smaller helpings of some main courses and children's meals. Besides Black Sheep and a guest such as Litton Potts Beck on handpump, they have a good range of sensibly priced wines by the glass (in a choice of sizes), and summer Pimms; piped music. This pretty village has a church with Brontë associations. *(Recommended by Malcolm Taylor, John Lane, Peter Burton, W K Wood, Karen Eliot, Paul Boot, Jo Lilley, Simon Calvert, John and Sylvia Harrop, R T and J C Moggridge)*

Free house ~ Licensee Emma Gillibrand ~ Real ale ~ Bar food (12-2(2.30 Sat, Sun), 6-9) ~

Restaurant ~ (01524) 274203 ~ Children welcome ~ Dogs allowed in bar ~ Live piano
music most Thurs nights ~ Open 11-3(3.30 Sat), 6-12(1 Sat); 12-3.30, 6-11 Sun; closed
Mon (exc bank hols), 25-26 Dec

UPPERMILL   SD9905   Map 7

Church Inn   ◖ £

**From the main street (A607), look out for the sign for Saddleworth Church, and turn
off up this steep narrow lane – keep on up!; OL3 6LW**

At this isolated and highly individual own-brew pub by the moors, local bellringers
practise on Wednesdays with a set of handbells that are kept here, while anyone is
invited to join the morris dancers who meet here on Thursdays. From a range of
eight to 12 real ales, fairly priced own-brewed Saddleworth beers are a big draw
(with prices from a staggeringly modest £1.20 a pint), and Ayrtons, Hopsmacker,
Saddleworth More, St Georges, Shaftbender and seasonal ales (including some
named after their children and which appear around their birthdays), as well as
guests like Greene King Old Speckled Hen, Hobgoblin and Thwaites Lancaster
Bomber are on handpump; continental wheat beer and dark lager on tap too. The
big unspoilt L-shaped main bar has high beams and some stripped stone; one
window at the end of the bar counter looks down over the valley, and there's also a
valley view from the quieter no smoking dining room; the conservatory is also no
smoking. The comfortable furnishings include settles and pews as well as a good
individual mix of chairs, and there are lots of attractive prints, staffordshire and
other china on a high delft shelf, jugs, brasses and so forth; TV (only when there's
sport on) and unobtrusive piped music. The horse-collar on the wall is worn by the
winner of their annual gurning (face-pulling) championship (part of the lively Rush
Cart Festival, usually held over the August bank holiday). Reasonably priced bar
food such as soup (£1.75), sandwiches (from £2.95), ploughman's (£3.25), steak
and ale pie (£5.95), roast beef (£6.25), 20-32oz jumbo cod (£8.95) and puddings
such as home-made cheesecake (£2.50); children's meals (from £3). There's a
delightful assortment of animals roaming around its garden or in view in the
adjacent field – rabbits, chickens, dogs, ducks, geese, horses and a couple of
peacocks, as well as an increasing army of rescued cats resident in an adjacent barn.
Children and dogs are made to feel very welcome. *(Recommended by John Fiander, the
Didler, Dennis Jones)*

Own brew ~ Licensee Julian Taylor ~ Real ale ~ Bar food (12-2.30, 5.30-9; 12-9 Sat-Sun) ~
Restaurant ~ (01457) 820902 ~ Well behaved dogs on leads welcome in bar ~ Open
12-12

WHEELTON   SD6021   Map 7

Dressers Arms   ◖ £

**2.1 miles from M61 junction 8; Briers Brow, off A674 Blackburn road from Wheelton
bypass (towards Brinscall); 3.6 miles from M65 junction 3, also via A674; PR6 8HD**

Nicely atmospheric with a series of cottagey low-beamed rooms, this enticingly
snug place has very good-value bar food as well as an interesting choice of beer. It's
much bigger than it looks from the outside, and the rooms are full of old oak and
traditional features, including a handsome old woodburning stove in the flagstoned
main bar. Candles on tables add to the welcoming feel, and there are newspapers
and magazines; two areas are no smoking (including one side of the bar); piped
music, juke box, pool table and games machine. They usually keep eight real ales
on at once, such as their own Big Franks (now brewed off the site) as well as the
more familiar Boddingtons and Tetleys and Timothy Taylors Landlord, plus five
guests such as Barnlsey Bitter, St Austell Tribute, Three Rivers Suitably Irish and
Northumberland Whitley Wobbler; also around 20 malt whiskies, and some well
chosen wines. Served all day at weekends, the good locally sourced bar food
includes soup (£2.95), sandwiches (from £3, toasted from £3.55), hot filled
baguettes (from £5.95), filled baked potatoes (£4.95), several vegetarian dishes such
as vegetable curry or mushroom risotto (£6.25), steak and kidney pie, sausage and

mash or paella (£6.95), 18oz battered cod and chips or trio of lamb chops (£7.95) and blackboard specials; good Sunday carvery (£8.95) and straightforward children's meals (£4.25, including an ice-cream); they also do three-course menus for £9.95 Monday to Thursday lunchtimes and early evenings from 5pm to 7.30pm. On the first floor is a cantonese restaurant. Lots of picnic-sets on a terrace in front of the pub, as well as a large umbrella with lighting and heaters; they have a very big car park, across the road. The licensees are great pet-lovers and welcome dogs. More reports please. *(Recommended by R T and J C Moggridge, Steve Whalley, R M Corlett, Mike and Linda Hudson, Jo Lilley, Simon Calvert)*

Own brew ~ Licensees Steve and Trudie Turner ~ Real ale ~ Bar food (12-2.30, 5-9; 12-9 weekends and bank hols) ~ (01254) 830041 ~ Children welcome, except in bar after 9pm ~ Dogs welcome ~ Open 11-12.30am(1am Sat)

WHITEWELL SD6546 Map 7

Inn at Whitewell ㉕ ★★ ⑪ ♀ ⇌

Most easily reached by B6246 from Whalley; road through Dunsop Bridge from B6478 is also good; BB7 3AT

With choice views over the adjacent River Hodder towards the high moors of the Forest of Bowland, this is a beautifully restful place to stay, though rooms are popular and you may need to book well in advance. The recently created riverside bar and adjacent terrace make the most of the view. Impressively furnished, the old-fashioned pubby main bar has antique settles, oak gateleg tables, sonorous clocks, old cricketing and sporting prints, roaring log fires (the lounge has a very attractive stone fireplace), and heavy curtains on sturdy wooden rails; one area has a selection of newspapers and magazines, local maps and guide books; there's a piano for anyone who wants to play, and even an art gallery. In the early evening, there's a cheerful bustle but once the visitors have gone, the atmosphere is tranquil and relaxing. Their good wine list contains around 180 wines (including a highly recommended claret), and they've beers from Copper Dragon, Timothy Taylor and Skipton Brewery on handpump. Besides lunchtime sandwiches (from £4.25), delicious, well presented food from the mostly traditional bar menu includes home-made soup (£3.50), fried chicken livers with a salad of flat mushrooms, roast onions and crispy bacon (£5.80), cumberland sausages and champ (£8.20), fish pie (£9.25), fish and chips (£9.50), braised shank of lamb (£11.50) and peppered rib-eye of beef with squash mash (£13), with specials such as mussels with white wine and cream (£5.50), prawn and smoky bacon chowder (£5.60), wild bowland venison sausages with black pudding mash (£9) and roast breast of goosnargh duckling, glazed plums with aubergine purée and roast garlic jus (£12.95); mouthwatering home-made puddings (£4.20) and british farmhouse cheeses (from £3.80); the staff are courteous and friendly. The dining room and one of the two bars are no smoking. You can get coffee and cream teas all day; they sell jars of home-made jam and marmalade. There's plenty of fell walking, they own several miles of trout, salmon and sea trout fishing on the Hodder, and with notice they'll even arrange shooting; they're happy to do picnic hampers for guests. *(Recommended by J S Burn, Karen Eliot, Revd D Glover, Brian Wainwright, Steve Whalley, Jo Lilley, Simon Calvert, Mr and Mrs A Curry, Steve Kirby, Peter and Jean Walker, Simon Cleasby, Anthony Longden, Michael and Deirdre Ellis)*

Free house ~ Licensee Charles Bowman ~ Real ale ~ Bar food (12-2, 7.30-9.30) ~ Restaurant ~ (01200) 448222 ~ Children welcome ~ Dogs welcome ~ Open 11(12 Sun)-11 ~ Bedrooms: £70B/£96B

Post Office address codings confusingly give the impression that some pubs are in Lancashire when they're really in Cumbria or Yorkshire (which is where we list them).

YEALAND CONYERS SD5074 Map 7

New Inn

3 miles from M6 junction 35; village signposted off A6; LA5 9SJ

This ivy-covered 17th-c village pub has excellent food served all day, and makes a handy stopping place from the nearby M6 or for exploring the area's wonderfully varied walks up Warton Crag and through Leighton Moss RSPB reserve. Inside, the simply furnished little beamed bar on the left has a cosy village atmosphere, with its log fire in the big stone fireplace. On the right, two communicating no smoking cottagey dining rooms have dark blue furniture, shiny beams and an attractive kitchen range. Robinsons Hartleys XB, one of their seasonal ales and perhaps another such as Unicorn on handpump and around 30 malt whiskies; piped music. The same menu runs through the dining rooms and bar, and some good vegetarian choices: as well as include soup (£3.65), sandwiches (from £3.85), filled baked potatoes (from £3.95) and warm baguettes (from £5.45), the menu includes starters such as cajun potato skins (£4.75) and mussels (£4.95), with main courses like cumberland sausage with garlic and mustard mash or spicy mexican bean chilli tortilla (£8.95), salmon fillet (£9.95) and 8oz fillet steak (£14.95), with more imaginative good specials such as rump of lamb marinated in garlic, rosemary and thyme, fillet of halibut poached in white wine, roast guinea fowl and pancake galette layered with cheese, fennel and tomato (from £9.95 to £12.95); they also do children's meals. A sheltered lawn at the side has picnic-sets among roses and flowering shrubs. *(Recommended by Dr D J and Mrs S C Walker, Tony and Caroline Elwood, Michael Doswell, Ann and Tony Bennett-Hughes, Peter Abbott, Jim Abbott, Alan Wilcock, Christine Davidson, Mr and Mrs A Dewhurst, Mrs Phoebe A Kemp, Maurice and Gill McMahon, Paul and Margaret Baker, Joan York, Peter and Eleanor Kenyon, Rhiannon Davies)*

Robinsons ~ Tenants Bill Tully and Charlotte Pinder ~ Real ale ~ Bar food (11.30(12 Sun)-9.30) ~ Restaurant ~ (01524) 732938 ~ Children welcome ~ Dogs allowed in bar ~ Open 11.30-11; 12-10.30 Sun

LUCKY DIP

Besides the fully inspected pubs, you might like to try these Lucky Dips recommended to us and described by readers (if you do, please send us reports: www.goodguides.co.uk).

ADLINGTON [SD6012]
Waggon & Horses PR7 4HE [Market St (A6)]: Pleasantly refurbished under newish licensees, enjoyable reasonably priced pubby food from sandwiches and baguettes up, real ales such as Greene King IPA and Old Speckled Hen and Wychwood Hobgoblin, conservatory restaurant *(Edward and Ann Marshall)*

AFFETSIDE [SD7513]
Pack Horse BL8 3QW [Watling St]: Attractive neatly kept moorland pub on Roman road, particularly well kept Hydes, big helpings of good value lunchtime bar food, snug pool room, restaurant early evenings (not Sun); big car park, good walking country, open all day wknds *(Peter Abbott, David R Brown, Norma and Noel Thomas, DJH)*

ARKHOLME [SD5872]
Bay Horse LA6 1AS [B6254 Carnforth—Kirkby Lonsdale]: Neatly kept and homely old three-room country pub popular for cheap generous food inc good value sandwiches, friendly service, a real ale such as Bass, Black Sheep or Everards Tiger, lovely inglenook, good atmosphere, pictures of long-lost London pubs; own bowling green, handy for charming

Lune valley walks, cl Mon *(MLR)*
ASHTON-UNDER-LYNE [SJ9399]
Station Hotel [Warrington St]: Doing well under current newish management, with lunchtime food, Holts (bargain price) and hefty Millstone True Grit *(G V Price)*
BEBINGTON [SJ3385]
Travellers Rest CH62 1BQ [B5151, not far from M53 junction 4; New Ferry Rd, Higher Bebington]: Friendly semi-rural corner pub with several areas around central bar and separate no smoking room, enjoyable reasonably priced bar lunches from good sandwiches to mixed grill (not Sun), up to eight real ales inc some from small breweries, efficient staff, alcoves, beams, brasses etc; no children, open all day *(MLR)*
BILSBORROW [SD5139]
Owd Nells PR3 0RS [off A6 N of Preston; at S end of village take Myerscough Coll of Agriculture turn into St Michaels Rd]: Nice pastiche of old rustic pub in busy expanding thatched canalside tourist complex inc hotel, craft and teashops and so forth, best for families; high pitched rafters each end, lower beams (and flagstones) by central bar counter,

wide choice of generous bar food (can take a while when really busy), half a dozen real ales, good value wines, tea and coffee, plenty of games, adjacent restaurant; children welcome, good play area outside (even cricket and bowls), comfortable bedrooms, open all day *(Emma Critchley, LYM)*

BIRKENHEAD [SJ3288]

Crown CH41 6JE [Conway St]: Friendly three-room alehouse with interesting changing ales inc Cains, Weston's farm cider, good value generous food all day till 6, good tilework; terrace tables, open all day *(the Didler)*

Dispensary CH41 5DQ [Chester St]: Comfortable pub with guest beers too, good value lunchtime food, handsome glass ceiling; handy for ferry, open all day *(the Didler)*

Stork CH41 6JN [Price St]: Early 19th-c, four well restored civilised rooms around island bar, polished mosaic floor, old dock and ferry photographs, several real ales, bargain basic food wkdy lunchtime and early evening, no smoking area, tiled façade; open all day (not Sun) *(the Didler, MLR, C J Fletcher)*

BLACKO [SD8641]

Rising Sun BB9 6LS [A682 towards Gisburn]: Welcoming traditional village pub now tied to Moorhouses, with their ales kept well, enjoyable well priced food, tiled entry, open fires in three rooms off main bar (no smoking one for families, with internet access); tables out on front terrace, open all day wknds *(MLR)*

BLACKPOOL [SD3136]

Ramsden Arms FY1 3AZ [Talbot Rd, opp Blackpool North station]: Large cheerful local with several panelled areas, masses of old prints and mainly beer-related bric-a-brac, helpful staff, good real ale range inc Blackpool, Jennings and Tetleys, perhaps one at bargain price, over 40 whiskies, may be lunchtime food, no smoking area; CD juke box, pool and games; good value bedrooms *(P Dawn, the Didler, John Dwane)*

BLACKROD [SD6011]

Thatch & Thistle BL6 5LA [Chorley Rd (A6 N)]: Thatched roadside pub with good value food inc popular Sun lunch, Bank Top real ale, friendly service *(Trevor and Sylvia Millum)*

BLACKSTONE EDGE [SD9716]

☆ *White House* OL15 0LG [A58 Ripponden—Littleborough, just W of B6138]: Beautifully placed largely no smoking moorland dining pub with remote views, emphasis on bargain hearty food from sandwiches up, prompt friendly service, Theakstons Best and changing ales such as Exmoor, Jennings and Timothy Taylors, belgian bottled beers, cheerful atmosphere, carpeted main bar with hot coal fire, other areas off, one with small settees, though most tables used (and often booked, wknd evenings) for food; children welcome, open for food all day Sun *(LYM, Mr and Mrs John Taylor, Dennis Jones)*

BOLTON [SD7109]

Hen & Chickens BL1 1EX [Deansgate]: Smart open-plan corner pub with popular hearty food, three changing real ales, efficient friendly service, traditional décor; open all day, cl Sun lunchtime *(Andy Hazeldine)*

Olde Man & Scythe BL1 1HL [Churchgate]: Interesting timbered local, largely 17th-c with cellar dating from 12th c, lively long low-beamed and flagstoned drinking area, two quieter bare-boards rooms, Boddingtons, cheap Holts and guest beers, two or more farm ciders, swift cheerful service, limited bargain lunchtime food (not Sun) such as sandwiches, or can bring in take-aways, darts and chess, sign language evenings; no children, piped music; delightful back terrace, handy for shopping area, open all day *(Andy Hazeldine, Nick Holding)*

Swan BL1 1HJ [Churchgate]: 19th-c (and partly 17th-c) hotel's comfortable bar with woody décor, real ales such as Bank Top, Moorhouses and Three Bs, belgian beers on tap and in bottle, no music; courtyard tables, bedrooms, open till 1am Thurs-Sat *(Andy Hazeldine)*

BRINDLE [SD5924]

☆ *Cavendish Arms* PR6 8NG [3 miles from M6 junction 29; A6 towards Whittle-le-Woods then left on B5256 (Sandy Lane)]: Comfortably worn-in extended village pub with good service, good value lunchtime food from sandwiches up, italian evening menu, Banks's and a guest beer such as Brains Rev James, several quaint little snugs, interesting stained-glass partitions and other decorations; no dogs; children welcome, picnic-sets in garden with terrace and rockery, tranquil little village with handsome stone church opposite, open all day wknds *(Dr D J and Mrs S C Walker, LYM, Graham Patterson)*

BROUGHTON [SD4838]

☆ *Plough at Eaves* PR4 0BJ [A6 N through Broughton, 1st left into Station Lane just under a mile after traffic lights, then bear left after another 1½ miles]: Two linked very low-beamed and comfortably old-fashioned front rooms with coal fire, back extension toning in, consistently enjoyable fairly priced home-made food (not Mon, all day wknds) from huge sandwiches up, Thwaites Bitter and a seasonal beer, lots of malt whiskies, decent house wines, good uniformed staff; small pool room, may be piped music; picnic-sets out in front, well equipped play area in good-sized peaceful garden behind *(LYM, Margaret Dickinson)*

BURNLEY [SD8332]

Inn on the Wharf BB11 1JG [Manchester Rd (B6240)]: Well run reliable pub by Leeds—Liverpool Canal, handy for centre, clean and spacious, with efficient staff, good choice from sandwiches up at all-day food bar (busy lunchtime), Hardys & Hansons, sensible prices, smart décor of beams, stripped stone and flagstones; waterside terrace, next to little Toll House Museum *(Margaret Dickinson)*

BURY [SD8007]

Blue Bell BL9 8DW [Manchester Rd (A56), handy for M60 junction 17, M62 and M66 junction 2 or 3]: Recently well renovated, with Holts, reasonably priced good standard pub food, quick service in bar and restaurant; popular and no bookings, so get there early, *(Brian Wainwright)*

Garsdale BL8 1BT [Woodhill Rd]: Welcoming traditional beamed pub with good value generous fresh food, good choice of wines by the glass, good attentive service, no smoking restaurant *(Anon)*

Trackside BL9 0EY [East Lancs Railway Station, Bolton St]: Busy station bar by East Lancs steam railway, great range of real ales and bottled imports, farm cider, bargain wkdy lunches (from breakfast time till 5 wknds); open all day *(P Dawn, the Didler)*

CARNFORTH [SD4970]

County Hotel LA5 9LD [Lancaster Rd (A6)]: Comfortable hotel with main bar well used by locals, reliable traditional food from good sandwiches to full meals in neat well divided informal restaurant/café off, good service; bedrooms, handy for Brief Encounter visitor centre *(Margaret Dickinson, Mrs Hazel Rainer)*

CATON [SD5364]

Ship LA2 9QJ [Lancaster Rd]: Roomy and reliable open-plan dining pub with good choice of reasonably priced food from sandwiches to generous fresh fish and Sun lunch, properly cooked veg, no smoking dining room, Thwaites ales and decent wines, efficient friendly staff, appealing nautical bric-a-brac, good fire in charming antique fireplace; subdued piped music; tables in garden, handy for Lune valley and Forest of Bowland *(Margaret Dickinson)*

CHEADLE [SU8586]

Griffin SK8 3BE [Wilmslow Rd (B5358, corner Finney Lane)]: Large 1960s local, good value straightforward lunchtime food inc popular Sun lunches, bargain Holts, huge divided main bar, games-oriented public bar *(Pete Baker)*

CLAUGHTON [SD5666]

☆ *Fenwick Arms* LA2 9LA [A683 Kirkby Lonsdale—Lancaster]: Welcoming black and white pub with enjoyable food inc fine yorkshire pudding, Black Sheep and Boddingtons, good range of wines, log fires, armchairs and cosy décor; piped music *(Karen Eliot, Jo Lilley, Simon Calvert)*

CLITHEROE [SD6642]

Craven Heifer BB7 3LX [Chipping Rd, Chaigley, off B6243 W]: Well run country dining pub with enthusiastic newish owners doing wide range of enjoyable food, friendly service, real ales such as Moorhouses Premier, good wine choice, large dining room, bar area with comfortable armchairs, sofas and big log fire, fine views *(Dennis Jones, Michael and Deirdre Ellis)*

New Inn BB7 2JN [Parson Lane]: Spotless traditional four-room pub with great range of real ales such as Black Sheep, Caledonian Deuchars IPA, Coach House ESB, Copper Dragon Orange Pippin, Moorhouses Pride of Pendle and Timothy Taylors Landlord from central bar, friendly and obliging expert staff, coal fires in both front rooms, no smoking room; open all day *(Steve Whalley)*

COCKERHAM [SD4652]

Manor LA2 0EF [not far from M6 junction 33]: Recently roomily refurbished under new ownership, strong flat-racing connections with associated memorabilia, food from massive sandwiches up, Moorhouses ales, good wine choice, friendly efficient service *(David and Katharine Cooke)*

COLNE [SD8940]

Hare & Hounds BB8 7EP [Skipton Old Rd, Foulridge]: Good value food inc some unusual dishes, pleasant service, relaxed unhurried atmosphere, Timothy Taylors ales, small no smoking restaurant; handy for canal and walks around lower reservoir *(F J Robinson, Stuart Paulley)*

COMPSTALL [SJ9690]

Andrew Arms SK6 5JD [George St (B6104)]: Enjoyable food inc bargain lunch Mon and other good deals, Robinsons real ale, enterprising choice of wines by the glass, busy no smoking back dining room; handy for Etherow Country Park *(Dennis Jones)*

CONDER GREEN [SD4556]

☆ *Stork* LA2 0AN [just off A588]: Fine spot where River Conder joins the Lune estuary among bleak marshes; cheery bustle and two blazing log fires in rambling dark-panelled rooms, generous popular food inc all-day sandwiches and light snacks, friendly efficient young staff, three real ales such as Black Sheep; pub games inc pool, juke box or piped music; children welcome, handy for Glasson Dock, comfortable bedrooms, open all day *(John Butterfield, LYM, Margaret Dickinson)*

Thurnham Mill Hotel LA2 0BD [signed off A588 just S]: Converted early 19th-c stone-built mill, comfortable beamed and flagstoned bar with good reasonably priced food, Everards and other ales, lots of whiskies, friendly staff and log fires, restaurant overlooking Lancaster Canal lock; tables out on terrace, comfortable bedrooms, good breakfast, open all day *(Ken Richards)*

COWAN BRIDGE [SD6277]

☆ *Whoop Hall* LA6 2HP [off A65 towards Kirkby Lonsdale]: Spacious and comfortable linked areas with wide choice of interesting quick food all day from 8am from popular buttery, smart service, real ales, decent wines; children welcome, garden well off road with back terrace and play area, well appointed bedrooms *(LYM, Margaret Dickinson)*

CROSTON [SD4818]

Crown PR26 9RN [Station Rd]: Busy beamed village pub with well priced food inc daily roasts, OAP wkdy lunches and fish and steak nights, hard-working young licensees, Thwaites; children welcome, lots of hanging baskets *(Jim and Maggie Cowell, John Cunningham, Mrs Y G Pearson)*

☆ *Wheatsheaf* PR26 9RA [Town Rd]: Convivial and chatty, with generous interesting food (usually all day) inc home-baked bread, reasonable prices, good friendly service, good changing range of real ales, hops and fresh flowers, 19th-c local photographs, stripped boards and quarry tiles, alcoves, no smoking

area; unobtrusive piped music; tables out on
sunny terrace, open all day
*(Margaret Dickinson, John Cunningham,
Tony and Caroline Elwood, Jim and
Maggie Cowell)*

DENTON [SJ9295]

Fletchers Arms M34 6EG [Stockport Rd]:
Spaciously refurbished beamed multi-room
pub with Robinsons full ale range, good choice
of wines by the glass, plentiful food inc
popular carvery, bookcases, flame-effect fires;
striking fairy-lit garden with fountain, pond
and lots of room for children to play *(Daniel
Jan Wejs)*

DOBCROSS [SD9906]

☆ *Swan* OL3 5AA [The Square]: Enjoyable
varied well priced home-made food inc
children's in low-beamed pub with three
interesting areas (one no smoking) off small
central bar, full Jennings ale range and guest
beers, attentive young staff, partitioned
alcoves, flagstones and traditional settles,
friendly atmosphere; Thurs folk night; tables
outside, attractive village below moors
(John Fiander, Pete Baker)

DOWNHAM [SD7844]

Assheton Arms BB7 4BJ [off A59 NE of
Clitheroe, via Chatburn]: Neatly kept partly no
smoking low-beamed L-shaped bar with pews,
big oak tables and massive stone fireplace, lots
of wines by the glass, wide range of generous
straightforward food from small open kitchen,
quick service, Marstons Bitter and Pedigree;
piped music; children and dogs welcome,
picnic-sets outside, prime spot in lovely village,
open all day Sun *(Len Beattie, John Kane,
LYM, Trevor and Sylvia Millum, Norma and
Noel Thomas)*

ECCLES [SJ7798]

Albert Edward M30 0LS [Church St]:
Refurbished Sam Smiths pub with their
bargain OB Bitter, corridor to small back no
smoking room and lounge; front bar can be
smoky; small sheltered terrace behind, open all
day *(the Didler)*

Grapes M30 7HD [Liverpool Rd, Peel Green;
A57 ½ mile from M63 junction 2]: Handsome
Edwardian local with superb etched glass, wall
tiling and mosaic floor, lots of mahogany, eye-
catching staircase, bargain Holts Bitter and
Mild with a good guest such as Bazens, fairly
quiet roomy lounge areas (children welcome
till 7) and smoke room, pool in classic billiards
room, vault with Manchester darts, drinking
corridor; tables outside, open all day
(the Didler, Pete Baker)

Lamb M30 0BP [Regent St (A57)]: Well
preserved Edwardian three-room local,
splendid etched windows, fine woodwork and
furnishings, extravagantly tiled stairway,
admirable trophies in display case, bargain
Holts Bitter and Mild and lunchtime
sandwiches, full-size snooker table in original
billiards room; popular with older people,
open all day *(the Didler)*

Royal Oak M30 0EN [Barton Lane]: Large
unspoilt Edwardian pub on busy corner,
several rooms off corridor, handsome tilework

and fittings, cheap Holts Bitter and Mild, good
licensees, pool; children allowed daytime in
former back billiards room (may be organ
singalongs), open all day *(the Didler)*

Stanley Arms M30 0QN [Eliza Ann
St/Liverpool Rd (A57), Patricroft]: Busy mid-
Victorian local with bargain Holts Bitter and
Mild, lunchtime filled rolls, popular front bar,
hatch serving lobby and corridor to small back
rooms, one with cast-iron range *(the Didler)*

White Lion M30 0ND [Liverpool Rd,
Patricroft, a mile from M63 junction 2]:
Welcoming Edwardian traditional local, clean,
tidy and popular with older people, with great
value Holts Bitter and Mild, games in lively
public bar, smoke room (wknd pianist) and
quiet lounge off tiled side drinking corridor
(the Didler, Pete Baker)

ECCLESTON [SD5117]

☆ *Original Farmers Arms* PR7 5QS [Towngate
(B5250, off A581 Chorley—Southport)]: Long
low-beamed pub/restaurant, wide choice of
consistently good competitively priced food all
day from open sandwiches and wkdy bargains
to huge mixed grill, tempting puddings
cabinets as you go in, cheery décor, several
changing real ales inc Tetleys, pleasant smartly
uniformed staff, darts; piped music and
machines (can be noisy), parking can be tight
when busy; good value bedrooms some with
own bathroom, open all day *(BB, T and P,
Margaret Dickinson, Norma and
Noel Thomas, W W Burke, Mike and
Linda Hudson)*

EDENFIELD [SD7919]

Original Coach & Horses BL0 0HJ [Market
St]: Locally popular for freshly made pubby
food from ploughman's and plenty of other
salads to steaks, nicely priced dishes for smaller
appetites, helpful friendly staff, decent wines,
tasteful extension; good new disabled facilities
(Rachel and Ross Gavin)

EDGWORTH [SD7416]

Rose & Crown BL7 0AR [Bury Rd]: Extended
17th-c local popular for its bargain wkdy
lunches and suppers, good range of food all
day from sandwiches, baguettes and baked
potatoes up inc carefully sourced meat, plenty
of vegetarian dishes, Sun carvery, friendly
service, cosy flagstoned bar divided by timbers,
no smoking dining area, Bass, Tetleys and
Timothy Taylors Landlord, reasonably priced
wines, darts; TV, games machine; children
welcome, good value bedrooms with own
bathrooms *(BB, Rachel and Ross Gavin,
Greg Yerbury)*

Spread Eagle BL7 0DS: Good choice of good
value food from italian chef, friendy staff *(Mr
and Mrs A Silver)*

ENTWISTLE [SD7217]

☆ *Strawbury Duck* BL7 0LU [signed off
Edgworth—Blackburn rd; by station]: Tucked-
away traditional beamed and flagstoned
country pub, Phoenix ales and one brewed for
the pub by Bank Top, hearty and enjoyable bar
food all day, friendly service, Victorian
pictures, some bare stone, no smoking room
and restaurant; pool, fruit machine, TV and

piped music; children welcome, tables outside, good for Pennine walks, open all day *(Mark Lowe, LYM, Miss Schofield, Mr Robinson, Andy Hazeldine)*

FENCE [SD8337]

☆ *Bay Horse* BB12 9EP [Wheatley Lane Rd]: Small country dining pub, cosy and spotless, with reliably good imaginative wide-ranging food inc fish specialities, Marstons Pedigree, Theakstons Best and a guest beer, lots of wines by the glass, friendly licensees and staff, restaurant, separate locals' tap room with darts, table football and pool; cl Mon *(Peter Abbott, Jim Abbott, Margaret Dickinson, Kevan Tucker)*

FLEETWOOD [SD3348]

☆ *North Euston* FY7 6BN [Esplanade, nr tram terminus]: Big architecturally interesting Victorian railway hotel dominating the seafront, extensive pubby bar giving great sea and hill views, particularly friendly helpful staff, good changing real ale choice such as Greene King, Timothy Taylors and Theakstons, enjoyable lunchtime food from sandwiches up, lots of separate-seeming areas inc large no smoking family room (till 7), café-bar and two restaurants; live music Fri-Sun; seats outside, comfortable bedrooms, open all day (Sun afternoon break) *(David and Ruth Hollands, BB, Margaret Dickinson, Keith and Chris O'Neill)*

GARSTANG [SD4943]

Bradbeer Bar PR3 1YE [Garstang Country Hotel & Golf Club; B6430 S]: Relaxed and spacious bar overlooking golfing greens, good value imaginative food, helpful well trained staff, huge woodburner; tables outside, bedrooms *(Margaret Dickinson)*

Royal Oak PR3 1ZA [Market Pl]: Comfortable and roomy small-town inn dating from 16th c, attractive panelling, several eating areas inc charming snug, reliably enjoyable generous food (all day Sun) inc imaginative specials, small helpings for children or OAPs, pleasant service (long in same family), Robinsons real ales, good value coffee, restaurant, spotless housekeeping; disabled access, comfortable bedrooms, open all day Fri-Sun *(Margaret Dickinson)*

☆ *Th'Owd Tithebarn* PR3 1PA [off Church St]: Rustic barn with big flagstoned terrace overlooking Lancaster Canal marina, Victorian country life theme with very long refectory table, antique kitchen range, masses of farm tools, stuffed animals and birds, flagstones and high rafters, simple food all day from filled baguettes up, Flowers IPA and Tetleys, lots of country wines, quieter parlour welcoming children; piped music in main bar may be loud, can get busy and smoky; open all day summer *(LYM, Bill Sykes, Margaret Dickinson)*

Wheatsheaf PR3 1EL [Park Hill Rd (one-way system northbound)]: Small and cosy neatly kept well-beamed pub with gleaming copper and brass, good range of well priced freshly cooked good food, cheerful friendly service even when busy, decent malt whiskies *(BB, Margaret Dickinson)*

GREAT HARWOOD [SD7331]

Victoria BB6 7EP [St Johns St]: Remarkable range of up to ten or so changing real ales, friendly regulars, unspoilt traditional Edwardian layout with five rooms off central bar, one with darts, one with pool, two quiet snugs (one no smoking), some handsome tiling; tables out behind, opens 4.30 (3 Fri, all day wknds), cl wkdy lunchtimes *(Pete Baker)*

HASLINGDEN [SD7823]

Griffin BB4 5AF [Hud Rake, off A680 at N end]: Friendly basic local brewing its own cheap Porters ales in the cellar, farm cider, L-shaped bar with views from comfortable lounge end, darts in public end; open all day *(Pete Baker)*

HAWKSHAW [SD7515]

☆ *Red Lion* BL8 4JS [Ramsbottom Rd]: Roomy, comfortable and attractive pub/hotel, friendly welcome and efficient cheerful service, good generous fresh local food in cosy bar and separate well run restaurant, good changing real ale range; comfortable if rather creaky bedrooms, quiet spot by River Irwell, open for food all day wknds *(Phil and Helen Holt, John and Sylvia Harrop, Ben Williams, Peter Abbott, Norma and Noel Thomas, Mark Butler)*

Waggon & Horses BL8 4JL [Bolton Rd]: New licensees doing short choice of good home-made food using fresh local ingredients (worth booking Fri/Sat evenings) in bar and small no smoking restaurant *(Rachel and Ross Gavin)*

HESKIN GREEN [SD5315]

☆ *Farmers Arms* PR7 5NP [Wood Lane (B5250, N of M6 junction 27)]: Cheerful country pub with wide choice of good value home cooking inc nicely cooked veg and good vegetarian choice in two-level dining area, friendly helpful staff, real ales inc John Smiths, heavy black beams, sparkling brasses and china, public bar with darts; piped music (even outside), SkyTV; picnic-sets in big colourful garden, good play area, more tables front and side, comfortable pretty bedrooms, open all day wknds *(Phil and Helen Holt, BB, Nick Holding)*

HEST BANK [SD4766]

☆ *Hest Bank Hotel* LA2 6DN [Hest Bank Lane; off A6 just N of Lancaster]: Picturesque three-bar coaching inn in attractive setting close to Morecambe Bay, plenty of tables out by Lancaster Canal, wide range of good fresh generous food all day from sandwiches, local potted shrimps and interesting salads to mixed grill and fresh local fish, bargain set menus, Boddingtons, Greene King IPA, Timothy Taylors Landlord and a monthly changing guest beer, decent wines, friendly and helpful young staff, comfortably worn in furnishings, separate restaurant area; children welcome *(Margaret Dickinson, Dr and Mrs S Donald, BB, Bill Sykes, Jo Lilley, Simon Calvert, Julian and Janet Dearden)*

HEYSHAM [SD4161]

Royal LA3 2RN [Main St]: Four changing real ales, well priced wines and decent food inc early evening bargains in early 16th-c quaint and low-beamed two-bar pub; dogs allowed (not at meal times), tables out in front and good-sized sheltered garden, pretty village with great views from interesting church *(Tony and Maggie Harwood, Margaret Dickinson)*

HOGHTON [SD6026]

Sirloin PR5 0DD [Station Rd]: Changing real ales, upmarket upstairs restaurant; handy for Hoghton Tower *(Jim and Maggie Cowell)*

HOLDEN [SD7749]

☆ *Copy Nook* BB7 4NL [the one up by Bolton by Bowland]: Roomy and attractive dining pub with helpful staff, wide choice of good popular reasonably priced food, particularly beef, lamb and fish, and specials inc plenty of game, real ales such as Marstons Pedigree, good wine choice, three dining rooms off main bar; piped music; children welcome, six bedrooms with own bathrooms *(Dudley and Moira Cockroft, BB, Norma and Noel Thomas, Mr and Mrs R B Berry)*

HORNBY [SD5868]

Royal Oak LA2 8JY [Main St]: Long low-beamed bar with food inc good fresh sandwiches, Thwaites, friendly service, pleasant décor with HMS *Royal Oak* memorabilia *(Pat and Robert Watt)*

HOSCAR [SD4611]

Railway L40 4BQ [Hoscar Moss Rd, off A5209 Parbold—Burscough]: Friendly refurbished country pub, attractively light and uncluttered, with Black Sheep, Jennings and Charles Wells Bombardier, usual food (also afternoon teas), efficient attentive staff *(J A Hooker)*

HURST GREEN [SD6837]

Shireburn Arms BB7 9QJ [Whalley Rd]: Quiet comfortable 17th-c hotel in idyllic setting with panoramic Ribble valley views from lovely neatly kept back garden and terrace, good reasonably priced food, Thwaites and other ales, armchairs and log fire in beamed lounge bar, light and airy restaurant, separate tea room; safe low-key play area, pretty Tolkien walk from here, bedrooms *(Margaret Dickinson)*

HYDE [SJ9495]

Cheshire Ring SK14 2BJ [Manchester Rd (A57, between M67 junctions 2 and 3)]: Tied to Cheshire's small Beartown brewery, their real ales at tempting prices, guest beers and imports on tap, farm cider, good house wines, warm welcome, good value lunchtime sandwiches; open all day (has been cl till 2 Mon-Weds) *(Dennis Jones, the Didler)*

Sportsman SK14 2NN [Mottram Rd]: Unpretentious Victorian local popular for its fine real ale range, good prices, welcoming licensees, open fires, memorabilia and plenty of atmosphere; children and dogs welcome *(the Didler, Greg Banks)*

INGLEWHITE [SD5440]

Green Man PR3 2LP [Silk Mill Lane; 3 miles from A6 – turn off nr Owd Nells, Bilsborrow]: Old-fashioned red plush in polished bar and dining room, good generous food served piping hot at attractive prices, good sandwiches, Charles Wells Bombardier, staff pleasant and attentive even when busy, log fire, lots of brasses

and cruet set collection; garden with unspoilt views nr Beacon Fell country park, camp site behind, bedrooms *(Margaret Dickinson)*

IRBY [SJ2586]

Irby Mill CH49 3NT [Irby Mill Hill, off Greasby rd]: Well kept Cains, Courage Directors, Greene King Ruddles County and Old Speckled Hen, John Smiths, Charles Wells Bombardier and changing guest beers, good value wines by the glass, decent food all day (can be a wait when it's busy), two low-beamed largely flagstoned rooms and carpeted lounge with comfortable pub furniture, coal-effect gas fire, interesting old photographs and history of the former mill; tables out on terraces and side grass, open all day *(MLR, BB, Tony Tollitt)*

KING'S MOSS [SD5001]

Colliers Arms WA11 8RD [Pimbo Rd (off B5205 W of Billinge)]: Traditional four-room country pub very popular for good reasonably priced food (not Sun evening) from sandwiches, baguettes and baked potatoes to steaks, good friendly service, three changing real ales; children welcome, garden tables, play area, open all day *(Julian and Janet Dearden)*

LANCASTER [SD4761]

☆ *Water Witch* LA1 1SU [parking in Aldcliffe Rd behind Royal Lancaster Infirmary, off A6]: Cheerful and attractive conversion of 18th-c canalside barge-horse stabling, flagstones, stripped stone, rafters and pitch-pine panelling, fine changing beer choice, lots of bottled beers, dozens of wines by the glass and good spirits range from mirrored bar, enjoyable stylishly cooked local food inc good cheese board, upstairs restaurant; children in eating areas, tables outside, open all day *(Jo Lilley, Simon Calvert, LYM, Mrs Hazel Rainer)*

LATHOM [SD4511]

☆ *Ship* L40 4BX [off A5209 E of Burscough; Wheat Lane]: Big pub tucked below embankment at junction of Leeds & Liverpool and Rufford Branch canals, several separate beamed rooms, some interesting canal memorabilia and naval pictures and crests, Moorhouses and several guest beers, some parts set for the fresh well priced unpretentious food from lunchtime sandwiches up (small helpings for children), prompt service even when busy, games room with pool, big-screen sports TV; children welcome, tables outside, open all day *(BB, MLR, Bill Sykes, Steve Whalley, Mrs Dilys Unsworth)*

LEIGH [SJ6699]

Waterside WN7 4EL [Twist Lane]: Civilised pub in converted 19th-c waterside warehouses handy for indoor and outdoor markets, wide choice of enjoyable reasonably priced food inc OAP deals, Hardys & Hansons, good friendly service, chatty atmosphere; plenty of tables by Leigh branch of Liverpool—Leeds Canal, lots of ducks and swans *(Ben Williams, John Fiander)*

LITTLE LEVER [SD7507]

Jolly Carter BL3 1BW: Bright and comfortable, with good value home-made food, Bank Top, Greene King Old Speckled

Hen and Timothy Taylors Landlord, modern décor, friendly helpful staff; handy for Bolton Branch of Manchester, Bolton & Bury Canal *(Ben Williams)*

LIVERPOOL [SJ4395]

☆ *Baltic Fleet* L1 8DQ [Wapping]: Interesting pub nr Albert Dock, full of nautical trappings, with big arched windows, lots of woodwork and nice mix of furnishings; marking time a bit because of the wholesale redevelopment all around, and may be refurbished itself in 2007, but well worth knowing meanwhile particularly for its Wapping ales brewed on the premises, with several interesting guest beers, short simple choice of bargain bar food, friendly service, no smoking room, upstairs restaurant; piped music, TV; children welcome in eating areas, dogs in bar, back terrace, open all day *(Paul Davies, the Didler, C J Fletcher, LYM, MLR, Eric Robinson, Jacqueline Pratt, Jack Clark)*

☆ *Cains Brewery Tap* L8 5XJ [Stanhope St]: Well restored Victorian pub with Cains full beer range (inc their good Mild) at attractive prices, guest beers from other small breweries, friendly efficient staff, good well priced wkdy food till 6 (2 Sat), nicely understated décor, wooden floors, plush raised side snug, interesting old prints and breweriana, handsome bar, flame-effect gas fire, daily papers, cosy relaxing atmosphere; sports TV; popular exceptional value brewery tour ending here with buffet and singing; open all day *(the Didler, C J Fletcher)*

Carnarvon Castle L1 1DS [Tarleton St]: Long and narrow, with compact bar and comfortable back lounge, Cains Bitter and Mild and a guest or two, lunchtime bar snacks, cabinet of Dinky toys and other eclectic collections, no music; open all day, cl Sun evening, Mon/Tues lunchtime (opens 8pm then) *(the Didler, Joe Green)*

☆ *Cracke* L1 9BB [Rice St]: Friendly backstreet local, bare boards and pews, lots of posters for local events and pictures of local buildings, unusual Beatles diorama in largest room, very cheap food till 6, Cains, Phoenix and guest beers, farm cider; juke box and TV, popular mainly with young people; open all day, sizeable garden *(the Didler, C J Fletcher, MLR, Eric Robinson, Jacqueline Pratt)*

Crown L1 1JQ [Lime St]: Well preserved art nouveau showpiece with fine tiled fireplace and copper bar front, plush banquettes, splendid ceiling in airy corner bar, smaller back room with another good fireplace, impressive staircase sweeping up under splendid cupola to handsome area with ornate windows, usual food inc some massive yet low-priced dishes, bargain real ales from small breweries *(C J Fletcher, Joe Green)*

☆ *Dispensary* L1 2SP [Renshaw St]: Small chatty central pub with Cains ales inc Mild and two guest beers, bottled imports, friendly staff, good value wkdy food 12-7, polished panelling, marvellous etched windows, bare boards, comfortable raised back bar, Victorian medicine bottles and instruments; open all day *(the Didler, C J Fletcher)*

☆ *Doctor Duncan* L1 1HF [St Johns Lane]: Neatly kept classic Victorian pub with particularly attentive staff, full Cains range and up to four guest beers, belgian beers on tap, convivial atmosphere (can get lively evenings), enjoyable food from sandwiches to economical main dishes till 7 (Tues curry night), pleasant helpful service, daily papers and magazines, several rooms inc impressive back area with pillared and vaulted tiled ceiling, no smoking family room; may be piped music, busy wknds; open all day *(the Didler, C J Fletcher, Mark Harrington)*

Globe L1 1HW [Cases St, opp station]: Chatty comfortably carpeted local, pleasant staff, Cains and guest beers, lunchtime filled cobs, cosy snug, tiny quiet sloping-floor back lounge, lots of prints of old Liverpool; may be piped music; open all day *(the Didler, Joe Green)*

Grapes L2 6RE [Mathew St]: Friendly open-plan local with Cains, Tetleys and guest beers, good value lunchtime bar food, pleasantly well worn cottagey décor (flagstones, old range, wall settles, no two chairs the same, gas-effect lamps); open all day *(the Didler)*

Lion L2 2BP [Moorfields, off Tithebarn St]: Ornate Victorian alehouse, sparkling etched glass and serving hatches in central bar, unusual wallpaper, big mirrors, panelling and tilework, two small back lounges one with fine glass dome, friendly atmosphere and landlord interested in the history, Lees, Caledonian Deuchars IPA and changing guest beers, lunchtime food inc splendid cheese and pie specialities, may be free bar nibbles, coal fire; open all day *(Paul Davies, the Didler, MLR, C J Fletcher, Pete Baker)*

Ma Boyles L3 1LG [Tower Gardens, off Water St]: Much modernised backstreet local with good value bar food (all day Sat) from dim sum and pies to galway oysters, Hydes and guest beers, quieter downstairs bar; open all day, cl Sat night and Sun *(the Didler, Joe Green)*

Ma Edgertons L1 1JA [Pudsey St, opp side entrance to Lime St Station]: Padded leather banquettes with bell pushes for service in handsomely old-fashioned lounge, Bass, John Smiths and Worthington *(Dave Braisted)*

Midland L1 1JP [Ranelagh St]: Well kept Victorian local with original décor, ornate lounge, long corner bar, nice etched glass, mirrors and chandeliers; keg beers *(the Didler)*

Peter Kavanaghs L8 7LY [Egerton St, off Catherine St]: Rambling shuttered pub with interesting décor in several small rooms inc old-world murals, stained glass and lots of bric-a-brac inc bicycle hanging from ceiling, Cains, Greene King Abbot and a guest beer, friendly staff; open all day *(the Didler, C J Fletcher)*

Poste House L1 6BU [Cumberland St]: Small comfortable early 19th-c backstreet local surrounded by huge redevelopment, Cains Bitter and Mild and guest beers, good wkdy lunches, friendly licensees, daily papers, room upstairs; open all day *(the Didler, Joe Green)*

Rigbys L2 2EZ [Dale St]: Great range of beers inc imports, reasonably priced hearty home-made food (with accompanying beer recommendations); tables and chairs outside *(Helen Slater)*

Roscoe Head L1 2SX [Roscoe St]: Three spotless little unspoilt rooms, chatty and civilised, with changing ales such as Jennings Cumberland and Tetleys Mild and Bitter, good value wkdy home-made lunches, amusing cartoons, tie collection, cribbage school Weds, Tues quiz night; open all day *(the Didler, C J Fletcher, David Martin, Joe Green)*

Ship & Mitre L2 2JH [Dale St]: Friendly gaslit local popular with university people, up to a dozen changing unusual real ales, imported beers, two farm ciders, good-humoured service, good value basic food lunchtime and early evening, pool, occasional beer festivals; piped music; open all day, cl Sun lunchtime *(the Didler, Joe Green)*

Swan L1 4DQ [Wood St]: Hydes, Phoenix, several guest beers and Weston's farm cider in busy bare-boards pub's ground-floor bar, good value cobs and home-cooked wkdy lunches, friendly staff, comfortable loft in second upstairs bar (open at busy times); good loud 1970s rock juke box; open all day *(the Didler)*

Vines L1 1JQ [Lime St]: Comfortable and friendly, with Victorian mahogany and mosaic tilework, handsome high-ceilinged room on right with stained glass; keg beer, can get very busy; open all day *(the Didler)*

White Star L2 6PT [Rainford Gdns, off Matthew St]: Welcoming traditional local with Bass, Bowland and changing guest beers, good service, lots of woodwork, boxing prints, White Star shipping line and Beatles memorabilia, big-screen sports TV in comfortable back lounge; open all day *(the Didler, C J Fletcher)*

LONGRIDGE [SD6137]
Corporation Arms PR3 2YJ [Lower Rd (B6243)]: Comfortably refurbished 18th-c pub with emphasis on largely traditional food all day, three or four changing guest beers, lots of malt whiskies, three small linked rooms and restaurant; five comfortable bedrooms with own bathrooms, plans for many more, open all day *(Graham and Doreen Holden, Jim and Maggie Cowell)*

LONGTON [SD4525]
Dolphin PR4 5JY [Marsh Lane, towards Longton Marsh]: Busy family pub with good cheap sensible food served 12-8 from sandwiches and baked potatoes to Sun roasts, pleasant speedy service, Boddingtons and several guest beers, occasional beer festivals with live music; lots of tables out behind, good play area *(Phil Berrill, Jim and Maggie Cowell)*

LYDIATE [SD3604]
Scotch Piper L31 4HD [Southport Rd]: Medieval thatched pub with heavy black beams, flagstones and thick stone walls, well kept Banks's and Marstons ales, darts in middle room off corridor, carpeted back snug, three coal fires, no food, music or machines; picnic-sets in large garden with aviary, chickens and donkey, open all day wknds *(the Didler, C J Fletcher)*

LYTHAM [SD3427]
Fairhaven FY8 1AU [Marine Drive]: Neatly kept extended modern pub with wide choice of generous fresh food from sandwiches and baguettes up, Boddingtons, Marstons Pedigree and Theakstons, helpful staff; handy for beach and Fairhaven Lake *(Ken Richards, Tina and Griff)*

MANCHESTER [SJ8284]
☆ *Ape & Apple* M2 6JP [John Dalton St]: Big friendly open-plan pub with bargain Holts and hearty bar food, comfortable seats in bare-boards bar with nice lighting and lots of old prints and posters, armchairs in upstairs lounge; piped music, TV area, games machines; unusual brick cube garden, bedrooms, open all day *(the Didler)*

Bar Centro M4 1LG [Tib St]: Two-floor café-bar with Hydes and a couple of local guest beers, continental draught beers, farm cider, up-to-date food, daily papers, local paintings for sale, nice woodwork; relaxed at lunchtime, popular with young people evenings – frequent live music and DJs, small dance floor; open all day (till very late Thurs-Sat) *(the Didler)*

Bar Fringe M4 5JN [Swan St]: Congenial bare-boards café-bar specialising in beers from the low countries, also four changing real ales from local small breweries such as Bank Top, farm cider, friendly staff, enjoyable food till 6 (4 Sat/Sun), daily papers, shelves of empty beer bottles, cartoons, posters and bank notes, polished motorcycle hung above door, games inc pinball, good music; tables out behind, open all day *(the Didler, Martin Grosberg)*

Beer House M4 4BR [Angel St, off Rochdale Rd]: Lively bare-boards open-plan pub with Phoenix House Blonde and half a dozen interesting changing ales, belgian beers, farm ciders, perry and country wines, robust cheap bar food (great sausage and mash Fri/Sat lunchtime), darts, good CD juke box, games machine, smaller upstairs bar with games and SkyTV; tables out in small area behind, open all day *(the Didler)*

☆ *Bridge St Tavern* M3 3BW [Bridge St]: Dining pub with enjoyable food (don't miss those tempting duck-fat chips) but also two good changing real ales, long narrow panelled room with two fine tiled and ironwork fireplaces, similar upstairs dining room *(GLD, Dennis Jones)*

Castle M4 1LE [Oldham St, about 200 yards from Piccadilly, on right]: Simple traditional front bar, small snug, full Robinsons range from fine bank of handpumps, games in well worn back room, nice tilework outside; no food, children allowed till 7, blues Thurs, open all day (cl Sun afternoon) *(the Didler)*

Circus M1 4GX [Portland St]: Two tiny rooms, back one panelled with leatherette banquettes, particularly well kept Tetleys from minute corridor bar (or may be table drinks service), friendly landlord, celebrity photographs, no music or machines; often looks closed but normally open all day (you may have to knock) *(the Didler)*

City Arms M2 4BQ [Kennedy St, off St Peters

Sq]: Five or six quickly changing real ales (awe-inspiring pumpclip collection), belgian bottled beers, occasional beer festivals, busy for bargain bar lunches inc sandwiches and baked potatoes, quick service, coal fires, bare boards and banquettes, prints and panelling, handsome tiled façade and corridor; good piped music, TV, games machine; wheelchair access but steps down to back lounge, open all day *(the Didler, Dennis Jones)*

Coach & Horses M45 6TB [Old Bury Rd, Whitefield; A665 nr Besses o' the Barn station]: Former early 19th-c coaching inn keeping several separate rooms, popular and friendly, with bargain Holts beers, table service, darts, cards; open all day *(the Didler)*

Crescent M5 4PF [The Crescent (A6), Salford – opp Salford Univ]: Three areas off central servery with up to eight changing real ales, farm ciders and lots of foreign bottled beers, friendly staff, buoyant local atmosphere (popular with students and university staff), low-priced food, open fire, homely unsmart décor, pool room, juke box; small enclosed terrace, open all day *(the Didler)*

Crown & Anchor M3 1SQ [Cateaton St]: Bargain Holts Bitter and Mild and enjoyable food, comfortable lounge area with soft chairs and thick carpets, more basic drinking area *(Dennis Jones)*

Crown & Kettle M4 5FF [Oldham Rd]: Recently comfortably refurbished and reopened after long closure, up to eight real ales in ornate high-ceilinged three-room Victorian pub with classic plasterwork, panelling from R100 airship in one room *(the Didler, BB)*

Dutton Arms M3 1EU [Park St, Strangeways]: Welcoming old-fashioned backstreet local almost in shadows of prison, three rooms with Hydes beers from central servery, plenty of bric-a-brac; open all day *(the Didler)*

Eagle M3 7DW [Collier St, Salford (keep on Greengate after it leaves B6182)]: Old-fashioned basic backstreet pub popular with older regulars, bargain Holts Bitter and Mild, friendly service, cheap filled rolls, bar servery to tap and passage with two smoke rooms, old Salford pictures; sports TV; open all day *(the Didler)*

Egerton Arms M3 5FP [Gore St, Salford; A6 by stn]: Several rooms, chandeliers, art nouveau lamps, low-priced Holts Bitter and Mild and guest beers, friendly service; open all day *(the Didler)*

Grey Horse M1 4QX [Portland St, nr Piccadilly]: Small traditional Hydes local, their Bitter and Mild, some unusual malt whiskies, panelled servery with colourful glazed gantry, lots of prints, photographs and plates, no juke box or machines; can bring in good sandwiches from next door, open all day *(the Didler, Dennis Jones)*

Hare & Hounds M4 4AA [Shudehill, behind Arndale]: Long narrow bar linking front snug and comfortable back lounge (with TV), notable tilework, panelling and stained glass, Holts and Tetleys, sandwiches, friendly staff;

games and machine, piano singalongs Weds and Sun perhaps with free chip butties, upstairs Fri folk club; open all day *(the Didler, Pete Baker)*

Jolly Angler M1 2JW [Ducie St]: Plain backstreet local, long a favourite, small and friendly, with Hydes ales, coal or peat fire; darts, pool and sports TV, informal folk nights Thurs and Sun; open all day Sat *(P Dawn, the Didler, Pete Baker, BB)*

Kings Arms M3 6AN [Bloom St, Salford]: Plain tables, bare boards and flagstones contrasting with opulent maroon and purple décor and stained glass, good changing real ale range, lunchtime food (not Sat); juke box, music, poetry or theatre nights upstairs; open all day (cl Sun evening) *(the Didler, Martin Grosberg)*

Knott Fringe M3 4LY [Deansgate]: Marble organic ales and guest beers, good range of continental imports, worthwhile food all day too inc good sandwiches; under railway arch, by Castlefield heritage site *(Dennis Jones)*

☆ *Mr Thomas Chop House* M2 7AR [Cross St]: Long Victorian city pub, bare boards, panelling and original gas lamp fittings in front bar with stools at wall and window shelves, back tiled eating area, period features inc wrought-iron gates for wine racks, good plain popular english lunchtime food, friendly staff, good wines by the glass, real ale, no smoking area; can get very busy lunchtime; open all day *(Revd D Glover, GLD, the Didler, Dennis Jones, Roger Huggins)*

Old Monkey M1 4GX [Portland St]: Holts showpiece recently built in traditional style, generous tasty food and their Bitter and Dark Mild, bargain prices, quick friendly service even when busy, etched glass and mosaic tiling, interesting memorabilia, upstairs lounge, wide mix of customers *(the Didler)*

☆ *Peveril of the Peak* M1 5JQ [Gt Bridgewater St]: Vivid art nouveau green external tilework, interesting pictures, lots of mahogany, mirrors and stained or frosted glass, changing real ales such as Boddingtons and Marstons Pedigree from central servery, cheap basic lunchtime food (not Sun), very welcoming family service, log fire, three sturdily furnished bare-boards rooms, pub games inc pool, busy lunchtime but friendly and homely evenings; TV; pavement tables, children welcome, cl wknd lunchtimes, open all day Fri *(Stephen and Jean Curtis, the Didler, LYM, Dennis Jones, Jack Clark)*

Plough M18 7FB [Hyde Rd (A57), Gorton]: Classic tiling, windows and gantry in unspoilt Robinsons local, wooden benches in large public bar, two quieter back lounges, small pool room and lots of pub games; TV; open all day *(the Didler)*

☆ *Queens* M8 8RG [Honey St, Cheetham; off Red Bank, nr Victoria Stn]: Welcoming licensees, interesting changing beers from small breweries, lots of belgian imports, farm ciders, simple enjoyable food (all day wknds), coal fire, bar billiards, board games, well preserved tiled façade; children welcome, unexpected views of Manchester across the industrialised Irk Valley and its railway lines from large back garden with good play area, open all day *(the Didler)*

☆ *Rain Bar* M1 5JG [Gt Bridgewater St]: Lots of woodwork and flagstones in former umbrella works, full range of Lees beers, masses of wines by the glass, good value food all day from 9am wknd breakfast through panini and light meals to fish and chips etc, friendly efficient service, relaxed atmosphere, daily papers, coal fire in small snug, large upstairs café-bar too; piped music may be loud; no under-21s or scruffs evenings, good back terrace overlooking spruced-up Rochdale Canal, handy for Bridgewater Hall, open all day *(the Didler, Dennis Jones)*

Sams Chop House M2 1HN [Back Pool Fold, Chapel Walks]: Small pleasant dining pub, offshoot from Mr Thomas Chop House, with thriving atmosphere, good beers, huge helpings of good plain english food, good wine choice, formal waiters, original Victorian décor *(Revd D Glover, Jo Lilley, Simon Calvert)*

☆ *Sinclairs* M3 1SW [2 Cathedral Gates, off Exchange Sq]: Charming no smoking low-beamed and timbered 18th-c pub (rebuilt here in redevelopment), bargain Sam Smiths OB, good all-day menu highlighting oysters, brisk friendly service, great atmosphere, upstairs bar with snugs and Jacobean fireplace; plastic glasses for the tables out by ultra-modern Exchange Sq, open all day *(LYM, the Didler, Dennis Jones)*

Smithfield M4 5JZ [Swan St]: Open-plan local with interesting changing guest beers, some in jugs from the cellar, inc one brewed for it by Phoenix, frequent beer festivals, bargain food from sandwiches up from open kitchen servery, daily papers, friendly staff and landlady; pool on front dais, games machine, juke box, sports TV in back lounge/eating area; good value bedrooms in nearby building, open all day *(the Didler, BB)*

White Lion M3 4NQ [Liverpool Rd, Castlefield]: Traditional Victorian pub, lots of dark wood, tables for eating up one side of three-sided bar, home-made food all day inc good hot beef sandwiches and children's helpings, changing ales inc Phoenix and Timothy Taylors Landlord, decent house wine, good tea, friendly service, real fire, lots of prints and Man Utd pictures, shelves of bottles and jugs; big-screen sports TV, nostalgic discos Fri-Sun; disabled access, children welcome, tables out among excavated foundations of Roman city overlooking fort gate, handy for Museum of Science and Industry and Royal Exchange Theatre, open all day *(the Didler)*

MARPLE [SJ9488]
Railway SK6 6EN [Stockport Rd]: Bright bustling good value pub, friendly and well run, with Robinsons and decent simple lunchtime food (children allowed then) from toasties to Sun roasts; handy for Middlewood Way, open all day *(David Hoult, Dennis Jones)*

MAWDESLEY [SD4915]
Black Bull L40 2QY [Hall Lane]: Attractive

rambling village pub said to date partly from 13th c, sporting prints and lots of nooks and crannies, real ales such as Black Sheep, Jennings Cumberland and a Mild, freshly made food from toasties up; tables outside, boules *(Rona Murdoch)*

MELLOR [SJ9888]
☆ *Devonshire Arms* SK6 5PP [Longhurst Lane; this is the Mellor nr Marple, S of Manchester]: Charming well run Robinsons pub, wide choice of enjoyable generous food, good value if not cheap, their Best and Mild with Old Tom in season, quick friendly service, three attractive rooms with Victorian fireplaces and unusual curved bar; picnic-sets out in front and in attractive back garden with lovely pergola and boules *(LYM, Roger Yates, Dennis Jones, David Hoult)*

MIDDLETON [SD8606]
Rose of Lancaster OL1 2TQ [Haigh Lane (B6195)]: Friendly post-war local with bargain Lees Bitter, wide range of food from baguettes up, lots of pine tongue-and-groove, conservatory dining room looking over fields to Rochdale Canal and moors beyond *(Ben Williams)*

MORECAMBE [SD4364]
Eric Bartholomew LA4 5DD [Euston Rd]: Wetherspoons named after Eric Morecambe, good value drinks and food, no smoking and family areas, plenty of wood and steel *(Mrs Hazel Rainer)*

PENDLETON [SD7539]
☆ *Swan With Two Necks* BB7 1PT: Welcoming olde-worlde pub in attractive streamside village below Pendle Hill, simply furnished, warm and tidy, with good blackboard range of inexpensive generous home cooking (not Mon), friendly service, local Moorhouses and changing ales; large garden, open all day Sun, cl Tues *(Pete Baker, LYM)*

PRESCOT [SJ4692]
Clock Face L34 3LL [Derby St]: Former mansion house with good value generous lunchtime food inc bargain platter big enough for two, cheap Thwaites beer from long bar counter, good welcoming service, comfortable seating in several areas; open all day summer *(Julian and Janet Dearden)*

PRESTON [SD5329]
Black Horse PR1 2EJ [Friargate]: Friendly and interesting unspoilt pub in pedestrian street, full Robinsons ale range, inexpensive lunchtime food, unusual ornate curved and mosaic-tiled Victorian main bar, panelling, stained glass and old local photographs, two quiet cosy comfortable enclosed snugs off, mirrored back area, upstairs 1920s-style bar, good juke box; no children, open all day from 10.30, cl Sun evening *(the Didler, Pete Baker, Nick Holding)*

RABY [SJ3179]
☆ *Wheatsheaf* CH63 4JH [off A540 S of Heswall; Raby Mere Rd]: Attractive thatched and timbered pub with unspoilt homely furnishings in chatty rambling bar inc high-backed settles making a snug around fine old fireplace, splendid choice of real ales and of

malt whiskies, nice wines, polite attentive service even when busy, spacious no smoking restaurant (evenings not Sun/Mon, and good Sun lunch) with conservatory; children and dogs allowed, picnic-sets on terrace and in pleasant back garden, pretty village, open all day *(A and B D Craig, MLR, Keith and Sue Campbell, Mr and Mrs M Stratton, LYM, A Harding, Dr Phil Putwain, Theocsbrian, Malcolm Ravenscroft)*

RADCLIFFE [SD7608]
Sparking Clog M26 3WY [Radcliffe Moor Rd]: Warmly welcoming staff, enjoyable food *(Louisa Lomax)*

ROCHDALE [SD8814]
Healey OL12 6LW [Shawclough Rd (B6377 NW of centre)]: Unspoilt stone-built pub with old film star photographs in main bar, separate no smoking lounge, Robinsons ale; attractive good-sized garden with boules; open all day from noon wknds (from 3 wkdys) *(Pete Baker)*

ROSSENDALE [SD8225]
Craven Heifer BB4 8HY [Burnley Rd (A682 N of Rawtenstall)]: Moorhouses pub with good range of their ales kept well, darts and several old photographs in good homely public bar, simple comfortable linked lounge; TV; cl lunchtime exc open all day Sun *(Pete Baker)*

RUFFORD [SD4517]
Rufford Arms L40 1SQ [Liverpool Rd (A59)]: Spick and span, with enjoyable food, charming well trained staff; tables outside (busy road) *(Margaret Dickinson)*

SCOUTHEAD [SD9605]
Three Crowns OL4 4AT [Huddersfield Rd]: Wide choice of enjoyable food from sandwiches to full meals inc imaginative dishes, cheerful efficient service, real ales, good thriving atmosphere; children welcome, inoffensive piped music *(Mrs Pauline Beckett)*

SILVERDALE [SD4574]
Silverdale Hotel LA5 0TP [Shore Rd]: Wide choice of good value generous food, Jennings Cumberland, quick pleasant service, four refurbished dining areas inc large conservatory and two no smoking rooms; children welcome, plenty of picnic-sets in attractive garden with limestone terrace, bedrooms, beautiful setting *(John Foord)*

SLAIDBURN [SD7152]
☆ *Hark to Bounty* BB7 3EP [B6478 N of Clitheroe]: Friendly old stone-built inn in charming Forest of Bowland village, neat rather modern décor in line of linked rooms, wide choice of good value generous food (lots of tables) inc old-fashioned puddings, good hospitable service, three real ales, decent wines and whiskies, comfortable chairs by open fire, games room with darts, pool and machines one end, well appointed restaurant the other; pleasant garden behind, good walks, bedrooms, open all day *(LYM, Len Beattie, Dennis Jones, Jeremy Whitehorn)*

SOUTHPORT [SD3315]
Falstaff PR8 1LG [King St]: Large open-plan pub, fresh and comfortable, with up to ten good ales, bargain food for most of the day (not Sun/Mon evenings) inc Sun roasts, friendly service, lots of 19th-c panelling and bric-a-brac; tables outside, open all day *(Dr B and Mrs P B Baker, Nick Holding)*
Scarisbrick PR8 1NZ [Lord St]: Comfortable armchairs and lots of real ales inc some rare for the area from central counter in hotel's relaxed and informal main bar done up as medieval baronial hall, adjoining café and bistro bar welcoming children, bargain food; bedrooms, open all day *(Dr B and Mrs P B Baker, BB)*

STOCKPORT [SJ8889]
Alexandra SK3 9NJ [Northgate Rd]: Large friendly backstreet local, reputedly haunted, with preserved Victorian interior, Robinsons Best and Mild; pool room *(the Didler)*
☆ *Arden Arms* SK1 2LX [Millgate St, behind Asda]: Good inventive freshly made lunchtime food in welcoming pub with fast cheerful service, full Robinsons ales range, well preserved traditional horseshoe bar, old-fashioned tiny snug through servery, two coal fires, longcase clocks, well restored tiling and panelling; tables out in courtyard sheltered by the original stables, open all day *(the Didler, Dennis Jones, Pete Baker, John C Gould)*
Armoury SK3 8BD [Shaw Heath]: Friendly two-bar local with Robinsons Best and Hatters Mild, perhaps Old Tom from a cask on the bar, lunchtime family room upstairs; open all day *(the Didler)*
Blossoms SK2 6LS [Buxton Rd (A6)]: Busy main-road Victorian local, very friendly, with Robinsons Best, Hatters Mild and (from bar-top cask) Old Tom, good home-made pies and other lunchtime food, three rooms of corridor inc pool room with pin table and attractive back lounge with handsome fireplace; open all day wknds *(the Didler)*
Crown SK4 1AR [Heaton Lane, Heaton Norris]: Partly open-plan Victorian local under arch of vast viaduct, huge real ale range inc Black Sheep and local Three Rivers, three cosy lounge areas (one no smoking) off gaslit bar, stylish décor, good value lunches Thurs-Sat, farm cider, pool, darts; TV, frequent live music; tables in cobbled courtyard, open all day Fri/Sat *(the Didler)*
Navigation SK4 1TY [Manchester Rd (B6167, former A626)]: Unpretentious pub run by friendly mother and daughter, with half a dozen or so local Beartown ales and a guest beer, several farm ciders tapped from cellar casks, continental bottled beers; open all day *(the Didler)*
Nursery SK4 2NA [Green Lane, Heaton Norris; off A6]: Very popular for enjoyable straightforward lunchtime food from servery on right with visible kitchen, good Sun lunch, friendly efficient service, good value Hydes ales, big bays of banquettes in panelled front lounge, brocaded wall banquettes in back one; children welcome if eating, on narrow cobbled lane at E end of N part of Green Lane, immaculate bowling green behind, open all day wknds *(BB, the Didler, Pete Baker)*
Olde Woolpack SK3 0BY [Brinksway, just off M60 junction 1 – junction A560/A5145]: Well

run three-room pub with Theakstons and interesting changing guest beers, good value home-made food, friendly landlord, traditional layout with drinking corridor; open all day wknds *(the Didler)*

Porters Railway SK1 2BZ [Avenue St (just off M63 junction 13, via A560)]: Their own Porters ales and three wknd guest beers, lots of foreign beers, farm cider, masses of whiskies and country wines, decent straightforward home-made food (not Sun), bargain prices throughout, friendly staff, bright and airy L-shaped bar with old Stockport prints and memorabilia, bar billiards; may be piped local radio; tables out behind, open all day *(the Didler, Dennis Jones)*

Queens Head SK1 1JT [Little Underbank (can be reached by steps from St Petersgate)]: Splendid Victorian restoration, long and narrow, with delightful separate snug and back dining area, rare brass cordials fountain, double bank of spirits taps and old spirit lamps, old posters and adverts, reasonably priced lunchtime snacks, bargain Sam Smiths, daily papers, good friendly bustle, bench seating and bare boards, no smoking area; famous tiny gents' upstairs, some live jazz; open all day *(the Didler, Dennis Jones)*

☆ *Red Bull* SK1 3AY [Middle Hillgate]: Steps up to friendly well run local, impressive beamed and flagstoned bar with dark panelling, substantial settles and seats, open fires, lots of pictures, mirrors and brassware, traditional island servery with Robinsons ales from nearby brewery, good value home-cooked bar lunches (not Sun); quiet at lunchtime, can get crowded evening, open all day (cl Sun afternoon) *(LYM, the Didler, David Hoult)*

Swan With Two Necks SK1 1RY [Princes St]: Traditional local, comfortable panelled bar, back skylit lounge and drinking corridor, Robinsons ales inc Old Tom, friendly efficient service, decent lunchtime food; handy for shops, open all day, cl Sun *(the Didler, Dennis Jones)*

Tiviot SK1 1TA [Tiviot Dale (E end of main shopping centre)]: Friendly and unspoilt Robinsons pub, four rooms off central bar inc good games-oriented public bar, lots of old local and steam locomotive photographs, simple inexpensive wkdy lunchtime food; open all day (not Sun evening) *(Pete Baker)*

TARBOCK GREEN [SJ4687]

Brickwall L35 1QG [Netherley Rd (B5179)]: Roomy and welcoming softly lit country pub, Burtonwood, Marstons and a weekly guest beer, food inc Sun carvery, friendly staff, old prints and china; sports TV, weekly entertainment; children welcome, large play area in garden behind *(Dr Rob Howard)*

THINGWALL [SJ2784]

Basset Hound CH61 1AS [Barnston Rd]: Bass Vintage Inn dining pub with comfortable mix of seating, generous food inc interesting dishes, good choice of wines by the glass; open all day *(Ann and Tony Bennett-Hughes)*

TYLDESLEY [SD6902]

Mort Arms M29 8DG [Elliott St]: Bargain

Holts Bitter and Mild in two-room 1930s pub, etched glass and polished panelling, comfortable lounge with old local photographs, friendly landlord and regulars, darts and dominoes, TV horseracing Sat; open all day *(the Didler)*

WALMER BRIDGE [SD4723]

Fox Cub PR4 5JT [Liverpool New Rd]: Attractively done Vintage Inn, new but traditional, with appealing furnishings and décor, their usual all-day food, professional service and fine choice of wines by the glass – lots of wine racks and bottles around; tables outside, open all day *(Margaret Dickinson)*

WEST KIRBY [SJ2186]

White Lion CH48 4EE [Grange Rd (A540)]: Interesting small 17th-c sandstone pub, several small beamed areas on different levels, Courage Directors, John Smiths, Theakstons and a guest beer, friendly staff, good value simple bar lunches inc wide choice of sandwiches, coal stove; no children even in attractive secluded back garden up steep stone steps, open all day *(MLR)*

WHALLEY [SD7335]

Dog BB7 9SP [King St]: Civilised, relaxing and roomy, four real ales such as Coach House Squires Gold and Okells Spring Ram, good value home cooking, attentive friendly service, quiet areas for eating and coffee inc no smoking family dining room, interesting bric-a-brac and Victorian prints *(Steve Whalley)*

WHEATLEY LANE [SD8338]

☆ *Old Sparrow Hawk* BB12 9QG [Wheatley Lane Rd]: Good fresh contemporary cooking strong on local produce, good sandwiches and rewarding children's menu too, in comfortable and civilised country dining pub, also pleasant for an early evening drink, with real ales such as Bass, Black Sheep, Moorhouses Blonde Witch, Tetleys and Charles Wells Bombardier, wheat beers on tap, lots of good wines by the glass, daily papers, attractive layout, dark oak panelling and timbers, stripped stonework and interesting furnishings, lots of snug corners inc nice area with fire and sofa under domed stained glass, buoyant relaxed atmosphere, friendly well trained staff; piped music may obtrude; children welcome in eating areas, tables out on roomy and attractive front terrace with views to moors beyond Nelson and Colne, open for food all day *(Andy Devanney, LYM, BB, Michael and Deirdre Ellis, Kevan Tucker)*

WIGAN [SD5806]

Royal Oak WN1 1XL [Standishgate (A49)]: Good Mayflower ales brewed and kept well here, good range of other beers inc Budvar, Erdinger and bottled imports, food till 6 Weds-Sat; brewery tours can be arranged; tables out behind, open all day, cl lunchtime Mon/Tues *(Andy Hazeldine)*

WOODFORD [SJ8882]

☆ *Davenport Arms* SK7 1PS [A5102 Wilmslow—Poynton]: Down-to-earth convivial country pub, largely no smoking, popular for enjoyable generous reasonably priced home cooking and Robinsons Best and Best Mild, good house wines, blazing coal fires, snug rooms, good games room; children allowed in back snug, tables on front terrace and in attractive back garden with play area, open all day Sat *(Tom Halsall, Dave Braisted)*

WORSLEY [SD7500]

Barton Arms M28 2ED [Stablefold; just off Barton Rd (B5211, handy for M60 junction 13)]: Recently built, with good value food, four real ales; children welcome *(Ben Williams)*

Bridgewater M28 2PD [Barton Rd (B5211, handy for M60 junction 13)]: Good atmosphere in big pub opp Bridgewater Canal and facing village green, standard food from light dishes up, changing real ales such as Banks's, Greene King and Phoenix, helpful staff *(Ben Williams)*

WREA GREEN [SD3931]

☆ *Grapes* PR4 2PH [Station Rd]: Busy Chef & Brewer with good layout of cosy olde-worlde linked areas, helpful service, enjoyable fresh food from good sandwiches to some imaginative specials, well kept Theakstons, Timothy Taylors Landlord and Charles Wells

Bombardier, good choice of wines by the glass, open fire and candles; tables out overlooking village green, picturesque church *(Spider Newth, Christine and Neil Townend, Tracey and Stephen Groves)*

WRIGHTINGTON [SD5011]

Rigbye Arms WN6 9QB [3 miles from M6 junction 27; off A5209 via Robin Hood Lane and left into High Moor Lane]: 16th-c inn in attractive moorland setting, relaxed atmosphere, good value generous food inc some interesting specials, good fresh veg, real ales inc Greene King Old Speckled Hen and Timothy Taylors Landlord, decent wines *(Mr and Mrs John Taylor, Norma and Noel Thomas, Jack Clark)*

WRIGHTINGTON BAR [SD5313]

☆ *Mulberry Tree* WN6 9SE [B5250, N of M6 junction 27]: Light, airy and stylish restaurant pub with good generous if not cheap imaginatively served food (best to book Sun lunch) from small sampler helpings to full meals, good wines, attentive polite staff, plenty of tables *(Christopher Mobbs, Karen Eliot)*

If a service charge is mentioned prominently on a menu or accommodation terms, you must pay it if service was satisfactory. If service is really bad you are legally entitled to refuse to pay some or all of the service charge as compensation for not getting the service you might reasonably have expected.

Leicestershire and Rutland

Many of the better pubs in this part of the world set their sights really high, aiming to do well on all counts. Over a third of them prepare food that is good enough to qualify for our Food Award, and this count is easily balanced out by the number with Beer Awards. The Olive Branch at Clipsham, with its genuinely warm welcome, and its sister pub the civilised Red Lion at Stathern, perhaps epitomise these high standards with their great range of drinks, combined with delicious carefully sourced food. Though simpler in décor, the Exeter Arms at Barrowden is worth a mention for the combination of its good value own-brew beers and up-to-date menu. The hospitable Italian chef/landlord at the Fox & Hounds at Exton is very deserving of his new Food Award this year, not least for his hand-thrown pizzas. New in this year, the unfussily modernised bustling Fox & Hounds at Knossington, looks set to do very well with its thoughtful menu, and another newcomer, the Crown & Plough at Long Clawson, is a fine all-rounder. It's the Olive Branch at Clipsham however that again wins the award of Leicestershire and Rutland Dining Pub of the Year. The Nevill Arms at Medbourne deserves a mention just for getting it spot-on as a great traditional pub, as does the happy Griffin at Swithland. In the Lucky Dip section at the end of the chapter, pubs gaining enthusiastic support in recent months include the Bell at Gumley, Bewicke Arms at Hallaton, Swan in Mountsorrel, Nags Head at Saltby and Royal Horseshoes at Waltham on the Wolds. The Bell at East Langton would have been a main entry this year, but the landlord was leaving in summer 2006 – the hope is that, with the same good chef, it will continue to be a particularly nice place for a meal out. Drinks prices tend to be a shade lower than the national norm. Apart from special local cases (our two main entries in Somerby, for example, which seem to vie with one another in keeping their beer prices low), Grainstore was the local beer that we found most often at good value prices in the area's pubs. Head for their down-to-earth tap in Oakham to taste the full range. Everards is the main local brewer, and smaller local brewers to note here include Belvoir, Brewsters, Langton and Parish.

AB KETTLEBY   SK7519   Map 7
Sugar Loaf
Nottingham Road (A606 NW of Melton); LE14 3JB

Food at this reworked country pub, although fairly straightforward, is well prepared and comes in remarkably generous helpings. As well as all-day snacks such as filled baked potatoes (from £4.45), filled baguettes with home-made chips (from £4.75) and burgers and ploughman's (from £4.95), there might be lunchtime choices such as soup (£3.75), pâté (£5.45), sausage and mash with red wine gravy (£6.75) and beef in ale pie (£7.95), with evening meals such as prawns and smoked salmon with lemon mayonnaise (£6.45), brie and cranberry wellington (£8.95), honey roast duck fillet with plum sauce (£12.95), and steaks (from £13.75). Relaxed and chatty (with friendly efficient service), the open-plan bar is comfortably modernised and warm, with big black and white photographs of Shipstones brewery dray horses and a variety of country prints on the ragged canary walls. A bare-boards end area (smoking in here only) with a coal-effect gas fire has darts, cribbage, dominoes, a quiet juke box and fruit machine. Good solid pale wood tables and chairs on the discreetly patterned carpet spread from here into a pleasant conservatory. The substantial carved bar counter, with well cushioned stools, has well kept Bass, Fullers London Pride and guests from brewers such as Belvoir, Charles Wells and Shepherd Neame on handpump; piped music. There are a few picnic-sets out by the road and car park. *(Recommended by Ruth Jeanes, Rob Darlington, Andrea and Guy Bradley, Phil and Jane Hodson)*

Free house ~ Licensees Josephine and Dennis Donovan ~ Real ale ~ Bar food (12-9.30) ~ Restaurant ~ (01664) 822473 ~ Children in eating area of bar ~ Open 11-11.30(12.30 Fri); 12-10.30 Sun

BARROWDEN   SK9400   Map 4
Exeter Arms
Main Street, just off A47 Uppingham—Peterborough; LE15 8EQ

A rewarding combination of their very fairly priced, own-brew Blencowe beers, and some rather upmarket freshly cooked food, are on offer at this peaceful 17th-c no smoking coaching inn. The beers are brewed in an old free-standing barn behind, and might include Beach Boys, Bevin Boy, Fun Boy Four and Boys with Attitude, alongside a couple of guests from brewers such as Freeminer and Grainstore. As well as lunchtime sandwiches (from £4.75) and ploughman's (£6.75) the contemporary menu (not such good value as the beers but tasty nevertheless) might include razor clam chowder topped with cornish yarg, lime and shaved truffle (£5.75), wild mushroom and cashew nut tart with mascarpone and red lentil gravy (£10.95), smoked quail stuffed with venison sausage, white truffle and apricot (£13.95), roast suckling pig cooked in cider, honey, garlic and herbs (£16.75), with puddings such as chestnut and chocolate cake with crème anglaise or rhubarb and elderflower bruschetta glazed in merlot syrup with honey and basil chantilly (£4.95). The long cheery yellow open-plan bar stretches away either side of a long central counter, and is quite straightforwardly furnished with wheelback chairs at tables at either end of the bar, on bare boards or blue patterned carpet. There's quite a collection of pump clips, beer mats and brewery posters; cribbage, dominoes, shove-ha'penny, piped music and boules. There are picnic-sets on a narrow front terrace overlooking the pretty village green, and ducks on the pond, with broader views stretching away beyond, and more well spaced picnic-sets in a big informal grassy garden at the back. We've been told there are red kites in the nearby Fineshades woods. *(Recommended by John Wooll, Noel Grundy, Duncan Cloud, the Didler, David Barnes, Barry Collett, Colin McKerrow, Keith Widdowson, Michael Doswell, Di and Mike Gillam, Mike and Sue Loseby, Jeff and Wendy Williams)*

Own brew ~ Licensee Martin Allsopp ~ Real ale ~ Bar food (not Sun evening, Mon) ~ Restaurant ~ (01572) 747247 ~ Children welcome away from the bar ~ Dogs allowed in bar ~ Open 12-2.30(3 Sat), 6-11; 12-3, 7-10.30 Sun; closed Mon lunchtime, also Sun evening in winter ~ Bedrooms: £35S/£70S

BREEDON ON THE HILL   SK4022   Map 7
Three Horse Shoes
Main Street (A453); DE73 1AN

This 18th-c stylish dining pub, opposite a quaint little conical village lock-up, has been simply restored to reveal the attractive period heart of the building. Heavy worn flagstones, a log fire, pubby tables, a dark wood counter and sludgy green walls and ceilings give a timeless feel to the clean cut central bar (with Caledonian Deuchars IPA, Marstons Pedigree and Theakstons XB on handpump, 30 malt whiskies, and good house wines). Beyond here on the left is a step up to a further eating room, with maroon walls, dark pews and cherry-stained tables. The two-room no smoking dining area on the right has a comfortably civilised chatty feel with big quite close-set antique tables on seagrass matting and colourful modern country prints and antique engravings on canary walls. Even at lunchtime there are lighted candles in elegant modern holders. Good interesting blackboard food, using local produce and suppliers, includes home-made soup (£4.50), club sandwich (£4.95), sausage and mash (£5.95), garlic and cream mushrooms or grilled goats cheese with cranberry dressing (£5.95), seared scallops with balsamic vinegar (£6.95), pasta with salmon and dill cream sauce (£7.95), aubergine, black olive and polenta layer with sun-dried tomato dressing (£11.95), chicken breast with stilton cream sauce (£14.95), beef, mushroom and red wine casserole (£15.50), monkfish with stir-fried oriental vegetables or lamb shank with mustard mash (£16.50), pheasant with savoy cabbage and whisky (£16.95), and puddings such as chocolate whisky trifle or an excellent treacle oat tart with custard (£4.95). *(Recommended by Clive and Fran Dutson, Ian and Jane Irving)*

Free house ~ Licensees Ian Davison, Jennie Ison, Stuart Marson ~ Real ale ~ Bar food (12-2, 5.30-9.15; not Sun) ~ Restaurant ~ (01332) 695129 ~ Children in restaurant ~ Dogs allowed in bar ~ Open 11.30-2.30, 5.30-11; 12-2.30, 7-10.30 Sun

CLIPSHAM SK9616 Map 8
Olive Branch ★ ⑪ ♀ ◀

Take B668/Stretton exit off A1 N of Stamford; Clipsham signposted E from exit roundabout; LE15 7SH

Leicestershire and Rutland Dining Pub of the Year

Everything is done to the highest possible standard at this very well run pub. It scores high on all fronts, leaving you to enjoy a comfortably civilised, relaxing visit. There's quite an emphasis on the beautifully prepared and presented food (served by friendly attentive staff) so it's worth booking in advance. The imaginative changing menu might include sandwiches (from £5.50), haricot bean and white truffle broth (£4.50), pork and stilton pie with their own piccalilli (half a pie £4.50; whole pie £8), tempura tiger prawns with sweet chilli dip (£7.75), super fish and chips with tomato sauce (£10.50), rigatoni pasta, rocket, pine nuts, olive oil and parmesan (£11), local sausages with mustard mash and spring greens (£11.50), grilled rib-eye (£14.95), confit duck leg and haricot bean cassoulet with chorizo (£13.95), roast bass with stuffed pepper, tagliatelle and red pepper coulis (£17.25), and puddings such as egg custard tart with mango salsa or chocolate roulade with black cherries and white ice-cream (from £5.75). Also interesting cheeses, good coffee, and lovely petit fours; three-course Sunday lunch (£18.50). A great range of drinks includes well kept Grainstore Olive Oil and a guest or two such as Holts on handpump, an enticing wine list (with about 18 by the glass), a fine choice of malt whiskies, armagnacs and cognacs, and 14 different british and continental bottled beers. The various smallish attractive rambling rooms have dark joists and beams, and there's a cosy log fire in the stone inglenook fireplace, an interesting mix of pictures (some by local artists) and country furniture. Many of the books were bought at antiques fairs by one of the partners, so it's worth asking if you see something you like, as much is for sale. The dining rooms are no smoking; shove-ha'penny and maybe unobtrusive piped music. Outside, there are tables, chairs and big plant pots on a pretty little terrace, with more on the neat lawn, sheltered in the L of its two low buildings. We'd like to hear about their new bedrooms so do please send us a report if you stay. *(Recommended by M and C Thompson, Barry Collett, P Dawn, Mike and Sue Loseby, John Saul, Nazeer Chowdhury, Peter Fitton, Tina and David Woods-Taylor, Les and Barbara Owen, Derek and Sylvia Stephenson, Jeff and Wendy Williams, Brian Wainwright, Malcolm and Jane Levitt, Robert Naylor, A G Marx)*

Free house ~ Licensees Sean Hope and Ben Jones ~ Real ale ~ Bar food (12-2(3 Sun), 7-9.30(9 Sun)) ~ Restaurant ~ (01780) 410355 ~ Children welcome ~ Dogs allowed in bar and bedrooms ~ Open 12-3, 6-11; 12-11(10.30 Sun) Sat ~ Bedrooms: £75S(£85B)/£85S(£95B)

We mention bottled beers and spirits only if there is something unusual about them – imported belgian real ales, say, or dozens of malt whiskies; so do please let us know about them in your reports.

EMPINGHAM SK9408 Map 4
White Horse
Main Street; A606 Stamford—Oakham; LE15 8PS

This big, well used, old stone-built dining pub is handy if you're visiting Rutland
Water. The bustling open-plan carpeted lounge bar has a big log fire below an
unusual free-standing chimney-funnel, and lots of fresh flowers. There are some
rustic tables among urns of flowers outside. Bar food includes soup (£3.25), garlic
mushrooms or cream cheese, walnut and celery pâté (£4.95), greek-style salad
(£8.25), ploughman's (£8.65), spicy vegetable crumble (£8.75), beef, mushroom
and ale pie (£8.95), fishcakes or home-made lasagne (£9.25), 10oz sirloin steak
with creamy stilton and bacon sauce (£14.95), and daily specials such as seared
scallops with tomato salsa (£5.75), chicken with celery and chervil cream sauce
(£9.95) and swordfish steak with ginger and sweet chilli dressing (£10.95). During
the afternoon they serve only sandwiches, baguettes and tea; most of the pub is no
smoking; TV, fruit machine and piped music. Well kept Adnams Best and Greene
King Abbot and Ruddles Best and possibly a guest such as Grainstore Triple B on
handpump, and around eight wines by the glass. Bedrooms are in a converted
stable block and they have wheelchair access. (Recommended by Duncan Cloud,
Fred Chamberlain, Howard and Margaret Buchanan, P S Hoyle, Barry Collett, Brian and
Ruth Archer, Paul and Annette Hallett, Martin and Sue Day, BOB, David Swift)

Enterprise ~ Lease Ian and Sarah Sharp ~ Real ale ~ Bar food (12-6, 7-9.30; 12-9 Sun) ~
(01780) 460221 ~ Children welcome away from bar ~ Dogs allowed in bedrooms ~
Open 11-11 ~ Bedrooms: £50B/£65B

EXTON SK9211 Map 7
Fox & Hounds 🍴
Signposted off A606 Stamford—Oakham; LE15 8AP

As the hospitable landlord at this handsome old country coaching inn is Italian, it's
not surprising that the menu includes quite a few italian dishes. As well as a vast
selection of handmade pizzas (Mon-Sat evenings only), in almost every combination
you could imagine (from £7.25), they have a good range of filled ciabattas or panini
(£5.95), and quite a few pasta and risotto dishes, such as tagliatelle with green
beans, pesto, potatoes and parmesan or gnocchi with butter, parmesan and sage
(£7.95) and fusilli with gorgonzola and walnuts (£8.25). Other very good well
presented food includes soup (£3.50), sandwiches (from £4.95), grilled halloumi
cheese on salad leaves (£4.25), sausages, mash and onion gravy (£8.95), lambs liver
and bacon (£9.75), fish pie (£10.25), gressingham duck breast with fruit of the
forest sauce (£11.95) and rack of lamb with apricots and rosemary (£11.25). The
comfortable high-ceilinged lounge bar is traditionally civilised, with some dark red
plush easy chairs, as well as wheelback seats around lots of pine tables, maps and
hunting prints on the walls, fresh flowers, a winter log fire in a large stone fireplace,
well kept Archers Best Bitter, Grainstore Ten Fifty, and Greene King IPA on
handpump, and a good range of wines by the glass; the restaurant and lounge are
no smoking; darts, dominoes, cribbage and piped music. Seats among large rose
beds on the pleasant well kept back lawn look out over paddocks, and the tranquil
village green with its tall trees out in front is most attractive. (Recommended by
Mike and Heather Watson, Colin McKerrow, A J W Smith, P Dawn, Roy Bromell, Bruce and
Penny Wilkie, Barry Collett, Jeff and Wendy Williams, A G Marx)

Free house ~ Licensees Valter and Sandra Floris ~ Real ale ~ Bar food (not Sun evening) ~
Restaurant ~ (01572) 812403 ~ Children welcome ~ Dogs allowed in bar ~ Open 11-3,
6-11; 12-3, 7-10.30 Sun ~ Bedrooms: £45B/£60(£70B)

KNOSSINGTON SK8008 Map 4

Fox & Hounds ⑪

Off A606 W of Oakham, taking Cold Overton Road out of Oakham just W of the railway crossing; Somerby Road; LE15 8LY

Though this handsome ivy-covered building is very much the village local, it's something more elaborate too, with the excellent food drawing in as many first-time visitors as regulars. At lunchtimes they do a particularly good two-course set menu for £9.95, with starters like stilton and broccoli soup or venison bresaola with parmesan, and main courses such as a tasty beef stew with lovely dumplings, pan-fried scallop salad or sausage and mash. Relying on seasonal local produce, the full menu might also include a tart of roasted aubergine, tomato, pepper and gorgonzola (£10.50), grilled salmon loin with thai green salad (£12.75), and roast chump of lamb with dauphinoise potatoes and buttered savoy (£16.25); two- or three-course Sunday lunches. The friendly staff take orders at the table – and bring fresh bread too; service is flexible, and they don't rush you at the end of the meal. Modernised in a simple, unfussy way, the relaxed knocked-through bar has a handful of big, light wooden tables, bright, stripy cushions on the wall-seats, a polished tiled floor, beams, and the odd standing timber; the windows are small so it's quite dimly lit, but pale green and cream painted walls help it feel lighter. There's a stuffed fox's head on one wall, and another stuffed animal next to a clock on the mantelpiece. At the opposite end is a more formal no smoking dining area, with another fireplace. They do bowls of olives at the bar, which has Fullers London Pride, Marstons Pedigree and a guest like Adnams on handpump. A big back garden has pétanque. They can get busy, so it may be worth booking, especially at weekends. (Recommended by Duncan Cloud, Barry Collett)

Free house ~ Licensees Brian Baker, Clare Ellis ~ Real ale ~ Bar food (12-2.30 (4 Sun), 7-9.30; not Sun evening; not Mon) ~ Restaurant ~ (01664) 454676 ~ Children welcome away from bar till 9pm ~ Dogs allowed in bar ~ Open 11-11; 12-10.30 Sun; closed 25 Dec

LONG CLAWSON SK7227 Map 7

Crown & Plough ♀ ◖

Village signposted off A606 NW of Melton Mowbray; East End; LE14 4NG

Reopened late in 2005 after attractive restoration, this is a good all-round pub. It's older than it looks from outside, dating from the 17th c, and dark flooring tiles, some strategic low bowed beams, stripped masonry and inglenooks have been exposed. Everything's been done with a careful eye to quality, so that the overall effect is of civilised good taste, with attractive fireplaces, carefully placed country prints on pastel walls, and a nice mix of chapel and country-kitchen chairs, cushioned pews and distinctive armed settles around unmatched scrubbed pine tables. There are also some comfortable armchairs and settees. The good enterprising food relies on local seasonal produce, and might include tempura mackerel niçoise (£5.50), chicken liver parfait and spiced poached figs (£5.75), pressed ham hock and foie gras terrine with blackberry dressing (£7.50), stilton risotto with wild mushrooms and asparagus (£12.50), cider-braised pork belly with black pudding, sage and bacon mash (£13), sirloin steak with béarnaise sauce (£16), half a lobster (£18.50), gooseberry fool with cinnamon shortbread or glazed lemon tart with raspberry sorbet (from £5); two-course lunch menu (£11.50). They bake their own bread, and make their own ice-creams. They have quickly changing real ales such as Adnams Sunflower, Everards Tiger, Hydes HPA and Marstons Pedigree on handpump, a good choice of reasonably priced wines by the glass, and decent coffee; service is welcoming and efficient. There are tables out in a sheltered courtyard. As we went to press they were working on six new bedrooms in the adjacent barn block; given the style of the place, we'd expect these to qualify for one of our Place to Stay Awards, and would be glad to hear from readers who have tried them. (Recommended by David Glynne-Jones)

W&D ~ Manager James Murphy ~ Real ale ~ Bar food (12-3, 5.30-9.30; not Sun evening or Mon) ~ Restaurant ~ (01664) 822322 ~ Children welcome ~ Dogs allowed in bar ~

Open 10-3, 5.30-11; 10am-1.30pm Sat; 10am-11pm Sun; closed Mon lunchtime ~
Bedrooms: /£80B

LYDDINGTON   SP8797   Map 4
Old White Hart 🍷
Village signposted off A6003 N of Corby; LE15 9LR

Attentive staff serving the particularly good food at this lovely old inn are caring
and friendly. As well as baguettes, the changing menu might include soup (£3.25),
salt and pepper duck wings with plum sauce (£5.95), seared foie gras with brioche
and figs (£8.95), roast pork with apple sauce or sausages wrapped in streaky bacon
with horseradish mash (£10.25), fillet steak (£16.95); side orders (from £2), with
puddings such as vanilla panna cotta with poached champagne rhubarb (£5.25)
and chocolate tart with orange sorbet (£6.25). Low ceilings, heavy bowed beams
and just four close-set tables in front of a glass shielded roaring log fire, in the softly
lit bar (the only place you can smoke) give it a welcoming local atmosphere. This
room opens into an attractive no smoking restaurant, and on the other side is
another tiled-floor room with rugs, lots of fine hunting prints, cushioned wall seats
and mate's chairs, and a woodburning stove. Greene King IPA, Abbot and Fullers
London Pride are well kept on handpump, and they may have freshly squeezed
orange juice; shove-ha'penny, cribbage and dominoes. Handy for Bede House, this
is a picturesque village with good nearby walks. The pretty walled garden (with
eight floodlit boules pitches) is very pleasant, and if you sit outside on Thursday
evening you may hear the church bell-ringers. *(Recommended by Duncan Cloud,
Jeff and Wendy Williams, Mr and Mrs G S Ayrton, Mike and Sue Loseby, Revd L and S Giller,
Ben and Helen Ingram, Mr and Mrs S Wilson, Barry Collett, Phil and Jane Hodson, Les and
Barbara Owen, Paul and Annette Hallett, Tracey and Stephen Groves, A G Marx)*

Free house ~ Licensees Stuart and Holly East ~ Real ale ~ Bar food (not Sun evening) ~
Restaurant ~ (01572) 821703 ~ Children welcome ~ Open 12-3, 6.30-11(7-10.30 Sun) ~
Bedrooms: £55B/£80B

MEDBOURNE   SP7993   Map 4
Nevill Arms ★ 🍽 £ 🛏
B664 Market Harborough—Uppingham; LE16 8EE

Readers enjoy the easy-going welcoming atmosphere, and good value food at this
handsome old inn. You get to it by a footbridge over the little duck-filled River
Welland, giving you time to take in its lovely stonework, imposing latticed
mullioned windows and large studded oak door. The inviting main bar has a
buoyant pubby feel, with a good mix of drinkers and diners, log fires in stone
fireplaces at either end, chairs and small wall settles around its tables, and a lofty
dark-joisted ceiling; a second smaller room has dark furniture and another open
fire; piped music. Much needed at busy times (it's worth getting here early), a
spacious back room by the former coachyard has pews around more tables, its own
bar, and children's toys. Popular traditional bar food includes sandwiches (from
£2.75; hot bacon and brie baguette £4.50), home-made soup (£2.95), filled baked
potatoes (from £3.95), ploughman's (£4.25), warm chicken salad, pork in honey
and ginger or asparagus and goats cheese parcel (£6.50), smoked haddock and
spinach bake (£6.95) and braised lamb shank (£7.95); friendly service. Well kept
Adnams Bitter, Fullers London Pride, Greene King Abbot and two changing guests
such as Nethergate on handpump, and about two dozen country wines; darts,
shove-ha'penny, cribbage, dominoes and carpet bowls. Look out for Truffles the
cat and the inquisitive great dane, Bertie. Seats outside by the dovecote overlook the
village green, and the church over the bridge is worth a visit. The bedrooms are in
two neighbouring cottages, and the first-class breakfasts are served in the pub's
sunny conservatory. *(Recommended by David and Ruth Hollands, David Field, Brian and
Jacky Wilson, Ian Stafford, P Dawn, the Didler, Mike and Sue Loseby, Rod and Chris Pring,
G Coates, Paul Humphreys, R T and J C Moggridge, Barry Collett, George Atkinson)*

Free house ~ Licensees Nicholas and Elaine Hall ~ Real ale ~ Bar food (12-2, 7-9.45) ~

(01858) 565288 ~ Children welcome ~ Dogs allowed in bar ~ Open 12-2.30(3 Sat), 6-11;
12-3, 7-10.30 Sun ~ Bedrooms: £50B/£65B

MOWSLEY SP6488 Map 4
Staff of Life ♀
Village signposted off A5199 S of Leicester; Main Street; LE17 6NT

Gleaming with polish, the roomy bar at this high-gabled early 20th-c house is quite
traditional with a panelled ceiling and comfortable seating, including some high-
backed settles on flagstones. The no smoking restaurant resembles a country barn;
piped music. They serve Banks and Marstons on handpump, and up to 15 wines by
the glass, but most people are here to enjoy the delicious food: one or two readers
mentioned that it wasn't cheap. As well as a good choice of lunchtime sandwiches
(£4.95), ploughman's (£5.95) and fish and chips or sausage and mash (£8.95), this
might include soup (£3.95), fried scallops with cream and basil thai noodles
(£7.95), pie of the day or parmesan potato cakes with wild mushrooms and spinach
and thai chive crème fraîche (£9.95), smoked pork belly with black pudding and
glazed apples with red wine gravy (£11.95), fried hake with tomato and garlic mash
with rocket purée and chorizo (£12.95) and beef fillet with red pesto and
caramelised shallots and tomatoes (£16.95); side orders (from £1.50). The rather
special puddings might include honeycomb and chocolate cheesecake or warm
blueberry and almond tart with white chocolate and apricot ice-cream (£4.95). The
back garden has a large pergola and teak furniture. *(Recommended by P Tailyour,
David Field, Ian Blackwell, Steph and Harry Short, Duncan Cloud, Phil and Jane Hodson,
Les and Barbara Owen, Gerry and Rosemary Dobson, Dennis and Gill Keen, Jeff and Wendy
Williams, Ian and Joan Blackwell)*

Free house ~ Licensee Spencer Farrell ~ Real ale ~ Bar food (12-2.30(3 Sun), 6.30-9.30
(6-8.30 Mon); 12-3 Sun; not Sun evening or Mon lunchtime) ~ Restaurant ~
(0116) 240 2359 ~ Children welcome but not in back garden ~ Open 12-3, 6-11; 12-10.30
Sun; closed Mon lunchtime except bank hols

NEWTON BURGOLAND SK3708 Map 4
Belper Arms
Village signposted off B4116 S of Ashby or B586 W of Ibstock; LE67 2SE

Although the original building has been very opened up, the many ancient interior
features, including heavy beams, changing floor levels and varying old floor and
wall materials, break this bustling place up into enjoyable little nooks and seating
areas. Parts are said to date back to the 13th c, and much of the exposed brickwork
certainly looks at least three or four hundred years old. A big freestanding central
chimney at the core of the building has a cottagey old black range on one side, and
open fire on the other, with chatty groups of nice old captain's chairs. There's
plenty to look at, from a suit of old chain mail, to a collection of pewter teapots,
some good antique furniture and, framed on the wall, the story of the pub ghost –
Five to Four Fred. They hold a beer festival during the August bank holiday, but
usually have well kept Marstons Pedigree, and three or four guests from brewers
such as Archers, Batemans and Wadworths on handpump, with ten wines by the
glass; piped music and dominoes. As well as lunchtime baguettes (from £5.50),
tasty bar food might include soup (£3.95), tempura prawns (£4.95), steak and ale
pie or curry of the day (£8.95), goats cheese gateau (£9.25), salmon fillet with sun-
dried tomato and basil (£11.75), sirloin steak (£11.95), and puddings such as
lemon meringue or chocolate fudge cake (£3.95); three-course Sunday lunch
(£11.95). The restaurant is very big, and service can slow down when they get busy.
A rambling garden has boules, cricket nets and a children's play area, and works its
way round the pub to teak tables and chairs on a terrace, and a steam-engine-
shaped barbecue; there's a good caravan site here too. *(Recommended by Derek and
Sylvia Stephenson, Duncan Cloud, C J Pratt, Dr and Mrs A K Clarke, the Didler, Mark Butler,
Michael Butler, Andy Chapman)*

Mercury Taverns ~ Manager Paul Jarvis ~ Real ale ~ Bar food (12-2.30, 7-9.30; 12-9.30

Fri-Sun) ~ Restaurant ~ (01530) 270530 ~ Children welcome ~ Dogs allowed in bar ~
Open 12-12(1 Fri, Sat)

OADBY   SK6200   Map 4
Cow & Plough ♨
Gartree Road (B667 N of centre); LE2 2FB

This interesting old place contains an extraordinary and ever-expanding collection
of brewery memorabilia, all lovingly assembled by the friendly landlord. The two
dark back rooms, known as the Vaults, are packed with items, and almost every
piece has a story behind it, from the enamel signs and mirrors advertising long-
forgotten brews, through the aged brass cash register, to the furnishings and fittings
salvaged from pubs and even churches (there's some splendid stained glass behind
the counter). The pub first opened about 16 years ago with just these cosily
individual rooms, but it soon tripled in size when an extensive long, light,
flagstoned conservatory was added to the front; it too has its share of brewery signs
and the like, as well as plenty of plants and fresh flowers, a piano, beams liberally
covered with hops, and a real mix of traditionally pubby tables and chairs, with lots
of green leatherette sofas, and small round cast-iron tables. One section has
descriptions of all Leicester's pubs. Named after the pub jack russell Billy, a star
feature here is the pair of Steamin Billy beers brewed for the landlord under licence
by Grainstore: Skydiver and Steamin Billy Bitter, which are well kept alongside a
good range of interesting guests such as Abbeydale Matins, Bartrams Bees Knees,
Fullers London Pride, Jennings and Oakham JHB, on handpump or tapped from
the cask; also six ciders and lots of country wines. Using local and organic
ingredients, the freshly prepared food might include huge lunchtime sandwiches
(from £3.95), home-made soup (£3.95), sweetcorn, chicken and parsnip fritters
with tomato salsa (£4.25), lamb steak braised in red wine and rosemary (£9.25),
battered cod and chips (£9.50) and chicken, spinach and wild mushroom roulade,
stuffed squid with indonesian sauce or sausage and mash (£9.95); they may offer an
early evening value meal and good value two-course lunches. The entire pub is no
smoking; piped music, darts, TV, shove-ha'penny, table skittles, bar billiards,
cribbage and dominoes. There are picnic-sets outside. *(Recommended by Duncan Cloud,
David Field, the Didler, Chris Evans, Barry Collett, John Fiander, Janice and Phil Waller)*

Free house ~ Licensee Barry Lount ~ Real ale ~ Bar food (12-3, 6-9 (not Mon evening);
12-5 Sun) ~ Restaurant ~ (0116) 272 0852 ~ Children in conservatory and restaurant ~
Dogs welcome ~ Jazz Sun and Weds ~ Open 11-111

OAKHAM   SK8508   Map 4
Grainstore ♨ £
Station Road, off A606; LE15 6RE

This somewhat masculine conversion of a three-storey Victorian grain station
warehouse is particularly popular for its own-brewed beers. Laid back or lively,
depending on the time of day, with noises of the brewery workings above, the
interior is plain and functional, with wide well worn bare floorboards, bare ceiling
boards above massive joists supported by red metal pillars, a long brick-built bar
counter with cast-iron bar stools, tall cask tables and simple elm chairs. Their fine
ales (they usually serve six of the full complement of nine) are served both
traditionally at the left end of the bar counter, and through swan necks with
sparklers on the right; the friendly staff are happy to give you samples. Decent good
value pubby food includes sandwiches, soup, baguettes, baked potatoes or burgers
(from £3.95), sausage and mash or chilli (£5.95) and burger, ploughman's, steak
and ale pie or all-day breakfast (£6.95). In summer they pull back the huge glass
doors that open on to a terrace with picnic-sets, often stacked with barrels; sporting
events on TV, fruit machine, bar billiards, cribbage, dominoes, darts, giant Jenga
and bottle-walking; disabled access. You can tour the brewery by arrangement,
they do take-aways, and hold a real ale festival with over 65 real ales and lots of
live music during the August bank holiday weekend. *(Recommended by Barry Collett,*

P Dawn, the Didler, Mike and Sue Loseby, Ian Stafford, Derek and Sylvia Stephenson, Di and Mike Gillam, J M Tansey, Tracey and Stephen Groves)

Own brew ~ Licensee Tony Davis ~ Real ale ~ Bar food (12-2.30; not evenings or Sun) ~ (01572) 770065 ~ Children welcome till 8pm ~ Dogs allowed in bar ~ Live jazz monthly Sun afternoon and blues and rock monthly Sun evening ~ Open 11-11(12 Sat)

PEGGS GREEN   SK4117   Map 7

New Inn £

Signposted off A512 Ashby—Shepshed at roundabout, then Newbold sign down Zion Hill; LE67 8JE

You really do have the sense that you've been welcomed into the home of the wholehearted Irish family who run this unspoilt little pub when you visit here. The laid-back friendly atmosphere, and group of regulars putting the world to rights around the old-fashioned booth bar, give it a lovely timeless and very human feel. Its two cosy tiled front rooms have an incredible collection of old bric-a-brac (it'll keep you busy for ages) which covers almost every inch of the walls and ceilings. The little room on the left, a bit like a kitchen parlour (they call it the Cabin), has china on the mantelpiece above a warm coal fire, lots of prints and photographs and little collections of this and that, three old cast-iron tables, wooden stools and a small stripped kitchen table. The room to the right has quite nice stripped panelling, and masses more appealing bric-a-brac. The small back 'Best' room, with a stripped wooden floor, has a touching display of old local photographs including some colliery ones. They serve filled baps all day (from £1.40), but otherwise, note the limited food serving times below. The very good value menu includes wholesome faggots and peas (£3.95), corned beef hash (£4.50), smoked haddock fillets or lasagne (£4.75) and a couple of specials such as fish bake (£4.50) or chicken, bacon and mushroom pie (£4.75); the licensees tell us they are thinking of allowing customers to bring in take-aways on the evenings when they don't serve food, but please check first if you plan to do so. Bass, Caledonian Deuchars IPA and Marstons Pedigree are well kept on handpump; piped music, cribbage and dominoes. There are tables out in the attractive cottage garden, which has a big lawn with plenty of room for children to let off steam. *(Recommended by Derek and Sylvia Stephenson, OPUS, the Didler, John Fiander, Robin and Tricia Walker, Peter and Jean Hoare, Ian and Joan Blackwell)*

Enterprise ~ Lease Maria Christina Kell ~ Real ale ~ Bar food (12-2; 6-8 Mon; not Tues-Sat evenings; not Sun) ~ No credit cards ~ (01530) 222293 ~ Well behaved children welcome ~ Dogs allowed in bar ~ Open 12-2.30, 5.30-11; 12-3, 6.30-11(7-10.30 Sun) Sat

SOMERBY   SK7710   Map 7

Stilton Cheese ✦

High Street; off A606 Oakham—Melton Mowbray, via Cold Overton, or Leesthorpe and Pickwell; can also be reached direct from Oakham via Knossington; LE14 2QB

Readers enjoy the cheery traditional welcome, reasonably priced tasty food and jolly decent range of beers at this bustling 17th-c village pub – even when very busy, the friendly staff make time for a chat. The comfortable hop-strung beamed bar/lounge has dark carpets, lots of country prints on its stripped stone walls, a collection of copper pots, a stuffed badger and plenty of restful seats. Five handpumps serve Grainstore Ten Fifty, Marstons Pedigree, Tetleys and a couple of thoughtfully sourced ales from brewers such as Belvoir and Brewsters, and they've cider on handpump, and over 25 malt whiskies; shove-ha'penny, cribbage and dominoes. The wide range of changing bar food includes soup (£2.95), stilton and cranberry parcels (£4.25), grilled sardines with garlic butter or smoked salmon and mascarpone roulade (£4.75), wild mushroom risotto (£6.95), game pie or rack of lamb with mint and redcurrant glaze (£7.95), duck breast with orange and ginger sauce (£8.45), plaice and spinach roulade with prawn butter sauce (£9.95), and good old-fashioned puddings such as ginger and walnut treacle tart, sherry trifle, and chocolate sponge with chocolate sauce (£3.25). The Farmers Bar is no smoking. There are seats and outdoor heaters on the terrace. *(Recommended by Rona Murdoch, I J and S A Bufton, Anthony Barnes, Robert Turnham, George Tucker, Phil and Jane Hodson, JJW, CMW, Derek and Sylvia Stephenson)*

Free house ~ Licensees Carol and Jeff Evans ~ Real ale ~ Bar food (12-2, 6-9) ~ (01664) 454394 ~ Children welcome ~ Dogs allowed in bedrooms ~ Open 12-3, 6(7 Sun)-11 ~ Bedrooms: £30/£40

Three Crowns 🍷 £

Off A606 Oakham—Melton Mowbray, via Cold Overton, or Leesthorpe and Pickwell; can also be reached direct from Oakham via Knossington; High Street; LE14 2PZ

You can get a very good value meal at this homely family run pub, especially on Tuesday and Friday when they do their two meals for £8 offer. They also do a two-course OAP lunch Wednesdays and Thursdays for £4.50, and their two-course Sunday lunch is only £5.95. Straightforward but tasty dishes include soup (£2.25), sandwiches (from £2.95), garlic mushrooms (£3.75), ploughman's or home-made vegetable curry (£4.95) and home-made steak and ale pie (£5.95), with puddings such as fruit pies (£2.50). The comfortable main bar has a happy mix of old-fashioned dining chairs around dark oak tables, and a good log fire in the big stone fireplace. Brick arches separate this room from the no smoking dining room. Bass, Greene King IPA, and Parish Bitter (brewed nearby) are well kept on handpump, and they hold a beer festival in May; fruit machine, darts, TV and piped music. An enclosed garden has benches and white plastic tables. As we went to press they were just finishing the refurbished bedrooms so couldn't give us a rate, but please write and tell us how you find them if you stay here. *(Recommended by Ian Stafford, Barry Collett, Phil and Jane Hodson, O K Smyth)*

Free house ~ Licensees Wendy and Mick Farmer ~ Real ale ~ Bar food (12-2, 7(6 Fri)-9 (5-7 Sun)) ~ Restaurant ~ (01664) 454777 ~ Children welcome ~ Dogs allowed in bar and bedrooms ~ Live bands first Sat in month ~ Open 12-2.30, 6.30(5.30 Fri)-11; 12-10.30 Sun ~ Bedrooms

STATHERN SK7731 Map 7
Red Lion 🍴 🍷 🍺

Off A52 W of Grantham via the brown-signed Belvoir road (keep on towards Harby – Stathern signposted on left); or off A606 Nottingham—Melton Mowbray via Long Clawson and Harby; LE14 4HS

Under the same ownership as the Olive Branch in Clipsham, and run along the same rather civilised lines and to the same high standards, this very popular dining pub, though placing much emphasis on the imaginative food, does nevertheless offer a splendid range of drinks too. Grainstore Olive Oil and changing guests such as Batemans XB, Greene King Abbot and Shepherd Neame Spitfire are well kept on handpump, alongside draught belgian beer and continental bottled beers, several ciders, a varied wine list with around a dozen by the glass, winter mulled wine and summer home-made lemonade. As at the Olive Tree, great care goes into the delicious bar food. Ingredients are sourced locally, they smoke their own meats, make their own preserves and pickles, and even have a kitchen shop where you can buy produce and fully prepared dishes. The changing menu might include soup (£3.95), smoked chicken caesar or coconut tempura prawns with sweet chilli dip (£5.95), main course £11.25), thai sweet potato curry with home-made naan bread or fish and chips with tartare sauce (£9.75), sausages with onion gravy (£9.75), sautéed calves liver with rösti, braised red cabbage and crispy bacon (£13.95), honey-glazed duck breast with beetroot mash, creamed leeks and caramelised apples (£14.95), baked halibut with chive mash and roast lobster bisque (£17.50), and puddings such as glazed lemon tart with raspberry sorbet, white chocolate cheesecake or vanilla crème brûlée with mixed berry compote (from £5.50). There's a relaxed country pub feel to the yellow room on the right, and a relaxing lounge has sofas, a fireplace, and a big table with books, paper and magazines; it leads off the smaller, more traditional flagstoned bar, with terracotta walls, another fireplace with a pile of logs beside it, and lots of beams and hops. Dotted around are various oddities picked up by one of the licensees on visits to Newark Antiques Fair: some unusual lambing chairs for example, and a collection of wooden spoons. A little room with tables set for eating leads to the long, narrow main dining room in what was once the pub's skittle alley, and out to a nicely arranged suntrap garden, with good hardwood furnishings spread over its lawn and terrace, and an unusually big play area behind the car park, with swings, climbing frames and so on. *(Recommended by David Glynne-Jones, Richard, Chris Evans, MP, Ian Stafford, Nazeer Chowdhury, Mr and Mrs Richard Osborne, Les and Barbara Owen, Peter and Jean Hoare, Bill and Marian de Bass)*

Free house ~ Licensees Sean Hope, Ben Jones, Marcus Welford ~ Real ale ~ Bar food (12-2, 7(6 Sat)-9.30; 12-4 Sun) ~ Restaurant ~ (01949) 860868 ~ Children welcome ~ Dogs allowed in bar ~ Open 12-3, 6-11; 12-11 Fri, Sat; 12-6.30 Sun; closed Sun evening

STRETTON SK9415 Map 8
Jackson Stops 🍴 ♀

Rookery Road; a mile or less off A1, at B668 (Oakham) exit; follow village sign, turning off Clipsham road into Manor Road, pub on left; LE15 7RA

Most customers visit this lovely old farmhouse for its superb interesting food. It's all beautifully presented, and might include minestrone with dark truffle oil (£4.50), pressed ham hock and mustard terrine with poached egg and hollandaise or filo baked camembert with rocket and pine nut salad (£5.50), deep-fried crab cake with sweet chilli sauce (£6.50), chicken parmigiana with pasta and tomato sauce (£10.95), roasted beetroot risotto with grilled goats cheese (£11.95), calves liver with pea purée and crisp onions (£12.95), whole lemon sole with nut brown butter (£13.50), half a roast duck with sautéed savoy cabbage and orange jus (£13.95), and puddings like pear tart tatin or hot chocolate fondant with white chocolate ice-cream (from £4.50). The thoughtful wine range includes around ten good wines by the glass, several enterprising half-bottles of pudding wine, and late-bottled vintage port by the glass, and the Oakham JHB and Timothy Taylors Landlord on handpump are very well kept. Down on the left, a homely black beamed country bar has some timbering in its ochre walls, just a couple of bar stools, a cushioned stripped wall pew and an elderly settle on its worn tile and brick floor, with a coal fire in the corner. The smarter main room, on the right, is light and airy, carpeted in dark blue, its stone walls mainly painted canary, and its half dozen well spaced stripped tables nicely mixing ancient and modern, with linen napkins in rings, big steel platters, and lit candles in brass sticks. This has another smokeless coal fire in its stone corner fireplace, and a couple of striking modern oils alongside a few tastefully disposed farm tools. Right along past the bar is a second dining room, older in style, with stripped stone walls, tiled floor, and an old open cooking range. Three dining rooms are no smoking. The unobtrusive piped music in the main dining room doesn't disturb the chatty and relaxed atmosphere. Service is efficient and attentive without being intrusive. As you might guess from the inn sign, this used to be called the White Horse; it got its present name years ago from an estate agent's sign, when it was waiting for a buyer. *(Recommended by M and C Thompson, B and M Kendall, Heather Couper, Malcolm and Jane Levitt, Robert Naylor)*

Free house ~ Licensee James Trevor ~ Real ale ~ Bar food (12-2, 7-10) ~ Restaurant ~ (01780) 410237 ~ Children in restaurant ~ Dogs allowed in bar ~ Open 12-2.30, 6.30-11; 12-3 Sun; closed Sun evening, Mon

Ram Jam Inn ♀ 🛏

Just off A1: heading N, look out for warning signs some 8 miles N of Stamford, turning off at big inn sign through service station close to B668; heading S, look out for B668 Oakham turn-off, inn well signed on left ¼ mile after roundabout; LE15 7QX

This big clean and comfortable dining stop is very handy if you're on the A1 as they serve food all day. It's recently been bought by a corporate chain so we're keeping our fingers crossed for it. As you go in, the first part of the big open-plan bar/dining area has terracotta-coloured walls decorated in one place with a spread of old breadboards, bentwood chairs and café tables, and sofas in a cosy panelled alcove with daily papers and a standard lamp. The counter on the left here has Greene King IPA and Marstons Pedigree on handpump, good house wines with about 11 by the glass, freshly squeezed orange juice and excellent fresh-ground coffee; faint piped music. This area spreads on back to a no smoking oak-boarded part with old prints and maps, more bentwood chairs, dining chairs, and (by a woodburning stove) another sofa and some wicker armchairs. On the right is a more formal dining layout, also no smoking, with big solid tables and attractive mediterranean photoprints by Georges Meris. Straightforward food might include light meals such as soup with home-made bread (£3.50), chicken liver pâté (£4.25), panini or door-step sandwiches (from £3.95), steakburger or penne and tomato sauce (£6.95), local sausages and mash (£8.95) and rib-eye steak (£12.95). *(Recommended by J F M and M West, Eithne Dandy, Comus and Sarah Elliott, Paul and Ursula Randall, John Coatsworth)*

London and Edinburgh Inns ~ Manager Julie Kirk ~ Real ale ~ Bar food (12-9.30; breakfast 7-11.30) ~ Restaurant ~ (01780) 410776 ~ Children welcome away from bar ~ Open 11-11; 12-10.30 Sun ~ Bedrooms: £52B/£62B

SWITHLAND   SK5413   Map 7
Griffin 🍺
Main Street; between A6 and B5330, between Loughborough and Leicester; LE12 8TJ

There's a sound family run atmosphere, decent food and a good choice of real ales at this attractively converted stone-built pub, which is handy for Bradgate Country Park, and walks in Swithland woods. The cheery landlord, friendly locals and helpful staff generate a happy village feel in the beamed communicating rooms, which have some panelling, and a nice mix of wooden tables and chairs and bar stools. Everards Beacon, Original and Tiger are well kept on handpump, with three guests such as Adnams, Bath Barnstormer and Marstons Pedigree. Also quite a few malt whiskies and a good wine list. Sensibly priced bar food includes a melton mowbray pork pie (£3.75), soup (£3.95), filled baguettes (from £2.75; steak and stilton £5.90), ploughman's (from £5.25), pie of the day (£7.95), trio of local sausages with onion gravy (£7.95), wild mushroom risotto (£8.50), medallions of pork tenderloin with apple mash (£9.25), steaks (from £10.95), and daily specials like chicken liver pâté (£4.50), battered haddock (£7.35), roast mediterranean vegetables with goats cheese (£8.95), and puddings such as treacle sponge or double mint and chocolate terrine (£3.95). The restaurant is no smoking. They also do cream teas and have speciality theme evenings; piped music, board games and skittle alley. The garden, overlooking open fields, is by a stream. *(Recommended by Duncan Cloud, BOB, Pete Baker, Brian and Ruth Archer, Phil and Jane Hodson, Chris Moore)*

Everards ~ Tenant John Cooledge ~ Real ale ~ Bar food (11-10; 12-8(9 in summer) Sun) ~ Restaurant ~ (01509) 890535 ~ Well supervised children welcome ~ Open 11-11; 12-10.30 Sun

THORPE LANGTON   SP7492   Map 4
Bakers Arms 🍴
Village signposted off B6047 N of Market Harborough; LE16 7TS

Emphasis at this well run, civilised pub is very much on the beautifully prepared imaginative food – it's definitely the place for a special meal out rather than a quick drink, and as the opening hours are somewhat limited, it is pretty essential to book well in advance. Dishes could include home-made soup (£4.50), mediterranean vegetable tartlet with goats cheese and pesto dressing (£5.95), fried scallops with black pudding and orange sauce (£7.95), baked avocado with confit of red onions and brie (£11.50), pork fillet filled with mozzarella and sage served with tomato jus (£11.95), stuffed chicken wrapped in parma ham (£13.50), calves liver with shallot and red wine jus (£14.95), halibut on mustard tagliatelle (£15.95), and puddings such as sticky toffee pudding or vanilla brûlée with orange in Cointreau and orange tuile biscuit (£4.50). Stylishly simple old-fashioned furnishings in the knocked-through cottagey beamed interior include stripped pine tables and oriental rugs on bare boards, and nice black and white photographs; no games or piped music. They've a good wine list with around five by the glass, well kept Langton Brewery Bakers Dozen on handpump, and in winter they do mulled wine too; the staff are friendly and attentive. There are picnic-sets in the garden. *(Recommended by Duncan Cloud, Gerry and Rosemary Dobson, Mike and Sue Loseby, P Tailyour, Les and Barbara Owen)*

Free house ~ Licensee Kate Hubbard ~ Real ale ~ Restaurant ~ (01858) 545201 ~ Children over 12 welcome ~ Open 6.30-11; 12-2.30, 6.30-11 Sat; 12-2.30 Sun; closed lunchtime Tues-Fri, Sun evening, Mon

WING SK8903 Map 4
Kings Arms ♀ ⇔
Village signposted off A6003 S of Oakham; Top Street; LE15 8SE

Even with its few modern touches, the attractively refurbished bar at this neatly kept 17th-c inn has a cosy traditional feel, with its origins showing in nice old beams, stripped stone and flagstone floors. Two large log fires, one in a copper-canopied central hearth, keep it cosy in winter. Friendly, helpful staff serve over 20 wines by the glass, as well as Grainstore Cooking, Marstons Pedigree, Timothy Taylors Landlord and possibly a guest on handpump; piped music and board games. The restaurant is no smoking. Bar food (one or two readers felt it wasn't cheap) might include mussels steamed in Pernod, white wine and cream (£5), burger or sausage and mash (£8.50), fish and chips (£10.50), seared bass and king scallops in lime, ginger and chilli with oriental vegetable and egg noodle stir fry or calves liver with pancetta, roast garlic, onions and sauté potatoes (£14.50), fillet steak with roasted shallots (£18.50), and puddings including tempting home-made ice-creams (£3), winter fruit and nut crumble (£3.50) and ginger and vanilla panna cotta with berry compote (£5.50); they may stay open all day if they are busy. There are seats out in front, and more in the sunny yew-sheltered garden, and there's a medieval turf maze just up the road. *(Recommended by Mrs Diane M Hall, Mark Farrington, Anthony R Locke, Ben and Helen Ingram, Derek and Sylvia Stephenson, Sally and Dave Bates, Jackie Coaker, Barry Collett, Di and Mike Gillam, Duncan Cloud, Robert F Smith, Michael Sargent, J S Rutter)*

Free house ~ Licensee David Goss ~ Real ale ~ Bar food (12-2, 6.30-9) ~ Restaurant ~ (01572) 737634 ~ Well supervised children welcome ~ Open 12-3, 6.30-11; closed Mon lunchtime ~ Bedrooms: £65B/£75B

LUCKY DIP

Besides the fully inspected pubs, you might like to try these Lucky Dips recommended to us and described by readers (if you do, please send us reports: www.goodguides.co.uk).

BARKBY [SK6309]
Malt Shovel LE7 3QG [Main St]: Thriving, civilised and friendly old village pub with U-shaped bar and no smoking room off, Greene King Abbot, Marstons Bitter and Pedigree, Tetleys and a guest beer, farm cider, fine choice of good value food; garden, hanging baskets galore and partly covered heated terrace *(Brian and Ruth Archer)*

BARNSDALE [SK9008]
☆ *Barnsdale Lodge* LE15 8AB [just off A606 Oakham—Stamford]: Hotel's extensive conservatory dining bar with good food choice, inventive, generous and attractively presented, charming décor, friendly attentive staff, good if not cheap range of real ales, pleasant sitting-roomish coffee lounge, cream teas; nice gardens, comfortable and attractive bedrooms, good breakfast, adjacent antiques centre and handy for Barnsdale Gardens *(BB, John and Sylvia Harrop)*

BARROW UPON SOAR [SK5716]
☆ *Navigation* LE12 8LQ [off South St (B5328)]: Good value freshly made standard food inc good baguettes and Sun roast in extended split-level pub based on former barge-horse stabling, good warm atmosphere, keen friendly licensees, changing ales such as local Belvoir, Marstons Pedigree and Timothy Taylors Landlord, daily papers, central open fire, unusual bar top made from old pennies, old local photographs, darts, skittle alley, family room; piped music, SkyTV, games machine; lovely canal view from small back terrace with

moorings, open all day *(Duncan Cloud, Comus and Sarah Elliott, Gwyn and Anne Wake, Brian and Ruth Archer)*

BELMESTHORPE [TF0410]
☆ *Blue Bell* PE9 4JG [Village signposted off A16 just E of Stamford]: This quaint olde-worlde beamed village pub was open for only very limited hours, and on the market as we went to press; no food; news please *(LYM)*

BELTON [SK4420]
Queens Head LE12 9TP [the one nr Loughborough, not the one over in Rutland; off A512/A453 between junctions 23 and 24, M1; Long St]: Former coaching inn with emphasis on up-to-date enjoyable food from ciabattas to popular lunches and imaginative blackboard dishes in log-fire dining area and more formal restaurant (not Sun evening), minimalist décor and leather seating, two bare-boards bar areas, Fullers London Pride, good wines and proper coffee, friendly uniformed staff; tables out on decking and lawn, attractive village, six bedrooms *(Derek and Sylvia Stephenson, Duncan Cloud, Sheelagh and John Morgan)*

BIRSTALL [SK5908]
Mulberry Tree LE4 4EF [White Horse Lane]: Relaxed and informal contemporary refurbishment, enjoyable food and good service, no smoking restaurant; disabled access, dogs welcome, tables in riverside garden, open all day *(Linda and John Backhouse)*

BRAUNSTON [SK8306]
☆ *Old Plough* LE15 8QT [off A606 in Oakham; Church St]: Welcoming black-beamed pub, comfortably opened up, with log fire, some emphasis on the beer side (not just their good Grainstore and fine range of guest ales, but beer-based dishes among their enjoyable food, and specific beers recommended for some dishes), friendly staff, appealing back dining conservatory (children allowed); tables in sheltered garden *(Barry Collett, LYM, Duncan Cloud)*

BRUNTINGTHORPE [SP6089]
☆ *Joiners Arms* LE17 5QH [Church Walk/Cross St]: More bistro restaurant than pub, largely no smoking, with good imaginative up-to-date food and popular Sun lunches in three beamed areas of open-plan dining lounge, Greene King IPA from small bar counter, good value wines, good friendly service, lots of china and brasses; cl Sun evening and Mon *(Jeff and Wendy Williams, Mike and Brenda Roberts)*

BUCKMINSTER [SK8822]
Tollemache Arms NG33 5SA [Main St]: Large rambling stone-built pub, recently refurbished to give smart open-plan bar with tables, chairs and a couple of sofas on its stripped boards, running into stylish and comfortable restaurant with interesting trendily presented food, good if not cheap (and veg extra), Grainstore real ale, friendly attentive staff; newly refurbished bedrooms, pretty village *(Barry Collett)*

BURBAGE [SP4294]
Anchor LE10 2DA [High St]: Open-plan red plush lounge with real ales such as Belhaven St Andrews, Hook Norton Old Hooky and

Marstons Pedigree, friendly staff, back dining area; side room with TV; garden behind, pleasant village *(Rona Murdoch)*

BURTON OVERY [SP6797]
☆ *Bell* LE8 9DL [Main St]: Interesting choice of consistently good food using local produce in welcoming L-shaped open-plan bar and newish dining room, Adnams, Bass, Greene King Old Speckled Hen and Marstons Pedigree, good log fire, comfortable settees, darts and games machine round corner; children welcome, good garden, lovely village, open all day wknds *(David Crews, Mrs L Aquilina, R L Borthwick)*

CASTLE DONINGTON [SK4426]
Nags Head DE74 2PS [Diseworth Rd/Hill Top; A453, S end]: Low-beamed bistro pub with wide food choice from lunchtime filled rolls and baked potatoes to more elaborate and expensive dishes, Banks's and related beers, good range of wines by the glass, large airy dining area with open-view kitchen, quarry-tiled bar opening into smaller back dining room; may be piped music *(Dave Braisted, Robert Garner, LYM)*

CHURCH LANGTON [SP7293]
Langton Arms LE16 7SY [B6047 about 3 miles N of Mkt Harborough; just off A6]: Civilised extended village pub with good choice of pubby food, friendly efficient service, Greene King IPA and Abbot or Ruddles County, decent wines, no smoking in restaurant or small side eating area; piped music, bar can be smoky; garden with play area *(Gerry and Rosemary Dobson, David Field)*

COTTESMORE [SK9013]
☆ *Sun* LE15 7DH [B668 NE of Oakham]: 17th-c thatched and stone-built village pub with stripped pine furnishings, inglenook log fire, good atmosphere and friendly service, Adnams Best, Everards Tiger and a couple of guest beers, bar food from lunchtime sandwiches up, one no smoking dining area; dogs and children welcome in bar, terrace tables, open all day wknds *(Derek and Sylvia Stephenson, LYM, Mrs Hazel Rainer)*

CROPSTON [SK5411]
Badgers Sett LE7 7GQ [Reservoir Rd]: Vintage Inn locally popular for good beers and wines by the glass and wide choice of food all day, efficient friendly staff, log fires; nice garden *(Adrian Johnson)*

CROXTON KERRIAL [SK8329]
Peacock NG32 1QR [A607 SW of Grantham]: New management (they say the ghost of a former landlord plays up when there are staff changes) in much modernised 17th-c former coaching inn, some emphasis on enjoyable straightforward food using good ingredients in big open-plan bare boards beamed bar with chunky stripped tables and separate small simple dining room and garden room, good service, real ales such as local Belvoir Star, decent wines, log fire; well behaved children welcome, picnic-sets in inner courtyard and pleasant sloping garden with views, bedroom block with own bathrooms *(John Wooll, Phil and Jane Hodson, BB)*

DADLINGTON [SP4097]

Dog & Hedgehog CV13 6JB [The Green]:
Comfortably extended, with friendly landlord,
attentive staff, emphasis on very wide choice of
generous sensibly priced food inc fish,
enormous grills and wkdy bargains, real ales
such as Chapel End and Hook Norton Old
Hooky, great views over Ashby Canal and
Bosworth Field; may be piped pop music
(Rob and Catherine Dunster, C J Pratt)

EAST LANGTON [SP7292]

Bell LE16 7TW [Off B6047; Main St]:
Appealing country pub with long low ceilinged
stripped-stone beamed bar, woodburning
stove, plain wooden tables; also tables on
sloping front lawn and good monthly changing
bar menu; new licensees may continue brewing
the well kept Langton Caudle produced in an
outbuilding here; good bedrooms *(P Tailyour,
Gerry and Rosemary Dobson, David Field,
John Saville, LYM, R V Peel, Brian and
Ruth Archer, Duncan Cloud, Mrs L Aquilina,
G Coates, Mr and Mrs S Oxenbury, Rob and
Catherine Dunster)*

FOXTON [SP6989]

Foxton Locks LE16 7RA [Foxton Locks, off
A6 3m NW of Market Harborough (park by
bridge 60/62 and walk)]: Reopened 2005 after
extensive rebuilding as joint venture by British
Waterways and Scottish & Newcastle, large no
smoking L-shaped bar with further room off,
usual food from baguettes up, prompt efficient
service, half a dozen real ales such as
Caledonian Deuchars IPA, Fullers London
Pride and Theakstons; picnic-sets on large
raised terrace and decking with canvas awning,
steps down to more picnic-sets on safely railed
waterside lawn – nice setting at foot of long
flight of canal locks *(Gerry and
Rosemary Dobson)*

GLASTON [SK8900]

☆ *Old Pheasant* LE15 9BP [A47 Leicester—
Peterborough, E of Uppingham]: Attractively
refurbished stone-built former Monckton
Arms, good interesting home-made food inc
some local produce, Greene King and a guest
beer from central servery, nice choice of wines
by the glass, spacious bar with alcoves, big
woodburner in inglenook and some
comfortable leather armchairs, restaurant;
children welcome, picnic-sets on sheltered
terrace, comfortable modern bedrooms
*(Barry Collett, LYM, Mike and
Margaret Banks)*

GREETHAM [SK9314]

☆ *Wheatsheaf* LE15 7NP [B668 Stretton—
Cottesmore]: Some comfortable new wicker
seating and new pictures in linked L-shaped
rooms, wide choice of good value generous
food, John Smiths and Tetleys, friendly service,
blazing open stove; soft piped music, end
games room with darts, pool and TV; dogs
welcome, wheelchair access, picnic-sets out on
front lawn and in tidy garden by back car park
beside pretty little stream, boules, popular
annexe bedrooms, open all day Sat
*(Michael and Jenny Back, BB, David and
Brenda Tew)*

GRIMSTON [SK6821]

☆ *Black Horse* LE14 3BZ [off A6006 W of
Melton Mowbray; Main St]: Proper village
pub thriving under new owners, welcoming
bar with Adnams and Marstons Pedigree, wide
choice of good value wholesome food inc
pigeon, lamb and hot-pot, log fire, darts;
attractive village with stocks and 13th-c church
(LYM, David Barnes)

GUMLEY [SP6890]

☆ *Bell* LE16 7RU [NW of Market Harboro;
Main St]: Cheerful neatly kept beamed village
pub with traditional country décor, good value
straightforward food (not Mon evening) from
sandwiches to steaks inc popular OAP
bargains, a good Sun lunch and splendid bread
and butter pudding, real ales such as Batemans
XB, Greene King IPA and Youngs, good soft
drinks choice, helpful friendly staff, open fire,
darts and cribbage, small no smoking dining
room (children over 5 allowed here),
interesting cricket memorabilia in lobby; pretty
terrace garden (not for children or dogs),
cl Sun evening *(P Tailyour, BB, Barry Collett,
George Atkinson, BB)*

HALLATON [SP7896]

☆ *Bewicke Arms* LE16 8UB [off B6047 or
B664]: Welcoming old thatched pub with
sensibly priced food from sandwiches to steak
and restaurant dishes, Adnams, Fullers and
Archers or Grainstore, friendly attentive
young staff, log fires, scrubbed pine tables,
orange paintwork, some interesting
memorabilia about the ancient local Easter
Monday inter-village bottle-kicking match;
darts, shove-ha'penny, piped music; children
in eating areas, stables tearoom/gift shop
across yard, big terrace overlooking paddock
and lake, bedrooms, open all day Sun
*(George Atkinson, Edmund Coan, Stuart and
Alison Ballantyne, David Field, LYM,
Duncan Cloud)*

Fox LE16 8UJ [North End]: Country pub with
good value food and wine, Bass and Tetleys,
compact no smoking dining room; children
welcome, sizeable attractive garden with duck
pond and playthings *(Barry Collett,
David Field)*

HATHERN [SK5021]

Dew Drop LE12 5HY [Loughborough Rd
(A6)]: Friendly traditional two-room beamed
local with Hardys & Hansons Bitter and Mild,
plenty of malt whiskies, coal fire, darts and
dominoes; tables outside *(the Didler)*

HEMINGTON [SK4527]

Jolly Sailor DE74 2RB [Main St]: Cheerful
village local with enjoyable fresh bar food
(not wkdy evenings or Sun), Bass, Marstons
Pedigree and two guest beers, summer farm
cider, decent wines by the glass, good range of
malt whiskies and other spirits, good log
fire each end, big country pictures, bric-a-
brac on heavy beams and shelves, candlelit
back restaurant Fri/Sat night, table skittles;
quiet piped music, games machines;
beautiful hanging baskets and picnic-sets
out in front, open all day wknds
(the Didler)

ILLSTON ON THE HILL [SP7099]

☆ *Fox & Goose* LE7 9EG [Main St, off B6047 Mkt Harboro—Melton]: Welcoming and individual two-bar local, plain, comfortable and convivial, with interesting pictures and assorted oddments, Everards ales and a guest beer, table lamps, good coal fire, no food *(LYM, the Didler)*

KEGWORTH [SK4826]

Britannia DE74 2EU [London Rd]: Friendly new management, wide choice of well priced food, Hardys & Hansons ales *(M J Winterton, the Didler)*

Red Lion DE74 2DA [a mile from M1 junction 24, via A6 towards Loughborough; High St]: Half a dozen or more good changing real ales and good range of whiskies and vodkas in four brightly lit traditional rooms around small servery, limited choice of good wholesome food (not Sun), assorted furnishings, coal and flame-effect fires, delft shelf of beer bottles, daily papers, darts and cards, no smoking family room; picnic-sets in small back yard, garden with play area, well equipped bedrooms with own bathrooms, open all day *(the Didler, BB, Pete Baker, G Coates, M J Winterton)*

KIBWORTH BEAUCHAMP [SP6894]

Coach & Horses LE8 0NN [A6 S of Leicester]: Popular turkey-carpeted local with friendly efficient staff, wide choice of good honest home-made food at very reasonable prices (mainly roasts on Sun), real ales such as Bass and Fullers London Pride, china and pewter mugs on beams, relaxing candlelit restaurant, no piped music *(P Tailyour, BB)*

KILBY [SP6295]

Dog & Gun LE18 3TD [Main St, off A5199 S of Leicester]: Welcoming much-extended pub locally popular for wide choice of enjoyable straightforward food from baguettes up, helpful service, Bass, Greene King Abbot, Marstons Pedigree and Websters (also the name of the lovely white cat), good wine choice, coal fire, attractive no smoking side restaurant with grandfather clock; disabled access, colourful back garden with terrace and pergola *(Michael and Jenny Back, Duncan Cloud)*

KNIPTON [SK8231]

☆ *Manners Arms* NG32 1RH [signed off A607 Grantham—Melton Mowbray; Croxton Rd]: Handsome Georgian hunting lodge beautifully renovated by the Duke and Duchess of Rutland, hunting prints and furniture from their Belvoir Castle, log fire, light bar dishes, changing guest beers and good choice of wines by the glass, wide range of interesting food using local produce in sizeable stylish restaurant with attractive conservatory, impeccable service, sumptuous lounge; open all day, terrace with ornamental pool, lovely views over pretty village, ten comfortable individually furnished bedrooms *(Tom and Marie Heffernan, BB)*

LANGHAM [SK8411]

☆ *Noel Arms* LE15 7HU [Bridge St]: Beams, flagstones and lots of pictures in long pleasant low-ceilinged bar/dining area, friendly service, enjoyable generous fairly priced food, Greene King Abbot and Tetleys, central log fire; may be piped music; children and well behaved dogs welcome, good tables on front terrace, new bedrooms *(LYM, J V Dadswell)*

LEICESTER [SK5804]

Ale Wagon LE1 1RE [Rutland St/Charles St]: Basic two-room 1930s interior, Hoskins and good range of changing guest beers, Weston's perry; handy for station, open all day *(the Didler)*

Black Boy LE1 6GD [Albion St/Chatham St]: Lively front bar with TV, quieter back area, real ales, good friendly atmosphere lunchtime and early evening; terrace tables *(Chris Evans)*

Black Horse LE3 5LT [Braunstone Gate/Foxon St]: Unspoilt late 19th-c two-room corner local with Everards Beacon, Tiger and wknd guest beers, farm cider, traditional layout (with outside lavatories), darts and dominoes, character back lounge; popular with students in term-time, frequent live music *(Pete Baker, G Coates)*

Criterion LE1 5JN [Millstone Lane]: Under same ownership as Swan & Rushes, with good value pizzas and tapas (till late Fri/Sat, not Sun) and decent changing choice of unusual beers, decent wines by the glass, rather wine-bar-like carpeted main room with close-set tables, dark wood and burgundy décor, relaxed room on left with games; reasonable wheelchair access (small front step) *(the Didler, G Coates)*

Forge LE3 8DG [Main St, Glenfield]: Large split-level open-plan pub, partly no smoking, with lots of woodwork, wide choice of bargain food, OAP deals (not Sun), four Everards ales; quiet piped music, games machines; children welcome, two terraces, open all day Sun *(JJW, CMW)*

☆ *Globe* LE1 5EU [Silver St]: Lots of woodwork in four old-fashioned uncluttered areas off central bar, charming more peaceful upstairs dining room, wrought-iron gas lamps, Everards and guest ales, low-priced honest food 12-7, helpful friendly staff; piped pop music (not in snug), very popular with young people wknd evenings; children allowed in some parts, open all day *(the Didler, LYM)*

☆ *Out of the Vaults* LE1 6RL [King St/New Walk]: Great quickly changing range of interesting real ales from a dozen handpumps in former wine bar, recently converted into alehouse, with friendly chatty landlady, enthusiast landlord, wkdy lunchtime cobs, baguettes and curries, decent reasonably priced wines by the glass, simple chairs and tables on bare boards; open all day *(the Didler)*

Swan & Rushes LE1 5WR [Oxford St/Infirmary Sq]: Good range of changing real ales inc Hardys & Hansons and Oakham JHB, several imported beers on tap and many dozens in bottle, farm cider, beer festivals, enjoyable food inc frequent continental theme nights; open all day *(the Didler)*

LEIRE [SP5290]

White Horse LE17 5HE [Main St]: Neat open-plan dining pub with wide choice of good food from interesting snacks up, good friendly licensees, Greene King Abbot and Tetleys, small bars and separate restaurant; children welcome, has been open all day wknds *(Michael J Caley, P Tailyour)*

LOUGHBOROUGH [SK5320]

Albion LE11 1QA [canal bank, about ¼ mile from Loughborough Wharf]: Cheerful and chatty canalside local with emphasis on at least three changing real ales inc one from local Wicked Hathern, friendly owners, cheap straightforward home-made food, coal fire, darts room; children welcome, occasional barbecues, budgerigar aviary in nice big courtyard *(Gwyn and Anne Wake, the Didler, Brian and Ruth Archer)*

☆ *Swan in the Rushes* LE11 5BE [A6]: Cheery down-to-earth bare-boards town local with wide range of carefully chosen changing real ales tapped from the cask, plenty of foreign bottled beers, farm cider, good value straightforward home-made food (not Sat/Sun evenings), daily papers, traditional games, open fire, three smallish high-ceilinged rooms; good juke box; children in eating areas, tables outside, bedrooms, open all day *(P Dawn, the Didler, Pete Baker, LYM, BB, Brian and Ruth Archer)*

Tap & Mallet LE11 1EU [Nottingham Rd]: Basic pub noted for five or six changing microbrews, foreign beers on tap, farm cider, occasional beer festivals; good juke box; walled back garden with play area, open all day wknds *(the Didler)*

LUTTERWORTH [SP5484]

Fox LE17 4BN [Rugby Rd; very handy for M1 junction 20]: Open-plan pub with four changing ales, low-priced traditional food, welcoming helpful service, coal fires, beams and woodstrip flooring, comfortable lounge area on right inc a cosy corner table for two, more of a public bar style on left; garden tables *(G Coates)*

Unicorn LE17 4AE [Church St, off A426; handy for M1 junction 20]: Welcoming town pub, banquettes in lounge and back restaurant, bargain food from sandwiches up inc children's dishes and popular OAP bargain lunches, nice log fire, Bass, Greene King IPA and Robinsons, more basic bar with traditional games inc hood skittles; sports TV, no credit cards *(Pete Baker, P Tailyour)*

LYDDINGTON [SP8797]

Marquess of Exeter LE15 9LT [Main St]: Comfortable series of well furnished rooms, wing armchairs by big inglenook log fire, black beams, neat friendly staff, real ales, good coffee, enjoyable food in bar's eating areas and restaurant; good-sized orchard garden with boules, good bedrooms *(LYM, R V T Pryor)*

MARKET BOSWORTH [SK4003]

☆ *Old Red Lion* CV13 0LL [Park St; from centre follow Leicester and Hinckley signs]: Cheerful and civilised black-beamed split-level pub with real ales such as Banks's Bitter and Mild, Marstons Pedigree and Theakstons XB and Old Peculier, sensibly priced food from

sandwiches and baked potatoes up inc proper steak and kidney pie, prompt efficient service, plushly tidy L-shaped bar; may be piped music; children welcome, tables and play area in sheltered courtyard, bedrooms, attractive village *(C J Fletcher, LYM, Pete Baker, Peter King)*

MARKET HARBOROUGH [SP7387]

Sugar Loaf LE16 7NJ [High St]: Popular Wetherspoons, smaller than many, with pleasant atmosphere, good choice of sensibly priced real ales, good value food all day, no smoking dining area, no piped music; children allowed, open all day *(Gerry and Rosemary Dobson, JJW, CMW)*

☆ *Three Swans* LE16 7NJ [High St]: Comfortable and handsome coaching inn now a Best Western conference hotel, beams and old local prints in plush and peaceful panelled front bar, no smoking flagstoned back dining lounge and fine courtyard conservatory (also no smoking, opened Weds-Fri evenings as good value bistro) in more modern part, friendly helpful staff, wide range of good value bar lunches from sandwiches up, some bar food early evenings, Courage Directors and a guest beer, decent wines, good coffee, more formal upstairs restaurant; piped music; attractive suntrap courtyard, good bedroom extension *(Gerry and Rosemary Dobson, George Atkinson, David and Ruth Hollands)*

MARKET OVERTON [SK8816]

Black Bull LE15 7PW [off B668 in Cottesmore]: This attractive thatched and low-beamed stone-built pub, well placed for Rutland Water, has now been sold to a small chain; children in eating areas, some tables out in front by small carp pool *(BB, Barry Collett)*

MELTON MOWBRAY [SK7519]

Anne of Cleves LE13 1AE [Burton St, by St Mary's Church]: Unpretentious pub in building of great potential – lovely medieval monks' chantry attached to parish church, chunky tables and character chairs and settles on flagstones, heavy Tudor beams and latticed mullioned windows, tapestries on burnt orange walls; Everards Tiger and Original and a guest beer, nice coffee, quick neat service, popular unpretentious food, small end dining room and no smoking room; piped music, no under-7s; tables in pretty little walled garden with flagstoned terrace, open all day, Sun afternoon closure *(Duncan Cloud, BOB, BB)*

Crown LE13 1AE [Burton St]: Handy central pub with Everards and a couple of guest beers, limited good value food (not Fri/Sat evening or Sun/Mon), friendly landlord and staff, good mix of customers, quiet no smoking lounge on right; garden behind *(Tony Hobden, Rona Murdoch)*

MOUNTSORREL [SK5715]

☆ *Swan* LE12 7AT [Loughborough Rd, off A6]: Warm and cosy inside, with log fires, old flagstones and stripped stone, friendly staff and locals, enjoyable food from baguettes and both traditional and contemporary light dishes to good full meals, Greene King Ruddles County,

Theakstons and a guest beer, good choice of wines, neat contemporary side dining area; pretty walled back garden leading down to canalised River Soar, self-contained accommodation, open all day Sat *(Heidi Rowe, Phil Merrin)*

NETHER BROUGHTON [SK6925]
Red House LE14 3HB [A606 N of Melton Mowbray]: Substantial and elegant extended Georgian house, emphasis on good popular no smoking restaurant on left past comfortable lounge bar with red leather settees and armchairs, also enjoyable sensibly priced bar food from sandwiches and local cheeses to steaks, bar on right with TV, changing real ales, fine range of spirits; garden picnic-sets, eight well equipped bedrooms *(P Dawn, Phil and Jane Hodson, BB)*

OADBY [SP6399]
Grange Farm LE2 4QZ [Florence Wragg Way, just off A6]: Roomy Vintage Inn based on attractive early 19th-c farmhouse, log fires, old local photographs, daily papers, wide food range from lunchtime sandwiches to steak, bass and Sun roast, friendly staff, good wine choice, real ales, good mix of customers, no smoking area; picnic-sets out in front *(David Field, Les and Barbara Owen)*
Old Library LE2 5DF [The Parade]: Conversion of three storey 19th-c house (once Council offices) in shopping area, generous reasonably priced food, good wine offers, real ales such as Archers and Marstons Pedigree, pool; quiet lunchtimes, can get crowded with young people evenings; picnic-sets on pleasant partly covered terrace *(Veronica Brown)*

OAKHAM [SK8508]
Horseshoe LE15 6LE [Braunston Rd]: 1960s pub doing well under newish management, pleasant open-plan lounge bar, smaller lounge leading to dining area, enjoyable fresh food inc two-for-one lunches Weds-Fri, Everards and guest beers, friendly service; some picnic-sets out in front, garden behind *(Barry Collett)*
Odd House LE15 6QT [Station Rd/Burley Rd]: Attractive old pub with good low-priced food inc gargantuan mixed grill, good service, dark décor *(Robert Turnham)*
Wheatsheaf LE15 6QS [Northgate]: Attractive three-room 17th-c local nr church, Everards and guest ales, enjoyable lunchtime pub food inc particularly good puddings, friendly helpful service, comfortable furnishings, open fire, plenty of bric-a-brac, conservatory (children welcome in it); pretty suntrap back courtyard with interesting and entertaining installation, nearby play park *(Barry Collett, Fiona McElhone)*
☆ *Whipper In* LE15 6DT [Market Pl]: Busy stone-built coaching inn with creaky boards, oak-beamed and panelled lounge opening into neatly kept attractive bistro area, good interesting food from sandwiches to popular Sun lunch, friendly staff, real ales, decent wines; comfortable bedrooms *(Ian Stafford, LYM)*

OLD DALBY [SK6723]
☆ *Crown* LE14 3LF [by school in village centre turn into Longcliff Hill; Debdale Hill]: Three

or four intimate little farmhouse rooms up and down steps, black beams, one or two antique oak settles among other seats, hunting and other rustic prints, open fires, real ales such as Belvoir, Courage Directors and Charles Wells Bombardier from homely servery, popular fresh locally sourced food (not Sun evening) from sandwiches and ciabattas up, no smoking snug, relaxed dining room, friendly cat, darts and cribbage; children and dogs welcome, nice tables in attractive garden with terrace, sheltered sloping lawn and boules, cl Mon lunchtime *(the Didler, LYM, G Coates, P T Sewell)*

PEATLING MAGNA [SP5992]
☆ *Cock* LE8 5UQ [off A5199 S of Leicester; Main St]: Two-room village pub with good value generous food (fills quickly for this in the evenings), may be help-yourself free cheddar and stilton Mon-Thurs evenings, Courage Directors and John Smiths, decent house wines, friendly staff, horsey pictures and plates above fire and on beams, cushioned wall benches, plush stools, neat country dining area, lots of events *(Ian Blackwell, LYM)*

QUENIBOROUGH [SK6412]
Britannia LE7 3DB: Enjoyable traditional home cooking inc Mon steak night, good choice of real ales, friendly helpful licensees, character beamed lounge, back no smoking restaurant, bar with TV *(Rona Murdoch)*

REDMILE [SK7935]
Windmill NG13 0GA [off A52 Grantham—Nottingham; Main St]: Wide choice of enjoyable good value home-made food from baguettes to steaks, wkdy meal deals and Sun roasts, real ales, good wines by the glass, good friendly service, comfortable and relaxed lounge extending into simple dining room, pleasant décor; children welcome *(Ellen Stephenson, Barry Collett)*

ROTHLEY [SK5812]
Woodmans Stroke LE7 7PD [Church St]: Popular and immaculate family-run pub with good value wkdy lunchtime bar food from sandwiches up, Greene King IPA, John Smiths and changing guest beers, lots of rugby and cricket memorabilia in two small areas; picnic-sets outside, open all day *(David Glynne-Jones)*

RYHALL [TF0310]
Millstone PE9 4HH [Bridge St]: Neatly kept, with recently upgraded no smoking restaurant, good generous food from baguettes to choice of Sun roasts, reasonable prices, Mansfield and Marstons ales, good wine choice, lots of malt whiskies, proper coffee, congenial licensees, comfortably plush lounge; main bar with pool, juke box and large sports TV; well behaved children welcome, tables in back garden *(Martin and Helen Ball, BB, Tim and Rosemary Wells)*

SADDINGTON [SP6591]
Queens Head LE8 0QH [S of Leicester between A5199 (ex A50) and A6; Main St]: Reasonably priced tasty food (not Sun evening) from baguettes to steaks and a fair amount of fish, Everards and guest ales, decent wines, quick polite service, daily papers, lots of knick-

knacks and plastic plants; no under-5s, steps from area to area; country and reservoir views from dining conservatory and tables in long sloping garden *(Gerry and Rosemary Dobson, LYM, George Atkinson, Dennis and Gill Keen)*

SALTBY [SK8426]

☆ *Nags Head* LE14 4RN [Back St]: Small beamed and stone-built pub thriving under friendly and enthusiastic hard-working landlady, relaxed chatty atmosphere, shortish blackboard choice of enjoyable home cooking using local supplies, bargain OAP lunches Tues/Thurs, choice of Sun roasts, Fri fish night, steaks on Sat, three changing ales (landlord won't stock more than he knows he can sell while still in top condition), three traditional rooms, each with own fireplace; soft piped music; dogs welcome, cl Sun evening, Mon lunchtime *(BB, R M Taylor, Orson Carte)*

SEATON [SP9098]

☆ *George & Dragon* LE15 9HU [Main St]: Comfortable stone-built pub opposite church, with good value generous food from sandwiches and baguettes to hot dishes cooked to order, Fri steak nights, Sun roasts, welcoming licensees, quick service, real ales such as Adnams Broadside, Black Sheep, Grainstore Ten Fifty and Marstons Pedigree, good wine choice, daily papers, nice solid fuel stove, two cosy bars, one no smoking with wide variety of sports memorabilia; piped jazz; tables outside, unspoilt village, good views of famous viaduct *(M and C Thompson, Rona Murdoch, BB, David Barnes, Gerry and Rosemary Dobson, Philip and Susan Philcox)*

SHACKERSTONE [SK3706]

☆ *Rising Sun* CV13 6NN [Church Rd, nr Bridge 52, Ashby Canal]: Relaxed olde-worlde canal-side pub, good enterprising food in panelled lounge bar and converted barn restaurant, good value house wine, changing real ales; tables outside, nr steam railway centre *(Duncan Cloud, Neil Kellett)*

SHAWELL [SP5480]

White Swan LE17 6AG [Main St; village signed down declassified rd (ex A427) off A5/A426 roundabout – turn right in village; not far from M6 junct 1]: Attractive 17th-c pub, beams, panelling and open fire, Greene King ales, good house wines, helpful landlord, decent food inc popular Sun lunch, no smoking restaurant; tables out in front, bedrooms, cl Sun evening, Mon, and lunchtime exc Sun *(Anthony Barnes, Kevin Blake, Gerry and Rosemary Dobson)*

SHEPSHED [SK4719]

Pied Bull LE12 9AA [handy for M1 junction 23; Belton St]: Nicely thatched two-bar local, neat and well organised, with enjoyable home-made food, cheerful accommodating staff, Banks's-related and guest ales from central bar, log fire in open-plan beamed lounge, back restaurant; children welcome, large garden behind, colourful and well kept *(Roger Noyes, Brian and Ruth Archer)*

SIBSON [SK3500]

☆ *Cock* CV13 6LB [A444 N of Nuneaton; Twycross Rd]: Ancient picturesque black and white timbered and thatched building run by its chefs, enjoyable food in bar and restaurant, Bass and Hook Norton Best, a dozen wines by the glass, low doorways, heavy black beams and genuine latticed windows, immense inglenook, three no smoking areas; piped music, games machine; children welcome, tables in courtyard and small garden, handy for Bosworth Field *(Ian and Jane Irving, LYM, Joan and Tony Walker, Kevin Blake)*

SILEBY [SK6015]

☆ *White Swan* LE12 7NW [Swan St]: Bright, cheerful and relaxed, with good choice of attractively priced home cooking (not Sun evening or Mon lunchtime) from home-baked rolls up, Marstons Pedigree, nice house wines, good friendly service and chatty locals, comfortable and welcoming dining lounge, small tasteful book-lined restaurant (booking needed) *(Dr Ann Henderson)*

SOUTH CROXTON [SK6810]

Golden Fleece LE7 3RL [Main St]: Large, clean and friendly, with enjoyable home-made food from good baguettes to popular Sun lunch, good-sized helpings, proper bar with some sofas, dark corners and attractive separate restaurant, good service, real ales such as Greene King Ruddles, good house wine, log fire; lovely area *(David Field)*

SOUTH LUFFENHAM [SK9401]

Coach House LE15 8NT [Stamford Rd (A6121)]: Pink walls, flagstones and much scrubbed pine furniture in good-sized bar, chef/landlord doing enjoyable and interesting food, changing real ales such as Greene King, quick cheerful young staff, elegant restaurant; comfortable bedrooms, good breakfast *(M and C Thompson, Michael Doswell)*

TINWELL [TF0006]

Crown PE9 3UF [Crown Lane]: Cosy and convivial, wide choice of good food, truly helpful landlord and very friendly service, real ales, decent wine *(MJB)*

UPPER HAMBLETON [SK9007]

Finches Arms LE15 8TL [off A606]: Outstanding views over Rutland Water from suntrap-back hillside terrace and no smoking picture-window modern restaurant at smart dining pub with stylish cane furniture on wooden floors, open fire in knocked-through front bar, imaginative food (not Sun evening), Greene King Abbot, Oakham JHB, Timothy Taylors Landlord and a guest beer; piped music; bedrooms, open all day *(Mike and Heather Watson, Gerry and Rosemary Dobson, M C and S Jeanes, Christopher Turner, Fred Chamberlain, Mike and Sue Loseby, Paul Humphreys, Tony and Margaret Cross, Phil and Jane Hodson, Derek and Sylvia Stephenson, Di and Mike Gillam, Robert F Smith, Philip and Susan Philcox)*

UPPINGHAM [SP8699]

Vaults LE15 9QH [Market Pl]: Attractive family-run pub next to church, reasonably priced fresh filling food inc good pies, helpful staff, Marstons ales, comfortable banquettes, pleasant upstairs dining room; piped music;

some tables out overlooking picturesque
square, bedrooms (*Barry Collett, Mr and
Mrs Bentley-Davies*)

WALTHAM ON THE WOLDS [SK8024]

☆ *Royal Horseshoes* LE14 4AJ [Melton Rd
(A607)]: Attractive thatched stone-built inn,
sturdily furnished and comfortable, with quick
friendly service, enjoyable food, Fullers
London Pride and Greene King Abbot, good
wines and fair range of malts, spotless
housekeeping, three open fires, interesting
aquarium (with albino frog) in no smoking
dining lounge; subtle piped music; children
welcome in eating area, tables outside,
bedrooms (*Derek and Sylvia Stephenson,
LYM, Phil and Jane Hodson*)

WESTON BY WELLAND [SP7791]

Wheel & Compass LE16 8HZ [Valley Rd]:
Comfortable banquettes in bar, popular
attractively priced food, five real ales inc Bass
and Marstons, friendly staff, back dining area
and separate restaurant; open all day wknds
(*Rona Murdoch*)

WHITWICK [SK4316]

Three Horseshoes LE67 5GN [Leicester Rd]:
Friendly and utterly unpretentious local, bar
and tiny smoke room, Bass, M&B Mild and
Marstons Pedigree, darts, dominoes and cards,
no food; outdoor lavatories (*the Didler,
Pete Baker*)

WIGSTON [SP6099]

William Wygston LE18 1DR [Leicester Rd]:
Roomy Wetherspoons, bright and airy, with
good value if limited food, well priced real ales,
quick helpful service; accessible books – not
exactly riveting except for specialists
(*Veronica Brown*)

WOODHOUSE EAVES [SK5313]

☆ *Wheatsheaf* LE12 8SS [Brand Hill; beyond
Main St, off B591 S of Loughborough]: Busy
open-plan beamed country pub with light and
airy upstairs dining area, good home-made
food here or in partly no smoking bar from
sandwiches up inc interesting specials,
changing ales such as Adnams, Hook Norton
Best and Timothy Taylors Landlord, good

house wines, friendly helpful staff, log fire,
motor-racing memorabilia; no motorcyclists or
children; dogs welcome, floodlit and heated
terrace tables (*Comus and Sarah Elliott,
P Dawn, Ian and Jane Irving, the Didler,
LYM, Les and Barbara Owen, Brian and
Ruth Archer*)

WYMESWOLD [SK6023]

☆ *Hammer & Pincers* LE12 6ST [East Rd
(A6006)]: Good if not cheap bar and
restaurant food (not Sun evening or Mon-
Tues) in smart restauranty dining pub, small
entrance bar with black leather settees and
armchairs around low tables, shallow steps up
to dark-carpeted linked eating areas with
chunky modern pine furniture, contemporary
lighting and big abstract artworks, decent
wines, neat polite staff; piped music, no real
ale; picnic-sets on sheltered well landscaped
back terrace, sturdy play area behind; cl Mon
(*Phil and Jane Hodson, Roger and
Maureen Kenning, JJW, CMW, BB*)

Three Crowns LE12 6TZ [45 Far St (A6006)]:
Snug and chatty 18th-c village pub with
impressive service from friendly staff, good
value food inc lots of specials, four or five real
ales such as Adnams, Belvoir and Marstons,
good soft drinks choice, attentive service,
pleasant character furnishings in beamed bar
and lounge with steps up to cosy no smoking
area, darts; picnic-sets out on decking
(*John and Sylvia Harrop, the Didler,
Roger and Maureen Kenning, JJW, CMW,
Brian and Ruth Archer*)

WYMONDHAM [SK8518]

Berkeley Arms LE14 2AG [Main St]: Attractive
old stone building with friendly helpful
landlord, good value fresh food from crusty
bread sandwiches up, Adnams, Marstons
Pedigree, Tetleys and a guest beer,
Addlestone's cider, good coffee, appealingly
pubby uncluttered décor with pine furniture,
good-sized main bar, dining lounge and
restaurant; well spaced picnic-sets in pleasant
garden, nice village (*David Barnes,
Michael Doswell*)

Post Office address codings confusingly give the impression that some pubs are in
Leicestershire, when they're really in Cambridgeshire (which is where we list them).

Lincolnshire

Lincolnshire is a county that respects tradition, and this is certainly the case with a lot of its pubs, which tend to be strongest in old-fashioned values. On the food side, for instance, the county's better pubs generally seem to score on attractive prices for tried and tested familiar favourites rather than anything really unusual. A handful though are starting to stretch themselves to produce more contemporary food. Both our new main entries this year, the smart Brownlow Arms at Hough-on-the-Hill and the gently modernised Inn on the Green at Ingham, fall into this category. The cheery Wheatsheaf at Dry Doddington is a great all-rounder, with its good range of beers and carefully sourced food, and the no smoking Blue Bell at Belchford has a good imaginative menu. The impeccable George at Stamford, however, stands out head and shoulders on all counts. It's a fabulous place for a very special meal out, and once again this year is Lincolnshire Dining Pub of the Year. Warmly recommended pubs in the Lucky Dip section at the end of the chapter include the Castle at Castle Bytham, Red Lion at Redbourne and Farmers Arms at Welton Hill. Drinks prices in the county are a little below the national average. Batemans is the county's long-established and family-run main brewer, and Tom Woods, much newer but increasingly available, is well worth looking out for too: both tend to be attractively priced. Interestingly, the beer we found most often offered as the cheapest here, in around a quarter of the better pubs, was an invader from Yorkshire, Black Sheep.

ALLINGTON   SK8540   Map 7
Welby Arms ♀ ◖ ⛏

The Green; off A1 N of Grantham, or A52 W of Grantham; NG32 2EA

We're happy to say that the friendly new licensees don't intend to change a thing at this bustling place, which is so handy for the A1. The large bar area is divided by a stone archway and has black beams and joists, log fires (one in an attractive arched brick fireplace), red velvet curtains and comfortable burgundy button-back wall banquettes and stools. The civilised back no smoking dining lounge (where they prefer you to eat) looks out on to tables in a sheltered walled courtyard with pretty hanging baskets in summer. A back courtyard formed by the restaurant extension and the bedroom block beyond has tables, with more picnic-sets out on the front lawn. A good choice of well kept real ales (served through a sparkler) might include Bass, John Smiths, Timothy Taylors Landlord and three guests such as Brewsters Hop a Doodle Doo, Phoenix Wobbly Bob and Shepherd Neame Spitfire, also 11 wines by the glass, and 20 malt whiskies; dominoes, cribbage, and piped music. Bar food is popular: soup (£3.25), wholemeal hoagies or filled baguettes (from £3.95; hot sirloin steak and stilton £4.95), home-made chicken liver pâté or garlic mushrooms (£4.25), chicken pasta, steak and mushroom in ale pie or home-made lasagne (all £7.95), chargrilled steaks (from £10.95), and specials such as pork and black pudding sausage or fresh grimsby haddock with mushy peas (£7.95), lambs liver and onions (£8.95) and lamb shank or poached plaice with prawn sauce (£10.95). Best to book to be sure of a table. *(Recommended by Michael and Jenny Back)*

Free house ~ Licensees Christine and John Thompson ~ Real ale ~ Bar food ~ Restaurant

~ (01400) 281361 ~ Well behaved children welcome at lunchtime ~ Open 12-2.30(3 Sat),
6-11(10.30 Sun) ~ Bedrooms: £48S/£60S

BARNOLDBY LE BECK   TA2303   Map 8
Ship ♀
Village signposted off A18 Louth—Grimsby; DN37 0BG

There's a calmly sedate atmosphere at this neatly kept little white painted pub,
which houses a delightful collection of beautifully kept Edwardian and Victorian
bric-a-brac. Charming items run from stand-up telephones and violins to a horn
gramophone as well as bowler and top hats, old racquets, crops and hockey
sticks and a lace dress. Heavy dark-ringed drapes swathe the windows, with
grandmotherly plants in ornate china bowls on the sills, and furnishings include
comfortable dark green plush wall benches with lots of pretty propped-up cushions
and heavily stuffed green plush Victorian-looking chairs on a green fleur de lys
carpet. Many of the tables are booked for dining. Enjoyable food could include
home-made soup (£3.95), sandwiches or filled baguettes (from £3.95), chicken liver
and brandy pâté with apple, ginger and plum chutney or salmon, prawns and white
fish crêpe (£4.95), grilled aubergine and tomato in tomato and basil sauce (£8.50),
beef in ale or fish pie (£8.95), seared salmon on citrus mash with red wine and
balsamic jus (£11.95), quite a few fresh fish specials such as skate (£13.50) or
turbot (£18.95), and puddings such as hot chocolate and brandy fudge cake
(£4.25). The restaurant is no smoking. Well kept Black Sheep and Timothy Taylors
Landlord on handpump, and several wines by the glass from a good wine list; piped
music. Out behind are a few picnic-sets under pink cocktail parasols and hanging
baskets in a fenced-off suntrap area. *(Recommended by Derek and Sylvia Stephenson,
Keith Rutter, Inga Davis, Alistair and Kay Butler, Kevin Blake)*

Inn Business ~ Lease Michele Hancock ~ Real ale ~ Bar food ~ Restaurant ~
(01472) 822308 ~ Children in restaurant ~ Open 12-3, 6-11(12 Sat, 10.30 Sun)

BELCHFORD   TF2975   Map 8
Blue Bell 🍴
**Village signposted off A153 Horncastle—Louth (and can be reached by the good
Bluestone Heath Road off A16 just under 1½ miles N of the A1104 roundabout);
Main Road; LN9 6LQ**

The emphasis at this cottagey 18th-c dining pub (now completely no smoking) is
very much on its imaginative modern food. From the changing menu, there might
be soup (£3.25), mussels with thai-style coconut sauce (£5.50), stilton, mushroom
and spinach spring rolls on sweet poached pear with walnut and basil dressing
(£5.95), scampi and chips or sausage and mash (£6.95), goats cheese with red
onion marmalade and red pepper coulis (£9.25), baked bass fillet stuffed with chilli,
spring onion, ginger, hoi sin and pak choi (£12.95), duck breast on thyme celeriac
purée with fig, lime and ginger jus (£13.50), lamb shank on bean and bacon
casserole (£13.95), 8oz fillet steak (£16.95), and puddings such as chocolate
roulade with pistachio ice-cream or vanilla and turkish delight panna cotta (£3.95);
cheeseboard (£4.95). The cosy comfortable bar has a relaxing pastel décor, some
armchairs and settees, as well as more upright chairs around good solid tables, and
well kept Black Sheep, Charles Wells Bombardier and a guest such as Everards
Original on handpump; friendly, prompt service. The neat garden behind, with a
terrace, has picnic-sets, and the pub is well placed for Wolds walks and the
Viking Way. *(Recommended by Keith Wright, Revd L and S Giller, Bill and Sheila McLardy,
Derek and Sylvia Stephenson, Mr and Mrs J Brown)*

Free house ~ Licensees Darren and Shona Jackson ~ Real ale ~ Bar food ~ Restaurant ~
(01507) 533602 ~ Children welcome ~ Open 11.30-2.30, 6.30-11; 12-4 Sun; closed Sun
evening, Mon and second and third weeks in Jan

> Prices of main dishes usually include vegetables or a side salad.

BILLINGBOROUGH   TF1134   Map 8
Fortescue Arms
B1177, off A52 Grantham—Boston; NG34 0PQ

This charmingly old-fashioned pub has several linked turkey-carpeted rooms with low beams, pleasant mainly Victorian prints, and big log fires in two cosy see-through fireplaces. Also, bay window seats, fresh flowers and pot plants, brass and copper, a stuffed badger and pheasant, and various quiz books in one place. Attractive no smoking dining rooms at each end have some stripped stone walls, flagstones and another open fire. Unusually, a long red and black tiled corridor runs right the way along behind the serving bar, making it an island. Here you'll find well kept Batemans XXXB, Ind Coope Burton, Greene King IPA and a guest such as Fullers London Pride on handpump. Under new licensees, bar food includes soup (£2.95), sandwiches (from £3.50), ham, egg and chips (£6.95), sausage and mash or beef suet pudding (£7.95) and roast lamb shank (£10.95). The car park is more like the gravelled drive of a country house, with picnic-sets on a lawn under apple trees on one side, and on the other a sheltered courtyard with flowers planted in tubs and a manger. More reports on the new regime please. *(Recommended by W M Paton, Beryl and Bill Farmer)*

Churchill Taverns ~ Managers Terry and Nicola Williams ~ Real ale ~ Bar food ~ Restaurant ~ (01529) 240228 ~ Children welcome ~ Open 12-3, 5.30-11(6-12 Sat); 12-11 Sun

CONINGSBY   TF2458   Map 8
Lea Gate Inn
Leagate Road (B1192 southwards, off A153 E); LN4 4RS

The three separate cosy areas at this traditional 16th-c inn are dimly lit and linked together around the corner bar counter, with heavy black beams supporting ochre ceiling boards. They are attractively furnished, with a cabinet holding a collection of ancient bottles, a variety of tables and chairs, including antique oak settles with hunting-print cushions, and two great high-backed settles making a snug around the biggest of the fireplaces. Another fireplace has an interesting cast-iron fireplace depicting the Last Supper; Charles Wells Bombardier and Theakstons XB and a guest such as Timothy Taylors Landlord on handpump; piped music. Quickly served, even when busy, the well liked bar food includes home-made soup (£2.70), lunchtime sandwiches (£2.95), garlic mushrooms (£3.25), mushroom stroganoff (£7.25), steak and kidney pie (£7.95), chicken breast with cider, apples, bacon and herbs (£9), chargrilled pork steak with stilton and creamy wholegrain mustard sauce or lamb rump with rosemary and madeira jus (£9.95), and beef wellington (£11.95); the restaurant is no smoking. The pub once stood by one of the perilous tracks through the marshes before the fens were drained, and outside the door, you can still see the small iron gantry that used to hold a lamp to guide travellers safely through the mist. The appealing garden has tables and an enclosed play area. *(Recommended by M C and S Jeanes, W K Wood, Martin and Alison Stainsby, Bill and Sheila McLardy, the Didler, Maurice and Gill McMahon)*

Free house ~ Licensee Mark Dennison ~ Real ale ~ Bar food (12-2, 6-9) ~ Restaurant ~ (01526) 342370 ~ Children welcome ~ Open 11(12 Sun)-3, 6-11 ~ Bedrooms: £55B/£75B

DRY DODDINGTON   SK8546   Map 8
Wheatsheaf
1½ miles off A1 N of Grantham; Main Street; NG23 5HU

Run by a landlord who clearly enjoys getting to know his customers, this largely 16th-c colourwashed village pub is buoyantly cheerful and busy, with friendly and efficient service. The front bar is basically two rooms, with a log fire, a variety of settles and chairs, and tables in the windows facing across to the green and the lovely 14th-c church with its crooked tower. The serving bar on the right has well kept Greene King Abbot, Timothy Taylors Landlord, Tom Wood's Best Bitter and a guest such as Phoenix Wobbly Bob on handpump, good hot drinks, and a nice choice of wines by the glass; you may smoke only in one part of the bar. A slight slope takes you back down to the comfortable and thickly carpeted smallish dining room with its relaxing red and cream décor. This part, once a cow byre, is even more ancient, perhaps dating from the 13th c. It's all spotlessly kept. Enjoyable food, cooked by the landlady and using local supplies where possible, includes light lunchtime choices such as filled baguettes (from £4.50), a good mixed salad platter (£6.95), and honey and mustard roasted ham and egg (£7.95), as well as home-made soup (£3.95), chicken liver pâté with orange marmalade or roasted peppers topped with melted goats cheese and drizzled with pesto dressing (£4.95), mediterranean-style haddock with ratatouille and mozzarella cheese topping (£10.95), roasted breast of duck with morello cherry and brandy sauce (£13.95), rack of english lamb with redcurrant and rosemary jus (£14.95), steaks (from £14.95) and daily specials such as sausages with bubble and squeak and onion gravy or steak, mushroom and ale pie or fresh grimsby haddock (£8.95), and spinach, brie and aubergine bake (£9.95); two-course Sunday lunch (£10.95). Disabled access at the side. The front terrace has neat dark green tables under cocktail parasols, among tubs of flowers. *(Recommended by Grahame Brooks, Michael and Jenny Back, Derek and Sylvia Stephenson, Di and Mike Gillam, Keith Wright)*

Free house ~ Licensees Bob and Josie Dyer ~ Real ale ~ Bar food (12-2(3 Sun), 7-9; not Sun evening) ~ Restaurant ~ (01400) 281458 ~ Children welcome in dining area till 8pm ~ Open 12-2.30(3 Sat, Sun), 5.30-11; closed Sun evening

HOUGH-ON-THE-HILL SK9246 Map 8
Brownlow Arms
High Road; NG32 2AZ

Rather akin to a country house hotel, this smartly upmarket inn is more restaurant-with-rooms than your traditional local, but they won't bat an eye if you just want a drink. A handsome stone building in a peaceful village, it has a comfortably refined air inside. The beamed bar has plenty of panelling, some exposed brickwork, local prints and scenes, a large mirror, and a pile of logs beside the big fireplace. Seating is on mismatched, elegant armchairs, and the carefully arranged furnishings make the room feel bigger than it is, giving the impression of several separate and surprisingly cosy areas; piped easy listening. Marstons Bitter and Pedigree and Timothy Taylors Landlord and a good choice of malt whiskies are served by friendly, impeccably polite staff. The very good food might include starters such as pan-roasted quail with buttered spinach, confit onions and red wine and thyme jus (£7.25) or baked cheese soufflé with roquefort, celery, walnuts and cream (£7.50), and main courses such as shoulder of lamb with crushed carrots, parsnips, swede, celeriac and rosemary jus (£12.95), braised blade of beef with bubble and squeak and shallots (£13.95) and panache of scallops, bass and salmon with leek mash and lemon and chive beurre blanc (£16.95), and they do a well liked Sunday lunch (two courses £15.45, three courses £18.45). The dining rooms (as you'd expect, both rather formal) are no smoking. In summer you can eat on the nicely landscaped back terrace. The well equipped bedrooms are attractive, and breakfasts are hearty. *(Recommended by Keith Wright, W W Burke, John and Ann Menzies, Dr A G Gibson)*

Free house ~ Licensee Paul L Willoughby ~ Real ale ~ Restaurant ~ (01400) 250234 ~ Open evenings only Tues-Sat (6.30-11); 12-3 Sun; closed all day Mon, 25-7 December, 1-20 January ~ Bedrooms: £65B/£96B

Bedroom prices normally include full English breakfast, VAT and any inclusive service charge that we know of. Prices before the '/' are for single rooms, after for two people in double or twin (B includes a private bath, S a private shower). If there is no '/', the prices are only for twin or double rooms (as far as we know there are no singles). If there is no B or S, as far as we know no rooms have private facilities.

INGHAM SK9483 Map 8
Inn on the Green
The Green; LN1 2XT

This welcoming and nicely modernised pub is thriving under its newish licensees, and on our early spring inspection every table was busy with people eating – no mean feat when the beamed and timbered dining room is spread over two floors. Though there's some emphasis on food, it feels like a proper pub, with a good chatty atmosphere throughout, and particularly in the stone-flagged locals' bar to the left of the entrance. The brick bar counter has home-made jams, marmalade and chutney for sale alongside the Black Sheep, Hop Back Summer Lightning and Thwaites Lancaster Bomber; opposite is a comfortably laid-back area with two red leather sofas. There's lots of exposed brickwork, and a mix of brasses, copper, local prints and bric-a-brac. The good food is all home-made using carefully sourced ingredients; as well as sandwiches, a typical menu might include fishcakes with sweet chilli jam (£4.35), duck and vegetable strudel (£4.50), caramelised pork fillet with a cider and apple sauce (£7.95), beef bourgignon or pan-fried breast of guinea fowl (£8.75) and rabbit and mustard stew with mash (£9.95); prompt friendly service. Readers have particularly praised the wines here. The dining room and lounge are no smoking. *(Recommended by Keith and Chris O'Neill, Mrs Brenda Calver)*

Free house ~ Licensees Andrew Cafferkey and Sarah Sharpe ~ Real ale ~ Bar food (12-2.15, 6.30-9.30 Mon-Sat, 12-7 Sun) ~ Restaurant ~ (01522) 730354 ~ Children allowed if eating, till 9pm ~ Open 11.30-3, 6-11; 12-10.30 Sun; closed Mon

LINCOLN SK9771 Map 8
Victoria 🗾 £
Union Road; LN1 3BJ

This basic early Victorian local, up a steep back street behind the castle, is popular for its fine choice of up to nine real ales, good value straightforward food and nice pubby atmosphere. Along with Batemans XB, Castle Rock Harvest Pale and Timothy Taylors Landlord, friendly staff serve five or six guests from brewers such as Hopback, Milestone and Ossett, as well as foreign draught and bottled beers, around 20 country wines, a farm cider on tap, and cheap soft drinks. They hold beer festivals in the last week in June and the first week in December. With a good mix of ages, the simply furnished little tiled front lounge has a coal fire and pictures of Queen Victoria; it's especially bustling at lunchtime and later on in the evening. Good value lunchtime food, from a short menu, includes filled cobs (from £1.50, big bacon ones £3.25) and all-day breakfast, beef stew, chilli, curry or ploughman's (from £4.75); the lounge is no smoking at lunchtime. Children are welcome in the restaurant which is open only on Sunday lunchtimes (Sunday roast £5.50). You can sit in the small conservatory or out in the gravelled side garden, which has good views of the castle. *(Recommended by David Carr, the Didler, Geoff and Kaye Newton, Mike and Linda Hudson, Keith and Chris O'Neill)*

Tynemill ~ Manager Neil Renshaw ~ Real ale ~ Bar food (12(11 Sat)-2.30(2 Sun)) ~ (01522) 536048 ~ Children welcome in one room only ~ Dogs allowed in bar ~ Open 11(12 Sun)-11(11.30 Fri, Sat)

Wig & Mitre ㉕ ★ ♀
Steep Hill; just below cathedral; LN2 1LU

It's incredibly useful to know that at almost any time of the day you can pop into this bustling café-style dining pub and get something to eat (though one or two readers have been a little startled by the prices). Spreading over a couple of floors, the building itself dates from the 14th c, and has plenty of period features. The big-windowed beamed downstairs bar has exposed stone walls, pews and gothic furniture on oak floorboards, and comfortable sofas in a carpeted back area. Upstairs, the calmer dining room is light and airy, with views of the castle walls and cathedral, shelves of old books, and an open fire. The walls are hung with antique prints and caricatures of lawyers and clerics, and there are plenty of newspapers and periodicals lying about – even templates to tempt you to a game of noughts and crosses. Food works its way up from breakfast menu (full english, £9.25 to caviar, £42.50). Other dishes might include soup (£4.50), sandwiches (from £5.50), smoked haddock and leek risotto (£6.95), cheese, mushroom, leek and pea soufflé with white truffle oil (£7.25), lasagne (£8.95), confit of pork belly with sage pot roasted potato and black pudding (£13.75), roast salt cod with clam chowder and pancetta (£14.95), aberdeen angus fillet steak (£21.95), puddings such as fig and frangipane tart with cornish clotted cream or terrine of dark chocolate with black cherry ice-cream (£4.95) and cheese platters (£6.50). They have 35 wines by the glass, lots of liqueurs and spirits and well kept Batemans XB and Black Sheep Bitter on handpump. *(Recommended by Sarah and Peter Gooderham, N R White, David Glynne-Jones, Kevin Blake, David Carr, Paul Boot, Richard, David and Ruth Hollands, Peter and Eleanor Kenyon, Keith and Chris O'Neill, Barry Collett, Anthony Barnes, W M Lien)*

Free house ~ Licensees Toby and Valerie Hope ~ Real ale ~ Bar food (8am-12pm) ~ Restaurant ~ (01522) 535190 ~ Children welcome ~ Open 8am-12pm

ROTHWELL   TF1499   Map 8

Blacksmiths Arms

Off B1225 S of Caistor; LN7 6AZ

Tidied up by new licensees, the pleasant heavily beamed bar at this long white painted pub is divided by a couple of arches, and has a relaxed atmosphere, a warm central coal fire, attractive wildlife prints, and comfortable chairs and tables. The spacious restaurant is no smoking. Bar food includes sandwiches (from £3.95), burgers (from £4.50), salmon and prawn salad (£4.95), lasagne or steak and ale pie (£7.95), battered haddock (£8.25), steaks (from £12.95); Sunday roast (£7.25). They also do a special offer early evening menu Mon-Fri, 5.30-7pm, two courses (£7.99). Black Sheep, Greene King Abbot and Tom Woods Shepherds Delight and a guest such as Batemans on handpump, and 15 malt whiskies; piped music, fruit machine, pool, darts and dominoes. There are plenty of tables outside. Take care coming out of the car park: it's a blind bend. More reports on the new regime please. *(Recommended by Derek and Sylvia Stephenson)*

Free house ~ Licensee Rachel Flello ~ Real ale ~ Bar food (12-2(3 Sun), 5.30(6 Sat, Sun)-9(9.30 Fri, Sat)) ~ Restaurant ~ (01472) 371300 ~ Children welcome ~ Open 12-3, 5-11.30; 12-11.30 Sat; 12-11 Sun

SOUTH WITHAM   SK9219   Map 8

Blue Cow 🍺

Village signposted just off A1 Stamford—Grantham (with brown sign for pub); NG33 5QB

Happily, the new landlord at this old stone-walled country pub plans to continue brewing the reasonably priced Blue Cow Best and Witham Wobbler. There's a nice pubby atmosphere in its two appealing rooms, which are completely separated by a big central open-plan counter. One dark-beamed room has bentwood chairs at big indonesian hardwood tables, wickerwork and panelling, and prettily curtained windows, and the second room has big black standing timbers and beams, partly stripped stone walls, shiny flagstones and a dark blue flowery carpet; piped music and darts. Basic but tasty bar food might include sandwiches (from £3.25), soup (£3.50) and baked potatoes (£3.75). The garden has tables on a pleasant terrace. *(Recommended by Comus and Sarah Elliott, the Didler, Kevin Thorpe, Keith and Chris O'Neill)*

Own brew ~ Licensee Simon Crathore ~ Real ale ~ Bar food (12-2.30, 6-9.30) ~ Restaurant ~ (01572) 768432 ~ Children welcome ~ Dogs welcome ~ Open 12-11 (10.30 Sun) ~ Bedrooms: £45S/£55B

Pubs in outstandingly attractive surroundings are listed at the back of the book.

STAMFORD TF0207 Map 8

George of Stamford ㉕ ★ ⑪ ♈ ☝

High Street, St Martins (B1081 S of centre, not the quite different central pedestrianised High Street); PE9 2LB

Lincolnshire Dining Pub of the Year

Exquisite attention to detail sets this beautifully preserved old coaching inn notches above your average place. It was built in 1597 for Lord Burghley (though there are visible parts of a much older Norman pilgrims' hospice, and a crypt under the cocktail bar that may be 1,000 years old); during the 18th and 19th c it was the hub of 20 coach trips a day each way from London and York (two of the front rooms are still named after these destinations). The atmosphere is smartly relaxed, with plenty of comfortably conversing customers enjoying a break from the busy A1, meeting friends for a drink or a meal or staying in the lovely bedrooms. Seats in its beautifully furnished rooms range through leather, cane and antique wicker to soft settees and easy chairs, while the central lounge has sturdy timbers, broad flagstones, heavy beams, and massive stonework. The other front room (the surprisingly pubby York Bar) is where you can get snacks such as soup (£4.65), sandwiches (from £4.95; steak £7.25), and chicken liver pâté with cumberland sauce or ploughman's (£6.45). More elaborate meals are served in the oak-panelled restaurant (jacket and tie required) and less formal Garden Lounge restaurant (which has well spaced furniture on herringbone glazed bricks around a central tropical grove). Made using high quality ingredients, food here has a continental lean (one of the licensees is Italian). Besides a cold buffet (£13.45), the menu includes several pasta dishes such as pasta strips with salmon and fresh peas in a saffron cream (£11.95), shellfish such as oysters (£7.50 for half a dozen), and dressed crab (£12.95), as well as caesar salad (£7.45), hot smoked salmon fishcakes with spring onion and coriander (£12.95), lamb shank with roast butternut squash and mint and chilli dressing (£12.45), home-made beefburger (£13.25), and puddings (£5.55); they do afternoon tea (£14). Well kept Adnams Broadside, Fullers London Pride and Greene King Ruddles County on handpump, an excellent choice of wines (many of which are italian and good value, with about 18 by the glass), freshly squeezed orange juice and malt whiskies. The staff are professional, with waiter drinks service in the charming cobbled courtyard at the back, which has comfortable chairs and tables among attractive plant tubs and colourful hanging baskets on the ancient stone buildings. There's also a neatly kept walled garden, with a sunken lawn where croquet is often played. *(Recommended by Richard Waller, Pauline Smith, Michael Dandy, David Carr, Derek Thomas, Alistair and Kay Butler, Fred Chamberlain, Les and Sandra Brown, Mike and Sue Loseby, the Didler, J F M and M West, Dr M A Turner, A J Bowen, Ian Phillips, Tina and David Woods-Taylor, Di and Mike Gillam, Grahame Brooks, Tracey and Stephen Groves, Michael Sargent)*

Free house ~ Licensees Chris Pitman and Ivo Vannocci ~ Real ale ~ Bar food (11-11) ~ Restaurant ~ (01780) 750750 ~ Children welcome ~ Dogs allowed in bar and bedrooms ~ Open 11-11; 12-11 Sun ~ Bedrooms: £78B/£115B

SURFLEET TF2528 Map 8

Mermaid

Just off A16 N of Spalding, on B1356 at bridge; PE11 4AB

The pretty garden at this old-fashioned pub has lots of seats and a terrace with thatched parasols and its own bar, and the children's play area is safely walled from the River Glen which runs beside the pub. Inside, a small central glass-backed bar counter (complete with original Babycham décor and well kept Adnams Broadside, Everards Original or Tiger and Greene King IPA on handpump, and quite a few malt whiskies) serves two high-ceilinged rooms, which have huge netted sash windows, green patterned carpets, red Anaglypta dado, navigation lanterns and horse tack on cream textured walls, and a mixture of banquettes and stools; cribbage and dominoes. Two steps down, the restaurant is decorated in a similar style; most of the pub is no smoking; piped music. Bar food includes filled ciabattas (from £3.25), soup (£3.50), sausage and mash (£8.25), ricotta and goats cheese tart with mediterranean vegetables or battered cod with chips and mushy peas (£8.95), roast duck with orange sauce (£11.95) and 10oz sirloin steak (£12.95). *(Recommended by Michael and Jenny Back, Ian Stafford, Roy Bromell, Gordon Neighbour, Beryl and Bill Farmer, Dr and Mrs R G J Telfer)*

Free house ~ Licensee Chris Bustance ~ Real ale ~ Bar food (12-3, 6-9.30) ~ Restaurant ~ (01775) 680275 ~ Children welcome ~ Open 11.30-11; 12-10.30 Sun; closed 3-5.30 in winter

WOOLSTHORPE   SK8435   Map 8

Chequers ♀

The one near Belvoir, signposted off A52 or A607 W of Grantham; NG32 1LU

With a good range of dishes, running from the fairly pubby to more imaginative, the tasty food at this 17th-c coaching inn might include soup (£4.50), red pepper, olive and feta sandwich (£5.50), risotto nero with calamari, red pepper and chilli tapenade (£7), sausage and mash (£9.50), pie of the day (£10.50), chicken breast with wild mushroom risotto (£12.50), fried calves liver with mash, sweet cured bacon and onion marmalade (£14.50), whole baby turbot with red onion and french bean salad (£16) and puddings such as crème brûlée or white chocolate cheesecake with peppered strawberries (from £5.50). There's a good value three-course evening menu (£15), and two-course Sunday lunch (£10.95). The heavy-beamed main bar has two big tables (one a massive oak construction), a comfortable mix of seating including some handsome leather chairs and leather banquettes, and a huge boar's head above a good log fire in the big brick fireplace. Among cartoons on the wall are some of the illustrated claret bottle labels from the series commissioned from famous artists, initiated by the late Baron Philippe de Rothschild. The lounge on the right has a deep red colour scheme, leather sofas, and big plasma TV, and on the left there are more leather seats in a dining area housed in what was once the village bakery; piped music. A corridor leads off to the light and airy main restaurant with contemporary pictures, and a second bar; smoking in the bar only. A good range of drinks includes well kept Brewsters Marquis and a guest such as Black Sheep on handpump, a selection of belgian beers, local fruit pressés, over 35 wines by the glass, over 20 champagnes, and 50 malt whiskies. There are nice teak tables, chairs and benches outside, and beyond some picnic-sets on the edge of the pub's cricket field; boules too, and views of Belvoir Castle. *(Recommended by Derek and Sylvia Stephenson, Barry Collett, W W Burke, Pat and Sam Roberts, Mrs E A Macdonald)*

Free house ~ Licensee Justin Chad ~ Real ale ~ Bar food (12-2.30, 6-9.30; 12-4, 6-8.30) ~ Restaurant ~ (01476) 870701 ~ Children welcome ~ Dogs allowed in bar and bedrooms ~ Open 12-3.30, 5.30-12; 12-1am Sat; 12-11 Sun ~ Bedrooms: £55B/£69B

LUCKY DIP

Besides the fully inspected pubs, you might like to try these Lucky Dips recommended to us and described by readers (if you do, please send us reports: www.goodguides.co.uk).

BICKER [TF2237]
☆ *Red Lion* PE20 3EF [A52 NE of Donnington]: Chatty and relaxing 17th-c village pub with real ales such as Adnams Broadside, Butcombe, Courage Directors and John Smiths, quick service even when busy, wide choice of good value generous food; bowed black beams and huge fireplace, separate restaurant; pool and games machine in main bar; tables on terrace and tree-shaded lawn *(Leon Shaw, LYM)*
BOSTON [TF3344]
Coach & Horses PE21 6SY [Main Ridge]: Friendly traditional one-bar pub with good

Batemans XB and XXB, good coal fire, pool and darts; cl wkdy lunchtimes *(the Didler)*
BOURNE [TF0920]
Nags Head PE10 9EF [Abbey Rd]: Recently redecorated (and soon to be no smoking), popular for bargain food lunchtime (with OAP deals) and Weds/Thurs steak nights *(Geoff and Pat Bell)*
Smiths PE10 9AE [North St]: Extensive shop conversion spreading through various bar areas and levels, pleasant décor with soft lighting, cosy corners and log fires, Fullers London Pride, Oakham JHB and two guest beers, food

all home made using local supplies – part no smoking at lunchtime; piped music – can get loud evenings; children welcome, large terrace with barbecues, open all day *(the Didler)*

BRANDY WHARF [TF0196]

☆ *Cider Centre* DN21 4RU [B1205 SE of Scunthorpe (off A15 about 16 miles N of Lincoln)]: No smoking cider haunt, up to 15 on draught, eight tapped from casks, many more in bottles and other smallish containers, also country wines and meads; simple bright main bar, dimly lit lounge bar with lots of cider memorabilia and jokey bric-a-brac, reasonably priced straightforward food (all day Sun); piped music, and housekeeping could be perked up; children in eating area, simple glazed verandah, tables and play area in meadows or by river with moorings and slipway, open all day wknds *(the Didler, David and Brenda Tew, A J Bowen, Keith and Chris O'Neill, LYM)*

CASTLE BYTHAM [SK9818]

☆ *Castle Inn* NG33 4RZ [off A1 Stamford—Grantham, or B1176]: Black-beamed village pub reopened after refurbishment by new licensees, enjoyable straightforward food from ciabattas up cooked to order by landlady, helpful friendly young staff, quickly changing real ales such as Exmoor Hound Dog and Camerons Strongarm, good hot drinks, comfortable armchairs and log fire, no smoking area, pub alsatian called Skye; disabled access by side door, cl Mon *(Michael and Jenny Back, LYM)*

CLEETHORPES [TA3008]

No 2 Refreshment Room DN35 8AX [Station Approach]: Well kept single-room platform bar with five changing ales from small breweries, friendly service, no food; tables out under heaters, open all day *(the Didler)*

☆ *Willys* DN35 8RQ [Highcliff Rd; south promenade]: Open-plan bistro-style seafront pub with panoramic Humber views, café tables, tiled floor and painted brick walls; visibly brews its own good beers, also Batemans and other changing ales, belgian beers, popular beer festival Nov, good value lunchtime home cooking (evening food too Mon/Tues and Thurs), friendly staff, nice mix of customers from young and trendy to weatherbeaten fishermen; quiet juke box; a few tables out on the prom, open all day *(the Didler)*

EWERBY [TF1247]

☆ *Finch Hatton Arms* NG34 9PH [Main St]: Handsome, well decorated and plushly furnished mock-Tudor pub with good food choice inc fresh fish and Sun lunch, helpful service, real ales inc a guest beer, coal fire, smart dining room, comfortable back locals' bar; eight bedrooms *(BB, Bill and Sheila McLardy)*

FROGNALL [TF1610]

Goat PE6 8SA [B1525, off A16 NE of Mkt Deeping]: Family-friendly pub with interesting changing real ales, lots of whiskies, enjoyable food from lunchtime sandwiches up, cheerful service, log fires, low 17th-c beams, stripped

stone, two dining rooms (one no smoking where children welcome); may be piped music; good wheelchair access, big garden with terrace and secure play area, separate part for under-5s *(Michael and Jenny Back, Geoff and Pat Bell)*

GAINSBOROUGH [SK8189]

Eight Jolly Brewers DN21 2DW [Ship Court, Silver St]: Small comfortable grown-up real ale pub with up to eight from small breweries inc its own Maypole, farm cider, simple lunchtime food (not Sun), friendly staff and locals, beams, bare bricks and brewery posters, quieter bar upstairs; folk club, open all day *(Michael and Maggie Betton, D A Bradford, the Didler)*

GEDNEY DYKE [TF4125]

☆ *Chequers* PE12 0AJ [off A17 Holbeach—Kings Lynn]: Fenland pub with food that's often good, from sandwiches with home-baked bread and chutney to interesting main dishes, Adnams and Greene King Abbot, simple bar with open fire, no smoking dining conservatory; piped music, friendly staff but service can sometimes suffer; children welcome, garden picnic-sets, cl Mon *(Comus and Sarah Elliott, June and Ken Brooks, John Wooll, Ken Marshall, K E and B Billington, Ryta Lyndley, Eddie and Lynn Jarrett, LYM)*

GRANTHAM [SK9135]

☆ *Angel & Royal* NG31 6PN [High St]: Comfortable hotel with elaborate carved 14th-c stone façade, ancient upstairs bars with formidable inglenook fireplaces and a charming little medieval oriel window seat jutting over the road, stylish downstairs bistro/bar with elegant modern tables, comfortable chairs on pale oak boards, up-to-date pastels and some ancient stripped stonework, two real ales, wide choice of modern food from good sandwiches up, grand-manner wknd restaurant; piped music, TV; children in eating areas, good if pricey bedrooms in modern back extension alongside narrow flagstoned inner coachway, good parking, open all day *(LYM, Phil and Jane Hodson)*

Beehive NG31 6SE [Castlegate]: Hive of bees in the good-sized back garden's lime tree has been this unpretentious pub's unique inn sign for a couple of centuries or more – same strain of bees all that time; real ales such as Everards and Newby Wyke, friendly service, coal fire; back games area with machines, juke box and TVs; children welcome till 7.30, open all day *(LYM, the Didler)*

☆ *Blue Pig* NG31 6RQ [Vine St]: Pretty jettied Tudor pub, low beams, panelling, stripped stone and flagstones, lots of pig ornaments, friendly unpretentious bustle, helpful staff, good range of interesting changing ales, good simple lunchtime food, open fire, daily papers, lots of prints and bric-a-brac; piped music, juke box, games machines, no children or dogs; tables out behind, open all day *(BB, the Didler)*

Nobody Inn NG31 6PR [Watergate]: Friendly bare-boards open-plan local with five or six good ales mainly from local breweries such as

Newby Wyke and Oldershaws; back games room with pool, table footer, SkyTV; open all day *(the Didler)*

GRIMSBY [TA2609]

Lincoln Castle DN31 1SY [Fishermans Wharf; follow Heritage Centre signs, behind Sainsburys]: Former Humber paddle-steamer converted to friendly and pleasant bar and lower deck restaurant, enjoyable inexpensive food inc Sun carvery, engines preserved and on view, cabinet showing ship's history, seats out on upper deck; games machine, piped music; handy for National Fishing Heritage Centre *(Mrs Hazel Rainer)*

GRIMSTHORPE [TF0422]

Black Horse PE10 0LY [A151 W of Bourne]: Extensive handsome no smoking grey-stone coaching inn refurbished by new licensees, with light and airy long narrowish bar and eclectic mix of furniture, Batemans and a guest beer, standard bar food; children welcome lunchtime only; bedrooms, cl Mon *(LYM)*

HALTON HOLEGATE [TF4165]

☆ *Bell* PE23 5NY [B1195 E of Spilsby]: Unchanging pretty village local, simple but comfortable and consistently friendly, with Batemans XB, Highwood Tom Woods Bomber County and guest beers, Lancaster bomber pictures, pub games, nice old golden labrador, low-priced generous food cooked by landlord; children in back eating area with tropical fish tank and restaurant *(LYM, the Didler, Michael and Jenny Back, Ian and Nita Cooper)*

HORNCASTLE [TF2669]

Bull LN9 5HU [Bull Ring]: Good pubby atmosphere in 16th-c country-town hotel, former posting inn, with attractively priced bar food from sandwiches up, helpful friendly staff, traditional décor, restaurant; tables in cobbled yard, comfortable bedrooms, substantial breakfast *(Alistair and Kay Butler)*

KIRKBY LA THORPE [TF0945]

Queens Head NG34 9NW [Boston Rd, backing on to A17]: Comfortably refurbished dining pub with large bar and small cosy no smoking restaurant, good choice of enjoyable food from well filled sandwiches and baguettes (home-baked bread) to fresh fish, pleasant service, Marstons, decent house wine; easy disabled access *(Bill and Sheila McLardy)*

LEADENHAM [SK9452]

Willoughby Arms LN5 0PP [High St; A17 Newark—Sleaford]: Comfortable bar, good food in two eating areas, friendly staff; good bedrooms *(Beryl and Bill Farmer)*

LINCOLN [SK9871]

Bull & Chain LN2 4AD [Langworthgate]: Popular unpretentious local with good value generous food inc OAP meals, good range of beers, wines and spirits, comfortable banquettes, no smoking areas, decorative plates, darts and dominoes; children welcome, big garden overlooking tennis court, not far from cathedral *(Gordon B Thornton)*

Golden Eagle LN5 8BD [High St]: Two-bar Tynemill town pub, up to half a dozen good value changing ales, good choice of country wines, cheap soft drinks, sensibly priced

lunchtime food, cheery back bar; tables outside, open all day *(the Didler)*

Morning Star LN2 4AW [Greetwellgate]: Friendly well scrubbed local handy for cathedral, enjoyable cheap lunches esp Fri specials, reasonably priced Bass, Greene King Abbot, Tetleys, Charles Wells Bombardier and guest beers, helpful service, coal fire, aircraft paintings, two bar areas and comfortable snug with sofas; enthusiastic singer/pianist Sat night; nice outside area, open all day exc Sun *(John Robertson, Pete Baker, the Didler, David and Ruth Hollands)*

Pyewipe LN1 2BG [Saxilby Rd; off A57 just S of bypass]: Much extended 18th-c waterside pub popular for its great position by Roman Fossdyke Canal (pleasant walk out from centre), wide range of decent food inc good fish choice, friendly attentive staff dealing with large numbers without becoming impersonal, real ales such as Timothy Taylors Landlord; pleasant tables outside, comfortable reasonably priced bedrooms *(M and C Thompson, David and Ruth Hollands, Alistair and Kay Butler)*

Sippers LN5 7HW [Melville St, opp bus station]: Two-bar pub with good value lunchtime food inc good Sun lunch (can book evening meals too), Hop Back real ales with others such as John Smiths and Marstons Pedigree; open all day (Sun afternoon break) *(the Didler)*

☆ *Strugglers* LN1 3BG [Westgate]: Friendly refurbished character local with particularly well kept ales such as Bass, Batemans, Black Sheep, Fullers London Pride and Timothy Taylors Landlord, above-average home-made food (not Sun/Mon), coal-effect fire in small back snug; heaters and canopy for terrace tables (no under-18s inside), open all day *(Kevin Blake, the Didler, David and Ruth Hollands, John Cross)*

Treaty of Commerce LN5 7AF [High St]: Tudor building with oak beams, grand old stained glass, antique etchings and panelling, lively pubby atmosphere, Batemans and guest beers, simple lunchtime food (not Sun/Mon), darts; open all day *(the Didler)*

LITTLE BYTHAM [TF0117]

☆ *Willoughby Arms* NG33 4RA [Station Rd, S of village]: Good Newby Wyke beers from back microbrewery, interesting guest beers, Weston's farm cider, frequent beer festivals, reasonably priced substantial food from sandwiches up, friendly staff and local atmosphere, daily papers, simple bar with wall banquettes, stripped tables and coal fire, pleasant no smoking end dining room; piped music, airy games room with pool and sports TV; good disabled access, children welcome, picnic-sets in pleasant good-sized back garden with quiet country views, bedrooms, open all day wknds *(BB, the Didler, Bill and Sheila McLardy, G Coates)*

LOUTH [TF3287]

Olde Whyte Swanne LN11 9NP [Eastgate]: Low 16th-c beams, coal or log fires in comfortable and relaxed front bar and dining room, good choice of enjoyable food all day using local produce, helpful friendly staff, real ales such as Black Sheep, Greene King and Theakstons; children welcome, open all day from 9.30, bedrooms *(the Didler, Ian and Nita Cooper)*

Wheatsheaf LN11 9YD [Westgate]: Cheerful early 17th-c low-beamed pub, coal fires in all three bars, changing real ales and a late May beer festival, decent lunchtime food (not Sun), old photographs; tables outside, open all day Sat *(the Didler)*

MARTIN [TF1259]

Royal Oak LN4 3QT [High St]: Recently refurbished, with bargain pubby food and pleasant staff *(Bill and Sheila McLardy)*

NEWTON [TF0436]

☆ *Red Lion* NG34 0EE [off A52 E of Grantham]: Old-fashioned seating, partly stripped stone walls with old farm tools and stuffed birds and animals, straightforward bar food inc daily cold carvery and hot carvery Fri/Sat evening and Sun lunchtime, Batemans XB and a guest beer, no smoking dining room; piped music, fruit machine; tables in sheltered back garden with terrace *(LYM)*

NORTH KELSEY [TA0401]

Butchers Arms LN7 6EH [Middle St; off B1434 S of Brigg]: Busy village local with five well kept Tom Woods Highwood beers, low ceilings, flagstones, bare boards, dim lighting, good value cold lunches, enthusiastic cheerful service, woodburner, pub games; tables outside, opens 4 wkdys, open all day wknds *(the Didler)*

NORTH THORESBY [TF2998]

New Inn DN36 5QS [Station Rd]: Attractive inn popular for consistently enjoyable reasonably priced food, good service, friendly atmosphere, roomy restaurant; pleasant terrace *(P Norton)*

PINCHBECK [TF2425]

Bull PE11 3RA [A16]: Enjoyable good value food inc fresh fish in bar and restaurant, good range of beers, friendly service *(John Cooke)*

REDBOURNE [SK9799]

☆ *Red Lion* DN21 4QR [Main Rd]: Welcoming traditional coaching inn with thriving atmosphere, enjoyable home-made food from lunchtime sandwiches and baguettes up inc some unusual dishes and specials, and nice cheeses; helpful staff, three or four real ales such as Greene King Abbot and Tetleys, open fires, flagstones, polished panelling and some duck ornamentation, no smoking garden room restaurant; dogs welcome, garden with terrace, decent bedrooms and breakfast, open all day *(Trevor and Sheila Sharman, BB, Michael Weston)*

SCAMPTON [SK9579]

Dambusters LN1 2SD [High St]: Beams, hops and masses of interesting Dambusters and other World War II memorabilia, reasonably priced simple food (not Sun/Mon evenings), pleasant nostalgic atmosphere, Greene King IPA, Abbot and Ruddles and guest beers, log fire, adjoining post office; very near Red Arrows runway viewpoint *(Mrs Carolyn Dixon, Keith and Chris O'Neill)*

SCOTTER [SE8800]

☆ *White Swan* DN21 3UD [The Green]: Comfortable well kept dining pub, varied well prepared generous food inc fish board and bargain three-course special, Black Sheep, John Smiths, Websters and interesting changing guest beers, several levels inc snug panelled area by one fireplace, friendly landlady and neat cheerful staff, big-windowed restaurant looking over lawn with picnic-table sets to duck-filled River Eau (best to book wknds); piped music, steps up to entrance; 14 comfortable bedrooms in modern extension, open all day Fri-Sun *(Keith Wright, BB, Alistair and Kay Butler)*

SILK WILLOUGHBY [TF0542]

Horseshoe NG34 8NZ [A15 S of Sleaford]: Pleasant décor, enjoyable good value food all day, real ale *(Geoff and Pat Bell)*

SKEGNESS [TF5661]

☆ *Vine* PE25 3DB [Vine Rd, off Drummond Rd, Seacroft]: Unspoilt small hotel based on late 18th-c country house, unpretentious well run bar with friendly staff, welcoming fire and Batemans XB, Mild and XXB, good bar food using local produce, imposing antique seats and grandfather clock in turkey-carpeted hall, inner oak-panelled room, restaurant; tables on big back sheltered lawn with swings, good reasonably priced bedrooms (plumbing could be quieter), peaceful suburban setting not far from beach and bird-watching *(BB, John Tavernor, the Didler, Brian and Ruth Archer, Maurice and Gill McMahon, Ian and Nita Cooper)*

SLEAFORD [TF0645]

Barge & Bottle NG34 7TR [Carre St]: Large busy open-plan pub handsomely done by local furniture-making family, impressive range of nine changing ales such as Batemans, Greene King, Highwood, Springhead and Tetleys, wide range of usual food from sandwiches and panini to full meals and Sun carvery, also children's dishes, teas and bargain early breakfasts, no smoking area and back no smoking restaurant/conservatory; shame about the piped music; riverside terrace, children welcome, handy for arts centre, open all day *(Tony and Wendy Hobden)*

SOUTH ORMSBY [TF3675]

☆ *Massingberd Arms* LN11 8QS [off A16 S of Louth]: Small village pub with welcoming and obliging landlord, John Smiths Magnet and a couple of interesting guest beers, short choice of enjoyable fresh food inc game and Sun lunch, restaurant; pleasant garden, good Wolds walks, cl Mon lunchtime *(the Didler, Ian and Nita Cooper)*

SOUTH THORESBY [TF4076]

☆ *Vine* LN13 0AS [about a mile off A16 N of Ulceby Cross]: Two-room village inn with small local pub part – tiny passageway servery, steps up to three-table lounge, separate pool room; wide choice of quickly served food, prompt welcoming service, Batemans XB, good value wines, nicely panelled no smoking dining room; bedrooms, tables in pleasant big garden *(the Didler, Ian and Nita Cooper)*

SPALDING [TF2422]
White Horse PE11 2RA [Churchgate]:
Attractive two-bar 17th-c thatched pub next to
High Bridge over River Welland, lively and
friendly, bargain Sam Smiths, pubby food inc
good value all-day Sun lunch in no smoking
dining room; open all day *(N R White,
John Honnor)*
STAMFORD [TF0306]
☆ *Bull & Swan* PE9 2LJ [High St, St Martins]:
Traditional pub with three low-beamed
connecting rooms, warmly welcoming
licensees, enjoyable food, real ales, good log
and coal fires, gleaming copper and brass;
children welcome, tables out in former back
coachyard, bedrooms, good breakfast
*(Josephine Messinger, Alistair and Kay Butler,
LYM)*
☆ *Crown* PE9 2AG [All Saints Pl]: Substantial
stone-built hotel, long a popular meeting point,
recently extraordinarily modernised in a way
that's quite unexpected from the outside;
spacious main bar (think nightclub or even
spaceship) with long leather-cushioned bar
counter, substantial pillars, a pinkish hue
thanks to the unusual lighting, step up to more
traditional flagstoned area with stripped stone
and lots of leather sofas and armchairs,
emphasis on good seasonal country cooking
using local produce, very friendly staff, four
changing real ales, decent wines and coffee;
fresh flowers, civilised dining room; heated
outdoor area for smokers, comfortable quiet
bedrooms, open all day *(M and C Thompson,
Derek Thomas, BB, the Didler, Mr and Mrs
B Jeffery)*
Green Man PE9 2YQ [Scotgate]: Half a dozen
or more changing ales inc Caledonian
Deuchars IPA and Theakstons, belgian beers,
farm ciders, friendly staff, good value
lunchtime food, sturdy scrubbed pale wood
tables on flagstones, log fire, steps up to back
room with good bottle collection and TV;
garden tables, comfortable bedrooms sharing
bathroom, open all day *(the Didler, G Coates,
Tracey and Stephen Groves)*
Lincolnshire Poacher PE9 1PG [Broad St]:
Handsome building with enjoyable food,
drinks and service *(Ron Deighton)*
Otters Pocket PE9 2PA [All Saints St]: Small
cosy bar and long back lounge, up to five
changing real ales, interesting bottled beers and
ciders, good service, wknd food; open all day
(P Dawn)
Periwig PE9 2AG [Red Lion Sq/All Saints Pl]:
Attractive façade, half a dozen good real ales,
good value food from baguettes up, gallery
above narrow split-level bar, bistro-style eating
area; piped music, sports TV and can get busy
with lively young people evenings – open till
late, esp Fri/Sat; open all day *(P Dawn)*
STOW [SK8881]
☆ *Cross Keys* LN1 2DD [B1241 NW of Lincoln]:
Reliable largely no smoking extended dining
pub nr Saxon minster church, prettily
presented fresh food inc lots of interesting
blackboard specials and good puddings,
Greene King, Highgate Tom Woods and

Theakstons ales, good range of wines, quick
friendly service, big woodburner in attractively
modernised bar; may be piped music; cl Mon
lunchtime *(BB, Bill and Sheila McLardy,
David and Ruth Hollands, Mrs Brenda Calver)*
SUSWORTH [SE8301]
☆ *Jenny Wren* DN17 3AS [East Ferry Rd]:
Popular family-run country pub in nice setting
with long partly divided bar/dining area
overlooking River Trent, wide choice of good
enterprising food at reasonable prices inc lots
of fish and local produce, panelling, stripped
brickwork, low beams and brasses, busy
décor and plenty of tables, real ales such as
John Smiths and Tom Woods, good wines by
the glass, two open fires; some tables on
terrace and more across quiet road by water;
monthly classic car rallies *(Mr and Mrs
G Sadie, BB)*
SWALLOW [TA1702]
Swallow LN7 6DL [Caistor Rd (A46)]: Large
dining pub with good service and good range
of food served all day *(Brian P White)*
SWINDERBY [SK8862]
Dovecote LN6 9HN [Newark Rd (A46)]:
Reopened after refurbishment, distinctive décor
with clever use of various artefacts, wide
choice of imaginative food from doorstep
sandwiches to lobster, Poachers real ales
(David and Ruth Hollands)
TATTERSHALL THORPE [TF2159]
Blue Bell LN4 4PE [Thorpe Rd; B1192
Coningsby—Woodhall Spa]: Attractive very
low-beamed pub said to date from 13th c and
used by the Dambusters, RAF memorabilia
and appropriate real ales such as Highgate
Tom Woods Bomber County and Poachers
Pathfinders, good choice of reasonably priced
bar food inc bargain pie, log fires and plenty of
character, small dining room; tables in garden,
impressive lavatera bushes, bedrooms
(the Didler, Bill and Sheila McLardy)
TEALBY [TF1590]
Olde Barn LN8 3YB [Cow Lane (B1203)]:
Neatly kept dining pub in extended former
barn, Highwood Best and a guest such as
North Yorkshire Flying Herbert,
extraordinarily wide choice of food, cheerful
service; big attractive back garden, handy for
Viking Way *(Val and Alan Green)*
TETFORD [TF3374]
☆ *White Hart* LN9 6QQ [East Rd, off A158 E of
Horncastle]: Interesting early 16th-c pub with
good choice of above-average food inc good
local beef, Adnams, Fullers London Pride and
Greene King, farm cider, old-fashioned curved-
back settles, slabby elm tables, red tiled floor
and log fire in pleasant quiet inglenook bar, no
smoking snug, basic games room; unobtrusive
piped music; tables on sheltered back lawn,
simple bedrooms, pretty countryside, cl Mon
lunchtime *(LYM, the Didler)*
TORKSEY [SK8479]
Castle LN1 2EQ [Station Rd]: Straightforward
pub which surprises with its good english and
portuguese food inc fresh fish from Hull
cooked by Portuguese landlady, helpful
landlord *(Wendy and Bob Needham)*

WAINFLEET [TF5058]

☆ *Batemans Brewery* PE24 4JE [Mill Lane, off A52 via B1195]: Not exactly a pub, but very pubby circular bar in brewery's ivy-covered windmill tower with Batemans ales in top condition, czech and belgian beers on tap, ground-floor dining area with unpretentious lunchtime food such as local sausages and pork pies, games room with plenty of old pub games (more of these outside), lots of brewery memorabilia and plenty for families to enjoy; entertaining brewery tours at 2.30, brewery shop (helpful service), tables out on terrace and grass, opens 11.30-3.30 *(the Didler, Gordon Neighbour)*

WALKERITH [SK7892]

Ferry House DN21 3DE [Walkerith Rd]: Substantial food inc popular Sun lunch, no smoking restaurant *(Peter and Eleanor Kenyon)*

WELBY [SK9738]

Crown & Anchor NG32 3LP: Attractive recently refurbished village pub with friendly local atmosphere in spacious bar area, enjoyable food here and in small dining room *(M and C Thompson)*

WELTON HILL [TF0481]

☆ *Farmers Arms* LN2 3RD [Market Rasen Rd (A46 NE of Lincoln)]: Well run and comfortable very spacious no smoking dining pub, hearty helpings of good fresh sensibly priced food from baguettes to popular Sun lunch, emphasis on top-notch local produce, lots of wine by the glass (wine-themed décor and events), changing ales such as Ringwood Bold Forester and local Tom Woods, prompt service from helpful friendly licensees and neat staff, panelling and some stripped brickwork, houseplants and fresh flowers; disabled access, very shallow steps to upper dining room *(R Pearce, BB, P W Baldwin,*

Mrs Brenda Calver)

WEST DEEPING [TF1009]

Red Lion PE6 9HP [King St]: Long low-beamed bar with plenty of tables, generous food from good bar snacks to full meals inc early evening offers in popular new back dining extension with goldfish tank, polite attentive service, Everards and other ales such as Nethergate or John Smiths, good coffee, roaring coal fire, stripped stone, brassware and pictures; disabled access and facilities, tables in back garden with attractive fenced play area, open all day *(Howard and Margaret Buchanan, Michael and Jenny Back)*

WHAPLODE ST CATHERINE [TF3419]

Blue Bell PE12 6SN [Cranesgate S – 3 miles down a country lane]: Welcoming village local brewing its own ales such as Old Session and Old Honesty, good value food in bar and well appointing dining room inc locally popular Sun carvery (worth booking ahead), good wine choice, log fire in lounge, pool in side room; cl wkdy lunchtimes *(Paul Stafford)*

WILSFORD [TF0043]

Plough NG32 3NS [Main St]: Neatly kept and properly pubby, with good value food, wider evening choice, pleasant service *(Bill and Sheila McLardy)*

WOODHALL SPA [TF1962]

Abbey Lodge LN10 6UH [B1192 towards Coningsby]: Family-run roadside inn with good genuine pubby feel mixing eating and drinking sides well, bustling discreetly decorated bar, Victorian and older furnishings, World War II RAF pictures, affable staff, good straightforward reasonably priced bar food from sandwiches up, Marstons Pedigree; children over 10 in restaurant, may be piped Radio 1; cl Sun *(LYM, Maurice and Gill McMahon, John Branston)*

Post Office address codings confusingly give the impression that a few pubs are in Lincolnshire, when they're really in Cambridgeshire (which is where we list them).

Norfolk

This is a prize part of the world for good pubs, with lots of places of real individuality and character. They range from no-nonsense little taverns to extremely civilised hotels with warmly inviting pubby bars, and a high percentage of them come up trumps as places to spend a few days in; many have Stay Awards. Several benefit from licensees who have looked after and developed them lovingly over many years, and there's plenty of genuine friendliness and informality. Good beer is a strong point, too, with the Fat Cat in Norwich leading the way (30 ales on at one time, and remarkably they keep them all in good condition – no doubt their really keen pricing encourages a quick turnover). Pubs doing particularly well here in recent months include the Kings Head at Bawburgh (moving steadily upmarket), the White Horse at Brancaster Staithe (a good mix of pub and restaurant), the Hoste Arms in Burnham Market (an amazing new underground cellar for their fine wines), the Lord Nelson at Burnham Thorpe (lots of Nelson memorabilia and a super atmosphere), the Saracens Head near Erpingham (gently eccentric in the best sort of way, and with good food), the Angel at Larling (a good mix of diners and drinkers), the Rose & Crown at Snettisham (ever-improving), the Crown at Stanhoe (unpretentious and friendly), the Red Lion at Stiffkey (enjoyable all round), the Hare Arms at Stow Bardolph (the licensees have now notched up 30 years there – they were already old hands when this *Guide* started), the Woolpack at Terrington St John (the boisterous landlady keeps things buzzing along), the Lifeboat at Thornham (doing well under its new licensees), the Old Ram at Tivetshall St Mary (a good place to stay), the Crown in Wells-next-the-Sea (much more pubby now, and with delicious food), and the Fur & Feather at Woodbastwick (next to the Woodfordes brewery and with plenty of their beers). These top pubs are joined by some really rewarding new entries this year, such the Jolly Sailors at Brancaster Staithe (brewing its own Brancaster ales), the smashing Victoria at Holkham (civilised and smart but informal, and certainly somewhere to spend a few days), the Anchor at Morston (a thriving atmosphere with a good mix of modern and old décor), the Gamekeeper at Old Buckenham (a pretty pub liked by a mix of customers), the Ostrich at South Creake (cheerfully informal and attractively laid out), and the Globe in Wells-next-the-Sea (sister pub to the Victoria at Holkham). There is some delicious food in the county, and plenty of fresh fish and seafood including local mussels, oysters, crabs and little brown shrimps. Particularly memorable meals this year have distinguished the Kings Head at Bawburgh, White Horse at Brancaster Staithe, Hoste Arms in Burnham Market, Saracens Head near Erpingham, Victoria at Holkham, Walpole Arms at Itteringham, Rose & Crown at Snettisham, and Crown in Wells-next-the-Sea. The Victoria at Holkham is Norfolk Dining Pub of the Year. Norfolk is one of those counties where we wish our pages were more elastic, as the Lucky Dip section at the end of the chapter is full of riches, too, with lots of pubs worth longer descriptions than we've room for. Prime examples are the Cock at Barford, Spread Eagle at Barton Bendish, Chequers at Binham, Buckinghamshire Arms at Blickling, Ostrich at Castle Acre, Crown at Colkirk, Windmill at Great Cressingham, Half Moon at

Rushall, Crown at Smallburgh, Chequers at Thompson, Stag at West Acre, Bell at Wiveton and Carpenters Arms at Wighton. Drinks prices in the area are on average fairly close to the national norm. The beers we found most often showing up as the cheapest on offer in good pubs here were the local Woodfordes and (from Suffolk) Adnams, with the region's dominant brewer Greene King also prominent. Other less common local ales to look out for include Wolf, Spectrum, Winters and Fox.

BAWBURGH TG1508 Map 5

Kings Head 🍴 ♀

Pub signposted down Harts Lane off B1108, which leads off A47 just W of Norwich; NR9 3LS

Moving steadily upmarket, this bustling old pub is particularly popular with our readers at lunchtime. There are wooden floors, leather sofas and seats, a mix of nice old wooden tables and wooden or leather dining chairs, low beams and some standing timbers, a warming log fire in a large knocked-through canopied fireplace, and a couple of woodburning stoves in the restaurant areas. Well presented and extremely good, the food might include bar snacks and lunchtime choices such as three-times cooked hand-cut chips with dutch mayo (£2.50), warm moroccan flat bread, hummous and black olive tapenade (£3.50), soup with home-made organic bread (£5), escabeche of whitebait, chilli, oregano and lime (£7.50), cumberland sausages with onion gravy, bruschetta, mozzarella, oak-roasted peppers and home-grown rocket pesto or smoked eel, scrambled eggs, watercress and parmesan (£8.50), home-made beefburger (£9.25), ham and free-range egg (£9.50), and crispy beef stir fry, pak choi, oyster mushrooms and crispy noodles or deep-fried cod with home-made tartare sauce (£10.50). Evening choices like caramelised red onion, thyme and goats cheese tart with rocket pesto (£7), farmhouse terrine with celeriac remoulade (£7.95), antipasti (£8.25), pasta with slow-cooked tomato ragoût and wild mushrooms (£11.50), and vietnamese marinated chicken or whole plaice with nut brown butter, brown shrimps and gremolata (£14.50), with puddings such as pine nut and honey tart with blackcurrant coulis, baked ginger pudding, chargrilled pineapple and ginger bread ice-cream or chocolate pod, chantilly cream and griottine cherries (£5.50). The restaurant and part of the bar area are no smoking. Well kept Adnams Bitter, Woodfordes Wherry and a guest such as Nethergate Augustinian on handpump, 20 wines by the glass, and freshly squeezed orange juice; piped music. Seats outside in the garden. *(Recommended by Anthony Barnes, Mark, Amanda, Luke and Jake Sheard, Margaret McPhee, Sally Anne and Peter Goodale, Ken Millar, Gerry and Rosemary Dobson, Peter and Jean Dowson, Chris and Diana Aylott)*

Free house ~ Licensee Anton Wimmer ~ Real ale ~ Bar food (12-2(2.30 Sun), 5.30-9.15; not Sun or Mon evenings) ~ Restaurant ~ (01603) 744977 ~ Children welcome ~ Dogs allowed in bar ~ Quiz night every second Mon ~ Open 11-11; 12-10.30 Sun; closed evening 25 Dec

BLAKENEY TG0243 Map 8

Kings Arms 🍺

West Gate Street; NR25 7NQ

This attractive white inn does get pretty crowded at peak times as it's just a stroll from the harbour. The three simply furnished, knocked-through pubby rooms have a good mix of locals and visitors, low ceilings, some interesting photographs of the licensees' theatrical careers, other pictures including work by local artists, and what must be the smallest cartoon gallery in England – in a former telephone kiosk. Look out for the brass plaque on the wall that marks a flood level. Two small rooms are no smoking, as is the airy garden room; darts, games machine, bar billiards, table skittles and board games. Adnams, Greene King Old Speckled Hen, Marstons

Pedigree and Woodfordes Wherry on handpump, and quite a few wines by the glass. Reasonably priced bar food includes sandwiches (from £1.80), soup (£2.95), filled baked potatoes (from £4.75), rough pork and garlic pâté (£4.95), vegetable burgers (£5.75), local mussels (winter only £6.50), battered haddock (£7.25), grilled gammon and egg (£7.95), daily pies or stews (from £8.50), and steaks (from £10.50). Lots of tables and chairs in the large garden; good nearby walks. *(Recommended by Ann and Colin Hunt, Geoff and Pat Bell, Alan Cole, Kirstie Bruce, Simon Cottrell, Roger Wain-Heapy, Dr and Mrs P Truelove, MDN, Sue and Graham Fergy, Keith and Chris O'Neill, Keith and Janet Morris)*

Free house ~ Licensees John Howard, Marjorie Davies and Nick Davies ~ Real ale ~ Bar food (12-9.30(9 Sun)) ~ (01263) 740341 ~ Children welcome ~ Dogs welcome ~ Open 11(11.30 Sun)-midnight; closed evening 25 Dec ~ Bedrooms: /£65S

White Horse
Off A149 W of Sheringham; High Street; NR25 7AL

Nicely set near the harbour, this busy little hotel is run by cheerful staff. The long main bar is predominantly green with a venetian red ceiling and restrained but attractive décor, including watercolours by a local artist. Many people, though, head for the big back no smoking dining conservatory. Well kept Adnams, Greene King IPA and Abbot, and Woodfordes Wherry on handpump, and a dozen wines by the glass. Enjoyable bar food includes a plate of crudités (£3.95), lunchtime sandwiches or filled ciabattas (from £3.95), home-made cockle chowder (£4.45), couscous with roasted aubergine and tagine dressing (£5.45; main course £8.95), caesar salad with crayfish tails (£5.95; main course £10.50), local crab salad (£6.25; main course £9.25), braised ham hock in cream sauce (£8.95), lunchtime fish pie (£9.95), maple-cured gloucester old spot pork chop with grain mustard and caper dressing (£10.95), breast of gressingham duck, asian coleslaw, wasabi oil and sweet potato crisps (£12.95), and fillet of black bream piri-piri (£13.95). There are tables in a suntrap courtyard and a pleasant paved garden. *(Recommended by Ann and Colin Hunt, MDN, Alan Cole, Kirstie Bruce, Minda and Stanley Alexander, Colin Goddard, John Wooll, Tracey and Stephen Groves, Mike and Shelley Woodroffe, Peter and Pat Frogley)*

Free house ~ Licensees Dan Goff and Simon Scillitoe ~ Real ale ~ Bar food (12-2.15, 6-9) ~ Restaurant ~ (01263) 740574 ~ Children allowed but must be away from bar area ~ Open 11(12 Sun)-11; closed second and third week in Jan ~ Bedrooms: /£60B

BRANCASTER STAITHE   TF7944   Map 8
Jolly Sailors
Main Road (A149); PE31 8BJ

This is prime bird-watching territory as the pub is set on the edge of thousands of acres of National Trust dunes and salt flats; walkers are welcome. It's unpretentious and simply furnished with three cosy rooms, a log fire, and a good mix of seats. Good bar food includes oysters and mussels from the harbour just across the road, soup (£3.95), smoked sprat pâté (£4.50), deep-fried whitebait (£4.95), local sausages made with beer, honey-glazed home-cooked ham and egg or steak and kidney pie (£8.50), haddock in beer batter or vegetarian spicy crispy tortilla pancake with tomato sauce (£8.95), locally smoked cod on buttered herb tagliatelle (£11.95), T-bone steak (£15.95), and home-made puddings; they are hoping to hold winter gourmet evenings. Both restaurants are no smoking. From their on-site microbrewery they produce Brancaster Staithe Brewery Old Les and IPA and keep a guest like Woodfordes Great Eastern on handpump. There's a sizeable garden and covered terrace, both with tables, and a children's play area. *(Recommended by Ann and Colin Hunt, John Wooll, Roger Wain-Heapy, Tracey and Stephen Groves, Eddie and Lynn Jarrett, Pat and Clive Sherriff)*

Free house ~ Licensee Mr Boughton ~ Real ale ~ Bar food (all day) ~ Restaurant ~ (01485) 210314 ~ Children welcome ~ Dogs allowed in bar ~ Open 11-11; 12-10.30 Sun; closed 25 Dec

White Horse ⑪ ♟ 🛏

A149 E of Hunstanton; PE31 8BY

Many customers come to this well run place to enjoy the very good food or stay overnight in the comfortable bedrooms, but the bar remains popular (particularly with locals) for a pint and a chat or a light lunchtime meal. It's all more or less open plan. The front bar has good local photographs on the left, with bar billiards and maybe piped music, and on the right is a quieter group of cushioned wicker armchairs and sofas by a table with daily papers and local landscapes for sale. This runs into the no smoking back restaurant with well spaced furnishings in unvarnished country-style wood, and some light-hearted seasidey decorations; through the big glass windows you can look over the sun deck to the wide views of the tidal marshes and Scolt Head Island beyond. Well kept Adnams, Fullers London Pride, Woodfordes Wherry, and a guest like Archers Swindon on handpump from the handsome counter, 15 malt whiskies and about a dozen wines by the glass from an extensive and thoughtful wine list. The lunch menu can be eaten in the bar or outside: soup such as purée of flageolet bean soup with crisp pancetta (£3.95), filled ciabattas (from £5.25; peppered minute steak with fried onions £6.50), smoked salmon and poached egg benedict with spinach and toasted croûte (£7.95), local mussels in white wine and cream (£6.25; main course £8.95), warm tartlet of goats cheese with balsamic onion confit (£9.25), baked seafood pasty with herb butter sauce (£10.50), and boiled bacon with grain mustard sauce (£11.50). In the restaurant and in the evening, there might be fried chicken livers with muscat grapes and port jus (£5.75), seared tuna niçoise salad with quail eggs (£5.95), roast fillet of black bream with shrimp, tomato and spinach broth (£11.95), roast rump of lamb with olive jus (£13.95), and fillet of bass with saffron, braised fennel and orange syrup (£14.25); nice breakfasts. You must book to be sure of a table. The coast path runs along the bottom of the garden. *(Recommended by Ann and Colin Hunt, Adele Summers, Alan Black, John Wooll, M and C Thompson, Derek and Sylvia Stephenson, Brian Root, Dr David Cockburn, Neil Ingoe, Mike and Sue Loseby, Giles and Annie Francis, Charles Gysin, David Field, Dr Ian S Morley, Louise English, Simon Jones, J L Nash, Hazel Morgan, Bernard Patrick, Peter and Liz Holmes, MDN, Peter Rozée, Michael Sargent, Mrs E Tyrrell, Adrian White, Simon Rodway)*

Free house ~ Licensees Cliff Nye and Kevin Nobes ~ Real ale ~ Bar food ~ Restaurant ~ (01485) 210262 ~ Children welcome but must be supervised ~ Dogs allowed in bar ~ Open 11-11; 12-10.30 Sun ~ Bedrooms: £75B/£120B

BURNHAM MARKET   TF8342   Map 8

Hoste Arms ⑪ ♟ 🛏

The Green (B1155); PE31 8HD

A fantastic new underground cellar has been created here to store their fine wines – you can see it through the conservatory and down the stairs. The new lavatories are quite something, too. It's all very smart and civilised with much emphasis on the thriving hotel and restaurant side, but the bar still retains the atmosphere of a village pub and there's a nice mix of chatty customers. This panelled bar is on the right and has a series of watercolours showing scenes from local walks, there's a bow-windowed bar on the left, a nice sitting room, a little art gallery in the staircase area, and massive log fires. The lovely walled garden has plenty of seats (you can enjoy full restaurant service here), or you can eat in the airy no smoking conservatory with its comfortable sofas; three restaurants are no smoking, another is partly smoking, and the lounge has a separate no smoking area. Imaginative food includes lunchtime filled ciabatta rolls (from £3.95), home-made soup (£4.50), oriental-style spicy salmon and potato cake with sweet chilli sauce, chicken caesar or shredded duck with thai-style salads, highland venison, celeriac and potato terrine with rhubarb compote or roast breast of local pigeon, spiced couscous and sultana dressing (all £6.25; main course £11.25), super oysters (from £7.50), real ale sausages with red onion jam or rump steak burger with crispy bacon and emmenthal cheese (£9.75), munster cheese and garlic shoot risotto (£10.50), sweet orange, red wine and chilli marinated beef stir fry (£13.50), mixed seafood in cockle and horseradish chowder (£14.50), herb-crusted lamb with minted mash and port jus (£16.75), and puddings such as sticky toffee pudding, toffee sauce, roasted pecan nuts and nutmeg ice-cream or orange crème caramel, orange sauce, mango and Grand Marnier sorbet (£5.75). Well kept Adnams Southwold, Greene King Abbot, and Woodfordes Nelsons Revenge and Wherry on handpump, 25 wines by the glass, and 25 malt whiskies. A big awning covers a sizeable eating area in the garden. *(Recommended by Jack Shonfield, Roger Wain-Heapy, Louise English, Jenny and Peter Lowater, Minda and Stanley Alexander, Michael Sargent, Giles and Annie Francis, Chris and Susie Cammack, Eric Robinson, Jacqueline Pratt, David Cosham, Pete Devonish, Ian McIntyre, Roy and Gay Hoing, Adrian White, Simon Rodway)*

Free house ~ Licensees Paul Whittome and Emma Tagg ~ Real ale ~ Bar food ~ Restaurant ~ (01328) 738777 ~ Children welcome with restrictions ~ Dogs allowed in bar and bedrooms ~ Open 11-11; 12-10.30 Sun ~ Bedrooms: £88S/£114B

BURNHAM THORPE   TF8541   Map 8
Lord Nelson 🍺
Village signposted from B1155 and B1355, near Burnham Market; PE31 8HL

With much character and a fine relaxing atmosphere, this friendly 17th-c pub is much enjoyed by our readers. There are plenty of pictures and memorabilia of Nelson (who was born in this sleepy village), and the little bar has well waxed antique settles on the worn red flooring tiles and smoke ovens in the original fireplace. An eating room has flagstones, an open fire, and more pictures of Nelson, and there are two no smoking rooms. Well kept Greene King IPA and Abbot, Woodfordes Nelsons Revenge and Wherry, and a guest such as Fox Nelsons Blood Bitter tapped from the cask, and 13 wines by the glass. They also have secret rum-based recipes called Nelson's Blood and Lady Hamilton's Nip; Nelson's Blood was first concocted in the 18th c and is passed down from landlord to landlord by word of mouth. At lunchtime, tasty bar food includes sandwiches (£5.75; soup and a sandwich £7.95), deep-fried herring roe with garlic and parsley butter, roast cherry tomato, red onion and mozzarella tart or fresh cromer crab salad (all £7.50), and mediterranean vegetable lasagne, braised lamb shank with red wine sauce or steak in ale pie (all £9.50); evening choices such as warm terrine of guinea fowl wrapped in parma ham on pear chutney with beetroot dressing (£6.50), a plate of cured meats with roasted artichoke or smoked salmon mascarpone and chive mousse with citrus and caviar salad (£6.95), roast provençale vegetables topped with grilled goats cheese and wilted spinach (£9.50), grilled fillet of cod on pesto mash with gorgonzola and walnut tortellini (£12.95), and roast loin of venison on grilled asparagus with port wine sauce (£16.95) and puddings such as iced terrine of nougat topped with chocolate sauce or banoffi pie with caramel suace and banana ice-cream (£5.50). The eating areas are no smoking. Cribbage, dominoes, chess, bar skittles and board games. There's a good-sized play area in the very big garden. *(Recommended by R E Dixon, Derek and Sylvia Stephenson, Brian Root, Tracey and Stephen Groves, D and J Allen, the Didler, Eric Robinson, Jacqueline Pratt, Barry Collett, Philip and Susan Philcox, Geoff and Carol Thorp, Anthony Longden, Mike Ridgway, Sarah Miles, Jeff and Wendy Williams)*

Greene King ~ Lease David Thorley ~ Real ale ~ Bar food (12-2(2.30 weekends), 6-9(9.30 Fri-Sun); not Sun evening or Mon in winter) ~ Restaurant ~ (01328) 738241 ~ Children welcome ~ Dogs allowed in bar ~ Live bands Thurs Sept-June ~ Open 11-3, 6(5 Fri)-11; 12-3, 6.30-10.30 Sun; 12-2.30, 6-11 weekdays in winter; closed Mon Sept-June (except school hols and bank hol Mon)

Real ale to us means beer which has matured naturally in its cask – not pressurised or filtered. We name all real ales stocked. We usually name ales preserved under a light blanket of carbon dioxide too, though purists – pointing out that this stops the natural yeasts developing – would disagree (most people, including us, can't tell the difference!)

CAWSTON TG1422 Map 8

Ratcatchers ♀

Eastgate, S of village – on B1149 from Norwich turn left towards Haveringland at crossroads ½ mile before the B1145 Cawston turn; NR10 4HA

The name of this dining pub is supposed to have originated at the turn of the century when the building was first converted to an inn, and the local ratcatcher was the first person to stay here. The L-shaped beamed bar has an open fire, nice old chairs, and a fine mix of walnut, beech, elm and oak tables; there's a quieter and cosier candlelit dining room on the right, and a conservatory (both of these rooms are no smoking). Bar food (with prices unchanged since last year) includes lunchtime sandwiches (from £3.95; not Sunday), bacon, mushrooms and cambozola cheese cooked in a pot with a puff pastry lid (£5.20), filled baked potatoes (from £6.25), ploughman's (£7.25), sausage and mash (£8.95), red thai vegetable curry (£9.25), home-made steak and kidney pie (£9.95), garlic chicken (£11.50), steaks (from £13.25), and daily specials. Well kept Greene King IPA, Hancocks HB, and Woodfordes Nelsons Revenge on handpump, and 20 malt whiskies; cribbage and piped music. The terrace has heaters for outdoor dining in cooler weather. *(Recommended by J S and S Chadwick, Sheila and Brian Wilson, David Twitchett, Anthony Barnes, Glenys and John Roberts, Mike and Chris Higgins, Barry Collett, Comus and Sarah Elliott, Dr and Mrs R G J Telfer, Philip and Susan Philcox, M and GR, Roy and Gay Hoing)*

Free house ~ Licensee Peter McCarter ~ Real ale ~ Bar food (12-2, 6-10; all day Sun) ~ Restaurant ~ (01603) 871430 ~ Children welcome ~ Open 12-3, 6-11; 12-11 Sun

ERPINGHAM TG1732 Map 8

Saracens Head ⑪ ♀ 🛏

At Wolterton – not shown on many maps; Erpingham signed off A140 N of Aylsham; keep on through Calthorpe, then where road bends right take the straight-ahead turn-off signposted Wolterton; NR11 7LZ

Well worth finding in the middle of nowhere, this gently civilised dining pub remains a fine place for special meal or overnight stay – and it's now been run by the charming Mr Dawson-Smith for 17 years. The two-room bar is simple and stylish, with high ceilings, terracotta walls, and red and white striped curtains at its tall windows – all lending a feeling of space, though it's not actually large. There's a mix of seats from built-in leather wall settles to wicker fireside chairs as well as log fires and flowers, and the windows look out on to a charming old-fashioned gravel stableyard with picnic-sets. A pretty six-table parlour on the right, in cheerful nursery colours, has another big log fire. Well kept Adnams Bitter and Woodfordes Wherry on handpump, an interesting wine list, local apple juice, and decent malt whiskies; the atmosphere is enjoyably relaxed. To be sure of a table, you'd be best to book and from the daily changing menu there might be local mussels with cider and cream, fricassee of wild and cultivated mushrooms, game and cranberry terrine or grilled halloumi on a lavender croûte with sunblush tomatoes and cream (from £5.25), main courses like roast leg of lamb with red and white beans, local pheasant with calvados, baked cromer crab with apple and sherry and fried scallops with rosemary and cream (from £11.50), and puddings such as treacle tart, brown bread and butter pudding or Baileys dark chocolate pot with orange jus (£4.95); there's also a two-course weekday lunch (£8). Smoking is only allowed after supper. The Shed next door (run by Mr Dawson-Smith's daughter Rachel) is a workshop and showcase for furniture and interior pieces. *(Recommended by John Wooll, David Twitchett, DF, NF, Paul Humphreys, T Walker, Peter and Jean Dowson, Dr and Mrs P Truelove, Philippe and Frances Gayton, Alan and Jill Bull, Philip and Susan Philcox, Pete Devonish, Ian McIntyre)*

Free house ~ Licensee Robert Dawson-Smith ~ Real ale ~ Bar food ~ Restaurant ~ (01263) 768909 ~ Children welcome but must be well behaved ~ Dogs allowed in bedrooms ~ Open 11.30-3.30, 6-11; 12-3.30, 7-10.30 Sun; closed 25 Dec and evening 26 Dec ~ Bedrooms: £45B/£85B

HOLKHAM   TF8943   Map 8
Victoria 🍴 ♟ 📷 🛏
A149 near Holkham Hall; NR23 1RG

Norfolk Dining Pub of the Year

This charmingly furnished small hotel cleverly doubles as an all-day pub. Virtually the whole of the ground floor is opened up into linked but quite individual areas. The main bar room, decorated in cool shades of green, has an eclectic mix of furnishings including deep low sofas with a colourful scatter of cushions, a big log fire, a dozen or so fat lighted candles in heavy sticks and many more tea lights, and some decorations conjuring up India (such as the attractive rajasthan cotton blinds for a triple bow window). This is quite upmarket, but very informally so: young women tucking their stockinged feet up into the cushions, people almost nodding off over the daily papers, good-natured young staff chatting to customers or among themselves – though this never delays the prompt service. Round at the back are smaller rooms, with more of a local feel in one bare-boards bar-propping area. The island servery has a decent range of wines by the glass as well as four well kept ales on handpump such as Adnams, Caledonian 80/-, Everards Tiger and Woodfordes Wherry, and good coffees and hot chocolate; there may be unobtrusive piped music. Two linked dining rooms continue the mood of faintly anglo-indian casual elegance. The good food includes produce from the owners' Holkham estate, with a 'wild' shoot – no artificially reared birds – so the game is excellent. The local seafood is also top-notch (if their mussels in red wine are on the menu, do try them). There's bar food such as sandwiches, garlic, lemon and chilli almonds or marinated olives (£2), soup (£5), chicken caesar salad (£7), antipasti (£8), and haddock with tartare sauce or ploughman's (£9), with more elaborate choices like terrine of corn-fed chicken and wild mushrooms with apple chutney (£6.95; main course £9.95), local oysters with pear salsa and crispy pickled ginger (six £7, a dozen £14), cromer crab with black pepper tuile (£7.25; main course £9.75), tomato and wild garlic risotto, confit yellow vine tomato (£12), 6oz estate venison burger (£12.50), organic salmon with red pepper and date couscous and lime beurre noisette (£15), estate rib-eye steak with mustard butter (£17), and puddings like chocolate fondant, brownie ice-cream, chocolate sauce or rhubarb rice pudding with nutmeg ice-cream (£6). Several separate areas outside with plenty of tables and picnic-sets include a sheltered courtyard with a high retractable awning and regular summer barbecues, and an orchard with a small play area. Just across the road is a walk down past nature-reserve salt marshes, alive with many thousands of geese and duck in winter, to seemingly endless broad beaches. As we went to press, the manager was leaving, but we are sure that with the Cokes (who own it as well as Holkham Hall itself) keeping an eye on things, all should continue to go well. *(Recommended by John Wooll, Tracey and Stephen Groves, Keith and Chris O'Neill, Eric Robinson, Jacqueline Pratt)*

Free house ~ Licensee Tom Coke ~ Real ale ~ Bar food ~ Restaurant ~ (01328) 711008 ~ Children welcome ~ Dogs allowed in bar ~ Open 11-11 ~ Bedrooms: £95S(£120B)/ £115S(£150B)

ITTERINGHAM   TG1430   Map 8
Walpole Arms 🍴 📷
Village signposted off B1354 NW of Aylsham; NR11 7AR

Rather civilised, the biggish open-plan bar in this popular dining pub has exposed beams, stripped brick walls, little windows, a mix of dining tables, and quietly chatty atmosphere. Well kept Adnams Bitter and Broadside and a beer named for the pub brewed for them by Wolf on handpump, 15 wines by the glass, Aspel's cider, and local apple juice. As well as a snack menu with occasional sandwiches, hummous, crostini and à la greque vegetables (£5), spiced mexican bean charros with cumin bread, sour cream, guacamole and tomato salsa (£8.75), and salmon, leek and dill fishcake with tartare sauce (£9), the ambitious food might include spicy sweet potato soup with coriander, yoghurt and coconut flakes (£5.75), home-made black pudding with bubble and squeak (£6.50), salad of white fin tuna, white beans, peppers, capers and olives (£6.75), local mussels steamed with curried lentils (£11.25), coddle of smoked haddock, spinach, creamy potatoes and gruyère (£11.50), home-made tortellini of smoked chicken in its own broth (£12.25), and daube of local venison (£15.50), with puddings such as baby brioche stuffed with apple and blackberry compote and brandy custard, pear, prune and frangipane tart with sweetened ricotta and baked white chocolate cheesecake with raspberry purée (from £4.75). Service can be stretched at peak times. The attractive restaurant is no smoking; piped music. Behind the pub is a two-acre landscaped garden and there are seats on the vine-covered terrace. *(Recommended by David Twitchett, Anthony Barnes, P Dawn, Helen and Ian Jobson, John and Bettye Reynolds, Mike and Shelley Woodroffe, Pete Devonish, Ian McIntyre, John Evans)*

Free house ~ Licensee Richard Bryan ~ Real ale ~ Bar food (not Sun evening) ~ Restaurant ~ (01263) 587258 ~ Children welcome ~ Dogs allowed in bar ~ Occasional live music Sun evenings ~ Open 12-3, 6-11; 12-3, 7-10.30 Sun

LARLING   TL9889   Map 5

Angel 🍴 🛏

If coming along A11, take B1111 turn-off and follow pub signs; NR16 2QU

There's a good mix of diners and those popping in for a pint and a chat in this neatly kept pub which creates a bustling and friendly atmosphere. It's been in the same family since 1913 and they still have the original visitors' books with guests from 1897 to 1909. The comfortable 1930s-style lounge on the right has cushioned wheelback chairs, a nice long cushioned and panelled corner settle, some good solid tables for eating and some lower ones, and squared panelling; also, a collection of whisky-water jugs on the delft shelf over the big brick fireplace, a woodburning stove, a couple of copper kettles, and some hunting prints. The dining room and breakfast room are no smoking. As well as snacks such as omelettes or filled baked potatoes (from £4.95), ploughman's (£6.50), home-made prime beefburgers (from £6.50), and ham and egg (£7.95), the popular food includes soup (£3.50), home-made pâté (£4.95), creamy mushroom pot (£5.25), vegetable korma (£7.95), spicy pork stir fry (£8.50), smoked haddock mornay (£8.95), chicken and mushroom stroganoff (£9.75), steaks (from £12.95), and daily specials like home-made steak and kidney pie or fresh battered cod (£7.95), roast beef or lamb (£7.50), and half a duck with orange gravy (£8.50); well liked breakfasts. Well kept Adnams Bitter and four changing guests on handpump, around 100 malt whiskies, and eight wines by the glass. The quarry-tiled black-beamed public bar has a good local atmosphere, with darts, dominoes, cribbage, juke box and piped music. A neat grass area behind the car park has picnic-sets around a big fairy-lit apple tree, and a safely fenced play area. Peter Beale's old-fashioned rose nursery is nearby. *(Recommended by Stuart and Alison Ballantyne, J F M and M West, Peter and Jean Dowson, Mike and Helen Rawsthorn, John and Elisabeth Cox, Simon Pyle, A J Murray)*

Free house ~ Licensee Andrew Stammers ~ Real ale ~ Bar food (all day Fri-Sun) ~ Restaurant ~ (01953) 717963 ~ Children welcome ~ Open 10-midnight ~ Bedrooms: £35B/£60B

MORSTON   TG0043   Map 8

Anchor

A149 Salthouse—Stiffkey; The Street; NR25 7AA

While the bar here has a snug and cheerily traditional feel, an airy new no smoking extension on the left is quite contemporary. So you can choose the latter's groups of deep leather sofas around low tables, with grey-painted country dining furniture, fresh flowers and fish pictures beyond; or turn right for three small rooms with pubby seating and tables on shiny black floors, coal fires, local 1950s beach photographs, lots of prints and bric-a-brac. The coffee lounge and second bar are no smoking. Whichever way you go, there's well kept Greene King Old Speckled Hen and local Winters Gold on handpump, decent wines by the glass, oyster shots (a local oyster in vodka), and daily papers. Besides sandwiches, the enjoyable and generously served food includes plenty of fish and local seafood from cod chowder (£4.95) or the village's famous mussels (£5.50 or £10.50) to monkfish or black bream with ginger, honey, soy and herbs (£11.95). They also have such things as home-made soup (£3.95), half-a-dozen local oysters (£7.95), kipper and whisky pâté (£5.50), spinach, mushroom and mozzarella strudel (£9.25), steakburger topped with crispy bacon and melting smoked cheddar (£9.75), cottage pie or honey-baked ham and eggs (£9.95), and daily specials like bangers and mash (£8.75), cassoulet (£10.20), chicken breast stuffed with mozzarella on a mild curry cream (£10.95), and locally caught grey mullet with fresh herbs (£13.50); good children's dishes. Service is pleasant and efficient. There are tables and benches out in front, with more tables on a side lawn. You can book seal-spotting trips here. *(Recommended by Brian Root, Tracey and Stephen Groves, Adele Summers, Alan Black)*

Free house ~ Licensee N J Handley ~ Real ale ~ Bar food (12-2.30, 6-9(9.30 Sat); 12-8 Sun) ~ Restaurant ~ (01263) 741392 ~ Children welcome ~ Dogs allowed in bar ~ Open 11-11(midnight Sat); 12-10.30 Sun

NORWICH TG2308 Map 5
Adam & Eve ㉕ ♀ £
Bishopgate; follow Palace Street from Tombland, N of cathedral; NR3 1RZ

Perhaps at its perkiest in warm weather when you can sit at one of the many picnic-sets and admire the award-winning and colourful tubs and hanging baskets, this old pub has quite a mix of customers. It's full of history and is thought to date back to at least 1249 (when it was used by workmen building the cathedral), and even has a Saxon well beneath the lower bar floor, though the striking dutch gables were added in the 14th and 15th c. The little old-fashioned bars have antique high-backed settles, cushioned benches built into partly panelled walls, and tiled or parquet floors; the snug and lower bar are no smoking. Good value, tasty bar food includes sandwiches or filled baguettes (from £3.25; lunchtime only and not Sunday), soup (£3.45; cheese and ale soup £4.95), spicy spinach and feta goujons with a honey and ginger dip (£5.45), elizabethan pork (£5.95), home-made chilli or ploughman's (£6.45), ham and egg (£6.75), king prawns in garlic butter or home-made lasagne (£6.95), and daily specials. Well kept Adnams, Greene King IPA, Theakstons Old Peculier and Charles Wells Bombardier on handpump, over 50 malt whiskies, quite a few wines by the glass, and Aspall's cider; piped music. On the last nine days of October, ghost walks start and end here and the pub might have barbecues then. *(Recommended by John Wooll, the Didler, Pat and Clive Sherriff, John Saville, N R White, MJVK, Revd R P Tickle)*

Unique (Enterprise) ~ Lease Rita McCluskey ~ Real ale ~ Bar food (12-7; 12-2.30 Sun; not Sun evening) ~ (01603) 667423 ~ Children in snug until 7pm ~ Open 11-11; 12-10.30 Sun; closed 25-26 Dec, 1 Jan

Fat Cat ◀
West End Street; NR2 4NA

With up to 30 quickly changing real ales on at any one time, this classic town pub 'is well worth the pilgrmage' said one reader. As well as their own beers (brewed at their sister pub, The Shed) Fat Cat Bitter, Honey Ale and Top Cat, the fantastic choice (on handpump or tapped from the cask in a still room behind the bar – big windows reveal all) might include Adnams Bitter, Arundel Fat Willy, Broadside and Explorer, Bass, Batemans XXXB, Brains SA, Burton Bridge Jules Gold, Caledonian Deuchars IPA, Coach House Gingernut, Dave Winters Storm Force, Elgoods Black Dog Mild, Fullers ESB and London Pride, Gales Prize Old Ale, Greene King Abbot and Old Speckled Hen, Hop Back Summer Lightning, Oakham Bishops Farewell, Shepherd Neame Spitfire, Spectrum Wizzard, Timothy Taylors Landlord, and Woodfordes Norfolk Nog and Wherry. You'll also find six draught belgian beers (two of them fruit), draught lagers from Germany and the Czech Republic, up to 15 bottled belgian beers, 15 country wines, and local farm cider. Open all day, with a good mix of customers, and a lively bustling atmosphere at busy times, with tranquil lulls in the middle of the afternoon. The no-nonsense furnishings include plain scrubbed pine tables and simple solid seats, lots of brewery memorabilia, bric-a-brac and stained-glass. Bar food consists of a dozen or so rolls (60p) and good pies (£1.60) at lunchtime (not Sunday). There are tables outside. *(Recommended by Roger Wain-Heapy, Ian Phillips, Ben Taylor, G Coates, Dr David Cockburn, P Dawn, the Didler, Comus and Sarah Elliott)*

Free house ~ Licensee Colin Keatley ~ Real ale ~ Bar food (available until sold out; not Sun) ~ No credit cards ~ (01603) 624364 ~ Children allowed in conservatory ~ Open 12-11; 11(12 Fri)-midnight Sat; 12-10.30 Sun; closed evening 31 Dec

OLD BUCKENHAM TM0691 Map 5
Gamekeeper
B1077 S of Attleborough; The Green; NR17 1RE

This civilised and pretty 16th-c pub has an appealing layout suiting both drinkers and diners. Service is welcoming, attentive and helpful – and Ollie the patadale terrier is friendly, too. The beamed bar, with two main areas, has a big open woodburning stove in a capacious inglenook fireplace, a pleasant variety of seating and tables including a couple of sturdy slabs of elm, and two unusual interior bow windows showing off rustic bygones including stuffed birds. The corner counter serves well kept Adnams Bitter and Broadside and a Wolf beer brewed for the pub on handpump, and a good range of wines by the glass. Tiffanyesque lamps over this counter, church candles and dried hops help towards a cosy pub atmosphere. Tasty seasonal food includes home-made soup (£3.95), sandwiches and filled baguettes (from £4.50), chicken liver pâté (£5.25), filled baked potatoes or omelettes (from £5.50), ham and eggs or red thai vegetable curry (£7.95), local sausages with rich onion gravy or steak in ale pie (£8.95), chicken in creamy stilton sauce (£10.95), steaks (from £11.95), and slow-braised shoulder of lamb (£12.95). Besides the comfortable main back dining area, which includes some stripped high-backed settles, there is a small separate room with a crushed raspberry colour scheme and two long rustic tables. Piped music is well reproduced and not irritating, though the central bar can be smoky; they have a discreetly placed fruit machine, skittle alley, darts and board games. Tables out on the back terrace have heaters, and there are picnic-sets on the grass beyond. We have not yet heard from readers who have stayed here. *(Recommended by TW, MW, Simon and Mandy King)*

Enterprise ~ Lease Keith and Val Starr ~ Bar food (12-2.30, 6.30-9; 12-3 Sun) ~ Restaurant ~ (01953) 860397 ~ Children allowed away from bar ~ Dogs allowed in bar and bedrooms ~ Open 11.45-11; 12-10.30 Sun; closed evenings 25 and 26 Dec ~ Bedrooms: £35/

RINGSTEAD TF7040 Map 8
Gin Trap
Village signposted off A149 near Hunstanton; OS Sheet 132 map reference 707403; PE36 5JU

Usefully open all day in July and August, this attractive white painted pub places firm emphasis on dining; best to book a table in advance. The neat bar has beams, a woodburning stove, captain's chairs and cast-iron-framed tables, and well kept Adnams Bitter, Woodfordes Wherry, and a guest on handpump, and eight wines by the glass. The small no smoking dining room is candlelit in the evening, and the top bar is also no smoking. Bar food includes grilled goats cheese brioche with sunblush tomato and chilli chutney (£4.50; main course £8), grilled sardines with rosemary, garlic and aïoli (£5; main course £11), thai salmon fishcake with crème fraîche and sweet chilli (£5.50; main course £9.50), mussels in white wine and cream or thai green curry sauce (£7; main course £11.95), pork and leek sausages with sweet onion sauce (£8.50), wild mushroom and pesto risotto (£9), beer-battered haddock (£9.50), braised lamb shank with caper sauce or calves liver with smoked bacon, celeriac purée and red wine sauce (£11), corn-fed chicken, chorizo and chilli polenta

(£11.25), and rib-eye steak (£15.95). Outside, a handsome spreading chestnut tree shelters the car park, and the neatly kept back garden has seats on the grass or small paved area, and pretty flowering tubs. There's an art gallery next door, and self-catering accommodation. The Peddar's Way is close by. *(Recommended by Ann and Colin Hunt, Mike and Shelley Woodroffe, Tracey and Stephen Groves, John Dwane, Keith and Avril Stringer, David Barnes, Ian Arthur, Chris and Susie Cammack, O K Smyth, Ben and Helen Ingram, Roy and Gay Hoing, Ian and Nita Cooper, Keith Eastelow)*

Free house ~ Licensee Margaret Greer ~ Real ale ~ Bar food ~ Restaurant ~ (01485) 525264 ~ Children allowed with restrictions ~ Dogs welcome ~ Open 11.30-3, 6-11(10.30 Sun); open all day July/Aug ~ Bedrooms: /£70S(£80B)

SNETTISHAM   TF6834   Map 8

Rose & Crown 🍽 ♀ ⇌

Village signposted from A149 King's Lynn—Hunstanton just N of Sandringham; coming in on the B1440 from the roundabout just N of village, take first left turn into Old Church Road; PE31 7LX

The improvements continue at this pretty white cottage. The friendly licensees are thrilled with their new, very well equipped bedrooms (and hope to start refurbishment on the older ones soon), the Garden Room should be finished by the time this book is published (inviting wicker-based wooden chairs, new tables, and careful lighting), and the front restaurant has a lovely oiled wooden floor, goldy green walls, new tables and chairs, and antique brass stable lamps. The garden has been re-landscaped, the terrace improved, and wheelchair ramps installed; it's the car park's turn next! There are two bars (the only places you can smoke), each with a separate character: an old-fashioned beamed front bar with black settles on its tiled floor and a big log fire, and a back bar with another large log fire and the landlord's sporting trophies and old sports equipment. Served by courteous staff and using local seasonal produce, the imaginative food might include soup such as leek and potato with fresh thyme and cheddar crostini (£4.25), sandwiches (from £4.95, toasted focaccia, home-made hummous, manchego and tomato and basil jam £5.50; lunchtimes, not Sunday), smoked haddock and salmon fishcakes with tarragon mayonnaise or local mussels (£5.95; main course £9.25), vietnamese crispy duck salad with toasted peanuts and lime and chilli dressing, pasta with oven-roasted peppers, confit red onions and basil or home-made prime beefburger, bacon and cheese (all £8.95), grilled lamb and stilton sausages, bubble and squeak, red wine and mint sauce (£9.25), seared cajun tuna loin, braised endive, soy and coriander dressing (£12.95), and puddings like dark chocolate mousse with raspberry cordial, pecan pie with clotted cream or baked passion fruit cheesecake (£4.95). Well kept Adnams Bitter, Bass, Fullers London Pride, and Greene King IPA on handpump, 20 wines by the glass, organic fruit juices and farm cider. Stylish café-style aluminium and blue chairs with matching blue tables under cream parasols on the terrace, and an outdoor heater. Disabled lavatories. *(Recommended by Ann and Colin Hunt, John Wooll, John Saville, DF, NF, Louise English, Paul Humphreys, A G Marx, Tracey and Stephen Groves, David Field, Dr Ian S Morley, J Jennings, Simon Jones, Keith and Margaret Kettell, Ryta Lyndley, Hazel Morgan, Bernard Patrick, Barry and Patricia Wooding, Comus and Sarah Elliott, Adrian White, Margit Severa, Jeff and Wendy Williams)*

Free house ~ Licensee Anthony Goodrich ~ Real ale ~ Bar food (12-2.30, 6.30-9.30) ~ Restaurant ~ (01485) 541382 ~ Children welcome ~ Dogs allowed in bar and bedrooms ~ Open 11-11; 12-10.30 Sun ~ Bedrooms: £60B/£90B

'Children welcome' means the pub says it lets children inside without any special restriction. If it allows them in, but to restricted areas such as an eating area or family room, we specify this. Places with separate restaurants often let children use them, hotels usually let them into public areas such as lounges. Some pubs impose an evening time limit – let us know if you find this.

SOUTH CREAKE   TF8635   Map 8

Ostrich 🍺

B1355 Burnham Market—Fakenham; NR21 9PB

Cheerfully informal and attractively laid out, this largely no smoking pub has friendly owners who work hard to keep both food and drink well up to scratch. With modern landscape prints on its apricot walls, the comfortable carpeted front bar has well kept Greene King IPA and Abbot, Woodfordes Wherry and an interesting guest beer such as Spectrum Light Fantastic on handpump, and a good choice of wines; they do an all-Norfolk beer festival in late summer. There are colourful scatter cushions on the dark leather sofa and armchairs in an area off on the left, which has some interesting books, an oriental rug on its bare boards, and a woodburning stove. Further areas include a maroon-walled dining room with white-painted tables and rush-seat chairs on very broad floor boards, and another spacious raftered dining room with similar décor. Food includes sandwiches, home-made soup (£3.95), home-made chicken liver and wild mushroom pâté (£4.95), mixed seafood salad (£6.25), honey-roast ham and egg (£7.50), creamy mushroom carbonara (£8.50; with bacon £9.25), pork goulash (£9.25), lambs liver and bacon or whole baked plaice with herb butter and capers (£10.50), beer-battered cod fillet (£11.95), and steaks (from £11.95). The Tuesday steak night is good value; board games. The sheltered and heated back gravel terrace has stylish furnishings under big canvas parasols, with a lively water feature. Children are very welcome inside, and we'd expect this to be a nice place to stay in, though we have not yet had readers' views of the bedrooms. The two beagles are friendly. Piped music can sometimes be rather intrusive (and if you ask for it to be turned down, they may just ask you to sit further away from it instead). *(Recommended by Mike and Shelley Woodroffe, Tracey and Stephen Groves)*

Free house ~ Licensees Simon and Emma Gardner ~ Real ale ~ Bar food ~ Restaurant ~ (01328) 823320 ~ Children welcome ~ Dogs allowed in bar ~ Open 12-11.30(midnight Sat); 12-3, 5-11.30 in winter ~ Bedrooms: /£60S

STANHOE   TF8036   Map 8

Crown

B1155 towards Burnham Mkt; PE31 8QD

Unpretentious and run by a genial and straight-talking ex-RAF landlord, this little open-plan country local has a relaxing, good-hearted atmosphere. It's clean and bright with aircraft pictures on the white walls, upholstered wall seats and wheelback chairs around dark tables on the carpet, and a central log fire. Beams and joists overhead – one beam densely studded with coins – and gas masks, guns and various military headgear behind the bar. Well kept Elgoods Cambridge and Greyhound on handpump, and decent house wines and coffee; piped music. A sensibly short choice of no-nonsense bar food includes sandwiches, soup, baked crab, or garlic mussels (£3.50-£4.80), ham and egg, steak and kidney pie, a vegetarian dish or braised liver (£6.80-£7.50), and puddings (£3.50). There are tables on a side lawn with a couple of apple trees, and a bigger lawn behind with room for caravans; fancy breeds of chicken may be running free. *(Recommended by John Wooll, R C Vincent, Tracey and Stephen Groves, Sue Crees, John Beeken, Jeff and Wendy Williams)*

Elgoods ~ Tenants Page and Sarah Clowser ~ Bar food (not Sun evening) ~ No credit cards ~ (01485) 518330 ~ Children allowed but must be well behaved ~ Dogs allowed in bar ~ Open 12-3.30, 6(7 Sun)-midnight; 12-3.30, 7-10.30 Sun

---

A few pubs try to make you leave a credit card at the bar, as a sort of deposit if you order food. This is a bad practice, and the banks and credit card firms warn you not to let your card go like this.

STIFFKEY   TF9743   Map 8

Red Lion

A149 Wells—Blakeney; NR23 1AJ

On a cold evening with torrential rain, one reader found this was an outpost of warmth and cheer. There's a bustling atmosphere, plenty of customers, and the oldest parts of the simple bars have a few beams, aged flooring tiles or bare floorboards, and big open fires; there's also a mix of pews, small settles and a couple of stripped high-backed settles, a nice old long deal table among quite a few others, and oil-type or lantern wall lamps. Well kept Woodfordes Nelsons Revenge and Wherry and a couple of guests on handpump, quite a few wines by the glass, and 30 malt whiskies; board games. Well liked bar food includes game (£3.95), deep-fried whitebait with lemon and parsley mayonnaise (£4.75), warm salad of confit rabbit, pickled wild mushrooms and beetroot (£4.95), mediterranean vegetables baked with feta cheese and pesto (£8.25), chicken with a tarragon scented sauce, steak and kidney pie or local mussels in creamy cider sauce (£8.95), line-caught cod, braised chicory and beurre blanc (£9.75), and puddings like Baileys crème brûlée, rich chocolate torte or sticky toffee pudding (£3.95). A back gravel terrace has proper tables and seats, with more on grass further up beyond; there are some pleasant walks nearby. Bedrooms should be open by February 2007. *(Recommended by John Wooll, Nigel and Sue Foster, Ann and Colin Hunt, Derek Field, Geoff and Pat Bell, Michael and Marilyn Switzer, Pat and Clive Sherriff, R C Vincent, the Didler, John and Bettye Reynolds, David Cosham, A G Marx, Dave Aldridge, Charles Gysin, Keith Easterlow, Graham and Rosemary Smith)*

Free house ~ Licensee Andrew Waddison ~ Real ale ~ Bar food (all day Sun) ~ (01328) 830552 ~ Children welcome ~ Dogs welcome ~ Open 12-midnight(11 Sun); 12-3, 6-11 winter

STOW BARDOLPH   TF6205   Map 5

Hare Arms ♀

Just off A10 N of Downham Market; PE34 3HT

A most welcome break from the A10, this neatly kept creeper-covered pub is a thoroughly enjoyable place with genuinely friendly service (the licensees have now been here for 30 years). The bustling bar has a proper village pub feel, bric-a-brac, old advertising signs, fresh flowers, plenty of tables around its central servery, and a good log fire. This bar opens into a spacious heated and well planted no smoking conservatory; the restaurant is also no smoking. Tasty bar food includes lunchtime sandwiches (from £3.25; crayfish tails with lemon crème fraîche £5.75), filled baked potatoes (from £4.75), and ploughman's (from £7.50), as well as home-made chilli (£7.75), home-made curry (£8), large salads (from £9), and daily specials such as mushroom stroganoff or sausages on cajun mash with barbecue sauce (£7.75), pork steak with honey and dijon mustard sauce or steak in a cream, brandy and black peppercorn sauce under pastry (£9), queenie scallops (£9.50), smoked haddock pie (£9.75), and slow-cooked lamb shank in rich mushroom sauce (£10.25); Sunday roast beef (£9). It's best to book for the restaurant (which has a more elaborate menu). Well kept Greene King IPA, Abbot and Old Speckled Hen, and a guest on handpump; a decent range of wines, and quite a few malt whiskies; fruit machine. There are plenty of seats in the large garden behind, and in the pretty front garden too, and chickens and peacocks roam freely. Church Farm Rare Breeds Centre is a two-minute walk away. *(Recommended by Ann and Colin Hunt, John Wooll, Brian Root, Anthony Barnes, Tracey and Stephen Groves, Stephen and Jean Curtis, Eric Robinson, Jacqueline Pratt)*

Greene King ~ Tenants David and Trish McManus ~ Real ale ~ Bar food (12-2, 6-10) ~ Restaurant ~ (01366) 382229 ~ Children allowed with restrictions ~ Open 11-2.30, 6-11; 12-2.30, 7-10.30 Sun

SWANTON MORLEY TG0117 Map 8
Darbys 🍺
B1147 NE of Dereham; NR20 4NY

Once two farm cottages, this creeper-covered local has a smashing choice of up to eight well kept real ales on handpump: Adnams Best and Broadside, Badger Tanglefoot, Fullers London Pride, Oulton Bitter, Shepherd Neame Spitfire, Smiles Best and Woodfordes Wherry. The long bare-boarded country-style bar has a comfortable lived-in feel, with lots of gin traps and farming memorabilia, a good log fire (with the original bread oven alongside), tractor seats with folded sacks lining the long, attractive serving counter, and maybe fresh flowers on the big stripped pine tables. A step up through a little doorway by the fireplace takes you through to the no smoking dining room. The children's room (also no smoking) has a toy box and a glassed-over well, floodlit from inside; piped music. Well liked bar food includes home-made soup (£3.25), filled ciabattas (from £4.50), garlic and stilton mushrooms (£5.50), burgers (from £5.85), ploughman's (£7), spinach and potato madras (£8.50), chicken thai green curry (£9.50), beef and smoked oyster in ale pie (£9.75), bass baked with garlic, olives and parsley (£10.95), and steaks (from £11.65). The garden has a children's play area, and the two dogs are called Boots and Dylan. Plenty to do locally (B&B is available in carefully converted farm buildings a few minutes away) as the family also own the adjoining 720-acre estate, and can arrange clay pigeon shooting, golf, fishing, nature trails and craft instruction. *(Recommended by R C Vincent, Michael and Jenny Back, Ian Phillips, Pat and Tony Martin, Mark, Amanda, Luke and Jake Sheard, Philippe and Frances Gayton, J G and P D Holdsworth, Stuart and Alison Ballantyne, MDN, Comus and Sarah Elliott)*

Free house ~ Licensees John Carrick and Louise Battle ~ Real ale ~ Bar food (12-2.15, 6.30-9.45) ~ Restaurant ~ (01362) 637647 ~ Children welcome ~ Dogs allowed in bar ~ Open 11.30-3, 6-11; 11.30-11 Sat; 12-10.30 Sun

TERRINGTON ST JOHN TF5314 Map 8
Woolpack
Village signposted off A47 W of King's Lynn; PE14 7RR

The landlady's lively and cheerful personality lifts this airy roadside pub right out of the ordinary. It's very popular locally and there's plenty of chatty banter between customers and the friendly staff. The rooms are decorated with Mrs Carter's bright modern ceramics and contemporary prints, and the bar has red plush banquettes and matching or wheelback chairs around its dark pub tables, a patterned red carpet, and terracotta pink walls; the large back no smoking dining room (which looks out on to the garden) has comfortable green seating, and an art deco décor punctuated by Mondrian prints. The reliably good value food, with efficient waitresses, also underpins the pub's popularity. As well as lunchtime sandwiches, baguettes and ciabattas (from £2.75), there might be home-made soup (£2.95), chicken liver pâté (£3.95), stuffed nutty aubergine or steak and kidney suet pudding (£6.95), honey and mustard home-cooked ham with eggs or cod and chips (£7.50), lambs liver and smoked bacon or chicken and bacon tower with creamy peppercorn sauce (£8.95), king prawn thai green curry (£9.75), steaks (from £11.95), daily specials like chicken tikka masala (£7.95) and roast duck breast with mozzarella and wild mushroom sauce (£11.95), and the famous pudding trolley with all manner of home-made cheesecake, crumbles, gateaux and tarts (£3.95). Well kept Greene King IPA, Slaters Shining Knight and Charles Wells Eagle on handpump; quiz machine and piped music; good disabled access. There are picnic-sets on neat grass by a herb garden and the car park (which has recycling bins including Planet Aid clothes and shoes). *(Recommended by John Wooll, Michael and Jenny Back, Duncan Cloud, Ian Stafford, Chris and Susie Cammack, Richard and Margaret McPhee, John and Bettye Reynolds, K Christensen, Mr and Mrs Bentley-Davies)*

Free house ~ Licensees Lucille and Barry Carter ~ Bar food ~ Restaurant ~ (01945) 881097 ~ Children allowed if eating and away from bar ~ Open 11.30-2.30, 6.30-11; 12-2.30, 7-10.30 Sun; closed 25 Dec

THORNHAM   TF7343   Map 8

Lifeboat ⇤

Turn off A149 by Kings Head, then take first left turn; PE36 6LT

Under a new licensee again this year but readers feel, happily, that little has
changed. It's a popular place with a good mix of locals and visitors, and the main
Smugglers bar is lit with antique paraffin lamps suspended among an array of traps
and yokes on its great oak-beamed ceiling. There are low settles, window seats,
pews, carved oak tables and rugs on the tiled floor, and masses of guns, swords,
black metal mattocks, reed-slashers and other antique farm tools. A couple of little
rooms lead off here, and all in all there are five open fires. No games machines or
piped music, though they still play the ancient game of 'pennies' which was
outlawed in the late 1700s, and dominoes. Up some steps from the no smoking
conservatory is a sunny terrace with picnic-sets, and further back is a children's
playground with fort and slide. Enjoyable bar food includes home-made soup
(£3.95), chicken and duck liver pâté (£5.50), caesar salad (£5.50; main course
£8.25), open baguettes (from £5.50), hickory pork ribs (£5.95; main course £9.95),
ploughman's (from £6.50), smoked salmon and crevettes (£6.80; main course
£11.75), puy lentil and butterbean chilli (£8.95), burger topped with bacon and
cheese (£9), fish pie (£9.50), venison sausages on horseradish mash with madeira
gravy (£9.95), steaks (from £13.75), and home-made puddings. The restaurant is
no smoking. Well kept Adnams, Burton Bridge Bridge Bitter, Greene King IPA and
Abbot, and Woodfordes Wherry on handpump, and ten wines by the glass. The inn
faces half a mile of coastal sea flats, and there are lots of lovely surrounding walks.
Most of the bedrooms have sea views. *(Recommended by Ann and Colin Hunt,
Mark, Amanda, Luke and Jake Sheard, Mike Ridgway, Sarah Miles, A J Murray, John Wooll,
Brian Root, Mark Farrington, Giles and Annie Francis, Louise English, A G Marx, Mike and
Sue Loseby, the Didler, Tracey and Stephen Groves, Eddie and Lynn Jarrett, Ian Arthur,
Stephen and Jean Curtis, Pat and Clive Sherriff, David Field, J Jennings, Eric Robinson,
Jacqueline Pratt, Simon Jones, Keith and Margaret Kettell, Keith and Janet Morris, W K Wood,
Hazel Morgan, Bernard Patrick, Alison anon and Pete, Chris Mawson, Adrian White,
Margit Severa, Jeff and Wendy Williams, Simon Rodway)*

Free house ~ Licensee Leon Mace ~ Real ale ~ Bar food (12-2.30, 6-9.30) ~ Restaurant ~
(01485) 512236 ~ Children welcome ~ Dogs allowed in bar and bedrooms ~ Open
11-11; 12-10.30 Sun ~ Bedrooms: £68B/£96B

TIVETSHALL ST MARY   TM1686   Map 5

Old Ram ♀ ⇤

A140 15 miles S of Norwich, outside village; NR15 2DE

Perhaps more of a small hotel and restaurant than a straighforward pub now, this
is an especially stylish and comfortable place to stay overnight and the food is very
good indeed. The spacious country-style main room has lots of stripped beams and
standing timbers, antique craftsmen's tools on the ceiling, a huge log fire in the
brick hearth, a turkey rug on rosy brick floors, and a longcase clock. It's ringed by
smaller side areas, and one dining room has striking navy walls and ceiling,
swagged curtains and an open woodburning stove; this leads to a second
comfortable dining room and gallery. Generous helpings of enjoyable bar food
includes sandwiches (from £4.95, until 6pm), chicken liver, brandy and herb pâté
or ricotta and spinach ravioli pasta with tomato and basil oil (£4.95), filled baked
potatoes (£5.95), fried scallops marinated in soy sauce and sherry with spring onion
and ginger (£7.50), sausages and mash with onion gravy (£8.95), escalopes of
roasted aubergine, celeriac, fennel, red pepper, a sunblush tomato and mozzarella
paste and a rosemary and garlic jus (£9.95), king prawn in green thai curry sauce
(£10.95), pork fillet with brandy and black pepper sauce and apple mash (£12.95),
fried medallions of aberdeen angus, roquefort, field mushrooms and port and
cranberry sauce (£15.95), and puddings such as crème brûlée with ginger
shortbread, bramley apple pie and clotted cream or fresh raspberry meringue
chantilly (£4.95). OAP two-course meal (£7.95; 11.30-6pm Monday-Friday). All

dining rooms are no smoking; courteous and attentive service. Unobtrusive fruit machine, TV and piped music. Well kept Adnams, Woodfordes Wherry and a couple of guests like Marstons Pedigree or Timothy Taylors Landlord on handpump, 28 wines by the glass, fresh orange, apple, pineapple and carrot juice, milkshakes, and 15 malt whiskies. The sheltered flower-filled terrace of this much extended pub is very civilised, with outdoor heaters and big green parasols. *(Recommended by Alan Cole, Kirstie Bruce, Liz and Brian Barnard, Ian and Nita Cooper, Chris and Marion Gardiner, Martin and Pauline Jennings, Bill and Marian de Bass, Michael Sargent, Alan and Jill Bull, Bryan and Mary Blaxall, Beryl and Bill Farmer)*

Free house ~ Licensee John Trafford ~ Real ale ~ Bar food (all day from 7.30am) ~ Restaurant ~ (01379) 676794 ~ Children allowed but must be over 7 after 8pm ~ Open 8am–midnight(1am Fri and Sat); closed 25 and 26 Dec ~ Bedrooms: £62.50B/£86B

WARHAM TF9441 Map 8
Three Horseshoes ★ 🍽 🛏

Warham All Saints; village signposted from A149 Wells-next-the-Sea—Blakeney, and from B1105 S of Wells; NR23 1NL

For those who like genuinely friendly, unspoilt and old-fashioned pubs, this is just the place to come. The simple interior with its gas lighting looks little changed since the 1920s, and parts of the building date back to the 1720s. There are stripped deal or mahogany tables (one marked for shove-ha'penny) on a stone floor, red leatherette settles built around the partly panelled walls of the public bar, royalist photographs, and open fires in Victorian fireplaces. An antique American Mills one-arm bandit is still in working order (it takes 5p pieces), there's a big longcase clock with a clear piping strike, and a twister on the ceiling to point out who gets the next round; darts, cribbage, shove-ha'penny and dominoes. Most people choose from the specials board: soups (£3.50), local mussels (£7), trout (£7.80), braised rabbit or pheasant (£8.20), steak and kidney or beef and stilton pies (£8.90), and puddings like golden syrup sponge or lemon cheesecake (£3.25); from the menu there might be beans on toast (£3.25), filled baked potatoes (from £4.20), chicken liver pâté (£4.80), ploughman's or home-cooked gammon (£6.80), and cheese and vegetable pie (£7.50). They don't take bookings, so it's a good idea to arrive early at busy times; the eating area of the bar is no smoking. Greene King IPA, Woodfordes Wherry and a weekly guest well kept on handpump or tapped from the cask, country wines, local summer cider, and home-made lemonade. One of the outbuildings houses a wind-up gramophone museum – opened on request. There's a courtyard garden with flower tubs and a well, and a garden. *(Recommended by Ann and Colin Hunt, John Beeken, Liz and Guy Marshlain, the Didler, Giles and Annie Francis, Barry Collett, Philip and Susan Philcox, Anthony Longden, Pam and David Bailey, Ben and Helen Ingram, M Mossman)*

Free house ~ Licensee Iain Salmon ~ Real ale ~ Bar food (12–1.45, 6–8.30) ~ No credit cards ~ (01328) 710547 ~ Children welcome ~ Dogs welcome ~ Open 11.30(12 Sun)–2.30, 6–11 ~ Bedrooms: £26/£56(£60S)

WELLS-NEXT-THE-SEA TF9143 Map 8
Crown 🏅 ♀ 🛏

The Buttlands; NR23 1EX

Even though this is a smart 16th-c coaching inn, there's now more of a pubby feel than there has been, which has pleased readers very much. The no smoking beamed bar is a friendly place with an informal mix of furnishings on the stripped wooden floor, local photographs on the red walls, a good selection of newspapers to read in front of the open fire, and well kept Adnams Bitter, Woodfordes Wherry and a guest on handpump; 15 wines by the glass. The sunny no smoking conservatory with wicker chairs on the tiled floor, beams and modern art is where families with well behaved children can sit, and there's a pretty restaurant; piped music and board games. Served by attentive staff, the good modern bar food might include hummous with bread (£1.40), soup (£3.95), super smoked haddock fritatta with cucumber pickle (£4.50), steamed local mussels with white wine, garlic and cream (£4.95; main course £10.10), fishcakes with tartare sauce (£7.75), club sandwich (£7.85), grilled pork chop with apple sauce and mustard mash (£8.35), lamb moussaka (£8.70), red onion and gorgonzola risotto (£8.95), salmon and ginger stir fry (£9.75), roast chicken breast with chorizo, black-eyed beans and haricot beans (£10.40), thai watermelon curry and market fish with coriander yoghurt (£10.75), and puddings such as steamed maple syrup sponge pudding, rhubarb crumble with warm anglaise sauce and chocolate brownie (from £4.25). You can sit outside on the sheltered sun deck. *(Recommended by R E Dixon, Graham and June Ward, John Wooll, Tracey and Stephen Groves, Mr and Mrs L Haines, Louise English, Keith and Chris O'Neill, Eric Robinson, Jacqueline Pratt, Adele Summers, Alan Black, John Evans, David and Sue Smith)*

Free house ~ Licensees Chris and Jo Coubrough ~ Real ale ~ Bar food (12-2.30, 6.30-9.30) ~ Restaurant ~ (01328) 710209 ~ Children welcome ~ Dogs allowed in bar ~ Open 11-11 ~ Bedrooms: £100B/£120B

Globe

The Buttlands; NR23 1EU

Recently taken over and revamped by the family who own Holkham Hall (and the Victoria there), this now has a spacious contemporary feel, and spreads well back from the front bar. Three big bow windows look over to a green lined by tall lime trees, there are well spaced tables on oak boards, walls in grey, cream or mulberry have moody local landscape photoprints, and the modern lighting is well judged. Bar food includes marinated olives (£2.50), sandwiches (from £4), chipolatas with mustard dip (£3.50), chicken caesar salad (£5.75; main course £8.75), garlic king prawns (£5.95), fish pie (£6.50), thai chicken curry (£7.50), toasted muffin with spinach, flat mushrooms, poached eggs and hollandaise (£8), lambs liver and bacon (£8.25), steaks (from £8.50), pies or deep-fried haddock with mushy peas (£8.75), and puddings (£4.25); they have bargain steaks on Wednesday evening, and Friday is thai night. Adnams Bitter, Broadside and winter Old and Woodfordes Wherry are kept well on handpump, and they do good coffee; piped music, TV, darts and board games. A nicely updated back coachyard has dark green cast-iron furniture on pale flagstones, among trellis tubs with lavender, roses and jasmine. *(Recommended by Steve Nye, Vicky Trumper, DF, NF, Paul Humphreys, Derek Field, Sarah Flynn, Tracey and Stephen Groves)*

Free house ~ Licensee Steve Loakes ~ Real ale ~ Bar food ~ (01328) 710206 ~ Children welcome ~ Dogs allowed in bar ~ Open 11-11; 12-10.30 Sun ~ Bedrooms: £75B/£105B

WEST BECKHAM   TG1339   Map 8
Wheatsheaf ◗

Off A148 Holt—Cromer; Church Road; NR25 6NX

There's a fine range of real ales in this flint-walled, pleasantly traditional pub. Tapped from the cask or on handpump they might include Greene King IPA, Shepherd Neame Spitfire, Smiles Best, and Woodfordes Wherry, Nelsons Revenge and Norfolk Nog. The bars have beams and cottagey doors, a roaring log fire in one part with a smaller coal one in another, comfortable chairs and banquettes, and perhaps, the enormous black cat. Light lunchtime snacks such as home-made soup (£3.50), sandwiches or filled baguettes (from £3.50; tortilla wraps or ciabattas £5.95), filled baked potatoes (from £4.25), and ploughman's (from £5.75); also, home-made chicken liver pâté (£4.50), home-made fishcakes with a creamy cheese and chive sauce (£4.95), ham and eggs (£6.95), home-made burger topped with bacon and cheese (£7.50), steak and kidney pudding (£8.95), daily specials like chicken tikka kebabs (£4.75), fresh cromer crab salad (£7.95), portabello mushroom risotto with brie (£8.95), leg of lamb steak with rosemary and redcurrant jus (£12.95), and puddings like home-made apple crumble, chocolate crème brûlée or mixed berry cheesecake (£4.25). The two dining rooms are no smoking. Darts, pool, cribbage, dominoes, fruit machine, juke box, TV and piped music. There are tables out in the partly terraced front garden, and an area for children with swings, some elusive rabbits, and chickens. *(Recommended by MDN, John Beeken, Derek Field, O K Smyth, R E Perry, Philip and Susan Philcox, Fred and Lorraine Gill, M Mossman)*

Free house ~ Licensees Clare and Daniel Mercer ~ Real ale ~ Bar food (not Sun evening) ~ Restaurant ~ (01263) 822110 ~ Children welcome ~ Dogs allowed in bar ~ Jazz days in summer ~ Open 11.30-3, 6.30-11; 12-3, 7-10.30 Sun; 12-2.30, 6.30-11 in winter

WINTERTON-ON-SEA   TG4919   Map 8
Fishermans Return   🍺 🛏️
From B1159 turn into village at church on bend, then turn right into The Lane; NR29 4BN

Friendly and busy, this attractive little pub is close to a sandy beach – liked by children and dogs. The cosily white-painted no smoking lounge bar has a roaring log fire, neat brass-studded red leatherette seats and vases of fresh flowers. The panelled public bar has low ceilings and a glossily varnished nautical air (good fire in here too), and the family room, dining room and small bar are no smoking. It's been well run for over 30 years by the same hospitable licensees, who keep a good choice of real ales on handpump: Adnams Bitter and Broadside, Woodfordes Wherry and Norfolk Nog and guests like Adnams Mayday and Archers St George. Several malt whiskies, Old Rosie cider, and wines by the glass. A sensibly short choice of tasty bar food includes toasties (from £3), filled baked potatoes (from £4), various burgers and omelettes (from £8.25), and daily specials like local fresh crab (£6.25), spinach stuffed cannelloni on a mushroom and pesto base (£8.25), whole fresh plaice (£9.75), and bass fillet with roasted red peppers, plum tomatoes and anchovies or slow-braised lamb shank (£10.75). Darts, pool, juke box and piped music. In fine weather you can sit on the attractive wrought-iron and wooden benches on a pretty front terrace with lovely views, or in the sheltered garden. *(Recommended by Anthony Barnes, Alan Cole, Kirstie Bruce, John Saville, Peter Meister, K Christensen, Nick Lawless, Pete and Sue Robbins, Ryta Lyndley)*

Free house ~ Licensees John and Kate Findlay ~ Real ale ~ Bar food ~ (01493) 393305 ~ Children welcome in no smoking garden room, dining room and one bar ~ Dogs welcome ~ Open 11-2.30, 6.30-11; 11-11 Sat; 12.10.30 Sun ~ Bedrooms: £50B/£70B

WOODBASTWICK   TG3315   Map 8
Fur & Feather   🍺
Off B1140 E of Norwich; NR13 6HQ

Seven of Woodfordes beers are tapped from the cask in this friendly and carefully converted thatched cottage – and as the brewery is next door, it's not surprising that they are in tip-top condition: Admirals Reserve, Great Eastern, Mardlers, Nelsons Revenge, Norfolk Nog, Headcracker and Wherry. You can also visit the brewery shop. The style and atmosphere are not what you'd expect of a brewery tap as it's set out more like a dining pub and the décor is modern. Bar food includes home-made soup (£3.75), sandwiches or filled baguettes (from £4.25), game pâté with port and redcurrant sauce (£4.50), smoked salmon and scrambled egg (£5), home-baked ham and eggs (£8), bangers with beer gravy or pure beef burger (£8.50), spicy bean casserole (£9), smoked haddock and spring onion fishcakes or home-made steak and kidney pudding (£9.25), pot-roasted venison in a giant yorky (£10), and sirloin steak (£12.95). Ten wines by the glass. You can smoke only in one small area of the bar; piped music. The pub forms part of a very attractive estate village and has tables out in a pleasant garden. *(Recommended by Comus and Sarah Elliott, Adele Summers, Alan Black, Alan Cole, Kirstie Bruce, R C Vincent, Alastair Gibson, the Didler, Stephen and Jean Curtis, Gerry and Rosemary Dobson, Pat and Clive Sherriff, Keith and Chris O'Neill, B N F and M Parkin, N R White, Pete Devonish, Ian McIntyre, Pete and Sue Robbins, Fred and Lorraine Gill)*

Woodfordes ~ Tenant Tim Ridley ~ Real ale ~ Bar food (12-2(3 Sun), 6-9) ~ Restaurant ~ (01603) 720003 ~ Children welcome ~ Open 11.30-11; 12-10.30 Sun; 11.30-3, 6-11 (10.30 Mon and Tues; still open all day Sun) in winter

LUCKY DIP

Besides the fully inspected pubs, you might like to try these Lucky Dips recommended to us and described by readers (if you do, please send us reports: www.goodguides.co.uk).

AYLSHAM [TG1926]
Black Boys NR11 6EH [Market Pl]: Friendly helpful staff, Adnams IPA, Greene King Abbot and IPA and a guest such as Woodfordes Wherry, good range of food from generous light dishes up, separate dining room, spacious and attractive 17th-c building; part of a popular small local group *(Keith Reeve, Marie Hammond, David Edwards)*
BARFORD [TG1107]
☆ *Cock* NR9 4AS [B1108 7 miles W of Norwich]: Nicely restored traditional main-road pub brewing its own good attractively priced Blue Moon ales, good food (freshly made, so may take a time) from large lunchtime sandwiches to interestingly cooked main dishes and plenty of fish, friendly helpful service and pleasantly relaxed atmosphere, good mix of candlelit tables, shove-ha'penny, smarter no smoking back dining room; well chosen piped music, occasional jazz *(BB, Rachel Abbott, Gerry and Rosemary Dobson)*
BARTON BENDISH [TF7105]
☆ *Spread Eagle* PE33 9DP [off A1122 W of Swaffham; Church Rd]: Attractive pub doing well under welcoming and enthusiastic newish licensees, enjoyable fresh food inc good soup, light lunches, inventive dishes and local game, decent wines inc champagne by the glass, real ales such as Adnams, service prompt even when busy, two neat and rather elegant small front rooms, back evening restaurant; pleasant garden, quiet village, cl all Mon, Tues/Weds lunchtime, open all day Sun till 6 *(BB, Anthony Barnes, Nicky Prentis, Mr and Mrs C Prentis)*
BINHAM [TF9839]
☆ *Chequers* NR21 0AL [B1388 SW of Blakeney]: 17th-c, now brewing its own good Front Street ales, also quickly changing guest beers and fine choice of bottled imports, decent house wines, enjoyable home-made food using local produce, prompt friendly service, long low-beamed bar, inglenook, sturdy plush seats, splendid coal fires each end, some nice old local prints, small no smoking dining area; picnic-sets out in front and on grass behind, interesting village with huge priory church *(MDN, Ann and Colin Hunt, BB, Tracey and Stephen Groves, Derek Field, Steve Nye, John Dwane, George Atkinson, John Knighton, Richard Lewis)*
BLAKENEY [TG0243]
☆ *Manor* NR25 7ND [The Quay]: Friendly and attractive hotel in own grounds with decorous bar, popular esp with older people for good fresh hearty waitress-served bar food, not expensive, from well filled crab sandwiches to attractive puddings, Adnams and Greene King Abbot, decent house wines, helpful attentive staff, conservatory; sunny tables in fountain courtyard and walled garden with bowling green, good big bedrooms; opp wildfowl reserve and sea inlet *(John Beeken, BB)*

BLICKLING [TG1728]
☆ *Buckinghamshire Arms* NR11 6NF [B1354 NW of Aylsham]: Handsome Jacobean inn by gates to Blickling Hall (NT), neat pews around stripped pine tables in lounge, banquettes in small front snug, wide choice of enjoyable carefully prepared food from baguettes and baked potatoes up, friendly helpful service, Adnams Best and Broadside and Woodfordes Wherry, local cider, good range of wines; well behaved children in restaurant, lots of tables out on big lawn with summer food servery, bedrooms with own bathrooms, may open all day in summer *(J F M and M West, Keith Reeve, Marie Hammond, Brian Root, LYM, Mike and Shelley Woodroffe, Dr and Mrs R G J Telfer, Philip and Susan Philcox)*
BRAMERTON [TG2905]
Woods End NR14 7ED [N of village, towards river]: Stunning spot with big windows overlooking bend of River Yare, wide choice of enjoyable food, real ale, good choice, much modernised high-ceilinged lounge, roomy L-shaped extension with pool table, restaurant; terrace tables by the grassy river banks (and hordes of ducks) *(Trevor and Sylvia Millum)*
BRISTON [TG0633]
☆ *John H Stracey* NR24 2JA [B1354, Aylsham end of village]: Cheerful well run country dining pub, wide choice of reasonably priced quickly served food inc fresh local crab in season, decent house wines, real ales, good coffee, comfortable seats, log fire, long-serving landlord, friendly obliging staff; popular pleasant restaurant, a few tables in small well kept garden; good value bedrooms, good breakfast *(R C Vincent)*
BURNHAM MARKET [TF8342]
Lord Nelson PE31 8EN [Creake Rd]: Wide range of generous traditional bar food from baguettes up, real ales inc Greene King IPA, some Nelson memorabilia, good choice of wines, games in public bar, small unpretentious no smoking restaurant; four attractive bedrooms, two in former outbuilding *(John Wooll, Brian Root, LYM, Mrs J C Pank, Michael and Marilyn Switzer)*
CASTLE ACRE [TF8115]
Albert Victor PE32 2AE [Stocks Green]: Big farmhouse tables and chairs, plush sofas, old prints and maps, good changing blackboard food choice, Greene King IPA and Abbot Ale, good range of wines by the glass; piped music; large attractive back garden and pergola *(Anthony Barnes)*
☆ *Ostrich* PE32 2AE [Stocks Green]: Prettily placed pub overlooking tree-lined green, which has been popular for friendly obliging service, unpretentious mix of utilitarian furnishings and fittings with some ancient beams, masonry and huge inglenook fireplace, Greene King ales, and cheap food with vegetarian emphasis, but talk of changes in 2006 – news please;

children welcome, picnic-sets in sheltered informal garden with doves and aviary, cheap plain bedrooms sharing shower (good breakfast), attractive village with castle and monastery remains, may be open all day at least summer Sats *(John Wooll, Brian Root, LYM, Charles Gysin, Philip and Susan Philcox, George Atkinson)*

CASTLE RISING [TF6624]
Black Horse PE31 6AG: Large comfortable dining pub, largely no smoking under two friendly new landladies, good furnishings inc sofas, two areas with plenty of tables, smarter back dining room, real ales such as Adnams, Elgoods, Marstons Pedigree and Woodfordes Wherry, decent choice of wines by the glass, reasonably priced standard food all day from baguettes and baked potatoes to steak and Sun lunch; piped music, no dogs; children particularly welcome, close-set tables out under cocktail parasols, by church and almshouses in pleasant unspoilt village, open all day *(Tracey and Stephen Groves, John Wooll, Mike Ridgway, Sarah Miles)*

CHEDGRAVE [TM3699]
White Horse : New licensees with new chef doing good food from home-baked bread sandwiches up using local produce, Adnams Bitter and Broadside, Flowers IPA and Timothy Taylors Landlord, good choice of wines by the glass and bottle, panelled tap room, new restaurant; children welcome *(Richard and Margaret McPhee)*

CLEY NEXT THE SEA [TG0443]
George NR25 7RN [High St, off A149 W of Sheringham]: Usefully placed Edwardian inn, sympathetically upgraded with contemporary décor and emphasis on food, welcoming new manager, enjoyable food, good choice of wines by the glass; sizeable garden over road, bedrooms *(Charles Gysin, LYM)*
☆ *Three Swallows* NR25 7TT [off A149; Newgate Green]: Cheery take-us-as-you-find-us pub doing straightforward food (all day wknds) from sandwiches up, banquettes around long high leathered tables, log fire, steps up to another small family eating area, second log fire in further no smoking stripped pine dining room on left, Adnams and Greene King IPA and Abbot from unusual richly carved bar, decent wines, nice photographs, dominoes, cribbage; children and dogs welcome, big garden with budgerigar aviary, surprisingly grandiose fountain, wooden climbing frame; handy for the salt marshes, simple bedrooms, open all day wknds and summer *(Geoff and Pat Bell, MDN, John Dwane, Pat and Tony Martin, Barry Collett, LYM)*

COLKIRK [TF9226]
☆ *Crown* NR21 7AA [off B1146 S of Fakenham; Crown Rd]: Unpretentious two-bar pub, spick and span and now all no smoking, with cheerful landlord and charming efficient service, solid country furniture and appealing décor, rugs and flooring tiles, open fires, splendid choice of wines by the glass, Greene King ales inc Ridleys Prospect, good coffee,

wide choice of enjoyable bar food, sunny dining room, pub games; good disabled access; children and dogs allowed, picnic-sets in garden with suntrap terrace *(Mark, Amanda, Luke and Jake Sheard, Comus and Sarah Elliott, R C Vincent, LYM, Tracey and Stephen Groves, Peter Rozée, George Atkinson)*

COLTISHALL [TG2719]
☆ *Kings Head* NR12 7EA [Wroxham Rd (B1354)]: Good dining pub close to river, imaginative food esp fish, generous bar snacks and good value lunch deals, Adnams, good wines, friendly helpful service, no smoking area, open fire, lots of fishing nets and several stuffed fish inc a 50lb pike (personable chef/landlord competes in international fishing contests); piped music; reasonably priced bedrooms, decent breakfast, moorings nearby *(BB, M J Bourke, J S and S Chadwick, Jill and Roger Hambling)*

CROMER [TG2242]
Red Lion NR27 9HD [off A149; Tucker St]: Proper pubby carpeted bar, friendly and unspoilt, in substantial Victorian seafront hotel with great sea views, stripped flint and William Morris wallpaper, old bottles and chamber-pots, lots of lifeboat pictures, Adnams and other ales, friendly staff, pleasant old-fashioned atmosphere (rather like that of the town itself); very wide range of reasonably priced bar food inc children's, restaurant with lots of fresh seafood; tables in back courtyard, comfortable bedrooms *(Fred and Lorraine Gill)*

DENVER SLUICE [TF5800]
Jenyns Arms PE38 0EQ [signed via B1507 off A1122 Downham Mkt bypass]: Extensive well laid out pub in fine spot by spectacular hydraulic sluices controlling Great Ouse, extensive generous straightforward food (not Sun evening), friendly helpful staff cope well with coach parties; Adnams and Greene King, light and airy games area, no smoking conservatory; piped music; children welcome, tables out by water with peacocks and chickens, self-catering *(BB, Louise English, Bill and Sheila McLardy)*

DERSINGHAM [TF6930]
☆ *Feathers* PE31 6LN [B1440 towards Sandringham]: Solid Jacobean sandstone inn with two relaxed modernised dark-panelled bars, Adnams, Bass and Black Sheep, log fires, wide choice of generous bar food from sandwiches up inc home-made pies and local game, friendly service, restaurant (not Sun evening), separate games room; children welcome and well catered for, large family garden with elaborate play area inc wendy house and outsize snakes and ladders, attractive secluded adults' garden with pond, comfortable well furnished bedrooms *(Mike Ridgway, Sarah Miles, LYM, Tracey and Stephen Groves)*

DICKLEBURGH [TM1682]
Crown IP21 4NQ [The Street]: Beamed Tudor pub with enjoyable food (not Mon) inc interesting dishes and real food for children, friendly atmosphere with armchairs, sofa,

candles and log fire, good short wine list and malt whiskies, Greene King and guest beers, separate pool/function area; children welcome, garden tables, open all day wknds *(Alan Cole, Kirstie Bruce)*

DOCKING [TF7637]

Railway Inn PE31 8LY [Station Rd]: Unpretentious local with wide choice of good sensibly priced home cooking inc fresh fish, generous helpings, polite attentive service, local Buffys Bitter and other ales such as Batemans XB and Woodfordes Admirals Reserve, good house wines, small chummy bar (can be smoky) with woodburner, pool and TV in little lounge behind, no smoking panelled and carpeted dining room with lots of fresh flowers and some rail prints and posters; small side garden with marquee, open all day wknds *(Derek and Sylvia Stephenson, Tracey and Stephen Groves, George Atkinson)*

EAST BARSHAM [TF9133]

White Horse NR21 0LH [B1105 3 miles N of Fakenham]: Attractive extended pub long popular for wide choice of straightforward food inc steak nights and bargain OAP lunches, big log fire in long beamed main bar, steps to other areas, real ales such as Adnams Bitter and Broadside and Charles Wells Bombardier, decent wine, good coffee, friendly attentive staff, two small attractive dining rooms; piped music, darts; children welcome, well priced bedrooms – a pleasant quiet place to stay *(R C Vincent)*

EAST RUSTON [TG3428]

Butchers Arms NR12 9JG [back rd Horning—Happisburgh, N of Stalham]: Comfortable village pub, friendly and well run, with generous enjoyable food inc bargain lunchtime dish of the day, real ales, two dining rooms; attractive garden, pretty hanging baskets, handy for Old Vicarage garden *(Alan M Pring, Michael Sargent)*

EATON [TG2006]

Red Lion NR4 7LD [Newmarket Rd]: More restaurant than pub (though it has real ales), well worth knowing for its enjoyable food at sensible prices; part of a popular small local group *(M J Bourke, Tony Middis)*

EDGEFIELD [TG0934]

Three Pigs NR24 2RL [Norwich Rd (B1149)]: Olde-worlde pub/restaurant with 18th-c smuggling connections, friendly licensees, good range of home-made food, chatty atmosphere, real ales, good coffee; attractive and secluded site for a few caravan tourers at the back, cl Mon *(Roy Bromell)*

GAYTON [TF7219]

Crown PE32 1PA [B1145/B1153]: Attractive flower-decked pub with some unusual old features and comfortable nooks and corners, good choice of sensibly priced food from good value sandwiches up (can be a wait at busy times), Greene King ales, limited but good wine choice, efficient service, good log fire, games room; tables in sheltered and attractive garden *(Hamish Breach, LYM)*

Rampant Horse PE32 1PA [Lynn Rd]: Locally popular food all day inc good value Sun lunch,

three real ales, friendly efficient staff; big garden with good play area *(R C Vincent)*

GREAT BIRCHAM [TF7632]

☆ *Kings Head* PE31 6RJ [B1155, S end of village (called and signed Bircham locally)]: Trendy contemporary retro décor, very good if pricey up-to-date meals inc simple interesting lunches but not bar snacks, friendly efficient young staff, four real ales, comfortable sofas in log-fire bar, light and airy modern dining room, much stainless steel, glass and plain dark wood, leather-walled back area, sumptuous lavatories; tables and chairs out front and back with rustic view, comfortable bedrooms, good breakfast *(LYM, Tracey and Stephen Groves, John Wooll)*

GREAT CRESSINGHAM [TF8401]

☆ *Windmill* IP25 6NN [village signed off A1065 S of Swaffham; Water End]: Masses of interesting pictures and bric-a-brac in warren of rambling linked rooms with plenty of cosy corners and no smoking areas, keenly priced fresh bar food from baguettes to steak, welcoming efficient service, log or coal fire, Adnams Bitter and Broadside, Greene King IPA, Windy Miller Quixote (brewed for the pub) and a couple of interesting guest beers, good coffee, decent sensibly priced wines, plenty of malt whiskies, well lit pool room, pub games; faint piped music, big sports TV in side snug; children and dogs welcome, picnic-sets and good play area in big garden, well screened caravan site *(MDN, Rita Scarratt, Charles Gysin, Minda and Stanley Alexander, LYM)*

GREAT YARMOUTH [TG5206]

Red Herring NR30 3HQ [Havelock Rd]: Welcoming unpretentious backstreet alehouse with at least six changing real ales at attractive prices, farm ciders, rock collection, old local photographs, books to read *(the Didler, Mrs M Hatwell)*

HAINFORD [TG2219]

Chequers NR10 3AY [Stratton Rd]: Comfortable and friendly rebuilt thatched cottage in charming setting, well prepared food from filled baguettes up, good choice of real ales, big airy bar area and rooms off, pleasant licensees; well arranged gardens with play area, children welcome *(M J Bourke)*

HAPPISBURGH [TG3831]

Hill House NR12 0PW [by village church]: Cheery heavy-beamed village pub with plush seats, woodburner in big inglenook, open fire other end, several changing real ales inc Adnams and Greene King, reasonably priced usual bar food from sandwiches up, darts and bar billiards, Sherlock Holmes memorabilia, separate no smoking restaurant; tables outside front and back, bedrooms, pleasant setting *(BB, Ian and Nita Cooper, John Beeken)*

HARPLEY [TF7825]

☆ *Rose & Crown* PE31 6TW [off A148 Fakenham—Kings Lynn; Nethergate St]: Simple refreshing contemporary décor with local artwork and old wooden tables, enjoyable food (not Mon) inc some interesting dishes as well as the usual pubby things, efficient friendly service without rushing you, Greene King IPA, good choice of wines by the glass, big log fire, no smoking dining room on left; tables in attractive garden *(John Wooll, Mark, Amanda, Luke and Jake Sheard, BB)*

HEACHAM [TF6737]

Bushel & Strike PE31 7DL [Malthouse Crescent]: Highly rated for children outside, with good big new play area, ride-on toys in separate toddlers' area, and child-sized picnic-sets, as well as normal ones in tree-shaded main garden; straightforward bar with juke box, games machine and big-screen TV, good value usual food, sensibly priced real ales such as Greene King IPA and Theakstons Old Peculier *(Mike Ridgway, Sarah Miles)*

HOLT [TG0738]

Feathers NR25 6BW [Market Pl]: Relaxed and unpretentious town hotel, bustling locals' bar comfortably extended around original panelled area with open fire, attractive entrance/reception area with antiques, helpful friendly staff, good value promptly served generous food, Greene King IPA and Abbot, decent wines, good coffee, calm dining room; piped music, can get smoky, busy on Sat market day; dogs welcome *(Geoff and Pat Bell, J S and S Chadwick, BB, Christine and Neil Townend, O K Smyth)*

Kings Head NR25 6BN [High St/Bull St]: Cheerful rambling pub, reasonably priced fresh food all day using local supplies, prompt friendly service, four real ales inc Adnams and Woodfordes, fair choice of wines, pleasant staff, pleasant no smoking dining conservatory; children welcome, some tables outside, may be afternoon closure winter wkdys *(John Wooll, Mr and Mrs A Langley, Keith and Janet Morris)*

HORSEY [TG4622]

☆ *Nelson Head* NR29 4AD [off B1159; The Street]: Experienced new landlady, friendly and chatty, putting more emphasis on the family dining side in nicely placed simple country local with usual bar food from baguettes up, Woodfordes Wherry and Nelsons Revenge, good log fire and shiny bric-a-brac, small pleasant no smoking side dining room, traditional games, small local pictures for sale; piped music; children welcome, picnic-sets in garden, good coast walks, open all day at least in summer *(Liz and Brian Barnard, LYM)*

HORSTEAD [TG2619]

☆ *Recruiting Sergeant* NR12 7EE [B1150 just S of Coltishall]: Spacious pleasantly refurbished village pub, part of a popular small local group, with enjoyable generous food inc good fish choice, friendly obliging service, real ales, impressive choice of wines by the glass, big open fire, brasses and muskets, music-free smaller room; children welcome *(M J Bourke)*

KING'S LYNN [TF6119]

Bradleys PE30 5DT [South Quay]: Long-closed pub now reopened as stylish bar/restaurant, smartly simple, with plenty of flowers and local artwork, good choice of wines by the glass, Adnams, friendly helpful staff, good value food, more expensive upstairs restaurant with lunch deals; quayside tables and small back garden, open all day *(John Wooll)*

Crown & Mitre PE30 1LJ [Ferry St]: Old-fashioned pub, soon if not already entirely no smoking, full of Naval and nautical memorabilia, constantly changing real ales, good value home-made food inc doorstep sandwiches and proper pies, river views from new back conservatory *(John Wooll)*

Dukes Head PE30 1JS [Tuesday Market Pl]: Imposing early 18th-c hotel with small bar on left and pubby food from baguettes up in informal dining room on right, pleasant efficient service, local pictures, sofas in inner lounge with small back bar and more formal restaurant; bedrooms *(John Wooll)*

Lloyds No 1 PE30 1EZ [King St/Tuesday Market Pl]: Spacious neatly kept good value Wetherspoons, two-for-one food bargains, good beer and wine choice, efficient friendly service; children welcome till 7, attractive back garden down to river, pleasant bedrooms, good value breakfast *(John Wooll, R C Vincent, Hazel Morgan, Bernard Patrick)*

No 3 Saturday Market Place PE30 5DQ [Saturday Market Pl]: Coffee/wine bar rather than pub, simple comfortable tables between window sofas and back bar, good value lunchtime sandwiches and up-to-date snacks, wider evening choice (and plans to extend kitchen), decent house wines and good coffee range, pleasant service; open all day from breakfast time but cl Mon-Weds evenings and Sun *(John Wooll)*

LESSINGHAM [TG3928]

Star NR12 0DN [School Rd]: Small and welcoming, with big inglenook and another open fire, comfortable armchairs, low ceilings, good beer and wine choice, good side restaurant where chef/landlord uses only local produce *(Luke Colby)*

LETHERINGSETT [TG0638]

Kings Head NR25 7AR [Holt Rd (A148)]: A boon for young families, with plenty of tables and lots of amusements for children on extensive lawn, summer brass or jazz bands, open-plan pub with sepia prints of Norfolk life, prominent Union flags, log fire, friendly landlord, small lounge, games room; piped music; dogs welcome, open all day *(R C Vincent, LYM, Ian Stafford)*

LITTLE PLUMSTEAD [TG3112]

Brick Kilns NR13 5JH [Norwich Rd (B1140)]: Friendly refurbished family pub with well done extension, enjoyable fresh food inc fish from Lowestoft; small garden *(M J Bourke)*

MUNDFORD [TL8093]

Crown IP26 5HQ [off A1065 Thetford—Swaffham; Crown Rd]: Unassuming heavily beamed 17th-c pub with huge fireplace, interesting local memorabilia, mainstream real ales, dozens of malt whiskies, spiral iron stairs to overflow club room and restaurant, games, TV and juke box in red-tiled locals' bar; children and dogs welcome, back terrace and garden with wishing well, bedrooms with own bathrooms, open all day *(LYM, Will Watson)*

NORTH WALSHAM [TG2928]
Scarborough Hill House NR28 9NA
[Yarmouth Rd]: Civilised and comfortable bar
with enjoyable food, good staff, and – at a
price – Adnams Broadside *(David Twitchett)*
NORWICH [TG2308]
Bell NR1 3QB [Orford Hill]: Big busy open-
plan Wetherspoons, good value, no music,
pleasant furnishings and atmosphere esp in
upper bar (favoured by customers of nearby
shopping mall – downstairs is more all-day
drinking), good choice of real ales inc Wolf,
friendly staff; open all day *(Ian Phillips)*
☆ *Eagle* NR2 2HN [Eagle Walk/Newmarket Rd
(A11)]: Attractively refurbished, comfortable
and welcoming, with sensible choice of good
fresh food cooked to order (so takes a while),
Adnams, Greene King and a guest beer,
friendly staff, upstairs restaurant; pleasant
lawned garden and play area *(M J Bourke,
Anthony Barnes)*
☆ *Kings Arms* NR1 3HQ [Hall Rd]: Traditional
woody pub with Adnams, Batemans, Wolf and
changing guest beers from the area, beer
festivals, dozens of malt whiskies and plenty of
wines, brewery memorabilia, good landlord
and atmosphere, may be lunchtime food (or
bring your own or order out – plates, cutlery
provided), light and airy garden room;
unobtrusive sports TV; vines in courtyard,
open all day *(Dr and Mrs A K Clarke)*
☆ *Ribs of Beef* NR3 1HY [Wensum St, S side of
Fye Bridge]: Warm, welcoming and well used
old pub, good range of real ales inc local
brews, farm cider, good wine choice, deep
leather settees and small tables upstairs,
attractive smaller downstairs room with river
view and some local river paintings, generous
cheap reliable food (till 5 Sat/Sun), quick
friendly service, long-serving licensees; river-
view terrace *(Keith Reeve, Marie Hammond)*
Take Five NR3 1HF [opp Cathedral gate]:
Cross between pub and café, moved here from
former home at Suckling Hall/Cinema City;
pleasant relaxed atmosphere, real ales inc
Woodfordes Wherry, farm cider, impressive
wine choice inc many organic by the glass,
good value cheerful food also largely organic
inc generous fresh light dishes and plenty for
vegetarians, helpful young staff *(Keith Reeve,
Marie Hammond)*
OLD HUNSTANTON [TF6842]
Ancient Mariner PE36 6JJ [part of L'Estrange
Arms Hotel, Golf Course Rd]: Relaxed and
cheerful rambling bar, dark low beams and
timbers, bare bricks and flagstones, several
little areas in conservatory and upstairs family
gallery, pleasant furnishings, four real ales
from Adnams and Woodfordes, good wines by
the glass, friendly service, popular menu, open
fires, papers and magazines; hotel in prime
spot, terrace and long sea-view garden down to
dunes, play area, nice bedrooms, open all day
Fri-Sun and summer *(Tracey and
Stephen Groves)*
Neptune PE36 6HZ [Old Hunstanton Rd]:
Friendly landlord and good service, log fire,
daily papers and magazines, local landscapes

and Lloyd Loom chairs in small front bar with
three real ales such as Greene King Abbot,
good wines by the glass, short good value
lunchtime food choice, equally short and
appealing if more pricey evening menu, small
pleasant side restaurant; seven bedrooms
(John Wooll, Ian Arthur)
OVERSTRAND [TG2440]
Sea Marge NR27 0AB [High St]: Substantial
sea-view hotel (former Edwardian country
house) with separate entrance to spacious bar
area, same food as in dining room; good-sized
garden, 22 comfortable bedrooms *(MDN)*
REEPHAM [TG0922]
Kings Arms NR10 4JJ [Market Pl]: Attractive
17th-c coaching inn, pleasant homely décor
with several areas, beams and stripped
brickwork, real ales such as Adnams and
Woodfordes Wherry, decent wines by the
glass, three open fires, wide choice of
reasonably priced food from sandwiches up,
cheerful willing service, games area one end,
steps to restaurant; tables out in sunny
courtyard, bedrooms *(Comus and
Sarah Elliott, MDN)*
☆ *Old Brewery House* NR10 4JJ [Market Sq]:
Georgian hotel with big log fire in no smoking
high-ceilinged panelled bar overlooking old-
fashioned town square, lots of farming and
fishing bric-a-brac, Greene King and a guest
such as Adnams, attentive friendly staff, good
value food from well filled sandwiches up,
carpeted lounge, no smoking conservatory;
piped music; children and dogs welcome, tables
in attractive courtyard with covered well and
garden with pond and fountain, bedrooms
with own bathrooms, open all day *(MDN,
John Wooll, LYM, the Didler, Dr and
Mrs R G J Telfer, George Atkinson)*
RINGLAND [TG1313]
Swan NR8 6AB [The Street]: Smartly
refurbished under enthusiastic young
Australian licensees, cheery friendly staff, lots
of dishes from Down Under, Adnams and
Woodfordes Wherry; piped music; plenty of
outside seating by River Wensum *(George
Atkinson)*
ROCKLAND ST MARY [TG3204]
New Inn NR14 7HP [New Inn Hill]: Over rd
from staithe, traditional local-feel core with
coal fire, sofas, darts and real ales such as
Adnams Broadside, more contemporary eating
area opening into attractive barn-style
restaurant extension with picture-window
views, reasonably priced enjoyable pubby food,
friendly service; children really welcome, good
disabled access, front terrace tables, back
garden, good walks to Rockland Broad and
bird hides *(Mark, Amanda, Luke and
Jake Sheard)*
RUSHALL [TM1982]
☆ *Half Moon* IP21 4QD [The Street]: Massive
helpings of hearty traditional food inc plenty of
fish and big puddings fill this main no
smoking pub most nights (two sittings, 6 and
8.30, if you book), with close-set tables on
bare boards or brick flooring in the chatty
beamed bar, more space in a picture-window

carpeted dining room (children welcome here), Adnams, Boddingtons and Woodfordes Wherry, good friendly service, hot inglenook log fire; unobtrusive piped music; back brick terrace, neat grass beyond, simple good value separate motel block *(BB, Ian and Nita Cooper, David Barnes, KC)*

SALTHOUSE [TG0743]

☆ *Dun Cow* NR25 7XA [A149 Blakeney—Sheringham]: Airy well used pub overlooking salt marshes, generous unpretentious food all day from good fresh crab sandwiches and baked potatoes to local fish, polite friendly staff, Adnams Broadside and Greene King IPA and Abbot, decent wines, open fires, stripped beams and cob walls in big barn-like main bar, no smoking family bar and games room with pool; piped radio; blues nights; coast views from big attractive walled front garden, sheltered courtyard with figs and apples, separate family garden with play area, good walks and bird-watching, bedrooms and self-catering *(Roger Wain-Heapy, Derek Field, BB, Tracey and Stephen Groves, John Evans, Ben and Helen Ingram)*

SCULTHORPE [TF8930]

Sculthorpe Mill NR21 9QG [inn signed off A148 W of Fakenham, opp village]: Rebuilt 18th-c mill conversion, comfortable dimly lit beamed bar with several rooms, enjoyable food from sandwiches and snack menu to full meals, Greene King ales, decent house wines; children in eating areas, spacious and appealing streamside garden, open all day wknds and summer, comfortable bedrooms, good breakfast *(LYM, Sue Crees, John Evans)*

SEDGEFORD [TF7036]

King William IV PE36 5LU [B1454, off A149 Kings Lynn—Hunstanton]: Friendly pub doing well under current licensees, inviting panelled bar with warm woodburner, two dining areas with good choice of inexpensive mainly traditional food, efficient service, Charles Wells Bombardier and Woodfordes Wherry, well chosen wines; attractive terrace and garden *(Tracey and Stephen Groves, Scott Emery)*

SHERINGHAM [TG1543]

Lobster NR26 8JP [High St]: Sizeable pub almost on seafront, seafaring décor in tidy panelled bar with old sewing-machine treadle tables and warm fire, Adnams, Greene King and interesting guest beers, farm cider, decent wines, enjoyable quickly served generous bar meals, no smoking restaurant with good seafood specials, pleasant staff, public bar with games inc pool, no piped music; dogs on leads allowed, two courtyards with summer hog roasts and heated marquee, open all day *(David and Sue Smith, Keith and Janet Morris, Fred and Lorraine Gill)*

Two Lifeboats NR26 8JR [promenade]: Comfortable sea-view lounge, cosier rooms behind, big helpings of good food from doorstep sandwiches up, Greene King IPA and Abbot, may be free bar nibbles, quick friendly young staff, no smoking restaurant; terrace tables, reasonably priced bedrooms *(Paul Humphreys, Michael Tack)*

SKEYTON [TG2524]

☆ *Goat* NR10 5DH [off A140 N of Aylsham; Long Rd]: Extended thatched and low-beamed pub with wide choice of reasonably priced food from baguettes and baked potatoes up in bar, long dark-raftered dining area and small no smoking restaurant (best to book Sat evening), Adnams and Woodfordes ales, good value wines, good coffees and hot chocolate, efficient friendly service, log-effect gas fire; piped local radio; pleasant terrace and tables under trees by pub's neat playing field – very quiet spot *(BB, Dr and Mrs R G J Telfer, Philip and Susan Philcox)*

SMALLBURGH [TG3324]

☆ *Crown* NR12 9AD: 15th-c thatched and beamed village inn with popular food in bar and upstairs dining room, welcoming old-fashioned landlord and good pub atmosphere, prompt service, Adnams, Caledonian Deuchars IPA and Greene King IPA and Abbot, good choice of wines by the glass, daily papers, darts; no dogs or children inside, smoking allowed throughout; picnic-sets in sheltered and pretty back garden, bedrooms, cl Mon lunchtime, Sun evening *(P B Morgan, Marguerite Pointer, BB, Philip and Susan Philcox)*

SOUTH WOOTTON [TF6622]

Farmers Arms PE30 3HQ [part of Knights Hill Hotel, Grimston Rd (off A148/A149)]: Olde-worlde conversion of barn and stables, wide choice of reliable food all day in bar and restaurant, puddings cabinet, good changing choice of real ales, good wines, abundant coffee, friendly prompt service; children welcome, tables outside, comfortable motel bedrooms, open all day *(R C Vincent)*

STALHAM [TG3424]

Wayford Bridge NR12 9LL [A149]: Enjoyable food inc good Sun lunch, real ales *(M J Bourke)*

STOKE HOLY CROSS [TG2302]

Wildebeest NR14 8QJ [Norwich Rd]: Dining pub with emphasis on good interesting bistro-style food but provision for drinkers too, good beer and wine by the glass, good cheerfully welcoming service, some unusual decorations inc african wooden masks *(Sheila and Brian Wilson)*

THOMPSON [TL9296]

☆ *Chequers* IP24 1PX [Griston Rd, off A1075 S of Watton]: Long, low and picturesque 16th-c thatched dining pub tucked away in attractive spot, good interesting food inc local game and lots of fresh fish in partly no smoking series of olde-worlde quaint rooms, Adnams, Fullers London Pride and Woodfordes, good modestly priced wine list, helpful staff and friendly atmosphere, low beams, inglenooks, some stripped brickwork, antique tools and traps; dogs allowed in bar, tables in good-sized garden with play area, good bedroom block *(R C Livesey, Rita Scarratt, LYM, Bill and Sheila McLardy)*

THORPE MARKET [TG2335]

Green Farm NR11 8TH [A149 N Walsham—Cromer]: Hotel based on 16th-c farmhouse, good value original food evenings and wknd lunchtimes in big pine-furnished lounge bar and smart restaurant, log fire, friendly attentive service, local Buffys and Wolf real ales; children welcome, attractive bedrooms, good breakfast *(J S and S Chadwick)*

TRUNCH [TG2834]

Crown NR28 0AH [Front St]: Small cheery village local with wide choice of low-priced pubby food (not Mon/Tues) from sandwiches and baguettes to steaks, Batemans and other ales, pleasant service, small dining room *(Alan M Pring, J S and S Chadwick, Richard Durrant)*

UPPER SHERINGHAM [TG1441]

Red Lion NR26 8AD [B1157; village signposted off A148 Cromer—Holt, and the A149 just W of Sheringham]: As we went to press, we heard that this nice pub had closed and might be relocating to a barn in the village; we'd be glad of news *(LYM)*

WELLS-NEXT-THE-SEA [TF9143]

☆ *Bowling Green* NR23 1JB [Church St]: Attractively refurbished and welcoming L-shaped bar, hearty traditional food at raised dining end (freshly made so may be a wait), friendly helpful service, Greene King IPA and Abbot and Woodfordes Wherry and Nelsons Revenge, two woodburners, panelling, flagstone and brick floor, simple furnishings; tables out on back terrace, quiet spot on outskirts *(John Wooll, Eddie and Lynn Jarrett, Michael and Marilyn Switzer, John Beeken)*

WEST ACRE [TF7815]

☆ *Stag* PE32 1TR [Low Rd]: Appealing pub tucked away in attractive spot in very quiet village, limited choice of good value home cooking using local produce from good value baguettes up, good choice of changing real ales in small bar, particularly cheerful and welcoming service, neat dining room; cl Mon *(BB, Colin McKerrow, Dr and Mrs R G J Telfer)*

WEYBOURNE [TG1143]

Ship NR25 7SZ [The Street (A149 W of Sheringham)]: Big comfortable bar, two no smoking dining rooms, wide food choice (not Sun evening) from plenty of sandwiches and baked potatoes up, real ales such as Adnams, decent wines by the glass, pleasant staff; unobtrusive piped music; garden tables and tearoom, cl Mon *(Roger Wain-Heapy, Keith and Janet Morris)*

WIGHTON [TF9439]

☆ *Carpenters Arms* NR23 1PF [High St – off main rd, past church]: Good modern cooking in 17th-c flint pub given contemporary redesign, bar with leather sofa and cheerily painted tables and chairs, welcoming service, Adnams, Marstons Pedigree and Woodfordes

Wherry and Nelsons Revenge, mulberry dining room; picnic-sets in informal back garden *(BB, Warren Marsh, Ian Arthur)*

WIMBOTSHAM [TF6205]

Chequers PE34 3QG [Church Rd]: Friendly local with enjoyable food, real ales, efficient cheerful service and good log fire *(Fred Farrow Pennsfields)*

WIVETON [TG0442]

☆ *Bell* NR25 7TL [Blakeney Rd]: Welcoming and relaxed open-plan dining pub, Danish landlord cooking wide choice of enjoyable food for bar and restaurant inc some danish dishes and interesting specials, Adnams Broadside and Woodfordes, good wines, helpful service, secondhand books, warm red décor and log fire, large carpeted no smoking conservatory, no music or machines; picnic-sets on lawn and garden behind, has been cl Mon lunchtime *(BB, Tracey and Stephen Groves, Derek Field)*

WROXHAM [TG2814]

☆ *Green Man* NR13 6NQ [Rackheath; A1151 towards Norwich]: Well kept and comfortable, with easy chairs, plush banquettes and other seats in open-plan bar, log fires, interesting World War II memorabilia (nearby air base), popular pubby food (two small dining areas can get crowded) inc generous Sun lunch, friendly landlord, Greene King and Woodfordes ales; children in eating areas, beautifully kept bowling green *(LYM, Brian and Jean Hepworth)*

WYMONDHAM [TG1101]

Feathers NR18 0PN [Town Green]: Traditional town pub with Elgoods and other ales, wide choice of bargain pub food, farm tools and other bric-a-brac; courtyard tables *(Tony Hobden)*

☆ *Green Dragon* NR18 0PH [Church Street]: Picturesque heavily timbered jettied 14th-c inn, cosy unsmart beamed and timbered back bar, log fire under Tudor mantelpiece, interesting pictures, bigger no smoking dining area (children allowed), Adnams Bitter and Broadside and a guest beer, friendly service; a shame they charge you for tap water; children and dogs welcome; modest bedrooms, nr glorious 12th-c abbey church *(Geoff and Pat Bell, the Didler, LYM, Michael B Griffith, Gerry and Rosemary Dobson)*

YAXHAM [TG0110]

Yaxham Mill NR19 1RP [Norwich Rd (B1135)]: Converted tower mill with particularly helpful willing staff, comfortable and attractive simple bar, pleasant restaurant, decent food, Adnams Broadside and Woodfordes Wherry; comfortable bedrooms with own bathrooms, good breakfast *(Peter and Lorely Murphy, David Harris, Ian Phillips)*

Post Office address codings confusingly give the impression that a few pubs are in Norfolk, when they're really in Cambridgeshire or Suffolk (which is where we list them).

Northamptonshire

Northamptonshire does well for good pubs. And with just under three-quarters of our main entries being free houses it's no surprise that there's plenty of individual character here. Quite a few are great all-rounders in the traditional sense, successfully relying on a genuinely cheery welcome, tasty pubby food and quite often a handful of thoughtfully sourced beers. The homely Windmill at Badby is one such, as are the very welcoming George at Kilsby, and the enjoyable Royal Oak at Eydon (among the main entries for the first time in many years), with its tasty food and handful of interesting real ales. The enthusiastically run Queens Head at Bulwick really gets this formula right, at the same time managing to take its imaginative food up a notch or two, and the Great Western Arms at Aynho is on a splendid roll. It's the rather special Falcon at Fotheringhay, however, with its most rewarding and inventive food, that is once again the clear winner of the title of Northamptonshire Dining Pub of the Year. Real ale gets a boost here in the shape of the lovely old Fox & Hounds at Great Brington, gaining a main entry with a beer award for its incredible range of nine real ales – and its food is tempting, too. In the Lucky Dip section at the end of the chapter, current favourites are the Stags Head at Maidwell, Malt Shovel in Northampton, Samuel Pepys at Slipton, Countryman at Staverton and Boat at Stoke Bruerne. Drinks prices in the county are close to the national average – if anything, very slightly higher. There are one or two local ales to look out for, such as Potbelly, Rockingham and Frog Island, but people after beers from specialist brewers are more likely to find ones from outside the immediate area, such as Adnams and Oakham.

AYNHO SP5133 Map 4
Great Western Arms
Just off B4031 W, towards Deddington; Aynho Wharf, Station Road; OX17 3BP

Don't be deterred by the unassuming exterior of this much enjoyed pub, which is sandwiched between a railway and the Oxford Canal. Its series of linked rambling rooms is divided enough to give a cosy intimate feel, and the golden stripped stone of some walling tones well with the warm cream and deep red plasterwork elsewhere. Attractive furnishings include good solid country tables and regional chairs on broad flagstones – a good log fire warms cosy seats in two of the areas. There are candles and fresh flowers throughout, daily papers and glossy magazines. Readers are very taken by the extensive collection of interesting GWR memorabilia including lots of steam locomotive photographs; the dining area on the right is rather elegant. Numerous seafood and fish dishes feature amongst the freshly made food, which might include fried sardines (£5.85), whitebait (£5.95), sausage and mash (£7.95), various pasta dishes (£8.95), vegetable risotto (£9.25), steak and kidney pie (£9.50), kedgeree (£10.75), grilled tuna with vegetable salsa (£12.95), bass with red pepper sauce (£13.95), and rack of lamb with honey and rosemary (£14.95). All dining areas are no smoking and they have piped music. They have well kept Hook Norton and a guest from a brewer such as Fullers on handpump, and good wines by the glass; service is welcoming and attentive. Opening out of the main bar, the former stable courtyard behind has white cast-iron tables and chairs; there are moorings and a marina nearby. (*Recommended by Gerry and*

Rosemary Dobson, George Atkinson, Gwyn and Anne Wake, Sir Nigel Foulkes, P and J Shapley, Susan and John Douglas, Charles and Pauline Stride, Ian Phillips, Eric George, John Saul, Iain R Hewitt, Stuart Turner, Michael Dandy)

Hook Norton ~ Lease Frank Baldwin ~ Real ale ~ Bar food ~ Restaurant ~
(01869) 338288 ~ Children welcome ~ Dogs allowed in bar ~ Open 12-3, 6-11(10 Sun);
closed Sun evening in winter

BADBY SP5559 Map 4
Windmill
Village signposted off A361 Daventry—Banbury; NN11 3AN

Bar food at this homely thatched dining pub is popular so it is worth booking: in addition to lunchtime sandwiches (from £3.50), they typically have soup of the day (£3.25), potato skins with yoghurt and mint or salsa dip (£3.95), vegetarian nut roast (£8.75), ploughman's or lasagne (£8.95), pie of the day (£9.25), roast salmon with thai marinade with dill mayonnaise (£11.50), and fillet steak topped with brandy and peppercorns (£15.25). On your way in, look out for Oscar, the large pub dog asleep in the corridor. Two beamed and flagstoned bars have a nice country feel with an unusual woodburning stove in an enormous tiled inglenook fireplace, simple country furnishings in good solid wood, and cricketing and rugby pictures. There's also a comfortably cosy lounge. The modern-feeling, brightly lit carpeted restaurant is no smoking. Bass, Flowers Original, Timothy Taylors Landlord and Wadworths 6X are well kept on handpump, with good fairly priced wines by the bottle; quiet piped music. Outside, there's a pleasant terrace by the green of the attractive ironstone village, and a nice path leads south through Badby Wood, carpeted with bluebells in spring, to a landscaped lake near Fawsley Hall. *(Recommended by Oliver Richardson, George Atkinson, Dr and Mrs T E Hothersall, Sally Anne and Peter Goodale, Rob and Catherine Dunster, Suzanne Miles, Les and Barbara Owen)*

Free house ~ Licensees John Freestone and Carol Sutton ~ Real ale ~ Bar food ~
Restaurant ~ (01327) 702363 ~ Children welcome ~ Dogs allowed in bar and bedrooms
~ Open 11.30-12; 12-11 Sun ~ Bedrooms: £59.50B/£72.50B

BULWICK SP9694 Map 4
Queens Head
Just off A43 Kettering—Duddington; NN17 3DY

Very friendly licensees inject a cheery enthusiasm for country life, food and real ale into this lovely 600-year-old stone cottage row. Whilst its unaltered appearance and character remain that of a delightfully traditional village local (bellringers pop in here after their Wednesday practice, and the darts and dominoes teams are very much active), there's something extra here too. Thoughtfully sourced beers – well kept and served from a stone bar counter – include Shepherd Neame Spitfire, with two or three interesting guests from brewers such as Burton Bridge, Newby Wyke and the very local Rockingham, and a good wine list includes interesting bin ends, with nine wines by the glass, and they've over 20 malt whiskies. A big draw is the changing choice of robustly flavoured food, which is cooked fresh to order, using local produce where possible: lunchtime sandwiches (from £4.95), soup (£4.95), pressed game terrine with cranberry and orange relish (£6.95), sweet potato, basil and parmesan risotto (£9.50), fettuccine with wild rabbit, tarragon and root vegetables in rabbit sauce (£12.50), grilled free-range pork cutlet marinated in lemon, garlic and sage with cassoulet (£13.95), grilled aberdeenshire fillet steak (£19.95), and puddings such as chocolate terrine with caramel sauce and crème fraîche or lemon polenta cake with lemon and vanilla syrup and crème fraîche (£5.95). The ancient two-room stone floored bar has beams, and a small fire in a stone hearth at each end, and the civilised dining area is no smoking; darts, shove-ha'penny, dominoes and piped music. There can be few more pleasant experiences than a summer evening on the garden terrace (with its own well) listening to swallows and martins, sheep in the adjacent field and bells ringing in the nearby church. This is an attractive bypassed village in an area where you may be lucky

enough to see red kites. *(Recommended by J C M Troughton, Michael and Jenny Back, Mike and Sue Loseby, Ian Stafford)*

Free house ~ Licensee Geoff Smith ~ Real ale ~ Bar food (12-2.30(3.30 Sun), 6-9.30; not Sun evening) ~ Restaurant ~ (01780) 450272 ~ Children in restaurant ~ Dogs allowed in bar ~ Open 12-3, 6-11(7-10.30 Sun); closed Mon

CRICK SP5872 Map 4

Red Lion 🍺 £

1 mile from M1 junction 18; A428; NN6 7TX

The cosy low-ceilinged bar at this welcoming old stone and thatched pub, though getting somewhat well worn these days, is nice and traditional, with lots of comfortable seating, some rare old horsebrasses, pictures of the pub in the days before it was surrounded by industrial estates, and a tiny log stove in a big inglenook; no smoking snug. The straightforward lunchtime menu is incredibly good value, making this a great break if you're on the M1: sandwiches (from £2), ploughman's (from £3.20), and hearty main courses such as chicken and mushroom pie, leek and smoky bacon bake, plaice or vegetable pancake rolls (all £4.50); they do a similarly bargain-price Sunday roast (£5). Prices go up a little in the evening when they offer a wider range of dishes that might include stuffed salmon fillet (£8.25), lamb shank (£8.50), half a roast duck (£12), and sirloin steak (£11); puddings such as lemon meringue pie (from £2.20). Four well kept beers on handpump include Charles Wells Bombardier, Greene King Old Speckled Hen, Websters and a guest from a brewer such as Everards. There are a few picnic-sets under cocktail parasols on grass by the car park, and in summer you can eat on the terrace in the old coachyard, which is sheltered by a Perspex roof; lots of pretty hanging baskets. *(Recommended by Ian and Nita Cooper, C J Pratt, Charles and Pauline Stride, Liz and Brian Barnard, Mrs M Wheatley, Ted George, Andrew Gardner, Susan and John Douglas, David and Ruth Shillitoe, Karen Eliot, Mrs Hazel Rainer, George Atkinson, Mike and Jayne Bastin, Brian P White, Stephen Funnell, Ian Stafford)*

Wellington ~ Lease Tom and Paul Marks ~ Real ale ~ Bar food (12-2, 6.30-9; not Sun evening) ~ (01788) 822342 ~ Children under 14 welcome lunchtimes only ~ Dogs welcome ~ Open 11-2.30, 6.15-11; 12-3, 7-10.30 Sun

EAST HADDON SP6668 Map 4

Red Lion 🍺

High Street; village signposted off A428 (turn right in village) and off A50 N of Northampton; NN6 8BU

There's a sedately old-fashioned feel at this rather smart substantially-built golden stone hotel. A neat lounge bar has antique furniture, including panelled oak settles, library chairs and a mix of oak, mahogany and cast-iron-framed tables. Little kegs, pewter, brass pots, swords and so forth are hung sparingly on a couple of beams, and there's attractive white-painted panelling with recessed china cabinets and old prints; piped music. Though a meal here might be a little more expensive than elsewhere, the good food, generous helpings and excellent service make it worth that little bit extra. Bar food includes soup (£4), sandwiches (from £4; not Saturday evening or Sunday lunchtime), chicken and smoked ham terrine (£7), loch fyne smoked salmon (£8), pie of the day or fish and chips (£10), farmer's platter (£12), honey-roast duckling with orange sauce (£13) and sirloin steak (£14); puddings (£5). The pretty no smoking restaurant overlooking the garden has a more elaborate menu. They serve very well kept Adnams Broadside, Charles Wells Bombardier and Eagle, and a guest such as St Austell Tribute on handpump, and decent wines including about ten by the glass; piped music. The walled side garden is pretty, with lilac, fruit trees, roses and neat flowerbeds, and leads back to the bigger lawn, which has well spaced picnic-sets. A small side terrace has more tables under cocktail parasols, and a big copper beech shades the gravel car park. *(Recommended by Michael Dandy, Gerry and Rosemary Dobson, Eric Robinson, Jacqueline Pratt, John Saville)*

Charles Wells ~ Lease Ian Kennedy ~ Real ale ~ Bar food (12-2, 7-9.30, not Sun evening)
~ Restaurant ~ (01604) 770223 ~ Children welcome in eating areas ~ Open 11-2.30,
6-11; 12-2.30, 7-10.30 Sun ~ Bedrooms: £60S/£75S

EYDON SP5450 Map 7
Royal Oak
Lime Avenue; village signed off A361 Daventry—Banbury, and from B4525; NN11 3PG

The room on the right at this enjoyable old stone village pub has low beams,
cushioned wooden wall benches built into alcoves, seats in a bow window, some
cottagey pictures, flagstones, and an open fire in an inglenook fireplace. The bar
counter, with bar stools, runs down a long central flagstoned corridor room and
links several other small idiosyncratic beamed rooms. An attractive covered terrace
with hardwood furniture is a lovely place for a meal in fine weather. Served by
friendly staff, the very tasty bar food, in nice substantial helpings, might include
tomato and apple soup with basil crème fraîche (£5), tempura avocado and tiger
prawns with lemon and coriander dipping sauce (£6.95), battered hake, pea purée
and chips (£9.50), seafood risotto with rocket salad (£13), roast rack of lamb with
tomato and herb crust, basil and olive mash with lamb and tomato jus (£14.50),
and fillet steak (£16.50). Well kept Fullers London Pride, Greene King IPA and a
couple of guests such as Archers Sunchaser and St Austell Tribute on handpump;
piped music, darts and table skittles. *(Recommended by Ruth Kitching, Sue and
Keith Campbell, John Baish, Mick Furn)*

Free house ~ Licensee Justin Lefevre ~ Real ale ~ Bar food (12-2, 7-9; not Mon) ~
Restaurant ~ (01327) 263167 ~ Children welcome ~ Dogs allowed in bar ~
Open 12-2.30, 6-11.30(12 Sat); 12-3, 6-10.30 Sun

FARTHINGSTONE SP6155 Map 4
Kings Arms 🍺
**Off A5 SE of Daventry; village signposted from Litchborough on former B4525 (now
declassified); NN12 8EZ**

The list of retail food produce on sale at this quirky gargoyle-embellished stone
18th-c country pub makes very tempting reading indeed. Products (including
cheeses, cured and fresh meat and cured and fresh fish) are sourced for their
originality of style, methods of rearing, smoking or organic farming methods.
Unfortunately bar food is only served weekend lunchtimes, but might include soup
(£3.95), british cheese platter or yorkshire pudding filled with steak and kidney or
game casserole (£6.50), ploughman's (£6.95), cumbrian wild boar sausage and
mash (£7.45), and loch fyne fish platter (£7.95). The timelessly intimate flagstoned
bar has plenty of character, as well as a huge log fire, comfortable homely sofas and
armchairs near the entrance, whisky-water jugs hanging from oak beams, and lots
of pictures and decorative plates on the walls. A games room at the far end has
darts, dominoes, cribbage, table skittles and board games. Batemans XB and
Youngs are well kept on handpump alongside a couple of guests such as Oakham
JHB and St Austell Tribute, the short wine list is quite decent, and they have a few
country wines; the outside gents' has an interesting newspaper-influenced décor.
Some visitors come specially to see the gardens, where there's always something
new and often wacky; in summer the hanging baskets are at their best, the tranquil
terrace is charmingly decorated with flower and herb pots and plant-filled painted
tractor tyres, and they grow their own salad vegetables and herbs too. The village is
picturesque, and there are good walks including the Knightley Way. It's worth
ringing ahead to check the limited opening and food serving times noted below as
the licensees are sometimes away. *(Recommended by Derek and Sylvia Stephenson, George
Atkinson, Pete Baker, David Hoult)*

Free house ~ Licensees Paul and Denise Egerton ~ Real ale ~ Bar food (12-2 Sat, Sun
lunchtime only) ~ No credit cards ~ (01327) 361604 ~ Children welcome ~ Dogs
welcome ~ Open 7(6.30 Fri)-11; 12-3.30, 7(9 Sun)-11 Sat; closed weekday lunchtimes and
Mon, Weds evenings

FOTHERINGHAY TL0593 Map 5

Falcon ★ ⊕ ♀

Village signposted off A605 on Peterborough side of Oundle; PE8 5HZ

Northamptonshire Dining Pub of the Year

Although the beautifully presented, inventive food at this civilised no smoking pub will probably be your main reason for visiting here, it does still have a thriving little locals' tap bar (and darts team) if you do just want a drink. It's the sort of knowledgeably run place where everything is done at top-notch level. A very good range of drinks includes well kept Adnams and Greene King IPA on handpump alongside a guest, good wines with 20 by the glass, organic cordials and fresh orange juice. Food takes in quite a few pub favourites and then works its way up to seasonally changing, quite intensely flavoured and heavily italian influenced specials: roast carrot, parsnip and coriander soup or chicken liver parfait with brioche and red onion jam (£4.95), open steak sandwich (£8.95), penne with purple sprouting broccoli, parmesan and garlic (£9.50), fisherman's pie or sausage and mash (£9.95), braised pork belly cooked in milk, lemon, bay and sage (£12.50), roast halibut with olive oil mash (£16.95), and puddings such as home-made ice-cream (£4.50) or walnut and ricotta or bitter chocolate espresso cake (from £4.95). The buzz of contented conversation fills the neatly kept little bar, which has cushioned slatback armchairs and bucket chairs, good winter log fires in a stone fireplace, and fresh flower arrangements. The conservatory restaurant is pretty, and if the weather's nice the attractively planted garden is particularly enjoyable. The vast church behind is worth a visit, and the ruins of Fotheringhay Castle, where Mary Queen of Scots was executed, are not far away. *(Recommended by Dr Brian and Mrs Anne Hamilton, Sarah Flynn, Edmund Coan, Alan Sutton, Michael Sargent, Mike and Sue Loseby, Jeff and Wendy Williams, O K Smyth, Howard and Margaret Buchanan, Sue and Keith Campbell, Les and Barbara Owen, Paul and Annette Hallett, Oliver and Sue Rowell)*

Huntsbridge ~ Licensee John Hoskins ~ Real ale ~ Bar food (12-2.15, 6.15-9.30) ~ Restaurant ~ (01832) 226254 ~ Children welcome ~ Dogs allowed in bar ~ Open 12-3, 6-11(10.30 Sun)

GREAT BRINGTON SP6664 Map 4

Fox & Hounds/Althorp Coaching Inn ⬛

Off A428 NW of Northampton, nr Althorp Hall; NN7 4JA

The ancient bar at this friendly golden stone thatched coaching inn has a lovely relaxed atmosphere with lots of old beams and saggy joists, an attractive mix of country tables (maybe with fresh flowers) and chairs on its broad flagstones and bare boards, plenty of snug alcoves, nooks and crannies, some stripped pine shutters and panelling, two fine log fires, and an eclectic medley of bric-a-brac from farming implements to an old typewriter and country pictures. The superb range of nine real ales (under light blanket pressure) includes Greene King IPA, Abbot and Old Speckled Hen, with up to five guests from a thoughtfully sourced range of brewers such as Archers, Cottage, Elgoods, Highgate and (local to them) Hoggleys, and they've about a dozen wines by the glass and a dozen malt whiskies. Very tasty bar food might include soup (£3.50), spicy chicken wings (£4.25), serrano ham with apricot and honey bread and olive (£4.85), wild rice and spinach honey roast (£9.25), garlic and rosemary tuna steak or seafood salad (£10.95), pork fillet medallions sautéed with mushrooms and sherry cream sauce (£12.95), sirloin steak (£14.75), and puddings such as spotted dick or chocolate and vanilla chocolate chip cheesecake (£3.95); the restaurant is no smoking; friendly service; piped music and TV. A cellarish games room down steps has a view of the casks in the cellar. A coach entry goes through to a lovely little paved courtyard with sheltered tables and tubs of flowers, and there are more, with a play area, in the side garden. *(Recommended by Sue and Keith Campbell, Michael Dandy, George Atkinson)*

Free house ~ Licensee Jacqui Ellard ~ Real ale ~ Bar food (12-2.30, 6.30-9.30) ~ Restaurant ~ (01604) 770164 ~ Children welcome ~ Dogs allowed in bar ~ Jazz, folk, R&B Tues evening ~ Open 11-11; 12-10.30 Sun

GREAT OXENDON SP7383 Map 4

George ♀ 🏠

A508 S of Market Harborough; LE16 8NA

The bar at this elegant and thoughtfully furnished 16th-c dining pub is cosy and clubby, with rather luxurious dark wallpaper, panelled dark brown dado, green leatherette bucket chairs around little tables, daily papers on poles, and a big log fire; the turkey-carpeted conservatory overlooks a shrub-sheltered garden. There may be piped easy-listening music; the conservatory and restaurant are no smoking. The entrance lobby has easy chairs and a former inn-sign, while the lavatories are entertainingly decked out with rather stylish naughty pictures. They put quite an emphasis on the food (you might want to book): soup (£4.25), mushrooms stuffed with spinach and pine nuts and topped with stilton (£8.25), steak sandwich (£8.95), pork and leek sausages and chive mash (£9.25), honey-roast lamb shank (£10.95), cod, chips and mushy peas (£11.95), roast rump of lamb with red wine sauce (£14.75), and puddings such as apple and blackberry pie or bread and butter pudding (£4.50); two-course Sunday lunch (£12.95). Well kept Adnams, Youngs Special and Greene King Old Speckled Hen on handpump, 15 wines by the glass and around 15 malts. *(Recommended by Duncan Cloud, David and Ruth Hollands, Anthony Barnes, Jeff and Wendy Williams, Richard Atherton, Steve Nye, Sheila and Peter Brown, Rob and Catherine Dunster, Gerry and Rosemary Dobson, K M Crook)*

Free house ~ Licensee David Dudley ~ Real ale ~ Bar food ~ Restaurant ~ (01858) 465205 ~ Dogs allowed in bedrooms ~ Open 11.30-3, 6.30-11; 12-3 Sun; closed Sun evenings ~ Bedrooms: £57.50B/£60B

KILSBY SP5671 Map 4

George

2½ miles from M1 junction 18: A428 towards Daventry, left on to A5 – look out for pub off on right at roundabout; CV23 8YE

The very cheery landlady keeps a good balance between the popular dining side of things, and the traditional public bar (it's one of just a handful of main entries that still has a pool table) at this nice welcoming stop. A cosy high-ceilinged bar on the right, with plush banquettes, dark panelling, a coal-effect gas stove and a big bay window, opens on the left into a smarter but relaxed attractive no smoking dining area with solidly comfortable furnishings. The long brightly decorated back public bar has a juke box, darts, that good pool table, fruit machine, table football and a large-screen TV. Fullers London Pride, Greene King IPA and Abbot and a guest such as Batemans Valiant are well kept on handpump, and they've a splendid range of malt whiskies, served in generous measures, and decent wines in big glasses; no smoking at the bars. Among the wholesome and reasonably priced bar food, the lighter lunch menu includes soup (£3.90), sandwiches (from £3), local sausages, egg and chips (£4.90), filled baguettes (from £4.90), ploughman's (£6.50) and home-made meat or vegetable lasagne (£7.90). The evening menu typically features home-made chicken liver pâté or deep-fried breaded brie wedges (£5.90), steak (from £7.90), salmon fillet (£8.50), beef and ale pie (£8.90) and lamb shank (£9.90), and readers recommend the children's menu here. It's best to book if you go for Sunday lunch (£7.90). There are wood picnic-sets out in the back garden, by the car park. *(Recommended by Ian and Nita Cooper, Simon and Amanda Baer, David and Pam Wilcox, Rob and Catherine Dunster, Ted George, P Dawn, Michael and Maggie Betton, Keith and Chris O'Neill, Michael and Alison Sandy, Neil and Brenda Skidmore, Ian Phillips, David and Ruth Shillitoe, Karen Eliot, Richard and Linda Ely)*

Punch ~ Lease Maggie Chandler ~ Real ale ~ Bar food (12-2, 6.30-9; 12-4 Sun; not Mon lunchtime or Sun evening) ~ Restaurant ~ (01788) 822229 ~ Well supervised children welcome ~ Dogs allowed in bar ~ Open 11.30-3, 5.30(6 Sat)-11; 12-5, 7.30-11 Sun ~ Bedrooms: £36/£52

It's very helpful if you let us know up-to-date food prices when you report on pubs.

LOWICK SP9780 Map 4

Snooty Fox

Signed off A6116 Corby—Raunds; NN14 3BH

You can watch the chefs at work in the kitchen through a glass partition while you dine at this neatly refurbished 16th-c inn. The good bar food they are preparing might include hot pork and apple sauce sandwich (£5.95), sausage, mash and cabbage or oxtail and kidney pudding (£9.50), lancashire hotpot (£9.95), roast lemon sole with garlic butter (£13) and roast monkfish tail (£16.50). You can pick your own steak (£1.70 per 25g) from the counter, and puddings might include hot banana tart with caramel sauce or vanilla panna cotta with citrus fruit salad (£5.50). The spacious interior has handsomely moulded dark oak beams, stripped stone walls and floors and a formidable monumentally carved bar counter with Greene King IPA and three guests from brewers such as Fullers and Ridleys Rumpus on handpump under a light blanket pressure. On wintry days a log fire roars away in the huge stone fireplace in the atmospheric lounge; piped music; the two smart dining rooms are no smoking. The softly lit picnic-sets on the grass in front are very inviting on a warm evening. *(Recommended by B N F and M Parkin, Ryta Lyndley, Judith and Oliver Stobart, Trevor and Sylvia Millum, K C Watson, Jeff and Wendy Williams, Emma Handley, Howard Dell, Mrs Phoebe A Kemp)*

Free house ~ Licensees Clive Dixon and David Hennigan ~ Real ale ~ Bar food (12-2, 6.30-9.30) ~ Restaurant ~ (01832) 733434 ~ Children welcome ~ Dogs allowed in bar ~ Open 12-11(10.30 Sun)

NETHER HEYFORD SP6558 Map 4

Olde Sun 🍴 £

1¾ miles from M1 junction 16: village signposted left off A45 westbound – Middle Street; NN7 3LL

Nooks and crannies in the several small linked rooms at this unpretentious 18th-c golden stone pub are packed with all sorts of curios, from gleaming brassware (one fireplace is a grotto of large brass animals), to colourful relief plates, 1930s cigarette cards, railway memorabilia and advertising signs, World War II posters and rope fancywork. There are beams and low ceilings (one painted with a fine sunburst), partly glazed dividing panels, steps between some areas, rugs on parquet, red tiles or flagstones, a big inglenook log fire – and up on the left a room with full-sized hood skittles, a fruit machine, darts, TV, cribbage, dominoes and sports TV. Furnishings are mostly properly pubby, with the odd easy chair; piped music. Well kept Banks's, Greene King Ruddles, Marstons Pedigree and a weekend guest such as Clarks Rams Revenge are served on handpump from two counters. The old cash till is stuck at one and a ha'penny. Pubby food includes sandwiches (£3.75), soup (£3.25), scampi and chips or chicken caesar salad (£4.75), steak pie or chicken stir fry (£9.75), battered cod and mushy peas (£9.95) and rump steak (£11.95); the dining areas are no smoking. The enjoyable collections of bygones and bric-a-brac continue outside, with blue-painted grain kibblers and other antiquated hand-operated farm machines, some with plants in their hoppers, standing beside a fairy-lit front terrace with picnic-sets. *(Recommended by Leigh and Gillian Mellor, Kevin Blake, George Atkinson, Mr and Mrs G Hughes, Peter and Jean Hoare)*

Free house ~ Licensees P Yates and A Ford ~ Real ale ~ Bar food (not Mon, Sun evenings) ~ Restaurant ~ (01327) 340164 ~ Children welcome in no smoking bar and restaurant ~ Dogs allowed in bar ~ Open 12-3, 5-11; 12-11 Sat; 12-10.30 Sun

OUNDLE TL0388 Map 5

Ship 🍴

West Street; PE8 4EF

The heavily beamed lounge bar at this bustling down-to-earth town pub (watch your head if you are tall) is made up of three areas that lead off the central corridor, one of them no smoking at lunchtime. Up by the street there's a mix of leather and other seats, with sturdy tables and a log fire in a stone inglenook, and down one end a charming little panelled snug has button-back leather seats built in around it. The wood-floored public side has a TV, fruit machine and a juke box. Oakham JHB, Theakstons XB and a guest or two from brewers such as Barnwell and Grainstore are under a light blanket pressure, and they've a good range of malt whiskies; piped music, TV, games machines, juke box and board games. Look out for Midnight, the companionable black and white pub cat. Enjoyable bar food in generous helpings is home made where possible, and might include soup (£3.95), vegetarian lasagne (£8), beef lasagne, haddock, chicken breast with mushroom sauce or pork curry (all £7.50) or rib-eye steak (£10.95); Sunday roast £8.50. The wooden tables and chairs out on the series of small sunny and sheltered terraces are lit at night. *(Recommended by the Didler, George Atkinson, Richard Waller, Pauline Smith)*

Free house ~ Licensees Andrew and Robert Langridge ~ Real ale ~ Bar food (12-3, 6-9; 12-9 Sat, Sun and bank hols) ~ (01832) 273918 ~ Children welcome away from bar ~ DJ Fri and some Sats ~ Open 11-11; 12-11 Sun ~ Bedrooms: £30(£35S)/£60(£70B)

SULGRAVE   SP5545   Map 4

Star 🛏

E of Banbury, signposted off B4525; Manor Road; OX17 2SA

New licensees are unlikely to make many major changes at this fine old 17th-c creeper-covered farmhouse. The peaceful bar is unpretentiously furnished with small pews, cushioned window seats and wall benches, kitchen chairs and cast-iron-framed tables, with polished flagstones in an area by the big inglenook fireplace, and red carpet elsewhere. Look out for the stuffed back end of a fox, seeming to leap into the wall. Framed newspaper front pages record memorable events such as Kennedy's assassination and the death of Churchill; Hook Norton Hooky and Old Hooky on handpump. Bar food includes soup or smoked trout pâté (£3.80), sausage and mash, thai chicken curry or salmon steak with watercress sauce (£6.50) and puddings such as lemon tart or chocolate brandy cream (£3.50); no smoking back dining room. In summer you can eat outside under a vine-covered trellis, and there are benches at the front, and in the back garden. The pub is a short walk from Sulgrave Manor, the ancestral home of George Washington, and is handy for Silverstone. *(Recommended by Michael Sargent, Michael Jones, Mick Furn, Iain R Hewitt, George Atkinson)*

Hook Norton ~ Tenant Andron Ingle ~ Real ale ~ Bar food (12-2(4 Sun), 7-9) ~ Restaurant ~ (01295) 760389 ~ Children welcome ~ Dogs allowed in bar ~ Open 10.30-3, 5-11.30; 11.30-4, 6-10.30 Sun ~ Bedrooms: £40S/£75S

WADENHOE   TL0083   Map 5

Kings Head

Church Street; village signposted (in small print) off A605 S of Oundle; PE8 5ST

This stone-built no smoking 16th-c country inn is in an idyllic setting by a big wooded meadow next to the River Nene, with views of the church, and if you're arriving by boat there's no charge for mooring here if you are using the pub. Picnic-sets among the willows and aspens on the sloping grass make pleasant vantage points, and this is a pretty village of up-and-down lanes and thatched stone cottages. Because of its lovely setting it does get very busy on summer days. There's an uncluttered simplicity to the very welcoming partly stripped-stone main bar, which has pleasant old worn quarry-tiles, solid pale pine furniture with a couple of cushioned wall seats, and a leather-upholstered chair by the woodburning stove in the fine inglenook. The bare-boarded public bar has similar furnishings and another fire; steps lead up to a games room with dominoes and table skittles, and there's yet more of the pale pine furniture in an attractive little beamed dining room. As well as Digifield Kings Head and Oakham JHB, a couple of interesting guests might be from brewers such as Barnwell and Potbelly, they've belgian fruit beers, and their 18 wines are all available by the glass. Pubby bar food might include filled lunchtime rolls with salad (from £4.95), soup (£3.95), goats cheese and caramelised red onion salad (£4.50), seafood salad (£4.75), vegetarian pizza (£7.95), sausage and mash (£8.50), fish and chips (£9.95) and puddings such as apple crumble (£4.95). *(Recommended by Michael Tack, Marion and Bill Cross, Dave and Jen Harley)*

Free house ~ Licensee Alex Burgess ~ Real ale ~ Bar food (12-2.30(3 Sun), 6.30-9) ~ Restaurant ~ (01832) 720024 ~ Children welcome ~ Dogs allowed in bar ~ Open 11-11; 12-10.30 Sun; closed Sun evening

WOODNEWTON TL0394 Map 5
White Swan
Main Street; back roads N of Oundle, easily reached from A1/A47 (via Nassington) and A605 (via Fotheringhay); PE8 5EH

A special treat at this nicely unpretentious village pub is the special beer, named Cocos Wisdom in honour of two great comics (Coco the Clown and Norman Wisdom) with local connections, that is brewed especially for the pub by Batemans. It's well kept on handpump alongside Adnams, Fullers London Pride and a changing guest from a brewer such as Archers; they also stock Aspell's farm cider. The enthusiastic licensees inject a genuinely friendly welcome that brings the fairly simple but spacious beamed bar and restaurant to life. Enjoyable bar food might include french onion soup (£3.95), grilled mushrooms with parmesan, tomato and basil stuffing (£4.25), chicken breast in hot red thai sauce with chinese noodles (£7.95), baked cod topped with thyme and ginger butter or rump steak with black pudding topped with Jamesons and peppercorn sauce (£8.95). The restaurant and part of the bar are no smoking; piped music and darts. The back lawn has tables and a boules pitch (league matches Tuesday evenings). More reports please. *(Recommended by Peter and Pat Frogley, Ben and Helen Ingram)*

Free house ~ Licensees Jenny Chalkley and Andrew Downing ~ Real ale ~ Bar food (not Sun evenings or Tues) ~ Restaurant ~ (01780) 470381 ~ Children welcome away from bar ~ Dogs allowed in bar ~ Open 12-2.30, 6-11; 12-3, 6-10.30 Sun; closed all day Mon and Tues lunchtime

---

LUCKY DIP

Besides the fully inspected pubs, you might like to try these Lucky Dips recommended to us and described by readers (if you do, please send us reports: www.goodguides.co.uk).

ARTHINGWORTH [SP7581]
Bulls Head LE16 8JZ [Kelmarsh Rd, just above A14 by A508 junction; pub signed from A14]: Much extended and recently developed pub with open fires in big beamed L-shaped bar, new no smoking dining room and kitchens, enjoyable straightforward family food from good value sandwiches to steaks, Everards Tiger, Charles Wells Eagle and two guest beers, quick cheery service; disabled access, terrace tables, bedrooms in separate block, open all day Sun and perhaps summer *(Gerry and Rosemary Dobson, Ian and Nita Cooper, J Jennings)*
ASHBY ST LEDGERS [SP5768]
Olde Coach House CV23 8UN [off A361]: Reopened a year or so ago, rambling linked rooms with bags of potential, big log fires, flagstones, nicely old-fashioned country furnishings and pictures, Everards Tiger and Old Original and Marstons Pedigree, good value baguettes and one or two hot dishes; big-screen TV, piped music; children welcome, disabled access, tables out among fruit trees, play area, interesting church nearby,

comfortable bedrooms, open all day in summer *(LYM, Rob and Catherine Dunster, Derek and Sylvia Stephenson)*
BARNWELL [TL0584]
☆ *Montagu Arms* PE8 5PH [off A605 S of Oundle, then fork right at Thurning, Hemington sign]: New licensees in attractive stone-built pub, good range of food from baguettes with enterprising fillings to good interesting meals, changing ales such as Adnams Bitter and Broadside and Potton Village Bike, decent wines, helpful cheerful staff, log fire, low beams, flagstones or tile and brick floors, neat back dining room; games room off yard, big garden with good well equipped play area, pleasant streamside village with good walks, open all day wknds *(BB, John Saul, Oliver and Sue Rowell)*
BRACKLEY HATCH [SP6441]
☆ *Green Man* NN13 5TX [A43 NE of Brackley (tricky exit)]: Spacious Chef & Brewer dining pub on busy dual carriageway nr Silverstone, comfortable old-look beamed lounge area and conservatory, big no smoking family restaurant, wide range of reliable food all day,

relaxed atmosphere, quick, friendly and helpful service, Courage Best, Theakstons Best and Charles Wells Bombardier, good wines and coffee, daily papers, log fires; piped music, games; tables on lawn, bedrooms in Premier Lodge behind, open all day *(Michael Dandy, BB, Phil and Jane Hodson, R T and J C Moggridge, George Atkinson)*

BRAFIELD-ON-THE-GREEN [SP8258]

☆ *Red Lion* NN7 1BP [A428 5 miles from Northampton towards Bedford]: Smart modern bistro-style Chef & Brewer, dark leather dining chairs and up-to-date brasserie food from fancy sandwiches and ciabattas up in two main rooms (one no smoking), small drinking area with a couple of settees, Fullers London Pride, Greene King Old Speckled Hen and Charles Wells Bombardier, good coffee and choice of wines by the glass, courteous attentive service; picnic-sets front and back, open all day *(Bruce and Sharon Eden, Michael Dandy, Mike Ridgway, Sarah Miles, Alan Sutton)*

BRIXWORTH [SP7470]

Coach & Horses NN6 9BX [Harborough Rd, just off A508 N of Northampton]: Warmly welcoming unpretentious 17th-c stone-built beamed pub, helpful staff, generous and enjoyable if not cheap food from wide choice of good sandwiches to fresh fish, seasonal game and popular Sun lunches, log fire, Adnams and Marstons Bitter and Pedigree, decent house wines, pink walls with lots of horsebrasses and pictures, small no smoking restaurant; piped music; children welcome, tables on small back terrace, attractive village with famous Saxon church *(Mrs M Wheatley, Michael Dandy, Gerry and Rosemary Dobson, George Atkinson, Mr and Mrs Bentley-Davies)*

BUGBROOKE [SP6756]

Wharf Inn NN7 3QB [The Wharf; off A5 S of Weedon]: Super spot by canal, plenty of tables on big lawn with moorings and summer boat trips; emphasis on big water-view restaurant, also bar and lounge with pleasant informal small raised eating area on either side, lots of stripped brickwork, wide choice of generous food from baguettes up (can be long waits when busy), four or five real ales inc Greene King IPA and local Frog Island Best, farm cider, nice fire; children very welcome, garden with boules *(George Atkinson, JJW, CMW, BB)*

CHACOMBE [SP4943]

☆ *George & Dragon* OX17 2JR [handy for M40 junction 11, via A361; Silver St]: Beams, flagstones, log fire in massive fireplace and even an old well, wide range of enjoyable food from baguettes and baked potatoes up, good modest service, Everards real ales, no smoking area in restaurant; darts, dominoes, TV and piped music; children in eating areas, bedrooms, pretty village with interesting church, open all day *(Chris Glasson, Oliver Richardson, Mick Furn, B M Eldridge, Les and Barbara Owen)*

CHAPEL BRAMPTON [SP7366]

☆ *Brampton Halt* NN6 8BA [Pitsford Rd, off A5199 N of Northampton]: Former stationmaster's house on Northampton & Lamport Railway well converted and extended inc new large no smoking restaurant, railway memorabilia and train theme throughout (some furnishings like railway carriages), popular generous food from sandwiches up, Everards Original, Fullers London Pride and Greene King IPA, games and TV in bar; piped music; children welcome, garden with awnings and heaters, pretty views over small lake, Nene Valley Way walks *(LYM, Eithne Dandy, Mike and Margaret Banks)*

Spencer Arms NN6 8AE [Northampton Rd]: Largely no smoking beamed Chef & Brewer family dining pub, go-ahead new manager bringing in interesting guest beers such as Camerons White Rabbit, Holts Fifth Sense and Timothy Taylors Landlord, prompt friendly service, plenty of stripped tables in long timber-divided L-shaped bar, two log fires, daily papers; piped music; tables outside *(Gerry and Rosemary Dobson, Eithne Dandy, Simon J A Powis)*

Windhover NN6 8AF [Welford Road (A5199)/Pitsford Rd]: Roomy well done Vintage Inn, largely no smoking, with Hook Norton Old Hooky and Charles Wells Bombardier, good choice of wines and soft drinks, food all day inc lunchtime sandwiches, feature log fire; piped music; picnic-sets on terrace, pleasant Brampton Valley Way walks *(Michael Tack, Eithne Dandy, Simon J A Powis)*

CHARWELTON [SP5356]

Fox & Hounds NN11 3YY [A361 S of Daventry]: Roomy bar with fox and hunting memorabilia, two real ales, good soft drinks choice, wide range of generous food inc OAP wkdy lunches, attentive service, darts, extended no smoking restaurant; piped music, TV, games machine *(JJW, CMW)*

COLLINGTREE [SP7555]

Wooden Walls of Old England NN4 0NE [1¼ miles from M1 junction 15; High St]: Low-beamed thatched stone-built village pub, Banks's Bitter and a seasonal ale, good choice of wines by the glass, freshly cooked pubby food (not Sun evening or Mon lunchtime) from sandwiches and baguettes up, quick helpful service, open fire, no smoking area down a few steps; piped music; children welcome, lots of picnic-sets and play area in nice big back garden with small terrace *(Michael Dandy, BB)*

COSGROVE [SP7942]

Barley Mow MK19 7JD [The Stocks]: Pleasant canalside village pub, cheerful service, good value food; big garden with terrace *(G Robinson)*

DUDDINGTON [SK9800]

☆ *Royal Oak* PE9 3QE [A43 just S of A47]: Attractive stone-built hotel, spotless and comfortable, with good log fire, fresh flowers, theatrical photographs and programmes and plush banquettes in bar areas, no smoking family section, dining room with gleaming brass shell cases and other memorabilia from nearby World War II airfield, wide choice of good value hearty food, welcoming efficient staff, real ales such as Robinsons Enigma and Timothy Taylors Landlord; quiet piped music; nice garden and terrace, six good bedrooms, pleasant village *(John Wooll, Tim and Rosemary Wells, George Atkinson)*

EASTCOTE [SP6853]

☆ *Eastcote Arms* NN12 8NG [off A5 N of Towcester]: Friendly unpretentious village pub, traditional furnishings and cottagey décor, good range of nicely served food from good sandwiches up, real ales such as Adnams, Black Sheep, Fullers London Pride and Greene King IPA, decent wines and malt whiskies, no smoking restaurant, two flame-effect gas fires, hood skittles in small back bar; unobtrusive piped music; neat back garden with picnic-sets and other tables, peaceful village *(Gerry and Rosemary Dobson, LYM, George Atkinson)*

ECTON [SP8263]

Worlds End NN6 0QN [A4500 Northampton—Wellingborough]: Extended 17th-c pub now putting emphasis on enjoyable imaginative food (pub snacks too), with good service, real ales such as Wadworths 6X, L-shaped bar and steps down to partly no smoking dining room; garden with terrace and play area *(Ryta Lyndley)*

EVENLEY [SP5834]

☆ *Red Lion* NN13 5SH [The Green]: Small villager-owned no smoking local, cheerful licensees and good service, Banks's, Marstons Pedigree and a guest such as Jennings, decent coffee and choice of wines, particularly good value sandwiches and wide choice of other food, relaxed atmosphere, cricketing books and other memorabilia, inglenook, beams and some flagstones; piped music; tables out in neatly kept garden, one or two seats out in front opp splendid village green *(Michael Dandy, George Atkinson)*

FLORE [SP6460]

Royal Oak NN7 4LL [A45 W of M1 junction 16; High St]: Stone-built pub with good choice of fresh food, friendly helpful staff, two linked bars, lots of wood, flame-effect fire and woodburner, two real ales, good coffee; darts and hood skittles in separate area; dogs welcome and fussed over, picnic-sets in garden with play area, pretty hanging baskets *(Revd Margaret Maclachlan)*

GEDDINGTON [SP8982]

Star NN14 1AD [just off A43 Kettering—Corby]: Leather chairs and log fire in attractive old-world bar yet with cosy new feel, enjoyable food esp fresh seafood in bar and restaurant; tables outside – pleasant village setting not far from picturesque packhorse bridge, handy for Broughton House *(Dave and Jen Harley)*

GRAFTON REGIS [SP7546]

White Hart NN12 7SR [A508 S of Northampton]: Thatched dining pub in thatched village, several linked rooms, Greene King IPA and Abbot, good wines by the glass, friendly hard-working helpful staff, popular pubby food (not Sun evening) inc lots of

splendid winter soups and fine range of baguettes, pensive african grey parrot, pub dog, bookings-only restaurant with open fire; piped music; good-sized garden (food not served there) with terrace tables, cl Mon exc bank hols *(Neil Kellett, Michael Dandy, Gerry and Rosemary Dobson, George Atkinson, BB)*

GREAT BILLING [SP8162]

Elwes Arms NN3 9DT [High St]: Thatched stone-built 16th-c village pub, two bars (steps between rooms), wide choice of good value food (all day Fri-Sun), three or four real ales, good soft drinks choice, pleasant no smoking dining room (children allowed here); may be piped music, TV, no dogs; tables and chairs in garden with covered terrace and play area *(JJW, CMW)*

GREAT DODDINGTON [SP8864]

Stags Head NN29 7TQ [High St (B573 S of Wellingborough)]: Old stone-built local with pleasant bar and split-level lounge/dining room, Adnams, Black Sheep and Wadworths 6X, good choice of soft drinks, cheery service, good value hearty pub food, also separate barn restaurant extension, public bar with pool and games; piped music may be rather loud; picnic-sets out in front and in garden *(Michael E Bridgstock, Michael Dandy, Mr and Mrs Bentley-Davies)*

GREAT HOUGHTON [SP7959]

Old Cherry Tree NN4 7AT [Cherry Tree Lane; a No Through Road off A428 just before the White Hart]: Thatched village pub with low beams, open fires, stripped stone and panelling, decent food from baguettes up (freshly made so can take a while), real ales such as Badger, Charles Wells and St Austell Tribute, good wine choice, steps up to restaurant, no smoking areas; quiet piped music; garden tables *(Michael Dandy, Sue and Keith Campbell, Gerry and Rosemary Dobson, JJW, CMW)*

White Hart NN4 7AF [off A428 Northampton—Bedford; High St]: Pleasantly unpretentious stone and thatch pub with four linked areas, enjoyable fresh food (not Mon evening), four or five real ales, good choice of wines and soft drinks, friendly helpful staff; piped music, TV, games machine, quite a few steps; attractive garden with terrace *(JJW, CMW)*

GRENDON [SP8760]

Half Moon NN7 1JW [Main Rd]: Thatched and stone-built 17th-c pub, long beamed bar with open fire, brasses, warming pan and games end, Charles Wells Eagle and Bombardier and a weekly guest beer, good choice of wines by the glass and soft drinks, reasonably priced traditional food (not Sun evening or Mon lunchtime) inc children's, no smoking area; piped music, no dogs, mobile phones or credit cards; quiz and music nights; small garden *(JJW, CMW, R Remidios)*

HACKLETON [SP8054]

White Hart NN7 2AD [B526 SE of Northampton]: Comfortably traditional 18th-c country pub with wide choice of generous food from sandwiches and baked potatoes up inc local produce and early evening bargains, Fullers London Pride, Greene King IPA and a guest beer, decent choice of other drinks, good coffee, dining area up steps from no smoking lounge, stripped stone, beamery and brickwork, illuminated well, brasses and artefacts, split-level flagstoned bar with flame-effect fire, pool and hood skittles; children welcome (not in bar after 5), garden with picnic-sets and goal posts, open all day *(JJW, CMW, Reg Falkner, Michael Dandy)*

HARLESTONE [SP7064]

☆ *Dusty Fox* NN7 4EW [A428, Lower Harlestone]: Attractive and relaxed Vintage Inn, small front bar and lounge, tasteful old-world furnishings, hops on beams, local photographs, mainly no smoking light and airy dining area and conservatory-style barn; enjoyable food all day from servery inc good sandwiches, Bass and Fullers London Pride or Greene King Old Speckled Hen, good wine and soft drinks range, prompt friendly attentive service, two log fires, no piped music; children welcome, tables in nice garden, handy for Althorp and Harlestone Firs walks, open all day *(Michael Dandy, Mr and Mrs Bentley-Davies, George Atkinson)*

HARPOLE [SP6960]

Bull NN7 4BS [High St; nr M1 junction 16]: Traditional village pub with good value food in comfortable front lounge and eating area, two or three real ales, log fire in big inglenook, brass and copperware, basic back bar and games room; garden with heated terrace and aviary *(JJW, CMW)*

HARRINGWORTH [SP9197]

☆ *White Swan* NN17 3AF [SE of Uppingham; Seaton Rd]: Eye-catching Tudor inn with limestone walls and imposing central gable, solid tables and elaborate hand-crafted oak counter in central bar, open fire dividing bar from roomy dining area with cottagey décor, bar food (not Sun evening), changing real ales, good wines by the glass, traditional games; piped music, games machine; terrace tables, six good bedrooms *(Dr B and Mrs P B Baker, LYM, Mike and Sue Loseby)*

HELLIDON [SP5158]

☆ *Red Lion* NN11 6LG [Stockwell Lane, off A425 W of Daventry]: Good popular OAP lunch in small wisteria-covered inn, wide choice of other good value food too inc some interesting dishes, softly lit no smoking low-ceilinged stripped stone dining area with lots of hunting prints, Fullers London Pride, Greene King IPA and Hook Norton Old Hooky, farm cider, helpful cheerful staff, cosy and comfortable lounge, bar with woodburner, hood skittles and pool in back games room; picnic-sets in front, beautiful setting by green of unspoilt village, good bedrooms, windmill vineyard and pleasant walks nearby *(George Atkinson)*

KETTERING [SP8778]

Alexandra Arms NN16 0BU [Victoria St]: Real ale pub, with ten changing so quickly that they keep in top condition (over 2,000 in the three

years they've been open, amazing collection of pump clips in front lounge), also their own Nobbys ale, may be sandwiches, back games bar with hood skittles; tables on back terrace, open all day (from 2 wkdys) *(Mick Furn)*

Trading Post NN15 7RH [Bignal Court]: New chain pub with Banks's and Marstons, good service, reliable food; tables outside with play area, open all day *(Karen Sharman)*

LAMPORT [SP7574]

Lamport Swan NN6 9EZ: Modern pub/bistro in imposing stone building, good-sized front bar with Greene King IPA, local Potbelly ales and good choice of wines by the glass, emphasis on large no smoking side restaurant with big flame-effect fire one end, some pubby as well as more bistroish dishes, daily papers; piped music; outside tables with good views *(Michael Dandy)*

LITTLE BRINGTON [SP6663]

☆ *Old Saracens Head* NN7 4HS [4½ miles from M1 junction 16, first right off A45 to Daventry; also signed off A428; Main St]: No smoking throughout, roomy U-shaped lounge with good log fire, flagstones, chesterfields and lots of old prints, book-lined eating room off and extended restaurant, good choice of enjoyable food from soup or baguettes up inc interesting dishes, Fullers London Pride, Greene King IPA and Timothy Taylors Landlord, good soft drinks range; piped music; tables in neat back garden, handy for Althorp House and Holdenby House *(Gerry and Rosemary Dobson, BB, JJW, CMW)*

LITTLE HARROWDEN [SP8671]

Lamb NN9 5BH [Orlinbury Rd/Kings Lane – off A509 or A43 S of Kettering]: Two-level lounge with log fire and brasses on beams, no smoking dining area, Charles Wells Eagle and Bombardier and a guest beer, good coffee, games bar with darts, hood skittles and machines; piped music; children welcome, small raised terrace and garden, delightful village *(Michael Dandy, JJW, CMW)*

LODDINGTON [SP8178]

Hare NN14 1LA [Main St]: 17th-c stone-built dining pub, carpeted throughout, with wide choice of enjoyable good value food from generous sandwiches and baguettes to game specialities in two eating areas, one no smoking, good-sized helpings, tablecloths and fresh flowers, Adnams and Fullers London Pride in small bar, good wine and soft drinks choice, good coffee, pleasant helpful service; piped music; picnic-sets on front lawn *(Michael Dandy)*

MAIDWELL [SP7477]

☆ *Stags Head* NN6 9JA [A508 Northampton—Mkt Harboro]: Wide choice of good value fresh food from baguettes to seasonal game in three largely no smoking areas, attractively light and airy, off small, spotless and comfortable beamed front bar with log fire and well chosen pictures, Fullers London Pride, Tetleys and a guest beer, good choice of wines and soft drinks, friendly bustling staff, log fire; piped music; disabled facilities, tables on terrace (dogs on leads allowed here) by neat back lawn with paddock beyond, bedrooms, not far from splendid Palladian Kelmarsh Hall in its parkland *(Gerry and Rosemary Dobson, Michael Dandy, George Atkinson, Mrs M Wheatley, P Tailyour, JJW, CMW)*

MEARS ASHBY [SP8466]

Griffins Head NN6 0DX [Wilby Rd]: Half a dozen or so good changing real ales, wide food choice from sandwiches, baguettes, baked potatoes and substantial OAP bargain wkdy lunches to much more ambitious dishes, attentive staff, front lounge with pleasant outlook, hunting prints and log fire in huge fireplace, small dining room with no smoking area, basic back bar with juke box; children welcome, neat flower-filled garden, open all day *(George Atkinson, W W Burke)*

MIDDLETON CHENEY [SP5041]

New Inn OX17 2ND [Main Rd, off A422 E of M40 junction 11]: Good choice of real ales in former 17th-c turnpike inn, popular food, welcoming service, bottle collection in bar and outer barn, no smoking back restaurant, mid-July beer festival; dogs welcome, good-sized neatly kept garden with aunt sally, open all day Sat *(Chris Glasson, Mick Furn)*

MOULTON [SP7866]

Artichoke NN3 7SP [Church St]: Large village pub, usual food plus wide choice of tapas-style starters (several could be shared as a full meal), sensibly priced ales inc Timothy Taylors Landlord, decent choice of wines, no smoking dining area *(Gerry and Rosemary Dobson)*

Telegraph NN3 7SB [West St]: Stone-built village pub with short choice of enjoyable food in front bar and restaurant extension, five changing ales, good soft drinks choice, locals' back bar with TV; piped music; garden picnic-sets *(Alan Sutton, Gerry and Rosemary Dobson)*

NASSINGTON [TL0696]

☆ *Black Horse* PE8 6QU [Fotheringhay Rd – 2½ miles S of A1/A47 interchange W of Peterboro]: Civilised olde-worlde 17th-c beamed and panelled dining pub in nice village, wide range of good food at sensible prices inc danish dishes (Danish landlord), real ales, good varied wine list, quick attentive service, splendid big stone fireplace, easy chairs and small settees in two rooms linked by bar servery; attractive garden, open all day summer wknds *(LYM, Steve, Paul Humphreys)*

NEWNHAM [SP5759]

Romer Arms NN11 3HB [The Green]: Pine panelling, mix of flagstones, quarry tiles and carpet, log fire, light and airy back dining conservatory, cheerful obliging licensees, reliably good generous home cooking (not Mon) inc some unusual dishes, Tues-Sat lunchtime bargains, good value Sun lunch (no snacks then), Greene King Old Speckled Hen, Charles Wells Eagle and a guest such as St Austell or Wadworths, good soft drinks choice, public bar with darts and pool; piped music; picnic-sets in enclosed back garden looking over fields, small attractive village *(George Atkinson)*

NORTHAMPTON [SP7862]

Bold Dragoon NN3 3JW [High St, Weston Favell; off A4500 Wellingborough Rd]: Well run two-bar pub with wide choice of generous enjoyable food inc imaginative dishes, real ales such as Batemans XXXB, Fullers London Pride, Greene King Abbot, Palmers Dorset Gold and St Austell Tribute, new world wines, friendly efficient staff, no smoking conservatory restaurant; disabled access, picnic-sets in garden with terrace *(June and Peter Shamash)*

Fish NN1 2AA [Fish St]: Large bare-boards pub in pedestrian area, half a dozen real ales inc unusual ones, farm cider, good wine choice, popular food till 6, daily papers, no smoking area; piped music, games machines; disabled access, bedrooms, open all day *(JJW, CMW, Richard Waller, Pauline Smith)*

☆ *Malt Shovel* NN1 1QF [Bridge St (approach rd from M1 junction 15); best parking in Morrisons opp back entrance]: Strong customer loyalty for its interesting choice of up to a dozen or so changing real ales inc three of their own, also Rich's farm cider, belgian bottled beers, over 50 malt whiskies, country wines, good soft drinks choice, occasional beer festivals, daily papers, breweriana inc some from Carlsberg Brewery opposite, open fire, darts, cheap pubby lunchtime food (not Sun); quiet piped music (live Weds); children welcome, picnic-sets on small back terrace, back disabled access *(JJW, CMW, Diane Hibberd, the Didler, Tony and Wendy Hobden, John Kearins, Andy Lickfold, Mick Furn)*

PITSFORD [SP7567]

☆ *Griffin* NN6 9AD [off A508 N of Northampton]: Now very popular for young chef/landlord's good reasonably priced food from lunchtime baguettes and bar dishes to wider restaurant choice, friendly helpful service, Fullers London Pride, Greene King IPA and Abbot and Youngs Special, good value wines, neat beamed bar, no smoking back lounge with steps up to small eating area and pleasant restaurant extension (also no smoking – book well ahead wknds), interesting pictures, old advertisements and so forth; pretty village nr Pitsford Water/Brixworth Country Park *(Gerry and Rosemary Dobson, Michael Dandy, George Atkinson, Revd R P Tickle)*

POTTERSPURY [SP7543]

Cock NN12 7PQ [High St; off A5]: Unassuming traditional pub with inglenook log fire, four real ales, good choice of soft drinks, wide choice of usual food (not Sun evening) inc OAP deals Mon-Thurs, friendly staff, games room with pool and darts, no smoking dining room; piped music, TV; terrace tables and small garden with picnic-sets *(JJW, CMW)*

Old Talbot NN12 7QD [A5; Watling St]: Family dining pub with chesterfields in small bar (also table football), pine furniture in large carpeted dining area behind, Greene King IPA and Abbot, reasonably priced food (not Sun evening) inc Sun carvery; piped music; neatly

fenced garden behind, open all day wknds
(Michael Dandy, JJW, CMW, LYM)

RAVENSTHORPE [SP6670]

☆ *Chequers* NN6 8ER [Chequers Lane]:
Refurbished and extended beamed local with
wide range of generous food from baguettes
and baked potatoes to steaks, Greene King
IPA, Fullers London Pride and three changing
guest beers, good soft drinks choice, friendly
attentive staff, pub cat, open fire, lots of mugs
and plates on stripped stone walls, no smoking
dining room, games room, may have free-range
eggs for sale; front bar can be smoky, piped
music, TV, games machine; children welcome,
small secluded back terrace and play area,
open all day Sat *(JJW, CMW, Michael Tack,
Michael Dandy, Gerry and Rosemary Dobson)*

RINGSTEAD [SP9875]

Axe & Compass NN14 4DW [Carlow Rd]:
Extended stone-built village pub, recently
redecorated bar and restaurant with flagstones
and lots of bric-a-brac, enjoyable fresh
straightforward food from sandwiches up,
friendly service, Banks's and Marstons
Pedigree; piped music; garden and play area
(Pete and Sue Robbins)

ROADE [SP7551]

Cock NN7 2NW [just off A508 S of M1
junction 15]: Cheerful family-run village pub
with enjoyable well presented reasonably
priced bar food (not Sun/Mon evenings),
Greene King IPA, Marstons Pedigree and a
guest beer, good soft drinks choice,
horsebrasses, woodburner and pine tables in
carpeted no smoking dining lounge; piped
music, TV; children in lounge, open all day
(Michael Dandy, JJW, CMW)

ROCKINGHAM [SP8691]

Sondes Arms LE16 8TG [Main St]: Nicely set
beamed pub with emphasis on enjoyable food
from light bar lunches to meals in large
separate no smoking restaurant, Adnams
Broadside and Charles Wells Bombardier,
efficient service; super views, tables out on
terrace, lovely village (except for the traffic)
(John and Sylvia Harrop)

RUSHDEN [SP9566]

Station Bar NN10 0AW [Station Approach]:
Not a pub, but part of station HQ of Rushden
Historical Transport Society (non-members can
sign in), restored in 1940s/60s style, with good
changing choice of interesting real ales, tea and
coffee, friendly staff, filled rolls (perhaps hot
dishes too, occasional barbecues), gas lighting,
enamelled advertisements, old-fangled
furnishings; authentic waiting room with piano,
also museum and summer trains and steam-ups;
cl wkdy lunchtimes *(P Dawn, the Didler)*

SIBBERTOFT [SP6782]

Red Lion LE16 9UD [Welland Rise, off A4303
or A508 SW of Mkt Harboro]: Enjoyable food
cooked by landlord in comfortable partly
panelled bar or light and airy bistro-style
beamed dining room with modern tables on
tiles, Bass and Youngs, splendid wine list,
sociable landlady; covered terrace tables, large
garden, two quiet well equipped bedrooms
with kitchens for do-it-yourself breakfast

*(Richard Pick, George Atkinson,
Ms E J Webster, Dr S Edwards, Gerry and
Rosemary Dobson)*

SLIPTON [SP9579]

☆ *Samuel Pepys* NN14 3AR [Slipton Lane – pub
well signed locally]: Smart and popular country
dining pub with informal eating area in long
low-beamed but airy main bar, some stripped
stone, neat no smoking restaurant and dining
conservatory, wide choice of good food using
fresh local supplies from doorstep sandwiches
to enterprising hot dishes, friendly helpful
service, local Potbelly ales with others such as
Digfield, Greene King IPA, Hook Norton,
Milton or Oakham, good wines by the glass
and hot drinks, colourful jars of preserves as
part of décor, log fire in locals' back bar (dogs
allowed here); piped music; disabled access,
country views from pleasant garden with
cocktail parasols and heaters *(Michael and
Jenny Back, Mark Butler, Andy Chapman)*

SPRATTON [SP7170]

Kings Head NN6 8HH [Brixworth Rd]: Large
stone-built village pub with flagstoned and
carpeted L-shaped bar, Caledonian Deuchars
IPA, Carlsberg Burton and Greene King IPA,
good soft drinks choice, good coffee, enjoyable
food from baguettes and baked potatoes
through pizzas and pasta to full meals, helpful
service, daily papers, woodburner and flame-
effect fire, new extension restaurant; TV,
games machine and hood skittles, separate
pool and darts area; picnic-sets by car park,
open all day *(Michael Dandy)*

STAVERTON [SP5461]

☆ *Countryman* NN11 6JH [Daventry Rd
(A425)]: Spotless beamed pub with carpeted
no smoking side and back dining areas, very
popular reasonably priced food from
sandwiches and baguettes to lots of fish, good
puddings range, smaller bar with games area,
Adnams, Fullers London Pride and Greene
King Ruddles Best, good coffee, good choice of
wines by the glass, friendly attentive staff;
piped music, should book Sun lunch and
Fri/Sat night; some tables outside and in small
garden *(George Atkinson, Kevin McPartlan,
JJW, CMW, Michael and Jenny Back)*

STOKE BRUERNE [SP7449]

☆ *Boat* NN12 7SB [3½ miles from M1 junction 15
– A508 towards Stony Stratford then signed on
right; Bridge Rd]: Appealing old-world
flagstoned bar in picturesque canalside spot by
beautifully restored lock, though main focus is
newly refurbished central-pillared back bar and
bistro without the views (children allowed in this
bit); real ales such as Marstons Bitter, Pedigree
and Old Empire and a guest such as Smiles Slap
& Tipple, prompt friendly service, good value
usual food from baguettes and baked potatoes
up, modern extension with all-day tearooms and
comfortable no smoking upstairs restaurant;
piped music; tables out by towpath opp British
Waterways Museum and shop, canal boat trips,
bar open all day summer Sats *(David and
Ruth Shillitoe, LYM, Doreen and
Haydn Maddock, Keith and Janet Morris,
George Atkinson, Michael Dandy)*

Navigation NN12 7SY: Large canalside pub, several levels and cosy corners, sturdy wood furniture, reasonably priced generous usual food from sandwiches up inc Sun lunch till 5, Marstons Pedigree and Hop Back Summer Lightning, good choice of wines by the glass, quick friendly young staff, separate family room, pub games; piped music; plenty of tables out overlooking water, big play area, open all day *(Michael Tack, Simon Jones, Michael Dandy)*

SUTTON BASSETT [SP7790]
Queens Head LE16 8HP [B664; village signed off A6 Mkt Harboro bypass]: Beamed village pub overlooking Welland Valley, comfortable banquettes in red and green lounge, Adnams and a guest beer, friendly service, enjoyable reasonably priced home cooking (all day wknds), back dining area; children welcome, some seats out beyond car park, open all day wknds and summer *(Dr B and Mrs P B Baker, Rona Murdoch)*

SYRESHAM [SP6341]
Kings Head NN13 5HW [off A43 Brackley—Towcester; Abbey Rd]: Family dining pub with enjoyable food from good sandwiches up, friendly landlord, Banks's and Marstons Pedigree, inglenook log fire, beams, brasses, pictures, motor-racing memorabilia, darts and TV in games room, no smoking restaurant; children welcome, picnic-sets in small garden, bedrooms *(JJW, CMW)*

SYWELL [SP8167]
Horseshoe NN6 0AW [off A43 NE of Northampton; Overstone Rd]: Large pleasantly decorated open-plan stone-built dining pub with traditional food from rolls and baked potatoes up, Greene King IPA and Old Speckled Hen and Wadworths 6X, prompt service, no smoking area; games area with pool, darts and machines; children welcome, largish garden with picnic-sets and play area *(Michael Dandy)*

THORNBY [SP6675]
☆ *Red Lion* NN6 8SJ [Welford Rd; A5199 Northampton—Leicester]: Relaxed and friendly old country local with half a dozen real ales inc Everards Original, Greene King IPA and Hook Norton Old Hooky, imaginative food choice from sandwiches up, old pictures and decorative china, pews, leather settee and armchairs, no smoking areas, flourishing houseplants, log fire, beamed dining area, good range of traditional games; dogs and children welcome, open all day wknds and bank hols *(Chris Evans, LYM)*

THORPE MANDEVILLE [SP5344]
☆ *Three Conies* OX17 2EX [off B4525 E of Banbury]: Attractive 17th-c stone-built pub doing well under current newish licensees, wide choice of enterprising food from good value sandwiches up, Hook Norton ales, beamed bar with some stripped masonry, flagstones and bare boards, log fires each end, mix of old dining tables, large family dining room; piped music; tables out in front and on lawn *(LYM, C J Pratt, George Atkinson, Mick Furn, Brian Englefield)*

TOWCESTER [SP7047]
Folly NN12 6LB [A5 S, opp racecourse]: Thatched pub, good choice of reasonably priced food from sandwiches up (no snacks Sun or race days), Charles Wells Eagle and Bombardier, friendly helpful landlord, steps up to no smoking dining area; quiet piped music; no dogs or children; garden with play area *(Michael Dandy, JJW, CMW)*

☆ *Red Lion* NN12 8LB [Foster's Booth (A5 3m N)]: Attractive 16th-c former posting inn, friendly and unpretentious, with Courage Directors, Fullers London Pride and a guest such as Exmoor, good value blackboard food from good sandwiches and baked potatoes up, hard-working licensees, daily papers, dark wood furniture in carpeted lounge bar/dining area with big inglenook fireplace, beams and bric-a-brac, copper and brass, another fire in chatty quarry-tiled public bar with hood skittles and darts in carpeted games room; quiet piped music, TV; children welcome, garden picnic-sets *(Michael Dandy, JJW, CMW, George Atkinson)*

Saracens Head NN12 6BX [Watling St W]: Substantially modernised coaching inn with interesting *Pickwick Papers* connections, high windows in thick walls and reworked cavernous fireplace in long comfortable partly no smoking three-level lounge and dining area, Greene King IPA and Old Speckled Hen, neat efficient staff, pub food from good choice of baguettes up; piped music, TV; children welcome, Victorian dining room in hotel part across attractive courtyard with tables, well equipped bedrooms *(Michael Dandy, LYM)*

UPPER BENEFIELD [SP9789]
Wheatsheaf PE8 5AN [Upper Main St]: Attractive country pub in pleasant rural area, good value food in bar and restaurant, friendly atmosphere, good choice of beers, fine house wines *(Mrs V Brown)*

WALGRAVE [SP8072]
Royal Oak NN6 9PN [Zion Hill, off A43 Northampton—Kettering]: Friendly old stone-built local with changing ales such as Adnams, Brains Rev James, Church End Vicars Ruin, Greene King Abbot and Village Champflower, good value food (not Sun evening) from sandwiches and baked potatoes to wild boar and swordfish, quick pleasant service, long three-part carpeted beamed bar with small lounge and restaurant extension behind; piped music; children welcome, small garden, play area, open all day Sun *(Val and Alan Green, Michael Dandy)*

WEEDON [SP6458]
☆ *Narrow Boat* NN7 4RZ [Stowe Hill (A5 S)]: Spacious terrace and big garden sloping down to canal (very popular in summer), small L-shaped bar with canal prints, sofa, easy chairs and low tables, high-raftered back restaurant extension with canal views, two no smoking rooms, wide food choice from generous baguettes and baked potatoes to good value Sun lunch (all afternoon) and tempting puddings, young well trained staff, Charles Wells ales, some good value wines, open fire;

fruit machine, skittles, quiet piped music; bedrooms in back motel extension, narrowboat hire next door *(LYM, George Atkinson, Gerry and Rosemary Dobson)*

WELFORD [SP6480]

Wharf NN6 6JQ [pub just over Leics border]: Castellated Georgian folly in delightful setting by two Grand Union Canal marinas, Banks's, Marstons Pedigree and three changing guest beers in compact locals' bar, enjoyable fresh standard food using local supplies, pleasant dining section; waterside garden *(John Moore)*

WELLINGBOROUGH [SP9069]

Locomotive NN8 4AL [Finedon Rd (A5128)]: Old-fashioned two-bar pub with friendly new landlord keeping up to half a dozen interesting changing real ales, lots of train memorabilia inc toy locomotive running above bar, huge lunchtime baguettes, log fire, daily papers, games room with pool, pin table and hood skittles; may be quiet piped music; dogs welcome, picnic-sets in small front garden, open all day (Sun afternoon break) *(JJW, CMW)*

WELTON [SP5866]

☆ *White Horse* NN11 2JP [High St; off A361/B4036 N of Daventry]: Welcoming new

management in two-bar beamed village pub, cosy dining areas inc one no smoking, changing real ales such as Greene King IPA, Shepherd Neame Spitfire, St Austell Tinners and Charles Wells Bombardier, decent house wines, big open fire, public bar with woodburner, darts, table skittles and pool room; attractively lit garden with play area, terrace and barbecue *(Andrew Gardner)*

YARDLEY HASTINGS [SP8656]

☆ *Red Lion* NN7 1ER [High St, just off A428 Bedford—Northampton]: Pretty thatched stone-built pub largely no smoking and set for good value food (not Sun/Mon evenings) from sandwiches up, wider evening choice, Charles Wells Eagle with guests such as Greene King Abbot and Robinsons Unicorn, good range of soft drinks, friendly staff (and cat), linked rooms with beams and stripped stone, lots of pictures, plates and interesting brass and copper, separate small annexe with hood skittles; quiet piped music, TV, no dogs; children welcome, picnic-sets in nicely planted sloping garden, and in front, open all day wknds *(Mike Ridgway, Sarah Miles, Michael Dandy, BB, JJW, CMW, George Atkinson)*

Northumbria
(County Durham, Northumberland and Tyneside)

The North East is a great place to find friendly and unpretentious pubs with generous food. Pubs here tend to be generous to their customers on price, too. Food is usually fairly priced, and drinks on average cost less than the national norm. There are plenty of thriving local brewers up here, producing distinctive ales that tend to be particularly good value in their home territory. The ones we found most frequently were Wylam, Hadrian & Border, Mordue, Big Lamp and Durham, with Hexhamshire, Camerons, Darwin and Northumberland also well worth keeping an eye open for. Two new main entries this year are the Battlesteads at Wark, a beautifully placed country inn given a real lift by the friendly personality of its new owners, and the Shiremoor Farm in New York, a well designed and smartly relaxed large dining pub. Other pubs in fine fettle here include the Manor House Inn at Carterway Heads (good food in nice surroundings, a fine all-rounder), the cheerful Dipton Mill Inn tucked away at Diptonmill (bargain food – and it's where that Hexhamshire beer comes from), the Feathers at Hedley on the Hill (good interesting food in unpretentious surroundings, and a fine choice of real ales), the comfortable Apple at Lucker (reliable food), the Keelman in Newburn (unorthodox building, with its own good Big Lamp beer and bargain food), the chatty Crown Posada in Newcastle (probably the city's most handsome pub building, with good real ales) and sympathetically refurbished Head of Steam there (bargain food and great drinks), the Ship idyllically placed at Newton-by-the-Sea (it does come under pressure from sheer force of numbers in the summer), the Cook & Barker Arms at Newton-on-the-Moor (a good handily placed restaurant-with-rooms, with a pubby bar too), the Olde Ship by the harbour in Seahouses (a great favourite), and the Pheasant up by Kielder Water at Stannersburn (a good all-rounder). New licensees seem to be settling in well at the Rat in Anick (very young and enthusiastic) and the Carts Bog Inn near Langley on Tyne. As we've said, several of the pubs mentioned above stand out for their food, but for a real treat with its excellent food changing daily it's the County in Aycliffe, County Durham, which wins the title of Northumbria Dining Pub of the Year. The Errington Arms near Corbridge, a very popular main entry in our last edition, was closed for rebuilding, following a fire, as we went to press with this new edition. It will be good to see it back in action. Incidentally, a lot of pubs up here have a much fresher atmosphere than they did just a few years ago, with the more food-oriented places now generally having good no smoking areas – or even going no smoking throughout, before the ban becomes compulsory. In the Lucky Dip section at the end of the chapter, pubs gaining particularly warm approval in recent months include the Red Lion in Alnmouth, Victoria at Bamburgh, Ancient Unicorn in Bowes, General Havelock at Haydon Bridge, Black Bull at Lowick, Magnesia Bank in North Shields, Wellington at Riding Mill, Newcastle Hotel at Rothbury, and Travellers Rest at Slaley. Newcastle upon Tyne has a fine clutch of entries, most with a good deal of genuine character and individuality.

ANICK NY9665 Map 10
Rat 🍺
Village signposted NE of A69/A695 Hexham junction; NE46 4LN

Tables out on the terrace and in the charming garden (with dovecote, statues and flowers) of this pleasantly relaxed country pub give charming views of the North Tyne valley in the area around Hexham. A coal fire blazes invitingly in the blackened kitchen range, and soft lighting gently illuminates lots of interesting knick-knacks: antique floral chamber-pots hanging from the beams, china and glassware, maps and posters, and framed sets of cigarette cards. Furnishings keep up the cosily traditional mood, with brocaded chairs around old-fashioned pub tables; piped music, daily papers and magazines. Besides the two no smoking small eating areas, the no smoking conservatory has pleasant valley views. From a changing blackboard menu, generous helpings of tasty pubby food might include soup (£2.90), open sandwiches (from £3.95), ploughman's (£4.50), their popular 'rat burger' (£6.50), chicken breast with creamy tomato and pesto sauce (£9.95), and tuna steak with lemon and dill sauce (£11.95), with enjoyable puddings such as home-made apple and raspberry crumble (£3.25); Sunday lunch (£6.95). Half a dozen changing real ales on handpump always include Caledonian Deuchars plus several local brews such as Hadrian & Border Farne Island, Mordue Workie Ticket or Wylam Gold Tankard. Parking is limited. The pub has recently changed hands; more reports on the new regime please. *(Recommended by Pat and Stewart Gordon, Paul Davies, Gerry Miller, Andy and Jill Kassube, Ann and Stephen Saunders, Tim and Suzy Bower, Mart Lawton)*

Freehouse ~ Lease Anthony Hunter ~ Real ale ~ Bar food ~ Restaurant ~ (01434) 602814 ~ Children welcome ~ Open 11-3, 6-11 Mon-Thurs; 11-11 Fri, Sat; 12-10.30 Sun

AYCLIFFE NZ2722 Map 10
County ㉕ 🍴 🍷 🍺
The Green, Aycliffe village; just off A1(M) junction 59, by A167; DL5 6LX

Northumbria Dining Pub of the Year

You can expect wonderful things to come out of the kitchen at this renowned dining pub: the talented chef/landlord, Andrew Brown, was the first Raymond Blanc scholarship winner back in 1995 and trained at such celebrated establishments as Le Manoir aux Quat' Saisons and the Petit Blanc. The civilised atmosphere is delightfully welcoming – and service is superbly attentive. Minimalist décor and blond wood floors are light and modern, and furnishings in the extended bar and no smoking bistro are definitely geared to dining. Food is prepared using mostly local produce. Delicious pubby bar food (served at lunchtime and in the early evening only) includes soup (£3.95), open sandwiches (£5.45), smoked salmon and scrambled egg toasted muffin (£5.95, or £8.95 as a main course), vegetable and mushroom stroganoff (£8.50), lambs liver and bacon with mash, scampi or cajun-spiced chicken with salsa (£8.95). Otherwise you can also eat from the more elaborate (and pricier) daily changing bistro menu, which might include starters such as beetroot and yorkshire blue cheese risotto (£6.95), crayfish and prawn salad (£7.50) or fried king scallops with crispy bacon (£7.95), and main courses like vegetable and goats cheese lasagne (£10.95), crispy duck leg (£14.50), fillet of salmon with crab and herb crust (£15.50), medallions of monkfish, mussel and crayfish broth or braised haunch of venison with chestnut and wild mushroom risotto (£16.95) or rib-eye steak with thick chips (£16.50); puddings might feature warm bitter chocolate tart or iced vanilla parfait with warm cherries and kirsch (£5). Dishes are freshly cooked, so there might be a bit of a wait, and booking is a good idea. As well as a good choice of wines by the glass, they've Charles Wells Bombardier alongside a couple of guests such as Barnsley Bitter and Greene King Old Speckled Hen; piped music. The green opposite is pretty. *(Recommended by Comus and Sarah Elliott, Michael Doswell, M A Borthwick, John and Sylvia Harrop, Judith and Edward Pearson, Mart Lawton)*

Free house ~ Licensee Andrew Brown ~ Real ale ~ Bar food ~ Restaurant ~
(01325) 312273 ~ Children welcome with restrictions ~ Open 12-3, 5.30(6.30 Sat)-11;
closed Sun

BLANCHLAND NY9750 Map 10
Lord Crewe Arms ㉕ 🛏
B6306 S of Hexham; DH8 9SP

You get immersed in history as you enter this remarkable building, originally a
guest-house built in 1235 for the neighbouring Premonstratensian monastery, in a
picturesque village built robustly enough to resist most border raiding parties; the
lovely walled garden was formerly the cloisters. Still separated from the rest of the
world by several miles of moors, rabbits and sheep, the building became home to
several distinguished families after the dissolution in 1536. An ancient-feeling bar is
housed in an unusual long and narrow stone barrel-vaulted crypt, its curving walls
being up to eight feet thick in some places. Plush stools are lined along the bar
counter on ancient flagstones, and next to a narrow drinks shelf down the opposite
wall; TV. Upstairs, the Derwent Room has low beams, old settles, and sepia
photographs on its walls, and the Hilyard Room has a massive 13th-c fireplace
once used as a hiding place by the Jacobite Tom Forster (part of the family who
had owned the building before it was sold in 1704 to the formidable Lord Crewe,
Bishop of Durham). Apart from the bar and some bedrooms, the whole of the hotel
is no smoking. Straightforward bar food includes soup (£2.75), filled rolls (from
£3.50), ploughman's (from £5.25), cumberland sausage with black pudding, apple
sauce and mash (£6.85) and a handful of daily specials. Black Sheep is on
handpump alongside a summer guest ale. *(Recommended by P and J Shapley, Dr and Mrs
T E Hothersall, Paul Davies, Chris and Sue Bax, Norma and Noel Thomas, Comus and Sarah
Elliott, M J Winterton)*

Free house ~ Licensees A Todd, Peter Gingell and Ian Press, Lindsey Sands ~ Real ale ~
Bar food ~ Restaurant ~ (01434) 675251 ~ Children welcome in no smoking areas ~
Dogs allowed in bar and bedrooms ~ Open 11-11 ~ Bedrooms: £80B/£120B

CARTERWAY HEADS NZ0552 Map 10
Manor House Inn 🍴 🍷 🍴 🛏
A68 just N of B6278, near Derwent Reservoir; DH8 9LX

Continuing to be a strong all-rounder for excellent food, well kept beer and well
chosen wine, not forgetting that this is also a thoroughly comfortable place to stay
(with good breakfasts, too), this popular and welcoming inn has sweeping views
towards the Derwent valley and reservoir. The highly praised food, using local
ingredients where possible, is served in generous helpings, and includes sandwiches
and a choice of two soups (£3.95), together with items such as sausage and mash
(£6.50), steak and ale pie (£7.95), pheasant or venison when in season (£11.95) and
a choice of up to five different fish dishes like fried scallops with chilli jam (£13.50);
among the home-made puddings are sticky toffee pudding and home-made ice-
cream (£3.95). The locals' bar has an original boarded ceiling, pine tables, chairs
and stools, old oak pews, and a mahogany counter. Picture windows in the
comfortable lounge bar (with woodburning stove) and from the partly no smoking
restaurant give fine views over moorland pastures, and rustic tables in the garden
have the same views; darts, dominoes, TV and piped music (only in the bar).
They've around 70 malt whiskies, farm cider and decent wines (with about a dozen
by the glass), along with Charles Wells Bombardier, Courage Directors, Theakstons
Best and a guest from a local brewer such as Greene King on handpump. You can
buy local produce, as well as chutneys, puddings and ice-cream made in the
kitchens from their own little deli. *(Recommended by Mr and Mrs John Taylor, Bruce and
Sharon Eden, Liz and Brian Barnard, J F M and M West, Alex and Claire Pearse, Michael Butler,
Will and Kay Adie, A Pickering, John Robertson, John Foord, Susan and John Douglas,
Andy and Jill Kassube, Christine and Keith Whale, M J Winterton)*

Free house ~ Licensees Moira and Chris Brown ~ Real ale ~ Bar food (12-9.30(9 Sun)) ~ Restaurant ~ (01207) 255268 ~ Well behaved children welcome away from bar ~ Dogs welcome ~ Open 11(12 Sun)-11 ~ Bedrooms: £38S/£60S

COTHERSTONE NZ0119 Map 10

Fox & Hounds 🛏

B6277 – incidentally a good quiet route to Scotland, through interesting scenery; DL12 9PF

This 18th-c country inn makes an excellent focal point to routes along the dramatic wooded Tees valley from Barnard Castle. The simple but cheery beamed bar has a good winter log fire, thickly cushioned wall seats, and local photographs and country pictures on the walls in its various alcoves and recesses. Using some local ingredients, bar food could include lunchtime sandwiches, soup (from £3.40), warm bacon, cotherstone cheese and apple salad (£6.20), pork, sage and apple pie (£6.80), chicken breast baked with cotherstone cheese in creamy mushroom and pancetta sauce (£10.45) and sirloin steak (£13.55), with specials like baked cod loin steak (£10.45), roast rack of lamb with redcurrant and rosemary jus (£15.50 or fried medallions of fillet steak in mushroom gravy on horseradish mash (£15.80); efficient service from the friendly staff; quoits. Both of the dining rooms and all the bedrooms are no smoking, and you may need to book. They've 13 wines by the glass, 15 malt whiskies from smaller distilleries, and Black Sheep Best and a guest such as Jennings Cocker Hoop are on handpump. Don't be surprised by the unusual lavatory attendant – an african grey parrot called Reva. *(Recommended by Sarah and Peter Gooderham, Peter and Jan Humphreys, I A Herdman, Pat and Tony Martin, Mike and Sue Loseby, M J Winterton)*

Free house ~ Licensees Nichola and Ian Swinburn ~ Real ale ~ Bar food (12-2, 7-8.30) ~ Restaurant ~ (01833) 650241 ~ Children in restaurant ~ Open 12-2.30, 6.45-11(10.30 Sun) ~ Bedrooms: £47.50B/£75B

DIPTONMILL NY9261 Map 10

Dipton Mill Inn 🍷 🗎 £

Just S of Hexham; off B6306 at Slaley, Blanchland and Dye House, Whitley Chapel signposts (and HGV route sign); not to be confused with the Dipton in Durham; NE46 1YA

Readers find it's well worth making the effort to find this own-brew ivy-clad pub, in a peaceful steep-sided wooded valley not far from Hexham race course. The cheery landlord is a brewer in the family-owned Hexhamshire Brewery, and Hexhamshire Shire Bitter, Devils Water, Devils Elbow, Old Humbug, Shire Bitter and Whapweasel are all well kept on handpump; also 18 wines by the glass (in two different sizes), 22 malt whiskies, and Weston's Old Rosie cider. Ideal with your pint, try one of their excellent ploughman's (£5-£6), with one of the great range of a dozen northumbrian cheeses they keep (or you can have cheese after your meal). Other straightforward but tasty bar food might include sandwiches (from £2), soup (from £2.25), tagliatelle with creamy basil sauce (£5.25), ratatouille with couscous (£5.50), salads (from £5.75), haddock baked with tomato and basil, or steak and kidney pie (£6.50), and lamb leg steak or chicken in sherry sauce (£7.30), with puddings such as bread and butter pudding or apple and pear crumble (from £2). The neatly kept, snug bar has dark ply panelling, low ceilings, red furnishings, a dark red carpet and two welcoming open fires. The back games room has darts, bar billiards, shove-ha'penny and dominoes. In fine weather it's pleasant to sit out on the sunken crazy-paved terrace by the restored mill stream, or in the attractively planted garden with its aviary. There's a pleasant walk through the woods along the little valley. *(Recommended by Bruce and Sharon Eden, Mr and Mrs Maurice Thompson, Alex and Claire Pearse, the Didler, Bob Richardson, Michael Doswell, Neil Whitehead, Victoria Anderson, Mike and Lynn Robinson, Gerry Miller, Dr D J and Mrs S C Walker, Comus and Sarah Elliott, MartLawton)*

Own brew ~ Licensee Geoff Brooker ~ Real ale ~ Bar food (12-2, 6.30-8.30) ~ No credit
cards ~ (01434) 606577 ~ Children welcome ~ Open 12-2.30, 6-11; 12-3 Sun; closed Sun
evening

DURHAM NZ2742 Map 10
Victoria 🍺 🛏

Hallgarth Street (A177, near Dunelm House); DH1 3AS

This evocative and immaculately kept city pub has changed little since it was built
in the closing years of Queen Victoria's reign, and celebrates her life with lots of
period prints and engravings, and staffordshire figurines of her and the Prince
Consort. Full of cheery bantering locals and presided over by a friendly landlord, it
has five interesting and very well kept real ales, which typically might include Big
Lamp Bitter, Darwin Ghost, Durham Magus, Hexhamshire Devils Elbow and
Mordue Five Bridge Bitter on handpump; also cheap house wines, around 50 malts
and a great collection of 36 irish whiskeys. The very traditional layout means three
little rooms lead off a central bar, with typically Victorian décor: mahogany, etched
and cut glass and mirrors, colourful William Morris wallpaper over a high panelled
dado, some maroon plush seats in little booths, some leatherette wall seats, long
narrow drinkers' tables, handsome iron and tile fireplaces for the coal fires, a piano,
and some photographs and articles showing a very proper pride in the pub;
dominoes; at lunchtime they do toasties (from £1.20). The good value bedrooms
are simple but pleasant; a hearty breakfast (good vegetarian one too) is served in
the upstairs dining room. *(Recommended by Blaise Vyner, the Didler, Pete Baker,
Tracey and Stephen Groves, Earl and Chris Pick, Peter Cleminson, C Sale)*

Free house ~ Licensee Michael Webster ~ Real ale ~ (0191) 386 5269 ~ Children
welcome ~ Dogs welcome ~ Open 11.45-3, 6-11; 12-2, 7-10.30 Sun ~ Bedrooms:
£40B/£58B

EGLINGHAM NU1019 Map 10
Tankerville Arms

B6346 Alnwick—Wooler; NE66 2TX

In an attractive village and with good views from the picnic-sets in the garden, this
pub has friendly service and an unhurried, cosy atmosphere. It's quite traditional,
with a coal fire at each end, black joists, some walls stripped to bare stone and
hung with brassware, and plush banquettes and captain's chairs around cast-iron-
framed tables on the turkey carpet. Well presented, enjoyable bar food might
include a choice of soups (£4), filled baguettes (£4.95), vegetarian dishes like bean
cassoulet or sweet potato, leek and brie strudel (£9.50), duck confit or slices of
pork loin with apple and onion confit (£10), salmon on herb-baked tomatoes with
melted gruyère cheese (£11) and cannon of venison on chunky black pudding with
roasted leeks (£12). They serve two or three real ales such as Black Sheep and
Hadrian & Border Secret Kingdom on handpump, as well as a decent selection of
wines and malt whiskies. The restaurant is no smoking; piped music. More reports
please. *(Recommended by Comus and Sarah Elliott, Jenny and Peter Lowater)*

Free house ~ Licensee J E Blackmore ~ Real ale ~ Bar food (12-2, 6.30-9) ~ Restaurant ~
(01665) 578444 ~ Children welcome ~ Open 12-2, 6.30-11.30(12.30 Sat);
12-3, 6.30-10.30 Sun; closed lunchtime Mon-Weds Jan-March

GREAT WHITTINGTON NZ0171 Map 10
Queens Head 🍴 🍺

Village signposted off A68 and B6018 just N of Corbridge; NE19 2HP

This well run and stylish dining pub, in rolling, solitary country just north of
Hadrian's Wall, produces beautifully presented food, and sources local meat and
fish fresh from the quay. Staff are attentive and well trained, paying attention to the
details, and all the dining areas are no smoking. Modern furnishings alongside

some handsome carved oak settles and log fires give its two fairly simple beamed rooms an elegantly comfortable feel. The room nearest the bar counter has a mural over its fireplace; perhaps unobtrusive piped music. Besides lunchtime sandwiches, imaginative bistro food (which you can eat in the bar) might include soup (£4.50), starters such as generous portions of steamed mussels (£4.50), tempura of black pudding with beetroot and red onion relish (£5.95) and cornets of smoked salmon and atlantic prawns (£7.95), and main courses such as roasted vegetable and goats cheese tart with tomato and basil coulis (£11.95), breast of chicken stuffed with gruyère cheese and fresh herbs (£13.95), sirloin steak (£16.95) and fillet of halibut on wilted greens with mustard beurre blanc (£18.95). They do a good-value two-course lunch (£12.50) and a three-course Sunday lunch (£17.50). Black Sheep and Queens Head (brewed for them by Wylam) are on handpump, and they've 30 malt whiskies and an extensive wine list. The small front lawn has half a dozen picnic-sets, and this attractive old building is in a smart stone-built village, surrounded by partly wooded countryside. They may close for holidays during October. *(Recommended by Nigel Cummings, M A Borthwick, Lawrence Pearse, JWAC, Alex and Claire Pearse, R Macfarlane, Mart Lawton)*

Free house ~ Licensee Ian Scott ~ Real ale ~ Bar food (12-2.30, 6-9) ~ Restaurant ~ (01434) 672267 ~ Children allowed at lunchtime if eating ~ Open 12-2.30(3 Sun), 6-11; closed Sun evening, Mon and perhaps during part of Oct

GRETA BRIDGE   NZ0813 Map 10
Morritt Arms ♀
Hotel signposted off A66 W of Scotch Corner; DL12 9SE

Around the nicely pubby bar of this country house hotel, where Charles Dickens stayed in 1838, runs a remarkable mural painted in 1946 by J V Gilroy – better known for his old Guinness advertisements, six of which are displayed on the walls here too. Big windsor armchairs and sturdy oak settles cluster around traditional cast-iron-framed tables, large windows look out on the extensive lawn, and there are nice open fires. Black Sheep, Timothy Taylors Landlord and Jennings Cumberland are well kept on handpump, and they've quite a few malt whiskies, and an extensive wine list. Straightforward bar food includes soup (£2.95), sandwiches (from £4, served all day), warm tart of tomato and local cheese (£5.50), steak and kidney pie (£8.95), wild mushroom and leek risotto (£9.95), and sirloin steak (£15). With a more elaborate menu, the no smoking bistro has wood floors and wrought iron, and is hung with paintings and prints (for sale) by local artists. The attractively laid out garden has some seats, with teak tables in a pretty side area looking along to the graceful old bridge by the stately gates to Rokeby Park, and swings, a slide and a wendy house at the far end. *(Recommended by Janet and Peter Race, C A Hall, Danny Savage, David Hall, Dr and Mrs R G J Telfer, Helen Clarke, A Pickering, J V Dadswell, Tom and Jill Jones, Barry Collett, David and Ruth Shillitoe, Mrs Jane Kingsbury, David and Jean Hall)*

Free house ~ Licensees Peter Phillips and Barbara Johnson ~ Real ale ~ Bar food (12-3, 6-9.30) ~ Restaurant ~ (01833) 627232 ~ Children welcome ~ Dogs allowed in bar and bedrooms ~ Open 11-11; 12-10.30 Sun ~ Bedrooms: £85B/£99B

HALTWHISTLE   NY7166 Map 10
Milecastle Inn
Military Road; B6318 NE – OS Sheet 86 map reference 715660; NE49 9NN

Within strolling distance of Winshields Crags and the most famous part of Hadrian's Wall, this 17th-c dining pub (now entirely no smoking) is a comforting haven to retreat to amid some energisingly wild scenery. The snug little rooms of the beamed bar are decorated with brasses, horsey and local landscape prints and attractive fresh flowers, and have two winter log fires; at lunchtime the small comfortable no smoking restaurant is used as an overflow. Friendly hard-working staff serve Big Lamp Bitter and Prince Bishop, and they have a fair collection of malt whiskies and a good wine list; piped music. Bar food, served in generous helpings, includes sandwiches, as well as soup (£3), hot and spicy chicken wings (£3.95), battered cod, battered haddock, and meat or vegetable lasagne (all £7.75), various home-made pies (£8.25), sirloin or fillet steak (£12.95), and daily specials like venison, pheasant or trout (all £8.25); children's menu (£4.25). It's worth getting here early for a table. The tables and benches out in a pleasantly sheltered big walled garden with a dovecote and rather stunning views are popular in summer, and there's a large car park. *(Recommended by Tony and Maggie Harwood, Edward Leetham, Alex and Claire Pearse, Ray and Winifred Halliday, Jane Massam, Molly Crozier, Christine and Neil Townend, Melanie Christie, Gerry Miller, Dr D J and Mrs S C Walker, Mark and Ruth Brock)*

Free house ~ Licensees Clare and Kevin Hind ~ Real ale ~ Bar food (12-9; 12-2.45, 6-8.45 in winter) ~ Restaurant ~ No credit cards ~ (01434) 321372 ~ Children welcome ~ Open 12-10(11 Sat); 12-3, 6-9(11 Sat) in winter

HEDLEY ON THE HILL NZ0759 Map 10
Feathers (🍴) ◀

Village signposted from New Ridley, which is signposted from B6309 N of Consett; OS Sheet 88 map reference 078592; NE43 7SW

Small-scale breweries are well represented at this quaint stone-built tavern – the selection of very well kept beers features Mordue Workie Ticket alongside three guests from brewers such as Big Lamp, Orkney and Wylam – and the home-made food is excellent too. With such a friendly welcome and comfortable pubby atmosphere it's not surprising that locals pop in for a drink, with others coming from further afield for the beautifully prepared and sensibly priced food (it's a good idea to book). A short but very appealing weekly changing menu might typically include stilton soup (£3.50), chicken liver pâté with red onion marmalade (£4.50), roast mediterranean vegetable and white wine risotto (£8.25), cumberland sausage with onion, cider and mustard sauce or cod and salmon cakes with chilli and ginger (£8.50), pork casseroled with fennel and orange (£10.95) and organic salmon fillet with salsa verde (£11.75), and puddings such as citrus tart or very tasty chocolate fudge pudding (£4.50). Three well kept turkey-carpeted traditional bars have an appealingly pubby atmosphere, with beams, open fires, stripped stonework, solid brown leatherette settles and old black and white photographs of local places and farm and country workers. They stock decent wines and around 30 malt whiskies. Shove-ha'penny, table skittles, cribbage and dominoes, and they hold a mini beer festival at Easter with over two dozen real ales (and a barrel race on Easter Monday). Picnic-sets in front are a nice place to sit and watch the world drift by. Note the restricted opening hours. *(Recommended by Alex and Claire Pearse, Lawrence Pearse, Chris and Sue Bax, Paul Davies, GSB, Keith Cohen, Mr and Mrs Pattison, Dr Richard Higgins)*

Free house ~ Licensee Marina Atkinson ~ Real ale ~ Bar food (7-9 Tues-Fri; 12-2.30, 7-9 Sat, Sun; not Mon except bank hols) ~ (01661) 843607 ~ Children welcome ~ Open 6-11; 12-3, 6-11(7-10.30 Sun) Sat; closed weekday lunchtimes

LANGLEY ON TYNE NY8160 Map 10
Carts Bog Inn

A686 S, junction B6305; NE47 5NW

Under new owners, this remote pub by the moors and dry-stone walled pastures above the Tyne valley is a welcoming place to come into, and the restaurant and tables in the garden make the most of the view. The neatly kept main black-beamed bar has a blazing log fire in the central stone fireplace, local photographs and horsebrasses, and windsor chairs and comfortably cushioned wall settles around the tables. It rambles about, with flagstones here, carpet there, and mainly white walls with some stripped stone. A side lounge (once a cow byre) with more wall banquettes has pool; piped music; darts; quoits pitch. Reasonably priced straightforward bar food includes sandwiches (from £3.50), soup (£4), baked avocado with stilton (£7), haddock (£8.50), sirloin steak (£14), and puddings such

Please use this card to tell us which pubs *you* think should or should not be included in the next edition of *The Good Pub Guide*. Just fill it in and return it to us – no stamp or envelope needed. Don't forget you can also use the report forms at the end of the *Guide*, or report through our web site: www.goodguides.co.uk

ALISDAIR AIRD

In returning this form I confirm my agreement that the information I provide may be used by The Random House Group Ltd, its assignees and/or licensees in any media or medium whatsoever.

YOUR NAME AND ADDRESS (BLOCK CAPITALS PLEASE)

☐ *Please tick this box if you would like extra report forms*

REPORT ON
(pub's name)

Pub's address

☐ **YES Main Entry**　　☐ **YES Lucky Dip**　　☐ **NO don't include**
Please tick one of these boxes to show your verdict, and give reasons and descriptive comments, prices etc

☐ Deserves FOOD award　　☐ Deserves PLACE-TO-STAY award

REPORT ON
(pub's name)

Pub's address

☐ **YES Main Entry**　　☐ **YES Lucky Dip**　　☐ **NO don't include**
Please tick one of these boxes to show your verdict, and give reasons and descriptive comments, prices etc

☐ Deserves FOOD award　　☐ Deserves PLACE-TO-STAY award

☐

THE GOOD PUB GUIDE

The Good Pub Guide
FREEPOST TN1569
WADHURST
E. SUSSEX
TN5 7BR

as apple crumble (£4). Mordue Five Bridge and a couple of guests such as Allendale Bitter and Big Lamp Bitter on handpump, and they've around 30 malt whiskies. More reports on the new regime please. *(Recommended by Brian Brooks, Di and Mike Gillam, Dr Graham Thorpe, Dr and Mrs R G J Telfer, Mart Lawton)*

Free house ~ Licensee Kelly Norman ~ Real ale ~ Bar food (12-2, 6.30-9) ~ (01434) 684338 ~ Children welcome ~ Dogs allowed in bar ~ Live folk second Thurs evening of month ~ Open 12-2.30, 5-11; 12-11 Sat; closed Mon lunchtime except bank hols

LUCKER   NU1631   Map 10
Apple
Village (and pub) well signposted off A1 N of Morpeth; NE70 7JH

Cheerful service and good food have generated strong reports for this village pub on the Duke of Northumberland's estate. The welcoming bar area has some walls stripped to show massive neatly dressed blocks of stone masonry, others painted a restful ochre, and some sturdy padded seats-for-two among other more usual pubby furnishings such as dark country-kitchen chairs and padded banquettes. The large brick-and-stone fireplace has a woodburning stove. Decoration is restrained, and the overall impression is of spacious civilised relaxation. The roomy and big-windowed side dining area on the left is fresh and airy, with flowers on the tables. The enjoyable bar food is given an uplift by quite a few individual touches, and vegetables are carefully cooked: soup (£3.25), sandwiches (from £3.75, toasted from £4.75), ploughman's or quiche of the day (£5.95), trio of fish goujons (£6.95), and asparagus and potato bake or salmon duo with prawns in a marie rose sauce (£8.95) and puddings such as vanilla cheesecake with black cherries or sticky toffee pudding (£3.85). The no smoking restaurant menu includes more ambitious dishes (evenings only). The short well chosen wine list is sensibly priced, with decent wines by the glass; it would be nice if they installed a cask-conditioned ale; piped music, darts, dominoes and board games. The campsite behind the pub is completely separate. *(Recommended by Dr Peter D Smart, Joan York, Michael Doswell, Bill and Sheila McLardy, Sheena W Makin, Mr and Mrs D W Mitchell, Bob and Louise Craft)*

Free house ~ Licensees Jane and Bob Graham ~ Bar food (12-2, 6.30-8.45; 12-8.45 Sun) ~ Restaurant ~ (01668) 213450 ~ Children welcome ~ Dogs allowed in bar ~ Open 12-3, 6.30-11; 12-10.30 Sun; closed Mon

NEW YORK   NZ3269   Map 10
Shiremoor Farm
Middle Engine Lane/Norham Road, off A191 bypass; NE29 8DZ

Former farm buildings have been imaginatively transformed into this large dining pub, which has a covered terrace with good electric heaters making it feasible to sit out even in late autumn and early spring. The spacious interior (all no smoking apart from the bar area) is furnished with a charming mix of interesting and comfortable furniture, a big kelim on the broad flagstones, warmly colourful farmhouse paintwork on the bar counter and several other tables, conical rafters of the former gin-gan, a few farm tools, and good rustic pictures such as mid-West prints, big crisp black and white photographs of country people and modern greek bull sketches. Gentle lighting in several well divided spacious areas cleverly picks up the surface modelling of the pale stone and beam ends. The wide blackboard choice of bar food is served all day, and could include hearty sandwiches (£1.95; hot sandwiches £3.95), starters like soup (£2.95), greek feta salad (£5.25) and tiger prawns (£5.45), with main courses that may typically feature vegetarian quiche (£6.45), and scampi or breast of chicken (£8.45) and beef medallions (£10.95); home-made puddings such as banana and chocolate pudding (from £3.50). Well kept Mordue Workie Ticket, Timothy Taylors Landlord, Theakstons Best and a guest such as Batemans XXXB; decent wines by the glass. The no smoking granary extension is pleasant for families. More reports please. *(Recommended by Mrs Carolyn Dixon, Mart Lawton)*

Free house ~ Licensee C W Kerridge ~ Real ale ~ Bar food (12-10) ~ 0191 2576302 ~
Children welcome away from main bar ~ Open 11-11; 11-10.30 Sun

NEWBURN   NZ1665   Map 10
Keelman ♨ £ ⇌

Grange Road: follow Riverside Country Park brown signs off A6085 (the riverside road
off A1 on Newcastle's W fringes); NE15 8ND

The bar counter's impressive array of eight handpumps here usually dispenses the
full range of the Big Lamp Brewery (itself on the same site), and as this is the
brewery tap the beers are in top condition and at attractive prices. If you're
confused about which one to go for, the neatly dressed staff will happily let you
sample a couple first – but beware of the aptly named Blackout, at 11%, it's very
strong; the Bitter (3.9%) is much easier to quaff. Built originally in 1854 as a
pumping station, and converted in 1996, this granite pub has an easy-going
atmosphere attracting a good mix of customers, the high-ceilinged bar has lofty
arched windows, making it light and airy, and it's not too crowded with tables
(access for wheelchairs is easy). There are more tables in an upper gallery, and the
modern all-glass no smoking conservatory dining area (pleasant at sunset) contrasts
stylishly with the original old building. Service is first-class, the hands-on landlord is
quick to help out when needed, and the whole place is kept spick and span.
Reasonably priced and served in generous helpings, straightforward food includes
soup (£2.25), sandwiches (from £3.70), baked potatoes (£3.75), vegetable lasagne
(£5.75), beef and ale pie or large fish and chips (£6.15), grilled trout (£6.25), and
10oz sirloin steak or a big mixed grill (£9.95); they do an early evening special on
weekdays from 5 till 7 (£4.75 for a selection of their main courses), and Sunday
roasts (£5.75); piped music. There are plenty of picnic-sets, tables and benches out
on the terraces, among flower tubs and beds of shrubs. This is a great base for
walks along the Tyne, with six up-to-date bedrooms in an adjoining block.
*(Recommended by Mike and Lynn Robinson, Liz and Brian Barnard, John Foord,
Michael Doswell, Alex and Claire Pearse, Andy and Jill Kassube, Prof and Mrs Tony Palmer,
T Stone, Mart Lawton, Mr and Mrs Maurice Thompson)*

Own brew ~ Licensee George Story ~ Real ale ~ Bar food (12-9) ~ Restaurant ~ (0191)
267 0772 ~ Children welcome in bar until 9pm and in dining area ~ Open 11-11; 12-10.30
Sun ~ Bedrooms: £45S/£64S

NEWCASTLE UPON TYNE   NZ2563   Map 10
Crown Posada ♨

The Side; off Dean Street, between and below the two high central bridges (A6125 and
A6127); NE1 3JE

Just for its architecture this easy-going and chatty alehouse (the second oldest in the
city) justifies a visit, although being in the centre of things means it can get very full.
A golden crown and magnificent pre-Raphaelite stained-glass windows add
grandeur to an already imposing carved stone façade, while inside highlights
include the elaborate coffered ceiling, stained glass in the counter screens, a line of
gilt mirrors each with a tulip lamp on a curly brass mount matching the great
ceiling candelabra. Fat low-level heating pipes make a popular footrest when the
east wind brings the rain off the North Sea. It's a very long and narrow room,
making quite a bottleneck by the serving counter; beyond that, a long soft green
built-in leather wall seat is flanked by narrow tables. There's a fruit machine, and
an old record player in a wooden cabinet provides mellow background music when
the place is quiet; dominoes. From half a dozen handpumps, Bass and Mordue Five
Bridge and Timothy Taylors Landlord are kept in top condition alongside
continually changing guests from brewers such as Marstons and Wylam. The
atmosphere is very friendly, and a good time to visit is during the week when
regulars sit reading the papers in the front snug; at the weekend it's usually packed,
but even then you'll get a warm welcome from the barmen. They don't do food, but
at lunchtime you can get a sandwich with a packet of crisps for £1.50. It's only a

few minutes' stroll to the castle. *(Recommended by Mike and Lynn Robinson, Eric Larkham, the Didler, P Dawn, Di and Mike Gillam, A Pickering, Pete Baker, Tracey and Stephen Groves, Tim and Ann Newell, Andy and Jill Kassube, Tony and Wendy Hobden, R T and J C Moggridge, Eric Robinson, Jacqueline Pratt)*

Sir John Fitzgerald ~ Licensee Derek Raisbeck ~ Real ale ~ No credit cards ~ (0191) 232 1269 ~ Open 11-11; 7-10.30 Sun; closed Sun lunchtime

Head of Steam @ The Cluny 🍺 £
Lime Street (which runs between A193 and A186 E of centre); NE1 2PQ

Doubling as an art gallery and studio for local artists and craftspeople and next door to the City Farm, this imaginatively converted whisky bottling plant makes an excellent place to sample a range of local beers, and the home-made food is good value too. Its back area has changing exhibitions of their paintings, sculptures and pottery, and for work by visiting artists. The friendly L-shaped bar is trendy and gently bohemian-feeling despite its minimalist décor, with slightly scuffed bare boards, some chrome seating and overhead spotlights. Around seven real ales are on offer, with usually four from local brewers such as Big Lamp, Camerons, Durham, Hadrian & Border, Mordue and Wylam, and three from further afield such as Batemans, Okells or Youngs; also two real ciders on handpump and rotating continental and american beers on tap, lots of bottled world beers, a good range of soft drinks, and a fine row of rums, malt whiskies, vodkas and banana smoothies. Simple bar food, served by cheerful staff, includes soup, sandwiches or toasties (£3), ploughman's, burgers, beef or spinach, chickpea and mushroom chilli (£5), daily specials like thai vegetable curry or crayfish with roasted peppers (£6), with puddings such as fudge cake (£2.50); Sunday roast (£6.50); it's all home-made so there may be a wait. A raised area looking down on the river (with much redevelopment work afoot) has comfortable seating including settees, with daily papers and local arts magazines. A separate room has a stage for live bands and comedy nights; disabled access and facilities, fruit machine and well reproduced piped music. To get here – opposite the Ship on Lime Street look out for a cobbled bank leading down to the Ouseburn, by the Byker city farm, and stretching down here, the pub (known to everyone locally as the Cluny) is below the clutch of bridges. *(Recommended by Mike and Lynn Robinson, Eric Larkham, Blaise Vyner, Tracey and Stephen Groves)*

Head of Steam ~ Licensee Dave Campbell ~ Real ale ~ Bar food (11.30-9) ~ (0191) 230 4474 ~ Children welcome until 7.30pm ~ Live bands from 8pm ~ Open 11.30-1am; 12-12 Sun

NEWTON-BY-THE-SEA   NU2424   Map 10
Ship
Village signposted off B1339 N of Alnwick; Low Newton – paid parking 200 metres up road on right, just before village (none in village); NE66 3EL

You'll need to book in the evening to eat at this popular pub, which has an enchanting coastal setting, in a row of converted fishermen's cottages, and looking across a sloping village green to a sandy beach just beyond. We recommend a phone call before your visit anyway as the opening times can vary, particularly in winter (but they are open every lunchtime except Christmas Day). Brilliantly simple cooking lets the marvellous quality of the fresh local, and quite often organic, ingredients shine through; service can be slow at times. A short lunchtime menu (when it's likely you'll be in the company of local walkers and their dogs) includes delicious local crab sandwiches (£3.50), warm goats cheese ciabatta or local kippers (£4.50), fishcakes and salad (£4.75), free-range ham stottie (£5.75) and ploughman's with local unpasteurised cheese (£6.95). In the evening, when the atmosphere shifts a gear gently, the menu might include crab salad (£9.50), venison rump steak with red wine and peppercorn sauce or grilled wild sea trout (£11.50), monkfish baked with coriander and red peppers (£13.50), scallops (£14.50), or local lobster (from £18.50), with puddings such as fruit crumble, sticky toffee pudding or good local ice-creams (£3.75). The plainly furnished bare-boards bar on the right has nautical charts on its dark pink walls, beams and hop bines. Another simple room on the left has some bright modern pictures on stripped-stone walls, and a woodburning stove in its stone fireplace; darts, dominoes. It's very quiet here in winter when they have just one or two local real ales. By contrast, they really only just cope when queues build up on hot summer days, and the beer range extends to up to four from mostly local brewers such as Hadrian & Border and Wylam; also decent wines, an espresso machine (colourful coffee cups, good hot chocolate), several malt whiskies and good soft drinks. Out in the corner of the square are some tables among pots of flowers, with picnic-sets over on the grass. There's no nearby parking, but there's a car park up the hill. *(Recommended by Joan York, Dr D J and Mrs S C Walker, Susan Hart, Ian Thurman, Comus and Sarah Elliott, the Didler, Will and Kay Adie, Mike and Sue Loseby, Di and Mike Gillam, Tim and Suzy Bower)*

Free house ~ Licensee Christine Forsyth ~ Real ale ~ Bar food (12-2.30, 7-8 Tues in school hols and Weds-Sat) ~ No credit cards ~ (01665) 576262 ~ Children welcome ~ Dogs welcome ~ Live bands during some weekends and bank hols ~ Open 11-11 in school holidays (phone for other periods)

NEWTON-ON-THE-MOOR NU1605 Map 10
Cook & Barker Arms 🍴 🛏
Village signposted from A1 Alnwick—Felton; NE65 9JY

There's a buoyant mood among the contented diners at this friendly stone-built inn, and it's a very comfortable place to stay. Though most people are here for the generously served food, the relaxed and unfussy long beamed bar feels distinctly pubby, with stripped stone and partly panelled walls, brocade-seated settles around oak-topped tables, brasses, a highly polished oak servery, and a lovely fire at one end with a coal-effect gas fire at the other. A no smoking eating area has oak-topped tables with comfortable leather chairs, and french windows leading on to the terrace; the lounge is also no smoking; piped music. The well cooked changing bar menu could include cream of vegetable soup (£2.95), salmon, prawn and crab risotto (£4.95), roast loin of pork or roast beef (£7.95), fried chicken with stilton, bacon and leeks (£8.25), mixed grill (£9.75), scallops, squid and tiger prawns in chilli, garlic and spinach butter (£10.95) and puddings (£3.95); at lunchtimes on Monday and Tuesday and from 5pm to 7pm on Wednesday and Thursday you can get two courses for £8; they also have more elaborate restaurant food. Up to four ales on handpump rotate between Bass, Black Sheep, Fullers London Pride, Marstons Pedigree, Theakstons XB and Best, and Timothy Taylors Landlord; their extensive wine list includes a dozen by the glass, and they've also local bottled beer, and quite a few malt whiskies. *(Recommended by Dr Peter D Smart, P and J Shapley, Joan York, R M Corlett, MJVK, Walter and Susan Rinaldi-Butcher, Comus and Sarah Elliott, Mr and Mrs M Porter, Mrs Jennifer Hurst, Tony Baldwin, Dr and Mrs R G J Telfer, Glenys and John Roberts, Christine and Phil Young, Mart Lawton)*

Free house ~ Licensee Phil Farmer ~ Real ale ~ Bar food (12-2, 6-10) ~ Restaurant (12-2, 7-9) ~ (01665) 575234 ~ Children welcome ~ Open 11-11; 12-10.30 Sun ~ Bedrooms: £47B/£75B

RENNINGTON NU2119 Map 10
Masons Arms 🛏
Stamford Cott; B1340 NE of Alnwick; NE66 3RX

A good place to stay for exploring the nearby coast, the bedrooms in this immaculately well cared for pub are in an adjacent stable block and annexe, and the breakfasts are good. The beamed lounge bar is pleasantly modernised and comfortable, with wheelback and mate's chairs around solid wood tables on a patterned carpet, plush bar stools, and plenty of pictures (some may be for sale), photographs and brass. The dining rooms have pine panelling and wrought-iron wall lights; piped classical music; the bar (until food finishes at 10pm) and dining area are no smoking. Hadrian & Border Secret Kingdom and a couple of guests such as Hadrian & Border RAF Boulmer and Northumberland St Patrick's Special on handpump. Straightforward bar food includes soup (£2.95), craster kipper pâté or jalapeno peppers stuffed with cream cheese (£4.75), curry of the day (£7.50), lemon sole (£8.25), roast duck with orange sauce (£9.95) and steak (from £12.95). There are sturdy rustic tables on the little front lavender-surrounded terrace, and picnic-sets at the back. *(Recommended by P and J Shapley, S and N McLean, Joan York, D Digby, Dr D J and Mrs S C Walker, Tony Baldwin, Alex and Claire Pearse, Michael J Caley, D S and J M Jackson, Bill Strang, Stuart Pearson)*

Free house ~ Licensees Bob and Alison Culverwell ~ Real ale ~ Bar food (12-2, 6.30-9) ~ Restaurant ~ (01665) 577275 ~ Children allowed in family and dining rooms ~ Dogs allowed in bedrooms ~ Open 12-11(10.30 Sun) ~ Bedrooms: £55B/£70B

ROMALDKIRK NY9922 Map 10
Rose & Crown ㉕ ★ ⑪ ♀ 🛏
Just off B6277; DL12 9EB

This gracious 18th-c country coaching inn in Upper Teesdale continues with its winning ways for civilised comfort, attentive and professional service and accomplished cooking. From lunchtime and evening menus that change about every six weeks (you do need to book), imaginative dishes might include lunchtime sandwiches (from £5.50) and ploughman's (£7.95), as well as soup (£4.25), smoked salmon soufflé (£5.75), welsh rarebit or creamed scrambled eggs with smoked salmon (£7.95), potato gnocchi gratin with blue wensleydale cheese (£9.50), fried pink pigeon with chestnut risotto (£10.50), steak, kidney and mushroom pie (£10.75), grilled rump of venison (£13.95) and halibut baked with cotherstone cheese, cream and red onion marmalade (£14.50), with puddings such as toasted almond and sherry trifle or chocolate and orange torte (£4.25); they also have a children's menu. The enthusiastic licensees even make their own marmalades, jams, chutneys and bread. The traditional cosy beamed bar has old-fashioned seats facing a warming log fire, a Jacobean oak settle, lots of brass and copper, a grandfather clock, and gin traps, old farm tools, and black and white pictures of Romaldkirk on the walls. Black Sheep and Theakstons Best are on handpump alongside 14 wines by the glass. The smart brasserie-style Crown Room (bar food is served in here) has large cartoons of French waiters on dark red walls, a grey carpet and smart high-back chairs. The hall has farm tools, wine maps and other interesting prints, along with a photograph (taken by a customer) of the Hale Bopp comet over Romaldkirk church. There's also an oak-panelled restaurant. Lovely in summer, tables outside look out over the village green, still with its original stocks and water pump. The village is close to the excellent Bowes Museum and the High Force waterfall, and has an interesting old church. *(Recommended by Pat and Stewart Gordon, Margaret and Roy Randle, Alex and Claire Pearse, Brian Brooks, Tony Baldwin, Lynda and Trevor Smith, Jack Clark, Mike Turner, Mike and Sue Loseby)*

Free house ~ Licensees Christopher and Alison Davy ~ Real ale ~ Bar food (12-1.45, 6.30-9.30) ~ Restaurant ~ (01833) 650213 ~ Children welcome but must be over 6 in restaurant ~ Dogs allowed in bar and bedrooms ~ Open 11-3, 5.30-11; 12-3, 7-10.30 Sun; closed 24-26 Dec ~ Bedrooms: £75B/£126B

SEAHOUSES NU2232 Map 10
Olde Ship ㉕ ★ 🍴 🛏
Just off B1340, towards harbour; NE68 7RD

Placed above the village's little harbour, the bar in this splendidly atmospheric hotel pays homage to the sea and seafarers with its assembly of maritime memorabilia. It's been in the hands of the same family for a century, and the collection has steadily accumulated. Besides lots of other shiny brass fittings, ship's instruments and equipment, and a knotted anchor made by local fishermen, there are sea pictures and model ships, including fine ones of the North Sunderland lifeboat, and Seahouses' lifeboat the *Grace Darling*. There's also a model of the *Forfarshire*, the paddle steamer whose passengers Grace Darling went to rescue in 1838 (you can read more of the story in the pub), and even the ship's nameboard. One clear glass window looks out across the harbour to the Farne Islands, and as dusk falls you can watch the Longstones lighthouse shine across the fading evening sky. The bar is gently lit by stained-glass sea picture windows, and it has an open fire in winter. Even the floor is scrubbed ship's decking and, if it's working, an anemometer takes wind speed readings from the top of the chimney. The low-beamed Cabin Bar and the restaurant are no smoking; piped music, TV. Up to eight ales are well kept on handpump – Bass, Black Sheep, Courage Directors, Greene King Old Speckled Hen and Ruddles County, Hadrian & Border Farne Island and Theakstons Best, with a guest such as Timothy Taylors Landlord; also around 30 malt whiskies and a good choice of wines. Very tasty bar food, from a changing menu, could include a well liked crab soup (£4), lunchtime main courses like beef stovies or fish stew (£7), chicken and mushroom casserole, fried plaice, smoked fish chowder or lamb curry (£8.50), with puddings such as chocolate trifle or steamed lemon pudding (£4.50). The pub is not really suitable for children though there is a little family room, and along with walkers, they are welcome on the battlemented side terrace (you'll even find fishing memorabilia out here). This and a sun lounge look out on the harbour. You can book boat trips to the Farne Islands Bird Sanctuary at the harbour, and there are bracing coastal walks, particularly to Bamburgh, Grace Darling's birthplace. *(Recommended by Ian and Jane Irving, Bruce and Sharon Eden, Joan York, Michael Doswell, Dr and Mrs T E Hothersall, Dr D J and Mrs S C Walker, Paul and Ursula Randall, Ian Thurman, Richard Tosswill, Comus and Sarah Elliott, N R White, Alan and Paula McCully, P Dawn, Will and Kay Adie, Christopher Turner, Di and Mike Gillam, John Robertson, Brian and Janet Ainscough, Mike and Lynn Robinson, Mark Walker, Dr and Mrs R G J Telfer, Peter D La Farge, Andrew Storey, the Didler, Keith and Chris O'Neill, Karen and Graham Oddey, DFL)*

Free house ~ Licensees Alan and Jean Glen ~ Real ale ~ Bar food ~ Restaurant ~ (01665) 720200 ~ Children in family room ~ Open 11(12 Sun)-11; 12-10.3 Sun ~ Bedrooms: £53S/£106B

STANNERSBURN   NY7286   Map 10

Pheasant

Kielder Water road signposted off B6320 in Bellingham; NE48 1DD

In the tranquil North Tyne Valley, with the vast plantations of Kielder Forest all around and very close to Kielder Water, this spotlessly kept and extremely welcoming village local has a streamside garden with picnic-sets, and a pony paddock behind. The low-beamed comfortable traditional lounge (no smoking) has ranks of old local photographs on stripped stone and panelling, red patterned carpets, and upholstered stools ranged along the counter. A separate public bar is similar but simpler, and opens into a further cosy seating area with beams and panelling. The evening sees a good mix of visitors and locals, when the small no smoking dining room can get quite crowded. Greene King Old Speckled Hen, Timothy Taylors Landlord and Wylam Gold are served by handpump or air pressure, and they've just over 30 malt whiskies, and a decent reasonably priced wine list. Home-made bar food could include lunchtime sandwiches (from £2.75) and ploughman's with several northumbrian cheeses (£7.50), also garlic chicken breast salad or lasagne (£7.50), with specials like cider-baked gammon with cumberland sauce (£7.95; the evening price is £10.50). In the evening, you can also choose from a handful of more elaborate dishes such as red onion and goats cheese tart (£4.95), roast northumbrian lamb with rosemary and redcurrant jus or home-made game pie (£10.95), grilled bass with lemon and parsley butter (£11.95) or confit of duck breast with port and raspberry glaze (£14.25). Puddings include brioche and marmalade bread and butter pudding (£3.95); roast Sunday lunch (£7.25); piped music. *(Recommended by Dr Peter Crawshaw, Dr Peter D Smart, Pat and Stewart Gordon, Richard and Karen Holt, Les and Sandra Brown, Alex and Claire Pearse, Lawrence Pearse, R Macfarlane, Ann and Stephen Saunders, Mark and Ruth Brock, David and Pauline Hambley)*

Free house ~ Licensees Walter and Robin Kershaw ~ Real ale ~ Bar food ~ Restaurant ~
(01434) 240382 ~ Children welcome until 9pm ~ Dogs allowed in bedrooms ~
Open 11-3, 6.30-11; 12-3, 7-11 Sun; closed Mon, Tues Nov-Mar ~ Bedrooms: £40S/£70S

STANNINGTON   NZ2279   Map 10
Ridley Arms
Village signposted just off A1 S of Morpeth; NE61 6EL

With food served all day, this efficiently run and relaxed pub ticks over nicely even
at the busiest of times. It's arranged into several separate areas, each slightly
different in mood and style from its neighbours. The front is a proper bar area, with
darts and a fruit machine, and stools along the counter. The beamed dining areas,
largely no smoking, lead back from here, with a second bar counter, comfortable
armchairs and upright chairs around shiny dark wood tables on polished boards or
carpet, with portraits and cartoons on cream, panelled or stripped stone walls,
careful lighting and some horsey statuettes. Six real ales on handpump feature Black
Sheep, Caledonian Deuchars and Timothy Taylors Landlord along with four guests
from brewers such as Greene King, Hebridean and Rudgate, and they've several
wines by the glass. Generously served bar food includes soup (£3.50), good
sandwiches (from £3.95), mussels cooked in cider (£4.50 starter, £8.50 main
course), asparagus tart with poached egg (£4.50 starter, £7.50 main course),
sausage and mash or fried haddock (£7.95), 10oz sirloin (£15), daily specials like
butternut and goats cheese risotto (£8) or calves liver (£11); puddings (from £4.25);
Sunday lunch (£8.25). Disabled access is good; unobtrusive piped music, games
machine, darts and dominoes. There are tables outside on a terrace. *(Recommended
by P Price, Dr Peter D Smart, Val and Alan Green, Comus and Sarah Elliott, Gerry Miller,
Keith Cohen, Mr and Mrs D S Price, Derek and Sylvia Stephenson)*

Sir John Fitzgerald ~ Managers Lynn and Gary Reilly ~ Real ale ~ Bar food (12-9.30(9 Sun))
~ (01670) 789216 ~ Children welcome ~ Open 11.30-11; 10.30-10.30 Sun

WARK   NY8677   Map 10
Battlesteads 🍺 ⌦
B6320 N of Hexham; NE48 3LS

This stone-built inn is flourishing under new licensees, and makes a splendid stop
on this scenic North Tynedale alternative to the A68 route north. It's warmly
welcoming, with a relaxed unhurried atmosphere (no piped music), and good
changing local ales such as Black Sheep, Durham Magus and Wylam Gold Tankard
from handpumps on the heavily carved dark oak bar counter. The nicely restored
carpeted bar has a log fire, with horsebrasses around the fireplace and on the low
beams, comfortable seats including some dark blue wall banquettes, floral
wallpaper above its dark dado, and double doors to a no smoking panelled inner
snug. The good value food uses prime local ingredients, including game, lamb from
their own sheep, and aberdeen angus beef. Besides sandwiches, it might include
soup (£3.25), baby sardines on salad (£3.95), fried lambs liver on toast (£4.25), cod
and chips or salmon baked with cajun spices with sweet chilli sauce (£8.95), lamb
joint with leek, rosemary and redcurrant jus (£11.50) and sirloin steak (£11.50).
The puddings, such as limoncella and strawberry panna cotta or apple and
blackberry pancake (£3.75) are particularly good, and sensibly they don't do
'children's dishes' but are happy to serve children with smaller helpings off the
normal menu. You can eat in the bar, or a restaurant beyond the snug. They do
good coffee (and a great breakfast if you're staying), and service is cheerful. Some
of the bedrooms are on the ground floor (with disabled access). There are picnic-
sets on a terrace in the walled garden, and fine walks nearby. *(Recommended by BOB)*

Free house ~ Licensees Richard and Dee Slade ~ Real ale ~ Bar food (12-3, 7-10) ~
Restaurant ~ (01434) 230209 ~ Children welcome ~ Dogs allowed in bar and bedrooms
~ Open 10(11 Sun)-11; 12-3, 6-11 in winter ~ Bedrooms: £45S/£80B

WELDON BRIDGE   NZ1399   Map 10

Anglers Arms 🛏

B6344, just off A697; village signposted with Rothbury off A1 N of Morpeth; NE65 8AX

Attached to this hotel is a former railway dining car that now functions as a light, airy no smoking restaurant, with crisp white linen and a pink carpet. Whether you dine in there or in the less formal surroundings of the bar, you'll need a very healthy appetite to eat your way through the massive helpings. Dishes might include home-made chicken liver pâté (£5.45), prawn and smoked salmon salad (£6.25), cod and chips or scampi (£7.95), mince and dumplings or northumbrian sausage casserole (£8.25), steak and ale pie (£8.75), chicken stuffed with asparagus and with mushroom sauce (£9.25), halibut (£11.75), and mixed grill or sirloin steak (£13.95), with puddings (£4.75); children's menu (£4.45). Nicely lit and comfortable, the traditional turkey-carpeted bar is divided into two parts: cream walls on the right, and oak panelling and some shiny black beams hung with copper pans on the left, with a grandfather clock and sofa by the coal fire, staffordshire cats and other antique ornaments on its mantelpiece, old fishing and other country prints, some in heavy gilt frames, a profusion of other fishing memorabilia, and some taxidermy. Some of the tables are lower than you'd expect for eating, but their chairs have short legs to match – different, and rather engaging. Timothy Taylors Landlord is on handpump alongside a couple of guests such as Black Sheep and Greene King Old Speckled Hen; also decent wines and an espresso machine. There are tables in the attractive garden with a good play area that includes an assault course; they have rights to fishing on a mile of the River Coquet just across the road. *(Recommended by Dr and Mrs S Donald, Comus and Sarah Elliott, Dr and Mrs R G J Telfer, Di and Mike Gillam, GSB, Dr Peter D Smart, David and Heather Stephenson, Mart Lawton, David and Sue Smith)*

Free house ~ Licensee John Young ~ Real ale ~ Bar food (12-9.30) ~ Restaurant ~ (01665) 570271 ~ Children welcome ~ Dogs allowed in bedrooms ~ Open 11-11; 12-10.30 Sun ~ Bedrooms: £37.50S/£60S

LUCKY DIP

Besides the fully inspected pubs, you might like to try these Lucky Dips recommended to us and described by readers (if you do, please send us reports: www.goodguides.co.uk).

ALLENHEADS [NY8545]

☆ *Allenheads Inn* NE47 9HJ [just off B6295]: Well placed high in wild former lead-mining country (and on the C2C Sustrans cycle route), this country local has new licensees again, too new for us to give a definite rating – so we'd be grateful for more reports; it's had Black Sheep, Greene King Abbot and local guest beers, straightforward pubby food at low prices, still some of the bric-a-brac which it used to be famous for, no smoking music room and country dining room, and darts and pool in the games room; piped music, TV; children welcome, tables out beside some agricultural antiques, pleasant bedrooms, open all day *(LYM)*

ALNMOUTH [NU2511]

Hope & Anchor NE66 2RA [Northumberland St]: Friendly bar and pleasant beamed dining room, reasonably priced home-made food inc imaginative dishes, Black Sheep ales, helpful cheerful young staff; dogs welcome, quietly appealing coastal village, attractive beaches, good coastal walks, cl winter wkdy lunchtimes *(Bill and Sheila McLardy, B Christie, Alan and Paula McCully)*

☆ *Red Lion* NE66 2RJ [Northumberland St]: Attractive 16th-c inn, relaxed and unpretentious, with cheerful staff, cosy old-fashioned panelled locals' bar full of theatre bills and memorabilia, real ales such as Black Sheep, Houston and Orkney, good choice of mainly new world wines by the glass, enjoyable modestly priced pubby food (not winter Mon evening) inc daily fresh fish, front bistro-style restaurant; may be piped music; children and dogs welcome, neat garden by alley with raised deck looking over Aln estuary, comfortable bedrooms, generous breakfast, open all day Sun *(Comus and Sarah Elliott, N R White, Alan and Paula McCully, Michael Doswell, Dr Roger Smith, Judy Nicholson, Bill and Sheila McLardy, Derek and Sylvia Stephenson)*

Saddle NE66 2RA [Northumberland St (B1338)]: Plainly furnished stone-built hotel rambling through several spacious eating areas, popular with older folk for wide choice of good value generous pubby food, choice of helpings size, pleasant efficient service even when busy, real ales such as Greene King Old Speckled Hen and Theakstons Best, well equipped games room, no smoking restaurant; unobtrusive piped music, parking may be a problem; children welcome, tables outside, open all day Sat, bedrooms *(Paul and Ursula Randall, N R White, Alan and Paula McCully, LYM, Dr Peter D Smart, Bill and Sheila McLardy)*

ALNWICK [NU1813]

John Bull NE66 1UY [Howick St]: Real ale pub with great changing range, also bottled imports and dozens of malt whiskies; cl wkdy lunchtime, open all day wknds *(the Didler)*

Olde Cross NE66 1JG [Narrowgate]: Unpretentious pub with friendly staff and customers, Hadrian & Border Farne Island, bar food; dogs and children welcome *(Dr D J and Mrs S C Walker)*

Plough NE66 1PN: High-ceilinged two-bar Victorian pub with friendly locals and staff, enjoyable home-made food, changing real ales, popular restaurant; bedrooms *(the Didler)*

BAMBURGH [NU1834]

Lord Crewe Arms NE69 7BL [Front St]: Small hotel prettily set in charming coastal village dominated by Norman castle, log fire and dark furniture inc some settles in two carpeted bar rooms, Bass and a guest beer such as Charles Wells Bombardier from penny-studded bar, good choice of wines by the glass, short choice of lunchtime bar food from sandwiches to monster fish and chips, good food in separate modern restaurant; dogs and children welcome, suntrap terrace, short walk from splendid sandy beach, comfortable bedrooms, good breakfast esp kippers *(Kevin Thorpe, Michael Dandy, LYM)*

☆ *Victoria* NE69 7BP [Front St]: Substantial hotel with lots of mirrors and pictures in comfortable two-part panelled bar, peaceful, light and airy, with smart more upmarket no smoking brasserie beyond, good quickly prepared food all day from sandwiches up, two rotating real ales from Black Sheep and/or Mordue, good wines by the glass, friendly young staff, young children's playroom; comfortable bedrooms (popular with coach parties), lovely setting, open all day *(Michael Dandy, Comus and Sarah Elliott, Michael Doswell)*

BARDON MILL [NY7466]

Twice Brewed NE47 7AN [Military Rd (B6318)]: Large pub with good choice of beers and malt whiskies, imaginative food, friendly bar staff; well placed for fell-walkers, and major Wall sites; warm bedrooms *(John and Gloria Isaacs)*

BEAMISH [NZ2153]

Beamish Mary DH9 0QH [off A693 signed No Place and Cooperative Villas, S of museum]: Up to ten good changing ales in friendly down-to-earth pub with 1960s-feel mix of furnishings, bric-a-brac, 1920s/30s memorabilia and Aga, Durham NUM banner in games room, attentive helpful staff, interesting choice of good value very generous bar food, good Sun lunch (best to book), coal fires; piped music, live music most nights in converted stables concert room, annual beer

festival; children allowed until evening, bedrooms *(Mark Walker, Mr and Mrs Maurice Thompson)*

BELFORD [NU1033]

Black Swan NE70 7ND [village signed off A1 S of Berwick; Market Pl]: Unpretentious beamed local with three friendly and comfortable olde-worlde bars (one at the back quieter), quick polite service, Jennings real ale, good plain home cooking in bar and dining room inc good sandwiches and good value three-course lunch, open fire; dogs welcome, bedrooms *(Dr D J and Mrs S C Walker)*

Blue Bell NE70 7NE [off A1 S of Berwick; Market Pl]: Substantial old coaching inn (hotel rather than pub) with decent fairly priced food from sandwiches up in pubby bar, log fire, friendly service, good choice of wines and whiskies, may be Theakstons Best, more elaborate food choice in either of two recently refurbished restaurant areas; piped music; children welcome, big garden, pleasant bedrooms *(P and J Shapley, LYM, Comus and Sarah Elliott, W K Wood, Dr and Mrs R G J Telfer, Bob and Louise Craft)*

BELSAY [NZ1277]

☆ *Highlander* NE20 0DN [A696 S of village]: Comfortable and roomy country dining pub, generous good value food from good lunchtime sandwiches up in extensively refurbished side bar and open-plan dining area, nice plain wood tables, plenty of nooks and corners for character, reasonable prices, welcoming helpful service, Black Sheep, Hadrian & Border and Timothy Taylors ales, good log fires, separate locals' bar; unobtrusive piped music; open all day, handy for Belsay Hall and Gardens *(Dr Peter D Smart, Comus and Sarah Elliott)*

BERWICK-UPON-TWEED [NT9952]

☆ *Barrels* TD15 1ES [Bridge St]: Convivial pub with thorough-going nautical décor in bar, car memorabilia and other bric-a-brac, Beatles pictures and eccentric furniture in lounge; good choice of real ales and malt whiskies, lunchtime filled rolls and imaginative evening food (perhaps not winter) from snacks and tapas to main dishes, friendly accommodating staff; live music downstairs, good juke box; open all day, cl midweek lunchtimes in winter *(Mike and Lynn Robinson, the Didler, Michael Butler)*

☆ *Foxtons* TD15 1AB [Hide Hill]: More chatty and comfortable two-level wine bar than pub, with wide choice of good imaginative food, prompt friendly service, real ales such as Caledonian Deuchars IPA and 80/- and Timothy Taylors Landlord as well as good range of wines, whiskies and coffees, lively side bistro; busy, so worth booking evenings, open all day, cl Sun *(John and Sylvia Harrop, Ian and Nita Cooper, Michael Butler, Comus and Sarah Elliott)*

Pilot TD15 1LZ [Low Green]: Small beamed and panelled bar full of old nautical photographs and knick-knacks, comfortable back lounge, Hadrian & Border and guest beers, welcoming landlady; garden tables, bedrooms, open all day Fri-Sun and summer *(the Didler)*

BOULMER [NU2614]

Fishing Boat NE66 3BP: Refurbished under new landlord, with pubby snacks and bar food wkdys, roast on Sun, Black Sheep and Hadrian & Border Farne Island; some tables outside, those at the back overlooking the sea – nice spot on Craster—Alnmouth coast walk *(Comus and Sarah Elliott)*

BOWES [NY9913]

☆ *Ancient Unicorn* DL12 9HL: Substantial stone inn with some 17th-c parts and interesting *Nicholas Nickleby* connection, warmly welcoming licensees who look after their real ales carefully (spring beer festival), good value generous fresh food from sandwiches and well filled baked potatoes to steak, pleasant atmosphere in spacious and comfortable open-plan bar with small but hot open fire, coffee shop; good-sized clean bedrooms in converted stables block around big cobbled courtyard *(Sarah and Peter Gooderham, Hilary Forrest, LYM, Jack Clark)*

CHATTON [NU0528]

☆ *Percy Arms* NE66 5PS [B6348 E of Wooller]: Stone-built inn with real ales such as Brakspears and Jennings, plenty of malt whiskies, cheerful efficient staff, popular food in bar and attractive panelled dining room from lunchtime baguettes up, lounge bar extending through arch, public bar with games; piped music; children in good family area and dining room, picnic-sets on small front lawn, bedrooms (12 miles of private fishing) *(Joan York, D Digby, Di and Mike Gillam, LYM, Bob and Louise Craft)*

CHESTER-LE-STREET [NZ2649]

Church Mouse DH2 3RJ [Front St (A167 S, Chester Moor)]: Well run and welcoming Vintage Inn, good helpings of filling food, good range of wines by the glass, efficient young staff, log fire, olde-worlde décor; tables out among attractive flower tubs, bedrooms in attached Innkeepers Lodge *(John Wooll, Dr Peter D Smart)*

CHRISTON BANK [NU2123]

Blink Bonny NE66 3ES: Newly refurbished country pub with enjoyable generous food inc fresh local fish and good Sun lunch, open fires; dogs and children welcome *(Dr D J and Mrs S C Walker)*

CORBRIDGE [NY9964]

Angel NE45 5LA [Main Street]: Small 17th-c hotel, no smoking at least at lunchtime, with good fresh food (not cheap by northern standards) from sandwiches to stylish restaurant meals, large modern bar and adjoining plush panelled lounge, Black Sheep and two local guest beers, good wines and coffees, prompt friendly service; big-screen TV; pleasant bedrooms, nr lovely bridge over River Tyne *(Michael Butler, LYM, Susan and John Douglas, Michael Doswell)*

Black Bull NE45 5AT [Middle St]: Neatly kept traditional pub with rambling linked rooms, largely no smoking, reasonably priced food all day from sandwiches and light lunches up,

brisk friendly service, four changing ales inc Black Sheep and Greene King IPA, good attractively priced wine choice, roaring fire, comfortable mix of seating inc traditional settles in stone-floored low-ceilinged bar; open all day *(Tony and Maggie Harwood, Michael Butler, John Foord, Gerry Miller, Peter and Eleanor Kenyon)*

☆ *Errington Arms* NE45 5QB [B6318/A68, N]: This friendly 18th-c stone-built pub, a very popular main entry, with lovely décor, good imaginative bistro-style food, decent wines and two or three real ales, was badly damaged by a fire in 2006; rebuilding work was under way as we went to press, and we look forward to its reopening *(LYM)*

☆ *Robin Hood* NE18 0LL [East Wallhouses, Military Rd (B6318 5 miles NE)]: Friendly and unpretentious, useful Hadrian's Wall stop, with generous reasonably priced food from good sandwiches to fish, steaks and hefty mixed grills, quick service even when busy, local real ales such as High House and Wylam, good short wine choice, great views from bay window in beamed lounge with blazing fires, lots of bric-a-brac and interesting carved settles, good-sized candlelit back restaurant, daily papers; piped music *(Michael Doswell, Gerry Miller)*

CRAMLINGTON [NZ2373]

Snowy Owl NE23 8AU [Blagdon Lane]: Large comfortable Vintage Inn, beams, flagstones, hop bines, stripped stone and terracotta paintwork, soft lighting and an interesting mix of furnishings and decorations, good choice of wines, Bass, reliable food inc popular Sun lunch, friendly efficient service, daily papers; may be piped music; bedrooms *(Dr Peter D Smart, Michael Doswell)*

CRASTER [NU2519]

Jolly Fisherman NE66 3TR [off B1339, NE of Alnwick]: Simple friendly take-us-as-you-find-us local in great spot, with picture window and picnic-sets on grass behind giving sea views over harbour and towards Dunstanburgh Castle (lovely clifftop walk); real ales such as Black Sheep and Greene King Old Speckled Hen, crab sandwiches, crab soup, seafood from smokery opp, games area with pool and juke box; children and dogs welcome, open all day in summer *(Dr D J and Mrs S C Walker, LYM, the Didler, Derek and Sylvia Stephenson, Elspeth Borthwick)*

CRAWCROOK [NZ1363]

Rising Sun NE40 4EE [Bank Top]: Roomy well refurbished suburban pub, bright décor, huge choice of reasonably priced usual food (all day Fri-Sun), quickly changing real ales from small breweries, cheerful staff, long bar with steps up to lounge, pool room, dining area and conservatory; neatly kept garden, open all day *(John Foord)*

CROOKHAM [NT9138]

Blue Bell TD12 4SH [Pallinsburn; A697 Wooler—Cornhill]: Small traditional bar, separate lounge and smart comfortably carpeted L-shaped dining area with enjoyable home-made food, friendly unpretentious atmosphere, good service, real ale; bedrooms, handy for Flodden Field (*N R White*)

DARLINGTON [NZ2814]

Quaker Coffee House DL3 7QF [Mechanics Yard, High Row (narrow passage by Binns)]: Small, narrow and cheerful, in one of town's most ancient buildings, cellar-bar feel from dim lighting and bare bricks (not to mention Ethel the ghost), nine interesting changing real ales and a farm cider, friendly staff, daily papers and magazines, bargain lunchtime food (not Sun or Tues) in upstairs restaurant with good choice of wines; lively bands Weds, open all day (not Sun lunchtime) (*John G Reed*)

DURHAM [NZ2642]

Colpitts DH1 4EG [Colpitts Terr/Hawthorn Terr]: Basic two-bar pub, friendly local atmosphere lubricated by particularly cheap Sam Smiths, sandwiches, open fires, pool; can be smoky, TV and machines, folk music most nights; seats out in little yard, open all day (*the Didler*)

Court Inn DH1 3AW [Court Lane]: Unpretentious traditional town pub with good generous home-made food all day from sandwiches to steaks and late-evening bargains, real ales such as Bass, Marstons Pedigree and Mordue, extensive no smoking stripped brick eating area, no mobile phones; bustling in term-time with students and teachers, piped pop music; seats outside, open all day (*BB, Pete Baker, Mr and Mrs Maurice Thompson*)

☆ *Dun Cow* DH1 3HN [Old Elvet]: Very welcoming and unspoilt traditional town pub in pretty 16th-c black and white timbered cottage, tiny chatty front bar with wall benches, corridor linking it to long narrow back lounge with banquettes, machines etc (can be packed with students), particularly well kept Castle Eden and other ales such as Boddingtons and local Hill Island, good value basic lunchtime snacks, friendly staff; piped music, can get smoky; children welcome, open all day Mon-Sat, Sun too in summer (*N R White, LYM, the Didler, Pete Baker, Tracey and Stephen Groves, Barry and Anne, C Sale*)

Stonebridge DH1 3RX [Stonebridge]: Welcoming rustic pub with conservatory, Black Sheep and Hop Back Summer Lightning, food inc Sun lunch (*Mr and Mrs Maurice Thompson*)

Woodman DH1 1QW: Unpretentious mainly no smoking local, good range of Durham and changing regional ales, pool; no children, juke box; tables out behind, open all day (*C Sale*)

EBCHESTER [NZ1054]

☆ *Derwent Walk* DH8 0SX [Ebchester Hill (B6309 outside)]: Friendly and interesting pub by the Gateshead—Consett walk for which it's named, wide range of consistently good value home-made food from unusual hot sandwiches through interesting dishes of the day to steaks, full Jennings range kept well and a guest beer, good wine range, good log fire and appealing old photographs, conservatory with fine Derwent Valley views; walkers welcome, pleasant heated terrace (*Andy and Jill Kassube, Michael Doswell, Prof and Mrs Tony Palmer*)

EDMONDBYERS [NZ0150]

Punch Bowl DH8 9NL: Homely and unpretentious, with welcoming landlord, Black Sheep, good range of reasonably priced bar food, big L-shaped bar with huge leather settee, pleasant conservatory restaurant, pool room popular with young people (their music may be loud); bedrooms with own bathrooms (*John Foord*)

ELLINGHAM [NU1625]

☆ *Pack Horse* NE67 5HA [signed off A1 N of Alnwick]: Compact stone-built country pub, neat and friendly, with modestly priced fresh food using local produce from ciabattas and substantial sandwiches up, wider evening choice, Black Sheep, good coffee, quick friendly attentive service, beams with a forest of jugs, may be local honey for sale, pretty dining room; bedrooms, peaceful village (*Comus and Sarah Elliott*)

ELWICK [NZ4532]

McOrville TS27 3EF [¼ mile off A19 W of Hartlepool]: Open-plan no smoking dining pub doing well under current licensees, good blackboard food, Black Sheep and a changing ale such as Caledonian Deuchars IPA, Shepherd Neame Spitfire or Timothy Taylors Landlord, carved panelling, slippers provided for walkers (*JHBS*)

ETAL [NT9239]

☆ *Black Bull* TD12 4TL [off B6354 SW of Berwick]: Pretty white-painted thatched cottage in nice spot nr castle ruins and light railway, spacious unpretentious open-plan beamed lounge bar popular for decent food from good value baguettes to good fish, steaks and good vegetarian choice, real ales such as Black Sheep, Marstons Pedigree and Theakstons, lots of malt whiskies, farm cider, quick friendly service; children in eating area, games room with darts, dominoes, pool, TV, juke box and piped music; open all day Sat, a few picnic-sets out in front; (*Val and Alan Green, Comus and Sarah Elliott, LYM, Mrs E E Sanders*)

GREAT LUMLEY [NZ2949]

Old England DH3 4JB [Front St]: Popular village local, friendly staff, enjoyable reasonably priced bar food, two changing real ales (*Anon*)

HALTWHISTLE [NY7064]

☆ *Black Bull* NE49 0BL [just off Market Sq, behind indian restaurant]: Particularly well kept Big Lamp Price Bishop, Jennings Cumberland and four quickly changing local guest ales, may have Weston's Old Rosie farm cider, enterprising food all day (not till 7 Mon) inc seafood, game and bargain winter lunches, welcoming landlord and locals, brasses on low beams, stripped stone with shelves of bric-a-brac, log fires, corridor to small dining room, darts and monthly quiz night; limited disabled access, dogs welcome in flagstoned part, attractive garden, open all day wknds and summer, cl Mon lunchtime (*Tony and Maggie Harwood, Edward Leetham*)

Twice Brewed NE47 7AN [B6318 NE]: Busy no smoking pub handy for the wall, local real ales such as High House and Redburn, attractively priced food from baguettes and burgers up; children allowed in restaurant; open all day, tables outside, comfortable bedrooms *(Andy and Jill Kassube)*

HARTLEPOOL [NZ5032]
Camerons Brewery TS24 7QS [Waldon St]: Small bar attached to brewery's heritage centre, friendly and quiet, full range of their beers at good prices; worthwhile brewery tour and brewing museum, cl evening *(Leon Shaw)*

HAWTHORN [NZ4145]
Stapylton Arms SR7 8SD [off B1432 S of A19 Murton exit]: Carpeted bar with lots of old local photographs, a real ale such as Shepherd Neame Spitfire, chatty ex-miner landlord, daughter and wife – she produces enjoyable food from sandwiches to steaks and Sun roasts; dogs on leads allowed, may be open all day on busy wknds, nice wooded walk to sea (joins Durham Coastal Path) *(JHBS)*

HAYDON BRIDGE [NY8364]
☆ *General Havelock* NE47 6ER [A69]: Civilised and individually furnished dining pub, open kitchen doing particularly good interesting food using local ingredients from baguettes and reasonably priced lunchtime dishes to more upmarket evening set menus, changing local real ales, good wines by the glass and coffee, relaxing leisurely atmosphere, open fires, smart and tranquil Tyne-view stripped stone back restaurant; children welcome, tables on terrace *(Tony and Maggie Harwood, LYM, Michael Doswell, Dr Peter D Smart)*
Railway NE47 6JG [Church St]: Friendly hard-working licensees, wide range of ales such as Caledonian Deuchars IPA, reasonably priced home-made meals (breakfast room serves as café for locals); low-priced bedrooms *(David Godfrey)*

HEDDON-ON-THE-WALL [NZ1367]
Three Tuns NE15 0BQ [Military Rd]: Attractively reupholstered and carpeted, friendly customers and polite obliging landlord, real ales such as Tetleys and Wychwood, home-made lunches; lively bank holiday entertainment *(John Foord)*

HEXHAM [NY9363]
Tap & Spile NE46 1BH [Battle Hill/Eastgate]: Congenial and cosy open-plan bare-boards pub with Caledonian Deuchars IPA, High House Nels Best and three or four quickly changing guest beers from central bar, country wines, good filling low-priced food from hot filled stotties up, no smoking lounge with warm coal-effect fire, cheerful attentive staff; children welcome, no dogs, some live music, open all day *(John Foord)*

HIGH HESLEDEN [NZ4538]
Ship TS27 4QD [off A19 via B1281]: No smoking pub popular for its five good changing ales such as Durham, Hadrian or Mordue, real fire and lots of sailing ship models inc big one hanging from bar ceiling, enjoyable food here or in capacious restaurant; yacht and shipping views from car park, cl Mon *(JHBS)*

HOLWICK [NY9126]
Strathmore Arms DL12 0NJ [back rd up Teesdale from Middleton]: Quiet and cosy unassuming country pub in beautiful scenery just off Pennine Way, good range of real ales, welcoming landlord, good home cooking at attractive prices, log fire, darts, piano; bedrooms and camp site, open all day *(Sarah and Peter Gooderham, Mr and Mrs Maurice Thompson)*

HOLY ISLAND [NU1241]
Crown & Anchor TD15 2RX [causeway passable only at low tide, check times (01289) 330733]: New management in comfortable pub/restaurant with compact bar and roomy and spotless no smoking modern back dining room, Black Sheep and Caledonian Deuchars IPA, lunchtime food from a good sandwich range inc crab ciabattas to a few pubby main dishes, wider evening choice running up to duck, salmon etc, pleasantly simple pink and beige décor with interesting rope fancy-work; garden picnic-sets looking across to castle, three bedrooms *(Michael Doswell)*
Ship TD15 2SJ [Marygate]: Nicely set pub very busy in tourist season, renovated bar with big stove, maritime/fishing memorabilia and pictures, no smoking bare-boards eating area, pubby food from filled stotties up, Hadrian & Border Holy Island in summer, good choice of whiskies; no dogs, even in sheltered garden; three comfortable Victorian-décor bedrooms, may close for a while Jan/Feb *(Michael Dandy, Val and Alan Green, N R White, Keith and Chris O'Neill, Mr and Mrs Staples)*

HORSLEY [NZ0965]
☆ *Lion & Lamb* NE15 0NS [B6528, just off A69 Newcastle—Hexham]: Good food from sandwiches to interesting dishes at reasonable prices, four changing local real ales such as High House Auld Hemp, Matfen Magic and Wylam Gold, cafetière coffee, friendly chatty service, main bar with scrubbed tables, stripped stone, flagstones and panelling, no smoking lounge with big sofas, small smart restaurant; under-21s with parent or guardian only, Tyne views from attractive garden with roomy terrace and particularly good adventure play area, open all day Fri-Sun *(Mike and Lynn Robinson, John Foord, Michael Doswell, Gerry Miller)*

HOUGHTON GATE [NZ2950]
Smiths Arms DH3 4HE [Castle Dene; off A183 Chester-le-Street—Sunderland via A1052 then Forge Lane]: Friendly traditional bar with open fire in old black kitchen range, three or four real ales, comfortable lounge with two log or coal fires, games room with another, decorative upstairs restaurant with new chef doing good interesting food inc set meal deals, lunchtime bar food; has been cl Mon-Thurs lunchtime *(Mike and Lynn Robinson)*

HUMSHAUGH [NY9171]
Crown NE46 4AG: Old pub in attractive village with very popular Weds bargain lunch, efficient friendly staff, organic real ale, decent wines, cheerful bar, comfortable separate dining room; dogs allowed exc at busy times,

bedrooms *(Bill and Sheila McLardy, Michael Doswell, John Oddey)*

LANGDON BECK [NY8531]
Langdon Beck Hotel DL12 0XP [B6277 Middleton—Alston]: Unpretentious isolated pub well placed for walks and Pennine Way, good choice of bar food, helpful friendly service, wonderful views from dining room; bedrooms *(Sarah and Peter Gooderham)*

LOW WORSALL [NZ3909]
Ship TS15 9PH: Good range of good value food, two real ales, friendly staff *(Malcolm M Stewart)*

LOWICK [NU0139]
☆ *Black Bull* TD15 2UA [Main St (B6353, off A1 S of Berwick-upon-Tweed)]: Nicely decorated village pub, bright and cheerful, with quick friendly service even when busy, good choice of plentiful modestly priced food using local produce from good soup and sandwiches up (take-aways too), Belhaven 60/- and 70/- and Theakstons (just one real ale at quiet seasons), comfortable main bar, small back bar, spotless big back dining room; children welcome, three attractive bedrooms, on edge of small pretty village *(John Foord, Comus and Sarah Elliott, Mr and Mrs Staples, Bill and Sheila McLardy)*

MIDDLETON-IN-TEESDALE [NY9425]
Teesdale DL12 0QG [Market Pl]: Pleasantly worn-in hotel bar with friendly prompt service, good range of bar food, good beer, reasonably priced wines, log fire; tables outside, comfortable bedrooms *(Sarah and Peter Gooderham, R V T Pryor)*

MORPETH [NZ1986]
☆ *Tap & Spile* NE61 1BH [Manchester St]: Consistently welcoming cosy and easy-going two-room pub, real ales such as Big Lamp and Mordue, farm cider and country wines, limited choice of good value lunchtime food (not Mon-Weds), stripped pine furniture, interesting old photographs, quieter back lounge with coal-effect gas fire; good local folk music Sun afternoon, Mon quiz night, sports TV in front bar, board games, dominoes, cards, darts, fruit machine, unobtrusive piped music; children welcome, open all day Fri-Sun *(Derek and Sylvia Stephenson)*

NETHERTON [NT9807]
Star NE65 7HD [off B6341 at Thropton, or A697 via Whittingham]: Neat and spartan local in superb remote countryside, many original features, Castle Eden tapped from cellar casks and served from hatch in small entrance lobby, large high-ceilinged room with panelled wall benches, charming service and welcoming regulars; no food, music or children; unfortunately rarely open – Weds, Fri and Sun evenings are the best bet *(Mike and Lynn Robinson, the Didler)*

NEWBIGGIN-BY-THE-SEA [NZ3188]
Queens Head NE64 6AT [High St]: Friendly talkative landlord an ambassador for real ales, massive display of pump clips is testament to the many hundreds he's had here in his first three years, several rooms, plenty of character

and thriving atmosphere – even at 10 in the morning; open all day *(the Didler)*

NEWCASTLE UPON TYNE [NZ2464]
☆ *Bacchus* NE1 6BX [High Bridge East, between Pilgrim St and Grey St]: Rebuilt just up the road from its former site, elegant and comfortable, with relaxed atmosphere, good modern lunchtime food (not Sun) from interesting doorstep sandwiches and ciabattas through unusual light dishes to more substantial things all at keen prices, half a dozen changing real ales and growing range of bottled imports, good photographs of the region's former industries; open all day but cl till 7 Sun *(Eric Larkham, Michael Doswell, Andy and Jill Kassube)*
Barcule NE6 1TW [St Peters Wharf]: Bar/bistro in good spot – nice outside seating *(Mike and Lynn Robinson)*
Bodega NE1 4AG [Westgate Rd]: Majestic Edwardian drinking hall next to Tyne Theatre, colourful walls and ceiling, snug front cubicles, spacious tiled back area with a handsome rug under two magnificent stained-glass cupolas; Big Lamp Prince Bishop, Durham Magus, Mordue Geordie Pride (sold here as No 9) and three quickly changing guest beers tapped from the cask, farm cider, friendly service, lunchtime food, table football; juke box or piped music, machines, big-screen TV, busy evenings; open all day *(Eric Larkham, the Didler, P Dawn, Tracey and Stephen Groves, Kevin Blake)*
☆ *Bridge Hotel* NE1 1RQ [Castle Sq, next to high level bridge]: Big cheery high-ceilinged room divided into several areas leaving plenty of space by the bar with replica slatted snob screens, particularly well kept Black Sheep, Caledonian Deuchars IPA, Durham, Mordue Workie Ticket and up to three or four guest beers, bargain lunchtime food and Sun afternoon teas, magnificent fireplace, great views of river and bridges from raised back no smoking area; sports TV, piped music, fruit machines, very long-standing Mon folk club upstairs; tables on flagstoned back terrace overlooking section of old town wall, open all day *(John Foord, Eric Larkham, the Didler, P Dawn, LYM, Mike and Lynn Robinson, Kevin Blake)*
☆ *Cooperage* NE1 3RF [The Close, Quayside]: Ancient building in good waterfront setting, thriving atmosphere in stripped stone bar and cosy beamed lounge, good changing real ale choice, hearty fresh sensibly priced lunchtime food, lively evenings with upstairs night club; pool, juke box; disabled facilities, cl Sun lunchtime *(LYM, the Didler)*
Cumberland Arms NE6 1LD [Byker Buildings]: Friendly traditional local with four particularly well kept changing local ales (tapped straight from the cask if you wish), farm cider, good value toasties, obliging staff; live music or other events most nights, tables outside overlooking Ouseburn Valley, cl wkdy lunchtimes, open all day wknds *(Eric Larkham, R T and J C Moggridge)*
Falcons Nest NE3 5EH [Rotary Way, Gosforth – handy for racecourse]: Roomy new

Vintage Inn in their comfortably relaxing traditional style of olde-worlde linked rooms, good choice of food from sandwiches and light dishes to fish, steaks and less usual things, good choice of wines by the glass, Worthington and several foreign beers; open all day *(Michael Doswell)*

Fitzgeralds NE1 6AF [Grey St]: Handsomely refurbished Victorian pub stretching a long way back from its narrow façade in elegant street on fringe of Bigg Market, lots of levels and alcoves (two short sets of steps between entrance, main area and lavatories), discreet lighting, red mahogany and polished brass, Black Sheep, Mordue Workie Ticket and two guest beers, wide range of good value lunchtime food (not Sun) inc freshly baked baguettes; can get very busy wknds, piped music, machines; open all day, cl Sun lunchtime *(Eric Larkham, Kevin Blake)*

Free Trade NE6 1AP [St Lawrence Rd, off Walker Rd (A186)]: Outstanding views up river to bridges and the Gateshead arts centres from its big windows and from terrace tables and seats on grass; thoroughly unpretentious and well worn in, with up to eight largely local changing ales from small brewers, warmly friendly atmosphere, good sandwiches, real fire, original Formica tables; eclectic free CD juke box, steps down to back room and lavatories; open all day *(Mike and Lynn Robinson, Eric Larkham)*

Head of Steam NE1 5EN [Neville St]: Unusual layout – stairs up to main bar with four changing real ales, stairs down to live music area with two ales (may be different), bare boards and carpet, some railway prints, reasonably priced lunchtime food inc two-course Sun lunch, friendly staff; very popular with students; children allowed, open all day *(Eric Larkham)*

Hotspur NE1 7RY [Percy St]: Cheerfully busy Victorian pub with half a dozen or more real ales largely from scottish brewers, farm cider, lots of bottled belgian beers, good value wine, sandwiches and hot snacks all day, big front windows and decorated mirrors; piped music, machines, big-screen sports TV, can get packed, esp pre-match, upstairs ladies'; open all day *(Mike and Lynn Robinson, Eric Larkham, GSB)*

New Bridge NE1 6PF [Argyle St]: Four changing real ales often from local small breweries, good value home-made food (not Thurs-Sun evenings) inc telephone take-aways, may be farm cider, large comfortably refurbished bar with separate areas and alcoves inc popular back dining lounge, photographs of Tyne Bridge abuilding; darts, piped music; open all day, view of Millennium Bridge from side entrance *(Eric Larkham)*

Newcastle Arms NE1 5SE [St Andrews St]: Open-plan pub on fringe of chinatown, several quickly changing real ales such as Black Sheep and Fullers, occasional farm cider (worth asking for if you don't see it) and mini beer festivals, friendly staff, decent food till 6 inc sandwiches, interesting old local photographs; piped music, big-screen sports TV, can get very busy esp on match days; open all day *(Eric Larkham, Mike and Lynn Robinson)*

Red House NE1 3JF [Sandhill]: Heavy unspoilt Victorian fittings and furnishings in stone-walled bar with two rooms off, generous helpings of low-priced food (kitchen shared with adjoining vegetarian Bob Trollopes), decent wine and beer *(John Wooll)*

Slug & Lettuce NE1 3DW [Love Lane, Quayside]: Relaxed atmosphere, Tyne view, enjoyable contemporary food, daily papers, good mix of customers *(Karen Eliot)*

Tanners NE1 2NS [Byker Bridge]: By Byker Bridge, two real ales and half a dozen interesting bottled ciders, wkdy bar snacks and Sun lunch, live music Sun evening, may be other evenings *(Eric Larkham)*

Tilleys NE1 4AW [Corner Westgate Rd and Thornton St]: Large bar next to Tyne Theatre and nr performing arts college and live music centre, so interesting mix of customers; half a dozen real ales, farm cider, good choice of bottled beers, enjoyable home-made food, artworks for sale; open all day *(Eric Larkham)*

Tyne NE6 1LP [Maling St]: Busy pub at end of quayside walk by confluence of Ouseburn and Tyne, plastered with band posters and prints, four local real ales, exotic hot or cold sandwiches all day, interesting free CD juke box, live music upstairs Sun lunchtime and evening, and midweek; fruit machine, sports TV, stairs up to lavatories; all-weather fairy-lit garden (loudspeakers out here too) under an arch of Glasshouse Bridge, also waterside picnic-sets, barbecues, open all day *(Mike and Lynn Robinson, Eric Larkham, P Dawn, Gerry Miller)*

NEWFIELD [NZ2035]

☆ *Fox & Hounds* DL14 8DF [Stonebank Terrace, off Long Lane at Queens Head]: Dining pub with good value light lunches (Tues-Fri) and elaborate full meals (Sat night booked well ahead), cosy beamed ante-room parlour with good fires in its old cream-coloured kitchen range, comfortable fairy-lit no smoking beamed dining area with dark pink timbered walls, friendly service, good choice of wines by the glass – no real ale; cl Sun evening, Mon *(LYM, M Lochore)*

NORTH SHIELDS [NZ3568]

☆ *Magnesia Bank* NE30 1NH [Camden St]: Lively and well run if not smart, roomy bar with raised eating areas, half a dozen or more real ales inc Black Sheep, Durham, Jarrow and Mordue in lined glasses, good wines and coffee, vast choice of cheerful home-made lunchtime food from cheap toasties to local lamb and fish, super puddings, good value all-day breakfast from 8.30am, attentive friendly uniformed staff and approachable chef, intriguing mix of customers, open fire, no smoking side restaurant (same menu); quiet piped pop music, TV, machines, upstairs comedy nights, live music Fri/Sat; children welcome, tables outside, open all day *(Mike and Lynn Robinson, P Dawn, Mr and Mrs M Brandrith, John and Gloria Isaacs, Pat Woodward)*

☆ **Wooden Doll** NE30 1JS [Hudson St]: Bare-boards pub with high view of fish quay and outer harbour from largely no smoking picture-window extension, enjoyable food from good sandwiches to fresh local fish, full Jennings range kept well, good service, informal mix of furnishings; disabled facilities, children welcome till 8, some live music, open all day Sat (Mike and Lynn Robinson, LYM, J H Bescoby)

PONTELAND [NZ1771]

Badger NE20 9BT [Street Houses; A696 SE, by garden centre]: Well done Vintage Inn, more character than most pubs in the area, relaxing rooms and alcoves, old furnishings and olde-worlde décor, flagstones, carpet or bare wood, timbered ceilings, stripped stone, brick and timbering, real fires and choice of real ales, good range of wines by the glass and good hot drinks, friendly attentive uniformed staff; quiet piped music, all-day food (GSB, BB, Dr Peter D Smart, Michael Doswell, Mrs E E Sanders)

RENNINGTON [NU2118]

☆ **Horseshoes** NE66 3RS: Comfortable flagstoned pub with good local feel, enjoyable generous food inc two-course lunch deals and good local meat and smoked fish, welcoming efficient service, Bass and Hadrian & Border Gladiator, simple neat bar with lots of horsebrasses, spotless compact restaurant with blue and white china; children welcome, tables outside, attractive quiet village nr coast (Michael Doswell)

RIDING MILL [NZ0161]

☆ **Wellington** NE44 6DQ [A695 just W of A68 roundabout]: Reliable and popular 17th-c Chef & Brewer, carefully refurbished in tune with its age, beams and candlelight, two big log fires and mix of tables and chairs, some upholstered, some not; vast good value blackboard food choice from hot ciabatta sandwiches to nice puddings, Courage Directors and Theakstons Bitter and Black Bull, good choice of wines by the glass, friendly service; piped classical music, can get busy; disabled access, children welcome, play area and picnic-sets outside, pretty village with nearby walks and river (Andy and Jill Kassube, Dr Peter D Smart, Mrs E E Sanders)

ROOKHOPE [NY9342]

Rookhope Inn DL13 2BG [off A689 W of Stanhope]: Friendly local on coast-to-coast bike route, three or four real ales such as Jennings Fish King and Timothy Taylors Landlord, simple home-made food, open fire; some live music; seats outside, bedrooms (Joan Kureczka)

ROTHBURY [NU0501]

☆ **Newcastle Hotel** NE65 7UT: Small solid Victorian pub/hotel at end of green, comfortably refurbished convivial lounge with separate dining area, second bar, friendly service, good reasonably priced food from filled baguettes to seasonal game and substantial Sun lunch, cheap high teas 3.30-5.30 Apr-Oct, toasties only winter Sun pm, Caledonian Deuchars IPA and Greene King

Abbot and Old Speckled Hen, no smoking upstairs dining room; piped music; good value comfortable bedrooms with own bathrooms, pretty village with river walks, handy for Cragside (NT), open all day (John Foord, Alex and Claire Pearse)

SEDGEFIELD [NZ3528]

Dun Cow TS21 3AT [Front St]: Large two-bar village inn with comfortable dining room, wide choice of enjoyable if not cheap food from well filled sandwiches to game, fresh whitby fish and unusual puddings, attentive service, Castle Eden and good range of guest beers, whiskies in great variety; children welcome; good bedrooms sharing bathrooms (John Coatsworth, T and P)

SLAGGYFORD [NY6754]

Kirkstyle CA8 7PB [Knarsdale]: Attractive pleasantly refurbished old inn with good atmosphere, friendly service and locals, wide range of good plain food, Black Sheep and decent wines, nice spot looking over South Tyne valley to hills beyond; comfortable bedrooms, handy for Pennine Way (David and Pauline Hambley)

SLALEY [NY9658]

☆ **Travellers Rest** NE46 1TT [B6306 S of Hexham (and N of village)]: Attractive and busy stone-built country pub, spaciously opened up inside, with farmhouse-style décor, beams, flagstones and polished wood floors, huge fireplace, comfortable high-backed settles forming discrete areas, popular food from simple low-priced hot dishes (12-5) to wider but still relatively cheap mealtime choice (not Sun evening) in bar and small pretty dining room, good children's menu, basic sandwiches, friendly staff, five real ales such as Black Sheep, Greene King, Mordue and Wylam, limited wines by the glass; dogs welcome, tables outside with well equipped adventure play area on grass behind, three good value bedrooms, open all day (Andy and Jill Kassube, Mr and Mrs C Walker, Dr D J and Mrs S C Walker, Peter and Jane Burton, Mart Lawton)

SOUTH SHIELDS [NZ3567]

Alum Ale House NE33 1JR [Ferry St (B1344)]: Relaxed 18th-c pub handy for ferry, big bars with polished boards, coal fire in old inglenook range, pictures and newspaper cuttings, Banks's, Camerons, Marstons and guest beers, hot drinks, good value basic lunchtime bar food; piped music, machines, some live music, good beer festivals; children welcome, open all day (Mike and Lynn Robinson, the Didler)

Bamburgh NE34 6SS [Bamburgh Ave]: Spacious open-plan bar with six real ales such as Black Sheep, Caledonian Deuchars IPA and Timothy Taylors, good value food lunchtime and early evening (Mr and Mrs Maurice Thompson)

Beacon NE33 2AQ [Greens Pl]: Pleasantly refurbished open-plan pub overlooking river mouth, with sepia photographs and bric-a-brac, central bar, stove in back room, obliging service, Adnams, Caledonian Deuchars IPA and Marstons Pedigree, good value lunchtime food, two raised eating areas, darts and dominoes; fruit machine, quiet piped music; open all day *(the Didler)*

Maltings NE33 4PG [Claypath Rd]: Good conversion tied to Jarrow brewery, full range of their ales, guest beers and a farm cider, bar food (not Fri-Sun evenings); open all day *(Eric Larkham)*

New Ship NE34 8DG [Sunderland Rd]: Pleasant roadside pub with wide choice of bar food in conservatory, bar or back room, Greene King Old Speckled Hen and Theakstons Cool Cask *(Mr and Mrs Maurice Thompson)*

Steamboat NE33 1EQ [Mill Dam/Coronation St]: Masses of interesting nautical bric-a-brac esp in split-level back room, friendly landlord, Black Sheep, Courage Directors, Greene King and local guest beers such as Jarrow, Mordue and Whitby, bargain stotties, pool in central area; usually open all day, nr river and market place *(Mike and Lynn Robinson, the Didler)*

STAMFORDHAM [NZ0772]
Bay Horse NE18 0PB [off B6309]: Long comfortable beamed bar, wide range of good value food from fresh lunchtime baguettes up, thoughtful children's dishes, three real ales, good coffee; dogs welcome, doubles as shop and post office, at end of green in attractive village *(Mike and Lynn Robinson, Bill and Sheila McLardy, Michael Doswell)*

STANLEY [NZ1753]
Harperley Hotel DH9 9TY [Harperley Country Park, 1½ miles W]: Good home cooking inc bargain three-course restaurant lunch and evening carvery, Courage Directors and Jennings or Greene King; extensive grounds, good walks *(Mike and Lynn Robinson)*

STOCKTON-ON-TEES [NZ4419]
Sun TS18 1SU [Knowles St]: Friendly town local specialising in Bass, well served at tempting price, quick service even when busy; folk night Mon, open all day *(the Didler)*

SUNDERLAND [NZ3956]
Fitzgeralds SR1 3PZ [Green Terr]: Busy two-bar city pub popular for up to ten real ales inc several from local Darwin, friendly atmosphere, generous cheap food from toasties, baguettes and ciabattas to basic hot dishes; children welcome lunchtime *(Mr and Mrs Maurice Thompson)*

THROPTON [NU0302]
☆ *Cross Keys* NE7 7HX [B6341]: Attractive little village pub, hearty food from good value baguettes to restaurant dishes inc plenty of fresh north shields fish, may be good bar nibbles, Bass, pleasant friendly staff, open fires in small cosy beamed bar with eating rooms off inc family room, darts; satellite TV; nice steeply terraced garden looking over village to the Cheviots, open all day at least in summer *(Pat and Stewart Gordon, LYM, Michael Doswell)*

☆ *Three Wheat Heads* NE65 7LR [B6341]: Comfortable 300-year-old village inn favoured by older people for its sedate dining atmosphere, good coal fires (one in a fine tall stone fireplace), straightforward bar food,

Black Sheep and Theakstons, no smoking restaurant, darts and pool; piped music; children welcome, garden with play area and lovely views to Simonside Hills, open all day wknds *(Dr Peter D Smart, June and Ken Brooks, Dr and Mrs T E Hothersall, Alan and Paula McCully, LYM, Stuart Orton, Dave Braisted, DFL)*

TRIMDON [NZ3734]
Red Lion TS29 6PG [Front North St]: Reopened 2005 (by local home-owner Tony Blair) after roomy refurbishment with maroon décor by new landlord, son cooks good choice of enjoyable food all day, Black Sheep and Shepherd Neame Spitfire, open fire; open all day *(JHBS)*

TYNEMOUTH [NZ3669]
Cumberland Arms NE30 4DX [Front St]: Small nautical-theme bar, more seats in upper bar, good range of Courage, Theakstons and other real ales, good value all-day food (till 5 wknds), back restaurant; back terrace with barbecues, open all day *(Mike and Lynn Robinson)*

WALL [NY9169]
☆ *Hadrian* NE46 4EE [Hexham—Bellingham/Rothbury Rd]: Two-room beamed lounge with interesting reconstructions of Romano-British life, woodburner, Jennings and guest beers, decent range of wines and whiskies, friendly attentive staff creating relaxed atmosphere, enjoyable generous food inc good Sun lunch, airy no smoking dining room; children welcome, unobtrusive piped music, games in public bar; neat garden, roomy comfortable bedrooms – back ones quieter, with good views *(BB, Bob Richardson)*

WARDEN [NY9166]
Boatside NE46 4SQ [½ mile N of A69]: New landlord and chef in extended and much modernised dining pub with enjoyable fresh food inc good sandwiches, pubby lunch popular with older people, good friendly service, Black Sheep and Jennings, pine dining room; children welcome, small neat enclosed garden, attractive spot by Tyne bridge *(Bill and Sheila McLardy, Michael Doswell, Dr D J and Mrs S C Walker)*

WARENFORD [NU1429]
☆ *White Swan* NE70 7HY [off A1 3 or 4 miles S of Belford]: This place, previously the Warenford Lodge and enjoyed despite its then limited opening hours for its good meals using local ingredients, warm fires and good value wines, reopened in summer 2006 after refurbishment under new ownership and this new name; news please *(LYM)*

WARKWORTH [NU2406]
Masons Arms NE65 0UR [Dial Pl]: Thriving village pub, good value generous home-made food inc local fish and bargain lunch, quick friendly helpful service, real ales such as Adnams Best, Caledonian Deuchars IPA and Theakstons XB, good coffee and wine choice, local pictures; disabled access and facilities, dogs welcome, attractive back flagstoned courtyard, appealing village not far from sea *(Dr D J and Mrs S C Walker, Mrs E E Sanders)*

Sun NE65 0UP [Castle Terr]: 17th-c hotel opp castle, homely convivial bar, real ales such as Northumberland, friendly helpful staff, enjoyable home-made food inc local fish; children and dogs welcome, useful parking, bedrooms with good views *(Mike and Lynn Robinson)*

Warkworth House NE65 0XB [Bridge St]: Hotel not pub, but unusual in having a proper friendly bar, recently nicely refurbished, with two changing guest ales, darts and bar billiards, as well as a wide choice of enjoyable and generous reasonably priced food, friendly helpful staff, a good range of spirits and of good value wines by the glass, proper coffee, and comfortable sofas; dogs welcome, good bedrooms, open all day *(Carole Jones, Comus and Sarah Elliott)*

WASHINGTON [NZ3054]

Courtyard NE38 8AB [Arts Centre Washington, Biddick Lane]: Relaxed open-plan bar with four changing real ales, bar food *(Mr and Mrs Maurice Thompson)*

WHITTONSTALL [NZ0757]

Anchor DH8 9JN [B6309 N of Consett]: Reliable stone-built beamed dining pub with comfortable banquettes in L-shaped lounge, dining area with high-raftered pitched roof, attractive décor, interesting old north-east photographs and facsimile posters, huge choice of good value generous food from good sandwich and baguette range through unusual hot dishes to popular Sun lunch, Courage Directors and Theakstons, good coffee; piped music; nice countryside *(Prof and Mrs Tony Palmer)*

WIDDRINGTON [NZ2596]

Widdrington Inn NE61 5DY [off A1068 S of Amble]: Recently redeveloped, with good service, real ale, all-day bar food; open all day *(Comus and Sarah Elliott)*

WOLSINGHAM [NZ0737]

Bay Horse DL13 3EX [Uppertown]: Recently renovated, with welcoming licensees and helpful attentive staff, good choice of beers, enjoyable food inc good value Sun lunch, traditional bar, smart dining room; seven bedrooms *(Judith and Edward Pearson)*

WYLAM [NZ1164]

☆ *Boathouse* NE41 8HR [Station Rd; across Tyne from village, handy for Newcastle—Carlisle rail line]: Thriving convivial riverside pub, emphasis more on contents than on appearance, with good range of northern real ales inc the local Wylam beers, keen prices and one cut-price bargain, good choice of malt whiskies, good cheap simple wknd bar lunches, bright low-beamed lounge bar with cheery open stove; can be smoky, poor disabled access, loud band nights; children and dogs welcome, seats outside, open all day *(Mike and Lynn Robinson, Mr and Mrs Maurice Thompson, the Didler, Tony and Wendy Hobden, Eric Larkham)*

Fox & Hounds NE41 8DL [Main Rd]: Immaculate recently refurbished local with roomy, bright and cheery bar, friendly newish licensees eager to please, Black Sheep and Jennings Cumberland, lunchtime and evening food; nr River Tyne, and George Stephenson's cottage is a short walk along the old railway track *(John Foord)*

Nottinghamshire

Perhaps the fact that this county is home territory for the good little Tynemill chain, with their emphasis on real ales, goes a little way to explaining why almost half the main entries here have a Beer Award. It's not uncommon to find up to a dozen real ales on tap at any one pub in this county. Hardys & Hansons of Kimberley has been the county's main brewer for many decades; it's now been bought by Greene King, and though as we went to press they had said nothing about closing the brewery, it may well not stay in production. Other local brews you'll find quite often here are Castle Rock (the Tynemill house beer) and Nottingham, with Caythorpe, Mallard and Milestone cropping up once or twice in our main entries. Local competition in the city of Nottingham itself throws a healthy factor into the mix, which is also reflected in the very reasonable food prices in that city. It really is a case of take your pick, with all the main entries here doing well and every one of them strong on real ale, from the interesting old Bell with its 11 real ales, and the Lincolnshire Poacher with its fantastic range of drinks, to the down-to-earth tap to next-door Castle Rock, the Vat & Fiddle with its total of ten beers. The civilised no smoking Cock & Hoop is very useful as it's our only main entry in Nottingham with bedrooms – indeed they're so nice it comes straight into the *Guide* with a Stay Award. Dining pubs don't feature overmuch in this county, but you can find good traditional food, and on the whole prices are sensible. The welcoming Victoria in Beeston is praiseworthy on this front, as well as for its splendid beer range. At the other end of the spectrum, both the Caunton Beck at Caunton and the no smoking Waggon & Horses at Halam offer imaginative menus in a civilised atmosphere and surroundings. It's the Caunton Beck (so usefully serving food all day) that wins the award of Nottinghamshire Dining Pub of the Year. In the Lucky Dip section at the end of the chapter, pubs to note on current form are Tom Browns at Gunthorpe, Nelson & Railway in Kimberley, Beehive at Maplebeck, Fox & Crown in Newark, Keanes Head in Nottingham, Pilgrim Fathers at Scrooby, Red Lion at Thurgarton, Red Lion in Underwood and Stratford Haven in West Bridgford. As a final thought, it looks to us as if the forthcoming ban on smoking in pubs – if our own inspection trips and recent reports from readers are anything to go by – will come as more of a change in Nottinghamshire than in most places.

BEESTON SK5338 Map 7

Victoria 🍽 ♀ 🍺

Dovecote Lane, backing on to railway station; NG9 1JG

Down to earth but very welcoming, this converted railway hotel stocks a hugely impressive choice of drinks, and serves enjoyable fairly priced food. It's run with real passion and commitment by former Tynemill director and chef Neil Kelso. Three unpretentious downstairs rooms have kept their original long narrow layout, and have simple solid traditional furnishings, very unfussy décor, stained-glass windows, stripped woodwork and floorboards (woodblock in some rooms), newspapers to read, and a chatty atmosphere. Service remains quick and polite even during very busy peak times; dominoes, cribbage and maybe piped music. The lounge and bar back on to the railway station, and a covered heated area outside has tables overlooking the platform, with trains passing just a few feet away. Running through as many as 500 different beers each year, widely sourced changing guests come from a great range of brewers such as Brewsters, Fullers, Hydes, Mighty Oak and Oakham, and are well kept alongside the house beers – Castle Rock Harvest and Elsie Mo and Everards Tiger. The full pump compliment is a dozen. They've also continental draught beers, farm ciders, over 100 malt whiskies, 20 irish whiskeys, and even over two dozen wines by the glass. A lively time to visit is during their two week beer and music festival at the end of July. Bar food is listed on a daily changing blackboard, and might include leek and potato soup (£3.95), sausage and mash (£6.95), mushroom and sweet pepper stroganoff (£7.95), salmon with dill mustard mayonnaise or braised beef in red wine and stilton (£9.50) and puddings such as apple crumble and dark chocolate fudge cake (£3.95). The much loved wolfhound–lurcher cross pub dog is called Fritz. Parking is limited and readers have warned us about active parking wardens in the area. *(Recommended by P T Sewell, David Eberlin, Simon and Mandy King, Andrew Beardsley, Alison Lawrence, Simon Pyle, the Didler, MP, C J Fletcher, Rona Murdoch, R M Taylor, Kevin Blake, Brian and Ruth Archer, Andy and Ali, Richard, Mark and Mary Fairman)*

Free house ~ Licensees Neil Kelso and Graham Smith ~ Real ale ~ Bar food (12-8.45(7.45 Sun)) ~ (0115) 925 4049 ~ Children in dining areas till 8pm ~ Dogs allowed in bar ~ Live music Sun evening and jazz Mon evenings Sept-May ~ Open 11(12 Sun)-11

CAUNTON SK7460 Map 7

Caunton Beck 🍴 ♀

Main Street; village signposted off A616 Newark—Ollerton; NG23 6AB

Nottinghamshire Dining Pub of the Year

You can get something to eat at most times of the day at this delightfully civilised dining pub, starting with a hearty english breakfast (£8.95) first thing, then later going on to delicious sandwiches (from £5.95), and a fairly elaborate quarterly changing menu (with a handful of daily specials) such as soup (£4.50), breaded whitebait (£5.25), devilled lambs kidneys with sautéed wild mushrooms (£6.95), sausage and mash (£9.50), roast chicken breast wrapped in parma ham with stilton and sage potatoes (£12.95), baked bass stuffed with chilli, coriander and pickled ginger (£14.25), fillet steak with tarragon and horseradish butter (£17.50), and puddings such as honeycomb and caramel crème brûlée or honey and whisky jelly with red berry compote (£4.75); no smoking restaurant. The lovely building itself is almost new, but as it was reconstructed using original timbers and reclaimed oak, around the skeleton of the old Hole Arms, it seems old. Scrubbed pine tables, clever lighting, an open fire and country-kitchen chairs, low beams and rag-finished paintwork in a spacious interior make for a relaxed atmosphere. With lots of flowers and plants in summer, the terrace is a nice place to sit when the weather is fine. About half the wines (around 35) on the very good wine list are available by the glass, and they've well kept Batemans XB and Black Sheep and a guest such as Milestone Loxley on handpump; also espresso coffee. Service is pleasant and attentive; daily papers and magazines, no music. *(Recommended by Gerry and Rosemary Dobson, Blaise Vyner, Richard, J R Ringrose, Derek and Sylvia Stephenson, Stephen Woad, Alison and Pete, Steve Harvey, Ray and Winifred Halliday, Adrian White)*

Free house ~ Licensee Julie Allwood ~ Real ale ~ Bar food (8am-11pm) ~ Restaurant ~ (01636) 636793 ~ Children welcome ~ Dogs allowed in bar ~ Open 8am-11pm

CAYTHORPE SK6845 Map 7

Black Horse 🍺

Turn off A6097 ¼ mile SE of roundabout junction with A612, NE of Nottingham; into Gunthorpe Road, then right into Caythorpe Road and keep on; NG14 7ED

'Straight from another era' is how one reader describes this quaintly old-fashioned little 300-year-old country local that has been run by the same family for many years. The timelessly uncluttered carpeted bar has just five tables, with brocaded wall banquettes and settles, a few bar stools hosting cheerful evening regulars, a warm woodburning stove, decorative plates on a delft shelf and a few horsebrasses on the ceiling joists. The landlady herself serves the tasty Caythorpe Dover Beck which is brewed here and is well kept alongside two changing guest beers such as Bass and Black Sheep. Off the front corridor is a partly panelled inner room with a wall bench running right the way around three unusual long copper-topped tables, and quite a few old local photographs; down on the left an end room has just one huge round table; darts and dominoes. Simple, but very enjoyable reasonably priced food from a shortish list includes soup (£2.75), prawn cocktail or cod roe on toast or king prawns in chilli sauce (£4), fried cod, haddock or plaice (£7), seafood salad (£8.75), fillet steak (£13), and puddings such as banana ice-cream cake and treacle sponge (from £3). Booking is essential. The entire pub is no smoking at lunchtime (except on Sunday). There are some plastic tables outside, and the River Trent is fairly close, for waterside walks. *(Recommended by P T Sewell, the Didler, J R Ringrose, Richard, Des and Jen Clarke)*

Own brew ~ Licensee Sharron Andrews ~ Real ale ~ Bar food (12-1.45, 7-8.30; not Sat evening, or Sun) ~ Restaurant ~ No credit cards ~ (0115) 966 3520 ~ Dogs allowed in bar ~ Open 12-3, 5(6 Sat)-11; 12-5, 8-10.30 Sun; closed Mon

ELKESLEY SK6975 Map 7
Robin Hood
High Street; village well signposted just off A1 Newark—Blyth; DN22 8AJ

The changing menu, with something for most tastes, is worth knowing about here. The food is not groundbreaking, but readers say it's well cooked and fairly priced. As well as good sandwiches, dishes might include soup (£3.50), baked egg with smoked haddock, leek and parmesan (£5), lamb curry, linguini bolognese or goats cheese bake with sweet peppers, roast beetroot and artichoke hearts (£8), sausage and mash or boeuf bourguignon (£9), fillet steak (£15), and puddings such as tiramisu or banana and toffee sponge (from £3.50). The neatly kept spacious dining room (no smoking) and lounge area have cheery yellow walls, and a pleasant mix of dark wood furniture on a patterned carpet; TV, piped music and board games. Marstons Pedigree is well kept on handpump. The garden (which is moderately well screened from the A1) has picnic-sets and a play area. *(Recommended by Edward and Deanna Pearce, Richard Cole, Brian Brooks, Jill and Julian Tasker, Christopher Turner, Mike and Linda Hudson, R T and J C Moggridge, Kevin Thorpe, Ian Phillips, MJB, Dr and Mrs R G J Telfer, Irene and Ray Atkin)*

Enterprise ~ Lease Alan Draper ~ Real ale ~ Bar food (12-2, 6.30-9) ~ Restaurant ~ (01777) 838259 ~ Children welcome ~ Dogs allowed in bar ~ Open 11.30-2, 6-11; 12-3 Sun; closed Sun evening, Mon lunchtime

HALAM SK6754 Map 7
Waggon & Horses 🍴
Off A612 in Southwell centre, via Halam Road; NG22 8AE

The inventive seasonally changing menu at this heavily oak-beamed civilised dining pub might include pea and watercress soup with mint crème fraîche (£4.50), feta cheese, red pepper jam and hummous (£6), seared scallops with cauliflower purée and crispy parma ham (£8), warm mushroom and brie tartlet with provençale vegetables (£11), grilled pork fillet with creamed leeks and baked apples (£12), baked cod fillet with roasted fennel and truffle cream or fried rib-eye steak with stilton and port sauce (£13.50). They also do a good value two-course offer (£11.50, lunchtimes (not Sun) and 6pm to 7pm Monday-Thursday). Spotlessly kept, the brightly congenial open-plan interior (no smoking throughout) has a pleasant dining atmosphere (though drinkers are welcome), and is nicely divided into smallish sections – an appealing black iron screen dividing off one part is made up of tiny african-style figures of people and animals. Good sturdy high-back rush-seat dining chairs are set around a mix of solid mainly stripped tables, there are

various wall seats, smaller chairs and the odd stout settle too, with lots of pictures
ranging from kitten prints to Spy cricketer caricatures on walls painted cream, brick
red and coffee; candles throughout give a pleasant night-time glow. Three Thwaites
beers are well kept on handpump; piped music. Out past a piano and grandfather
clock in the lobby are a few roadside picnic-sets by the pretty window boxes.
*(Recommended by David Glynne-Jones, Colin Fisher, Mike and Mary Carter, R and M Tait,
Derek and*
Sylvia Stephenson, Michael Doswell, Richard, Peter and Jean Hoare)

Thwaites ~ Tenants Rebecca and William White and Roy Wood ~ Real ale ~ Bar food
(12-2.30(3 Sun), 6-9.30; not Sun evening) ~ Restaurant ~ (01636) 813109/816228 ~
Children welcome ~ Open 11.30-3, 5.30-11; 11.30-11 Sat; 11.30-10.30 Sun

LAXTON   SK7267   Map 7
Dovecote 🛏️
Signposted off A6075 E of Ollerton; NG22 0NU

This very welcoming red-brick free house manages to maintain a pubby
atmosphere, despite the popularity of the food (you may need to book). Served by
very friendly and courteous staff, fairly priced dishes come in big helpings and
might include soup (£3.25), sandwiches (from £3.75), grilled goats cheese salad
(£4.50), garlic prawns (£5.95), steak and kidney pie (£6.99), mushroom
stroganoff (£8.50) and scampi (£8.25), with specials such as chicken and
mushroom cream pie (£8.99), battered cod (£8.99), bass stuffed with prawns
(£11.50) and pork medallions in mushroom and brandy cream (£10.99). The
puddings, such as cheesecake (£3.50), are made by Aunty Mary, the landlord's aunt,
who lives in the village. The central lounge has dark wheelback chairs and tables on
wooden floors, and a coal-effect gas fire. This opens through a small bay (the former
entrance) into a carpeted dining area. Around the other side, another little lounge
leads through to a pool room (smoking in here only) with darts, fruit machine, pool,
dominoes and piped music. Three changing beers on handpump might be from
brewers such as Batemans, Charles Wells and Marstons, and they've around ten
wines by the glass. There are wooden tables and chairs on a small front terrace by a
sloping garden, which has a disused white dovecote. It's handy for the A1, and as
well as the two bedrooms, they have a site and facilities for six caravans. The pub
stands next to three huge medieval open fields as Laxton is one of the few places in
the country still farmed using the traditional open field system. Every year in the
third week of June the grass is auctioned for haymaking, and anyone who lives in the
parish is entitled to a bid – and a drink. You can find out more at the visitor centre
behind the pub. *(Recommended by David and Ruth Hollands, J R Ringrose, Richard Cole,
Keith and Chris O'Neill, Ian Phillips, Comus and Sarah Elliott, T and P, Peter and Jean Hoare)*

Free house ~ Licensees Lisa and Betty Shepherd ~ Real ale ~ Bar food (12-2, 6.30-9) ~
Restaurant ~ (01777) 871586 ~ Children welcome in restaurant ~ Dogs allowed in bar ~
Open 11-3, 6.30(6 Sat)-11(10.30 Sun) ~ Bedrooms: £35B/£50B

MORTON   SK7251   Map 7
Full Moon
**Pub and village signposted off Bleasby—Fiskerton back road, SE of Southwell;
NG25 0UT**

Tucked away in a remote hamlet not far from the River Trent, this friendly place is
a jolly decent village dining pub. L-shaped and beamed, the main part is
traditionally decorated with pink plush seats and cushioned black settles around a
variety of pub tables, and wheelback chairs in the side dining area, and a couple of
fireplaces. Fresh flowers and the very long run of Christmas plates on the walls add
a spot of colour; look out for the two sociable pub cats. Charles Wells Bombardier,
Greene King Ruddles (which they call Full Moon), Nottingham Legend and a
changing guest such as Theakstons XB are well kept on handpump; piped music
(which can at times be a little loud), TV, games machines and board games. Lots of
effort has gone into the garden which comprises a peaceful shady back terrace with

picnic-sets, with more on a sizeable lawn, and some sturdy play equipment. As well as daily specials, sensibly priced enjoyable food includes soup (£3.25), home-made pâté with cumberland sauce or whitebait (£4.50), steak and kidney pie (£8.50), red thai chicken curry (£9.50), parsnip and chestnut bake or grilled sea bream (£9.95), mixed grill (£13.95) and puddings such as lemon brûlée or treacle sponge pudding (£3.95); two-course OAP bargain lunch (£6.95). *(Recommended by Keith Wright, Gordon Prince, the Didler, Derek and Sylvia Stephenson, Richard Greenwood, Ian and Nita Cooper, J R Ringrose, Simon Pyle, Eric Robinson, Jacqueline Pratt, Richard, Phil and Jane Hodson, Michael Doswell)*

Free house ~ Licensees Clive and Kim Wisdom ~ Real ale ~ Bar food (12-2, 6.30-10) ~ Restaurant ~ (01636) 830251 ~ Children welcome ~ Open 11-3, 6-11(12 Sat); 12-10.30 Sun

NOTTINGHAM   SK5640   Map 7
Bell 🍺 £
Angel Row, off Market Square; NG1 6HL

The labyrinthine cellars (tours 7.30pm Tues) of this ancient pub are about ten metres down in the sandstone rock, and the efforts of the hardworking Norman monks who are said to have dug them is still much appreciated as they keep a great range of 11 real ales down here. These include the full Hardys & Hansons complement, alongside three or four guests from thoughtfully sourced brewers such as Burton Bridge, Castle Rock and Nottingham. Friendly young staff also serve 11 wines by the glass, quite a few malt whiskies and a farm cider. A little dwarfed by the office tower next door, this atmospheric 500-year-old building is reputed to have formed part of a Carmelite friary. Its venerable age is clearly evident throughout – some of the original timbers have been uncovered, and in the front Tudor bar you can see patches of 300-year-old wallpaper (protected by glass). With quite a café feel in summer, this room is perhaps the brightest, with french windows opening to tables on the pavement, and bright blue walls. The room with the most historical feel is the very pubby and sometimes quite smoky low-beamed Elizabethan Bar, with its half-panelled walls, maple parquet floor and comfortable high-backed armchairs. Upstairs, at the back of the heavily panelled Belfry (usually open only at lunchtime, when it functions as a family restaurant), you can see the rafters of the 15th-c crown post roof, and you can look down on the busy street at the front; TV, fruit machine and piped music. Reasonably priced straightforward bar food includes soup (£1.90), burgers (from £1.99), ploughman's (£3.99), steak and kidney pudding (£4.99), red pepper and mushroom lasagne or cod in parsley sauce (£5.99), 8oz rump (£7.99) and puddings such as jam roly-poly (£2.99) and lots of ice-cream sundaes (£3.79). *(Recommended by the Didler, David Carr, C J Fletcher, Rona Murdoch, Ian and Nita Cooper, R M Taylor, Martin and Sue Day)*

Hardys & Hansons ~ Manager Brian Rigby ~ Real ale ~ Bar food (12-8 (6 Sun)) ~ Restaurant ~ (0115) 947 5241 ~ Children in restaurant ~ Live jazz Sun lunchtime and Mon, Tues evenings, rock Weds, covers band Thurs ~ Open 10am-12 midnight(12.30 Fri, Sat); 11am-12 midnight Sun

Cock & Hoop 🛏
Lace Market Hotel, High Pavement; NG1 1HF

Civilised and completely no smoking, this carefully restored pub is in the heart of the Lace Market, opposite the former courthouse and jail, and is a welcome alternative to the somewhat louder bars that at weekends characterise this area of town. It's part of Nottingham's nicest hotel, but feels quite separate, with its own entrance, leading into a tiny front bar. There are a few tables and comfortable armchairs in here, as well as a small pewter-topped counter serving Caledonian Deuchars IPA, Fullers London Pride, and three guests like Charles Wells Bombardier, Morlands Old Speckled Hen and Nottingham Rock; cheery service. A corridor and stairs lead off to the most distinctive part of the pub – the big downstairs cellar bar, a long, windowless stone-flagged room with part panelled and part exposed brick walls, leatherette sofas and upholstered chairs and stools, and, on one side, several tiny alcoves each with a single table squeezed in. The wall lights have unusual cone-shaped shades; piped music. Good bar food includes soup (£4.95), smoked haddock, chive and parmesan risotto (£7.95), sautéed calves liver with smoked bacon and mashed potatoes (£8.50), home-made beefburger or roast salmon tournedos with warm potato and caper salad and aged balsamic dressing (£8.95), and Sunday roasts (£9.95). It can get busy at lunchtimes. Bedrooms are smart and comfortably upmarket (the ones overlooking the street can be noisy at weekends); breakfasts are good. *(Recommended by the Didler, P Dawn)*

Free house ~ Licensee Mark Cox ~ Real ale ~ Bar food (12-7 Mon-Sat, 12-9 Sun) ~ Restaurant ~ (0115) 852 3231 ~ Children allowed in cellar bar till 7pm if eating ~ Dogs allowed in bar and bedrooms ~ Open 12-11; 12 noon-2am Sat; 12-10.30 Sun; closed 25 and 26 Dec, 1 Jan ~ Bedrooms: £90S/£119B

Fellows Morton & Clayton ◗ £

Canal Street (part of inner ring road); NG1 7EH

A buzzy town pub atmosphere fills the spreading interior of this former canal warehouse, which is popular with local workers at lunchtime, and a younger set in the evening (when it can get smoky). The softly lit downstairs bar has dark red plush seats built into alcoves on shiny blonde wood floors, lots of exposed brickwork, a glossy dark green high ceiling, more tables on a raised carpeted area, and a rack of daily newspapers; piped pop music, big TVs. From a big window in the quarry-tiled, no smoking glassed-in area at the back you can see the little brewery where they brew the tasty Samuel Fellows, which is served alongside Post Haste (now brewed for them by Nottingham), as well as Castle Eden, Fullers London Pride, Mallard Duckling and Timothy Taylors Landlord. Outside, a large decked terrace overlooking the water at the back is a great place for a summer evening drink. Popular good value pub staples might include soup (£2.85), seasonal pâté (£3.50), sandwiches or wraps (from £5.25), haddock and chips or niçoise salad (£6.25), beefburger in ciabatta (£6.50), sausage and mash (£6.95), steak and kidney pie (£7.25) and 8oz sirloin (£9.95). They also do a Saturday and Sunday morning breakfast 10-11.30am (£5.25); service is prompt and friendly and a reader tells us there is disabled access, and parking at the back. *(Recommended by Andrew Beardsley, Alison Lawrence, the Didler, G Coates, David Carr, Veronica Brown)*

Own brew ~ Licensees Les Howard and Keely Willans ~ Real ale ~ Bar food (11(10 Sat)-9; 10-6 Sun) ~ Restaurant ~ (0115) 950 6795 ~ Live music Friday ~ Open 11-11(12 Fri, Sat); 12-10.30 Sun

Lincolnshire Poacher ◗ £

Mansfield Road; up hill from Victoria Centre; NG1 3FR

The dozen real ales at this popular two-room pub include Batemans XB and XXXB and the local Castle Rock Nottingham Gold and Harvest Pale, which are well kept alongside guests from a thoughtfully sourced range of brewers such as Caythorpe, Downton, Newby Wyke, Oldershaws or Ossett, Wentworth. Their impressive range of drinks is rounded out with five continental draught beers, and around 20 continental bottled beers, good farm cider, around 70 malt whiskies and ten irish ones, and very good value soft drinks. The traditional big wood-floored front bar has a cheerfully bustling atmosphere, wall settles, plain wooden tables and breweriana, and opens on to a plain but lively room on the left, with a corridor that takes you down to the chatty panelled no smoking back snug, with newspapers, cribbage, dominoes, cards and backgammon. A conservatory overlooks tables on a large terrace behind. It can get very busy in the evening, when it's popular with a younger crowd. Simple but very good value tasty bar food includes greek platter or braised vegetables in Harvest Pale (£5.50), mushroom stroganoff or vegetable sag curry (£5.75), roast pork loin in cherry beer (£5.95), sausage and mash (£6.25) and lamb and mushroom stroganoff (£6.50). *(Recommended by Richard, the Didler, David Carr, R M Taylor, Bruce Bird, Eric Robinson, Jacqueline Pratt, Des and Jen Clarke)*

Tynemill ~ Manager Karen Williams ~ Real ale ~ Bar food (12(10 Sat)-8(6 Sat, Sun)) ~
(0115) 941 1584 ~ Children away from bar areas till 8pm ~ Dogs welcome ~ Live music
Sun evening from 8.30 ~ Open 11-11(12 Fri); 10am-12pm Sat; 12-11 Sun

Olde Trip to Jerusalem ㉕ ★ 🍴 £

Brewhouse Yard; from inner ring road follow The North, A6005 Long Eaton signpost
until you are in Castle Boulevard, then almost at once turn right into Castle Road; pub
is up on the left; NG1 6AD

Some say this ancient place is the oldest pub in the country (it does feel suitably
well worn). Whether or not that's true, it's probably quite unlike any other you'll
visit. Its name refers to the 12th-c crusaders who used to meet at this site on their
way to the Holy Land – pub collectors of today still make their own crusades to
come here. Parts are darkly built into caverns burrowed into the sandstone rock
below the castle, and the siting of the current building is attributed to the days
when a brewhouse was established here to supply the needs of the castle above. The
panelled walls of the unusual upstairs bar (thought to have served as cellarage for
that earlier medieval brewhouse) soar narrowly into a dark cleft above, and also
mainly carved from the rock, the downstairs bar has leatherette-cushioned settles
built into dark panelling, tables on flagstones, and snug banquettes built into low-
ceilinged rock alcoves; there's also a no smoking parlour/snug, and two more caves
open to visitors. If you prefer not to visit with the crowds, it's best to go early
evening or on a winter lunchtime, but staff do cope efficiently with the busy mix of
tourists, conversational locals and students (it can get smoky). They keep their real
ales in top condition, and you'll find Hardys & Hansons Kimberley Best, Mild,
Olde Trip and monthly beer, alongside a couple of very quickly rotating guests
from brewers such as Leatherbritches and Oldershaw on handpump. Attractively
priced straightforward bar food includes soup (£1.99), burgers or baguettes (from
£1.99), tortilla wraps (from £3.50), steak and kidney pudding (£5.10), lasagne
(£5.90), red pepper and mushroom lasagne (£5.99), and rump steak (£7.99).
They've ring the bull and a fruit machine, and there are some seats in a small
courtyard. The museum next door is interesting. *(Recommended by A P Seymour,
Andrew Beardsley, Alison Lawrence, Derek and Sylvia Stephenson, the Didler, Kevin Blake,
Geoff and Kaye Newton, Mike and Linda Hudson, David Carr, R M Taylor, Anthony Barnes,
Colin Gooch)*

Hardys & Hansons ~ Manager Allen Watson ~ Real ale ~ Bar food (12-7(6 Sun)) ~
(0115) 9473171 ~ Children allowed until 7pm ~ Open 10.30am-11pm(12 midnight Thurs-
Sat); 11-11 Sun

Vat & Fiddle 🍴

Queens Bridge Road, alongside Sheriffs Way (near multi-storey car park); NG2 1NB

'I always feel a warm glow when I leave here – and it is not just the excellent beers,'
says one reader about this plain little brick pub. Down to earth, chatty and relaxed
and relying more on genuine character perhaps than other Nottingham main
entries, the fairly functional open-plan interior has a strong unspoilt 1930s feel,
with cream and navy walls and ceiling, varnished pine tables and bentwood stools
and chairs on parquet and terrazzo flooring, patterned blue curtains, and some
brewery memorabilia. An interesting display of photographs depicts demolished
pubs in a nearby area. Also magazines and newspapers to read, piped music some
of the time, a fruit machine, and Kipper the cat. As well as four Castle Rock beers
(the pub is right next door to the brewery and you'll probably see some comings
and goings), they serve half a dozen interesting guests from brewers such as
Archers, Burton Bridge, Black Sheep, Hop Back, Newby Wyke and Oakham. They
also have around 65 malt whiskies, a changing farm cider, a good range of
continental bottled beers, several polish vodkas and good value soft drinks, and
have occasional beer festivals too. Chilli (£5.50) is served at lunchtime, and rolls
(from £1.60) are available until they run out. Work has started, and was then
suspended, on a new restaurant so at some point in the future they may extend the

range of food. There are picnic-sets in front by the road; the train and bus stations are both just a short walk away. *(Recommended by the Didler, P Dawn, Rona Murdoch, David Carr, R M Taylor, Des and Jen Clarke)*

Tynemill ~ Manager Sarah Houghton ~ Real ale ~ Bar food (rolls all day) ~ (0115) 985 0611 ~ Children welcome away from bar ~ Dogs allowed in bar ~ Afternoon jazz last Sun in month ~ Open 11-11(12 Fri, Sat); 12-11 Sun

RANBY SK6580 Map 7

Chequers

Ranby signposted off A620 Retford—Worksop, just E of A1; DN22 8HT

This extensive open-plan pub is right next to the Chesterfield Canal, and has tables on a small terrace behind, where you may well see a colourful narrowboat mooring; there is some noise out here from the A1 traffic beyond. Inside, the main area (partly no smoking) opens into three neatly kept more or less self-contained carpeted side bays, each with an appealingly homely feel – particularly the front one on the right, which is like a pleasantly kitsch parlour with its deeply cushioned sofa and wing armchairs, dolls, nice lamps and coal-effect fire in an attractive panelled surround. Other furnishings are more orthodox, good and solid in a pleasant variety of styles, and the walls are coloured and textured. Generous attractively priced food includes soup, duck and cranberry terrine or battered onions and dips (£3.95), lobster soup (£4.25), prawn cocktail (£4.50), lunchtime sandwiches (from £4.50), omelettes (from £4.95), sausage and mash (£5.95), lamb in cinnamon and apricot sauce (£7.50), poached salmon with hollandaise or cherry tomato and red onion tart (£7.95), chicken curry (£8.25), scampi (£9.95) and 5oz rib-eye steak (£9.95); Sunday roast (£6.50). They have well kept Black Sheep, Everards Tiger and Timothy Taylors Landlord on handpump, and Burts good crisps; there may be piped music. The ladies' has all sorts of hand creams and such. *(Recommended by P Jeffries, Richard Cole, Anne and Paul Horscraft)*

Enterprise ~ Lease Christopher Jessop ~ Real ale ~ Bar food (12-2, 6-10; 12-10 Sat, Sun) ~ Restaurant ~ (01777) 703329 ~ Well behaved children welcome ~ Open 11.30-3, 5.30-11; 11.30-11.30 Sat; 12-10.30 Sun; closed Mon in winter

---

LUCKY DIP

Besides the fully inspected pubs, you might like to try these Lucky Dips recommended to us and described by readers (if you do, please send us reports: www.goodguides.co.uk).

AWSWORTH [SK4844]
Gate NG16 2RN [Main St, via A6096 off A610 Nuthall—Eastwood bypass]: Friendly old traditional local with Hardys & Hansons Best and Mild, coal fire in quiet comfortable lounge, small pool room; nr site of once-famous railway viaduct – photographs in passage *(the Didler)*

BAGTHORPE [SK4751]
Dixies Arms NG16 5HF [2 miles from M1 junction 27; A608 towards Eastwood, then first right on to B600 via Sandhill Rd, then first left into School Rd; Lower Bagthorpe]: Unspoilt 18th-c beamed and tiled-floor local, good fire in small part-panelled parlour's fine fireplace, entrance bar with tiny snug next to counter serving real ales such as Batemans XXXB, Bass, Greene King Abbot and Theakstons Best, longer narrow room with toby jugs and darts, wknd folk music, Sun quiz night; unobtrusive fruit machine, rarely used juke box; good big garden with play area and football pitch, own pigeon, gun and morris

dancing clubs; open 2-11, all day wknds *(the Didler, Kevin Blake, Derek and Sylvia Stephenson, Andy and Jill Kassube)*
Shepherds Rest NG16 5HF [2 miles from M1 junction 27, via A608 towards Eastwood, then off B600; Lower Bagthorpe]: Extensively refurbished old pub with pleasant staff, three changing real ales, good range of other drinks, wide choice of enjoyable home-made food (not Sun or Mon evening), no smoking restaurant; piped music; children welcome, garden with play area, pretty surroundings, open all day *(JJW, CMW)*

BEESTON [SK5236]
Crown NG9 1FY [Church St]: Beamed traditional local with Hardys & Hansons inc seasonal ales, small bar with high-backed settles, settles and darts in larger panelled room, comfortable lounge; open all day *(the Didler)*

BINGHAM [SK7039]
☆ *Horse & Plough* NG13 8AF [off A52; Long Acre]: Low beams, flagstones and stripped

brick, prints and old brewery memorabilia, comfortable open-plan seating inc pews, Caledonian Deuchars IPA, Charles Wells Bombardier and several guest beers inc a Mild (may offer tasters), good wine choice, generous wkdy lunchtime sandwiches and normally three or four hot bar dishes, popular upstairs evening grill room (Tues-Sat, and Sun lunch) with polished boards, hand-painted murals and open kitchen; piped music, can be smoky; open all day *(the Didler, P Dawn, BB, Hugh Roberts, David Glynne-Jones)*

BLEASBY [SK7149]

Waggon & Horses NG14 7GG [Gypsy Lane]: Comfortable banquettes in country pub's carpeted lounge, coal fire in character bar with pub games, pleasant chatty landlord, wife makes good value fresh lunchtime food from snacks up, Fri fish and chips night, Banks's and related ales inc Mansfield; piped music; back lobby with play area and comfortable chairs to watch over it, tables outside, small camping area behind *(the Didler, J R Ringrose)*

BRAMCOTE [SK5037]

White Lion NG9 3HH [just off A52 W of Nottingham; Town St]: Genuine end-terrace local with wider-than-local appeal, particularly well kept reasonably priced Hardys & Hansons ales, bar serving two split-level adjoining rooms, dominoes and darts; tables in garden behind *(Alan Bowker, MP)*

BUNNY [SK5829]

Rancliffe Arms NG11 6QT [Nottingham—Loughborough]: Popular village pub opp church, reasonably priced food and wines, carvery and curry nights, good changing ales, friendly efficient staff *(John and Sylvia Harrop)*

CAYTHORPE [SK6846]

Old Volunteer NG14 7EB [Caythorpe Rd]: Cheerful old village pub, two real ales, good fresh cobs and baguettes, daily papers, coal fire, fresh flowers, pool; TV, bar can get smoky; dogs welcome; garden tables *(JJW, CMW)*

CHILWELL [SK5135]

Cadland NG9 5EG [High Rd]: Well divided open-plan pub with good choice of wines by the glass, Bass, Worthington and guest beers, good value popular food all day, open fires, friendly staff; open all day *(the Didler)*

COLLINGHAM [SK8361]

Kings Head NG23 7LA [High St]: Modern no smoking pub behind unpretentious Georgian façade, Timothy Taylors Landlord and a guest beer from long steel bar, abstracts on light and airy dining area's colourwashed walls, bar sandwiches, good restaurant dishes with unusual touches, takeaways too, ad lib coffee; garden tables, cl Sun evening *(Kevin Thorpe)*

COLSTON BASSETT [SK6933]

☆ *Martins Arms* NG12 3FD [School Lane]: Upmarket country dining pub with formal uniformed service, good food (not winter Sun evenings) at a price, elegant restaurant (children welcome here and in family room), antiques and warm log fires in Jacobean fireplaces in comfortable bar, no smoking snug, good range of wines, malt whiskies and

cognacs, seven real ales; they may try to keep your credit card while you eat outside; antiques shop in their converted stables, sizeable attractive garden (summer croquet) backing on to parkland *(the Didler, P Dawn, Ian and Nita Cooper, Derek and Sylvia Stephenson, Richard, LYM)*

COSSALL [SK4843]

Gardeners NG16 2RZ [Awsworth Lane]: Neat open-plan local with good value Hardys & Hansons Bitter, Mild and seasonal beers, good choice of lunchtime food, end games area with pool and sports TV; pleasant tables outside *(the Didler)*

COTGRAVE [SK6435]

Rose & Crown NG12 3HQ [Main Rd, off A46 SE of Nottingham]: Comfortable and well kept village pub, with consistently good value food all day inc mid-week and early evening bargains, also more elaborate evening/wknd dishes, young helpful staff, friendly atmosphere, four changing real ales such as Caledonian Deuchars IPA, good soft drinks choice, log fires, no smoking back eating area with fresh flowers and candles; front public bar can be rather smoky; children welcome, garden picnic-sets *(Sally and Dave Bates, Richard and Jean Green, JJW, CMW)*

EASTWOOD [SK4846]

Foresters Arms NG16 2DN [Main St, Newthorpe]: Relaxed open-plan local, friendly and chatty, with Hardys & Hansons real ales, darts, dominoes, open fire, old local photographs, wknd organ singalong; TV; nice garden, occasional barbecues *(the Didler)*

EDWINSTOWE [SK6266]

Forest Lodge NG21 9QA [Church St]: 17th-c, with smiling efficient service, good range of enjoyable reasonably priced home-made food in welcoming pubby bar or restaurant, real ale, log fire; children welcome, comfortable bedrooms, handy for Sherwood Forest, open all day *(Mike Bini)*

EPPERSTONE [SK6548]

Cross Keys NG14 6AD [Main St]: Two-bar village pub with comfortably refurbished lounge/eating area popular for its home-made food (not Mon/Tues) inc bargain OAP wkdy lunch, Hardys & Hansons beers, good value house wine, prompt careful service; pretty village, pleasant countryside *(David Glynne-Jones, J R Ringrose)*

FARNSFIELD [SK6456]

Plough NG22 8EA [Main St, E end]: Warm and friendly, with attractive and comfortable L-shaped beamed lounge, good value lunchtime and (not wknds) early evening traditional food inc good Sun roasts, Marstons real ale, good fireplace; may be quiet piped music, darts, pool, TV and video games, Mon quiz night; garden with play area, open all day wknds *(Kevin Blake, Jenny Mollinson)*

GRANBY [SK7436]

☆ *Marquis of Granby* NG13 9PN [Village signposted off A52 E of Nottingham; Dragon Street]: Standing out for its seven or more quickly changing guest beers served from the chunky yew bar counter, good value food and

friendly service, this 18th-c local would have
been a main entry this year, but was up for sale
as we went to press; the two small flagstoned
rooms have had a comfortably old-fashioned,
lived-in feel, with faded rugs, low beams
covered with hundreds of pump clips, books to
read, a piano, log fire, and an open kitchen;
simple outside lavatories; wheelchair access
(and a welcome for dogs), has been cl Mon-
Weds lunchtimes, open all day Sat *(BB)*

GUNTHORPE [SK6843]

☆ *Tom Browns* NG14 7FB [Old School House,
Trentside; off A6097 E of Nottingham]:
Comfortably modern restauranty dining bar
over road from River Trent, enjoyable up-to-
date food inc good Sun lunch and early
evening bargains, splendid choice of wines,
changing real ales (and a few seats for having
just a drink), friendly staff and easy-going
atmosphere, log fire; well reproduced pop
music, no dogs; seats outside, pleasant walks
(Mr and Mrs Gerry Price, BB)

HARBY [SK8870]

Bottle & Glass NG23 7EB [High St]:
Reopened after long closure as smart dining
pub under new owners, enjoyable and
imaginative food in bar and restaurant, choice
of real ales; tables outside *(David and
Ruth Hollands)*

HOVERINGHAM [SK6946]

☆ *Reindeer* NG14 7JR [Main St]: Comfortably
unspoilt and unpretentious low-beamed
Tynemill pub with particularly friendly staff,
four or five good changing ales such as Black
Sheep, Castle Rock and Fullers London Pride,
good wines by the glass, good short choice of
enjoyable food, fair value if not cheap, from
pubby things to enterprising dishes, coal fires
in bar and no smoking dining lounge/back
restaurant, daily papers; children welcome,
picnic-sets outside, cl Sun evening, Tues
lunchtime and Mon, open all day Sat, and Sun
till 5 *(the Didler, J R Ringrose, JJW, CMW,
Phil and Jane Hodson)*

HUTHWAITE [SK4659]

Miners Arms NG17 2RF [off M1 junction 28]:
Large friendly bar with two real ales, good soft
drinks range, good choice of fairly priced food,
attentive service, games machines, no smoking
conservatory restaurant, pub cat; piped music
(can be turned down); children welcome,
picnic-sets in small garden *(JJW, CMW)*

KIMBERLEY [SK4944]

☆ *Nelson & Railway* NG16 2NR [Station Rd;
handy for M1 junction 26 via A610]: Cheery
and chatty beamed Victorian local with plans
for bigger no smoking dining area and kitchen
(so may expand food – currently bargain
simple range from sandwiches and hot rolls
up), particularly well kept Hardys & Hansons
ales (fragrant brewery opposite – if Greene
King keep it open), welcoming service, mix of
Edwardian-looking furniture, brewery prints
and railway signs, traditional games inc alley
and table skittles; piped music, fruit machine,
juke box; dogs allowed in bar, children in
restaurant, tables and swings in good-sized
cottage garden, good value bedrooms, open

all day *(the Didler, Pete Baker, Geoff and
Angela Jaques, Ian Stafford, Roy Branson,
LYM, Dr D and Mrs B Woods, Dr Alan and
Mrs Sue Holder, Karen Eliot)*
Stag NG16 2NB [Nottingham Rd]: Friendly
16th-c traditional local kept spotless by
devoted landlady, two cosy rooms, small
central counter and corridor, low beams, dark
panelling and settles, real ales inc Adnams,
Black Sheep, Caledonian Deuchars IPA,
Marstons Pedigree and Timothy Taylors
Landlord, vintage working penny slot
machines and Shipstones brewery
photographs; attractive back garden with play
area, cl wkdy lunchtime (opens 5; 1.30 Sat,
12 Sun) *(the Didler, P Dawn)*

LANGAR [SK7234]

Unicorns Head NG13 9HE [Main St]: Dining
pub popular with business and older people,
children's menu too, sensible prices *(MP)*

LANGLEY MILL [SK4248]

Thorn Tree NG16 4HG [Nottingham Rd]:
Great views over rountry, real ales,
enjoyable reasonably priced food
(Richard Greenwood)

LINBY [SK5351]

Horse & Groom NG15 8AE [Main St]:
Picturesque and unpretentious, with several
rooms and pleasant colour scheme, wide
choice of decent straightforward food, several
changing real ales such as Theakstons and
Charles Wells Bombardier, friendly staff,
inglenook log fire, conservatory, no piped
music or mobile phones; tables outside, big
play area, attractive village nr Newstead
Abbey, open all day *(the Didler,
Richard Greenwood)*

LOWDHAM [SK6746]

Magna Charta NG14 7DQ [Southwell Rd]:
Big Hardys & Hansons pub with good friendly
staff, good beers and choice of wines and soft
drinks, popular for good range of good value
standard food all day from sandwiches, wraps
and baked potatoes to steaks, different linked
areas inc no smoking ones; they may try to
keep your credit card while you eat, piped
pop music, big-screen sports TV; special
children's lavatory, garden *(Gerry and
Rosemary Dobson, JJW, CMW)*

☆ *Old Ship* NG14 7BE [nr A612/A6097; Main
St]: Friendly beamed country pub with good
blackboard food choice, large no smoking
two-level dining area up steps, comfortable
furnishings from traditional built-in settles to
plush banquettes, some big round tables, up to
five real ales such as John Smiths, coal fire, lots
of pictures for sale, plates, copper and brass;
piped music, separate public bar can get
smoky; picnic-sets on heated verandah and
neat sheltered back lawn, bedrooms, pleasant
walks nearby *(JJW, CMW, BB)*
Worlds End NG14 7AT [Plough Lane]: Small
village pub with reasonably priced food inc
popular OAP lunches in recently refurbished
restaurant area, several real ales, good soft
drinks choice, log fire in pubby beamed bar;
piped music; children welcome, picnic-sets,
some under awning, in garden *(Richard)*

MANSFIELD [SK5260]
Nell Gwynne NG18 5EX [A38 W of centre]:
Former gentlemen's club with the look of a
private house, two well kept usually quite
strong changing ales, chatty landlady, homely
lounge with log-effect gas fire, old colliery
plates and mementoes of old Mansfield pubs,
games room; sports TV, piped music, nearby
parking can be difficult; cl Mon-Thurs
lunchtimes *(the Didler, Derek and
Sylvia Stephenson)*
Railway Inn NG19 8AD [Station St; best
approached by viaduct from nr market pl]:
Friendly traditional pub with long-serving
landlady, attractively priced Batemans XB and
a seasonal beer, bargain home-made lunches,
divided main bar and separate room; handy for
Robin Hood Line stn, normally open all day,
cl Sun evening *(the Didler, Pete Baker)*
MANSFIELD WOODHOUSE [SK5463]
Greyhound NG19 8BD [High St]: Popular
village local with Banks's Mansfield, Greene
King IPA, Theakstons Mild, Websters and one
or two guest beers, cosy lounge, darts,
dominoes and pool in busy bar; quiz nights
Mon and Weds; open all day *(the Didler,
P Dawn)*
MAPLEBECK [SK7160]
☆ *Beehive* NG22 0BS [signed down pretty
country lanes from A616 Newark—Ollerton
and from A617 Newark—Mansfield]: Cosy
and unspoiled beamed country tavern in nice
spot, chatty landlady, tiny front bar, slightly
bigger side room, traditional furnishings, coal
or log fire, free antique juke box, changing real
ales such as local Milestone; tables on small
terrace with flower tubs and grassy bank
running down to little stream, play area with
swings, barbecues; no food, may be cl wkdy
winter lunchtimes, very busy wknds and bank
hols *(LYM, the Didler, J R Ringrose)*
NEWARK [SK7953]
Castle & Falcon NG24 1TW [London Rd]:
Former coaching inn now a friendly bustling
local, John Smiths and guest beers, comfortable
back lounge and family conservatory; lively
games bar with darts, dominoes, pool and TV;
terrace tables and skittle alley, evening
opening 7, cl lunchtime Tues-Thurs
(David Carr, the Didler)
☆ *Fox & Crown* NG24 1JY [Appleton Gate]:
Convivial bare-boards open-plan Tynemill
pub, chatty and relaxed, with Castle Rock ales
and several interesting guest beers from central
servery, Stowford Press cider, lots of whiskies,
vodkas and other spirits, good coffee and
decent wines by the glass, friendly obliging
staff, cheap simple fresh food from filled rolls,
baguettes, panini and baked potatoes up,
several side areas inc no smoking ones
(children allowed); parts can get smoky, piped
pop music may be loudish; good wheelchair
access, open all day (till 12 Fri/Sat) *(Gwyn and
Anne Wake, the Didler, Andy Booth,
David and Ruth Hollands, BB,
Mrs Hazel Rainer)*
Mail Coach NG24 1TN [London Rd, nr
Beaumond Cross]: Friendly open-plan

Georgian local, three candlelit separate areas,
lots of chicken pictures, hot coal fires and
comfortable chairs, Caledonian Deuchars IPA,
Flowers IPA and Original and two or more
local guest beers, pleasant staff, lunchtime food
(not Mon); May beer festival, pub games,
frequent live music Thurs, upstairs ladies';
tables on back terrace *(the Didler, Kevin Blake,
Di and Mike Gillam)*
Navigation NG24 4TS [Mill Gate]: Lively
open-plan bar in converted warehouse, big
windows on to River Trent, bare
boards and iron pillars, Everards Tiger, bar
food, nautical decorations; weekly live music
(David and Ruth Hollands)
Old Malt Shovel NG24 1HD [North Gate]:
Welcoming and comfortably opened-up, with
enjoyable food from doorstep sandwiches to
restaurant dishes, several good changing ales
such as Timothy Taylors Landlord and Charles
Wells Bombardier, choice of teas, open fire,
lots of books and bottles on shelves, cheerfully
laid-back atmosphere and service, pub games,
skittle alley; wheelchair access, terrace tables,
open all day Weds-Sun *(the Didler,
David Carr)*
NEWSTEAD [SK5252]
Station Hotel NG15 0BZ [Station Rd]: Busy
basic red-brick village local opp station on
Robin Hood rail line, bargain Barnsley Bitter
and Robinsons Old Tom Mild, fine old railway
photographs; no food Sun *(the Didler)*
NORMANTON ON TRENT [SK7969]
☆ *Square & Compass* NG23 6RN [East Gate;
signed off B1164 S of Tuxford]: Low-beamed
pub reopened under new management after
being closed for a while, good sensibly priced
food, good choice of beers; children welcome
in eating areas, small play area out behind,
motel-style bedrooms, open all day
(J V Dadswell, LYM)
NORTH MUSKHAM [SK7958]
Muskham Ferry NG23 6HB [Ferry Lane,
handy for A1 (which has small sign to pub)]:
Traditional pub in splendid location on River
Trent, relaxing views from bar/restaurant,
varied food from sandwiches up, changing real
ales, attentive staff; children very welcome,
waterside terrace *(LYM, Peter Bloodworth,
Susan Knight)*
Muskham Inn NG23 6HN [off A1 N of
Newark, by B6325 exit roundabout]: This
handy pub, a useful main entry for its civilised
bar with lots of soft dark leather settees, log
fire and good choice of cold and hot drinks,
and spacious and relaxed dining area with
good food, was closed as we went to press,
with the possibility of a complete change of
style; tables out on a sheltered terrace behind,
under cover, well equipped modern bedrooms
in separate block; news please *(LYM)*
NOTTINGHAM [SK5739]
Bunkers Hill NG1 1FP [Hockley, next to Ice
Stadium]: Stylish and imposing high-beamed
and panelled bank conversion with half a
dozen real ales such as Batemans, Mallard,
Nottingham Rock and Springhead, espresso
machine and good wine choice, enjoyable up-

to-date food (not Sun evening), some live music upstairs; pleasant terrace tables, open all day – till 1am Fri/Sat *(the Didler)*

Canal House NG1 7EH [Canal St]: Big conversion of wharf building, bridge over indoors canal spur complete with narrowboat, lots of bare brick and varnished wood, huge joists on studded steel beams, long bar with good choice of house wines (two glass sizes) and changing real ales, lots of standing room; good upstairs restaurant and second bar, masses of solid tables out on attractive waterside terrace; piped music (live Sun), popular with young people at night; open all day – till midnight Thurs, 1am Fri/Sat *(the Didler, David Carr, BB)*

Cast Bar NG1 5AL [Wellington Circus, nr Playhouse Theatre]: Adjoining theatre, more wine bar/restaurant than pub, cool, sophisticated and relaxed, with lots of chrome and glass, decent range of wines by the glass, real ale such as Castle Rock or Nottingham (the handpumps hide below the counter), good value light menu, more adventurous restaurant meals (the blue seats are no smoking – children allowed here), good integral all-day deli; plenty of tables out on notable courtyard terrace by huge Anish Kapoor *Sky Mirror*, open all day *(Patrick Renouf, Richard)*

Coopers Arms NG3 6JH [Porchester Rd, Thornywood]: Solid Victorian local with three unspoilt rooms, Black Sheep, Theakstons and guest ales, small family room in skittle alley; cl Weds lunchtime *(the Didler)*

Falcon NG7 3JE [Canning Circus/Alfreton Rd]: Two small friendly rooms with old pictures and flame-effect fire in attractive fireplace, Adnams Bitter and Broadside and a guest beer, good choice of wines, pleasant upstairs restaurant serving indian food inc takeaways; TV may obtrude, needs a no smoking area; terrace tables and barbecues, open all day *(the Didler, MP)*

Fox & Crown NG6 0GA [Church St/Lincoln St, Old Basford]: Good range of Alcazar beers brewed at back of unpretentious open-plan pub (window shows the brewery, tours Sat, new next-door beer shop), also guest beers, good continental bottle choice, enjoyable fresh food inc thai and wide choice of early evening home-made pizzas, helpful staff and Canadian landlord; good piped music, games machines, Tues quiz night, frequent beer festivals, big-screen sports TV; disabled access possible (lavatories difficult), tables out behind, open all day *(the Didler, Kevin Blake, P Dawn, R M Taylor)*

Gladstone NG5 2AW [Loscoe Rd, Carrington]: Properly pubby two-room local, local Nottingham EPA and several other ales such as Timothy Taylors Landlord, good range of malt whiskies, helpful landlord and friendly staff, cosy comfortable lounge with reading matter, basic bar with darts and sports TV; upstairs folk club Weds, quiz Thurs; tables in yard with lots of hanging baskets, cl wkdy lunchtimes, open all day wknds (from 3 Fri) *(Richard, the Didler)*

Globe NG2 3BQ [London Rd]: Light and airy roadside pub with attractively priced fresh straightforward food all day inc good Sun lunch, six real ales mainly from local breweries, farm cider, coal fire; handy for cricket or football matches, open all day *(the Didler, R M Taylor, Des and Jen Clarke)*

Horse & Groom NG7 7EA [Radford Rd, New Basford]: Unpretentious and well run partly open-plan pub by former Shipstones brewery, still with their name and other memorabilia, friendly (if sometimes a little smoky) atmosphere, eight good changing ales, good value fresh straightforward food from sandwiches to Sun lunches, daily papers, nice snug, wknd live music; open all day *(the Didler, Kevin Blake, R M Taylor)*

☆ *Keanes Head* NG1 1QA [St Marys Gate]: Comfortable and cheerily unpretentious no smoking one-room Tynemill pub, good range of enjoyable food, lots for vegetarians, all home-made (the jam too), all day from breakfast till late, changing choice of carefully selected ales, with some emphasis on local Castle Rock, two dozen wines by the glass, draught belgian beers, interesting variety of bottled beers and soft drinks, lots of coffees and teas (can take these away); simple wooden furnishings, exposed brickwork, low sofa by big window overlooking street, daily papers; piped music, and may try to keep your credit card while you eat; open all day *(the Didler, Andy and Ali, P Dawn, BB, MP, Val and Alan Green)*

☆ *Lion* NG7 7FQ [Lower Mosley St, New Basford]: Three or four Batemans ales and half a dozen interesting changing guest beers kept in one of city's deepest cellars (glass viewing panel – and can be visited at quiet times), farm cider, ten wines by the glass, wide choice of good value wholesome home-made food all day inc doorstep sandwiches, children's helpings and summer barbecues; open plan but the feel of separate areas, bare bricks and polished dark oak boards, coal or log fires, daily papers; live music Fri/Sat, jazz Sun lunchtimes; well behaved children welcome, pleasant terrace, open all day *(the Didler, Kevin Blake, P Dawn, R M Taylor, Brian and Ruth Archer, Andy Lickfold)*

News House NG1 7HB [Canal St]: Friendly two-room Tynemill pub with attractive blue exterior tiling, eight well kept changing ales inc bargain Castle Rock, belgian and czech imports on tap, Weston's Old Rosie farm cider, good wine and hot drinks choice, enjoyable fresh food inc Sun lunch, mix of bare boards and carpet, one room filled with local newspaper front pages spanning years of events and personalities; sports TV; open all day *(the Didler)*

Old Moot Hall NG3 2DG [Carlton Rd, Sneinton]: Now tied to Tom Woods Highwood, with a fine choice of guest beers and wines by the glass too, good friendly staff, enjoyable wholesome food, coal-effect gas fire, polished boards and striking décor, upstairs bar with pool; big-screen sports TV; open all day *(A and P Lancashire, the Didler)*

☆ *Pit & Pendulum* NG1 2EW [Victoria Street]: Dark and dramatic gothick theme bar with ghoulish carving and creeping ivy lit by heavy chandeliers and (electronically) flaring torches, all sorts of other more or less cinematic horror allusions in the décor, all-day bar food, friendly staff, well reproduced piped music; keg beers, and there may be changes as the tenant has left; good wheelchair access, open all day *(David Carr, LYM)*

☆ *Plough* NG7 3EN [St Peters St, Radford]: Unpretentious two-room 19th-c pub brewing its own interesting Nottingham ales, also a guest beer and farm ciders, good bargain food inc fresh rolls and popular Sun lunch (live jazz then), bargain curries Tues evening, two coal fires, traditional fittings and nice windows, bar billiards and other traditional games (competitions Weds), Thurs irish music night (may be free chilli); Sun barbecues, open all day Thurs-Sun *(the Didler, P Dawn, R M Taylor)*

☆ *Salutation* NG1 7AA [Hounds Gate/Maid Marion Way]: Proper pub, with beams, flagstones and cosy corners inc two small quiet rooms and no smoking area in ancient lower back part, plusher modern front lounge, good range of real ales and bottled beers, helpful staff, enjoyable plain quickly served food till 7; piped music; open all day *(David Carr, BB, Val and Alan Green, R M Taylor)*

Sherwood Manor NG5 2FX [Mansfield Rd, Sherwood]: Recently refurbished Hardys & Hansons pub with their ales kept well, several eating and drinking areas *(Patrick Renouf)*

ORSTON [SK7741]

Durham Ox NG13 9NS [Church St]: Country local opp church, Fullers London Pride, Greene King IPA, Marstons Pedigree and guest beers, good soft drinks choice, good value filled rolls (no hot food), comfortable split-level open-plan bar with hot coal fire, interesting RAF/USAF memorabilia, collection of whisky bottles; may be piped music or TV; terrace tables, nice garden, pleasant countryside, open all day Sat *(the Didler)*

OXTON [SK6250]

Olde Bridge NG25 0SE [Nottingham Rd (B6386)]: Large well kept pub with three or more real ales inc Everards, good soft drinks range, good value food, daily papers, popular no smoking restaurant area; piped music, games machines; disabled facilities, children welcome, large garden, cl Mon, open all day Sat *(JJW, CMW, J R Ringrose)*

RADCLIFFE ON TRENT [SK6439]

Black Lion NG12 2FD [Main Rd (A52)]: Popular for good choice of good value food all day from filled rolls to full meals, Courage Directors, Everards and three quickly changing guest beers, farm cider, good soft drinks choice, big comfortable lounge, half no smoking, with games machine and coal fire, friendly bar with pool and big-screen sports TV; beer festivals; big enclosed garden, barbecues and play area, open all day *(the Didler, JJW, CMW)*

Trent NG12 1AE [Shelford Rd]: Reopened late 2005 after extensive refurbishment, all no smoking, well run and comfortable, with wide food choice inc wkdy lunchtime OAP bargains, changing ales such as Batemans, Greene King, Ringwood BB and Theakstons XB, well chosen wines, friendly efficient service; extensive decking with colourful flowers *(David Glynne-Jones)*

RETFORD [SK6980]

☆ *Market Hotel* DN22 7SN [off West Carr Rd, Ordsall; follow Leisure Centre signs from A620, then just after industrial estate sign keep eyes skinned for pub sign on left]: In same family for over 40 years, with eight well chosen and kept changing ales (up to 40 in autumn beer festival), comfortable plush banquettes, generous straightforward food (not Sun evening) from sandwiches and rolls up, popular Sun carvery lunch, friendly helpful service, no smoking area, occasional jazz; children welcome till early evening, tables outside, bedrooms, open all day Sat *(LYM, Tony Hobden, Tony and Wendy Hobden)*

SCROOBY [SK6590]

☆ *Pilgrim Fathers* DN10 6AT [Great North Rd (A638 S of Bawtry)]: Well kept beamed pub with good freshly made food inc nice puddings, Greene King Abbot, John Smiths and Timothy Taylors Landlord, good coffee, friendly and unobtrusively efficient service, leather wing armchair and panelled window seat among other furnishings in comfortable carpeted main bar, small homely end dining area, simpler separate public bar, lots of games such as shove-ha'penny and bagatelle, sizeable conservatory; unobtrusive piped music, games machine; dogs welcome, garden tables *(Derek and Sylvia Stephenson, Dave and Liz Cubbon, BB)*

SELSTON [SK4553]

Horse & Jockey NG16 6FB [handy for M1 junctions 27/28; Church Lane]: Charming 17th-c interior on three levels, low beams and flagstones, several real ales such as Abbeydale Absolution, Bass, Greene King IPA and Timothy Taylors Landlord on handpump or in jugs from the cellar, friendly staff, coal fire in cast-iron range, cosy snug off lower bar area, darts and pool in top room *(the Didler, R T and J C Moggridge)*

SOUTH LEVERTON [SK7881]

Plough DN22 0BT [Town St]: Tiny local doubling as morning post office, basic trestle tables and benches, real fire, Greene King Ruddles County and a guest beer, traditional games; tables outside, open 2ish-11, all day wknds *(the Didler)*

SOUTHWELL [SK7053]

Bramley Apple NG25 0HQ [Church St (A612)]: Light and airy long bar with front room off, friendly newish licensees, good value food, Springhead and changing guest ales, attentive service; bedrooms, open all day Sat/Sun *(the Didler, BB)*

SUTTON IN ASHFIELD [SK5059]

King & Miller NG17 4JP [Kings Mill Rd E]: Comfortable and relaxed family pub, play areas inside and out, huge range of low-priced enjoyable food, warm welcome, decent wines, Hardys & Hansons beers, alcove seating in lounge with old local pictures and shelves of bric-a-brac, restaurant *(Kevin Blake)*

THURGARTON [SK6949]

Coach & Horses NG14 7GY [Main St]: Smart and pleasantly laid out, with good value often interesting changing ales, wines classified by grape, helpful staff under new licensees, well priced bar menu *(J R Ringrose)*

☆ *Red Lion* NG14 7GP [Southwell Rd (A612)]: Cheery 16th-c inn with consistently good freshly cooked food (all day wknds and bank hols) inc fresh fish and some adventurous dishes in brightly decorated split-level beamed bars and restaurant, good friendly service, real ales such as Black Sheep, Caledonian Deuchars IPA and Mansfield, comfortable banquettes and other seating, flame-effect fire, lots of nooks and crannies, big windows to attractive good-sized two-level back garden with well spaced picnic-sets (dogs on leads allowed here); unobtrusive fruit machine, steepish walk back up to car park; children welcome *(David Glynne-Jones, Derek and Sylvia Stephenson, BB, J R Ringrose)*

UNDERWOOD [SK4751]

☆ *Red Lion* NG16 5HD [off B600, nr M1 junction 27; Church Lane]: Reliable sensibly priced family food inc OAP lunches, other bargains and good fresh fish in welcoming 17th-c split-level beamed village pub, Caledonian Deuchars IPA, Marstons Pedigree and guests such as Archers and Timothy Taylors Landlord, good service, spacious open-plan quarry-tiled bar with open fire, some cushioned settles, pictures and plates on dressers, penny arcade machine, no piped music; children welcome, picnic-sets and large adventure playground in big garden with terrace and barbecues, attractive setting, open all day Fri-Sun *(the Didler, Kevin Blake, Derek and Sylvia Stephenson, Andy and Jill Kassube)*

WALKERINGHAM [SK7692]

Three Horse Shoes DN10 4HR [High St]: This pub, once famous for its floral displays, and more recently still enjoyed for good value food and drink, has closed, with plans for housing on the site *(LYM)*

WATNALL CHAWORTH [SK5046]

☆ *Queens Head* NG16 1HT [3 miles from M1 junction 26: A610 towards Nottingham, left on B600, then keep right; Main Rd]: Cosy and tastefully extended old pub with great fish and chips and wide range of other good value food (all day summer), Greene King IPA, Theakstons and guest beers, efficient friendly service, beams and stripped pine, coal fire, intimate snug, dining area; piped music; picnic-sets in spacious and attractive back garden with big play area, open all day Fri/Sat *(the Didler, Derek and Sylvia Stephenson)*

Royal Oak NG16 1HS [Main Rd; B600 N of Kimberley]: Friendly beamed village local with interesting plates and pictures, Hardys & Hansons, guest beers and beer festivals, fresh

cobs, woodburner, back games room and pool room, upstairs lounge open Fri-Sun; sports TV; open all day *(the Didler)*

WELLOW [SK6666]

Olde Red Lion NG22 0EG [Eakring Rd, just off A616 E of Ollerton]: Welcoming low-beamed and panelled 16th-c pub by green with towering maypole, chatty licensees, attractively priced Caledonian Deuchars IPA, Fullers London Pride and Charles Wells Bombardier, good value food from sandwiches to steak and bargain Sun roasts, no smoking restaurant and dining area, no piped music; children welcome, picnic-sets outside *(LYM, J R Ringrose)*

WEST BRIDGFORD [SK5838]

Southbank NG2 5GJ [Trent Bridge]: Bright well run sports bar with polished wood floors, sofas, real ales such as Boddingtons, Fullers London Pride, Mallard and Nottingham, wide choice of lagers and soft drinks, coffee, good all-day food choice from baguettes and light dishes to mixed grills, Mon curry night, friendly efficient staff; several big screens and lots of other sports TVs; big garden overlooking river, handy for cricket ground and Notts Forest FC, open all day *(the Didler, P Dawn)*

☆ *Stratford Haven* NG2 6BA [Stratford Rd, Trent Bridge]: Busy and chatty Tynemill pub, bare-boards front bar leading to linked areas inc airy skylit and carpeted yellow-walled back part with relaxed local atmosphere, Castle Rock and good changing guest beers, exotic bottled beers, farm ciders, ample whiskies and wines, good value simple home-made food all day, daily papers; some live music (nothing too noisy), can get crowded; handy for cricket ground and Nottingham Forest FC, tables outside, open all day *(the Didler, Kevin Blake, P Dawn, MP, BB, R M Taylor, Derek and Sylvia Stephenson, Des and Jen Clarke)*

Test Match NG2 5LP [Gordon Sq, West Bridgford]: Handsome art deco décor with revolving door, high ceiling and sweeping staircase up to lounge, unpretentious furnishings, big cricketing prints, some signed bats, full range of Hardys & Hansons beers, friendly staff, bar food, no smoking room, separate sports and games bar; live music Sun; disabled access and facilities, tables outside *(Kevin Blake, P Dawn, Sarah Cunningham)*

WEST LEAKE [SK5126]

☆ *Star* LE12 5RQ [Melton Lane, off A6006]: Comfortable oak-panelled lounge with good central log fire, pewter mugs, china, pictures, attractive table lamps and side eating area, traditional beamed and quarry-tiled country bar on left with wall settles, plenty of character and traditional games, good value home-made food (not Sun evening) from substantial baps to cheap steaks, Bass, Caledonian Deuchars IPA and changing guest beers, good coffee, jovial landlord, helpful service, no piped music or machines; children in eating area, picnic-sets on front terrace (quiet spot) and in garden with play area, bedrooms, open all day *(the Didler, P Dawn, LYM, Brian and Ruth Archer)*

WEST MARKHAM [SK7273]
Mussel & Crab NG22 0PJ [Sibthorpe Hill; B1164 nr A1/A57/A638 roundabout N of Tuxford]: Pub/restaurant specialising in good fish and seafood fresh daily from Brixham, other enjoyable dishes on vast array of blackboards, interesting bar and two roomy dining areas (beams and stripped stone, or more flamboyant pastel murals), welcoming attentive staff, good wines by the glass (wine racks around the room), Tetleys, good coffee; good disabled access, picnic-sets on terrace, play area, views over wheatfields *(M and C Thompson)*

WIDMERPOOL [SK6429]
☆ *Pullman* NG12 5PR [1st left off A606 coming towards Nottingham from A46 junction; Kinoulton Lane]: Thriving family dining pub in well converted and extended station building, abundant locomotive and train paintings, friendly helpful service, big helpings of good food inc fish and carvery nights, two real ales,

good wine choice; piped music; tables and picnic-sets outside *(John and Sylvia Harrop, Andrew Beardsley, Alison Lawrence, Phil and Jane Hodson)*

WOODBOROUGH [SK6347]
Nags Head NG14 6DD [Main St]: Village pub recently reopened and refurbished by Hardys & Hansons, clean and smart, with comfortable atmosphere, good service and wide choice of mainly pubby food *(J R Ringrose)*

WYSALL [SK6027]
Plough NG12 5QQ [Keyworth Rd; off A60 at Costock, or A6006 at Wymeswold]: Welcoming and attractive 17th-c beamed village pub, changing real ales, generous enjoyable food inc popular Sun lunch, two rooms on either side of central bar with nice mix of furnishings, soft lighting, big log fire; can get a bit smoky when busy; french doors to pretty terrace with flower tubs and baskets *(Gwyn and Anne Wake, Brian and Ruth Archer)*

Post Office address codings confusingly give the impression that a few pubs are in Nottinghamshire, when they're really in Derbyshire (which is where we list them).

Oxfordshire

This year we have lost quite a few former main entries in this county, with licensee changes, changes in management style and performance, and even outright closures moving all too many former favourites to the small print section. However, the swings and roundabouts have been working rather well, and we have a good clutch of tempting new finds to make up. The Chequers at Aston Tirrold, the Radnor Arms at Coleshill, the Cherry Tree at Kingston Blount, the Bell at Langford, the Baskerville Arms in Shiplake and the Masons Arms at Swerford all serve good, even very good, food, and represent a surprisingly wide range of different styles. Another nice new entry (in fact returning to the *Guide* after a very long absence) is the well run Trout at Godstow; here, it's character and position which count above all else. Given how well this county scores for pub food, it's quite a surprise that so many of the best pubs here are chattily unspoilt places rather than smart restauranty dining pubs. Pubs on great form include the Reindeer in Banbury (a congenial and interesting town local), the super little Horse & Groom at Caulcott (though sadly the licensees are thinking of selling up), the Chequers in Chipping Norton (this unspoilt town tavern is quite a favourite with readers), the Merrymouth at Fifield (a nice place to stay), the popular Falkland Arms in the lovely village of Great Tew (a charming building with plenty of real ales), the Anchor in Henley (another unspoilt town pub with a friendly landlady), the Gate Hangs High and the Sun, both in Hook Norton, the Plough at Kelmscott (a peaceful setting by the Thames), the Rose & Crown and Turf Tavern in Oxford (both are busy and very well run), and the enjoyable Royal Oak at Ramsden. For a special meal out, notable pubs offering excellent food include the Chequers at Aston Tirrold, the White Hart at Fyfield, the Gate Hangs High near Hook Norton, and the Baskerville Arms in Shiplake. Two of these are new entries this year (which underlines the continuing rapid pace of improvement in Oxfordshire's pub food), and one of them, the Baskerville Arms in Shiplake, takes the title of Oxfordshire Dining Pub of the Year. Pubs to pick out in the Lucky Dip section at the end of the chapter are the Saye & Sele Arms at Broughton, Tite at Chadlington, Bell in Charlbury, Crown at Church Enstone, Barley Mow at Clifton Hampden, Bat & Ball at Cuddesdon, Deddington Arms in Deddington, Catherine Wheel and Miller of Mansfield, both in Goring, Rose Revived at Newbridge, Lamb at Satwell, Bell at Shenington, Shaven Crown at Shipton-under-Wychwood, Duck on the Pond at South Newington, Cherry Tree and Crooked Billet, both at Stoke Row, Flowing Well at Sunningwell, Six Bells at Warborough and Kings Head at Wootton. There's no shortage of decent pubs in Oxford – or, perhaps more surprisingly, in Burford. Drinks prices in the county are higher than the national average. Often, the cheapest beer sold by a pub here turns out to be the local Hook Norton, always worth looking out for. The county's other famous beer, Brakspears, tends not to be cheap; and three other local breweries also supplying some good pubs here are Loddon, White Horse and Wychwood.

ALVESCOT SP2704 Map 4
Plough
B4020 Carterton—Clanfield, SW of Witney; OX18 2PU

Some changes here this year include new carpets and a Victorian fireplace for the bar and additional dining space created, a new back terrace, and the removal of the pool table. The dogs have been replaced by two cats, Dino and Boo, and the fruit machine is now a quiz machine. The neatly kept bar has a good pubby atmosphere, a collection of aircraft prints and a large poster of Concorde's last flight, as well as plenty of cottagey pictures, china ornaments and house plants, a big antique case of stuffed birds of prey, sundry bric-a-brac, and a log fire. Comfortable seating includes cushioned settles, a nice armchair, and of course the bar stools bagged by cheerful regulars in the early evening; tropical fish tank. The dining area is no smoking. From a wide menu, the food might include home-made soup (£3.95), egg mayonnaise (£4.25), brussels pâté (£4.50), cottage cheese and pineapple, chicken kiev or cumberland sausage and mash (£7.25), ham and eggs, battered cod or brie, almond and courgette crumble (£7.50), home-made beef and mushroom in ale pie or a combination starter for two (£7.95), lamb cobbler (£8.25), and steaks (from £10.95); two meals for £10 (Monday-Saturday lunchtimes only) and Sunday roast (£6.50). Wadworths IPA and 6X on handpump. There's a proper public bar with TV and darts; piped music and skittle alley. Two picnic-sets stand out in front below particularly colourful hanging baskets by the quiet village road, with more behind under trees, by a bird table and play area; aunt sally. (Recommended by KN-R, Marjorie and David Lamb, Peter and Audrey Dowsett, Ian Phillips, Karen and Graham Oddey)

Wadworths ~ Tenant Kevin Robert Keeling ~ Real ale ~ Bar food (12-3, 7-9) ~ (01993) 842281 ~ Children allowed but no under-5s after 8pm ~ Dogs allowed in bar ~ Open 11.30-3, 6-11; 12-3, 7-10.30 Sun

ASTON TIRROLD SU5586 Map 2
Chequers 🍴 ♀
Village signposted off A417 Streatley—Wantage; Fullers Road; OX11 9EN

This charming hybrid has two signs – the Chequers of course, and also the Sweet Olive – and formally it calls itself the Sweet Olive at the Chequers. The double naming gives a very good clue to its character: the shape and atmosphere of a welcoming village pub, combined with the heart and soul of a rustic french restaurant. The food is very good. They have quite a variety of baguettes (they bake their own bread, using organic flour), such as crispy duck, sausage, venison burger (£6, or £7.50 with chips), and one or two snacks such as goats cheese salad (£6.75), with a full menu changing daily. Starters might include home-made gravadlax or duck pâté (£6.50), crispy duck salad (£6.65) and lamb sweetbreads with spinach and wild mushrooms or cornish mussels done with coriander (£7.95); main dishes might include chicken breast with mushroom sauce and pasta (£9.95), skate with lime butter (£13.95), venison in port sauce with creamed cabbage (£14.95) or seared scallops with wild mushroom and parmesan risotto (£15.50). They make nice puddings such as nougat ice-cream with fresh raspberry coulis. Service is unobtrusively stylish in the best french manner, and meals come with a slate of olives and good breads as well as a handsomely ringed linen napkin. Yet the feel of the place is relaxed and chattily pubby. The main room has a proper bar counter, complete with sturdy bar stools (and people using them), and Caledonian Deuchars IPA and Hook Norton Hooky on handpump, as well as good coffees and a nice range of french wines by the glass, including a pudding wine. It has grass matting over its quarry tiles, six or seven sturdy stripped tables with mate's chairs and cushioned high-backed settles against the walls, a small fireplace, and plain white walls. There are two or three wine cartoons, and wine box-ends, mainly claret and sauternes, panel the back of the servery. A second rather smaller room, set more formally as a restaurant, has a similarly restrained décor of pale grey dado, white-panelled ceiling and red and black flooring tiles. There may be soft piped music. A charming small cottagey garden, well sheltered by flowering shrubs, angles around the pub, with picnic-sets under cocktail parasols and a play tree; it has aunt sally. They will be totally no smoking by March 2007. *(Recommended by Dr D Scott, Roderick Braithwaite, Hunter and Christine Wright, B H and J I Andrews)*

Enterprise ~ Lease Olivier Bouet and Stephane Brun ~ Real ale ~ Bar food ~ Restaurant ~ (01235) 851272 ~ Children welcome ~ Dogs allowed in bar ~ Open 12-3, 6-midnight; closed Weds; Sun evening Oct-Apr; all Feb

BANBURY SP4540 Map 4

Reindeer £

Parsons Street, off Market Place; OX16 5NA

The atmosphere in this pubby town local is relaxed and friendly and there are plenty of chatty regulars and shoppers enjoying one of the well kept real ales on handpump: Hook Norton Best Bitter, Hooky Dark and Double Stout, and maybe Mordue Workie Ticket and Wadworths 6X. Readers like the warmly welcoming front bar with its heavy 16th-c beams, very broad polished oak floorboards, magnificent carved overmantel for one of the two roaring log fires, and traditional solid furnishings. It's worth looking at the handsomely proportioned Globe Room – used by Cromwell as his base during the Battle of Edgehill in 1642. Quite a sight, it still has some wonderfully carved 17th-c dark oak panelling. Served only at lunchtime, straightforward bar food in generous helpings might include soup (£2.50), well liked omelettes or good filled baked potatoes (from £4), sandwiches (from £4.10), all day breakfast (£4.50), bubble and squeak (£4.95), and changing daily specials. Country wines, several whiskies, and even snuffs and clay pipes for the more adventurous; board games and skittle alley. A smaller back room up steps is no smoking at lunchtime. The little back courtyard has tables and benches under parasols, aunt sally, and pretty flowering baskets. No under-21s (but see below). *(Recommended by the Didler, Ted George, Ian Phillips, Iain R Hewitt, David Green, George Atkinson, BOB, Klaus and Elizabeth Leist)*

Hook Norton ~ Tenants Mr and Mrs Puddifoot ~ Real ale ~ Bar food (11-2.30) ~ (01295) 264031 ~ Children in Globe Room ~ Dogs welcome ~ Open 11-11; 12-4 Sun; closed Sun evening

CAULCOTT SP5024 Map 4

Horse & Groom 🍽

Lower Heyford Road (B4030); OX25 4ND

Although early days, we heard as we went to press that the friendly licensees here are thinking of retiring. This will be a considerable blow to all the many customers who so enjoy the warm welcome and chatty atmosphere they have created. It's not a huge place: an L-shaped red-carpeted room angles around the servery, with plush-cushioned settles, chairs and stools around a few dark tables at the low-ceilinged bar end, framed racehorse cigarette cards, and a blazing fire in the big inglenook, with brassware under its long bressumer beam; shove-ha'penny and board games. The far end, up a shallow step, is set for dining (and is no smoking; best to book), with lots of decorative jugs hanging on black joists, and some decorative plates. There are some lovely watercolours and original drawings dotted around, including a charming one of Harvey the west highland terrier who greets everyone on arrival; look out too for the nice old poster of the auction of the pub in 1899. Well kept Hook Norton Best and three guests like Downton Chimera Gold, Orkney Dragonhead Stout and York Yorkshire Terrier on handpump; decent house wines. They serve a good selection of O'Hagan speciality sausages, with flavours such as chorizo, pork and red wine, somerset scrumpy, creole, and drunken duck (all £7.50); also, sandwiches and toasties (from £3.40), home-made soup (£3.95), filled baked potatoes (from £3.90), ham and egg (£6.25), daily specials such as a pint of jumbo prawns (£9.25), chicken breast (£9.25), steaks (from £11.95), and beef wellington (£13.95), with puddings (£4.25). There is a small side sun lounge and picnic-sets under cocktail parasols on a neat side lawn. *(Recommended by David Twitchett, D P and M A Miles, Guy Vowles, Dave Lowe, Barbara and Peter Kelly, Ken and*

Barbara Turner, Dick and Madeleine Brown, Tracey and Stephen Groves, Kevin Blake, Susan and Nigel Wilson, Mrs Hazel Rainer, Sue Demont, Tim Barrow)

Free house ~ Licensees Chris and Celestine Roche ~ Real ale ~ Bar food ~ Restaurant ~ (01869) 343257 ~ Children in dining area only ~ Open 11-3, 6-11; 12-3, 7-10.30 Sun; closed evenings 25 Dec and 1 Jan

CHECKENDON   SU6684   Map 2
Black Horse
Village signposted off A4074 Reading—Wallingford; coming from that direction, go straight through village towards Stoke Row, then turn left (the second turn left after the village church); OS Sheet 175 map reference 666841; RG8 0TE

After enjoying some of the very attractive surrounding countryside, cyclists and walkers often drop into this unpretentious and simple local for a snack and a pint. The same family have been in charge for a hundred years and there's a refreshingly relaxed atmosphere in the back still room, where three changing West Berkshire beers are tapped from the cask. The room with the bar counter has some tent pegs ranged above the fireplace, a reminder that they used to be made here; a homely side room has some splendidly unfashionable 1950s-look armchairs, and there's another room beyond that. They keep pickled eggs and usually do very simple filled rolls (from £2). There are seats out on a verandah and in the garden. *(Recommended by the Didler, Pete Baker, Susan and John Douglas, Torrens Lyster, Richard Greaves)*

Free house ~ Licensees Margaret and Martin Morgan ~ Real ale ~ No credit cards ~ (01491) 680418 ~ Children allowed but must be very well behaved ~ Open 12-2(2.30 Sat), 7-11; 12-3, 7-10.30 Sun; closed evening 25 Dec

CHIPPING NORTON   SP3127   Map 4
Chequers ★ ♀ 🍺
Goddards Lane; OX7 5NP

Open all day and full of customers of all ages, this is a friendly, busy and unpretentious town pub. The three softly lit beamed rooms have no frills, but are clean and comfortable, with low ochre ceilings, plenty of character, and blazing log fires. Efficient staff serve very well kept Fullers Chiswick, London Pride, ESB and seasonal brews from handpump – unusual to have the full Fullers range around here – and they have good house wines (with 18 by the glass, including champagne), espresso and cappuccino coffee. As well as lunchtime sandwiches (from £3.25) and ploughman's (£5.95), well liked bar food includes soup with garlic bread (£3.95), chicken liver pâté (£4.50), wild mushroom risotto (£4.75; main course £6.95), honey and cider roast ham with free-range eggs (£7.95), goats cheese and tomato filo tart or pork and leek sausages with onion gravy (£8.50), fresh haddock in beer batter or a daily thai curry (£8.95), chicken stir fry (£9.25), daily specials, and rib-eye steak (£10.95). The no smoking restaurant at the back was converted from an old barn adjacent to the courtyard. The pub is very handy for the town's Victorian theatre. *(Recommended by Chris Glasson, the Didler, Sean A Smith, Miss A G Drake, Paul Goldman, Keith and Sue Ward, Richard Greaves, Alan Sadler, Rod Stoneman, A G Marx, J Iorwerth Davies, Peter Bailey, Tracey and Stephen Groves)*

Fullers ~ Lease Josh and Kay Reid ~ Real ale ~ Bar food (12-2.30, 6-9.30; 12-5 Sun; not Sun evening) ~ Restaurant ~ (01608) 644717 ~ Children in bar during the day and in restaurant until 9pm ~ Dogs allowed in bar ~ Open 11-11; 12-10.30 Sun; closed 25 Dec

---

Stars after the name of a pub show exceptional quality. One star means most people (after reading the report to see just why the star has been won) would think a special trip worth while. Two stars mean that the pub is really outstanding – for its particular qualities it could hardly be bettered.

CLIFTON SP4831 Map 4
Duke of Cumberlands Head ♀
B4031 Deddington—Aynho; OX15 0PE

The low-beamed turkey-carpeted lounge in this attractive thatched and stone pub
has a good log fire in a vast stone fireplace, attractive paintings by the landlord's
mother of lilies and rhododendrons grown by her on the west coast of Scotland,
and mainly sturdy kitchen tables, with a few more through in the little no smoking
dining room, which has some stripped stone; none of the walls or ceilings is
straight. Bar food might include home-made soup (£3.50), chicken liver pâté
(£4.50), local sausages or deep-fried haddock fillet (£6 small helping, £9 large),
steak and kidney pie (£7 small helping, £10 large), spinach and ricotta cannelloni,
wild boar with wine, cream and apples or chicken dijonnaise (£10), steaks (from
£14), and puddings such as white chocolate and raspberry torte or crème caramel
(£4). Black Sheep, Hook Norton Best, and maybe Adnams Southwold on
handpump, plenty of wines to choose from and 30 malt whiskies. Picnic-sets out on
the grass behind. The canal is a short walk away. *(Recommended by Val and
Alan Green, Simon Collett-Jones, Sean A Smith, Sir Nigel Foulkes, Andrew Shore,
Maria Williams, A G Marx, Simon Jones, Ian Phillips, Michael Dandy, Gerry and
Rosemary Dobson, Mark O'Sullivan, Pam and John Smith)*

Free house ~ Licensee Nick Huntington ~ Real ale ~ Bar food (not Sun evening or Mon
lunchtime) ~ Restaurant ~ (01869) 338534 ~ Children welcome ~ Dogs allowed in bar ~
Open 12-2.30(3 Sat), 6-11; 12-3 Sun; closed Sun evening and Mon lunchtime ~ Bedrooms:
£50S(£50B)/£65B

COLESHILL SU2393 Map 4
Radnor Arms ♀ ◧
B4019 Faringdon—Highworth; village signposted off A417 in Faringdon and A361 in
Highworth; SN6 7PR

This pub, like the attractive village itself, is owned by the National Trust, and for
the last few months has been blossoming under splendid new management – the
new tenants have previously made the Trout at nearby Tadpole Bridge very popular
with readers. They take great care in tracking down prime ingredients for their
food, often local and sometimes even from Mr Green's father's farm. Besides
soup (£3.95), it might include lunchtime baguettes (£4.95), ploughman's or
meatballs with tagliatelle (£7.95), and local sausages (£8.95), plus home-cured
gravadlax (£4.95), home-smoked duck breast (£5.25), tiger prawns with chilli and
ginger (£6.25), scallops with black pudding or meat balls with tomato sauce and
tagliatelle (£7.95), pork fillet with black pudding (£12.95), organic chicken
jardinière (£13.95), rack of lamb (£16.95), and puddings such as crème brûlée or
chocolate pot (£4.95). Service is friendly and quick. Despite the quality of the food,
this remains very much a pub in atmosphere. The small welcoming carpeted bar has
Goffs Galahad and Youngs tapped from casks behind the counter, which like as not
has a couple of locals chatting over their pints; a good range of wines by the glass is
fairly priced, they make good coffees, and in summer they do a fine Pimms, and
elderflower pressé. This room has a couple of cushioned settles as well as its
comfortable plush carver chairs, and a woodburning stove; a back alcove has a few
more tables. Steps take you down into the main no smoking dining area, once a
blacksmith's forge: with a lofty beamed ceiling, this has kept its brick chimney stack
angling up (with a log fire now), and its canary walls are decorated with dozens of
forged tools and smith's gear. A small garden out behind, with a big yew tree, has
picnic-sets under cocktail parasols; there is plenty of good walking nearby.
(Recommended by D R Ellis, Peter and Audrey Dowsett)

Free house ~ Licensees Chris Green and Shelley Crowhurst ~ Real ale ~ Bar food (no
food Sun evening) ~ Restaurant ~ (01793) 861575 ~ Children welcome ~ Dogs welcome
~ Open 11.30-3, 6-11; 12-3, 7-10.30 Sun; closed Mon

CROWELL   SU7499   Map 4
Shepherds Crook ✿
B4009, 2 miles from M40 junction 6; OX39 4RR

There's plenty of character in this bustling village pub – a lot of it down to the straight-talking landlord who is not afraid to have opinions. The well kept real ales are quite a draw too: Bathams Best Bitter, Otter Bitter, Westerham British Bulldog, Youngs Bitter, and a guest on handpump. Wines come from small producers (like the Lebanon) and they have farm cider. The bar is unpretentious (but not scruffy), and cheerfully pubby, with beams and exposed brickwork, stone-flagged floors, books on shelves and in a case, and a big fire in a brick fireplace; standing timbers divide it from a partly no smoking dining area with high wooden rafters, sporting prints and chunky tables. As well as popular fish and chips, the well liked food might include sandwiches, home-made soup (£4.50), rustic pâté with home-pickled plums (£4.95), omelette arnold bennett or grilled goats cheese on a croûton with a honey dressing (£5.95), scallops with a light garlic glaze (£6.95; main course £12.95), steak and kidney pie (£8.25), local sausages with mustard mash and onion gravy or home-made lamb and potato curry (£8.95), fillet of cornish cod topped with tomatoes and bubbling cheese (£10.50), and puddings like mocha mousse or apricot and cinnamon torte (£4.50). The golden retriever is called Compton, and has now been joined by Sobers the labrador. No music or machines; dominoes, cribbage. There are a few tables in front on the green, and decent walks nearby. *(Recommended by Mr and Mrs John Taylor, Torrens Lyster, Tracey and Stephen Groves)*

Free house ~ Licensees Steve and Elizabeth Scowen ~ Real ale ~ Bar food (12-2.30, 7-9.30; 12-3, 7-9 Sun) ~ Restaurant ~ (01844) 351431 ~ Children allowed but must be well behaved ~ Dogs allowed in bar ~ Open 11.30-3, 5-11; 11.30-11 Sat; 12-10.30 Sun

EAST HENDRED   SU4588   Map 2
Eyston Arms
Village signposted off A417 E of Wantage; High Street; OX12 8JY

The several separate seeming areas in this neatly kept pub are attractively laid out and refurbished in a modern country style and although a lot of emphasis is placed on the good food, you are just as welcome to drop in for a drink. There are nice tables and chairs on the flagstones, some cushioned wall-seats, stripped timbers, particularly low ceilings and beams, and a piano; an attractive inglenook has winter log fires. The bar counter has olives to pick at, and even on a sunny day the candles may be lit. The food can be very good indeed and at lunchtime might include ciabatta bread rolls with filling such as brie, bacon and cranberry or rare rib of beef (£5.50), local sausages with caramelised onion gravy (£8.95), caesar salad with hot chicken or king prawns (from £10.95), wild mushroom risotto (£11.95), and hot smoked salmon with lemon mayonnaise (£13.75); evening choices like seared pavé of smoked haddock with a poached egg and velouté of fennel and chervil (£6.25), carpaccio of beef with salsa verde (£7.50), caramelised breast of chicken with sherry glazed chicken livers and smoked bacon (£14.25), fillet of bream with confit of tomato, saffron, braised fennel and a black olive dressing (£15.75), roast piece of beef with a wild mushroom and smoked bacon jus (£15.95), and puddings such as chocolate and griottine cherry mousse with kirsch or banana parfait with caramelised banana and white chocolate sauce (£4.75). An area is no smoking – though some readers feel this is too small to be effective. Well kept Adnams and Wadworths 6X on handpump, good wines, friendly helpful service; maybe piped easy-listening music, cribbage, chess, dominoes. A couple of outside tables overlooks the pretty village lane. *(Recommended by Peter and Jan Humphreys, Sir John Palmer, Paul Butler, Peter Brown, Dr D Scott, Susan and John Douglas, Terry Miller, Franklyn Roberts, Peter Titcomb)*

Free house ~ Licensee George Dailey ~ Real ale ~ Bar food ~ Restaurant ~ (01235) 833320 ~ Children allowed but with restrictions ~ Dogs allowed in bar ~ Open 11-11; 12-10.30 Sun

FIFIELD SP2318 Map 4

Merrymouth

A424 Burford—Stow; OX7 6HR

Readers enjoy staying in the quaint, well cared for bedrooms here. It's a family run place dating back to the 13th c and the Domesday Book mentions an inn on this site (its name comes from the Murimuth family who once owned the village). The simple but comfortably furnished L-shaped bar has nice bay-window seats, flagstones, horsebrasses and antique bottles hanging from low beams, some walls stripped back to the old masonry, and an open fire in winter. Except for five tables in the bar, the pub is no smoking; piped classical music. Popular bar food includes light lunches such as filled baguettes (from £4.95), mixed cheese platter (£5.25), sausage and mash with onion gravy (£7.95), and smoked haddock with welsh rarebit topping (£8.95), as well as home-made soup (£3.95), blue cheese and walnut pâté (£4.95), tipsy mushrooms (£5.50), cold home-baked ham and salad (£7.95), steak and kidney pie (£9.50), cajun chicken (£9.95), steaks (from £11.95), loin of venison with bacon, whisky and cream (£13.50), daily specials like lamb and apricot casserole (£9.50), grilled gilt-head sea bream with fennel and tomato (£11.50), and guinea fowl with orange sauce (£12.95), and home-made puddings such as white chocolate flan or cherry and rum trifle (£4.50). Well kept Timothy Taylors Landlord and Wychwood Hobgoblin on handpump, and decent wines. There are tables on a terrace and in the back garden (there may be a little noise from fast traffic on the road). *(Recommended by Neil and Angela Huxter, Dennis Jones, Noel Grundy, B Brewer, Martin and Pauline Jennings, B and F A Hannam, Colin McKerrow, KN-R)*

Free house ~ Licensees Andrew and Timothy Flaherty ~ Real ale ~ Bar food (12-2, 6.30-9; not winter Sun evenings) ~ Restaurant ~ (01993) 831652 ~ Children welcome ~ Dogs allowed in bar and bedrooms ~ Open 11-3, 6-11(7-10.30 Sun); closed Sun evening in winter ~ Bedrooms: £45S/£65B

FYFIELD SU4298 Map 4

White Hart 🍴 ♀ 🍺

In village, off A420 8 miles SW of Oxford; OX13 5LW

This former chantry house was built in 1442 to house priests and almsmen who were required to pray for the soul of the founder of the chapel, Sir John Golafre, lord of Fyfield Manor. It's an impressive and civilised place and well worth wandering around. The bustling main room is a grand hall with soaring eaves, huge stone-flanked window embrasures and flagstoned floors and is overlooked by a minstrel's gallery on one side and several other charming and characterful side rooms on the other. In contrast, the side bar is cosy with a large inglenook fireplace at its centre and a low beamed ceiling. The new licensees try to source all their ingredients locally and make everything themselves – including bread and pasta: jerusalem artichoke soup with a truffle cream (£4.95), potted brown shrimps (£5.95), pumpkin and amaretti ravioli with sage butter (£6.95), coarse pork and herb terrine with home-made piccalilli (£6.25), italian braised oxtail with roasted garlic mash (£12.95), baked whole john dory with chilli, cannellini beans and thyme (£16.95), fried duck breast with roasted sweet potato and rhubarb sauce (£14.75), slow-roasted pork belly with black pudding and mustard mash (£14.25), and puddings such as passion fruit crème caramel, warm chocolate fondant with vanilla bean ice-cream and pears poached in red wine and cinnamon with crème anglaise (£4.95). Beware that they add an automatic service charge for parties of more than eight. Well kept Batemans XB, Hook Norton Old Hooky, White Horse Oxfordshire Bitter and a guest beer on handpump, and a dozen wines by the glass (including champagne); they hold an annual beer festival on the August bank holiday weekend. You can smoke in only one section of the bar; piped music and board games. There are elegant metal seats around tables under smart umbrellas on the really big terrace, and flower-edged lawns. Plenty to do nearby. *(Recommended by Colin and Janet Roe, Ken and Barbara Turner, David and Cathrine Whiting, Ian Phillips, Geoffrey Tyack, Clive and Kathryn Brimsom, Jeremy Woods, Mark and Ruth Brock, A P Seymour)*

Free house ~ Licensee Mark Chandler ~ Real ale ~ Bar food (12-2.30, 7-9.30; 12-4 Sun;
not Sun evening) ~ Restaurant ~ (01865) 390585 ~ Children welcome ~
Open 11.30-3, 6-11; 11.30-11 Sat; 12-10.30 Sun; 12-3, 6-11 Mon-Sat in winter

GODSTOW SP4809 Map 4

Trout

**Off A34 Oxford bypass northbound, via Wytham, or A40/A44 roundabout via
Wolvercote; OX2 8PN**

It's the lovely riverside position that makes this pretty medieval pub so special –
best enjoyed on a sunny day – and there are plenty of seats on the terrace
overlooking a clear stream filled with fat fish; several strolling peacocks wander the
grounds. Inside, the beamed main bar has plenty of character, with cushioned old
settles on the flagstones and bare floorboards, old Oxford views and sporting prints
on the walls, and a big stone fireplace; piped music. There's a separate beamed no
smoking restaurant and a more modern extension bar. Adnams Bitter and Bass on
handpump, and bar food such as sandwiches (from £4.50; not Sunday), chicken
skewers with peanut sauce (£4.50), sardines on toasted ciabatta with tomato and
garlic dressing (£4.75), gammon and egg or mushroom, spinach and parmesan
lasagne (£6.95), steak in ale pie (£7.25), liver and bacon (£9.50), and chargrilled
cajun swordfish (£10.95). *(Recommended by Alain and Rose Foote, Paul and Shirley White,
P and J Shapley, A Rees, Martin and Karen Wake, Andy Trafford, Louise Bayly, Meg and
Colin Hamilton, David Glynne-Jones)*

Vintage Inns ~ Manager Robert Maher ~ Real ale ~ Bar food (all day) ~ Restaurant ~
(01865) 302071 ~ Children allowed but must be very well behaved ~ Open 11-11(10.30
Sun)

GREAT TEW SP3929 Map 4

Falkland Arms 🍺

Off B4022 about 5 miles E of Chipping Norton; The Green; OX7 4DB

The fifth Viscount Falkland (whose family owned the manor here until the end of
the 17th c), was treasurer of the navy in 1690 and gave his name to the Falkland
Islands – as well as to this classic country inn. This is a lovely village and the pub is
just one of the untouched golden-stone cottages; it can get very busy. The unspoilt
and partly panelled bar has high-backed settles and a diversity of stools around
plain stripped tables on flagstones and bare boards, one, two and three-handled
mugs hanging from the beam-and-board ceiling, dim converted oil lamps, shutters
for the stone-mullioned latticed windows, and a fine inglenook fireplace with a
blazing fire in winter. A smashing choice of real ales on handpump such as
Wadworths IPA, 6X and a seasonal ale plus maybe Batemans Jester, Hydes
Original, Ringwood Forester and Youngs Kew Brew. The counter is decorated with
tobacco jars and different varieties of snuff which you can buy, and you'll also find
45 malt whiskies, 16 country wines, and farm cider; darts, cribbage and dominoes.
Lunchtime bar food includes soup (£3.95), filled baguettes (from £4.50),
ploughman's (from £6.25), and changing daily specials like beef and ale pie,
smoked haddock chowder and mushroom and herb stroganoff (from £7.50); in the
evenings bar snacks are limited to their hand-raised pork pies, but the no smoking
restaurant does more sophisticated meals (you'll need to book). You have to go out
into the lane and then back in again to use the lavatories. There are tables out in
front of the pub, and picnic-sets under cocktail parasols in the garden behind. Dogs
must be on a lead. Small good value bedrooms (no under-16s). No mobile phones.
*(Recommended by Nick Lawless, Mr and Mrs W D Borthwick, John Saville, the Didler,
M J Winterton, Dr David Cockburn, Dave Lowe, Trevor and Judith Pearson, Bob Ellis,
Michael Dandy, Tracey and Stephen Groves, Kevin Blake, DP and RA Pascoe, Andy Trafford,
Louise Bayly, A P Seymour, K H Frostick, Mr and Mrs G Hughes)*

Wadworths ~ Managers Paul Barlow-Heal and S J Courage ~ Real ale ~ Bar food (12-2,
7-8; not Sun evening) ~ Restaurant ~ (01608) 683653 ~ Children in restaurant lunchtimes
only ~ Dogs allowed in bar ~ Live folk Sun night ~ Open 11.30-2.30(3 winter Sat), 6-11;

11.30-11 summer Sat; 12-10.30 Sun; 12-3, 7-10.30 Sun in winter; closed evening 25 Dec ~
Bedrooms: £50S/£80S(£110B)

HENLEY   SU7882   Map 2
Anchor 🍺

Friday Street; coming in over bridge, first left towards A4155 then next right; RG9 1AH

Run by a friendly and charming landlady and her staff, this old-fashioned and
homely local makes a pleasing contrast to the rest of this rich little town. The two
traditionally furnished main rooms have a slightly cluttered and nicely lived-in feel,
and the beams in the dark ochre ceiling are thickly hung with chamber-pots, steins,
whisky-water jugs, copperware and so forth; interesting pictures too. Mainly local
river photographs in the left room and a mix of antique sporting, ship and comical
prints on the right, which has a piano and TV; shove-ha'penny, backgammon,
cribbage, dominoes, large Jenga and winter darts. Throw rugs, scatter cushions,
chintz curtains, some venerable wall boarding and dim lighting add to the cottagey
feel; much of the pub is no smoking. A simply furnished back dining room has lots
of rowing photographs, and a cage with a cockatiel; behind is a charming informal
terrace surrounded by lush vegetation and hanging vines. Besides an impressive
choice of lunchtime open sandwiches, filled baked potatoes, baguettes, ciabattas or
ploughman's (£6), there might be salads, fish pie, thai green curry, and changing
specials such as winter stews and hotpots, steak and kidney pie, somerset chicken
and liver and bacon (all £8.50). Well kept Brakspears Bitter and Special and a
seasonal ale on handpump, and a good range of malt whiskies and new world
wines by the glass. Ruger the friendly chocolate labrador is still much in evidence.
(Recommended by Tony and Tracy Constance, the Didler, Tim and Ann Newell, Ian Phillips,
Barry and Anne, Tracey and Stephen Groves, Brian P White)

Brakspears ~ Tenant G A Ion-Savage ~ Real ale ~ Bar food (not Sun or Mon evenings) ~
(01491) 574753 ~ Well behaved children in restaurant until 8.30pm ~ Open 11-11;
12-10.30 Sun; closed evening 25 Dec

HIGHMOOR   SU6984   Map 2
Rising Sun

Witheridge Hill, signposted off B481; OS Sheet 175 map reference 697841; RG9 5PF

With a new licensee yet again, this pretty black and cream pub has seen a few
changes recently. The back garden now has some tables amongst the herbs and
flowers, there's a delicatessen selling home-grown and home-made and local
produce, and they've started doing tapas and cream teas. On the right by the bar,
there are stripped wooden tables and chairs and a sofa on the stripped wooden
floors, cream and terracotta walls, an open fire in the big brick inglenook fireplace,
and Brakspears Bitter and Special and a guest beer on handpump. The main area
spreading back from here has shiny bare boards and a swathe of carpeting, with
well spaced tables and attractive pictures on the walls; piped music and board
games. Interesting bar food includes boiled egg and bread soldiers (£1.50 or £2 for
two eggs), soup (from £2), sandwiches (from £3.50), wild rabbit rillette with plum
compote (£4), pheasant satay (£4.25), butternut squash, blue cheese and walnut
risotto with steeped pears and sweet red onions (£4.50; main course £7.50),
ploughman's (from £6), english toulouse sausage and three-bean stew (£7.50),
chicken casserole (£8.50), home-made faggots (£9), smoked haddock with mustard
mash and a poached egg (£10), and puddings such as hot date cake with toffee
sauce or rice pudding with home-made strawberry jam (from £3.95). The eating
areas are no smoking. Boules in the garden. *(Recommended by John Roots, P Price,*
Bob and Margaret Holder, Ron Deighton, Philip and June Caunt, Tracey and Stephen Groves,
Jeremy Woods)

Brakspears ~ Tenant Judith Bishop ~ Real ale ~ Bar food (12-2.30, 7-9.30; 12-5(4 winter)
Sun; no food Sun evening) ~ Restaurant ~ (01491) 640856 ~ Children allowed if eating
and must be strictly supervised by parents ~ Dogs allowed in bar ~ Open 12-3, 6-11;
12-11 Sat; 12-10.30(9.30 in winter) Sun

HOOK NORTON SP3533 Map 4

Gate Hangs High 🍽 ♀ 🍺

Banbury Road; a mile N of village towards Sibford, at Banbury—Rollright crossroads;
OX15 5DF

Readers have enjoyed staying in the newish barn bedrooms here and the breakfasts
are very good. It's a friendly place with efficient staff and is popular for both its real
ales and food. The bar has joists in the long, low ceiling, a brick bar counter, stools
and assorted chairs on the carpet, baby oil lamps on each table, a gleaming copper
hood over the hearth in the inglenook fireplace, and hops over the bar counter.
Well kept Hook Norton Best, Old Hooky and a monthly guest on handpump,
bottled beers, and decent wines. Particularly nice food includes sandwiches (£4.50),
black pudding rösti with poached egg and bacon (£5.95), lambs kidneys with onion
and bacon (£9.95), braised rabbit with mustard and cider (£10.95), half a duck
with orange marmalade sauce (£13.50), and rack of lamb with mint and pear
(£13.95); there are also set weekday menus (two courses £9.50, three courses
£11.50). You'll need to book for Saturday evening and Sunday lunch in the slightly
chintzy no smoking side dining extension. Piped music, dominoes and cards.
There's a pretty courtyard garden and seats on a broad lawn behind, with holly and
apple trees and fine views; the flower tubs and wall baskets are very colourful.
*(Recommended by Stuart Turner, Sir Nigel Foulkes, Andrew Shore, Maria Williams, A G Marx,
G T Cannon, Michael Dandy, Simon Jones, Iain R Hewitt, Pam and David Bailey, M and GR)*

Hook Norton ~ Tenant Stephen Coots-Williams ~ Real ale ~ Bar food (12-2.30, 6-11; all
day Sat and Sun) ~ Restaurant ~ (01608) 737387 ~ Children welcome ~ Dogs allowed in
bar ~ Open 11.30-3, 6-11; 11.30-11 Sat; 12-11 Sun; closed evening 25 Dec ~ Bedrooms:
£40B/£60B

Sun 🍺 🛏

High Street; OX15 5NH

This is rather a good all-rounder. It's a nice place to stay, the food is very well
thought of, and there's a proper pubby atmosphere. The relaxed front bar has a
huge log fire, flagstones, hop-strung beams, well kept Hook Norton Best, Old
Hooky and seasonal ales on handpump, and ten wines by the glass; dominoes,
darts and alley skittles. Behind the central servery, a cosy carpeted room with
comfortable banquettes and other seats leads into the attractive no smoking
restaurant. Bar food includes a new fish menu which changes daily and includes up
to a dozen fish and seafood choices on a first come first served basis. Also, home-
made soup (£3.75), filled baked potatoes (from £5.25), filled baguettes, chicken
liver pâté or cod and prosciutto fishcake (£5.95), fresh crab and crayfish in lemon
and dill mayonnaise served on a potato pancake (£6.95), ploughman's (£7.40),
nachos with chilli beef, jalapeno peppers and mozzarella cheese and finished with
sour cream (£7.95), tempura-fried vegetables with couscous and sweet and sour
sauce (£9.25), tandoori chicken on caesar salad (£10.95), lamb shank with smashed
root vegetables (£12.75), fillet tails of beef with wholegrain mustard cream sauce
(£15.50), and puddings such as apple and almond tart or lemon brûlée custard
torte (£4.75). There are tables on the street in front (as well as on a back terrace)
that give a pleasantly continental feel on summer evenings. Good wheelchair access
and disabled facilities. *(Recommended by Chris Glasson, Darren and Jane Staniforth,
Mrs G A Wilson Bett, Brian Wainwright, Alan Meakin, Pete Baker, Michael Clatworthy,
Richard Greaves, Michael Dandy, Simon Jones, George Atkinson)*

Hook Norton ~ Tenant Stuart Rust ~ Bar food ~ Restaurant ~ (01608) 737570 ~
Children allowed in eating areas only ~ Dogs allowed in bar ~ Open 11-3, 6-11(midnight
Sat); 12-3, 7-11 Sun ~ Bedrooms: £45B/£65B

Post Office address codings confusingly give the impression that some pubs are in
Oxfordshire, when they're really in Berkshire, Buckinghamshire, Gloucestershire or
Warwickshire (which is where we list them).

KELMSCOTT   SU2499   Map 4

Plough 🛏

NW of Faringdon, off B4449 between A417 and A4095; GL7 3HG

This pretty pub is in a lovely spot in a peaceful hamlet by the upper Thames. The small traditional beamed front bar has ancient flagstones and stripped stone walls, along with a good log fire and the relaxed chatty feel of a real village pub. Most of the bar food is served in a choice of small and large helpings, from a menu that takes in a good choice of substantial sandwiches (£5.50), home-made soup (£4.50/£6.50), devilled kidneys or ploughman's (£6.50/£8.50), ham and eggs (£5.50/£7.50), smoked haddock, crème fraîche and dill fishcakes (£7.50/£10.50), chicken caesar or greek salads or roast belly pork with apple mash and onion gravy (£7.90/£9.50), and sizzling stir fries (£8.50/£12.50). The pleasant no smoking dining area has attractively plain and solid furnishings. Archers Best, Hook Norton Best, Timothy Taylors Landlord and Wychwood Hobgoblin on handpump, and Black Rat farm cider; piped music, pool, TV and darts. The garden is pretty, with seats among plantings of unusual flowers, and aunt sally; there are picnic-sets under cocktail parasols out in front. The Oxfordshire Cycleway runs close by.
(Recommended by Dr Paull Khan, Richard and Sheila Fitton, Ian Phillips, Angus and Rosemary Campbell, Gordon and Jay Smith, Ian and Nita Cooper, Charles and Pauline Stride, Tony and Wendy Hobden, R Huggins, D Irving, E McCall, T McLean, Paul Butler, Ann and Colin Hunt, Karen and Graham Oddey, A P Seymour)

Free house ~ Licensee Martin Platt ~ Real ale ~ Bar food (12-2.30, 7-9; all day weekends) ~ Restaurant ~ (01367) 253543 ~ Children welcome ~ Dogs allowed in bar and bedrooms ~ Live entertainment Sat evening ~ Open 11-midnight(2am Sat) ~ Bedrooms: £45S/£75B

KINGSTON BLOUNT   SU7399   Map 4

Cherry Tree

1.9 miles from M40 junction 6: B4009 towards Chinnor; Park Lane; OX39 4SL

After the unassuming brick façade, the cheerful up-to-date style of this nicely reworked Brakspears pub comes as a warm surprise. The long uncluttered single-room bar has light school chairs around chunky tables on its stripped wood floor, with soft leather sofas facing each other beside a small brick fireplace at one end. The cool décor of cream and olive-beige, set off by fresh flowers, big modern abstracts and contemporary lighting, makes for a light and airy feel. This relaxed chatty atmosphere continues into the good-sized popular back no smoking dining room. Big chalkboards set out the menu, which might include home-made soup (£3.50), field mushrooms grilled with blue cheese and bacon (£5.50), coarse duck and cherry pâté with red onion marmalade (£5.75), lambs liver and crispy bacon (£8.75), warm chicken and bacon salad with a green peppercorn dressing (£9.25), wild mushroom, asparagus and mascarpone cheese pancakes (£9.75), salmon and seafood tagliatelle in a herb cream sauce (£10.95), honey-roast shoulder of lamb with rosemary jus (£14.50), and Sunday roasts (£8.95). They have three Brakspears ales on handpump, and a good choice of wines by the glass; staff take their cue well from the friendly young licensees. There may be piped music. *(Recommended by Tracey and Stephen Groves, Torrens Lyster, Heather Couper)*

Brakspears ~ Tenant Sharon Dallacosta ~ Real ale ~ Bar food (12-2.30, 7-9.30; 12-8.30 Sun) ~ Restaurant ~ (01844) 352273 ~ Children in restaurant ~ Dogs allowed in bar ~ Open 12-11(10.30 Sun); closed 1 Jan ~ Bedrooms: £70B/£80B

LANGFORD   SP2402   Map 4

Bell ♀ 🍷

Village signposted off A361 N of Lechlade, then pub signed; GL7 3LF

Tucked away near the church in a quiet and charming village, this little country dining pub is a really relaxing and civilised spot for a leisurely lunch. The simple low-key furnishings and décor add to the appeal: the main bar has just five sanded and sealed mixed tables on grass matting, a variety of chairs, three nice cushioned window seats, am attractive carved oak settle, polished broad flagstones by a big stone inglenook fireplace with a good log fire, low beams and butter-coloured walls with two or three antique engravings. A second even smaller room on the right is similar in character and is no smoking. The small back servery has Hook Norton Hooky, Timothy Taylors Landlord and Charles Wells Bombardier on handpump, with a good interesting range of wines by the bottle, and good coffees; daily papers on a little corner table back here. The good food is unquestionably the main thing. The regular menu might include lunchtime baguettes (from £4.50), goats cheese and mediterranean vegetable salad (£5.95; main course £9.95), sausage with wholegrain mustard mash (£7.95), home-made steak and kidney or chicken, ham and mushroom pies or gammon and egg (£8.95), thai green chicken curry (£9.95), calves liver and bacon (£13.95), and puddings such as hot chocolate fondant with coffee ice-cream or sticky toffee pudding (£4.75). There are also half a dozen or more fresh fish dishes changing each day, which might for example include seared scallops with cauliflower and coriander purée (£7.95/£14.95), plaice (£11.95), and halibut with creamy cabbage and bacon or bass with beans, leeks and mushrooms (£13.95); service is friendly and efficient. There may be inoffensive piped music. There are two or three picnic-sets out in a small garden with a play house. They hope to open bedrooms this year. Dogs must be on a lead. *(Recommended by Noel Grundy, Mrs Linda Ferstendik, Barry and Anne Cooper, Karen and Graham Oddey)*

Free house ~ Licensees Paul and Jackie Wynne ~ Real ale ~ Bar food ~ Restaurant ~ (01367) 860249 ~ Children welcome ~ Dogs welcome ~ Open 12-3, 7-11; closed Sun evening, all day Mon

LEWKNOR SU7198 Map 4

Olde Leathern Bottel

Under a mile from M40 junction 6; just off B4009 towards Watlington; OX49 5TW

Happily unchanging, this is a pleasant country pub with a cheery welcome and good service. There are heavy beams and low ceilings in the two bar rooms (both no smoking), as well as rustic furnishings, open fires, and an understated décor of old beer taps and the like; the family room is separated only by standing timbers, so you won't feel segregated from the rest of the pub. Bar food includes lunchtime filled baguettes or ploughman's with chips and salad (from £6.25), ham and eggs (£6.95), and daily specials like cheese and onion quiche (£6.95), chicken balti (£7.95), and grilled halibut with herb crust or roasted duck breast with plum sauce £10.95), with home-made puddings such as chocolate mousse or raspberry cheesecake £3.90). Well kept Brakspears Bitter and Special on handpump, and all their wines are available by the glass. The attractive sizeable garden has plenty of picnic-sets under parasols, and a children's play area. *(Recommended by Ian Phillips, Howard Dell, Chris Smith, Dr D J and Mrs S C Walker, Brian Wainwright, John and Jill Perkins)*

Brakspears ~ Tenant L S Gordon ~ Real ale ~ Bar food (12-2, 7-9.30) ~ (01844) 351482 ~ Children in restaurant and family room ~ Dogs allowed in bar ~ Open 10.30-2.30(3 Sat), 6-11; 12-3, 7-10.30 Sun

LONGWORTH SU3899 Map 4

Blue Boar

Off A420/A415; Tucks Lane; OX13 5ET

Even in rotten weather, this 17th-c thatched stone local is likely to be full of chatty customers. The three low-beamed, characterful little rooms are warmly traditional with well worn fixtures and furnishings, and two blazing log fires, one beside a fine old settle. Brasses, hops and assorted knick-knacks like skis and an old clocking-in machine line the ceilings and walls, there are fresh flowers on the bar and scrubbed wooden tables, and faded rugs on the tiled floor; benches are firmly wooden rather than upholstered. The main eating area is the no smoking red-painted room at the end and this year they've added a no smoking restaurant extension. Plenty of blackboards listing things like lunchtime sandwiches (from £3.95), soup (£4.25), antipasti (£6.95), standard dishes like steak in Guinness pie or burgers (£7.50), a good range of vegetarian meals, and more interesting changing weekend specials; meals are promptly served, in good-sized helpings. Brakspears, Greene King Ruddles Best and Timothy Taylors Landlord on handpump, 25 malt whiskies, and a wide choice of wines, several by the glass. The licensee has been here for 28 years, though his friendly young team are generally more in evidence. There are tables in front, and the Thames is a short walk away. More reports please. *(Recommended by BOB)*

Free house ~ Licensee Paul Dailey ~ Real ale ~ Bar food (12-2(2.30 Sat, 3 Sun), 7-10 (9 Sun)) ~ Restaurant ~ (01865) 820494 ~ Children welcome ~ Dogs allowed in bar ~ Open 12-midnight(1am Sat); 12-11 Sun; closed 25 Dec, 1 Jan

OXFORD SP5106 Map 4
Rose & Crown

North Parade Avenue; very narrow, so best to park in a nearby street; OX2 6LX

A great deal of originality and atmosphere are given to this rather straightforward but congenial local by its licensees. They have been here for over 20 years and the sharp-witted Mr Hall makes both locals and strangers alike very welcome. The front door opens into little more than a passage by the bar counter, with a piano in the small room on the left (Mr Hall enjoys people playing if they're good – but is quick to give his opinion if not). The panelled back room, with traditional pub furnishings and decorated with pennants, hockey sticks and the like, is slightly bigger, and you'll find reference books for crossword buffs; one room is no smoking. There's a blessed freedom from mobile phones (though not always from smoke), as well as from piped music and machines – and not too many undergraduates, though graduate students from St Anthony's like it. Well kept Adnams Bitter and Broadside, and Hook Norton Old Hooky on handpump, around 25 malt whiskies and a large choice of wines. Traditional but enjoyable lunchtime food might include sandwiches (from £3.95; the hot salt beef with dill pickles is very popular £5), baked potatoes (£5.95), ploughman's (£6.75), main courses such as gammon and egg, whole trout, rump steak and daily specials like cottage pie or warm chicken salad (all from around £7), and puddings such as sticky toffee or apple pie (£3.95). The pleasant walled back yard can be completely covered with a huge awning, and was one of the first places in Britain to have belgian-style outdoor heaters, well over ten years ago; at the far end is a little overflow eating room. The lavatories are pretty basic. No children inside. *(Recommended by Chris Glasson, the Didler, Torrens Lyster)*

Punch ~ Tenants Andrew and Debbie Hall ~ Real ale ~ Bar food (12-2.15(3.15 Sun), 6-9; not 25, 26 or 31 Dec) ~ No credit cards ~ (01865) 510551 ~ Children in courtyard weekend lunchtimes only ~ Open 10am-midnight(1am Sat); 12-10.30 Sun; closed 25 and 26 Dec

Turf Tavern 🐼 🍺

Tavern Bath Place; via St Helen's Passage, between Holywell Street and New College Lane; OX1 3SU

Mentioned by Hardy in *Jude the Obscure*, this notoriously hard to find pub is secluded from the modern bustle of the city behind high stone walls. There's quite a mix of customers in the two dark-beamed and low ceilinged little bars – students usually play a major part – though there are many more who, whatever the time of year, prefer to sit outside in the three attractive walled-in flagstoned or gravelled courtyards (one has its own bar); in winter, they have coal braziers, so you can roast chestnuts or toast marshmallows, and there are canopies with lights and heaters. Up to a dozen real ales are well kept on handpump: Bath Gem, B&T Black Dragon Mild, Caledonian Deuchars IPA, Greene King Ruddles Best, Lees Dragons Fire, Tom Wood Hop & Glory, Wentworth Needles Eye and three from the White Horse Brewery (including one named for the pub). Regular beer festivals,

Weston's Old Rosie cider and winter mulled wine. Well liked bar food includes good soup (£3.05), ciabatta sandwiches (from £3.25), caesar salad (£4.95, with chicken £6.45), sausage and mash (£5.95), mediterranean risotto or tagliatelle carbonara (£6.45), thai green curry or fish and chips (£6.95), steak in ale pie (£7.45), fish and chips (£7.45), and puddings such as apple and blackberry crumble (£3.25); the top food area is no smoking. Service is generally bright and knowledgeable, but can be stretched when busy (which it often is). (Recommended by LM, the Didler, Michael Dandy, Tracey and Stephen Groves, Dave Lowe, R Huggins, D Irving, E McCall, T McLean, Peter Dandy, Kevin Blake, R E Perry, A G Marx, Ann and Colin Hunt, Chris Glasson, Michael and Alison Sandy, Jeremy Whitehorn)

Greene King ~ Manager Darren Kent ~ Real ale ~ Bar food (12-7.30) ~ (01865) 243235 ~ Live music Thurs evening ~ Open 11-11; 12-10.30 Sun

RAMSDEN SP3515 Map 4
Royal Oak ♀ ◧
Village signposted off B4022 Witney—Charlbury; OX7 3AU

Readers have enjoyed their visits to this well run and unpretentious village inn over the last year. The landlord and his staff are friendly and helpful, there's no music or machines, and the atmosphere is relaxed and chatty. The basic furnishings are comfortable, with fresh flowers, bookcases with old and new copies of Country Life and, when the weather gets cold, a cheerful log fire. Well kept Hook Norton Best, White Horse Oxfordshire Bitter and maybe Hereford IPA or Youngs Special on handpump, and a splendid choice of 40 wines by the glass from Languedoc and Roussillon; several armagnacs and farm ciders. Very good bar food includes lunchtime ploughman's (£5.50), club sandwich (£6.25), smoked salmon and scrambled egg (£6.50), and sausages with thick onion gravy (£6.95), as well as home-made soup (£3.50), smoked haddock cooked with whisky and cream topped with cheese (£5.25; main course £9.95), pie of the week (£7.95), home-made burgers (from £7.95), stilton, leek and mushroom puff (£8.95), mediterranean-style lamb casserole (£11.50), daily specials like plump pacific oysters (half a dozen £7.50, a dozen £14), italian meatballs on pasta with a piquant tomato sauce (£9.25), wild mushroom and truffle pasta (£9.95), and fillet of roast cod with tapenade crust with a sweet pepper sauce (£14), and home-made puddings; Thursday evening special rump steak, pudding and glass of house wine (£13.95). The dining room is no smoking. There are tables and chairs out in front and on the terrace behind the restaurant (folding back doors give easy access); outdoor heaters. The bedrooms are in separate cottages. (Recommended by Chris Glasson, Mr and Mrs Billy Rideout, William Bakersville, Brian T Smith, Mr and Mrs P Dolan, Rainer Zimmer, Richard Atherton, Dennis Dort, Comus and Sarah Elliott, Pierre Boyer, Chris Wood, Keith and Maureen Trainer, Paul Duthrie, Ann and Colin Hunt, Nigel and Sue Foster, John Cook, Franklyn Roberts)

Free house ~ Licensee Jon Oldham ~ Real ale ~ Bar food (11.30-2, 7-10) ~ Restaurant ~ (01993) 868213 ~ Children in dining room with parents ~ Dogs allowed in bar ~ Open 11.30-3, 6.30-11; 12-3, 7-10.30 Sun; closed 25 and 26 Dec ~ Bedrooms: £40S/£60S

ROKE SU6293 Map 2
Home Sweet Home
Village signposted off B4009 Benson—Watlington; OX10 6JD

The two warmly welcoming smallish bar rooms in this tiled old house are pleasantly relaxed. There's a particularly striking big log fire, heavy stripped beams and traditional furniture, and on the right, a carpeted room with low settees and armchairs that leads through to the no smoking restaurant. Good well presented bar food includes lunchtime filled baguettes and ploughman's, chicken liver and Cointreau pâté (£4.95), fried salt and pepper squid (£5.50), fresh cornish crab cake with home-made tartare sauce (£5.95), pancakes filled with leeks, cheese and white wine (£7.95), wild boar and apple sausages with onion gravy or beef in ale pie (£8.75), chicken supreme with parma ham and a rocket and cream sauce (£11.95), half a crispy duck with redcurrant and red wine sauce (£12.95), slow-cooked shoulder of lamb with a roasted garlic and port gravy (£13.95), daily specials and home-made puddings; they also do popular spit-roasts on Wednesday, Friday and Sunday during the winter, and fish and curry evenings. Well kept Adnams Best and Black Sheep and Loddon Brewery Hoppit on handpump (there's a family connection to the Loddon Brewery). Also, up to 14 wines by the glass (champagne as well), and several malt whiskies; friendly service, no music or machines. There are lots of flowers around tables out by the well and a low-walled front garden. They hope to open up bedrooms soon. *(Recommended by Richard Marjoram, John Baish, Susan and John Douglas, Geoff and Teresa Salt, Margaret and Roy Randle, Heather Couper, Roy and Gay Hoing)*

Free house ~ Licensee Andy Hearn ~ Real ale ~ Bar food (12-2(3 Sun), 7-9.30; not Sun evening) ~ Restaurant ~ (01491) 838249 ~ Children welcome ~ Dogs allowed in bar ~ Open 11.30-2.30, 6.30-11; 12-3 Sun; closed Sun evening; 25 and 26 Dec

SHIPLAKE   SU7779   Map 2
Baskerville Arms ⓦ
Station Road, Lower Shiplake (off A4155 just S of Henley); RG9 3NY
Oxfordshire Dining Pub of the Year

The hardworking, professional and friendly licensees who run this neat brick house are no strangers to the pages in this *Guide*. They ran another Oxfordshire pub for many years, culminating in that pub becoming the county's Dining Pub of the Year – so their award this year is a case of history repeating itself, but a bit more quickly this time around. There's a nice, partly no smoking bar with blue armchairs, darts and piles of magazines where locals gather for a chat and a pint of well kept Fullers London Pride, Loddon Hoppit and Timothy Taylors Landlord on handpump – but mostly, it's laid out for eating with much space given over to the restaurant; a couple of other comfortable areas, too. Apart from the wooden flooring around the light, modern bar counter, it's all carpeted and there are a few beams, pale wooden furnishings (lit candles on all the tables), plush red banquettes around the windows, and a brick fireplace with plenty of logs next to it. A fair amount of sporting memorabilia and pictures, especially old rowing photos (the pub is very close to Henley), plus some maps of the Thames are hung on the red walls, and there are flowers and large houseplants dotted about. It all feels quite homely, but in a smart way, with some chintzy touches such as a shelf of china dogs. Bar food is extremely good with absolutely nothing that is not made on the premises: soup (£4.50; their stilton soup is much liked, £5.50), muffins with toppings like their own organic gravadlax, pickled quail eggs, marinated anchovies and mustard sauce (from £6.50), open omelettes (from £6.50), open sandwiches made with their own bread (from £6.95), salad such as thai-style tiger prawns with a lime and coconut dressing or niçoise with fresh tuna and fresh anchovies (from £6.95), herbed sausages with rich onion gravy (£7.90), honey-baked gammon with two free-range eggs (£8.50), steak and kidney pie (£8.90), and hand-made burger (£8.95); also, more elaborate choices like tomato, basil and shallot summer pudding with crème fraîche (£6), chargrilled saffron and garlic polenta cake with tarka dhal and minted raita (£9.50), and roulade of corn-fed chicken supreme filled with prawn and chive mousse or citrus steamed hake fillet with a mango and avocado salsa (£12.95). The pretty garden has a proper covered barbecue area and smart teak furniture under huge parasols. *(Recommended by Paul Humphreys)*

Enterprise ~ Lease Graham and Mary Cromack ~ Real ale ~ Bar food ~ Restaurant ~ (0118) 940 3332 ~ Children welcome but with restrictions ~ Dogs allowed in bar ~ Open 11.30-2.30, 6-11; 12-4.30, 7-10.30 Sun ~ Bedrooms: £45S/£75S

Please keep sending us reports. We rely on readers for news of new discoveries, and particularly for news of changes – however slight – at the fully described pubs. No stamp needed: The Good Pub Guide, FREEPOST TN1569, Wadhurst, E Sussex TN5 7BR or send your report through our web site: www.goodguides.co.uk

STANTON ST JOHN SP5709 Map 4

Star

Pub signposted off B4027, in Middle Lane; village is signposted off A40 heading E of Oxford (heading W, you have to go to the Oxford ring-road roundabout and take unclassified road signposted to Stanton St John, Forest Hill etc); OX33 1EX

Not easy to find, this pleasant old place is popular locally and run by a friendly landlord. It is appealingly arranged over two levels, with the oldest parts two characterful little low-beamed rooms, one with ancient brick flooring tiles, and the other quite close-set tables. Up some stairs is an attractive extension on a level with the car park, with old-fashioned dining chairs, an interesting mix of dark oak and elm tables, rugs on flagstones, bookshelves on each side of an attractive inglenook fireplace (good blazing fires in winter), shelves of good pewter, terracotta-coloured walls with a portrait in oils, and a stuffed ermine. Decent bar food includes sandwiches (from £3.75, soup and sandwich £6.50), chicken liver pâté (£5.95), ploughman's (from £5.95), battered haddock, spinach and mushroom strudel or steak in Guinness pie (£8.75), chicken kiev or seafood pasta (£8.95), lamb shank in redcurrant and rosemary (£12.50), and 10oz rib-eye steak (£13.25). Well kept Wadworths IPA and 6X on handpump. The rather straightforward family room and conservatory are no smoking; piped music, darts, shove-ha'penny, cribbage, chess and draughts. The walled garden has seats among the rockeries and children's play equipment. *(Recommended by JJW, CMW, Simon and Sally Small, Ian Phillips, Douglas and Ann Hare, Paul Humphreys, KC, Mr and Mrs John Taylor, Roy and Gay Hoing)*

Wadworths ~ Tenant Michael Urwin ~ Real ale ~ Bar food (not Sun evening) ~ (01865) 351277 ~ Children in family room and lower bar area only ~ Dogs welcome ~ Open 11-2.30, 6.30-11; 12-2.30, 7-10.30 Sun

STEEPLE ASTON SP4725 Map 4

Red Lion

Off A4260 12 miles N of Oxford; OX25 4RY

Now owned by Hook Norton, this little stone village pub also has a new landlord. The comfortable partly panelled bar is welcoming and pubby, with beams, an antique settle and other good furnishings, and Hook Norton Best, Old Hooky and a seasonal beer on handpump. The newish back dining extension is no smoking. Bar food at lunchtime now includes ciabatta sandwiches (from £4), ham and egg (£6.50), triple sausage and mash (£6.95), vegetarian pasta (£7.50), and a pie of the day (£8.95), with evening choices such as soup (£3.50), pâté (£3.95), kedgeree (£5.50), baked cod fillet with parsley sauce or chicken breast wrapped in bacon with stilton sauce (£8.95), roast loin of pork with sage and redcurrant sauce (£9.75), and puddings such as treacle sponge or apple and rhubarb crumble (£3.50). The suntrap front terrace has lovely flowers and shrubs. More reports please. *(Recommended by BOB)*

Hook Norton ~ Tenant Melvin Phipps ~ Real ale ~ Bar food (not Sun evening, not Mon except bank hols) ~ Restaurant ~ (01869) 340225 ~ Children in eating area of bar and restaurant ~ Dogs allowed in bar ~ Open 12-3, 6-11; 12-11 Sat; 12-5.30, 7-10.30 Sun; 12-4, 6-11 Sat in winter; closed evenings 25 and 26 Dec and 1 Jan

SWERFORD SP3830 Map 4

Masons Arms

A361 Banbury—Chipping Norton; OX7 4AP

Since taking over this popular dining pub, Mr Leadbeater the chef/patron has been drawing customers in to enjoy the well liked refurbishments and very good food. A new dining extension has been built that is light and airy, and the bar has pale wooden floors with rugs, a carefully illuminated stone fireplace, thoughtful spotlighting, and comfortable blue armchairs around big round tables in light wood. Doors open on to a small terrace with a couple of stylish tables, while steps lead down into a cream-painted room with chunky tables and contemporary pictures. Round the other side of the bar is another roomy dining room with great views by day, candles at night, and a relaxed civilised feel. Using local ingredients and rare breed, traceable meats, the food at lunchtime includes sandwiches (from £4.50), country pork terrine (£5.25), caesar salad (£5.50; with chicken £9.95), greek salad (£5.70), home-baked ham and free-range eggs (£6.50), polenta-fried hake fillet with caper mayo (£6.90), ploughman's (£7.50), and chicken korma (£7.70); there's also a menu of the day – one course £6.95, two courses £9.95 and three courses £10.95. Evening choices such as home-made soup (£4.50), smoked venison, peppered cream cheese, redcurrant and watercress salad (£6.95), crab and endive salad with lime and passion fruit dressing (£7.95), butternut squash and spinach roulade, garlic fried beans, tomato bruschetta (£11.95), baby back ribs, barbecue sauce, radicchio coleslaw (£12.95), seared fillet of red snapper with harissa dressing (£13.90), and pot-roasted shoulder of lamb with caper mash and onion purée (£14.50), with puddings like belgian chocolate pot with pistachio ice-cream or raspberry, honey and Drambuie brûlée (£5.50). Well kept Brakspears Special and Hook Norton Best on handpump, seven wines by the glass, elderflower pressé, real apple juice and iced tea. Behind is a neat square lawn with picnic-sets and views over the Oxfordshire countryside. *(Recommended by Hugh Spottiswoode, David Glynne-Jones, Chris Glasson, Robert Gomme, Nigel and Sue Draper, Iain R Hewitt, M and GR, Michael Dandy)*

Free house ~ Licensee Bill Leadbeater ~ Real ale ~ Bar food ~ Restaurant ~ (01608) 683212 ~ Children welcome ~ Open 10-3, 6-11; 11-4, 7-10.30 Sun; closed 24-26 Dec

TADPOLE BRIDGE   SP3300   Map 4
Trout
Back road Bampton—Buckland, 4 miles NE of Faringdon; SN7 8RF

Just as we went to press, we heard that this comfortably upmarket inn was about to change hands. But as this is a lovely spot and we know the new people have a country house hotel background, we're hoping that things here will not change too much. The L-shaped bar has plenty of seats and some rugs on flagstones, a modern wooden bar counter with terracotta wall behind, some stripped stone, a woodburning stove, and a large stuffed trout; the restaurant is no smoking, and it's all appealingly candlelit in the evenings. Food has been extremely good and real ales have included Butts Traditional, Ramsbury Bitter and Youngs Bitter on handpump; maybe a dozen wines by the glass. The well kept garden is a lovely place to sit in summer, with small fruit trees, attractive hanging baskets and flower troughs. They sell day tickets for fishing on a two-mile stretch. More reports on the new regime, please. *(Recommended by Charles Artley, Jane Skerrett, Bob and Margaret Holder, Peter Titcomb, Dave Braisted, David and Ruth Hollands, Mr and Mrs G S Ayrton, Di and Mike Gillam, David and Cathrine Whiting, Jeff and Wendy Williams, T and P, Mary Rayner, Susan Loppert, Jane Caplan, Norman and Sarah Keeping, Keith and Maureen Trainer, Ian Phillips, Mrs C Hamilton, David Ellis, Tony and Tracy Constance, Mrs Phoebe A Kemp, Karen and Graham Oddey, A P Seymour, Jonathan Aquilina, Mr and Mrs D S Price)*

Free house ~ Licensees Gareth and Helen Pugh ~ Real ale ~ Bar food (not Sun evening) ~ Restaurant ~ (01367) 870382 ~ Children welcome ~ Dogs welcome ~ Open 12-3, 6-11; 12-3 Sun ~ Bedrooms: £55B/£80B

Bedroom prices normally include full English breakfast, VAT and any inclusive service charge that we know of. Prices before the '/' are for single rooms, after for two people in double or twin (B includes a private bath, S a private shower). If there is no '/', the prices are only for twin or double rooms (as far as we know there are no singles). If there is no B or S, as far as we know no rooms have private facilities.

LUCKY DIP

Besides the fully inspected pubs, you might like to try these Lucky Dips recommended to us and described by readers (if you do, please send us reports: www.goodguides.co.uk).

ABINGDON [SU4996]
Broad Face OX14 3HR [Bridge St]: Friendly dining pub nr Thames with thoughtful choice of freshly made modern food all day inc plenty for vegetarians, lunchtime menu with sandwiches, baked potatoes, pasta and so forth, good choice of wines by the glass, Greene King and Wadworths ales; children welcome, small side terrace *(Tom and Ruth Rees)*

ADDERBURY [SP4735]
Plough OX17 3NL [Aynho Rd]: Attractively furnished medieval thatched pub, friendly cottagey atmosphere and log fire in small L-shaped bar, enjoyable bar lunches from wide choice of sandwiches and baguettes to half a dozen bargain home-made hot dishes, helpful staff, Charles Wells Eagle and Bombardier and a guest such as Butcombe, larger separate restaurant with broad menu; piped music, TV, games; tables outside *(Michael Dandy)*

☆ *Red Lion* OX17 3NG [The Green; off A4260 S of Banbury]: Attractive and congenial, with three linked bar rooms, big inglenook log fire, panelling, high stripped beams and stonework, old books and Victorian and Edwardian pictures, Greene King ales, good wine range and coffee, helpful friendly staff, daily papers, popular pubby food (all day wknds) from baguettes, ciabattas and baked potatoes to steak; games area on left; piped music; children in eating area, picnic-sets out on new roadside terrace, 12 comfortable bedrooms, open all day summer *(Michael Dandy, George Atkinson, Fred Chamberlain, LYM, E A and D C T Frewer)*

ARDINGTON [SU4388]
☆ *Boars Head* OX12 8QA [signed off A417 Didcot—Wantage]: Enjoyable restaurranty food at one end of civilised low-beamed pub with attractively simple country décor, good wines, real ales, locals' end with traditional games; TV, piped music; children welcome, cl Sun evening, peaceful attractive village *(Oliver Richardson, LYM)*

ASTHALL [SP2811]
Maytime OX18 4HW [off A40 at W end of Witney bypass, then 1st left]: Genteel dining pub with good food choice from sandwiches and snacks up (just set lunch on Sun), slightly raised plush dining lounge neatly set with tables, airy conservatory restaurant with family area, proper bar with two changing real ales, good wine range, prompt service, interesting pictures, small bar with flagstones and log fire; piped music; in tiny hamlet, nice views of Asthall Manor and watermeadows from garden, attractive walks, quiet comfortable bedrooms around charming back courtyard *(Stuart Turner, BB, E A and D C T Frewer)*

BANBURY [SP4540]
Exchange OX16 5LA [High St]: Popular well run Wetherspoons with their usual value-oriented food and beer, family eating area well away from bar; open all day *(Ted George)*

BARNARD GATE [SP4010]
☆ *Boot* OX29 6XE [off A40 E of Witney]: Stone-tiled dining pub with stout standing timbers and stub walls with latticed glass, huge log fire, solid country tables and chairs on bare boards, attractive décor majoring on masses of celebrity footwear, Brakspears and Hook Norton Best, decent wines, usual food from sandwiches up, piano – they like you to play if you can; children welcome, tables out in front, open all day wknds *(Ian Phillips, Bruce and Penny Wilkie, LYM)*

BECKLEY [SP5611]
☆ *Abingdon Arms* OX3 9UU [signed off B4027; High St]: Interesting old pub in unspoilt village with good food from sandwiches to nicely presented main dishes inc some imaginative things, friendly staff, Brakspears, bare boards, lots of beams and stripped stone, two real fires, a variety of seating inc pews, board games, separate dining room; extensive pretty garden dropping away from floodlit terrace to orchard with superb views over RSPB Otmoor reserve – good walks *(Brian Root, David Morgan, LYM, Dr and Mrs R Booth, Canon Michael Bourdeaux)*

BERRICK SALOME [SU6294]
Chequers OX10 6JN: Large 18th-c Brakspears pub transformed by new licensees and their chef, very popular for food and atmosphere *(John Braker)*

BICESTER [SP5822]
Swan OX26 6AY [Church St]: Small 17th-c Brakspears pub done up in contemporary bistro style, good value lunch deals and other food, cheerful young staff; piped music *(E A and D C T Frewer)*

BINFIELD HEATH [SU7479]
☆ *Bottle & Glass* RG9 4JT [off A4155 at Shiplake; between village and Harpsden]: Chocolate-box thatched black and white timbered Tudor cottage with emphasis on good value food from sandwiches up, bleached pine tables, low beams, flagstones, fine fireplace, black squared panelling, Brakspears and Wychwood, good choice of wines by the glass, no smoking dining area, shove-ha'penny, dominoes; no children or dogs inside; lovely big garden with tables under little thatched roofs *(Rebecca Knight, the Didler, LYM, Paul Humphreys, Susan and John Douglas)*

BLEWBURY [SU5385]
Red Lion OX11 9PQ [Nottingham Fee – narrow turning N from A417]: Beamed tiled-floor downland village pub under welcoming new landlords, Brakspears with a guest such as Hook Norton Dark, enjoyable food, big log fire, cribbage, dominoes, no piped music or machines, restaurant (children allowed); terrace tables in nice back garden, pretty surroundings *(LYM, C Harris)*

BRIGHTWELL BALDWIN [SU6594]
☆ *Lord Nelson* OX49 5NP [off B480
Chalgrove—Watlington, or B4009 Benson—
Watlington]: Thriving civilised dining pub with
wide range of enjoyable food esp duck and
game, stylish décor, careful lighting, dining
chairs around invitingly big candlelit tables,
nice silverware, helpful friendly service and
spotless housekeeping, real ales and decent
house wines, good log fires, snug armchair
area, plenty of Nelson memorabilia; children
and dogs welcome, front verandah, attractively
updated back garden *(Peter and Giff Bennett,
LYM, Geoff and Teresa Salt)*

BRITWELL SALOME [SU6793]
☆ *Goose* OX49 5LG [B4009 Watlington—
Benson]: Attractive country pub which has
been popular for good interesting restaurant
food using local produce in two small back
dining rooms, and small comfortable log-fire
dining room, but reopened under new
ownership after refurbishment summer 2006,
just too late for us to form any view; garden
tables; reports on new regime please *(Anon)*

BROUGHTON [SP4238]
☆ *Saye & Sele Arms* OX15 5ED [B4035 SW of
Banbury]: Thriving after refurbishment under
new management, changing real ales such as
Adnams, Archers, Slaters, Wadworths and
White Horse from long bar, several wines by
the glass, good choice of pubby food at value
prices, good-humoured efficient service even
when busy, low beams, flagstones, stripped
stone and terracotta walls, pleasant dining area
and small popular restaurant (best to book),
interesting photographs in exemplary
lavatories; handy for Castle (open pm Weds,
Sun and bank hols exc winter, also pm Thurs
in summer) *(K H Frostick, P and J Shapley,
A G Roby)*

BUCKLAND [SU3497]
Lamb SN7 8QN [off A420 NE of Faringdon]:
Smart 18th-c stone-built dining pub with
popular food (not Mon) from lunchtime
special deals to grander and more expensive
evening menus, Hook Norton Best, good
choice of wines by the glass, lamb motif
everywhere, formal no smoking restaurant;
piped music, service can slow when busy;
children welcome, pleasant tree-shaded garden,
good walks nearby, comfortable bedrooms,
cl Sun evening and over Christmas/New Year
*(Philip and June Caunt, Sue Demont,
Tim Barrow, the Didler, LYM, David Ellis,
Di and Mike Gillam, Mary Rayner,
Richard Wyld, J Crosby, A P Seymour,
Ian Phillips)*

BUCKNELL [SP5525]
Trigger Pond OX27 7NE [handy for M40
junction 10; Bicester Rd]: Neat stone-built pub
opp the pond, good range of popular sensibly
priced food from bar snacks up (must book
Sun lunch), friendly young licensee happy to
try 'off menu' requests, welcoming atmosphere,
full Wadworths beer range, good value wines,
no smoking restaurant; pleasant terrace and
garden *(John and Joyce Snell, E A and
D C T Frewer, Trevor and Judith Pearson)*

BURFORD [SP2512]
Cotswold Arms OX18 4QF [High St]: Cosy
bar and larger back dining area, wide choice of
enjoyable pubby food from baguettes and
ploughman's to steak, Courage Best and
Theakstons XB, pleasant staff, beautiful
stonework, two flame-effect stoves; tables out
in front and in back garden *(Ian Phillips,
K Turner, Michael Dandy)*
Golden Pheasant OX18 4QA [High St]: Small
early 18th-c hotel with friendly helpful staff,
settees, armchairs and well spaced tables in
flagstoned split-level bar, enjoyable imaginative
food from interesting sandwiches to wide
choice of restaurant dishes, Greene King IPA
and Old Speckled Hen, reasonably priced
wines, daily papers, board games, stuffed
pheasant above woodburner, back dining
room down some steps; piped music, bar can
be smoky; children welcome, pleasant back
terrace, open all day *(Ian Phillips, C and
R Bromage, Michael Dandy, R Huggins,
D Irving, E McCall, T McLean, Guy Vowles,
BB, Mrs Pat Crabb, Sue Hiscock)*
☆ *Lamb* OX18 4LR [Sheep St (B4425)]: There's
still a lot to enjoy in the fabric and furnishings
of this 500-year-old stone-built inn with its
broad flagstones, polished oak boards and fine
log fireplace, but in recent months reports on
the food, service and atmosphere have been
less unanimously favourable – and it's far from
cheap; Brakspears and Hook Norton, no
smoking restaurant; children welcome, teak
furniture on pretty garden's suntrap terrace,
good bedrooms, open all day *(Paul and
Shirley White, Susan and Nigel Wilson,
Ian Phillips, the Didler, Michael Dandy,
R Huggins, D Irving, E McCall, T McLean,
Martin and Karen Wake, R Halsey, LYM,
Mr and Mrs Martin Joyce, Karen and
Graham Oddey, A P Seymour,
Penny Sheppard, David Glynne-Jones)*
☆ *Mermaid* OX18 4QF [High St]: Handsome
jettied Tudor dining pub with attractive long
narrow bar, beams, flagstones, panelling and
stripped stone, good log fire, Greene King ales,
lots of wines by the glass, nice winter mulled
wine, enjoyable sensibly priced food from
lunchtime baguettes up, good fresh veg,
prompt friendly service, bay seating around
row of dining tables on the left, further airy
back dining room and no smoking upstairs
restaurant; piped music, games machine;
children in eating areas, picnic-sets under
cocktail parasols outside, open all day
*(Stuart Turner, Guy Vowles, K Turner,
Michael Dandy, Peter and Audrey Dowsett,
LYM, Karen and Graham Oddey)*
Old Bull OX18 4RG [High St]: Handsome
building well reconstructed in the 1980s with
beams, panelling and big fireplaces, then
smartly refurbished in wine bar/bistro style,
settees and open fire, steps down to no
smoking eating area, restaurant behind, Greene
King ales with a guest such as Brakspears,
decent wines, wide choice of usual food from
sandwiches up; piped music; children welcome,
open all day, tables out in front or back

through old coach entry, comfortable bedrooms *(LYM, Michael Dandy)*

☆ *Royal Oak* OX18 4SN [Witney St]: Relaxed and homely 17th-c stripped stone local with long-serving friendly landlord, Wadworths from central servery, good range of generous good value food using local produce from filled rolls up, good service, over a thousand beer mugs and steins hanging from beams, antlers over big log fire (underfloor heating too), some comfortable sofas as well as pine tables, chairs and benches on flagstones, more in carpeted back room (no smoking at lunchtime) with bar billiards; terrace tables, sensibly priced bedrooms off garden behind *(Ted George, Pete Baker, Ian Phillips, Michael Dandy, E A and D C T Frewer, Martin and Pauline Jennings, Revd R P Tickle)*

CANE END [SU6879]
Fox RG4 9HE [A4074 N of Reading]: Welcoming and helpful staff and good choice of food inc interesting dishes, proper separate bar area *(Hugh Spottiswoode)*

CHADLINGTON [SP3222]
☆ *Tite* OX7 3NY [off A361 S of Chipping Norton, and B4437 W of Charlbury; Mill End, slightly out of village – at garage turn towards Churchill, then left at playground]: No smoking traditional pub with good home-made food from sandwiches to lovely puddings, some unusual dishes, vine-covered back restaurant evenings and Sun lunchtime, Youngs and interesting west country ales, good house wines, farm perry or cider, cheerful long-serving landlord, good service, big log fire in huge fireplace, settles, wooden chairs, prints, rack of guide books, daily papers and magazines; piped classical music – and they have the uproarious village pantomime here; children and dogs welcome, superb garden full of shrubs, some quite unusual, with stream running under pub, good walks nearby, cl Mon *(BB, Mick Furn, Sean A Smith, Richard Greaves, Stuart Turner, Guy Vowles, David Glynne-Jones)*

CHARLBURY [SP3519]
☆ *Bell* OX7 3PP [Church St]: Welcoming and relaxed old-fashioned atmosphere in small olde-worlde 17th-c hotel's attractive civilised two-room bar, flagstones, stripped stonework and huge inglenook log fire, good bar lunches (not Sun) from sandwiches to short choice of imaginative dishes, friendly attentive service, Greene King ales with a guest such as Everards Original, good value wines, wide choice of malt whiskies, pleasant restaurant; children welcome in eating area, dogs in bar, pleasant garden tables, comfortable quiet bedrooms, good breakfast *(George Atkinson, LYM, Diana Campbell, Sue Hiscock)*

CHIPPING NORTON [SP3127]
Blue Boar OX7 5NP [High St/Goddards Lane]: Spacious and cheerful two-bar stone-built pub divided by arches and pillars, wide choice of sensibly priced food from separate servery inc generous Sun roasts, Hook Norton and Marstons Pedigree, beamed back restaurant by long light and airy flagstoned dining

conservatory; piped pop music, games machines; children welcome, open all day Sat *(Keith and Sue Ward)*

☆ *Off the Beaten Track* OX7 5AQ [Horsefair]: Good food inc authentic italian dishes, nice atmosphere and furnishings, real ales *(Amy Chef)*

CHRISTMAS COMMON [SU7193]
☆ *Fox & Hounds* OX49 5HL [off B480/B481]: Upmarket Chilterns pub in lovely countryside, Brakspears and Wychwood, proper coffee, cheerful staff, two compact beamed rooms simply but comfortably furnished, bow windows, red and black tiles and big inglenook, snug little back room, some emphasis on the food side with front barn restaurant; children and dogs welcome, rustic benches and tables outside, open all day wknds *(Heather Couper, the Didler, LYM, Torrens Lyster, Richard Greaves, Derek Harvey-Piper, Susan and John Douglas)*

CHURCH ENSTONE [SP3725]
☆ *Crown* OX7 4NN [Mill Lane; from A44 take B4030 turn-off at Enstone]: Popular and attractive old pub, smart and uncluttered, with congenial bar, good enterprising fresh food (not Mon night) from tasty lunchtime baguettes to good Sun lunch, friendly staff, Hook Norton Best, Shepherd Neame Spitfire and Wychwood Hobgoblin, decent wines by the glass, log fire in brass-fitted stone fireplace, beams, stripped stone and sisal matting, good-sized light modern dining area and roomy conservatory; may be piped music, may be cl Mon lunchtime; garden tables *(Mr and Mrs J Curtis, Pam Adsley, Guy Vowles, Dave Lowe, LYM, Chris Glasson)*

CHURCHILL [SP2824]
☆ *Chequers* OX7 6NJ [B4450 Chipping Norton—Stow; Church Rd]: This airy open-plan dining pub has been hugely popular with us and with readers thanks to its legendarily welcoming licensees, Assumpta and Peter Golding – but they've decided to sell, and told us they planned to go be gone before this edition is in the shops; it has been good all round, with enjoyable food, good wines by the glass, Hook Norton and a guest ale, farm cider and a good inglenook log fire, so fingers crossed for the future; reports on the new regime please *(LYM)*

CLIFTON HAMPDEN [SU5495]
☆ *Barley Mow* OX14 3EH [towards Long Wittenham, S of A415]: Interesting and welcoming thatched Chef & Brewer dining pub, plenty of atmosphere with very low ancient beams, some appropriate furniture and nice dark corners, oak-panelled family room, real ales such as Adnams Broadside and Charles Wells Bombardier, good choice of wines by the glass, efficient service by friendly young staff, log fire, decent food all day from sandwiches up, restaurant; piped music; no dogs inside, tables on pleasant terrace and in well tended waterside garden, short stroll from the Thames; open all day *(Chris Glasson,*

LYM, D J and P M Taylor, John Saville, B M Eldridge, Rob and Catherine Dunster, Mel Smith, Albert Nicolas)

COMBE [SP4115]

Cock OX29 8NT [off A4095 at Long Hanborough; The Green]: Country pub in idyllic spot facing green of charming village, good-sized congenial bar, friendly helpful service, Greene King ales, bar food from good home-made soup and baguettes up, restaurant *(Guy Vowles)*

CRAYS POND [SU6380]

White Lion RG8 7SH [B471 nr junction with B4526, about 3 miles E of Goring]: Welcoming low-ceilinged pub popular for honest food from good value fresh baguettes to good fish choice, good beer and relaxed casual atmosphere, hands-on licensees, open fire, attractive conservatory; big garden with play area, lovely countryside *(Rob Winstanley, Paul Suter)*

CROPREDY [SP4646]

Brasenose OX17 1PW [Station Rd]: Welcoming new family settling in well in village inn nr Oxford Canal, good choice of enjoyable pub food at pine tables in attractively refurbished no smoking dining room, Hook Norton ales, long bar with woodburner; comfortable bedrooms, decent breakfast, has been open all day Fri-Sun *(Charles and Pauline Stride, Chris Glasson, BB, Martin and Alison Stainsby, JJW, CMW, Roger and Pauline Pearce)*

Red Lion OX17 1PB [off A423 N of Banbury]: Rambling old thatched stone-built pub charmingly placed opp pretty village's churchyard, enjoyable food from sandwiches and baguettes up (two rooms set for eating), low beams, inglenook log fire, high-backed settles, brass, plates and pictures, friendly staff, changing ales such as Greene King IPA, Marstons Pedigree, Oxfordshire Marshmellow and Shepherd Neame Spitfire, games room; piped music, limited parking; children allowed in dining part, picnic-sets under cocktail parasols on back terrace by car park *(Mr and Mrs B A R Frost, LYM, Bob and Laura Brock, George Atkinson, Simon Jones)*

CUDDESDON [SP5902]

☆ *Bat & Ball* OX44 9HJ [S of Wheatley; High St]: Civilised pub full of all sorts of interesting cricketing memorabilia, low beams, some flagstones, well liked food from baguettes to elaborate dishes (evening concentration on this, big no smoking dining extension), Banks's LBW, Marstons Pedigree and a guest beer, decent wines, friendly attentive young staff; cribbage, dominoes, piped music; children welcome, pleasant back terrace with good views, aunt sally, comfortable annexe bedrooms (some small), open all day *(Penny and Peter Keevil, Brian Root, Paul Humphreys, LYM, Mel Smith, A P Seymour)*

CUMNOR [SP4604]

Vine OX2 9QN [Abingdon Rd]: Cosy and welcoming beamed pub refurbished and largely no smoking under new ownership, real ales

such as Adnams, Hook Norton Old Hooky and Charles Wells Bombardier, enjoyable unpretentious food from baguettes and light dishes up, back dining area and conservatory, games room (smoking allowed here) with darts and pool; occasional live music; well behaved children and dogs welcome, picnic-sets in attractive back garden with aunt sally, open all day *(David Howe)*

CURBRIDGE [SP3208]

Lord Kitchener OX29 7PD [Lew Rd (A4095 towards Bampton)]: Bustling easy-going local atmosphere, good value food inc two-for-one lunch deals in neat, light and roomy no smoking dining extension, old local photographs, big log fire, real ales, quick efficient service by chirpy NZ family; piped music; garden with play area, open all day *(Peter and Audrey Dowsett, Howard and Margaret Buchanan, Marjorie and David Lamb)*

CUXHAM [SU6695]

☆ *Half Moon* OX49 5NF [B480, not far from M40, junction 6]: The gifted French chef/landlord whose good if pricey restauranty food made such an impact left this charming 16th-c thatched Brakspears pub just as we went to press, and the menu is back to more familiar pubby staples; besides the two main eating areas (both no smoking), there's also a small red and black-tiled bar, with oak benches and tables, stripped beams and a brick fireplace; good-sized back garden *(LYM)*

DEDDINGTON [SP4631]

☆ *Deddington Arms* OX15 0SH [off A4260 (B4031) Banbury—Oxford; Horse Fair]: Beamed and timbered hotel with emphasis on its sizeable smartly refurbished back eating area with contemporary furniture on stripped wood and much ochre paintwork, popular food from good sandwiches and light dishes up inc good value seasonal offers, friendly attentive young staff, pleasant bar with mullioned windows, good log fire, Greene King IPA and Abbot, good choice of wines by the glass; unobtrusive piped music; open all day, comfortable chalet bedrooms around courtyard, good breakfast, attractive village with lots of antiques shops *(Mr and Mrs John Taylor, Hugh Spottiswoode, LYM, P and J Shapley, Trevor and Judith Pearson, E A and D C T Frewer, Michael Dandy)*

Red Lion OX15 0SE [Market Pl]: Smart and spotless bar and bistro, inviting modern décor with new tables on bare boards, Brakspears and Fullers London Pride, good choice of wines by the glass, good inexpensive coffee, reasonably priced food from lunchtime sandwiches and baked potatoes up, friendly staff, daily papers; piped music, games; back courtyard tables *(Michael Dandy)*

☆ *Unicorn* OX15 0SE [Market Pl]: Cheerful 17th-c inn run by helpful hands-on mother and daughter, good value generous food (not Sun evening) from sandwiches and baked potatoes up in freshly decorated clean-cut L-shaped bar and beamed dining areas off, plenty of fish and

separate evening menu, Hook Norton and
Fullers London Pride, good choice of wines by
the glass, proper coffee, quick courteous young
staff, daily papers, inglenook fireplace, no
smoking areas, pub games; dogs welcome in
bar, cobbled courtyard leading to lovely walled
back garden, open all day (from 9 Sat for
farmers' market), good bedrooms
*(Michael Dandy, BB, Trevor and Judith
Pearson, Richard Tosswill, George Atkinson)*

DORCHESTER [SU5794]

George OX10 7HH [just off A4074
Maidenhead—Oxford; High St]: Handsome
well cared-for timbered hotel in lovely village,
roaring log fire and charming furnishings in
smart beamed bar, enjoyable fairly priced bar
food, Brakspears, good wines, cheerful
landlord; piped music; children in restaurant,
bedrooms, open all day *(LYM, Susan Loppert,
Jane Caplan, Craig Turnbull)*

DRAYTON [SP4241]

Roebuck OX15 6EN [Stratford Rd (A422 W
of Banbury)]: Comfortable creeper-covered
16th-c pub with Hook Norton ales, reasonably
priced wines, good choice of realistically priced
usual food in bar and restaurant, friendly
family service *(Alun Howells, Mr and Mrs
P Tonsley)*

DUCKLINGTON [SP3507]

☆ *Bell* OX29 7UP [off A415, a mile SE of
Witney; Standlake Rd]: Pretty thatched local
with wide choice of generous good value
home-made food (not Sun eve) inc particularly
good sandwiches, Greene King ales, good
house wines, friendly service; big stripped stone
and flagstoned bar with scrubbed tables, log
fires, glass-covered well, old local photographs,
farm tools, hatch-served public bar, roomy and
attractive well laid out back restaurant, its
beams festooned with bells; cards and
dominoes, no piped music; small garden
behind with play area, colourful hanging
baskets, nine bedrooms *(BB, Pete Baker,
Peter and Audrey Dowsett)*

EATON [SP4403]

☆ *Eight Bells* OX13 5PR [signed off B4017 SW
of Oxford]: Tudor pub recently reopened by
friendly and obliging new licensees, small
choice of particularly good food, proper pubby
atmosphere in two small low-beamed bars
with real ales and open fires, dining room off
cosy lounge; tables in front garden, nice walks
(LYM, Hannah Selinger)

ENSLOW [SP4818]

Rock of Gibraltar OX5 3AY [A4095 about
1½ miles SW of Kirtlington]: Tall friendly pub
with three real ales such as Hook Norton, well
prepared reasonably priced food, beams,
stripped stone, bright narrowboat paintwork,
modern dining extension overlooking Oxford
Canal, upper conservatory with even better
view; popular Thurs folk night; dogs welcome,
lots of picnic-sets under cocktail parasols in
pretty waterside garden *(Chris Glasson,
Pete Baker)*

EWELME [SU6491]

Shepherds Hut OX10 6HQ [off B4009 about
6 miles SW of M40 junction 6; High St]:

Cheery unpretentious country local with
landlady cooking good weekly-changing choice
of fresh good value food (not Sun evening) inc
some unusual dishes and good Sun lunch,
friendly landlord, Greene King and guest ales,
decent coffee, small restaurant; big-screen
sports TV; children welcome, small pleasant
garden with terrace and barbecues, open all
day *(David Glynne-Jones, Geoff and
Teresa Salt, BB, Marjorie and David Lamb,
Susan Loppert, Jane Caplan)*

EYNSHAM [SP4309]

Newlands OX29 4LD [Newland St]:
Unpretentiously comfortable beamed and
flagstoned bar, wide choice of generous
enjoyable food from impressive sandwiches up,
quick friendly service, real ales, decent wine,
big inglenook log fire, stripped early 18th-c
pine panelling, pretty restaurant on left; very
busy and bustling wknds, may be piped music
(David Handforth)

FERNHAM [SU2991]

☆ *Woodman* SN7 7NX [B4508, off A420 SW of
Oxford]: Heavily beamed 17th-c country pub
carefully refurbished to keep the good pubby
atmosphere of its rambling character bar, real
ales tapped from the cask, good if not cheap
food (not Sun) from sandwiches and baguettes
up, massive log fire, good restaurant area, no
piped music; children welcome, good walks
below the downs *(Peter and Audrey Dowsett,
LYM, Dick and Madeleine Brown, Tony and
Tracy Constance)*

FINSTOCK [SP3616]

Plough OX7 3BY [just off B4022 N of Witney;
High St]: Rambling thatched and low-beamed
village local under new management, long
divided bar with armchair by open
woodburner in massive stone inglenook, good
new limited lunch menu, real ales such as
Adnams, Brakspears and Hook Norton, small
choice of decent wines, pleasant service, games
area with bar billiards, stripped-stone dining
room; children welcome, sizeable garden with
old-fashioned roses and aunt sally, good walks
(Chris Glasson, S Crowe, LYM)

FRINGFORD [SP6028]

Butchers Arms OX27 8EB [off A421 N of
Bicester]: Bustling village pub with wide choice
of generous pubby food from sandwiches and
ciabattas up, Adnams Broadside, Caledonian
Deuchars IPA and Marstons Pedigree, good
soft drinks choice, darts and TV in L-shaped
bar, separate smaller dining room; piped
music; a few tables outside *(Michael Dandy,
E A and D C T Frewer, JJW, CMW)*

FRITWELL [SP5229]

George & Dragon OX27 7PX [East St; signed
off B4100; quite handy for M40 junction 10]:
Welcoming village local refurbished under
newish licensees, enjoyable home-made food,
good drinks choice inc changing real ales
(Daniel Woodard)

FULBROOK [SP2512]

Carpenters Arms OX18 4BH [Fulbrook Hill]:
Old Cotswold stone pub with beams, windsor
chairs and oak settles, good generous english
food freshly made (meat from landlord's farm),

a real ale and wines by the glass from long bar serving tap room and lounge, large separate restaurant; children welcome, disabled access and facilities, tables in garden behind, good play area *(E A and D C T Frewer)*

GALLOWSTREE COMMON [SU7081]
☆ *Greyhound* RG9 5HT [Gallowstree Rd, Shiplake Bottom; off B481 at N end of Sonning Common]: Low-beamed 17th-c pub in lovely setting nr green, reopened 2005 as pub/restaurant, small proper bar with big fireplace and real ales such as Fullers London Pride and West Berkshire Good Old Boy, good choice of wines by the glass, friendly unpretentious service, neatly ranked modern tables in good-sized casual dining area and more formal barn restaurant, particularly good meals inc Mon-Thurs lunchtime and early evening bargains; children welcome, tables out in front and at side, charming garden with terrace and arbour *(Rob Winstanley)*

GARSINGTON [SP5802]
Three Horseshoes OX44 9DF [The Green; off B480 SE of Oxford]: Popular home-made food (not Sun/Mon evenings) using local supplies in traditional two-bar village pub carefully rebuilt after fire damage and reopened 2005, leather sofas, log fire and flagstones, friendly hard-working licensees, changing Greene King ales, good wines by the glass, no smoking restaurant with Sun carvery; tables in garden with aunt sally, pleasant outlook *(Anon)*

GORING [SU5980]
☆ *Catherine Wheel* RG8 9HB [Station Rd]: Smart and well run, with friendly landlord and good informal atmosphere in two neat and cosily traditional bar areas, especially the more individual lower room with its low beams and big inglenook log fireplace; well priced and generous straightforward home-made food inc Tues steak night, Brakspears, Hook Norton and Wychwood ales, Stowford Press cider, decent wine, good coffee; back restaurant (children welcome here), notable door to gents'; nice courtyard and garden behind, handy for Thames Path, attractive village, open all day *(Andy and Jill Kassube, Rob Winstanley, the Didler, Paul Humphreys, BB)*
John Barleycorn RG8 9DP [Manor Rd]: Quiet and unpretentious low-beamed cottagey local with prints in cosy little lounge bar, attractive adjoining eating area, Brakspears and Wychwood, good sandwiches and other food, good service, pool in end room; children welcome, simple bedrooms *(Rob Winstanley, the Didler, Paul Humphreys, Jeremy Woods)*
☆ *Miller of Mansfield* RG8 9AW [High St]: Reopened after complete contemporary refurbishment, now all no smoking, very dark green décor, lots of easy chairs and log fires in three linked areas of large bow-windowed bar, good if not cheap bar food all day, Butts Jester, Marlow Rebellion and West Berkshire Good Old Boy, friendly young staff, up-to-date meals in large smart and airy back restaurant; well reproduced piped pop music; children

welcome, good tables under big canopy on heated terrace, open all day *(Rob Winstanley, Paul Suter, BB)*

GREAT HASELEY [SP6301]
Old Plough OX44 7JQ [handy for M40 junction 7; Rectory Rd]: Small friendly thatched pub very popular for good inventive food from bar snacks to leisurely evening meals (they bake their own bread, too), good wines by the glass, Shepherd Neame Spitfire, helpful staff, buoyant pubby atmosphere with thriving darts and cribbage teams; attractive garden with aunt sally, quiet area *(Tim Lumb)*

HAILEY [SU6485]
☆ *King William IV* OX10 6AD [the Hailey nr Ipsden, off A4074 or A4130 SE of Wallingford]: Attractive 16th-c pub in charming peaceful countryside, some concentration on wide choice of good generous mainly traditional food, friendly talkative landlord and helpful staff, thriving atmosphere, Brakspears and Wychwood, beams, bare bricks and tiled floor (carpet in middle room), big inglenook log fire, clean fresh décor and well kept traditional furnishings, extended dining room; outstanding views from pub and tables on front terrace *(the Didler, LYM, Barry Collett)*

HAILEY [SP3512]
Lamb & Flag OX29 9UB [B4022 a mile N of Witney; Middletown]: Rambling beamed and stone-built 17th-c village local with some ancient flagstones, woodburner in inglenook fireplace, friendly helpful service, modestly priced fresh food, Greene King IPA and Abbot, good choice of wines by the glass, bright lighting, darts, bar billiards; good garden for children *(BB, E A and D C T Frewer)*

HANWELL [SP4343]
Moon & Sixpence OX17 1HN [Main St]: Dining pub with wide choice of good food inc good value set lunch in comfortable bar and dining area (often booked up), friendly efficient staff, Hook Norton, decent wines by the glass; small terrace, pretty location *(Dick Withington, Zac Webster)*

HENLEY [SU7682]
Angel on the Bridge RG9 1BH [Thameside, by the bridge]: Worth knowing for prime spot by Thames, with nice waterside terrace (plastic glasses for this), small front bar with open fire, back bar and adjacent bistro restaurant with settles, Brakspears beer, good choice of wines by the glass, food from sandwiches and usual pubby lunchtime dishes to midweek meal deals and more elaborate evening menu *(Michael Dandy, Paul Humphreys)*
Catherine Wheel RG9 2AR [Hart St]: Big Wetherspoons with two bars, large no smoking family area, usual inexpensive food, Courage Directors, Fullers London Pride, Greene King, Loddon and Marstons Pedigree; pleasant terrace with nice tables under parasols, good bedrooms in hotel part above (parking for hotel guests), open all day *(Ian Phillips)*
☆ *Three Tuns* RG9 2AA [Market Pl]: Heavy-beamed front bar with old-fashioned seating inc traditional settles, coal-effect gas fire,

Brakspears and Wychwood, decent wines, fresh imaginative food, friendly young staff, neat rustic panelled back dining area; may be piped music; tables in small attractive back courtyard *(Michael Dandy, LYM, the Didler)*

HETHE [SP5929]

Whitmore Arms OX27 8ES [Main St]: A couple of steps up to large low-ceilinged open-plan bar, Brakspears, Fullers London Pride and Hook Norton from oak counter, small blackboard choice of sensibly priced home-made food, pleasantly relaxed service, inglenook log fire, rustic bygones, games area on right; lovely village, cl wkdy lunchtimes *(Guy Vowles)*

HIGHMOOR [SU7084]

Dog & Duck RG9 5DL [B481]: Unspoilt country pub with rather too frequent management changes recently, and 'in between' as we go to press in summer 2006; we hope things will settle back, as it's a nice place, with a tiny beamed bar with space for barely three tables, piano and coal fire, not much larger flagstoned dining room with hatch service and an eclectic mix of old prints and pictures, and no smoking family room leading off, decent food, Brakspears ales; children and dogs welcome, long garden with some play equipment, plenty of surrounding walks *(the Didler, LYM, Roger Yates)*

HOOK NORTON [SP3533]

☆ *Pear Tree* OX15 5NU [Scotland End]: Pleasant village pub with full Hook Norton beer range kept well from nearby brewery, country wines, usual bar food (not Sun evening) from doorstep sandwiches and baked potatoes up, attentive staff, partly no smoking chatty knocked-together bar area with country-kitchen furniture, wood log fire, daily papers and magazines; TV; children and dogs welcome, sizeable attractive garden with outdoor chess, wendy house and play area, bedrooms, open all day *(Chris Glasson, K H Frostick, LYM, Robert Gomme, Michael Dandy, Dennis Jenkin)*

KIDLINGTON [SP4914]

Kings Arms OX5 2AJ [The Moors, off High St (not the Harvester out on the Bicester Rd)]: Friendly local with enjoyable wkdy lunchtime food from sandwiches up, Greene King IPA and a couple of other changing ales, homely lounge, games in proper public bar; children welcome, courtyard tables with occasional barbecues, open all day wknds *(Anon)*

Squire Bassett OX5 1EA [Oxford Rd (A4260)]: Big pub with newish management doing good value Sun roasts and other food, good service; tables in large garden *(Claire Friend, David Adams)*

KINGHAM [SP2523]

Tollgate OX7 6YA [Church St]: Upscale refurbishment, with good choice of well cooked food from light meals up, good if not cheap Sun lunch, friendly landlord *(Keith and Sue Ward)*

KINGSTON LISLE [SU3283]

Blowing Stone OX12 9QL [signed off B4507 W of Wantage]: Friendly pub/restaurant with good food choice from sandwiches, wraps and baked potatoes to steaks, West Berkshire real ale, daily papers, log fire, comfortable lounge, cheerful modernised bar and attractive dining conservatory; children welcome, tables out in lovely garden with goldfish pond, pretty bedrooms, handy for Uffington Castle hill fort and the downs *(LYM, C and E Henry, Pat and Tony Martin)*

KIRTLINGTON [SP4919]

Oxford Arms OX5 3HA [Troy Lane]: Oak-beamed dining pub with enjoyable generous if not cheap food from proper sandwiches and imaginative starters to traditional english main dishes, charming young staff, good reasonably priced wines by the large glass, Hook Norton Best and two other ales from central bar with small standing area, leather settees and open fire one end, smaller no smoking area with fresh wood furniture off main eating area; small sunny back garden *(E A and D C T Frewer, C Cottrell-Dormer)*

LONG WITTENHAM [SU5493]

Plough OX14 4QH [High St]: Friendly refurbished pub with good value food (all day wknds, with OAP bargains Mon-Thurs lunchtimes), low beams and lots of brass, inglenook log fires, Greene King ales, good value coffee, good service, no smoking dining room, games in public bar, Weds folk night; dogs welcome, Thames moorings at bottom of long spacious garden with aunt sally, bedrooms *(Nick and Lynne Carter, Chris Glasson)*

LONGWORTH [SU3897]

Lamb & Flag OX13 5HN [off W end of A420 Kingston Bagpuize bypass]: Good choice of good value food inc popular all-day carvery in big smart no smoking restaurant area with unusual wattle ceiling, lots of interesting bric-a-brac, good-sized bar area with open fire, friendly service, pool in games room; children welcome, tables outside *(Peter and Audrey Dowsett)*

LOWER ASSENDON [SU7484]

Golden Ball RG9 6AH [B480]: Friendly new licensees in cosy and attractive 16th-c beamed pub, rustic traditional interior with two blazing log fires, enjoyable home-made food, fine choice of wines by the glass, Brakspears; children welcome, nice big garden behind *(Heather Couper, Martin and Karen Wake)*

LOWER HEYFORD [SP4824]

Bell OX25 5NY [Market Sq]: Charming creeper-clad building in small village square of thatched cottages, nice layout with uncluttered refurbished rooms around central beamed bar, cheerful helpful staff, good range of generous enjoyable food freshly cooked to order inc some interesting dishes, mainstream ales such as Flowers IPA and Greene King Ruddles County; disabled access and facilities, bedrooms, nearby Oxford Canal walks *(Trevor and Judith Pearson, K H Frostick, Meg and Colin Hamilton)*

MAIDENSGROVE [SU7288]

☆ *Five Horseshoes* RG9 6EX [off B480 and B481, W of village]: Country dining pub reopened after refurbishment, on lovely common high in the Chilterns beechwoods, rambling bar with low ceiling and log fire, friendly atmosphere, particularly helpful service, enjoyable bar food from sandwiches up, Brakspears, good choice of wines by the glass, airy no smoking conservatory restaurant with its own menu; children and dogs welcome, plenty of tables outside (yet another – good but rather pricey – wknd barbecue menu for these), good walks, open all day summer wknds, cl winter Sun evening *(Julia and Richard Tredgett, Martin and Karen Wake, LYM)*

MARSH BALDON [SU5699]

Seven Stars OX44 9LP [the Baldons signed off A4074 N of Dorchester]: Popular generous food in small beamed pub on attractive village green, two bar areas with comfortable settees as well as tables and chairs, a real ale, decent wines by the glass, good coffee, small dining room *(E A and D C T Frewer)*

MIDDLETON STONEY [SP5323]

☆ *Jersey Arms* OX25 4AD [Ardley Rd (B430/B4030)]: Small 19th-c stone-built hotel with nicely countrified bow-windowed bar, beams, oak flooring and some stripped stone, attractive tables, sofa and daily papers, good inglenook log fire, home-made fresh food from well filled baguettes up (sandwiches too if you ask), friendly owner and staff, good range of wines and spirits, good coffee, Bass or Wadworths 6X, attractive largely no smoking two-level dining room; piped music, TV, car park across road; tables in courtyard and garden, comfortable bedrooms *(BB, Michael Dandy, E A and D C T Frewer, Cathryn and Richard Hicks, Mr and Mrs Bentley-Davies)*

MILCOMBE [SP4034]

☆ *Horse & Groom* OX15 4RS [off A361 SW of Banbury]: Bustling village local with friendly chatty licensees, good reasonably priced bar lunches (soup, sandwiches and baguettes) and pubby evening meals, Hook Norton Old Hooky and Youngs, good wine and coffee choice, settee and inglenook woodburner in appealing low-beamed and flagstoned bar, back restaurant, pub games; piped music, occasional live; children welcome, lots of picnic-sets out in front, bedrooms (they can organise fishing), handy for Wigginton Heath waterfowl and animal centre *(BB, Michael Dandy)*

MILTON [SP4535]

Black Boy OX15 4HH [off Bloxham Rd; the one nr Adderbury]: Inglenook, oak beams, flagstones, bare boards and stripped stone in former coaching inn, enjoyable and affordable home-made food, friendly young licensees and good service, Adnams and Fullers London Pride, cricket memorabilia, candlelit restaurant; dogs welcome in bar, tables outside with plenty of space *(Chris Glasson)*

MINSTER LOVELL [SP3111]

New Inn OX29 0RZ [Burford Rd]: Extensively reworked, with enjoyable food from antipasti, lunchtime sandwiches and light dishes to major meals, good choice of wines by the glass, Hook Norton and Wadworths 6X, friendly efficient service, impressive views over pretty Windrush valley; children welcome, terrace tables, lovely setting *(David Glynne-Jones)*

Old Swan OX29 0RN [just N of B4047 Witney—Burford]: Intriguing old building with variety of secluded seating areas, deep armchairs and rugs on flagstones, Hook Norton ales, log fire, enjoyable lunchtime snacks and light meals, efficient young staff, carvery restaurant; piped music, and more an adjunct to the adjacent Old Mill Conference Centre than an individual pub; tables in lovely garden, bedrooms, idyllic village *(David Glynne-Jones, LYM, E A and D C T Frewer, Mr and Mrs R W Allan)*

MURCOTT [SP5815]

Nut Tree OX5 2RE [off B4027 NE of Oxford]: Charming open-plan beamed and thatched medieval building, fairly priced food from substantial lunchtime sandwiches up, more elaborate evening dishes, real ales inc Hook Norton, good wines by the glass, neat friendly young staff, log fire, small back conservatory-style no smoking restaurant; pretty garden with terrace, pond and aunt sally, bedrooms *(Dr R H Wilkinson, Mrs Jane-Ann Jones, Chris Smith, LYM, Richard Greaves)*

NEWBRIDGE [SP4001]

Maybush OX29 7QD [A415 7 miles S of Witney]: Low-beamed dining pub in lovely Thamesside setting and handy for Thames Path, obliging service, Greene King ales; children truly welcome, pretty and neatly kept waterside garden and terrace *(LYM, David and Cathrine Whiting, Comus and Sarah Elliott, A P Seymour, Meg and Colin Hamilton)*

☆ *Rose Revived* OX29 7QD [A415 7 miles S of Witney]: Roomy and well reworked pub with comfortable settees, attractive prints and photographs, central log-effect fire between two dining areas, beamed side areas, enjoyable quickly served food from good soup and sandwiches up all day, cheerful young staff, Greene King ales, good coffee; some live music; children welcome, lovely big lawn by the upper Thames, prettily lit at night (good overnight mooring free), comfortable bedrooms *(Dick and Madeleine Brown, LYM, Charles and Pauline Stride, Comus and Sarah Elliott, Ann and Colin Hunt, Meg and Colin Hamilton)*

NORTH MORETON [SU5689]

Bear at Home OX11 9AT [off A4130 Didcot—Wallingford; High St]: Dating from 16th c and doing well under attentive new licensees, enjoyable reasonably priced food served piping hot, good choice of wines by the glass, Timothy Taylors Landlord, snugly traditional bar one end, conservatory the other; attractive garden overlooking cricket pitch *(Roderick Braithwaite)*

NORTHMOOR [SP4202]

Red Lion OX29 5SX [B4449 SE of Stanton Harcourt]: Refurbished 15th-c stone-built village pub with thriving local atmosphere, busy lunchtime for good choice of down-to-earth food cooked to order, low prices and big helpings, Greene King ales with a guest such as Batemans, friendly landlord and locals, good log fires each end, heavy beams, stripped stone, small no smoking dining room; walkers welcome, no dogs, no credit cards, Thurs morning post office; garden *(P and J Shapley)*

NUFFIELD [SU6787]
Crown RG9 5SJ [A4130/B481]: Attractive building with country furniture and inglenook log fire in beamed lounge bar, friendly helpful staff, enjoyable inexpensive food from sandwiches up, Brakspears ales; walkers welcome (good walks nearby), children in small family room, pleasant garden with tables outside front and back *(John Roots, LYM)*

OXFORD [SP5206]
Angel & Greyhound OX4 1AB [St Clements St]: Unpretentious Youngs pub with their ale, good atmosphere, good range of food (not Sun evening), scrubbed pine tables on bare boards; front picnic-sets and tables on back terrace, open all day *(Tim and Ann Newell)*
☆ *Bear* OX1 4EH [Alfred St/Wheatsheaf Alley]: Two small low-ceilinged and partly panelled 16th-c rooms, not over-smart and often packed with students, thousands of vintage ties on walls and beams, simple reasonably priced lunchtime food most days inc sandwiches, four changing real ales from centenarian handpumps on pewter bar counter, no games machines; upstairs ladies'; tables outside, open all day summer *(LYM, Tim and Ann Newell, R Huggins, D Irving, E McCall, T McLean, the Didler)*
Bookbinders Arms OX2 6BT [Victor St]: Mellow little local, friendly and unpretentious, with good range of beers, reasonably priced simple food, darts, cards and shove ha'penny *(Gwyn Jones)*
Cock & Camel OX1 2AE [George St]: Café-feel Youngs pub in shop conversion, good choice of wines by the glass, their real ales, pub food from sandwiches to steak, breakfast from 10, small no smoking area, sizeable evening cellar bar too; piped music; bedrooms, open all day *(Michael Dandy)*
☆ *Eagle & Child* OX1 3LU [St Giles]: Attractive panelled front bar, compact mid-bars full of actors' and Tolkien/C S Lewis memorabilia, tasteful stripped-brick modern back dining extension with no smoking conservatory, friendly service, bargain range of pubby food from sandwiches up, Brakspears, Caledonian Deuchars IPA, Fullers London Pride and Hook Norton, good choice of wines by the glass, newspapers, events posters; piped music, busy at lunchtime, bar can get rather smoky; open all day *(BB, the Didler, Dick and Madeleine Brown, Michael Dandy, Revd R P Tickle, Chris Glasson, Ned Kelly, Ann and Colin Hunt)*
Harcourt Arms OX2 6DG [Cranham Terr]: Friendly local with proper landlord and some character, pillars dividing it, good value snacks, Fullers ales, two log fires, well

reproduced piped jazz, good choice of board games *(P S Hoyle)*
☆ *Kings Arms* OX1 3SP [Holywell St]: Bustling 16th-c Youngs pub with their full beer range, guest beers and fine choice of wines by the glass, cosy comfortably worn in partly panelled side and back rooms (one no smoking), daily papers, relaxed atmosphere; children in all-day eating area with counter servery doing usual food (all day wknds) from sandwiches up, a few tables outside, open all day *(the Didler, Michael Dandy, Dave Lowe, Peter Dandy, Simon Jones, Pat and Tony Martin, Colin and Janet Roe, Tim and Ann Newell, Kevin Blake, LYM, Ann and Colin Hunt, P S Hoyle)*
Lamb & Flag OX1 3JS [St Giles/Banbury Rd]: Old pub owned by nearby college, modern airy front room with big windows over street, more atmosphere in back rooms with exposed stonework and low panelled ceilings, changing ales such as Fullers London Pride, Palmers Best and a beer they brew for the pub (L&F Gols), Shepherd Neame Spitfire and Skinners Betty Stogs, good value well served food from baguettes and ciabattas up, cheerful service; can be packed with students *(Michael Dandy, Richard Greaves)*
Marlborough House OX1 4LG [Western Rd, just off Abingdon Rd S of Folly Bridge]: Small friendly side-street local, Adnams Bitter and Broadside, Caledonian Deuchars IPA and Greene King IPA, inexpensive lunchtime snacks such as filled rolls, charming little snug off corridor, simple main bar with darts and juke box *(Pete Baker)*
☆ *Watermans Arms* OX2 0BE [South St, Osney (off A420 Botley Rd via Bridge St)]: Tidy and unpretentious riverside local tucked away nr Osney Lock, welcoming landlord, Greene King ales inc Morlands Original, good generous home cooking; tables outside, open all day *(Alan Kilpatrick, Mr and Mrs B A R Frost, Anthony Ellis)*
Wharf House OX1 1TT [Butterwyke Pl/Speedwell St]: Half a dozen or so changing real ales such as Fullers London Pride, Hook Norton Best, Shepherd Neame Spitfire and Timothy Taylors Landlord in small bare-boards early Victorian local with knowledgeable, friendly and helpful landlord, two farm ciders, imported bottled beers with their proper glasses, rickety old tables and chairs, darts, cards, elderly bull terrier; occasional vinyl records played, old TV brought out for sports, some impromptu singing; open all day Sat *(Derek and Sylvia Stephenson, Pete Baker)*
☆ *White Horse* OX1 3BB [Broad St]: Bustling and studenty, squeezed between bits of Blackwells bookshop, small narrow bar with snug one-table raised back alcove, low beams and timbers, ochre ceiling, beautiful view of the Clarendon building and Sheldonian, good lunchtime food (the few tables reserved for this) from sandwiches up, changing real ales such as Brakspears, Caledonian Deuchars IPA, Hook Norton Old Hooky and M&B Brew XI, Addlestone's cider, friendly staff *(Giles and*

Annie Francis, the Didler, Michael Dandy, BB, Dave Lowe, R Huggins, D Irving, E McCall, T McLean)

PISHILL [SU7190]

☆ *Crown* RG9 6HH [B480 Nettlebed—Watlington]: Popular dining pub in wisteria-covered ancient building, black beams and timbers, good log fires and candlelight, amiable landlord, wholesome home-made food from good baguettes up inc carefully chosen ingredients and local venison, Brakspears and Wychwood; children welcome in no smoking restaurant, pleasant bedroom in separate cottage, picnic-sets on attractive side lawn, pretty country setting – lots of walks *(the Didler, LYM, Howard Dell, Paul Humphreys, Peter Abbott, Susan and John Douglas)*

PLAY HATCH [SU7476]

Crown RG4 9QN: Olde-worlde heavily beamed 16th-c dining pub, two bars and several rooms inc barn restaurant and big modern no smoking conservatory, Brakspears ales tapped from the cask, extensive choice of decent wines, log fires, smartly dressed young antipodean staff; piped music; big pleasant garden with play area *(John Baish, BB, Julia and Richard Tredgett, Mr and Mrs D J Pickles, A P Seymour)*

RADCOT [SU2899]

Swan OX18 2SX [A4095 2½ miles N of Faringdon]: Welcoming Thames-side pub with enjoyable food from generous baguettes to hearty Sun roast, friendly efficient staff, log fire, Greene King ales, lots of stuffed fish; children in eating area; piped music; pleasant waterside garden, summer boat trips (lift to bring wheelchairs aboard), four good value bedrooms *(LYM, Tim Venn, A P Seymour)*

ROTHERFIELD GREYS [SU7282]

Maltsters Arms RG9 4QD: Old Brakspears pub with their Bitter and Best, good choice of food from rolls and panini to piping hot specials (best to book wknds), helpful friendly landlord, lots of cricket memorabilia; not far from Greys Court (NT), lovely country views *(Philip and June Caunt, John A Barker, Roy and Gay Hoing)*

SATWELL [SU7083]

☆ *Lamb* RG9 4QZ [2 miles S of Nettlebed; follow Shepherds Green signpost]: Cosy and attractive little 16th-c low-beamed cottage, previously popular with readers for its cheerful unpretentious style and generous simple lunchtime food, with plain pine furniture on its tiled floors, huge log fireplace and a small carpeted family dining room, has recently reopened as more of a bistro dining pub – we'd be grateful for more reports; tables out in prettily reworked garden, nice spot *(LYM, Dick and Madeleine Brown)*

SHENINGTON [SP3742]

☆ *Bell* OX15 6NQ [2 miles NW of Banbury]: Hospitable 17th-c two-room pub well worth knowing for landlady's consistently good reasonably priced home cooking, good sandwiches too, low-priced Hook Norton Best, good wine choice, informal service, relaxed

atmosphere, heavy beams, some flagstones, stripped stone and pine panelling, coal fire, friendly dogs, cribbage, dominoes; children in eating areas, tables out in front, small attractive back garden, charming quiet village, good surrounding walks, bedrooms, cl Mon (and alas sometimes other wkdy) lunchtimes *(LYM, Sir Nigel Foulkes, Graham and Nicky Westwood, K H Frostick, Michael and Jeanne Shillington, John Kane)*

SHILTON [SP2608]

Rose & Crown OX18 4AB [off B4020 S of Burford]: Mellow 17th-c low-beamed stone-built village pub, small beamed and tiled bar with inglenook log fire, neat small dining room, interesting choice of reasonably priced food (should book for Sun roasts), Greene King ales, warm civilised atmosphere, quick friendly service, darts; tables in lovely garden, nice setting opp pond in pretty village *(Mrs Angela Brown)*

SHIPLAKE [SU7678]

Plowden Arms RG9 4BX [Reading Rd (A4155)]: Neat and friendly, with three linked rooms and side dining room, good range of home-made food from well filled baguettes up, Brakspears, good coffee, friendly staff, log fire; handy for Thames walk *(Paul Humphreys)*

SHIPLAKE ROW [SU7478]

White Hart RG9 4DP [off A4155 W of Shiplake]: Three simple and friendly linked rooms mainly set for good choice of food (just roasts Sun lunchtime), cheerful attentive service, Brakspears, decent house wines, log fires; interestingly planted back garden, nice location, fine views, boules, good walks *(Betty Laker)*

SHIPTON-UNDER-WYCHWOOD [SP2717]

Lamb OX7 6DQ [off A361 to Burford]: Neat dining pub with friendly current management, enjoyable if not cheap food from light dishes to daily fresh fish, Greene King ales and perhaps a guest beer, some stripped stone and log fire, no smoking restaurant in Elizabethan core; piped music, jazz Sun night; children and dogs welcome, tables outside, five attractive bedrooms (some over bar which can stay lively till late), good breakfast *(Stuart Turner, LYM, Colin McKerrow, M and GR, R Huggins, D Irving, E McCall, T McLean, Derek Stafford)*

☆ *Shaven Crown* OX7 6BA [High St (A361)]: Ancient building, well worth a look for the hotel part's hall – magnificent lofty medieval rafters and imposing double stairway; separate friendly back bar more work-a-day; with booth seating, enjoyable food, Hook Norton, several wines by the glass and traditional games, no smoking restaurant; piped music; children and dogs welcome, peaceful courtyard with outside heaters, bowling green *(Chris Glasson, Ian Phillips, LYM, Howard and Margaret Buchanan, Mrs Phoebe A Kemp, Jane Taylor, David Dutton)*

SHRIVENHAM [SU2488]

☆ *Prince of Wales* SN6 8AF [High St; off A420 or B4000 NE of Swindon]: Bustling 17th-c stone-built local with hearty food (not Sun evening) inc Sun roasts, warm-hearted atmosphere, real ales inc Wadworths and Charles Wells Bombardier, good soft drinks choice, spotless low-beamed lounge, pictures, lots of brasses, log fire and candles, small dining area, side bar with darts, board games and machines; may be quiet piped music, no dogs; children welcome, picnic-sets and heaters in secluded back garden *(Gordon and Jay Smith, A P Seymour)*

SHUTFORD [SP3840]

☆ *George & Dragon* OX15 6PG [Church Lane]: Ancient stone-built pub with prompt obliging service, decent food inc good ploughman's and Sun lunches, Hook Norton Best and changing ales such as Everards Original, fine choice of wines by the glass, comfortable flagstoned L-shaped bar with impressive fireplace, and oak-panelled beamed dining room; children and dogs welcome, small garden, pretty village, cl Mon, open all day Sun *(BB, Guy Vowles, Chris Glasson)*

SIBFORD GOWER [SP3537]

Bishop Blaize OX15 5RQ [just off B4035 W of Banbury; Burdrop]: The cheerful licensees who made this stone-built old local so popular have moved on; it's still worth knowing, for its unpretentious heavily beamed partly panelled bar with inglenook log fire and big windows overlooking the spacious sloping lawn and lower terrace with their splendid rural pastoral views; Hook Norton real ale, food from baguettes up with plans to expand the dining side *(LYM)*

☆ *Wykham Arms* OX15 5RX [signed off B4035 Banbury—Shipston on Stour; Temple Mill Rd]: Pretty and cottagey thatched and flagstoned restauranty dining pub doing good meals inc good value set lunch, Hook Norton Best, good wines by the glass and coffee, comfortable open-plan low-beamed stripped-stone lounge, nice pictures, table made from glass-topped well, inglenook tap room, friendly efficient staff; children welcome; country views from big well planted garden, lovely manor house opp; has been cl Mon lunchtime *(Steve and Liz Tilley, Guy Vowles, LYM, Simon Jones, Iain R Hewitt)*

SOULDERN [SP5231]

Fox OX27 7JW [off B4100; Fox Lane]: New licensees in charming small open-plan beamed pub, Brakspears and good choice of wines by the glass, big log fire, settles and chairs around oak tables, oriental prints, good baguettes with soup, salad or proper chips, full menu of other dishes, no piped music; delightful village *(E A and D C T Frewer)*

SOUTH NEWINGTON [SP4033]

☆ *Duck on the Pond* OX15 4JE: Thriving dining pub with tidy modern-rustic décor in small flagstoned bar and linked no smoking carpeted eating areas up a step with fresh flowers and lit candles, wide choice of generous enjoyable food from wraps, melts and other light dishes to steak and mixed grill, real ales such as Adnams, Hook Norton, Loddon Hullabaloo and Wychwood, accommodating landlord and

neat and friendly young staff; piped pop music; lots of tables out on deck and lawn, pretty pond, open all day *(Chris Glasson, Ted George, Keith and Sue Ward, BB, Michael Dandy)*

SOUTHMOOR [SU3998]

Waggon & Horses OX13 5BG [Faringdon Rd just W of Kingston Bagpuize (off A420 Oxford—Faringdon)]: Welcoming traditional two-bar pub with beams and open fire, enjoyable food from baguettes and good soup up, friendly staff, Greene King IPA and Old Speckled Hen, more elaborate dining room in former bars; picnic-sets on roadside terrace and in garden *(Dick and Madeleine Brown)*

STADHAMPTON [SU6098]

Crazy Bear OX44 7UR [signed off A329 in village; Bear Lane]: Stylishly updated 16th-c dining pub, stuffed bears, log fire, flagstones and polished bar, good if not cheap food from oysters up, Greene King IPA, good range of wines (and champagne) by the glass, frozen vodkas, friendly staff; tables outside, bedrooms *(Hunter and Christine Wright)*

STANFORD IN THE VALE [SU3393]

Horse & Jockey SN7 8NN [Faringdon Rd]: Popular old local in racehorse country, low ceilings, flagstones and woodburner in big fireplace, good drawings and paintings of horses and jockeys, friendly landlord, Batemans XXB and Greene King ales, limited bar food and charming restaurant; dogs welcome, play area *(Peter and Audrey Dowsett, Ian Phillips)*

STANTON ST JOHN [SP5709]

☆ *Talk House* OX33 1EX [Middle Rd/Wheatley Rd (B4027 just outside)]: Peacefully placed 17th-c pub with enjoyable carefully prepared food, Hook Norton Best, Wadworths 6X and a guest beer, helpful service, Oxford academia prints on partly stripped stone walls, lots of oak beams, flagstones and tiles, simple but solid rustic furnishings, pleasant area by log fire; children welcome in restaurant, tables in sheltered courtyard, comfortable bedrooms, has been open all day in summer *(Sue Demont, Tim Barrow, LYM, Heather Couper)*

STEVENTON [SU4791]

☆ *Cherry Tree* OX13 6RZ [B4017 (High St); village signed off A34 S of Abingdon via A4130]: Well kept Wadworths ales and others such as Butcombe and Charles Wells Bombardier in rambling updated 18th-c pub with open-plan beamed areas around island bar, flagstones and bare boards, mix of furniture inc heavily carved settles and brocaded dining chairs, dark green walls, open fires and old prints, good value generous food served quickly from good sandwiches up, decent wines, friendly staff, no smoking area; pool and big-screen sports TV in back room, folk night 3rd Sun in month; disabled facilities, tables out on terrace, three bedrooms, open all day Fri-Sun *(BB, G Coates, Marjorie and David Lamb, Dick and Madeleine Brown)*

☆ *North Star* OX13 6SG [Stocks Lane, The Causeway, central westward turn off B4017]: Carefully restored old-fangled village pub with tiled entrance corridor, main area with ancient high-backed settles around central table, Greene King Morlands Original on handpump and two guest ales tapped from the cask in small tap room off (no bar counter), hatch service to side room with plain seating, a couple of tables and good coal fire, simple lunchtime food, mainly inexpensive sandwiches, ploughman's and hot-filled baguettes, friendly staff and three-legged cat; sports TV; tables on side grass, front gateway through living yew tree *(the Didler, Pete Baker, LYM)*

STOKE LYNE [SP5628]

☆ *Peyton Arms* OX27 8SD [from minor road off B4110 N of Bicester fork left into village]: Largely unspoilt stone-built pub with Hook Norton beers (full range) tapped from casks behind small corner bar in sparsely decorated front snug, tiled floor, inglenook log fire, hops on beam, food may use home-grown veg, bigger refurbished games room with darts and pool, charity book store; well behaved children and dogs welcome, pleasant garden with aunt sally, open all day wknds *(Mick Furn, the Didler, Pete Baker, JJW, CMW)*

STOKE ROW [SU6884]

☆ *Cherry Tree* RG9 5QA [off B481 at Highmoor]: Contemporary dining pub with good if not cheap food (freshly made so can take a while at busy times), Brakspears ales, good choice of wines by the glass, helpful smiling young staff, fresh minimalist décor in four linked rooms with solid new rustic furniture, stripped wood, heavy low beams and some flagstones; TV in bar; good seating in attractive newly done garden, nice nearby walks, five good bedrooms in new block, good breakfast *(Rob Winstanley, BB, Susan and John Douglas, Julie Woolmer, Jim Cooper, P Price, Roy and Gay Hoing, Karen and Graham Oddey, Howard Dell)*

☆ *Crooked Billet* RG9 5PU [Nottwood Lane, off B491 N of Reading – OS Sheet 175 map ref 684844]: A favourite of ours, but restaurant not pub (so not eligible for the main entries – you can't have just a drink); rustic pub layout though, with heavy beams, flagstones, antique pubby furnishings and great inglenook log fire as well as crimsonly Victorian dining room; wide choice of well cooked interesting meals using local produce inc good value lunch (you can have just a starter), particularly helpful friendly staff, Brakspears tapped from the cask (no bar counter), good wines, relaxed homely atmosphere – like a french country restaurant; children truly welcome (they actually cook for the lucky local primary school, too), occasional live music, big garden by Chilterns beechwoods *(Bob and Judy Smitherman, Mr and Mrs Bentley-Davies, Heather Couper, Penny and Peter Keevil, Rob Winstanley, the Didler, LYM, Paul Humphreys, Mrs E A Macdonald, Karen and Graham Oddey)*

Rising Sun RG9 5PF [Witheridge Hill, Highmoor, E of village]: Country pub doing well under current licensees, proper bar area and separate dining area with enjoyable very generous food, also tapas-style smaller dishes, Brakspears ales; idyllic spot *(Torrens Lyster)*

STRATTON AUDLEY [SP6026]

Red Lion OX27 9AZ [off A421 NE of Bicester; Church St]: Thatched local with big inglenook log fire in L-shaped bar, stripped stone, low beams and small adjacent eating area, quick generous food from baguettes and baked potatoes up with wider evening choice, Caledonian Deuchars IPA, Greene King Ruddles County and Shepherd Neame Spitfire, friendly service, good atmosphere, antique sale posters, old varnished wooden furniture; TV; children and dogs welcome, pavement tables, more on heated terrace in small colourful garden, pretty village *(Michael Dandy, E A and D C T Frewer, JJW, CMW)*

SUNNINGWELL [SP4900]

☆ *Flowing Well* OX13 6RB [just N of Abingdon]: Cheerfully relaxed, with unpretentious furnishings and warm décor in attractive timbered building, good enterprising home-made food from baguettes to restaurant dishes and wicked puddings, Greene King Abbot and Morlands and Wadworths 6X, good wine choice inc many organic ones, plus organic coffees and juices, remarkable collection of rare rums, big no smoking area, pool; TV, gentle live jazz and blues nights (at other times piped jazz can be loud); they may try to keep your credit card while you eat; garden with small well and picnic-sets under cocktail parasols *(Derek Goldrei, BB)*

SWINBROOK [SP2812]

Swan OX18 4DY [back rd a mile N of A40, 2 miles E of Burford]: This prettily set country pub, listed as a main entry in our last edition, closed after that edition was sent to the printers, but before it was published; as we go to press in 2006 there is still no sign of its reopening; news please *(LYM)*

TACKLEY [SP4619]

Sturdys Castle OX5 3EP [Banbury Rd (A4260)]: Renovated roadside inn with mezzanine bar, two rooms either side, one with stripped stone, Wadworths 6X, daily papers, games, ground-floor restaurant; piped music, TV; tables outside, bedrooms around pleasant courtyard, open all day *(Michael Dandy)*

TETSWORTH [SP6801]

Red Lion OX9 7AS [A40, between M40 junctions 6 and 7]: New management for attractive bistro-feel pub overlooking big village green, several spacious areas around central bar counter with pale wood floors, Greene King Abbot and a guest beer, bar food and library/conservatory restaurant (children welcome, though this bit has not always been open recently), board games; open all day *(LYM)*

Swan OX9 7AB [A40, not far from M40 junction 7]: Thriving bar doubling as restaurant and afternoon teashop for antiques centre in other parts of this rambling 15th-c coaching inn, appropriate furnishings, gilt-framed paintings and masses of character, good upmarket food, pleasant atmosphere and helpful service, good log fire in massive fireplace; keg beer *(Susan and John Douglas)*

THAME [SP7005]

☆ *Bird Cage* OX9 3DX [Cornmarket]: Elaborate recent refurbishment making the most of striking 15th-c black and white beamed and timbered dining pub, attractive front bar and smart dining room served by new kitchen, good if not cheap food, continental beer on tap as well as real ale, good coffee, friendly staff, daily papers; piped music, no children or dogs inside; pavement tables *(LYM, Tim and Ann Newell, Ron Deighton)*

Six Bells OX9 2AD [High St]: Gently upmarket open-plan bar with log fire, cosier no smoking back rooms, candlelit tables, relaxed atmosphere, interestingly varied food, Fullers ales; dogs welcome, large terrace *(Tim and Ann Newell)*

Swan OX9 3ER [Upper High St]: Pubby atmosphere in heavily beamed 16th-c coaching inn under new management, changing real ales such as Archers, Hanby, Hook Norton Best and Timothy Taylors Landlord, food from sensibly priced sandwiches up, friendly informal service, individual furnishings and bric-a-brac, big log fire, upstairs restaurant with medieval ceiling; children and dogs welcome, open all day *(LYM, Derek and Sylvia Stephenson, Tim and Ann Newell)*

THRUPP [SP4815]

☆ *Boat* OX5 1JY [off A4260 just N of Kidlington]: Cheerful accommodating licensees getting everything right in stone-built pub particularly popular in summer for its attractive position by Oxford Canal, sensible choice of good value freshly made food from good baguettes up, Greene King ales, decent wine, coal fire, old canal pictures and artefacts, bare boards and stripped pine, restaurant, no piped music; nice safely fenced garden behind with plenty of tables, some in shade *(Sue Demont, Tim Barrow, Pete Baker, A Darroch Harkness, Charles and Pauline Stride, Meg and Colin Hamilton)*

TOOT BALDON [SP5600]

Mole OX44 9NG: Light bright open-plan dining pub with enjoyable food, good wines by the glass, attentive service, woodburners, conservatory; garden tables *(Richard Atherton)*

WALLINGFORD [SU6089]

Cross Keys OX10 0DB [High St]: Small two-bar brick-built low-beamed local, welcoming landlord, Brakspears, character customers, traditional games, interesting live music; tables outside with play area, open all day Fri-Sun *(Luke Johnson)*

WANTAGE [SU3987]

☆ *Royal Oak* OX12 8DF [Newbury St]: Welcoming two-bar local with lots of ship photographs and naval hatbands, friendly landlord well informed about his particularly well kept ales such as Bass or Marstons Pedigree, Wadworths 6X and two beers brewed for him by West Berkshire; table football, darts, cribbage; cl wkdy lunchtimes, bedrooms *(BB, the Didler)*

Shoulder of Mutton OX12 8AX [Wallingford St]: Friendly and chatty local, coal fire and racing TV in bar, passage to two small snug back rooms, changing real ales; tables on back terrace, not open till 3.30 (noon wknds) *(the Didler, Pete Baker)*

WARBOROUGH [SU5993]

Cricketers Arms OX10 7DD [Thame Rd (off A329)]: Good value fresh food (booking recommended Sun) in neat and pleasantly decorated pub with good friendly service, Greene King IPA and Abbot, proper bar and dining area; tables outside, has been cl wkdy lunchtimes and Sun-Tues evenings *(Marjorie and David Lamb)*

☆ *Six Bells* OX10 7DN [The Green S; just E of A329, 4 miles N of Wallingford]: Friendly new young licensees in thatched 16th-c pub facing cricket green, attractive country furnishings in linked small areas off bar, good fresh food, Brakspears ales and a guest such as Wychwoods, decent wines, good service, big log fire, daily papers, low beams and stripped stone, scrubbed farmhouse tables, antique photographs and pictures; dogs welcome, tables in pleasant orchard garden *(LYM, Ian Phillips, Barry Collett, Martin and Karen Wake)*

WENDLEBURY [SP5619]

Red Lion OX25 2PW [a mile from M40 junction 9; signposted from A41 Bicester—Oxford]: Friendly and attentive new licensees in spacious low-beamed stone-built pub with traditional furnishings and big log fire, two comfortable dining areas, straightforward food from sandwiches and baguettes up, Fullers London Pride and Charles Wells Bombardier, several wines by the glass; large garden *(E A and D C T Frewer)*

WEST HANNEY [SU4092]

☆ *Plough* OX12 0LN [Church St]: Unspoilt and pretty thatched pub with attractive timbered upper storey, original timbers and uneven low ceilings, homely and welcoming panelled lounge with good log fire in stone fireplace, genial landlord, good value food from sandwiches and baguettes up using local ingredients, changing ales such as Adnams, Brakspears, Marstons Pedigree, Timothy Taylors Landlord and Youngs, interesting whiskies, no smoking dining room, darts in public bar; children and dogs welcome, tables in back garden *(Dr Williams, Helene Grygar)*

WITNEY [SP3509]

Angel OX28 6AL [Market Sq]: Wide choice of bargain food from good sandwiches up inc OAP specials in comfortably bustling 17th-c town local, real ales such as Courage Best, Hook Norton Best and Charles Wells Bombardier, daily papers, welcoming unpretentious surroundings and hot coal fire, quick friendly service even when packed; piped music, can get smoky, big-screen sports TV, pool room, coffee bar, bingo nights; parking nearby can be difficult *(Peter and Audrey Dowsett, MDN, Derek Allpass)*

Fleece OX28 4AZ [Church Green]: Wide choice of enjoyable if not cheap food in smart and civilised town pub on green, Greene King ales; piped music; children welcome, tables outside *(Jane Taylor, David Dutton)*

☆ *Three Horseshoes* OX28 6BS [Corn St, junction with Holloway Rd]: Good welcoming and attentive service in attractive 16th-c stone-built pub with thoughtful choice of good home-made food from filled baguettes, ciabattas and other pubby lunchtime food to more imaginative restauranty dishes, Greene King Abbot and Morlands Original and a guest beer, decent house wines, heavy beams, flagstones, log fires, well polished and comfortable old furniture, separate dining room *(LYM, John Stanbury, KN-R)*

Windrush OX28 6DJ [Burford Rd; A4095, outskirts]: Smartly kept sizeable roadside pub with affordable food, two or three real ales, large no smoking restaurant; quiet piped music *(Peter and Audrey Dowsett)*

WOLVERCOTE [SP4909]

Plough OX2 8AH [First Turn/Wolvercote Green]: Lots of comfortably well worn in pubby linked areas, with friendly helpful service, bustling atmosphere, armchairs and Victorian-style carpeted bays in main lounge, real ales, decent wines, good value usual food in flagstoned ex-stables dining room and library (children allowed here), traditional snug, woodburner; picnic-sets on front terrace looking over rough meadow to canal and woods *(BB, R T and J C Moggridge, Alan and Carolin Tidbury)*

Red Lion OX2 8PG [Godstow Rd]: Big plush no smoking dining extension with coal-effect fires, good value food inc carveries, curry nights and popular Sun lunch, several real ales, friendly atmosphere, original bar with lots of photographs, prints and memorabilia; quiet piped music; lots of garden tables, play area *(Peter and Audrey Dowsett)*

WOODSTOCK [SP4416]

Bear OX20 1SZ [Park St]: Small heavy-beamed bar at front of smart hotel, cosy alcoves, immaculate and tastefully casual mix of antique oak, mahogany and leather furniture, paintings and sporting trophies, blazing inglenook log fire, Stones, good fresh sandwiches and hot bar lunches (not cheap), quick friendly service, restaurant; tables in back courtyard, good bedrooms, open all day *(Michael Dandy, BB, DFL, Mr and Mrs J Hutton)*

Crown OX20 1TE [High St (A44)]: Large comfortable L-shaped bar with Greene King IPA and Abbot and a guest such as Gales, baguettes, daily papers, log fire, roomy restaurant with conservatory doing pizzas and pasta, popular prices; piped music, sports TV one end; bedrooms, open all day *(Derek and Sylvia Stephenson, Michael Dandy)*

Feathers OX20 1SX [Market St]: Not a pub but a formal cotswold hotel with attractive period furnishings, and does have enjoyable though pricey bar food, good wines by the glass and daily papers in small comfortable back bar with nice log fire, opening on to charming sunny courtyard garden with heaters; piped music; children welcome, good bedrooms *(Michael Dandy, LYM)*

☆ *Kings Arms* OX20 1SU [Market St/Park Lane]:

Good interesting food, pleasant furnishings and friendly helpful landlord and staff in roomy pub/hotel with two small bars and attractive back brasserie, good value wines, Marstons Pedigree and Theakstons, open fire; piped music; children welcome, comfortable nicely refurbished bedrooms, good breakfast, open all day *(Michael Dandy, David Glynne-Jones, Guy Vowles)*

Star OX20 1TA [Market Pl]: Big cheerful beamed town pub, Tetleys and Wadworths 6X, good value wines, decent food all day from good filled baguettes up, popular family Sun lunch, bare boards, some stripped stone, daily papers, open fires; piped music, TV; pleasant pavement tables and more in back courtyard, good-sized bedrooms, good breakfast *(Derek and Sylvia Stephenson, BB)*

Woodstock Arms OX20 1SX [Market St]: 16th-c heavy-beamed stripped-stone pub, lively and stylish, with above-average food showing real care in preparation, prompt service by young friendly staff, Greene King IPA, Abbot and Old Speckled Hen, good wine choice, daily papers, log-effect gas fire in splendid stone fireplace, long narrow bar, end eating area; piped music; tables out in yard, bedrooms, open all day *(Michael Dandy, John Holroyd, Paul Goldman, Chris Glasson)*

WOOLSTONE [SU2987]

☆ *White Horse* SN7 7QL [village signed off B4507]: Plushly refurbished partly thatched 16th-c pub with steep Victorian gables, two big open fires in spacious and eclectically decorated beamed and part-panelled room, wide choice of enjoyable quickly served bar food, friendly relaxed staff and black labrador, Arkells ales, decent wines, lots of whiskies, good coffee, log fire, evening restaurant; quiet piped music, no visiting dogs; children allowed in eating area, sheltered garden, four charming good value bedrooms, big breakfast, secluded interesting village handy for White Horse and Ridgeway walkers *(Mrs Rosemary Bayliss, BB, Mary Rayner)*

WOOTTON [SP4320]

☆ *Killingworth Castle* OX20 1EJ [Glympton Rd; B4027 N of Woodstock]: Striking three-storey 17th-c coaching inn with cheerful hard-working landlord and lively local atmosphere, Greene King ales, decent house wines, wide choice of generous food, long narrow main bar with pine furnishings, parquet floor, candles, lots of brasses and log fire with books above it, daily papers, bar billiards, darts and shove ha'penny in smaller games end, attractive garden; soft piped music, frequent live music nights; bedrooms *(Craig Adams, Felicity Davies, Pete Baker, BB)*

☆ *Kings Head* OX20 1DX [off B4027 N of Woodstock; Chapel Hill]: Upmarket and rather formal no smoking 17th-c inn enjoyed by many for its interesting but not over-elaborate choice of good if not cheap fresh food using local and even home-grown ingredients, Greene King Ruddles County and Hook Norton Old Hooky tapped from the cask, good wines, armchairs, sofas and old oak settles and chairs in elegant and peaceful beamed lounge bar with log fire, larger back dining area; children not welcome; immaculate bedrooms, good breakfast, cl Sun evening and Mon *(Howard Dell, Mrs Rosemary Bayliss, Bernard Stradling, Sir Nigel Foulkes, LYM, Colin and Bernardine Perry)*

YARNTON [SP4812]

Turnpike OX5 1PJ [A44 N of Oxford]: Large Vintage Inn pub/restaurant with good atmosphere in spacious low-ceilinged bar areas, wide range of promptly served food all day, Bass, friendly helpful staff, log fire *(Chris Glasson, Nigel and Sue Foster)*

Shropshire

Shropshire has some particularly nice pubs to stay in, and with such lovely countryside in this part of the world it makes a delightful place for a short break. Bishop's Castle does particularly well from a pub lover's point of view, and a stay at the distinctive old Castle Hotel would give you the chance to tour the brewery at the cheery Six Bells, and taste the John Roberts beers brewed across the yard from the sociable Three Tuns, all in the same town. Another good place to stay (and for a meal) is the very civilised and no smoking Inn at Grinshill, which gains a new Stay Award this year for its rather charming rooms. It's notable that two of the new main entries in Shropshire this year are completely no smoking, with the kindly new licensees at the family-friendly Ragleth in Little Stretton being particularly concerned for the health of their staff; at the lovely old Crown at Munslow the smoke-free environment makes the most of a rewarding and very carefully sourced menu. Our other new entry here, the handsomely reworked Fox at Chetwynd Aston, comes out of the almost infallible Brunning & Price stable, and goes straight into the *Guide* with both Beer and Wine Awards (and is clearly well in the running for a Food Award). From the same enterprising small group, the Armoury at Shrewsbury was a strong contender for Shropshire Dining Pub of the Year, but the award goes to the meticulously run Burlton Inn at Burlton with its slightly more sophisticated food – just the place for a special occasion. Several pubs making a splash in the Lucky Dip section at the end of the chapter are the Mytton & Mermaid at Atcham, Railwaymans Arms in Bridgnorth, Jolly Frog at Leintwardine, and Loggerheads and Three Fishes, both in Shrewsbury. Drinks tend to be rather cheaper than the national average here, with several local small breweries offering good value. Chief among them is Hobsons, and others to look out for include Woods, John Roberts and Hanby. It's also worth keeping an eye open for good value beers from just outside the county, such as Wye Valley and Holdens. And of course there are the bargain brews from the Six Bells in Bishop's Castle.

BISHOP'S CASTLE   SO3289   Map 6

Castle Hotel 🛏

Market Square, just off B4385; SY9 5BN

This splendid early 18th-c stone coaching inn is full of creaky charm, and the warm welcome from staff makes it a particularly pleasant place to stay. Neatly kept and attractively furnished, the clubby little beamed and panelled bar, glazed off from the entrance, has a good coal fire, old hunting prints and sturdy leather chairs on its muted carpet. It opens into a much bigger room, with maroon plush wall seats and stools, big Victorian engravings, and another coal fire in an attractive cast-iron fireplace. The lighting in both rooms is gentle and relaxing, and the pub tables have unusually elaborate cast-iron frames; shove-ha'penny, dominoes, cribbage and board games. Hobsons Best, local Six Bells Big Nevs and possibly a guest are well kept on handpump, they've decent wines, and over 30 malt whiskies. Made with good quality ingredients, a short choice of enjoyable bar food might include soup (£3.50), smoked trout pâté (£5.45), breaded fish and chips (£6.25), sausages, bubble and squeak (£6.50), salmon fillet poached in white wine with tarragon and cream (£9.25), beef and ale pie (£9.45), fillet steak (£13.95). The handsome no smoking panelled dining room is open in the evening and on Sunday lunchtime. The old-fashioned bedrooms are spacious, and they do good breakfasts. It is especially lovely in summer, when the pub is festooned with pretty hanging baskets, and there are picnic-sets in the back garden, which has terraces with blue chairs on either side of a large formal raised fish pond, pergolas and climbing plants, and stone walls; it looks out over the town rooftops to the surrounding gentle countryside. A new extension links the garden to the bars, with access for the disabled, via a lower courtyard. *(Recommended by John Wooll, Greta and Christopher Wells, Tracey and Stephen Groves, the Didler, Ian Phillips, P Dawn, John and Gloria Isaacs, Reg Fowle, Helen Rickwood, David Field, Paul and Gloria Howell)*

Free house ~ Licensees David and Nicky Simpson ~ Real ale ~ Bar food (12-1.45, 6.30 (7 Sun)-8.45) ~ (01588) 638403 ~ Children welcome but with restrictions ~ Dogs welcome ~ Open 12-2.30, 6-11(7-10.30 Sun) ~ Bedrooms: £40B/£70S

Six Bells 🍺
Church Street; SY9 5AA

The really friendly easy-going welcome and the tasty beers which are brewed here are the main reasons for visiting this cheerfully chatty former coaching inn. You can arrange a tour of the brewery, and they have a beer festival on the second full weekend in July. Big Nevs is most people's favourite, and you'll also find Cloud Nine and Goldings Best, and they also keep a wide range of country wines. The no frills bar is really quite small, with an assortment of well worn furniture and old local photographs and prints. The second, bigger room has bare boards, some stripped stone, a roaring woodburner in the inglenook, plenty of sociable locals on the benches around plain tables, and lots of board games (you may find people absorbed in Scrabble here in winter). The service is very friendly. Good value tasty bar food includes soup (£3.50), sandwiches (£3.70), quiche (£5.90), with additional lunchtime dishes such as sausage and mash (£8.50) and duck breast with rosemary and red wine sauce (£12), and puddings such as blackberry crumble or chocolate mousse (£4); the dining area is no smoking. It can be packed here on the weekend. *(Recommended by Rona Murdoch, MLR, Paul Davies, the Didler, Ian Phillips, P Dawn, Guy Vowles, David Field, Paul and Gloria Howell, Bruce Bird)*

Own brew ~ Licensee Neville Richards ~ Real ale ~ Bar food (12-2, 6.30-9; not Sun evening or Mon) ~ No credit cards ~ (01588) 630144 ~ Children welcome if well behaved ~ Dogs allowed in bar ~ Open 12-2.30, 5-11; 12-11(10.30 Sun) Sat; 12-4, 7-10.30 Sun in winter; closed Mon lunchtime

Three Tuns 🍺
Salop Street; SY9 5BW

The four-storied Victorian John Roberts brewhouse across the yard from this no-frills pub supplies the well kept beers you'll find here: John Roberts XXX, Clerics Cure, Golden Nut and Three 8 are served from old-fashioned handpumps. They always have a farm cider or perry on too. They do carry-out kegs, and the brewery (which is a separate business) sells beer by the barrel; a popular annual beer festival takes place in July. Full of friendly conversation and undisturbed by piped music, the beamed rooms at this sociable pub are very simply furnished with low-backed settles and heavy walnut tables, with newspapers left out for customers to read. Bar food includes sandwiches (from £3.25), soup (£3.50), devilled whitebait (£4.25), fish and chips (£7.50), glazed ham (£7.95), red bean and lentil chilli (£8.25), thai green curry (£8.50) and beef and wild mushrooms in beer (£8.95). *(Recommended by Paul Davies, Pat and Tony Martin, Tracey and Stephen Groves, the Didler, Ian Phillips, P Dawn, Mike and Lynn Robinson, Guy Vowles, MLR, JMM, Paul and Gloria Howell)*

John Roberts ~ Tenant Tim Curtis-Evans ~ Real ale ~ Bar food (12-3, 7-9; not Sun evening) ~ Restaurant ~ (01588) 638797 ~ Children welcome ~ Dogs allowed in bar ~ Live music every weekend ~ Open 12-11(10.30 Sun) ~ Bedrooms: /£60B

BRIDGES SO3996 Map 6

Horseshoe 🍺

Near Ratlinghope, below the W flank of the Long Mynd; SY5 0ST

You will need to get here early as quite a crowd (often including walking groups) manages to find its way to this remote pub, which is in splendid country in the Shropshire hills. The interior has light oak beams, log burners and lots of rustic bygones, and the down-to-earth yet comfortable bar has interesting windows, lots of farm implements, pub mirrors and musical instruments, and well kept Six Bells Big Nev, Cloud Nine and Wood Quaff on handpump, and they've also Old Rosie farm cider. A small no smoking dining room leads off from here; cribbage, darts and dominoes, Scrabble (Monday evenings) and occasional, discreet piped music. Home-made bar food might include sandwiches (from £3.95), soup (£2.95), farmhouse sausage and mash, meat lasagne, spinach and marscarpone lasagne or steak and kidney pie (£7.50), cod and home-made chips (£8.50), 16oz rump steak (£12), with puddings such as apple pie or bread and butter pudding (£3.50). On Wednesday evenings they have a 'feast for a fiver', with themed food such as curry or mexican for just £5. Tables are placed out by the little River Onny; the Long Mynd rises up behind. *(Recommended by Des and Ursula Weston, Richard, Gerry and Rosemary Dobson, John and Gloria Isaacs, Reg Fowle, Helen Rickwood)*

Free house ~ Licensees Bob and Maureen Macauley ~ Real ale ~ Bar food (12-2.45, 6-8.45; 12-8.45 Sat; 12-4 Sun) ~ No credit cards ~ (01588) 650260 ~ Children welcome till 8.45pm ~ Dogs welcome ~ Open 12(4 Mon)-12

BROMFIELD SO4877 Map 6

Clive/Cookhouse 🍷 🛏

A49 2 miles NW of Ludlow; SY8 2JR

This handsome and immaculately kept Georgian brick house (once home to Clive of India) is known in full as the Clive Restaurant with Rooms and Cookhouse Café Bar; it scores well for both food and accommodation, and is an interesting contemporary take on the traditional inn. The front section has been brightly modernised in minimalist city style, but the back part is more traditional – though still with a modern edge. During the day the focus is on the dining room, café-bar in style, with modern light wood tables, and a big open kitchen behind the end stainless steel counter. A door leads through into the bar, sparse but neat and welcoming, with round glass tables and metal chairs running down to a sleek, space-age bar counter with fresh flowers, newspapers and spotlights. Then it's down a step to the Clive Arms Bar, where traditional features like the huge brick fireplace (with woodburning stove), exposed stonework, and soaring beams and rafters are appealingly juxtaposed with wicker chairs, well worn sofas and new glass tables. The restaurant and café-bar are no smoking; piped jazz, daily papers. Besides sandwiches (from £3.95), good bar food includes soup (£4.25), goats cheese tart with honey-roast shallots (£5.95), sausage and mash (£6.95), cod and chips (£7.95), sun-dried tomato and fennel risotto (£8.95), smoked haddock rarebit with tomato and basil salad or lamb shank with thyme jus and garlic herbed butter beans (£9.95), duck breast with orange and rosemary sauce with braised red cabbage (£11.95) and fillet steak (£14.95). They do two courses for £12.50, and have a more expensive restaurant menu. The good wine list includes nearly 20 by the glass, and Hobsons Best is well kept on handpump; they also have a range of coffees and teas. An attractive secluded terrace has tables under cocktail parasols and a fish pond. They have 15 stylishly modern, good-sized no smoking bedrooms, and breakfast is excellent. *(Recommended by Liz and Tony Colman, Des and Ursula Weston, Mr and Mrs M Stratton, Richard, Ian Phillips, Therese Flanagan, Mike and Mary Carter, Bruce and Sharon Eden, Jo Lilley, Simon Calvert, Michael Sargent)*

Free house ~ Licensee Paul Brooks ~ Real ale ~ Bar food (12-3, 6.30-9.30; 12-9.30 Sat, Sun) ~ (01584) 856565 ~ Children welcome ~ Open 11-11; 12-10.30 Sun ~ Bedrooms: £75B/£95B

BURLTON   SJ4626   Map 6

Burlton Inn   🍴 🍺 🛏

A528 Shrewsbury—Ellesmere, near junction with B4397; SY4 5TB

Shropshire Dining Pub of the Year

Attention to detail is the watch-word at this extremely welcoming and attractively refurbished old pub, where everything seems meticulously arranged and well cared for, from the pretty flower displays in the brick fireplace or beside the neatly curtained windows, to the piles of interior design magazines in the corner. There are a few sporting prints, spurs and brasses on the walls, open fires in winter and dominoes and cribbage. Service is just as thoughtful, and kind, and the food here continues to deserve high praise. Dishes from the menu and specials board might include soup (£3.95), thai mussels (£6.50), venison terrine (£6.95), four-cheese tortellini with creamy butternut and roasted garlic and black pepper sauce (£9.50), steak, kidney and beer pie (£9.95), shallot and blue cheese tarte tatin with sweet moroccan spinach (£10.95), grilled bass on pea, goats cheese and pancetta risotto (£13.95), 10oz beef fillet with shallot and merlot gravy (£16.95), and puddings such as rich orange torte with raspberry crème fraîche (£4.95); there may be two set-time evening sittings in the restaurant, part of which is no smoking. French windows lead from the garden dining room to the pleasant terrace, with its smart wooden furniture; the snug has comfortable seats, great for sinking into with a drink – maybe one of their dozen wines by the glass, or a pint of Banks's, which is well kept alongside three continually changing guests from brewers such as Burton Bridge, Greene King and Salopian. They have facilities for the disabled. There are tables on a small lawn behind, with more on a strip of grass beyond the car park. *(Recommended by Tom and Jill Jones, Andy Sinden, Louise Harrington, Ian Phillips, Mark Blackburn, JCW, Noel Grundy, Derek and Sylvia Stephenson, Mr and Mrs F Carroll, Neil Kellett, Tony and Caroline Elwood, Rosemary Cladingbowl, John and Jane Hayter)*

Free house ~ Licensee Gerald Bean ~ Real ale ~ Bar food (12-2, 6.30-9.45(7-9.30 Sun)) ~ Restaurant ~ (01939) 270284 ~ Well behaved children welcome ~ Dogs welcome ~ Open 11-3, 6-11; 12-3.30, 7-10.30 Sun; closed bank hol Mon lunchtimes ~ Bedrooms: £50B/£80B

CARDINGTON   SO5095   Map 4

Royal Oak ㉕

Village signposted off B4371 Church Stretton—Much Wenlock, pub behind church; also reached via narrow lanes from A49; SY6 7JZ

The rambling, low-beamed bar at this ancient place has a roaring winter log fire, cauldron, black kettle and pewter jugs in its vast inglenook fireplace, the old standing timbers of a knocked-through wall, and red and green tapestry seats solidly capped in elm; darts and dominoes. A comfortable no smoking dining area has exposed old beams and studwork. Hobsons, Greene King Old Speckled Hen and a couple of guests such as Wye Valley Butty Bach and Woods Devils Delight are well kept on handpump. Big helpings of tasty bar food from the menu and specials board might include soup (£2.95), garlic mushrooms (£3.95), baguettes (from £3.50), filled baked potatoes (from £4), ploughman's (£5), mushroom stroganoff (£7.95), thai green chicken curry (£8.20), fidget pie (£8.45), grilled trout (£8.50), steaks (from £9.95) and bass in lemon butter or venison steak with honey and mustard sauce (£10.95). Tables in the front courtyard make the most of the delightful landscape round here, which wavers between lowland and upland. A mile or so away to the west – from the track past Willstone (ask for directions at the pub) – you can walk up Caer Caradoc Hill, which has great views. *(Recommended by Gloria Bax, Des and Ursula Weston, C and R Bromage, TOH, A H Gordon Clark, MLR, A G Roby, David and Gilly Wilkins, Nigel Long)*

Free house ~ Licensees Steve Oldham and Eira Williams ~ Real ale ~ Bar food (not Sun evening) ~ Restaurant ~ (01694) 771266 ~ Children welcome ~ Open 12-3, 7-12(1 Fri, Sat); closed Mon except bank hols

CHETWYND ASTON   SJ7517   Map 7
Fox ♀ ☕

Village signposted off A41 and A518 just S of Newport; TF10 9LQ

This roomy extended 1920s building, previously the Three Fishes, has now been handsomely reworked as a thriving dining pub by the small Brunning & Price group. As usual, they've used good materials, and the style will be familiar to anyone who has tried their other pubs, though in a good way – not at all mass-produced. A series of linked semi-separate areas, mainly no smoking and one with a broad arched ceiling, has plenty of tables in all shapes and sizes, some quite elegant, and a vaguely matching diversity of comfortable chairs, all laid out in a way that's fine for eating but serves equally well for just drinking and chatting. There are masses of attractive prints, three open fires, a few oriental rugs on parquet or boards, some floor tiling; big windows and careful lighting help towards the relaxed and effortless atmosphere (though no doubt the easy-going nature of people in from nearby Harper Adams agricultural college and the Lilleshall Sport England centre helps too). A good range of food includes leek and potato soup (£4.25), interesting sandwiches (from £4.50), tomato and basil sardines (£4.95), ploughman's (£7.95), pesto, olive and artichoke linguini (£8.95), burger with grilled bacon and mozzarella (£9.25), cold meat plate (£9.95), fried chicken breast with tarragon crust, braised potato and onion and garlic butter sauce (£11.95), braised shoulder of lamb with roast potatoes and mediterranean vegetables (£12.95) and puddings such as baked vanilla cheesecake with plum compote or dark chocolate torte with mandarin sorbet (£4.95). The handsome bar counter, with a decent complement of bar stools, serves an excellent changing range of about a dozen wines by the glass, and has Thwaites Original, Timothy Taylors Landlord, Shropshire Gold and three guests from brewers such as Cottage, Oakham and Phoenix on handpump. The staff, mainly young, are well trained, cheerful and attentive. Disabled access and facilities are good (no push chairs or baby buggies, though). There are picnic-sets out in a good-sized garden with quiet country views from the sunny terrace, or shade from some mature trees. *(Recommended by J S Burn, John Whitehead)*

Brunning & Price ~ Manager Sam Cornwall-Jones ~ Real ale ~ Bar food (12-10.30(9.30 Sun)) ~ (01952) 815940 ~ Children welcome till 7pm ~ Dogs allowed in bar ~ Open 12-11(10.30 Sun)

GRINSHILL   SJ5223   Map 7
Inn at Grinshill 🛏

Off A49 N of Shrewsbury; SY4 3BL

The civilised 19th-c bar at the front of this attractively refurbished and well cared for completely no smoking early Georgian inn reflects the pub's former name: the Elephant and Castle. Greene King Ruddles, Hanbys Drawell and Theakston XB, plus a guest from a brewer such as Batemans are well kept on handpump; TV, piped music, dominoes, and an evening pianist on Friday. The spacious contemporary styled main restaurant has a view straight into the kitchen, and doors into the rear garden, which is laid out with tables and chairs. Prepared with care, the very good food might include soup (£4.50), almond-coated shrimp cakes with soy lime mayonnaise (£6), caesar salad (£6.50), seared king scallops with green mango slaw or penne puttanesca (£9), braised lamb with chickpea and mixed bean cassoulet (£11), wild mushroom and butternut risotto (£12.50), fillet steak with leek mashed potato and roast plum tomatoes (£16), and puddings such as coconut panna cotta with sesame tuile and lime leaf syrup or summer pudding (from £5.50). At lunchtime and before 7.30 during weekdays you can take advantage of the 'lunchtime and early bird menu', with three courses for £9.95. Beautifully decorated bedrooms have wide-screen TV and broadband access. Though not at all high, the nearby hill of Grinshill has an astonishingly far-ranging view. *(Recommended by Derek and Sylvia Stephenson, Poppy Laight, A J Bowen, J S Burn, M Joyner, TOH, Geoffrey Parker, Noel Grundy)*

Free house ~ Licensees Kevin and Victoria Brazier ~ Real ale ~ Bar food (12-2.30, 6.30-
9.30; not Sun evening) ~ Restaurant ~ (01939) 220410 ~ Children welcome ~ Dogs
allowed in bar ~ Open 11-3, 6-11; 12-4 Sun; closed Sun evening ~ Bedrooms: £60S/£120B

IRONBRIDGE   SJ6704   Map 6
Malthouse   ♀ 🍺
The Wharfage (bottom road alongside Severn); TF8 7NH

The spacious bar at this 18th-c former malthouse is broken up by white-painted
iron pillars that support the heavy pine beams. A mix of scrubbed light wooden
tables with candles, cream-painted banquettes and bright pictures keeps it light and
airy; piped music. Boddingtons, Scottish Courage Best and Directors are well kept
on handpump, and they've a wide choice of wines including around ten by the
glass, and quite a few malt whiskies. Appropriately informal, the bar menu includes
dishes such as soup (£3.50), cream stilton mushrooms (£4.95), baked salmon fillet
with lemon and caper butter (£8.50), lamb tagine, mint and lemon couscous with
grilled pitta bread or casserole of the day (£8.95), hand-made burger (£9.50),
grilled rib-eye steak (£11.95) and puddings such as glazed lemon tart with
raspberry coulis or brandy basket with vanilla marinated fruit (£4.50). The
atmosphere is quite different in the recently refurbished restaurant (along with the
eating area of the bar, it's no smoking), which has a much more elaborate menu.
There are a few tables outside in front (beware, they retain your credit card if you
eat in the bar) by the car park. (*Recommended by M Joyner, Pamela and Merlyn Horswell,
BOB*)

Malthouse Pubs Ironbridge Ltd ~ Lease Alex and Andrea Nicoll ~ Real ale ~ Bar food ~
Restaurant ~ (01952) 433712 ~ Children welcome, not in bar after 7.30pm ~ Live jazz
Weds-Sat evenings ~ Open 11-11(12 Sat) ~ Bedrooms: /£79B

LITTLE STRETTON   SO4492   Map 6
Ragleth
Village signposted off A49 S of Church Stretton; Ludlow Road; SY6 6RB

This completely no smoking family friendly pub has been nicely opened up and
refurbished by very friendly new licensees. The bay-windowed front bar, with a
warming fire in winter, is now lighter and airier with fresh plaster and an eclectic
mix of light wood old tables and chairs, and some of the original wall brick and
timber work has been exposed. The heavily beamed brick-and-tile-floored public
bar has a huge inglenook; darts and juke box; piped music. Courage Directors,
Hobsons Best and an Archers guest are well kept on handpump. Served by friendly
young staff, the good reasonably priced bar food might include baguettes (from
£3.25), soup (£3.50), fried garlic and lemon king prawns (£5.95), ploughman's
(£7.25), crispy duck, mango and cashew nut salad (£8.50), spinach, nut and cheese
roast with tomato and basil sauce or steak and ale pie (£8.95) and puddings such as
banoffi pie or cherry cheesecake (£3.25). Tables on the lawn (where there's a tulip
tree) look across to a thatched and timbered church, and there's a good play area.
(*Recommended by C and R Bromage, TOH*)

Free house ~ Licensees Chris and Wendy Davis ~ Real ale ~ Bar food (12-2.30, 6.30-9.30
(9 Sun)) ~ Restaurant ~ (01694) 722711 ~ Children welcome ~ Dogs allowed in bar ~
Open 12-3, 6.30-11; 12-11 Sat; 12-10.30 Sun; 12-3, 6.30-10.30 Sun in winter

---

Post Office address codings confusingly give the impression that some pubs are in
Shropshire, when they're really in Cheshire (which is where we list them).

LUDLOW SO5174 Map 4

Church Inn 🍺

Church Street, behind Butter Cross; SY8 1AW

A lively urban buzz rolls through the rooms of this much-liked old town centre inn, which is owned by a former mayor, and is popular with a good cross-section of customers. Appealingly decorated, with comfortable banquettes in cosy alcoves off the island bar, and pews and stripped stonework from the church (part of the bar is a pulpit), the interior is divided into three areas; hops hang from the heavy beams; daily papers and piped music. There are displays of old photographic equipment, plants on windowsills, and church prints in the no smoking side room; a long central area with a fine stone fireplace (good winter fires) leads to lavatories. The more basic side bar has old black and white photos of the town. The civilised no smoking upstairs lounge has vaulted ceilings and long windows overlooking the church, display cases of glass, china and old bottles, and musical instruments on the walls, along with a mix of new and old pictures. They serve a great choice of eight well kept real ales from brewers such as Hobsons, Hook Norton, Three Tuns, Weetwood and Wye Valley, as well as 14 malt whiskies and country wines. In summer you can get three different types of Pimms, while in winter there's mulled wine and hot toddy, and they do a roaring trade in tea and coffee too. Enjoyable sensible food (they make good use of local suppliers) could include sandwiches (from £3.50, baguettes from £3.95), soup (£3.70), filled baked potatoes (£4.95), courgette and broccoli quiche, battered cod or chicken chasseur (£7.95) and 8oz sirloin steak (£10.45). The bedrooms are simple but comfortable; good breakfasts. Car parking is some way off. *(Recommended by Richard Waller, Pauline Smith, Des and Ursula Weston, Chris Flynn, Wendy Jones, Joan York, Richard, Tracey and Stephen Groves, Rob and Catherine Dunster, Roger and Anne Newbury, P Dawn, N R White, Mike and Lynn Robinson, Reg Fowle, Helen Rickwood, JoLilley, Simon Calvert, Di and Mike Gillam, JMM, Paul and Gloria Howell, Gwyn and Anne Wake, Joe Green)*

Free house ~ Licensee Graham Willson-Lloyd ~ Real ale ~ Bar food (12-2.30(3.30 Sat), 6.30-9; 12-3, 6-8.30 Sun) ~ Restaurant ~ (01584) 872174 ~ Children welcome ~ Dogs welcome ~ Open 11-11; 12-10.30 Sun ~ Bedrooms: £35B/£60B

Unicorn

Corve Street – the quiet bottom end, beyond where it leaves the main road to Shrewsbury; SY8 1DU

This white-fronted 17th-c inn is prettily placed adjoining a row of black and white cottages (parking in this picturesque town may be tricky), and tables on the terrace shelter pleasantly among willow trees by the modest River Corve. Inside, the solidly beamed and partly panelled bar, with its huge log fire in a big stone fireplace, gives a real feel of age. A new landlord was taking over just as we went to press but he told us he plans to keep Timothy Taylors Landlord as a house beer, with a couple of guests such as Black Sheep and a local beer. Bar food is likely to include soup (£3.25), sandwiches (from £3.60), whitebait (£4.50), seafood ravioli with seafood sauce (£5.50), nut roast with stilton sauce (£8.95), pork tenderloin with wholegrain mustard sauce (£11.25), lamb stew (£13.50), bass fillets with basil butter (£13.95), fillet medallions (£15.75) and puddings such as fruit cake ice-cream or fruit crumble (£3.75); Sunday roast (£7.50). The timbered candlelit dining areas are no smoking. *(Recommended by Joan York, Tracey and Stephen Groves, Chris Flynn, Wendy Jones, Ian Phillips, Dave Braisted, Di and Mike Gillam, Dr Graham Thorpe, Jo Lilley, Simon Calvert, A G Roby, TOH, Andy Hazeldine, Paul and Gloria Howell, Joe Green)*

Enterprise ~ Tenant Graham Moore ~ Real ale ~ Bar food (12-2.30, 6-9.30) ~ Restaurant ~ (01584) 873555 ~ Children welcome ~ Dogs allowed in bar ~ Open 12-3, 6-11; 12-11 Sat; 12-10.30 Sun

MUCH WENLOCK   SO6299   Map 4
George & Dragon 🍺
High Street (A458); TF13 6AA

The cosy rooms at this friendly town local are home to an impressive array of pub paraphernalia, including old brewery and cigarette advertisements, bottle labels and beer trays, and George-and-the-Dragon pictures, as well as around 500 jugs hanging from the beams. Furnishings such as antique settles are among more conventional seats, and there are a couple of attractive Victorian fireplaces (with coal-effect gas fires). At the back is the no smoking restaurant; piped music. Greene King Abbot and IPA, Hobsons Town Crier, Timothy Taylors Landlord and a guest such as Hop Back Crop Circle are well kept on handpump, and they also have country wines and farmhouse cider. Enjoyable bar food could include soup (£4.25), sandwiches (£4.50), ploughman's (£5.25), spinach, mozzarella and tomato pasta bake, salmon fillet poached in dill or thai chicken curry (£9.95), 8oz sirloin (£11.45), with puddings such as crumble of the day or crème brûlée (£4.25). *(Recommended by Pete Baker, Reg Fowle, Helen Rickwood, Mr and Mrs A B Moore, Paul and Gloria Howell)*

Punch ~ Lease Milton Monk ~ Real ale ~ Bar food (12-2, 6-9 (not Weds, Sun evenings)) ~ Restaurant ~ (01952) 727312 ~ Children welcome ~ Occasional live music ~ Open 12-11(10.30 Sun)

MUNSLOW   SO5287   Map 2
Crown 🍺
B4368 Much Wenlock—Craven Arms; SY7 9ET

A cosy Tudor interior with oak beams and nooks and crannies is tucked behind the imposing Georgian façade of this completely no smoking old court house. The split-level lounge bar has a pleasantly old-fashioned mix of furnishings on its broad flagstones, a collection of old bottles, country pictures, and a bread oven by its good log fire. There are more seats in a traditional snug with its own fire, and the eating area has tables around a central oven chimney, stripped stone walls, and more beams and flagstones; piped music. Holdens Black Country, Golden Glow and John Roberts XXX are well kept on handpump alongside a local farm cider. The rather good imaginative food is produced with thought, using lots of carefully sourced local produce. As well as lunchtime sandwiches (from £4), the changing menu might include soup (£4.50), confit of duck leg with warmed beetroot chutney, glazed shallots and port wine syrup (£5.50), leek and truffle oil risotto with pine nuts and parmesan (£5.75), roast chicken wrapped in pancetta with chorizo and wild mushroom cream sauce (£12.50), roast rump of lamb with sweet potato mash and caper and mint jus (£14.95), griddled monkfish with roast vegetables, griddled polenta and basil cream sauce (£16.95), and puddings such as crème brûlée with caramelised fig and ice-cream or warm spiced carrot cake with toffee sauce cinnamon ice-cream (£4.95). Look out for Jenna, the boxer who usually makes her rounds at the end of the evening. *(Recommended by Joan York, R A P Cross, A Harding)*

Free house ~ Licensees Richard and Jane Arnold ~ Real ale ~ Bar food ~ Restaurant ~ (01584) 841205 ~ Children welcome in restaurant and seated in bar early evening ~ Dogs allowed in bar ~ Open 12-3, 6.30-11(6.15-10.30 Sun); closed Mon ~ Bedrooms: £45S/£65B

NORBURY   SO3692   Map 6
Sun 🛏
Off A488 or A489 NE of Bishop's Castle; OS Sheet 137 map reference 363928; SY9 5DX

To avoid disappointment, do check the unusual opening times (see below) of this charmingly civilised dining pub with rooms, which is worth a visit for its well prepared food and lovely location below the Stiperstones. The blackboard bar menu is fairly short, but might typically include baguettes (£4.95), cumberland sausage (£7.50), ploughman's (£8.50), smoked trout or scampi (£8.75) and rump steak (£10.75). The elegantly furnished no smoking dining room has a different menu. A proper tiled-floor bar has settees and Victorian tables and chairs, cushioned stone seats along the wall by the gas stove, and a few mysterious implements (the kind that it's fun to guess about) on its neat white walls. The restaurant side has a charming lounge with button-back leather wing chairs, easy chairs and a chesterfield on its deep-pile green carpet, as well as a welcoming log fire, nice lighting, willow-pattern china on a dark oak dresser, fresh flowers, candles and magazines; service is friendly. Wye Valley Bitter and maybe a guest such as Woods are kept on handpump under a light blanket pressure, and they have several malts and decent house wines. There are tables outside in a delightful garden by a pond. *(Recommended by Paul Davies, Reg Fowle, Helen Rickwood, Brian and Jacky Wilson)*

Free house ~ Licensee Carol Cahan ~ Real ale ~ Bar food (7-9.30; 12-2 Sun only) ~ Restaurant ~ (01588) 650680 ~ Children welcome Sunday lunchtime only ~ Open 7-11; 12-3, 7-10.30 Sun; closed lunchtimes (except Sun) and all day Mon, Tues ~ Bedrooms: /£90S

NORTON SJ7200 Map 4
Hundred House ♀
A442 Telford—Bridgnorth; TF11 9EE

This carefully kept place is run by a keen family of four, each taking a hand in a different aspect of the business. Sylvia Phillips puts particular effort into the lovely garden, with its old-fashioned roses, herbaceous plants, and big working herb garden that supplies the kitchen – you can buy bags of their herbs for £1 and the money goes to charity. Inside, bunches of fresh flowers brighten the tables and counter in the neatly kept bar, and there are hops and huge bunches of dried flowers and herbs hanging from beams. Handsome fireplaces have log fires or working coalbrookdale ranges (one has a great Jacobean arch with fine old black cooking pots), and a variety of interesting chairs and settles with some long colourful patchwork leather cushions set out around sewing-machine tables. Steps lead up past a little balustrade to a partly panelled eating area, where the stripped brickwork looks older than that elsewhere. The main dining room and one other room are no smoking; piped music. Davenports Bitter, Heritage Bitter and Mild (the last two brewed especially for them by a small brewery) are well kept on handpump alongside a guest such as Highgates Saddlers, and they've also an extensive wine list with house wines by the carafe, half carafe and big or small glass. Bar food includes soup (£3.95), greek salad (£5.95/£9.95), lasagne (£7.95), sausage and mash or steak and kidney pie (£8.95), 10oz rib-eye steak (£12.95). Readers report that service can seem to slow down, even where there are only a few customers. *(Recommended by David Edwards, Des and Ursula Weston, David and Ruth Hollands, Lynda and Trevor Smith, Simon Jones, Pamela and Merlyn Horswell, Rosemary Cladingbowl, A Darroch Harkness, JMC)*

Free house ~ Licensees Henry, Sylvia, Stuart and David Phillips ~ Real ale ~ Bar food (12-2.30, 6-9.30(7-8.45 Sun)) ~ Restaurant ~ (01952) 730353 ~ Dogs allowed in bedrooms ~ Open 11-3, 5.30-11(11.30 Sat); 12-4, 7-10.30 Sun ~ Bedrooms: £69B/£99B

PICKLESCOTT SO4399 Map 6
Bottle & Glass
Village signposted off A49 N of Church Stretton; SY6 6NR

The jovial character of the whimsical bow-tied landlord ensures a cheery welcoming atmosphere at this really lovely old 16th-c pub. He works hard to make sure everyone is happy, easily running the bar and striking up conversations with customers – ask him to tell you about the antics of the resident ghost of the former landlord, Victor. Much to the delight surely of the two resident cats, Hello and Cookie, the fire rarely goes out in the small low beamed and quarry-tiled cosy candlelit no smoking bar. The lounge, dining area and library area (for dining or sitting in) have open fires too. Hobsons, Woods Shropshire Lad and a changing guest beer such as Fullers London Pride are well kept on handpump Very good home-made bar food (promptly served, in hearty helpings) might include soup (£3.50), stilton, pork and celery pâté (£4.50), sausage and mash, roast of the day or battered cod (£7.50), steak, kidney and Guinness pie or fish pie (£10.50) and rosemary and garlic-crusted rack of lamb with red wine, honey and redcurrant sauce (£14.50), and very tasty puddings such as sticky toffee pudding or chocolate mint roulade (£4); unobtrusive piped music. There are picnic-sets in front and the pub has a lovely position 1,000 feet above sea level and near the Long Mynd. *(Recommended by Angus Johnson, Carol Bolden, TOH, Phil Merrin, Pete Yearsley, Ken Marshall, J C Brittain-Long)*

Free house ~ Licensees Paul and Jo Stretton-Downes ~ Real ale ~ Bar food ~ Restaurant ~ (01694) 751345 ~ Children welcome with restrictions ~ Dogs allowed in bar ~ Open 12-3.30, 6-12; closed Sun evening, Mon

SHREWSBURY   SJ4912   Map 6
Armoury 🍽 � 🍺
Victoria Quay, Victoria Avenue; SY1 1HH

The spacious open-plan interior, with its long runs of big arched windows with views across the broad river, at this 18th-c former warehouse can make quite an impression when you first arrive. It's light and airy, but the eclectic décor, furniture layout and lively bustle give a personal feel. Mixed wood tables and chairs are grouped on expanses of stripped wood floors, a display of floor-to-ceiling books dominates two huge walls, there's a grand stone fireplace at one end, and masses of old prints mounted edge to edge on the stripped brick walls. Colonial-style fans whirr away on the ceilings, which are supported by occasional green-painted standing timbers, and glass cabinets display collections of explosives and shells. The long bar counter has a terrific choice of drinks with up to eight real ales from brewers such as Abbeydale, Derwent, Greene King and Salopian, a great wine list (with 16 by the glass), around 50 malt whiskies, a dozen different gins, lots of rums and vodkas, a variety of brandies, and some unusual liqueurs. Superbly cooked bar food, from an interesting menu, includes tasty soup (£3.95), sandwiches with imaginative fillings (from £4.25), black pudding with red onion gravy or rollmop herrings (£5.25), warm tiger prawn and melon salad (£6.50), ploughman's or tomato and spinach risotto (£8.95), vegetarian moussaka (£9.50), roast pork belly with baked apple and cider gravy (£10.95), seared tuna with fennel, olive and parmesan salad (£12.95), 10oz rump steak with mushroom and dijon mustard sauce (£14.95), and puddings such as warm chocolate brownie with white chocolate sauce or hot waffle with black cherry compote (£4.95). Tables at one end are laid out for eating, and part of the eating area is no smoking. The massive uniform red brick exteriors are interspersed with hanging baskets and smart coach lights at the front, and there may be queues at the weekend. The pub doesn't have its own parking, but there are plenty of places nearby. *(Recommended by Des and Ursula Weston, Martin and Karen Wake, Sue Holland, Dave Webster, Mrs Suzy Miller, Derek and Sylvia Stephenson, Paul and Gloria Howell, Joe Green)*

Brunning & Price ~ Manager Andy Barker ~ Real ale ~ Bar food (12-9.30(9 Sun)) ~ (01743) 340525 ~ Children welcome till 8pm ~ Open 12-11(10.30 Sun)

WENTNOR   SO3893   Map 6
Crown 🛏
Village and pub signposted (not very clearly) off A489 a few miles NW of junction with A49; SY9 5EE

Though much of the main bar area at this 16th-c country inn is laid for eating (you will need to book at weekends), they do reserve a couple of tables for drinkers, and do get a few locals in. Greene King Old Speckled Hen, Hobsons Best, John Roberts XXX and Woods Shropshire Lad are well kept on handpump, and they have decent wines and a good choice of malt whiskies; dominoes, cribbage, newspapers and magazines. One end has a snug area with pictures and fixed seating, there are good log fires and the restaurant is surprisingly large. Attentive staff serve the tasty bar food, which might include sandwiches (from £3.75), soup (£2.95), chicken with leek and stilton sauce or cod (£6.95), salads or scampi (£7.25), home-made pie such as venison or minced lamb (£7.95), battered cod and chips (£8.50), roast duck (£12.95) and home-made puddings such as lemon cheesecake or chocolate and ginger truffle slice (£3.50); some dishes may come in smaller helpings. Seats on the back lawn give charming views over the Long Mynd, and the location and the good value pretty bedrooms make this a nice place for a night's stay. (Recommended by Reg Fowle, Helen Rickwood, TOH, Philip and Susan Philcox, Steve Whalley)

Free house ~ Licensees Mike and Chris Brown ~ Real ale ~ Bar food (12-2, 6-9) ~ Restaurant ~ (01588) 650613 ~ Open 12-3, 6-12; 12-12 Sat; 12-11 Sun ~ Bedrooms: £35S/£60S

LUCKY DIP

Besides the fully inspected pubs, you might like to try these Lucky Dips recommended to us and described by readers (if you do, please send us reports: www.goodguides.co.uk).

ALL STRETTON [SO4595]
Yew Tree SY6 6HG [Shrewsbury Rd (B4370)]: Pleasant old pub with houseplants and lots of interesting watercolours, decent food (not Mon, and may take a while at busy times) from revamped kitchen, small helpings available, Fullers London Pride, Hobsons Best and a changing Wye Valley ale, helpful service, good log fire, bookable dining room (not always open), lively nicely worn in bar with darts, two big dogs; no credit cards; children welcome, small village handy for Long Mynd, cl Tues (Sarah and Peter Gooderham, MDN, TOH, Reg Fowle, Helen Rickwood, Margaret Dickinson)
ATCHAM [SJ5409]
☆ *Mytton & Mermaid* SY5 6QG: Comfortable hotel rather than pub, but with really nice friendly atmosphere, good food from panini to guinea fowl in bar and relaxed easy-going restaurant, speedy service and helpful staff, Greene King Ruddles and Woods Shropshire Lad, good wine choice, some theme nights; pleasant Severn-view bedrooms, nice setting opp entrance to Attingham Park (NT) (Des and Ursula Weston, Mrs Suzy Miller, Mr and Mrs F Carroll, Francis Johnston, Bruce and Sharon Eden)
BRIDGNORTH [SO7193]
Bell & Talbot WV16 4QU [Salop St (former A458 towards Shrewsbury)]: Charming early 19th-c stone building with Hobsons, Holdens and other local beers, log fires each end of L-shaped main room, record sleeves, guitars and other instruments covering ceiling, smaller room off and interesting back conservatory, no machines; well chosen piped music, live bands wknds; bedrooms, cl wkdy lunchtimes (Gill and Tony Morriss, Ian and Liz Rispin, Paul and Gloria Howell)
☆ *Railwaymans Arms* WV16 5DT [Severn Valley station, Hollybush Rd (off A458 towards Stourbridge)]: Bathams, Hobsons and other good value local ales in chatty old-fashioned converted waiting-room at Severn Valley steam

railway terminus, bustling on summer days; coal fire, station nameplates, superb mirror over fireplace, tables out on platform; may be simple summer snacks and good baguettes, children welcome, wheelchair access; the train to Kidderminster (another bar there) has an all-day bar and bookable Sun lunches (Richard Waller, Pauline Smith, Gill and Tony Morriss, the Didler, Ian and Liz Rispin, LYM, Paul and Gloria Howell)
White Lion WV16 4AB [West Castle St]: Good value carvery with OAP deals, good beer; tables outside (Caroline and Michael Abbey)
CALVERHALL [SJ6037]
Old Jack SY13 4PA [New St Lane]: New licensees doing enjoyable home-made food (best to book wknds), beamed bar with log fire and button-back banquettes, arches to separate dining area opening on to terrace (Susan Brookes)
CHURCH STRETTON [SO4593]
Bucks Head SY6 6BX [High St]: Popular town pub with friendly responsive staff, enjoyable fresh food, Three Tuns ale, relaxed atmosphere, no smoking open-plan eating area off bar (MDN)
CLEEHILL [SO5875]
Royal Oak SY8 3PE [Ludlow Rd (A4117)]: Friendly unassuming pub dating from 17th c, surprisingly wide-ranging choice of daily-changing food, all freshly made (they are helpful with special requests), seasonal game and fish, charming staff, real ales; good view from the front (Mrs F Denham-Bowyer, Mrs E Westley)
CLUN [SO3080]
Sun SY7 8JB [High St]: Beamed and timbered Tudor pub with some sturdy antique furnishings, modern paintings and older prints, enormous open fire in lively flagstoned public bar with darts, cards and dominoes, larger carpeted lounge bar, Banks's Bitter, Hobsons Best and Marstons Pedigree, charming landlady; children allowed in eating area, terrace tables in back garden, lovely village,

nice bedrooms, has been cl Weds lunchtime
(Rona Murdoch, the Didler, BB)

☆ *White Horse* SY7 8JA [Market Sq]: Well run
low-beamed open-plan local dating from
18th c, helpful friendly service, good value
food inc particularly good Sun lunch, half a
dozen well priced changing ales such as
Hobsons, Salopian, Six Bells and Wye Valley,
Weston's farm cider, good coffee, daily papers,
inglenook and open woodburner, country bric-
a-brac, pool and juke box in panelled games
end; children welcome, pavement tables in
front, small back garden, bedrooms, open all
day *(Gill and Tony Morriss, Theocsbrian,
MLR, Nigel Long, Bruce Bird)*

COALBROOKDALE [SJ6604]

☆ *Coalbrookdale Inn* TF8 7DX [Wellington Rd,
opp Museum of Iron]: Handsome dark brick
18th-c pub with half a dozen quickly changing
real ales from square counter in simple
convivial tiled-floor bar, good value food using
local meats, cheeses etc here or in quieter
refurbished dining room, farm ciders, country
wines, good log fire, local pictures, piano,
naughty beach murals in lavatories; bar can be
smoky, long flight of steps to entrance; dogs
welcome, a few tables outside, opens noon
*(DC, the Didler, BB, Richard Tosswill,
Fred and Lorraine Gill, M Joyner)*

COALPORT [SJ6902]

☆ *Boat* TF8 7LS [Ferry Rd, Jackfield; nr Mawes
Craft Centre]: Long but cosy 18th-c quarry-
tiled bar, coal fire in lovely range, reasonably
priced fresh food inc meat, game and cheeses
and good value Sun lunch, welcoming service,
Banks's Bitter and Mild and related beers,
Weston's farm cider, darts; summer barbecues
on big tree-shaded lawn, in delightful if
floodable part of Severn Gorge, footbridge
making it handy for Coalport China Museum,
may be cl wkdy lunchtimes *(Martin and
Karen Wake, BB, the Didler, Fred and
Lorraine Gill)*

COCKSHUTT [SJ4329]

☆ *Leaking Tap* SY12 0JQ [A528 Ellesmere—
Shrewsbury]: Comfortable and attractive, with
good varied food (Sun lunch very popular),
reasonable prices, friendly licensees, good beer
and wines by the glass *(J M Sparrow, Mr and
Mrs J Carroll)*

CORFTON [SO4985]

☆ *Sun* SY7 9DF [B4368 Much Wenlock—Craven
Arms]: Very welcoming chatty landlord (if he's
not busy in the back brewery) in unsmart two-
bar country local with its own Corvedale ales
and a guest beer, lots of breweriana, public bar
with internet access as well as darts and pool,
sensibly priced food using local produce from
generous baguettes to bargain Sun lunch,
dining room with no smoking area and
covered well, tourist information; piped music;
particularly good disabled access throughout,
tables on terrace and in good-sized garden with
good play area *(MLR, BB, Paul and
Gloria Howell, Gwyn and Anne Wake)*

CRESSAGE [SJ5704]

Riverside SY5 6AF [A458 NW, nr Cound]:
Spacious pub/hotel, light and airy, with

pleasant mix of furnishings, enjoyable food
from lunchtime baguettes to salmon and steak,
reasonable prices, interesting wine choice, local
and guest real ales, lovely Severn views from
roomy conservatory; french windows to big
terraced garden with wandering rare-breed
chickens, good value bedrooms, good
breakfast, open all day wknds *(LYM,
Mike and Mary Carter)*

DORRINGTON [SJ4703]

Bridge Inn SY5 7ED [A49 N]: Enjoyable
wholesome food inc bar snacks and bargain
lunches, Sun carvery lunch booked well ahead,
in streamside pub with settees and armchairs as
well as plenty of tables and chairs in roomy
lounge bar, well spaced tables in conservatory
restaurant; tables outside, caravan spaces in
paddock behind *(TOH)*

EDGERLEY [SJ3517]

☆ *Royal Hill* SY10 8ES [off A5 following MoD
Nesscliff Training Camp signs, then Melverley
signs]: Nicely unspoilt 17th-c beamed country
local tucked away in quiet spot, worn tiled
corridor behind tall settles forming snug
around coal fire, little parlour with settee, easy
chair, rocking chair and TV, back bar with
two Salopian beers and Worthington,
occasional plain food; children welcome, long
old-fashioned benches out in front, picnic-sets
over lane on banks of River Severn, pleasant
caravan/camp site, cl winter wkdy lunchtimes,
open all day wknds *(Noel Grundy, BB,
the Didler)*

ELLESMERE [SJ3934]

Black Lion SY12 0EG [Scotland St; back car
park on A495]: Bargain simple substantial
food, relaxed beamed bar with interesting
décor and some nice unusual features such as
the traditional wood-and-glass screen along its
tiled entrance corridor, quiet and comfortable
roomy dining room; piped music; bedrooms,
handy car park, not far from canal wharf
*(Peter and Audrey Dowsett, BB, Rita and
Keith Pollard)*

GLEDRID [SJ2936]

Poachers Pocket LL14 5DG [B5070, handy
loop through Chirk off new A5]: Pretty family
pub with reasonably priced quite interesting
food, good choice of beers, several small
rooms with bare boards, lots of stuffed and
artificial animals, comical hunting prints and
memorabilia; seats out by flower tubs
overlooking canal *(Donald and
Maureen Barber)*

HALFWAY HOUSE [SJ3311]

Seven Stars SY5 9DG [A458 Shrewsbury—
Welshpool]: Spotless and unspoilt small bar
with two high-backed settles by the gas fire,
real ales such as Banks's or Marstons Pedigree
tapped from casks in the friendly licensees'
kitchen area, no food or music *(the Didler)*

HAMPTON LOADE [SO7486]

River & Rail WV16 6BN: Welcoming pub
with wide choice of enjoyable and interesting
fresh food inc tempting puddings, attentive
family service, real ale and country wines,
modern surroundings; big garden with plenty
of under-cover seating overlooking River

Severn and steam railway, Apr-Oct ferry from station *(Caroline and Michael Abbey, Juliet Browning)*

HINSTOCK [SJ6927]

Falcon TF9 2TA [just off A41 9 miles N of Newport; Wood Lane]: Friendly service, interesting choice of the area's real ales, enjoyable and interesting reasonably priced food in no smoking entrance bar and dining room from generous open sandwiches up, decent wines and malt whiskies, woodburner *(Margaret and Allen Marsden, Bill and Celia Witts)*

HODNET [SJ6128]

☆ *Bear* TF9 3NH [Drayton Rd (A53)]: Small beamed quarry-tiled bar with log fire, broad arch to rambling open-plan carpeted main area with blond seats and tables set for the good range of reasonably priced food from sandwiches up (can take a while), well filled puddings cabinet, snug end alcoves with heavy 16th-c beams and timbers, friendly helpful staff, good wines by the glass, Courage Directors, Theakstons Best and Youngs Special; may be faint piped radio; children welcome (high chairs and child-size cutlery), six good value bedrooms, opp Hodnet Hall gardens and handy for Hawkstone Park, open all day *(J M Sparrow, BB, Francis Johnston)*

HOPTON WAFERS [SO6376]

☆ *Crown* DY14 0NB [A4117]: Attractive 16th-c beamed and creeper-covered inn (under new management and much extended since our 2006 edition – more reports on new regime please), with big inglenook, light and comfortable décor and furnishings, Hobsons Best, Timothy Taylors Landlord and Wood Shropshire Lad, good choice of wines, no smoking dining areas; children welcome, dogs welcome in bar and pretty bedrooms, inviting garden with duck pond, stream and terraces, open all day *(Carol Broadbent, Walter and Susan Rinaldi-Butcher, LYM, Andy Sinden, Louise Harrington, Lynda and Trevor Smith, Ian and Jane Irving, Martin and Pauline Jennings, Mike and Lynn Robinson)*

IRONBRIDGE [SJ6603]

Swan TF8 7NH [Wharfage]: Friendly ex-warehouse with dark woodwork and lots of alcoves, decent food from baguettes up, friendly efficient service, real ales and a continental beer on tap, separate candlelit red-décor dining area; tables outside *(Martin and Karen Wake, Fred and Lorraine Gill, M Joyner)*

LEEBOTWOOD [SO4798]

☆ *Pound* SY6 6ND [A49 Church Stretton—Shrewsbury]: Thatched 16th-c building now extensively remodelled as dining pub, former bar now new kitchen for smart expanded no smoking restaurant, promptly served good food inc upmarket dishes as well as ham and eggs and so forth, pleasant staff, Greene King Abbot, decent wines; garden tables *(BB, TOH, Tom and Jill Jones)*

LEINTWARDINE [SO4175]

☆ *Jolly Frog* SY7 0LX [Toddings; A4113 out towards Ludlow]: Restauranty pub/bistro with new landlord and fresh décor (we'd like more

reports), French chef keen to make an impression with frequently changing menus specialising in daily fresh fish, not cheap but lunchtime and early evening better value set meals, cooking imaginative without being fussy or pretentious, welcoming relaxed atmosphere, mix of table sizes (high chairs for small children), log fire, good wine list and coffees, real ale; good views from tables out on decking *(Christopher Woodward)*

LONGVILLE [SO5393]

☆ *Longville Arms* TF13 6DT [B4371 Church Stretton—Much Wenlock]: Two neat and spacious bars with beams, stripped stone and some oak panelling, good service, Courage and Woods ales, bar food and large comfortable no smoking restaurant, adult games room with juke box, darts and pool; piped music; disabled facilities, children and dogs welcome, terraced side garden with good play area, lovely countryside, bedrooms, open all day wknds *(TOH, Reg Fowle, Helen Rickwood, LYM)*

LUDLOW [SO5174]

Bull SY8 1AD [Bull Ring]: 15th-c timbered building with long low-beamed traditional bar, Banks's and Marstons Pedigree, sizeable back seating area; courtyard through side arch *(Mike and Lynn Robinson)*

Charlton Arms SY8 1PJ [Ludford Bridge]: Former coaching inn in great spot overlooking River Teme and the town, now extensively refurbished by landlord of the Church Inn (see main entries) and so very promising, though we've had no reports since completion – during the works they had only limited food, but good beers such as Three Tuns; waterside garden and terrace, bedrooms (may be traffic noise), open all day; news please *(Paul and Gloria Howell, Joe Green)*

Feathers SY8 1AA [Bull Ring]: Superb timbered building, elegantly refurbished inside with Jacobean panelling and carving, fine period furnishings; for a snack or drink you'll probably be diverted to a less distinguished side café-bar, which has bar food and Woods real ale; good parking, lift to comfortable bedrooms, not cheap *(the Didler, LYM, Mike and Lynn Robinson, Francis Johnston)*

MADELEY [SJ6934]

All Nations TF7 5DP [Coalport Rd]: Simple 18th-c pub up steps from road, refurbished but unspoilt, with distinctive Worfield Dableys Ale, Gold and Mild from small bar, bargain hefty filled rolls, rooms each side with coal fires; picnic-sets on heated terrace, handy for Blists Hill (you may find actor/staff from there, in full Victorian costume), open all day Fri-Sun *(Martin and Karen Wake)*

MAESBURY MARSH [SJ3125]

Navigation SY10 8JB: Pub bistro and restaurant in great location towards the limit of navigation on partially restored Montgomery Canal, good enterprising food (no chips), three changing real ales *(Bob and Laura Brock)*

MINSTERLEY [SJ3705]

Bridge Hotel SY5 0BA: Enjoyable food inc bargain ploughman's, open fire, comfortable bar, good value beer *(Robin W Buckle)*

MUCH WENLOCK [SO6299]

☆ *Talbot* TF13 6AA [High St (A458)]: Ancient inn once part of Wenlock Abbey with several neatly kept areas, low ceilings, red tapestry button-back wall banquettes, prints of fish and brewery memorabilia, art deco-style lamps and gleaming brasses, Bass, Woods Shropshire Lad and a guest beer, standard bar food and more elaborate evening menu, no smoking dining area; quiet piped music; children welcome, courtyard with metal and wood tables and pretty flower tubs, bedrooms, open all day Sat *(Margaret Dickinson, MDN, Blaise Vyner, Brian and Jacky Wilson, John Oates, Denise Walton, Mrs Catherine Draper, A G Roby)*

NEWCASTLE [SO2482]

☆ *Crown* SY7 8QL [B4368 Clun—Newtown]: Pretty village pub with reasonably priced good beers such as Hobsons and Timothy Taylors Landlord, friendly licensees, settees and woodburner in smart stripped stone lounge with some well spaced tables in two dining areas, good coffee, attractively priced standard food from sandwiches to steak, locals' bar and games room; piped music; tables outside, charming well equipped bedrooms above bar, attractive views and walks, open all day Sat *(Rona Murdoch, LYM)*

OSWESTRY [SJ2929]

Fox SY11 2SU [Church St/Cross St]: Ancient black and white timbered façade, little entrance bar down a step, attractive low-beamed and panelled main room with dark oak furniture (friendly landlord may be sitting with locals at one of the long tables), good plain décor, fox theme, ample straightforward food and good Banks's and related ales, blazing log fire, no smoking area, no TV or juke box; open all day (Mon afternoon break) *(J R Ringrose)*

PORTH-Y-WAEN [SJ2623]

☆ *Lime Kiln* SY10 8LX [A495, between village and junction with A483, S of Oswestry]: Good food in neatly kept stripped pine pub with pews and big pine tables (Sun lunch is popular), friendly service, Banks's, Marstons Pedigree and a guest beer, good value wines; children in eating areas, picnic-sets out in side garden with boules and terraced lawn, open all day wknds *(Roy Payne, John Hanby, LYM, Mr and Mrs Peter Longland)*

PULVERBATCH [SJ4202]

☆ *White Horse* SY5 8DS [off A49 at N end of Dorrington]: Rambling country pub under new chef/landlord, wide choice of popular food using fresh local supplies and fresh-delivered fish, friendly service, good choice of real ales and of wines by the glass, contemporary colour scheme and attractive country pictures along with black beams, heavy timbering and open coalburning range, fabric-covered high-backed settles and brocaded banquettes; some live music; seats in front loggia *(LYM)*

QUEENS HEAD [SJ3326]

☆ *Queens Head* SY11 4EB [just off A5 SE of Oswestry, towards Nesscliffe]: Emphasis on wide choice of generous good value food (all day Fri and wknds) from speciality sandwiches to lots of fish and steaks, four or five

Theakstons and other real ales, prompt friendly helpful service, two dining areas with hot coal fires, one no smoking with nice roomy conservatory overlooking restored section of Montgomery Canal; picnic-sets under cocktail parasols in suntrap waterside garden, country walks *(Alex and Claire Pearse)*

SHIFNAL [SJ74508]

White Hart TF11 8BH [High St]: Half a dozen or more interesting changing real ales such as Bathams, Black Sheep and Enville in friendly timbered 17th-c pub, quaint and old-fashioned, separate bar and lounge, comfortable without pretension, wide range of sandwiches and promptly served good value home-made hot dishes, good choice of wines by the glass, welcoming staff; couple of steep steps at front door *(the Didler, Pamela and Merlyn Horswell)*

SHREWSBURY [SO4912]

Coach & Horses SY1 1NF [Swan Hill/Cross Hill]: Friendly old-fashioned Victorian local, panelled throughout, with main bar, cosy little side room and back dining room, good value fresh food inc daily roast and some unusual dishes, Bass, Goodalls Gold (brewed for pub by Salopian) and a guest beer, relaxed atmosphere, prompt helpful service even when busy, interesting prints; pretty flower boxes outside, open all day *(Pete Baker, Sue Holland, Dave Webster, the Didler, Joe Green, John Tavernor)*

Lion SY1 1UY [follow City Centre signposts across the English Bridge]: Grand largely 18th-c coaching inn with bargain bar lunches inc succulent hot sandwiches, tea or coffee and cakes other times, Bass and Boddingtons, civilised service, cosy oak-panelled bar and sedate series of high-ceilinged rooms opening off; children welcome, comfortable bedrooms *(Ian Phillips, LYM, Francis Johnston)*

☆ *Loggerheads* SY1 1UG [Church St]: Friendly and gossipy old-fashioned local, panelled back room with flagstones, scrubbed-top tables, high-backed settles and coal fire, three other rooms with lots of prints, flagstones and bare boards, quaint linking corridor and hatch service of Banks's Bitter and Mild, related beers and a guest beer, friendly and meticulously professional bar staff, bargain lunchtime food (not Sun) inc doorstep sandwiches, baked potatoes and good steak pie with great chips; darts, dominoes, poetry society, occasional live music; open all day *(Pete Baker, Sue Holland, Dave Webster, the Didler, Joe Green)*

Red Barn SY3 7HS [Longden Rd]: Warm and welcoming, with wide choice of good if not cheap food, a couple of real ales; overlooks Quarry Park and River Severn *(John Tavernor)*

☆ *Three Fishes* SY1 1UR [Fish St]: Well run timbered and heavily beamed 16th-c pub with no smoking and no mobiles, Caledonian Deuchars IPA, Fullers London Pride, Salopian, Timothy Taylors Landlord and interesting guest beers, good value wines, fairly priced simple hearty bar food (not Sun evening) from baguettes and filled baked potatoes up, good friendly service even when busy, old pictures; open all day Fri/Sat *(Dr John Worthington, John Coatsworth, Derek and Sylvia Stephenson, Sue Holland, Dave Webster, Tracey and Stephen Groves, the Didler, LYM, Dr B and Mrs P B Baker, Theo, Anne and Jane Gaskin, Jeff and Sue Evans, Hugh Roberts, Paul and Gloria Howell, Joe Green, Helen McLagan)*

STIPERSTONES [SJ3600]

☆ *Stiperstones Inn* SY5 0LZ [signed off A488 S of Minsterley; OS Sheet 126 map ref 364005]: Simple bargain fresh food all day in welcoming walkers' pub (they sell maps) with Six Bells or Woods Parish, small modernised lounge bar, comfortable leatherette wall banquettes, lots of brassware on ply-panelled walls, decent wine, real fire, darts in plainer public bar, restaurant; may be unobtrusive piped music; tables outside, cheap bedrooms (small dogs welcome), good breakfast *(Roy Payne, BB, Guy Vowles, John and Gloria Isaacs)*

STOTTESDON [SO6782]

☆ *Fighting Cocks* DY14 8TZ [High St]: Delightful old half-timbered pub in unspoilt countryside, good substantial home cooking using local produce (not Mon), warm welcome, Hobsons ales, local farm cider, log fire, low ceiling, equestrian pictures, no smoking dining room; doubles as village vegetable and bread shop; nice views from garden tables, open all day wknds, cl wkdy lunchtimes *(Ian and Liz Rispin)*

TELFORD [SJ7012]

Bulls Head TF2 7AL [Plough Rd, off Wrockwardine Wood Way (between A518 exit roundabout of A442 and B5060 roundabout)]: Newly restored Victorian pub, public bar with local Maws tilework throughout, fine etched glass, warmly welcoming licensees, enjoyable food and good beers *(Johnny Themans)*

WELLINGTON [SJ6410]

Old Orleton TF1 2HA [Holyhead Road (B5061, off M54 Junction 7)]: Sympathetically modernised old coaching inn with Hobsons beers, Weston's farm cider and enjoyable food *(David Field)*

WELSHAMPTON [SJ4335]

Sun SY12 0PH [A495 Ellesmere—Whitchurch]: Friendly village inn with good service, good value food, Tetleys and a guest beer, no smoking restaurant; big back garden, 15-minute walk to Llangollen/Shropshire Union Canal *(A Harding)*

WENLOCK EDGE [SO5696]

Wenlock Edge Inn TF13 6DJ [B4371 Much Wenlock—Church Stretton]: Pretty country dining pub in lovely spot, welcoming service, enjoyable generous reasonably priced home-made food from baguettes up (three menus

kept separate for public bar/outside, lounge bar and more modern no smoking dining extension), Hobsons and Wychwood real ale, pleasant décor, open fire and inglenook woodburner; children welcome in eating areas, dogs in bar, terrace tables front and back, cosy attractive bedrooms, lots of walks; may be cl winter wkdy lunchtimes *(Gloria Bax, C and R Bromage, LYM, Rodney and Norma Stubington, Richard and Jean Green)*

WHITCHURCH [SJ5345]

☆ *Willey Moor Lock* SY13 4HF [signed off A49 just under 2 miles N]: Large pub in picturesque spot by Llangollen Canal, linked rooms with low beams, countless teapots, two log fires, cheerful chatty atmosphere, half a dozen changing ales from small breweries, around 30 malt whiskies, good value quickly served simple food from sandwiches and baked potatoes up; fruit machine, piped music, several dogs and cats; children welcome away from bar, terrace tables, secure garden with big play area *(LYM, MLR, Gwyn and Anne Wake)*

WISTANSTOW [SO4385]

☆ *Plough* SY7 8DG [off A49 and A489 N of Craven Arms]: Simple high-raftered pub, informally welcoming tap for Woods brewery, with their good beers at low prices, hearty lunchtime food from baguettes to steak, wider evening choice, quick service, interesting collection of Royal wedding commemorative beers, games area with darts, dominoes and pool, small bar and larger restaurant; piped music; children and dogs welcome, cl Mon evening in winter *(Mrs Phoebe A Kemp, Tracey and Stephen Groves, Paul and Gloria Howell)*

WORFIELD [SO7595]

☆ *Dog* WV15 5LF [off A454 W of Bridgnorth; Main St]: Pretty pub in beautiful unspoilt stone-built village, three sprucely decorated areas with emphasis on food from good value baguettes to plenty of seafood, several real ales inc a guest beer, good house wines, log fire; children welcome *(Carol Broadbent, Mrs E A O'Byrne)*

YORTON [SJ5023]

Railway SY4 3EP: Same family for over 60 years, friendly and chatty mother and daughter, unchanging atmosphere, plain tiled bar with hot coal fire, old settles and a modicum of railway memorabilia, big back lounge (not always open) with fishing trophies, Woods Bitter and Shropshire Lad and other mainly local ales such as Holdens and Salopian, may do simple sandwiches if you ask, darts and dominoes – no piped music or machines; seats out in yard *(Martin Grosberg, the Didler)*

Please tell us if any Lucky Dips deserve to be upgraded to a main entry – and why.
No stamp needed: The Good Pub Guide, FREEPOST TN1569,
Wadhurst, E Sussex TN5 7BR.

Somerset

In this chapter we include Bristol, as well as Bath. Pubs on particularly fine form here in recent months are the friendly and unspoilt Old Green Tree in Bath (great range of real ales), the civilised Bear & Swan in Chew Magna (very good food in appealing and welcoming surroundings), the Cat Head at Chiselborough (nice combination of enjoyable food and great atmosphere), the unspoilt and individual Crown at Churchill (quite a favourite, with a very good range of real ales), the Ring o' Roses at Holcombe (a neat and well run dining pub, with comfortable bedrooms, and qualifying this year for our coveted Food Award), the Kingsdon Inn at Kingsdon (an appealing dining pub, also gaining a Food Award under its helpful new licensees – it has bedrooms now, too), the Three Horseshoes at Langley Marsh (now completely no smoking, and warmly enjoyed for its food, beer and atmosphere), the Pilgrims Rest at Lovington (restaurant but relaxed, with a gifted chef/landlord), the Royal Oak at Luxborough (a welcoming place to stay, with enjoyable food), the Talbot at Mells (interesting layout, good food and service), and the Montague Inn at Shepton Montague (a nice all-rounder, its friendly and helpful newish licensees settled in very well now). Four pubs are back in the main entries this year, after a break: the Queens Arms in Bleadon, a thriving all-rounder; the Strode Arms at Cranmore, on great form under newish licensees who win plenty of plaudits for their food and welcome; the Kings Arms at Litton, a fascinating old place enjoying a surge of popularity under excellent new licensees; and the Notley Arms at Monksilver, an attractive all-rounder with generous enjoyable food using named local suppliers. We also have half a dozen entirely new main entries this year: the King William in Bath, enterprising food in the informal surroundings of an unpretentious town pub; the Sexeys Arms at Blackford, an attractive country pub with Award-quality food from its French landlord; the upmarket yet relaxed Queens Arms at Corton Denham, with a wide range of drinks and good unusual food; Woods in Dulverton, striking a nice balance between enjoyable dining and a relaxed atmosphere for just dropping in for a drink or a coffee; the Helyar Arms at East Coker, a splendid place, good all round – for atmosphere, food, drink, service and bedrooms; and the idyllically placed Tarr Farm overlooking Tarr Steps. Good food is a major factor in the appeal of so many of the best Somerset pubs that it's easy to find places here for a special meal out. It also means that there's plenty of competition for our top title of Somerset Dining Pub of the Year – which says a great deal for the quality offered by this year's winner, the Bear & Swan in Chew Magna. The Lucky Dip section at the end of this Somerset chapter is particularly well provided with good pubs. Ones deserving a special mention are the Ring o' Bells at Ashcott, White Horse at Bradford-on-Tone, Adam & Eve in Bristol, Wheatsheaf at Combe Hay, George at Croscombe, Rose & Crown at East Lambrook, Lord Poulett Arms at Hinton St George, Hope & Anchor at Midford, Phelips Arms in Montacute, Fleur de Lys at Norton St Philip, Exmoor Forest Hotel at Simonsbath, Greyhound at Staple Fitzpaine, Lowtrow Cross Inn at Upton, Cotley Inn at Wambrook, restauranty Fountain in Wells, Holman Clavel near Widcombe and Royal Oak at Winsford. Drinks prices are close to the national average. In a Somerset pub, you'll probably find a local beer the best value: Butcombe is the most likely, with Exmoor, Cotleigh, Bath, RCH, Abbey and Cottage also providing the cheapest beer in some of our main entries. Cheapest of all for beer was the splendidly individual Black Horse at Clapton-in-Gordano, which was selling a national brew for comfortably under £2 a pint.

APPLEY ST0621 Map 1

Globe 🍽

Hamlet signposted from the network of back roads between A361 and A38, W of B3187 and W of Milverton and Wellington; OS Sheet 181 map reference 072215; TA21 0HJ

Hidden in a maze of pretty country lanes, this 500-year-old pub is a delightfully unchanging place, well liked for its very good meals. The simple beamed front room has a built-in settle and bare wood tables on the brick floor, and another room has a GWR bench and 1930s railway posters; there's a further room with easy chairs and other more traditional ones, open fires, and a collection of model cars, art deco items and *Titanic* pictures; skittle alley. A brick entry corridor leads to a serving hatch with Palmers Copper and Wadworths 6X on handpump, and Heck's farm cider. Tasty bar food (with most prices unchanged since last year) includes sandwiches, home-made soup (£3.25), chicken liver pâté (£5.50), seafood pancake (£7.95), vegetable pasta topped with stilton (£8.50), chicken curry (£9.50), home-made steak and kidney in ale pie (£8.95), steaks (from £10.50), daily specials such as russian lamb casserole with suet dumplings (£9.50), fillet steak rossini with chicken liver pâté and madeira sauce or whole cornish lemon sole (£11.95), and puddings like sticky ginger pudding with ginger ice-cream (£4.75); Sunday roast (£6.50). The restaurant and parts of the bar are no smoking. Seats, climbing frame and swings outside in the garden; the path opposite leads eventually to the River Tone. *(Recommended by Bob and Margaret Holder, the Didler, Brian and Anita Randall, Michael Rowse, John and Fiona McIlwain)*

Free house ~ Licensees Andrew and Liz Burt ~ Real ale ~ Bar food ~ Restaurant ~ (01823) 672327 ~ Children welcome ~ Open 11-3, 6.30-12; 12-3, 7-10.30 Sun; closed Mon except bank hols

---

ASHILL ST3116 Map 1

Square & Compass

Windmill Hill; off A358 between Ilminster and Taunton; up Wood Road for 1 mile behind Stewley Cross service station; OS Sheet 193 map reference 310166; TA19 9NX

The well worn edges of this nicely remote simple pub are very much part of the appeal. It's in an assuming spot, with sweeping views over the rolling pastures around Neroche Forest from the upholstered window seats in the little bar; there are other seats and an open winter fire – and perhaps the pub cats Daisy and Lilly. Butcombe, Exmoor Ale, Flowers IPA and St Austell HSD on handpump; skittle alley. Very generously served bar food includes good sandwiches, soup (£3.50), cauliflower cheese topped with mushrooms (£6.50), lasagne or steak and ale pie (£7.95), breast of chicken in a creamy stilton and bacon sauce (£10.95), and duck with a port and cranberry sauce (£12.95). The piped music is often classical. There's a garden with picnic-sets, and regular live music in their Barn. *(Recommended by Mr and Mrs Colin Roberts, R T and J C Moggridge, John and Fiona McIlwain, Pat and Tony Martin, B J Harding)*

Free house ~ Licensees Chris, Janet and Beth Slow ~ Real ale ~ Bar food (not Tues, Weds or Thurs lunchtimes) ~ (01823) 480467 ~ Children welcome ~ Dogs welcome ~ Monthly live music in separate barn ~ Open 12-2.30, 6.30-11; 12-2.30, 7-10.30 Sun; closed Tues, Weds and Thurs lunchtimes; 25 and 26 Dec

AXBRIDGE ST4255 Map 1

Lamb

The Square; off A371 Cheddar—Winscombe; BS26 2AP

Readers enjoy the friendly feel of this ancient place, well positioned on the market square so usually busy with a mix of regulars and shoppers. The big rambling bar is full of heavy beams and timbers, cushioned wall seats and small settles, an open fire in one great stone fireplace, and a collection of tools and utensils including an unusual foot-operated grinder in another. Butcombe Bitter, Blonde and Gold and a changing guest like Shepherd Neame Spitfire on handpump from a bar counter built largely of bottles, and local cider; shove-ha'penny, cribbage, dominoes, table skittles and skittle alley. Good value bar food includes lunchtime sandwiches and filled baguettes (from £3), as well as home-made soup (£2.75), chicken liver pâté with fruit chutney (£4.25), deep-fried brie with redcurrant jelly (£4.50), filled baked potatoes (from £4.75), home-cooked ham and eggs (£6.25), leek and potato bake (£6.50), a good daily curry or popular beef in ale pie (£7.45), steaks (from £8.95), and daily specials such as faggots and mash (£7.25), pork medallions in mustard sauce (£8.25), and fresh bass (£9.25); children's meals (£4.25), and they do a two-course lunch for OAPs Tues-Fri (£6.25). Nearly half the pub is no smoking. Although the sheltered back garden is not big, it's prettily planted with rock plants, shrubs and trees. The National Trust's medieval King John's Hunting Lodge is opposite. *(Recommended by Mr and Mrs B Hobden, Matthew Shackle, Peter Mack Wilkins, Len Clark, Dr A J and Mrs Tompsett, Steve Kirby)*

Butcombe ~ Manager Alan Currie ~ Real ale ~ Bar food (12-2.30, 6.30-9; not Sun evening) ~ (01934) 732253 ~ Children in eating area of bar ~ Dogs allowed in bar ~ Open 11.30-3, 6-11 Mon-Weds, 11.30-11 Thurs and Fri;; 11.30-11.30 Sat; 12-10.30 Sun

BABCARY ST5628 Map 2

Red Lion ♀

Off A37 south of Shepton Mallett; 2 miles or so north of roundabout where A37 meets A303 and A372; TA11 7ED

Properly pubby despite its emphasis on food, this golden stone thatched pub is run by an enthusiastic and personable young landlord. With a reliance on local produce, lunchtime meals might include soups with a warm fresh loaf on its own little breadboard (£3.95), sandwiches (from £4.95), roasted red pepper, goats cheese pastry tart and shaved fennel salad (£5.25), crispy pork belly, preserved lemon noodles and honey soy dressing (£5.50), ploughman's with elderflower chutney (£6.75), ham, poached duck egg, fried hen egg and chips (£6.95), and burger with tomato relish (£7.95), with evening choices such as chicken liver parfait with grape compote and toasted brioche (£5.50), warm duck pancakes, spring onions, and hoi sin dipping sauce (£5.75), roasted wild garlic, toasted almonds, salami and mascarpone risotto (£9.50), chicken breast with tagliatelle, red pepper, artichokes and pesto crème fraîche (£10.75), and herb-crusted rack of lamb, colcannon, cracked pepper pumpkin and coffee jus (£13.95); fish dishes are listed on a specials board, and for children they will gladly prepare any dish in smaller helpings. It's a popular place, so service may be stretched at busier times. Several distinct areas work their way around the well refurbished bar, though all share the same feeling of unhurried well-being. To the left of the entrance is a longish room with dark pink walls, a squashy leather sofa and two housekeeper's chairs by a low table and a woodburning stove, just a few well spaced tables and captain's chairs including a big one in a bay window with built-in seats. There are elegant rustic wall lights, some clay pipes in a cabinet, and local papers to read; board games and gardening magazines too. Leading off here with lovely dark flagstones is a public bar area with a panelled dado, a high-backed old settle and more straightforward chairs; darts, dominoes, cribbage, shove-ha'penny and table skittles. The good-sized smart no smoking dining room has a large stone lion's head on a plinth above the open fire (with a huge stack of logs to one side), a big rug on polished bare boards, and properly set tables. O'Hanlon's Yellowhammer and Teignworthy beers like

Reel Ale and Springtide on handpump or tapped from the cask, seven good wines by the glass, fresh fruit cocktails, summer smoothies and iced tea, and a proper bloody mary. There's a long informal garden with picnic tables and a play area with slide for children; they have plans for a barbecue area and bar out here. More reports please. *(Recommended by Michael Doswell, Jane Legate, Guy Vowles, Ian Phillips, Bob and Margaret Holder, Tom Evans, Clare West)*

Free house ~ Licensee Charles Garrard ~ Real ale ~ Bar food (12-2.30, 7-9.30) ~ Restaurant ~ (01458) 223230 ~ Children welcome ~ Dogs allowed in bar ~ Open 12-2.30(3 Sat), 6-11; 12-3 Sun; closed Sun evening

BATCOMBE   ST6838   Map 2
Three Horseshoes 🍴 ♔ ♈
Village signposted off A359 Bruton—Frome; BA4 6HE

Very much a dining pub, with a wide range of thoughtfully prepared food, this well placed and attractive honey-coloured stone house now has bedrooms – we look forward to reports on these from readers. Smartly traditional, the longish narrow main room has beams, local pictures on the lightly ragged dark pink walls, built-in cushioned window seats and solid chairs around a nice mix of old tables, a woodburning stove at one end, and a big open fire at the other; at the back on the left, the snug has dark panelled walls, tiled floors and old pictures. The menu might typically include lunchtime ciabattas (£6.75), soup (£4.25), pan-fried organic chicken livers en croûte with a brandy, bacon and parsley cream sauce (£6.25), local sausages and mash (£9.50), vegetable and blue cheese lattice, confit of duck cassoulet, or home-cured beef brisket pot with root vegetables (£10.50), battered fish and chips in newspaper (£11.95), seared salmon fillet on linguini with tomato butter sauce (£12.25), slow-braised shoulder of lamb on buttered mash and red wine jus (£14.75), seasonal game specials and, nice for those who can't decide what to choose, three different miniature traditional puddings (£5.50). They plan to introduce duck spit roasts by the time this edition hits the shops. The no smoking, stripped stone dining room is pretty (no mobile phones allowed). They recommend booking at weekends, and you may otherwise find all the tables reserved. Butcombe Bitter and Bats in the Belfry (brewed for the pub) and Wadworths 6X on handpump, and ten wines by two sizes of glass. The back terrace has picnic-sets, with more on the grass, outdoor heaters, and a pond with koi carp. The pub is on a quiet village lane by the church which has a very striking tower. *(Recommended by Paul and Annette Hallett, Susan and Nigel Wilson, Mr and Mrs R B Berry, Roger Wain-Heapy, Peter Craske, Michael Doswell, Mr and Mrs Peter Llewellyn, Julian and Jennifer Clapham)*

Free house ~ Licensees Bob Wood and Shirley Greaves ~ Real ale ~ Bar food (not Mon) ~ Restaurant ~ (01749) 850359 ~ Children in eating area of bar and restaurant lunchtimes only; must be over 12 evenings ~ Dogs allowed in bar ~ Guitarist/singer Thurs night ~ Open 12-3, 6.30-11; 12-3, 7-10.30 Sun; closed all day Mon; evening 25 Dec ~ Bedrooms: £50B/£75B

BATH   ST7565   Map 2
King William ♈
Thomas Street, corner with A4 London Road – may be no nearby parking; BA1 5NN

This little corner pub has good food (and drink), and seems all the better for being not at all smart. Its two plain rooms have simple seating and just three chunky old tables each on dark bare boards, and big windows looking out on the busy street; at night heavy curtains can keep out the lights of the traffic. It's certainly a place where people are comfortable just dropping in for a drink or a chat. They have Blindmans Golden Spring, Otter and Palmers Copper on handpump, and a fine choice of good wines in two glass sizes, including good sherries and ports. However, the special draw here is the good individual food. This includes super hearty soups such as lentil and bacon (£6) or smoked haddock chowder (£6.50), half a dozen main dishes such as mackerel cooked with bacon (£10), wild mushroom risotto (£11.50) and pigeon done with wild garlic or organic bath chaps (salted pig's cheeks cooked long and very slow – delicious here; £12), and homely puddings such as a good rhubarb crumble (£5). They also do a good generous beef sandwich (£5) or a plate of cheeses (£7). Helpful informal service by nice young staff, daily papers, a few lighted church candles, and perhaps a big bunch of lilies on the counter. Steep stairs go up to a simple and attractive dining room, used mainly on Wednesday to Saturday evenings, decorated with Jane Grigson *British Cooking* prints. *(Recommended by Mark O'Sullivan, Richard and Lynn Seers)*

Free house ~ Licensees Charlie and Amanda Digney ~ Real ale ~ Bar food (12-2.30, 6-10; not Sun evening) ~ Restaurant ~ (01225) 428096 ~ Children welcome ~ Dogs allowed in bar ~ Open 12-3, 5-11(12 Fri); 12-12 Sat; 12-11 Sun

Old Green Tree ◖

12 Green Street; BA1 2JZ

This traditional little pub has been extraordinarily popular with readers this year – one of whom says the atmosphere was exactly as he found it on his last visit, 28 years ago. It's always busy (sometimes packed), but keeps a cheerily relaxed feel – as well as a splendid choice of six real ales on handpump, a typical choice including Butcombe Blond, Cottage Brewery Jack and the Dragon, RCH Pitchfork, Wickwar Brand Oak and Mr Perretts Traditional Stout, and a beer named for the pub. Also, a dozen wines by the glass from a nice little list with helpful notes, 35 malt whiskies, winter hot toddies, and a proper Pimms. It's laid-back and cosy rather than particularly smart, the three small oak-panelled and low wood-and-plaster ceilinged rooms including a comfortable lounge on the left as you go in, its walls decorated with wartime aircraft pictures in winter and local artists' work during spring and summer, and a no smoking back bar (the other bars can feel a little smoky at times); the big skylight lightens things up attractively. Popular lunchtime bar food includes soup and sandwiches (from £4.50), ploughman's (from £5.50), bangers and mash with cider or beer and onion sauce (£7), an enjoyable rare roast beef platter (£8.50), and daily specials such as mushroom and leek risotto, curry of the day, and smoked trout and asparagus (all £7.50); friendly service. Tables are tiny and highly prized, so arrive early if you're planning to eat, especially at weekends. No music or machines; chess, cribbage, dominoes, backgammon, shut the box, Jenga. The gent's is down steep steps. No children. *(Recommended by Dr and Mrs M E Wilson, Pete Baker, Gaynor Gregory, Susan and Nigel Wilson, Alain and Rose Foote, Malcolm Ward, Tom and Ruth Rees, W W Burke, Bruce and Penny Wilkie, Dr and Mrs A K Clarke, Donna and Roger, Peter Craske, Mike Pugh, the Didler, Dennis Jones, John Saville, Colin and Peggy Wilshire, Michael Butler, Mary Rayner, Bill and Jessica Ritson, Clare Rosier, Edward Mirzoeff)*

Free house ~ Licensees Nick Luke and Tim Bethune ~ Real ale ~ Bar food (lunchtime until 3) ~ No credit cards ~ Dogs allowed in bar ~ Open 11-11; 12-10.30 Sun; closed 25 and 26 Dec

Star ◖

23 Vineyards; The Paragon (A4), junction with Guinea Lane; BA1 5NA

On a street of undeniably handsome if well worn stone terraces, this honest old town pub has a historic interior that hasn't changed for years. It's the brewery tap for Abbey Ales, so among the three or four well kept real ales you'll always find Abbey Bellringer – and Bass tapped stright from the cask. Not smart, the four (well, more like three and a half) small linked rooms are served from a single bar, separated by sombre panelling with glass inserts. They are furnished with traditional leatherette wall benches and the like – even one hard bench that the regulars call Death Row – and the lighting's dim, and not rudely interrupted by too much daylight. With no machines or music, chat's the thing here – or perhaps cribbage, dominoes and shove-ha'penny. Food is limited to filled rolls only (from £1.70; served throughout opening hours during the week) – though they have rather unusual bar nibbles Sunday lunchtime and Thursday evening; friendly staff and customers. The pub can get busy at weekends. *(Recommended by Pete Baker, Andy and Jill Kassube, Dr and Mrs A K Clarke, the Didler, Dr and Mrs M E Wilson, N R White, Rob Stevenson)*

Punch ~ Lease Paul Waters and Alan Morgan ~ Real ale ~ Bar food (see text) ~ (01225) 425072 ~ Dogs allowed in bar ~ Open 12-2.30, 5.30-12; 12-12 Sat; 12-10.30 Sun

BLACKFORD ST4147 Map 1
Sexeys Arms 🍴
B3139 W of Wedmore; BS28 4NT

This pretty roadside cottage dates from the 1400s, with three or four linked bar rooms – beams and log fires (one in an inglenook), careful lighting, a nice mix of seating around dining and scrubbed kitchen tables, some handsome old flagstones and a proper basic public bar area. Under the keen young French chef/landlord and his friendly wife, food is a strong point here, all cooked to order and with many things available in two sizes of helpings. As well as sandwiches, the changing menu might include pork and leek sausages with bubble and squeak and onion gravy or chicken, leek and mushroom pie with creamy mash and spiced turnips (£8), salmon, dill and chilli fishcake with creamed spinach and tartare sauce (£10), pan-roasted tenderloin of pork on turmeric and raisin mash with cider sauce and coriander seed-glazed carrots (£12.50), griddled fresh yellowfin tuna steak on crushed new potatoes, capers and roasted tomato, with marinated roasted vegetables (£15.50), and rare roast fillet of local venison wrapped in pancetta on garlic mash with port jus and braised red cabbage (£16.50). They do a two-course lunchtime menu for £13; three courses £17. Cheerful helpful staff will do starters with bread as a lighter alternative, and they have Butcombe and a guest like Greene King Old Speckled Hen on handpump, and good value wines by the glass; there may be unobtrusive piped music. On the right, a stripped-stone restaurant has country furnishings on its ceramic tiles. The dining room and lounge are no smoking. There are picnic-sets under cocktail parasols outside. *(Recommended by R K Phillips, Comus and Sarah Elliott, Dr and Mrs C W Thomas, Peter Mack Wilkins)*

Punch ~ Lease Thierry and Philippa Lacassin ~ Bar food (12-2 (3 Sat/Sun), 7-9 (9.30 Sat); not Sun evenings, or Mon) ~ (01934) 712487 ~ Children in eating area of bar and restaurant ~ Dogs allowed in bar ~ Open 12-3 (2 in winter), 7-11; 12-11(as weekdays in winter) Sat; 12-10.30 Sun; closed Mon (exc bank hols), and in winter Suns from 6

BLEADON ST3457 Map 1
Queens Arms 🍺
Just off A370 S of Weston; Celtic Way; BS24 0NF

Opened up inside, this 16th-c pub has carefully divided separate areas that still let the comfortably chatty and convivial atmosphere run right through. Plenty of distinctive elements include the dark flagstones of the terracotta-walled restaurant and back bar area (both no smoking), candles on sturdy tables flanked by winged settles, old hunting prints, a frieze of quaint sayings in Old English print, and above all, the focal servery where up to half a dozen well kept changing ales are tapped from the cask: Bath Ales Gem Bitter, Butcombe Bitter, Gold, and Blonde, Newmans Bite IPA, St Austell Charlies Angels, and Youngs Waggledance; several wines by the glass. Well liked bar food at lunchtime includes sandwiches and filled baguettes or panini (from £3.50; brie and grape panini £5.50; triple decker club toastie £5.25), soup (£3.95), filled baked potatoes (from £4.25), caesar salad (£5.25), moules marinière (£5.95), roasted rack of ribs in barbecue sauce (£5.50), vegetable lasagne (£6.45), home-made faggots (£6.50), honey-roasted ham and eggs (£6.95), home-made pie of the day (£7.45), and home-made beer battered cod (£7.95), with evening choices such as asparagus and wild mushroom risotto (£5), king scallops on a black pudding salad with a creamy dijon sauce (£8.50), goats cheese, potato and red onion tarte tatin (£9.95), corn-fed chicken breast stuffed with goats cheese and pear and wrapped in back bacon with a white wine and mushroom sauce or bass fillet on braised fennel and cherry tomatoes with a white wine and tarragon cream (£12.95), and home-made puddings like crème brûlée of the day or chocolate torte (£4.50). There is a big solid fuel stove in the main bar, with another woodburning stove in the stripped-stone back tap bar; games machine and darts. There's a new and pretty terrace surrounded by shrubs and flowers with a pergola, outdoor heaters and picnic-sets on flagstones. *(Recommended by Brian Root, Michael Rowse, Comus and Sarah Elliott, Peter Mack Wilkins, Dr Martin Owton, Grahame Brooks, M G Hart, Dr and Mrs C W Thomas, John Coote, Tom Evans)*

Butcombe ~ Managers Daniel Pardoe, Jessica Perry, Guy Newell ~ Real ale ~ Bar food (12-2, 6-9) ~ Restaurant ~ (01934) 812080 ~ Children welcome away from bar ~ Dogs allowed in bar ~ Open 11-3, 5.30-11; 11.30-11 Fri and Sat; 12-10.30 Sun

CHEW MAGNA ST5763 Map 2
Bear & Swan 🍽️ ♀
B3130 (South Parade), off A37 S of Bristol; BS40 8SL
Somerset Dining Pub of the Year

Very well liked by readers for its excellent food and warm welcome, this carefully laid-out open-plan pub splendidly mixes the traditional with the modern – though its appealingly up-to-date feel comes as something of a surprise in such an austerely traditional-looking building. The left hand end, beyond a piano, is an L-shaped no smoking dining room, with stripped stone walls, dark dining tables, a woodburning stove, bare boards and an oriental rug. The other half, also bare boards with the odd oriental rug, has various sizes of pine tables, pews and raffia-seat dining chairs. In this part a relaxed and civilised mix of customers runs from young men chatting on the bar stools through smart lunching mums sipping champagne to older people reading the racing form; there may also be a friendly golden labrador. Décor is minimal, really just plants in the windows with their heavy dark blue curtains, and some china above the huge bressumer beam over a splendid log fire; a wide-screen TV may be on with its sound turned down; cribbage. Changing every day, with a manageably short blackboard choice, the good food might include baguettes filled with anything from egg mayonnaise to goats cheese and chorizo (lunchtime only, not Sunday; from £4.25), home-made soup such as spicy pumpkin (£3.50), aubergine and ham roulade with spiced apricot chutney (£6), mushroom risotto (£6.50), spinach and ricotta tortellini with white wine and parmesan (£6.75), cumberland sausage on mustard mash with onion gravy (£7.50), bass with a prawn spring roll and soy and sesame oil dressing (£14), and puddings such as summer pudding or pecan tart (from £4). The food is so popular booking is recommended to be sure of a table.The long bar counter has Bath Gem, Butcombe Bitter and Courage Best on handpump, and around 15 wines by the glass. The car park is small, and street parking needs care (and patience). *(Recommended by Michael Doswell, BOB, Dr and Mrs A K Clarke, Dr and Mrs C W Thomas, Gaynor Gregory, M G Hart, Julian and Jennifer Clapham, Angus and Rosemary Campbell)*

Free house ~ Licensees Nigel and Caroline Pushman ~ Real ale ~ Bar food (12-2(3 Sun), 7-9.45; not Sun evening) ~ Restaurant ~ (01275) 331100 ~ Well behaved children welcome ~ Dogs allowed in bar ~ Open 11am-12.30am ~ Bedrooms: £50S/£80S

CHISELBOROUGH ST4614 Map 1
Cat Head
Take the slip road off A303 at Crewkerne A356 junction; TA14 6TT

Lots of very high praise from readers this year for both the food and the welcome at this neatly kept and friendly country pub. Handy from the main road, it's a particularly nice stop in summer when there are plenty of colourful plants around the picnic-sets in the attractive gardens; nice views over the peaceful village, too. The spotless, traditional flagstoned rooms have light wooden tables and chairs, some high-backed cushioned settles, flowers and plants, a woodburning stove, and curtains around the small mullioned windows; most areas are no smoking. The pub often gets busy in the evenings (particularly at weekends), but at lunchtime you may have its peaceful charms almost to yourself. Served in good-sized helpings, the popular food at lunchtime might include soup (£3.90), ploughman's (£4.80), smoked loin of pork and pine nut salad or lambs kidney in madeira sauce (£4.90), baked cornish crab and scallops mornay (£6.10), chicken breast suffed with dorset blue cheese (£10.40), venison casseroled in a red wine and juniper sauce (£11.80), and half a crispy duck with scrumpy sauce (£13.80), with daily specials like wild rabbit with thyme and mustard (£7.60), and seasonal game, with evening dishes such as grilled bass fillets with chive butter (£12.20) and fillet of monkfish with Pernod and cream (£12.80). Well kept Butcombe, Fullers London Pride and Otter Bitter on handpump, a good wine list, and Thatcher's cider; soft piped music, darts, alley skittles, shove-ha'penny, cribbage and dominoes. *(Recommended by Geoff and Sylvia Donald, M Carr, Revd D E and Mrs J A Shapland, Mary Ellen Cummings, Frank Willy, Charles Gysin, Richard Endacott, Ian and Nita Cooper, Theo, Anne and Jane Gaskin, Marianne and Peter Stevens, Guy Vowles, Mary Stokes, Norman and Sarah Keeping, Richard Wyld, Mrs A P Lee, Mrs A Macartney, Mrs S J Frost)*

Enterprise ~ Lease Duncan and Avril Gordon ~ Real ale ~ Bar food ~ Restaurant ~ (01935) 881231 ~ Children welcome ~ Open 12-3, 6(7 Sun)-11; closed 25 Dec

CHURCHILL   ST4560   Map 1
Crown 🍺 £
The Batch; in village, turn off A368 into Skinners Lane at Nelson Arms, then bear right; BS25 5PP

Unspoilt and characterful, this bustling little cottage is a real favourite with some readers, particularly those who like their pubs simple and unpretentious rather than pristine and modern. For some the atmosphere is the main draw, but others come for the excellent range of well kept real ales, with up to ten tapped from the cask, usually including Bass, Bath Spa, Cotleigh Batch, Hop Back GFB, Palmers IPA, RCH Hewish and PG Steam, and two changing guests; also farm ciders. Especially busy at weekends, the small and rather local-feeling stone-floored and cross-beamed room on the right has a wooden window seat, an unusually sturdy settle, and built-in wall benches; the left-hand room has a slate floor, and some steps past the big log fire in a big stone fireplace lead to more sitting space. No noise from music or games (except perhaps dominoes), just a steady murmur of happy chat. Straightforward lunchtime bar food includes sandwiches (£3.80), good soup (£3.75), filled baked potatoes (£4.25), ploughman's (£5.75), salads (£7.25), home-made daily specials like cauliflower cheese or chilli (£4.75), broccoli and cheese bake (£5.25), and beef casserole (£6.25), with puddings such as a well liked treacle pudding (£3.90). Outside lavatories. There are garden tables on the front and a smallish back lawn, and hill views; the Mendip Morris Men come in summer. Good walks nearby. *(Recommended by John and Gloria Isaacs, Michael Doswell, Tom Evans, Joan and Tony Walker, Peter Mack Wilkins, the Didler, Andrea and Guy Bradley, Alan and Paula McCully, Geoff and Carol Thorp, John Urquhart, Rod and Chris Pring, R T and J C Moggridge)*

Free house ~ Licensee Tim Rogers ~ Real ale ~ Bar food (12-2.30; not evenings) ~ No credit cards ~ (01934) 852995 ~ Children welcome away from bar ~ Dogs welcome ~ Open 11-11; 12-11 Sun

CLAPTON-IN-GORDANO   ST4773   Map 1
Black Horse
4 miles from M5 junction 19; A369 towards Portishead, then B3124 towards Clevedon; in N Weston opposite school turn left signposted Clapton, then in village take second right, maybe signed Clevedon, Clapton Wick; BS20 7RH

Especially pretty in summer, when the pub and its pretty little flagstoned garden are liberally festooned with flowers, this unspoilt old place dates back to the 14th c, though it's the early years of the last century that it recalls inside. The partly flagstoned and partly red-tiled main room has winged settles and built-in wall benches around narrow, dark wooden tables, window seats, a big log fire with stirrups and bits on the mantelbeam, and amusing cartoons and photographs of the pub. A window in an inner snug is still barred from the days when this room was the petty-sessions gaol; high-backed settles – one a marvellous carved and canopied creature, another with an art nouveau copper insert reading East, West, Hame's Best – lots of mugs hanging from its black beams, and plenty of little prints and photographs. There's also a simply furnished no smoking room (which is the only place families are allowed; several have been disappointed to be so cut off from the jolliness of the rest of the pub); piped music, darts, cribbage and dominoes. Straightforward bar food (lunchtime only) includes filled hot and cold baguettes (from £4.25), ploughman's (£5.25), and a few hot dishes like soup (£3.25), lamb hotpot (£6.50) and leek and smoky bacon bake or fisherman's pie (£6.75); friendly service. Butcombe Bitter, Courage Best, Shepherd Neame Spitfire, Wadworths 6X and Websters Green Label on handpump or tapped from the cask; also Thatcher's cider. There are some old rustic tables and benches in the garden, with more to one side of the car park. Paths from the pub lead up Naish Hill or along to Cadbury Camp. *(Recommended by Tom Evans, Dave Braisted, Peter Mack Wilkins, the Didler, Gaynor Gregory, Gloria Bax)*

Inntrepreneur ~ Tenant Nicholas Evans ~ Real ale ~ Bar food (not evenings, not Sun) ~ No credit cards ~ (01275) 842105 ~ Children in very plain family room only ~ Dogs welcome ~ Live music Mon evening ~ Open 11-11; 12-10.30 Sun; closed 2.30-5 weekdays in winter

COMPTON MARTIN   ST5457   Map 2
Ring o' Bells 🍺
A368 Bath—Weston; BS40 6JE

Overlooked by the Mendip Hills, this bustling family-friendly country pub is in an attractive position, and there's a friendly welcome from the landlord and his staff. The cosy, traditional front part of the bar has rugs on the flagstones and inglenook seats right by the log fire, and up a step is a spacious carpeted back part with largely stripped stone walls and pine tables. Well kept Butcombe Bitter, Blond and Gold and a guest like Bath Gem on handpump; darts, cribbage and dominoes in the public bar. The lounge and eating areas are no smoking; a family room has blackboards and chalks, a Brio track, and a rocking horse. Bar food includes sandwiches (from £2.95), home-made soup (£3.75), filled baked potatoes (from £4.50), ham and eggs (small £4.25; large £5.45), omelettes (from £4.95), ploughman's (from £5.50), broccoli, mushroom and almond tagliatelle (£6.75), beef in ale or lasagne (£6.95), and steaks (from £10.50). The big garden has swings, a slide and a climbing frame. Blagdon Lake and Chew Valley Lake are not far away. *(Recommended by Tom Evans, Peter Mack Wilkins, Basil and Jarvis, Geoff and Carol Thorp, Gaynor Gregory)*

Butcombe ~ Manager Roger Owen ~ Real ale ~ Bar food ~ Restaurant ~ (01761) 221284 ~ Children in family room ~ Dogs allowed in bar ~ Open 11.30-3, 6-11; 12-3, 6.30-10.30 Sun

CONGRESBURY   ST4464   Map 1
White Hart
Wrington Road, which is off A370 Bristol—Weston just E of village – keep on; BS49 5AN

The L-shaped main bar of this pleasant country dining pub has a few heavy black beams in the bowed ceiling of its longer leg, along with country-kitchen chairs around good-sized tables, and a big stone inglenook fireplace at each end, with woodburning stoves and lots of copper pans. The short leg of the L is more cottagey, with wooden games and other bric-a-brac above yet another fireplace and on a delft shelf, lace and old-gold brocaded curtains, and brocaded wall seats. A roomy family Parlour Bar, open to the main bar, is similar in mood, though with lighter-coloured country-style furniture, some stripped stone and shiny black panelling, and big bright airy conservatory windows on one side; the restaurant is no smoking. Promptly served home-made bar food includes soup (£4.25), ploughman's (£4.25), deep-fried cheese with cranberry sauce (£5.25), ham and eggs (£6.50), broccoli and brie pie (£8.25), steak pie (£8.95), chicken in stilton (£9.50), andalusian lamb (£13.25), and puddings such as fruit crumbles (£4.25); decent children's menu, and they're happy to help with dietary requirements such as gluten or dairy-free dishes. Badger Fursty Ferret, Gold and Tanglefoot on handpump; shove-ha'penny, cribbage, dominoes and table skittles. There are picnic-sets under an arbour on the terrace behind, and in the big landscaped garden (fom which, beyond the tall trees, you may see the Mendips). *(Recommended by Bob and Margaret Holder, Brian Root, Colin Morgan)*

Badger ~ Tenants Paul Merrick and Rebecca North ~ Real ale ~ Bar food (12-2, 6-9.30(9 Sun); maybe longer in summer) ~ Restaurant ~ (01934) 833303 ~ Children allowed away from bar, but not late at night ~ Dogs welcome ~ Open 11.30-2.30, 6-11; 12-3, 6-10.30 Sun; closed 25 Dec

CORTON DENHAM   ST6322   Map 2

Queens Arms 🛏️

Village signposted off B3145 N of Sherborne; DT9 4LR

Tucked away in a very quiet village near Cadbury Castle hill fort, with good views too from Corton Ridge, this Georgian inn built of attractive honey-coloured stone is rather hard to classify under its enthusiastic newish owners. One reader had described it as Barnes coming to the deep country, which did strike a chord with us on our early evening inspection visit. The plain high-beamed partly flagstoned bar, with a woodburning stove in the inglenook, was a little smoky and as full of regulars as you'd expect of any good west country local, some with dogs and some in very well worn rustic clothes (muddy boots are welcome here). Yet their accents and chatter suggested something altogether smarter, and that squares up with what's on offer here. Expect nice touches like pistachios, good marinated olives and hand-raised pork pies on the bar counter, and a big bowl of flowers. The young staff go out of their way to be helpful, and the food using local supplies is worth the wait for fresh cooking. It might include fresh asparagus and goats cheese with hollandaise sauce (£4.70), unusual salads like quail egg, paw paw and roast nectarine (£8.70), calves liver and mash with red onion marmalade and rich gravy (£8.90), stinging nettle risotto with parmesan shavings (£9.20), line-caught beer-battered cod (£9.70), roast duck with rhubarb and orange compote and red cabbage (£10.20), and puddings like deep-fried christmas pudding ice-cream with warm rum sauce (£3.90) or butterscotch and roasted almond pavlova (£4.20). They have a good children's menu (and crayons and toys to keep younger visitors happy). People like their sandwiches, such as rare roast beef or rib-eye steak. On the left the comfortable dining room, dark pink with crisp white paintwork, has good oak tables and a log fire. They have an extraordinary range of good bottled beers from around the world, as well as Butcombe, Timothy Taylors Landlord and guest beers such as Otter and Harveys Sussex on handpump, an interesting choice of wines by the glass, a good few malt whiskies, and Cheddar Valley farm cider. A south-facing back terrace has teak tables and chairs under cocktail parasols (or heaters if it's cool), with colourful flower tubs. The village lane has some parking nearby, though not a great deal. *(Recommended by OPUS, Clare West, Mark Flynn, B and F A Hannam, Robert and Christina Jones)*

Free house ~ Licensees Rupert and Victoria Reeves ~ Real ale ~ Bar food (12-3, 6-10) ~ Restaurant ~ (01963) 220317 ~ Children welcome ~ Dogs allowed in bar ~ Open 11-3, 6-11; 11-11 Sat; 12-10.30 Sun ~ Bedrooms: £60S(£70B)/£75S(£90B)

CRANMORE ST6643 Map 2
Strode Arms ⑪ ♀
Off A361 Frome—Shepton Mallet; BA4 4QJ

Enthusiastically recommended by several readers in recent months, this pretty former farmhouse returns to the main entries thanks to its very good, well presented food. Home-made using fresh local ingredients, the choice includes baguettes (from £3.80), soup (£3.95), ploughman's (from £5), liver, bacon and onions in gravy (£6.75), steak and kidney pie (£7.45), asparagus and saffron risotto (£7.75), paella (£7.95), green thai vegetable curry (£8.50), excellent bass fillet with sauce vierge (£9.95), and daily specials such as moroccan lamb with couscous (£7.50), smoked haddock with spinach and cheese sauce (£8.50), and scallops with smoked bacon, butternut squash risotto and fish sauce (£11). Smartened up under the current licensees, the rooms have charming country furnishings, fresh flowers, pot plants, a grandfather clock on the flagstones, remarkable old locomotive engineering drawings and big black and white steam train murals in a central lobby, newspapers to read, and lovely log fires in handsome fireplaces. The bar area and restaurant are no smoking; attentive, friendly service. Wadworths 6X, IPA and seasonal brews on handpump, as well as an interesting choice of wines by the glass from a thoughtful menu, lots more by the bottle, and quite a few liqueurs and ports. The pub is an attractive sight in summer with its neat stonework, cartwheels on the walls, pretty tubs and hanging baskets, and seats under umbrellas on the front terrace, looking across to the village pond; more seats in the back garden. The East Somerset Light Railway is nearby. *(Recommended by Gaynor Gregory, Mrs Pat Crabb, Pat and Robert Watt, Sylvia and Tony Birbeck, Richard Fendick, Geoffrey Kemp)*

Wadworths ~ Tenants Tim and Ann-Marie Gould ~ Real ale ~ Bar food (till 10pm Fri and Sat; not Sun evening (exc bank hol weekends)) ~ Restaurant ~ (01749) 880450 ~ Children allowed in restaurant ~ Dogs allowed in bar ~ Open 11.30-3, 6-11; 12-3, 7-10.30 Sun; closed Sun evening Oct-Mar

CROWCOMBE ST1336 Map 1
Carew Arms
Village (and pub) signposted just off A358 Taunton—Minehead; TA4 4AD

A nicely located 17th-c beamed inn, with a genuinely friendly welcome from the family in charge. The front bar has long benches and a couple of old long deal tables on its dark flagstones, a high-backed antique settle by the woodburning stove in its huge brick inglenook fireplace, and a thoroughly non-PC collection of hunting trophies to remind you that this is the Quantocks. (Another reminder is the freedom dogs enjoy throughout the pub.) A back room behind the bar is a carpeted and gently updated version of the front one, and on the right is a library, and residents' lounge. The smart no smoking dining room has doors to one side leading to an outside terrace where you can eat in fine weather. Exmoor Ale and either Fox, Gold or Hart on handpump, along with a changing beer from the Cottage Brewery, eight wines by the glass, Lane's strong farm cider, and a dozen malt whiskies. Dominoes, cribbage, darts, skittle alley, fruit machine, and piped music (only in the Garden Room); several dogs. Particularly enjoyable bar food includes sandwiches, soup (£4.50), filled baked potatoes (£5), mushroom stroganoff (£7.75), home-cooked gammon with hot garlic potatoes (£8), sausages with bubble and squeak and onion gravy (£8.25), daily specials such as slow-braised breast of lamb or garlic-roasted vegetables in red pepper jus (£8.50), prime cod fillet baked with cheddar and cream (£12), bream baked with garlic and tarragon (£12.50), and evening dishes like griddled calves liver with bacon and madeira gravy (£13.50) or king scallops with hot garlic butter (£14.50). Some dishes may run out at busy times, and the informal service can seem erratic at times – some readers find this all part of the charm, but a few do not. Though the jazz is usually monthly, it may be more frequent in summer. Picnic-sets out on the back grass look over rolling wooded pasture, and the attractive village at the foot of the hills has a fine old church and church house.

*(Recommended by Bob and Margaret Holder, John A Barker, Colin Chapman,
Claire Hardcastle, Mike Dean , Lis Wingate Gray, Peter Mack Wilkins, MP, the Didler, MLR,
David R Brown, Hugh Roberts, Henry and Fiona Dryden, Bob and Marilyn Baylis, Comus and
Sarah Elliott)*

Free house ~ Licensees Simon and Reg Ambrose ~ Real ale ~ Bar food (not winter Sun evenings) ~ Restaurant ~ (01984) 618631 ~ Children allowed in restaurant ~ Dogs welcome ~ Live jazz monthly, Sun lunchtime ~ Open 11-3.30, 5-12; 11-1am Sat; 11-midnight Sun; closed weekend afternoons in winter ~ Bedrooms: £49B/£79B

DOULTING ST6445 Map 2
Waggon & Horses ♀

**Doulting Beacon, 2 miles N of Doulting; eastwards turn off A37 on Mendip ridge N of
Shepton Mallet, just S of A367 junction; pub is also signed from A37 at Beacon Hill
crossroads and from the A361 at Doulting and Cranmore crossroads; BA4 4LA**

The big walled garden at this bustling pub is very enjoyable on a fine day, with tables and chairs on a terrace, picnic-sets out on the grass, and perennials and flowering shrubs interspersed in a pretty and pleasantly informal way. There's a wildlife pond, several rabbits, and a climber for children. Inside, the rambling bar has studded red leatherette seats and other chairs, a homely mix of tables including antiques, Butcombe Bitter, Greene King IPA and Wadworths 6X on handpump, and quite a few wines by the glass. Half the pub is no smoking. Bar food includes sandwiches or baguettes (from £3.25), soup (£3.50), leek and mushroom bake (£7.90), tomato, pepper and courgette lasagne (£8.20), local ham and eggs from their own chickens (£8.50; you can buy the eggs to take away too), beer-battered cod and chips (£8.90), italian-style chicken casserole (£9.20), a choice of sausages with mash and onion gravy (£9.50), marinated trio of grilled lamb chops (£9.90), and daily specials. The new licensees appear to be settling in well, and they still have music nights organised by the previous landlord. *(Recommended by MRSM, Susan and Nigel Wilson, Colin and Janet Roe, Richard Fendick, Jenny and Brian Seller, Peter Meister)*

InnSpired ~ Lease Simon Cooke and Clare Wilson ~ Real ale ~ Bar food (11.30-2.30, 6.30-9.30) ~ Restaurant ~ (01749) 880302 ~ Children tolerated but must be well behaved and quiet ~ Dogs allowed in bar ~ Jazz first Fri of month ~ Open 11.30-3, 6-11; 12-3, 7-11 Sun

DULVERTON SS9127 Map 1
Woods ♀

Bank Square; TA22 9BU

Originally a baker's and café known some decades ago as Woods Refreshment and Chocolate House, this reopened in 2004 after rebuilding as a comfortable bar with some emphasis on good interesting food. At lunchtime this might include rustic rolls (£4.50), caesar salad (£5.50), a melt-in-the-mouth carpaccio cut from local beef (one of the best we have ever tasted, £6.50), ploughman's (£6.95), battered hake and chips (£8.50), wild mushroom risotto with truffle oil (£9.50) and calves liver and bacon with port wine sauce or chicken supreme with bourguignon garnish (£11.50). They take particular care with their puddings, such as panna cotta and pear Belle-Hélène. The evening menu is rather more elaborate and might include twice-baked gruyère cheese soufflé (£6.) and roast turbot on white bean, chorizo and herbs (£16.50). The atmosphere is comfortably relaxed, mildly upmarket in a country way, and very Exmoor – plenty of good sporting prints on the salmon pink walls, some antlers, other hunting trophies and stuffed birds, and a couple of salmon rods. There are bare boards on the left by the bar counter, which has four changing local ales from brewers such as Exmoor, Otter, St Austell and O'Hanlons on handpump and Cheddar Valley farm cider. You can order any of the 400 or so wines from the amazing wine list by the glass, and the landlord also keeps an unlisted collection of about 500 old new world wines which he will happily chat about; they have daily papers. Its tables partly separated by stable-style timbering and masonry dividers, the bit on the right is carpeted and has a woodburning stove in the big fireplace set into its end wall, which has varnished plank panelling. There may be unobjectionable piped music. Big windows keep you in touch with what's going on out in the quiet town centre (or you can sit out on the pavement at a couple of metal tables). A small suntrap back courtyard has a few picnic-sets. *(Recommended by Lyn Dixon, Len Clark, Jeremy Whitehorn)*

Free house ~ Licensee P Groves ~ Real ale ~ Bar food (12-2, 6-9.45(7-9.30 Sun)) ~ Restaurant ~ (01398) 324007 ~ Children welcome ~ Dogs allowed in bar ~ Open 11-3, 6-12(1 Sat); 12-3, 7-10.30 Sun

EAST COKER ST5412 Map 2
Helyar Arms ♀ 🛏

Village signposted off A37 or A30 SW of Yeovil; Moor Lane; BA22 9JR

Very well run, this neatly kept heavy-beamed pub has a spacious and comfortable turkey-carpeted bar carefully laid out to give a degree of intimacy to its various candlelit tables, helped by soft lighting, a couple of high-backed settles, and squashy leather sofas at each end. There are lots of hunting and other country pictures, and a log fire. Good fresh imaginative food uses local produce from named farms, and they have home-pickled eggs (plain or balsamic), and do a weekday lunchtime beer-and-a-sandwich deal for £5. Other dishes might include soups like roasted yellow pepper and sweetcorn (£4), lunchtime sandwiches (£5) and ploughman's (£7), chicken liver parfait with toasted brioche and red onion marmalade (£6), sweet potato and spinach cakes with vegetable ribbons and ratatouille (£9), chargrilled pork sausages with marrowfat peas and mash (£10), glazed slow-roasted pork belly with green beans, roasted sweet potato and parsnip crisps (£12), grilled spring lamb chops with carrot and swede mash, dauphinoise potatoes and rosemary jus (£13), calves liver and bacon with caramelised shallots, mash, and deep-fried sage leaves (£14), specials such as braised beef and carrots with watercress mash or baked pepper stuffed with herb couscous and spinach (£9), and home-made ice-creams; choice of Sundy roasts (from £11). There are steps up to a good-sized back high-raftered dining room with well spaced tables. Service is welcoming and helpful, and they have Butcombe, Greene King IPA and Sharps Doom Bar on handpump, local farm cider, reasonably priced wines (pretty much all available by the glass), and daily papers; piped music. There are a few picnic-sets out on a neat lawn, and they have a skittle alley. *(Recommended by Gill Elston, John A Barker, Paul and Annette Hallett, Christina Dowsett, Theo, Anne and Jane Gaskin, John and Diana Head, Charles Gysin)*

Punch ~ Tenant Ian McKerracher ~ Real ale ~ Bar food (12-2.30, 6.30-9.30(9 Sun); not 25 Dec) ~ Restaurant ~ (01935) 862332 ~ Children welcome ~ Dogs welcome ~ Open 11-3, 6-11; 12-10.30 Sun ~ Bedrooms: £59S/£79S

EXFORD SS8538 Map 1
White Horse 🛏

B3224; TA24 7PY

The hands-on licensee and helpful staff have both been praised by readers visiting this substantial creeper-covered coaching inn in recent months. It's a pretty spot in summer, with the River Exe running past; there are tables outside to enjoy the view. The more or less open-plan bar has windsor and other country kitchen chairs, a high-backed antique settle, scrubbed deal tables, hunting prints, photographs above the stripped pine dado, and a good winter log fire; it can get very busy. Up to five real ales on handpump (fewer in winter), usually Exmoor Ale, Fox and Gold, Fullers London Pride and Greene King Old Speckled Hen, and a fine collection of malt whiskies, currently standing at around 150, but aiming for 200 by the end of 2006. Straightforward but very good value bar food includes sandwiches (from £2.25; filled baguettes from £3.50), home-made soup (£2.95), filled baked potatoes (from £3.25), ploughman's (from £4.25), cornish pasty (£4.65), breaded haddock (£4.75), smoked ham and egg (£4.95), steak in ale pie (£6.45), local trout (£8.25), steaks (from £8.95), specials like lamb shanks or poacher's pie (£6.95), and home-made puddings (£3.50); children's menu, three-course Sunday lunch (£11.95). They

do cream teas all day. The restaurant and eating area of the bar are no smoking.
They run daily Landrover 'safaris' of Exmoor's wildlife. Note the price we quote
for bedrooms is their standard rate – they often have cheaper rooms so it's worth
checking. Though the old coach road climbs from here up over Exmoor, the
attractive village itself is sheltered; the village green with children's play equipment
is next to the pub. *(Recommended by A and B D Craig, A S and M E Marriott, Stan and
Hazel Allen, Bob and Margaret Holder, Howard and Lorna Lambert, Lynda and Trevor Smith,
Rod and Chris Pring, Phil and Sally Gorton, Klaus and Elizabeth Leist, George Atkinson)*

Free house ~ Licensees Peter and Linda Hendrie ~ Real ale ~ Bar food (12-2.30, 6-9.30) ~
Restaurant ~ (01643) 831229 ~ Children welcome ~ Dogs allowed in bar and bedrooms
~ Open 11-11(12 Sat) ~ Bedrooms: £63B/£126B

FAULKLAND   ST7354   Map 2
Tuckers Grave ★ £
A366 E of village; BA3 5XF

Still claiming the title of Smallest Pub in the *Guide*, this very special place has an
atmosphere all of its own, and it's little wonder that so many of our most seasoned
correspondents consider it one of their all-time favourites. It's basic but warmly
friendly cider house, where nothing has changed for many years: the flagstoned
entry opens into a teeny unspoilt room with casks of Bass and Butcombe Bitter on
tap and Thatcher's Cheddar Valley cider in an alcove on the left. Two old cream-
painted high-backed settles face each other across a single table on the right, and a
side room has shove-ha'penny. There are winter fires and maybe newspapers to
read; also a skittle alley, and lots of tables and chairs on an attractive back lawn
with good views. Food is limited to sandwiches and ploughman's at lunchtime.
Several readers have commented on the attentiveness of the landlady, but it's also
the kind of place where the the locals are a key part of the pub's unique charms.
*(Recommended by Pete Baker, R Huggins, D Irving, E McCall, T McLean, Dr and Mrs
M E Wilson, Dr and Mrs A K Clarke, MLR, the Didler, Ian Phillips, Mike Ridgway, Sarah Miles)*

Free house ~ Licensees Ivan and Glenda Swift ~ Real ale ~ No credit cards ~
(01373) 834230 ~ Children in family room ~ Open 11.30-3, 6-11; 12-3, 7-10.30 Sun;
closed 25 Dec

HOLCOMBE   ST6649   Map 2
Ring o' Roses 🍴 🛏
Village signposted off A367 by War Memorial in Stratton-on-the-Fosse, S of Radstock;
BA3 5EB

Taking its name from the nursery-rhyme reminder of the plague that almost wiped
out the original village, this quietly placed and extensively modernised country pub
is well liked for its food and attentive, friendly service. The bar has flagstones, two
woodburning stoves, some orthodox cushioned captain's chairs around cast-iron-
framed pub tables, and a handsome counter facing attractively cushioned window
seats; behind is a gently lit parlourish area with sofas and cushioned chairs around
low tables. There are more easy chairs in a pleasant panelled lounge on the right,
and a good-sized dining area is nicely divided by balustrades and so forth, and has a
mix of old local scenes and more modern prints on the walls. Bar food is served at
lunchtimes only, from a sensibly organised menu where the choices cost the same –
starters like soup or beef and wild mushroom pâté are £4.95, sandwiches and
panini are £5.95, light meals such as chargrilled goats cheese brioche or asparagus
and gruyère tart are £6.95, and the main courses like pork stroganoff, sausage and
mash, honey-roasted ham with free-range egg, beer-battered haddock with broccoli
purée, and 8oz organic rump steak are all £8.95. The evening menu in the no
smoking restaurant has some of the same dishes (perhaps slightly more expensive)
as well as things like apricot-glazed roast duck with caramelised apples (£12.50)
and whole baked bass with tomato and herb compote (£13.50). Otter Ale and
Bitter on handpump, several wines by the glass, daily papers and piped music.
There are peaceful farmland views from picnic-sets on a terrace and on the lawn

around the side and back, with nice shrub plantings and a small rockery. The chocolate labrador is called Sam. Some bedrooms have good views – and readers have enjoyed their breakfasts. *(Recommended by M G Hart, Steve and Liz Tilley, Bruce and Sharon Eden, John A Barker, JCW, Doreen and Haydn Maddock, Ian Phillips, Malcolm Ward, Vince Lewington, S G N Bennett)*

Free house ~ Licensee Richard Rushton ~ Real ale ~ Bar food ~ Restaurant ~ (01761) 232478 ~ Children welcome ~ Dogs allowed in bar and bedrooms ~ Open 11.30-11; 11.30-2.30, 7-11 Sat; 12-2.30, 7-10.30 Sun; closed 26 Dec ~ Bedrooms: £65S(£65B)/£85B

HUISH EPISCOPI   ST4326   Map 1

Rose & Crown
Off A372 E of Langport; TA10 9QT

Known locally as 'Eli's' after the friendly landlady's father, this very unspoilt thatched pub has been in the same family for well over 140 years. It's a real step back in time, with a determinedly unpretentious atmosphere and character: there's no bar as such – to get a drink, you just walk into the central flagstoned still room and choose from the casks of Teignworthy Reel Ale and guests such as Hop Back GFB and Sharps Doombar. Also offering several farm ciders (and local cider brandy), this servery is the only thoroughfare between the casual little front parlours with their unusual pointed-arch windows – and genuinely friendly locals. Food is home-made, simple and cheap and uses local produce (and some home-grown fruit and vegetables): generously filled sandwiches (from £2.30), home-made soup (£2.90), filled baked potatoes (from £3.70), ploughman's (from £4.70), a vegetarian tart like stilton and broccoli (£6.25), cottage pie (£6.50), pork, cider and apple cobbler, chicken breast in a creamy white wine sauce or steak in ale pie (£6.75), and puddings such as sticky toffee pudding (£3.25); good helpful service. Shove-ha'penny, dominoes and cribbage, and a much more orthodox big back extension family room has pool, darts, fruit machine and juke box; skittle alley and popular quiz nights. One room is no smoking. There are tables in a garden, and a second enclosed garden with a children's play area. The welsh collie is called Bonny. Summer morris men, good nearby walks, and the site of the Battle of Langport (1645) is close by. *(Recommended by Pete Baker, Philip Kingsbury, Donna and Roger, the Didler, MLR, Steve and Liz Tilley, Lucy Osborn, Bruce Horsefield)*

Free house ~ Licensee Mrs Eileen Pittard ~ Real ale ~ Bar food (12-2, 5.30-7.30; not Sun evening) ~ No credit cards ~ (01458) 250494 ~ Children welcome ~ Dogs welcome ~ Folk singers every third Sat and Irish night fourth Thurs in month Sept-May ~ Open 11.30-2.30, 5.30-11; 11.30-11 Fri and Sat; 12-10.30 Sun; closed evening 25 Dec

KINGSDON   ST5126   Map 2

Kingsdon Inn 🍴
At Podimore roundabout junction of A303, A372 and A37 take A372, then turn right on to B3151, right into village, and right again opposite post office; TA11 7LG

Arriving at this very pretty old thatched cottage is rather like visiting a private house – you even walk up a path through the garden to a neatly painted door with a brass knocker. The newish licensees have settled in well: they've added a couple of bedrooms, and enthusiastic new reports have commented favourably on everything from the food to the welcome and the good, professional service (though we've not yet heard anything about the new bedrooms). There are four charmingly decorated, low-ceilinged rooms; on the right are some very nice old stripped pine tables with attractive cushioned farmhouse chairs, more seats in what was a small inglenook fireplace, a few low sagging beams, fresh flowers and newspapers, and an open woodburning stove. Down three steps through balustrading is a light, airy room with cushions on stripped pine built-in wall seats, more stripped pine tables, and a winter open fire, while a similarly decorated room has more tables and another fireplace. Well kept Butcombe, Otter and a guest like Bath Barnstormer on handpump, local cider, and up to a dozen wines by the glass. Well presented and generously served, good lunchtime meals might include tomato and basil soup (£3.80), grilled goats cheese salad (£5.50), ploughman's (£6.50), steak and kidney pie, chicken in cider, mushroom and cream sauce, poached salmon in parsley sauce or braised oxtail (all £7.95), and grilled rump steak (£10.50); in the evening things go up a notch, with things like leek and goats cheese bake (£9.20), wild rabbit in a dijon mustard sauce (£11.50), venison casseroled in red wine and junipers (£12.50), and seared fillet of bass in a fennel and cream sauce (£12.95). The Sunday lunch menu has a shorter choice (£7.40 one course, £9.90 two courses, £12.60 three courses). They take bookings only for big groups so it's worth arriving early for a table. The dining area and part of the bar are no moking. With picnic-sets on the grass in font, the pub is handy for Lytes Cary (National Trust) and the Fleet Air Arm Museum. *(Recommended by Gareth Lewis, Mike and Heather Watson, R G Trevis, Clare West, Ian Phillips, Julie Walton, Mike Gorton, KC, Edward Mirzoeff, Colin and Peggy Wilshire, Mrs Angela McArt, M G Hart, Liz and Tony Colman, Sylvia and Tony Birbeck, Mrs Ann Webb, Lucy Osborn, Bruce Horsefield, Simon Jones, Charles Gysin, Stuart Paulley, John and Angela Main, Malcolm Ward, Mr and Mrs A Silver, John and Jane Hayter, Brian P White, Michael Doswell)*

Free house ~ Licensees Bob and Carole Horler ~ Real ale ~ Bar food ~ Restaurant ~ (01935) 840543 ~ Children in restaurant ~ Open 12-3.30, 6.30-11.30; 12-3.30, 7-10.30 Sun; closed 1 Jan ~ Bedrooms: £45S(£45B)/£70S(£70B)

LANGLEY MARSH ST0729 Map 1
Three Horseshoes ㉕ ◖
Village signposted off B3227 from Wiveliscombe; TA4 2UL

Already completely no smoking, this nicely old-fashioned and traditional red sandstone pub is tucked away in the Somerset hills. The back bar has low modern settles and polished wooden tables, dark red wallpaper, planes hanging from the ceiling, bank notes papering the wall behind the bar counter, a piano, and a local stone fireplace. Well kept Otter Bitter, Palmers IPA, St Austell Tribute and Youngs Bitter tapped from the cask, and farm cider. Highly praised by readers in recent months, the bar food includes sandwiches, soups like courgette and mushroom or broccoli and stilton (£3), baguette-style pizzas (from £5.50), steaks (from £9.75), and daily specials such as cheesy leek stuffed courgette (£6.75), pork tenderloin in port and stilton or free-range chicken breast topped with mozzarella in a herby white wine sauce (£8.75), lamb steak with fresh mint and yoghurt (£9.25), pan-fried scallops with mushrooms, wine and garlic sauce (£10.25), and seared tuna loin on a bed of spiced pasta and smoked vegetables (£11.25). The dining area has antique settles, tables and benches; dominoes, cribbage, shove-ha'penny, table skittles, separate skittle alley and piped music. You can sit on rustic seats on the verandah or in the attractive sloping back garden; in fine weather there are often vintage cars outside. They offer self-catering (and maybe bed and breakfast if they are not already booked up). *(Recommended by Bob and Margaret Holder, Irene King, the Didler, J Stickland, Brian Monaghan, Peter Mack Wilkins)*

Free house ~ Licensee John Hopkins ~ Real ale ~ Bar food (12-1.45, 7-9; in winter not Mon or Sun evening) ~ (01984) 623763 ~ No children under 8 inside ~ Open 12-2.30, 7-11; 12-2.30, 7-10.30 (9 in winter) Sun; closed winter Mons; plus first two weeks of July

LITTON ST5954 Map 2
Kings Arms
B3114, NW of Chewton Mendip on A39 Bath—Wells; BA3 4PW

Mr and Mrs Nicholls successfully ran one of our Somerset main entries a few years back, so we are pretty confident that this partly 15th-c pub is in very good hands. There's a big entrance hall with polished flagstones, and bars lead off to the left with low heavy beams and more flagstones; a nice bit on the right beyond the huge fireplace has a big old-fashioned settle and a mix of other settles and wheelback chairs. Throughout there are nice paintings, four open fires, a full suit of armour in one alcove and the rooms are divided up into areas by standing timbers. Popular bar food at lunchtime and early evening includes ploughman's, ham and eggs, sirloin baguette, lamb and coriander burger, sausage and onion gravy or faggots and mash (all £7.95 – though from Monday to Thursday in the early evening, the time you order is the price you pay); there's also chicken caesar salad (£6.45; main course £13.95), chargrilled loin of fresh yellowfin tuna niçoise (£7.95; main course £14.95), seared szechuan peppered foie gras, griottine and toasted citrus brioche (£9.95), butternut squash risotto (£11.95), chicken or beef curry (£12.95), pork loin on raisin mash, bramley sauce and cinnamon apple fritters (£13.95), aberdeen angus fillet steak with caramelised shallots and claret thyme jus (£18.95), and home-made puddings like lavender panna cotta with strawberry and rose petal syrup, dark chocolate and raspberry brownie with chocolate ice-cream and raspberry coulis and sticky toffee pudding with toffee ice-cream (£5.95). The eating areas are no smoking; piped music. Greene King IPA, Abbot and Ruddles County on handpump. The terrace overlooking the River Chew has plenty of wooden tables and chairs; pétanque. *(Recommended by Liz and Tony Colman, Chris and Ann Coy, Rod and Chris Pring)*

Greene King ~ Lease Will and Mary Nicholls ~ Real ale ~ Bar food (12-2(3 Sun), 7-9(6.30-9.30 summer weekends)) ~ Restaurant ~ (01761) 241301 ~ Children welcome ~ Dogs allowed in bar ~ Open 11.30-11; 12-10.30 Sun

LOVINGTON ST5930 Map 2

Pilgrims Rest 🍴 ♀

B3153 Castle Cary—Keinton Mandeville; BA7 7PT

With the emphasis very much on the top quality food cooked by the landlord, this quietly placed and civilised country bar/bistro is rather upmarket, but not in a stuffy way: there's a relaxed, chatty atmosphere, and a nice unhurried feel – even on busy nights they won't rush you with your food. Totally no smoking, the bar has a few stools by a corner counter, a rack of daily papers, nice wines by the glass and Cottage Champflower on handpump, from the nearby brewery. A cosy little dark green inner area has sunny modern country and city prints, a couple of shelves of books and china, a cushioned pew, a couple of settees and an old leather easy chair by the big fireplace. With flagstones throughout, this runs into the compact eating area, with candles on tables and some stripped stone; piped music. Using local produce and daily fresh fish, the lunchtime menu might include open sandwiches or soup (£5), a tart of various mushrooms sautéed in garlic, white wine and mascarpone (£6), good cheeses with biscuits or a hunk of their own bread (£7), a hearty fish soup (£8), and wild boar and herb sausages with savoy cabbage and bacon, with à la carte dishes such as vegetarian paella (£12), sirloin steak with green peppercorn and anchovy butter (£16), grilled and flambéed lemon sole with a dash of Noilly Prat (£17), rack of lamb with a rich redcurrant gravy (£19), and monkfish and scallops sautéed with smoked bacon and wild mushrooms (£23); they do smaller helpings of most things, including their two-course Sunday lunch (£16 full helping, £12 smaller). There's also a separate, more formal carpeted dining room. The landlady's service is efficient and friendly. The enclosed garden has tables, chairs and umbrellas on a decked terrace. The car park exit has its own traffic lights – on your way out line your car up carefully or you may wait for ever for them to change. *(Recommended by Roger White, Mrs J H S Lang, Brenda and Stuart Naylor, A Warren, Ian and Nita Cooper, Michael Doswell, John and Diana Head, Paul and Annette Hallett, Julian and Jennifer Clapham)*

Free house ~ Licensees Sally and Jools Mitchison ~ Real ale ~ Bar food (see opening hours) ~ Restaurant ~ (01963) 240597 ~ Children welcome ~ Dogs allowed in bar ~ Open 12-2.30, 7-11; closed Sun evening, all day Mon and Tues, plus first week of May and first two weeks of October

---

Half pints: by law, a pub should not charge more for half a pint than half the price of a full pint, unless it shows that half-pint price on its price list.

LUXBOROUGH   SS9837   Map 1

Royal Oak 🛏

Kingsbridge; S of Dunster on minor roads into Brendon Hills – OS Sheet 181 map reference 983378; TA23 0SH

In the heart of Exmoor, this is a fine place to stay, with enjoyable food and a particularly warm welcome from staff who go out of their way to make visits special. Recently sensitively refurbished, the bar rooms date back to the 14th c, and have beams and inglenooks, good log fires, flagstones in the front public bar, a fishing theme in one room, and a real medley of furniture; the three dining rooms are no smoking. Well kept Cotleigh Tawny, Exmoor Gold and Palmers IPA and 200 on handpump, local farm ciders and a good range of malt whiskies. Lunchtime bar food might include filled baguettes or rustic herb bread (from £4.95), ploughman's (£5.95), lamb kofta kebabs with mint yoghurt (£6.75), and deep-fried dahl cakes (£7.25), while the fuller menu has daily specials such as roast fillet of salmon with steamed mussels and parsnip crisps (£13.25), grilled rib-eye steak with stilton sauce or roast chicken breast wrapped in streaky bacon with pea and ham purée (£13.75), seared cornish scallops with sweet chilli sauce (£13.95), and venison and foie gras wellington with redcurrant sauce (£14.95). No music or machines; darts, dominoes and board games. If you're staying, expect comfortable bedrooms and good, generous breakfasts. There are tables out in the charming back courtyard, and lots of surrounding walks, notably the recently opened Coleridge Way. *(Recommended by A S and M E Marriott, C J Pratt, David Crook, Bob and Margaret Holder, the Didler, John and Gloria Isaacs, Mr and Mrs Peter Larkman, Mrs Ann Webb, Peter Mack Wilkins, Helen Sharpe, Paul and Sue Dix)*

Free house ~ Licensees James and Sian Waller and Sue Hinds ~ Real ale ~ Bar food ~ Restaurant ~ (01984) 640319 ~ Children in dining rooms and bedrooms only ~ Dogs allowed in bar and bedrooms ~ Open 12-2.30, 6 (7 Sun)-11; closed 25 Dec ~ Bedrooms: £55B/£60(£65B)

MELLS   ST7249   Map 2

Talbot 🛏

W of Frome; off A362 W of Buckland Dinham, or A361 via Nunney and Whatley; BA11 3PN

Another favourite with readers, this interesting old inn opens on to a very pleasant cobbled courtyard and vine-covered pergola. The public bar is in a carefully restored tithe barn opposite here, with old beams under the high ceiling, banners on the stone walls, and a big mural behind the counter. Butcombe, and in summer Fullers London Pride, are tapped from the cask, and there's shove ha'penny, darts and cribbage. Back in the main building, the attractive no smoking dining room has stripped pews, mate's and wheelback chairs, fresh flowers and candles in bottles on the mix of tables, and sporting and riding pictures on the walls, which are partly stripped above a broad panelled dado, and partly rough terracotta-colour. A small corridor leads to a nice little reception with an open fire, and on to restaurant rooms with solid oak tables, high-backed settles and wheelback chairs on a rough pine floor. The good food at lunchtime might include home-made soup (£4.75), chicken liver parfait with red onion marmalade (£6.50), ploughman's (£8.50), ham and free-range eggs (£8.65), and confit leg of barbary duck on celeriac mash with peppercorn and cranberry sauce (£10.95), with evening choices such as caramelised shallot tart with grilled goats cheese (£12.50), rabbit, pork and cider pie (£13.95), pan-fried calves liver with horseradish mash, smoked bacon and red wine and shallot jus (£14.25), roast fillet of pork with braised red cabbage and chilli plum sauce (£15.75), and fish specials like whole baked bream with spring onions, ginger and garlic (£14.25) and grilled lemon sole (£16.50); choice of Sunday roasts (the beef comes rare). Friendly service from hard-working staff. The village was purchased by the Horner family of the 'Little Jack Horner' nursery rhyme and the direct descendants still live in the manor house next door. *(Recommended by Ian Phillips, Kath and Ted Warren, Richard and Lynn Seers, Gaynor Gregory, Martin Hatcher,*

Clive and Geraldine Barber, David Hoult, Anthony Barnes, Clare Rosier, Graham Holden, Julie Lee)

Free house ~ Licensee Roger Stanley Elliott ~ Real ale ~ Bar food (12-2, 6.30-9) ~ Restaurant ~ (01373) 812254 ~ Children welcome ~ Dogs allowed in bedrooms ~ Open 12-2.30, 6.30-11; 12-3, 6.30-10.30 Sun ~ Bedrooms: £75B/£95B

MONKSILVER ST0737 Map 1

Notley Arms

B3188; TA4 4JB

The good, generously served food at this bustling nicely set pub has a real emphasis on fresh, local produce, and the menu lists the suppliers of everything from their meats, fish and cheese to the ice-cream, potatoes and eggs. A typical choice includes soups like sweet potato and horseradish (£3.95), half a pint of smoked prawns (£5.95), hot stuffed pitta breads (£6.25), panini (£6.50), ham, egg and chips with piccalilli or apple chutney (£7.50), local cheddar and caramelised onion tart or toad in the hole (£7.65), good steaks (£10.75), ostrich steak (£13.95), and changing specials like spicy bean and spinach burgers, venison and red wine casserole, or chicken, coconut and lime curry (£8.95), and pesto and pecorino cheese salmon fillet with fresh local asparagus (£10.50). Good service from the friendly staff and attentive landlord. They can get busy, even midweek and out of season. The beamed and L-shaped bar has small settles and kitchen chairs around the plain country wooden and candlelit tables, original paintings on the ochre-coloured walls, fresh flowers, and a couple of woodburning stoves. Bath Ale, Exmoor Ale and Wadworths 6X on handpump, and farm ciders; cribbage, dominoes and alley skittles. There's a bright no smoking little family room (an area near the food servery is no smoking too). The immaculate garden has plenty of tables, and runs down to a swift clear stream. This is a lovely village. *(Recommended by Peter and Margaret Glenister, the Didler, Mrs D W Privett, Karen Eliot, Mr and Mrs D J Nash, Jeremy Whitehorn, George Atkinson)*

Unique (Enterprise) ~ Lease Russell and Jane Deary ~ Real ale ~ Bar food ~ (01984) 656217 ~ Children in family room if well behaved ~ Dogs welcome ~ Open 12-2.30, 6.30-11; 12-2.30, 7-10.30 Sun; closed Mon lunchtime (all day Mon in winter)

NORTH CURRY ST3225 Map 1

Bird in Hand

Queens Square; off A378 (or A358) E of Taunton; TA3 6LT

Despite its reputation for food, this well run village pub always has seats for drinkers. The bustling but cosy main bar has some nice old pews, settles, benches and old yew tables on the flagstones, original beams and timbers, some locally woven willow work, and a cheerful atmosphere; cricketing memorabilia, and a log fire in the inglenook fireplace. Readers have been impressed by the friendly welcome and service over the last year. As well as sandwiches, and ploughman's with three west country cheeses (£5.95), the daily changing blackboard menus might include bubble and squeak (£5.75), moules marinière or pan-fried scallops and bacon salad (£7.50), mediterranean vegetable kebabs with tomato and basil sauce (£7.75), pork fillet medallions with grain mustard sauce (£10.95), grilled marlin with lime, chilli and coriander (£13.95), rack of lamb with hot mint and red wine sauce or venison steak in a port, orange and redcurrant sauce (£14.95), home-made puddings, and Sunday roasts; meals are generously served. The restaurant is no smoking. Otter Ale and a couple of guests like Badger Fursty Ferret and Fullers London Pride on handpump, Rich's farm cider, and eight wines by the glass. Piped music and fruit machine. *(Recommended by Roger Wain-Heapy, Brian and Bett Cox, Dennis and Gill Keen, Bob and Margaret Holder, Dr and Mrs M E Wilson, Di and Mike Gillam, John and Gloria Isaacs, Stephen and Jean Curtis)*

Free house ~ Licensee James Mogg ~ Real ale ~ Bar food ~ Restaurant ~ (01823) 490248 ~ Children welcome ~ Dogs allowed in bar ~ Open 12-3, 6-11.30; 12-4, 6-12 Sat; 12-3, 7-11.30 Sun; closed evening 25 Dec

NORTON ST PHILIP   ST7755   Map 2

George 🛏

A366; BA2 7LH

The building itself is the main draw here; a pub for nearly 600 years, it's a remarkable old place, very impressive as you approach, and no less interesting inside. The central Norton Room, which was the original bar, has really heavy beams, an oak panelled settle and solid dining chairs on the narrow strip wooden floor, a variety of 18th-c pictures, an open fire in the handsome stone fireplace, and a low wooden bar counter. Wadworths IPA, 6X and perhaps a seasonal guest on handpump, and pleasant service. As you enter the building, there's a room on the right with high dark beams, squared dark half-panelling, a broad carved stone fireplace with an old iron fireback and pewter plates on the mantelpiece, a big mullioned window with leaded lights, and a round oak 17th-c table reputed to have been used by the Duke of Monmouth who stayed here before the Battle of Sedgemoor – after their defeat, his men were imprisoned in what is now the Monmouth Bar. The Charterhouse Bar is mostly used by those enjoying a drink before a meal: a wonderful pitched ceiling with trusses and timbering, heraldic shields and standards, jousting lances, and swords on the walls, a fine old stone fireplace, high backed cushioned heraldic-fabric dining chairs on the big rug over the wood plank floor, and an oak dresser with some peweter. Bar food includes moussaka, sausages and mash, ham and egg, chicken curry, and a cold meat or cheese platter with pickles (all £7.50), while the full menu takes in home-made soup (£4.95), goats cheese and caramelised onion tartlet (£5.45), mixed nut and red lentil roast (£9.95), home-made steak and mushroom in ale pie (£10.95), fillet of local trout with toasted almonds (£11.95), and half a duck with sage and onion stuffing or rib-eye steak marinated in tabasco and chilli (£13.95). The no smoking dining room (a restored barn with original oak ceiling beams, a pleasant if haphazard mix of early 19th-c portraits and hunting prints, and the same mix of vaguely old-looking furnishings) has a good relaxing, chatty atmosphere. The bedrooms are very atmospheric and comfortable – some reached by an external Norman stone stair-turret, and some across the cobbled and flagstoned courtyard and up into a fine half-timbered upper gallery (where there's a lovely 18th-c carved oak settle). A stroll over the meadow behind the pub (past the picnic-sets on the narrow grass pub garden) leads to an attractive churchyard around the medieval church whose bells struck Pepys (here on 12 June 1668) as 'mighty tuneable'. *(Recommended by Alain and Rose Foote, Klaus and Elizabeth Leist, R Huggins, D Irving, E McCall, T McLean, Donna and Roger, the Didler, Rod and Chris Pring, W K Wood, Ian Phillips, Michael Hasslacher, H W Roberts, Mark and Mary Fairman, J Stickland, Warren Marsh)*

Wadworths ~ Managers David and Tania Satchell ~ Real ale ~ Bar food ~ Restaurant ~ (01373) 834224 ~ Well behaved children welcome ~ Dogs allowed in bar ~ Open 11.30-2.30, 5.30-11; 11-11 Sat; 12-10.30 Sun; closed evenings 25 Dec and 1 Jan ~ Bedrooms: £60B/£80B

OAKE   ST1526   Map 1

Royal Oak

Hillcommon, N; B3227 W of Taunton; if coming from Taunton, ignore signpost on left for Oake and go 200 yards, pub is on left directly off B3227; TA4 1DS

This neatly kept country pub is particularly busy at lunchtime on Tuesdays, Thursdays and Sundays when they have a very good value carvery, with reductions for OAPs. The spacious bar has several separate-seeming areas around the central servery; on the left is a little tiled fireplace, with a big woodburning stove on the other side. The windows have smart curtains, there are plenty of fresh flowers, and lots of brasses on the beams and walls. At the back is a long dining area which leads out to a pleasant sheltered garden. Tables are candlelit in the evenings. Cotleigh Tawny, RCH Pitchfork, Sharps Doombar and a guest like Archers Special on handpump, and several wines by the glass; cheerful service. Lunchtime bar food includes baguettes (from £4.95), filled baked potatoes (from £5.25), ploughman's

(£6.95), breaded plaice and home-made curry or lasagne (£7.95), and a good few
daily specials, with evening choices such as sausages with cheese and spring onion
mash (£8.95), cajun chicken on onion and lime marmalade or thai fishcakes (£9.95),
and steaks (from £10.95); children's menu. Skittle alley in winter, and piped music.
*(Recommended by Bob and Margaret Holder, Christine and Neil Townend, Andy and Jill Smith,
Theo, Anne and Jane Gaskin, John and Fiona McIlwain, Richard and Sheila Brooks)*

Free house ~ Licensee Angela Gibbons ~ Real ale ~ Bar food (12-2, 6.30-9) ~
(01823) 400295 ~ Children in restaurant ~ Open 12-3, 6-11; 12-11.30 Sat; 12-11 Sun

PITNEY ST4428 Map 1
Halfway House 🍺
Just off B3153 W of Somerton; TA10 9AB

A warmly friendly, traditional village local, this busy place has an excellent range of
changing real ales, with between eight and ten on at any one time; regular beers
tapped from the cask include Branscombe Vale Branoc, Butcombe Bitter, Hop Back
Crop Circle and Summer Lightning, and Teignworthy Reel Ale, with guests like
Archers Golden, Bath Spa and Otter Bright. They also have 20 or so continental
bottled beers, Wilkins' farm cider, and a dozen malt whiskies; cribbage, dominoes
and board games. There's a good mix of people chatting at communal tables in the
three old-fashioned rooms, all with roaring log fires and a homely feel underlined
by a profusion of books, maps and newspapers; it can get a bit smoky. Good simple
filling food includes sandwiches (from £2.95), soup (£3.50), filled baked potatoes
(from £3.45), a fine ploughman's with home-made pickle (£5.50) and specials like
lamb stew with dumplings (£6.95), and fish pie (£7.50); in the evening they do
about half a dozen home-made curries (from £7.95). There are tables outside.
*(Recommended by Guy Vowles, John and Gloria Isaacs, the Didler, Theo, Anne and Jane
Gaskin, Mrs Ann Webb, Lucy Osborn, Bruce Horsefield, Peter Meister)*

Free house ~ Licensee Julian Lichfield ~ Real ale ~ Bar food (not Sun) ~ (01458) 252513 ~
Children welcome ~ Dogs allowed in bar ~ Open 11.30-3, 5.30-11(12 Sat); 12-3, 7-11 Sun;
closed 25 Dec

PORTISHEAD ST4777 Map 1
Windmill 🍺
3.7 miles from M5 junction 19; A369 into town, then follow 'Sea Front' sign off left and into Nore Road; BS20 6JZ

Once a golf club-house, this bustling three-level family dining pub has a marvellous
view in fine weather from the wall of picture windows on the top and bottom
floors, looking out over the Bristol Channel to Newport and Cardiff (with the
bridges on the right). An efficient mealtime stop from the motorway, it's by no
means a traditional village pub and is hardly undiscovered: when the car park fills
up you have to park in a nearby field. The bottom floor is a simple easy-going no
smoking family area, the top one a shade more elegant with its turkey carpet,
muted green and cream wallpaper and dark panelled dado. The middle floor, set
back from here, is quieter and (with its black-painted ceiling boards) more softly lit.
A third of the building is no smoking; fruit machine. To eat, you find a numbered
table, present yourself at the order desk (by a slimline pudding show-cabinet), pay
for your order, and return to the table with a tin (well, stainless steel) tray of
cutlery, condiments and sauce packets. It works well: the good value generous food
then comes quickly, and might include home-made soup (£3.25), sandwiches (from
£3.50), filled baked potatoes (from £3.95), ploughman's (£4.95), spinach and red
pepper lasagne (£7.50), home-made steak and mushroom in ale pie (£8.25), daily
specials such as faggots (£6.95), lambs liver (£7.25), home-made curry (£7.75), and
lamb shank (£9.50); there are dishes for smaller appetites (from £3.65) and early
bird offers. Unexpectedly, they have six quickly changing real ales on handpump,
such as Bass, Butcombe Gold, Courage Best, RCH Pitchfork and two guest beers.
Out on the seaward side are picnic-sets on three tiers of lantern-lit terrace.
(Recommended by P Price, Tom Evans, B and M Kendall, Andrea and Guy Bradley)

Free house ~ Licensee J S Churchill ~ Real ale ~ Bar food (all day) ~ (01275) 843677 ~
Children in eating area of bar and family room ~ Dogs allowed in bar ~ Open 11-11;
12-10.30 Sun

SHEPTON MONTAGUE   ST6731   Map 2

Montague Inn ♀
Village signposted just off A359 Bruton—Castle Cary; BA9 8JW

This busy little country pub is doing well under its newish licensees, who readers
have particularly praised for their friendly welcome and helpful service. Recently
redecorated, the rooms are simply but tastefully furnished with stripped wooden
tables and kitchen chairs, and a log fire in the attractive inglenook fireplace; the
restaurant has french windows overlooking the pretty back terrace and gardens,
now tidied up with clearer views. Using regional and often organic ingredients, the
bar food is made fresh every day (they don't have a freezer), and might include
lunchtime sandwiches and ploughman's, soup (£3.95), good seared scallops with
avocado and bacon salad (£8.75), confit of duck (£13.50), 10oz rump steak
(£16.50), and a daily special like hotpot or chicken and ham pie (£6.95).
Butcombe, Greene King IPA and a local guest like Hidden Brewery Hidden Quest
tapped from the cask, local cider and a big varied wine list, with a good choice by
the glass. *(Recommended by Katharine Cowherd, Clare West, Mrs Christa Sansom, Colin and
Janet Roe, Paul and Annette Hallett, Mrs J H S Lang, Dennis and Gill Keen, David and
Ruth Hollands, Fergus Dowding, Edward Mirzoeff, OPUS, Glen and Nola Armstrong,
H G H Stafford)*

Free house ~ Licensee Sean O'Callaghan ~ Bar food (not Sun evening, Mon) ~ Restaurant
~ (01749) 813213 ~ Children welcome ~ Dogs allowed in bar ~ Open 12-3, 6-11;
closed evenings Sun and all day Mon ~ Bedrooms: /£75S

STANTON WICK   ST6162   Map 2

Carpenters Arms 🍴 ♀ 🛏
Village signposted off A368, just W of junction with A37 S of Bristol; BS39 4BX

In peaceful countryside, with pretty flowerbeds and lovely hanging baskets and tubs
outside, this attractive and neatly kept low tile-roofed inn is a civilised dining pub
with a helpful, friendly landlord. At lunchtimes during the week (when it may be
worth booking), it's full of mostly retirement-age diners enjoying food such as
home-made soup (£3.95), sandwiches (from £5.50), caesar salad with anchovy
dressing (£5.50), warm smoked duck with poached pear and stilton (£5.95),
lunchtime sausages and mash or smoked haddock and spinach omelette (£7.95),
steak, mushroom and ale pie or roast pepper filled with mediterranean vegetables
and topped with goats cheese (£9.95), baked salmon on linguini with tomato, red
onion, garlic and oregano (£10.50), thai chicken curry or roast pork loin on apple
mash with cider and sage jus (£11.95), and specials like roast lamb with mint jus
(£10.95) or seared fillet of sesame tuna with rocket and bacon salad (£12.95). They
may ask you to leave your credit card behind the bar. All areas except the bar are
now no smoking. The Coopers Parlour on the right has one or two beams, seats
around heavy tables, and attractive curtains and plants in the windows; on the
angle between here and the bar area there's a fat woodburning stove in an opened-
through corner fireplace. The bar has wood-backed built-in wall seats and some
leather fabric-cushioned stools, stripped stone walls, and a big log fire. There's also
a snug inner room (lightened by mirrors in arched 'windows') and a refurbished
restaurant with leather sofas and easy chairs in a comfortable lounge area.
Butcombe, Courage Best and Wadworths 6X on handpump, ten wines by the glass,
and a dozen malt whiskies; fruit machine and TV. There are picnic-sets on the front
terrace. *(Recommended by MRSM, Richard and Judy Winn, Dr and Mrs A K Clarke, Dr and
Mrs C W Thomas, Andrew Shore, Maria Williams, M G Hart, Ian Phillips, John and
Fiona McIlwain, Peter Mack Wilkins, Alan and Paula McCully, Barry and Anne, B N F and
M Parkin, Pat and Tony Martin, Angus and Rosemary Campbell)*

Buccaneer Holdings ~ Manager Simon Pledge ~ Real ale ~ Bar food (12-2, 7-10;

12-2.30, 7-9.30 Sun) ~ Restaurant ~ (01761) 490202 ~ Children welcome ~ Dogs allowed
in bar ~ Pianist Fri and Sat evenings ~ Open 11-11; 12-10.30 Sun; closed evenings
25 and 26 Dec ~ Bedrooms: £67S(£67B)/£95S(£95B)

STOKE ST GREGORY   ST3527   Map 1

Rose & Crown 🍴 ☲

Woodhill; follow North Curry signpost off A378 by junction with A358 – keep on to
Stoke, bearing right in centre, passing church and follow lane for ½ mile; TA3 6EW

A thriving family business, this bustling country pub has a cheerful, friendly feel,
and is well liked for its food. Not smart (even some of its staunchest supporters this
year felt a tidying-up was probably in order), the cosy bar is decorated in a pleasant
stable theme: dark wooden loose-box partitions for some of the interestingly angled
nooks and alcoves, lots of brasses and bits on the low beams and joists, stripped
stonework, a wonky floor, and appropriate pictures including a highland pony
carrying a stag. Many of the wildlife paintings on the walls are the work of the
landlady, and there's an 18th-c glass-covered well in one corner. The two rooms of
the dining area lead off here with lots of country prints and paintings of hunting
scenes, animals and birds on the walls, more horsebrasses, jugs and mugs hanging
from the ceiling joists, and candles in bottles on all tables. At lunchtime, the food
includes soup (£3.75), good sandwiches on home-made granary bread (from
£4.25), ploughman's (from £4.75), home-cooked ham and eggs (£5.95), beer-
battered haddock with mushy peas (£7.25), salads and steaks (from £7.50), grilled
lambs liver and bacon (£8.50), and daily specials; evening choices such as goats
cheese and pecan salad with honey and mustard vinaigrette (£5.25), crab cakes
with sweet chilli (£6.50), vegetable stroganoff (£8.50), chicken breast with a port,
stilton and cream sauce (£11.50), half a crispy duck with plum and apricot sauce
(£13.50), red snapper fillet with a spicy cream and lemon sauce (£14.50), and
home-made puddings like apple and blackberry crumble (from £3.75); helpful,
polite service. The restaurants are no smoking. Butcombe, Exmoor Ale and Otter
on handpump, and decent wines; piped music and fruit machine. Under cocktail
parasols by an apple tree on the sheltered front terrace are some picnic-sets.
Readers who've stayed in the modest bedrooms don't rate them as highly as they do
the food or atmosphere. The pub is in an interesting Somerset Levels village with
willow beds still supplying the two basket works. (Recommended by Paul and Sue Dix,
Bob and Margaret Holder, Geoff and Sylvia Donald, Revd D E and Mrs J A Shapland,
Donna and Roger, Peter Mack Wilkins, Duncan Cloud, Ken Marshall, Mrs Ann Webb,
Michael Hasslacher, Theo, Anne and Jane Gaskin)

Free house ~ Licensees Stephen, Sally, Richard and Leonie Browning ~ Real ale ~
Bar food ~ Restaurant ~ (01823) 490296 ~ Children welcome ~ Dogs allowed in bar ~
Open 11-3, 6.30-11; 12-3, 7-10.30 Sun; closed evening 25 Dec ~ Bedrooms:
£36.50(£46.50B)/£53(£73B)

TARR   SS8632   Map 1

Tarr Farm 🛏

Tarr Steps – rather narrow road off B3223 N of Dulverton, very little nearby parking
(paying car park quarter-mile up road); OS Sheet 181 map reference 868322 – as the
inn is on the E bank, don't be tempted to approach by car from the W unless you can
cope with a deep ford; TA22 9PY

The setting is glorious, an Exmoor hillside looking down on Tarr Steps just below –
that much-photographed clapper bridge of massive granite slabs for medieval
packhorses crossing the River Barle as it winds through this lightly wooded combe.
Given the site, the inn does get very busy even out of season, but they work hard
here to keep their customers happy. The pub part consists of a line of compact and
unpretentious rooms, with plenty of good views, slabby rustic tables, stall seating,
wall seats and pub chairs, a woodburning stove at one end, salmon pink walls, nice
game bird pictures and a pair of stuffed pheasants. The serving bar up a step or two
has Exmoor Ale and St Austell on handpump, eight wines by the glass and a good

choice of other drinks. A wide range of food includes sandwiches such as local cheese or bacon and brie (from £3.95), soup (£3.95), caesar salad (£5.95), gnocchi with roasted vegetables, parmesan and tomato sauce (£7.95), lamb tagine (£9.95), rib-eye steak (£13.95) and puddings such as apple and gooseberry crumble or poached pear with chocolate mousse (£3.50). They do popular cream teas. The residents' end has a smart little evening restaurant, and a pleasant log-fire lounge with dark leather armchairs and sofas. Outside, lots of chaffinches hop around between slate-topped stone tables above the steep lawn. *(Recommended by JJW, CMW, Stan and Hazel Allen, John and Jackie Chalcraft, Gavin and Helen Griggs, Dr Ian S Morley)*

Free house ~ Licensees Richard Benn and Judy Carless ~ Real ale ~ Bar food (12-3; cream teas 11-5) ~ Restaurant ~ (01643) 851507 ~ Children over 10 in bedrooms and evenings ~ Dogs allowed in bar and bedrooms ~ Open 11-11; closed one week beginning Feb ~ Bedrooms: £80B/£130B

TRISCOMBE ST1535 Map 1
Blue Ball 🍴 ♗

Village signposted off A358 Crowcombe—Bagborough; turn off opposite sign to youth hostel; OS Sheet 181 map reference 155355; TA4 3HE

The current licensees of this 15th-c thatched stone-built building will have been here only about a year when this edition of the *Guide* is published, but already they've won several regional awards for their food. The emphasis these days is more than ever on the dining side (leaving some readers who've visited before slightly disappointed), so you'll generally find most tables given over to eating – and at busy times like weekends you may need to book to be sure of getting one. On the first floor of the original stables, it's a smart place, sloping down gently on three levels, each with its own fire, and cleverly divided into seating by hand-cut beech partitions. Relying very much on carefully sourced ingredients from smaller local farms (suppliers are listed on the menu), the changing choice of food might at lunchtime include soups like pumpkin and white onion (£3.95), filled rolls (from £5.50), ploughman's (£6.95), venison sausages with mash and redcurrant jam (£8.95), tomato tarte tatin with goats cheese (£10.95), pork with pan haggerty and Cotleigh Tawny juices (£12.50), and pigeon breast with creamed savoy and carrots (£12.95), with evening dishes such as organic salmon fillet with spinach and fennel cream (£12.95), and cannon of lamb with turnip gratin and red wine juices (£14.95); Sunday lunches. All dining areas are no smoking. The food is cooked to order, and some readers have experienced delays. Cotleigh Tawny, and a couple of guests like Exmoor Gold, Otter or St Austell HSD, and good wines by the glass. The decking at the top of the woodside, terraced garden makes the most of the views. As we went to press they told us they were hoping to open on Mondays soon. *(Recommended by Mr and Mrs D Scott, Bob and Margaret Holder, Gaynor Gregory, Gordon and Jay Smith, Michael and Catherine Mills, Canon Michael Bourdeaux, Peter and Giff Bennett, Peter Mack Wilkins, Trevor and Diane Waite, Pete Devonish, Ian McIntyre, John and Jane Hayter, Mrs Jill Wyatt, Rod and Chris Pring)*

Free house ~ Licensees Sue and Gerald Rogers ~ Real ale ~ Bar food (12-1.45, 7-8.45; not Sun evening or Mon) ~ Restaurant ~ (01984) 618242 ~ Well behaved children welcome ~ Dogs allowed in bar ~ Open 12-3, 7-11(10.30 Sun); closed Mon (exc bank hols) but see text ~ Bedrooms: £40B/£60B

WELLS ST5545 Map 2
City Arms ⚑

High Street; BA5 2AG

Opening early for breakfast, then usefully serving food for the rest of the day, this 16th-c building was originally a jail, and you can still see a couple of small, barred windows in the courtyard. It's been extensively refurbished in recent years, with a new first floor terrace in the cobbled courtyard, and plenty of new furnishings. The main bar operates as a café-bar/patisserie during the day and a bistro at night, and they have two kitchens to cope with demand. Bar food includes sandwiches (from

£2.80), home-made soup (£2.95), home-made chicken liver pâté with home-made bread (£3.95), grilled goats cheese with chargrilled aubergine and balsamic dressing (£5.75), fish pie (£6.50), pan-fried lambs liver with smoked bacon or chargrilled cajun chicken (£7.95), steak and ale pie (£8.45), aberdeen angus steaks (from £10.50), evening extras like pork loin with apple and cider cream sauce, and fish specials such as shetland trout with cracked black pepper butter (£6.95) and monkfish medallions in prawn and ginger sauce (£8.95). They keep six real ales on handpump: Butcombe Bitter, Gold and Blond, Greene King Abbot, Moles Rucking Mole, Sharps Doom Bar or Wadworths IPA. Also, 15 wines by the glass, 30 malt whiskies, and four draught ciders; various coffees. The restaurant and main bar are no smoking; piped music, cribbage and dominoes. More reports please.
(Recommended by Hugh Roberts, Henry and Fiona Dryden)

Free house ~ Licensee Jim Hardy ~ Real ale ~ Bar food (all day till 10pm Mon-Thurs, 6pm Fri-Sun) ~ Restaurant ~ (01749) 673916 ~ Children allowed in no smoking Keepers Bar ~ Dogs allowed in bar ~ Open 8am-11pm (midnight Sat)

Crown 🛏

Market Place; BA5 2RF

A useful meeting point for visitors to this attractive little city (it's in the Market Place, overlooked by the cathedral), this brightly modernised former coaching inn has a very clean, contemporary feel. The walls in the various bustling bar areas are painted white or blue, there's light wooden flooring, and plenty of matching chairs and cushioned wall benches; up a step is a comfortable area with a sofa, and newspapers. A sunny back room (where children tend to go) has an exposed stone fireplace, GWR prints, and a couple of fruit machines and TV; it opens on to a small courtyard with a few tables. Reliable bar food at lunchtime includes sandwiches and panini (from £3.75), soup (£3.95), ploughman's or crispy battered cod (£5.75), lamb stew, salmon fishcake, thai vegetable stir fry or honey-roast ham and egg (all £5.95); early evening extras such as tagliatelle with mushrooms, spinach and pesto (£9.95) and rib-eye steak with béarnaise butter (£11.95); the pleasant staff usually keep up even at the busiest of times. Butcombe Bitter and Blond, Greene King Old Speckled Hen and Smiles Best on handpump, and a dozen wines by the glass (though readers worn down by sightseeing have gone for the half-carafes). The restaurant and part of the Penn Bar are no smoking; piped music (sometimes loud), fruit machine and TV. William Penn is said to have preached from a window here in 1685. This is a nice place to stay. *(Recommended by Rob Bowran, B J Harding, M G Hart, Anthony Barnes, Mrs C Peters, Henry and Fiona Dryden, Minda and Stanley Alexander, Michael H Legge, Colin and Janet Roe)*

Free house ~ Licensee Adrian Lawrence ~ Real ale ~ Bar food (12-10 in summer; winter 12-2, 6-10) ~ Restaurant ~ (01749) 673457 ~ Children welcome in restaurant any time and in bar till 8pm ~ Dogs allowed in bedrooms ~ Open 10am-11pm(midnight Fri and Sat); closed 25 Dec ~ Bedrooms: £60S/£90S

WITHYPOOL SS8435 Map 1

Royal Oak 🛏

Village signposted off B3233; TA24 7QP

Tucked down below some of the most attractive parts of Exmoor, this country local has a nicely old-fashioned beamed interior and a particularly welcoming atmosphere. There's a fine raised log fireplace in the lounge, as well as comfortably cushioned wall seating and slat-backed chairs, and sporting trophies and paintings, and various copper and brass ornaments on its walls. The locals' bar has some old oak tables, and plenty of character. Exmoor Ale and a guest like Courage Best or Exmoor Gold on handpump, and several wines by the glass. Bar food includes lunchtime sandwiches, home-made soup (£4.95), home-made game pâté (£5.75), beer-battered cod and chips (£8.95), pan-seared peppered tuna loin with roasted mediterranean vegetables (£10.95), baked bass fillet with mussel, parsley and pea purée (£13.95), and fillet steak with blue cheese and mushroom sauce (£15.95).

The dining room is no smoking. R D Blackmore stayed in this country village inn while writing *Lorna Doone*. There are wooden benches on the terrace, and just up the road, some grand views from Winsford Hill. The River Barle runs through the village itself, with pretty bridleways following it through a wooded combe further upstream. *(Recommended by Tracey and Stephen Groves, Bob and Margaret Holder, Nigel Long, A S and M E Marriott, George Atkinson, Brian and Anita Randall, Sheila Topham, Mrs M Ainley, Dr Ian S Morley, S Topham, Alex Mason, Phil and Sally Gorton, Duncan Cloud, Bob and Marilyn Baylis, Paul Humphreys, Jeremy Whitehorn, Mrs Ann Webb, Peter Titcomb)*

Coast & Country Inns ~ Managers Helga Tarttaglione and James Allen ~ Real ale ~ Bar food (12-2, 6.30-9) ~ (01643) 831506 ~ Children in eating area of bar and restaurant ~ Dogs allowed in bar and bedrooms ~ Open 11-11; 12-10.30 Sun; closed 25 Dec ~ Bedrooms: £65B/£110B

WOOKEY   ST5145   Map 2
Burcott 🍺
B3139 W of Wells; BA5 1NJ

Popular with both locals and visitors, this neatly kept roadside pub has been refurbished over the last year. Welcoming and old-fashioned, the two simply furnished small front bar rooms now have exposed flagstoned floors, a new woodburner, and lantern-style lights on the walls. The lounge has a square corner bar counter, fresh flowers at either end of the mantelpiece above the tiny stone fireplace, Parker-Knollish brocaded chairs around a couple of tables, and high bar stools; the other bar has beams (some willow pattern plates on one), a solid settle by the window and a high backed old pine settle by one wall, cushioned mate's chairs and fresh flowers on the mix of nice old pine tables, and a hunting horn on the bressumer above the fireplace. A little no smoking room on the right has darts, shove-ha'penny, cribbage and dominoes, neat built-in wall seats, and small framed advertisements, and there's a roomy back no smoking restaurant with black joists, stripped stone walls and sea-green check tablecloths; piped music. Good, proper home cooking includes chicken liver pâté or salmon and dill fishcake (£3.95), sandwiches or filled baked potatoes (from £4.25), ploughman's (£5.25), honey-roast ham and eggs (£6.45), lasagne or vegetable and cashew nut bake (£6.95), steak in ale pie (£7.45), apricot chicken breast (£9.75), steamed salmon in lemon, garlic and thyme (£10.45), steaks (from £11.45), and daily specials like lamb cutlets (£9.45) or beef wellington (£15.75); efficient, friendly service. Archers Golden, Hop Back Summer Lightning and RCH Pitchfork on handpump, and several wines by the glass. The window boxes and tubs in front of the building are pretty in summer, and a sizeable garden has picnic-sets, plenty of small trees and shrubs, and Mendip Hill views; there's a paddock beyond. By the time this edition hits the shops they should have opened some bedrooms in the former stables. *(Recommended by Tom Evans, Peter Mack Wilkins, Phil and Sally Gorton, Alan and Paula McCully, Anthony Barnes)*

Free house ~ Licensees Ian and Anne Stead ~ Real ale ~ Bar food (12-2, 6.30-9; not Sun or Mon evenings) ~ Restaurant ~ (01749) 673874 ~ Well behaved children in restaurant ~ Open 11.30-2.30, 6-11; 12-3, 6-11 Sat; 12-3, 7-10.30 Sun; closed 25 and 26 Dec, 1 Jan

---

LUCKY DIP

Besides the fully inspected pubs, you might like to try these Lucky Dips recommended to us and described by readers (if you do, please send us reports: www.goodguides.co.uk).

ABBOTS LEIGH [ST5473]
☆ *George* BS8 3RP [A369, between M5 junction 19 and Bristol]: Main-road dining pub under newish management, tidy and comfortable, with attractively presented reasonably priced food from snacks up, Fullers London Pride and Sharps Doom Bar and Cornish Coaster, two log fires; pleasant enclosed garden *(LYM, Adrian Johnson)*

ASHCOTT [ST4436]
Pipers TA7 9QL [A39/A361, SE of village]: Welcoming dining pub with large beamed lounge, good range of mainstream and other ales, Addlestone's cider, prompt helpful service, wide food choice from sandwiches to steaks inc children's, woodburner, leather armchairs, pictures for sale and potted plants, prettily set no smoking beamed dining area;

unobtrusive piped music; pleasant roadside garden *(Dr and Mrs C W Thomas)*

☆ *Ring o' Bells* TA7 9PZ [High St; follow Church and Village Hall signs off A39 W of Street]: Neatly kept comfortably modernised local, steps up and down making snug areas (at least for the able-bodied), quickly changing real ales, Wilkins' farm cider, wide choice of good value wholesome home-made food from fresh sandwiches and rolls up, separate no smoking stripy pink dining room, decent wines, helpful service, inglenook woodburner; piped pop music, fruit machines, skittle alley; attractively planted back garden with play area and shaded terrace, camping *(S J and B S Highmore, Dr A J and Mrs Tompsett, Peter Mack Wilkins, BB, Andy and Jill Smith, Christine and Neil Townend)*

AXBRIDGE [ST4354]

Crown BS26 2BN [St Marys St]: Good value unpretentious food, three Skinners ales, pleasant staff, plenty of locals *(Hugh Roberts)*

BARRINGTON [ST3918]

Royal Oak TA19 0JB: Newish licensees in roomy old stone-built pub, recently sensitively refurbished, with solid modern furnishings in light and airy no smoking lounge bar (children welcome here), enjoyable food from enterprising sandwiches to steaks and speciality fish (veg may come from nearby Barrington Court), real ales inc Bass and Butcombe, friendly prompt service, no piped music; large outdoor area, opp church in beautiful village *(Revd L J and Mrs Melliss, P and D Carpenter)*

BARROW GURNEY [ST5367]

Princes Motto BS48 3RY [B3130, just off A370/A38]: Cosy and well run, with unpretentious local feel in traditional tap room, long refurbished lounge/dining area up behind, real ales such as Butcombe and Wadworths, good value wkdy lunchtime food, log fire, some panelling, cricket team photographs, jugs and china; pleasant garden with terrace, open all day *(Dr A J and Mrs Tompsett, LYM, Dr and Mrs M E Wilson)*

BATH [ST7564]

Ale House BA1 1NG [York St]: Quiet and unassuming city-centre local with big windows to street, helpful friendly landlord, Courage Best, Fullers London Pride and Sharps Cornish Coaster, flame-effect fire, Bath RFC memorabilia, bargain lunchtime food from baked potatoes up in rambling cellar bar, more seating upstairs *(Michael and Alison Sandy, Ian Phillips)*

Bell BA1 5BW [Walcot St]: Eight regular real ales and interesting guest beers in long narrow split-level dark-ceilinged pub with lots of pump clips and gig notices, good value baguettes, bar billiards; calm at lunchtime, packed and lively with loud piped music evenings, frequent live music *(Dr and Mrs A K Clarke, Pete Baker, Rob Stevenson, Clare Rosier)*

Boater BA2 4BQ [Argyle St, by Pulteney Bridge]: Simple pub in good spot near river, nice view of weir from main bar upstairs, neat cellar bar mainly for younger people, Bass and

Courage, good value food inc enterprising filled rolls, friendly staff; no children inside; tables in good-sized floodlit courtyard *(Alain and Rose Foote, Dr and Mrs M E Wilson, Dr and Mrs A K Clarke)*

Boathouse BA1 3NB [Newbridge Rd]: Large riverside pub nr Kennet & Avon marina on outskirts, rugs on wooden floor, apple-theme and riverside decorations, good value food from filled ciabattas to steaks and restaurant dishes, efficient courteous service, Brains ales, decent house wines; children very welcome, wicker furniture and potted plants in conservatory on lower level, picnic-sets out in neat garden with steps up to waterside balcony *(Dr and Mrs A K Clarke, Betsy and Peter Little)*

☆ *Coeur de Lion* BA1 5AR [Northumberland Pl; off High St by W H Smith]: Tiny single-room pub, perhaps Bath's prettiest, simple, cosy and friendly, with real ales such as Adnams and Jennings, candles and log-effect gas fire, good mulled wine at Christmas, lunchtime filled rolls in summer; may be piped music, stairs to lavatories; tables out in charming flower-filled flagstoned pedestrian alley, open all day *(LYM, Dr and Mrs A K Clarke, the Didler, Dr and Mrs M E Wilson)*

☆ *Cross Keys* BA2 5RZ [Midford Rd (B3110)]: Pleasant dining lounge with smarter end restaurant (best to book, high chairs for children), good food cooked to order from sandwiches in home-baked bread up inc popular pies and great choice of puddings, real ales such as Everards, friendly service, locals' bar; big garden with prettily populated aviary – great attraction for children *(Meg and Colin Hamilton, Dr and Mrs A K Clarke)*

Crystal Palace BA1 1NW [Abbey Green]: Cheerfully busy two-room modernised pub, dark panelling and tiled floors, freshly prepared straightforward food (not Sun evening) inc lunchtime snacks, speedy friendly service, real ales at a price, log fire, family room and conservatory; piped music and games; sheltered heated courtyard with lovely hanging baskets *(LYM, Dr and Mrs M E Wilson)*

☆ *George* BA2 6TR [Bathampton, E of Bath centre, off A36 or (via toll bridge) off A4; Mill Lane]: Big well reworked and extended Chef & Brewer dining pub in nice canalside spot, good-sized bar opening through arches into pleasantly rambling beamed no smoking rooms with soft lighting, candles on nice mix of tables, rugs on polished boards, dark panelling, period portraits and plates, three log fires, wide blackboard food choice all day at good range of prices from baguettes to duck and fresh fish (can be long delays when it's busy), Courage Best and Directors, Greene King Old Speckled Hen and Charles Wells Bombardier, good range of wines by the glass, plenty of young uniformed staff; may be quiet piped music; children welcome, picnic-sets on enclosed terrace and out on grass (shorter menu for outside) *(Chris and Ann Coy, Dr and Mrs A K Clarke, Dr and Mrs M E Wilson,*

*Betsy and Peter Little, Meg and
Colin Hamilton, Alain and Rose Foote)*

Hare & Hounds BA1 5TJ [Lansdown Rd,
Lansdown Hill]: Elegant stone building with
superb views over Charlcombe and the
Swainswick Valley from big garden and
terrace, attractive and comfortably furnished
long well divided bar, Abbey Bellringer and
Courage, enjoyable food, friendly staff, leaded
lights in mullioned windows, lots of
woodwork, hanging bird cages and shelves of
bric-a-brac, roomy eating area and
conservatory *(Dr and Mrs M E Wilson)*

☆ **Hop Pole** BA1 3AR [Albion Buildings, Upper
Bristol Rd]: Bustling Bath Ales pub, also farm
cider, decent wines by the glass and good soft
drinks, good if pricey food Tues-Sun
lunchtimes from sandwiches through modern
recipes using good fresh ingredients to juicy
steak in bar and former skittle alley restaurant,
traditional settles and other pub furniture on
bare boards in four tastefully reworked linked
areas inc no smoking area, lots of black
woodwork and ochre walls, no juke box or
pool; children welcome while food served,
attractive two-level back courtyard with
boules, terrace tables, fairy-lit vine arbour and
summer houses with heaters, opp Victoria Park
with its great play area, open all day Fri-Sun
*(Colin and Peggy Wilshire, BB, Ian Phillips,
Michael Doswell)*

Olde Farmhouse BA1 5EE [Lansdown Rd]:
On hill overlooking Bath, Abbey Bellringer
from neighbouring microbrewery, Butcombe
and Wadworths, real fire, L-shaped parquet-
floor bar with wall seats, panelling, stained-
glass lamps and bar gantry, big jazz pictures;
juke box, big-screen TV; jazz some evenings,
open all day *(the Didler, Rob Stevenson)*

Pig & Fiddle BA1 5BR [Saracen St]: Lively pub
with several sensibly priced real ales inc Abbey
and Bath, two big open fires, clocks set to
different time zones, bare boards and cheery
red and yellow walls and ceiling, good value
home-made food inc takeaways lunchtime till
early evening, steps up to darker bustling
servery and little dining area, games area and
several TVs; lots of students at night, good
piped trendy pop music then; picnic-sets on big
heated front terrace, open all day *(Dr and
Mrs M E Wilson, Dr and Mrs A K Clarke,
the Didler, BB)*

Pulteney Arms BA2 6ND [Daniel St/Sutton St]:
Cosy cheerful local with gas lamps and two gas
fires, friendly staff, Bath Gem, Fullers London
Pride, Wadworths 6X and Youngs from casks
behind capacious three-sided bar counter, food
inc good big chip baps, daily papers, old
furniture on wooden floors, jug collection,
books, lots of Bath RFC memorabilia;
unobtrusive piped music, TV; pavement tables
*(Pete Baker, Dr and Mrs M E Wilson,
Colin and Peggy Wilshire, Michael Dandy,
Ian Phillips)*

Raven BA1 1HE [Queen St]: Small, friendly
and civilised, with four changing mainly west
country ales, cheerful helpful staff, good
lunchtime food choice inc magic speciality pies

and sausages, open fire, charity bookshelves,
some stripped stone, no smoking room upstairs
*(Terry Buckland, Dr and Mrs A K Clarke,
Dr and Mrs M E Wilson)*

Richmond Arms BA1 5PZ [Richmond Pl, off
Lansdown Rd]: Relaxed informal atmosphere
in small 18th-c house converted into two-room
pub off the tourist track, bright smiling service,
good imaginative food, good wine choice, Bass
and Butcombe, bare boards, pine tables and
chairs, attractive pastel décor, some aboriginal
artefacts and pictures; children welcome, tables
in enclosed pretty front garden
(Bernard Stradling, Dr and Mrs A K Clarke)

Ring o' Bells BA2 4JT [Widcombe Parade]:
Small warmly welcoming pub/bistro, good
fresh and individual sensibly priced food inc
good value lunch deal, relaxed surroundings,
Bass and foreign beers on tap, good coffee;
worth the walk – don't expect to park nearby
(Michael Doswell, Roger Wain-Heapy)

Salamander BA1 2JL [John St]: Traditional
town-centre pub tied to Bath Ales, service not
flawless but their full range and guest beers
kept well, bare boards, dark woodwork and
dark ochre walls, popular bar lunches from
sandwiches up, two rooms downstairs, no
smoking open-kitchen upstairs restaurant,
decent wines, daily papers *(Dr and Mrs M E
Wilson, Guy Vowles, Dr and Mrs A K Clarke,
Colin and Peggy Wilshire, BB)*

Sam Weller BA1 1RH [Upper Borough Walls]:
Reopened under new management after short
closure, decent food and choice of ales and
wines by the glass, sensible prices, big window
for watching world go by, no smoking back
room *(Dr and Mrs M E Wilson)*

BECKINGTON [ST8051]

☆ **Woolpack** BA11 6SP [Warminster Rd, off A36
bypass]: Well refurbished and civilised old inn
with charming helpful staff, imaginative and
well prepared if not cheap food from well filled
ciabattas up, Greene King Abbot and John
Smiths, decent wines, big log fire and chunky
candlelit tables in flagstoned bar, attractive
smarter no smoking oak-panelled dining room
and conservatory; children welcome,
comfortable period bedrooms with own
bathrooms (but avoid the attic), open all
day *(Dr and Mrs A K Clarke, LYM,
Michael Butler, Henry and Fiona Dryden)*

BISHOP'S WOOD [ST2512]

Candlelight TA20 3RS [off A303/B3170 S of
Taunton]: Roomy and busy yet cosy, wide
choice of good value food from sandwiches to
bargain wkdy lunches, pleasant dining room,
cheerful staff, spotless housekeeping, Butcombe
and Cottage or Otter, warm fire, no smoking
areas *(Bob and Margaret Holder, Dr and Mrs
M E Wilson)*

BLAGDON [ST5058]

☆ **New Inn** BS40 7SB [off A368; Park Lane]: No
smoking pub with some comfortable antique
settles among more modern furnishings in old-
fashioned beamed bar, two inglenook log fires,
enjoyable well priced food from filled rolls and
baked potatoes up (even Sun evening), quick
friendly service, Wadworths; piped music; nice

views from tables outside looking down to Blagdon Lake and beyond *(LYM, M G Hart, Michael and Judy Buckley, Ian and Rose Lock, Angus and Rosemary Campbell)*

BRADFORD-ON-TONE [ST1722]

☆ *White Horse* TA4 1HF [fairly nr M5 junction 26, off A38 towards Taunton]: Neatly kept and comfortable stone-built local in quiet village, wide choice of good reasonably priced standard food in straightforward bar eating area and cheerfully decorated dining room, big helpings, welcoming landlord and staff, Badger Tanglefoot and Cotleigh Tawny, decent wines, armchairs by ornate woodburner, hunting cartoons, bar billiards; piped music; back garden with fairy-lit arbour and picnic-sets on lawn, skittle alley *(Geoff and Sylvia Donald, BB, Christine and Neil Townend, Brian and Bett Cox)*

BRENDON HILLS [ST0334]

Raleghs Cross TA23 0LN [junction B3190 with declassified Elsworthy—Winsford rd]: Busy family-friendly upland inn, views to Wales on clear days, huge comfortably modernised bar with rows of plush banquettes, back restaurant, wide choice of popular generous food (some tables no smoking), good puddings, Cotleigh, Exmoor and Sharps Doom Bar, efficient service; children in restaurant and family room, no dogs; open all day summer, plenty of tables outside with play area, good walking country, 17 comfortable bedrooms *(Nigel Long, Stan and Hazel Allen, LYM)*

BRISTOL [ST5672]

☆ *Adam & Eve* BS8 4ND [Hope Chapel Hill, Hotwells]: Quietly tucked away pub with good inexpensive creative food changing daily, interesting recipes and organic ingredients, friendly staff, organic wines and juices, belgian beers, good country-pub atmosphere, log fire, dark bare boards, café chairs and wall settles, quaint nooks and corners; gentle piped music, not much parking nearby *(Gaynor Gregory, Mark O'Sullivan, BB)*

Bag o' Nails BS1 5UW [St Georges Rd, by B4466/A4 Hotwells roundabout]: Popular for its half a dozen or so changing real ales and lots of bottled beers, with a Nov beer festival; piped music; open all day Fri-Sun *(the Didler, Catherine Pitt)*

Brewery Tap BS2 8DJ [Upper Maudlin St/Colston St]: Four well kept sensibly priced real ales and a farm cider in chatty and relaxed unpretentious pub, interesting décor, plain tables and seating, panelling and bare boards, log fire in no smoking half, good value simple food (not Sun evening) from decent sandwiches up, unusual continental bottled beers; may be quiet piped music; tables on good-sized heated terrace, open all day *(Jeremy King, the Didler, Bob and Margaret Holder, Simon and Amanda Southwell, Rob Stevenson)*

Bridge Inn BS2 0JF [Passage St]: Neat little one-bar city pub nr floating harbour, good friendly service, lots of film stills and posters, Bath and guest ales, lunchtime sandwiches and limited hot food, padded wall seats; well reproduced piped music; tables outside, open all day *(Donna and Roger, the Didler)*

☆ *Commercial Rooms* BS1 1HT [Corn St]: Spacious Wetherspoons with lofty domed ceiling and snug cubicles along one side, gas lighting, comfortable quieter no smoking room with ornate balcony; wide changing choice of good real ales, their sensibly priced food all day, friendly chatty bustle, wind indicator; good location, very busy wknd evenings, side wheelchair access *(the Didler, Rob Stevenson)*

Cottage BS1 6XG [Baltic Wharf, Cumberland Rd]: Attractively converted stone-built and panelled harbour master's office nr Maritime Heritage Centre, fine views of Georgian landmarks and Clifton suspension bridge; comfortable, roomy, welcoming and civilised, with big helpings of wholesome and attractively priced plain home-made food (can take a while) all day from sandwiches and baked potatoes up, obliging landlord and pleasant service, three Bristol ales and Flowers IPA (they may give tasters), lots of old local photographs; piped music; waterside terrace tables, neighbouring camp/caravan site, access through sailing club, on foot along waterfront, or by round-harbour ferry, open all day *(Neil and Anita Christopher)*

Highbury Vaults BS2 8DE [St Michaels Hill, Cotham]: Small partly dark-panelled rooms with old-fashioned furniture and prints, Youngs and a guest ale, cheap bar food (not Sat/Sun evenings), bar billiards, dominoes, cribbage; busy with Uni students and teachers, steep steps to lavatories; children welcome, attractive back terrace with heated arbour, open all day *(Donna and Roger, the Didler, LYM, Simon and Amanda Southwell)*

Hope & Anchor BS8 1DR [Jacobs Wells Rd, Clifton]: Pleasant atmosphere in bare-boards 18th-c pub with large shared pine tables, changing real ales from small breweries, two belgian beers, good service, good value substantial food inc lots of sandwiches, interesting dishes and sumptuous ploughman's – very popular lunchtime; piped music, occasional live, can get crowded late evening; disabled access, summer evening barbecues in good-sized tiered back garden with interesting niches *(Len Clark, Bob and Margaret Holder, Catherine Pitt)*

☆ *Kings Head* BS1 6DE [Victoria St]: Friendly relaxed 17th-c pub with big front window and splendid mirrored bar back, corridor to cosy panelled bar snug with serving hatch, Bass and Courage Best, toby jugs on joists, old-fashioned local prints and photographs, interesting gas pressure gauge, generous reasonably priced food wkdy lunchtimes (get there early if you want a seat); no credit cards; pavement tables, cl Sat lunchtime, open all day Weds-Fri *(Pete Baker, Pete Walker, the Didler, BB, Susan and Nigel Wilson, Di and Mike Gillam, Meg and Colin Hamilton)*

Lion BS8 4TX [Church Lane, Clifton]: Good value bistro-type food and good beer in two bare-boards bars, friendly welcome; some live music; cl lunchtimes Mon-Thurs, open all day Fri-Sun *(Paul Williams)*

Llandoger Trow BS1 4ER [off King St/Welsh Back]: By docks, interesting as the last timber-framed building built here, and making the most of its picturesque past with its impressive flower-decked façade and cosy collection of cleverly lit small alcoves and rooms with original fireplaces and carvings around central servery, reasonably priced bar food inc daytime bargains, real ales inc Greene King Old Speckled Hen, friendly staff, good mix from students to tourists; tables out on cobbled pedestrian street, bedrooms in adjacent Premier Lodge *(Neil and Anita Christopher)*

Naval Volunteer BS1 4EF [King St]: Well done re-creation of traditional city pub in genuinely ancient building, locals' front snug, long bar buzzing with conversation, nice dark wood décor with small well furnished rooms and relaxed civilised atmosphere (more lively wknd evenings), several changing national and local ales, enjoyable limited lunchtime food from sandwiches to good fish and chips, steaks and popular Sun lunch, prompt friendly service *(Donna and Roger)*

Nova Scotia BS1 6XJ [Baltic Wharf, Cumberland Basin]: Unspoilt old pub on S side of Floating Harbour, views to Clifton and Avon Gorge, Bass, Courage Best, Wickwar Tom and a guest beer, Thatcher's farm cider, good value blackboard food from filling baguettes to fresh fish and moroccan dishes, wooden seats in four linked areas, nautical charts as wallpaper; plenty of tables out by water, bedrooms *(Hywel Bevan)*

Port of Call BS8 2YE [up very narrow steep rd off to left at top of Whiteladies Rd, Clifton]: Small welcoming traditional pub with fine choice of up to ten or so changing real ales, good value pub food, nautical décor; can get crowded wknds, no children; tables on back terrace, cl Sun evening, open all day Sat *(Len Clark)*

Robin Hoods Retreat BS7 8BG [Gloucester Rd, Bishopston]: Smartly refurbished horseshoe bar with eight real ales inc Hook Norton Old Hooky, cheerful staff, appealing menu, small no smoking dining area *(Matthew Shackle)*

Wellington BS7 8UR [Gloucester Rd, Horfield (A38)]: Lively and roomy 1920s pub done up in traditional unpretentious style by Bath Ales, their beers served by friendly knowledgeable staff, comfortable bar seating, large horseshoe bar and no smoking side room, enjoyable simple fresh food inc generous Sun roasts; jazz and blues nights, very busy on home match days for Bristol RFC or Bristol Rovers; small terrace, open all day Sun, and Fri/Sat in summer *(Barry and Anne, Dr and Mrs A K Clarke, Matthew Shackle, Len Clark, R Huggins, D Irving, E McCall, T McLean, Rob Stevenson)*

BROMPTON REGIS [SS9531]

☆ *George* TA22 9NL: 17th-c ex-farmhouse in quiet remote village, warmly welcoming and attentive chef/landlord, wide choice of reasonably priced home-made food inc imaginative dishes and good Sun roast, Cotleigh Tawny and/or Barn Owl and Exmoor, organic wines, woodburners, no juke box or machines, skittle alley; may be quiet piped music; children and dogs welcome, Exmoor views from pleasant garden by churchyard, good walks, cl Mon *(Jeremy Whitehorn)*

BRUTON [ST6834]

Sun BA10 0AH [High St]: Quaint old two-bar local with warm welcome, Greene King real ales and giant pub dog – an english mastiff *(Robert Hilton)*

BUCKLAND DINHAM [ST7551]

☆ *Bell* BA11 2QT [High St (A362 Frome—Radstock)]: 16th-c pub with friendly atmosphere in narrow beamed main bar, pine furnishings inc booth settles, interesting décor, woodburner in huge inglenook; generous good value food inc local speciality sausages and pies, helpful service, Butcombe Bitter and Gold and Fullers London Pride, quite a few malt whiskies, children allowed in partly no smoking two-level dining room; cribbage, dominoes, piped music; dogs welcome, sheltered garden with side terraces *(Dave Braisted, LYM, Ian Phillips, Jenny Garrett)*

BURTLE [ST4042]

Burtle Inn TA7 8NG [Catcott Rd]: Friendly country local with real ales inc Bass and Boddingtons, good value food inc special offers, log fire, two dining rooms, neat staff; children welcome *(Rod and Chris Pring, Peter Mack Wilkins)*

CASTLE CARY [ST6432]

George BA7 7AH [just off A371 Shepton Mallet—Wincanton; Market Pl]: Thatched country-town hotel, quiet and civilised, with big inglenook in small front bar, inner no smoking lounge off main central reception area, decent food from sandwiches and filled baked potatoes up, Greene King ales, decent house wines, no smoking restaurant; children welcome, 16 bedrooms, open all day *(LYM, Phil and Sally Gorton, Meg and Colin Hamilton)*

CATCOTT [ST3939]

Crown TA7 9HQ [off A39 W of Street; Nidon Lane, via Brook Lane]: Quietly set country pub under newish licensees putting emphasis on the food side, meals rather than snacks, with roomy no smoking dining areas, wide choice of wines by the glass and a couple of real ales; may be piped music; children welcome, picnic-sets and play area out behind, bedrooms *(Dr and Mrs A K Clarke, Philip Lane, LYM, Colin and Janet Roe, Peter Meister)*

CHEDDAR [ST4553]

Bath Arms BS27 3AA [Bath St]: Roomy pub with good value food all day from breakfast on (quite a few dishes using cheddar cheese), Bass, Courage Best and Greene King Old Speckled Hen, decent wines, friendly atmosphere, public bar and no smoking lounge; children welcome, comfortable bedrooms, open all day *(Darren Toner)*

☆ *Gardeners Arms* BS27 3LE [Silver St]: Comfortably modernised pub tucked quietly away in the old part of the town, Adnams, Butcombe and Courage Best, attractive no smoking two-room beamed dining area, pubby food all day; children and dogs welcome, picnic-sets with playthings and a wendy house in quiet back garden, open all day *(Liz and Tony Colman, Rod and Chris Pring, Dr and Mrs A K Clarke, LYM, Comus and Sarah Elliott)*

CHILCOMPTON [ST6451]
Somerset Wagon BA3 4JW [B3139; Broadway]: Cosy and friendly, with enjoyable food inc good value baps and good range of home-made pies, Butcombe and Wadworths, pleasant olde-worlde areas off central bar, lots of settles, log fire; small front garden *(Mark Flynn)*

CLUTTON HILL [ST6360]
Hunters Rest BS39 5QL [off A39 Bristol— Wells]: Extended pub with tasteful mix of stone and plaster walls, black beams and joists, Butcombe, Matthews, Otter and a guest beer, Thatcher's farm cider, wide choice of enjoyable bar food from interestingly filled home-baked rolls and pastries to hearty home cooking, family room, no smoking area, log fires, restaurant, no piped music; disabled facilities, big garden with play area and view to Mendips, bedrooms *(Mark O'Sullivan)*

COMBE FLOREY [ST1531]
☆ *Farmers Arms* TA4 3HZ [off A358 Taunton— Williton, just N of main village turn-off]: Neat and popular newly refurbished dining pub, picturesquely thatched and beamed, with smiling chatty service, traditional pubby specials and wider more original menu choice, Exmoor and guest ales, log fire in comfortable bar, woodburner in dining area; plenty of tables in attractive garden, by summer steam line *(David and Pauline Brenner, Geoff and Sylvia Donald, Mr and Mrs Tucker, BB, E V Lee)*

COMBE HAY [ST7359]
☆ *Wheatsheaf* BA2 7EG [off A367 or B3110 S of Bath]: Low-beamed pub reopened under new ownership after extensive (and expensive) refurbishment with much more emphasis on the food side, interesting well balanced choice, more restaurantly in evenings; fresh and airy décor and stylish light modern furnishings but keeping big log fire and good real ales, quick friendly service; children in eating areas, tables on spacious terraced lawn overlooking church and steep valley, dovecotes built into the walls, plenty of good nearby walks, comfortable bedrooms in outbuildings, cl Mon *(Dr and Mrs A K Clarke, LYM)*

COMPTON DUNDON [ST4832]
Castlebrook Inn TA11 6PR [Castlebrook]: Cheerful two-bar village local, warm and friendly, with super flagstone floors, blazing fire, Sharps Doom Bar, good value Sun carvery in big back simple family restaurant; tables on big lawn behind with play area *(Edward Mirzoeff, Steve and Liz Tilley)*

CORSTON [ST6764]
Wheatsheaf BA2 9HB [A39 towards Marksbury]: Big helpings of good value fresh

pub food from lunchtime sandwiches, baguettes and baked potatoes up, competitive prices, friendly staff, Butcombe, farm cider, log fires in both bars, stripped pine, bare boards, local prints on stripped stone walls *(Nicki Coll, Basil and Jarvis, Nigel Long)*

CREWKERNE [ST4508]
Old Stagecoach TA18 8AL [Station Rd]: Good choice of food inc beer-based belgian dishes, Fullers London Pride and changing local ales, fine range of belgian beers, good-humoured Belgian landlord keen on classic motor-cycles; comfortable motel-style bedrooms behind, cl Sat lunchtime *(Oliver Richardson)*

CROSCOMBE [ST5844]
☆ *George* BA5 3QH [Long St]: Relaxed and friendly village atmosphere, good home-made food freshly made by landlady from reasonably priced sandwiches up, good seasonal veg, welcoming efficient Canadian landlord and young staff, three real ales and two or three local farm ciders, good short choice of sensibly priced wines, log fire, chatty locals, darts, unusual table games, back skittle alley, stylish and attractive no smoking dining room with local artwork or photographs; attractive garden behind *(Len Clark, Hugh Roberts, Phil and Sally Gorton, Sylvia and Tony Birbeck)*

CROSS [ST4254]
New Inn BS26 2EE [A38 Bristol—Bridgwater, junction A371]: Done-up roadside pub with good choice of weekly-changing ales, reasonably priced sustaining food in pleasant dining area, friendly staff, fine views, upstairs games room *(Hugh Roberts, Peter Mack Wilkins)*
White Hart BS26 2EE [not far from A38; Old Coach Rd]: Attractive and relaxing old two-bar local, beams, pillars and big log fires, generous bar food inc good fish and chips, good service, nice wines and beer *(Peter Mack Wilkins, Henry and Fiona Dryden)*

DINNINGTON [ST4013]
Dinnington Docks TA17 8SX [aka Rose & Crown; Fosse Way]: Good cheery atmosphere in large attractive country local, unspoilt and welcoming, with good inexpensive genuine home cooking, Butcombe and guest beers such as Archers, Burrow Hill farm cider, log fire, friendly attentive staff, lots of memorabilia to bolster the myth that there was once a railway line and dock here, sofas in family room, skittle alley; large garden behind with solid climber and play tractor *(MLR)*

DITCHEAT [ST6236]
☆ *Manor House* BA4 6RB [signed off A37 and A371 S of Shepton Mallet]: Pretty village inn with enjoyable home-made food from bar snacks to both hearty and more sophisticated main dishes, Butcombe and two guest beers, keen young manager and staff, open fires, unusual arched doorways linking big flagstoned bar to comfortably relaxed lounge and restaurant, skittle alley; children welcome, tables on back grass, upgraded bedrooms *(BB, Peter Mack Wilkins, Michael Sargent)*

DONYATT [ST3314]
George TA19 0RW [A358, a mile S of A303]:
Well run pub, friendly and civilised, with
relaxing traditional décor, Butcombe and
Fullers London Pride, decent choice of wines
by the glass, interesting choice of reasonably
priced enjoyable food from well filled rolls to
plenty of fish; games machine in smaller side
room *(David and Pauline Brenner)*

DOULTING [ST6444]
☆ *Poachers Pocket* BA4 4PY [Chelynch Rd, off
A361]: Cheerful and popular modernised local,
flagstones with some carpet, log fire in
stripped-stone end wall (not always lit),
plentiful good value food from sandwiches
through good specials to Sun roasts,
welcoming quick service, Butcombe, Cotleigh,
Wadworths 6X and a guest beer, local farm
cider (a spring cider festival, as well as an
autumn beer one), well spaced tables, pub
games and piano, friendly cat and dog;
children in eating area and large family
room/skittle alley, back garden with country
views *(B and K Hypher, LYM, Susan and
Nigel Wilson)*

DRAYCOTT [ST4750]
Strawberry Special BS27 3TQ [off A371;
Station Rd]: Carefully improved village local
with high-backed settles, huge open fire, good
choice of beers, very welcoming landlord and
American landlady *(Ken Flawn)*

DULVERTON [SS9127]
Lion TA22 9BU [Bank Sq]: Charmingly old-
fashioned two-bar country-town hotel popular
with locals from surrounding villages, rambling
bar with big log fire, cheerful staff, Exmoor
real ale, decent wine and coffee, sensibly priced
pub food, no music; children welcome away
from main serving bar, 14 bedrooms with own
bathrooms, pleasant setting *(George Atkinson)*

DUNSTER [SS9943]
☆ *Luttrell Arms* TA24 6SG [High St; A396]:
Small hotel in 15th-c timber-framed abbey
building, unpretentious high-beamed back bar
hung with bottles, clogs and horseshoes, stag's
head and rifles on walls above old settles and
more modern furniture, big log fires, fairly
priced and imaginative bar food inc
substantial sandwiches with home-baked
bread, small helpings available, Cotleigh
Tawny and Exmoor Fox, good wines in three
glass sizes; dogs welcome in bar, ancient
glazed partition dividing off small galleried
and flagstoned courtyard, upstairs access to
quiet attractive garden with Civil War
cannon emplacements and great views,
comfortable bedrooms *(D W Stokes, A and
B D Craig, BB, John and Gloria Isaacs,
Mrs M Ainley, Michael Rowse, S Topham,
Peter Titcomb, Peter and Margaret Glenister,
H O Dickinson)*

EAST LAMBROOK [ST4218]
☆ *Rose & Crown* TA13 5HF: Neatly kept
attractive stone-built pub sympathetically
extended from compact 17th-c core with
inglenook log fire, friendly atmosphere and
welcoming staff, good inexpensive food freshly
made using local supplies from baguettes and

bar snacks up inc fish specialities, full Palmers
real ale range, farm cider, decent wines by the
glass, restaurant extension showing old well
through central glass floor panel
*(Guy Consterdine, R Gutteridge, A S and
M E Marriott)*

EAST LYNG [ST3328]
Rose & Crown TA3 5AU [A361 about 4 miles
W of Othery]: Charming coaching inn with
lovely rural views from pretty back garden
(lots of seats out here), has been popular main
entry but as we went to press was changing
hands for second time in quick succession;
open-plan beamed lounge with log fire and
some nice features inc unusual bow window
seat, skittle alley; reports on new regime please
(LYM)

EAST WOODLANDS [ST7944]
☆ *Horse & Groom* BA11 5LY [off A361/B3092
junction]: Small pub tucked away down
country lanes, pews and settles in flagstoned
bar, woodburner in comfortable lounge, big
no smoking dining conservatory, enjoyable
competitively priced fresh food worth waiting
for (not Sun evening), Archers Golden,
Branscombe Vale Branoc and Butcombe Bitter
tapped from the cask, choice of wine glass
sizes, traditional games; dogs welcome away
from restaurant, children in eating areas,
disabled access, picnic-sets in nice front garden
with more seats behind, handy for Longleat
*(Richard Fendick, LYM, N F C Phillips,
the Didler, Gaynor Gregory, Mr and Mrs
A H Young)*

EASTON-IN-GORDANO [ST5175]
Kings Arms BS20 0PS [St Georges Hill; handy
for M5 junction 19 via A369 E]: Rambling
pub with pleasant local feel, friendly staff,
decent quickly served food; attractive garden
(Richard Fendick)
Rudgleigh Inn BS20 0QD [A369 a mile from
M5 junction 19]: Two-bar refurbished
roadside pub popular for enjoyable promptly
served food at sensible prices from baguettes
up, big helpings (doggy bags provided),
Courage ales, extension restaurant suiting
families, welcoming service; piped music; big
well tended enclosed garden with willows,
tamarisks, play area and cricket-field view,
open all day wkdys *(LYM, Donald Godden)*

ENMORE [ST2434]
☆ *Tynte Arms* TA5 2DP: Cheerful open-plan pub
with west country real ales from long bar, wide
choice of good generous food cooked by
landlady inc lots of fish, good puddings and
good value set menus, pleasant staff, plenty of
dining tables, attractive décor and low beams;
car park over road, good walking country
*(Richard Wyld, Bob and Margaret Holder,
B M Eldridge)*

EXFORD [SS8538]
Crown TA24 7PP [The Green (B3224)]:
Attractive Exmoor inn with hospitable
landlord, relaxed two-room bar with hunting
décor, old local photographs and big stone
fireplace, Exmoor Ale and Gold and a guest
beer, Thatcher's farm cider, ambitious bar
food, restaurant; piped music, TV; dogs and

children welcome, charming waterside garden behind, smaller terraced side garden overlooking village and green, bedrooms, has been open all day wknds *(George Atkinson, LYM)*

FAILAND [ST5171]

Failand Inn BS8 3TU [B3128 Bristol—Clevedon]: Simply furnished old coaching inn with tasty reasonably priced popular food, cheerful efficient service, real ales, comfortable dining extension; may be piped music *(Mr and Mrs John Taylor, Richard and Judy Winn, A D Lealan)*

FARMBOROUGH [ST6660]

Butchers Arms BA2 0AE [Timsbury Rd]: Comfortable two-bar village pub with friendly staff and atmosphere, three real ales, varied restauranty food inc bargain Sun lunch; children and dogs welcome *(Dr and Mrs A K Clarke)*

New Inn BA2 0BY [Bath Rd (A39)]: Roomy roadside pub/restaurant with Greene King Morlands Original, friendly staff, bar snacks and interesting restaurant food *(Dr and Mrs A K Clarke)*

FAULKLAND [ST7354]

☆ *Faulkland Inn* BA3 5UH: Welcoming modernised L-shaped country local with good value food from interesting hot or cold filled sandwiches to wider evening choice inc modern starter/light dishes and good carefully cooked fresh fish, good staff, Butcombe Bitter and Gold and Otter or Palmers Dorset Gold, decent wines, contemporary colours alongside beams, flagstones and some stripped stone, dining area on left, games area in public end; piped music; children welcome, picnic-sets on small back lawn, four good value bedrooms, pretty village *(Dr and Mrs A K Clarke, BB, Ian Phillips)*

FRESHFORD [ST7960]

☆ *Inn at Freshford* BA2 7WG [off A36 or B3108]: Comfortably modernised and roomy beamed stone-built dining pub, very busy for Tues OAP lunch, Butcombe, Courage Best, Wadworths 6X and a guest beer, usual pub food from sandwiches, baguettes and filled baked potatoes up, friendly staff, no smoking restaurant; piped music; children and dogs welcome, picnic-sets in pretty garden, attractive spot by river *(Susan and Nigel Wilson, Meg and Colin Hamilton, Roger Wain-Heapy, Dr and Mrs A K Clarke, LYM, MRSM, Jason Caulkin, Tony and Wendy Hobden)*

FROME [ST7748]

Griffin BA11 3DB [Milk St]: Unpretentious and civilised bare-boards room, long bar with several good Milk Street beers brewed by the friendly landlord, open fires, easy-going mixed crowd; occasional live music, cl lunchtime *(MLR, B M Eldridge)*

GLASTONBURY [ST4938]

King Arthur BA6 9NB: Great atmosphere in friendly recently refurbished pub with fine range of real ales at good prices, farm ciders, good live music Fri; tables in nice outside area *(David Ellerington, D M Paterson)*

HALSE [ST1428]

New Inn TA4 3AF [off B3227 Taunton—Bampton]: Traditional 17th-c stone-built inn refurbished by new landlord, with its own Taunton Vale ales and guest beers, local farm ciders, enjoyable generous home cooking, friendly service, woodburner in big inglenook, oak beams, no smoking dining room, separate games area and skittle alley; tables in garden, lovely village *(MLR, Peter Mack Wilkins)*

HARDINGTON MANDEVILLE [ST5111]

☆ *Mandeville Arms* BA22 9PQ [off A30 SW of Yeovil]: Enjoyable fresh pubby food at reasonable prices, Butcombe and weekly guest beers such as Shepherd Neame Spitfire and Thwaites Lancaster Bomber, good wines by the glass, helpful and welcoming new landlady, thriving atmosphere in comfortable bar and restaurant, skittle alley; pleasant garden, attractive quietly set village *(LYM, Mark and Lynette Davies)*

HARDWAY [ST7234]

☆ *Bull* BA10 0LN [off B3081 Bruton—Wincanton at brown sign for Stourhead and King Alfred's Tower; Hardway]: Charming beamed country dining pub popular locally, esp with older people wkdy lunchtimes, for fine choice of reliably good generous food in comfortable bar and character dining rooms, pleasant long-serving licensees, quick friendly obliging service, Butcombe and Wadworths, good wines by the glass, farm cider, log fire; unobtrusive piped music; tables and barbecues in new garden behind, more in rose garden over road, bedrooms *(Colin and Janet Roe, Sylvia and Tony Birbeck)*

HEWISH [ST3964]

Full Quart BS24 6RT [nr M5 junction 21; A370 towards Congresbury]: Recently refurbished roadside pub with pleasant dark-wood décor in beamed bar, open fire, Bass and Fullers London Pride, all-day food, young enthusiastic staff; lots of picnic-sets in family garden and on front and side terraces, open all day *(Alan and Paula McCully)*

HILLFARRANCE [ST1624]

Anchor TA4 1AW: Comfortably modernised pub with friendly hard-working staff, enjoyable usual food in eating areas off attractive two-part bar, pleasant atmosphere, Butcombe and Exmoor, family room; garden with play area, lots of flower tubs, bedrooms, caravan site, holiday apartments *(Bob and Margaret Holder)*

HINTON BLEWETT [ST5956]

☆ *Ring o' Bells* BS39 5AN [signed off A37 in Clutton]: Charming low-beamed stone-built country local opp village green, good value wholesome food (not Sun evening) from sandwiches to some interesting main dishes, obliging service, Butcombe and guest beers, good wines by the glass and cafetière coffee, log fire; children welcome, pleasant view from tables in sheltered front yard *(LYM, John and Gloria Isaacs)*

HINTON CHARTERHOUSE [ST7758]

Rose & Crown BA2 7SN [B3110 about 4 miles S of Bath]: Roomy partly divided pub with Bass, Butcombe and two or three other ales tapped from casks, wide choice of good value generous home-made food inc plenty of fish (be sure to check out all the scattered blackboards), efficient staff, reasonably priced wines, no smoking area, nice panelling, ornate stone fireplace, rugby memorabilia, restaurant, skittle alley; children welcome, small terrace, bedrooms, open all day Sat *(BB, Meg and Colin Hamilton, Dr and Mrs M E Wilson, Peter Mack Wilkins, Ian Phillips)*

☆ *Stag* BA2 7SW [B3110 S of Bath; High St]: Attractively furnished bustling ancient pub very popular for good sensibly priced straightforward food in cosy log-fire bar and stripped-stone no smoking dining area, real ales such as Bass and Butcombe, friendly helpful service, no piped music; provision for children, tables outside, has been open all day *(Dr and Mrs M E Wilson, LYM, Meg and Colin Hamilton)*

HINTON ST GEORGE [ST4212]

☆ *Lord Poulett Arms* TA17 8SE [off A30 or A356 NW of Crewkerne; High St]: Attractive and substantial 17th-c thatched pub with cosy linked areas, flagstones, open fires and lovely solid furnishings inc some antiques, good choice of enjoyable upmarket food with small helpings available, local and organic ingredients, friendly relaxed service and civilised atmosphere, Butcombe and good guest beers tapped from the cask in small plain public bar, farm cider, good value wines, skittle alley with darts, gent's worth seeing; needs a no smoking area; children and dogs welcome, good disabled access, tables in prettily planted back garden, rare very old fives court, charming stone village with good walks, four attractive character bedrooms, cl Mon lunchtime *(OPUS, MLR, Bob and Margaret Holder, David Howell, Fergus Dowding)*

HORFIELD [ST5977]

Inn on the Green BS7 0PA [Filton Rd]: Two-bar pub with half a dozen or more changing real ales, tasters offered, good menu, friendly service, games area inc pool tables in former skittle alley, big-screen sports TVs *(Len Clark)*

HUNTWORTH [ST3134]

Boat & Anchor TA7 0AQ [just off M5 junction 24; local rd off exit roundabout, then turn right towards narrow canal bridge]: Good choice of enjoyable pub food inc consistently good steaks, good service and nice house wines; lovely canalside garden, simple bedrooms *(Lucien Perring, Andy Sinden, Louise Harrington)*

ILCHESTER [ST5222]

Ilchester Arms BA22 8LN [Church St]: Hotel with Butcombe in small pine-panelled bar on right, bistro with reasonably priced mediterranean-leaning food, restaurant; comfortable bedrooms *(Michael Doswell)*

ILMINSTER [ST3514]

Dolphin TA19 0DR [Silver St]: Simple neatly kept pub with attentive landlord and welcoming helpful staff, food inc notable nut

roast and lots of country puddings, good farm cider; some tables outside *(John and Elisabeth Cox)*

George TA19 0DG [North St, opp central butter market]: New licensees doing straightforward pubby food from lunchtime sandwiches and baked potatoes up, in neat little front bar and larger no smoking back restaurant area, Otter and Shepherd Neame Spitfire, good wines by the glass; children and dogs welcome, cl Sun evening *(Bruce and Penny Wilkie, Mrs Jill Wyatt, Theo, Anne and Jane Gaskin, LYM)*

KEWSTOKE [ST3263]

Commodore BS22 9UZ [Beach Rd]: Hotel at end of Sand Bay, beach and dune walks, attractive beamed bar with no smoking part and nautical bric-a-brac, neat dark tables, welcoming service, Courage and John Smiths from small counter, reasonably priced food inc carvery, two for one lunches popular with older people (younger customers evenings), aquarium; bedrooms *(Dr and Mrs C W Thomas)*

KEYNSHAM [ST6669]

☆ *Lock-Keeper* BS31 2DD [A4175]: Bustling and popular, in lovely spot on Avon island with lots of picnic-sets on big heated deck and shady garden by lock, marina and weir; full Youngs range kept well, appealing well priced food served promptly from sandwiches, panini and baked potatoes to more upmarket dishes, friendly helpful young staff, small room by bar, arches to unpretentious main divided room with rust and dark blue décor, black beams and bare boards, barrel-vaulted lower area, conservatory; boules *(BOB, Michael Doswell, Dr and Mrs M E Wilson, M G Hart)*

KILVE [ST1442]

☆ *Hood Arms* TA5 1EA [A39 E of Williton]: Friendly attentive service, enjoyable good value bar food cooked to order (no sandwiches), real ales such as Exmoor, cosy little plush lounge, woodburner in bar, no smoking restaurant; skittle alley, tables on sheltered back terrace by pleasant children's garden, nice bedrooms – back are quietest *(Bob and Margaret Holder, LYM)*

LEIGH UPON MENDIP [ST6947]

Bell BA3 5QQ [Leigh St]: Friendly L-shaped pub with good value food from baguettes up, efficient service, five real ales inc Butcombe and Wadworths 6X, monthly vintage sports car meeting first Tues; garden *(Martin Hatcher)*

LONG SUTTON [ST4625]

Devonshire Arms TA10 9LP [B3165 Somerton—Martock, just off A372 E of Langport]: Tall gabled stone inn with settees on right, partly no smoking restaurant area on left, lots of sporting and country prints, courteous young staff, interesting blackboard food from enterprising sandwiches up, real ale, quite a few wines by the glass, homely flagstoned back bar with darts and TV; may be piped music; children in eating areas, open all day, bedrooms *(LYM, Brian and Pat Wardrobe, Brian Small)*

MARSTON MAGNA [ST5922]
☆ *Red Lion* BA22 8DH [Rimpton Rd]: Warmly welcoming and helpful newish licensees, Butcombe and Hidden ales, honest good value food using local supplies, relaxed wine-bar feel with squashy sofas and high ceilings, simple dining area; children welcome, scent-filled garden *(OPUS, Dr and Mrs P Clark)*

MARTOCK [ST4619]
Nags Head TA12 6NF [East St]: Thriving and appealing local with great staff, good choice of good value food, Badger ales, coal-effect gas fire, games room *(John A Barker)*

MIDFORD [ST7660]
☆ *Hope & Anchor* BA2 7DD [Bath Rd (B3110)]: Good attractively presented interesting food from light dishes to mouth-watering more elaborate things and imaginative puddings in civilised bar and heavy-beamed and flagstoned candlelit restaurant end, Bath Gem, Butcombe Gold and a guest such as Sharps Cornish Coaster, good house wines, proper coffee, pleasantly informal atmosphere, log fire; teak tables on sheltered back terrace, picnic-sets on next level up, pleasant walks on disused Somerset & Dorset railway track *(Gaynor Gregory, Roger Wain-Heapy, M G Hart, BB, Michael Doswell, Andy Lickfold)*

MIDSOMER NORTON [ST6654]
White Hart BA3 2HQ [The Island]: Chatty and individualistic Victorian local with several rooms, Bass and Butcombe tapped from the cask, old local coal-mining photographs and memorabilia, enjoyable bar snacks; open all day, bedrooms *(Dr and Mrs A K Clarke, the Didler)*

MILBORNE PORT [ST6718]
Queens Head DT9 5DQ [A30 E of Sherborne]: Friendly helpful staff, quick service, wide range of enjoyable food from sandwiches up, real ales such as Butcombe, Greene King Old Speckled Hen and Wadworths 6X, farm ciders, decent wines, neat beamed lounge, restaurant and no smoking conservatory, games in public bar, skittle alley, live music nights; provision for children and quiet dogs, reasonable disabled access, tables in sheltered courtyard and garden with play area, three cosy good value bedrooms *(LYM, Dennis Jenkin)*

MINEHEAD [SS9746]
Red Lion TA24 5UJ [Quay St (seafront)]: Pleasant town pub with real ales and good value home cooking *(Dave Braisted)*

MONTACUTE [ST4916]
☆ *Phelips Arms* TA15 6XB [The Borough; off A3088 W of Yeovil]: Good manageable daily-changing choice of interesting fresh food from filled crusty rolls to more restaurchy main dishes in roomy and airy open-plan bar and smart yet relaxed restaurant, attentive landlord and friendly efficient service even when busy, Palmers ales, fine choice of wines by the glass, farm cider, good coffee, nice fireplace and old-fashioned décor; children and dogs welcome, skittle alley, tables in attractive walled garden behind, comfortable bedrooms, pretty square next to Montacute House *(Paul and*

Annette Hallett, BB, John A Barker, Peter Titcomb, Shirley Mackenzie, Chris Wall)

MUDFORD [ST5719]
Half Moon BA21 5TF [A359 N of Yeovil]: Enjoyable generous food all day, real ales inc RCH Pitchfork, welcoming service, carefully restored bar with plenty of character, large dining area with stripped pine tables; tables in courtyard, good value bedrooms, open all day *(J Stickland, Guy Vowles, M Payne)*

NAILSEA [ST4469]
Blue Flame BS48 4DE [West End]: Small well worn 19th-c unspoilt farmers' local, two rooms with mixed furnishings, Bass, RCH and guest beers such as Abbey and Bath, Thatcher's farm cider, filled rolls and doorstep sandwiches, coal fire, pub games; children's room, sizeable informal garden with barbecue, open all day summer wknds *(the Didler)*
Old Farmhouse BS48 2PF [Trendlewood Way, off B3130]: Roomy pub with connected stone-built barn, good value inventive food, carvery Fri-Sun, friendly staff, olde-worlde bric-a-brac; disabled facilities, tables outside with barbecues and good play area *(Richard Fendick)*

NETHER STOWEY [ST1939]
Rose & Crown TA5 1LJ [St Mary St]: Local bustle in 16th-c former posting inn, Cotleigh, Palmers and Otter, Thatcher's farm cider, enjoyable food (not Sun evening – the specials go quickly), separate public bar, restaurant (not Mon/Tues); dogs and children welcome, garden tables, bedrooms, open all day *(R M Corlett)*

NEWTON ST LOE [ST7065]
☆ *Globe* BA2 9BB: Roomy and popular, attractively split into smaller areas by dark wood partitions, pillars and timbers giving secluded feel, accent on enjoyable food all day, good atmosphere, friendly helpful service, good beer, large no smoking area *(Dr and Mrs M E Wilson, Dr and Mrs A K Clarke)*

NORTH BREWHAM [ST7236]
☆ *Old Red Lion* BA10 0JL [off A359 Frome—Bruton]: Flagstoned low-beamed former farmhouse with enjoyable blackboard food, real ales such as Butcombe, Fullers and Greene King ales, good coffee, log fire, friendly efficient service, spacious bar, comfortable dining room; handy for King Alfred's monument, bedrooms *(Colin and Janet Roe)*

NORTON ST PHILIP [ST7755]
☆ *Fleur de Lys* BA2 7LG [High St]: Flourishing chatty local in 13th-c stone cottages stitched together centuries ago, steps and pillars giving cosy feel of separate rooms in the beamed and flagstoned areas around the central servery, good log fire in huge fireplace, Butcombe and Wadworths beers, friendly landlord, good value home-made food from baguettes through sausages and mash etc to steak; children very welcome, skittle alley *(R K Phillips, Dr and Mrs M E Wilson, Dr and Mrs A K Clarke, the Didler, BB, Ian Phillips)*

NUNNEY [ST7345]
☆ *George* BA11 4LW [Church St; signed off A361 Shepton Mallet—Frome]: Rambling

much modernised open-plan bar with panelling and stripped stone, log fire, helpful efficient staff, Black Sheep and a changing ale such as Thwaites Lancaster Bomber, sound food in bar and restaurant – can cater for large numbers; piped music, pool in public bar, no dogs; streamside picnic-sets by car park, rare gallows inn-sign spanning road, in quaint village with ruined castle; children allowed in side room, comfortable bedrooms *(Ian Phillips, Susan and Nigel Wilson, BB, Howard C R Shaw)*

PITMINSTER [ST2219]
Queens Arms TA3 7AZ [off B3170 S of Taunton (or reached direct); nr church]: Village pub keeping pub layout yet with skilled chef doing good choice of upmarket bistro food (can take a while at busy times), real ales inc Cotleigh and Otter, interesting wines, log fires, simple wooden bar furniture, pleasant dining room; bedrooms with own bathrooms *(Alyson Hartley, Colin and Alma Gent)*

PORLOCK [SS8846]
Ship TA24 8QD [High St]: Picturesque thatched partly 13th-c pub with low beams, flagstones and big inglenook log fires, small locals' front bar, Cotleigh and guest beers, farm cider, food from sandwiches to familiar hot dishes with plenty for children, back dining room, pub games and pool; children very welcome, attractive split-level sunny garden with decking, nearby nature trail to Dunkery Beacon, bedrooms *(Tracey and Stephen Groves, LYM, Edward Leetham)*

PORLOCK WEIR [SS8846]
☆ *Ship* TA24 8QD [separate from but run in tandem with neighbouring Anchor Hotel]: Prettily restored and friendly old inn in wonderful spot by peaceful harbour (so can get packed), with tables in terraced rose garden and good walks (but no views to speak of from bars); nets and chalked beams in touristy Mariners Bar, four ales inc Cotleigh Barn Owl and Exmoor, Inch's cider, good soft drinks choice, huge log fire, usual food from thick sandwiches up, no smoking back family room; piped music, big-screen TV, young staff, little free parking but pay & display opposite; children and dogs welcome, attractive bedrooms *(Tracey and Stephen Groves, D W Stokes, Heather Couper, Stan and Hazel Allen, David Crook, Cathy Robinson, Ed Coombe, LYM, Dr Peter Crawshaw, J Stickland, Geoff and Teresa, Edward Leetham, Ian and Joan Blackwell, George Atkinson)*

PORTBURY [ST4975]
Priory BS20 7TN [Station Rd, ½ mile from A369 (just S of M5 junction 19)]: Reliable much extended Vintage Inn dining pub, several beamed rooms, some no smoking, with nice mix of solid furnishings in alcoves, obliging service, wide choice of nicely presented usual food inc good steaks all day till 10pm, decent beer and good range of house wines; piped music; bedrooms, open all day *(Dr A J and Mrs Tompsett, DAV, Dr and Mrs C W Thomas)*

PORTISHEAD [ST4475]
Ship BS20 8JT [the one on Down Rd (coast rd to Walton in Gordano)]: Modern pub with limited low-priced lunchtime food (pleasant Edwardian-style dining lounge), changing ales such as Bass, Butcombe and Sharps Doom Bar, lots of Royal Navy memorabilia, good views across to Newport and Cardiff *(Tom Evans)*

PRIDDY [ST5450]
Hunters Lodge BA5 3AR [from Wells on A39 pass hill with TV mast on left, then next left]: Welcoming and unchanging walkers' and pothoiers' inn above ice-age cavern, in same family for generations, Butcombe and Exmoor tapped from casks behind the bar, Weston's farm cider, good plain food inc bread and local cheeses, low prices, log fire, flagstones; garden picnic-sets, bedrooms *(LYM, Jon Barnfield, Gaynor Gregory)*
☆ *Queen Victoria* BA5 3BA [village signed off B3135; Pelting Drove]: Relaxed character country pub with Butcombe Bitter and Gold and Wadworths 6X tapped from the cask, three good log fires (one open on two sides), organic beers, farm ciders and perries, good coffee, basic low-priced wholesome food such as filled rolls, ploughman's and cottage pie, stripped stone and flagstones, interesting bric-a-brac, collected furnishings inc miscellaneous tables and old pews, welcoming licensees; good garden for children over road, great walks, cl lunchtime Oct-Apr exc hols, open all day wknds and high season *(John Hillman, Phil and Sally Gorton)*

RODE [ST8053]
☆ *Bell* BA11 6PW [Frome Rd (A361)]: Comfortable, spotless and roomy, with friendly licensees and quick obliging service, good atmosphere, wide and interesting choice of enjoyable generous food from good hot-filled sandwiches up, Courage Best and three Butcombe beers, roomy sparely decorated bar on left with a couple of armchairs as well as pleasantly practical furnishings, step up to good-sized pool room, smaller lounge bar on right leading to busy attractively set no smoking restaurant; dogs welcome, plenty of tables on spreading lawn *(John and Joan Nash, Ted George)*
Mill BA11 6AG: Family food pub in beautifully set former watermill, smart layout and up-to-date décor and artwork, upstairs no smoking area, children's room with impressive games; live music Fri may be loud; garden and decks overlooking river, big play area *(Dr and Mrs M E Wilson, Angus and Rosemary Campbell)*

ROWBERROW [ST4458]
☆ *Swan* BS25 1QL [off A38 S of A368 junction]: Spacious and efficiently set up dining pub opp pond, olde-worlde beamery and so forth (most atmosphere in bar part), popular food from substantial lunchtime sandwiches, baguettes and baked potatoes to good chargrills, Bass and Butcombe Bitter, Blond and Gold, good choice of wines by the glass, Thatcher's cider, good log fires; dogs welcome, no children *(Gaynor Gregory, Bob and Margaret Holder,*

Andrew Shore, Maria Williams, Hugh Roberts, LYM, John and Fiona McIlwain, Peter Mack Wilkins, Alan and Paula McCully, M G Hart)

RUDGE [ST8251]

☆ *Full Moon* BA11 2QF [off A36 Bath—Warminster]: Black-beamed 17th-c inn with friendly and flexible staff, good value food, Butcombe and other ales, local ciders, nice mix of furnishings in cottagey front bars, inglenook fireplace, flagstoned tap room, back no smoking restaurant extension, traditional games and skittle alley; children welcome, pretty gardens with plenty of seats, comfortable modern bedroom building, swimming pool, open all day *(Derek and Brenda Lamont, Pamela and Douglas Cooper, LYM)*

SALTFORD [ST6867]

Bird in Hand BS31 3EJ [High St]: Comfortable and friendly, with lively local feel in front bar, good range of beers such as Abbey Bellringer, Butcombe and Courage, farm cider, attractive back conservatory dining area popular locally for good value fresh food from mini-ploughman's to daily roast, huge omelettes and whitby fish, quick service even when quite a queue for food, lots of bird pictures, small family area; live entertainment; picnic-sets down towards river, handy for Bristol—Bath railway path *(Dr and Mrs A K Clarke, Meg and Colin Hamilton)*

Jolly Sailor BS31 3ER: Great spot by lock and weir on River Avon, with garden tables and own island between lock and pub; standard food, friendly service, real ales, restaurant; children welcome *(W J Simpson)*

SIDCOT [ST4256]

Sidcot Hotel BS25 1NN [Bridgwater Rd (A38)]: Clean and bright Brewers Fayre conversion of old hotel, decent choice of wines and other drinks, good staff, promptly served food; open all day *(Comus and Sarah Elliott, Mick and Moira Brummell)*

SIMONSBATH [SS7739]

☆ *Exmoor Forest Hotel* TA24 7SH [B3223]: Exmoor inn recently renovated under new owners and now completely no smoking, relaxed atmosphere, log fires, Exmoor and St Austell, lots of whiskies, interesting if not cheap freshly prepared local food in bar or spacious upper dining area, capable service, hunting prints and trophies; dogs welcome and well looked after, comfortable bedrooms, good breakfast, nine miles of good trout fishing for residents *(LYM, Rona Murdoch, Mrs D Wilford, Gordon and Jay Smith)*

SOUTH CADBURY [ST6325]

Camelot BA22 7EX [Chapel Rd]: Recently refurbished and extended in modern rural style by the Montgomerys (famous for their prized cheddar), interesting food and beer, skittle alley, plenty of locals; just below Cadbury Castle *(Revd D E and Mrs J A Shapland, Mrs J H S Lang, Pat and Robert Watt, OPUS)*

SOUTH CHERITON [ST6924]

White Horse BA8 0BL [A357 Wincanton—Blandford]: Friendly and pleasant inside, with

good service, small choice of well cooked nicely served food at reasonable prices, small individual dining areas, family room with games *(Mark Flynn, J C Burgis)*

SOUTH PETHERTON [ST4316]

Brewers Arms TA13 5BW [St James St]: Substantially refurbished 17th-c stone-built inn with generous enjoyable food from hearty favourites to interesting dishes at pine tables in elegant russet-walled dining lounge, jovial landlord, helpful staff, good choice of changing real ales inc Badger and Butcombe, decent wines, games in big public bar; picnic-sets in neatly kept garden, useful A303 diversion *(Mike Gorton)*

SOUTH STOKE [ST7461]

☆ *Pack Horse* BA2 7DU [off B3110, S edge of Bath]: Intriguing and unspoilt medieval pub, a former priory (central passageway still a public right of way to the church), with heavy beams, handsome inglenook log fire, antique settles, Butcombe, Courage Best and Wadworths 6X, plenty of farm cider, willing staff, decent food, shove-ha'penny tables; piped music; children welcome, tables in spacious back garden, boules, open all day wknds *(R Huggins, D Irving, E McCall, T McLean, Dr and Mrs A K Clarke, LYM, Jane and Graham Rooth)*

SPARKFORD [ST6026]

Sparkford Inn BA22 7JH [just W of Wincanton; High St]: Big softly lit low-beamed rambling pub which can divide opinions sharply over its beetroot and dark brown décor, its queuing system for drinks then food, its lunchtime carvery and its staff, but does please most, with a pleasant mix of furnishings, a variety of other pubby food, Courage Directors, a welcome for children and dogs, tables and decent play area outside, and well equipped bedrooms; open all day *(Steve Jones, B J Harding, LYM, Michael Rowse, Dr and Mrs M E Wilson, Clive and Vivienne Locks, June and Robin Savage, Mr and Mrs D S Price, Ian and Nita Cooper, Brian P White)*

STAPLE FITZPAINE [ST2618]

☆ *Greyhound* TA3 5SP [off A358 or B3170 S of Taunton]: Rambling country pub with good choice of enjoyable food, changing real ales, good wines by the glass, welcoming atmosphere and friendly service, flagstones, inglenooks, pleasant mix of settles and chairs, log fires throughout, olde-worlde pictures, farm tools and so forth; children welcome, good bedrooms in modern extension *(LYM, Brian and Bett Cox)*

STOGUMBER [ST0937]

☆ *White Horse* TA4 3TA [off A358 at Crowcombe]: Proper village pub with enjoyable food from good sandwiches to proper Sun roasts, reasonable prices, Cotleigh Tawny, Greene King Old Speckled Hen and Marstons Pedigree, welcoming service and atmosphere, long near bar, old village photographs with more recent ones for comparison, good log fires, no smoking dining area, games room and skittle alley; children welcome away from bar, quiet garden,

bedrooms, open all day wknds and summer
(Bob and Margaret Holder, LYM)

STOKE ST MARY [ST2622]

Half Moon TA3 5BY [from M5 junction 25
take A358 towards Ilminster, 1st right, right in
Henlade]: Roomy much-modernised village
pub, several neat open-plan main areas, wide
choice of hearty food from sandwiches to
steaks, no smoking restaurant, pleasant staff,
Butcombe, Boddingtons, Fullers London Pride
and Greene King Abbot, nice coffee, quite a
few malt whiskies, pleasant local atmosphere,
bar billiards; children welcome, picnic-sets in
well tended garden *(Bob and Margaret Holder,
LYM, Brian and Genie Smart)*

STOKE SUB HAMDON [ST4717]

Prince of Wales TA14 6RW [Ham Hill]: On
top of Ham Hill with superb views, good value
food and good choice of real ales; children,
dogs and muddy boots welcome *(Guy Vowles)*

STREET [ST4836]

Two Brewers BA16 0HB [Leigh Rd]:
Welcoming and popular dining pub, pleasant
décor, wide choice of well cooked fairly priced
food from bargain sandwiches up, Courage
Best and Directors and interesting guest beers;
garden with play area *(Colin and Janet Roe)*

TAUNTON [ST2525]

☆ *Hankridge Arms* TA1 2LR [Hankridge Way,
Deane Gate (nr Sainsbury); just off M5
junction 25 – A358 towards city, then right at
roundabout, right at next roundabout]: 16th-c
former farm reworked as well appointed old-
style dining pub in modern shopping complex,
buoyant atmosphere and quick friendly service,
generous enjoyable food from interesting
soups, sandwiches and baguettes through
sensibly priced pubby things to restaurant
dishes, largely no smoking dining room,
Badger ales, decent wines, big log fire; piped
music; dogs welcome, plenty of tables in
pleasant outside area *(Chris Glasson, Gill and
Keith Croxton)*

TIMBERSCOMBE [SS9542]

Lion TA24 7TP [Church St]: Good new
landlord in thoroughly refurbished Exmoor-
edge former coaching inn dating from 15th c,
thriving village-pub atmosphere in comfortable
flagstoned main bar and three rooms off, wide
choice of enjoyable honest pub food from
good fresh baguettes up, Exmoor Gold and
St Austell Tribute tapped from the cask,
reasonable prices, good log fire; dogs welcome,
bedrooms *(Brian and Anita Randall,
Michael Rowse)*

TINTINHULL [ST5019]

☆ *Crown & Victoria* BA22 8PZ [Farm St, village
signed off A303]: Roomy, light and airy main
bar, pleasant conservatory, wide choice of
generous fairly priced food cooked to order,
Butcombe and Wadworths, prompt helpful
service; disabled facilities, well kept big garden
with play area, bedrooms, handy for Tintinhull
House (NT) *(LYM, Dave Braisted)*

Lamb BA22 8PY [Vicarage St]: Welcoming
village pub with good value straightforward
food inc two-course bargains (must book for
no smoking restaurant), helpful staff, Courage

Directors, good choice of other drinks; well
kept garden behind, handy for Tintinhull
Manor (NT) *(Teresa Pritchard)*

TRUDOXHILL [ST7443]

☆ *White Hart* BA11 5DP [off A361 SW of
Frome]: Enjoyable food from good open
sandwiches and baguettes to interesting main
dishes, good choice of changing ales,
Thatcher's farm cider, interesting sensibly
priced wine choice, mainly table seating with a
couple of easy chairs by one of the two log
fires, beams and stripped stone; no dogs,
children in eating area, picnic-sets in flower-
filled sheltered side garden *(MRSM, Pat and
Robert Watt, the Didler, LYM, Hugh Roberts)*

TRULL [ST2122]

Winchester Arms TA3 7LG [Church Rd]: Cosy
village local with friendly attentive staff,
enjoyable varied food inc good value set menu
and lots of puddings, Exmoor ales, small
dining room; bedrooms *(Bob and Margaret
Holder, David and Teresa Frost)*

TYTHERINGTON [ST7645]

Fox & Hounds BA11 5BN: 17th-c, with
roomy and tidy L-shaped stripped-stone bar,
small no smoking dining area, generous
interesting food (not Mon) inc unusual curries
and Sun roasts, Bass, Butcombe and a guest
beer tapped from the cask, farm ciders,
welcoming landlord and atmosphere; tables
outside, comfortable bedrooms, good breakfast
(MRSM)

UPTON [ST0129]

☆ *Lowtrow Cross Inn* TA4 2DB: Good fresh
home-made food in character low-beamed bar
and more straightforward no smoking back
restaurant, Badger, Bass and Cotleigh, friendly
landlord and staff, efficient service, relaxed
pubby atmosphere, nice rugs on bare boards or
flagstones, enormous inglenook; no dogs;
children welcome, attractive surroundings,
bedrooms *(Richard and Anne Ansell, LYM,
Jeremy Whitehorn)*

VOBSTER [ST7049]

☆ *Vobster Inn* BA3 5RJ [Lower Vobster]:
Relaxed and roomy old stone-built dining pub
particularly popular with older people
(children welcomed too), good food choice
from smart sandwiches and range of local
cheeses to fish fresh daily from Cornwall in
three comfortable open-plan areas with antique
furniture, friendly licensees from Australia,
helpful young staff, Fullers London Pride, good
new world wines by the glass (plenty of room
if you just want a drink); tables on side lawn
with boules, peaceful views, adventure
playground behind *(Liz and Tony Colman,
Gaynor Gregory, BB, Sylvia and
Tony Birbeck)*

WAMBROOK [ST2907]

☆ *Cotley Inn* TA20 3EN [off A30 W of Chard;
don't follow the small signs to Cotley itself]:
Well run stone-built pub, smartly
unpretentious, good competitively priced
food cooked to order from light dishes to fish
and steaks, cheerful efficient staff, Otter and
Wadworths 6X, nice ambiance, simple
flagstoned entrance bar opening on one side

into small plush bar, several open fires, popular two-room no smoking dining area (best to book, children allowed here); pool, piped music, skittle alley; seats and play area in nice garden, well refurbished bedrooms, quiet spot with plenty of surrounding walks *(Bob and Margaret Holder, Mr and Mrs W Mills, LYM)*

WATCHET [ST0643]

Star TA23 0BZ [Mill Lane (B3191)]: Old low-beamed cottagey pub nr seafront, wooden furniture, lots of bric-a-brac and pleasantly homely atmosphere, cheerful efficient service, good log fire, straightforward reasonably priced food, four good changing real ales; picnic-sets out in front and in garden *(JJW, CMW, Ian and Joan Blackwell)*

WELLOW [ST7358]

☆ *Fox & Badger* BA2 8QG [signed off A367 SW of Bath]: Cheerful flagstoned lounge with snug alcoves, small winged settles, woodburner in massive hearth, flowers on tables, Badger, Bass and Butcombe ales, Thatcher's farm cider, wide range of good value bar food, warmly welcoming service, good village atmosphere, family dining room; games and piped music in cosy bare-boards public bar; children and dogs welcome (pub sealyham and springer spaniel), picnic-sets in covered courtyard with barbecues, open all day Fri-Sun *(LYM, Dr and Mrs A K Clarke, Ian Phillips)*

WELLS [ST5546]

☆ *Fountain* BA5 2UU [St Thomas St]: Comfortable and very friendly big-windowed dining pub, now laid as a restaurant on both floors, with tablecloths on half the tables in the downstairs dining bar (which has a good log fire), and steep stairs up to the original dining room; popular sensibly priced food from filled baguettes and wkdy lunchtime bargains to fresh fish, interesting dishes and a good Sun lunch, attentive staff, Butcombe and Courage Best, good choice of wines, good coffee, daily papers; can be fully booked even wkdys, may be piped music; children welcome, right by cathedral and moated Bishop's Palace *(Gaynor Gregory, Peter Mack Wilkins, BB, Terry Buckland, Henry and Fiona Dryden, Douglas and Ann Hare)*

WEST CHINNOCK [ST4613]

Muddled Man TA18 7PT [Lower St]: Friendly unassuming local with attractively priced straightforward food using good local meat, interesting local ales, farm cider, unobtrusive small pool area off simple single bar; attractive rustic village, open all day Fri-Sun, cl winter Mon lunchtime *(Pete Baker, Guy Vowles)*

WEST HATCH [ST2719]

Farmers TA3 5RS [W of village, at Slough Green; from A358 head for RSPCA centre and keep past]: Spacious and friendly 16th-c beamed dining pub, renamed (was Farmers Arms) perhaps to reflect shift upscale on the food side, with good new French chefs; Otter ales tapped from the cask, good service, open fires, bleached wood furniture, stylishly simple modern décor, no smoking restaurant; children welcome, garden with nice herb garden, small terrace and play area *(Bob and Margaret Holder)*

WESTON-SUPER-MARE [ST3562]

Golden Lion BS22 6ET [High St, Worle]: Enjoyable low-priced food from baguettes and baked potatoes up inc lunchtime bargains for two, good value wines, good beers, friendly helpful staff; picnic-sets outside *(Ken Flawn)*

Regency BS23 2AG [Lower Church Rd]: Comfortable, spacious and civilised, with good real ales, particularly local ones, good value lunchtime food from sandwiches and baguettes up; seats out in front *(Peter Mack Wilkins)*

WHATLEY [ST7347]

Sun BA11 3LA: Well updated by current licensees, good décor, new floors, new kitchen doing enjoyable generous food inc proper pies, changing daily and using only fresh local produce, local real ales; spectacular views from tables outside *(D P and M A Miles)*

WHEDDON CROSS [SS9238]

☆ *Rest & Be Thankful* TA24 7DR [A396/B3224, S of Minehead]: Spotless comfortably modern two-room bar with warm welcome, Exmoor and a guest beer such as Cotleigh or St Austell, good soft drinks choice, two good log fires, huge jug collection, wide range of usual food from sandwiches up (can be a wait if busy), no smoking restaurant, games area with pool and darts, skittle alley; piped music, no dogs; tables out in courtyard adjoining Exmoor public car park (with lavatory for the disabled), four good bedrooms and breakfast, good walking country *(Nigel Long, LYM, Dave Braisted, JJW, CMW, John and Jackie Chalcraft, Geoff Calcott)*

WIDCOMBE [ST2216]

☆ *Holman Clavel* TA3 7EA [Culmhead, by ridge rd W of B3170 2 miles S of Corfe]: Charmingly unspoilt deep-country local dating from 14th c and named after the massive holly chimney-beam over its huge log fire, comfortable dining area, good sensibly priced home cooking strong on fish and seafood, friendly informal staff, Butcombe Bitter and Gold and Fullers London Pride, colourful wine list, nice atmosphere with fresh local produce for sale, original skittle alley; dogs welcome, small garden, handy for Blackdown Hills, open all day *(BB, Lee and Liz Potter, Michael Rowse, David and Helen Sawyer, Anthony Double)*

WINSCOMBE [ST4257]

Woodborough BS25 1HD [Sandford Rd]: Big beamed dining pub, smart, comfortable and busy, with good range of above-average food inc local produce and good veg, helpful friendly staff, Butcombe and Wadworths 6X, good wine choice, separate drinking areas *(Ken Flawn, John and Susan Fysh)*

WINSFORD [SS9034]

☆ *Royal Oak* TA24 7JE [off A396 about 10 miles S of Dunster]: Rather smart and prettily placed thatched Exmoor inn with beams and big stone fireplace in attractively furnished lounge bar, big bay-window seat looking across towards village green and foot and packhorse bridges over River Winn, more eating space in second bar, several pretty and comfortable lounges, three no smoking rooms, good choice of enjoyable food (now all day, at least in summer) from baguettes to restaurant dishes, Brakspears and Butcombe tapped from the cask, nice pub labrador; children and dogs welcome, good bedrooms *(Mr and Mrs W Mills, A S and M E Marriott, LYM, Gordon and Jay Smith, Dr Peter Crawshaw, Peter and Giff Bennett, David and Sheila Pearcey, George Atkinson)*

WITHAM FRIARY [ST7440]
☆ *Seymour Arms* BA11 5HF [signed from B3092 S of Frome]: Well worn in rustic flagstoned local, two simple rooms off hatch-service corridor, one with darts, the other with central table skittles; Bass and Cottage, Rich's local farm cider, open fire, cards and dominoes – no juke box or machines; good-sized attractive garden by main rail line *(Pete Baker, MLR, the Didler)*

WORTH [ST5145]
Pheasant BA5 1LQ [B3139 Wells—Wedmore]: Cheerful pub with newish licensees doing enjoyable food in simple bar and attractively unpretentious dining area, real ales, decent house wines, smiling service; skittle alley, garden *(Ann Sutton)*

WRANTAGE [ST3022]
Canal Inn TA3 6DF [A378 E of M5 junction 25]: Welcoming and neatly kept three-room country pub with friendly and helpful young licensees, enjoyable fresh food (not Sun evening) in bar and dining room, all local sourcing plus daily brixham fish, changing real ales, farm cider, log fires, parrot; surcharge for credit cards; dogs welcome, good-sized garden with play area, chickens and goats, cl Mon lunchtime *(John and Wendy Dodds, Gordon Kenworthy, David Clark)*

WRAXALL [ST4971]
Old Barn BS48 1LQ [just off Bristol Rd (B3130)]: Rustic gabled barn conversion with scrubbed tables, school benches and soft sofas under oak rafters, stripped boards, flagstones

and festoons of dried flowers; welcoming atmosphere, five real ales inc Bass and local brews tapped from the cask, friendly service; two TV screens, Sun quiz night; garden with good play area and barbecues on cobbled terrace *(Philip Lane, the Didler)*

WRINGTON [ST4762]
Plough BS40 5QA [2½ miles off A370 Bristol—Weston, from bottom of Rhodiate Hill]: Large popular beamed pub rambling around central servery with Smiles and Youngs, interesting wines and cocktails, good value food (all day Sun) inc tapas, traditional pubby décor, step up to long no smoking dining area, two coal or log fires; two TVs, fruit machine and cash machine; lots of picnic-sets out on sloping grass, more under cover on heated terrace, open all day *(Bob and Margaret Holder, BB, Alan and Paula McCully, Ken Marshall, Peter Mack Wilkins)*

YARLINGTON [ST6529]
☆ *Stags Head* BA9 8DG [Pound Lane]: Interesting old flagstoned and low-ceilinged country pub tucked away in rustic hamlet, Bass and Otter from small central locals' bar, woodburner, chapel chairs and mixed pine tables on left, carpeted room on right with big log fire, modern landscape prints and a collection of old seats and tables, friendly welcome, enjoyable food, decent wines; picnic-sets in sheltered back garden with small flagstoned back terrace and barbecue; cl Sun evening and Mon *(BB, Mary Kirman and Tim Jefferson)*

YEOVIL [ST5516]
Armoury BA20 1DY [The Park]: Old-fashioned, with pubby food, Wadworths and a guest beer, farm cider, darts, pool, table football, bar skittles and skittle alley; bedrooms *(Leon Shaw)*
Fleur de Lys BA21 4NP [Mudford Rd]: Friendly new landlord keeping five real ales, good range of pubby food; children and dogs welcome, good-sized garden *(Geoff Wheating)*

Staffordshire

This county has a great line in unpretentious and properly pubby pubs, many of them unspoilt and traditional in the best possible way. What's more, they represent really good value for money, for both their food and their beer. This is one of the cheapest areas in Britain for pub drinks. The Yew Tree at Cauldon, with its remarkable collections from odd well worn bric-a-brac to impressive antiques, sets a fine example with its particularly low drinks prices, but beer prices in the county are generally well below the national average. Burton upon Trent has for many years been a brewing centre, with Marstons (who now also brew Bass) the main brewer based there. The Burton Bridge Inn there, a cheerful main *Guide* entry, produces its own good value Burton Bridge ales which can also be found elsewhere, and other local brews we found in our main entries were Blythe, Enville and Kinver. A good batch of nicely varied new main entries this year consists of the Blue Bell on the edge of Kidsgrove (great for real ale lovers with its thoughtfully sourced changing beers), the Cat at Enville (a fine old place, wonderful if you're a sausage and mash fan), and the Meynell Ingram Arms at Hoar Cross (a bustling place with a wide range of great food). Other pubs on notable form here include the Goats Head in Abbots Bromley (good food in nice surroundings), the unfussy George at Alstonefield, now in the second generation of the same family (its hearty meals, welcoming atmosphere and sensible pricing just right for the Peak District), and the Holly Bush at Salt (very popular for its attractively priced food). Not many counties in the *Guide* can boast a dining pub of the year with a full range of imaginative main courses under the £10 mark, but you can experience exactly that admirable situation at the Staffordshire Dining Pub of the Year – the carefully run Boat in Lichfield, which really deserves praise for selling such beautifully prepared dishes at such fair prices. In the Lucky Dip section at the end of the chapter, pubs showing well in recent months include the Queens at Freehay near Cheadle and Manifold Inn at Hulme End.

ABBOTS BROMLEY   SK0824   Map 7
Goats Head
Market Place; WS15 3BP

Famous for its annual horn dance, this is a charmingly unspoilt village, and this nicely atmospheric old black and white timbered pub fits in beautifully. The opened up cream-painted interior has attractive oak and stone floors, with furniture running from the odd traditional oak settle to comfy leather sofas, and a big inglenook has a warm fire. Served by attentive staff, the carefully prepared good value bar food might include soup or sandwiches (£3.95), thai-style fishcakes (£4.95), cottage pie (£5.95), pizzas (from £6.95), lasagne (£7.50), salmon fillet with hollandaise (£8.95), 8oz sirloin (£8.95), and some more interesting daily specials; no smoking restaurant. Fullers London Pride, Greene King Abbot and Marstons Pedigree are well kept on handpump, and you can have any of the wines on their good wine list (Tanners of Shrewsbury) by the glass; piped music, TV. Picnic-sets and teak tables out on a neat sheltered lawn look up to the church tower behind; more reports please. *(Recommended by Derek and Sylvia Stephenson, Tony and*

Wendy Hobden, BOB, Neil and Brenda Skidmore, J A Hooker, Matthew Hegarty)

Punch ~ Lease Dawn Skelton ~ Real ale ~ Bar food (12-2, 6-9; 12-9 Sun) ~ Restaurant ~ (01283) 840254 ~ Children welcome in restaurant ~ Open 12-2, 5-11; 12-11 Sun; closed Mon lunchtime

ALSTONEFIELD SK1355 Map 7
George
Village signposted from A515 Ashbourne—Buxton; DE6 2FX

This stone-built Peak District pub has been handed down a generation since the last edition of the *Guide*, and the good news is that little is expected to change. All sorts of people, from sightseers and campers, to cyclists and walkers (though no muddy boots) enjoy its charming simplicity and cheery local atmosphere. It's in a peaceful farming hamlet by the green, and fine weather makes it a real pleasure to sit out on wooden benches beneath the inn-sign and watch the world go by, or in the big sheltered stableyard behind the pub which has picnic-sets by a pretty rockery. For a longer stay you can arrange with the landlord to camp on the croft. The unchanging straightforward low-beamed bar has locals' pewter tankards hanging by the copper-topped bar counter (well kept Burtonwood Bitter, Marstons Pedigree and a guest such as Jennings Snecklifter on handpump), a collection of old Peak District photographs and pictures, a roaring coal fire on chilly days and cribbage and dominoes. The spacious no smoking family/dining room has plenty of tables and wheelback chairs. Tasty no nonsense home-made food, very much geared towards hikers, is good value and includes sandwiches (£2.95), ploughman's (£5.50), meat and potato pie (£6.75), lasagne (£7.50), fillet steak (£12.95), a couple of daily specials, and delicious home-made puddings such as apple bakewell pudding (£3); you order food from the friendly staff at the kitchen door. *(Recommended by Theocsbrian, I J and S A Bufton, Richard, the Didler, W W Burke, Paul Robinshaw, Colin Buckle, Michael B Griffith, Geoff and Linda Payne, John Tavernor, John Saul, Dr David Clegg)*

Union Pub Company ~ Tenants Richard and Sue Grandjean ~ Real ale ~ Bar food (12-2, 7-9) ~ (01335) 310205 ~ Children welcome in dining room ~ Dogs allowed in bar ~ Open 11-3, 6-11; 11-11 Sat; 12-10.30 Sun

BURTON UPON TRENT SK2423 Map 7
Burton Bridge Inn 🍴 £
Bridge Street (A50); DE14 1SY

Gloriously unchanged from one year to the next, this straightforward bustling old brick local is as genuinely friendly and cheerily down-to-earth as ever. It's the tap for Burton Bridge Brewery (out in the long old-fashioned yard at the back) which produces the Bitter, Festival, Golden Delicious, Gold Medal and Porter that are well kept and served on handpump here, alongside a guest such as Timothy Taylors Landlord. They also keep around 25 whiskies and over a dozen country wines. The simple little front area leads into an adjacent bar, separated from a no smoking oak-panelled lounge by the serving counter. The bar has wooden pews, plain walls hung with notices, awards and brewery memorabilia, and the lounge has oak beams, a flame-effect fire and old oak tables and chairs. Simple but hearty bar snacks include filled cobs, such as roast beef and pork (from £1.60), filled yorkshire pudding (from £3.40) and ploughman's (£3.60); the panelled upstairs dining room is open only at lunchtime. A blue-brick patio overlooks the brewery. *(Recommended by Pete Baker, the Didler, David Carr, C J Fletcher, Theo, Anne and Jane Gaskin)*

Own brew ~ Licensees Kevin and Jan McDonald ~ Real ale ~ Bar food (lunchtime only, not Sun) ~ No credit cards ~ (01283) 536596 ~ Dogs welcome ~ Open 11.30-2.15, 5-11; 12-2, 7-10.30 Sun; closed bank hol Mon lunchtime

---

Our web site is at: .www.goodguides.co.uk

CAULDON SK0749 Map 7

Yew Tree ㉕ ★★ £

Village signposted from A523 and A52 about 8 miles W of Ashbourne; ST10 3EJ

The charming landlord at this timelessly idiosyncratic place has amassed a museum's-worth of curiosities over the years, and for most readers the dust and wear and tear here just add to the atmosphere, though some are not quite so sure. The most impressive pieces are perhaps the working polyphons and symphonions – 19th-c developments of the musical box, often taller than a person, each with quite a repertoire of tunes and elaborate sound-effects; take plenty of 2p pieces to work them. But there are also two pairs of Queen Victoria's stockings, ancient guns and pistols, several penny-farthings, an old sit-and-stride boneshaker, a rocking horse, swordfish blades, dominoes and cribbage, a little 800 BC greek vase, and even a fine marquetry cabinet crammed with notable early staffordshire pottery. Soggily sprung sofas mingle with 18th-c settles, plenty of little wooden tables and a four-person oak church choir seat with carved heads which came from St Mary's church in Stafford; above the bar is an odd iron dog-carrier (don't ask how it works!). As well as all this, there's an expanding choir of fine tuneful longcase clocks in the gallery just above the entrance, a collection of six pianolas (one of which is played most nights) with an excellent repertoire of piano rolls, a working vintage valve radio set, a crank-handle telephone, a sinuous medieval wind instrument made of leather, and a Jacobean four-poster which was once owned by Josiah Wedgwood and still has his original wig hook on the headboard. Clearly it would be almost an overwhelming task to keep all that sprucely clean. The drinks here are very reasonably priced (so no wonder it's popular with locals), and you'll find well kept Bass, Burton Bridge and Grays Dark Mild on handpump or tapped from the cask, along with about a dozen interesting malt whiskies; piped music (probably Radio 2), darts, shove-ha'penny, table skittles, dominoes and cribbage. Simple good value tasty snacks include pork pies (from 70p), meat and potato pies, chicken and mushroom or steak pies (85p), hot big filled baps and sandwiches (from £1.50), quiche, smoked mackerel or ham salad (£3.50), and home-made puddings (£1.50). When you arrive here don't be put off by the plain exterior, or the fact that the pub is tucked unpromisingly between enormous cement works and quarries and almost hidden by a towering yew tree. (Recommended by Richard, the Didler, Mark Flynn, P Dawn, Rona Murdoch, Mike and Mary Carter, W W Burke, Simon Cleasby)

Free house ~ Licensee Alan East ~ Real ale ~ Bar food ~ No credit cards ~ (01538) 308348 ~ Children in polyphon room ~ Dogs welcome ~ Folk music first Tues in month ~ Open 10-2.30(3 Sat), 6-12; 12-3, 7-12 Sun

ENVILLE SO8286 Map 4

Cat

A458 W of Stourbridge; DY7 5HA

The nicest part of this pub is the bar closest to the road, where its 17th-c origins seem clearest. Here, two linked carpeted rooms with a slight step between have heavy black beams, ancient timbers showing in the walling, a log fire in a small brick fireplace, cast-iron framed and other pub tables, and brocaded wall seats with comfortable matching oak carver chairs – the tabby cat may have its eye on one, but the quiet collie wouldn't dare. The bar counter has changing Enville real ales on handpump, brewed on the other side of the estate, using honey to add to their distinctive tastes: typically Ale, White and Ginger or Phoenix on handpump. Three or four guests from brewers might be from Hop Back, Kinver and Wye Vallley – if they're new to you, the landlord can help with your choice. He does mulled wine in winter, and keeps a range of country wines. A speciality here is the sausage mix and mash menu (£7). The sausages are made for the pub by a local butcher, and you get to choose from a list of ten. Then there's a list of eight mashes and eight gravies, in any combination you want – you might go for olde english sausages with bacon and leek mash and Guinness and mushroom gravy or tomato and garlic sausages with pesto mash and balsamic reduction gravy. Other bar food includes sandwiches (from £3.50), hot baguettes (from £4.50), vegetarian pasta of the day (£6.75), battered cod or steak and ale pie (£6.95), and daily specials such as butternut and baby corn tartlet (£6.75), tuna steak with olives and citrus fruits (£7.50); the family room and restaurant are no smoking. A comfortable back area has plush wall banquettes and dark tables, and there is a restaurant upstairs; piped music, games machines and darts. You come into the pub through a splendidly old-fashioned paved yard alongside a monumentally tall and massive estate wall, and back here there are picnic-sets on a gravel terrace. The estate has attractive lakeside grounds, and the pub is also on the Staffordshire Way, so popular with walkers. Until 2004 Sunday walkers went dry here, as it was only in that year that the estate lifted a 300-year ban on Sunday drinking. *(Recommended by Guy Vowles, the Didler, Paul and Gloria Howell, John and Helen Rushton)*

Free house ~ Licensee Guy Ayres ~ Real ale ~ Bar food (12-2(2.30 Fri, 3 Sun)), 7-9.30; not Sun evening or Mon) ~ Restaurant ~ (01384) 872209 ~ Children in family room and main lounge ~ Dogs allowed in bar ~ Open 12-2.30(3 Sat), 7(6.30 Fri, Sat)-11; 12-5.30 Sun; closed Sun evening

HOAR CROSS   SK1323   Map 7
Meynell Ingram Arms
Abbots Bromley Road, off A515 Yoxall—Sudbury; DE13 8RB

Well regarded for its very good, locally sourced food, this is an attractive, bustling place, with an enjoyably buoyant feel on our Friday night visit; it's a pub that appeals to drinkers as much as diners. The big car park fills up fast, as do the several neat little rooms that ramble round the central bar counter. It's been carefully extended in recent years, with the smartest area the brightly painted no smoking room leading to the dining room, with its elegant red curtains and coal effect fire. Elsewhere there's a traditional red-tiled room with a brick fireplace, hunting pictures and a bespectacled fox's head, comfortably upholstered seats, a few beams and brasses, and yellow walls displaying local notices and certificates praising the food. Marstons Pedigree, Timothy Taylors Landlord and a changing guest like Burton Bridge Golden Delicious on handpump (though not necessarily all from the same side of the bar); good wines too, and helpful young staff. The wide choice of food might include lunchtime sandwiches (from £3.75) and hot filled cobs (from £4.75), soup (in two sizes – from £3.45), home-made mango and brie filo pastry parcels with sweet chilli sauce (£5.50), ploughman's and salads, roasted vegetable tagliatelle carbonara (£7.95), pan-fried chicken breast stuffed with black pudding and apricot on a bed of sautéed mediterranean vegetables (£9.15), baked red snapper fillet on gingered red cabbage and apple (£9.35), and puddings such as jam or syrup sponge (£4.25). There are tables in a courtyard behind, and some on the grass in front; it's a pretty spot in summer. *(Recommended by Pete Baker, David Martin, Ian Tolfts)*

Free house ~ Licensees Jane and Mike Chappell ~ Real ale ~ Bar food (not Sun evening) ~ Restaurant ~ (01283) 575202 ~ Open 12-11(12 Sat); 12-10.30 Sun

KIDSGROVE   SJ8354   Map 7
Blue Bell ◧
25 Hardings Wood; off A50 NW edge of town; ST7 1EG

They take beer very seriously at this simple little pub, converted from two cottages at the junction of the Trent & Mersey and Macclesfield canals. The constantly changing range of six real ales is carefully selected from smaller, often very unusual brewers, typically including Acorn, Crouch Vale, Oakham, Townhouse and Whim. More than two thousand brews have passed through the pumps over the last eight years; current and forthcoming choices are listed on the pub's website, www.bluebellkidsgrove.co.uk. They don't stock beers from the bigger producers, and lagers are restricted to czech or belgian brews; there's also usually a draught continental beer, at least one farm cider, a good range of bottled beers, and various teas, coffees and soft drinks. Service is friendly and knowledgeable. The four small, carpeted rooms are unfussy and straightforward, with only a few tables in each, and blue upholstered benches running around the white-painted walls; there's a coal fire, and maybe soft piped music. In fine weather there are tables in front, and more on a tiny back lawn. Bar food is limited to filled rolls, at weekends only. Note the limited opening hours, and they may not always open on time: on our sping evening visit quite a crowd was patiently waiting before the doors finally opened. *(Recommended by Sue Holland, Dave Webster, the Didler)*

Free house ~ Licensees Dave and Kay Washbrook ~ Real ale ~ No credit cards ~ (01782) 774052 ~ Well behaved children until 9pm ~ Dogs welcome ~ Impromptu folk Sun evenings ~ Open evenings only on weekdays, 7.30-11; 1-4, 7-11 Sat; 12-10.30 Sun; closed Mon

LICHFIELD SK0705 Map 4
Boat 🍴

2.7 miles from M6 Toll, junction T6: B5011 S, then left on A5, then at Muckley Corner roundabout head SW on A461 Walsall Road; WS14 0BU

Staffordshire Dining Pub of the Year

Readers are delighted to find such top-notch food at such terribly fair prices at this very well run modern pub. Dishes, which are imaginative, very well prepared and beautifully presented, might include starters such as soup (£2.95), crispy chicken and noodles with plum sauce (£4.95), fried scallops with rocket salad (£7.25), and main courses such as caramelised onion tart with rocket and plum tomatoes (£7.50), roast ham hock with parsley sauce or mackerel fillet on chive mash with mustard sauce (£8.50), roast shoulder of lamb with redcurrant and mint or fried duck breast with caramelised orange and red wine sauce (£9), sirloin steak (£10.95) and puddings such as toffee and banana crumble or warm chocolate tart (£3.95). The pub is immaculately kept and staff are cheerful and tremendously attentive. Well lit from above by a big skylight, the first area as you enter is the most contemporary, with bright plastic flooring, views straight into the kitchen, striking photoprints, blue and russet café furniture and potted palms, all of which is dominated by huge floor-to-ceiling food blackboards. A dining area to the left has views on to the canal (currently undergoing restoration), and to the right the solid light wood bar counter has three constantly changing thoughtfully sourced real ales from brewers such as Blythe and Youngs on handpump, and around ten wines by the glass. Further round to the right a plainer area has sturdy modern pale pine furniture on russet pink carpets and prints on white walls; faint piped music and the restaurant and part of the bar are no smoking. A landscaped area outside is paved with a central raised decking area. There is good wheelchair access throughout. *(Recommended by Karen Eliot, Bren and Val Speed, Colin Fisher, Clifford Blakemore, John and Hazel Williams, Brian and Jacky Wilson, Phil and Jane Hodson, Peter Robinson, Ian and Jane Irving, P Burns, Arthus, Jo Lilley, Simon Calvert, Neil Kellett, John and Yvonne Davies)*

Free house ~ Licensee Ann Holden ~ Real ale ~ Bar food (12-2.30, 6-9.30; 12-8.30 Sun) ~ Restaurant ~ (01543) 361692 ~ Well behaved children welcome ~ Dogs allowed in bar ~ Open 12-2.30, 6-11; 12-11 Sun

SALT SJ9527 Map 7
Holly Bush

Village signposted off A51 S of Stone (and A518 NE of Stafford); ST18 0BX

As they serve food all day, and it does draw the crowds, you may want to aim for a slightly off peak visit (or at the least get here early for a table) when you visit this very lovely white-painted 14th-c house. Inside is as delightful as the charming deep thatched, flower bedecked exterior will lead you to expect. The oldest part has a heavy beamed and planked ceiling (some of the beams are attractively carved), a salt cupboard built in by the coal fire, and other nice old-fashioned touches such as an antique pair of clothesbrushes hanging by the door, attractive sporting prints and watercolours, and an ancient pair of riding boots on the mantelpiece. Several cosy areas spread off from the standing-room serving section, with comfortable settees as well as more orthodox seats. A modern back extension blends in well, with beams, stripped brickwork and a small coal fire. About half the pub is no smoking. Adnams, Marstons Pedigree and a guest such as Black Sheep are well kept on handpump, and served by really cheerful staff. This year the helpful landlord tells us he's added a commercial smoking oven, which allows them to make their own smoked meats and fish, and an 18th-c-styled wood-fired oven (in the beer garden) for pizzas, hearth breads and other interesting dishes. The menu features traditional english food in the main, made where possible from locally sourced products, and they make their own sausages. Served in generous helpings, and very reasonably priced, there might be soup (£2.95), blue cheese stuffed pears or warm watercress, potato and bacon salad (£3.95), battered cod or champagne and mash sausages or pork, plum and mulled wine sausages with bubble and squeak (£7.95), chicken breast in red wine with raisins and apricots or steak and ale pie (£8.95), braised venison with celery and chestnuts (£9.25), 8oz sirloin steak (£10.50), puddings such as crumbles (from £3.45), and a british cheeseboard (£4.95). The back of the pub is beautifully tended, with rustic picnic-sets on a big lawn, and they may have traditional jazz and a hog roast in summer and a fireworks display on 5 November. The pub operates a type of locker system for credit cards, which they will ask to keep if you are running a tab. *(Recommended by Michael and Jenny Back, Dr and Mrs T E Hothersall, Robert Garner, Sue Holland, Dave Webster, Dr and Mrs A K Clarke, M G Hart, Simon and Sally Small, Pat and Tony Martin, Ian and Ruth Laurence, Dave Braisted, Maurice and Gill McMahon)*

Pyramid ~ Licensees Geoffrey and Joseph Holland ~ Real ale ~ Bar food (12-9.30) ~ (01889) 508234 ~ Children welcome away from counter area ~ Open 12-11.30

STOURTON   SO8485   Map 4
Fox

A458 W of junction with A449, towards Enville; DY7 5BL

Standing alone with well spaced picnic-sets on a big stretch of sloping grass and surrounded by woodland, this isolated roadside pub is well placed for Kinver Country Park walks, and the Staffordshire Way. Inside, several cosily small areas ramble back from the small serving bar by the entrance, with its well kept Bathams Best and a guest such as Wye Valley Butty Bach on handpump (and a noticeboard of hand-written travel offers). Tables are mostly sturdy and varnished, with pews, settles and comfortable library or dining chairs; there is green carpet here, dark blue there, bare boards beyond, with a good positive colour scheme picked up nicely by the curtains, and some framed exotic menus and well chosen prints (jazz and golf both feature). The woodburning stoves may be opened to give a cheery blaze on cold days. They put out big bunches of flowers, and the lighting (mainly low voltage spots) has been done very carefully, giving an intimate bistro feel in the areas round on the right, but the warm atmosphere is largely down to the welcoming family who've been running it for over 30 years. Bar food includes lunchtime sandwiches (from £3.25), as well as soup (£3.50), tomato and basil pasta (£6.75), mediterranean risotto (£9.25), battered cod or fish pie (£9.50), steak and stout pie (£9.95) and 8oz sirloin steak (£7.95); it's a good idea to book if you want to go to one of their fortnightly fish evenings; no smoking dining areas including a smart conservatory which has neat bentwood furniture and proper tablecloths; piped music. *(Recommended by Chris Glasson, Theo, Anne and Jane Gaskin)*

Free house ~ Licensee Stefan Caron ~ Real ale ~ Bar food (till 5 Sun, not Sun evening) ~ Restaurant ~ (01384) 872614 ~ Open 11-11; 12-10.30 Sun; 11-3, 4.30-11 weekdays in winter

---

Post Office address codings confusingly give the impression that some pubs are in Staffordshire, when they're really in Cheshire or Derbyshire (which is where we list them).

WETTON SK1055 Map 7

Olde Royal Oak

Village signposted off Hulme End—Alstonefield road, between B5054 and A515; DE6 2AF

Nestling as it does in the heart of lovely National Trust countryside, with Wetton Mill and the Manifold Valley nearby, and a croft behind the pub for caravans and tents, it's not surprising that this aged white-painted and shuttered stone-built village house is popular with walkers, with boot covers at both doors. There's a good convivial atmosphere in the bar, which has black beams with white ceiling boards above, small dining chairs around rustic tables, an oak corner cupboard, and a coal fire in the stone fireplace. The bar extends into a more modern-feeling area, which in turn leads to a carpeted sun lounge looking out over the small garden; piped music, darts, TV, shove-ha'penny, cribbage and dominoes. The family room is no smoking. You can choose from more than 30 whiskies, and they've well kept Greene King Abbot, Theakstons Best and a guest from a brewer such as Belvoir on handpump. Reasonably priced bar food includes soup (£2.50), beefburger, breaded mushrooms or spicy chicken dippers (£2.95), battered cod or vegetarian dish of the day (£6.45), gammon with pineapple and egg or chicken tikka (£6.95), steaks (from £9.45) and puddings such as treacle sponge or strawberry ice-cream sundae (£2.95); more reports please. (Recommended by Richard, the Didler)

Free house ~ Licensees Brian and Janet Morley ~ Real ale ~ Bar food (not Mon, Tues in winter) ~ (01335) 310287 ~ Children in sun lounge ~ Dogs allowed in bar ~ Open 12-2.30(3 Sat, Sun), 7-11; closed Tues lunchtime, and Mon lunchtime in winter ~ Bedrooms: 1£40S

LUCKY DIP

Besides the fully inspected pubs, you might like to try these Lucky Dips recommended to us and described by readers (if you do, please send us reports: www.goodguides.co.uk).

ABBOTS BROMLEY [SK0824]
Coach & Horses WS15 3BN [High St]: Comfortable Tudor village pub with wide choice of enjoyable food in attractive beamed bar and restaurant (worth booking), good range of real ales, friendly helpful staff; pleasant garden, good value bedrooms *(John Wooll, David Green, Tony and Wendy Hobden, John and Yvonne Davies)*
ALREWAS [SK1715]
Crown DE13 7BS [Post Office Rd]: Friendly and cosy local with three real ales such as Bass and Charles Wells Bombardier, enjoyable pub food inc OAP deals and good value Sun lunch, welcoming staff, decent wines, small comfortable dining room; tables out in front and in pleasant back garden *(John Tavernor, Brian and Jacky Wilson)*
☆ *George & Dragon* DE13 7AE [off A38; Main St]: Three friendly low-beamed linked rooms with Banks's, Marstons Pedigree and a guest beer, good value generous simple food inc fresh veg and children's dishes, efficient staff, attractive paintings; piped music; pleasant partly covered garden with good play area, children welcome in eating area; opens 5pm wkdys *(LYM, Francis Johnston, John Tavernor)*
ALSTONEFIELD [SK1255]
☆ *Watts Russell Arms* DE6 2GD [Hopedale]: Cheerful light and airy beamed pub handy for Dovedale and the Manifold (can get busy wknds), Black Sheep, Timothy Taylors Landlord and an occasional guest beer, decent range of soft drinks, low-priced straightforward food from sandwiches up, traditional games; children welcome, picnic-sets under parasols on sheltered tiered terrace and in garden, cl Mon and winter Sun evening *(the Didler, W W Burke, LYM)*
ALTON [SK0742]
Bulls Head ST10 4AQ [High St]: Greene King Abbot, good value bar lunches, nice staff; shame about the piped music; children welcome *(Mark Flynn)*
ANSLOW [SK2024]
☆ *Burnt Gate* DE13 9PY [Hopley Rd]: Comfortable largely no smoking country pub with good Sun lunches, some imaginative dishes and other fresh home-made food using local produce, friendly efficient staff, Bass and Marstons Pedigree, separate restaurant *(John and Yvonne Davies, C J Fletcher)*
ARMITAGE [SK0716]
☆ *Plum Pudding* WS15 4AZ [Rugeley Rd (A513)]: Canalside pub and brasserie with modern warm colour scheme, good contemporary food inc good value set menu, sandwiches and light dishes, Greene King Old Speckled Hen, Marstons Pedigree and Bass or Tetleys, decent wines (choice of large or giant glasses), friendly service; no dogs, loud live

music Fri; tables on waterside terrace and narrow canal bank (moorings available), bedrooms in neighbouring cottage *(Bren and Val Speed, BB, John Rushton)*

BALTERLEY [SJ7450]

Broughton Arms CW2 5PY [Newcastle Rd (A531/B5500, Balterley Heath)]: Well run family dining pub, clean and airy, with lots of prints, ornaments and central fire in bar, friendly staff, real ales inc Black Sheep; wide choice of good value home-made food inc sandwiches and children's dishes (all tables kept for dining on Sun – very busy then, with food all day), comfortable banquettes and no smoking section in dining balcony; back pergola facing open countryside *(Jenny and Brian Seller)*

BLYTHE BRIDGE [SJ9640]

Black Cock ST11 9NT [Uttoxeter Rd (A521)]: Warmly welcoming and helpful, with enjoyable freshly made food making the most of good local produce, good beer and wine choice, great 50s and Beatles memorabilia *(Tony and Maggie Harwood)*

BRADLEY [SJ8717]

Red Lion ST18 9DZ [off A518 W of Stafford; Smithy Lane]: Friendly old-world 16th-c village pub, Bass and good guest beers, good reasonably priced straightforward food inc OAP midweek bargains and good Sun lunch, decent wine choice, no smoking dining room *(John Tavernor, Neil and Brenda Skidmore)*

BRANSTON [SK2221]

Bridge Inn DE14 3EZ [off A5121 just SW of Burton; Tatenhill Lane, by Trent & Mersey Canal Bridge 34]: Cosy low-beamed canalside pub with Italian landlord doing good reasonably priced pizzas and pastas (and a rather special tiramisu), friendly staff and atmosphere, Marstons Pedigree, warm log fire; tables in waterside garden, good moorings, basic supplies for boaters and caravanners *(C J Fletcher, B M Eldridge)*

BREWOOD [SJ8808]

Bridge Inn ST19 9BD [High Green; by Shrops Union Canal Bridge 14]: Friendly and comfortable two-bar pub with changing ales such as Brakspears, Mansfield, Marstons Bitter and Double Drop, Shepherd Neame Spitfire and White Star Titanic, generous usual food at bargain prices (very popular wknds), dining extension; no credit cards; picnic-sets out high over canal *(Ian Phillips, Keith and Maureen Trainer, John and Helen Rushton)*

BURSTON [SJ9330]

Greyhound ST18 0DR [just off A51 Sandon—Stone]: Busy dining pub, largely no smoking, extended from 17th-c core, with wide choice of good value food (all day wknds), three sensibly priced real ales, quick friendly service, spacious dining areas behind rambling traditional bar *(Dr and Mrs T E Hothersall, John Tavernor)*

BURTON UPON TRENT [SK2523]

Burton Bar DE14 1YQ [part of Coors Museum of Brewing, Horninglow St]: Reconstructed Edwardian bar, comfortable, with unusual local real ales; the brewing museum is an interesting outing *(PL, Tony and Wendy Hobden)*

Coopers Tavern DE14 1EG [Cross St]: Change of management (though we hope not of direction) for traditional pub with coal fire in homely no smoking front parlour, real ales tapped from casks in counterless back room with cask tables, lunchtime food; reports on new regime please *(Pete Baker, LYM, David Carr, C J Fletcher, the Didler)*

Derby Inn DE14 1RU [Derby Rd]: Unspoilt and well worn in friendly local with particularly good Marstons Pedigree, long-serving landlord, local produce for sale wknd, brewery glasses collection in cosy panelled lounge, lots of steam railway memorabilia in long narrow bar; sports TV; dogs welcome, open all day Fri/Sat *(the Didler, C J Fletcher)*

Devonshire Arms DE14 1BT [Station St]: Two-bar pub with good range of Burton Bridge ales and of continental bottled beers, also country wines, decent food (all day Fri/Sat, not Sun), lots of snug corners – some no smoking; pleasant back terrace with water feature, open all day Fri/Sat *(the Didler, C J Fletcher)*

Old Cottage Tavern DE14 2EG [Rangemoor St/Byrkley St]: Tied to local small brewery Old Cottage, interesting ales from them and guest breweries, good value food (not Sun evening) inc bargain specials and good Sun lunch, solid fuel stove, four rooms inc no smoking room, games room and pleasant little back restaurant; open all day *(the Didler, C J Fletcher)*

Wetmore Whistle DE14 1SH [Wetmore Rd]: Former Crown & Anchor reopened and renamed by Tynemill, tastefully renovated with plenty of individual touches, two unpretentiously comfortable linked areas and back café, good value simple nourishing food all day inc good breakfast from 8am, Castle Rock Harvest Pale, Marstons Pedigree and two or more guest beers tapped from the cask, continental beers on tap or by bottle, farm ciders, good choice of wines by the glass, good landlady and staff; open all day *(the Didler, C J Fletcher)*

CANNOCK WOOD [SK0412]

Park Gate WS15 4RN [Park Gate Rd, S side of Cannock Chase]: Good atmosphere, Banks's and Worthington ales, enjoyable food (not Sat evening) from sandwiches and bargain lunchtime hot dishes to wide restaurant choice, friendly efficient service, cushioned chairs and pews, lots of woodwork, woodburner, extensive no smoking dining area and conservatory; plenty of picnic-sets and play area outside, by Castle Ring Iron-Age fort, good Cannock Chase walks *(John Tavernor, Anton Mans)*

CHEADLE [SK0342]

☆ *Queens at Freehay* ST10 1RF [Counslow Rd, SE]: Friendly no smoking family dining pub with wide range of good mainly familiar food inc attractively priced light lunchtime dishes, Bass and Worthington, swift attentive service by well turned out staff, arch to neat and airy dining area from comfortable lounge; tables and chairs in attractive back garden *(Mr and Mrs D Collard, Mr and Mrs J Morris, LYM, John Tavernor, Martin and Alison Stainsby, Dr David Clegg)*

CODSALL [SJ8603]
Codsall Station WV8 1BY [Chapel Lane/Station Rd]: Pub in simply restored listed waiting room and ticket office (station still used by trains) with added conservatory, good range of Holdens beers inc one brewed for the pub, lots of railway memorabilia, good value basic food from sandwiches and baked potatoes to wknd specials; terrace tables, open all day wknds *(Robert Garner, Blaise Vyner, the Didler)*

CONSALL [SK0049]
☆ *Black Lion* ST9 0AJ [Consall Forge, OS Sheet 118 map ref 000491; best approach from Nature Park, off A522, using car park ½ mile past Nature Centre]: Traditional take-us-as-you-find-us tavern tucked away in rustic old-fashioned canalside settlement by restored steam railway station, enjoyable generous unpretentious food freshly cooked by landlord from huge baguettes to good fish choice, good coal fire, Marstons Best and Pedigree; piped music, no muddy boots; busy wknd lunchtimes, good walking area *(the Didler, LYM, Ian and Ruth Laurence, Bob and Laura Brock)*

CRESSWELL [SJ9739]
☆ *Izaak Walton* ST11 9RE [off A50 Stoke—Uttoxeter via Draycott in the Moors; Cresswell Lane]: Wide food choice all day from sandwiches, filled rolls and light dishes to steaks and mixed grill in attractive country inn with prints and panelling, several small rooms and larger upstairs area, real ales such as Adnams Best, Bass and Fullers London Pride, good wines by the glass, attentive welcoming service; well behaved children welcome, disabled facilities (but some steps), attractive back garden, open all day *(LYM, John Tavernor, Joan and Tony Walker)*

DOVEDALE [SK1450]
☆ *Izaak Walton* DE6 2AY [follow Ilam sign off A52, or Thorpe off A515, NW of Ashbourne]: Relaxing, informal and pleasantly individual low-beamed bar in sizeable hotel, walkers welcome, some distinctive antique oak settles and chairs, good log fire in massive central stone chimney; real ales, decent wines by the glass, good food priced as you'd expect in bar and restaurant, morning coffee and afternoon tea; very tranquil spot – seats on two spreading well kept lawns by sheep pastures, superb views; bedrooms comfortable *(LYM, John Tavernor)*

ECCLESHALL [SJ8329]
☆ *George* ST21 6DF [A519/B5026]: Beams, flagstones, coal fire in splendid central inglenook, cosy alcoves, well worn in unassuming furnishings, Slaters beers, good wines by the glass, farm cider, quick cheerful service, generous food from lunchtime sandwiches, baguettes and baked potatoes up in brightly lit dining area (all day wknds), reasonable prices; may be piped music, bar can be smoky; children in eating areas, dogs welcome, open all day *(Stan and Hazel Allen, LYM, Sue Holland, Dave Webster, Richard, John Tavernor, Paul and Ursula Randall,*

David Howell, Robert Garner, Derek and Sylvia Stephenson)

GNOSALL [SJ8221]
Royal Oak ST20 0BL [Newport Rd]: Small, civilised and friendly two-bar pub with nice atmosphere, Greene King IPA and Abbot, Highgate Mild and a weekly guest beer, enjoyable home-made food (all day till 8 Sun, not Tues) inc wide vegetarian choice; dogs welcome, good-sized garden *(Justin O'Doherty)*

GRINDON [SK0854]
☆ *Cavalier* ST13 7TP [signed off B5033 N of A523]: 16th-c character pub with roaring fires in smallish front bar and larger room behind, Theakstons and guest beers, hearty food from soup and fresh sandwiches up, obliging service, separate games room; pleasant informal garden, attractive walking countryside *(LYM, David and Sue Atkinson)*

HANLEY [SJ8847]
Coachmakers Arms ST1 3EA [Lichfield St]: Friendly traditional town pub, three small rooms and drinking corridor, several changing ales, darts, cards and dominoes, original seating and local tilework; open all day, cl lunchtime Sun *(the Didler)*

HARTSHILL [SJ8645]
Jolly Potters ST4 7NH [Hartshill Rd (A52)]: Traditional local with changing real ales from central servery, corridor to public bar (with TV) and three small homely lounges; open all day *(Pete Baker, the Didler)*

HAUGHTON [SJ8620]
Bell ST18 9EX: Choice of real ale, good value food inc Sun roasts, good friendly service even when busy *(Deb and John Arthur)*

HIGH OFFLEY [SJ7725]
Anchor ST20 0NG [off A519 Eccleshall—Newport; towards High Lea, by Shrops Union Canal, Bridge 42; Peggs Lane]: Real boaters' pub, little changed in the century or more this family have run it, two small simple rooms behind partition, Marstons Pedigree and Wadworths 6X in jugs from cellar, Weston's farm cider, may be lunchtime toasties; on Shrops Union Canal, outbuilding with small shop and semi-open lavatories, lovely garden with great hanging baskets and notable topiary anchor, caravan/campsite; occasional wknd singalongs, cl Mon-Thurs winter *(Angus Johnson, Carol Bolden, the Didler, Ian and Ruth Laurence, Nick and Lynne Carter)*

HILDERSTONE [SJ9437]
Spotgate ST15 8RP [Spot Acre; B5066 N]: Friendly service, Marstons Pedigree, reasonably priced wines, enjoyable bar food, also good value meals in two opulent 1930/40s Pullman dining coaches behind *(Terry Gurd)*

HIMLEY [SO8990]
☆ *Crooked House* DY3 4DA [signed down rather grim lane from B4176 Gornalwood—Himley, OS Sheet 139 map ref 896908]: Extraordinary sight, building thrown wildly out of kilter (mining subsidence), with slopes so weird things look as if they roll up not down them; otherwise a basic well worn low-priced pub,

mainly no smoking, with Banks's Bitter and Mild and guest beers, Weston's Old Rosie cider, straightforward food (all day in summer), some local antiques in level more modern extension, conservatory; children in eating areas, big outside terrace, open all day wknds and summer *(Paul and Gloria Howell, Ian Phillips, the Didler, LYM, R T and J C Moggridge)*

HOPWAS [SK1704]

Tame Otter B78 3AT [Hints Rd (A51 Tamworth—Lichfield)]: Cosily rustic Vintage Inn with usual beams, nooks and alcoves, three log fires, easy chairs, settles, dining chairs, old photographs and canalia, friendly well trained staff, reasonably priced food all day, good choice of wines, Bass; huge car park *(Colin Gooch, W M Lien)*

HULME END [SK1059]

☆ *Manifold Inn* SK17 0EX [B5054 Warslow—Hartington]: Attractive 18th-c country pub nr river, real ales such as Bass, Marstons Pedigree and Whim Hartington (check that you're paying the locals' price), wide choice of generous good value food using local produce, good sandwiches, helpful service, cosy soft seating in neat lounge bar, log-effect gas fires and some stripped stone, separate light and airy dining room and new conservatory, both no smoking; children and cyclists welcome, disabled facilities, tables outside, camp site, bedrooms in converted stone smithy off secluded back courtyard *(I J and S A Bufton, BB, John Beeken, B M Eldridge, Paul and Margaret Baker)*

KINGSBURY []

Royal Oak B78 2LP [Coventry Rd]: Split-level village pub with dark wood, beams and open fires, Marstons beers, attentive young staff, wide range of bargain food inc children's helpings; tables outside, play area *(Colin Gooch)*

KINVER [SO8483]

Constitutional Social Club DY7 6HL [High St]: A club, but ring the bell and speak to the steward to be signed in, fine changing choice of bargain real ales, friendly staff and members, pool, restaurant; open evenings and wknds *(the Didler)*

Plough & Harrow DY7 6HD [High St (village signed off A449 or A458 W of Stourbridge); aka the Steps]: Friendly old split-level Bathams local with their Best, Mild and XXX on top form, good choice of ciders and malt whiskies, plain bar food (filled rolls even Sun lunchtime), low prices, film star pictures; proper public bar with darts, dominoes etc, lounge with nostalgic juke box, sports TV and games machine; children allowed in some parts, tables in back courtyard, open all day wknds *(Pete Baker, the Didler, Paul and Gloria Howell)*

KNIGHTON [SJ7240]

White Lion TF9 4HJ [B5415 Woore—Mkt Drayton]: Roomy unpretentious local, friendly licensees and staff, three log or coal fires, three good changing ales, nice choice of generous home-made food (not Mon), cosy dining area, conservatory and restaurant; large adventure playground *(Anon)*

LEEK [SJ9856]

Den Engel ST13 5HG [Stanley St]: Belgian-style bar in largely no smoking high-ceilinged former bank, many dozens of beers from there inc lots on tap, three or four changing british real ales, three dozen genevers; piped classical music; tables on back terrace, open all day Weds-Sun, cl Mon/Tues lunchtimes *(the Didler)*

☆ *Swan* ST13 5DS [St Edward St]: Bustling old pub popular for cheap lunchtime food from sandwiches and baguettes up, quick helpful service even when busy, changing real ales such as Bass, Fullers London Pride and Jennings Snecklifter, occasional beer festivals, lots of malt whiskies, choice of coffees, pleasant no smoking front lounge; two bars behind central servery can get smoky; downstairs wine bar, folk club, seats in courtyard *(I J and S A Bufton, the Didler)*

☆ *Three Horseshoes* ST13 8TW [A53 NNE, on Blackshaw Moor]: Friendly family-run inn with emphasis on reliable generous food from sandwiches to roasts, brasserie and candlelit beamed restaurant – Sat dinner-dance; lots of nooks and crannies, open fire, no smoking area, good service, Courage Directors, Greene King Old Speckled Hen and Theakstons XB, sensible prices, children's area; no dogs, bedrooms *(Martin and Alison Stainsby, Dr D J and Mrs S C Walker)*

☆ *Wilkes Head* ST13 5DS [St Edward St]: Convivial three-room local dating from 18th c (still has back coaching stables), tied to Whim with their ales and interesting guest beers, good choice of whiskies, farm cider, friendly chatty landlord, welcoming regulars and dogs, filled rolls, pub games, gas fire, lots of pump clips; juke box in back room, Mon music night; children allowed in one room (but not really a family pub), fair disabled access, tables outside, open all day *(Pete Baker, the Didler)*

LICHFIELD [SK1010]

Hedgehog WS13 8JB [Stafford Rd (A51)]: Large Vintage Inn with lots of tables and plenty of nooks and corners, good choice of well prepared food, Marstons Pedigree, friendly attentive staff; children welcome, picnic-sets outside, bedrooms *(Colin Gooch)*

Kings Head WS13 6PW [Bird St]: Part 17th-c, part even older, beams and old prints, friendly new landlord, real ales such as Marstons Pedigree and Titanic, good range of bar snacks and bargain lunches, coachyard conservatory *(Colin Gooch)*

☆ *Queens Head* WS13 6QD [Queen St]: Attractive old-fashioned alehouse décor with comfortable aged furniture on stripped boards, self-choice counter of unusual cheeses in huge helpings (doggy bags provided) at very reasonable prices with free pickles, onions and gherkins, short but interesting range of bargain home-made hot dishes, real ales such as Marstons Pedigree and Timothy Taylors Landlord, friendly staff *(Simon Fox)*

LONGNOR [SK0864]

Crewe & Harpur Arms SK17 0NS: Doing well under newish ownership, with six real ales and good food from ambitious kitchen brigade, service coping well with busy nights; bedrooms *(Chris Brooks)*

Olde Cheshire Cheese SK17 0NS: 14th-c building, a pub for 250 years, Robinsons real ales, friendly service, tasty nourishing food, plenty of bric-a-brac and pictures in traditional main bar and two attractive dining rooms with their own separate bar; hikers welcome, bedrooms *(John Dwane, Theocsbrian)*

MEERBROOK [SJ9960]

Lazy Trout ST13 8SN: Wide choice of food from traditional bar dishes to restaurant meals, good friendly service under current newish landlady, interesting guest beers, decent wines, two small comfortable bars and dining room; plenty of tables in pleasant garden behind, attractive setting *(Brian and Jean Hepworth, Mr and Mrs John Taylor)*

MILWICH [SJ9533]

Red Lion ST15 8RU [Dayhills; B5027 towards Stone]: Old-fashioned bar at end of working farmhouse, old settles, tiled floor, inglenook log or coal fire, Bass and one or two guest beers tapped from the cask, friendly welcome, darts, dominoes and cribbage; cl lunchtimes exc Sun, cl Sun evening *(the Didler)*

MUCKLEY CORNER [SK0806]

Olde Corner House WS14 0BG [A5/A461]: Comfortably homely hotel-cum-pub, pleasantly relaxed, with good generous sensibly priced food in two restaurants (the smarter one is no smoking), Marstons Pedigree and Wadworths 6X, wide choice of wines, friendly service; good value bedrooms *(Colin Fisher)*

NEWCASTLE-UNDER-LYME [SJ8547]

New Smithy ST5 0EH [Church Lane, Wolstanton]: Friendly bustling local with good mix of ages and consistently well kept ales *(Sue Holland, Dave Webster)*

PENKRIDGE [SJ9214]

Boat ST19 5DT [Penkridge Lock, Cannock Rd (B5012), by Staffs & Worcs Canal, Bridge 86]: Comfortably old-fashioned pub by canal (not very scenic here, but quite busy with boaters), welcoming staff and pleasant layout, good value generous food from sandwiches to steak, Greene King Abbot, two gentle great danes; piped music, no children; picnic-sets outside *(Colin Gooch, Nick and Lynne Carter)*

☆ *Star* ST19 5DJ [Market Pl]: Charming open-plan local with lots of low black beams and button-back red plush, Banks's ales, limited lunchtime bar food from chip butties to cheap main dishes, friendly prompt service, open fires; piped music, sports TV; open all day, terrace tables *(Colin Gooch, BB, Ian and Ruth Laurence)*

RAWNSLEY [SK0311]

Rag WS12 0QD [Ironstone Rd]: Unassuming woods-view country pub with enjoyable food inc interesting dishes at good prices, wider evening choice, friendly service, Ansells and Greene King Abbot and Old Speckled Hen, good value wines, warm pleasant décor, no smoking lounge and restaurant, locals' bar; tables out on grass with summer evening barbecues, handy for Castle Ring and Cannock Chase walks *(Bren and Val Speed)*

ROUGH CLOSE [SJ9239]

Swynnerton Arms ST3 7PP [Windmill Hill]: Wide choice of good value food, friendly staff, pleasant location; children welcome *(J Metcalfe)*

SANDON [SJ9429]

Dog & Doublet ST18 0DJ: Some emphasis on the dining side, with enjoyable food, but still a place where the locals play dominoes *(R J Herd)*

SHENSTONE [SK1104]

Bulls Head WS14 0JR [Birmingham Rd; A5127 Lichfield—Sutton Coldfield]: Roomy rambling 18th-c Vintage Inn, low beams, flagstones, bare bricks, panelling, close-set old pine tables and mixed chairs in narrow rooms, good value food, welcoming quick food service even when busy, real ales and good wine choice; children welcome, disabled facilities *(W M Lien)*

STAFFORD [SJ9222]

Picture House ST16 2HL [Bridge St/Lichfield St]: Grade II listed art deco cinema well converted by Wetherspoons keeping ornate ceiling plasterwork and stained-glass name sign, bar on stage with good real ales at competitive prices, farm cider, friendly efficient service, seating in stalls, circle and upper circle, no smoking areas, good choice of food all day, lively atmosphere, film posters, Peter Cushing mannequin in preserved ticket box; good disabled facilities, spacious terrace overlooking river, open all day *(John Tavernor, R T and J C Moggridge)*

Stafford Arms ST16 2DS [Railway St; turn right at main entrance outside station, 100 yards down]: Open-plan modern feel with clever wall lighting, big solid tables, nautical décor, four real ales such as Greene King Abbot and Old Speckled Hen, no smoking area up a couple of steps; open all day exc Sun afternoon *(John Tavernor, Martin Grosberg, Paul and Gloria Howell)*

STANLEY [SJ9352]

Travellers Rest ST9 9LX [off A53 NE of Stoke]: Large popular restaurant/bar area with Marstons Pedigree and interesting guest beers such as Brewsters Daffys Elixir, Lancaster JSB and Mauldons Pickwick from central servery, reasonably priced food inc bargain Sun lunch, friendly service; tables out in front *(C and R Bromage)*

STOKE-ON-TRENT [SJ8745]

Bulls Head ST6 3AJ [St Johns Sq, Burslem]: Titanic and guest beers in two-room town pub with good service even when busy, coal fire, bar billiards; cl till 3 wkdys, open all day Fri-Sun *(the Didler)*

Potter ST4 3DB [King St]: Unpretentious town local with several real ales such as Coach House and Greene King; sports TV; open all day *(the Didler)*

STOWE [SK0027]

Cock ST18 0LF [off A518 Stafford—Uttoxeter]: Nicely laid out bistro-style conversion of village local, good value light lunches, pleasant efficient service *(Mark Flynn)*

SWYNNERTON [SJ8535]
Fitzherbert Arms ST15 0RA [village signposted
off A51 Stone—Nantwich]: Olde-worlde
beamed pub with friendly efficient service,
enjoyable food inc special deals for two
(Susan Brookes)

TAMWORTH [SK2104]
Albert B79 7JS [Albert Rd]: Small cosy town
pub with Banks's beers, wide range of good
value pubby food, friendly fast service, pool;
juke box, games machine; terrace tables,
bedrooms *(Colin Gooch)*
Three Tuns B78 3QN [Lichfield St, Fazeley]:
Proper busy and welcoming local by Coventry
Canal, Everards Tiger and Marstons Pedigree,
reasonably priced home-made food inc Sun
roasts, pour-and-serve coffee, large back dining
room; small front bar can be a bit smoky, juke
box; informal garden *(Gerry Price)*
Tweeddale Arms B79 7JS [Albert Rd/Victoria
Rd]: Substantial building with modern airy
atmosphere, daily papers, pleasant spacious
restaurant with reasonably priced food inc
good steaks, attentive service, Marstons
Pedigree; games machines *(Colin Gooch,
John and Yvonne Davies)*

TATENHILL [SK2021]
✩ *Horseshoe* DE13 9SD [off A38 W of Burton;
Main St]: Reliable food (all day Sat) from
sandwiches to steaks inc more ambitious
dishes and proper children's food in cheery
pub with tiled-floor bar, cosy no smoking side
snug with woodburner, two-level restaurant
and back family area, Marstons ales, good
wine range, quick polite service; pleasant
garden, good play area with pets corner
(C J Fletcher, LYM)

THORNCLIFFE [SK0158]
Red Lion ST13 7LP: Comfortable and
attractively homely 17th-c pub with good
choice of enjoyable fresh food from sandwiches
up, Thurs steak night, all-day Sun roasts,
prompt service, good atmosphere, log fires,
wide range of wines and beers, new no
smoking dining room, games area with pool;
children welcome *(Mr and Mrs B Jones,
Brian and Jean Hepworth, Pauline and
Terry James, Howson and Janet Adams,*

Brenda Pauline, Pam Haines)

TRYSULL [SO8594]
Bell WV5 7JB [Bell Rd]: Extended red brick
village local, softly lit lounge with lots of table
lamps, big grandfather clock, inglenook fire
and good chatty atmosphere, many original
features in cosy bar with brasses and
locomotive number-plates, Holdens Bitter,
Special and Golden Glow, Bathams Best and a
guest beer, interesting bar food from
sandwiches up at fair prices, evening restaurant
Weds-Sat; open all day wknds *(the Didler,
Paul and Gloria Howell)*

TUTBURY [SK2128]
✩ *Olde Dog & Partridge* DE13 9LS [High St; off
A50 N of Burton]: Good Chef & Brewer in
handsome Tudor inn, rambling extensively
back with heavy beams, timbers, various small
rooms, nooks and corners, their usual food inc
generous snacks, several real ales such as
Greene King Old Speckled Hen, attentive
cheerful staff, good log fire, thriving
atmosphere; comfortable well equipped
bedrooms, open all day *(Colin Fisher,
LYM, Dennis Jones, Michael J Caley,
Francis Johnston)*

WARSLOW [SK0858]
Greyhound SK17 0JN [B5053 S of Buxton]:
Closed down *(Ian and Gill Everett,
Rona Murdoch, LYM)*

WHITTINGTON [SK1608]
Dog WS14 9JU [the one nr Lichfield; Main St]:
Welcoming family-run village local very
popular lunchtime for wide choice of good
value food from sandwiches and baked
potatoes to steaks, Adnams, Marstons Pedigree
and Timothy Taylors Landlord, friendly
efficient service, lots of beams, brassware, old
prints and team photographs, no smoking
area; small terrace, bedrooms *(Ian and
Jane Irving, Colin Gooch)*

WRINEHILL [SJ7547]
Hand & Trumpet CW3 9BJ [A531
Newcastle—Nantwich]: Large newly
refurnished pub with wide choice of well
cooked good value family food; splendid
garden with pond and ducks, good value
bedrooms *(Anon)*

The letters and figures after the name of each town are its Ordnance Survey map
reference. *Using the Guide* at the beginning of the book explains how it helps you find a
pub, in road atlases or on large-scale maps as well as on our own maps.

Suffolk

This is an enjoyable county with plenty of really good pubs – a lot of them are by the waterside, and so are particularly popular with visitors. Waterside or not, what often stands out is genuine friendliness and lack of pretension. As well as tiny little town pubs and unspoilt locals, there are some very well run dining pubs in lovely rambling buildings. These tend to have menus that reflect excellent produce and sound basics rather than over-ambitious restauranty dishes. Whatever their claim to fame, pubs on top-notch form here include the Queens Head in Bramfield (the hard-working licensees are always offering some sort of event), the quaint and tiny Nutshell in Bury St Edmunds, the exceptionally busy Old Cannon there (good own brewed beers too), the very nice Queens Head in Erwarton, the civilised Beehive in Horringer, the Angel in Lavenham (a great favourite of many readers), the Anchor at Nayland (it's worth looking at their Heritage Farm next door), the unspoilt and chatty Jolly Sailor in Orford (best to visit before the super licensees retire), the Plough at Rede (the sort of place you want to come back to), the St Peters Brewery at South Elmham (own brew beers and a stunning medieval building), the Crown, Harbour Inn and Lord Nelson all in Southwold (very different places but all deserving their huge popularity), and the smartly contemporary Crown at Stoke-by-Nayland. Half a dozen newcomers join this vanguard of top Suffolk pubs: the Dog at Grundisburgh, taken in hand by two brothers who have turned it into a charmingly civilised and relaxed all-rounder; the cheerful Five Bells at Hessett, with nice cooking by the landlord's wife; the handsomely upmarket Black Lion in Long Melford (back in the *Guide* after a break); the Fox at Newbourne, enjoyable food in a proper village-pub atmosphere; the Ravenwood Hall at Rougham (this handsome country house hotel's secret is its thoroughly welcoming all-day bar); and the Anchor in Walberswick, a rather special find, with its enterprising new licensees doing good food well matched to interesting beers. Fish features strongly in Suffolk, even in places where food is perhaps pretty straightforward. Places that stand out for special meals include the Queens Head at Bramfield, the Crown at Buxhall, the Beehive at Horringer, the Angel in Lavenham, the Plough at Rede, the Crown in Snape, the Crown in Southwold, the Angel at Stoke-by-Nayland, and the Anchor in Walberswick. The Angel at Stoke-by-Nayland is Suffolk Dining Pub of the Year. In the Lucky Dip section at the end of the chapter, pubs to note include the Sorrel Horse at Barham, Peacock at Chelsworth, Froize at Chillesford (restaurant rather than pub, so excluded from the main entries), Eels Foot at Eastbridge, Station Hotel in Framlingham, Angel in Halesworth, Fat Cat in Ipswich, Bull in Long Melford, Ramsholt Arms at Ramsholt, Plough & Sail in Snape, Angel at Wangford and Cherry Tree on the edge of Woodbridge. In general, pub food is not cheap here, and drinks prices tend to be rather higher than the national norm. This is home territory for Greene King, one of the country's main brewers, though you are at least as likely to find a beer from the much smaller local firm of Adnams being sold as a good pub's cheapest offering here. Mauldons and Nethergate also crop up fairly frequently here, and you may come across Cox & Holbrook.

BRAMFIELD TM4073 Map 5

Queens Head 🍴

The Street; A144 S of Halesworth; IP19 9HT

During the winter months, there are regular fun dining events held in this bustling, well run pub – and even a birthday club, too. They make their own preserves (which you can buy) and bread, and many of the ingredients they use come from small local organic farms; you can get a list of their suppliers in the lobby. As well as filled baguettes, the good, popular food might include home-made soup (£3.95), chicken liver pâté or grilled dates wrapped in bacon on a mild mustard sauce (£4.95), mushrooms baked in cream and garlic and topped with cheese (£5.95), grilled goats cheese with a mustard crumb topping on a roast beetroot salad (£6.95), home-made free-range pork sausages with onion gravy (£8.95), curried nut loaf with spicy tomato sauce, free-range chicken, leek and bacon crumble or steak and kidney in ale pie (£9.95), smoked haddock fillet topped with welsh rarebit (£10.95), and lamb à la grecque (£12.95), with puddings such as warm apricot frangipane tart, vanilla crème brûlée with shortbread or rich chocolate pot (£4.35). Well kept Adnams Bitter and Broadside, a decent wine list with seven by the glass, local apple juice and home-made elderflower cordial. The high-raftered lounge bar has scrubbed pine tables, a good log fire in its impressive fireplace, and a sprinkling of farm tools on the walls; a separate side bar has light wood furnishings; half the pub is now no smoking. Cheerful blue-painted picnic-sets under blue and white umbrellas in the pretty garden, a dome-shaped bower made of willow, and a family of bantams. The church next door is rather lovely. *(Recommended by Neil Powell, John Wooll, A J Murray, Charles and Pauline Stride, John and Bettye Reynolds, J F M and M West, Pat and Tony Hinkins, Comus and Sarah Elliott, Simon Cottrell, TW, MW, Richard and Margaret McPhee, Clive and Vivienne Locks, M and GR, MJVK, Bryan and Mary Blaxall, Philip and Susan Philcox)*

Adnams ~ Tenants Mark and Amanda Corcoran ~ Real ale ~ Bar food (12-2, 6.30-10(7-9 Sun)) ~ (01986) 784214 ~ Children welcome until 9pm unless dining ~ Dogs welcome ~ Open 11.45-2.30, 6.30-11; 12-3, 7-10.30 Sun; closed 26 Dec

BURY ST EDMUNDS TL8564 Map 5

Nutshell

The Traverse, central pedestrian link off Abbeygate Street; IP33 1BJ

Quaint and really tiny, this bare-boards local dates from the 17th c, and has been selling beer since 1873. The timeless interior contains a short wooden bench along its shop-front corner windows, one cut-down sewing-machine table, an elbow rest running along its rather battered counter, and well kept Greene King IPA and Abbot on handpump served by the chatty landlord. A mummified cat, which was found walled up here (something our ancestors did quite commonly to ward off evil spirits) hangs from the dark brown ceiling, along with stacks of other bric-a-brac, from bits of a skeleton through vintage bank notes, cigarette packets and military and other badges to spears and a great metal halberd; piped music, cribbage and dominoes. The modern curved inn sign is appealing. No children. *(Recommended by David Carr, the Didler)*

Greene King ~ Lease Martin Baylis ~ Real ale ~ No credit cards ~ (01284) 764867 ~ Dogs allowed in bar ~ Open 11(12 winter weekdays)-11; 12-10.30 Sun

Old Cannon 🍺

Cannon Street, just off A134/A1101 roundabout N end of town; IP33 1JR

Run by a sociable landlord and his helpful staff, this looks more like a stylish private town house than a pub. It's very busy most nights of the week, so best to get here early if you want a seat. The bar has miscellaneous chairs around a few tables on dark bare boards, dark red or ochre walls, one with a big mirror, and plenty of standing space; a fanciful touch is that where you'd expect a ceiling there is instead a sort of floorless upper room complete with radiator, table and chairs.

On the left, another dark red-walled and bare-boards room has neat slat-backed dining chairs around tables; it opens at the back into the neat kitchen. On the right in the bar are two gleaming stainless steel brewing kettles, often gently burbling, that produce the pub's own good reasonably priced Old Cannon Best, Gunners Daughter and Blonde Bombshell. They also have a couple of guest beers from brewers such as Adnams and Bath on handpump, a farm cider and continental beers. Bar food includes home-made soup (£4), sandwiches (from £4.50, baguettes from £4.95), toad in the hole, ham, egg and chips, venison burger, moroccan lamb curry, roast mushrooms and peppers with penne in spinach, ricotta and asparagus cream sauce or cod and chips (all £7.95), with puddings such as lime and chocolate cheesecake or cappuccino mousse (£3.75); the menu for the smarter no smoking evening restaurant is more elaborate. Piped music. Behind, through the old side coach arch, is a good-sized cobbled courtyard neatly set with planters and hanging baskets, with rather stylish metal tables and chairs in bays at the back. *(Recommended by Keith Reeve, Marie Hammond, John Robertson, Mike and Mary Carter)*

Free house ~ Licensee Carole Locker ~ Real ale ~ Bar food (not Sun evening or all day Mon) ~ Restaurant ~ (01284) 768769 ~ Open 12-3, 5-11(7-10.30 Sun); closed Mon lunchtime ~ Bedrooms: £55S/£69S

BUXHALL TM0057 Map 5
Crown ⑪ ♀

Village signposted off B1115 W of Stowmarket; fork right by post office at Gt Finborough, turn left at Buxhall village sign, then second right into Mill Road, then right at T junction; IP14 3DW

This 17th-c timber framed pub is tucked away near a windmill down a quiet country lane. It's now totally no smoking, and the intimate little bar on the left has an open fire in a big inglenook, a couple of small round tables on a tiled floor, and low hop-hung beams. Standing timbers separate it from another area with pews and candles, and flowers in summer on beech tables with leather chairs, and there's a further light and airy room which they call the Mill Restaurant. As well as Cox & Holbrook Old Mill (brewed just two minutes away), they have Greene King IPA, Tindalls Best and Woodfordes Wherry on handpump, and 25 whiskies. Well liked bar food includes sandwiches, soup (£5.50), mussels steamed in white wine, cream, garlic and ginger (£5.75; main course £11.50), warm chicken and anchovy caesar salad (£5.95; main course £10.95), lightly spiced fried goats cheese on garlic crostini with sweet red pepper, rocket and balsamic syrup (£6.95), warm mushroom risotto (£8.95), deep-fried haddock in beer batter (£9.50), steak and mushroom pie or spicy chicken and chorizo casserole (£10.95), and duck breast with a rhubarb and ginger sauce (£13.45). Plenty of seats and solid wood tables under parasols on the heated terrace, and they've a pretty garden, with nice views over gently rolling countryside. A large enclosed side garden has wooden decking and raised flowerbeds. *(Recommended by Derek Field, J F M and M West, Pamela Goodwyn, M and GR, Adele Summers, Alan Black, Tina and David Woods-Taylor, Sheila Stothard)*

Greene King ~ Lease Trevor Golton ~ Real ale ~ Bar food (not Sun evening or Mon) ~ Restaurant ~ (01449) 736521 ~ Children welcome if well behaved ~ Dogs allowed in bar ~ Open 12-3.30, 6.30-11.30; 12-3.30 Sun; closed Sun evening, Mon, 25 and 26 Dec

CHELMONDISTON TM2038 Map 5
Butt & Oyster ㉕

Pin Mill – signposted from B1456 SE of Ipswich; IP9 1JW

Through the bay windows of this simple old bargeman's pub there's a fine view of the ships coming down the River Orwell from Ipswich and of the long lines of moored black sailing barges; the suntrap terrace shares the same view. The half-panelled timeless little smoke room is pleasantly worn and unfussy and has model sailing ships around the walls and high-backed and other old-fashioned settles on the tiled floor; ferocious beady-eyed fish made by a local artist stare at you from the walls. Good bar food includes sandwiches (from £3.90), soup (£3.95), home-made seafood terrine (£5.25), local duck breast and crispy bacon salad (£5.50), fresh deep-fried fish and chips (£8.45), and home-made steak in ale pie, chicken in three mustard sauce and grilled fresh plaice or halibut (all £9.95). As space is limited, you might need to arrive early at the weekend to get a seat. The dining room is no smoking. Adnams Best and Broadside, and Greene King IPA on handpump or tapped from the cask; board games, dominoes and bar skittles. The annual Thames Barge Race (end June/beginning July) is fun. *(Recommended by JDM, KM, Peter and Jean Dowson, David Carr, Ken Millar, the Didler, Pamela Goodwyn)*

Punch ~ Lease Steve Lomas ~ Real ale ~ Bar food (all day weekends) ~ Restaurant ~ (01473) 780764 ~ Children in dining rooms ~ Dogs allowed in bar ~ Open 11-11; 12-11 Sun

COTTON   TM0467   Map 5
Trowel & Hammer ♀
Mill Road; take B1113 N of Stowmarket, then turn right into Blacksmiths Lane just N of Bacton; IP14 4QL

Even when busy, which it usually is, the landlady and her staff in this civilised thatched pub remain very pleasant and efficient. The spreading series of quiet rooms has fresh flowers, lots of beamery and timber baulks, a big log fire, and plenty of wheelbacks and one or two older chairs and settles around a variety of tables; half the public bar is no smoking. Quite a choice of good bar food includes soup (£4.25), filled baked potatoes (from £4.25), sandwiches (from £4.50; panini £6.50), garlic mushrooms (£4.75), duck and port pâté or burgers £5.25), antipasti (£5.95), pizzas (£6.50), full english breakfast (£7.25), mushroom stroganoff (£7.50), gammon and egg (£8.25), curries, steak and kidney pie or lasagne (£8.95), chicken dijonnaise (£9.50), beer-battered haddock (£9.75), and puddings like treacle sponge (£4.25); they serve tapas all day. The restaurant is no smoking. Adnams Broadside, Greene King IPA and Abbot, and Mauldons Suffolk Pride on handpump, and decent wines. Piped music, pool, games machine, TV and a juke box. The back garden is pretty with colourful flowers and there are seats and tables under thatched umbrellas, and large ornamental elephants; swimming pool and croquet. More reports please. *(Recommended by Ian and Nita Cooper, Alan Jefferson)*

Free house ~ Licensee Sally Selvage ~ Real ale ~ Bar food (12-2, 6-9 (tapas served all day); 12-9 Sun) ~ Restaurant ~ (01449) 781234 ~ Children welcome ~ Live music every second summer weekend and some Sun afternoons ~ Open 12-11(10.30 Sun)

DENNINGTON   TM2867   Map 5
Queens Head
A1120; IP13 8AB

Set by the church, this is one of Suffolk's most attractive pub buildings. It's a lovely Tudor place and the arched rafters in the steeply roofed part of the bar are reminiscent of a chapel – in fact, it was owned for centuries by a church charity. The main neatly kept L-shaped room has carefully stripped wall timbers and beams, a handsomely carved bressumer beam, and comfortable padded wall seats on the partly carpeted and partly tiled floor. Adnams Bitter and a guest such as Woodfordes Wherry on handpump and local cider; piped music. Quite a choice of bar food might include lunchtime sandwiches (from £2.30) and ploughman's (from £5.15), as well as home-made soup (£3.25), deep-fried whitebait (£3.95), thai fishcakes with sweet chilli dip (£4.25), roast beef or pork (£7.15), mushroom stroganoff (£7.50), liver, sausage and bacon casserole (£7.75), home-made pie of the day (£8.25), salmon fillet in lemon and cream sauce (£8.95), shank of lamb (£9.50), steaks (from £10.45), and home-made puddings such as fruit pie of the day or treacle tart (£3.75). You may smoke only in the bar. There are some seats on a side lawn, attractively planted with flowers and sheltered by some noble lime trees, and the pub backs on to Dennington Park which has swings and so forth for children. More reports please. *(Recommended by David and Jean Hall, Keith Berrett, Michael Clatworthy, John Saul, P and J Shapley, George Atkinson)*

Free house ~ Licensees Hilary Cowie, Peter Mills ~ Real ale ~ Bar food (9-11 for breakfast, 12-2, 6.30-9) ~ Restaurant ~ (01728) 638241 ~ Children allowed with restrictions ~ Open 11-3, 6-11; 12-3, 6-10.30 Sun; closed 25 and 26 Dec

DUNWICH TM4770 Map 5
Ship ㉕
St James Street; IP17 3DT

In what is left of a charming village (coastal erosion has put most of it under the sea), this old brick pub is useful for a drink while enjoying all the surrounding walks and lovely coastal scenery. The RSPB reserve at Minsmere and nearby Dunwich Museum are certainly worth visiting. The traditionally furnished main bar has benches, pews, captain's chairs and wooden tables on its tiled floor, a woodburning stove (left open in cold weather) and lots of sea prints and nautical memorabilia. From the handsomely panelled bar counter, you can get Adnams Bitter and Broadside and maybe Mauldons served from antique handpumps; fruit machine, dominoes and cribbage. A simple conservatory looks on to a back terrace, and the large garden is very pleasant, with its well spaced picnic-sets, two large anchors, and enormous fig tree. Bar food is fairly standard; the restaurant is no smoking. More reports please. *(Recommended by Carolyn Browse, Rob and Catherine Dunster, MDN, W K Wood, Mrs Joyce Robson, Comus and Sarah Elliott, Mike and Sue Loseby, Peter Meister, J C Mann, Edward Mirzoeff, Robert Lorimer, Alan Sadler, Eric Robinson, Jacqueline Pratt, Richard and Margaret McPhee, Clive and Vivienne Locks, Stephen and Jean Curtis, H and P Cate, Louise English, A J W Smith)*

Free house ~ Licensee Brett Stephenson ~ Real ale ~ Bar food (12-3, 6-9) ~ Restaurant (evening only) ~ (01728) 648219 ~ Children welcome away from bar ~ Dogs allowed in bar and bedrooms ~ Open 11-11; 12-10.30 Sun ~ Bedrooms: /£75B

EARL SOHAM TM2363 Map 5
Victoria 🍺 £
A1120 Yoxford—Stowmarket; IP13 7RL

It's certainly worth coming to this unpretentious place to enjoy the three Earl Soham beers from the brewery right across the road: Albert, Victoria and Sir Rogers Porter on handpump; farm cider too. There's an easy-going local atmosphere in the well worn bar, which is fairly basic and sparsely furnished, with stripped panelling, kitchen chairs and pews, plank-topped trestle sewing-machine tables and other simple scrubbed pine country tables, tiled or board floors, an interesting range of pictures of Queen Victoria and her reign, and open fires. Fair value bar food such as sandwiches (from £2.50), soup (£3.75), ploughman's (from £4.25), corned beef hash (£5.75), vegetarian pasta dishes (£6.25), lamb curry (£7.50), and puddings (£3.95). There are seats on the raised back lawn, with more out in front. The pub is quite close to a wild fritillary meadow at Framlingham, and a working windmill at Saxtead. More reports please. *(Recommended by Pete Baker, Comus and Sarah Elliott, Stephen P Edwards, Pam and David Bailey)*

Free house ~ Licensee Paul Hooper ~ Real ale ~ Bar food (12-2, 7-10) ~ (01728) 685758 ~ Children welcome ~ Dogs allowed in bar ~ Open 11.30-3, 6-11; 12-3, 7-10.30 Sun

ERWARTON TM2134 Map 5
Queens Head ♀ 🍺
Village signposted off B1456 Ipswich—Shotley Gate; pub beyond the attractive church and the manor with its unusual gatehouse (like an upturned salt-cellar); IP9 1LN

A nice place to sit here is at tables by the window which look across fields to the Stour estuary – but best to get here early, especially at the weekend when it can get busy. The friendly bar has bowed black oak beams in its shiny low yellowing ceiling, comfortable furnishings, several sea paintings and photographs, and a cosy coal fire. Adnams Bitter and Broadside, Greene King IPA, and maybe Palmers Tally

Ho! on handpump, a decent wine list, local cider and apple juice, and several malt whiskies. Good bar food includes sandwiches, home-made soup (£3.25), whitebait (£4.25), ploughman's (£5.75), a trio of sausages (£5.95), home-cooked ham and eggs (£7.25), vegetable curry or chicken in peach and almond sauce (£7.95), steak and kidney pudding (£8.50), and steaks (from £10.50), with daily specials such as cheesy leek and horseradish bake, tagliatelle carbonara, somerset pork or rabbit casserole (all £7.95), and lamb and apricot casserole, chicken breast wrapped in bacon with a stilton sauce or salmon and prawn mornay (£8.95). The no smoking conservatory dining area is pleasant; darts, bar billiards, shove-ha'penny, cribbage and dominoes, and maybe piped music. The gents' has quite a collection of navigational charts. There are picnic-sets under summer hanging baskets in front. *(Recommended by Judi Bell, Pamela Goodwyn, Tony and Shirley Albert, Mike and Mary Carter, A J Murray)*

Free house ~ Licensees Julia Crisp and G M Buckle ~ Real ale ~ Bar food ~ Restaurant ~ (01473) 787550 ~ Children allowed away from bar areas ~ Open 11-3, 6.30-11; 11.30-3, 6.30-10.30 Sun; closed 25 Dec

GREAT GLEMHAM   TM3361   Map 5
Crown 🍺

Between A12 Wickham Market—Saxmundham and B1119 Saxmundham—Framlingham; IP17 2DA

As we went to press we heard that this immaculately kept pub was on the market, so by the time this edition is published, there might be new people at the helm. There's a big entrance hall with sofas on rush matting, and an open-plan beamed lounge with wooden pews and captain's chairs around stripped and waxed kitchen tables, local photographs and interesting paintings on cream walls, fresh flowers, and some brass ornaments; log fires in two big fireplaces. A fair choice of good pubby food might include sandwiches (from £3.75), roasted vegetable or meaty lasagne (£8.95), east anglian pork chop (£9.75), and steak and kidney pie, carbonnade of beef or fish and chips (£9.95). Adnams Bitter and Broadside are served from old brass handpumps, and they've seven wines by the glass. A tidy, flower-fringed lawn, raised above the corner of the quiet village lane by a retaining wall, has some seats and tables under cocktail parasols; disabled access. The pub is in a particularly pretty village. *(Recommended by Neil Powell, Simon Cottrell, Comus and Sarah Elliott, Ian and Nita Cooper, Pamela Goodwyn, Charles and Pauline Stride, Clive and Vivienne Locks, Pete and Sue Robbins, Simon Rodway)*

Free house ~ Licensees Barry and Susie Coote ~ Real ale ~ Bar food (not Mon) ~ (01728) 663693 ~ Children welcome ~ Dogs allowed in bar ~ Open 11.30-3, 6.30-11; 12-3, 7-10.30 Sun; closed Mon except bank hols; maybe 2 weeks Oct

GRUNDISBURGH   TM2250   Map 5
Dog ♀

Off A12 via B1079 from Woodbridge bypass; The Green – village signposted; IP13 6TA

Run by two brothers and attractively placed near the village green, this pink-washed pub has a softly lit and relaxing carpeted lounge bar on the left, with comfortable seating around dark oak tables, antique engravings on its crushed raspberry walls, and unusual flowers in the windows. It links with a similar bare-boards dining room, with some attractive antique oak settles – no smoking here on Friday to Sunday evenings or Sunday lunchtime. Carefully cooked by James Rogers and using local produce and seasonal game (or even fish caught by them using their nearby boat), seasonal food might include filled organic baguettes or baked potatoes (from £3.50), a choice of soups such as leek and potato, asparagus or pigeon and bacon (£3.75), squid with sweet chilli sauce (£4), chicken liver pâté (£4.25; main course £7), vol au vent filled with goats cheese and red onion, honey and pesto dressing (£4.50; main course £7.50), gnocchi with fresh herbs and tomato (£7.50), lasagne (£7.75), beef casserole (£8), sweet chilli roast salmon fillet (£8.25), daily specials such as venison sausages with redcurrant gravy (£7.95), roast pheasant breast with red wine and spring onion mash (£8.50), and puddings like warm chocolate brownie pudding, raspberry fool with almond biscuits or hot toffee and butterscotch pudding (from £3). They have good espresso coffee and an interesting range of wines, plus well kept Adnams Best and Broadside and Shepherd Neame Spitfire on handpump; good, friendly service, and a relaxed and civilised atmosphere. A separate tiled-floor bar on the right has darts, a fruit machine and video game; the young jack russell is called Poppy. There are a few picnic-sets out in front, and the fenced back garden has a play area. *(Recommended by Anthony Rickards Collinson, J B and M E Benson)*

Punch ~ Lease Charles and James Rogers ~ Real ale ~ Bar food ~ Restaurant ~ (01473) 735267 ~ Children may be allowed away from bar and if accompanied by an adult ~ Dogs allowed in bar ~ Open 12-3, 5.30-11 Mon-Weds; 12-11pm Thurs, Fri and Sat; 12-10.30 Sun; 12-3, 5.30-11 Thurs in winter

HESSETT   TL9361   Map 5
Five Bells
Off A14 E of Bury; The Street; IP30 9AX

Just a little way down the road from a spectacular square-towered flint-built Norman church, this friendly open-plan building – a pub for at least 250 years – has a strong local following and a pleasantly relaxed atmosphere. With one or two black beams in its rather low shiny ochre ceiling, it has a good log fire in the carpeted area on the left, and big rugs on red flooring tiles over on the right. There's a pleasant mix of tables, and country prints above the panelled dado. The friendly landlord's wife cooks enjoyable food using as much local and seasonal produce as possible: sandwiches or filled baguettes (from £2.50; rump steak £4.95), chicken tikka sticks with mango chutney (£4.25), toasted brie with olives and sun-dried tomatoes (£4.50), three-cheese ploughman's (£5.25), pesto and goats cheese tortellini (£6.50), toulouse sausages braised in mixed beans and vegetable stew (£7.25), curries (from £7.25), battered cod and chips (£7.95), smoked haddock, cod, prawn and salmon gratin (£8.50), home-made steak and kidney in ale pie (£8.95), duck and noodle salad (£9.25), duck breast with red wine, sage and redcurrant sauce (£10.25), and puddings such as honey-baked peaches with mascarpone or sticky toffee pudding (from £3.50). They also offer a take-away service; Sunday lunch is popular. They have Greene King IPA and Abbot with a guest such as Ridleys Prospect on handpump, piped music, darts and cribbage. The sheltered garden behind has a boules pitch. *(Recommended by Derek Field, Mrs Kay Dewsbury, Joan Astley Cooper, J W Russell)*

Greene King ~ Tenant John Muir ~ Real ale ~ Bar food (12-2.30(3 Sun), 6.30-9.30; not Sun evening, not Mon) ~ Restaurant ~ (01359) 270350 ~ Children welcome ~ Dogs allowed in bar ~ Open 12-3, 5(6 Sat)-11; 12-4, 7-11 Sun; closed Mon lunchtime except bank hols

HORRINGER   TL8261   Map 5
Beehive 🍴 ♆
A143; IP29 5SN

It's a treat to come here, feel several readers, and this civilised, no smoking pub offers a warm welcome and enjoyable food to all its customers. The rambling series of little rooms is furnished with good quality old country furniture on coir or flagstones and there's a cottagey feel, largely because they've refrained from pulling walls down to create the usual open-plan layout. Despite some very low beams, stripped panelling and brickwork, good chalky heritage wall colours keep it fairly light and airy. Changing daily, the interesting food might include cream of watercress soup (£4.50), salmon and gurnard roulade with sorrel dressing or bruschetta of roast peppers and melting goats cheese (£5.50), a plate of french cheeses, pickle and apple (£6.50), warm tartlet of wild mushrooms and cheese or ham with french bread and chutneys (£8.95), home-made pork and paprika sausages (£9.50), chargrilled fresh tuna on niçoise salad (£10.50), sauté of sweetbreads with a sage glaze and braised rice (£10.95), tasty slow-roast belly of pork with bubble and squeak or seared scallops with teriyaki dressing (£11.95), and puddings such as floating island meringue with fruit compote, chocolate and Cointreau mousse or sticky toffee pudding (£4.50); to be sure of a table, it's best to book. Greene King IPA, Abbot and Old Speckled Hen on handpump, and several wines by the glass. An attractively planted back terrace has picnic-sets and more seats on a raised lawn. Their friendly, well behaved dog Muffin is a great hit with readers and has now been joined by Skye the friendly yorkshire terrier – other dogs are not really welcome. *(Recommended by Simon Cottrell, G D Baker, John Saville, Mr and Mrs Martin Joyce, Jo Lilley, Simon Calvert, Pam and David Bailey, Jeremy Whitehorn, Eamonn and Natasha Skyrme)*

Greene King ~ Tenants Gary and Dianne Kingshott ~ Real ale ~ Bar food (not Sun evening) ~ Restaurant ~ (01284) 735260 ~ Children welcome ~ Open 11.30-3, 7-11.30; 12-3, 7-10.30 Sun; closed 25 and 26 Dec

LAVENHAM   TL9149   Map 5
Angel ★ 🍽 ♀ 🍺 🛏
Market Place; CO10 9QZ

Certainly a comfortable place to stay, this attractive Tudor inn remains very popular with our readers. It's totally no smoking and very well run and service is friendly and helpful. The light and airy long bar area has plenty of polished dark tables, a big inglenook log fire under a heavy mantelbeam, and some attractive 16th-c ceiling plasterwork – even more elaborate pargeting in the residents' sitting room upstairs. Round towards the back on the right of the central servery is a further dining area with heavy stripped pine country furnishings. They have shelves of books, dominoes, lots of board games, and classical piped music. You can eat the enjoyable food in the bar or the restaurant. At lunchtime, this might include roast pepper and butternut squash soup (£3.95), chicken liver pâté (£5.25), grilled sardine fillets with basil pesto (£5.75), fish pie or tomato, mozzarella and basil tart (£7.25), steak in ale pie or baked pepper stuffed with celeriac, tomatoes and thyme (£9.25), corn-fed chicken breast with carrot and coriander purée and white wine sauce or roast salmon fillet with courgette, chilli and lemon (£10.75), and marinated pork fillet with honey-roast parsnips (£11.95); evening choices such as pork, chicken and pistachio terrine (£5.75), king prawns with garlic, chilli and lime (£6.75), roast rump of lamb (£12.95), and fillet steak with green peppercorn sauce (£16.95), and puddings like apricot and passion fruit syllabub, chocolate charlotte or steamed syrup pudding (£4.50). Well kept Adnams Bitter and Broadside, Greene King IPA and Nethergate Suffolk County on handpump, ten wines by the glass, and 23 malt whiskies. Picnic-sets out in front overlook the former market square, and there are tables under parasols in a sizeable sheltered back garden; it's worth asking if they've time to show you the interesting Tudor cellar. *(Recommended by MJB, Dr and Mrs R G J Telfer, Mrs Carolyn Dixon, MDN, Mike Gorton, David Carr, David Twitchett, Walter and Susan Rinaldi-Butcher, DFL, the Didler, Pamela Goodwyn, Victoria Taylor, Margaret and Roy Randle, Richard Pitcher, P and J Shapley, Pam and Alan Neale, I A Herdman, John Saville, Adele Summers, Alan Black, Pam and David Bailey, Paul and Margaret Baker)*

Free house ~ Licensees Roy Whitworth and John Barry ~ Real ale ~ Bar food (12-2.15, 6.45-9.15) ~ Restaurant ~ (01787) 247388 ~ Children welcome ~ Dogs allowed in bedrooms ~ Classical piano Fri evenings ~ Open 11-11; 12-10.30 Sun; closed 25 and 26 Dec ~ Bedrooms: £55B/£80B

LAXFIELD   TM2972   Map 5
Kings Head ★ 🍺
Behind church, off road toward Banyards Green; IP13 8DW

New licensees have taken over this unspoilt 15th-c pub. The charmingly old-fashioned rooms have plenty of character and a warmly welcoming atmosphere, and there's now a no smoking dining room. Lots of people like the front room best, with a high-backed built-in settle on the tiled floor, and an open fire. Two other equally unspoilt rooms – the card and tap rooms – have pews, old seats, scrubbed deal tables, and some interesting wall prints. There's no bar; instead, the licensees potter in and out of a cellar tap room to pour pints of Adnams Best, Broadside and Explorer and Fullers London Pride straight from the cask; piped music, cards, and board games. Bar food now includes sandwiches (from £2.95; toasties or filled baguettes £4.50), home-made soup or baked banana and stilton cream (£3.95), ploughman's (£5.50), sausage and mash (£5.95), vegetarian tortellini (£6.95), smoked chicken breast with sun-dried tomatoes, pine nuts and raspberry vinaigrette (£7.50), home-cooked ham with coarse grain mustard sauce (£8.50), steak in ale pie (£8.95), and daily specials. Outside, the garden has plenty of benches and tables, there's an arbour covered by a grape and hop vine, and a small pavilion for cooler evenings. They have a self-contained flat to rent. *(Recommended by Pete Baker, Comus and Sarah Elliott, Ian and Nita Cooper, the Didler, Michael Clatworthy, Alan Sadler, Pam and David Bailey)*

Adnams ~ Tenant Ros Puffett ~ Real ale ~ Bar food (12-2(4 Sun), 7-9) ~ Restaurant ~ (01986) 798395 ~ Children welcome with restrictions ~ Dogs welcome ~ Open 12-3(4.30 Sun), 6-11

LIDGATE TL7257 Map 5

Star ♀

B1063 SE of Newmarket; CB8 9PP

There's quite an emphasis in this village dining pub on the food now. The main room has handsomely moulded heavy beams, a good big log fire, candles in iron candelabra on good polished oak or stripped pine tables, bar billiards, dominoes, darts and ring the bull, and some antique catalan plates over the bar; piped music. Besides a second similar room on the right, there's a cosy little no smoking dining room on the left. The landlady is Spanish, and the interesting (but not cheap) menu reflects this: fish soup, boquerones, grilled squid or catalan salad (£5.90), paella, roast lamb in garlic and wine or lambs kidneys in sherry (£15.50), cod in garlic mousseline, wild boar in strawberry sauce or monkfish marinière (£15.50), puddings such as strawberry cream tart and chocolate roulade (£4.95) or an unusual cheeseboard (£5.50). They also do a two-course lunch (£12.50). Well kept Greene King IPA, Abbot and Ruddles County on handpump, and decent house wines Tables are out on the raised lawn in front, and in a pretty little rustic back garden. Dogs may be allowed with permission from the landlady. More reports please. *(Recommended by M and GR)*

Greene King ~ Lease Maria Teresa Axon ~ Real ale ~ Bar food (not Sun evening) ~ Restaurant ~ (01638) 500275 ~ Children welcome ~ Open 12-3, 6(7 Sun)-11; closed evening 25 Dec, 1 Jan

LONG MELFORD TL8646 Map 5

Black Lion ♀ 🛏

Church Walk; CO10 9DN

Comfortable and civilised, this 400-year-old hotel faces the village green and there are seats and tables under terracotta parasols on the terrace that make the most of the view; more, too in the appealing Victorian walled garden. Inside, one side of the oak serving counter is decorated in ochre and, besides bar stools, has deeply cushioned sofas, leather wing armchairs and antique fireside settles, while the other, in shades of terracotta, has leather dining chairs around handsome tables set for the good modern food. This might include carrot and coriander soup with herb croûtons (£4.25), pressed terrine of ham hock (£5.75), warm caramelised shallot and spinach fritatta with tomato vinaigrette (£5.75; main course £9.95), lime, honey and minted seared scallops (£6.25; main course £11.50), courgette and ricotta cheese dumplings with a tomato and basil sauce (£10.95), seared salmon fillet, home-made pesto tagliatelle and lemon oil (£13.95), duo of rabbit wrapped in herbs and parma ham, confit of leg, and saffron and parsley risotto (£15.75), chargrilled tuna with white bean and black olive salsa (£15.95) and puddings such as chocolate tart with cherries in red wine syrup or iced honeycomb parfait and milk chocolate sauce (£4.95). The restaurant is no smoking. Big windows with swagged-back curtains have a pleasant outlook over the green, and there are large portraits, of racehorses and of people. Service by neatly uniformed staff is friendly and efficient; piped music. Adnams Best and Broadside tapped from the cask, ten wines by the glass (and local ones), and 20 malt whiskies. *(Recommended by Comus and Sarah Elliott, Derek and Sylvia Stephenson)*

Ravenwood Group ~ Manager Yvonne Howland ~ Real ale ~ Bar food (till 10pm Fri and Sat) ~ Restaurant ~ (01787) 312356 ~ Children welcome ~ Dogs allowed in bar and bedrooms ~ Open 9am-midnight ~ Bedrooms: £87.50B/£120B

NAYLAND   TL9734   Map 5
Anchor ♀
Court Street; just off A134 – turn off S of signposted B1087 main village turn; CO6 4JL

You can certainly be sure that the produce used in the cooking here is fresh. Their own farm, Heritage Farm, is next to this neat, no smoking dining pub, and using traditional farming methods, produces free-range eggs, vegetables and home-reared lambs, pigs, beef, game, trout, and venison from the estate; they also have their own smokehouse. The pub is light and sunny inside, with interesting old photographs of pipe-smoking customers and village characters on its pale yellow walls, farmhouse chairs around a mix of tables, and coal and log fires at each end. Behind, a room with similar furniture and another fire leads into a small carpeted sun room. As well as lunchtime nibbles such as pickled free-range egg, sliced cured sausage or nut assortment (from 50p), home-made soup (£3.50), and filled huffers (triangular bread rolls, from £4), the good food might include chicken terrine with tomato chutney (£5), a selection of fish, meat and cheese from their smoke house (£5; main course £8), shellfish risotto (£5.50), spinach and ricotta cannelloni or a home-made sausage of the day with bubble and squeak and bacon gravy (£7.50), cider-battered fish (£8.50), kid curry with onion bhaji (£10), rolled lamb fillet with caper jus or roast fillet of monkfish with sorrel butter sauce (£11), and puddings such as sweet rice pudding with spiced date compote, pistachio crème brûlée or chocolate fondant (from £3.50). The separate restaurant, similarly light and airy, is up quite steep stairs. Well kept Adnams and Greene King IPA, Mild and Triumph on handpump, and several wines by the glass. The bare-boards front bar is liked by regulars who gather for a pint and a chat; piped music. There are picnic-sets on the back terrace looking across to the peaceful River Stour and its quacking ducks. The farmland next door is being worked by suffolk punch horses using traditional farming methods. The suffolk punch is a seriously endangered species and visitors are welcome to watch these magnificent animals or maybe try their hands at the reins. *(Recommended by Ray J Carter, Richard Siebert, Charles and Pauline Stride, Clive and Vivienne Locks, Bryan and Mary Blaxall, Derek Thomas)*

Free house ~ Licensee Daniel Bunting ~ Real ale ~ Bar food (12-2.30, 6.30-9(9.30 Fri and Sat); 10-3, 4.30-10.30 Sun) ~ Restaurant ~ No credit cards ~ (01206) 262313 ~ Children welcome ~ Open 11-3, 5-11; 11-11 Sat; 10am-10.30pm Sun

NEWBOURNE   TM2743   Map 5
Fox
Off A12 at roundabout 1.7 miles N of A14 junction; The Street; IP12 4NY

As you come in, you're left in no doubt that food has pride of place here – an eye-catching array of some two or three dozen little black hanging panels shows, in white writing, one dish to each, what's on offer. Besides good generous lunchtime baps which take even a hungry man some getting through, such as smoked chicken and salad, this might include home-made soup (£3.65), caesar salad with smoked chicken (£4.95), mushroom and spinach lasagne (£7.25), fresh haddock fillet or greek-style lamb (£7.95), steaks (from £8.95), seared fresh tuna steak with a sweet chilli sauce (£9.95), and daily specials; there's also a 'small eater' menu with fresh cod, ham and egg, sausages, and 4oz rib-eye steak (from £4.45). The atmosphere is pleasantly relaxed and pubby, with a few shiny black beams in the low rather bowed ceiling, slabby elm and other dark tables on the bar's tiled floor, a stuffed fox sitting among other decorations in an inglenook, and a warm décor in orange and crushed raspberry. A comfortable carpeted dining room with a large modern artwork and several antique mirrors on its warm yellow walls opens off on the left. They have Adnams and Greene King IPA and Abbot on handpump and decent wines by the glass, and service is prompt and friendly. There are picnic-sets out in front, with more in an attractive garden with a pond; it's a quiet spot. (Recommended by Comus and Sarah Elliott, Pamela Goodwyn, Alan Payne)

Punch ~ Lease Steve and Louise Lomas ~ Real ale ~ Bar food (all day weekends) ~ Restaurant ~ (01473) 736307 ~ Children welcome ~ Dogs allowed in bar ~ Open 11-11

ORFORD TM4250 Map 5
Jolly Sailor ㉕ £
Quay Street; IP12 2NU

Some time during this year, the straight-talking (but very much liked by our readers) landlord and his charming wife will be retiring, so we're obviously hoping that the brewery won't change too much. It's an unspoilt 17th-c brick pub, built mainly from wrecked ships' timbers, and the several snugly traditional rooms have lots of exposed brickwork, and are served from counters and hatches in an old-fashioned central cubicle. There's an unusual spiral staircase in the corner of the flagstoned main bar – which also has 13 brass door knockers and other brassware, local photographs, two cushioned pews and a long antique stripped deal table, and an open woodburning stove in the big brick fireplace (with nice horsebrasses above it); a small room is popular with the dominoes and cribbage players. Well kept Adnams Bitter and Broadside on handpump, and a short choice of straightforward food in generous helpings could include tasty battered local cod, skate or rock eel with chips, home-made pies, omelettes or home-cooked ham (all £6.50), with weekend evening specials such as pasta with various home-made sauces (£7), spicy chicken stir fry (£7.50), and mixed grill (£8.50). The dining room and some tables in the bar are no smoking. There are lovely surrounding coastal walks and plenty of outside pursuits; several picnic-sets on grass at the back have views over the marshes. (Recommended by David and Linda Holmes, Neil Powell, David Carr, R J Snell, Mike and Shelley Woodroffe, Sarah Flynn, Ray J Carter)

Adnams ~ Tenant Philip Attwood ~ Real ale ~ Bar food (not Mon evening, nor Mon-Thurs evenings Nov-Mar) ~ No credit cards ~ (01394) 450243 ~ Dogs allowed in bar ~ Open 11.30-2.30, 7-11; 12-2.45, 7-10.30 Sun ~ Bedrooms: /£50

REDE TL8055 Map 5
Plough 🍴 ♈
Village signposted off A143 Bury St Edmunds—Haverhill; IP29 4BE

This is the sort of friendly and enjoyable pub that readers tend to come back to again and again. It's family run and simple and traditional, and the bar has low black beams, decorative plates on a delft shelf and surrounding the solid-fuel stove in its brick fireplace, and red plush button-back built-in wall banquettes. Featuring quite a lot of game and roundly robust flavours, the changing food is very well cooked: rabbit wrapped in bacon with mustard sauce, venison pancetta casserole, oxtail braised in wine, sea bream with a béarnaise sauce, and simmered basil and tomato chicken (all £10.95), and lamb shank with chick peas, wild boar and wild mushroom stew or monkfish creole (£11.95); efficient, friendly service. Best to book to be sure of a table; the restaurant is no smoking. Greene King IPA and Old Speckled Hen kept under light blanket pressure and lots of wines by the glass; piped music. There are picnic-sets in front, and a sheltered cottage garden at the back. (Recommended by Adele Summers, Alan Black, Helen and Christopher Roberts, Judi Bell, Philip and Susan Philcox)

Greene King ~ Tenant Brian Desborough ~ Real ale ~ Bar food (not Sun evening) ~ Restaurant ~ (01284) 789208 ~ Children welcome but with restrictions ~ Open 11-3, 6-midnight; 12-3, 7-10.30 Sun

ROUGHAM TL9063 Map 5

Ravenwood Hall ♀ ⇌

Just off A14 E of Bury St Edmunds; IP30 9JA

A peaceful and civilised escape from the nearby trunk road, this country house hotel has a thoroughly welcoming all-day bar which does a pub's job better than any of the pubs that are handy for this stretch of the A14. Basically two fairly compact rooms, it has tall ceilings, gently patterned wallpaper, and heavily draped curtains for big windows overlooking a sweeping lawn with a stately cedar. The part by the back serving counter is set for food, its nice furnishings including well upholstered settles and dining chairs, sporting prints and a log fire. As well as sandwiches, there might be mussel, spinach and wild mushroom soup (£4.95), slow-roasted tomato tartlet with white onion cream (£5.25), their own smoked quail terrine with thyme jelly (£6.25), beer-battered cod (£8.95), basil gnocchi with tomato, aubergine and caper ragoût (£12.95), wild rod-caught scotch salmon with lime hollandaise (£15.95), rib-eye steak with cracked black pepper and cognac crème fraîche (£15.95), and puddings such as pineapple carpaccio with coconut ice-cream or stem ginger pudding (£4.95). They smoke their own meats and fish, make their own preserves, and use as much local produce as possible. Well kept Adnams Bitter and Broadside on handpump, good wines by the glass, mulled wine around Christmas, and freshly squeezed orange juice; neat unobtrusive staff give good service. The other end of the bar has horse pictures, several sofas and armchairs with lots of plump cushions, one or two attractively moulded beams, and a good-sized fragment of early Tudor wall decoration above its big inglenook log fire. There may be piped local radio. They have a more formal quite separate restaurant. Outside, teak tables and chairs, some under a wooden shelter, stand around a swimming pool, and out in the wooded grounds big enclosures by the car park hold geese and pygmy goats. *(Recommended by J F M and M West, Comus and Sarah Elliott)*

Free House ~ Licensee Craig Jarvis ~ Real ale ~ Bar food (till 10pm Fri and Sat) ~ Restaurant ~ (01359) 270345 ~ Children welcome ~ Dogs allowed in bar and bedrooms ~ Open 9am-midnight ~ Bedrooms: £98.50B/£135B

SNAPE TM3959 Map 5

Crown ⑪ ♀ ⇌

B1069; IP17 1SL

Run by a friendly landlady and her staff, this busy inn is handy for the Maltings. The attractive bar is furnished with striking horseshoe-shaped high-backed settles around a big brick inglenook with a log fire, spindleback and country kitchen chairs, and nice old tables on some old brick flooring; an exposed panel shows how the ancient walls were constructed, and there are lots of beams in the various small side rooms. Popular bar food might include toasted goats cheese, pesto and caramelised onions (£5.50), smooth duck pâté and chutney or potted shrimps (£5.95), mussels with wine, cream and garlic (£6.95), pasta with tomatoes, aubergine and feta cheese (£10.25), thai salmon fishcakes with chilli jam (£10.50), chicken curry (£11.95), confit of duck with honey glaze or calves liver and bacon (£13.50), fillet steak (£14.95), and puddings such as crème brûlée, chocolate marquise or sticky toffee pudding (£3.95). The dining room is no smoking. The wine list is thoughtful, with 15 wines by the glass (including champagne and pudding wine), and they've Adnams Bitter, Broadside and a seasonal ale on handpump. Readers enjoy staying here but it should be noted that the bedrooms are up very steep stairs; the beams and sloping floors and doorways you may have to stoop under are not for everyone, and furnishings are simple and old-fashioned. Seats and tables in pretty roadside garden. No children. *(Recommended by Mike and Heather Watson, Michael Dandy, Neil Powell, Simon Cottrell, David and Jean Hall, MDN, Comus and Sarah Elliott, W K Wood, Steve Barnes, Ali Henderson, John and Enid Morris, Mr and Mrs L Haines, Pamela Goodwyn, Charles and Pauline Stride, Mrs Jane Kingsbury, Peter and Pat Frogley, Roy and Lindsey Fentiman, Barry Collett, Clive and Vivienne Locks, Mrs S Lyons, Vanessa Young, Ryta Lyndley, Simon Rodway, Rob and Catherine Dunster)*

Adnams ~ Tenant Diane Maylot ~ Real ale ~ Bar food ~ (01728) 688324 ~ Open 12-3, 6-11; 12-3, 7-10.30 Sun; closed 25 Dec, evening 26 Dec ~ Bedrooms: £70B/£80B

SOUTH ELMHAM   TM3389   Map 5
St Peters Brewery 🍺

St Peter S Elmham; off B1062 SW of Bungay; NR35 1NQ

Much enjoyed by our readers, this is a lovely medieval manor with the added attraction that it brews its own beers. St Peter's Hall, to which the brewery is attached, itself dates back to the late 13th c but was much extended in 1539 using materials from the recently dissoved Flixton Priory. Genuinely old tapestries and furnishings make having a drink in the small main bar feel more like a trip to a historic home than a typical pub outing, but the atmosphere is relaxed and welcoming, with candles and fresh flowers on the dark wooden tables, and comfortable seats – from cushioned pews and settles to a 16th-c French bishop's throne. Their beers are made using water from a 100-metre (300-ft) bore hole, in brewery buildings laid out around a courtyard; tours on Saturday, Sunday and bank holiday Monday 12-4 (no need to book unless there are more than five of you); gift shop, too. On handpump and served by warmly friendly staff, the three real ales might include St Peters Best Bitter, Golden Ale and a dark beer, and the others are available by bottle. There's a particularly dramatic high-ceilinged dining hall with elaborate woodwork, a big flagstoned floor and an imposing chandelier, as well as a couple of other appealing old rooms reached up some steepish stairs. Bar food includes home-made soup (£3.95), duck liver parfait (£4.95), panini (from £4.95), steak in ale pie or ham and free-range eggs (£8.95), chicken, bacon and tarragon parcel or roast vegetables and goats cheese strudel (£9.25), sirloin steak with pepper sauce (£10.50), and puddings (£4.25). Outside, tables overlook the original moat where there are black swans. *(Recommended by John Saville, Charles and Pauline Stride, Mike Gorton, Richard and Margaret McPhee, M and GR, David Barnes, Ken Millar, Ian and Nita Cooper, the Didler, Adele Summers, Alan Black, Peter Meister, Jonathan Brown, John Wooll, P and J Shapley, Martin and Pauline Jennings, Marion and Bill Cross, Mrs M Hatwell)*

Own brew ~ Licensees John Murphy and Janet Fogg ~ Real ale ~ Bar food ~ Restaurant ~ (01986) 782288 ~ Children welcome ~ Dogs allowed in bar ~ Open 11-11; 12-10.30 Sun

SOUTHWOLD   TM5076   Map 5
Crown 🍽 🍷 🍺

High Street; IP18 6DP

As popular as ever, this is a rather smart, no smoking old hotel with quite an emphasis on the extremely good food – though they do keep Adnams Bitter, Broadside, Explorer and Oyster on handpump (at a price). The extended elegant beamed main bar has a relaxed atmosphere and a good mix of customers, a stripped curved high-backed settle and other dark varnished settles, kitchen chairs and some bar stools, pretty flowers on the tables, and a carefully restored and rather fine carved wooden fireplace; maybe newspapers to read. The smaller back oak-panelled locals' bar has more of a traditional pubby atmosphere, with red leatherette wall benches and a red carpet; shove-ha'penny, dominoes and cribbage. Using as much local, organic produce as possible, the menu might include sandwiches, fish soup with rouille croûte (£4.50), goats cheese and spinach brûlée and tomato chutney (£5.50), salmon and cod fishcake with tartare sauce (£5.95; main course £11), home-made corned beef hash topped with a poached egg (£6), clam linguini with plum tomato, garlic, chilli and parsley cream (£7; main course £13), wild mushroom risotto (£12.95), honey-glazed lamb shank with parsnip mash and roasted root vegetables (£13), pot-roasted pork belly with local apple compote or roast fillet of hake with beery rarebit (£13.50), and rib-eye steak with café de paris butter (£16.50). There's a splendid wine list, with a monthly changing choice of 20 interesting varieties by the glass or bottle, and quite a few malt whiskies. Tables out in a sunny sheltered corner are very pleasant. *(Recommended by*

Tracey and Stephen Groves, MJVK, John Wooll, David and Jean Hall, W K Wood, Robert and
Susan Phillips, Mike Gorton, David Carr, Comus and Sarah Elliott, John and Enid Morris,
Mike and Sue Loseby, John and Elisabeth Cox, John Saul, J Jennings, Richard Pitcher, Clive and
Vivienne Locks, Michael Dandy, H and P Cate, the Didler, Pam and David Bailey, M and GR,
David and Sue Atkinson, Simon Rodway, Rob and Catherine Dunster)

Adnams ~ Manager Francis Guildea ~ Real ale ~ Bar food (7.30am-2, 6.30-9(9.30 Fri and
Sat)) ~ Restaurant ~ (01502) 722275 ~ No children under 5 in restaurant ~
Open 11-3.30, 6-11(10.30 Sun) ~ Bedrooms: £90B/£140B

Harbour Inn 🍺

Blackshore, by the boats; from A1095, turn right at the Kings Head, and keep on past
the golf course and water tower; IP18 6TA

Many of our readers prefer this waterside pub during the quieter months of the
year, but there's no doubt that its position amongst the small black fishing huts and
seats out in front, where you can watch all the activity on the busy Blyth Estuary
quay, are very appealing in warm weather. As the friendly licensee is a lifeboatman,
the nautical character here is pretty genuine. The back bar has a wind speed
indicator, model ships, a lot of local ship and boat photographs, smoked dried fish
hanging from a line on a beam, a lifeboat line launcher, and brass shellcases on the
mantelpiece over a stove; also, rustic stools and cushioned wooden benches built
into its stripped panelling. The tiny, low-beamed, tiled and panelled front bar has
antique settles and there's a no smoking dining extension. Their fish and chips tend
to sell out pretty fast so get there early if this is what you want: haddock (£9.75),
cod (£9.95), and plaice (£10.95). This is served wrapped in paper on Friday
evenings. Also, sandwiches, home-made soup (£4.25), moules marinière (£4.50;
main course £9), chicken caesar salad (£5.75; main course £11.50), vegetable and
three-cheese tartlet (£10.50), sirloin steak (£13.50), and puddings such as home-
made mango cheesecake with a duo of fruit coulis or white chocolate tart (from
£4.65). Well kept Adnams Bitter, Broadside and Explorer and maybe a guest on
handpump; piped music. On former marshland, the back garden has lots of tables
and a little terrace with fine views across marshy fields towards the town and the
lighthouse; look out for the 1953 flood level marked on the outside of the pub.
(Recommended by Pete Baker, KC, David and Jean Hall, Fiona McElhone, Mike Gorton,
Mike and Sue Loseby, the Didler, Eddie and Lynn Jarrett, Peter and Pat Frogley, Barry Collett,
Paul and Ursula Randall, Michael Dandy, Philip and Susan Philcox)

Adnams ~ Tenant Colin Fraser ~ Real ale ~ Bar food (12-2.30, 6-9) ~ (01502) 722381 ~
Children in bottom bar and restaurant ~ Dogs allowed in bar ~ Open 11-11; 11-10.30 Sun

Lord Nelson 🍺

East Street, off High Street (A1095); IP18 6EJ

With a friendly, ever-present licensee and chatty locals, this lively seaside pub does
get extremely busy at peak times, but it is so well run that there's never any sense of
strain, and the good-natured service is always quick and attentive. The partly
panelled bar and its two small side rooms are kept spotless, with a small but
extremely hot coal fire, light wood furniture on the tiled floor, lamps in nice nooks
and corners, and some interesting Nelson memorabilia, including attractive nautical
prints and a fine model of HMS *Victory*. Well kept Adnams Bitter, Broadside,
Explorer and maybe Oyster Stout on handpump, and good wines by the glass.
Tasty bar food includes sandwiches (from £2.35), home-made soup (£2.75),
ploughman's (from £4.85), home-made cheese and bacon quiche (£5.75), home-
made curry (£6.50), lots of salads (from £6.50), cod in beer batter or ham and
chips (£6.85), a couple of daily specials, and puddings such as home-made sticky
toffee pudding (£3.10). Daily papers but no piped music or games machines. There
are nice seats out in front with a sidelong view down to the sea and more in a
sheltered back garden, with the brewery in sight (and often the appetising fragrance
of brewing in progress). The seafront is just moments away. Disabled access is not
perfect but is possible, and they help. *(Recommended by Pete Baker, Derek Field,*

Rob and Catherine Dunster, Comus and Sarah Elliott, Mike Gorton, David Carr, Mike and Sue Loseby, the Didler, Keith and Janet Morris, Charles and Pauline Stride, Dr and Mrs M E Wilson, Michael Dandy, Pam and David Bailey)

Adnams ~ Tenant John Illston ~ Real ale ~ Bar food ~ No credit cards ~ (01502) 722079 ~ Children in family room and snug ~ Dogs welcome ~ Open 10.30(12 Sun)-11

STOKE-BY-NAYLAND   TL9836   Map 5

Angel 🍽 ♀

B1068 Sudbury—East Bergholt; also signposted via Nayland off A134 Colchester—Sudbury; CO6 4SA

Suffolk Dining Pub of the Year

We are always heartened to come across a place – such as this elegant inn – that manages to appeal to a wide cross-section of customers. It's not an easy thing to do but it's clear that visitors hoping for a delicious meal and locals in for a chat and a pint are all made extremely welcome. The comfortable main bar area has handsome Elizabethan beams, some stripped brickwork and timbers, a mixture of furnishings including wing armchairs, mahogany dining chairs, and pale library chairs local watercolours, modern paintings and older prints, attractive table lamps, and a huge log fire. Round the corner is a little tiled-floor stand-and-chat bar. Neatly uniformed smiling staff serve well kept Greene King IPA, Abbot and a guest on handpump and ten wines by the glass. Another room has a low sofa and wing armchairs around its woodburning stove, and mustard-coloured walls. From a changing menu, the extremely good food might include home-made soup (£3.25), sauté of chicken livers with treacle-cured black bacon and coarse-grained mustard dressing (£4.75), prawn and avocado tian with dill and lemon dressing (£4.95), marinated seafood salad (£6.75), good seared king scallops with a florida salad (£6.95; main course £14.50), polenta and dolcelatte cake on rich tomato sauce (£7.75), confit of duck leg with blackberry sauce and bubble and squeak cake (£9.95), griddled mackerel with beetroot relish and horseradish cream (£10.50), slow-braised shank of gammon with parsley and mustard sauce and sugar-glazed carrots (£12.60), and pork wellington with an apple and cider sauce (£13.50). People may smoke in the village bar only. There are seats and tables on a sheltered terrace. *(Recommended by Dr and Mrs R G J Telfer, Dr and Mrs T E Hothersall, W K Wood, Michael Hasslacher, MDN, M and GR, N R White, David Twitchett, Norman Fox, Charles Gysin, Eric Robinson, Jacqueline Pratt, Mike and Shelley Woodroffe)*

Horizon Inns ~ Manager Neil Bishop ~ Real ale ~ Bar food (12-2, 6-9.30; all day Sun) ~ Restaurant ~ (01206) 263245 ~ Children welcome ~ Dogs allowed in bar ~ Open 11-11(10.30 Sun) ~ Bedrooms: £70B/£85B

Crown ★ ♀

Park Street (B1068); CO6 4SE

An unusual feature in this rather smart dining pub is the glass-walled wine 'cellar' in one corner. From around 200 wines on their list, you can choose from two dozen by the glass plus champagne; they also sell wines by the half-case to take away. Most of the pub is open to the three-sided bar servery, yet it's well divided, and with two or three more tucked-away areas too. The main area, with a big woodburning stove, has quite a lot of fairly closely spaced tables, in a variety of shapes, styles and sizes. Elsewhere, several smaller areas have just three or four tables each. Seating varies from deep armchairs and sofas to elegant dining chairs and comfortable high-backed woven rush seats – and there are plenty of bar stools. This all gives a good choice between conviviality and varying degrees of cosiness and privacy. With a subtle scheme of several gentle toning colours, cheerful wildlife and landscape paintings, quite a lot of attractive table lamps and carefully placed gentle spotlighting, low ceilings (some with a good deal of stripped old beams), and floors varying from old tiles through broad boards or dark new flagstones to beige carpet, the overall feel is of relaxation. There is a table of daily papers. Adnams Bitter and Greene King IPA and a couple of guests on handpump, and nicely served coffee. Well liked, interesting food includes prawn, white bean, wild mushroom and cockle chowder (£4.50; main course £9.50), spicy quail, puy lentils, pancetta and baby spinach salad (£5.95), smoked eel, new potato and beetroot salad, soft boiled egg and horseradish cream (£6.95; main course £10.50), mutton stew with stuffed savoy cabbage (£8.95), slow-roasted tomatoes, artichoke hearts, fennel, winter leaves, garlic croûtons and shaved wensleydale (£9.50), calves liver, celeriac chips, bacon, crispy onions and balsamic jus (£11.50), garlic and herb-stuffed suckling pig with bacon and herb cream (£14.50), fresh fish dishes, and puddings such as steamed chocolate chip pudding, frozen lime soufflé or pecan pie (£4.95); Sunday roast. Half the pub is no smoking (the division is the wall and fireplace); good service. A sheltered (and heated) back terrace, with cushioned teak chairs and tables under big canvas parasols, looks out over a neat lawn to a landscaped shrubbery that includes a small romantic ruined-abbey folly. There are many more picnic-sets out on the front terrace. Disabled access is good, and the car park is big. *(Recommended by Will Watson, Mr and Mrs Foulston, MDN, Ken Millar, David Twitchett, J F M and M West, Pamela Goodwyn, Alan Sadler, Derek Thomas)*

Free house ~ Licensee Richard Sunderland ~ Real ale ~ Bar food (12-2.30, 6-9.30 (10 Fri, Sat); 12-9 Sun) ~ (01206) 262001 ~ Children allowed away from bar ~ Dogs allowed in bar ~ Open 11-11; 12-10.30 Sun; closed 25 and 26 Dec, 1 Jan

SWILLAND   TM1852   Map 5
Moon & Mushroom   ♀ ◖

Village signposted off B1078 Needham Market—Wickham Market, and off B1077; IP6 9LR

The entrance to this cosy pub is through an archway of grapevines and roses, and there are two terraces with outside heaters, retractable awnings and lots of flowers. The homely interior is mainly quarry-tiled, with a log fire, old tables (board games in the drawers) arranged in little booths made by pine pews, and cushioned stools along the bar. A fine choice of at least six real ales is tapped from casks functionally racked up behind the long counter: Crouch Vale Brewers Gold, Nethergate Umbel Ale, Wolf Bitter and Golden Jackal, and Woodfordes Norfolk Nog and Wherry. Also, quite a few wines by the glass and 23 malt whiskies. Bar food includes home-made soup (£2.95), home-made duck liver or smoked mackerel pâté (£3.50), ploughman's with home-cooked ham, vegetarian chilli (£7.95), cajun dusted salmon, slow-cooked belly of pork in cider, wild rabbit pie, beef in ale with dumplings, and pheasant breast cooked with chorizo (all around £8.95), and puddings such as treacle pudding or rhubarb pie (£3.95). Two-course lunch (£6.95; Tuesday-Saturday). Some people who have known and liked the pub for a long time regret the passing of the row of Le Creuset hot-pots with help-yourself vegetables alongside. The dining room is no smoking. *(Recommended by Pam and David Bailey, Ian and Nita Cooper, the Didler, Charles and Pauline Stride, Jonathan Brown, M G Hart, Clive and Vivienne Locks, Mrs Carolyn Dixon, Pamela Goodwyn, Adele Summers, Alan Black)*

Free house ~ Licensees Nikki Gavin and Martin Burgess ~ Real ale ~ Bar food (12-2.30, 7.15-8.45 Sun) ~ Restaurant ~ (01473) 785320 ~ Children welcome ~ Dogs welcome ~ Folk music Sun evening ~ Open 11.30-2.30, 6-11; 12-3.15, 7-10.30 Sun; closed Mon lunchtime

WALBERSWICK   TM4974   Map 5
Anchor   ⑪ ♀ ◖

Village signposted off A12; The Street (B1387); IP18 6UA

Stylishly reworked by the couple who have made such a success of the White Horse on Parsons Green in West London, this brings out to the Suffolk coast that pub's civilised atmosphere, warmly welcoming service and clever coupling of a fine range of drinks with good individual food. The big-windowed comfortable front bar has heavy stripped tables on its dark blue carpet, sturdy built-in wall seats cushioned in green leather, nicely framed black and white photographs of local fishermen and their boats on the varnished plank panelling, and log fires in the chimneybreast which divides it into two snug halves. They have loads of bottled beers from all over the world and a remarkable range of interesting wines by the glass (sensibly served in 125ml glasses) including two sweet ones, as well as well kept Adnams Bitter, Broadside and another Adnams beer such as Flagship on handpump. They do good coffee, attractively served, and have daily papers. A short menu using fresh local seafood and other local supplies suggests a particular wine and beer to go with each dish. It might include soup (£4.50), mixed charcuterie with cornichons and olives (£5.75), wild mushroom and truffle risotto cake (£6.25; main course £8.95), seared scallops with artichoke purée and streaky bacon (£6.75; main course £10.25), ham, bubble and squeak with free-range poached eggs and mustard cream (£8.75), beer-battered local cut with jalapeno tartare sauce and pease pudding (£9.25), vegetable and chestnut pithivier with spicy red cabbage or portuguese black bean and pork stew (£9.75), venison casserole (£11.25), rib-eye steak (£12.75), and puddings such as steamed marmalade pudding or vanilla and rosemary panna cotta (£4.25). Quite an extensive no smoking dining area stretching back from a more modern-feeling small lounge on the left is furnished much like the bar, with a gentle blue-grey décor, and looks out on a good-sized sheltered and nicely planted garden. The pub is right by the coast path, and there's a pleasant walk across to Southwold – in season you can also cross by a pedestrian ferry. Welcoming service, enjoyable real food inc fresh local seafood and other local supplies, good guidance on drinks inc well kept Adnams Bitter, Broadside and Fisherman tapped from the cask and some good wines, special events inc beer and food matching evenings, comfortably refurbished bar, roomy, airy and bright, with pine furnishings, no smoking area, cosy log fires; dogs welcome, neat garden behind, bedrooms (Recommended by Charles and Pauline Stride, Roger and Pauline Pearce, Comus and Sarah Elliott, Dr and Mrs M E Wilson)

Adnams ~ Lease Mark and Sophie Dorber ~ Real ale ~ Bar food (12-3, 6-9) ~ Restaurant ~ (01502) 722112 ~ Children welcome with restrictions ~ Dogs allowed in bar and bedrooms ~ Open 11(12 Sun)-4, 6-11 ~ Bedrooms: /£90B

Bell ♀ 🛏
Just off B1387; IP18 6TN

A novel but nice way to get to this busy pub is on the little ferry from Southwold, ending with a short walk. It's in a great setting close to the beach (most of the well appointed bedrooms look over the sea or river), and tables on the sizeable lawn are sheltered from the worst of the winds by a well placed hedge. Inside, there are brick floors, well worn uneven flagstones and wonky steps, and oak beams that were here 400 years ago when the sleepy little village was a flourishing port. The rambling traditional bar has curved high-backed settles, tankards hanging from oars above the counter, and a woodburning stove in the big fireplace; a second bar has a very large open fire. Up to five Adnams ales are kept on handpump, there are around ten wines by the glass, and several malt whiskies. As well as lunchtime sandwiches (from £4), the seasonal menu might include soup (£3.95), chicken liver pâté with pear chutney or potted prawns (£4.95), locally smoked sprats (£5.25), hot, spicy chilli or vegetable curry (£7.50), cumberland sausage with mushroom gravy (£7.95), chicken supreme with sage and onion stuffing (£8.25), a pie of the day or proper fish pie (£8.50), burger of the day with cheese in toasted ciabatta (£8.95), and puddings such as bread and butter pudding or bakewell tart (from £3.95); Sunday roast (£8.95). They call out your number when your food is ready. One bar area and the dining room are no smoking; darts, shove-ha'penny, cribbage and dominoes; boules outside. The landlady's daughter runs a ceramics business from a shed in the garden. Perhaps the best time to come here is out of season when it's less busy – particularly as they don't take bookings for bar food, and there are usually queues at peak times. (Recommended by MJVK, Louise English, David and Jean Hall, Comus and Sarah Elliott, John and Enid Morris, Blaise Vyner, Mike and Sue Loseby, John Saul, the Didler, Victoria Taylor, Alan Sadler, J Jennings, H and P Cate, Charles and Pauline Stride, Ryta Lyndley, Simon Rodway)

Adnams ~ Tenant Sue Ireland Cutting ~ Real ale ~ Bar food (12-2(2.30 Sun), 7(6 Fri, Sat, and every day July, Aug)-9) ~ Restaurant ~ (01502) 723109 ~ Children allowed in one bar area only ~ Dogs allowed in bar and bedrooms ~ Open 11-11(midnight Fri and Sat); 12-10.30 Sun; 11-3, 6-11 Mon in winter ~ Bedrooms: /£80S(£100B)

WALDRINGFIELD TM2844 Map 5
Maybush
Off A12 S of Martlesham; The Quay, Cliff Road; IP12 4QL

The many tables on the verandah outside this busy family pub are snapped up quickly in fine weather by customers keen to watch the boats and birds on the River Deben. Inside, the spacious bar has quite a nautical theme, with lots of old lanterns, pistols and so forth, as well as aerial photographs, an original Twister board, and fresh flowers; though it's all been knocked through, it's divided into separate areas by fireplaces or steps; games machine and piped music. A glass case has an elaborate ship's model, and there are a few more in a lighter, high-ceilinged extension. Some of the dark wooden tables are set for eating and it can fill quickly at lunchtime (particularly in summer). Adnams Best, Broadside and Explorer on handpump, and a fair choice of wines by the glass. Besides lunchtime sandwiches, straightforward bar food includes soup (£3.95), brussels pâté (£4.95), burgers (from £7.45), spinach and ricotta cannelloni or home-made lasagne (£8.45), battered cod, haddock, plaice or skate (from £8.45), steak, mushroom and Guinness pie (£8.75), steaks (from £8.95), lamb shank (£9.95), and daily specials. The dining rooms are no smoking. River cruises are available nearby. *(Recommended by David Carr, Michael Clatworthy, Louise English, Tracey and Stephen Groves, J F M and M West)*

Punch ~ Lease Steve and Louise Lomas ~ Real ale ~ Bar food (12-2, 7-9; all day weekends and bank hols) ~ (01473) 736215 ~ Children welcome ~ Dogs allowed in bar ~ Open 11(12 Sun)-11

LUCKY DIP

Besides the fully inspected pubs, you might like to try these Lucky Dips recommended to us and described by readers (if you do, please send us reports: www.goodguides.co.uk).

ALDEBURGH [TM4656]
Cross Keys IP15 5BN [Crabbe St]: Well worn in 16th-c pub extended from low-beamed core with antique settles, Victorian prints, woodburners, Adnams ales (the full range) and wines, friendly landlord and staff, simple food, Sunday papers; can be crowded, games machine; open all day July/Aug, children in eating areas, picnic-sets in sheltered back yard by promenade and beach; elegant bedrooms with own bathrooms *(Comus and Sarah Elliott, Ryta Lyndley, LYM, MDN)*
Mill IP15 5BJ [Market Cross Pl, opp Moot Hall]: Small 1920s seaside pub, friendly and relaxing, with good value fresh food from sandwiches and baguettes to very local fish and crabs, good service (humorous landlord), Adnams ales, decent coffee, locals' bar, lots of pictures, cosy no smoking beamed dining room with *Gypsy Queen* model, sea view and strong RNLI theme, cream teas July/Aug; fruit machine; dogs welcome, open all day wknds, bedrooms *(Derek and Sylvia Stephenson, the Didler, Clive and Vivienne Locks, Michael Dandy, Keith and Janet Morris)*
Wentworth IP15 5BB [Wentworth Rd]: Hotel

not pub, useful for enjoyable reasonably priced bar lunches in a choice of welcoming areas, Adnams and a good choice of wines by the glass; conservatory, seafront terrace tables, bedrooms *(Pamela Goodwyn, Pam and David Bailey, Simon Rodway)*
BARHAM [TM1251]
☆ *Sorrel Horse* IP6 0PG [Old Norwich Rd]: Thriving local atmosphere in open-plan pub with good log fire in central chimneybreast, black beams and timbers, Adnams, Shepherd Neame Spitfire and Theakstons Best, friendly landlord and staff, ample wholesome home cooking, two dining areas off; piped local radio; well behaved children allowed, picnic-sets on side grass with big play area, eight comfortable bedrooms in converted barn, open all day Weds-Sun *(Ian and Nita Cooper, BB, J F M and M West, David Eberlin)*
BECCLES [TM4290]
Bear & Bells NR34 9AP [Old Market]: Attractive bright façade, welcoming inside, with enjoyable attractively presented food *(R L Borthwick)*
Kings Head NR34 9HA [New Market]: Hospitable hotel, Tudor behind handsome

18th-c red brick front and pleasantly refitted in uncluttered unfussy style, with cheerful small bar, Adnams and guest beers, helpful staff, good range of reasonably priced pub food, peaceful and comfortable no smoking restaurant; in central pedestrian area, bedrooms *(Keith and Janet Morris)*

BEYTON [TL9363]

White Horse IP30 9AB [signed off A14 and A1088; Bury Rd]: Village-green pub very popular with older lunchers, helpful landlady and staff, good home-made food inc particularly good vegetarian choice, Greene King IPA and Abbot, no music *(J F M and M West, Mr and Mrs Staples)*

BILDESTON [TL9949]

☆ *Crown* IP7 7EB [B1115 SW of Stowmarket]: Picturesque and impressively refurbished 15th-c timbered country inn, smart new furnishings in beamed main bar with inglenook log fire, Adnams ales, good choice of wines by the glass, kind relaxed service, good if not cheap upmarket food, no smoking dining room; children welcome, nice tables out in courtyard, more in large attractive garden, quiet newly refitted bedrooms *(MDN, LYM, Hunter and Christine Wright)*

BLYTHBURGH [TM4575]

☆ *White Hart* IP19 9LQ [A12]: Open-plan family dining pub with fine ancient beams, woodwork and staircase, full Adnams ale range and good range of wines in two glass sizes, good coffee, friendly efficient service, robust sensibly priced blackboard food inc game and fish; children in eating area and restaurant, open all day, spacious lawns looking down on tidal marshes (barbecues), magnificent church over road, bedrooms *(B J Harding, Comus and Sarah Elliott, LYM)*

BOXFORD [TL9640]

☆ *Fleece* CO10 5DX [Broad St]: Unpretentious partly 15th-c pub with particularly friendly landlord, good home-made food, Adnams, cosy panelled bar on right, airy lounge bar with wonderful medieval fireplace, armchairs and some distinctive old seats among more conventional furnishings *(LYM, PL, Paul and Angela Acton)*

BRENT ELEIGH [TL9348]

☆ *Cock* CO10 9PB [A1141 SE of Lavenham]: Relaxed and unspoilt thatched local with piano in clean and cosy snug, benches, table and darts in second small room, antique flooring tiles, lovely coal fire, ochre walls with old photographs of local villages (the village church is well worth a look), Adnams and Greene King IPA and Abbot, organic farm cider, obliging landlord, no food beyond crisps and pickled eggs; picnic-sets up on side grass with summer hatch service, attractive inn-sign, bedrooms *(BB, the Didler)*

BROME [TM1376]

Cornwallis IP23 8AJ [Rectory Road; after turning off A140 S of Diss into B1077, take first left turn]: Nice old and antique furnishings, glazed-over well and handsome woodburner in 19th-c hotel's beamed and timbered bar, Adnams and St Peters ales, quite

a few wines by the glass, board games, ambitious bar food, nicely planted Victorian-style conservatory and elegant no smoking restaurant; piped music; children welcome, splendid grounds, comfortable bedrooms, open all day *(LYM, Simon Cottrell, Peter and Jean Dowson, Richard and Margaret McPhee)*

BROMESWELL [TM3050]

☆ *Cherry Tree* IP12 2PU [Orford Rd, Bromeswell Heath]: Neat beamed pub refurbished under new landlord, good choice of enjoyable wide-ranging food, Adnams and Greene King, open fire; tables outside, big adventure playground, charming inn-sign *(BB, Lew and Dot Hood)*

BUNGAY [TM3389]

Castles NR35 1AF [Earsham St]: Dining pub with open fire and comfortable informal atmosphere in black-beamed front restaurant area, pubby back bar (can be smoky), decent food, Greene King IPA, friendly efficient staff; four well equipped bedrooms *(KC, J C Mann)*

BURY ST EDMUNDS [TL8564]

Angel IP33 1LT [Angel Hill]: Thriving long-established country-town hotel with good food from bar snacks to beautifully presented meals in elegant Regency restaurant and terrace rooms, helpful friendly service, Adnams in rather plush bar, cellar grill room; comfortable bedrooms *(David Carr)*

Fox IP33 1XX [Eastgate St]: Enjoyable fresh food, choice of real ales, staff welcoming even at busy Sat lunchtime, no smoking areas *(Stuart and Alison Ballantyne)*

Linden Tree IP33 1JQ [Out Northgate/Station Hill]: Reliable family dining pub with wide choice of generous good value food from good baguettes up, friendly quick service, good choice of real ales, decent wines in two glass sizes, stripped pine bar, popular no smoking conservatory restaurant; good well kept garden *(Paul Humphreys, Julian and Janet Dearden)*

Rose & Crown IP33 1NP [Whiting St]: Unassuming town local with affable landlord, bargain simple lunchtime home cooking (not Sun), particularly well kept Greene King ales and a guest beer, pleasant lounge with lots of piggy pictures and bric-a-brac, good games-oriented public bar with darts, cards and dominoes, rare separate off-sales counter; may be piped local radio; open all day wkdys *(Pete Baker, J C Mann)*

CAMPSEY ASH [TM3356]

Dog & Duck IP13 0PT [Station Rd]: Attractive family-friendly pub, good range of enjoyable food, welcoming helpful staff, Adnams and Woodfordes Wherry tapped from the cask; tables out in front, nice garden with good play area, five bedrooms with own bathrooms *(Derek and Sylvia Stephenson, Pamela Goodwyn, the Didler)*

CAVENDISH [TL8046]

☆ *Bull* CO10 8AX [A1092 Long Melford—Clare]: Attractive 16th-c open-plan pub with friendly new landlady (let's hope she stays – there have been rather frequent management changes), new chef doing enjoyable food inc good value wkdy lunches, real ales such as

Adnams or Nethergate, decent wines by the glass, heavy beams and timbers and fine fireplaces; children in eating areas, tables in garden, summer barbecues, car park (useful in this honeypot village) *(LYM, Marianne and Peter Stevens, PL, Marion and Bill Cross)*

☆ *George* CO10 8BA [The Green]: Attractively laid out as more restaurant than pub, good food from interesting lunchtime sandwiches and light dishes to a nice slant on pubby favourites such as steak and kidney pudding, good atmosphere and charming efficient service, beamed and bow-windowed no smoking front part, further good-sized eating area, good value wines, good coffees and teas; tables out in garden behind *(Marianne and Peter Stevens, BB, Tony and Margaret Cross, Sarah Flynn)*

CHELSWORTH [TL9848]

☆ *Peacock* IP7 7HU [B1115 Sudbury—Needham Mkt]: Attractive and prettily set old dining pub with new chef doing good food inc Weds steak night, Thurs regional dishes and (booked far ahead) monthly thai and jazz nights, some more economical simpler dishes, good friendly service, well spaced comfortable tables, pubby bar with real ales, big inglenook log fire and lots of Tudor brickwork and exposed beams; nice small garden, pretty village *(MDN, Tessa van Rossum, LYM, R A P Cross)*

CHILLESFORD [TM3852]

☆ *Froize* IP12 3PU [B1084 E of Woodbridge]: Largely no restaurant rather than pub (open only when they serve food, ie not Mon, nor Sun-Weds evenings), good country cooking in pleasantly decorated bar and restaurant, good value two-course buffet-style lunch, wide choice of more elaborate evening meals, local pork, game and venison, generous Sun lunch, original puddings, Adnams, decent wines by the glass, warmly welcoming service; may be cl Feb for hols *(LYM, Kerry and Tricia Thomas, Tony and Shirley Albert, Pamela Goodwyn, Gordon Neighbour, Simon Rodway)*

CLARE [TL7645]

☆ *Bell* CO10 8NN [Market Hill]: Large timbered inn with comfortably rambling beamed lounge, splendidly carved black beams, old panelling and woodwork, Greene King IPA and local Nethergate Suffolk Best, decent wines and food from sandwiches up, dining room with feature fireplace, conservatory opening on to terrace; darts, pool, games machine and TV in public bar; nice bedrooms off back courtyard (very special village, lovely church), open all day Sun *(Michael Dandy, LYM)*

☆ *Swan* CO10 8NY [High St]: Much modernised early 17th-c beamed and timbered village pub with lots of copper and brass and huge log fire in main room, public bar with World War II memorabilia (dogs allowed here), no smoking dining room, friendly service, low-priced food from sandwiches and baked potatoes up, Greene King ales, good choice of wines by the glass; big-screen sports TV; good tables on back terrace among lovely flower tubs *(Michael Dandy, BB)*

CREETING ST MARY [TM1155]

Highwayman IP6 8PD [A140, just N of junction with A14]: Much modernised two-bar pub with pleasant barn extension, relaxed atmosphere, keen and welcoming newish landlord, Ukrainian wife cooks good interesting food, Adnams, Fullers London Pride and Woodfordes Wherry, decent wines, gallery overflow; unobtrusive piped music; tables on back lawn with small pond, cl Mon and Tues/Weds lunchtime *(Ian and Nita Cooper, Mrs Carolyn Dixon, Pamela Goodwyn)*

CRETINGHAM [TM2260]

Bell IP13 7BJ [The Street]: New owners and management for this attractive and formerly well liked pub, comfortably modernised lounge bar, quarry-tiled public bar with several real ales, lots of beams and timbers, fine old fireplace; attractive garden with rustic tables on sheltered grass in front and more on lawn by rose bushes and fine old oak tree; more reports please *(LYM)*

DALHAM [TL7261]

☆ *Affleck Arms* CB8 8TG [Brookside]: Well kept thatched pub by stream (dry in some summers), log fire in cosy low-beamed locals' bar, more comfortable and intimate rambling dining bar on right opening into two small back no smoking dining rooms, good value food from good baguettes up, Greene King and other ales, good welcoming service; picnic-sets out in front and across stream, more on back terrace, pretty village, cl Mon/Tues lunchtimes, open all day Sun *(Adele Summers, Alan Black, LYM, Paul Humphreys, Ron Deighton)*

EARSHAM [TM3289]

Queens Head NR35 2TS [Station Rd]: Good value bar food and beer brewed at the pub, two or three other reasonably priced real ales *(Pam and David Bailey)*

EAST BERGHOLT [TM0734]

☆ *Kings Head* CO7 6TL [Burnt Oak, towards Flatford Mill]: Attractively extended and good value, with more ambitious food choice turning out well, well kept beamed lounge with comfortable sofas, interesting decorations, Greene King and guest ales, decent wines and coffee, friendly staff and atmosphere, exemplary new lavatories; piped classical music; lots of room in pretty garden, flower-decked haywain, baskets and tubs of flowers in front *(Tony and Shirley Albert, Mike and Mary Carter, Edward Leetham)*

EASTBRIDGE [TM4566]

☆ *Eels Foot* IP16 4SN [off B1122 N of Leiston]: Cheerful beamed country pub, Adnams ales, good cider, light modern furnishings, wide choice of food from good value hot-filled rolls up, obliging service, log fire, darts in side area, neat back dining room; famously long-running sing-song (now Thurs); walkers, children and dogs welcome, pleasant garden with tables and swings, pretty village handy for Minsmere bird reserve (nice 2½ mile walk from sluice); bedrooms, open all day in summer *(LYM, Charles and Pauline Stride, John Beeken, Simon Rodway)*

EASTON [TM2858]
White Horse IP13 0ED [N of Wickham Market on back rd to Earl Soham and Framlingham]: Neatly kept pink-washed two-bar country pub, bigger than it looks, with wide choice of popular food in bar and dining room, Adnams, welcoming staff, open fires; children in eating area, nice garden *(LYM, Gordon Neighbour)*

FELIXSTOWE FERRY [TM3237]
☆ *Ferry Boat* IP11 9RZ: Relaxed and cottagey extended and much modernised 17th-c family pub tucked between golf links and dunes nr harbour, martello tower and summer rowing-boat ferry, impressive blackboard choice of good value food from snacks to fresh fish, Adnams Best and Greene King IPA and Old Speckled Hen, welcoming helpful service, good log fire; piped music; dogs welcome, tables out in front, on green opposite, and in securely fenced garden, busy summer wknds, good seaside walks *(MLR, Charles and Pauline Stride, LYM, Comus and Sarah Elliott)*

☆ *Victoria* IP11 9RZ: Child-friendly riverside pub, substantial good value no-nonsense food inc local fish, cheerful efficient staff, Adnams and Greene King ales, tempting liqueur coffees, good log fire in snug, sea views from no smoking upstairs dining area *(Mike and Mary Carter, Ryta Lyndley, Pamela Goodwyn)*

FELSHAM [TL9457]
Six Bells IP30 0PJ [Church Rd]: Open-plan rural local with good mix of locals, darts players and people eating, nice décor and fresh flowers, Greene King ales, friendly relaxed licensees – he does the cooking, which is good and inventive, using fresh local ingredients, and bakes his own bread; children welcome *(Mrs Kay Dewsbury)*

FLIXTON [TM3187]
Buck NR35 1NZ [The Street]: Several refurbished bars, big restaurant, good beer range, good value food inc Sun carvery; quiet spot, handy for Aviation Museum *(Adele Summers, Alan Black)*

FRAMLINGHAM [TM2863]
Castle Inn IP13 9BP [Castle St]: Small and smartly decorated, next to the castle (which has no food itself), with wide range of decent food from baguettes and baked potatoes up, cream teas too, Adnams and Greene King IPA, good service even when busy; children welcome, front picnic-sets overlooking duckpond, more on back terrace *(Mrs Joyce Robson, J F M and M West)*

☆ *Station Hotel* IP13 9EE [Station Rd (B1116 S)]: High-ceilinged big-windowed bar with pine tables and chairs on stripped boards, imaginative and generous food inc good fish dishes (an emphasis on smoked), four Earl Soham ales and a guest beer, good choice of house wines, welcoming service, informal relaxed atmosphere, plenty of train pictures, small tiled-floor back snug; children welcome, picnic-sets in good-sized pleasant garden *(Pete Baker, BB, MLR, Gordon Neighbour)*

FRESSINGFIELD [TM2677]
Swan IP21 5PE [B1116 Harleston—Framlingham]: Welcoming village pub with linked areas inc one for families and another with pool, Adnams and good house wines, decent food, separate no smoking area with leather sofas leading to modern restaurant extension *(KC)*

FRISTON [TM4160]
Old Chequers IP17 1NP [just off A1094 Aldeburgh—Snape]: Attractively refurbished dining pub, welcoming and civilised, with good enterprising reasonably priced food inc fish, game and Sun carvery, OAP lunches Mon-Thurs, Adnams Best and Broadside, good wines and whiskies, friendly efficient landlord, big woodburner; piped music may obtrude; children welcome, good walk from Aldeburgh *(Tracey and Stephen Groves, John Beeken, LYM)*

HALESWORTH [TM3877]
☆ *Angel* IP19 8AH [Thoroughfare (now pedestrianised)]: Civilised, comfortable and substantial, with lounge bar (no smoking at lunchtime) looking out on pedestrianised main street from tall windows, more tables in roofed-in galleried coachyard with Act of Parliament clock, three reasonably priced Adnams ales, nice wines, busy espresso machine, good log fire, friendly efficient staff, sandwiches and baps all day, cheap traditional bar dishes and pizzas, sizeable no smoking restaurant; piped pop music, small inner bar with fruit machines; children welcome, seven well equipped bedrooms with good bathrooms, car park – useful here, open all day *(John Wooll, BB, Peter and Jean Dowson, Robert Lorimer, Steve Nye)*

HARTEST [TL8352]
☆ *Crown* IP29 4DH [B1066 S of Bury St Edmunds]: Pink-washed pub by church behind pretty village green, smartly minimalist décor with quality tables and chairs on tiled floor, good log fire in impressive fireplace, wide choice of enjoyable food from baguettes up, Greene King IPA, Abbot and Old Speckled Hen, quick friendly service, two no smoking dining rooms and conservatory; piped music; children and dogs welcome, tables on big back lawn and in sheltered side courtyard, good play area *(Adele Summers, Alan Black, LYM, Marianne and Peter Stevens, Chris and Ali Charman)*

HITCHAM [TL9851]
White Horse IP7 7NQ [The Street (B1115 Sudbury—Stowmarket)]: Friendly local with obliging service, Greene King Abbot, log fire, two bars (one no smoking), restaurant; dogs welcome, cl Mon/Tues *(Francis Nicholls)*

HOLBROOK [TM1636]
Compasses IP9 2QR [Ipswich Rd]: Roomy and tidy pub with nice range of good value food from good baguettes up, prompt cheerful service, Adnams and Greene King ales, big log fire, restaurant area; garden with play area, nice spot on Shotley peninsula *(Charles and Pauline Stride, Keith Berrett, Pamela Goodwyn)*

HOXNE [TM1877]

☆ *Swan* IP21 5AS [off B1118, signed off A140 S of Diss; Low St]: Outstanding well restored late 15th-c building, broad oak floorboards, handsomely carved timbering in the colour-washed walls, armchairs by deep-set inglenook log fire, no smoking snug, another huge log fire in dining room, Adnams Bitter and Broadside and good guest beers tapped from the cask, bank hol beer festivals, enjoyable bar food from baguettes and light dishes up, friendly landlord, hard-working cheerful staff, lighted candles; children welcome, sizeable attractive garden behind, summer barbecues *(TW, MW, Comus and Sarah Elliott, LYM, Michael Clatworthy, Peter and Jean Dowson)*

HUNDON [TL7247]

☆ *Plough* CO10 8DT [Brockley Green, SW towards Kedington]: Friendly neatly kept knocked-through bar, beams, timbers and stripped brick, scrubbed tables and open fire, enjoyable if not cheap food from lunchtime sandwiches to some enterprising dishes (can take a while if they're busy), cheerful staff, Greene King IPA, Woodfordes Wherry and a guest beer, good choice of wines by the glass and malt whiskies, no smoking restaurant; children and dogs welcome, extensive attractive grounds with croquet, good tables and terrace, comfortable bedrooms *(Adele Summers, Alan Black, Frank W Gadbois, Dave Braisted, Alan Sadler, LYM, P and J Shapley, Eric Robinson, Jacqueline Pratt)*

IPSWICH [TM1844]

☆ *Fat Cat* IP4 5NL [Spring Rd, opp junction with Nelson Rd]: Neatly kept pastiche of basic bare-boards pub with 15 or more interesting ales mainly from small breweries, belgian imports, farm ciders, helpful friendly service and cheery regulars, snacks such as scotch eggs, filled rolls and pasties (plates and cutlery if you bring your own food on busy nights – chinese takeaway opp), lots of enamel beer advertisements, no music or machines, cat called Dave; very little daytime parking nearby; back conservatory and terrace with summer thai barbecues, open all day *(Ian and Nita Cooper, Danny Savage, BB, the Didler)*

Milestone IP4 2EA [Woodbridge Rd]: Open-plan pub with up to a dozen or so real ales, farm ciders, several dozen whiskies, home-made food lunchtime and Mon-Weds evening; big-screen sports TV, live bands; large front terrace, open all day wknds *(the Didler)*

IXWORTH [TL9370]

☆ *Pykkerel* IP31 2HH [High St; just off A143 Bury—Diss]: Friendly and attractive Elizabethan pub with several rooms off central servery, good value food (not Sun evening) from sandwiches to a dozen or more local fish dishes, Greene King ales, big fireplaces, antique tables and comfortable old settles, oriental rugs on polished boards, beams, stripped brickwork, panelling and paintings, restaurant; children and dogs welcome, comfortable bedrooms *(LYM, Paul Humphreys, Pam and David Bailey)*

KENTFORD [TL7066]

Cock CB8 7PR [Bury Rd, just off A14]: Comfortable and attractive, with inglenook log fire and beautiful carved beams, good interesting range of food, friendly service, Greene King real ales, airy restaurant; neat garden *(M and GR)*

KERSEY [TM0044]

☆ *Bell* IP7 6DY [signed off A1141 N of Hadleigh; The Street]: Well kept flower-decked Tudor building in notably picturesque village, friendly obliging staff, wide choice of good value pubby food from sandwiches and bar lunches to more elaborate evening dishes, Adnams and Greene King IPA, decent house wines, tastefully modernised low-beamed bar with log fire, two dining rooms; children allowed, open all day, sheltered back terrace with fairy-lit side canopy *(Will Watson, LYM, Judi Bell, Philip and Susan Philcox)*

KIRTLING [TL6856]

Red Lion CB8 9PD [The Street]: Good choice of enjoyable home-made food in bar and restaurant, pleasant service, two real ales; cl Sun evening and Mon *(Margaret and John Corbett)*

KNODISHALL [TM4361]

Butchers Arms IP17 1UQ [Leiston Rd]: Good value wholesome food inc interesting dishes in straightforward local with pleasant airy dining room, Adnams, darts, cribbage etc; garden with terrace *(Simon Rodway)*

LAVENHAM [TL9148]

Cock CO10 9SA [Church St]: Comfortable and attractive thatched village pub with generous reasonably priced food from baguettes and salads up, plush lounge, separate family dining room, basic bar (popular with young people wknds), Adnams and Greene King ales, good wine choice; no dogs; seats out in front and back garden, nice view of church *(Adele Summers, Alan Black, MLR, the Didler, P and D Carpenter)*

Swan CO10 9QA [High Street]: Smart, well equipped and by no means cheap hotel incorporating handsome medieval buildings, well worth a look for its appealing network of beamed and timbered alcoves and more open areas, inc peaceful little tiled-floor inner bar with leather chairs and memorabilia of its days as the local for US 48th Bomber Group, Adnams and a guest beer, fairly short lunchtime bar menu, morning coffee, afternoon tea, good young staff, lavishly timbered no smoking restaurant; children welcome, sheltered courtyard garden *(LYM, the Didler, MDN, David Barnes)*

LAYHAM [TM0340]

☆ *Marquis of Cornwallis* IP7 5JZ [Upper St (B1070 E of Hadleigh)]: Beamed 16th-c pub with current management putting more emphasis on carefully prepared food (two evening sittings), quick attentive service, Greene King and Woodfordes, good wines and coffee, buoyant evening atmosphere, pleasant pine furniture, warm coal fire, separate restaurant; good valley views, picnic-sets in extensive riverside garden, open all day Sat in summer, cl Sun evening *(MDN, Judi Bell, David Barnes)*

LEVINGTON [TM2339]

☆ *Ship* IP10 0LQ [Gun Hill/Church Lane]: Nautical décor and pictures in charming old pub with cosy flagstoned dining room, very popular tasty food inc sensibly priced fresh fish and seafood, good choice of wines by the glass, Adnams and Greene King, two no smoking areas; no children inside, front picnic-sets with a bit of a sea view, attractive surroundings, good walks, cl Sun evening *(Ian and Nita Cooper, LYM, Pamela Goodwyn)*

LONG MELFORD [TL8645]

☆ *Bull* CO10 9JG [Hall St (B1064)]: Lovely medieval great hall, now a hotel, with beautifully carved beams in old-fashioned timbered front lounge, antique furnishings, blazing log fire in huge fireplace, visitors' more spacious back bar with sporting prints, very friendly helpful staff, Greene King IPA and Abbot, good range of bar food from good filled huffers to one-price hot dishes inc imaginative salads and fresh fish, daily papers, no smoking restaurant; children welcome, courtyard tables, comfortable bedrooms, open all day Sat/Sun *(Derek and Sylvia Stephenson, LYM)*

Cock & Bell CO10 9JR [Hall St]: Attractive dining pub, roomy and comfortable, with welcoming efficient staff, enjoyable good value food all day inc interesting fish choice and sumptuous puddings, Greene King IPA and reasonably priced wines, no smoking area *(David and Sue Smith, Adele Summers, Alan Black)*

LOWESTOFT [TM5593]

Triangle NR32 1QA [St Peters St]: Jovial pub brewing its own good range of Green Jack ales, several guest beers and often a farm cider, open fire you can cook on, frequent live music and all-day jam sessions, pool and juke box in back bar; open all day *(Leon Shaw)*

MARKET WESTON [TL9777]

☆ *Mill* IP22 2PD [Bury Rd (B1111)]: Opened-up pub with attractively priced lunches using local produce, OAP discounts, thoughtful evening menu, Adnams, Greene King IPA, Woodfordes Wherry and an Old Chimneys beer from the village brewery, local farm cider, enthusiastic effective service, two log fires, dominoes; children welcome, small well kept garden *(Derek Field)*

MARTLESHAM [TM2446]

Black Tiles IP12 4SP [off A12 Woodbridge—Ipswich]: Spotless and spacious family dining pub with pleasantly decorated bistro-style garden-room restaurant (children allowed here), big woodburner in appealing old bar, wide choice of good inexpensive generous home-made food served quickly by smart helpful staff, daily roast, Adnams Bitter and Broadside and a guest beer; garden tables, open all day *(Charles and Pauline Stride, LYM, Pamela Goodwyn)*

MELTON [TM2850]

Wilford Bridge IP12 2PA [Wilford Bridge Rd]: Light, roomy and well organised, with emphasis on good value food from good sandwiches to local fish in two spacious bars and restaurant, steak nights Mon/Tues, takeaways, Adnams and Greene King Old Speckled Hen, good wines by the glass, prompt friendly service; nearby river walks *(Pamela Goodwyn)*

MIDDLETON [TM4267]

Bell IP17 3NN [off B1125 Leiston—Westleton; The Street]: Traditional pub, part thatched and beamed, full Adnams range tapped from the cask, enjoyable cheap food inc children's, woodburner in comfortable lounge, small back dining room, darts and open fire in small low-ceilinged public bar (dogs allowed); impromptu folk nights Weds; garden picnic-sets, pretty setting nr church, camping, handy for RSPB Minsmere and coast *(BB, Comus and Sarah Elliott)*

ORFORD [TM4249]

Crown & Castle IP12 2LJ: Restaurant with rooms and small smart italian-chair bar with Greene King IPA and good though pricey wines by the glass (used mainly but not solely for pre-dinner drinks); well worth knowing for good if not cheap food (not a large choice at lunchtime) with a strong streak of individuality, pleasant service; tables outside (mainly for diners), residents' garden, good bedrooms *(Michael Dandy, Tom Gondris, A J Murray, Tracey and Stephen Groves)*

☆ *Kings Head* IP12 2LW [Front St]: Compact bar and adjacent airy no smoking dining room with ancient bare boards and stripped brickwork, Adnams ales, good coffee, good reasonably priced food from sandwiches and baguettes up, proper children's specials, friendly efficient staff; live music Fri, seats outside and nearby pub garden, attractive character bedrooms with own bathrooms *(Michael Dandy, LYM, Jonathan and Gillian Shread, N R White)*

OTLEY [TM1852]

White Hart IP6 9NS [Helmingham Rd (B1079)]: Reopened summer 2006 after closure for several months, tasteful redecoration, enjoyable home-made food, good Earl Soham beers; sizeable pretty garden, handy for Helmingham Hall gardens *(J F M and M West)*

PAKENHAM [TL9267]

Fox IP31 2JU [signed off A1088 and A143 S of Norwich]: Neatly kept beamed village pub with good value pub food, Greene King IPA and Abbot, good choice of wines by the glass, log fire, compact dining room; quiet piped jazz; children welcome, nice tables in streamside garden with barbecue, boules and summer bar, cl Mon *(Derek Field, John and Bettye Reynolds)*

PETTISTREE [TM2954]

Greyhound IP13 0HP [off A12 just S of Wickham Mkt]: Picturesque 15th-c village pub with bistro-style food, Earl Soham ale, friendly landlord, comfortable lounge with sofas, armchairs and lots of horsey memorabilia, pleasant dining room; cl wkdy lunchtimes and Mon evening *(Comus and Sarah Elliott)*

POLSTEAD [TL9938]
☆ *Cock* CO6 5AL [signed off B1068 and A1071 E of Sudbury, then pub signed; Polstead Green]: Black beams and timbers, dark pink walls, woodburner and open fire, random mix of unassuming furniture, good-natured local atmosphere, real ales such as Adnams Broadside, Greene King IPA and Woodfordes Wherry, good choice of wines and malt whiskies, good coffee, friendly young staff, bargain Fri steak night, other bar food from big filled lunchtime rolls up, smarter no smoking light and airy barn restaurant; bar can get smoky, piped music; good disabled access and facilities, children and dogs welcome, picnic-sets out overlooking quiet green, side play area, cl Mon *(BB, David Barnes, Pamela Goodwyn)*

PRESTON [TL9450]
Six Bells CO10 9NG [just NE of Lavenham; The Street]: Neatly refurbished ancient manor-owned pub with central bar between dining end and good-natured games end; simple generous inexpensive food, Greene King IPA and Old Speckled Hen, decent wines; tables out on grass *(MDN)*

RAMSHOLT [TM3041]
☆ *Ramsholt Arms* IP12 3AB [signed off B1083; Dock Rd]: Lovely isolated spot, with well used nautical bars overlooking River Deben, handy for bird walks and Sutton Hoo; quickly served wholesome food inc plenty of good value seafood and game, two sittings for Sun lunch, Adnams Best and Broadside with a seasonal guest such as Nethergate, decent wines by the glass, winter mulled wine, easy-going contented bar (one of the dogs can let himself in) with good log fire, no smoking restaurant; longish steep walk down from car park, busy summer wknds; children very welcome, tables outside with summer afternoon terrace bar (not Sun), roomy bedrooms with stunning view, open all day *(J F M and M West, LYM, Comus and Sarah Elliott, Pamela Goodwyn, Stephen and Jean Curtis, P and J Shapley, Tracey and Stephen Groves)*

RENDHAM [TM3564]
White Horse IP17 2AF [B1119 Framlingham—Saxmundham]: No smoking open-plan pub with good simple traditional home cooking inc Sun lunch, generous helpings and named local sources, friendly family atmosphere, Earl Soham Bitter on handpump with changing ales such as Marstons Burton, Moultons Suffolk, Nethergate Three Point and Timothy Taylors Landlord tapped from the cask, two open fires; local walks leaflet, lovely spot opp 14th-c church *(Mr Biagioni, John Beeken)*

REYDON [TM4977]
Randolph IP18 6PZ [Wangford Rd]: Light and airy contemporary décor, light wood furniture on parquet and blinds for the big windows, polite and helpful young staff, good food choice from local ham and chutney sandwiches to plenty of fish and interesting puddings, Adnams beers and wines; children welcome in dining area, garden tables, good value

bedrooms *(Tracey and Stephen Groves, Comus and Sarah Elliott)*

SAXON STREET [TL6759]
Reindeer CB8 9RS [The Street]: Smart and friendly dining pub with enjoyable food prepared to order, Adnams ales; picnic-sets outside *(Mike and Jennifer Marsh, M and GR)*

SHOTTISHAM [TM3244]
Sorrel Horse IP12 3HD [Hollesley Rd]: Charming two-bar thatched Tudor local, Greene King ales tapped from the cask, limited tasty home-made food from granary baguettes up, helpful service, good log fire in tiled-floor bar, attractive dining room; tables out on green of tucked-away village *(the Didler, Comus and Sarah Elliott, Geoff and Carol Thorp)*

SIBTON [TM3570]
White Horse IP17 2JJ [Halesworth Rd]: 16th-c former farmhouse under new owners, attractive two-room layout with lots of beams, big brick fireplaces and upper gallery, enjoyable food, friendly staff; attractive big garden, bedrooms being upgraded *(David Roberts, LYM, Edward Gregory)*

SNAPE [TM4058]
Golden Key IP17 1SA [Priory Lane]: Comfortable and attractively worn in old pub with cheerful landlord, wide choice of quickly served simple pubby food, Adnams Bitter and Broadside, extensive no smoking low-beamed restaurant; no dogs (two pub dogs); children welcome, good disabled access, tables on front terrace, sheltered flower-filled garden, comfortable bedrooms *(Mike and Heather Watson, Michael Dandy, David Roberts, LYM, Pamela Goodwyn, Pam and David Bailey, Alan Payne)*
☆ *Plough & Sail* IP17 1SR [the Maltings]: Pleasant layout with good space for drinkers inc attractive original core with sofas, settles and log fires, Adnams ales, decent wines, light and airy eating areas with enjoyable up-to-date food from generous sandwiches and baguettes to restaurant meals, genial barman and fast professional food service; children welcome, teak tables out in big enclosed flower-filled courtyard, open all day in summer, lovely surroundings with good walks *(Tracey and Stephen Groves, Comus and Sarah Elliott, LYM, Andy Lickfold, Pamela Goodwyn, Keith and Janet Morris, Clive and Vivienne Locks, A J Murray)*

SOMERLEYTON [TM4797]
Dukes Head NR32 5QR [Slugs Lane (B1074)]: Thriving and stylish stripped-stone pubby bar with Adnams ales and occasional beer festivals, enjoyable seasonal food using local produce, family dining extension; regular live music; tables out on grass, country views, a stiff walk up from River Waveney *(Kate Abbot, Dr and Mrs M E Wilson)*

SOMERSHAM [TM0848]
☆ *Duke of Marlborough* IP8 4QA [off A14 just N of Ipswich; Main Rd]: Pub/restaurant with good service and atmosphere, good fresh food from lunchtime baguettes and baked potatoes to some interesting hot dishes, Greene King IPA and Old Speckled Hen, decent wines, good

coffee, pleasant efficient young staff, sturdy pine tables on stripped boards in big open room, attractive country prints and 16th-c inglenook, light and airy turkey-carpeted dining room (BB, Pamela Goodwyn, J F M and M West)

SOUTHWOLD [TM5076]

☆ Red Lion IP18 6ET [South Green]: Good atmosphere, warm friendly service, reasonably priced wholesome food from sandwiches up inc good fish and chips, Adnams ales, big windows looking over green to sea, pale panelling, ship pictures, lots of brassware and copper, pub games, no smoking dining room; children and dogs welcome, lots of tables outside, right by the Adnams retail shop; bedrooms small but comfortable (BB, Mike Gorton, Dr and Mrs M E Wilson, Michael Dandy, Pam and David Bailey)
Sole Bay IP18 6JN [East Green]: Bright and stylish café/bar décor and light wood furnishings, lively local atmosphere, Adnams ales, cheerful and efficient smartly dressed staff, good simple food from impressive doorstep sandwiches up, conservatory; live music Fri; tables on side terrace, moments from sea and lighthouse (Comus and Sarah Elliott, David Carr, LYM, Dr and Mrs M E Wilson, Paul and Ursula Randall, MDN)

☆ Swan IP18 6EG [Market Pl]: Relaxed and comfortable back bar in smart hotel, Adnams and Broadside, full range of their bottled beers, fine wines and malt whiskies, good bar lunches (not cheap, but worth it) from enormous baguettes and ciabattas to ten or so main dishes, pleasant staff, pricey coffee and teas in luxurious chintzy front lounge; good bedrooms inc garden rooms where (by arrangement) dogs can stay too (Mike and Heather Watson, LYM, Martin and Pauline Jennings, Dr and Mrs M E Wilson, Michael Dandy, George Atkinson)

STOWUPLAND [TM0759]

Crown IP14 4BQ [Church Rd (A1120 just E of Stowmarket)]: Traditional main bar with brasses and farm tools, Greene King IPA, reliable solid pub food inc imaginative curries and meats from good local butcher, locals' lively back bar with darts, pool and big-screen sports TV (J F M and M West, Stephen P Edwards)

STUTTON [TM1434]

Gardeners Arms IP9 2TG [Manningtree Rd, Upper Street (B1080)]: Adnams, Greene King and a guest beer, friendly landlord, enjoyable fresh home-made food inc good value Sun lunch in separate dining room; open all day (Andrew Scarr, Edward Leetham)

SUDBURY [TL8741]

☆ Waggon & Horses CO10 1HJ [Church Walk]: Comfortable compact bar with good choice of reasonably priced fresh food inc good sandwiches and proper pies, good beers and house wines, good welcoming service, interesting décor, log fire; pleasant walled garden with picnic-sets, handy for Gainsborough House (David Miles-Dinham, Charles Gysin)

THEBERTON [TM4365]

Lion IP16 4RU [B1122]: Unpretentious village local with changing real ales such as Adnams Best, Greene King Abbot, Nethergate and Woodfordes Wherry, good value food, welcoming licensees, no smoking lounge, comfortable banquettes, lots of old local photographs, pictures, copper, brass, plates and bric-a-brac, fresh flowers, games area with darts and pool; back garden with picnic-sets and small terrace, camp site with showers (John Beeken, Comus and Sarah Elliott, Jonathan Brown)

THORNHAM MAGNA [TM1070]

Four Horseshoes IP23 8HD [off A140 S of Diss; Wickham Rd]: Extensive thatched pub with dim-lit rambling well divided bar, very low heavy black beams, mix of chairs and plush banquettes, country pictures and farm tools, big log fireplaces, inside well, no smoking areas; Greene King ales, wide food choice inc Sun lunch, competent young staff; piped music, games machine; handy for Thornham Walks and interesting thatched church, picnic-sets on big sheltered lawn, bedrooms, open all day (Ian and Nita Cooper, LYM, David Barnes, N R White)

THORPENESS [TM4759]

☆ Dolphin IP16 4NB: Attractive almost scandinavian décor, light and bright, very busy lunchtime for enjoyable food from sandwiches up, Adnams, good wine range, welcoming landlord and relaxed helpful service, interesting photographs of this quaint purpose-built seaside holiday village with its boating lake; children and dogs welcome, large attractive garden with summer bar and barbecue, three comfortable and appealingly decorated bedrooms with own bathrooms (Tracey and Stephen Groves, W K Wood, Pamela Goodwyn, Comus and Sarah Elliott)

TOSTOCK [TL9563]

Gardeners Arms IP30 9PA [off A14 or A1088]: Useful low-beamed village pub, Greene King and a guest ale, good-sized helpings of substantial pubby food inc fresh fish, reasonable prices, log fire, games in tiled public bar, no smoking dining area; picnic-sets in nicely planted sheltered garden (Ian and Nita Cooper, LYM, John and Bettye Reynolds, Robert F Smith, J F M and M West, Tim and Suzy Bower)

WANGFORD [TM4679]

Angel NR34 8RL [signed just off A12 by B1126 junction; High St]: Good unusual food inc upmarket dishes in handsome 17th-c village inn with well spaced tables in light and airy bar, real ales, decent wines; children in no smoking dining room, comfortable bedrooms (the church clock sounds on the quarter), open all day (LYM, Pete and Sue Robbins)

WESTLETON [TM4469]

Crown IP17 3AD [B1125 Blythburgh—Leiston]: Extended and recently refurbished coaching inn with some nice old settles and big log fire, above-average bar and more exotic restaurant food, real ales such as Adnams, Mauldons and Woodfordes, carpeted no smoking dining conservatory, traditional games; piped music; charming garden, good walks nearby *(Comus and Sarah Elliott, LYM)*

☆ *White Horse* IP17 3AH [Darsham Rd, off B1125 Blythburgh—Leiston]: Homely and friendly traditional pub with generous straightforward food inc good value sandwiches, OAP bargain lunch and take-away fish and chips, Adnams, friendly service, unassuming high-ceilinged bar with lots of bric-a-brac, steps down to attractive no smoking Victorian back dining room; quiet piped music; children in eating area, picnic-sets in cottagey back garden with climbing frame, more out by village duckpond, bedrooms *(Tracey and Stephen Groves)*

WOODBRIDGE [TM2748]

☆ *Anchor* IP12 1BX [Quay St]: High-ceilinged plainly furnished bar with quick cheerful service even when busy, buoyant atmosphere, good value prompt usual food inc sandwiches, good pies and well priced fresh local fish, Greene King IPA and Abbot, lots of nautical character, nice mix of boating and local paintings (some for sale), separate eating area *(Charles Gysin)*

☆ *Cherry Tree* IP12 4AG [opp Notcutts Nursery, off A12; Cumberland St]: Continuing improvements at this nicely refurbished open-plan 17th-c inn, good daily-changing pubby food at sensible prices (they do breakfast too, from 7.30), Adnams and guest ales helpfully described, welcoming helpful staff, beams and two log fires, pine furniture, old local photographs and aircraft prints; children

welcome, garden with play area, three good bedrooms in adjoining barn conversion, open all day wknds *(Jenny and Brian Seller, Danny Savage, Tony and Shirley Albert, Gill Kegel, MDN)*

Olde Bell & Steelyard IP12 1DZ [New St, off Market Sq]: Unusual and unpretentious olde-worlde pub, steelyard still overhanging the street, good friendly mix of drinking and dining in bar, Greene King ales, short varied blackboard choice of home-made food from good filled baguettes to local fish, good service *(Ian and Nita Cooper, David Carr, Barry Collett)*

Seckford Hall IP13 6NU [signed off A12 bypass, N of town; Seckford Hall Rd, Great Bealings]: Civilised Tudor country-house hotel not pub, but its dark and friendly comfortable bar has good bar snacks, Adnams and good wines inc lots of half bottles, also good value though not cheap fixed-price meals; garden with lake, leisure centre and swimming pool, good bedrooms *(J F M and M West, Pamela Goodwyn, Comus and Sarah Elliott)*

YOXFORD [TM3969]

☆ *Griffin* IP17 3EP [High St]: Happy 14th-c village pub with log fire and nice corner sofa in appealing main bar, good value generous food using local supplies, Adnams and changing guest beers, decent reasonably priced wines, friendly attentive staff, charming log-fire restaurant; comfortable beamed bedrooms, good breakfast *(Comus and Sarah Elliott, Keith and Janet Morris)*

Post Office address codings confusingly give the impression that some pubs are in Suffolk, when they're really in Cambridgeshire, Essex or Norfolk (which is where we list them).

Surrey

Surrey's pubs are among the country's most expensive, with both food and drinks prices well above average. If you don't know your way around, you can easily be paying top whack without getting top quality here. So it's almost more important than usual to know which pubs are really worth while. The six new entries we have found for this year all, in their different ways, make you feel that your money is well spent: the Plough just outside Cobham, combining a warm-hearted pubby atmosphere with a good value french bistro; the Mill at Elstead, a particularly well converted watermill with landscaping that makes the most of its lovely surroundings; the Stephan Langton tucked away in the woodland hamlet of Friday Street, with notable bar lunches and a fine evening restaurant; the Seven Stars at Leigh, filling quickly at lunchtime with people who know about its good value food; the Surrey Oaks at Newdigate, with its enthusiastic landlord tracking down rewarding real ales; and the traditional Barley Mow at West Horsley, with its attentive and personal service and attractive garden. Other pubs on fine form here include the smart and very civilised Withies at Compton (at a price), the attractive and prettily set Stag at Eashing, Marneys in Esher (interesting pub and food, in surprising surroundings), the Parrot in its enviable position at Forest Green (their enjoyable food includes some meat from their own farm), the Hare & Hounds on the edge of Lingfield (good food in unpretentious surroundings), the King William IV at Mickleham (very good all round, with a charming hillside garden), the gently upmarket Running Horses on the other side of the same village (good food and bedrooms), and the stylish Inn at West End (interesting food and super wines). As you can see, good food is part of the appeal of many of these; however, it is one of the new entries, the Stephan Langton at Friday Street, which takes the top award of Surrey Dining Pub of the Year. The Lucky Dip section at the end of the chapter includes several other recommended pubs in the same small local Auberge group as the Plough near Cobham, sharing its general style; other pubs to note particularly include the Crown at Chiddingfold, Ramblers Rest at Chipstead, Queens Head at East Clandon, White Horse at Hascombe, Hurtwood at Peaslake, Good Intent at Puttenham and White Horse in Shere. The main local beer to look out for is Hogs Back, and besides Leith Hill (brewed at the Plough at Coldharbour) we found Surrey Hills ales at one or two of our main entries.

BETCHWORTH TQ2149 Map 3
Dolphin ㉕ ♀

Turn off A25 W of Reigate opposite B2032 at roundabout, and keep on into The Street; opposite the church; RH3 7DW

Now open all day and under new licencees, this 16th-c village pub is a character-laden stopping point if you're walking the Greensand Way, and on Tuesdays you can hear the bell-ringers practising in the church opposite. The neat and homely front bar has kitchen chairs, gas lights over the inglenook and plain tables on the 400-year-old scrubbed flagstones, as does the carpeted smaller bar. The candlelit, no smoking restaurant bar has oak panelling, a blazing fire and a chiming grandfather clock. Youngs Bitter, Special and maybe a seasonal guest are on handpump; decent wines, with several by the glass. It's best to arrive early, or book a table beforehand if you want to enjoy the home-made food, which includes soup (£3.95), sandwiches (from (£3.50), ploughman's (from £5.95), a range of main courses from around £8.95 such as a trio of cumberland sausage, curry or cod, and more expensive dishes like lamb shank (£12.95). There are some seats in the small west-facing front courtyard, and picnic-sets in the rear garden. Morris men dance one weekend a month here from May to September. Parking can be difficult in the small car park, but there's space along the lanes or perhaps in the car park behind the church. More reports on the new regime please. *(Recommended by DWAJ, Tina and David Woods-Taylor, the Didler, Ian Phillips, Alan Sadler, Ron and Sheila Corbett, PL)*

Youngs ~ Managers Chris and Melanie Gowers ~ Real ale ~ Bar food (12-2.30, 6-9.30; 12-6 Sun) ~ (01737) 842288 ~ Children in restaurant ~ Dogs allowed in bar ~ Open 11-11; 12-10.30 Sun

BLACKBROOK   TQ1846   Map 3
Plough ㉕ ♀

On by-road E of A24, parallel to it, between Dorking and Newdigate, just N of the turn E to Leigh; RH5 4DS

The licensees have recently celebrated 25 years at this neatly kept white-fronted pub, which is nicely placed by oak woods. The no smoking red saloon bar has fresh flowers on its tables and on the sills of its large windows (which have new green and gold curtains). Down some steps, the public bar has brass-topped treadle tables, old saws on the ceiling, and bottles and flat irons; shove-ha'penny, cribbage and dominoes. Bar food includes lunchtime snacks such as local spicy sausage and chips (£4.75), ploughman's or grilled ham steak with chips (£5.75), nice bagels with fillings such as warm pastrami or smoked salmon and cream cheese (£5.95), scampi (£7.45), steak sandwich (£7.75), and blackboard specials (some available in smaller portions) such as watercress, leek and potato soup (£4.25), ratatouille (£7.45), moussaka, lasagne or chilli con carne (£8.95), mild chicken and lime curry (£9.25), steak (from £14.95) and steamed bass with crab stuffing (£15.95), with puddings like strawberry Sunday or raspberry crème brûlée (£4.75; platter for two £7.45); wide-ranging children's menu including filled baked potatoes (£3.75) and mini ploughman's or hot lunch (£4.25), and children get a free ice-cream if they finish their meal. They now do a Sunday roast too, and may be serving food on Sunday evenings, as well as summer cream teas on Sunday afternoons in summer. Badger Best, K&B Sussex and Tanglefoot, and a guest such as Gribble Fursty Ferret on handpump and 18 wines by the glass, with hot toddies in winter, as well as speciality teas and freshly ground coffees. The outside is prettily adorned with hanging baskets and window boxes; there are tables and chairs outside on the terrace and a little swiss playhouse furnished with little tables and chairs in the secluded garden. More reports please. *(Recommended by Neil Hardwick, John Evans, Cathryn and Richard Hicks, Debbie and Neil Hayter, Jack and Sandra Clarfelt)*

Badger ~ Tenants Chris and Robin Squire ~ Real ale ~ Bar food (12-2, 7-9; Sun 12-4; not Sun or Mon evenings) ~ (01306) 886603 ~ Children welcome until 9pm ~ Dogs allowed in bar ~ Open 11-3, 6-11; 12-10 Sun; closed 1 Jan, 25-26 Dec

CHARLESHILL   SU8944   Map 2
Donkey

B3001 Milford—Farnham near Tilford; coming from Elstead, turn left as soon as you see pub sign; GU10 2AU

On the edge of woodlands, this beamed, cottagey 18th-c place has been a pub since 1850 and takes its name from donkeys that were once kept to transport loads up the hill opposite: even today you might meet two friendly donkeys here, called Pip and Dusty. The pub puts a firm accent on food, using locally sourced ingredients wherever possible, and with a good fish selection. Friendly staff serve lunchtime sandwiches (from £3.95; club sandwiches £6.50), and other menu items include soup (£3.75), liver and brandy pâté (£5.95), scallops (£8.95 starter, £13.95 main course), salads, scampi or gammon and eggs (£8.95), steak and Guinness pie or asparagus and stilton pancake (£10.95), breast of chicken stuffed with mango and with mild curry sauce (£11.95), steak (from £12.95), roast gressingham duck (£14.95), baked whole bass (£16.95), and daily specials. They also do two-course lunches from Monday to Thursday (£10.95), and Friday and Saturday (£14.95), as well as a Sunday roast (£10.50). The bright saloon has lots of polished stirrups, lamps and watering cans on the walls, and prettily cushioned built-in wall benches, while the lounge has a fine high-backed settle, highly polished horsebrasses, and swords on the walls and beams; the dining areas are no smoking. All their wines (including champagne) are available by the glass, and you'll also find any three of Greene King IPA, Abbot, Triumph and Old Speckled Hen on handpump; piped music. There's a wendy house; the attractive garden also has a terrace and plenty of seats. Attractive local walking areas through heathlands include Thursford Common, and there are paths into the woods around the pub. More reports please. *(Recommended by Tom and Ruth Rees, James Price, John and Joyce Snell)*

Greene King ~ Lease Lee and Helen Francis ~ Real ale ~ Bar food (12-2.30(4 Sun), 6-9.30(8.30 Sun)) ~ Restaurant ~ (01252) 702124 ~ Children welcome ~ Dogs allowed in bar ~ Open 11-3, 6-12; 11am-12 midnight Sat; 12-10.30 Sun; 12-3, 6-10.30 Sat and Sun in winter

COBHAM TQ1059 Map 3

Plough ♀

3.2 miles from M25 junction 10; A3, then right on A245 at roundabout; in Cobham, right at Downside signpost into Downside Bridge Road; Plough Lane; KT11 3LT

This is a cheerful and civilised country local, brought new life by the french bistro at one end. The thriving low-beamed bar has a relaxed atmosphere, with Courage Best (just as when we drank here more than 20 years ago), Fullers London Pride, Hogs Back TEA and a guest such as Wadworths 6X on handpump, a fine choice of wines by the glass including champagne, and good coffee – served with hot milk. A separate servery takes food orders. The bar menu might include sandwiches (from £3.60), chicken liver parfait (£4.95), baguettes (from £5.95), fish soup, cheese and spinach crêpe or ravioli, or mushroom risotto (all £5.95), pork chop or good lambs liver and bacon (£6.95), fish and chips (£7.95), and puddings (£4.95) such as fig tatin and good ice-creams; at these prices, the quality represents very good value. Service is swift and good-natured; the lavatories are stylishly modern, and there are disabled access and facilities. Round on the right is a cosy parquet-floored snug with cushioned seats built into nice stripped pine panelling, and horse-racing prints. The main part is carpeted, with a mix of pubby furnishings, and past some standing timbers a few softly padded banquettes around good-sized tables by a log fire in the ancient stone fireplace. The restaurant part rambles around behind this – pews, bare boards, white table linen. Behind the pretty brick house, which is thought to date back some 500 years, a terrace has picnic-sets sheltering beside a very high garden wall. If you enjoy the Plough, you will probably also like this small Auberge group's other pubs, run on similar principles, which include the Hare & Hounds in Claygate, Wire Mill at Newchapel, Onslow Arms at West Clandon and Queens Head in Weybridge (see the Lucky Dip entries at the end of this chapter). *(Recommended by Geoffrey Kemp, Tom and Ruth Rees, Ian Phillips, Shirley Mackenzie)*

Free house ~ Licensee Joe Worley ~ Real ale ~ Bar food (12-2.30, 7-9.30(not Fri/Sat evening)) ~ Restaurant ~ (01932) 589790 ~ Children welcome ~ Dogs allowed in bar ~ Open 11-11; 12-10.30 Sun

---

Post Office address codings confusingly give the impression that some pubs are in Surrey when they're really in Hampshire or London (which is where we list them). And there's further confusion from the way the Post Office still talks about Middlesex – which disappeared in 1965 local government reorganisation.

COLDHARBOUR   TQ1543   Map 3
Plough 🍺
Village signposted in the network of small roads around Leith Hill; RH5 6HD

The excellent own-brew ale makes this scenically placed inn a popular destination
for walkers: it's high up in the Surrey hills in a peaceful hamlet, and there's some of
the best walking in the county around here, with paths up to the tower and
viewpoint on Leith Hill and further afield to Friday Street and Abinger Common.
From the pub's own Leith Hill Brewery, they serve well kept Crooked Furrow,
Hoppily Ever After and Tallywhacker on handpump, along with a couple of guests
such as Ringwood Fortyniner and Shepherd Neame Spitfire; also Biddenden farm
cider and several wines by the glass; at busy times it may be hard to find
somewhere to sit if you're not dining. The two bars (each with a lovely open fire)
have stripped light beams and timbering in the warm-coloured dark ochre walls,
with quite unusual little chairs around the tables in the snug red-carpeted games
room on the left (with darts, board games and cards), and little decorative plates on
the walls; the one on the right leads through to the no smoking candlelit restaurant.
Bar food includes soup (£4.50); deep-fried herring roe with horseradish (£5.95),
chilli con carne (£7.95), sausages and mash or cajun spiced salmon (£10.95), steak
(from £10.95) and confit of duck on mash with orange and burgundy jus (£13.95);
puddings such as chocolate and walnut brownie or apple crumble (£4.50); children's
menu. The front and the terraced gardens have picnic-sets, tubs of flowers and a
fishpond full of water-lilies. *(Recommended by Mike Buckingham, Andy Booth,
A J Longshaw, Dick Pyper, C and R Bromage, Andy Trafford, Louise Bayly, A G Roby,
R A Rosen, Peter Lewis, Mike and Mary Carter, Paul Humphreys, Brian and Janet Ainscough)*

Own brew ~ Licensees Richard and Anna Abrehart ~ Real ale ~ Bar food (12-2.30(3 Sun),
6-9.30(9 Sun)) ~ Restaurant ~ (01306) 711793 ~ Small children not allowed in restaurant
~ Dogs allowed in bar ~ Open 11(12 Sun)-12 midnight(1am Sat); closed 25-26 Dec
evenings, 1 Jan evening ~ Bedrooms: £59.50S/£69.50S(£95B)

COMPTON   SU9546   Map 2
Withies
Withies Lane; pub signposted from B3000; GU3 1JA

Smart yet atmospheric, with emphasis on the restaurant side, this civilised 16th-c
pub preserves a genuinely pubby low-beamed bar. It has some fine 17th-c carved
panels between the windows, and a splendid art nouveau settle among the old
sewing-machine tables; you'll find a good log fire in a massive inglenook fireplace;
piped music. They do good straightforward bar food such as soup (£3.75),
sandwiches or filled baked potatoes (from £4.50; 6oz sirloin steak sandwich £9.50),
quiche or smoked salmon pâté (£4.75), ploughman's (£5.75), cumberland sausages
with mash and onion gravy (£5.50) and seafood platter (£11.50). The no smoking
restaurant is more formal, with an elaborate, and expensive, menu and is very
popular with a well heeled local set. Even when it's busy, the pleasant uniformed
staff remain helpful and efficient, though unfortunately they may try to keep your
credit card while you eat bar meals (though this rule does not apply to the
restaurant). Badger K&B, Fullers London Pride, Greene King IPA and Hogs Back
TEA are on handpump. A mass of flowers borders the neat lawn in front, and
weeping willows overhang the immaculate garden, where there are dining tables
under an arbour of creeper-hung trellises, more on a crazy-paved terrace and others
under old apple trees. Polsted Manor and Loseley Park are a pleasant walk up the
lane from here. *(Recommended by R Lake, James Price, R T and J C Moggridge, Derek and
Heather Manning, John Evans, Gene and Kitty Rankin, Mrs Margo Finlay, Jörg Kasprowski,
Ian Phillips, Bob and Margaret Holder, Nigel B Thompson, Wendy Arnold, Alec and
Joan Laurence)*

Free house ~ Licensees Brian and Hugh Thomas ~ Real ale ~ Bar food (12-2.30, 7-10) ~
Restaurant ~ (01483) 421158 ~ Children welcome ~ Open 11-3, 6-11; 12-3 Sun; closed
Sun evening

EASHING   SU9543   Map 2

Stag

Lower Eashing; Eashing signposted off A3 southbound, S of Hurtmore turn-off; or
pub signposted off A283 just SE of exit roundabout at N end of A3 Milford bypass;
GU7 2QG

Readers enjoy sitting out in the riverside garden here, under mature trees and by a
millstream; picnic-sets and tables under cocktail parasols are set out on a terrace
and in a lantern-lit arbour. The pub (also known as the Stag on the River) is older
than its Georgian brick façade suggests and dates back in part to the 15th c: inside
you'll find an attractively opened-up interior with a charming old-fashioned locals'
bar on the right with red and black flooring tiles by the counter. They serve
Courage Best, Fullers London Pride and Shepherd Neame Spitfire on handpump,
and about 14 wines by the glass. A cosy gently lit room beyond has a low white
plank ceiling, a big stag print and stag's head on the dark-papered walls, some
cookery books on shelves by the log fire, and sturdy cushioned housekeeper's chairs
grouped around dark tables on the brick floor. An extensive blue-carpeted area
rambles around on the left, with similar comfortable dark furniture, some smaller
country prints and decorative plates on pink Anaglypta walls, and round towards
the back a big woodburning stove in a capacious fireplace under a long
mantelbeam. It's all rather smart yet cosily traditional; there is a table of
conservative daily papers, and they are kind to visiting dogs. Lunchtime bar snacks
include soup (£3.85), hot baguettes (from £6.35), ploughman's (£6.55) and toad in
the hole (£8.50), with blackboard specials such as a starter of thai fishcakes
(£7.25), wild mushroom filo parcel with cherry tomato and thyme sauce (£9.50),
slow-roast belly of pork (£13.50), fillet of trout with bisque sauce (£13.55) and
scottish sirloin steak (£17.95); Sunday roasts (£10.25). Prices on the evening menu
(available in the bar or restaurant) are more expensive and include dishes like
home-made game pie (£13.50), half a roast duck stuffed with caramelised apples
(£14.95) and fillet of beef on dauphinoise potatoes with wild mushroom thyme
sauce (£18.95); no smoking restaurant. *(Recommended by Ian Phillips, C J Roebuck,
Susan and John Douglas, Geoffrey Kemp, Tom and Jill Jones, Ann and Colin Hunt)*

Punch ~ Lease Marilyn Lackey ~ Real ale ~ Bar food (12-2.30(3 Sun), 6-9.30; not Sun, Mon
evenings) ~ Restaurant ~ (01483) 421568 ~ Children welcome ~ Dogs allowed in bar ~
Open 11-11; 12-10.30 Sun

ELSTEAD   SU9044   Map 2

Mill at Elstead ♀ 🍴

Farnham Road (B3001 just W of village, which is itself between Farnham and Milford);
GU8 6LE

The long cobbled drive, crossing a bridge and then winding between tall trees and a
spreading meadow, makes clear that you are heading for something out of the
ordinary. And there it is ahead: a stately four-storey brick-built watermill, largely
18th-c, straddling the River Wey. Inside, you are greeted by a great internal
waterwheel, and the gentle rush of the stream turning it below your feet. The
building has been converted most sympathetically, making for a good rambling
series of linked bar areas on the ground floor, and further seating including a no
smoking restaurant area upstairs. There are so many different spaces that you can
pick an area to suit almost any mood: brown leather armchairs and antique
engravings by a longcase clock; neat modern tables and dining chairs on pale
woodstrip flooring; big country tables and rustic prints on broad ceramic tiles; dark
boards and beams, iron pillars and stripped masonry; a log fire in a huge inglenook,
or a trendy finned stove with a fat black stovepipe. Throughout, big windows make
the most of the charming surroundings – broad millpond, swans, weeping willows.
Service is commendably helpful, friendly and personal (not always the case in a
chain pub – this one is owned by Fullers). They have Fullers Discovery, London
Pride, ESB and a seasonal beer on handpump, a good range of wines by the glass in
two glass sizes, and nice coffee, and the good value food includes soup (£3.95),

baked camembert and mixed berries (£5.75), sausages and mash (£7.50), battered cod and chips (£7.95), steak burger (£8.50), organic salmon salad (£10.95), sirloin steak (£11.95) and daily specials such as thai breaded chicken and salad (£10.95) and venison steak on mushroom and mint toast (£13.95), with a carvery on Sunday. There are plenty of picnic-sets in a variety of appealing waterside seating areas outside, with flares and good floodlighting at night. *(Recommended by Susan and John Douglas, R Lake, Tracey and Stephen Groves, D Marsh)*

Fullers ~ Managers Carol and Brian Jewell ~ Real ale ~ Bar food (12-9.30(10 Fri, Sat; 9 Sun)) ~ (01252) 703333 ~ Children welcome ~ Open 11-11; 11.30-10.30 Sun

ESHER   TQ1566   Map 3
Marneys ♀

Alma Road (one way only), Weston Green; heading N on A309 from A307 roundabout, after Lamb & Star pub turn left into Lime Tree Avenue (signposted to All Saints Parish Church), then left at T junction into Chestnut Avenue; KT10 8JN

This cottagey place is a pleasant surprise, by a nicely rural-feeling common and near a duckpond. The owner is Norwegian, and proudly displays his country's flags and even national anthem inside, and the chatty low-beamed and black and white plank-panelled bar has shelves of hens and ducks and other ornaments, small blue-curtained windows, and perhaps horse racing on the unobtrusive corner TV; piped music; no smoking at the bar. On the left, past a little cast-iron woodburning stove, a dining area (somewhat roomier but still small) has big pine tables, pews and pale country kitchen chairs, with attractive goose pictures; this leads on to a recently added decking area with seating and large tables. The well liked food tends towards the scandinavian style: the sensibly small choice features baguettes (from £5.75), scandinavian meatballs and red cabbage, chilli con carne or good soused herring fillets (£8.25), frikadeller (danish meatcakes) (£8.50), and home-made puddings such as apple crumble (£4); they usually have around nine specials on the board, such as mediterranean penne pasta (£8.75), cod fishcakes (£9.50) or calves liver (£9.95); they are happy to provide children's portions. Courage Best, Fullers London Pride and a guest such as Charles Wells Bombardier on handpump, 11 wines and pink champagne by the glass, enterprising soft drinks, norwegian schnapps and good coffee. Service by friendly uniformed staff is quick and efficient; and they have daily papers on sticks. The pleasantly planted sheltered garden has a bar, black picnic-sets and tables under green and blue canvas parasols, and occasionally a Spanish guitarist playing under the willow tree; the front terrace has dark blue cast-iron tables and chairs under matching parasols, with some more black tables too, with table lighting. *(Recommended by John Millwood, Ian Phillips, Ron and Sheila Corbett, Jennie George, Martin and Karen Wake, Susan and John Douglas, Ellen Weld, David London)*

Free house ~ Licensee Henrik Platou ~ Real ale ~ Bar food (12-(12.30 Sun)-2.30; 12-2.30, 6-9 Thurs-Sat) ~ (020) 8398 4444 ~ Children welcome (not after 9pm in bar) ~ Dogs welcome ~ Open 11-11; 12-10.30 Sun

FOREST GREEN   TQ1241   Map 3
Parrot

B2127 just W of junction with B2126, SW of Dorking; RH5 5RZ

The owners of this quaint, rambling pub have their own farm not far away at Coldharbour, and the pork and lamb that appear on the menu are their own. Comfortably civilised, the pub has a particularly attractive bar, with its profusion of heavy beams, timbers and flagstones, and huge inglenook fireplace. There's plenty of space, with a couple of cosy areas hidden away behind the fireplace, and some more spread out tables opposite the long brick bar counter, which has a few unusual wooden chairs in front. Five or six real ales include Ringwood Best and Youngs, and guests from brewers such as Greene King, Ringwood, St Georges and Shepherd Neame on handpump; freshly squeezed orange juice, and 14 wines (including champagne) by the glass; newspapers are laid out for customers. A brass parrot sits beside a brick fireplace with a stove, then beyond here is a big, no smoking restaurant, less distinctive than the bar (part of which is also no smoking), but with the same enjoyably relaxed atmosphere. You can eat anywhere, from a frequently changing menu which might include lunchtime sandwiches, soup (£4), smoked mackerel salad (£4.75), roasted middlewhite pork belly (£9.25), roast guinea fowl (£9.85), herb-crusted rack of lamb (£11.75), sirloin steak (£13); puddings (£4.50); they do a choice of good, popular Sunday roasts. Outside there's lots of room, with tables in front and among several attractive gardens, one with apple trees and rose beds; they plan to turn the rather run-down play area into a vegetable garden. The pub faces the village cricket field and is handy for the good woodland walks in the hills around Abinger. *(Recommended by Mike and Lynn Robinson, Fr Robert Marsh, John Branston, Pamela and Alan Neale, Gordon Stevenson, Susan and John Douglas, R Lake, Evan Davies)*

Free house ~ Licensee Charles Gotto ~ Real ale ~ Bar food (12-3(4 Sun), 6-9 (10 Fri, Sat); no food Sun evening) ~ Restaurant ~ (01306) 621339 ~ Children welcome with restrictions ~ Dogs allowed in bar ~ Open 11(12 Sun)-11

FRIDAY STREET   TQ1245   Map 3
Stephan Langton ⓦ
Signed off B2126, or from A25 Westcott—Guildford; RH5 6JR
Surrey Dining Pub of the Year

With a growing reputation for imaginative food, this prettily placed pub in deeply rural woodlands and a few steps away from a much-frequented lake has more of a restauranty feel in the evening, but by day it's very much a pub, with very good bar food (booking is strongly advised at weekends when it gets extremely busy). The lounge bar has tobacco-coloured walls and is hung with gilded antique mirrors and framed classic menus, and there's a sunflower print above the fireplace; no piped music or games machines. Available at lunchtime only, bar food is all home-made (even the bread, ice-cream, chutney and pasta) and typically includes onion and cider soup with goats cheese toast (£5), panini (£4.50), ploughman's (£5.75), starters like sweet-cured herrings with beetroot, horseradish and crème fraîche (£5.75) or chicken livers, pigeon and bacon with pumpkin chutney (£6.50) and main courses like braised cuttlefish fino with red pepper and paprika potatoes (£9), smoked haddock and leek pie (£9.50) or chargrilled rib-eye steak (£14); puddings might include buttermilk pudding with poached rhubarb and strawberries or chocolate brownie crème fraîche (£4.50); in the evening there is a more elaborate menu for the no smoking restaurant. Adnams Best, Fullers London Pride and Hogs Back TEA are on handpump, and they have a well chosen selection of wines, with about ten by the glass; Weston's Old Rosie farm cider. There are plenty of tables in a front courtyard, with more on a back tree-surrounded stream-side terrace. It's surrounded by good walks – Leith Hill is particularly rewarding, and the tiny village is so unspoilt they prefer you to leave your car in a free car park just outside, but if you don't fancy the lovely stroll there are a few spaces in front of the pub itself. *(Recommended by Paul Humphreys, Sheila Topham, Edward Mirzoeff)*

Free house ~ Licensee Cynthia Coomb ~ Real ale ~ Bar food (12.30-2.45) ~ Restaurant (7-10) ~ (01306) 730775 ~ Children until 8pm ~ Dogs allowed in bar ~ Open 11-3, 5.30-11; 11-11 Sat; 11-9 Sun; closed Mon lunchtime

LALEHAM   TQ0568   Map 3
Three Horseshoes ⓨ
5 miles from M25 junction 13; A30 E, then at roundabout turn on to A308 (signposted Kingston, Sunbury), then at roundabout after another 1.3 miles turn right on to B377; in Laleham turn right on to B376 (Shepperton Road); TW18 1SE

Wisteria and hanging baskets adorn the front of this 13th-c tavern, which was a favourite bolt-hole for Edward VII when he was Prince of Wales. The flagstoned bar is airy with gentle lighting, cream walls, farmhouse tables, comfortable settees, newspapers to read, a fireplace with an open fire and some intimate little corners, and widescreen TV. A feng shui consultation determined the placing of the red, blue and green carpets. Bar food is served in generous helpings and includes soup (£3.95), sandwiches (from £3.95), ham, egg and chips (£7.50), steak and ale pie (£7.50), vegetable curry (£6.95), grilled cajun chicken with caesar salad (£8.25), chicken breast stuffed with onion and cheese (£9.95), steak (from £13.95) and home-made and bought-in puddings (£3.95); fish specials might include halibut (£12.95) or bass (£13.50). Five parts – the conservatory, two restaurant areas and two other rooms – are no smoking. Efficient bar staff serve Courage Best, Fullers London Pride, Youngs Special and a couple of guests such as Adnams Broadside and Caledonian Deuchars on handpump and over a dozen wines by the glass; piped music (which can be obtrusive). Close to a pleasant stretch of the Thames, Thorpe Park and the intersection of the M3 and M25, it does get busy here on summer days. *(Recommended by Simon Collett-Jones, John Robertson, JMM, Martin and Alison Stainsby)*

Unique (Enterprise) ~ Lease Sean Alderson ~ Real ale ~ Bar food (12-3(10 Fri, Sat, 9 Sun)) ~ Restaurant ~ (01784) 455014 ~ Children welcome ~ Open 11am-12 midnight (11.30 Sun)

LEIGH   TQ2147   Map 3
Seven Stars
Dawes Green, S of A25 Dorking—Reigate; RH2 8NP

An ancient sign painted on the wall inside this tile-hung country pub reads '...you are Wellcome to sit down for your ease, pay what you call for and drink what you please': today it's just as welcoming here as it seems it was when it opened in 1637, though it's strongly recommended you book a table if you want to eat. It's also free of piped music and games machines. The comfortable saloon bar has a 1633 inglenook fireplace with the royal coat of arms in the smoke-blackened brick. The plainer public bar has an alley set aside for darts. There's also a sympathetically done no smoking restaurant extension at the side, with 17th-c floor timbers imported from a granary. From the lunchtime and evening menus tasty bar food includes welsh rarebit ciabatta (£2.95), soup (from £3.95), warm goats cheese salad with roasted beetroot, peppers and walnuts (£5.50 starter, £8.95 main course), whitebait (£5.95), ham off the bone with eggs and chips (£7.95), hotpot with braised cabbage or roasted camembert fondue (£8.95), curry (£9.50) cured gravadlax or game burger (£10.95) or braised shank of lamb with chunky irish stew (£13.50); puddings (from £4.50); they have a tapas evening on Tuesdays, with about 15 dishes from £2.95 to £4.95; three-course Sunday lunches (£14-£16.50). Greene King Old Speckled Hen, Fullers London Pride and Youngs Ordinary, as well as decent wines with several by the glass. In warmer months there's plenty of room outside, in the beer garden at the front, on the terrace and in the side garden. *(Recommended by Mike and Heather Watson, DWAJ, Jenny and Brian Seller)*

Punch ~ Lease David and Rebecca Pellen ~ Real ale ~ Bar food (12-2.30(4 Sun), 6-9(6.30-9.30 Fri and Sat); not Sun evening) ~ Restaurant ~ (01306) 611254 ~ Dogs allowed in bar ~ Open 12-11(9 Sun); closed 25 Dec, 1 Jan

LINGFIELD   TQ3844   Map 3
Hare & Hounds 🍴
Turn off B2029 N at Crowhurst and Edenbridge signpost, into Lingfield Common Road; RH7 6BZ

There's a nicely relaxed, unsmartened tone to this eclectically furnished and sophisticated dining pub. The smallish open-plan bar (mostly no smoking) is light and airy by day, with soft lighting and nightlights burning on a good mix of different-sized tables at night – when it's full of the chatter of happy customers, some drinking, some eating, all mixing comfortably. Partly bare boards and partly flagstones, it has a variety of well worn scatter-cushioned dining chairs and other seats from pews to a button-back leather chesterfield, black and white pictures of jazz musicians on brown tongue-and-groove panelling; perhaps piped music. The bar opens into a quieter no smoking dining area with big abstract-expressionist paintings. They make their own soda bread, ice-cream and pasta, and the well presented, daily changing bar food (not cheap) might include starters such as sweet potato, chilli, ginger and coconut soup (£3.95) and tiger prawn and mushroom crostini (£6.95), and main courses like fresh penne with creamy mushroom sauce (£7.50), cumberland sausages with cheddar mash (£8.50), smoked haddock fishcakes with chilli roast tomato salsa (£8.95), confit leg of duck with sweet potato mash and balsamic roast red onions (£12.95) and fillet steak with lemon and cheddar stuffed baked potato, swiss chard and roast shallot jus (£15.95); side dishes are an extra £2.95. Fullers London Pride, Youngs Bitter and Greene King Abbot are on handpump, and there are decent wines. Tables are set out in a pleasant split-level garden, some on decking. This is good walking country near Haxted Mill; walkers can leave their boots in the porch, guarded by a life-size great dane statue. They hold irish theme and cabaret nights around every two months and quiz nights every Monday. *(Recommended by Jill Franklin, Tony and Wendy Hobden, Sharon and Alan Corper, Paul A Moore, Derek Thomas)*

Pubmaster ~ Lease Fergus Greer ~ Real ale ~ Bar food (12-2.30, 7-9(9.30 Fri, Sat); not Sun evening) ~ Restaurant ~ (01342) 832351 ~ Children welcome ~ Dogs allowed in bar ~ Open 12-1(8 Sun)

MICKLEHAM TQ1753 Map 3
King William IV 🍴 📷

Byttom Hill; short but narrow steep track up hill just off A24 Leatherhead—Dorking by partly green-painted restaurant – public car park down here is best place to park; OS Sheet 187 map reference 173538; RH5 6EL

Originally an alehouse for Lord Beaverbrook's estate staff, this hillside pub within strolling distance of Box Hill is a fair walk up from the public car park at the bottom of the hill (which you may need to use as there's not much room in the lane), but you are rewarded with lovely views over the Mole valley. Needless to say, such an idyllic spot does draw the crowds on a sunny day and as they don't take bookings during the summer you will need to get here early to secure a table, and be aware that you will have to queue to place your order, but service should be quick enough after that. The snug plank-panelled front bar shares the same panoramic views as the garden. The more spacious back bar is quite brightly lit, with kitchen-type chairs around its cast-iron-framed tables, log fires, fresh flowers on all the tables, and a serviceable grandfather clock. There's a friendly atmosphere throughout. Very enjoyable bar food in huge helpings includes sandwiches (not at weekends), filled baked potatoes (from £6.75), ploughman's (£6.95), roast chestnut and cranberry risotto with melted goats cheese (£8.95), steak and kidney pie or fisherman's pie (£9.95), half a roast pheasant with an onion, bacon and red wine sauce (£12.75), baked butterfish steak with spinach and ricotta cheese topping (£12.95), fillet steak (£15.95), with puddings such as fruit crumble or hot chocolate fudge cake (£4.50). The choice is more limited on Sundays and bank holidays. Adnams Best, Badger Best, Hogs Back TEA and a monthly changing guest from a brewery such as Badger on handpump; light piped music. The lovely terraced garden at the back is neatly filled with sweet peas, climbing roses and honeysuckle, and plenty of tables (some in an extended open-sided wooden shelter with gas heaters). *(Recommended by Andy Trafford, Louise Bayly, James Price, Derek and Heather Manning, C and R Bromage, Grahame Brooks, Cathryn and Richard Hicks, T R and B C Jenkins, LM, Alan Sadler, Catherine and Richard Preston, Tracey and Stephen Groves, Ian Phillips, Clive and Janice Sillitoe, Rosemary and Tom Hall, N R White)*

Free house ~ Licensees Chris and Jenny Grist ~ Real ale ~ Bar food (12-2, 7-9.30; 12-5 Sun) ~ (01372) 372590 ~ Children over 12 ~ Open 11-3, 6-11; 12-10.30 Sun

Running Horses ⊕ ♀ ☞

Old London Road (B2209); RH5 6DU

An elegant place for a meal, this upmarket inn maintains very high standards for its food and professional service, but is still a place where you feel perfectly at ease if you just want to enjoy a drink. It has two calmly relaxing bar rooms, neatly kept and spaciously open plan, with fresh flowers (in summer) in an inglenook at one end, lots of race tickets hanging from a beam, some really good racing cartoons, hunting pictures and Hogarth prints, dark carpets, cushioned wall settles and other dining chairs around straightforward pubby tables and bar stools. Brakspears, Fullers London Pride, Greene King Abbot and Youngs are on handpump alongside good, if pricey, wines by the glass, from a serious list; piped music. There is a tempting choice of bar food such as soup (£4.50), very well filled lunchtime chunky sandwiches (from £4.60), devilled kidneys with toast (£6.50), filled baguettes or club sandwich (£7.25), parma ham, parmesan and rocket (£7.95), tempura fish or vegetables and pineapple (£9.50) and steak, Guinness and mushroom pudding (£12.50). For a special meal out you would probably be more interested in the more elaborate and more expensive restaurant menu, which might include a starter helping of dressed crab (£6.95), chargrilled pheasant breasts (£15.95) and baked monkfish with crayfish tails (£17.50), and puddings such as sticky date and sultana pudding with butterscotch sauce and toffee ice-cream or passion fruit cheesecake with strawberry coulis (£5.25). You can eat from this menu in the pubby bar part, but might prefer the extensive no smoking restaurant area. This leads straight out of the bar and, although it is set out quite formally with crisp white cloths and candles on each table, it shares the thriving atmosphere of the bar. There are picnicsets on a terrace in front by lovely flowering tubs and hanging baskets, with a peaceful view of the old church with its strange stubby steeple. *(Recommended by Andrew York, S Topham, Susan and John Douglas, Norma and Noel Thomas, C J Roebuck, Gordon Stevenson, Paul Humphreys)*

Punch ~ Lease Steve and Josie Slayford ~ Real ale ~ Bar food (12-2.30(3 Sat, Sun), 7-9.30(9 Sun)) ~ Restaurant ~ (01372) 372279 ~ Children allowed in part of restaurant area ~ Dogs allowed in bar ~ Open 11.30-11; 12-10.30 Sun ~ Bedrooms: £85(£85S)(£95B)/£95(£95S)(£130B)

NEWDIGATE   TQ2043   Map 3

Surrey Oaks ◖

Off A24 S of Dorking, via Beare Green; Parkgate Road; RH5 5DZ

The welcoming landlord at this cottagey 16th-c country pub is a real ale enthusiast and holds beer festivals over the May Whitsun and August bank holiday weekends. He serves five well kept real ales on handpump, with Harveys Sussex Best, Surrey Hills Ranmore and Timothy Taylors Landlord alongside constantly rotating guests such as Hambleton Goldfield or Naylors Gonzo Porter; there are also belgian bottled beers, several wines by the glass and farm cider. The atmosphere is pubby, and families feel particularly welcome here; no smoking throughout. The pub is interestingly divided into four areas; in the older part locals gather by a coal-effect gas fire in a snug little beamed room, and a standing area with unusually large flagstones has a woodburning stove in an inglenook fireplace. Rustic tables are dotted around the light and airy main lounge to the left, and there's a pool table in the separate games room; fruit machine and piped classical music. Reasonably priced tasty bar food includes filled baguettes (from £4), ploughman's (from £5.50), ham, eggs and chips or battered fish of the day (£7), with home-made specials such as sausage of the day and mash (£7.50), fish pie (£8), steak and ale pie (£8.50) and calves liver, bacon and onion gravy (£9.50); children's meals; also occasional food theme evenings. There's a nicely complicated garden with a terrace, and a rockery with pools and a waterfall – the play area and two goats help keep children amused. *(Recommended by Tracey and Stephen Groves, Louise English, C and R Bromage)*

Free house ~ Licensee Ken Proctor ~ Real ale ~ Bar food (12-2.30(2.15 Sat, Sun), 6.30(7 Sat)-9; not Sun, Mon evenings) ~ Restaurant ~ (01306) 631200 ~ Children welcome ~ Dogs allowed in bar ~ Open 11.30-2.30, 5.30-11; 11.30-3, 6-11 Sat; 12-10.30 Sun

OTTERSHAW TQ0263 Map 3
Castle ◀

2.6 miles from M25 junction 11; heading S on A320, after A319 roundabout pass church on right, then after another 350 yards or so take sharp left turn into Brox Road; KT16 0LW

Blazing winter log fires, rustic paraphernalia on black ceiling joists and walls hung with horse tack exemplify the rustic feel in the two bars of this pleasantly unpretentious early Victorian local. There are small pictures and some stripped brickwork (including little stub walls making two or three snugly cushioned side booths); the bar on the right opens into a dining area and small side conservatory. Under quite an armoury of venerable guns, the servery between the two separate bars has half a dozen ales with a guest like Shepherd Neame Spitfire alongside Fullers London Pride, Greene King Abbot, Harveys Sussex Best, Timothy Taylors Landlord and Youngs on handpump, Addlestone's cider and nine wines by the glass. A range of home-made food runs from good value lunchtime sandwiches (from £2.75) and panini (£5.50) and soup (£3.75) to other pubby dishes such as ploughman's (£6.95), curry, chilli con carne or fish pie (£8.95), steak and ale pie (£9.95), and puddings such as apple crumble (£3.95); Sunday roast (£8.95). In the left-hand bar a low table made from a smith's bellows has a good collection of upmarket magazines; piped music. The sheltered garden has tables, and the front terrace is set well back from the fairly quiet road. Most of the pub, including one bar and the conservatory, is no smoking; note there are no high chairs or children's meals. *(Recommended by Ian Phillips, JMM)*

Punch ~ Lease John Olorenshaw ~ Real ale ~ Bar food (12-2, 6.30-9.30; 12-4 Sun; not Sun evening) ~ (01932) 872373 ~ Children (not babies) in conservatory ~ Dogs allowed in bar ~ Open 11-2.30, 5.30-11; 11-11 Sat; 12-10.30 Sun

REIGATE HEATH TQ2349 Map 3
Skimmington Castle

3 miles from M25 junction 8: through Reigate take A25 towards Dorking, then on edge of Reigate turn left past Black Horse into Flanchford Road; after ¼ mile turn left into Bonny's Road (unmade, very bumpy track); after crossing golf course fork right up hill; RH2 8RL

Popular with walkers and horse-riders (there's a hitching rail for horses at the front), this prettily situated rural pub has plenty of sitting space outside for enjoying the view in fine weather. The bright main front bar leads off a small room with a central serving counter, with dark simple panelling and lots of keys hanging from the beams. There's a miscellany of chairs and tables, shiny brown plank panelling, a brown plank ceiling; Adnams, Greene King Old Speckled Hen and Harveys Sussex Best, with a guest ale such as Hop Back Summer Lightning are on handpump, with 17 wines by the glass, Addlestone's farm cider and even some organic spirits. The cosy back rooms are partly panelled too, with old-fashioned settles and windsor chairs; one has a big brick fireplace with its bread-oven still beside it – the chimney is said to have been used as a highwayman's look-out. Steps take you down to just three tables in a small but pleasant no smoking room at the back; ring the bull and piped music. The bar food is good and popular, so you need to get here early for a table as they don't take bookings. Swiftly served dishes could include sandwiches (from £3.85), ploughman's or baked potatoes (from £5.25), home-made fish pie (£6.95), steak and kidney pie (£7.50), rack of lamb (£9.25), crayfish and cured salmon salad (£9.50), beef wellington (£11.50) and duck breast or peppered steak (£12.50), with puddings (from £3.95). There's a crazy-paved front terrace and tables on the grass by lilac bushes. More tables at the back overlook the meadows and the hillocks (though you may find the views blocked by trees in summer). No children. More reports please. *(Recommended by Gordon Stevenson, PL, James Price, DWAJ,*

Fr Robert Marsh, John and Elisabeth Cox, Andy and Yvonne Cunningham, Ian Phillips, GHC)

Punch ~ Tenants Anthony Pugh and John Davidson ~ Real ale ~ Bar food (12-2(2.30 Sun),
7-9.30(9 Sun)) ~ (01737) 243100 ~ Dogs welcome ~ Open 11-3, 5.30(6 Sat)-11;
12-10.30 Sun; closed 25 Dec, 26 Dec evening

WEST END SU9461 Map 2
Inn at West End 🍽 ♀

Just under 2½ miles from M3 junction 3; A322 S, on right; GU24 9PW

With gastronomic evenings and wine tastings on the pub's calendar, this is a place
that takes its food and drink very seriously, and a full list of their events is on the
'what's on?' section of their website (www.the-inn.co.uk), which also lists such
things as bank holiday boules contests (held by the terrace) and pub quizzes
(inevitably with fiendish food and drink rounds). Knowledgeably chosen house
wines include ten by the glass, several sherries and dessert wines, and as the
landlord is a wine merchant they can supply by the case. Food is not cheap but uses
locally sourced ingredients, and could include soup (£4.75), sandwiches (from £5),
grilled goats cheese on pesto croûte with rocket and tomato salad or lightly curried
smoked haddock kedgeree with poached egg (£7.75 starter, £11.75 as a main
course), salmon in cream, lemon, dill and garlic sauce (£9.75), wild mushroom,
walnut and blue cheese risotto (£13.50), pan-roasted maize-fed chicken supreme
with wild mushroom and tarragon cream (£16.50) and roasted rump of lamb
wrapped in bacon, buttered spinach and red wine jus (£18.95); they also do two-
course set menus at various prices. Appealingly up-to-date, the pub is open plan,
with bare boards, attractive modern prints on canary yellow walls above a red
dado, and a line of dining tables with crisp white linen over pale yellow tablecloths
on the left. The bar counter, straight ahead as you come in, is quite a focus, with
chatting regulars on the comfortable bar stools, Courage Best and Fullers London
Pride on handpump; good coffee. The area on the right has a pleasant relaxed
atmosphere, with blue-cushioned wall benches and dining chairs around solid pale
wood tables, broadsheet daily papers, magazines and a row of reference books on
the brick chimneybreast above a woodburning stove. This opens into a garden
room, which in turn leads to a pergola-covered (with grapevine and clematis)
terrace. *(Recommended by Guy Consterdine, Mrs Ann Gray, Mayur Shah, David and
Sue Smith, Ian Phillips, A Warren, KC, B and M Kendall, David and Ruth Shillitoe)*

Enterprise ~ Lease Gerry and Ann Price, Lee Watts and Vicky Wolfe ~ Real ale ~ Bar food
(12-2.30, 6-9.30; 12-3, 6-9 Sun) ~ Restaurant ~ (01276) 858652 ~ Well behaved children
over 5 welcome in restaurant if dining ~ Dogs allowed in bar ~ Open 12-2.30, 5-11; 12-11
Sat; 12-10.30 Sun

WEST HORSLEY TQ0853 Map 3
Barley Mow

Off A246 Leatherhead—Guildford at Bell & Colvill garage roundabout; The Street;
KT24 6HR

Tucked behind a handsome horse chestnut tree, this attractive traditional country
pub is distinguished by particularly attentive and good-humoured service, under a
charming black-waistcoated Spanish manager. The low-beamed bar has Fullers
London Pride, Greene King IPA, Shepherd Neame Spitfire and Youngs on
handpump, decent wines and spirits, and daily papers; there may be unobtrusive
piped music. Bar food includes soup (£3.95), sandwiches (from £4.50),
ploughman's (£5.75), broccoli and stilton bake or sausage, mash and leek and
onion gravy (£7.95), steak and ale pie (£9.95), salmon fillet with balsamic
reduction (£10.95), 8oz sirloin steak (£13.95) and puddings such as strawberry
gateau or apple crumble (£3.95). The flagstoned part on the right probably dates
from the 16th c, and with its big log fire under an unusual domed smoke canopy is
quite a magnet for dogs and their owners at weekends. The left-hand side is
carpeted, with comfortable library chairs, flowers on its pubby tables (two of them
copper-topped and framed with cast iron), cottagey lantern lighting, and another

fireplace. The vintage and classic racing-car prints in a less ancient front extension are a sign of the pub's popularity with motor enthusiasts – when they meet here you might find all sorts of treasures in the car park. On the left, the comfortable and softly lit restaurant, with white tablecloths and more fresh flowers, includes what looks like a former barn, with pitched rafters. The good-sized garden, sheltered, well planted and neatly kept, has picnic-sets. *(Recommended by Colin Christie, Ian Phillips, Tony Hobden, C J Roebuck, Susan and John Douglas)*

Punch ~ Lease John and Juliette Andon ~ Real ale ~ Bar food (12-2.30, 6-9(9.30 Fri, Sat); 12-4.30 Sun, not Sun evening) ~ Restaurant ~ (01483) 282693 ~ Well supervised children welcome ~ Dogs allowed in bar ~ Open 11-11; 12-10.30 Sun

WORPLESDON   SU9854   Map 3
Jolly Farmer 🍺

Burdenshott Road, off A320 Guildford—Woking, not in village – heading N from Guildford on the A320, turn left after Jacobs Well roundabout towards Worplesdon Station; OS Sheet 186 map reference 987542; GU3 3RN

There's an appealingly fresh look to this stylishly done dining pub, with modern furnishings nicely setting off the woodwork and beams. The bar retains a pubby feel, and offers Fullers Discovery and London Pride, and Gales HSB on handpump, plus one or two guests such as Rebellion IPA, and a large wine list with a good number by the glass. You can eat here, or in a no smoking dining extension with stripped brickwork and well spaced tables. The menu ranges from soup (£3.50), welsh rarebit (£4.50) and large open sandwiches (from £5, though they'll happily make more standard-size normal ones on request) to home-made beefburger (£7.95), cassoulet of butter beans, red beans and chickpeas (£ 8.25), chicken, leek, mushroom and ale pie (£9.95), ploughman's (£10.25), and sirloin steak (£14.25), with specials such as fried fillet of bass on crab and prawn risotto (£13.95) and rump of lamb marinated in rosemary and garlic (£14.95); Sunday roasts (£10.95-£12.95). In summer they have occasional barbecues and hog roasts in the large, sheltered back garden, which has grape vines and fruit trees, and picnic-sets under cocktail parasols. The car park is shared with Whitmore Common, and there are walks from here into the surrounding woods. *(Recommended by KC, James Price, Mayur Shah, C J Roebuck, Martin and Alison Stainsby)*

Fullers ~ Managers Monica and John Howard ~ Real ale ~ Bar food (12-3, 6-9.30; 12-9.30 Fri, Sat;12-8 Sun) ~ Restaurant ~ (01483) 234658 ~ Children welcome ~ Open 12-11(12 Sat)

LUCKY DIP

Besides the fully inspected pubs, you might like to try these Lucky Dips recommended to us and described by readers (if you do, please send us reports: www.goodguides.co.uk).

ABINGER COMMON [TQ1146]
☆ *Abinger Hatch* RH5 6HZ [off A25 W of Dorking, towards Abinger Hammer]: Beautifully placed woodland pub nr pretty church and pond, heavy beams and flagstones, log fires, pews forming booths around oak tables in carpeted side area, popular pub food (not Sun evening) from generous ciabattas up, friendly and attentive young junior staff, plenty of space (it gets very busy wknds); piped music, children allowed only in plain extension; dogs welcome, tables and friendly ducks in nice garden, summer barbecues, open all day *(Edward Mirzoeff, LYM, Mike and Lynn Robinson, Barry Steele-Perkins, N R White)*

ALBURY [TQ0447]
Drummond Arms GU5 9AG [off A248 SE of Guildford; The Street]: Tidily kept traditional country pub with several real ales, attentive helpful staff, attractive dining room, conservatory (children allowed here); piped music; pretty streamside back garden with duck island, tables by willows, fountain, covered terrace and barbecue, bedrooms, attractive village, pleasant walks nearby *(LYM, Mrs Frances Pennell)*
ALBURY HEATH [TQ0646]
William IV GU5 9DG [Little London, off A25 Guildford—Dorking – OS Sheet 187 map ref 065468]: Welcoming country local with big log fire in rustic low-beamed flagstoned bar,

enjoyable and generous sensibly priced food from sandwiches up, local Hogs Back and Surrey Hills ales, simple dining area, close-set tables in upstairs restaurant, small games room; children welcome, tables in pretty front garden, good walks (LYM, Bruce Bird)

ASH VALE [SU8952]

Swan GU12 5HA [Hutton Rd, off Ash Vale Rd (A321) via Heathvale Bridge Rd]: Big friendly three-room Chef & Brewer on the workaday Basingstoke Canal, huge blackboard choice of decent food all day (can take a while when very busy), good sandwiches, Courage Directors, Youngs and a guest beer, good reasonably priced wines by the glass, good cheerful staff inc chefs in tall white hats, large log fire; piped classical music; children welcome, attractive garden, well kept heated terraces and window boxes, open all day (KC, Mrs Pam Mattinson, Philip and June Caunt)

BANSTEAD [TQ2659]

Mint SM7 3DS [Park Rd, off High St towards Kingswood]: Comfortably opened up with several nicely decorated areas, friendly service by helpful considerate staff, good value food (not Sun evening) from sandwiches and ciabattas up, real ales and good choice of wines by the glass (Jenny and Brian Seller)

BETCHWORTH [TQ2150]

Red Lion RH3 7DS [Old Rd, Buckland]: Restaurtany dining pub, light and airy, with wide choice of enjoyable food, steps down to stylish long flagstoned room and no smoking rather Tuscan-seeming candlelit dining room, modern furnishings, Adnams Broadside and guest beers; children welcome, picnic-sets on lawn with play area and cricket ground beyond, dining terrace, bedroom block, open all day (John Evans, DWAJ, LYM, Mike and Heather Watson)

BISLEY [SU9459]

Hen & Chickens GU24 9DJ [Guildford Rd]: Modernised cosy local with masses of Tudor beams at varying heights, warm friendly welcome, Courage Best and Directors, Fullers London Pride and Hogs Back TEA, good value pubby food from enterprising sandwiches up, daily papers; small garden (Ian Phillips)

BLETCHINGLEY [TQ3250]

☆ *Prince Albert* RH1 4LR [Outwood Lane]: Unpretentious country local with linked beamed rooms, panelling and simple furnishings, vintage car pictures, enjoyable food from baguettes to quite a range of fish, Itchen Valley and guest beers, decent house wines, friendly staff, smallish restaurant; may be piped pop music, big-screen sports TV, and can get loud and smoky evenings; dogs and children welcome, open all day Sun (also Weds-Sat in summer), tables on terrace and in pretty garden (Colin McKerrow, N R White, Ian Phillips, LYM, Geoffrey Kemp, B J Harding)

Whyte Harte RH1 4PB [2½ miles from M25 junction 6, via A22 then A25 towards Redhill]: Low-beamed open-plan pub with old prints and big inglenook log fire, decent food, Charles Wells Bombardier, reasonably priced

wines; seats outside, comfortable bedrooms (LYM, Geoffrey Kemp)

☆ *William IV* RH1 4QF [3 miles from M25 junction 6; Little Common Lane, off A25 on Redhill side of village]: New landlord settling in well in tile-hung and weatherboarded country local down pretty lane, promising food, good friendly service, real ales inc Adnams, Fullers London Pride and Greene King IPA, good wines, two separate bar rooms and comfortably old-fashioned little back no smoking dining room; two-level garden (Ian Phillips, Martin Pearson, LYM, N R White)

BRAMLEY [TQ0044]

☆ *Jolly Farmer* GU5 0HB [High St]: Unpretentious rambling pub with five changing ales inc Badger Best and Hogs Back TEA, czech beers on tap, proper coffee, pleasant staff, two log fires, wide choice of generous food inc carvery, beer mat, banknote and splendid farm tool collections among other bric-a-brac, big dining area; comfortable bedrooms, open all day (LYM, Geoff and Carol Thorp)

BUCKLAND [TQ2250]

Jolly Farmers RH3 7BG [A25 nr Reigate]: Completely refurbished under new licensees, putting emphasis on their good meals (a few sandwiches too, and a couple of real ales); thriving if not pubby atmosphere, pleasant staff, integral farm shop (Mike and Heather Watson)

BYFLEET [TQ0661]

Plough KT14 7QT [High Rd]: Medley of furnishings in friendly local with Courage Best, Fullers London Pride and several guest beers, attractively priced straightforward food from sandwiches up, two log fires, lots of farm tools, brass and copper, dominoes; picnic-sets in pleasant back garden (Ian Phillips)

CATERHAM [TQ3355]

Olde King & Queen CR3 5UA [High St]: 16th-c Fullers local with ochre walls, flagstoned bar, room off with open fire, books and brass ornaments, small partly panelled eating area with very low boarded ceiling, good beers, friendly young landlord, small menu of good value basic food (not Sun) from sandwiches up; terrace tables, open all day (Tony Hobden)

CHARLTON [TQ0868]

Harrow TW17 0RJ [Charlton Rd, Ashford Common; off B376 Laleham—Shepperton]: Popular thatched 17th-c pub with Indian licensees doing generous good value food inc good indian dishes (Sat food is all indian), massive helpings – can take a while when busy; picnic-sets out in front (Mayur Shah)

CHERTSEY [TQ0466]

Crown KT16 8AP [London St (B375)]: Traditional Youngs pub with button-back banquettes in spreading high-ceilinged bar, tall and very sonorous longcase clock, real ales, decent wines by the glass, no-nonsense food from sandwiches and baked potatoes up, cheerful attentive staff, neatly placed darts; big-screen sports TV each end, fruit machines; children and dogs welcome, garden bar with conservatory, tables in courtyard and garden

with pond; smart 30-bedroom annexe
(Ian Phillips, Geoffrey Kemp)
Golden Grove KT16 9EN [Ruxbury Rd,
St Anns Hill (nr Lyne)]: Low beam and plank
ceiling, bare boards, stripped wood and coal-
effect gas fire giving this busy local a snug
welcoming feel, bargain straightforward home-
made food from sandwiches up (not Sat-Mon
evenings) in pine-tabled eating area, Fullers
London Pride, Tetleys and Wadworths 6X,
cheerful service; piped music, fruit and games
machines; big pretty sloping garden with
picnic-sets under grape-laden vine, play area,
tree-shaded pond *(Ian Phillips)*
Kingfisher KT16 8LF [Chertsey Bridge Rd]:
Big popular Vintage Inn in delightful spot by
Thames lock, repro period décor and
furnishings in spreading series of small intimate
areas, Greene King IPA and Wadworths 6X,
good wine choice, reasonably priced food,
friendly service, good log fires, daily papers,
large-scale map for walkers; soft piped music;
families welcome if eating (otherwise no under-
21s), riverside garden by road, open all day
*(Ian Phillips, Simon Collett-Jones, Ron and
Sheila Corbett)*

CHIDDINGFOLD [SU9635]

☆ *Crown* GU8 4TX [The Green (A283)]:
Impressive and picturesque medieval inn under
good new management, fine carving,
Elizabethan plaster ceilings, massive beams,
lovely inglenook log fire, surprisingly
reasonably priced real ales such as Adnams, fff
and Fullers London Pride, some interesting
lagers, enjoyable bar food, tapestried panelled
restaurant; children welcome, tables out on
verandah, attractive village-green surroundings,
good bedrooms *(LYM, Phil and Sally Gorton)*
☆ *Mulberry* GU8 4SS [Petworth Rd (A283 S)]:
Relaxed country inn with welcoming fire in
huge inglenook, attractive rambling panelled
bar, light and airy by day, candlelit at night,
couple of steps down to appealing carpeted
dining area, sofas by second back log fire with
plenty of reading, enjoyable if not cheap food
from sandwiches and baguettes up, Greene
King IPA and Hogs Back TEA, good choice of
wines by the glass, friendly attentive staff; tables
on covered verandah, picnic-sets among fruit
trees on neat lawn with wendy house and play
area, well equipped bedrooms in separate
block, open all day wknds *(Nathan Tough, BB)*
☆ *Swan* GU8 4TY [A283 S]: Attractive dining
pub, comfortable and smartly up to date, with
good choice of food from tempting if not
cheap sandwich range up in light and airy
dining bar and restaurant, several real ales,
thoughtful wine choice, friendly relaxed
service, no smoking area; good bedrooms
*(Martin and Karen Wake, LYM, John and
Rosemary Haynes, Gerry and
Rosemary Dobson, Michael B Griffith)*

CHIPSTEAD [TQ2757]

☆ *Ramblers Rest* CR5 3NP [Outwood Lane
(B2032)]: Picturesque aggregation of partly
14th-c buildings, recently reopened after
refurbishment and now all no smoking, airy
and spacious, with panelling, flagstones, log

fires and low beams, Fullers London Pride and
Pilgrim, good wines by the glass, good varied
up-to-date food inc interesting dishes, friendly
efficient service, daily papers; children and
dogs welcome, big pleasant garden behind,
attractive views, good walks nearby, open all
day *(BB, Melanie Eskenazi, C and R Bromage,
N R White, Grahame Brooks, S Topham)*
Well House CR5 3SQ [Chipstead signed with
Mugswell off A217, N of M25 junction 8]:
Partly 14th-c, cottagey and comfortable, with
lots of atmosphere, good value food (not Sun
evening) from hefty sandwiches and baguettes
to some interesting blackboard specials,
efficient friendly staff, log fires in all three
rooms (one bar is no smoking), real ales such
as Adnams, Everards Tiger, Fullers London
Pride, Hogs Back Hair of the Hog and
Wadworths 6X; dogs allowed; large attractive
hillside garden with well reputed to be
mentioned in Domesday Book, delightful
setting *(John Branston, LYM, N R White)*
White Hart CR5 3QW [Hazelwood Lane]:
Reworked pub with some emphasis on the
food side, with enjoyable and distinctive food
from bar meals to added restaurant; sheltered
walled garden *(John Branston)*

CHOBHAM [SU9761]

Sun GU24 8AF [High St, off A319]: Pleasant
low-beamed timbered pub with Courage
Directors, Fullers London Pride and Hogs Back
TEA, indian-based food, friendly staff, lots of
daily papers, two log fires, shining brasses
(LYM, Ian Phillips)

CHURT [SU8538]

Crossways GU10 2JE: Sound down-to-earth
village pub, small and friendly, with good
value usual food, interesting choice of up to
seven or eight changing real ales at reasonable
prices, two distinct bar areas *(R B Gardiner)*

CLAYGATE [TQ1563]

Hare & Hounds KT10 0JL [The Green]:
Typical Victorian/Edwardian pub now putting
some emphasis on good value lunches in its
french restaurant; same small group as Plough,
Cobham – see main entries *(Geoffrey Kemp)*

COBHAM [TQ1058]

☆ *Cricketers* KT11 3NX [Downside Common,
S of town past Cobham Park]: Popular olde-
worlde pub with low beams and standing
timbers, blazing log fire, horsebrasses and
simple furnishings. Fullers London Pride, Gales
and Greene King Old Speckled Hen, pricey bar
food, restaurant; children welcome, neat
garden with heated terrace and village-green
views, open all day *(Evelyn and Derek Walter,
Ian Phillips, LYM, Roy and Lindsey Fentiman)*

COMPTON [SU9546]

Harrow GU3 1EG [B3000 towards Godalming
off A3]: Upmarket country local popular for
enjoyable if not cheap home-made food inc
some interesting dishes, good service, real ales,
good wines by the glass, simple décor; children
welcome, picnic-sets outside, bedrooms, open
all day *(LYM, R B Gardiner)*

DORKING [TQ1649]

☆ *Kings Arms* RH4 1BU [West St]: Rambling
16th-c pub in antiques area, masses of timbers

and low beams, nice lived-in furniture in olde-worlde part-panelled lounge, warm relaxed atmosphere, mainstream and interesting guest ales, friendly efficient service, good choice of low-priced home-made food from sandwiches and baked potatoes to roasts and a good pie of the day, prompt polite service, attractive old-fashioned back dining area; piped music; open all day (Fr Robert Marsh, Andy Trafford, Louise Bayly, Edna Jones)

Watermill RH4 1NN [Reigate Rd]: Attentive efficient service and some good interesting if not cheap food as well as more pubby dishes in busy partly no smoking dining area, well arranged with some adults-only tables (Ian and Julia Beard)

DUNSFOLD [TQ0036]

Sun GU8 4LE [off B2130 S of Godalming]: Elegantly double-fronted pub with scrubbed pine furniture, log fire in inglenook, good mix of locals and visitors, Adnams, Fullers London Pride and Harveys, decent wines, enjoyable generous food, eating area and smarter restaurant, traditional games; seats out on terrace and overlooking quiet village green (LYM, Gordon Stevenson)

EAST CLANDON [TQ0551]

☆ *Queens Head* GU4 7RY [just off A246 Guildford—Leatherhead; The Street]: Rambling dining pub under hands-on new licensees, more of a restaurant feel to the good but not cheap food and atmosphere now though they still do baguettes and light dishes, emphasis on local produce (veg charged extra), good friendly service even if busy, Hogs Back TEA and Youngs Bitter and Special from fine old elm bar counter, small, comfortable and spotless connecting rooms, big inglenook log-effect fire; children welcome, picnic-sets on pretty front terrace and in quiet side garden, handy for two NT properties (John Evans, LYM, Mike and Heather Watson, Ian Phillips)

EFFINGHAM [TQ1153]

☆ *Plough* KT24 5SW [Orestan Lane]: Friendly and well run Youngs pub, largely no smoking, with consistently well kept ales from traditional bar with handbag hooks, good choice of food and of wines by the glass (two glass sizes), friendly antipodean staff, two coal-effect gas fires, beamery, panelling, old plates and brassware in long lounge, small smoking area; plenty of tables on forecourt and in attractive garden with play area, handy for Polesdon Lacey (NT) (Sue and Mike Todd, Gordon Stevenson, John Evans, Martin and Karen Wake, Stephen Funnell)

Sir Douglas Haig KT24 5LU [off A246 Leatherhead—Guildford]: Large open-plan beamed pub, recently pleasantly refurbished, enjoyable nicely served food, real ales inc Fullers London Pride, good choice of coffees; piped music; children in eating area, open all day, tables on attractive terrace and back lawn, decent bedrooms (DWAJ, LYM)

ELLENS GREEN [TQ0936]

Wheatsheaf RH12 3AS [B2128 N of Rudgwick]: Current good licensees putting emphasis on enjoyable fairly priced food using fresh local supplies, Harveys and a guest beer, good choice of wines by the glass inc champagne, friendly helpful service, no piped music; pleasant garden (Shirley Mackenzie, Simon and Jan Brook)

ELSTEAD [SU9043]

Woolpack GU8 6HD [B3001 Milford—Farnham]: Wide range of enjoyable generous food from sandwiches up, Brakspears and Greene King Abbot tapped from the cask, good choice of wines by the glass, efficient friendly service, high-backed settles in long airy main bar, open fires each end, country décor, darts in back room; children allowed, garden with picnic-sets, open all day wknds (Gordon Stevenson, Mrs Ann Gray, Liz and Brian Barnard, Joan and Tony Walker, LYM, Michael Sargent)

ENGLEFIELD GREEN [SU9872]

☆ *Fox & Hounds* TW20 0XU [Bishopsgate Rd, off A328 N of Egham]: Welcoming 17th-c bare-boards pub by Windsor Park and a very short stroll from Savill Garden, bar food, Brakspears, Hogs Back TEA and guest beers, fine choice of wines and malt whiskies, cheerful log fire, attractive candlelit back restaurant; may be piped music; children welcome, tables on pretty front lawn and back terrace, open all day (afternoon break Jan-Easter) (Derek and Sylvia Stephenson, Kevin Thomas, Nina Randall, LYM, Ian Phillips, Martin and Karen Wake, Robert Hay, Ellen Weld, David London, N R White)

Sun TW20 0UF [Wick Lane, Bishopsgate]: Well used local, nothing too fancy, Courage Best, Fullers London Pride and Greene King Abbot, good blackboard wine choice, long-serving landlord and efficient young staff, enjoyable food from good sandwiches and baguettes to Sun lunch, reasonable prices, daily papers, lovely log fire in back conservatory, biscuit and water for dogs, interesting beer bottle collection; quiet garden with aviary, handy for Savill Garden and Windsor Park (Ian Phillips)

EPSOM [TQ2158]

☆ *Derby Arms* KT18 5LE [Downs Rd, Epsom Downs]: Comfortable dining pub very popular lunchtimes with older people for wide choice of reasonably priced food from good sandwich range up, efficient service even when busy, decent wines, Fullers London Pride and Shepherd Neame Spitfire, log fires, no smoking area; open all day Sun, nice tables outside, good views – opp racecourse grandstand (yet surprisingly little racing memorabilia) (MRSM, C and R Bromage)

Rubbing House KT18 5LJ [Epsom Downs]: Nicely appointed dining pub popular at lunchtime for good value promptly served food, pleasant efficient service even when busy, Fullers London Pride, large no smoking area (DWAJ, C and R Bromage)

ESHER [TQ1364]

Bear KT10 9RQ [High St]: Thriving Youngs pub with their full range kept well, good choice of wines by the glass, good service, popular food from sandwiches to fish and steak in bar and no smoking dining end, big-screen sports TV, two landmark life-size bears behind roof parapet; bedrooms, open all day *(Craig Turnbull)*

Prince of Wales KT10 8LA [West End Lane; off A244 towards Hersham, by Princess Alice Hospice]: Victorian pub tudorised as warm and homely Chef & Brewer dining pub, wide choice of reasonably priced food from sandwiches up, cosy candlelit corners, log fires, turkey carpets, old furniture, prints and photographs, real ales such as Greene King Old Speckled Hen and Charles Wells Bombardier, good wine choice, daily papers; big shady garden, lovely village setting nr green and pond *(Geoffrey Kemp, Ian Phillips)*

FRIMLEY GREEN [SU8856]
Old Wheatsheaf GU16 6LA [Frimley Green Rd (B3411, was A321)]: Quick friendly service and lots of sensibly priced sandwiches as well as baguettes, ploughman's and a few substantial bargain daily specials in informal proper pub with Greene King IPA, wheelback chairs, banquettes and country prints in opened-up bar, evening restaurant; terrace tables *(Mrs S M Prince, R T and J C Moggridge)*

GODSTONE [TQ3551]
Bell RH9 8DX [under a mile from M25 junction 6, via B2236]: Enjoyable if not cheap up-to-date and more traditional food in open-plan updated beamed and bare-boards dining pub, modern furnishings and lighting, good-sized restaurant, separate bar with one draught beer; tables in attractive garden *(Grahame Brooks, LYM)*

Hare & Hounds RH9 8LN [handy for M25 junction 6; A25 towards Bletchingley]: Pleasant and comfortable traditional pub with Badger K&B, Fullers London Pride and Youngs Special, reasonably priced food from sandwiches up *(Ian Phillips)*

White Hart RH9 8DU [handy for M25 junction 6; High St]: Attractive beamed and timbered former coaching inn opp pretty village pond, emphasis on the food side with good choice in bar and restaurant, Fullers London Pride and Wadworths 6X, decent choice of wines by the glass, games room; suntrap courtyard *(BB, Tony and Wendy Hobden)*

GOMSHALL [TQ0847]
Compasses GU5 9LA [A25]: Plain bar (open all day) and much bigger neat and comfortable no smoking dining area, good value food from sandwiches and baked potatoes to steak, good service, real ales and decent wines by the glass; may be piped music; children welcome, pretty garden sloping down to roadside mill stream, open all day *(Gordon Prince, LYM)*

GUILDFORD [SU9949]
Keystone GU2 4BL [Portsmouth Rd]: Generous good value food (not Fri-Sat evenings), Black Sheep, Wadworths 6X and a guest beer, friendly young staff, bistro atmosphere with simple décor and furnishings inc a couple of settles; tables on heated back

terrace, open all day *(Mr and Mrs B Hobden)*

Rodboro Buildings GU1 4RY [Bridge St]: Wetherspoons in converted Dennis automotive factory and later Rodboro Print Works, wide range of well priced ales such as Batemans Dark Lord, Brakspears, Itchen Godfather, Marstons, Titanic Lifeboat and Youngs, good value coffee, usual food *(Ian Phillips)*

White House GU2 4AJ [High St]: Waterside pub with friendly efficient young staff, Fullers ales and Gales HSB, tasty bar food, unusual upstairs no smoking gallery, side sun lounge; terrace by River Wey, pretty setting, good canal walks, open all day *(Bruce Bird)*

HAMBLEDON [SU9639]
☆ *Merry Harriers* GU8 4DR [off A283; just N of village]: Charmingly old-fashioned and homely country local popular with walkers, huge inglenook log fire, dark wood with cream and terracotta paintwork, pine tables, impressive collection of chamber-pots hanging from beams, Greene King IPA and Abbot, Hogs Back TEA and Hop Back Crop Circle, farm cider, decent wines and coffee, attentive staff, reasonably priced fresh simple food from sandwiches up, daily papers and classic motorcycle magazines, pool room; big back garden in attractive walking countryside near Greensand Way, picnic-sets in front and over road – caravan parking *(N R White, Phil and Sally Gorton, Susan and John Douglas)*

HASCOMBE [TQ0039]
☆ *White Horse* GU8 4JA [B2130 S of Godalming]: Picturesque old rose-draped pub with attractively simple beamed public bar, traditional games and quiet small-windowed alcoves, more traditional dining bar (children allowed), good bar food from sandwiches and baguettes up, Adnams and Harveys, prompt service, good wine list, log fires or woodburners; small front terrace, spacious sloping back lawn, pretty village with good walks from the pub, open all day wknds *(Gerry and Rosemary Dobson, LYM, C J Roebuck, Jenny and Brian Seller)*

HEADLEY [TQ2054]
Cock KT18 6LE [Church Lane]: Contemporary refurbishment (pub actually dates back to the 15th c), with several light and airy dining areas, good value up-to-date food, real ales, sophisticated décor; tables outside – attractive setting, good walks *(Mark Percy, Lesley Mayoh, Mike and Heather Watson)*

HINDHEAD [SU8736]
Woodcock GU26 6PD [Churt Rd (A287)]: Welcoming licensees, good value food inc good Sun carvery, Gales HSB; handy for Frensham Ponds *(Klaus and Elizabeth Leist)*

HOLMBURY ST MARY [TQ1144]
Kings Head RH5 6NP: Relaxed bare-boards pub in popular walking country (leave muddy boots in porch), real ales inc Kings, enjoyable bar food using local supplies, friendly young licensees, two-way log fire; pretty spot with seats out facing village green, more in big sloping back garden, has been open all day wknds and summer *(Barry Steele-Perkins, Susan and Erik Falck-Therkelsen)*

HORSELL [SU9859]

Cricketers GU21 4XB [Horsell Birch]: Friendly local with long neatly kept bar, quietly comfortable end sections, extended back eating area, carpet and shiny boards, good straightforward food (all day Sun and bank hols) from sandwiches up, Courage Best, Fullers London Pride and a guest beer, cheerful service, children well catered for; big well kept garden, seats out in front overlooking village green *(Ian Phillips)*

Plough GU21 4JL [Cheapside]: Small friendly pub overlooking wooded heath, pubby food from sandwiches and baguettes up, Adnams, Badger K&B, Lees Green Gate and Wadworths 6X, quiet dining area one side of L, machines and TV the other *(Ian Phillips)*

Red Lion GU21 4SS [High St]: Welcoming comfortably renovated pub with good if not cheap food, Courage Best, Fullers London Pride and Greene King IPA, decent wines, friendly staff, picture-filled converted barn where children allowed; can sometimes get smoky; ivy-clad passage to garden with picnic-sets under cocktail parasols and pleasant terrace, good walks nearby *(N R White, Ian Phillips)*

HORSELL COMMON [TQ0160]

Bleak House GU21 5NL [Chertsey Rd, The Anthonys; A320 Woking—Ottershaw]: Pleasant upscale gastropub now calling itself Sands at Bleak House, grey split sandstone for floor and face of bar counter, tasteful mushroom and white décor with black tables, sofas and stools, good food from baguettes to aberdeen angus steak, Hogs Back TEA and Hop Garden Gold and Charles Wells Bombardier, lots of smart yet friendly uniformed staff; shame about the piped music – and the acoustics are very lively; tables in pleasant back garden merging into woods with good shortish walks to sandpits which inspired H G Wells's *War of the Worlds* *(Guy Consterdine, Ian Phillips)*

IRONS BOTTOM [TQ2546]

Three Horseshoes RH2 8PT [Sidlow Bridge, off A217]: Friendly country local with good value carefully made food from hot baguettes up, Fullers London Pride and guest beers, thoughtful service, darts; tables outside, summer barbecues *(Mike and Heather Watson)*

KINGSWOOD [TQ2456]

☆ *Kingswood Arms* KT20 6EB [Waterhouse Lane]: Attractive old pub, big and busy, with good atmosphere in rambling bar, enjoyable generous food from good sandwiches up, helpful friendly staff, good range of beers inc Fullers London Pride, Shepherd Neame Spitfire and Theakstons Old Peculier, hanging plants in pleasant light and airy conservatory dining extension; spacious rolling garden with play area *(Mike and Heather Watson)*

LALEHAM [TQ0470]

☆ *Anglers Retreat* TW18 2RT [B376 (Staines Rd)]: Well appointed 1930s pub rejuvenated with emphasis on family dining, French chef doing wide choice (all day wknds) inc lots of fresh fish, pale panelling, big tropical aquarium set into wall, even larger one in smart no smoking restaurant area extended into conservatory, two bright coal fires, Brakspears and a guest beer, decent wines; unobtrusive piped music, fruit machine, no dogs; children welcome, seats out in front, play area in back garden, open all day *(LYM, Geoffrey Kemp)*

LEATHERHEAD [TQ1656]

Edmund Tylney KT22 8AW [High St]: Cosy Wetherspoons with good value food, big roasting fire in upstairs library-style dining room; open all day *(Edna Jones)*

Running Horse KT22 8BZ [Bridge St]: Small pleasant local with Fullers London Pride, Greene King IPA and Old Speckled Hen, Timothy Taylors Landlord and Youngs, good value pubby food inc lots of sandwiches, no smoking eating area; close to River Mole *(Fr Robert Marsh, Andy Trafford, Louise Bayly)*

LEIGH [TQ2246]

☆ *Plough* RH2 8NJ [3 miles S of A25 Dorking—Reigate; Church Rd]: Weatherboarded village-green pub with low beams and lots of games, Badger real ales, good all day from sandwiches up (may need to book wknds); limited nearby parking; children welcome, garden tables, open all day *(LYM, N R White)*

LIMPSFIELD CHART [TQ4251]

Carpenters Arms RH8 0TG [Tally Rd]: Much modernised open-plan pub in delightful setting by village common, friendly atmosphere and service, real ales, decent coffee, nice range of home-made food, unpretentious furnishings, darts one end (dogs welcome), eating area the other; picnic-sets in small garden, lovely walks, handy for Chartwell *(N R White)*

LITTLE BOOKHAM [TQ1254]

Olde Windsor Castle KT23 3AA: Spacious well extended Chef & Brewer family dining pub with lots of timbers, old-style country furniture and log fire, good choice of food from sandwiches to full meals, lots of decent wines by the glass, Courage Best, Hogs Back TEA and a guest beer, friendly staff, no smoking area; tables in huge garden with terrace and popular play area *(Edna Jones)*

LYNE [TQ0166]

Royal Marine KT16 0AN [Lyne Lane]: Friendly and cosy little pub, neat as a new pin, real ales such as Archers King George V, Hogs Back TEA and Charles Wells Bombardier, unpretentious well presented reasonably priced home-made food, lots of nautical bric-a-brac and fine collection of pewter mugs; some picnic-sets out in front, most attractive small back garden, cl Sun evening *(Ian Phillips)*

MARTYRS GREEN [TQ0857]

Black Swan KT11 1NG [handy for M25 junction 10; off A3 S-bound, but return N of junction]: Extended pub, as we went to press in summer 2006 being refurbished as open-plan dining pub by small London-based Geronimo group (so no reports yet); plenty of tables in big woodside garden with particularly good play area, handy for M25 junction 10 and for RHS Wisley Garden, has been open all day *(Anon)*

MILFORD [SU9442]
White Lion GU8 5BB [Portsmouth Rd]: Good value home-made food inc Sun roasts, good choice of real ales *(Roger and Pauline Pearce)*
MOGADOR [TQ2453]
Sportsman KT20 7ES [from M25 up A217 past 2nd roundabout, then Mogador signed; edge of Banstead Heath]: Interesting, relaxed and welcoming low-ceilinged pub with enterprising food from foreign cheeses to wild boar and exotic imaginatively prepared fish, Fullers London Pride and Youngs, friendly service, fresh flowers in dining room; dogs welcome if not wet or muddy, tables out on common, on back lawn, and some under cover (some M25 noise out here), on Walton Heath – a magnet for walkers and riders *(C and R Bromage, N R White)*
NEWCHAPEL [TQ3641]
Wire Mill RH7 6HJ [Wire Mill Lane; off A22 just S of B2028 by Mormon Temple]: Spacious big-windowed two-storey pub in same small Auberge group as Plough, Cobham (see main entries), weatherboarded mill said to have been built with 16th-c ship's timbers, low beams and olde-worlde décor, real ales such as Shepherd Neame Spitfire and Charles Wells Bombardier, up-to-date home-made food from baguettes and omelettes up; lots of tables out on terrace by watersports lake (can be noisy speedboats), bedrooms, open all day *(N R White, Michael and Ann Cole)*
NEWDIGATE [TQ1942]
Six Bells RH5 5DH: Good atmosphere in refurbished local with good range of real ales, four blackboards of good value food in the popular and pleasant eating section (marquee added in summer), friendly service and cheery landlord; children really welcome, plenty of tables in pleasant garden, lovely outlook over wooden-towered church *(Mark Killman, DWAJ)*
OCKHAM [TQ0756]
☆ *Hautboy* GU23 6NP [Ockham Lane – towards Cobham]: Remarkable red stone Gothick folly, emphasis on upstairs brasserie bar like a 19th-c arts & crafts chapel, darkly panelled and high-vaulted, with medieval-style murals, minstrels' gallery and Greene King Old Speckled Hen, Hogs Back TEA and Ringwood Best, friendly helpful young staff, imaginative choice of enjoyable food from sandwiches, ciabattas and baked potatoes up in fun bargain two-course lunch; children welcome, tables on cricket-view terrace and in secluded orchard garden with play area, bedrooms; currently the best lunch place within easy reach of RHS Wisley *(LYM, Ian Phillips, P and J Shapley)*
OCKLEY [TQ1439]
☆ *Kings Arms* RH5 5TS [Stane St (A29)]: Attractive 17th-c country inn bought by small group and now operating more as restaurant with rooms than as pub (though you can have just a drink – Bass, Flowers IPA, Greene King Old Speckled Hen and Marstons Pedigree, good choice of wines by the glass); heavy beams and timbers, low lighting, comfortable olde-worlde décor inc masses of antique prints,

good inglenook log fire, food (not cheap) from sandwiches to steaks; children welcome, discreetly placed picnic-sets in immaculate big back garden, good bedrooms *(LYM)*
☆ *Punchbowl* RH5 5PU [Oakwood Hill, signed off A29 S]: Cosily old-fashioned country pub, smart and clean, with cheerful relaxed atmosphere, wide choice of imaginative inexpensive food, Badger ales, friendly helpful service, daily papers, huge inglenook, polished flagstones, lots of low beams and hunting décor, restaurant off on one side, public bar with darts and pool the other; children allowed in dining area, picnic-sets on side terrace and in pretty front garden, quiet spot with good walks inc Sussex Border Path *(LYM, C and R Bromage, Susan and John Douglas)*
OUTWOOD [TQ3246]
Bell RH1 5PN [Outwood Common, just E of village; off A23 S of Redhill]: Attractive extended and neatly kept 17th-c pub/restaurant, mildly upmarket food in olde-worlde beamed bar and sparser restaurant area, Fullers London Pride, good wines by the glass, log fires; children and dogs welcome, piped music; summer barbecues and cream teas, pretty fairy-lit garden with country views, handy for windmill *(LYM, Geoffrey Kemp)*
Castle RH1 5QB [Millers Lane]: Welcoming panelled and carpeted pub with real ales inc Adnams and Harveys, short interesting choice of lunchtime food from ciabattas up, log fire and old wooden tables; large terrace *(Terry Buckland, GHC)*
OXTED [TQ3852]
☆ *George* RH8 9LP [High St, Old Oxted]: Recently refurbished, keeping chatty atmosphere and attractive prints in two front bar areas, and opening up the restaurant for more of a bistro style, enjoyable home-made food, good choice of wines by the glass, real ales, open fire; new tables out on back decking *(LYM, Derek Thomas)*
Royal Oak RH8 0RR [Caterfield Lane, Staffhurst Wood, S of town]: Comfortable and unchanging traditional bar, good range of real ales, decent house wine, good bar food, wider choice in added back dining room with country views, emphasis on fish, choice of Sun roasts *(N R White, GHC)*
PEASLAKE [TQ0844]
☆ *Hurtwood* GU5 9RR [off A25 S of Gomshall; Walking Bottom]: Homely and warmly welcoming pre-war country hotel, comfortable bar and lounge with Hogs Back TEA, Kings Horsham Best and two Surrey Hills ales, good range of wines by the glass, coffee and malt whiskies, reasonably priced bar food from sandwiches up, helpful staff, daily papers and magazines, two coal-effect fires, sizeable interesting restaurant; dogs welcome, good walks from the door, bedrooms, good breakfast *(BB, Barry Steele-Perkins, Ian Phillips, Paul Humphreys)*
PUTTENHAM [SU9347]
☆ *Good Intent* GU3 1AR [signed off B3000 just S of A31 junction; The Street/Seale Lane]: Bustling beamed village local, unspoilt and

welcoming, with hands-on landlord and cheerful efficient staff, real ales such as Hogs Back TEA, Theakstons Old Peculier and Youngs Special, good range of reasonably priced generous fresh food (not Sun/Mon evenings) from sandwiches and baked potatoes up, farm cider, decent wine choice, handsome log fire in cosy front bar with alcove seating, pool, old photographs of the pub, simple dining area; can get smoky; dogs welcome, no children, picnic-sets in small sunny garden, good walks, open all day wknds *(Phil Hanson, Phil and Sally Gorton, BB, Dennis Jenkin, Ian Phillips)*

PYRFORD LOCK [TQ0559]
Anchor GU23 6QW [3 miles from M25 junction 10 – S on A3, then take Wisley slip rd and go on past RHS Garden]: Busy modern pub included for its honeypot position by bridge and locks on River Wey Navigation; low-priced food counter popular lunchtime with families and older people, real ales inc Courage Best and Fullers London Pride, big conservatory extension, upstairs room (not always open) with narrow-boat memorabilia, splendid terrace; juke box, sports TV, machines etc; open all day in summer *(DWAJ, LYM, Jenny and Brian Seller)*

RIPLEY [TQ0556]
☆ *Anchor* GU23 6AE [High St]: Former 16th-c almshouse, three interesting cool dark low-beamed connecting rooms and small no smoking restaurant, wide choice of tasty promptly served thai food, also ciabattas, baked potatoes and other pub staples, Fullers London Pride and Greene King IPA, daily papers, nautical memorabilia and photographs of Ripley's cycling heyday, coal-effect stove; disabled facilities, tables in coachyard *(C and R Bromage, Ian Phillips, BB, KC)*

SEND [TQ0156]
New Inn GU23 7EN [Cartbridge]: Well placed by Wey Navigation canal, long bar decorated to suit, Adnams Broadside, Fullers London Pride, Greene King Abbot, Ringwood Best and a guest beer, reasonably priced popular food from toasted sandwiches up, two log-effect gas fires; smoking throughout; picnic-sets in front by road and in garden by canal path *(Ian Phillips, KC)*

SENDMARSH [TQ0455]
Saddlers Arms GU23 6JQ [Send Marsh Rd]: Friendly and unpretentious low-beamed local with creeper-covered porch, Fullers London Pride, Greene King Old Speckled Hen, Shepherd Neame Spitfire and Youngs, enjoyable home-made pub food, open fire, no smoking area, toby jugs, brassware etc; well behaved dogs welcome, picnic-sets out front and back *(Ian Phillips)*

SHALFORD [SU9946]
Parrot GU4 8DW [Broadford]: Big neatly kept canalside pub with nice décor, good value bar food from good sandwiches up, Fullers London Pride, Greene King Abbot, Hogs Back TEA and Itchen Valley Fagins, quick friendly staff, pleasant conservatory grill restaurant; attractive garden *(Gordon Stevenson, Fr Robert Marsh)*

SHERE [TQ0747]
☆ *White Horse* GU5 9HF [signed off A25 3 miles E of Guildford; Middle St]: Well run Chef & Brewer, a lovely place to take foreign visitors – uneven floors, massive beams and timbers, Tudor stonework, olde-worlde décor with oak wall seats and two log fires, one in a huge inglenook, several rooms off small busy bar, good choice of reasonably priced food all day from sandwiches and baguettes up, nice staff and warm atmosphere, real ales such as Adnams, Gales Butser and Greene King IPA, lots of wines by the glass; good-sized children's area, dogs welcome, picnic-sets in big back garden, beautiful film-set village, open all day *(Ian Phillips, Mark Percy, Lesley Mayoh, LYM, Norma and Noel Thomas, Andy Trafford, Louise Bayly, Mike and Heather Watson, A and B D Craig)*

STAINES [TQ0371]
Bells TW18 4ZB [Church St]: Quietly comfortable and friendly local, Youngs real ales, decent wines, prompt and reasonably priced home-made lunchtime food from good sandwiches to popular good value Sun lunch, central fireplace, darts; tables in garden with terrace *(Ian Phillips)*

STOKE D'ABERNON [TQ1259]
Old Plough KT11 3BN [Station Rd, off A245]: Pleasantly refurbished, popular at lunchtime for good choice of enjoyable proper food, Courage Best and interesting guest beers, helpful staff, airy conservatory restaurant; sizeable garden, open all day *(BB, DWAJ, Stephen Funnell)*

SUNBURY [TQ1068]
Flower Pot TW16 6AA [Thames St, Lower Sunbury; handy for M3 junction 1, via Green St off exit roundabout]: Pleasant 18th-c inn with comfortable local feel, good home-made food in bar and small restaurant with emphasis on fish and seasonal produce, Brakspears Bitter and Special, Fullers London Pride and a guest beer, good choice of wines by the glass, helpful cheerful young staff; simple comfortable bedrooms *(Ian Barker)*

SUTTON GREEN [TQ0054]
Olive Tree GU4 7QD [Sutton Green Road]: Welcoming modern dining pub with good honest food inc fish and seafood, cheaper bar menu, Timothy Taylors Landlord and two other real ales, good choice of wines by the glass, relaxing dining room with minimalist décor *(Barry Steele-Perkins, R Lake, Mrs S M Prince, C A Hall)*

TADWORTH [TQ2355]
Dukes Head KT20 5SL [Dorking Rd (B2032 opp Common and woods)]: Wide range of low-priced enjoyable food (not Sun evening) from formidable sandwiches up, attentive service, good choice of real ales and of wines by the glass, two big inglenook log fires; garden, open all day *(C and R Bromage)*

THAMES DITTON [TQ1567]
Albany KT7 0QY [Queens Rd, signed off Summer Rd]: Thameside chain pub included for its lovely position, nice balconies and lots of tables on terrace and lawn with great views

across river; thoroughly modern inside (leather sofas and teak furniture on woodblock floors, up-to-date lighting), friendly staff, usual food served piping hot at good prices, good choice of wines by the glass, log fire, daily papers, river pictures, waitress-service restaurant; moorings, open all day *(R Lake, Tom and Ruth Rees, Jennie George, Ian Phillips, A Rees, John and Glenys Wheeler)*

TILFORD [SU8742]

Duke of Cambridge GU10 2DD [Tilford Rd]: Well run and civilised, with enjoyable food and efficient friendly service; garden tables, play area *(Wendy Arnold, R B Gardiner)*

VIRGINIA WATER [TQ9768]

Wheat Sheaf GU25 4QF [London Rd]: Good welcoming service in large pub with several bar and dining areas; garden tables (traffic noise), by wooded entry to lake area *(Gloria Bax)*

WALLISWOOD [TQ1138]

Scarlett Arms RH5 5RD [signed from Ewhurst—Rowhook back rd, or off A29 S of Ockley]: Smartly unpretentious country pub, low black oak beams, flagstones, simple furniture, two log fires (huge inglenook), Badger ales, good coffee, decent food with separate evening menu, pleasant efficient staff, back dining room; peaceful benches in front, garden tables under cocktail parasols, good walks *(LYM, C and R Bromage)*

WARLINGHAM [TQ3658]

Hare & Hounds CR6 9DZ [Limpsfield Rd (A269)]: Clean and spacious, with Fullers London Pride, Larkins and a beer brewed for the pub, wide range of pubby food all day (till 4 Sun) from hot baguettes up; piped music may obtrude; pretty summer flowers, play area *(Tony Brace)*

WEST CLANDON [TQ0451]

☆ *Bulls Head* GU4 7ST [A247 SE of Woking]: Friendly and comfortably modernised, based on 1540s timbered hall house, very popular esp with older people lunchtime for reliable hearty food from sandwiches, ploughman's and baked potatoes through home-made proper pies to steak, small lantern-lit beamed front bar with open fire and some stripped brick, contemporary artwork for sale, older local prints and bric-a-brac, steps up to simple raised back inglenook dining area, efficient service, Courage Best, Greene King Old Speckled Hen and Wadworths 6X, good coffee, no piped music, games room with darts and pool; no credit cards; children and dogs on leads welcome, tables and good play area in pleasant garden, convenient for Clandon Park, good walking country *(R Lake, Ian Phillips, DWAJ, Jenny and Brian Seller, C J Roebuck)*

☆ *Onslow Arms* GU4 7TE [A247 SE of Woking]: Popular partly 17th-c country pub in same small Auberge group as Plough, Cobham (see main entries); rambling through dark nooks and corners, heavy beams and flagstones, warm seats by inglenook log fires, lots of brass and copper, good value food (not Sun evening) from baguettes to main dishes inc two-course lunch deals in partly no smoking french brasserie, real ales such as Courage Directors,

Fullers London Pride and Charles Wells Bombardier, decent wines; children welcome (and dogs in bar), great well lit garden, open all day *(R A Rosen, Mike and Heather Watson, Barry Steele-Perkins, LYM, Geoffrey Kemp)*

WEST HORSLEY [TQ0752]

King William IV KT24 6BG [The Street]: Comfortable early 19th-c pub, largely no smoking, with very low-beamed open-plan rambling bar, reasonably priced proper food from sandwiches up here and in updated conservatory restaurant, good choice of wines by the glass, Courage Best and Directors and Gales HSB, good coffee, log fire, board games; children and dogs very welcome, good disabled access, small garden and terrace with gorgeous hanging baskets *(Ian Phillips, Kate Foulger Moorby)*

WESTHUMBLE [TQ1751]

Stepping Stones RH5 6BS [just off A24 below Box Hill]: Comfortable mainly no smoking dining pub (drinks brought to table) with consistently good sensibly priced straightforward lunchtime food and more elaborate evening menu, good friendly service even when busy, circular bar with Fullers London Pride, Greene King Abbot and a guest beer, clean uncluttered décor, open fire, no music; children and walkers welcome, terrace and garden with summer barbecue and play area *(DWAJ, Mike and Heather Watson, Sue and Mike Todd)*

WEYBRIDGE [TQ0765]

☆ *Old Crown* KT13 8LP [Thames St]: Friendly and comfortably old-fashioned three-bar pub dating from 16th c, very popular lunchtime for good value food from sandwiches and baked potatoes up esp fresh grimsby fish (served evening too), good specials; Courage Best and Directors and Youngs, service good even when busy, no smoking family lounge and conservatory, coal-effect gas fire; may be sports TV in back bar; children welcome, suntrap streamside garden *(DWAJ, Mark Percy, Lesley Mayoh, Ian Phillips, JMM)*

☆ *Prince of Wales* KT13 9NX [Cross Rd/Anderson Rd off Oatlands Drive]: Congenial and attractively restored, reasonably priced generous blackboard food inc interesting dishes and Sun lunch with three roasts, real ales such as Adnams, Boddingtons, Fullers London Pride, Tetleys and Wadworths 6X, ten wines by the glass, relaxed lunchtime atmosphere, friendly service, log fire in right-hand bar, daily papers, candlelit stripped pine dining room down a couple of steps; big-screen TVs for major sports events; well behaved children welcome *(David and Heather Stephenson, Minda and Stanley Alexander)*

Queens Head KT13 8XS [Bridge Rd]: In same small Auberge group as Plough, Cobham (see main entries); good architectural mix of old and new, and good practical mix of proper pub and french restaurant, comfortable and welcoming, with real ales, friendly staff and authentic cooking; tables out in front *(Hunter and Christine Wright)*

WINDLESHAM [SU9464]

☆ *Brickmakers* GU20 6HT [Chertsey Rd (B386, W of B383 roundabout)]: Bistro-feel dining pub with enjoyable fresh seasonal food from good interesting ciabattas up, flagstones, pastel colours and different areas, one room with sofas and low tables, Brakspears, Courage Best, Fullers London Pride and Marstons Pedigree, good choice of wines by the glass, nice coffee, friendly service, log fire, conservatory; may be quiet piped classical music; well behaved children allowed, attractive courtyard with flower-filled pergola, heater, boules and barbecues *(Ian Phillips, Martin and Karen Wake, Robert Hay)*

☆ *Half Moon* GU20 6BN [Church Rd]: Popular family pub with reliable food inc Sun lunch, half a dozen interesting changing ales alongside Brakspears and Fullers London Pride, Weston's farm cider, decent wines, good range of children's drinks, cheerful efficient staff, friendly labrador called Boddington, log fires, World War II pictures, modern furnishings, attractive barn restaurant out along covered flagstoned walkway; piped music, silenced fruit machine; children welcome, picnic-sets in huge well kept garden with two new terraces and well used play area *(Guy Consterdine, R Lake, Robert Hay)*

WITLEY [SU9439]

White Hart GU8 5PH [Petworth Rd]: Attractive beamed Tudor local doing well under current energetic landlord, Shepherd Neame real ales, enjoyable home-made food, fair prices, daily papers, good oak furniture and log fire in cosy panelled inglenook snug where George Eliot drank, games in public bar, restaurant; piped music; tables on flower-filled cobbled terrace, lower meadow with picnic-sets and play area *(Phil and Sally Gorton, LYM, Michael B Griffith)*

WOKING [TQ0158]

Maybury Inn GU22 8AB [Maybury Hill/Old Woking Rd (B382)]: Popular locally for good value food from baguettes up, Courage Best and Greene King IPA, log fire, large dining conservatory; plenty of tables outside *(Ian Phillips)*

Mayford Arms GU22 9QT [Guildford Rd, Mayford (A320)]: Roomy pub with good value generous pubby food, Greene King IPA and Abbot, friendly staff, log fire, no smoking dining area; garden with play area *(Ian Phillips)*

Wetherspoons GU21 5AJ [Chertsey Rd]: Civilised retreat, with lots of intimate areas and cosy side snugs, good range of food all day and of real ales and coffees, fair prices, friendly helpful staff, daily papers, interesting old local pictures, no music; open all day *(Ian Phillips, Tony Hobden)*

WOOD STREET [SU9550]

Royal Oak GU3 3DA [Oak Hill]: Brightly lit popular pub, comfortably unpretentious and friendly, with good changing ale range such as Courage Best, Hogs Back TEA, Pilgrim Surrey

and Shere Drop, good moderately priced plain cooking with lots of fresh veg and nice puddings *(Liz and Brian Barnard, Ian Phillips)*

WOODHAM [TQ0361]

Victoria KT15 3QE [Woodham Lane]: Cheery local with changing ales such as Caledonian Deuchars IPA and Shepherd Neame Spitfire and Bishops Finger, decent wines by the glass, popular generous food in back dining area, friendly staff, daily papers, lots of team events; piped music and machines may obtrude; big back balcony/terrace, pretty window boxes, sheltered garden with play area *(Jason Muxworthy)*

WORPLESDON [SU9654]

Fox GU3 3PP [Fox Corner]: Modernised pub/restaurant with wicker chairs and pine tables, Courage Best and Greene King IPA, good if not cheap food, good service, proper bar area too; big pretty garden with picnic-sets under dark green parasols, heated terrace *(Ian Phillips)*

WOTTON [TQ1247]

☆ *Wotton Hatch* RH5 6QQ [A25 Dorking—Guildford]: Attractive and well run Vintage Inn family dining pub, welcoming largely no smoking rambling rooms around 17th-c core, interesting furnishings and log fire, good generous reasonably priced food (all day Thurs-Sun and summer), hearty sandwiches till 5 (not Sun), real ales, good choice of decent wines, generous soft drinks, hospitable landlord and staff, daily papers, conservatory; gentle piped music, no dogs; impressive views from neat garden, open all day *(R Lake, Gordon Prince, LYM, Gordon Stevenson, Mark Percy, Lesley Mayoh, Alan M Pring, C and R Bromage)*

WRECCLESHAM [SU8344]

☆ *Bat & Ball* GU10 4SA [approach from Sandrock Hill and Upper Bourne Lane then narrow steep lane to pub]: Neatly refurbished local tucked away in hidden valley, wide range of above-average pubby and more upmarket food (small helpings available) inc good puddings, up to half a dozen or more changing ales such as one brewed for them by Hampshire, good choice of wines by the glass, friendly staff, no smoking areas; they may try to keep your credit card while you eat, sports TV; disabled facilities, dogs and children allowed in one area with games machines, tables out on heated terrace and in garden with substantial play fort, open all day wknds *(R Lake, BB, D Marsh)*

Sandrock GU10 4NS [Sandrock Hill Road]: Popular and unpretentious real ale tavern with Bathams Best, Enville White, Holdens Special, Surrey Hills and several interesting changing guest beers, reasonably priced food from huge lunchtime sandwiches, pittas and ciabattas through pubby standards to steaks and a good fish stew, good choice of sensibly priced wines by the glass, friendly knowledgeable staff, real fire, bar billiards in games room, annual beer festival; children and dogs welcome, pleasant garden, open all day *(Tony Smith)*

Sussex

Sussex has a splendid choice of pubs that combine real country charm with enjoyable food and drink. And the area certainly has a bumper crop of cottagey and unspoilt pubs, some that have been in the same family for many years. Doing well this year are the lovely little Rose Cottage at Alciston, the delightful Cricketers Arms in Berwick, the very popular Basketmakers Arms and the foody Greys, both in Brighton, the Black Horse in Byworth (enjoyed by both locals and visitors), the Fox Goes Free at Charlton, the Royal Oak hidden down a track at Chilgrove (a new entry for this appealing traditional country all-rounder), the contrasting White Horse there (altogether smarter, but welcoming diners and walkers alike), the ancient George & Dragon near Coolham (another new main entry, warm-hearted and good value), the comfortably rustic Horse & Groom at East Ashling, the Tiger at East Dean (its village green position is charming), the upmarket Griffin at Fletching, the Star just outside Heathfield (a proper country local), the extremely well run Queens Head at Icklesham, the Cock at Ringmer (newly back in the *Guide* after a break of several years), and the proudly old-fashioned Royal Oak at Wineham. Pubs doing particularly well on the food front include the Curlew at Bodiam, the Greys in Brighton, the White Horse at Chilgrove, the tucked away Jolly Sportsman at East Chiltington, the Griffin at Fletching, and the Star & Garter at East Dean. For a special meal out, our choice for Sussex Dining Pub of the Year is the Griffin at Fletching. The Basketmakers Arms in Brighton also deserves an honourable mention, for the pocket-friendly pricing of its enjoyable food. In the Lucky Dip section at the end of the chapter, pubs showing great form in recent months include the Sportsmans at Amberley, Spotted Cow in Angmering, Swan in Arundel, Anchor Bleu at Bosham, Evening Star in Brighton, Old House at Home at Chidham, Coach & Horses at Danehill, Huntsman at Eridge Station, Anglesey Arms at Halnaker, Woodmans Arms at Hammerpot, Duke of Cumberland Arms at Henley, Noahs Ark at Lurgashall, Rising Sun at Milland, Inkerman Arms at Rye Harbour, White Lion at Thakeham, Horse Guards at Tillington and Cat at West Hoathly. Drinks prices tend to be higher in Sussex pubs than in most parts of the country. The main local brewer is Harveys, and you are more likely to find beer from them than from any other brewer as the cheapest on offer in the county's better pubs. Other good local beers to look out for include Arundel, Weltons, Ballards, Kings, Dark Star and Hepworths; the so-called K&B Sussex is actually brewed down in Dorset by Badger.

ALCISTON   TQ5005   Map 3
Rose Cottage
Village signposted off A27 Polegate—Lewes; BN26 6UW

'I just wish this was my local' is a phrase we often hear about this old-fashioned little cottage. The same friendly family have been running it for more than 40 years and it remains just what you imagine a country pub to be. There's a good mix of locals and ramblers, cosy winter log fires, half a dozen tables with cushioned pews under quite a forest of harness, traps, a thatcher's blade and lots of other black ironware, and more bric-a-brac on the shelves above the stripped pine dado or in the etched-glass windows; in the mornings you may also find Jasper the parrot (he gets too noisy in the evenings and is moved upstairs). There's a lunchtime overflow into the no smoking restaurant area. Using fresh fish, free-range meat and poultry and as much organic produce as possible – and local honey, rabbits and seasonal game – the good, home-made food at lunchtime includes soup (£3.75), ploughman's (£6.50), honey-roast ham with poached egg and chips (£6.95), and pork sausages from the local butcher (£7.45), with evening extras such as pâté (£4.50), steaks (from £10.25), and half a roast duckling with a sauce of the month (£13.95), and daily specials like steak in ale pie or vegetarian pancake filled with spinach, cream cheese and pine nuts topped with tomato sauce and parmesan (£7.95), rabbit and bacon pie (£8.50), fish pie with salmon and tiger prawns or chicken with a chestnut, mushroom, lemon and sage cream sauce (£8.95), braised lamb shank (£10.95), and grilled bass with chilli, rosemary and garlic (£11.25); the Friday night mussels (£8.50) are usually a sell-out. Well kept Harveys Best and a guest from Kings on handpump, a good little wine list with fair value house wines and a few nice bin ends, and local farm cider; the landlord is quite a plain-speaking character. There are gas heaters outside for cooler evenings (and a new boules pitch), and the small paddock in the garden has ducks and chickens. Nearby fishing and shooting. The charming little village (and local church) are certainly worth a look. They only take bedroom bookings for two nights. *(Recommended by PL, Jenny and Peter Lowater, Mary Rayner, D Marsh, Michael Hasslacher, R and S Bentley, the Didler, Michael and Ann Cole, John Beeken, C J Roebuck, Richard May, Mrs Phoebe A Kemp, John and Jill Perkins, Jude Wright)*

Free house ~ Licensee Ian Lewis ~ Real ale ~ Bar food ~ Restaurant ~ (01323) 870377 ~ Children allowed if over 10 ~ Dogs allowed in bar ~ Open 11.30-3, 6.30-11; 12-3.30, 6.30-10.30 Sun; closed 25 and 26 Dec and evening 1 Jan ~ Bedrooms: /£50S

ALFRISTON   TQ5203   Map 3
George
High Street; BN26 5SY

This lovely village is a tourist honeypot and well liked by ramblers – two long-distance paths (the South Downs Way and Vanguard Way) cross here and Cuckmere Haven is close by. The long no smoking bar in this 14th-c timbered inn has massive low beams hung with hops, appropriately soft lighting, and a log fire (or summer flower arrangement) in a huge stone inglenook fireplace that dominates the room, with lots of copper and brass around it. Sturdy stripped tables have settles and chairs about them, and there's Greene King IPA, Abbot and Old Speckled Hen, and maybe Ridleys Prospect on handpump; decent wines, champagne by the glass, board games and piped music. Bar food at lunchtime includes soup (£4.25), salami and chorizo plate with capers and olives or potted prawns in paprika butter (£5.95), ploughman's (£7.95), and baked ham and free-range eggs (£8.50); there's also a vegetarian risotto of the day (£10.50), breast of chicken filled with spinach and lentils (£12.95), baked shank of lamb or pork pot roast (£13.25), and salmon supreme with rosemary, lemon and white wine sauce (£13.50). The no smoking restaurant is cosy and candlelit – or you can sit out in the charming flint-walled garden behind. *(Recommended by Ian and Nita Cooper, Len Beattie, David and Karen Cuckney, Dr David Cockburn, W A Evershed, Glenwys and Alan Lawrence)*

Greene King ~ Lease Roland and Cate Couch ~ Real ale ~ Bar food (12-2.30, 7-9 (10 Fri and Sat)) ~ Restaurant ~ (01323) 870319 ~ Children welcome ~ Dogs allowed in bar and bedrooms ~ Open 12-11; 12-midnight Fri and Sat; 12-11 Sun; closed 25 and 26 Dec ~ Bedrooms: £50S/£100B

Bedroom prices are for high summer. Even then you may get reductions for more than one night, or (outside tourist areas) weekends. Winter special rates are common, and many inns cut bedroom prices if you have a full evening meal.

AMBERLEY SO8401 Map 3
Black Horse
Off B2139; BN18 9NL

After a walk along the South Downs Way, the restful garden of this pretty pub with its fine views is just the place to relax with a drink. The main bar has high-backed settles on flagstones, beams over the serving counter festooned with sheep bells and shepherd's tools (hung by the last shepherd on the Downs), and walls decorated with a mixture of prints and paintings. The lounge bar has many antiques and artefacts collected by the owners on their world travels; there are log fires in both bars and two in the no smoking restaurant. Bar food (they tell us prices have not increased this year) includes soup (£3.45), chicken liver pâté (£3.95), deep-fried brie and camembert with cumberland sauce (£4.55), sandwiches with salad and chips or ploughman's (£5.95), lasagne or broccoli and pasta bake (£8.95), steak in ale pie (£8.95), and various curries (£9.95). Greene King IPA and Charles Wells Bombardier on handpump; piped music. More reports please. *(Recommended by Barry Collett, Mayur Shah, David H T Dimock, Jude Wright)*

Punch ~ Lease Gary Tubb ~ Real ale ~ Bar food (12-3, 6-9.30(10 Sat); all day Sun) ~ Restaurant ~ (01798) 831552 ~ Children allowed but must be well supervised at all times ~ Dogs allowed in bar ~ Open 11-midnight; 12-midnight Sun

ARLINGTON TQ5407 Map 3
Old Oak
Caneheath, off A22 or A27 NW of Polegate; BN26 6SJ

Part of this building was first used as an ale and cider house for local agricultural and brick-making workers. It was built in 1733 and first became a pub in the early 1900s. The open-plan, L-shaped bar has heavy beams, well spaced tables and comfortable seating, log fires, and Badger Best, Harveys Best and a guest such as Adnams Broadside tapped from the cask; several malt whiskies, piped music, darts, toad in the hole (a Sussex coin game) and dominoes. Straightforward bar food includes filled baguettes and ploughman's as well as home-made soup (£3.95), duck and orange pâté (£5.75), ham and eggs (£6.95), vegetable lasagne (£7.50), home-made curry (£7.95), and home-made steak and mushroom in ale pie or a roast of the day (£8.95); Sunday roast. The garden is attractive and peaceful. More reports please. *(Recommended by Fr Robert Marsh, Alan Sadler, Michael and Ann Cole, M and R Thomas, Ron Gentry, Paul A Moore)*

Free house ~ Licensees Mr J Boots and Mr B Slattery ~ Real ale ~ Bar food (12-2.30, 6.30-9.30; all day weekends) ~ Restaurant ~ (01323) 482072 ~ Children welcome ~ Dogs allowed in bar ~ Open 11-11

BALLS CROSS SU9826 Map 2
Stag
Village signposted off A283 at N edge of Petworth, brown sign to pub there too; GU28 9JP

The tiny flagstoned bar in this unspoilt little 16th-c pub has a winter log fire in its huge inglenook fireplace, just a couple of tables, a window seat, and a few chairs and leather-seated bar stools; on the right a second room with a rug on its bare boards has space for just a single table. Beyond is an appealing old-fashioned no smoking dining room, carpeted, with quite a few horsey pictures. There are yellowing cream walls and low shiny ochre ceilings throughout, with soft lighting from little fringed wall lamps, and fishing rods and country knick-knacks hanging from the ceilings. On the left a separate carpeted room with a couple of big Victorian prints has table skittles, darts and board games. Badger Best, Sussex and a guest on handpump, decent wines by the glass, summer cider, and some nice malt whiskies. A fair choice of good value food using meat from a local butcher and game bagged by the landlord includes filled rolls (from £4.75), ploughman's (from £6), filled baked potatoes (£5.50), ham and egg (£7.50), mediterranean vegetable lasagne or a well liked full breakfast (£8), seasonal pheasant casserole (£9), and calves liver and bacon or fish pie (£9.50). The good-sized garden behind, divided by a shrubbery, has teak or cast-iron tables and chairs, picnic-sets, and in summer a couple of canvas awnings; there are more picnic-sets out under green canvas parasols in front, and the hitching rail does get used. The veteran gents' (and ladies') are outside. *(Recommended by Jude Wright, David Cosham, Susan and John Douglas, Mrs J A Sales, Peter Lewis, Phil and Sally Gorton, Jeremy Whitehorn, R B Gardiner)*

Badger ~ Tenant Hamish Barrie Hiddleston ~ Real ale ~ Bar food (not Sun evening) ~ Restaurant ~ (01403) 820241 ~ Children in dining area or games room but must be well behaved ~ Dogs allowed in bar and bedrooms ~ Open 11-3, 6-11; 12-3, 7-10.30 Sun ~ Bedrooms: £30/£60

BERWICK TQ5105 Map 3
Cricketers Arms
Lower Road, S of A27; BN26 6SP

This is a little gem. It's in a quiet village close to the downs and perhaps at its best on a warm sunny day when you can sit in the old-fashioned front garden amidst small brick paths and mature flowering shrubs and plants; there are more seats behind the building. Inside, the three small cottagey rooms are all similarly furnished rooms (two are no smoking) with simple benches against the half-panelled walls, a pleasant mix of old country tables and chairs, a few bar stools, and some country prints; quarry tiles on the floors (nice worn ones in the middle room), two log fires in little brick fireplaces, a huge black supporting beam in each of the low ochre ceilings, and (in the end room) some attractive cricketing pastels; some of the beams are hung with cricket bats. Good straightforward bar food includes home-made soup, garlic mushrooms (£5.95), country pâté (£6.25), local sausages (£6.50), filled baked potatoes or ploughman's (£6.75), gammon and egg (£8.25), chicken, bacon and mushroom warm salad (£8.95), steaks (from £13.95), and daily specials. Well kept Harveys Best and two seasonal ales tapped from the cask, and decent wine; cribbage, dominoes and an old Sussex coin game called toad in the hole. The wall paintings in the nearby church done by the Bloomsbury Group during WWII are worth a look. *(Recommended by Joel Dobris, Alan Cowell, Fr Robert Marsh, Mike Gorton, Richard Pitcher, the Didler, Kevin Thorpe, Paul Hopton, Percy and Cathy Paine, Mrs Phoebe A Kemp, Michael Sargent, M and R Thomas)*

Harveys ~ Lease Peter Brown ~ Real ale ~ Bar food (12-2.15, 6.30-9; all day weekends) ~ (01323) 870469 ~ Children in side room ~ Dogs welcome ~ Open 11-3, 6-11 (all day July/August); 11-11 Sat; 12-10.30 Sun; closed 25 Dec

BLACKBOYS TQ5220 Map 3
Blackboys Inn
B2192, S edge of village; TN22 5LG

A new licensee has taken over this pretty 14th-c pub and there's to be some refurbishment. The bustling locals' bar has a good, chatty atmosphere and the other old-fashioned and unpretentious little rooms have dark oak beams, bare boards or parquet, antique prints, copious curios (including a collection of keys above the bar), and usually, a good log fire in the inglenook fireplace. Bar food now includes home-made soup (£3.75), moules marinière (£4.75); main course £8.75), local sausage and egg (£5.25), home-made burger (from £5.50), ploughman's (£6.50), wild mushroom risotto (£9.75), mackerel filled with cream cheese and horseradish and baked in cider (£9.50), pork and vegetable pie (£9.75), steaks (from £10.50), chicken in a creamy white wine and tarragon sauce (£10.75), and calves liver and bacon on mustard mash (£12.50). The restaurant is no smoking. Harveys Best and Pale Ale, and a couple of guests on handpump and several wines by the glass; piped music and darts. The garden has plenty of rustic tables overlooking the pond, with more under the chestnut trees. The Vanguard Way passes the pub, the Wealdway goes close by, and there's the Woodland Trust opposite. More reports on the new regime, please. *(Recommended by Ann and Colin Hunt, Len Beattie, Jude Wright,*

R M Corlett, Michael and Ann Cole, Angus Johnson, Carol Bolden, Susan and John Douglas, Tom and Jill Jones)

Harveys ~ Tenant Paul James ~ Real ale ~ Bar food (all day) ~ Restaurant ~ (01825) 890283 ~ Children welcome ~ Dogs allowed in bar ~ Open 10am-11pm (midnight Fri and Sat)

BODIAM   TQ7825   Map 3
Curlew 🍴

B2244 S of Hawkhurst, outside village at crossroads with turn-off to Castle; TN32 5UY

Most customers come to this well run dining pub to enjoy the very good food – though they do keep Badger Best and Everards Tiger on handpump. The main bar has timbered walls and ceilings and a woodburning stove, and off to the right is a smaller no smoking room with more timbering in the red walls and neat napkinned tables. Attractively presented, the food at lunchtime might include greek salad with kalamata olives and feta cheese (£6.95), filled baguettes (from £6.95), smoked haddock risotto with poached egg and hollandaise sauce (£7.95), pasta with roasted red peppers, cherry tomatoes and parmesan (£8.50), saltimbocca of chicken with pesto mash (£9.95), fish and chips in light batter (£9.95), chicken curry with coconut cream or sausage of the day with onion chutney (£10.95), and calves liver and bacon with garlic mash and caramelised onion gravy (£11.95); also, daily specials such as halibut steamed with lemon grass and japanese soba noodles (£14.95), herb-coated rump of lamb (£15.50), and extra mature fillet steak (£18.95), and puddings like orange and Grand Marnier crème brûlée or white and dark chocolate truffle with wasabi and ginger ice-cream (£5.95). Eight wines by the glass from a fine list and local Biddenden cider. The restaurant is no smoking. The terraced garden is pretty in summer and there are lots of flowering baskets and troughs. *(Recommended by Mrs J Ekins-Daukes, JMC, Peter Meister, John Bell, Laurence Manning, Gene and Kitty Rankin, Mr and Mrs Hale, Richard Mason, Paul A Moore, Steve Godfrey)*

Free house ~ Licensee Simon Lazenby ~ Bar food (not Sun evening or Mon) ~ Restaurant ~ (01580) 861394 ~ Children welcome away from bar but must be well behaved ~ Dogs allowed in bar ~ Open 11.30-11(11.30 Sat); 12-4 Mon and Sun; 11.30(12 Sun)-3.30, 5.30-11 in winter; closed Sun and Mon evening

BRIGHTON   TQ3105   Map 3
Basketmakers Arms £

Gloucester Road – the E end, near Cheltenham Place; off Marlborough Place (A23) via Gloucester Street; BN1 4AD

With a good mix of customers and a really bustling, chatty atmosphere, this little back street corner pub remains on excellent form. The two small low-ceilinged rooms have brocaded wall benches and stools on the stripped wood floor, lots of interesting old tins all over the walls, cigarette cards on one beam with whisky labels on another, beermats, and some old advertisements, photographs and posters; piped music. Good value enjoyable bar food includes lots of sandwiches (from £2.75; brie and avocado £3.50; steak in french bread £4.25), particularly good home-made meaty and vegetarian burgers (£3.25), baked potatoes with fillings such as beef, chilli and yoghurt (from £3.60), ploughman's (£4.75), and specials such as seafood chowder (£5.75), spicy sweet potato pie (£6.25), steak in ale pie or lamb and spinach curry (£6.50), and Friday beer-battered fish (£6.50); popular Sunday roasts. Well kept Fullers London Pride, Gales Butser Bitter, Festival Mild and HSB, and guests like Adnams Broadside and Fullers ESB on handpump, good wines (house wines come in three different glass sizes), 90 malt whiskies, a dozen irish whiskeys and good coffees; they do a splendid Pimms and staff are helpful and friendly. There are three metal tables out on the pavement. *(Recommended by Mayur Shah, Bruce Bird, Ann and Colin Hunt, MLR, Janet Whittaker, Torrens Lyster, the Didler, Andy Trafford, Louise Bayly, Tony Hobden, Tracey and Stephen Groves, Jude Wright)*

Gales (Fullers) ~ Tenants P and K Dowd, A Mawer, J Archdeacon ~ Real ale ~ Bar food
(12-3, 5.30-8.30; 12-7 Sat; 12-5 Sun; not Sun evening) ~ (01273) 689006 ~ Children
welcome until 8pm ~ Dogs allowed in bar ~ Open 11-11(midnight Thurs-Sat); 12-11 Sun;
closed 26 Dec

Greys 🍴 ♀

Southover Street, off A270 Lewes Road opposite The Level (public park); BN2 9UA

It's not so much the description of the layout and furnishings that is important here,
but the really enjoyable buoyant and informal atmosphere, the easy-going mix of
drinkers and diners – and the very good food. It boils down to a good little
restaurant sharing one small L-shaped room with an unabashed pubby local.
Furnishings are basic, with simple wall seats and stools around mixed pub tables on
bare boards and flagstones, ochre walls, and some varnished plank panelling
around a flame-effect stove below a big metal canopy; piped music is at a
reasonable level. The serving bar is on the right, with well kept Harveys Best and
Timothy Taylors Landlord on handpump, Leffe and Hoegaarden on tap, a
considerable range of belgian bottled beers, and a cheery local crowd on the bar
stools and at the nearby tables. The five or six tables on the left, each with a little
vase of flowers and lighted tea lamp, are the food bit – one corner table is snugged
in by a high-backed settle, and another at the back is tucked into a quiet corner.
The stair wall is papered with posters and flyers from bands, singers and poets who
have performed here. Served by smiling, efficient staff, the interesting food from a
shortish menu that changes every couple of months might include duck liver foie
gras with warm brioche, haggis with neeps and creamy tatties or thai fishcakes with
a little siamese salad and sweet chilli and soy dipping suace (all £4.50), stuffed
peppers (£9.50), fish pie with scallops, prawns, salmon, hake, white burgundy and
cream (£10.50), organic pork cutlet with a gherkin, tongue, hard boiled egg and
white wine sauce (£11), rich game stew with some dark chocolate (£11.75), grilled
sirloin steak with a shallot, claret and marrow sauce (£12.25), and puddings such
as blueberry and raspberry cheesecake, rhubarb fool with stem ginger, and home-
made strawberry and cherry ice-cream with cherry and kirsch (£4.50); masses of
vegetables and potatoes are served separately. The house wines, from Burgundy, are
excellent value. There is not much daytime parking on this steep lane or the nearby
streets. No children inside. *(Recommended by MLR, Ann and Colin Hunt, Guy Vowles,
Tony and Wendy Hobden)*

Free house ~ Licensees Chris Taylor and Gill Perkins ~ Real ale ~ Bar food (12-2(3 Sun),
6-9; not Mon or Fri or Sun evenings) ~ (01273) 680734 ~ Dogs allowed in bar ~ Live
music Sun and Mon evenings ~ Open 12-11 (midnight Fri/Sat; 10.30 Sun); closed Mon
lunchtime (but open 5.30-11.30)

BURPHAM   TQ0308   Map 3
George & Dragon 🍺

Warningcamp turn off A27 outside Arundel: follow road up and up; BN18 9RR

Built in 1736, this popular dining pub is in an attractive setting at the end of the
village between the partly Norman church (which has some unusual decoration)
and cricket ground. The front part is a proper bar with old pale flagstones and a
woodburning stove in a big inglenook on the right, a carpeted area with an old
wireless set, nice scrubbed trestle tables, and bar stools along the counter serving
King Red River Ale, Triple fff Moondance and Youngs Special on handpump; you
may smoke only at the bar. A couple of tables share a small light flagstoned middle
area with the big blackboard that lists changing dishes such as seafood platter
(£7.95; large helping £14.95), pork and apple sausages with wholegrain mustard
sauce on chive mash (£10.95), slow-cooked lamb shank with a mint and apricot
glaze (£13.95), and seared king scallops in a creamy white wine sauce (£16.95); at
lunchtime there are sandwiches and filled baguettes (from £4.95; fresh crab
sandwich £5.95), and filled baked potatoes and ploughman's (£6.95). The
conservatory extension overlooks the garden. The back part of the pub, angling

right round behind the bar servery, with a further extension beyond one set of internal windows, has solid pale country-kitchen furniture on neat bare boards, and a fresh and airy décor, with a little bleached pine panelling and long white curtains. The garden has picnic-sets under cocktail parasols. The pub gets extremely busy on Goodwood race days. *(Recommended by Martin and Karen Wake, Sue Demont, Tim Barrow, R T and J C Moggridge, Cathryn and Richard Hicks, Ian and Jane Irving, Martin O' Keefe, Peter Lewis, Elizabeth)*

Free house ~ Licensees Alastair and Angela Thackeray ~ Real ale ~ Bar food (not Sun evening) ~ Restaurant ~ (01903) 883131 ~ Children welcome ~ Open 11-11; 12-4 Sun; 11-3, 6-11 winter; closed Sun evening

BYWORTH SU9820 Map 2
Black Horse ◗
Off A283; GU28 0HL

This is a proper country pub that now serves food all day. There's a quietly chatty atmosphere and large open fires, and the simply furnished though smart bar has pews and scrubbed wooden tables on its bare floorboards, pictures and old photographs on the walls, and newspapers to read. The back dining room has lots of nooks and crannies and upstairs is a games room with pool, bar billiards and darts; lovely views of the downs. As well as lunchtime filled baguettes and ciabattas (from £4.25), filled baked potatoes (£4.75), and ploughman's (£5.95), the tasty food might include avocado stuffed with tuna and melted brie (£4.95), sausage and mash with onion gravy, chicken caesar salad or chilli nachos with sour cream and guacamole (£8.95), home-made fishcakes on beef tomato and basil salad (£9.25), honey-roast ham hock and mash (£9.45), lamb shank on root vegetables (£9.95), and scallops in mint and lemon (£10.50). Well kept Cheriton Best Bitter, Fullers London Pride, Hidden Quest and Skinners Betty Stogs on handpump; juke box and board games. The particularly attractive garden has tables on a steep series of grassy terraces sheltered by banks of flowering shrubs that look across a drowsy valley to swelling woodland. *(Recommended by John Beeken, Gordon Neighbour, Bruce Bird, Kevin Thorpe, Dave Lowe, David Coleman, Phil and Sally Gorton, Colin McKerrow, David Cosham, Mr and Mrs G Hughes, Rosemary and Tom Hall, Jude Wright)*

Free house ~ Licensee Mark Robinson ~ Real ale ~ Bar food (11.30-9.30 Mon-Sat; 12-9 Sun) ~ Restaurant ~ (01798) 342424 ~ Children welcome ~ Dogs allowed in bar ~ Open 11.30-11; 12-10.30 Sun

CHARLTON SU8812 Map 2
Fox Goes Free
Village signposted off A286 Chichester—Midhurst in Singleton, also from Chichester—Petworth via East Dean; PO18 0HU

This bustling pub has been a meeting place for the last 300 years and in 1915 was the site of the first Women's Institute gathering. Throughout, there are old irish settles, tables and chapel chairs, and the first of the dark and cosy series of separate rooms is a small bar with an open fireplace. Standing timbers divide a larger beamed bar which has a huge brick fireplace with a woodburning stove, and old local photographs on the walls. A dining area with hunting prints looks over the garden and the South Downs beyond. The family extension is a clever conversion from horse boxes and the stables where the 1926 Goodwood winner was housed; darts and fruit machine. Well kept Arundel Gauntlet, Ballards Best and Ringwood Boondoggle on handpump and eight wines by the glass. Using as much fresh local produce as possible, the enjoyable food includes home-made soup (£4.95), chicken liver parfait with apple chutney (£5.95), filled baguettes (from £6.50), king prawns in garlic butter (£6.95), ham and eggs (£8), steak and kidney pie (£9.50), a curry of the day (£9.95), specials such as salmon with basil mash (£14.95), braised lamb shoulder (£15), and home-made puddings such as Baileys crème brûlée with honeycomb ice-cream or chocolate brownie with chocolate fudge sauce (£4.95). Best to book to be sure of a table. The attractive garden has plenty of picnic-sets among fruit trees and the terrace has fine downland views. Goodwood Racecourse is not far away (on race days it does get very busy); it's also handy for the Weald and Downland Open Air Museum, and there are some fine surrounding walks. *(Recommended by Wendy Arnold, R G Trevis, Gene and Kitty Rankin, Ann and Colin Hunt, Tony and Jill Radnor, Gordon Neighbour, Mrs S Gardner, MLR, Ian Wilson, Dave Yates, Mrs J A Sales, Keith and Maureen Trainer, Jenny Garrett, W A Evershed, Paul and Shirley White)*

Free house ~ Licensee David Coxon ~ Real ale ~ Bar food (12-2.30, 6.30-10; all day weekends) ~ (01243) 811461 ~ Children in dining rooms ~ Dogs allowed in bar ~ Live music Weds evenings ~ Open 11-11(midnight Sat); 12-10.30 Sun ~ Bedrooms: £50S/£80S

CHIDDINGLY TQ5414 Map 3
Six Bells ★ £
Village signed off A22 Uckfield—Hailsham; BN8 6HE

Cheerily old-fashioned with a good bustling atmosphere, this is a very well run pub where you can be sure of a genuinely friendly welcome from the long-standing landlord. The bars have log fires as well as solid old wood furnishings such as pews and antique seats, lots of fusty artefacts and interesting bric-a-brac, and plenty of local pictures and posters. A sensitive extension provides some much needed family space; dominoes and cribbage. Particularly for this part of the country, the bar food is a bargain: straightforward but tasty, there might be french onion soup (£2.50), shepherd's or steak and kidney pies (£3.30), filled baked potatoes (from £4), ploughman's (from £4.25), chilli nachos with sour cream (£5.30), lentil, leek and mushroom loaf, chicken curry or spare ribs in barbecue sauce (£5.50), garlic mussels (£5.95), and hock of ham (£6.95). Well kept Courage Directors, Harveys Best and a guest such as 1648 Signature on handpump. The top bar is no smoking. Outside at the back, there are some tables beyond a big raised goldfish pond, and a boules pitch; the church opposite has an interesting Jefferay monument. Vintage and Kit car meetings outside the pub every month. This is a pleasant area for walks. More reports please. *(Recommended by R M Corlett, Michael and Ann Cole, Susan and John Douglas)*

Free house ~ Licensees Paul Newman and Emma Bannister ~ Real ale ~ Bar food (12-2, 6-9.30; all day Fri-Sun) ~ (01825) 872227 ~ Children in family room ~ Dogs allowed in bar ~ Live music Fri and Sat evenings and Sun lunchtime ~ Open 11-3, 6-11; 11am-midnight Sat; 11-11 Sun

CHILGROVE SU8116 Map 2
Royal Oak
Off B2141 Petersfield—Chichester, signed Hooksway down steep single track; PO18 9JZ

Tucked away down a little wooded track, this isolated and friendly white cottage is in the heart of the Downs and popular with walkers; the South Downs Way is close by. It's simply furnished with plain country-kitchen tables and chairs and there are huge log fires in the two cosy rooms of the partly brick-floored beamed bar. The cottagey dining room and plainer family room are both no smoking. Well liked traditional bar food includes home-made soup or pâté (£4.50), filled baked potatoes (£4.95), ploughman's (£5.50), sausage and chips (£5.75), chilli (£7.75), pasta tuna bake (£7.95), gammon and egg or home-made mixed mushroom and chestnut or steak and kidney pies (£8.95), salmon fillet with creamy watercress sauce (£9.90), half shoulder of lamb with red wine and rosemary gravy or mixed grill (£12.45), and puddings (£3.95). Exmoor Beast, Gales HSB, Hampshire Hooksway and a guest such as Arundel ASB or Timothy Taylors Landlord on handpump; piped music. There are plenty of picnic-sets under parasols on the grass of the big, pretty garden. *(Recommended by Torrens Lyster, Prof and Mrs S Barnett, Ann and Colin Hunt, Michael B Griffith, Bruce Bird, Martin Richardson, W A Evershed, R B Gardiner)*

Free house ~ Licensee Dave Jeffery ~ Real ale ~ Bar food (not Sun evening or Mon) ~ Restaurant ~ (01243) 535257 ~ Children in family room ~ Dogs allowed in bar ~ Live music second Fri evening of the month ~ Open 11.30-2.30, 6-11; 12-3 Sun; closed Sun evening and all day Mon; two weeks Oct

White Horse 🍴 🍸 🛏

B2141 Petersfield—Chichester; PO18 9HX

Handy for Goodwood, this civilised and quietly upmarket inn is a super place to stay and enjoy the particularly good food. But there are still plenty of tables for drinkers at the front and walkers and their dogs are very welcome (lots of fine walks nearby). No smoking throughout. There are dark brown deco leather armchairs and a sofa grouped on dark boards near the bar counter, and on either side are three or four well spaced good-sized sturdy tables with good pale spindleback side and elbow chairs on lighter newer boards. The light and airy feeling is helped by uncluttered cream walls, clear lighting and a big bow window. The bar counter is made up from claret, burgundy and other mainly french wooden wine cases, and good wines by the glass, with an impressive range by the bottle, are a big plus here – in fact, every dish from the restaurant menu has a recommended wine to go with it; Ballards on handpump and well reproduced piped music. As well as filled baked potatoes and warm baguettes (£7.95), the interesting (but pricey) menu might include home-made soup (£5.95), black pudding mousse and bubble and squeak or warm goats cheese and sweet pepper tartlet (£8.50), tian of hand-picked selsey crab, avocado and tomato (£9.95), terrine of foie gras and toasted brioche (£11.50), butternut squash and red onion risotto (£14.95), wild bass with puréed cauliflower and gravadlax sauce (£16.95), organic lamb rump on madeira jus (£17.95), and puddings like Valrhona chocolate filled with white chocolate mousse with home-made chocolate ice-cream, orange and mascarpone cheesecake or burnt citrus cream (£6.95). The bar has a woodburner on one side, and a log fire on the other. Past here, it opens into a restaurant with comfortable modern seats and attractively laid tables – as in the bar, generously spaced out. Outside, one neat lawn has white cast-iron tables and chairs under an old yew tree, and another has wooden benches, tables and picnic-sets under a tall flag mast. Comfortable bedrooms in separate annexe and super continental breakfasts brought to your room in a wicker hamper. *(Recommended by John Evans, Phyl and Jack Street, Tracey and Stephen Groves, Stephen and Anne Atkinson, Ann and Colin Hunt)*

Free house ~ Licensee Charles Burton ~ Real ale ~ Bar food (not Sun evening or Mon) ~ Restaurant ~ (01243) 535219 ~ Children welcome ~ Dogs allowed in bar and bedrooms ~ Piano Sat evening in restaurant ~ Open 10.30-3, 6-11; 12-3 Sun; closed Sun evening, Mon ~ Bedrooms: £65B/£95B

COMPTON SU7714 Map 2
Coach & Horses 🍺

B2146 S of Petersfield; PO18 9HA

This is a pleasant village with attractively wooded hilly countryside nearby so there's usually a good mix of walkers and locals in this 17th-c local. The roomy front public bar has an open fire and the Village Bar has pine shutters, panelling, and an original pitch-pine block floor. It is here that the enjoyable food, cooked by the landlord, is served: sandwiches (from £3.90), home-made soup (£4.10), filled baguettes (from £4.10), lamb sweetbreads on spinach (£5.75), black pudding, bacon and poached egg salad (£6.75), chicken and mushroom pie (£9.50), and baked aubergine with chargrilled peppers and brie or chicken breast with grain mustard and almond sauce (£9.75). The charming little plush beamed lounge bar serves as a relaxing ante-room to the attractive no smoking restaurant. Ballards Best, Cheriton Diggers Gold, Fullers ESB, Triple fff Moondance and Welton Pride 'n' Joy on handpump; bar billiards and games machine. There are tables out by the square in front; it's not far from Uppark (NT). *(Recommended by Tracey and Stephen Groves, Ann and Colin Hunt, Geoff and Linda Payne)*

Free house ~ Licensees David and Christiane Butler ~ Real ale ~ Bar food ~ Restaurant ~ (023) 9263 1228 ~ Children welcome ~ Dogs allowed in bar ~ Open 11.30-11; 12-10.30 Sun; closed 25 Dec

COOLHAM TQ1423 Map 3
George & Dragon
Dragons Green, Dragons Lane; pub signed just off A272, about 1½ miles E of village; RH13 8GE

This welcoming old tile-hung cottage has a small snug bar with heavily timbered walls, a partly woodblock and partly polished-tile floor, unusually low and massive black beams (see if you can decide whether the date cut into one is 1677 or 1577), simple chairs and rustic stools, some brass, and a big inglenook fireplace with an early 17th-c grate. There's also a smaller back bar and restaurant. Badger K&B Sussex and summer Fursty Ferret or winter Festive Feasant on handpump; kind service and a relaxed atmosphere. Well liked home-made bar food includes lunchtime sandwiches (from £4.50), filled baked potatoes (from £5.50), and ploughman's (£6.75), as well as soup (always vegetarian, £3.75), salmon and crab thai fishcakes with dipping sauce (£4.25; main course £8.90), pork ribs in barbecue sauce (£4.25; main course £9.95), chicken liver pâté (£4.95), ham, eggs and home-made chips or field mushrooms stuffed with goats cheese and herbs (£7.75), breaded chicken breast with herb and garlic butter (£8.75), steak, stilton and mushroom pie with a suet crust (£8.95), and puddings such as Baileys crème brûlée or chocolate slice (£3.95). Stretching away behind the pub, the big grassy orchard garden is neatly kept with lots of picnic-sets, shrubs and pretty flowers; the little front garden has a sad 19th-c memorial to the son of a previous innkeeper. *(Recommended by John Beeken, Terry Buckland, Ron Gentry)*

Badger ~ Tenant Jemma Ford ~ Real ale ~ Bar food ~ Restaurant ~ (01403) 741320 ~ Children welcome ~ Dogs allowed in bar ~ Open 12-3, 6-11; 11-11 Sat; 12-10.30 Sun; open from 6 weekday evenings in winter

COWBEECH TQ6114 Map 3
Merrie Harriers
Village signed from A271; BN27 4JQ

This is a white clapboarded village inn in the heart of the Weald. The beamed and panelled bar has a log fire in the brick inglenook, quite a mix of tables and chairs, and Harveys Sussex Best, Timothy Taylors Landlord and a changing guest from Kings on handpump; nine wines by the glass. Bar food includes sandwiches (from £4.50), baked ham with piccalilli (£7.95), sausages with apple mash and red onion gravy (£8.95), and beer-battered local cod (£9.95), with more elaborate dishes such as butternut squash ravioli with sage butter sauce (£9.95), fried scallops on fennel risotto or roast tenderloin of pork with cider and shallot sauce (£14.95), and fillet of local beef with wild mushroom ravioli and oxtail gravy (£17.95), with puddings such as warm dark chocolate brownie or orange and passionfruit cheesecake (£4.50). The brick-walled and oak-ceilinged back restaurant is no smoking; piped music. There are rustic seats amongst colourful shrubs and pots in the terraced garden, and country views. They are licensed to hold weddings here. More reports please. *(Recommended by PL)*

Free house ~ Licensee Roger Cotton ~ Real ale ~ Bar food ~ Restaurant ~ (01323) 833108 ~ Children allowed with restrictions ~ Dogs allowed in bar ~ Monthly jazz ~ Open 11.30-3(4 Sat), 6-11; 12-4, 6-10.30 Sun

DITCHLING TQ3215 Map 3
Bull ♀
High Street (B2112); BN6 8TA

This 14th-c place was originally a coaching inn and also served as a local court. The invitingly cosy main bar on the right is quite large, rambling and pleasantly traditional with well worn old wooden furniture, beams and floorboards, and a blazing winter fire. To the left, the nicely furnished rooms have a calm, restrained mellow décor and candles, and beyond that there's a snug area with chesterfields around a low table; piped music. Half the pub is no smoking. Harveys Sussex Best and Timothy Taylors Landlord with a couple of guests such as Hogs Back Hair of the Hog and Kings Red River on handpump, and 14 wines by the glass. As well as bar snacks and lunchtime sandwiches, bar food includes soup (£4.50), parsnip fritters with a walnut and blue cheese whip (£6), pancetta, black pudding and red chard salad with a soft poached egg (£7), local sausages with oxtail gravy or aubergine, courgette and pepper lasagne (£9.50), beer-battered haddock (£10), moroccan spiced lamb tagine with fruity couscous (£11.50), slow-roasted pork belly with apple sauce (£13), and roasted duck breast with marsala sauce (£14.50), and daily specials like smoked salmon fishcake with a carrot butter sauce (£9.50), and sauté of crayfish with saffron, olives, spinach and cherry tomatoes (£14.50). Picnic-sets in the good-sized pretty downland garden which is gently lit at night look up towards Ditchling Beacon, and there are more tables on a suntrap back terrace; good wheelchair access. The charming old village is a popular base for the South Downs Way and other walks. More reports please. *(Recommended by J P Humphery, Mr and Mrs John Taylor, N R White)*

Free house ~ Licensee Dominic Worrall ~ Real ale ~ Bar food (12-2.30(4 Sat), 7-9.30; 12-6 Sun) ~ (01273) 843147 ~ Children welcome ~ Dogs allowed in bar ~ Open 11-11; 12-11 Sun ~ Bedrooms: /£80B

DONNINGTON   SU8502   Map 2
Blacksmiths Arms

Turn off A27 on to A286 signposted Selsey, then almost immediately left on to B2201; PO20 7PR

For families, the big garden here is quite a plus. There's a play area with swingboats, a climbing frame, two rabbits called Barnham and Blu, three miniature schnauzers (Tess, Cleo, and Alfie), a cat (Amber), and four tortoises (only allowed in the garden on special occasions), and plenty of picnic-sets. Inside, the small low-ceilinged rooms are prettily decorated and have Victorian prints on the walls, solid, comfortable furnishings, and a relaxed atmosphere; the lounge is no smoking, as is the pleasant back restaurant. Bar food includes sandwiches and baguettes, lunchtime specials like ham and egg (£7.95) or scampi or vegetable tartlets (£9.95) – as well as home-made soup (£4.95), tempura-battered pork (£5.95), wild mushrooms in brandy and cream on a toasted brioche (£6.95), a vegetarian dish of the day or sausages (£9.95), gressingham duck with a sweet chilli plum sauce (£13.95), steaks (from £15.95), fish dishes and daily specials. Fullers London Pride, Greene King Abbot, Oakleaf Bitter and Charles Wells Bombardier on handpump. *(Recommended by Bob and Margaret Holder, David Carr, Ann and Colin Hunt, Susan and John Douglas, Ian Phillips, Tony and Shirley Albert, Bruce Bird)*

Punch ~ Tenants George and Lesley Ward ~ Real ale ~ Bar food (12-2.30, 6-8.30(8 Sun)) ~ Restaurant ~ (01243) 783999 ~ Children welcome ~ Dogs allowed in bar ~ Open 11.30-3(4 Sat), 6-11; 12-4, 6-10.30 Sun

EAST ASHLING   SU8207   Map 2
Horse & Groom   ♀ ■

B2178 NW of Chichester; PO18 9AX

If you're popping into this bustling country pub for just a drink, the best place to head for is the front part with its old pale flagstones and a woodburning stove in a big inglenook on the right or the carpeted area with its old wireless set, nice scrubbed trestle tables, and bar stools along the counter serving well kept Brewsters Hophead, Harveys Sussex Best, Hop Back Summer Lightning and Youngs on handpump. Several wines by the glass; piped music and board games. A couple of tables share a small light flagstoned middle area with the big blackboard that lists daily changing dishes: sandwiches and filled baguettes (from £3.95), filled baked potatoes (from £4.25), ploughman's (from £5.95), home-cooked ham and eggs (£6.50), cajun chicken (£10.25), steak in ale pie or lamb cutlets with rosemary jus (£10.95), whole baked plaice with lemon butter (£11.25), king prawns in parsley butter (£12.95), and puddings (£4.95); perhaps Sunday lunchtime nibbles. The restaurant is no smoking. The back part of the pub, angling right round behind the bar servery, with a further extension beyond one set of internal windows, has solid pale country-kitchen furniture on neat bare boards, and a fresh and airy décor, with a little bleached pine panelling and long white curtains. French windows lead out to a garden with picnic-sets under cocktail parasols. The pub gets extremely busy on Goodwood race days. *(Recommended by Ann and Colin Hunt, Tony and Wendy Hobden, Bruce Bird, Tracey and Stephen Groves, Cathy Robinson, Ed Coombe, S G N Bennett, Barry Ashton, Walter and Susan Rinaldi-Butcher, Tony and Shirley Albert, Gordon Neighbour, Paul and Shirley White)*

Free house ~ Licensee Michael Martell ~ Real ale ~ Bar food (12-2(2.30 Sun), 6-9; not Sun evening) ~ Restaurant ~ (01243) 575339 ~ Children welcome but must leave bar by 9pm ~ Dogs allowed in bar and bedrooms ~ Open 11-3, 6-11; 11-6 Sun; closed Sun evening ~ Bedrooms: £40.50B/£60.75B

EAST CHILTINGTON   TQ3715   Map 3

Jolly Sportsman 🍴 ♀

2 miles N of B2116; Chapel Lane – follow sign to 13th-c church; BN7 3BA

This is a top-notch place and, although very foody, does still have some pubbiness. There are a couple of chairs in the chatty little bar by the fireplace set aside for drinkers, and a mix of furniture on the stripped wood floors. Well kept Dark Star Hophead, Triple fff Altons Pride and a guest tapped from the cask, a remarkably good wine list with nine by the glass, farm cider, over 50 malt whiskies, and quite a few cognacs and armagnacs. Most people do head, though, for the smart but informal no smoking restaurant with contemporary light wood furniture, and modern landscapes on green-painted walls. As well as a set two-course (£12.50) and three-course (£15.95) lunch menu, there might be nibbles such as pickled cornish mussels, pickled anchovies or an oyster bloody mary shooter (from £2.50), home-made soup (£4.85), slow-braised ox cheek, shallot purée, and red wine (£5.95), smoked haddock, crispy bacon and salsify salad (£6.45), hot cornish crab tart (£6.85), cod in beer batter with tartare sauce (£12.45), seared organic salmon fillet with brown shrimp and herb salsa (£12.95), slow-braised shoulder of mutton (£14.85), and grilled scottish angus rib-eye with fresh horseradish crème fraîche (£15.75), with puddings like pineapple carpaccio with orange ice-cream, chocolate tart or apricot, walnut, ginger and toffee pudding (from £5.45). There are rustic tables and benches under gnarled trees in a pretty cottagey front garden with more on the terrace and the front bricked area, and the large back lawn with a children's play area looks out towards the South Downs; good walks nearby. More reports please. *(Recommended by Michael and Ann Cole, Tracey and Stephen Groves, Roger Hancock, Tony Curtis, Alison Stewart)*

Free house ~ Licensee Bruce Wass ~ Real ale ~ Bar food (till 10 Fri and Sat; 12.15-3 Sun; not Sun evening) ~ Restaurant ~ (01273) 890400 ~ Children welcome ~ Dogs welcome ~ Open 12-2.30, 6-11; 12-11 Sat; 12-4.30 Sun; closed Sun evening, all day Mon (except bank hols), three days Christmas

EAST DEAN   SU9012   Map 2

Star & Garter 🍴 ♀

Village signposted with Charlton off A286 in Singleton; also signposted off A285; note that there are two East Deans in Sussex (this one is N of Chichester) – OS Sheet 197 map reference 904129; PO18 0JG

In a peaceful village at the bottom of the Downs – and on the South Downs Way – this brick and flint pub is mainly set for dining, though some readers do feel drinkers are still made welcome. It is more or less one roomy square area, with sturdy and individual mainly stripped and scrubbed tables in various sizes and an interesting variety of seating from country-kitchen chairs through chunky modern dining chairs to cushioned pews and some handsome 17th-c or 18th-c carved oak seats; broad stripped boards, a few stripped beams, and some stripped panelling and masonry. The high ceiling, big windows and uncluttered walls give a light and airy feel, and tables over on the right-hand side can be booked; helpful, welcoming owners, an easy-going atmosphere, a rack of daily papers by the entrance, and piped music. The bar counter (with a few bar stools, often used for those reading menus) is over on the left, with a dozen or so well chosen wines by the glass, well kept Arundel Gaunlet and Ballards Best and Nyewood Gold tapped from casks in a back stillroom, a couple of farm ciders such as Weston's and Whitehead's, a dozen malt whiskies, and an espresso machine. As well as lunchtime filled baguettes, the good food might include home-made soup (£6), warm salad of black pudding, smoked bacon and balsamic dressing or sauté of wild mushrooms with crispy saffron risotto cake (£6.50; main course £11.50), pasta in a roasted pepper and tomato sauce (£9.50), beer-battered cod with home-made tartare sauce (£10.50), locally caught black bream baked with pesto and pine nuts (£14), breast of barbary duck with rhubarb and port sauce or rib-eye steak (£14.50), and roast rump of lamb with rosemary and redcurrant jus (£15.50). The restaurant is no smoking. The sheltered terrace behind has teak tables and chairs with big canvas parasols and heaters; steps go up to a walled lawn with picnic-sets (there are also a few steps up to the front door). *(Recommended by Cathy Robinson, Ed Coombe, M and GR, OPUS, Ann and Colin Hunt, Mr and Mrs Gordon Turner, Janet Whittaker, Bruce and Penny Wilkie, Richard Haw, Mrs J A Sales, Mrs Brenda Calver, J P Humphery, W A Evershed)*

Free house ~ Licensee Oliver Ligertwood ~ Real ale ~ Bar food (12-2.30, 6.30-10; all day weekends) ~ Restaurant ~ (01243) 811318 ~ Children welcome away from bar area ~ Dogs allowed in bar ~ Open 11-3, 6-11; 11-11 Fri and Sat; 12-10.30 Sun; closed evening 25 Dec ~ Bedrooms: £60S(£70B)/£80S(£100B)

EAST DEAN   TV5597   Map 3

Tiger ♀

Pub (with village centre) signposted – not vividly – from A259 Eastbourne—Seaford; note that there's another East Dean in Sussex, over near Chichester, see above entry; BN20 0DA

In summer particularly, this long, low tiled pub is a lovely place to visit and you can sit outside by the pretty window boxes and flowering climbers and look over the delightful cottage-lined green. Inside, there are just nine tables in the two smallish rooms (candlelit at night) so space at peak times is very limited; best to arrive early for a table as they don't, in the best pub tradition, take bookings. There are low beams hung with pewter and china, polished rustic tables and distinctive antique settles, and old prints and so forth. Harveys Best with guests such as Adnams Broadside and Kings Horsham Best Bitter on handpump, and a good choice of wines with a dozen by the large glass; board games. They get their fish fresh from Hastings, their lamb from the farm on the hill, all vegetables and eggs from another local farm, and meat from the local butcher. From a sensibly short but ever-changing menu, the imaginative food at lunchtime might include welsh rarebit ciabatta (£4.95), a choice of around 14 or more different ploughman's or a bowl of vegetable stew (£6.50), a bowl of feta, hummous, black olives and cherry tomato salad, haddock and leek mornay, downland rabbit with cider and cream or hot smoked salmon and dill fishcakes (all £8.95), rich beef casserole (£9.95), calves liver (£10.95), and fresh whole local lobster (£14.95). At lunchtimes on hot days and bank holidays they usually have only cold food. The South Downs Way is close by so the pub's naturally popular with walkers, and the lane leads on down to a fine stretch of coast culminating in Beachy Head. No children inside. *(Recommended by Kevin Thorpe, Pete Walker, Prof and Mrs S Barnett, Alan Sadler, Michael and Ann Cole, Michael B Griffith, C J Roebuck, Geoff and Molly Betteridge, Ann and Colin Hunt)*

Free house ~ Licensee Nicholas Denyer ~ Real ale ~ Bar food ~ (01323) 423209 ~ Dogs allowed in bar ~ Open 11-3, 6-11; 11-11 Sat; 12-10.30 Sun

EAST HOATHLY TQ5116 Map 3

Foresters Arms

Village signposted off A22 Hailsham—Uckfield (take south-easternmost of the two turn-offs); South Street; BN8 6DS

The new licensees have carried out major refurbishments in this village pub. The small counter between the two small linked rooms has been removed to create more space and there are just a handful of tables (one in a bow window) and dark woodwork; the one on the right has a small art nouveau fireplace under a big mirror. Back from here is a bigger room with a new extended carved wooden bar counter and attractive etched glass mirrors. Piped music, TV, darts and board games. Bar food at lunchtime now includes home-made soup (£3.50), ploughman's (£5.50), brunch or chilli (£6.95), mediterranean pasta (£7.65), and steak in ale pie (£8.95), with evening choices such as smoked duck breast on warm plum sauce (£5.10), moules marinière (£5.95; main course £7.95), battered cod (£7.10), thai vegetable curry (£7.95), tiger prawns provençale (£10.75), beef stroganoff (£13.50), and half a barbary duck (£13.95). The newly carpeted restaurant is no smoking. Harveys Best Bitter, Old and Armada on handpump and up to 15 wines by the glass. The garden has been restructured and there's new furniture under parasols. Full disabled facilities. More reports on the changes, please. *(Recommended by Neil Hardwick, John Beeken)*

Harveys ~ Tenants Ernest and Sandra Wright ~ Real ale ~ Bar food (12-2.30, 6-9.30; not Sun evening) ~ Restaurant ~ (01825) 840208 ~ Children welcome with restrictions ~ Dogs allowed in bar ~ Occasional live music Fri evening ~ Open 11-3, 5-11; 11-11 Sat; 12-10.30 Sun

ELSTED SU8119 Map 2

Three Horseshoes 🍺

Village signposted from B2141 Chichester—Petersfield; also reached easily from A272 about 2 miles W of Midhurst, turning left heading W; GU29 0JY

Now totally no smoking, this 16th-c pub is extremely popular and very well run. Although cosy inside in winter, the garden in summer is lovely with free-roaming bantams, plenty of tables, pretty flowers and stunning views. It's all very friendly and cheerful and the snug little rooms have ancient beams and flooring, antique furnishings, log fires, fresh flowers on the tables, attractive prints and photographs, candlelight, and a very congenial atmosphere. Well liked bar food includes home-made soup (£4.50), a generous ploughman's with a good choice of cheeses or mozzarella and bacon salad or avocado and stilton with mushroom sauce and topped with bacon (£6.95), chicken breast with wild mushrooms and madeira, cottage pie or butternut squash and brie lasagne (all £9.95), seasonal game pie or lamb with apples and apricots (£10.50), and puddings like treacle tart or various cheesecakes (£4.95). Well kept changing ales racked on a stillage behind the bar counter might include Archers Swindon, Ballards Best, Hop Back Summer Lightning and the local Langham Brewery Halfway to Heaven; summer cider; dominoes. *(Recommended by Michael B Griffith, Ann and Colin Hunt, Peter Lewis, Geoff and Linda Payne, W A Evershed, Adrian Wilkes, Paul and Shirley White, R B Gardiner)*

Free house ~ Licensee Sue Beavis ~ Real ale ~ Bar food ~ (01730) 825746 ~ Well behaved children in eating areas ~ Dogs allowed in bar ~ Open 11-2.30, 6-11; 12-3, 7-10.30 Sun

---

'Children welcome' means the pub says it lets children inside without any special restriction. If it allows them in, but to restricted areas such as an eating area or family room, we specify this. Some pubs may impose an evening time limit. We do not mention limits after 9pm as we assume children are home by then.

FITTLEWORTH   TQ0118   Map 2

Swan 🛏

Lower Street; RH20 IEL

In good weather, this pretty tile-hung inn gets very busy. There's a big back lawn with plenty of well spaced tables and flowering shrubs, and benches in front by the village lane; good nearby walks in beech woods. The beamed main bar is comfortable and relaxed with windsor armchairs and bar stools on the part-stripped wood and part-carpeted floor, there are wooden truncheons over the big inglenook fireplace (which has good winter log fires), and Fullers London Pride and Youngs on handpump. The restaurant is no smoking; piped music. Bar food includes lunchtime sandwiches (from £5.95) and ploughman's (£6.75), as well as home-made soup (£4.50), home-made parfait of the day (£5.95), smoked haddock with a rarebit topping on bubble and squeak topped with a poached egg or bangers and mash (£9.95), cajun chicken (£11.95), home-made vegetable samosas (£13.95), and steaks (from £15.95). The pub was about to change hands as we went to press, so any news on the new licensees would be welcome. *(Recommended by BOB)*

Enterprise ~ Real ale ~ Bar food ~ Restaurant ~ (01798) 865429 ~ Children welcome with restrictions ~ Dogs allowed in bar ~ Open 10.30-3, 5-11; 12-4, 7-10.30 Sun ~ Bedrooms: £50B/£85B

FLETCHING   TQ4223   Map 3

Griffin ★ 🍴 🍷 🛏

Village signposted off A272 W of Uckfield; TN22 3SS

Sussex Dining Pub of the Year

By the time this edition is published, the licensees will have bought the house next door, refurbished it, and opened up five extra stylish bedrooms. It's a gently upmarket and civilised old inn and has beamed and quaintly panelled bar rooms with blazing log fires, old photographs and hunting prints, straightforward close-set furniture including some captain's chairs, and china on a delft shelf. There's a small bare-boarded serving area off to one side, and a snug separate bar with sofas and TV; the restaurant is no smoking. As well as weekday lunchtime hot ciabattas (from £5.95), the very good modern cooking might include home-made soup like sweet potato and chilli (£4.95), chicken liver parfait with date and apricot chutney or risotto of pancetta, spinach and pine nuts (£6.50), deep-fried flounder goujons with home-made tartare sauce (£7.50), thai curry with butternut squash, spinach and coconut (£8.50), slow-roasted lamb shanks with champ mash or pasta with chorizo, chilli and tomato and rosemary sauce (£9.50), moules frites (£9.95), local beer-battered cod or wild boar sausages on chorizo and chickpea stew (£10.50), honey-glazed confit of duck, puy lentils, coriander, sweet potato and spinach (£12.50) and rib-eye steak with home-made chips and red onion confit (£15.95), with puddings such as pear tarte tatin, vanilla and grappa panna cotta with spiced apricot and almond compote or sticky toffee pudding with caramel sauce (£4.95). Well kept Badger Tanglefoot, Harveys Best and Kings Horsham Best Bitter on handpump, and a fine wine list with 14 (including champagne) by the glass; efficient, friendly young service. The two acres of garden behind the pub look across fine rolling countryside towards Sheffield Park, and there are plenty of seats here and on the sandstone terrace with its woodburning oven. *(Recommended by Tom and Ruth Rees, Joel Dobris, David Cosham, Mike Gorton, Grahame Brooks, Andy Booth, Mike and Mary Carter, Ann and Colin Hunt, Philip Vernon, Kim Maidment, Uta and John Owlett, Susan May, N R White, Kenneth Gervase-Williams, Edward Faridany, Simon Rodway)*

Free house ~ Licensees J Pullan, T Erlam, M W Wright ~ Real ale ~ Bar food (12-2.30, 7-9.30) ~ Restaurant ~ (01825) 722890 ~ Children welcome ~ Dogs allowed in bar ~ Duo Fri evening and Sun lunchtime ~ Open 12-1am(1.30am Fri and Sat); 12-midnight Sun; closed 25 Dec and evening 1 Jan ~ Bedrooms: £60B/£95B

HEATHFIELD   TQ5920   Map 3
Star ㉕ ◣

Old Heathfield – head East out of Heathfield itself on A265, then fork right on to B2096; turn right at signpost to Heathfield Church then keep bearing right; pub on left immediately after church; TN21 9AH

With a warm welcome from the cheerful staff and a really good chatty and pubby atmosphere, it's not surprising that this fine old pub is so popular. There's always a good mix of locals and visitors and the L-shaped beamed bar has a roaring winter log fire in the inglenook fireplace, panelling, built-in wall settles and window seats, and just four or five tables; a doorway leads into a similarly furnished smaller room. The tables are candlelit at night. Chalked up on boards, the well liked food (with prices unchanged since last year) might include home-made soup (£4.75), home-made chicken liver or smoked mackerel pâté (£5.75), moules marinière (£6.50; main course £8.50), home-cooked ham and two free-range eggs (£7.95), cold meats and bubble and squeak (£8.50), home-made steak and mushroom pie or local fish and chips (£8.75), cumberland sausage with red wine and onion gravy (£9.50), pasta tossed with smoked salmon, sun-dried tomatoes, greek olives, basil, garlic and cream (£10.25), half a shoulder of lamb in rosemary, garlic and redcurrant (£13.95), and half a free-range duckling with tangy honey and orange sauce (£14.95); efficient, courteous service. You must book to be sure of a table (and get there early to bag a parking space in the car park). Well kept Harveys Best, Shepherd Neame Best Bitter and a guest such as Welton Old Harry on handpump, half a dozen wines by the glass, Pimms by the jug, and a good bloody mary; piped music, shove-ha'penny, cribbage and bar billiards. The garden is very prettily planted, there's rustic furniture under smart umbrellas, and lovely views of rolling oak-lined sheep pastures. Turner thought it fine enough to paint. *(Recommended by Kevin Thorpe, Mr and Mrs Hale, Susan and John Douglas, Nigel Bowles, Ron Gentry)*

Free house ~ Licensees Mike Chappell and Fiona Airey ~ Real ale ~ Bar food (12-2.15, 7-9.30) ~ Restaurant ~ (01435) 863570 ~ Children in eating area of bar ~ Dogs welcome ~ Open 11.30-3, 5.30-11; 12-4, 7-10.30 Sun; closed evenings 25 and 26 Dec

HERMITAGE   SU7505   Map 2
Sussex Brewery

A259 just inside Sussex boundary, by Thorney Island turn just W of Emsworth; PO10 8AU

There's usually quite a mix of customers in this cheerful pub, just a stroll from the waterside. The bar is quite small, with sawdust (yes, real sawdust) on bare boards, an old wing armchair by the huge brick fireplace (with a good winter log fire – there's a second little blue-tiled Victorian fireplace opposite it, also used), simple seats, four tables (two painted as inn signs, one as thrown-down playing cards), and small brewery mirrors on yellowing walls. Well kept Youngs Bitter, Special, Waggle Dance and a seasonal beer, and guests such as Marstons Pedigree and St Austell Tribute on handpump from the dark brick counter, and quite a few wines by the glass. At the end of the bar, a little flagstoned snug with small polished pews around just two tables is kept food-free at night; piped music, darts and cribbage. Down a flagstoned passage, a small pink-walled carpeted back no smoking dining room has comfortable plush chairs, and there's a second little no smoking dining room overlooking the garden. The main event on the menu is the speciality sausages, over 40 different and often unusual varieties such as chicken, orange and walnut, ostrich, duck with cognac and port, pigeon, brandy, herbs and quince jelly, and local pork with real ale, cheese and grain mustard (from £6.10). Also, filled baked potatoes (from £4.25), ploughman's (from £5.95), steak and mushroom in ale pudding (£7.25), poached smoked haddock (£10.90), and steaks (from £14.50). There are picnic-sets in a small enclosed back courtyard, with one or two more out by the side. More reports please. *(Recommended by Ian Phillips, Steve Whalley, Tracey and Stephen Groves, Ann and Colin Hunt, John Beeken, Mike and Mary Carter)*

Youngs ~ Tenant David Roberts ~ Real ale ~ Bar food (12-2.30, 7-10(9.30 Sun)) ~ Restaurant ~ (01243) 371533 ~ Children welcome ~ Dogs allowed in bar ~ Open 11-11; closed evening 25 Dec

HORSHAM   TQ1730   Map 3
Black Jug ♀
31 North Street; RH12 1RJ

Now totally no smoking, this is an airy, open-plan, turn-of-the-century-style room with a large central bar. There's a nice collection of sizeable dark wood tables and comfortable chairs on a stripped wood floor, the cream walls are crammed with interesting old prints and photographs above a dark wood panelled dado, and there's a warm terracotta ceiling. A spacious conservatory has similar furniture and lots of hanging baskets; piped music. Well kept Adnams Broadside, Camerons Strongarm, Greene King Old Speckled Hen, Hydes Jekylls Gold Premium, and Weltons Bitter on handpump, 40 malt whiskies, lots of gins, vodkas and rums; most wines on the list are available by the glass. Bar food includes soup (£3.90), chicken liver and port pâté (£5.50), smoked haddock and salmon kedgeree with poached egg or ploughman's (£6.95), chicken caesar salad, bangers and mash or home-baked ham and eggs (£8.95), grilled pork chop with stilton and bitter rarebit with black pudding mash (£9.95), roast breast of corn-fed chicken with crispy potato cake and creamy lentils (£10.50), roasted rump of lamb with rosemary cream (£14.95), and home-made puddings such as crème brûlée with home-made shortbread or chocolate fondant with blackcurrant compote (£4.95). The pretty flower-filled back terrace has plenty of garden furniture by outside heaters. The small car park is for staff and deliveries only but you can park next door in the council car park. More reports please. (*Recommended by Mark Killman, Dave Lowe*)

Brunning & Price ~ Manager Myles Abell ~ Real ale ~ Bar food (all day) ~ (01403) 253526 ~ Well behaved children allowed but no prams; no under-21s in evening ~ Dogs allowed in bar ~ Open 12-11; 12-10.30 Sun

ICKLESHAM   TQ8716   Map 3
Queens Head ♀ ◧
Just off A259 Rye—Hastings; TN36 4BL

This is an extremely well run place and even when really busy – which it deservedly often is – the staff remain friendly and efficient. The open-plan areas work round a very big serving counter which stands under a vaulted beamed roof, the high beamed walls and ceiling of the easy-going bar are lined with shelves of bottles and covered with farming implements and animal traps, and there are well used pub tables and old pews on the brown patterned carpet. Other areas (two are no smoking and popular with diners) have big inglenook fireplaces, and the back room is decorated with old bicycle and motorbike prints. Well kept Courage Directors and Greene King IPA and Abbot, with guests like Tring Ridgeway, Westerham British Bulldog and Whitstable Wheat Beer on handpump, Biddenden cider, and a dozen wines by the glass. Reasonably priced, decent home-made bar food includes sandwiches (from £2.75), soup (£3.95), filled baked potatoes (from £4.50), chicken liver pâté (£4.75), ploughman's (from £5.50), ham and eggs (£6.50), roasted vegetable and lentil gratin (£7.25), lasagne (£7.95), steak and mushroom in ale pie or leek and haddock mornay (£8.45), curry (£9.25), and steaks (from £10.95). Shove-ha'penny, dominoes, cribbage, darts, games machine and piped music. Picnic-sets look out over the vast, gently sloping plain of the Brede Valley from the little garden, and there's an outside children's play area, and boules. Good local walks. (*Recommended by Kevin Thorpe, Ian and Nita Cooper, Peter Meister, Stephen Harvey, N R White, E D Bailey, Christopher Turner, Michael and Ann Cole, Bruce Bird, Steve Godfrey, Lucien Perring*)

Free house ~ Licensee Ian Mitchell ~ Real ale ~ Bar food (12-2.30, 6-9.30; all day Sat, Sun and bank hols; not 25 or 26 Dec) ~ (01424) 814552 ~ Well behaved children in eating area of bar until 8.30pm ~ Dogs welcome ~ Open 11-11; 12-10.30 Sun; closed 25 and 26 Dec

LODSWORTH SU9223 Map 2
Halfway Bridge Inn ♀ ⇋
Just before village, on A272 Midhurst—Petworth; GU28 9BP

New licensees again for this civilised inn. The three or four bar rooms are
comfortably furnished with good oak chairs and an individual mix of tables, and
down some steps is the no smoking restaurant area; one of the log fires is contained
in a well polished kitchen range. Arundel Gold, Ringwood Best and Skinners Betty
Stogs on handpump and 14 wines by the glass; piped music. From a sensibly short
menu, the bar food now includes soup (£4.95), lunchtime sandwiches (£5.25), tuna
and sweet potato fishcakes with fresh mango salsa (£6.50), fillet of beef and pâté
filo parcel on a lightly spiced cauliflower purée (£9.95), butternut squash and wild
mushroom risotto (£10), lamb kofta burger (£10.50), fillet of salmon in black
sesame seeds with a ginger, soy and coriander sauce on stir-fried noodles or calves
liver and bacon (£13), scottish rib-eye steak with pink peppercorn sauce (£14.95),
and puddings such as coconut crème brûlée or baked blueberry cheesecake drizzled
with a sharp lime syrup (from £5.25). At the back there are seats on a small terrace.
More reports on the new regime, please. *(Recommended by Darren and Jane Staniforth,
Mrs L Aquilina, Colin McKerrow, Martin and Karen Wake, Ann and Colin Hunt)*

Free house ~ Licensee Paul Carter ~ Real ale ~ Bar food ~ Restaurant ~ (01798) 861281
~ Children welcome ~ Dogs allowed in bar ~ Open 11-11; 12-10.30 Sun ~
Bedrooms: £65B/£100B

OVING SU9005 Map 2
Gribble Inn 🍺
**Between A27 and A259 just E of Chichester, then should be signposted just off village
road; OS Sheet 197 map reference 900050; PO20 2BP**

There's a cottagey feel in the several linked rooms of this 16th-c thatched pub –
each with huge winter log fires. The chatty bar has lots of heavy beams and
timbering and old country-kitchen furnishings and pews, and as the pub is owned
by Badger, you might find the own brewed real ales from here at other pubs owned
by the brewery as well. Their own brews include Gribble Ale, Pigs Ear, Plucking
Pheasant, Reg's Tipple, and winter Wobbler, and they also keep Badger First Gold
and Fursty Ferret on handpump. Decent wine and farm cider. The dining room and
family room are no smoking. Bar food includes lunchtime sandwiches (from £4.95),
ploughman's (£5.75), ham and eggs (£7.25), vegetarian pasta (£8.50), sausage and
mash, beer-battered fish or steak, ale and mushroom pie (£8.95), steaks (from
£11.95), and puddings (£4.25). Cribbage, dominoes, and a separate skittle alley.
Seats outside under a covered area, and more chairs in the pretty garden with apple
and pear trees; at the end of the garden are some rabbits and a hamster.
*(Recommended by Val and Alan Green, R G Trevis, Susan and John Douglas, PL,
David H T Dimock, Mike and Lynn Robinson, Ann and Colin Hunt, Roy and Lindsey Fentiman,
Peter Titcomb)*

Own brew ~ Tenants Dave and Linda Stone ~ Real ale ~ Bar food (12-2.30, 6-9.30; all day
Sun) ~ Restaurant ~ (01243) 786893 ~ Children welcome away from bar ~ Dogs allowed
in bar ~ Jazz first Tues of month, live bands last Fri of month ~ Open 11-3, 5.30-11; 11-11
Sat; 12-10.30 Sun

PETWORTH SU9921 Map 2
Welldiggers Arms
Low Heath; A283 towards Pulborough; GU28 0HG

Under the eye of the long-serving, hands-on landlord, this remains a well run
country pub with an unassuming style and appearance. The smallish L-shaped bar
has low beams, a few pictures (Churchill and gun dogs are prominent) on shiny
ochre walls above a panelled dado, a couple of very long rustic settles with tables to
match, and some other stripped tables (many are laid for eating); a second rather
lower side room has a somewhat lighter décor. No music or machines. Youngs on

handpump, and decent wines. Popular home-made food includes sandwiches (from £3.50), ploughman's (£6.50), salmon and herb fishcakes with chilli dressing (£5.95; main course £12.95), bangers and mash with giant onion rings or aubergine stuffed with roasted vegetables and topped with brie (£8.95), bass fillets with braised fennel, crispy bacon and lemon hollandaise (£12.95), and calves liver (£14.50). Outside, screened from the road by a thick high hedge, are plenty of tables and chairs on pleasant lawns and a terrace, looking back over rolling fields and woodland. *(Recommended by Terry Buckland, Mrs D W Privett, Mrs J A Sales, Peter Lewis, James Marchant)*

Free house ~ Licensee Ted Whitcomb ~ Real ale ~ Bar food (see opening hours) ~ Restaurant ~ (01798) 342287 ~ Children welcome ~ Dogs welcome ~ Open 11-3.30, 6-11; closed Mon; closed Tues, Weds and Sun evenings

RINGMER   TQ4313   Map 3
Cock
Uckfield Road – blocked-off section of road off A26 N of village turn-off; BN8 5RX

Whether you are dining or popping into this 16th-c coaching house for a pint and a chat, the friendly licensees will make you welcome. The unspoilt, heavily beamed bar has traditional pubby furniture on flagstones, a log fire in the inglenook fireplace, and well kept Harveys Sussex Best and Mild (or Old in season) with guests like Fullers London Pride or Marstons Pedigree on handpump and ten wines by the glass. Enjoyable, reasonably priced bar food includes filled sun-dried tomato and olive oil rolls (from £3), home-made soup (£3.75), home-made chicken liver pâté (£3.95), grilled fresh sardines (£4.50), ploughman's (£4.75), ham and egg (£5.75), chicken curry, steak and kidney pudding or mixed nut roast (£7.50), pork fillet in a creamy mustard sauce (£8.50), steaks (from £8.95), fresh tuna steak with a tomato and basil sauce (£9.75), half a crispy duck with cumberland sauce (£12.95), and puddings such as rhubarb crumble, sticky toffee, date and walnut sponge or white and dark chocolate terrine (£3.95). The dining areas are no smoking; piped music. The ruby king charles cavalier is called Fred. There are lots of picnic-sets on the terrace and in the garden and views across open fields to the South Downs. *(Recommended by Tony and Wendy Hobden, John Beeken, P W Taylor, Steve Godfrey)*

Free house ~ Licensees Ian and Matt Ridley ~ Real ale ~ Bar food (12-2, 6-9.30; all day Sun) ~ Restaurant ~ (01273) 812040 ~ Children welcome ~ Dogs allowed in bar ~ Open 11-3, 6-11.30; 11am-11.30pm Sun

RUSHLAKE GREEN   TQ6218   Map 3
Horse & Groom
Village signposted off B2096 Heathfield—Battle; TN21 9QE

Now owned by Shepherd Neame and stocking their beers, this country pub is in an attractive setting by the village green. The little L-shaped bar has low beams (watch your head) and is simply furnished with high bar stools and bar chairs, red plush cushioned wall seats and a few brocaded cushioned stools, and there's a brick fireplace with some brass items on the mantelpiece; horsebrasses, photographs of the pub and local scenes on the walls. A small room down a step has jockeys' colours and jockey photographs and watercolours of the pub. To the right of the entrance is the heavily beamed no smoking restaurant with guns and hunting trophies on the walls, plenty of wheelback chairs around pubby tables, and a log fire. Listed on boards by the entrance to the bar, the large choice of popular bar food (at prices unchanged since last year) might include home-made soup (£4.50), home-made chicken liver pâté (£5.50), asparagus sautéed with crispy pancetta and a smoked mozzarella croûton (£6.95), fresh scallops with spring onions, bacon and buttery oyster sauce in a puff pastry shell (£7.95), steak and kidney in Guinness pudding (£10.95), organic salmon fishcakes (£11.95), red thai tiger prawn curry (£12.95), and marinated chump of lamb on dauphinoise potatoes with port wine sauce (£15.95). Well kept Shepherd Neame Master Brew and Spitfire on handpump, and several wines by the glass; piped music. The cottagey garden has oak seats and tables made by the landlord and pretty country views. More reports please. *(Recommended by John Bell, Ron Gentry, William Ruxton)*

Shepherd Neame ~ Tenants Mike and Sue Chappel ~ Real ale ~ Bar food ~ Restaurant ~ (01435) 830320 ~ Children welcome ~ Dogs welcome ~ Open 11.30-3, 5.30(6 Sat)-11; 12-3, 7-10.30 Sun; closed evening 25 Dec

RYE   TQ9220   Map 3
Mermaid ♀ 🛏
Mermaid Street; TN31 7EY

The sign outside this lovely black and white timbered hotel says 'rebuilt in 1420', and the cellars are two or three centuries older than that. It's extremely civilised with prices to match, and the little bar is where those in search of a light lunch and a drink tend to go: a fair mix of quite closely set furnishings such as Victorian gothic carved oak chairs, older but plainer oak seats, and a massive deeply polished bressumer beam across one wall for the huge inglenook fireplace. Three antique but not ancient wall paintings show old English scenes. Well kept Courage Best and Greene King Old Speckled Hen on handpump, a good wine list, and a short choice of bar food such as sandwiches (from £6), open goats cheese and spinach omelette or moules marinière (£8.50), minute steak with blue cheese salad (£10.50), seafood platter for two (£29), and puddings (£6). The smart (expensive) restaurant is no smoking; piped music (bar only), dominoes and cribbage. Seats on a small back terrace overlook the car park – where there are morris dancers on bank holiday weekends. *(Recommended by Nick Lawless, Joel Dobris, N R White, the Didler)*

Free house ~ Licensees Robert Pinwill and Mrs J Blincow ~ Real ale ~ Bar food (12-2.30, 7-9.30) ~ Restaurant ~ (01797) 223065 ~ Children in main bar only ~ Open 12-11 ~ Bedrooms: £85S(£90B)/£180B

SALEHURST   TQ7424   Map 3
Salehurst Halt ♀
Village signposted from Robertsbridge bypass on A21 Tunbridge Wells—Battle Road; TN32 5PH

Two local families have bought this little pub and have redecorated it and renovated the kitchen. It's now totally no smoking and the L-shaped beamed bar has sofas and chairs by the little open brick fireplace on the right, and to the left are plain wooden tables and chairs on the new oak floor; a half wall leads to the dining area. They were still finding their feet with regards to the food as we went to press, but might include baguettes (£4), lamb goujons (£4.50), ploughman's (£6), ham and eggs, local sausages or popular home-made pork pie (£6.50), and fishcakes with home-made tartare sauce (£7); a set two-course (£13) and three-course (£17) menu might have spicy courgette and chickpea burger or braised shin of beef with field mushrooms. Well kept Harveys Best and maybe a guest beer on handpump; piped music and board games. The charming and pretty back garden now has an extended terrace giving more space for eating. More reports on the changes, please. *(Recommended by Ian and Nita Cooper, Brian Root, Pamela and Douglas Cooper, Kevin Thorpe, M Sage)*

Free house ~ Licensee Andrew Augarde ~ Real ale ~ Bar food (not Mon) ~ Restaurant ~ (01580) 880620 ~ Children welcome ~ Dogs allowed in bar ~ Open 12-3, 6.30-11 (10.30 Sun); 12-11 Sat; closed Mon

---

Cribbage is a card game using a block of wood with holes for matchsticks or special pins to score with; regulars in cribbage pubs are usually happy to teach strangers how to play.

SINGLETON   SU8713   Map 2

Partridge

Just off A286 Midhurst—Chichester; heading S into the village, the main road bends sharp right – keep straight ahead instead; if you miss this turn, take the Charlton road, then first left; PO18 0EY

This pretty black and white pub dates from the 16th c. There are polished wooden floors, flagstones and daily papers, some small rooms with red settles and good winter log fires, and a roomy back dining extension. Much of the pub is no smoking. As well as lunchtime dishes such as home-made soup (£5.50), pâté or cheese platter with pickles (£7.50), pasta of the day (£9.95), lambs liver and bacon or gammon with mustard and rosemary (£10.50), and steak in ale pie (£10.95), there are daily specials such as bean cassoulet or salmon and cornish crab fishcakes (£9.95), pork loin steak with cheese and home-grown crab apple jelly (£10.50), and duck breast with a port and citrus sauce (£11.95), with puddings like home-made chocolate brownies, raspberry pavlova and spotted dick (£4.50). Fullers London Pride, Hepworths Sussex, and Ringwood Best on handpump, and decent wines by the glass; piped music. There's a terrace and a big walled garden with colourful flowerbeds and fruit trees. The Weald & Downland Open Air Museum is just down the road, and Goodwood Racecourse is not far away. *(Recommended by Tom and Ruth Rees, Sue and Mike Todd, Dick and Madeleine Brown, Ann and Colin Hunt, Prof and Mrs S Barnett, Lionel and Sylvia Kopelowitz, W A Evershed)*

Enterprise ~ Lease Tony Simpson ~ Real ale ~ Bar food (all day weekends) ~ Restaurant ~ (01243) 811251 ~ Children welcome with restrictions ~ Dogs allowed in bar ~ Trad jazz third Tues of month ~ Open 11.30-3, 6-11; 11.30-11 Sat; 12-11 Sun

TROTTON   SU8323   Map 2

Keepers Arms

A272 Midhurst—Petersfield; pub tucked up above road, on S side; GU31 5ER

There's certainly plenty of interest in this individually decorated, no smoking pub. A north african-style room has a cushioned bench around all four walls, a large central table, rare ethnic fabrics and weavings, and a big moroccan lamp. The walls throughout are decorated with some unusual pictures and artefacts that reflect Jenny's previous long years of travelling the world, and the beamed L-shaped bar has timbered walls and some standing timbers, sofas by the big log fire, and ethnic rugs scattered on the oak floor. Elsewhere, there are a couple of unusual adult high chairs at an oak refectory table, two huge Georgian leather high-backed chairs around another table, an interesting medley of old or antique seats, and dining tables decorated with pretty candelabra, and bowls of fruit and chillis. Interesting piped music (which they change according to the customers) ranges from Buddha bar-type music to classical. Bar food includes deep-fried camembert with hot cranberry sauce or home-made soup (£4.50), thai-style fishcake with chilli dipping sauce (£5), home-made duck liver and foie gras pâté (£6), lunchtime cheese and hot ham platter (for two people, £7 each), moules marinière or sausage and egg (£7.50), chargrilled chicken fillet (£8), and chargrilled fillet steak rossini (£16.50). Ballards Best, Cheriton Pots Ale and Ringwood Fortyniner on handpump, and decent wines. Plenty of seats on the attractive, almost mediterranean-feeling south facing front terrace. Dogs lunchtime only. *(Recommended by Liz and Brian Barnard, Mrs L Aquilina, M and GR, John Evans, Prof and Mrs S Barnett, Michael and Ann Cole, Martin and Karen Wake, Karen Eliot, Mrs Phoebe A Kemp, W A Evershed)*

Free house ~ Licensee Jenny Oxley ~ Real ale ~ Bar food (not Sun evening, Mon) ~ Restaurant ~ (01730) 813724 ~ Children welcome ~ Dogs welcome ~ Open 12-3, 6.30-11; 12-3 Sun; closed Sun evening, all Mon (except bank hols); 24 Dec; first Tues in Jan

---

If you stay overnight in an inn or hotel, they are allowed to serve you an alcoholic drink at any hour of the day or night.

WARTLING TQ6509 Map 3
Lamb ♀

Village signposted with Herstmonceux Castle off A271 Herstmonceux—Battle;
BN27 1RY

Locals tend to gather for a pint and a chat in the little entrance bar of this pleasant pub: brocaded settles and stools and just a few tables on the green patterned carpet, a big blackboard with specials of the day, and a woodburning stove with logs stacked to one side. A narrow tiled floor area runs along the carved bar counter, and leads to the snug (mind your head on the low entrance beam) with a mix of cushioned chairs and more brocaded settles around straightforward pubby tables, and beams and timbering. The lounge has a mix of sofas and armchairs around low tables by the fireplace, and there's a restaurant, too. Doors from here lead up steps to a back terrace with green picnic-sets, climbers on the gazebo, and flowering tubs and pots. Gribble Toffs, Harveys Sussex Best, and a guest from Kings on handpump, ten wines by the glass (including champagne), and friendly, helpful staff. Well liked bar food might include soup with herb croûtons (£4.25), tartlet of fresh crab and gruyère cheese with a sweet chilli dressing (£6.25), vegetable casserole (£9.95), braised lamb shank with rosemary mash (£11.95), chicken with a smoked bacon and mushroom cream sauce or duck cassoulet (£12.95), local lamb cutlets with a madeira and herb jus (£15.50), fresh fish dishes, and puddings such as chocolate and praline bread and butter pudding or blackcurrant and vanilla crème brûlée (£4.95). The eating areas are no smoking; best to book to be sure of a table. There are seats out in front. *(Recommended by Jenny and Peter Lowater, Ian and Nita Cooper, Geoff and Marion Cooper, Sue Demont, Tim Barrow, David Thompson, Tony and Wendy Hobden, Roy and Lindsey Fentiman, Colin and Janet Roe)*

Free house ~ Licensees Robert and Alison Farncombe ~ Bar food (11.45-2.15, 6.45-9) ~ Restaurant ~ (01323) 832116 ~ Children in eating areas ~ Dogs allowed in bar ~ Open 11(12 Sun)-3, 6-11

WILMINGTON TQ5404 Map 3
Giants Rest

Just off A27; BN26 5SQ

This comfortable no smoking pub is watched over by the impressive chalk-carved Long Man of Wilmington at the foot of the South Downs; it's a popular place to come after a walk. The long wood-floored bar and adjacent open areas, one with a log fire, are simply furnished with old pews and pine tables – each with its own bar game or wooden puzzle; well kept Harveys Best, Hop Back Summer Lightning and Timothy Taylors Landlord on handpump. Popular bar food includes soup (£3.50), baked field mushroom with goats cheese, pesto and garlic or garlic king prawns with lemon and lime salsa (£5), baked camembert in a box with crusty bread (for two, £6.50), filled baked potatoes or ploughman's (from £6.50), spinach, peanut and sweet potato stew (£8.50), hake, coriander, chilli, ginger and spring onion fishcakes, rabbit pie or home-cooked ham with bubble and squeak with home-made chutney (all £8.50), rack of lamb with a pistachio crust and red wine gravy (£12), and home-made puddings like sticky date and walnut pudding or apple and blackberry crumble (£4). Sunday lunchtime is especially busy and there may not be much space for those just wanting a drink as most of the tables are booked by diners; piped music. Plenty of seats in the front garden, and Elizabeth David the famous cookery writer is buried in the churchyard at nearby Folkington; her headstone is beautifully carved and features mediterranean vegetables and a casserole. More reports please. *(Recommended by PL, Fr Robert Marsh, Kevin Thorpe, Guy Vowles, Grahame Brooks, John Beeken, M and R Thomas, Paul Hopton, Anthony Longden)*

Free house ~ Licensees Adrian and Rebecca Hillman ~ Real ale ~ Bar food ~ Restaurant ~ (01323) 870207 ~ Children welcome ~ Dogs welcome ~ Open 11-3, 6-11; 11-11 Sat; 12-10.30 Sun

WINEHAM   TQ2320   Map 3
Royal Oak £
Village signposted from A272 and B2116; BN5 9AY

One reader was delighted to find this welcoming and old-fashioned local quite unchanged since his last visit in 1966. It's been in the same family for over 50 years, and still has no fruit machines, piped music or even beer pumps. Logs burn in an enormous inglenook fireplace with a cast-iron Royal Oak fireback, and there's a collection of cigarette cards showing old English pubs, a stuffed stoat and crocodile, a collection of jugs, ancient corkscrews decorating the very low beams above the serving counter, and racing plates, tools and a coach horn on the walls; maybe a nice tabby cat, and views of quiet countryside from the back parlour. Well kept Harveys Best with a guest such as Wadworths 6X tapped from the cask in a still room; darts and board games. Bar snacks are limited to home-made winter soup (£2.75), simple sandwiches (from £2.50), and ploughman's (from £5). There are some picnic-sets outside – picturesque if you are facing the pub. *(Recommended by Richard May, Terry Buckland, Barry and Sue Pladdys, Lucy Wild, N R White, Jude Wright)*

Punch ~ Tenant Tim Peacock ~ Real ale ~ Bar food (served during opening hours) ~ No credit cards ~ (01444) 881252 ~ Children allowed away from main bar ~ Dogs allowed in bar ~ Open 11-2.30, 5.30(6 Sat)-11; 12-3, 7-10.30 Sun

---

LUCKY DIP

Besides the fully inspected pubs, you might like to try these Lucky Dips recommended to us and described by readers (if you do, please send us reports: www.goodguides.co.uk).

ALFRISTON [TQ5203]
☆ *Olde Smugglers* BN26 5UE [Waterloo Sq]: Cottagey low-beamed décor with big inglenook in white-panelled bar, plenty of bric-a-brac and smuggling mementoes, good value bar food from sandwiches to steaks, Courage Directors, Harveys and interesting guest beers, good choice of wines by the glass, good friendly service; can get crowded as this lovely village draws many visitors; children allowed in eating area and conservatory, nice well planted back suntrap terrace *(LYM, MLR, Tracey and Stephen Groves, Michael and Ann Cole)*
☆ *Star* BN26 5TA [High St]: Fascinating fine painted medieval carvings outside, heavy-beamed old-fashioned bar (busy lunchtime, quiet evenings) with some interesting features inc medieval sanctuary post, antique furnishings and big log fire in Tudor fireplace, easy chairs in comfortable lounge, Bass, Fullers London Pride and Harveys Best, decent wines by the glass, good coffee and service, daily papers and magazines, more space behind for eating, food from sandwiches and baked potatoes to restaurant dishes; good modern bedrooms in up-to-date part behind, open all day summer *(LYM, the Didler, Mr and Mrs John Taylor, Ann and Colin Hunt)*
AMBERLEY [TQ0313]
☆ *Sportsmans* BN18 9NR [Crossgates; Rackham Rd, off B2139]: Great views over Amberley Wild Brooks, enjoyable reasonably priced food cooked to order (so may be a wait), sandwiches too, welcoming well organised staff, changing real ales such as Harveys Best and Hogs Back TEA, lots of wines by the glass,

three bars and pretty little back conservatory; piped music; children welcome, good walks, bedrooms *(Sue Demont, Tim Barrow, LYM, Richard May, Tony and Wendy Hobden, Martin and Karen Wake, David H T Dimock, Francis Vernon, Cathy Robinson, Ed Coombe, Ron Gentry, Jason Caulkin, C and R Bromage)*
ANGMERING [TQ0604]
Lamb BN16 4EQ [The Square]: Helpful staff in relaxed and friendly village pub with well spaced tables, lots of bric-a-brac and big fireplace, enjoyable reasonably priced bar food inc sandwiches and lots of specials (not Sun-Tues evenings), Harveys Best, Shepherd Neame Spitfire and Youngs, low-priced coffee; unobtrusive piped music, live Sat *(Bruce Bird, Tony and Wendy Hobden)*
☆ *Spotted Cow* BN16 4AW [High St]: Good interesting generous food (very popular wkdy lunchtimes with older people) from sandwiches up, several real ales such as Fullers, Greene King, Harveys, Marstons Pedigree and Ringwood, good choice of wines by the glass, friendly and enthusiastic chef/landlord, smallish bar on left, long dining area with large no smoking conservatory on right, two log fires, smuggling history, sporting caricatures, no piped music; children welcome, big garden with boules and play area; open all day Sun, afternoon jazz sometimes then, lovely walk to Highdown hill fort *(Derek and Heather Manning, W W Burke)*
ARDINGLY [TQ3429]
Ardingly Inn RH17 6UA [Street Lane, off B2028]: Spacious and comfortable brightly lit lounge, warm and friendly, with big central log fire, full Badger ale range, good choice of wines

by the glass, attractively presented plentiful food from sandwiches and baguettes to interesting restaurant dishes and Sun lunch, attentive service, restaurant, second bar with pool; piped music; dogs allowed, reasonably priced bedrooms *(Kim Lo, Tony Hobden, Ron Gentry)*

Gardeners Arms RH17 6TJ [B2028 2 miles N]: Olde-worlde food pub reopened after extensive refurbishment, linked rooms with standing timbers and inglenooks, scrubbed pine furniture on flagstones and broad boards, lots of old local photographs, daily papers, Badger beers from new bar counter, pleasant efficient service, hearty reasonably priced pub food, new back dining area (former kitchen) with appropriate mural; attractive wooden furniture on pretty terrace, lots of picnic-sets in side garden, opp S of England show ground and handy for Borde Hill and Wakehurst Place, open all day at least at wknds *(Susan and John Douglas, BB, David Coleman)*

ARLINGTON [TQ5407]

Yew Tree BN26 6RX [off A22 nr Hailsham, or A27 W of Polegate]: Neatly modernised two-bar Victorian village local popular for generous food (can ask for smaller helpings) from hot filled rolls and small range of starters to much wider choice of main dishes, Harveys Best (not cheap here), log fires, prompt service even when busy, darts, no smoking conservatory; children welcome, good big garden with play area by paddock with farm animals, good walks *(Graham and Carol Uren, BB, Fr Robert Marsh, John Beeken, Andy Seares)*

ARUNDEL [TQ0208]

☆ *Black Rabbit* BN18 9PB [Mill Rd, Offham; keep on and don't give up!]: Long nicely refurbished riverside pub very popular with families – lovely spot nr wildfowl reserve, lots of tables outside, timeless views of water-meadows and castle; enjoyable food range, Badger real ales, good choice of decent wines by the glass, friendly service, log fires; doubles as summer tea shop, with summer boat trips, good walks, open all day *(Susan and John Douglas, LYM)*

☆ *Swan* BN18 9AG [High St]: Smart but relaxed open-plan L-shaped bar with attractive woodwork and matching fittings, friendly efficient young staff, good choice of good value food from baguettes and baked potatoes to restaurant meals, Fullers London Pride and Gales BB and HSB, sporting bric-a-brac and old photographs, beaten brass former inn-sign on wall, restaurant; good bedrooms, open all day *(Paul Rampton, Bruce Bird, LYM, Sue and Mike Todd)*

ASHURST [TQ1816]

☆ *Fountain* BN44 3AP [B2135 S of Partridge Green]: Attractive and well run 16th-c country local with fine old flagstones, friendly rustic tap room on right with some antique polished trestle tables and housekeeper's chairs by inglenook log fire, second inglenook in opened-up heavy-beamed snug, attentive young staff, interesting blackboard food as well as pub

staples, Fullers London Pride, Harveys and Kings Horsham; dogs welcome, no under-10s, prettily planted garden with duck pond *(David Field, LYM, Pete Walker, Terry Buckland, PL, M Sage)*

BARCOMBE [TQ4416]

Anchor BN8 5BS [Barcombe Mills]: Nice for summer, with lots of lawn tables by winding River Ouse (boat or canoe hire), ice-creams, quiet walks; two beamed bars carefully reworked in pleasant simple style, Badger Best and Tanglefoot and Harveys Best, unpretentious food inc enjoyable specials, restaurant (bookings only), traditional games, small front conservatory; open all day *(Ann and Colin Hunt, LYM, Sue Demont, Tim Barrow)*

BERWICK [TQ5206]

Berwick Inn BN26 6SZ [by station]: Genial hands-on landlord who doesn't forget faces in roomy and rambling pub with cheery family emphasis and partly no smoking eating areas, good choice of decent food all day, Harveys Best, quick helpful service, log fire, pool in upper front games room, conservatory; piped music; large garden behind with good playground and attractive Perspex-roofed garden bar *(Paul A Moore, LYM)*

BILLINGSHURST [TQ0830]

☆ *Blue Ship* RH14 9BS [The Haven; hamlet signposted off A29 just N of junction with A264, then follow signpost left towards Garlands and Okehurst]: Unpretentious pub in quiet country spot, beamed and brick-floored front bar with blazing inglenook log fire, scrubbed tables and wall benches, Badger ales served from hatch, limited home-made food, two small carpeted back rooms (no smoking), darts, bar billiards, shove-ha'penny, cribbage, dominoes, reasonably priced traditional bar food (not Sun or Mon evenings), no mobile phones; no credit cards; children in one back room, seats by trees or tangle of honeysuckle around front door *(Phil and Sally Gorton, LYM, the Didler, Roy and Lindsey Fentiman, S G N Bennett, Peter Lewis)*

BOARSHEAD [TQ5332]

Boars Head TN6 3HD [Eridge Rd, off A26 bypass]: Attractive old unspoilt pub with good friendly service, good value fresh food, Adnams, Fullers London Pride and Harveys Best, separate restaurant; nice grounds, picturesquely ageing outbuildings *(Michael and Ann Cole, Ian Phillips)*

BOGNOR REGIS [SZ9298]

Waverley PO21 2QA [Marine Drive West, Aldwick]: Full Youngs beer range kept well and enjoyable food in neatly kept beamed pub with lots of prints, efficient young staff, no smoking area (children allowed here), games; big terrace with sea-view decking *(Bruce Bird)*

BOSHAM [SU8003]

☆ *Anchor Bleu* PO18 8LS [High St]: Helpful and friendly new licensees for beautifully placed waterside pub, two nicely simple period rooms, changing ales such as Courage Best, Gales, Greene King IPA and John Smiths, reasonably priced straightforward food inc seafood and steaks from cafeteria-style servery; little terrace outside massive wheel-operated bulkhead door to ward off high tides (cars parked on seaward side often submerged), sea and boat views, charming village, open all day *(W W Burke, LYM, OPUS, Judy Bow, Arnold Rose, George and Elizabeth Storton, Ann and Colin Hunt, Ian Phillips)*

BRAMBER [TQ1810]

Castle Hotel BN44 3WE [The Street]: Roomy olde-worlde quiet lounge, full choice of reasonably priced bar food from baguettes and filled baked potatoes up, Bass, Fullers London Pride and Harveys Best; lovely back garden, charming village and views, bedrooms *(Ian Phillips, Des and Jen Clarke)*

BRIGHTON [TQ3105]

Bugle BN2 3HJ [St Martins St]: Lively three-room local with Irish licensees, posters and live music, Harveys, Timothy Taylors Landlord, Youngs and a guest beer, real fire; picnic-sets out in front and in good-sized back terrace garden – perhaps with summer evening live irish music *(MLR)*

Chimney House BN1 5DF [Upper Hamilton Rd]: Attractive building nicely restored under new ownership and now opened as no smoking pub, good choice of real ales and of enjoyable fresh up-to-date food at sensible prices *(Judy Bow, Arnold Rose)*

☆ *Cricketers* BN1 1ND [Black Lion St]: Cheerful and genuine town pub, friendly bustle at busy times, good relaxed atmosphere when quieter, cosy and darkly Victorian with loads of interesting bric-a-brac – even a stuffed bear; attentive quick service, Greene King Old Speckled Hen, Harveys, Charles Wells Bombardier and Youngs tapped from the cask, good coffee, usual well priced lunchtime bar food with fresh veg in upstairs bar, restaurant (where children allowed) and covered ex-stables courtyard bar; piped music; open all day *(Ann and Colin Hunt, Mayur Shah, LYM)*

☆ *Evening Star* BN1 3PB [Surrey St]: Chatty tap for good Dark Star microbrewery, with several of their own good beers and changing beers from other small breweries – about ten in all, interesting bottled belgian beers too, enthusiastic landlord (may let you sample before you buy), changing farm ciders and perries, lots of country wines, good lunchtime baguettes (rolls Sun), simple pale wood furniture on bare boards, good mix of customers; unobtrusive piped music, some live; pavement tables, open all day *(MLR, BB, Bruce Bird, Tony Hobden)*

Hand in Hand BN2 1JN [Upper St James's St, Kemptown]: Busy local brewing its own unusual Kemptown beers and lagers, also Badger Best and Tanglefoot, Stowford Press cider, good value wkdy lunchtime snacks such as sandwiches, pies and pizzas, Sun roast potatoes, cheerful service, dim-lit bar with tie collection and newspaper pages all over walls, nice photographs on ceiling, colourful mix of customers; veteran fruit machine, TV, good piped music; open all day wknds, from mid-afternoon wkdys *(MLR)*

King & Queen BN1 1UB [Marlborough Pl]: Chain pub notable for its surprising medieval-style lofty main hall with original décor, Theakstons Best and XB from long bar, generous good value food inc good Sun roasts, friendly service, pool table; several TV screens; flagstoned courtyard, open all day Sun *(Mayur Shah, LYM)*

Lord Nelson BN1 4ED [Trafalgar St]: Friendly four-room town pub with good value lunchtime food from sandwiches to fresh fish, Harveys ales inc Mild, farm cider, log fire, daily papers, old football photographs and theatre and cinema posters, back conservatory; pub games, sports TV, Tues quiz night; open all day *(MLR, Bruce Bird)*

Prestonville BN1 5DN [Hamilton Rd, off A23]: Appealing two-level corner local with enjoyable food, several Gales ales; seats in pleasant courtyard *(MLR)*

Sir Charles Napier BN2 9UE [Southover St]: Well run corner pub, relaxing and civilised, with Fullers/Gales ales, limited food (all day wknds), interesting local memorabilia; steep steps to small pleasant back terrace garden, cl till 4 wkdys, open all day Fri-Sun *(MLR, Guy Vowles)*

Sussex Cricketer BN3 3AF [Eaton Rd, Hove, by cricket ground]: Ember Inn with welcoming layout and comfortable sofas, reasonably priced standard food all day from baguettes up, some small helpings available, Greene King Old Speckled Hen, Harveys Best, Timothy Taylors Landlord and Youngs, decent wines by the glass *(Andy and Jill Kassube, Tony and Wendy Hobden)*

Sussex Yeoman BN1 3LU [Guildford Rd]: Friendly local with enjoyable wkdy evening food, welcoming staff, good choice of wines by the glass; smallish bar can get loud and smoky *(Rosanna Luke, Matt Curzon)*

Waggon & Horses BN1 1UD [Church St]: Well run town pub, bare boards and basic wall seating, real ales inc Harveys, lunchtime food *(MLR)*

BUCKS GREEN [TQ0733]

Fox RH12 3JP [Guildford Rd (A281 W of Rudgwick)]: Ancient open-plan inglenook bar with good-sized restaurant specialising in good generous fish, Badger beers, decent wines by the glass, welcoming efficient service by cheerful staff; play area *(J P Humphery, Keith and Inga Crabtree)*

BURWASH [TQ6724]

☆ *Bell* TN19 7EH [A265 E of Heathfield]: Pretty tile-hung pub with interesting bric-a-brac and good log fire in well used L-shaped bar, friendly service, Greene King and Wadworths 6X, decent house wines, pub games, usual food (not Sun evening) from sandwiches up, cosy and attractive no smoking dining room; music quizzes, TV, piped music, children and dogs welcome; roadside picnic-sets facing Norman church, bedrooms sharing bathrooms, charming village, open all day wknds *(LYM, Ian Phillips)*

☆ *Rose & Crown* TN19 7ER [inn sign on A265]: Welcoming low-beamed timbered local tucked away down lane in pretty village, enjoyable food inc lots of seafood from fresh crab sandwiches up, well kept Harveys IPA and Best, decent wines, fine log fire in bar, pleasant restaurant area with woodburner, young obliging licensees and good service; tables out in small quiet garden, bedrooms *(BB, Pamela and Douglas Cooper, Gwyn Jones)*

BUXTED [TQ4923]

White Hart TN22 4DP [Station Rd (A272)]: Welcoming roadside pub with real ales such as Wadworths 6X, decent pubby food, chatty regulars, main bar divided by timbering, big brick fireplace, red leatherette seats, left-hand dining bar, big light and airy conservatory with light wooden furniture on wood-strip floor; may be piped music; pleasant garden with plenty of seats *(Terry Buckland)*

CHAILEY [TQ3919]

☆ *Five Bells* BN8 4DA [A275 9 miles N of Lewes]: Attractive rambling roadside pub, spacious and interesting, with Fullers London Pride, Greene King Old Speckled Hen and Harveys Best, decent wine choice, smallish but interesting range of enjoyable food, well trained friendly young staff, lots of different rooms and alcoves leading from low-beamed bar area with fine old brick floor, brick walls and inglenook, candles and fresh flowers, leather sofas and log fire, dining extension; Fri jazz nights; picnic-sets in pretty garden with play area *(R V Peel, BB, J Stickland)*

CHICHESTER [SU8605]

Bell PO19 6AT [Broyle Rd]: Friendly helpful service, changing real ales such as Adnams and Ringwood Fortyniner, interesting wines, generous reasonably priced food from separate counter inc good puddings, daily papers, bric-a-brac on high beams, comfortable seating, no smoking dining area; bar can get smoky; children welcome, pleasant partly covered terrace, handy for Festival Theatre *(Bruce Bird, Tony Hobden, Ann and Colin Hunt)*

Dolphin & Anchor PO19 1QD [West St]: Well run no smoking Wetherspoons in former hotel opp cathedral, good value food from 9am breakfast on, six low-priced real ales; small family area till 7 (not wknds), very busy with young people Sat night, doorman and queues to get in; disabled access, pleasant back terrace, open all day *(Tony Hobden, Craig Turnbull)*

Four Chestnuts PO19 7EJ [Oving Rd]: Large open-plan bar with helpful enthusiastic staff, Caledonian Deuchars IPA, Tetleys and an interesting guest beer, generous basic lunchtime food, games room, skittle alley, some live music; open all day *(Tony Hobden, Bruce Bird)*

George & Dragon PO19 1NQ [North St]: Bustling simply refurbished bare-boards bar with good beers and wines, wholesome plentiful food, pleasant service, conservatory; tables out on back terrace, bedrooms *(Richard Waller, Pauline Smith, David H T Dimock, Ann and Colin Hunt)*

Old Cross PO19 1LP [North St]: Open-plan dining pub in pleasantly modernised building

dating from 16th c, wide blackboard food choice all day inc speciality pies, Courage Best and Directors and Charles Wells Bombardier, good choice of wines by the glass, friendly efficient service, no smoking areas; dogs welcome, open all day *(Mike and Lynn Robinson)*

☆ *Park Tavern* PO19 1NS [Priory Rd, opp Jubilee Park]: Comfortably reworked pub in attractive spot opp Priory Park, cheerful friendly service, enjoyable lunchtime food using fresh local produce and the day's fish, also good value baguettes, sandwiches and some thai dishes, Gales BB, HSB, a seasonal beer and a guest such as Wadworths 6X, relaxing smallish front bar (no smoking on right, with huge mirrors) and extensive back eating area with crisp white tablecloths *(BB, R T and J C Moggridge)*

Waterside PO19 8DT [Stockbridge Rd]: Family-run pub with enjoyable interesting home-made food, friendly unhurried atmosphere, no swearing policy; tables out by canal basin *(Mr Abbott)*

CHIDHAM [SU7804]

☆ *Old House at Home* PO18 8SU [off A259 at Barleycorn pub in Nutbourne; Cot Lane]: Cheerful and welcoming old cottagey pub, enjoyable food esp good local fish, Adnams Broadside, Fullers London Pride, Ringwood Best and Youngs, low beams and timbering, log fire, windsor chairs and long wall seats, partly no smoking restaurant, no piped music or machines; children in eating areas, tables outside, remote unspoilt farm-hamlet location, nearby walks by Chichester Harbour, open all day wknds *(R G Trevis, LYM, Charles and Pauline Stride, Roger and Pauline Pearce, Paul A Moore, Tony and Shirley Albert, Ann and Colin Hunt, Mrs Stephanie Carson)*

CLAPHAM [TQ1105]

Coach & Horses BN13 3UA [Arundel Rd (A27 Worthing—Arundel)]: Large pleasantly improved roadside pub, bar food inc well filled fresh baguettes and good fresh specials, quick friendly service, Fullers London Pride, Greene King Abbot, Harveys Best and a guest beer, decent coffee, log fire, lots of brass and china, second back bar, extended dining area and family room; piped music; children welcome, Tues quiz night, jazz first Mon, well kept garden with lots of tables and play area *(Val and Alan Green)*

CLAYTON [TQ2914]

Jack & Jill BN6 9PD [A273 N of Brighton]: Friendly country pub with good range of enjoyable food from ploughman's to duck confit, impressive service, changing real ales *(Fr Robert Marsh)*

CLIMPING [TQ0001]

Black Horse BN17 5RL: Friendly good value dining pub with wide choice of standard dishes from sandwiches and baked potatoes up, very popular Sun lunch (best to book), Courage Best and Directors, good choice of wines by the glass, pleasant attentive service, country views from the back; tables out behind, walk to beach *(B S Gill, Fr Robert Marsh)*

Oystercatcher BN17 5RU [A259/B2233]:
Thatched Vintage Inn dining pub, largely no
smoking and pleasantly back-dated with hops
and bric-a-brac, friendly young well trained
staff, their usual reasonably priced food all day
from sandwiches and starters doubling as light
dishes up, Bass and Harveys Best, good choice
of wines by the glass, nicely served coffee,
log fires; disabled lavatories *(Tony and
Wendy Hobden)*

COLEMANS HATCH [TQ4533]

☆ *Hatch* TN7 4EJ [signed off B2026, or off
B2110 opp church]: Quaint and attractive little
weatherboarded Ashdown Forest pub dating
from 1430, big log fire in quickly filling
beamed bar, small back dining room with
another log fire, very wide choice of good
generous food from sandwiches, baked
potatoes and giant ploughman's through
imaginative salads to bass and steak, Harveys
Best, Larkins Best and one or two guest beers,
friendly quick young staff, good mix of
customers inc families and dogs; not much
parking so get there early; picnic-sets on front
terrace and in beautifully kept big garden, open
all day Sun and summer Sat *(Debbie and
Neil Hayter, Pamela and Douglas Cooper,
LYM, Neil Hardwick)*

COLGATE [TQ2233]

Dragon RH12 4SY [Forest Rd]: Small
unpretentious two-bar pub with good value
home-made food from interesting sandwiches
to local game, log fire, good service, Badger
ales, dining area; big garden, pleasant and
secluded – good for children *(Ivan Turner)*

COOLHAM [TQ1223]

Selsey Arms RH13 8QJ [A272/B2139]: Chatty
local with hospitable service even when quite
busy, Fullers London Pride and Harveys Best,
enjoyable blackboard food from sandwiches
and baked potatoes up, two linked areas with
plates, prints and blazing log fires; garden
fenced off from road in front, another behind
with lots of trees *(Bruce Bird, Peter Lewis,
Stephen Harvey)*

COUSLEY WOOD [TQ6533]

☆ *Old Vine* TN5 6ER [B2100 Wadhurst—
Lamberhurst]: Popular and attractive dining
pub with lots of old timbers and beams, wide
range of generous enjoyable food inc good fish,
good house wines, Greene King IPA and
Harveys, rustic pretty restaurant on right,
pubbier bare-boards or brick-floored area with
woodburner by bar; they like things done their
way and may try to keep your credit card
while you eat, but otherwise good friendly
service; dogs welcome, a few tables out behind
*(Steve Harvey, B J Harding, Ian Phillips, BB,
Robert Rice, Oliver and Sue Rowell,
Jamie May)*

COWFOLD [TQ2122]

Coach House RH13 8BT [Horsham Rd]:
Smart and comfortable, with enjoyable food,
good coffee and service; open all day *(Ann and
Colin Hunt)*

Hare & Hounds RH13 8DR [Henfield Rd
(A281 S)]: Good friendly landlord and
attentive staff, Harveys Bitter and Mild, Kings

Horsham Best and small-brewery guest beers,
generous food from well filled baguettes to lots
of specials, decent wines, log fire, daily papers,
some flagstones and bric-a-brac inc lots of
pewter mugs, no smoking family area, darts;
unobtrusive piped music; back terrace
*(Tony and Wendy Hobden, Jackie and
Alan Moody, Paul Humphreys, Bruce Bird)*

CRAWLEY [TQ2836]

Snooty Fox RH10 1LX [Haslett Ave, opp
Three Bridges Stn]: Comfortable Steak & Ale
pub, low-priced food inc two-for-one bargains,
Bass and Charles Wells Bombardier, no
smoking area; big-screen sports TV
(Tony Hobden)

CROWBOROUGH [TQ5130]

Blue Anchor TN6 1BB [Beacon Rd (A26)]:
Shpeherd Neame pub with their real ales, good
friendly service, food from sandwiches up
(Ian Phillips)

CUCKFIELD [TQ3024]

White Harte RH17 5LB [South St; off A272 W
of Haywards Heath]: Pretty partly medieval
pub, comfortable beamed and timbered lounge
with polished floorboards and ancient brick
flooring, sturdy furnishings in public bar with
blazing inglenook log fire and traditional
games, Badger Best, K&B and Tanglefoot;
piped music, TV; dogs in bar, children
welcome, tables in back yard *(LYM,
Francis Vernon, W A Evershed)*

DALLINGTON [TQ6619]

☆ *Swan* TN21 9LB [Woods Corner, B2096 E]:
Cosy low-beamed country local with enjoyable
blackboard food inc interesting dishes and
local fish, also lunchtime sandwiches and
panini, Harveys Best and a guest beer, good
wines by the glass and coffee, friendly staff,
warm log fire in softly lit bare-boards bar with
a couple of sofas and tea lights, small
comfortable back dining room with far views
to Beachy Head; steps down to smallish garden
(BB, N R White, Mike Gorton)

DANEHILL [TQ4128]

☆ *Coach & Horses* RH17 7JF [off A275, via
School Lane towards Chelwood Common]:
Well run dining pub in attractive countryside,
good if not cheap restaurany food (not Sun
evening) served with style – and linen napkins,
Harveys Best and Wychwood Shires, good
wines by generous glass, little hatch-served
public bar with simple furniture on highly
polished boards and small woodburner, main
bar on the left with big Victorian prints and
mix of chairs around attractive old tables on
fine brick floor, no smoking dining extension;
may try to keep your credit card while you eat
outside; well behaved children and dogs
allowed, plenty of tables in big attractive
garden with terrace under huge maple
*(Karen Eliot, R M Yard, Mr and Mrs
R A Bradbrook, Alan Cowell, Pete Walker,
Pamela Goodwyn, Alan Sadler,
Pierre Richterich, B J Harding, Roger Fox,
N R White, Martin and Karen Wake, LYM)*

DELL QUAY [SU8302]

☆ *Crown & Anchor* PO20 7EE [off A286 S of
Chichester – look out for small sign]:

Modernised 15th-c pub in splendid spot on site of Roman quay overlooking Chichester Harbour – best at high tide and quiet times, can be packed on sunny days; comfortable bow-windowed lounge bar, panelled public bar (dogs welcome), two log fires and lots of beams, Courage Directors and Theakstons Best or John Smiths and Charles Wells Bombardier, very wide choice of wines by the glass, good popular food from all-day servery; terrace picnic-sets, nice walks *(Derek and Heather Manning, OPUS, BB, Colin McKerrow, Mrs Sheela Curtis, Ann and Colin Hunt, W A Evershed)*

DENTON [TQ4502]

☆ *Flying Fish* BN9 0QB [Denton Rd]: Attractive 17th-c flint village pub by South Downs Way, recently refurbished keeping plenty of individuality and tiled floors throughout, two smaller rooms off bar, Shepherd Neame ales, French chef/landlord doing good well priced food from interesting baguettes up inc seasonal food esp game and fresh fish from nearby Newhaven, friendly prompt service, comfortable high-ceilinged no smoking dining room with bric-a-brac; attractive sloping garden behind, more tables on long deck and out in front, bedrooms *(John Beeken, the Didler, Emily Mottram)*

DITCHLING [TQ3215]

White Horse BN6 8TS [West St]: Popular village local nr church, Harveys and a changing guest beer, unpretentious food from sandwiches up, quick service, log fire, games area; unobtrusive piped music *(MLR)*

DUNCTON [SU9517]

☆ *Cricketers* GU28 0LB [set back from A285]: Pretty little white country pub under new licensees and back to its roots as a cheerful pubby local (even selling local papers and produce), bar food from sandwiches to Sun roast and lots of fish (prices down), Ballards and Youngs ales, several decent wines by the glass, inglenook fireplace, cricketing pictures and bats on walls, steps down to no smoking room, shove-ha'penny, cribbage and dominoes; piped music, Sun morning market/boot sale and barbecue; children and dogs welcome, picnic-sets in charming garden behind with creeper-covered bower and proper barbecue, open all day (till 8 Sun) *(David Cosham, Jude Wright, LYM)*

EARTHAM [SU9309]

☆ *George* PO18 0LT [signed off A285 Chichester—Petworth, from Fontwell off A27, from Slindon off A29]: Friendly pub with good blackboard range of enjoyable home-made food at sensible prices, Greene King ales and well listed wines, log fire, light wood furnishings in comfortable lounge, attractive public bar with games, old farm tools and photographs, darts, backgammon, no smoking restaurant; piped music; easy disabled access, children welcome in eating areas, large pretty garden, attractive surroundings, open all day summer wknds *(Jude Wright, Nicholas and Dorothy Stephens, LYM, W A Evershed)*

EASEBOURNE [SU8922]

☆ *White Horse* GU29 0AL [off A272 just NE of Midhurst]: Comfortable and relaxing beamed village pub, fireside armchairs in tasteful and well divided mainly bare-boards bar with small no smoking dining area, convivial landlord, efficient friendly service, traditional food from baked potatoes up (worth booking wknds), Greene King IPA and Abbot, two open fires, no piped music; children and dogs welcome, tables on back grass and in courtyard *(T O'Brien, LYM, Jeremy Whitehorn)*

EAST HOATHLY [TQ5216]

Kings Head BN8 6DR [High St]: 1648 ales brewed here inc Bee Head (not just a pun on the battleaxe over one big fireplace – it's a honeyed beer), also Harveys Best, in long friendly and comfortably worn in open-plan bar with some dark panelling and old local photographs, good value bar food, good service, restaurant; TV; tables in garden up steps behind *(John Beeken, Kevin Thorpe, Bruce Bird)*

EAST LAVANT [SU8608]

☆ *Royal Oak* PO18 0AX [signed off A286 N of Chichester; Pook Lane]: Restaurant dining pub, not cheap but good value, with appealing relaxed atmosphere, prompt friendly service, candlelight and scrubbed tables, rugs on bare boards and flooring tiles, two open fires and a woodburner, racing prints, several Badger ales tapped from the cask, country wines, good house wines; attractively planted gardens inc secluded terrace with bookable tables (quiet exc for wknd light planes using Goodwood airfield), good walks; comfortable bedrooms, cl Sun pm *(Richard Waller, Pauline Smith, LYM, Christopher and Elise Way, Dr D and Mrs B Woods, Lionel and Sylvia Kopelowitz)*

EASTBOURNE [TV6198]

Buccaneer BN21 4BW [Compton St, by Winter Gardens]: Popular open-plan bar shaped like a galleon, raised no smoking side, Bass, Greene King, Tetleys and guest beers, bar food, theatre memorabilia; open all day *(the Didler)*

☆ *Lamb* BN21 1HH [High St]: Two main heavily beamed traditional bars off pretty Tudor pub's central servery, spotless antique furnishings (but not too smart), good inglenook log fire, Harveys ales, good generous fair-priced food and well organised service, upstairs dining room (Sun lunch); by ornate church away from seafront, popular with students in evenings *(Michael and Ann Cole)*

Terminus BN21 3NS [Terminus Rd]: Busy unpretentious L-shaped bar with Harveys ales, helpful staff, very reasonably priced lunchtime food, comfortable no smoking restaurant, bric-a-brac and railway prints; children welcome *(Bruce Bird)*

ELSTED [SU8320]

Elsted Inn GU29 0JT [Elsted Marsh]: Attractive two-bar country pub with home-made food inc very popular sensibly priced Sun lunch, four real ales such as Ballards, Flower Pots and Timothy Taylors Landlord, nice country furniture, wooden floors, old railway photographs, log fires, traditional games; lovely enclosed downs-view garden with big terrace and summer barbecues, well appointed adjacent bedroom block *(LYM, David Cosham, Ann and Colin Hunt, W A Evershed)*

ERIDGE STATION [TQ5434]

Huntsman TN3 9LE [Eridge Rd]: Small unpretentious country local with changing daily choice of good value home-made food (worth booking wknds) from fat fresh filled soft rolls to some innovative dishes, huge helpings, quietly friendly landlord with considerable wine expertise, also three Badger ales on top form, farm cider, good coffee, Tues evening motorcycle meeting (and bike show and barbecue probably first Sun in Aug); walkers and dogs welcome, picnic-sets on good-sized covered front and back terraces and in big garden behind with tall trees, cl Mon, open all day wknds *(Paul A Moore, Ian Phillips, Pete Walker, BB, Fr Robert Marsh, Robert A Dean, Bill and Pauline Harvey)*

FAIRWARP [TQ4626]

Foresters Arms TN22 3BP [B2026]: Ashdown Forest local handy for Vanguard Way and Weald Way, comfortable lounge bar, wide food choice from baguettes and light dishes to steak and Sunday lunch, Badger ales, farm cider, woodburner; piped music; children in eating area, tables out on terrace and in garden, play area on small village green opp, has been open all day summer *(Neil Hardwick, LYM, Gwyn Jones)*

FERNHURST [SU8926]

☆ *Kings Arms* GU27 3HA [A286 towards Midhurst]: Attractive low-beamed 17th-c dining pub with updated décor and new furnishings, big inglenook fireplace in one eating area, woodburner in bar; has been very popular for good sensible food, real ales such as Hogs Back TEA and Crop Circle, Kings Horsham Best, fff Moondance and Ringwood Fortyniner and a nice choice of wines by the glass, but changing hands summer 2006, too late for us to find out anything about the new people – so reports please; pleasant fair-sized garden *(LYM)*

FERRING [TQ0903]

Henty Arms BN12 6QY [Ferring Ln]: Modest two-bar pub with half a dozen changing ales such as Caledonian Deuchars IPA and Youngs, attractively priced food even Sun evening, friendly local atmosphere, no smoking back dining area, separate public bar with games and TV; garden tables *(Tony and Wendy Hobden)*

Tudor Close BN12 5NQ [Ferringham Lane, S Ferring]: Thatched and high-raftered 16th-c former barn with some emphasis on enjoyable reasonably priced food from lunchtime sandwiches and baked potatoes up (very popular with older people at lunchtime), Badger and Greene King ales, no smoking restaurant end, upper gallery overlooking bar the other end, imposing intricately carved fireplace, ornate lamp stands, suit of armour,

conservatory; open all day Fri-Sun *(Tony and Wendy Hobden)*

FINDON [TQ1208]

☆ *Gun* BN14 0TA [High St]: Civilised low-beamed village pub, friendly atmosphere, traditional main bar, pine-floored no smoking dining area, good attractively presented food from lunchtime sandwiches to modern light and main dishes, sensible prices, quick service, Adnams, Fullers London Pride, Gales HSB and Harveys BB, range of foreign beers; attractive sheltered lawn, pretty village in horse-training country below Cissbury Ring *(LYM, Des and Jen Clarke)*

Snooty Fox BN14 0TA [bar of Findon Manor Hotel]: Hospitable and comfortable, with Black Sheep, Greene King Abbot and Ruddles and Harveys Best, good coffee, enjoyable food from sandwiches up (no smoking at meal times), 16th-c beams, wall settles, hunting caricatures and other foxy decorations, old advertisements and local photographs; pleasant lawn *(Tony and Wendy Hobden, Bruce Bird, Des and Jen Clarke)*

FIRLE [TQ4607]

☆ *Ram* BN8 6NS [village signed off A27 Lewes—Polegate]: 17th-c village pub reopened after being closed for a few months, nice chatty local atmosphere, pleasant décor with pictures on carefully contrasting coloured walls, good mix of unassuming furnishings inc some big comfortable armchairs, log fires, good if not cheap food from sandwiches up, Harveys Best and seasonal Old, helpful staff (though service can slow when busy); end public bar can get rather smoky; children and dogs welcome, tables in big walled garden behind, open all day *(BB)*

FISHBOURNE [SU8304]

☆ *Bulls Head* PO19 3JP [Fishbourne Rd (A259 Chichester—Emsworth)]: Relaxing and comfortable beamed village pub with pretty window boxes, fair-sized main bar, Fullers London Pride and Gales ales, good varied quickly served food often using local produce (not Sun evening – Sun lunch very popular), sandwiches and small helpings available too, sensible prices, friendly neatly dressed staff, good log fire, daily papers, children's area, restaurant with no smoking area, exemplary lavatories; skittle alley, terrace picnic-sets, bedrooms *(Richard Waller, Pauline Smith, Dr Alan and Mrs Sue Holder, David H T Dimock, Bruce Bird, C and R Bromage, Mrs Angela Bromley-Martin, Ann and Colin Hunt, Ian Phillips)*

FLETCHING [TQ4223]

☆ *Rose & Crown* TN22 3ST [High St]: Proper 16th-c village pub, well run and unpretentious, with friendly atmosphere, good value home-made food in bar and small restaurant, good service, real ales, beams, inglenooks and log fires; tables in pretty garden *(Ron Gentry, D Ray)*

FLIMWELL [TQ7131]

Royal Oak TN5 7PJ [A21 S of Lamberhurst]: Well run, with good value bar food (all day Sat), Sun roasts 12-6, comfortable leather settees and big block leather stools at new tables on bare boards, partly no smoking dining area, locals' bar with high tables and big-screen sports TV; tables outside *(BB)*

FORD [SU0003]

Ship & Anchor BN18 0BJ [Station Rd]: Local Arundel beers and a guest such as Skinners Betty Stogs, sensibly priced pubby food all day from baguettes and baked potatoes up, friendly staff and locals, no smoking area, games room and family area; by small marina, open all day *(Mr and Mrs B Hobden)*

FRANT [TQ5835]

Abergavenny Arms TN3 9DB [A267 S of Tun Wells]: Welcoming and helpful landlord putting heart into mock-Tudor main-road pub, two bars, log fire, real ales such as Adnams Broadside, Fullers London Pride, Harveys Best and Wye Valley Golden, good choice of wines by the glass, wide choice of reasonably priced popular food from open sandwiches and baked potatoes up, bar billiards, three-legged dog; children welcome, bedrooms *(Ian Phillips)*

FULKING [TQ2411]

Shepherd & Dog BN5 9LU [off A281 N of Brighton, via Poynings]: Bow-windowed pub in beautiful spot below downs, with pretty streamside garden and upper play lawn; now a Badger dining pub, and refurbished with modern tables and chairs, painted panelling, new granite bar counter; wide food choice (all day wknds), their real ales, good wine choice, log fire; open all day *(LYM)*

FUNTINGTON [SU7908]

Fox & Hounds PO18 9LL: Cheerful beamed family pub with wide food choice from sandwiches to popular Sun roasts (best to book wknds), cottagey rooms, comfortable and attractive dining extension, welcoming service, Badger Best, K&B and Tanglefoot, reasonably priced wines, good coffee, huge log fire, no music; garden behind, pair of nice inn signs – one a pack of hounds, the other a family of foxes *(Nicholas and Dorothy Stephens, Ian Phillips, Peter and Audrey Dowsett)*

GLYNDE [TQ4508]

Trevor Arms BN8 6SS: Well kept Harveys ales and bargain food from ploughman's and baked potatoes to good Sun roasts, congenial landlord, small bar with corridor to no smoking room and big dining room, Glyndebourne posters and photographs; tables in large garden with downland backdrop, Glyndebourne musicians may play out here on summer Suns *(John Beeken, Tony and Wendy Hobden)*

GODDARDS GREEN [TQ2820]

Sportsman BN6 9LQ: Family dining pub with wide choice of popular usual food from open sandwiches and baked potatoes up, friendly efficient waitress service, Badger ales, decent house wines, no smoking restaurant extension; children and dogs welcome *(Tony and Wendy Hobden, Ron Gentry)*

GORING-BY-SEA [TQ1002]

Bull BN12 5AR [Goring St]: Old and attractively beamed, small linked areas with larger no smoking barn-style dining room,

warm relaxed atmosphere, efficient staff, reasonably priced bar food inc wknd roasts (discounts 2.30-6), Courage Directors, Harveys Best and two guest beers, pictures and old photographs; large walled garden *(Tony and Wendy Hobden)*

GRAFFHAM [SU9217]

Foresters Arms GU28 0QA: Friendly smallish two-room 17th-c pub, heavily timbered, with stripped brick, big log fire in fine old fireplace, country sports pictures, changing ales such as Ballards Poms Delight, Ringwood Best and Youngs Special, good wine choice, home-made meals, efficient service, daily papers and magazines, old pulpit as feature of small pretty no smoking restaurant (can be fully booked); tables in big pleasant garden, bedrooms, good walks *(Richard Waller, Pauline Smith, John Beeken, Bruce Bird, Prof and Mrs S Barnett)*

GUN HILL [TQ5614]

☆ *Gun* TN21 0JU [off A22 NW of Hailsham, or off A267]: Big welcoming country dining pub, several interesting rambling areas either side of large central bar, beams and log fires, generous straightforward food, real ales, good wines, efficient pleasant service; children allowed in two no smoking rooms, lovely garden with play area, right on Wealden Way *(M and R Thomas, LYM)*

HAILSHAM [TQ5809]

Grenadier BN27 1AS [High St (N end)]: Striking early 19th-c pub with warm welcome, traditional games in nice panelled locals' bar, comfortable lounge bar, simple lunchtime meals, full Harveys ale range; children welcome in lounge, dogs in public bar *(Pete Baker)*

HALNAKER [SU9008]

☆ *Anglesey Arms* PO18 0NQ [A285 Chichester—Petworth]: Charmingly unpretentious bar with friendly new licensees and helpful staff, Adnams Best, Youngs and a guest such as Caledonian Deuchars IPA, decent wines, good generous imaginative food inc local organic produce and Selsey fish, simple but smart no smoking L-shaped dining room with woodburners, stripped pine and some flagstones (children allowed), traditional games; tables in large tree-lined garden *(Ann and Colin Hunt, Nicholas and Dorothy Stephens, Tony and Wendy Hobden, LYM, Ewart McKie, W W Burke, Bruce Bird)*

HAMMERPOT [TQ0605]

☆ *Woodmans Arms* BN16 4EU: Pretty thatched and timbered pub comfortably rebuilt after 2004 fire, in its former 16th-c layout but with bigger fireplace, more headroom for the big beams, a more contemporary feel, and extension giving extra no smoking dining room; Gales ales and a guest such as Wadworths 6X from longer bar counter, enjoyable pubby food from sandwiches and baked potatoes up, quick service; piped music; tables outside with summer marquee, open all day Fri/Sat and summer Sun, may be cl Sun evening *(Val and Alan Green, Tony and Wendy Hobden, LYM, Brad Featherman,*

Bruce Bird, Don and Thelma Anderson, Ann and Colin Hunt, Mark Weber, John Beeken)

HANDCROSS [TQ2529]

Royal Oak RH17 6DJ [Horsham Rd (A279, off A23)]: Two smallish low-beamed areas divided by big log-effect gas fire, friendly atmosphere and good prompt service, enjoyable and interesting food from light dishes to seasonal game, Fullers London Pride, Harveys and a guest such as Shepherd Neame Spitfire, winter mulled wine, old photographs and curios; comfortable tables on terrace with pleasant arbour overlooking fields and woods, handy for Nymans (NT) *(Brian Root, Terry Buckland, J P Humphery, C and R Bromage, N R White)*

Wheatsheaf RH13 6NZ [B2110 W]: Warm welcome, Badger ales, good range of generous good value home-made food using local produce from sandwiches to steaks inc children's, two simply furnished bars with lots of horse tack and farm tools, no smoking dining area; large garden with piped music and big play area, handy for Nymans (NT) and Leonardslee gardens *(Graham Breen, Terry Buckland)*

HARTFIELD [TQ4735]

Haywaggon TN7 4AB [High St (A264)]: Friendly and busy, with two big log fires, pews and lots of large tables in spacious beamed bar, wide range of blackboard bar food and good value former bakehouse restaurant, real ales inc Harveys, good choice of wines by the glass, nice dog; picnic-sets outside *(Pamela and Douglas Cooper, Bill and Pauline Harvey)*

HASSOCKS [TQ3115]

Thatched BN6 8DH [Ockley Lane/Grand Avenue]: Good choice of generous food in bar and no smoking restaurant, Fullers London Pride and Greene King IPA from central servery *(Paul A Moore, Tony and Wendy Hobden)*

HASTINGS [TQ 8109]

Jenny Lind TN34 3EW [High St]: Two rooms with interesting memorabilia in back bar, friendly welcome, good local beers and quickly served generous lunchtime sandwiches; no under-21s *(M Joyner)*

HENFIELD [TQ2116]

Plough BN5 9HP [High St]: Hospitable licensees, wide choice of reliable beers inc Kings, reasonably priced enjoyable food inc tapas; pavement tables *(Bill Shelton, Terry Buckland)*

White Hart BN5 9HP [High St (A281)]: Friendly 16th-c village pub with interesting tiled roof, cheery landlord, efficient service, Badger beers, large civilised dining area with home-cooked food inc tempting puddings, decent wines with choice of glass sizes, comfortable L-shaped lounge and big no smoking area, log fire, lots of panelling, tools hanging from low beams, horsebrasses, paintings, prints, photographs and fresh flowers; children welcome, small back area with terrace and play things *(Terry Buckland, Ron Gentry)*

HENLEY [SU8925]

☆ *Duke of Cumberland Arms* GU27 3HQ [off A286 S of Fernhurst]: Rather special wisteria-covered 15th-c stone-built pub with big scrubbed pine or oak tables in two small rooms each with a log fire, low ceilings, white-painted wall boards and rustic decorations, hands-on licensees, real ales tapped from the cask such as Adnams Broadside, Brakspears, Hook Norton Best, Shepherd Neame Spitfire and Youngs Special, Rich's farm cider, good wine choice; pricey food (not Sun evening) from sandwiches up, can be quite a queue to order – which regulars may aggravate by bypassing; children and dogs welcome, beautiful hill views from gnarled seats in charming big sloping garden criss-crossed by stream and trout ponds, open all day *(Paul A Moore, Edwina Messer, Phil and Sally Gorton, Torrens Lyster, A J Longshaw, J P Humphery, LYM, John Evans, Alasdair Stark)*

HERSTMONCEUX [TQ6312]

Brewers Arms BN27 4LB [Gardner S]: Neatly kept two-bar pub with attentive efficient service, Caledonian Deuchars IPA and Greene King ales, good value pub food, dining area with pleasant outlook over garden *(C and R Bromage)*

HOOE [TQ6708]

Lamb TN33 9HH [A259 E of Pevensey]: Quick friendly young staff in prettily placed olde-worlde Vintage Inn with lots of stripped brick and flintwork, one snug area around huge log fire and lots of other seats, big tables, Bass and Harveys, good range of house wines, very wide food choice from sandwiches and baguettes up *(M and R Thomas)*

HORSHAM [TQ1629]

Boars Head RH13 0AD [Worthing Rd (B2237)]: No smoking flagstoned country pub doing well under current licensees, enjoyable food and atmosphere, helpful staff, Badger ales, log fire, back restaurant; downs view from nice garden *(J Sumoter)*

ICKLESHAM [TQ8716]

· *Robin Hood* TN36 4BD [Main Rd]: Friendly down-to-earth local with fortnightly summer Sun car boot sale, cheerful staff, enjoyable standard food, Fullers London Pride and other beers *(Tom and Jill Jones)*

ISFIELD [TQ4417]

Laughing Fish TN22 5XB: Simply modernised Victorian local with good value fresh straightforward food, four or five Greene King ales, friendly staff, traditional games, no smoking bar; entertaining beer race Easter bank hol Mon; children and dogs welcome, tables in small pleasantly shaded walled garden with enclosed play area, right by Lavender Line *(John Beeken, Ron Gentry, BB, the Didler)*

JEVINGTON [TQ5601]

☆ *Eight Bells* BN26 5QB: Busy and neatly kept, fast friendly service, good value hearty home-made food (all day Sun) from good unusual lunchtime filled rolls and baked potatoes up, Adnams Broadside, Flowers Original and

Harveys Best and winter Old, simple furnishings, beams, parquet floor, flame-effect fire in inglenook; piped music, fruit machine; walkers welcome, South Downs Way, Weald Way and 1066 Trail all nearby, quiet village with interesting church; tables under cocktail parasols on front terrace, secluded downs-view garden with some sturdy tables under cover, open all day *(David Cosham, BB, Kevin Thorpe, John Beeken)*

KINGSTON NEAR LEWES [TQ3908]

Juggs BN7 3NT [village signed off A27 by roundabout W of Lewes]: Ancient rose-covered pub with heavy 15th-c beams and very low front door, lots of neatly stripped masonry, sturdy wooden furniture on bare boards and stone slabs, smaller eating areas inc no smoking family room off, good choice of bar food from baguettes and baked potatoes up, Shepherd Neame ales, good coffee and wine list, log fires, dominoes and shove-ha'penny; piped music; nice seating areas outside, compact well equipped play area *(PL, LYM, John Beeken, Ann and Colin Hunt, Ian Phillips)*

KIRDFORD [TQ0126]

☆ *Half Moon* RH14 0LT [opp church, off A272 Petworth—Billingshurst]: 17th-c tile-hung upmarket bar/restaurant, picturesque and charmingly set, with linen-laid tables in immaculate roomy and rambling largely no smoking low-beamed dining area, good wines by the glass, kind professional service, Fullers London Pride from curved counter in attractive partly quarry-tiled bar with log fire; tables in pretty back garden and out in front *(LYM, Derek and Maggie Washington, Derek Thomas, J P Humphery)*

LANCING [TQ1704]

Crabtree BN15 9NQ [Crabtree Lane]: Friendly pub with good landlord and staff, changing independent ales such as Archers and Hop Back, games area in large public bar, comfortable Spitfire lounge with unusual 30s ceiling, art deco lights, model planes and old photographs, food inc evening thai buffets, Sun roast and hot counter; garden with downs views and play area *(Bruce Bird)*

LAVANT [SU8508]

Earl of March PO18 0BQ [A286, Mid Lavant]: Reopened after smart refurbishment, lots of Goodwood car and aircraft photographs, comfortable alcove lounge, helpful staff, Hop Back Crop Circle, Ringwood Best and several guest beers tapped from the cask, usual food; piped music can obtrude; good views from garden, good local walks – handy for Centurion Way cycle path *(Bruce Bird)*

LEWES [TQ4109]

Brewers Arms BN7 1XN [High St]: Neatly kept local with obliging friendly staff, good choice of attractively priced food all day till 6.30, Harveys Best and two interesting guest ales, local photographs and clay pipe collection in front bar, quiet lounge, back sports-theme bar with pool and sports TV in games room; open all day *(Anne and Tim Locke,*

Tony Hobden, Bruce Bird, the Didler, Quentin and Carol Williamson)

Elephant & Castle BN7 2DJ [White Hill]: Friendly bare-boards local with smoking allowed throughout, large main room and side room with pool and some settles, real ales inc Black Sheep and Brakspears, lunchtime food inc organic local burgers *(Tony Hobden)*

Gardeners Arms BN7 2AN [Cliffe High St]: Traditional small local, light, airy and quiet, with Harveys and interesting changing ales and farm ciders, good value lunchtime sandwiches and ploughman's, good friendly service (with helpful opinions on the beers), plain scrubbed tables on bare boards around three sides of bar, daily papers and magazines, Sun bar nibbles; can be smoky *(Anne and Tim Locke)*

John Harvey BN7 2AN [Bear Yard, just off Cliffe High St]: Tap for nearby Harveys brewery (with separate good brewery shop), all their beers inc seasonal kept perfectly, some tapped from the cask, generous decent value food from lunchtime sandwiches, baked potatoes and ciabattas up, efficient young staff, basic dark flagstoned bar with one great vat halved to make two towering 'snugs' for several people, lighter room on left; piped music and machines; a few tables outside, open all day, breakfast from 10am *(Anne and Tim Locke, BB, Bruce Bird)*

☆ *Lewes Arms* BN7 1YH [Castle Ditch Lane/Mount Pl – tucked behind castle ruins]: Unpretentious corner local built into castle ramparts, nostalgic chatty and friendly atmosphere, old-fashioned layout with small front bar and hatchway, larger lounge with eating area off, Greene King IPA and XX Mild and Harveys Best, good value wine, bargain simple lunchtime food from good baguettes and tapas up, weekly curry night, daily papers, local pictures, darts, toad in the hole and board games, no music or mobiles; can be rather smoky; small heated terrace, open all day *(Sue Demont, Tim Barrow, BB, Tony Hobden, John Beeken, Phil and Sally Gorton)*

Snowdrop BN7 2BU [South St]: Two spacious well worn in bar areas with the cliffs as a backdrop and a maritime décor with figureheads, ship lamps etc, fairly straightforward bar food, Adnams Broadside, Harveys Best and a guest beer, dominoes, spiral stairs up to more seats and pool; piped music, no nearby parking if pub's small space full; local bands Sat evening, children and dogs welcome, open all day *(Ann and Colin Hunt, Sue Demont, Tim Barrow, Guy Vowles, LYM)*

LICKFOLD [SU9226]

☆ *Lickfold Inn* GU28 9EY [NE of Midhurst, between A286 and A283]: Attractive dining pub with Tudor beams, ancient flooring bricks and big log fire in huge inglenook, simple pale wooden furnishings in bar and back dining room, smarter restaurant (tablecloths, sofas and rugs on bare boards) upstairs, good choice of wines by the glass, imaginative food, welcoming efficient staff; no children in main bar, shame about the piped music; sleek tables under big parasols on terrace, picnic-sets in interestingly laid out garden *(Tom and Jill Jones, LYM, John Evans)*

LINDFIELD [TQ3425]

Bent Arms RH16 2HP [High St]: Nice layout segueing gently from bar through eating area to restaurant, antique and art deco furnishings and stained glass, decent home-made food, Badger Tanglefoot, prompt friendly service; back flower garden *(LYM, Terry Buckland)*

Witch RH16 2AB [Sunte Ave]: New chef doing interesting and generous food using local and organic ingredients, particularly imaginative vegetarian options – and they're happy just to serve a bowl of chips; garden with play area *(Jane Songi)*

LITTLEHAMPTON [TQ0202]

☆ *Arun View* BN17 5DD [Wharf Rd; W towards Chichester]: Roomy and comfortable 18th-c pub in lovely spot right on harbour with river directly below windows, worth booking for its interesting food with good fresh fish (very popular lunchtime with older people, a younger crowd evenings), sandwiches too, Ringwood Best and Old Thumper and Youngs Special, good wine list, cheerful helpful service, lots of drawings, caricatures and nautical collectables, flagstoned and panelled back public bar, large no smoking conservatory and flower-filled terrace both overlooking busy waterway and pedestrian bridge; disabled facilities, summer barbecues evenings and wknds, winter live music, bright and modest good value bedrooms *(David Carr, Bruce Bird, Ian and Jane Irving, Mrs Sue Barlow, Craig Turnbull, Tony and Wendy Hobden)*

LODSWORTH [SU9223]

☆ *Hollist Arms* GU28 9BZ [off A272 Midhurst—Petworth]: Cheerful and civilised village pub overlooking small green, Kings Horsham Best, Timothy Taylors Landlord and Youngs, good wines by the glass and coffee, good range of generous enjoyable bar food inc fresh fish and shellfish, popular Sun lunch, relaxed atmosphere, lively landlord and prompt charming service, interesting books and magazines, country prints, sofas by log fire for no smoking dining room (must book for Sat night), outside lavatories; may be piped classical music; children welcome, nice tree-lined back garden, good walks *(Ron Gentry, Denis Dutton, Gerry and Rosemary Dobson, Mrs J A Sales, Martin and Karen Wake, Peter Lewis)*

LOWER BEEDING [TQ2225]

Crabtree RH13 6PT [Brighton Rd]: Good 16th-c pub/restaurant with fine inglenook log fire in beamed Belloc bar, Badger beers inc K&B *(LYM, Birgit Bartlett, Michael Sargent)*

LOXWOOD [TQ0331]

Onslow Arms RH14 0RD [B2133 NW of Billingshurst]: Popular local with Badger ales, good house wines, plenty of coffees and teas, lovely old log fireplaces, enjoyable food inc light dishes and smaller helpings, friendly informal service, daily papers; dogs welcome, picnic-sets in good-sized pleasant garden sloping to river and nearby newly restored

Wey & Arun canal, good walks and boat trips *(Mike and Lynn Robinson, Lucien Perring)*

LURGASHALL [SU9327]

☆ *Noahs Ark* GU28 9ET [off A283 N of Petworth]: Convivial 16th-c country local, two neat beamed bars with log fires (one in a capacious inglenook), muted canary walls with small windows looking out over churchyard or village cricket green, Greene King IPA, Abbot and Old Speckled Hen, sandwiches, wraps, filled baked potatoes and enjoyable simple hot bar food (not Sun evening), restaurant, darts; may be soft piped music; dogs and children welcome, picnic-sets on front grass, more in back garden, cl winter Sun evening *(Mike and Lynn Robinson, Alison and Graham Hooper, Jude Wright, Cathy Robinson, Ed Coombe, LYM, Klaus and Elizabeth Leist, Michael B Griffith, Jeremy Whitehorn, R B Gardiner)*

LYMINSTER [TQ0204]

Six Bells BN17 7PS [Lyminster Rd, Wick]: Warmly welcoming, with good-sized helpings of unusual and enjoyable elegantly presented food from sandwiches and baguettes up, popular two-course lunches, friendly helpful service, Greene King Abbot and Fullers London Pride in small central part between bar dining area and no smoking restaurant, open fire *(Tony and Wendy Hobden, Carol and Dono Leaman, David and Cherie Cheetham)*

MILLAND [SU8328]

☆ *Rising Sun* GU30 7NA [Iping Rd junction with main rd through village]: Light and airy no smoking main bar with friendly service, generous interesting food inc fresh fish, some recipes from Normandy and good french country puddings, Gales Butser, BB, HSB and a guest beer, classic bar skittles table, smoking area too; picnic-sets in good-sized neatly kept garden, good walking area *(Mike Edwards, Mike Friend, BB, Michael B Griffith)*

MILTON STREET [TQ5304]

Sussex Ox BN26 5RL [off A27 just E of Alfriston – brown sign to pub]: Attractive country pub with magnificent downs views, smallish beamed and brick-floored bar with roaring woodburner, real ales, friendly and enthusiastic young licensees, separate restaurant; piped music; children allowed in good no smoking family room (book well ahead in summer), big lawn, lots of good walks *(Jenny and Peter Lowater, LYM, Michael B Griffith)*

NETHERFIELD [TQ7118]

Netherfield Arms TN33 9QD [just off B2096 Heathfield—Battle]: Friendly and unpretentious low-ceilinged country pub with wide choice of enjoyable home-made food, Fullers London Pride, decent wines, inglenook log fire, no smoking area, cosy restaurant, no music; lovely back garden *(BB)*

NEWICK [TQ4121]

☆ *Bull* BN8 4LA [A272 Uckfield—Haywards Heath]: Attractive and welcoming rambling dining pub in 16th-c former coaching inn, wide range of generous food in sizeable eating area, good service, real ales such as Greene King and

Harveys Best, inglenook log fires, lots of beams and old-world character; bedrooms in adjacent building *(BB, Ann and Colin Hunt, Tony Hobden)*

Royal Oak BN8 4JU [Church Rd]: Neat, friendly and comfortable, on lovely village green, food inc enjoyable Sun roasts with local veg, Harveys Best, decent coffee, good service; tables out in front, open all day wknds *(Ann and Colin Hunt)*

NUTBOURNE [TQ0718]

Rising Sun RH20 2HE [off A283 E of Pulborough; The Street]: Unspoilt creeper-covered village pub dating partly from 16th c, beams, bare boards and scrubbed tables, friendly young landlord, Fullers London Pride, Greene King Abbot and Ruddles Best and a changing guest beer, good value usual bar food, big log fire, daily papers, enamel advertising signs and 1920s posters, chess and cosy games room, no smoking beamed back restaurant; children and dogs allowed, two garden areas with small back terrace under apple tree, handy for Nutbourne vineyard *(Bruce Bird, Tony and Wendy Hobden, John Beeken)*

NUTHURST [TQ1926]

☆ *Black Horse* RH13 6LH [off A281 SE of Horsham]: Convivial 17th-c country pub with low black beams, flagstones, inglenook log fire and plenty of character in its several small rooms, attentive landlord and friendly efficient service, Harveys Best, Kings, Timothy Taylors Landlord and a guest beer, good range of wines by the glass, no smoking snug and restaurant; may be piped music; children and dogs welcome, attractive woodland streamside back garden, more seats on front terrace *(Mike and Lynn Robinson, C and R Bromage, LYM, Mrs Margo Finlay, Jörg Kasprowski)*

OFFHAM [TQ3912]

☆ *Blacksmiths Arms* BN7 3QD [A275 N of Lewes]: Popular open-plan dining pub, open sandwiches, baked potatoes, ploughman's and usual pubby things as well as good fresh fish and other specials, Harveys Best, good professional service, huge end inglenook fireplace; french windows to terrace with picnic-sets, four bedrooms with own bathrooms *(Fr Robert Marsh, Ann and Colin Hunt, LYM, Mr and Mrs Peter Chance, Ron Gentry, Geoff and Molly Betteridge, Mrs J A Jackson)*

Chalk Pit BN7 3QF [A275 N of Lewes]: Bright and pleasant pub under friendly new licensees, Harveys Best and Old, good range of standard food all day (same chef), good Sun roasts, neat no smoking restaurant; bedrooms, open all day *(Tony and Wendy Hobden, Ann and Colin Hunt, Terry Buckland)*

PAGHAM [SZ8998]

Lamb PO21 4NJ [Pagham Rd]: Rambling flower-decked pub with lots of beams, timbers and paintings, Fullers London Pride, Greene King Abbot and Youngs Bitter and Special, generous enjoyable food, polite efficient service even when busy, large no smoking area, restaurant; garden tables *(Bruce Bird)*

PATCHING [TQ0705]

Fox BN13 3UJ [signed off A27 eastbound just W of Worthing]: Friendly efficient staff, enjoyable reasonably priced generous food freshly made from imaginative sandwiches, baguettes and baked potatoes up, popular Sun roasts (book ahead for these), Harveys Best, Shepherd Neame Spitfire and a guest beer, good wine choice, daily papers, large no smoking dining area off roomy panelled bar, hunting pictures; quiet piped music, nice big tree-shaded garden with play area, small caravan site, open all day wknds *(Bruce Bird, Cathryn and Richard Hicks, Tony and Wendy Hobden)*

PETT [TQ8713]

Royal Oak TN35 4HG [Pett Rd]: Particularly generous enjoyable food from sandwiches up inc OAP lunches in well run friendly local, roomy bars, real ales, separate dining area *(Pamela and Douglas Cooper, Michael and Ann Cole)*

PETWORTH [SU9719]

☆ *Badgers* GU28 0JF [Station Rd (A285 1½ miles S)]: Small drinking area by entrance, but most customers come to eat the up-to-date rather upmarket food, served generously at well spaced tables with mix from old mahogany to waxed stripped pine, charming wrought-iron lamps, log fires, friendly staff, Badger Best and K&B, a good range of wines; may be faint piped music; children in eating area of bar if over 5, stylish tables and seats out on terrace by water lily pool, bedrooms, cl winter Sun evenings *(Pat Woodward, Peter Mueller, Pamela and Merlyn Horswell, Walter and Susan Rinaldi-Butcher, LYM)*

New Star GU28 0AH [Market Sq]: Busy roomy pub in centre, Fullers ESB, freshly made food (so may take a while) daily papers, large no smoking area *(Terry Buckland)*

Stonemasons GU28 9NL [North St]: Welcoming new licensees in attractive old beamed pub, enjoyable food with some enterprising dishes, local beer, comfortable roomy eating areas (opp Petworth House so best to book in summer); pleasant garden and terrace, nine comfortable bedrooms, good breakfast *(Pam and David Bailey, Cathy Robinson, Ed Coombe)*

PLAYDEN [TQ9121]

Playden Oasts TN31 7UL [Rye Rd]: Attractive converted oast house with comfortable bar and restaurant, helpful licensee, friendly homely atmosphere, Harveys Best *(Marion and Bill Cross)*

PLUMPTON [TQ3613]

Half Moon BN7 3AF [Ditchling Rd (B2116)]: Long friendly bar with lots of beams and timbering, Harveys Best and Weltons, reasonably priced pubby food from baked potatoes and baguettes up, good log fire with unusual flint chimneybreast, jug collection and painting of regulars, games area, small dining area; children welcome, tables in wisteria front courtyard and big back downs-view garden with big play area, good walks *(John Beeken)*

POYNINGS [TQ2611]
Royal Oak BN45 7AQ [The Street]: Large darkly beamed chatty bar with wide choice of enjoyable food (can book tables), good service, Courage Directors, Greene King Old Speckled Hen and Harveys from three-sided servery, no smoking area, woodburner, no piped music; big attractive garden with barbecue, climbing frame and country/downs views *(N R White, Mr and Mrs John Taylor, J Varey)*

PUNNETTS TOWN [TQ6220]
Barley Mow TN21 9DL [B2096]: Recently reopened traditional pub with cheery young chef doing enjoyable fresh food from sandwiches and ploughman's to pubby favourites and plenty of fresh fish, restaurant with fine Weald views to distant sea, pool in games room *(Diana Brumfit)*
☆ *Three Cups* TN21 9LR [B2096 towards Battle]: Welcoming and relaxed low-beamed country local with log fire in big fireplace, small partly no smoking back dining room, enjoyable home-made food (not Sun evening or Mon) from pubby favourites to several foreign dishes, four Greene King ales, traditional games; piped music, small TV by bar; children and dogs welcome, tables outside, great walks, open all day wknds *(Kevin Thorpe, LYM)*

PYECOMBE [TQ2912]
Plough BN45 7FN [London Rd (A23)]: Smartly refurbished extended pub with huge helpings of largely italian food in back conservatory restaurant, good short wine choice, real ales such as Harveys and Shepherd Neame Bishops Finger in small front bar which still attracts locals, friendly and efficient staff all in black; children welcome, handy for South Downs Way walks *(Chris Wall, D and M T Ayres-Regan)*

RINGMER [TQ4415]
Old Ship BN8 5RP [Uckfield Rd (A26 Lewes—Uckfield, outside village S of Isfield turn-off)]: Tastefully refurbished olde-worlde beamed pub back to its proper name after a spell as the Stewards Enquiry, friendly helpful staff, wide choice of enjoyable fresh food using local supplies, real ales such as Courage Directors and Harveys Best, farm cider; good-sized attractive garden with play area *(Iain Forbes, Ben Burdass)*

ROBERTSBRIDGE [TQ7323]
Ostrich TN32 5DG [Station Rd]: Cheerful open-plan former station hotel, enjoyable food from filled rolls up, Adnams, Harveys Best and a guest beer, coal fire, eye-catching artworks; games room; tables in attractive garden, bedrooms, open all day *(the Didler)*

RODMELL [TQ4105]
Abergavenny Arms BN7 3EZ [back rd Lewes—Newhaven]: Open-plan beamed and raftered village pub, largely no smoking, with some interesting bric-a-brac and furnishings, generous food from ploughman's to sensible hot dishes, Harveys Best and guest beers such as Dark Star and Hogs Back, quick friendly service, log fire, small no smoking section; piped music may obtrude; dogs on leads

welcome, large two-level back terrace, good walks and handy for Virginia Woolf's Monks Cottage *(Bruce Bird, Sue Demont, Tim Barrow, Tony and Wendy Hobden, Paul Hopton)*

ROGATE [SU8023]
☆ *White Horse* GU31 5EA [East St; A272 Midhurst—Petersfield]: Rambling heavy-beamed local, civilised and friendly, with Harveys full range particularly well kept, relaxed atmosphere, flagstones, stripped stone, timbers and big log fire, step down to attractive no smoking candlelit dining area, good generous reasonably priced food (not Sun eve or Mon), hands-on licensees, traditional games (and quite a collection of trophy cups), no music or machines; quiz and folk nights; some tables on back terrace, open all day Sun *(LYM, Bruce Bird, Pamela and Merlyn Horswell, Geoff and Linda Payne, J Stickland)*

RUSTINGTON [TQ0503]
Windmill BN16 3JN [Mill Lane (B2187)]: Courage Best and several local ales such as Arundel, Dark Star, Hammerpot and Kings, generous enjoyable food (not Sun evening) ordered from separate counter inc Thurs OAP lunches, efficient friendly service, no smoking restaurant (plans to extend this); large pleasant garden with neat lawn, miniature windmill, boules and play area *(Tony and Wendy Hobden, Bruce Bird)*

RYE [TQ9120]
Old Bell TN31 7EN [The Mint, High St]: Ancient beamed and panelled two-room pub with old prints and photographs, good service, real ales, decent coffee, good value food, no smoking area; small garden with lovely wisteria *(Ann and Colin Hunt)*
Ship TN31 7DB [The Strand]: Lots of space, wooden tables on bare boards, Harveys and Youngs, usual food at reasonable prices; bedrooms *(Paul Rampton)*
Union TN31 7JY [East St]: Attractive beamed pub with newish licensees doing enjoyable fresh home-made food, Harveys ale, good atmosphere; children welcome *(Mrs Tay Abhyankar)*
☆ *Ypres Castle* TN31 7HH [Gun Garden; steps up from A259, or down past Ypres Tower]: Nicely placed, with informal traditional bars, lots of artworks (though it's not a smart place), log fire, Adnams Broadside, Harveys Best and Charles Wells Bombardier, good choice of wines by the glass, food inc local fish, comfortable no smoking restaurant area; service, usually good and friendly, can be a bit offhand; children welcome lunchtime, dogs in bar, tables outside, open all day summer Sats, cl Tues in winter and Sun evening *(Louise English, Gwyn Jones, Sarah Hapgood, Peter Meister, LYM, Stephen Harvey, B and M Kendall, Barry Ashton, Tim Maddison)*

RYE HARBOUR [TQ9419]
☆ *Inkerman Arms* TN31 7TQ [Rye Harbour Rd]: Friendly unpretentious pub nr nature reserve, stools around the bar but otherwise mainly tables for the wide choice of good food

inc lots of low-priced fresh local fish, fine home-made pies and old-fashioned puddings, Greene King IPA, Harveys Best and a guest such as Weltons Sussex Pride, no smoking area; tables out in small sheltered back area, cl Mon evening and winter Mon lunchtime *(Peter Meister, Stephen Harvey, Pete Taylor, Mr and Mrs S Wilson, B J Harding)*

SEAFORD [TV5199]
Golden Galleon BN25 4AB [Exceat, A259 E]: Vintage Inns family dining pub in fine position, handy for the level walk down the valley to the sea, with plenty of tables outside, usual food all day *(LYM, Michael and Ann Cole, Ron Gentry, Karen Eliot)*
White Lion BN25 2BJ [Claremont Rd]: Friendly new management taking care over food quality, good range from sandwiches and baguettes to local fish and Sun roasts, children's helpings, Fullers London Pride and Harveys, no smoking conservatory; bedrooms, open all day *(Fr Robert Marsh)*

SELHAM [SU9320]
Three Moles GU28 0PN [village signed off A272 Petworth—Midhurst]: Small simple old-fashioned pub tucked away in woodland village, quietly relaxing atmosphere, friendly enthusiastic landlady, Skinners Betty Stogs and unusual guest beers collected direct from small breweries (one always a Mild, others often west country), farm cider, daily papers, darts, bar billiards, plenty of board games, a few oil lamps and pictures, no mobile phones; steep steps up to bar, no food or children, monthly singsongs, June beer festival; garden tables, nice walks, open all day wknds *(Kevin Thorpe, Bruce Bird)*

SELSEY [SZ8692]
Lifeboat PO20 0DJ [Albion Rd, nr seafront]: Congenial unpretentious bar (dogs allowed) with dining extension, wide choice of low-priced food from sandwiches to local fish and crab, Fullers London Pride, friendly helpful staff; tables out on big verandah – only main courses served at hatch here *(David H T Dimock, Phil and Sally Gorton, LM, Tony and Shirley Albert)*

SHIPLEY [TQ1321]
☆ *Countryman* RH13 8PZ [SW of village, off A272 E of Coolham]: Nicely updated early 19th-c pub, welcoming timbered and flagstoned bar with inglenook log fire, comfortable lounge with big leather sofas, wide choice of enjoyable food from warm baguettes and baked potatoes through tapas to interesting main dishes, real ales such as Bass, Kings Horsham Best and Youngs Special, friendly efficient staff, large carpeted dining area; may be piped music; picnic-sets and play equipment in pretty garden, horse park, handy for Shipley windmill and D-Day Airfield at Coolham *(Mrs Jennifer Hurst, Siri Burton)*

SHOREHAM-BY-SEA [TQ2105]
Royal Sovereign BN43 5DP [Middle St]: Comfortable backstreet L-shaped local with part laid out for dining, low-priced lunchtime food from sandwiches to a few main meals,

Castle Eden and Timothy Taylors Landlord, good choice of wines by the glass *(Tony and Wendy Hobden)*

SIDLESHAM [SZ8599]
Anchor PO20 7QU [Selsey Rd]: Well spaced bar seating (dogs allowed in), Courage Best and Directors and Greene King Old Speckled Hen, good choice of reasonably priced food from separate servery inc fresh local fish, no smoking dining room; nice terrace, handy for wildlife centre *(Tony and Wendy Hobden)*
Crab & Lobster PO20 7NB [Mill Lane; off B2145 S of Chichester]: This nicely sited country pub, with pretty back garden looking over to the bird reserve of silted Pagham Harbour and popular for its friendly individuality, good drinks, small choice of bar food from local crab sandwiches up, traditional layout with log fire in regulars' bar and side dining lounge, was closed for major refurbishment in summer 2006, with talk of turning into a restaurant; news please *(LYM)*

SOMPTING [TQ1605]
Marquis of Granby BN15 0AP [West St]: Big 1930s pub with large sofas and raised dining area in pleasantly updated lounge, thriving family atmosphere, Harveys Best and Shepherd Neame Spitfire, good choice of sensibly priced food, pool in public bar; big-screen TV; garden tables *(Val and Alan Green)*

SOUTH HARTING [SU7819]
Ship GU31 5PZ [North Lane (B2146)]: Well kept Ballards, Flower Pots and Palmers in welcoming 17th-c pub, unpretentious and informal, with good choice of good value food (not Sun evening, when there are bar nibbles) from sandwiches up in dimly lit main bar, fine log fire, old photographs, friendly helpful licensees and staff, plain wooden settles in locals' bar with log fire and dominoes; unobtrusive piped music; nice setting in pretty village *(MLR, Rona Murdoch, Ann and Colin Hunt, W A Evershed, Brian and Janet Ainscough)*

SOUTHWATER [TQ1528]
Bax Castle RH13 0LA [Two Mile Ash, a mile or so NW]: Popular early 19th-c flagstoned country pub pleasantly extended with ex-barn no smoking restaurant, big log fire in back room, Brakspears, Harveys and Kings Best, good value generous bar food inc good Sun lunch (best to book), two no smoking areas, no music or machines; picnic-sets on two pleasant lawns, play area, near Downs Link Way on former rail track *(Bruce Bird, Ian Phillips)*

ST LEONARDS [TQ7608]
Bull TN38 8AY [Bexhill Rd (A259)]: Well run local, cheerful and unpretentious, with Shepherd Neame ales, usual pub food from sandwiches up, prompt polite service, fairly large no smoking dining room *(Stephen Harvey)*

STAPLEFIELD [TQ2728]
☆ *Jolly Tanners* RH17 6EF [Handcross Rd, just off A23]: Spotless and comfortable, good honest home-made food inc popular Sun roasts, real ales such as Elgoods Black Dog, Fullers Chiswick and London Pride and

Harveys Best, helpful efficient staff, two good
log fires, lots of china, brasses and old
photographs, no smoking room; piped music;
attractive nicely kept garden with lots of space
for children, terrace tables under cocktail
parasols and picnic-sets on grass, by cricket
green, quite handy for Nymans (NT)
*(Tony and Wendy Hobden, Bruce Bird,
Fred Chamberlain, C and R Bromage)*

STEYNING [TQ1711]
White Horse BN44 3YE [High St]: Rambling
creeper-covered inn, recently refurbished, with
enjoyable food and Greene King ales; tables on
spacious terrace *(Roger Price, Des and
Jen Clarke)*

STOPHAM [TQ0318]
☆ *White Hart* RH20 1DS [off A283 E of village,
W of Pulborough]: Interesting old heavily
timbered, beamed and panelled pub with log
fire and sofas in one of its three snug rooms,
Fullers London Pride, Greene King Old
Speckled Hen and Weltons Kid, wide food
choice from baguettes and baked potatoes
through pubby staples to venison, friendly
young enthusiastic staff, no smoking
restaurant; piped music; children welcome,
play area over road, tables out by River Arun
*(Bruce Bird, John Beeken, LYM, E H and
J I Wild)*

STOUGHTON [SU8011]
Hare & Hounds PO18 9JQ [signed off B2146
Petersfield—Emsworth]: Airy recently
renovated pine-clad country dining pub with
emphasis on standard food, four real ales, big
open fires; children in eating areas, tables on
pretty front terrace and in back garden, lovely
setting nr Saxon church, good walks nearby
(LYM, Ann and Colin Hunt, W A Eversbed)

THAKEHAM [TQ1017]
☆ *White Lion* RH20 3EP [off B2139 N of
Storrington; The Street]: Heavily beamed two-
bar 16th-c pub, truly welcoming with friendly
staff and locals, real ales such as Fullers
London Pride, Harveys Best and Kings, good
choice of wines by the glass, robust home-
made food (not Sun-Weds evenings) from open
kitchen, friendly informal service, big log fire,
bare boards and traditional furnishings inc
corner settles, small no smoking bar and
pleasant separate eating area; dogs welcome,
terrace tables, more on small lawn, small pretty
village *(Terry Buckland, Bruce Bird,
Mrs M Rice)*

TICEHURST [TQ6830]
Bell TN5 7AS [High St]: Splendidly
unchanging and unsmart, with Harveys Best,
chatty veteran landlady who was born here,
some fine old empire and Victorian prints and
posters, old cash register, lots of bric-a-brac,
barrel chairs and tables, big log fire, piano; TV,
open all day *(Kevin Thorpe)*
Bull TN5 7HH [Three Legged Cross; off
B2099 towards Wadhurst]: Attractive 14th-c
hall house with two big log fires in very heavy-
beamed old-fashioned simple two-room bar,
contemporary furnishings and new floor in
light and airy dining extension, new chef doing
enjoyable food, real ales; charming front

garden with fish pond, bigger back one with
play area *(LYM)*

TILLINGTON [SU9621]
☆ *Horse Guards* GU28 9AF [off A272
Midhurst—Petworth]: Enthusiastic young new
licensees in prettily set 18th-c dining pub with
log fire and country furniture in neat beamed
front bar, lovely views from bow window, no
smoking dining room, enjoyable enterprising
food using local produce, generous helpings,
Gales HSB, Greene King Old Speckled Hen
and Youngs, good choice of wines by the glass;
may be piped music; terrace tables and
sheltered garden behind, attractive ancient
church opposite, bedrooms in pub and
adjoining cottage *(Mrs L Aquilina, LYM,
David Collison, Kevin Thorpe)*

TURNERS HILL [TQ3435]
☆ *Red Lion* RH10 4NU [Lion Lane, just off and
parallel with B2028]: Warmly welcoming
traditional local with great range of customers,
proper landlord, Harveys PA, Best and
seasonal beers, good choice of wines by the
glass, good value food from filled rolls through
simple hot dishes to good reasonably priced
Sun roast, narrow high-beamed bar with small
fire, three steps up to smallish low-ceilinged
dining area with inglenook log fire, cushioned
pews and built-in settles, lots of photographs
(one reader visiting after long absence was
startled to find one of himself in 1973 world
marbles championship); can be a bit smoky,
live music Fri; children and well behaved dogs
welcome, picnic-sets in quiet side garden
(Richard May, BB, J Cross, Terry Buckland)

UDIMORE [TQ8519]
Kings Head TN31 6BG: Traditional chatty
village pub with Fullers London Pride and
Harveys from long bar, good-sized helpings of
low-priced pubby food in dining area, long-
serving licensees, open fires, low beams, plain
tables and chairs on bare boards
(Peter Meister)
☆ *Plough* TN31 6AL [Cock Marling (B2089
W of Rye)]: Civilised and popular, with good
fresh home-made food, Greene King and a
guest beer, reasonably priced wines, relaxed
friendly service, woodburner, books for sale,
open fire and country prints in small dining
area; tables on good-sized suntrap back terrace
(Peter Meister, V Brogden)

UPPER DICKER [TQ5409]
Plough BN27 3QJ [Coldharbour Rd]: Under
new licensees and much extended from ancient
core, with Shepherd Neame Kents Best and
Spitfire, fairly priced food inc good specials (all
day wknds), friendly service, armchairs and
sofas in no smoking lounge, darts and big-
screen TV in public bar, woodburners,
restaurant; garden tables *(Fr Robert Marsh,
Paul A Moore)*

WALBERTON [SU9705]
Holly Tree BN18 0PH [The Street]: Pleasant
staff, wide choice of enjoyable good value food
from baguettes and baked potatoes up, Fullers
London Pride and Charles Wells Bombardier,
no smoking part; attractive hanging baskets
and flower tubs *(J F M and M West)*

WALDERTON [SU7910]
☆ *Barley Mow* PO18 9ED [Stoughton rd, just off
B2146 Chichester—Petersfield]: Flagstoned
country pub popular for good choice of good
value generous food from baguettes up, real
ales such as Fullers, Ringwood and Youngs,
quick cheerful service even on busy wknds,
two log fires and rustic bric-a-brac in U-shaped
bar with roomy dining areas, no music;
children welcome, skittle alley, nice furniture in
big pleasant streamside garden with fish pond,
aviary and swings, good walks, handy for
Stansted House (*W A Evershed, R B Gardiner*)

WALDRON [TQ5419]
Star TN21 0RA [Blackboys—Horam side
road]: Lively village local with big inglenook
log fire in panelled bar, Harveys Bitter and
seasonal Old, reliable food from good ham
baguettes up, friendly helpful service, no music,
separate back dining room; pleasant garden,
seats out in front overlooking pretty village
(*Phil and Sally Gorton, BB, PL*)

WARNHAM [TQ1533]
☆ *Sussex Oak* RH12 3QW [just off A24
Horsham—Dorking; Church St]: Cheerful
country pub with friendly staff, big inglenook
log fireplace, mix of flagstones, tiles, wood and
carpeting, heavy beams and timbers,
comfortable sofas, Adnams, Fullers London
Pride, Timothy Taylors Landlord, Youngs and
a guest beer from carved servery, plenty of
wines by the glass, popular food (not Sun/Mon
evenings) from sandwiches and baked potatoes
to steaks, high-raftered no smoking restaurant,
bar billiards; piped music; children and dogs
welcome, picnic-sets in pleasant garden, open
all day (*LYM, Malcolm Pearce, Ron Gentry,
Peter Lewis, Brian Mathers*)

WARNINGLID [TQ2425]
☆ *Half Moon* RH17 5TR [The Street]:
Traditional village pub with enjoyable and
reasonably priced fresh country food using
local supplies with some nice imaginative
touches in distinct eating side, Black Sheep,
Harveys and Shepherd Neame Spitfire, good
wines, friendly and hard-working young
licensees, cheerful fire, soft lighting and old
pews; pleasant good-sized garden behind
(*Elizabeth Turrell, Don Scarff,
Terry Buckland, Liz and Brian Barnard,
J P Humphery*)

WASHINGTON [TQ1213]
Frankland Arms RH20 4AL [just off A24
Horsham—Worthing]: Wide choice of
unpretentious food all day from warm
baguettes to good puddings, take-aways too,
Flowers Original, Fullers London Pride and a
guest beer, good value wines by the glass, log
fires, pleasant prompt service, well used
bar/lounge (dogs welcome) and large
comfortable no smoking dining area, TV and
pool; disabled facilities, Post Office in
outbuilding, tables in neat garden below
Chanctonbury Ring (*Tony and
Wendy Hobden, Des and Jen Clarke*)

WEST CHILTINGTON [TQ0917]
Five Bells RH20 2QX [Smock Alley, off B2139
SE]: Large open-plan beamed and panelled bar

with old photographs, unusual brass bric-a-
brac, real ales inc Arundel Dark Mild, Harveys
and guests from small breweries, farm cider,
pubby food (not Sun evening or Mon) inc good
ploughman's, friendly enthusiastic landlord,
log fire, daily papers, big pleasant conservatory
dining room, no piped music; peaceful garden
with terrace, bedrooms (*Bruce Bird,
John Beeken*)

WEST DEAN [SU8512]
Selsey Arms PO18 0QX [A286 Midhurst—
Chichester]: Large welcoming late 18th-c pub
with smart no smoking dining bar, plentiful
enjoyable food inc good home-made crisps,
Greene King IPA and Fullers London Pride,
decent wines, friendly service, log fire,
traditional public bar (*Richard Waller,
Pauline Smith, Ann and Colin Hunt*)

WEST HOATHLY [TQ3632]
☆ *Cat* RH19 4PP [signed from A22 and B2028 S
of E Grinstead; North Lane]: Attractive dining
pub doing well under new owners with good
track record in other pubs, beams, panelling,
fresh flowers and inglenook log fires, real ales
such as Black Sheep, Fullers London Pride,
Harveys and Shepherd Neame Spitfire, decent
wines, enjoyable food from sandwiches to
interesting main dishes, helpful polite service
even when they're busy; tables outside, quiet
view of church (*Don Scarff, LYM,
Terry Buckland, JMM, Jane Saunders,
Amanda Harries*)
Intrepid Fox RH19 4QG [Hammingden
Lane/North Lane, towards Sharpthorne]:
Former Vinols Cross Inn, now a comfortably
up-to-date restauranty pub, warm and
welcoming, with genial landlord, enjoyable
generous food, good wine (*Mrs Tester,
Selina Knight, Mrs F Reynolds*)
White Hart RH19 4RA [Ardingly Rd]: Cosy
bar with affable helpful new landlord, log fire,
Adnams and Harveys Best and short choice of
pub food, wider choice for huge timbered
Sussex barn restaurant area and conservatory,
lounge with sofas; handy for Wakehurst Place
(*C and R Bromage*)

WEST ITCHENOR [SU7901]
Ship PO20 7AH [The Street]: Large panelled
pub in good spot nr Chichester Harbour,
tables outside, good long walk to W Wittering
or foot ferry to Bosham Hoe; generous
changing food from good baguettes to
restaurant dishes inc local fish, good friendly
service, Ballards, Gales, Itchen Valley and
Ringwood, two log fires, lots of bric-a-brac inc
many chamber-pots, lots of bare wood inc
scrubbed tables and seats made from old boat,
marine pictures, children in pleasant eating
area with well spaced tables; open all day, said
to be able to get supplies for yachtsmen
(nearest shop is two miles away) (*BOB*)

WEST MARDEN [SU7713]
Victoria PO18 9EN [B2146 2 miles S of
Uppark]: Doing well after light refurbishment
by popular new owners, now no smoking, with
new chef doing short choice of good food in
bar and small back candlelit restaurant, three
real ales such as Harveys, Ringwood and

Timothy Taylors Landlord, good choice of reasonably priced wines, old Royal wedding photographs, pleasant end alcove with old-fashioned sofa by log fire, friendly attentive staff, no piped music; pleasant garden, good walks nearby, bedrooms *(Ann and Colin Hunt, Bruce Bird, Jon and Penny Barnes)*

WEST WITTERING [SZ8099]

Lamb PO20 8QA [Chichester Rd; B2179/A286 towards Birdham]: Several rooms (some no smoking) neatly knocked through in 18th-c country pub, clean smart furnishings, rugs on tiles, blazing fire, Badger ales, decent wines, reasonably priced food from separate servery inc full bar menu on Sun lunchtime; dogs on leads allowed, lots of tables out in front and in small sheltered back garden with terrace - good for children; busy in summer - handy for beach *(David H T Dimock, BB, Klaus and Elizabeth Leist)*

WHATLINGTON [TQ7619]

Royal Oak TN33 0NJ [A21]: Two long welcoming and relaxing beamed rooms with stripped pine tables and chairs, log fire, nooks and corners, feature well edged with flowers, generous enjoyable traditional food with good veg, decent wine, efficient welcoming service; tables in back garden *(J N Davidson, Brian Root, BB, Pamela and Douglas Cooper, Veronica Ford, M and R Thomas)*

WHITEMANS GREEN [TQ3025]

Ship RH17 5BY [B2115/B2114]: Caledonian Deuchars IPA, Courage Best and Kings Horsham Best, lunchtime food inc good value sandwiches, cheerful landlord, pub dalmatian, two facing sofas in lounge, dining area beyond central open fire, side games room; dogs welcome *(Tony Hobden)*

WINCHELSEA [TQ9017]

Bridge TN36 4JT [The Strand (A259)]: Wide choice of enjoyable food inc fresh local fish in bar and no smoking dining lounge, genial welcoming landlord, relaxing atmosphere, Fullers London Pride and Harveys *(Paul Rampton)*

☆ *New Inn* TN36 4EN [German St; just off A259]: Rambling open-plan beamed areas with emphasis on the enjoyable food from good sandwiches to hearty traditional dishes and fresh local fish, Greene King ales, decent wines and malt whiskies, obliging helpful staff, log fire, Georgian décor with turkey carpet and some slate flagstones, back public bar with darts and machines; piped music may obtrude; children in eating area, pleasant walled garden, six pretty bedrooms (some sharing bathrooms), delightful setting opp pretty church - Spike Milligan buried in graveyard *(Joel Dobris, Peter Meister, Grahame Brooks, LYM, Andrew Richard Smith, John Beeken)*

WISBOROUGH GREEN [TQ0526]

Cricketers Arms RH14 0DG [Loxwood Rd, just off A272 Billingshurst—Petworth]: Very low beams, bare boards and timbering in attractive open-plan old pub, two big woodburners, pleasant mix of country furniture, five or six real ales, no smoking stripped brick dining area on left, cheerful

staff; piped music; tables out on terrace and across lane from green *(Mike and Lynn Robinson, LYM)*

☆ *Three Crowns* RH14 0DX [Billingshurst Rd (A272)]: Neatly kept elongated pub with real ales such as Badger, Ballards and Kings from end bar, good range of standard food from sandwiches and baguettes up, friendly helpful service, heavy beams and stripped brick in no smoking dining area, good coffee; disabled facilities, sizeable tree-shaded back garden *(Mike and Lynn Robinson, DWAJ, John Beeken, Peter Lewis, David A Hammond)*

WITHYHAM [TQ4935]

☆ *Dorset Arms* TN7 4BD [B2110]: 16th-c pub handy for Forest Way walks, cheerful young landlord and good service, enjoyable traditional food from filled rolls up, reasonable prices, Harveys full beer range, decent wines inc local ones, good log fire in Tudor fireplace, sturdy tables and simple country seats on wide oak boards (sometimes a bit uneven - beware of wobbles), darts, dominoes, shove-ha'penny, cribbage, pretty no smoking restaurant; piped pop music, fruit machine; dogs welcome, white tables on brick terrace by small green *(Michael and Ann Cole, LYM, Angus Johnson, Carol Bolden, Peter Meister, Debbie and Neil Hayter)*

WORTHING [TQ1404]

Cricketers BN14 9DE [Broadwater St W, Broadwater Green (A24)]: Extended panelled local with welcoming staff, Bass, Fullers London Pride, Harveys and two guest beers, log fires, reasonably priced popular food, friendly staff, steps down to small lounge with no smoking dining room beyond; garden with bouncy castle *(Jude Wright, Tony and Wendy Hobden)*

Hare & Hound BN11 1QG [Portland Rd, N of Marks & Spencer]: Thriving extended local with five real ales from several different breweries from central brass and oak bar, good value promptly served straightforward food (not Fri-Sun evenings) from sandwiches and baked potatoes up, helpful staff, jazz night Tues; canopied courtyard *(P Dawn, Tony and Wendy Hobden)*

John Seldon BN13 2HN [Lower Salvington]: Refurbished Victorian local, friendly young staff, straightforward lunchtime food from sandwiches to bargain hot dishes, Fullers London Pride, Greene King Abbot and Tetleys, spacious saloon hung with hops and tankards, smaller public bar with darts; tables in big courtyard and on side terrace *(Tony and Wendy Hobden)*

Old House at Home BN14 9AD [Broadwater St E]: Quiet panelled lounge with friendly young staff, Greene King IPA, Harveys Best and Shepherd Neame Spitfire, good choice of good value food, open fires, bric-a-brac and old photographs, no smoking conservatory; children welcome, terrace tables *(Bruce Bird)*

Selden Arms BN11 2DB [Lyndhurst Rd, between Safeway and hospital]: Friendly local with up to half a dozen good real ales inc

Ringwood Fortyniner and Youngs, farm cider, lively landlady and locals, generous good value lunchtime food inc popular doorstep sandwiches, log fire, lots of old pub photographs; open all day *(P Dawn, Tony and Wendy Hobden, Bruce Bird)*
Sir Timothy Shelley BN11 1EG [Chapel Rd]:

One of the smaller Wetherspoons, mainly no smoking, with internal conservatory, real ales inc bargain guests, decent economical food, friendly efficient service, silenced big-screen TV news; children welcome in family area till 6, handy for Connaught theatre, open all day *(Tony and Wendy Hobden)*

A very few pubs try to make you leave a credit card at the bar, as a sort of deposit if you order food. They are not entitled to do this. The credit card firms and banks which issue them warn you not to let them out of your sight. If someone behind the counter used your card fraudulently, the card company or bank could in theory hold you liable, because of your negligence in letting a stranger hang on to your card. Suggest instead that if they feel the need for security, they 'swipe' your card and give it back to you. And do name and shame the pub to us.

Warwickshire
(with Birmingham and West Midlands)

Food figures strongly in this area's best pubs. Foody pubs on particularly good form this year include the Bell at Alderminster (a neatly kept Georgian pub), the Fox & Goose in Armscote (a clever cross between dining pub and local), the Kings Head in Aston Cantlow (new licensees offering unusual and interesting dishes that have been going down extremely well with readers), the Inn at Farnborough (very restauranty, and with no real ale now), the Howard Arms at Ilmington (a real favourite with readers for its super food), the Crabmill at Preston Bagot (a stylish conversion of an ancient cider mill), and the Bell at Welford-on-Avon (a charming old place with good real ales and modern cooking). The Kings Head in Aston Cantlow now heads this fine contingent, as Warwickshire Dining Pub of the Year. Other pubs doing well include the Old Joint Stock in Birmingham (surprisingly opulent and most enjoyable), the Turf in Bloxwich (in the same friendly family for 130 years), the Vine in Brierley Hill (a well liked no-nonsense Black Country pub), the Case is Altered at Five Ways (quite unchanged for decades), the Malt Shovel at Gaydon (a good clutch of real ales, and handy for the M40), the Duck on the Pond at Long Itchington (an interesting bistro-type feel), the Old Swan in Netherton (our one new main entry this year, splendidly traditional, brewing its own bargain beers, with bargain food to match), and the Holly Bush at Priors Marston (a well run, lively country local). In the Lucky Dip section at the end of the chapter, pubs currently giving particular pleasure include the Bartons Arms and Tap & Spile in Birmingham, Dun Cow at Dunchurch (a Vintage Inn – this is rather a good area for pubs belonging to the better chains), Red Lion at Long Compton, Bell at Monks Kirby, Horseshoe in Shipston-on-Stour, Garrick in Stratford (several other decent pubs here too), Plough at Stretton-on-Fosse and Great Western in Wolverhampton. Drinks and indeed food prices show quite a sharp divide between Warwickshire proper, where they are more or less in line with the national average, and the more urban parts of the West Midlands, where they tend to be significantly cheaper. Beer prices in the West Midlands are among the lowest in Britain, and as well as interesting own-brew pubs such as the Netherton Old Swan and the Beacon in Sedgley, there are highly pocket-friendly local brewers, most notably Bathams and Holdens. Banks's is the main West Midlands brewer, and you may also find Highgate. Out in the countryside, local beers we found in the main entries included Shakespeares, Church End and Frankton Bagby, though you are more likely to find beers from just outside the county, most notably Hook Norton.

Looking for a pub with a really special garden, or in lovely countryside, or with an outstanding view, or right by the water? They are listed separately, at the back of the book.

ALDERMINSTER SP2348 Map 4

Bell ⑪ ⚲

A3400 Oxford—Stratford; CV37 8NY

Neatly kept and popular, this Georgian inn places much emphasis on its good food. The communicating rooms of the bar are spacious and open plan and there are stripped slatback chairs around wooden tables on flagstones and beautifully polished wooden floors, little vases of flowers, a counter fronted with rough timber from wine crates, and a solid fuel stove in a stripped brick inglenook. The green walls are hung with huge modern prints. As well as filled baguettes (from £4.50) and little dishes like soup (£4.25), smoked haddock and prawns au gratin (£5.95), duck livers fried with spiced apple and Grand Marnier (£6.95), and mixed hors d'oeuvres (£7.25), the menu might include leek and cheese croquettes (£8.25), stir-fried chicken, smoked bacon and avocado salad (£9.95), sausage and mash (£10.50), steak and kidney pudding (£11.95), seared lambs liver with black pudding and bacon (£12.25), daily specials such as minted lamb kebab with cucumber chilli salsa (£5.25), creamy crab tartlet (£5.95), home-made lasagne (£9.25), bass fillet on roasted artichokes (£12.95), and braised shank of local lamb with redcurrant jus (£13.95), and puddings such as apple and blackberry crumble, treacle tart or raspberry fool (£5.25). Greene King IPA and Old Speckled Hen on handpump and a fine range of around 20 wines by the glass. A conservatory and terrace overlook the garden and Stour Valley. *(Recommended by Carol Broadbent, David and Ruth Shillitoe, David and Jean Hall, K H Frostick, Bruce and Penny Wilkie, Bernard Stradling, Clive and Fran Dutson, Carol and David Havard, Mrs Philippa Wilson, M Joyner, Pat and Clive Sherriff, Joan Crane, Eileen White, Les and Barbara Owen, Margaret Best, Michael and Jeanne Shillington, Dr P M O'Donnell, Iain R Hewitt, David Tett, H O Dickinson)*

Free house ~ Licensees Keith and Vanessa Brewer ~ Real ale ~ Bar food ~ Restaurant ~ (01789) 450414 ~ Children welcome ~ Dogs allowed in bar and bedrooms ~ Open 11.30-2.30, 6.30-11(10.30 Sun); closed evenings 24-30 Dec ~ Bedrooms: £32(£45S)(£60B)/£48(£55S)(£85B)

ARMSCOTE SP2444 Map 4

Fox & Goose ⑪ ⚲ 🛏

Off A3400 Stratford—Shipston; CV37 8DD

Enjoyable and very busy, this stylishly simple blacksmith's forge is an interesting mix of gastro pub and local. The small flagstoned bar has red-painted walls, bright crushed velvet cushions plumped up on wooden pews, a big gilt mirror over a log fire, polished floorboards and black and white etchings. In a quirky tableau above the dining room's woodburning stove a stuffed fox stalks a big goose. Not cheap, but nevertheless very good, the bar food is listed on a daily changing blackboard, and as well as sandwiches (£4.95), there might be home-made chicken liver parfait with red onion marmalade or cherry tomato and mozzarella salad with a balsamic glaze (£5.50), smoked fish platter with cracked black pepper and fresh lime juice (£5.75), sweet pepper and caramelised onion risotto with a goats cheese topping (£10.50), beer-battered haddock (£10.95), bass stuffed with spinach, cherry tomatoes and toasted almonds (£16), beef fillet with red wine jus (£17.95), and puddings such as a trio of miniature crumbles (£4.95); helpful service from charming young staff. Hook Norton Best and a guest such as Shepherd Neame Spitfire on handpump, well chosen wines and maybe winter mulled wine and summer Pimms. Bedrooms, which are named after characters in *Cluedo*, are mildly quirky, stylishly decorated and comfortable. Outside, the garden has an elegant vine-covered deck area overlooking a big lawn with tables, benches and fruit trees, and several of the neighbouring houses boast splendid roses in summer. *(Recommended by John Kane, Margaret and Allen Marsden, Keith and Sue Ward, Rob and Catherine Dunster, A Warren, Susan and John Douglas, KC, Rod Stoneman, Michael and Jeanne Shillington, Iain R Hewitt, Stephen Woad, Robin and Yvonne Calvert, D M Heath)*

Free house ~ Licensee Sarah Watson ~ Real ale ~ Bar food ~ Restaurant ~
(01608) 682293 ~ Children allowed away from bar area ~ Dogs allowed in bar ~
Open 12-2.30, 6-midnight; 12-midnight Sun and Sat; 12-2.30, 6-midnight in winter ~
Bedrooms: £60B/£100B

ASTON CANTLOW   SP1359   Map 4
Kings Head 🍴 ♀
Village signposted just off A3400 NW of Stratford; B95 6HY
Warwickshire Dining Pub of the Year
In summer particularly, this lovely old black and white timbered Tudor pub is quite
a sight with its colourful hanging baskets and wisteria. It's the sort of place that
customers enjoy coming back to again and again for the very good (and very
popular) food, gently civilised atmosphere, and welcoming, attentive service. Under
the new licensees, the interesting, regularly changing dishes might include
sandwiches, soup (£3.95), spicy courgette fritters layered with smoked salmon and
dill crème fraîche (£5.45), chicken ballotine on celeriac and walnut salad or satay of
minced rabbit on lemongrass stick with chilli and raisin jam (£5.95), french bean
and parmesan risotto with basil sauce (£9.95), white crab meat and coriander
fishcake with soy and sweet chilli (£10.75), chicken tandoori with marsala sauce
(£11.25), pork tenderloin marinated in coffee (£12.50), chargrilled rib-eye steak
with melted horseradish butter (£14.75), their famous duck supper (£14.95), and
puddings such as chargrilled banana with rum and raisin ice-cream and Kahlua,
upside-down fig pudding with port and lemon sorbet or triple-decker cake with
dark and white chocolate fudge (£5.95). The restaurant is no smoking. The clean
and comfortable village bar on the right is a nice mix of rustic surroundings with a
subtly upmarket atmosphere, flagstones, low beams, and old-fashioned settles
around its massive inglenook log fireplace. The chatty quarry-tiled main room has
attractive window seats and oak tables. Greene King Abbot, M&B Brew XI and a
guest beer on handpump and decent wines; piped jazz. The garden is lovely, with a
big chestnut tree. This is a very pretty village; the pub is not far from Mary Arden's
house in Wilmcote, and Shakespeare's parents are said to have married in the
church next door. *(Recommended by Paul and Gloria Howell, John Kane, Caroline Shaw,
Stephen Woad, P Dawn, Rob and Catherine Dunster, Mrs Philippa Wilson, Therese Flanagan,
Mike Gorton, Charles and Isabel Cooper, Les and Barbara Owen, Dr D Scott, Di and
Mike Gillam, Susan and John Douglas, John Saul, Des and Jen Clarke, David J Cooke)*

Enterprise ~ Lease Peter and Louise Sadler ~ Real ale ~ Bar food (11-3, 5.30-11; all day Fri
and Sat) ~ Restaurant ~ (01789) 488242 ~ Children welcome ~ Dogs allowed in bar ~
Open 11-3, 5.30-11(midnight in summer); 11-midnight Sat; 12-10.30(maybe 11.30) Sun

BIRMINGHAM   SP0686   Map 4
Old Joint Stock ◖
Temple Row West; B2 5NY
This is a well run and enjoyable city centre pub opposite the cathedral. It does get
busy, particularly with local office workers, but effortlessly absorbs what seem like
huge numbers of people. The interior is quite a surprise: chandeliers hang from the
soaring pink and gilt ceiling, gently illuminated busts line the top of the ornately
plastered walls, and there's a splendid if well worn cupola above the centre of the
room. Drinks are served from a handsome dark wood island bar counter, and big
portraits and smart long curtains create an air of unexpected elegance. Around the
walls are plenty of tables and chairs, some in cosy corners, with more on a big
balcony overlooking the bar, reached by a very grand wide staircase. A separate
room with panelling and a fireplace has a more intimate, clubby feel. This is the
only pub we know of N of Bristol to be owned by the London-based brewer
Fullers; it stocks their Chiswick, ESB, London Pride and one of their seasonal beers,
which are well kept alongside a guest from the local Beowulf, and they have a
decent range of about a dozen wines by the glass; helpful friendly service, teas,
coffees. Usefully served all day, a nice variety of very fairly priced bar food includes

soup (£2.75), sandwiches (from £3.75), bangers of the week (£6.50), lots of pies such as steak in ale or with stilton, cheesy leek and mushroom or chicken and mushroom (from £6.50), and fish and chips (£7.50). Daily papers, TV, games machine, and piped music. A small back terrace has some cast-iron tables and chairs. *(Recommended by Richard Waller, Pauline Smith, Colin Gooch, Graham and Glenis Watkins, Tim and Ann Newell, Rob and Catherine Dunster, Steve and Liz Tilley, Susan and John Douglas, John and Fiona McIlwain, Kevin Blake, Barry Collett, Tony and Wendy Hobden)*

Fullers ~ Manager Alison Turner ~ Real ale ~ Bar food (12-8; not Sun) ~ (0121) 200 1892 ~ Open 11-11; closed Sun and bank hols

BLOXWICH   SJ9902   Map 4

Turf 🍺

Wolverhampton Road, off A34 just S of A4124, N fringes of Walsall; aka Tinky's; WS3 2EZ

From the outside you could be forgiven for thinking that this quite unspoilt and old-fashioned local – in the same family for over 130 years – is no longer in business, as it appears to be a rather run-down terraced house. Once through the front door it still doesn't immediately look like a pub, but more like the hall of a 1930s home; the public bar is through a door on the right. Reminiscent of a waiting room, it has wooden slatted benches running around the walls, with a big heating pipe clearly visible underneath; there's a tiled floor, three small tables, and William Morris curtains and wallpaper around the simple fireplace. What's particularly nice is that even though the unspoilt rooms are Grade II listed, it's far more than just a museum piece. It's alive and chatty with friendly locals happy to tell you the history of the place, and the particularly impressive changing range of beers, always very well kept, draws in a wider range of customers than you might expect. The bar counter has four changing real ales from brewers such as Bathams, Beowulf, Holdens, RCH and Titanic. There's hatch service (friendly and chatty) out to the hall, on the other side of which is the smoking room, slightly more comfortable, with unusual padded wall settles with armrests. There's also a tiny back parlour with chairs around a tiled fireplace. It almost goes without saying that there's no music or machines. The pub's basic charms won't appeal to those who like their creature comforts; the no-frills lavatories are outside, at the end of a simple but pleasant garden, and they don't do food. *(Recommended by Pete Baker, Paul and Gloria Howell, Ian and Liz Rispin, the Didler, Mike Begley)*

Free house ~ Licensees Doris and Zena Hiscott-Wilkes ~ Real ale ~ No credit cards ~ (01922) 407745 ~ Open 12-3, 7-11(10.30 Sun)

BRIERLEY HILL   SO9187   Map 4

Vine 🍺 £

Delph Road; B4172 between A461 and (nearer) A4100; DY5 2TN

As this no-nonsense Black Country pub is the tap for the next-door Bathams brewery, the Bitter and Mild, and perhaps Delph Strong in winter, are in top condition and very cheap. The down-to-earth landlord and his staff are friendly and welcoming and the place is usually very busy. It's known locally as the Bull & Bladder in reference to the good stained-glass bull's heads and very approximate bunches of grapes in the front bow windows. The plainer front bar has wall benches and simple leatherette-topped oak stools; the extended and comfortable snug on the left (partly no smoking) has solidly built red plush seats; and the back bar has brass chandeliers – as well as darts, dominoes and a big-screen TV. A couple of tables and games machines stand in a corridor. Some of the memorabilia here, including one huge pair of horns over a mantelpiece, relates to the Royal Ancient Order of Buffalos, who meet in a room here. Simple but tasty fresh lunchtime snacks such as sandwiches and baguettes (from £1). There are tables in a back yard, and the car park is opposite. *(Recommended by Paul and Gloria Howell, Gill and Tony Morriss, P Dawn, the Didler, Theo, Anne and Jane Gaskin, Martin Grosberg)*

Bathams ~ Manager Melvyn Wood ~ Real ale ~ Bar food (12-2 Mon-Fri) ~ No credit cards ~ (01384) 78293 ~ Children in family room ~ Dogs allowed in bar ~ Open 12-11(10.30 Sun)

EASENHALL   SP4679   Map 4

Golden Lion ⇔

Village signposted from B4112 Newbold—Pailton, and from B4455 at Brinklow; Main Street; CV23 0JA

In a peaceful village, this expanding and comfortable no smoking place has all the comforts of a modern hotel with the added charm of a 17th-c pub. The spotlessly kept tiled and flagstoned bar still has many of its original features, including low beams, timbers and a fine carved settle. Yellow walls have occasional stencilled lion motifs or latin phrases, while a slightly raised area has a comfortable little alcove with padding overhead; the lower level has a brick fireplace. Highgates Davenports Bitter and Wychwood Hobgoblin on handpump and several wines by the glass. As well as hot help-yourself buffet dishes (from £5.95; Monday-Saturday lunchtimes), the well liked bar food includes sandwiches, soup (£3.50), chicken liver pâté (£5.10), continental meat platter (£5.95), goats cheese and onion tartlet with chive hollandaise (£8.25), red thai chicken curry (£8.95), bangers with mustard mash and onion gravy (£9.75), steamed fillet of scottish salmon with chive sauce (£10.25), and puddings such as chocolate and black cherry roulade or sticky toffee pudding with hot toffee sauce (£4.65); two-course Sunday lunch (£13.90). There are tables at the side, and a good few picnic-sets on a spacious lawn. *(Recommended by Gerry and Rosemary Dobson, Stuart and Alison Ballantyne, Alan Johnson, Rob and Catherine Dunster, Clive and Fran Dutson, Simon Cottrell, Ian Phillips)*

Free house ~ Licensee James Austin ~ Real ale ~ Bar food (12-2, 6-9.30) ~ Restaurant ~ (01788) 832265 ~ Children in eating area of bar ~ Open 11-11 ~ Bedrooms: £52B/£72.50B

EDGE HILL   SP3747   Map 4

Castle

Off A422; OX15 6DJ

This crenellated octagon tower (also known as the Round Tower or Radway Tower) is a folly that was built in 1749 by a Gothic Revival enthusiast to mark the spot where Charles I raised his standard at the start of the Battle of Edge Hill. The big attractive garden has lovely glimpses down through the trees of the battlefield, and it's said that after closing time you can hear ghostly sounds of battle – a phantom cavalry officer has even been seen galloping by in search of his severed hand. Inside, there are arched doorways, and the walls of the lounge bar, which has the same eight sides as the rest of the main tower, is decorated with maps, pictures and a collection of Civil War memorabilia. Hook Norton Best Bitter, Old Hooky and Hooky Dark plus a monthly guest on handpump and 40 malt whiskies; piped music, games machine, TV, darts, pool and aunt sally. Bar food includes lunchtime home-made soup (£3.50), sandwiches (£3.75), filled baked potatoes (£4.15), and ploughman's (£5.75), as well as sausage and egg (£4.50), cottage pie (£5.95), battered cod (£6.25), roasted vegetable lasagne (£6.50), home-made steak in ale pie (£6.95), gammon and egg (£7.95), rack of pork ribs in barbecue sauce (£8.95), and puddings (from £3.95). Upton House is nearby on the A422, and Compton Wynyates, one of the most beautiful houses in this part of England, is not far beyond. *(Recommended by Rob and Catherine Dunster, Gill and Tony Morriss, Iain R Hewitt, B Brewer, John Dwane)*

Hook Norton ~ Lease Tony, Susan and Rory Sheen ~ Real ale ~ Bar food (12-2, 6.30-9; snacks available all day in summer) ~ (01295) 670255 ~ Children welcome ~ Dogs allowed in bar ~ Open 12-3, 6-midnight; 11-midnight Sun and Sat; 12-3, 6-midnight in winter; closed 25 Dec ~ Bedrooms: /£60S

FARNBOROUGH SP4349 Map 4

Inn at Farnborough 🍴 ♉

Off A423 N of Banbury; OX17 1DZ

This year, the emphasis on food at this elegant old golden stone house is even more pronounced as they have stopped serving real ale – they tell us this is due to lack of demand. The stylishly refurbished interior is a pleasant mix of the traditional and contemporary, with plenty of exposed stonework, and thoughtful lighting. The beamed and flagstoned bar has neat blinds on its mullioned windows, a chrome hood over a warm log fire in the old stone fireplace, plenty of fresh flowers on the modern counter, candles on wicker tables, and smartly upholstered chairs, window seats and stools. A stable door leads out to chic metal furnishings on a decked terrace. The no smoking dining room has a comfortably roomy seat in a fireplace, nice wooden floors, and a good mix of mismatched tables and chairs. Using plenty of local produce, the very good food might include soup (£5.50), lunchtime focaccias (£5.95) and ploughman's (£6.95), somerset brie, field mushroom and caramelised onion bruschetta (£5.95; main course £10.95), salmon fishcakes with baby spinach and hollandaise sauce (£6.95; main course £12.95), foie gras and duck terrine with orange muscat chutney (£8.50), seared king scallops with crispy parma ham and toasted hazelnut and tarragon dressing (£10.95; main course £19.95), organic beefburgers (from £10.95), roast pork with cheese and leek mash and tomato and thyme jus (£13.95), grilled monkfish with tiger prawn ratatouille and fennel lime sauce (£16.95), and specials such as garlic sautéed chicken and pancetta caesar salad or thai-style steamed mussels (£6.95; main course £12.95). They also offer a fixed course menu: two courses £10.95, three courses £12.95. Carefully chosen wines with 19 by the glass. Service is professional and courteous; piped music. The landscaped garden is really delightful with a lovely sloping lawn and plenty of picnic-sets (one under a big old tree). *(Recommended by John Kane, Nicky McNeill, Simon Jones, Mrs Philippa Wilson, Arnold Bennett, Iain R Hewitt, KN-R, Heather Couper, George Atkinson)*

Free house ~ Licensees Anthony and Jo Robinson ~ Bar food (12-3, 6-10; all day weekends) ~ Restaurant ~ (01295) 690615 ~ Children welcome ~ Dogs allowed in bar ~ Open 12-3.30, 6-11; 12-midnight(11pm Sun)Sat; closed 25 Dec

FIVE WAYS SP2270 Map 4

Case is Altered 🍺

Follow Rowington signposts at junction roundabout off A4177/A4141 N of Warwick, then right into Case Lane; CV35 7JD

The bar in this tiled white-painted brick cottage has been licensed to sell beer for over three centuries: Greene King IPA, Hook Norton Old Hooky and a guest like Brewsters Hop A Doodle Doo or Frankton Bagby Squires Brew are all served by a rare type of handpump mounted on the casks that are stilled behind the counter. You can be sure of a warm welcome from the friendly landlady and the old-fashioned rooms are filled with the sound of happy conversation – no noisy games machines, music or children (and no food either). A door at the back of the building leads into a modest small room with a rug on its tiled floor and an antique bar billiards table protected by an ancient leather cover (it takes pre-decimal sixpences). From here, the simple little main bar has a fine old poster showing the old Lucas Blackwell & Arkwright brewery (now flats) and a clock with its hours spelling out Thornleys Ale – another defunct brewery; there are just a few sturdy old-fashioned tables, with a couple of stout leather-covered settles facing each other over the spotless tiles. Behind a wrought-iron gate is a little brick-paved courtyard with a stone table. Full disabled access. *(Recommended by Pete Baker, Kerry Law, Simon Smith, the Didler, Mike Begley)*

Free house ~ Licensee Jackie Willacy ~ Real ale ~ No credit cards ~ (01926) 484206 ~ Open 12-2.30, 6-11; 12-2, 7-10.30 Sun

GAYDON SP3654 Map 4
Malt Shovel 🍺

Under a mile from M40 junction 12; B4451 into village, then over roundabout and across B4100; Church Road; CV35 0ET

So handy for the M40, this bustling pub is now totally no smoking. Its slightly unusual layout sees a sort of pathway in mahogany-varnished boards running through bright carpeting to link the entrance, the bar counter on the right and the log fire on the left. The central area has a high pitched ceiling, milk churns and earthenware containers in a loft above the bar, and well kept Adnams Best, Fullers London Pride, Everards Tiger, Hook Norton Best Bitter and Wadworths 6X with maybe a guest like Brains Rev James on handpump; several wines by the glass. Three steps take you up to a snug little space with some comfortable sofas overlooked by a big stained-glass window and reproductions of classic posters. At the other end is a busy lower-ceilinged dining area with flowers on the mix of kitchen, pub and dining tables. Enjoyable food, cooked by the chef-landlord, includes good lunchtime sandwiches, home-made soup (£3.25), pâté with plum and apple chutney (£4.45), salads such as roasted peppers, goats cheese and olives or tarragon chicken and bacon (starters from £3.75; main course from £7.15), three-egg omelettes or ham and egg (from £5.95), leek and mushroom pancakes (£6.95), wild boar and apple sausages braised in calvados and cider (£8.95), home-cured duck leg with thyme (£9.95), grilled bass fillets with tomato salsa (£10.95), steaks (from £11.95), and puddings like rhubarb pie or sticky toffee pudding (from £3.50). Service is friendly and efficient; piped music, darts and games machine. The springer spaniel is Rosie, and the jack russell is Mollie. *(Recommended by Mark and Ruth Brock, Bruce and Sharon Eden, Karen Eliot, Jill Bickerton, Ian Phillips, Gordon Prince, Tina and David Woods-Taylor, Mr Tarpey, Liz and Brian Barnard, David and Katharine Cooke, J V Dadswell, Anne Mallard, Michael and Judy Buckley, Craig Turnbull, Roger, Debbie and Rebecca Stamp, Rob and Catherine Dunster, Fergus Dowding, J Stickland, Neil Ingoe, George Atkinson)*

Enterprise ~ Lease Richard and Debi Morisot ~ Real ale ~ Bar food (12-2, 6.30-9) ~ Restaurant ~ (01926) 641221 ~ Children welcome ~ Dogs allowed in bar ~ Open 11-3, 5-11; 11-11 Fri and Sat; 12-10.30 Sun

GREAT WOLFORD SP2434 Map 4
Fox & Hounds

Village signposted on right on A3400 3 miles S of Shipston-on-Stour; CV36 5NQ

New licensees were just taking over this 16th-c stone inn as we went to press and were still finding their feet. The cosy low-beamed bar has a nice collection of chairs and old candlelit tables on spotless flagstones, antique hunting prints, and a roaring log fire in the inglenook fireplace with its fine old bread oven. An old-fashioned little tap room serves Hook Norton and a guest beer on handpump, and over 100 malt whiskies; piped music. Bar food now includes sandwiches (from £5.50), confit duck and green peppercorn terrine with hazelnut salad and apple and apricot chutney or grilled mackerel fillet with watercress sauce and horseradish (£6.75), ploughman's with home-made bread and local ham, beef and cheese (£7.50), spinach, red pepper and local blue cheese quiche (£8), free-range chicken, dry cured bacon and mushroom pie with home-made chips (£8.50), local sausages with a tomato and bean ragoût (£8.75), steaks (from £15.50), wild bass fillet on spring onion mash with red wine and thyme jus (£18), and puddings like lemon and lime posset with strawberries and shortbread and sticky toffee pudding with butterscotch sauce (£5.50). The dining area is no smoking. A terrace has solid wood furniture and a well. More reports on the new regime, please. *(Recommended by K H Frostick, Chris Glasson, Susan and John Douglas, Mrs Philippa Wilson, Margaret and Roy Randle, Iain R Hewitt, Les and Barbara Owen, R Huggins, D Irving, E McCall, T McLean)*

Free house ~ Licensees Gill, Jamie and Sioned ~ Real ale ~ Bar food (not Sun evening or Mon) ~ (01608) 674220 ~ Well behaved children welcome ~ Dogs allowed in bar ~ Open 12-3, 6-midnight; 12-3, 7-10.30 Sun; closed Mon ~ Bedrooms: £45B/£70B

ILMINGTON SP2143 Map 4

Howard Arms ⑪ ♚ ⌂

Village signposted with Wimpstone off A3400 S of Stratford; CV36 4LT

Readers very much enjoy staying overnight in the comfortable bedrooms of this totally no smoking golden-stone inn – and the breakfasts are particularly good. The stylishly simple interior is light and airy, with a few good prints on attractively painted warm golden walls, rugs on broad polished flagstones, and a nice mix of furniture from hardwood pews to old church seats. Well kept Everards Tiger, Hook Norton 303 and Shakespeares Noble Fool on handpump, organic soft drinks and cider, and 18 wines by the glass. The imaginative menu changes two or three times a week, and is carefully written on boards above a huge stone inglenook (with a log fire that burns most of the year). Given the tremendous quality of the freshly prepared food, prices are fair: home-made soup (£3.75), chicken liver parfait with onion marmalade (£5.50), smoked duck, honey grilled fig and roast beetroot salad or seared scallops, spiced lentils and curry crème fraîche (£6.50), beef, ale and mustard pie or butternut squash and thyme risotto cakes with roast roots and gruyère sauce (£9.50), sage-crumbed pork escalopes, sherry cream sauce (£11.50), chargrilled rib-eye steak, café de paris butter (£13.50), roast duck breast with fresh cherry sauce (£14), grilled whole lemon sole with crab and parsley butter (£14.50), and puddings such as steamed spotted dick, caramel chocolate pot or warm pear and walnut tart with nutmeg ice-cream (from £4.50); you will need to book – and beware that they are very strict about food serving times. The garden is lovely in summer with fruit trees sheltering the lawn, a colourful herbaceous border, and a handful of tables on a neat york stone terrace; the chocolate-spotted dalmatian is called Loulou, and her wirehaired german pointer companion is Nola. The pub is nicely set beside the village green, and there are lovely walks on the nearby hills (as well as strolls around the village outskirts). *(Recommended by Bernard Stradling, Mr and Mrs G S Ayrton, John Kane, K H Frostick, David and Jean Hall, Dr David Cockburn, Revd L and S Giller, Paul Humphreys, Alec and Barbara Jones, Clive and Fran Dutson, Nicholas and Dorothy.Stephens, Mrs Philippa Wilson, Therese Flanagan, Nigel and Sue Foster, Les and Barbara Owen, Di and Mike Gillam, Anthony Moody, Roger Braithwaite, David Handforth, Ian and Joan Blackwell, Karen and Graham Oddey, Theo, Anne and Jane Gaskin, David and Ruth Shillitoe, W M Lien, Jonathan Aquilinailina)*

Free house ~ Licensees Rob Greenstock and Martin Devereux ~ Real ale ~ Bar food ~ Restaurant ~ (01608) 682226 ~ Children welcome till 8pm ~ Open 11-3, 6-11; 12-3.30, 6.30-10.30 Sun; closed 25 Dec ~ Bedrooms: £80B/£105B

LITTLE COMPTON SP2630 Map 4

Red Lion

Off A44 Moreton-in-Marsh—Chipping Norton; GL56 0RT

New licensees have taken over this traditional 16th-c cotswold stone local – a handy base for exploring the Cotswolds. The simple plush lounge is comfortably old-fashioned and low-beamed with snug alcoves and a couple of little tables by the log fire. The plainer public bar has another log fire, Donnington BB and SBA on handpump and several wines by the glass; darts, pool, games machine, TV, juke box and piped music. Bar food now includes lunchtime sandwiches or filled baguettes (from £5.25), filled baked potatoes (£6.25), and omelettes (£7.75), as well as home-made soup (£4), home-made chicken and duck liver terrine with tomato chutney (£5.25), moules marinière (£5.75; main course £10), gammon and organic eggs (£8.75), roast rump of lamb with cumberland sauce (£9.50), roast beef with yorkshire pudding, thai chicken curry or tomato and basil pasta parcels with roasted sweet peppers (all £9.75), and puddings such as chocolate, brandy, pecan and date truffle or home-made sticky toffee pudding (£4). The restaurant is no smoking. The garden is well enclosed and rather pretty; aunt sally. More reports please. *(Recommended by Paul Goldman, Margaret and Roy Randle, R Huggins, D Irving, E McCall, T McLean, Michael Dandy)*

Donnington ~ Tenants Ian and Jacqui Sergeant ~ Real ale ~ Bar food ~ Restaurant ~
(01608) 674397 ~ Children allowed but must be away from public bar after 8pm ~
Dogs allowed in bar ~ Open 12-3, 6-11; 12-11 Sun and Sat; 12-2.30, 6-11 winter ~
Bedrooms: £50S/£60S

LONG ITCHINGTON SP4165 Map 4

Duck on the Pond

Just off A423 Coventry—Southam; The Green; CV47 9QJ

The surprisingly eclectic interior of this spacious no smoking dining pub is vaguely
reminiscent of a 1970s french bistro. The central bar has dark wooden floorboards
with a few scattered rugs, dark pine ceiling planks, royal blue banquettes, some
barrel tables, bacchanalian carvings around its coal fire and some big wading bird
decoys. Wicker panels provide an unusual frontage to the bar counter, which has
Charles Wells Bombardier and maybe Adnams Broadside on handpump, and
several wines by the glass. Service is friendly and attentive. On each side of the bar,
sizeable dining areas have pine furniture (some tables painted in light red chequers),
a wall of wine bottles, big Edwardian prints on sienna red walls, a crystal
chandelier and a grandfather clock. Enjoyable bar food includes various nibbles
(from £3.25), home-made soup (£3.95), home-cured sambuca and lemongrass
salmon with citrus potato salad or home-made chicken liver pâté with red onion
marmalade (£5.95), bacon and melting brie on a light orange salad (£5.95; main
course £9.95), roasted mediterranean vegetable pasta with tomato, basil and cream
sauce (£9.95), sausages of the week with onion gravy (£10.95), pork fillet stuffed
with nettles on apple mash with cider cream sauce (£12.95), spiced marinated fresh
tuna loin on couscous with coconut chutney (£13.95), and steaks with wild
mushrooms and a béarnaise or peppercorn sauce (from £14.95). Well produced
piped pop or jazzy soul music. Tables and chairs in front look down on a pond,
which does indeed have ducks; the main road is quite busy. (Recommended by
Darren and Jane Staniforth, Suzanne Miles, Keith Moss, George Atkinson, Dennis and Gill Keen)

Charles Wells ~ Lease Andrew and Wendy Parry ~ Real ale ~ Bar food (12-2, 6.30-9.30;
all day weekends; not Mon) ~ Restaurant ~ (01926) 815876 ~ Children allowed but not
after 7pm Fri or Sat ~ Open 12-3, 5-11; 12-11(10.30 Sun) Sat; closed Mon except bank
hols

NETHERTON SO9387 Map 4

Old Swan 🍽 £

Halesowen Road (A459 just S of centre); DY2 9PY

With very good own-brewed beers and plenty of friendly, chatty locals, it's not
surprising that this characterful local is so popular. As well as a seasonal guest, the
ales include Old Swan Original, Dark Swan, Entire, and Bumble Hole. The original
bar is traditionally furnished, with mirrors behind the bar engraved with the swan
design, an old-fashioned cylinder stove with its chimney angling away to the wall,
and a lovely patterned ceiling with a big swan centrepiece. The cosy back bar is
fitted out very much in keeping with the rest of the building, using recycled bricks
and woodwork, and even matching etched window panels. Bar food is restricted to
lunchtime filled cobs (£1) and home-made soup (£1.95). The evening restaurant
menu includes daily fresh fish dishes as well as home-made steak and kidney pie or
gammon and egg (£4.95). There's a good car park at the back of the pub. No
under-16s. (Recommended by Pete Baker, Kerry Law, Simon Smith, Ian and Liz Rispin,
the Didler, Martin Grosberg, Paul and Gloria Howell)

Own brew ~ Licensee Tim Newey ~ Real ale ~ Bar food (12-2, 6-9; not Sun evening) ~
Restaurant ~ (01384) 253075 ~ Dogs allowed in bar ~ Open 11-11; 12-4, 7-10.30 Sun

---

Half pints: by law, a pub should not charge more for half a pint than half the price of a
full pint, unless it shows that half-pint price on its price list.

PRESTON BAGOT SP1765 Map 4
Crabmill ⊕

B4095 Henley-in-Arden—Warwick; B95 5EE

A very stylish transformation of an old cider mill, this rambling place has a smart two-level lounge area with a good relaxed feel, soft leather settees and easy chairs, low tables, big table lamps and one or two rugs on bare boards. There's also an elegant and roomy low-beamed dining area (no smoking), with candles and fresh flowers, and a beamed and flagstoned bar area with some stripped pine country tables and chairs, snug corners and a gleaming steel bar serving Greene King Abbot, Tetleys and Wadworths 6X on handpump and eight wines by the glass. Terrific modern food includes sandwiches, soup (£3.95), bresaola with horseradish remoulade and beetroot pesto (£5.95), smoked haddock brandade, soft fried egg and chive beurre blanc (£6.25), ham and pea macaroni cheese with truffle oil (£6.50), duck and armagnac prune terrine with orange and parsley brioche (£6.95), braised faggots with pea mash, honey-roast carrots and onion jam (£10.95), toulouse sausage with bean cassoulet, olive oil mash and crispy onions (£11.25), moroccan chicken breast with spiced potatoes and cucumber yoghurt relish or seared salmon with crab, chilli and lemon crème fraîche linguini (£12.95), and specials such as sugar-cured beef and feta with hummous, smoked red pepper and asparagus (£5.50), seared scallops with bacon, avocado and raspberry dressing (£7.50), pancetta wrapped free-range chicken breast, tarragon and lemon mousse with parmesan mash and creamed leeks (£12.95), and chargrilled swordfish with carpaccio of vegetables and saffron verde dressing (£14.25); lunchtime items like barbecue chicken and bacon panini, cheeses with chutney, celery and biscuits, and cornish pasty (all £5.95). Piped music is well chosen and well reproduced. There are lots of tables, some of them under cover, out in a large attractively reworked garden with a play area. More reports please. (Recommended by Gavin and Helen Griggs, Denise Greenhalgh, David Morgan, P and J Shapley, Mrs P Burvill, Susan and John Douglas, George Atkinson)

Enterprise ~ Lease Sarah Robinson ~ Real ale ~ Bar food (12-2.30(3.30 Sun), 6.30-9.30) ~ Restaurant ~ (01926) 843342 ~ Children welcome ~ Dogs allowed in bar ~ Open 11-11; 12-6 Sun; closed Sun evening; 25 Dec

PRIORS MARSTON SP4857 Map 4
Holly Bush

Village signposted from A361 S of Daventry (or take the old Welsh Road) from Southam); from village centre follow Shuckburgh signpost, then take first right turn by phone box; CV47 7RW

'An unusually good pub' is how one reader describes this golden stone inn, and others agree heartily. It's particularly well run with very good service, enjoyable food, and well kept beers. The building has plenty of character, and the main part is divided into small beamed rambling rooms by partly glazed timber dividers, keeping a good-sized bar as well as the main dining area, and there are flagstones, some bare boards, a good deal of stripped stone, and good sturdy tables in varying sizes. A log fire blazes in the big stone hearth at one end, and the central lounge area has a woodburning stove. Beside a second smaller and smarter no smoking dining area is a back snug with temptingly squashy leather sofas and a woodburning stove. Good food might include soup (£3.95), baguettes (£5.95), chicken, bacon and avocado salad (£8.25), steak in ale pie (£8.95), rump steak with green peppercorn sauce (£12.95), daily specials such as baked tuna fillet (£7.95), beef bourguignon (£8) or roasted mediterranean vegetables in a basil and shallot sauce (£8.95), and popular Wednesday curry night dishes (£3.00). Fullers London Pride, Hook Norton Old Hooky and a guest like Wychwood England's Ale on handpump and eight wines by the glass; pool, TV and board games. The sheltered garden behind has tables and chairs on the lawn, and this is an attractive village. (Recommended by Mr and Mrs B A R Frost, A Darroch Harkness)

Free house ~ Licensee Richard Saunders ~ Real ale ~ Bar food (12-2.30, 6.30-9.30; 12-3, 7-9 Sun) ~ Restaurant ~ (01327) 260934 ~ Children welcome ~ Dogs allowed in bar and

bedrooms ~ Open 12-2.30, 5.30-11(midnight Fri); 12-3, 6-midnight Sat; 12-3, 7-10.30 Sun
~ Bedrooms: £45S/£55B

SEDGLEY   SO9193   Map 4
Beacon   ★   🍺
Bilston Street (no pub sign on our visit, but by Beacon Lane); A463, off A4123
Wolverhampton—Dudley; DY3 1JE

It's worth tracking down this plain-looking old brick pub for two very good
reasons: the good unusual beers brewed on the premises, and the well preserved
Victorian layout. The front door opens into a plain quarry-tiled drinking corridor
where you may find a couple of cheery locals leaning up against the walls going up
the stairs, chatting to the waistcoated barman propped in the doorway of his little
central serving booth. Go through the door into the little snug on your left and you
can easily imagine a 19th-c traveller tucked up on one of the wall settles, next to the
imposing green-tiled marble fireplace with its big misty mirror, the door closed for
privacy and warmth and a drink handed through the glazed hatch. The dark
woodwork, turkey carpet, velvet and net curtains, heavy mahogany tables, old
piano and little landscape prints all seem unchanged since those times. Another
simple snug on the right has a black kettle and embroidered mantel over a
blackened range, and a stripped wooden wall bench. The corridor then runs round
the serving booth, past the stairs and into a big well proportioned dark-panelled
smoking room with sturdy red leather wall settles down the length of each side, gilt-
based cast-iron tables, a big blue carpet on the lino, and dramatic sea prints. Round
a corner (where you would have come in from the car park) the conservatory is
densely filled with plants, and has no seats. The well kept Sarah Hughes (a former
landlady) beers served here include Dark Ruby, Pale Amber and Surprise Bitter
(brewed in the traditional Victorian brewery at the back; you can arrange to look
round) plus guests such as Church End Vicars Ruin and Dark Star IPA. The only
food served is cheese and onion cobs (£1). A children's play area in the garden has a
slide, climbing frame and roundabout. No children inside. *(Recommended by
Pete Baker, Paul and Gloria Howell, Kerry Law, Simon Smith, Ian and Liz Rispin, the Didler,
Mark and Diane Grist)*

Own brew ~ Licensee John Hughes ~ Real ale ~ No credit cards ~ (01902) 883380 ~
Dogs welcome ~ Open 12-3, 5.30(6 Sat)-11; 12-3, 6-11 Sat; 12-3, 7-10.30 Sun

SHIPSTON-ON-STOUR   SP2540   Map 4
White Bear
High Street; CV36 4AJ

New licensees have taken over this lively town local but had made no major
changes as we went to press. The long narrow front bar on the left has massive
stripped settles and attractive lamps, and interesting pictures from charming pen
and wash drawings of Paris café society, through sporting and other cartoons of
Alken and Lawson Wood, and bright modern ones by Tibb on the rag-rolled
walls. The back lounge is more plainly furnished and decorated, with comfortable
modern furniture, and big Toulouse-Lautrec and other prints of french music-hall
life. A separate bar on the right has a woodburning stove in a big painted stone
fireplace. Adnams, Bass, Hook Norton Old Hooky and a guest on handpump. Bar
food now includes sandwiches, soup (£3.50), chicken liver pâté with spicy onion
chutney (£4.95), fried lambs kidneys and bacon in sherry sauce (£5.20), warm
salad of chicken, bacon and avocado with a chive vinaigrette (£5.50; main course
£7.95), spinach and ricotta cannelloni with tangy tomato sauce (£8.95), steak,
onion and Guinness pie or pork fillet with a mushroom and marsala cream sauce
(£9.95), and rack of lamb with sweet potato, rosemary and redcurrant jus or
chargrilled rib-eye steak (£12.50). The restaurant is no smoking; games machine,
juke box and TV. There are tables on the pavement outside. More reports please.
(Recommended by P Dawn, Michael and Jeanne Shillington, Mr and Mrs D S Price)

Punch ~ Lease Steve Jones ~ Real ale ~ Bar food (12-3, 7-10; not Sun evening) ~ Restaurant ~ (01608) 661558 ~ Children welcome ~ Dogs allowed in bar and bedrooms ~ Live music Sun evening ~ Open 11-11 ~ Bedrooms: £40S/£65B

SHUSTOKE SP2290 Map 4

Griffin 🍺 £

5 miles from M6 junction 4; A446 towards Tamworth, then right on to B4114 and go straight through Coleshill; pub is at Church End, a mile E of village; B46 2LB

A smashing choice of up to ten real ales is well kept on handpump in this unpretentious country local. Dispensed from a servery under a very low heavy beam, they come from an enterprising range of brewers such as Banks's, Bathams, Everards, Exmoor, Fullers, Holdens, Hook Norton, RCH and Stonehenge. Also lots of english wines, farm cider, and mulled wine and hot punch in winter. Usually busy with a cheery crowd, the low-beamed L-shaped bar has log fires in two stone fireplaces (one's a big inglenook). Besides one nice old-fashioned settle the décor is fairly simple, from cushioned café seats (some quite closely packed) to sturdily elm-topped sewing trestles, lots of old jugs on the beams, beer mats on the ceiling and a games machine. Lunchtime bar food includes sandwiches (from £2.25), pie and chips, broccoli bake, and cod, chips and mushy peas (from £5.50), and daily specials such as chicken and ham pie or pork with paprika (£6.50). There are old-fashioned seats and tables outside on the back grass, a play area and a large terrace with plants in raised beds. *(Recommended by Richard Waller, Pauline Smith, Carol Broadbent, John Saville, Brian and Jacky Wilson, John Dwane, David Green)*

Free house ~ Licensee Michael Pugh ~ Real ale ~ Bar food (12-2; not Sun or evenings) ~ No credit cards ~ (01675) 481205 ~ Children in conservatory but must be accompanied by parents ~ Dogs welcome ~ Open 12-2.30, 7-11; 12-2.45, 7-10.30 Sun

WELFORD-ON-AVON SP1452 Map 4

Bell 🍴 🍺

Off B439 W of Stratford; High Street; CV37 8EB

Usefully open all day at weekends, this charming 17th-c place puts quite an emphasis on its popular food, but with five real ales on handpump it remains very much a proper pub. The attractive interior is divided into five comfortable areas, each with its own character, from the cosy terracotta-painted bar to the light and airy gallery room with its antique wood panelling, solid oak floor and contemporary Lloyd Loom chairs. Flagstone floors, stripped, well polished antique or period-style furniture, and three real fires (one in an inglenook) give it a relaxed, informal feel. Flowers Original and London Pride, Hobsons, Hook Norton Old Hooky and Wadworths 6X on handpump, and they've 14 wines including champagne and locally grown wine by the glass; piped music. Using local suppliers – which they list on the menu – the enjoyable food might include soup (£4.25), sandwiches (from £4.75; hot steak with horseradish crème fraîche ciabatta £5.75), deep-fried brie with a ginger and apricot compote (£4.95), ploughman's (£7.50), home-made lasagne (£9.25), gammon and local free-range eggs (£9.50), beer-battered fresh cod (£9.95), minty lamb curry (£10.25), specials such as smoked salmon and red pepper roulade (£5.95), pork and leek sausages on cheddar mash with red onion chutney (£9.75), tomato, spinach and parmesan risotto or steak in ale pie (£9.95), and sweet and sour monkfish with an asian risotto cake (£13.95), and puddings like chocolate pot or coconut rice pudding with pineapple (£4.75); most of the pub is no smoking. In summer the creeper-covered exterior is hung with lots of colourful baskets, and there are tables and chairs on a vine-covered dining terrace. The riverside village has an appealing church and pretty thatched black and white cottages. *(Recommended by Gerry and Rosemary Dobson, Oliver Richardson, K H Frostick, Keith and Sue Ward, Di and Mike Gillam, Martin O' Keefe, John Kane, Martin and Pauline Jennings, Les and Barbara Owen, Michael and Jeanne Shillington)*

Laurel (Enterprise) ~ Lease Colin and Teresa Ombler ~ Real ale ~ Bar food (11.45-2.30, 6-9.30(10 Fri and Sat); 12-9.30 Sun) ~ Restaurant ~ (01789) 750353 ~ Children welcome ~ Open 11.30-3, 6(6.30 weekdays in winter)-11; 11.30-11 Sat; 12-10.30 Sun; 11.30-3, 6-11 Sat in winter

LUCKY DIP

Besides the fully inspected pubs, you might like to try these Lucky Dips recommended to us and described by readers (if you do, please send us reports: www.goodguides.co.uk).

ALCESTER [SP0957]
☆ *Holly Bush* B49 5QX [Henley St]: Warren of unpretentious 17th-c panelled rooms off central bar, good relaxed atmosphere, hard-working landlady and pleasant staff, enjoyable fair-priced food (not Mon) from baguettes and simple dishes to some interesting blackboard items, enterprising changing range of real ales such as Cannon Royall, Enville and Uley, farm cider, dozens of whiskies, steps down to no smoking area, June and Oct beer festivals, no piped music; disabled access, pleasant sheltered back garden, open all day *(Pete Baker, G Coates, Gill and Tony Morriss, Derek and Sylvia Stephenson, B M Eldridge, Des and Jen Clarke)*

ALLESLEY [SP2981]
Elms CV5 9TZ [Birmingham Rd (A4114, at B4076/B4106 roundabout)]: Big Brewers Fayre (once a children's home), with good atmosphere in many linked rooms, their usual food, Bass; large outside area *(Andrea and Guy Bradley)*
Rainbow CV5 9GT [Birmingham Rd]: Busy local in lopsided ancient building (which eventually became a pub in the 1950s), brewing its own real ale, other ales too, good value generous straightforward food (not wknd evenings), friendly helpful landlord, two small beamed rooms and small servery; big-screen sports TV, can be crowded with young people at night; sunny terrace, open all day Sun *(Donna and Roger)*

ARDENS GRAFTON [SP1153]
Golden Cross B50 4LG [off A46 or B439 W of Stratford, OS Sheet 150 map ref 114538; Wixford rd]: Neat stone-built dining pub with welcoming staff, generous mildly upmarket food from lunchtime baguettes up in flagstoned bar with log fire or comfortable dining room with well spaced tables, attractive décor, light wood and good lighting, real ales such as Hook Norton and Timothy Taylors Landlord, decent wines; wheelchair access, tables in charming garden, nice views *(Stephen Woad, Des and Jen Clarke)*

AVON DASSETT [SP4049]
Avon CV47 2AS [off B4100 Banbury—Warwick; aka the Avon]: Pleasant décor, friendly and relaxing atmosphere, good value fresh food from sandwiches up inc great variety of sausages and mash, Courage, Hook Norton and a guest beer, several wines by the glass, interesting Civil War memorabilia, nice restaurant with plenty of fish; wet and muddy walkers welcome – bar's flagstones cope well;

tables in side garden, attractive small village on edge of country park *(Gill and Keith Croxton)*

BAGINTON [SP3375]
☆ *Old Mill* CV8 3AH [Mill Hill]: Olde-worlde Chef & Brewer conversion of old watermill nr airport (and Lunt Roman fort), heavy beams, timbers and candlelight in warm and roomy rustic-theme main bar, good wine choice, Courage Best and Directors, Greene King Old Speckled Hen and Theakstons Old Peculier, neat and friendly uniformed staff, restaurant; lovely terraced gardens leading down to River Sower, 28 bedrooms *(Richard Tosswill, LYM, Susan and John Douglas, Rob and Catherine Dunster)*

BARFORD [SP2660]
Granville Arms CV35 8DS [Wellesbourne Rd (A429 S of Warwick)]: Recently refurbished beamed dining pub, seasonal food with plenty of fresh fish, Hook Norton and changing guest beers, open fire in no smoking dining lounge, some leather armchairs and settees, separate bar and no smoking dining room; children welcome, tables in good-sized garden with terrace *(Anon)*

BARNT GREEN [SP0074]
☆ *Barnt Green* B45 8PZ [Kendal End Rd]: Large Elizabethan pub with comfortable and eclectic new look inside (Bali meets Manhattan, as one reader puts it), clubby seating in panelled front bar, large brasserie area, good innovative food from breads with dipping oils through wood-fired pizzas to rotisserie, relaxed atmosphere, plenty of adept young staff for busy nights, good choice of real ales; tables outside, handy for Lickey Hills walks *(Caroline and Michael Abbey, Mike and Mary Carter, D Halle)*

BARSTON [SP2078]
☆ *Bulls Head* B92 0JU [from M42 junction 5, A4141 towards Warwick, first left, then signed down Barston Lane]: Unassuming and genuine partly Tudor village pub, comfortable lounge with pictures and plates, oak-beamed bar with a little buddy Holly memorabilia, fine changing ale choice such as Adnams, Hook Norton, Hydes and Timothy Taylors Landlord, friendly efficient service, enjoyable traditional food from sandwiches to good fresh fish and Sun lunch, log fires, separate dining room; good-sized secluded garden alongside, hay barn behind, open all day wknds *(Pete Baker, Clive and Fran Dutson, P Dawn, Bob Ellis)*
Malt Shovel B92 0JP [Barston Lane]: Attractive dining pub, light and airy, with generous brasserie-style food inc interesting

starters, three real ales, good choice of wines, helpful young staff, stylish country-modern décor, converted barn restaurant; pleasant garden *(Mrs Philippa Wilson)*

BERKSWELL [SP2478]

Bear CV7 7BB [off A452 W of Coventry; Spencers Lane, junction with Coventry Rd, Meriden Rd and Lavender Hall Lane]: Attractive timbered 16th-c Chef & Brewer all-day dining pub in nice setting near interesting church, rambling areas with beams, bric-a-brac and log fires, Courage Directors, Charles Wells Bombardier and a guest beer, good range of wines by the glass, rarely used games bar upstairs; children welcome, tables on pleasant tree-sheltered back lawn, Crimean War cannon in front, open all day *(Alun Howells, LYM)*

BILSTON [SO9496]

Trumpet WV14 0EP [High St]: Holdens and a guest beer, good free nightly jazz bands (quiet early evening before they start), trumpets and other instruments hang from ceiling, lots of musical memorabilia and photographs, back conservatory *(the Didler)*

White Rose WV14 0NU [Temple St]: Friendly and lively traditional town pub well worth knowing for up to a dozen or so interesting real ales, also belgian beers and unusual lagers, reasonably priced substantial food all day inc Sun carvery, long narrow bar, no smoking eating area; children welcome, tables outside, open all day, Sun afternoon break *(Paul and Gloria Howell, Ian and Liz Rispin)*

BINLEY WOODS [SP3977]

Cocked Hat CV3 2AX [A428 Coventry—Warwicks]: Two-bar pub dating from 17th c, enjoyable changing bar food, Bass and M&B Brew XI, some live music inc Sun lunchtime jazz, quiz nights, restaurant; no children or dogs; terrace and garden, bedrooms, open all day wknds *(Anon)*

BIRMINGHAM [SP0788]

☆ *Bartons Arms* B6 4UP [High St, Aston (A34)]: Magnificent Edwardian landmark, a trouble-free oasis in rather a daunting area, imposing series of well restored richly decorated rooms from the palatial to the snug, original tilework murals, stained glass and mahogany, decorative fireplaces, sweeping stairs to handsome rooms upstairs, well kept Oakham and guest beers from ornate island bar with snob screens in one section, interesting imported bottled beers and frequent mini beer festivals, good choice of well priced thai food (not Mon), good young australian staff; open all day *(Richard Waller, Pauline Smith, Kerry Law, Simon Smith, Ian and Liz Rispin, the Didler, Steve Jennings)*

Bennetts B2 5RS [Bennetts Hill]: Attractively converted opulent bank with egyptian/french theme, big mural, high carved domed ceiling, snugger side 'board room' and 'library' with lots of old pictures, ironwork and wood, relaxed atmosphere, comfortable seats inc armchair and leather settee, well kept ales inc Banks's and Marstons Pedigree, decent house wines, good coffee, friendly staff, dining area;

piped music; good wheelchair access, but parking restrictions *(Dr and Mrs A K Clarke, Kevin Blake, John and Yvonne Davies, Mrs Hazel Rainer)*

Brasshouse B1 2HP [Broad St]: Handsome and comfortable bank conversion with lots of dark oak and brass, enjoyable reasonably priced food from chip butties to steaks, real ales such as Greene King Old Speckled Hen, unusual collection of builders' hard hats, attractive dining area; very handy for National Sea Life Centre and convention centre *(Colin Gooch, John and Yvonne Davies)*

Lord Clifden B18 6AA [Gt Hampton St]: Popular food from sandwiches to steaks and good value generous Sun roasts, real ales such as Timothy Taylors Landlord, prompt friendly service, contemporary artwork and sporting memorabilia; Thurs quiz night, live music Sat; plenty of tables out behind *(Anon)*

Old Fox B5 4TD [Hurst St (follow Hippodrome signs)]: Traditional two-room high-ceilinged pub with island bar and original early 19th-c features, changing ales such as Greene King Old Speckled Hen, Marstons Pedigree and Tetleys, bargain simple lunchtime food, friendly staff, interesting old photographs and theatre prints; pavement tables *(Tony and Wendy Hobden)*

Pennyblacks B1 1RQ [Mailbox shopping mall, Wharfside St]: Good atmosphere and service in well run spacious pub with mix of contemporary and old furnishings on wood and slate floors, appealing up-to-date décor, enjoyable food and beer, good spot by canal *(D Halle)*

☆ *Tap & Spile* B1 2JT [Gas St]: Nicely placed with picnic-sets by Gas Street canal basin, attractive back-to-basics yet quite cottagey décor, stripped brickwork, bare boards and reclaimed timber, old pine pews and settles, lots of prints, three levels, thriving atmosphere, real ales such as Fullers London Pride, Greene King Old Speckled Hen, Charles Wells Bombardier and Youngs, low-priced lunchtime bar food from baguettes up; piped music, darts, dominoes, fruit machine, no children; open all day *(LYM, Colin Gooch, Nigel and Sue Foster, Dave Braisted)*

Trocadero B2 5BG [Temple St]: Well run traditional pub with old-fashioned décor, usual bar food such as baked potatoes, M&B Brew XI, low prices *(Dave Braisted)*

Villa Tavern B7 5PD [Nechells Park Rd]: Two-bar local popular for its Ansells Bitter and Mild and Marstons Pedigree and wkdy lunchtime food, darts, dominoes and pool, Victorian décor inc stained glass; open all day Fri-Sun *(the Didler)*

Woodman B5 5LG [Albert St]: Victorian etched windows and fittings in friendly and lively L-shaped main bar, hatch service to relaxing back smoke room with original tiling and coal fire, Ansells Mild, Courage Directors, Greene King and a guest beer, friendly unhurried service, interesting juke box; open all day, cl Sun evening *(Pete Baker, the Didler)*

BRINKLOW [SP4379]

Bulls Head CV23 0NE [A427, fairly handy for M6 junction 2]: Enjoyable family pub with play areas indoors and outdoors, generous popular food from fresh sandwiches up inc plenty for children, particularly friendly bar staff, real ales such as Badger Best, Flowers Original, Hook Norton Best and Marstons Pedigree, collection of old pub signs, no smoking area, shove-ha'penny and table skittles; heated terrace, good bedrooms *(Mrs Lindsay, Alan Johnson, R Lindsay, Mrs S Gaade)*

BROOM [SP0853]

Broom Tavern B50 4HL [High St; off B439 in Bidford]: Attractive and comfortable 16th-c timber-framed pub in pretty village by River Arrow, relaxed and welcoming, with Greene King IPA and Timothy Taylors Landlord, attentive young staff, decent wines and ample food inc OAP lunches, big log fire, heavy beams, hunting and country-life cartoons, two-room restaurant; children welcome, handy for Ragley Hall *(Phyllis McCombie, Des and Jen Clarke)*

BROWNHILLS [SK0504]

Royal Oak WS8 6DU [Chester Rd]: Good village-local atmosphere, particularly well kept ales such as Greene King IPA and Abbot and Holdens Golden Glow, friendly efficient staff, no smoking back eating area with good choice of low-priced standard food from sandwiches to steaks inc children's from open kitchen, comfortable art deco lounge with Clarice Cliff pottery etc, 1930s-feel public bar; reasonable disabled access, pleasant garden *(Clifford Blakemore)*

BUBBENHALL [SP3672]

Three Horseshoes CV8 3BD [Spring Hill]: Pleasantly updated pub/restaurant with good range of mid-priced home-made food from good baguettes up, M&B Brew Xl, Hook Norton Old Hooky and Charles Wells Bombardier, large restaurant; piped music; bedrooms *(Alan Johnson, Nigel and Sue Foster, Mrs S Gaade)*

CHERINGTON [SP2836]

☆ *Cherington Arms* CV36 5HS [off A3400]: Old-fashioned creeper-covered stone house with enjoyable food (not Sun evening) inc interesting dishes, real ales inc Hook Norton, farm cider, good value wines, cafetière coffee, efficient friendly service, nice beamed bar with piano and blazing log fire, separate dining room; dogs welcome in bar, big garden behind with trees and tables, good nearby walks, has been cl Mon lunchtime *(K H Frostick, BB, Chris Glasson)*

COVENTRY [SP3379]

Gatehouse CV1 4AN [Hill St/Berger St, by S end of Leigh Mills car park]: Gatehouse for the former Leigh Mills worsted factory, reworked as pub with three changing real ales, good wkdy doorstep sandwiches, stained glass decorations; two big-screen TVs for rugby; attractive terrace, open all day Thurs-Sun *(P Dawn)*

Old Windmill CV1 3BA [Spon Street]: Well

worn timber-framed 15th-c pub which unlike other buildings in this reconstituted medieval street has always been here; lots of tiny old rooms, exposed beams in uneven ceilings, carved oak seats on flagstones, inglenook woodburner, Courage Directors, Greene King IPA and Old Speckled Hen, Theakstons Old Peculier, Wychwood Hobgoblin and a changing guest beer, basic lunchtime bar food (not Mon) served from the kitchen door, partly no smoking restaurant; popular with students and busy at wknds, fruit machine and juke box, no credit cards; open all day *(LYM, P Dawn, the Didler, Susan and John Douglas, the Gray family)*

Town Wall CV1 4AH [Bond St, among car parks behind Belgrade Theatre]: Busy Victorian town local with Adnams Bitter and Broadside, Bass and M&B Brew XI, farm cider, nice hot drinks choice, good generous lunchtime doorstep sandwiches, filled rolls and cheap hot dishes, unspoilt basic front bar and tiny snug, engraved windows and open fires, bigger fresher back lounge with actor and playwright photographs; big-screen sports TV; open all day *(BB, Alan Johnson, Suzanne Miles, Ted and Lyn Clarkson)*

☆ *Whitefriars* CV1 5DL [Gosford St]: Pair of well preserved medieval town houses, restored 2000 – three genuinely old-fashioned and dark historic rooms on both floors, the nicest downstairs at the front, with lots of ancient beams, timbers and furniture, flagstones, cobbles and real fires; up to nine well kept changing ales (more during beer festivals) – Church End prominent, daily papers; basic food, frequent live music Sun, folk on Weds, quiz nights, special offers for students (university nearby); no children (but shelter on good-sized terrace behind), open all day *(BB, Alan Johnson, Ian and Joan Blackwell)*

DORRIDGE [SP1674]

Railway B93 8QA [Grange Rd (A4023, ¼ mile from station)]: Small friendly family-run local with some emphasis on good value home cooking, popular sandwiches too, Bass, M&B Brew XI and guest beers, airy carpeted two-part lounge, coal fire and darts in public bar, no music or machines; small garden overlooking village green, play area, open all day wknds *(P Dawn)*

DUDLEY [SO9487]

Park DY2 9PN [George St/Chapel St]: Welcoming and pleasantly updated tap for adjacent Holdens brewery, their beers kept well and priced attractively, as is the good straightforward lunchtime food inc hot beef, pork and chicken sandwiches, conservatory, small games room; sports TV; attractive octagonal conservatory *(the Didler, Colin Fisher)*

DUNCHURCH [SP4871]

☆ *Dun Cow* CV22 6NJ [A mile from M45 junction 1: on junction of A45 and A426]: Good landlady and plenty of pleasant efficient young staff in handsomely beamed largely no smoking Vintage Inn with massive log fires and other traditional features, good range of wines by the glass, real ales such as Banks's, Hook Norton and Bass from small bar counter, reasonably priced standard food all day; piped music; children welcome, tables out in attractive former coachyard and on sheltered side lawn, comfortable bedrooms, open all day *(David Green, Suzanne Miles, P M Newsome, Michael and Alison Sandy, LYM, Dr D Jeary, Les and Barbara Owen)*

EATHORPE [SP3968]

☆ *Plough* CV33 9DQ [car park off B4455 NW of Leamington Spa]: Big helpings of good value pub food cooked by landlord inc wkdy bargain lunches in long neat split-level dining room, attentive landlady and helpful friendly service, good wine choice and coffee, Greene King Abbot, open fire in small bar *(Carol and David Havard, Rob and Catherine Dunster)*

ETTINGTON [SP2748]

White Horse CV37 7SU [A429 Warwick—Moreton-in-Marsh]: Pretty building based on 16th-c farm cottages, cosy lounge/restaurant and pleasant bar area, food inc good fresh fish, attentive service, several real ales and wines by the glass, lovely back garden, four bedrooms *(K H Frostick)*

FILLONGLEY [SP2787]

Cottage CV7 8EG [Black Hall Lane]: Recently refurbished dining pub with consistently enjoyable reasonably priced food, unpretentious yet with plenty of interesting touches, Church End, Marstons and Tetleys ales, pleasant rather restauranty atmosphere *(Tim Phillips, Alun Howells)*

GRANDBOROUGH [SP4966]

Shoulder of Mutton CV23 8DN [off A45 E of Dunchurch; Sawbridge Rd]: Well refurbished creeper-covered dining pub with attractive pine furnishings, beams and panelling, enjoyable fresh food (should book Fri/Sat evening and Sun lunch), friendly helpful staff, relaxed atmosphere, Adnams Broadside, Fullers London Pride and Greene King IPA, good coffee, no music; garden with play area, cl Mon *(P M Newsome)*

HALESOWEN [SO9683]

Hawne Tavern B63 3UG [Attwood St]: Up to nine interesting real ales from sidestreet local's rough-cut central servery, bar with cushioned pews, piano and darts and pool in games area, lounge with leatherette-backed velvet wall banquettes, good value cheap food inc big baguettes, good staff; small terrace, cl till 4.30 wkdys, open all day wknds *(G Coates, the Didler)*

King Edward VII B63 3UP [Stourbridge Rd; next to Halesowen FC]: Two-bar pub with good value food, Banks's and Everards Tiger; some disabled access, open all day Sat *(G Coates)*

Lighthouse B62 8AF [Coombes Rd, Blackheath]: Distinctive nautical-theme local, outside painted with lighthouse, L-shaped bar, two small lounge areas behind, enjoyable and generous pubby food, Banks's and guest ales, friendly atmosphere; garden tables *(G Coates)*

Somers Club B62 0JH [The Grange, Grange Hill (B4551 S)]: Early Georgian mansion, now a friendly sports and social club – visitors can sign in; comfortable bar with up to a dozen changing real ales from long counter inc Banks's, Bathams and Old Swan, simple snacks; bowling green in grounds behind *(the Didler)*

Waggon & Horses B63 3TU [Stourbridge Rd]: Bathams and up to a dozen or so interesting changing ales from small independent brewers in long narrow bare-boards bar and more spacious lounge, country wines and belgian brews, chatty regulars, good snacks, brewery memorabilia; TV, Tues music night; open all day *(the Didler, Martin Grosberg)*

HAMPTON IN ARDEN [SP2080]

White Lion B92 0AA [High St; handy for M42 junction 6]: Beamed pub restored to traditional format by new landlord, with open fires, brasses and local memorabilia in carpeted bar, good friendly service, real ales such as Black Sheep and Hook Norton, enjoyable straightforward food in bar and separate back restaurant; seven bedrooms, attractive village, handy for NEC *(LYM, P M Newsome)*

HAMPTON LUCY [SP2557]

Boars Head CV35 8BE [Church St, E of Stratford]: Hard-working and friendly young couple in low-beamed two-bar local next to lovely church, good range of promptly served lunchtime baguettes and other food from interesting light meals up, good choice of wines by the glass, log fire, lots of brasses; picnic-sets in neat and attractive secluded back garden, pretty village nr Charlcote House *(Joan and Tony Walker)*

HARBOROUGH MAGNA [SP4779]

Old Lion CV23 0HL [3 miles from M6 junction 1; B4122]: Busy village local with friendly staff, Greene King ales, good helpings of food from sandwiches, baguettes and baked potatoes up inc OAP lunches, bar with pool etc, no smoking dining area off, more formal restaurant; children welcome, family events, open all day wknds *(Alan Johnson)*

HATTON [SP2367]

Falcon CV35 7HA [Birmingham Rd, Haseley (A4177, not far from M40 junction 15)]: Rambling relaxing rooms around island bar, lots of stripped brickwork and low beams, tiled and oak-planked floors, prints, old photographs, nice mix of stripped and waxed tables and various chairs, more formal no smoking barn-style back restaurant, several real ales, food all day wknds; children welcome, picnic-sets and play area out on side and back lawns, open all day *(P Price, LYM, Jack Clark, Stephen Dadswell)*

KENILWORTH [SP2872]

Clarendon Arms CV8 1NB [Castle Hill]: Busy traditional pub opp castle, huge helpings of good value food in several rooms, some no smoking, off long partly flagstoned bustling bar, largish peaceful upstairs dining room, plenty of atmosphere, efficient and friendly obliging staff, good range of beers, wines and other drinks; best to book wknds *(Alan Johnson, John and Yvonne Davies, Roger Huggins, David Glynne-Jones)*

Clarendon House CV8 1LZ [High St]: Ancient timber building with leather armchairs and sofas in large redecorated front lounge with new wooden floor, contemporary prints and displays of china, Greene King ales and decent wines from long serving counter, daily papers, interesting choice of snacks (all day) and meals, back no smoking area and dining room; piped music; comfortable bedrooms, open all day *(Joan and Tony Walker, LYM)*

Old Bakery CV8 1LZ [High St, nr A429/A452 junction]: Pleasant hotel with charming bar, quiet and friendly, real ales such as Hook Norton and Timothy Taylors Landlord; comfortable bedrooms *(Andy and Jill Kassube)*

Virgin & Castle CV8 1LY [High St]: Maze of intimate rooms off inner servery, small snugs by entrance corridor, flagstones, heavy beams, lots of woodwork inc booth seating, coal fire, quick friendly service, Adnams, Everards Beacon and Tiger and Charles Wells Bombardier, good coffee, bar food from generous sandwiches and baked potatoes up, no smoking room, upstairs games bar, restaurant; disabled facilities, children in eating area, tables in sheltered garden, open all day *(Anne Wickens, LYM, Rona Murdoch)*

KNOWLE [SP1876]

☆ *Herons Nest* B93 0EE [Warwick Rd S]: Vintage Inn dining pub in former hotel, dining tables in several individual rooms inc no smoking areas, some flagstones and high-backed settles, hops on beams, interesting décor, open fires, wide choice of sensibly priced food inc children's helpings, attentive staff, plenty of good value wines by the glass, real ales; tables in garden by Grand Union Canal, moorings, bedrooms, open all day *(Carol Broadbent, Edward Leetham, R T and J C Moggridge, David Green, Lynn Elliott)*

LAPWORTH [SP1871]

☆ *Boot* B94 6JU [Old Warwick Rd (B4439, by Warwickshire Canal)]: Upmarket dining pub with good contemporary brasserie menu from baguettes and interesting light dishes up, nice choice for children, more traditional Sun lunch too, fast friendly service by smart young staff, upscale wines (big glasses), Wadworths 6X, lots of board games, cartoons, charming raftered dining room; piped nostalgic pop music; good lavatories, beautifully done waterside garden, pleasant walks *(Edward Leetham, Mrs Philippa Wilson, B M Eldridge, M Joyner, Susan and John Douglas, George Atkinson, Lawrence Bacon, Jean Scott)*

☆ *Navigation* B94 6NA [Old Warwick Rd (B4439 S)]: Busy well worn in two-bar beamed pub by Grand Union Canal, cheery atmosphere, high-backed winged settles on flagstones, built-in window seats, warm coal fire and some bright canal ware, modern no smoking back dining room, straightforward bar food, Bass, M&B Brew XI and a guest, around 30 malt whiskies; TV, and they may try to keep your credit card while you eat; children and dogs welcome, hatch service to terrace making the most of the pretty waterside setting, open all day *(Paul and Gloria Howell, Jean Barnett, David Lewis, P Price, Charles and Pauline Stride, LYM, Dr D J and Mrs S C Walker, M Joyner, Richard Endacott, Lynn Elliott, Mrs Joyce Robson, Steve Kirby)*

LEAMINGTON SPA [SP3165]

Benjamin Satchwell CV32 4AQ [The Parade]: Well laid out Wetherspoons, tidy and airy, with their reliable food all day, quick service, good choice of low-priced beers, two levels, some cosy seating, cheerful relaxed atmosphere; disabled access and facilities, open all day *(Ted George)*

LONG COMPTON [SP2832]

☆ *Red Lion* CV36 5JS [A3400 S of Shipston-on-Stour]: Relaxing layout and atmosphere, with old-fashioned built-in settles among other pleasantly assorted old seats and tables, stripped stone, bare beams, panelling, flagstones, old prints and team photographs, good value food from good generous sandwiches through substantial well cooked main dishes to delicious puddings in bar and restaurant, children's helpings, real ales such as Adnams Broadside and Hook Norton, good welcoming service, log fires and woodburners, simple public bar with pool; dogs and children welcome, big back garden with picnic-sets and climber, newly refurbished bedrooms *(LYM, Chris Glasson, Mike and Mary Carter, George Atkinson, KC)*

LONG ITCHINGTON [SP4165]

Blue Lias CV47 8LD [Stockton Rd, off A423]: Fine setting on Grand Union Canal, good choice of ales inc Adnams Broadside and Greene King Abbot and Old Speckled Hen, pleasant staff, snug booth seating in eating area; plenty of tables in waterside grounds, also a separate outbuilding bar with tables under a dome *(Rob and Catherine Dunster, Charles and Pauline Stride)*

Buck & Bell CV47 9PH [The Green]: Reopened 2005 as well furnished country dining pub, linked rooms on two levels with lots of stripped brick and woodburners, good up-to-date food with separate menus for light and full meals, real ales such as Banks's, Hook Norton Old Hooky and Marstons Pedigree, ample wine choice, efficient helpful uniformed staff, one small segregated smoking room; piped music *(Suzanne Miles, A G Marx, Rob and Catherine Dunster)*

Two Boats CV47 9QZ [A423 N of Southam, by Grand Union Canal]: Lively canal views from waterfront terrace and alcove window seats in long cheery picture-filled main room, generous well priced usual food, Hook Norton and changing ales; piped music; moorings, open all day *(Meg and Colin Hamilton, BB, Charles and Pauline Stride)*

LOWER GORNAL [SO9291]

Black Bear DY3 2AE [Deepdale Lane]: Simple friendly local based on former 18th-c farmhouse, Shepherd Neame and three or four changing beers, good choice of whiskies, open all day wknds, cl wkdy lunchtimes *(the Didler)*

Fountain DY3 2PE [Temple St]: Lively two-room local with helpful landlord and staff, well kept Enville, RCH and up to six changing ales (beer festivals Easter and Oct), two farm ciders, country wines and imported beers, enjoyable inexpensive food all day (not Sun evening), back dining area, pigs-and-pen skittles; piped music can be loud; open all day *(the Didler, Paul and Gloria Howell)*

Old Bulls Head DY3 2NU [Redhall Rd]: Victorian local with its own Black Country ales from back microbrewery, busy front bar with raised no smoking area, may be good filled cobs, pub games behind; some live music; open all day wknds (from 4 wkdys) *(the Didler)*

LOWSONFORD [SP1868]

Fleur de Lys B95 5HJ [off B4439 Hockley Heath—Warwick; Lapworth St]: Prettily placed by Warwickshire Canal, no smoking throughout, with simple décor in varying-sized linked beamed rooms, log fires, good seating inc sofas, Greene King ales, good choice of wines by the glass, wide choice of quickly served good value usual food, helpful service; large waterside garden, open all day *(LYM, Charles and Pauline Stride, Mick and Moira Brummell, Paul and Margaret Baker)*

LOXLEY [SP2552]

☆ *Fox* CV35 9JS [signed off A422 Stratford—Banbury]: Cheerful and welcoming, with good value inventive generous food from sandwiches to fish specialities, real ales such as Hook Norton and Charles Wells Bombardier, quick service, partly divided lounge with panelling, a few pictures and plates, settles and brocaded banquettes, pleasant dining area; piped music; tables in good-sized garden behind, sleepy village handy for Stratford *(Nigel and Sue Foster, Mr and Mrs G Hughes)*

MIDDLETON [SP1798]

Green Man B78 2AN [Church Lane]: Busy pleasantly laid out Vintage Inn, decent food all day, well kept Bass and guest beer, plenty of atmosphere; open all day *(W M Lien)*

MONKS KIRBY [SP4682]

☆ *Bell* CV23 0QY [just off B4027 W of Pailton]: Hospitable long-serving Spanish landlord enlivening this dimly lit pub, dark beams, timber dividers, flagstones and cobbles, very wide choice of good value largely spanish food inc starters doubling as tapas, fine range of spanish wines and of brandies and malt whiskies, relaxed informal service, Bass and Flowers Original, plenty of brandies and malt whiskies, no smoking dining area, enjoyably appropriate piped music; children and dogs welcome, streamside back terrace with country view, may be cl Mon *(Ian and Nita Cooper, LYM, Jill and Julian Tasker, Tim West, Julie Hill, Jane Davies)*

☆ *Denbigh Arms* CV23 0QX [Main St]: Generous reliable food inc OAP bargain in small friendly 17th-c beamed pub opp church, Greene King Abbot, Timothy Taylors Landlord and Theakstons XB, good wine choice, old photographs and interesting 18th-c pew seating, no smoking family room; upstairs folk club 2nd Sun of month; play area

(Ian and Nita Cooper, June and Ken Brooks, Alan Johnson, Rob and Catherine Dunster, Mrs S Fairbrother)

NEWBOLD ON STOUR [SP2446]

☆ *Bird in Hand* CV37 8TR [A3400 S of Stratford]: Neatly kept L-shaped bar with comfortable well spaced dining tables, bow windows, charming friendly service, enjoyable food inc low-priced basic and snack menu and interesting more elaborate one, Hook Norton and guest beers, good tea and coffee, log fire, pool in side public bar *(BB, Colin Fisher, Pete Baker)*

White Hart CV37 8TS [A3400 S of Stratford]: Dining pub doing good fresh midweek fish and popular Sun lunch (no food Sun evening), long and airy beamed and tiled bar divided by stub walls and big stone fireplace (good log fire), big bay windows, welcoming service, roomy back games bar, Adnams and M&B Brew XI, separate dining room; children welcome, picnic-sets and boules outside, open all day Sat *(K H Frostick, LYM)*

NEWTON REGIS [SK2707]

Queens Head B79 0NF [Main Rd]: Roomy local in attractive duck-pond village, good choice of real ales inc Fullers London Pride and Charles Wells Bombardier, good value bar food, friendly staff; tables out in front and in small suntrap garden *(Ian and Jane Irving)*

OLD HILL [SO9686]

Waterfall B64 6RG [Waterfall Lane]: Good value unpretentious local, friendly staff, good Holdens, good value plain home-made food from hot filled baguettes with chips to Sun lunch, tankards and jugs hanging from boarded ceiling, lounge with no smoking eating area; piped music; children welcome, back garden with play area, open all day wknds *(Gill and Tony Morriss, the Didler)*

OLDBURY [SO9989]

Waggon & Horses B69 3AD [Church St, nr Savacentre]: Copper ceiling, original etched windows, open fire and Black Country memorabilia in busy town pub with Enville, Old Swan and two or three guest beers, wide choice of generous lunchtime food (not Sun) from sandwiches and baguettes up inc lots of puddings, decent wines, friendly efficient service even when busy, ornate Victorian tiles in corridor to lively comfortable no smoking back lounge with tie collection, side room with high-backed settles and big old tables, bookable upstairs bistro; open all day *(the Didler, Pete Baker)*

PRINCETHORPE [SP4070]

Three Horseshoes CV23 9PR [High Town; junction A423/B4453]: Friendly old beamed village pub with plates, pictures, comfortable settles and chairs, real ales such as Greene King Ruddles Best, Marstons Pedigree and Charles Wells Bombardier, good choice of food, no smoking eating area, open fire; pleasant big garden with terrace and play area, bedrooms *(Anon)*

RIDGE LANE [SP2994]

Church End Brewery Tap CV10 0RD [2 miles SW of Atherstone]: No smoking home of good

Church End beers, equipment on view (interesting brewery tour, (01827) 713080 to book), lunchtime food Fri/Sat; tables outside, open all day Fri-Sun, has been cl other days *(Alain and Rose Foote)*

RUGBY [SP5373]

Bell CV21 4HD [Hillmorton]: Well decorated no smoking lounge, public bar, hard-working young licensees and friendly service, popular restaurant *(Ted George)*

RYTON-ON-DUNSMORE [SP3872]

Old Bull & Butcher CV8 3EP [Oxford Rd]: Roomy refurbished pub with usual food inc bargain lunches, two real ales, no smoking restaurant and conservatory; no dogs; children welcome, good-sized garden with play area, open all day *(Anon)*

SHIPSTON-ON-STOUR [SP2540]

☆ *Black Horse* CV36 4BT [Station Rd (off A3400)]: 16th-c thatched pub with good inglenook log fire in spotless low-beamed bar, welcoming service, enjoyable home-made food (not Sun evening) inc wkdy OAP bargain lunches, Greene King and local guest beers, good choice of wines by the glass, friendly staff and locals, interesting bric-a-brac, side room with darts, small dining room; back garden with terrace and barbecue, comfortable bedrooms, good breakfast *(JHBS, Kevin and Jane O'Mahoney)*

☆ *Horseshoe* CV36 4AP [Church St]: Good generous food (not Sun evening) from baguettes and baked potatoes to interesting specials, OAP discounts and popular Sun carvery, in pretty timbered inn with open-plan largely modern bar, lots of maroon plush, coal-effect fire in big fireplace with copper pans above, appealing no smoking chintzy restaurant, friendly staff, three changing ales such as Greene King Ruddles County and local Wizard Apprentice, decent wines and coffee, darts, no piped music (live Fri); children very welcome, small flower-decked back terrace, bedrooms pretty, bright and clean *(BB, JHBS, Michael Dandy, John and Bridget Levick, Sharon Redshaw)*

SHREWLEY [SP2167]

☆ *Durham Ox* CV35 7AY [off B4439 Hockley Heath—Warwick]: Spacious upmarket country dining pub with good food from interesting sandwiches and up-to-date snacks to particularly well presented and enterprising main dishes, attentive service; pleasant garden, open all day *(BB, Jason Caulkin)*

SOLIHULL [SP1780]

Boat B91 2TJ [Hampton Lane, Catherine de Barnes]: Recently converted Chef & Brewer, their usual food, quick efficient service, good range of beers *(Alun Howells)*

STOURBRIDGE [SO9083]

Shrubbery Cottage DY8 1RQ [Heath Lane, Old Swinford (B4186 S)]: Refurbished L-shaped local with full Holdens ale range, welcoming staff and regulars, darts one end, people playing cards and dominoes the other; central wide-screen sports TV *(Pete Baker)*

STRATFORD-UPON-AVON [SP2054]

Dirty Duck CV37 6BA [Waterside]: Bustling

16th-c pub nr Memorial Theatre, lots of signed RSC photographs, open fire, interesting choice of enjoyable food, decent prices, Flowers Original and Greene King IPA, good choice of wines by the glass, modern conservatory restaurant; children allowed in dining area, attractive small terrace looking over riverside public gardens which tend to act as summer overflow *(Mrs Ann Gray, LYM, BOB, Michael and Alison Sandy, Michael Dandy, Carolyn Browse, Kevin Blake)*

☆ *Garrick* CV37 6AU [High St]: Bustling ancient pub, no smoking throughout, with heavy beams and timbers, odd-shaped rooms and simple furnishings on bare boards, good-natured efficient staff, Greene King IPA, Old Speckled Hen and a guest such as Timothy Taylors Landlord, decent wines by the glass, food from sandwiches and light dishes up all day, small air-conditioned back restaurant; piped music, TV, games machine; children welcome, open all day *(Paul and Gloria Howell, John Millwood, Val and Alan Green, Liz and Brian Barnard, Sue Dibben, Michael Dandy, Derek and Sylvia Stephenson, Ted George, A J Knight, LYM, Frank and Chris Sharp, Edward Mirzoeff, David Glynne-Jones, Neil and Anita Christopher)*

Pen & Parchment CV37 6YY [Bridgefoot, by canal basin]: Shakespeare theme and pleasant pubby atmosphere in L-shaped split-level lounge and snug, rustic-style beams, balusters, bare boards and tiles or flagstones, small alcoves and no smoking area, big open fire in old fireplace, prompt helpful service, good wine choice, Greene King IPA and Abbot and Timothy Taylors Landlord, wide choice of good value usual food; tables out among shrubs and ivy, pretty hanging baskets, good canal basin views (busy road), open all day *(Roger and Anne Newbury, Charles and Pauline Stride, Derek and Sylvia Stephenson, Meg and Colin Hamilton, Dave Braisted)*

Shakespeare Hotel CV37 6ER [Chapel St]: Smart hotel based on handsome lavishly modernised Tudor merchants' houses, compact character bar (which can get rather smoky) and comfortable lounge with plush settees and armchairs, beams and huge log fire, grandfather clock in hallway, good attentive staff, good choice of wines by the glass, drinks come with nibbles, sandwiches and light bar meals, good restaurant; tables in sheltered courtyard, bedrooms comfortable and well equipped *(Michael Dandy, LYM, Kevin Blake)*

☆ *West End* CV37 6DT [Bull St]: Attractively modernised old pub away from main part, friendly service, thriving atmosphere, fine changing real ale range inc Hook Norton and Uley, good value nicely presented seasonal food, good wine choice and interesting soft drinks range inc plenty of coffees, nice film star photographs; well chosen piped music; appealing terrace *(Derek and Sylvia Stephenson, Maurice Ribbans, Margaret and Roy Randle, M C and S Jeanes)*

☆ *Windmill* CV37 6HB [Church St]: Cosy and

civilised old pub with town's oldest licence, beyond the attractive Guild Chapel; very low black beams, attractive carpeted front room, varnished boards in main one, big log fire, wide choice of good value food from sandwiches to substantial Sun lunch and some unusual main dishes, friendly efficient staff, well kept sensibly priced Flowers Original and Greene King IPA, carpeted dining area; piped music, sports TV; tables outside, open all day from noon (Ted George, Paul and Gloria Howell, John and Yvonne Davies)

STRETTON-ON-FOSSE [SP2238]

☆ *Plough* GL56 9QX [just off A429]: Good new landlady in olde-worlde 17th-c village pub, French chef doing enjoyable food from baguettes through OAP lunches to more adventurous dishes, inglenook log fire, happy local atmosphere, Hook Norton and interesting guest beers, small bar and larger lounge, stripped stone and some flagstones, jugs and mugs on oak beams, small attractive candlelit dining room on right, darts, dominoes and cribbage, folk nights every other Sun; dogs welcome, a few tables outside, has been cl Mon lunchtime (K H Frostick, BB, J C Burgis)

SUTTON COLDFIELD [SP1198]

Halfway House B74 2UD [Lichfield Rd (A5127), Mere Green]: Popular Ember Inn with roomy open bar areas, good range of food, changing mainly local real ales, efficient service (Clifford Blakemore)

TEMPLE GRAFTON [SP1355]

☆ *Blue Boar* B49 6NR [a mile E, towards Binton; off A422 W of Stratford]: Extended country dining pub with above-average generous food from imaginative sandwiches up, fair prices, popular Sun lunch, prompt service, changing ales such as Brakspears, Greene King Old Speckled Hen, Hook Norton and Theakstons XB, good coffee and wine choice, beams, stripped stonework and log fires, comfortable partly no smoking dining room (past glass-top well with golden carp) with attractive farmhouse-kitchen mural, traditional games in flagstoned side room; can get smoky; children and dogs welcome, picnic-sets outside, pretty flower plantings, comfortable well equipped bedrooms, open all day summer wknds (A G Marx, LYM, William Ruxton, Dennis Jenkin, Michael and Jeanne Shillington, Grahame Brooks, Des and Jen Clarke, John and Hazel Williams)

TIPTON [SO9792]

Rising Sun DY4 7NH [Horseley Rd (B4517, off A461)]: Friendly staff and regulars in Victorian pub with particularly well kept Banks's, Oakham JHB and guest beers in lined glasses, farm ciders, back lounge with coal fires, alcoves and original bare boards and tiles, lunchtime food; tables outside, open all day Fri/Sat (the Didler)

TREDINGTON [SP2543]

White Lion CV36 4NS [A3400]: Comfortably modernised pub with enjoyable food inc speciality sausages, two real ales; open all day (Susan and John Douglas)

UFTON [SP3762]

White Hart CV33 9PJ [just off A425 Daventry—Leamington, towards Bascote]: Friendly old pub with big L-shaped lounge, beams, brasses and stripped stone, pictures and polo equipment, usual food inc cheap OAP wkdy lunches (several steps down to no smoking back dining part), real ales such as Adnams, Tetleys and Charles Wells Bombardier, even stocks the rare Manns Brown Ale; unobtrusive piped music; hatch service to hilltop garden with boules and panoramic views (Tannoy food announcements out here) (DC)

UPPER GORNAL [SO92921]

☆ *Britannia* DY3 1UX [Kent St (A459)]: 19th-c local popular for its old-fashioned character and particularly well kept Bathams Best and Mild (bargain prices), tiled floors, coal fires in front bar and time-trapped no smoking back room down corridor; sports TV; nice flower-filled back yard, cl lunchtimes Mon-Thurs, open all day Fri/Sat (Kerry Law, Simon Smith, the Didler, Paul and Gloria Howell)

Jolly Crispin DY3 1UL [Clarence St (A459)]: Friendly well run 18th-c local with up to ten or so interesting quickly changing ales, two farm ciders or perry, compact front bar, wall seats and mixed tables and chairs on tiled floor, lots of aircraft pictures in larger back room, beer festivals; open all day Fri/Sat, cl lunchtime Mon-Thurs (Paul and Gloria Howell, Ian and Liz Rispin, the Didler)

WALSALL [SP0198]

Arbor Lights WS1 1SY [Lichfield St]: Modern bar and restaurant, relaxed and friendly, with wide choice of wines, real ales, freshly made food all day from sandwiches up, good service (Anon)

WARMINGTON [SP4147]

Plough OX17 1BX [just off B4100 N of Banbury]: Traditional village pub, several real ales inc Greene King, friendly service, unpretentious bar with big fireplace, ancient settle, nice chairs and jugs and mugs on heavy beams, generous popular food (not Sun evening), extended dining room; children and dogs welcome, delightful village with interesting church (John Coatsworth, LYM, MLR, John Dwane)

WARWICK [SP2967]

Saxon Mill CV34 5YN [Guy's Cliffe, A429 just N]: Pleasantly refurbished converted mill, included chiefly for its lovely setting; wheel turning slowly behind glass, mill race under glass floor-panel, contemporary chairs and tables on polished boards and flagstones below the beams, cosy corners with leather armchairs and big rugs, real ales such as Hook Norton, Timothy Taylors Landlord or Charles Wells Bombardier, standardised food such as pizzas (pay up front), upstairs restaurant; teak tables out on terraces by broad willow-flanked river, bridge to more tables on far side, delightful views across to Grade I ruins of Guy's Cliffe House, open all day (Andy and Jill Kassube, Susan and John Douglas, LYM, Dr W I C Clark)

☆ **Zetland Arms** CV34 4AB [Church St]: Cosy town pub with short choice of good interesting sensibly priced food (not wknd evenings) with fresh veg, friendly quick service even when busy, Marstons Pedigree and Tetleys, decent wines in generous glasses, neat but relaxing small panelled front bar with toby jug collection and sports TV, comfortable larger L-shaped back eating area with small conservatory; children welcome, interestingly planted sheltered garden, bedrooms sharing bathroom *(LYM, Peter and Jean Hoare)*

WELFORD-ON-AVON [SP1452]

Four Alls CV37 8PW [Binton Rd]: Scarcely a pub now, more a trendy restaurant, with attractive light modern décor and furnishings in large L-shaped no smoking dining area; reasonably priced food, Shepherd Neame Spitfire and Wadworths 6X, good wines by the glass, cheerful antipodean service; pleasant terrace with heaters, fine spot by River Avon *(Andrew Richardson, W W Burke, Martin and Pauline Jennings)*

WELLESBOURNE [SP2755]

Kings Head CV35 9LT: Vintage Inn dining pub with contemporary furnishings in high-ceilinged lounge bar, log fire and smaller areas leading off, lively public bar with games room, wide choice of keenly priced wines, Bass, good value food from wraps and sandwiches up, friendly staff; piped music, no dogs; proper tables and chairs on small front terrace, more in prettily placed back garden facing church, bedrooms (handy for Stratford but cheaper), open all day *(Martin and Karen Wake, Gordon Prince, LYM)*

WHARF [SP4352]

Wharf Inn CV47 2FE [A423 Banbury—Southam, nr Fenny Compton]: Open-plan pub with great potential, by Bridge 136 on South Oxford Canal – and has its own moorings; good contemporary layout and furnishings, small central flagstoned bar with Adnams Broadside, Brakspears and Charles Wells Bombardier, wide food choice, several no smoking areas; piped music, games machine; dogs welcome in bar, children away from bar, disabled access and facilities, waterside garden with picnic-sets and playhouse, open all day *(Simon Jones, LYM)*

WHATCOTE [SP2944]

☆ **Royal Oak** CV36 5EF: Dating from 12th c, quaint and unpretentious low-beamed small room with Civil War connections and lots of knick-knacks and curios, wide choice of good value fresh food from nice baguettes to venison and good steaks, cheery landlord, pub dog called Pip, Hook Norton ales and a guest such as Bath, decent wines, good log fire in huge inglenook, pleasant no smoking dining room; children welcome, picnic-sets in informal garden *(LYM, Clive and Fran Dutson, Michael and Jenny Back, Kevin Blake)*

WHICHFORD [SP3134]

Norman Knight CV36 5PE: Welcoming two-room pub with four interesting changing beers from its back Wizard brewery, enterprising landlord, nicely priced straightforward food

(lunchtime not Mon/Tues, and Fri/Sat evening) from appealing sandwiches to good Sun roasts, darts and dominoes, flagstones and stone walls; some live music; dogs welcome, tables out in front by attractive village green, small back campsite, cl Mon lunchtime *(Pete Baker, Tina and David Woods-Taylor, Stuart Turner)*

WILLOUGHBY [SP5267]

Rose CV23 8BH [just off A45 E of Dunchurch; Main St]: Partly thatched beamed pub pleasantly opened up and refurbished without losing character, Greene King Abbot, Hook Norton Best and Timothy Taylors Landlord, enthusiastic landlord, welcoming cheerful staff, good range of baguettes and limited lunchtime hot dishes, evening restaurant; lots of outside seating at front and in garden with play area, flowers everywhere *(George Atkinson)*

WITHYBROOK [SP4384]

Pheasant CV7 9LT [B4112 NE of Coventry, not far from M6 junction 2]: Friendly and comfortable dining pub with very wide choice of generous usual food from sandwiches up, Courage Directions, John Smiths and Theakstons, good coffee, big log fires, lots of dark tables with plush-cushioned chairs; piped music; children welcome, tables under lanterns on brookside terrace, open all day Sun *(LYM, Ken Richards, Alan Johnson)*

WIXFORD [SP0854]

Fish B49 6DA [B4085 Alcester—Bidford]: Enjoyable reasonably priced food inc lots of chargrills and bargain roasts for two, friendly helpful staff, good choice of changing ales, roomy L-shaped bar and snug, beams, polished panelling, carpets over flagstones, log fire, stuffed fish, and quite an art gallery in corridor to lavatories; piped music; lovely riverside setting, nice on a summer's evening *(Carol Broadbent, Des and Jen Clarke)*

Three Horseshoes B49 6DG [B4085 off A46 S of Redditch, via A422/A435 Alcester roundabout, or B439 at Bidford]: Roomy and neatly renovated L-shaped dining pub, wide choice (esp wknds, when it can get crowded), helpful service, good beer choice, bric-a-brac from blowtorches to garden gnomes; pleasant seating areas outside *(Des and Jen Clarke)*

WOLLASTON [SO8884]

Unicorn DY8 3NX [Bridgnorth Rd (A458)]: Cosy and friendly traditional local with well kept low-priced Bathams Bitter and Mild, unpretentious L-shaped bar and unspoilt back parlour, lots of brasses and knick-knacks, good sandwiches; tables outside, open all day, Sun afternoon break *(the Didler)*

WOLVERHAMPTON [SO9098]

Combermere Arms WV3 0TY [Chapel Ash (A41 Tettenhall rd)]: Cosy old-fashioned three-room local with friendly new licensees, Banks's and guest beers, decent wines, lunchtime food from bargain sandwiches up, bare boards and quaint touches, Wolves photographs, bar billiards; tree growing in gents', courtyard and secluded garden, open all day wknds *(Ian and Liz Rispin)*

☆ **Great Western** WV10 0DG [Corn Hill/Sun St, behind BR station]: Well run and down to earth, tucked interestingly away by cobbled lane down from main line station to GWR low-level one, with particularly well kept Bathams, Holdens Bitter, Golden Glow, Special and perhaps Sham Rock Stout, winter mulled wine (no tea or coffee), friendly and very prompt service, cheap hearty home-made lunchtime food (not Sun) inc good big baguettes and fish and chips, interesting railway and more recent motorcycle photographs, traditional front bar, other rooms inc separate no smoking bar and neat dining conservatory; SkyTV; picnic-sets in yard with good barbecues, open all day (Sun afternoon break) *(Pete Baker, Robert Garner, BB, Ian and Liz Rispin, John Tav, the Didler, Paul and Gloria Howell)*

Mitre WV6 9AH [Lower Green, Tettenhall Rd (A41)]: Small and comfortable, with good atmosphere, decent food and ales, Spanish guitarist Sat night; setting overlooking green is a pleasant oasis *(Ian and Liz Rispin, Richard Corfield)*

Moseley Park WV10 6TA [Greenfield Lane; handy for M54 junction 2, first left off A449 S]: Large and comfortable new Brewers Fayre, well laid out to give private-feeling spaces, Banks's Original and Marstons Pedigree; bedrooms in adjoining Travel Inn *(Ian Phillips)*

Posada WV1 1DG [Lichfield St]: Ornate tile and glass frontage, three rooms sympathetically refurbished with lots of wood, brass and glass, nooks and crannies, semicircle central bar with changing ales inc Jennings, Shelley memorabilia and genuine old Wolverhampton prints, friendly locals, helpful staff, back room with games; open all day, cl Sun *(Ian and Liz Rispin)*

Wiltshire

New entries here this year are the attractive and civilised Flemish Weaver in the centre of Corsham, the lively Bath Arms at Crockerton where the chef/patron does the appealing cooking, the Fox Hounds near East Knoyle (the friendly New Zealand landlord does the cooking here, too), and the friendly Beckford Arms on the edge of a fine parkland estate at Fonthill Gifford. Other pubs on great form are the Red Lion at Axford (quite a bit of emphasis on the restaurant food), the quirky Dandy Lion in Bradford-on-Avon (which is changing hands shortly), the Compasses at Chicksgrove (a lovely place to stay, and they are kind to children and dogs, too), the Two Pigs in Corsham (a cheerfully eccentric little pub), the Three Tuns at Great Bedwyn (given a special lift by its hard-working and convivial licensees), the bustling Neeld Arms at Grittleton (again, its friendly licensees are a big plus), the Old Royal Ship at Luckington (slightly ramshackle and well liked by both locals and visitors), the Malet Arms at Newton Tony (the cricket-loving landlord shoots his own game for cooking), the Vine Tree at Norton (particularly well run and with super food), and the Pear Tree at Whitley (an exceptional all-rounder). There's no shortage of places here for a special meal out. For super food, we'd look to the Boot at Berwick St James, the Compasses at Chicksgrove, the Forester at Donhead St Andrew, the Linnet at Great Hinton, the Malet Arms at Newton Tony, the Vine Tree at Norton, the George & Dragon at Rowde, and the Pear Tree at Whitley. In a very close-run contest between two outstanding contenders, the Vine Tree at Norton (last year's winner) and the Pear Tree at Whitley, it's the Pear Tree at Whitley which carries off the top title of Wiltshire Dining Pub of the Year. Drinks prices in the county are closely in line with the national average. There is plenty of choice of good local beers here. Wadworths of Devizes is generally available and provides far more of the county's better pubs with their cheapest beer than any other brewer. Other local brewers which also supply some of our main entries with their best-priced ale are Archers, Moles, Stonehenge and Wessex. Hop Back, Ramsbury, Hidden and Downton are also well worth looking out for. A good many of the pubs and inns in the Lucky Dip section at the end of this chapter are really well worth knowing. Ones on particularly good form include the Castle Inn in Castle Combe, Ivy at Heddington, Calley Arms at Hodson, Millstream at Marden, Victoria and Albert at Netherhampton, Rattlebone at Sherston, White Horse at Winterbourne Bassett and Bell at Wylye.

AXFORD   SU2370   Map 2

Red Lion ♀

Off A4 E of Marlborough; on back road Mildenhall—Ramsbury; SN8 2HA

There's no doubt that the main emphasis in this pretty and welcoming flint-and-brick pub is placed on the imaginative restaurant-style food but they do offer bar snacks and keep Downton Quadhop, Hook Norton Best and Ramsbury Gold on handpump, 15 wines by the glass and 24 malt whiskies. The beamed and pine-panelled bar has a big inglenook fireplace, and a pleasant mix of comfortable sofas, cask seats and other solid chairs on the parquet floor; the pictures by local artists are for sale. There are lovely views over a valley from good hardwood tables and chairs on the terrace outside the no smoking restaurant, and you get the same views from picture windows in the restaurant and lounge. As well as lunchtime filled bloomers (from £4.95; brie and bacon £6.25), bar snacks include home-made soup (£4.50), home-baked ham and egg (£7.75), and chilli con carne, sausages with onion gravy, and steak and kidney, fish or vegetable pies (all £8.50). You can also eat from the more elaborate restaurant menu in the bar: smoked pigeon breast with berry compote (£5.25), crab and prawn fishcakes with cucumber, yoghurt and dill dressing (£5.75), sautéed prawns with pawpaw, orange and coconut (£6.50), mixed bean and pulse tagine with herb-infused couscous (£12.95), grilled mackerel fillets with smoked paprika and capsicum mash (£13.25), calves liver with a balsamic and cream reduction (£13.95), half a roast guinea fowl with a kumquat, brandy and thyme sauce (£14.75), and steaks (from £14.95); piped music. The sheltered garden has picnic-sets under parasols. *(Recommended by Mary Rayner, Bernard Stradling, Alan and Paula McCully, Mr and Mrs Peter Llewellyn, Alec and Barbara Jones, Peter Titcomb)*

Free house ~ Licensee Seamus Lecky ~ Real ale ~ Bar food ~ Restaurant ~ (01672) 520271 ~ Children welcome ~ Dogs allowed in bar ~ Open 12-2.30, 6.30-11; 12-3, 7-10.30 Sun; closed 25 Dec

BERWICK ST JAMES   SU0639   Map 2
Boot ⍟

B3083, between A36 and A303 NW of Salisbury; SP3 4TN

There's a good mix of customers in this flint and stone pub. The partly carpeted and flagstoned bar has a huge winter log fire in the inglenook fireplace at one end, sporting prints over a small brick fireplace at the other, and houseplants on its wide window sills. A small back dining room has a nice mix of dining chairs around four tables, and deep pink walls with an attractively mounted collection of celebrity boots. Using local produce where possible (vegetables may even come from the garden), the well liked bar food includes good, tasty lunchtime baguettes (from £5.50) and ploughman's (£5.95), soup (£4.95), breaded brie with raspberry coulis (£5.75), baked goats cheese with date compote (£8.50), chilli con carne (£8.95), red thai chicken curry (£9.95), trout supreme on pak choi with ginger and soy sauce or sauté of pigeon breast with raspberry dressing (£10.95), valentine of pork loin with grainy mustard sauce (£11.95), steaks (from £14.95), and puddings (£4.95). Wadworths IPA and 6X and maybe a guest such as Archers Best on handpump; piped jazz. The neat sheltered side lawn has pretty flowerbeds and some well spaced picnic-sets. *(Recommended by D P and M A Miles, Gwyn and Anne Wake, Amanda De Montjoie, Sheila Manchester, Alistair Forsyth, Tonya Govender, Mrs Joyce Robson, Dr Michael Smith)*

Wadworths ~ Tenant Kathie Duval ~ Real ale ~ Bar food (12-2.30, 6.30-9.30; not Sun evening or Mon) ~ Restaurant ~ (01722) 790243 ~ Children welcome ~ Dogs welcome ~ Open 12-3, 6-11.30; 12-3, 7-10.30 Sun; closed Mon lunchtime

BERWICK ST JOHN   ST9422   Map 2
Talbot

Village signposted from A30 E of Shaftesbury; SP7 0HA

The unspoilt, heavy-beamed bar in this friendly Ebble Valley pub is simply furnished with cushioned solid wall and window seats, spindleback chairs, a high-backed built-in settle at one end, and a huge inglenook fireplace with a good iron fireback and bread ovens. Reasonably priced bar food at lunchtime includes home-made soup (£3), sandwiches (from £3), filled baguettes (from £5), ploughman's (from £5.50), chilli beef nachos (£5), sausage and onion gravy (£6.50), hot chicken and bacon salad (£7), and ham and eggs or home-made lasagne (£7.50); there's also deep-fried brie with redcurrant jelly (£4), butterfly prawns with sweet chilli dip (£4.50), vegetable bourguignon with herb dumplings (£6.50), salmon and broccoli mornay (£7.75), cajun-style chicken (£7.95), and mixed grill (£13.50). Sunday roasts (£7.50). Bass, Ringwood Best, Wadworths 6X and a guest such as Wadworths JCB on handpump; darts and cribbage. There are seats outside, and this is a peaceful and pretty village, surrounded by thatched old houses. More reports please. *(Recommended by D and J Ashdown, David and Elizabeth Briggs)*

Free house ~ Licensees Pete and Marilyn Hawkins ~ Real ale ~ Bar food (not Sun evening, or Mon) ~ (01747) 828222 ~ Children in eating area of bar ~ Dogs allowed in bar ~ Open 12-2.30, 6.30-11; 12-4 Sun; closed Sun evening, Mon

BOX ST8369 Map 2
Quarrymans Arms
Box Hill; coming from Bath on A4 turn right into Bargates 50 yards before railway bridge, then at T junction turn left up Quarry Hill, turning left again near the top at grassy triangle; from Corsham, turn left after Rudloe Park Hotel into Beech Road, then third left on to Barnetts Hill, and finally right at the top of the hill; OS Sheet 173 map reference 834694; SN13 8HN

This is not the smartest of pubs, but beautifully sweeping views from big windows in the no smoking dining room are usually enough to distract visitors from the mild untidiness. Once the local of the Bath stone miners, it has quite a lot of mining-related photographs and memorabilia dotted around the interior, and the friendly licensees run interesting guided trips down the mine itself. One modernised room with an open fire is entirely set aside for drinking, with well kept Butcombe Bitter, Moles Best, Wadworths 6X and maybe a guest on handpump, as well as good wines and up to 60 malt whiskies. The fairly priced menu includes sandwiches (£2.50), soup (£2.95), macaroni cheese (£5.25), ham, egg and chips or all-day breakfast (£5.95), moules marinière (£5.25; £9.50 main course), spaghetti carbonara (£7.95), various stir fries (£8.25), and daily specials such as liver and bacon (£5.95). The pub is ideally placed for cavers, potholers and walkers, and the atmosphere is easy-going; piped music, games machine and board games. An attractive outside terrace has picnic-sets; boules. *(Recommended by Gene and Kitty Rankin, Dr and Mrs A K Clarke, Dr and Mrs M E Wilson, Amanda De Montjoie, M Sage, Clare Rosier)*

Free house ~ Licensees John and Ginny Arundel ~ Real ale ~ Bar food (11-3, 6-10 (but you must make bookings after 9pm)) ~ Restaurant ~ (01225) 743569 ~ Children welcome ~ Dogs allowed in bar ~ Open 11-3, 6-11.30 Mon-Thurs; 11-midnight Fri, Sat and Sun ~ Bedrooms: £25(£35B)/£50(£65B)

BRADFORD-ON-AVON ST8261 Map 2
Dandy Lion
35 Market Street; BA15 1LL

As we went to press, we heard that this thriving town pub would have new licensees by the time this book is published. It's been much enjoyed by our readers so we are keeping our fingers crossed that things don't change too much. There's been an enjoyably continental feel and a good mix of customers and big windows on either side of the door look out on to the street – each with a table and cushioned wooden armchair. Further in, the pleasantly relaxed long main bar has nice high-backed farmhouse chairs, old-fashioned dining chairs, a long brocade-cushioned settle on the stripped wooden floor (a couple of rugs, too), sentimental and gently erotic pictures on the panelled walls, an overmantel with brussels horses, and fairy-lit hops over the bar counter. Up a few steps at the back, a snug little bare-boarded room has a lovely high-backed settle and other small ones around sturdy tables, a big mirror on a mulberry wall, and a piano; piped jazz. The upstairs restaurant is candlelit at night, and has an area with antique toys and baskets of flowers; it's no smoking in here (as is the back bar at lunchtimes). Butcombe Bitter, Wadworths IPA, 6X and a guest on handpump, several wines by the glass, and good coffees; welcoming service. Bar food has included home-made soup (£4.50), filled baked potatoes (£5.95), filled baps (from £6.50), chicken liver pâté (£6.75), vegetarian pasta (£6.95), niçoise salad (£7.25), fish and chips (£7.50), sirloin steak

(£12.95), and daily specials. More reports on the new regime, please. *(Recommended by Ian Phillips, Susan and Nigel Wilson, Dr and Mrs A K Clarke, Dr and Mrs M E Wilson, Colin and Janet Roe, David and Pam Wilcox, Michael Butler, Mrs Margo Finlay, Jörg Kasprowski, Douglas and Ann Hare, David Crook, Mike Gorton)*

Wadworths ~ Real ale ~ Bar food (12-2.15(3 Sun), 7-9.30(9.15 Sun)) ~ Restaurant ~ (01225) 863433 ~ Children allowed but away from bar ~ Open 10.30-3, 6-11(11.30 Fri); 10.30-11.30 Sat; 11.30-4, 6.30-11 Sun

BREMHILL ST9772 Map 2

Dumb Post

Off A4/A3102 just NW of Calne; Hazeland, just SW of village itself, OS Sheet 173 map reference 976727; SN11 9LJ

This is run by and for people who like their pubs unpretentious and brimming with genuine character – but it may not suit those with fussier tastes. The main lounge is a glorious mix of mismatched, faded furnishings, vivid patterned wallpaper, and stuffed animal heads, its two big windows boasting an unexpectedly fine view down over the surrounding countryside; not huge (it has a half dozen or so tables), it has something of the air of a once-grand hunting lodge. There's a big woodburner in a brick fireplace (not always lit) and a log fire on the opposite side of the room, comfortably-worn armchairs and plush banquettes, a standard lamp, mugs, bread and a sombrero hanging from the beams, and a scaled-down model house between the windows; in a cage is an occasionally vocal parrot, Oscar. The narrow bar leading to the lounge is more dimly lit, but has a few more tables, exposed stonework, and quite a collection of toby jugs around the counter; there's a plainer third room with a pool table, darts, games machine, and piped music. Wadworths 6X and a couple of summer guests like Archers Best or Butcombe Gold on handpump, and friendly service. The lunchtime bar food is simple, hearty and well liked by locals: toasted sandwich (£2.40), soup (£3.10), sausage, egg and chips (£4.90), steak and kidney pudding (£5.55), and ham and egg (£5.80); the dining room is no smoking. There are a couple of picnic table sets outside, and some wooden play equipment. A peaceful spot in good walking country. Note the limited lunchtime opening times. *(Recommended by JJW, CMW, Kevin Thorpe)*

Free house ~ Licensee Mr Pitt ~ Real ale ~ Bar food (12-2) ~ No credit cards ~ (01249) 813192 ~ Children welcome ~ Dogs allowed in bar ~ Open 12-2 (not Mon-Weds), 7-11(11am Sat); 12-3, 7-midnight Sun; closed Mon-Weds lunchtimes

BRINKWORTH SU0184 Map 2

Three Crowns ♀

The Street; B4042 Wootton Bassett—Malmesbury; SN15 5AF

With five real ales on handpump, this busy place could hardly be called a restaurant but the emphasis on their popular food is steadily growing and prices in the evening are pretty steep for a pub. The bar part of the building is the most traditional, with big landscape prints and other pictures, some horsebrasses on dark beams, a dresser with a collection of old bottles, stripped deal table, and a couple made from gigantic forge bellows, big tapestry-upholstered pews and blond chairs, and log fires; sensibly placed darts, shove-ha'penny, dominoes, cribbage, board games, games machine and piped music. Archers Best, Camerons Castle Eden Bitter, Fullers London Pride, Greene King IPA and Wadworths 6X on handpump, over 20 wines by the glass, and home-grown apple juice. The elaborate menu covers an entire wall and as well as lunchtime double-decker rolls (from £6.45), filled baked potatoes (from £6.95), ploughman's (from £6.95), bangers and mash (£8.95), home-made curry (£10.95), and seafood pancake (£11.95), there might be home-made steak and kidney pie (£14.95), mussels with a rich creamy white wine sauce (£15.95), wild boar with shallots, sun-dried apricots and button mushrooms flamed with apricot wine (£17.95), steaks (from £17.95), half a duck with a cassis, redcurrant jelly and cream sauce (£18.95), rack of lamb with pear and rosemary jelly (£19.95), and puddings such as white chocolate and raspberry brûlée, hot chocolate brownie layered with home-made Baileys ice-cream or strawberry and champagne cheesecake (from £5.65). Most people choose to eat in the no smoking conservatory or in the light and airy garden room. There's a terrace with outdoor heating to the side of the conservatory. The garden stretches around the side and back, with well spaced tables and a climbing frame, and looks over a side lane to the church, and out over rolling prosperous farmland. *(Recommended by Tom and Ruth Rees, Richard and Sheila Fitton, June and Peter Shamash, John Baish, Dr and Mrs A K Clarke, Gordon Neighbour, Andrew Shore, Maria Williams, Ian Phillips, Malcolm Ward, Martin and Karen Wake)*

Enterprise ~ Lease Anthony Windle ~ Real ale ~ Bar food (12-2(3 Sun), 6-9.30; not 25 or 26 Dec) ~ Restaurant ~ (01666) 510366 ~ Well behaved children in dining area until 7pm ~ Dogs allowed in bar ~ Open 11-3(4 Sat), 6-11; 12-4.30, 6-11 Sun; closed 25 and 26 Dec

CHICKSGROVE ST9729 Map 2
Compasses ★ (🏠) 🍷 🛏️

From A30 5½ miles W of B3089 junction, take lane on N side signposted Sutton Mandeville, Sutton Row, then first left fork (small signs point the way to the pub, in Lower Chicksgrove; look out for the car park); SP3 6NB

This is a smashing place to stay with lovely surrounding walks and plenty to do in the area. You can be sure of a friendly welcome from the landlord and his family and staff and they are happy to allow children and dogs too. The bar has old bottles and jugs hanging from beams above the roughly timbered counter, farm tools and traps on the partly stripped stone walls, and high-backed wooden settles forming snug booths around tables on the mainly flagstoned floor. Bass, Chicksgrove Churl (brewed for the pub by Wadworths), Wadworths 6X and a guest like Hidden Quest on handpump, several wines by the glass, and ten malt whiskies. Super bar food includes lunchtime filled onion loaves (from £4.95), ham and egg, 6oz rib-eye steak or smoked salmon omelette (£6.95), and lamb and apricot pie or salmon steak with new potatoes (£8.95), as well as broccoli, stilton and walnut soup (£4.95), duck liver parfait with a fennel compote or goats cheese, sun-dried tomato and pesto tartlet (£5.45), mussels cooked in bacon, cream, garlic and white wine (£5.95), baked red peppers stuffed with wild mushrooms and garlic (£9.95), pork tenderloin with a vinny, cider and cream sauce (£13.95), a warm salad of scallops with chorizo and crayfish (£14.95), lamb fillet on crispy pancetta with an anchovy and basil jus (£15.95), and fillet of beef on horseradish and sweet potato rösti with red wine sauce (£16.95). The dining room is no smoking. The quiet garden, terraces and flagstoned farm courtyard are very pleasant places to sit. *(Recommended by Frogeye, Mike Dean, Lis Wingate Gray, Richard May, Ingrid Baxter, Tony and Jill Radnor, Mrs J H S Lang, John Robertson, M Sage, Mike and Brenda Roberts, Mary Kirman and Tim Jefferson, Phyl and Jack Street, Paul Humphreys, Richard and Nicola Tranter, Robert Blevin, Bill and Jessica Ritson, Andrew Hollingshead, Helen and Brian Edgeley, Bob and Margaret Holder)*

Free house ~ Licensee Alan Stoneham ~ Real ale ~ Bar food (not Sun evenings or Mon exc bank hols) ~ (01722) 714318 ~ Children welcome ~ Dogs welcome ~ Open 12-3, 6-11; 12-3, 7-8.30 Sun; closed Mon exc bank hols (when closed the next day instead) ~ Bedrooms: £55B/£75B

CORSHAM ST8770 Map 2
Flemish Weaver
High Street; SN13 0EZ

Built in the early 17th c, originally to house drovers in the wool trade, this is an attractive and civilised mellow stone building in the heart of the town. The three bars are sensitively modernised, but keeping many original features, with patterned blue banquettes and matching chairs on slate floors, flowers on the tables, and tealights in the fireplaces; old black and white photographs on the walls. Using local produce and organic and free-range meat, the well liked bar food includes lunchtime baguettes, soup (£3.75), pheasant and pork terrine with pickles (£5.25), local ham and egg (£6.75), cauliflower and broccoli cheese bake (£7.70), free-range gammon with pineapple (£8.50), smoked haddock, cod, salmon, prawns and leeks in parsley sauce with crumble topping (£8.75), steak and onions braised in beer (£10.99), shin of veal in tomatoes, peppers and olives (£12.50), and puddings such as pear and almond tart or spotted dick (£4.50). Banks's Original, Bath Ales Gem Bitter and SPA, and Shepherd Neame Spitfire on handpump or tapped from the cask, Thatcher's cider, several malt whiskies, and eight wines by the glass from a carefully chosen list; piped music. They have a parsons terrier and a doberman. There are tables in the back courtyard, and the pub is handy for Corsham Court. *(Recommended by D P and M A Miles, Michael Doswell, Mr and Mrs P R Thomas)*

Enterprise ~ Lease Nathalie Bellamy and Jeremy Edwards ~ Real ale ~ Bar food (12-2.30, 7-9.30; not Sun evening) ~ Restaurant ~ (01249) 701929 ~ Children welcome away from bar ~ Dogs allowed in bar ~ Open 11-3, 5.30-11; 12-3.30, 7-10.30 Sun

Two Pigs 🍺
A4, Pickwick; SN13 0HY

The cheerfully eccentric feel at this friendly little beer lover's pub owes much to the individualistic landlord, and the place is probably at its liveliest on Monday nights, when live blues draws a big crowd into the narrow and dimly lit flagstoned bar. There's a zany collection of bric-a-brac including enamel advertising signs on the wood-clad walls, pig-theme ornaments, and old radios. A good mix of customers gathers around the long dark wood tables and benches, and friendly staff serve well kept Hop Back Summer Lightning and Stonehenge Pigswill, along with a couple of changing guests such as Abbey Bellringer and Stonehenge Dynamite; piped blues. A covered yard outside is called the Sty. Beware of their opening times – the pub is closed every lunchtime, except on Sunday; no food (except crisps) or under-21s. *(Recommended by R Huggins, D Irving, E McCall, T McLean, Dr and Mrs A K Clarke, Mr and Mrs P R Thomas, Catherine Pitt, P R and D Thomas, Kevin Thorpe)*

Free house ~ Licensees Dickie and Ann Doyle ~ Real ale ~ No credit cards ~ (01249) 712515 ~ Blues Mon evening ~ Open 7-11; 12-2.30, 7-10.30 Sun

CROCKERTON   ST8642   Map 2
Bath Arms
Just off A350 Warminster—Blandford; BA12 8AJ

This attractive old dining pub is very appealing from outside with plenty of picnic-sets in various garden areas. Inside, it's warmly welcoming with a thriving informal atmosphere, lots of well spaced tables on the parquet floor in the long two-roomed bar, beams in the whitewashed ceiling, and brasses; there's a restaurant at one end and a log fire in a stone fireplace at the other end. Sharps Cornish Coaster, Wessex Crockerton Classic and a couple of guest beers on handpump and quite a few wines by the glass; piped music. Cooked by the chef/landlord and using local produce, the good, attractively presented food might include creamed onion soup with herb croûtons (£4), ravioli bolognese (£4.95); main course £9.95), confit of tuna with pickled endive (£5.75), filled baguettes (from £5.75), seared scallops with tomato and crab (£6.95), cumberland sausages and champ or gammon and poached eggs (£9.95), grilled vegetable bruschetta (£10.95), sticky beef with braised red cabbage or fishcake with cornish crab and broad beans (£11.25), mixed grill (£13.95), and puddings such as white chocolate cannelloni with mixed berries or lemon curd cheesecake (from £3.50); Sunday roast. The restaurant is no smoking. Longleat is not far away. *(Recommended by Edward Mirzoeff, Bob Monger)*

Wellington ~ Lease Dean Carr ~ Real ale ~ Bar food (12-2.30, 6.30-9) ~ Restaurant ~ (01985) 212262 ~ Children in restaurant ~ Dogs allowed in bar ~ Open 11-3, 6-11; 11-11 Sat; 12-10.30 Sun ~ Bedrooms: /£75S

Pubs close to motorway junctions are listed at the back of the book.

DEVIZES SU0061 Map 2

Bear ♀ ◖

Market Place; SN10 1HS

This old coaching inn is comfortable and pleasant with some proper character and it has provided shelter to distinguished guests as diverse as King George III and Dr Johnson. The big main carpeted bar has log fires, black winged wall settles and muted cloth-upholstered bucket armchairs around oak tripod tables; the classic bar counter has shiny black woodwork and small panes of glass. Separated from the main bar by some steps, a room named after the portrait painter Thomas Lawrence (his father ran the establishment in the 1770s) has dark oak-panelled walls, a parquet floor, a big open fireplace, shining copper pans, and plates around the walls; it's partly no smoking. Well kept Wadworths IPA, 6X and a seasonal guest on handpump, as well as a good choice of wines (including 16 by the glass), and quite a few malt whiskies. Decent straightforward bar food includes sandwiches (from £3; freshly baked filled baguettes from £4.45), soup (£3.25), double egg and chips (£4), three-egg omelettes or filled baked potatoes (from £4.75), ham and egg (£5.15), ploughman's (from £5.25), breakfast (£6.25), beer-battered fish (£6.75), and warm chicken breast with mexican salad (£7.25). There are buffet meals in the Lawrence Room, and you can eat these in the bar too. A mediterranean-style courtyard with olives trees, hibiscus and bougainvillea has some outside tables. It's only a stone's throw from here to Wadworths brewery, where you can buy beer in splendid old-fashioned half-gallon earthenware jars. *(Recommended by Mike and Lynn Robinson, Blaise Vyner, Dr and Mrs A K Clarke, the Didler, Tina and David Woods-Taylor, Ian Phillips, Alan Sadler, Mary Rayner, D H Lloyd, Bill and Jessica Ritson)*

Wadworths ~ Tenant Andrew Maclachlan ~ Real ale ~ Bar food (11.30-2.30, 7-9.30) ~ Restaurant ~ (01380) 722444 ~ Children welcome ~ Dogs allowed in bar ~ Live jazz/blues Fri and Sat in cellar bar ~ Open 10am-11pm(10.30pm Sun); closed 25 and 26 Dec ~ Bedrooms: £70B/£95B

DONHEAD ST ANDREW ST9124 Map 2

Forester ⏏ ♀

Village signposted off A30 E of Shaftesbury, just E of Ludwell; Lower Street; SP7 9EE

In a charming village, this 14th-c thatched pub has fine country views from a good-sized terrace where there are plenty of seats. Inside, the appealing bar has a warmly welcoming atmosphere, stripped tables on wooden floors, a log fire in its big inglenook fireplace, and usually a few locals chatting around the servery: Ringwood Best, Wadworths 6X and maybe Sharps Doom Bar on handpump, and 18 wines (including champagne) by the glass. The comfortable main no smoking dining room has country-kitchen tables in varying sizes, nicely laid out with linen napkins, and attractive wrought-iron candlesticks – they sell these, if you like the design; there's also a second smaller and cosier (and also no smoking) dining room. Using fresh local produce, the good food includes pubby dishes like filled ciabattas (from £4.95), croque monsieur (£5.50), chicken caesar salad (£6.95 or £8.95), fresh tagliatelle with duck livers and dijon mustard sauce (£6.95), and a trio of sausages with caramelised onion gravy or chicken, ham and leek pie (£8.95), as well as more elaborate choices such as cured bresaola with fresh figs, cantaloupe melon and taleggio (£6.50), tomato tarte tatin with red pepper chutney (£6.95), foie gras terrine with sauternes jelly, fine beans and toasted brioche (£8.25), fresh pasta with pesto, pine nut, roquefort and parmesan (£10.95), corn-fed chicken breast with truffle and thyme stuffing and a merlot glaze (£12.95), bass fillet with aïoli dressing (£13.95), and poached and grilled saddle of wild rabbit with tarragon cream (£14.95). Service is pleasant and helpful, and there are no machines or piped music. Good walks nearby, for example to the old and 'new' Wardour castles. The neighbouring cottage used to be the pub's coach house. *(Recommended by Liz and Tony Colman, Michael Doswell, Roger White, Dennis and Gill Keen, Sue Demont, Tim Barrow, OPUS, Mary Kirman and Tim Jefferson, Roger Wain-Heapy, Richard and Nicola Tranter, J D O Carter)*

Free house ~ Licensee Martin Hobbs ~ Real ale ~ Bar food (12-2(3 Sun), 7-9(9.30 Fri and Sat)) ~ Restaurant ~ (01747) 828038 ~ Children welcome but must be accompanied by adults at all times ~ Dogs allowed in bar ~ Open 11-3(3.30 summer Sat), 6-11; 12-3.30(3 in winter), 7-10.30 Sun ~ Bedrooms: £57.50S/£65S

EAST KNOYLE   ST8731   Map 2
Fox Hounds ♀

Village signposted off A350 S of A303; The Green (named on some road atlases), a mile NW at OS Sheet 183 map reference 872313; or follow signpost off B3089, about ½ mile E of A303 junction near Little Chef; SP3 6BN

It's best to come here on a clear day, not just to navigate the little lanes, but primarily to get the bonus of remarkable views right over into Somerset and Dorset – and you might also enjoy a walk in the nearby woods. The pub itself is a pretty sight, an ancient thatched building dating from the 16th c and facing the green where you get the best views, with picnic-sets outside. Inside has the warmly welcoming feel of a proper long-established pub (rather than a more formal pub/restaurant), and the New Zealand licensees are particularly friendly. It does have a small light-painted conservatory restaurant, and three linked areas on different levels around a central horseshoe-shaped servery, with a big log fire in one cosy area and a log-effect gas fire in another, plentiful oak woodwork and flagstones, comfortably padded dining chairs around big scrubbed tables with vases of flowers, and a couple of leather settees; the furnishings are all very individual and uncluttered. The landlord's cooking of carefully sourced often local ingredients is now a big draw here: lunchtime clay oven pizzas (from £4.75), filled ciabattas (from £5.25; not Sunday), and ploughman's (from £5.75), as well as chicken and wild mushroom pâté (£4.95), a greek mezze plate for sharing (£7.95), fresh fish and chips (£8.25), local ham and free-range eggs or rare-breed pork sausages (£8.45), popular thai green chicken curry, home-made steak or chicken and ham pies (£8.95), lots of fresh fish such as lemon sole, organic salmon and lobster (from £10.95), steaks (from £12.95), and puddings such as warm banana bread with vanilla ice-cream, blackberry and apple crumble and pavlovas (£3.95). Service is smiling and helpful, and they have Bass, Wessex Golden Delirious, Youngs Bitter and a guest like Butcombe Bitter on handpump, farm cider, and a good choice of wines by the glass, quite a few from New Zealand. (Recommended by Nick and Elaine Cadogan, David Stranack, J Philip Geary, Dr and Mrs M E Wilson, Edward Mirzoeff, Mrs H E Cunliffe)

Free house ~ Licensees Murray and Pam Seator ~ Real ale ~ Bar food (12-2.30, 6-9.30) ~ (01747) 830573 ~ Children welcome ~ Dogs welcome ~ Open 12-2.30, 6-11

EBBESBOURNE WAKE   ST9824   Map 2
Horseshoe ★ 🍽 🛏

On A354 S of Salisbury, right at signpost at Coombe Bissett; village is around 8 miles further on; SP5 5JF

Visitors and locals alike are welcomed in this charmingly unspoilt old country pub, tucked away in fine downland. The neatly kept bar has fresh home-grown flowers on the tables, lanterns, a large collection of farm tools and other bric-a-brac crowded along its beams, and an open fire; a conservatory extension seats ten people. Archers Bouncing Bunny, Otter Ale and Ringwood Best tapped from the cask, farm cider, country wines and several malt whiskies. Well liked bar food includes lunchtime sausages (£5.25), ploughman's (from £6.50), and ham and eggs (£6.75), as well as chicken and broccoli bake (£9.75), watercress and mushroom lasagne (£9.50), venison and mushroom pie (£9.95), home-made fish bake or beef and shallots in red wine (£10.25), half a roast duck with a choice of sauces (£15), lamb and blackcurrant pie (£9.95), and home-made puddings like treacle tart (£4.25). Booking is advisable for the small no smoking restaurant, especially at weekends when it can fill quite quickly. There are pleasant views over the steep sleepy valley of the River Ebble from seats in its pretty little garden, three goats in a paddock at the bottom of the garden, and two jack russells; good nearby walks. *(Recommended by Noel Grundy, Douglas and Ann Hare, the Didler, Sue Demont, Tim Barrow, Pat and Robert Watt, OPUS, Colin and Janet Roe, Keith and Jean Symons, Anthony Longden, Rosemary and Tom Hall, H W Roberts, Dr Michael Smith, Mike and Linda Hudson, Pam and DavidBailey)*

Free house ~ Licensees Tony and Pat Bath ~ Real ale ~ Bar food (not Sun evening or Mon) ~ Restaurant ~ (01722) 780474 ~ Children welcome but with restrictions ~ Open 12-3, 6.30-11; 12-4 Sun; closed Sun evening and Mon lunchtime ~ Bedrooms: /£65B

FONTHILL GIFFORD ST9231 Map 2
Beckford Arms 🛏️
Off B3089 W of Wilton at Fonthill Bishop; SP3 6PX

On the edge of a fine parkland estate with a lake and sweeping vistas, this country house has an enjoyably civilised atmosphere. The smartly informal rooms are big, light and airy, with stripped bare wood, a parquet floor and a pleasant mix of tables with church candles. In winter, a big log fire burns in the lounge bar, which leads into a light and airy back garden room with a high pitched plank ceiling and picture windows looking on to a terrace. Locals tend to gather in the straightforward games room: darts, games machine, pool, board games and piped music. Good, interesting food includes home-made soup (£4.50), apple, courgette, fennel and pine nut salad with apple olive oil or roasted baby goats cheese in breadcrumbs with red onion marmalade (£6.25), filled focaccias (from £6.25), smoked duck breast with a nectarine compote (£6.95), fennel, spring onion and english asparagus risotto with basil oil and parmesan (£10.25), chicken and grilled aubergine on mixed pepper couscous and aged lemon oil (£12.50), fillet of scottish beef with a blue cheese glaze, coriander and a red wine reduction (£16.95), daily fresh fish dishes, and puddings such as sticky toffee pudding with butterscotch sauce or strawberry millefeuille (£5.95); Sunday roasts (from £9.50). Fullers London Pride, Greene King Abbot, Hidden Fantasy and Timothy Taylors Golden Best on handpump, and several wines by the glass. *(Recommended by Peter Salmon, Mr Walker, Pat and Robert Watt, Owen Upton, M Sage, Penny Simpson, M C Stephenson, A P Seymour)*

Free house ~ Licensees Karen and Eddie Costello ~ Real ale ~ Bar food (not 25 Dec or 1 Jan) ~ (01747) 870385 ~ Well behaved children welcome ~ Dogs welcome ~ Open 12-11; 12-10.30 Sun; closed 25 Dec, evening 1 Jan ~ Bedrooms: £45S/£75B

GREAT BEDWYN SU2764 Map 2
Three Tuns
Village signposted off A338 S of Hungerford, or off A4 W of Hungerford via Little Bedwyn; High Street; SN8 3NU

Cheerful, hard-working licensees run this thriving village pub and despite the emphasis on the good food, there's a genuinely pubby atmosphere and you won't feel out of place if you just want a pint. The traditional décor is lifted out of the ordinary by some quirky touches, such as life-size models of the Blues Brothers at separate tables in the beamed, bare-boards front bar, and a similarly incongruous female mannequin in the back restaurant. Almost every inch of the walls and ceiling is covered by either the usual brasses, jugs, hops and agricultural implements, or more unusual collections such as ribbons from ships' hats, showbiz photos, and yellowing cuttings about the royal family, all of which reflect stages of the landlord's career. There's a profusion of chalked-up quotes and pithy comments (mostly from the licensees), as well as an inglenook fireplace, and lighted candles in the evenings. It does get busy at weekends, particularly on Sunday lunchtimes when locals gather for the weekly meat raffle. Black Sheep, Flowers IPA and Fullers London Pride on handpump (the cellar was once the village morgue), ten wines by the glass, 40 malt whiskies, and a good bloody mary; friendly, helpful service, piped music and board games. Enjoyable bar food includes sandwiches, home-made soup (£3.95), salad of cashel blue cheese with black grapes and roasted pine nuts or coconut breaded torpedo prawns with sweet chilli dipping sauce (£5.95), home-made thai-style crab cakes with ginger, coriander, red onion and rocket salad (£6.95), home-made steak and kidney pie or home-made burger (£9.95), cassoulet of chorizo, pork and duck (£10.95), baked cod with a mild green thai curry sauce (£11.95), slow-roasted half shoulder of lamb with redcurrant jus (£13.95), and daily specials such as moules marinière (£6.95; main course £10.95), popular spanish-style rabbit (£10.95) or irish stew (£11.95). Good Sunday roasts, and they also do a take-away menu. The restaurant is no smoking. The whitewashed building has quite a few plants in front, and a pleasant raised garden behind. More reports please. (Recommended by Penny Simpson, Ian Phillips, N R White)

Punch ~ Lease Alan and Janet Carr ~ Real ale ~ Bar food (not Sun evening) ~ Restaurant ~ (01672) 870280 ~ Children welcome with restrictions ~ Dogs allowed in bar ~ Open 11.30(12 Sat)-3, 6-11; 12-3 Sun; closed Sun evening

GREAT HINTON ST9059 Map 2
Linnet 🍴

3½ miles E of Trowbridge, village signposted off A361 opposite Lamb at Semington; BA14 6BU

Such is the reputation for the food in this attractive brick pub, that you have to book a few weeks in advance to be sure of a table. Everything on the menu is home-made, from the bread to the sausages and ice-cream. Served by attentive staff in the little bar or restaurant, the changing menu might include at lunchtimes filled focaccia or salads (from £6.95), roast red onion, mushroom and brie tart with parsnip crisps (£7.95), crispy duck and herb couscous spring rolls on asparagus salad with mustard dressing or honey-roast ham ploughman's (£8.50), prawn and crab tagliatelle with parsley and sweetcorn cream sauce (£8.75), and grilled rib-eye steak with thyme ketchup (£12.95), with evening choices such as poached sole on cherry tomato caesar salad (£5.95), honey and soy marinated duck breast stuffed with pak choi and rolled in sesame seeds with sweet and sour sauce (£6.25), baked aubergine stuffed with courgettes, leek and pine nuts, glazed with goats cheese, and a tomato and basil sauce (£13.25), baked tenderloin of pork filled with prunes and spinach wrapped in smoked bacon on a wild mushroom sauce (£13.95), and fried lemon sole fillets with crab and dill dumplings and langoustine sauce (£15.50). Puddings like milk chocolate and orange torte with mint ice-cream or banoffi bread and butter pudding with almond cream (from £4.95) and two-course Sunday lunch (£13.25). The bar to the right of the door has a cream carpet and lots of photographs of the pub and the brewery, and there are bookshelves in a snug end part. The no smoking restaurant is candlelit at night. Wadworths IPA and 6X on electric pump, around two dozen malt whiskies, and several wines by the glass; piped music. In summer, the flowering tubs and window boxes with seats dotted among them are quite a sight. More reports please. (Recommended by Bernard Stradling, Mr and Mrs Peter Llewellyn, Glenwys and Alan Lawrence, Michael Doswell)

Wadworths ~ Tenant Jonathan Furby ~ Real ale ~ Bar food (not Mon) ~ Restaurant ~ (01380) 870354 ~ Children welcome ~ Dogs allowed in bar ~ Open 11-2.30, 6-11; 12-3, 7-10.30 Sun; closed Mon; 25 and 26 Dec, 1 Jan

GRITTLETON ST8680 Map 2
Neeld Arms 🍷 🍽 🛏

Off A350 NW of Chippenham; The Street; SN14 6AP

Friendly, helpful licensees run this cheerful 17th-c black-beamed pub, now totally no smoking. It's largely open plan, with a convivial and chatty atmosphere, some stripped stone, and a log fire in the big inglenook on the right and a smaller coal-effect fire on the left. Flowers on tables and a pleasant mix of seating from windsor chairs through scatter-cushioned window seats to some nice arts and crafts chairs and a traditional settle. The parquet-floored back dining area has yet another inglenook, with a big woodburning stove; even back here, you still feel thoroughly part of the action. Brains SA, Moles Best and Wadworths IPA and 6X on handpump at the substantial central bar counter, and a good choice of reasonably priced wines by the glass; piped music, board games, cribbage and dominoes. Well liked bar food at lunchtime includes soup (£2.95), filled ciabattas (£4.25), ham and egg (£5.95), home-made burger or chicken caesar salad (£6.95), salmon fishcakes (£7.25), and a pie of the week (£7.50), with evening choices such as local sausage and mash (£7.50), venison steak or pork fillets wrapped in bacon strips with asparagus (£10.95), shoulder of lamb (£11.25), and mixed grill (£12.95); Sunday roast beef (£7.25). There's an outdoor terrace, with pergola. The golden retriever is called Soaky. *(Recommended by Kevin Thorpe, Dr and Mrs A K Clarke, Richard Stancomb, R Huggins, D Irving, E McCall, T McLean, Ian Phillips, Dr Alan and Mrs Sue Holder, Andrew Scarr, Pete Devonish, Ian McIntyre, Michael Doswell, Colin and Peggy Wilshire)*

Free house ~ Licensees Charlie and Boo West ~ Real ale ~ Bar food (12-2(2.30 weekends), 7-9.30) ~ Restaurant ~ (01249) 782470 ~ Children welcome ~ Dogs welcome ~ Open 12-3(3.30 Sat), 5.30(5 Fri)-midnight; 12-3.30, 7-11 Sun ~ Bedrooms: £40S(£40B)/£60S(£70B)

HINDON ST9132 Map 2
Lamb
B3089 Wilton—Mere; SP3 6DP

Perhaps more of a hotel nowadays, this smart and civilised place has a big welcoming log fire, friendly, polite staff, and four real ales. The two flagstoned lower sections of the roomy long bar have a very long polished table with wall benches and chairs, blacksmith's tools set behind a big inglenook fireplace, high-backed pews and settles, and at one end, a window seat (overlooking the village church) with a big waxed circular table. Deep red walls add to the comfortable, relaxed feel. Up some steps a third, bigger area has lots more tables and chairs – though it can fill up fast and at busy times you may not be able to find a seat. Blackboards list the enjoyable bar food, which might include soup (£4.50), baguettes (from £4.50), a huge ploughman's (£7.95), beer-battered fish with minted peas (£9.25), a changing vegetarian dish of the day (£9.25), a pie of the day (£9.95), smoked haddock with black pudding, Guinness and a mustard seed dressing (£11.95), free-range chicken wrapped in parma ham with a wild mushroom and herb risotto and salsa verde (£13.50), 21-day matured local steaks (from £15.75), local game, and puddings such as iced chocolate parfait with white chocolate sauce (£5); you may be able to get cream teas throughout the afternoon. From the polished dark wooden counter, pleasant staff serve Youngs Bitter, Special and a seasonal brew, and maybe Hop Back Summer Lightning on handpump, and a good choice of wines by the glass; the extensive range of whiskies includes all the malts from the Isle of Islay, and they have a wide choice of Havana cigars. There are picnic-sets across the road (which is a good alternative to the main routes west); parking is limited. *(Recommended by B J Harding, Colin and Janet Roe, W W Burke, Bernard Stradling, Dr and Mrs M E Wilson, Mike Gorton, E V Lee, Ian Phillips, Mrs J H S Lang)*

Free house ~ Licensee Nick James ~ Real ale ~ Bar food (12-2.30, 6.30(7 Sun)-9.30 (9 Sun)) ~ Restaurant ~ (01747) 820573 ~ Children welcome ~ Dogs allowed in bar and bedrooms ~ Open 11(12 Sun)-11 ~ Bedrooms: £65B/£90B

HORTON SU0363 Map 2
Bridge Inn 🍺
Signposted off A361 Beckhampton road just inside the Devizes limit; Horton Road; SN10 2JS

In 1810, this well run place was extended to include a flour mill and bakery using grain transported along the Kennet & Avon Canal; the pub now has its own moorings. Inside, there are old black and whites of brightly dressed bargee families and their steam barges among other old photographs and country pictures on the red walls above a high panelled dado. In the carpeted area on the left all the sturdy pale pine tables are set for food: staples such as filled rolls (from £3.75; soup and a roll from £6.50), ploughman's (from £3.75), sausages and eggs (£6.50), and burger or large battered cod (£6.75), plus rosemary and garlic-crusted brie with raspberry coulis (£5.50), ardennes pâté with caramelised onion and cranberry chutney or spicy chicken wings (£5.65), cod and prawn crumble (£7.50), butternut squash and ginger bake (£8.25), minted lamb pudding (£8.75), chicken tikka masala (£9.65), and steaks (from £10.75). The no smoking dining room has a log fire in the front area. On the right of the bar is a pubbier bit with similar country-kitchen furniture on reconstituted flagstones, and some stripped brickwork, with superbly kept Wadworths IPA, 6X and a seasonal ale tapped straight from the cask, and eight decent wines by the glass. Service by the helpful staff is well organised; disabled lavatories, piped music. The safely fenced garden has picnic-sets, and an aviary with two or three dozen white fantail doves. *(Recommended by Paul A Moore, Sheila and Robert Robinson, Mark and Joanna, Sarah and Peter Gooderham, Michael Doswell, Keith and Sally Jackson, Howard and Margaret Buchanan)*

Wadworths ~ Tenants Sue Jacobs and Kevin Maul ~ Real ale ~ Bar food ~ Restaurant ~ (01380) 860273 ~ Children under parental guidance all the time and away from bar ~ Dogs allowed in bar ~ Open 11.30-3(2.30 in winter), 6.30-11; 12-3, 6.30-10.30 Sun

KILMINGTON ST7736 Map 2
Red Lion £ 🛏

B3092 Mere—Frome, 2½ miles S of Maiden Bradley; 3 miles from A303 Mere turn-off; BA12 6RP

Stourhead Gardens are only a mile from here and this down-to-earth ivy-covered country inn is owned by the National Trust. It's popular with both locals and visitors and there's a good convivial atmosphere in the snug low-ceilinged bar. Pleasant furnishings such as a curved high-backed settle and red leatherette wall and window seats on the flagstones, photographs of locals pinned up on the black beams, and a couple of big fireplaces (one with a fine old iron fireback) with log fires in winter. A newer big-windowed no smoking eating area is decorated with brasses, a large leather horse collar, and hanging plates. Darts, shove-ha'penny and board games. Butcombe, Butts Jester, Wessex Kilmington Best and a guest on handpump, Thatcher's Cheddar Valley cider and several wines by the glass. Served only at lunchtime, the straightforward bar menu includes soup (£1.50), sandwiches (from £3.25; toasties £3.50), ploughman's (from £4.50), pasties (from £4.70), steak and kidney or fish pie (from £5.40), meat or vegetable lasagne (£7.50), and a couple of daily specials such as chicken casserole or cottage pie (£5.95). There are picnic-sets in the big attractive garden (look out for Kim the labrador). A gate gives on to the lane which leads to White Sheet Hill, where there are riding, hang gliding and radio-controlled gliders. *(Recommended by Peter Titcomb, Gloria Bax, Steve Jackson, Mike Gorton)*

Free house ~ Licensee Chris Gibbs ~ Real ale ~ Bar food (12-1.50; not evening) ~ No credit cards ~ (01985) 844263 ~ Children welcome in eating area of bar till 8.30pm ~ Dogs allowed in bar ~ Open 11.30-2.30, 6.30-11; 12-3, 7-11 Sun; closed evening 25 Dec

LACOCK ST9168 Map 2
George

West Street; village signposted off A350 S of Chippenham; SN15 2LH

Even when busy – which this cosy old pub usually is – the long-standing landlord and his staff remain cheerful and efficient. It dates back to 1361 and is one of the oldest buildings in this lovely village. The low-beamed bar has upright timbers in the place of knocked-through walls making cosy rambling corners, candles on close-set tables (even at lunchtime), armchairs and windsor chairs, seats in the stone-mullioned windows, and flagstones just by the counter; piped music. The treadwheel set into the outer breast of the original great central fireplace is a talking point – worked by a dog, it was used to turn a spit for roasting. Wadworths IPA, JCB and 6X on handpump. Bar food might include lunchtime sandwiches (from £3.75), baguettes (from £5.75) and ploughman's (£5.95), as well as soup (£3.95), wild rice, honey and spinach roast (£8.50), home-made steak in ale pie (£8.95), smoked haddock florentine (£9.50), chicken with leeks and stilton (£10.95), and puddings such as bread and butter pudding or apple and raspberry crumble (£4.50). The barn restaurant is no smoking. Outside, there are picnic-sets with umbrellas in the attractive back garden and a good children's play area. *(Recommended by Andy and Jill Kassube, Anne Morris, B J Harding, Dr and Mrs M E Wilson, Paul and Shirley White, Dr and Mrs Ewing, Rod and Chris Pring, Michael Doswell, Tom and Ruth Rees, Alan Sadler, John and Joan Nash, Colin and Janet Roe, Phil and Sally Gorton, Kevin Thorpe)*

Wadworths ~ Manager John Glass ~ Real ale ~ Bar food ~ Restaurant ~ (01249) 730263 ~ Children welcome ~ Open 10am-11pm(10.30pm Sun)

Red Lion

High Street; SN15 2LQ

New licensees again for this imposing National Trust-owned Georgian inn. The long and airy pink-painted bar has heavy dark wood tables and tapestried chairs, turkey rugs on the partly flagstoned floor, a fine old log fire at one end, aged-looking paintings, branding irons hanging from the ceiling, and a nice pubby atmosphere. The cosy snug has comfortable leather armchairs. Wadworths IPA, 6X and a seasonal beer on handpump, country wines, and several malt whiskies; games machine and piped music. Lunchtime bar food includes sandwiches (from £3.95), filled baked potatoes (from £4.50), ploughman's (£5.95), home-cooked ham and egg (£6.75), salmon and broccoli fishcake (£7.95), and filo king prawns with sweet chilli dip (£8.50), with evening choices such as creamy stilton mushrooms (£4.25), home-made pâté with grape chutney (£4.50), broccoli, stilton and potato bake (£7.50), chicken breast in a creamy blue cheese and bacon sauce (£9.75), venison in a rich red wine sauce (£11.50), and steaks (from £11.75). The restaurant and part of the bar are no smoking. In fine weather, seats outside are a pleasant place for a drink. The pub is handy for Lacock Abbey and the Fox Talbot Museum. More reports please. *(Recommended by Mr and Mrs John Taylor, John and Joan Nash)*

Wadworths ~ Managers Paul and Sarah Haynes ~ Real ale ~ Bar food (12-2.30, 6-9) ~ (01249) 730456 ~ Children welcome ~ Dogs allowed in bar ~ Open 11.30-11; 11.30-11 Sat; 12-10.30 Sun ~ Bedrooms: £55B/£80B

Rising Sun 🍺

Bewley Common, Bowden Hill – out towards Sandy Lane, up hill past Abbey; OS Sheet 173 map reference 935679; SN15 2PP

New licensees have taken over this unpretentious stone pub but have not made any major changes. The three welcoming little rooms are knocked together to form one simply furnished area, with a mix of old chairs and basic kitchen tables on stone floors, country pictures, and open fires. Welcoming staff serve Moles Best Bitter, Tap, Rucking Mole, Capture and a seasonal guest on handpump; piped music. Bar food now includes filled baguettes (from £4.25), potato boats filled with mushrooms, bacon and stilton (£4.95), smoked chicken salad with honey and mustard dressing (£5.25), home-made broccoli and cheese lasagne (£7.95), home-made beef in ale pie (£8.25), thai chicken curry (£8.25), devilled pork (£9.50), and puddings such as apple and blackberry flapjack (£4.50). The garden is delightful with its big two-level terrace offering views extending up to 25 miles over the Avon valley; marvellous sunsets. More reports on the new regime, please. *(Recommended by Theocsbrian, Paul and Shirley White, Dr and Mrs M E Wilson, Kevin Thorpe, Jane and Mark Hooper, A P Seymour)*

Moles ~ Managers Patricia and Tom Russell ~ Real ale ~ Bar food (12-2, 6-9) ~ Restaurant ~ (01249) 730363 ~ Children welcome ~ Dogs allowed in bar ~ Live entertainment every Weds evening ~ Open 12-3, 6-11; 12-11 Sun

LOWER CHUTE SU3153 Map 2
Hatchet
The Chutes well signposted via Appleshaw off A342, 2½ miles W of Andover;
SP11 9DX

This neat and friendly thatched 16th-c house is one of the county's most attractive
pubs. The very low-beamed bar has a splendid 17th-c fireback in the huge fireplace
(and a roaring winter log fire), a mix of captain's chairs and cushioned wheelbacks
around oak tables, and a peaceful local feel. Fullers London Pride, Otter Bitter and
Timothy Taylors Landlord on handpump; cards, chess, board games and piped
music. Thursday night is curry night, when you can eat as much as you like (£7.75).
Other bar food includes lunchtime baguettes (from £4.95), ploughman's (£6.50),
liver and bacon, smoked haddock florentine and mushroom tortellini with sun-
dried tomatoes and pesto (all £7.95), and daily specials such as well liked mussels
(£4.95 or £8.95), mushroom and red pepper stroganoff (£8.25), and lamb shank
(£8.75). The restaurant and part of the bar are no smoking. There are seats out on
a terrace by the front car park, or on the side grass, and there's a children's sandpit.
*(Recommended by Mrs J H S Lang, Mr and Mrs G N Davies, Bill and Jessica Ritson, Mr and
Mrs R Davies, Peter and Jean Hoare)*

Free house ~ Licensee Jeremy McKay ~ Real ale ~ Bar food (12-2.15, 7-9.45) ~ Restaurant
~ (01264) 730229 ~ Children in restaurant and end bar only ~ Dogs allowed in bar ~
Open 11.30-3, 6-11; 12-3.30, 7-10.30 Sun ~ Bedrooms: /£60S

LUCKINGTON ST8384 Map 2
Old Royal Ship
Off B4040 SW of Malmesbury; SN14 6PA

Locals and visitors alike are very fond of this bustling, partly 17th c pub. It's
pleasantly opened up, making in effect one long bar divided into three areas. The
central servery has Archers Village, Bass, Wadworths 6X and a changing guest on
handpump, farm cider, and ten decent wines by the glass. On the right are neat
tables, spindleback chairs and small cushioned settles on dark bare boards, with a
small open fireplace and some stripped masonry. On the left, past an area with
corks packed into its ceiling, there is more of a mix of tables and chairs, and a small
step up to a carpeted section partly divided by rubber plants and dracaenas; in here,
an extraordinary trompe l'oeil stone staircase disappears up into a fictitious turret.
Flowers on the tables, some rather lively yellow paintwork, and bright curtains add
quite a touch of colour. Decent bar food includes sandwiches (from £4.25), deep-
fried whitebait (£5.75; main course £8.75), deep-fried chicken goujons with chilli
dip (£5.95), breaded plaice (£8.25), gammon and egg (£9.95), chicken caesar salad
(£10.50), and steaks (from £13.75). The restaurant is no smoking, and service is
welcoming and helpful; skittle alley and piped music. The garden beyond the car
park has boules, a play area with a big wooden fort, and plenty of seats on the
terrace or grass. It does get very busy during the Badminton horse trials.
(Recommended by Mrs Jill Wyatt, Richard Stancomb, J L Wedel, Colin and Peggy Wilshire)

Free house ~ Licensee Helen Johnson-Greening ~ Real ale ~ Bar food (12-2.30, 6-9.30) ~
Restaurant ~ (01666) 840222 ~ Children allowed until 9.30pm ~ Jazz second Weds of
month March-Nov ~ Open 11.30-3, 6-11; 11.30-11 Sat; 12-4, 7-11 Sun; closed evening
25 Dec

MALMESBURY ST9287 Map 2
Smoking Dog ◖
High Street; SN16 9AT

With interesting and temptingly priced beers and a friendly, bustling atmosphere,
it's not surprising that this double-fronted mid-terrace 17th-c pub is so popular –
and especially so on the spring bank holiday weekend when they hold their annual
sausage and beer festival. The two smallish front bars have a sociable local feel,
with flagstones, dark woodwork, cushioned bench seating, big pine tables and a

blazing log fire. A flagstoned corridor with notices on the walls leads to a bare-boards no smoking restaurant. Archers Best, Brains Revd James and Buckleys Best, with guests like Exmoor Hound Dog and Timothy Taylors Landlord on handpump or tapped from the cask, and eight wines by the glass; attentive young staff. Good, reasonably priced bar food includes home-made soup (£3.50), smoked haddock and spring onion fishcake with lemon mayonnaise (£3.95), roast field mushrooms with caramelised red onions and a rich red wine sauce (£4.25), sandwiches using garlic and rosemary or lemon and pepper flatbread or traditional bread (from £4.75), chargrilled chicken burger with green pesto mayonnaise or tasty speciality sausages of the day (£6.50), beer-battered haddock or meatballs in a rich tomato, garlic and basil sauce with tagliatelle (£7.95), a pie of the day (£8.25), parmesan and basil-crusted cod loin with roast cherry vine tomatoes and a tomato and coriander sauce (£9.95), 10oz chargrilled rump steak (£11.95), and puddings such as crème brûlée or crisp chocolate tart (£4.25); Sunday roast £8.50. The garden has pleasant views out over the town. *(Recommended by Deborah Boyle,*
Amanda De Montjoie, Tom and Ruth Rees, Baden and Sandy Waller, Christine and
Neil Townend, R M Corlett, DAV, Mike Pugh, R Huggins, D Irving, E McCall, T McLean,
Paul A Moore)

Brains ~ Manager Martin Bridge ~ Real ale ~ Bar food (12-2.30, 7-9.30) ~ Restaurant ~ (01666) 825823 ~ Children allowed but must be away from bar by 7pm ~ Dogs allowed in bar ~ Live music occasionally ~ Open 12-11(midnight Fri and Sat; 10.30 Sun)

NEWTON TONY SU2140 Map 2
Malet Arms 🍴 🍺
Village signposted off A338 Swindon—Salisbury; SP4 0HF

This is a proper village pub opposite the playing field and run by a landlord who is mad about cricket (and coaches the local schoolchildren). The two low-beamed interconnecting rooms have nice furnishings including a mix of different-sized tables with high winged wall settles, carved pews, chapel and carver chairs, and there are lots of pictures, mainly from imperial days. The main front windows are said to have come from the stern of a ship, and there's a log and coal fire in a huge fireplace. The homely back dining room is no smoking. Chalked up on a blackboard, the good changing food might include home-made soup (£4.25), olives and antipasti with hot ciabatta (£4.95), lemon breaded sardine fillets with saffron mayonnaise (£5.75), home-made cornish pasty (£8.50), fettucine with mushrooms, white wine, cream and parmesan (£8.75), wild boar and apple sausages (£8.95), wild rabbit in cider, mustard and cream (£9.50), large grilled gammon steak with free-range eggs (£10.50), supreme of chicken braised in white wine with celery, garlic and shallots or popular saddle of local venison (shot by the landlord usually, £12), and super puddings made by the landlady such as Mars Bar cheesecake, walnut and honey tart or dark chocolate mousse (£4.50). Well kept Archers Special, Butts Barbus Barbus, Stonehenge Heelstone, and maybe one from Butcombe, Palmers or Ramsbury on handpump, farm cider, several malt whiskies, and ten wines by the glass. There's an african grey parrot called Steerpike. The small front terrace has old-fashioned garden seats and some picnic-sets on the grass there, and there are more in the back garden along with a wendy house. There's also a little aviary, and a horse paddock behind. Getting to the pub takes you through a ford and it may be best to use an alternative route in winter as it can be quite deep. *(Recommended by M G Hart, Dave Braisted, Kevin Thorpe, Grahame Brooks,*
Gillian Rodgers, Evelyn and Derek Walter, Ian Phillips, Patrick Hall, J Stickland,
Michael Doswell, Pat and Tony Martin, M B Manser)

Free house ~ Licensee Noel Cardew ~ Real ale ~ Bar food (12-2.30, 6.30-10 (7-9.30 Sun)) ~ (01980) 629279 ~ Children allowed but not in bar area ~ Dogs allowed in bar ~ Open 11-3, 6-11; 12-3, 7-10.30 Sun; closed 25 and 26 Dec, 1 Jan

Places with gardens or terraces usually let children sit there – we note in the text the very few exceptions that don't.

NORTON ST8884 Map 2

Vine Tree 🍴 ⚓

4 miles from M4 junction 17; A429 towards Malmesbury, then left at Hullavington,
Sherston signpost, then follow Norton signposts; in village turn right at Foxley signpost,
which takes you into Honey Lane; SN16 0JP

Once they've discovered it, customers tend to become enthusiastic regulars at this
civilised dining pub. It's extremely well run and despite the emphasis on the
imaginative food, there's a buoyant atmosphere and drinkers do pop in for a drink
and a chat. Three beautifully kept little rooms open together: old beams, some old
settles and unvarnished wooden tables on the flagstone and oak floors, big cream
church altar candles, a woodburning stove at one end of the no smoking restaurant
and a large open fireplace in the central bar, limited edition and sporting prints, and
a mock-up mounted pig's mask (used for a game that involves knocking coins off its
nose and ears); look out for Clementine, the friendly and docile black labrador. One
side of the inn is no smoking. Using seasonal and traceable local produce, fish from
Brixham and Cornwall, and beef from their next door neighbour's farm, the
regularly changing and very good food might include filled ciabattas, soups such as
mussel and saffron, white bean and thyme with truffle oil or mushroom minestrone
(from £3.95), creamy parfait of foie gras and chicken livers with grape and sauterne
jelly (£5.95), a rich brûlée of cornish beer crab (£4.95), goats cheese soufflé (£5.50),
seared pigeon breast with chestnuts, smoked bacon, lardons and puy lentils (£6.25;
main course £12), moules marinière or various caesar salads (£6.25; main course
£12.50), pumpkin ravioli with walnut sauce (£9.95), freshly minced burger with or
without a spicy blood mary (from £11.75), venison and juniper pie (£11.95), roast
saddle and leg of wild rabbit (£12.95), corn-fed chicken stuffed with mixed seafood
with a mild red thai curry cream (£13.95), chargrilled fillet of beef with vichy carrot
purée (£15.50), wild bass fillet with a scallop, leek and herb risotto and vanilla bean
jus (£15.75), and puddings such as pink champagne and strawberry jelly with a
sabayon of white peach, white and dark chocolate torte or burnt tarte au citron with
a seville orange sorbet (from £5.15); super cheeses (£5.95 for three, £7.95 for five)
with home-made apricot and ginger chutney, celery sticks and savoury biscuits, and
proper children's meals. It's best to book if you want to eat here, especially at
weekends. Butcombe Bitter, Fullers London Pride, and St Austell Tribute on
handpump, around 35 wines by the glass from an impressive list (they do monthly
tutored tastings), and quite a choice of malt whiskies and armagnacs; helpful,
attentive staff. There are picnic-sets and a children's play area in a two-acre garden
plus a pretty suntrap terrace with teak furniture under big cream umbrellas, a lion
fountain, lots of lavender and box hedging. They have a busy calendar of events,
with outdoor music in summer, vintage car rallies and lots going on during the
Badminton horse trials. Many things to do and see nearby. That said, it's not the
easiest place to find, so it can feel more remote than its proximity to the motorway
would suggest. *(Recommended by John and Gloria Isaacs, Rob Winstanley, Richard and
Sheila Fitton, Richard Stancomb, Andy and Claire Barker, Mike and Helen Rawsthorn,
Mary Rayner, Rod Stoneman, Simon Collett-Jones, Mrs Pat Crabb, Mr and Mrs Peter Llewellyn,
Matthew Shackle, Andrea and Guy Bradley, Adelle Wheeler, Guy Vowles, Deborah Weston)*

Free house ~ Licensees Charles Walker and Tiggi Wood ~ Real ale ~ Bar food (12-2(2.30
Sat, 3.30 Sun), 7-9.30(10 Fri/Sat)) ~ Restaurant ~ (01666) 837654 ~ Children welcome ~
Dogs welcome ~ Live jazz and blues once a month but during summer, every Sun ~
Open 12-3(3.30 Sat), 6-midnight; 12-midnight Sun; closed 25 Dec

PITTON SU2131 Map 2

Silver Plough ⚓

Village signposted from A30 E of Salisbury (follow brown tourist signs); SP5 1DU

There's a good bustling atmosphere and a wide mix of customers at this pleasant
country dining pub. The comfortable front bar has plenty to look at since the black
beams are strung with hundreds of antique boot-warmers and stretchers, pewter
and china tankards, copper kettles, toby jugs, earthenware and glass rolling pins,

painted clogs, glass net-floats, and coach horns and so forth. Seats include half a
dozen cushioned antique oak settles (one elaborately carved, beside a very fine
reproduction of an Elizabethan oak table), and the timbered white walls are hung
with Thorburn and other game bird prints, original Craven Hill sporting cartoons,
and a big naval battle glass-painting. The back bar is simpler, but still has a big
winged high-backed settle, cased antique guns, substantial pictures, and – like the
front room – flowers on its tables. There's a skittle alley next to the snug bar; piped
music. Well liked bar food includes various salads such as black pudding,
mushrooms and apples or smoked chicken caesar (from £5.95; they do two sizes),
home-made vegetable lasagne or steak and kidney pie (£4.95; larger £8.95), and
home-made thai red chicken curry (£5.95; larger £9.95), with evening choices such
as spinach and brie filo parcel on wine and dill sauce (£6.50), pasta with
mediterranean vegetables (£10.95), chicken stuffed with brie and wrapped in bacon
on a dijon sauce (£13.95), and roast half a shoulder of lamb with mint and garlic
gravy (£14.50), and daily specials like scallops in saffron sauce (£6.95), a trio of
sausages with onion gravy (£9.95), and sirloin steak (£12.95). On Sunday the menu
is more limited, and they do a choice of roasts. The restaurant and snug bar are no
smoking. Badger Gold, Sussex Bitter, Tanglefoot and a seasonal brew on
handpump kept under light blanket pressure, quite a few country wines, and nine
wines by the glass. A quiet lawn has picnic-sets and other tables under cocktail
parasols. The pub is well placed for good downland and woodland walks.
*(Recommended by Bernard Stradling, James Price, Phyl and Jack Street, Noel Grundy,
Clifford Blakemore, N R White, Fr Robert Marsh, Edward Mirzoeff, John Robertson,
Michael Butler, Anthony Longden, Kevin Blake, Peter Neate, Patrick Hall)*

Badger ~ Tenants Hughen and Joyce Riley ~ Real ale ~ Bar food (12-2, 6-9; 12-2.15,
6.30-8.30 Sun) ~ Restaurant ~ (01722) 712266 ~ Small children allowed in snug bar ~
Dogs allowed in bar ~ Open 11-3, 6-11(midnight Sat); 12-3, 6-11 Sun; closed 25 Dec and
evening 26 Dec ~ Bedrooms: /£50S

POULSHOT   ST9559   Map 2
Raven 🍺
Village signposted off A361 Devizes—Seend; SN10 1RW

The setting here is pretty – it's just across from the village green. The two cosy
black-beamed rooms are well furnished with sturdy tables and chairs and
comfortable banquettes; the lounge and dining room are no smoking. Wadworths
IPA, 6X and maybe a seasonal ale are tapped straight from the cask; obliging
service. Bar food includes devilled whitebait or creamy garlic mushrooms (£4.85),
filled ciabattas (from £5.20), ham and eggs (£8.10), vegetable curry (£8.20),
battered cod (£8.80), home-made steak and kidney pie (£9.25), pork tenderloin
with onions and mushrooms in brandy and cream (£12.40), daily specials like
home-made soup (£3.50), sausage hotpot (£8.35), home-made salmon fishcakes
with sweet chilli sauce (£9.25), and stilton chicken (£9.65), and puddings such as
crème brûlée or home-made chocolate fudge cake (£3.75). The gents' is outside.
More reports please. *(Recommended by Paul A Moore, Mr and Mrs J Brown)*

Wadworths ~ Tenants Philip and Susan Henshaw ~ Real ale ~ Bar food (not Mon) ~
Restaurant ~ (01380) 828271 ~ Children allowed but must be accompanied by an adult at
all times ~ Dogs allowed in bar ~ Open 11-2.30, 6.30-11; 12-3, 7-10.30 Sun; closed Mon,
25 Dec and evenings 26 and 31 Dec

RAMSBURY   SU2771   Map 2
Bell
Signed off B4192 NW of Hungerford, or A4 W; SN8 2PB

As we went to press we heard that this neatly kept dining pub had suffered dreadful
fire damage. They were managing to keep the bar open but could not offer food – but
all this will change by the time this edition is published. The airy bar has exposed
beams, cream-washed walls, two woodburning stoves, and a chatty, relaxed
atmosphere. Victorian stained-glass panels in one of the two sunny bay windows look

out on to the quiet village street. The friendly landlord and staff serve local Ramsbury Gold and one of their guests such as Bitter, Flint Knapper or Kennet Valley and Sharps Doom Bar on handpump. There are picnic-sets on the raised lawn; roads lead from this quiet village into the downland on all sides. We'd be grateful for news on the refurbishments. *(Recommended by Mark and Ruth Brock, Alan and Paula McCully)*

Free house ~ Licensee Jeremy Wilkins ~ Real ale ~ Bar food (not Sun evening) ~ Restaurant ~ (01672) 520230 ~ Children welcome ~ Dogs allowed in bar ~ Open 12-3, 5.30-11; 12-3, 7-10.30 Sun

ROWDE   ST9762   Map 2
George & Dragon 🍽 ♈
A342 Devizes—Chippenham; SN10 2PN

Behind the imposing black front door in this attractive no smoking dining pub are two low-ceilinged rooms with large wooden tables, antique rugs, and walls covered with old pictures and portraits; the atmosphere is pleasantly chatty. As well as fish and seafood delivered daily from Cornwall, the menu might include roast tomato, onion and basil soup (£5), caesar salad with fresh anchovies and garlic croûtons (£7.50), wild mushroom, parmesan and black truffle oil risotto or devilled lambs kidneys with grainy mustard cream sauce (£7.50; main course £9.50), roast chicken breast with dauphinoise potatoes or chargrilled sirloin steak with a blue cheese and herb crust (£14.50), roast rack of lamb with spring onion and new potato compote (£15.50), and puddings like apple and blueberry crumble or crème brûlée (£5.50); three-course Sunday lunch (£15.50). Butcombe Bitter on handpump and nine wines by the glass; board games. A pretty garden at the back has tables and chairs; the Kennet & Avon Canal is nearby. More reports please. *(Recommended by Oliver Richardson, Tina and David Woods-Taylor, Mary Rayner, Mr and Mrs F J Parmenter)*

Free house ~ Licensees Philip and Michelle Hale, Christopher Day ~ Real ale ~ Bar food (12-3, 7-10 Tues-Fri; 12-4, 6.30-10 Sat; 12-4 Sun; not Sun evening, Mon lunchtime) ~ Restaurant ~ (01380) 723053 ~ Children welcome ~ Dogs allowed in bar ~ Open 12-3(4 Sat and Sun), 7-11; closed Sun evening, Mon lunchtime, first week Jan

SALISBURY   SU1429   Map 2
Haunch of Venison ㉕
Minster Street, opposite Market Cross; SP1 1TB

This interesting old pub was built 650 years ago as the church house for St Thomas's, just behind. The two tiny downstairs rooms are quite spit-and-sawdust in spirit, with massive beams in the white ceiling, stout oak benches built into the timbered walls, black and white floor tiles, and an open fire. A tiny snug (popular with locals, but historically said to be where the ladies drank) opens off the entrance lobby. Courage Best, Wadworths 6X and a guest such as Hop Back Summer Lightning on handpump from a pewter bar counter, and there's a rare set of antique taps for gravity-fed spirits and liqueurs. They've also 55 malt whiskies, decent wines, and a range of brandies. Halfway up the stairs is a panelled no smoking room they call the House of Lords, which has a small-paned window looking down on to the main bar, and a splendid fireplace that dates back to the building's early years; behind glass in a small wall slit is the smoke-preserved mummified hand of an 18th-c card sharp still clutching his cards. Lunchtime bar snacks such as venison sausage or scampi and aïoli (£5.50) and turkey ballotine (£6.90), as well as a three-course menu (taken in the upstairs no smoking restaurant) with dishes such as oak-smoked salmon with wasabi mayonnaise, salmon fishcakes with prawn antipasto, baked mustard and brown sugar ham or goats cheese and caramelised onion tartlet (£9.90). *(Recommended by Mike and Lynn Robinson, David Carr, Ann and Colin Hunt, N R White, Pete Walker, the Didler, Howard and Margaret Buchanan, Kevin Blake, Ken and Joyce Hollis, Bill and Jessica Ritson)*

Scottish Courage ~ Lease Anthony Leroy, Rupert Willcocks ~ Real ale ~ Bar food (12-2.30, 6-9.30) ~ Restaurant ~ (01722) 411313 ~ Children in restaurant ~ Dogs allowed in bar ~ Open 11-11; closed 25 Dec and 1 Jan

SEEND ST9461 Map 2

Barge

Seend Cleeve; signposted off A361 Devizes—Trowbridge, between Seend village and signpost to Seend Head; SN12 6QB

The neatly kept waterside garden here is an excellent place to watch the bustle of boats on the Kennet & Avon Canal – old streetlamps let you linger there after dark, and moorings by the humpy bridge are very useful for thirsty bargees. The bar has an unusual barge-theme décor, and intricately painted Victorian flowers cover the ceilings and run in a waist-high band above the deep green lower walls. A distinctive medley of eye-catching seats includes milk churns, unusual high-backed chairs (made from old boat-parts), a seat made from an upturned canoe, and the occasional small oak settle among the rugs on the parquet floor, while the walls have big sentimental engravings. The watery theme continues with a well stocked aquarium, and there's also a pretty Victorian fireplace, big bunches of dried flowers, and red velvet curtains for the big windows; piped music. Butcombe and Wadworths IPA and 6X on handpump, quite a few malt whiskies, and a good choice of wines by the glass. Uniformed staff serve well liked lunchtime bar food such as sandwiches (£4.95; soup and a sandwich £5.95), filled baked potatoes (from £5.25), ploughman's (£6.90), home-cooked ham and eggs (£8.50), baked field mushroom topped with goats cheese and a herb crust with spicy plum sauce or beer-battered cod (£9), and steak, kidney and mushroom in ale pie (£9.50), with evening choices such as chicken liver parfait with red onion chutney (£5.95), crab and cod fishcakes with dijon mayonnaise (£6.75), spinach roulade with cherry tomato and fennel dressing (£9.25), cajun salmon fillet with red pepper salsa (£12), and barbary duck breast with a port and redcurrant sauce (£13); Sunday roast (from £9.50). The restaurant extension (and the canal room) are no smoking. *(Recommended by Mike and Lynn Robinson, Kevin Thorpe, Paul and Shirley White, Richard and Liz Dilnot, R T and J C Moggridge, Christine and Neil Townend, Keith and Sally Jackson, Mark Flynn, Alan Sadler, Ian Moody, Dr and Mrs M E Wilson, Mrs Joyce Robson, Mark and Mary Fairman, Peter Titcomb)*

Wadworths ~ Tenant Christopher Moorley Long ~ Real ale ~ Bar food ~ Restaurant ~ (01380) 828230 ~ Children must be well behaved and away from bar area ~ Dogs allowed in bar ~ Open 11-3, 6-11; 11-11 Sat; 12-10.30 Sun; 11-3, 6-11 Sat in winter. They may close some evenings over the Christmas period

STOURTON ST7734 Map 2

Spread Eagle

Church Lawn; follow Stourhead brown signs off B3092, N of junction with A303 just W of Mere; BA12 6QE

The setting for this civilised old place is rather grand amongst other elegant stone buildings at the head of Stourhead Lake; all are owned by the National Trust. The interior has an old-fashioned feel with antique panel-back settles, a mix of new and old solid tables and chairs, handsome fireplaces with good winter log fires, smoky old sporting prints, prints of Stourhead, and standard lamps or brass swan's-neck wall lamps. One room by the entrance has armchairs, a longcase clock and a corner china cupboard. Two bars are no smoking. Butcombe, Wadworths 6X and a guest like Wessex Kilmington Best on handpump, farm ciders and seven wines by the glass. Lunchtime bar food includes soup (£4.50), chicken liver and wild mushroom pâté with onion jam (£5.95), free-range chicken salad, avocado, stilton and bacon (£5.95; main course £10.50), ploughman's (£6.95), ham and free-range eggs (£9.25), wild mushroom and asparagus pie (£9.50), and beef in ale pie (£10.25), with evening choices such as spider crab cakes with lemon and tarragon mayonnaise (£5.75), goats cheese mousse, butternut squash and beetroot salad (£5.95), fish pie (£9.95), old spot pork loin, organic cider and parsnip crisps (£13.50), sirloin steak glazed with stilton (£14.95), and puddings like sticky toffee pudding with caramel sauce (£4.95). There are benches in the courtyard behind. A bonus when staying here is that you can wander freely around the gardens outside their normal opening times – a nice way of enjoying them away from the crowds. *(Recommended by Tracey and Stephen Groves, Meg and Colin Hamilton, B J Harding, Sheila Topham, John Robertson, Colin and Janet Roe, Dr and Mrs M E Wilson, Ian Phillips, S Topham, Gill and Keith Croxton, P R and D Thomas, Mike Turner, John and Joan Nash, David Hoult, Paul Humphreys, Edward Mirzoeff)*

Free house ~ Licensees Stephen Ross, Karen Lock ~ Real ale ~ Bar food (12-10) ~ Restaurant (evening) ~ (01747) 840587 ~ Children welcome ~ Open 11-11; closed 25 Dec ~ Bedrooms: £60B/£90B

WEST LAVINGTON   SU0052   Map 2
Bridge Inn 🍴
A360 S of Devizes; Church Street; SN10 4LD

With a good mix of customers and enjoyable food, this quietly civilised and no smoking village pub is well liked by our readers. The light, spacious bar comfortably mixes contemporary features such as spotlights in the ceiling with firmly traditional fixtures like the enormous brick inglenook that may be filled with big logs and candles; at the opposite end is a smaller modern fireplace, in an area set mostly for eating. Pictures on the cream-painted or exposed brick walls are for sale, as are local jams, and there are plenty of fresh flowers on the tables and bar; timbers and the occasional step divide the various areas. Attractively presented, the food might include fish soup (£4.50), seared marinated pigeon in rosemary and port with crispy bacon and garlic croûtons (£5.30), chicken liver and pork terrine with apple and cider brandy chutney (£5.75), tian of crab and sun-dried tomato (£6.25), steaks (from £8.50), blue cheese, leek and basil pesto soufflé (£9.95), free-range chicken breast marinated in lemon sauce with stir-fried teriyaki vegetables (£12.95), specials such as salmon, cod and dill fishcakes (£4.95; main course £8.95), seared tiger prawns with a honey and coriander dressing (£5.50; main course £9.95), ham and free-range eggs (£6.95 lunchtime only), and haddock in beer batter (£8.25); puddings like chocolate brownie topped with a chocolate and caramel mousse and vanilla sauce or honey cheesecake with an Amaretti biscuit base, served with a sharp raspberry coulis (£5.10). Brakspears, Ringwood Best and Shepherd Neame Spitfire on handpump, and 11 wines by the glass; piped music in the evenings. At the back is a nice raised lawn area with several tables under a big tree; boules. *(Recommended by B and F A Hannam, Trevor Swindells, Jo and Mark Wadman, Bill and Jessica Ritson)*

Enterprise ~ Lease Cyrille and Paula Portier, Dave Hamilton ~ Real ale ~ Bar food (not Sun evening or Mon) ~ Restaurant ~ (01380) 813213 ~ Well behaved children welcome ~ Open 12-3, 6-11; 12-3 Sun; closed Sun evening and all day Mon; two weeks Feb

WHITLEY   ST8866   Map 2
Pear Tree 🍴 ♗ 🛏
Off B3353 S of Corsham, at Atworth 1½, Purlpit 1 signpost; or from A350 Chippenham—Melksham in Beanacre turn off on Westlands Lane at Whitley 1 signpost, then left and right at B3353; SN12 8QX

Wiltshire Dining Pub of the Year

This is a really smashing place and cleverly manages to appeal to those just wanting a drink, others out for a special meal (the food is exceptionally good), and as a place to stay – the bedrooms are very comfortable and well appointed and the breakfasts are excellent. And on top of this the staff are genuinely friendly and helpful. The front bar has quite a pubby feel, with cushioned window seats, some stripped shutters, a mix of dining chairs around good solid tables, a variety of country pictures and a Wiltshire Regiment sampler on the walls, a little fireplace on the left, and a lovely old stripped stone one on the right. Candlelit at night, the popular but unhurried big back no smoking restaurant (best to book) has green dining chairs, quite a mix of tables, and a pitched ceiling at one end with a quirky farmyard theme – wrought-iron cockerels and white scythe sculpture. From an imaginative menu, the modern food might include lunchtime toasties (£5.95), as well as soups such as jerusalem artichoke with truffle oil or fish soup with salt cod pasta parcels (£4.50), game terrine with pear and apple chutney and toasted sourdough (£5.50), devon blue, chestnut and pear ravioli with butter sauce and parmesan (£6.50; main course £10.50), hand-picked cornish crab, mayonnaise, deep-fried avocado and toast (£7.10), diver-caught scallops with celeriac purée, crispy pancetta and saffron butter sauce (£8), home-made pork, apple and herb sausages with bubble and squeak and slow-cooked shallots in red wine sauce (£11.50), roast cod with marinated borlotti beans, courgettes, butternut squash, parsley and extra virgin olive oil (£14.95), breaded cutlets of lamb with orange and mint couscous and spiced aubergine (£16.95), fillet of local beef with wild mushrooms, potato and pancetta torte with spinach and red wine sauce (£18.50), and puddings such as blood orange jelly with spiced chocolate orange caramel and chocolate ice-cream, sticky gingerbread with quince and cardamom ice-cream or rhubarb fool with tuile biscuits (£5.50); two-course set lunch (£13.50), three-course (£16). Moles Best, Stonehenge Pigswill and Wadworths 6X on handpump and ten wines by the glass. A bright spacious garden room opens on to a terrace with good teak furniture and views over the carefully maintained gardens, which are prettily lit at night to show features like the ruined pigsty; more seats on the terrace, and boules. *(Recommended by Craig Adams, Felicity Davies, Dr and Mrs T E Hothersall, W W Burke, Amanda De Montjoie, Joyce and Maurice Cottrell, Dr and Mrs M E Wilson, P and J Shapley, Therese Flanagan, Sebastian Snow, Paul and Ursula Randall, Alan Sadler, M and G R, Mr and Mrs Peter Llewellyn, Mr and Mrs A H Young, John and Jane Hayter, A P Seymour, Bill and Jessica Ritson)*

Free house ~ Licensees Martin and Debbie Still ~ Real ale ~ Bar food (12-2.30, 6.30-9.30(10 Fri and Sat); 12-3, 7-9 Sun) ~ Restaurant ~ (01225) 709131 ~ Children in eating area of bar and restaurant ~ Dogs allowed in bar ~ Open 12-11; closed 25 and 26 Dec, 1 Jan ~ Bedrooms: £75B/£110B

LUCKY DIP

Besides the fully inspected pubs, you might like to try these Lucky Dips recommended to us and described by readers (if you do, please send us reports: www.goodguides.co.uk).

ALDBOURNE [SU2675]
☆ *Blue Boar* SN8 2EN [The Green (off B4192)]: Homely and relaxed, with friendly service even when packed, very generous inexpensive food from baguettes up, three Wadworths ales, good choice of wines and soft drinks, farm tools, boar's head and flame-effect woodburner in traditional bar with darts, extensive more modern back dining room; may be quiet piped music; children welcome, terrace overlooking pretty village green nr church, open all day *(Guy Vowles, Mary Rayner, John Downham)*

ALVEDISTON [ST9723]
Crown SP5 5JY [off A30 W of Salisbury]: 15th-c thatched inn with new licensees yet again, three very low-beamed partly panelled rooms, deep pink paintwork, two inglenook fireplaces, no smoking dining area, enjoyable home-made food, good wines by the glass, Ringwood Best and guest beers, darts, cribbage, dominoes; piped music; children welcome, pretty views from neatly kept attractive garden, good bedrooms *(J S Phillips, LYM, Pat and Robert Watt)*

BADBURY [SU1980]
Bakers Arms SN4 0EU [a mile from M4 junction 15, off A346 S]: Comfortable and friendly three-room village pub with Arkells ales, wide choice of good value food from speciality sandwiches to indian and chinese dishes, coal fire, no smoking area, pool; piped music; no dogs or small children, garden tables, lovely flowers *(Bill Leckey, Peter and Audrey Dowsett)*

Plough SN4 0EP [A346 (Marlborough Rd) just S of M4 junction 15]: Large friendly rambling bar area, cheerful efficient staff, Arkells 2B, 3B and Kingsdown, decent wines, good value changing food inc afternoon snacks and all-day Sun roasts, light and airy no smoking dining room (children allowed) looking over road to Vale of the White Horse with pianola and papers to read, darts; piped music; children welcome, play area in sunny garden above, handy for Great Western Hospital, open all day *(Mark and Ruth Brock, Brian and Maggie Woodford, R T and J C Moggridge, Mrs Pat Crabb, Dr and Mrs A K Clarke)*

BARFORD ST MARTIN [SU0531]
☆ *Barford Inn* SP3 4AB [B3098 W of Salisbury (Grovely Rd), just off A30]: Panelled front bar with big log fire, other chatty interlinking rooms and bars, no smoking restaurant, friendly staff, enjoyable food inc good fresh fish, Badger Best and K&B, disabled access and lavatories, children welcome, dogs allowed in bar, terrace tables, more in back garden, charming cheerful bedrooms, open all day (has been cl Sun afternoon) *(LYM, Klaus and Elizabeth Leist, M G Hart)*

BECKHAMPTON [SU0868]

☆ *Waggon & Horses* SN8 1QJ [A4
Marlborough—Calne]: Handsome old stone-
and-thatch pub handy for Avebury, old-
fashioned settles and comfortably cushioned
wall benches in open-plan beamed bar, no
smoking dining area, sensible food (not Sun
evening), Wadworths IPA, JCB, 6X and a guest
beer, pool and pub games; piped music;
children in restaurant, pleasant garden with
good play area, open all day, bedrooms
*(Mike and Lynn Robinson, LYM, Sheila and
Robert Robinson, Dr and Mrs A K Clarke,
Paul A Moore)*

BOX [ST8268]

Bear SN13 8NJ [High St (A4)]: 18th-c, with
real ales such as Wadworths 6X and Wickwar
Cotswold Way, welcoming staff, log fires,
lively locals' bar with cards and dominoes,
quiet lounge set for enjoyable reasonably
priced food; bedrooms, backs on to cricket
ground *(Dr and Mrs A K Clarke)*

Queens Head SN13 8NH [High St]: Civilised
open-plan local with old-world dark wood
décor, prompt friendly service, three real ales,
bargain food from snacks and light dishes such
as baked potatoes up, valley views *(Dr and
Mrs A K Clarke, Guy Vowles)*

BRADFORD LEIGH [ST8362]

Plough BA15 2RW [B2109 N of Bradford]:
Emphasis on meals in extended and smartened
up dining area (no baps or sandwiches),
friendly service, Moles and
Wadworths 6X, log fire; darts and pool;
children welcome, nice seats outside, play area
(Dr and Mrs A K Clarke, MRSM)

BRADFORD-ON-AVON [ST8260]

Barge BA15 2EA [Frome Rd]: Four real ales,
pleasant atmosphere, well priced food from
lunchtime sandwiches and baguettes to some
interesting dishes and choice of Sun roasts,
leather sofas in window; soft piped music;
children welcome, steps up to waterside tables
and more on own barge, softly coloured lamps
out here *(Dr and Mrs M E Wilson, Dr and
Mrs A K Clarke, Keith and Sally Jackson,
John and Joan Nash)*

Beehive BA15 1UA [A363 out towards
Trowbridge]: Yet another change of landlord
for old-fashioned L-shaped pub nr canal on
outskirts, helpful service, real ales such as
Butcombe, reasonably priced food, good range
of wines, cosy log fires, candlelit tables, 19th-c
playbills, cricketing prints and cigarette cards,
darts; children and dogs welcome; attractive
good-sized back garden, play area, barbecues
*(Pete Baker, BB, Mike Gorton, Dr and Mrs
A K Clarke)*

Bunch of Grapes BA15 1JY [Silver St]: Dim-lit
wine-bar style décor, cask seats and rugs on
bare boards in small front room, bigger tables
on composition floor of roomier main bar,
good real ales, range of wines and malt
whiskies, good choice of interesting reasonably
priced food in bar and upstairs eating area
(BB, Dr and Mrs A K Clarke)

Cross Guns BA15 2HB [Avoncliff, outside
town]: Listed for its position, with floodlit

gardens steeply terraced above the bridges,
aqueducts and river (dogs allowed out here);
stripped-stone low-beamed bar with 16th-c
inglenook, upstairs river-view restaurant, four
real ales, lots of malt whiskies and country
wines; loudspeaker announcements, piped
music, and the pub can get very busy indeed,
though service normally stays commendably
quick and friendly; children welcome, open all
day *(Meg and Colin Hamilton, D P and
M A Miles, LYM, Angus Johnson,
Carol Bolden, Dr and Mrs A K Clarke,
Ian Phillips, Roger Wain-Heapy,
Wendy Straker)*

Three Horseshoes BA15 1LA [Frome Rd, by
station car park entrance]: Comfortable and
chatty old proper pub with quickly served
good food from tapas to substantial dishes,
Butcombe and Wadworths 6X, friendly
service, plenty of nooks and corners, small
restaurant; tables on terrace with big barbecue
(Ted George, Dr and Mrs A K Clarke)

BRATTON [ST9152]

Duke BA13 4RW [B3098 E of Westbury]:
Comfortable, neat and civilised open-plan pub
with restaurant area off traditional bar, very
good generous food (freshly cooked, so may
take a while) inc lunchtime bargains, Moles
real ale, quick pleasant service, exemplary
lavatories; darts and fruit machine in public
area, piped music; ancient whalebone arch to
enclosed side garden, nearby walks, bedrooms
(Geoff and Brigid Smithers, BB)

BROUGHTON GIFFORD [ST8764]

Bell on the Common SN12 8LX [The
Common]: Imposing rose-draped stone-built
pub on huge informal village green, traditional
furnishings, long-serving landlord and friendly
staff, Wadworths from handpumps on back
wall, big coal fire, enjoyable homely food,
dining lounge full of copper and old country
prints, rustic bar with local photographs old
and new, small pool room with darts and juke
box, popular quiz night; children welcome,
charming flower-filled crazy-paved garden
(occasional pig roasts and live music), bowls
club next door *(Dr and Mrs M E Wilson,
Michael Doswell, Dr and Mrs A K Clarke)*

Fox & Hounds SN12 8PN [The Street]:
Traditional timbered pub, welcoming helpful
staff, good varied bar food cooked fresh, so
can take a while *(MRSM)*

BULKINGTON [ST9458]

Tipsy Toad SN10 1SJ [High St]: Friendly and
straightforward, with cheerful licensees,
Wadworths 6X and a couple of guest beers,
good value generous fresh food inc choice of
Sun roasts; skittle alley *(Mr and Mrs A Curry)*

BURCOMBE [SU0631]

Ship SP2 0EJ [Burcombe Lane]: Cosy two-level
dining pub with unpretentious bistro
atmosphere, low beams, panelling and window
seats, two log fires, pleasant décor, candles and
soft lighting, young chef/landlord doing good
choice of good value fresh food inc enterprising
dishes, friendly efficient staff, Wadworths 6X,
decent wines, no smoking area; unobtrusive
piped music; children welcome, tables on front

terrace and in peaceful riverside garden, pretty village *(John Coatsworth, Pat and Robert Watt, James Blood)*

CASTLE COMBE [ST8477]

☆ *Castle Inn* SN14 7HN: Smart and attractive old-world country hotel with friendly and obliging antipodean staff, good atmosphere and plenty of individual touches in comfortable and pleasantly furnished beamed bar, enjoyable food from ciabattas and ploughman's up, Bass and Moles best, afternoon teas, upstairs dining room and conservatory with tented ceiling; tables and chairs out in front and on sheltered pretty terrace, beautiful village, 13 good bedrooms *(J Roy Smylie, Cathy Robinson, Ed Coombe, Ian Phillips, Mrs Ann Gray, Peter and Audrey Dowsett)*

Salutation SN14 7LH [The Gibb; B4039 Acton Turville—Chippenham, nr Nettleton]: Roomy old pub with plenty of beamery, choice of seating areas inc comfortable lounge and locals' bar, huge handsome fireplace, prompt welcoming service, real ales such as Abbey Bellringer, Fullers London Pride, Moles and Wadworths 6X, good choice of wines, enjoyable food from big baguettes up, separate raftered thatched and timbered restaurant; children welcome, pretty garden with pergola, open all day *(Dr and Mrs A K Clarke, MRSM)*

White Hart SN14 7HS [signed off B4039 Chippenham—Chipping Sodbury]: Attractive ancient stone-built pub, friendly and relaxed, with beams, panelling, flagstones, seats in stone-mullioned window, lots of old local photographs, Wadworths ales, nice staff, log fires, wide food choice, smaller lounge, family room, games room; walkers welcome (handy for Macmillan Way), tables on pavement and in sheltered courtyard; in centre of this honeypot village, so can be very busy *(LYM, Ian Phillips, Phyl and Jack Street, Peter and Audrey Dowsett)*

CHARLTON [ST9688]

☆ *Horse & Groom* SN16 9DL [B4040 towards Cricklade]: Appealing stone-built inn, smart and relaxing, with fine old furnishings, stripped stone and log fire, simpler right-hand bar with hops on beams, wide choice of good freshly made food in bar and restaurant, real ales, friendly and obliging young landlord knowledgeable about wine; dogs welcome, tables out under trees, good bedrooms *(K H Frostick, LYM, Mark and Joanna, R Huggins, D Irving, E McCall, T McLean)*

CHILMARK [ST9732]

Black Dog SP3 5AH [B3089 Salisbury—Hindon]: 15th-c beamed village pub with several smallish rooms, a log fire in each (armchairs by one and fossil ammonite in another's fireplace), new landlord aiming higher on the food side, sandwiches and baguettes too, Wadworths ales, good value house wines, good local atmosphere; rows of picnic-sets in good-sized roadside garden with terrace *(Dr and Mrs M E Wilson, LYM, Mrs J H S Lang, Colin and Janet Roe)*

CHIPPENHAM [ST9073]

Kingfisher SN14 0JL [Hungerdown Lane]: Welcoming local with Wadworths 6X, interesting malt whiskies and brandies, good lunchtime sandwiches and salads, fine old prints; soft piped music, board games, frequent music and good quiz nights; tables outside *(Dr and Mrs A K Clarke)*

Old Road Tavern SN15 1JA [Old Rd, by N side of station]: Thriving town pub, very friendly, with games-oriented public bar, two-part lounge, Courage Best, Fullers London Pride, Greene King Old Speckled Hen and a guest beer, cheap lunchtime food from sandwiches up; frequent wknd live music; pleasant secluded little back garden *(Pete Baker, Dr and Mrs A K Clarke)*

CHITTERNE [ST9843]

☆ *Kings Head* BA12 0LJ [B390 Heytesbury—Shrewton]: Relaxed and understated Salisbury Plain oasis, despite out-of-the-way setting well liked for food from short choice of good bar lunches to inventive evening meals inc good fish; Butcombe and Wadworths 6X, friendly service, good log fire, simple traditional décor with wooden floors, panelled dado and chunky old pine tables with lighted candles, no music or machines; lovely hanging baskets, tables on back terrace, pretty village, good walks *(Kit Stallard, BB, J Stickland, John and Elisabeth Cox)*

CLYFFE PYPARD [SU0776]

Goddard Arms SN4 7PY: Cheery 16th-c local with log fire and raised dining area in split-level main bar, small sitting room with another fire and two old armchairs, down-to-earth chatty and welcoming licensees, Wadworths 6X and guest beers like local Ramsbury, good value straightforward fresh food, daily papers, artwork for sale, pool room with darts, cribbage etc; sports TV, no credit cards; picnic-sets in back courtyard, bedrooms, also bunkhouse in former skittle alley, tiny pretty thatched village in lovely countryside, open all day wknds *(Pete Baker, BB, Mrs Pat Crabb)*

CODFORD [ST9639]

George BA12 0NG [just off A36 W of A303 intersection; High St]: Old inn with amiable staff, knocked-through L-shaped bar, stripped brickwork, well spaced tables, big house plants, contemporary art and lighting, log fire, Timothy Taylors Landlord, some good cooking; piped music; well behaved children welcome, tables on narrow front terrace overlooking road, bedrooms, cl Sun evening and Tues *(Julia and Richard Tredgett, LYM, Richard J Mullarkey, John A Barker)*

COLLINGBOURNE DUCIS [SU2453]

☆ *Shears* SN8 3ED [Cadley Rd]: Popular racing-country thatched pub reopened after stylishly simple refurbishment under new chef/landlord, good fresh imaginative food in bar and restaurant, local ingredients, Brakspears; attractive courtyard garden, six nice bedrooms *(J Stickland)*

COMPTON BASSETT [SU0372]

White Horse SN11 8RG: Cheerful welcome, good choice of food from baguettes and pubby dishes to more elaborate short restaurant menu, good friendly service, Wadworths 6X and guest beers *(J R Bieneman)*

CORSTON [ST9284]

Radnor Arms SN16 0HD [A429, N of M4 junction 17]: Large L-shaped bar, good value food inc speciality sausages, interesting changing ales such as Hadrian & Border, Hook Norton and Youngs, log fire one end, darts the other; good-sized garden, open all day *(Kevin Thorpe)*

CRICKLADE [SU1093]

Red Lion SN6 6DD [off A419 Swindon—Cirencester; High St]: Fine old 16th-c former coaching inn with great range of good real ales – Moles Best, Wadworths 6X and several guests such as Ramsbury, two farm ciders, good choice of malt whiskies, friendly landlord and helpful staff, sandwiches and simple hot dishes (not Mon/Tues), generous Sun carvery (the roasts are well done), log fire, interesting signs and bric-a-brac in large yet cosy bar, local artwork for sale, no music or mobile phones; neat garden, bedrooms, open all day *(Mr and Mrs G S Ayrton, Pete Baker, R Huggins, D Irving, E McCall, T McLean, MLR, Martin and Karen Wake)*

CRUDWELL [ST9592]

Plough SN16 9EW [A429 N of Malmesbury]: Nice timeless local feel, friendly attentive service, quiet lounge and raised dining area, Adnams Broadside, Archers Golden, Caledonian Deuchars IPA and Timothy Taylors Landlord, good value food, open fires, end pool room, bar with TV and games machines; pleasant side garden *(KC, R Huggins, D Irving, E McCall, T McLean)*

DERRY HILL [ST9570]

Lansdowne Arms SN11 9NS [Church Rd]: Stately stone-built pub opposite one of Bowood's grand gatehouses, several civilised areas with relaxed period flavour, hearty log fire and candles in bottles, Wadworths ales, good value wines by the glass, prompt attentive cheerful service, wide food choice from good range of huge sandwiches with chips up in bar and restaurant; faint piped music; fine views, picnic-sets in neat side garden, good play area *(BB, Meg and Colin Hamilton)*

DOWNTON [SU1721]

Wooden Spoon SP5 3PG [High St (A338 S of Salisbury)]: Convivial family-run pub with welcoming attentive service, good sensibly priced food from sandwiches and baguettes to wide choice of hot dishes using local produce, inc some interesting dishes, good steaks and popular Sun lunch, John Smiths, Ringwood and a guest such as Shepherd Neame Spitfire, good value wines, public bar on left; children welcome *(W W Burke, Tony Shepherd, Mark Barker, Glen and Nola Armstrong)*

EAST KNOYLE [ST8830]

☆ *Seymour Arms* SP3 6AJ [The Street; just off A350 S of Warminster]: Warmly welcoming creeper-covered stone-built pub, good freshly made generous food inc interesting specials, attentive service, Wadworths IPA, 6X and JCB, spotless and comfortable rambling bar areas,

cosy beamed part with high-backed settle by log fire; tables in garden with play area, good bedrooms *(Mrs J Cooper, BB, Pam Parkinson)*

EASTON ROYAL [SU1961]

Bruce Arms SN9 5LR [Easton Rd]: Unchanging 19th-c local with benches by two long scrubbed antique pine tables on bar's brick floor, homely carpeted and curtained parlour with easy chairs, old pictures, flowers and piano, Wadworths IPA and 6X, Pewsey organic cider, good filled rolls only (despite the menu's claim of 'duck à l'orange £13.95 – sold out'), darts, extension with pool and TV; camping field, open all day Sun *(the Didler, Kevin Thorpe, Phil and Sally Gorton)*

EDINGTON [ST9353]

☆ *Lamb* BA13 4PG [Westbury Rd (B3098)]: Open-plan beamed village pub with assorted pine furniture on bare boards, cheerful helpful new licensees, log fire, real ales such as Butcombe, Otter and Wadworths 6X, wide food choice from good generous panini up, dining room; pleasant garden tables (access to pretty village's play area beyond), great views, good walks *(Dr and Mrs M E Wilson)*

ENFORD [SU1451]

Swan SN9 6DD [Long St, off A345]: Thatched village-owned dining pub, relaxed and friendly, with wide choice of good enterprising food, friendly helpful staff, local real ales; dogs welcome *(Mrs C Sleight)*

FARLEIGH WICK [ST8063]

Fox & Hounds BA15 2PU [A363 Bath—Bradford, 2½ miles NW of Bradford]: Well extended low-beamed rambling pub with large comfortable dining area; attractive garden *(MRSM)*

FORD [ST8474]

☆ *White Hart* SN14 8RP [off A420 Chippenham—Bristol]: Comfortable stone-built country inn in attractive stream-side grounds, new carpets and a discreet lick of paint while keeping its attractive old-world style with heavy black beams and a good log fire in its ancient fireplace, wide choice of restaurant food (all day Sun), bar food too, good choice of wines by the glass, real ales such as Abbey Bellringer, Courage and Wadworths 6X, attentive service; piped music; children in restaurant, tables outside, pleasant bedrooms, good breakfast, open all day wknds *(Tom and Ruth Rees, John and Gloria Isaacs, Dr and Mrs M E Wilson, Hugh Roberts, Dr and Mrs A K Clarke, LYM, A P Seymour, Nigel and Sue Foster)*

FOXHAM [ST9777]

Foxham Inn SN15 4NQ [NE of Chippenham]: Small country dining pub with appealingly simple traditional décor, real ales such as Bath Gem, Hop Back Odyssey and Wadworths 6X, enterprising food from ciabattas and baguettes to sensibly priced main dishes and puddings (with pudding wines), good wine choice, woodburner, compact more contemporary no smoking back restaurant; provision for dogs and children, terrace tables with pergola, extensive views from front, peaceful village, cl Mon *(Michael Doswell)*

FROXFIELD [SU2968]
Pelican SN8 3JY [A4]: Extended former coaching inn with friendly landlord and staff, relaxed atmosphere, several real ales, moderately priced food, pleasant clean décor in bars and dining area; attractive streamside garden with dovecot and duck pond, Kennet & Avon Canal walks, ten bedrooms with own bathrooms *(Gavin Oclee Brown, Ian Phillips)*

GIDDEAHALL [ST8574]
✩ *Crown* SN14 7ER [A420 Chippenham—Ford; keep eyes skinned as no village sign]: Interesting Tudor pub with attractive and comfortably worn in rambling beamed and flagstoned bar, smarter dining areas in several small rooms on various levels, wide choice of enjoyable food, friendly staff, changing real ales; some live music; comfortable bedrooms *(LYM, Peter and Audrey Dowsett, Michael Doswell)*

GREAT CHEVERELL [ST9854]
Bell SN10 5TH [off B3098 Westbury—Mkt Lavington]: New licensees in friendly 18th-c dining pub with enjoyable reasonably priced food from familiar favourites to more inventive dishes, Wadworths IPA and 6X and a guest beer, good choice of wines by the glass, log fire, comfortable chairs and settles, cosy little alcoves, beamed restaurant; attractive village *(Mike and Lynn Robinson, Mrs C D West)*

GREAT DURNFORD [SU1337]
✩ *Black Horse* SP4 6AY [follow Woodfords sign from A345 High Post traffic lights]: Cheery pub with some nice alcoves and two no smoking rooms, one with ship pictures, models and huge ensigns, the other with a large inglenook woodburner, masses of bric-a-brac, Fullers London Pride, Ringwood and other ales, genial staff, food from baguettes up, darts, shove-ha'penny, table skittles, pinball, cribbage, dominoes and ring the bull; piped blues and jazz; children and dogs welcome, picnic-sets in big informal riverside garden with play area and barbecues, decent bedrooms, cl Sun evening and Mon in winter *(Ian Phillips, LYM)*

GREAT WISHFORD [SU0735]
✩ *Royal Oak* SP2 0PD [off A36 NW of Salisbury]: Emphasis on enjoyable food in appealing two-bar pub with big family dining area and restaurant, prompt service by friendly helpful young staff, three real ales such as Ringwood (useful tasting notes), decent wines, pleasant décor with beams, panelling, rugs on bare boards and log fires; pretty village *(LYM, S E Milton-White, Simon Jones)*

HEDDINGTON [ST9966]
✩ *Ivy* SN11 0PL [off A3102 S of Calne]: Picturesque and friendly thatched 15th-c village pub with good inglenook log fire in simple old-fashioned L-shaped bar, heavy low beams, timbered walls, assorted furnishings on parquet floor, brass and copper, Wadworths IPA, 6X and a seasonal beer tapped from the cask, promptly served good plain fresh home-made food (not Sun-Weds evenings) from great lunchtime club sandwiches up, back family eating room, sensibly placed darts, piano, dog and cat; may be piped music; disabled access, open all day wknds, picnic-sets in front garden, attractively set hamlet *(Pete Baker, LYM, the Didler, Gordon and Jay Smith, Guy Vowles, Dr and Mrs M E Wilson, George Atkinson)*

HEYTESBURY [ST9242]
✩ *Angel* BA12 0ED [just off A36 E of Warminster; High St]: Upmarket dining pub in quiet village just below Salisbury Plain, comfortable lounge opening into restaurant (children allowed here) with courtyard garden, left-hand beamed bar with open fire, straightforward furnishings and some attractive prints and old photographs, Greene King IPA and Morlands Original, good wines by the glass; piped music; bedrooms, open all day *(Brian Dean, D P and M A Miles, LYM, Hugh Roberts, Keith and Jean Symons, M G Hart, Dr and Mrs A K Clarke, MRSM, Jeremy Whitehorn)*

HIGHWORTH [SU1891]
Freke Arms SN6 7RN [Swanborough; B4019, a mile W on Honnington turning]: Airy, smart and relaxed, four comfortable rooms on different levels, real ales inc Arkells 2B and 3B, reasonably priced blackboard food inc good sandwiches and puddings, friendly landlord, no smoking areas; quiet piped music; picnic-sets in small garden with play area, nice views *(Peter and Audrey Dowsett)*
✩ *Saracens Head* SN6 7AG [High St]: Civilised and relaxed rambling bar, wide choice of reasonably priced blackboard food, several real ales inc Arkells 2B and 3B tapped from casks in bar area, good soft drinks choice, comfortably cushioned pews in several interesting areas around great four-way central log fireplace, timbers and panelling, no mobile phones; piped music; children in eating area, tables in sheltered courtyard, comfortable bedrooms, open all day wkdys *(LYM, Peter and Audrey Dowsett)*

HINDON [ST9032]
Angel SP3 6DJ [B3089 Wilton—Mere]: 18th-c flagstoned coaching inn, real ales such as Archers from chrome bar counter, decent wines, big fireplace, no smoking lounge, pleasant staff, enjoyable food from lunchtime snacks inc good baguettes up, main emphasis on long cream restaurant with huge window showing kitchen; piped music; children in eating areas, tables outside, spacious comfortable bedrooms, good breakfast, open all day in summer *(John Evans, Dr and Mrs M W A Haward, LYM, Peter Dixon, Colin and Janet Roe)*

HODSON [SU1780]
✩ *Calley Arms* SN4 0QG [not far from M4 junction 15, via Chiseldon; off B4005 S of Swindon]: Relaxed and friendly village pub with new licensees doing wide range of enjoyable freshly made food, attentive cheerful service, Wadworths ales, good choice of other drinks, open fire in lounge area, neat dining area; children welcome, picnic-sets in garden with dovecote, plenty of good walks *(Nick Duffy, Sheila and Robert Robinson)*

HOLT [ST8561]

☆ *Toll Gate* BA14 6PX [Ham Green; B3107 W of Melksham]: Appealing individual décor and furnishings and generally good fresh food inc imaginative dishes in bar and high-raftered ex-chapel restaurant up steps, five good interesting changing ales, good choice of wines by the glass, farm cider and good coffee, friendly attentive service, log fire; piped music may obtrude; dogs welcome, no under-12s, picnic-sets out on back terrace, compact bedrooms, cl Sun evening, Mon *(Dr and Mrs M E Wilson, Ian Phillips, Mr and Mrs P R Thomas, Mr and Mrs A H Young, LYM, Norman and Sarah Keeping, W F C Phillips, David and Jean Hall, Mrs Jill Wyatt)*

HORNINGSHAM [ST8041]

☆ *Bath Arms* BA12 7LY [by entrance to Longleat House]: Civilised old stone-built inn on sloping green, cosy and well appointed, with lots of old woodwork, interesting local photographs, wide choice of good value home-made food from sandwiches up inc children's menu, Youngs ales, good wine choice, friendly service, daily papers, side restaurant and conservatory; attractive garden with neat terrace, good bedrooms, pretty village, cl Mon *(BB, John Coatsworth)*

KINGTON LANGLEY [ST9277]

☆ *Hit or Miss* SN15 5NS [handy for M4 junction 17, off A350 S; Days Lane]: Cottagey and friendly, with delightfully chatty landlady and welcoming landlord, emphasis on left-hand restaurant with good log fire, also small rather plush low-beamed cricket-theme bar with no smoking area, appetising food from good baguettes (not Sun) through familiar pub dishes and popular Sun lunch to more exotic dishes, Fullers London Pride and Timothy Taylors Landlord, darts and pool in room off; tables out in front *(Dr and Mrs M E Wilson, John and Gloria Isaacs, Michael Doswell, BB)*

LEA [ST9586]

Rose & Crown SN16 9PA: Smart Victorian dining pub with red and white tiles by bar, some rather individual decorations, comfortable sofas by big log fire, two small attractive dining areas off with period prints and photographs on dark red walls, helpful family-friendly staff, 2B, 3B and a seasonal ale, decent wines choice, daily papers; may be unobtrusive piped music; tables outside *(Peter and Audrey Dowsett)*

LIMPLEY STOKE [ST7861]

☆ *Hop Pole* BA2 7FS [off A36 and B3108 S of Bath]: Largely panelled 16th-c stone-built two-bar pub with Butcombe, Courage Best and Marstons Pedigree, wide choice of reasonably priced bar food (may be fully booked wknds), quick friendly service, log fire, traditional games; TV; children in eating areas, nice enclosed garden behind *(LYM, Dr and Mrs M E Wilson, Angus Johnson, Carol Bolden, John and Gloria Isaacs, Peter and Audrey Dowsett)*

LOCKERIDGE [SU1467]

Who'd A Thought It SN8 4EL [signed just off A4 Marlborough—Calne just W of Fyfield]: Friendly local under newish management, two

linked rooms set for good plentiful sensibly priced food from good value baguettes up, small side drinking area, Wadworths and a guest beer, good choice of decent wines by the glass, coal or log fire, interesting well illustrated and annotated collection of cooperage tools, family room; unobtrusive piped music; pleasant back garden with play area, delightful quiet scenery, lovely walks *(Mark and Ruth Brock, Jenny and Brian Seller, BB, Angus and Rosemary Campbell)*

LUDWELL [ST9022]

Grove Arms SP7 9ND [A30 E of Shaftesbury]: Hotel's bright and roomy bar with linked dining area, welcoming licensees and friendly well trained staff, good varied food from generous lunchtime sandwiches and other snacks to attractively priced main meals, real ales, spotless housekeeping, restaurant; children welcome, good value bedrooms *(Colin and Janet Roe, D G T Horsford, Pat and Robert Watt)*

MAIDEN BRADLEY [ST8038]

Somerset Arms BA12 7HW [Church St]: New management for relaxed and nicely restored two-bar village pub, emphasis on mainly traditional food inc Sun roasts, wkdy lunchtime sandwiches, baguettes and hot dishes from ham and eggs up, Wadworths real ales, daily papers; pleasant garden, bedrooms *(Colin and Janet Roe)*

MALMESBURY [ST9387]

Old Bell SN16 0BW: Impressive Grade I listed 13th-c small hotel looking across churchyard to Norman abbey, snug little bar with wooden chairs and settles, log fires, good service, good choice of wines by the glass, Courage Directors, limited choice of good food; attractively old-fashioned garden courtyard providing well for children, bedrooms *(Ian Phillips, LYM)*

Whole Hog SN16 9AS [Market Cross]: Homely basic furnishings on bare boards, market cross view from bar stools at window counter, piggy theme, friendly efficient service, Archers and Youngs ales, enjoyable reasonably priced pub food, daily papers, separate dining room (not Sun evening); games machines, popular with young people evenings *(Robert Gomme, R Huggins, D Irving, E McCall, T McLean)*

MANTON [SU1768]

Oddfellows Arms SN8 4HW [High St, signed off A4 Marlborough—Devizes]: Newly reopened village pub, roomy and comfortable, with lots of nooks and crannies, good value fresh food inc popular Sun lunch (best to book this), good choice of wines by the glass, real ales such as Wadworths Bishops Tipple, cheerful willing service; children welcome, big garden *(Robin and Tricia Walker, Mr and Mrs A Curry)*

MARDEN [SU0857]

☆ *Millstream* SN10 3RH [off A342]: Pleasantly refurbished and extended upmarket bar/restaurant with enjoyable changing food inc their own bread and ice-creams, fresh local organic ingredients, Wadworths real ales and great wine choice inc champagne by the glass, beams, flagstones, open fires and woodburners, attentive service, maps and guides as well as daily papers; children and well behaved dogs welcome, pleasant garden with tables on neat terrace, cl Mon *(James and Karen Oliver, Bill and Jessica Ritson, Michael Doswell)*

MARLBOROUGH [SU1869]

Castle & Ball SN8 1LZ [High St]: Georgian coaching inn with plenty of atmosphere in comfortably worn in lounge bar, unusually wide choice of decent generous food inc good speciality pie, quieter and slightly simpler no smoking eating area, Greene King ales, good range of well listed wines by the glass, young enthusiastic staff; seats out under projecting colonnade, good value bedrooms *(W W Burke, Neil and Anita Christopher, Paul Humphreys, A P Seymour, Michael Sargent)*

Sun SN8 1HF [High St]: Quaint old-fashioned 15th-c pub, small bar with heavy sloping beams, wonky floors, dim lighting, log fire, benches built into black panelling, food from sandwiches to steaks, Greene King Abbot and Wadworths 6X, daily papers, no smoking dining area; piped music; simple bedrooms, small back courtyard *(LYM, Jacques and Huguette Laurent)*

MARSTON MEYSEY [SU1297]

Old Spotted Cow SN6 6LQ [off A419 Swindon—Cirencester]: L-shaped cotswold stone pub with welcoming licensees, real ales such as Milk Street, Wadworths and Youngs, decent wines, bar lucnhes and (Tues-Fri) enjoyable evening meals, raised stone fireplace, light wood furniture on bare boards, plants and cow pictures, parquet-floored dining room; quiet piped music; open all day wknds, spacious garden with picnic-sets on terrace and lots of play equipment, adjacent camp site *(J E Hutchinson, R Huggins, D Irving, E McCall, T McLean)*

MILDENHALL [SU2169]

☆ *Horseshoe* SN8 2LR: Relaxed and neatly kept traditional 17th-c thatched pub with good value food from sandwiches up, quick friendly service even when busy, real ales such as Archers and Wadworths, good value wines, three attractive partly partitioned beamed rooms, small no smoking dining room; bedrooms, picnic-sets out on grass, pleasant village setting, good Kennet Valley and Savernake Forest walks *(Mary Rayner, Angus and Rosemary Campbell)*

MINETY [SU0390]

White Horse SN16 9QY [Station Rd (B4040)]: Friendly pub with unusual two-storey layout, around four real ales such as Adnams and Wadworths 6X from central servery in stripped brick and stone bar, good baguettes and innovative choice of hot dishes, good range of wines by the glass, daily papers, pleasant no smoking evening restaurant with sofas and armchairs on landing, impressive décor, upmarket without being pretentious, games bar too; children very welcome, heated balcony tables overlooking pond below, bedrooms *(Chris and Ann Coy, JJW, CMW)*

NETHERHAMPTON [SU1129]

☆ *Victoria & Albert* SP2 8PU [just off A3094 W of Salisbury]: Cosy black-beamed bar in simple thatched cottage with welcoming licensees and staff, good generous food from nicely presented sandwiches up, sensible prices and local supplies, changing ales such as Fullers London Pride and Palmers, farm cider, decent house wine, nicely cushioned old-fashioned wall settles on ancient floor tiles, no smoking restaurant; children welcome, hatch service for sizeable garden behind, handy for Wilton House and Nadder Valley walks *(Ian and Sandra Thornton, Tony Orman, Colin and Janet Roe, LYM, James Blood)*

NORTH WROUGHTON [SU1482]

Check Inn SN4 9AA [Woodland View (A4361 just S of Swindon)]: Extended real ale pub with interesting changing choice of up to ten, lots of bottled imports, farm cider, good soft drinks choice, helpful friendly service even when crowded, good value generous food, log fire, glossy pine furniture, various comfortable areas inc children's and large no smoking area; darts, games machine; children and dogs welcome, disabled access, heated front terrace, garden bar, boules, bedrooms, open all day Fri-Sun *(Tim and Rosemary Wells, JJW, CMW)*

NUNTON [SU1526]

☆ *Radnor Arms* SP5 4HS [off A338 S of Salisbury]: Pretty ivy-clad village pub very popular for its food inc fish and local game, friendly staff (very helpful with wheelchairs), Badger real ales, three pleasantly decorated and furnished linked rooms inc cheerfully busy yet relaxing bar and staider restaurant, log fires; wknd booking essential; attractive garden good for children *(Don and Thelma Anderson, J H Vaughan-Johnson)*

OAKSEY [ST9993]

Wheatsheaf SN16 9TB: Village pub with newish chef/landlord earning praise for his cooking (even the bread's home-baked), changing ales such as Bath Gem, Hook Norton and Wye Valley, cosy snug with padded wall seats, separate dining area, local artwork for sale; tables outside *(Michael Dallas)*

OARE [SU1563]

White Hart SN8 4JA [A345 S of Marlborough]: Unassuming pub in nice village with lovely gardens, interesting choice of good value home-made food, Wadworths; bedrooms *(Theocsbrian)*

PEWSEY [SU1561]

French Horn SN9 5NT [A345 towards Marlborough; Pewsey Wharf]: Pleasantly refurbished old pub just taken over by new licensees, Wadworths IPA and 6X, good choice of wines by the glass, two-part back bar divided by log fire open to both sides, steps down to pleasant and rather smart flagstoned front dining area (children allowed here); piped music; picnic-sets on back terrace, many more in well fenced wood-chip area with robust timber play area above barges moored on Kennet & Avon Canal *(BB, Neil and Anita Christopher)*

Waterfront Café SN9 5NU [Pewsey Wharf

(A345 just N)]: Unpretentious bar upstairs in converted wharf building, warm and cosy, with panelling, canalia, corner woodburner, comfortable chairs, windows on Kennet & Avon Canal on three sides, jovial landlord, Greene King IPA, Abbot and Old Speckled Hen, food from baguettes to full meals provided by downstairs café; garden tables, usually open 10-8 in season *(Dr and Mrs M E Wilson, Nick and Lynne Carter)*

SALISBURY [SU1430]

☆ *Avon Brewery* SP1 3SP [Castle St]: Long and narrow city bar, busy and friendly, with dark mahogany, frosted and engraved bow windows, friezes and attractive pictures, two open fires, sensibly priced food (not Sun evening) from sandwiches up, mainstream real ales, decent wines; piped music; long sheltered courtyard garden overlooking river, open all day *(David Carr, Colin and Janet Roe, LYM)*
Chough SP1 1DA [Blue Boar Row]: Comfortable former Beefeater in ancient building (said to be haunted), redone with some big sofas as well as proper dining tables, wide food choice, real ales; wknd DJs and bands *(Anon)*
Kings Head SP1 2ND [Bridge St]: Wetherspoons Lloyds No 1 on site of former hotel, variety of seating in large bar with separate TV area (and piped music), no smoking gallery upstairs, their usual low-priced menu (inc breakfast); bedrooms *(Craig Turnbull, Ann and Colin Hunt)*
New Inn SP1 2PH [New St]: Ancient pub with massive beams and timbers, quiet cosy alcoves, leather chairs and inglenook log fire, Badger beers, decent house wines, good friendly service, usual food from sandwiches to grills, large no smoking area; unobtrusive piped music, children welcome, walled garden with striking view of nearby cathedral spire, open all day summer wknds *(Sue and Mike Todd, N R White, LYM)*
Old Ale House SP1 2QD [Crane St]: Long open-plan bare-boards pub with hotch-potch of old sofas, seats and tables, cosy lighting, entertainingly cluttered décor, inexpensive generous lunchtime food (not Sun), real ales such as Courage Best, Ringwood Best and Wadworths 6X tapped from the cask, efficient cheerful service, pub games; big-screen TV, machines and piped music; children welcome away from the bar till 5, picnic-sets in small back courtyard, open all day *(Mike and Lynn Robinson, LYM)*

☆ *Old Mill* SP2 8EU [Town Path, W Harnham]: Charming 17th-c pub/hotel in glorious tranquil out-of-centre setting, pleasant beamed bars with prized window tables, enjoyable bar food from sandwiches and focaccia up, helpful staff, real ales, good wines and malt whiskies, good value lunch in attractive restaurant showing mill race; children welcome, picnic-sets in small floodlit garden by duck-filled millpond, delightful stroll across water-meadows from cathedral (classic view of it from bridge beyond garden), bedrooms *(P R and D Thomas, David Carr, Tony and Jill Radnor, LYM)*

☆ *Wig & Quill* SP1 2PH [New St]: Low-beamed softly lit 16th-c former shop with rugs, worn leather armchairs, stuffed birds and low arches to connecting rooms, friendly landlord, Wadworths and guest beers tapped from the cask, decent wines and interesting long summer drinks, standard food (not winter evenings) from sandwiches up, tiled back eating room; dogs allowed, nice small courtyard behind with cathedral views, open all day *(John and Gloria Isaacs, David Carr, Ann and Colin Hunt, Tony and Jill Radnor)*
Wyndham Arms SP1 3AS [Estcourt Rd]: Friendly modern corner local with Hop Back beers (originally brewed here, now from Downton), country wines, simple bar food, small no smoking front room, longer main bar; children welcome in front room, open all day wknds, cl lunchtime other days *(the Didler)*

SEMINGTON [ST9259]

☆ *Lamb* BA14 6LL [The Strand; A361 Devizes—Trowbridge]: Busy dining pub with good blackboard choice of consistently good food inc fresh fish in attractive linked rooms, reasonable prices, carefully chosen wines, Butcombe, Ringwood Best and a guest beer, good coffee, buoyant atmosphere, good friendly service, log fires each end; children in eating area, helpful with wheelchairs, attractive walled garden, cl Sun evening *(Miss M W Hayter, Mr and Mrs A Curry, LYM)*
Somerset Arms BA14 6JR [off A350 bypass 2 miles S of Melksham]: Cosy 16th-c coaching inn, heavy-beamed long bar, real and flame-effect fires, high-backed settles, plenty of tables, lots of prints and brassware, wide range of reasonably priced food in bar and restaurant from sandwiches and chips to some imaginative dishes, good atmosphere, cheerful service, Badger beers, good coffee; piped music; pleasant garden behind, short walk from Kennet & Avon Canal, open all day summer wknds *(Matthew Shackle, Colin McKerrow)*

SEMLEY [ST8926]

☆ *Benett Arms* SP7 9AS [off A350 N of Shaftesbury]: Bustling character village inn across green from church, welcoming long-serving licensees and good relaxed atmosphere, real ales such as Brakspears, Ringwood Best and Youngs, decent wines and good range of other drinks, enjoyable fairly priced food, log fire, traditional games, no music, restaurant; children and well behaved dogs allowed, pleasant tables outside *(LYM, Dr and Mrs M E Wilson, Dr Alan and Mrs Sue Holder)*

SHAW [ST8765]

Golden Fleece SN12 8HB [Folly Lane (A365 towards Atworth)]: Attractive former coaching inn with good atmosphere in bright and clean low-ceilinged L-shaped bar and long sympathetic front dining extension, good range of food inc generous bargain lunches – very popular with older people, good welcoming service, real ales such as Bass, Fullers London Pride and Moles, farm cider, flame-effect fires; garden tables *(Brian Pearson, Dr and Mrs M E Wilson)*

SHERSTON [ST8586]

Carpenters Arms SN16 0LS [Easton (B4040)]:
Cosy small-roomed low-beamed pub doing
well under present landlord, settles and shiny
tables, log fire, real ales, decent wines, good
choice of reasonably priced food, welcoming
service, attractive modern conservatory and
dining rooms; no piped music; TV in locals'
bar; tables in pleasant garden with play area
(*Richard Stancomb, Andrew Scarr, Peter and
Audrey Dowsett, John and Gloria Isaacs*)

☆ *Rattlebone* SN16 0LR [Church St (B4040
Malmesbury—Chipping Sodbury)]: Rambling
beamed and stone-walled 17th-c village pub
thriving under welcoming new licensees,
popular food from baguettes up, Youngs real
ales, decent wines inc interesting bin-ends, log
fire, cosy corners with pews, settles and
country-kitchen chairs, public bar with pool
and other games; no smoking area could be
improved; children in restaurant, skittle alley,
picnic-sets in back garden, has been open all
day (*Guy Vowles, Richard Stancomb, Paul and
Shirley White, Bernard Stradling, Jane and
Graham Rooth, LYM, Andrew Scarr,
Peter and Audrey Dowsett*)

SHRIVENHAM [SU2488]

Blue Strawberry SN6 8AN [High St]: Former
Crown renamed, enjoyable food and friendly
service (*Anon*)

SOUTH WRAXALL [ST8364]

Long Arms BA15 2SB [Upper S Wraxall, off
B3109 N of Bradford on Avon]: Cheerful
cosily refurbished country local dating from
17th c, friendly landlord, good value popular
food in bargain daily roast and homely
puddings, Wadworths, good range of wines by
the glass, character dark décor with flagstones
and some stripped stone, log fire; pretty garden
(*Mark Flynn, Michael Doswell*)

STAPLEFORD [SU0636]

Pelican SP3 4LT [Warminster Rd (A36)]: Long
bar with large dining area, Banks's and related
real ales, decent food, nice atmosphere,
friendly service; big riverside garden, pleasant
despite nearby road (*Dr D Smith*)

STEEPLE LANGFORD [SU0437]

Rainbows End SP3 4LZ [just off A36 E of
A303 junction]: Attractive and popular dining
pub with large comfortable bar, wide choice of
enjoyable fresh food inc fish, friendly landlord,
staff and dog, three changing real ales inc local
brews; nice lake and Wylye Valley views from
sunny conservatory and terrace, picnic-sets on
lawn (*Richard Fendick*)

STIBB GREEN [SU2262]

☆ *Three Horseshoes* SN8 3AE [just N of
Burbage]: Compact old-world local with
welcoming landlord, good honest home
cooking (not Sun evening or Mon) by
landlady – pies are her speciality; sensible
prices and quick service, Wadworths IPA and
6X, farm cider, inglenook log fire in
comfortable beamed front bar, second no
smoking bar, railway memorabilia and
pictures (landlord is an enthusiast), dining
room; attractive garden, cl Mon (*R T and
J C Moggridge, Pete Baker*)

SWALLOWCLIFFE [ST9627]

☆ *Royal Oak* SP3 5PA [signed just off A30
Wilton—Shaftesbury; Common Lane]: Pretty
little partly 16th-c partly thatched pub with
current licensees (both chefs) doing good
interesting frequently changing food, fine range
of wines, modest choice of good real ales, good
mix of chairs around varying-sized solid tables
in pink-walled carpeted bar with sofa by log
fire, cosy bistro beyond; picnic-sets under
cocktail parasols in big sheltered back garden,
good walks (*H G H Stafford, BB*)

SWINDON [SU1383]

Running Horse SN1 4NQ [Wootton Bassett
Rd (A3102)]: Big modernised pub with Arkells
2B and 3B, sensibly priced usual food from
baked potatoes up, some panelling, back
restaurant area; pleasant back garden with
stream beyond (*Ian Phillips*)

TISBURY [ST9429]

Boot SP3 6PS [High St]: Ancient unpretentious
village local with jovial landlord, good choice
of real ales tapped from the cask, good value
food, thriving atmosphere, smashing fireplace
(*John and Mary Ling, Douglas and Ann Hare*)

TROWBRIDGE [ST8557]

Sir Isaac Pitman BA14 8AL [Castle Pl]: Useful
Wetherspoons well done out in elm-coloured
wood, comfortable alcoves and different levels
below cupola, the shorthand Sir Isaac invented
along the beams, no smoking area, good value
beer and food, pleasant staff (*Dr and Mrs
M E Wilson*)

UPPER CHUTE [SU2953]

Cross Keys SP11 9ER: Early 18th-c village pub
newly reopened (after enthusiastic help from
local volunteers) under welcoming new ex-
farmer landlord, sofas around big log fire,
good fairly priced straightforward food using
local seasonal ingredients, pleasant
atmosphere, real ale, good wines by the glass;
rustic views from picnic-sets out under
flowering cherries on charming south-facing
terrace, interesting area for walking, bedrooms
(*K Louden*)

UPPER WOODFORD [SU1236]

☆ *Bridge Inn* SP4 6NU: Good sensibly priced
food using good fresh ingredients (best to book
wknds), wide menu and blackboard choice,
quick friendly service, Hop Back ales, good
house wines, upmarket newspapers, big flower
prints and contemporary décor, log fire, neat
country-kitchen tables on expanse of newish
wooden flooring, rather smart games room
with pool and leather chesterfields; attractive
riverside garden across road, lots of ducks (*BB,
Richard Stancomb, Howard and
Margaret Buchanan, Richard Fendick*)

UPTON LOVELL [ST9441]

☆ *Prince Leopold* BA12 0JP: Prettily tucked
away in quiet thatched village, with cheerful
staff, good food from interesting ciabattas up,
Ringwood and John Smiths, good value wines,
dark Victorian bar décor, airy newish dining
extension with river views from end tables;
tables in small attractive garden beside the
clear Wylye trout stream, comfortable quiet
bedrooms (*Richard Fendick*)

UPTON SCUDAMORE [ST8647]
Angel BA12 0AG [off A350 N of Warminster]:
Stylish and roomy contemporary dining pub
with airy bustling upper part, sofas and
armchairs by more traditionally furnished
lower dining area, interesting food from open
kitchen, Butcombe, Wadworths 6X and a guest
beer, good changing wine choice, courteous
and caring young staff, artwork for sale, daily
papers, pub games; piped music, TV; sheltered
flagstoned back terrace with big barbecue,
bedrooms in house across car park *(LYM,
Dr and Mrs M E Wilson, Mr and Mrs
Peter Llewellyn, Mike and Mary Carter)*
WANBOROUGH [SU2183]
Harrow SN4 0AE [3 miles from M4 junction
15; Lower Wanborough signed off A346]:
Pretty thatched pub with long low-beamed
stepped bar, big inglenook log fire, pine
panelling, candles in bottles, settles and bay
window alcoves, real ales such as Greene King
Old Speckled Hen, Hook Norton Old Hooky
and Youngs Special, good value wines by the
glass, friendly staff, sensibly priced food (not
Sun evening) from baguettes up, daily papers,
no piped music, simple beamed and flagstoned
stripped stone dining room with another open
fire; live music Sun night, cast-iron tables and
picnic-sets outside *(Paul Humphreys, BB,
A P Seymour)*
WESTBURY [ST8751]
Westbury Hotel BA13 3DQ [Market Pl]:
Under newish management, with sofas and low
tables in attractive beamed bar, cheerful
friendly staff, Bass and Charles Wells
Bombardier, good choice of enjoyable food in
bistro area with scrubbed tables or smart
dining room; bedrooms *(Alan and
Paula McCully)*
WESTWOOD [ST8159]
New Inn BA15 2AE [off B3109 S of Bradford-
on-Avon]: New management for traditional
country pub with several linked rooms, beams
and stripped stone, scrubbed tables on newish
slate floor, log fires, generous popular food in
bar and no smoking restaurant, Wadworths
IPA and 6X; piped radio; a few tables out
behind, lovely hanging baskets, walks nearby,
pretty village, has been cl Sun evening and
Mon; more reports on new regime please *(BB)*
WHADDON [SU1926]
Three Crowns SP5 3HB [off A36 SE of
Salisbury]: Pleasant friendly bar, real ale,
appealing choice of good food; lovely
downland walks with fine views, comfortable
and individual bedrooms *(Amanda Rushton)*
WILTON [SU0931]
☆ *Pembroke Arms* SP2 0BH [Minster St (A30)]:
Elegant Georgian hotel handy for Wilton
House with big sash windows in roomy and
comfortable bar, excellent licensees and
friendly service, tasty fresh lunchtime ciabattas,
good wines by the glass, a Badger beer, good
coffee, open fire, plenty of daily papers and
magazines, fresh flowers and candles, good
more expensive no smoking restaurant; some
outside tables, attractive bedrooms with
marble bathrooms *(Edward Mirzoeff, BB)*

Swan SN8 3SS [the village S of Gt Bedwyn]:
Warm and friendly simple pub with stripped
pine tables and bright décor, wide variety of
enjoyable food with some mexican touches,
changing real ales such as Greene King Old
Speckled Hen and Wadworths 6X; children
welcome, garden with small play area,
picturesque village with windmill, handy for
Crofton Beam Engines *(Dave Braisted)*
WINGFIELD [ST8256]
☆ *Poplars* BA14 9LN [B3109 S of Bradford-on-
Avon (Shop Lane)]: Attractive country pub
very popular for good sensibly priced
interesting food, especially with older people at
lunchtime, Wadworths real ales, friendly fast
service even when busy, warm atmosphere, no
juke box or machines, light and airy no
smoking family dining extension; tables out by
own cricket pitch *(Dr and Mrs M E Wilson,
LYM, Susan and Nigel Wilson)*
WINSLEY [ST7960]
Seven Stars BA15 2LQ [off B3108 bypass W
of Bradford-on-Avon (pub just over Wilts
border)]: Big stripped-stone open-plan pub,
welcoming and relaxed, with low beams, soft
lighting, snug alcoves, log-effect gas fires, Bass,
Butcombe, Wadworths 6X and a guest beer,
good wine choice, enjoyable food inc good
vegetarian choice, friendly attentive service, no
smoking dining area; discreet piped music;
picnic-sets out on pleasant terrace, attractive
village *(Dr and Mrs M E Wilson, MRSM,
Meg and Colin Hamilton)*
WINTERBOURNE BASSETT [SU1075]
☆ *White Horse* SN4 9QB [off A4361 S of
Swindon]: A favourite with many readers for
its wide choice of reliable fresh generous food
inc several fish dishes, good bargain lunches
Mon-Sat and good Sun roast, in neat and well
cared for big-windowed attractively extended
bar, comfortable dining room and warm
conservatory, cheerful warmly welcoming
licensees and efficient service, Wadworths and
a guest beer, good sensibly priced wines by the
glass and coffee, goldfish tank and
woodburner; quiet piped music; tables on
good-sized side lawn, lovely hanging baskets,
pleasant setting *(P A Pillinger, Mr and Mrs
I Pillinger, William Booth-Davey, Sheila and
Robert Robinson, M J Collie, Dr M Yates,
Mrs Jill Wyatt, MJ Winterton, BB, Baden and
Sandy Waller, Tony Baldwin, JJW, CMW)*
WINTERBOURNE MONKTON [SU1072]
New Inn SN4 9NW [A361 Avebury—
Wroughton]: Small friendly village pub with
local real ales such as Ramsbury, helpful staff,
decent pub food, separate restaurant; subdued
piped music; children welcome, comfortable
bedrooms in converted barn *(Tim and
Rosemary Wells)*
WOODBOROUGH [SU1159]
Seven Stars SN9 6LW [off A345 S of
Marlborough; Bottlesford]: Pretty thatched
pub doing enjoyable meals, Fullers London
Pride, Wadworths 6X and a changing guest
beer, good choice of wines, friendly staff,
hunting prints, attractively moulded panelling,
hot coal fire in the old range at one end, big

log fire the other, nice mix of antique settles and country furniture, cosy nooks, no smoking dining extension; piped music turned off on request; children and dogs welcome, extensive riverside gardens, open all day Sun *(H Frank Smith, Mary Rayner, Ron Shelton, Lawrence Pearse, Guy Vowles, LYM, A P Seymour, Bill and Jessica Ritson)*

WOOTTON BASSETT [SU0982]

Sally Pusseys SN4 8ET [A3102 just SW of M4 junction 16]: Bright and spacious bar/dining lounge with pleasant modern cream and beige décor, various extensions inc good-sized lower restaurant, Arkells 2B and 3B, wide food range from baguettes and baked potatoes to Sun carvery, helpful staff, lots of pictures; may be piped music; picnic-sets in sizeable garden (M-way noise) *(Gary Marchant, Mr and Mrs I Pillinger, Ian Phillips)*

WOOTTON RIVERS [SU1963]

Royal Oak SN8 4NQ [off A346, A345 or B3087]: Attractive 16th-c beamed and thatched pub, wide range of reliable if not cheap food from lunchtime sandwiches, ciabattas and baguettes up, L-shaped dining lounge with woodburner, timbered bar with

small games area, Fullers London Pride, Wadworths 6X and perhaps a guest beer, good wine list; children welcome, tables out in yard, pleasant village, bedrooms in adjoining house *(LYM, Neil and Anita Christopher, Ned Kelly, A P Seymour, Mrs J H S Lang, Peter Titcomb)*

WYLYE [SU0037]

☆ *Bell* BA12 0QP [just off A303/A36; High St]: Friendly new management in spotlessly spruced up and peacefully set 14th-c village pub, four local Hidden ales, big log fire, daily papers and magazines, sturdy rustic furnishings on new carpets, black beams and timbers, good value food from sandwiches up, agreeable staff, no smoking restaurant; may be piped music; pleasant walled terrace and attractive back garden, fine downland walks nearby, bedrooms *(LYM, Dr and Mrs M E Wilson, Douglas and Ann Hare, Ian Phillips)*

YATTON KEYNELL [ST8676]

Bell SN14 7BG [B4039 NW of Chippenham]: Cosy village pub with good value home-made food, real ales inc Bass, nicely decorated bar and no smoking country-feel dining area; well spaced picnic-sets in good-sized fenced garden *(Michael Doswell, Jennifer Banks)*

'Children welcome' means the pub says it lets children inside without any special restriction. If it allows them in, but to restricted areas such as an eating area or family room, we specify this. Places with separate restaurants often let children use them, hotels usually let them into public areas such as lounges. Some pubs impose an evening time limit – let us know if you find this.

Worcestershire

Quite a few Worcestershire pubs serve both great food and a good range of beers in a nice traditional environment. The bustling Admiral Rodney at Berrow Green, particularly well run, is just such a place, with four thoughtfully sourced real ales and an imaginative fairly priced bar menu. The welcoming landlord's honest simple cooking gives real value at the Walter de Cantelupe at Kempsey, in the chatty atmosphere of a proper pub. The Bell at Pensax is another particularly enjoyable pub with tasty bargain-priced food and local ciders and perrys, and the rambling Talbot at Knightwick adds its own temptingly priced Teme Valley own-brew beer and a nicely quirky dash of individuality to the mix. The ancient Fleece at Bretforton with its bags of atmosphere is a classic country pub of great charm, with the bonus of a fine choice of half a dozen real ales. The Swan at Hanley Swan (a new entry) is a complete contrast in its appealing contemporary layout, but has all the traditional virtues of an all-round good pub – including comfortable bedrooms. The increased range of changing real ales at the cheerily traditional Nags Head at Malvern has astonished us this year – their 16 taps are likely to get through around 1,000 different beers a year. If you're looking for somewhere for a special dining experience you won't go wrong with the very well run Bell & Cross at Holy Cross, with its delicious changing bar food served in the unspoilt small rooms of a timeless country tavern. It's the completely no smoking and cheerfully welcoming Bear & Ragged Staff at Bransford that wins this year's high accolade of Worcestershire Dining Pub of the Year, for its beautifully prepared and presented imaginative food. More than half the entries in the Lucky Dip section at the end of the chapter are new to this year's edition; the section's stars include the Queens at Belbroughton, Gate at Bournheath, Greyhound at Eldersfield, Peacock at Forhill, Old Bull at Inkberrow, Royal Oak at Leigh Sinton, Coach & Horses at Weatheroak Hill and Anchor at Welland. The riverside Anchor at Wyre Piddle is normally a main entry, but we've had no chance yet to judge the new management. Drinks prices in the county tend to be a little below the national norm – very much below, in the case of the entertaining King & Castle in Kidderminster station. Good value local brews to look out for include Wyre Piddle, Cannon Royall, Mayfields and St Georges, with beers from Hook Norton and other small brewers in neighbouring counties, such as Hobsons, Wye Valley and Stanway, also often cheaper than the national brands. Banks's is the main regional brewer.

BAUGHTON   SO8742   Map 4

Jockey ♀

4 miles from M50 junction 1; A38 northwards, then right on to A4104 Upton—Pershore; WR8 9DQ

Now with welcoming new licensees, this no smoking dining pub is open plan but partly divided by stripped brick and timbering, with a mix of good-sized tables, a few horse-racing pictures on the butter-coloured walls, and a cream Rayburn in one brick inglenook; piped music. As well as lunchtime sandwiches (from £4.50, not Sundays), bar food includes soup (£3.95), cajun mushrooms with garlic mayonnaise dip (£4.50), king prawns in garlic butter (£6.95), battered haddock or lasagne (£8.95), roast duck breast with orange sauce (£10.95), daily specials such as baked chicken in stilton sauce (£9.95), bass fillet stuffed with onions and thai herbs (£12.95), and Sunday roast (£8.95). Courage Directors and John Smiths are well kept alongside a changing guest such as Greene King Old Speckled Hen, and they've a rewarding choice of wines, with ten by the glass. There are picnic-sets out in front, with an array of blue flowers (out here, but not inside, you can hear the motorway in the distance). *(Recommended by John and Sarah Webb, Ken Marshall)*

Free house ~ Licensee Colin Clarke ~ Real ale ~ Bar food (12-2, 6-9; 12-2.30, 7-9 Sun) ~ Restaurant ~ (01684) 592153 ~ Children welcome ~ Open 11.30-3, 6-11; 11.30-11 Sat; 12-10.30 Sun; 11.30-4, 6-11 Sat and 11.30-4, 7-10.30 Sun in winter ~ Bedrooms: /£40B

BERROW GREEN SO7458 Map 4
Admiral Rodney 🍴 🛏
B4197, off A44 W of Worcester; WR6 6PL

Welcoming licensees run this enjoyable country inn with forethought and attention to detail. Pleasantly light and roomy throughout, the bare-boards entrance bar is still a place you can just enjoy a drink; with high beams and a sunny bow window, it has big stripped kitchen tables and cushioned chairs, a traditional winged settle, and a woodburning stove in a fireplace that opens through to the comfortable no smoking lounge area. This has some carpet on its slate flagstones, dark red settees, a table of magazines and rack of broadsheet newspapers, quite a few board games, and prints of the Battle of the Saints, where Lord Rodney obliterated the french fleet in the Caribbean. A separate skittle alley has pool; also darts and board games. Bar food here is very good, and indeed, there's quite an emphasis on the very nicely balanced menu, which includes soup (£3.95), lunchtime sandwiches or ciabattas (from £3.95), platter of cured meats or spicy thai beef salad (£4.95), roast pepper and butternut risotto with coriander and mediterranean vegetables (£7.50), malaysian lamb curry or battered cod (£7.95), lamb shank with red onion mash and redcurrant thyme gravy (£8.25) and a british plate – roast pork belly with apple sauce, mini cottage pie, corned beef hash and black pudding (£10.50). They also have some interesting daily fish specials such scallops on minted mash (£5.75), bass steamed with wild mushroom and cream sauce (£12.50), black bream baked with lime, herbs, chilli and potato (£13.75). A rebuilt barn stepping down through three levels forms a charming end restaurant (mostly no smoking and with a more elaborate menu). Alongside well kept Wye Valley Bitter, they've three changing guests from brewers such as Beartown, Goffs and Youngs and you'll find a tempting choice of wines and malt whiskies, and local perry and apple juice. A new terrace has outdoor heating and a retractable canopy, and neat green, solid tables and chairs look over the Lower Teme valley (two of the three bedrooms share the views), and this is good walking country. *(Recommended by Martin and Pauline Jennings, Denys Gueroult, Nick and Lynne Carter, Richard, Dave Braisted, Noel Grundy, John and Patricia White, Mr Tarpey)*

Free house ~ Licensees Gillian and Kenneth Green ~ Real ale ~ Bar food (12-2(2.30 Sun), 6.30-9(9.30 Sat)) ~ Restaurant ~ (01886) 821375 ~ Children welcome ~ Dogs allowed in bar and bedrooms ~ Folk night first Weds of month ~ Open 11-3, 5-11; 11-11 Sat; 12-10.30 Sun; closed Mon lunchtime ~ Bedrooms: /£65B

BEWDLEY SO7875 Map 4
Little Pack Horse 🍴
High Street; no nearby parking – best to park in main car park, cross A4117 Cleobury road, and keep walking on down narrowing High Street; DY12 2DH

Gently refurbished since the last edition of the *Guide*, this interesting old timber-framed pub has been given a bit of extra character with the addition of reclaimed oak panelling and floor boards. It's all nicely warmed by a woodburning stove, and a splendid miscellany of old advertisements, photos and other memorabilia should amuse you for a while. Food is reasonably priced, comes in a wide choice, and lots of dishes are available in two sizes: sandwiches (from £3.20), moroccan vegetable and chickpea couscous (£4.30, £5.60 large), tasty pies (from £5.20), scampi and chips (£5.85, £7.25 large), cajun chicken breast (£7.20), and steaks (from £11.25), with three or four quite interesting specials such as fried tuna on niçoise salad or pork fillet stuffed with mango, apricot and pecan nuts (£8.75), steamed bass with lime juice and herbs (£9.15), and puddings such as home-made apple and rhubarb crumble (£3); the dining area is no smoking. Alongside Greene King IPA, a couple of guest ales (the new landlord is hoping to expand the range to four guests) might be from brewers such as Adnams, Batemans and Shepherd Neame; piped music; the dining areas are no smoking. It's best to leave your car in the public car park near the river in this rewarding old town, and walk up. *(Recommended by Paul and Gloria Howell, T R and B C Jenkins, Richard, Martin and Pauline Jennings, Ian and Jane Irving, Stuart Paulley)*

Punch ~ Lease Mark Payne ~ Real ale ~ Bar food (12-3, 6-10; 12-10 Sat, Sun) ~ Restaurant ~ (01299) 403762 ~ Children welcome ~ Dogs allowed in bar ~ Open 12-3, 6-11.30; 12-12 Fri, Sat; 12-10.30 Sun

BIRTSMORTON   SO7936   Map 4
Farmers Arms 🍺 £
Birts Street, off B4208 W; WR13 6AP

Little changes from year to year at this peacefully old-fashioned and fairly straightforward half-timbered village local. Quietly free of piped music or games machines, the neatly kept big room on the right (with no smoking area), rambles away under very low dark beams, with some standing timbers, and flowery-panelled cushioned settles as well as spindleback chairs; on the left an even lower-beamed room seems even cosier, and in both the white walls have black timbering; the local cribbage and darts teams play here, and you can also play shove-ha'penny or dominoes. Sociable locals gather at the bar for Hook Norton Hooky and Old Hooky, which are well kept on handpump, alongside a changing guest from a brewer such as Wye Valley. Unhurried staff serve the very good value simple bar food, which typically includes sandwiches (from £1.80), soup (£2.20), ploughman's (from £3.15), tasty macaroni cheese (£3.75), fish and chips (£4.95), chicken and vegetable curry (£4.95), steak and kidney pie (£5.95), steak (£8.50), with good puddings such as apple pie or spotted dick (from £2.30). You'll find seats out on the large lawn (though one reader thought they were getting a bit rickety), and the pub is surrounded by plenty of walks. Please treat the opening hours we give below as approximate – they may vary according to how busy or quiet things are. *(Recommended by the Didler, Ian and Nita Cooper, Steve Bailey, Pam and David Bailey, Martin and Pauline Jennings, Alec and Joan Laurence)*

Free house ~ Licensees Jill and Julie Moore ~ Real ale ~ Bar food (12-2, 6.30(7 Sun)-9.30) ~ No credit cards ~ (01684) 833308 ~ Children welcome ~ Dogs welcome ~ Open 11-4, 6-11; 12-4, 7-10.30 Sun

BRANSFORD   SO8052   Map 4
Bear & Ragged Staff 🍴 ♀
Off A4103 SW of Worcester; Station Road; WR6 5JH

Worcestershire Dining Pub of the Year

Now completely no smoking, this happy place is doing very well at the moment, with the food, the very friendly welcome, and good accommodating service scoring well. They make much use of local produce, and the tempting bar specials (carefully prepared and attractively presented) might typically include smoked haddock and leek tart (£5.50), home-made faggots, haddock and chips or curry of the day (£9.95), roast cod with red wine, bacon and mushroom velouté or fried black bream with almonds, lemon and capers in brown butter (£13), and puddings such as blackberry and vanilla crème brûlée with lavender tuile biscuit or chocolate or date panettone bread and butter pudding with butternut crunch ice-cream (£4.75); they also do lunchtime sandwiches with dressed salad and crisps (from £4.75; not

Sunday). The cheerful interconnecting rooms give fine views over rolling country, and in winter you'll find an open fire; cribbage, and piped music. In fine weather, the garden and terrace are enjoyable places to sit (pleasant views from here too). There are proper tablecloths, linen napkins and fresh flowers on the tables in the restaurant, which has a more expensive menu. They've a good range of wines to choose from too, with about ten by the glass, lots of malt whiskies, quite a few brandies and liqueurs, and Bass and St Georges Best are well kept on handpump. Good disabled access and facilities. *(Recommended by Mr and Mrs P H Griffiths, Mr and Mrs B Jeffery, A J Wright, Roger Braithwaite, JCW, Denys Gueroult, Chris Flynn, Wendy Jones, Mr and Mrs J Tout, Sallie Hammond, Rodney and Norma Stubington, Jeff and Wendy Williams)*

Free house ~ Licensees Lynda Williams and Andy Kane ~ Real ale ~ Bar food (12-2, 6.30-9; not Sat evening; 12-2.30, 7-8.30 Sun) ~ Restaurant ~ (01886) 833399 ~ Children welcome ~ Open 11.30-2.30, 6(6.30 Sat)-11; 12-3, 7-10.30 Sun

BREDON SO9236 Map 4
Fox & Hounds
4½ miles from M5 junction 9; A438 to Northway, left at B4079, then in Bredon follow signpost to church and river on right; GL20 7LA

Nice to know as a pleasant all-rounder, this 15th-c stone and timber thatched pub stands by the village church, and is especially pretty in summer, when it's decked with brightly coloured hanging baskets; some of the picnic-sets are under Perspex. The open-plan carpeted bar has low beams, stone pillars and stripped timbers, a central woodburning stove, upholstered settles, a variety of wheelback, tub and kitchen chairs around handsome mahogany and cast-iron-framed tables, dried grasses and flowers and elegant wall lamps. There's a smaller no smoking side bar. Friendly efficient staff serve Banks's Bitter and Greene King Old Speckled Hen along with a guest such as Caledonian 80/- on handpump and eight wines by the glass; piped music. A fairly short lunchtime snack menu includes baguettes (from £4.95), soup (£3.95), whitebait (£4.75), ploughman's (from £6.50), beer-battered cod (£8.95), beef bourguignon (£10.95) and steak (from £11.50), or you can choose from the à la carte menu, which includes a few additional dishes such as warm leek and smoked mackerel tart (£5.50), oriental vegetable stir fry (£9.50), and herb-crusted pork cutlet with roasted apple and red wine reduction (£11.95); on Sunday they do a choice of roasts (from £8). *(Recommended by Andy and Claire Barker, A G Marx, Chris Flynn, Wendy Jones, Simon Jones, Di and Mike Gillam, W H and E Thomas, John and Hazel Williams, Mrs Hazel Rainer)*

Enterprise ~ Lease Cilla and Christopher Lamb ~ Real ale ~ Bar food ~ Restaurant ~ (01684) 772377 ~ Children welcome ~ Dogs allowed in bar ~ Open 12-3, 6(6.30 winter)-11

BRETFORTON SP0943 Map 4
Fleece ★ £
B4035 E of Evesham: turn S off this road into village; pub is in centre square by church; there's a sizeable car park at one side of the church; WR11 7JE

Before becoming a pub in 1848 this enchanting medieval part-thatched pub was a farm, owned by the same family for nearly 500 years, and eventually left to the National Trust in 1977. Many of the furnishings, such as the great oak dresser that holds a priceless 48-piece set of Stuart pewter, are heirlooms passed down through that family for many generations, and now back in place. The rooms have massive beams and exposed timbers, and marks scored on the worn and crazed flagstones were to keep out demons. There are two fine grandfather clocks, ancient kitchen chairs, curved high-backed settles, a rocking chair, and a rack of heavy pointed iron shafts, probably for spit roasting (though there have been all sorts of esoteric guesses), in one of the huge inglenook fireplaces, and two more log fires. Plenty of oddities include a great cheese-press and set of cheese moulds, and a rare dough-proving table; a leaflet details the more bizarre items, and look out for the photographs of the terrible fire that struck this place a couple of years ago. A great choice of beers includes well kept Hook Norton Best and Uley Pigs Ear, with around four changing guests from breweries such as Bathams, Salopian, Woods and Wye Valley from handpump, along with farm cider and fruit wines. They have darts, cribbage, dominoes, shove-ha'penny and various board games, but no piped music or fruit machines. A shortish choice of very fairly priced bar food includes soup (£2.95), chicken and duck liver parfait with orange syrup (£3.25), sandwiches (from £3.50), faggots and mash (£5.95), ploughman's, baked mushrooms with spinach and cream cheese topping or scampi (£6.75), steak and ale pie (£7.50) and puddings such as chocolate brandy cake with raspberry purée or apple crumble (from £3.25). Most of the pub is no smoking. They hold the annual asparagus auctions (end of May) and village fête (August bank holiday Monday), there's sometimes morris dancing, and the village silver band plays here regularly too; in summer, musical and theatrical events are performed on a stage in the garden. The lawn around the beautifully restored thatched and timbered barn is a lovely place to sit, among the fruit trees, and at the front by the stone pump-trough; there are more picnic-sets in the front courtyard. The pub gets very busy in summer. *(Recommended by Carol Broadbent, Rob Weeks, Andy and Claire Barker, Dave Braisted, Eithne Dandy, W W Burke, Michael and Alison Sandy, George Atkinson, Keith and Sue Ward, Pat and Tony Martin, Paul Humphreys, Martin and Pauline Jennings)*

Free house ~ Licensee Nigel Smith ~ Real ale ~ Bar food (12-2.30(4 Sun), 6.30-9; not Sun evening) ~ (01386) 831173 ~ Children welcome ~ Open 11-12; 11-3, weekdays 6-12 winter; 12-11 Sun

BROADWAY   SP0937   Map 4
Crown & Trumpet   ✍
Church Street; WR12 7AE

The helpful landlord at this cheerfully bustling, down-to-earth 17th-c golden stone pub is both a music and real ale fan. Seasonal beers (one for each season) are brewed for the pub by the local Stanway Brewery, and he also keeps Greene King Old Speckled Hen (in summer), Hook Norton Old Hooky and Timothy Taylors Landlord; also hot toddies and mulled wine. The pub hosts regular live music and has a range of pub games, including darts, shove-ha'penny, cribbage, dominoes, ring-the-bull and evesham quoits; they've also a fruit machine, TV and piped music. The relaxed beamed and timbered bar has antique dark high-backed settles, good big tables and a blazing log fire (one reader found the pub a bit smoky). Outside hardwood tables and chairs among flowers on a slightly raised front terrace are popular with walkers – even in adverse weather. Straightforward bar food includes wraps (from £3.95), ploughman's (from £6.45), various pies (from £6.95), vegetable lasagne (£7.25), puddings (£3.45), and Sunday roasts (£7.45). Dogs are welcome outside food service times. *(Recommended by Paul and Gloria Howell, Pam Adsley, Donna and Roger, W W Burke, Roger and Pauline Pearce, Hugh Pollard)*

Laurel (Enterprise) ~ Lease Andrew Scott ~ Real ale ~ Bar food (12-2.15(3.30 Sat, Sun), 6-9.15) ~ (01386) 853202 ~ Children welcome ~ Live music Sat evening, blues monthly Thurs, jazz monthly Thurs ~ Open 11-3, 5-11(11-11 July, Aug); 11-11 Sat, Sun ~ Bedrooms: £43S(£48B)/£58S(£65B)

CHILDSWICKHAM   SP0738   Map 4
Childswickham Inn   ♀
Village signposted off A44 just NW of Broadway; WR12 7HP

This rather formal dining pub has been carefully expanded, and the main area, largely no smoking, is for eating in, with a mix of chairs around kitchen tables, big rugs on boards or broad terracotta tiles, more or less abstract contemporary prints on walls painted cream and pale violet or mauve, candlesticks in great variety, a woodburning stove and a piano; piped music. Off to the right is a modern-style lounge-like bar (snacks only, such as baguettes, in here), light and airy, with Greene King Old Speckled Hen and Hook Norton Hooky on handpump (from a counter that seems made from old doors), a good choice of over 50 french, italian and other wines (with ten sold by the glass), and good coffee in elegant cups; service is friendly and attentive. This small carefully lit room has a similarly modern colour-scheme with paintings by local artists, leather armchairs and sofas, and bamboo furniture. The entrance lobby has the biggest doormat we have ever seen – wall to wall – with good disabled access and facilities. Although there's a new licensee this year, the chef who's been responsible for the eclectic restaurant food here over the last three years is still in charge of the kitchen. As well as fairly straightforward lunchtime snacks such as baguettes (£6.95), macaroni cheese (£7.95) or chicken chasseur (£8.95), the broad-ranging menu might include breaded brie with cranberry and port wine jelly (£5.25), grilled sardines in garlic, lemon and herbs (£5.75), sausage and mash (£12.50), chicken breast with spring onion, ginger and sherry vinegar dressing (£14.50) and T-bone steak (£17.50). A large sunny deck outside has tables, and the garden is nicely cottagey, with a lawn and borders. *(Recommended by Bernard Stradling, Paul and Gloria Howell, Mike and Mary Carter)*

Punch ~ Lease Carol Marshall ~ Real ale ~ Bar food ~ Restaurant (not Sun evening or Mon lunch) ~ (01386) 852461 ~ Children welcome with restrictions ~ Dogs allowed in bar ~ Open 12-3, 5.30-11; 12-3 Sun; closed Sun evening, Mon

CLENT SO9279 Map 4
Fountain
Off A491 at Holy Cross/Clent exit roundabout, via Violet Lane, then turn right at T junction; Adams Hill/Odnall Lane; DY9 9PU

It's worth making a table reservation if you are planning to visit this very restauranty no smoking pub, as it's very popular and can get heavily booked up. Although drinkers are welcome to stand at the bar, or sit if there is a table free, you may not feel terribly at home after a hard day's hiking in the nearby breezy Clent Hills. As well as interesting lunchtime sandwiches (from £4.50), the menu and specials board might include generous helpings of home-made soup (£3.95), chicken liver pâté (£4.75), devilled whitebait (£4.95), fried plaice and chips (£8.95), roast duck braised in red wine (£8.95), mixed bean chilli (£10.95), filo rack of lamb stuffed with apricot and mixed nuts (£15.85), and rather tasty-sounding puddings such as raspberry fool or spotted dick (from £4.65); service by uniformed staff is courteous, friendly and efficient. With a buoyant atmosphere, the long carpeted dining bar – four knocked-together areas – is filled mainly by sturdy pine tables and country-kitchen or mate's chairs, with some comfortably cushioned brocaded wall seats. There are nicely framed local photographs on the ragged pinkish walls above a dark panelled dado, pretty wall lights, and candles on the tables. Three or four changing real ales might be from brewers such as Adnams, Banks, Marstons and Shardlow, and they've decent wines served in cut glass, and ten malts; also a choice of speciality teas and good coffees, and freshly squeezed orange juice; alley skittles; piped music. There are a few picnic-sets out in front. Note that they may close in the evening on winter Sundays. *(Recommended by Ian Phillips, Miss Glynis Hume, Theo, Anne and Jane Gaskin, Lynda and Trevor Smith, J and P Blake, J C Churchill-Wood, Mrs Pat Crabb)*

Union Pub Company ~ Lease Richard and Jacque Macey ~ Real ale ~ Bar food (12-2(4.30 Sun), 6-9 (9.30 Fri, Sat); not Sun evening) ~ Restaurant ~ (01562) 883286 ~ Children welcome till 7.30 ~ Open 11-11; 12-10.30 Sun

CROWLE SO9256 Map 4
Old Chequers ♀
2½ miles from M5 junction 6; A4538 towards Evesham, then left after ½ mile; then follow Crowle signpost right to Crowle Green; WR7 4AA

This well run pub is a very handy stop for a meal if you are on the motorway. Generously served, well prepared food includes soup (£3.50), ploughman's (£6.50), thai chicken curry (£11.50), loin of lamb with sauce of the day (£14.50), rib-eye steak with sauce of the day (£15.50) and daily specials. Much modernised, the pub rambles extensively around an island bar, with plush-seated mate's chairs around a mix of pub tables on the patterned carpet, some brass and copper on the swirly-plastered walls, lots of pictures for sale at the back, and a coal-effect gas fire at one end (there's central heating too). A big square extension on the right, with shinily varnished rustic timbering and beamery, has more tables. Banks's Bitter and Timothy Taylors Landlord are well kept on handpump with a guest such as Hook Norton Hooky, and they've good value house wines. Disabled access; piped music; one bar area is no smoking. Outside, there are picnic-sets on the grass behind, among shrubs and small fruit trees – a pleasant spot, with pasture beyond. *(Recommended by Dave Braisted, Paul Boot, David Green, Jill and Julian Tasker, M G Hart, John and Gloria Isaacs, Mr and Mrs F E Boxell, Mr and Mrs A H Young, M Joyner, Stuart Paulley, Alistair and Kay Butler, Rod Stoneman, John and Jill Perkins, Malcolm and Kate Dowty)*

Free house ~ Licensees Steven and Ian Thomas ~ Real ale ~ Bar food (12-2(2.30 Sun), 7-9.45) ~ (01905) 381275 ~ Open 12-2, 7-11; 12-3 Sun; closed Sun evening

DEFFORD   SO9042 Map 4
Monkey House
A4104 towards Upton – immediately after passing Oak public house on right, there's a small group of cottages, of which this is the last; WR8 9BW

Suspended in something of a time-warp, and really only for those who like very simple unspoilt places, this enchantingly unchanged black and white thatched cider-house has been in the same family for some 150 years. With no inn sign, at first sight it hardly resembles a pub at all. Very cheap Bulmer's Medium or Special Dry cider is tapped from barrels, poured by jug into pottery mugs (some locals have their own) and served from a hatch beside the door. As a concession to modern tastes, beer is sold too, in cans. Apart from crisps and nuts they don't do food, but you can bring your own. In the summer you could find yourself sharing the garden with the hens and cockerels that wander in from an adjacent collection of caravans and sheds; there's also a pony called Mandy, Tapper the jack russell, and Marie the rottweiler. Alternatively you can retreat to a small and spartan side outbuilding with a couple of plain tables, a settle and an open fire. The pub's name comes from the story of a drunken customer who, some years ago, fell into bramble bushes and swore that he was attacked by monkeys. Please note the limited opening times below. *(Recommended by Pete Baker, the Didler, Annabel Viney)*

Free house ~ Licensee Graham Collins ~ No credit cards ~ (01386) 750234 ~ Open 11-2, 6-10.30; 12-2, 7-10.30 Sun; closed Mon evening, Tues, lunchtimes Weds-Thurs

HANLEY SWAN   SO8142 Map 4
Swan 🍴 🛏
B4209 Malvern—Upton; WR8 0EA

Much changed since we'd last seen it a few years earlier, this prettily set pub now has an attractively contemporary new layout and décor – and rather more room than we'd remembered. It has two main areas, the extended back part now set for dining, with french windows looking out over the picnic-sets on the good-sized side lawn and its play area, and the front part more of a conventional bar; each area has its own servery. Good sturdy dining tables have comfortably high-backed chairs, and one part of the bar has dark leather bucket armchairs and sofas brightened up by scatter cushions. It's all been given a fresh and up-to-date country look, with cream paintwork, some attractive new oak panelling contrasting with older rough timbering, well chosen prints, some stripped masonry and bare boards, a log fire, and stylishly rustic lamps. They have three changing real ales on handpump, typically Adnams, Charles Wells Bombardier and Shepherd Neame Spitfire. As well as a good choice of sandwiches (£4.95) and a help yourself baked potato counter (£5.50), the food includes soup (£3.95), ploughman's (£6.75), roast spicy couscous stuffed peppers (£7.50), battered cod and chips (£8.50), lamb and leek minted casserole (£8.95) and puddings (£3.95). On Sundays virtually the whole pub is devoted to their popular Sunday lunch (£8.25). People like the way that a platter with a small loaf of fresh bread, oil and butter is brought at the start of a meal. The young staff are cheerful, attentive and helpful; disabled access and facilities. The five bedrooms are new. This is charming countryside, and the inn, handy for the Malvern show ground and set well back from the road, faces a classic green complete with duck pond and massive oak tree. *(Recommended by P Dawn, Chris Flynn, Wendy Jones, M Joyner, Colin Fisher, GSB, Martin and Pauline Jennings, Ron and Val Broom, Pat and Graham Williamson)*

Punch ~ Lease Michelle Steggles and Adrian Bowden ~ Real ale ~ Bar food (12-2.30, 6.30-9) ~ Restaurant ~ (01684) 311870 ~ Children in restaurant ~ Dogs allowed in bedrooms ~ Open 11-3, 6-11(10.30 Sun), all day summer weekends ~ Bedrooms: £50B/£65B

HOLY CROSS SO9278 Map 4
Bell & Cross 🍴 ♀

4 miles from M5 junction 4: A491 towards Stourbridge, then follow Clent signpost off on left; DY9 9QL

Unanimous praise from readers means this distinctively well run pub is unlikely to disappoint, and though they serve terrific food, it's still the sort of place where you can pop in for just a drink. With a classic unspoilt early 19th-c layout, the five small rooms and kitchen open off a central corridor with a black and white tiled floor: they give a choice of carpet, bare boards, lino or nice old quarry tiles, a variety of moods from snug and chatty to bright and airy, and an individual décor in each – theatrical engravings on red walls here, nice sporting prints on pale green walls there, racing and gundog pictures above the black panelled dado in another room. Two of the rooms have small serving bars, with well kept Banks's Bitter, Hook Norton, Timothy Taylors Landlord and maybe a guest such as Hook Norton Hooky on handpump. You'll find over 50 wines (with 14 sold by the glass), a variety of coffees, daily papers, coal fires in most rooms, perhaps regulars playing cards in one of the two front ones, and piped music; all dining areas are no smoking. Delicious dishes, from a changing menu, include lunchtime snacks (not Sunday) such as sandwiches (from £4.50, baguettes and panini from £4.95), fish cakes with white wine, prawn and chive sauce (£6), and oak-smoked salmon (£7), with other dishes such as mushroom and white bean soup (£4.50), spring vegetable tarte tatin with poached egg and mustard glaze (£10.75), seared salmon fillet with king prawns and oriental egg noodles or chicken breast with roasted pepper and chorizo ragoût (£11.95) and grilled rib-eye steak with baked stuffed tomato (£13.95). Puddings might include banoffi cheesecake or raspberry panna cotta with peach melba sauce (£4.95); Sunday roast (£10.95). You get pleasant views from the garden terrace. The pub cat is called Pumba. *(Recommended by Pete Baker, Ian Phillips, Drs E J C Parker, Margaret and Allen Marsden, Clifford Blakemore, John Street, KC, J and P Blake, J C Churchill-Wood, Mike and Linda Hudson, Roy and Lindsey Fentiman, Karen Eliot)*

Enterprise ~ Lease Roger and Jo Narbett ~ Real ale ~ Bar food (12-2, 6.30-9.15(9.30 Fri-Sat); 12-2.30, 7-9 Sun) ~ Restaurant ~ (01562) 730319 ~ Children welcome away from bar ~ Dogs allowed in bar ~ Open 12-3(3.30 Sat), 6-11; 12-4, 7-10.30 Sun

KEMPSEY SO8548 Map 4
Walter de Cantelupe ♀ 🛏

A38, handy for M5 junction 7 via A44 and A4440; WR5 3NA

The interesting choice of well kept real ales on handpump at this welcoming pub includes Cannon Royall Kings Shilling, Hobsons Best, Timothy Taylors Landlord and a guest such as Mayfields Naughty Nell. For non-beer drinkers they have locally grown and pressed apple juices, wines from a local vineyard, half a dozen wines by the glass, and in summer they also have a farm cider. Boldly decorated in red and gold, the bar area has an informal and well worn in mix of furniture, an old wind-up HMV gramophone and a good big fireplace. The dining area has various plush or yellow leather dining chairs, an old settle, a sonorous clock, and candles and flowers on the tables; piped music and board games. Cooked by the friendly landlord, using lots of local produce, good value enjoyable bar food includes lunchtime sandwiches (from £3), home-made soup (£3.60), very good ploughman's (£5.60), sausages and mash (£7.25; with vegetarian sausages £6.50), chicken balti (£7.50), and gammon, egg and chips (£7.60), with specials such as home-made baked beans in a real tomato and Guinness sauce served on toast (£3.95), chicken liver pâté (£4), beef and ale pie (£8.50), and poached salmon salad (£8.75), with puddings such as sticky ginger pudding with ginger wine and toffee sauce (£3.95); you can buy jars of home-made chutney and marmalade. The entire pub is no smoking on Saturday nights, at other times just the dining area and counter are; cribbage, dominoes and table skittles. There's a pretty suntrap walled garden at the back; the sociable labrador is called Monti. *(Recommended by Paul Kemp, Andy and Jill Kassube, P Dawn, M G Hart, Dr A J and Mrs Tompsett, David Morgan, Theocsbrian, Pat and Tony Martin, Rhiannon Davies)*

Free house ~ Licensee Martin Lloyd Morris ~ Real ale ~ Bar food (12-2(3 Sun), 6-9.30; 12-2.30, 6.30-10 Fri, Sat; not Sun evening) ~ Restaurant ~ (01905) 820572 ~ Children in restaurant until 8.15 ~ Dogs welcome ~ Open 12-2.30(3 Sat), 6-11; 12-3, 7-10.30 Sun; closed Mon ~ Bedrooms: £44.50S(£49.50B)/£55S(£77B)

KIDDERMINSTER SO8376 Map 4
King & Castle 🍺 £
Railway Station, Comberton Hill; DY10 1QX

Great fun to visit, this is a detailed re-creation of a better-class Edwardian station refreshment room, and steam trains hissing by the platform immediately outside evoke the great age of the railways at the terminus of the Severn Valley Railway. With beer at around only £1.20 a pint, your pocket will feel it's made a journey back in time too! The atmosphere is lively and sometimes noisily good-humoured, with a good mix of customers, though it can get rather smoky. Furnishings are solid and in character, and there's the railway memorabilia that you'd expect. Bathams and Wyre Piddle Royal Piddle are superbly kept alongside a couple of changing guests from brewers such as Enville, Harviestoun and Hobsons on handpump, and they've ten malt whiskies. The reasonably priced straightforward menu includes toasties (from £2.50), basket meals such as sausage and chips (£2.75), all-day breakfast (£4.75), broccoli and cream cheese bake, scampi or chicken kiev (£5.25), and traditional puddings such as lemon sponge (£2.50); they also do Sunday roasts (£4.75), and children's meals (£2.75). The cheerful landlady and friendly staff cope well with the bank holiday and railway gala day crowds (you'll be lucky to find a seat then). You can use a Rover ticket to shuttle between here and the Railwaymans Arms in Bridgnorth (see Shropshire chapter). *(Recommended by Paul and Gloria Howell, Gill and Tony Morriss, P Dawn, John Tav, Theocsbrian, B M Eldridge, Theo, Anne and Jane Gaskin)*

Free house ~ Licensee Rosemary Hyde ~ Real ale ~ Bar food (12-2(2.30 Sat-Sun), 6-8 Fri-Sat, 7-9 Sun; not Mon-Thurs evenings) ~ Restaurant ~ No credit cards ~ (01562) 747505 ~ Children welcome with restrictions ~ Dogs welcome ~ Open 11-3, 5-11; 11-11 Sat; 12-10.30 Sun

KNIGHTWICK SO7355 Map 4
Talbot 🍷 🍺 🛏
Knightsford Bridge; B4197 just off A44 Worcester—Bromyard; WR6 5PH

This extensive 15th-c white painted coaching inn is a jolly decent welcoming all-rounder. With a good log fire in winter, the heavily beamed and extended carpeted lounge bar opens on to a terrace and an arbour with roses and clematis in summer. There is a variety of traditional seats from small carved or leatherette armchairs to the winged settles by the tall bow windows, and a vast stove squats in the big central stone hearth. The well furnished back public bar has pool on a raised side area, darts, fruit machine, video game and juke box; dominoes and cribbage. Well kept on handpump and fairly priced, This, That, Wot and T'other ales are brewed in their own microbrewery from locally grown hops. They also have a guest such as

Hobsons Bitter and sometimes a farm cider, as well as ten different wines by the glass and 15 malt whiskies. There are some old-fashioned seats in front of the pub, with more on a good-sized lawn over the lane by the River Teme (they serve out here too). Freshly prepared with local ingredients (some of the vegetables are grown in the pub's organic garden), good bar food, served by cheerfully attentive staff, might include cream of carrot and coriander soup (£4.50), preserved fish salad with caper mayonnaise (£6.50), sweet potato and red lentil casserole (£13), stuffed breast of lamb with stir-fried gourds or shin of beef in ale with garlic mash (£14) and mullet fillet with oyster sauce (£15); the restaurant is no smoking. Some of the bedrooms are above the bar. They hold a farmers' market here on the second Sunday in the month. *(Recommended by Carol Broadbent, Andy and Claire Barker, Howard Dell, P Dawn, Cathryn and Richard Hicks, Noel Grundy, Dick and Madeleine Brown, Pat and Tony Martin)*

Own brew ~ Licensees Wiz and Annie Clift ~ Real ale ~ Bar food ~ Restaurant ~ (01886) 821235 ~ Children welcome ~ Dogs allowed in bar and bedrooms ~ Open 11-11(11.30 Sat, 10.30 Sun) ~ Bedrooms: £48S/£82B

MALVERN SO7845 Map 4

Nags Head 🍺

Bottom end of Bank Street, steep turn down off A449; WR14 2JG

They keep an astonishing range of 16 real ales on handpump at this welcoming old inn. Along with Banks's, Bathams, Greene King IPA, Marstons Pedigree and Woods Shropshire Lad, you'll find changing guests (last year they got through over 1000) from brewers such as Cairngorm, Cottage, Dark Star, Fullers, Sharps and Three Rivers, to name but a few. If you're having trouble making a choice they will happily give you a taste first. They also keep a fine range of malt whiskies, belgian beers and decent wines by the glass. The pub attracts a good mix of customers (with plenty of locals), and the mood is chatty and easy-going, with friendly young staff. There's a good variety of places to sit: a series of snug individually decorated rooms with one or two steps between, all sorts of chairs including leather armchairs, pews sometimes arranged as booths, a mix of tables with sturdy ones stained different colours, bare boards here, flagstones there, carpet elsewhere, and plenty of interesting pictures and homely touches such as house plants and shelves of well thumbed books; there's a coal fire opposite the central servery; broadsheet newspapers and a good juke box; piped music, shove-ha'penny, cribbage and dominoes. Bar food (now served in the evening too) might include goats cheese ciabatta (£4.95), soup (£4), sausages and mash (£6.80), battered haddock (£7.50) and steak and stilton pie (£8). In the evenings they do meals only in the extension barn dining room. Outside are picnic-sets and rustic tables and benches on the front terrace and in a garden, there are heaters, and umbrellas for wet weather. *(Recommended by Ray and Winifred Halliday, Theocsbrian, Chris Flynn, Wendy Jones, Dave Braisted, Brian Banks, Mike Pugh, Ian and Nita Cooper, Richard, Dr and Mrs Jackson, Andy Trafford, Louise Bayly, Barry Collett, Mike and Mary Clark, David and Sue Smith)*

Free house ~ Licensee Duncan Ironmonger ~ Real ale ~ Bar food (12-2, 6.30-8.30) ~ Restaurant ~ (01684) 574373 ~ Children welcome with restrictions ~ Dogs allowed in bar ~ Open 11-11.15(11.30 Sat); 12-11 Sun

PENSAX SO7368 Map 4

Bell 🍺 £

B4202 Abberley—Clows Top, SE of the Snead Common part of the village; WR6 6AE

Enjoyable and extremely welcoming, this mock-Tudor local attracts a nice mix of customers and is a good all-rounder. As well as Hobsons, four well kept changing real ales on handpump might be from brewers such as Archers, Hook Norton, Three Tuns and Timothy Taylor, and they've three local ciders and a local perry on handpump too; over the last weekend of June they hold a beer festival. The L-shaped main bar has a restrained traditional décor, with long cushioned pews on its bare boards, good solid pub tables, and a woodburning stove. Beyond a small area on the left with a couple more tables is a more airy dining room, with french windows opening on to a wooden deck; the pub has a log fire for our more usual weather. Besides good value lunchtime weekday specials such as steak and ale pie, vegetable stir fry, cornish pasty or sausage and mash (all £5.50), hearty enjoyable dishes, using locally sourced meat and vegetables, could include generous sandwiches (£3.50), faggots, chips and mushy peas (£6.95), pork chop with dijon sauce (£9.50), and steaks (from £11.95); Sunday roast (£6.95); children's menu (£4.50); the dining room is no smoking. Picnic-sets in the back garden look out over rolling fields and copses to the Wyre Forest. *(Recommended by Gill and Tony Morriss, Dave Braisted, MLR, David Eberlin, Lynda and Trevor Smith, Guy Vowles, Phil and Sally Gorton)*

Free house ~ Licensees John and Trudy Greaves ~ Real ale ~ Bar food (12-2(3 Sun), 6-9; not Sun evening) ~ Restaurant ~ (01299) 896677 ~ Children welcome away from the bar ~ Dogs welcome ~ Open 12-2.30, 5-11; 12-10.30 Sun; closed Mon lunch

---

LUCKY DIP

Besides the fully inspected pubs, you might like to try these Lucky Dips recommended to us and described by readers (if you do, please send us reports: www.goodguides.co.uk).

ABBERLEY [SO7567]
Manor Arms WR6 6BN: Comfortable country inn nicely tucked away in a quiet village backwater, façade emblazoned with coats of arms, warm welcome, quick friendly service, good generous plain cooking, Timothy Taylors Landlord and Wye Valley HPA, two bars and restaurant, interesting collection of toby jugs; ten reasonably priced bedrooms *(Alec and Susan Hamilton)*
BECKFORD [SO9835]
☆ *Beckford Hotel* GL20 7AN [A435]: Colourfully modernised by good new landlady, pleasant bar and no smoking snug, Adnams and Greene King real ales, wide choice of enjoyable traditional bar food from sandwiches up, friendly service, attractive cream-décor no smoking restaurant, airy and roomy; large well kept garden with terrace tables, comfortable bedrooms *(Mrs Pauline Wakeman, Martin and Pauline Jennings, Bob Richardson)*
BELBROUGHTON [SO9177]
☆ *Queens* DY9 0DU [Queens Hill (B4188 E of Kidderminster)]: 18th-c pub by Belne Brook, thriving under current landlord, several linked areas with nice mix of comfortable seating, 19th-c oak and other tables in varying sizes, enjoyable food with plentiful veg and interesting puddings, Banks's, Marstons Pedigree and good guest beers, good choice of wines by the glass, friendly efficient service, no smoking family area, fresh flowers; picnic-sets on small roadside terrace, pleasant village *(Clifford Blakemore, David Green, John Westley)*
BERROW [SO7835]
Duke of York WR13 6JQ [junction A438/B4208]: Two comfortable linked rooms, good value pub food from good sandwiches up, real ales, farm cider, cheerful young staff, 15th-c beams, nooks and crannies, friendly atmosphere, good log fire, dominoes, cribbage, partly no smoking back restaurant; piped music; children welcome, picnic-sets in big

attractive back garden, handy for Malvern Hills *(Dr A J and Mrs Tompsett, BB)*
BEWDLEY [SO7875]
Mug House DY12 2EE [Severn Side N]: Pleasantly renovated 18th-c pub in charming spot by River Severn, friendly service, pubby bar food from sandwiches to pasta, fish and chips and so forth, good range of real ales such as Hobsons and Wye Valley, log fire, restaurant; terrace tables, bedrooms, open all day *(Andrew York)*
BIRLINGHAM [SO9343]
Swan WR10 3AQ [off A4104 and B4080 S of Pershore; Church St]: Friendly village pub thriving under current management, increasingly popular for its enjoyable food; nice garden (and snowdrops in village churchyard well worth seeing in season) *(Theocsbrian, John Street)*
BOURNHEATH [SO9474]
☆ *Gate* B61 9JR [handy for M5 junction 4, via A491 and B4091; Dodford Rd]: Country dining pub with long-serving licensees, wide choice of attractively priced good fresh food from lunchtime and early evening bargains to all sorts of exotic dishes, good value Sun lunch, friendly staff helpful with special diets, quick service even though busy, real ales in cosy partitioned-off bar, attractive open dining area inc no smoking conservatory; nice garden *(David Edwards, Kevin Connor, Isabel York)*
☆ *Nailers Arms* B61 9JE [4 miles from M5 junction 4; Doctors Hill]: Minimalist modern open-plan bistro-style lounge and restaurant, comfortable light wood chairs and tables on stripped floors, some sofas, good food from lunchtime sandwiches through up-to-date starters, main dishes and puddings to hefty Sun lunch, attentive helpful service, Enville White, Greene King Old Speckled Hen and two changing guest beers, good choice of wines by the glass, country wines, daily papers, more traditional tiled-floor locals' back bar with log fire; children really welcome, smart outdoor

eating area, open all day *(David Edwards, Richard and Jean Phillips)*

BROADWAY [SP0937]

☆ *Lygon Arms* WR12 7DU [High St]: Stately top-rank Cotswold hotel, strikingly handsome, with interesting old rooms rambling away from attractive oak-panelled bar, splendid restaurant, helpful staff; adjoining bar/brasserie has good imaginative food, quick attentive service, good wines; children welcome, tables in prettily planted courtyard (dogs allowed here), well kept gardens, smart comfortable bedrooms, open all day in summer *(LYM, Dennis Jenkin)*

CALLOW END [SO8349]

Old Bush WR2 4TE [Upton Rd]: Friendly pub with pleasant staff, Banks's and Marstons Bitter and Pedigree, good choice of bar food *(P Dawn, Colin Fisher)*

CHADDESLEY CORBETT [SO8973]

Fox DY10 4QN [A448 Bromsgrove—Kidderminster]: Popular and friendly, with several eating and drinking areas, bargain carvery, four real ales inc Enville and Hobsons Town Crier; can seem quite loud *(Gill and Tony Morriss, Mr and Mrs B Thomas, V Wood)*

Talbot DY10 4SA [off A448 Bromsgrove—Kidderminster]: Comfortably refurbished and neatly kept late medieval timbered pub in quiet village street, friendly staff, changing ales inc Banks's, enjoyable bar food – good chips; comfortable outside area, attractive village and church *(Alan and Pat Newcombe)*

CROPTHORNE [SO9944]

New Inn WR10 3NE [B4084 (former A44) Evesham—Pershore]: Popular welcoming food pub, partly no smoking, with Hook Norton and Tetleys, paintings for sale; children welcome, large garden *(Tony and Wendy Hobden)*

CUTNALL GREEN [SO8868]

☆ *Chequers* WR9 0PJ [Kidderminster Rd]: Some recent comfortable and stylish refurbishment in beamed country dining pub with comprehensive choice of enjoyable food inc some good italian dishes; pleasant atmosphere, scrubbed tables, good wine choice, real ales *(R J Herd)*

DODFORD [SO9372]

Dodford Inn B61 9BG [Whinfield Rd]: As we go to press threat of closure over this friendly unpretentious walkers' pub in extensive grounds, quiet spot overlooking wooded valley, lots of footpaths; relaxed peaceful atmosphere, traditional décor and simple furnishings, good value hearty home-made food, two interesting changing real ales, central fire, darts; children and dogs welcome, disabled access (though tables close together) and facilities, garden with terrace and play area *(G Coates)*

DRAKES BROUGHTON [SO9248]

☆ *Plough & Harrow* WR10 2AG [A44 NW of Pershore]: Well run dining pub with partly no smoking extended and refurbished restaurant area, comfortable and attractive rambling lounge, attentive service, two or three changing ales, sensible prices and cut-price small

helpings for the elderly, log fire; may be two sittings on busy days; good disabled access, pleasant terrace, big orchard-side garden with play area, open all day *(Chris Flynn, Wendy Jones, Mr and Mrs F E Boxell)*

DRAYTON [SO9075]

Robin Hood DY9 0BW [off B4188]: Comfortably old-fashioned early 19th-c dining pub with inglenook log fire, low beams and lovely stained glass in large lounge, handsome wooden furniture, cheerful landlady and friendly efficient service, real ales inc guest beers, good value varied bar food, regulars' pictures all over cosy bar; garden with trampoline and pets' corner, attractive surroundings, good walks; open all day wknds *(Dave Braisted)*

DROITWICH [SO9063]

Hop Pole WR9 8ED [Friar St]: Beamed 16th-c pub with bargain home-made lunches inc Sun roasts, Wye Valley beers, welcoming staff, pool; loud music Thurs-Sun evenings, otherwise quiet; wicker furniture in partly canopied back garden, open all day *(Dr B and Mrs P B Baker)*

DUNHAMPSTEAD [SO9160]

☆ *Fir Trees* WR9 7JX [just SE of Droitwich, towards Sale Green – OS Sheet 150 map ref 919600]: Pretty and attractively refurbished country dining pub with good bar food, Hook Norton and Timothy Taylors Landlord, comfortable no smoking dining conservatory; tables on flower-filled terrace and in small grassy garden, nice spot not far from canal – good walks *(LYM, Dave Braisted, Lynda and Trevor Smith)*

EARLS CROOME [SO8642]

Yorkshire Grey WR8 9DA [A38, N of M50 junction 1]: Bustling entirely no smoking pub, stylish contemporary décor (think Yorkshire Mauve), friendly atmosphere, fair-priced enjoyable food inc some enterprising dishes, Greene King Old Speckled Hen, sensibly priced wines, log fire, candlelit restaurant; disabled access, garden tables *(Paul Kemp, Denys Gueroult, Mrs S Lyons, Reg Fowle, Helen Rickwood)*

ELDERSFIELD [SO8131]

☆ *Greyhound* GL19 4NX [signed from B4211; Lime St (don't go into Eldersfield itself), OS Sheet 150 map ref 815314]: Unspoilt country local, already largely no smoking, with welcoming young licensees, good inexpensive country cooking (not Mon) by landlord, real ales such as Butcombe and Woods Parish tapped from the cask, big woodburner and friendly tabby cat in appealing black-beamed ochre-walled public bar, horse-racing pictures in candlelit carpeted no smoking room, lively skittle alley, strikingly modern lavatories with interesting mosaic in gents'; picnic-sets in small front garden, swings and dovecote out behind *(the Didler, BB, Dr A J and Mrs Tompsett)*

FAIRFIELD [SO9475]

Swan B61 9NG [B4091; marked PH on OS map]: Friendly typical Banks's pub, good value food from hot pork sandwiches to interesting specials, good guest beers *(Dave Braisted)*

FECKENHAM [SP0061]

☆ *Lygon Arms* B96 6JE [B4090 Droitwich—Alcester]: Welcoming licensees, good sensible food using fresh ingredients inc fish delivered daily, small helpings of main courses available, three or four real ales, reasonably priced wines, traditional bar, attractive and popular two-room no smoking dining conservatory *(Martin and Pauline Jennings, Dave Braisted)*

FLADBURY [SO9946]

Chequers WR10 2PZ [Chequers Lane]: Attractive upmarket dining pub dating from 14th c, huge old-fashioned range with log fire at end of long bar, lots of local prints, short but nicely varied choice of good generous food from sandwiches up, Hook Norton and other ales, willing staff, charming beamed back restaurant with new conservatory; children welcome, large pleasant garden with play area, peaceful pretty village, comfortable well equipped bedroom extension *(M S Catling, Martin and Pauline Jennings, Mr and Mrs F E Boxell)*

FLYFORD FLAVELL [SO9754]

☆ *Boot* WR7 4BS [off A422 Worcester—Alcester; Radford Rd]: Georgian-fronted country pub under new management, good value traditional food from lunchtime sandwiches up, friendly staff, real ales, log fire in ancient heavily beamed and timbered partly no smoking back core now mainly for dining, comfortable modern conservatory, little old-world beamed front bar with small inglenook log fire, cards and pool, up to half a dozen real ales; piped music, games machine; children welcome, pretty garden with heaters and lighting, comfortable bedrooms, open all day Sun *(Mike Dean, Lis Wingate Gray, David Collison, Mike and Mary Carter, Theo, Anne and Jane Gaskin, LYM)*

Flyford Arms WR7 4DA [Old Hill (A422)]: Adnams Best, Broadside and Explorer, Fullers London Pride and a house beer from central bar, welcoming staff, enjoyable food from baguettes up, light and airy carpeted back dining area, pleasant country views *(Michael and Jenny Back)*

FORHILL [SP0575]

☆ *Peacock* B38 0EH [handy for M42 junctions 2 and 3; pub at junction Lea End Lane and Icknield St]: Appealing, quietly placed and well run no smoking Chef & Brewer with wide range of generous enjoyable food, plenty of tables in comfortably fitted knocked-through beamed rooms, woodburner in big inglenook, Enville, Hobsons Best, Theakstons Old Peculier and two changing ales, friendly prompt helpful service; piped classical music; children welcome, picnic-sets on back terrace and front grass, open all day *(Stan and Hazel Allen, LYM, R T and J C Moggridge, Nigel and Sue Foster, Dennis and Gill Keen, M G Hart)*

HADLEY [SO8662]

Bowling Green WR9 0AR [Hadley Heath; off A4133 Droitwich—Ombersley]: Pleasantly refurbished 16th-c inn, beams and big log fire, huge sofas in back lounge, wide range of good value food from enterprising filled baguettes to popular Sun carvery (packed with families then), friendly staff, Banks's Bitter and Mild, Marstons Pedigree and Hook Norton, good value wines, attractive restaurant; children welcome, tables out overlooking its bowling green (UK's oldest), comfortable bedrooms, pleasant walks nearby *(Jane and Emma Macdonald)*

HANBURY [SO9262]

Eagle & Sun WR9 7DX [B4090 Hanbury—Droitwich; Hanbury Rd, by Worcester & Birmingham Canal]: Neatly laid out, with Banks's and John Smiths, popular good value carvery, dining extension overlooking canal and wharf *(Dave Braisted)*

HANLEY CASTLE [SO8342]

☆ *Three Kings* WR8 0BL [Church End, off B4211 N of Upton upon Severn]: By no means smart or particularly house-proud, even a little unkempt, but much loved by those who put unspoilt character and individuality above all else; friendly and homely, with huge inglenook and hatch service in little tiled-floor tap room, consistently well kept Butcombe, Hobsons Best and two or three changing beers from small breweries usually inc a Mild, Nov beer festival, farm cider, dozens of malt whiskies, two other larger rooms, one with fire in open range, low-priced food (not Sun evening – singer then; be prepared for a possibly longish wait other times), seats of a sort outside; family room, bedroom *(Pete Baker, Gill and Tony Morriss, Carol Broadbent, P Dawn, the Didler, LYM, MLR)*

INKBERROW [SP0157]

☆ *Old Bull* WR7 4DZ [off A422 – note that this is quite different from the nearby Bulls Head]: Photogenic Tudor pub with lots of Archers memorabilia (it's the model for the Ambridge Bull), friendly service, good value generous pubby food inc bargain Fri night fish and chips, real ales, big log fire in huge inglenook, bulging walls, flagstones, oak beams and trusses, some old-fashioned high-backed settles among more modern furnishings; children allowed in eating area, plenty of tables outside *(LYM, Gill and Keith Croxton)*

KINGTON [SO9855]

Red Hart WR7 4DD [Cockshot Lane]: Smart contemporary décor in old pub, good value enjoyable food, friendly and attentive young staff, attractive restaurant *(Mrs M D Lawson, Jason Withers)*

LEIGH SINTON [SO7850]

☆ *Royal Oak* WR13 5DZ [Malvern Rd]: Well run dining pub with cheerful cartoons in low-beamed bar, careful service by relaxed and responsive staff, reliably enjoyable and remarkably cheap home cooking very popular with older lunchers, notable Sun lunch and bargain Mon buffet, two or three real ales, short choice of reasonably priced wines, plenty of locals, attractive restaurant; charming flower-filled garden behind with covered seating *(Denys Gueroult, Chris Flynn, Wendy Jones)*

LONGLEY GREEN [SO7250]

Nelson WR6 5EF: Pleasant and comfortable

lounge bar, good friendly staff, good range of reliable home-made food, three real ales; tables outside, good walks nearby *(Jason Caulkin)*

MALVERN [SO7746]

Foley Arms WR14 4QS [Worcester Rd]: Substantial Georgian hotel with bar in spacious modern extension, Bass, Fullers London Pride and an occasional guest beer, good enterprising bar food lunchtime and evening, helpful uniformed staff, nice atmosphere in hotel lounges and smarter restaurant; sunny terrace with splendid views, bedrooms – back ones have the view *(D W Stokes)*

Malvern Hills Hotel WR13 6DW [opp British Camp car park, Wynds Point; junction A449/B4232 S]: Red plush banquettes, turkey carpet and open fire in extensive dark-panelled lounge bar, very popular wknds, decent bar food, Black Sheep, Hobsons, Greene King Old Speckled Hen and Wye Valley Butty Bach, quite a few malt whiskies, good coffee, downstairs pool room, smart more expensive restaurant; well reproduced piped music; dogs welcome, great views from terrace picnic-sets, bedrooms small but comfortable, open all day – fine position high in the hills *(Guy Vowles, BB)*

OMBERSLEY [SO8463]

Cross Keys WR9 0DS [A449, Kidderminster end]: Smart and comfortable beamed front bar, enjoyable attractively presented food from light bar meals to the conservatory restaurant's fish specialities, Hook Norton ales, good value wines by the glass *(Paul and Gloria Howell, Colin Fisher, Mr and Mrs F E Boxell)*

Kings Arms WR9 0EW [A4133]: Imposing black-beamed and timbered Tudor pub with comfortable rambling rooms, cosy wood-floored nooks and crannies with rustic bric-a-brac, one room with Charles II's coat of arms decorating its ceiling, four open fires, enjoyable food, friendly staff, Banks's Bitter, Marstons Pedigree and a guest beer, good coffee; good disabled access, children welcome, colourful tree-sheltered courtyard, open all day Sun *(LYM, Paul and Gloria Howell, M and C Thompson, Mike and Mary Carter, W M Lien)*

PERSHORE [SO9545]

☆ *Brandy Cask* WR10 1AJ [Bridge St]: Plain high-ceilinged bow-windowed bar, back courtyard brewery producing their own attractively priced real ales, guest beers too, Aug beer festival, quick friendly helpful service, coal fire, food from sandwiches to steaks, quaintly decorated no smoking dining room; well behaved children allowed; long attractive garden down to river (keep a careful eye on the children), with terrace, vine arbour and koi pond *(BB, John Street, the Didler)*

SEDGEBERROW [SP0238]

Queens Head WR11 7UE [Main St (B4078, just off A46 S of Evesham)]: Welcoming village pub with enjoyable traditional pub food, Wickwar Cotswold Way and one or two guest beers, farm cider, no smoking dining end allowing children, central area where the locals congregate, far end with piano, darts and comfortable settees

among more usual pub furnishings, collection of old 3-D relief advertisements; open all day wknds *(Pete Baker)*

SEVERN STOKE [SO8544]

Rose & Crown WR8 9JQ [A38 S of Worcester]: Attractive 16th-c black and white pub, low beams, knick-knacks and good fire in character front bar, Banks's and Marstons, good value food from generous hot-filled baguettes with chips up, friendly staff, back room where children allowed; nice big garden with picnic-sets and play area *(Carol Broadbent, Dave Braisted, R T and J C Moggridge)*

SHATTERFORD [SO7981]

☆ *Bellmans Cross* DY12 1RN [Bridgnorth Rd (A442)]: French-mood dining pub popular with business people at lunchtime, interesting and attractively presented bar food from sandwiches up, good Sun lunch, smart tasteful restaurant, French chefs and bar staff, pleasant deft service, neat timber-effect bar with Bass, Greene King Old Speckled Hen and a guest beer, good choice of wines by the glass inc champagne, teas and coffees; picnic-sets outside, handy for Severn Woods walks, open all day wknds *(BB, Theo, Anne and Jane Gaskin, Dave Braisted)*

STOCK GREEN [SO9959]

Bird in Hand B96 6SX: Proper old-fashioned pub with Banks's, Boddingtons and a guest beer such as Wye Valley Butty Bach, good cheap lunchtime rolls *(Dave Braisted)*

STOKE PRIOR [SO9666]

Gate Hangs Well B60 4HG [Woodgate Rd, off B4091 Hanbury Rd via Moorgate Rd]: Much extended dining pub, open plan but well divided, keeping balance between its popular carvery (and other good value generous food) and its bar side, with good local atmosphere, Banks's special brews and guest beers, friendly service, conservatory and country views *(Dave Braisted)*

STOKE WHARF [SO9468]

Navigation B60 4LB [Hanbury Rd (B4091), by Worcester & Birmingham Canal]: Friendly good value pub popular for good food inc Thurs paella night and (by prior arrangement) fantastic seafood platter, changing real ales, newly refurbished lounge *(Dave Braisted)*

STOKE WORKS [SO9365]

Boat & Railway B60 4EQ [Shaw Lane, by Bridge 42 of Worcester & Birmingham Canal]: Popular and unpretentious, with happy old-fashioned atmosphere, efficient service with a smile, Banks's and related ales, bargain generous lunchtime food, carvery restaurant in former skittle alley; pretty hanging baskets, pleasant waterside terrace *(Bob and Bridget Attridge, Dave Braisted)*

Bowling Green B60 4BH [a mile from M5 junction 5, via Stoke Lane; handy for Worcester & Birmingham Canal]: Attractively and comfortably refurbished, with good range of sensibly priced traditional food, Banks's Bitter and Mild, good atmosphere; big garden with beautifully kept bowling green *(Dave Braisted)*

STOURPORT ON SEVERN [SO8071]
Bridge DY13 8UX [Bridge St]: Friendly town
pub with cheap basket meals, Banks's and
St Austell Tribute; pleasant terrace, good
position *(Dave Braisted)*
Old Rose & Crown DY13 9PA [Worcester
Rd]: Banks's pub with interestingly carved bar
counter, reasonably priced food; handy for
Hartlebury Common Countryside Park
(Dave Braisted)

TENBURY WELLS [SO6168]
☆ *Peacock* WR15 8LL [Worcester Rd, Newnham
Bridge (A456 about 1½ miles E – so inn
actually in Shrops)]: Attractive 14th-c dining
pub under new management, good choice of
enjoyable food and of wines by the glass, good
friendly service, real ales, several separate
rooms, heavy black beams, big log fire in
panelled front lounge, comfortable kitchen
chairs and ex-pew settles, back family room,
pleasant dining room; terrace picnic-sets, lovely
setting by River Teme, good bedrooms *(LYM,
Chris Flynn, Wendy Jones)*
☆ *Pembroke House* WR15 8EQ [Cross St]:
16th-c upmarket beamed and timbered dining
pub, good atmosphere in well divided open-
plan layout, well above average reasonably
priced fresh food (not Sun evening or Mon)
from sandwiches up, generous helpings with
lots of veg, booking recommended evenings,
more elaborate menu then, friendly helpful
staff, Hobsons and a guest beer, woodburner;
open all day wknds *(Mr and Mrs J L Hall,
MLR, David and Lesley Elliott)*

UPHAMPTON [SO8464]
Fruiterers Arms WR9 0JW [off A449 N of
Ombersley]: Homely country local (looks like a
private house with a porch) brewing its own
good Cannon Royall ales, also farm cider,
inexpensive fresh lunchtime sandwiches, simple
rustic Jacobean panelled bar serving lounge
with comfortable armchairs, beamery, log fire,
lots of photographs and local memorabilia; no
music, plain pool room; garden, some seats out
in front *(Pete Baker)*

UPTON UPON SEVERN [SO8540]
Swan WR8 0JD [Waterside]: Popular low-
beamed main bar in charming riverside setting,
Banks's, Marstons Pedigree and guest beers,
two open fires and boating memorabilia,
quieter separate hotel lounge bar with sizeable
dining room off, good value generous standard
food, attentive staff; waterside garden with
summer barbecues, bedrooms *(P Dawn, BB,
Nick and Lynne Carter)*
White Lion WR8 0HJ [High St]: Good value
well presented food and good changing real
ales in family-run hotel's pleasant bar,
comfortable lounge and restaurant, warm and
relaxing atmosphere, sofas, stag's head and old
prints; covered courtyard, bedrooms *(Nick and
Lynne Carter, BB)*

WEATHEROAK HILL [SP0574]
☆ *Coach & Horses* B48 7EA [Icknield St –
coming S on A435 from Wythall roundabout,
filter right off dual carriageway a mile S, then
in village turn left towards Alvechurch; not far
from M42 junction 3]: Roomy and cheery

country pub brewing its own good
Weatheroak beers, also good choice of others
from small breweries, farm ciders, plush-seated
low-ceilinged two-level dining bar, tiled-floor
proper public bar, bargain lunches, also
modern restaurant with well spaced tables;
piped music; children allowed in eating area,
plenty of seats out on lawns and upper terrace,
open all day wknds *(Pete Baker,
Dave Braisted, LYM, W H and E Thomas)*

WELLAND [SO8039]
☆ *Anchor* WR13 6LN [Drake St (A4104 just
over ½ mile E of B4208 crossroads)]: Pretty
flower-covered Tudor cottage with wide choice
of enjoyable food from baguettes and baked
potatoes up, chatty L-shaped bar with some
armchairs, comfortable and nicely set
spreading no smoking dining area with fine
views, five or six real ales, all wines available
by the glass (large measures for wine and
spirits), shove-ha'penny, dominoes, chess,
Jenga; may be unobtrusive piped music, and
service, normally friendly and efficient, may
falter on busy evenings; children in restaurant,
charming garden, field for tents or caravans,
appealingly furnished bedrooms (normally no
access outside opening hours), cl Sun evening
*(Bernard Stradling, Dennis and Gill Keen,
Julia and Richard Tredgett, David and
Ruth Shillitoe, Chris Flynn, Wendy Jones,
Sara Fulton, Roger Baker, LYM, Barry Collett,
Sue Holland, Dave Webster, Dave Braisted,
Canon George Farran)*

WILDMOOR [SO9675]
Wildmoor Oak B61 0RB [a mile from M5
junction 4 – 1st left off A491 towards
Stourbridge; Top Rd]: Busy friendly local with
Adnams, good choice of reasonably priced
generous food, separate eating area; some live
music, no under-5s; small sloping terrace and
garden *(Ian and Sharon Shorthouse)*

WILLERSEY [SP1039]
New Inn WR12 7PJ [Main St]: Friendly and
attractive old stone-built local, good value
straightforward food all day from good range
of sandwiches up, Donnington ales, ancient
flagstones, darts and raised end area in simple
main bar, pool in separate public bar
(Pete Baker)

WORCESTER [SO8554]
Cardinals Hat WR1 2NA [Friar Street; just off
A44 near cathedral]: Several small ancient-
feeling rooms with great character, service
quick and friendly even when busy, real ales
(LYM, Sarah Ling)
Green Man WR1 1JL [The Tything]: Recently
renovated building dating from 15th c, décor
and fittings to reflect its age, varied food at
upmarket prices (it's just across from the Law
Courts), five real ales, extensive wine list,
friendly service, front bar, back dining area,
second upstairs dining room; jazz and blues
Sun night *(Chris Flynn, Wendy Jones)*
Plough WR1 2HN [Fish St]: Cosy local
reopened under friendly new licensees, two
rooms off entrance lobby, good simple wkdy
food 12-5.30 (not Sun/Mon) using local
produce, home-baked bread for sandwiches,

four good changing real ales, farm cider; tables out on new decking in pleasant back courtyard, open all day *(Pete Baker, Dr B and Mrs P B Baker, Sarah Ling)*

WYRE PIDDLE [SO9647]

☆ *Anchor* WR10 2JB [off A4538 WNW of Evesham]: Riverside pub with new covered back decking and lots of tables on the floodlit lawn (River Avon moorings), big airy back bar, Banks's Bitter, Marstons Pedigree,

Timothy Taylors Landlord and local Wyre Piddle, neat little lounge with comfortable new leather sofas and armchairs and flame-effect gas fire in the inglenook, no smoking dining area, popular food (not Sun evening) from baguettes up; children and dogs welcome, open all day (till 1 Sat); reports on new management please *(Paul and Gloria Howell, John Saville, Theo, Anne and Jane Gaskin, Dennis Jenkin)*

Post Office address codings confusingly give the impression that some pubs are in Worcestershire, when they're really in Gloucestershire, Herefordshire, Shropshire, or Warwickshire (which is where we list them).

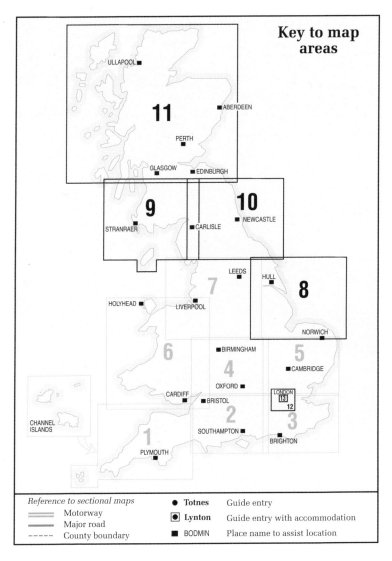

Key to map areas

ULLAPOOL

11

ABERDEEN

PERTH

GLASGOW

EDINBURGH

9

STRANRAER

10

CARLISLE

NEWCASTLE

LEEDS

HULL

8

HOLYHEAD

7

LIVERPOOL

NORWICH

6

BIRMINGHAM

5

OXFORD

CAMBRIDGE

CARDIFF

BRISTOL

LONDON
13
12

4

2

3

CHANNEL
ISLANDS

1

SOUTHAMPTON

BRIGHTON

PLYMOUTH

Reference to sectional maps

———— Motorway
———— Major road
– – – – County boundary

● **Totnes**   Guide entry
◉ **Lynton**   Guide entry with accommodation
■ **BODMIN**   Place name to assist location

MAPS IN THIS SECTION

For Maps 1 – 7 see earlier colour section

10

● **Thwing**

■ BRIDLINGTON

A614

A166

A165

North Dalton
◉

SE

Lund ●

A164

● **South Dalton**

● **Beverley**

EAST YORKSHIRE

A165

M62

A63

● **Hull**

SCUNTHORPE

M180

A180

■ GRIMSBY

A18

A46

● **Barnoldby le Beck**

A159

GAINSBOROUGH

A631

SK

A631

■ LOUTH

● **Rothwell**

A16

Ingham ●

A57

A46

A158

A158

● **Belchford**

A16

Lincoln ●

LINCOLNSHIRE

A158

■ MABLETHORPE

■ SKEGNESS

A155

TF

NEWARK ON TRENT

A15

◉ **Coningsby**

A16

A52

Dry Doddington
●

◉ **Hough-on-the-Hill**

BOSTON ■

A17

Allington
◉

A52

A17

A16

THE WASH

GRANTHAM

A52

Brancaster Staithe

Burnham Market

Holkham

◉ ● ◉

Woolsthorpe
◉

A1

● **Billingborough**

Thornham ◉

Ringstead ◉ **Stanhoe**

Burnham Thorpe
●

● **Surfleet**

SPALDING ■

A17

Snettisham ◉

South Creake
◉

LEICS

South Witham
◉

A151

A16

A149

A148

NORFOLK

Stretton ◉ ● **Clipsham**
◉

● **Stamford**

■ KINGS LYNN

Exton
◉

Terrington St John
●

WISBECH

A47

A10

5

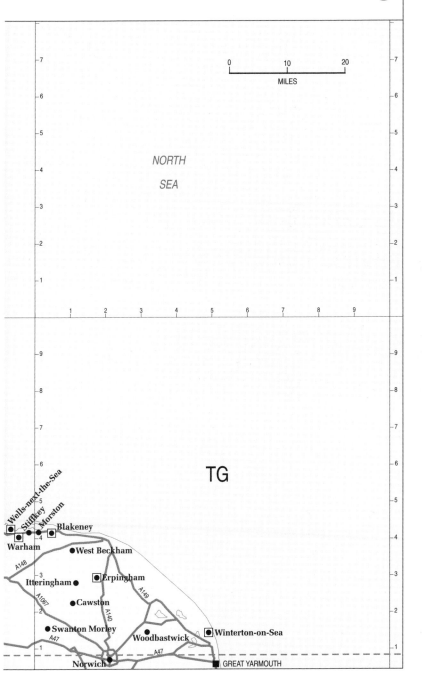

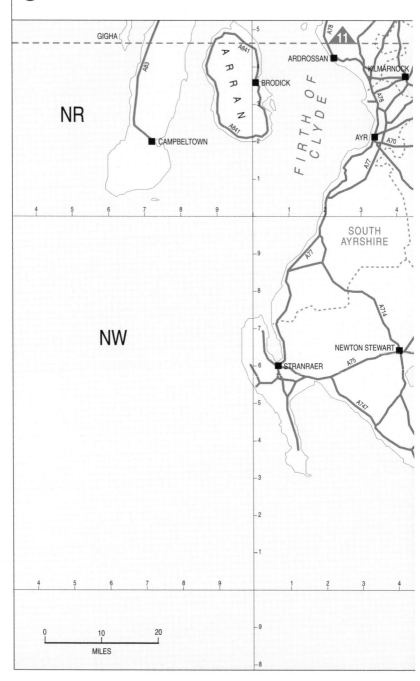

GIGHA

A83

A R R A N

A841

BRODICK

A841

NR

CAMPBELTOWN

ARDROSSAN

KILMARNOCK

11

A78

A78

F I R T H   O F   C L Y D E

AYR

A70

A77

SOUTH AYRSHIRE

A77

A714

A77

NEWTON STEWART

A75

STRANRAER

A747

NW

0   10   20
MILES

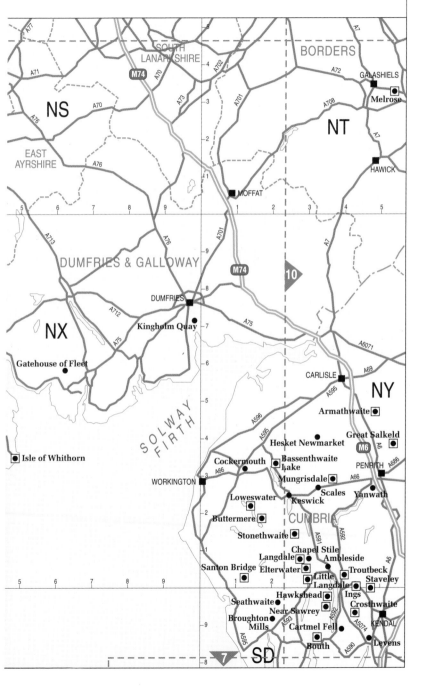

10

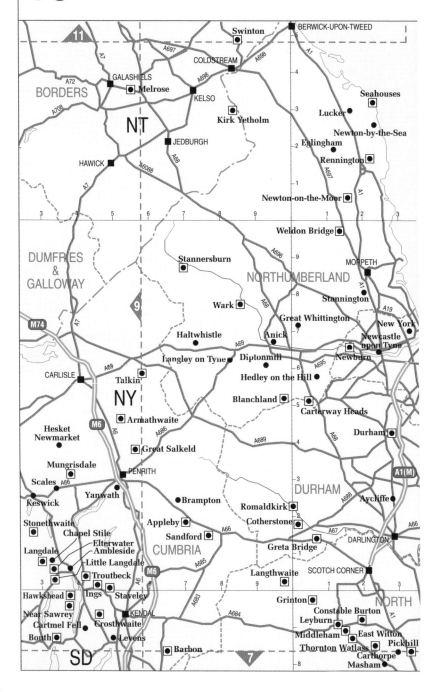

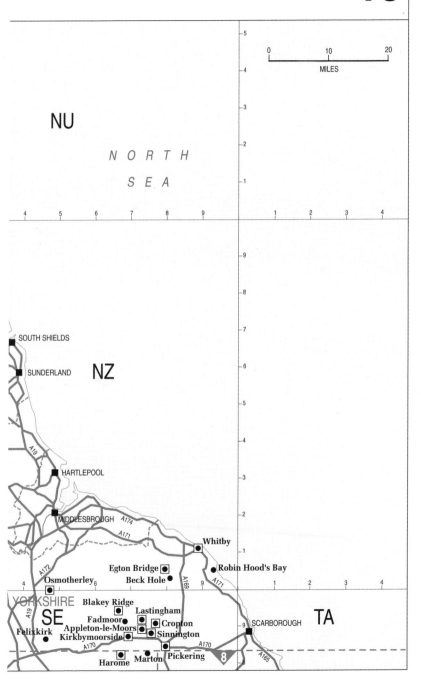

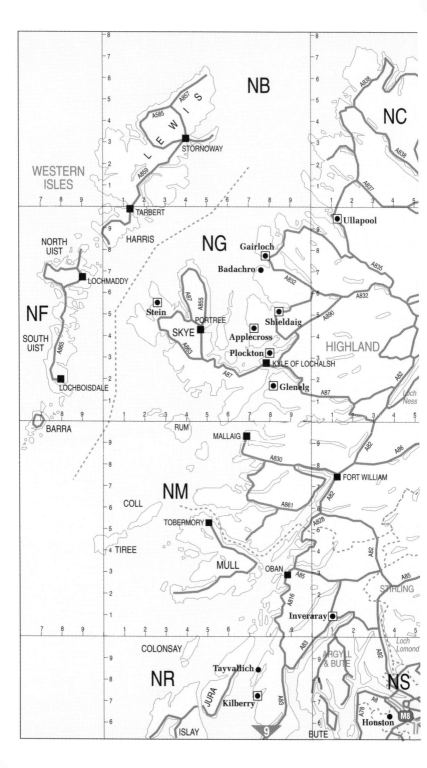

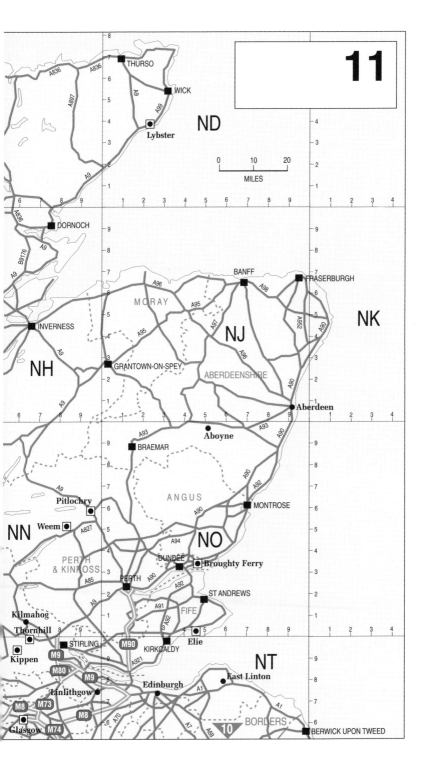

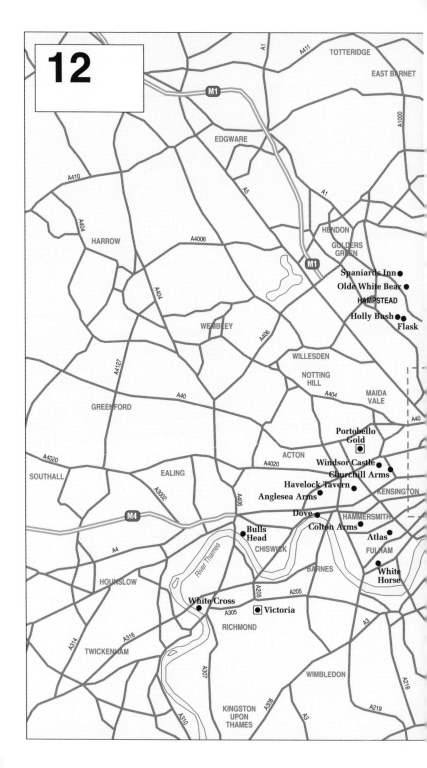

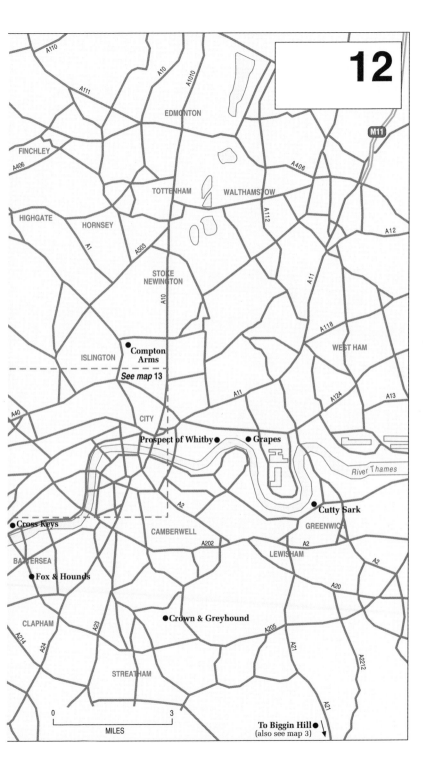

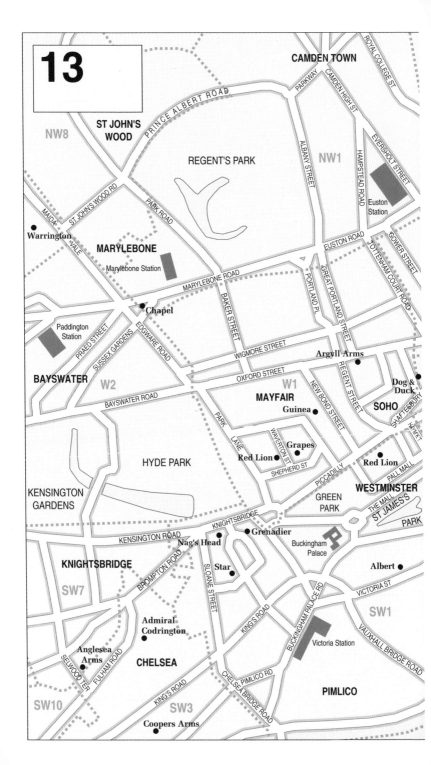

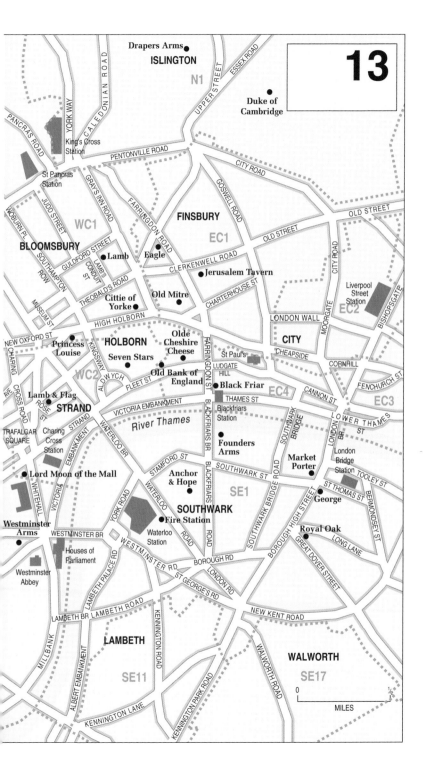

'Since I've discovered *The Good Pub Guide* I haven't had to suffer a bad pub again'
Simon Heptinstall, Mail on Sunday

'Easily the best.'
Time Out

'*The Good Pub Guide* is to alcohol what *Wisden* is to cricket.'
The Times

✳ Since it was first published 25 years ago, *The Good Pub Guide* has received many fabulous recommendations because, unlike other guide books, it is totally independent. We never take payment for entries.

✳ Pubs are inspected anonymously by the editorial team, and we rely on reports from readers to tell us whether pubs deserve to be in the next edition.

✳ Don't forget to report to us on any pubs you visit over the coming year. You can use the card in the middle of the book, the tear-out forms at the back, or you can send reports via our website: www.goodguides.co.uk

Write and tell us about your favourite pub!

We'll send you more forms (free) if you wish.
You don't need a stamp in the UK.
Simply write to us at:

The Good Pub Guide,
FREEPOST TN1569, WADHURST,
East Sussex TN5 7BR

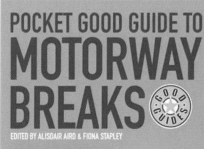

POCKET GOOD GUIDE TO
MOTORWAY BREAKS

EDITED BY ALISDAIR AIRD & FIONA STAPLEY

GOOD GUIDES

OVER 650 PLACES TO EAT, VISIT AND STAY

EASILY ACCESSIBLE FROM THE UK's MAIN ROADS

'Superb...contains hundreds of restaurants, cafés and places to stay that are in easy driving distance of the motorway'
Daily Express

'Saved my sanity... with a charming little eaterie just off the main drag'
Mail on Sunday

✳ Over 650 easy-to-reach, value-for-money places to eat, drink and visit

✳ Organised by major motorways and A-roads, with maps to show you how to get there

A brilliantly useful guide to good places to eat, drink, stay and visit – all easily accessible from motorways and main A-roads. Make life easier. Make life better. Buy your car a copy of the *Pocket Good Guide to Motorway Breaks*.

If you would like to order a copy of
Pocket Good Guide to Motorway Breaks (£5.99 each)
direct from Ebury Press (p&p free), please call our credit-card hotline on
01206 255 800
or send a cheque/postal order made payable to Ebury Press to
Cash Sales Department, TBS Direct,
Frating Distribution Centre, Colchester Road,
Frating Green, Essex CO7 7DW

Yorkshire

Even though this is such a massive area, we're always surprised to find quite such a diversity of interesting and worthwhile pubs here. One common factor seems to be the genuine friendliness of the landlords and landladies. This permeates not just simple walkers' pubs in fantastic scenery, and lively city pubs with a splendid range of ales, but also comfortable country inns, and smart, civilised dining places with ambitious food to match. Those on top form and much enjoyed by our readers this year include the Moors at Appleton-le-Moors (bustling and friendly, with a nice landlady), the Birch Hall at Beck Hole (unique sweetie-shop-cum-pub), the White Horse in Beverley (basic and gaslit), the Lion up on Blakey Ridge (well run and with lovely views and walks all around), the Wyvill Arms at Constable Burton (a popular dining pub with friendly staff), the White Lion at Cray (superb walking country and a warm welcome for all), the Tempest Arms at Elslack (bustling and enjoyable, with a new bedrooms extension this year), the Plough at Fadmoor (well run, neatly kept and very busy), the Carpenters Arms at Felixkirk (a smashing pub with quite a choice of interesting food), the General Tarleton at Ferrensby (some refurbishment enhancing this smart, civilised place), the Star at Harome (they still manage to keep a pubby bar despite much emphasis on the food and bedroom side), the Angel at Hetton (some changes but still very popular), the Olde White Harte in Hull (full of history – and cheap prices), the Queens Head at Kettlesing (with that subtle hidden ingredient that brings people back regularly), the Bay Horse at Kirk Deighton (very good food at this new entry), the Charles Bathurst at Langthwaite (a particular favourite – readers love staying here), the Chequers at Ledsham (elaborately described but enjoyable food), the Whitelocks in Leeds (unspoilt Victoriana), the Sair in Linthwaite (the own-brewed beers draw the crowds at weekends), the Queens Arms at Litton (a lovely little pub, full of charm, brewing its own good beers), the Maypole at Long Preston (this family-run new entry is a good warm-hearted all-rounder), the White Swan in Pickering (a smart coaching inn but with a proper pubby bar), the New Barrack in Sheffield (lots going on at weekends and with a fine range of beers), the Three Acres at Shelley (extremely popular for its restauranty food, but lacking any pretensions), the Fox & Hounds at Sinnington (a friendly welcome and enjoyable food), the Pipe & Glass at South Dalton (yet another new entry, reopened in spring 2006 with most enjoyable food), the St Vincent Arms at Sutton upon Derwent (a fine choice of real ales and hearty food in a particularly well run local), and the Sportsmans Arms at Wath in Nidderdale (the charming landlord has now been there 29 years; a super place to stay). There's no shortage of excellent food in Yorkshire pubs. More than two dozen have now qualified for our Food Award. For really special meals out you could head for the Plough at Fadmoor, the Carpenters Arms at Felixkirk, the General Tarleton at Ferrensby, the Shibden Mill in Halifax, the Star at Harome, the Bay Horse at Kirk Deighton, the Charles Bathurst at Langthwaite, the Sandpiper in Leyburn, the Wellington at Lund, the White Swan in Pickering, the Three Acres at Shelley, the Fox & Hounds at Sinnington, the Pipe & Glass at South Dalton, the Sportsmans Arms at Wath in Nidderdale, and the Blacksmiths at Westow. But it's the Three Acres at Shelley that takes the top title of Yorkshire Dining Pub of the Year. In the Lucky Dip section at the end of the chapter, pubs to note include the Fleece at Addingham, White Swan at Ampleforth, Craven Arms at Appletreewick, Falcon at Arncliffe, Kings Arms at Askrigg, Hare & Hounds at Burton Leonard (only an absence of recent reader reports keeps this nice pub out of the main entries this year), Falcon at Cloughton, Olde Sun at Colton, George at Easingwold, Coverbridge Inn at East Witton, Black Horse at Giggleswick, Royal Oak at Gillamoor, Kings Head in Kettlewell, Blind Jacks in Knaresborough, Fox & Rabbit at Lockton, Farmers Arms at Muker, Old Bore at Rishworth, Tan Hill Inn, Blue Bell at Weaverthorpe, restauranty Wensleydale Heifer at West Witton, Golden Ball at Whiston, and Ackhorne, Black Swan and Blue Bell among York's other many good pubs. Drinks prices in the area are well below the national average, with Sam Smiths the Tadcaster brewery setting a notable low-pricing example. Quite a few pubs here brew their own good value beers, and there is a large number of local brewers. The one you'll find most commonly supplying the area's better pubs is Black Sheep, with Theakstons (owned by other branches of the same family) also common. Other local brewers which we found supplying at least some of our main entries with their cheapest beers were Timothy Taylor, Clarks, Brown Cow, Wold Top and Copper Dragon. The national brands John Smiths, Courage and Tetleys are produced in Yorkshire.

ALNE SE4965 Map 7
Blue Bell
Off A19 NW of York; Main Street; YO61 1RR

Doing particularly well at the moment, this no smoking and rather restauranty dining pub has two linked front areas with neatly set tables, a coal fire on the left and a coal-fired stove on the right, old engravings on cream walls, and stripped joists in the dark red ceiling. The furnishings are an appealing mix of styles and periods; on the left there's a splendid big bow-window seat around one good-sized round table. Behind is a small sun lounge with a sofa, and beyond that, forming an L, what looks an older part of the building, with dark tables on quarry tiles; a little dickensian bow window opens on to a sort of external corridor around the angle of this L. Black Sheep, John Smiths and Timothy Taylors Landlord on handpump, and friendly, helpful service. Popular food includes an early bird menu (weekdays between 6 and 7pm; two-course £10, three-course £12), as well as home-made soup or chicken liver pâté (£4.50), black pudding tower with caramelised apple and fruit chutney (£4.75), pies such as steak and mushroom in ale or chicken and leek (£8.95), thai fishcakes with pineapple, coriander and apple salsa (£9.75), cheese and vegetable strudel, pork fillet with leeks and bacon or baked cod fillet with a fresh herb crust and parsley sauce (£9.95), slow-braised lamb shoulder with minted gravy (£11.95), twice-roasted half duckling with caramelised orange and marmalade sauce (£12.50), beef stroganoff (£12.95), and puddings such as well liked lemon and ginger crunch. A neat garden behind has metal tables and chairs on a small terrace, and some pretty arbour seats. *(Recommended by Pat and Graham Williamson, Jon and Siobhan Brier, Mr and Mrs P M Jennings, John Knighton)*

Free house ~ Licensee Michael Anson ~ Real ale ~ Bar food (6-9; 12-8 Sun) ~ Restaurant ~ (01347) 838331 ~ Children welcome ~ Open 12-2, 6-11; 12-8 Sun; closed Mon and Tues lunchtimes

---

If we don't specify bar meal times for a main entry, these are normally 12-2 and 7-9; we do show times if they are markedly different.

APPLETON-LE-MOORS SE7388 Map 10

Moors

Village N of A170 just under 1½ miles E of Kirkby Moorside; YO62 6TF

Now totally no smoking, this little stone-built pub is a very nice place to stay
with super breakfasts, cosy bedrooms, and a welcoming, helpful landlady. It's all
strikingly neat and surprisingly bare of the usual bric-a-brac. Sparse decorations
include just a few copper pans and earthenware mugs in a little alcove, a couple
of plates, one or two pieces of country ironwork, and a delft shelf with miniature
whiskies; the whiteness of walls and ceiling is underlined by the black beams and
joists, and the bristly grey carpet. Perfect for a cold winter evening, there's a nice
built-in high-backed stripped settle next to an old kitchen fireplace, and other
seating includes an unusual rustic seat for two cleverly made out of stripped
cartwheels; plenty of standing space. The games room has been converted into an
extra dining area. To the left of the bar, you'll probably find a few regulars
chatting on the backed padded stools: Black Sheep and Theakstons Black Bull on
handpump, and quite a few malt whiskies. Darts and board games. Well liked
food could include home-made soup (£2.95), home-made chicken liver pâté
(£3.95), lasagne (£8.45), celeriac and blue cheese pie (£8.50), pheasant casserole
(£8.95), fresh tuna steak with tomato salsa (£9.25), lemon and saffron chicken or
pork medallions with a ginger sauce (£9.50), lamb shoulder with an apricot
stuffing and a honey and mint glaze (£9.75), steaks (from £11.95), daily specials,
and home-made puddings (from £3.50). There are tables in the walled garden
with quiet moors views, and moors walks straight from here to Rosedale Abbey
or Hartoft End, as well as paths to Hutton-le-Hole, Cropton and Sinnington.
(Recommended by Michael and Ann Cole, Lynda Lloyd, Colin and Dot Savill,
Roger Hobson)

Free house ~ Licensee Janet Frank ~ Real ale ~ Bar food (see opening hours) ~ Restaurant
~ No credit cards ~ (01751) 417435 ~ Children welcome ~ Dogs allowed in bar and
bedrooms ~ Open 7-11; 12-2, 7-11 Fri, Sat and Sun; closed all day Mon in winter; closed
Mon, Tues, Weds, Thurs lunchtimes all year ~ Bedrooms: £35B/£56B

ASENBY SE3975 Map 7

Crab & Lobster ♀ 🛏

Village signposted off A168 – handy for A1; YO7 3QL

This bustling and interesting place is handy for the A1. It's totally no smoking this
year, and the rambling, L-shaped bar has an interesting jumble of seats from
antique high-backed and other settles through settees and wing armchairs heaped
with cushions, to tall and rather theatrical corner seats; the tables are almost as
much of a mix, and the walls and available surfaces are quite a jungle of bric-a-
brac, with standard and table lamps and candles keeping even the lighting
pleasantly informal. There's also a dining pavilion with big tropical plants,
nautical bits and pieces, and Edwardian sofas. Good bar food includes thai crab
cakes with oriental slaw and noodle salad or risotto of artichoke, fennel and
button mushrooms with parmesan-crusted chicken fingers (£5.50; main course
£11), terrine of duck confit and ham hock and foie gras with pear and saffron
chutney (£6.30), mussels with ale, cabbage and bacon or a lunchtime club
sandwich (£7), baked queenie scallops with gruyère, cheddar, garlic and lemon
(from £7.50), natural cured haddock, bacon and cheese mash, poached egg, black
pudding fritters and wholegrain mustard (£13.50), breast of chicken stuffed with
wild mushrooms, local cheese and a wrapping of leek and courgette (£14), pesto-
roasted loin of lamb with a warm salad of italian vegetables (£16), and honey and
peppered breast of goosnargh duck with a parcel of leg meat and sweet onions and
port gravy (£17). Copper Dragon Golden Pippin and 1816 and John Smiths on
handpump, and quite a few wines by the glass; piped music. The gardens have
bamboo and palm trees lining the paths, there's a gazebo at the end of the
walkways, and seats on a mediterranean-style terrace. The opulent bedrooms
(based on famous hotels around the world) are in the surrounding house which

has seven acres of mature gardens, and 180-metre golf hole with full practice facilities. More reports please. *(Recommended by Michael Doswell, Peter and Lesley Yeoward, Jack Morley)*

Vimac Leisure ~ Licensee Mark Spenceley ~ Real ale ~ Bar food ~ Restaurant ~ (01845) 577286 ~ Children welcome ~ Dogs allowed in bar and bedrooms ~ Lunchtime jazz Sun ~ Open 11.30-midnight ~ Bedrooms: /£150B

BECK HOLE   NZ8202   Map 10
Birch Hall
Signed off A169 SW of Whitby, from top of Sleights Moor; YO22 5LE

Happily unchanging and unique, this pub-cum-village-shop is in a beautiful steep valley and surrounded by marvellous walks; you can walk along the disused railway line from Goathland, and part of the path from Beck Hole to Grosmont is surfaced with mussel shells. There are two rooms (one is no smoking) with the shop selling postcards, sweeties and ice-creams in between, and hatch service to both sides. Furnishings are simple – built-in cushioned wall seats and wooden tables (spot the one with 136 pennies, all heads up, embedded in the top) and chairs on the floor (flagstones in one room, composition in the other), some strange items such as french breakfast cereal boxes and a tube of Macleans toothpaste priced 1/3d, and Black Sheep Bitter and Archers Foxy Lady and York Yorkshire Terrier on handpump; several malt whiskies. Bar snacks like locally made pies (£1.50), butties (£2.20), and home-made scones and cakes including their lovely beer cake (from 90p); friendly, welcoming staff; dominoes and quoits. Outside, an ancient oil painting of the view up the steeply wooded river valley hangs on the pub wall, there are benches out in front, and steps up to a little steeply terraced side garden. They have a self-catering cottage attached to the pub. *(Recommended by Paul Newberry, Michael and Ann Cole, Christopher Turner, John Fiander, P Dawn, the Didler, A Pickering, Pete Baker, Sue Demont, Tim Barrow, Pat and Tony Martin, David Carr, C E Reid)*

Free house ~ Licensee Glenys Crampton ~ Real ale ~ Bar food (available during all opening hours) ~ No credit cards ~ (01947) 896245 ~ Children in small family room ~ Dogs allowed in bar ~ Open 11-11; 12-10.30 Sun; 11-3, 7.30-11 in winter; closed winter Mon evening

BEVERLEY   TA0340   Map 8
White Horse   £
Hengate, close to the imposing Church of St Mary's; runs off North Bar; HU17 8BN

Quite without frills, this is a pub for those who like determinedly traditional and unspoilt places. It is known locally as 'Nellies' and has a carefully preserved Victorian feel, with the basic but very atmospheric little rooms huddled together around the central bar: brown leatherette seats (high-backed settles in one little snug) and basic wooden chairs and benches on bare floorboards, antique cartoons and sentimental engravings on the nicotine-stained walls, a gaslit pulley-controlled chandelier, a deeply reverberating chiming clock, and open fires – one with an attractively tiled old fireplace. Well kept and very cheap Sam Smiths OB on handpump, and simple food such as sandwiches, bangers and mash or pasta provençale (£3.95), steak in ale pie (£4.50), lasagne (£4.95), beef goulash or somerset pork (£5.50), and puddings like spotted dick and custard (£2). A separate games room has darts, games machine, trivia, bar billiards and two pool tables; skittle alley. Upstairs, there's a large no smoking area with a sideboard full of children's toys and an open fire. John Wesley preached in the back yard in the mid 18th c. *(Recommended by Len Beattie, John Wooll, David Carr, the Didler, Pete Baker, Mark Walker)*

Sam Smiths ~ Manager Anna ~ Real ale ~ Bar food (10.30-2.45 Mon-Sat; no food Sun) ~ No credit cards ~ (01482) 861973 ~ Children welcome away from bar and adjacent lounge area until 8pm ~ Dogs allowed in bar ~ Open 11-11; 12-10.30 Sun

BLAKEY RIDGE   SE6799   Map 10

Lion ▧ ⇔

From A171 Guisborough—Whitby follow Castleton, Hutton le Hole signposts; from A170 Kirkby Moorside—Pickering follow Keldholm, Hutton le Hole, Castleton signposts; OS Sheet 100 map reference 679996; YO62 7LQ

As this busy pub is open all day it makes a useful stop for thirsty walkers – there are plenty of surrounding hikes and some stunning views; the Coast to Coast Footpath is close by. If you are thinking of staying you must book weeks in advance. The beamed and rambling bars have warm open fires, a few big high-backed rustic settles around cast-iron-framed tables, lots of small dining chairs, a nice leather settee, and stone walls hung with some old engravings and photographs of the pub under snow (it can easily get cut off in winter). Generous helpings of good basic bar food include lunchtime sandwiches (from £3.45) and filled baked potatoes (from £3.45), as well as soup or giant yorkshire pudding with gravy (£2.50), home-cooked ham and egg, home-made lasagne, beef curry, battered cod or leek and mushroom crumble (all £7.95), daily specials such as home-made steak in ale pie (£7.95), duckling with peach and apricot stuffing (£8.95), and beef stroganoff (£10.95), and puddings like hot chocolate fudge cake or treacle roly-poly (£3.25); the dining rooms are no smoking. Greene King Old Speckled Hen, John Smiths, and Theakstons Best, Old Peculier, Black Bull and XB on handpump; piped music and games machine. *(Recommended by Mark and Ruth Brock, Dr David Cockburn, Sarah and Peter Gooderham, Dr D J and Mrs S C Walker, Cathryn and Richard Hicks, Tony and Penny Burton, Peter Coxon, Sylvia and Tony Birbeck)*

Free house ~ Licensee Barry Crossland ~ Real ale ~ Bar food (12-10) ~ Restaurant ~ (01751) 417320 ~ Children welcome ~ Dogs allowed in bar and bedrooms ~ Open 10am-11pm ~ Bedrooms: £18(£38.50B)/£50(£62B)

BOROUGHBRIDGE   SE3966   Map 7

Black Bull ♀

St James Square; B6265, just off A1(M); YO51 9AR

For many centuries, this attractive old town pub has been looking after people travelling between Scotland and England – it's handy for the A1. The main bar area has a big stone fireplace and brown leather seats, and is served through an old-fashioned hatch; there's also a cosy snug with traditional wall settles. The restaurant and tap room are no smoking. Well liked bar food includes soup (£3.25), sandwiches (from £3.25; hot cajun chicken with sweet chilli and mustard mayo £5.50), deep-fried mushrooms with a blue cheese dressing (£5.95), smoked salmon and scrambled eggs on toasted brioche (£6.95), beef curry (£7.75), thai beef strips with egg noodles and stir-fried vegetables in a hot and sour sauce (£7.95), tuna loin (£10.25), steaks (from £14.25), daily specials, and puddings like jam sponge or dark treacle tart (£3.25). John Smiths, Theakstons and Timothy Taylors Landlord on handpump, ten wines by the glass and quite a few malt whiskies; dominoes and chess. The two borzoi dogs are called Charlie and Sadie, and the cat Mimi; the local mummers perform here on New Year's Day. The hanging baskets are lovely. *(Recommended by Ian and Nita Cooper, Anthony Barnes, the Didler, J V Dadswell, Janet and Peter Race)*

Free house ~ Licensees Anthony and Jillian Burgess ~ Real ale ~ Bar food (12-2(2.30 Sun), 6-9) ~ Restaurant ~ (01423) 322413 ~ Children welcome ~ Dogs allowed in bar and bedrooms ~ Open 11-11; 11am-midnight Fri and Sat; 12-10.30 Sun ~ Bedrooms: £40S/£60S

We accept no free drinks, meals or payment for inclusion. We take no advertising, and are not sponsored by the brewing industry – or by anyone else.
So all reports are independent.

BRADFIELD SK2392 Map 7

Strines Inn

From A57 heading E of junction with A6013 (Ladybower Reservoir) take first left turn (signposted with Bradfield) then bear left; with a map can also be reached more circuitously from Strines signpost on A616 at head of Underbank Reservoir, W of Stocksbridge; S6 6JE

In an area known as Little Switzerland, this isolated moorland inn was originally built as a manor house in 1275; superb scenery and surrounding walks. The main bar has a welcoming atmosphere and a good mix of customers, black beams liberally decked with copper kettles and so forth, quite a menagerie of stuffed animals, homely red-plush-cushioned traditional wooden wall benches and small chairs, and a coal fire in the rather grand stone fireplace. A room off on the right has another coal fire, hunting photographs and prints, and lots of brass and china, and on the left is another similarly furnished room; two rooms are no smoking. Good bar food includes sandwiches (from £2.25; panini from £3.80), home-made soup (£2.95), filled baked potatoes (from £3.60), garlic mushrooms (£4.10), filled giant yorkshire puddings (from £6.25), liver and onions (£6.95), three-cheese and broccoli pasta (£6.95), pie of the day (£7.35), steaks (from £9.25), daily specials such as sweet chilli pork stir fry (£7.25), home-made fish pie (£7.50), and honey and dijon mustard chicken (£8.50), and puddings like apple and rhubarb crumble or chocolate roulade (£3.30). Adnams Broadside, Mansfield Bitter and Marstons Pedigree on handpump, and several malt whiskies; piped music. The bedrooms have four-poster beds (one has an open log fire) and a dining table, as breakfast is served in your room. Fine views from the picnic-sets, a safely fenced in children's playground, and wandering peacocks. *(Recommended by Gerry Miller, the Didler, Peter F Marshall, JJW, CMW, Trevor and Judith Pearson, John and Joan Calvert, Greta and Christopher Wells, BOB)*

Free house ~ Licensee Bruce Howarth ~ Real ale ~ Bar food (12-2.30, 6-9 winter weekdays; all day weekends and summer weekdays) ~ (0114) 285 1247 ~ Children welcome ~ Dogs welcome ~ Open 10.30am-11pm; 10.30-3, 6-11 weekdays in winter; closed 25 Dec ~ Bedrooms: /£70B

BREARTON SE3261 Map 7

Malt Shovel 🍺

Village signposted off A61 N of Harrogate; HG3 3BX

To be sure of a seat, you must arrive at this 16th-c village pub promptly as they don't take reservations. Several heavily beamed rooms radiate from the attractive linenfold oak bar counter with plush-cushioned seats and a mix of tables, an ancient oak partition wall, tankards and horsebrasses, an open fire, and paintings by local artists (for sale) and lively hunting prints on the walls. The dining area is no smoking. Bar food includes specials such as a cheese board (£4.50), thai chicken curry (£7.95), bass (£9.50), and venison (£10.50), as well as pubby things like sandwiches (from £3.75), ploughman's (£6), meaty or vegetarian lasagne (£6.25), and sausage and mash (£6.95). Black Sheep Bitter, Daleside Bitter, Timothy Taylors Landlord and a couple of guests on handpump and 30 malt whiskies. You can eat outside on the small terrace where they have outdoor heaters. More reports please. *(Recommended by Peter Burton, Keith Wright, Ian and Nita Cooper, Pierre Richterich, Blaise Vyner, Paul Boot, G Dobson, Yana Pocklington, Patricia Owlett, Tony and Penny Burton, Mr and Mrs Staples, Mike Tucker, Jo Lilley, Simon Calvert, Peter and Jean Dowson)*

Free house ~ Licensees Jamie and Hayley Stewart ~ Real ale ~ Bar food (not Sun evening or Mon) ~ (01423) 862929 ~ Children welcome ~ Dogs welcome ~ Open 11.45-3, 6.45(7 Sun)-11; closed Mon; first two weeks Jan

---

Virtually all pubs in this book sell wine by the glass. We mention wines if they are a cut above the average.

BURN   SE5928   Map 7

Wheatsheaf 🍺 £

A19 Selby—Doncaster; Main Road; YO8 8LJ

There's masses to look at in this roadside mock-Tudor pub and it is all very nicely done up: gleaming copper kettles, black dagging shears, polished buffalo horns and the like around its good log and coal fire (and a drying rack with bunches of herbs above it), decorative mugs above one bow-window seat, and cases of model vans and lorries on the cream walls. The highly polished pub tables in the partly divided open-plan bar have comfortable seats around them, and the atmosphere is welcoming and chatty, with a friendly landlord and neat efficient young staff. Good value food might include sandwiches or burgers (£2.25), ploughman's (£2.95), lamb rogan josh, vegetarian dishes, lasagne, and chilli con carne (all £5.25), and sirloin steak (£6.95); notable fish and chips (OAPs £2.95; medium £4.50; jumbo £5.50), daily specials such as seafood platter or lamb shank (£5.95) and mixed grill (£8.95), and Sunday lunch (from £4.50). Brown Cow Bitter, Copper Dragon Golden Pippin, Ossett Pale Gold, John Smiths, and Timothy Taylors Landlord on handpump at attractive prices, over 50 malt whiskies, and australian wines at exceptionally low mark-ups. A pool table is out of the way on the left, cribbage, dominoes, games machine, TV, and there may be unobtrusive piped music. A small garden behind has picnic-sets on a heated terrace. *(Recommended by Matt Waite)*

Free house ~ Licensee Andrew Howdall ~ Real ale ~ Bar food (12-2 daily and 6.30-8.30 Thurs-Sat) ~ Restaurant ~ (01757) 270614 ~ Children welcome ~ Dogs welcome ~ Local live bands and theatre companies Weds or Sat evenings every two months ~ Open 12-11(midnight Sat and Sun)

CARTHORPE   SE3184   Map 10

Fox & Hounds 🍽 ☼

Village signposted from A1 N of Ripon, via B6285; DL8 2LG

With a friendly welcome and good food, it's not surprising that this neatly kept extended dining pub is so popular; best to book to be sure of a table. The cosy L-shaped bar has quite a few mistily evocative Victorian photographs of Whitby, a couple of nice seats by the larger of its two log fires, plush button-back built-in wall banquettes and chairs, plates on stripped beams, and some limed panelling; piped light classical music. There is some theatrical memorabilia in the corridors and an attractive high-raftered no smoking restaurant with lots of neatly black-painted farm and smithy tools. Bar food includes home-made soup (£3.45), grilled black pudding with caramelised apple and onion marmalade (£4.95), smoked salmon pâté (£5.25), fresh crab tartlet (£5.95), chicken filled with coverdale cheese in a creamy sauce (£10.95), pheasant breast with a pear and thyme stuffing wrapped in bacon with a red wine sauce (£11.95), fried bass on potato rösti with red pepper sauce (£12.95), daily specials like salmon fishcakes with a tomato salsa (£4.95), honey-roast ham hock terrine with home-made piccalilli (£5.25), steak and kidney pie (£9.45), half a guinea fowl with parsley and thyme stuffing, apple sauce and a bacon and rich gravy sauce (£10.95), and seafood platter (£14.95), and home-made puddings such as sticky ginger pudding with toffee sauce and honeycomb ice-cream, white chocolate and irish cream cheesecake with chocolate mocha ice-cream or iced apricot and pineapple soufflé (from £4.85). On Tuesdays to Thursdays they also offer a two-course (£12.95) and three-course (£14.95) set meal. Black Sheep and Worthingtons on handpump or tapped from the cask, and an extensive wine list. More reports please. *(Recommended by Janet and Peter Race, Jill and Julian Tasker, Peter Hacker)*

Free house ~ Licensees Vince and Helen Taylor, Howard and Bernie Fitzgerald ~ Real ale ~ Bar food (not Mon) ~ Restaurant ~ (01845) 567433 ~ Children in restaurant ~ Open 12-3, 7-11; closed Mon

CHAPEL LE DALE SD7477 Map 7

Hill Inn 🍺

B5655 Ingleton—Hawes, 3 miles N of Ingleton; LA6 3AR

You can be sure of a warm welcome from the friendly licensees here – but it is essential you phone and check their opening hours. There are old pine tables and benches on the stripped wooden floors, nice pictures on the walls, stripped-stone recesses, a warm log fire, and Black Sheep Best, Dent Aviator and Rambrau, and Theakstons Best on handpump. The dining room is no smoking, and there's a well worn-in sun lounge. Cooked by the licensees, the enjoyable food might include home-made soup (£3.65), ratatouille of mediterranean vegetables and chickpeas topped with grilled goats cheese (£9.50), chicken in a white wine, cream and tarragon sauce (£10.95), pork cooked with cider, apples and mushrooms or beef in ale casserole (£11.25), duck breast with a prune, orange, redcurrant and port jus (£12.95), and puddings such as warm chocolate pudding with a white chocolate sauce and home-made vanilla ice-cream, crème brûlée with an orange salad with home-made orange and yoghurt ice-cream and lemon tart with a raspberry coulis (£5.25). Fine views to Ingleborough and Whernside and wonderful remote walks. More reports please. *(Recommended by J Conti-Ramsden, Rona Murdoch, Paul and Anita Holmes)*

Free house ~ Licensee Sabena Martin ~ Real ale ~ Bar food (not Mon) ~ Restaurant ~ (015242) 41256 ~ Children have been allowed in restaurant but best to phone and check ~ Dogs welcome ~ Open 6.30-11(but you must ring to check these times); closed all Mon and maybe Tues-Fri lunchtimes ~ Bedrooms: /£65S

CONSTABLE BURTON SE1791 Map 10

Wyvill Arms 🍴 🍷 🍺

A684 E of Leyburn; DL8 5LH

The emphasis in this popular, no smoking dining pub is on the very good food but they do have a small bar area with a mix of seating, a finely worked plaster ceiling with the Wyvill family's coat of arms, and an elaborate stone fireplace. The second bar, where food is served, has semicircled, upholstered alcoves, hunting prints, and old oak tables; the reception area of this room includes a huge chesterfield which can seat up to eight people, another carved stone fireplace, and an old leaded church stained-glass window partition. Both rooms are hung with pictures of local scenes. Served by friendly, efficient staff, the enjoyable food includes lunchtime filled baguettes, soup (£3.50), smoked ham and three-cheese terrine with pear and apple chutney (£5.10), spicy noodles with suckling pig and asian greens (£5.45; main course £8.75), thai green pea and spinach risotto or vegetarian pasta (£5.65; main course £9), rarebit of smoked haddock with roast cherry tomatoes (£5.75), steak and onion pie (£9.45), gammon with eggs or with an orange, rum and raisin sauce (£9.75), fish and chips with home-made mushy peas (£9.25), thai green chicken curry with coconut rice (£10.50), slow-roast lamb shank (£12.95), and steaks (from £14.95). Black Sheep, John Smiths Bitter, Theakstons Best and a guest like Thwaites Lancaster Bomber on handpump and ten wines by the glass; darts, chess and dominoes, board games, and piped music. Several large wooden benches under large white parasols for outdoor dining. Constable Burton Gardens are opposite and worth a visit. *(Recommended by P and J Shapley, E D Fraser, Ian and Nita Cooper, John and Sylvia Harrop, G Dobson, B and M Kendall, Richard and Anne Ansell, Ben and Helen Ingram, Jack Morley, Mike and Jayne Bastin)*

Free house ~ Licensee Nigel Stevens ~ Real ale ~ Bar food ~ Restaurant ~ (01677) 450581 ~ Children welcome but with restrictions ~ Dogs allowed in bar and bedrooms ~ Open 11-3, 5.30-11 ~ Bedrooms: £50B/£75B

CRAY   SD9379   Map 7
White Lion 🍺 🛏

B6160, Upper Wharfedale N of Kettlewell; BD23 5JB

After a hike in the superb surrounding countryside, walkers and their well behaved dogs are made welcome in this no smoking former drovers' hostelry; the landlord can also advise about other walks in the area. The simply furnished bar has an open fire, seats around tables on the flagstone floor, shelves of china, iron tools, old painted metal adverts for animal feed and so forth, and a high dark beam-and-plank ceiling; there's also a back room. As well as lunchtime filled yorkshire puddings (from £3.30), filled baguettes (from £3.75), and ploughman's (£5), the enjoyable bar food might include home-made soup (£3.50), home-made chicken liver pâté (£3.95), home-made steak and mushroom casserole or baked goats cheese pie (£8.50), pork fillet in a honey and spiced mustard cream (£9.95), and home-made game casserole (£10.50); evening extras such as good smoked trout pâté or home-made chicken goujons with garlic mayonnaise (£4.25), lambs liver and onions with mustard mash (£8.50), roast duck breast with a white wine and red berry sauce (£10.50), and whole bass (£11.50), and puddings such as nice lemon meringue; best to book to be sure of a table in the bar. If you eat between 5.45 and 6.15pm you get a 20% discount on some items. Well kept Moorhouses Bitter, Timothy Taylors Landlord, and maybe Copper Dragon Golden Pippin and 1816 on handpump, nine wines by the glass, and around 20 malt whiskies; board games, ring the bull and giant Jenga. In fine weather, you can sit at picnic benches above the very quiet steep lane or on the great flat limestone slabs in the shallow stream which tumbles down opposite. *(Recommended by Mr and Mrs Maurice Thompson, Blaise Vyner, G Dobson, the Didler, Walter and Susan Rinaldi-Butcher, Tony and Betty Parker, Dr and Mrs M E Wilson, Richard, Peter F Marshall, Ann and Tony Bennett-Hughes, Lynda and Trevor Smith, W K Wood, Paul and AnitaHolmes)*

Free house ~ Licensees Kevin and Debbie Roe ~ Real ale ~ Bar food (12-2, 5.45-8.30) ~ (01756) 760262 ~ Children welcome ~ Dogs allowed in bar and bedrooms ~ Open 11-11; closed 25 Dec ~ Bedrooms: £50S/£65S

CRAYKE   SE5670   Map 7
Durham Ox

Off B1363 at Brandsby, towards Easingwold; West Way; YO61 4TE

The tale is that this is the hill which the Grand Old Duke of York marched his men up; the view from the hill opposite is marvellous. The old-fashioned lounge bar has an enormous inglenook fireplace, pictures and photographs on the dark red walls, interesting satirical carvings in its panelling (Victorian copies of medieval pew ends), polished copper and brass, and venerable tables and antique seats and settles on the flagstones. In the bottom bar is a framed illustrated account of the local history (some of it gruesome) dating back to the 12th c, and a large framed print of the original famous Durham Ox which weighed 171 stones. Bar food includes bar bites (not available Saturday evening or Sunday lunchtime) such as sandwiches (from £5.95), sticky ribs (£6.50), moules marinière (£6.95; main course £11.95), burgers (from £7.50), bangers and mash with onion gravy (£7.95), and haddock and chips (£8.95); also, home-made soup (£3.95), grilled black pudding with apple chutney and poached egg (£5.95), basil and ricotta gnocchi (£12.95), grilled free-range chicken breast (£14.45), steaks (from £16.95), daily specials like baked queen scallops with garlic and gruyère cream (£6.95; main course £10.95) and roast monkfish wrapped in pancetta with chorizo, ratatouille and mediterranean pesto (£16.95), and puddings such as marmalade bread and butter pudding or baked rhubarb and ginger cheesecake (from £4.95). The main bar and restaurant are no smoking; piped music and board games. Theakstons Best, Coopers Butt and IPA on handpump and 12 wines by the glass. There are seats outside on a terrace and in the courtyard, and the comfortable bedrooms are in converted farm buildings. *(Recommended by Andy and Jill Kassube, Brian and Pat Wardrobe, Peter Burton)*

Free house ~ Licensee Michael Ibbotson ~ Real ale ~ Bar food (12-2.30, 6-9.30(10 Sat; 8.30 Sun); not 25 Dec) ~ Restaurant ~ (01347) 821506 ~ Children welcome ~ Dogs allowed in bedrooms ~ Open 12-3, 6-11; 12-11 Sat and Sun ~ Bedrooms: £60B/£80B

CROPTON   SE7588   Map 10

New Inn 🍺 🛏️

Village signposted off A170 W of Pickering; YO18 8HH

Friendly staff, own-brew beers and tasty food continue to draw customers to this comfortably modernised village inn. The traditional village bar has Victorian church panels, terracotta and dark blue plush seats, lots of brass, and a small fire. A local artist has designed historical posters all around the no smoking downstairs conservatory that doubles as a visitor centre during busy times. Well kept Cropton Endeavour Ale, Honey Gold, King Billy, Monkmans Slaughter, Two Pints and Yorkshire Moors Bitter, and a guest like Theakstsons Best on handpump; several malt whiskies and wines by the glass. Bar food includes lunchtime sandwiches or ciabatta rolls (from £4.75), soup (£3.95), home-made salmon fishcakes with caper and lemon mayonnaise (£4.95), broccoli and stilton quiche (£7.95), ploughman's (from £8.25), beef and root vegetable pie or a sausage ring made with their own beer (£8.95), fish pie (£9.25), chicken tortilla wrap (£9.95), pork medallions in a calvados cream sauce (£10.25), and steaks (from £12.95). The elegant no smoking restaurant has locally made furniture and paintings by local artists. Darts, pool, juke box, TV and piped music. There's a neat terrace, a garden with a pond, and a brewery shop. *(Recommended by Michael and Ann Cole, Rosanna Luke, Matt Curzon, D Weston, Dr David Cockburn, Esther and John Sprinkle, O K Smyth, Christine and Phil Young, John and Sylvia Harrop, Sylvia and Tony Birbeck)*

Own brew ~ Licensee Philip Lee ~ Real ale ~ Bar food (12-2, 6-9) ~ Restaurant ~ (01751) 417330 ~ Children in family room, restaurant and pool room ~ Dogs allowed in bar and bedrooms ~ Open 11-11; 12-10.30 Sun ~ Bedrooms: £41B/£70B

EAST WITTON   SE1586   Map 10

Blue Lion 🍽️ 🍷 🛏️

A6108 Leyburn—Ripon; DL8 4SN

Not really the place for a casual drink, this dining pub is smart and rather civilised. The big squarish bar has high-backed antique settles and old windsor chairs on the turkey rugs and flagstones, ham-hooks in the high ceiling decorated with dried wheat, teazles and so forth, a delft shelf filled with appropriate bric-a-brac, several prints, sporting caricatures and other pictures on the walls, a log fire, and daily papers; the friendly labrador is called Archie. We and readers have very high expectations of the Blue Lion as it has been such a favourite for so long, but this year there have been two or three isolated reports of unsatisfactory service and even disappointing food. We trust that things will quickly be taken in hand so we can again take the highest standards for granted here. From a changing menu, the food might include sandwiches, home-made tagliatelle carbonara (£4.80; main course £9.80), chicken liver parfait or moules marinière (£5.25), warm onion and blue wensleydale cheese tart with tomato chutney (£5.85), salad of black pudding, smoked bacon and shallot topped with a poached egg (£6.25), beef and onion suet pudding with dark onion sauce (£12.95), poached fillet of smoked haddock with leek and mushroom sauce topped with gruyère cheese (£14.25), free-range chicken breast wrapped in parma ham with tarragon butter or slow-braised lamb shank (£14.95), and puddings such as raspberry crème brûlée or rich chocolate and hazelnut tart topped with Baileys cream (from £4.95). The restaurant is no smoking. Black Sheep Bitter, Theakstons Best and Worthingtons on handpump, and an impressive wine list with quite a few by the glass. Picnic-sets on the gravel outside look beyond the stone houses on the far side of the village green to Witton Fell, and there's a big, pretty back garden. Three new bedrooms were being added as we went to press. *(Recommended by S and N McLean, Anthony Longden, Blaise Vyner, Ian and Nita Cooper, Jon Forster, the Didler, David Hall, Stephen Woad, Peter Hacker,*

*Lynda and Trevor Smith, Rod Stoneman, Christopher J Darwent, Dr and Mrs T E Hothersall,
I A Herdman, Peter Abbott, Dr Peter Crawshaw, Jane Taylor, David Dutton, Neil and
Angela Huxter)*

Free house ~ Licensee Paul Klein ~ Real ale ~ Bar food ~ Restaurant ~ (01969) 624273 ~
Children welcome ~ Dogs allowed in bar and bedrooms ~ Open 11-11 ~
Bedrooms: £59.50S/£79S(£89B)

EGTON BRIDGE   NZ8005   Map 10

Horse Shoe

**Village signposted from A171 W of Whitby; via Grosmont from A169 S of Whitby;
YO21 1XE**

In summer particularly, the position of this charmingly placed inn is quite a draw.
It's a peaceful spot and the attractive gardens have pretty roses and mature
redwoods, and there are comfortable seats on a quiet terrace and lawn beside a
little stream (where there are ducks). Fishing is available on a daily ticket from
Egton Estates. The bar has old oak tables, high-backed built-in winged settles, wall
seats and spindleback chairs, a big stuffed trout (caught near here in 1913), pictures
on the walls, and a warm log fire; the restaurant is no smoking. Using some home-
grown produce, bar food includes lunchtime sandwiches (from £3.50; hot brie and
bacon baguette £5.50) and ploughman's (£6.50), as well as soup (£3.40), home-
made chicken liver pâté (£4.50), fish pie or lasagne (£8.90), bacon chops with
peach sauce (£9.20), steaks (from £14.25), and daily specials. Black Sheep and John
Smiths with guests from Copper Dragon and Durham on handpump, and 35 malt
whiskies; the area around the bar is no smoking. Darts, dominoes, board games,
and piped music. A different way to reach the pub is to park by the Roman
Catholic church, walk through the village and cross the River Esk by stepping
stones. Not to be confused with a similarly named pub up at Egton. *(Recommended
by Matt and Vicky Wharton, Greta and Christopher Wells, R Pearce, John Dwane, Pete Baker,
David Carr, Richard and Karen Holt, Mark and Angela Stephens, Derek and Sylvia Stephenson,
John and Yvonne Davies, Dr and Mrs R G J Telfer)*

Free house ~ Licensees Tim and Suzanne Boulton ~ Real ale ~ Bar food (not 25 Dec) ~
Restaurant ~ (01947) 895245 ~ Children in restaurant and small back family room only ~
Dogs allowed in bar ~ Open 11.30-3, 6.30-11; 11.30-11 Sat and Sun; 11.30-3, 6.30-11
winter Sat; 12-4, 7-10.30 Sun in winter ~ Bedrooms: /£50(£60S)

ELSLACK   SD9249   Map 7

Tempest Arms 🍽 ♀ 🍺

Village signposted just off A56 Earby—Skipton; BD23 3AY

A major bedroom extension is being added to this friendly pub that will include
luxury suites with balconies. It's a bustling, popular place with a genuinely warm
welcome and helpful, efficient staff. The series of quietly decorated areas has three
log fires (one in a dividing fireplace), comfortable plum or chocolate plush
cushioned armchairs, cushioned built-in wall seats, stools, and lots of tables; there's
also quite a bit of stripped stonework, prints on the cream walls, and perhaps
Molly the friendly black labrador. Several parts of the bar and the dining room are
no smoking; piped music in one area only, and winter darts and dominoes. Well
kept Black Sheep, Tetleys, Theakstons Best, Timothy Taylors Best, and guests like
Copper Dragon Golden Pippin and Wharfedale Folly Ale on handpump, ten wines
by two sizes of glass from a good list, and several malt whiskies. Very good food
from a menu that can be used for both the bar and restaurant might include soup
(£3.50), lunchtime sandwiches (from £4.75; breakfast ciabatta £7.50; bacon
muffin, fresh spinach, poached eggs and hollandaise £8.50), jellied rabbit with
smoked bacon, cumberland sauce and toasted brioche (£5.95), tiger prawns in beer
batter with warming curried dip (£6.50), steak and mushroom or fish pie, roast
vegetable suet pudding with caramelised onion gravy or local cumberland sausage
toad in the hole with rich gravy (all £8.95), chicken breast filled with blue cheese
and served with a leek and apple mousse and creamy mustard sauce (£9.95),

steaks (from £10.50), and daily specials such as crispy yorkshire pudding with rich onion gravy (£3.25), smoked haddock topped with sage rarebit (£6), aberdeen angus burger (£8.50), lambs liver and onion on bubble and squeak (£8.95), vegetable moussaka (£9.50), and beef curry (£9.95). Tables outside are largely screened from the road by a raised bank. *(Recommended by Mrs R A Cartwright, Karen Eliot, G Dobson, Steve Whalley, Trevor and Sylvia Millum, Jill and Julian Tasker, Fred and Lorraine Gill, Jo Lilley, Simon Calvert, Graham and Doreen Holden, Sheila Stothard)*

Free house ~ Licensees Martin and Veronica Clarkson ~ Real ale ~ Bar food (12-2.30, 6-9(9.30 Sat); 12-7.30 Sun) ~ Restaurant ~ (01282) 842450 ~ Children welcome ~ Dogs allowed in bedrooms ~ Open 11-11; 12-10.30 Sun ~ Bedrooms: £59.95B/£74.95B

FADMOOR SE6789 Map 10

Plough ⊕ ♀

Village signposted off A170 in or just W of Kirkbymoorside; YO62 7HY

As popular as ever, this is a well run and neatly kept dining pub with friendly licensees. The elegantly simple little rooms have richly upholstered furnishings, yellow walls, rugs on seagrass, Black Sheep Best and Tetleys on handpump, and an extensive wine list. Very good, interesting food includes home-made soup (£4.95; the chowder is super), home-made pressed farmhouse pork terrine with home-made fruit chutney (£5.50), fried black pudding with caramelised onions and sweet tomato coulis, fresh crab and prawn timbale with guacamole dip or fresh mango and brie puff pastry tartlet (£5.95), cod and pancetta fishcakes with sweet chilli and ginger dip or thai green vegetable curry (£8.95), breast of chicken stuffed with cream cheese, ham, garlic and herbs on fresh tagliatelle with a creamy basil sauce (£11.50), grilled seafood kebab with a spring onion and white wine sauce (£12.50), roast pork loin stuffed with spinach, bacon and wensleydale cheese (£12.95), griddled venison steak on redcurrant risotto rice with port jus (£14.50), and puddings such as home-made chocolate Baileys cheesecake with mango coulis, caramelised lemon tart with blueberry and crème fraîche ice-cream or banoffi pie drizzled with brandy caramel (£4.95); two-course set meal (£12.95; not Saturday evening or Sunday lunchtime). The dining area is no smoking; piped music. There are seats on the terrace. *(Recommended by David and Jane Hill, Walter and Susan Rinaldi-Butcher, Terry and Linda Moseley, R Pearce, Peter and Eleanor Kenyon, Stephen Woad, Christopher Turner)*

Holf Leisure Ltd ~ Licensee Neil Nicholson ~ Real ale ~ Bar food (12-1.45, 6.30-8.45; 12-1.45, 7-8.30 Sun) ~ Restaurant ~ (01751) 431515 ~ Children allowed but must eat early in evening ~ Open 12-2.30, 6.30-11; 12-2.30, 7-10.30 Sun; closed 25 and 26 Dec, 1 Jan

FELIXKIRK SE4785 Map 10

Carpenters Arms ⊕ ♀

Village signposted off A170 E of Thirsk; YO7 2DP

In a picturesque small moors-edge village, this is a smashing pub – totally no smoking now – run by warmly friendly licensees. There are three or four cosy areas that ramble around the bar counter (made partly from three huge casks), with dark beams and joists hung with carpentry tools and other bric-a-brac, comfortable seats around tables with check tablecloths and little lighted oil burners, and a couple of huge japanese fans by the stone fireplace; one area is no smoking. Good, enjoyable food includes sandwiches, a bistro menu with all dishes at £8.95 (not Saturday evening or Sunday lunchtime) such as home-made salmon fishcake with wilted spinach and fish cream sauce, indonesian clay-baked chicken, bacon with almonds and sultanas, spinach and field mushroom pasta, and home-made steak and mushroom in ale pie; there's also potted duck, spiced apple chutney and toasted sourdough bread (£4.95), twice-baked cheese soufflé (£5.95), cracked wheat, roasted red pepper and fennel salad with olives and mint (£9.95), fillet of bream with a prawn, herb and parmesan risotto (£12.25), roast rump of lamb, grilled aubergine, rocket, chilli and preserved lemon (£14.50), daily specials like a warm salad of chicken livers and bacon (£4.95), confit of duck with home-made black pudding with toffee apples and oranges (£8.95), home-made fish pie (£9.95), and chargrilled rib-eye steak with chorizo (£13.95), and puddings such as vanilla crème brûlée, chocolate nemesis or apple jelly with rhubarb (£4.50). Set lunch menu – two courses £10.95, three courses £12.95. Black Sheep, Moorhouses Premium Bitter, John Smiths and Timothy Taylors Landlord on handpump, and a good wine list. The two dalmatians are called Lola and Lloyd. The church is prettily floodlit at night. *(Recommended by J Crosby, Judith and Edward Pearson, Peter and Jean Dowson, Edward and Deanna Pearce, Walter and Susan Rinaldi-Butcher, Michael Butler, Dr Ian S Morley)*

Free house ~ Licensee Karen Bumby ~ Real ale ~ Bar food (not Sun evening or Mon) ~ Restaurant ~ (01845) 537369 ~ Children welcome ~ Open 11.30-3, 6.30-11; 12-3 Sun; closed Sun evening, Mon and 25 Dec

FERRENSBY   SE3761   Map 7

General Tarleton 🍴 🍷 🛏

A655 N of Knaresborough; HG5 0QB

The good, interesting food remains the chief draw to this rather smart and comfortable old coaching inn – totally no smoking this year. The beamed and carpeted bar has brick pillars dividing up the several different areas to create the occasional cosy alcove, some exposed stonework, and neatly framed pictures of staff on the red walls; there are new leather chairs around wooden tables, a big open fire, and a door leading out to a pleasant tree-lined garden – which also has new furniture; seats in a covered courtyard, too. Enjoyable dishes include parfait of chicken livers and foie gras with cumberland sauce (£4.95), crisp tomato tart with grilled goats cheese (£5.75), queenie scallops with gruyère and cheddar cheese, garlic, chilli, lemon and pine nuts (£6.70; main course £9.95), sausages with savoury pudding (£8.50), roast butternut squash and pumpkin cannelloni with a carrot and lemongrass broth or lunchtime open sandwiches (£8.95), beer-battered fish with tartare sauce (£9.95), confit of dales lamb with thyme and tomato jus (£12.50), rib-eye steak with béarnaise sauce, daily specials such as half a dozen oysters (£8.95), seared tuna steak with tuscan vegetables and salsa verde (£11.75), and dressed whitby crab salad with lemon mayonnaise (£12.75), and puddings like lemon tart or chocolate sponge layer with pralines and a coffee bean sauce (from £4.95). Black Sheep Best and Timothy Taylors Landlord on handpump, over 20 good wines by the glass, and quite a few coffees. The bedrooms are being refurbished. *(Recommended by R E Dixon, June and Ken Brooks, Michael Butler, Blaise Vyner, Janet and Peter Race, A Allcock, Judith and Edward Pearson, David and Pam Lewis)*

Free house ~ Licensee John Topham ~ Real ale ~ Bar food (12-2.15, 6-9.15(8.30 Sun)) ~ Restaurant ~ (01423) 340284 ~ Children welcome ~ Dogs allowed in bedrooms ~ Open 12-3, 6-11(10.30 Sun) ~ Bedrooms: £85B/£97B

GOOSE EYE   SE0240   Map 7

Turkey 🍺

Just S of Laycock on road to Oakworth and Haworth, W of Keighley; OS Sheet 104 map reference 028406; BD22 0PD

It's worth the trip to reach this pleasant pub tucked away down high-walled lanes at the bottom of a steep valley. There are various cosy and snug alcoves, roaring winter log fires, brocaded upholstery, walls covered with pictures of surrounding areas, and a friendly landlord and locals; the restaurant is no smoking. You can visit their microbrewery – they ask for a donation for Upper Wharfedale Fell Rescue: Turkey Bitter, John Peel and winter Dark Mild; they have these and three changing guest beers on handpump. Over 40 whiskies. Generous helpings of decent, straightforward bar food include home-made soup (£2.75), sandwiches (from £3.75), home-made pie (£6.75), steaks (from £8), home-made daily specials (from £6), and puddings (from £2.40); two-course Sunday lunch (£7.40). Piped music, and a separate games area with pool, games machine and TV. More reports please. *(Recommended by Greta and Christopher Wells)*

Own brew ~ Licensee Harry Brisland ~ Real ale ~ Bar food (12-2, 6-9; all day Sun; not Mon or Tues lunchtimes) ~ Restaurant ~ (01535) 681339 ~ Children welcome until 8.30pm ~ Dogs allowed in bar ~ Live entertainment first and third Sun of month ~ Open 12-3, 5.30-11; 12-11 Fri, Sat and Sun; closed Mon and Tues lunchtimes

GRINTON SE0598 Map 10
Bridge Inn 🍺 🛏️
B6270 W of Richmond; DL11 6HH

As this pretty Swaledale village is surrounded by good walks, the sign here welcoming dogs and muddy boots is much appreciated. The cheerful gently lit red-carpeted bar has bow window seats and a pair of stripped traditional settles among more usual pub seats, all well cushioned, a good log fire, Jennings Cumberland, Dark Mild, Cocker Hoop and a guest on handpump, nice wines by the glass, and a good collection of malt whiskies. On the right a few steps take you down into a dark red room with darts, TV, board games, a well lit pool table, and piped music. As well as lunchtime filled baguettes (£4.95) and filled baked potatoes (from £4.25), the well liked food includes soup (£3.10), crispy whitebait with a sherry salsa (£3.95), chicken liver pâté with spicy red onion marmalade (£4.95), cumberland sausage with onion gravy (£7.25), cod in cider and dill batter, chicken in beer masala with onion bhajis, steak in ale pie or aubergine and wild mushroom tower (all £7.95), gammon and egg (£8.95), sirloin steak (£14.25), and specials such as lamb casserole with minted dumplings (£8.95), roast pheasant with bacon and whisky cream (£11.25), and fresh water king prawns in garlic butter with tomato couscous (£13.95). Friendly, helpful service. On the left is an extensive, no smoking two-part dining room, past leather armchairs and a sofa by a second log fire (and a glass chess set); the décor is in mint green and shades of brown, with a modicum of fishing memorabilia. There are picnic-sets outside, and the inn is right opposite a lovely church known as the Cathedral of the Dales. The bedrooms are neat and simple, with a good breakfast. (Recommended by Blaise Vyner, David Hall, Tony and Betty Parker, Dave Braisted, Clive Gibson, Karina Spero, Edward and Deanna Pearce)

Jennings (W & D) ~ Lease Andrew Atkin ~ Real ale ~ Bar food (all day) ~ Restaurant ~ (01748) 884224 ~ Children welcome ~ Dogs allowed in bar and bedrooms ~ Open 12-midnight(1am Sat) ~ Bedrooms: £42S/£64S

HALIFAX SE1026 Map 7
Shibden Mill 🍽️ 🍷
Off A58 into Kell Lane at Stump Cross Inn, near A6036 junction; keep on, pub signposted from Kell Lane on left; HX3 7UL

This tucked-away restored mill is run by helpful and friendly people. The rambling bar has cosy side areas with enticing banquettes heaped softly with cushions and rugs; tables and chairs are well spaced, but candles in elegant iron holders give a feeling of real intimacy. There are old hunting prints, country landscapes and so forth, and a couple of big log fireplaces. John Smiths, Theakstons XB, a beer brewed for them by Moorhouses, and guests such as Everards Sunchaser and Wards Best Bitter on handpump, and 14 wines by the glass. Good, enjoyable bar food includes home-made soup (£3.75), home-made fishcakes with poached egg and mayonnaise (£4.75; main course £8.75), sandwiches on home-made bread (from £5.15), terrine of free-range chicken (£5.75), smoked venison, parsnip risotto and chocolate oil (£6.45), ploughman's or cold flaked ham hock with eggs (£8.25), pork and black pudding sausages with onion gravy (£8.75), chicken or shepherd's pie (£8.95), venison burger with redcurrant compote (£9.95), grilled tuna steak niçoise (£12.95), maize-fed chicken wrapped in serrano ham with a chorizo, tomato and olive stew (£13.75), confit of gressingham duck leg with plum sauce (£14.75), and puddings such as treacle and cinnamon tart or bitter chocolate torte with blood orange ice-cream (£4.95). The upstairs restaurant is no smoking; piped music. There are plenty of seats and chairs (some a bit wobbly) out on an attractive terrace, with lots of heaters; the building is prettily floodlit at night. (Recommended

by Paul Leason, Geoffrey and Brenda Wilson, Greta and Christopher Wells, Revd D Glover,
Ian and Nita Cooper, Alan Bowker, Jo Lilley, Simon Calvert)

Free house ~ Licensee Glen Pearson ~ Real ale ~ Bar food (12-2, 6-9.30; all day Sun) ~
Restaurant ~ (01422) 365840 ~ Children welcome ~ Dogs allowed in bar ~
Open 12-2.30, 5.30-11; 12-11(10.30 Sun) Sat ~ Bedrooms: £68B/£85B

HAROME   SE6582   Map 10

Star ★ (𝔜𝔜) ♀ ◖ ⇌

Village signposted S of A170, E of Helmsley; YO62 5JE

Not surprisingly, the emphasis in this pretty, thatched 14th-c inn is on the first class,
restaurant-style food, though the bar does have a proper pubby atmosphere. This has
a dark bowed beam-and-plank ceiling, well polished tiled kitchen range, plenty of
bric-a-brac, interesting furniture (this was the first pub that 'Mousey Thompson' ever
populated with his famous dark wood furniture), a fine log fire, and daily papers and
magazines; as they don't take bar reservations, it's best to arrive early to get a seat.
There's also a private dining room and a popular coffee loft in the eaves, and a
separate no smoking restaurant. The inventive food uses fish that is delivered daily
from Hartlepool, local hen, duck, and guinea fowl eggs, three types of honey from the
village, and their own herbs and vegetables; lots of british cheeses, too. Changing
daily and cooked by the young chef/patron, the menu might include home-made soup
(£4.50), soused hartlepool halibut with crushed pink fir apples, dill vodka and soda
bread toasts (£8.50), sandwiches (from £8.50), ploughman's (£9.95), grilled black
pudding with fried foie gras, watercress, apple and vanilla chutney and scrumpy cider
reduction (£9.95; main course £15.95), grilled scottish queen scallops with leeks and
mature wensleydale and 'hot house' salmon salad (£11.95; main course £16.95),
bangers and mash with thyme and onion gravy (£12.50), posh local wild rabbit pie
with morel mushrooms and spring truffle shavings (£17.50), fried pork loin with
pease pudding, peppered swede gratin, pancetta and sauce poivrade (£18.50), daily
specials such as cullen skink soup with poached quail egg and parsley oil (£4.50),
dressed whitby crab with green herb mayonnaise (£8.50), roast gloucester old spot
suckling pig with celeriac purée, apple and black pudding and home-brewed cider
juices (£18.50), fillet of turbot with boiled ham knuckle, pea risotto, grain mustard
and lovage velouté (£19.95), and puddings like steamed ginger savarin with a warm
rhubarb compote, ripple ice-cream and hot spiced syrup or irish coffee mousse with
Jameson 'sugar cubes' and baked oatcakes (from £7.50); cheeses with biscuits, grape
chutney and celery (from £4.50). John Smiths, Theakstons and a couple of guests
from Copper Dragon or Hambleton on handpump, 17 wines by the glass, home-
made fresh fruit juices and fruit liqueurs, gooseberry gin, rhubarb schnapps, farm
cider, coffees, teas and hot chocolate with marshmallows and home-made chocolates.
The restaurant is no smoking; piped music. Their bakery/delicatessen, The Corner
Shop, selling take-away meals and snacks as well as all manner of delicious goodies, is
doing very well indeed. There are some seats and tables on a sheltered front terrace
with more in the garden with fruit trees. Eight superbly equipped, stylish bedrooms in
converted farm buildings plus three suites in a thatched cottage, and there's a private
dining room, too. They have a village cricket team. They run a café in the Walled
Garden at Scampston Hall and also own a traditional butcher in the Market Place in
Helmsley which specialises in home-made terrines, british cheeses, cooked meats and
so forth. *(Recommended by Michael and Ann Cole, David Thornton, Oliver Richardson, M and
C Thompson, Cathryn and Richard Hicks, Geoff and Angela Jaques, David and Ruth Hollands,
Walter and Susan Rinaldi-Butcher, Paul and Ursula Randall, Ian and Rose Lock, C E Reid,
Dr D Scott, Adrian White, W K Wood, Neil Ingoe)*

Free house ~ Licensees Andrew and Jacquie Pern ~ Real ale ~ Bar food (11.30-2, 6.15-
9.30; 12-6 Sun; not Mon) ~ Restaurant ~ (01439) 770397 ~ Children welcome ~
Open 11.30-3, 6.15-11; 12-11 Sun; closed Mon and two weeks late winter/early spring ~
Bedrooms: /£140B

Tipping is not normal for bar meals, and not usually expected.

HEATH SE3519 Map 7

Kings Arms

Village signposted from A655 Wakefield—Normanton – or, more directly, turn off to the left opposite Horse & Groom; WF1 5SL

Sunny benches outside this very old-fashioned pub face the village green and you'd never believe that this is in the industrial heartland of West Yorkshire. There are also picnic-sets on a side lawn, and a nice walled flower-filled garden. Inside, the gas lighting adds a lot to the atmosphere, and the original bar has a fire burning in the old black range (with a long row of smoothing irons on the mantelpiece), plain elm stools and oak settles built into the walls, and dark panelling. A more comfortable extension has carefully preserved the original style, down to good wood-pegged oak panelling (two embossed with royal arms), and a high shelf of plates; there are also two other small flagstoned rooms, and the conservatory opens on to the garden. Good value bar food includes sandwiches (from £2.95; hot sausage and onion £3.25), home-made soup (£3.25), mushroom stroganoff, liver and onions in rich gravy or beef in ale pie (all £6.95), rump steak (£8.95), and puddings like treacle sponge and custard (£2.95). Well kept Clarks Classic Blonde, Tetleys, Timothy Taylors Landlord and a seasonal guest from Clarks on handpump. The landlord tells us that with four exits to the pub, customers do leave without paying, so they ask for ID – though most people prefer to leave their credit card in the till. *(Recommended by Richard and Karen Holt, the Didler, Greta and Christopher Wells, Dave Braisted)*

Clarks ~ Manager Alan Tate ~ Real ale ~ Bar food ~ Restaurant ~ (01924) 377527 ~ Children allowed away from bar areas ~ Open 11.30-11(midnight Sat); 12-11 Sun; 11.30-3, 5.30-11 weekdays in winter

HETTON SD9558 Map 7

Angel 🍴 ♀

Just off B6265 Skipton—Grassington; BD23 6LT

As good as ever, this popular no smoking dining pub remains a reliable place for an enjoyable meal. The snug is being refurbished to create a private dining room, but there are still four timbered and panelled rambling rooms with lots of cosy alcoves, comfortable country-kitchen chairs or button-back green plush seats, Ronald Searle wine snob cartoons and older engravings and photographs, log fires, and in the main bar (which readers feel has the pubbiest atmosphere), a Victorian farmhouse range in the big stone fireplace. Good bar food includes confit chicken, thyme, shi-itake mushroom and leek terrine or little moneybags (seafood baked in crispy pastry with lobster sauce, £5.95), home-made black pudding with pear and apple compote and organic foie gras (£8.25), spicy pasta with chorizo, mussels, tomato and chilli (also available without the chorizo or mussels), sausages with grain mustard and apple mash and onion gravy or lambs liver and bacon (all £8.95), roast goosnargh chicken breast wrapped in potato with celeriac purée and mushroom sauce (£12.95), wild venison with jerusalem artichoke purée (£14.75), daily specials such as silver hake with creamed leeks, crayfish tail and parsley sauce (£10.75), roast local wood pigeon with wild mushrooms and thyme jus (£10.95), or wild bass with seared queenies, rissole potatoes and lobster sauce (£14.50), and puddings like white chocolate and lemon mousse or sticky toffee pudding with butterscotch sauce (from £4.75). Black Sheep Bitter and Timothy Taylors Landlord on handpump, 25 wines by the glass, including champagne, and quite a few malt whiskies; quite a few teas, infusions and coffees, too. This year, there's a new decking area outside with canopies and outdoor heaters. *(Recommended by Pierre Richterich, Roger Thornington, A Darroch Harkness, Yana Pocklington, Patricia Owlett, Karen Eliot, Margaret and Jeff Graham, Dr Ian S Morley, Mr and Mrs A Curry, Tim Nicoll, W K Wood, J S Burn, Adrian White)*

Free house ~ Licensees Bruce Elsworth and Luc Daguzan ~ Real ale ~ Bar food (12-2.15 (2.30 Sun), 6-9) ~ Restaurant ~ (01756) 730263 ~ Children welcome ~ Dogs allowed in bedrooms ~ Open 12-3, 6-11; 12-2.30(3 Sun), 6-10.30(10 Sun, 11 Sat) in winter; closed 25 Dec, 1 Jan ~ Bedrooms: /£130B

HULL   TA0927   Map 8

Minerva ◗

Park at top of pedestrianised area at top of Queen's Street and walk over Nelson Street or turn off Queen's Street into Wellington Street, right into Pier Street and pub is at top; no parking restrictions weekends, 2-hour stay Mon-Fri; HU1 1XE

This busy pub is at the heart of the attractively restored waterfront and bustling marina, and handy for nearby The Deep (Europe's deepest aquarium); there are seats out in front from which you can watch the passing boats – you can also watch them from the piers on each side, too. Inside, several rooms ramble all the way round a central servery, and are filled with comfortable seats, quite a few interesting photographs and pictures of old Hull (with two attractive wash drawings by Roger Davis) and a big chart of the Humber. A tiny snug has room for just three people, and a back room (which looks out to the marina basin) houses a profusion of varnished woodwork; two coal fires in winter. They hold three beer festivals a year – at Easter, mid-July, and whenever the Sea Shanty Festival is on – August/September. Otherwise, they keep Tetleys with guests like Greene King IPA, Shepherd Neame Spitfire, Tetleys and Timothy Taylors Landlord on handpump. Bar food includes soup (£2.25), sandwiches or filled baked potatoes (from £3.45), burger (£4.85), ham and eggs (£6.45), vegetarian pasta (£7.25), beef in ale pie (£7.95), chicken with barbecue sauce and bacon (£8.95), minted lamb shoulder (£9.95), and puddings (£3.25). The bar and restaurant are no smoking. Fruit machine, TV, darts and piped music. *(Recommended by Paul and Ursula Randall, David Carr, J R Ringrose, the Didler, John Robertson)*

Spirit Group ~ Manager Adam Brailsford ~ Real ale ~ Bar food (all day) ~ Restaurant ~ (01482) 326909 ~ Children in restaurant if eating ~ Open 10am-midnight; closed 25 Dec

Olde White Harte ★

Off 25 Silver Street, a continuation of Whitefriargate; pub is up narrow passage, and should not be confused with the much more modern White Hart nearby; HU1 1JG

This historic old place used to be known as a fine place for eating hull cheese (an 18th-c euphemism for enjoying a great deal to drink – the town was known then for its very strong ales). It's tucked away in a cosy courtyard amongst narrow alleyways, and the three bars have some fine features. The downstairs one has attractive stained-glass windows that look out above the bow window seat, carved heavy beams support black ceiling boards, and there are two big brick inglenooks with a frieze of delft tiles. The curved copper-topped counter serves Caledonian Deuchars IPA, McEwans 80/-, Theakstons Old Peculier and a changing guest on handpump, 55 malt whiskies, and good value bar food: home-made soup (£1.95), filled baguettes or panini (from £2.75), stilton and vegetable crumble (£4.35), home-made steak pie or gammon and egg (£4.95), daily specials and puddings like home-made apple crumble (£2.25). The restaurant is no smoking. It was in the heavily panelled room up the oak staircase that in 1642 the town's governor Sir John Hotham made the fateful decision to lock the nearby gate against Charles I, depriving him of Hull's arsenal; it didn't do him much good, as in the Civil War that followed, Hotham, like the king, was executed by the parliamentarians. There are seats in the courtyard, and outside heaters. *(Recommended by Paul and Ursula Randall, W W Burke, David Carr, the Didler)*

Scottish Courage ~ Lease Bernard Copley ~ Real ale ~ Bar food (12-5 but 12-2 Tues) ~ Restaurant ~ (01482) 326363 ~ Children in restaurant only ~ Dogs allowed in bar ~ Open 11-midnight(1am Fri and Sat); 12-midnight Sun

---

Real ale to us means beer which has matured naturally in its cask – not pressurised or filtered. We name all real ales stocked. We usually name ales preserved under a light blanket of carbon dioxide too, though purists – pointing out that this stops the natural yeasts developing – would disagree (most people, including us, can't tell the difference!)

KETTLESING SE2256 Map 7

Queens Head ◖

Village signposted off A59 W of Harrogate; HG3 2LB

Totally no smoking now, this friendly stone-built pub remains popular for its good food. The L-shaped, carpeted main bar is decorated with Victorian song sheet covers, lithographs of Queen Victoria, little heraldic shields, and a delft shelf of blue and white china. There's also a quietly chatty atmosphere, and lots of quite close-set elm and other tables around its walls, with cushioned country seats. Nicely presented, the bar food at lunchtime includes soup (£3.50), sandwiches (from £3.75; grilled steak £6.50), filled yorkshire puddings (from £3.95), home-made burger (£4.95), salads (from £5.25), and omelettes or brunch (£6.95), with evening choices such as home-made chicken liver pâté or garlic mushrooms (£4.50), wensleydale and bacon salad with croûtons (£4.95), gammon with egg or pineapple (£8.95), jumbo haddock in home-made batter (£9.50), steaks (from £13.95), and mixed grill (£14.95), and daily specials such as home-made steak in ale pie (£7.95), seafood bake (£8.95) and lamb rump with minted gravy (£9.95); there may be a good value lunchtime OAP menu, too. Coal or log fires at each end and maybe unobtrusive piped radio. A smaller bar on the left, with built-in red banquettes, has cricketing prints and cigarette cards, coins and banknotes, and in the lobby there's a life-size portrait of Elizabeth I. Black Sheep Bitter, Theakstons Old Peculier and a quickly changing guest like Roosters Hooligan on handpump. Seats in the neatly kept suntrap back garden, and benches in front by the lane. *(Recommended by Peter Burton, Peter Hacker, G Dobson, Brian and Janet Ainscough, Roger and Anne Newbury)*

Free house ~ Licensees Louise and Glen Garbutt ~ Real ale ~ Bar food (11.30-2, 6.30-9; 12-9 Sun) ~ (01423) 770263 ~ Children welcome ~ Open 11-3, 6-11; 12-10.30 Sun ~ Bedrooms: £73.50S(£55B)/£88S(£65B)

KIRK DEIGHTON SE3950 Map 7

Bay Horse ◖▯ ♀

B6164 N of Wetherby; Main Street; LS22 4DZ

The licensees, who formerly had a popular Boston Spa restaurant, have turned this into an attractive dining pub. There's a small flagstoned bar by the entrance if you want just a drink, with changing real ales on handpump such as Black Sheep, John Smiths and Timothy Taylors Landlord, good wines by the glass, and good coffees, from a solid mahogany bar counter with proper brass foot and elbow rails. The main dark terracotta no smoking dining area is not large, with perhaps a dozen or so candlelit tables, comfortable banquettes and other seats, rugs on flagstones, beams and pictures; throughout, there's a warm happy atmosphere – expectant or contented, depending on what stage of the meal people are at. Blackboards show the suppliers of the carefully sourced – and equally carefully prepared – food, which at lunchtime might include home-made soup (£3.75; crab £4.95), pork dim sum, smoked haddock risotto, basil and spinach gnocchi, thai salmon fishcakes or tempura prawns (all £5.50; main course £10.95), queenie scallops with garlic butter and gruyère (£5.75; main course £11.95), seafood pancake, beer-battered fish or bangers and mash (£7.95), thai chicken and seafood stir fry or monkfish with bacon, prawns and mussels (£13.95), and a range of other fish such as turbot (around £14.50); there's also a set lunch menu, one course £9.95 and two courses £13.95. Their lunchtime sandwiches (£4.50) are made with home-baked bread, and the puddings are tempting – though judging by our readers' experience few people finish their meal with enough room left for one; they make all their own jams and preserves, too. It's worth booking even quite well ahead, especially for evenings or weekends. Service is friendly and efficient; piped music and games machine. *(Recommended by Michael Doswell, OPUS, Danny Savage, Howard and Margaret Buchanan, Michael and Maggie Betton, Brian and Janet Ainscough, Les and Sandra Brown, Derek and Sylvia Stephenson)*

Enterprise ~ Lease Karl and Amanda Maney ~ Real ale ~ Bar food (12-2.15(3 Sun), 6-9) ~ Restaurant ~ (01937) 580058 ~ Children welcome ~ Dogs allowed in bar ~ Open 12-3, 5-11; closed Mon lunchtime

KIRKBYMOORSIDE   SE6987   Map 10

George & Dragon
Market Place; YO62 6AA

In a pretty little town, this handsome white-painted 17th-c coaching inn has a
bustling atmosphere in its convivial front bar. Also, leather chesterfields, brass-
studded solid dark red leatherette armchairs set around polished wooden tables,
burgundy and cream walls and panelling stripped back to its original pitch pine,
horsebrasses hung along the beams, newspapers to read, and a blazing log fire;
piped music. There's an attractive beamed bistro and a no smoking restaurant.
Enjoyable bar food includes home-made soup (£3.50), cajun chicken liver pâté with
mango, lime and coconut chutney (£4.75), confit duck leg with spicy sausage
(£5.95), chicken supreme in white wine, mushrooms, tomatoes and thyme (£9.50),
duo of salmon and haddock with a saffron, leek and prawn velouté (£11.95),
braised lamb shank with redcurrant and rosemary sauce (£12.95), steaks (from
£13.95), daily specials such as stilton pâté, button mushrooms in a cheddar and
bacon cream sauce or a plate of antipasti (£4.75), shepherd's pie or vegetable
lasagne (£7.95), cajun salmon with pink peppercorn cream sauce or lamb curry
(£8.95), pork chop on black pudding with grain mustard sauce (£9.95), and whole
bass with prawn, caper and herb butter (£13.95); Sunday roast (£6.50; two courses
£9.50). Black Sheep Bitter, Tetleys, and Timothy Taylors Landlord on handpump,
ten wines by the glass, and 25 malt whiskies. There are seats under umbrellas in the
back courtyard and a surprisingly peaceful walled garden for residents to use.
Market day is on Wednesdays. *(Recommended by Mark and Ruth Brock, Dr David
Cockburn, Sarah and Peter Gooderham, Pat and Tony Martin, Sue Demont, Tim Barrow,
Derek and Sylvia Stephenson)*

Free house ~ Licensee Elaine Walker ~ Real ale ~ Bar food (12-2.15, 6.30(7 Sun)-9.15) ~
Restaurant ~ (01751) 433334 ~ Children welcome ~ Dogs allowed in bar and bedrooms
~ Open 10-1am ~ Bedrooms: £54B/£89B

KIRKHAM   SE7466   Map 7

Stone Trough ♀ ◧
Kirkham Abbey; YO60 7JS

The several beamed and cosy rooms in this bustling country inn have warm log fires,
Black Sheep Bitter, Tetleys, Timothy Taylors Landlord, and a couple of guests such
as Suddabys Double Chance and Theakstons Old Peculier on handpump, and 11
wines by the glass; the snug room in the bar and the restaurant are no smoking. Well
liked bar food includes lunchtime sandwiches (from £4.95) as well as soup (£4.25),
chicken liver and foie gras parfait with pear and apricot chutney (£5.50), salmon and
crab cakes with sweet basil and noodle salad (£5.75), cumberland sausage ring on
sage mash with red onion marmalade (£7.75), spicy mexican meatballs (£8.50),
roast chicken breast with a shallot and bacon sauce (£9.95), lamb and apricot suet
pudding with rosemary jus (£10.50), rib-eye steak with a peppercorn dressing
(£13.75), and puddings such as hot chocolate pot with fresh fruit and marshmallow
or scotch pancakes with apple and raisins and calvados ice-cream (£4.50). Games
machine, piped music, and TV in the pool room. From the seats outside, there are
lovely views down the valley, and the inn is handy for Kirkham Abbey and Castle
Howard. *(Recommended by Mike Dean, Lis Wingate Gray, Christopher Turner, Colin and
Dot Savill, Michael Doswell, Pat and Graham Williamson, J Crosby)*

Free house ~ Licensees Sarah and Adam Richardson ~ Real ale ~ Bar food (12-2, 6.30-
8.30; not Mon except bank hols) ~ Restaurant ~ (01653) 618713 ~ Well behaved children
welcome ~ Open 12-2.30, 6-11; 12-11(10.30 Sun) Sat; closed Mon except bank hols;
25 Dec

Ring the bull is an ancient pub game – you try to lob a ring on a piece of string
over a hook (occasionally a bull's horn) on wall or ceiling.

LANGTHWAITE NY9902 Map 10

Charles Bathurst 🍴 🍺 🛏

Arkengarthdale, a mile N towards Tan Hill; generally known as the CB Inn; DL11 6EN

This is a lovely spot with fine views over Langthwaite village and Arkengarthdale, and the pub remains extremely popular with our readers. As well as a friendly welcome and a good mix of customers, there's a long bar with light pine scrubbed tables, country chairs and benches on stripped floors, plenty of snug alcoves, and a roaring fire; the wooden floored dining room (with views of Scar House, a shooting lodge owned by the Duke of Norfolk), is no smoking, as are the other dining areas. The island bar counter has Black Sheep Bitter and Riggwelter, John Smiths and Theakstons Best on handpump, and nine wines by the glass. Piped music, darts, pool, TV and dominoes. Cooked by the licensee and his team, the imaginative food might include lunchtime filled baguettes, broccoli and stilton soup with sun-dried tomato bread (£3.85), chicken leg, ham hock and black pudding terrine with cumberland sauce (£4.95), crab and avocado in a filo basket with lime and coriander dressing (£5.30), goats cheese, tomato and red onion tartlet (£8.95), breast of chicken wrapped in smoked bacon on roquefort macaroni (£10.50), fillet of pork with apple and celeriac boulangère and tomato, caper and madeira sauce (£10.95), breast of duck with stir-fried vegetables and noodles, confit duck leg spring roll and hoisin sauce (£12.85), fillet of beef on oxtail terrine with green peppercorn sauce and foie gras (£16.50), and puddings such as chocolate tart with raspberry coulis, white chocolate marquise with apricot compote or Southern Comfort and honey crème brûlée (£3.95). Best to book to be sure of a table. The bedrooms are pretty and comfortable. *(Recommended by Bruce and Sharon Eden, Mark and Ruth Brock, Pat and Robert Watt, Lynda and Trevor Smith, Dr Alan and Mrs Sue Holder, Jill and Julian Tasker, Richard, Professors Alan and Ann Clarke, Anthony Barnes, David Hall, Helen Clarke, Dr and Mrs M E Wilson, Benand Helen Ingram, Ellen and Jeremy Clark-King, J Crosby, Rod Stoneman, Jo Lilley, Simon Calvert, Peter and Anne-Marie O'Malley, Dr and Mrs T E Hothersall, David and Jean Hall, Peter J and Avril Hanson)*

Free house ~ Licensees Charles and Stacy Cody ~ Real ale ~ Bar food ~ (01748) 884567 ~ Children welcome ~ Dogs welcome ~ Open 11-midnight; closed 25 Dec ~ Bedrooms: /£85B

LASTINGHAM SE7391 Map 10

Blacksmiths Arms 🍺

Off A170 W of Pickering at Wrelton, forking off Rosedale road N of Cropton; or via Appleton or Hutton-le-Hole; YO62 6TL

In the National Park at the foot of the moors, this neatly kept and comfortable stone inn usually has plenty of walkers keen for refreshment. The cosily old-fashioned beamed bar has a log fire in an open range, traditional furnishings, Theakstons Best and a couple of changing guests from breweries like Daleside, Phoenix, Roosters and York on handpump and ten wines by the glass. The two dining rooms are no smoking. Decent bar food at lunchtime includes filled rolls or hot toasted panini (£4.95; soup and a filled roll £6.95), home-made steak in ale pie, tomato and lentil lasagne or beer-battered cod (£7.95), and yorkshire hotpot or lamb casserole (£8.95), with evening dishes such as crispy garlic mushrooms, home-made soup or yorkshire pudding with onion gravy (from £2.95), mushroom and stilton pancake, slow-roast lamb shank, fish pie or steaks (from £7.95), and home-made puddings (£3.65); best to book at weekends. There are seats in the back garden and the village is very pretty. It's worth a visit to the church as it has a unique Saxon crypt built as a shrine to St Cedd. *(Recommended by Mike Dean, Lis Wingate Gray, Dr David Cockburn, Sarah and Peter Gooderham, Dr and Mrs Jackson, C E Reid, Jane Taylor, David Dutton)*

Free house ~ Licensee Peter Trafford ~ Real ale ~ Bar food (not winter Tues lunchtime or 6-22 Nov) ~ Restaurant ~ (01751) 417247 ~ Children allowed away from bar area ~ Open 12-11(10.30 Sun); 12-2.30, 6-11 Mon-Thurs in winter; closed winter Tues lunchtime ~ Bedrooms: £45S/£60B

LEDSHAM   SE4529   Map 7
Chequers ✵

1.5 miles from A1(M) junction 42: follow Leeds signs, then Ledsham signposted; also some 4 miles N of junction M62; Claypit Lane; LS25 5LP

Run by a long-standing and popular landlord, this friendly stone-built village pub is always busy with a good mix of customers. The old-fashioned little central panelled-in servery has several small, individually decorated rooms leading off with low beams, lots of cosy alcoves, a number of toby jugs, log fires, and well kept Brown Cow Bitter, John Smiths, Theakstons Best, Timothy Taylors Landlord and a guest beer on handpump. The lounge and restaurant are no smoking. There are some bar snacks but the emphasis is on the more elaborate dishes: sandwiches (from £4.95; steak sandwich or crisp bacon and somerset brie baguette £5.85), smoked salmon and scrambled eggs (£6.85), and sausage and mash or tasty home-made steak and mushroom pie (£9.85). Also, home-made soup (£4.65), slivers of smoked duck breast on garlicky new potatoes (£7.65), steamed mussels in white wine, garlic, fine leek strips and pesto (£7.85), filo basket with mushrooms cooked in dijon mustard cream and chilli (£13.95), slow-cooked lamb shank with apple mash and redcurrant and rosemary jus (£14.45), monkfish tail wrapped in pancetta on garlicky tomatoes (£15.65), sirloin steak glazed with Dubonnet and sweet pepper strips (£15.95), venison steak on parsnip matchsticks with a cranberry and orange marmalade (£16.95), and puddings such as fudgy walnut tart with a scoop of liquorice ice-cream, lemon drizzle sponge, and chocolate and Baileys cheesecake (from £4.65). A sheltered two-level terrace behind the house has tables among roses, and the hanging baskets and flowers are very pretty. *(Recommended by Kevin Thorpe, David Thornton, Bob Broadhurst, Roger and Pauline Pearce, Mike Dean, Lis Wingate Gray, Peter Hacker, OPUS, R M Corlett, the Didler, Peter and Eleanor Kenyon, Paul and Ursula Randall, Simon Jones, Christine and Neil Townend, Lawrence Pearse, Richard Cole, Di and Mike Gillam, K M Crook, Alison and Pete, JWAC, Bill and Marian de Bass)*

Free house ~ Licensee Chris Wraith ~ Real ale ~ Bar food (12-9 Mon-Sat; not Sun) ~ Restaurant ~ (01977) 683135 ~ Well behaved children allowed ~ Dogs allowed in bar ~ Open 11-11; closed Sun

LEEDS   SE3033   Map 7
Whitelocks ㉕ ★ ✵ £

Turks Head Yard; alley off Briggate, opposite Debenhams and Littlewoods; park in shoppers' car park and walk; LS1 6HB

It's best to arrive at this beautifully preserved pub early as it does get packed with quite a mix of customers. It has hardly changed since Victorian times and the long and narrow old-fashioned bar has polychrome tiles on the bar counter, stained-glass windows and grand advertising mirrors, and red button back plush banquettes and heavy copper-topped cast-iron tables squeezed down one side. Under the new licensee, bar food includes sandwiches and filled baguettes (from £3.75), and hot dishes like a home-made pie of the day, sausage and mash and fish and chips (all £6.45). Well kept Caledonian Deuchars IPA, John Smiths, Theakstons Best and Old Peculier and York Guzzler on handpump. There are some tables in the narrow courtyard outside. *(Recommended by David Carr, Ann and Tony Bennett-Hughes, Jeremy King, the Didler, Neil Whitehead, Victoria Anderson, Chris Parsons, Jo Lilley, Simon Calvert, David and Nina Pugsley, B and M Kendall, Mrs Maricar Jagger)*

Spirit ~ Manager Dave Scholey ~ Real ale ~ Bar food (12-7 Mon-Sat, 12-4 Sun) ~ Restaurant ~ (0113) 245 3950 ~ Children in restaurant if eating ~ Open 11-11; 12-10.30 Sun

---

Pubs with outstanding views are listed at the back of the book.

LEYBURN SE1191 Map 10

Sandpiper 🍴 ⚲

Just off Market Place; DL8 5AT

Although there is a small cosy bar used by locals (and our readers enjoy it too), most of the emphasis in this extremely likeable, no smoking 17th-c cottage is on the very good food. This little bar has a couple of black beams in the low ceiling, antlers, brass jugs, and a few tables and chairs, and the back room up three steps has attractive Dales photographs; get here early to be sure of a seat. Down by the nice linenfold panelled bar counter there are stuffed sandpipers, more photographs and a woodburning stove in the stone fireplace; to the left is the restaurant. At lunchtime, the menu might include sandwiches (from £4; croque monsieur £4.75), caesar salad (£5.50; main course £8.50), country terrine with chutney (£6), fishcakes with a fine herb sauce (£6.25; main course £11.50), beer-battered fish, cottage pie or pasta with wild mushrooms and spinach (£8.95), and grilled rib-eye steak (£13.95); evening choices such as fish soup with rouille (£5.50), pressed ham hock, chicken and mushroom terrine (£6), black pudding with caramelised apple and foie gras (£7.25), roasted vegetable risotto with parmesan curls (£9.95), moroccan spiced chicken with couscous or crispy duck leg with plum and orange sauce (£11.50), halibut on a spaghetti of courgette and lobster sauce (£16), and puddings such as warm Valrhona chocolate tart, crème brûlée or sticky toffee pudding with butterscotch sauce (from £4.95). Well kept Black Sheep Best Bitter and guests from Copper Dragon and Hambleton on handpump, over 100 malt whiskies, a decent wine list with eight by the glass, and friendly, cheerful staff under the supervision of the amiable, attentive landlord; piped music. There are green cast-iron tables on the front terrace amidst the lovely hanging baskets and flowering climbers. *(Recommended by M S Catling, Michael Butler, Barbara and Peter Kelly, Richard and Anne Ansell, Terry and Linda Moseley, Karen Eliot, A Jones, Michael Doswell, David Hoult, Keith and Avril Stringer, J Crosby, Malcolm and Lynne Jessop)*

Free house ~ Licensees Jonathan and Michael Harrison ~ Real ale ~ Bar food (12-2.30 (2 Sun), 6.30(7 Sun)-9(9.30 Fri and Sat); not Mon) ~ Restaurant ~ (01969) 622206 ~ Children welcome ~ Dogs allowed in bar ~ Open 11.30-3, 6.30-11; 12-3, 6.30-10.30 Sun; closed Mon ~ Bedrooms: £65S(£70B)/£75S(£80B)

LINTHWAITE SE1014 Map 7

Sair 🍺

Hoyle Ing, off A62; 3½ miles after Huddersfield look out for two water storage tanks (painted with a shepherd scene) on your right – the street is on your left, burrowing very steeply up between works buildings; OS Sheet 110 map reference 101143; HD7 5SG

Particularly at weekends, this unspoilt and old-fashioned pub – with some improvements this year – does get very busy. It's the large choice of own-brewed beers on handpump that remains the main draw: Linfit Bitter, Dark Mild, Special, Swift, Gold Medal, Autumn Gold, Old Eli, English Guineas Stout, Leadboiler, Enochs Hammer, and occasional brews like Smoke House Ale, Springbok Bier, Xmas Ale and Ginger beer. Weston's farm cider and a few malt whiskies; weekend sandwiches. The four rooms are furnished with pews or smaller chairs on the rough flagstones or wooden floors, and there are open fires in every room; the room to the left of the entrance is no smoking and has dominoes, a juke box, shove-ha'penny and cribbage; piano players welcome. In summer, there are plenty of seats and tables in front of the pub that have a striking view across the Colne Valley. The Huddersfield Narrow Canal is restored through to Ashton; in the 3½ miles from Linthwaite to the highest, deepest and longest tunnel in Britain, there are are 25 working locks and some lovely countryside. *(Recommended by J R Ringrose, the Didler)*

Own brew ~ Licensee Ron Crabtree ~ Real ale ~ No credit cards ~ (01484) 842370 ~ Children welcome ~ Dogs welcome ~ Open 5-11; 12-11 Sat; 12-10.30 Sun; closed weekday lunchtimes

LINTON SE3946 Map 7
Windmill

Leaving Wetherby W on A661, fork left just before hospital and bear left; also signposted from A659, leaving Collingham towards Harewood; LS22 4HT

The small beamed rooms in this pleasant pub have walls stripped back to bare stone, polished antique oak settles around copper-topped cast-iron tables, pots hanging from the oak beams, a high shelf of plates, and log fires; the sizeable restaurant is no smoking. Well presented, decent bar food at lunchtime includes sandwiches (from £3.95), chicken liver parfait with plum and apple chutney (£4.95), goats cheese and mediterranean vegetable tart (£5.95), filled baked potatoes (from £5.95), lemon-battered scampi (£7.95), and rump steak with chorizo and mozzarella (£10.95); evening choices such as wild mushroom risotto with parmesan crisps (£4.95), steamed mussels with garlic and tomatoes (£5.95), salmon with garlic vegetables and a watercress velouté (£9.95), and gressingham duck breast with an apricot and ginger sauce (£11.95). John Smiths, Theakstons Best and a couple of guests like Jennings Golden Host and Youngs Bitter on handpump, and several wines by the glass; piped music and TV. The pear tree outside was raised from seed brought back from the Napoleonic Wars, and there are seats in the sheltered garden and on the sunny terrace at the back. *(Recommended by GSB, OPUS, A S and M E Marriott, Jeremy King, Tony and Penny Burton, Richard Cole, Kevin Blake, Alex and Claire Pearse)*

Scottish Courage ~ Lease Janet Rowley and John Littler ~ Real ale ~ Bar food (12-2(2.30 Sat. 3.30 Sun), 5.30-9; not Sun evening) ~ Restaurant ~ (01937) 582209 ~ Children allowed until 7.30pm unless eating in the dining room ~ Dogs allowed in bar ~ Open 11-3, 5-11; 11-11 Sat; 12-10.30 Sun; closed 1 Jan

LINTON IN CRAVEN SD9962 Map 7
Fountaine

Just off B6265 Skipton—Grassington; BD23 5HJ

In a delightful hamlet, this bustling pub looks down over the village green to a narrow stream and there are some fine surrounding walks in the Dales. Inside, it's been given a refurbishment under the newish licensees and now has more of a wine bar-ish feel but still keeping Black Sheep, Copper Dragon Scotts 1816, Litton Ale, John Smiths and Tetleys on handpump and several wines by the glass. Cooked by the licensee, the imaginative food includes home-made soup (£3.50), lunchtime sandwiches (from £4.95), grilled baby black pudding on bubble and squeak (£5.50), fish platter (£5.95; main course £7.95), home-made steak and mushroom in ale pie (£8.50), braised brisket with garlic mash (£9.50), old spot pork with crackling and seed mustard sauce (£9.95), thai tuna (£11.50), and puddings such as white chocolate cheesecake or chocolate fudge brownies (£4.20). The restaurant and one other room are no smoking. More reports please. *(Recommended by Paul Humphreys, G Dobson, Richard, Tony and Penny Burton, Simon and Mandy King, Fred and Lorraine Gill, Alyson and Andrew Jackson, Lynda and Trevor Smith, Len Beattie)*

Individual Inns ~ Manager Christopher Gregson ~ Real ale ~ Bar food (all day) ~ Restaurant ~ (01756) 752210 ~ Children welcome ~ Dogs allowed in bar ~ Open 11-11; 12-10.30 Sun

LITTON SD9074 Map 7
Queens Arms ㉕ ◖

From B6160 N of Grassington, after Kilnsey take second left fork; can also be reached off B6479 at Stainforth N of Settle, via Halton Gill; BD23 5QJ

'Unmissable' and 'a gem' are just two descriptions readers have used for this super little inn. It's got plenty of local charm, own-brewed beers, and a lovely setting. In fine weather you can make the most of the seats outside; the views over the fells are stunning, and there's a safe area for children in the two-level garden. The main bar on the right has a good coal fire, stripped rough stone walls, a brown beam-and-plank ceiling, stools around cast-iron-framed tables on the stone and concrete floor, a seat built into the stone-mullioned window, and signed cricket bats. The left-hand room is an eating area with old photographs of the Dales around the walls. You may only smoke in the bar. As well as Litton Ale, they also offer one other – Dark Star, Potts Beck Ale or Litton Light on handpump from their own microbrewery. Good, popular bar food includes home-made soup (£2.90), sandwiches (from £4.50; the sausage baguette is well liked), filled baked potatoes (from £4.95), home-made rabbit pie (£8.60), gammon and egg (£8.95), daily specials such as local blue cheese, onion, mushroom and black olive tart (£8.95), local leg of lamb (£9.95), teriyaki tuna (£10.95), and venison haunch on haggis with a red wine jus (£12.95), and puddings like rhubarb crumble, bread and butter pudding or syrup tart (£4). Darts, board games and piped music. Plenty of surrounding walks – a track behind the inn leads over Ackerley Moor to Buckden, and the quiet lane through the valley leads on to Pen-y-ghent. Walkers enjoy staying here very much – and there is a walkers' room (price on request). *(Recommended by Mr and Mrs Maurice Thompson, Andy and Jill Kassube, Tony and Penny Burton, Greta and Christopher Wells, B and M Kendall, D W Stokes)*

Own brew ~ Licensees Tanya and Neil Thompson ~ Real ale ~ Bar food (not Mon or Jan) ~ (01756) 770208 ~ Children welcome away from bar ~ Dogs allowed in bar and bedrooms ~ Open 12-3, 6.30-11; closed Mon (except bank hols) and all Jan ~ Bedrooms: /£75S

LONG PRESTON SD8358 Map 7

Maypole 🍺 🛏️

A65 Settle—Skipton; BD23 4PH

Handy for this busy road (and a good base for walking in the Dales), the Maypole gets a warm-hearted feel not just from its log fires but also from its welcoming and obliging licensees – who have been the longest serving landlords here since 1700. The carpeted two-room bar has sporting prints and local photographs and a list of landlords dating back to 1695 on its butter-coloured walls, a delft shelf with whisky-water jugs and decorative plates, a couple of stags' heads, and good solid pub furnishings – heavy carved wall settles and the like, and heavy cast-iron framed pub tables with unusual inset leather tops. A good range of attractively priced and substantial food might include sandwiches (from £2.50; bacon and egg baguette £4.75), vegetable soup (£2.95), chicken liver pâté (£4.25), filled baked potatoes (£4.75), ploughman's (from £5.50), fennel and chestnut casserole (£6.50), ham and eggs (£8.25), escalope of pork in Pernod, cream, mushrooms and basil (£10.50), steaks (from £11.75), and daily specials such as chilli con carne (£5.95), turkey curry or kidneys turbigo (£6.50), chicken in orange and brandy sauce (£7.50), and good rabbit pie with proper shortcrust pastry (£8.50). There is a separate country dining room. They have Moorhouses Premier, Timothy Taylors Landlord and two changing ales such as Copper Dragon Scotts 1816 and Charles Wells Bombardier on handpump, and serve good strong coffee. Wines by the glass are reasonably priced. There's a piano in the room on the left, also darts, a games machine and dominoes; piped music only for major events. Out behind is a terrace with a couple of picnic-sets under an ornamental cherry tree, with another picnic-set on grass under a sycamore. If you're staying, they do a good breakfast. *(Recommended by Pete Yearsley, Michael Butler, Dudley and Moira Cockroft, Brian and Janet Ainscough)*

Enterprise ~ Lease Robert Palmer ~ Real ale ~ Bar food (12-2, 6.30-9(9.30 Fri); 12-9.30 Sat; 12-9 Sun) ~ Restaurant ~ (01729) 840219 ~ Children welcome but not in bars after 9pm ~ Dogs allowed in bar and bedrooms ~ Open 12-2.30, 6-midnight; 12-midnight (11 Sun) Sat ~ Bedrooms: £29S/£55B

'Children welcome' means the pubs says it lets children inside without any special restriction; readers have found that some may impose an evening time limit – please tell us if you find this.

LOW CATTON SE7053 Map 7
Gold Cup
Village signposted with High Catton off A166 in Stamford Bridge or A1079 at Kexby Bridge; YO41 1EA

At weekends, this white-rendered house usefully serves food all day. There are comfortable, communicating rooms with a fire at one end, plush wall seats and stools around good solid tables, some decorative plates and brasswork on the walls, and a relaxed atmosphere; the back bar has a woodburning stove in a brick fireplace. From a changing menu, the well liked meals might include sandwiches, creamed stilton mushrooms (£3.75), prawn cocktail (£4), chicken chasseur and roast beef or lamb (£6.95), popular home-cooked ham with leek and stilton sauce (£7.25), cajun chicken or grilled cheesy gammon with pineapple (£7.75), and puddings such as mocha crème brûlée or poached pear (£3.50); they also offer a Sunday-Wednesday evening two-course special (£11). The restaurant is no smoking (as is the area at the bar) and has solid wooden pews and tables, said to be made from a single oak tree, and pleasant views of the surrounding fields. Black Sheep and John Smiths on handpump; piped music, pool, games machine and TV. The garden has a grassed area for children, and the back paddock houses a goat and some horses. They also own Boris and Marilyn (retired greyhounds), and have fishing rights on the adjoining River Derwent. (Recommended by Pat and Tony Martin, Mr and Mrs P M Jennings, Debbie Reynolds)

Free house ~ Licensees Pat and Ray Hales ~ Real ale ~ Bar food (12-2, 6-9.30; all day weekends; not Mon lunchtime) ~ No credit cards ~ (01759) 371354 ~ Children welcome ~ Dogs allowed in bar ~ Open 12-2.30, 6-11; 12-11(10.30 Sun) Sat; closed Mon lunchtime; evenings 25 and 26 Dec

LUND SE9748 Map 8
Wellington ⑪ ♀
Off B1248 SW of Driffield; YO25 9TE

There's a good mix of drinkers and diners in this smart, bustling pub. The restaurant is supported by a back dining area where you cannot reserve a table – this seems to work well and the main bar in the evening remains a haven for drinkers only. The most atmospheric part is the cosy Farmers Bar, a small heavily beamed room with an interesting fireplace and some old agricultural equipment; the neatly kept main bar is much brighter, with a brick fireplace and bar counter, well polished wooden banquettes and square tables, dried flowers, and local prints on the textured cream-painted walls; two areas are no smoking. Off to one side is a plainer flagstoned room, while at the other a york-stoned walkway leads to a room with a display case showing off the village's Britain in Bloom awards. Good enjoyable bar food at lunchtime includes home-made soup (£3.95), smoked haddock fishcakes with a mild curried apple sauce (£5.45), chicken liver parfait with redcurrant and orange sauce (£5.50), beer-battered local haddock (£9.95), chicken, bacon and blue cheese salad (£7.95), calves liver and bacon (£11.95), and breast of chicken on warm potato, rocket and parmesan salad or fresh half pound skipsea crab salad with fresh herb mayonnaise (£12.95); evening choices such as devilled lambs kidney and mushroom hotpot (£5.95), warm home-smoked breast of gressingham duck, grapefruit, lemon balm and leaf salad (£6.95), king scallops with smoked bacon and garlic risotto (£9.45), lamb and apricot suet pudding or fried chicken breast, toasted goats cheese, sun-dried tomato and basil lemon butter sauce (£13.95), monkfish poached in a vegetable and vermouth cream ragoût (£15.95), loin of wild local venison with redcurrant and juniper reduction (£18.95), and puddings like warm chocolate and pear frangipane tart with vanilla bean ice-cream or rum and raisin crème caramel (£4.25). Well kept Black Sheep, John Smiths, and Timothy Taylors Landlord with a changing local guest like Copper Dragon Golden Pippin on handpump, a good wine list with a helpfully labelled choice by the glass, and 30 malt whiskies. Piped music, darts, pool, TV and games machine. A small courtyard beside the car park has a couple of benches. More reports please.

(Recommended by Michael Butler, June and Ken Brooks, Roger A Bellingham, Paul and Ursula Randall, Peter and Caroline Barker, Derek and Sylvia Stephenson, Keith and Margaret Kettell, J Crosby, Fred and Lorraine Gill, David Field)

Free house ~ Licensees Russell Jeffery and Sarah Jeffery ~ Real ale ~ Bar food (not Sun evening or Mon) ~ Restaurant (Tues-Sat evenings) ~ (01377) 217294 ~ Children welcome but must be over 12 in evening ~ Open 12-3, 6.30-11; 12-3, 7-11 Sun; closed Mon lunchtime

MARTON SE7383 Map 10
Appletree 🍴 🍷 🍺
Village signposted off A170 W of Pickering; YO62 6RD

This year, the dining space in this neatly kept pub has been reduced and a new kitchen, cellar and back entrance created. The relaxed beamed lounge bar has comfortable settees in red or blue around polished low tables, an open fire in the stone fireplace, and a modicum of carefully placed decorations on the eau de nil walls; there's also a smaller bar with Suddabys Double Chance, Wold Top Bitter, York Stonewall and a guest like Archers Billy No Mates or Timothy Taylors Golden Best on handpump, 14 wines by the glass plus two champagnes and five sweet wines, and maybe winter mulled wine. Many customers head for the terracotta-walled dining room, which has well spaced farmhouse tables, fresh flowers, and masses of candles at night. Both dining areas are no smoking and tables here can be pre-booked. Good interesting food cooked by the landlord might include sandwiches (in the bar only), truffled mushroom soup (£4), smoked salmon and scrambled egg (£6.90), sautéed king scallops (£7.50), caramelised onion tarte tatin (£9.50), roast tenderloin of pork with black pudding, sweet potato purée and grainy mustard sauce (£12.90), daube of beef with horseradish cream (£13), roast rump of lamb with pea risotto (£14.50), and puddings such as marbled chocolate mousse with griottine cherries or sticky toffee pudding (from £3.90); Sunday evening posh pie and pea supper (£6.50). They continue to grow some of their own herbs and vegetables, and produce their own flavoured breads, chutneys, preserves, flavoured oils and butters and so forth. There are cast-iron tables and chairs out on a sheltered flagstoned courtyard behind. More reports on the changes please.
(Recommended by Jane Johnston)

Free house ~ Licensees Melanie and T J Drew ~ Bar food (12-2, 6.30(7 Sun)-9.30(9 Sun); not Mon or Tues) ~ Restaurant ~ (01751) 431457 ~ Children welcome away from bar ~ Open 12-2.30, 6.30-11; 12-3, 7-11 Sun; closed Mon and Tues

MASHAM SE2381 Map 10
Black Sheep Brewery 🍺
Crosshills; HG4 4EN

Well worth a detour from the A1 – even if this bustling place is pretty far from being a pub. A huge upper warehouse room has a bar serving well kept Black Sheep Best, Emmerdale Ale, Riggwelter and Special on handpump, good wines by the glass, and a good choice of soft drinks. Well liked lunchtime food includes home-made soup (£3.75), sandwiches (from £3.95; minute steak baguette £5.75), filled baked potatoes (from £4.50), home-made fishcakes (£4.95), hot crispy duck, black pudding and bacon salad (£5.50), omelettes (from £5.50), pork and ale sausages (£5.95), and ploughman's or steak in ale pie (£7.95); evening dishes such as chicken supreme with wensleydale cheese, wrapped in bacon and topped with a tomato and sage sauce (£9.95), lemon sole with prawns and a lime and chive butter (£10.95), and braised lamb shank in ale (£11.95); cream teas (£3.75), plus cakes and tray bakes, milk shakes, lots of coffees and hot chocolates, and an ice-cream menu. Most of the good-sized tables have cheery american-cloth patterned tablecloths and brightly cushioned green café chairs but there are some modern pubbier tables near the bar. There's a good deal of bare woodwork, with some rough stonework painted dark red or dark green, and green-painted steel girders and pillars. This big area is partly divided up by free-standing partitions and some big plants; there's a thriving easy-going mix of ages and service is prompt and friendly. You may smoke only near the bar; piped music. Interesting brewery tours and a shop selling beers and more or less beer-related items from pub games and T-shirts to pottery and fudge. A glass wall lets you see into the brewing exhibition centre. Picnic-sets out on the grass. *(Recommended by Mr and Mrs Maurice Thompson, Neil and Angela Huxter, Tony and Penny Burton, Gerry and Rosemary Dobson)*

Free house ~ Licensee Paul Theakston ~ Real ale ~ Bar food (12-2.30(3 Sun); they do only evening food Thurs-Sat) ~ Restaurant ~ (01765) 680100 ~ Children welcome ~ Open 10.30-5 Mon-Weds and Sun; 10.30-midnight Thurs, Fri and Sat; best to phone for opening hours in winter

MIDDLEHAM   SE1288   Map 10

Black Swan
Market Place; DL8 4NP

As this 17th-c stone inn is in the heart of racing country, it is popular with local trainers and stable staff. The immaculately kept heavy-beamed bar has high-backed settles built in by the big stone fireplace, racing memorabilia on the stripped stone walls, horsebrasses and pewter mugs, and Hambleton Fabulous Filly, John Smiths, Theakstons Best, Black Bull and Old Peculier, and Wensleydale Tony's Tipple on handpump; a decent little wine list with several by the glass, and piped music, TV, bar skittles, dominoes, cribbage and board games. Bar food includes lunchtime soup (£3.50) and sandwiches or filled baguettes (from £3.50), as well as mushroom and spinach lasagne (£7.50), several varieties of sausage (£6.95), home-made steak pie (£7.50), beef in ale or chicken curry (£7.95), evening steaks (from £12.95), and daily specials such as local pheasant (£9.95), roasted squash and pepper strudel (£10.25), salmon fillet in lime and coriander butter (£10.95), and moroccan lamb (£11.95). The dining rooms and area by the bar are no smoking. There are tables on the cobbles outside and in the sheltered back garden. The bathrooms have all been refurbished this year. Good walking country. *(Recommended by R E Dixon, DC, Jon Forster, John Unsworth, Catherine Smith, Stephen R Holman, K M Crook)*

Free house ~ Licensees John and James Verbeken ~ Real ale ~ Bar food (12-2.30, 6.30-9) ~ Restaurant ~ (01969) 622221 ~ Children welcome ~ Dogs allowed in bar and bedrooms ~ Open 11-midnight; 11-1am Sat; 12-11 Sun; 11-3.30, 6-11 weekdays in winter ~ Bedrooms: £35S/£65S(£70B)

White Swan ♀ ⇌
Market Place; DL8 4PE

The new dining room here (which was the old post office next door) is now up and running and is light, spacious and modern with some popular window tables, a large fireplace, and in an area opposite the bar, some contemporary leather chairs and sofa. The beamed and flagstoned entrance bar has a relaxed pubby atmosphere, a long dark pew built into a big window, a mix of chairs around a handful of biggish tables, Black Sheep Best Bitter and Emmerdale Ale, John Smiths and Theakstons Best on handpump from the curved counter, 17 wines by the glass, and 20 malt whiskies; a good inglenook log fire. Another beamed room has a red oriental rug on its black boards and, like the first room, is candlelit. Piped music, cards and dominoes. From a sensibly smallish menu, the food might include sandwiches, home-made soup (£3.25), potted chicken liver parfait with red onion marmalade and apple chutney (£4.25), thai crab cakes with chilli jam (£4.75), pizzas (from £5.50), moules marinière (£5.75), home-made tagliatelle with wild mushrooms and thyme (£6.95), battered cod with home-made chips (£8.25), home-made chicken or steak in ale pie (£8.95), chicken breast stuffed with mozzarella and sun-dried tomato with pesto risotto (£9.75), and puddings such as iced liquorice terrine with caramel sauce or banoffi pie (£4.25); they also serve morning coffee and afternoon tea. *(Recommended by B and M Kendall, Janet and Peter Race, Dr and Mrs M W A Haward, Michael Butler, Richard, John Unsworth, Catherine Smith, Ian and Nita Cooper, Ben and Helen Ingram, Peter Burton)*

Free house ~ Licensees Andrew Holmes and Paul Klein ~ Real ale ~ Bar food (12-2.30, 6.30-9.30) ~ Restaurant ~ (01969) 622093 ~ Children allowed but not near bar area ~ Dogs allowed in bar ~ Open 11-midnight; 12-11.30 Sun ~ Bedrooms: £55B/£69B

MILL BANK SE0321 Map 7

Millbank 🍽 ♀

Mill Bank Road, off A58 SW of Sowerby Bridge; HX6 3DY

From the outside, this dining pub is cottagey and traditionally Pennine but once inside, there's a clean-cut minimalist modern décor and local photographs for sale. The interior is divided into the tap room, bar and no smoking restaurant, with Tetleys and Timothy Taylors Landlord on handpump, and 20 wines by the glass including champagne, port and pudding wines; also, a specialised gin list. Discreet background music of a jazzy flavour. Daily changing interesting food might include pea and mint soup (£4.95), sandwiches (from £4.95; available until 7pm), six oysters in cider batter with raita and chilli sauce (£8.95), chorizo and goats cheese flan with marinated beetroot or ham hock faggot with cheese mash and grape chutney (£5.95), saffron-marinated monkfish with warm niçoise-style salad (£5.95; main course £11.95), beer-battered haddock with pea purée or calves liver with sage and onion sauce (£9.95), lamb hotpot with hot and sour cabbage (£11.50), braised oxtail with root vegetables (£12.95), steaks (from £12.95), roast suckling pig with polenta fritters and spiced honey sauce (£13.95), and puddings like chocolate fondant cake with peanut butter ice-cream or lemongrass crème brûlée with raspberry sorbet (£5.50); they also have a two-course set menu (£11.95, not Sunday). Outside, the terrace has a glass roof and fold-away windows that make the most of the glorious setting overlooking an old textile mill. Below this is a garden adorned with metal sculptures made from old farm equipment. The Calderdale Way is easily accessible from the pub. More reports please.
(Recommended by Walter and Susan Rinaldi-Butcher)

Timothy Taylor ~ Licensee Joe McNally ~ Real ale ~ Bar food (12-2.30, 6-9.30(10 Sat); 12-4.30, 6-8 Sun; not Mon lunchtime) ~ Restaurant ~ (01422) 825588 ~ Children welcome ~ Dogs allowed in bar ~ Open 12-3, 5.30-11; 12-10.30 Sun; closed Mon lunchtime; first two weeks Oct, first week Jan

NORTH DALTON SE9352 Map 8

Star

B1246 Pocklington—Driffield; YO25 9UX

Now leased to Enterprise and with new licensees, this 18th-c brick-built pub is set for some changes. By the time this edition is published bedrooms will have been opened, a new kitchen created, and the bar doubled in size. It's a civilised place in a relaxed gently upmarket country style, with a mix of candlelit tables in the main right-hand eating area, and some deeply comfortable seats with a good coal fire in the smart but properly pubby bar; there's still a growing collection of breweriana. John Smiths plus Black Sheep, Timothy Taylors Landlord and a beer from Copper Dragon on handpump, and several wines by the glass; piped music. Bar food now includes home-made soup (£3.95), goats cheese, banana and toasted walnut salad with a honey dressing (£5.95), smoked duck breast, apple and redcurrant salad with scrumpy dressing (£6.95), fresh local crab and pawpaw salad with a zappy lemon coulis (£7.50), charred halloumi, red pepper and aubergine stack with fried wild mushrooms and truffle oil (£13.95), roast pork fillet wrapped in smoked bacon on colcannon potato cake with cider jus (£14.95), calves liver, pancetta and sage polenta and grain mustard and rioja sauce (£15.50), baked halibut with a kiwi, cherry tomato, spring onion and chilli salsa (£17.95), and puddings such as muscovado ginger sponge, cider syrup and vanilla ice-cream, individual chocolate crusted cheesecake with fresh raspberry coulis (£5.50), and passion fruit crème brûlée with home-made biscuits (from £5.50). The no smoking restaurant was originally a victorian pig sty. They have a bar quiz on Sunday evenings. More reports on the changes, please. *(Recommended by Dr Ian S Morley, C A Hall, Michael Swallow)*

Enterprise ~ Lease John Hall ~ Real ale ~ Bar food ~ Restaurant ~ (01377) 217688 ~
Children allowed if eating and well behaved ~ Open 12-2.30, 6-midnight; 12-3, 6-midnight
Sun ~ Bedrooms

NOSTERFIELD   SE2780   Map 7
Freemasons Arms ⬤
B6267; DL8 2QP

There's lots to look at in this popular, bustling pub. The low black beams are hung
with gas masks, steel helmets, miners' lamps, pewter tankards and so forth, there
are big prints of Queen Victoria, many old enamel advertising signs, and union
flags propped in corners; the cosy feel is boosted by the warm lighting, the candles
on the tables, and the hot coal fires. Using only local produce, the well liked bar
food includes sandwiches (from £3.95), caesar salad (£4.25), baked goats cheese
with rocket salad and red onion jam (£4.95), salmon fillet wrapped in parma ham
with roasted mediterranean vegetables (£12.50), 12oz free-range pork chop with
thyme mash and cider jus or rump of lamb with creamed savoy cabbage and
smoked bacon (£12.95), and puddings such as eton mess (£3.95). The main bar
area has just two or three tables with close wooden booth seating on its flagstones;
there are more tables with pews and settles in the carpeted room on the left. Black
Sheep, Theakstons Best, Timothy Taylors Landlord and a changing guest on
handpump and ten wines by the glass; piped music and dominoes. There are a few
picnic-sets out in front, with pretty flower tubs and baskets. They now have a self-
catering flat to let. More reports please. *(Recommended by Mr and Mrs
Maurice Thompson, Pete Baker, Janet and Peter Race)*

Free house ~ Licensee Kris Stephenson ~ Real ale ~ Bar food (not Mon) ~
(01677) 470548 ~ Children allowed but must be well behaved ~ Dogs allowed in bar ~
Open 12-3, 6-11; 12-10.30 Sun; closed Mon

NUNNINGTON   SE6779   Map 7
Royal Oak 🍴
Church Street; at back of village, which is signposted from A170 and B1257; YO62 5US

After a visit to Nunnington Hall (National Trust), this neatly kept and attractive
little pub is just the place to head for. The bar has high black beams strung with
earthenware flagons, copper jugs and lots of antique keys, one of the walls is
stripped back to the bare stone to display a fine collection of antique farm tools,
and there are open fires; carefully chosen furniture such as kitchen and country
dining chairs or a long pew around the sturdy tables on the turkey carpet, and a
lectern in one corner. The dining room is no smoking and staff are genuinely
friendly and helpful. Good bar food includes home-made soup (£4.35), sandwiches
(from £4.95), chicken liver pâté with home-made chutney (£5.75), mushrooms
stuffed with garlic butter and stilton (£5.95), seafood hors d'oeuvres (£6.50),
ploughman's (£7.50), delicious steak pie (£9.50), lasagne, sweet and sour
vegetables, steak and kidney casserole with herb dumpling, pork fillet in barbecue
sauce or chicken breast in cheesy mustard sauce (all £9.95), fisherman's pot
(£10.25), crispy roast duckling with orange sauce (£11.95), 12oz sirloin
steak (£14.95), daily specials such as local sausages with red onion gravy (£8.95),
salmon in dill sauce (£9.50), fresh battered cod (£9.95), and fillet steak au poivre
(£17.50), and nice puddings (£4.75). Black Sheep, Tetleys, and Theakstons Old
Peculier on handpump; piped music. *(Recommended by Mike Dean, Lis Wingate Gray,
Miss J E Edwards, Peter Burton, Roger A Bellingham, Michael J Caley, Pat and
Graham Williamson, Mr and Mrs P M Jennings)*

Free house ~ Licensee Anthony Simpson ~ Real ale ~ Bar food (not Mon) ~
(01439) 748271 ~ Children welcome with restrictions ~ Open 12-2.30, 6.30-11;
12-2.30, 7-10.30 Sun; closed Mon

The knife-and-fork award distinguishes pubs where the food is of exceptional quality.

OSMOTHERLEY   SE4499   Map 10

Golden Lion ◀

The Green, West End; off A19 N of Thirsk; DL6 3AA

By the time this edition is published, the bedrooms in this old stone-built pub
should be up and running. The courtyard is to be adapted to offer a covered dining
area. The roomy beamed bar on the left, simply furnished with old pews and just a
few decorations on its white walls, has a pleasantly lively atmosphere, candles on
tables, Hambleton Bitter, Timothy Taylors Landlord and John Smiths or York
Yorkshire Terrier on handpump and 45 malt whiskies; one side of the pub is no
smoking. On the right, a similarly unpretentious and well worn-in eating area offers
bar food such as soup (£3.95), goats cheese and red pepper terrine with onion and
apricot relish (£5.50), mussels in wine and cream (£6.50), home-made burgers using
beef, chicken or lamb (£6.50), king prawns in garlic butter or spinach, ricotta and
pine nut lasagne (£7.95), salmon fishcake with creamy sorrel sauce (£8.75), home-
made chicken kiev or steak and kidney pie (£9.95), calves liver and onions
(£11.95), daily specials like pork stroganoff (£9.95) or roast duck with marsala,
mushroom and tarragon sauce (£14.95), and puddings such as crème brûlée or
middle eastern orange cake with marmalade cream (£3.95). You must book to be
sure of a table and it does get pretty packed. There's also a separate dining room,
mainly open at weekends; piped music. Benches out in front look across the village
green to the market cross. As the inn is the start of the 44-mile Lyke Wakes Walk
on the Cleveland Way and, quite handy for the Coast to Coast Walk, it is naturally
popular with walkers. More reports please. *(Recommended by Martin and
Alison Stainsby, Blaise Vyner, David Carr, A Pickering, Roger Noyes, Pat and Tony Martin,
Dr and Mrs R G J Telfer)*

Free house ~ Licensee Christie Connelly ~ Real ale ~ Bar food (12-3, 6-9) ~ Restaurant ~
(01609) 883526 ~ Children welcome if eating ~ Dogs allowed in bar ~ Open 12-3.30,
6-11; 12-midnight(11 Sun) Sat; closed 25 Dec ~ Bedrooms: /£70B

PICKERING   SE7983   Map 10

White Swan 🍽 ♀ 🛌

Market Place, just off A170; YO18 7AA

This smart old coaching inn has particularly comfortable, well appointed bedrooms
and very good, interesting restaurant-style food – but the small bar remains
properly pubby with a charming country atmosphere, panelling, a log fire and just
three or four tables. Opposite, a bare-boards room with a few more tables has
another fire in a handsome art nouveau iron fireplace, a big bow window, and pear
prints on its plum-coloured walls. The restaurant has flagstones, a fine open fire,
rich tweed soft furnishings, comfortable settles and gothic screens. You may smoke
only in the bar. Using the best local produce, the attractively presented food at
lunchtime might include sandwiches (from £5.95; club sandwich £7.95), soup with
home-made bread (£4.25), baked free-range eggs with brown shrimps and parsley
cream (£5.95), potted whitby crab with dressed celeriac (£5.95), pressed ham
knuckle with potato and chive salad (£6.95), posh fish and chips with home-made
sauces (£10.95), blue cheese and leek stuffed aubergine with saffron risotto
(£11.95), and belly pork with mustard mash and apple sauce (£14.95); there's also
a two-course (£10.95) and three-course (£12.95) set lunch. Evening choices such as
seared pigeon breast with red wine risotto (£6.95), carpaccio of wild venison with
blue cheese, rocket and loganberries (£7.95), hand-dived king scallops with capers,
york ham and garlic butter (£8.95), jerusalem artichoke, spinach and grilled goats
cheese pasta with red onion marmalade (£12.95), roast free-range chicken breast
with vegetable stew and crisp smoked bacon (£13.95), baked turbot with nut
brown butter (£16.95), and puddings like crème brûlée with fruit and nut biscotti,
chocolate cake with chocolate sauce or glazed lemon tart with boozy cherries
(£5.50). Black Sheep, Cropton Yorkshire Moors and Timothy Taylors Landlord
tapped from the cask, good house wines (by two sizes of glass; pudding wines and
superb list of old St Emilions), and several malt whiskies. The old coach entry to the

car park is very narrow. *(Recommended by Paul Humphreys, David Carr, A Pickering, Sylvia and Tony Birbeck, Christopher Turner, Judith and Edward Pearson, J Crosby)*

Free house ~ Licensees Marion and Victor Buchanan ~ Real ale ~ Bar food ~ Restaurant ~ (01751) 472288 ~ Children in lounge and restaurant ~ Dogs allowed in bar and bedrooms ~ Open 10-4, 6-11; 10am-11pm Mon and Sat; 12-3, 7-10.30 Sun ~ Bedrooms: £89B/£139B

PICKHILL SE3584 Map 10
Nags Head ⊕ ♀ ⇔
Take the Masham turn-off from A1 both N and S, and village signposted off B6267 in Ainderby Quernhow; YO7 4JG

Most people come to this busy dining pub to enjoy the good food and indeed, apart from the bar, the tables are laid for eating. If it is just a drink you're after, head for the bustling tap room on the left (which is the only place you may smoke): beams hung with jugs, coach horns, ale-yards and so forth, and masses of ties hanging as a frieze from a rail around the red ceiling. The smarter lounge bar has deep green plush banquettes on the matching carpet, pictures for sale on its neat cream walls, and an open fire. The well liked food might include sandwiches, home-made soup (£3.50), smoked haddock, cod and salmon fishcakes with chilli jam (£5.25), chicken liver pâté with pear chutney or fried wild pigeon breast with apple salad and raspberry vinaigrette (£5.50), bangers and mash with onion gravy (£8.95), wild rocket and toasted pine nut risotto with blue buffalo cheese (£9.50), curried chicken breast on saag aloo potatoes and an onion bhaji (£11.95), game casserole with herb dumpling (£12.95), roast chump of local lamb with caramelised apple and mint juices (£13.95), roast fillet of halibut on savoy cabbage with lemon butter and shellfish bisque (£14.95), steaks (from £15.95), and puddings such as Baileys cheesecake with a mango compote and butterscotch sauce or iced rhubarb parfait with sweet ginger shortbreads (£4.95); good breakfasts. There's also a library-themed restaurant. Black Sheep, Hambleton Bitter, Theakstons Best and Village White Boar on handpump, a good choice of malt whiskies, vintage armagnacs, and a carefully chosen wine list with several by the glass. One table is inset with a chessboard, and they also have cribbage, dominoes and shove-ha'penny. There's a front verandah, a boules and quoits pitch, and nine-hole putting green. *(Recommended by Val and Alan Green, David Miles-Dinham, Charles and Pauline Stride, J F M and M West, Phil and Helen Holt, Tony and Tracy Constance, Jill and Julian Tasker, Ginny Barbour, Alan Jefferson, Walter and Susan Rinaldi-Butcher, Michael and Anne Brown, Mr and Mrs John Taylor, Alison and Pete, Barry and Anne)*

Free house ~ Licensee Edward Boynton ~ Real ale ~ Bar food ~ Restaurant ~ (01845) 567391 ~ Children in bistro bar and dining room until 7.30pm ~ Dogs allowed in bedrooms ~ Open 11-11; closed 25 Dec ~ Bedrooms: £50S(£55B)/£75B

RIPLEY SE2861 Map 7
Boars Head ⊕ ♀ ▨ ⇔
Off A61 Harrogate—Ripon; HG3 3AY

The friendly, no smoking bar here is attached to a smart and comfortable hotel but it still manages to keep a relaxed atmosphere, local customers, and Black Sheep, Hambleton White Boar, Theakstons Old Peculier and Timothy Taylors Landlord on handpump; an excellent wine list (with ten or so by the glass), and around 20 malt whiskies. It's a long flagstoned room with green checked tablecloths and olive oil on all the tables, most of which are arranged to form individual booths. The warm yellow walls have jolly little drawings of cricketers or huntsmen running along the bottom, as well as a boar's head (part of the family coat of arms), an interesting religious carving, and a couple of cricket bats. From a menu that changes every two weeks, the well liked food might include sandwiches, soup (£3.50), a plate of british cheeses with celery and grapes (£3.75), chicken mousseline or a plate of smoked salmon with lemon and dill mascarpone (£5.50; main course £10.50), asparagus, garlic and pepper linguini (£8.95), venison sausages on mustard mash with red wine jus, braised rump of lamb with apricot and thyme crushed new potatoes and madeira gravy or salmon topped with guacamole with a watercress dressing (£9.95), and puddings such as dark chocolate crème brûlée, mixed berry parfait with cassis sauce, and sticky toffee pudding with butterscotch sauce (£3.75); efficient staff even when very busy. Piped music and TV. Some of the furnishings in the hotel came from the attic of next door Ripley Castle, where the Ingilbys have lived for over 650 years. A pleasant little garden has plenty of tables. *(Recommended by Martin and Pauline Jennings, Geoff and Teresa Salt, Keith Wright, Michael Butler, Comus and Sarah Elliott, Andrew and Samantha Grainger, G Dobson, the Didler, Stephen R Holman, David and Ruth Hollands, Michael Doswell, M J Winterton, Dr D Scott)*

Free house ~ Licensee Sir Thomas Ingilby ~ Real ale ~ Bar food ~ Restaurant ~ (01423) 771888 ~ Children welcome ~ Dogs allowed in bedrooms ~ Open 11-11(10.30 Sun); 11-3, 5-11 winter ~ Bedrooms: £105B/£125B

RIPPONDEN SE0419 Map 7
Old Bridge ♀ ◨

From A58, best approach is Elland Road (opposite Golden Lion), park opposite the church in pub's car park and walk back over ancient hump-backed bridge; HX6 4DF

This 15th-c pub is by the medieval pack-horse bridge over the little River Ryburn and there's a little garden overlooking the water. Inside, the three communicating rooms are each on a slightly different level – the bottom one is no smoking. There's a relaxed atmosphere, oak settles built into the window recesses of the thick stone walls, antique oak tables, rush-seated chairs, a few well chosen pictures and prints, and a big woodburning stove. On weekday lunchtimes, bar food includes only sandwiches (from £3) and soup together with the popular help-yourself carvery and salad buffet (£10.50). At weekends and in the evening, there might be dolcelatte cheesecake with pickled pear (£4.50), country-style terrine with apricot chutney (£4.75), meat and potato pie (£7.50), smoked haddock and spinach pancakes (£7.75), gressingham duck on oriental noodles (£8.50), slow-roast shoulder of lamb with rosemary, red wine and garlic (£10.95), sirloin steak with madeira sauce (£10.95), and puddings (£3.50). Black Sheep Emmerdale Ale, Copper Dragon Black Gold and Timothy Taylors Best, Golden Best and Landlord on handpump, a dozen wines by the glass, 30 malt whiskies, and a good choice of foreign bottled beers. More reports please. *(Recommended by Matt Waite, Mrs Yvette Bateman, GSB)*

Free house ~ Licensees Tim and Lindsay Eaton Walker ~ Real ale ~ Bar food (12-2, 6.30-9.30; not Sat or Sun evening) ~ (01422) 822595 ~ Children in eating area of bar until 8pm but must be well behaved ~ Open 12-3, 5.30-11; 12-11 Sat; 12-10.30 Sun; closed 25 Dec

ROBIN HOOD'S BAY NZ9505 Map 10
Laurel ◨

Village signposted off A171 S of Whitby; YO22 4SE

At the heart of one of the prettiest and most unspoilt fishing villages on the north east coast is this charming little pub. The beamed and welcoming main bar is neatly kept, and is decorated with old local photographs, Victorian prints and brasses, and lager bottles from all over the world; the snug is no smoking, there's a roaring open fire, and sandwiches are served on winter Saturday lunchtimes only. Well kept Caledonian Deuchars IPA, and Theakstons Best and Old Peculier on handpump; darts, board games and piped music. In summer, the hanging baskets and window boxes are lovely. They have a self-contained apartment for two people. More reports please. *(Recommended by John Dwane, David Carr)*

Free house ~ Licensee Brian Catling ~ Real ale ~ Bar food ~ No credit cards ~ (01947) 880400 ~ Children in snug bar only ~ Dogs welcome ~ Open 12-11; 12-10.30 Sun; weekday opening time 2pm in winter

---

Pubs brewing their own beers are listed at the back of the book.

SAWLEY   SE2568   Map 7

Sawley Arms ♀

Village signposted off B6265 W of Ripon; HG4 3EQ

For 37 years Mrs Hawes has been at the helm of this spotlessly kept, no smoking dining pub. It is particularly popular with older customers and is ultra-civilised in an old-fashioned, decorous sort of way. The small turkey-carpeted rooms have log fires and comfortable furniture ranging from small softly cushioned armed dining chairs and settees, to the wing armchairs down a couple of steps in a side snug; maybe daily papers and magazines to read, piped music. There's also a conservatory. Restaurant food includes lunchtime sandwiches, home-made soup with croûtons (£3.50), salmon mousse (£5.50), plaice mornay (£8.95), home-made steak pie (£10.50), corn-fed chicken breast in a mushroom and herb sauce (£11.50), and daily specials; good house wines. In fine weather there are tables and chairs in the pretty garden, and the flowering tubs and baskets are lovely; two stone cottages in the grounds for rent. Fountains Abbey (the most extensive of the great monastic remains – floodlit on late summer Friday and Saturday evenings, with a live choir on the Saturday) – is not far away. *(Recommended by G Dobson, Brian Wainwright, Bryan and Mary Blaxall)*

Free house ~ Licensee Mrs June Hawes ~ Bar food (not Mon evening or winter Sun evening) ~ Restaurant ~ (01765) 620642 ~ Well behaved children over 9 only ~ Dogs allowed in bedrooms ~ Open 11.30-3, 6.30-10.30; 12-3, 6-10 Sun; Sun evening in winter; closed Mon evening all year

SHEFFIELD   SK3687   Map 7

Fat Cat ♪ £

23 Alma Street; S3 8SA

The upstairs room here has been refurbished and a new TV system installed for sport. But it's the downstairs pubby rooms that most customers head for – keen to enjoy the own-brewed Kelham Island beers and six guests all well kept on handpump. There's a Brewery Visitor's Centre (you can book brewery trips (0114) 249 4804). There are framed beer mats, pump clips and prints on the walls, and Kelham Island Bitter, Pale Rider, and two of their own guests, plus guests from Archers, Copper Dragon, Station House, Timothy Taylors and Woodfordes. Also, foreign bottled beers, two belgian draught beers, fruit gin, country wines and farm cider. Incredibly cheap, enjoyable bar food includes sandwiches, soup (£2), ploughman's, cheese and cauliflower hotpot or spicy beef casserole (all £3.50), aubergine and tomato or steak pie (£4), and puddings like spotted dick or apple crumble (£1.50). The two small downstairs rooms have brewery-related prints on the walls, coal fires, simple wooden tables and cushioned seats around the walls, and jugs, bottles and some advertising mirrors; the one on the left is no smoking; cribbage and dominoes and maybe the pub cat wandering around. There are picnic-sets in a fairylit back courtyard. *(Recommended by Kevin Blake, David Carr, the Didler, Mark and Diane Grist, C J Fletcher, Keith and Chris O'Neill, BOB, James A Waller, Pete Baker)*

Own brew ~ Licensee Stephen Fearn ~ Real ale ~ Bar food (not 25 or 26 Dec or 1 Jan) ~ No credit cards ~ (0114) 249 4801 ~ Children welcome away from bar ~ Dogs welcome ~ Open 12-3, 5.30-11; 12-midnight Fri and Sat; 12-3, 7-11 Sun; closed 25 Dec

New Barrack ♪ £

601 Penistone Road, Hillsborough; S6 2GA

The lively atmosphere in this really friendly, sizeable pub is helped by regular live music, a curry night (Tuesday), a weekly quiz evening (Wednesday), and up to ten real ales. Well kept on handpump, there are regulars such as Abbeydale Moonshine, Acorn Barnsley Bitter and Castle Rock Harvest Pale and a seasonal beer, and six constantly changing guests; also, real cider, a range of bottled belgian beers, and 28 malt whiskies. The comfortable front lounge has soft upholstered seats, old pine floors, a woodburning stove, and collections of decorative plates and of bottles, and there are two smaller rooms behind – one with high ceilings and benches, stools and tables around the edges, and the third room (no smoking) is more set up for eating; TV, darts, cribbage, dominoes and piped music. Tasty bar food now includes sandwiches (from £1.90; fresh baked baguettes from £3.95; steak sandwich £5.75), burgers (from £2.10), all-day breakfast (£3.75), pie and peas (£4.35), pizzas (from £4.60; 50p per extra topping), spicy vegetable gumbo or chicken piri piri (£5.50), chilli (£5.95), and mixed grill (£9.95). Daily papers and magazines to read; maybe quiet piped radio. There's a small walled back garden. Local parking is not easy. More reports please. *(Recommended by David Carr, B and M Kendall, the Didler, Mark and Diane Grist)*

Tynemill ~ Manager Kevin Woods ~ Real ale ~ Bar food (11-3, 5-9; 12-3, 7-9 Sun) ~ (0114) 234 9148 ~ Children welcome until 9pm ~ Dogs welcome ~ Live music Fri, Sat and Sun evenings ~ Open 11-11; 11-midnight Fri and Sat; 12-11 Sun

SHELLEY SE2112 Map 7

Three Acres 🏮 ♀ 🍴 🛏️

Roydhouse (not signposted); from B6116 heading for Skelmanthorpe, turn left in Shelley (signposted Flockton, Elmley, Elmley Moor) and go up lane for 2 miles towards radio mast; HD8 8LR

Yorkshire Dining Pub of the Year

Now totally no smoking, this civilised former coaching inn is still on top form and remains exceedingly popular for its stylish food. The roomy lounge bar has a relaxed, friendly atmosphere, tankards hanging from the main beam, button-back leather sofas, old prints and so forth, and Black Sheep, Caledonian Deuchars IPA, Tetleys and Timothy Taylors Landlord on handpump, over 40 whiskies and a fantastic (if not cheap) choice of wines, with at least 17 by the glass. To be sure of a place, you must book (quite a way ahead) – try to get a table with a view; piped music. Even the sandwiches are special here: vegetarian club, prawns and langoustines with avocado, sun-blush tomatoes and seafood sauce or open hot toulouse sausage, dijon mustard and caramelised peppers on onion bread with chilli onion rings (all £5.95), and open steak on toasted olive and tomato bread with caramelised sweet pepper marmalade topped with mustard and horseradish butter (£8.95). Also, french onion soup baked with a gruyère croûton (£4.95), potted shrimps or chinese beef, ginger and spring onion dumplings with fragrant noodles (£6.95), coquilles of smoked fish with spinach and sorrel cream glazed with parmesan (£7.95), steak, kidney and mushroom pie with a pot of home-made brown sauce or roast mediterranean vegetables with gratin of goats cheese, fresh sage pasta and garlic ciabatta (£13.95), fresh haddock in a crisp tomato and basil butter with home-made tartare sauce or a lunchtime roast (£14.95), open ravioli of squab pigeon and wild mushrooms on buttered cabbage and pancetta lardons (£15.95), honey-roast half a crispy gressingham duck, sage and onion stuffing and bramley apple jus (£16.95), and puddings such as prune and armagnac sticky toffee pudding with toffee sauce, green apple and grapefruit bavarois with mango sorbet and apple crisp or chocolate marquise with crème de menthe ice-cream and griottine cherries (£6.50). There's a delicatessen next door with take-home meals; helpful, welcoming service, even when really pushed. Fine views across to Emley Moor. *(Recommended by W K Wood, J R Ringrose, Trevor and Judith Pearson, Hunter and Christine Wright, Anthony Moody, M and GR, Peter Fitton, Mr and Mrs J Hutton, Richard Cole, Dr Michael Smith, Martin and Sue Day, Michael Butler)*

Free house ~ Licensees Neil Truelove and Brian Orme ~ Real ale ~ Bar food (12-2, 6.30-9.30) ~ Restaurant ~ (01484) 602606 ~ Children welcome ~ Open 12-3, 6-11(10.30 Sun); closed 25 Dec-2 Jan ~ Bedrooms: £60B/£80B

If we know a pub does sandwiches we always say so – if they're not mentioned, you'll have to assume you can't get one.

SINNINGTON SE7485 Map 10
Fox & Hounds 🍴 ♟ 🛏️
Just off A170 W of Pickering; YO62 6SQ

Although the food in this welcoming and neat 18th-c coaching inn is very good,
they've cleverly managed to retain a pubby image, too. The beamed bar has various
pictures and old artefacts, a woodburning stove and comfortable wall seats and
carver chairs around the tables on its carpet. The curved corner bar counter has
Black Sheep Special and Theakstons Best on handpump, several wines by the glass
and some rare malt whiskies. At lunchtime, the well liked bar food might include
home-made soup (£4.25), sandwiches (from £4.50), chicken liver parfait with
madeira jelly (£5.25), twice-baked stilton, dried tomato and cheddar soufflé with
black grape compote (£5.45; main course £9.45), crab cakes with red pepper pesto
(£5.95; £8.95 main course), local sausages with spinach and onion gravy (£7.45),
chargrilled minute steak with paprika and tomato chutney (£8.50), beer-battered
fresh haddock with home-made tartare sauce (£9.45), and roast breast and leg of
chicken with mushrooms, smoked bacon and red wine sauce (£9.95); evening
extras such as hot smoked salmon with blinis, horseradish and shallot cream
(£6.75), black pudding, seared foie gras, spinach, quail egg and apple rösti (£6.95),
filled vegetarian savoury choux ring (£9.75), slow-cooked shoulder of lamb with
rosemary and thyme sauce (£13.25), and fillet of pork wellington, sweet beetroot
casserole and calvados cream (£13.50), and puddings like lemon tart with raspberry
coulis, white chocolate bavarois, brandy snap basket and dark chocolate ice-cream
and bread and butter pudding with apricot glaze (£4.65). The lounge bar and
restaurant are no smoking; piped music and dominoes. Picnic-sets out in front and
in the garden. This is a quiet and charming village. (*Recommended by Janet and
Peter Race, Matthew Shackle, Cathryn and Richard Hicks, Sarah and Peter Gooderham,
C A Hall, Mark Walker, Alison and Pete, Michael Butler*)

Free house ~ Licensees Andrew and Catherine Stephens ~ Real ale ~ Bar food ~
Restaurant (evening) ~ (01751) 431577 ~ Children allowed until 8.15pm ~ Dogs allowed
in bar and bedrooms ~ Open 12-2, 6(6.30 in winter)-11(midnight Sat); 12-2, 6.30-11 Sun;
closed 25 and 26 Dec ~ Bedrooms: £59S(£69B)/£90S(£100B)

SOUTH DALTON SE9645 Map 8
Pipe & Glass 🍴 ♟
West End; brown sign to pub off B1248 NW of Beverley; HU17 7PN

This charmingly set tucked-away dining pub has been given a thorough shake-up
by new licensees who have the very best of credentials – both played big parts in
making the Star at Harome so special. It's a pretty, tiled building, and they have
kept its traditional bar, beamed and bow-windowed, with a log fire, some old
prints and even high-backed settles. Beyond that, all is airy and comfortably
contemporary, angling around past some soft modern dark leather sofas into a light
restaurant area overlooking Dalton Park, with comfortable dining chairs around
well spaced country tables on bare boards. You may smoke only in the bar; piped
music. The decorations – a row of serious cookery books, and framed big-name
restaurant menus – show how high the chef/landlord aims. Changing daily and
using top quality local produce, the imaginative food includes lunchtime dishes like
boiled bacon shank and parsley terrine with piccalilli purée (£4.95; main course
£7.95), home-smoked roe deer with celeriac coleslaw, crispy quail egg and roast
hazelnut dressing (£5.45), sandwiches (from £5.45), a little jar of potted shrimps
with watercress and baby caper salad (£5.95), a proper ploughman's (£6.95), and
mature cheddar omelette with scallion salad or good sausages, bubble and squeak
and onion gravy (£8.95); also, tomato and avocado salad with peppered goats
cheese and cumin crisps (£5.45; main course £9.95), three-onion quiche with wild
rocket, parmesan and a salad with soubise cream (£9.95), grilled barnsley chop,
devilled kidneys and a nettle and mint sauce or coq au vin with girolle mushrooms,
garlic and oregano mash (£12.95), sirloin steak with thyme sautéed potatoes, roast
shallots and blue cheese fritter (£14.95), daily specials such as salmon fishcakes

with cullen skink stew (£5.45; main course £9.95), whitby crab risotto with asparagus (£5.95; main course £9.95), chicken kiev or dry cure gammon steak with chips (£9.95), roast monkfish with braised fennel, oxtail and green lentils (£14.95), grilled whole dover sole, samphire, smoked eel and capers or gressingham duck breast with scrumpy potato, crispy black pudding and apple sauce (£15.95), and puddings like warm chocolate fondant with goats milk ice-cream, pear and almond tart or sticky toffee pudding with demerara butterscotch sauce (£4.95). John Smiths and a couple of changing guests like Copper Dragon Golden Pippin and Daleside Blonde on handpump, ten wines by the glass, and Old Rosie cider. Service is friendly and prompt, by bright and attentive young staff who have obviously been well trained; disabled access. There are tables out on the garden's peaceful lawn beside the park; people say the yew tree is some 500 years old. The village is charming, and its elegant Victorian church spire, 62 metres (204 ft) tall, is visible for miles around. They hope to open bedrooms some time this year. *(Recommended by Jonathan Laverack, John Saul, Kevin Blake)*

Free house ~ Licensees James Mackenzie and Kate Boroughs ~ Real ale ~ Bar food (12-2, 6.30-9.30; 12-4 Sun; no food Sun evening) ~ Restaurant ~ (01430) 810246 ~ Children welcome ~ Open 12-3, 6.30-11; 12-10.30 Sun; closed Mon

SUTTON UPON DERWENT   SE7047   Map 7
St Vincent Arms   🍽 ♀ 🍺
B1228 SE of York; YO41 4BN

Happily unchanging and always with a good, bustling atmosphere, this is a really enjoyable local run by friendly people. The parlour-like panelled front bar has traditional high-backed settles, a cushioned bow-window seat, windsor chairs and a gas-effect coal fire; another lounge and separate dining room open off. To be sure of a seat, it's best to get here early. At lunchtime, the tasty food includes sandwiches (from £3.80; sirloin steak in ciabatta £6.50), salads (from £7; griddled chicken caesar £8), home-made lasagne (£7.90), home-made steak and mushroom in ale pie or large haddock and chips (£8.20), and steaks (from £12); evening choices such as home-made soup (£3.50), baked mushrooms topped with goats cheese and pesto dressing (£5), cornish crab mayonnaise (£5.50), vegetable stir fry (£7), mixed grill (£9), thai chicken breast or beef stroganoff (£10.50), rack of lamb with mini shepherd's pie (£13.50), and puddings like home-made tiramisu, apple pie or treacle tart (from £3.80). All rooms, except the bar, are no smoking. A super choice of beers on handpump: Fullers Chiswick, London Pride, ESB, and seasonal ales, Marstons Pedigree, Old Mill Bitter, Timothy Taylors Landlord, Charles Wells Bombardier and York Yorkshire Terrier; nine wines by the glass, and several malt whiskies. There are seats in the garden. The pub is named after the admiral who was granted the village and lands by the nation as thanks for his successful commands – and for coping with Nelson's infatuation with Lady Hamilton. Handy for the Yorkshire Air Museum. *(Recommended by Roger A Bellingham, David Carr, Paul and Ursula Randall, Andy and Jill Kassube, Pat and Tony Martin, Peter and Anne-Marie O'Malley, Brian P White, Derek and Sylvia Stephenson)*

Free house ~ Licensees Phil, Simon and Adrian Hopwood ~ Real ale ~ Bar food ~ Restaurant ~ (01904) 608349 ~ Children welcome ~ Open 11.30-3, 6-11; 12-3, 7-10.30 Sun

SUTTON-ON-THE-FOREST   SE5864   Map 7
Rose & Crown   🍽 ♀
B1363 N of York; YO61 1DP

A new conservatory and large decked terrace with thatched outside tables and a sizeable heated thatched gazebo have been added to this neatly kept beamed pub; there's a garden, too. Inside on the right is a small parquet-floored bar with old engravings on sage green walls, Black Sheep, Timothy Taylors Landlord, and a changing guest on handpump from an intricately carved counter, 14 wines by the glass from an interesting list, old-fashioned pub seating, a couple of dimpled copper tables, and some bric-a-brac on the mantelpiece. The L-shaped, newly decorated no smoking dining room on the left is bigger and now has proper dining chairs and tables on its polished boards, more etchings on its cream walls, and a former inglenook, There's quite an emphasis on fish and seafood: prawn caesar salad (£4.95), mussels in white wine, cream and garlic (£5.95; main course £10.95), king scallops with garlic butter and gruyère (£6.50; main course £12.50), giant prawns with tomato mayonnaise (£8.95), chunky roast whitby cod, natural smoked haddock with creamed savoy cabbage and black pudding or fillet of plaice with spinach and a rich cheese sauce (all £13.50), a cold seafood platter (£19.50), and lobster thermidor (half £17.50; whole £26); daily specials, meaty options like sirloin steak with peppercorn sauce (£14.95) and loin of lamb with pea and mint risotto (£15.95), and puddings such as crème brûlée or sticky toffee pudding (£4.50); coffee is good. More reports please. *(Recommended by Mr and Mrs P M Jennings, Michael Doswell, Pat and Graham Williamson)*

Free house ~ Licensee Mr Middleton ~ Real ale ~ Bar food (12-2(3 Sun), 6-9; not Sun vening or Mon) ~ Restaurant ~ (01347) 811333 ~ Children welcome ~ Open 12-2, 6-11; 12-11 Sat; 12-2.30 Sun; closed Sun evening, all day Mon

THORNTON IN LONSDALE   SD6976   Map 7

Marton Arms 🍺 🛏

Off A65 just NW of Ingleton (or can be reached direct from Ingleton); LA6 3PB

It's not surprising that this place is so popular – they have around 350 malt whiskies and up to 15 real ales. It's now totally no smoking and the beamed bar has stools on black boards by the long counter, lots of stripped pine tables, pews and built-in wall seats in the light and airy main part and biggish black and white local photographs; some train memorabilia. A curtained-off flagstoned public bar has bar billiards, darts and piped music, and both seating areas have open log fires. On handpump, the beers come from breweries like Batemans, Black Sheep, Brains, Copper Dragon, Cropton, Dent, Elgoods, Hydes, Jennings, Lancaster, Moorhouses, Theakstons, Timothy Taylors and Wychwood; four-pint take-aways, too. Also, Stowford Press and Weston's farm cider, all sorts of unusual spirits, a decent choice of wines, and an enterprising range of soft drinks, as well as proper tea and coffee. Bar food, generously served, includes home-made soup (£3.75), pâté (£4.35), sandwiches (from £4.65), burgers (from £5.10), home-made pizzas (from £6.50), cumberland sausage with onion gravy (£7.95), home-made meaty or vegetarian lasagne (£8.25), battered haddock (£9.20), steak and kidney pudding (£9.45), gammon and egg (£10.95), steaks (from £13.50), daily specials, and puddings (£3.50); Sunday roast (£9.50) and friendly service. There are picnic-sets out on the front terrace, with more behind. Two of the bedrooms are equipped for disabled people; good breakfasts, which suit this great walking country. The 13th-c church opposite is where Sir Arthur Conan Doyle was married. *(Recommended by Rob Razzell, Andy and Jill Kassube, David and Sue Smith, Len Beattie, Jo Lilley, Simon Calvert, John and Sylvia Harrop, Alex and Claire Pearse)*

Enterprise ~ Lease Graham Wright ~ Real ale ~ Bar food (not Mon-Thurs lunchtimes in winter) ~ (0152 42) 41281 ~ Children allowed until 9pm ~ Open 12-2.30, 5.30-11; 12-11 Fri and Sat; 12-10.30 Sun; closed Mon-Thurs lunchtimes in winter ~ Bedrooms: £46S/£72S

THORNTON WATLASS   SE2486   Map 10

Buck 🍺 🛏

Village signposted off B6268 Bedale—Masham; HG4 4AH

The bedrooms and ladies' lavatories have been newly refurbished this year and the hard-working licensees have now been here 20 years. It remains a genuine, friendly local and the pleasantly traditional right-hand bar has upholstered old-fashioned wall settles on the carpet, a fine mahogany bar counter, a high shelf packed with ancient bottles, several mounted fox masks and brushes, and a brick fireplace. The dining room is no smoking. The Long Room (which overlooks the cricket green) has large prints of old Thornton Watlass cricket teams, signed bats, and cricket balls and so forth. As well as specials that change every two weeks such as salmon mousse (£5.95), thai green chicken curry (£8.95), chargrilled chicken breast with a tomato, garlic and red wine sauce (£9.95), and braised lamb shank with rosemary jus (£10.95), there might be soup (£3.75), greek salad (£4.75; large £6.75), potted shrimps (£4.95), ploughman's (£6.25), omelettes (£6.50), lasagne (£7.50), steak and kidney pie (£7.95), battered whitby cod (£8.50), gammon and egg (£9.95), and steaks (from £10.95); there's also a set lunch menu for those with smaller appetites – two courses (£7.95) and three courses (£8.95). Black Sheep Bitter and John Smiths and guests like Barngates Westmoreland Gold, Durham Bedes Gold and Theakstons Best on handpump, over 40 interesting malt whiskies, and seven wines by the glass; darts, cribbage and dominoes. The sheltered garden has an equipped children's play area and summer barbecues, and they have their own cricket team; quoits. (Recommended by J R Ringrose, Adrian Barker, John Unsworth, Catherine Smith, Matthew Hall, Anthony Barnes, Mrs P Wynne)

Free house ~ Licensees Michael and Margaret Fox ~ Real ale ~ Bar food (12-2(3 Sun), 6.30-9.30) ~ Restaurant ~ (01677) 422461 ~ Children welcome ~ Dogs allowed in bedrooms ~ Jazz alternate Sun lunchtimes ~ Open 11-midnight; closed evening 25 Dec ~ Bedrooms: £55S/£65(£75B)

THWING TA0570 Map 8
Falling Stone
Off B1253 W of Bridlington; Main Street; YO25 3DS

Open only at lunchtime at the weekends, this pub brews its own beer on a farm a few miles away: Wold Top Gold and Falling Stone are kept well on handpump, and there might be a guest, too. The carpeted bar on the right has attractively upholstered stools, bar stools and wall seats, with some button-back banquettes, a modicum of china on its cream walls, and steps up to a comfortable back pool room. Friendly service and a relaxed atmosphere. On the left is an extensive no smoking dining area, part conservatory, with white table linen neatly contrasting with the grey carpet; the cheerful street-scene pictures are by the landlady. Tasty bar food includes fishcakes with home-made tartare sauce or crab chowder (£4.95), sandwiches (from £5), duck pancakes (£5.95), chicken with mozzarella and sun-dried tomato wrapped in parma ham with a tomato sauce, wild bass with capers or whole baked crab with chilli and herbs (all around £11), local lamb rump (£12), steaks (from £13), and puddings such as rhubarb cheesecake, Malteser parfait or sticky toffee pudding (£5). More reports please. (Recommended by C A Hall, Fred and Lorraine Gill, Dr Ian S Morley, Marlene and Jim Godfrey)

Wold Top ~ Lease Richard Ferebee ~ Bar food (12-2, 6-10; no food weekday lunchtimes (see opening hours)) ~ Restaurant ~ (01262) 470403 ~ Children in eating area of bar ~ Open 6-11; 12-2.30, 6-11 Sat and Sun; closed all day Mon and Tues and lunchtimes Weds-Fri

WASS SE5679 Map 7
Wombwell Arms 🛏
Back road W of Ampleforth; or follow brown tourist-attraction sign for Byland Abbey off A170 Thirsk—Helmsley; YO61 4BE

This is a thoroughly nice pub in a pretty village run by friendly people. The two character bars, both with log fires, are cosy and neatly kept and the two no smoking restaurants are incorporated into a 17th-c former granary. Enjoyable and popular food might include sandwiches, soup (£3.95), pâté with home-made sweet chutney (£4.95), crayfish and avocado (£6.25), mussels in a lightly spiced cream sauce (£6.95), filled baked pepper (£9), steak, mushroom and Guinness pie (£9.50), lamb casserole with raisins and sherry (£10.75), chicken and basil tagliatelle (£10.95), monkfish in parma ham and rosemary with vine tomatoes (£12.95), gressingham duck with orange or brandy plum sauce (£15.25), daily specials such as red mullet (£9.95) and tournedos rossini (£16.95), and home-made puddings (£4.25). Black Sheep Bitter, Timothy Taylors Landlord and maybe a beer from

Copper Dragon on handpump, several malt whiskies, and seven wines by the glass; darts. *(Recommended by W K Wood, P and J Shapley, Sue Holland, Dave Webster, Comus and Sarah Elliott, Dr and Mrs R G J Telfer, Mr Knarlson, Dr and Mrs P Truelove, Paul and Ursula Randall, Pat and Stewart Gordon, J Crosby, Patricia and Brian Copley)*

Free house ~ Licensees Steve and Mary Wykes ~ Real ale ~ Bar food (12-2, 6.30-8.30; 12-2.30, 6.30-9 Sat and Sun) ~ Restaurant ~ (01347) 868280 ~ Children welcome ~ Dogs allowed in bar ~ Open 12-2.30(4 Sat and Sun), 6.15-11(10.30 Sun); closed Sun evening and all day Mon ~ Bedrooms: £42S/£70S

WATH IN NIDDERDALE   SE1467   Map 7
Sportsmans Arms 🍴 ♀ 🛏️

Nidderdale road off B6265 in Pateley Bridge; village and pub signposted over hump-back bridge on right after a couple of miles; HG3 5PP

There is a welcoming bar in this very well run and civilised 17th-c sandstone inn and locals do drop in for just a drink, but most customers are here to enjoy the particularly good food – and many stay overnight, too. It's been run by the charming Mr Carter for 29 years now and you can be sure of a genuinely warm welcome from both him and his courteous and friendly staff. Using the best local produce – game from the moors, fish delivered daily from Whitby, and nidderdale lamb, pork and beef – the changing food might include lunchtime sandwiches, freshly made soup with assorted breads (£4), local black pudding with a red onion jus (£4.85), a plate of tapas (£7.50), king scallops with garlic butter and a gruyère glaze (£8.50), local trout with almonds, capers and brown butter or slow-cooked venison with button onions and mushrooms (£11.50), grilled rib-eye steak with aïoli (£12.50), braised calves liver with pancetta and a light onion sauce (£12.95), and escalope of halibut with beurre blanc (£13.95). The restaurant is no smoking. Black Sheep and a guest such as Wharfedale Folly Ale on handpump, a very sensible and extensive wine list with 15 by the glass (including champagne), over 30 malt whiskies and several russian vodkas; open fires and quiet piped music. Benches and tables outside. Seats in the pretty garden. As well as their own fishing on the River Nidd, this is an ideal spot for walkers, hikers and ornithologists, and there are plenty of country houses, gardens and cities to explore. *(Recommended by Bill and Sheila McLardy, Edward Mirzoeff, Pat and Tony Hinkins, Keith Moss, Terry and Linda Moseley, Hunter and Christine Wright, Peter and Lesley Yeoward, Mr and Mrs D J Nash, John Saul, David and Ruth Hollands, Lynda and Trevor Smith, T Walker, Stephen Woad)*

Free house ~ Licensee Ray Carter ~ Real ale ~ Bar food ~ Restaurant ~ (01423) 711306 ~ Children allowed with restrictions ~ Dogs allowed in bar ~ Open 12-2.30, 6.30-11; closed 25 Dec and evening 26 Dec ~ Bedrooms: £70B/£110B

WESTOW   SE7565   Map 7
Blacksmiths 🍴 ♀ 🛏️

Off A64 York—Malton; Main Street; YO60 7NE

Friendly new licensees have taken over this bustling dining pub and were just about to complete the refurbishment of a six bedroom barn converstion as we went to press. There's quite an emphasis on the very good food, but the locals haven't been left out: there's often a group of them on the left of the small black-beamed bar area, perhaps watching football on TV. There are traditional high-backed settles around sturdy stripped tables, each with a fat candle, a big open woodburning stove in the capacious brick inglenook, and a few small engravings (farm animals, scenes from *Mr Sponge's Sporting Tour* and the like) on the cream walls. A brightly lit focal serving bar has John Smiths, Tetleys and Timothy Taylors Landlord on handpump, and they have a carefully chosen wine list with several by the glass and a wine of the month; 20 malt whiskies and a range of belgian beers; piped music. The main, no smoking dining area on the right, open to the bar, is basically two linked smallish rooms, with a medley of comfortable dining chairs including some distinctive antiques around candlelit stripped dining tables; mixed old cutlery on linen napkins and nice glassware and china set the tone. They make all their own bread and ice-creams and have home-made free crisps on the bar. Changing daily and using local produce, the interesting modern dishes might include soups like cream of butternut squash and watercress (£3.95), grilled black pudding, fried egg, pickled shallot hash and home-baked beans, steamed mussels with leeks, cider and cream or potted gressingham duck and foie gras with black grape chutney (all £5.50), home-made fishcakes with a plum tomato velouté (£11.95), saddle of local rabbit filled with ham hock and a truffle cream (£13.50), spiced free-range pork belly, cider potato, purée of parsnips, black pudding faggot and scrumpy and sage juices (£14.50), venison haunch steak, mini venison cottage pie, black trompette and green lentils and thyme (£16.50), roasted monkfish with biarritz potatoes, deep-fried calamari and brown shrimp and caper butter (£17.50), and puddings such as baked egg custard tart, nutmeg ice-cream and fresh blackberries, bramley apple and rhubarb crumble or sticky toffee pudding with dark muscovado sauce (from £5.50); two-course early bird menu Wednesday-Friday evenings (£12.95) and three courses (£14.95). There are picnic-sets in a side rockery. *(Recommended by Christopher Turner, Dr Ian S Morley, Sue Ashton, David and Lyndsay Lewitt, John H Smith, Tim and Suzy Bower)*

Free house ~ Licensees Gary and Sarah Marshall ~ Bar food (not Mon or Tues; not lunchtimes except Sat and Sun) ~ Restaurant ~ (01653) 618365 ~ Children welcome ~ Dogs allowed in bar ~ Open 6-11; 12-2, 6-11 Sat; 12-4 Sun; closed Mon; closed lunchtimes except Sun; closed Sun evening (but may be open in summer) ~ Bedrooms: £40S/£70S

WHITBY NZ9011 Map 10
Duke of York
Church Street, Harbour East Side; YO22 4DE

From the windows in this bustling pub, there's a splendid outlook over the harbour entrance and the western cliff. It's also close to the famous 199 Steps that lead up to the abbey. The comfortable beamed no smoking lounge bar has plenty of atmosphere and fishing memorabilia – including the pennant numbers of local trawlers that are chalked on the beams; best to arrive early to be sure of a table. Quickly served straightforward food such as good crab sandwiches (£3.50), home-made steak in ale or fish pies (£6.50), and large local cod or haddock or crab salad (£6.95). Black Sheep, Courage Directors and Caledonian Deuchars IPA on handpump, decent wines by two sizes of glass, and quite a few malt whiskies; piped music (which some customers feel is unnecessary), TV, darts and games machine. Try to get a bedroom overlooking the water – it's also quieter. There is no nearby parking. *(Recommended by Michael and Ann Cole, Paul Humphreys, Richard, David Carr, the Didler, John Fiander, Christine and Neil Townend, Stuart Orton, LS, Kevin Thorpe, Steve Whalley)*

Enterprise ~ Lease Lawrence Bradley ~ Real ale ~ Bar food (all day) ~ (01947) 600324 ~ Children allowed until 9pm ~ Live music Mon ~ Open 11-11(midnight Sat); 12-11 Sun; closed 25 Dec ~ Bedrooms: /£50B

WIDDOP SD9531 Map 7
Pack Horse ▣
The Ridge; from A646 on W side of Hebden Bridge, turn off at Heptonstall signpost (as it's a sharp turn, coming out of Hebden Bridge road signs direct you around a turning circle), then follow Slack and Widdop signposts; can also be reached from Nelson and Colne, on high, pretty road; OS Sheet 103 map reference 952317; HX7 7AT

Usefully included for its position, this is an isolated and traditional pub high up on the moors; leave your boots and backpacks in the porch. The bar has warm winter fires, window seats cut into the partly panelled stripped stone walls that take in the moorland view, sturdy furnishings, horsey mementoes, and Black Sheep, Greene King Old Speckled Hen, Thwaites Bitter and a changing guest on handpump, around 130 single malt whiskies and some irish ones as well, and eight wines by the glass. Bar food includes home-made pâté (£3.50), sandwiches or baps (from £3.50), home-made steak and kidney pie, ploughman's or vegetable bake (£5.95), steaks (from £9.95), roast rack of lamb (£11.95), and specials such as lambs liver and onions (£7.95), venison and pheasant pie (£9.95), and slow-baked lamb shank with rosemary gravy (£10.95). The restaurant is open only on Saturday evenings. The friendly golden retrievers are called Paddy and Murphy and there's a third dog called Holly. Seats outside and pretty summer hanging baskets. More reports please. *(Recommended by Greta and Christopher Wells, Ann and Tony Bennett-Hughes, Ian and Nita Cooper, Martin and Sue Day)*

Free house ~ Licensee Andrew Hollinrake ~ Real ale ~ Bar food (not Mon or weekday winter lunchtimes) ~ Restaurant ~ (01422) 842803 ~ Children in eating area of bar until 8pm ~ Dogs welcome ~ Open 12-3, 7-11; 12-11 Sun; closed weekday lunchtimes in winter; closed Mon ~ Bedrooms: /£48B

YORK SE5951 Map 7

Maltings ♠ ▮ £

Tanners Moat/Wellington Row, below Lendal Bridge; YO1 6HU

As one reader put it, 'this is just what a good old city pub should be'. There's a really good mix of customers, a friendly and lively atmosphere, good value food and a fine range of real ales. The tricksy décor is entirely contrived and strong on salvaged somewhat quirky junk: old doors for the bar front and much of the ceiling, enamel advertising signs for the rest of it, what looks like a suburban front door for the entrance to the ladies', partly stripped orange brick walls, even a lavatory pan in one corner. As well as Black Sheep and a beer from Roosters, the jovial landlord keeps five guest ales on handpump and holds frequent special events. He also has two or three continental beers on tap, up to four farm ciders, a dozen or so country wines, and more irish whiskeys than you normally see. In generous helpings, the well liked food might include sandwiches (from £2.85), extremely good, truly home-made chips (£2.50; with chilli or curry £3.50), filled baked potatoes (from £3.75), haddock (£4.95), and beef in ale pie or stilton and leek bake (£5.25); get there early to be sure of a seat. The day's papers are framed in the gents'; games machine. Nearby parking is difficult; the pub is very handy for the Rail Museum and the Yorkshire Eye. *(Recommended by Martin Grosberg, David Carr, D L Parkhurst, the Didler, Andy and Jill Kassube, David Hoult, Neil Whitehead, Victoria Anderson, Tracey and Stephen Groves, Fred and Lorraine Gill, Esther and John Sprinkle, Mark Walker, Andy Lickfold, Eric Larkham, Mrs Hazel Rainer)*

Free house ~ Licensee Shaun Collinge ~ Real ale ~ Bar food (12-2 weekdays, 12-4 weekends; not evenings) ~ No credit cards ~ (01904) 655387 ~ Children allowed after food service and must be well behaved ~ Dogs welcome ~ Blues Mon, folk Tues ~ Open 11-11; 12-10.30 Sun; closed 25 Dec

LUCKY DIP

Besides the fully inspected pubs, you might like to try these Lucky Dips recommended to us and described by readers (if you do, please send us reports: www.goodguides.co.uk).

ADDINGHAM [SE0749]
☆ *Fleece* LS29 0LY [Main St]: Tastefully refurbished and extended, good value home-made food from hearty sandwiches to generous blackboard meals using fresh local meat, whitby fish and smoked fish, popular Sun roasts (all day then) and some unusual dishes, friendly efficient staff, Black Sheep, Timothy Taylors Landlord and Theakstons, good choice of wines by the glass, low ceilings, flagstones, candles and log fire, no smoking dining area, tap room with darts and dominoes; very busy wknds; children welcome, tables outside *(David Crook, Mrs R A Cartwright, Richard Crabtree, Tina and David Woods-Taylor)*

AINDERBY QUERNHOW [SE3480]
Black Horse YO7 4HX: Friendly licensees, good variety of plentiful appetising food, spacious well refurbished bar with coal fire *(H Bramwell)*
ALDBOROUGH [SE4166]
☆ *Ship* YO51 9ER [off B6265 just S of Boroughbridge, close to A1]: Attractive creeper-clad 14th-c village pub under yet another new licensee, heavy beams, some old-fashioned seats around cast-iron framed tables, lots of copper and brass, coal fire in stone inglenook, straightforward food, John Smiths, Theakston and Timothy Taylors Landlord; piped music; children welcome, tables on front

terrace, handy for Roman remains and museum, comfortable bedrooms, open all day wknds *(LYM, Tony and Penny Burton)*

ALLERSTON [SE8783]

Cayley Arms YO18 7PJ [A170 Pickering—Scarborough]: Well cooked and served food in spacious dining areas, cosy main bar, pool room, no piped music; seats out by brook, bedrooms *(R J Collis)*

AMPLEFORTH [SE5878]

White Horse YO62 4DX [West End]: Imaginative choice of good generous freshly made food in well appointed no smoking dining room, good genial service, relaxed atmosphere, Tetleys, interesting wines by the glass, open fires, usual games (no fruit machines or piped music); sunny terrace, three bedrooms with own bathrooms *(Michael Butler, Michael Sargent)*

☆ *White Swan* YO62 4DA [off A170 W of Helmsley; East End]: Relaxed atmosphere in three separate interestingly furnished and decorated rooms, good generous food from sandwiches up in bar and no smoking candlelit restaurant, nice home-made puddings, friendly efficient staff, Black Sheep and Timothy Taylors Landlord, good wines by the glass, blazing log fires, comfortable squashy seating, sporting prints, public bar with darts and dominoes; children welcome, attractive back terrace *(Martin and Alison Stainsby, LYM, Dr and Mrs R G J Telfer, Lily Hornsby Clark)*

APPLETREEWICK [SE0560]

☆ *Craven Arms* BD23 6DA [off B6160 Burnsall—Bolton Abbey]: Attractively placed creeper-covered 17th-c beamed pub with comfortably down-to-earth settles, flagstones and brown-painted ply panelling, coal fire in the old range, good service, up to five real ales such as Black Sheep and Wharfedale, good choice of wines by the glass, enjoyable reasonably priced home-made food from good baguettes up, small no smoking dining room (back extension being built summer 2006), no piped music; walking boots welcome (plenty of surrounding walks), nice views from front picnic-sets, more seats in back garden *(LYM, Mr and Mrs T Stone, Fred and Lorraine Gill, Mr and Mrs Staples, Michael Butler, Lawrence Pearse)*

ARNCLIFFE [SD9371]

☆ *Falcon* BD23 5QE [off B6160 N of Grassington]: Ideal setting on moorland village green for a favourite basic country tavern, same family for generations, no frills, coal fire in small bar with elderly furnishings, Timothy Taylors Landlord tapped from cask to stoneware jugs in central hatch-style servery, generous plain lunchtime and early evening sandwiches and snacks from old family kitchen with range, interesting photographs and humorous sporting prints, simple back sunroom (children allowed here lunchtime) looking on to pleasant garden; cl winter Thurs evenings; plain bedrooms (not all year), good breakfast and evening meal *(B and M Kendall, Neil and Angela Huxter, Karen Eliot, the Didler, LYM, Fred and Lorraine Gill, Clare Rosier)*

ARTHINGTON [SE2644]

Wharfedale LS21 1NL [A659 E of Otley (Arthington Lane)]: Good value food from sandwiches and pub staples to restaurant dishes, Black Sheep, Timothy Taylors Landlord and Tetleys, several wines by the glass, mix of tables, chairs and banquettes in roomy and comfortably refurbished open-plan bar, intimate alcoves, soft lighting, half-panelling and Yorkshire landscapes, separate restaurant; disabled access and facilities, three new bedrooms *(Tony and Penny Burton)*

ASKRIGG [SD9491]

Crown DL8 3HQ [Main St]: Neatly kept open-plan local in popular and attractive James Herriot village, several separate areas off main bar with blazing fires inc old-fashioned range, relaxed atmosphere, cheap and cheerful home-made food inc cut-price small helpings, good value Sun lunch and good puddings choice, helpful friendly staff, Black Sheep and Theakstons XB; can get smoky; children, dogs and walkers welcome, tables outside *(Dudley and Moira Cockroft, M Greening, Alan and Carolin Tidbury, Peter Abbott, D W Stokes)*

☆ *Kings Arms* DL8 3HQ [signed from A684 Leyburn—Sedbergh in Bainbridge]: Early 19th-c coaching inn, cracking atmosphere in flagstoned main bar with roaring log fire, attractive traditional furnishings and décor, small snug well used by locals, real ales such as Black Sheep, John Smiths, Theakstons Best and Old Peculier, decent wines by the glass, good choice of malt whiskies, good interesting food choice from good sandwiches up, quick friendly service, another log fire in no smoking dining room, pool in barrel-vaulted former beer cellar; dogs welcome, tables out in pleasant courtyard, bedrooms run separately as part of Holiday Property Bond complex behind *(Pat and Robert Watt, Michael Tack, LYM, G D Baker, Terry and Linda Moseley, Alvin Morris, Mrs E M Richards, John and Joan Calvert, M Greening, Mike and Jayne Bastin, Revd John E Cooper)*

AUSTWICK [SD7668]

☆ *Game Cock* LA2 8BB [just off A65 Settle—Kirkby Lonsdale]: Prettily placed below the Three Peaks, friendly barman and good log fire in homely old-fashioned beamed bare-boards back bar, Timothy Taylors Landlord, Thwaites and Charles Wells Bombardier, nice coffee, most space devoted to the food side, with good fairly priced choice from sandwiches up inc good game pie, two dining rooms and modern front conservatory-type extension; dogs welcome, tables out in front with good play area, neat bedrooms, good walks all round *(BB, Len Beattie, Michael Butler, Mr and Mrs P Eastwood, Margaret Dickinson, Karina Spero)*

AYSGARTH [SE0088]

George & Dragon DL8 3AD [just off A684]: Upmarket 17th-c posting inn with good imaginative though not cheap food, good choice of wines by the glass, Black Sheep Bitter, John Smiths and Theakstons Best, small appealing bar, log fire, beams and panelling, polished hotel lounge with antique china, attractive no smoking dining areas; may be piped music; children welcome, rather mediterranean-style furniture in paved garden (the coconut-straw shaded tables look a bit surprising on a snowbound night), lovely scenery, open all day, compact bedrooms with own bathrooms *(Terry and Linda Moseley, LYM, Nigel Bowles)*

Palmer Flatt DL8 3SR: Moorland hotel doing well with friendly new licensees, comfortable eating areas, some interesting ancient masonry at the back recalling its days as a pilgrims' inn, generally most enjoyable food and welcoming accommodating service (one reader hit an out-of-season Sunday with a staff-shortage glitch), great scenery nr broad waterfalls; tables outside, fishing rights, space for caravans, bedrooms *(Michael and Maggie Betton, LYM, Mr and Mrs Maurice Thompson)*

BAINBRIDGE [SD9390]
☆ *Rose & Crown* DL8 3EE: Comfortable hotel with friendly and pubbily old-fashioned front bar overlooking moorland village green, beams, oak panelling, old settles and big log fire, good range of enjoyable food from good baguettes up in bar and spacious no smoking restaurant, welcoming service, Black Sheep and Websters, good coffee, reasonably priced wines by the glass; children welcome, busy back extension popular with families, bedrooms, open all day *(Michael and Maggie Betton, Alistair and Kay Butler, LYM, Peter Abbott, Mr and Mrs Maurice Thompson)*

BARKISLAND [SE0416]
Brown Cow HX4 0DZ: Relaxed stone-built pub in lovely Pennine setting, good reasonably priced blackboard food inc interesting dishes (best to book Fri-Sun), friendly landlord and staff, Timothy Taylors Landlord and changing guest beers, good choice of wines by the glass, tastefully simple contemporary country décor with two candlelit no smoking dining rooms off lively open-plan flagstoned bar, three open woodburners, rugged moorland views from front bay window, some unusual artwork; tables out on teak deck, cl Mon and lunchtime Tues-Sat, open all day Sun *(Dr Ian S Morley, John Proud)*

BECKWITHSHAW [SE2853]
Pine Marten HG3 1UE [Otley Rd, Beckwith Knowle; B6162 towards Harrogate]: Vintage Inn based on rambling Victorian house, big comfortable rooms and cosy nooks, mullioned windows, panelling, settles and open fires, sensibly priced food all day from sandwiches up, efficient polite service, Tetleys, decent wines, no smoking areas; handy for Harlow Carr gardens, Innkeepers Lodge bedrooms *(David Crook, Mike Turner)*

BEVERLEY [TA0339]
☆ *Corner House* HU17 9EY [Norwood]: Open-plan largely bare-boards pub with some leather settees and easy chairs each end as well as pews and stripped solid tables, modern prints and some blue and pink décor, soft lighting, good value fresh up-to-date food from baguettes up, popular wknd breakfast from 10, long counter with real ales such as Black Sheep, Fullers London Pride, Greene King Abbot, Roosters Yankee, Timothy Taylors Landlord and Tetleys, good wines, farm cider, wide range of fresh fruit juices, coffee top-ups, daily papers; piped pop music; disabled access and facilities, tables outside, open all day Fri-Sun *(Len Beattie, Fred and Lorraine Gill, David Carr, BB)*

Woolpack HU17 8EN [Westwood Rd, W of centre]: Small welcoming pub in 19th-c former cottage pair, jovial landlady and cheerful efficient service, limited choice of good value fresh generous food Weds-Sat evenings and Sun lunchtime (best to book), Burtonwood and guest beers, decent wines by the glass, cosy snug, real fires, simple spotless furnishings, no pretensions, brasses, teapots, prints and maps; subdued piped music, no nearby parking; open all day Sun, has been cl Mon-Thurs lunchtimes *(Len Beattie, David Carr, Paul and Ursula Randall, J Crosby)*

BILBROUGH [SE5346]
☆ *Three Hares* YO23 3PH [off A64 York—Tadcaster]: Village pub with good food, imaginative if not cheap (and there may be a wait), from sandwiches up, take-away regional delicacies too, good choice of wines by the glass, Black Sheep and Timothy Taylors Landlord, relaxing atmosphere, sofas and log fire; has been cl Mon *(Mr and Mrs P M Jennings, Roger A Bellingham, G Dobson, Andy and Jill Kassube, Dr Ian S Morley)*

BINGLEY [SE1039]
☆ *Brown Cow* BD16 2QX [Ireland Bridge; B6429 just W of junction with A650]: Genuine and unpretentious, open-plan but snugly divided, with good coal fires, easy chairs, toby jugs, lots of pictures, panelling, good range of beers inc Timothy Taylors, good reasonably priced food from sandwiches to steaks, no smoking restaurant, friendly staff; may be piped music; children welcome, tables on sheltered terrace, pleasant spot by river *(LYM, Tim and Sue Halstead, Mrs Dilys Unsworth)*

Dick Hudsons BD16 3BA [Otley Rd, High Eldwick]: Comfortable and appealingly old-world Vintage Inn, with popular food, Bass and Tetleys, good choice of wines by the glass, quick service; tables out by cricket field, tremendous views and good walks, open all day *(Pat and Graham Williamson, Neil Whitehead, Victoria Anderson, Stuart Paulley)*

BIRSTALL [SE2126]
☆ *Black Bull* WF17 9HE [Kirkgate, off A652; head down hill towards church]: Medieval stone-built pub opp part-Saxon church, dark panelling and low beams in long row of five small linked rooms, traditional décor complete with stag's head and lace curtains, lively local atmosphere, good cheap home-made food inc bargain early meals and good value Sun lunch, good service, Boddingtons, upstairs former courtroom (now a function room, but they may give you a guided tour); children welcome, quiz night Mon *(Michael Butler, BB)*

BISHOPTHORPE [SE5947]
Ebor YO23 2RB [Main St]: Popular and welcoming local nr main entrance to Archbishop of York's Palace (hence name), big lounge opening into no smoking dining area, helpful attentive staff, Sam Smiths OB, generous traditional food inc enjoyable Sun lunch, lots of china and brass; pool and TV in bar; children welcome, beautiful hanging baskets and big well planted back garden with play area *(JJW, CMW)*

BOROUGHBRIDGE [SE3967]
Grantham Arms YO51 9BW [Milby]: Friendly pub, helpful staff, Greene King IPA, John Smiths and Tetleys, good Sun lunch, evening meals (not Sun); eight bedrooms, opens 4 wkdys, open all day wknds *(Mr and Mrs Gerry Price)*
Malt Shovel YO51 9AR [St James Sq]: Bright and attractively modernised, with Boddingtons, Caledonian Deuchars IPA and John Smiths, enjoyable interesting food from reasonably priced sandwiches and panini up, friendly staff, alcoves off bare-boards central bar *(Val and Alan Green)*
Three Horseshoes YO51 9LF [Bridge St]: Spotless unspoilt pub/hotel run by same family that opened it in 1930s, friendly landlord and staff, huge fire in lounge, darts, dominoes and cards in public bar (not always open), original features inc slide-down snob screens, good plain home cooking from sandwiches to steaks in bars and restaurant, Camerons Strongarm and Tetleys, splendidly tiled ladies'; bedrooms, open all day Sun *(the Didler, Pete Baker)*

BRADFORD [SE1633]
Cock & Bottle BD3 9AA [Barkerend Rd, up Church Bank from centre]: Taken over and reopened as base for Greenwoods real ales, interesting guest beers too, carefully restored Victorian décor, deep-cut and etched windows and mirrors enriched with silver and gold leaves, stained glass, enamel intaglios, heavily carved woodwork and traditional furniture, open fire *(BB, the Didler)*
Fighting Cock BD7 1JE [Preston St (off B6145)]: Busy bare-boards alehouse by industrial estate, a dozen changing real ales inc Theakstons and Timothy Taylors, foreign bottled beers, farm ciders, all-day doorstep sandwiches and simple lunchtime hot dishes, low prices, coal fires; open all day *(Andy and Jill Kassube, the Didler)*
Haigys BD8 7QU [Lumb Lane]: Friendly and distinctive local with cosy lounge area, cracking evening atmosphere, fine changing range of beers inc Ossett, Phoenix and Rooster, revolving pool table, music area; open till 1am Fri/Sat, cl lunchtime *(the Didler)*
New Beehive BD1 3AA [Westgate]: Robustly old-fashioned and unspoilt Edwardian inn with a mixed crowd of faintly alternative customers, several rooms inc good pool room and no smoking room, huge range of beers, gas lighting, candles and coal fires; basement music nights; nice back courtyard, bedrooms, open all day (till 2am Fri/Sat) *(the Didler)*
Symposium BD10 9PY [Albion Rd, Idle]: No smoking Market Town Tavern with good

choice of ales and wines, foreign bottled beers, enjoyable inexpensive food inc popular Sun lunch, back dining snug; terrace tables, open all day Fri-Sun *(Bren and Val Speed)*

BRAMHAM [SE4242]
Swan LS23 6QA [just off A1 2 miles N of A64]: Unspoilt three-room country local with engaging long-serving landlady, super mix of customers, John Smiths and Theakstons, no food or music *(Les and Sandra Brown)*

BRIDGE HEWICK [SE3370]
Black-a-moor HG4 5AA [Boroughbridge Rd (B6265 E of Ripon)]: Dining pub locally very popular for its enjoyable food using local produce, well trained cheerful and willing young staff, pleasant landlord, Black Sheep ales, good coffee; bedrooms *(Roy Bromell, Roger Noyes, Janet and Peter Race)*

BRIDLINGTON [TA1867]
Marine Bar YO15 2LS [Expanse Hotel, N Marine Dr]: Plush seating, modern artwork, real ales inc guest beers, plentiful low-priced fresh food such as filled baked potatoes and local haddock; overlooks North Sea, bedrooms in hotel part *(Kevin Blake, Colin Gooch)*
Pavilion Bar YO15 2PB [Jeromes, Esplanade]: Wicker chairs, modern art, huge lamps, lots of glass and iron pillars in former Floral Hall Theatre, attentive friendly staff, Marstons Pedigree and John Smiths, usual food lunchtime and early evening; piped music; good disabled access and facilities, children welcome (indoor play area – small fee), small stage for entertainment, tables outside *(Kevin Blake, Colin Gooch)*

BRIGHOUSE [SE1323]
Red Rooster HD6 2QR [Brookfoot; A6025 towards Elland]: Flagstoned pub popular for real ales such as Caledonian Deuchars IPA, Moorhouses, Ossett, Roosters Yankee, Salamander, Timothy Taylors Landlord and new or esoteric guest beers, country wines, coffee, open fire, separate areas inc one with pin table, brewery memorabilia; small terrace, opens 3 (12 wknds) *(Andy and Jill Kassube, J R Ringrose, the Didler)*

BROUGHTON [SD9450]
Bull BD23 3AE: Neatly modernised and well run old-fashioned pub with good wholesome food – all home-made, even the chutneys – in bar and restaurant, cheerfully friendly staff, pleasant busy atmosphere, polished brass and china, Black Sheep, Tetleys and a beer brewed for the pub, good wines by the glass *(LYM, John and Sylvia Harrop, Hunter and Christine Wright, Mr and Mrs A Silver)*

BURNSALL [SE0361]
☆ *Red Lion* BD23 6BU [B6160 S of Grassington]: Popular 16th-c inn in lovely spot by River Wharfe, looking across village green to Burnsall Fell, tables out on front cobbles and on big back terrace; attractively panelled sturdily furnished no smoking front dining rooms with log fire, more basic back public bar, several real ales inc Timothy Taylors Landlord, interesting wine choice by glass or bottle (they import direct), good imaginative but pricey bar food, friendly management,

conservatory; leave boots in entrance even if clean, they may try to keep your credit card while you eat, service can slow; children welcome, tables outside, comfortable bedrooms (dogs allowed in some and bar), open all day, fishing permits *(Len Beattie, Robert Wivell, LYM, Keith and Margaret Kettell, Neil Whitehead, Victoria Anderson, Simon and Mandy King, Alyson and Andrew Jackson)*

BURTON LEONARD [SE3263]

☆ *Hare & Hounds* HG3 3SG [off A61 Ripon—Harrogate, handy for A1(M) exit 48]: Well organised country pub popular for decent reasonably priced food and pleasant service, large carpeted main area divided by log fire, traditional furnishings, Black Sheep, Tetleys and Timothy Taylors Landlord from long counter, several wines by the glass and 30 malt whiskies, no smoking end and restaurant, bright little room with sofa and easy chairs; children in eating areas, pretty back garden, cl Tues *(R E Dixon, Jo Lilley, Simon Calvert, LYM)*

BURYTHORPE [SE7964]

Bay Horse YO17 9LJ [5 miles S of Malton]: New licensees doing well in welcoming linked rooms, pictures, books and armchairs in small 'study', large civilised no smoking dining area, emphasis on good value generous food (not Sun/Mon evenings), good range of real ales such as Timothy Taylors; nice Wolds-edge village *(David Barnes)*

BYLAND ABBEY [SE5478]

☆ *Abbey Inn* YO61 4BD [brown Abbey sign off A170 Thirsk—Helmsley]: By the beautiful abbey ruins and very popular under previous owners; now taken over by English Heritage, still plenty of character despite the intrusive piped music, and physically unchanged, with good tables, settles, carved oak seats, big fireplaces, polished boards and flagstones and attractive décor in two no smoking front rooms, library room, big back room with lots of rustic bygones, Black Sheep and a beer named for the pub, bar food; children welcome, no dogs, plenty of room out on terrace and in garden, comfortable bedrooms, has been cl Sun evening and Mon lunchtimes; more reports on the new regime, please *(Dr Peter Crawshaw, LYM)*

CALDER GROVE [SE3017]

Navigation WF4 3DS [just off M1 junction 39; A636 signposted Denby Dale, then 1st right – Broad Cut Rd]: Good motorway break – cheery waterside stone-built local with interesting old canal photographs, two or three real ales in summer (real ale only towards wknd in winter), good pubby food, low prices, steps up to panelled main bar with coal fire and impressive U-shaped wall banquette, flat access to no smoking family room; TV and fruit machine; tables outside with play area, walks by Calder & Hebble Canal *(G Coates, LYM, JHBS)*

CALDWELL [NZ1613]

Brownlow Arms DL11 7QH: Appealing small flower-decked pub with carefully cooked food inc some unusual dishes as well as pubby

favourites, friendly service, dining area and pool area; isolated village, good walks *(Mrs C Crawshaw)*

CARLTON [SE0684]

☆ *Foresters Arms* DL8 4BB [off A684 W of Leyburn]: Welcoming pub with new management doing good food inc local game and venison, good service, Black Sheep, John Smiths and the pub's own Wensleydale ale, decent wines by the glass, log fire, low beams and flagstones, no smoking restaurant; children welcome, picnic-sets out among tubs of flowers, pretty village at the heart of the Yorkshire Dales National Park, comfortable bedrooms, lovely views *(LYM, Gerry Miller, the Didler, Mr and Mrs Maurice Thompson)*

CARLTON MINIOTT [SE4081]

Vale of York YO7 4LX: Enjoyable food from early-evening bargains and robust traditional dishes to more exotic things, good real ales; good value bedrooms, quite handy for Thirsk racecourse *(Andy and Jill Kassube)*

CARLTON-IN-CLEVELAND [NZ5203]

Lord Stones TS9 7JH: Looks ancient but recently built from reclaimed stone and timber, moorland pub handy for Cleveland Way walkers, useful blackboard menu, Theakstons Old Peculier; open all day 9-5, plus summer evenings *(JHBS)*

CARPERBY [SE0089]

☆ *Wheatsheaf* DL8 4DF [a mile NW of Aysgarth]: Attractive traditional inn in quiet village, friendly helpful service under welcoming landlord, old-fashioned locals' bar, wide range of enjoyable bar food inc good sandwiches and ploughman's, good puddings choice, reasonable prices, Black Sheep, John Smiths and Websters, darts and dominoes, dining room; bedrooms *(Pat and Robert Watt, R L Borthwick, Barry and Anne)*

CAWOOD [SE5737]

Castle YO8 3SH [Wistowgate]: Comfortable pub with log fires, good choice of sensibly priced wines by the glass, Black Sheep, John Smiths and a weekly guest beer, wide range of home-made pubby food served piping hot inc children's and smaller-appetite helpings, friendly landlady and efficient service, air-conditioned no smoking dining areas; back caravan standing *(John and Sheila Coggrave)*

CHAPELTOWN [SK3596]

Commercial S35 2XF [Station Rd]: Friendly three-room tap for Wentworth ales, quickly changing guest beers too, lots of pump clips in small no smoking snug, good choice of good value generous food all day (not Sun evening) inc good roasts and hot meat sandwiches on Sun, pictures and fans in lounge/dining room, games room with pool off L-shaped bar; no music or dogs, picnic-sets in small garden, open all day Fri/Sat *(the Didler, Jo Lilley, Simon Calvert)*

CHOP GATE [SE5599]

Buck TS9 7JL: Hospitable old-world stone-built pub with usual food, real ales, prompt service, restaurant; big garden with play area and Bilsdale views, good bedrooms, handy for walks *(Sarah and Peter Gooderham)*

CLAPHAM [SD7469]
New Inn LA2 8HH [off A65 N of Settle]:
Welcoming riverside inn in famously pretty
village, landlady's tapestries and
caving and other cartoons in small comfortable
lounge, changing real ales such as Black Sheep,
Copper Dragon and Thwaites, good honest
food in bars and restaurant, friendly service,
public bar with pool in games area; handy for
round walk to Ingleborough Cavern and more
adventurous hikes, comfortable bedrooms
(Roy and Lindsey Fentiman, Len Beattie)

CLIFTON [SE1622]
☆ *Black Horse* HD6 4HJ [Westgate/Coalpit
Lane; signed off Brighouse rd from M62
junction 25]: 17th-c pub/hotel with pleasant
décor featuring racing, golf, football and
former star performers at Batley Variety Club,
front dining rooms (one no smoking) focused
on wide choice of popular generous food from
interesting ciabattas and other good lunchtime
snacks to full meals inc fine fish stew,
imaginative puddings and good value set
dinners, smaller back area by bar counter
mainly just standing room, beam and plank
ceiling, open fire, real ales such as Black Sheep
and Timothy Taylors Landlord, decent wines;
21 comfortable bedrooms, pleasant village
(Michael Butler, BB, Pat and Tony Martin)

CLOUGHTON [SE9798]
☆ *Falcon* YO13 0DY [pub signed just off A171
out towards Whitby]: Big dependable open-
plan bar, neatly kept and well divided, light
and airy, with comfortable banquettes and
other seats on turkey carpet, good value honest
fresh food in quantity (no booking, but worth
the wait for a table), John Smiths and
Theakstons Best and XB, good friendly family
service, log fire in big stone fireplace, cheerful
regulars, distant sea view from end windows;
piped music; picnic-sets on walled lawn, good
bedrooms with own bathrooms
(Danny Savage, BB, DJH)

COLTON [SE5444]
☆ *Olde Sun* LS24 8EP [off A64 York—
Tadcaster]: Immaculate 17th-c beamed pub
with some emphasis on its wide choice of good
food, Caledonian Deuchars IPA, John Smiths,
Timothy Taylors Landlord and Tetleys, good
choice of wines by the glass, good service
(young couple trying hard to please), several
linked low-ceilinged rooms with nice collection
of old chairs inc an antique settle around good
solid tables, log fires, good delicatessen
specialising in local produce; picnic-sets on
quiet front terrace, has been cl Mon
*(Michael Swallow, Les and Sandra Brown,
Tony and Penny Burton, Mrs Jean Mitchell,
BB)*

CONONLEY [SD9846]
New Inn BD20 8NR [Main St/Station Rd]:
Busy village pub with good value food inc
bargain mixed grill, Timothy Taylors real ales;
worth booking evenings *(Dudley and
Moira Cockroft)*

CRACOE [SD9760]
Devonshire Arms BD23 6LA [B6265
Skipton—Grassington]: Olde-worlde pub with
good value food in bar and restaurant, four
real ales reasonably priced, efficient staff, log
fire, solidly comfortable furnishings, old
pictures, polished flooring tiles with rugs here
and there, low shiny beams supporting
creaky white planks; darts, dominoes,
cribbage, piped music; children in eating areas,
picnic-sets on terrace with well kept
flowerbeds, more seating on lawn, comfortably
refurbished bedrooms, open all day, cl Mon
(Dudley and Moira Cockroft, LYM)

CRATHORNE [NZ4407]
Crathorne Arms TS15 0BA: Large dining pub
under friendly and helpful new licensees, good
range of enjoyable generous food inc some
interesting recipes and splendid Sun lunch (very
popular then), Black Sheep and Hambleton,
thriving atmosphere; pleasant village
(Alyson and Andrew Jackson)

CRIGGLESTONE [SE3217]
Red Kite WF4 3BB [Denby Dale Rd, Durkar
(A636, by M1 junction 39)]: Vintage Inn done
like a Georgian house adjoining a cottage row,
pleasant atmosphere and décor, their usual
food and wide range of wines by the glass,
Bass, Greene King Old Speckled Hen, John
Smiths and Tetleys, log fire, daily papers; lots
of tables outside, bedrooms in adjacent
Holiday Inn Express *(Michael Butler,
Richard and Karen Holt)*

DACRE BANKS [SE1961]
☆ *Royal Oak* HG3 4EN [B6451 S of Pateley
Bridge]: Solid and comfortable stone-built pub
with Nidderdale views, good value food from
enterprising sandwiches to good three-course
speciality nights, friendly staff (helpful over
special diets), Rudgate ales and Tetleys, good
wine choice, good log fire in no smoking
dining area, interesting old photographs, pool,
dominoes, cribbage; TV and piped music;
children in eating areas, terrace tables and
informal back garden, three good value
character bedrooms, good breakfast *(LYM,
Geoff and Teresa Salt, Steve Kirby,
Dr Peter Crawshaw, Alison and Pete,
Pat and Tony Martin)*

DARLEY [SE1959]
Wellington HG3 2QQ [B6451 S of Pateley
Bridge]: Large comfortable stone-built country
inn under newish chef/landlord, wide choice of
imaginative blackboard food, welcoming
capable staff, partly no smoking bar and large
no smoking dining area, real ales, log fires;
12 good reasonably priced bedrooms, good
breakfast *(Mrs Pat Crabb)*

DEIGHTON [SE6244]
White Swan YO19 6HA [A19 N of Escrick]:
Friendly pub locally popular for good value
unpretentious food from sandwiches and
ploughman's up, welcoming service, two
comfortable bars, separate restaurant, good
choice of real ales and wines by the glass; seats
outside (some traffic noise) *(Pat and
Graham Williamson)*

DEWSBURY [SE2622]
Huntsman WF12 7SW [Walker Cottages,
Chidswell Lane, Shaw Cross – pub signed]:
Cosy converted cottages alongside urban-fringe

farm, low beams, lots of brasses and
agricultural bric-a-brac, friendly locals, Black
Sheep, John Smiths and Timothy Taylors
Landlord, hot log fire, small no smoking front
extension; no food evening or Sun/Mon
lunchtime, busy evenings *(Michael Butler)*
Leggers WF12 9BD [Robinsons Boat Yard,
Savile Town Wharf, Mill St E (SE of B6409)]:
Friendly if basic wharfside hayloft conversion
by marina, low-beamed upstairs bar with
Everards Tiger, several sensibly priced guest
and bottled belgian beers, farm cider, pies and
sandwiches or filled rolls all day, real fire,
helpful staff, daily papers, lots of old brewery
and pub memorabilia, pool; picnic-sets outside,
open all day, and they do Calder boat trips
*(Michael Butler, J R Ringrose, the Didler,
Tony Hobden)*
Shepherd's Boy WF13 2RP [Huddersfield Rd,
Ravensthorpe]: Four Ossett ales and four
interesting guest beers such as Pictish, good
range of foreign lagers and good choice of
bottled beers, no food yet *(Andy and
Jill Kassube)*
☆ **West Riding Licensed Refreshment Rooms**
WF13 1HF [Station, Wellington Rd]: Busy
three-room early Victorian station bar on
southbound platform, particularly well kept
Anglo Dutch (from the related local brewery),
Black Sheep, Timothy Taylors and other
changing ales, farm ciders, bargain wkdy
lunchtime food on scrubbed tables, popular pie
night Tues and curry night Weds, daily papers,
friendly staff, coal fire, lots of steam
memorabilia inc paintings by local artists, jazz
nights; disabled access, open all day *(Andy and
Jill Kassube, the Didler, Richard and
Karen Holt, Tony Hobden)*

DONCASTER [SE5702]
Corner Pin DN1 3AH [St Sepulchre Gate W,
Cleveland St]: Plushly refurbished beamed
lounge with old local pub prints, welsh dresser
and china, John Smiths and interesting guest
beers, good value traditional food from fine
hot sandwiches to cheap Sun roast, friendly
landlady and locals, cheery bar with darts,
games machine and TV; open all day
(the Didler)
Hare & Tortoise DN4 7PB [Parrots Corner,
Bawtry Rd, Bessacarr (A638)]: Relaxed and
civilised Vintage Inn pub/restaurant suiting all
ages, varying-sized antique tables in eight small
rooms off bar, sensibly priced food all day,
friendly efficient young staff, choice of real ales
and good range of wines by the glass, log fire
(Stephen Woad, Mrs Hazel Rainer)
Leopard DN1 3AA [West St]: Lively and
friendly, with superb tiled façade, John Smiths,
local Glentworth and guest beers, cheap basic
lunchtime food, lounge with lots of bric-a-brac,
children's games and nostalgic juke box, basic
bar area with pool and darts; TV and games
machine, good live music upstairs, can get very
busy; disabled access, open all day *(the Didler)*
Plough DN1 1SF [W Laith Gate, by
Frenchgate shopping centre]: Old-fashioned
small local with low-priced ales such as Bass
and Blackpool, old town maps, friendly staff

and chatty regulars, bustling front room with
darts and dominoes (and sports TV), quieter
back lounge; tiny central courtyard, open all
day (Sun afternoon break) *(the Didler,
Pete Baker)*
DORE [SK3081]
Dore Moor Inn S17 3AB [A625 Sheffield—
Castleton]: Busy extended Vintage Inn on edge
of Peak District looking down on Sheffield,
popular for early evening family meals; good
value ample food, fine choice of wines by the
glass, good coffee with refills, Bass and Tetleys,
hard-working friendly staff, superb central log
fires, lots of stripped pine, nice flower
arrangements; tables outside
(Revd John Hibberd, BOB)
DUNNINGTON [SE6751]
Windmill YO19 5LP [Hull Rd (A1079)]:
Welcoming and unpretentious no smoking
dining pub, large and fairly modern, popular
for good value hearty food, with swift friendly
service, good range of beers and cider, busy
new back dining conservatory, quieter small
raised dining area; open all day Sun, new
bedrooms *(David Barnes, Mr and Mrs
P M Jennings)*
EASINGWOLD [SE5270]
☆ **George** YO61 3AD [Market Pl]: Neat, bright
and airy market town hotel popular with older
people, pleasant bustle though quiet corners
even when busy, carefully presented food in
bar and no smoking dining room inc generous
sandwiches, good service by cheerful staff, five
real ales such as Black Sheep, Golcar Pennine
Gold, Moorhouses and Timothy Taylors
Landlord, warm fire, interesting bric-a-brac;
comfortable bedrooms, good breakfast
*(Janet and Peter Race, Roger A Bellingham,
Andy and Jill Kassube, David Greene,
Philip and June Caunt, J Crosby)*
EAST MORTON [SE0941]
Busfeild Arms BD20 5SP [Main Rd]: Attractive
stone-built village pub, partly no smoking,
with smallish bar, coal fire in comfortable low-
beamed lounge, John Smiths, Timothy Taylors
Landlord and Tetleys, good range of wines,
good value food (not wknd evenings),
interesting local historical prints, games room
with pool and TV; Thurs quiz night
(Michael Butler)
EAST WITTON [SE1487]
☆ **Coverbridge Inn** DL8 4SQ [A6108 out
towards Middleham]: Homely and welcoming
unspoilt 16th-c country local with two small
character bars, good home-made food from
tasty sandwiches to massive meals and prime
local steak in eating area, changing real ales
such as Black Sheep, Copper Dragon Golden
Pippin, Salamander Old Hooker, John Smiths,
Timothy Taylors Landlord and Theakstons
Best, log or coal fires; pleasant garden tables,
bedrooms, open all day *(the Didler, LYM,
Mr and Mrs Maurice Thompson)*
ELLAND [SE1021]
☆ **Barge & Barrel** HX5 9HP [quite handy for
M62 junction 24; Park Rd (A6025, via A629
and B6114)]: Large welcoming pub, several
good changing ales inc Black Sheep and local

E&S Elland, farm cider, pleasant staff, limited but generous low-priced tasty lunchtime food (not Mon), real fire, family room (with air hockey); piped radio, some live music; seats by Calder & Hebble Canal, limited parking, open all day (J R Ringrose, the Didler)

EMBSAY [SE0053]

Cavendish Arms BD23 6QT [Skipton Rd]: Pleasant pub next to steam railway station, with Black Sheep, John Smiths and Theakstons, good value pubby food from sandwiches up, warmly welcoming landlady (M S Catling)

ESCRICK [SE6342]

Black Bull YO19 6JP [E of A19 York—Selby]: Neat open-plan pub divided by arches and back-to-back fireplaces, flagstones one side, mix of wooden tables with benches, stools and chairs (in winter the ones near the good fires are at a premium), good value lunches, John Smiths, Tetleys and a guest beer, back dining room, efficient staff (C A Hall)

FINGHALL [SE1889]

☆ *Queens Head* DL8 5ND [off A684 E of Leyburn]: Warm and comfortable, with good log fires each end, some panelling, low black beams and lit candles, settles making stalls around big tables, friendly helpful young licensees, enjoyable reasonably priced food, Black Sheep, Johns Smiths and Theakstons, interesting range of well priced wines, good soft drinks, elegant and roomy no smoking back Wensleydale-view restaurant, cards and dominoes; no dogs; children welcome, wheelchair access, disabled facilities, garden tables sharing view, open all day (Julie Woffendin, Fiona Salvesen, Leslie J Lyon, Mrs Hilary Nicholson, BB)

FLAMBOROUGH [TA2270]

North Star YO15 1BL [N Marine Rd]: Sizeable hotel with comfortable and pleasantly pubby bar and eating area, decent choice of enjoyable bar food inc game and fresh fish, no smoking restaurant; tables in pleasant garden, comfortable bedrooms (Patricia and Brian Copley)

☆ *Seabirds* YO15 1PD [Tower St (B1255/B1229)]: Pretty recently redecorated village pub with shipping-theme bar, woodburner and local pictures in comfortable lounge, enjoyable food from sandwiches up with some emphasis on fresh fish, good cheerful service, John Smiths and a guest beer, decent wine list, smart light and airy no smoking dining extension; piped music; children and dogs welcome, tables in sizeable garden (Dr and Mrs T E Hothersall, Carol and Dono Leaman, LYM, Dr Alan and Mrs Sue Holder, Patricia and Brian Copley)

FLAXTON [SE6762]

Blacksmiths Arms YO60 7RJ [off A64]: Small traditional pub on attractive village green, two cosy bars and simple dining room, enjoyable food, good beer (Jane Taylor, David Dutton)

GANTON [SE9877]

Greyhound YO12 4NX [Main Rd (A64 Malton—Scarboro)]: Comfortable well run pub with friendly attentive staff, good value

standard pub food from sandwiches up inc separate pie menu, Black Sheep and John Smiths, uncluttered décor, light and airy no smoking conservatory restaurant; well placed for the championship golf course (Colin and Dot Savill, DB)

GARGRAVE [SD9253]

Masons Arms BD23 3NL [Church St/Marton Rd (off A65 NW of Skipton)]: Attractive and well run, friendly and homely, good choice of generous quickly served sensibly priced food from good sandwiches up, Boddingtons, Timothy Taylors Landlord and Tetleys, copper-canopied log-effect gas fire dividing two open-plan areas, one no smoking; well behaved children welcome, tables in garden, bowling green behind – charming village on Pennine Way, between river and church and not far from Leeds & Liverpool Canal (J R Ringrose, Geoffrey and Brenda Wilson)

GARSDALE HEAD [SD7992]

☆ *Moorcock* LA10 5PU [junction A684/B6259; marked on many maps, nr Garsdale station on Settle—Carlisle line]: Isolated stone-built inn with Black Sheep and its own Moorcock ale brewed down in Hawes, good value food from overstuffed sandwiches to good hot dishes, welcoming landlord, log fire, pleasantly informal décor with non-matching furniture, no smoking lounge bar with cosy corners; occasional live music, tables outside with views of viaduct and Settle—Carlisle railway, bedrooms (Pat and Robert Watt, Len Beattie, John Keeler, Mr and Mrs Maurice Thompson)

GIGGLESWICK [SD8164]

☆ *Black Horse* BD24 0BE [Church St]: Quaint 17th-c village pub crammed between churchyard and pretty row of cottages, spotless cosy bar with lots of bric-a-brac and gleaming brasses, good simple reasonably priced food from sandwiches and baked potatoes up in bar or intimate dining room, nice home-made puddings, Jennings, Tetleys and Timothy Taylors, hands-on landlord and son, good friendly service, coal fire; three comfortable bedrooms (Martin and Alison Stainsby, Neil Whitehead, Victoria Anderson, Keith and Margaret Kettell)

GILLAMOOR [SE6890]

☆ *Royal Oak* YO62 7HX [off A170 in Kirkbymoorside]: Traditional stone-built village inn with some emphasis on the good value food side, good welcoming young staff under friendly hands-on landlady, Black Sheep Bitter and Riggwelter, John Smiths and Tetleys, good coffee and reasonably priced wines, roomy turkey-carpeted bar, heavy dark beams, log fires in two tall stone fireplaces (one with a great old-fashioned iron kitchen range), flowers and candles throughout, no music; comfortable bedrooms, good breakfast, attractive village handy for Barnsdale Moor walks, may be cl wkdy lunchtimes (David and Jane Hill, BB, R Pickles, C A Hall)

GILLING EAST [SE6176]

☆ *Fairfax Arms* YO62 4JH [Main St (B1363)]: Attractive and comfortable stone-built country inn with friendly staff, Black Sheep, enjoyable reasonably priced food in bar and restaurant, good wine choice, log fire; picnic-sets on streamside front lawn, pleasant village with castle and miniature steam railway, good newly reworked bedrooms *(Mr and Mrs P M Jennings, Walter and Susan Rinaldi-Butcher, Colin and Dot Savill, Michael Sargent)*

GLUSBURN [SD9944]

Dog & Gun BD20 8DS [Colne Rd (A6068 W)]: Recently refurbished traditional pub very popular for its wide choice of enjoyable bargain food, good service, Timothy Taylors ales *(Geoffrey and Brenda Wilson)*

GRANGE MOOR [SE2215]

☆ *Kaye Arms* WF4 4BG [A642 Huddersfield—Wakefield]: Very good family-run eating place, too restaurant for the main entries but well up to that standard: civilised, friendly and busy, enterprising proper food, sandwiches too (they bake and sell their own bread), courteous efficient staff, exceptional value house wines from imaginative list, hundreds of malt whiskies, no smoking room; handy for Yorkshire Mining Museum, cl Mon lunchtime *(LYM)*

GRASSINGTON [SE0064]

Black Horse BD23 5AT [Garrs Lane]: Comfortable and cheerful open-plan pub, very popular in summer, with wide choice of enjoyable food from good sandwiches and snacks up inc children's, Black Sheep Bitter and Special, Tetleys and Theakstons Best and Old Peculier, friendly service, modern furnishings, open fires, darts in back room, no smoking area and small attractive restaurant; sheltered terrace, bedrooms comfortable, well equipped and good value, open all day *(BB, Len Beattie)*

☆ *Devonshire* BD23 5AD [The Square]: Handsome small hotel with good window seats and tables outside overlooking sloping village square, good range of well presented generous food from well filled sandwiches and hot snacks to bargain two-course lunches in big popular restaurant, interesting pictures and ornaments, beams and open fires, pleasant family room, good service from cheerful chatty uniformed staff even though it's busy, buoyant mix of locals and visitors, real ales inc Black Sheep Best and Timothy Taylors Landlord, decent wines, top-up coffee; comfortable bedrooms, open all day Sun *(LYM, Paul Humphreys, Tony and Penny Burton, Rod Stoneman, B and M Kendall)*

Foresters Arms BD23 5AA [Main St]: Locally popular opened-up old coaching inn with friendly efficient staff, five changing ales such as Black Sheep, Tetleys Mild and Timothy Taylors Landlord, good value straightforward food, log fire, dining room off on right; pool and sports TV on left; children welcome, reasonably priced bedrooms, open all day *(the Didler, Richard, Fred and Lorraine Gill)*

GREAT HABTON [SE7576]

☆ *Grapes* YO17 6TU: Homely and cosy traditionally refurbished dining pub in small village, good cooking by chef/landlord, fresh local fish, game and tender meat, warm-

hearted service, relaxing atmosphere, appealing comfortably old-world dining room with interesting bric-a-brac, proper bar; attractive country walks *(Richard Kilvington, Colin and Dot Savill)*

GREAT HATFIELD [TA1842]

Wrygarth HU11 4UY [Station Rd]: Cosy local, friendly licensees with chef/landlord doing short choice of good fresh food, Black Sheep and a weekly guest beer, comfortably furnished lounge and restaurant, children's room; tables outside, country views, open all day *(Fred and Lorraine Gill)*

GREAT OUSEBURN [SE4461]

☆ *Crown* YO26 9RF [off B6265 SE of Boroughbridge]: Cheerful country pub very popular for wide choice of good generous elegantly presented food (all afternoon Sat/Sun) from baguettes to some interesting dishes and big steaks, early evening bargains, tip-top cheeses, Black Sheep, Hambleton, John Smiths and Theakstons, good choice of wines, good friendly service, lots of Edwardian pictures and assorted bric-a-brac, no smoking back dining extension; may be piped music; well behaved children welcome, tables in garden with enclosed terrace and play area, cl wkdy lunchtimes, open all day wknds and bank hols *(David Hall, LYM, Michael Doswell)*

GREWELTHORPE [SE2376]

☆ *Crown* HG4 3BS [back rd NW of Ripon]: Log fires in warm and friendly two-room Dales bar, comfortable furnishings, good value enterprising and generous food (not Mon lunchtime but all day Fri-Sun), Jennings real ales, separate back dining room, pub cat; some good live music; children welcome, picnic-sets out in front, pleasant small village, good walks nearby *(Mrs M Granville-Edge, M J Winterton)*

GUNNERSIDE [SD9598]

Kings Head DL11 6LD [B6270 Swaledale rd]: Small open-plan flagstoned local in pretty riverside Dales village, friendly staff, Black Sheep and Hambleton, good value simple home-made food, old village photographs; unobtrusive piped music; children welcome, some tables out by bridge, good walks nearby, open all day *(David Hall, Tim and Rosemary Wells)*

HACKNESS [SE9788]

Everley YO13 0BT [NW of Scarborough]: Comfortable lounge bar in prettily set stone-built hotel, real ales such as Greene King Ruddles County, landlady (who taught at catering college) cooks good food specialising in puddings, beautiful valley views from restaurant; bedrooms *(Colin and Dot Savill)*

HALIFAX [SE0925]

Barum Top HX1 1NH [Rawson St]: Wetherspoons handy for cheap food all day, good range of beers and wines by the glass, balcony and family mezzanine; open all day *(John Wooll)*

☆ *Shears* HX3 9EZ [Paris Gates, Boys Lane; OS Sheet 104 map ref 097241]: Down steep cobbled lanes among tall working textile mill buildings, roomy locals' bar with bays of plush banquettes and plenty of standing space, Copper Dragon and Timothy Taylors ales, competent cheerful staff, good cheap generous lunchtime food from hefty hot-filled sandwiches up, local sports photographs; big-screen sports TV; seats out above the Hebble Brook *(Sam and Christine Kilburn, J R Ringrose, BB, the Didler)*

HAMPSTHWAITE [SE2558]

Joiners Arms HG3 2EU [about 5 miles W of Harrogate; High St]: Popular updated local with good reasonably priced fresh food, Rudgate Viking and John Smiths, decent wines, friendly landlord, efficient staff, big fireplace, decorative plates on lounge beams, public bar and barrel-vaulted snug, spacious and airy back dining extension with dozens of sauceboats on beams and corner chest of joiner's tools; unobtrusive piped music; tables out in front and pleasant back garden, attractive village *(Neil and Anita Christopher)*

HARDROW [SD8691]

Green Dragon DL8 3LZ: Traditional Dales pub, stripped stone, antique settles and bric-a-brac, beamed snug with coal fire in old iron range, log fire in big main bar, Black Sheep and other changing ales, decent food from baguettes up, small neat restaurant; gives access (for a small fee) to Britain's highest single-drop waterfall; children welcome, bedrooms *(LYM, Peter Bloodworth, Susan Knight)*

HAREWOOD [SE3245]

Harewood Arms LS17 9LH [A61 opp Harewood House]: Busy hotel, former coaching inn, two comfortable rooms off spacious L-shaped lounge bar, good value food from sandwiches up (also breakfast and bacon and sausage sandwiches served till 11.30, and afternoon teas), friendly courteous staff, cheap Sam Smiths OB, decent house wines, good coffee, attractive dark green décor with Harewood family memorabilia, leisurely old-fashioned no smoking restaurant; back disabled access, bedrooms *(Stuart Paulley)*

HARROGATE [SE3155]

Coach & Horses HG1 1BJ [West Park]: Welcoming pub with local ales such as Daleside, Timothy Taylors and Tetleys, reasonably priced bar food inc charity nights, no piped music; can get smoky on busy wknds; open all day *(the Didler)*

Gardeners Arms HG1 4DH [Bilton Lane (off A59 either in Bilton itself or on outskirts towards Harrogate – via Bilton Hall Dr)]: Small stone-built house converted into friendly old-fashioned local, tiny bar and three small rooms, flagstone floors, panelling, old prints and little else; very cheap Sam Smiths OB, decent bar lunches (not Weds), big log or coal fire in stone fireplace, dominoes; children welcome, tables and play area in good-sized surrounding streamside garden, lovely peaceful setting near Nidd Gorge *(Michael Butler, the Didler)*

☆ *Hales* HG1 2RS [Crescent Rd]: Classic Victorian décor in 18th-c town local close to Pump Rooms, gas lighting (and counter flare lighter), stuffed animals, comfortable saloon

and tiny snug, Bass and Daleside, simple good value lunchtime bar food inc Sun roast *(Giles and Annie Francis)*

☆ *Old Bell* HG1 2SZ [Royal Parade]: No smoking two-bar Market Town Taverns pub with handsome bar counter and friendly knowledgeable staff helpful at choosing from their eight real ales such as Black Sheep, Copper Dragon Golden Pippin, Daleside, Roosters Yankee and Timothy Taylors Landlord, lots of continental bottled beers, impressive choice of wines by the glass, enjoyable fresh food inc popular Fri fish night, quiet upstairs no smoking evening restaurant, no music or machines; no children; open all day *(the Didler, Mr and Mrs P Eastwood, Jo Lilley, Simon Calvert, Mr Tarpey, T and P, J Stickland, Drs M J and P M Cox)*

Tap & Spile HG1 1HS [Tower St]: Friendly bare-boards local, central bar with two pleasant rooms off (one no smoking), up to ten changing ales such as Hambleton, Roosters and Theakstons, helpful staff, good value basic lunchtime food, daily papers, old photographs, stripped stone and panelling; open all day *(the Didler)*

Winter Gardens HG1 2RR [Royal Baths, Crescent Rd]: Notable Wetherspoons transformation of former ballroom in landmark building, comfortable sofas in lofty hall, upper no smoking gallery, cheap well kept Theakstons and other ales; very busy late evening; attractive terrace, open all day *(John Fiander, David Crook)*

HARTHILL [SK4980]

Beehive S26 7YH [Union St]: Smart two-bar village pub opp attractive church, welcoming service, chef/landlord doing wide choice of enjoyable well priced food (not Mon lunchtime) inc proper pies and Sun lunch, Fullers London Pride, Timothy Taylors Landlord and Tetleys, good choice of wines and soft drinks, lounge no smoking at meal times; games room with pool, fruit machine, piped music; children welcome, picnic-sets in attractive garden, walks nearby *(R T and J C Moggridge, Tony Hobden)*

HARTOFT END [SE7493]

☆ *Blacksmiths* YO18 8EN [Pickering—Rosedale Abbey rd]: Civilised and relaxing 16th-c moorland pub, originally a farmhouse and gradually extended, three linked rooms with lots of original stonework, brasses, cosy nooks and crannies, good bar food inc fresh fish and veg, wider evening choice, John Smiths and Theakstons, good wines, friendly staff, open fires, attractive restaurant with cane furnishings; sports TV; children welcome, comfortable bedrooms *(R M Corlett)*

HAWES [SD8789]

☆ *White Hart* DL8 3QL [Main St]: Old-fashioned local bustling wknds and Tues market day, quieter on left, wide choice of good value generous food from sandwiches to some interesting hot dishes in beamed bar and dining room, hot fire, Black Sheep on good form, decent carafe wines, cheerful helpful staff, brisk service, daily papers, darts and dominoes, juke box; occasional craft fairs upstairs, good value bedrooms, good breakfast *(BB, Michael Tack, John Fiander, Mr and Mrs Maurice Thompson, George Atkinson)*

HAWNBY [SE5489]
Hawnby Hotel YO62 5QS [off B1257 NW of Helmsley]: Attractive pub with good choice of consistently enjoyable generous food inc imaginative up-to-date dishes in spotless inn, real ales inc Black Sheep and John Smiths, helpful welcoming service, owl theme in lounge, darts in tap room; views from pleasant garden tables, lovely village in picturesque remote walking country *(Sarah and Peter Gooderham)*

HAWORTH [SE0336]
Haworth Old Hall BD22 8BP [Sun St]: Friendly open-plan 17th-c beamed and panelled building with valley views, three eating areas off long bar, log fire, stripped stonework, appropriately plain furnishings, up to five Jennings ales plus Tetleys, generous food from good sandwiches up, quick service by well trained cheerful staff; piped music; plenty of tables out in front, bedrooms, good breakfast, open all day *(the Didler, Peter F Marshall)*
Old White Lion BD22 8DU [West Lane]: Wide choice of good value home-made food (all day Sun), Tetleys and Theakstons Best, friendly attentive staff, warm comfortable carpeted lounge with plush banquettes and TV, beamed dining area; children welcome, very handy for museum, open all day, spotless comfortable bedrooms *(George Atkinson)*

HEADINGLEY [SE2736]
Arcadia LS6 2UE [Arndale Centre]: Small bank conversion, half a dozen or more good changing ales and lots of continental bottled beers, knowledgeable staff, bar food; a Market Town Tavern, open all day *(E Woodshed)*

HEBDEN BRIDGE [SE0027]
Hare & Hounds HX7 8TN [Billy Lane/Lands End Lane, Wadsworth – above E end of town]: Friendly and well worn in traditional pub with enjoyable generous pub food inc Sun roasts, Timothy Taylors Landlord, Best, Golden Best and a seasonal beer, roaring fire, playful boxer called George, local artwork for sale; tables on terrace with lovely views, plenty of good walks (not to mention the walk up from the town), good bedrooms, cl wkdy lunchtimes, open all day wknds *(Bruce Bird)*
☆ *White Lion* HX7 8EX [Bridge Gate]: Solid stone-built inn with busy comfortable bar and country-furnished no smoking bare-boards back area with coal fire, good choice of sound reasonably priced home cooking all day (just lunchtime Sun), fish specialities, Boddingtons, Timothy Taylors Landlord and a guest beer, pleasant service; disabled access and facilities, attractive secluded riverside garden, comfortable bedrooms *(John Fiander, G Coates, David and Sue Smith)*
White Swan HX7 8EX: Proper local with bargain home-made food, friendly old-fashioned landlady, Black Sheep and Jennings; tables outside *(Ann and Tony Bennett-Hughes)*

HELMSLEY [SE6183]
☆ *Crown* YO62 5BJ [Market Pl]: Simple, welcoming and pleasantly furnished beamed front bar opening into bigger unpretentious central dining room, separate no smoking dining room with conservatory area, good choice of substantial usual food from sandwiches up, real ales, good wines by the glass, efficient staff, roaring fires; tables in sheltered garden behind, pleasant bedrooms *(BB, Sarah and Peter Gooderham)*
☆ *Royal Oak* YO62 5BL [Market Pl]: Neatly updated two-bar inn with three real ales from impressive central servery, good value simple substantial food from sandwiches to Sun lunch, different evening menu, welcoming landlord, quick service even though busy, plenty of breweriana, pool in bare-boards back games area; piped music, TV; picnic-sets out behind, open all day, good bedrooms, big breakfast *(R N Lovelock)*

HIGH BRADFIELD [SK2890]
Nags Head S6 6SJ [Stacey Bank (B6077)]: Stone-built country pub, four real ales, good soft drinks range, enjoyable food (not Sun-Tues evenings) from sandwiches up using local meat and produce, nautical décor with pictures, telescope, ships in bottles, games room with pool and machine; picnic-sets on heated terrace *(JJW, CMW)*

HOLME [SE1005]
☆ *Fleece* HD9 2QG [A6024 SW of Holmfirth]: Cosy pleasant L-shaped bar, Adnams Broadside and Marstons Pedigree, good coffee, popular fresh pub food inc OAP bargains and some special nights (best to book), warmly welcoming jovial landlord, pleasant staff, real fire, conservatory with nice flowers, pool/darts room; quiet piped music, Thurs quiz night; tables out in front, attractive village setting just off Pennine Way below Holme Moss TV mast, great walks (they have plenty of leaflets, even walking socks and gloves for sale) *(Christine and Neil Townend, Stuart Paulley, Michael Butler)*

HOLME-ON-SPALDING-MOOR [SE8138]
Red Lion YO43 4AD [Old Rd]: Friendly, fresh and comfortable L-shaped pub under new licensees, generous wholesome food giving value in bar and restaurant; sunny terrace with big water feature, comfortable bedrooms in cottages behind *(Mr and Mrs P M Jennings)*

HOLMFIRTH [SD1408]
Old Bridge HD9 7DA [Market Walk]: Roomy and comfortable modernised beamed bar in small hotel, Batemans ales, extensive wine list, wide choice of usual food all day from sandwiches and hot baguettes up, good cheerful service even on a hectic summer's day; riverside tables outside, bedrooms, open all day *(George Atkinson)*
Rose & Crown HD9 2DN [aka The Nook; Victoria Sq]: Family-run stone-built local, friendly and basic, with several rooms, low beams, tiled floor, Moorhouses Black Cat Mild, Timothy Taylors Best and Landlord and a guest beer, coal fire, pool room; occasional folk nights, tables outside, open all day *(the Didler)*

HORBURY [SE2918]

Boons WF4 6LP [Queen St]: Lively, chatty and comfortably unpretentious flagstoned local, Clarks, John Smiths, Timothy Taylors Landlord and three or four quickly changing guest beers, bare walls, Rugby League memorabilia, back tap room with pool and TV; can get crowded, no children; courtyard tables *(Michael Butler)*

Bulls Head WF4 5AR [Southfield Lane]: Large relaxed pub well divided into more intimate areas, panelling and wood floors, library room, no smoking snug, popular food in bar and restaurant (busy wknds), Black Sheep and John Smiths, lots of wines by the glass; big car park *(Michael Butler)*

HOVINGHAM [SE6675]

Malt Shovel YO62 4LF [Main St (B1257 NW of Castle Howard)]: Attractive and comfortably unpretentious, with friendly staff, enjoyable generous sensibly priced food using their own veg, Sam Smiths, good coffee with cream jug, cosy dining room; children welcome, appealing village setting *(Mr and Mrs John Taylor, Shirley and Clive Pickerill, John and Jill Perkins)*

☆ *Worsley Arms* YO62 4LA [High St]: Smart inn in pretty village handy for Castle Howard, good value well prepared food in friendly and welcoming back bar and separate restaurant (different menu), real ales, good wines and coffee, friendly attentive staff, lots of yorkshire cricketer photographs esp from 1930s and 40s; nice tables out by stream, pleasant bedrooms, some in cottages across green *(BB, Adrian White)*

HUBBERHOLME [SD9278]

George BD23 5JE: Beautifully placed ancient Dales inn with River Wharfe fishing rights, heavy beams, flagstones and stripped stone, simple bar food from plump sandwiches to steak and local lamb, Black Sheep Bitter and Special and a guest beer, dominoes; children welcome, tables outside, bedrooms, cl Mon in winter *(Michael and Maggie Betton, LYM, Blaise Vyner, Robert Wivell, Malcolm and Lynne Jessop, David and Jean Hall)*

HUDDERSFIELD [SE1416]

Head of Steam HD1 1JF [Station, St Georges Sq]: Railway memorabilia, model trains, cars, buses and planes for sale, pies, ciabattas, baked potatoes and good value Sun roasts, four rooms inc comfortable no smoking eating area by platform, hot coal fire, front room with breweriana, long bar with up to eight changing ales such as Black Sheep, Coach House, Holts (rare to find this in Yorks) and Phoenix, lots of bottled beers, farm ciders, fruit wines; jazz nights, can be very busy; open all day *(Martin Grosberg, J R Ringrose, Andy and Jill Kassube, John Fiander)*

High Park HD2 1PX [Bradley Rd, Bradley]: Neatly kept dining pub, attractively done and keeping plenty of room for drinking and chatting, with Hardys & Hansons beers (unusual around here), good value typical food, quick friendly service, no smoking family area *(J R Ringrose, John Fiander)*

Star HD1 3PJ [Albert St, Lockwood]: Changing real ale rota inc Timothy Taylors Landlord, continental beers, farm cider, several well organised beer festivals, bric-a-brac and customers' paintings, no juke box, pool or machines – or food (may be pie and peas Tues); cl Mon, and lunchtime Tues-Thurs *(J R Ringrose, Andy and Jill Kassube)*

HUGGATE [SE8855]

☆ *Wolds Inn* YO42 1YH [Driffield Rd]: Traditional 16th-c village pub cheerfully blending locals' bar and games room with civilised and comfortable panelled lounge and decorous dining room, wide range of good generous food (meats especially well chosen), friendly family service, Greene King Old Speckled Hen, Timothy Taylors Landlord and Tetleys, pool and darts; benches out in front and pleasant garden behind with delightful views; cl lunchtime Mon-Thurs, bedrooms compact but clean and nicely appointed – lovely village, good easy walks, handy for Wolds Way *(Mr and Mrs P M Jennings)*

HULL [TA1029]

Bay Horse HU2 8AH [Wincolmlee]: Popular unassuming corner local tied to Batemans, their beers kept well, good value basic food inc good home-made pies, pleasant licensees, big log fire, raftered extension lounge/dining room, interesting brewery memorabilia; open all day *(the Didler)*

Green Bricks HU1 1TB [Humber Dock St]: Recently redecorated early 19th-c open-plan pub overlooking marina, two or three changing real ales, Weston's farm cider and perry, good value meals and snacks all day, settees as well as dining tables; tables outside, open all day from late lunchtime on *(Paul and Ursula Randall)*

Olde Black Boy HU1 1PS [High St, Old Town]: Appealing little black-panelled low-ceilinged front room with carved fireplace, lofty 18th-c back vaults bar with leather seating, interesting Wilberforce-related posters etc, good value food lunchtime (not Sun) and late afternoon (not wknds), also Sun breakfast, friendly service, several changing real ales such as Caledonian Deuchars IPA, country wines, old jugs and bottles, upstairs pool room and overflow wknd bar; darts, piano Thurs, games machine; children allowed, open all day *(the Didler, BB, David Carr)*

Olde Blue Bell HU1 1RQ [alley off Lowgate; look out for huge blue bell over pavement]: Friendly traditional 17th-c local with bargain Sam Smiths OB, good value simple lunchtime food, three rooms off corridor, remarkable collection of bells, coal fire; open all day (Sun afternoon break) *(David Carr, the Didler, BB)*

Pave HU5 3QA [Princes Avenue, nr Thoresby St]: Comfortable minimalist café-bar with two Theakstons ales and a guest beer, belgian beers, low-priced interesting food from all-day breakfast to tapas, friendly staff, sofas as well as dining tables, open fire in iron stove, pleasant décor; some live jazz *(Fred and Lorraine Gill)*

HUNTON [SE1892]
Countrymans DL8 1PY: Welcoming and
comfortable village inn, beams and panelling,
interesting and enjoyable food, four real ales
mainly from Masham, reasonably priced
wines, no smoking dining room; seven
bedrooms *(Ian Vipond)*

HUTTON-LE-HOLE [SE7089]
Crown YO62 6UA [The Green]: Attractive
bustling pub overlooking pretty village green
with wandering sheep in classic coach-trip
country, opened-up bar with adjoining dining
area, good sandwiches and huge helpings of
no-fuss food (all day Sun), efficient friendly
service, Black Sheep, lots of whisky-water jugs;
children and dogs welcome, near Folk Museum
and handy for Farndale walks *(Edward and
Deanna Pearce, Dr and Mrs R G J Telfer,
Sarah and Peter Gooderham, Michael Butler)*

ILKLEY [SE1147]
Bar t'at LS29 9DZ [Cunliffe Rd]: No smoking
bare-boards pub with six real ales inc several
from small Yorkshire breweries, good wine
choice, good value brasserie food, quick polite
service, plenty of atmosphere, spiral stairs
down to light and airy no smoking bar, daily
papers; dogs welcome, tables on heated back
terrace, open all day *(David Crook)*
Cow & Calf LS29 8BT [Hangingstone Rd
(moors rd towards Hawksworth)]: Vintage Inn
in stunning spot with lovely views over Ilkley
and Wharfedale, their usual reliable food with
good touches, Bass and Tetleys and fine choice
of wines by the glass, courteous young staff,
old-world décor, log fire in food-free snug;
children welcome, good bedrooms
(Geoffrey and Brenda Wilson, Karen Eliot)

INGBIRCHWORTH [SE2106]
Fountain S36 7GJ [off A629 Shepley—
Penistone; Welthorne Lane]: Beamed country
dining pub under new tenants late 2005,
enjoyable home-made food, real ales such as
Black Sheep, John Smiths and Tetleys, roomy
red plush lounge, cosy front bar, open fires,
comfortable family room; well reproduced
piped music; tables in sizeable garden
overlooking reservoir with pretty walks,
comfortable bedrooms *(Nigel and Sue Foster,
Phil and Helen Holt, BB)*

INGLETON [SD6973]
Wheatsheaf LA6 3AD [High Street]: Useful
17th-c coaching inn in attractive village, long
open-plan bar, usual food, real ales such as
Black Sheep, Moorhouses and Timothy
Taylors, quite a few whiskies, big log fire, two
no smoking dining rooms; piped music; seats
in back garden, nine bedrooms with own
bathrooms, open all day wknds at least in
season *(Andy and Jill Kassube, Mike Dean,
Lis Wingate Gray, Karen Eliot, LYM, Mr and
Mrs John Taylor)*

JACKSON BRIDGE [SE1607]
White Horse HD9 1LY [Scholes Rd, signed off
A616]: Low-ceilinged small-roomed pub with
blue plush wall seats and dining chairs, masses
of *Last of the Summer Wine* photographs (the
pub featured), Black Sheep and Tetleys, soup
and sandwiches, tea and coffee, friendly

landlord, pool room looking out on charming
waterfall and ducks behind *(Michael Butler)*

KEIGHLEY [SE0641]
Boltmakers Arms BD21 5HX [East Parade]:
Split-level open-plan local with particularly
well kept Timothy Taylors Landlord, Best,
Golden Best and guest beers, good value basic
food all day, friendly landlord and staff, coal
fire, nice brewing pictures; sports TV; short
walk from Worth Valley Railway, open all day
(the Didler)
Globe BD21 4QR [Parkwood St]: Comfortable
local by Worth Valley steam railway track,
wkdy lunches, Timothy Taylors ales; open all
day *(the Didler)*

KETTLEWELL [SD9672]
Bluebell BD23 5QX [Middle Lane]: Roomy
and friendly knocked-through 17th-c pub with
snug simple furnishings, low beams and
flagstones, good Copper Dragon ales, good
wine choice, sensibly priced enjoyable food
from sandwiches up in bar and attractive
restaurant, daily papers, some no smoking
tables, children's room; pool room, piped
music; picnic-sets out on cobbles facing Wharfe
bridge, more on good-sized back terrace,
decent bedrooms mainly in annexe *(Mr and
Mrs Maurice Thompson, JJW, CMW, LYM,
Len Beattie, Margaret and Roy Randle,
Michael Butler)*
☆ *Kings Head* BD23 5RD: Cheerful and
welcoming old local tucked away near church,
lively flagstoned main bar with log fire in big
inglenook, comfortable tartan-carpeted snug
around corner, discreet dining room, Black
Sheep, local Litton ales and Tetleys, Stowford
Press cider, interesting wines, reliable good
value straightforward food from good
baguettes up, friendly helpful staff; four
comfortable bedrooms with own bathrooms
*(Edmund Coan, DC, BB, Robert Wivell,
Len Beattie, O K Smyth, B and M Kendall,
Dr D and Mrs B Woods, Guy Vowles)*
☆ *Racehorses* BD23 5QZ [B6160 N of Skipton]:
Comfortable, civilised and friendly, with
generous good value food from substantial
lunchtime rolls and baguettes to local game,
Timothy Taylors real ales, good wine choice,
efficient helpful staff, log fires; dogs welcome
in front bar, picnic-sets on attractive terrace,
well placed for Wharfedale walks, good
bedrooms with own bathrooms, open all day
*(Mr and Mrs Maurice Thompson, DC, BB,
Len Beattie, Sam and Christine Kilburn,
Margaret and Roy Randle, Dr D and Mrs
B Woods)*

KILBURN [SE5179]
☆ *Forresters Arms* YO61 4AH [between A170
and A19 SW of Thirsk]: Next to Thompson
furniture workshops (visitor centre opp) in
pleasant village, handsomely furnished by
them; big log fire, good home-made food from
good value baguettes to enterprising specials,
welcoming father-and-son licensees, real ales
such as Hambleton, John Smiths and Tetleys,
side eating area, bar with TV and pool room,
restaurant; well behaved children welcome,
suntrap seats out in front, good value cheerful

bedrooms, open all day *(LYM, Andy and Jill Kassube)*

KILNSEA [TA4016]

☆ *Crown & Anchor* HU12 0UB [Kilnsea Rd]: Welcoming family-friendly pub in great remote location overlooking eroding Spurn Point nature reserve and Humber estuary, single bar opening into two beamed lounges and linen-set restaurant, prints and bric-a-brac, friendly staff, Timothy Taylors Landlord and Tetleys, low-priced wines, above-average reasonably priced generous pub food inc good fresh fish; piped music; picnic-sets in back garden and out in front facing Humber estuary, four bedrooms with own bathrooms, open all day *(Paul and Ursula Randall, DC, J Crosby)*

KILNSEY [SD9767]

☆ *Tennants Arms* BD23 5PS: Immaculately kept pub dramatically placed in good Wharfedale walking area, views of spectacular overhanging crag from restaurant, good range of good food, Black Sheep, Tetleys and Theakstons Best and Old Peculier, log fire, prompt friendly service, several rooms, interesting decorations, unusual cartwheel-back seats, exemplary lavatories; piped music; comfortable good value bedrooms *(Ian Blake, Neil Whitehead, Victoria Anderson)*

KIRKBY MALZEARD [SE2374]

Henry Jenkins HG4 3RY [NW of Fountains Abbey]: Spotless pub in attractive village, decent generous bar food at reasonable prices in small comfortable lounge bar with beams and brasses, real ales, nice-looking restaurant; the man the pub's named for is said to have lived in the village from 1500 right through to 1670 *(Bill and Sheila McLardy)*

KIRKBYMOORSIDE [SE6986]

Kings Head YO62 6AT [High Market Pl]: 16th-c inn with well priced home-made food inc local fish, game and meat, interesting vegetarian menu, friendly service, Jennings ales, good log fire, cosy lounge and pleasant conservatory; children welcome, sheltered courtyard and attractive garden, comfortable good value bedrooms *(Sue Demont, Tim Barrow, Judith and Edward Pearson)*

KNARESBOROUGH [SE3556]

☆ *Blind Jacks* HG5 8AL [Market Pl]: Charming and friendly multi-floor traditional tavern in 18th-c building, simple but attractive furnishings, brewery posters etc, particularly well kept Black Sheep, Timothy Taylors (inc their great Dark Mild) and other changing ales such as Copper Dragon, farm cider and foreign bottled beers, bubbly atmosphere downstairs, quieter up – one room there no smoking; well behaved children allowed away from bar, open all day wknds, cl Mon till 5.30; Beer Ritz two doors away sells all sorts of rare bottled beers *(Andrew Hewitt, LYM, the Didler, J R Ringrose)*

LANGSETT [SE2100]

Wagon & Horses S36 4GY [A616 Stocksbridge—Huddersfield]: Welcoming and comfortable main-road moors pub, blazing log fire, stripped stone and woodwork, enjoyable food inc good value Sun lunch, Theakstons,

magazines to read *(Trevor and Judith Pearson, James A Waller)*

LANGTHWAITE [NZ0002]

☆ *Red Lion* DL11 6RE [just off Reeth—Brough Arkengarthdale rd]: Homely unspoilt 17th-c pub, so individual and relaxing as to be quite a favourite, in charming Dales village with ancient bridge; basic cheap nourishing lunchtime food, Black Sheep Bitter and Riggwelter and John Smiths, country wines, tea and coffee, character firm-viewed landlady; well behaved children allowed lunchtime in very low-ceilinged side snug; the ladies' is a genuine bathroom; seats outside, good walks all around, inc organised circular ones from the pub – maps and guides for sale *(Anthony Barnes, LYM, Dr and Mrs M E Wilson, Ann and Tony Bennett-Hughes)*

LEALHOLM [NZ7607]

Board YO21 2AJ [off A171 W of Whitby]: In wonderful moorland village spot by wide pool of River Esk, two tidy refurbished and unpretentious bars, one for locals with darts, and one with dining tables, stripped stone, welcoming licensees, Jennings Cumberland, Theakstons Black Bull and a guest beer, big log fire, restaurant; TV; secluded riverside garden, bedrooms, open all day Sat, cl wkdy winter lunchtimes *(John H Smith, Kevin Thorpe)*

LEAVENING [SE7863]

Jolly Farmers YO17 9SA [Main St]: Welcoming and pleasantly unpretentious village local, good choice of changing real ales such as Timothy Taylors Landlord, good value popular food (not Sun evening or Mon/Tues), lots of fresh veg, friendly licensees, smallish front bar with eating area behind and separate no smoking dining room, games room with pool and TV; cl Mon evening *(Christopher Turner, David Barnes)*

LEEDS [SE3033]

Adelphi LS10 1JQ [Hunslet Rd]: Thoroughly refurbished (but they've kept the handsome Edwardian mahogany screens, panelling, tiling, cut and etched glass and impressive stairway), Tetleys and guest ales, decent lunchtime food, prompt friendly service; live jazz Sat *(the Didler)*

Beulah LS12 5EP [Tong Rd, Farnley]: Hilltop spot with good views, Tetleys and other changing ales, enjoyable home-made food from bar meals to three-course Sun lunch *(James Brown)*

Cross Keys LS11 5WD [Water Lane]: Recently opened designer bar with polished wood floors, stripped brick, metal and timbers, several real ales from small breweries such as Black Sheep, Copper Dragon and Roosters, good choice of imported bottled beers, up-to-date food (not Sun evening); tables under big canvas parasols in sheltered courtyard, open all day *(Andy and Jill Kassube)*

Duck & Drake LS2 7DR [Kirkgate, between indoor market and Parish Church]: A dozen or more interesting reasonably priced real ales from well worn in two-bar pub's central servery, farm cider too, good coal fires, basic furniture, bare boards and beer posters and mirrors, low-priced wkdy lunchtime bar snacks, games room with Yorkshire doubles dartboard as well as pool etc; juke box, big-screen TV, games machines; open all day *(the Didler, Pete Baker, Martin Grosberg)*

Garden Gate LS10 2QB [Whitfield Pl, Hunslet]: Basic well used local interesting for its untouched flagstoned Victorian layout and intricate glass, ceramics and woodwork, with various rooms off central drinking corridor, Tetleys Bitter and Mild, farm cider, no food; open all day *(BB, the Didler)*

Grove LS11 5PL [Back Row, Holbeck]: Unspoilt 1930s-feel local, three or four rooms off drinking corridor, up to eight changing ales inc Adnams, Caledonian Deuchars IPA, Theakstons and Charles Wells Bombardier, farm cider; open all day *(the Didler, Mark and Diane Grist)*

Palace LS2 7DJ [Kirkgate]: Pleasantly uncityfied, with polished wood, unusual lighting from electric candelabra to mock street lamps, lots of old prints, friendly helpful staff, good value lunchtime food from sandwiches up inc two-for-one bargains and popular Sun roasts in no smoking dining area, fine changing choice of real ales, may be bargain wine offers; games end with pool, TV, good piped music; tables out in front and in small heated back courtyard, open all day *(the Didler)*

Roundhay Fox LS8 2JL [by Roundhay Park, Princes Avenue]: Popular Vintage Inn in former stone-built stables by Canal Gardens, plenty of space, pleasant atmosphere, friendly staff, good range of sensibly priced food, guest beers, log fire; courtyard tables *(David Carr, A S and M E Marriott, DAV, M Joyner)*

Scarborough LS1 5DY [Bishopgate St, opp station]: Ornate art nouveau tiled curved façade, bare boards, barrel tables, lots of wood and stone, shelves of Victoriana, showy fireplace, half a dozen or more interesting changing real ales, farm cider, wide choice of cheap wkdy lunchtime food inc occasional special offers, friendly helpful staff, music-hall posters; very busy lunchtime and early evening, machines, big-screen sports TV; open all day *(the Didler)*

Viaduct LS1 6ER [Lower Briggate]: Pleasantly furnished long narrow bar, lots of wood, Tetleys and guest ales, popular lunchtime food, friendly helpful staff, no smoking area; actively caters for disabled customers, attractive back garden, open all day exc Sun afternoon *(the Didler)*

☆ *Victoria* LS1 3DL [Gt George St, just behind Town Hall]: Opulent bustling early Victorian pub with grand cut and etched mirrors, impressive globe lamps extending from the majestic bar, imposing carved beams, booths with working snob-screens in lounge, smaller rooms off, changing ales such as Black Sheep and Timothy Taylors, friendly efficient service by smart bar staff, reasonably priced food 12-6 from sandwiches and light dishes up in luncheon room with end serving hatch, no smoking room; open all day *(the Didler, David Carr, M and GR)*

LELLEY [TA2032]
Stags Head HU12 8SN [Main St; NE of Preston]: Stylishly refurbished bar with sofas and a couple of high-stool tables, dining area on one side and comfortable restaurant the other, enjoyable enterprising fresh food, long-serving landlady and cheerful well turned out staff, Marstons Pedigree and John Smiths, decent wines by the glass; TV *(Paul and Ursula Randall)*

LEVISHAM [SE8390]
Horseshoe YO18 7NL [off A169 N of Pickering]: Cosy and welcoming, more restaurant than pub, civilised service, limited choice of stylishly served good if not cheap food, beams and simple comfortable old wooden furniture, log fire in stone fireplace, no smoking dining area, Theakstons, good wine choice; no dogs or children, quiet piped classical music; picnic-sets on attractive green, delightful unspoilt village a steep walk up from station, plenty of good walks *(Michael and Ann Cole, Richard, LYM, Andrew Given)*

LEYBURN [SE1190]
Black Swan DL8 5AS [Market Pl]: Thriving old open-plan stone-built local with decent range of food inc popular Sun carvery, real ales such as Black Sheep, Marstons Pedigree, John Smiths and Timothy Taylors Landlord, genial landlord and quick service; children and dogs welcome, good disabled access, terrace tables, nine bedrooms, open all day *(the Didler, Michael Tack)*

LOCKTON [SE8488]
☆ *Fox & Rabbit* YO18 7NQ [just off A169 N of Pickering]: Smart and neatly kept by young brothers, one cooks enjoyable imaginative food, good sandwiches too, friendly efficient service, Black Sheep and Timothy Taylors Landlord, plush banquettes, brasses, real fires, busy locals' bar, good views from comfortable no smoking separate restaurant; tables outside and in sun lounge, nice spot on moors edge *(Richard, Sarah and Peter Gooderham, Colin and Dot Savill, LYM, Brian and Pat Wardrobe, John H Smith, Ian Ward)*

LONG MARSTON [SE5051]
Sun YO26 7PG [B1224 Wetherby—York]: Friendly new landlady, good value food, bargain Sam Smiths, log fire and several pleasant areas; garden with big play area *(Tony and Penny Burton, Judith and Edward Pearson)*

LOW BENTHAM [SD6469]
Punch Bowl LA2 7DD: Enjoyable home-made food inc Fri bargain and popular Sun lunch, log fire, no smoking dining room *(Karen Eliot)*

LOW BRADFIELD [SK2691]
Plough S6 6HW [New Rd]: Popular no smoking pub, attractively restored, with good value fresh food, good changing ales inc Caledonian Deuchars IPA, comfortable banquettes, lots of brass and copper, old lamps and bric-a-brac, two fires (one in an inglenook), restaurant; children welcome, picnic-sets in attractive garden, lovely scenery *(Matthew Lidbury, Peter F Marshall)*

MALHAM [SD9062]
Buck BD23 4DA [off A65 NW of Skipton]:
Popular country inn, wide range of quickly
served enjoyable generous home-made food
from reasonably priced sandwiches up, Black
Sheep, Tetleys, Theakstons Best and a guest
beer, good value wines, good service, big log
fire in plush panelled lounge, big basic hikers'
bar, elegant candlelit dining room; picnic-sets
in small yard, picture-book village, many good
walks from the door, ten decent well equipped
bedrooms *(Len Beattie)*
Listers Arms BD23 4DB [off A65 NW of
Skipton]: Creeper-covered stone-built inn in
nice spot by river, good walking country; easy-
going open-plan lounge, busy wknds, good
value food from bowl of chips and hot-filled
ciabattas up, small helpings available, changing
real ales such as Black Sheep, Caledonian
Deuchars IPA and Timothy Taylors Landlord,
lots of continental beers, malt whiskies and
soft drinks, friendly service, roaring fire, big-
windowed bare-boards lower room good for
families; bar can get smoky; children and dogs
welcome, seats out overlooking small green,
more in back garden, comfortable modern
bedrooms with own bathrooms *(David Crook,
Paul Graham, R T J and J J Hubbard,
Alun Howells)*

MALTON [SE8871]
Crown YO17 7HP [Wheelgate – aka Suddabys
and signed as that not Crown]: In same family
for generations, chatty basic town bar with
strong horse-racing links, racing TV on bar,
Malton Crown ales (now brewed elsewhere, no
longer brewed on site) and guest beers, daily
papers; lots of local notices, beer festivals June
and Dec; children welcome in back courtyard
nicely redone as conservatory (occasional live
music here), good value bedrooms *(BB,
David Carr, Alan Brayshaw, John Tav,
Roger A Bellingham)*

MARSDEN [SE0411]
☆ *Riverhead* HD7 6BR [Peel St, next to Co-op;
just off A62 Huddersfield—Oldham]: Busy
basic pub in converted grocer's, spiral stairs
down to microbrewery (tours available)
producing interesting beers named after local
reservoirs, the higher the reservoir, the higher
the strength (March Haigh is a favourite), farm
cider; unobtrusive piped music; wheelchair
access, streamside tables, cl wkdy lunchtimes,
open from 4pm, all day wknds, handy for
Huddersfield Broad Canal and moorland
walks *(J R Ringrose, the Didler, John Fiander)*
Tunnel End HD7 6NF [Reddisher Rd (off A62
via Peel St)]: Pleasant setting overlooking mouth
of restored Standedge Canal Tunnel – at three
miles under the Pennines, the UK's longest; very
warm welcome, real ales such as Black Sheep
and Timothy Taylors Landlord, simple generous
well made food from sandwiches to Sun roasts,
reasonable prices, four good-sized but homely
rooms (one no smoking), hot log fire in back
room *(Joan York, Dr Michael Smith)*

MASHAM [SE2280]
☆ *Kings Head* HG4 4EF [Market Pl]: Handsome
stone inn in good position, two linked rooms

with imposing fireplace and clock, Theakstons
Best, Black Bull, XB, and Old Peculier and up
to 20 wines by the glass, bar food (all day
wknds), no smoking restaurant; piped music,
games machine, TV; children in eating areas,
good bedrooms in back courtyard area (some
for disabled), open all day *(LYM, Richard and
Anne Ansell, Janet and Peter Race, Dr and
Mrs Jackson, Jack Morley, K M Crook,
Mike and Jayne Bastin)*
☆ *White Bear* HG4 4EN [Wellgarth, Crosshills;
signed off A6108 opp turn into town]: Bright
and cheerful beamed and stone-built pub, small
lino-floor public bar with darts, comfortable
larger bare-boards lounge with coal fire,
Caledonian Deuchars IPA, Theakstons and a
changing guest beer, decent wines by the glass,
good fairly priced food choice (not Sun
evening) from sandwiches up, neat efficient
staff; piped radio; metal tables and chairs out
on terrace, open all day *(Janet and Peter Race,
the Didler, BB)*

MEXBOROUGH [SK4799]
Concertina Band Club S64 9AZ [Dolcliffe
Rd]: Friendly pubby club happy to sign in
visitors and brewing its own good changing
ales (may allow brewery tour at quiet times),
also guest beers; large bar with stage and small
games area with pool, other games and SkyTV;
cl Sun lunchtime *(the Didler)*

MIDDLETON [SE7885]
Middleton Arms YO18 8PB [Church Lane]:
Cosy and welcoming no smoking
pub/restaurant with good sensibly priced food
from local farms, lovely log fire, friendly
attentive service, good value wines, nice coffee
(Susan Hosker)

MIRFIELD [SE2019]
Flower Pot WF14 8NN [Calder Rd]: Cosy
restaurant, attractively presented quickly
served enjoyable food, efficient service
(Julian Lewington)
Navigation WF14 8NL [Station Rd]:
Canalside pub, enjoyable home-made food
from sandwiches to some enterprising dishes
using locally sourced meat, Theakstons ales,
new restaurant section *(Andy and Jill Kassube)*

MOULTON [NZ2303]
☆ *Black Bull* DL10 6QJ [just off A1 nr Scotch
Corner]: The long-serving owners have recently
sold this interesting black-beamed dining pub,
long a favourite of many readers, with its
individual furnishings, big log fire, dark-
panelled side seafood bar with high seats at
marble-topped counter, polished conservatory
restaurant and even a Brighton Belle dining
car, and courtyard tables under trees; reports
on new regime, please – fingers crossed that
they'll add a real ale to the good wines and
spirits *(Jill and Julian Tasker, LYM)*

MUKER [SD9097]
☆ *Farmers Arms* DL11 6QG [B6270 W of
Reeth]: Basic family-friendly walkers' pub in
beautiful valley village, well placed both for
rewarding walks and interesting drives, warm
open fire, friendly staff and locals, Black Sheep
and Theakstons, wines, teas and coffees,
enjoyable straightforward food from

sandwiches to generous pies, casseroles and so forth, flagstones and carpeting, darts and dominoes; tables outside, self-catering studio flat *(LYM, the Didler, David Hall, A Pickering, Ben and Helen Ingram, Ann and Tony Bennett-Hughes, Michael Gallagher, David and Jean Hall, J P Humphery)*

MYTHOLMROYD [SE0126]
Dusty Miller HX7 5LH [Burnley Rd]: Newly refurbished, with new young chef doing good generous food at appealing prices, international dishes with true Yorkshire appeal *(Anon)*

NABURN [SE5945]
Blacksmiths Arms YO19 4PN [Main St]: Newish brother and sister licensees in country pub with several linked rooms, pleasant nooks and corners, sizeable dining area, wide choice of enjoyable food from sandwiches to Sun carvery, real ales and fairly priced wines, log fire; includes small village shop, baking own bread; garden tables, lovely village *(Christine and Phil Young)*

NEW MILL [SE1708]
Crossroads HD9 7JL: Spacious and attractive rambling pub with Mansfield ale, proper coffee, wide choice of good value food, open fire in bar, kitchen range and darts in smaller tiled-floor room leading off, adjoining raftered partly no smoking dining barn; nice garden with play area and country views *(Michael Butler)*

NORTHALLERTON [SE3794]
Tithe Bar DL6 1DP [Friarage St]: Half a dozen quickly changing real ales such as Black Sheep, Caledonian Deuchars IPA and Timothy Taylors, masses of continental bottled beers, friendly staff, enjoyable food lunchtime and early evening, traditional settle and armchairs in one area, two rooms with tables and chairs on bare boards (not unlike a belgian bar), upstairs restaurant; a Market Town Tavern, open all day *(Mr and Mrs Maurice Thompson)*

NORWOOD GREEN [SE1326]
☆ *Olde White Beare* HX3 8QG [signed off A641 in Wyke, or off A58 Halifax—Leeds just W of Wyke; Village St]: Large 17th-c building well renovated and extended, with character tap room, larger split-level lounge, beams and panelling, brasses, good personal service, Boddingtons and Timothy Taylors, good service, bar food inc tapas, bargain early suppers and popular Sun lunch, handsome barn restaurant; tables out in front and in back garden with barbecue, Calderdale Way and Brontî Way pass the door *(Len Beattie, Michael Butler)*

NUN MONKTON [SE5057]
Alice Hawthorn YO26 8EW [off A59 York—Harrogate; The Green]: Modernised standard dining pub on broad village green with pond and lovely avenue to church and Rivers Nidd and Ouse; lots of brass etc in bar with big brick inglenook fireplace, another open fire in restaurant, several changing real ales, big helpings of reasonably priced home-made food *(Tony and Penny Burton, BB, Alex and Claire Pearse)*

OAKWORTH [SE0138]
☆ *Grouse* BD22 0RX [Harehills, Oldfield; 2 miles towards Colne]: Comfortable old Timothy Taylors pub well altered and extended, their ales kept well, wide range of enjoyable generous food all day, good service, lots of bric-a-brac, gleaming copper and china, prints, cartoons and caricatures, charming evening restaurant; undisturbed hamlet in fine moorland surroundings, Pennine views, open all day *(Margaret Dickinson, Geoffrey and Brenda Wilson)*

OLDSTEAD [SE5380]
Black Swan YO61 4BL [Main St]: Unpretentious beamed and flagstoned country pub, friendly landlord, enjoyable food inc enterprising vegetarian dishes, Black Sheep and John Smiths, pretty valley views from two big bay windows and picnic-sets outside, restaurant up steps (level with car park); children welcome, bedrooms in modern back extension, beautiful surroundings *(Andy and Jill Kassube, BB)*

OSMOTHERLEY [SE4597]
Queen Catherine DL6 3AG [West End]: Welcoming family pub, friendly and unpretentious, with old local prints and roomy modern décor, Tetleys and a guest beer such as Hambleton, hearty helpings of popular food all day, log fire, separate dining area; children welcome, simple comfortable bedrooms, good breakfast *(Danny Savage, David Carr, Michael Butler)*

OSSETT [SE2719]
☆ *Brewers Pride* WF5 8ND [Low Mill Rd/Healey Lane (long cul-de-sac by railway sidings, off B6128)]: Warmly friendly basic local with Rooster, Timothy Taylors and its own Ossett beers (now brewed nearby – the pub may still occasionally brew ales itself), cosy front room and bar both with open fires, brewery memorabilia and flagstones, small games room, enjoyable lunchtime food (not Sun); Thurs folk night; big back garden with local entertainment summer wknds, nr Calder & Hebble Canal, open all day wknds *(the Didler)*

OTLEY [SE2047]
Spite LS21 2EY: Low-beamed traditional pub with good value food from sandwiches to carvery roasts in bar and restaurant, several real ales, good wines, well organised service, good log fire; children in eating area, tables out in neat well lit rose garden, beautiful setting *(LYM, Geoffrey and Brenda Wilson)*

OUTLANE [SE0818]
Swan HD3 3YJ [just off A640 Huddersfield—Rochdale by M62 junction 23, handy for junction 24 too]: Comfortable and genuine open-plan pub with good range of sensibly priced home cooking inc hot and cold sandwiches, bargain specials and (all afternoon) good value Sun lunch, Black Sheep and Timothy Taylors, jovial landlord and keen staff, no smoking area; unobtrusive piped music, pool table in side area *(J R Ringrose, Stuart Paulley)*

OVERTON [SE2516]
Black Swan WF4 4RF [off A642 Wakefield—Huddersfield; Green Lane]: Traditional local,

two knocked-together low-beamed rooms with lots of brasses and bric-a-brac, John Smiths; Thurs quiz night (may be free food) *(Michael Butler)*

PATRINGTON [TA3022]

Station Hotel HU12 0NE [Station Rd]: Light airy décor, good range of enjoyable food from baguettes up all day in bar and restaurant, real ales inc Tetleys; open all day *(C A Hall)*

PENISTONE [SE2402]

Cubley Hall S36 9DF [Mortimer Rd, out towards Stocksbridge]: Rambling centre for functions, weddings and so forth as well as family meals and drinks, panelling, elaborate plasterwork, mosaic tiling and plush furnishings, roomy conservatory, wide choice of bar food all day, Greene King Abbot and Old Speckled Hen, Marstons Pedigree and Charles Wells Bombardier, decent wines, no smoking room; piped music, fruit machine, TV; children welcome (whatever happened to being seen and not heard?), big garden with plenty of tables, good playground and distant views, bedrooms with own bathrooms, open all day *(RJH, LYM, Trevor and Judith Pearson, Matthew Lidbury)*

PINCHINTHORPE [NZ5714]

Pinchinthorpe Hall TS14 8HG [A173 W of Guisborough]: Partly medieval hotel/restaurant, not pub, brewing its own good North Yorkshire organic ales, with good sensibly priced fresh food (may be a wait) in bistro; bedrooms *(Blaise Vyner)*

POOL [SE2445]

☆ *White Hart* LS21 1LH [just off A658 S of Harrogate, A659 E of Otley]: Reliable largely no smoking Vintage Inn all-day family dining pub which has long been popular with readers, but closed for extensive refurbishment as we go to press: news please *(LYM)*

RAMSGILL [SE1171]

☆ *Yorke Arms* HG3 5RL [Nidderdale]: Upmarket small hotel (not a pub), small smart bar with some heavy Jacobean furniture and log fires, Black Sheep Special, a fine wine list, good choice of spirits and fresh juices, good if pricey full meals in classy no smoking restaurant; piped music, no under-12s even in restaurant; comfortable bedrooms, good quiet moorland and reservoir walks *(LYM, Peter and Lesley Yeoward)*

REETH [SE0399]

☆ *Black Bull* DL11 6SZ [B6270]: Proper village pub in fine spot at foot of broad sloping green, Black Sheep, John Smiths and Theakstons, well prepared unpretentious reasonably priced food, friendly helpful staff, traditional dark beamed and flagstoned L-shaped front bar cosy at night with open fires, lovely Dales views from dining room; piped music in pool room; children welcome, tables outside, comfortable bedrooms (also with views), good breakfast *(Martin and Alison Stainsby, LYM, Dr and Mrs M E Wilson, Ann and Tony Bennett-Hughes)*

Buck DL11 6SW: Welcoming and comfortable, with friendly efficient staff, good value food in bar and restaurant, Black Sheep Bitter, Best

and Special and Theakstons Old Peculier; annual jazz festival; very popular with hikers, with a few tables out in front, bedrooms, good breakfast *(Jill and Julian Tasker)*

Kings Arms DL11 6SY [Market Pl (B6270)]: Friendly beamed village pub with dining area facing green, reasonably priced food, Black Sheep, full Theakstons range and a guest beer, pine pews around walls, log fire in 18th-c stone inglenook, quieter room behind; may be piped music; children very welcome, tables outside, bedrooms *(Dr and Mrs M W A Haward, Mr and Mrs Maurice Thompson)*

RIBBLEHEAD [SD7678]

Station Hotel LA6 3AS [B6255 Ingleton—Hawes]: Alone on the moors by Ribblehead Viaduct (Settle—Carlisle trains), kind licensees, good log fire in woodburner, Black Sheep, Copper Dragon Golden Pippin and an interesting guest beer, low-priced wine, substantial food from sandwiches to steaks, basic pub furnishings, central pool table, darts, dining room with viaduct mural (the bar has relevant photographs, some you can buy); piped music or juke box, TV; open all day in season, some picnic-sets outside, good value simple bedrooms and next-door bunkhouse, good wholesome breakfast *(JJW, CMW, BB, Dr D J and Mrs S C Walker, JHBS)*

RILLINGTON [SE8574]

Coach & Horses YO17 8LH [Scarborough Rd]: Homely village local with vast china cat collection in spotless lounge, generous straightforward home-made food at bargain prices inc fine steak and kidney pie and Sun roast, friendly landlord, Black Sheep and Theakstons XB *(Colin and Dot Savill)*

RIPON [SE3071]

Dog & Duck HG4 2PT [Skellbank]: Bright and spacious, with attentive service and good value food *(Janet and Peter Race)*

☆ *One-Eyed Rat* HG4 1LQ [Allhallowgate]: No-frills friendly bare-boards pub with fine changing range of interesting real ales, farm cider, lots of bottled beers and country wines, log or coal fire, cigarette cards, framed beer mats, bank notes and old pictures, bar billiards (no food, juke box or music); tables in pleasant outside area, open all day Sat, cl Mon-Weds lunchtimes *(Maggie Ainsley, Mr and Mrs P G Mitchell, Jack Clark)*

Turf HG4 2BU [Ripon Spa Hotel, Park St]: Comfortable bar with reliable bar food, good range of real ales; bedrooms in parent hotel *(Janet and Peter Race)*

RISHWORTH [SE0316]

☆ *Old Bore* HX6 4QU [Oldham Rd (A672)]: Plenty of bric-a-brac, old prints on individualistic wallpaper, flagstones and mixed furnishings in comfortably and stylishly extended newish bar/restaurant with good if not cheap food, enthusiastic young staff, Tetleys, Timothy Taylors and guest ales; cl Mon *(David and Cathrine Whiting, John Proud)*

ROBIN HOOD'S BAY [NZ9504]

Bay Hotel YO22 4SJ [The Dock, Bay Town]: Unpretentious old village inn with fine sea views from cosy picture-window upstairs bar (downstairs open only at busy times), friendly staff, three real ales, log fires, good value generous food in bar and separate dining area; tables outside, cosy bedrooms, open all day *(Edward Leetham, A Pickering)*

ROECLIFFE [SE3765]

Crown YO51 9LY [W of Boroughbridge]: Thriving pub with helpful thoughtful service, good choice of well presented enjoyable food from enterprising sandwiches and snack lunches to interesting full meals, Black Sheep, John Smiths and Timothy Taylors Landlord, flagstoned bar, lounge with caricatures of famous Yorkshire folk, spacious dining room; front benches overlook quaint village green, lovely village, bedrooms, unobtrusive touring caravan site *(Michael Doswell, Judith and Edward Pearson)*

ROTHERHAM [SK4292]

Blue Coat S60 2DJ [The Crofts]: Wetherspoons where the friendly staff really care for the good range of real ales; no smoking area upstairs, open all day *(Leon Shaw)*

SANDHUTTON [SE3882]

Kings Arms YO7 4RW: Good value food in pleasant village-edge pub, small convivial dining room *(Janet and Peter Race)*

SANDSEND [NZ8612]

Hart YO21 3SU [East Row]: Good helpings of good food from fine crab sandwiches through lots of fish to tempting puddings in shoreside pub with log fire in nicely unmodernised downstairs bar, upstairs no smoking dining room, good welcoming service, real ale; pleasant garden *(Hugh Bower)*

SCAGGLETHORPE [SE8372]

Ham & Cheese YO17 8DY: Hospitable new owners doing well in friendly and comfortable country dining pub, changing real ales, enjoyable pubby food from baguettes to good steaks, separate smartly appointed no smoking restaurant *(Colin and Dot Savill)*

SCARBOROUGH [TA0387]

Cellars YO11 2LX [Valley Rd]: Lively bar in basement of Victorian mansion (now holiday flats), four interesting ales such as Acorn, Archers, Black Sheep and Boggart Hole Clough, good value food, snug comfortable seating; live music nights *(Andy and Jill Kassube)*

Lord Rosebery YO11 1JW [Westborough]: Large handsome Wetherspoons in former Co-op (and once the local Liberal HQ), very busy and lively evenings, in traffic-free central shopping area; galleried upper bar, good beer range, enjoyable quickly served food inc Sun roast, obliging staff, no smoking area, local prints, disabled facilities, open all day *(David Carr, Colin Gooch, Kevin Blake)*

Scarborough Arms YO11 1HU [North Terr]: Comfortable mock-Tudor pub, walls decorated with weaponry, good value filling meals (not Sun evening), Marstons, John Smiths Bitter and Magnet and a guest beer, helpful landlady, friendly staff, warm open range, darts, pool; children welcome, good outside seating, open all day *(David Carr, LS)*

Tap & Spile YO12 5AZ [Falsgrave Rd]: Up to a dozen or more real ales in three-room pub with good value home-made food lunchtime and early evening, efficient good-humoured staff, bare boards or flagstones, no smoking room; sports TV, some live music; terrace with barbecues, open all day *(the Didler)*

Valley YO11 2LX [Valley Rd]: Bargain simple food using local produce inc popular speciality nights such as curry on Fri, changing real ales such as Brown Cow, Hambleton and Wold Top, friendly staff *(Andy and Jill Kassube)*

SCAWTON [SE5483]

☆ *Hare* YO7 2HG [off A170 Thirsk—Helmsley]: Attractive dining pub with enterprising rather upmarket food, Black Sheep, Jennings Cumberland and John Smiths, good wines, well spaced stripped pine tables, heavy beams and some flagstones, old-fashioned range and woodburner, appealing prints, no smoking restaurant (allowing children) and part of bar; open all day summer, cl Mon *(Michael and Ann Cole, Walter and Susan Rinaldi-Butcher, Peter and Anne Hollindale, LYM, Edward and Deanna Pearce)*

SCRUTON [SE3092]

Coore Arms DL7 0QP [off A1 via A684; Station Rd]: Old family-run inn with reliable good value food from good vegetarian dishes to a very substantial lamb speciality, friendly helpful staff *(Sheila Stothard)*

SETTLE [SD8163]

☆ *Golden Lion* BD24 9DU [B6480 (main rd through town), off A65 bypass]: Thriving atmosphere in old-fashioned market town inn with surprisingly grand staircase sweeping down into spacious baronial-style high-beamed hall bar, log fire in enormous fireplace, comfortable settles, plush seats, brass, prints and chinese plates on dark panelling; local and guest ales, decent wines by the glass, well priced food (all day wknds) inc popular pizzas and interesting specials, splendid dining room; music video, public bar with darts, pool, fruit machine and TV; children in eating area, 12 recently well refurbished spacious bedrooms, hearty breakfast, open all day *(Michael Butler, Richard and Anne Ansell, Michael and Maggie Betton, LYM, Karen Eliot, Sue Demont, Tim Barrow)*

SHEFFIELD [SK3487]

Bath S3 7QL [Victoria St, off Glossop Rd]: Two small colourfully restored bare-boards rooms (one no smoking) with nice woodwork, tiles and glass, Abbeydale Moonshine, Acorn Barnsley, Tetleys or Timothy Taylors Landlord from central servery, lunchtime bar food (not Sat); open all day, cl Sun lunchtime *(C J Fletcher, the Didler, Mrs Hazel Rainer, Pete Baker)*

☆ *Cask & Cutler* S3 7EQ [Henry St; Shalesmoor tram stop right outside]: Unpretentious and relaxed real ale pub with fine changing range of up to ten ten interesting newcomers and occasional Port Mahon beers brewed on the premises, dutch and belgian bottled beers, farm ciders and perry, coal fire in no smoking lounge on left, friendly licensees and cat called

Magus (the dog's Holly), appropriate posters, daily papers, pub games, good Nov beer festival; wheelchair access, tables in nice back garden, open all day Fri/Sat, cl Mon lunchtime *(the Didler, Pete Baker)*

Castle S17 4PT [Twentywell Rd, Bradway]: Two-bar extended stone-built pub in attractive spot, sensibly priced food (not Sun evening) inc Sun carvery, five real ales such as Boddingtons, Timothy Taylors Landlord and Tetleys, good soft drinks choice, friendly service and atmosphere, books to read, no smoking restaurant; quiet piped music; children welcome, picnic-sets out in front, open all day *(JJW, CMW)*

Cobden View S10 1HQ [Cobden View Rd, Crookes]: Friendly two-bar local with Black Sheep, Caledonian Deuchars IPA and guest beers at reasonable prices, bar snacks, pew seating, games room; dogs welcome, tables outside *(BOB)*

☆ *Devonshire Cat* S1 4HG [Wellington St (some local parking)]: Bright and airy contemporary café/bar with plenty of room inc no smoking area, polished light wood, some parquet, big modern prints, friendly staff knowledgeable about the dozen mainly Yorkshire real ales inc Abbeydale and Kelham Island, some tapped from the cask, eight foreign beers on tap, masses of bottled beers in glass-walled cool room, two farm ciders, tea and coffee, good value food more interesting than usual from end servery, plenty of board games, good smoke extraction; well reproduced piped music, wide-screen TV, silenced games machine, ATM, live music Weds, quiz night Mon; good disabled access and facilities, open all day *(C J Fletcher, the Didler, Mrs Jane Kingsbury, David Carr, Bob, BB)*

Fagans S1 4BS [Broad Lane]: Welcoming old pub with long bar, real ales, plenty of malt whiskies, friendly staff, fresh lunchtime food; good folk night Fri *(Bob)*

Gardeners Rest S3 8AT [Neepsend Lane]: Timothy Taylors Landlord, Dark Mild and Golden Best, Wentworth WPA and several guest beers tapped from the cask (often the full range from one microbrewery), farm cider, continental beers on tap and in bottle, welcoming beer-enthusiast landlord, no smoking lounge with old brewery memorabilia, lunchtime food, daily papers, games inc bar billiards, changing local artwork; Thurs folk night, poetry/story-telling nights, Oct beer festival; disabled access and facilities, back conservatory and tables out overlooking River Don, open all day *(David Carr, the Didler, Pete Baker)*

☆ *Hillsborough* S6 2UB [Langsett Rd/Wood St; by Primrose View tram stop]: Largely no smoking pub-in-hotel with its own Crown, Edale and Wellington ales at attractive prices, also lots of guest beers, friendly staff, bare-boards bar, lounge, open fire, daily papers, good filled rolls, views to ski slope from attractive back conservatory and terrace tables; TV; good value bedrooms with own bathrooms, covered parking, real ale bar open

evenings only, not Mon, from 6 (4.30 Thurs-Sat) *(the Didler, JJW, CMW)*

Holly Bush S6 5GQ [Hollins Lane]: Stone-built pub with comfortable partly no smoking lounge, Greene King Abbot and Tetleys, good soft drinks choice, generous enjoyable food (not Sun-Weds evenings), freshly made so may be a wait, inc OAP bargains, chatty landlord, public bar with TV and machines; piped music, no dogs or credit cards; children welcome, picnic-sets outside, garden with play area, good walks nearby, open all day *(JJW, CMW)*

☆ *Kelham Island Tavern* S3 8RY [Kelham Island]: Very popular backstreet local, friendly and comfortable, with well kept Acorn Barnsley, Pictish Brewers Gold and several interesting beers from other small brewers, continental imports, farm cider, nice artwork, filled cobs and other lunchtime food (not Sun), good-sized no smoking room, Sun folk night; disabled facilities, open all day (Sun afternoon break) *(the Didler, Kevin Blake, David Carr, C J Fletcher)*

Lions Lair S1 2HF [Burgess St]: Thriving atmosphere and smart décor, leather banquettes on bare boards, Black Sheep Bitter, decent wine choice, enjoyable sensibly priced food; can get a bit smoky; pleasant back terrace with decking and greenery *(Anon)*

Norfolk Arms S4 7LJ [Carlisle St]: New management doing sensibly short choice of enjoyable food, changing real ales; fine views from garden, on road out to moors and NT Langshaw Estate *(DC)*

Red Deer S1 4DD [Pitt St]: Thriving backstreet local among Univ buildings, plenty of real ales from central bar, wide choice of good value simple wkdy lunchtime food, extended lounge with pleasant raised back area; open all day, cl Sun lunchtime *(BOB, the Didler, David Carr, Mrs Hazel Rainer)*

Red Lion S1 2ND [Charles St, nr stn]: Traditional local, comfortable rooms off welcoming central bar, ornate fireplaces and coal fires, attractive panelling and etched glass, good simple lunchtime food, small back dining room, pleasant conservatory *(Kevin Flack, the Didler, Pete Baker, BOB)*

Rutland Arms S1 2BS [Brown St/Arundel Lane]: Convivial pub handy for the Crucible (and station), several sensibly priced changing real ales, also bottle-conditioned Wentworth, good wine and soft drinks, plentiful good value home-made food early evening and wknd lunchtimes from cheap basic snacks to more substantial meals, handsome façade; piped music; tables in prettily kept compact garden, bedrooms, open all day (Sun afternoon break) *(Mrs Hazel Rainer)*

Sheaf View S2 3AA [Gleadless Rd, Heeley Bottom]: Recently attractively refurbished in unpretentious 1960s/70s style, wide range of changing ales inc local Abbeydale, Barnsley and Wentworth, farm cider, spotless unusually shaped bar, pleasant staff; disabled facilities, tables outside, open all day wknds, cl Mon lunchtime *(David Carr)*

Walkley Cottage S6 5DD [Bole Hill Rd]:
Warm-hearted 1930s pub, a surprise for the
area and popular for half a dozen or so real
ales and limited range of decent well priced
food (not Sun evening) inc bargain OAP lunch
Mon-Thurs and good Sun roast, some take-
aways, farm cider, good coffee and other
drinks choice, daily papers, no smoking dining
area, games room; piped music; children and
dogs welcome (pub dog called Max), views
from picnic-sets in small back garden with play
area, lovely hanging baskets, open all day
(JJW, CMW, Bob)

SHERIFF HUTTON [SE6566]
Highwayman YO60 6QZ [The Square]: Cosy
old coaching inn nr Castle Howard, welcoming
landlord, enjoyable standard food from good
sandwiches to delicious puddings and good
value Sun lunch, Boddingtons and Tetleys,
decent house wines, log fires, oak beams in
lounge and dining room, homely snug bar;
good wheelchair access, big garden, attractive
village with 12th-c church *(Martin and
Alison Stainsby)*

SHIPLEY [SE1437]
Fannys Ale & Cider House BD18 3JN
[Saltaire Rd]: Interesting gaslit two-room
roadside local with up to nine changing ales inc
Timothy Taylors, foreign beers on tap and in
bottle, farm cider; open all day, cl Mon
lunchtime *(the Didler)*
Old Tramshed BD18 4DH [Bingley Rd]: Smart
and roomy new open-plan bar and cottagey
restaurant area, real ales such as Black Sheep
and Timothy Taylors Landlord from curved
bar, steps down to sofas and armchairs, more
up in carpeted galleries, enjoyable food inc set
meal deals; open all day, cl Mon *(Andy and
Jill Kassube)*

SKIPTON [SD9851]
Cock & Bottle BD23 1RD [Swadford St]: Old-
fashioned open-plan local in former coaching
inn, real ales, simple good food, welcoming
licensees, open fire, beams and bare boards;
small play area out behind *(BOB)*
☆ *Narrow Boat* BD23 1JE [Victoria St; pub
signed down alley off Coach St]: No smoking
town pub nr canal in small Market Town
Taverns group, half a dozen or so real ales
from mainly yorkshire small breweries inc
local Copper Dragon and a Mild (they may
give you tasters), belgian beers too, fairly
priced food (not Fri/Sat evening) from
ciabattas and potato wedges up, good wine
choice, friendly service, dark woodwork and
upper gallery, no piped music; no children,
some jazz and folk music; tables outside,
open all day *(Kevin Blake, the Didler,
Andy and Jill Kassube, Rona Murdoch,
Tony Hobden, Mrs Hazel Rainer)*
☆ *Royal Shepherd* BD23 1LB [Canal St; from
Water St (A65) turn into Coach St, then left
after bridge over Leeds & Liverpool Canal]:
Convivial old-fashioned local with big bustling
bar, snug and dining room, open fires, local
Copper Dragon ales, decent wine, unusual
sensibly priced whiskies, cheery landlord and
brisk service, low-priced standard food from

sandwiches and baked potatoes up,
photographs of Yorks CCC in its golden days;
games and piped music; children welcome in
side room, tables out in pretty spot by canal
*(the Didler, Stephen R Holman, Meg and
Colin Hamilton, George Atkinson)*
☆ *Woolly Sheep* BD23 1HY [Sheep St]: Big
bustling largely no smoking town pub with
fully range of Timothy Taylors ales, prompt
friendly enthusiastic service, daily papers, two
beamed bars off flagstoned passage, exposed
brickwork, stone fireplace, lots of sheep prints
and bric-a-brac, roomy comfortable lunchtime
dining area, usual cheap generous food (plenty
for children); unobtrusive piped music;
spacious pretty garden, six good value
bedrooms, good breakfast *(J R Ringrose,
Dr and Mrs M E Wilson, Clive Flynn,
Tim and Rosemary Wells)*

SKIPWITH [SE6638]
Drovers Arms YO8 5SF [follow Escrick sign
off A163 NE of Selby]: Comfortable two-room
country pub in smart village by Skipwith
Common nature reserve, Black Sheep and
Shepherd Neame Spitfire, enterprising good
value home-made food from proper
sandwiches to upmarket dishes and good Sun
roasts, cheerful young licensees, obliging
service, fine range of house wines, good log
fires, separate dining room; wheelchair access
(Rita and Keith Pollard, Daniel Reid)

SLAITHWAITE [SE0712]
White House HD7 5TY [Chain Rd (B6107
Meltham—Marsden)]: Attractive moorland inn
with enjoyable home-made food, real ales such
as Timothy Taylors Landlord, good choice of
wines by the glass, good service, small bar with
log fire, comfortable lounge on right, pleasant
restaurant area on left; children welcome,
tables out on front flagstones *(J R Ringrose,
Anna Prior)*

SOUTH ANSTON [SK5183]
Leeds Arms S25 5DT [Sheffield Rd (B6059, off
A57)]: Comfortable no smoking café-bar with
basic bargain all-day food from sandwiches up,
two Greene King ales, several wines by the glass;
TVs, games end with pool and juke box, quiet
piped music; children welcome *(JJW, CMW)*

SOUTH CAVE [SE9231]
☆ *Fox & Coney* HU15 2AT [Market Pl
(A1034)]: Pleasant pub with real ales such as
Caledonian Deuchars IPA and Timothy
Taylors Landlord from central servery,
generous enjoyable standard food from
baguettes to steaks, friendly efficient staff, coal
fire, bright and comfortable warmly Victorian
open-plan main bar and dining areas;
bedrooms in adjoining hotel *(DC, Dr D J and
Mrs S C Walker, Steve Whalley)*

SOWERBY BRIDGE [SE0623]
Rams Head HX6 2AZ [Wakefield Rd]: Brews
its own good well priced Ryburn ales, open fire
in well divided stripped stone lounge bar, good
value home-made food in no smoking
L-shaped dining area *(Pete Baker, G Coates,
Tony and Wendy Hobden)*
White Horse HX6 2TW [Spring Gardens
(A646 N)]: Friendly local with public bar and

lounge off main serving area, Tetleys and local guest beers (Pete Baker)

Works [Hollins Mill Lane]: Recently opened bareboards pub in converted joinery workshop, seating from pews to comfortable sofas, at least eight real ales, lunchtime food planned by the time this edition comes out (Pat and Tony Martin)

SPOFFORTH [SE3650]

Railway Inn HG3 1BW [A661 Harrogate—Wetherby; Park Terr]: Simple pub with well kept Sam Smiths, straightforward furnishings in basic locals' bar and unfussy no smoking lounge, real fires, usual food; tables and swing in garden behind (BB, Stuart Paulley, B and M Kendall)

SPROTBROUGH [SE5301]

☆ *Boat* DN5 7NB [3½ miles from M18 junction 2, less from A1(M) junction 36 via A630 and Mill Lane; Nursery Lane]: Roomy stone-built Vintage Inn dining pub, sensibly priced food from sandwiches and crusty buns to steak all day till 10, several snug flagstoned areas, log fires in big stone fireplaces, latticed windows, dark beams, Black Sheep, John Smiths and Tetleys, plenty of wines by the glass, prompt friendly uniformed service; can be smoky, unobtrusive piped music, games machine, no dogs; tables in big sheltered prettily lit courtyard, River Don walks, open all day (Mr and Mrs Gerry Price, DC, GSB, LYM, Trevor and Judith Pearson, Stephen Woad)

Ivanhoe DN5 7NS [quite handy for A1(M)]: Large mock-Tudor Sam Smiths pub, friendly and chatty, with their OB at an appealing price, bargain pubby food (not Sun evening) from hot servery inc popular Sun carvery, three linked rooms with conservatory extension overlooking cricket ground, uniformed waitresses, games bar with pool; children in eating areas, tables out on flagstoned terrace with play area, open all day (Mr and Mrs Gerry Price)

STAMFORD BRIDGE [SE7055]

☆ *Three Cups* YO41 1AX [A166 W of town]: Spacious Vintage Inn family dining pub in timbered country style, glass-topped 20-metre well in bar, reliable food all day, good range of wines by the glass, real ales, good welcoming staff and relaxed atmosphere; good disabled access, children welcome, good play area behind, bedrooms, open all day (LYM, David Carr, Roger A Bellingham, Pat and Graham Williamson)

STANBURY [SE0037]

☆ *Old Silent* BD22 0HW [Hob Lane]: Neatly rebuilt moorland dining pub near Ponden reservoir, friendly atmosphere, enjoyable reasonably priced fresh food inc particularly good meat, real ales such as Timothy Taylors, attentive helpful service, character linked rooms with beams, flagstones, mullioned windows and open fires (it's easy to believe there's a ghost), games room, restaurant and conservatory; children welcome, bedrooms (BB, Andy and Jill Kassube)

STARBOTTON [SD9574]

Fox & Hounds BD23 5HY [B6160]: Small popular Dales inn in pretty village, friendly landlord, big log fire in attractively traditional beamed and flagstoned bar, compact no smoking dining room, Black Sheep and guest beers, usual bar food (gets busy, so there may be quite a wait for a meal); may be piped music, dogs allowed in bar; children welcome, cl Mon (LYM, Len Beattie, the Didler)

STOCKTON ON THE FOREST [SE6556]

Fox YO32 9UW [off A64 just NE of York]: Attractive village pub, now with chain menu but chef's own enjoyable specials, welcoming staff, three cosy and comfortable linked rooms and separate dining room, Tetleys, good choice of wines by the glass; tables outside with lots of hanging baskets (Jane Taylor, David Dutton, Roger A Bellingham)

STOKESLEY [NZ5208]

☆ *White Swan* TS9 5BL [West End]: Good Captain Cook ales brewed in attractive and neatly kept pub, interesting changing guest beers, great ploughman's, welcoming staff, three seating areas, top one no smoking, log fire, lots of brass on elegant dark panelling, lovely bar counter carving, hat display, unusual clock; cl Tues lunchtime (Blaise Vyner, the Didler)

TADCASTER [SE4843]

☆ *Angel & White Horse* LS24 9AW [Bridge St]: Tap for Sam Smiths brewery, their ale at low price, generous bargain lunchtime food counter, quick friendly service, big bar with alcoves at one end, fine oak panelling and solid furnishings; restaurant (children allowed there); piped music; brewery tours can be arranged (01937) 832225, open all day Sat (Dr Alan and Mrs Sue Holder, LYM)

TAN HILL [NY8906]

☆ *Tan Hill Inn* DL11 6ED [Arkengarthdale rd Reeth—Brough, at junction Keld/W Stonesdale rd]: Basic old stone pub in wonderful remote setting on Pennine Way – Britain's highest pub, full of bric-a-brac and pictures inc interesting old photographs, simple sturdy furniture, flagstones, ever-burning big log fire (with prized stone side seats); chatty atmosphere, friendly staff, Black Sheep and Theakstons ales (in winter the cellar does chill down – whisky with hot water's good then), cheap generous food from good sandwiches to usual hot dishes and hearty yorkshire puddings, help-yourself coffee, pool in family room; may be piped radio, often snowbound, can get overcrowded; swaledale sheep show here last Thurs in May; children and dogs welcome, bedrooms, inc some in extension with own bathrooms, open all day (N R White, LYM, Michael Tack)

TERRINGTON [SE6770]

☆ *Bay Horse* YO60 6PP [W of Malton]: Country pub under good new landlord, cosy log-fire lounge bar, good thai food in handsome no smoking dining area and back family conservatory with old farm tools, Theakstons Black Bull, Timothy Taylors Landlord and a guest beer, over 100 whiskies, traditional public bar with darts, shove-ha'penny, cribbage and dominoes; children welcome in eating areas, garden tables, unspoilt village (Christopher Turner, LYM)

THIXENDALE [SE8461]
Cross Keys YO17 9TG [off A166 3 miles N of Fridaythorpe]: Unspoilt welcoming country pub in deep valley below the rolling Wolds, cosy L-shaped bar with fitted wall seats, relaxed atmosphere, Jennings, Tetleys and a guest beer, sensible home-made blackboard food; large pleasant garden behind, popular with walkers, handy for Wharram Percy earthworks, bedrooms *(the Didler)*

THORGANBY [SE6941]
☆ *Jefferson Arms* YO19 6DA [off A163 NE of Selby, via Skipwith]: Pleasant bistro feel in dining pub with above-average food, Marstons Pedigree, Timothy Taylors Landlord and perhaps a guest beer, armchairs, sofas and log fires as well as the attractive dining rooms' marble-topped tables and bentwood chairs, two conservatories (they may cut grapes for your cheese board); piped music; children welcome, comfortable bedrooms, cl Mon *(Comus and Sarah Elliott, Janet and Peter Race, Barbara and Derek Thompson, David and Cathrine Whiting, LYM)*

THORNE [SE6713]
John Bull DN8 4JQ [Waterside, just off M18 junction 6]: Enjoyable reasonably priced food inc generous bargain carvery all week (not Mon), real ales such as Timothy Taylors Landlord, decent wine by the glass, no smoking dining area and bar with chatting locals *(Miss J E Edwards, Sue and Neil Dickinson)*

THORNTON [SE0933]
☆ *Ring o' Bells* BD13 3QL [Hill Top Rd, off B6145 W of Bradford]: 19th-c moortop dining pub very popular for wide choice of reliably good home cooking inc fresh fish, speciality pies, superb steaks, good puddings, bargain early suppers, separate-sittings Sun lunch (best to book), Black Sheep, Courage Directors and Websters Green Label, crisp efficient service, spotless pleasant bar, popular air-conditioned no smoking restaurant and pleasant conservatory lounge; wide views towards Shipley and Bingley *(Pierre Richterich, Andy and Jill Kassube)*

THORNTON-LE-CLAY [SE6865]
☆ *White Swan* YO60 7TG [off A64 York—Malton; Low St]: Good fresh generous food in comfortably old-fashioned beamed dining pub, homely and peaceful, with Black Sheep and a local guest beer, decent wines, reasonable prices, friendly attentive long-serving landlord, fine log fire, shining brasses, plenty of board games and even toys; well chosen piped music; children welcome, neatly kept grounds with terrace tables, duck pond, herb garden and rescued donkeys, attractive countryside nr Castle Howard; cl Mon lunchtime *(Oliver Richardson)*

THRESHFIELD [SD9863]
Old Hall Inn BD23 5HB [B6160/B6265 just outside Grassington]: Olde-worlde atmosphere in three knocked-together rooms, high beam-and-plank ceiling, cushioned wall pews, tall well blacked kitchen range, log fires, limited choice of enjoyable sensibly priced food in bar

and restaurant, Marstons Pedigree, Timothy Taylors Landlord and Theakstons; children in eating area, neat garden *(Janet and Peter Race, LYM)*

TICKHILL [SK5992]
Carpenters Arms DN11 9NE [Westgate]: Two-bar pub with three real ales, enjoyable food freshly made (so may be a wait), no smoking family conservatory; no credit cards; attractive garden, picturesque village *(JJW, CMW)*

TOSSIDE [SD7655]
Dog & Partridge BD23 4SQ: Well refurbished under new licensees, short choice of good simple home cooking, reasonable prices, changing real ales such as Black Sheep, Copper Dragon, Moorhouses and Thwaites Lancaster Bomber, charming staff, chunky modern light oak furniture on bare boards, stripped beams, clean fresh pink décor; pleasant tables out in front, attractive spot overlooking Trough of Bowland, cl Mon-Weds *(Richard Crabtree, Michael and Deirdre Ellis, Margaret Dickinson)*

TOTLEY [SK3080]
Cricket S17 3AZ [signed from A621; Penny Lane]: Attractive stone-built pub with fresh well presented food (not Sun/Mon evening) from lunchtime snacks to unusual evening restaurant dishes, homely interior with open fire and bay-window views of rustic cricket field, two log fires, two real ales, good choice of other drinks; piped pop music may obtrude; children welcome, terrace tables, open all day wknds *(JJW, CMW)*
Crown S17 3AX [Hillfoot Rd]: Old-fashioned country pub, partly no smoking, with two rooms off central bar, friendly landlord and good staff, four or five real ales and good choice of other drinks, short choice of good plain home-cooked food (not Sun/Mon evenings), fresh flowers, pictures for sale, wknd jazz; TV, dogs welcome, no children; picnic-sets outside *(JJW, CMW, James A Waller)*
Shepley Spitfire S17 4HD [Mickley Lane]: Comfortable modern open-plan L-shaped pub with raised no smoking dining area one end (Sun carvery), Hardys & Hansons Olde Trip, good soft drinks range, games end with pool, TV and machines; quiet piped music; children welcome, picnic-sets, play area and pets in garden, nearby walks, open all day *(JJW, CMW)*

WAKEFIELD [SE3320]
Fernandes Brewery Tap WF1 1UA [Avison Yard, Kirkgate]: Upper floor of 19th-c malt store, Fernandes ales brewed here and interesting guest beers, farm cider, unusual breweriana, friendly atmosphere, bare boards and rafters; cl Mon-Thurs lunchtime, open all day Fri-Sun with lunchtime soup and sandwiches then, brewery shop *(the Didler, Tony Hobden)*
Henry Boons WF2 9SR [Westgate]: Clarks in fine fettle from next-door brewery, and Black Sheep, Timothy Taylors and Tetleys, in two-room bare-boards local, friendly staff, barrel tables and breweriana, side pool area; gets busy late on with young people, juke box,

machines, live bands; open all day (till 1am Fri/Sat) *(the Didler)*

Redoubt WF2 8TS [Horbury Rd, Westgate]: Busy and friendly traditional pub, four compact rooms off long corridor, Timothy Taylors Landlord, Tetleys and guest beers, Rugby League photographs and memorabilia, pub games; family room till 8, open all day *(the Didler)*

Wakefield Labour Club WF1 1QX [Vicarage St]: Red wooden shed rather like a works canteen inside, small and chatty – it is a club, but you can just sign in; changing keenly priced real ales usually inc Ossett, belgian beers; picnic-sets outside, cl lunchtime Mon-Thurs and Sun evening *(the Didler)*

WALES [SK4782]
Duke of Leeds S26 5LQ [Church St]: Comfortable 18th-c stone-faced village pub with good range of fresh food (all day Sun), early evening and wkdy OAP bargains, John Smiths, Theakstons and two or three guest beers, good wine and soft drinks choice, quick friendly service, long no smoking dining lounge and smaller room where smoking allowed, lots of brass and copper, flame-effect gas fire; quiet piped music, often cl Sat lunchtime for private functions; children welcome, nearby walks *(JJW, CMW)*

WALKINGTON [SE9937]
☆ **Ferguson-Fawsitt Arms** HU17 8RX [East End; B1230 W of Beverley]: Wide choice of enjoyable food in airy no smoking flagstone-floored food bar, good friendly service, real ale, decent wine, interesting mock-Tudor bars; tables out on terrace, delightful village *(June and Ken Brooks, LYM)*

WALTON [SE4447]
Fox & Hounds LS23 7DQ [Hall Park Rd, off back rd Wetherby—Tadcaster]: Popular dining pub with enjoyable food (should book Sun lunch), thriving atmosphere, John Smiths and a guest beer such as Black Sheep or Caledonian Deuchars IPA *(OPUS, Les and Sandra Brown)*
New Inn WF2 6LA [Shay Lane]: Village pub with real ales such as Caledonian Deuchars IPA, Jennings Cumberland and Timothy Taylors Landlord, good range of good value food, friendly welcome, dining extension *(Michael Butler)*

WEAVERTHORPE [SE9670]
☆ **Blue Bell** YO17 8EX: Attractive country dining pub with beautifully presented good food, fine choice of wines and Black Sheep real ale, pre-meal home-made crisps and dips, cosy and cheerful bar covered with a mass of wine bottles and other drinks packaging, intimate no smoking back restaurant also with wine décor, charming efficient waitresses; bedrooms, good breakfast *(Louise Medcalf, C A Hall, Stanley and Annie Matthews)*

WELBURN [SE7168]
Crown & Cushion YO60 7DZ [off A64]: Cosy village pub with good home cooking from fresh sandwiches and ploughman's up, busy landlord and good service, Camerons and Tetleys, decent wine, games in public bar, restaurant, children in eating areas, amusing pictures in gents'; piped

music, and some talk of the cheerful warmly welcoming landlord retiring, as we went to press; attractive small back garden with terrace, handy for Castle Howard *(LYM, Peter and Anne Hollindale, Walter and Susan Rinaldi-Butcher, Jane Taylor, David Dutton)*

WELL [SE2682]
Milbank Arms DL8 2PX [Bedale Rd]: Beautifully refurbished, with consistently good pub food and wide choice of beers; bedrooms *(Ian Vipond)*

WENTWORTH [SK3898]
☆ **George & Dragon** S62 7TN [3 miles from M1 junction 36; Main St]: Friendly staff in rambling split-level bar, Timothy Taylors Landlord, local Wentworth and wide range of guest beers, good choice of generous good value food all cooked to order (worth the wait), flagstones and assorted old-fashioned furnishings, ornate stove in lounge; high chairs provided; may be piped music, small back games room with darts and machine; benches in front courtyard, tables out on big back lawn, crafts and antiques shop – pleasant village *(Nigel and Sue Foster, LYM, Jo Lilley, Simon Calvert)*

WEST BURTON [SE0186]
Fox & Hounds DL8 4JY [on green, off B6160 Bishopdale—Wharfedale]: Friendly local on long green of idyllic Dales village, good friendly service, Black Sheep and Copper Dragon, wide choice of generous usual food inc good sandwiches and cheese or pâté ploughman's, pleasant evening dining room; nearby caravan park; children and dogs welcome, good modern bedrooms, lovely walks and waterfalls nearby *(Martin and Alison Stainsby, Brian and Janet Ainscough, Gerry Miller, Keith and Avril Stringer, B and M Kendall)*

WEST WITTON [SE0588]
☆ **Wensleydale Heifer** DL8 4LS [A684 W of Leyburn]: Reworked by new owners as stylish restaurant-with-rooms rather than pub, good food with emphasis on fresh fish and seafood, cosy informal food bar as well as extensive main formal restaurant, leather armchairs in big-windowed front bar with log fire in huge fireplace, daily papers and showcased malt whiskies; nice comfortable bedrooms (back ones quietest), good big breakfast *(Dr Alan and Mrs Sue Holder, BB)*

WETHERBY [SE4048]
Muse Café LS22 6NQ [Bank St]: Very popular no smoking café-bar with enjoyable reasonably priced fresh food, four yorkshire ales, continental lagers on tap, young friendly helpful staff, restaurant on right; open all day *(Danny Savage)*

WHASHTON [NZ1506]
Hack & Spade DL11 7JL: New licensees doing good individual food inc proper puddings in small pretty village pub's attractive bar and dining area, Theakstons, good wine choice *(Jenny and Brian Seller)*

WHISTON [SK4489]
☆ **Golden Ball** S60 4HY [nr M1 junction 33, via A618; Turner Lane, off High St]: Good atmosphere in charming extended Ember Inn,

wide choice of enjoyable reasonably priced food, real ales such as Adnams, Caledonian Deuchars IPA, John Smiths, Stones and Timothy Taylors Landlord, several wines by the glass, good soft drinks choice, daily papers, log fire, no smoking room; quiet piped music, machines, quiz nights, no children inside; picnic-sets outside, open all day *(Nigel and Sue Foster, JJW, CMW, Derek and Sylvia Stephenson)*

WHITBY [NZ8911]

Elsinore YO21 3BB [Flowergate]: Comfortable and well kept, lifeboat and Whitby fishing boat photographs on dark panelling, Camerons Strongarm and John Smiths, capable old-fashioned landlord, lunchtime food; may be unobtrusive piped music *(Steve Whalley)*

Endeavour YO22 4AS [Church St]: Bare-boards one-room local with real ales such as Adnams Broadside and Caledonian Deuchars IPA, settles and coal fire, nautical memorabilia and Frank Sutcliffe Whitby photographs *(Geoff Ziola)*

Middle Earth Tavern YO22 4AE [Church St]: Well used pub in quiet spot facing river and harbour, Black Sheep and Tetleys, bar food; tables outside *(David Carr)*

WHIXLEY [SE4457]

Anchor YO26 8AG [New Rd]: Family-friendly pub just outside village, traditional generous food inc bargain lunchtime carvery particularly popular with OAPs, friendly young staff, John Smiths and Tetleys, straightforward main eating extension, original core with some character and coal fire in small lounge *(Alistair and Kay Butler)*

WIGGLESWORTH [SD8056]

☆ *Plough* BD23 4RJ [B6478, off A65 S of Settle]: Friendly dining pub with wide range of good reasonably priced bar food (not Sun evening or Mon in winter) from baguettes to fish and steaks inc takeaways and good Sun lunch, efficient service, Black Sheep and Tetleys, attractive bar with log fire, little rooms off, some simple yet cosy, others more plush, inc no smoking panelled dining room, snug and attractive newly refurbished conservatory restaurant with panoramic Dales views; pleasant garden, homely and comfortable bedrooms also with views *(MLR, Norma and Noel Thomas, Geoffrey and Brenda Wilson)*

WOMBLETON [SE6683]

Plough YO62 7RW: Local with good blackboard choice of pubby food, John Smiths, Theakstons and Worthington, bar eating area and restaurant *(Martin and Alison Stainsby)*

WYKE [SE1426]

Wyke Lion BD12 8LL [A641 Bradford—Brighouse, just off A58]: Popular Vintage Inn, with their usual good value food inc enjoyable specials, good wines by the glass and real ales, friendly staff *(Geoffrey and Brenda Wilson)*

YORK [SE5951]

☆ *Ackhorne* YO1 6LN [St Martins Lane, Micklegate]: Good pub feel, not over-modernised, with changing real ales from small brewers, up to four farm ciders, perry, country wines, foreign bottled beers and good coffee;

beams and bare boards, leather wall seats, Civil War prints, bottles and jugs, carpeted snug one end, good value basic food, not Sun, from good choice of sandwiches up (fresh chillies in the chilli), friendly landlord and family, helpful service, open fire, daily papers, traditional games, silenced games machine; Sun quiz night; new suntrap back terrace (steps a bit steep), open all day *(Roger A Bellingham, the Didler, David Carr, Esther and John Sprinkle, Peter Coxon, Alison and Pete, Pat and Tony Martin, Eric Larkham)*

☆ *Black Swan* YO1 7PR [Peaseholme Green (inner ring road)]: Striking timbered and jettied Tudor building, compact panelled front bar, crooked-floored central hall with fine period staircase, black-beamed back bar with vast inglenook, great atmosphere, real ales such as Fullers London Pride, Greene King Abbot, John Smiths and York Yorkshire Terrier, cheerful service, basic low-priced food from baked potatoes and baguettes up, decent wines; piped music, jazz and folk nights; useful car park *(Heidi Rowe, Kevin Blake, the Didler, LYM, Paul and Ursula Randall, Alison and Pete)*

☆ *Blue Bell* YO1 9TF [Fossgate]: Delightfully old-fashioned Edwardian pub with real ales such as Adnams, Caledonian Deuchars IPA, Jennings Cumberland, Ossett Silver King and Timothy Taylors Landlord, good value sandwiches and tapas all day, chatty locals and landlady, daily papers, tiny tiled-floor front bar with roaring fire, panelled ceiling, stained glass, bar pots and decanters, corridor to back smoke room not much bigger, hatch service to middle bar, lamps and flickering candles, pub games; may be piped music; open all day *(Michael Dandy, the Didler, Kerry Law, Simon Smith, Pete Baker, Tracey and Stephen Groves, Alison and Pete, Eric Larkham)*

Brigantes YO1 6JX [Micklegate]: Recently opened no smoking Market Town Taverns bar/bistro, eight real ales and good range of bottled beers, farm cider, good wines and coffee, enjoyable food from panini up; open all day *(Andy and Jill Kassube, Fred and Lorraine Gill)*

Golden Ball YO1 6DU [Cromwell Rd/Bishophill]: Unspoilt and buoyant 1950s local feel in friendly and well preserved four-room Edwardian pub, enjoyable straightforward wkdy lunchtime food, changing ales such as Caledonian Deuchars IPA, Marstons Pedigree, John Smiths and Charles Wells Bombardier, bar billiards, cards and dominoes; TV, can be lively evenings, live music Thurs; pleasant small walled garden, open all day Fri-Sun *(the Didler, Pete Baker, Peter Coxon, Alison and Pete)*

Golden Fleece YO1 9UP [Pavement]: Black Sheep, Greene King IPA and Timothy Taylors Landlord, usual bar food from sandwiches up all day (till 5 Sun), long corridor from bar to back lounge (beware the sloping floors – it dates from 1503), interesting décor with quite a library, lots of pictures and ghost stories, pub games; piped music; children welcome, bedrooms *(Michael Dandy, Kevin Blake, Esther and John Sprinkle)*

Golden Lion YO1 8BG [Church St]: Big comfortable open-plan pub done up in bare-boards Edwardian style (in fact first licensed 1771), beams, plenty of lamps, old photographs and brewery signs, John Smiths, Theakstons and half a dozen changing ales such as Daleside Blonde, Goffs White Knight and Wentworth Bumble, wide choice of sensible food all day from good sandwiches up, good range of wines by the glass, pleasant young staff; piped music can be obtrusive; open all day *(Pat and Tony Martin, Peter Coxon)*

Golden Slipper YO1 7LG [Goodramgate]: Dating from 15th c, renovated carefully to keep distinctively old-fashioned almost rustic local feel in its neat unpretentious bar and three small rooms, one lined with books, good cheap plain lunchtime food from sandwiches, baguettes and baked potatoes to tender Sun roast beef, Caledonian Deuchars IPA, Greene King IPA and Old Speckled Hen and John Smiths, cheerful staff; tables in back courtyard *(Paul and Ursula Randall, David Carr)*

Hansom Cab YO1 8SL [Market St]: Lively dark-panelled bar, long and narrow, with low-priced Sam Smiths, enjoyable cheap quick food counter, plenty of tables, wall seats, wing chairs, side alcoves, interesting ceiling (like a glass pyramid surrounded by plants); children allowed lunchtime *(R N Lovelock)*

Hole in the Wall YO1 7EH [High Petergate]: Rambling much modernised open-plan pub handy for Minster, low beams, panelling and stripped masonry, lots of prints, turkey carpeting, plenty of low plush stools, real ales such as Highgate Fatz Catz, Mansfield Riding and Marstons Owd Rodger, good wine choice and coffee, very busy lunchtime for wide choice of well priced food noon onwards from sandwiches to generous Sun lunch, friendly service; juke box, games machines, piped music not too loud, live some nights; children welcome, open all day *(Martin and Sarah, Michael Dandy, LYM, Tracey and Stephen Groves, Esther and John Sprinkle)*

Kings Arms YO1 9SN [King's Staithe, by Clifford St]: Fine riverside position (so can get flooded), bowed black beams, flagstones, straightforward furnishings, good lunchtime food from sandwiches up; CD juke box can be loud, keg beers; open all day, nice picnic-sets out on cobbled waterside terrace *(David Carr, LYM)*

☆ *Last Drop* YO1 8BN [Colliergate]: Basic traditional York Brewery pub with several of their own beers and one or two expertly kept guests, decent wines and country wines, enthusiastic landlord and friendly helpful young staff, big windows overlooking pavement, bare boards, barrel tables and comfortable seats (some up a few steps), no music, machines or children, nice simple fresh food 12-4 inc sandwiches, panini and good salads; piped music, no children, can get very

busy lunchtime, attic lavatories; tables out behind, open all day *(Michael Dandy, David Carr, Dr and Mrs P Truelove, David R Brown, Fred and Lorraine Gill, Mark Walker, Esther and John Sprinkle)*

☆ *Lendal Cellars* YO1 8AA [Lendal]: Cheerful bustling split-level ale house down steps in broad-vaulted 17th-c cellars carefully spotlit to show up the stripped brickwork, stone floor, interconnected rooms and alcoves, good choice of fairly priced changing real ales, farm cider, decent coffee, good range of wines by the glass, foreign bottled beers, daily papers, cheerful staff, children allowed for good plain food 11.30-7(5 Fri/Sat); good piped music, popular with students; open all day *(the Didler, LYM)*

Masons Arms YO10 4AB [Fishergate]: 1930s local, two fires in panelled front bar with blow lamps and pig ornaments, no smoking second room, attractive fireplaces, good range of beers inc guests, generous interesting home-made food, friendly service; comfortable bedroom block with own bathrooms (no breakfast), tables out in front and on back riverside terrace *(Kevin Blake, Martin and Sarah, Eric Larkham)*

Olde Starre YO1 8AS [Stonegate]: City's oldest licensed pub, a big tourist draw, with 'gallows' sign across York's prettiest street, original panelling and prints, green plush wall seats, several other little carpeted rooms off porch-like lobby, changing real ales such as Fullers ESB, Theakstons Best and Charles Wells Bombardier from long counter, cheerful young staff, low-priced food, daily papers; piped music, games machines; open all day, children welcome away from bar, flower-filled back garden and front courtyard with Minster glimpsed across the rooftops *(Michael Dandy, David Carr, LYM, Dr and Mrs Jackson)*

Rook & Gaskill YO10 3WP [Lawrence St]: Tied to York Brewery, with all their beers and lots of guests, traditional décor, dark wood tables, banquettes, chairs and high stools, cheerful knowledgeable service, limited bar food (not wknd evenings); no children; open all day *(the Didler, Peter Coxon)*

☆ *Royal Oak* YO1 7LG [Goodramgate]: Comfortably worn in three-room black-beamed 16th-c pub simply remodelled in Tudor style 1934, blazing log fire in front room, prints, swords, busts and old guns, bargain generous pubby dishes (limited Sun evening) 11.30-8, sandwiches with home-baked bread after 3, speedy service from cheerful bustling young staff, Greene King Abbot and Caledonian Deuchars IPA, decent wines, good coffee; no smoking family room, games; piped music, can get crowded, outside gents'; handy for Minster, open all day *(Michael Dandy, Kevin Blake, BB)*

Snickleway YO1 7LS [Goodramgate]: Interesting little open-plan pub behind big shop-front window, cosy and comfortable, lots of antiques, copper and brass, good coal or log fire, Black Sheep, Greene King Old Speckled Hen and John Smiths, good value fresh well filled doorstep sandwiches, baked potatoes and a coupe of hot dishes lunchtimes, cheerful landlord, prompt service, splendid cartoons in gents', exemplary ladies'; unobtrusive piped music *(Michael Dandy, Kevin Blake, Paul and Ursula Randall, David Carr, Esther and John Sprinkle)*

Swan YO23 1JH [Bishopgate St, Clementhorpe]: Unspoilt 1950s feel, friendly and chatty, hatch service to lobby for two small rooms off main bar, great staff, several changing ales inc Caledonian Deuchars IPA and Timothy Taylors Landlord; can be smoky, busy with young people wknds; small pleasant walled garden, nr city walls, open all day wknds *(the Didler, Fred and Lorraine Gill, Pete Baker, Peter Coxon, Richard)*

☆ **Tap & Spile** YO31 7PB [Monkgate]: Friendly open-plan late Victorian pub with Roosters and other interesting changing real ales, farm cider and country wines, decent wines by the glass, bookshelves, games in raised back area, cheap straightforward lunchtime bar food (not Mon); children in eating area, tables on heated terrace and in garden, open all day *(LYM, the Didler, Paul and Ursula Randall)*

☆ **Three Legged Mare** YO1 7EN [High Petergate]: Bustling open-plan light and airy modern café-bar with York Brewery's full beer range kept well, good range of belgian Trappist beers, quick cheerful service (staff know about beers), generous interesting sandwiches and one or two basic lunchtime hot dishes, some comfortable sofas, back conservatory; no children, can be smoky; disabled facilities (other lavatories down noisy spiral stairs), tables in back garden with replica of the original three-legged mare – a local gallows used for multiple executions *(Michael Dandy, David Carr, Fred and Lorraine Gill, Esther and John Sprinkle, Paul and Ursula Randall, Eric Larkham)*

☆ **York Arms** YO1 7EH [High Petergate]: Cheerful Sam Smiths pub by Minster, quick helpful service, good value sandwiches and simple hot dishes lunchtime to early evening (not Sun-Tues), snug little basic panelled bar (beware the sliding door), big modern back lounge, cosier partly panelled no smoking parlour full of old bric-a-brac, prints, brown-cushioned wall settles, dimpled copper tables and an open fire, pub games, no piped music; open all day *(Michael Dandy, Kevin Blake, BB, Esther and John Sprinkle)*

York Brewery Tap YO1 6JT [Toft Green, Micklegate]: Upstairs lounge at York Brewery, their own full cask range in top condition, also bottled beers, nice clubby atmosphere with friendly staff happy to talk about the beers, lots of breweriana and view of brewing plant, comfortable settees and armchairs, magazines and daily papers; no food, brewery tours by arrangement, shop; children allowed, open 11.30-7, cl Sun, annual membership fee £3 unless you live in York or go on the tour *(the Didler, Esther and John Sprinkle, Paul and Ursula Randall, Eric Larkham)*

Yorkshire Terrier YO1 8AS [Stonegate]: York Brewery pub hiding behind traditional shop front (look for the brewery memorabilia in the window), their full beer range from smallish bar, dining room behind front brewery shop, another no smoking room upstairs, soup, sandwiches and limited range of other good value food noon till 4 inc Sun *(Andy and Jill Kassube, Paul and Ursula Randall, Fred and Lorraine Gill)*

Bedroom prices normally include full English breakfast, VAT and any inclusive service charge that we know of. Prices before the '/' are for single rooms, after for two people in double or twin (B includes a private bath, S a private shower). If there is no '/', the prices are only for twin or double rooms (as far as we know there are no singles). If there is no B or S, as far as we know no rooms have private facilities.

LONDON
SCOTLAND
WALES
CHANNEL ISLANDS

London

Over the years we have considered well over 2,000 London pubs, filing many thousands of reports on them from readers, and carrying out anonymous inspections of many hundreds that have shown the most promise. So this 25th anniversary edition's selection of London's best pubs is a well tried and tested distillation. Among the main entries, current favourites include in Central London the Argyll Arms (very busy and well placed for visitors, yet surprisingly individual), the Cittie of York (full of interest and character), the smart old Grenadier, the Jerusalem Tavern (a recently done yet most impressive evocation of a traditional City tavern), the cheerful Lamb & Flag (great atmosphere in this fine old place), the Lord Moon of the Mall (so useful for good value food and drink all day – and all day here means from 9am till 11pm), the distinctive and unspoilt Nags Head, the stylish Old Bank of England (perhaps best in daytime), the charming and intriguing Olde Cheshire Cheese, the beautifully preserved Red Lion in Duke of York Street (a little gem), and the Seven Stars (this nicely individual all-rounder getting a bit more space by expanding next door – and gaining a Food Award this year). In North London, the Chapel and Drapers Arms are scoring highly on the food side, the Holly Bush combines commendable food, drink and service with tremendous atmosphere, and the Spaniards Inn is appealing both inside and out. South London is becoming one of the capital's best areas for good pubs: its current stars include the Anchor & Hope (for its food – a surprise to find such high quality in such a determinedly ordinary sort of pub), the nicely placed Cutty Sark (good all round), the Market Porter with its magnificent range of real ales (it's a London favourite of quite a few readers), the Royal Oak (traditional alehouse in style, with enjoyable food and Harveys good Sussex ales) and an entirely new entry, the Victoria (good if not cheap food and drink in attractive surroundings – good bedrooms, too). West London's prime pubs include the riverside Bulls Head (plenty of character and individuality in this Chef & Brewer with its decent all-day food), the cheerful Churchill Arms under its ebullient Irish landlord, the delightfully unspoilt Colton Arms (well worth a special visit), the Dove (another Thamesside pub on good current form), the lively Portobello Gold (good food, wide drinks range and lots going on), and the Windsor Castle (cosy and atmospheric inside, lovely garden out). The number of London entries with the fork-and-knife symbol that signifies particularly good food has now climbed well into double figures, showing how much food standards in London pubs have risen over the last few years. In any of these, you can be sure of a good meal, though in many of the trendier gastropubs the atmosphere might strike you as too informally pubby (not to say scruffy) to suit a special occasion, despite really interesting top-quality food. The Seven Stars in Carey Street, Central London, is undeniably and proudly a proper pub, and sets a great example with its good carefully cooked equally proper food, at fair prices, served in friendly and light-hearted surroundings; the Seven Stars is London Dining Pub of the Year. On the drinks side, most London pubs suffer the disadvantage of being seriously overpriced. It's getting very hard indeed to find beer for under £2 a pint here. However, there are bargains to be found, for example in Wetherspoons pubs. And the Yorkshire brewer Sam Smiths keeps its prices right down to pocket-friendly Yorkshire levels in its fine London pubs – including three Central London main entries, the Cittie of York, Princess Louise and Olde Cheshire Cheese. Other beers from outside London that quite often crop up as the cheapest that a good pub has on sale – though at nothing like as good a price as Sam Smiths – are Adnams and Harveys. Now that Youngs has announced a merger with Charles Wells of Bedford and the closure of its Wandsworth brewery, Fullers is left as the single main London brewer. The much smaller and newer London brewer, Pitfield, specialises in organic beers and is worth looking out for. The Lucky Dip section at the end of the chapter is divided into Central, East, North, South and West (with the pubs grouped by postal district). Outer London suburbs come last, by name, after the numbered postal districts. In this section, Central London pubs currently showing particularly well include the Hand & Shears (EC1), Morpeth Arms (SW1), Audley and Clachan (W1), Victoria (W2), and Cross Keys and Salisbury (WC2); in East London, the Dickens Inn (E1); in North London, the House (N1), Flask (N6), and Rising Sun (NW7); in South London, the Greenwich Union (SE10), Angel (SE16) and Idle Hour (SW13); and in West London, the City Barge (W4).

CENTRAL LONDON   Map 13
Admiral Codrington ♀
Mossop Street; ⊖ South Kensington; SW3 2LY

The chief draw at this popular pub remains the sunny back dining room, mainly because of the excellently prepared food, but also because of its design – particularly impressive in fine weather when the retractable glass roof slides open. With something of an emphasis on fish, the menu in this part might include salmon and smoked haddock fishcakes (£10.75), cod baked with tomatoes and mushrooms in a soft herb crust (£11.75), thyme and lemon steamed red snapper (£13.95), seared breast of barbary duck (£14.95), and good puddings or farmhouse cheeses (£5.25); it's worth booking, particularly at weekends. The more pubby bar was elegantly reworked by designer Nina Campbell; it's an effective mix of traditional and chic, with comfortable sofas and cushioned wall seats, neatly polished floorboards and panelling, spotlights in the ceiling and lamps on elegant wooden tables, a handsome central counter, sporting prints on the yellow walls, and houseplants around the big bow windows. There's a model ship in a case just above the entrance to the dining room. A separate lunchtime bar menu might include soups like broccoli and goats cheese (£4.50), eggs benedict (£5.75 starter; £7.75 main course), caesar salad (from £6.95; with smoked salmon and quail egg £8.75), risotto of radicchio with wild sorrel (£8.25), cornish crab tagliatelle with fresh chilli and lemon dressing (£9.25), and rib-eye burgers (£9.95); Sunday roasts. At weekends they serve brunch from 11. Charles Wells Bombardier and Greene King IPA on handpump (not cheap, even for round here), and an excellent wine list, with nearly all available by the glass; various coffees, and a range of havana cigars, friendly service from smartly uniformed young staff. There may be piped pop or jazz – though in the evenings especially it will be drowned out by the sound of animated conversation; the dining room is quieter. At the side is a nice little terrace with tables, benches and heaters. They now have a bridge club upstairs. The pub is right in the heart of Chelsea, and though it's the kind of place where half the customers arrive by taxi, the clientele can be rather more varied than you might expect. More reports please. *(Recommended by Joel Dobris, Heather McQuillan)*

Punch ~ Lease Langlands Pearse ~ Real ale ~ Bar food (12-2.30 (3.30 Sat, 4.30 Sun), 7-11) ~ Restaurant ~ (020) 7581 0005 ~ Children in eating area of bar and restaurant ~ Dogs allowed in bar ~ Open 11.30am-midnight; 12-11 Sun; closed 25-26 Dec

Albert

Victoria Street; ⊖ St James's Park; SW1H 0NP

Considering its location, this bustling 19th-c pub is surprisingly good value for food
and drink – and the architecture is worth a look too. It still has some of its original
Victorian fixtures and fittings – notably the heavily cut and etched windows which
run along three sides of the open-plan bar, giving the place a surprisingly airy feel.
Always busy – especially on weekday lunchtimes and after work – it also has some
gleaming mahogany, an ornate ceiling, and good solid comfortable furnishings. A
wonderfully diverse mix of customers takes in tourists, civil servants and even the
occasional MP: the division bell is rung to remind them when it's time to get back to
Westminster. Service from the big island counter is efficient, friendly, and particularly
obliging to people from overseas. Charles Wells Bombardier, Courage Best, Fullers
London Pride, and a guest like Greene King IPA on handpump, and a good choice of
wines by the glass. Usefully served all day, the promptly served bar food includes soup
(£2.95), sandwiches (from £3.95), burgers (from £5.45, including vegetarian), sausage
and mash (£6.45), fish and chips or a pie of the day (£6.95), and changing hot
specials like turkey casserole or sweet and sour chicken (£5.95) from a servery. The
no smoking upstairs restaurant has a better than average carvery (all day inc Sunday,
£16.50 for three courses and coffee, £12.65 for two); it may be worth booking ahead.
The handsome staircase that leads up to it is lined with portraits of Prime Ministers.
The back bar is no smoking, other areas can feel smoky at times; piped music, fruit
machine. Handily placed between Victoria and Westminster, the pub was one of the
few buildings in this part of Victoria to escape the Blitz, and is one of the area's most
striking sights (though it's now rather dwarfed by the surrounding faceless cliffs of
dark modern glass). *(Recommended by John Branston, Kevin Blake, Ian Phillips, R T and
J C Moggridge, Michael Butler, Michael Dandy, GHC)*

Spirit Group ~ Manager Liz Cairns ~ Real ale ~ Bar food (11-10) ~ Restaurant ~
(020) 7222 5577 ~ Children in eating area of bar till 9.30 ~ Open 11-12 (11 Sun, and
every day in winter); closed 25 Dec

Argyll Arms 🍺

Argyll Street; ⊖ Oxford Circus, opposite tube side exit; W1F 7TP

Really individual pubs are hard to find in this part of town, so this bustling
Victorian place is a welcome surprise – and a useful retreat from the Oxford Street
crowds. Particularly unusual are the three atmospheric and secluded little cubicle
rooms at the front, essentially unchanged since they were built in the 1860s. All
oddly angular, they're made by wooden partitions with remarkable frosted and
engraved glass, with hops trailing above. A long mirrored corridor leads to the
spacious back room. Black Sheep, Fullers London Pride, Timothy Taylors
Landlord, Youngs, and maybe a changing guest on handpump; also several malt
whiskies. Served all day, the decent value straightforward bar food might include
doorstep sandwiches (from £3.90), an all-day breakfast (£5.25), fish and chips
(£6.95, or £9.95 for an especially big helping), and beef and ale pie (£7.50). Service
is generally prompt and friendly; newspapers to read, two fruit machines, piped
music. The quieter upstairs bar overlooks the pedestrianised street – and the
Palladium theatre if you can see through the impressive foliage outside the window;
divided into several snugs with comfortable plush easy chairs, it has swan's-neck
lamps, and lots of small theatrical prints along the top of the walls. The pub can get
very crowded (and can seem less distinctive on busier evenings), but there's space
for drinking outside. *(Recommended by Ian Phillips, Derek Thomas, N R White, the Didler,
Tracey and Stephen Groves, Mrs Hazel Rainer)*

Mitchells & Butlers ~ Manager Greg Porter ~ Real ale ~ Bar food (12-10) ~
(020) 7734 6117 ~ Children in upstairs bar till 9pm ~ Open 11-11; 12-10.30 Sun; closed
25 Dec

We say if we know a pub allows dogs.

Black Friar ⑳

Queen Victoria Street; ⊖ ⇌ Blackfriars; EC4V 4EG

A must-see for its unique and quite extraordinary décor – which includes some of the best Edwardian bronze and marble art nouveau work to be found anywhere – this distinctive old favourite is now entirely no smoking. The inner back room has big bas-relief friezes of jolly monks set into richly coloured florentine marble walls, an opulent marble-pillared inglenook fireplace, a low vaulted mosaic ceiling, gleaming mirrors, seats built into rich golden marble recesses, and tongue-in-cheek verbal embellishments such as Silence is Golden and Finery is Foolish. See if you can spot the opium-smoking hints modelled into the fireplace of the front room. The Adnams, Fullers London Pride and Timothy Taylors Landlord are often joined by some unusual guest beers, and there's a decent range of wines by the glass; fruit machine. Served all day, straightforward bar food might include sandwiches (from £4.25), ham, egg and chips (£6.45), a vegetarian dish of the day, toad in the hole or fish and chips (£6.95), and sirloin steak (£9.95); prompt, friendly service. The pub does get busy, and in the evenings lots of people spill out on to the wide forecourt, near the approach to Blackfriars Bridge; there's some smart new furniture out here (and in spring some rather impressive tulips). If you're coming by Tube, choose your exit carefully – it's all too easy to emerge from the network of passageways and find yourself on the wrong side of the street, or marooned on a traffic island. *(Recommended by Darren Le Poidevin, N R White, Donna and Roger, the Didler, Susan and John Douglas, Dr and Mrs A K Clarke, Andy Trafford, Louise Bayly, Eithne Dandy, Kevin Blake, Alison and Pete, R Huggins, D Irving, E McCall, T McLean)*

Mitchells & Butlers ~ Manager David Tate ~ Real ale ~ Bar food (12-9) ~ (020) 7236 5474 ~ Open 11-11; 12-11(10.30 Sun)Sat; 11.30-11 winter

Cittie of Yorke ◀

High Holborn – find it by looking out for its big black and gold clock; ⊖ Chancery Lane; WC1V 6BN

Readers are always delighted by the refreshingly cheap real ale at this unique old place (if only they had more than one type!) but it's the remarkable back bar that really impresses. Like a vast baronial hall, it has thousand-gallon wine vats resting above the gantry, big bulbous lights hanging from the soaring high-raftered roof, and an extraordinarily extended bar counter stretching off into the distance. A favourite with lawyers and City types, it can get busy in the evenings, but there's plenty of space to absorb the crowds – and indeed it's at the busiest times that the pub is at its most magnificent (it never feels quite right when it's quiet). Most people tend to congregate in the middle, so you should still be able to bag one of the intimate, old-fashioned and ornately carved booths that run along both sides. The triangular Waterloo fireplace, with grates on all three sides and a figure of Peace among laurels, used to stand in the Hall of Grays Inn Common Room until less obtrusive heating was introduced (thanks to the readers who sent us more thorough notes on its history). Sam Smiths OB on handpump (at around a pound less than the typical cost of a London pint); fruit machine. A smaller, comfortable panelled room has lots of little prints of York and attractive brass lights, while the ceiling of the entrance hall has medieval-style painted panels and plaster York roses. Served from buffet counters in the main hall and no smoking cellar bar, bar food includes sandwiches, soup (£4), and half a dozen daily-changing hot dishes such as pies like steak and kidney or spinach, potato and tomato, and turkey parmigiana (all between £5.50 and £6.95). As in other Sam Smiths pubs, readers have noted unusual brands of spirits rather than the more familiar names. A pub has stood on this site since 1430, though the current building owes more to the 1695 coffee house erected here behind a garden; it was reconstructed in Victorian times, using 17th-c materials and parts. *(Recommended by John Evans, Ian Phillips, Tracey and Stephen Groves, N R White, David and Sue Smith, Pete Walker, Dr and Mrs M E Wilson, Keith and Chris O'Neill, Donna and Roger, the Didler, John and Gloria Isaacs, Catherine and Richard Preston, Barry Collett, Peter Coxon, Kevin Blake, Joe Green)*

Sam Smiths ~ Manager Stuart Browning ~ Real ale ~ Bar food (12-3, 5-9; all day Sat) ~ (020) 7242 7670 ~ Children in eating area of bar ~ Open 11.30(12 Sat)-11; closed Sun, bank holidays, 25-26 Dec

Coopers Arms

Flood Street; ⊖ Sloane Square, but quite a walk; SW3 5TB

Brightened up in recent months with a fresh coat of paint, this spacious open-plan pub is a useful retreat fom the bustle of the Kings Road, with a relaxed and properly pubby atmosphere. Interesting furnishings include kitchen chairs and some dark brown plush chairs on the floorboards, a mix of nice old good-sized tables, and a pre-war sideboard and dresser; also, LNER posters and maps of Chelsea and the Thames on the walls, an enormous railway clock, a fireplace with dried flowers and a tusky boar's head, and tea-shop chandeliers. Youngs Bitter, Special and seasonal St Georges or Waggle Dance on handpump, with 14 wines by the glass. Bar food might include soup (£4.50), grilled goats cheese and red pepper crostini with wild rocket (£5.50), bangers and mash or fish and chips (£8.50), and chargrilled organic chicken, avocado and bacon salad (£8.95). The pub has become a managed house since our last edition, and reports so far suggest the service is not always up to the high standards of before. *(Recommended by Sue Demont, Tim Barrow)*

Youngs ~ Real ale ~ Bar food (11-10 (9 Sun)) ~ (020) 7376 3120 ~ Children in eating area of bar ~ Dogs allowed in bar ~ Open 11-11; 12-10.30 Sun; closed 25 Dec

Cross Keys

Lawrence Street; ⊖ Sloane Square, but some distance away; SW3 5NB

The distinctive style and décor of this bustling Victorian pub is down to designer Rudy Weller, best known for his Horses of Helios in Piccadilly Circus. You can tell he had fun with this: there's an unusual array of brassware hanging from the rafters, including trumpets and a diver's helmet, as well as animal-skin prints on the furnishings, and quite a mix of sculptures, paintings and objects. The roomy high-ceilinged flagstoned bar also has an island servery, a roaring fire, lots of atmosphere, and a good range of customers; there's a light and airy conservatory-style back restaurant, with an ironic twist to its appealing gardening décor. A short choice of good bar food includes soup (£4.50), feta cheese and spinach tart (£5.50), various ciabattas and wraps (from £5.90), sausages and mash with caramelised red onions or pasta of the day (£6.50), and salmon and prawn fishcakes with cream spinach sauce (£6.90), while the conservatory has things like roasted pork belly with apple and sage, colcannon and calvados jus (£12.50), and seared king scallops wrapped in parma ham (£15.90). Courage Best and Directors on handpump (not cheap, even for this area), and a good choice of wines by the glass. Attentive young staff; piped music. Like most pubs round here, this can be busy and lively on Saturday evenings. *(Recommended by Esther and John Sprinkle, David and Nina Pugsley, Derek Thomas)*

Free house ~ Licensee Chris Chatou ~ Bar food (12-3, 6-8 (not weekends)) ~ Restaurant ~ (020) 7349 9111 ~ Children under parental supervision welcome ~ Dogs allowed in bar ~ Open 12-11; 12-10.30 Sun; closed bank holidays

Dog & Duck ◼

Bateman Street, on corner with Frith Street; ⊖ Tottenham Court Road, Leicester Square; W1D 3AJ

A cheery Soho landmark, this pint-sized corner house hasn't really changed in the last 40 years. In the evenings it can be very busy indeed, packing a lot of atmosphere into a small space, so afternoons are probably the best time to fully appreciate the décor, which has some interesting detail and individual touches. On the floor near the door is an engaging mosaic showing a dog with its tongue out in hot pursuit of a duck; the same theme is embossed on some of the shiny tiles that frame the heavy old advertising mirrors. There are some high stools by the ledge along the back wall, and further seats in a slightly roomier area at one end; the piped music is usually drowned out by the good-natured chatter. Friendly staff behind the unusual little bar counter serve well kept Adnams, Fullers London Pride, Timothy Taylors Landlord and a guest like O'Hanlons Yellow Hammer; also Addlestone's cider, and decent wines by the glass. There's a fire in winter. Served all day, good value bar snacks include sausage sandwiches (£4.50), summer salads, and fish and chips (£6.95). In good weather especially, most people tend to spill on to the bustling street, though even when the pub is at its busiest you may find plenty of space in the rather cosy upstairs bar. The pub is said to be where George Orwell celebrated when the American Book of the Month Club chose *Animal Farm* as its monthly selection. Ronnie Scott's jazz club is near by. *(Recommended by LM, Donna and Roger, the Didler, Mike Gorton, Ian Phillips, C J Fletcher, Tracey and Stephen Groves, Tim Maddison, B and M Kendall)*

Mitchells & Butlers ~ Real ale ~ Bar food (12-9) ~ (020) 7494 0697 ~ Open 11-11; 12-10.30 Sun; closed 25 Dec

Eagle 🍽 🍷

Farringdon Road; opposite Bowling Green Lane car park; ⊖ ⇌ Farringdon, Old Street; ECIR 3AL

It's busy, noisy, and you'll be lucky to bag an empty table without a wait, but this is still one of London's very best pubs for food, the distinctive mediterranean meals as impressive now as they were when this was the capital's original gastro-pub. Despite the emphasis on eating, the atmosphere always feels chatty and pubby, with a buzzing informality that belies the quality of the cooking. Served from an open kitchen that dominates the busy single room, typical dishes might include a rich tuscan tomato and bread soup (£5), casarrecia pasta with organic egg, pancetta, chilli and rosemary (£7), marinated rump steak sandwich (£8.50), grilled mackerel with tabbouleh and chilli jam (£9), paella or grilled lamb chops with grilled aubergines, coriander and hummous (£12), and a handful of tapas dishes like chorizo, brandy and a soft boiled egg (£5); they also do unusual spanish, sardinian or goats milk cheeses (£6.50), and portuguese custard tarts. On weekday lunchtimes especially, dishes from the blackboard menu can run out or change fairly quickly, so it really is worth getting here as early as you possibly can if you're hoping to eat. Furnishings are basic but stylish – school chairs, a random assortment of tables, a couple of sofas on bare boards, and modern paintings on the walls (there's an art gallery upstairs, with direct access from the bar). During the week it's generally very busy indeed around meal times (and can occasionally be slightly smoky then), so isn't the sort of place you'd go for a quiet dinner, or a smart night out; it's generally quieter at weekends. Well kept Charles Wells Eagle and Bombardier on handpump, good wines including around 20 by the glass, decent coffee, and properly made cocktails; piped music (sometimes loud). *(Recommended by Tony and Jill Radnor)*

Free house ~ Licensee Michael Belben ~ Real ale ~ Bar food (12.30-3(3.30 weekends), 6.30-10.30 (not Sun)) ~ (020) 7837 1353 ~ Children welcome ~ Dogs allowed in bar ~ Open 12-11(5 Sun); closed Sun evening, bank holidays and a week at Christmas

Grapes

Shepherd Market; ⊖ Green Park; W1J 7QQ

Genuinely atmospheric and engagingly old-fashioned, this characterful pub is enjoyable at lunchtime when you can more easily take in its traditional charms, but is perhaps at its best when it's so very busy in the evenings, and the cheery bustle rather adds to the allure. The dimly lit bar has plenty of plush red furnishings, stuffed birds and fish in glass display cases, wooden floors and panelling, a welcoming coal fire, and a snug little alcove at the back. A good range of six or seven well kept beers on handpump (as in most Mayfair pubs fairly pricey), usually takes in Bass, Boddingtons, Flowers IPA, Fullers London Pride, Marstons Pedigree, and Timothy Taylors Landlord on handpump, with a guest like Charles Wells Bombardier tapped from the cask; fruit machine. No food, but, very appealingly, they say that customers are welcome to bring in their own if they're buying drinks. Service can sometimes slow down at the busiest times, and it can get smoky then; you'll generally see smart-suited drinkers spilling onto the square outside. The ladies' lavatory has received some criticism this year. The pub is in the heart of Shepherd Market, one of central London's best-kept secrets. *(Recommended by Darren Le Poidevin, N R White, the Didler, Dr and Mrs M E Wilson, Eric Robinson, Jacqueline Pratt, Ian Phillips, Jeremy Whitehorn, GHC)*

Free house ~ Licensees Gill and Eric Lewis ~ Real ale ~ Dogs allowed in bar ~ Open 11(12 Sat)-11; 12-10.30 Sun

Grenadier

Wilton Row; the turning off Wilton Crescent looks prohibitive, but the barrier and watchman are there to keep out cars; walk straight past – the pub is just around the corner; ⊖ Knightsbridge; SW1X 7NR

Said to be London's most haunted pub, this snugly characterful place is patriotically painted in red, white and blue, a reminder of the days when it was the mess for the officers of the Duke of Wellington. His portrait hangs above the fireplace, alongside neat prints of guardsmen through the ages. It doesn't take many people to fill up the tiny bar, but even at the busiest of times the mood is good-natured and smartly civilised, and you should generally be able to plonk yourself on one of the stools or wooden benches. Adnams, Charles Wells Bombardier, Fullers London Pride and Youngs from handpumps at the rare pewter-topped bar counter, though on Sundays especially you'll find several of the customers here to sample their famous bloody marys, made to a unique recipe. The bar menu (and the manager) were about to change as we went to press, but they have done good sandwiches (from £4.75), sausage and mash (£7.75), aberdeen angus burger with goats cheese and red onion relish (£8.50), fish and chips (£8.75), and Sunday roasts – as well as bar snacks like a pork and leek sausage, or bowls of chips and nachos. At the back is an intimate restaurant. There's a single table outside in the peaceful mews. *(Recommended by Paul and Marion Watts, Kevin Blake, N R White, Jo Lilley, Simon Calvert, Ian Phillips, GHC)*

Spirit Group ~ Real ale ~ Bar food (12-2.30, 6-9.30(9 weekends)) ~ Restaurant ~ (020) 7235 3074 ~ Dogs allowed in bar ~ Open 12-11(10.30 Sun)

Guinea

Bruton Place; ⊖ Bond Street, Green Park, Piccadilly Circus, Oxford Circus; W1J 6NL

The prize-wining steak and kidney pies served on weekday lunchtimes are the main draw to this old-fashioned little pub – almost standing room only inside, with plenty of people spilling onto the smart mews, even in winter. The look of the place is appealingly simple, with bare boards, yellow walls, old-fashioned prints, and a red-planked ceiling with raj fans, but the atmosphere is chatty and civilised, with a good few suited workers from Mayfair offices (it's quieter at the weekend). Three cushioned wooden seats and tables are tucked to the left of the entrance to the bar, with a couple more in a snug area at the back, underneath a big old clock; most people tend to prop themselves against a little shelf running along the side of the small room. Beyond the pies (which easily live up to the hype), the menu is limited to a vegetarian sandwich (£4.95) and a couple of elaborate grilled ciabattas (£6.95; these have won awards too). Youngs Bitter, Special, and seasonal brews from the striking bar counter, which has some nice wrought-iron work above it; the landlord is friendly. Take care to pick the right entrance – it's all too easy to walk into the quite separate upscale Guinea Grill which takes up much of the same building; uniformed doormen will politely redirect you if you've picked the door to that by mistake. *(Recommended by Darren Le Poidevin, the Didler, Andy and Jill Kassube)*

Youngs ~ Manager Carl Smith ~ Real ale ~ Bar food (12.30-2.30 Mon-Fri only) ~ Restaurant ~ (020) 7409 1728 ~ Children in restaurant ~ Open 11-11; 6-11 Sat; closed Sat lunchtime, all day Sun, bank holidays

Jerusalem Tavern ★ ⬛

Britton Street; ⊖ ⇌ Farringdon; EC1M 5UQ

One of our most popular London main entries, this carefully restored old coffee house is the only place to stock the whole range of brews from the Suffolk-based St Peter's other than the brewery itself, with half a dozen tapped from casks behind the little bar counter, and the rest available in their elegant, distinctively shaped bottles. Depending on the season you'll find St Peters Best, Fruit Beer, Golden Ale, Grapefruit, Strong, Porter, Wheat Beer, Winter, and Spiced ales, and you can buy them to take away too. Particularly inviting when it's candlelit on a cold winter's evening, the pub is a vivid re-creation of a dark 18th-c tavern, seeming so genuinely old that you'd hardly guess the work was done only a few years ago. The current building was developed around 1720, originally as a merchant's house, then becoming a clock and watchmaker's. It still has the shop front added in 1810, immediately behind which is a light little room with a couple of wooden tables and benches, a stack of *Country Life* magazines, and some remarkable old tiles on the walls at either side. This leads to the tiny dimly lit bar, which has a couple of unpretentious tables on the bare boards, and another up some stairs on a discreetly precarious-feeling though perfectly secure balcony – a prized vantage point. A plainer back room has a few more tables, a fireplace, and a stuffed fox in a case. There's a relaxed, chatty feel in the evenings, although these days it's getting harder to bag a seat here then, and it can feel crowded at times. Blackboards list the simple but well liked lunchtime food, the choice depending on what the helpful staff have picked up fom the local markets that day: good big doorstep sandwiches (from £5), and a couple of changing hot dishes such as chicken, bacon and asparagus pie, tuna niçoise salad, or stuffed aubergines (all between £6 and £8). Food service can be slow at times. There may be a couple of tables outside. Note the pub is closed at weekends. The brewery's headquarters in South Elmham is a main entry in our Suffolk chapter. *(Recommended by Gordon Prince, Darren Le Poidevin, the Didler, Sue Demont, Tim Barrow, Giles and Annie Francis, Nigel and Sue Foster, Mike Gorton, Esther and John Sprinkle, Andy and Jill Kassube, Jo Lilley, Simon Calvert, Anthony Longden, R Huggins, D Irving, E McCall, T McLean, Joe Green, Ian Phillips)*

St Peters ~ Manager Steve Medniuk ~ Real ale ~ Bar food (12-3) ~ (020) 7490 4281 ~ Children welcome ~ Dogs allowed in bar ~ Open 11-11; closed weekends and bank holidays

Lamb ㉕ ★ ⬛

Lamb's Conduit Street; ⊖ Holborn; WC1N 3LZ

Readers take a great deal of pleasure from a visit to this well run old favourite, one of London's most famous pubs. It stands out for its unique Victorian fittings and atmosphere, with the highlight the bank of cut-glass swivelling 'snob-screens' all the way around the U-shaped bar counter. Sepia photographs of 1890s actresses on the ochre panelled walls, and traditional cast-iron-framed tables with neat brass rails around the rim add to the overall effect. Consistently well kept Youngs Bitter, Special and seasonal brews like St Georges and Waggle Dance on handpump, and a good choice of malt whiskies. Now served all day, bar food still includes their popular hot ham rolls (£4.95), plus well-liked traditional dishes such as fish and chips (£7.95) and beef and ale pie (£8.75); Sunday roasts (£6.95). No machines or music, but shove-ha'penny, cribbage and dominoes. A couple of areas are no smoking, including the snug room at the back. There are slatted wooden seats in front, and more in a little courtyard beyond. It can get very busy, especially in the evenings, but can be rather peaceful after lunch. Like the street, the pub is named for the Kentish clothmaker William Lamb who brought fresh water to Holborn in 1577. Note they don't allow children. *(Recommended by B and M Kendall, David and Sue Smith, the Didler, Sue Demont, Tim Barrow, Tracey and Stephen Groves, James A Waller, Anthony Longden, Kevin Blake, Dr and Mrs M E Wilson, Joe Green, GHC)*

Youngs ~ Manager Suzanne Simpson ~ Real ale ~ Bar food (12-9) ~ (020) 7405 0713 ~ Open 11-midnight; 12-10.30 Sun

Lamb & Flag ㉕ ▉ £

Rose Street, off Garrick Street; ⊖ Leicester Square; WC2E 9EB

Unspoilt and in places rather basic, this historic Covent Garden pub buzzes with atmosphere: it's easily the area's most characterful pub, with a lively and well documented history. Dryden was nearly beaten to death by hired thugs outside, and Dickens made fun of the Middle Temple lawyers who frequented it when he was working in nearby Catherine Street. Enormously popular with after-work drinkers and visitors (it can be empty at 5pm and cheerfully heaving by 6), it always has an overflow of people chatting in the little alleyways outside, even in winter. The more spartan front room leads into a snugly atmospheric low-ceilinged back bar, with high-backed black settles and an open fire; in Regency times this was known as the Bucket of Blood thanks to the bare-knuckle prize-fights held here. Half a dozen well kept real ales typically include Adnams, Courage Best and Directors, Greene King IPA and Youngs Bitter and Special; also, a good few malt whiskies. The upstairs Dryden Room is often less crowded than downstairs, and has jazz every Sunday evening. The bar food served up here – lunchtimes only – is simple but very good value, including soup (£2.50), filled baked potatoes (£4.50), a few daily changing specials like steak and kidney pie, sausage casserole or fish and chips (£5.25), and a choice of roasts (£6.50). Service remains prompt and pleasant even at the busiest times. There's a TV in the front bar. *(Recommended by Neil Powell, David Carr, LM, Donna and Roger, the Didler, Barry and Anne, Mike Gorton, Derek Thomas, Mrs Hazel Rainer, Fr Robert Marsh, Anthony Longden, B and M Kendall, N R White)*

Free house ~ Licensees Terry Archer and Adrian and Sandra Zimmerman ~ Real ale ~ Bar food (11-3.30 weekdays, 12-5 weekends) ~ (020) 7497 9504 ~ Children in upstairs dining room 11-5 only ~ Jazz Sun evenings ~ Open 11-11; 12-10.30 Sun; closed 25-26 Dec, 1 Jan

Lord Moon of the Mall ▉ £

Whitehall; ⊖ Charing Cross; SW1A 2DY

This efficiently run and nicely converted former bank now opens for meals and drinks from 9am, allowing one surprised reader to enjoy his first pint of the day shortly after a breakfast meeting in Downing Street. More individual than many Wetherspoons pubs, it's a useful pit-stop for families and visitors touring the nearby sights, not least because the all-day food is far cheaper than you'll find anywhere else in the area. The impressive main room has a splendid high ceiling and quite an elegant feel, with old prints, big arched windows looking out over Whitehall, and a huge painting that seems to show a well-to-do 18th-c gentleman; in fact it's Tim Martin, founder of the Wetherspoons chain. Once through an arch the style is more recognisably Wetherspoons, with a couple of neatly tiled areas and bookshelves opposite the long bar; silenced fruit machines, trivia and a cash machine. They usually have up to nine real ales, with the regulars Fullers London Pride, Greene King Abbot, Marstons Pedigree and Shepherd Neame Spitfire; the guests can be quite unusual, and the prices for all of them are much less than the London norm. They have occasional beer festivals, and also keep Weston's cider. Bar food is from the standard Wetherspoons menu: sandwiches (from £2.69), bangers and mash (£5.89), five bean chilli (£6.09), aberdeen angus steak pie (£6.39), a big italian platter for sharing (£7.99), and children's meals; after 2pm (and all day weekends) they usually have a two-for-one meal offer for £7.50. The terms of the licence rule out fried food. Service can slow down at lunchtimes, when it does get busy. The back doors (now only an emergency exit) were apparently built as a secret entrance for the bank's account holders living in Buckingham Palace (Edward VII had an account here from the age of three); the area by here is no smoking. As you come out, Nelson's Column is immediately to the left, and Big Ben a walk of ten minutes or so to the right. *(Recommended by Ian Phillips, Darren Le Poidevin, Dr and Mrs A K Clarke, Stuart and Alison Ballantyne, Pete Walker, Keith and Chris O'Neill, Dr and Mrs M E Wilson, Barry Collett, Meg and Colin Hamilton, Mrs Hazel Rainer, B Shelley, Joe Green)*

Wetherspoons ~ Manager Mathew Gold ~ Real ale ~ Bar food (9am-11pm) ~ (020) 7839 7701 ~ Children welcome till 7pm if eating ~ Open 9am-11.30pm (12 Fri/Sat; 11 Sun)

Nags Head ㉕ 🍺

Kinnerton Street; ⊖ Knightsbridge; SW1X 8ED

'A country pub in town,' says one reader, neatly summing up the appeal of this
quirky little gem; it feels so much like an old-fashioned local in a sleepy village that
you can scarcely believe you're only minutes from Harrods and the hordes of
Knightsbridge. One of London's most unspoilt pubs (and indeed one of our own
favourites), it's hidden away in an attractive and peaceful mews, and rarely gets too
busy or crowded. There's a snugly relaxed, cosy feel in the small, panelled and low-
ceilinged front room, where friendly regulars sit chatting around the unusual
sunken bar counter. There's a log-effect gas fire in an old cooking range (seats by
here are generally snapped up pretty quickly), then a narrow passage leads down
steps to an even smaller back bar with stools and a mix of comfortable seats.
Adnams Best, Broadside and seasonal brews are pulled on attractive 19th-c china,
pewter and brass handpumps, while other interesting old features include a 1930s
what-the-butler-saw machine and a one-armed bandit that takes old pennies. The
piped music is rather individual: often jazz, folk or 1920s-40s show tunes, and
around the walls are drawings of actors and fading programmes from variety
performances. There are a few seats and sometimes a couple of tables outside. Bar
food (less distinctive than the rest of the pub) includes sandwiches (from £4),
ploughman's or salads (from £6.50), sausage, mash and beans or chilli con carne,
daily specials, and a choice of roasts (£6.95); there's a £1.50 surcharge added to all
dishes in the evenings, and at weekends. It can get smoky at times. Most readers are
delighted by their fairly hard-line policy on mobile phone use. *(Recommended by
Kevin Thomas, Nina Randall, Kevin Blake, R T and J C Moggridge, the Didler, Pete Baker,
Sue Demont, Tim Barrow, Giles and Annie Francis, Michael Butler, Phil and Sally Gorton, LM,
Ian Phillips, John and Gloria Isaacs, GHC, B and M Kendall)*

Free house ~ Licensee Kevin Moran ~ Real ale ~ Bar food (11-9.30 (12-8.30 Sun)) ~
No credit cards ~ (020) 7235 1135 ~ Open 11-11; 12-10.30 Sun

Old Bank of England ♀

Fleet Street; ⊖ Temple; EC4A 2LT

It's worth visiting this spectacularly converted former branch of the Bank of
England at quieter times if you want to fully appreciate the work that went into its
transformation – the opulent décor can take your breath away when seen for the
first time. Of course it's no less dramatic when the pub is at its busiest (usually
straight after work), but the noise and bustle can sometimes leave as deep an
impression then. The soaring, spacious bar has three gleaming chandeliers hanging
from the exquisitely plastered ceiling, high above an unusually tall island bar
counter, crowned with a clock. The end wall has big paintings and murals that look
like 18th-c depictions of Justice, but in fact feature members of the Fuller, Smith
and Turner families, who run the brewery the pub belongs to. There are well
polished dark wooden furnishings, plenty of framed prints, and, despite the
grandeur, some surprisingly cosy corners, with screens between some of the tables
creating an unexpectedly intimate feel which readers really enjoy. Tables in a
quieter galleried section upstairs offer a birds-eye view of the action, and some
smaller rooms (used mainly for functions) open off; several areas are no smoking.
Well kept Fullers Chiswick, ESB, London Pride and seasonal brews on handpump,
a good choice of malt whiskies, and a dozen wines by the glass; service is prompt
and friendly. Available all day, the good bar food has an emphasis on home-made
pies such as sweet potato and goats cheese (£7.25) and chicken, bacon and leek or
steak and ale (£7.95), but also includes soup (£3.50), sandwiches (from £3.75),
bangers and mash (£6.95), liver and bacon (£7.25), beer-battered cod (£8.25), and
bacon and brie chicken (£8.95); they do full afternoon teas. At lunchtimes the piped
music is generally classical or easy listening; it's louder and livelier in the evenings.
In winter the pub is easy to spot by the Olympic-style torches blazing outside the
rather austere Italianate building. Note they don't allow children, and are closed at
weekends. Pies have a long if rather dubious pedigree in this area; it was in the
vaults and tunnels below the Old Bank and the surrounding buildings that Sweeney

Todd butchered the clients destined to provide the fillings in his mistress
Mrs Lovett's nearby pie shop. *(Recommended by Darren Le Poidevin,
Ian Phillips, Stuart and Alison Ballantyne, Barry Collett, Dr and Mrs M E Wilson, the Didler,
Kevin Blake)*

Fullers ~ Manager James Carman ~ Real ale ~ Bar food (12-9(8 Fri)) ~ Restaurant ~
(020) 7430 2255 ~ Open 11-11; closed weekends, bank holidays

Olde Cheshire Cheese

Wine Office Court, off 145 Fleet Street; ↻ ≩ Blackfriars; EC4A 2BU

There's something especially convivial about this atmospheric 17th-c former chop
house, and we often hear from people who've struck up interesting conversations
with strangers in its warren of dark, historic rooms. Over the years Congreve, Pope,
Voltaire, Thackeray, Dickens, Conan Doyle, Yeats and perhaps Dr Johnson have
called in, and many parts appear hardly to have changed since. It can get busy
with tourists, but there are plenty of hidden corners to absorb the crowds. The
unpretentious rooms have bare wooden benches built in to the walls, bare boards,
and, on the ground floor, high beams, crackly old black varnish, Victorian
paintings on the dark brown walls, and big open fires in winter. A particularly snug
room is the tiny one on the right as you enter, but the most rewarding bit is the
Cellar Bar, down steep narrow stone steps that look as if they're only going to lead
to the loo, but in fact take you to an unexpected series of cosy areas with stone
walls and ceilings, and some secluded alcoves. Sam Smiths OB on handpump, as
usual for this brewery, extraordinarily well priced (almost £1 less than beers in
some other London pubs); helpful service from smartly dressed staff. With some
choices available all day, the reliable bar food includes a good value lunchtime pie
and mash buffet served in the cellar bar (12-2 only, £4.95), as well as sandwiches or
panini (from £3.50), and main dishes like steak and kidney pudding or fish and
chips (£7.75); part of the cellar bar is no smoking at lunchtimes. It's much quieter
at weekends than during the week. In the early 20th c the pub was well known for
its famous parrot that for over 40 years entertained princes, ambassadors and other
distinguished guests; she's still around today, stuffed and silent, in the restaurant on
the ground floor. *(Recommended by Darren Le Poidevin, Tracey and Stephen Groves,
Richard Marjoram, Barry Collett, Donna and Roger, the Didler, N R White, Simon and
Sally Small, Barry and Anne, Mike Gorton, Andy Trafford, Louise Bayly, Bruce Bird, Jo Lilley,
Simon Calvert, Anthony Longden, Tich Critchlow, Alison and Pete)*

Sam Smiths ~ Manager Gordon Garrity ~ Real ale ~ Bar food (12-10 Mon-Fri; 12-8.30 Sat;
not Sun (though restaurant open then)) ~ Restaurant ~ (020) 7353 6170 ~ Children in
eating area of bar and restaurant ~ Open 11-11; 12-3 Sun; closed Sun evening

Olde Mitre ㉕ ◖ £

**Ely Place; the easiest way to find it is from the narrow passageway beside 8 Hatton
Garden; ↻ Chancery Lane; EC1N 6SJ**

This splendidly atmospheric old tavern is a real hidden treasure – and notoriously
difficult to find; it's best approached from Hatton Garden, where an easily missed
sign on a lamppost points the way down a narrow alley. The cosy small rooms have
lots of dark panelling, as well as antique settles and – particularly in the popular
back room, where there are more seats – old local pictures and so forth. It gets
good-naturedly packed between 12.30 and 2.15, filling up again in the early
evening, but in the early afternoons and by around 9pm becomes a good deal more
tranquil. An upstairs room, mainly used for functions, may double as an overflow
at peak periods. Adnams Bitter and Broadside, Caledonian Deuchars IPA, and a
carefully chosen guest like Highgate Irish Whisky Ale on handpump; smart service
from obliging staff. No music, TV or machines – the only games here are darts,
cribbage and dominoes. Served all day, bar snacks are limited to pickled eggs and
gherkins (60p), scotch eggs or pork pies (£1), and really good value toasted
sandwiches with cheese, ham, pickle or tomato (£1.50). There's some space for
outside drinking with some pot plants and jasmine in the narrow yard between the

pub and St Ethelreda's church. Note the pub doesn't open weekends. The iron gates that guard one entrance to Ely Place are a reminder of the days when the law in this district was administered by the Bishops of Ely. *(Recommended by Neil Powell, N R White, Dr and Mrs M E Wilson, the Didler, Peter Coxon, Tracey and Stephen Groves, Joe Green)*

Punch ~ Managers Eamon and Kathy Scott ~ Real ale ~ Bar food (11.30-9.30) ~ (020) 7405 4751 ~ Open 11-11; closed weekends, bank holidays

Princess Louise
High Holborn; ⊖ Holborn; WC1V 7EP

Every letter we receive about this splendid Victorian gin-palace highlights a different part of its extraordinary décor, created by the finest craftsmen of the day and surviving essentially intact. The gloriously opulent main bar includes magnificent etched and gilt mirrors, brightly coloured and fruity-shaped tiles, and slender Portland stone columns soaring towards the lofty and deeply moulded crimson and gold plaster ceiling. Quieter corners have comfortable orange plush seats and banquettes. Its architectural appeal is unique (even the gent's has its own preservation order) but the pub also scores for its friendly, bustling atmosphere, and good value food and drink. Very nicely priced Sam Smiths OB on handpump from the long main bar; good, prompt service. Hot food is served upstairs (open only on weekdays), with things like home-made lasagne, various pies, hotpot and breaded plaice (all £5.50), but downstairs sandwiches, baguettes and ploughman's (£5.25) are available pretty much all day. Though it can get crowded during the week (especially in winter), it's usually quieter later on in the evening, or on a Saturday lunchtime. *(Recommended by Ian Phillips, Bruce Bird, Donna and Roger, the Didler, Simon Collett-Jones, C J Fletcher, Tracey and Stephen Groves)*

Sam Smiths ~ Licensee Campbell Mackay ~ Real ale ~ Bar food (12-2.30, 6-8.30 Mon-Fri; only sandwiches at weekends, but served all day) ~ (020) 7405 8816 ~ Dogs allowed in bar ~ Open 11-11; 12-11 Sat; 12-10.30 Sun; closed 25-26 Dec, 1 Jan

Red Lion ㉕ ◖
Waverton Street; ⊖ Green Park; W1J 5QN

In one of Mayfair's quietest and prettiest corners, the sudden appearance of what appears to be a smart village local is a real but welcome surprise. Standing out for its very relaxed but distinctly un-London atmosphere, this is a comfortably civilised pub that gets very busy indeed in the early evenings, but always keeps its warmly cosy feel. The main L-shaped bar has small winged settles on the partly carpeted scrubbed floorboards, and carefully framed London prints below the high shelf of china on the well polished, dark-panelled walls. Charles Wells Bombardier, Fullers London Pride, Shepherd Neame Spitfire and Youngs Ordinary on handpump, and they do rather good bloody marys (with a Very Spicy option); also a dozen malt whiskies, and around 14 wines by the glass. Good, honest bar food (served from a corner at the front) includes sandwiches (from £3.65; toasted from £4), soup (£2.95), ploughman's (£5.50), cumberland sausage and mash (£6.35), battered haddock (£6.65), scampi (£6.95), cottage pie (£7.25), and daily specials; friendly, smiling service. The restaurant is no smoking. The gent's usually has a copy of *The Times* at eye level. On Saturday evenings they generally have a pianist. *(Recommended by Dr and Mrs A K Clarke, Barry Collett, B and M Kendall, Michael Dandy, Dr and Mrs M E Wilson, Ian Phillips, Tracey and Stephen Groves, Revd R P Tickle)*

Punch ~ Manager Greg Peck ~ Real ale ~ Bar food (11.30-3 (not Sat), 6-9.30) ~ Restaurant ~ (020) 7499 1307 ~ Children in restaurant ~ Dogs welcome ~ Piano Sat evening ~ Open 11.30-11; 6-11 Sat; 12-3, 6-10.30 Sun; closed Sat am, all day 25-26 Dec, 1 Jan

---

Please let us know of any pubs where the wine is particularly good.

Red Lion 🍺

Duke of York Street; ⊖ Piccadilly Circus; SW1Y 6JP

Perhaps central London's most perfectly preserved Victorian pub, this fills up fast thanks to its busy location in the heart of the West End. When the pub was built its profusion of mirrors was said to enable the landlord to keep a watchful eye on local prostitutes, but the gleaming glasswork isn't the only feature of note: the series of small rooms also has a good deal of polished mahogany, as well as crystal chandeliers and cut and etched windows, and a striking ornamental plaster ceiling. Adnams, Caledonian Deuchars IPA, Fullers London Pride and Greene King IPA on handpump, and simple lunchtime snacks like sandwiches (from £3) and fish and chips (£6.50) – though one reader has found there may be days when they don't serve these. Diners have priority on a few of the front tables, and there's a minuscule upstairs eating area. It can be very crowded at lunchtime (try inching through to the back room where there's sometimes more space); many customers spill out on to the pavement, in front of a mass of foliage and flowers cascading down the wall. The piped music can be loud at times, and the atmosphere is generally bustling; come at opening time to appreciate its period charms more peacefully. No children inside. *(Recommended by Darren Le Poidevin, Dr and Mrs M E Wilson, Michael Dandy, the Didler, N R White, LM, Ian Phillips, Mike Gorton, Sue Demont, Tim Barrow, Andrew Wallace)*

Mitchells & Butlers ~ Real ale ~ Bar food (12-3) ~ Restaurant ~ (020) 7321 0782 ~ Open 11.30(12 Sat)-11; closed Sun, bank holidays

Seven Stars 🍴 🍺

Carey Street; ⊖ Holborn (just as handy from Temple or Chancery Lane, but the walk through Lincoln's Inn Fields can be rather pleasant); WC2A 2JB

London Dining Pub of the Year

Run with a light touch and a healthy dose of eccentricity, this cosy little pub facing the back of the Law Courts has expanded into the next door building, formerly a secondhand legal wig shop, but kept the original frontage intact, so there's still a neat display of wigs in the window. Partly hidden behind are very welcome extra tables and seating, though one can't help wondering if this is the kind of place that absorbs whatever space is available, as this new, no smoking area fills up just as fast as the original two unspoilt rooms. The pub has long been a favourite with lawyers and reporters covering notable trials nearby, so there are plenty of caricatures of barristers and judges on the red-painted walls, along with posters of legal-themed British films, big ceiling fans, and a relaxed, intimate atmosphere; checked tablecloths add a quirky, almost continental touch. Several of the tables are set for eating the good bar food. The landlady is quite an authority (she's even presented a BBC food series), and this year the pub's thoroughly honest rather than trendily fanciful cooking gains a Food Award. Served all day from a changing blackboard menu, the food might include things like welsh rarebit (£8), spiced pork back ribs (£8.50), beef stew or roast guinea fowl and mash (£8.75), chargrilled rib-eye steak (£13.50), plenty of seasonal game, and various cheeses (£7); at times you may also find vintage port with fruit cake. Adnams Best and Broadside on handpump, with a couple of changing guests like Dark Star Best and Hophead; service is prompt and very friendly. The pub can fill up very quickly, and on busy evenings customers sometimes spill out on to the quiet road in front; it generally quietens down after 8pm. The Elizabethan stairs up to the lavatories are rather steep, but there's a good strong handrail. Tom Paine, the large and somewhat po-faced pub cat, is very much a centre of attention: blackboards outside often recount his latest news, and he may take umbrage if you move the newspaper he likes to sleep on (indeed some have described the pussy as pushy). The licensees now have a second pub, the Bountiful Cow, on Eagle Street near Holborn, which specialises in beef; we have not yet had reports on this from readers – do let us know if you've tried it. *(Recommended by Ian and Nita Cooper, N R White, Ian Phillips, Dr and Mrs M E Wilson, the Didler, Sue Demont, Tim Barrow, Tracey and Stephen Groves, Mike Gorton, Barry Collett)*

Free house ~ Licensee Roxy Beaujolais ~ Real ale ~ Bar food (12-9) ~ (020) 7242 8521 ~ Well behaved children welcome ~ Open 11-11; 12-11.30 Sat; 12-11 Sun; closed some bank holidays (usually including Christmas)

Star ◀

Belgrave Mews West; behind the German Embassy, off Belgrave Square; ⊖ Knightsbridge; SW1X 8HT

With a restful local feel outside peak times (when it can be busy), this timeless pub impresses in summer with its astonishing array of hanging baskets and flowering tubs. The small bar has stools by the counter and tall windows, and an arch leading to the main seating area, with swagged curtains, well polished wooden tables and chairs, heavy upholstered settles, globe lighting, and raj fans. The seasonally changing bar menu at lunchtime might include broccoli and cauliflower gratin (£5.75), and beef stew or breaded cod (£5.95), with evening dishes such as mushroom and parmesan risotto (£8.45), confit duck leg with braised red cabbage (£9.95), and 28 day-hung rib-eye steak (£14.75). Fullers Chiswick, ESB, London Pride and seasonal brews on handpump; efficient service. The pub (which can get smoky in the evenings) is said to be where the Great Train Robbery was planned. *(Recommended by N R White, Ian Phillips, Dr Martin Owton, the Didler, Sue Demont, Tim Barrow, Mike Tucker, GHC)*

Fullers ~ Managers Jason and Karen Tinklin ~ Real ale ~ Bar food (12-2.30, 6-9.30; no food weekends) ~ (020) 7235 3019 ~ Dogs allowed in bar ~ Open 11-11; 12-10.30 Sun; closed 25-26 Dec, 1 Jan

Westminster Arms ◀

Storey's Gate; ⊖ Westminster; SW1P 3AT

There's a real mix of regulars at this friendly and unpretentious Westminster local – it's the nearest pub to both the Abbey and the Houses of Parliament, and can be packed after work with government staff and researchers. If you hear something a bit like a telephone bell, it's the Division Bell, reminding MPs to go back across the road to vote. A good range of seven real ales takes in Adnams Best and Broadside, Fullers London Pride, Greene King Abbot, Youngs and guests like Smiles Best and Thwaites Lancaster Bomber; they also do decent wines, and several malt whiskies. The plain main bar has simple old-fashioned furnishings, with proper tables on the wooden floors, a good deal of panelling, and a fruit machine; there's not a lot of room, so come early for a seat. Bar food is served in the downstairs wine bar (a good retreat from the ground-floor bustle), with some of the tables in cosy booths; typical dishes include filled baguettes (£4), various salads or ploughman's (£6.50), steak and kidney pie or fish and chips (£7.95), and daily specials; you can get most of the same things in the more formal upstairs restaurant, but they may be slightly more expensive. Both these areas are no smoking at lunchtime, and there's piped music (but not generally in the main bar). There are a couple of tables by the street outside. *(Recommended by Peter Dandy, Ian Phillips, the Didler, Jarrod and Wendy Hopkinson, Mike Begley, Sue Demont, Tim Barrow)*

Free house ~ Licensees Gerry and Marie Dolan ~ Real ale ~ Bar food (12-8 weekdays, 12-4 Sat/Sun) ~ Restaurant (weekday lunchtimes (not Weds)) ~ (020) 7222 8520 ~ Children in eating area of bar and restaurant ~ Open 11-11; 11-7 Sat; 12-5 Sun; closed 25 Dec

EAST LONDON   Map 12
Grapes ㉕

Narrow Street; ⊖ Shadwell (some distance away) or Westferry on the Docklands Light Railway; the Limehouse link has made it hard to find by car – turn off Commercial Road at signs for Rotherhithe tunnel, then from the Tunnel Approach slip road, fork left leading into Branch Road, turn left and then left again into Narrow Street; E14 8BP

Charles Dickens used this warmly welcoming 16th-c tavern as the basis of his Six
Jolly Fellowship Porters in *Our Mutual Friend*, describing it as a place that
'softened your heart', and presciently predicting it would 'outlast many a better-
trimmed building, many a sprucer public house'. Almost exactly as he would have
known it (all the more remarkable considering the ultra-modern buildings that
surround it), the Grapes remains one of London's most engaging riverside pubs, in
a peaceful spot well off the tourist route. The back part is the oldest (and in winter
when the fire is lit perhaps the cosiest), with the small back balcony a fine place for
a sheltered waterside drink; steps lead down to the foreshore. The chatty, partly
panelled bar has lots of prints, mainly of actors, and old local maps, as well as some
elaborately etched windows, plates along a shelf, and newspapers to read. Well kept
Adnams, Marstons Pedigree and Timothy Taylors Landlord on handpump, a
choice of malt whiskies, and a good wine list; efficient, friendly service. Good bar
food includes soup (£3.25), sandwiches (from £3.25), ploughman's (£4.75), a pint
of shell-on prawns (£5.25), bangers and mash (£6.25), home-made fishcakes with
caper sauce (£6.50), dressed crab (£7.75), and a highly regarded, generous Sunday
roast (no other meals then, when it can be busy, particularly in season). The river
end of the bar is no smoking, as is the very good upstairs fish restaurant, which has
fine views of the river (the pub was a favourite with Rex Whistler, who used it as
the viewpoint for his rather special river paintings). Shove-ha'penny, table skittles,
cribbage, dominoes, chess, backgammon; there may be piped classical or jazz. As
we went to press the pub was to become a leasehold rather than a managed house,
with some uncertainty as to who would be in charge – fingers crossed the current
rather characterful manager remains at the helm. *(Recommended by Kurt Hollesen,
Tracey and Stephen Groves, John and Gloria Isaacs, N R White)*

Spirit Group ~ Manager Barbara Haigh ~ Real ale ~ Bar food (not Sun evening) ~
Restaurant ~ (020) 7987 4396 ~ Dogs allowed in bar ~ Open 12-3, 5.30-11; 12-11 Sat;
12-10.30 Sun; closed 25-26 Dec, 1 Jan

Prospect of Whitby
Wapping Wall; ⊖ Wapping; E1W 3SH

As we went to press this entertaining pub was about to reopen with a new manager
after a short closure for refurbishment. But it's the kind of place where all that
means is a sort of tidy-up rather than drastic changes; it claims to be the oldest pub
on the Thames (dating back to 1543), so its whole appeal is based around its
unspoilt old fittings and colourful history. For a long while it was better known as
the Devil's Tavern, thanks to its popularity with smugglers and other ne'er-do-
wells, and some of the capital's best-known figures were frequent callers: Pepys and
Dickens both regularly popped in, Turner came for weeks at a time to study the
scene, and in the 17th c the notorious Hanging Judge Jeffreys was able to combine
two of his interests by enjoying a drink at the back while looking down over the
grisly goings-on in Execution Dock. The tourists who flock here lap up the
colourful tales of Merrie Olde London (it's an established favourite on evening
coach tours), but only the most unromantic of visitors could fail to be carried along
by the fun. Plenty of bare beams, bare boards, panelling and flagstones in the
L-shaped bar (where the long pewter counter is over 400 years old), and an
unbeatable river view towards Docklands from tables in the waterfront courtyard.
They have had Charles Wells Bombardier, Fullers London Pride and Greene King
Old Speckled Hen on handpump, and a wide range of standard dishes is usually
available all day. *(Recommended by Derek Thomas, the Didler, N R White, Dr and Mrs
M E Wilson, Tracey and Stephen Groves, Eric Robinson, Jacqueline Pratt, D J and P M Taylor,
Jeremy Whitehorn)*

Spirit Group ~ Manager Chris Buckley ~ Real ale ~ Bar food (12-9.30) ~ Restaurant ~
(020) 7481 1095 ~ Children welcome ~ Dogs welcome ~ Open 12-11; 12-10.30 Sun

---

Children – if the details at the end of a main entry don't mention them, you
should assume that the pub does not allow them inside.

NORTH LONDON   Map 13

Chapel ⑪ ♀

Chapel Street; ⊖ Edgware Road; NW1 5DP

Consistently good food continues to be the hallmark of this much-modernised child-friendly gastropub, with readers very impressed by the meals they've had here in recent months. It does get busy, particularly in the evenings when it can be a little noisy, but service remains smiling and efficient, and the staff really know their stuff. The choice of well presented meals changes every day, but might include soups such as broccoli and pancetta (£4.50), moules marinière or baked goats cheese with honey and rosemary (£5.50), puff pastry parcel of roast squash and ricotta cheese (£8.50), fried pork chop with sauté potatoes, celeriac, sage and cider (£11.50), braised chicken with ginger and coconut (£12), grilled gilt-head bream with olive mash, asparagus and light tartare sauce (£13), and grilled bison fillet with french beans, haricots blancs, rosemary and balsamic jus (£14). The atmosphere is always cosmopolitan – perhaps more relaxed and civilised at lunchtime, when it's a favourite with chic local office workers, then altogether busier and louder in the evenings. Light and spacious, the cream-painted rooms are dominated by the open kitchen; furnishings are smart but simple, with plenty of plain wooden tables around the bar, a couple of comfortable sofas at the lounge end, and a big fireplace. You may have to wait for a table during busier periods. On days when it all feels a little frenetic, it's nice to bag a spot on the spacious and rather calming outside terrace. Well kept Adnams and Greene King IPA on handpump, a decent choice of wines by the glass, cappuccino and espresso, fresh orange juice, and a choice of tisanes such as peppermint or strawberry and vanilla. In the evening, trade is more evenly split between diners and drinkers, and the music is more noticeable then, especially at weekends. A couple of readers have found it a little smoky at times. *(Recommended by Dr and Mrs M E Wilson, Sue Demont, Tim Barrow, Steve Harvey, Ian Phillips, Heather McQuillan)*

Punch ~ Lease Lakis Hondrogiannis ~ Real ale ~ Bar food (12-2.30(12.30-3 Sun), 7-10) ~ (020) 7402 9220 ~ Children welcome ~ Dogs welcome ~ Open 12-11(10.30 Sun); closed 25-26 Dec, Easter

Compton Arms £

Compton Avenue, off Canonbury Road; ⊖ Highbury & Islington; N1 2XD

The very pleasant back terrace of this tiny, well run pub is an unexpected bonus, with tables among flowers under a big sycamore tree; there may be heaters in winter, and barbecues in summer. Like an appealing village local, the unpretentious low-ceilinged rooms are simply furnished with wooden settles and assorted stools and chairs, with local pictures on the walls; there's a TV for sport, but the only games are things like chess, Jenga and battleships. Well kept Greene King Abbot and IPA and a couple of changing guests on handpump; friendly service. Decent bar food such as baguettes (£3.95), filled baked potatoes (£3.95), various burgers (£4.95), fish and chips or steak and ale pie (£5.95), and eight different types of sausage served with mashed potato and home-made red onion gravy (£5.95); their Sunday roasts come in two sizes, normal (£4.95), and large (£5.95). The pub is hidden away in a peaceful mews, though as it's deep in Arsenal country can get busy on match days. More reports please. *(Recommended by Sue Demont, Tim Barrow, Joe Green)*

Greene King ~ Managers Scott Plomer and Eileen Shelock ~ Real ale ~ Bar food (12-2.30, 6-8.30 weekdays; 12-4 Sat/Sun; no food (except soup) Mon) ~ (020) 7359 6883 ~ Children welcome in back room ~ Open 11am-11.30pm (10.30 Sun)

Drapers Arms ⑪ ♀

Far west end of Barnsbury Street; ⊖ ⇌ Highbury & Islington; N1 1ER

The fresh, carefully judged flavours and tempting presentation make a meal at this top-notch gastro-pub a particularly rewarding and memorable experience (if not exactly cheap). The choice might include lunchtime sandwiches (from £5.95), creamed white onion soup with thyme chantilly (£5), warm salmon and leek tart with celeriac remoulade (£6), beef carpaccio with radish, parmesan and truffle oil (£7.50), spaghetti with mussels, chilli and lemon oil (£11), squash risotto cake with broccoli and parmesan fritters (£13), slow-cooked lamb shank with rosemary and lentil jus and creamed savoy cabbage (£13.50), fried bream with crab mash and caper butter (£14), and moroccan chicken with spiced squash, chickpea purée and tzatziki (£14.50), with good puddings like caramelised fig and almond tart or a first-rate sticky toffee (£5.50). Service is helpful and unobtrusive. Big colourful bunches of flowers, inset shelves of paperbacks and board games, and a couple of groups of sofas and armchairs offset what might otherwise seem rather a severe open-plan layout and décor, with high-backed dining chairs or booths on dark bare boards, high ceilings, a few big drapery prints on dusky pink walls, and a pair of large fireplaces and mirrors precisely facing each other across the front area; the overall effect is not unlike a bright, elegant wine bar. The choice of wines by the glass (including champagne) is excellent, and they have Courage Best and Greene King Old Speckled Hen on handpump, with a guest like Caledonian Deuchars IPA, and a dozen malt whiskies; there may be piped jazz and swing. The dining room is no smoking. The pub is a striking Georgian townhouse, in a quiet residential street away from Islington's main drag; perhaps its slightly hidden location explains why we don't receive more reports on what in our view is now London's best pub for a special meal out. *(Recommended by Dr and Mrs M E Wilson, Bob and Maggie Atherton)*

Free house ~ Licensees Mark Emberton and Paul McElhinney ~ Real ale ~ Bar food (12-3, 7-10.30 (6.30-9.30 Sun)) ~ Restaurant ~ (020) 7619 0348 ~ No children after 6pm unless family eating a full meal ~ Dogs allowed in bar ~ Open 12-11; 12-10.30 Sun; closed 25-26 Dec, 1 Jan

Duke of Cambridge 🍴 ♀ 🍺

St Peter's Street; ⊖ Angel, though some distance away; N1 8JT

This trailblazing cornerhouse was London's first organic pub, and the excellent range of impeccably sourced drinks and food is still the main draw. It may cost more than you'd pay for a non-organic meal, but it's usually worth the extra to enjoy choices and flavours you won't find anywhere else. Changing twice a day, the blackboard menu might include soups like sweetcorn chowder or wild garlic with stilton croûtons (£4), sardines on toast with lemon, tomato and olive paste or home-smoked mackerel and caper pâté with pickles (£7), root vegetable, cauliflower and chickpea curry (£11), butternut squash stuffed with couscous, spinach, red onion and gorgonzola cream (£12.75), slow-braised ham hock with spring greens (£13.75), venison and chocolate stew with red cabbage and celeriac dauphinoise or diver-caught scallops with buttered leeks and white wine baked in puff pastry (£14.75), crispy pork belly with apple, watercress and mangetout (£15), and puddings like thyme crème brûlée with rhubarb compote (£6); helpings aren't always huge. They make all their own bread, pickles, ice-cream and so on. On handpump are four organic real ales such as Eco Warrior, SB and Shoreditch Stout from London's small Pitfield Brewery, and St Peters Best, and they also have organic draught lagers and cider, organic spirits, and a very wide range of organic wines, many of which are available by the glass. The full range of drinks is chalked on a blackboard, and also includes good coffees and teas, and a spicy ginger ale. The atmosphere is warmly inviting, and it's the kind of place that somehow encourages conversation, with a steady stream of civilised chat from the varied customers. The big, busy main room is simply decorated and furnished, with lots of chunky wooden tables, pews and benches on bare boards, a couple of big metal vases with colourful flowers, daily papers, and carefully positioned soft lighting around the otherwise bare walls. A corridor leads off past a few tables and an open kitchen to a couple of smaller candlelit rooms, more formally set for eating, and a conservatory. Most of the pub is no smoking. It's worth arriving early to eat, as they can get very busy. *(Recommended by Tony and Jill Radnor, Alistair Forsyth, Susan May)*

Free house ~ Licensee Geetie Singh ~ Real ale ~ Bar food (12.30-3(3.30 Sat/Sun), 6.30-10.30(10 Sun)) ~ Restaurant ~ (020) 7359 3066 ~ Children welcome ~ Dogs allowed in bar ~ Open 12-11(10.30 Sun); closed 24-26 Dec

Flask ♀
Flask Walk; ⊖ Hampstead; NW3 1HE

Relaxed, simple, and unassuming, this peaceful old local has a properly old-fashioned and rather villagey feel, and is a popular haunt of Hampstead artists, actors and characters. The snuggest and most individual part is the cosy lounge at the front, with plush green seats and banquettes curving round the panelled walls, a unique Victorian screen dividing it from the public bar, and an attractive fireplace. A comfortable orange-lit room with period prints and a few further tables leads into a rather smart dining conservatory, which with its plants, prominent wine bottles and neat table linen feels a bit like a wine bar. A couple of white iron tables are squeezed into the tiny back yard. Youngs Bitter, Special and seasonal brews on handpump, around 16 wines by the glass, and decent coffees – they have a machine that grinds the beans to order. Bar food might include sandwiches, soup, daily changing specials like chicken casserole, lamb curry or spiced minced beef pie with a cheese and leek mash topping (from £5.50), and good fish and chips (£6.50). A plainer public bar (which you can get into only from the street) has leatherette seating, cribbage, backgammon, lots of space for darts, fruit machines, trivia and big-screen SkyTV. There are quite a few tables out in the alley. Small dogs are allowed in the front bar only. The pub's name is a reminder of the days when it distributed mineral water from Hampstead's springs. *(Recommended by Darren Le Poidevin, the Didler, Steve Harvey, Derek Thomas, N R White, Tim Maddison, Ian Phillips)*

Youngs ~ Manager John Cannon ~ Real ale ~ Bar food (12-8.30) ~ Restaurant ~ (020) 7435 4580 ~ Dogs allowed in bar ~ Open 11-11(12 Fri/Sat); 12-10.30 Sun

Holly Bush ㉕ ♀ ◧
Holly Mount; ⊖ Hampstead; NW3 6SG

With an atmosphere described by readers as 'magical', this timeless old favourite is on particularly fine form at the moment. Originally the stable block of a nearby house, it's well liked for its food and range of drinks, but it's the unique mood of the place that's really special, particularly in the evenings, when the old-fashioned and individual front bar has a distinctive gloom that's welcoming even in the height of summer, and there's a good mix of chatty locals and visitors. Under the dark sagging ceiling are brown and cream panelled walls (decorated with old advertisements and a few hanging plates), open fires, bare boards, and cosy bays formed by partly glazed partitions. Slightly more intimate, the back room, named after the painter George Romney, has an embossed red ceiling, panelled and etched glass alcoves, and ochre-painted brick walls covered with small prints; piped music, and lots of board and card games. With carefully sourced ingredients (most of their meat is organic), bar food includes half a pint of prawns (£4), welsh rarebit (£5.50), various sausages with cheddar mash and gravy (from £8.50), pies like chicken, mushroom and London Pride (£9) or beef and Harveys (£9.50), roast chicken in beer and paprika sauce (£10.50), slow-roasted lamb shank (£11.50), and some good, unusual cheeses (£7). Well kept Adnams Broadside, Fullers London Pride, Harveys Sussex and a couple of guests like Everards Buddings and Hop Back Crop Circle on handpump, plenty of whiskies, and a good, seasonally changing wine list; friendly service. The back bar and the upstairs dining room (with table service Weds-Sun) are no smoking. There are tables on the pavement outside. The pub is reached by a delightful stroll along some of Hampstead's most villagey streets. *(Recommended by the Didler, Tracey and Stephen Groves, Steve Harvey, Jo Lilley, Simon Calvert, Tim Maddison, Derek Thomas, Ian Phillips)*

Punch ~ Lease Nicolai Outzen ~ Real ale ~ Bar food (12-4, 6.30-10 weekdays; 12-10 Sat, 12-9 Sun) ~ Restaurant ~ (020) 7435 2892 ~ Children in eating area of bar and restaurant ~ Dogs allowed in bar ~ Open 12-11(10.30 Sun); closed 1 Jan

---

There are report forms at the back of the book.

Olde White Bear

Well Road; ⊖ Hampstead; NW3 1LJ

Reckoned by many to be Hampstead's friendliest pub, this neo-Victorian place has a wonderfully clubby feel that attracts a splendidly diverse mix of customers. The dimly lit knocked-through bar is smart but relaxed, with elegant panelling, wooden venetian blinds, and three separate-seeming areas: the biggest has lots of Victorian prints and cartoons on the walls, as well as wooden stools, cushioned chairs, a couple of big tasselled armchairs, a flowery sofa, a handsome fireplace and an ornate Edwardian sideboard. A brighter section at the end has elaborate brocaded pews, while a central area has dried flower arrangements and signed photographs of actors and playwrights. Bar food is served all day, from a range including soups like broccoli and stilton (£4), good elaborate sandwiches (from £5), greek salad or home-made moussaka or burger (£7), salmon fishcakes with saffron sauce or sausages and mash (£8), beef in Guinness pie (£8.50), and rosemary lamb shank in red wine gravy with mash (£9); their choice of roasts on Sundays is very popular. A third of the pub is no smoking. Adnams, Fullers London Pride, Greene King Abbot, and Youngs on handpump; over a dozen wines by the glass, and a decent range of whiskies. There are a few tables in front, and more in a courtyard behind. Regular visitors feel the piped music is louder in the evenings these days – perhaps reflecting its popularity then with a younger crowd; cards, chess, TV and excellent Thursday quiz nights. Parking nearby is mostly permits only (there are no restrictions on Sundays), but the pub sells visitors' permits for up to two hours. The Heath is close by. (Recommended by Darren Le Poidevin, the Didler, Tracey and Stephen Groves, Sue Demont, Tim Barrow, N R White, Tim Maddison, Ian Phillips)

Punch ~ Lease Christopher Ely ~ Real ale ~ Bar food (12-9) ~ (020) 7435 3758 ~ Children welcome ~ Dogs allowed in bar ~ Thurs quiz night (starts 9) ~ Open 11-11; 11-11 Sat; 12-10.30 Sun

Spaniards Inn ㉕ 🍺

Spaniards Lane; ⊖ Hampstead, but some distance away, or from Golders Green station take 220 bus; NW3 7JJ

Famed for its tales of hauntings and highwaymen (some of which are best taken with a large dose of salt), this busy former toll house dates back to 1585, and the low-ceilinged oak-panelled rooms of the attractive main bar are full of character, with open fires, genuinely antique winged settles, candle-shaped lamps in shades, and snug little alcoves. But for many it's the charming garden that's the main draw, nicely arranged in a series of areas separated by judicious planting of shrubs. A crazy paved terrace with slatted wooden tables and chairs opens on to a flagstoned walk around a small raised area with roses, and a side arbour of wisteria, clematis and hops; you may need to move fast to bag a table. There's an outside bar, and regular barbecues out here in summer. The range of drinks is impressive, with between five and eight real ales at a time, typically including Adnams, Caledonian Deuchars IPA, Fullers London Pride, Marstons Old Empire and a guest like Roosters Leg Horn, some unusual continental draught lagers, and 22 wines by the glass – though in summer you might find the most favoured drink is their big jug of Pimms. Served all day, the popular bar food might include soup (£3.45), lunchtime sandwiches (from £4.50) and ploughman's (£5.85), mussels with bacon and cider (from £5.90), a daily pasta dish (£6), goats cheese and butternut squash lasagne (£7.50), pork, cider and apple sausages with mash (£8.90), fish and chips (£10), and 8oz sirloin steak (£10.50); service is helpful and friendly. The food bar and the georgian Turpin bar upstairs are no smoking. The pub is believed to have been named after the Spanish ambassador to the court of James I, who had a private residence here. It's fairly handy for Kenwood. The car park fills up fast, and other parking nearby is difficult. (Recommended by Ian Phillips, John Saville, Jo Lilley, Simon Calvert, Tracey and Stephen Groves)

Mitchells & Butlers ~ Manager David Nichol ~ Real ale ~ Bar food (11.30-10) ~ (020) 8731 6571 ~ Children welcome ~ Dogs welcome ~ Open 11-11(open from 10 at weekends)

SOUTH LONDON   Map 13

Anchor & Hope 🕮 ♀

The Cut (B300, turning E off A301 Waterloo Road, S of Waterloo station);
⊖ ⇌ Waterloo; SE1 8LP

It looks a bit scruffy, and the atmosphere is determinedly informal, but the top-notch cooking has made this vibrant bare-boards gastropub one of London's most fashionable places to eat, its unusual meals thoughtfully prepared using excellent seasonal ingredients. Very highly thought of in foody circles, the blackboard menu changes twice a day and might include a seasonal garlic soup (£4.80), pressed chicken and bacon terrine (£5.80), snails, bacon and laverbread on duck fat toast (£6.60), foie gras ballotine (£9.80), stewed rabbit and polenta or roast pigeon with semolina gnocchi and ceps (£11.80), skate, leeks and brown shrimps or cod, white beans and mussels (£13), roast middlewhite pork with baker's potatoes and apple sauce (£15), several dishes for sharing such as ox cheek and dumplings (for two, £29), and puddings like polenta cake and blood oranges (£5). It's very much of the Eagle school (open kitchen and absolutely no booking – even well known faces have been made to wait), and perhaps appeals to the same sort of people, but here there's a separate dining room, and on arrival you can add your name to the list to be seated there. Alternatively you can join the throng in the bar, which shares the same menu, but the dining room tables are better for an unhurried meal; those in the bar are rather low and small. There's a piano in one corner, and a big mirror behind the counter, but otherwise the bar is fairly plain, with dark red-painted walls and big windows that open up in summer. On the other side of a big curtain, the dining room is similar, but with contemporary paintings on the walls; it's no smoking in here. Well kept Charles Wells Bombardier and Eagle on handpump, along with a guest like Everards Tiger (again, not cheap); there's a good wine list, served in tumblers and carafes rather than smart glasses, but a popular choice before dinner is one of their sherries. The atmosphere is relaxed and unstuffy – it's the kind of place where strangers cheerfully ask what you're eating; at busy times there can be a slight air of chaos, and service, though generally friendly, can be confused then. There are a few metal tables in front on the street. *(Recommended by Dr and Mrs M E Wilson, Tony and Jill Radnor, Mayur Shah, Derek Thomas, Sue Demont, Tim Barrow)*

Charles Wells ~ Lease Robert Shaw ~ Real ale ~ Bar food (12-2.30 (not Mon), 6-10.30) ~ Restaurant ~ (020) 7928 9898 ~ Children welcome ~ Dogs welcome ~ Open 11-12 (closed till 5 Mon); closed Sun; closed bank holidays and Christmas

Crown & Greyhound

Dulwich Village; ⇌ North Dulwich; SE21 7BJ

One of this big, relaxed Victorian pub's main draws is the very pleasant back garden, with smart new tables shaded by a chestnut tree, and barbecues on summer weekends. The fence has been cheerfully brightened up by murals painted by local schoolchildren, and they've added french boules and over-sized versions of games like Connect Four and dominoes. A big back dining room and conservatory open on to here, leading from the pleasantly furnished roomy main bar at the front. Refurbished but retaining many of its original features, this has some quite ornate plasterwork and lamps over on the right, and a variety of nicely distinct seating areas, some with traditional upholstered and panelled settles, others with stripped kitchen tables on stripped boards; there's a coal-effect gas fire and some old prints. As well as Fullers London Pride they have three rotating real ales like Adnams, Timothy Taylors Landlord and Youngs Special, and an unusual guest such as Nethergate Cross Border; beer festivals at Easter and perhaps some other bank holidays. The menu might include sandwiches (from £3.95), various types of sausage or their well liked burgers (from £6.90, including vegetarian), and specials like 21-day-hung rib-eye steak (£13.50). Best to arrive early for their popular Sunday carvery (£8.90), as they don't take bookings; the pub can be popular with families then. Known locally as the Dog, it was built at the turn of the century to

replace two inns that had stood here previously, hence the unusual name. Busy in
the evenings, but quieter during the day, it's handy for walks through the park, and
for the Dulwich Picture Gallery. More reports please. *(Recommended by
Dave W Holliday, Dr and Mrs M E Wilson)*

Mitchells & Butlers ~ Manager Duncan Moore ~ Real ale ~ Bar food (12-10(9 Sun)) ~
(020) 8299 4976 ~ Children in restaurant ~ Dogs welcome ~ Open 11-11(12 Thurs-Sat);
12-10.30 Sun

Cutty Sark

**Ballast Quay, off Lassell Street; ≠ Maze Hill, from London Bridge; or from the river
front walk past the Yacht in Crane Street and Trinity Hospital; SE10 9PD**

You can almost imagine smugglers and blackguards with patches over their eyes in
the dark, flagstoned bar of this late 16th-c white-painted house, well liked by
readers at the moment not just for the characterful building, but also for its well
presented food. The unspoilt bar has a genuinely old-fashioned feel, with rough
brick walls, wooden settles, barrel tables, open fires, low lighting and narrow
openings to tiny side snugs; there's an elaborate central staircase. Adnams
Broadside, Black Sheep, Fullers London Pride, St Austell Tribute and Timothy
Taylors Landlord on handpump, with a good choice of malt whiskies, and a range
of organic wines; fruit machine, juke box. In a roomy eating area, the good,
promptly served bar food includes well liked sandwiches (from £3.95), and
changing hot dishes like bangers and mash (£7.95), sweet chilli salmon on a bed of
noodles (£9.95), and garlic peppered rib-eye steak (£11.95); service is friendly and
efficient. There are splendid views of the Thames and the Millennium Dome from
the busy terrace across the narrow cobbled lane (where the concrete tables strike a
slightly incongruous note), or, better still, from the upstairs room with the big bow
window – itself notable for the way it jetties over the pavement. The pub is alive
with young people on Friday and Saturday evenings, but can be surprisingly quiet
some weekday lunchtimes. Morris dancers occasionally drop by. Parking is limited
nearby – though, unusually for London, if you can bag a space it's free.
*(Recommended by Simon and Mandy King, N R White, the Didler, Jo Lilley, Simon Calvert,
John Saville, Andy Trafford, Louise Bayly, GHC, B and M Kendall)*

Free house ~ Licensee Katie Jackson ~ Real ale ~ Bar food (12-9(10 Sat)) ~ Restaurant ~
(020) 8858 3146 ~ Children upstairs till 9pm ~ Dogs allowed in bar ~ Open 11-11;
12-10.30 Sun

Fire Station ♀

Waterloo Road; ⊖ ≠ Waterloo; SE1 8SB

Exciting plans are afoot to revamp the food at this bustling conversion of the
former LCC central fire station, which changed hands just as we went to press.
When it first opened as a pub back in the mid-1990s there was a real freshness to
the menu offered in the spacious back dining room, and it's those glory days that
the new manager is hoping to re-create, with a shorter, daily changing menu that
will rely on fresh, local ingredients. All should be ready by the time this edition hits
the shops, though already there's been a change to the bar menu (and the hours it's
served), which now offers substantial sandwiches (from £6) and pizzas (from
£7.95) all day. The atmosphere is vibrantly busy on weekdays after work, with
loud chat and music combining in a cheery cacophony that most readers
thoroughly enjoy, but some find a little overpowering. Though some original
features remain, the building looks rather like a cross between a warehouse and a
schoolroom, with plenty of wooden pews, chairs and long tables (a few spilling on
to the street), some mirrors and rather incongruous pieces of dressers, and brightly
red-painted doors, shelves and modern hanging lightshades. Adnams, Fullers
London Pride, Shepherd Neame Spitfire, Youngs and a guest on handpump, as well
as a number of European bottled beers, variously flavoured teas, several malt
whiskies and a good choice of wines. It's calmer at lunchtimes, and at weekends;
TV for rugby and football. It's very handy for the Old Vic and Waterloo station.

(Recommended by Darren Le Poidevin, Ian Phillips, Sue Demont, Tim Barrow, Paul A Moore, Michael Butler, R T and J C Moggridge, Keith and Chris O'Neill, Mrs Hazel Rainer, Mayur Shah, Nina Randall, Giles and Annie Francis, GHC)

W&D~ Manager Tom Alabaster ~ Real ale ~ Bar food ~ Restaurant ~ (020) 7620 2226 ~ Children in eating area of bar and restaurant ~ Open 11am-midnight(11 Sun-Tues); closed 25-26 Dec

Founders Arms

Hopton Street (Bankside); ⊖ ⇌ Blackfriars, and cross Blackfriars Bridge; SE1 9JH

The views from the waterside terrace of this big, modern place are among the best from any pub along the Thames, particularly in the City, with fine views of the river, St Paul's, and the Millennium Bridge; it's no wonder most people sit outside, and there are plenty of picnic-sets to take it all in. Rather like a huge conservatory, this is the handiest pub for visiting Tate Modern, and Shakespeare's Globe is a short stroll away. If you're inside, the lighting is nice and unobtrusive so that you can still see out across the river at night. It can get busy, particularly on weekday evenings, when it's popular with young City types for an after-work drink. Youngs Bitter, Special and seasonal brews from the modern bar counter angling along one side; also, coffee, tea and hot chocolate. Available all day (starting at 9 for breakfast), the promptly served bar food is useful rather than outstanding, with things like sandwiches and panini (from £4.95), sausages and mash, fish and chips, or pasta with artichokes, peppers, pesto and cream (£7.95), steak and ale pie (£8.95), and daily specials; Sunday roasts. Efficient, cheerful service. One raised area is no smoking; piped music, fruit machine. Like many City pubs, it may close a little early on quieter nights. *(Recommended by John Wooll, Ian Phillips, N R White, D J and P M Taylor, the Didler, Susan and John Douglas, Mrs Pat Crabb, Dr and Mrs M E Wilson)*

Youngs ~ Manager Paul Rayner ~ Real ale ~ Bar food (brunch 10-12; full menu 12-10) ~ (020) 7928 1899 ~ Children in eating area of bar until 8.30 ~ Open 10am(9 Sat/Sun)-11 (midnight Fri/Sat)

Fox & Hounds 🍴 ♀

Latchmere Road; ⇌ Clapham Junction; SW11 2JU

It's the excellent mediterranean cooking that makes this otherwise unremarkable big Victorian local worth a detour. The second of the small group run by the two brothers who transformed the Atlas (see West London, below), it has a very similar style and menu. Changing every day (though note they don't do food weekday lunchtimes), a typical choice might include butternut squash, sweet potato and courgette soup (£4.50), chicken and spinach terrine with cream cheese, almonds and dill wrapped in parma ham with mango chutney (£8), octopus and baby prawn risotto with lemon, coriander, saffron and olive oil (£8.50), spanish chicken casserole or pan-roasted marinated pork chop with lemon, rosemary, crispy mustard polenta and tomato chilli jam (£11), grilled rib-eye steak with new potato and beetroot mash and red onion marmalade (£13), vanilla and lime cheesecake (£4.50), and unusual cheeses with apple and grilled bread (£5.50). The pub can fill quickly, so you may have to move fast to grab a table. The spacious, straightforward bar has bare boards, mismatched tables and chairs, two narrow pillars supporting the dark red ceiling, photographs on the walls, and big windows overlooking the street (the view partially obscured by colourful window boxes). There are fresh flowers and daily papers on the bar, and a view of the kitchen behind. Two rooms lead off, one more cosy with its two red leatherette sofas. Well kept Caledonian Deuchars IPA, Fullers London Pride and Harveys Sussex on handpump; the carefully chosen wine list (which includes a dozen by the glass) is written out on a blackboard. It's still very much the kind of place where locals happily come to drink – and they're a more varied bunch than you might find filling the Atlas; the piped music fits in rather well. The garden has been extensively refurbished, with plenty of new planting and big parasols and heaters for winter.

The same team has another two similarly organised pubs: the Cumberland Arms near Olympia, and the Swan in Chiswick. *(Recommended by Keith and Chris O'Neill)*

Free house ~ Licensees Richard and George Manners ~ Real ale ~ Bar food (7-10.30(10 Sun), plus 12.30-2.30 Fri, and 12.30-3 Sat/Sun (no lunch Mon-Thurs)) ~ (020) 7924 5483 ~ Children welcome in eating area till 7pm ~ Dogs welcome ~ Open 12-3 (not Mon), 5-11 Mon-Thurs; 12-11 Fri-Sat; 12-10.30 Sun; closed Mon lunchtime; 24 Dec-1 Jan; Easter Sat and Sun

George ㉕ ★ ◧

Off 77 Borough High Street; ⊖ ⇄ Borough or London Bridge; SE1 1NH

Perhaps the country's best example of a historic coaching inn (and now preserved by the National Trust), this splendid-looking place dates from the 16th c, but was rebuilt to the original plan after the great Southwark fire of 1676. The tiers of open galleries look down over a bustling cobbled courtyard with plenty of picnic-sets, and maybe morris men and even Shakespeare in summer. Inside, the row of no-frills ground-floor rooms and bars all have square-latticed windows, black beams, bare floorboards, some panelling, plain oak or elm tables and old-fashioned built-in settles, along with a 1797 'Act of Parliament' clock, dimpled glass lantern-lamps and so forth. The snuggest refuge is the room nearest the street, where there's an ancient beer engine that looks like a cash register. Two rooms are no smoking at lunchtimes. In summer they open a bar with direct service into the courtyard. Greene King Abbot and IPA, and a beer brewed by them for the pub, as well as Wadworths 6X and a changing guest on handpump; mulled wine in winter, tea and coffee. Good value lunchtime bar food includes baguettes (from £4.25) and wraps (from £4.75), soup (£2.95), filled baked potatoes (from £3.50), ham, egg and chips or scampi (£5.45), spinach and mixed mushroom cannelloni (£5.95), sausage and mash (£5.95), fish and chips (£6.45), and steak and ale pie (£6.75); they do a Sunday carvery (£9.95). An impressive central staircase goes up to a series of dining rooms and to a gaslit balcony; darts, trivia. What survives today is only a third of what it once was; the building was 'mercilessly reduced' as E V Lucas put it, during the period when it was owned by the Great Northern Railway Company. Unless you know where you're going (or you're in one of the many tourist groups that flock here in summer) you may well miss it, as apart from the great gates and sign there's little to indicate that such a gem still exists behind the less auspicious-looking buildings on the busy high street. *(Recommended by Andy and Jill Kassube, Ian Phillips, the Didler, N R White, Derek and Sylvia Stephenson, B and M Kendall, Jo Lilley, Simon Calvert, Peter Coxon, R Huggins, D Irving, E McCall, T McLean, W W Burke)*

Greene King ~ Manager Scott Masterson ~ Real ale ~ Bar food (12-5) ~ Restaurant (5-10 (not Sun)) ~ (020) 7407 2056 ~ Children in eating area of bar ~ Open 11-11(12 Fri/Sat); 12-10.30 Sun

Market Porter ◧

Stoney Street; ⊖ ⇄ London Bridge; SE1 9AA

We've had more reports on this busily pubby place than for any other London pub this year, with all overwhelmed by the biggest and most interesting range of real ales you're likely to come across. They usually have around a dozen to choose from, with most of them brews you've never heard of, let alone tried. The range changes every day, but a typical visit might turn up Battersea Power Station Porter, Burton Bridge Damson Porter, Cairngorm Wild Cat, Castle Rock Mayfly, Everards Svengal Tiger, Exmoor Silver Stallion, Goose Eye No Eye Deer, Grainstore Steaming Billy, Harveys Copperwheat, Oakham Mompesson Gold, Potton Shambles and Salamander Golden Goal, all perfectly kept and served. Their website (www.themarketporter.co.uk) lists the latest range. The pub opens between 6 and 8.30 on weekday mornings to serve the workers and porters from Borough Market (they do breakfasts then), and the only criticism we've heard in recent years is that it's sometimes so busy you can't read the names of the beers on the pumps. They doubled the size of the place last year, but even so at lunchtimes it still feels very bustling indeed, and can be noisy with chatter; it's usually quieter in the afternoons (or in the upstairs restaurant). The main part of the bar has rough wooden ceiling beams with beer barrels balanced on them, a heavy wooden bar counter with a beamed gantry, cushioned bar stools, an open fire, and 20s-style wall lamps; it gets more old-fashioned the further you venture in. Sensibly priced lunchtime bar food includes sandwiches (from £2.95), panini (from £3.95), caesar salad (£4.95), sausages and mash (£5.75), a changing home-made pie (£6.25), fish and chips (£6.50), and sirloin steak (£7.95); good Sunday roasts. Obliging, friendly service; darts, fruit machine, TV and piped music. The company that owns the pub has various others around London; ones with similarly unusual beers (if not quite so many) can be found in Stamford Street and Seymour Place. *(Recommended by Rob Razzell, Darren Le Poidevin, Ian Phillips, Pete Walker, Derek Thomas, the Didler, Mike and Sue Loseby, N R White, Sue Demont, Tim Barrow, Ian and Julia Beard, R T and J C Moggridge, R Huggins, D Irving, E McCall, T McLean, Nigel and Sue Foster, Dr and Mrs M E Wilson, Valerie Baker, Susan and John Douglas, GHC, Andrew Wallace)*

Free house ~ Licensee Nick Turner ~ Real ale ~ Bar food (12-3 (not Sat)) ~ Restaurant ~ (020) 7407 2495 ~ Children in restaurant ~ Open 6-8.30am weekdays, then 11-11; 12-11 Sat; 12-10.30 Sun

Old Jail

Jail Lane, Biggin Hill (first turn E off A233 S of airport and industrial estate, towards Berry's Hill and Cudham); no station near; TN16 3AX

Formerly a mainstay of RAF pilots based at nearby Biggin Hill, this interesting old pub feels so much in the heart of the countryside it's easy to forget you're only ten minutes or so away from the bustle of Croydon and Bromley. A highlight is the lovely big garden, with well spaced picnic-sets on the grass, several substantial trees, and a nicely maintained play area; it's a popular spot for families on fine weekends. Inside, several traditional beamed and low-ceilinged rooms ramble around a central servery, with the nicest parts the two cosy little areas to the right of the front entrance; divided by dark timbers, one has a very big inglenook fireplace with lots of logs and brasses, and the other has a cabinet of Battle of Britain plates (it can be smoky in here at busy times). Other parts have wartime prints and plates too, especially around the edge of the dining room, up a step beyond a second, smaller fireplace. There's also a plainer, flagstoned room; discreet fruit machine, low piped music. Greene King IPA, Harveys and Shepherd Neame Spitfire on handpump; friendly, efficient service. A standard menu takes in sandwiches (from £2.50), soup (£3.30), filled baked potatoes (from £3.50), and ploughman's (£6.45), but the food to go for is the wide choice of good, blackboard specials, which might include local sausages with mash and red onion gravy (£8.50), chicken tarragon with bacon and onion potato cake (£8.95), slow-cooked beef with new potatoes and swede mash (£9.95), roast spiced duck with parmentier potatoes and lemongrass jus (£11.95), and rib-eye steak (£12.85); they do a choice of roasts on Sundays. With nice hanging baskets in front on the narrow leafy lane, the attractive building wasn't itself part of any jail, but was a beef shop until becoming a pub in 1869. *(Recommended by GHC, N R White)*

Punch ~ Lease Richard Hards ~ Real ale ~ Bar food (12-2.30(3 Sat/Sun), 7-9.30 (not Sun evening)) ~ (01959) 572979 ~ Children welcome ~ Dogs allowed in bar ~ Open 11.30-3, 6-11 (all day Fri in summer); 11.30-11 Sat; 12-10.30 Sun

Royal Oak 🍺

Tabard Street; ⊖ ⇌ Borough; SE1 4JU

A real mix of people actively seeks out this wonderfully evocative Victorian corner house, despite it being slightly off the beaten track. The relaxed, chatty atmosphere and old-fashioned feel are part of the draw – but so is the full range of impeccably kept beers from Sussex brewer Harveys. Best-loved among these is perhaps their Sussex Best, but you'll also find their stronger Armada, as well as Mild, Pale Ale, and changing seasonal brews. The brewery transformed the pub when they took over, and painstakingly re-created the look and feel of a traditional London alehouse – so successfully that you'd never imagine it wasn't like this all along. Two busy little L-shaped rooms meander around the central wooden servery, which has a fine old clock in the middle. They're done out in a cosy, old-fashioned style: patterned rugs on the wooden floors, plates running along a delft shelf, black and white scenes or period sheet music on the red-painted walls, and an assortment of wooden tables and chairs. It almost goes without saying, but there's no music or machines. Well liked by readers, good honest bar food includes impressive doorstep sandwiches, and generously served daily specials such as vegetable hotpot (£5.50), lamb and apricot pie (£5.75), game pie (£7.25), or fillets of bass (£8.75). *(Recommended by B and M Kendall, Pete Walker, the Didler, Mike and Sue Loseby, Susan and John Douglas, Derek and Sylvia Stephenson, Tracey and Stephen Groves, C J Fletcher, C M Harnor, Sue Demont, Tim Barrow)*

Harveys ~ Tenants John Porteous, Frank Taylor ~ Real ale ~ Bar food (12-2.45 (not Sat), 6-9.15; 12-4.45 Sun) ~ (020) 7357 7173 ~ Dogs allowed in bar ~ Open 11-11; 6-11 Sat; 12-6 Sun; closed bank holidays

Victoria 🍴 ⌂ 🛏

West Temple Sheen; ⇌ Mortlake; SW14 7RT

A short stroll from Richmond Park's Sheen Gate, this once-incongruous local has been radically reworked over the last few years, and is now a stylish gastro-pub with rooms, very well regarded for its superior food and as a peaceful place to stay. The management's pedigree in some of London's most famous kitchens quickly becomes obvious, but that doesn't make it at all stuffy or self-important – in fact quite the opposite: though firmly upmarket, it still has the air of a favourite neighbourhood drop-in eating place. At lunchtimes it's popular with families, when children can enjoy the sheltered play area in the back garden while parents supervise from the charming no smoking back conservatory, but it's in the evenings that we've enjoyed it most. This last summer, the garden has been a sought-after evening refuge in the hot spells. And indoors it's particularly civilised and sophisticated then, when the huge glass room at the back seems especially stunning. Leading into that is essentially one big thoughtfully designed room, with wooden floors and armchairs, and separate-seeming areas with a fireplace, sofas, and plenty of contemporary touches. They open at 8.30 for breakfast and after that the kitchen doesn't really close, serving morning coffee, lunch, tea and cake, and finally dinner. The menu changes every day, but might include things like piquillo peppers stuffed with smoked haddock brandade and salsa verde (£6.95), serrano ham with celeriac remoulade and truffle oil (£7.95), penne with roast walnut sauce, wilted rocket and pecorino (£9.95), braised wild rabbit with red wine, bacon and mushrooms (£11.95), and grilled bass with basil mash, bouillabaisse sauce and rouille (£15.95). Their tapas plate is a popular starter (£8.95), and they have a weekend brunch menu with dishes such as pumpkin gnocchi with parmesan cream and crisp sage (£4.95 small, £6.95 large), wild boar and apple sausages with mash and onion gravy (£5.95 small, £7.95 large), and duck confit hash with a fried egg, bacon and their own herb ketchup (£7.95). The wine list is very good, with plenty by the glass (including champagne), and they have various unusual sherries and malts; also Brakspears (not cheap). Bedrooms (in a secluded annexe) are simple and smart. *(Recommended by Pat Woodward, Martin and Karen Wake, Bob and Maggie Atherton)*

Enterprise ~ Lease March Chester ~ Real ale ~ Bar food (5-9(8 Fri, Sat, Sun)) ~ Restaurant ~ (020) 8876 4238 ~ Children welcome ~ Open 11(12 Sun)-11 ~ Bedrooms: £108.50B/£108.50B

Bedroom prices normally include full English breakfast, VAT and any inclusive service charge that we know of. Prices before the '/' are for single rooms, after for two people in double or twin (B includes a private bath, S a private shower). If there is no '/', the prices are only for twin or double rooms (as far as we know there are no singles).

White Cross ♀

Water Lane; ⊖ ⇌ Richmond; TW9 1TH

At its best in summer when the busy paved garden in front is packed with people enjoying the river views, this perfectly-set Thameside pub can feel rather like a cosmopolitan seaside resort, and there's an outside bar to make the most of the sunshine (they may use plastic glasses for outside drinking). Inside, the two chatty main rooms have something of the air of the hotel this once was, with local prints and photographs, an old-fashioned wooden island servery, and a good mix of variously aged customers. Two of the three log fires have mirrors above them – unusually, the third is below a window. A bright and airy upstairs room has lots more tables, and a pretty cast-iron balcony opening off, with a splendid view down to the water, and a couple more tables and chairs. Now available all day, bar food includes sandwiches (from £3), salads (from £5.95), a variety of sausages (£7), and plenty of daily-changing specials, including a roast. Youngs Bitter, Special and seasonal beers on handpump, and a dozen or so carefully chosen wines by the glass; fruit machine, dominoes. It pays to check the tide times if you're leaving your car by the river; the water can rise rapidly, and you might return to find it marooned in a rapidly swelling pool of water; it's not unknown for the water to reach right up the steps into the bar. Boats leave from immediately outside for Kingston and Hampton Court. *(Recommended by Derek Thomas, the Didler, Barry Collett)*

Youngs ~ Managers Ian and Phyl Heggie ~ Real ale ~ Bar food (12-9.30) ~ (020) 8940 6844 ~ Children in garden area only ~ Dogs welcome ~ Open 11-12; 12-10.30 Sun; closed 25 Dec (except open 12-2)

WEST LONDON   Map 12

Anglesea Arms ⓘⓘ ♀

Wingate Road; ⊖ Ravenscourt Park; W6 0UR

This buzzing gastro-pub changed hands late last year but early reports on the new regime suggest it's absolutely business as usual, with no change to the quality of the superior food. Served in the bustling eating area at the back, the imaginative choice changes every lunchtime and evening, with the big blackboard typically including starters such as cauliflower soup (£4.50), duck liver parfait with onion marmalade and poilane toast (£5.50), sautéed squid with chickpeas, chorizo, chilli, parsley and olive oil (£6.75), and half a dozen rock oysters with shallot relish and soda bread (from £7.95), and main courses like asparagus and field mushroom risotto with mascarpone and parmesan (£8.50), spanish black pudding with mash, green beans and apple sauce (£8.95), confit duck leg with duck gizzard potato cake, carrot purée and spinach (£9.95), and fillet of gilt-head bream with rosemary and hazelnut couscous and bloody mary sauce (£11.95); good puddings like chocolate bavarois with banana and cardamom caramel (£5.25) and some unusual farmhouse cheeses (£5.95). They usually do a set menu on weekday lunchtimes (two courses £9.95, three courses £12.95). Though the dining room leads off the bar it feels quite separate, with skylights, closely packed tables, and a big modern painting along one wall; directly opposite is the kitchen, with several chefs frantically working on the meals. It's no smoking in here, and you can't book, so best to arrive early for a table, or be prepared to wait – it gets very busy after around 7.30. It feels a lot more restaurant than, say, the Eagle, though you can also eat in the bar: rather plainly decorated, but cosy in winter when the roaring fire casts long flickering shadows on the dark panelling. Neatly stacked piles of wood guard either side of the fireplace (which has a stopped clock above it), and there are some well worn green leatherette chairs and stools. Adnams Broadside, Fullers London Pride, Greene King Old Speckled Hen and Timothy Taylors Landlord on handpump, with a wide range of carefully chosen wines listed above the bar (20 served by the glass), and a good few malt whiskies. Several tables outside overlook the quiet street (not the easiest place to find a parking space). *(Recommended by Richard Siebert, the Didler, Paul A Moore)*

Enterprise ~ Lease Michael Mann and Jamie Wood ~ Real ale ~ Bar food (12.30-2.45 (3 Sat, 3.30 Sun), 7-10.30 (9.30 Sun)) ~ Restaurant ~ (020) 8749 1291 ~ Children in restaurant ~ Dogs allowed in bar ~ Open 11-11; 12-10.30 Sun; closed 24-30 Dec

Anglesea Arms 🍴

Selwood Terrace; ⊖ South Kensington; SW7 3QG

Characterful and genuinely old-fashioned, the bar of this bustling pub has something of the feel of a late Victorian local. Often very busy indeed, it's long been renowned for its enjoyably chatty, traditional atmosphere but these days the food stands out too, with a sensible choice of carefully prepared home-made meals. There's a mix of cast-iron tables on the bare wood-strip floor, panelling, and big windows with attractive swagged curtains; at one end several booths with partly glazed screens have cushioned pews and spindleback chairs. If there weren't so many people, there might be an air of slightly faded grandeur, heightened by some heavy portraits, prints of London and large brass chandeliers. On particularly busy days – when well heeled young locals are very much part of the mix – you'll need to move fast to grab a seat, but most people seem happy leaning on the central elbow tables. A good choice of real ales takes in Adnams Bitter and Broadside, Brakspears Special, Fullers London Pride, Youngs and a weekly changing guest like Hogs Back Tea; also a few bottled belgian beers, around 20 whiskies, and a varied wine list, with everything available by the glass. At lunchtime you can eat in either the bar or the no smoking dining room, down some steps, with a Victorian fireplace; the shortish menu changes every day but might include roast red pepper and tomato soup (£4.25), sandwiches with their home-made chips (from £5.95), pan-fried black pudding with mustard mash, apple sauce and crisp sage (£5.95), pork and apricot burger with grain mustard mayonnaise, battered haddock with pea purée or fettuccine with smoked sunblush tomatoes, pine nuts, olives and parmesan (£9.95), slow-braised lamb shank with roast baby onions, spring greens and rosemary (£12.95), and pan-fried veal chop on the bone with roquefort butter and roast plum tomatoes. In the evenings the menu is similar, but only available in the dining room (when there's table service, and usually much more space than upstairs), though you can usually get snacks such as mini fishcakes in the bar. It's worth booking in advance for their good all-day Sunday roasts (from £9.95). Service is friendly and helpful. In summer the place to be is the leafy front patio (with outside heaters for chillier evenings). *(Recommended by the Didler, Brian and Janet Ainscough, Revd R P Tickle, Dr and Mrs M E Wilson, Paul A Moore)*

Free house ~ Licensee Jenny Podmore ~ Real ale ~ Bar food (12-3, 6.30-10 weekdays; 12-5, 6-10(9.30 Sun) weekends) ~ Restaurant ~ (020) 7373 7960 ~ Children welcome in dining room all day, but not in bar in evenings ~ Dogs allowed in bar ~ Open 11-11; 12-10.30 Sun; closed 25-26 Dec

Atlas 🍴 🍷

Seagrave Road; ⊖ West Brompton; SW6 1RX

The innovative food at this souped-up local really is excellent, with a creative combination of flavours that results in a very satisfying, enjoyable meal. Influenced by recipes from North Africa, Turkey and Italy, the menu changes twice a day but might include things like celeriac and parsnip soup with leek, chestnuts and cream (£4.50), very good antipasti (£7.50), goats cheese and sage risotto with caramelised shallots and parmesan (£8.50), grilled tuscan sausages with fennel and black pepper, parmesan polenta, and braised sweet peppers with olives (£9.50), pan-roast marinated chicken breast with paprika, couscous salad with toasted almonds, red onions, sultanas, coriander and lime, and yoghurt and mint salsa (£11), roast saddle of lamb with garlic, rosemary, puy lentils, and tomato and red wine salsa verde (£12), and grilled tuna steak with mangetout and cucumber salad and black olive tapenade (£13); their delicious chocolate and almond cake (£4.50) is usually the only pudding, though they also have italian cheese with apple and grilled bread (£5.50). A downside is simply the place's popularity – tables are highly prized, so if you're planning a meal, arrive early, or swoop quickly. With a pleasantly bustling feel in the evenings (it's maybe not the place for a quiet dinner), the long, simple knocked-together bar has been well renovated without removing the original features; there's plenty of panelling and dark wooden wall benches, a couple of brick fireplaces, a mix of school chairs, and well spaced tables. Smart young people figure prominently in the mix, but there are plenty of locals too, as well as visitors to the Exhibition Centre at Earls Court (one of the biggest car parks is next door). Well kept Adnams Broadside, Caledonian Deuchars IPA and Fullers London Pride on handpump, and a very good, carefully chosen wine list, with plenty by the glass; big mugs of coffee; friendly service. The piped music is unusual – on various visits we've come across everything from salsa and jazz to vintage TV themes; it can be loud at times. Down at the end, by a hatch to the kitchen, is a TV (though big sports events are shown in a room upstairs). Outside is an attractively planted narrow side terrace, with an overhead awning; heaters make it comfortable even in winter. This was the first of a small group of pubs set up by two brothers; another, the Fox & Hounds, is a main entry in the South London section. *(Recommended by Joel Dobris, Robert Lester, Derek Thomas, Dr and Mrs M E Wilson, Tim Maddison)*

Free house ~ Licensees Richard and George Manners, James Gill, Toby Ellis ~ Real ale ~ Bar food (12.30-3, 7-10.30(10 Sun)) ~ (020) 7385 9129 ~ Children welcome till 7pm ~ Dogs allowed in bar ~ Open 12-11(10.30 Sun); closed 24 Dec-1 Jan, and Easter Sat/Sun

Bulls Head

Strand-on-the-Green; ≈ Kew Bridge; W4 3PQ

Very much enjoyed by readers for its Thameside setting and cosily atmospheric dark, beamed rooms, this busy Chef & Brewer pub has also impressed recently with its choice of real ales. They now have six on handpump, typically including Adnams, Bass, Charles Wells Bombardier, Greene King Old Speckled Hen, Shepherd Neame Spitfire, and maybe something more unusual like Titanic English Glory; good service from friendly uniformed staff. If you get here early enough you should be able to bag one of the highly prized tables by the little windows, with nice views past attractively planted hanging flower baskets to the river. The series of comfortably refurbished rooms rambles up and down steps, with plenty of polished dark wood and beams, and old-fashioned benches built into the simple panelling.The black-panelled alcoves make useful cubby-holes (especially snug on chilly autumn days), and there are lots of empty wine bottles dotted around. Served all day, the big menu takes in everything from good sandwiches and filled baguettes (£4.99), through fish and chips (£6.25) and beef and ale pie (£6.95), to plenty of fresh fish, delivered daily; popular Sunday roasts. Most of the pub is now no smoking. The pub can fill up fast. They do pitchers of Pimms in summer, and newspapers are laid out for customers. The original building served as Cromwell's HQ several times during the Civil War. *(Recommended by John Saville, Darren Le Poidevin, N R White, Sue Demont, Tim Barrow, Roger Thornington, Mayur Shah)*

Spirit Group ~ Manager Andy Cockram ~ Real ale ~ Bar food (12-10) ~ (020) 8994 1204 ~ Children welcome ~ Open 11-11; 12-10.30 Sun

Churchill Arms 🍴

Kensington Church Street; ⊖ Notting Hill Gate/Kensington High Street; W8 7LN

In summer every inch of the space outside this bustling old favourite is covered with colourful hanging baskets and window boxes. The wonderfully cheery atmosphere owes a lot to the genial Irish landlord, who's very much in evidence, delightedly mixing with customers as he threads his way through the evening crowds. It feels like a friendly local, and even when it's very busy (which it usually is on weekdays after work), you can quickly feel at home. One of the landlord's hobbies is collecting butterflies, so you'll see a variety of prints and books on the subject dotted around the bar. There are also countless lamps, miners' lights, horse tack, bedpans and brasses hanging from the ceiling, a couple of interesting carved figures and statuettes behind the central bar counter, prints of american presidents and lots

of Churchill memorabilia. Fullers Chiswick, ESB, London Pride and seasonal beers
on handpump, with a good choice of wines. The spacious and rather smart plant-
filled dining conservatory may be used for hatching butterflies, but is better known
for its big choice of excellent authentic thai food, such as a very good, proper thai
curry, or various rice, noodle or stir-fried dishes (all £6); it's no smoking in here.
They do food all day, with other choices including lunchtime baguettes, and a good
value Sunday roast (£6). Fruit machine, TV; they have their own cricket and
football teams. There can be quite an overspill on to the street, where there are
some chrome tables and chairs. Even early in the week this isn't really a place for a
quiet pint; it can get a bit smoky too. Look out for special events and decorations
around Christmas, Hallowe'en, St Patrick's Day and Churchill's birthday (30
November) – along with more people than you'd ever imagine could feasibly fit
inside. *(Recommended by Pete Walker, the Didler, LM, John Saville, Ian Phillips, Andy and
Jill Kassube, Mrs Hazel Rainer)*

Fullers ~ Manager Jerry O'Brien ~ Real ale ~ Bar food (12-10) ~ Restaurant ~
(020) 7727 4242 ~ Children in restaurant ~ Dogs allowed in bar ~ Open 11-11(12 Thurs-
Sat); 12-10.30 Sun; closed evening 25 Dec

Colton Arms

Greyhound Road; ⊖ Barons Court; W14 9SD

Readers visiting here invariably tell us first of all about the unprepossessing walk
from the underground, and how it led them to expect disappointment, then go on
to express astonishment that such an unspoilt little gem has survived intact. That it
has is down to the friendly, dedicated landlord who has kept it exactly the same for
the last 40 years. Like an old-fashioned country pub in town, the main U-shaped
front bar has a log fire blazing in winter, highly polished brasses, a fox's mask,
hunting crops and plates decorated with hunting scenes on the walls, and a
remarkable collection of handsomely carved 17th-c oak furniture. That room is
small enough, but the two back rooms are tiny; each has its own little serving
counter, with a bell to ring for service. Well kept Caledonian Deuchars IPA, Fullers
London Pride and Greene King Old Speckled Hen on handpump (when you pay,
note the old-fashioned brass-bound till); the food is limited to sandwiches (weekday
lunchtimes only, from £3). Pull the curtain aside for the door out to a charming
back terrace with a neat rose arbour. The pub is next to the Queens Club tennis
courts and gardens *(Recommended by Darren Le Poidevin, Ian Phillips, Tracey and
Stephen Groves, Susan and John Douglas)*

Enterprise ~ Tenants N J and J A Nunn ~ Real ale ~ Bar food (12-2 weekday lunchtimes
only) ~ No credit cards ~ (020) 7385 6956 ~ Children welcome lunchtimes only ~ Dogs
welcome ~ Open 12-3, 5.30(6.30 Sat)-11; 12-4, 7-10.30 Sun; closed evening 25 Dec,
all day 26 Dec and Easter Sat

Dove ㉕

Upper Mall; ⊖ Ravenscourt Park; W6 9TA

On good form at the moment, this famous old riverside pub has seen so many
writers, actors and artists pass through its doors over the years that a framed list on
the wall of the bar is the only way to keep up with all the names. Perhaps its best
claim to fame is that 'Rule Britannia' is said to have been composed in one of the
upstairs rooms, but it was also a favourite with Turner, who painted the view of
the Thames from the delightful back terrace. The main flagstoned area out here,
down some steps, has a verandah and some highly prized tables looking over the
low river wall to the Thames reach just above Hammersmith Bridge. There's a tiny
exclusive area up a spiral staircase, a prime spot for watching the rowing crews out
on the water. By the entrance from the quiet alley, the front bar (said to be Britain's
smallest) is cosy and traditional, with black panelling, and red leatherette cushioned
built-in wall settles and stools around dimpled copper tables; it leads to a bigger,
similarly furnished room, with old framed advertisements and photographs of the
pub. They stock the full range of Fullers beers, with ESB, London Pride and

seasonal beers on handpump, and maybe a guest like Gales HSB: no games
machines or piped music. Well liked bar food includes lunchtime sandwiches (from
£5.95), roast vegetable korma curry (£6.95), sausage and mash (£8.25), steak and
ale pie or fish and chips (£8.95), a proper ploughman's (£9.95), 8oz sirloin steak
(£10.95), and daily specials. The pub isn't quite so crowded at lunchtimes as it is in
the evenings. A plaque marks the level of the highest-ever tide in 1928.
*(Recommended by Tracey and Stephen Groves, Ian Phillips, Darren Le Poidevin, the Didler,
N R White)*

Fullers ~ Manager Nick Kiley ~ Real ale ~ Bar food (12-3, 5-9 weekdays; 12-9 Sat;
12-5 Sun) ~ (020) 8748 9474 ~ Dogs allowed in bar ~ Open 11-11; 12-10.30 Sun

Havelock Tavern 🍴 ♀
Masbro Road; ⊖ ⇄ Kensington (Olympia); W14 0LS

A disastrous fire last year saw this well regarded gastro-pub close for nine months
while it was painstakingly restored; it reopened shortly before this edition went to
press, happily much the same as before, but a little more shiny around the edges,
spanking new of course, and feeling lighter and more airy than before. It looks
rather ordinary from the outside, and it's the classy food that's very much the
centre of attention, particularly in the evenings. Changing every day, the menu
might include things like courgette, fennel and chilli soup (£4), warm leek, spinach
and goats cheese tart (£8), fillets of red mullet wrapped in parma ham with baby
spinach, green beans and salsa verde (£8.50), smoked haddock kedgeree with sweet
chilli sauce (£9), thai red beef curry (£9.50), grilled leg of lamb with spinach, roast
potatoes, peppers, aubergine, fennel and tzatziki (£9.50), and some unusual cheeses
served with apple chutney (£6); you can't book tables. Until 1932 the blue-tiled
building was two separate shops (one was a wine merchant, but no one can
remember much about the other), and it still has huge shop-front windows along
both street-facing walls. The L-shaped bar is welcoming but plain and unfussy: bare
boards, long wooden tables, a mix of chairs and stools, a few soft spotlights, and a
fireplace. A second little room with pews leads to a small paved terrace, with
benches, a tree, and wall climbers. Brakspears, Fullers London Pride and Marstons
Pedigree on handpump from the elegant modern bar counter (not cheap), and a
good range of well chosen wines, with around a dozen by the glass; mulled wine in
winter, and in May and June perhaps home-made elderflower soda. No music or
machines, but backgammon, chess, Scrabble and other board games. Plenty of
chat from the mostly smart customers – at busy times it can seem really quite noisy
(and can be a little smoky). You may have to wait for a table in the evenings (when
some dishes can run out quite quickly), but it can be quieter at lunchtimes, and in
the afternoons can have something of the feel of a civilised private club. On
weekdays, nearby parking can be limited, though restrictions stop at 5.
*(Recommended by Derek Thomas, Ian Phillips, Jack Clark, Mayur Shah, Karen and
Graham Oddey)*

Free house ~ Licensees Peter Richnell, Jonny Haughton ~ Real ale ~ Bar food (12.30-
2.30(3 Sun), 7-10(9.30 Sun)) ~ No credit cards ~ (020) 7603 5374 ~ Children welcome ~
Dogs welcome ~ Open 11-11; 12-10.30 Sun; closed 22-26 Dec

Portobello Gold ♀
Portobello Road; ⊖ Notting Hill Gate; W11 2QB

There's always something new at this unique Notting Hill stalwart – an engaging
combination of pub, hotel, restaurant and even Internet café. A typical week might
find the enterprising licensees reintroducing live music sessions, revamping the
bewildering array of menus, or changing the art or photographs on the walls
(currently showcasing the work of music photographer David Redfern). Our
favourite part is the rather exotic-seeming back dining room, with big tropical
plants, an impressive wall-to-wall mirror, comfortable wicker chairs, stained
wooden tables, and a cage of vocal canaries adding to the outdoor effect. In the old
days – when we remember this being a Hells Angels hangout – this was the pub

garden, and in summer they still open up the sliding roof. The smaller front bar has a nice old fireplace, cushioned banquettes, daily papers and, more unusually, several Internet terminals (which disappear in the evening). The atmosphere is cheerful and relaxed (at times almost bohemian), though they can get busy in the evenings. The Gold was the first place in the UK to serve oyster shooters (a shot glass with an oyster, parmesan, horseradish, crushed chillies, Tabasco and lime), and the good bar food still has something of an emphasis on oysters and seafood. The menu typically includes soup (£4.25), sandwiches (from £5), cajun jumbo shrimp (from £5.50), various salads (from £5.75; cold roast meat salad £7.95), half a dozen irish rock oysters (£6.95), cumberland sausage on parsley mash with red onion and tomato gravy or spicy lamb burger (£7.95), chicken fajitas (£8.55), fish and chips (£9.95), and puddings like chocolate and amaretti torte (£4.50). You can eat fom the seasonally changing restaurant menu too, with dishes such as aubergine and marrow parmigiana (£8.95) or roast loin of pork with black pudding and cider, apple and plum tomato sauce (£11.50), and at lunchtime they do a good value set menu, with two courses for £10 (three courses £13); also, popular Sunday roasts, children's helpings and cream teas. Opening at 10 for coffee and fresh pastries, the bar has Fullers London Pride and a changing guest like Hogs Back TEA, as well as several draught belgian beers, Thatcher's farm cider, a good selection of bottled beers from around the world and a wide range of interesting tequilas and other well sourced spirits; the wine list is particularly good (the landlady has written books on matching wine with food). They also have a cigar menu and various coffees. Polite, helpful young staff; piped music, TV, chess and backgammon. There are one or two tables and chairs on the pretty street outside, which, like the pub, is named in recognition of the 1769 battle of Portobello, fought over control of the lucrative gold route to Panama. A lively stall is set up outside during the Notting Hill Carnival. Parking nearby is metered; it's not always easy to find a space. The price we quote for bedrooms is for the cheapest; all rooms have free Internet access, and there's a spacious apartment with rooftop terrace (and putting green). *(Recommended by Ian Phillips, Stephen R Holman, John Saville, Brian and Janet Ainscough)*

Unique (Enterprise) ~ Lease Michael Bell and Linda Johnson-Bell ~ Real ale ~ Bar food (all day; till 9.30 Sun) ~ Restaurant ~ (020) 7460 4910 ~ Children welcome ~ Dogs allowed in bar ~ Live music Sun 6-8 ~ Open 10am (9 Sat)-midnight (12.30 Fri/Sat); 10-11 Sun; closed 25-31 Dec, except to residents ~ Bedrooms: £60S/£65S

Warrington ♀ ◀ £
Warrington Crescent; ⊖ Maida Vale; W9 1EH

The main bar of this striking late Victorian gin palace is well worth a look for its opulent art nouveau décor, with a highlight the splendid marble and mahogany bar counter, topped by an extraordinary structure that's rather like a cross between a carousel and a ship's hull, with cherubs thrown in for good measure. The drawings of nubile young women here and above a row of mirrors on the opposite wall are later additions, very much in keeping with the overall style, and hinting at the days when the building's trade was rather less respectable than it is today. Throughout are elaborately patterned tiles, ceilings and stained glass, and a remarkable number of big lamps and original light fittings; there's a small coal fire, two exquisitely tiled pillars, and high ceiling fans for summer. At the end a particularly comfortable area has tables around a long curved cushioned wall seat, and alcoves with elegant light fittings in the shape of dancers. It's very much a bustling local, with a real buzz of conversation from the broad mix of customers; some areas can get smoky at times. There's a similar but simpler public bar, with darts and a big-screen TV for sports. Caledonian Deuchars IPA, Fullers ESB and London Pride, Youngs Special and a changing guest on handpump; 24 wines are available by the glass, and the bottles are displayed around the top of the bar counter. Service is friendly and efficient. Though it looks thoroughly english, the upstairs evening restaurant is a very good value thai, with main courses at around £6, and specials rarely more than £7.85; it's no smoking in here. The same food is available in the bar at lunchtimes. No music, but quite a few games machines. There are plenty of picnic sets to the side of the pub, overlooking the street, with heaters for winter. *(Recommended by Rob Razzell, Russell Lewin, Tracey and Stephen Groves, Alan and Carolin Tidbury)*

Free house ~ Licensee John Brandon ~ Real ale ~ Bar food (12-2.30 (1-3.30 Sat/Sun), 6-10.30) ~ Restaurant (6-10.30) ~ (020) 7286 2929 ~ Dogs allowed in bar ~ Open 11-11(midnight Fri/Sat); 12-10.30 Sun

White Horse ♀ ◖

Parsons Green; ⊖ Parsons Green; SW6 4UL

They take their drinks very seriously at this particularly well run pub, and real thought is put into the expertly selected range. They're keen to encourage people to match the right drink to their food (and to select beers as they might wines), so every item on the menu, whether it be scrambled egg or raspberry tart, has a suggested accompaniment listed beside it, perhaps a wine, perhaps a bottled beer. Looking very smart these days, the stylishly modernised U-shaped bar has plenty of sofas, wooden tables, huge windows with slatted wooden blinds, and winter coal and log fires, one in an elegant marble fireplace. The pub is usually busy (and can feel crowded at times), but there are enough smiling, helpful staff behind the solid panelled central servery to ensure you'll rarely have to wait too long to be served. Six perfectly kept real ales might include Adnams Broadside, Gales HSB, Harveys Sussex, O'Hanlons Wheat Beer, Oakham JHB and Roosters Yankee; they also have five well chosen draught beers from overseas such as Sierra Nevada Pale Ale or Alaskan Smoked Porter, as well as 15 Trappist beers, around 100 other foreign bottled beers, 15 or so malt whiskies and a constantly expanding range of good, interesting and reasonably priced wines. The good bar food might include sandwiches, pea and mint risotto (£5.75 starter, £9.75 main), salmon and dill fishcake or pork, leek and pepper sausages with mash and onion jam (£9.25), steak and porter pie or moroccan fish stew (£10.25), lamb burger with mint yoghurt and pickled aubergine (£11.75), and prime scotch beef rib-eye steak (£13.75). At weekends they do a good brunch menu, and in winter they do a popular Sunday lunch. The back and upstairs restaurants are no smoking. On summer evenings the front terrace overlooking the green has something of a continental feel, with crowds of people drinking al fresco; in spring and summer you'll usually find an excellent barbecue out here Fri-Sun, when the pub's appeal to smart young people is more apparent than ever. They have quarterly beer festivals, often spotlighting regional breweries. *(Recommended by LM, the Didler, Martin and Karen Wake, Ian Phillips, Sue Demont, Tim Barrow, Tracey and Stephen Groves)*

Mitchells & Butlers ~ Manager Mark Dorber ~ Real ale ~ Bar food (12(11 Sat/Sun)-10.30) ~ Restaurant ~ (020) 7736 2115 ~ Children welcome ~ Dogs allowed in bar ~ Open 11-midnight (12.30 Sat); 11-11 Sun; closed 25 Dec

Windsor Castle

Campden Hill Road; ⊖ Holland Park/Notting Hill Gate; W8 7AR

So impressive is the wealth of dark oak furnishings inside this warmly characterful Victorian pub that one reader likens it to being below deck on an old wooden galleon. The series of tiny unspoilt rooms with their time-smoked ceilings oozes genuine atmosphere – each has its own entrance from the street, but it's much more fun trying to navigate through the minuscule doors between them inside. Finding people you've arranged to meet can be quite a challenge; more often than not they'll be hidden behind the high backs of the sturdy built-in elm benches. A cosy pre-war-style dining room opens off, and soft lighting and a coal-effect fire add to the old-fashioned charm. It's especially cosy in winter, but the pub's appeal is just as strong in summer, thanks to the big, tree-shaped garden behind, easily one of the best pub gardens in London. It's always busy out here when the sun's shining, but there's quite a secluded feel thanks to the high ivy-covered sheltering walls. The garden has its own bar in summer, as well as heaters for cooler days, and lots of tables and chairs on the flagstones. Served pretty much all day, bar food includes ciabattas (from £5.30), steamed mussels in white wine and cream (£5.90), chicken caesar salad (£7.80), beefburger with home-cut chips and red onion relish (£8), fish and chips or various sausages with mash, sweet red onions and gravy (£9), and specials like roast bass with spicy couscous (£13.50); they do a choice of roasts on Sunday (£9.95), when the range of other dishes may be more limited. Adnams Broadside, Fullers London Pride, Timothy Taylors Landlord and maybe a guest like Smiles Sunchaser on handpump, decent house wines, various malt whiskies, jugs of Pimms in summer, and perhaps mulled wine in winter; they have occasional beer festivals. No fruit machines or piped music. Usually fairly quiet at lunchtime, the pub is packed most evenings, and you'll need to move fast to bag a table; one area is no smoking. Service can be a little variable, and an evening here is rarely a cheap night out. The bones of Thomas Paine are said to be buried in the cellar, after his son sold them to the landlord to settle a beer debt. *(Recommended by Gwyn and Anne Wake, David and Sue Smith, the Didler, Ian Phillips, Mark Percy, Lesley Mayoh)*

Mitchells & Butlers ~ Manager Richard Bell ~ Real ale ~ Bar food (12-3, 5-10 weekdays, 12-10 Sat, 12-9 Sun) ~ (020) 7243 9551 ~ Dogs welcome ~ Open 12-11(10.30 Sun)

LUCKY DIP

Besides the fully inspected pubs, you might like to try these Lucky Dips recommended to us and described by readers (if you do, please send us reports: www.goodguides.co.uk).

CENTRAL LONDON

EC1

☆ *Bishops Finger* EC1A 9JR [W Smithfield, opp Bart's]: Comfortable and civilised, with big windows and close-set elegant tables on polished boards, full Shepherd Neame beer range kept particularly well, good choice of wines by the glass, several ports and champagnes, decent coffee, daily papers, lunchtime food from open kitchen inc sandwiches, speciality sausages and steaks, friendly service, more room upstairs; big-screen TV; children welcome, a couple of tables outside, open all day, cl wknds *(Michael Dandy, LYM, Ian Phillips)*

Butchers Hook & Cleaver EC1A 9DY [W Smithfield]: Attractive bank conversion, now a Fullers Ale & Pie House, their full ale range, good value food from nibbles and baguettes up, wkdy breakfast from 7.30am, friendly staff, relaxed atmosphere, nice mix of chairs inc some button-back leather armchairs, wrought-iron spiral stairs to pleasant mezzanine with waitress service; big-screen sports TV; open all day *(Michael Dandy, BB)*

☆ *Hand & Shears* EC1A 7JA [Middle St]: Traditional Smithfield pub dating from 16th c, three rooms around central servery, bustling at lunchtime, quiet evenings, Courage Best and Directors and Theakstons, quick friendly service, interesting bric-a-brac, reasonably priced food from filled rolls and baked potatoes up – evening too; open all day but cl weekends *(Michael Dandy, N R White, LYM, Tracey and Stephen Groves)*

Melton Mowbray EC1N 2LE [Holborn]: Large busy pastiche of Edwardian pub with Fullers ales, good food service (Melton Mowbray pies among other dishes), lots of woodwork, etched glass, front button-back banquettes, back booths below small mezzanine gallery; opens out in summer to pavement café tables) *(Dr and Mrs M E Wilson)*

One Tun EC1N 8QS [Saffron Hill]: Unpretentious pub with good choice of real ales such as Adnams Greene King and Youngs, Thai cooks doing good value curries and stir-fries, speedy service, upstairs dining room *(John Coatsworth)*

☆ *Peasant* EC1V 4PH: Elaborate, imaginative food in strikingly furnished upstairs bistro or welcoming if rather loud downstairs bar, still with some reminders of its days as a more traditional corner house inc tiled picture of St George and Dragon, helpful service, mosaic floor, dim lighting *(Peter and Jean Hoare)*

Sekforde Arms EC1R 0HA [Sekforde St]: Small and comfortably simple corner local with friendly licensees, full Youngs beer range, wide choice of well priced standard food (busy at lunchtime), nice pictures inc Spy caricatures, upstairs restaurant, darts, cards and board games; pavement tables *(the Didler, Andy and Jill Kassube)*

Sutton Arms EC1M 6EB [Carthusian St]: Small high-ceilinged Victorian with small tables on bare boards and little décor beyond big brewery mirrors and four large busts, refurbished dining room upstairs with a few sofas, friendly staff, Adnams and Fullers London Pride and Trafalgar, good choice of wines by the glass, lunchtime sandwiches and a few basic hot dishes *(Michael Dandy, Tracey and Stephen Groves)*

EC2

☆ *Dirty Dicks* EC2M 4NR [Bishopsgate]: Busy re-creation of traditional City tavern with booths and barrel tables in bare-boards bar, interesting old prints inc one of Nathaniel Bentley the weird original Dirty Dick, Youngs full beer range, enjoyable food inc open sandwiches, baguettes and reasonably priced hot dishes, pleasant service, cellar wine bar with wine racks overhead in brick barrel-vaulted ceiling, further upstairs area too; games machines and TV, but otherwise loads of character – fun for foreign visitors; cl wknds *(LYM, Ian Phillips, the Didler, Tracey and Stephen Groves)*

☆ *Fox* EC2A 4LB [Paul St]: Good enterprising fixed-price lunches in intimate upstairs dining room with friendly helpful service and appealing canopied terrace, bustling downstairs bare-boards bar with Charles Wells Bombardier, decent wines, good coffee; may be piped jazz; dogs welcome, open all day, cl wknds *(LYM, Richard Siebert)*

☆ *Hamilton Hall* EC2M 7PY [Bishopsgate; also entrance from L'pool St station]: Big busy Wetherspoons with flamboyant Victorian baroque décor, plaster nudes and fruit mouldings, chandeliers, mirrors, good-sized no smoking mezzanine, comfortable groups of seats, reliable food all day, lots of real ales inc interesting guest beers, decent wines and coffee, good prices; silenced machines, can get crowded; tables outside, open all day *(LYM, Ian Phillips)*

EC3
East India Arms EC3M 4BR [Fenchurch St]: Archetypal City pub, real ales inc Fullers London Pride and Youngs, good service even with the lunchtime crowds, bar stools and standing room *(Ian Phillips)*

Elephant EC3M 5BA [Fenchurch St]: Small ground floor bar, larger basement lounge, full range of Youngs beers, good sandwiches and other lunchtime food, friendly efficient staff *(Ian Phillips)*

Jamaica Wine House EC3V 9DS [St Michael's Alley, Cornhill]: In a warren of small alleys, refurbished in traditional style with booths, benches and bare boards, Courage and Charles Wells Bombardier, wide choice of wines, limited well cooked and presented food in downstairs lunchtime dining area, friendly helpful service; can get smoky when crowded, quietens after 8; cl wknds *(N R White, John Saville, Ian Phillips)*

☆ *Lamb* EC3V 1LR [Grand Ave, Leadenhall Mkt]: Well run traditional stand-up bar, bustling atmosphere (can get very busy – full of sharp lads from Essex who have made it in the City), Youngs ales, friendly service, engraved glass, plenty of ledges and shelves, spiral stairs up to small light and airy no smoking carpeted gallery overlooking market's central crossing, corner servery doing good hot carvery rolls; also basement bar with shiny wall tiling and own entrance *(Ian Phillips, N R White, Dr and Mrs M E Wilson, Derek Thomas)*

Swan EC3V 1LY [Ship Tavern Passage, off Gracechurch St]: Bustling narrow flagstoned bar, larger carpeted upstairs room, neatly kept Victorian panelled décor, friendly chatty landlord, generous lunchtime sandwiches, particularly well kept Fullers and perhaps a guest beer; quiet corner TV, can get packed early wkdy evenings; usually closes at 9, cl wknds *(N R White, Tracey and Stephen Groves)*

EC4
Centre Page EC4V 5BH [Knightrider St]: Row of window booths in narrow entrance room, more space beyond, Dickensian style and subdued lighting, pleasant efficient staff, simple appetising menu, well kept Fullers London Pride and Marstons Pedigree, good tea; piped music *(N R White, Tim and Ann Newell)*

Old Bell EC4Y 1DH [Fleet St, nr Ludgate Circus]: 17th-c traditional tavern backing on to St Brides (the wedding-cake church); heavy black beams, brass-topped tables, stained-glass bow window, good changing choice of real ales from island servery, friendly service, good value standard food, coal fire, lively atmosphere, some tables tucked away to give a sense of privacy; can get smoky when crowded *(BB, the Didler, N R White)*

Punch EC4Y 1DE [Fleet St]: Newly refurbished, with eclectic international mix of styles, colourful cushions and modern tables alongside Victorian features such as superb tiled entrance with mirrored lobby, pleasant informal atmosphere, Timothy Taylors Landlord, good choice of wines by the glass, home-made lemonade, bar nibbles, good service by friendly young staff, very wide choice of fresh food from lunchtime roasts, casseroles and lots of salads to all sorts of foreign dishes; children welcome, open all day *(N R White)*

Samuel Pepys EC4V 3PT [Brooks Wharf; Stew St, off Upper Thames St]: Enjoyable food in recently stylishly refurbished two-level pub with interesting views over Thames to Globe Theatre and Tate Modern, especially from its two breezy balconies, friendly helpful staff *(BB, Christine Brown)*

Williamsons EC4M 9EH [Groveland Court, off Bow Lane]: Well priced food all day (very busy wkdy lunchtimes) and Fullers London Pride, Shepherd Neame Spitfire, Charles Wells Bombardier and Youngs in two-bar pub with interesting Jacobean décor, well rebuilt in 1960s using old timbers; third bar downstairs, open all day *(Anthony Double)*

SW1
☆ *Buckingham Arms* SW1H 9EU [Petty France]: Well run 18th-c local, chatty and welcoming, with elegant mirrors and woodwork, unusual long side corridor fitted out with elbow ledge for drinkers (and SkyTV for motor sports), Youngs ales, good value food lunchtime and evening, reasonable prices, good service even when busy, friendly pub dog, no music; dogs welcome, handy for Buckingham Palace, Westminster Abbey and St James's Park, open all day *(LYM, N R White, the Didler, Mike Tucker)*

Cardinal SW1P 1DN [Francis St]: Well priced Sam Smiths beers from big horseshoe bar, good value back food counter with plenty of space for eating, good upstairs area; big-screen sports TV; behind Westminster cathedral *(Mark Doughty)*

Cask & Glass SW1E 5HN [Palace St]: Inviting panelled room overflowing into street in summer – colourful flowers then; good range of Shepherd Neame ales, friendly staff and chatty local atmosphere, good value lunchtime sandwiches, old prints and model aircraft; handy for Queen's Gallery *(N R White, R T and J C Moggridge)*

☆ **Fox & Hounds** SW1W 8HR [Passmore St/Graham Terr]: Small cosy bar with real ales such as Adnams, Bass, Greene King IPA and Harveys, bar food, friendly staff, wall benches, big hunting prints, old sepia photographs of pubs and customers, some toby jugs, hanging plants under attractive skylight in back room, coal-effect gas fire and organ; can be very busy Fri night, quieter wkdy lunchtimes *(the Didler)*

Gallery SW1V 3AS [Lupus St, opp Pimlico tube station]: Light and airy atrium one end with stairs up to gallery, attractive prints and bric-a-brac, no smoking area, Bass, Courage Best, Greene King Abbot and Shepherd Neame Spitfire, reliable varied food; disabled access and lavatories (conventional ones down stairs) *(Dr and Mrs M E Wilson, Mark Doughty)*

Golden Lion SW1Y 6QY [King St]: Imposing bow-fronted Victorian pub opp Christies auction rooms, Adnams Broadside, Fullers London Pride and Youngs from decorative servery, decent wines by the glass, good value food, friendly atmosphere, ornate décor; shame about the piped music; seats and tables usually available in passageway alongside or upstairs theatre bar *(Tracey and Stephen Groves, Craig Turnbull)*

Jugged Hare SW1V 1DX [Vauxhall Bridge Rd/Rochester Row]: Popular Fullers Ale & Pie pub in impressive former colonnaded bank with balustraded balcony, chandelier, prints and busts; their real ales, friendly efficient service, reasonably priced traditional food from sandwiches up, no smoking back area; fruit machine, unobtrusive piped music; open all day *(BB, the Didler, Mark Doughty, Andy and Jill Kassube)*

☆ **Morpeth Arms** SW1P 4RW [Millbank]: Roomy and comfortable nicely preserved Victorian pub facing MI6 HQ across River Thames, some etched and cut glass, old books and prints, photographs, earthenware jars and bottles, full Youngs beer range, good choice of reasonably priced food from sandwiches up, good choice of wines, welcoming landlord and staff, good service even when it's packed at lunchtime (useful overflow upstairs), quieter evenings; seats outside (a lot of traffic), handy for Tate Britain *(BB, Dr and Mrs M E Wilson, the Didler, R T and J C Moggridge, John Saville, Mike Gorton, Mark Doughty)*

Orange Brewery SW1W 8NE [Pimlico Rd]: Friendly panelled bar, all-day cheap food inc various pies and good sausages, Fullers London Pride and Greene King Abbot, no smoking eating area; some seats outside *(LYM, Sue Demont, Tim Barrow, Roger Thornington)*

Red Lion SW1Y 6PP [Crown Passage, behind St James's St]: Thriving early Victorian local tucked down narrow passage nr St James's Palace, dark oak panelling, settles and leaded lights, real ales such as Adnams and Courage Directors, busy lunchtime (popular sandwiches), room upstairs *(Dr and Mrs M E Wilson, BB)*

Red Lion SW1A 2NH [Parliament St]: Congenial pub by Houses of Parliament, used by Foreign Office staff and MPs – has Division Bell; parliamentary cartoons and prints, decent wines by the glass, real ales, good range of food from good panini up, efficient staff who welcome visitors, also cellar bar and small narrow no smoking upstairs dining room *(Dr and Mrs M E Wilson, John and Gloria Isaacs)*

Royal Oak SW1P 4BZ [Regency St/Rutherford St]: Compact one-bar Youngs pub with good choice of wines by the glass as well as their real ales, good value home-made wkdy lunchtime bar food, friendly mainly antipodean staff; handy for Vincent Sq *(David Sizer, Mark Doughty)*

Sanctuary House SW1H 9LA [Tothill St]: Recently done up pub/hotel with plenty of room, ornate exterior scrollwork, nice stools and armchairs, raised and balustraded back area with monkish mural, Fullers ales, cheerful helpful staff; piped music; children welcome, 30 or more bedrooms, open all day *(Dr and Mrs M E Wilson)*

☆ **St Stephens Tavern** SW1A 2JR [Parliament St]: Elegantly refurbished two-bar Victorian pub opp Houses of Parliament and Big Ben, lofty ceilings with brass chandeliers, tall windows with etched glass and swagged gold curtains, gleaming mahogany, four Badger ales from handsome counter with pedestal lamps, pleasant staff, usual food, Division Bell for MPs; open all day *(Dr and Mrs M E Wilson, N R White, BB)*

Talbot SW1X 7AL [Little Chester St]: Good range of beers, friendly management *(B J Harding)*

Three Crowns SW1Y 6HD [Babmaes St]: Smart and cheerful, comfortable armchairs, button-back settees and bentwood chairs, dark oak panelling and ceiling, friendly staff, five real ales such as Adnams, Courage and Charles Wells Bombardier *(Dr and Mrs M E Wilson)*

Wetherspoons SW1V 1JT [Victoria Station]: Cheap changing ales inc interesting guest beers, wide choice of reasonably priced food all day, decent wines, prompt friendly service; glass-walled upper level and tables outside overlooking the main concourse and platform indicators *(Sue Demont, Tim Barrow)*

White Swan SW1V 2SA [Vauxhall Bridge Rd]: Roomy T&J Bernard pub handy for the Tate, good value set menu, good choice of wines by the glass and range of beers, no smoking area *(BB, Mark Doughty)*

Wilton Arms SW1X 8ED [Kinnerton St]: Pleasant civilised local with good choice of reasonably priced food, unusual real ales, good friendly service even when busy; back conservatory, open all day *(Russell Lewin, BB)*

SW3

Hour Glass SW3 2DY [Brompton Rd]: Small well run pub handy for V&A and other nearby museums, Fullers London Pride, freshly squeezed fruit juice, good value food (not Sun), welcoming landlady and quick young staff; sports TV, can get a bit smoky; pavement picnic-sets *(LM)*

☆ *Pigs Ear* SW3 5BS [Old Church St]: Former Front Page, now civilised gastro-pub, interesting food with flashes of real talent, good choice of wines by the glass inc champagne, Uley Pigs Ear ale, good coffee and service, solid wooden furnishings, white-painted panelling, huge windows and big ceiling fans for airy feel *(LYM, Bob and Maggie Atherton)*

W1

☆ *Audley* W1K 2RX [Mount St]: Classic Mayfair pub, classy and relaxed, with opulent red plush, mahogany panelling and engraved glass, chandelier and clock hanging in lovely carved wood bracket from ornately corniced ceiling, good choice of real ales from long polished bar, friendly efficient service, good standard food (reasonably priced for the area) and service, good coffee, upstairs panelled dining room, large no smoking area; pavement tables, open all day *(Tracey and Stephen Groves, N R White, LYM, Catherine and Richard Preston, Kevin Blake)*

Barley Mow W1U 6QW [Dorset St]: Chatty 18th-c pub, its small basic front bar made unusual by the three swiftly-bagged 19th-c cubicles opening on to serving counter (where poor farmers pawned their watches to the landlord in privacy); Adnams Broadside, Greene King IPA, Marstons Pedigree and Charles Wells Bombardier, all-day panini, good value lunchtime two-for-one offers, wooden floors and panelled walls, old pictures, tiny back parlour; can get rather smoky, piped music, TV; pavement café tables *(Tracey and Stephen Groves, BB, the Didler, Dr and Mrs M E Wilson, Nick Holding, Sue Demont, Tim Barrow)*

☆ *Clachan* W1B 5QH [Kingly St]: Ornate plaster ceiling supported by two large fluted and decorated pillars, comfortable screened leather banquettes, smaller drinking alcove up three or four steps, Adnams, Fullers London Pride, Timothy Taylors Landlord and Charles Wells Bombardier from handsome counter, good service, decent food from sandwiches up; can get busy, but very relaxed in afternoons *(PL, BB, Sue Demont, Tim Barrow)*

Cock W1W 8QE [Great Portland St]: Big corner local with enormous lamps over picnic-sets outside, florid Victorian/Edwardian décor with handsome wood and plasterwork, some cut and etched glass, high tiled ceiling and mosaic floor, velvet curtains, coal-effect gas fire, cheap Sam Smiths OB from all four handpumps, popular food (not Fri-Sun evenings) in upstairs lounge with two more coal-effect gas fires, ploughman's downstairs too 12-6, friendly efficient service *(the Didler, Nick Holding, Ian Phillips)*

Dover Castle W1G 7EQ [Weymouth Mews]: Comfortably old-fashioned and well worn in, with dark panelling, old prints and plenty of bric-a-brac, charming back snug, cheap Sam Smiths OB, chatty landlord, good range of bar food inc substantial all-day breakfast *(Angus Lyon, Nick Holding, John and Gloria Isaacs)*

Fitzroy W1T 2LY [Charlotte St]: Traditional pub with grand mahogany servery, maroon leather and handsome frosted glass and mirrors, photographs of customers Augustus John, Dylan Thomas and the young Richard Attenborough, George Orwell's NUJ card and so forth, quieter carpeted downstairs bar with white-painted brickwork, wooden settles, a couple of snugs and occasional poetry and other readings, low-priced Sam Smiths OB, good value food inc filled baguettes, expert friendly staff; may be piped music; plenty of tables out under cocktail parasols, popular in summer *(Rob Razzell)*

Fullers Ale Lodge W1X 9HA [Avery Row]: Friendly barman who cares for his beers (full Fullers range), basic woody chalet/coffee house setup, nice high chairs by window-side table; cl Sun *(Tracey and Stephen Groves)*

Goat W1S 4RP [Albemarle St]: Handsome and bustling Edwardian local, plushly carpeted and mirrored, with four real ales *(Tracey and Stephen Groves)*

☆ *Golden Eagle* W1U 2NY [Marylebone Lane]: Well updated Victorian pub with good St Austell ales from elegant curving bar with plenty of bar stools, relaxing perimeter seating, friendly barman, lunchtime pasties, blue and yellow décor, fresh flowers; popular informal piano singalong Thurs and Fri *(Tracey and Stephen Groves, Tim Maddison)*

King & Queen W1W 6DL [Foley St]: Small friendly corner pub now run by previous long-serving landlord's son and daughter, real ales such as Adnams, St Austell Tribute and Charles Wells Bombardier, decent wines and enthusiast's spirits range, enjoyable wkdy lunchtime food inc fresh sandwiches and pubby hot dishes with good chunky chips, reasonable prices; open all day *(Tony Galcius)*

Red Lion W1B 5PR [Kingly St]: Narrow rather dark front bar with deep leather banquettes, back bar with darts, well kept low-priced Sam Smiths, bargain simple lunchtime food from baguettes up in comfortable upstairs lounge *(Ian Phillips, Peter Dandy, BB)*

St Georges Hotel W1B 2QS [take express lift in far corner of hotel lobby]: By no means a pub, but the 15th-floor bar is a most civilised place for a drink with a breathtaking view – worth the extra cost; good choice of wines by the glass and cocktails, efficiently served, restaurant, bedrooms; open all day, best visited at twilight to watch the lights coming on *(BB, Sue Demont, Tim Barrow)*

Stags Head W1W 6XW [New Cavendish St]: 1930s-style décor, Courage and Fullers London Pride, friendly staff, decent bar food; TV for football *(Angus Lyon)*

W2

Archery Tavern W2 2SD [Bathurst St]: This comfortable old pub beside the stables, much enjoyed by readers and a popular main entry, closed early in 2006 and was still for sale as we went to press in the summer; news please *(LYM)*

Kings Head W2 4AH [Moscow Rd]: Large open-plan T&J Bernard pub, bright and cheery, with their usual no-nonsense generous well priced food, prompt helpful service, good choice of real ales, dark panelled dado and lots of old London pictures, *(Gwyn and Anne Wake)*

Mad Bishop & Bear W2 1HB [Paddington Stn]: Up escalators from concourse, well used bar that must need refurbishment more often than its accountants would like, full Fullers ale range and a guest beer from long counter, good wine choice, friendly neat staff, wide choice of good value food from breakfast (7.30 on) and sandwiches to Sun roasts, city-pub décor in cream and pastels, ornate plasterwork, etched mirrors and fancy lamps inc big brass chandeliers, parquet, tiles and carpet, booths with leather banquettes, lots of wood and prints, big no smoking area, train departures screen; soft piped music, fruit machine; open all day, tables out overlooking concourse *(Dr and Mrs A K Clarke, Pete Walker, BB, Dr and Mrs M E Wilson, Roger Huggins)*

☆ *Victoria* W2 2NH [Strathearn Pl]: Interesting and well preserved corner local, lots of Victorian pictures and memorabilia, cast-iron fireplaces, wonderful gilded mirrors and mahogany panelling, brass mock-gas lamps above horseshoe bar, bare boards and banquettes, relaxed atmosphere, friendly attentive service, full Fullers ale range, good choice of wines by the glass, well priced food counter; upstairs has leather club chairs in small library/snug (and, mostly used for private functions now, replica of Gaiety Theatre bar, all gilt and red plush); quiet piped music, TV (off unless you ask); pavement picnic-sets, open all day *(LYM, Sue Demont, Tim Barrow)*

WC1

Calthorpe Arms WC1X 8JR [Grays Inn Rd]: Relaxed and civilised corner pub with plush wall seats, Youngs beers, big helpings of popular food upstairs lunchtime and evening, good staff under friendly long-serving landlord; nice pavement tables, open all day *(the Didler)*

Dolphin WC1R 4PF [Red Lion St]: Small and cottagey, high stools and wide shelves around the walls, old photographs, horsebrasses, hanging copper pots and pans and so forth inside, simple wkdy lunchtime food, and real ales such as Bass, Boddingtons, Brakspears and Fullers London Pride; seats and flower-filled window boxes outside, open all day wkdys, plus Sat lunchtime *(the Didler)*

Mabels WC1H 9AZ [just off Euston Rd]: Cosy open-plan pub with reasonably priced food from sandwiches and baguettes up, Shepherd Neame ales, good wine choice, friendly staff; pavement tables, open all day *(C J Fletcher)*

Penderels Oak WC1V 7HJ [High Holborn]: Vast Wetherspoons pub with their usual food, but otherwise quite distinctive, with attractive décor and woodwork, lots of books, pew seating around central tables, no smoking area, huge choice of real ales at sensible prices, charming staff; open all day *(John Coatsworth)*

Plough WC1A 1LH [Museum St/Little Russell St]: Neatly kept and welcoming two-bar Bloomsbury local with Adnams, Fullers London Pride, Charles Wells Bombardier and Youngs, upstairs no smoking room with ploughman's and simple reasonably priced hot food; tables outside *(Stephen R Holman, Ian Phillips)*

Rugby WC1N 3ES [Great James St]: Sizeable corner pub with Shepherd Neame ales inc their seasonal beer from central servery, decent usual food, good service, darts, appropriate photographs; tables on pleasant terrace *(the Didler)*

WC2

☆ *Chandos* WC2N 4ER [St Martins Lane]: Busy downstairs bare-boards bar with snug cubicles, lots of theatre memorabilia on stairs up to more comfortable lounge with opera photographs, low wooden tables, panelling, leather sofas, orange, red and yellow leaded windows; cheap Sam Smiths OB, prompt cheerful service, generous reasonably priced food from sandwiches to Sun roasts, air conditioning, darts and pinball; can get packed early evening, piped music and games machines; note the automaton on the roof (working 10-2 and 4-9); children upstairs till 6, open all day from 9 (for breakfast) *(Susan and Nigel Wilson, LYM, Craig Turnbull, Bruce Bird, GHC)*

Cheshire Cheese WC2R 3LD [Little Essex St/Milford Lane]: Small cosy panelled pub dating from 17th c, leaded bow windows, tankards hanging from beams, high-backed settles, friendly staff, thriving local atmosphere (can get smoky), cheap food, Courage, Charles Wells Bombardier and guest beers, decorative butter dishes, basement overflow; piped music; cl wknds *(N R White)*

Coach & Horses WC2E 7BD [Wellington St]: Small irish pub with imported Dublin Guinness (at a price) from old-fashioned copper-topped bar, Fullers London Pride and Marstons Pedigree, lots of whiskeys, good lunchtime hot roast beef baps, irish sports mementoes and cartoons; can get crowded, handy for Royal Opera House *(John and Gloria Isaacs, Ian Phillips, the Didler, Giles and Annie Francis)*

Coal Hole WC2R 0DW [Strand]: Pleasant and comfortable, softly lit and relaxed no smoking downstairs dining bar with wall reliefs, mock-baronial high ceiling and raised back balcony, chatty front bar (can get crowded and smoky), good range of beers, decent house wine, well priced sandwiches, baked potatoes, good sausages and mash etc *(BB, N R White, GHC)*

Cove WC2E 8HB [Piazza, Covent Garden]: Cornish-style nautical-theme bar up steep stairs, good pasties from shop below, Skinners Cornish Knocker and Betty Stogs and St Austell HSD and Tribute, wood and flagstones; small, may be crowded; seats out on balcony overlooking cobbled piazza with its entertainers *(Meg and Colin Hamilton, Catherine Pitt)*

☆ **Cross Keys** WC2H 9EB [Endell St/Betterton St]: Relaxed and chatty retreat, masses of photographs and posters inc Beatles memorabilia, brassware and tasteful bric-a-brac on dark dim-lit walls, bargain food inc impressive range of lunchtime sandwiches and a few hot dishes, Courage Best and guests such as Charles Wells Bombardier and Youngs, decent wines by the glass, quick friendly service even at busy times; small upstairs bar, often used for functions; fruit machine, gents' down stairs; picnic-sets out on cobbles tucked behind a little group of trees, pretty flower tubs and hanging baskets, open all day *(LYM, the Didler, David Crook, Sue Demont, Tim Barrow, Ian Phillips)*

Marquis of Granby WC2N 4HS [Chandos Pl]: Long narrow pub with high window stools overlooking street, Adnams, Fullers London Pride and Greene King IPA, reasonably priced pub food, daily papers; open all day *(the Didler, Ian Phillips)*

☆ **Porterhouse** WC2E 7NA [Maiden Lane]: London outpost of Dublin's Porterhouse microbrewery, their interesting if pricey unpasteurised draught beers inc Porter and two Stouts (they do a comprehensive tasting tray), also their TSB real ale and a guest, lots of bottled beers, good choice of wines by the glass, reasonably priced food 12-9 from soup and open sandwiches up with some emphasis on rock oysters, shiny three-level maze of stairs, galleries and copper ducting and piping, some nice design touches, sonorous openwork clock, neatly cased bottled beer displays; piped music, irish live music, big-screen sports TV (repeated in gents'); tables on front terrace, open all day *(BB, G Coates)*

☆ **Salisbury** WC2N 4AP [St Martins Lane]: Lavish Victorian décor, gilded figurines and gleaming mahogany, theatrical sweeps of red velvet, huge sparkling mirrors and cut and etched glass, well upholstered banquettes, Courage Directors, Charles Wells Bombardier and Youngs Bitter and Special, decent house wines, friendly helpful staff, pubby food from sandwiches and ploughman's up, no smoking back room; open all day *(BB, the Didler, Mike Gorton, Susan and John Douglas, Ian Phillips, Peter Coxon, John and Gloria Isaacs)*

☆ **Sherlock Holmes** WC2N 5DB [Northumberland St; aka Northumberland Arms]: Fine collection of Holmes memorabilia, inc complete model of his apartment, also silent videos of black and white Holmes films; Greene King ales and a beer brewed for the pub, usual furnishings, sandwiches and basic main dishes and puddings served quickly from good value lunchtime food counter, friendly young staff,

upstairs restaurant; busy lunchtime, can get smoky; tables out in front *(Ross Balaam, Dr and Mrs A K Clarke, Ian Phillips, N R White, BB, John Saville)*

☆ **Ship & Shovell** WC2N 5PH [Craven Passage, off Craven St]: Four Badger real ales from hop-hung bar, decent reasonably priced food from wide range of baguettes, bloomers and ciabattas up, good friendly service, bright lighting, pleasant décor inc interesting prints, mainly naval (to support a mythical connection between this former coal-heavers' pub properly called Ship & Shovel with Sir Cloudesley Shovell the early 18th-c admiral), open fire, compact back section; TV, and can get crowded and smoky, but separate no smoking partitioned bar on opposite side of alley; open all day *(John and Gloria Isaacs, the Didler, N R White, Ian Phillips, Sue Demont, Tim Barrow, Ian and Nita Cooper)*

EAST LONDON

E1

Black Bull E1 1DE [Whitechapel Road]: Spotless and comfortable, with several Nethergate ales from handsome bar counter, friendly efficient service, green-lamp-and-dark-panelling décor, some cosy corners; big-screen TV; open all day *(Tracey and Stephen Groves)*

Captain Kidd E1W 2NE [Wapping High St]: Great Thames views from large open-plan nautical-theme pub's jutting bay windows in renovated Docklands warehouse stripped back to beams and basics, good choice of hot and cold food all day inc themed puddings, cheap Sam Smiths keg beers, obliging bow-tied staff, lively bustle; sports TV; chunky tables on roomy back waterside terrace *(N R White, Eric Robinson, Jacqueline Pratt)*

☆ **Dickens Inn** E1W 1UH [Marble Quay, St Katharines Way]: Outstanding position looking over smart docklands marina to Tower Bridge, bare boards, baulks and timbers, wide choice of enjoyable food from separate servery (or pizza/pasta upstairs, and smarter restaurant above that), real ales such as Adnams, Greene King Old Speckled Hen and Charles Wells Bombardier, decent wines by the glass, friendly prompt service; piped music, machines; popular with overseas visitors, attractive flower-filled façade, tables outside *(John Saville, GHC, the Didler, N R White, LYM, Dr and Mrs M E Wilson, Andy Trafford, Louise Bayly)*

Pride of Spitalfields E1 5LJ [Heneage St]: Convivial East End local with Fullers London Pride and changing guests such as Crouch Vale Diggers Gold from central servery, friendly staff and chatty regulars, nice lighting, interesting prints and comfortable banquettes in lounge *(Tracey and Stephen Groves)*

Shooting Star E1 7JF [Middlesex St]: Full range of Fullers beers, friendly service *(Ian Phillips)*

Town of Ramsgate E1W 2PN [Wapping High St]: Interesting old-London Thameside setting, with restricted but evocative river view from small back floodlit terrace and wooden deck; long narrow bar with squared oak panelling, real ales inc Adnams, friendly service, good choice of food inc daily specials; piped music; open all day *(BB, N R White)*

E4
Royal Forest E4 7QH [Rangers Rd (A1069)]: Large recently refurbished timbered Brewers Fayre backing on to Epping Forest and dating partly from 17th c, friendly atmosphere, good value separate restaurant; play area *(Robert Lester)*

E8
LMNT E8 3NH [Queensbridge Rd, Hackney]: Opera-theme bar dominated by huge 3D sphinx head, individually posed tables (one above the bar, one in a giant urn, one rather like being on board ship), good food at sensible prices inc three-course deals (cheapest at lunchtime), mythology nudes in lavatories; open all day *(Pat and Tony Martin)*

E10
Bakers Arms E10 7EQ [Lea Bridge Rd]: Large pub recently reopened after winebar-feel refurbishment, enjoyable food; big-screen TV *(Ron Deighton)*

E11
Duke of Edinburgh E11 2EY [Nightingale Lane]: Comfortably unspoilt two-bar mock-Tudor local, warm and friendly, with bargain generous home cooking from hot sandwiches up lunchtime (not Sun) and all afternoon, Adnams and Youngs, decent wine, cheerful helpful staff, lots of prints and plates, darts, cards and shove-ha'penny; sports TV; garden tables, open all day *(Pete Baker)*

E14
Gun E14 9NS [Cold Harbour, Canary Wharf]: Trendy and very popular, well restored early 19th-c building, dark wood, white walls, bottles stacked to the ceiling, two back Thames-view bar rooms with good log fires, comfortable leather armchairs and chesterfields, Adnams Broadside, good choice of wines by the glass inc champagne, good coffees, ambitious bar food, small expensive restaurant; attractive riverside terrace with good tables and chairs and fascinating views, open all day *(Bob and Maggie Atherton)*
Narrow Street Pub & Dining Room E14 8DQ [Narrow St]: Stylish up-to-date pastel décor, leather sofas, pale floors, contemporary fireplaces, stainless bar and open kitchen doing good value upmarket bar snacks and more expensive restaurant meals, menus changing daily, friendly efficient service, interesting imported beers on tap, great Thames views; piped music may obtrude evenings; children welcome, big heaters for picnic-sets on spacious if breezy terrace, open all day *(N R White, Tracey and Stephen Groves)*

NORTH LONDON

N1
Eagle N1 7LB [Shepherdess Walk]: Batemans XXXB, Fullers London Pride and Greene King IPA, decent home-made food – very popular at lunchtime; cl till noon *(Ian Phillips)*
☆ *House* N1 2DG [Canonbury Rd]: Stylish and thriving restauranty pub with carefully crafted tables and unusual chairs around art deco central servery, sofas and daily papers by a couple of fireplaces, back partly no smoking dining area (you can eat anywhere), welcoming helpful service, good mainly modern food inc good value lunchtime and early evening set meals, wide choice of wines, pricey Adnams Broadside, quite a selection of hot drinks; piped music; children welcome, roadside terrace, open all day, cl Mon lunchtime *(Bob and Maggie Atherton, BB)*
☆ *Island Queen* N1 8HD [Noel Rd]: High-ceilinged Victorian pub handy for Camden Passage antiques area, Fullers London Pride, a guest beer, lots of imported beers and good value wines from island bar, sensibly short choice of fresh often unusual food, pleasant staff, dark wood and decorative big mirrors, upstairs room; children welcome *(John Wooll, LYM)*
Kings Head N1 1QN [Upper St]: Convivial high-ceilinged Victorian pub in good spot, Adnams, Tetleys and Youngs from horseshoe bar with fine old cash register, bar food (via ancient dumb waiter) and popular bistro, decent coffee, green décor, big windows and large mirrors, hot solid fuel fires, theatre lighting, even some pensioned-off row seats, and lots of dated theatre photographs; an oasis of calm on wkday lunchtimes, can get packed evenings and wknds; singer most nights, good theatre in back room (but hard seats there) *(BB, Tracey and Stephen Groves)*

N4
Faltering Fullback N4 3HB [Perth Rd/Ennis Rd]: Comfortable small corner pub, two softly lit bars, friendly staff and locals, Fullers London Pride, enjoyable thai food in back room; may be quiet piped music, silenced sports TV; nice outside area *(Darren Le Poidevin)*

N6
☆ *Flask* N6 6BU [Highgate West Hill]: Comfortable Georgian pub, mostly modernised but still has intriguing up-and-down layout, sash-windowed bar hatch, panelling and high-backed carved settle in snug no smoking lower area with nice log fire, quick friendly service, changing beers such as Adnams Broadside, Hop Back Summer Lightning, Moorhouses Blond Witch and Timothy Taylors Landlord and Golden Best, Addlestone's cider, several continental beers on tap, enjoyable all-day food (limited Sun) from soup and sandwiches up; Mon quiz night, very busy Sat lunchtime; well behaved children allowed, close-set picnic-sets out in attractive heated front courtyard with

barbecues, handy for strolls around Highgate village or Hampstead Heath *(Ian Phillips, LYM, Russell Lewin)*

N16

Shakespeare N16 8RY [Allen Rd]: Friendly and relaxed bare-boards local with classical figures dancing on walls, Fullers and interesting continental lagers from imposing mirrored Victorian horseshoe bar serving three linked areas; tables out on narrow side terrace *(Tracey and Stephen Groves, Tim Maddison)*

N19

St Johns N19 5QU [Junction Rd]: Well run dining pub, good value wines, good service even when busy *(Howard and Lorna Lambert)*

NW1

☆ *Engineer* NW1 8JH [Gloucester Ave]: Mix of foodies and drinkers in big informal L-shaped bar, lively and popular, with good interesting food (not cheap but worth it), enterprising wine list, Greene King IPA, handsome original woodwork and rather unusual décor, individual more ornate candlelit rooms upstairs (may need to book); children welcome, attractive garden, handy for Primrose Hill *(BB, Susan Loppert, Jane Caplan, Derek Thomas)*

Euston Flyer NW1 2RA [Euston Rd, opp British Library]: Spacious and comfortable open-plan pub opp British Library, full Fullers beer range, decent food from big well filled fresh sandwiches up, relaxed lunchtime atmosphere, plenty of light wood, tile and wood floors, smaller more private raised areas, big doors open to street in warm weather; piped music, big-screen TVs, can get packed early evening, then again later; open all day, cl 8.30 Sun *(Stephen and Jean Curtis)*

☆ *Head of Steam* NW1 2DN [Eversholt St]: Sold to Fullers in spring 2006, reopened after short refurbishment and still stocking the wide changing range of real ales from other brewers which previously made it very popular with many readers, also farm cider and lots of bottled beers; virtually part of Euston station, up stairs from bus terminus and overlooking it, with friendly helpful service, good value food, pleasantly nostalgic atmosphere, railway and other transport memorabilia, downstairs restaurant; discreet sports TV; note that there may be a change of name during 2006; open all day *(BB)*

Ice Wharf NW1 7DB [Suffolk Wharf, Jamestown Rd]: Comfortable modern Wetherspoons Lloyds No 1 with usual good value food and real ales such as Courage Best, Greene King IPA, Salopian Shropshire Gold, Shepherd Neame Spitfire and Tom Woods Shepherds Delight, plenty of lagers inc czech imports, daily papers; live music Weds, Fri and Sat; shiny french-look metal tables and chairs out on big canalside terrace by pretty little footbridge, right on the lock, extensive canal views *(Ian Phillips)*

Lock 17 NW1 8AL [11 East Yard]: Large modern two-level café-bar with some leather sofas, Tetleys and several continental lagers, good coffee and choice of wines by the glass, low-priced usual food from sandwiches to steak, daily papers; piped music, live some nights; large terrace overlooking canal *(Michael Dandy)*

Metropolitan NW1 5LA (Baker St station, Marylebone Rd]: Wetherspoons in ornate Victorian hall, big enough inside for some tranquillity (if not on Fri night), lots of tables on one side, very long bar the other, their usual good beer choice and prices, good coffee, inexpensive food, no smoking areas; open all day *(Ian Phillips, Pete Walker, Tracey and Stephen Groves)*

Queens NW1 8XD [Regents Park Rd]: Long narrow bare-boards bar, chatty and smart, with mahogany, stained glass and african art, secluded corners inc quiet enclosed area up a few steps, ornate end mirrors, Youngs Bitter and Special, lots of wines by the glass, upstairs restaurant with outdoor terrace and open kitchen doing innovative food inc asian dishes, pleasant service; dogs welcome *(Ian Phillips)*

Somerstown Coffee House NW1 1HS [Chalton St]: Recently converted to french-run dining pub, good value brasserie food in pubby atmosphere *(Sue Demont, Tim Barrow)*

Windsor Castle NW1 4SH [Park Rd, by Regents Park]: Good atmosphere in downstairs bar with Fullers and guest ales such as Adnams and Orkney Dark Island, good bar menu, stylish restaurant upstairs *(Ian Phillips)*

NW3

Duke of Hamilton NW3 1JD [New End]: Attractive Fullers local with proper hands-on landlord, good range of seating, tall Edwardian central servery, interesting prints, bric-a-brac and signed cricket bats, farm cider and malt whiskies; raised back suntrap terrace, next to New End Theatre, open all day *(the Didler, N R White, Tracey and Stephen Groves)*

NW4

Greyhound NW4 4JT [Church End]: Friendly three-bar local with Youngs ales, bar lunches, some wknd evening meals; dogs welcome, open all day *(Jean Barnett, David Lewis)*

NW5

Assembly House NW5 2TG [Kentish Town Rd/Leighton Rd]: Grandiose tall building, spacious and comfortable, with cut glass windows, stained glass coachlight dominating back bar area, Greene King Old Speckled Hen, bar food; quiet piped music, sports TV *(Giles and Annie Francis, Ian Phillips)*

NW6

Hugos NW6 6RA [Lonsdale Rd]: Trendy and popular if not cheap ochre-décor café-bar/restaurant with open front and tables out among flowers, enterprising if not cheap food using organic produce, good choice of wines by the glass *(Ian Phillips)*

NW7

☆ **Rising Sun** NW7 4EY [Marsh Lane/Highwood Hill, Mill Hill]: Beautiful wisteria-covered local dating from 17th c, nicely worn in cottagey bar and tiny low-ceilinged candlelit snug on right, lots of dark panelling, timber and coal fires, antique tables, prints and old local photographs, big plainer lounge on left, Adnams, Greene King Abbot and Youngs Special, good wines by the glass and malt whiskies, enjoyable quickly served food from sandwiches up, charming helpful staff; children welcome, picnic-sets on suntrap back terrace, good walks nearby, open all day *(John Wooll, Tracey and Stephen Groves, Ian Phillips, Tim Maddison)*

NW8

Lords Tavern NW8 8QP [St Johns Wood Rd]: Next to Lords Cricket Ground, light and airy with lots of glass and modern bare-boards décor, Fullers London Pride and Youngs, good wine choice, decent if not cheap food from sandwiches up, friendly service; tables out on decking *(BB, Michael Dandy)*

SOUTH LONDON

SE1

Anchor SE1 9EF [Bankside]: Much refurbished riverside pub, now mainly a biggish two-level open bar (also creaky little black-panelled beamed rooms and passageways, now often closed off), Courage Best and Directors, a dozen wines by the glass, jugs of Pimms, winter mulled wine, various teas and coffees, ready-made baguettes, all-day simple low-priced hot dishes upstairs, some parts no smoking; great Thames views from outside tables, summer barbecues, children in top restaurant and family room, bedrooms in Premier Lodge behind, open all day *(R E Dixon, LYM, the Didler, N R White, Michael Butler, Mrs Pat Crabb, GHC)*

Barrow Boy & Banker SE1 9QQ [Borough High St, by London Bridge station]: Smart and civilised banking hall conversion with biggish upper gallery, full Fullers beer range kept well, decent wines, good manageress and efficient young staff, sensibly priced sandwiches; right by Southwark cathedral *(Charles Gysin, Ian Phillips, Valerie Baker)*

Bridge House SE1 2UP [Tower Bridge Rd]: Relaxed upmarket Adnams bar with modern décor and sofas, their full ale range and good wine choice, reliable generous food at fair prices, friendly efficient service, no smoking downstairs dining area *(Richard Siebert, N R White)*

Charles Dickens SE1 0LH [Union St]: Bustling pub with half a dozen real ales such as Adnams Bitter and Old, Cotswold Spring Olde English Rose and Sharps Doom Bar, sensibly priced pubby food *(Ian Phillips)*

Hole in the Wall SE1 8SQ [Mepham St]: Popular no-frills haunt in railway arch virtually underneath Waterloo – rumbles and shakes with the trains; Adnams Bitter and Broadside, Battersea Bitter, Fullers London Pride and Youngs Bitter and Special, bargain basic food all day, small front bar, well worn mix of tables set well back from long bar in back room; loudish juke box, pinball and games machines; open all day, cl wknd afternoons *(Ian Phillips, LYM)*

☆ **Horniman** SE1 2HD [Hays Galleria, off Battlebridge Lane]: Spacious, bright and airy Thameside drinking hall with lots of polished wood, comfortable seating inc a few sofas, no smoking area upstairs, Adnams, Fullers London Pride and Greene King IPA, choice of teas and coffees at good prices, lunchtime bar food from soup and big sandwiches up, snacks other times, efficient service coping with large numbers after work; unobtrusive piped music; fine river views from picnic-sets outside, open all day *(N R White, LYM)*

Kings Arms SE1 8TB [Roupell St]: Proper corner local, bustling and friendly, traditional bar and lounge, both distinctive and curved, Fullers London Pride and Youngs Special, cheap and cheerful thai food at long trestle tables in back bar extension/conservatory with attractive prints, good friendly service; can get a bit smoky; open all day *(Sue Demont, Tim Barrow, Tracey and Stephen Groves, Andrew Wallace)*

☆ **Lord Clyde** SE1 1ER [Clennam St]: Unpretentious panelled L-shaped local, Adnams Best, Fullers London Pride, Greene King IPA, Shepherd Neame Spitfire and Youngs Special, good value straightforward home-made food wkdy lunchtimes and early evenings, welcoming staff, darts in small hatch-service back public bar; striking tiled façade, open all day *(Sat early evening break, cl 7 Sun)* *(Mike and Sue Loseby, Pete Baker, C J Fletcher)*

☆ **Old Thameside** SE1 9DG [Pickfords Wharf, Clink St]: Good 1980s pastiche of ancient tavern beside dock with replica *Golden Hind*, two floors, hefty beams and timbers, pews, flagstones, candles; splendid river view upstairs and from charming waterside terrace, Tetleys, Marstons Pedigree and a guest beer, friendly staff, fresh baguettes from salad bar, lunchtime hot buffet; pool down spiral stairs, piped music, service can slow when busy after work; open all day but closes at 3 at wknds *(LYM, N R White)*

Ring SE1 8HA [Blackfriars Rd/The Cut, opp Southwark tube station]: Neat, cosy and bright, with stripped pale boards, lots of boxing photographs and memorabilia, thai food, Bass and Fullers London Pride *(Mayur Shah, Ian Phillips)*

Shipwrights Arms SE1 2TF [Tooley St]: Traditional nautical-theme pub surrounded by modern development, changing real ales such as Adnams, Fullers London Pride and Charles Wells Bombardier from island counter serving four comfortable areas, bargain straightforward bar lunches, friendly efficient service; quiet piped music; handy for London Dungeon and HMS *Belfast*, open all day *(Pete Baker, GHC)*

Studio Six SE1 9PP [Gabriel's Wharf, Upper Ground]: Bustling South Bank bar/bistro in two linked timber-framed buildings, glazed all round, picnic-sets on two terraces (one heated), good well priced modern food all day inc mezze and lots of fish, good choice of belgian beers on tap, decent wines, Boddingtons, efficient service; soft piped music; children welcome, great location, open all day *(BB, Sue Demont, Tim Barrow)*

Wellington SE1 8UD [Waterloo Rd, opp Waterloo station]: Thriving late Victorian pub with large high-ceilinged linked rooms, light wood panelling, enormous stirring Battle of Waterloo murals on wall and ceiling, Fullers London Pride, Marstons Pedigree and Youngs from ornate bar counter, food all day, armchairs and sofas, attractive tables, friendly service; can get packed, noisy and smoky, piped music, pool, machines and sports TV; has had deaf people's night every other Fri, bedrooms, open all day *(Dr and Mrs M E Wilson)*

Windmill SE1 8LW [The Cut]: Big vibrant theatre-theme pub with publicity photographs, ceiling play posters, huge mirror, cast-iron framed tables on bare boards, thai food *(Mayur Shah)*

SE3

Crown SE3 0BS [Tranquil Vale]: Now a popular T&J Bernard pub, with friendly efficient service, real ales, side no smoking area; picnic-sets out by pavement *(N R White)*

Hare & Billet SE3 0QJ [Eliot Cottages, Hare & Billet Rd]: Pleasant and chatty open-plan traditional pub dating from 16th c, panelling, bare boards, good solid furniture and open fire, raised middle section, good value food inc interesting dishes and (till 7) Sun lunch, real ales such as Adnams, Bass, Fullers London Pride and Wadworths 6X, good choice of wines, view over Blackheath, no smoking area; open all day *(BB, N R White)*

SE5

Phoenix SE5 8BB [Windsor Walk, Denmark Hill]: Interesting lofty Victorian railway hall converted to civilised contemporary pub, spiral stairs to upper gallery, Adnams Broadside, Charles Wells Bombardier and Youngs, good coffee, helpful service, up-to-date food all day from ciabattas and focaccia through light dishes to enjoyable main courses and traditional puddings, wide mix of furnishings from stripped tables to sofas; piped music *(Michael Dandy, LYM, Steve Harvey)*

SE10

Ashburnham Arms SE10 8UH [Ashburnham Grove]: Friendly Shepherd Neame local with good pasta and other food (not Mon); pleasant garden with barbecues *(the Didler)*

☆ *Greenwich Union* SE10 8RT [Royal Hill]: Tied to small Meantime brewery in nearby Charlton, with their own very good interesting keg and bottled beers (sold in Sainsbury's as Taste the Difference) and a real ale, friendly helpful staff, enjoyable fresh rather upmarket food (not Sun evening) inc tapas and two-sitting Sun lunch, modern yellow décor, flagstones, some button-back leather chairs and settees, relaxing atmosphere, daily papers and pub games, may be free nibbles, small back conservatory; well reproduced piped music (live Tues and fortnightly Weds); children welcome, picnic-sets on small pleasant back terrace, open all day *(the Didler, N R White, Ben Bacon, Andrew Wallace)*

☆ *Plume of Feathers* SE10 9LZ [Park Vista]: Well run low-ceilinged Georgian local with cheerful efficient service, good value food from sandwiches, baguettes and well filled baked potatoes up inc good curries and kebabs, Adnams, Fullers London Pride and a couple of guest beers from central bar, good coffee, flame-effect fire in large attractive fireplace, lots of pictures and plates on ochre walls, back dining area; SkyTV sports; children welcome, play room across walled back garden (Greenwich Park playground nearby too), handy for Maritime Museum *(LM, Pete Baker, Esther and John Sprinkle, N R White)*

☆ *Richard I* SE10 8RT [Royal Hill]: Old-fashioned pubby atmosphere in friendly and well run traditional two-bar local with Youngs ales, food inc notable sausages, good staff, no piped music, bare boards, panelling; picnic-sets out in front, lots more in pleasant back garden with wknd barbecues – busy summer wknds and evenings *(the Didler, N R White, Humphry and Angela Crum Ewing)*

☆ *Trafalgar* SE10 9NW [Park Row]: Substantial 18th-c building with river views from big windows in four elegant rooms inc pleasant no smoking end dining room and central bar, careful colour schemes and soft lighting, oak panelling and good maritime prints, Fullers ales, good house wines, warmly welcoming and helpful young staff, good atmosphere, popular food inc speciality whitebait and some imaginative dishes; bar can get noisy and smoky when packed Fri/Sat evenings, may be piped music; handy for Maritime Museum *(Gloria Bax, S Topham, N R White, Mr and Mrs A H Young, Ian Phillips)*

SE16

☆ *Angel* SE16 4NB [Bermondsey Wall E]: Handsomely refurbished and reopened by Sam Smiths, Thameside pub with superb views to Tower Bridge and the City upstream, and the Pool of London downstream, from back lounge, upstairs restaurant, balcony supported above water by great timber piles, and from picnic-sets in garden alongside; softly lit front bars with two public areas on either side of snug, low-backed settles, old local photographs and memorabilia, etched glass and glossy varnish; food from baguettes to impressive main meals and good Sun roast, cheap Sam Smiths, kind friendly service; nr remains of Edward III's palace, interesting walks round Surrey Quays *(LYM, N R White)*

SE22

Bishop SE22 8EW [Lordship Lane]: Smart and cool new contemporary dining pub with good food and attentive staff; children and dogs welcome *(Philippe and Frances Gayton)*

Palmerston SE22 8EP [Lordship Lane]: Popular dining pub with thriving atmosphere, good food choice, prime ingredients; children and dogs welcome *(Philippe and Frances Gayton)*

SE24

Commercial SE24 0JT [Railton Rd (opp Herne Hill station)]: Roomy and relaxed, with sofas and comfortable chairs, decent beer, daily papers; SkyTV *(Giles and Annie Francis)*

Half Moon SE24 9HU [Half Moon Lane]: Edwardian local, the last in London still to keep its boxing gym upstairs; traditional layout, original cut glass; sports TV *(Giles and Annie Francis)*

SE26

☆ *Dulwich Wood House* SE26 6RS [Sydenham Hill]: Well worn in extended Youngs pub in Victorian lodge gatehouse complete with turret, decent wines, nice local atmosphere, friendly service, straightforward food cooked to order (can take a while); steps up to entrance (and stiff walk up from station), can get smoky when crowded, lots of tables in big pleasant back garden (no dogs, which are allowed inside – children aren't) with old-fashioned street lamps and barbecues, handy for Dulwich Wood walks – unless you have both dogs and children *(Dave W Holliday, R T and J C Moggridge, Pete Walker, Ian and Nita Cooper, N R White)*

SW5

O'Neills SW5 9BQ [Earls Court Rd/Old Brompton Rd]: Large open-plan pub with good value food, friendly service, irish prints, upstairs restaurant; live bands Fri *(Robert Lester)*

SW8

Canton Arms SW8 1XP [South Lambeth Rd]: Large airily modernised corner pub, cheery efficient service, Fullers London Pride and Greene King IPA, decent wines, enjoyable generous pub food, mixed elderly dining tables and chairs on stripped boards, sofa and daily papers in quiet far corner, nice wall paintings of swiss cantonal coats of arms, good architectural prints; picnic-sets out in front *(Ian Phillips)*

Grelha D'Ouro SW8 1XN [South Lambeth Rd]: Genuine portuguese feel (and customers) with portuguese beer on tap at bar with tall stools, open-fronted café section on left, toasted sandwiches and bargain authentic hot dishes, swing doors to back restaurant with fuller menu and prices *(Ian Phillips)*

SW11

Eagle SW11 6HG [Chatham Rd]: Attractive old backstreet local, real ales such as Flowers IPA, Fullers London Pride and Timothy Taylors Landlord, friendly helpful service, leather sofas in fireside corner of L-shaped bar; big-screen sports TV; back terrace with marquee, small front terrace too *(Sue Demont, Tim Barrow)*

SW12

☆ *Nightingale* SW12 8NX [Nightingale Lane]: Cosy and civilised early Victorian local, small woody front bar opening into larger back area and attractive family conservatory, half a dozen real ales from central servery, wide food choice from sandwiches to fresh fish, sensible prices, friendly staff, no smoking area; small secluded back garden *(Pete Baker, BB, Sue Demont, Tim Barrow)*

SW13

☆ *Idle Hour* SW13 0PQ [Railway Side (off White Hart Lane between Mortlake High St and Upper Richmond Rd)]: Friendly and well named tucked-away organic gastropub, very good individually cooked food at reasonable prices inc splendidly served choice of Sun roasts, good range of organic soft drinks and great wine list, nice chunky old tables on bare boards, relaxed atmosphere, daily papers and magazines, a profusion of wall clocks, comfortable sofa by small fireplace; chill-out piped music, no children; if driving, park at end of Railway Side and walk (road gets too narrow for cars); tables with candles and cocktail parasols out in small pretty yard behind, elaborate barbecues, cl wkdy lunchtimes *(Jack Crofts, BB)*

Red Lion SW13 9RU [Castelnau]: Big smartly refurbished Fullers pub with impressive Victorian woodwork, enjoyable food inc children's helpings and particularly popular Sun lunch, good choice of reasonably priced wines by the glass, good atmosphere, polite service, three separate areas; big garden with good play area and barbecue *(Peter Rozée, BB)*

SW14

Ship SW14 7QR [Thames Bank]: Comfortable pub with prompt friendly service, good range of reasonably priced generous pubby food from sandwiches up, Fullers London Pride, Greene King IPA and Charles Wells Bombardier, good Thames view from conservatory; terrace tables, not on river side *(Anon)*

SW15

☆ *Boathouse* SW15 2JX [Brewhouse Lane, Putney Wharf; [U] Putney Bridge, then cross the Thames – from the bridge you can see the pub on your left]: Very busy Thameside pub in new development, Youngs real ales from long bar in tall glazed extension from former Victorian vinegar factory, low modern seating, young chatty atmosphere, quieter panelled room on another level behind, cosy upstairs panelled no smoking restaurant with another bar (and wider range of customers); piped pop music; children in eating areas, glass-sided balcony and attractive riverside terrace, open all day *(Peter Dandy, LYM, John and Elisabeth Cox, Peter Rozée)*

Coat & Badge SW15 1NL [Lacy Rd]: Good interesting food at appealing prices, enterprising wines by the glass, real ales, perhaps a wheat beer on tap, good service and atmosphere, contemporary décor; unobtrusive piped music; pleasant well shaded terraced garden with barbecues *(K and M Graville)*

☆ **Dukes Head** SW15 1JN [Lower Richmond Rd]: Classic big Victorian pub, light and airy civilised lounge with ceiling fans, tables by window with great Thames view, Youngs ales, 20 wines by the glass, good value fresh lunchtime food, pleasant service, coal fires, smaller more basic locals' bar; plastic glasses for outside *(Peter Dandy, BB, Susan and John Douglas)*

SW16

Leigham Arms SW16 2BT [1-3 Wellfield Rd]: Friendly local just off Streatham High Rd, basic pub food, Fullers London Pride *(R T and J C Moggridge)*

SW18

Alma SW18 1TF [York Road, SW18; [U] Wandsworth Town]: The licensees who made this big pub a popular main entry for many years have now moved out to the Parrot at Forest Green in Surrey, so we are unsure how things will fare here; décor has been light and airy, with a simple mix of unpretentious furniture around brightly repainted walls, a couple of sofas, gilded mosaics of the 19th-c Battle of the Alma; Youngs ales from island bar counter, house wines, coffee, less pubby dining room overlooking ornamental garden; has been open all day; reports on new regime please *(LYM)*

Royal Standard SW18 1AL [Ballantine St]: Good-natured corner local, Greene King IPA; popular with young people *(Roger Wain-Heapy)*

SW19

Alexandra SW19 7NE [Wimbledon Hill Rd]: Busy refurbished Youngs pub with three of their ales and good choice of wines by the glass from central bar, carpeted front rooms (middle one no smoking) with games and TVs, efficient service, contemporary bare-boards dining areas behind; attractive roof terrace, tables also out in mews *(Peter Dandy, N R White)*

Crooked Billet SW19 4RQ [Wimbledon Common]: Olde-worlde pub popular for its position by common, lovely spot in summer; full Youngs range, friendly efficient service, daily papers, lots of old prints, nice furnishings inc high-backed settles on broad polished oak boards, restaurant in 16th-c barn behind; plastic glasses for outdoor drinking; open all day *(Kevin Blake, Colin McKerrow, Edward Mirzoeff, N R White)*

Hand in Hand SW19 4RQ [Crooked Billet]: Cheerful U-shaped bar serving several small areas, some tiled, others carpeted, Youngs full ale range, good wine choice, straightforward food inc home-made pizzas and huge burgers, friendly efficient service, log fire; rather spartan no smoking family annexe with bar billiards, darts etc; tables out in front courtyard with vine and hanging baskets, benches out by common (plastic glasses there); can be crowded with young people on summer evenings *(Kevin Blake, BB, N R White)*

☆ **Rose & Crown** SW19 5BA [Wimbledon High St]: Well run quiet comfortably refurbished 17th-c pub with alcove seating in roomy bar, full range of Youngs ales, enjoyable food, friendly attentive staff, old prints inc interesting religious texts and drawings, no smoking back dining conservatory; tables in neat partly covered former coachyard, bedrooms *(LYM, Bruce Bird, Colin McKerrow, Kevin Blake, MRSM, N R White)*

WEST LONDON

SW6

Fulham Mitre SW6 7DU [Dawes Rd]: Stylish contemporary décor, imaginative food, good choice of wines by the glass, conservatory; delightful south-facing walled garden *(Nick Davis)*

Harwood Arms SW6 1QP [Walham Grove]: Bare-boards pub with Fullers London Pride and Shepherd Neame Spitfire, friendly helpful bar staff, separate eating area, board games *(Robert Lester)*

SW7

Hoop & Toy SW7 2HQ [Thurloe Pl]: Friendly staff, Fullers Chiswick and London Pride, Greene King IPA and Abbot and Marstons Pedigree, decent food; can get smoky when crowded; handy for museums *(Val and Alan Green)*

W4

Bell & Crown W4 3PF [Strand on the Green]: Big busy Fullers local with their standard beers, sensibly priced food, good service, log fire, great Thames views from no smoking back bar and from conservatory (can get smoky); picnic-sets on terrace out by towpath, good walks, open all day *(N R White)*

Bollo House W4 5LR [Bollo Lane]: Spacious modern bar/bistro with sofas, comfortable banquettes, big refectory tables and amber walls above pale dado, up-to-date tasty food (you can share dishes), good service and relaxed atmosphere, Greene King IPA and Abbot, good choice of wines inc reasonably priced champagne by the glass, daily papers, board games; tables outside *(Bob and Maggie Atherton)*

☆ **City Barge** W4 3PH [Strand on the Green]: Small panelled riverside bars, not over-modernised and with nice original features, in picturesque and welcoming front part (reserved for diners lunchtime), also airy newer back part done out with maritime signs and bird prints; friendly service, sensibly priced bar food (not Sun) from sandwiches up, Fullers London

Pride and Charles Wells Bombardier, back conservatory, winter fires, waterside picnic-sets – lovely spot to watch sun set over Kew Bridge *(Darren Le Poidevin, LYM, N R White, Mayur Shah)*

Devonshire House W4 2JJ [Devonshire Rd]: Spacious made-over contemporary dining pub with comfortable dining chairs and banquettes on bare boards, good interesting up-to-date food, friendly atmosphere and attentive service; cl Mon, open all day *(Simon Rodway)*

Pilot W4 4BZ [Wellesley Rd]: Interesting food and friendly service in dining pub which keeps a proper bar; pleasant garden *(Simon Rodway)*

W5

Ealing Park Tavern W5 4RL [South Ealing Rd]: Sensibly short blackboard choice of enjoyable frequently changing modern dishes from end kitchen in large open-plan dining room, large bar too, Youngs ales, decent wines, pleasant service *(Simon Rodway)*

W6

Blue Anchor W6 9DJ [Lower Mall]: Well worn in panelled pub right on Thames, two linked areas with oars and other rowing memorabilia, banquette seating, cheap generous bar lunches, real ales, pleasant river-view upstairs restaurant; riverside tables, busy wknds *(BB, Tracey and Stephen Groves)*

Grove W6 0NQ [Hammersmith Grove]: Popular dining pub with enjoyable food, younger customers – can get quite loud *(Simon Rodway)*

Latymers W6 7JP [Hammersmith Rd]: Big lively café/bar with minimal décor, lots of steel and glass inc ornate mirrored ceiling, well kept Fullers ales and friendly bar staff; three TV screens, may be unobtrusive piped music; good authentic thai food, generous and inexpensive, in comfortable and spacious back restaurant with cheerful attentive staff in thai dress, take-aways too *(Susan and John Douglas)*

Queens Head W6 7BL [Brook Green]: Attractive pub dating from early 18th c, lots of cosy rooms, beams, candlelight, fires, country furniture and pictures in keeping with period, wide food choice with unusual dishes alongside favourites (veg almost too al dente), good wines by the glass, Courage Directors; tables out in front overlooking green with tennis courts, secret garden behind *(Gloria Bax)*

Thatched House W6 0ET [Dalling Rd]: Spacious dining pub with generous enjoyable food, stripped pine, modern art, big armchairs, well kept Youngs and good wine list, good service, conservatory; open all day wknds *(BB, Simon Rodway)*

W7

Fox W7 2PJ [Green Lane]: Friendly open-plan 19th-c local in quiet cul de sac nr Grand Union Canal, several real ales, decent wines, good value wholesome pub lunches from good toasties, baguettes and baked potatoes to home-made hot dishes inc Sun roasts, dining area, panelling and stained glass one end,

wildlife pictures and big fish tank, farm tools hung from ceiling, darts end; dogs welcome, small side garden, occasional wknd barbecues, towpath walks *(Jean Barnett, David Lewis)*

W8

Kensington Arms W8 6AH [Abingdon Rd]: Recently renovated, with fresh food inc cornish pasties and lots of fish, Fullers London Pride, Sharps Doom Bar and a guest beer, reasonable prices; four big-screen sports TVs *(Matthew Stewart, Pippa Sellars)*

☆ *Scarsdale* W8 6HE [Edwardes Sq]: Busy Georgian pub in lovely leafy square, stripped wooden floors, two or three fireplaces with good coal-effect gas fires, lots of nick-nacks, ornate bar counter, good choice of enjoyable blackboard food from ciabattas to chargrilled steaks, plenty of light dishes, charming service, Fullers London Pride and Charles Wells Bombardier, good wine choice; tree-shaded front courtyard with impressive show of flower tubs and baskets, open all day *(Gloria Bax, LYM, Joel Dobris)*

☆ *Uxbridge Arms* W8 7TQ [Uxbridge St]: Small friendly backstreet local with three linked areas, changing ales such as Brakspears and Fullers, good choice of bottled beers, china, prints and photographs; sports TV; open all day *(the Didler)*

W10

Station Tavern W10 6SZ [Bramley Rd]: Spacious dining pub with good choice, comfortable unhurried atmosphere; pleasant garden *(Simon Rodway)*

W11

Prince of Wales W11 4NJ [Princedale Rd (back on to Pottery Lane)]: Fullers and other ales such as Abbey Bellringer, good choice of wines by the glass, welcoming good-humoured landlord, relaxed atmosphere, pleasantly mixed furnishings and décor; charming hidden garden *(Christine Brown)*

W12

Eagle W12 9AZ [Askew Rd]: Relaxing and smartly revamped, sofas, table lamps, dark carpet and drapes, interesting if not cheap food, friendly service, Youngs, lots of imported beers; attractive well shaded back two-level terrace *(Tracey and Stephen Groves)*

W14

Radnor Arms W14 8PX: Classic pub architecture, interesting windows, plenty of character, rare outlet for Everards, usually a guest beer too, friendly staff who are real ale enthusiasts, good choice of whiskies, pub games; open all day *(the Didler)*

Warwick Arms W14 8PS [Warwick Rd]: Early 19th-c, with lots of woodwork, comfortable atmosphere, friendly regulars (some playing darts or bridge), good service, Fullers ales from elegant Wedgwood handpumps, limited tasty food (not Sun evening), sensible prices; tables outside, handy for Earls Court and Olympia, open all day *(the Didler)*

OUTER LONDON

ARKLEY [TQ2295]

Arkley EN5 3EP [Barnet Rd (A411 W of Barnet)]: Former Big Steak pub, now a useful Ember Inn, comfortable and friendly, with Black Sheep, Fullers London Pride and a seasonal guest beer, low-priced standard food from baguettes up, daily papers, log fire; attractive conservatory, tables outside *(Ian Phillips)*

BARKING [TQ4484]

Britannia IG11 8PR [Tanner St/Church Rd]: Large softly lit yet airy Youngs pub with their real ales and a guest beer, good value food from sandwiches and baked potatoes up inc bargain wkdy lunches and very popular Sun lunch, friendly family service, pool; tables outside *(Carole and John Smith)*

BARNET [TQ2195]

Gate at Arkley EN5 3LA [Barnet Rd (A411, nr Hendon Wood Lane)]: Efficient friendly service, good value lunchtime baguettes and wide choice of other enjoyable generous food all day, Adnams, Greene King Abbot and Wadworths 6X, reasonably priced wines, several comfortable areas with three blazing log fires, small no smoking conservatory; well behaved children welcome, attractive sheltered garden, open all day *(Piotr Chodzko-Zajko, BB)*

BECKENHAM [TQ3769]

Jolly Woodman BR3 6NR [Chancery Lane]: Small chatty traditional local with friendly atmosphere, real ales such as Fullers/Gales and Harveys, good value changing lunchtime food; can get crowded evenings; picnic-sets out in flower-filled back yard and tiny street *(N R White)*

BRENTFORD [TQ1777]

Griffin TW8 0NP [Brook Rd S]: Welcoming home of Griffin Brewery, at one corner of what we think is the only UK football ground with a pub on all four corners *(Keith and Chris O'Neill)*

BROMLEY [TQ4069]

Red Lion BR1 1LG [North Rd]: Chatty traditional backstreet local, soft lighting, shelves of books and heavy green velvet curtains, good range of Greene King and other ales, good service; picnic-sets on front terrace *(N R White)*

Two Doves BR2 8HD [Oakley Rd (A233)]: Popular local notable for its picturesque garden with terrace tables; plenty of character inside, with friendly service, good beer and no smoking back conservatory *(LM, N R White)*

CARSHALTON [TQ2764]

☆ *Greyhound* SM5 3PE [High St]: Handsomely refurbished 18th-c coaching inn opp duck ponds in picturesque outer London 'village', comfortable panelled front lounge bar with log fire, dining and no smoking areas, friendly service, Youngs ales, wide choice of enjoyable food from interesting sandwiches and ciabattas up; TV in large public bar; picnic-sets out by road, bedrooms *(N R White)*

CHELSFIELD [TQ4963]

☆ *Bo-Peep* BR6 7QL [Hewitts Rd, off exit roundabout from M25 junction 4]: Friendly new licensees doing good reasonably priced straightforward food from sandwiches to steaks in small refurbished traditional pub dating from 16th c, magnificent Tudor fireplace, low beams and lots of brasses, Courage and Greene King IPA, no smoking sheep-theme beamed dining room; unobtrusive piped music; lots of tables out in garden with new terrace, quiet spot, open all day wknds *(Anna Prior, N R White, GHC)*

CHISLEHURST [TQ4470]

Bulls Head BR7 6NR [Royal Parade]: Substantial pub/hotel with several rooms, one with comfortable armchairs and big log fire, thriving civilised atmosphere, generous bar food and roomy back restaurant, Youngs ales, good choice of wines by the glass, daytime family room; tables in garden, nr pleasant nature reserve *(Andrew Wallace)*

Ramblers Rest BR7 5ND [Mill Place; just off Bickley Park Rd and Old Hill, by Summer Hill (A222)]: White weatherboarded local in picturesque hillside setting on edge of Chislehurst Common, friendly staff, real ales, pleasant unpretentious atmosphere, upper and lower bars; can get smoky; garden behind, grassy slope out in front (plastic glasses for there), handy for Chislehurst Caves *(N R White)*

Sydney Arms BR7 6PL [Old Perry St]: Friendly atmosphere, brisk service even when busy, good range of good value food even on Sun, well kept real ales, big conservatory; pleasant garden good for children, almost opp entrance to Scadbury Park, country walks *(B J Harding, GHC)*

Tigers Head BR7 5PJ [Watts Lane/Manor Park Rd (B264 S of common, opp St Nicholas Church)]: Pleasantly airy Chef & Brewer overlooking church and common, dating from 18th c and pleasantly divided into cosy low-beamed areas, polite friendly staff, wide food choice inc variety of fish and Sun lunch, good wine list, real ales; smart casual dress code, no under-21s; side terrace tables, good walks nearby *(N R White)*

CROYDON [TQ3265]

Ship CR0 1QD [High St]: Wide choice of good value food, panelling and stained glass, very varied customers – even ghosts, they say; sports TV *(Ian and Julia Beard)*

DOWNE [TQ4361]

Queens Head BR6 7US [High St]: Civilised and comfortable, with green and cream décor, latticed windows, lanterns and hops, Darwin texts and splendid log fire in lounge, good value food from sandwiches to popular Sun roasts, Adnams Bitter and Broadside, friendly staff, plush dining room; big-screen TV in public bar, well equipped children's room; picnic-sets on pavement, more in small pleasant back courtyard, handy for Darwin's Down House, good walks, open all day *(N R White)*

GREEN STREET GREEN [TQ4563]

Rose & Crown BR6 6BT [Farnborough Way (A21)]: Civilised family-run pub with simple choice of good value bar food, good friendly

service, real ales such as Courage Best and
Shepherd Neame Spitfire, restaurant; big child-
friendly garden *(GHC)*

HAMPTON COURT [TQ1668]

Kings Arms KT8 9DD [Hampton Court Rd, by
Lion Gate]: On the edge of Hampton Court
grounds, a relaxed winter retreat, with good
open fires in linked rooms, oak panelling,
beams and stripped brickwork, Badger beers,
good choice of wines by the glass, attractively
priced pubby food from sandwiches up,
pleasant efficient service; piped music; children
and dogs welcome, picnic-sets roadside front
terrace, open all day *(Ian Phillips, LYM,
Susan and John Douglas)*

HILLINGDON [TQ0682]

Red Lion UB8 3QP [Royal Lane, Hillingdon
Hill (A4006 towards Uxbridge)]: Large
rambling old Fullers pub, low beams, real
fires, scrubbed tables on bare boards, cosy
welcoming traditional atmosphere, good real
ales, enjoyable food with good specials, staff
who cope easily with large numbers; unusually,
still has back funeral parlour; well decorated
new bedrooms, good breakfast *(Tracey and
Stephen Groves)*

ILFORD [TQ4188]

Red House IG4 5BG [Redbridge Lane E]:
Smartly refurbished multi-level Beefeater with
good service, large good value restaurant;
bedrooms in adjoining Travelodge
(Robert Lester)

KEW [TQ1977]

Coach & Horses TW9 3BH [Kew Green]:
Open-plan Youngs pub with their full beer
range and good coffees, decent food from
pubby staples to exotics, no smoking
restaurant area; sports TV; tables on front
terrace, nice setting *(Jeremy King, LM)*

MALDEN RUSHETT [TQ1763]

☆ *Star* KT22 0DP [Kingston Rd (A243 just N of
M25 junction 9)]: Reliable family dining pub on
Surrey border, good reasonably priced food from
baguettes and baked potatoes to a good range of
hot dishes, friendly service and atmosphere, nice
log fire; quiet piped music *(DWAJ)*

ORPINGTON [TQ4963]

Rock & Fountain BR6 7PJ [Rock Hill, past
Chelsfield Park Hospital (and just inside Kent);
quite handy for M25 junction 4]: Comfortably
extended family pub, large dining bar and side
dining room, good value pubby food from
sandwiches to steak, two or three real ales,
friendly prompt service, quiz night; children
welcome, picnic-sets out on back terrace and
lawn, quiet country lane *(N R White)*

OSTERLEY [TQ1578]

☆ *Hare & Hounds* TW7 5PR [Windmill Lane
(B454, off A4 – called Syon Lane at that
point)]: Large light and airy suburban pub,
wide choice of enjoyable food from sandwiches
up, prompt friendly service, Fullers ales,
pleasant dining extension; spacious terrace and
good mature garden, nice setting opp beautiful
Osterley Park *(Anon)*

PINNER [TQ1289]

Queens Head HA5 5PJ [High St]: Traditional
panelled pub dating from 16th c, welcoming

bustle, interesting décor, four real ales such as
Marstons Pedigree and Youngs Special, good
value fresh bar lunches; useful car park
(Quentin and Carol Williamson)

RICHMOND [TQ1874]

Britannia TW9 1HH [Brewers Lane]: Open-
plan pub with big Georgian windows
overlooking the passers-by, welcoming helpful
staff, good value food inc some generous
modern dishes, real ales such as Charles Wells
Bombardier, heroic pictures, nice upstairs room;
tables in small back courtyard *(Mayur Shah)*

Orange Tree TW9 2NQ [Kew Rd]: Big open-
plan room with good reasonably priced food
from sandwiches up, pleasant attentive service,
Youngs from central bar; piped music, sports
TV; open all day, lots of tables out in front,
small back covered terrace *(LYM,
Mayur Shah)*

Rose & Crown TW9 3AH [Kew Green]:
Popular 18th-c Chef & Brewer handy for Kew
Gardens, dark interior with panelling, old
prints and cosy corners, their usual food, real
ale, friendly service; raised front terrace
overlooking cricket green, tree-shaded back
terrace *(Mayur Shah, N R White)*

White Swan TW9 1PG [Old Palace Lane]:
Civilised old pub with dark-beamed open-plan
plush bar, relaxed and chatty, Charles Wells
Bombardier, good freshly cooked wholesome
bar lunches, coal-effect gas fires, popular
upstairs restaurant; piped music may obtrude;
children allowed in conservatory, pretty little
walled back terrace below railway, barbecues
(LYM, N R White)

White Horse TW10 6DF [Worple Way, off
Sheen Rd]: Large open-plan bare-boards
Fullers pub doing well under current
management, their real ales and good choice of
wines from long aluminium bar, leather settees
one end, plenty of tables for daily-changing
imaginative modern food from upmarket
sandwiches to restauranty meals, friendly
helpful service; terrace with new heated
canopy, backs on to residential area and
playground *(Huw Bassett)*

TEDDINGTON [TQ1671]

Teddington Arms TW11 8EW [High St]: Big-
windowed pub conversion, leather sofas and
rugs on bare boards, half a dozen changing
real ales, good malt whiskies and brandies,
home-made food from lunchtime sandwiches
to restaurant dishes, light and airy no smoking
panelled dining room; children welcome, open
all day *(Anon)*

Tide End Cottage TW11 9NN [Broom
Rd/Ferry Rd, nr bridge at Teddington Lock]:
Friendly low-ceilinged local in Victorian
cottage terrace, lots of river, fishing and
rowing memorabilia and photographs in two
rooms united by big log-effect gas fire, Greene
King ales, good reasonably priced
straightforward bar food from baguettes and
tapas to huge Sun roasts served 12-5 (can get
busy then); back dining extension now, but still
fills quickly at lunchtime, sports TV in front
bar, minimal parking; children welcome till
8.30, no river view, but does have circular

picnic-sets outside *(LM, Rob Keenan, Sue Demont, Tim Barrow)*

TWICKENHAM [TQ1673]

Eel Pie TW1 3NJ [Church St]: Busy and unpretentious, Badger and other real ales, foreign beers in their individual branded glasses, usual bar food (lunchtime not Sun), friendly service even on busy match days, lots of Rugby caricatures, bar billiards and other pub games; piped music; tables outside, children allowed till 6, open all day *(Steve Derbyshire, LYM)*

White Swan TW1 3DN [Riverside]: Unpretentious take-us-as-you-find-us 17th-c Thameside house up steep anti-flood steps, little waterside lawn across quiet lane, traditional bare-boards bar with big rustic tables and blazing fires, back room full of Rugby memorabilia, Courage Directors, Greene King IPA and Shepherd Neame Spitfire, good choice of wines by the glass, winter

mulled wine, sandwiches, one or two pubby hot dishes and simple summer wkdy lunchtime salad bar; backgammon, cribbage, piped blues or jazz, winter Weds folk night; children welcome, open all day summer *(LYM, Sue Demont, Tim Barrow, Roger Huggins)*

UXBRIDGE [TQ0582]

Load of Hay UB8 2PU [Villier St, off Cleveland Rd opp Brunel University]: Cheap food inc good steak and kidney pudding and popular Sun roast in rambling low-key local with mixed bag of furniture, four rotating real ales, impressive fireplace in no smoking back part; dogs welcome, flower-filled back garden, pergola with vine *(John and Glenys Wheeler)*

WOODFORD GREEN [TQ4091]

Castle IG8 0XG [High Rd (A104)]: Massive well refurbished Harvester almost opp the green, reasonably priced food inc early bargains, Bass in proper bar area *(Robert Lester)*

If a pub tries to make you leave a credit card behind the bar, be on your guard. The credit card firms and banks which issue them condemn this practice. After all, the publican who asks you to do this is in effect saying: 'I don't trust you'. Have you any more reason to trust his staff? If your card is used fraudulently while you have let it be kept out of your sight, the card company could say you've been negligent yourself — and refuse to make good your losses. So say that they can 'swipe' your instead, but must hand it back to you. Please let us know if a pub does try to keep your card.

Scotland

Quite a few readers this year have commented on the extra appeal gained by scottish pubs, now that – ahead of England and Wales – they are already all no smoking throughout. And we have also noticed two related developments which will no doubt follow south of the border, too: the first is that outdoor seating areas are now visibly appreciated by smokers – not perhaps ideal for the rest of us on a balmy summer's evening; and the second is that some pubs have been going out of their way to provide extra shelter outside, with overhead cover, and sometimes enclosure of up to two sides, which still counts as 'outside' for the smoking rules. Leaving that aside, pubs and inns which have been marking up strong scores in the last few months include the beautifully placed Applecross Inn (excellent seafood, and even the drive there is a plus in fine weather), the cheerful Fishermans Tavern in Broughty Ferry, the superbly Victorian Café Royal in Edinburgh (doing well under new licensees), the warm-hearted Masonic Arms in Gatehouse of Fleet (a splendid new entry, good drinks, service and cooking – so good, in fact, that it comes straight in with a Food Award), the Bon Accord in Glasgow (the city's best beer pub, with its impressive bank of rapidly changing real ales), the Glenelg Inn (good food, fine views, and it now has a real ale), the Lade at Kilmahog (friendly new owners bringing it back into the main entries on fine form), the welcoming dark-panelled Cross Keys in Kippen, the Border at the end of the Pennine Way in Kirk Yetholm (local ingredients for its popular food), the well run Burts Hotel in Melrose (good food and bedrooms, dozens of malt whiskies), the Plockton Hotel in its spectacular waterside setting, and the upmarket Wheatsheaf at Swinton, a serious good food destination. We have been so impressed by its combination of cheerful informality on the bar side with imaginative cooking that we name one of the newcomers, the Masonic Arms at Gatehouse of Fleet, as Scotland Dining Pub of the Year. It's this style, we believe, which is pointing the way forward for the future of the best pubs not just in Scotland but in the whole UK. Pubs looking particularly good in the Lucky Dip section at the end of the chapter include, in Argyll, the Oyster at Connel and Clachaig in Glencoe; in Inverness-shire, the Old Forge at Inverie (if you can manage to get there); in Peeblesshire, the Traquair Arms in Innerleithen; in Perthshire, the Byre at Brig o' Turk and Glenisla Hotel at Kirkton of Glenisla; in Ross-shire, the Anderson in Fortrose; and in Stirlingshire, the Portcullis in Stirling itself. Both Glasgow and, particularly, Edinburgh are filled with interesting and rewarding pubs. Drinks prices are in general rather higher than the norm in England (let alone Wales). The Counting House in Glasgow had by far the cheapest real ales of any of our main entries, and the Moulin in Pitlochry and Fox & Hounds in Houston both sold their own good brews fairly cheaply. The local beer most often on sale as a good pub's cheapest beer is Caledonian, with Isle of Skye supplanting it in parts of the west coast. Other scottish beers which we found at least some of our main entries offering as their cheapest were Inveralmond, Belhaven, Harviestoun, Fyne, Sulwath and Broughton. There are many other small breweries worth looking out for in Scotland. Ones we found in our main entries this year were Orkney, Atlas, Cairngorm, An Teallach, Arran, Black Isle, Highland and Stewart.

ABERDEEN NJ9305 Map 11

Prince of Wales 🍺 £

St Nicholas Lane; AB10 1HF

A good range of eight real ales is served at this individual old tavern in a narrow cobbled lane in the city centre, with Caledonian 80/-, Theakstons Old Peculier, and a Prince of Wales ale named for the pub from Inveralmond, along with guests from brewers such as Atlas, Isle of Skye and Orkney. The bar counter in a cosy central flagstoned area is said to be the longest in Scotland. Screened booths are furnished with pews and other wooden furniture, while a smarter main lounge has some panelling and a fruit machine. Friendly staff serve generous helpings of good value bar food such as sandwiches and filled rolls (from £1.30, served all day until they run out), filled baguettes or baked potatoes (£3.50), macaroni cheese (£4), steak pie (£4.50), and breaded haddock or curry (£4.80), with puddings such as chocolate fudge cake (£1.50). At lunchtime a busy mix of locals and visitors often makes for standing room only. Sunday evening folk nights are jam sessions where anyone can bring along an instrument and play. *(Recommended by Pete Walker, the Didler, Mark Walker)*

Free house ~ Licensee Kenny Gordon ~ Real ale ~ Bar food (11.30(12 Sun)-2.30(4 Sat, Sun)) ~ (01224) 640597 ~ Children allowed in eating area of bar at lunchtime ~ Traditional folk music Sun evening, quiz night Mon ~ Open 10am-midnight; 12-12 Sun

ABOYNE NO5298 Map 11

Boat 🍺

Charlestown Road (B968, just off A93); AB34 5EL

As you step inside this pleasantly pubby waterside inn you are greeted by a model train, often chugging around just below the ceiling, making appropriate noises. There are also scottish pictures and brasses and an openable woodburning stove in the two areas downstairs, a bar counter that runs down the narrower linking section, and games along in the public-bar end; piped music, TV. Spiral stairs take you up to a roomy additional dining area. Pleasantly served by prompt, friendly staff, lunchtime bar food includes soup (£2.50), sandwiches (from £3), mince, tatties and skirlie (£6.50), lasagne, very good fresh battered haddock (£7.95), and daily specials (including turbot, halibut, duck, venison and salmon), while in the evening they add things like baked aubergine layered with peppers and goats cheese with tomato salsa and toasted pine nuts (£8.75) and beef daube (£10.95); puddings (£4.50); children's meals. They use plenty of fresh local produce, and are happy to accommodate special requests. Bass along with a couple of real ales from scottish brewers such as Caledonian, Harviestoun, Houston, Inveralmond and Isle of Skye; also 40 malt whiskies. The pub used to serve the ferry that it's named for; outside there are tables, and they have a self-catering flat, sleeping four people, at £55 a night. *(Recommended by J F M and M West, Susan and John Douglas, Michael Lamm, Lucien Perring)*

Free house ~ Licensee Wilson Forbes ~ Real ale ~ Bar food (12-2(2.30 Sat, Sun), 5.30-9(9.30 Fri, Sat)) ~ Restaurant ~ (01339) 886137 ~ Children welcome ~ Dogs allowed in bar ~ Open 11-2.30, 5-11(12 Fri); 11-midnight Sat; 11-11 Sun

APPLECROSS NG7144 Map 11

Applecross Inn ★ 🍽 🛏

Off A896 S of Shieldaig; IV54 8ND

Readers thoroughly enjoy the remoteness of this pub and its magnificent waterside view across to the Cuillin Hills on Skye, and the journey to reach it over the Pass of the Cattle (Beallach na Ba) is undoubtedly one of Britain's greatest scenic drives. The alternative route, along the single-track lane winding round the coast from just south of Shieldaig, has equally glorious sea loch and then sea views nearly all the way. Tables in the nice shoreside garden are perfect for soaking it all in. One reader arrived to find an RNLI fund-raising event in full flow and the place humming. The fresh seafood is a big draw, and most of the ingredients they use are local. Up on chalkboards, the menu might include starters such as home-made soup or chowder (£2.50-3.50), half a dozen local oysters (£6.95), followed by local venison sausage with onion gravy and bubble and squeak, ploughman's or generous portions of haddock in a light batter (£7.95), crab salad (£8.95), chicken breast with home-made balinese sauce (£9.95), king scallops with garlic and crispy bacon on wild rice (£12.95), sirloin steak (£13.95), with home-made puddings such as raspberry cranachan or fruit crumble (£3.95); they also do very good sandwiches. With a friendly mix of locals and visitors, the no-nonsense bar has a woodburning stove, exposed stone walls, and upholstered pine furnishings on the stone floor; Isle of Hebridean Gold and Red Cuillin, and over 50 malt whiskies. There are lavatories for the disabled and baby changing facilities; pool (winter only), board games and juke box (musicians may take over instead). *(Recommended by Jarrod and Wendy Hopkinson, JDM, KM, Dr D E Granger, Michael Lamm, Peter Meister, Barry Collett, Mr and Mrs M Stratton, A J Bowen, Alistair and Kay Butler, W Holborow, G D Brooks, Karen Eliot, Edna Jones, Bill Strang, Stuart Pearson)*

Free house ~ Licensee Judith Fish ~ Real ale ~ Bar food (12-9) ~ (01520) 744262 ~ Children welcome until 8.30pm ~ Dogs allowed in bar and bedrooms ~ Live music Thurs evenings in summer ~ Open 11-11.30(11.45 Sat); 12.30-11 Sun; closed 25 Dec, 1 Jan ~ Bedrooms: £30/£60(£80B)

BADACHRO NG7773 Map 11

Badachro Inn ⑨

2½ miles S of Gairloch village turn off A832 on to B8056, then after another 3¼ miles turn right in Badachro to the quay and inn; IV21 2AA

This extremely welcoming pub makes the most of its lovely waterside setting on the southern shore of Loch Gairloch; they've recently installed heaters on the newly installed decking, with a covered area (where people can smoke) done in a nautical style with sail and rigging. Inside, the dining conservatory also overlooks the bay. There's an appealing local atmosphere in the bar, and gentle eavesdropping suggests that some of the yachtsmen have been calling in here annually for decades – the talk is still very much of fishing and boats. There are some interesting photographs and collages on the walls, and they put out the Sunday newspapers. The quieter dining area on the left has big tables by a huge log fire. Friendly staff serve a couple of beers from the An Teallach, Caledonian or Isle of Skye breweries on handpump, and they've over 50 malt whiskies, and a good changing wine list, with several by the glass. Look out for the sociable pub spaniel Casper. Enjoyable food – with the good fresh fish earning the place its Food Award – includes snacks such as sandwiches (from £3.65), baked potatoes (from £3.35), beef and spring onion burger (£4.50) and ploughman's (£6.75), with changing specials such as soup (£3.35), grilled goats cheese and salad (£6.95), locally smoked haddock topped with welsh rarebit (£10.25), roast rib of scottish beef or baked chicken breast with potato, celeriac and garlic mash (£10.95) and locally caught langoustines or monkfish kebab (£13.95), and home-made puddings such as chocolate marquise (£4.95). The pub is in a tiny village, and the quiet road comes to a dead end a few miles further on at the lovely Redpoint beach. The bay is very sheltered, virtually landlocked by Eilean Horrisdale just opposite. There are three pub moorings (free for visitors), and showers are available at a small charge. Usefully, there's Internet access. *(Recommended by Michael Lamm, Peter Meister, A J Bowen, Bill Strang, Stuart Pearson)*

Free house ~ Licensee Martyn Pearson ~ Real ale ~ Bar food (12(12.30 Sun)-3, 6-9) ~ (01445) 741255 ~ Children welcome with restrictions ~ Dogs allowed in bar ~ Open 12-12; 12.30-11 Sun; closed Sun evening in winter

BROUGHTY FERRY NO4630 Map 11

Fishermans Tavern ♀ ◖

Fort Street; turning off shore road; DD5 2AD

A pleasant waterfront place for enjoying an interesting range of beer, this has been a pub since 1827, when it was converted from a row of fishermen's cottages. They have half a dozen brews on handpump changing almost every day; their website (www.fishermans-tavern-hotel.co.uk) has updates about which are currently on – you might typically find Belhaven Sandy Hunters, Caledonian Deuchars IPA, Inveralmond Lia Fail, Timothy Taylors Landlord and guests from brewers such as Greene King and Samuel Smiths. They also have some local country fruit wines, draught wheat beer, and a good range of malt whiskies. There's an enjoyable atmosphere, and the staff and locals are friendly. A little carpeted snug on the right has nautical tables, light pink soft fabric seating, basket-weave wall panels and beige lamps, and is the more lively bar; on the left is a secluded lounge area with an open coal fire. The carpeted back bar (popular with diners) has a Victorian fireplace; dominoes, TV and fruit machine, and a coal fire. On summer evenings there are tables on the front pavement, and they might have barbecues in the secluded walled garden (where they hold an annual beer festival on the last weekend in May). As well as toasties, the enjoyable bar food might include soup (£2.25), sandwiches (from £3.40), quorn chilli or venison casseroled in red wine (£7.50), smokie pie or seafood crêpes with parmesan (£7.90), and plenty of fresh fish specials (not Mon); children's meals (from £4.75); the early evening menu includes soup (£2.75), prawn and egg salad (£5.75), casserole of steak and ale with puff pastry topping (£8.50), lemon sole stuffed with prawns in mornay sauce (£9.50) and seafood platter (£9.95), with puddings like apple pie (£3.75). They do a two-course lunch for £8.90, and have disabled lavatories, and baby changing facilities. Modern and comfortably equipped, the bedrooms extend into the neighbouring cottages; the residents' lounge has a sea view (the bay is just around the corner). Breakfast is served until 8.45am on weekdays and 9.30am at weekends. The landlord has another pub nearby, and also runs the well preserved Speedwell Bar in Dundee. (*Recommended by Charles and Pauline Stride, Peter Abbott, Steve Whalley, Alistair and Kay Butler*)

Free house ~ Licensee Jonathan Stewart ~ Real ale ~ Bar food (12-2.30 and 5-7.30 (weekdays), 12.30-3 and 5-7 (Sat, Sun)) ~ Restaurant ~ (01382) 775941 ~ Accompanied children welcome until 7pm ~ Dogs allowed in bar ~ Scots fiddle music Thurs night from 10 ~ Open 11am-midnight(1 Sat); 12.30-12 Sun ~ Bedrooms: £39B/£62B

EAST LINTON NT5977 Map 11

Drovers ◖

Bridge Street (B1407), just off A1 Haddington—Dunbar; EH40 3AG

An inviting place to spend the evening chatting over a beer, the main bar here feels like someone's living room. It has wooden floors, a basket of logs in front of the woodburning stove, and comfortable armchairs. There's a goat's head on a pillar in the middle of the room, fresh flowers and newspapers, lighted candles, and a mix of prints and pictures on the half panelled, half magenta-painted walls; piped music. A similar room leads off, and a door opens out on to a walled lawn with tables. Well kept Adnams Broadside, Belhaven Best, Caledonian Deuchars IPA and sometimes a guest are on handpump. Bar food takes in starters like soup (£3.50), haggis with creamy brandy sauce (£4.10) and goats cheese and honey croûtons (£4.25), and main courses such as vegetable lasagne (£6.95), cumberland sausage with thyme mash (£7.25), steak and ale pie (£7.95) and grilled salmon fillet with sun-dried tomato cream (£9.95); also specials such as beef stroganoff (£9.25) or half a roast chicken with brandy cream sauce (£10.50); the restaurant upstairs has piped music. The pub is on a pretty village street; readers have enjoyed its window boxes in spring. (*Recommended by Comus and Sarah Elliott, Steve Whalley, Michael Butler*)

London & Edinburgh Inns ~ Manager Bob Gordon ~ Real ale ~ Bar food (12.30-2.30, 6-9;
12.30-4, 6-9.30 Sat, Sun) ~ Restaurant ~ (01620) 860298 ~ Children welcome in dining
areas ~ Dogs welcome ~ Open 11-11(1am Sat); 12-12 Sun

EDINBURGH   NT2574   Map 11

Abbotsford ◖

Rose Street; E end, beside South St David Street; EH2 2PR

Under new owners since early in 2006, this nicely traditional city-centre pub offers
five changing real ales from brewers like Atlas, Broughton, Fyne and Orkney,
served from a set of air pressure tall founts, along with nearly 60 malt whiskies.
The single bar has dark wooden half-panelled walls, an impressive highly polished
Victorian island bar counter, long wooden tables and leatherette benches, and a
welcoming log-effect gas fire. There are prints on the walls, a rather handsome
plaster-moulded high ceiling, and a nicely old-fashioned atmosphere; games
machine and TV. Reliable and good value, lunchtime bar food includes sandwiches
(£1.75), soup (£2.25), pie of the day, a daily roast or haggis, neeps and tatties
(£6.95), and good home-made puddings (£3.75); in the evenings they have a more
elaborate menu for the restaurant only. Dogs allowed in the bar only after 3pm.
More reports on the new regime please. *(Recommended by Ian and Nita Cooper,
the Didler, Joe Green, Esther and John Sprinkle, Janet and Peter Race)*

Free house ~ Licensee Paul Tilsley ~ Real ale ~ Bar food (12-3) ~ Restaurant (12-2.15,
5.30-9.30) ~ (0131) 225 5276 ~ Children welcome ~ Dogs allowed in bar ~ Open 11-11;
closed 25 Dec, 1 Jan

Bow Bar ★ ◖

West Bow; EH1 2HH

Tucked away below the castle, this handsome, character-laden alehouse retains tall
founts dating from the 1920s made by Aitkens, Mackie & Carnegie as well as an
impressive carved mahogany gantry housing over 140 malts, including cask
strength whiskies. Busy and friendly with a good chatty atmosphere, the simple,
neatly kept rectangular bar has a fine collection of appropriate enamel advertising
signs and handsome antique trade mirrors, sturdy leatherette wall seats and heavy
narrow tables on its wooden floor, and café-style bar seats. Eight superbly kept
beers include Belhaven 80/-, Caledonian Deuchars IPA, Timothy Taylors Landlord
and various changing guests like Fyne Vital Spark, Harviestoun Bitter & Twisted,
Highland Scapa Special and Moorhouses Black Cat. There's a good choice of rums
and gins too. The only food they serve is tasty pies (from £1.40) and toasties (from
£1.60). More reports please. *(Recommended by the Didler, Joe Green, Mark Walker)*

Free house ~ Licensee Helen McLoughlin ~ Real ale ~ (0131) 226 7667 ~ No children ~
Dogs welcome ~ Open 12-11.30; 12.30-11 Sun; closed 25-26 Dec, 1-2 Jan

Café Royal

West Register Street; EH2 2AA

It's a good idea to pay a visit to this dazzlingly ornate Victorian building on a quiet
afternoon, when its listed interior can be best appreciated, as it does get very busy
at meal times. It was built with what at the time were state-of-the-art plumbing and
gas fittings; its floor and stairway are laid with marble, chandeliers hang from the
magnificent ceilings, and the big island bar is graced by a carefully re-created
gantry. The high-ceilinged café rooms have a particularly impressive series of highly
detailed doulton tilework portraits of historical innovators Watt, Faraday,
Stephenson, Caxton, Benjamin Franklin and Robert Peel (forget police – his
importance here is as the introducer of calico printing). There are some fine original
fittings in the downstairs gents', and the stained-glass well in the seafood and game
restaurant is well worth a look. Alongside a decent choice of wines, with a dozen
by the glass, they've 15 malt whiskies, and Caledonian Deuchars IPA and 80/- on
handpump, with perhaps a couple of scottish guests like Arran Blonde and Orkney

Dark Island; there's a TV (for major sports events) and piped music. The restaurant specialises in seafood and game, so the bar menu has plenty of these too; as well as sandwiches (from £3.95), you might find mussels (half a kilo £7.50, or a kilo – that's a lot of mussels – for £10.95), oysters (from £7.25), good sausage and mash (£7.50), steak and ale pie (£7.95), several fish specials such as seared swordfish steak or tuna steak (£9.95), and puddings such as chocolate tart with raspberry sorbet (from £3.75). *(Recommended by Alistair and Kay Butler, Pat and Stewart Gordon, Bruce and Penny Wilkie, P Dawn, Christine and Neil Townend, the Didler, Geoff and Pat Bell, Joe Green, Esther and John Sprinkle, Mark Walker, John and Fiona McIlwain, Janet and Peter Race, P and D Carpenter)*

Punch ~ Manager Amar Campbell ~ Real ale ~ Bar food (11(12.30 Sun)-10) ~ Restaurant ~ (0131) 556 1884 ~ Children in restaurant ~ Open 11(12.30 Sun)-11(12 Thurs; 1 Fri, Sat)

Guildford Arms ◗

West Register Street; EH2 2AA

Step inside this pub and you are greeted by a sumptuous Victorian interior, its main bar resplendent with painted plasterwork, mahogany fittings, original advertising mirrors and heavy swagged velvet curtains at the arched windows. The snug little upstairs gallery restaurant gives a dress-circle view of the main bar (notice the lovely old mirror decorated with two tigers on the way up). They have ten beers on handpump – Caledonian Deuchars IPA and 80/-, Harviestoun Bitter & Twisted and Orkney Dark Island, together with a range of guests from brewers such as Broughton, Cairngorm and Stewart; the helpful, friendly staff may offer a taste before you buy. Also, 16 wines by the glass, and a good choice of malt whiskies. The menu includes sandwiches, starters like soup (£2.95), breaded brie with raspberry coulis (£4.35) and prawn fritters with sweet chilli dip (£5.95), and main courses such as penne pasta bolognese (£6.50, home-made steakburger (£6.95), fajitas (£6.95-£8.45) and steak and ale pie (£7.75); the daily specials feature a fish of the day, and dishes such as lamb chops with rosemary gravy (£9.50), cajun tuna steak (£10.50) and sirloin steak with pepper sauce (£13.95); in the evenings food from the same menu is served only in the gallery restaurant. There are board games, a TV, a fruit machine and piped music. This is the flagship of a small regional group of pubs and bars. *(Recommended by Pat and Stewart Gordon, P Dawn, the Didler, Geoff and Pat Bell, Joe Green, Nigel Espley, Liane Purnell, Peter Abbott, Esther and John Sprinkle, Mark Walker, John and Fiona McIlwain, Janet and Peter Race)*

Free house ~ Licensee Scott Wilkinson ~ Real ale ~ Bar food (12-2.30(3 Sun), 6-9.30 (10 Fri), 12-10 Sat) ~ Restaurant (12(12.30 Sun)-2.30, 6-9.30(10 Fri/Sat)) ~ (0131) 556 4312 ~ No children or dogs ~ Open 11(12.30 Sun)-11(midnight Fri/Sat); closed 25-26 Dec, 1-2 Jan

Kays Bar ◗ £

Jamaica Street W; off India Street; EH3 6HF

The quality and range of the beer continue to make this backstreet pub a popular haunt, and on wintry days a cosy open fire in the main bar is a warming sight. They have an interesting range of up to eight superbly kept real ales on handpump, including Caledonian Deuchars IPA, McEwans 80/-, Theakstons Best and guests from brewers such as Arundel, Atlas, Greene King and Harviestoun. The choice of whiskies is impressive too, with more than 50 malts between eight and 50 years old, and ten blended whiskies. The cosy interior is decked out with various casks and vats, old wine and spirits merchant notices, gas-type lamps, well worn red plush wall banquettes and stools around cast-iron tables, and red pillars supporting a red ceiling. A quiet panelled back room leads off, with a narrow plank-panelled pitched ceiling and a collection of books ranging from dictionaries to ancient steam-train books for boys; lovely warming coal fire in winter. In days past, the pub was owned by John Kay, a whisky and wine merchant; wine barrels were hoisted up to the first floor and dispensed through pipes attached to nipples which can still be seen around the light rose. Service is friendly and obliging; TV, dominoes and cribbage, Scrabble

and backgammon. Straightforward but good value lunchtime bar food includes soup
(£1.25), haggis and neeps or mince and tatties, steak pie and filled baked potatoes
(£3.50), and lasagne, beefburger and chips or chicken balti (£3.95). *(Recommended by
Peter F Marshall, the Didler, John and Fiona McIlwain, Tich Critchlow)*

Free house ~ Tenant David Mackenzie ~ Real ale ~ Bar food (12-2.30, Mon-Sat; not on
rugby international days) ~ (0131) 225 1858 ~ No children ~ Dogs welcome ~
Open 11-12(1 Fri, Sat); 12.30-11 Sun

Starbank ♀ ◖ £

Laverockbank Road, off Starbank Road, just off A901 Granton—Leith; EH5 3BZ

The waterside views from the long light and airy bare-boarded bar over the Firth of
Forth alone justify a visit to this comfortably elegant and friendly pub. Its
impressive range of drinks includes eight real ales, with Belhaven 80/- and Sandy
Hunters, Caledonian Deuchars IPA and Timothy Taylors Landlord alongside guests
from breweries all over Britain such as Everards, Greene King, Harviestoun and
Robinsons. Nearly all of their wines are served by the glass, and there's a tempting
selection of malt whiskies. Good-value bar food includes soup (£2), herring rollmop
salad (£2.75), a daily vegetarian dish (£5), ploughman's or seafood salad (£5.75),
steak and ale pie (£6), haddock mornay or poached salmon (£6.50), minute steak
(£7.50) and puddings (£3). You can eat in the conservatory restaurant, and there's
a sheltered back terrace; TV. Parking on the adjacent hilly street. *(Recommended by
Pat and Stewart Gordon, Ken Richards, Ian and Nita Cooper, Peter Abbott, Mark O'Sullivan,
Paul Hopton, R N Lovelock, R M Corlett, Maurice and Gill McMahon)*

Free house ~ Licensee Valerie West ~ Real ale ~ Bar food (12-2.30, 6-9; 12(12.30 Sun)-9
weekends) ~ Restaurant ~ (0131) 552 4141 ~ Children welcome till 8.30pm ~ Dogs
allowed in bar ~ Live music first Sat evening of month, and jazz second Sun afternoon of
month ~ Open 11-11(12 Thurs-Sat); 12.30-11 Sun

ELIE NO4900 Map 11

Ship 🛏

The Toft, off A917 (High Street) towards harbour; KY9 1DT

Oystercatchers and gulls are very much in earshot from the terrace outside this
welcoming harbourside pub, which looks over a wide sandy bay enclosed by
headlands. The unspoilt, villagey beamed bar has a buoyantly nautical feel, with
friendly locals and staff, warming winter coal fires, and partly panelled walls
studded with old prints and maps. There's also a simple carpeted back room; cards,
dominoes and shut the box. Very well liked bar food includes good soup (£2.50),
home-made potato skins or liver pâté with oatcakes (£4), haddock and chips or
smoked haddock crêpe (£8), sausages and mash or steak and ale pie (£8.50), steak
(£15-£17) and daily specials, including fresh fish; they do a good Sunday lunch, and
lunchtime panini (£5.50); children's menu (£4.50); puddings (£4). In summer they
have a seafood lunch menu served in the garden, with things like mussels (£6), or
smoked haddock and gruyère quiche (£8), seafood platter (£12) and a catch of the
day (£13). On summer Sundays you can watch the progress of their cricket team
(they have regular barbecues then too). Caledonian Deuchars IPA, several wines by
the glass, and half a dozen malt whiskies. The comfortable bedrooms are in a
guesthouse next door. *(Recommended by David and Katharine Cooke, Peter and
Anne Hollindale, Michael Butler, A P Ross)*

Free house ~ Licensees Richard and Jill Philip ~ Real ale ~ Bar food (12-2.30, 6-9(9.30 Fri,
Sat); 12.30-3, 6-9 Sun) ~ Restaurant ~ (01333) 330246 ~ No children in front bar if under
14 ~ Dogs allowed in bar ~ Open 11-12(1 Fri, Sat); 12.30-12 Sun; closed 25 Dec ~
Bedrooms: £45B/£70B

GAIRLOCH NG8077 Map 11

Old Inn 🍴 ♟ 🍺 🛏

Just off A832/B8021; IV21 2BD

Barely a few steps away from a little fishing harbour and nicely tucked away from
the main shoreside road, this 18th-c inn is well placed for strolls up Flowerdale
valley to a waterfall. Picnic-sets are prettily placed outside by the trees that line the
stream as it flows past under the old stone bridge; you might spot eagles over the
crags above. The changing beers are a big draw, with usually around four or five on
offer: a typical selection might be Adnams, Black Sheep, Cairngorms Tradewinds,
and Isle of Skye Red Cuillin and Blind Piper (a blend of Isle of Skye ales made for
the pub and named after a famed 17th-c local piper). They have a lot of fairly
priced wines by the glass, a decent collection of 30 malt whiskies, and you can get
speciality coffees. The food is popular, and fresh locally landed fish is a speciality,
with bouillabaisse, seared scallops, and langoustines commonly on the board, and
mussels, crabs, lobster, skate, haddock and hake often cropping up too. The regular
bar menu includes cullen skink (£3.95), home-made game pâté (£4.25), game
casserole (£7.95), fish pie (£8.50), dressed crab (£11.50), roasted monkfish
(£13.50), 12oz sirloin steak (£17.95) with specials like mussels (£5.25 as a starter,
£13.50 as a main course), venison steak (£12.95) and halibut (£13.50), with
puddings such as clootie dumpling and custard (£3.75); they also do lunchtime
open sandwiches (from £4.50). The landlady makes her own chutneys and
preserves – and grows many of the herbs they use (they also track down organic
vegetables). Credit (but not debit) cards incur a surcharge of £1.75. It's nicely
decorated with paintings and murals on exposed stone walls, and the cheerfully
relaxed public bar has chatty locals; darts, TV, fruit machine, pool, and juke box.
More reports please. *(Recommended by Peter Meister, Michael Lamm, Mr and Mrs
M Stratton, Alistair and Kay Butler, Edna Jones)*

Free house ~ Licensees Alastair and Ute Pearson ~ Real ale ~ Bar food (12-2.30
(weekends), 5-8.30 in winter; 12-9.30 in summer) ~ Restaurant ~ 01445 712006 ~
Children allowed in some rooms ~ Dogs allowed in bar and bedrooms ~ Live music
summer weekends ~ Open 11-1(12 Sat); 12.30-11.30 Sun ~ Bedrooms: £40B/£75B

GATEHOUSE OF FLEET NX6056 Map 9

Masonic Arms 🍴 ♟ 🍺

Ann Street, off B727; DG7 2HU

Scotland Dining Pub of the Year

A few years ago, when Chris and Sue Walker ran the Creebridge House Hotel over
near Newton Stewart, they made it very popular with our readers for good food
from Chris and his head chef, fine real ales, and the cheerful atmosphere fostered by
Sue. They have now done the same trick here, this time in a pub which they have
transformed through a careful refurbishment (and they have the same head chef).
The comfortable two-room beamed bar is indeed a proper bar, with Masonic Boom
(brewed for them by Sulwath) and a good changing guest like Black Sheep,
Caledonian Deuchars IPA or Hook Norton Old Hooky on handpump, and a good
choice of whiskies and wines by the glass. There's traditional seating, pictures on
lightly timbered walls, and blue and white plates on a delft shelf. Service is friendly
and efficient, with everything kept spick and span, and there is a relaxed warm-
hearted atmosphere. Good generous interesting food includes lunchtime sandwiches
(from £3.95) and melts (£5.95), as well as home-made soup (£3.10), smooth pâté
of chicken livers with boozy beetroot pickle on toasted brioche (£4.75), haggis and
tattie scone tower with Drambuie sauce (£4.95), king scallop tempura on fresh
linguini with sweet chilli sauce (£5.25), crab salad with cucumber jelly and grainy
mustard vinaigrette, bangers and mash with caramelised red onions and port or
posh fish and chips (£8.95), roasted chunky ratatouille and mixed bean lasagne
(£10.95), escalope of chicken with swiss cheese, crayfish, white wine cream and
mushrooms (£11.95), fillet of salmon with creamy curried prawn and mussel
risotto (£12.95), super steaks using grass-fed beef (from £12.95), and puddings

such as raspberry and white chocolate cheesecake finished with macerated strawberries and green ginger, mango brûlée with coconut sorbet and a coconut tuile or sticky toffee banana pudding (£4.25). They also offer set evening menus: two courses (from £16) and three courses (from £20). The bar opens into an attractive and spacious conservatory, with stylish and comfortable cane bucket chairs around good tables on its terracotta tiles, pot plants, and colourful pictures on one wall; it's airy even in bright sunlight (good blinds and ventilation). The conservatory also opens through into a smart contemporary restaurant, with high-backed thickly padded chairs around neat modern tables on bare boards. There are picnic-sets under cocktail parasols out in the neatly kept sheltered garden, and seats out in front of the flower-decked black and white building; this is an appealing small town, between the Solway Firth and the Galloway Forest Park. *(Recommended by Stan and Hazel Allen, Dr and Mrs R G J Telfer, Nick Holding, Christine and Phil Young, Chris Smith)*

Free house ~ Licensee Chris and Sue Walker ~ Real ale ~ Bar food (12-2 and 6-9) ~ Restaurant ~ (01557) 814335 ~ Children welcome ~ Dogs allowed in bar ~ Open 11.30-2.30, 5.30-11.30; closed Mon and Tues Nov-Mar

GLASGOW   NS5965   Map 11

Babbity Bowster 🍴 ♀

Blackfriars Street; G1 1PE

This city-centre pub is a lively blend of scottish and continental, traditional and modern both in its ambience and its good-value food. On Saturday evenings traditional scottish music is played, while at other times you may find games of boules in progress outside. A big ceramic of a kilted dancer and piper in the bar illustrates the mildly cheeky 18th-c lowland wedding pipe tune (Bab at the Bowster) from which the pub takes its name – the friendly landlord or his staff will be happy to explain further. The simply decorated light interior has fine tall windows, well lit photographs and big pen-and-wash drawings of the city, its people and musicians, dark grey stools and wall seats around dark grey tables on the stripped wooden boards, and a peat fire. The bar opens on to a pleasant terrace with tables under cocktail parasols, trellised vines and shrubs; they may have barbecues out here in summer. You'll find Caledonian Deuchars IPA and a couple of guests like Hampshire Mayhem and Houston Peter's Well on air pressure tall fount, and a remarkably sound collection of wines, malt whiskies and farm cider; good tea and coffee too. A short but interesting bar menu includes scottish and french items such as hearty home-made soup (from £3.25), cullen skink (£4.25), potted rabbit (£4.50), croques monsieur or haggis, neeps and tatties (£4.95; they also do a vegetarian version), panini (from £5.65), stovies (£5.75), mussels (£6.50), cauliflower and mungbean moussaka (£6.95) and gravadlax or a platter of scottish smoked salmon (£7.25), roast leg of duck on a bed of haricot beans and sautéed potatoes (£11.75), with daily specials, and a different main course dish on offer for each day of the week (£6.50-£8.50). The airy upstairs restaurant has more elaborate meals. *(Recommended by Nick Holding, Tracey and Stephen Groves, Tony and Wendy Hobden, Stephen and Jean Curtis)*

Free house ~ Licensee Fraser Laurie ~ Real ale ~ Bar food (12-10.30) ~ Restaurant ~ (0141) 552 5055 ~ Children welcome ~ Live traditional music on Sat ~ Open 11am(12.30 Sun)-midnight; closed 25 Dec ~ Bedrooms: £40S/£55S

Bon Accord 🍴 £

North Street; G3 7DA

With pot plants everywhere and a friendly atmosphere, this neatly kept pub is a welcoming place for a drink. There are ten changing beers on handpump, featuring an interesting range from smaller breweries around Britain; among some 600 different brews on offer each year, the range might typically include beers from Brakspears, Broughton, Caledonian, Durham, Hop Back, Fullers, Harviestoun, Houston, Kelham Island and Marstons. Whisky drinkers have lots to keep them happy too, with over 160 malts to choose from, and all 13 of their wines are available by the glass. There's a friendly atmosphere, and you'll find a good mix of customers (women find it welcoming here). The interior is neatly kept, partly polished bare-boards and partly carpeted, with a mix of tables and chairs, terracotta walls, and pot plants throughout; TV, fruit machine, cribbage, chess and piped music. Reasonably priced bar food includes baked potatoes or baguettes (£2.95), lasagne (£4.65), scampi (£4.80), and steak (£7.95); they do a two-course special (£3.95). It's open mike night on Tuesday, there's a quiz on Wednesday and a band on Saturday. *(Recommended by Nick Holding)*

Scottish Courage ~ Tenant Paul McDonagh ~ Real ale ~ Bar food (12(12.30 Sun)-7 (8 Weds)) ~ (0141) 248 4427 ~ Children welcome ~ Open 11am-midnight; 12.30-11 Sun

Counting House 🍴 £
St Vincent Place/George Square; G1 2DH

Built as a glorious temple to commercialism, this imaginatively converted former bank is now a bustling, atmospheric Wetherspoons pub that stays civilised and efficient even when it's crowded. The imposing interior is stunning, rising into a lofty, richly decorated coffered ceiling which culminates in a great central dome, with well lit nubile caryatids doing a fine supporting job in the corners. You'll also find the sort of decorative glasswork that nowadays seems more appropriate to a landmark pub than to a bank, as well as wall-safes, plenty of prints and local history, and big windows overlooking George Square. Away from the bar, several areas have solidly comfortable seating, while a series of smaller rooms – once the managers' offices – lead around the perimeter of the building. Some of these are surprisingly cosy, one is like a well stocked library, and a few are themed with pictures and prints of historical characters such as Walter Scott or Mary, Queen of Scots. The central island servery has fairly priced Cairngorms Wildcat, Caledonian 80/-, Deuchars IPA and Greene King Abbot, along with guests such as Fullers London Pride, Houstons Barochan and Timothy Taylors Landlord on handpump. They also do a good choice of bottled beers and malt whiskies, and a dozen wines by the glass; fruit machines. Friendly efficient staff serve the usual straightforward Wetherspoons food, with sandwiches and wraps (from £2.99), haggis, neeps and tatties (£3.99), chilli con carne, breaded scampi or sausages and mash (£5.49), chicken tikka masala (£5.89), steaks (from £7.19), specials, Sunday roasts, and children's meals (£3.59); they do two meals from a limited range for £6.99. Tuesday is steak night, and Thursday curry night. The pub is a handy place to wait if catching a train from Queen Street station. *(Recommended by David Crook, Dave Braisted, Andrew York, Doug Christian, Tony and Wendy Hobden, Nick Holding)*

Wetherspoons ~ Manager Stuart Coxshall ~ Real ale ~ Bar food (9am-11pm) ~ (0141) 225 0160 ~ Children in eating area of bar till 7pm ~ Open 9am-12pm

GLENELG NG8119 Map 11
Glenelg Inn 🍴
Unmarked road from Shiel Bridge (A87) towards Skye; IV40 8JR

Endowed with lovely views across the water to Skye, this delightfully placed inn is memorably reached by a single-track road climbing dramatically past heather-blanketed slopes and mountains with spectacular views to the lochs below. Feeling a bit like a mountain cabin (and still decidedly pubby given the smartness of the rest of the place), the unpretentious green-carpeted bar gives an overwhelming impression of dark wood, with lots of logs dotted about, a big fireplace, and only a very few tables and well worn cushioned wall benches – when necessary crates and fish boxes may be pressed into service as extra seating. Black and white photographs line the walls at the far end around the pool table, and there are various jokey articles and local information elsewhere; winter pool and maybe piped music (usually scottish). A real ale from Isle of Skye is on handpump, and there's a good collection of malt and cask strength whiskies; the locals are welcoming. At lunchtime they do only snacks such as soup (£2.50), huge filled granary rolls (£7), smoked salmon salad (£12.50) or prawn salad (£20; also available in the evening), while in the evening there's a big range of dishes all for £10 such as roast guinea fowl stuffed with haggis, venison casserole, deep-fried monkfish, scampi and chargrilled local lamb, with puddings such as maple and pecan cheesecake (£3). They also do an outstanding four-course evening meal in the dining room (£35). The friendly staff or rather forthright landlord can organise local activities, and there are plenty of enjoyable walks nearby. On a sunny day it is very inviting to sit at tables in the beautifully kept garden, Some of the bedrooms have great views; more are planned, and they do bargain rates in winter. Glenelg is the closest place on the mainland to the island, and there's a little car ferry across in summer. *(Recommended by JDM, KM, Alistair and Kay Butler, W Holborow, G D Brooks, Edna Jones)*

Free house ~ Licensee Christopher Main ~ Real ale ~ Bar food (12-2, 6-9; not Sun evening) ~ Restaurant ~ (01599) 522273 ~ Children welcome ~ Dogs allowed in bar and bedrooms ~ Open 12-2.30, 5-11(11.30 or 12.30 Sat); 12-2.30 Sun; closed lunchtime in winter; closed 25 Dec ~ Bedrooms: /£100B

HOUSTON NS4166 Map 11
Fox & Hounds ◀
South Street at junction with Main Street (B789, off B790 at Langbank signpost E of Bridge of Weir); PA6 7EN

A window in the bar of this welcoming village pub allows you to look into the pub's own Houston Brewery, which now sends its award-winning cask and bottled beers throughout the UK. Their tasty Barochan, Killellan, Peters Well and Warlock Stout are kept in top condition and served by handpump alongside a seasonal brew such as Houstons Auld Copperheid and a guest such as Greene King IPA. You'll also find 12 wines by the glass, around 100 malt whiskies and freshly squeezed orange juice. The clean plush hunting-theme lounge has comfortable seats by a fire and polished brass and copper; piped music. Popular with a younger crowd, the lively downstairs bar has a large-screen TV, pool, juke box and fruit machines; board games, piped music; they have a quiz on Tuesdays. Served upstairs (downstairs they do only sandwiches), a good choice of enjoyable bar food might include soup (£2.95), smoked trout, rocket and home-made potato salad (£4.95), and main courses such as chargrilled venison sausages with mash and onion gravy or home-made irish stew with creamy mash (£6.95), steak, mushroom and ale pie or large baked mushrooms stuffed with herb ratatouille (£7.50), apple, celery and mushroom stroganoff (£7.95), their own beer-battered scampi or cold seafood salad (£9.50) and steaks (from £12.95); specials might include soups such as lentil broth or cullen skink (£3.50), crisp-fried wild mushrooms (£3.95), charred breast of chicken with wild rice, smoked bacon and leek cream (£10.95) and half a lobster gilled with garlic butter (£13.95). The same family has been in charge for nearly 30 years. *(Recommended by Stephen and Jean Curtis, Martin and Sue Day)*

Own brew ~ Licensee Jonathan Wengel ~ Real ale ~ Bar food (12-2.30, 5.30-10; 12-10 Sat, Sun) ~ Restaurant ~ (01505) 612448 ~ Children welcome ~ Dogs allowed in bar ~ Regular live music; quiz on Tues ~ Open 11-12(1am Fri, Sat); 12-12 Sun

INVERARAY NN0908 Map 11
George £ 🛏
Main Street E; PA32 8TT

Pleasantly placed in the centre of this handsome little Georgian town, near Inveraray Castle and the shore of Loch Fyne, this comfortably modernised inn is a civilised place to stay. It is also well placed for walks and the great Argyll woodland gardens, best for their rhododendrons in May and early June. Run by the same family since 1860, the George has a bustling dark bar that oozes character from its bare stone walls, and shows plenty of age in its exposed joists, old tiles and big flagstones. There are antique settles, cushioned stone slabs along the walls, carved wooden benches, nicely grained wooden-topped cast-iron tables, lots of curling club and ships' badges, and a cosy log fire in winter. Swiftly served by friendly staff (you order at the table), generously served enjoyable bar food includes soup (£2.65), ploughman's (from £5.25), haggis, neeps and tatties (£5.75), steak pie or spaghetti bolognese (£5.95), scampi (£6.95), and evening dishes like crispy duck pancakes (£5.25 as a starter or £9.95 as a main course), vegetarian dish of the day (£5.75), haddock and chips (£6.95), lamb fillet with kale mash, pea purée and red wine sauce (£10.95), and steaks (from £14), with home-made puddings such as crumble or warm chocolate cake (£4.50); proper children's meals (£3.75). There's a conservatory restaurant, and tables in a very pleasant, well laid-out garden. Two beers include one from Fyne along with Caledonian Deuchars IPA on handpump, and they've over 60 malt whiskies; darts, board games, piped music and TV, but no bar games in summer. The individually decorated bedrooms (reached by a grand wooden staircase) have jacuzzis or four-poster beds. You may glimpse seals or even a basking shark or whale in the loch. *(Recommended by Paul Leason, Derek and Sylvia Stephenson, BOB, OPUS)*

Free house ~ Licensee Donald Clark ~ Real ale ~ Bar food (12-9) ~ Restaurant ~ (01499) 302111 ~ Children welcome ~ Dogs welcome ~ Open 11(12 Sun)-12.30am ~ Bedrooms: £35B/£70B

ISLE OF WHITHORN   NX4736   Map 9
Steam Packet 🍽 ♀ 🛏
Harbour Row; DG8 8LL

This is an appealing place to stay or just pop in for a drink, and there's no piped music, fruit machines or other similar intrusions: from the big picture windows of this welcoming modernised inn you look out on to a restful scene of an attractive working harbour, with a crowd of yachts and fishing boats. The comfortable low-ceilinged bar is split into two: on the right, plush button-back banquettes and boat pictures, and on the left, green leatherette stools around cast-iron-framed tables on big stone tiles, and a woodburning stove in the bare stone wall. Bar food can be served in the lower-beamed dining room, which has excellent colour wildlife photographs, rugs on its wooden floor, and a solid fuel stove, and there's also a small eating area off the lounge bar, as well as a conservatory. Swiftly served by helpful but unfussy staff, the food features changing lunchtime specials such as sweet potato and roasted red pepper soup (£2.75), chicken, stilton and macademia tartlet on mixed leaves (£4.25), beer-battered haddock and chips (£6.50) and mushroom, tarragon and red onion risotto or wild boar honey and mustard sausages and mash (£6.95), and evening specials such as smoked salmon fillet on roasted vegetable and feta couscous (£8.25), loch fyne langoustines (£8.50 as a starter or £17 as a main course), and poached monkfish and scallops in white wine sauce (£13.25); other dishes might include filled rolls (from £2.75), haggis-stuffed mushroom (£4.25), steamed mussels (£6.95 as a starter or £11.25 as a main course), stir-fried vegetables in sweet and sour sauce (£6.25), curry (£7.50) and steaks (from £12.95), with puddings such as chocolate torte or apple, honey and cinnamon tart (£3.50); they do children's meals (£2.50). Theakstons XB is kept on handpump, along with a guest such as Houston Peters Well, and they've two dozen malt whiskies and a good wine list; TV, pool and board games. There are white tables and chairs in the garden. Several of the recently refurbished bedrooms have good views. Boat trips leave from the harbour; you can walk up to the remains of St Ninian's Kirk, on a headland behind the village. *(Recommended by Dr and Mrs T E Hothersall, JWAC, John and Angie Millar, Julian and Linda Cooke, Stan and Hazel Allen, Andrew Wallace)*

Free house ~ Licensee John Scoular ~ Real ale ~ Bar food (12-2, 6.30-9) ~ Restaurant ~ (01988) 500334 ~ Children welcome except in bar ~ Dogs allowed in bar and bedrooms ~ Open 11-11(12 Sat); 12-11 Sun; closed 2.30-6 winter ~ Bedrooms: £30B/£60B

Smoking is not allowed in any part of a pub in Scotland.

KILBERRY NR7164 Map 11

Kilberry Inn 🛏

B8024; PA29 6YD

The owners of this remotely placed inn (actually a former post office) have made considerable efforts with the food that's on offer to those who make the tortuous drive along a single-track road. Typical items on the lunch and dinner menus include starters like cumin-spiced parsnip soup (£4), smoked haddock chowder (£4.95) and blue cheese tartlet with red onion marmalade (£5.25), and main courses such as cottage pie with braised red cabbage (£9.95), beef cooked in ale with buttery mash (£10.50), fillets of bass grilled with fennel (£12.75), and warm salad of king scallops and monkfish (£12.95). The small beamed dining bar, tastefully and simply furnished, is relaxed and warmly sociable, with a good log fire; piped music. There's no real ale, but they do Fyne bottled beers and have a selection of malt whiskies (with quite a few local ones). The bedrooms are stylishly attractive. You'll know you've arrived when you spot the old-fashioned red telephone box outside the low corrugated-roof building. *(Recommended by J D G Isherwood, Christine and Neil Townend, Mrs Ruth McCaul, Catherine Kent, Colin Baigent)*

Free house ~ Licensees Clare Johnson and David Wilson ~ Bar food (12.30-2.30, 6.30-9) ~ Restaurant ~ (01880) 770223 ~ Children in restaurant and family room ~ Dogs allowed in bedrooms ~ Open 12.30-2.30, 6.30-11; closed Mon, and in winter also closed Tues-Thurs and all Jan-Mar ~ Bedrooms: £39.50S/£79S

KILMAHOG NN6008 Map 11

Lade ♀ 🍺

A84 just NW of Callander, by A821 junction; FK17 8HD

An enthusiastic hands-on family run this lively pubby inn, which is a great place to visit at the weekend if you want to hear some traditional scottish music. Another great feature is the organic beers brewed here – WayLade, LadeBack and LadeOut, which are well kept alongside a guest such as Broughton Clipper, eight wines by the glass and about 25 malts. By the time this edition is published they hope to have opened a little shop selling a range of about 100 bottled scottish real ales. Several small beamed areas are cosy with red walls, panelling and stripped stone, and decorated with highland prints and a cigarette card collection; piped music. Straightforward bar food includes soup (£3.75), sandwiches (£4.75), ploughman's (£7.50), caesar salad (£8) and battered haddock (£8.50). A conservatory restaurant (with more ambitious dishes) opens on to a terrace with pleasant garden and three fish ponds. *(Recommended by Darren and Jane Staniforth)*

Own brew ~ Licensees Frank and Rita Park ~ Real ale ~ Bar food (12(12.30 Sun)-9; 12-3, 5-9 winter weekdays) ~ Restaurant ~ (01877) 330152 ~ Children welcome till 8pm ~ Dogs allowed in bar ~ Ceilidhs Fri and Sat evenings ~ Open 12-11; 12-1am Sat; 12.30-10.30 Sun

KINGHOLM QUAY NX9773 Map 9

Swan

B726 just S of Dumfries; or signposted off B725; DG1 4SU

In good weather there are plenty of things to enjoy outside here, with a small garden equipped with tables and a play area, and a pleasant two-mile walk or cycle ride from Dumfries along the River Nith using the tarmacked cycle path; it's also handy for the Caerlaverock nature reserve with its multitude of geese. Popular with families, it can get busy on Sundays. A short selection of pubby food is promptly served in the well ordered lounge with its little coal fire, or at busy times in the restaurant, from a menu that typically includes soup (£2.75), haggis with melted cheese (£3.75), liver and bacon (£6.25), steak pie or chicken with leeks and white wine (£6.95) and battered haddock (£6.95), with evening specials such as rack of ribs or seafood risotto (£8.75) and steaks (from £8.50); puddings might include sticky toffee pudding (£3.20). Many dishes can be served in half helpings. The neat and nicely furnished public bar has Theakstons Best on handpump, and good house wines; TV and quiet piped music. *(Recommended by Mr and Mrs P R Thomas, Nick and Meriel Cox, Nick Holding, Joe Green, Maurice and Gill McMahon, Michael and Marion Buchanan)*

Free house ~ Licensees Billy Houliston, Tracy Rogan and Alan Austin ~ Real ale ~ Bar food (5-8.45 (9 Fri/Sat); 11.45-12.15, 4.45-8.45 Sun) ~ (01387) 253756 ~ Children welcome ~ Open 11.30-2.30, 5-10(11Thurs-Sat); 11.30-11 Sun

KIPPEN   NS6594   Map 11
Cross Keys 🛏

Main Street; village signposted off A811 W of Stirling; FK8 3DN

'Timeless and atmospheric,' commented one reader on this cosy and unpretentious 18th-c village inn, which has dark panelling and subdued lighting; the friendly licensees really make an effort to help you feel at home. It has a strong local following, but extends a warm welcome to visitors. The straightforward lounge has a good log fire, and there's a coal fire in the attractive family dining room. Generously served and making good use of fresh, local produce, the enjoyable bar food includes soups like leek and potato (£3), smoked salmon and prawn marie rose parcel (£4.95), main courses such as home-made lasagne or baked ham salad (£7.25) and lamb casserole (£7.95), with puddings such as clootie dumpling (£4.50); they also do sandwiches (from £2.95), and you can get smaller helpings. Harviestoun Bitter & Twisted on handpump, and they've more than 30 malt whiskies; cards, dominoes, TV, and maybe a radio in the separate public bar; they hold a quiz night on the last Sunday of the month. Tables in the garden have good views towards the Trossachs. *(Recommended by Pat and Stewart Gordon, Mr and Mrs M Stratton, Dr A McCormick, Tracey and Stephen Groves)*

Free house ~ Licensees Mr and Mrs Scott ~ Real ale ~ Bar food (12-2, 6-9; 12.30-8.45 Sun; not 25 Dec, 1 Jan and some Mons in winter) ~ Restaurant ~ (01786) 870293 ~ Children welcome ~ Dogs allowed in bar and bedrooms ~ Open 12-2.30, 5.30-11(12 Fri); 12-12 Sat; 12.30-11 Sun ~ Bedrooms: /£70S

KIRK YETHOLM   NT8328   Map 10
Border 🛏

Village signposted off B6352/B6401 crossroads, SE of Kelso; The Green; TD5 8PQ

Readers remark on the warm and friendly welcome as well as the imaginative use of carefully sourced fresh local ingredients at this comfortable hotel that makes a particularly cheering landmark for walkers at the end of the 256-mile Pennine Way National Trail. If you have done the full walk, and have with you a copy of the guide to the walk written and drawn by Alfred Wainwright, they will give you a free pint of beer. Originally Wainwright left some money at the inn, to pay for walkers claiming just a half-pint, but that's long gone, and the hotel now foots the bill itself. It's by no means just walkers who will enjoy the pub. Under its friendly chef/landlord and his wife, the food is careful and inventive without being at all pretentious. It might include open sandwiches using locally made pickles (from £4.25), starters such as home-made soup (£2.95), grilled black pudding with caramelised apple (£4.95) and crayfish cocktail (£5.95) and main courses like roasted peppers stuffed with spicy vegetable risotto (£6.45), venison and red wine sausages on creamed potatoes with gravy (£8.45), smoked haddock risotto or pork loin stack (£8.95) and steaks (from £9.95); the specials board might include smoked langoustines from Eyemouth (£5.95), roast of the day (£6.95), fish and chips or scottish steak pie (£7.95) and pot-roast guinea fowl or tweed valley pheasant breast with pear and thyme stuffing (£8.45); home-made puddings like cranachan or bread and butter pudding (£3.95); plenty of autumn game and summer fish. The public bar has been gently freshened up, but is still cheerfully unpretentious, with snug side rooms. It has beams, flagstones and a log fire, and a signed photograph of Wainwright and various souvenirs of the Pennine Way, as well as appropriate borders scenery etchings and murals. They have Caledonian Deuchars IPA and a changing scottish guest beer on handpump, decent wines by the glass, a good range of malt whiskies, and a water bowl for dogs; service is warm and efficient. There's a roomy pink-walled dining room, a comfortably refurbished lounge with a second log fire, and a neat conservatory; TV, darts, pool, board games, and children's games and books. A sheltered back terrace has more picnic-sets, and the colourful window boxes and floral tubs make a very attractive display outside. The pub experienced quite a bad fire just as we were going to press. The bar area was unaffected, but cooking is now being done from a temporary kitchen, and they don't expect the bedrooms to be open again until Spring 2007. *(Recommended by Carolyn Reid, Mr D J Crawford, Julie Wilson, Prof and Mrs S Lockley, Mairi Reynolds, Joe Green, Adam Peters, Mathew Horsman)*

Free house ~ Licensees Philip and Margaret Blackburn ~ Real ale ~ Bar food (12-2, 6-9, unless booked for weddings) ~ Restaurant ~ (01573) 420237 ~ Children welcome ~ Dogs allowed in bar and bedrooms ~ Open 11-11 ~ Bedrooms: £45B/£80B

LINLITHGOW NS9976 Map 11

Four Marys 🍺 £

High Street; 2 miles from M9 junction 3 (and little further from junction 4) – town signposted; EH49 7ED

Dating from the 16th c and close to the ruin of Linlithgow Palace, this pub takes its name from the four ladies-in-waiting of Mary, Queen of Scots, who was born at the palace in 1542. Accordingly the pub is stashed with mementoes of the ill-fated queen, such as pictures and written records, a piece of bed curtain said to be hers, part of a 16th-c cloth and swansdown vest of the type she's likely to have worn, and a facsimile of her death-mask. Eight real ales are kept on handpump, with changing guests such as Greene King Triumph, Ossetts Silver King and Orkney Red MacGregor joining the regular Belhaven 80/- and St Andrews and Caledonian Deuchars IPA; they also have a good range of malt whiskies (including a malt of the month) and several wines by the glass. During their May and October beer festivals they have 20 real ale pumps and live entertainment. The L-shaped bar also has mahogany dining chairs around stripped period and antique tables, a couple of attractive antique corner cupboards, and an elaborate Victorian dresser serving as a bar gantry. The walls are mainly stripped stone, including some remarkable masonry in the inner area; piped music. Readers recommend the haggis, neeps and tatties (£5.95), while other generously served good value bar food includes warm baguettes and baked potatoes (from £3.95), soup (£2.10; good cullen skink £2.50), spicy potato wedges (£3.25), lasagne (£5.95, burgers (from £5.25), home-made steak pie or curry (£6.25), chicken and haggis roulade (£6.95), steaks (from £10.95) and specials like braised lamb shanks, smoked haddock mornay or vegetable lasagne (all £7.95; other specials range from £5.95 to £10.95); children's menu. Service is charming. Parking can be difficult. In earlier times the building was an apothecary's shop, where David Waldie experimented with chloroform – its first use as an anaesthetic. *(Recommended by P Price, Peter F Marshall)*

Belhaven (Greene King) ~ Managers Eve and Ian Forrest ~ Real ale ~ Bar food (12-3, 5-9 weekdays, 12(12.30 Sun)-9 weekends) ~ Restaurant ~ (01506) 842171 ~ Children in restaurant ~ Open 12(12.30 Sun)-11(11.45 Thurs/Fri, 12 Sat)

LYBSTER ND2436 Map 11

Portland Arms 🛏️

A9 S of Wick; KW3 6BS

At a busy little fishing port and in an area celebrated for its prehistoric sites and spectacular coastal scenery, this welcoming hotel (our most northerly main entry) makes a useful base, and the staff can arrange fishing trips too. One area has been attractively laid out as a cosy country kitchen room with an Aga, pine furnishings and farmhouse crockery; the smart bar-bistro has warm colours and fabrics, solid dark wood furnishings, softly upholstered chairs and a cosy fire. Straightforward bar food includes soup (£2.50), sandwiches (£3, £3.50 toasted), ploughman's

(£5.50), macaroni cheese (£6.50), fish and chips or steak pie (£8.00) and salmon steak (£9.00). They serve a good selection of malt whiskies (the beers are keg); board games, piped music. *(Recommended by Dr A McCormick, Alan Wilcock, Christine Davidson)*

London & Edinburgh Inns ~ Licensee Robert Reynolds ~ Bar food (12-3, 5-9, 12-9 Sun; daily 12-10 May-Sept) ~ Restaurant ~ (01593) 721721 ~ Children welcome until 8pm except in bar area ~ Open 12-11(12 Sat); 12-3, 5-11 weekdays in winter; closed 31 Dec-3 Jan ~ Bedrooms: £70B/£86B

MELROSE NT5434 Map 9
Burts Hotel ⑤ ⑪ ⇦
B6374, Market Square; TD6 9PL

In the market square at the heart of this conspicuously attractive border town and a few steps away from the abbey ruins, this comfortable 200-year-old inn is the ideal place to stay and discover the area's charms. The inviting lounge bar has lots of cushioned wall seats and windsor armchairs, and scottish prints on the walls. There are 90 malt whiskies to choose from, and Caledonian Deuchars IPA and 80/- and a guest such as Timothy Taylors Landlord are kept on handpump; there's a good wine list too, with seven by the glass; space for those just wanting a drink is fairly limited. Excellent, swiftly served food might include soup (£3.25), thai chicken parcel (£5.25), salads (from £7.50), vegetable chilli tortilla (£8.25), steak and ale pudding (£8.95), supreme of chicken stuffed with parma ham and tarragon (£10.95), braised highland venison, button mushroom and onion casserole (£12.50), king prawn oriental stir fry or kebab of monkfish, salmon and prawn (£13.50) and steaks (from £14.50), with puddings such as banana crème brûlée or steamed chocolate pudding (£5.25); efficient friendly service. In summer you can sit out in the well tended garden. *(Recommended by Ian and Jane Irving, Dr Peter Crawshaw, Pat and Stewart Gordon, Mrs J H S Lang, Edward Perrott, John and Sylvia Harrop, Peter Abbott, Mark Walker, Julian and Linda Cooke, Nick Holding, Lucien Perring)*

Free house ~ Licensees Graham and Anne Henderson ~ Real ale ~ Bar food (12-2, 6-9.30) ~ Restaurant ~ (01896) 822285 ~ No children under 8 in restaurant ~ Dogs allowed in bedrooms ~ Open 11-2.30, 5-11; 12-2.30, 6-11 Sun; closed 26 Dec, 3-5 Jan ~ Bedrooms: £56B/£106B

PITLOCHRY NN9459 Map 11
Moulin ⑪ ⇦
Kirkmichael Road, Moulin; A924 NE of Pitlochry centre; PH16 5EH

A strong attraction of this inviting flower-bedecked 17th-c inn is its excellent home-brewed beers, actually brewed in the little stables across the street, and it's an enjoyable place to stay, with an excellent range of walks close at hand. Ale of Atholl, Braveheart, Moulin Light and the stronger Old Remedial are superbly kept on handpump, and they also have around 40 malt whiskies, and a good choice of wines by the glass and carafes of house wine available by the litre and half litre. Although it has been much extended over the years, the bar, in the oldest part of the building, still seems an entity in itself, nicely pubby, with plenty of atmosphere. Above the fireplace in the smaller room is an interesting painting of the village before the road was built (Moulin used to be a bustling market town, far busier than upstart Pitlochry), while the bigger carpeted area has a good few tables and cushioned banquettes in little booths divided by stained-glass country scenes, another big fireplace, some exposed stonework, fresh flowers, and golf clubs and local and sporting prints around the walls; games include bar billiards and board games. The extensive bar menu includes soup (£2.75), deep-fried haggis with piquant sauce (£4.65) and a platter of local smoked meats (£5.75), with main courses such as steak and ale pie (£6.95), stuffed peppers with pine nuts, mushrooms, onions and cheddar (£7.45), game casserole or lamb shank (£7.95), seafood pancake (£8.25), local venison fried with mushrooms (£8.75) and 8oz sirloin steak (£11.95), and daily specials, with puddings such as home-made apple pie (£3.30); from 12 till 6pm they also serve baked potatoes and sandwiches (from £4.45), and they do children's meals. In the evening, readers enjoy eating in the restaurant. Service is friendly; the landlord is a historic motor rallying fan. Surrounded by tubs of flowers, picnic-sets outside look across to the village kirk. The rooms are comfortable and breakfasts are good; they offer good value three-night breaks out of season. *(Recommended by Pat and Stewart Gordon, Andy and Jill Kassube, Paul and Ursula Randall, Charles and Pauline Stride, R N Lovelock, Alistair and Kay Butler, Alex and Claire Pearse, Mr and Mrs Maurice Thompson)*

Own brew ~ Licensee Heather Reeves ~ Real ale ~ Bar food (12-9) ~ Restaurant ~ (01796) 472196 ~ Children welcome ~ Dogs allowed in bar ~ Open 12-11(11.45 Sat) ~ Bedrooms: £45B/£55B

PLOCKTON   NG8033   Map 11
Plockton Hotel ★ ⑪ 🛏
Village signposted from A87 near Kyle of Lochalsh; IV52 8TN

'Welcoming and friendly as ever – the staff remember you from year to year,' enthuses one reader of this charmingly friendly and much-liked family-run hotel, and the food is highly rated too. Forming part of a long, low terrace of stone-built houses, the inn is set in a lovely National Trust for Scotland village. Tables in the front garden look out past the village's trademark palm trees and colourfully flowering shrub-lined shore, and across the sheltered anchorage to the rugged mountainous surrounds of Loch Carron; a stream runs down the hill into a pond in the landscaped back garden. With a buoyant, bustling atmosphere, the welcoming comfortably furnished lounge bar has window seats looking out to the boats on the water, as well as antiqued dark red leather seating around neat Regency-style tables on a tartan carpet, three model ships set into the woodwork, and partly panelled stone walls. The separate public bar has darts, pool, board games, TV and piped music, and on Wednesday evenings they have live traditional folk music. Well cooked, using lots of fresh local ingredients such as shellfish and red meat (they also hold a Scottish Healthy Choices Award and indicate healthy eating options on the menu), the food might include lunchtime sandwiches, soup (£2.75, with home-made bread; cream of smoked fish soup £3.85), haggis starter with a tot of whisky (£4.25), smoked salmon platter with home-made bread (£5.25), home-made lasagne (£7.50), herring in oatmeal (£7.75), seafood bake (£6.95), venison casserole (£8.75), langoustines (£9.25 starter, £18.50 main), supreme of chicken stuffed with argyle smoked ham and cheese in sun-dried tomato, garlic and basil sauce (£10.75), good steaks (from £13.25), monkfish and bacon brochettes (£13.50), and fish specials such as hand-dived scallops and steamed local mussels; they also do children's meals; some of the same items on the lunch menu are a pound or so cheaper. It's a good idea to book at busy times (when service can slow down). Caledonian Deuchars IPA and Isle of Skye Hebridean Gold on handpump, and bottled beers from the Isle of Skye brewery, along with a good collection of malt whiskies, and a short wine list. Most of the comfortable bedrooms are in the adjacent building – one has a balcony and woodburning stove, and they now have a few superior rooms, including one with a four-poster; half of them have extraordinary views over the loch; expect good breakfasts. A hotel nearby changed its name a few years ago to the Plockton Inn, so don't get the two confused. *(Recommended by Les and Sandra Brown, JDM, KM, Joan and Tony Walker, Jeff and Wendy Williams, J D Taylor, Brian McBurnie, Carol and Phil Byng, Ian and Jane Irving, Tracey and Stephen Groves, John and Claire Pettifer, W Holborow, Alistair and Kay Butler, Edna Jones)*

Free house ~ Licensee Tom Pearson ~ Real ale ~ Bar food (12(12.30 Sun)-2.30, 6-9.15) ~ Restaurant ~ (01599) 544274 ~ Children welcome ~ Traditional folk music Weds evenings ~ Open 11-12(12.30 Sat); 12.30-11 Sun ~ Bedrooms: £55B/£90B

SHIELDAIG   NG8154   Map 11
Tigh an Eilean Hotel ⏚
Village signposted just off A896 Lochcarron—Gairloch; IV54 8XN

Tables in a sheltered little courtyard of this civilised hotel are well placed to enjoy the gorgeous position at the head of Loch Shieldaig (which merges into Loch Torridon), beneath some of the most dramatic of all the highlands peaks, and looking out to Shieldaig Island – a sanctuary for a stand of ancient caledonian pines. Their new bar extension has been delayed and they now hope to complete it by early 2007; in the meantime they have incorporated a sizeable internal porch area into the main bar area and have installed larger, more comfortable tables. Fresh fish and seafood, all hand-dived or creel-caught by local fishermen, feature heavily on the bar menu, and particularly among the daily specials, which might take in whole local langoustines with a lemongrass, chilli and coriander dipping sauce (£2 each), razor clam fritters with romesco sauce (£4.95), home-made steak pie or venison liver with red wine gravy (£7.50), grilled bream with lemon and garlic butter (£9.50), and their popular seafood stew (12.95); other dishes include burgers (from £3.25), venison sausages and mash (£7.25) and scampi (£7.75), and they do soup with home-made bread (£2.50) and sandwiches all day; children's meals (£3). Isle of Skye Black Cuillin and Red Cuillin on handpump, along with maybe Plockton ales or a summer guest from the Black Isle brewery, as well as up to ten wines by the glass, and several malt whiskies; winter darts. The Beinn Eighe nature reserve isn't too far away. *(Recommended by Charles and Pauline Stride, Peter Meister, Bill Strang, Stuart Pearson)*

Free house ~ Licensees Cathryn and Christopher Field ~ Real ale ~ Bar food (12-2.30, 7-8.30) ~ (01520) 755251 ~ Children welcome in restaurant and eating areas of bar till 9pm ~ Dogs allowed in bedrooms ~ Traditional live folk music at some weekends and holidays ~ Open 11-11; 12-10 Sun; closed 3-5 weekdays in winter ~ Bedrooms: £68B/£144B

STEIN   NG2656   Map 11
Stein Inn ⏚
End of B886 N of Dunvegan in Waternish, off A850 Dunvegan—Portree; OS Sheet 23 map reference 263564; IV55 8GA

A comfortable spot to stay, this 18th-c inn has an extremely restful location by the water's edge on a far-flung northern corner of Skye. The tables outside are an ideal place to sit with a malt whisky (they've over 100 to choose from), and watch the sunset. Inside, the original public bar has great character, with its sturdy country furnishings, flagstone floor, beam and plank ceiling, partly panelled stripped-stone walls and peat fire. The atmosphere can be surprisingly buzzing, and there's a good welcome from the owners and the evening crowd of local regulars (where do they all appear from?). Good service from the smartly uniformed staff. There's a games area with pool table, dominoes and cribbage, and maybe piped music. Caledonian Deuchars IPA and Isle of Skye Reeling Deck (specially brewed for the pub) are kept on handpump, along with a guest like Isle of Skye Blaven or Orkney Northern Light; in summer they have several wines by the glass. Making good use of local fish and highland meat, the short choice of bar food includes good value sandwiches (from £1.85), various salads (from £5.95), steak pie (£6.85), battered haddock (£7.50), and 8oz sirloin steak (£11.50), langoustines (£12.95), with specials such as home-made soup (£2.40), feta cheese and spinach pastry parcels or venison pie (£6.85), and fresh fillet of sea trout with parsley butter (£9.75); puddings include rich chocolate sponge (£4.30), and local cheeses (£4.95). There's a lively children's inside play area, and showers for yachtsmen. Some of the bedrooms have sea views, and breakfasts are good – readers tell us it's well worth pre-ordering the tasty smoked kippers if you stay here. Useful campsites nearby. *(Recommended by Walter and Susan Rinaldi-Butcher, Joan and Tony Walker, John Robertson, Ian and Jane Irving, Tracey and Stephen Groves, Gill Cathles, Mrs Jane Kingsbury, Mr and Mrs M Stratton)*

Free house ~ Licensees Angus and Teresa Mcghie ~ Real ale ~ Bar food (12(12.30 Sun)-4,

6-9.30(9 Sun)) ~ Restaurant ~ (01470) 592362 ~ Children welcome until 8pm if dining ~
Dogs allowed in bedrooms ~ Open 11-12(12.30 Sat); 11.30-11 Sun; 4-11weekdays,
12-12 Sat, 12.30-11 Sun winter; closed 25 Dec, 1 Jan ~ Bedrooms: £26S/£52S(£72B)

SWINTON NT8448 Map 10
Wheatsheaf ⓐ ♀ 🛏
A6112 N of Coldstream; TD11 3JJ

This inn puts the emphasis very much on dining and very comfortable
accommodation, and friendly staff make it a very civilised base for exploring the
nearby River Tweed. The carefully thought-out main bar area has an attractive
long oak settle and comfortable armchairs, with sporting prints and plates on the
bottle-green wall covering; a small lower-ceilinged part by the counter has pubbier
furnishings, and small agricultural prints on the walls, especially sheep. A further
lounge area has a fishing-theme décor (with a detailed fishing map of the River
Tweed). The front conservatory has a vaulted pine ceiling and walls of local stone.
There's plenty of choice on the imaginative changing menu, and food is skilfully
prepared with fresh local ingredients. Lunchtime dishes might include starters like
soup (£3.65), caramelised red onion and goats cheese tart (£5.60) or breast of
woodpigeon on black pudding with redcurrant and port sauce (£6.20), with main
courses like organic pork and leek meatballs in cider gravy (£7.70), lambs liver
with mash (£8.20), battered haddock with hand-cut chips or mushroom, leek and
ricotta filo pastry strudel (£8.50) or sirloin steak in balsamic vinegar (£12.95);
evening meals might include the same starters as on the lunchtime menu, with
more expensive main courses like seared salmon and poached egg with watercress
dressing (£14.30), breast of maize-fed duck on roast sweet potato (£16.35), roast
loin of wild highland venison on braised red cabbage and juniper (£16.90) or
medallions of beef fillet on oyster mushroom and roasted shallot sauce with white
truffle oil (£18.95); the puddings and Sunday roasts are highly praised. It's a good
idea to book, particularly from Thursday to Saturday evening. Caledonian
Deuchars IPA and a guest such as Broughton Reiver are kept on handpump, and
they have around 40 malt whiskies, and a fine choice of 150 wines (with ten by
the glass). Readers especially enjoy staying here, and the breakfasts are good, with
freshly squeezed orange juice. *(Recommended by Dr and Mrs S Donald, Carol Broadbent,
John and Sylvia Harrop, Dr Peter D Smart, Carol and Phil Byng, R Macfarlane,
Mrs Ellen Wort)*

Free house ~ Licensees Chris and Jan Winson ~ Real ale ~ Bar food (12-2, 6-9(8.30 Sun))
~ Restaurant ~ (01890) 860257 ~ Children under 6 until 7pm in dining room ~
Open 11-2.30, 6-11; 12-2.30, 6-10.30 Sun; closed Sun evening in Dec-Feb; 25-27 Dec ~
Bedrooms: £67B/£102B

TAYVALLICH NR7386 Map 11
Tayvallich Inn ⓐ
B8025, off A816 1 mile S of Kilmartin; or take B841 turn-off from A816 2 miles N of
Lochgilphead; PA31 8PL

A pleasant place to make for on a sunny day, this dining pub has sliding glass doors
opening on to a terrace with decking and awning, and getting lovely views over the
yacht anchorage. Service is friendly, and people with children are made to feel
welcome. Inside are exposed ceiling joists, pale pine chairs, benches and tables on
the quarry-tiled floors, and local nautical charts on the cream walls; piped music.
The good food focuses on the fresh seafood caught by the fishing boats out on Loch
Sween, and the daily specials depend very much on what they've landed. Typical
items might include roast red peppers stuffed with goats cheese (£5.95), fish and
chips (£8.95), mussels from Loch Etive (£11.95), king scallops (£16.95) and 12oz
scottish sirloin (£17.95); they serve fresh milk shakes. Malt whiskies include a full
range of Islay malts, and they have Loch Fyne Maverick and Pipers Gold on
handpump. Until it was turned into a restaurant in the early 1970s, this was the
village bus station. *(Recommended by BOB)*

Free house ~ Licensee Roddy Anderson ~ Real ale ~ Bar food (12-2, 6-9) ~ Restaurant ~ (01546) 870282 ~ Children welcome till 8pm ~ Dogs allowed in bar ~ Live music two Sats a month ~ Open 11-11(1 Sat); 12-12 Sun; 12-3, 5.30-11 in winter, when also closed Tues lunchtimes and all day Mon

THORNHILL   NS6699   Map 11

Lion & Unicorn

A873; FK8 3PJ

With its old walls, beamed ceiling and blazing fire, this characterful pub dates in part back to 1635, and readers enjoy its bar food. The carpeted open-plan front room has comfortable seating; the restaurant still has its original massive fireplace, almost big enough to drive a car into. Friendly obliging staff serve a couple of real ales on handpump such as Caledonian Deuchars IPA and Harviestoun Bitter & Twisted – it's cheaper in the public bar than it is in the lounge. Served all day, bar food includes soup (£2.95), starters such as haggis wontons or chinese spare ribs (£5.45), baked potatoes (from £5.75), steak pie or battered haddock (£7.25), scampi (£7.50), four vegetarian dishes such as stir-fried vegetables (£7.95) or home-made vegetable lasagne (£8.25) and puddings such as apple and cinnamon crumble (from £3.95); speciality coffees. Juke box, pool, fruit machine, TV, darts, board games, quiz nights and piped music. There's a play area in the garden. *(Recommended by John Urquhart, Nick Holding, Michael Butler)*

Free house ~ Licensees Fiona and Bobby Stevenson ~ Real ale ~ Bar food (12-9) ~ Restaurant ~ (01786) 850204 ~ Children welcome ~ Open 11-midnight(1am Sat); closed 1 Jan ~ Bedrooms: £55B/£75B

ULLAPOOL   NH1294   Map 11

Ferry Boat 🍺

Shore Street; coming from the S, keep straight ahead when main A835 turns right into Mill Street; IV26 2UJ

Take a pair of binoculars here and you might spot seals from this nicely chatty 18th-c inn. The unassuming pubby bar has big windows with good views over Loch Broom, yellow walls, brocade-cushioned seats around plain wooden tables, quarry tiles by the corner serving counter and patterned carpet elsewhere, a stained-glass door hanging from the ceiling, and a fruit machine; cribbage, dominoes, board games and piped music, and they have a ceilidh band on Thursday nights. A smaller more peaceful room has a coal fire, and a delft shelf of copper measures and willow-pattern plates. Hearty bar food might include sandwiches, home-made fishcakes (£7.95), home-made steak pie (£8.25), vegetarian nut roast (£9.95), local haddock topped with tomato, cheese and herb crust (£10.95) and chicken stuffed with haggis with creamy white wine sauce (£12.95). Dogs are allowed in the bar outside food serving times. There are up to three changing real ales from breweries such as An Teallach, Belhaven and Greene King on handpump. In summer you can sit on the wall across the road and take in the fine views to the tall hills beyond the attractive fishing port, with its bustle of yachts, ferry boats, fishing boats and tour boats for the Summer Isles. *(Recommended by N R White, Peter Meister, Mr and Mrs M Stratton, Mike and Sue Loseby)*

Punch ~ Tenant Terry Flower ~ Real ale ~ Bar food (12-7) ~ (01854) 612366 ~ Children in eating area of bar and restaurant ~ Dogs allowed in bar ~ Ceilidh band Thurs nights ~ Open 11-11(10.30 Sun) ~ Bedrooms: £40S/£80B

Real ale to us means beer which has matured naturally in its cask – not pressurised or filtered. We name all real ales stocked. We usually name ales preserved under a light blanket of carbon dioxide too, though purists – pointing out that this stops the natural yeasts developing – would disagree (most people, including us, can't tell the difference!)

WEEM   NN8449   Map 11

Ailean Chraggan 🍴 ⛄ 🛏

B846; PH15 2LD

Small and friendly, this family-run hotel is a lovely place to stay, with well liked food (worth booking at busy times) and a couple of beers from the local Inveralmond Brewery, usually Lia Fail, Independence, Ossian or Thrappledouser on handpump. You're likely to find chatty locals in the bar; winter darts and board games. You can eat in either the comfortably carpeted modern lounge or the dining room, and good changing dishes might include sandwiches (from £2.65), soup (£2.95), a range of starters such as stuffed pepper, smoked fillet of beef with parmesan and green bean salad or wood pigeon with black pudding and bacon (£4.95), mussels marinière with garlic toast (£5.35 starter, £9.95 main course), spinach and goat cheese parcel (£7.95), chargrilled lamb chops with haggis mash (£12.65), fillet of scottish salmon (£12.95), perthshire venison steak with sautéed wild mushrooms (£13.45), sirloin steak (£14.95), seared west coast scallops with basil pesto and roast pine nut risotto (£15.45) and puddings like glazed lemon tart or profiteroles (from £4.25); they do children's meals too (£3.95). There's also a very good wine list, with several wines by the glass, and you can choose from around 100 malt whiskies. The owners can arrange fishing nearby. From here you look to the mountains beyond the Tay from its two outside terraces, sweeping up to Ben Lawers (the highest peak in this part of Scotland). *(Recommended by Walter and Susan Rinaldi-Butcher, Paul and Ursula Randall, Mark Flynn, Charles and Pauline Stride, Mr and Mrs M Stratton)*

Free house ~ Licensee Alastair Gillespie ~ Real ale ~ Bar food ~ Restaurant ~ (01887) 820346 ~ Children welcome ~ Dogs allowed in bar and bedrooms ~ Open 11-11; closed 1-2 Jan, 25-26 Dec ~ Bedrooms: £55B/£90B

LUCKY DIP

Besides the fully inspected pubs, you might like to try these Lucky Dips recommended to us and described by readers (if you do, please send us reports: www.goodguides.co.uk).

ABERDEENSHIRE

ABERDEEN [NJ9305]
Grill AB11 6BA [Union St]: Old-fashioned traditional local with real ales such as Caledonian 80/-, Courage and Isle of Skye Red Cuillin, enormous range of malt whiskies, polished dark panelling, match-strike metal strip under bar counter, basic snacks; open all day *(the Didler, Graham Watson)*
BRAEMAR [NO1591]
Fife Arms AB35 5YN: Big tartan-carpeted Victorian hotel balancing catering for coach parties with serving as a local pub, good selection of malt whiskies, reasonably priced self-service pub food, huge log fire, comfortable sofas; children and dogs welcome, piped music; bedrooms warm and comfortable with mountain views, pleasant strolls in village *(Susan and John Douglas)*
CRATHIE [NO2293]
Inver AB35 5UL [A93 Balmoral—Braemar]: Sensitively refurbished 18th-c inn by River Dee, stripped stone bar and upstairs lounge, open fires, sensible choice of enjoyable home-made food, decent wine by the glass, lots of whiskies; bedrooms *(J F M and M West)*
ECHT [NO7005]
Midmar AB51 7LX [Midmar; W on B9119]:

New wood floors, changing real ales from new bar counter, comfortable chairs in separate red-carpeted lounge, enjoyable food from new kitchen; ceilidh Thurs *(David and Betty Gittins)*
MUIR OF FOWLIS [NJ5612]
Muggarthaugh AB33 8HX [Tough, just off A980]: Above-average food interestingly cooked using good ingredients (made from fresh so may be a wait), good friendly service, small neat bar with coal fire, TV and games room off, simple restaurant, Caledonian Deuchars IPA and a guest from Cairngorm or Tomintoul, nice wine choice; bedrooms, open for most of day at least in summer, handy for Craigievar (which has no catering), cl Mon *(David and Betty Gittins, Lucien Perring)*
OLDMELDRUM [NJ8127]
☆ *Redgarth* AB51 0DJ [Kirk Brae]: Good-sized comfortable lounge, traditional décor and subdued lighting, changing real ales such as Isle of Skye Red Cuillin, good range of malt whiskies, nicely presented satisfying food inc some interesting dishes and good puddings, more intimate restaurant, cheerful and attentive landlord and staff; gorgeous views to Bennachie, immaculate bedrooms *(David and Betty Gittins)*

ANGUS

MEMUS [NO4259]

Drovers DD8 3TY: Quaint bar interestingly restored with kitchen range, quarry tiles and lots of memorabilia, cosy lounge with duck pictures, real ales such as Orkney Dark Island, wide choice of whiskies, traditional food inc popular Sunday high teas, pleasantly formal softly lit two-room restaurant divided by woodburner, large dining conservatory looking over charming garden with peaceful country views, impressive adventure play area and Sun barbecues; cl Mon evening (*Susan and John Douglas*)

ARGYLL

ARDFERN [NM8004]

Galley of Lorne PA31 8QN [B8002; village and inn signposted off A816 Lochgilphead—Oban]: Cosy bar with warming log fire, big navigation lamps by counter, unfussy assortment of furniture, Caledonian Deuchars IPA and a local guest beer, dozens of malt whiskies, enjoyable home-made bar food inc local seafood, darts, dominoes and board games, spacious restaurant (children welcome here); games machine, TV, piped music; good sea and loch views from sheltered terrace and comfortable bedroom extension, open all day (*Dave Braisted, LYM*)

CAIRNBAAN [NR8390]

Cairnbaan Hotel PA31 8SQ [B841, off A816 N of Lochgilphead]: Charming spot overlooking busy canal lock and swing bridge, with walk to four central locks; cheerful efficient service, delightful small bar, warm and welcoming, with bare boards, bookshelves and immaculate restful décor, enjoyable bar food in carpeted conservatory, Fyne real ale, good stylish restaurant; tables on flagstoned terrace, attractive and comfortable bedrooms, open all day (*Richard J Holloway*)

CLACHAN SEIL [NM7819]

☆ *Tigh an Truish* PA34 4QZ [linked by bridge via B844, off A816 S of Oban]: Friendly and interesting unsmart 18th-c pub nr lovely anchorage, pine-clad walls and ceiling, bay windows overlooking inlet, prints and oil paintings, woodburner in one room, open fires in others, home-made bar food inc good fresh seafood (all day in summer), dining room, Fyne Somerled and McEwans 80/-, good choice of malt whiskies, locals dropping in for a wee dram, darts and dominoes; TV, piped music; children in restaurant, plenty of tables outside inc some in small suntrap side garden, good value bedrooms, open all day summer (*Jenny and Brian Seller, LYM*)

CONNEL [NM9034]

☆ *Oyster* PA37 1PJ: Cosy 18th-c inn opp former ferry slipway, lovely view across the water, attractive bar and restaurant, good thriving Highland atmosphere, enjoyable well prepared standard food, helpful friendly service even when busy, keg beers but good range of wines by the glass and of malt whiskies; comfortable bedrooms (*Charles and Pauline Stride, Topher Nairn, Ian Fleming, Maurice and Gill McMahon*)

DUNBEG [NM8833]

Wide Mouthed Frog PA37 1PX [Dunstaffnage Marina]: Long bar with enjoyable food, Fyne Highlander, decent wines; verandah and huge covered terrace overlooking marina, bay and Dunstaffnage Castle, bedrooms in same complex (*J V Dadswell*)

EASDALE [NM7317]

Puffer PA34 4TB [Easdale Island – park at end of B844 on Easdale itself and sound horn for passenger ferry]: Corridor to back bar from front tea room, Caledonian Deuchars IPA, bar food; centre of island activities (*Dave Braisted*)

ELLENABEICH [NM7417]

Oyster Brewery PA34 4RQ [Harbour; Seil]: Opened 2004, brewing its own ales such as IPA Easd'Ale, also Thistle Tickler, Red Pearl, Old Tosser and Oyster Gold, food from crab sandwiches through yorkshire puddings to full seafood meals; lovely setting (*Jenny and Brian Seller, Dave Braisted*)

GLENCOE [NN1058]

☆ *Clachaig* PH49 4HX [old Glencoe rd, behind NTS Visitor Centre]: Extended inn doubling as mountain rescue post and cheerfully crowded with outdoors people in season, with mountain photographs in basic flagstoned walkers' bar (two woodburners and pool), quieter pine-panelled snug and big modern-feeling dining lounge – service better in here, and hot plates for the hearty all-day bar food, wider evening choice, great real ale choice inc four locally brewed ones, unusual bottled beers, over 120 malt whiskies, annual beer festival, children in restaurant; live music Sat; simple bedrooms, spectacular setting surrounded by soaring mountains (*LYM, Dr Peter Crawshaw, Richard and Anne Ansell, Andy and Cath Pearson*)

OBAN [NM8529]

Aulays PA34 5SQ [Airds Crescent]: Attractive flower-decked façade, nice bustling pubby atmosphere, good value straightforward food, simple compact eating area, murals and lots of maritime pictures; piped music, keg beer; 5 minutes' walk from ferries (*George Atkinson*)

Barn PA34 4SE [off A816 S – follow Ardoran Marine sign]: Friendly converted barn in lovely remote-feeling countryside nr sea, wide choice of good changing chip-free home-made food esp Fri local seafood (great shortbread for sale, too), reasonable prices, real ale, wooden tables and settles, scottish music nights; children very welcome (dogs too), beautiful views from terrace, play area, donkeys, rabbits and hens all around; part of chalet holiday complex (*Linda Battison*)

☆ *Oban Inn* PA34 5NJ [Stafford St, nr North Pier]: Cheery 18th-c harbour-town local breathing easier since the smoking ban, pubby beamed and slate-floored downstairs bar, Caledonian Deuchars IPA, 45 malt whiskies, partly panelled upstairs dining bar (good value food all day) with button-back banquettes around cast-iron-framed tables, coffered woodwork ceiling, little stained-glass false windows and family area; fruit machine, juke box, piped music; dogs allowed in bar, open all day *(LYM, N R White, Susan and John Douglas, C J Fletcher, Simon Jones)*

STRACHUR [NN0802]

Creggans PA27 8BX [Creggans; A815]: Welcoming small hotel in lovely countryside by Loch Fyne, tweedy lounge bar, lively locals' bar with games room, popular good value bar food inc local seafood, good choice of malt whiskies and wines, restaurant and conservatory; children welcome, comfortable bedrooms, open all day *(Dr Peter Crawshaw, LYM)*

TARBERT [NR8768]

Columba PA29 6UF [Pier Rd]: Civilised and well preserved 1900s pub named for the then daily ferry from Glasgow, attractive and congenial bar, enjoyable food using local fish and fresh produce here, small room off, and charming restaurant; seven comfortable bedrooms *(A and B D Craig, Richard J Holloway)*

Victoria PA29 6TW [Barmore Rd]: Bright yellow pub with conservatory overlooking beautiful harbour, wide choice of enjoyable food using local seafood, venison and so forth *(D W Walker)*

AYRSHIRE

AYR [NS3320]

Abbotsford KA7 2ST [Corsehill Rd, just off B7024]: Small hotel run by welcoming family, cosy and comfortable bar, enjoyable sensibly priced bar food, helpful service, McEwans 80/- *(Mr and Mrs Colin Roberts)*

West Kirk KA7 1BX [Sandgate]: Outstanding Wetherspoons conversion of a former church, keeping its original stained glass, pulpit, balconies, doors and so forth; good real ales and their usual food *(Nick Holding)*

SORN [NS5526]

Sorn Inn KA5 6HU [Main St]: Unexpectedly smart restaurant-with-rooms in tiny conservation village, good bar food in chop house, imaginative cooking in upmarket restaurant, reasonable prices; comfortable bedrooms *(Roy Bromell)*

BANFFSHIRE

PORTSOY [NJ5866]

Shore AB45 2QR [Church St]: Small harbourside pub, bare-boards L-shaped bar with dark bentwood seats, masses of nautical and other bric-a-brac, prints and pictures, good value food, straightforward but cooked with flair, real ale such as Cairngorm Smugglers or Caledonian Deuchars IPA, cheerful chatty regulars, darts; subdued piped music, small TV *(David and Betty Gittins)*

BERWICKSHIRE

AUCHENCROW [NT8560]

☆ *Craw* TD14 5LS [B6438 NE of Duns; pub signed off A1]: Attractive cottagey beamed country pub with new French landlord cooking enjoyable good value food inc good fish, good service by his friendly wife, two changing real ales, good wines by the glass, woodburner, back eating areas; children welcome, tables on back terrace and out on green, bedrooms, open all day wknds *(BB, Comus and Sarah Elliott, Dr Jim Craig-Gray)*

DUNS [NT7853]

Black Bull TD11 3AR [Black Bull St]: Small country inn with landlord cooking enjoyable interesting food (helpful with special diets), good wine choice, pleasant unpretentious atmosphere, entertaining electronic cuckoo clock in dining room; bedrooms *(Dr Jim Craig-Gray)*

LAUDER [NT5347]

☆ *Black Bull* TD2 6SR [Market Pl]: Comfortably refurbished 17th-c inn with good choice of interesting food served in three linked areas, good beer and service; children welcome, open all day, comfortable bedrooms *(David and Jane Hill, Pat and Stewart Gordon, LYM, Mr and Mrs H Hine)*

PAXTON [NT9352]

Cross TD15 1TE: Smart village pub with enterprising newish landlady, real ales such as Mordue or Wylam, farm cider, good food selection at modest prices *(Comus and Sarah Elliott, Stanley and Annie Matthews)*

RESTON [NT8762]

Red Lion TD14 5JP [Main St (B6438)]: Neatly kept family-run pub, cheery bar with blazing log fire and collection of old cameras, enjoyable food cooked to order, wider evening choice; pretty garden, cl Mon, open wkdy lunchtimes out of season, open till late wknds *(Catherine Ferguson)*

DUMFRIESSHIRE

DUMFRIES [NX9776]

Cavens Arms DG1 2AH [Buccleuch St]: Caledonian Deuchars IPA, Greene King Abbot and up to half a dozen changing guest beers, friendly landlord, enjoyable food (not Mon) inc pubby standards and imaginative dishes, entertainingly silly pub newspaper, civilised outer air-conditioned bar with lots of wood; no children, open all day *(Nick Holding, Joe Green)*

MOFFAT [NT0805]

☆ *Black Bull* DG10 9EG [Churchgate]: Attractive and well kept small hotel, plush dimly lit bar with Burns memorabilia, enjoyable unpretentious food from sandwiches and light dishes up using local meats, service efficient even though the coach parties from the nearby Woollen Mill gift shop can put some strain on it, Caledonian Deuchars IPA, McEwans 80/- and Theakstons XB, several dozen malt whiskies, friendly public bar across courtyard with railway memorabilia and good open fire, simply furnished tiled-floor dining room; decent piped music, side games bar with juke box, big-screen TV for golf; children welcome, tables in courtyard, 12 comfortable good value bedrooms, open all day *(Dave Braisted, LYM,*

Stephen R Holman, Nick Holding, David and Heather Stephenson, Bill Strang, Stuart Pearson)

NEW ABBEY [NX9666]

Abbey Arms DG2 8BX [The Square]: Always welcoming, with enjoyable pubby food from generous baguettes up, good service, a changing real ale such as Black Sheep, decent wines by the glass, dark pink dining room; dogs welcome *(Stan and Hazel Allen, R T and J C Moggridge)*

THORNHILL [NX8795]

☆ *Buccleuch & Queensberry* DG3 5LU [Drumlanrig St (A76)]: Substantial red sandstone Georgian former coaching inn with comfortable banquettes in traditional main beamed bar, good coal fire, friendly service, food from interesting sandwiches and baked potatoes to some good value main dishes, Caledonian 80/- and a changing guest beer; access to three miles of fishing on the River Nith – the inn is popular with sporting folk; children welcome, comfortable bedrooms with good breakfast, attractive small town *(LYM, Nick Holding, JWAC)*

DUNBARTONSHIRE

ARROCHAR [NN2903]

Village Inn G83 7AX [A814, just off A83 W of Loch Lomond]: Friendly staff and changing ales inc english guests as well as ones such as Orkney Dark Island, simple all-day dining area with heavy beams, bare boards and big open fire, steps down to unpretentious bar, several dozen malt whiskies, good coffee, fine sea and hill views; piped music, juke box, can be loudly busy Sat in summer; children welcome in eating areas till 8, tables out on deck and lawn, comfortable bedrooms inc spacious ones in former back barn, good breakfast, open all day *(LYM, M G Hart, Tracey and Stephen Groves)*

KILCREGGAN [NS2380]

Kilcreggan Hotel G84 0JP [Argyll Rd]: Recently renovated old small hotel overlooking Loch Long/ Firth of Clyde, good choice of beers, locally popular for good cheap food *(Dr Peter Crawshaw)*

EAST LOTHIAN

GIFFORD [NT5368]

Goblin Ha' EH41 4QH [Main St]: Recently refurbished hotel with contemporary décor and colour scheme in roomy and civilised front dining lounge, lively stripped-stone public bar with games area, varied food from simple bar lunches to more exotic or elaborate things, friendly quick service, real ales such as Caledonian Deuchars IPA, Hop Back Summer Lightning, Marstons Pedigree and Timothy Taylors Landlord, airy back conservatory; children welcome in lounge and conservatory, tables and chairs in good big garden with small play area, bedrooms, open all day Fri-Sun *(Ken Richards, Steve Whalley, Mrs K J Betts)*

Tweeddale Arms EH41 4QU [S of Haddington; High St (B6355)]: White-painted

hotel under new ownership, modernised lounge bar with several malt whiskies and modestly priced wines, bar food from sandwiches up, lively public bar with games machine and darts, relaxing hotel lounge with antique tables and paintings, chinoiserie chairs and chintzy easy chairs, three-course meals in restaurant; children welcome, overlooks attractive village green, comfortable bedrooms, open all day *(Archie and Margaret Mackenzie, LYM)*

PRESTONPANS [NT3874]

Prestoungrange Gothenberg EH32 9BE [High St]: Interesting pub/restaurant on the sea road, brewing its own Fowlers 70/-, 80/- and IPA, eclectic fairly priced food, friendly young staff, good wines *(Stephen Funnell)*

FIFE

ANSTRUTHER [NO5603]

Dreel KY10 3DL [High St W]: Cosy low 16th-c building in attractive spot with garden overlooking Dreel Burn, plenty of gleaming brass, low beams and timbers, small two-room bar with pleasant conservatory eating area, good value generous varied bar food inc fresh fish, real ales such as Batemans XB, Harviestoun and Tetleys, welcoming efficient staff, open fire in stripped-stone dining room, back pool room; dogs welcome, open all day *(Susan and John Douglas, Michael Butler)*

CERES [NO4011]

Ceres Inn KY15 5NE [The Cross]: Early 18th-c traditional village pub, good friendly service, Caledonian Deuchars IPA, wide choice of inexpensive pub food from standard lunchtime dishes to some stylish modern cooking using fresh local ingredients, small helpings available, OAP lunches, wknd high teas, small attractive stripped-stone and tartan-carpeted bar and linked lounge area with log fire, tankards on low beams, panelled dado, high-backed settles, horse tack, antlers and bric-a-brac, games area with pool and TV, small separate dining room downstairs; picnic-sets out behind by burn, across from pretty village green *(Susan and John Douglas, Lucien Perring)*

Meldrums KY15 5NA [Main St]: Small hotel popular for good choice of enjoyable reasonably priced bar lunches in roomy clean and attractive beamed dining lounge, well kept Caledonian Deuchars IPA, pleasant atmosphere, good friendly service even when busy (as it is for Sun lunch), cottagey parlour bar; seven well appointed bedrooms, charming village nr Wemyss Pottery *(Lucien Perring, Michael Butler)*

INVERNESS-SHIRE

AVIEMORE [NH8912]

☆ *Old Bridge* PH22 1PU [Dalfaber Rd, southern outskirts off B970]: Busy well kept inn with stripped stone and wood, local books and memorabilia, roaring open fire, good value food from sandwiches to carvery in bar with short but enterprising lunchtime choice, enjoyable meals in large restaurant extension (best to book for Tues ceilidh), cheerful landlady and friendly staff, changing ales such as Caledonian Deuchars IPA and 80/- and Isle of Skye Red Cuillin, decent wines; quiet piped music; children welcome, pleasant surroundings *(Andy and Jill Kassube, Topher Nairn, Christine and Neil Townend, Christine and Phil Young, Jarrod and Wendy Hopkinson)*

DRUMNADROCHIT [NH5029]
Fiddlers Elbow IV63 6TX: Enjoyable carefully cooked traditional food using good produce (must book evenings in high season), good value sandwiches served through the afternoon too, at least in summer, friendly atmosphere and good service, good real ale choice, affordable wines, original little girl effigy at entrance; two comfortable spotless bedrooms in the pub, more across the road, handy for Urquhart Castle *(David and Sheila Hawkes)*

FORT WILLIAM [NN1073]
Ben Nevis Bar PH33 6DG [High St]: Roomy raftered converted barn with imaginative choice of good value food, prompt cheery service, McEwans 80/-, harbour views from restaurant; TV, games, live music nights; bunk house below *(Michael and Maggie Betton, Dave Braisted, Sarah and Peter Gooderham)*

GLEN SHIEL [NH0711]
☆ *Cluanie Inn* IV63 7YW [A87 Invergarry—Kyle of Lochalsh, on Loch Cluanie]: Welcoming inn in lovely isolated setting by Loch Cluanie (good walks), big helpings of good freshly prepared bar food inc some interesting dishes in three knocked-together rooms with dining chairs around polished tables, overspill into restaurant, friendly efficient staff, good fire; children welcome, big comfortable modern bedrooms nicely furnished in pine, stunning views – great breakfasts for non-residents too *(Mrs J Main)*

INVERIE [NG7500]
☆ *Old Forge* PH41 4PL: Utterly remote waterside pub with fabulous views, comfortable mix of antique furnishings, lots of charts and sailing prints, buoyant atmosphere, open fire, good reasonably priced bar food inc fresh local seafood, even two real ales in season, also lots of whiskies and good wine choice; restaurant extension, open all day, late wknds, occasional live music and ceilidhs; the snag's getting there – boat (jetty moorings), Mallaig ferry three days a week, or 15-mile walk through Knoydart from nearest road *(Michael and Maggie Betton)*

INVERNESS [NH6446]
☆ *Clachnaharry Inn* IV3 8RB [High St, Clachnaharry (A862 NW of city)]: Congenial and cosily dim beamed bar, simple top lounge, more comfortable bottom lounge with picture windows looking over Beauly Firth, warm chatty atmosphere, plenty of friendly efficient staff, bargain freshly cooked food all day from big baked potatoes up, half a dozen real ales, great log fire as well as gas stove; children welcome, tables out overlooking railway,

lovely walks by big flight of Caledonian Canal locks, open all day *(Graham MacDonald, Joe Green)*
Harlequin IV2 4SA [1-2 View Pl, top of Castle St]: Relaxed downstairs bar with enjoyable lunchtime food, good restaurant upstairs; terrace with castle view *(Graham MacDonald)*
Heathmount IV2 3JT [Kingsmill Rd]: Two smart bars, enjoyable food, real ales, good friendly atmosphere; stylish bedrooms *(Graham MacDonald)*
Hootananny IV1 1ES [Church St]: Basic studenty music pub, dark walls, candlelight and scottish musicians sitting around playing – truly atmospheric; Black Isle real ale *(Graham MacDonald)*
Phoenix IV1 1LX [Academy St]: Several changing real ales in bare-boards 1890s bar with much dark brown varnish and granite trough at foot of island servery, neat adjoining dining room with some booth seating; sports TVs *(Graham MacDonald, Joe Green)*
Snow Goose IV2 7PA [Stoneyfield, about ¼ mile E of A9/A96 roundabout]: Useful Vintage Inn dining pub, the most northerly of this chain, well laid out with country-feel room areas, beams and flagstones, several log fires, soft lighting, interesting décor, their standard food and decent wines by the glass; comfortable bedrooms in adjacent Travelodge *(J F M and M West, Pamela and Merlyn Horswell, Walter and Susan Rinaldi-Butcher)*

KIRKHILL [NH5644]
Old North IV5 7PX [Inchmore (A862 Inverness—Beauly)]: Transformed by newish owners, now charming proper pub with log fires, good yet unpretentious home-made food using top local suppliers, real ales and good choice of malt whiskies, exemplary service *(Graham MacDonald)*

CATTERLINE [NO8678]
☆ *Creel* AB39 2UL: Good generous imaginative food esp soups and local fish and seafood in big but cosy lounge with woodburner, plenty of tables, real ales such as Caledonian Deuchars IPA and Maclays 70/-, welcoming service, small second bar, compact seaview restaurant (same menu, booking advised); bedrooms, old fishing village, cl Tues *(Brian McBurnie)*

FETTERCAIRN [NO6573]
Ramsay Arms AB30 1XX: Substantial small hotel with wholesome reasonably priced bar and restaurant food, friendly service; children welcome, garden tables, attractive village, bedrooms *(Anon)*

STONEHAVEN [NO8595]
☆ *Lairhillock* AB39 3QS [Netherley; 6 miles N of Stonehaven, 6 miles S of Aberdeen, take the Durris turn off from the A90]: Good fresh food from baguettes to aberdeen angus steaks in smartly extended pub's cheerful traditional beamed bar and spacious separate lounge, thoughtful children's choice, enterprising range of real ales, wines by the glass and malt

whiskies, good atmosphere and log fires, panoramic views from conservatory, cosy well regarded adjacent restaurant; children and dogs allowed, open all day wknds (*LYM, Brian McBurnie*)

AUCHENCAIRN [NX8249]
☆ *Balcary Bay Hotel* DG7 1QZ [about 2½ miles off A711]: Beautifully placed hotel with reasonably priced food from soup and open sandwiches to good imaginative hot dishes (huge child's helpings) in civilised friendly bar and small conservatory with idyllic views over Solway Firth, prompt friendly service even when busy; tables on terrace and in gardens in peaceful seaside surroundings, comfortable bedrooms (*Lucien Perring*)

CASTLE DOUGLAS [NX7662]
Crown DG7 1AA [King St]: Lively locals and tourists, good food, beer wine and service (*Stan and Hazel Allen*)

COLVEND [NX8555]
Clonyard House DG5 4QW: Small hotel nr Solway coast; efficient friendly service, decent food, half price for children for most dishes, reasonably priced wine by the glass, three bar rooms well used by locals, conservatory restaurant; dogs welcome, tables outside with play area (and said to be an enchanted tree in the pleasant wooded grounds), bedrooms and cosy log-cabin chalets (*Stan and Hazel Allen, Lucien Perring*)

DALRY [NX6281]
☆ *Clachan* DG7 3UW [A713 Castle Douglas—Ayr]: Cheerful bar, attractively refurbished yet pleasantly traditional with plenty of dark wood and log fires, friendly willing service, Greene King Abbot, good inexpensive wine list, fine selection of malts, enjoyable straightforward food using local meat, game and fish, from good sandwiches and toasties up, also breakfast 8-12, another log fire in beamed and timbered restaurant, interesting fishing and shooting frieze; bedrooms, on Southern Upland Way (baggage-transport service for walkers), open all day wknds (*Nick Holding, Edward and June Sulley, Mrs Maureen Robertson*)

HAUGH OF URR [NX8066]
Laurie Arms DG7 3YA [B794 N of Dalbeattie]: Warmly welcoming village pub with log fires in both bars, three or four changing real ales such as Black Sheep, Greene King, Houston or Harviestoun, enjoyable reasonably priced bar food from sandwiches to good steaks, more adventurous choice in adjacent restaurant with own bar, decent wine, good robust landlord and helpful staff, attractive décor with various knick-knacks, Bamforth comic postcards in the lavatories; tables outside (*Nick Holding, Joe Green, Mark O'Sullivan, Chris Smith*)

KIPPFORD [NX8355]
Anchor DG5 4LN [off A710 S of Dalbeattie]: Popular waterfront inn in lovely spot overlooking big natural harbour and peaceful

hills, efficient service, enjoyable food from sandwiches up, local Sulwath beers, lots of malt whiskies, coal fire in traditional back bar (dogs allowed in one area here), lounge bar, simple dining room; piped music, TV and machines; children welcome, tables outside, good walks and birdwatching, open all day in summer (*Stan and Hazel Allen, Derek and Sylvia Stephenson, David and Heather Stephenson, LYM*)
Mariner DG5 4LN: Neatly kept pub with ship décor, friendly staff, ample good value food (*Stan and Hazel Allen*)

KIRKCUDBRIGHT [NX6851]
Royal DG6 4DY [St Cuthbert St]: Well used local with hearty food in two friendly bars and restaurant, decent beer and wines, efficient service; dogs welcome (*Stan and Hazel Allen*)

BIGGAR [NT0437]
Crown ML12 6DL [High St (A702)]: Two real ales and above-average food all day (new back dining extension), coal fire in front bar, old-fashioned panelled back lounge with old local pictures; open all day (*J V Dadswell, Nick Holding*)

GLASGOW [NS5965]
Rogano G1 3AN [Exchange Pl]: Smart sophisticated downstairs café-bar with good food, cocktails and wines, cushioned booth seating, big ceiling fan, outstanding 1930s deco woodwork and chromium; piped jazz; good if pricey mainly seafood restaurant upstairs (*OPUS, LYM*)

TWEEDSMUIR [NT1026]
Crook ML12 6QN [A701 a mile N]: Unusual mix of 17th c (as in simple flagstoned back bar) with 1936 art deco (airy lounge, classic lavatories, all sorts of 1930s details to look out for); log fires, bar food, sometimes Broughton real ale, good choice of malt whiskies, restaurant, traditional games; children welcome, tables outside, play area, garden over road, bedrooms, Tweed trout fishing, open all day (*Nick Holding, LYM*)

BALERNO [NT1566]
Johnsburn House EH14 7BB [Johnsburn Rd]: Lovely old-fashioned beamed bar in 18th-c former mansion with masterpiece 1911 ceiling by Robert Lorimer; Caledonian Deuchars IPA and interesting changing ales, coal fire, panelled dining lounge with good food inc shellfish and game, more formal evening dining rooms; children and dogs welcome, open all day wknds, cl Mon (*the Didler*)

EDINBURGH [NT2574]
☆ *Bennets* EH3 9LG [Leven St]: Ornate Victorian bar with original glass, mirrors, arcades, panelling and tiles, friendly service, real ales inc Caledonian Deuchars IPA from tall founts, over a hundred malt whiskies, bar snacks and bargain homely lunchtime hot dishes (not Sun; children allowed in eating area), second bar

with counter salvaged from old ship; open all day *(LYM, the Didler)*

☆ *Caledonian Ale House* EH12 5EZ [Haymarket Terr, by Stn]: Long convivial Victorian-style bar with Caledonian and scottish guest beers, imported beers on tap and in bottle, simple furnishings on bare boards, good range of enjoyable food in upstairs bistro (booking recommended wknd evenings), good service; sports TVs *(P Dawn, John and Julie Moon)*

☆ *Canny Man's* EH10 4QU [Morningside Rd; aka Volunteer Arms]: Great bustling atmosphere and utterly individual and distinctive, saloon, lounge and snug, all sorts of fascinating bric-a-brac, ceiling papered with sheet music, good bar food inc formidable open sandwiches and smorgasbord served with panache, huge choice of whiskies, real ales such as Caledonian Deuchars IPA and Fullers London Pride, cheap children's drinks, very friendly staff; courtyard tables *(Bruce and Penny Wilkie, Dr and Mrs R G J Telfer)*

Cask & Barrel EH1 3RZ [Broughton St]: Bare-boards traditional drinkers' pub, half a dozen mainly scottish real ales inc Caledonian 80/- from U-shaped bar, helpful service, good value bar food esp stovies Mon-Fri; sports TVs *(P Dawn, BB, R M Corlett)*

Cloisters EH3 9JH [Brougham St]: Friendly and interesting ex-parsonage alehouse with Caledonian Deuchars and 80/- and half a dozen or so interesting guest beers, 70 malt whiskies, several wines by the glass, decent food till 3 (4 Sat) from toasties to Sun roasts, plenty for vegetarians, breakfast too, pews and bar gantry recycled from redundant church, bare boards and lots of brewery mirrors; lavatories down spiral stairs, folk music Fri/Sat; dogs welcome, open all day *(the Didler, Mark and Lynette Davies)*

Doric EH1 1DE [Market St]: Plenty of atmosphere, Caledonian Deuchars IPA and McEwans 80/-, decent wines, good value bar food, friendly young staff, good upstairs bistro *(Nigel Espley, Liane Purnell, Janet and Peter Race)*

☆ *Kenilworth* EH2 3JD [Rose St]: Edwardian pub with ornate high ceiling, carved woodwork and tiles, huge etched brewery mirrors and windows, red leather seating around tiled wall; central bar with Caledonian Deuchars IPA and three guest beers, good choice of hot drinks and wines by the glass, good value food lunchtime and evening, quick friendly attentive service, back family room; piped music, discreetly placed games machines, TV; tables outside, open all day *(BB, P Dawn, the Didler)*

☆ *Milnes* EH2 2PJ [Rose St/Hanover St]: Well reworked traditional city pub rambling down to several areas below street level and even in yard; busy old-fashioned bare-boards feel, dark wood furnishings and panelling, cask tables, lots of old photographs and mementoes of poets who used the 'Little Kremlin' room here, wide choice of real ales, open fire, reasonably priced bar food *(BB, the Didler, J M Tansey, R M Corlett)*

Oxford EH2 4JB [Young St]: Friendly unspoilt pub with two built-in wall settles and unchanging regulars in tiny bustling front bar, quieter back room, lino floor, Caledonian Deuchars IPA and Belhaven Best and 80/-, cheap filled cobs; lavatories up a few steps *(Peter F Marshall, Joe Green, Nigel Espley, Liane Purnell, J M Tansey)*

☆ *Peacock* EH6 4TZ [Lindsay Rd, Newhaven]: Good honest food all day esp fresh fish in hefty helpings in neat plushly comfortable pub with several linked areas inc conservatory-style back room leading to garden, McEwans 80/- and a guest such as Orkney Dark Island, efficient service; very popular, best to book evenings and Sun lunchtime; children welcome, open all day *(Charles and Pauline Stride, Mr and Mrs M Shirley, LYM)*

Steading EH10 7DU [Hill End, Biggar Rd (A702)]: Popular modern pub, several cottages knocked together at foot of dry ski slope, a dozen changing scottish and english real ales inc Timothy Taylors Landlord, friendly staff, reasonably priced usual food 10-10 in cheerful bar, upstairs restaurant and conservatories *(Christine and Neil Townend)*

White Hart EH1 2JU [Grassmarket]: One of Edinburgh's oldest pubs, small, basic and easy-going, with relaxed atmosphere, good friendly young staff, Caledonian Deuchars and other real ales, enjoyable food all day; piped music, some live; pavement tables, open all day *(Bruce and Penny Wilkie, Mark Walker)*

Worlds End EH1 1TB [High St (Royal Mile)]: Small hospitable pub in 17th-c building, plenty of atmosphere and interesting nooks to sit in, Caledonian 80/-, good breakfast *(Bruce and Penny Wilkie, Esther and John Sprinkle)*

MUSSELBURGH [NT3372]

Volunteer Arms EH21 6JE [N High St; aka Staggs]: Same family since 1858, unspoilt busy bar, dark panelling, old brewery mirrors, great gantry with ancient casks, Caledonian Deuchars IPA and 80/- and a quickly changing guest beer; dogs welcome, open all day *(the Didler, Joe Green)*

MORAYSHIRE

FINDHORN [NJ0464]

☆ *Kimberley* IV36 3YG: Unpretentious wood-floored seaside pub with good generous food inc particularly good fresh seafood collected by landlord from early morning Buckie fish market, friendly staff, weekly changing guest beers, loads of whiskies, jovial company, log fire; children and dogs welcome, heated terrace tables looking out to sea *(Graham MacDonald)*

PEEBLESSHIRE

EDDLESTON [NT2447]

☆ *Horseshoe* EH45 8QP [A703 Peebles—Penicuik]: Civilised newly renovated old beamed pub, French chef doing good imaginative mix of french and scottish cooking for bar and restaurant, friendly helpful staff, soft lighting, comfortable seats, Bass and good choice of wines and whiskies; eight well equipped bedrooms in annexe (LYM, Archie and Margaret Mackenzie)

INNERLEITHEN [NT3336]

☆ Traquair Arms EH44 6PD [B709, just off A72 Peebles—Galashiels]: Under new management and well run, with warm fire in unpretentious bar, good bar food all day, three real ales inc one from nearby Traquair House, another open fire in spacious dining room; piped music; children and dogs welcome, good bedrooms (some in annexe), open all day (Derek and Sylvia Stephenson, R M Corlett, LYM, Anthony Barnes, Graham Findlay)

WEST LINTON [NT1451]

☆ Gordon Arms EH46 7DR [Dolphinton Rd (A702 S of Edinburgh)]: Friendly and unpretentious L-shaped bar with a couple of leather chesterfields and more usual pub furniture, log fire, decent food (all day wknds) in bar and restaurant from massive open sandwiches to good local lamb, good service, Caledonian Deuchars IPA and a guest beer; children welcome, dogs on leads too (biscuits for them), tables outside, bedrooms (Nick Holding, Ian Mcfarlane, BB)

PERTHSHIRE

AUCHTERARDER [NN9412]

Glendevon PH3 1AF [High St]: Good friendly service, good value bar food, pleasant surroundings (G Dobson)

BLAIR ATHOLL [NN8765]

☆ Atholl Arms PH18 5SG: Sizeable hotel's stable-theme pubby bar in lovely setting nr the castle, full range of Moulin real ales (same ownership), well priced good food all day from sandwiches to interesting dishes and local wild salmon and meat, helpful friendly staff; 31 good value bedrooms, open all day (Andy and Jill Kassube, Paul and Ursula Randall, Mr and Mrs Maurice Thompson, Karen Eliot)

BRIG O' TURK [NN5306]

☆ Byre FK17 8HT [A821 Callander—Trossachs, just outside village]: Beautifully placed byre conversion with hard-working and welcoming chef/landlord doing generous helpings of good simple inexpensive food inc unsual dishes, attentive service, Tetleys, cast-iron framed tables and log fire in flagstoned bar, roomier high-raftered restaurant above; tables out on extensive decking, three bedrooms, good walks, open all day, has been cl Thurs in winter (LYM, Susan and John Douglas, Maurice and Gill McMahon, Michael Butler)

CHAPELHILL [NO0030]

Chapelhill Inn PH1 3TH [B8063]: Unpretentious-looking two-bar pub in beautiful countryside, good friendly service, immaculate housekeeping, enjoyable food from simple things to enterprising dishes using fresh local produce, good fresh veg, restaurant; cl Mon (David Kerr)

COMRIE [NN7722]

Royal PH6 2DN [Melville Sq]: Pleasant country hotel with good value bar food, good

dining room menu, lounge and separate public bar; bedrooms (Dr Jim Craig-Gray)

DUNNING [NO0114]

Kirkstyle PH2 0RR [B9141, off A9 S of Perth; Kirkstyle Sq]: Friendly olde-worlde streamside pub with log fire in unpretentious bar, good choice of beers and whiskies, good service, enjoyable home-made food inc interesting dishes (must book in season), charming back restaurant with flagstones and stripped stone walls (Susan and John Douglas)

KENMORE [NN7745]

☆ Kenmore Hotel PH15 2NU [A827 W of Aberfeldy]: Civilised small hotel in pretty 18th-c village by Loch Tay, comfortable traditional front lounge with warm log fire and long poem pencilled by Burns himself on the chimney-breast, dozens of malt whiskies helpfully arranged alphabetically, polite uniformed staff, restaurant; bar food from sandwiches and baguettes up in light and airy back bar and terrace overlooking River Tay, pool and winter darts back here, also juke box, TV, fruit machine, and entertainment Weds and Sun; children and dogs welcome, back terrace overlooking River Tay, good bedrooms, open all day (LYM, Susan and John Douglas, Graham Findlay, Michael Butler)

KIRKTON OF GLENISLA [NO2160]

☆ Glenisla Hotel PH11 8PH [B951 N of Kirriemuir and Alyth]: Friendly newish owners working hard to please customers, real ales such as Houston and Inveralmond and initiatives such as small beer festivals with folk groups, freshly made food using local produce, good service, lively local atmosphere and good log fire in beamed bar, comfortable sunny lounge and attractive high-ceilinged dining room, games area in converted stable block; piped music; children and dogs welcome (big pub dog), decent bedrooms, good walks, open all day in season (Les and Sandra Brown, Alistair and Kay Butler, LYM, Lucien Perring)

LOCH TUMMEL [NN8160]

Loch Tummel Inn PH16 5RP [B8019 4 miles E of Tummel Bridge]: Lochside former coaching inn with great views over water to Schiehallion, lots of walks and local wildlife, big woodburner in cosy partly stripped stone dining bar, good food inc game and home-smoked salmon here and in residents' converted hayloft restaurant, changing ales (at a hefty price) such as Isle of Skye, Moulin or Williams Fraoch, good choice of wines and whiskies, no music or machines; prompt bar closing time; attractive loch-view bedrooms with log fires, even an open fire in one bathroom, good breakfast, fishing free for residents; cl winter (Andy and Jill Kassube, Paul and Ursula Randall, LYM, J F M and M West)

MEIKLEOUR [NO1539]

☆ Meikleour Hotel PH2 6EB [A984 W of Coupar Angus]: Two quietly well furnished lounges, one with stripped stone and flagstones, another more chintzy, both with open fires, welcoming landlord, polite helpful staff, three real ales such as Fyne and

Inveralmond, local bottled water, good reasonably priced bar food inc fine sandwiches, back public bar; understated pretty building, picnic-sets in pleasant garden with tall pines and distant Highland view, comfortable bedrooms, good breakfast *(Susan and John Douglas, Christine and Neil Townend)*

PERTH [NO1223]

☆ *Greyfriars* PH2 8PG [South St]: Small and comfortable, with pretty décor, good value lunchtime food from baguettes and baked potatoes up, four changing real ales inc good Friars Tipple brewed for them by local Inveralmond, friendly staff and core of local regulars; small restaurant upstairs *(Christine and Neil Townend)*

Old Ship PH1 5TJ [High St]: Compact and neatly refurbished, with real ales such as Caledonian Deuchars IPA, Greene King Abbot and Inveralmond Ossian, good coffee and tea, low-priced lunchtime soup, baguettes and light meals, comfortable banquettes and chairs, landlord's geological samples and his father's interesting World War II merchant seaman's history alongside the usual prints and photographs, handsome preserved former inn sign; no children *(Paul and Ursula Randall)*

PITLOCHRY [NN9163]

☆ *Killiecrankie Hotel* PH16 5LG [Killiecrankie, off A9 N]: Comfortable and splendidly placed country hotel with extensive peaceful grounds and dramatic views, attractive panelled bar (may have piped music), airy conservatory extension, good choice of reasonably priced enjoyable food here and in rather formal restaurant, extensive wine list; children in bar eating area, bedrooms, open all day in summer *(LYM, Joan and Tony Walker)*

ROSS-SHIRE

ACHILTIBUIE [NC0208]

☆ *Summer Isles* IV26 2YQ: Popular small bar attached to hotel, fresh food from good sandwiches up inc seafood and organic supplies from nearby Hydroponicum, real ales such as Isle of Skye Cuillin Red or Orkney Raven, good wines by the glass, friendly service, lovely views of the Summer Isles from small terrace; hotel side warm, friendly and well furnished, with pretty watercolours and flowers, bedrooms comfortable and good value, though the cheapest are not lavish *(N R White, Christine and Phil Young)*

CROMARTY [NH7867]

☆ *Royal* IV11 8YN [Marine Terrace]: Pleasant old-fashioned harbourside hotel with cheerful helpful management, reasonably priced food esp fish, lots of malt whiskies (keg beers), sleepy sea views across Cromarty Firth to Ben Wyvis from covered front verandah, games etc in separate locals' bar; children and dogs welcome, comfortable up-to-date bedrooms (not all have the view), good breakfast, open all day *(N R White, LYM)*

CULBOKIE [NH6059]

Culbokie Inn IV7 8JH: Village inn with popular bar and small restaurant, Wadworths

6X, pleasant service, well presented good value food, panelling; tables in small garden with excellent mountain and loch views *(Neil and Anita Christopher)*

FORTROSE [NH7256]

☆ *Anderson* IV10 8TD [Union St, off A832]: Good small 19th-c hotel which takes its pub side seriously, with approaching 200 malt whiskies, good Cairngorm real ale, dozens of bottled belgian beers, settees by the log fire, friendly knowledgeable landlord, and enterprising food with a scottish touch in bar and restaurant; children welcome (games for them), comfortable bedrooms, open all day *(Ruth Green, Christopher J Darwent)*

KYLE OF LOCHALSH [NG7627]

Lochalsh Hotel IV40 8AF [Ferry Rd]: Large friendly hotel's lounge bar with civilised armchairs and sofas around low tables, plainer eating area, good simple bar food from generous double sandwiches to dishes of the day, pleasant Skye Bridge views, quick friendly service, good coffee; picnic-sets on spreading front lawns, bedrooms *(Joan and Tony Walker, George Atkinson)*

LOCHCARRON [NG9039]

Rockvilla IV54 8YB: Good choice of reasonably priced food inc sandwiches and some local specialities in small hotel's light and comfortable bar, helpful owners and quick friendly service, Isle of Skye real ale, loch view; comfortable bedrooms *(Jane and David Hill, G D Brooks)*

MUNLOCHY [NH6453]

Munlochy Hotel IV8 8NL [Millbank Rd]: Large bar with panelling, stripped wood and stone, pleasant service, Black Isle real ale, seafood, venison and other dishes in airy dining room *(Neil and Anita Christopher)*

PLOCKTON [NG8033]

Plockton Inn IV52 8TW [Innes St; unconnected to Plockton Hotel]: Fresh substantial well cooked food inc good fish, congenial bustling atmosphere even in winter, friendly efficient service, real ales, good range of malt whiskies; some live traditional music, comfortable bedrooms *(Andrew Birkinshaw)*

SHIEL BRIDGE [NG9319]

Kintail Lodge IV40 8HL: Lots of varnished wood in large plain bar adjoining hotel, convivial bustle in season, plenty of malt whiskies, Isle of Skye Black Cuillin, particularly good food from same kitchen as attractive conservatory restaurant with magnificent view down Loch Duich to Skye and its mountains, local game, wild salmon and own smokings, also children's helpings; good value big bedrooms, bunkhouse *(Dave Braisted, Bill Strang, Stuart Pearson)*

ULLAPOOL [NH1294]

Argyll IV26 2UB [Argyle St]: Cheerful modern lounge bar with wide choice of enjoyable food, reasonable prices, friendly efficient staff, local An Teallach real ale, good range of whiskies, small locals' bar; bedrooms *(N R White)*

☆ *Ceilidh Place* IV26 2TY [West Argyle St]: Arty celtic café/bar with art gallery, bookshop and coffee shop, regular jazz, folk and classical music, informal mix of furnishings, woodburner, wide choice of food from side servery, conservatory restaurant with some emphasis on fish; children welcome in eating areas, terrace tables, comfortable bedrooms, open all day *(LYM, Kevin Flack)*

Seaforth IV26 2UE [Quay St]: Roomy open-plan harbour-view bar with Hebridean and Isle of Skye ales, good range of malt whiskies, wide choice of enjoyable local seafood from end food counter, friendly chatty efficient staff, simple décor, upstairs evening restaurant; live music most nights, open till late *(Joan and Tony Walker)*

ROXBURGHSHIRE

ST BOSWELLS [NT5930]

☆ *Buccleuch Arms* TD6 0EW [A68 just S of Newtown St Boswells]: Civilised sandstone hotel with calm unchanging feel, wide choice of enjoyable inexpensive bar food (inc Sun), sandwiches all day, real ale, efficient uniformed staff, Georgian-style plush bar with light oak panelling, restaurant; children welcome, tables in attractive garden behind with new self-service plant centre, bedrooms *(Susan and John Douglas, LYM)*

SELKIRKSHIRE

ETTRICKBRIDGE [NT3824]

Cross Keys TD7 5JN: Good atmosphere, better-than-average pub food, friendly efficient staff; bedrooms *(Bob Ellis)*

TUSHIELAW [NT3018]

☆ *Tushielaw Inn* TD7 5HT [Ettrick Valley, B709/B7009 Lockerbie—Selkirk]: Former coaching inn in lovely spot by River Ettrick, unpretentiously comfortable little bar attracting an interesting mix of customers, open fire, local prints and photographs, home-made bar food inc good aberdeen angus steaks, friendly family service, decent house wines, a good few malt whiskies, darts, cribbage, dominoes, shove-ha'penny and liar dice, dining room; children welcome, terrace tables, bedrooms, open all day Sat in summer, cl Sun night and in winter all day Mon *(LYM, Nick Holding, Bob Ellis)*

STIRLINGSHIRE

PORT OF MENTEITH [NN5801]

☆ *Lake of Menteith* FK8 3RA: Recently refurbished, with good food from traditional favourites to contemporary dishes in comfortable bar overlooking lake, breakfast 8-10 too, excellent choice of wines by the glass, Caledonian Deuchars IPA and Harviestoun Bitter & Twisted, well trained friendly staff, imaginative more expensive meals in adjoining restaurant; plenty of tables outside, comfortable bedrooms *(Maurice Heron, Archie and Margaret Mackenzie)*

STIRLING [NS7993]

☆ *Portcullis* FK8 1EG [Castle Wynd]: Attractive former 18th-c school below castle, overlooking town and surroundings, entry through high-walled courtyard, spacious and elegant high-ceilinged stripped-stone bar with inglenooks and brocades, friendly helpful staff, pleasant atmosphere, nice choice of sandwiches and very generous pubby hot dishes (not Mon evening, best to book other evenings), Isle of Skye Red Cuillin and Orkney Dark Island from handsome bar counter, good choice of whiskies, log fire; lush sheltered terrace garden, good bedrooms and breakfast *(J F M and M West, Tracey and Stephen Groves, Tom McLean)*

SUTHERLAND

DORNOCH [NH7989]

Dornoch Castle Hotel IV25 3SD [Castle St]: Chatty bar in hotel once part of 16th-c fortified bishop's palace, real ales such as Caledonian Deuchars IPA or Isle of Skye, log fire and sofas, bar snacks, upmarket restaurant; pretty garden behind, comfortable bedrooms *(N R White, J D Taylor)*

KYLESKU [NC2333]

☆ *Kylesku Hotel* IV27 4HW [A894, S side of former ferry crossing]: New owners and friendly accommodating staff in remote NW coast hotel, pleasant local bar facing glorious mountain and sea view, with seals and red-throated divers often in sight (tables outside too); short choice of reasonably priced wonderfully fresh local seafood, also sandwiches and soup, three dozen malt whiskies, more expensive sea-view restaurant extension; five comfortable and peaceful if basic bedrooms, good breakfast, boatman does good loch trips; in winter may be open only wknds, just for drinks *(Christine and Phil Young, Mike and Penny Sutton)*

WIGTOWNSHIRE

BLADNOCH [NX4254]

Bladnoch Inn DG8 9AB: Bright and cheerful small local under friendly new Irish owners, obliging service, enjoyable pubby food from sandwiches and baked potatoes up, Theakstons, dining area with dog pictures; children and dogs welcome, picturesque riverside setting across from Bladnoch distillery (tours available), comfortable bedrooms *(Richard J Holloway, Mr Pusill)*

PORTPATRICK [NW9954]

Crown DG9 8SX [North Crescent]: Waterside hotel in delightful harbourside village, good atmosphere and warm fire in rambling old-fashioned bar with cosy nooks and crannies, several dozen malt whiskies, decent wine by the harvestoun, pleasant staff, food from good crab sandwiches up, attractively decorated early 20th-c dining room opening through quiet conservatory into sheltered back garden; TV, games machine, piped music; children and dogs welcome, tables out in front, open all day *(Stan and Hazel Allen, LYM, Michael Lamm, Chris Smith)*

SCOTTISH ISLANDS

ARRAN

BLACKWATERFOOT [NR8928]
Blackwaterfoot Lodge KA27 8EU: Beautifully
set hotel with friendly licensees, satisfying food,
Arran and Orkey Dark Island real ale, nice bar
with leather sofa and armchairs and interesting
books, dining conservatory; tables outside,
bedrooms, cl winter *(David Edwards)*

CATACOL [NR9049]
Catacol Bay KA27 8HN: Welcoming
walkers' and climbers' pub, totally
unpretentious, in wonderful setting yards from
the sea with bay window looking across to
Kintyre, bright décor (lots of notices), unusual
beers inc local Arran, home-made food; tables
outside, decent bedrooms – the ones at the
front have the view *(Andrew Wallace,
Alistair and Kay Butler)*

WHITING BAY [NS0425]
Eden Lodge KA27 8QH: Hotel's public bar,
enjoyable fresh blackboard food inc good local
steaks and fine collection of whiskies in partly
stone-floored bar with cheerful atmosphere,
airy modern décor and big contemporary
pictures; next to bowling green, great sea and
mainland views from beachside terrace picnic-
sets and attractive modern bedrooms, open all
year *(Andrew Wallace)*

HARRIS

RODEL [NG0483]
☆ *Rodel Hotel* HS5 3TW [A859 at southern tip
of South Harris (hotel itself may be unsigned)]:
Attractive and comfortably refurbished hotel
with well done contemporary woodwork and
local art in two bars and dining room,
enjoyable bar lunches, keg beer; four bedrooms
and self-catering, beautiful setting in small
harbour *(Walter and Susan Rinaldi-Butcher,
Stephen R Holman)*

ISLAY

BRIDGEND [NR3362]
Bridgend Hotel PA44 7PJ: Country house
hotel with comfortable tartan-carpet cocktail
bar, interesting prints and maps, open fire, fine
range of food with commendable emphasis on
scottish dishes; bedrooms
(Richard J Holloway)

PORT CHARLOTTE [NR2558]
☆ *Port Charlotte Hotel* PA48 7TU [Main St]:
Roaring log or peat fire and lovely sea loch
views in charming smallish traditional bar,
lots of wood, piano and charcoal prints,
nicely furnished back lounge with books on
the area, dozens of rare Islay malts and real
ales such as Adnams, Black Sheep and Islay,
wide choice of bar food lunchtime and
evening esp good local seafood, good
welcoming service, local art and sailing ship
prints in comfortable restaurant, good
wines; folk nights; good bedrooms
(Richard J Holloway)

JURA

CRAIGHOUSE [NR5266]
Jura Hotel PA60 7XU: Superb position next to
the famous distillery, looking east over the
Small Isles to the mainland, enjoyable
inexpensive home-made bar food, agreeable
owner, good restaurant; tables and seats in
garden down to water's edge, bedrooms – the
island is great for walkers, birdwatchers and
photographers *(Richard J Holloway)*

ORKNEY

LONGHOPE [ND3089]
Stromabank KW16 3PA [Hoy]: Recent school
conversion, Orkney Red MacGregor in locally
popular bar, enjoyable basic pub food with
emphasis on local ingredients, conservatory
dining extension with lovely sea views, pool
room doubles as breakfast room; bedrooms
(Peter Meister)

WESTRAY [HY4348]
Pierowall Hotel KW17 2BZ: Comfortable
pub/hotel nr ferry, friendly main bar largely
given over to eating, from sandwiches and
light snacks up inc good freshly landed fish,
bottled Orkney and Shetland beers, pool
room and separate dining area; nine
spacious bedrooms with bay or hill views
(Peter Meister)

SHETLAND

SUMBURGH [HU4009]
Sumburgh Hotel ZE3 9JN [Virkie]: Pleasant
efficient service, enjoyable food from good
range of snacks up in bar and restaurant,
Belhaven and McEwans beer; handy for
Sumburgh Head bird reserve, Jarleshoff
archaeological site and airport, nice bedrooms
(Gordon Neighbour)

SKYE

CARBOST [NG3731]
☆ *Old Inn* IV47 8SR [B8009]: Unpretentious
simply furnished bare-boards bar in idyllic
peaceful spot close to Talisker distillery,
friendly staff, limited bar food inc good fresh
langoustines, perhaps a real ale such as Isle of
Skye Red Cuillin, peat fire, darts, pool,
cribbage and dominoes; TV, piped traditional
music; children welcome, terrace with fine
Loch Harport and Cuillin views (bar's at the
back though), sea-view bedrooms in annexe
(breakfast for non-residents too if you book
the night before), bunkhouse and showers for
yachtsmen, open all day, cl midwinter
afternoons *(LYM, Stephen R Holman,
David and Betty Gittins, Tracey and
Stephen Groves)*

ISLE ORNSAY [NG7012]
☆ *Eilean Iarmain* IV43 8QR [off A851
Broadford—Armadale]: Bar adjunct to smart
hotel in beautiful location, with tolerant
willing staff inc students at the island's gaelic
college, enjoyable often interesting bar food
from same kitchen as charming sea-view

restaurant, good choice of vatted (blended) malt whiskies inc its own Te Bheag, open fire; piped gaelic music; children welcome, very comfortable bedrooms *(Joan and Tony Walker, LYM, John and Elspeth Howell, Mrs Jane Kingsbury, W Holborow)*

PORTREE [NG4744]

Portree House IV51 9LX [Home Farm Rd]: Hotel's comfortable lounge bar with three Isle of Skye ales and friendly attentive staff, separate coffee/snack bar and upstairs restaurant, decent snacks and main dishes inc local venison, wild salmon and other fish, home-made ice-creams; bedrooms *(George Atkinson)*

SKEABOST [NG4148]

☆ *Skeabost House Hotel* IV51 9NR [A850 NW of Portree, 1½ miles past junction with A856]: This opulent place in its extensive grounds overlooking Loch Snizort, formerly a popular main entry, has now been taken over as a Swallow hotel, and the best parts are now mainly for residents (who also have good salmon fishing and a golf course); there is a more ordinary public bar, with Isle of Skye real ale, over 100 malt whiskies, and decent reasonably priced bar food from sandwiches up; children and dogs allowed, comfortable bedrooms, open all day, cl lunchtimes in winter; reports on new regime please *(LYM)*

'Children welcome' means the pub says it lets children inside without any special restriction. If it allows them in, but to restricted areas such as an eating area or family room, we specify this. Places with separate restaurants often let children use them, hotels usually let them into public areas such as lounges. Some pubs impose an evening time limit – let us know if you find this.

Wales

Pubs generating a lot of attention here this year are the stylish and sophisticated Harbourmaster in Aberaeron (good food and a lovely place to stay in), the Olde Bulls Head in Beaumaris (nice combination of character old bar and good food in modern brasserie), the well run Pen-y-Bryn in Colwyn Bay (good all round), the Bear in Crickhowell (another all-rounder, a favourite of many though not all), the Griffin at Felinfach (good food and wines, and gaining a Place to Stay Award this year), Kilverts in Hay-on-Wye (rather a different sort of pub, suiting this town's character well) and the Old Black Lion there (doing well under its new licensee), the beautifully set Hand at Llanarmon Dyffryn Ceiriog (a new entry – peaceful and happy to stay in, and nice to drop in too, for good food and drinks in appealing surroundings), the friendly White Lion at Llanelian-yn-Rhos (back in the *Guide* after quite a break, with a wide range of enjoyable food and an attractive bar), the interesting Corn Mill making the most of its great riverside setting in Llangollen (chatty and well run, good all round), the Glasfryn in Mold (good food and service), the Cross Foxes at Overton Bridge (good all round – from the same stable as the previous two pubs), the no smoking Sloop in its lovely waterside setting at Porthgain (very good for families), the charmingly simple Goose & Cuckoo perched up at Rhyd-y-Meirch, the rather smart Bell at Skenfrith (its good food is not cheap, but certainly worth it), the nice old thatched Bush in St Hilary (perhaps even better than ever under its newish people), the Groes at Ty'n-y-Groes (great atmosphere, good locally sourced food, nice setting) and the Nags Head in Usk (warmly welcoming family in charge, good food – particularly the seasonal game). It's an Anglesey pub which takes the top title of Wales Dining Pub of the Year: the Olde Bulls Head in Beaumaris, with good food in either its up-to-date brasserie or for a special occasion its smart upstairs restaurant. We have listed the Lucky Dip entries at the end of the chapter under the various regions (rather than the newer administrative areas which have replaced them). We'd particularly pick out, on Anglesey, the Sailors Return in Beaumaris; in Clwyd, the White Horse at Cilcain; in Dyfed, the Old Point House at Angle, Druidstone Hotel at Broad Haven, Dyffryn Arms at Cwm Gwaun, Georges in Haverfordwest, Castle in Little Haven, Butchers Arms at Llanddarog, Cambrian in Solva and Stackpole Inn at Stackpole; in Gwent, the Hunters Moon at Llangattock Lingoed, Abbey Hotel at Llanthony, Greyhound at Llantrisant Fawr, Moon & Sixpence at Tintern and Royal Hotel in Usk; in Gwynedd, the Ty Gwyn in Betws-y-Coed and Castle Hotel in Conwy; and in Powys, the Lion in Berriew, Royal Oak at Gladestry, Tai'r Bull at Libanus and Star at Talybont-on-Usk. Welsh pub drinks prices are slightly lower than the UK average. Brains is the main local brewer, and it or the Hancocks beer it brews for the Coors brewing combine are the local beers you are most likely to find on offer as a pub's cheapest. Other local beers we found at good prices were Breconshire, Felinfoel, Plassey, Rhymney and Tomos Watkins (as were the own brews produced in the Nags Head at Abercych), and beers from Bryn Cyf, Conwy and Purple Moose also turned up at one or two of our main entries.

ABERAERON SN4562 Map 6
Harbourmaster 🍴 ☶ 🛏
Harbour Lane; SA46 0BA

Appealingly chic and wonderfully comfortable, this stylish blue-painted hotel isn't as pubby as some of the area's more traditional locals, but it makes a splendidly civilised alternative, especially if you're staying. Boasting a prime spot on the yacht-filled harbour, among a charming array of colourwashed buildings, it's open all day (except Sundays in winter), and is usually buzzing with locals and visitors. Modern rustic in style, the wine bar (which may be a bit smoky) has dark wood panelling, sofas, and chunky blocks of wood as low tables or stools on dark wood floors; piped music. Brains SA and Buckleys Best on handpump, and a good wine list, with a constantly changing selection sold by the glass. Tapas dishes served in here might include grilled mackerel or grilled aubergines with pesto (£5.50), serrano ham with roasted chicory (£6.50), grilled crevettes in chilli butter (£7.50) and mixed tapas (£12). The owners are chatty and welcoming, and service is good. In the no smoking restaurant, new light wood furniture looks stylishly modern on light wood floors against light and dark blue walls. Here, the good, fashionable food has an emphasis on local produce, and typically takes in soup (£4), fishcakes or moules marinière (£6.50), half a dozen oysters (£7.50), duck pâté (£5.50), antipasti platter for two (£12), lemon sole with sweet potato chips and red pepper coulis (£14.50), chargrilled welsh black beef fillet (£17.50), and blueberry and brazil nut brûlée with hazelnut ice-cream (£4.95). Some bedrooms have panoramic views – and powerful showers. (*Recommended by Geoff and Angela Jaques, Andy Sinden, Louise Harrington, Graham and Glenis Watkins, Dr A McCormick, Blaise Vyner, Glenys and John Roberts, Di and Mike Gillam, Mike and Mary Carter*)

Free house ~ Licensees Glyn and Menna Heulyn ~ Real ale ~ Bar food (12-2, 6-9; not Mon lunchtime, or winter Sun evenings) ~ Restaurant ~ (01545) 570755 ~ Children welcome but not in bar after 7pm ~ Open 11-11 (11-5 winter Suns); closed 24 Dec-10 Jan ~ Bedrooms: £55S/£105B

ABERCYCH SN2441 Map 6
Nags Head 🍺
Off B4332 Cenarth—Boncath; SA37 0HJ

Beautifully set next to a river, this traditional ivy-covered local impresses with its much-enjoyed Old Emry's beer, made in their own brewery and named after one of the regulars; they also keep Greene King Abbot and Old Speckled Hen, and a guest. The dimly lit beamed and flagstoned bar has a comfortable old sofa in front of the big fireplace, clocks showing the time around the world, stripped wood tables, a piano, photographs and postcards of locals, and hundreds of beer bottles displayed around the brick and stone walls – look out for the big stuffed rat. A plainer no smoking small room leads down to a couple of big dining areas (one of which is also no smoking), and there's another little room behind the bar; piped music and TV. Served in huge helpings (described as daunting by one reader), the bar food might include home-made cawl with crusty bread (£3.50), breaded brie wedges with home-made pear and ginger chutney (£4.25), vegetable chilli (£6.95), battered cod or lasagne (£7.25), steak and kidney pudding (£7.50), and daily specials such as lamb and mint sausages with spring onion mash (£6.95), dressed local crab (£8.95), and coracle-caught sewin (sea trout) (£9.95); they do smaller helpings of some dishes (from £4.95) and children's meals. Service is pleasant and efficient. Lit by fairy lights in the evening, the pub is tucked away in a little village; tables under cocktail parasols across the quiet road look over the water, and there are nicely arranged benches, and a children's play area. They sometimes have barbecues out here in summer. (*Recommended by John and Enid Morris, Gene and Kitty Rankin, Colin Moore, David and Nina Pugsley*)

Own brew ~ Licensee Samantha Jamieson ~ Real ale ~ Bar food (12-2, 6-9 (not Mon)) ~ Restaurant ~ (01239) 841200 ~ Children welcome ~ Dogs allowed in bar ~ Open 11.30-3, 6-11.30; 12-10.30 Sun; closed Mon

ABERDOVEY SN6296 Map 6

Penhelig Arms 🍴 ♀ 🛏

Opposite Penhelig railway station; LL35 0LT

Particularly popular in summer, when you can sit outside by the harbour wall looking over the Dyfi estuary, this splendidly located 18th-c hotel has quite a reputation for its food – and especially the fresh fish, delivered daily from the local fishmonger. It's also renowned for its wines: they have a selection of some 300, with around 30 sold by the glass. Good log fires in the small original beamed bar make it especially cosy in winter, and there's nothing in the way of fruit machines or piped music. In addition to lunchtime sandwiches (from £2.95), the daily lunch and dinner menus (which they serve in the dining area of the bar and restaurant, both of which are no smoking) could include spring cabbage and coriander soup (£3.50), dressed crab (£6.95), home-made faggots or mushroom ravioli (£7.95), chargrilled lambs liver or haddock and chips (£9.50), roast loin of cod with parmesan crust and salsa verde or grilled fillet of hake with anchovies, capers, tomato and mozzarella (£12.50), monkfish stew with chorizo (£12.95), and chargrilled welsh black rib-eye steak with port and stilton sauce (£13.50); they do a two-course lunch menu for £12.50. It's worth booking, as they can get very busy (which might explain the rare wobbles in service experienced by a couple of readers this year). Brains Reverend James, Hancocks HB and Greene King Abbott on handpump, two dozen malt whiskies, fruit and peppermint teas, and various coffees; dominoes. The bedrooms are comfortable (some have balconies overlooking the estuary) but the ones nearest the road can be noisy; breakfasts varied and good. *(Recommended by C J Pratt, Prof Keith and Mrs Jane Barber, Mike and Mary Carter, Colin Moore, Earl and Chris Pick, Di and Mike Gillam, Comus and Sarah Elliott, David Glynne-Jones, Ian and Jane Irving)*

Free house ~ Licensees Robert and Sally Hughes ~ Real ale ~ Bar food ~ Restaurant ~ (01654) 767215 ~ Children welcome ~ Dogs allowed in bar ~ Open 11-3.30, 6-11.30; 11-4, 5.30-11.30 Sat; 12-4, 5.30-11 Sun; usually close slightly earlier in winter; closed 25-26 Dec ~ Bedrooms: £49S/£78S

ABERGORLECH SN5833 Map 6

Black Lion

B4310 (a pretty road roughly NE of Carmarthen); SA32 7SN

Readers who've made the detour to this welcoming 17th-c coaching inn enjoy the little touches like the gravy boat that came with the steak and kidney pudding, and the jug of custard served with the bread pudding. It's delightfully placed in a tranquil spot in the wooded Cothi Valley; the picnic-tables, wooden seats and benches have lovely views, and the garden slopes down towards the River Cothi where there's a Roman triple-arched bridge. The plain but comfortably cosy stripped-stone bar is traditionally furnished with oak tables and chairs, and high-backed black settles facing each other across the flagstones by the gas-effect log fire. There are horsebrasses and copper pans on the black beams, old jugs on shelves, and fresh flowers and paintings by a local artist. The dining extension has french windows opening on to a landscaped enclosed garden. Good value freshly cooked bar food (there may be a wait at busy times) includes soup (£2.75), sandwiches (from £2.75), sausage, egg and chips (£4.95), a good ploughman's (£5.50), curry or vegetable and stilton crumble (£6.50), on some evenings their own pizzas, and changing specials like chicken and leek pudding (£6.95) or game casserole (£7.95); also Sunday lunch (one course £5.95, two courses £7.95, and three £9.95), children's meals (from £3.50), and in summer they do afternoon teas. The one or two real ales are likely to come from Merthyr Tydfil's Rhymney Brewery, and are kept under a light blanket pressure on handpump; also Welsh whiskey, mulled wine in winter and lots of fruit juices. Daily papers, sensibly placed darts, chess, cribbage, dominoes, draughts, monthly quiz nights and piped music. The pub is a good place to head for if you're visiting the nearby Dolaucothi Gold Mines at Pumsaint, or the plantations of Brechfa Forest. *(Recommended by Mrs Edna M Jones, Pete Yearsley,*

Norman and June Williams, David and Lin Short, JWAC, Martin Frith, Annabel Viney, Richard Siebert)

Free house ~ Licensees Michelle and Guy Richardson ~ Real ale ~ Bar food ((not Mon)) ~ Restaurant ~ (01558) 685271 ~ Well behaved children welcome in eating areas until 9pm ~ Dogs allowed in bar ~ Open 12-3, 7-11; 12-11(10 Sun) Sat; closed Mon exc bank hols

BEAUMARIS SH6076 Map 6

Olde Bulls Head 25 🍴 ⛾ 🛏

Castle Street; LL58 8AP

Wales Dining Pub of the Year

On especially good form at the moment, this roomy 15th-c inn has a delightful beamed bar that can't have changed much since Charles Dickens popped in for a drink in 1859, but also scores highly for the good food served in the altogether more contemporary brasserie. The bar has plenty of interesting reminders of the town's past, with a rare 17th-c brass water clock, a bloodthirsty crew of cutlasses and even an oak ducking stool tucked among the snug alcoves; also, lots of copper and china jugs, comfortable low-seated settles, leather-cushioned window seats, a good log fire, and Bass, Hancocks and a guest like Purple Moose Glaslyn on handpump. Quite a contrast, the busy brasserie behind is lively and modern, with piped music and a menu that includes soup (£3.50), lamb broth with barley and vegetables (£3.95), sandwiches (from £4.95), salads (from £5.50), home-made sausage with apple and onion compote and red cabbage (£7.25), pasta in a creamy pesto sauce (£7.50), seared calves liver with black pepper mash, spinach and red onion sauce (£8.75), grilled black bream with lyonnaise potato cake (£9.45), ragoût of venison with herb potato gnocchi (£9.50), smoked haddock and chive risotto with poached egg (£9.95), and marinated 10oz rump steak with tomato, herb and shallot sauce and potato and beetroot rösti (£14.60); small but decent children's menu (from £4.60). They don't take bookings in here, but do for the smart restaurant upstairs; both are no smoking. The brasserie wine list incudes a dozen available by the glass; the restaurant list runs to 120 bottles. The entrance to the pretty courtyard is closed by what is listed in *The Guinness Book of Records* as the biggest simple-hinged door in Britain (11 feet wide and 13 feet high). Named after characters in Dickens's novels, the bedrooms are very well equipped; some are traditional, and others more up to date. *(Recommended by Dr A McCormick, Clive Watkin, John and Enid Morris, Donald Mills, Neil Whitehead, Victoria Anderson, J Roy Smylie, Andy Sinden, Louise Harrington, Dr and Mrs M E Wilson, A J Law, Gerry and Rosemary Dobson, Revd D Glover, W W Burke)*

Free house ~ Licensee David Robertson ~ Real ale ~ Bar food (12-2, 6-9; not 25 Dec or evening 1 Jan) ~ Restaurant ~ (01248) 810329 ~ Children welcome in brasserie but no under-7s in loft restaurant ~ Open 11-11; 12-10.30 Sun; closed evening 25 Dec ~ Bedrooms: £75B/£98.50B

CAPEL CURIG SH7258 Map 6

Bryn Tyrch

A5 W of village; LL24 0EL

Readers enjoy the pleasantly informal feel of this isolated inn, very much in the heart of Snowdonia; if you stay, you may even see other residents lighting the fire. Wholesome food, with an emphasis on vegetarian and vegan dishes, is generously served to meet the healthy appetite of anyone participating in the local outdoor attractions – very much what this place is about. Big picture windows run the length of one wall, with views across the road to picnic-sets on a floodlit patch of grass by a stream running down to a couple of lakes, and the peaks of the Carneddau, Tryfan and Glyders in close range. Comfortably relaxed, the bar has several easy chairs round low tables, some by a coal fire with magazines and outdoor equipment catalogues piled to one side, and a pool table in the plainer hikers' bar; the dining room and part of the main bar are no smoking. The good, hearty bar food includes soup (from £3.95), lunchtime sandwiches (£5.50) and panini (£5.95), welsh rarebit (£6.25), ploughman's (£6.95), spicy vegetable and bean couscous, mediterranean roast vegetable lasagne, local lamb and leek sausages or navarin of lamb (all £8.95), beef and ale stew or smoked haddock, prawn and mushroom pie (£9.50), and home-made puddings such as apple and raisin crumble (£4.50). You can also pop in here for a cup of one of the many coffee blends or Twinings teas that are listed on a blackboard, and served with a piece of vegan cake. Camerons Castle Eden, Flowers IPA and Greene King Old Speckled Hen on handpump, and quite a few malt whiskies, including some local ones; pool, shove-ha'penny and dominoes. There are tables on a steep little garden at the side. Bedrooms are simple but clean, and some have views; £10 cleaning charge for dogs. You could hardly be closer to the high mountains of Snowdonia, with some choice and challenging walking right on the doorstep. *(Recommended by Andy Sinden, Louise Harrington, Peter Craske, Rona Murdoch)*

Free house ~ Licensee Rita Davis ~ Real ale ~ Bar food (12-3, 5-9.30 weekdays; 12-9.30 weekends) ~ Restaurant ~ (01690) 720223 ~ Children welcome ~ Dogs welcome ~ Open 12-11; closed lunchtime Mon-Thurs in winter ~ Bedrooms: £40(£45B)/£56(£65S)(£65B)

COLWYN BAY   SH8478   Map 6
Pen-y-Bryn ♀
B5113 Llanwrst Road, on S outskirts; when you see the pub turn off into Wentworth Avenue for its car park; LL29 6DD

From the outside this modern building looks as far removed from a pub as you could imagine (even they say it could be a doctor's surgery), but the light and airy open-plan interior is really quite attractive. The main draws though are the terrific views over the bay and the Great Orme (it's worth booking a window table), and the consistently reliable, very good food, served all day; several readers enjoy making regular return visits here. On a typical day the menu might include sandwiches (from £4.25), leek and potato soup (£4.50), chicken, leek and ham terrine with spiced pineapple chutney (£5.95), potato pancakes with ham, poached egg and hollandaise sauce (£7.35), ploughman's with welsh cheeses or potato gnocchi with spinach, broad beans and blue cheese (£8.75), sausages with mustard mash and onion gravy (£8.95), fried salmon fillet with caesar salad (£10.95), fish stew (£11.95), and braised shoulder of lamb with root vegetable mash and rosemary sauce or braised shin of beef with fondant potatoes, parsnips and red wine sauce (£12.95), and puddings such as black cherry sponge with chocolate sauce or bara brith bread pudding (£4.95); efficient service from friendly staff. Two thirds of the pub is no smoking. Working around the three long sides of the bar counter, the mix of seating and well spaced tables, oriental rugs on pale stripped boards, shelves of books, welcoming coal fires, profusion of pictures, big pot plants, careful lighting and dark green school radiators are all typical of the pubs in this small chain. Besides Flowers Original, Thwaites and Timothy Taylors Landlord, you'll find three changing guests such as Bryn Cyf, Conwy Honey Fayre and Phoenix March Hare on handpump. They also have well chosen good value wines including just over a dozen by the glass, 60 malts and several irish whiskeys, proper coffee and freshly squeezed orange juice; cribbage, dominoes, chess, faint piped music. Outside there are sturdy tables and chairs on a side terrace and a lower one, by a lawn with picnic-sets. *(Recommended by Paul Boot, Donald Mills, Joan York, William Ruxton, R T J and J J Hubbard, Alan and Paula McCully, KC)*

Brunning & Price ~ Managers Graham Arathoon and Graham Price ~ Real ale ~ Bar food (12-9.30(9 Sun)) ~ (01492) 533360 ~ Children under 14 welcome till 7.30pm ~ Open 11.30-11; 12-10.30 Sun; closed 25-26 Dec

---

Post Office address codings confusingly give the impression that some pubs are in Gwent or Powys, Wales when they're really in Gloucestershire or Shropshire (which is where we list them).

CRESSWELL QUAY   SN0406   Map 6
Cresselly Arms
Village signposted from A4075; SA68 0TE

Covered in creepers and facing the tidal creek of the Cresswell River, this marvellously unchanged ale house is like stepping back to the early days of the last century. Often full of locals, the two simple and comfortably old-fashioned comunicating rooms have a relaxed and jaunty air, as well as red and black floor tiles, built-in wall benches, kitchen chairs and plain tables, an open fire in one room, a working Aga in the other, and a high beam-and-plank ceiling hung with lots of pictorial china. A third red-carpeted no smoking room is more conventionally furnished, with red-cushioned mate's chairs around neat tables. Well kept Worthington BB and a winter guest beer are tapped straight from the cask into glass jugs by the landlord, whose presence is a key ingredient of the atmosphere; fruit machine. No children. If you time the tides right, you can arrive by boat, and seats outside make the most of the view. *(Recommended by Phil and Sally Gorton, Pete Baker, the Didler, R M Corlett)*

Free house ~ Licensees Maurice and Janet Cole ~ Real ale ~ No credit cards ~ (01646) 651210 ~ Open 12-3, 5-11; 11-11 Sat; 12-3, 5(7 winter)-10.30 Sun

CRICKHOWELL   SO2118   Map 6
Bear ★ 🍴 ♀ 🍺 🛏
Brecon Road; A40; NP8 1BW

One couple tell us they like to visit this old favourite every winter, when they find it hard to prise themselves off the sofas by the fire. A civilised old coaching inn in the centre of this delightful little town, the Bear manages to blend traditional charms with efficient service, and is a welcoming place to stay. The comfortably decorated, heavily beamed lounge has fresh flowers on tables, lots of little plush-seated bentwood armchairs and handsome cushioned antique settles, and a window seat looking down on the market square. Up by the great roaring log fire, a big sofa and leather easy chairs are spread among rugs on the oak parquet floor. Other good antiques include a fine oak dresser filled with pewter and brass, a longcase clock, and interesting prints. All areas except the main bar are now no smoking. Bass, Brains Rev James, Courage Directors and and Greene King Ruddles Best on handpump, as well as 24 malt whiskies, vintage and late-bottled ports, unusual wines (with ten by the glass) and liqueurs (with some hops tucked in among the bottles) and local apple juice. Good, honest bar food includes sandwiches (from £2.50; baguettes from £3.50), soup (£3.50), chicken liver parfait with cumberland sauce and toasted brioche (£5.25), goats cheese and fried onion pie, sausages and mash or diced lamb with cumin and apricots and savoury rice (£7.95), salmon fishcakes (£8.25), chicken supreme in thai marinade with shredded vegetables and coconut rice (£9.50), and daily specials like grilled trout with mash and a white wine and chive sauce or braised oxtail with puy lentils (£8.95), with puddings such as dark chocolate and orange mousse or bread and butter pudding (£4.25); they do a popular three-course Sunday lunch for £16.95. You can eat in the garden in summer; disabled lavatories. A refurbishment programme is under way.
(Recommended by David Edwards, Bob and Valerie Mawson, Tom and Ruth Rees, Jarrod and Wendy Hopkinson, Ann and Colin Hunt, Roger Smith, W W Burke, Dr A McCormick, David and Sheila Pearcey, Mrs Phoebe A Kemp, R Halsey, LM, Giles and Liz Ridout, Donna and Roger, Colin McKerrow, Barry and Anne, Di and Mike Gillam, Brian and Jacky Wilson, Mrs D W Privett, Colin Moore, Basil and Jarvis, B P Abrahams, Anthony Barnes, Mike Pugh, Jo Lilley, Simon Calvert, Colin Morgan, A S and M E Marriott, David and Nina Pugsley, Mike and Mand Mary Carter, Peter Titcomb, Dr Phil Putwain, R Michael Richards)

Free house ~ Licensee Judy Hindmarsh ~ Real ale ~ Bar food (12-2, 6-10; 12-2, 7-9.30 Sun) ~ Restaurant ~ (01873) 810408 ~ Children in family lounge and over 8 in restaurant ~ Dogs allowed in bar and bedrooms ~ Open 11-3, 6-11; 12-3, 7-10.30 Sun ~ Bedrooms: £65S/£80S(£90B)

Nantyffin Cider Mill ♀

1½ miles NW, by junction A40/A479; NP8 1LP

All the meat at this stylish pink-washed brasserie comes from the licensee's farm a few miles away. The food has a deservedly high reputation, and though it is very much the focus, there's a smartly traditional pubby atmosphere too. You can see the old cider press that gives the pub its name in the raftered barn that has been converted into the striking no smoking dining room; appropriately, they still serve farm cider. From a seasonally changing menu, the food might include hand-rolled fresh pasta ravioli filled with smoked chicken and leeks with roasted garlic sauce (£6), thai green vegetable curry (£11.95), confit of lamb with creamed herb mash (£12.95), roast loin of pork with bubble and squeak and tarragon and grain mustard sauce (£14.50), half a duck with braised rhubarb, ginger and honey (£14.95), and daily specials like smoked haddock fishcakes with buttered spinach, curry sauce and poached egg (£8.50) or bass fillets with potato rösti (£15.50); vegetable side dishes (£2.50). On weekdays they do a two-course meal for £12.95, and their Sunday lunches are good. With warm grey stonework, the bar has fresh flowers, good solid comfortable tables and chairs and a woodburner in a fine broad fireplace. The counter at one end of the main open-plan area has Felinfoel Double Dragon and Wadworths IPA and 6X on handpump, as well as thoughtfully chosen new world wines (a few by the glass or half bottle), Pimms and home-made lemonade in summer, and hot punch and mulled wine in winter. The River Usk is on the other side of a fairly busy road, and there are charming views from the tables out on the lawn above the pub's neat car park; a ramp makes disabled access easy. *(Recommended by Bob and Valerie Mawson, Bernard Stradling, Mike Pugh, R T and J C Moggridge, David and Nina Pugsley)*

Free house ~ Licensees Glyn Bridgeman and Sean Gerrard ~ Real ale ~ Bar food (12-2.30, 6.30-9.30; not Mon) ~ Restaurant ~ (01873) 810775 ~ Children welcome ~ Dogs allowed in bar ~ Open 12-3, 6-11(12 Sat); closed Mon

EAST ABERTHAW   ST0367   Map 6

Blue Anchor ◖

B4265; CF62 3DD

Back to normal and looking splendid after its enforced restoration in 2004, this charming medieval thatched pub is full of character. The warren of snug low-beamed rooms dates back to 1380, and has massive stone walls and tiny doorways, and open fires everywhere, including one in an inglenook with antique oak seats built into its stripped stonework. Other seats and tables are worked into a series of chatty little alcoves, and the more open front bar still has an ancient lime-ash floor. Friendly, helpful staff serve Brains Bitter, Theakstons Old Peculier, Wadworths 6X and Wye Valley Hereford Pale Ale on handpump, alongside a changing guest from a brewer such as Tomos Watkin; fruit machine, darts, trivia machine and dominoes. As well as lunchtime baguettes (£3.95), and filled baked potatoes (£4.95), enjoyable bar food might include soup (£3.25), home-made chicken liver parfait (£3.75), sun-dried tomato, mascarpone and wild rocket risotto or faggots and mushy peas (£6.95), welsh beef casserole or deep-fried cod (£7.50), daily specials like roast butternut squash with a mediterranean vegetable ratatouille (£7.50), grilled plaice (£8.50), and loin of venison with a confit of pancetta, potato and onions (£9.50); piped music in the no smoking restaurant. Some of the fruit and vegetables come from the garden of the landlord's father. Rustic seats shelter peacefully among tubs and troughs of flowers outside, with more stone tables on a newer terrace. From here a path leads to the shingly flats of the estuary. The pub can get very full in the evenings and on summer weekends. *(Recommended by J R Ringrose, Norman and Sarah Keeping, R Michael Richards, Ian Phillips)*

Free house ~ Licensee Jeremy Coleman ~ Real ale ~ Bar food (12-2, 6-8; not Sat evening, not Sun lunchtime) ~ Restaurant ~ (01446) 750329 ~ Children welcome away from bar ~ Dogs allowed in bar ~ Open 11-11; 12-10.30 Sun

FELINFACH SO0933 Map 6
Griffin ⏺ ♀ 🛏
A470 NE of Brecon; LD3 0UB

Contempory and classy, but not at all pretentious, this restauranty dining pub is a delightfully civilised place for a good meal – or even better, a relaxing break. The back bar is quite pubby in an up-to-date way, with three leather sofas around a low table on pitted quarry tiles, by a high slate hearth with a log fire, and behind them mixed stripped seats around scrubbed kitchen tables on bare boards, and a bright blue-and-ochre colour scheme. It has a few modern prints, and some nice photoprints of a livestock market by Victoria Upton. An upright piano stands against one wall – the acoustics are pretty lively, with so much bare flooring and uncurtained windows. The two smallish no smoking front dining rooms, linking through to the back bar, are attractive: on the left, mixed dining chairs around mainly stripped tables on flagstones, and white-painted rough stone walls, with a cream-coloured Aga in a big stripped-stone embrasure; on the right, similar furniture on bare boards, with big modern prints on terracotta walls, and good dark curtains. There may be piped radio in the bar. The good food might include lunchtime dishes such as jerusalem artichoke and tomato soup (£4.90), morel mushroom risotto with poached egg and almond foam (£6.95), welsh cheese ploughman's or pork and leek sausages and mash (£7.95), and calves liver with leek colcannon and thyme sauce, breast of woodpigeon with mash, red cabbage and huckleberry sauce or fresh salted cod with aubergine caviar (£9.95). Evening dishes might be local rib-eye steak (£15.95), and rack of lamb with spring vegetables, dauphinoise potatoes and red pepper jus (£16.50). The licensees take great pride in sourcing local ingredients, and grow most of the vegetables themselves. They have a good choice of wines including ten by the glass, welsh spirits, and Evan Evans, Tomos Watkins OSB and Tw Cwrw Braf on handpump. Wheelchair access is good, and there are tables outside. Though they generally close for the afternoon, they may stay open all day so it's worth checking. Bedrooms are comfortable and tastefully decorated, and the hearty breakfasts nicely informal: you make your own toast on the Aga and help yourself to home-made marmalade and jam.
(Recommended by K H Frostick, Bob and Valerie Mawson, Euryn Jones, J P Humphery, Mrs Philippa Wilson, Andy Sinden, Louise Harrington, Rodney and Norma Stubington)

Free house ~ Licensees Charles and Edmund Inkin ~ Real ale ~ Bar food (12.30-2.30, 6.30-9.30(9 Sun); not Mon lunch (exc bank hols)) ~ Restaurant ~ (01874) 620111 ~ Children welcome ~ Dogs allowed in bar and bedrooms ~ Open 12-3, 6-11(10.30 Sun); closed Mon lunchtime except bank hols ~ Bedrooms: £67.50B/£97.50B

GRESFORD SJ3555 Map 6
Pant-yr-Ochain ⏺ ♀
Off A483 on N edge of Wrexham: at roundabout take A5156 (A534) towards Nantwich, then first left towards the Flash; LL12 8TY

Now totally no smoking, this elegant 16th-c country house has rebuilt its conservatory since our last edition, the new slate roof insulating it so the room is a popular dining extension in the winter as well as summer. In attractive grounds and with its own lake, the pub is run with flair and attention to detail, and has been thoughtfully refurbished inside. The light and airy rooms are stylishly decorated, with a wide range of interesting prints and bric-a-brac on walls and on shelves, and a good mix of individually chosen country furnishings, including comfortable seats for relaxing as well as more upright ones for eating. There is a good open fire, and one area is set out as a library, with floor to ceiling bookshelves. Good food, from a well balanced daily changing menu, might typically include sandwiches (from £3.95), soups such as sweet potato and coconut (£4.25), local goats cheese and red onion filo parcel with walnut dressing (£5.50), ploughman's (£7.25), moroccan chickpea cakes in warm pitta bread (£7.95), lambs liver with bacon and mustard mash or local ham and free-range egg (£8.95), spinach gnocchi with roast shallots and salsa verde (£9.25), lamb and vegetable casserole (£11.25), whole farm trout

with dauphinoise potatoes and hazelnut butter (£12.95), and game and steak suet
pudding with red cabbage (£13.50), with puddings such as orange and chestnut
panna cotta with chocolate sauce (£4.95). Caledonian Deuchars IPA, Flowers
Original and Timothy Taylors Landlord on handpump, along with changing guests
like Lancaster Blonde, Ossett Snowdrop and locally brewed Plassey Bitter, and they
have a good range of decent wines (strong on up-front new world ones), and more
than 60 malt whiskies. Disabled access is good; piped music, board games and
dominoes. *(Recommended by Dr R A Smye, Ian Phillips, Clive Watkin, Paul Boot,
Esther and John Sprinkle, John and Helen Rushton, Susan Brookes, David Glynne-Jones,
Bruce and Sharon Eden)*

Brunning & Price ~ Licensee Lindsey Douglas ~ Real ale ~ Bar food (12-9.30(9 Sun)) ~
(01978) 853525 ~ Children welcome away from bar till 6pm ~ Open 12-11(10.30 Sun)

HAY-ON-WYE SO2342 Map 6
Kilverts 🛏

Bullring; HR3 5AG

A particularly friendly hotel in the centre of town, this comfortable place is now
completely no smoking. Open all day, it has a pleasantly unrushed feel, and you
can watch the world go by from tables in a small front flagstoned courtyard (with
outdoor heaters) or while away the hours by the fountain in a pretty terraced back
garden. Enjoyable bar food from a sensibly balanced menu is served in very
generous helpings, and includes lunchtime sandwiches (from £3.75), home-made
soup (£3.95), about a dozen pizzas (from £5.75), spaghetti carbonara (£7.75),
sautéed scallops with a bacon and Pernod cream sauce (£7.95), curry and rice or
beer-battered haddock and chips (£9.25), beef and ale casserole (£9.95), grilled bass
with fennel, lime and tarragon glaze (£10.25), baked filo parcel stuffed with sautéed
red peppers, leeks, olives and welsh brie, with balsamic red onion marmalade
(£11.95), baked chicken breast stuffed with wilted baby spinach, smoked garlic,
parma ham and nutmeg with a vermouth cream sauce (£12.95), and 12oz sirloin
steak (£13.95); good service from genial staff. Calm and understated, the airy high-
beamed bar has some stripped stone walls, *Vanity Fair* caricatures, a couple of
standing timbers, candles on well spaced mixed old and new tables, and a pleasant
variety of seating. They've an extensive wine list with about a dozen by the glass, as
well as three well kept real ales such as Brains Rev James, Hancocks HB and Wye
Valley Butty Bach on handpump, a decent choice of wines by the glass, a dozen
malt whiskies, and good coffees; piped music. There's a £5.50 cleaning charge for
dogs in the comfortable bedrooms. *(Recommended by Alun Howells, Peter and
Jean Hoare, Ian Phillips, Mike and Mary Carter, Andy and Jill Kassube, Sue Demont,
Tim Barrow, Mrs Philippa Wilson, MLR, Mrs Hazel Rainer, Jeremy Whitehorn)*

Free house ~ Licensee Colin Thomson ~ Real ale ~ Bar food (12-2, 6.15(6.30 Fri-Sat)-
9.30) ~ Restaurant ~ (01497) 821042 ~ Children welcome in eating area of bar until 9pm
~ Dogs welcome ~ Open 9am-11pm; closed 25 Dec ~ Bedrooms: £50S/£70S(£80B)

Old Black Lion 🍽 🍺 🛏

Lion Street; HR3 5AD

A new landlady has arrived at this characterful and neatly kept old hotel since our
last edition, but not much has changed, including the chef, so the high standard of
cooking remains exactly the same. Dating back in part to the 13th c, it's right in the
heart of town, and there's a snugly enveloping atmosphere in the comfortable low-
beamed bar, which has crimson and yellow walls, nice old pine tables, and an
original fireplace. You can eat from either the bar or restaurant menu throughout,
with a typical choice including soup (£4.95), lunchtime sandwiches, baked garlic
bread with sunblushed tomatoes and mozzarella (£5.25), creamy chicken and pesto
tagliatelle (£7.95), moroccan lamb with couscous and apricot and fig compote
(£10.50), grilled plaice with herb butter or wild mushroom and leek crêpes with
cheese sauce (£12.50), and duck breast with honey and five spice glaze on braised
red cabbage with apples and sultanas (£16.50); no smoking restaurant. As well as

Old Black Lion (a good beer brewed for them by Wye Valley) on handpump, they have Brains Reverend James and good value wines; service is polite and briskly efficient. There are tables out behind on a sheltered terrace. Comfortably creaky bedrooms make this an atmospheric place to stay. *(Recommended by MLR, David and Jean Hall, Mrs Phoebe A Kemp, Nick and Meriel Cox, Ian Phillips, Andy and Jill Kassube, DFL, Sue Demont, Tim Barrow, Richard, Mrs Philippa Wilson, Tony Hall, Melanie Jackson, Mrs Hazel Rainer, Colin Morgan, Alistair and Kay Butler, Pamand David Bailey, Jeremy Whitehorn)*

Free house ~ Licensee Mrs Leighton ~ Real ale ~ Bar food (12-2.30, 6.30-9.30) ~ Restaurant ~ (01497) 820841 ~ Children welcome lunchtimes only; no under-5s after 7.30pm ~ Open 11-11; 12-10.30 Sun ~ Bedrooms: £50S(£42.50B)/£80B

LLANARMON DYFFRYN CEIRIOG   SJ1532   Map 6
Hand ⇔
On B4500 from Chirk; LL20 7LD

The black-beamed carpeted bar on the left of the broad-flagstoned entrance hall has a good log fire in its inglenook fireplace, a mixture of comfortable armchairs and settees, and old prints on its cream walls, with bar stools along the modern bar counter, which has Weetwood Best on handpump, a dozen or so whiskies, and reasonably priced wines by the glass; happy and welcoming staff help towards the warm atmosphere. Round the corner, the largely stripped stone dining room, with a woodburning stove and parquet floor, has a seasonally changing menu, with an emphasis on local ingredients. Besides lunchtime sandwiches (from £3.95), the good food might include soup with home-made bread (£4.50), chicken liver pâté (£4.50), ploughman's with welsh cheeses (£6.95), steak and kidney pie (£8), herb pancake filled with fresh vegetables, risotto and parmesan (£8.50), whole grilled trout with lemon and tarragon butter (£9.50), free-range chicken breast with creamed leeks and black pudding (£13), roast loin of free-range pork with coriander and pearl barley risotto and roast apple garnish (£13.50), and daily specials such as herb-crusted lamb shank with vegetable and red wine sauce (£14.95) or rump steak with glazed cheese (£16.50). If you are staying, they do a good country breakfast, and the residents' lounge on the right is comfortable and attractive. There are tables out on a crazy-paved front terrace, with more in the garden, which has flowerbeds around another sheltered terrace. Beyond the back lawn sheep pasture stretches up into the Berwyn Hills – it's a very quiet spot in this pretty valley, and the River Ceiriog runs through the village. Much of the building has been redecorated in the last year, and they have plans to revamp the bar – and even to open their own microbrewery. *(Recommended by Mr and Mrs J Jennings, Patrick Renouf)*

Free house ~ Licensees Gaynor and Martin de Luchi ~ Bar food (12-2.30(12.30-2.45 Sun), 6.30-9) ~ Restaurant ~ (01691) 600666 ~ Children welcome away from bar ~ Dogs allowed in bar and bedrooms ~ Open 11(12 Sun)-11(12.30 Sat) ~ Bedrooms: £45B/£70B

LLANBERIS   SH6655   Map 6
Pen-y-Gwryd ㉕ £ ⇔
Nant Gwynant; at junction of A498 and A4086, ie across mountains from Llanberis – OS Sheet 115 map reference 660558; LL55 4NT

In a spectacularly remote position among the peaks of Snowdonia, and run by the same family for years, this characterful old inn doubles up as a mountain rescue post. The team that first climbed Everest in 1953 used it as a training base, leaving their fading signatures scrawled on the ceiling. One snug little room in the homely slate-floored log cabin bar has built-in wall benches and sturdy country chairs to let you gaze at the surrounding mountain landscapes – like precipitous Moel Siabod beyond the lake opposite. A smaller room has a worthy collection of illustrious boots from famous climbs, and a cosy panelled smoke room has more fascinating climbing mementoes and equipment; darts, pool, shove-ha'penny, bar billiards and dominoes. The landlady hopes to have redecorated at least some areas by the time this edition hits the shops. There's a sociable atmosphere, and alongside Bass, they've home-made lemonade in summer, mulled wine in winter, and sherry from their own solera in Puerto Santa Maria. The short choice of simple good-value home-made lunchtime bar food (you order it from a hatch) could include soup with home-made bread (£3.25), chicken liver pâté or sweet-cured herrings in a sherry marinade (£4.95), vegetable and cheddar tart or fish pie (£5.95), and steak and mushroom pie, roast welsh black beef or slow-braised local pork with mushrooms, cream and mustard (all £6.25). Staying here can be quite an experience: a gong at 7.30 signals the prompt start of service in the no smoking evening restaurant, but they don't hang around – if you're late, you'll miss it, and there's no evening bar food. The excellent, traditional breakfast is served at 8.50; again, they're not generally flexible with this. Comfortable but basic bedrooms, dogs £2 a night. The inn has its own chapel (built for the millennium and dedicated by the Archbishop of Wales), and sauna. (*Recommended by John and Enid Morris, Donald Mills, Edna Jones, Tony and Maggie Harwood, Rona Murdoch, John and Joan Nash*)

Free house ~ Licensee Jane Pullee ~ Real ale ~ Bar food (lunchtime only) ~ Restaurant (evening) ~ No credit cards ~ (01286) 870211 ~ Children welcome ~ Dogs allowed in bar ~ Open 11-11; closed all Nov-Dec, and Mon-Thurs Jan and Feb ~ Bedrooms: £35(£40S)(£40B)/ £70(£80S)(£80B)

LLANDDAROG   SN5016   Map 6
White Hart ✊

Just off A48 E of Carmarthen, via B4310; aka Yr Hydd Gwyn; SA32 8NT

Well over 600 years old, this thatched pub is often busy with tourists drawn by its pretty exterior and the many tales attached to its history. But the main attraction today is the range of beers they make using water from their own 300-foot bore hole. Named after the family in charge, the small Coles brewery produces ales such as Cwrw Blasus and Llanddarog, as well as a barley stout and a lager. The rooms are packed with bric-a-brac, lots of 17th-c welsh oak carving, a tall grandfather clock, stained glass, a collection of hats and riding boots, china, brass and copper on walls and dark beams, antique prints and even a suit of armour. The heavily carved fireside settles by the huge crackling log fire are the best place to sit. There are steps down to the high-raftered dining room, also interestingly furnished; table skittles, shove-ha'penny and piped music. Generous helpings of bar food from the servery include sandwiches (from £3.25), toasties and baked potatoes (from £3.50), pizza (from £4.95), faggots, peas and gravy (£5.75), ploughman's (from £6), plaice and chips or pie of the day (£6.75), various curries (£6.95), and daily specials and roasts; the restaurant menu (which you can also eat from in the bar) includes japanese prawns (£5.75), cheese and broccoli bake (£10.95), salmon fillet or pork loin (£11.95), steaks (from £13), and puddings (£3.95). Two small niggles: the 5% surcharge on credit cards, and the 50p charge for a pint of tap water (unless you're eating). There are picnic-sets out on a terrace and a children's play area; they can put a ramp in place for disabled access. Look out for Zac the macaw. (*Recommended by Mike Pugh, MDN, P Price, Dave Irving, David and Nina Pugsley*)

Own brew ~ Licensees Marcus and Cain Coles ~ Real ale ~ Bar food (11.30-2, 6.30-10; 12-2, 7-9.30 Sun) ~ (01267) 275395 ~ Children welcome ~ Open 11.30-3, 6.30-11; 12-3, 7-10.30 Sun; closed 25-26 Dec

LLANDUDNO JUNCTION   SH8180   Map 6
Queens Head 🍽 ♀

Glanwydden; heading towards Llandudno on B5115 from Colwyn Bay, turn left into Llanrhos Road at roundabout as you enter the Penrhyn Bay speed limit; Glanwydden is signposted as the first left turn off this; LL31 9JP

Though this looks like an unassuming village pub, don't be fooled – the very good food makes it a real draw, with some visitors travelling quite a distance for a meal here. With an emphasis on fresh local produce, the well presented and efficiently served dishes could include soup (£4.10, tasty fish soup £4.50), open sandwiches (from £6.25), a generous seafood platter (£7.50 starter; £16.50 main), pumpkin and chestnut risotto or sausage and mash (£8.95), steak and mushroom pie or green thai chicken curry (£9.25), confit of belly pork and black pudding with creamed savoy cabbage (£10.50), steak (from £12.50), rack of lamb (£13.25), monkfish and prawn kebab or queen scallops pan-fried in garlic and topped with melted caerphilly (£13.50), and daily specials. Part of the dining room is no smoking. Despite the emphasis on eating, locals do pop in for a drink, and you'll find Greene King Abbot, Marstons Pedigree and guests like Cwrw Glaslyn or Weetwoods Old Dog on handpump, as well as decent wines (including some unusual ones and 15 by the glass), a dozen malt whiskies and good coffee. The spaciously comfortable modern lounge bar – partly divided by a white wall of broad arches – has brown plush wall banquettes and windsor chairs around neat black tables, and there's a little public bar; unobtrusive piped music. There are some tables out by the car park and you can rent the stone cottage across the road. *(Recommended by Donald Mills, GLD, Mr and Mrs Colin Roberts, KC, Peter Fitton, Mr and Mrs A B Moore, Revd D Glover, Dodie and Cliff Rutherford)*

Free house ~ Licensees Robert and Sally Cureton ~ Real ale ~ Bar food (12-2, 6-9; 12-9 Sun) ~ Restaurant ~ (01492) 546570 ~ Children over 5 in restaurant ~ Open 11.30-3, 6-11; 11.30-10.30 Sun; closed 25 Dec

LLANELIAN-YN-RHOS SH8676 Map 6

White Lion

Signed off A5830 (shown as B5383 on some maps) and B5381, S of Colwyn Bay; LL29 8YA

Several readers this year have particularly praised the friendly welcome at this picturesque old place (one describing it as exemplary), and we know of one couple who enjoy an annual lunchtime visit even though the round trip is 120 miles. The pub has two distinct parts, each with its own personality, linked by a broad flight of steps. Up at the top is a neat and very spacious no smoking dining area, while down at the other end is a traditional old bar, with antique high-backed settles angling snugly around a big fireplace, and flagstones by the counter where they serve Brains Rev James and Marstons Bitter and Pedigree; on the left, another dining area has jugs hanging from the beams, and teapots above the window. A wide choice of good, generously served food cooked by the landlord might include soup (£3.25), black pudding and smoked bacon salad with honey and mustard dressing (£5.25), roasted mediterranean vegetables on a garlic croûton topped with goats cheese or vegetable rogan josh (£8.50), chicken in a garlic and cream sauce (£8.95), grilled gammon steak or salmon and prawns in a cream and cheese sauce (£9.50), and changing specials such as roast loin of pork with creamy pepper sauce and home-made stuffing (£8.95), and steak and kidney pie or baked trout topped with grilled mixed nuts (£9.95); Sunday roasts (£7.50). Prompt service from helpful staff, good wine list and lots of malt whiskies; dominoes, cribbage and piped music. Outside, an attractive courtyard between the pub and the church has sheltered tables (it's also used for parking). There's good walking in the pasture hills around. *(Recommended by Michael and Jenny Back, Mr and Mrs B Hobden, GLD, Donald Mills)*

Free house ~ Licensee Simon Cole ~ Real ale ~ Bar food (12-2, 6-9(9.30 Fri-Sat); not Mon (exc bank hols)) ~ (01492) 515807 ~ Children welcome ~ Live jazz every Tues evening, bluegrass Weds ~ Open 11.30-3, 6-11(11.30 Sat); 12-4, 6-10.30 Sun; closed Mon (exc bank holidays)

LLANFERRES SJ1860 Map 6

Druid 🏠

A494 Mold—Ruthin; CH7 5SN

Originally a farmhouse, this extended 17th-c whitewashed inn in the Alyn valley has glorious views across to the Clwydian Range; you can enjoy the setting from tables outside at the front and from the broad bay window in the civilised, smallish plush lounge. You can also see the hills from the bigger beamed and characterful back bar, with its two handsome antique oak settles as well as a pleasant mix of more modern furnishings. There's a quarry-tiled area by the log fire, and a three-legged cat, Chu. Jennings Golden Host, Marstons Pedigree and a guest like Smiles April Fuel on handpump, and around two dozen malt whiskies. Welcoming staff serve a wide range of generously plated bar food such as soup (£3.25), filled baps (£3.95), mussels (£4.95), home-made lamb and leek pie (£8.50), mixed vegetables in a creamy chilli sauce or asparagus wrapped in ham with cheese sauce (£8.95), steak and oyster pie or chicken fillet with creamy chilli sauce (£9.95), thai-style fish curry or whole bass with coriander butter (£10.95), braised shoulder of welsh lamb with mint and tarragon gravy (£13.95), and a good few daily specials, including fresh fish. The attractive dining room is no smoking. A games room has darts and pool, along with dominoes, cribbage, shove-ha'penny, bagatelle, board games, also TV and perhaps piped music. The bedrooms have recently been refurbished. *(Recommended by KC, Gareth Mo Owen, John and Helen Rushton, G T Harding)*

Union Pub Company ~ Lease James Dolan ~ Real ale ~ Bar food (12-2.30, 6-9; 12-9 weekends and bank hols) ~ Restaurant ~ (01352) 810225 ~ Children welcome ~ Dogs allowed in bar and bedrooms ~ Open 12-3, 5.30-12; 12-12 weekends; closed evening 25 Dec ~ Bedrooms: £40S/£65S

LLANFRYNACH SO0725 Map 6
White Swan ♀
Village signposted from B4558, off A40 E of Brecon – take second turn to village, which is also signed to pub; LD3 7BZ

More upmarket perhaps than it was when we first knew it, this pretty black and white dining pub is supremely well placed for hefty climbs up the main Brecon Beacons summits, or for undemanding saunters along the towpath of the Monmouthshire and Brecon Canal. The good food is very much the centre of attention, with at lunchtimes a short choice of things like soup (£4.95), roasted red pepper and pesto tart with goats cheese and sweet red onion marmalade (£6.25), wild mushroom risotto with blue cheese or local venison sausages with a rich port sauce (£8.95), grilled local trout with almond butter (£9.95), chicken breast stuffed with baby leeks in a welsh mustard and cheese sauce (£10.95), and grilled 8oz sirloin steak with pink peppercorn and brandy cream sauce (£12.95); you can have any starter and main course for £14.95. Service is cheerful and attentive. The original part of the beamed bar has stripped stone and flagstones, with sturdy oak tables and nice carver chairs in a polished country-kitchen style, a woodburning stove, and leather sofas and armchairs in groups around low tables; it opens into an apricot-walled high-ceilinged extension, light and airy, with bare boards and different sets of chairs around each table. Breconshire Brecon County and Hancocks HB on handpump, good wines (a dozen by the glass) and coffees; piped music. The charming secluded back terrace has stone and wood tables with a good choice of sun or shade, and is attractively divided into sections by low plantings and climbing shrubs, with views out over peaceful paddocks. More reports please. *(Recommended by Bob and Valerie Mawson, Mrs C Sleight, Elven Money, David and Nina Pugsley)*

Free house ~ Licensee Richard Griffiths ~ Real ale ~ Bar food (12-2, 7-9) ~ Restaurant ~ (01874) 665276 ~ Children welcome ~ Open 12-3(4 Sun), 7-11

LLANGEDWYN SJ1924 Map 6
Green Inn
B4396 ¾ mile E of Llangedwyn; SY10 9JW

On a well used scenic run from the Midlands to the coast, this country pub gets busy in summer, but that's when it's at its best, with the attractive garden across the road really coming into its own. Picnic-sets run down towards the river, and they sometimes have spit roasts or a marquee with live music. The bar is nicely laid out with various snug alcoves, nooks and crannies, a good mix of furnishings including oak settles and attractively patterned fabrics, and a blazing log fire in winter. Besides well kept Tetleys, they've usually three changing guests such as Charles

t and Weetwood Ambush on handpump, and
, fruit machine and piped music.
p (£3.25), lunchtime sandwiches, steak and
stuffed with broccoli and brie (£8.45), and
or braised lamb with root mash and
; Sunday roasts (£11.95 for three courses)
oking restaurant upstairs opens in the
ilable to customers – day permit £4. More
ther and John Sprinkle)

d Scott Currie ~ Real ale ~ Bar food (12-2, 6-9;
01691) 828234 ~ Children in eating area of bar
e music every first Friday of the month ~
un

of bridge; LL20 8PN

imaginatively converted watermill
ushes over rocks below; across the river you
nearby station and maybe a horse-drawn
with decking and teak tables and chairs is
t of the mill machinery remains – most
ing – but the place has been interestingly

gleaming timber and tensioned steel rails, and mainly stripped stone walls. A lively
bustling chatty feel greets you, with quick service from plenty of neat young staff,
good-sized dining tables, big rugs, nicely chosen pictures (many to do with water)
and lots of pot plants; a couple of areas are no smoking. One of the two serving
bars, away from the water, has a much more local feel, with pews on dark slate
flagstones, daily papers, and regulars on the bar stools. Five changing beers like
Archers Mild, Caledonian Deuchars IPA, Flowers IPA, Phoenix White Monk and
Woodlands Stout on handpump, around 50 malt whiskies and a decent wine choice
that includes pudding wines. Good food – served all day – could include cream of
chicken soup with crusty bread (£3.75), sandwiches (from £4.25), pressed ham
terrine or black pudding topped with welsh rarebit and with spiced apple sauce
(£4.75), pressed ham terrine with piccalilli and crusty bread (£4.75), salmon and
smoked haddock fishcakes (£7.95), ploughman's or welsh pork and herb sausage
with spring onion mash (£8.25), pasta with artichoke hearts, sweet roast shallots
and tomatoes (£9.25), stuffed pork loin with cider and leek sauce (£9.95), fried
free-range chicken breast (£10.95), and 10oz rib-eye steak (£14.50), with puddings
such as strawberry cheesecake (£4.25) or double chocolate muffin (£4.50). The pub
can get busy, so it might be worth booking if you're planning to eat. (Recommended
by John Wooll, Peter and Audrey Dowsett, Pete Yearsley, J R Ringrose, Gwyn and Anne Wake,
Clive Watkin, John Whitehead, David and Sue Atkinson, Esther and John Sprinkle,
Brian Brooks, Mrs Hazel Rainer, W Andrew, Lawrence Pearse, Mrs S E Griffiths,
Bruce and Sharon Eden)

Brunning & Price ~ Licensee Andrew Barker ~ Real ale ~ Bar food (12-9.30(9 Sun)) ~
(01978) 869555 ~ Children in eating areas till 7.30pm ~ Open 12-11(10.30 Sun); closed
25-26 Dec

LLANNEFYDD SH9871 Map 6

Hawk & Buckle

Village well signposted from surrounding main roads; one of the least taxing routes is
from Henllan at junction of B5382 and B5429 NW of Denbigh; LL16 5ED

Enjoying a splendid, peaceful position high up in the hills above Rhyl and
Prestatyn, this pleasant little 17th-c coaching inn is a nicely traditional place,
slightly off the beaten track but well liked for its food. The long knocked-through

black-beamed lounge bar has comfy upholstered settles around its walls and facing
each other across the open fire, and a neat red carpet in the centre of its tiled floor.
The buzzy locals' side bar has pool and unobtrusive piped music. The good bar
food might include dishes such as soup (£3.25), steak pie (£7.95), fried chicken
breast with leeks, mushroom and smoked bacon (£8.95), shoulder of roast lamb
(£10.50), and half a roast duck (£13.95), with home-made puddings (£3.75); the
dining room is no smoking. Brains SA on handpump, and an extensive wine list.
The good views stretch some distance; on a clear day, if you know where to look,
you may be able to see as far as the Lancashire coast – and even spot Blackpool
Tower, some 40 miles away. Note they no longer do bedrooms. More reports
please. *(Recommended by Clive Watkin, Donald Mills, Ian Saunders)*

Free house ~ Licensees David Topping and David Corlus ~ Bar food (not Sun evenings, or
Mon) ~ Restaurant ~ (01745) 540249 ~ Children in restaurant ~ Open 6-11; 12-3,
7-10.30 Sun; closed Mon

MOLD   SJ2465   Map 6

Glasfryn   ⑪ ♀

N of the centre on Raikes Lane (parallel to the A5119), just past the well signposted
Theatr Clwyd; CH7 6LR

Just across the road from Theatr Clwyd, this upbeat bistro-style pub maintains the
winning formula that has made it a real hit with readers. A bonus is that the full
choice of good, well prepared food is available all day, but the great range of drinks,
attractive layout, and enthusiastic licensees also help to explain its appeal. Open-plan
rooms have both spaciousness and nice quiet corners, with an informal and attractive
mix of country furnishings, and interesting decorations; two large eating areas are no
smoking. Besides a good variety of around a dozen wines by the glass and around
100 whiskies, they've well kept Bryn Cyf (brewed locally), Flowers IPA, Thwaites,
Timothy Taylors Landlord, and swiftly changing guests like Batemans XXXB,
Caledonian Deuchars IPA and Weetwood Old Dog on handpump. The menu might
include tomato and basil soup (£4.25), sandwiches (from £4.95), smoked trout and
poached egg muffin (£5.95), cheese and onion quiche with pickle or coconut and chilli
tiger prawns with rice (£7.95), ploughman's with welsh cheeses (£8.50), smoked
haddock and salmon fishcakes (£8.75), bean cassoulet with chive soda bread (£9.25),
free-range chicken with tomato, black olives and tagliatelle (£11.95), braised shoulder
of lamb with mash and cabbage (£13.95), whole trout with feta and mint butter
(£14.95), and puddings like baked cinnamon apple with vanilla ice-cream and
butterscotch sauce or chocolate bread and butter pudding with clotted cream (£4.75).
Outside, sturdy timber tables on a big terrace give superb views to the Clwydian Hills
– idyllic on a warm summer's evening. *(Recommended by John Wooll, June and
Ken Brooks, KC, Clive Watkin, Chris Flynn, Wendy Jones, Maurice and Della Andrew,
Esther and John Sprinkle, Brian Brooks, Dodie and Cliff Rutherford)*

Brunning & Price ~ Manager James Meakin ~ Real ale ~ Bar food (12-9.30(9 Sun)) ~
(01352) 750500 ~ Children welcome away from bar until 6pm ~ Dogs allowed in bar ~
Open 11.30-11; 12-10.30 Sun; closed 25-26 Dec

MONKNASH   SS9270   Map 6

Plough & Harrow   ◖ £

Signposted Marcross, Broughton off B4265 St Brides Major—Llantwit Major – turn left
at end of Water Street; OS Sheet 170 map reference 920706; CF71 7QQ

Originally part of a monastic grange, and dating back almost nine centuries, this
white-painted cottage is one of those pubs worth visiting just to see the building.
Built with massively thick stone walls, its dimly lit unspoilt main bar used to be the
scriptures room and mortuary; instantly welcoming and genuinely atmospheric, it
seems hardly changed over the last 70 years. The heavily black-beamed ceiling has
ancient ham hooks, an intriguing arched doorway to the back, and a comfortably
informal mix of furnishings that includes three fine stripped pine settles on the
broad flagstones. There's a log fire in a huge fireplace with a side bread oven large

n the left has lots of Wick rugby club
ily papers, piped music. Up to eight well kept
n the cask might include Archers Golden, Wye
n BB and thoughtfully sourced guest ales
m Island and RCH; helpful service from
ckboards, the daily changing bar food could
rom £4.95), three-cheese ploughman's or
ess or gammon, egg and chips (£7.95) and
95). It can get crowded at weekends, when
en's helpings). There are picnic-sets in the
nd they hold barbecues out here in
but not while food is being served. In a
Nash Point, it's an enjoyable walk from
up a fine stretch of the coastal path along
full of blow holes and fissures.
n Phillips, John and Joan Nash)

~ Bar food (12-2.30, 6-9) ~ Restaurant ~
allowed in bar ~ Live music Sun evening ~

or in Walton; LD8 2RH

In   vhy they don't open weekday
lu   -built pub is on a hill looking across to
th   .csт. In the evening and at weekends chatty locals gather in
the ...a iasmoned brownstone public bar, which has high-backed settles, an antique
reader's chair and other elderly chairs around a log fire; cribbage, dominoes. The
snug slate-floored lounge has a handsome curved antique settle and another log fire
in a fine inglenook, and there are lots of local books and guides for residents.
There's usually at least one bargain real ale (two in summer) from brewers such as
Wilds of Weobley, and they have just over a dozen malt whiskies; friendly, helpful
service. Fairly simple bar food might include soup (£3.50), filled baguettes
(from £3.95), ploughman's, home-made faggots or pork and herb sausages and
mash (£5.95), cod and chips (£6.95), chicken wrapped in bacon with stilton sauce
(£9.25), rump steak (£10.95), and specials like lambs liver and bacon (£7.95) or
pork loin with wholegrain mustard sauce (£9.25), with puddings such as home-
made sticky toffee pudding (£3.50); it can be worth booking on busy evenings.
Note they don't allow large dogs in the bedrooms, which are generally much
enjoyed by readers (though one had trouble with the hot taps in the top room); they
also have a self-catering bungalow next door. Outside, there's plenty of seating –
either under the big sycamore tree, or on the grass. The impressive church is worth
a look for its interesting early organ case (Britain's oldest), fine rood screen and
ancient font. _(Recommended by Reg Fowle, Helen Rickwood, David and Jacque Hart,
the Didler, Anne Morris)_

Free house ~ Licensees Erfyl Protheroe and Heather Price ~ Real ale ~ Bar food (7-9,
plus 12-2 weekends; not Mon (exc bank holidays)) ~ Restaurant ~ (01544) 350655 ~
Children welcome ~ Dogs allowed in bar ~ Open 6-11; 12-3, 6-11(10.30 Sun) Sat; 7pm
evening opening winter; closed weekday lunchtimes, all day Mon (exc bank holidays) ~
Bedrooms: £35(£40S)(£40B)/£58(£68S)(£68B)

OVERTON BRIDGE   SJ3542   Map 6
Cross Foxes 🍴 ♈

A539 W of Overton, near Erbistock; LL13 0DR

An attractive waterside spot, this very well run 18th-c coaching inn certainly makes
the most of its position, but doesn't depend on it: there are plenty of other draws,
not least the wide choice of imaginative food. Served all day, the changing choice

Anne Newbury, Mike and Mary Carter, Mark and Lynette Davies, Bruce and Sharon Lack,

Brunning & Price ~ Manager Paul Fletcher ~ Real ale ~ Bar food (12-9.30(9 Sun)) ~
(01978) 780380 ~ Children under 5 until 7pm and under 10 until 8pm, in dining areas only
~ Dogs allowed in bar ~ Open 12-11(10.30 Sun)

PEMBROKE FERRY SM9603 Map 6

Ferry Inn

Nestled below A477 toll bridge, N of Pembroke; SA72 6UD

A nice spot in summer, this old sailors' haunt is attractively set by the Cleddau estuary under the bridge, with tables on a terrace by the water. It's where the old ferry used to stop years ago, and aptly enough has quite a nautical feel, with lots of seafaring pictures and memorabilia, a lovely open fire and good sea views. Some of the comfortable seating areas are painted a cosy red. Bass, Felinfoel Double Dragon and a guest such as Shepherd Neame Spitfire on handpump; fruit machine, board games and unobtrusive piped music. With something of an emphasis on fresh fish, the bar food might include natural smoked haddock with poached eggs or salmon in filo pastry with dill butter (£8.95), steak and ale pie (£9.50), local lamb stuffed with caerphilly and leeks (£9.95), whole fresh brill (£11.95) and whole bass (£12.95); as the menu depends on market supplies, the fish dishes can quickly sell out. Note that the all day opening hours are limited to the summer holiday. *(Recommended by Jim Abbott, JJW, CMW, Mayur Shah, Norman Lewis, Prof H G Allen)*

Free house ~ Licensee Jayne Surtees ~ Real ale ~ Bar food (12-2, 7-9.30; 12-1.30, 7-9 Sun)
~ (01646) 682947 ~ Children in snug area only ~ Dogs allowed in bar ~ Open 11.30-11;
12-10.30 Sun; 11.30-3(12-2.30 Sun), 6.30-11(7-10.30 Sun) in winter; closed 25-26 Dec

PORTHGAIN SM8132 Map 6

Sloop

Off A487 St Davids—Fishguard; SA62 5BN

Readers very much enjoy visiting this wonderfully positioned white-painted old pub, whether in the madness of summer (when the staff cope remarkably well with the visiting hordes) or on quieter, misty winter evenings. On the Pembrokeshire Coast Path and in a tiny harbour village tucked into a cove, it's crammed with seafaring memorabilia; the walls of the plank-ceilinged bar are hung with lobster pots and fishing nets, ships' clocks and lanterns, and even relics from wrecks along this stretch of the shoreline. Down a step, another room leads round to a decent-sized eating area, with simple wooden chairs and tables, cushioned wall seats, and a freezer with ice-creams for children. Bass and Brains Rev James on handpump, and wine by the glass in three different sized glasses. Rather than having a number for food service, many of the tables are named after a wrecked ship. Straightforward promptly served bar food includes soup (£3.80), lunchtime baguettes (from £4.40), moules marinière (£5.90), vegetable lasagne (£6.90), ploughman's (£7.45), crab salad (£11.90, if available), steak (from £13.75), and good daily specials (perhaps unavailable during the summer holiday) such as cumberland sausages and mash (£7.50), seared tuna with coriander and sweet pepper salsa or sea bass with cherry tomato confit (£13.95); there are children's helpings for many dishes, and the dining area is no smoking. There's a well segregated games room (used mainly by children) which has a couple of games machines, juke box, pool, dominoes and Scrabble. At the height of summer they may extend food serving times. Tables on the terrace overlook the harbour, with outdoor heaters for cooler weather. *(Recommended by Ian and Deborah Carrington, Jim Abbott, Blaise Vyner, Trevor and Judith Pearson, MDN, Glenwys and Alan Lawrence, Mike Pugh, Pat and Stewart Gordon, Mark and Mary Fairman, Conus and Sarah Elliott, Geoff and Brigid Smithers)*

Free house ~ Licensee Matthew Blakiston ~ Real ale ~ Bar food (12-2.30, 6-9.30; not 25 Dec) ~ (01348) 831449 ~ Children welcome ~ Open 9.30-11; closed part of 25 Dec

PRESTEIGNE SO3265 Map 6
Radnorshire Arms
High Street; B4355 N of centre; LD8 2BE

Built in Elizabethan times for Christopher Hatton, one of Elizabeth I's favourite courtiers, this striking half-timbered house is part of a small group of hotels, but is full of individuality and historical charm; it's a great place for a peaceful morning coffee or afternoon tea. Past renovations have revealed secret passages and priest's holes, with one priest's diary showing he was walled up here for two years. The relaxed bar's discreet worn-in modern furnishings blend in well with venerable dark oak panelling, latticed windows, and elegantly moulded black oak beams (some decorated with horsebrasses). Around the fireplace are polished copper pans and measures, and a handful of armchairs, and there's a plush red carpet throughout; piped music. You'll find three beers on handpump such as Evan Evans Cwrw, Felinfoel Double Dragon and Greene King Abbot, and they've wine from Herefordshire as well as several malt whiskies. Friendly staff serve dishes from a bar menu which includes soup (£3.55), triple sandwiches (£3.95), welsh rarebit (£4.85), warm brie and redcurrant tartlet (£5.25), and a daily carvery (£7.95; £9.95 with pudding; Sunday lunch (£9.95 for three courses), and an indian buffet on Monday evenings (£5). The bar and restaurant are completely no smoking. There are lots of tables on an elegant sheltered flower-bordered lawn, which used to be a bowling green. *(Recommended by Ian Phillips, Reg Fowle, Helen Rickwood, Chris Smith)*

Free house ~ Licensee Philip Smart ~ Real ale ~ Bar food ~ Restaurant ~ (01544) 267406 ~ Children in eating area of bar and restaurant ~ Open 11-3, 5-11.30; 11am-midnight Sat; 12-10.30 Sun ~ Bedrooms: £68B/£86B

RAGLAN SO3608 Map 6
Clytha Arms 🍴 🍺 🛏
Clytha, off Abergavenny road – former A40, now declassified; NP7 9BW

This fine old country inn stands in its own extensive well cared for grounds on the edge of Clytha Park – a mass of colour in spring. With long verandahs and diamond paned windows, it's comfortable, light and airy, with scrubbed wood floors, pine settles, big faux fur cushions on the window seats, a good mix of old country furniture and a couple of warming fires. Don't miss the murals in the lavatories. Run by charming licensees, it's the sort of relaxed place where everyone feels welcome, from locals who've walked here for a pint, to diners in the contemporary linen-set restaurant. The good bar menu includes sandwiches, soup

(£5.25), cider-baked ham with warm potato salad (£6.95), mussels (£7.50), wild boar sausages with potato pancakes (£7.95), wild mushroom omelette or chicken breast with parmesan crust (£8.50), smoked haddock with y-fenni cheese (£9.25), and daily specials like stuffed lambs hearts (£7.50) or rabbit and cider pie (£8.90). The restaurant menu is pricier and more elaborate; Sunday lunch (£14.95 for two courses, £17.95 for three). An impressive choice of drinks includes Bass, Felinfoel Double Dragon and Hook Norton Hooky, three swiftly changing guest beers from brewers such as Caledonian, Carters and Fullers, an extensive wine list with about a dozen or so by the glass, a good choice of spirits, farm cider and even home-made perry. They have occasional cider and beer festivals. The restaurant and lounge are no smoking; darts, shove-ha'penny, boules, table skittles, bar billiards, cribbage, dominoes, draughts and chess. The two friendly labradors are Beamish and Stowford and there's an english setter. Quite a few readers this year have found the service less efficient than on previous visits, and a couple felt the loos could do with sprucing up. The bedrooms are comfortable, with good welsh breakfasts. *(Recommended by Ian Phillips, Tom and Ruth Rees, William Orchard, Glenys and John Roberts, Donna and Roger, Pete Baker, Mike Pugh, Mike and Mary Carter, Simon Jones, the Didler, MLR, John and Joan Nash, Geoff and Marianne Millin, David and Nina Pugsley, Andy Trafford, Louise Bayly, Simon Cleasby, Karen Eliot)*

Free house ~ Licensees Andrew and Beverley Canning ~ Real ale ~ Bar food (12.30-2.30, 7-9.30; not Sun evening or Mon lunch) ~ Restaurant ~ (01873) 840206 ~ Children welcome ~ Dogs allowed in bar ~ Open 12-12; 12-11 Sat, Sun; closed Mon lunchtime; evening 25 Dec ~ Bedrooms: £60B/£80B

RED WHARF BAY SH5281 Map 6

Ship ♀ ◖

Village signposted off B5025 N of Pentraeth; LL75 8RJ

The superb setting and views are perhaps the main draw at this slate-roofed seaside pub on Anglesey's north coast, but they do mean it's hardly undiscovered. You'll need to get here early on a sunny day for a table, but if you can bag one of the benches placed against the white walls you'll be rewarded with a stunning sweeping view of the big bay, with vast tidal sands enclosed by dunes and rounded headlands. Inside is old-fashioned and interesting, with lots of nautical bric-a-brac in big rooms on each side of the busy stone-built bar counter, both with long cushioned varnished pews built around the walls, glossily varnished cast-iron-framed tables and roaring fires. Most areas are now no smoking; piped Classic FM (in lounge only). Adnams, Brains and Tetleys and a guest like Black Sheep on handpump, more than 50 malt whiskies, and a wider choice of wines than is usual for the area (with about ten by the glass). The bar menu might include soup (£3.50), lunchtime sandwiches (from £4.10), welsh cheeses with fruit chutney, celery, apple salad and tomato bread (£6.95), sausages with spring onion and blue cheese mash and roasted tomato sauce (£8.95), wild mushroom, spinach and brie lasagne (£9.50), calves liver with roasted sweet potato, crispy pancetta and onion gravy (£10.50), and pan-fried fillet of sea trout (£10.95); they do children's meals (from £4.55) and a two-course set menu Mon-Thursday lunchtimes (£30 for two people, including a bottle of wine). Quite a few readers this year felt the helpings could be more generous. If you want to run a tab they'll ask to keep your credit card behind the bar in a locked numbered box (to which you are given the key). *(Recommended by J R Ringrose, Joan York, R T J and J J Hubbard, J Roy Smylie, Dr and Mrs M E Wilson, Tony and Maggie Harwood, Gerry and Rosemary Dobson)*

Free house ~ Licensee Neil Kenneally ~ Real ale ~ Bar food (12-2.30, 6-9; 12-9 Sat-Sun) ~ (01248) 852568 ~ Children in family areas till 9pm ~ Open 11-11(12 Sat)

If a service charge is mentioned prominently on a menu or accommodation terms, you must pay it if service was satisfactory. If service is really bad you are legally entitled to refuse to pay some or all of the service charge as compensation for not getting the service you might reasonably have expected.

RHYD-Y-MEIRCH SO2907 Map 6
Goose & Cuckoo ◀

Upper Llanover signposted up narrow track off A4042 S of Abergavenny; after ½ mile take first left, then keep on up (watch for hand-written Goose signs at the forks); NP7 9ER

Well positioned for walks along the nearby Monmouthshire and Brecon Canal towpath or over the hilltops towards Blorenge and Blaenavon, this remote and simple place is essentially one small rustically furnished room with a woodburner in an arched stone fireplace, but what makes it special, apart from the setting, is the warmth of welcome you get from the friendly licensees. They have well kept Evans and Jones Premium Welsh, Youngs, and an often unusual guest on handpump, as well as more than 80 whiskies and good coffees; daily papers, cribbage, darts, dominoes, draughts, shove-ha'penny, quoits and boules. With everything made on the premises and cooked in the Aga (including the bread), the choice of enjoyably simple food includes filled rolls (from £1.80), very good bean soup (£2.40), a variety of ploughman's (£6), turkey and ham pie, liver and bacon casserole, spaghetti bolognese or chilli con carne (all £6.50), with specials such as steak and kidney pie or corned beef pie (£6.50) and home-made puddings (£2.50); you'll need to book for their Sunday lunch. Readers particularly like the home-made ice-creams. A small picture-window extension makes the most of the view down the valley. There is a variety of rather ad hoc picnic-sets out on the gravel below, and the licensees keep sheep, geese and chickens. They may have honey for sale. The bedroom has two single beds, and they hope to have completed a new self-catering bungalow by the New Year. *(Recommended by Reg Fowle, Helen Rickwood, Louise Barrett, John Fiander, John and Gloria Isaacs, Guy Vowles, Mike Pugh, R T and J C Moggridge)*

Free house ~ Licensees Michael and Carol Langley ~ Real ale ~ Bar food (12-2.30, 7-9; not Mon) ~ No credit cards ~ (01873) 880277 ~ Dogs welcome ~ Open 11.30-3, 7-11; 11.30-11 Sat; 12-10.30 Sun; closed Mon exc bank holidays ~ Bedrooms: £25S/£50S

ROSEBUSH SN0729 Map 6
Tafarn Sinc

B4329 Haverfordwest—Cardigan; SA66 7QU

Built in 1876 as a rudimentary hotel for a halt of the adjacent long abandoned railway, this maroon-painted corrugated iron shed is a quirky place, basic but with bags of atmosphere – and don't be surprised if everyone, including the staff, is speaking welsh. The halt itself has been more or less re-created, even down to life-size dummy passengers waiting out on the platform, and the sizeable garden is periodically enlivened by the sounds of steam trains chuffing through – actually broadcast from a replica signal box. Though not exactly elegant, inside is really interesting, almost a museum of local history, with sawdust on the floor and an appealingly buoyant feel. The bar has plank panelling, an informal mix of chairs and pews, woodburners, and Cwrw Tafarn Sinc (brewed specially for the pub), and a weekly changing guest such as Sharps Doom Bar on handpump; piped music, darts and TV. Basic food includes home-made faggots with onion gravy, vegetable lasagne, or lamb burgers (all £7.90), steaks (from £9.90), and puddings (£3.90). There's a no smoking dining room. *(Recommended by Phil and Sally Gorton, John and Enid Morris, the Didler, Alan and Paula McCully)*

Free house ~ Licensee Brian Llewelyn ~ Real ale ~ Bar food (12-2, 6-9) ~ Restaurant ~ (01437) 532214 ~ Children in eating areas till 9pm ~ Open 12-11(midnight Sat, 10.30 Sun); closed Mon

SAUNDERSFOOT SN1304 Map 6
Royal Oak ♀ ◀

Wogan Terrace (B4316); SA69 9HA

Tables outside this well run village local overlook the harbour, and have heaters – they're highly prized in summer, when a good many people come for the fresh fish specials. The choice and price depend on the time of year but you might find a pint of prawns (£6.95), beer-battered haddock (£9.25), tuna steak topped with garlic prawns (£13.95), hake (£14.95) and grilled whole bass (£17.95). Other food includes lunchtime sandwiches (from £3.95), home-made lasagne, local pork and garlic sausages or curry (£8.95), and 8oz fillet steak (£17.95), with puddings such as cheesecake of the day or lemon mousse (from £3.95); two-course Sunday lunch (£8.50, three courses £10.50). Service is pleasant and attentive. There's a cheerful atmosphere in the dining area and carpeted lounge bar, which has captain's chairs and wall banquettes. Frequented by chatty locals, the small public bar has a TV; piped music. Five real ales on handpump include one named for the pub, Greene King Abbot and Old Speckled Hen, and a couple of guests such as Felinfoel Double Dragon; they've also over 30 malt whiskies and an interesting choice of wines (lots of new world ones), with about a dozen by the glass. Several areas are no smoking. *(Recommended by David Eberlin, the Didler, P Price, Brian and Ruth Archer, Alastair Stevenson)*

Free house ~ Licensees T S and T L Suter ~ Real ale ~ Bar food (12-2.30, 5.30-9.30; 12-4 Sun (longer in summer)) ~ Restaurant ~ (01834) 812546 ~ Children welcome ~ Dogs allowed in bar ~ Open 10.30am-12.30am

SHIRENEWTON   ST4894   Map 6

Carpenters Arms

Mynydd-bach; B4235 Chepstow—Usk, about ½ mile N; NP16 6BU

Popular with locals (especially for Sunday lunch), this quaint stone-built pub was originally a smithy, and one of the unusual interconnecting rooms still has blacksmith's bellows hanging from the planked ceiling. Other interesting features include an array of chamber-pots, an attractive Victorian tiled fireplace, and a collection of chromolithographs of antique royal occasions. Furnishings run the gamut too, from one very high-backed ancient settle to pews, kitchen chairs, a nice elm table, several sewing-machine trestle tables and so forth; shove-ha'penny, cribbage, dominoes, backgammon and piped pop music. Bass, Fullers London Pride, Marstons Pedigree and Shepherd Neame Spitfire on handpump with an occasional seasonal guest. The wide choice of popular food, written up on blackboards, takes in everything from sandwiches and filled baked potatoes (from £4) to unusual meats like kangaroo (£10.95) and a big mixed grill (from £15.95). There are tables outside at the front, under hanging baskets in summer. *(Recommended by Dr and Mrs C W Thomas, BOB, Steve Bailey, Mr and Mrs J Brown, Stephen and Jean Curtis, Ian Phillips)*

Punch ~ Lease Gary and Sandra Hayes ~ Real ale ~ Bar food (12-9.30; 12-3, 6-9.30 in winter) ~ Restaurant ~ (01291) 641231 ~ Children welcome ~ Dogs welcome ~ Open 12-12; 11-10.30 Sun; 12-3.30, 5.30-12 (10.30 Sun) in winter

SKENFRITH   SO4520   Map 6

Bell ♀ ⇌

Just off B5421, NE of Abergavenny and N of Monmouth; NP7 8UH

Though they've grown their own herbs for a while, the licensees of this gently upmarket country inn are now developing a kitchen garden with organic fruit and vegetables. Their consistently good food is the place's main draw, and though it's certainly not cheap, readers agree it's worth it – this is a good choice for that celebratory splurge. Using named local suppliers of carefully chosen fresh ingredients, the menu might include roasted butternut squash soup (£4.50), lunchtime open sandwiches (from £7), glazed red onion, sunblush tomato, red onion and mozzarella tart, with red chard and walnut salad (£14), pork and leek sausages with mustard mash and braised red cabbage (£13), pan-seared scallops with broad bean and saffron risotto and lemon-glazed rocket (£15.50), and whole baked bass with pesto roast potatoes and courgette chips (£16). The owners are welcoming and enthusiastic, and service is cheerful and efficient. The big back bare-boards dining area is very neat, light and airy, with dark country-kitchen chairs and rush-seat dining chairs, church candles and flowers on the dark tables, canary walls and a cream ceiling, and brocaded curtains on sturdy big-ring rails. The flagstoned bar on the left has a rather similar décor, with old local and school photographs, and a couple of pews as well as tables and café chairs; Breconshire Golden Valley, Freeminer and Timothy Taylors Landlord on handpump from an attractive bleached oak bar counter. They have good wines by the glass and half-bottle, and make good coffee. The lounge bar on the right, opening into the dining area, has a nice Jacobean-style carved settle and a housekeeper's chair by a log fire in the big fireplace. The atmosphere is relaxed but smart (the lavatories are labelled Loos), and the pub is now entirely no smoking. There are good solid round picnic-sets as well as the usual rectangular ones out on the terrace, with steps up to a sloping lawn; it's a quiet spot. The bedrooms are comfortable, with thoughtful touches. Across the access road is a pretty bridge over the River Monnow. *(Recommended by Duncan Cloud, Bernard Stradling, Alec and Barbara Jones, Tom and Ruth Rees, R T and J C Moggridge, Ron and Sheila Corbett, Mark and Mary Fairman)*

Free house ~ Licensees William and Janet Hutchings ~ Real ale ~ Bar food (12-2.30, 7-9.30(9 Sun)) ~ Restaurant ~ (01600) 750235 ~ Children welcome in eating areas till 7pm, then over-8s only ~ Dogs allowed in bar and bedrooms ~ Open 11-11; 12-10.30 Sun; closed all day Mon in winter; last week Jan/first week Feb ~ Bedrooms: /£100B

ST HILARY   ST0173   Map 6
Bush

Village signposted from A48 E of Cowbridge; CF71 7DP

In a delightful spot not far from Cardiff, tucked behind the village church, this cosily old-fashioned 16th-c stone and thatch pub has been much enjoyed in recent months for its good food and particularly friendly welcome. Comfortable in a quietly stylish way, it has a lovely big log fire (leading some to describe this as their favourite winter pub), stripped old stone walls, and farmhouse tables and chairs in the low-beamed carpeted lounge bar, while the other bar is pubbier with old settles and pews on aged flagstones, and a pleasant mix of locals and visitors. Bass, Greene King Old Speckled Hen, Hancocks HB and a guest on handpump or tapped from the cask; TV, cribbage, dominoes and subdued piped music. The well presented bar food might include lunchtime sandwiches, soup (£3.95), pork and leek sausages with mash and onion gravy (£6.95), ploughman's (£7.50), fish and chips, steak and ale pie or thai chicken curry (£7.50), and chargrilled sirloin of welsh beef (£12); also available in the bar, the restaurant menu might have pan-fried fillets of bass with wild mushroom risotto (£13) and rack of lamb with dauphinoise potatoes and cassoulet of beans (£15). The Sunday lunch, with organic meats and very good vegetables, is well liked. The restaurant and lounge are no smoking. There are tables and chairs in front, and more in the back garden; reasonable disabled access. *(Recommended by Mark and Deb Ashton, Malcolm and Faith Thomas, P Price, Glenwys and Alan Lawrence, David and Nina Pugsley, Ian Phillips)*

Punch ~ Tenant Phil Thomas ~ Real ale ~ Bar food (12-2.30(3 Sun), 6.30-9.30; not Sun evening) ~ Restaurant ~ (01446) 772745 ~ Children welcome ~ Dogs allowed in bar ~ Open 12-11(10.30 Sun)

TINTERN   SO5200   Map 6
Cherry Tree ◧

Pub signed up narrow Raglan road off A466, beside Royal George; parking very limited; NP16 6TH

The approach to this late-16th-c stone cottage is delightful, across a little stone slab bridge over a tiny stream. Not especially smart (when readers have said it's disorganised, we know they mean that as a compliment), it's a characterful place very much at the heart of the local community – even more so now the building takes in the village shop and post office. It's been sympathetically extended in recent years, but not in a way that's altered its appeal: the well kept Hancocks HB and two and four guests like Hereford Pale Ale, Sharps Doom Bar and Wye Valley

Butty Bach are still tapped straight from the cask, and they also serve farm ciders from the barrel, along with a good few wines by the glass, and home-made country wines; warmly welcoming service. The original beamed and stone-built bar has a walnut serving counter in one area and a good open fire in another, and leads into the slate-floored extension; cribbage, darts, cards, dominoes and piped music. Good value food, in big helpings and made with fresh local ingredients, might include sandwiches (from £1.85), soup (£3.95), omelettes (from £3.95, prawn and spinach £4.95), tagliatelle with mushroom and tomato sauce (£4.95), local beef chilli or lamb stew with herby dumplings (£5.95), pork chop with chutney sauce (£8.95), daily specials, and a choice of Sunday roasts (£5.95); decent children's menu (from £2.50). Readers have found them reluctant to take credit cards for smaller amounts. The pub is in a quiet and attractive spot, yet only half a mile or so from the honey-pot centre of Tintern, and there are tables out in a charming garden, and on a nicely refurbished patio; disabled access is difficult. They have two beer and cider festivals a year. *(Recommended by Tim and Ann Newell, Tony and Wendy Hobden, James Read, Ginette Medland, R T and J C Moggridge, Pete Baker, the Didler, John and Gloria Isaacs, Piotr Chodzko-Zajko, LM, A S and M E Marriott, Bruce Bird)*

Free house ~ Licensees Jill and Steve Pocock ~ Real ale ~ Bar food (12-3, 6-9 (8.30 Sun); not winter Sun evenings) ~ Restaurant ~ (01291) 689292 ~ Children in restaurant only ~ Dogs allowed in bar ~ Occasional live music ~ Open 12-11(10.30 Sun); 12-6 Sundays in winter ~ Bedrooms: /£60S(£60B)

TRELLECK SO5005 Map 6

Lion ◀

B4293 6 miles S of Monmouth; NP25 4PA

Popular with a mix of locals, walkers and visitors, this stone-built pub has the feel of a chatty local – and an extraordinarily wide range of food. The menu includes baguettes (from £3.25), filled baked potatoes (from £3.50), omelettes (from £3.95), ploughman's (from £6), ham, egg and chips (£7.50), vegetarian hotpot (£7.80), pasta carbonara or battered plaice (£8), chicken tikka (£8.75), cottage pie (£8.65) gammon steak with egg or pineapple, weekly specials, and various hungarian specialities like erdö pulyka – fried diced turkey in creamy dill sauce (£11.25) or chicken breast filled with apricots, cherries and cheese, wrapped in bacon and served with parsley potatoes (£14); children's menu. Unpretentious and traditional, the open-plan bar has one or two black beams in its low ochre ceiling, a mix of furnishings including some comfortable brocaded wall seats and tub chairs, a hop-hung window seat, varying-sized tables, and log fires in two fireplaces opposite each other. A small fish tank occupies a wall recess, and there's another bigger one in the lobby by the lavatories; piped music, cribbage, dominoes, shove-ha'penny and bar skittles. A colourful galaxy of pump clips in the porch and on a wall shows the range of rapidly changing guest beers such as Rhymney Bevans Bitter or Stonehenge Nine Lives that are kept alongside Wye Valley Butty Bach; they have an annual beer festival, as well as nearly two dozen malt whiskies, and traditional cider. Readers who've found the pub rather smoky will be pleased to hear that much of the public bar is now no smoking, as well as the restaurant. There are some picnic-sets and an aviary out on the grass, and a new side courtyard overlooking the church. The bedrooms are in a spearate cottage. Close by is a group of prehistoric standing stones. *(Recommended by Theocsbrian, LM, Mike Pugh, Piotr Chodzko-Zajko, Derek and Sylvia Stephenson, Bruce Bird, Guy Vowles, R T and J C Moggridge)*

Free house ~ Licensee Debbie Zsigo ~ Real ale ~ Bar food (12-2(2.30 weekends), 6(7 Mon)-9.30; not Sun evening) ~ Restaurant ~ (01600) 860322 ~ Children welcome ~ Dogs allowed in bar ~ Live music on evening of bank holiday Sats ~ Open weekdays 12-3, 6(7 Mon)-11(12 Thurs/Fri); 12-12 (12-3, 6.30-12 in winter) Sat; 12-5(4 in winter) Sun; closed Sun evening, all day 1 Jan, and evening 25 Dec ~ Bedrooms: £40S/£65S

Information about no smoking areas is for the period before smoking becomes illegal throughout Welsh pubs.

TY'N-Y-GROES   SH7672   Map 6

Groes 🍴 ♀ 🛏

B5106 N of village; LL32 8TN

Though it's the wonderfully relaxing atmosphere that's most impressed readers over the last few months, this elegantly romantic hotel stands out too for its very good food. They make excellent use of local ingredients, such as lamb and salmon from the Conwy Valley, and game birds from local shoots, and bake their own bread and grow their own herbs. Said to have been the first welsh pub to be properly licensed – in 1573 – it enjoys magnificent views over the Vale of Conwy and the distant mountains. Past the hot stove in the entrance area, the spotlessly kept series of rambling, low-beamed and thick-walled rooms is nicely decorated with antique settles and an old sofa, old clocks, portraits, hats and tins hanging from the walls, and fresh flowers. A fine antique fireback is built into one wall, perhaps originally from the formidable fireplace in the back bar, which houses a collection of stone cats as well as cheerful winter log fires. The restaurant and family room are no smoking, as is the airy and verdant conservatory. Well presented dishes might include soup (£4.25), sandwiches (from £4.75), freshly made linguini pasta, smoked chicken and carbonara sauce (£6.75), sausages, bacon and mash or welsh hill lamb shepherd's pie (£7.95), haddock, prawn and mushroom mornay (£8.75), poached salmon with hollandaise sauce (£11.50), and steaks (from £13.95), with daily specials such as game casserole (£11.25), and local lamb steak or bass (£12.50). As well as puddings such as white chocolate and vanilla bean panna cotta or sticky toffee pudding (from £4.75), they do delicious home-made ice-creams, with a few unusual flavours such as rose petal, or lemon curd and poppy seed. Ind Coope Burton and Tetleys on handpump, and they've a good few malt whiskies, kir, and a fruity Pimms in summer; light classical piped music at lunchtimes, nostalgic light music at other times and a live harpist every now and then. The neatly kept, well equipped bedroom suites (some have terraces or balconies) have gorgeous views, and in summer it's a pleasure to sit outside in the pretty back garden with its flower-filled hayricks; there are more seats on the flower-decked roadside. They also rent out a well appointed wooden cabin, idyllically placed nearby. (*Recommended by Spider Newth, Terry and Linda Moseley, Mike and Mary Carter, Clive Watkin, Donald Mills, Margaret and Jeff Graham, Joan York, Sarah and Peter Gooderham, J F M and M West, Neil Whitehead, Victoria Anderson, Andy Sinden, Louise Harrington, Jo Lilley, Simon Calvert*)

Free house ~ Licensee Dawn Humphreys ~ Real ale ~ Bar food (12-2.15, 6.30(6 Sat, Sun)-9) ~ Restaurant ~ (01492) 650545 ~ Children in family room till 7pm ~ Dogs welcome ~ Open 12-3, 6.30-11 (all day summer weekends); closed 25 Dec ~ Bedrooms: £79B/£95B

USK   SO3801   Map 6

Nags Head 🍴 ♀

The Square; NP15 1BH

The family that runs this old coaching inn has been here almost 40 years, and its their friendly welcome that has once again impressed readers the most this year; first-time visitors can be treated like long-established locals, and one correspondent tells how the landlord drove him home when a thunderstorm began unexpectedly. With a friendly chatty atmosphere, the beautifully kept traditional main bar has lots of well polished tables and chairs packed under its beams (some with farming tools), lanterns or horsebrasses and harness attached, as well as leatherette wall benches, and various sets of sporting prints and local pictures – look out for the original deeds to the pub. Tucked away at the front is an intimate little corner with some african masks, while on the other side of the room a passageway leads to a new dining area converted from the old coffee bar. There may be prints for sale, and perhaps a knot of sociable locals. Popular, generously served food (concentrating on local produce) includes soup (£3.90), frog legs in hot provençale sauce or whitebait (£6), steak pie (£7), several vegetarian dishes like cheese and leek sausages or vegetable bake (£7.95), delicious rabbit pie (£8), and seasonal game specials (lovely on a cold winter evening) such as wild boar steak in apricot and brandy sauce (£13), pheasant in port (£14), and a brace of boned quail (£15.50). You can book tables, some of which may be candlelit at night; nice proper linen napkins, and quiet piped classical music. They do 15 wines by the glass, along with well kept Brains SA, Buckleys Best and Rev James on handpump, 12 malt whiskies and Thatcher's Gold farm cider. Two rooms are no smoking. The centre of Usk is full of pretty hanging baskets and flowers in summer, and the church is well worth a look. *(Recommended by M G Hart, Tim and Ann Newell, Ian Phillips, Sue and Ken Le Prevost, Donna and Roger, Terry and Linda Moseley, Peter Craske, Roy and Lindsey Fentiman, Mike Pugh, Prof Keith and Mrs Jane Barber, Dr and Mrs C W Thomas, Mr and Mrs A Williams, A S and M EMarriott, Pam and Alan Neale, Bruce Bird, Eileen McCall, Eryl and Keith Dykes)*

Free house ~ Licensee the Key family ~ Real ale ~ Bar food (12-2, 6-9.30) ~ Restaurant ~ (01291) 672820 ~ Children welcome ~ Dogs allowed in bar ~ Open 10.30-3, 5.30-11; closed 25 Dec

LUCKY DIP

Besides the fully inspected pubs, you might like to try these Lucky Dips recommended to us and described by readers (if you do, please send us reports: www.goodguides.co.uk).

ANGLESEY

BEAUMARIS [SH6076]

☆ *Sailors Return* LL58 8AB [Church St]: Bright cheery partly divided open-plan bar with comfortable banquettes and open fire, some emphasis on generous good value food from sandwiches and baguettes up inc a dish of the day, smiling helpful service, Bass and perhaps one or two other real ales, decent wines, bookable tables in no smoking dining area; unobtrusive piped music; children welcome in eating area, dogs in bar, comfortable bedrooms *(Phil Merrin, LYM, Neil Whitehead, Victoria Anderson, John and Helen Davey, Gerry and Rosemary Dobson, J C Brittain-Long)*

MARIANGLAS [SH5084]

Parciau Arms LL73 8PH: Decent bar food from sandwiches up, light and airy family dining lounge with log fire, four real ales inc a Mild, good range of other drinks, cheerful service, comfortable built-in banquettes and other seating, old coaching prints, interesting bric-a-brac inc lots of gleaming brass, pub games in busy bar; terrace and good-sized garden with excellent play area, open all day *(John Tav)*

MENAI BRIDGE [SH5773]

☆ *Gazelle* LL59 5PD [Glyngarth; A545, half way towards Beaumaris]: Outstanding waterside situation looking across to Snowdonia, extensive comfortable refurbishment making the most of the views, enjoyable food inc fresh fish, real ale, helpful staff, lively main bar, smaller rooms off and restaurant; children welcome, steep and aromatic mediterranean garden behind, good bedrooms *(J Roy Smylie, LYM, Peter and Liz Holmes)*

CLWYD

BANGOR IS Y COED [SJ3845]

Royal Oak LL13 0BU [High St]: Attractive pub by ancient bypassed bridge over River

Dee, Black Sheep, Boddingtons, Greene King Old Speckled Hen and Stones, helpful landlady, impressive range of generous food, long low-beamed bar with neatly set dining tables and no smoking end, armchairs in back snug, bright brasses and full suit of armour; nice back terrace with awning and roses *(Michael and Jenny Back)*

BERSHAM [SJ3149]

Black Lion LL14 4HN [Ddol]: Friendly local in former industrial area, good Hydes ales, welcoming staff and inexpensive straightforward bar food, darts, cards and pool in public bar, TV in lounge for racing; a few tables outside *(Pete Baker)*

BODFARI [SJ0970]

☆ *Dinorben Arms* LL16 4DA [off A541, near church]: Attractive black and white hillside pub nr Offa's Dyke, three well worn beamed and flagstoned rooms, old-fashioned settles, three open fires, a glassed-over old well, lots of hanging whisky-water jugs, over 250 malt whiskies, popular food from sandwiches and bar snacks to restaurant dishes, carvery (Fri/Sat night, Sun lunch), welcoming landlord, efficient young staff, Banks's, Marstons Pedigree and a guest beer, good wines, darts and pool, light and airy garden room; fruit machine, TV, piped classical music; children welcome, grassy play area, charming views from pretty brick terraces, open all day wknds *(Donald Mills, LYM, Esther and John Sprinkle, KC)*

CADOLE [SJ2062]

Colomendy Arms CH7 5LL [just off A494 Mold—Ruthin]: Four attractively priced and well chosen real ales from small corner bar, two small rooms, coal fire, lots of interesting lead-mining memorabilia, cheery landlord and landlady; dogs and children welcome, handy for Loggerheads Country Park *(Phil Merrin)*

CARROG [SJ1143]

Grouse LL21 9AT [B5436, signed off A5

, games inc pool in
...the bar (also piped music, games machine,
juke box, quiz nights); tables on front terrace,
bright window boxes *(KC, LYM)*

CROSS LANES [SJ3746]
Cross Lanes Hotel LL13 0TF [Bangor Rd
(A525 Wrexham—Bangor-is-y-coed)]: Good
atmosphere and Plassey real ales in hotel bar
with good adjoining brasserie; bedrooms
(Donald Mills, Esther and John Sprinkle)

DYSERTH [SJ0579]
New Inn LL18 6ET [Waterfall Rd (B5119)]:
Welcoming helpful service, several rooms
served from central bar inc tables for drinkers
(real ales such as Banks's Original, Mansfield
Cask and Marstons Pedigree and Burton) and
for the very popular good reasonably priced
home-made food with proper pastry for the
pies – best to book *(Joan York, Pete and
Kate Holford)*

GRESFORD [SJ3455]
Griffin LL12 8RG [The Green (B5373, just off
A483 Chester—Wrexham)]: Fine traditional
village pub, homely and unspoilt, well divided
single bar with piano in one bit, darts in
another, chatty regulars, real ales such as Black
Sheep and Everards; cl till 4 (3 wknds)
(Pete Baker)

GWYTHERIN [SH8761]
Lion LL22 8UU [B5384 W of Denbigh]:
Isolated small village pub recently reopened
after refurbishment by new owners, log fire in
attractive main bar, pleasant small restaurant
area with another log fire, wide choice of
interesting food, good wines by the glass and
real ale; five good bedrooms *(Anon)*

LLANDEGLA [SJ2051]
Plough LL11 3AB [Ruthin Rd]: Cosy and
couth dining pub, wide choice of enjoyable

food all day inc two-for-one bargains, efficient
staff, Robinsons, large dining room, no
smoking area; unobtrusive piped music;
nr Offa's Dyke Path *(KC)*

LLANDYRNOG [SJ1065]
White Horse LL16 4HG: Friendly pub popular
for its enjoyable food inc some interesting
dishes *(J R Ringrose)*

LLOC [SJ1476]
Rock CH8 8RD [St Asaph Rd (A5151)]: Bright
décor, interesting choice of enjoyable generous
food in busy bar with good log fire or (if you
have a main dish) dining room – freshly made
so can take a while *(KC)*

MOLD [SJ2364]
Bryn Awel CH7 1BL [A541 Denbigh Rd nr
Bailey Hill]: Hillside modern hotel with
welcoming attentive service, reliable choice of
satisfying good value food from interesting
snacks up, big helpings, sensibly priced wines,
cheerful bustling carpeted lounge bar,
comfortable woodstrip-floor restaurant
extension with picture-window country views,
good no smoking area; may be piped music
(KC)

PONTBLYDDYN [SJ2761]
New Inn CH7 4HR [A5104, just S of A541 3
miles SE of Mold]: Interesting choice of good
food in unassuming building's attractive
upstairs dining room, good service; piped
music *(KC)*

RHEWL [SJ1160]
Drovers Arms LL15 2UD [A525 2 miles N of
Ruthin]: Old-fashioned low-beamed pub with
enjoyable food using local produce, roomy and
spotless eating areas inc new no smoking back
conservatory, pleasant staff, real ales such as
Fullers and Youngs, no piped music, pool
room; children welcome, attractive garden,
open all day wknds *(Donald Mills)*

RHYDTALOG [SJ2354]
Liver CH7 4NU: Small busy pub with
decent food, good staff, no piped music; lacks
a no smoking area *(KC)*

RUTHIN [SJ1258]
Wynnstay Arms LL15 1AN [Well St]: No
smoking contemporary refurbishment with
wide choice of reasonably priced food from
sandwiches, panini and pubby favourites to
up-to-date dishes in café/bar and brasserie; six
bedrooms *(AJ)*

ST ASAPH [SJ0673]
Farmers Arms LL17 0DY [The Waen; B5429
between A55 and Tremeirchion]: Charming
little country pub, cosy lounge with log-effect
gas fire, good food inc some local specialities,
interesting wines by the glass, local beer tapped
from the cask, friendly efficient service
(Kenneth and Mary Davies)

ST GEORGE [SH9775]
Kinmel Arms LL22 9BP [off A55 nr Abergele]:
17th-c former posting inn in attractive village,
interesting building with several refurbished
rooms, nice mix of tables and chairs, rugs on
stripped wood, wide range of reasonably
priced interesting modern food from lunchtime
baguettes and dutch-style open sandwiches up,
changing ales such as Greene King Old

Speckled Hen, Brains Rev James and Wychwood Shires, good choice of wines by the glass, friendly staff, conservatory; cl Mon *(Anon)*

TAL-Y-CAFN [SH7871]

☆ *Tal-y-Cafn Hotel* LL28 5RR [A470 Conway—Llanrwst]: Cheerful bustle in comfortable lounge bar with jugs hanging from ceiling and log fire in big inglenook, wide choice of good value satisfying home cooking in huge helpings, Bass, Boddingtons and Tetleys; children welcome, seats in spacious garden, pleasant surroundings, handy for Bodnant Gardens *(KC, LYM)*

DYFED

ABERAERON [SN4462]

Royal Oak SA46 0JG [North Rd (A487)]: Good atmosphere in big invitingly cosy and popular front lounge, good food with some interesting specials, friendly prompt service, good beers, good choice of wines by the glass *(P Price, Jackie and Alan Moody, Andy Sinden, Louise Harrington)*

ANGLE [SM8703]

☆ *Old Point House* SA71 5AS [signed off B4320 in village, along long rough waterside track; East Angle Bay]: Dating from 14th c, unspoilt, comfortable and in idyllic spot overlooking Milford Haven, with friendly down-to-earth atmosphere, good food (almost all fresh local fish), Felinfoel Double Dragon, flagstoned bar with open fire, small lounge bar, lots of charm and character, run by local lifeboat coxswain – many photographs and charts; plenty of tables and ancient slate seats out by the shore *(Matthew Shackle, Blaise Vyner, Glenwys and Alan Lawrence, Douglas and Ann Hare)*

BONCATH [SN2038]

☆ *Boncath Inn* SA37 0JN [B4332 Cenarth—Eglwyswrw]: Good home-made food inc tasty specials running up to lobster in large, friendly and attractively traditional village pub, four or five changing real ales (not cheap), woodburner, farm tools and photographs of former railway; prominent pool table; open all day *(Brian and Carole Polhill, Colin Moore, Helene and Richard Lay)*

BOSHERSTON [SR9694]

☆ *St Govans Country Inn* SA71 5DN [off B4319 S of Pembroke]: Cheerful, friendly and comfortably modernised, with helpful service, changing real ales such as Adnams, Brains Rev James, Fullers London Pride and Tetleys, good climbing photographs and murals of local beauty spots in big open-plan bar, log fire in large stone fireplace, no smoking dining area, dominoes, board games, pool (winter only), cheap unpretentious food; piped music, TV, fruit machine; children and dogs welcome, picnic-sets on front terrace, good value spotless bedrooms (car park if you stay), good breakfast, handy for water-lily lakes, beach and cliffy coast *(P Price, LYM, Mike Pugh, Richard Haw, John R Muller, Comus and Sarah Elliott)*

BRECHFA [SN5230]

Ty Mawr SA32 7RA [B4310]: New Tap Room added to upmarket small country hotel, single large and simple quarry-tiled stone building open to the rafters, and including its own new microbrewery with the brewing process on display, good choice of wines by the glass too, good attractively priced blackboard food; bedrooms, well placed for walkers *(Chris Wall)*

BROAD HAVEN [SM8614]

☆ *Druidstone Hotel* SA62 3NE [N of village on coast rd, bear left for about 1½ miles then follow sign left to Druidstone Haven – inn a sharp left turn after another ½ mile; OS Sheet 157 map ref 862168, marked as Druidston Villa]: Cheerfully informal, the family's former country house in a grand spot above the sea, individualistic and relaxed, ruled out of the main entries only by its club licence (you can't go for just a drink and have to book to eat or stay there); terrific views, inventive home cooking with fresh often organic ingredients, folksy cellar bar with Worthington BB tapped from the cask, good wines, country wines and other drinks, ceilidhs and folk events, chummy dogs (dogs welcomed), all sorts of sporting activities from boules to sand-yachting; attractive high-walled garden, spacious homely bedrooms, even an eco-friendly chalet, cl Nov and Jan, restaurant cl Sun evening *(Blaise Vyner, John and Enid Morris, LYM, Colin Moore, Mike Pugh)*

BURTON [SM9805]

Jolly Sailor SA73 1NX: Great views of River Cleddau, toll bridge and Milford Haven beyond, riverside garden with well spaced tables, good choice of plentiful pubby food, friendly staff; can moor a small boat at the jetty *(Prof H G Allen)*

CAIO [SN6739]

Brunant Arms SA19 8RD [off A482 Llanwrda—Lampeter]: Unpretentious and interestingly furnished village pub, five changing real ales, good log fire, wide food choice from baguettes up (can take a while), stripped stone public bar with games inc pool; juke box, TV; children and dogs welcome, small Perspex-roofed verandah and lower terrace, has been open all day wknds *(LYM, Richard Siebert, Chris Smith)*

CAREW [SN0403]

☆ *Carew Inn* SA70 8SL [A4075, just off A477]: Cheerful old beamed pub with back garden overlooking spectacular castle ruins, outdoor heaters and summer marquee, good play area, more tables out in front, unpretentious old-fashioned furnishings inside, with interesting prints, real ales such as Brains and Worthington, reasonably priced food, friendly service, cosy no smoking upstairs dining room, traditional games; very busy in summer, piped music, live Thurs and summer Sun; children and dogs welcome, open all day wknds and summer *(V Brogden, LYM, the Didler, Colin Moore, Brian and Jacky Wilson)*

CENARTH [SN2641]

White Hart SA38 9JL [A484 Cardigan—Newcastle Emlyn]: Attractive 16th-c pub by famous River Teifi waterfalls and nr coracle centre, quickly served generous straightforward food in bar and restaurant, a couple of real ales, central bar and two separate rooms, simple pleasant furnishings; outside tables *(Pete Yearsley)*

CILGERRAN [SN1942]

Pendre Inn SA43 2SL [off A478 S of Cardigan; High St]: Friendly local with pleasant atmosphere and service, straightforward food, real ale, massive medieval stone walls and broad flagstones *(LYM, Colin Moore)*

CILYCWM [SN7540]

☆ *Neuadd Fawr Arms* SA20 0ST: Welcoming traditional village local in interesting building with simple old-world furnishings, good range of real ales, good choice of reasonably priced fresh homely food in bar and dining room, friendly landlady, staff and lots of cheerful welsh-speaking regulars; good spot by churchyard above river Gwenlas, among lanes to Llyn Brianne *(Mr and Mrs M Stratton, BB, Pat and Stewart Gordon)*

CROESGOCH [SM8430]

Artramont Arms SA62 5JP [A487 Fishguard—St David's, by Porthgain turn]: Friendly roadside pub, light and bright, with efficient service, good choice of sensibly priced fresh food, Brains SA and Felinfoel Double Dragon, daily papers, large bar with pool, small snug, separate dining area with charming conservatory; dogs welcome, good enclosed garden for children *(Mike Pugh, Alan and Paula McCully)*

CWM GWAUN [SN0333]

☆ *Dyffryn Arms* SA65 9SE [Cwn Gwaun and Pontfaen signed off B4313 E of Fishguard]: Classic unspoilt country tavern, virtually the social centre for this lush green valley, very relaxed, basic and idiosyncratic, with veteran landlady (her farming family have run it since 1840, and she's been in charge for over one-third of that time); 1920s front parlour with plain deal furniture inc rocking chair and draughts boards inlaid into tables, coal fire, Bass, Carlsberg Burton or Tetleys served by jug through a sliding hatch, pickled eggs, low prices, World War I prints and posters, darts; pretty countryside, open more or less all day (may close if no customers) *(Phil and Sally Gorton, LYM, the Didler, Colin Moore, Giles and Annie Francis)*

FELINDRE FARCHOG [SN0939]

Olde Salutation SA41 3UY [A487 Newport—Cardigan]: Smart and spacious sympathetically modernised pub with Brains Rev James, Felinfoel Double Dragon and a guest beer, good value food from toasties and baguettes to bass, local beef and seasonal local sea trout, wide choice in good evening restaurant, genial landlord, pool in public bar; disabled access and facilities, eight comfortable bedrooms in new extension, good breakfast, fishing and good walks by nearby River Nevern *(Blaise Vyner, Colin Moore, Paul A Moore)*

FISHGUARD [SM9537]

☆ *Fishguard Arms* SA65 9HJ [Main St (A487)]: Tiny front bar with a couple of changing real ales served by jug at unusually high counter, warmly friendly staff, open fire, rugby photographs, traditional games in back room; open all day Sun, cl Mon, also perhaps lunchtime Tues and Sat *(LYM, the Didler, Brian and Ruth Archer, Patrick Renouf)*

Royal Oak SA65 9HA [Market Sq, Upper Town]: Darkly beamed and stripped stone front bar leading through panelled room to big no smoking picture-window dining extension, pictures commemorating defeat here of bizarre french raid in 1797, Brains and changing guest beers from bar counter carved with welsh dragon, decent well priced generous food, woodburner; bar billiards, games machine; pleasant terrace, open all day *(BB, Mike Pugh, the Didler, Anne Morris)*

HAVERFORDWEST [SM9515]

☆ *Georges* SA61 1NH [Market St]: Behind front eclectibles shop and small coffee bar/teashop area is long narrow celtic-theme bar with small stable-like booths – not a pub, but has Brains SA or Rev James and a guest beer, interesting reasonably priced wines esp New World, pleasantly relaxed and helpful service even when busy, informal and idiosyncratic atmosphere underlined by fancy mirrors, glistening stones and dangly hangings; larger upstairs restaurant, generous interesting home-made food using good meat, fresh veg and good fish and vegetarian ranges; no dogs; back crafts shop/showroom, lovely walled garden, open 10.30-5.30 Mon-Thurs, 10.30-10.30 Fri/Sat *(V Brogden, Mike Pugh)*

Pembroke Yeoman SA61 1QQ [High St]: Limited choice of enjoyable imaginative food, five real ales from unusual small breweries, good landlord, plenty of chat *(Mike Pugh)*

LITTLE HAVEN [SM8512]

☆ *Castle* SA62 3UF: Good value open-plan pub well placed by green looking over sandy bay (lovely sunsets), prompt friendly service even when busy, good reasonably priced food in bare-boards bar and carpeted dining area inc tasty cawl and local fish, Brains, beams and stripped stone, big oak tables, castle prints, pool; children welcome, tables outside *(Geoff and Angela Jaques, Ian and Celia Abbott)*

☆ *St Brides Hotel* SA62 3UN [in village itself, not St Brides hamlet further W]: Compact and unassuming stripped-stone bar and linking dining area, good range of enjoyable popular food (busy evenings even into Oct), Brains Rev James and Worthington, good wine choice, friendly staff, open fire, no piped music, interesting well in back corner grotto may be partly Roman; Pay & Display parking; big good value bedrooms, some in annexe over rd by sheltered sunny terraced garden, short stroll from the sea *(LYM, Trevor and Judith Pearson, Roger and Cynthia Calrow)*

LLANDDAROG [SN5016]

☆ *Butchers Arms* SA32 8NS: Ancient heavily black-beamed local with three smallish eating areas rambling off small central bar, cheerily welcoming atmosphere, generous home cooking from sandwiches through hearty country dishes to some interesting specials (menu willingly adapted for children), friendly helpful staff, Felinfoel Best and Double Dragon tapped from the cask, good wines by the glass, conventional pub furniture, fairylights and candles in bottles, woodburner in biggish fireplace; piped pop music; tables outside, delightful window boxes *(A S and M E Marriott, BB, Tom Evans, JWAC, J Iorwerth Davies)*

LLANDEILO [SN6226]

☆ *Angel* SA19 7LY [Salem; unclassified rd N, off B4302]: Attractive open-plan U-shaped bar, busy and well run, with thriving country-house atmosphere, young chef/landlord doing good reasonably priced home-made food using fresh produce from baguettes, well filled pitta breads and lunchtime bargain specials to wide range of fish, imaginative dishes in back bistro, friendly helpful young staff, Brains and local real ales; tables outside, lovely country setting opp castle *(D and C Dampier, John Stirrup, Mike Pugh, Anne Morris)*

Castle SA19 6EN [Rhosmaen St (A483)]: Has been popular for its nicely renovated traditional layout, several changing real ales and wide food choice, but recent licensee/management changes have left it for periods either without food or even completely closed; we hope it will settle down again – news please *(LYM)*

☆ *Cottage* SA19 6SD [Pentrefelin (A40 towards Carmarthen – brown sign from Llandeilo)]: Large smart open-plan beamed dining pub, comfortable and welcoming, with huge log fire and lots of horsey prints, plates and brasses, good generous well priced food from good baguettes to some local fish and welsh black beef, Brains SA and Fullers London Pride, decent house wines, attentive landlord, well appointed back dining room; piped music *(Michael and Alison Sandy, Tom Evans)*

White Horse SA19 6EN [Rhosmaen St]: Friendly 16th-c local with several rooms, popular for its real ales such as Breconshire and Charles Wells Bombardier, occasional live music; tables outside front and back *(the Didler)*

LLANDOVERY [SN7634]

Red Lion SA20 0AA [Market Sq]: One basic welcoming room with no bar, Brains Buckleys and a guest beer tapped from the cask, jovial landlord; cl Sun, may close early evening if no customers *(BB, the Didler)*

LLANEGWAD [SN5321]

☆ *Halfway* SA32 7NL [A40 Llandeilo—Carmarthen]: Popular dining pub (worth booking in season, esp at wknds), with imaginative elegantly presented food, good wine choice, fair prices, energetic landlord and efficient friendly staff, two large dining areas; cl Sun evening and Mon *(R Davies)*

LLANYCHAER [SM9835]

Bridge End SA65 9TB [Bridge St (B4313 SE of Fishguard)]: Former watermill in attractive hamlet, friendly enthusiastic staff, one or two real ales, good choice of food from lunchtime

snacks to full evening meals inc popular roast Sunday lunches *(Colin Moore)*

LLWYNDAFYDD [SN3755]

☆ *Crown* SA44 6BU [off A486 S of Newquay]: Stripped stone, red plush banquettes and copper-topped tables, Flowers IPA and Original and one or two guest beers, friendly helpful service, big woodburner, popular bar food, darts in winter, simple dining room; piped music; children in family room, picnic-sets and terrace in pretty garden with good play area and winter darts, lane down to attractive cove, cl Sun evening in winter *(Pete Yearsley, Gene and Kitty Rankin, B and M Kendall, LYM)*

MANORBIER [SS0697]

Castle Inn SA70 7TE: Interesting old black and white building with lots of small linked rooms leading to back bar, unpretentious food from good sanwiches up, real ale, games room with pool; idyllic tree-sheltered back garden with rustic furniture and cottage flowers, handy for beach and coast path, open all day in summer *(Matthew Shackle)*

MATHRY [SM8831]

☆ *Farmers Arms* SA62 5HB [Brynamlwg, off A487 Fishguard—St David's]: Creeper-covered no smoking pub with beams, flagstones and dark woodwork in carefully renovated homely bar, enjoyable low-priced pubby food freshly made by landlady from good crab sandwiches to reasonably priced hot dishes esp fish, cheerful welcoming landlord and staff, Brains Rev James, Felinfoel Double Dragon and a guest beer, fair range of reasonably priced wines, log fire, children welcome in large no smoking dining vine-covered conservatory; piped music; tables in small walled garden, open all day, cl till 4 Mon-Weds in winter *(Trevor and Judith Pearson, Ian and Deborah Carrington, Alan and Paula McCully, Patrick Renouf)*

NEVERN [SN0839]

☆ *Trewern Arms* SA42 0NB: Extended welcoming inn in delightful peaceful setting nr notable church and medieval bridge over River Nyfer, lively family area merging into appealing dark stripped-stone slate-floored bar, rafters hung with rural bric-a-brac, high-backed settles, plush banquettes, Wadworths 6X, friendly helpful service, enjoyable bar food from sandwiches up prepared in open servery, good value attractive Thurs-Sat restaurant; TV in bar, games room, no dogs; tables in pretty garden, bright comfortable bedrooms, big breakfast *(Dr A McCormick, LYM)*

NEWPORT [SN0539]

Castle SA42 0TB [Bridge St]: Rambling local with some interesting home-made specials as well as generous pubby standards, real ales, pleasant service; handy for Parrog Estuary walk (esp for birdwatchers) *(Mike Pugh)*

☆ *Royal Oak* SA42 0TA [West St (A487)]: Bustling and well run sizeable pub with friendly helpful landlady and staff, good choice of good generous food inc lunchtime light dishes, local lamb and lots of authentic curries, Tues OAP lunch, Greene King Old Speckled

Hen and guest beers, children welcome in no smoking lounge with eating areas, separate stone and slate bar with pool and games, upstairs dining room; some tables outside, an easy walk from the beach and coast path *(Colin Moore, Helene and Richard Lay)*

PONTRHYDFENDIGAID [SN7366]

Black Lion SY25 6BE [B4343 Tregaron—Devils Bridge]: Simple informal country pub with friendly service, good basic food; good value bedrooms, good breakfast *(Sarah and Peter Gooderham)*

RHANDIRMWYN [SN7843]

Royal Oak SA20 0NY: Friendly 17th-c stone-built inn in remote and peaceful walking country, comfortable bar with log fire, up to six changing real ales, reasonably priced straightforward food (welsh black beef recommended), big dining area (can book); 60s music on free juke box; dogs and children welcome, plenty of hanging baskets and flowering tubs, hill views from front garden and from good big bedrooms, handy for Brecon Beacons *(David Eberlin, Mr and Mrs M Stratton, BB, JWAC)*

ROCH [SM8621]

Victoria SA62 6AW [A487 Haverfordwest—Newgale]: Lively good value local with five real ales, good cooking by landlady using fresh local ingredients, OAP bargains, welcoming landlord *(Mike Pugh)*

SOLVA [SM8024]

☆ *Cambrian* SA62 6UU [Lower Solva; off A487 Haverfordwest—St Davids]: Attractive neatly kept civilised dining pub much enjoyed by older people, enjoyable if not cheap food inc authentic pasta, fresh fish (good crispy chips) and popular Sun lunch in bar and restaurant, decent italian wines, real ales such as Brains Revd James and local Ceredigion Red Kite, courteous efficient service, log fires; piped music, no dogs or children; nice spot nr harbour and art and crafts shops *(Geoff and Angela Jaques, David and Jean Hall)*

Harbour Inn SA62 6UT [Main St]: Staff helpful to families and cope well with the holiday crowds in basic three-bar beamed pub, wide choice of reasonably priced food from quickly served sandwiches up, Brains ale, lots of local pictures, children's area with pool table; piped music; plenty of tables on suntrap terrace, delightful setting by small sailing harbour, splendid views, bedrooms, open all day *(Geoff and Angela Jaques, Mike Pugh, Norma and Noel Thomas)*

ST DAVID'S [SM7525]

☆ *Farmers Arms* SA62 6RF [Goat St]: Bustling old-fashioned low-ceilinged pub by cathedral gate, cheerful and unpretentiously pubby, mainly drinking on the left and eating on the right, central servery with real ales such as Brains Rev James and Worthington, wide choice of good value straightforward food from baguettes and ploughman's with local cheeses to steaks and Sun lunch, busy young staff, chatty landlord and locals, pool room; they may try to keep your credit card while you eat, TV for rugby; cathedral view from

large tables on big back suntrap terrace, and lack of car park means no tour bus groups, open all day *(Geoff and Angela Jaques, P Price, Dave Irving, Michael and Alison Sandy, Giles and Annie Francis)*

ST DOGMAELS [SN1646]

Ferry SA43 3LF: Old stone building with spectacular views of Teifi estuary and hills from picture-window dining extension, Brains and guest ales, decent wines, good value food from sandwiches up (in summer best to book for evenings and popular Sun lunch), pleasant service, character bar, pine tables, nice clutter of bric-a-brac with many old advertising signs; children welcome, plenty of tables out on decking *(LYM, Colin Moore, Helene and Richard Lay)*

STACKPOLE [SR9896]

☆ *Stackpole Inn* SA71 5DF [off B4319 S of Pembroke]: Good L-shaped dining pub on four levels, partly no smoking, with wide choice from baguettes and pubby staples to wok dishes, plenty of local produce, Brains Rev James and Felinfoel Best and Double Dragon, welcoming service, neat uncluttered décor with light oak furnishings and ash beams in low ceilings, shove-ha'penny and dominoes; piped music; children welcome, disabled access and facilities, tables out in attractive gardens, good woodland and coastal walks in the Stackpole estate, open all day (Sun afternoon break), new four-bedroom annexe *(P Price, Ron Gentry, LYM, Ian and Deborah Carrington, Comus and Sarah Elliott)*

TENBY [SN1300]

Imperial SA70 7HR [The Paragon]: Substantial hotel on cliffs, reasonably priced bar food from sandwiches and baked potatoes to good fish and chips, decent beer range, superb view of Caldy Island from bar and particularly terrace; comfortable bedrooms *(MDN)*

Plantagenet House SA70 7BX [Quay Hill]: Well renovated early medieval building, marvellous old chimney, stripped stonework, tile and board floors, downstairs bar, good upstairs restaurant with cane furniture, candles on tables; piped music, fine Victorian lavatories; open all day in season, has been cl lunchtime out of season *(Matthew Shackle)*

TRESAITH [SN2751]

☆ *Ship* SA43 2JL: Tastefully decorated bistro-style pub on Cardigan Bay with magnificent views of sea, beach, famous waterfall, perhaps even dolphins and seals; good generous home-made food from ploughman's with local cheeses to local fish, speciality paella, take-away pizzas, Buckleys and two changing guest beers often from Ceredigion, good photographs, no smoking dining area, cheerful staff (but they may try to keep your credit card while you eat); tables with heaters out on decking stepped down to garden *(Pete Yearsley, David and Nina Pugsley, Helene and Richard Lay)*

WOLFS CASTLE [SM9526]

Wolfe SA62 5LS [A40 Haverfordwest—Fishguard]: Good fresh home-made food (not

Sun or Mon evenings in winter) from reasonably priced bar lunches to more upmarket restaurant dishes, friendly service, comfortable brasserie dining lounge, garden room and conservatory, two real ales, good wine choice, log fire, board games; children welcome, attractively laid-out garden, bedrooms *(ff, LYM, J and J Palmer)*

GWENT

ABERGAVENNY [SO2914]
Angel NP7 5EN [Cross St, by Town Hall]: Nicely cleaned up by new local owners, thriving atmosphere, efficient pleasant bar staff, some big comfortable settees, lovely bevelled glass behind servery, good service, popular restaurant and adjacent lounge areas *(Graham and Glenis Watkins, Pamela and Merlyn Horswell)*
Coliseum NP7 5PE [Lion St/Frogmore St]: Steps up to modest Wetherspoons cinema conversion, very light and spacious, with low-priced real ales and good coffee, pleasant service, their usual food, lots of panelling, raised areas one end; wheelchair lift *(Mike Pugh)*
Hen & Chickens NP7 5EG [Flannel St]: Unpretentious and relaxed traditional local, Bass, Brains and guest beers from bar unusually set against street windows, basic wholesome cheap lunchtime food (not Sun), mugs of tea and coffee, friendly efficient staff, interesting side areas, popular darts, cards and dominoes; TV, very busy on market day *(Pete Baker, the Didler)*
ABERSYCHAN [SO2603]
White Hart NP4 7BQ [Broad St (A4043 Pontypool—Blaenavon)]: Unchanged front parlour, basic but cosy, with Brains Buckleys, perhaps a guest beer and summer farm cider, friendly local feel, pool in one of two back rooms; meeting place for several local societies *(Pete Baker)*
BRYNGWYN [SO4008]
☆ *Cripple Creek* NP15 2AA [Abergavenny Rd; off old A40 W of Raglan]: Smartly extended and civilised old country dining pub with wide range of good reasonably priced food from simple things to more elaborate meals inc fresh fish and choice of four Sun roasts, obliging enthusiastic landlord and efficient cheerful staff, real ales such as Adnams Broadside, Brains and Tetleys, decent wines, teas and coffees, pleasant no smoking restaurant; country views from small terrace, play area, open all day *(Mike Pugh, Pamela and Merlyn Horswell, Rhiannon Davies)*
CAERLEON [ST3693]
Wheatsheaf NP18 1LT [Llanhennock, N]: Unspoilt ancient-seeming pub with Usk Valley views, cosy and friendly bar and snug, good collection of small plates and mugs, bargain wkdy lunches, Bass and a guest beer, log fire; children welcome, garden tables, boules on Sat *(Ian Barker)*
CROSS ASH [SO3919]
Three Salmons NP7 8PB [B4521 E of Abergavenny]: Small and unpretentious, with

wide choice of good value home-made food, local beers *(R A Rosen)*
GROSMONT [SO4024]
Angel NP7 8EP: 17th-c village pub recently taken over by village co-operative, Tomos Watkins ales, farm cider, enjoyable straightforward bar food, friendly local atmosphere, pool room with darts; a couple of tables and boules pitch behind, seats out by ancient market cross on attractive steep single street within sight of castle *(BB, R T and J C Moggridge)*
LLANGATTOCK LINGOED [SO3620]
☆ *Hunters Moon* NP7 8RR [off B4521 just E of Llanvetherine]: Attractive tucked-away pub dating from 13th c, nicely refurbished keeping beams, dark stripped stone and flagstones, welcoming service, Wye Valley Cwrw Dewi Sant tapped from the cask, good country cooking, pleasant mildly eccentric fairy-lit dining room décor; dogs and children welcome, tables out on deck and in charming dell, comfortable bedrooms with own bathrooms, glorious country nr Offa's Dyke *(Dave Irving, LYM, Neil Kellett)*
LLANISHEN [SO4703]
Carpenters Arms NP16 6QH: Small cottage pub with enjoyable usual bar food in comfortable bar/lounge, Timothy Taylors Landlord, helpful landlady and friendly staff, coal fire, pool table in back area; stone seats and small chrome tables and chairs on back flagstoned terrace, small side lawn up a few steps, a couple of front picnic-sets *(Theocsbrian, LM)*
LLANTHONY [SO2827]
☆ *Abbey Hotel* NP7 7NN [Llanthony Priory; off A465, back rd Llanvihangel Crucorney—Hay]: Magical setting for plain bar in dim-lit vaulted flagstoned crypt of graceful ruined Norman abbey, lovely in summer, with lawns around and the peaceful border hills beyond; real ales such as Black Sheep and Felinfoel, farm cider in summer, good coffee, simple lunchtime bar food, evening restaurant; no children, occasional live music; bedrooms in restored parts of abbey walls, open all day Sat and summer Sun, cl winter Mon-Thurs and Sun evening, great walks all around *(LYM, Barry and Anne, MLR, the Didler, Mark and Mary Fairman)*
Half Moon NP7 7NN: Basic dog-friendly country inn with flagstoned bar and carpeted lounge, decent well priced plain food, Bullmastiff beers inc power-packed Son-of-a-Bitch, bar billiards; big back paddock (on the pony treks), gorgeous views from nice back garden, bedrooms not luxurious but clean and comfortable, unspoilt valley with great walks, cl Tues lunchtime, other lunchtimes out of season (though usually open wknds then) *(MLR)*
LLANTILIO CROSSENY [SO3815]
Hogs Head NP7 8TA: New pub opened in converted barn as farm diversification, enjoyable food and real ale *(T B Noyes)*
LLANTRISANT FAWR [ST3997]
☆ *Greyhound* NP15 1LE [off A449 nr Usk]: Prettily set and popular 17th-c country inn

with relaxed homely feel in three linked bar rooms of varying sizes, steps between two, nice mix of furnishings and rustic decorations, wide choice of consistently good home cooking at sensible prices, good sandwiches and baguettes too, Bass, Flowers Original, Greene King Abbot and a weekly guest beer, decent wines by the glass, friendly helpful staff, log fires, colourful prints in pleasant grey-panelled dining room; picnic-sets in attractive garden with big fountain, hill views, adjoining pine shop, good bedrooms in small attached motel *(Graham and Glenis Watkins, BB, B M Eldridge, Colin McKerrow)*

MONMOUTH [SO5012]

Kings Head NP25 3DY [Agincourt Sq]: Wetherspoons in former substantial coaching inn, plenty of well spaced seating with extensive central no smoking family area, their usual good deals all day on food (using some local produce) and on drink, pleasant service, lots of books inc interesting ones *(PRT, B M Eldridge)*

PANDY [SO3322]

Pandy Inn NP7 8DR [A465 Abergavenny—Hereford]: Welcoming old slate-built family pub, good reasonably priced bar food, good service, changing ales such as Wye Valley Hereford, comfortable modern settles, 3D Brecons maps, good Sun night nostalgic pianist; adjacent walkers' bunkhouse *(R T and J C Moggridge)*

PANTYGELLI [SO3017]

Crown NP7 7HR [Old Hereford Rd, N of Abergavenny]: Real ales such as Shepherd Neame Spitfire (charming licensees have not forgotten their Kent roots), Stowford Press farm cider, good wine choice, interesting and enjoyable lunchtime food, more extensive evening menu, plenty of local produce, bowls of mixed nuts sold, dark woody interior with nice old furnishings; immaculate seats out in front, bedroom extension in hand *(Mike Pugh, Colin McKerrow, Guy Vowles)*

PONTYPOOL [ST2998]

Sebastopol Social Club NP4 5DU [Wern Rd, Sebastopol]: At least five real ales at tempting prices, sandwiches and rolls, bar and lounge; big-screen sports TV; well behaved dogs welcome – it is a club, but you can sign in for a small fee *(Gwyneth and Salvo Spadaro-Dutturi)*

RAGLAN [SO4107]

Beaufort Arms NP15 2DY [High St]: Former coaching inn by church, friendly helpful new owners, good real ales, good range of food, log fire, comfortable and roomy character beamed bars; piped music; children welcome, 15 bedrooms *(Graham and Glenis Watkins)*

ST ARVANS [ST5196]

Piercefield NP16 6EJ: Modern décor and setting, nice choice of innovative enjoyable food, friendly efficient service *(Mike and Mary Carter)*

TINTERN [SO5300]

Anchor NP16 6TE: Appealing if touristy pub right by abbey arches, reasonably priced usual food, medieval cider press in main bar;

comfortable newly decorated bedrooms *(Linda and Rob Hilsenroth)*
☆ *Moon & Sixpence* NP16 6SG [A466 Chepstow—Monmouth]: Attractively furnished largely smoke-free flower-decked pub with good choice of good value generous food inc curry specialities, good range of real ales from back bar, friendly helpful service, lots of stripped stone, beams and steps, one room with sofas and wicker armchairs, natural spring feeding indoor goldfish pool; quiet piped music; children welcome, terrace tables under arbour look along River Wye to abbey, good walks *(R T and J C Moggridge, Tony and Wendy Hobden, BB, Tim and Ann Newell, Bruce Bird)*
Wye Valley Hotel NP16 6SQ [A466 at Catbrook junction]: Pubby bar with decent food, Wye Valley Bitter and Butty Bach, delft shelves with beer bottles in variety, adjacent no smoking restaurant; bedrooms *(Tony and Wendy Hobden)*

USK [SO3700]

Cross Keys NP15 1BG [Bridge St]: Small friendly two-bar pub dating from 14th c, oak beams, interesting Last Supper tapestry, log fire, popular food, good range of drinks; comfortable new bedrooms, good breakfast *(Ian Phillips)*
Kings Head NP15 1AL [Old Market St]: Good chatty atmosphere, Fullers London Pride and Timothy Taylors Landlord, enjoyable food, friendly staff, huge log fire in superb fireplace; sports TV; open all day, bedrooms *(Terry and Linda Moseley, Mike Pugh, Ian Phillips)*
☆ *Royal Hotel* NP15 1AT [New Market St]: Comfortably and genuinely traditional, with old china and pictures, old-fashioned fireplaces, wide choice of good value home cooking (not Sun evening; worth booking Sat and Sun lunch), three changing real ales from deep cellar, friendly service; may be piped music; well behaved children welcome, has been cl Mon lunchtime *(Peter and Audrey Dowsett, LYM, Chris Flynn, Wendy Jones, Mike Pugh)*
Three Salmons NP15 1RY [Porthycarne St/Bridge St]: Smart hotel dating from early 17th c, comfortable front bar and small bustling back public bar, impeccable service, Bass, Flowers IPA and Greene King Abbot, enjoyable food in bar and from big leatherbound restaurant menu; good disabled access and bedrooms *(Pamela and Merlyn Horswell, Ian Phillips)*

GWYNEDD

ABERDOVEY [SN6196]

Dovey LL35 0EF [Sea View Terr]: Bay-window estuary views from bright clean front rooms, big helpings of good moderately priced imaginative food, helpful polite staff; three terraces, comfortable bedrooms, good breakfast *(Anon)*

ABERGYNOLWYN [SH6706]

Railway LL36 9YW [Tywyn—Talyllyn pass]: 16th-c two-bar village pub in lovely setting, friendly staff, enjoyable honest food from sandwiches up inc good lunchtime specials, Brains SA, Greene King Ruddles and Tetleys, big inglenook fire in welcoming lounge, small no smoking dining room, friendly labrador called Winston; nice outside seating but close to the road, handy for good walks and Talyllyn railway *(C J Pratt, Di and Mike Gillam, J V Dadswell)*

BALA [SH9235]

White Lion Royal LL23 7AE [High St]: Timbered coaching inn, character beamed bar with settles and inglenook fireplace, leather settees and armchairs in lounge, Bass, Marstons and local beer, good whisky choice, varied well presented food in bars and restaurant, attentive staff; comfortable bedrooms *(M J Winterton)*

BEDDGELERT [SH5848]

Saracens Head LL55 4UY [Caernarfon Rd]: Cheerful hotel with Robinsons beers, decent wines, good value food, welcoming prompt service, big lounge bar with small dining area, compact back bar decorated with coffee pans; tables on partly covered terrace, small garden opposite river, comfortable bedrooms *(J V Dadswell)*

BETWS-Y-COED [SH7856]

Pont y Pair LL24 0BN: Small hotel with welcoming mix of diners and local drinkers, Greene King Abbot, Marstons Pedigree and Tetleys, good reasonably priced food (freshly made, so may be a wait if busy) from lunchtime soup and sandwiches up in small cosy bar and separate no smoking dining room (not always open), decent wine, no piped music; bedrooms *(KC, W W Burke)*

☆ *Ty Gwyn* LL24 0SG [A5 just S of bridge to village]: Restaurant with rooms rather than pub (you must eat or stay overnight to be served alcohol – disqualifying it from our main entries), but pubby feel in beamed lounge bar with ancient cooking range, easy chairs, antique prints and interesting bric-a-brac, really good interesting meals (they do sandwiches too), real ales such as Adnams, Brains Rev James and Greene King Old Speckled Hen, friendly professional service, partly no smoking restaurant; piped music; children welcome (high chair and toys), cl Mon-Weds in Jan *(Nigel and Sheila Mackereth, LYM, Jon Floyd, Jack Clark, Revd D Glover)*

CAERNARFON [SH4762]

Black Boy LL55 1RW [Northgate St]: Busy traditional pub by castle walls, attractively renovated, with cheery fire, beams from ships wrecked here in 16th c, bare floors, food all day from filled baguettes and doorstep sandwiches up, prompt friendly service, Brains ale, cosy lounge bar, restaurant, public bar with TV; a couple of pavement picnic-sets, bedrooms *(Alastair Stevenson, Neil Whitehead, Victoria Anderson, Mike and Mary Carter, Tony and Maggie Harwood, Revd D Glover)*

CONWY [SH7877]

☆ *Castle Hotel* LL32 8DB [High St]: Plenty of well spaced tables in interesting old building's

cosy sympathetically refurbished bars, good substantial food all day here and in restaurant, three real ales, decent wines, friendly atmosphere and good informed service; own car parks (which helps here), 29 bedrooms with own bathrooms *(Keith and Sue Ward, J F M and M West, Peter Cole)*

DOLGELLAU [SH7318]

Royal Ship LL40 1AR [Queens Sq]: Traditional small central hotel, pleasantly redecorated, with helpful and friendly young staff and good value food, compact bar, lounge with dining area, more formal restaurant *(Mike and Mary Carter, Rona Murdoch)*

GELLILYDAN [SH6839]

Bryn Arms LL41 4EN [just off A487 W of A470 junction]: Functional modern building well worth knowing for enjoyable cheap bar food from sandwiches up, Wye Valley Butty Bach, helpful friendly service, enterprising landlord; children welcome, tables outside with play area *(Michael and Judy Buckley, Mike and Mary Carter)*

GLANDWYFACH [SH4843]

Goat LL51 9LJ [A487]: Thick slate walls, good choice of home-made food all freshly prepared, reasonable prices, real ale, pleasant atmosphere, friendly family service; garden *(GLD)*

LLANBERIS [SH5661]

Lake View LL55 4EL [A4086]: Hotel in beautiful situation overlooking lake, interesting antiques, old books for sale, good food; comfortable quiet bedrooms *(Edna Jones)*

LLANDWROG [SH4556]

Harp LL54 5SY [½ mile W of A499 S of Caernarfon]: Welcoming lounge bar with good helpful service, good value food, local and other real ales, daily papers and magazines, irregular layout giving cosy corners, plenty of board games and Jenga, parrot that's bilingual if it's feeling chatty, cheerful separate dining room; picnic-sets among fruit trees overlooking quiet village's imposing church, well equipped cottagey bedrooms, good breakfast, cl Mon *(BB, K Hutchinson)*

LLANFROTHEN [SH6141]

Brondanw Arms LL48 6AQ [aka Y Ring; B4410]: Friendly helpful staff, enjoyable reasonably priced food from good bacon baps to full meals inc Sun lunch, and real ales such as Black Sheep and Marstons Pedigree in welsh-speaking pub (welsh piped music too) with plenty of room, interesting bric-a-brac; folk night alternate Sats; picnic-sets and play area outside, good walking area *(Myke and Nicky Crombleholme)*

LLANUWCHLLYN [SH8730]

☆ *Eagles* LL23 7UB [aka Eryrod; A494/B4403]: Good reasonably priced food from sandwiches to traditional and more enterprising dishes (bilingual menu), helpful and courteous young staff, thriving atmosphere in small front bar and plush back lounge, neat décor with beams and some stripped stone, no smoking dining area, back picture-window view of mountains with Lake Bala in distance, limited wine list, strong coffee, no music; disabled access, picnic-sets under cocktail parasols on flower-filled back terrace *(Michael and Jenny Back, Jacquie and Jim Jones, KC)*

LLANYSTUMDWY [SH4738]

Tafarn y Plu LL52 0SH: Beamed two-bar pub opp Lloyd George's boyhood home and museum, thoroughly welsh ethos with Felinfoel and Evan Evans real ales, a welsh lager, Ralph's welshy cider and even welsh wines, spirits and liqueurs; enjoyable bar food from sandwiches to steaks most days, small restaurant; large peaceful garden *(Ian Parri)*

MAENTWROG [SH6640]

Grapes LL41 4HN [A496; village signed from A470]: Rambling old stripped stone inn popular with families in summer for very wide choice of reasonably priced generous food inc good fish, Greene King Old Speckled Hen and two or three changing guest beers, over 30 malt whiskies and decent wine choice, lots of stripped pine (pews, settles, panelling, pillars and carvings), good log fires, intriguing collection of brass blowlamps, lovely views from conservatory dining extension, pleasant back terrace and walled garden; they may try to keep your credit card while you eat, juke box in public bar; disabled facilities, dogs welcome, open all day *(Mike and Mary Carter, LYM, Julian and Janet Dearden)*

MORFA NEFYN [SH2939]

Bryncynan LL53 6AA: Modernised pub concentrating (particularly in summer) on reasonably priced largely grilled or fried food, real ales such as Greene King Old Speckled Hen and Wadworths 6X, quick friendly service even when busy with family groups, quiet in winter with good log fire in the partly tiled bar, restaurant; electronic table game; children allowed, rustic seats outside, has been cl Sun *(Pete Devonish, Ian McIntyre, Donald Mills, M G Hart, LYM, John Mitchell)*

PENMAENPOOL [SH6918]

☆ *George III* LL40 1YD [just off A493, nr Dolgellau]: Attractive well set inn, light lunches as well as other food from baguettes up in no smoking lower bar with beams, flagstones and stripped stone, real ales such as Bass, good choice of wines by the glass, lovely views over Mawddach estuary from civilised partly panelled upstairs bar opening into cosy inglenook lounge, with same food, and separate restaurant; may be piped music downstairs; sheltered terrace, good walks, good if not always well lit bedrooms inc some (allowing dogs) in quiet and interesting conversion of former station on disused line now a walkway, open all day *(Mike and Mary Carter, Jacquie and Jim Jones, Peter Craske, LYM, GSB, Stephen Woad, Comus and Sarah Elliott)*

PORTHMADOG [SH5738]

Spooners LL49 9NF [Harbour Station]: Virtually a museum of railway memorabilia inc full-size narrow-gauge locomotive, particularly well kept Marstons Bitter and Pedigree and quickly changing unusual guest beers, good value pub lunches inc good filled baguettes, Thurs-Sat evening meals, popular Sun lunch,

overflow into no smoking station buffet; children welcome, tables out on steam railway platform, open all day *(Tony Hobden, J V Dadswell)*

ROWEN [SH7571]

Ty Gwyn LL32 8YU [off B5106 S of Conwy]: Friendly and pretty local in charming village, good basic food, Lees real ale, pleasant service; cheap bedrooms, good walking country *(Mrs Jane Kingsbury)*

TALYLLYN [SH7210]

☆ *Tynycornel* LL36 9AJ [B4405, off A487 S of Dolgellau]: Civilised hotel reopened after major extension, great setting below mountains with picture windows overlooking attractive lake, comfortable sofas and armchairs, central log fire, nice pictures, enjoyable bar lunches from sandwiches up, no smoking restaurants and conservatory; service can slow, keg beer; children welcome, prettily planted side courtyard, open all day, boat hire for fishermen, good bedrooms *(Des and Ursula Weston, C J Pratt, Mike and Mary Carter, Jacquie and Jim Jones, LYM, Peter Cole)*

TREFRIW [SH7863]

Old Ship LL27 0JH: Friendly local atmosphere, enjoyable generous food, changing real ales inc Banks's and Marstons Pedigree *(Donald Mills, Jane Smith)*

TUDWEILIOG [SH2336]

☆ *Lion* LL53 8ND [Nefyn Rd (B4417), Lleyn Peninsula]: Cheerfully busy village inn with wide choice of good value straightforward food in bar and no smoking family dining conservatory (small helpings for children, who have a pretty free rein here), quick friendly service, mainstream real ales well described by helpful landlord, dozens of malt whiskies, decent wines, games in lively public bar; pleasant front garden, good value bedrooms with own bathrooms *(Sally and Dave Bates, LYM, J V Dadswell)*

MID GLAMORGAN

BRYNCETHIN [SS9184]

Masons Arms CF32 9YR: Enjoyable generous food inc some interesting dishes, efficient prompt restaurant service, decent wines, good choice of real ales; piped music may be loud in big main bar, pool in locals' bar; nine bedrooms *(John and Gloria Isaacs)*

CAERPHILLY [ST1586]

Courthouse CF83 1FN [Cardiff Rd]: 14th-c pub listed here for its superb view of classic castle from light and airy modern back café/bar and picnic-sets on grassy terrace above its moat; a real ale such as Shepherd Neame Spitfire, lots of lagers, cheap food all day (not Sun evening, not after 5.30 Mon, Fri or Sat); piped pop music, virtually no nearby parking; children welcome in eating areas, open all day *(LYM, Ian Phillips)*

GROES-FAEN [ST0781]

Dynevor Arms CF72 8NS [handy for M4 junction 34 via A4119]: Quick food and bar service even though busy, good food and beer choice, no smoking dining room *(Norman and Sarah Keeping)*

KENFIG [SS8081]

☆ *Prince of Wales* CF33 4PR [2¼ miles from M4 junction 37; A4229 towards Porthcawl, then right when dual carriageway narrows on bend, signed Maudlam and Kenfig]: Interesting ancient pub among sand dunes, Bass and a wknd guest beer tapped from the cask, good choice of malt whiskies and decent wines, enjoyable straightforward food, stripped stone and log fire, lots of wreck pictures, traditional games, small upstairs dining room for summer and busy wknds; big-screen TV; children and (in non-carpet areas) dogs welcome, handy for nature-reserve walks (awash with orchids in June) *(Phil and Sally Gorton, LYM, John and Joan Nash, Ian Phillips, the Didler)*

LLANWONNO [ST0395]

☆ *Brynffynon* CF37 3PH [off B4275, B4273 or B4277 in Ferndale – into valley at Commercial Hotel S-bend]: Unpretentious isolated mountain pub with solid furnishings in plain and welcoming high-ceilinged bar, good value genuine food inc good specials, a real ale, friendly obliging service; good base for walks in the largely forested surrounding hills, children and dogs welcome till 9pm, occasional live music *(Edward Gregory, LYM)*

MISKIN [ST0480]

Miskin Arms CF72 8JQ [handy for M4 junction 34, via A4119 and B4264]: Friendly and roomy newly tastefully extended village pub with changing ales such as Everards Tiger and Hancocks HB, good value bar food, popular restaurant Sun lunch and Tues-Sat evenings *(Colin Moore)*

PONTYPRIDD [ST0790]

Bunch of Grapes CF37 4DA [off A4054; Ynysangharad Rd]: Stripped-down pub with French chef doing good choice of enteprising eclectic food (not Sun evening) from good sandwiches up, rewarding children's choice, Bass, Hereford PA and guest beers, interesting bottled beers from around the world, reasonably priced wines, bare boards and simple décor, small easy-chair lounge, large no smoking dining area opening into grape-vine conservatory, public bar, coal fire; extension planned to pretty cottage behind, tables out on two terraces, open all day *(Pamela and Merlyn Horswell)*

PORTHCAWL [SS8377]

Ancient Briton CF36 5NT [Clevis Hill]: Well kept Brains, reasonably priced food inc enjoyable Sun lunch *(Anon)*

Lorelei CF36 3YU [Esplanade Ave]: Good food, atmosphere and service in comfortable hotel bar with Bass and guest ales such as Archers, Brains, Tomos Watkins or Wye Valley, evening restaurant; comfortable bedrooms *(Jon Barnfield)*

RUDRY [ST2087]

☆ *Maenllwyd* CF83 3EB [off A468 Newport—Caerphilly in Lower Machen, halfway towards Caerphilly on minor rd]: Rambling olde-worlde Tudor Chef & Brewer with plenty of character and atmosphere, low beams,

panelling, huge log fireplace, easy access between its different levels, decent food all day, attentive polite staff, at least two real ales, good choice of wines; piped music, can be very busy Fri/Sat; nice spot on the edge of Rudry Common, open all day from noon *(Mark and Deb Ashton, LYM, David and Nina Pugsley)*

TREHARRIS [ST0996]

Glan Taff CF46 5AH [Quakers Yard; over bridge off A4054 Merthyr Tydfil—Ystrad Mynach]: Solidly comfortable, plenty of tables inc a couple in nice end nook, friendly licensees, good range of real ales and of decent food at sensible prices *(Michael and Alison Sandy)*

ABEREDW [SO0847]

☆ *Seven Stars* LD2 3UW [just off B4567 SE of Builth Wells]: Cosy and attractive local doubling as post office, good generous honest food from sandwiches up with wider evening choice, Wadworths 6X and guest beers such as Woods Shropshire Lad, friendly butcher landlord and efficient service, low beams and stripped stone, log fire, local pictures and antiques, small games room with darts and bar billiards, pleasant bustling restaurant (booking advised); disabled facilities, three good newly done bedrooms *(W W Burke)*

BERRIEW [SJ1800]

☆ *Lion* SY21 8PQ [B4390; village signed off A483 Welshpool—Newtown]: Friendly and comfortable village inn with nicely old-fashioned inglenook public bar and partly stripped stone lounge bar with open fire, enjoyable home-made food (not Sun evening) here or in restaurant from sandwiches and baguettes to good fresh fish choice, character landlady, Banks's and Marstons real ales, decent house wines, dominoes and cribbage; piped music, TV; children and dogs welcome, comfortable bedrooms with own bathrooms, open all day, nice riverside village with lively sculpture gallery *(Mark Killman, J M Sparrow, Simon Lawson, P Bottomley, LYM, Rodney and Norma Stubington, J V Dadswell)*

BLEDDFA [SO2068]

Hundred House LD7 1PA [A488 Knighton—Penybont]: Doing well under appealing enthusiastic new young couple, appealing menu and real ales, small relaxed lounge with log fire in huge stone fireplace, L-shaped main bar with attractively flagstoned lower games area, cosy dining room with another vast fireplace; tables in peaceful garden dropping steeply behind to small stream, lovely countryside *(Theocsbrian, BB)*

BRECON [SO0428]

Boars Head LD3 9AL [Watergate, nr R Usk Bridge]: Several real ales inc Breconshire Red Dragon and Ramblers Ruin, enjoyable bar food from toasties up, pool table; terrace overlooking River Usk *(Andy and Jill Kassube)*

Bulls Head LD3 7LS [The Struet]: Friendly pub in attractive setting, Breconshire and three quickly changing guests from small breweries (hundreds of pump clips on show), knowledgeable waistcoated landlord, reasonably priced food with vegetarian leanings (some vegan dishes), unusual music-theme lounge with sheet music and instruments; bedrooms, cl Mon lunchtime *(Mike Evans, Bruce Bird)*

Inn on the Avenue LD3 9BN [The Avenue]: Warmly friendly new family management, very wide food choice, two real ales, fine range of malt whiskies *(Edmund Coan)*

BWLCH [SO1522]
New Inn LD3 7RQ [A40]: Friendly mix of locals and visitors, real ales such as Brains, Cottage and Dunn Plowman, welcoming fire one end of flagstoned bar, tables for eating at the other – simple food lunchtime and evening inc bargain filled rolls; good walks *(MLR)*

BWLCH-Y-CIBAU [SJ1717]
Stumble Inn SY22 5LL: Attractively refurbished inn in quiet village, reopened under enthusiastic new couple (both ex-RAF chefs), with good imaginative food in comfortable and friendly lounge bar or restaurant, Hook Norton Old Hooky; tables in neat garden *(John Andrew)*

CARNO [SN9696]
Aleppo Merchant SY17 5LL [A470 Newtown—Machynlleth]: Good value popular food from good sandwiches to steaks, friendly helpful service, Boddingtons and Marstons Pedigree, tapestries in plushly modernised stripped stone bar, peaceful no smoking lounge on right with open fire, restaurant (well behaved children allowed here), refurbished back games room with big-screen TV; piped music; steps up to tables in attractively enlarged garden, bedrooms, nice countryside *(Michael and Jenny Back, LYM)*

CILMERY [SO0051]
Prince Llewelyn LD2 3NU: Home-made food using local supplies, good real ales, welcoming staff *(Susie Hughes)*

CLYRO [SO2143]
Baskerville Arms HR3 5RZ: Long comfortable panelled lounge with assorted metalwork, small log fire one end, bigger one up stone steps the other, welcoming new landlord, Wye Valley ales, enjoyable reasonably priced food, friendly service, fresh flowers, cartoons of well known phrases; TV; picnic-sets under cocktail parasols in pleasant garden, good bedrooms *(Bruce Bird)*

CWMDU [SO1823]
☆ *Farmers Arms* NP8 1RU [A479 NW of Crickhowell]: Friendly 18th-c country local, popular with walkers, with good hearty home cooking inc good local lamb, beef and cheeses, three changing real ales such as Shepherd Neame Spitfire, decent wines by the glass, attractive prints and stove in unpretentious partly flagstoned bar's big stone fireplace, plush restaurant; TV; children welcome, tables in garden, comfortable bedrooms with good breakfast, campsite nearby *(BB, Colin and Wendy John, Paul and Sue Dix)*

FELINDRE [SO1836]
Three Horseshoes LD3 0SU [Velindre on some maps – the one on the hill rd Hay-on-Wye—

Talgarth]: New licensees doing well in pleasant 17th-c country pub below Black Mountains, enjoyable food from bar snacks to good steaks, attractive dining room *(Patricia Davies)*

GARTH [SN9449]
Garth Inn LD4 4AG [A483]: Converted mill with tasty low-priced food, Boddingtons, Buckleys and Youngs, country décor, farm shop *(Dave Braisted)*

GLADESTRY [SO2355]
☆ *Royal Oak* HR5 3NR [B4594 W of Kington]: Charming small two-bar beamed and flagstoned walkers' and locals' pub with no unnecessary airs and graces, young welcoming new owners, warm log fire, three changing ales such as Brains Rev James, Hancocks HB and Wye Valley Butty Bach, enjoyable honest food from sandwiches up inc popular Sun roasts, picnic-sets in secluded garden behind, quiet village on Offa's Dyke Path, family bedroom, cl Mon *(Theocsbrian, Duncan Cameron, Peter Edwards, MLR, LYM, T B Noyes, Guy Vowles)*

HAY-ON-WYE [SO2242]
Blue Boar HR3 5DF [Castle St/Oxford Rd]: Good choice of generous home cooking (not Sun evening) in light and airy long no smoking dining room with food counter, lots of pictures for sale, bright tablecloths and cheery décor, big sash windows, good coffees and teas, also breakfasts; relaxed candlelit panelled medieval bar with pews and country chairs, real ales such as Brains SA and Timothy Taylors Landlord, interesting bottled ciders inc organic, decent wines, log fire; may be quiet well chosen piped music; children welcome *(BB, Sue Demont, Tim Barrow)*
Swan HR3 5DQ [Church St]: Pleasant hotel bars (one with pool table), helpful new management, Brains real ale, enjoyable bar food and good restaurant; good smart bedrooms, good breakfast *(Andy and Jill Kassube)*
Wine Vaults HR3 5DF [Castle St]: New bar with nice atmosphere, enjoyable food, good choice of wines by the glass, real ales inc Bass and Breconshire Red Dragon *(Andy and Jill Kassube)*

KNIGHTON [SO2872]
Horse & Jockey LD7 1AE [Wylcwm Pl]: Several cosy and friendly areas, one with log fire, good traditional and innovative food in bar and adjoining restaurant, several real ales; tables in pleasant courtyard, handy for Offa's Dyke *(Joan York)*

LIBANUS [SN9926]
☆ *Tai'r Bull* LD3 8EL [A470 SW of Brecon]: Lovely atmosphere in friendly old well run pub, generous food from large ciabattas to good up-to-date restaurant dishes with delicate sauces, local venison, pheasant and gloucester old spot pork, Brains SA and a guest such as Rhymney Export, attentive young licensees and charming springer called Charlie, woodburner, light and airy no smoking restaurant, great views of Pen-y-Fan out in front; bedrooms well appointed and comfortable, good breakfast – good base for walking *(Giles and Liz Ridout,*

*Stephen Funnell, Anthony Ellis,
Melanie Edwards)*

LLANFIHANGEL-NANT-MELAN [SO1958]
☆ *Red Lion* LD8 2TN [A44 10 miles W of
Kington]: Good value stripped-stone 16th-c
roadside dining pub with welcoming licensees
and good obliging service, good fresh food
from sandwiches up in roomy main area
beyond standing timbers on right, smaller
room with small pews around tables, changing
real ale such as Woods Parish, nice wine
choice, some tables in front sun porch, back
bar with pool; comfortable simple chalet
bedrooms, handy for Radnor Forest walks, nr
impressive waterfall, has been cl Tues-Thurs
lunchtime, Tues evening *(M G Hart, BB,
Rodney and Norma Stubington)*

LLANGYNIDR [SO1519]
☆ *Coach & Horses* NP8 1LS [Cwm Crawnon Rd
(B4558 W of Crickhowell)]: Tidy and roomy
flower-decked dining pub with wide choice of
generous enjoyable food from sandwiches and
baguettes up, plenty of cheerful young staff,
Courage Best and Directors, Greene King
Ruddles County and Wadworths 6X,
comfortable banquettes and stripped stone,
nice big log fire ideal for winter nights, large
attractive restaurant with no smoking area;
pub games, piped music, TV; children and
dogs welcome, picnic-sets across road in safely
fenced pretty sloping garden by lock of
Newport & Brecon Canal; three good value
comfortable bedrooms, good breakfast, lovely
views and walks, open all day *(Ann and
Colin Hunt, LYM, John and Joan Nash,
R T and J C Moggridge)*

LLANGYNOG [SJ0526]
New Inn SY10 0EX [B4391 S of Bala]:
Comfortable neatly kept pub with several
linked areas, friendly helpful staff, bargain
generous food in bar and restaurant; disabled
access *(Michael and Jenny Back)*

LLYSWEN [SO1337]
Griffin LD3 0UR [A470, village centre]:
Attractive country pub with sensible choice of
enjoyable home-made food, Brains real ales,
decent wines, attentive welcoming staff, fine
log fire in easy-going bar; piped music; children
welcome in eating areas, tables out by road,
comfortable bedrooms *(Terry and
Linda Moseley, LYM)*

MACHYNLLETH [SH7400]
☆ *White Lion* SY20 8DN [Heol Pentrerhedyn;
A489, nr clock tower and junction with A487]:
Friendly and comfortably worn in country-
town bar with pink and maroon décor, plush
seats, shiny copper-topped tables, big bay
window seats overlooking main street,
inglenook log fire, end eating area with
enjoyable usual food all day from sandwiches
to roasts, Banks's Bitter and Mild and
Marstons Pedigree, decent wines by the glass,
service brisk and cheerful even on busy Weds
market day; piped music, can get smoky,
silenced fruit machine; children welcome,
pretty views from picnic-sets in attractive back
garden, some tables out by road too, neat
stripped pine bedrooms *(Pete Devonish,*

Ian McIntyre, BB, Christine and Phil Young)
☆ *Wynnstay Arms* SY20 8AE [Maengwyn St]:
Well established market-town hotel with good
sandwiches and interesting snacks in busy and
welcomingly pubby annexe bar, friendly
service, three real ales, good choice of wines by
the glass, comfortable and relaxed hotel lounge
and good restaurant; courtyard tables,
bedrooms *(Mike and Mary Carter, Mr and
Mrs Richard Osborne, Rodney and
Norma Stubington)*

MALLWYD [SH8612]
Brigands SY20 9HJ: Attractive stone-built
Tudor-style hotel with spick and span central
bar and dining rooms either side, good range
of reasonably priced food from sandwiches
and chips up inc good local beef and lamb,
three real ales and good wine choice; tables on
extensive neatly kept lawns with play area,
comfortable bedrooms, lovely views, three
miles of sea trout fishing on River Dovey
*(Ian and Deborah Carrington, John and
Joan Nash)*

MONTGOMERY [SO2296]
Dragon SY15 6PA [Market Sq]: Tall timbered
17th-c hotel with attractive prints and china in
pleasant beamed bar, good wines and coffee,
Woods Special and guest beer, reasonably
priced food, board games, restaurant;
unobtrusive piped music, jazz most Weds;
comfortable well equipped bedrooms and
swimming pool, very quiet town below ruined
Norman castle, open all day *(LYM,
Marion and Bill Cross, Mark Percy,
Lesley Mayoh)*

NEW RADNOR [SO2160]
Radnor Arms LD8 2SP [Broad St]:
Unpretentious village local with enjoyable
reasonably priced home cooking from baked
potatoes to popular Sun carvery, children's
dishes, two real ales such as Archers and Six
Bells, choice of ciders, friendly staff; open all
day wknds *(MLR)*

PENTRE BACH [SN9032]
☆ *Shoemakers Arms* LD3 8UB [off A40 in
Sennybridge]: Simple country pub in the middle
of nowhere, well refurbished by consortium of
local people, enjoyable lunchtime home
cooking from good sandwiches up, reasonable
prices, obliging service from helpful cheerful
staff, changing real ales such as Thwaites
Lancaster Bomber, small restaurant Sun
lunchtime and Weds-Sat evenings; tables
outside, good walks, open all day Sun,
cl Mon/Tues lunchtime *(Annabel Pfeiffer,
R Michael Richards, David Cosham)*

RHAYADER [SN9668]
☆ *Triangle* LD6 5AR [Cwmdauddwr; B4518 by
bridge over Wye, SW of centre]: Interesting
mainly 16th-c pub, small and spotless, with
good value home-made food lunchtime and
early evening, Greene King IPA and Abbot and
Hancocks HB, small selection of reasonably
priced wines, quick friendly helpful service,
separate dining area with view over park to
Wye, darts and quiz nights; three tables on
small front terrace *(Lucien Perring, Mike and
Mary Carter)*

TALYBONT-ON-USK [SO1122]

☆ *Star* LD3 7YX [B4558]: Fine choice of changing real ales inc local Breconshire, usually about four in winter and more in summer, in relaxed and unpretentious stone-built local, straightforward food from good cheap filled rolls to some tasty main dishes, friendly attentive service, good log fire in fine inglenook with bread oven, Dunkerton's farm cider, three bustling plain rooms off central servery inc brightly lit games area, lots of beermats, bank notes and coins on beams, monthly band night, winter quiz Mon; dogs and children welcome, picnic-sets in sizeable tree-ringed garden below Monmouth & Brecon Canal, bedrooms, open all day Sat and summer *(LYM, MLR, Andy and Jill Kassube, Pete Baker, the Didler, R Michael Richards, Elven Money, Neil and Anita Christopher)*

Travellers Rest LD3 7YP: Beautiful setting with valley views, changing ales such as Brains Rev James, Rhymney and Wadworths, small stripped-floor bar with low beams, soft lighting and big sofa, above-average generous upmarket food here or in big separate restaurant up a few steps; piped music; good sloping garden by Monmouthshire & Brecon Canal towpath, front terrace too, bedrooms *(Anon)*

TRE'R-DDOL [SN6592]

Wildfowler SY20 8PN [A487]: Good value fresh food and friendly service, no smoking area, games area with darts, pool and big-screen TV; disabled access, children and dogs welcome, tables outside with play area *(Mike and Mary Carter)*

SOUTH GLAMORGAN

CARDIFF [ST1776]

☆ *Cayo Arms* CF11 9LL [Cathedral Rd]: Friendly, relaxed and spick and span, with real ales such as Bass, Brains Rev James and several from Tomos Watkins, good value food all day from ciabattas and baked potatoes to full meals inc Sun lunch, quick service, daily papers, pubby front bar with comfortable side area in Edwardian style, more modern back dining area; piped music, big-screen TV in one part, very busy wknds; tables out in front, more in yard behind (with parking), open all day *(Michael and Alison Sandy, Roger Huggins, Ian Phillips, Andy and Jill Kassube)*

Monkstone CF3 4LL [Newport Rd, Rumney]: Under new ownership and comfortably refurbished, good value fresh food, four real ales, good choice of wines *(Peter Hufton)*

Old Butchers Arms CF14 6NB [Heol Y Felin, Rhiwbina]: Enjoyable reasonably priced food inc afternoon bargains, Brains, Greene King Old Speckled Hen and changing guest beers, no smoking area *(R J Collis)*

Pantmawr Inn CF14 7TL [Tyla Teg, off Pantmawr Rd, Rhibwina; handy for M4 junction 32]: Small comfortable country-feel pub in attractive former period farmhouse, friendly licensees, Bass and Hancocks HB, decent wines by the glass, enjoyable food; sizeable secure garden with play area, in 1960s housing estate *(Anon)*

COWBRIDGE [SS9974]

☆ *Bear* CF71 7AF [High St, with car park behind off North St; signed off A48]: Well run and busy old coaching inn in smart village, Bass, Hancocks HB and two guest beers, usually one from Wye Valley, decent house wines, friendly efficient young staff, three bars with flagstones, bare boards or carpet, some stripped stone and panelling, big hot open fires, enjoyable usual bar food from sandwiches up, barrel-vaulted cellar restaurant; children welcome, CCTV in car park, bedrooms quiet and comfortable *(LYM, David and Nina Pugsley, Ian Phillips)*

CRAIG PENLLYN [SS9777]

Barley Mow CF71 7RT: Pleasant surroundings, good home-made standard food in generous helpings, Hancocks HB and a guest beer, friendly staff, log fires, no smoking dining room; children welcome, tables outside, open all day (till late Fri/Sat) *(Mark and Deb Ashton)*

GWAELOD-Y-GARTH [ST1183]

Gwaelod y Garth Inn CF15 9HH [Main Rd]: Locally very popular for its food *(Raymond Bonifay)*

LLANTWIT MAJOR [SS9668]

☆ *Old Swan* CF61 1SB [Church St]: Unusual dark medieval building with lancet windows, candles even midday, good log fires in big stone fireplaces, wide choice of enjoyable usual food from baguettes up in bar and restaurant, changing real ales such as Fullers London Pride and local Cwmbran, lively public bar; tables outside, open all day *(LYM, Ian Phillips)*

PENARTH [ST1871]

Windsor CF64 1JE [Windsor Rd]: Convivial bare-boards pub with about eight interesting changing real ales, good value end restaurant; jazz Weds, pop Sat, folk Sun *(Pete Baker)*

PENDOYLAN [ST0576]

Red Lion CF71 7UJ [2½ miles S of M4 junction 34]: Welcoming, quiet and comfortable, with new landlord doing unusually good interesting restaurant food, friendly professional service, pleasant bar with real ale; good garden with play area, next to church in pretty vale *(Virginia Porter)*

ST FAGANS [ST1277]

☆ *Plymouth Arms* CF5 6DU: Stately Victorian pub sympathetically reworked as rambling Vintage Inn with plenty of dark wood and nice touches in bustling linked areas inc log fires, good range of generous food all day, Bass and Hancocks HB, decent wines by the glass at reasonable prices, prompt friendly service, daily papers; lots of tables on extensive back lawn, water bowls outside for dogs, handy for Museum of Welsh Life *(Ian and Deborah Carrington, Pamela and Merlyn Horswell, Michael and Alison Sandy)*

WEST GLAMORGAN

BLACK PILL [SS6190]

Woodman SA3 5AS [Mumbles Rd (A4067 Swansea—Mumbles)]: Attractive seafront dining pub with good value food all day from good sandwiches and baguettes to fresh local fish (can take a while at peak times), Courage Directors and guests such as Adnams and Greene King Old Speckled Hen, good choice of wines by the glass in two sizes, friendly helpful staff, several sensibly furnished linked areas opening out of bar, hundreds of wine bottles above panelled dado, airy restaurant and conservatory; car park across busy road; children welcome in some areas, next to beautiful Clyne Gardens (great rhododendrons in May) *(Anne Morris, Michael and Alison Sandy, Dave Braisted)*

RHOSSILI [SS4188]

Worms Head Hotel SA3 1PP: Stunning views over Rhossili Bay and three-mile sweep of beach from clifftop terrace tables or plain and comfortable compact bar, cheerful helpful staff, good value hearty food from baked potatoes to local fresh fish, Tomos Watkins Cwrw Braf; 17 bedrooms *(Guy Consterdine, John and Joan Nash, Dr C C S Wilson)*

THREE CROSSES [SS5694]

Poundffald Inn SA4 3PB [Tirmynydd Rd, NW end]: 17th-c beamed and timbered pub popular for generous good value food all day (children's last orders 6.30), cheerful helpful landlord, prompt service, changing real ales, good coal fires, stuffed birds and animals; sports TV in separate public bar; smart tables on attractive side terrace, pretty hanging baskets and raised beds *(Norman Lewis)*

Channel Islands

Guernsey's best pub by far, indeed the best pub on the Channel Islands, is the civilised and gently upmarket Fleur du Jardin at King's Mills, which moves confidently from strength to strength each year. The tasty and imaginative food here earns the Fleur du Jardin at King's Mills the accolade of Channel Islands Dining Pub of the Year. On Jersey, the Old Portelet in St Brelade, though it can get quite busy, is a great place for families, with its happy bustling atmosphere and various amusements for children. We will be watching the Town House in St Helier with interest, as the charming new licensees there should add a bundle of quality and character. As usual, the Lucky Dip section at the end of the chapter includes quite a few other places which have been capturing readers' attention recently. Two strong tips are the Black Dog bar of the Waters Edge Hotel in Trinity on Jersey, and the Harbour Lights at Newtown on Alderney. And we're always keen to add new discoveries here, so do please send us any suggestions. The islands no longer have a clear price advantage over the mainland on drinks; beer prices are still a bit lower than the mainland average, but they are now higher than the cheapest mainland areas. For value, your best bet is the locally brewed Tipsy Toad beer.

KING'S MILLS Map 1
Fleur du Jardin 🍴 🍷 🛏

King's Mills Road; GY5 7JT

Channel Islands Dining Pub of the Year

Readers thoroughly enjoy this lovely old hotel which is peacefully set in good-sized gardens, with picnic-sets among colourful borders, shrubs, bright hanging baskets and flower barrels. Comfortably civilised, its cosy relaxing rooms have low beams and thick granite walls, a good log fire in the public bar (popular with locals), and individual country furnishings in the hotel lounge bar. Fullers London Pride and Tipsy Toad Sunbeam are well kept on handpump, alongside a good wine list (with around 15 by the glass) and a local cider. A well balanced menu with quite a few choices includes beautifully prepared dishes such as soup (from £3.25), sandwiches (from £2.95), sautéed scallops with mango and coconut relish in a filo basket (£6.50), italian meat platter (£6.95), lasagne (£6.95), lamb curry (£8.75), fish and chips (£8.75), steak, kidney and ale pudding (£9.95), local scallops sautéed with white wine, shallots, garlic and herbs (£14.75), 8oz fillet (£14.95) and daily specials such as fried hake with onion marmalade and tomato coulis (£13.25), potato gnocchi with mushroom, cream, basil and sweet pepper sauce (£14.25) and fried veal cutlet coated with dijon mustard with white wine and shallot sauce (£15.50); three-course Sunday lunch (£12.95). The restaurant menu amalgamates some bar menu items with other pricier more elaborate dishes; friendly efficient service; piped music. They have a large car park and there is a swimming pool for residents. *(Recommended by Theocsbrian, Gordon Neighbour, Stephen R Holman)*

Free house ~ Licensee Keith Read ~ Real ale ~ Bar food (12-2, 7-9.30(9 Sun)) ~ Restaurant ~ (01481) 257996 ~ Children welcome ~ Open 10-11.45; 12-11 Sun ~ Bedrooms: £70B/£116B

We say if we know a pub has piped music.

ROZEL Map 1
Rozel
La Vallee De Rozel; JE3 6AJ

Tucked away at the edge of a sleepy little fishing village and just out of sight of the sea, this friendly inn has a very pleasant steeply terraced and partly covered hillside garden. Inside, the bar counter (Bass, Charles Wells Bombardier and Courage Directors under light blanket pressure) and tables in the traditional-feeling and cosy little dark-beamed back bar are stripped to their original light wood finish, and there are dark plush wall seats and stools, an open granite fireplace, and old prints and local pictures on the cream walls. Leading off is a carpeted area with flowers on big solid square tables. Piped music, and TV, games machine, juke box, darts, pool, cribbage and dominoes in the games room; the lounge bar is no smoking. Food from a good value menu is served in generous helpings and includes dishes such as soup (£2.95), sandwiches (from £2.95), filled ciabattas (from £4.95, steak £5.25), half a dozen oysters (£5.50), salads and burgers (from £6.95), tempura cod (£8.25), braised lamb shank or fresh fish platter (£8.95), daily specials such as tagliatelle with creamy tomato sauce (£6.95), fillet steak (£14.50) and puddings such as iced parfait or sticky toffee (£3.95); Sunday roast (£8.95). The upstairs restaurant has a relaxed rustic french atmosphere, and a menu with up to ten fish dishes a day, and good value specials. *(Recommended by BOB)*

Free house ~ Licensee Trevor Amy ~ Real ale ~ Bar food (12-2.15, 6-8.45) ~ Restaurant (not Sun evening) ~ (01534) 869801 ~ Children welcome ~ Dogs allowed in bar ~ Open 11-11

ST AUBIN Map 1
Old Court House Inn 🛏
Harbour Boulevard; JE3 8AB

This very popular 15th-c hotel is rather gloriously positioned with views over the tranquil harbour and on past St Aubin's fort right across the bay to St Helier. Both the conservatory and decking in front make the most of the delightful outlook. The pubby downstairs bar has cushioned wooden seats built against its stripped granite walls, low black beams, joists in a white ceiling, a turkey carpet, and an open fire. A dimly lantern-lit inner room has an illuminated rather brackish-looking deep well, and beyond that is the spacious cellar room which is open in summer. The Westward Bar is elegantly constructed from the actual gig of a schooner and offers a restauranty menu with prices to match. The front rooms here were once the home of a wealthy merchant, whose cellars stored privateers' plunder alongside more legitimate cargo, and the upstairs restaurant still shows signs of its time as a courtroom. Bar food includes soup (£3), ciabattas (from £5.25), starters such as sautéed squid and chorizo with fresh chilli or pork and apple terrine with chickpea and shallot salsa (£6.25), and main courses such as vegetable lasagne (£4.95), lasagne (£5.50), sausage and mash (£8.95), fish and chips (£11.50), fruits de mer cocktail (£9.95), local plaice (£10.50) and grilled dover sole (£19.95). One or two well kept beers might be Bass and Jersey on handpump; piped music, TV. It can be difficult to find parking near the hotel. *(Recommended by Phil and Helen Holt)*

Free house ~ Licensee Jonty Sharp ~ Real ale ~ Bar food (12.30-2.30, 7-9.30) ~ Restaurant ~ (01534) 746433 ~ Well behaved children welcome ~ Dogs allowed in bar ~ Open 11-11.30 ~ Bedrooms: £60B/£120B

Please keep sending us reports. We rely on readers for news of new discoveries, and particularly for news of changes – however slight – at the fully described pubs. No stamp needed: The Good Pub Guide, FREEPOST TN1569, Wadhurst, E Sussex TN5 7BR or send your report through our website: www.goodguides.co.uk

ST BRELADE   Map 1
Old Portelet Inn   £
Portelet Bay; JE3 8AJ

You can get a very good value meal at this enjoyable 17th-c farmhouse, and as there's plenty to keep children occupied it's particularly good for families too. There's a supervised indoor play area (half an hour 60p), another one outside, board games in the wooden-floored loft bar, and even summer entertainments arranged by the pub; also TV, pool, cribbage, dominoes and piped music. From a short snack menu, generous helpings of food served by neatly dressed attentive staff include sandwiches (from £2.30), soup (£2.75), filled baked potatoes (from £5.15), macaroni cheese (£5.20), ploughman's (£5.20), steak and mushroom pie (£6.45), and half a roast chicken or chicken curry (£6.95). The pub is well placed at the head of a long flight of granite steps, giving views across Portelet (Jersey's most southerly bay) as you walk down to a sheltered cove. There are picnic-sets on the partly covered flower-bower terrace by a wishing well, and seats in the sizeable landscaped garden, with lots of scented stocks and other flowers. The low-beamed downstairs bar has a stone bar counter (well kept Bass and a guest such as Flowers Original kept under light blanket pressure and reasonably priced house wine), a huge open fire, gas lamps, old pictures, etched glass panels from France, and a nice mixture of old wooden chairs on bare oak boards and quarry tiles. It opens into the big timber-ceilinged no smoking barn restaurant, with standing timbers and plenty of highchairs; disabled and baby-changing facilities. It can get very busy, but does have its quiet moments too. *(Recommended by Phyl and Jack Street, Stephen R Holman, Philip and June Caunt)*

Randalls ~ Manager Sarah Pye ~ Real ale ~ Bar food (12-2, 6-9(snack menu 2.30-5.30)) ~ Restaurant ~ (01534) 741899 ~ Children in restaurant and family room ~ Dogs allowed in bar ~ Open 11am-1pm

Old Smugglers
Ouaisne Bay; OS map reference 595476; JE3 8AW

The welcoming bar at this straightforward pub has thick walls, black beams, log fires and cosy black built-in settles, with well kept Bass and two guests from brewers such as Charles Wells and Ringwood on handpump, and a farm cider; sensibly placed darts, cribbage and dominoes. A glassed porch running the width of the building takes in interesting views over one of the island's many defence towers. Bar food includes soup (£3.25), vegetarian spring roll with sweet chilli dip (£4.95), filled baguettes (from £4.75), prawn cocktail (£5.45), steak and Guinness pie or battered haddock (£7.25), chicken curry or lasagne (£7.50), duck breast with orange and brandy sauce (£7.75), king prawns with garlic butter or black bean sauce (£9.25), steaks (from £9.75) and daily specials such as seafood risotto (£9.75) or dover sole (£14.25). The entire restaurant is no smoking. *(Recommended by BOB)*

Free house ~ Licensee Nigel Godfrey ~ Real ale ~ Bar food (12-2, 6-9; not Sun evening Nov-Mar) ~ Restaurant ~ (01534) 741510 ~ Children welcome ~ Dogs allowed in bar ~ Open 11am-11.30pm

ST HELIER   Map 1
Town House
New Street; JE2 3RA

Charming new licensees have taken over this big 1930s pub, which is much more attractive inside than its unassuming old cinema style exterior suggests. Popular with locals, its two main bars are divided by heavy but airy glass and brass doors. The sports bar on the left has two giant TV screens, darts and pool and a juke box. To the right, the lounge area has parquet flooring, some attractive panelling and upholstered armchairs at low round glass tables. Bar food currently includes soup (£2.95), sandwiches (from £3.55), burgers (from £4.50), fish and chips (£5.75), steak and ale pie (£5.95) and puddings such as Baileys bread and butter pudding

(£3.95) but they are planning to expand the food range with a wider choice of daily specials, such as baked cod with basil, mozzarella and tomatoes and chicken with onions, mushrooms and cheese topping (£9.50). Well kept Tipsy Toad Jimmys on handpump, and sound house wines; piped music. *(Recommended by BOB)*

Jersey ~ Managers Duncan Carse and Andy James ~ Real ale ~ Bar food (12-2, 6-9; not Mon evening or Sun) ~ Restaurant ~ (01534) 615000 ~ Children welcome in dining areas ~ Open 11-11

ST JOHN   Map 1
Les Fontaines
Le Grand Mourier, Route du Nord; JE3 4AJ

The cheery bustle of happy families and locals livens up this enjoyable former farmhouse, which is in a pretty spot on the north coast, and a nice place for a pint after a walk (well kept Bass and Charles Wells Bombardier). As you go in, look out for a worn, unmarked door at the side of the building, or as you go down the main entry lobby towards the bigger main bar go through the tiny narrow door on your right. These entrances take you into the best part, the public bar (where you might even hear the true Jersey patois), which has very heavy beams in the low dark ochre ceiling, massively thick irregular red granite walls, cushioned settles on the quarry-tiled floor and antique prints. The big granite-columned fireplace with a log fire warming its unusual inglenook seats may date back to the 16th c, and still sports its old smoking chains and side oven. The quarry tiled main bar is a marked contrast, with plenty of wheelback chairs around neat dark tables, and a spiral staircase leading up to a wooden gallery under the high pine-raftered plank ceiling; the dining area is no smoking; piped music and board games. A bonus for families is Pirate Pete's, a play area for children. Bar food includes sandwiches (from £2.95), soup (£2.95), ploughman's (from £5.95), battered cod (£6.90), cumberland sausage (£6.95), baked lamb shank with mash (£8.35) and specials such as cajun salmon fillet with spinach sauce (£8.50), scallop and bacon kebab (£9.50), baked bass stuffed with asian greens (£13). Seats on a terrace outside have good views. *(Recommended by Ron Gentry)*

Randalls ~ Manager Hazel O'Gorman ~ Real ale ~ Bar food (12-2.15(2.45 Sun), 6-9(8.30 Sun)) ~ (01534) 862707 ~ Children welcome ~ Dogs allowed in bar ~ Open 11.30-11

ST OUENS BAY   Map 1
La Pulente
Start of Five Mile Road; OS map reference 562488; JE3 8HG

Marvellous terrace views across the endless extent of Jersey's longest beach are reason enough to visit this bustling seaside pub. Inside, the carpeted lounge (with ragged walls and scrubbed wood tables) and the conservatory share the same sweeping views. Well kept Bass on handpump; piped music. Bar food, served by friendly staff, includes sandwiches (from £2.50), soup (£2.50), baked potatoes (from £3.50), ploughman's (from £5), battered cod (£6.75), steak and ale pie (£6.95), thai chicken curry (£7.95), swordfish steak niçoise (£9), monkfish and king prawn kebab (£10), 8oz sirloin (£10.95) and daily specials such as roast duck breast or local plaice (£11.50) and grilled lemon sole (£12.50). *(Recommended by John Evans, Phil and Helen Holt, Keith Eastelow)*

Randalls ~ Manager Julia Wallace ~ Real ale ~ Bar food (12-2.15(2.45 Sun in winter), 6-9(8.30 Sun); not Sun evening in winter) ~ Restaurant ~ (01534) 744487 ~ Children welcome ~ Open 11-11

The letters and figures after the name of each town are its Ordnance Survey map reference. *Using the Guide* at the beginning of the book explains how it helps you find a pub, in road atlases or on large-scale maps as well as on our own maps.

LUCKY DIP

Besides the fully inspected pubs, you might like to try these Lucky Dips recommended to us and described by readers (if you do, please send us reports: www.goodguides.co.uk).

ALDERNEY

NEWTOWN

☆ *Harbour Lights* GY9 3YR: Welcoming, clean and well run pub adjoining family-run hotel in a quieter part of this quiet island, comfortably refurbished bar with limited choice of good well presented bar food (not Sun nor wkdy lunchtime) from ploughman's with home-baked bread and home-made pickles to top-class fresh local fish and seafood, attractive prices, real ales such as Badger and Courage Directors, reasonably priced wines; caters well for families, sunny terrace in pleasant garden, bedrooms *(Donald Godden)*

ST ANNE

Moorings GY9 3XT [Braye Beach]: Open sunny pub with good range of pub food, friendly staff; large bay-view terrace *(Kevin Flack)*

GUERNSEY

GRANDE HAVRE

☆ *Houmet* GY6 8JR [part of Houmet du Nord Hotel; Rte de Picquerel]: Friendly and well run, with good choice of reasonably priced food inc good fresh local fish and scampi, big picture windows overlooking rock and sand beach; bedrooms *(BB, Gordon Neighbour)*

ST MARTIN

Ambassador GY4 6SQ [Sausmarez Rd]: Good sensibly priced food inc good fresh fish, obliging service, good local beer, pleasant surroundings; gets busy evenings; pretty garden, bedrooms *(Theocsbrian)*

ST PETER PORT

Ship & Crown GY1 2NB [opp Crown Pier, Esplanade]: Bustling town pub with bay windows overlooking harbour, very popular with yachting people and smarter locals, sharing building with Royal Guernsey Yacht Club; interesting photographs (esp concerning World War II German Ooccupation, also boats and ships), good value food from sandwiches through fast foods to steak, two or three real ales, welcoming prompt service even when busy; TVs rather detract from the atmosphere; open all day from 10am *(LYM, GHC)*

ST SAVIOUR

St Saviours Tavern GY7 9PW [Grande Rue]: Popular with locals for good choice of reasonably priced food from baked potatoes to local seafood and steak *(Gordon Neighbour)*

TORTEVAL

☆ *Imperial* GY8 0PS [Pleinmont (coast rd, nr Pleinmont Point)]: Good choice of enjoyable meals inc good seafood and traditional Guernsey bean jar in dining room which like the neat and tidy bar has a great sea view over Rocquaine Bay, Randalls beers; tables in suntrap garden, bedrooms in hotel part separate from the pub, handy for good beach *(Theocsbrian, Gordon Neighbour)*

HERM

HERM

☆ *Mermaid* GY1 3HR [linked to White House Hotel]: Lovely spot on idyllic island, very friendly service, big nautical-theme panelled bar with nice coal fire, snack bar (with cream teas), children's games area, large conservatory; Randalls Patois, bar food from bacon rolls up, restaurant dishes running up to duck, fish and seafood, also good barbecues; pleasant bedrooms, ranks of picnic-sets in spacious courtyard – best at peaceful times, can be busy on fine days *(GHC)*

JERSEY

GOREY

Castle Green JE3 6DR [steep climb to castle, above]: French-run dining pub up above the village, enjoyable food using fresh local produce, good choice of wines by the glass, cosy inside; steps up to picnic-sets on deck with superb views over bay *(Phyl and Jack Street)*
Village Pub JE3 9EP [Gorey Common]: Friendly and comfortably refurbished, light and cheerful, very popular locally for good value straightforward food (not Sun) all day inc good fresh fish, no smoking room *(Keith Eastelow)*

ST BRELADE

Landmark JE3 8EP [La Marquanderie Hill]: Very friendly, with tasty food and good disabled access and lavatories *(Paul Goldman)*

ST HELIER

☆ *Admiral* JE2 3QZ [St James St]: Friendly atmosphere in heavily beamed candlelit pub with lots of shiny dark wood panelling, attractive and spotless solid country furniture, plenty of bric-a-brac inc an old penny 'What the Butler Saw' machine and enamel advertising signs (many more in small suntrap back courtyard), reasonably priced bar food (something available all afternoon), perhaps Boddingtons and a monthly guest beer, daily papers, dominoes, cribbage; TV, piped music; children welcome, open all day *(Ron Gentry, LYM)*

TRINITY

☆ *Waters Edge* JE3 5AS [Bouley Bay]: Spacious and comfortable modern hotel with well kept waterside grounds and picture-window sea views; 17th-c core has relaxed and welcoming stripped-stone Black Dog bar (no view from here), with lots of panelling and ornate carvings, old-world furnishings and décor, Mary Ann and Tetleys beers, good value house wines, good service by neat staff, wide choice of good bar food inc fresh local seafood; comfortable bedrooms, open all day, cl Mon in winter *(LYM, Roger Thornington)*

Overseas Lucky Dip

We're always interested to hear of good bars and pubs overseas – preferably really good examples of bars that visitors would find memorable, rather than transplanted 'British pubs'. A star marks places we would be confident would deserve a main entry. It's common for good bars overseas, if they serve food, to serve it all day (a pleasant contrast to the UK, where most pubs outside big cities actually close for much of the day, let alone serve food all day). In many foreign bars, partly thanks to the fairly strong £, drinks are relatively cheap – note that this is not the case in Hong Kong, nor (surprisingly) in Dublin. On the other hand, the Republic of Ireland's ban on smoking in pubs is now having a real effect. For this reason, we have this year separated the Ireland pubs listed into Republic (smoking ban) and Northern (no ban yet).

ARGENTINA

BUENOS AIRES

Biela [Ave Quintana]: At the gates of cemetery where Evita is buried, wide food choice, assorted beers, afternoon tea, motor-racing photographs esp Fangio; lots of tables out under vast ancient rubber tree *(Ian Phillips)*

Whiskeria La Rambla [Posedas 1602]: Intimate corner café/bar oasis ideal for sitting out on the street and watching the world go by, beer, light snacks, good coffee, afternoon tea *(Ian Phillips)*

CALAFATE

Casablanca [Av Libertador 1202]: Draught beer in tall litre glasses, good empanadas, pizzas etc, Bogarde and Bergman theme; pavement tables – can be too windy in this lakeside town, springboard for glacier tours *(Ian Phillips)*

Whirra: Small corner café and bar nr the nature reserve and lake, charming English proprietor, microbrewery making its own lager and dark beer, bar snacks; live music evenings; picnic-sets out in front, open all day, cl Tues *(Ian Phillips)*

PUERTO MADRYN

Margarita [Ave Roca 331]: Draught beer, decent wines, good fairly priced food; music may be rather loud *(Ian Phillips)*

Yoaquina: Super location in this town founded by the Welsh, with verandah right on beach overlooking vast bay – you may see whales from your table; usual beers, good seafood *(Ian Phillips)*

AUSTRIA

SEEFELD

Wildmoosalm [on plateau above – short bus ride from centre]: Picturesque family-run bar alone in the winter snowfields, three rooms full of striking stuffed birds of prey and animals, walls festooned with football shirts, fresh flowers on the tables, good beer, enjoyable food,

really friendly bustling atmosphere; in summer the terrace is great *(John and Joan Nash)*

ZELL AM ZEE

Crazy Daisy [Brucker Bundestrasse 9]: In winter full of snowboarders, skiers and ski instructors, in summer board sailors and watersports – with appropriate video in corner; dark and noisy, with lively atmosphere, carefully served Guinness, good range of food *(John and Joan Nash)*

BELGIUM

BRUGES

Craenenburg [Markt]: Large bar with own little turret, quiet and refined, Leffe, Hoegaarden and Jupiter brought to table by efficient long-serving staff from splendid back counter, good coffee, cakes and good value waffles, pasta and salads, daily papers, leather and light wood panelling, stained-glass medallions in big picture windows looking over square; pavement tables *(Steve Whalley)*

CUBA

HAVANA

Hotel Nacional: Hotel built in 1930 as casino; flamboyant Spanish Colonial style, included for its Bar of Fame, hundreds of former customers from Winston Churchill to Nat King Cole, Yuri Gagarin to the Manic Street Preachers, pictured in floor-to-ceiling paintings in decade order around the bar, good range of drinks in cocktail-bar atmosphere, amazing range of cigars in all sorts of sizes, pubby food in another bar downstairs; bedrooms, open all day and night *(Keith and Chris O'Neill)*

CZECH REPUBLIC

PRAGUE

Cerneho Vola [Loretanske Namesti 1]: Up

steps above castle, unspoilt, friendly and jolly, with beams, leaded lights, long dark benches or small stand-up entrance bar, good Kozel Pale and Dark 12 black beer, and Velkopopovicky Korel lager, local snacks; can get very busy (though rarely too touristy), cl 9 *(the Didler, J M Tansey)*

Fleku [Kremencova 11, Nove Mesto]: Brewing its own strong tasty black Flekovsky Dark 13 since 1843 (some say 1499); helpful waiters will try to sell you a schnapps with it – say Ne firmly; huge, with benches and big refectory tables in two big dark-beamed rooms – tourists on right with ten-piece oompah band, more local on left (music here too), also courtyard after courtyard; good basic promptly served food – sausages, pork, goulash with dumplings; open early morning to late night, can be very busy and noisy with tourists *(Bruce Bird, the Didler, John Dwane)*

Medvidku [Na Perstyne 5, Stare Mesto]: Superb old building in red light district, namesake bears etched in stone over entry, lots of copper in left bar, bigger right room more for eating, Budvar Budweiser on tap *(Myke and Nicky Crombleholme, the Didler)*

Novomestsky Pivovar [Vodickova 20, Nove Mesto]: Fine brewpub opened 1994 in unlikely spot off shopping arcade, rambling series of basement rooms (some no smoking) with interesting old copper brewing equipment, lots of substantial bric-a-brac and old posters, their own unfiltered Novomestsky light and dark beers, good promptly served cheap food esp goulash; open all day *(Bruce Bird)*

Pivovarsky Dum [Lipova 15]: Brewpub with big windows showing fermentation room and brewing equipment, smart modern green décor and woodwork, interesting range inc wheat, banana, cherry and even coffee and champagne beers as well as classic lager (tempting brewing aromas out on the street), served by the gallon stick with its own tap if you wish, low prices, good choice of english-style foods, friendly service; open all day *(the Didler, John Dwane)*

Vejvodu [Jilska 4]: Carefully rebuilt and extended next door, with thriving atmosphere, good service, well presented food, good value Pilsner Urquell; roomy but can get busy, handy for old town square *(the Didler, Myke and Nicky Crombleholme)*

☆ *Zlateho Tygra* [Husova 17, Stare Mesto]: 13th-c cellars with superb Pilsner Urquell 12 and eponymous Golden Tiger served by white-coated waiters; sometimes a queue of locals even before 3pm opening, and no standing allowed, but worth the wait (don't be put off by Reserved signs as the seats, mainly long wooden benches, aren't usually being used till later – and they do make tourists feel welcome) *(the Didler)*

FALKLAND ISANDS

STANLEY

Harbour Lights [Mare Harbour, Mt Pleasant Airfield; an hour from Stanley]: Friendly and enjoyable club/pub for port staff and users, open only a few nights a week, well worth a

visit if for instance you are on a marine sightseeing trip – and you can phone home buying a C&W phone card *(Bruce and Penny Wilkie)*

GERMANY

COLOGNE

Café Reichard [Unter Fettenhannen 11]: Attractively decorated large café with decent food from light dishes through pasta to hearty main dishes, usual drinks inc mainly white and rosé wines by the glass; great cathedral views from terrace *(Christine and Neil Townend, Michael Dandy)*

IRELAND (NORTHERN)

BELFAST

☆ *Crown* [Gt Victoria St, opp Europa Hotel]: Well preserved ornate 19th-c National Trust gin palace, lively and bustling, with pillared entrance, opulent tiles outside and in, elaborately coloured windows, almost church-like ceiling, handsome mirrors, lots of individual snug booths with little doors and bells for waiter service (some graffiti too now, alas), gas lighting, mosaic tiled floor, pricey Whitewater real ale from imposing granite-top counter with colourful tiled facing, good lunchtime meals till 5 upstairs inc oysters; can be smoky, very wide and sometimes noisy range of customers (can take their toll on the downstairs gents'), and shame about the TV; open all day *(Tracey and Stephen Groves, C J Fletcher, Joe Green)*

John Hewitt [Donegall St]: Popular restaurant with good food by day, vibrant bar with live music by night *(Keith and Chris O'Neill)*

IRELAND (REPUBLIC)

BALLYVAUGHAN

Monks [Co Clare]: Traditional village pub with bay view close to quay, seafood specials and other food all day inc delicious ice-cream, peat fire in bar, woodburners in other rooms; TV or piped music may be loud, traditional live music wknds; children welcome, disabled facilities (but steps in pub), courtyard picnic-sets *(JJW, CMW)*

BRAY

Porterhouse [Strand Rd; Co Wicklow]: Large dimly lit rather rambling seafront pub with various areas off large central bar, their own-label beers and Porters and lots of foreign bottled beers, enjoyable food all day from fairly priced menu inc some unusual dishes; piped music, TV *(JJW, CMW)*

DOOLIN

Gus O'Connors [Co Clare]: Large yet cosy, with several areas, real fire, good choice of generous food all day inc lots of fish at reasonable prices, one own brew as well as usual drinks; TV, games machines in back lobby, live irish music nightly; children and dogs welcome, disabled access *(JJW, CMW)*

Macdermotts [off R478/479; Co Clare]: Three rooms with real fire, reasonably priced food all day in dining area; piped music, several TVs,

very busy, esp for live traditional music late evening; children welcome *(JJW, CMW)*
McGanns [Co Clare]: Usual food and drink, very busy for late evening live traditional music (get there much earlier for a table); TV; children welcome till 8pm, bedrooms *(JJW, CMW)*

DUBLIN

Brazen Head [Lower Bridge St]: Charming bar, said to be oldest here, maze of dimly lit cosy unspoilt rooms off attractive red and white tiled passage, with old beams, mirrors, old settles inc one given by Thin Lizzy's Phil Lynnot, interesting memorabilia and local-hero pictures, open fires; lunchtime bar food from filled cobs to carvery, evening restaurant, well served Guinness; peaceful front smokers' cobbled courtyard, sheltered and covered, good traditional music each night, main bar very busy Sun lunchtime with music too *(David Crook, Carol Broadbent, Keith and Chris O'Neill)*
Fitzsimons [East Essex St, Temple Bar]: Very comfortable and welcoming if not genuine 'old Dublin', highly geared to tourists esp downstairs – traditional music, periodic dancers; real ales, enjoyable food inc carvery, fast friendly service, lots of varnished wood, polished floor and bar counter; three sports TV screens, becomes a nightclub after last orders *(Carol Broadbent)*
☆ *Gravity Bar* [St James Gate Guinness Brewery]: Great 360° views from huge round glass-walled tasting bar on top floor – effectively Dublin's highest vantage-point; Guinness at its best, culmination of up-to-date exhibition on firm's history, brewing and advertising campaigns, also lower Storehouse bar with lunchtime food and gift shop *(Dr and Mrs M W A Haward, Keith and Chris O'Neill, Bruce and Penny Wilkie, David Crook)*
Kielys of Donnybrook [Donnybrook Rd]: Great atmosphere, enjoyable food, perfectly served Guinness, friendly skilled staff *(Bruce and Penny Wilkie)*
Madigans [O'Connell St/N Earl St]: Plenty of atmosphere in relaxed traditional pub very near the historic GPO of the 1916 Easter Rising, long magnificently panelled bar with seats both sides, good choice of snacks and light meals, good friendly service, usual drinks, good tea; may be traditional music *(JJW, CMW, Keith and Chris O'Neill, Bruce and Penny Wilkie)*
Messrs Maguires [O'Connell Bridge, S side]: Well restored early 19th-c splendour, four floors with huge staircase, superb woodwork and ceilings, flame-effect gas fires, tasteful décor inc contemporary irish prints and functioning library; good own-brewed keg beers inc Stout, Extra Stout, Red Ale, Rusty Ale and lager, good coffee, enjoyable reasonably priced food from interesting sandwiches through very popular lunchtime carvery to top-floor gourmet restaurant; two TVs; irish music Sun-Tues from 9.30 *(JJW, CMW, Phil and Sally Gorton, J M Tansey)*
O'Neills [Suffolk St]: Hospitable and congenial spreading early Victorian pub, lots of dark panelling and cubby-holes off big lively bar,

more rooms upstairs, good lunchtime carvery (all day Sun) and good value sandwich bar, quick efficient service, well served Guinness; main tourist information centre in converted church opp *(Bruce and Penny Wilkie, Keith and Chris O'Neill)*
Oliver St John Gogarty [Anglesea St, Temple Bar]: Bustling bare-boards bars on three floors, bric-a-brac inc bicycle above counter, generous good if not cheap food in fairly small cosy upper-floor restaurant (former bank, interesting preserved features) and at lunchtime in main bar, pleasant lively atmosphere and friendly efficient service, good wine and Guinness; rambles through into adjoining Left Bank bar which has integral heated terrace tables; live music upstairs *(David Crook, Dr and Mrs M W A Haward, Keith and Chris O'Neill, J M Tansey)*
Porterhouse [Parliament St, nr Wellington Quay]: Vibrant three-storey modern pub, lots of pine and brass for café-bar feel, brewing half a dozen good beers inc several good Porters and usually a cask-conditioned real ale, praiseworthy sample trays, guest beers, dozens of foreign bottled beers, friendly efficient service, lots of anti-Guinness propaganda; high tables and equally high seats, good food from ciabatta sandwiches to steaks, upstairs restaurant; piped music, nightly live music, can be standing room only wknds *(Rob Winstanley, J M Tansey)*
Temple Bar [Temple Bar]: Rambling multi-levelled, many-roomed pub on corner of two cobbled streets, more modern back extension, lively mix of tourists and loyal locals, throbbing on wknd nights, quick friendly service even when crowded; tables out in big yard, good live music from 4pm *(Bruce and Penny Wilkie, Keith and Chris O'Neill)*

GLENCULLEN

Johnnie Foxs [about 4 miles NW of Enniskerry; Co Dublin]: Primarily a dining pub, with wide choice of food, not cheap but good, inc fine seafood and excellent bread; very friendly service, good buzzy atmosphere, good wines and well served Guinness, interesting décor with antique settles, scrubbed tables, beams, stripped stone and a forest of bric-a-brac, traditional music and irish dancing till midnight (must book wknds) *(Dr and Mrs M W A Haward)*

INAGH

Biddy Early [Co Clare]: Good lager, ale and stout from next-door brewery (tours available), food all day, chatty friendly landlord, darts and pool in second room; TV *(JJW, CMW)*

KENMARE

Purple Heather [Henry St; Co Kerry]: Red walls and ceiling, framed tapestries and old photographs, comfortable alcoves, plenty of tables, large reasonably priced menu from sandwiches to steaks inc three kinds of soup, well served Guinness, plenty of wines by the glass, cheerful waitresses stay calm even when it's crowded; open all day till 7, then their next-door restaurant takes over *(Peter and Pat Frogley)*

KILBRITTAIN
Pink Elephant [Harbour View (R600); Co Cork]: Pleasant pub/restaurant with bay views from inside and breezy picnic-sets, limited drinks choice, short choice of enjoyable food esp fish; quiet piped irish music, may be a pianist later; children welcome *(JJW, CMW)*

LAHINCH
Mrs O'Brien's Kitchen [Co Clare]: Long friendly bar with informal furnishings and décor, lots of bric-a-brac inc old 78s on ceiling and first-day covers on walls, tasty food all day (can take a while if busy), bottled beers from Biddy Early as well as usual drinks, corner internet access; piped music, live three nights a week *(JJW, CMW)*

LISDOONVARNA
Roadside Tavern [Co Clare]: Three linked rooms with pine tables, fish-oriented food all day, two real fires, usual drinks; TV; good nightly traditional music *(JJW, CMW)*
Royal Spa [N67; Co Clare]: Food all day, pizzas till midnight, usual drinks (tea, coffee and milk popular too); unobtrusive piped traditional music, some live *(JJW, CMW)*

RAMSGRANGE
Hollow [R733, S of New Ross; Co Wexford]: Friendly pub/restaurant, usual drinks, enjoyable food; quiet piped music; open all day *(JJW, CMW)*

RATHCOOLE
An Poitin Stil [N7 Dublin—Naas; Co Dublin]: Big busy rambling main-road two-bar former coaching inn, recently refurbished and moving upmarket, generous reasonably priced food until 10pm, usual drinks, downstairs restaurant; piped music, live three nights a week; children welcome, picnic-sets outside *(JJW, CMW)*

ISLE OF MAN

DOUGLAS [SC3876]
Cornerhouse [Ridgeway St, between Lord St bus station and Peel Rd railway station]: Reopened after open-plan refurbishment, now one very large room with pool one side, tables for the lunchtime food, drinking area in front of bar (which has reasonably priced wine quarter-bottles), friendly staff; live music; open all day, useful location between bus terminus and steam railway station *(Dr J Barrie Jones)*

NEW ZEALAND
CROMWELL
Golden Gate: Big newish pub and hotel in new town, usual drinks, good food, friendly welcome, no piped music; pleasant outdoor tables *(JJW, CMW)*

DEVONPORT
Patriot [14 Victoria Rd]: English-run no smoking pub in former bank, lots of wines as well as usual drinks, good choice of food all day; service can slow when busy, quiz night, TV, pool, piped and occasional live music; upstairs verandah, interesting area for antiques and secondhand books *(JJW, CMW)*

FRANZ JOSEF
Alice May [Cowan St/Crow St]: Good choice of drinks and generous food, reasonable prices, pool, bric-a-brac, no piped music; silent TV *(JJW, CMW)*

QUEENSTOWN
Speights Old Ale House [Stanley St]: Copper dome and stone fireplace, high bar stools, good friendly service, full range of their beers on tap (the sort of place you might have problems remembering leaving), massive helpings of enjoyable food such as liver and bacon with their own bread, no smoking; piped music may be loud, SkyTV; old tractor seats as outside seating *(JJW, CMW, Steve Nye, David Crook)*

ROTORUA
Pig & Whistle [Tutanekai/Haupapa St; North Island]: Former police station, rare example of 1940s architecture, good local beers on tap inc Speights Gold, lots of wines, enjoyable generous simple meals, reasonably priced, and all-day snacks; piped pop, live music wknds; children welcome, large covered outdoor seating area with heaters *(JJW, CMW, David Crook)*

POLAND
KRAKOW
Bankowa [opp St Mary's Church in Main Sq]: Small coffee shop and bar, carved glass shop front, ornate wall frieze above very tall glass cabinets of bottles and glasses, draught and bottled beers, coffered gold ceiling; tables with large umbrellas outside *(Ian Phillips)*
Europejska [Rynek Glowney]: Comfortable window seats looking out over beautiful market square, high ceilings, horse pictures and musical instruments on stripe-papered walls, limited choice of enjoyable food, daily papers, old red british telephone box in corner, two back rooms, one with longcase clock; unobtrusive piped music *(Donna and Roger)*
Kacpra [Slawkowska off Rynek Glowny]: Dim-lit cellar bar just off Main Sq, posters of Bob Marley, Miles Davis and the like, dummy in evening dress in one alcove, cartwheels and horse tack, higher and lower seating areas off one end, friendly staff, local beers on tap, separate pool room *(Donna and Roger)*

SINGAPORE
SINGAPORE
Penny Black [Boat Quay]: Popular no smoking open-plan waterside Victorian pub replica, fish and chips and so forth, keg Bass and Guinness; TV, piped or live music *(JJW, CMW)*

USA
TOPSHAM
Maine Sea Dog [Main St]: Big mill conversion, arched windows, huge beams and timbers, bare boards, good food and ten or so of their interesting Sea Dog beers, friendly service, pool room; tables out on side deck overlooking Androscoggin River rapids *(Dr and Mrs M E Wilson)*

Special Interest Lists

The pubs listed here have bigger or more beautiful gardens, grounds or terraces than are usual for their areas. Note that in a town or city this might be very much more modest than the sort of garden that would deserve a listing in the countryside.

BEDFORDSHIRE
Bletsoe, Falcon
Bolnhurst, Plough
Milton Bryan, Red Lion
Northill, Crown
Old Warden, Hare & Hounds
Riseley, Fox & Hounds

BERKSHIRE
Aldworth, Bell
Ashmore Green, Sun in the Wood
Frilsham, Pot Kiln
Hurst, Green Man
Inkpen, Crown & Garter
Knowl Hill, Royal Oak
Shinfield, Magpie & Parrot
White Waltham, Beehive
Winterbourne, Winterbourne Arms

BUCKINGHAMSHIRE
Bennett End, Three Horseshoes
Bovingdon Green, Royal Oak
Denham, Swan
Dorney, Palmer Arms
Ford, Dinton Hermit
Grove, Grove Lock
Hawridge Common, Full Moon
Hedgerley, White Horse
Mentmore, Stag
Oving, Black Boy
Penn, Crown
Skirmett, Frog

CAMBRIDGESHIRE
Elton, Black Horse
Fowlmere, Chequers
Heydon, King William IV
Madingley, Three Horseshoes

CHESHIRE
Aldford, Grosvenor Arms
Bunbury, Dysart Arms
Haughton Moss, Nags Head
Macclesfield, Sutton Hall Hotel

CORNWALL
Lostwithiel, Globe
Philleigh, Roseland
St Agnes, Turks Head
St Kew, St Kew Inn
St Mawgan, Falcon
Tresco, New Inn

CUMBRIA
Barbon, Barbon Inn

Bassenthwaite Lake, Pheasant
Bouth, White Hart
Staveley, Eagle & Child

DERBYSHIRE
Hathersage, Plough
Melbourne, John Thompson
Woolley Moor, White Horse

DEVON
Avonwick, Turtley Corn Mill
Broadhembury, Drewe Arms
Clayhidon, Merry Harriers
Clyst Hydon, Five Bells
Cornworthy, Hunters Lodge
Exeter, Imperial
Exminster, Turf Hotel
Haytor Vale, Rock
Lower Ashton, Manor Inn
Lydford, Castle Inn
Newton Abbot, Two Mile Oak
Newton Ferrers, Dolphin
Poundsgate, Tavistock Inn
Sidbury, Hare & Hounds
Torbryan, Old Church House

DORSET
Cerne Abbas, Royal Oak
Chideock, George
Marshwood, Bottle
Nettlecombe, Marquis of Lorne
Osmington Mills, Smugglers
Plush, Brace of Pheasants
Shave Cross, Shave Cross Inn
Shroton, Cricketers
Tarrant Monkton, Langton Arms

ESSEX
Castle Hedingham, Bell
Chappel, Swan
Fyfield, Queens Head
Great Henny, Henny Swan
Great Yeldham, White Hart
Hastingwood, Rainbow & Dove
Mill Green, Viper
Peldon, Rose
Stock, Hoop

GLOUCESTERSHIRE
Blaisdon, Red Hart
Ewen, Wild Duck
Frampton on Severn, Bell
Nailsworth, Egypt Mill
Prestbury, Royal Oak
Upper Oddington, Horse & Groom

HAMPSHIRE
Bramdean, Fox
Exton, Shoe
Ovington, Bush
Steep, Harrow
Stockbridge, Grosvenor
Tichborne, Tichborne Arms

HEREFORDSHIRE
Aymestrey, Riverside Inn
Hoarwithy, New Harp
Sellack, Lough Pool
Ullingswick, Three Crowns
Woolhope, Butchers Arms

HERTFORDSHIRE
Ashwell, Three Tuns
Chapmore End, Woodman
Potters Crouch, Holly Bush
Preston, Red Lion
Sarratt, Cock

ISLE OF WIGHT
Hulverstone, Sun
Shorwell, Crown

KENT
Biddenden, Three Chimneys
Bough Beech, Wheatsheaf
Boyden Gate, Gate Inn
Brookland, Woolpack
Chiddingstone, Castle Inn
Dargate, Dove
Groombridge, Crown
Newnham, George
Penshurst, Bottle House
Selling, Rose & Crown
Stowting, Tiger
Ulcombe, Pepper Box

LANCASHIRE
Newton, Parkers Arms
Whitewell, Inn at Whitewell

LEICESTERSHIRE AND RUTLAND
Barrowden, Exeter Arms
Exton, Fox & Hounds
Lyddington, Old White Hart
Medbourne, Nevill Arms
Peggs Green, New Inn
Stathern, Red Lion

LINCOLNSHIRE
Billingborough, Fortescue Arms
Coningsby, Lea Gate Inn
Lincoln, Victoria
Stamford, George of Stamford

NORFOLK
Brancaster Staithe, Jolly Sailors
Burnham Thorpe, Lord Nelson
Holkham, Victoria
Ringstead, Gin Trap
Snettisham, Rose & Crown
Stanhoe, Crown
Stow Bardolph, Hare Arms
Woodbastwick, Fur & Feather

NORTHAMPTONSHIRE
Bulwick, Queens Head
East Haddon, Red Lion
Farthingstone, Kings Arms
Wadenhoe, Kings Head

NORTHUMBRIA
Anick, Rat
Blanchland, Lord Crewe Arms
Diptonmill, Dipton Mill Inn
Greta Bridge, Morritt Arms
Newburn, Keelman

Weldon Bridge, Anglers Arms

NOTTINGHAMSHIRE
Caunton, Caunton Beck

OXFORDSHIRE
Aston Tirrold, Chequers
Clifton, Duke of Cumberlands Head
Fyfield, White Hart
Highmoor, Rising Sun
Hook Norton, Gate Hangs High
Kelmscott, Plough
Stanton St John, Star
Swerford, Masons Arms
Tadpole Bridge, Trout

SHROPSHIRE
Bishop's Castle, Castle Hotel, Three Tuns
Chetwynd Aston, Fox
Norton, Hundred House

SOMERSET
Axbridge, Lamb
Chiselborough, Cat Head
Compton Martin, Ring o' Bells
Litton, Kings Arms
Monksilver, Notley Arms
Shepton Montague, Montague Inn

STAFFORDSHIRE
Salt, Holly Bush
Stourton, Fox

SUFFOLK
Dennington, Queens Head
Lavenham, Angel
Laxfield, Kings Head
Long Melford, Black Lion
Newbourne, Fox
Rede, Plough
Rougham, Ravenwood Hall
Stoke-by-Nayland, Crown
Walberswick, Anchor, Bell
Waldringfield, Maybush

SURREY
Charleshill, Donkey
Coldharbour, Plough
Compton, Withies
Eashing, Stag
Elstead, Mill at Elstead
Forest Green, Parrot
Laleham, Three Horseshoes
Leigh, Seven Stars
Lingfield, Hare & Hounds
Mickleham, King William IV
Newdigate, Surrey Oaks
Ottershaw, Castle
West End, Inn at West End
West Horsley, Barley Mow
Worplesdon, Jolly Farmer

SUSSEX
Alfriston, George
Amberley, Black Horse
Balls Cross, Stag
Berwick, Cricketers Arms
Blackboys, Blackboys Inn
Byworth, Black Horse
Coolham, George & Dragon
Elsted, Three Horseshoes
Fittleworth, Swan

Fletching, Griffin
Heathfield, Star
Oving, Gribble Inn
Ringmer, Cock
Rushlake Green, Horse & Groom
Singleton, Partridge
Wineham, Royal Oak

WARWICKSHIRE
Edge Hill, Castle
Farnborough, Inn at Farnborough
Ilmington, Howard Arms
Preston Bagot, Crabmill
Priors Marston, Holly Bush

WILTSHIRE
Berwick St James, Boot
Brinkworth, Three Crowns
Chicksgrove, Compasses
Ebbesbourne Wake, Horseshoe
Horton, Bridge Inn
Kilmington, Red Lion
Lacock, George, Rising Sun
Norton, Vine Tree
Seend, Barge
Whitley, Pear Tree

WORCESTERSHIRE
Bretforton, Fleece
Hanley Swan, Swan

YORKSHIRE
East Witton, Blue Lion
Egton Bridge, Horse Shoe
Halifax, Shibden Mill
Heath, Kings Arms
South Dalton, Pipe & Glass
Sutton upon Derwent, St Vincent Arms

LONDON
Central London, Cross Keys
East London, Prospect of Whitby
North London, Spaniards Inn
South London, Crown & Greyhound,
   Founders Arms, Old Jail, Victoria
West London, Colton Arms, Dove,
   Windsor Castle

SCOTLAND
Badachro, Badachro Inn
Edinburgh, Starbank
Gairloch, Old Inn
Gatehouse of Fleet, Masonic Arms
Glenelg, Glenelg Inn
Kilmahog, Lade
Thornhill, Lion & Unicorn

WALES
Colwyn Bay, Pen-y-Bryn
Crickhowell, Bear, Nantyffin Cider Mill
Gresford, Pant-yr-Ochain
Llanfrynach, White Swan
Llangedwyn, Green Inn
Llangollen, Corn Mill
Mold, Glasfryn
Old Radnor, Harp
Presteigne, Radnorshire Arms
Raglan, Clytha Arms
Rosebush, Tafarn Sinc
Skenfrith, Bell
St Hilary, Bush

Tintern, Cherry Tree
Ty'n-y-groes, Groes

CHANNEL ISLANDS
King's Mills, Fleur du Jardin
Rozel, Rozel

WATERSIDE PUBS

The pubs listed here are right beside the sea, a
sizeable river, canal, lake or loch that contributes
significantly to their attraction.

BEDFORDSHIRE
Bletsoe, Falcon

BERKSHIRE
Kintbury, Dundas Arms

BUCKINGHAMSHIRE
Grove, Grove Lock

CAMBRIDGESHIRE
Sutton Gault, Anchor

CHESHIRE
Chester, Old Harkers Arms
Wrenbury, Dusty Miller

CORNWALL
Bodinnick, Old Ferry
Malpas, Heron
Mylor Bridge, Pandora
Polkerris, Rashleigh
Polperro, Blue Peter
Port Isaac, Port Gaverne Inn
Porthleven, Ship
Porthtowan, Blue
Portmellon Cove, Rising Sun
Sennen Cove, Old Success
St Agnes, Turks Head
Tresco, New Inn

CUMBRIA
Brampton, New Inn
Staveley, Eagle & Child
Ulverston, Bay Horse

DERBYSHIRE
Hathersage, Plough

DEVON
Buckfast, Abbey Inn
Culmstock, Culm Valley
Exminster, Turf Hotel
Newton Ferrers, Dolphin
Noss Mayo, Ship
Torcross, Start Bay
Tuckenhay, Maltsters Arms

ESSEX
Burnham-on-Crouch, White Harte
Chappel, Swan
Fyfield, Queens Head
Great Henny, Henny Swan

GLOUCESTERSHIRE
Ashleworth Quay, Boat

HAMPSHIRE
Exton, Shoe
Ovington, Bush
Portsmouth, Still & West
Wherwell, Mayfly

HEREFORDSHIRE
Aymestrey, Riverside Inn

ISLE OF WIGHT
Bembridge, Crab & Lobster
Cowes, Folly
Seaview, Seaview Hotel
Ventnor, Spyglass

KENT
Oare, Shipwrights Arms

LANCASHIRE
Little Eccleston, Cartford
Manchester, Dukes 92
Whitewell, Inn at Whitewell

NORFOLK
Brancaster Staithe, White Horse

NORTHAMPTONSHIRE
Wadenhoe, Kings Head

NORTHUMBRIA
Newcastle upon Tyne,
   Head of Steam @ The Cluny
Newton-by-the-Sea, Ship

NOTTINGHAMSHIRE
Ranby, Chequers

OXFORDSHIRE
Godstow, Trout
Tadpole Bridge, Trout

SHROPSHIRE
Ludlow, Unicorn
Shrewsbury, Armoury

SOMERSET
Churchill, Crown
Compton Martin, Ring o' Bells
Portishead, Windmill

SUFFOLK
Chelmondiston, Butt & Oyster
Nayland, Anchor
Southwold, Harbour Inn
Waldringfield, Maybush

SURREY
Eashing, Stag
Elstead, Mill at Elstead

WILTSHIRE
Horton, Bridge Inn
Seend, Barge

WORCESTERSHIRE
Knightwick, Talbot

YORKSHIRE
Hull, Minerva
Whitby, Duke of York

LONDON
East London, Grapes, Prospect of Whitby
South London, Cutty Sark, Founders Arms
West London, Bulls Head, Dove

SCOTLAND
Aboyne, Boat
Badachro, Badachro Inn
Edinburgh, Starbank
Elie, Ship
Gairloch, Old Inn

Glenelg, Glenelg Inn
Isle of Whithorn, Steam Packet
Kingholm Quay, Swan
Plockton, Plockton Hotel
Shieldaig, Tigh an Eilean Hotel
Stein, Stein Inn
Tayvallich, Tayvallich Inn
Ullapool, Ferry Boat

WALES
Aberaeron, Harbourmaster
Abercych, Nags Head
Aberdovey, Penhelig Arms
Abergorlech, Black Lion
Cresswell Quay, Cresselly Arms
Llangedwyn, Green Inn
Llangollen, Corn Mill
Overton Bridge, Cross Foxes
Pembroke Ferry, Ferry Inn
Red Wharf Bay, Ship
Skenfrith, Bell

CHANNEL ISLANDS
St Aubin, Old Court House Inn
St Ouens Bay, La Pulente

PUBS IN ATTRACTIVE SURROUNDINGS

These pubs are in unusually attractive or
interesting places – lovely countryside, charming
villages, occasionally notable town surroundings.
Waterside pubs are listed again here only if their
other surroundings are special, too.

BEDFORDSHIRE
Old Warden, Hare & Hounds

BERKSHIRE
Aldworth, Bell
Frilsham, Pot Kiln

BUCKINGHAMSHIRE
Bovingdon Green, Royal Oak
Hawridge Common, Full Moon
Skirmett, Frog
Turville, Bull & Butcher

CAMBRIDGESHIRE
Elton, Black Horse
Reach, Dyke's End

CHESHIRE
Barthomley, White Lion
Bunbury, Dysart Arms

CORNWALL
Altarnun, Rising Sun
Blisland, Blisland Inn
Helston, Halzephron
Polperro, Blue Peter
St Agnes, Turks Head
St Kew, St Kew Inn
St Mawgan, Falcon
Tresco, New Inn
Zennor, Tinners Arms

CUMBRIA
Bassenthwaite Lake, Pheasant
Bouth, White Hart
Broughton Mills, Blacksmiths Arms
Buttermere, Bridge Hotel
Cartmel, Kings Arms

Chapel Stile, Wainwrights
Crosthwaite, Punch Bowl
Elterwater, Britannia
Hawkshead, Drunken Duck, Kings Arms
Hesket Newmarket, Old Crown
Ings, Watermill
Langdale, Old Dungeon Ghyll
Levens, Strickland Arms
Little Langdale, Three Shires
Loweswater, Kirkstile Inn
Mungrisdale, Mill Inn
Santon Bridge, Bridge Inn
Scales, White Horse
Seathwaite, Newfield Inn
Stonethwaite, Langstrath
Troutbeck, Queens Head
Ulverston, Bay Horse

DERBYSHIRE
Alderwasley, Bear
Brassington, Olde Gate
Foolow, Bulls Head
Froggatt Edge, Chequers
Hardwick Hall, Hardwick Inn
Hathersage, Plough, Scotsmans Pack
Hayfield, Lantern Pike
Kirk Ireton, Barley Mow
Ladybower Reservoir, Yorkshire Bridge
Litton, Red Lion
Monsal Head, Monsal Head Hotel
Over Haddon, Lathkil
Sheldon, Cock & Pullet
Woolley Moor, White Horse

DEVON
Branscombe, Fountain Head
Buckland Monachorum, Drake Manor
Culmstock, Culm Valley
East Budleigh, Sir Walter Raleigh
Exminster, Turf Hotel
Haytor Vale, Rock
Holne, Church House
Horndon, Elephants Nest
Iddesleigh, Duke of York
Kingston, Dolphin
Lower Ashton, Manor Inn
Lustleigh, Cleave
Lydford, Castle Inn
Molland, London
Parracombe, Fox & Goose
Peter Tavy, Peter Tavy Inn
Postbridge, Warren House
Rattery, Church House
Sandy Park, Sandy Park Inn
Slapton, Tower
Widecombe, Rugglestone
Wonson, Northmore Arms

DORSET
East Chaldon, Sailors Return
Marshwood, Bottle
Nettlecombe, Marquis of Lorne
Osmington Mills, Smugglers
Pamphill, Vine
Plush, Brace of Pheasants
Worth Matravers, Square & Compass

ESSEX
Mill Green, Viper

GLOUCESTERSHIRE
Ashleworth Quay, Boat
Bisley, Bear
Bledington, Kings Head
Chedworth, Seven Tuns
Chipping Campden, Eight Bells
Eastleach Turville, Victoria
Frampton on Severn, Bell
Guiting Power, Hollow Bottom
Miserden, Carpenters Arms
Nailsworth, Weighbridge
Newland, Ostrich
Sapperton, Bell

HAMPSHIRE
Fritham, Royal Oak
Hawkley, Hawkley Inn
Lymington, Kings Head
Ovington, Bush
Tichborne, Tichborne Arms

HEREFORDSHIRE
Aymestrey, Riverside Inn
Dorstone, Pandy
Hoarwithy, New Harp
Sellack, Lough Pool
Titley, Stagg
Walterstone, Carpenters Arms
Woolhope, Butchers Arms

HERTFORDSHIRE
Aldbury, Greyhound
Frithsden, Alford Arms
Sarratt, Cock

ISLE OF WIGHT
Hulverstone, Sun

KENT
Brookland, Woolpack
Chiddingstone, Castle Inn
Groombridge, Crown
Newnham, George
Selling, Rose & Crown
Stowting, Tiger

LANCASHIRE
Bury, Lord Raglan
Little Eccleston, Cartford
Newton, Parkers Arms
Sawley, Spread Eagle
Tunstall, Lunesdale Arms
Uppermill, Church Inn
Whitewell, Inn at Whitewell

LEICESTERSHIRE AND RUTLAND
Barrowden, Exeter Arms
Exton, Fox & Hounds

LINCOLNSHIRE
Dry Doddington, Wheatsheaf

NORFOLK
Blakeney, White Horse
Brancaster Staithe, Jolly Sailors
Burnham Market, Hoste Arms
Holkham, Victoria
Thornham, Lifeboat
Woodbastwick, Fur & Feather

NORTHUMBRIA
Blanchland, Lord Crewe Arms
Diptonmill, Dipton Mill Inn

Great Whittington, Queens Head
Haltwhistle, Milecastle Inn
Langley on Tyne, Carts Bog Inn
Newton-by-the-Sea, Ship
Romaldkirk, Rose & Crown
Stannersburn, Pheasant
Wark, Battlesteads

NOTTINGHAMSHIRE
Halam, Waggon & Horses
Laxton, Dovecote

OXFORDSHIRE
Checkendon, Black Horse
Coleshill, Radnor Arms
Great Tew, Falkland Arms
Kelmscott, Plough
Langford, Bell
Oxford, Turf Tavern

SHROPSHIRE
Bridges, Horseshoe
Cardington, Royal Oak
Picklescott, Bottle & Glass

SOMERSET
Appley, Globe
Axbridge, Lamb
Batcombe, Three Horseshoes
Cranmore, Strode Arms
Crowcombe, Carew Arms
Exford, White Horse
Luxborough, Royal Oak
Tarr, Tarr Farm
Triscombe, Blue Ball
Wells, City Arms

STAFFORDSHIRE
Alstonefield, George
Stourton, Fox

SUFFOLK
Dennington, Queens Head
Dunwich, Ship
Lavenham, Angel
Newbourne, Fox
Walberswick, Bell

SURREY
Blackbrook, Plough
Esher, Marneys
Forest Green, Parrot
Friday Street, Stephan Langton
Lingfield, Hare & Hounds
Mickleham, King William IV
Reigate Heath, Skimmington Castle

SUSSEX
Alfriston, George
Amberley, Black Horse
Burpham, George & Dragon
Chilgrove, Royal Oak, White Horse
Ditchling, Bull
East Dean, Tiger
Fletching, Griffin
Heathfield, Star
Rye, Mermaid
Wineham, Royal Oak

WARWICKSHIRE
Edge Hill, Castle
Priors Marston, Holly Bush

WILTSHIRE
Axford, Red Lion
Donhead St Andrew, Forester
East Knoyle, Fox Hounds
Ebbesbourne Wake, Horseshoe
Lacock, Rising Sun
Newton Tony, Malet Arms
Stourton, Spread Eagle

WORCESTERSHIRE
Berrow Green, Admiral Rodney
Broadway, Crown & Trumpet
Hanley Swan, Swan
Kidderminster, King & Castle
Knightwick, Talbot
Pensax, Bell

YORKSHIRE
Beck Hole, Birch Hall
Blakey Ridge, Lion
Bradfield, Strines Inn
Chapel le Dale, Hill Inn
Cray, White Lion
East Witton, Blue Lion
Grinton, Bridge Inn
Halifax, Shibden Mill
Heath, Kings Arms
Langthwaite, Charles Bathurst
Lastingham, Blacksmiths Arms
Linton in Craven, Fountaine
Litton, Queens Arms
Lund, Wellington
Middleham, Black Swan
Osmotherley, Golden Lion
Ripley, Boars Head
Robin Hood's Bay, Laurel
Shelley, Three Acres
South Dalton, Pipe & Glass
Thornton in Lonsdale, Marton Arms
Thornton Watlass, Buck
Wath in Nidderdale, Sportsmans Arms
Widdop, Pack Horse

LONDON
Central London, Olde Mitre
North London, Spaniards Inn
South London, Crown & Greyhound

SCOTLAND
Applecross, Applecross Inn
Gairloch, Old Inn
Kilberry, Kilberry Inn
Kilmahog, Lade
Kingholm Quay, Swan
Kirk Yetholm, Border
Stein, Stein Inn

WALES
Abergorlech, Black Lion
Capel Curig, Bryn Tyrch
Crickhowell, Nantyffin Cider Mill
Llanarmon Dyffryn Ceiriog, Hand
Llanberis, Pen-y-Gwryd
Llangedwyn, Green Inn
Old Radnor, Harp
Red Wharf Bay, Ship
Rhyd-y-Meirch, Goose & Cuckoo
Tintern, Cherry Tree

CHANNEL ISLANDS
St Brelade, Old Portelet Inn, Old Smugglers
St John, Les Fontaines

PUBS WITH GOOD VIEWS

These pubs are listed for their particularly good views, either from inside or from a garden or terrace. Waterside pubs are listed again here only if their view is exceptional in its own right – not just a straightforward sea view for example.

BUCKINGHAMSHIRE
Oving, Black Boy
Penn, Crown

CHESHIRE
Higher Burwardsley, Pheasant
Langley, Hanging Gate

CORNWALL
Falmouth, 5 Degrees West
Sennen Cove, Old Success
St Agnes, Turks Head
St Anns Chapel, Rifle Volunteer

CUMBRIA
Cartmel Fell, Masons Arms
Hawkshead, Drunken Duck
Langdale, Old Dungeon Ghyll
Loweswater, Kirkstile Inn
Mungrisdale, Mill Inn
Stonethwaite, Langstrath
Troutbeck, Queens Head
Ulverston, Bay Horse

DERBYSHIRE
Alderwasley, Bear
Foolow, Bulls Head
Monsal Head, Monsal Head Hotel
Over Haddon, Lathkil

DEVON
Brixham, Maritime
Newton Ferrers, Dolphin
Portgate, Harris Arms
Postbridge, Warren House
Sidbury, Hare & Hounds
Strete, Kings Arms

DORSET
Worth Matravers, Square & Compass

ISLE OF WIGHT
Bembridge, Crab & Lobster
Hulverstone, Sun
Ventnor, Spyglass

KENT
Tunbridge Wells, Beacon
Ulcombe, Pepper Box

LANCASHIRE
Bury, Lord Raglan
Newton, Parkers Arms
Sawley, Spread Eagle
Uppermill, Church Inn

NORFOLK
Brancaster Staithe, White Horse

NORTHUMBRIA
Anick, Rat
Seahouses, Olde Ship

OXFORDSHIRE
Swerford, Masons Arms

SOMERSET
Portishead, Windmill

Shepton Montague, Montague Inn
Tarr, Tarr Farm

SUFFOLK
Erwarton, Queens Head

SURREY
Mickleham, King William IV

SUSSEX
Byworth, Black Horse
Elsted, Three Horseshoes
Fletching, Griffin
Icklesham, Queens Head

WILTSHIRE
Axford, Red Lion
Box, Quarrymans Arms
Donhead St Andrew, Forester
East Knoyle, Fox Hounds
Lacock, Rising Sun

WORCESTERSHIRE
Malvern, Nags Head
Pensax, Bell

YORKSHIRE
Blakey Ridge, Lion
Bradfield, Strines Inn
Kirkham, Stone Trough
Langthwaite, Charles Bathurst
Litton, Queens Arms
Shelley, Three Acres
Whitby, Duke of York

LONDON
South London, Founders Arms

SCOTLAND
Applecross, Applecross Inn
Badachro, Badachro Inn
Edinburgh, Starbank
Glenelg, Glenelg Inn
Kilberry, Kilberry Inn
Shieldaig, Tigh an Eilean Hotel
Stein, Stein Inn
Ullapool, Ferry Boat
Weem, Ailean Chraggan

WALES
Aberdovey, Penhelig Arms
Capel Curig, Bryn Tyrch
Colwyn Bay, Pen-y-Bryn
Llanberis, Pen-y-Gwryd
Llanferres, Druid
Llangollen, Corn Mill
Llannefydd, Hawk & Buckle
Mold, Glasfryn
Old Radnor, Harp
Overton Bridge, Cross Foxes
Rhyd-y-Meirch, Goose & Cuckoo
Ty'n-y-groes, Groes

CHANNEL ISLANDS
St Aubin, Old Court House Inn

PUBS IN INTERESTING BUILDINGS

Pubs and inns are listed here for the particular interest of their building – something really out of the ordinary to look at, or occasionally a building that has an outstandingly interesting historical background.

BUCKINGHAMSHIRE
Aylesbury, Kings Head
Forty Green, Royal Standard of England

DERBYSHIRE
Kirk Ireton, Barley Mow

DEVON
Dartmouth, Cherub
Rattery, Church House

ESSEX
Great Yeldham, White Hart

LANCASHIRE
Liverpool, Philharmonic Dining Rooms

LINCOLNSHIRE
Stamford, George of Stamford

NORTHUMBRIA
Blanchland, Lord Crewe Arms
Newcastle upon Tyne, Crown Posada

NOTTINGHAMSHIRE
Nottingham, Olde Trip to Jerusalem

OXFORDSHIRE
Banbury, Reindeer
Fyfield, White Hart

SOMERSET
Norton St Philip, George

SUFFOLK
Laxfield, Kings Head

SURREY
Elstead, Mill at Elstead

SUSSEX
Rye, Mermaid

WILTSHIRE
Salisbury, Haunch of Venison

WORCESTERSHIRE
Bretforton, Fleece

YORKSHIRE
Hull, Olde White Harte

LONDON
Central London, Black Friar, Cittie of Yorke, Red Lion
South London, George

SCOTLAND
Edinburgh, Café Royal, Guildford Arms

PUBS THAT BREW THEIR OWN BEER

The pubs listed here brew their own beer on the premises; many others not listed have beers brewed for them specially, sometimes an individual recipe (but by a separate brewer). We mention these in the text.

CAMBRIDGESHIRE
Peterborough, Brewery Tap

CUMBRIA
Cockermouth, Bitter End
Hawkshead, Drunken Duck
Hesket Newmarket, Old Crown
Loweswater, Kirkstile Inn

DERBYSHIRE
Derby, Brunswick
Melbourne, John Thompson

DEVON
Branscombe, Fountain Head

HAMPSHIRE
Cheriton, Flower Pots

HEREFORDSHIRE
Hereford, Victory

KENT
West Peckham, Swan on the Green

LANCASHIRE
Bury, Lord Raglan
Little Eccleston, Cartford
Manchester, Marble Arch
Uppermill, Church Inn
Wheelton, Dressers Arms

LEICESTERSHIRE AND RUTLAND
Barrowden, Exeter Arms
Oakham, Grainstore

LINCOLNSHIRE
South Witham, Blue Cow

NORTHUMBRIA
Diptonmill, Dipton Mill Inn
Newburn, Keelman

NOTTINGHAMSHIRE
Caythorpe, Black Horse
Nottingham, Fellows Morton & Clayton

SHROPSHIRE
Bishop's Castle, Six Bells

STAFFORDSHIRE
Burton upon Trent, Burton Bridge Inn

SUFFOLK
South Elmham, St Peters Brewery

SURREY
Coldharbour, Plough

WARWICKSHIRE
Sedgley, Beacon

WORCESTERSHIRE
Knightwick, Talbot

YORKSHIRE
Cropton, New Inn
Goose Eye, Turkey
Linthwaite, Sair
Litton, Queens Arms
Sheffield, Fat Cat

SCOTLAND
Houston, Fox & Hounds
Kilmahog, Lade
Pitlochry, Moulin

WALES
Abercych, Nags Head
Llanddarog, White Hart

We list here all the pubs that have told us they
plan to stay open all day, even if it's only Saturday.
We've included the few pubs which close just for
half an hour to an hour, and the many more,
chiefly in holiday areas, which open all day only in
summer. The individual entries for the pubs
themselves show the actual details.

BEDFORDSHIRE
Bletsoe, Falcon
Henlow, Engineers Arms
Old Warden, Hare & Hounds
Stanbridge, Five Bells
Steppingley, French Horn

BERKSHIRE
Bray, Hinds Head
East Ilsley, Crown & Horns
Frilsham, Pot Kiln
Hurst, Green Man
Reading, Hobgoblin
Remenham, Little Angel
Ruscombe, Royal Oak
White Waltham, Beehive
Winterbourne, Winterbourne Arms
Yattendon, Royal Oak

BUCKINGHAMSHIRE
Aylesbury, Kings Head
Bennett End, Three Horseshoes
Bovingdon Green, Royal Oak
Chalfont St Giles, White Hart
Denham, Swan
Dorney, Palmer Arms
Easington, Mole & Chicken
Ford, Dinton Hermit
Forty Green, Royal Standard of England
Grove, Grove Lock
Hawridge Common, Full Moon
Hedgerley, White Horse
Ley Hill, Swan
Mentmore, Stag
Penn, Crown
Skirmett, Frog
Soulbury, Boot
Stoke Mandeville, Woolpack
Turville, Bull & Butcher
Wooburn Common, Chequers

CAMBRIDGESHIRE
Cambridge, Eagle
Elton, Black Horse
Godmanchester, Exhibition
Hemingford Grey, Cock
Huntingdon, Old Bridge Hotel
Kimbolton, New Sun
Longstowe, Red House
Peterborough, Brewery Tap, Charters

CHESHIRE
Aldford, Grosvenor Arms
Astbury, Egerton Arms
Aston, Bhurtpore
Barthomley, White Lion
Bunbury, Dysart Arms
Chester, Albion, Old Harkers Arms
Cotebrook, Fox & Barrel
Eaton, Plough
Haughton Moss, Nags Head

Higher Burwardsley, Pheasant
Langley, Hanging Gate
Macclesfield, Sutton Hall Hotel
Mobberley, Roebuck
Peover Heath, Dog
Prestbury, Legh Arms
Tarporley, Rising Sun
Wettenhall, Boot & Slipper
Wincle, Ship
Wrenbury, Dusty Miller

CORNWALL
Altarnun, Rising Sun
Blisland, Blisland Inn
Bodinnick, Old Ferry
Lostwithiel, Royal Oak
Mitchell, Plume of Feathers
Mithian, Miners Arms
Mylor Bridge, Pandora
Polkerris, Rashleigh
Polperro, Blue Peter
Port Isaac, Port Gaverne Inn
Porthleven, Ship
Porthtowan, Blue
Portmellon Cove, Rising Sun
Sennen Cove, Old Success
St Agnes, Turks Head
Tregadillett, Eliot Arms
Tresco, New Inn
Truro, Old Ale House
Zennor, Tinners Arms

CUMBRIA
Ambleside, Golden Rule
Armathwaite, Dukes Head
Bouth, White Hart
Brampton, New Inn
Broughton Mills, Blacksmiths Arms
Buttermere, Bridge Hotel
Cartmel, Kings Arms
Cartmel Fell, Masons Arms
Chapel Stile, Wainwrights
Cockermouth, Bitter End
Crosthwaite, Punch Bowl
Elterwater, Britannia
Hawkshead, Kings Arms, Queens Head
Ings, Watermill
Keswick, Dog & Gun
Langdale, Old Dungeon Ghyll
Levens, Strickland Arms
Little Langdale, Three Shires
Loweswater, Kirkstile Inn
Mungrisdale, Mill Inn
Near Sawrey, Tower Bank Arms
Santon Bridge, Bridge Inn
Scales, White Horse
Seathwaite, Newfield Inn
Staveley, Eagle & Child
Stonethwaite, Langstrath
Troutbeck, Queens Head
Ulverston, Bay Horse, Farmers Arms
Yanwath, Gate Inn

DERBYSHIRE
Alderwasley, Bear
Beeley, Devonshire Arms
Derby, Alexandra, Brunswick, Olde Dolphin
Fenny Bentley, Coach & Horses
Foolow, Bulls Head

Froggatt Edge, Chequers
Hardwick Hall, Hardwick Inn
Hathersage, Plough, Scotsmans Pack
Hayfield, Lantern Pike, Royal
Holbrook, Dead Poets
Hope, Cheshire Cheese
Ladybower Reservoir, Yorkshire Bridge
Litton, Red Lion
Monsal Head, Monsal Head Hotel
Over Haddon, Lathkil
Sheldon, Cock & Pullet
Wardlow, Three Stags Heads
Woolley Moor, White Horse

DEVON

Avonwick, Turtley Corn Mill
Branscombe, Masons Arms
Buckfast, Abbey Inn
Buckland Monachorum, Drake Manor
Cockwood, Anchor
Culmstock, Culm Valley
Dartmouth, Cherub
Exeter, Imperial
Exminster, Turf Hotel
Haytor Vale, Rock
Holbeton, Dartmoor Union
Iddesleigh, Duke of York
Lustleigh, Cleave
Lydford, Castle Inn
Marldon, Church House
Newton Abbot, Two Mile Oak
Nomansland, Mount Pleasant
Noss Mayo, Ship
Postbridge, Warren House
Poundsgate, Tavistock Inn
Rockbeare, Jack in the Green
Sandy Park, Sandy Park Inn
Sidbury, Hare & Hounds
Stoke Gabriel, Church House
Torbryan, Old Church House
Torcross, Start Bay
Tuckenhay, Maltsters Arms
Winkleigh, Kings Arms
Wonson, Northmore Arms
Woodbury Salterton, Diggers Rest
Woodland, Rising Sun
Yealmpton, Rose & Crown

DORSET

Cerne Abbas, Royal Oak
East Chaldon, Sailors Return
Middlemarsh, Hunters Moon
Mudeford, Ship in Distress
Osmington Mills, Smugglers
Poole, Cow
Sherborne, Digby Tap
Tarrant Monkton, Langton Arms
Worth Matravers, Square & Compass

ESSEX

Burnham-on-Crouch, White Harte
Castle Hedingham, Bell
Chappel, Swan
Chelmsford, Alma
Clavering, Cricketers
Dedham, Sun
Fingringhoe, Whalebone
Great Henny, Henny Swan
Great Yeldham, White Hart

Langham, Shepherd & Dog
Little Braxted, Green Man
Little Walden, Crown
Mill Green, Viper
Peldon, Rose
Rickling Green, Cricketers Arms
Stock, Hoop
Stow Maries, Prince of Wales
Youngs End, Green Dragon

GLOUCESTERSHIRE

Almondsbury, Bowl
Awre, Red Hart
Barnsley, Village Pub
Bledington, Kings Head
Box, Halfway House
Brimpsfield, Golden Heart
Chedworth, Seven Tuns
Chipping Campden, Eight Bells, Volunteer
Cowley, Green Dragon
Didmarton, Kings Arms
Dursley, Old Spot
Ewen, Wild Duck
Fairford, Bull
Ford, Plough
Guiting Power, Hollow Bottom
Littleton-upon-Severn, White Hart
Lower Oddington, Fox
Miserden, Carpenters Arms
Nailsworth, Egypt Mill, Weighbridge
Oldbury-on-Severn, Anchor
Prestbury, Royal Oak
Tetbury, Gumstool, Snooty Fox
Upper Oddington, Horse & Groom

HAMPSHIRE

Bank, Oak
Bentley, Bull
Bentworth, Sun
Boldre, Red Lion
Braishfield, Wheatsheaf
Chalton, Red Lion
Chawton, Greyfriar
Easton, Chestnut Horse
Fritham, Royal Oak
Littleton, Running Horse
Lower Wield, Yew Tree
Lymington, Kings Head
Monxton, Black Swan
Portsmouth, Still & West
Rotherwick, Falcon
Rowland's Castle, Castle Inn
Southsea, Wine Vaults
Stockbridge, Grosvenor
Wherwell, Mayfly
Winchester, Wykeham Arms

HEREFORDSHIRE

Bodenham, Englands Gate
Dorstone, Pandy
Hereford, Victory
Hoarwithy, New Harp
Ledbury, Feathers
Lugwardine, Crown & Anchor
Walford, Mill Race
Walterstone, Carpenters Arms

HERTFORDSHIRE

Aldbury, Greyhound, Valiant Trooper
Ashwell, Three Tuns

Batford, Gibraltar Castle
Chapmore End, Woodman
Cottered, Bull
Frithsden, Alford Arms
Hertford, White Horse
Royston, Old Bull
Sarratt, Cock

ISLE OF WIGHT
Arreton, White Lion
Bembridge, Crab & Lobster
Cowes, Folly
Hulverstone, Sun
Seaview, Seaview Hotel
Ventnor, Spyglass

KENT
Bough Beech, Wheatsheaf
Brookland, Woolpack
Chiddingstone, Castle Inn
Groombridge, Crown
Hawkhurst, Queens
Hollingbourne, Windmill
Langton Green, Hare
Newnham, George
Penshurst, Bottle House
Pluckley, Mundy Bois
Selling, Rose & Crown
Shipbourne, Chaser
Stodmarsh, Red Lion
Tunbridge Wells, Beacon, Sankeys
West Peckham, Swan on the Green

LANCASHIRE
Barnston, Fox & Hounds
Belmont, Black Dog
Bispham Green, Eagle & Child
Bury, Lord Raglan
Chipping, Dog & Partridge
Fence, Fence Gate
Goosnargh, Horns
Great Mitton, Three Fishes
Lancaster, Sun
Little Eccleston, Cartford
Liverpool, Philharmonic Dining Rooms
Longridge, Derby Arms
Lydgate, White Hart
Lytham, Taps
Manchester, Britons Protection, Dukes 92,
    Marble Arch
Newton, Parkers Arms
Ribchester, White Bull
Rimington, Black Bull
Stalybridge, Station Buffet
Uppermill, Church Inn
Wheelton, Dressers Arms
Whitewell, Inn at Whitewell
Yealand Conyers, New Inn

LEICESTERSHIRE AND RUTLAND
Ab Kettleby, Sugar Loaf
Clipsham, Olive Branch
Empingham, White Horse
Knossington, Fox & Hounds
Long Clawson, Crown & Plough
Mowsley, Staff of Life
Newton Burgoland, Belper Arms
Oadby, Cow & Plough
Oakham, Grainstore
Somerby, Three Crowns

Stathern, Red Lion
Stretton, Ram Jam Inn
Swithland, Griffin
Wing, Kings Arms

LINCOLNSHIRE
Lincoln, Victoria, Wig & Mitre
Rothwell, Blacksmiths Arms
South Witham, Blue Cow
Stamford, George of Stamford
Surfleet, Mermaid
Woolsthorpe, Chequers

NORFOLK
Bawburgh, Kings Head
Blakeney, Kings Arms
Brancaster Staithe, Jolly Sailors, White Horse
Burnham Market, Hoste Arms
Cawston, Ratcatchers
Holkham, Victoria
Larling, Angel
Morston, Anchor
Norwich, Adam & Eve, Fat Cat
Old Buckenham, Gamekeeper
Ringstead, Gin Trap
Snettisham, Rose & Crown
Swanton Morley, Darbys
Thornham, Lifeboat
Tivetshall St Mary, Old Ram
Wells-next-the-Sea, Crown
Winterton-on-Sea, Fishermans Return
Woodbastwick, Fur & Feather

NORTHAMPTONSHIRE
Badby, Windmill
Great Brington, Fox & Hounds/Althorp
Kilsby, George
Lowick, Snooty Fox
Nether Heyford, Olde Sun
Oundle, Ship
Wadenhoe, Kings Head
Woodnewton, White Swan

NORTHUMBRIA
Anick, Rat
Blanchland, Lord Crewe Arms
Carterway Heads, Manor House Inn
Greta Bridge, Morritt Arms
Haltwhistle, Milecastle Inn
Langley on Tyne, Carts Bog Inn
Lucker, Apple
New York, Shiremoor Farm
Newburn, Keelman
Newcastle upon Tyne, Crown Posada,
    Head of Steam @ The Cluny
Newton-by-the-Sea, Ship
Newton-on-the-Moor, Cook & Barker Arms
Seahouses, Olde Ship
Stannington, Ridley Arms
Wark, Battlesteads
Weldon Bridge, Anglers Arms

NOTTINGHAMSHIRE
Beeston, Victoria
Caunton, Caunton Beck
Halam, Waggon & Horses
Morton, Full Moon
Nottingham, Bell, Fellows Morton & Clayton,
    Lincolnshire Poacher, Olde Trip to Jerusalem,
    Vat & Fiddle

OXFORDSHIRE
Banbury, Reindeer
Chipping Norton, Chequers
Crowell, Shepherds Crook
East Hendred, Eyston Arms
Fyfield, White Hart
Godstow, Trout
Great Tew, Falkland Arms
Henley, Anchor
Highmoor, Rising Sun
Kelmscott, Plough
Kingston Blount, Cherry Tree
Oxford, Turf Tavern

SHROPSHIRE
Bishop's Castle, Six Bells, Three Tuns
Bridges, Horseshoe
Bromfield, Clive/Cookhouse
Chetwynd Aston, Fox
Ironbridge, Malthouse
Little Stretton, Ragleth
Ludlow, Church Inn, Unicorn
Much Wenlock, George & Dragon
Shrewsbury, Armoury
Wentnor, Crown

SOMERSET
Axbridge, Lamb
Bath, Old Green Tree, Star
Bleadon, Queens Arms
Chew Magna, Bear & Swan
Churchill, Crown
Clapton-in-Gordano, Black Horse
Congresbury, White Hart
Crowcombe, Carew Arms
Exford, White Horse
Holcombe, Ring o' Roses
Huish Episcopi, Rose & Crown
Norton St Philip, George
Portishead, Windmill
Stanton Wick, Carpenters Arms
Wells, City Arms, Crown
Withypool, Royal Oak

STAFFORDSHIRE
Abbots Bromley, Goats Head
Alstonefield, George
Hoar Cross, Meynell Ingram Arms
Lichfield, Boat
Salt, Holly Bush
Stourton, Fox

SUFFOLK
Bury St Edmunds, Nutshell
Chelmondiston, Butt & Oyster
Cotton, Trowel & Hammer
Dunwich, Ship
Lavenham, Angel
Long Melford, Black Lion
Nayland, Anchor
Rougham, Ravenwood Hall
South Elmham, St Peters Brewery
Southwold, Harbour Inn, Lord Nelson
Stoke-by-Nayland, Angel, Crown
Walberswick, Bell
Waldringfield, Maybush

SURREY
Betchworth, Dolphin
Blackbrook, Plough

Charleshill, Donkey
Cobham, Plough
Coldharbour, Plough
Eashing, Stag
Elstead, Mill at Elstead
Esher, Marneys
Forest Green, Parrot
Friday Street, Stephan Langton
Laleham, Three Horseshoes
Lingfield, Hare & Hounds
Mickleham, King William IV, Running Horses
Newdigate, Surrey Oaks
Ottershaw, Castle
Reigate Heath, Skimmington Castle
West End, Inn at West End
West Horsley, Barley Mow
Worplesdon, Jolly Farmer

SUSSEX
Alfriston, George
Amberley, Black Horse
Arlington, Old Oak
Berwick, Cricketers Arms
Blackboys, Blackboys Inn
Brighton, Greys
Burpham, George & Dragon
Charlton, Fox Goes Free
Chiddingly, Six Bells
Coolham, George & Dragon
Ditchling, Bull
Donnington, Blacksmiths Arms
East Dean, Star & Garter, Tiger
East Hoathly, Foresters Arms
Fittleworth, Swan
Fletching, Griffin
Hermitage, Sussex Brewery
Horsham, Black Jug
Icklesham, Queens Head
Lodsworth, Halfway Bridge Inn
Oving, Gribble Inn
Rye, Mermaid
Singleton, Partridge
Wilmington, Giants Rest

WARWICKSHIRE
Aston Cantlow, Kings Head
Birmingham, Old Joint Stock
Brierley Hill, Vine
Easenhall, Golden Lion
Edge Hill, Castle
Farnborough, Inn at Farnborough
Gaydon, Malt Shovel
Long Itchington, Duck on the Pond
Netherton, Old Swan
Preston Bagot, Crabmill
Shipston-on-Stour, White Bear
Welford-on-Avon, Bell

WILTSHIRE
Box, Quarrymans Arms
Devizes, Bear
Fonthill Gifford, Beckford Arms
Hindon, Lamb
Lacock, George, Red Lion, Rising Sun
Luckington, Old Royal Ship
Malmesbury, Smoking Dog
Norton, Vine Tree
Salisbury, Haunch of Venison
Seend, Barge

Stourton, Spread Eagle
Whitley, Pear Tree

WORCESTERSHIRE
Baughton, Jockey
Berrow Green, Admiral Rodney
Bewdley, Little Pack Horse
Bretforton, Fleece
Broadway, Crown & Trumpet
Clent, Fountain
Hanley Swan, Swan
Kempsey, Walter de Cantelupe
Kidderminster, King & Castle
Knightwick, Talbot
Malvern, Nags Head
Pensax, Bell

YORKSHIRE
Asenby, Crab & Lobster
Beck Hole, Birch Hall
Beverley, White Horse
Blakey Ridge, Lion
Boroughbridge, Black Bull
Bradfield, Strines Inn
Burn, Wheatsheaf
Cray, White Lion
Crayke, Durham Ox
Cropton, New Inn
East Witton, Blue Lion
Elslack, Tempest Arms
Ferrensby, General Tarleton
Goose Eye, Turkey
Grinton, Bridge Inn
Halifax, Shibden Mill
Harome, Star
Heath, Kings Arms
Hull, Minerva, Olde White Harte
Kettlesing, Queens Head
Kirkbymoorside, George & Dragon
Langthwaite, Charles Bathurst
Lastingham, Blacksmiths Arms
Ledsham, Chequers
Leeds, Whitelocks
Linthwaite, Sair
Linton, Windmill
Linton in Craven, Fountaine
Low Catton, Gold Cup
Masham, Black Sheep Brewery
Middleham, Black Swan, White Swan
Mill Bank, Millbank
Osmotherley, Golden Lion
Pickering, White Swan
Pickhill, Nags Head
Ripley, Boars Head
Ripponden, Old Bridge
Robin Hood's Bay, Laurel
Sheffield, Fat Cat, New Barrack
South Dalton, Pipe & Glass
Thornton in Lonsdale, Marton Arms
Thornton Watlass, Buck
Whitby, Duke of York
Widdop, Pack Horse

LONDON
Central London, Admiral Codrington, Albert,
Argyll Arms, Black Friar, Cittie of Yorke,
Coopers Arms, Cross Keys, Dog & Duck, Eagle,
Grapes, Grenadier, Guinea, Jerusalem Tavern,
Lamb, Lamb & Flag, Lord Moon of the Mall,
Nags Head, Old Bank of England,
Olde Cheshire Cheese, Olde Mitre,
Princess Louise, Red Lion (both pubs),
Seven Stars, Star, Westminster Arms
East London, Grapes, Prospect of Whitby
North London, Chapel, Compton Arms,
Drapers Arms, Duke of Cambridge, Flask,
Holly Bush, Olde White Bear, Spaniards Inn
South London, Anchor & Hope,
Crown & Greyhound, Cutty Sark, Fire Station,
Founders Arms, Fox & Hounds, George,
Market Porter, Royal Oak, Victoria,
White Cross
West London, Anglesea Arms (both pubs),
Atlas, Bulls Head, Churchill Arms, Dove,
Havelock Tavern, Portobello Gold, Warrington,
White Horse, Windsor Castle

SCOTLAND
Aberdeen, Prince of Wales
Aboyne, Boat
Applecross, Applecross Inn
Badachro, Badachro Inn
Broughty Ferry, Fishermans Tavern
East Linton, Drovers
Edinburgh, Abbotsford, Bow Bar, Café Royal,
Guildford Arms, Kays Bar, Starbank
Elie, Ship
Gairloch, Old Inn
Glasgow, Babbity Bowster, Bon Accord,
Counting House
Houston, Fox & Hounds
Inveraray, George
Isle of Whithorn, Steam Packet
Kilmahog, Lade
Kingholm Quay, Swan
Kippen, Cross Keys
Kirk Yetholm, Border
Linlithgow, Four Marys
Lybster, Portland Arms
Pitlochry, Moulin
Plockton, Plockton Hotel
Shieldaig, Tigh an Eilean Hotel
Stein, Stein Inn
Swinton, Wheatsheaf
Tayvallich, Tayvallich Inn
Thornhill, Lion & Unicorn
Ullapool, Ferry Boat
Weem, Ailean Chraggan

WALES
Aberaeron, Harbourmaster
Abercych, Nags Head
Abergorlech, Black Lion
Beaumaris, Olde Bulls Head
Capel Curig, Bryn Tyrch
Colwyn Bay, Pen-y-Bryn
Cresswell Quay, Cresselly Arms
East Aberthaw, Blue Anchor
Gresford, Pant-yr-Ochain
Hay-on-Wye, Kilverts, Old Black Lion
Llanarmon Dyffryn Ceiriog, Hand
Llanberis, Pen-y-Gwryd
Llandudno Junction, Queens Head
Llanferres, Druid
Llangedwyn, Green Inn
Llangollen, Corn Mill
Mold, Glasfryn
Monknash, Plough & Harrow
Overton Bridge, Cross Foxes

Pembroke Ferry, Ferry Inn
Porthgain, Sloop
Presteigne, Radnorshire Arms
Raglan, Clytha Arms
Red Wharf Bay, Ship
Rhyd-y-Meirch, Goose & Cuckoo
Rosebush, Tafarn Sinc
Saundersfoot, Royal Oak
Shirenewton, Carpenters Arms
Skenfrith, Bell
St Hilary, Bush
Tintern, Cherry Tree
Ty'n-y-groes, Groes

CHANNEL ISLANDS
King's Mills, Fleur du Jardin
Rozel, Rozel
St Aubin, Old Court House Inn
St Brelade, Old Portelet Inn, Old Smugglers
St Helier, Town House
St John, Les Fontaines
St Ouens Bay, La Pulente

PUBS WITH NO SMOKING AREAS

We have listed all the pubs which told us they were already completely no smoking when the *Guide* went to press. Don't forget that all pubs in Scotland are now completely no smoking.

BEDFORDSHIRE
Bolnhurst, Plough
Keysoe, Chequers
Old Warden, Hare & Hounds
Woburn, Birch

BERKSHIRE
Ashmore Green, Sun in the Wood
Bray, Crown, Hinds Head
Frilsham, Pot Kiln
Kintbury, Dundas Arms
Remenham, Little Angel
Stanford Dingley, Bull, Old Boot
White Waltham, Beehive
Winterbourne, Winterbourne Arms
Yattendon, Royal Oak

BUCKINGHAMSHIRE
Aylesbury, Kings Head
Cadmore End, Old Ship
Dorney, Palmer Arms
Haddenham, Green Dragon
Oving, Black Boy

CAMBRIDGESHIRE
Cambridge, Cambridge Blue, Free Press
Fen Ditton, Ancient Shepherds
Fordham, White Pheasant
Hemingford Grey, Cock
St Neots, Chequers
Sutton Gault, Anchor
Thriplow, Green Man

CHESHIRE
Eaton, Plough

CORNWALL
Lanlivery, Crown
St Agnes, Turks Head
Tresco, New Inn

CUMBRIA
Beetham, Wheatsheaf
Bouth, White Hart
Buttermere, Bridge Hotel
Cartmel Fell, Masons Arms
Crosthwaite, Punch Bowl
Hawkshead, Drunken Duck
Little Langdale, Three Shires
Loweswater, Kirkstile Inn
Near Sawrey, Tower Bank Arms
Scales, White Horse
Stonethwaite, Langstrath
Yanwath, Gate Inn

DERBYSHIRE
Beeley, Devonshire Arms
Froggatt Edge, Chequers
Hardwick Hall, Hardwick Inn
Hassop, Eyre Arms
Hathersage, Plough

DEVON
Avonwick, Turtley Corn Mill
Branscombe, Fountain Head
Broadhembury, Drewe Arms
Haytor Vale, Rock
Lustleigh, Cleave
Marldon, Church House
Noss Mayo, Ship
Topsham, Bridge Inn

DORSET
Cerne Abbas, Royal Oak
Osmington Mills, Smugglers
Pamphill, Vine
Worth Matravers, Square & Compass

ESSEX
Clavering, Cricketers
Fingringhoe, Whalebone

GLOUCESTERSHIRE
Ashleworth, Queens Arms
Ashleworth Quay, Boat
Barnsley, Village Pub
Chipping Campden, Eight Bells
Nailsworth, Egypt Mill
Poulton, Falcon
Prestbury, Royal Oak
Sapperton, Bell

HAMPSHIRE
Bank, Oak
Bentley, Bull
Littleton, Running Horse
Rowland's Castle, Castle Inn

HEREFORDSHIRE
Ullingswick, Three Crowns

ISLE OF WIGHT
Bembridge, Crab & Lobster
Shalfleet, New Inn

KENT
Boyden Gate, Gate Inn
Langton Green, Hare

LANCASHIRE
Great Mitton, Three Fishes

LEICESTERSHIRE AND RUTLAND
Barrowden, Exeter Arms
Oadby, Cow & Plough

LINCOLNSHIRE
Belchford, Blue Bell

NORFOLK
Wells-next-the-Sea, Globe

NORTHAMPTONSHIRE
Fotheringhay, Falcon
Wadenhoe, Kings Head

NORTHUMBRIA
Haltwhistle, Milecastle Inn
Newton-by-the-Sea, Ship

NOTTINGHAMSHIRE
Halam, Waggon & Horses
Nottingham, Cock & Hoop

OXFORDSHIRE
Swerford, Masons Arms

SHROPSHIRE
Grinshill, Inn at Grinshill
Little Stretton, Ragleth
Munslow, Crown

SOMERSET
Langley Marsh, Three Horseshoes
Lovington, Pilgrims Rest

STAFFORDSHIRE
Kidsgrove, Blue Bell

SUFFOLK
Buxhall, Crown
Horringer, Beehive
Southwold, Crown

SURREY
Newdigate, Surrey Oaks

SUSSEX
Chilgrove, White Horse
Elsted, Three Horseshoes
Horsham, Black Jug
Salehurst, Salehurst Halt

WARWICKSHIRE
Easenhall, Golden Lion
Gaydon, Malt Shovel
Ilmington, Howard Arms
Long Itchington, Duck on the Pond

WILTSHIRE
Corsham, Flemish Weaver
Grittleton, Neeld Arms
Rowde, George & Dragon

WORCESTERSHIRE
Baughton, Jockey
Clent, Fountain

YORKSHIRE
Alne, Blue Bell
Appleton-le-Moors, Moors
Asenby, Crab & Lobster
Constable Burton, Wyvill Arms
Cray, White Lion
Felixkirk, Carpenters Arms
Ferrensby, General Tarleton
Hetton, Angel
Kettlesing, Queens Head
Leyburn, Sandpiper
Ripley, Boars Head
Shelley, Three Acres
Thornton in Lonsdale, Marton Arms

LONDON
Central London, Black Friar

WALES
Gresford, Pant-yr-Ochain
Hay-on-Wye, Kilverts
Presteigne, Radnorshire Arms
Tintern, Cherry Tree

CHANNEL ISLANDS
King's Mills, Fleur du Jardin

PUBS CLOSE TO MOTORWAY JUNCTIONS

The number at the start of each line is the number of the junction. Detailed directions are given in the main entry for each pub. In this section, to help you find the pubs quickly before you're past the junction, we give the name of the chapter where you'll find the text.

M1
13: Woburn, Birch (Beds) 3.5 miles
16: Nether Heyford, Olde Sun (Northants) 1.8 miles
18: Crick, Red Lion (Northants) 1 mile; Kilsby, George (Northants) 2.6 miles
29: Hardwick Hall, Hardwick Inn (Derbys) 3 miles

M3
3: West End, Inn at West End (Surrey) 2.4 miles
5: Rotherwick, Falcon (Hants) 4 miles
9: Easton, Chestnut Horse (Hants) 3.6 miles
10: Winchester, Black Boy (Hants) 1 mile

M4
7: Dorney, Pineapple (Bucks) 2.4 miles; Dorney, Palmer Arms (Bucks) 2.7 miles
8: Oakley Green, Olde Red Lion (Berks) 4 miles
9: Bray, Crown (Berks) 1.75 miles; Bray, Hinds Head (Berks) 1.75 miles
11: Shinfield, Magpie & Parrot (Berks) 2.6 miles
13: Winterbourne, Winterbourne Arms (Berks) 3.7 miles
17: Norton, Vine Tree (Wilts) 4 miles

M5
4: Holy Cross, Bell & Cross (Worcs) 4 miles; Crowle, Old Chequers (Worcs) 2 miles
7: Kempsey, Walter de Cantelupe (Worcs) 3.75 miles
9: Bredon, Fox & Hounds (Worcs) 4.5 miles
13: Frampton on Severn, Bell (Glos) 3 miles
16: Almondsbury, Bowl (Glos) 1.25 miles
19: Portishead, Windmill (Somerset) 3.7 miles; Clapton-in-Gordano, Black Horse (Somerset) 4 miles
26: Clayhidon, Merry Harriers (Devon) 3.1 miles
28: Broadhembury, Drewe Arms (Devon) 5 miles
30: Topsham, Bridge Inn (Devon) 2.25 miles; Woodbury Salterton, Diggers Rest (Devon) 3.5 miles

M6
4: Shustoke, Griffin (Warwicks) 5 miles
T6: Lichfield, Boat (Staffs) 2.7 miles
16: Barthomley, White Lion (Cheshire) 1 mile
33: Bay Horse, Bay Horse (Lancs) 1.2 miles
35: Yealand Conyers, New Inn (Lancs) 3 miles
36: Levens, Strickland Arms (Cumbria) 4 miles
40: Yanwath, Gate Inn (Cumbria) 2.25 miles

M9

3: Linlithgow, Four Marys (Scotland) 2 miles

M11

7: Hastingwood, Rainbow & Dove (Essex) 0.25 miles

8: Birchanger, Three Willows (Essex) 0.8 miles

9: Hinxton, Red Lion (Cambs) 2 miles

10: Thriplow, Green Man (Cambs) 3 miles

M20

8: Hollingbourne, Windmill (Kent) 1 mile

11: Stowting, Tiger (Kent) 3.7 miles

M25

8: Reigate Heath, Skimmington Castle (Surrey) 3 miles

10: Cobham, Plough (Surrey) 3.2 miles

11: Ottershaw, Castle (Surrey) 2.6 miles

13: Laleham, Three Horseshoes (Surrey) 5 miles

16: Denham, Swan (Bucks) 0.75 miles

18: Chenies, Red Lion (Bucks) 2 miles

21A: Potters Crouch, Holly Bush (Herts) 2.3 miles

M27

1: Fritham, Royal Oak (Hants) 4 miles

M40

2: Hedgerley, White Horse (Bucks) 2.4 miles; Forty Green, Royal Standard of England (Bucks) 3.5 miles

6: Lewknor, Olde Leathern Bottel (Oxon) 0.5 miles; Kingston Blount, Cherry Tree (Oxon) 1.9 miles; Crowell, Shepherds Crook (Oxon) 2 miles

12: Gaydon, Malt Shovel (Warwicks) 0.9 miles

M48

1: Littleton-upon-Severn, White Hart (Glos) 3.5 miles

M50

1: Baughton, Jockey (Worcs) 4 miles

3: Upton Bishop, Moody Cow (Herefs) 2 miles

M53

3: Barnston, Fox & Hounds (Lancs) 3 miles

M61

8: Wheelton, Dressers Arms (Lancs) 2.1 miles

M65

13: Fence, Fence Gate (Lancs) 2.6 miles

M66

1: Bury, Lord Raglan (Lancs) 2 miles

REPORT FORMS

REPORT FORMS

Please report to us: you can use the tear-out forms on the following pages, the card in the middle of the book, or just plain paper – whichever's easiest for you, or you can report to our website, **www.goodguides.co.uk**. We need to know what you think of the pubs in this edition. We need to know about other pubs worthy of inclusion. We need to know about ones that should not be included. And we need to know that vital factor – how good the landlord or landlady is.

The atmosphere and character of the pub are the most important features – why it would, or would not, appeal to strangers, so please try to describe what is special about it. In particular, we can't consider including a pub in the Lucky Dip section unless we know something about what it looks like inside, so that we can describe it to other readers. And obviously with existing entries, we need to know about any changes in décor and furnishings, too. But the bar food and the drink are also important – please tell us about them.

If the food is really quite outstanding, tick the FOOD AWARD box on the form, and tell us about the special quality that makes it stand out – the more detail, the better. And if you have stayed there, tell us about the standard of accommodation – whether it was comfortable, pleasant, good value for money. Again, if the pub or inn is worth special attention as a place to stay, tick the PLACE-TO-STAY AWARD box.

If you're in a position to gauge a pub's suitability or otherwise for **disabled people**, do please tell us about that.

Please try to gauge whether a pub should be a main entry, or is best as a Lucky Dip (and tick the relevant box). In general, main entries need qualities that would make it worth other readers' while to travel some distance to them; Lucky Dips are the pubs that are worth knowing about if you are nearby. But if a pub is an entirely new recommendation, the Lucky Dip may be the best place for it to start its career in the *Guide* – to encourage other readers to report on it.

The more detail you can put into your description of a Lucky Dip pub that's only scantily described in the current edition (or not in at all), the better. A description of its character and even furnishings is a tremendous boon.

It helps enormously if you can give the full address for any new pub – one not yet a main entry, or without a full address in the Lucky Dip sections. In a town, we need the street name; in the country, if it's hard to find, we need directions. Even better for us is the post code. If we can't find out a pub's post code, we no longer include it in the *Guide* – and the Post Office directories we use will not yet have caught up with new pubs, or ones which have changed their names. With any pub, it always helps to let us know about prices of food (and bedrooms, if there are any), and about any lunchtimes or evenings when food is not served. We'd also like to have your views on drinks quality – beer, wine, cider and so forth, even coffee and tea; and do let us know about bedrooms.

If you know that a Lucky Dip pub is open all day (or even late into the afternoon), please tell us – preferably saying which days.

When you go to a pub, don't tell them you're a reporter for the *Good Pub Guide*; we do make clear that all inspections are anonymous, and if you declare yourself as a reporter you risk getting special treatment – for better or for worse!

Sometimes pubs are dropped from the main entries simply because very few readers have written to us about them – and of course there's a risk that people may not write if they find the pub exactly as described in the entry. You can use the forms at the front of the batch of report forms just to list pubs you've been to, found as described, and can recommend.

When you write to The Good Pub Guide, FREEPOST TN1569, WADHURST, East Sussex TN5 7BR, you don't need a stamp in the UK. We'll gladly send you more forms (free) if you wish.

Though we try to answer all letters, please understand if there's a delay (particularly in summer, our busiest period). We now edit and inspect throughout the year, so reports are valuable at any time. Obviously it's most useful of all if you write soon after a pub visit, while everything's fresh in your mind, rather than storing things up for a later batch.

We'll assume we can print your name or initials as a recommender unless you tell us otherwise.

I have been to the following pubs in *The Good Pub Guide 2007* in the last few months, found them as described, and confirm that they deserve continued inclusion:

Continued overleaf

PLEASE GIVE YOUR NAME AND ADDRESS ON THE BACK OF THIS FORM

Pubs visited continued...

Your own name and address *(block capitals please)*

Postcode

Please return to
The Good Pub Guide,
FREEPOST TN1569,
WADHURST,
East Sussex
TN5 7BR

IF YOU PREFER, YOU CAN SEND US
REPORTS THROUGH OUR WEBSITE:
www.goodguides.co.uk

I have been to the following pubs in *The Good Pub Guide 2007* in the last few months, found them as described, and confirm that they deserve continued inclusion:

Continued overleaf

PLEASE GIVE YOUR NAME AND ADDRESS ON THE BACK OF THIS FORM

Pubs visited continued...

Your own name and address *(block capitals please)*

Postcode

**Please return to
The Good Pub Guide,
FREEPOST TN1569,
WADHURST,
East Sussex
TN5 7BR**

IF YOU PREFER, YOU CAN SEND US
REPORTS THROUGH OUR WEBSITE:
www.goodguides.co.uk

REPORT ON (PUB'S NAME)

Pub's address

☐ **YES** MAIN ENTRY   ☐ **YES** LUCKY DIP   ☐ **NO** DON'T INCLUDE
Please tick one of these boxes to show your verdict, and give reasons and descriptive
comments, prices etc

☐ DESERVES **FOOD** award   ☐ DESERVES **PLACE-TO-STAY** award   2007:1

PLEASE GIVE YOUR NAME AND ADDRESS ON THE BACK OF THIS FORM

✂ -

REPORT ON (PUB'S NAME)

Pub's address

☐ **YES** MAIN ENTRY   ☐ **YES** LUCKY DIP   ☐ **NO** DON'T INCLUDE
Please tick one of these boxes to show your verdict, and give reasons and descriptive
comments, prices etc

☐ DESERVES **FOOD** award   ☐ DESERVES **PLACE-TO-STAY** award   2007:2

PLEASE GIVE YOUR NAME AND ADDRESS ON THE BACK OF THIS FORM

Your own name and address *(block capitals please)*

In returning this form I confirm my agreement that the information I provide may be used by
The Random House Group Ltd, its assignees and/or licensees in any media or medium whatsoever.

DO NOT USE THIS SIDE OF THE PAGE FOR WRITING ABOUT PUBS

✂ ....

Your own name and address *(block capitals please)*

In returning this form I confirm my agreement that the information I provide may be used by
The Random House Group Ltd, its assignees and/or licensees in any media or medium whatsoever.

DO NOT USE THIS SIDE OF THE PAGE FOR WRITING ABOUT PUBS

IF YOU PREFER, YOU CAN SEND US REPORTS THROUGH OUR WEBSITE:
www.goodguides.co.uk

REPORT ON (PUB'S NAME)

Pub's address

☐ **YES** MAIN ENTRY ☐ **YES** LUCKY DIP ☐ **NO** DON'T INCLUDE
Please tick one of these boxes to show your verdict, and give reasons and descriptive comments, prices etc

☐ DESERVES **FOOD** award ☐ DESERVES **PLACE-TO-STAY** award 2007:3
PLEASE GIVE YOUR NAME AND ADDRESS ON THE BACK OF THIS FORM

✂

REPORT ON (PUB'S NAME)

Pub's address

☐ **YES** MAIN ENTRY ☐ **YES** LUCKY DIP ☐ **NO** DON'T INCLUDE
Please tick one of these boxes to show your verdict, and give reasons and descriptive comments, prices etc

☐ DESERVES **FOOD** award ☐ DESERVES **PLACE-TO-STAY** award 2007:4
PLEASE GIVE YOUR NAME AND ADDRESS ON THE BACK OF THIS FORM

Your own name and address *(block capitals please)*

In returning this form I confirm my agreement that the information I provide may be used by
The Random House Group Ltd, its assignees and/or licensees in any media or medium whatsoever.

DO NOT USE THIS SIDE OF THE PAGE FOR WRITING ABOUT PUBS

✂ ....

Your own name and address *(block capitals please)*

In returning this form I confirm my agreement that the information I provide may be used by
The Random House Group Ltd, its assignees and/or licensees in any media or medium whatsoever.

DO NOT USE THIS SIDE OF THE PAGE FOR WRITING ABOUT PUBS

IF YOU PREFER, YOU CAN SEND US REPORTS THROUGH OUR WEBSITE:
www.goodguides.co.uk

REPORT ON _____ (PUB'S NAME)

Pub's address _____

☐ **YES** MAIN ENTRY   ☐ **YES** LUCKY DIP   ☐ **NO** DON'T INCLUDE
Please tick one of these boxes to show your verdict, and give reasons and descriptive comments, prices etc

☐ DESERVES **FOOD award**   ☐ DESERVES **PLACE-TO-STAY award**   2007:5

PLEASE GIVE YOUR NAME AND ADDRESS ON THE BACK OF THIS FORM

✂ - - - - - - - - - -

REPORT ON _____ (PUB'S NAME)

Pub's address _____

☐ **YES** MAIN ENTRY   ☐ **YES** LUCKY DIP   ☐ **NO** DON'T INCLUDE
Please tick one of these boxes to show your verdict, and give reasons and descriptive comments, prices etc

☐ DESERVES **FOOD award**   ☐ DESERVES **PLACE-TO-STAY award**   2007:6

PLEASE GIVE YOUR NAME AND ADDRESS ON THE BACK OF THIS FORM

Your own name and address *(block capitals please)*

In returning this form I confirm my agreement that the information I provide may be used by
The Random House Group Ltd, its assignees and/or licensees in any media or medium whatsoever.

DO NOT USE THIS SIDE OF THE PAGE FOR WRITING ABOUT PUBS

✂

Your own name and address *(block capitals please)*

In returning this form I confirm my agreement that the information I provide may be used by
The Random House Group Ltd, its assignees and/or licensees in any media or medium whatsoever.

DO NOT USE THIS SIDE OF THE PAGE FOR WRITING ABOUT PUBS

IF YOU PREFER, YOU CAN SEND US REPORTS THROUGH OUR WEBSITE:
www.goodguides.co.uk

REPORT ON (PUB'S NAME)

Pub's address

☐ **YES** MAIN ENTRY ☐ **YES** LUCKY DIP ☐ **NO** DON'T INCLUDE
Please tick one of these boxes to show your verdict, and give reasons and descriptive
comments, prices etc

☐ DESERVES **FOOD award** ☐ DESERVES **PLACE-TO-STAY award** 2007:7

PLEASE GIVE YOUR NAME AND ADDRESS ON THE BACK OF THIS FORM

REPORT ON (PUB'S NAME)

Pub's address

☐ **YES** MAIN ENTRY ☐ **YES** LUCKY DIP ☐ **NO** DON'T INCLUDE
Please tick one of these boxes to show your verdict, and give reasons and descriptive
comments, prices etc

☐ DESERVES **FOOD award** ☐ DESERVES **PLACE-TO-STAY award** 2007:8

PLEASE GIVE YOUR NAME AND ADDRESS ON THE BACK OF THIS FORM

Your own name and address *(block capitals please)*

In returning this form I confirm my agreement that the information I provide may be used by
The Random House Group Ltd, its assignees and/or licensees in any media or medium whatsoever.

DO NOT USE THIS SIDE OF THE PAGE FOR WRITING ABOUT PUBS

✄ ···

Your own name and address *(block capitals please)*

In returning this form I confirm my agreement that the information I provide may be used by
The Random House Group Ltd, its assignees and/or licensees in any media or medium whatsoever.

DO NOT USE THIS SIDE OF THE PAGE FOR WRITING ABOUT PUBS

IF YOU PREFER, YOU CAN SEND US REPORTS THROUGH OUR WEBSITE:
www.goodguides.co.uk

REPORT ON (PUB'S NAME)

Pub's address

☐ **YES** MAIN ENTRY ☐ **YES** LUCKY DIP ☐ **NO** DON'T INCLUDE
Please tick one of these boxes to show your verdict, and give reasons and descriptive
comments, prices etc

☐ DESERVES **FOOD** award ☐ DESERVES **PLACE-TO-STAY** award 2007:9

PLEASE GIVE YOUR NAME AND ADDRESS ON THE BACK OF THIS FORM

✂ ···

REPORT ON (PUB'S NAME)

Pub's address

☐ **YES** MAIN ENTRY ☐ **YES** LUCKY DIP ☐ **NO** DON'T INCLUDE
Please tick one of these boxes to show your verdict, and give reasons and descriptive
comments, prices etc

☐ DESERVES **FOOD** award ☐ DESERVES **PLACE-TO-STAY** award 2007:10

PLEASE GIVE YOUR NAME AND ADDRESS ON THE BACK OF THIS FORM

Your own name and address *(block capitals please)*

In returning this form I confirm my agreement that the information I provide may be used by
The Random House Group Ltd, its assignees and/or licensees in any media or medium whatsoever.

DO NOT USE THIS SIDE OF THE PAGE FOR WRITING ABOUT PUBS

By returning this form, you consent to the collection, recording and use of the information you submit, by The Random House Group Ltd. Any personal details which you provide from which we can identify you are held and processed in accordance with the Data Protection Act 1998 and will not be passed on to any third parties. The Random House Group Ltd may wish to send you further information on their associated products. Please tick box if you do not wish to receive any such information.

✂ ··

Your own name and address *(block capitals please)*

In returning this form I confirm my agreement that the information I provide may be used by
The Random House Group Ltd, its assignees and/or licensees in any media or medium whatsoever.

DO NOT USE THIS SIDE OF THE PAGE FOR WRITING ABOUT PUBS

By returning this form, you consent to the collection, recording and use of the information you submit, by The Random House Group Ltd. Any personal details which you provide from which we can identify you are held and processed in accordance with the Data Protection Act 1998 and will not be passed on to any third parties. The Random House Group Ltd may wish to send you further information on their associated products. Please tick box if you do not wish to receive any such information.

IF YOU PREFER, YOU CAN SEND US REPORTS THROUGH OUR WEBSITE:
www.goodguides.co.uk

REPORT ON _____ (PUB'S NAME)

Pub's address _____

☐ **YES** MAIN ENTRY   ☐ **YES** LUCKY DIP   ☐ **NO** DON'T INCLUDE

Please tick one of these boxes to show your verdict, and give reasons and descriptive comments, prices etc

☐ DESERVES **FOOD** award ☐ DESERVES **PLACE-TO-STAY** award 2007:11

PLEASE GIVE YOUR NAME AND ADDRESS ON THE BACK OF THIS FORM

✂ -

REPORT ON _____ (PUB'S NAME)

Pub's address _____

☐ **YES** MAIN ENTRY   ☐ **YES** LUCKY DIP   ☐ **NO** DON'T INCLUDE

Please tick one of these boxes to show your verdict, and give reasons and descriptive comments, prices etc

☐ DESERVES **FOOD** award ☐ DESERVES **PLACE-TO-STAY** award 2007:12

PLEASE GIVE YOUR NAME AND ADDRESS ON THE BACK OF THIS FORM

Your own name and address *(block capitals please)*

In returning this form I confirm my agreement that the information I provide may be used by
The Random House Group Ltd, its assignees and/or licensees in any media or medium whatsoever.

DO NOT USE THIS SIDE OF THE PAGE FOR WRITING ABOUT PUBS

✂ ....

Your own name and address *(block capitals please)*

In returning this form I confirm my agreement that the information I provide may be used by
The Random House Group Ltd, its assignees and/or licensees in any media or medium whatsoever.

DO NOT USE THIS SIDE OF THE PAGE FOR WRITING ABOUT PUBS

IF YOU PREFER, YOU CAN SEND US REPORTS THROUGH OUR WEBSITE:
www.goodguides.co.uk

REPORT ON (PUB'S NAME)

Pub's address

☐ **YES** MAIN ENTRY ☐ **YES** LUCKY DIP ☐ **NO** DON'T INCLUDE
Please tick one of these boxes to show your verdict, and give reasons and descriptive comments, prices etc

☐ DESERVES **FOOD** award ☐ DESERVES **PLACE-TO-STAY** award 2007:13

PLEASE GIVE YOUR NAME AND ADDRESS ON THE BACK OF THIS FORM

✂

REPORT ON (PUB'S NAME)

Pub's address

☐ **YES** MAIN ENTRY ☐ **YES** LUCKY DIP ☐ **NO** DON'T INCLUDE
Please tick one of these boxes to show your verdict, and give reasons and descriptive comments, prices etc

☐ DESERVES **FOOD** award ☐ DESERVES **PLACE-TO-STAY** award 2007:14

PLEASE GIVE YOUR NAME AND ADDRESS ON THE BACK OF THIS FORM

Your own name and address *(block capitals please)*

In returning this form I confirm my agreement that the information I provide may be used by
The Random House Group Ltd, its assignees and/or licensees in any media or medium whatsoever.

DO NOT USE THIS SIDE OF THE PAGE FOR WRITING ABOUT PUBS

✂ ···

Your own name and address *(block capitals please)*

In returning this form I confirm my agreement that the information I provide may be used by
The Random House Group Ltd, its assignees and/or licensees in any media or medium whatsoever.

DO NOT USE THIS SIDE OF THE PAGE FOR WRITING ABOUT PUBS

IF YOU PREFER, YOU CAN SEND US REPORTS THROUGH OUR WEBSITE:
www.goodguides.co.uk

REPORT ON (PUB'S NAME)

Pub's address

☐ **YES** MAIN ENTRY ☐ **YES** LUCKY DIP ☐ **NO** DON'T INCLUDE

Please tick one of these boxes to show your verdict, and give reasons and descriptive comments, prices etc

☐ DESERVES **FOOD award** ☐ DESERVES **PLACE-TO-STAY award** 2007:15

PLEASE GIVE YOUR NAME AND ADDRESS ON THE BACK OF THIS FORM

✂ ···

REPORT ON (PUB'S NAME)

Pub's address

☐ **YES** MAIN ENTRY ☐ **YES** LUCKY DIP ☐ **NO** DON'T INCLUDE

Please tick one of these boxes to show your verdict, and give reasons and descriptive comments, prices etc

☐ DESERVES **FOOD award** ☐ DESERVES **PLACE-TO-STAY award** 2007:16

PLEASE GIVE YOUR NAME AND ADDRESS ON THE BACK OF THIS FORM

Your own name and address *(block capitals please)*

In returning this form I confirm my agreement that the information I provide may be used by
The Random House Group Ltd, its assignees and/or licensees in any media or medium whatsoever.

DO NOT USE THIS SIDE OF THE PAGE FOR WRITING ABOUT PUBS

✄ ....

Your own name and address *(block capitals please)*

In returning this form I confirm my agreement that the information I provide may be used by
The Random House Group Ltd, its assignees and/or licensees in any media or medium whatsoever.

DO NOT USE THIS SIDE OF THE PAGE FOR WRITING ABOUT PUBS

IF YOU PREFER, YOU CAN SEND US REPORTS THROUGH OUR WEBSITE:
www.goodguides.co.uk